ALSO BY JOHN F. KASSON

Civilizing the Machine:
Technology and Republican Values in America, 1776–1900

Rudeness and Civility:
Manners in Nineteenth-Century Urban America

Amusing the Million:
Coney Island at the Turn of the Century

HOUDINI, TARZAN,

AND

THE PERFECT MAN

HOUDINI, TARZAN,

AND

THE PERFECT MAN

THE WHITE MALE BODY AND

THE CHALLENGE OF MODERNITY IN AMERICA

JOHN F. KASSON

HILL AND WANG

A DIVISION OF FARRAR, STRAUS AND GIROUX

NEW YORK

Hill and Wang
A division of Farrar, Straus and Giroux
18 West 18th Street, New York, 10011

Printed in the United States of America
Published in 2001 by Hill and Wang
First paperback edition, 2002

The Library of Congress has cataloged the hardcover edition as follows:
Kasson, John F., 1944–
    Houdini, Tarzan, and the perfect man : the white male body and the challenge of
modernity in America / John F. Kasson.— 1st ed.
        p. cm.
    Includes bibliographical references and index.
    ISBN-13: 978-0-8090-8862-1 (alk. paper)
    ISBN-10: 0-8090-8862-2 (alk. paper)
        1. Men in popular culture—United States—History.   2. Masculinity in popular
culture—United States—History.   3. Body, Human—Social aspects—United States.
4. Sandow, Eugen, 1867–1925.   5. Houdini, Harry, 1874–1926.   6. Tarzan (Fictitious
character).   I. Title.

HQ1090.3 .K39 2001
305.31—dc21

                                                                                00053669

Paperback ISBN-13: 978-0-8090-5547-0
Paperback ISBN-10: 0-8090-5547-3

Designed by Jonathan D. Lippincott

www.fsgbooks.com

*For
Joy, Peter, and Laura,
who give me strength,
and for Peter Filene,
who led the way*

ACKNOWLEDGMENTS

I am grateful to many individuals and institutions for help in writing this book. The University of North Carolina at Chapel Hill provided crucial support, including fellowships and grants from the Institute for the Arts and Humanities, the Pogue Research Fund, the University Research Council, the Office of the Dean of Arts and Sciences, and the Department of History. A fellowship from the John Simon Guggenheim Memorial Foundation sped the work's completion.

I would also like to thank the following librarians for their assistance and for permission to quote from and to reproduce unpublished materials in special collections: Annette Fern and Jason Radalin at the Harvard Theatre Collection; Wallace Finley Dailey at the Theodore Roosevelt Collection, Harvard College Library; Joan F. Higbee at the Rare Book Collection, Library of Congress; Melissa Miller and Esther L. Mes at the Theatre Arts Collection, Harry Ransom Humanities Research Center, The University of Texas at Austin; Matthew Carpenter at the Houdini Historical Center, Appleton, Wisconsin; Rita Belda at the Wisconsin Center for Film and Theater Research; Josephine Matthews at the Image Library, The National Archives, Public Record Office, U.K.; Therese Babineau at the Phoebe A. Hearst Museum of Anthropology, University of California at Berkeley; Scott S. Taylor at Georgetown University Library; and George McWhorter and Linda Buie at the Edgar Rice Burroughs Memorial

Collection, University of Louisville. I am also especially grateful to Danton Burroughs for his kind permission to quote from manuscripts and to reproduce photographs owned by Edgar Rice Burroughs, Inc.

In conducting research for this book, I benefited from the help of David Avitabile, Matthew Brown, Eric Combest, Jason Dash, Joshua Guthman, Daniel Jolley, Emily Kelley, Michael Kramer, Ethan Kytle, Thomas Newsome, Michael Sistrom, Jill Snider, Shirley Taylor, and Adam Tuchinsky. A host of friends and colleagues also provided encouragement, criticism, and hospitality. Let me thank especially Gavin Campbell, Charles Capper, Michael Claxton, James W. Cook, Jr., the late Robert Crunden, Ann Fabian, Leon Fink, Alison Isenberg, Michael Kammen, Susan Levine, David Lubin, Jennifer Ritterhouse, Daniel Rodgers, Joan Shelley Rubin, Bill Stott, Alan Trachtenberg, and Keith Wailoo. Kent Plemmons gave valuable technical advice on computer hardware and software.

Although I have recorded specific scholarly debts in the endnotes, I wish to acknowledge my three principal subjects' major biographers: David L. Chapman, the late Irwin Porges, and Kenneth Silverman.

Hill and Wang, with which I have worked for a quarter century, remains my ideal publisher. Arthur W. Wang cheered my first stumbling efforts, and Elisabeth Sifton's brilliance and enthusiasm kept me going. Nina Ball-Pesut provided assistance with unfailing grace. Ingrid Sterner's copyediting was impeccable.

Peter Filene, a pioneer in the history of masculinity, has been an incomparable friend, giving encouragement, advice, and insight every step of the way.

And my family has been superb. My brother and sister-in-law, Jim and Betty Kasson, generously supplied computer equipment at critical moments. My children, Peter and Laura, sustained me with their love and sharpened my prose with their suggestions. My wife, Joy, has been indispensable to the project—as she has been to my life.

CONTENTS

CONTENTS

HOUDINI, TARZAN,

AND

THE PERFECT MAN

INTRODUCTION

In 1904 a balding, compactly built banker in Muncie, Indiana, posed for the camera on his forty-fifth birthday. It was not a conventional birthday portrait, however. For the occasion he stripped to the waist, flexed his biceps, and had himself photographed from behind. His business life was sedentary, but during the next forty years he kept up various physical regimens, ranging from lifting light weights to deep-breathing exercises. His name was Albert G. Matthews, and he was my great-grandfather; he died nine days before I was born.

I first saw this portrait in a family album as a child, and it prompted questions that fascinate me still. My initial response was surprise: What was he doing? Other male relatives in photographs showed their bodies, if at all, only in swim trunks as they squinted at the camera, usually holding a fish. Later I wondered, What was his sense of his body, and how was it shaped by the technologies and culture of his time? What models of strength did he admire? What dreams and anxieties did this image contain? Family photographs were one of the earliest ways by which I learned the importance of visual evidence in history, and in retrospect, I can see that this photograph was the first historical fragment that led to this book.

Many years later, I sifted through some thirteen thousand photo-

Albert G. Matthews on his forty-fifth birthday, 1904

graphs at Harvard University devoted to the most famous of all Albert Matthews's contemporaries (ten months his senior), the man who was president when his birthday portrait was made in 1904, Theodore Roosevelt. Here the sense of theatricality that I had first glimpsed with my ancestor burst forth on a colossal scale. Crucial to Roosevelt's success was his ability to turn prized characteristics of manliness into spectacle, literally to embody them. The camera and the pen were essential aids in that effort. Born in 1858 to one of the richest and most socially prominent families in New York, Roosevelt created his own stirring drama of childhood adversity overcome in an account of how he transformed his "sickly, delicate," asthmatic body into the two-hundred-pound muscular, barrel-chested figure of a supremely strong and energetic leader. His *Autobiography*, first published in 1913, included illustrations of Roosevelt in positions of executive authority (assistant secretary of the navy, governor of New York, president of the United States) carefully balanced with portraits of him active and outdoors (on horseback, returning from a bear hunt in Colorado, with hand on hip as Rough Rider colonel in the Spanish-American War, and holding a rifle "in winter riding costume").[1]

The photographic archive showed that Roosevelt had practiced

such poses assiduously, and no American of his generation or president before or since—not Lincoln, not Kennedy, not Reagan—developed a broader repertoire. Once past his childhood, when he was pictured in the unisex white dress, long hair, and bonnet worn by upper-class children of the time, he seems to have determined never to appear before the camera in a pampered guise again. In a routine physical examination as a Harvard undergraduate, he learned from Dr. Dudley A. Sargent, the college physician and the nation's leading authority on physical education, that he had "heart trouble" and should lead a sedentary life, taking care not even to run up stairs. Roosevelt replied that he could not bear to live that way and intended to do precisely the opposite.[2] A photograph from about this time shows him outside the Harvard boathouse wearing rowing togs, bare-chested and barefoot, his jaws filled out with a beard, his biceps bulged by his fists.

Theodore Roosevelt as a Harvard undergraduate in rowing attire. Theodore Roosevelt Collection, Harvard College Library

From his college days to the end of his life, Roosevelt appears to have considered no hunting trip complete without recording it either in the field or in a photographer's studio. For his first book, *Hunting Trips of a Ranchman* (1885), based on his adventures in the Dakota Territory, he struck various attitudes, holding a rifle and wearing a fringed buckskin outfit in the style of Buffalo Bill and sporting the holsters, pistols, chaps, and broad-brimmed hat of the ranchman. In 1898, upon his return from Cuba, where he had led his regiment of Rough Riders in victorious charges up Kettle Hill and San Juan Hill, he instantly memorialized his achievements in portraits that displayed a commanding martial bearing. In 1904, the year my great-grandfather posed for his birthday portrait, Roosevelt repeatedly jumped a fence on horseback until a *Harper's Weekly* photographer caught just the right dynamic image for the upcoming presidential campaign.[3] After his presidency, a stage of life in which most of his successors have done nothing more strenuous than golf, he threw himself into new activities—with photographers always at the ready. He recorded his exploits as big-game hunter and explorer (including obligatory poses with animal trophies) in Africa in 1909. Four years later, after his fiercely energetic but unsuccessful "Bull Moose" campaign against William Howard Taft and Woodrow Wilson, he headed for uncharted wilderness and big game once again, this time in Brazil, where he nearly lost his life. He spent his last years, also before the camera, stumping on behalf of the U.S. military effort during the Great War and itching to be in the thick of battle himself.

Many historians exploring manliness in this period have stopped with Roosevelt. But my pursuit has taken me further. And it has led to three immensely popular artists who entertained Americans in the two decades between 1893 and 1914: the strongman Eugen Sandow (1867–1925), the escape artist Harry Houdini (1874–1926), and the author of *Tarzan of the Apes*, Edgar Rice Burroughs (1875–1950). Sandow, Houdini, and Burroughs's Tarzan all acquired immense national and international fame. They literally became part of our language, which suggests that the cultural need for the metaphors they supplied was great, as was the power with which they entered into the lives of their audiences. Viewed in conjunction, these figures assume still greater significance: they expressed with special force and

clarity important changes in the popular display of the white male body and in the challenges men faced in modern life.

Although Sandow's name is no longer a household word, he is still revered as the father of modern bodybuilding and a pioneer of physical culture. In his heyday as a vaudeville performer, his position was even more exalted. Physical-fitness experts and journalists alike hailed him as the "perfect man," and his unclad body became the most famous in the world. He established a new paradigm of muscular development and attracted countless followers, ranging from the reformed "ninety-seven-pound weakling" Charles Atlas to the poet William Butler Yeats. His significance for cultural history is still greater. His display of his physique provides a fresh point by which we can assess the changing standards of male strength and beauty that may have inspired men like Albert Matthews to inspect their own bodies in private.

Sandow's celebrity has faded, but Houdini's hold on the popular imagination remains strong even today, though the nature of his feats and the context of his career have been obscured. For the general public, his name dominates the history of magic—to the intense annoyance of many conjurers and magic historians, who rank others superior. Wildly erroneous myths about him persist, such as that he died performing his "Chinese Water Torture Cell" escape (as does Tony Curtis's character in the 1953 Paramount film *Houdini*). Meanwhile, there has been little effort to place him in full historical and cultural context as not only the most brilliant escape artist in the history of illusion but also a magus of manliness, known for some of the most audacious displays of the male body in his time.

Burroughs's fictional character Tarzan is best known of all, but, again, in ways that obscure the significance of his creation. As the subject of twenty-four books written by Burroughs over thirty-five years, and of roughly fifty films, four major television series, a radio serial, and comic books, Tarzan and his adventures have been adapted in ways that hardly resemble the original. The persistence of his popularity testifies to enduring cultural fantasies about manly freedom and wildness. And an examination of the cultural milieu at his first appearance in Frank Munsey's *All-Story* magazine in 1912 illuminates important, if forgotten, aspects of American life a century

ago. It reveals why a story about an immensely strong, incomparably free, indomitably wild noble savage could so entrance men who felt locked in the "iron cage" of modern urban, corporate life.[4]

The spectacles of the male body mounted by these three figures built on values embodied in men such as Theodore Roosevelt. In fact, at various points in their careers, all three sought to associate themselves directly with Roosevelt. As a confused young man in 1898, Burroughs wrote to Roosevelt to volunteer for the Rough Riders; he received a gracious but firm refusal. In 1905, at the height of his international prestige, Sandow met with Roosevelt, then president, to discuss their mutual support of the physical-fitness cause. As for Houdini, after entertaining the ex-president on a transatlantic voyage in 1914, he eagerly distributed hundreds of copies of a photograph of himself and his new "pal," in which five other men had been carefully airbrushed away.[5]

Nonetheless, the popular spectacles created by Sandow, Houdini, and Burroughs take us far beyond Roosevelt's performances of manliness, expressing even deeper fantasies and anxieties. All three laid great stress on the unclad male body in ways that Roosevelt would have found unimaginable. This element was crucial to their novelty and impact. They contributed to a new popular interest in the male nude as a symbol of ideals in peril and a promise of their supremacy, as a monument to strength and a symbol of vulnerability, as an emblem of discipline and an invitation to erotic fantasy. In the guise of entertaining, they reasserted the primacy of the white male body against a host of challenges that might weaken, confine, or tame it. Popular spectacles of the female body in this period usually revolved around issues of subordination and transgression, but the overriding theme for these three men concerned metamorphosis. They repeatedly dramatized the transformation from weakness to supreme strength, from vulnerability to triumph, from anonymity to heroism, from the confinement of modern life to the recovery of freedom.

These images of manliness were obviously images of whiteness as well. Neither Sandow, nor Houdini, nor Burroughs was a racial extremist by the lights of his era, any more than Roosevelt himself, who famously invited Booker T. Washington to dine with him at the White House (and infamously issued dishonorable discharges to 170 African American soldiers in the "Brownsville affair"). Yet like Roosevelt, all

Harry Houdini and
Theodore Roosevelt
on board the liner
Imperator, June 1914 . . .

Taken on Board the
Hamburg American Liner "Imperator"
In Mid Ocean June 23. 1914.

. . . with their fellow passengers.

three shared—and to various degrees contributed to—the highly
racialized views that mark and mar this period. In science, popular literature, art, and daily life, the bodies of African American and Native
American men had been frequently displayed, even fetishized, while
their dignity and worth were denied. Significantly, the popular exaltation of the white male body took place at the very time when Plains
Indians, supposedly a "vanishing race" following the massacre at
Wounded Knee in 1890, were forced onto reservations little better
than prisons and African Americans were brutally subjected to segregation, disfranchisement, and lynchings. It is as if white American
men sought to seize the "primitive" strength, freedom, wildness, and
eroticism that they ascribed to these darker bodies to arm themselves
for modern life.

Manliness is a cultural site that is always under construction, of
course, but in this period it seems to have been undermined on a
number of fronts and demanded constant work in new arenas to remain strong. Many men born too late for the Civil War wondered how
they would fare in a similar test of courage, and some, like Roosevelt,
plunged into the Spanish-American and Philippine-American Wars as
opportunities to prove themselves and to build American manhood.[6]
Alarmed by the "new immigration" from southern and eastern Europe, composed principally of Catholics and Jews, some Americans
worried that the "enterprising, thrifty, alert, adventurous, and courageous" immigrants of past generations were being replaced by
"beaten men from beaten races; representing the worst failures in the
struggle for existence."[7] At the same time, reports warned that Americans of Anglo-Saxon stock were declining markedly in physical vigor
and, by failing to reproduce themselves in sufficient numbers, might
ultimately commit "race suicide."[8] Keenly aware of the passing of the
frontier, many Americans believed that a nation of farmers was rapidly becoming a nation of city dwellers. Roosevelt's fervent commitment to conservation represented one attempt among many to stay
close to the wild lest it be extinguished. Even those such as he who
occupied the most privileged positions often worried that society's
comforts might weaken their bodies and their wills. Anglo-Saxon
Protestants from refined and intellectually cultivated classes were
thought to be especially susceptible to neurasthenia, that distinctively modern, characteristically American disease of nervous weak-

ness and fatigue. The founder of this medical specialty, George M. Beard, placed high among its manifold causes excessive brain work, intense competition, constant hurry, rapid communications, the ubiquitous rhythm and din of technology. At the turn of the century, neurasthenia appeared to be reaching epidemic proportions.[9]

Above all, perceptions of manliness were drastically altered by the new dynamics created by vast corporate power and immense concentrations of wealth. Fundamental to traditional conceptions of American manhood had been autonomy and independence, which had to be recast in a tightly integrated economy of national and international markets. Titanic corporations arose with incredible swiftness in all areas of industry: Standard Oil, United States Steel, Pennsylvania Railroad, General Electric, Consolidated Coal, American Telephone and Telegraph, International Harvester, Weyerhaeuser Timber, U.S. Rubber, Pittsburgh Plate Glass, International Paper, Du Pont de Nemours, American Sugar Refining, Armour, United Fruit, American Can, Central Leather, and Eastman Kodak. By 1904, about three hundred industrial corporations had gained control of more than 40 percent of all manufacturing in the United States.[10]

And at the head of these new companies stood a greatly expanded, highly bureaucratized managerial class. Clerical workers, no more than 1 percent of the workforce in 1870, had swelled to more than 3 percent by 1900 and nearly 4 percent by 1910. These nascent "organization men" (and some women) increasingly worked in large buildings where the offices were as hierarchical and rule-bound as armies. A writer in *The Independent* worried, "The middle class is becoming a salaried class, and rapidly losing the economic and moral independence of former days."[11]

Factory workers, for their part, were the foot soldiers in this expanding industrial force. The period 1890–1914 was pivotal in the struggle between them and management over control of production within factories. Skilled workers had treasured a certain autonomy in setting the pace, organization, and distribution of wages for their work, an autonomy they had earned because of their superior knowledge of their craft. As Big Bill Haywood of the Industrial Workers of the World liked to boast: "The manager's brains are under the workman's cap."[12] The new corporate industrial order massively assaulted this power and the ethic of manly pride and brotherhood among

workers that sustained it. Through intense mechanization, division of labor, and "scientific management," industrialists endeavored to dominate all aspects of production and to reduce the workers' bodies to components in a gigantic machine.

Americans were in the forefront of this corporate revolution. Whereas in 1870 Britain provided 32 percent of the world's industrial output (followed by the United States at 23 percent and Germany at 13 percent), in 1913 the United States provided an immense 36 percent (Germany and Britain distantly trailed at 16 percent and 14 percent, respectively).[13] Yet to contemporaries, this industrial growth felt not like an orderly process but like a wild, careening ride. Wall Street panics in 1873 and 1893 began two of the greatest depressions in American history, and smaller depressions in 1885 and 1907 jolted the economy. By the mid-1880s supporters of labor and capital alike had come to fear that the strains of the new industrial society might erupt in large-scale riots, even a class-based civil war.

Industrialization accelerated major demographic shifts that were also altering the arenas in which manliness might be exercised. The nation's population continued to be the fastest growing in the world, leaping from fewer than forty million in 1870 to roughly sixty-three million in 1890 and nearly ninety-two million in 1910. This increase was partly due to unprecedented numbers of immigrants, amounting to 16 percent of the population in 1881–1900 and a staggering 24 percent in 1901–1920.[14] The new arrivals clustered mostly in America's cities, particularly along the manufacturing belt from the Northeast to the upper Midwest. In 1910 in New York, Chicago, Boston, Cleveland, Detroit, and Providence, more than one in three residents was foreign-born.[15]

Yet even as the population grew, more and more men deferred marriage; in fact, one historian has called this period "the age of the bachelor." In 1890 an estimated two-thirds of all men aged fifteen to thirty-four were unmarried, a proportion that changed little through the first two decades of the twentieth century. In cities the proportion was higher still, forming the basis for a flourishing urban bachelor culture that included a growing gay subculture. In many respects, this bachelor culture represented a pocket of resistance to—or at least a refuge from—the responsibilities of family and community, the demands of women, the discipline of work, and the pressures of a more

regulated society. In boisterous play and aggressive competition, bachelors could enjoy a continuity between boyhood and manhood. They played or watched sports and reveled in contests of physical skill and decisive triumph. At the beginning of this period, their great hero was no exponent of manly rectitude such as Roosevelt became, but boxing's brawling heavyweight champion John L. Sullivan. In newspapers and pulp fiction, they avidly read adventure stories about other heroic men, from Eugen Sandow to Tarzan. Many also indulged in pursuits that more respectable elements condemned: heavy drinking, swearing, gambling, engaging in casual sex with women—or other men.[16]

These urban bachelors had several female counterparts, including the working-class "tough girl," the radical needleworker, the shop clerk, the typist, and the "New Woman." The last was a capacious term for middle- and upper-class women who in various ways conducted themselves with a new independence and assertiveness, whether by shopping in department stores, smoking in public, playing tennis, expressing interest in sexuality, earning advanced degrees, entering traditionally male professions, calling for social and political reforms, or agitating for the ballot. Self-development, not self-sacrifice, was the New Woman's watchword. As one woman writer succinctly put it, "The question now is, not 'What does man like?' but 'What does woman prefer?'" Although neither the term "feminism" nor its full expression emerged until the end of this period, it was already clear that many women were refusing to be bound by traditional notions of women's domestic sphere.[17]

As the structure of both work and urban life changed dramatically, so too did the forms of leisure and communications by which people found release from and perspective on their worlds. Many commercial enterprises offered attractions calculated to appeal to broad popular tastes across different classes, ethnicities, and genders, and they grew into big businesses with some of the same characteristics of systematization, centralization, and managerial control that defined corporate industries. As they intersected, they created the conditions for a new society of spectacle that seemed to ease some of the deep divisions in America's new urban, industrial life. It is here that Sandow, Houdini, and Burroughs flourished.

Vaudeville theater, one of the most popular new entertainments

and the springboard for both Sandow's and Houdini's careers, emerged in the 1880s. It represented an extraordinarily successful effort to unite a fragmented theatergoing public: it combined the format of the variety show with standards of morality and settings of refinement that placed it decisively apart from the concert saloons and burlesque houses where variety shows had flourished. With as many as ten or twelve acts, sometimes in continuous performance throughout the day, vaudeville triumphed by offering "something for everyone." "If one objects to the perilous feats of the acrobats or jugglers," observed a critic in 1899, "he can read his programme or shut his eyes for a few moments and he will be compensated by some sweet bell-ringing or sentimental or comic song, graceful or grotesque dancing, a one-act farce, trained animals, legerdemain, impersonations, clay modeling, the biograph [moving] pictures, or the stories of the comic monologuist."[18] Whether in small-time houses or big-time theaters, vaudeville performers prided themselves on being able to engage diverse audiences of men, women, and children from both working-class and middle-class backgrounds in cities and towns across America. Even so, theirs was an industrialized art in which the vaudevillians worked along regional circuits that were dominated after 1900 by the United Booking Office, which spanned the continent.

Sport experienced a similar transformation into commercial entertainment. As once local, informal, and unregulated games became big business, they were systematized and put under managerial control. Yet they did not succumb to bureaucratic rationalization; the most popular sports, boxing and baseball, offered stirring dramas of individual prowess and communal aspiration that some fans treasured for their lifetimes. These professional sports, as well as college football, were heavily freighted with ambitions to revitalize American manhood. Even while seeking to reform their abuses, elite spokesmen extolled the value of these sports in instilling strength, skill, toughness, endurance, and courage. Writing in the dignified pages of *The North American Review* in 1888, Duffield Osborne simultaneously advocated replacing bare-knuckle fighting with regulated glove boxing and defended pugilism, with its "high manly qualities," as a bulwark against the emasculating tendencies of modern life. Without such antidotes to "mawkish sentimentality," he warned, civilization would degenerate into "mere womanishness."[19] Four years later,

"Gentleman Jim" Corbett defeated John L. Sullivan in the first heavyweight championship bout fought with padded gloves and timed rounds under the Marquis of Queensberry Rules. When the African American Jack Johnson won the title in 1908, however, it became abundantly clear that many fans thought revitalization should be for whites only. They raised an insistent call for a "Great White Hope" who could defeat Johnson, which was finally answered by the hulking Jess Willard in 1915.[20]

The transformations in popular theater and sport were sustained by profound changes in journalism. In the country as a whole from 1892 to 1914, the number of daily newspapers rose by more than a third, from 1,650 to 2,250, an all-time high; and their size expanded and circulation doubled. In the vanguard of change marched the great metropolitan newspapers. In 1892 ten papers in four cities had circulation bases higher than 100,000; in 1914 more than thirty papers in a dozen cities could make such a claim. Publishers, led by Joseph Pulitzer and William Randolph Hearst, increasingly encouraged the practice of what was called the New Journalism, by which they hoped to attract as diverse a readership as possible. They offered at low prices a bulging combination of sensational stories (such as those about Houdini's flamboyant escapes), serious news coverage, reportorial stunts, personal interviews (often with vaudeville and sports celebrities), civic crusades, and lavish illustrations. When newspapers were organized into spaces and departments devoted to sports, fashion, Sunday magazine supplements, and special columns, they acquired a variety format that resembled a vaudeville bill. And like vaudeville, these newspapers self-consciously aspired to be the "voice of the city," speaking for as well as to its myriad residents. They expressed this ambition both in their publications and, frequently, in their very offices, exemplified by the Pulitzer Building, which, upon its completion in 1890, surpassed Trinity Church as the tallest structure in New York City.[21]

The birth of the modern metropolitan daily and Sunday newspaper was accompanied by that of the modern, low-priced, mass-circulation magazine. Previously, inexpensive magazines had enjoyed only fleeting success. But in 1893 S. S. McClure founded an illustrated monthly magazine bearing his name that offered both fiction and articles and sold for only fifteen cents rather than the thirty-five

charged by his self-consciously genteel rivals. Other magazines, such as *Cosmopolitan* and *Munsey's*, cut their prices still further, and a host of new ten-cent magazines followed in their wake. In 1896, on the strength of his success, Frank Munsey revamped his story weekly, *The Argosy*, printed it on cheap, porous wood-pulp paper, and launched the modern pulp-fiction magazine. In the next few years he created a stable of such magazines, including *The All-Story*, in which *Tarzan* first appeared. By 1903 Munsey could fairly estimate that the ten-cent magazines had gained 85 percent of the entire magazine circulation in the country. Offering a wide variety of stories and articles, abundant illustrations, and a lively tone, such magazines represented a significant cultural challenge to established competitors. The editor of *The Independent* snobbishly defended his magazine's concentration on the "comparatively cultivated class" in magazines and newspapers, saying it was "the only audience worth addressing, for it contains the thinking people." But publishers such as McClure, Munsey, Pulitzer, and Hearst, like vaudeville impresarios such as B. F. Keith and F. F. Proctor, staked their fortunes on their ability to hold a mass following by giving the people plenty of varied materials at low prices.[22]

A number of factors held down the costs of mass-circulation magazines and newspapers, including technological breakthroughs in papermaking, typesetting, printing, and binding. But in their development, revenues from advertising were indispensable. Between 1892 and 1914 advertising in newspapers and periodicals increased by roughly 350 percent, and most of it was from local sources, especially the new department stores. Yet magazines, long the messengers for correspondence courses and patent nostrums, now were key sites for national advertising of standard brands from Victrolas to Grape-Nuts. Older "polite" magazines had once prided themselves on avoiding advertising, but for mass-circulation magazines in the early twentieth century the situation was fundamentally different. "There is still an illusion to the effect that a magazine is a periodical in which advertising is incidental," explained an advertising executive in 1907. "But we don't look at it that way. A magazine is simply a device to induce people to read advertising."[23]

Associated with these transformations in the popular theater, sports, and the press, as well as with the expansive commercial culture as a whole, was the continuing proliferation of photographic im-

Recovering classical manhood through Grape-Nuts, an advertisement in *The All-Story*, December 1911. The University of North Carolina at Chapel Hill

ages. The passion for studio portraits, awakened with the rise of photography, not only seized people of all classes but helped to make possible a new celebrity culture. Innovations in photographic reproduction and display changed individuals' very apprehension of themselves and the world. In 1888 George Eastman introduced his Kodak camera, initially a toy for the wealthy but a device that quickly demonstrated its potential to make virtually everyone an amateur photographer. At about the same time, between 1885 and 1910, the halftone, a new, cheaper technique of photoengraving that permitted the direct reproduction of photographs in newspapers, magazines, and books, effected a visual revolution.[24] Finally, the new mass medium of the movies grew with dazzling speed from Thomas Edison's peephole kinetoscope of 1893 (in which Sandow made an appearance), to large-scale motion-picture projection in 1896 (which was frequently the concluding diversion on vaudeville programs), to D. W. Griffith's controversial two-and-a-half-hour epic of white supremacy, *The Birth of a Nation*, in 1915. What had begun as a novelty became a consuming national pastime.

These popular spectacles were crucial in both maintaining and subverting gender categories. Indeed, one of the most striking elements was that men's and women's bodies were displayed and dramatized as never before in popular theater, sports, photography, fiction, film, and advertisements. Recent studies have highlighted aspects of this process, especially as it affected women. In the popular theater, for example, spectacle could be used to address quite different audiences for vastly different purposes. Burlesque, expelled from "legitimate" theaters and vaudeville houses, offered leg shows for working-class and lower-middle-class men. By contrast, vaudeville theaters, looking to attract middle-class families as well as members of the bachelor subculture, offered women a broader range of roles. Many of these were constraining, but others allowed for freedom, independence, and self-expression that laid the groundwork for an emergent feminism. By the second decade of the twentieth century, protesting women, including socialists, trade unionists, and suffragists, had taken this sense of theatricality from the stage to the streets to gather support for their causes.[25]

Historians have paid less attention to the importance of the *male* body in popular spectacles—and, especially, challenges to the ex-

posed white male body—as expressing the meaning of manliness in this emergent urban, industrial order. That subject lies at the heart of this book. My approach is highly selective. I have chosen to focus on Sandow, Houdini, and Burroughs in order to see how they reveal popular aesthetic and cultural patterns. In a context dominated by the rise of corporate capitalism, the changing character of work, the advent of a skyscraper civilization, and the emergence of the New Woman, they helped to create the Revitalized Man. As a model of wholeness and strength, this figure ostensibly stood above the political conflict and class strife of the period, inviting a broad and diverse public of men and women, blue-collar and white-collar workers, to celebrate common gender ideals. The appeal of Sandow, Houdini, and Tarzan could unite followers of John L. Sullivan and Theodore Roosevelt; readers of newspapers as diverse as Richard Kyle Fox's *National Police Gazette*, Hearst's and Pulitzer's metropolitan dailies, and the socialist *Masses*; admirers of Burt L. Standish's *Frank Merriwell at Yale* and Jack London's *The Call of the Wild*; and fans of the illustrator J. C. Leyendecker's Arrow Collar Man and the painter George Bellows's savage boxers.

Sandow, Houdini, and Burroughs's Tarzan can thus illuminate much about the place of popular culture at the advent of modern society. They help us to understand more about how the shift to an advancing technological civilization was communicated to and apprehended by publics in North America and abroad. They tell us about how modernity was understood in terms of the body and how the white male body became a powerful symbol by which to dramatize modernity's impact and how to resist it. They reveal the degree to which thinking about masculinity in this period meant thinking about sexual and racial dominance as well. They also tell us that hopes and fears, aspirations and anxieties are often difficult to distinguish. Perhaps every dream is the sunny side of some nightmare; perhaps every cultural wish has a dark lining of fear.

WHO IS THE PERFECT MAN?

EUGEN SANDOW AND

A NEW STANDARD FOR AMERICA

Images of male muscular development and bodily perfection have both a distinguished lineage and a troubled history in Western culture. Though securely established in classical Greece and Rome, their position afterward became highly precarious, particularly in the context of a Christian pursuit of spiritual perfection that denied the body. In response, artists from the Renaissance on have been remarkably resourceful in attaching both male and female nudes to classical, biblical, ideal, or exotic subjects. In addition, beginning in the 1840s, the new medium of photography offered an expanding range of images of the nude in more and less acceptable guises: academic studies for artists; records of medical and scientific subjects; ethnographic evidence of exotic peoples; and pornography. Still, even in the late nineteenth century, to display the unclad male figure, let alone the female one, bereft of divine, allegorical, or alien trappings—not as a god, virtue, ruler, hero, exotic figure, or scientific specimen but simply as a person—was to risk falling from the lofty plane of the nude to the shameful one of the merely naked.[1]

Given this context, the emergence of the unclad male body from the realms of high art, science, and low life into the broader culture toward the turn of the twentieth century demands historical investi-

Sandow dressed in fig leaf and Roman sandals, 1894. Photograph by Benjamin J. Falk. Library of Congress

gation. That body did not simply walk free. It faced suspicious inquiries as to its status. And it carried heavy aesthetic and cultural baggage, into which were stuffed a multitude of claims and aspirations, fantasies and anxieties. This baggage bore various tags, sometimes prominently, about manliness, heroism, power, virility, and eroticism. The figure who could lift them all would be regarded as not an ordinary but a perfect man.

This was perhaps the weightiest baggage that accompanied Eugen Sandow when he disembarked from the liner *Elbe* in New York in June 1893, and it only increased during his appearances across the United States in the next year. Sandow arrived at a key moment: just a month earlier, the stock market had crashed, slowly pulling the economy into a deep depression that profoundly threatened the sense of independence and control once enjoyed by men. Already bankers and businessmen feared ruin; soon millions of workers were unemployed, and tens of thousands of tramps drifted around the country. The depression intensified a widespread sense of gender malaise. To many, manhood seemed no longer a stable condition—absolute and unproblematic—but rather an arduous, even precarious achievement that had to be vigilantly defended. Supposedly a biological category, manhood was also a *performance*.[2] And Sandow quickly emerged as the most brilliant performer of manhood of the 1890s. In his live appearances at vaudeville theaters, in widely circulated photographs, newspaper and magazine illustrations, and in some of the very first moving pictures, Sandow's unclad body became the most famous in the world and his name a synonym for muscular development. He helped to reshape notions of what male bodily perfection—and masculinity itself—might be in modern industrial society. And for all his active participation in this process, this "perfect man" was not simply a figure waiting to be discovered. In significant respects he was created out of the cultural demands of his time.

FROM ADONIS TO HERCULES

An acrobatic strongman on the English music-hall stage, Sandow made his American debut on June 12, 1893, at the Casino Roof Garden at Broadway and Thirty-ninth Street in New York City. He was

an unusual attraction for the Casino, whose manager took pride in its being among the most refined variety theaters in the country, offering comic operas and other stylish acts in a theater of fantastic Moorish design. Sandow's six-week run came during the slack season, one made worse by a heat wave that baked the city and by the economy's plunge into depression. After the stock market's collapse in May, credit had tightened like a fist. Businesses failed daily. The Erie Railroad went bankrupt in July, and other railroads rapidly followed. Rich, middle-class, and laboring men alike had reason to feel tense about the future and uncertain about themselves. Depending on their class and political position, they would cast the blame on labor agitators or greedy capitalists, Democrats or Republicans. All were receptive to a man who embodied strength and confidence—as were many women of all classes. The wealthy saw Sandow first, but instantly newspapers and illustrated magazines made him a household name.[3]

Sandow went onstage immediately after a performance of William Gill's musical spoof *Adonis*, one of the most popular American plays of the time. In retrospect, we can see the two acts not simply as diverting offerings on a single variety bill but as contending performances of masculinity, the first of a series of such contrasts that Sandow's American tour entailed. To appreciate the effect of Sandow's performance, we need to watch the previous act closely.

The title role of Adonis, the perfection of male beauty, was taken by a handsome, trim matinee idol named Henry Dixey. *Adonis*, first produced in 1884, when he was twenty-five, had made his career. Dixey was a "master of pantomime," in the words of one critic, and had made "his body . . . a thoroughly trained instrument of expression, of which he has perfect and complete control." He was so successful at embodying this popular theatrical ideal of physical perfection that he was virtually trapped in the role, performing it more than seven hundred times in New York alone, in addition to tours around the country and an acclaimed run in London.[4]

Adonis was a late-Victorian burlesque lampooning the conventions of melodrama, society plays, and gender roles as it presented women in aggressive competition for and pursuit of an irresistibly beautiful man. Gill's play turned inside out the Greek myth of Pygmalion and Galatea, in which a sculptor falls in love with his female creation, whom Aphrodite brings to life. (The Pygmalion story was being

freshly popularized at the time both in comic treatments, including a play by W. S. Gilbert performed in New York in 1881, and in paintings by the British artists G. F. Watts and Edward Burne-Jones and the Frenchman Jean-Léon Gérôme.) In Gill's play a sculptress has created in her statue of Adonis a "perfect figure." Indeed, he is so beautiful and alluring that she cannot bear to sell him as promised to a wealthy duchess. Seeing Adonis, the duchess, together with her four daughters, is instantly and passionately smitten as well. The daughters try to conceal their ardor as each offers a refined observation about the figure's artistic merits: "Isn't it lovely." "What grace in that nostril." "What symmetry in that eyebrow." "What indications of strength in those biceps." Until the fourth sighs, "And what lovely calves."

To resolve the question of ownership, an obliging goddess brings the statue to life. Theatrical photographs suggest how Dixey comically achieved this metamorphosis. The determinedly absurd plot combined the spirit of Gilbert and Sullivan's *Iolanthe* (in which Dixey had earlier played) and a college farce. The pursuit of Adonis rapidly becomes entangled with three figures who are burlesques of stock characters of melodrama: the Marquis de Baccarat, a quintessential "polished villain"; Rosetta, a self-declared simple and poor "village beauty . . . pursued by all the lordly vilyuns for miles around"; and Rosetta's rustic father, Bunion Turke, who, doubting his daughter's virtue, repeatedly declaims the necessity of shutting against her his "poor but honest door" and "poor but honest heart"—even as he attempts to steal Adonis's lunch. To heighten the absurdity (and the gender inversion), Adonis ludicrously assumes the disguise of a village maid and is briefly courted by the Marquis. For her part, Rosetta, who promptly falls in love with Adonis and who boasts that she weighs 120 pounds, was played by the hefty Amelia Summerville. (In an earlier production she had been played by the 300-pound George K. Fortesque in drag.) Ultimately, Adonis is cornered by all his female pursuers, who demand that he choose among them. Instead, he beseeches the goddess who gave him life, "Oh take me away and petrify me—place me on my old familiar pedestal—and hang a placard round my neck:—'HANDS OFF.' " Thus, exhausted by his stint as a flesh-and-blood object of desire, Dixey as Adonis reassumed the pose of a perfect work of art as the curtain fell.

Dixey's metamorphoses in *Adonis*.
Photographs by Napoleon Sarony. Theatre
Arts Collection, Harry Ransom Humanities
Research Center, The University of
Texas at Austin

Dixey's Adonis as a village maid.
Photograph by Napoleon Sarony.
Harvard Theatre Collection

Adonis pointed to a new set of attitudes governing gender relations and bodily display, in which genteel women were assuming some of the prerogatives that earlier in the century had been reserved for men.[5] That a man might be the construction and possession of women, valued solely for his beauty, his body openly admired and aggressively pursued by them (as well as courted by his own sex)—such was the stuff of both male fantasies and male anxieties. In its farcical way, *Adonis* played with the meaning of gender in modern life and with the question of whether anatomy indeed determined destiny or merely offered a pretext for roles and disguises. Still, if at the end of the play anyone in the audience were asked who best portrayed the perfect man, the answer would undoubtedly have been Henry Dixey.

Then it was Sandow's turn. When the curtain rose again, Sandow, clad only in a loincloth and Roman sandals, had assumed the statue's pose in Dixey's stead—and the contrast made the audience gasp. One observer wrote, "New York has come to look upon Dixey as a fairly well-made young man. When New York has seen Sandow after Dixey, however, New York will realize what a wretched, scrawny creature the

usual well-built young gentleman is compared with the perfect man."
Slowly, this new statue came to life as Sandow struck classical poses
and moved his "forest of muscles" at will. For almost a decade, Dixey
had successfully played the part of a beautiful classical statue come to
life, but Sandow took on the dual roles of sculptor and masterpiece.
He instantly eclipsed Dixey. In the words of one journalist at the time
of his debut: "It was hard for the spectators . . . to believe that it was
indeed flesh and blood that they beheld. Such knots and bunches and
layers of muscle they had never before seen off the statue of an
Achilles, a Discobolus, or a fighting gladiator." Another reporter marveled: "He postures so as to bring the muscles more prominently before the audience, and he appears to be able to make them rise and
fall just as easily as he can open and shut his eyes."[6]

In the second part of his act Sandow demonstrated his strength
and dexterity. With a crisp, military manner and to piano accompaniment, he performed a series of feats with two fifty-six-pound dumbbells, repeatedly exceeding what the audience thought possible.
Holding a dumbbell in each hand, he turned a back flip; he did the
same feat with his ankles tied together and his eyes blindfolded.
Then, with a great show of exertion, eight men brought onstage a
huge barbell with a basket holding a man at each end. Using only one
hand, Sandow lifted the two men over his head, stopping momentar-
ily to hold the barbell straight out from his shoulder as a further proof
of his strength. In still another feat displaying his powerful abdominal
and dorsal muscles, he had his knees fastened to a Roman column
and then bent backward to lift two men over his head.

The finale of Sandow's half-hour performance was the human
bridge. Making his body into an arch with his chest upraised and his
hands and feet on the floor in the "Tomb of Hercules" position, he
supported a wooden platform on his shoulders, chest, and knees.
Then three trained horses (actually ponies), with an advertised combined weight of twenty-six hundred pounds, stepped onto the platform and stayed there for about five seconds supported by Sandow,
whose "every muscle . . . stood out like whipcord."[7]

From the moment of his New York debut, Sandow was seen not
simply as a remarkable figure of strength and showmanship but also
as a new ideal of the male body which brought to the fore a host of
personal and cultural issues. At the height of his career, from 1893 to

1906, he repeatedly toured the United States (the total duration of his visits amounted to nearly seven years, far more time than he spent in his adopted home of England or anywhere else), but already by the end of his second American tour, in 1894, his presence had dramatically altered the discussion. His appearance shattered the prevailing image of the strongman: the thickset, barrel-chested performer in circuses, dime museums, and beer halls who might be mistaken for a blacksmith but never for a gentleman, let alone an Adonis. Sandow brilliantly succeeded in winning the applause of elite theatergoers even before he gained the attention of the broader middle and working classes. To them all, he represented a new standard of male fitness, beauty, strength, and potency. Starkly exposed and thoroughly publicized as he was, he became an icon of the hypermasculine who with his extraordinary muscular development literally embodied characteristics that many men and women believed were threatened by modern life.

Spectators viewed Sandow's body as both an attraction and a challenge, a model of strength and an object of desire, an inspiration, a rebuke, and a seduction. He simultaneously incited superlatives and stirred disquieting controversies and ambiguities. He was touted as the "strongest man in the world" and the "perfect man," yet he was pursued by challengers, imitators, and impostors who claimed they could duplicate or better his feats. He was celebrated as a monument not only of strength but also of classical beauty, yet his body was criticized as abnormal, even decadent. He cultivated prestige in both medical science and sport, yet he was supremely a creature of the vaudeville stage, the newspaper interview, and the photographer's studio. He presented himself as a modern gladiator with a heroic aura, yet he aroused charges of fabrication and deception. He was ostensibly an apostle of asexual health and strength, yet he implicitly promised to restore lost virility. He never acknowledged himself as an object of erotic interest, yet he enlarged the boundaries of the display of the male nude in live exhibitions and in photographs that elicited intense interest from women and especially from men at a time when the categories of heterosexuality and homosexuality did not squeeze so tightly as to inhibit a man's frank admiration of another man's body.[8] He claimed to embody an ancient heroic ideal of manhood that had been lost in the modern world, yet he turned his body into a com-

mercial spectacle and a commodity whose image was widely reproduced and sold.

THE RECOVERY OF LOST MANHOOD

Superlatives and ambiguities began with Sandow's accounts of his upbringing and training. At the outset of his American tour, he concocted an autobiography that emphasized his eminently respectable
origins and heroic achievements, and he reiterated it throughout his
career in interviews, articles, and amply padded books (beginning
with *Sandow on Physical Training*, a compendium of physical instruction, biography, press clippings, photographs, and line drawings.[9] In
the process he changed his name from Friedrich Wilhelm Müller to a
version of his mother's maiden name, Sandov (frequently Anglicizing
his new given name of Eugen to Eugene as well). He preserved his
background in Prussia, where he was born on April 2, 1867, but elevated his father from a fruit and vegetable seller in the markets of
Königsberg to a successful jeweler and merchant. At the same time he
shrewdly insisted his strength was not a gift of nature but an attainment strenuously earned. Indeed, the more he retold the story, the
more his health as a youth declined. In some of his earlier newspaper
interviews during his first American tour, as well as in his first book,
he was "healthy," though less strong than his fellows; in later accounts he grew "very slight and sickly" as a child, and "my parents, as
well as the physician, had serious doubts as to whether I would
live."[10]

In this way Sandow struck chords about masculine strength and
self-determination that have been played by many exemplars of
American manhood from his time down to our own. Making his body
became a sign of a man's ability to make his way in the world against
all adversaries, strictly on his own merits. A strong, muscular body was
an emblem of strong character and command. The message could be
used equally well to validate the achievements of men from obscure
and privileged backgrounds.

Born in the lap of the upper class, Theodore Roosevelt wrote that
the turning point of his boyhood was his resolve to remake his "sickly,
delicate," and asthmatic body into the strong, vigorous frame of a

fearless leader. Significantly, he determined to do so at the age of fourteen after a trip to Maine on which two boys taunted him unmercifully and he discovered himself helpless to lay a blow on either. His transformation was no seven-day wonder, but years of boxing lessons and exercise paid off. A decade later, in the Dakota Territory, when a profane, two-gunned barroom bully called Roosevelt "four eyes" and goaded him beyond endurance, the eastern dude met the challenge decisively: "As I rose, I struck quick and hard with my right just to one side of the point of his jaw, hitting with my left as I straightened out, and then again with my right. . . . When he went down he struck the corner of the bar with his head . . . he was senseless."[11]

From the other end of the social spectrum, the leading American exemplars of physical culture in the early twentieth century credited Sandow for their own youthful conversions of body and will. The once frail and tubercular Bernarr Macfadden (1868–1955) saw Sandow perform in Chicago in 1893 and almost immediately began posing in classical and muscular attitudes himself. In 1899 Macfadden launched a monthly magazine, *Physical Culture*, which crusaded for health, fit-

Bernarr Macfadden posing as Mercury. Photograph by F. W. Guerin. Library of Congress

ness, exercise, and nutrition—as well as the "inspiration" of the muscular male (and occasionally female) body—with what might be regarded as missionary zeal, huckster's effrontery, or both. "Weakness is a crime," the magazine darkly warned readers. "Don't be a criminal."

A decade later, in 1909, sixteen-year-old Angelo Siciliano, a self-described "ninety-seven-pound weakling" and target of sand-kicking beach bullies, fastened a picture of Sandow on his dresser mirror and determined to emulate his hero. Within a few years he was performing as a strongman, first in sideshows at Coney Island, then on the vaudeville circuit. Having adopted the name Charles Atlas, he was proclaimed, in contests sponsored by Macfadden, the "World's Most Beautiful Man" in 1921 and "America's Most Perfectly Developed Man" the following year. For the next four decades, Atlas ruled as the most prominent physical-culture entrepreneur in the nation.[12]

All these men emphasized how, by dint of determination and method, they had transformed themselves from puny boys to men of strength, confidence, and command. The theme of metamorphosis lies at the heart of bodybuilding; and a longing for male metamorphosis lay deep in the culture of the United States and much of western Europe at the advent of the modern age. Sandow invoked it again and again.

Sandow dated his own conversion (almost certainly inauthentic) to the age of ten while on a studious Italian holiday with his father. By Sandow's account, in Rome he and his father pondered in art galleries the magnificently sculpted figures of ancient warriors and athletes "bespeaking power and energy in every limb." Sandow claimed to have asked his father not about the attainment of male power and virility but about their loss: "How is it that these men were so strong?" Why were men today so inferior in strength and stature? His father explained: "The heroes of old, my little Eugen, . . . never lolled at ease in a carriage or a railway train." Modern civilization marked the ascendancy of the brain over the body, but the price was "world-wide degeneration in health and strength."[13] Enraptured by this classical ideal, or so he later maintained, Sandow resolved to reclaim for himself, for men, and ultimately for humanity the health and strength they had lost.

But how? In Sandow's account he avidly acquired every book on athletics and exercise that "I could persuade my generous parents to

purchase" and spent every spare moment at the gymnasium, all without much success. Only when he began to study anatomy seriously and to devise his own system of exercises to develop each and every muscle did he find "the key to the secret I had been endeavoring to solve." Here, it appeared, was a wholly individual achievement of almost Promethean proportions: to bring strength to the weak and health to the ill. From Sandow's account, one would never know of the enormously influential gymnastic movement founded by Friedrich Ludwig Jahn (1778–1852) to revive German manhood after the humiliating defeats of the Napoleonic Wars or of the vast revival of enthusiasm for the classical Greek ideal of the male nude dating back to Johann Winckelmann in the mid-eighteenth century.[14]

In this way Sandow appropriated the prestige both of science and of classical art in his career as a bodybuilder pioneering the display of the nearly nude body. Here again, he was not entirely original. Among men, self-declared "professors" of physical culture grew commonplace in variety shows, music halls, and dime museums; and, especially among women, "living sculptures," "*tableaux vivants*," and "model artist" shows had for half a century borrowed classical subjects as the thinnest of pretexts for the display of the female body.[15] Yet Sandow cultivated an air of bourgeois respectability that lifted him above these low entertainments. Though he admitted he served apprenticeships in circuses and wrestling matches on the European continent, he asserted that they came only after he dropped out of medical studies and the resulting rift with his father forced him to support himself. Throughout his career he cannily sought the appearance and demeanor of a gentleman, if a rather flamboyant one. Sandow early sensed, as would Edgar Rice Burroughs in *Tarzan of the Apes*, the importance of social credentials as well as great physical strength. Both Sandow and Burroughs were aware that a privileged class standing was vital in the new ideal of the male body, that class remained inscribed on the body, even the nude body. Class and, in Sandow's case, the incessant cultivation of classicism provided social and aesthetic cover that saved the body from mere nakedness.[16]

While knocking about the Continent in circuses and as an occasional artists' model (labors converted to picaresque adventures in his reminiscences), Sandow met one of the most successful professional strongmen, "Professor Louis Attila" (Ludwig Durlacher; 1844–1924),

The defeated French strongman
Charles A. Sampson. Harvard Theatre
Collection

Sandow triumphant, 1893.
Photograph by Benjamin J. Falk.
Library of Congress

then living in Brussels. A canny self-promoter, Attila eventually claimed among his students Tsar Alexander III, King George of Greece, and Britain's King Edward VII. Under the professor's tutelage, Sandow vastly developed his physique through progressive weight training, and, even more important, he honed his abilities as a showman.[17] Attila also orchestrated Sandow's first great breakthrough: his successful challenge in London for the title "strongest man on earth."

Challenges were a mainstay of stage strongmen, as they were of other stage performers (as we shall see with Harry Houdini) and of prizefighters such as John L. Sullivan. Formal challenges—including standing offers to best all comers and published challenges (known as cards) aimed at a specific rival—flourished on both sides of the Atlantic. These challenges, borrowing elements of the aristocratic duel, gave working- and middle-class men occasions to participate vicariously in dramas of strength, courage, and honor. And, of course, they contributed considerably to publicity and box-office receipts.[18]

In the fall of 1889 a French strongman who had taken the name Charles A. Sampson packed London's Royal Aquarium music hall as he nightly reiterated a dramatic challenge. Appearing with his protégé Cyclops (the Pole Franz Bienkowski), he offered a cash prize of five hundred pounds—as well as his self-awarded title, the "strongest man on earth"—to anyone who could duplicate his feats. In earlier appearances Sampson had performed such prodigies of strength as lifting a barbell that supposedly weighed an imperial ton (2,240 pounds) and raising a platform that supported an elephant. Yet like most stage strongmen, he accomplished these exploits far less through strength than through showmanship, deception, and special equipment that blurred the line between strongman and magician. A successful challenger to his title would need not only strength but also cunning.

With Attila's aid, on October 29, 1889, the unknown Sandow rose from the audience at the music hall to accept Sampson's challenge. He first surpassed Cyclops in a series of lifts. The following week he triumphed over Sampson himself, duplicating, if not as gracefully, the Frenchman's tricks of bending an iron bar, snapping a wire by expanding his chest, and breaking a chain with his arms.[19] With this triumph Sandow supplanted Sampson as the leading strongman on the

British music-hall circuit, a position he retained until his debut in the
United States almost four years later made him an international star.

THE CHALLENGE OF SANDOW'S BODY

Sandow was not simply an athlete but also an actor, a man of the theater even more than of the gymnasium, and it is no accident that his
career flourished during the great age of the music hall in England
and of vaudeville in the United States, both of which placed a pre-
mium on specialty acts that could be reproduced for broad audiences
night after night in a kind of industrialization of the theater. Onstage
and off, he performed compressed dramas of masculine strength,
agility, and physical development. These demanded great skill and
training, to be sure, those not merely of sport but of showmanship.
(Even his bent-press lifts might be regarded as less a proof of strength
than a spectacular balancing act. Modern bodybuilding has continued
to exist uneasily between sport and spectacle.) He offered his body
not so much as an instrument of his achievements but as an achievement in itself: a heroic sculpture come to life. For muscular strength,
development, control, and proportion, that body seemed instantly to
set a new standard. To an unprecedented degree, Sandow made his
body a subject of immense popular attention and cultural debate from
the moment of his New York debut, as his press coverage clearly attests.

His extraordinary body fascinated observers, first, because it could
be so successfully cloaked in a mantle of ordinariness. A Bar-
numesque giant who could lift a five-hundred-pound weight with his
middle finger, break iron rods across his arms and legs, perform a regulation army drill with a good-sized man instead of a musket, or defeat three large and expert wrestlers at once would be impressive
enough. That these and equally prodigious feats were achieved by a
handsome young man of middle height who, when conventionally
dressed, easily blended into a crowd seemed almost incredible.
Sandow learned to cultivate this surprise and to startle spectators with
the speed of his transformation from late-Victorian man-about-town
to modern Hercules. When he had emerged from the music-hall audience to challenge Sampson in London, he had come onstage sporting

SANDOW.

13 AND 15 WEST 24TH ST. N.Y.

•MADISON SQUARE•

Sandow as a well-dressed gentleman. Photograph by Benjamin J. Falk. Harvard Theatre Collection

a monocle and evening clothes especially designed to be whisked off, like the unveiling of an artist's masterpiece, to reveal his powerful, sculpted body. So American viewers repeatedly marveled how this genial blond man, who was "nothing like so formidable in appearance as many men one [met] on the street every day," could reveal a body of almost superhuman development.[20] Thus, to his gradual transformation from sickly youth to strongman Sandow added a second, virtually instantaneous metamorphosis: from man of the crowd to marvel of muscle. This simultaneously placed Sandow in a class by himself and appealed to fantasies of self-transformation in boys and men, much as Clark Kent was to inspire later generations to dream of stripping off their street clothes and eyeglasses in a telephone booth and turning into Superman.

With his triumph over Sampson, Sandow claimed the title "strongest man on earth," and upon his arrival in America, he immediately won a new title: the "perfect man." Bodybuilding stresses muscle mass, definition, symmetry, and proportion, and Sandow embodied these to an unprecedented degree. His body's combination of well-proportioned, articulated, and extraordinary measurements fascinated trained observers and novices alike. By Sandow's own report, he stood five feet eight and a half inches and weighed 190 pounds. He boasted a neck of "18½ inches; biceps, 19½ inches; forearm, 17 inches; chest, normal, 52 inches; contracted, 46 inches; expanded, 58 inches; waist, 29 inches; thigh, 26⅔ inches; calf, 18 inches." These numbers prompted one reporter to observe that Sandow's waist was "not much bigger around than" the renowned beauty Lillie Langtry's, while his chest was "a good deal bigger . . . than [President] Grover Cleveland's." A century later, in a world of specialized equipment, systematic training, sophisticated diets, and anabolic steroids, Sandow's measurements would not earn even a second glance from experienced observers, but in 1893 they were staggering. Still more impressive was his overall muscular strength, control, and definition; before the names of the major muscle groups were common parlance, Sandow seemed a walking anatomic chart. "With the fond pride of a mother displaying a large family of children," he showed off his "collection of muscles one at a time and . . . [dwelled] modestly but lovingly upon their merits." A reporter exclaimed over his triceps ("much bigger than the calf in an ordinary strong man's leg"), the ex-

ternal obliques covering his ribs (each "twice as big around as a man's thumb"), and the erectors, lats, and other muscles on his back ("so thick, so deep, that the backbone, which is quite invisible, runs along at the bottom of a deep gorge"). Sandow proudly exhibited his trapezius muscles ("as thick through as the back of a man's hand is broad, and thicker in some places") and his abdominal muscles ("each about as big as a man's wrist"), which gave the impression of a corrugated washboard.[21]

He delighted still more in examinations by physicians and other experts, stripping for their inspection even as he shrewdly wrapped himself in their scientific and social prestige. The day before his public debut at New York's Casino Theatre, Sandow offered a private demonstration before a group of two hundred, including many physicians. Perhaps the most knowledgeable among them, Dr. Ramon Guiteras, a member of the New York Athletic Club and a former amateur boxer, declared him far stronger and faster than Sullivan, as well as "about the most perfectly developed specimen of a man I have ever seen."[22]

Mention of Sullivan reminds us that while Henry Dixey stood (especially among middle-class theatergoers) as one contender for the title "perfect man," because of his physical beauty, John L. Sullivan for a decade claimed that title (especially among working-class men), on account of his violent physical strength and fighting skill. Heavyweight boxing champion from 1882 until his loss to James Corbett ten years later, Sullivan attracted a greater following than any previous sports figure in American history. He early earned the nickname the "Boston Strong Boy," which stemmed from such feats as lifting barrels of flour and kegs of nails above his head; and during his boxing career he acquired numerous other appellations—"the Boston Hercules," "the Boston Miracle of huge muscles, terrific chest, and marvellous strength," "the finest specimen of physical development in the world."[23]

Born in Boston in 1858 to an Irish hod carrier, Sullivan worked as a plumber's apprentice, a tinsmith, then a mason, all before he was out of his teens. He was quarrelsome and restless. By temperament and physique as well as by class and culture, he proudly displayed the tough, manly bearing by which workers sought to affirm their independence in a time of shrinking respect and autonomy. His frequent

disputes and occasional fights lost Sullivan his early jobs, but his aggressiveness and bravado were to distinguish him as a boxer and to make him a beloved hero to the working class.

In Sullivan's career as a boxer, as in Sandow's as a strongman, sport and stage melded in intense performances of manliness. Sullivan began his boxing career at the age of nineteen, slugging in exhibitions at local variety theaters and music halls. Though he catapulted to fame on the basis of bare-knuckle prizefights, generally fought outside the law, his fortune and following were sustained by stage bouts in which he challenged all comers to last four gloved rounds of three minutes apiece. "My name's John L. Sullivan," he would boom from the stage, "and I can lick any son-of-a-bitch alive." (However, in an era of growing racial segregation, Sullivan refused to fight black contenders such as the Australian heavyweight champion Peter Jackson.) If there were no takers, he sparred with a fellow member of the troupe. On other tours he did not box at all but posed or acted. Exploiting the enthusiasm for "living statues," which Sandow would transform, Sullivan struck poses as "the biggest undressed heroes of antiquity": "the Dying Gladiator," "Hercules at Rest," "Cain Killing Abel," and so on.

Dudley A. Sargent. Library of Congress

In 1890–1891 he played the part of a virtuous Irish blacksmith in the tailor-made melodrama *Honest Hearts and Willing Hands*. With Sullivan's ascendancy, prizefighting moved from the shady pursuit of gamblers and saloon keepers to a more respectable mass entertainment that attracted solidly middle-class and professional patrons as well as the working classes.[24]

In 1892, as the thirty-four-year-old Sullivan trained for his championship bout with the Californian James Corbett, his celebrated body was rigorously examined by the nation's leading figure in physical education, Dudley A. Sargent. Sargent was best qualified to determine who the perfect man was from a purely physical standpoint, and, because he also examined Eugen Sandow the following year, he is best qualified to help us compare the two figures.

Sargent was both a scientist keenly interested in the possibilities of bodily perfection and a onetime circus acrobat who knew firsthand the kind of theaters in which both Sullivan and Sandow got their start. After a brief stint as a performer in his teens, he left such entertainments behind for the life of a college athletic instructor. He took charge of the Bowdoin College gymnasium in his native Maine at the age of twenty, two years before he enrolled as a freshman. He went on to receive a medical doctorate from Yale, transforming that college's gymnastic instruction in the process. Since 1879, as director of Harvard's Hemenway Gymnasium, he had trained numerous teachers of physical education and devised an array of muscle "developers," equipment sold throughout the country.[25] He also took detailed body measurements of all Harvard and Radcliffe students. The distribution of variants among these measurements formed a bell-shaped, or normal, curve, which to Sargent, as to many would-be scientists in the nineteenth and twentieth centuries, seemed an empirical revelation of natural law. If the statistically "typical" man stood at the absolute mean, or center, of the bell curve, then, Sargent believed, the "ideal" man possessed equally symmetrical measurements while improving all, so that not only was each element strong and well developed in itself but together they plotted a straight line in their relation to the typical man. Anthropometry proved, according to Sargent, "[t]here is a perfect form or type of man, and the tendency of the race is to attain this type." Yet one price of civilization, he believed, had been the contravention of this law. The specialization of tasks in modern life,

as well as the use of conveniences, discouraged balanced exercise of the whole body and contributed to improper physical development and, with it, disease. Furthermore, because bodily health and moral vigor were interconnected, this imbalance and debility inevitably invited moral decline as well.[26]

Sargent was thus John the Baptist of fitness, preaching the gospel of physical education and longing for the coming of a messiah, a "perfect man" who would show forth the way to all. He had beheld this vision in classical "statues of the Gladiator, the Athlete, Hercules, Apollo, and Mercury," and as he composed his anthropometric charts on thousands of young men, he eagerly awaited the second coming.[27]

It was not Sullivan. Sargent examined the heavyweight champion twice during the summer of 1892, first on June 2, at the beginning of training for the match with Corbett, and again on August 13, a month before the fight. Like other physical educators of the period, Sargent believed that concentration on a single activity or sport created a physical imbalance and, with it, a potential moral distortion. He claimed that he not only could identify a gymnast or a baseball player by his distinctive muscular development but also could tell his particular event or position.[28] So Sargent's perfect man would have no mark of specific endeavor or work. Not surprisingly, he found that Sullivan had the body—and presumably the morals—of a slugger. (Although Sullivan was toasted for his lordly generosity at the bar, he was notorious for drunken rages and flagrant affairs.[29]) In fact, the dissipation of the Boston Strong Boy was starkly evident in the first examination. Standing five feet ten and a half inches, he weighed 236 pounds, 20 of which he managed to shed in the next two months. Nor did his bodily measurements present the model of symmetry that the physical educator so esteemed. (The measurements of Sandow, who was two inches shorter and at least twenty-six pounds lighter, are included in the table for comparison.)

Sullivan	June 2	August 13	(Sandow)
Neck:	17.1	16.5	(18.5)
Chest:	46.1	44.5	(52)
Waist:	42.1	38.2	(29)
Hips:	46.1	42.9	(—)
Thighs:	26.4	25	(26.67)
Knees:	—	17.5	(—)

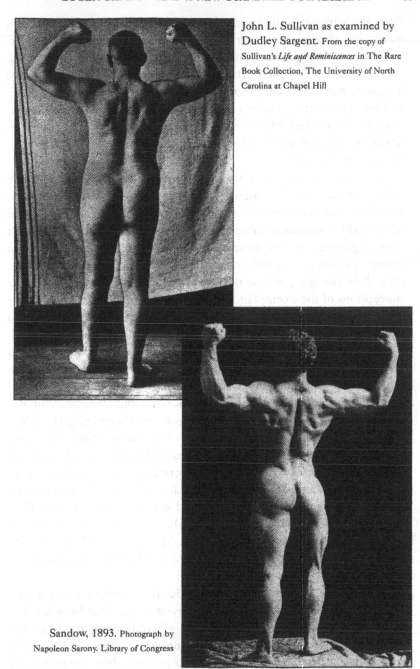

John L. Sullivan as examined by Dudley Sargent. From the copy of Sullivan's *Life and Reminiscences* in The Rare Book Collection, The University of North Carolina at Chapel Hill

Sandow, 1893. Photograph by Napoleon Sarony. Library of Congress

Even the trimmer Sullivan of the second examination had a girth in waist, hips, thighs, and knees that approached and in one instance exceeded any comparable measurements in Sargent's extensive tables. Sargent tried to put the best face on these figures. Euphemistically, he commended Sullivan's "large trunk" as "a reservoir of vital action" and his "powerful . . . thighs as a basis of support." Sullivan, he concluded, exemplified "the brawn and sinew that conquers both opponents and environments and sustains the race."[30] But he was certainly not the perfect man.

Most telling of all were the full-length photographs of the nude Sullivan at the second examination, showing him with arms at his side and with arms raised and muscles flexed, when he was supposedly in fighting trim. Sargent emphasized that they displayed the champion's "strong points," and Sullivan and his book publishers were proud enough of them to include them in his *Life and Reminiscences*. Still, they show the great divide that was just opening between different conceptions of the exemplary male body and how Sullivan was on the verge of losing not just his championship but also his centrality as a manly physical ideal.

No one could mistake Sullivan for a classical nude; he is merely a man undressed. He is massive and powerful but markedly lacks both the proportion and the articulation of musculature that Sandow would do so much to popularize. He has a thick waist, big buttocks, solid but undefined legs. His body is a blunt instrument, shaped to give and receive hard blows and difficult to topple. With some effort, a present-day reader may imagine why in his prime Sullivan could be called a Hercules. But it takes no effort to understand why he was never regarded as an Adonis or Apollo. With Sandow's New York debut ten months later, however, a figure emerged who was hailed as both Hercules *and* Apollo, even as Sargent's prophesied "perfect man." So it is also not hard to understand why, when asked by Joseph Pulitzer's *New York World* to conduct an examination of Sandow, Sargent jumped at the chance.

For Sandow, this examination was in an important sense a title bout, and he went to it eagerly. He arrived at the Broadway hotel in which Sargent had assembled an array of equipment, shed his cutaway coat and steel-gray suit, and presented himself to the physician. Sargent had already made clear his skepticism about mere muscle

size in discussing his examination of Sullivan: "We often read of seventeen inch biceps, and seventeen inch calves, but these proportions are more likely to be found on dime museum freaks than on well developed athletes."[31] Nonetheless, Sargent was immediately struck by Sandow's muscular development, especially in the upper arms and back. The first measurements—of height and weight—must have disappointed Sandow. He tipped the scales at only 180 pounds (10 pounds less than his reported weight) and measured five feet eight inches—a half inch shorter than he claimed. (Undaunted, Sandow would later maintain that he stood over five feet nine inches.[32]) But once past these preliminaries, Sandow excelled in the tests, including those measuring both his reaction time and his strength.

Even so, moving an indicator up a scale hardly satisfied Sandow's sense of drama, and he proposed tests of his own. Searching for the heaviest man in the room, he chose the 175-pound Sargent. The strongman knelt down behind the physician and had him step with one foot onto Sandow's open palm. Then with his arm straight, Sandow lifted the surprised Sargent up and placed him on a table. He performed other feats of strength with Sargent, including one that might have been billed "The Human Trampoline." Sandow lay on the floor and asked Sargent to stand on his abdomen. With the doctor in place, Sandow kept his abdominal muscles relaxed for a moment, then suddenly contracted them, popping Sargent into the air. Sandow concluded by making the muscles on his arms and legs dance as Sargent marveled at his control.

Sargent had at last found the figure whom he had so long sought. His enthusiastic judgment was a press agent's dream:

> Sandow is the most wonderful specimen of man I have ever seen. He is strong, active and graceful, combining the characteristics of Apollo, Hercules, and the ideal athlete. There is not the slightest evidence of sham about him. On the contrary, he is just what he pretends to be. His behavior under the tests was admirable. I might add that he combines with his other qualities that of a perfect gentleman. He has a considerable knowledge of anatomy, and can call the muscles by their proper names. I shall be glad to have him come and lecture before the students of Harvard.[33]

The "perfect man" was also the "perfect gentleman." With Sargent's examination all Sandow's claims had been authoritatively verified. Having defeated the lightweight Henry Dixey, he had now knocked out the heavyweight champion John L. Sullivan just as assuredly as had Corbett in the ring.[34]

Ultimately, however, the challenge posed by Sandow's body affected much more than perceptions of public figures such as Dixey and Sullivan. His supposed recovery of the classical ideal made men reevaluate their modern bodies in private and look in the mirror with new eyes. A reporter found Sandow "not only inspiring because of his enormous strength, but absolutely beautiful as a work of art as well. . . . One look at him is enough to make the average young man thoroughly disgusted with himself, and to make him give up his nightly habit of standing in front of the [looking] glass in his pajamas [the sense of the passage suggests without pajamas] and swelling his chest with pride." More immediately and intensely than any figure before him, Sandow aroused a desire among men to emulate another man's body, a desire that, depending on the individual, might be more or less mixed with an erotic impulse to possess it. As if to shake off this ambiguous desire, the reporter thrilled to imagine how that manly power might prove itself in a fight: "There is . . . no doubt that he could kill any man with a blow very easily. He could crush in the chest, break the neck, or fracture the skull of any man, and not use one-half his strength."[35] Sandow always emphasized his composure and restraint, even when others picked a fight, but he would not have disagreed with the reporter's assessment. Here was a figure who combined the qualities of Adonis and Hercules.

ASSAULTS ON MANHOOD

This image as Adonis and Hercules was one that Sandow and his managers carefully promoted, and it proved enduring. Yet it was never uncontested. Questions and controversy started to swirl around Sandow within weeks of his debut at the Casino. They began, perhaps surprisingly given the newspapers' stress on Sandow's great strength and potentially murderous capacities, with a violent assault on the vaunted strongman. Still more surprising, the assault came at the hands of a woman.

As Sandow left the Casino after his nightly performance on July 1, 1893, a woman in her thirties stepped from the crowd of admirers and demanded to speak to him. He tried to move past her, whereupon she struck him several times with a horsewhip, cutting his face. This was an act of contempt, an effort to reduce Sandow to the level of a beast. White with anger, Sandow raised his walking stick as if to retaliate. Three bystanders leaped forward and held him. The woman was immediately arrested and charged with assault and blackmail.

Almost as quickly as the bystanders leaped forward, the press seized on the incident. The assault on the "perfect man" fascinated them. It was already a familiar theme. The *National Police Gazette*, the most popular men's weekly of the era and a staple of barbershops, specialized in exuberantly illustrated stories of women attacking men, whether in a good cause or not. Accounts of women horsewhipping husbands, lovers, and slanderers frequently emblazoned its pages, together with stories of (preferably young, ideally scantily clad) women,

"Horsewhipped an Editor," in *National Police Gazette*, April 1, 1893. Library of Congress

ranging from "plucky" to "insane," who punched, bit, stabbed, slashed, bludgeoned, and shot men. Plainly, these accounts aroused male readers, who found such gender-crossing punishments both provocative and disturbing. Already in the 1890s, it was clear that some women were not content to rely on male protectors, either at the ballot box or in the bedroom, but would assert their own claims vigorously, even violently. Thus the female attack on the "strongest man in the world," the "perfect man," had crucial if unspoken sexual implications. If Sandow was a Hercules, who was this queen of the Amazons?

The day after the horsewhipping, an excited press identified Sandow's attacker as "Lurline, the Water Queen." A "vigorous woman" who "looks as if she could wield a cowhide with considerable effect," she had been born in Boston "as plain Miss Sarah E. Swift." Lurline, as the press insisted on calling her, had acquired her sobriquet as an aquatics performer in a revealing costume, and her association with Sandow dated back to his beginnings as a strongman under the tutelage of Attila in Belgium. He was, in her account, a lowly servant in a circus and occasional artists' model when she advanced the money for lessons and clothes to transform him into a strongman and gentleman. Besides bankrolling his success, Lurline maintained, she had given him crucial assistance when he triumphed over Sampson in London: as Sandow passed around the chains and coins that he proposed to break in his competition, she deftly switched them with others made to snap easily. She had now come forth to remind Sandow—and, because he had turned a deaf ear, the public—of his debt. Not only did she cast him as a charlatan in his feats against Sampson, but also Lurline and her lawyers appeared eager to bring forth details from Sandow's past, including his family history, that would undermine his claims to respectability. Their insinuation that Sandow had no money, no clothes, and nothing to eat when he came to Lurline for aid made him hardly better than a beggar, perhaps even a kept man.[36]

Feeding the controversy, Lurline brought Sandow's former mentor, Attila, to New York. Whether Lurline intended to blackmail Sandow, as seems probable, or to humiliate him and so be revenged, it was hardly in his interest to keep the story alive and in the papers. The two settled matters privately, and the blackmail charge was dropped.

If Lurline represented an obvious threat to male power and dominance, others were more insidious. The genital power that men were encouraged to see as the core of their identity could, it was believed, be easily sapped by the temptations and strains of modern life: from overwork to overindulgence, from solitary masturbation to the perils of the brothel, including the venereal diseases that afflicted more than one man in ten. Sandow's splendidly self-made physique must be understood in relation to the anxieties of men who often felt unmade and unworthy. The pages of the *National Police Gazette* that carried stories of vengeful women and strongmen such as Sandow bulged with advertisements addressed to "WEAK MEN" that offered cures for various symptoms of impotence, or "lost manhood," and other afflictions, ranging from the supposed effects of "self-abuse" to syphilis. These home remedies, in the golden age of patent medicine, were purportedly devised by fellow sufferers and extended in a philanthropic spirit:

FREE CURE I was Quickly and Permanently CURED of Nightly Emissions, Complete Impotency, Varicocele and Small, Wasted and Shrunken Organs caused by Self-Abuse. Thousands have been fully restored through me. I will mail the means of this UNFAILING SELF-CURE (sealed) FREE . . .

CERTAIN PARTS Of Body Enlarged. Beware of Bogus Free Cures. Send for the common sense method. Surest and safest developing tonic known! Cures all weak men. Increases Sexual Power. Sealed information Free . . .

WEAK MEN suffering from Lost Manhood. Youthful Errors, Spermatorhoea, Gonorrhea, Gleet, Syphilis, and all Private Diseases, should read my 64 p. Book and learn how to cure themselves quietly at home . . .

ELECTRICITY FOR WEAK MEN Only cure for lost manhood, emissions, debility, weakness of man or woman, varicocele. I will send you Dr. Judd's Electric Belt and Battery combined . . .[37]

Whereas some men were anxious about their ability to perform sexually, others worried about the loss of sexual power that intercourse itself might entail. In a diary entry of 1898 a young Virginian, Stephen D. Boyd, expressed conventional medical wisdom when he steeled himself against the temptation of sex with a young woman: "There would be a great drain of nerve force and much useful time and energy would be more than wasted. . . . It is only a momentary physical pleasure, and where indulged in with high nervous excitement causes certain sclerotic changes in the spinal cord and exhaustion of the brain and injury to the medulla."[38]

Such advertisements and reflections suggest some of the deeper fears about manly power and virility, and the keen sense of shame that attended them, to which Sandow's body so eloquently spoke. The average young man's "nightly habit of standing in front of the glass" might not involve "swelling his chest with pride" so much as an anxious self-appraisal. And Sandow's body both highlighted other men's inadequacies and, together with the photographs, exercises, books, and muscle developers he sold, offered another self-help restorative for lost manhood.

LOOKING AND TOUCHING

After his successful New York run, Sandow performed at Boston's Tremont Theatre in July, where he followed a light opera in a program that *The Boston Daily Globe* called "Mirth and Muscle." In a city concerned about artistic and moral propriety, Sandow achieved a noteworthy triumph. One reporter wrote, "It was very agreeable to observe the delighted enthusiasm with which ladies and gentlemen of the highest culture and refinement witnessed an exhibition of animal strength which had not the remotest suggestion of vulgarity."[39] Yet he was still not the stupendous attraction he was to be a month later in Chicago.

The lavish world's fair, the Columbian Exposition, which had opened on May 1 and was ultimately to attract 21.5 million admissions, was then at its height at Jackson Park, six miles from downtown Chicago. Its exhibits created a special context for anyone purporting to be a "perfect man." At the fair various human "types" were on dis-

play in both formal and commercial settings. The colossal sideshow that formed the Midway presented peoples and cultures from around the globe with the intention of suggesting a hierarchy beginning with the most westernized nations and stretching on to the least "civilized," such as the Dahomey Village. Then, in the Anthropology Building at the fair proper, visitors could survey an even greater range of types from prehistoric times to the present, beginning with North American native peoples. Fair goers might then consider "typical" modern American men and women in relation to these, as exemplified by "anthropometric statues" based on Dudley Sargent's measurements and photographs of thousands of Harvard and Radcliffe freshmen. Many visitors paid a small fee to have their bodies measured and compared with the standards Sargent had devised. In this way, fair goers might consider exotic bodies, typical bodies, and their own bodies during a single visit.

But where stood a model of white male perfection? Not in the "White City" of the fair or along the Midway. Yet such a marvel

Sandow supporting the Trocadero Vaudevilles. Florenz Ziegfeld sits directly above him. Wisconsin Center for Film and Theater Research

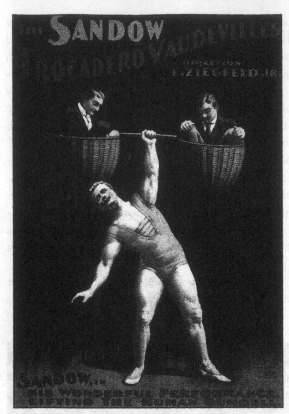

Sandow lifting the "Human Dumbell," c. 1894. Library of Congress

awaited the fair goer willing to travel to downtown Chicago: "The perfection of physical manhood," "the strongest man on earth!" "the sensation of the century," "the modern Hercules." On August 1, Sandow began a three-month run at the Trocadero Theatre, as well as an immensely profitable three-year partnership with the impresario who so trumpeted his abilities. The Trocadero owner's twenty-six-year-old son, Florenz Ziegfeld, Jr., would make the stylish display of bodily perfection a specialty, although he would soon concentrate on female beauty. Sandow was the springboard for his extraordinary career as a theatrical producer, which lasted four decades until his death in 1932.

Billed as "America's only refined European theatre," the Trocadero offered a range of tickets (fifty cents for general admission; seventy-five cents and one dollar for reserved seats) and a diverse

program of exotic attractions: songs, dances, specialty acts (later including "Scott, the calculating collie"), and bands. But it quickly became apparent that to lure tourists from the fairgrounds to Michigan Avenue, near the Art Institute, the theater needed a headliner. The young Ziegfeld had taken notice of the strongman's success in New York and, in a bold gamble, engaged him to play at the Trocadero for the last three months of the fair.

Sandow's performance as the tenth act on the bill served as the grand finale of the evening's entertainment. Keeping alive the drama of challenge that had distinguished the strongman's career from the outset, Ziegfeld offered ten thousand dollars "to any athlete duplicating his performance."[40] Ziegfeld spent lavishly on advertising. He cultivated publicity both in high society and in the press, emphasizing Sandow's dashing figure and erotic appeal, and he added greater showmanship to Sandow's feats of strength. When his musical accompanist came onstage with his piano, Sandow effortlessly lifted the man with one hand and then lifted the piano. The snug silk shorts he wore in the opening portion of his act may have been more modest than those he had favored in New York or Europe, but his body and his feats so captivated spectators that they sometimes forgot to applaud. Ziegfeld also arranged private receptions for specially invited guests, including, in addition to all the reporters he could muster, scientists and physicians qualified to authenticate Sandow's muscular development, athletes prepared to admire his feats, artists and sculptors educated to appreciate the classical beauty of his body, and Chicago's leading socialites to ogle and swoon over it. Among these last were Harriet S. Pullman, wife of the sleeping-car manufacturer and civic leader George Pullman, and Bertha Honoré Palmer, wife of the merchant and real-estate magnate Potter Palmer and herself a leading force behind the Columbian Exposition.

Sandow eagerly invited their inspection. Even more than in New York or Boston, spectators remarked on his extraordinary combination of strength and beauty. The drama critic for the *Chicago Daily News*, Amy Leslie, meticulously inventoried his "blue eyes and wealth of golden, close-cut curls," "pink and white" skin, "red lips," "even, shiny, and white" teeth, and "soft" face "lighted by a smile that is just short of girlish." "Mr. Sandow," she concluded, "is a dangerously handsome young man." Others marveled over Sandow's fair com-

plexion, too. One Chicago spectator remembered his skin as "velvety and most extraordinary," "a transparent white without blemish."[41] Sandow heightened the effect by shaving his body hair to display his musculature (as have bodybuilders ever since).

Sandow's skin was an emblem in two respects. Its whiteness testified to his status as a gentleman whose body had not been exposed to the sun. Still more important, it was a sign of racial purity. Sandow represented not simply a male physical ideal but a *white* European male ideal. Appropriately for one whose career was inspired by classical European statues, he was selected in 1901 as the model for a statue of the "perfect type of a European man," and his body arduously cast. One statue thus cast was enshrined in the British Museum, and a duplicate was exhibited in the lobby of B. F. Keith's vaudeville theater in Boston, then presented by Sandow to Dudley Sargent on behalf of Harvard University.[42] In later travels in India and elsewhere, Sandow extolled the virtues of physical culture to people of color. Yet a clear sense of racial hierarchy remained. In accounts of his first American tour, he cheerfully related how he punished an impudent "nigger" bellhop by dangling him over a stairwell sixteen stories high.[43] Sandow's anecdote was in keeping with a period of blatant racism. (The Supreme Court decision enshrining segregation in *Plessy v. Ferguson* was only three years away.) Beginning in Chicago, with the ethnographic displays as a sort of backdrop, he became, in an important sense, the great white hope, a figure whose ideal physique confirmed the place of white European men on the top of the racial hierarchy.

Sandow appealed not just to the eye but also to the touch. He would strip to his tights to display his muscular development and control, make gnarls of muscle bulge and disappear at will over his body, and, at his receptions, urge spectators to feel the size and hardness of his muscles for themselves. The result was a curious mixture of intimacy and distance. Earlier, in New York, a male journalist had described such an experience: "He took my hand while I was in his dressing room and rubbed it across his abdominal muscles, and the feeling was just about the same as it would be rubbing the hand over an old fashioned washboard."[44] With women, the encounter was much more charged. Ostensibly an invitation to verify his muscular development, it carried obvious if unspoken erotic elements. In

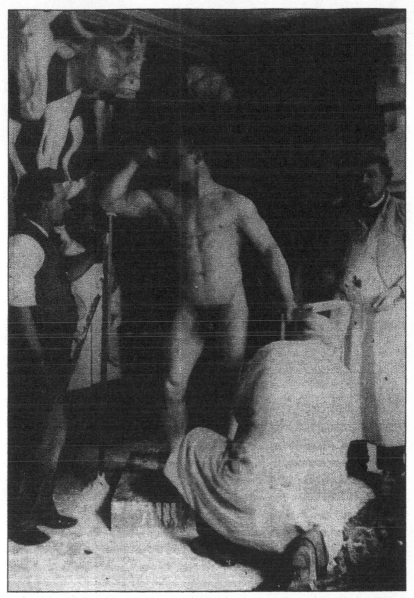

Sandow posing for the cast of a statue of European man, 1901. Image Library, The National Archives, Public Record Office, U.K.

"The Ladies Idolize Sandow,"
in *National Police Gazette*,
January 27, 1894. Library of
Congress

THE LADIES IDOLIZE SANDOW,
THE STRONG MAN EXHIBITS HIS FORM AT SELECT RECEPTIONS TO THE PRETTY CREATURES.

Chicago, Amy Leslie reported how Sandow "walked over to me and threw out a stack of corded muscles under the white, smooth skin of his chest in a sort of mechanical way that rather stunned me." When she did not immediately feel his chest, Sandow took her gloved hand and "said amiably, 'hit me hard; you will not hurt me.' " Mrs. Potter Palmer was less shy. Reportedly, she stroked Sandow's massive chest and declared she was "thrilled to the spine."[45]

These receptions became an established part of Sandow's appearances on his early American tours and fortified his image as an irresistible ladies' man.[46] The *National Police Gazette* portrayed one such event with all its erotic titillation, more powerful because never overtly declared, in an article the following year. The writer emphasized Sandow's dominance and his female admirers' timidity as the strongman bade each to touch his body. "I want you to feel how hard these muscles are," he urged them. "As I stop before you, I want each

of you to pass the palm of your hand across my chest." The first woman he approached drew back timidly. "Oh, please," she remonstrated. "Never mind." "Ah, but you must," Sandow replied. "These muscles, madam, are hard as iron itself, I want you to convince yourself of the fact." The reporter described Sandow tenderly taking the woman's gloved hand in his own and passing it slowly over his muscle. "It's unbelievable!" she gasped, staggering backward, and an attendant rushed to her aid with smelling salts. It is as if the phallic power of Sandow's body toppled her with a touch.

The drawing that accompanied this article, in all likelihood a product of the illustrator's imagination rather than direct observation, set forth its own fantasy of phallic power and female response. Its fashionable young women are far from timid. They surround the shirtless strongman and vie for the pleasure of feeling his muscles and appraising his body. Conceivably, the seated woman on the left represents the overcome figure described in the article, but she may have taken a chair to gain a better view of the strongman's massive chest. Here is a scene recalling the pursuit of Dixey's character in *Adonis*, the only instance we have seen thus far where the erotic appeal of the male body was openly (if comically) recognized. In this illustration Sandow performs a double legitimation: of the unclad muscular male as an object of desire and of women as active admirers.[47]

A more searching and provocative study of these receptions appeared in a drawing and unsigned article in *Frank Leslie's Illustrated Weekly*. The fact that the artist clearly based his drawing of Sandow on an earlier studio photograph where the pose is identical, then elaborated it as the text and his fancy dictated, undermines its status as reportage but makes it all the more revealing of responses to Sandow's body. Here Sandow stands at the center foreground, dumbbells on the floor behind him. He wears Roman sandals as a token of classicism—and almost nothing else. So lightly drawn are his shorts that they seem to fit like a second skin. In contrast to his virtual nudity, the spectators are all in evening dress. The picture thus shows a confrontation between two kinds of power: social and financial power, signaled by the viewers' clothes; and physical power, signaled by Sandow's naked muscularity, which commands the attention of men and women alike.

People cluster around him, approaching with a frank curiosity and

admiration as if he were a classical statue or scientific specimen—two models of viewership to which he appealed. A half century earlier even exhibitions of nude sculpture, such as Hiram Powers's acclaimed *Greek Slave*, often included special showings for women, so that they would not have to view undraped works in mixed company. Male nudity in art was more easily accommodated, but the issue of the exposed male body in daily life remained highly charged. Although men frequently swam naked among themselves, for example, they would wear tank tops for mixed bathing at least into the 1920s; and as late as 1934 men were arrested, fined, and rebuked for appearing topless on a Coney Island beach.[48] Yet here, before a live seminude subject, women and men peer eagerly. To the extreme right, a woman holds a lorgnette to her eyes. A second feels Sandow's bare forearm with her gloved hand. Sandow himself returns her gaze as he offers himself for her inspection. Both his fists are clenched, his arm muscles hard. To the left, a bespectacled older man leans forward, intently examining his body. No one speaks.

This is a study of male exhibition—perhaps tinged with exhibitionism. The scene crackles with tension between the genteel disavowal of erotic interest in the male body and the obvious (if unspecified) gratifications of gazing on and touching this essentially nude man. The success of the event depends on the preservation of its ambiguities. The woman feeling Sandow's bulging arm and marveling at its hardness, the spectators appraising his body—all seem to participate in a connoisseurship that, to be sustained, cannot permit the nature of its interest to be clearly defined. An essential attribute of the ideal nude was its impersonality; that is what saved it from mere nakedness. But is it here a work of art (or subject of science) that these spectators consider or a specific individual in a state of undress?[49]

On another level, the scene becomes a study in a different set of ambiguities between the natural and the artificial, between physical development and social decadence. Although Sandow presented himself as reclaiming from the degeneration and torpor of modern life a classical masculine ideal in heroic action, the text accompanying the illustration sounded a dissenting note. Both aesthetically and morally, the author recoiled from the spectacle of Sandow's body and of its admirers. Instead, the writer interpreted Sandow as an instance of "ab-

Sandow, 1893. Photograph by Napoleon Sarony. Library of Congress

"The Latest Society Fad," drawing by B. West Clinedinst, in *Frank Leslie's Illustrated Weekly*, March 29, 1894. The University of North Carolina at Chapel Hill

normal development" and his success as part of a modern hunger "for the *outré*." Sandow's body struck him as not beautiful but grotesque, reminding him "of some great, massive, gnarled oak, petrified and as relentless as stone." When he thought of ancient Rome, he remembered its decadence: "when the nobles of both sexes visited the gladiators in their quarters and admiringly examined their brawn and sinews" before they placed their bets.[50]

Thus article and illustration left the relationship between Sandow and his admirers ambiguous. Were they "fans" courting him "at his private levee," as the headline implied? If so, it might attest to how male physical development was superior to all social hierarchies. Or were those hierarchies still intact, and was Sandow the spectators' pet, their plaything, ultimately their victim, as were the ancient gladiators? And if he was a gladiator, what contest was at issue? Sandow versus contenders for the title "perfect man"? Virility, embodied by Sandow, versus the debilitating tendencies of modern life, epitomized by his admirers? Sandow as the male representative in the war between the sexes? Sandow as the great white hope? Sandow was extraordinary in his ability to stand center stage simultaneously in these multiple arenas.[51]

By means of these illustrations and texts, the circles of men and women who looked at and, in imagination at least, felt Sandow's body widened to tens of thousands of readers and were extended still further by drawings of his body that accompanied newspaper articles and advertisements describing his exploits. In intimate detail, his body became better known to more people than that of any previous man in history, apart from those depicted in religious art. Important as the illustrator was in this process, the crucial role was played by the commercial photographer.

From its inception in 1839, photography stimulated and satisfied demand for intimate knowledge of the body, and beginning in the late 1850s, souvenir photographs became a major industry throughout North America and Europe. Would-be celebrities of all sorts—stage performers, writers, and politicians—came to depend on the work of studio photographers. For Sandow and for the nascent bodybuilding business, the photographer was essential. The camera captured moments from Sandow's onstage performances, of course, just as it recorded conventional actors in their roles; but it also permitted him

Sandow showing how he won the title "strongest man on earth," 1889. Photograph by London Stereoscopic Company. Harvard Theatre Collection

Sandow in leotard, flexing his
right arm. Photograph by Napoleon
Sarony. Library of Congress

Sandow seated, wearing a fig leaf.
Photograph by Napoleon Sarony. Library
of Congress

to display far more of his body than even his scanty stage costume would permit—and it allowed each viewer to examine it singly and anonymously, to view Sandow not in public but in private.

From the moment of his 1889 triumph over Sampson, Sandow posed often for leading theatrical studio photographers. That same year, equipped with assorted weights, he made one series of photographs for the London Stereoscopic Company and another in classical poses, wearing only a fig leaf, for the London photographer Henry Van der Weyde. During his first American tours, he made still more, including a series for the foremost theatrical photographer in the country, Napoleon Sarony, and for one of his leading competitors, Benjamin J. Falk, both of New York, as well as for the Los Angeles photographer George Steckel.

Sandow carefully distanced himself from circus performers and human oddities, the subjects of popular photographs, and made pic-

Sandow in a leopard-skin leotard.
Photograph by Benjamin J. Falk. Library of Congress

tures that showed he wanted to be ranked with leading actors and even works of art. He offered himself in a number of roles—as classical ideal, polished gentleman, and thoroughly modern athlete—and assumed various guises: he posed in tights (adorned with a medal), in leopard skins (secured by a belt), in evening dress (sporting a boutonniere), and in the nude (shielded only by a fig leaf). He flexed an array of muscles, lifted weights, demonstrated exercises, and dreamily stared into space; he reclined against Roman columns, and he rode a bicycle. In classical poses that still figure prominently in bodybuilding, he struck a range of attitudes from the triumphantly erect (the Farnese Hercules) to the submissively prostrate (the Dying Gaul).[52] He held his emotions within relatively narrow limits: pensive rather

Sandow seated, wearing a leotard and medals.
Photograph by Napoleon Sarony.
Library of Congress

Sandow as the Farnese Hercules. Photograph by Napoleon Sarony. Harvard Theatre Collection

Sandow exercising with dumbbells. Photograph by Napoleon Sarony. Theatre Arts Collection, Harry Ransom Humanities Research Center, The University of Texas at Austin

Sandow performing a provocative push-up. Photograph by Napoleon Sarony. Theatre Arts Collection, Harry Ransom Humanities Research Center, The University of Texas at Austin

Sandow as the Dying Gaul. Photograph by Benjamin J. Falk. Library of Congress

than weary as the Farnese Hercules, elegiac rather than tortured as the Dying Gaul. Just as photographic reproductions of classical sculpture were helping to disseminate ancient conceptions of the ideal body, photographs of modern muscled men in classical poses offered compelling, apparently objective proof that these ideals could indeed be achieved. In the photographer's studio, makeup and lighting enhanced muscle definition and created a monumental physical presence. Careful retouching and printing in the darkroom did the rest. The smooth, monochromic print completed the process of abstraction and idealization and placed the contemporary body on a plane with classical sculpture. Multiple perspectives on Sandow's body furthered the parallel, giving the viewer the impression of appraising a statue from various angles.[53]

These images were sold at theaters, hotels, and photographers' studios and by mail in various sizes, including the popular cabinet format on stiff cardboard (roughly four by six inches when mounted) for perhaps $.35 and the larger panel size (roughly seven by thirteen inches) for $1.50.[54] And as the basis for newspaper and magazine illustrations, they were widely circulated and took Sandow from the theatrical spotlight into the hands and imaginations of countless thousands of individual owners, who could amass their own collections.

These images of muscular display were (one suspects intentionally) left open to the widest range of constructions and responses, allowing viewers to make of them what they pleased. They attracted women, inviting thousands to participate in intimate encounters with Sandow and to gaze on his body with all its thrilling force and eroticism. A Frenchman visiting the summer resort of Newport, Rhode Island, was startled to discover Sandow's nude portrait displayed in fashionable ladies' sitting rooms. But in all likelihood, these photographs fascinated men even more, with an exhibition of muscularity that sustained many fantasies about physical prowess, virility, strength, and eroticism across a broad spectrum of sexual orientation. All the while Sandow managed to skirt censorship, even though its sentries were especially vigilant. In 1883 Anthony Comstock, the organizer and secretary of the New York Society for the Suppression of Vice, had listed photographs of classical nudes among the many immoral "traps" for the unwary. In a similar spirit, in 1910 a judge upheld the Sandow-inspired health reformer Bernarr Macfadden's

conviction for sending obscene materials through the mails, basing his ruling in good part on a magazine cover showing the Venus de Milo, the Discus Thrower, and the Flying Mercury.[55] By avoiding any declared erotic intent and by cultivating an urbane dignity, Sandow became the first great male pinup in modern history.

MODERN GLADIATORS

Among all Sandow's poses, the gladiator deserves special remark. The role of the gladiator, in which Sandow frequently cast himself and was cast by others, underwent a revival in the late nineteenth century. To be sure, the gladiator had been a complex and controversial figure even in ancient Rome, and (as the piece on Sandow in *Frank Leslie's Illustrated Weekly* has already shown) in the late nineteenth century he could easily be associated with the brutality and decadence that led to the ancient empire's decline and fall. Yet the gladiator remained a compelling positive figure as well, which legitimated and popularized the unclad muscular male body in situations of violent and often primitive combat. (Gladiator movies did the same for the bodybuilder Steve Reeves in the 1950s and 1960s, making him the first bodybuilder since Sandow to become an international celebrity.[56])

This positive image was congenial to a growing celebration of America's historic encounter with the primitive. In July 1893, less than three weeks before Sandow's Chicago debut, the young historian Frederick Jackson Turner delivered his famous address in that city, "The Significance of the Frontier in American History." For Turner, the frontier, the "meeting point between savagery and civilization," was the historic site not only of American individualism and democracy but also (though he did not make this claim explicit) of American manhood:

> The wilderness masters the colonist. It finds him a European in dress, industries, tools, modes of travel, and thought. It takes him from the railroad car and puts him in the birch canoe. It strips off the garments to civilization and arrays him in the hunting shirt and the moccasin. . . . Before long he has gone to planting Indian corn and plowing with a sharp stick; he shouts

the war cry and takes the scalp in orthodox Indian fashion. . . .
Little by little he transforms the wilderness, but the outcome is
not the old Europe. . . . The fact is, that here is a new product
that is American.[57]

So when Turner added that the frontier had, as of the 1890 census,
vanished, and with its passing an era in American history had closed,
a fair inference was that an era of American manhood was passing as
well.

The frontier might be gone, but Americans might still savor the
spectacle of gladiatorial combat in other realms of history and contemporary life through art. The French artist Jean-Léon Gérôme explored both its heroic and its brutal dimensions in a number of
paintings and sculptures of warriors and martyrs in the Roman Colosseum. Some of the most famous of these, including *Pollice Verso*, popularly known as "Thumbs Down" (1872), were quickly purchased,
even commissioned, by American collectors; and they became still
more widely known and admired through reproductions.[58] In addition, several of Gérôme's American students at the École des Beaux-
Arts carried this interest back to the United States. Preeminent
among these was the great Philadelphia artist Thomas Eakins, who
found modern analogies to the gladiatorial arena in the surgical clinic
(*The Gross Clinic*, *The Agnew Clinic*) and the boxing ring (*Between
Rounds*, *Taking the Count*, *Salutat*). Such works evinced the hunger for
a modern heroic warrior who, contending in the arena and commanding the eyes of the multitude, could achieve a splendor and purity
akin to the combatants of old.[59]

As promoters of modern boxing and wrestling did their best to
reach larger audiences in the late nineteenth century and to distance
themselves from their rowdy working-class antecedents, figures involved in both sports cultivated the gladiatorial analogy. Contestants
were often referred to as gladiators and given the names of ancient
warriors by the press. Among the many nicknames bestowed on John
L. Sullivan, for example, was "Spartacus Sullivan," and his 1892 autobiography was grandly titled *Life and Reminiscences of a 19th Century
Gladiator*.[60] Similarly, the New York policeman turned Greco-Roman
wrestling champion William Muldoon adopted the studded breechcloth and high-laced sandals of the Roman gladiator for his matches

William Muldoon as the Fighting
Gaul. Photograph by Benjamin J. Falk.
Library of Congress

and added still more gladiatorial props for publicity photographs.
Like Sandow, he found in Roman models of strength, muscular development, and courage a fit manly context for displaying his body.

Sandow disdained many of these competitors for the gladiatorial
ideal, particularly professional boxers. "A man cannot fight a prize
fight," he sniffed, "and be a gentleman." At the same time, he told
stories to show that although he was slow to anger or respond to
provocation, if forced he could teach any bully a lesson he would
never forget. Even as Sandow modestly denied he was a perfect man,
he added, "If any man thinks he is stronger than I—well, then, I
should try to be nearer perfection than he when we meet."[61]

Indeed, much as Sandow endeavored to stand alone as a resurrection of the ancient gladiatorial ideal, he attracted both challengers and
counterfeits. The first impostor claiming to be Sandow reportedly
preceded the strongman to America, though his feats were decidedly
inferior. In Chicago, as Sandow appeared at the Trocadero, another
strongman, Sebastian Miller, twisted horseshoes at the nearby Grotto

Theatre but aroused scant interest. The Grotto then booked Sandow's former rival Charles Sampson, who persisted in claiming the title the "strongest man on earth." Sampson specialized in breaking chains and bending coins, but he challenged Sandow to a competition involving any feats of strength, adding accusingly, "providing trickery is not employed."[62] Sandow ignored these taunts, and Sampson quickly sank back into obscurity.

When Sandow arrived with Ziegfeld's Trocadero company in San Francisco in the spring of the following year, 1894, he discovered another impostor appearing under the name Sandowe already performing at the Orpheum Theatre. Imitating Sandow's latest feat, the pretender balanced a grand piano and four musicians on his upraised shoulders, chest, and knees. More galling still, he affected the appearance of the Prussian strongman right down to the cut and curls of his hair. Ziegfeld obtained a court injunction, forbidding Sandowe (alias Irving Montgomery, a Birmingham, England, strongman) to appear in the area under his assumed name. When Montgomery violated the injunction, the matter went to court. As in the earlier contretemps with Lurline, the Water Queen, the case hugely amused the press but did

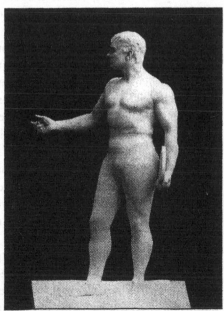

A Sandow Impostor: Irving
Montgomery as a Discobolus.
Harvard Theatre Collection

Sandow little good, even though he was vindicated. Inevitably, it identified him as a man of the theater rather than a self-made titan of strength and beauty, and his feats appeared more as stage tricks than as heroic accomplishments.

More profoundly, Sandow's great appeal lay in his claim to being an original, a man who stood apart from the crowd. Although his achievement may have been based on his imitation of classical models, he seemed to have attained his ideals to an unparalleled degree. All his accolades—the "strongest man," the "perfect man"—rested on that foundation. Of course, Sandow encouraged emulation and purported to share his methods. (He advocated the use of five-pound weights, but this would not have achieved his muscular bulk.) Nonetheless, followers were meant to understand there could be only one Sandow. And the extent to which his body and his feats might be successfully duplicated, even counterfeited, destroyed his mystique. From the lost world of manly strength and heroism, he sank into the modern world, where there were no longer originals, only copies.

Perhaps in part goaded by the controversy with Montgomery, at the end of his San Francisco appearance in May 1894, Sandow promised to pursue the gladiatorial ideal in an audacious spectacle: he would wrestle a lion with his bare hands. The proposition recalled not only the one-sided contests between lions and Christians in the Roman Colosseum but also the first labor of Hercules, in which he slays the Nemean lion (to which Sandow often alluded in his poses). Under Ziegfeld's management, the event was ballyhooed as "the sensation of the century," and Sandow expertly stoked the fires of prefight publicity. "The lion is a coward" before a man, Sandow sneered. He claimed to have earlier killed two wild lions in hand-to-paw combat for the pleasure of the Turkish sultan.[63] But the San Francisco event was to be a wrestling match rather than a duel to the death. In consideration of Sandow, Commodore, representing the king of beasts, was to be muzzled and his claws covered with leather mittens. In consideration of the lion, the "perfect man" was to carry no weapons and had agreed to a bar on strangleholds.

On the night of the contest, the press reported, three thousand spectators, including "prominent citizens" and "ladies of wealth and fashion . . . burning up with eagerness to see Sandow, the modern Sampson, twist the daylights out of the four footed athlete," gathered

in a large tent in Golden Gate Park. But from the start, something was clearly wrong, and "the sensation of the century" quickly turned into a ludicrous farce. Only after attendants poked and prodded the lion did the "aged," "worn and weary," "moth-eaten" creature limp out of his box. "As soon as Commodore found himself in the arena he lost heart and fell down." The intrepid Sandow, clad in pink tights, strode boldly forward and eyed his opponent. For his part, "Commodore . . . tried to bury his face in the sawdust." The reporter for the *San Francisco Chronicle* gave a blow-by-blow account of how Sandow tugged Commodore's ear, shook him by the mane, pulled his whiskers, slung him by the tail, raised him by the neck, and generally rolled him to and fro in an effort to arouse some response. But the lion was either too old, too sedated, or too abused, possibly all three, to offer resistance. Shouts of "fake" and hisses erupted from the crowd. To pose as gladiator required a ferocious antagonist, a worthy natural opponent by which to measure the qualities of civilized man. Now the heroic ideal fizzled. Perhaps lions had degenerated even faster than human beings! When officials at last intervened and Sandow was congratulated "for his gallantry in entering this den of wild beasts," the crowd laughed derisively. Sandow departed with his winnings as fast as he could and never "fought" a lion again.[64]

Despite this debacle, Sandow's position as a celebrity was secure. Changing his act little, he continued to tour extensively in the United States until 1906, when he was nearly forty. In 1894 he recorded some of his vaudeville feats on brief filmstrips for Thomas Edison's kinetoscope. Two years later, he made two similar projected film shorts for W. K. L. Dickson, an erstwhile Edison assistant, at the Biograph Company. Both films concluded with his astonishing back flip. Nonetheless, they lacked the immediacy of his live performances and the intimacy of his still photographs.

In ensuing years he endeavored to build on his success as a performer in both England and the United States by encouraging men and women to embrace physical fitness through his sponsored gymnasiums, special equipment (for example, "Sandow's Patent Spring Grip Dumb Bells"), magazines, and mail-order course. A 1903 advertisement for the last, issued in conjunction with the opening of his College of Physical Culture in Boston, broadened his targeted audience to anyone seeking relief from such ailments of modern life as "consti-

Sandow in an Edison kinetoscope, 1894. Library of Congress

pation, indigestion, or disordered nerves." He also revisited Dudley Sargent, who reiterated his abiding conviction that Sandow was "the most perfectly developed man the world has ever seen."[65]

In 1906 Sandow formally became a British subject and thereafter concentrated on affairs in England. Although he was appointed "Professor of Scientific and Physical Culture" to King George V in 1911, the honor did not altogether shield him from anti-German sentiment during the Great War. In response, the old master of self-invention claimed his mother's Russian heritage rather than his father's Prussian stock. He also pressed physical fitness into the war effort, seconding Prime Minister David Lloyd George's concern about the "lost army of the rejected," the dismaying number of men who failed the army's physical examination. Indeed, in his zeal he contended that by following his methods, society could virtually eradicate disease.[66] When Sandow died in 1925 at the age of fifty-eight, newspapers attributed his death to an injury sustained in a final feat of strength. Sometime earlier, after a road accident, he had, single-handed, lifted a car out of a ditch. The strain reportedly resulted in a burst blood vessel in his brain. Obituaries sealed his legend: the "weakling" who became the "world's most perfect man," the extraordinary individual who had devised a program of training whereby "the average man" could also "become strong and vigorous."[67]

Sandow's success was filled with ironies that illuminate the passage from Victorian to modern culture. He helped many Americans (as well as countless others, especially in the English-speaking world) to negotiate this transition, not by clearly delineating what was at stake but by keeping ambiguities suspended. In the name of ancient ideals, he adroitly tapped antimodernist sentiments and fears of an emasculating civilization. Yet ultimately he raised a new, potentially more punishing "scientific" standard against which to measure one's inadequacy. The concept of a perfect body, ostensibly devised in opposition to modern industrial society, in fact capitulated to the presumption that perfection lay in materially defined, standardized, and repeatable processes and products. He helped to displace the Victorian conception of the body as a moral reservoir and instrument of productive labor with a modern conception of the body as an ex-

pression of individual desire and site of pleasure. In place of pride in manly bearing and competence in the workplace, he exemplified a compensatory "working out," a concentration on manly strength and beauty off the job. At a time when the nascent field of "scientific management" was pressing for workers as specialized in their bodies as the work they performed, Sandow offered a vision of the reintegrated male body—yet one that might easily become a product in its own right. Elevating his background and presenting himself as a gentleman, he fortified the ideal of manly dominance based on the body, but in the process he surrendered the assertions of working-class power that had frequently accompanied this ideal. On the music-hall and the vaudeville stage, he adapted older traditions of manly physical challenge to promote a new mass culture of entertainment. And as he made the exposed male body a compelling spectacle in live performance, he also drew on classical art traditions to pioneer its dissemination in still and moving pictures. Lastly, Sandow revealed how the erotics of the male body could be broadly exposed precisely because it was never explicitly mentioned. Studious concentration on antique sculpture and muscular development provided the crucial fig leaf.

Ultimately, Sandow's success as a performer of masculinity suggested the changing status of gender in the modern world. His physique was widely interpreted not simply as an individual achievement but as a reaffirmation of male identity at a time when it seemed to be losing authority and coherence. By stressing the potential for strength, control, heroism, and virility in the male physique, he reassured a broad public of the continuation of these qualities—and their potential for further development—in the modern world. Yet for many who scrutinized Sandow's body and its meaning, nature and artifice were hard to separate. A triumph of man's natural potential to some eyes, his body appeared the epitome of the artificial to others. If his manliness was a performance that impostors could counterfeit, what were the deeper implications for gender imposture? Even as Sandow claimed to return to ancient ideals of male strength as the core of male identity, the possibilities of gender as a repertoire of assumed roles and cultivated performances rushed in.

THE MANLY ART OF ESCAPE

THE METAMORPHOSES

OF EHRICH WEISS

The period from the 1890s to the mid-1920s was not only the golden age of vaudeville, in which Sandow excelled, but also the end of the golden age of stage magic that flourished in vaudeville's format and settings: live performances of specialized acts before a diverse public. Just as we might ask why the exhibition of masculine strength and physical perfection became so compelling at a time in which the practical need for such strength was lessening, we need to inquire why demonstrations of magic gripped audiences just when modern science and technology were supposedly supplanting the need to believe in magic at all. "Magic is dominant when control of the environment is weak," declared the pioneering anthropologist Bronislaw Malinowski in the 1920s. It was "to be expected and generally to be found whenever man comes to an unbridgeable gap, a hiatus in his knowledge or in his powers of practical control, and yet has to continue in his pursuit." With the rise of more powerful, rational procedures and mechanisms, in science and technology especially, Malinowski confidently asserted, reliance on magic withered away.[1]

Whatever the strengths and shortcomings of Malinowski's functionalist explanation of the place of magic in "primitive" societies, ironically it illuminates some of the lure of stage magic in his own cul-

Houdini stripped and chained. Library of Congress

ture and time. By the 1890s, several generations of stage magicians had forsworn the pretensions of wizardry for demonstrations of "scientific" or "rational" magic, and many had taken special aim at those who used conjuring skills to claim supernatural powers. Still, as entertainers, modern magicians (overwhelmingly male) appealed to people's hunger for the semblance of miracles in a disenchanted world. Much as Western "man" (in the collective sense in which Malinowski used the term) might claim to control events, the individual male frequently faced "an unbridgeable gap" between his powers and his ambitions. By performing amazing feats of mastery over objects and situations, the magician became an exemplary masculine figure to complement the strongman. Both spoke to dreams of dominance and authority in the modern world.

The career of Harry Houdini must be understood in this context. What allowed him to become one of the most celebrated performers of the twentieth century was his skill in making themes of risk and control, helplessness and mastery central to his art and to the male body. A number of talented rivals bested him in straight magic and sleight of hand, including Howard Thurston (1869–1936) and, later, Harry Blackstone (Harry Boughton [1885–1965]), but none approached Houdini in his specialty. He was indisputably the greatest escape artist in the history of illusion. Much has been written describing his extraordinary feats: How he freed himself from the most cunningly designed handcuffs and leg irons. How he escaped from massive packing crates and zinc-lined piano cases, from office safes and bank vaults, from the jail cells of notorious criminals and from entire prisons, from straitjackets, first onstage and then suspended upside down high above city streets. How he extricated himself from a padlocked can filled with water, milk, and even beer, then from an even more spectacular "water torture cell." How, wrapped with chains and ropes or locked inside a weighted box, he plunged into rivers and harbors and swam free. How, lashed against the open barrel of a cannon with a time fuse, he vowed to free himself or "be blown to Kingdom Come." How he consented to be buried alive under six feet of earth and clawed his way back from the grave.[2] Devotees of magic have long discussed how he managed to perform these and other feats.[3] Biographers have probed the personal issues that drove him to do them in the first place.[4] Yet cultural historians have paid lit-

tle attention to the larger meanings of his tricks and the significance of his career.

When Sandow was making his American debut at the most prestigious variety theaters in the summer of 1893, the nineteen-year-old Houdini was a struggling magician in dime museums. Yet beginning in 1899, his career climbed like a steeplejack, and he soon became not only a leading vaudeville and music-hall entertainer across North America and Europe but an international celebrity. Just as Sandow was the most brilliant popular performer of manliness in the 1890s and his unclad body the most famous in the world, Houdini might be accorded this title for the decade and a half preceding the Great War. The gender meaning of escape art is less obvious, though no less profound, than that of bodybuilding. But Houdini dramatized his naked body as audaciously as any performer of his time. And, naked or clothed, fully exposed or hidden from sight, he relentlessly explored issues of the body and of masculinity. He adapted Romantic and melodramatic themes of the nineteenth century in compelling ways to modern life at the beginning of the twentieth. Although some of his feats have been performed at different times, before his day and since, the way he presented them, as well as his special appeal and fame, was deeply embedded in the cultural needs of his time. In part these needs were epitomized in Houdini himself: he was driven to his performances of manliness by intensely personal issues, which he brilliantly converted into popular art. In addition, as with Sandow, his career is best understood as an intense interaction between the performer and his public in which he learned to select and refine his feats according to his audiences' responses.

ORIGINS OF AN ILLUSIONIST

Like Sandow, Houdini was a self-made man with a self-bestowed name and a keen desire to escape, first and foremost, from his humble, at times humiliating, origins. Over the course of his career, he gave many versions of his family history and his youthful beginnings, almost all embellished and some wholly fictitious. He was born Erik Weisz (later spelled Ehrich Weiss) in Budapest in 1874, the third son of Cecilia and Mayer Samuel Weisz. Two years later, his father immi-

Rabbi Mayer Samuel Weiss, Houdini's father. Boldt Collection, Houdini Historical Center, Appleton, Wisconsin

grated to the United States to take a position as rabbi of a small German Jewish congregation in Appleton, Wisconsin. Mayer Samuel's wife and five sons, including one by an earlier marriage, joined him in 1878. Soon one of the greatest waves of Jewish immigration in history, totaling more than two million people by the time of the Great War, surged after them to the United States.

At first, the family's passage from Budapest to small-town Wisconsin, buoyed by the father's education and prospects, seemed in stark contrast to the more common plunge from eastern European *shtetl* to urban tenement. But in 1882, Weiss (as his name was now spelled) lost his honored position as rabbi to a newly emigrated German evidently more to the congregation's liking. At the age of fifty-three, still speaking little English (the language of his household and congregation was German), now with seven children, he found that the American ladder pointing upward to success also descended toward failure. Rapidly he slipped down the rungs from shabbiness to want to despair. He moved his family to Milwaukee, which had a larger Jewish community than Appleton, and tried to support them by conducting occasional services without a formal congregation, by offering private

lessons in Hebrew and perhaps German, and by working as a *shocher*, or kosher butcher, and as a *moyel* performing ritual circumcisions. Soon the family, pursued by creditors, was shuffling among furnished rooms. On at least one occasion, they appealed to the local Hebrew Relief Society for coal and grocery money to survive the winter. As Houdini later summarized this period: "Such hardships and hunger came our lot that the less said on the subject, the better."[5]

In 1886, the Weiss family moved to New York, where the once exalted father again desperately sought any rabbinic occupation at hand, printing business cards that offered "all religious services," including weddings, *brises*, and funerals. Evidently, he achieved no more success than in Milwaukee. Houdini remembered these as "hard and cruel years when I rarely had the bare necessities of life."[6] Ultimately, like many other Jewish immigrants, both literate and illiterate, the elder Weiss was reportedly reduced to working in a necktie factory on a bench alongside Ehrich. He died of cancer in 1892 at the age of sixty-three when Ehrich was eighteen. He left, in addition to Ehrich and two older sons (the first son had died of tuberculosis), three children ages sixteen, thirteen, and ten and a fifty-one-year-old widow. "*Weiss, Weiss*," Houdini recalled his mother, Cecilia, exclaiming at the time of her husband's death, "*du hast mich verlassen mit deiner Keinder!!! Was hast du gethan?*" [Weiss, Weiss, you've left me with your children!!! What have you done?][7]

If in Houdini's recollections his father was a revered but failed rabbi, his mother was a figure of transcendent love and selfless devotion, an "angel." "I am what would be called a Mothers-boy [*sic*]," he later acknowledged, and despite his five siblings, Houdini would claim throughout his life a special relationship to her, as, apparently, she did to him.[8] To cite but two examples: her pet name for him was "Tateleh" (Little Papa), and she would insist that even as a baby, he never cried. If he started to fret, she would hold him to her breast, and the sound of her heartbeat soothed him. Well into his adult life, Houdini and his mother would gratify each other by reenacting this embrace. Houdini spoke of it as one of those "little peculiarities that mean so much to a mother and son when they love each other as much as we did."[9] But in 1913, when she was seventy-two, her heart stopped beating; and upon receiving the news, he immediately fainted. Until his own death thirteen years later, he would extrava-

gantly mourn her absence and try to reconstitute her presence, even making efforts to speak with her through spiritualist mediums— and when they offered only bogus messages, he would rage against them.[10]

His father's decline and his mother's vulnerability appear to have been shaping experiences of Ehrich's childhood. Many stories he later told of his father have a strong compensatory quality: exaggerating his education and degrees, supplying a romantic past (including a victorious duel with a nobleman that supposedly impelled him to emigrate in the first place), and stressing the special bond that united father and son in the protection of Houdini's mother. Houdini claimed that in moments of crisis, including once when Ehrich was twelve and again on the father's deathbed, Mayer Samuel made his trusted son (his siblings are notably absent from these memories) solemnly promise to take care of his mother as long as she lived.[11]

Yet such a pledge—whether made to his father or only to himself—might put Ehrich in a double bind in which he surpassed his father if he succeeded and let down mother and father both if he failed. At the age of twelve, Ehrich ran away from home in what may have

Houdini with his mother and his wife, 1907. Library of Congress

been a confused response to his father's plight and to the pressures he felt. A postcard to his mother, mailed from Missouri, announced his intention to proceed to Galveston, Texas, and to "be home in about a year." It was signed "Your truant son, Ehrich Weiss." In fact, it appears that he was gone only several months and spent most of this time about fifty miles from Milwaukee, in Delavan, Wisconsin. Working as a shoeshine boy and calling himself Ehrich White (his first tentative shedding of his Jewish name and racial identity in favor of a more generalized whiteness), he was taken in by a couple who thought him homeless. Houdini later offered various explanations for this escapade, perhaps reflecting the confusion he felt at the time: that he "ran away from home to earn some money" (and so was a dutiful son after all); that he sought to "seek my fortune" (like the younger son in a folktale); that he intended to "join a small circus" (under the spell of which he had already fallen and styled himself "Ehrich, the Prince of the Air"); and, more vaguely, that he "resolved to see the world."[12] In such an incident one glimpses both the future Houdini's fierce independence and his wish to be seen as not really a truant but an exemplary and devoted son. Much of Houdini's tremendous desire for success sprang from the painful sight of his father's failure and the ambitions kindled by the warmth of his mother's embrace.

THE ROLE OF THE MAGICIAN

Houdini claimed to have seen his first magic show as a boy in Milwaukee, accompanied by his father. It was, in his recollection, a performance by the celebrated English conjurer Dr. H. S. Lynn (1831–1899).[13] The trick called "Palingenesia" (regeneration) especially impressed him; in fact, he recalled it vividly in his diary three decades later and still later incorporated a version of it into his own act.[14] In this trick, Dr. Lynn (or possibly an imitator) administered chloroform to a man onstage, secured him in a cabinet, then sharpened a butcher knife with the blade of a scimitar and exuberantly dissected his victim, lopping off first a leg, then an arm, and, finally, the head. "I really believed that the man's arm, leg, and head were cut off," Houdini remembered. As the audience gasped, the magician

calmly gathered the body parts inside the cabinet and drew the curtain; within seconds the man stepped forward intact.[15]

Such a performance might fascinate anyone, but it appears to have struck a special chord with the future Houdini. Like many magic tricks, Dr. Lynn's unorthodox surgery offered a form of playacting about bodily risk and miraculous recovery that might give expression to unconscious fears and forbidden desires. In Dr. Lynn's role as a coolly ironic assailant ("another man cut up tonight," his advertisements promised), he tapped spectators' fears of mutilation and their aggressive urges. Witnessing this magic show with his father—who like the magician was a wielder of knives (as a *moyel* and *shocher*) and was also a figure of esoteric learning (as a rabbi), though one who could no longer command an audience—Ehrich may have found the illusion particularly powerful. He may have felt he was seeing, in displaced but recognizable form, elements of his subconscious come to life. For whatever reason, the drama of bodily risk and recovery, mutilation and integration, death and rebirth consumed him throughout his career.

During Ehrich's adolescence in Manhattan, as he toiled on the bench at the necktie factory, the dream of being a circus acrobat gave way to the dream of being a magician. With a friend and fellow worker, Jacob Hyman, his younger brother Theo, and others, he spent hours practicing magic tricks, including rope tying and escape—with Ehrich usually taking the role of the bound victim. It is of course impossible to say what private meanings such games held for them. In such play, magic can overlap with adolescent male "damage games," in which participants enact fantasized scripts of bodily privation and injury in order to reassure themselves of their phallic mastery and integrity. Like other acts of exhibitionism, this play, with its demonstration of invulnerability, might soothe the uncertain sense of self that is characteristic of adolescence.[16] Such an interpretation is obviously highly speculative. But what can be said with certainty is that Ehrich discovered in magic more than an intriguing diversion: it gave him a powerful identity.

The turning point seems to have come when Ehrich read a secondhand copy of the memoirs of the great French conjurer Jean-Eugène Robert-Houdin (1805–1871).[17] Packed with adventures and triumphs, this book chronicled the extraordinary career of the father

of modern magic. (Like many such accounts, including Houdini's later autobiographical statements, it also mixed fact and fiction in a powerful act of self-invention.) The son of a humble clock maker, Robert-Houdin was from boyhood fascinated by ingenious mechanisms and magical feats. Though his father wanted him to enter a respectable profession such as law or medicine, the son followed his bent and ultimately became a mesmerizing performer who astounded multitudes and monarchs throughout Europe. Rejecting the trappings of wizardry, Robert-Houdin produced apparently supernatural marvels such as the "Floating Boy" (in which he suspended his son in midair) and "Second Sight" (an illusion of thought transference and clairvoyance) by what he emphasized were entirely rational means. He capped his memoirs with a thrilling account of how, on behalf of French colonial rulers, he single-handedly bested the sorcery of Marabouts and thus quelled an incipient Muslim revolt in Algiers. In his hands, modern magic was both a source of wonder and a tool of Western imperialism and "enlightenment."

Robert-Houdin's colorful account and commanding persona seized Ehrich's imagination. Houdini later recalled that he "re-read his works until I could recite passage after passage from memory."[18] The memoirs offered Ehrich an irresistible example of one who had created a profession combining science and spectacle, rationality and illusion. In his performances Robert-Houdin fed a public hungry for the uncanny, the inexplicable, and the miraculous. And for Ehrich Weiss, he did more than this: he provided a romantic father figure who, in contrast to Ehrich's own father, offered him an opportunity to claim a charismatic identity that might lead to fame and fortune.[19] "A conjurer is not a juggler," Robert-Houdin famously declared, distinguishing himself from the low carnival performer; "he is an *actor* playing the role of a magician."[20] As Ehrich Weiss grew up, he adapted the theatrical possibilities of this role, along with Robert-Houdin's name, to his own professional and personal needs.

Of course, magic held an attraction for many adolescent boys at this time and since, which publishers explicitly recognized in titles such as *The Boy's Own Conjuring Book*.[21] Even so, everything we know about Ehrich Weiss's childhood and future life and career suggests that for him magic held a special fascination. In its play with appearance and reality, deception and illusion, imposture and grandiosity,

magic offered a means by which he could negotiate his anxieties and fantasies about manliness in a household in which he both desired and feared to take his father's place.[22] The magician was a role by which he could sustain a fantasized self of miraculous powers. More specifically, it offered a grandiose *masculine* role by which Ehrich could proclaim his complete independence, even invulnerability. This was, in addition, an *assimilated* role. The downward spiral of his father's career would not be his. Tricking others could fortify his sense of mastery and of mental and bodily integrity. The line between an actor playing the role of a magician and a boy imagining an imposture as a masculine hero might for Ehrich Weiss have been a fine one.

His first and crucial feat as a magician, then, was to reinvent himself. Beginning on a part-time basis in 1891 (the year before his father's death), and soon as a full-time performer, Ehrich Weiss metamorphosed into Harry Houdini—the given name deriving from his nickname Ehrie, the surname from the great French master.

Here was a kind of escape art in itself. Shedding his Jewish name gave him additional means to throw off the burden of his father's fate. More generally, with the name change, he proclaimed a new identity that would not be confined by Old World conceptions of what it meant to be a Jew. Rejecting any suggestion of weakness or effeminacy, he emphasized his masculine toughness, fearlessness, and invincibility for the rest of his life. In his performances, he came to radiate confidence and command. The trace of an accent remained, but in time he shed his guttural voice for the stentorian, bell-shaped tones of a polished orator. Playing the role of magician allowed him to transmute rabbinic failure into assimilated success. He dressed in refined evening clothes to perform stunning illusions on a secular stage while disavowing supernatural means altogether. Although he never denied his Jewishness, he defined himself first and foremost as a free man and only incidentally as a Jew. Yet the ease with which he was mistaken for a Christian occasionally exposed him to the depths of anti-Semitism, particularly in Europe. He once wrote from Munich, "It is awful what I hear from people that are Jew Haters and don't know that I am a Sheeney."[23] And behind his back, even in the United States, detractors occasionally muttered their regret that "this low-minded Jew has any claim on the word American."[24]

Bess and Harry Houdini, 1894. Library of Congress

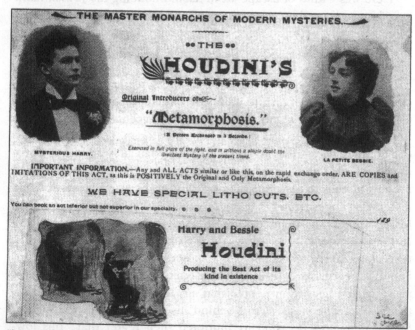

"Mysterious Harry" and "La Petite Bessie," "The Master Monarchs of Modern Mysteries," promoting their act. Library of Congress

At the beginning, he was half of the Brothers Houdini, though initially not with an actual brother but with his friend Jacob Hyman. Styling themselves "The Modern Monarchs of Mystery," they performed in dime museums and cheap variety theaters around New York and in the Midwest alongside minor blackface minstrels, Wild West imitators, fat ladies, giants, midgets, and legless wonders. Most of the performers, like themselves, had scrambled onstage from immigrant or working-class families, lured by dreams of success. For white performers with talent and drive, and bereft of education and capital, the institutions of mass entertainment offered tempting rewards—at very long odds. Minnie Marx, mother of the Marx Brothers, spoke for their ambitions when she explained why she sent her children into show business: "Where else can people who don't know anything make so much money?"[25] In the summer of 1893, shortly before Sandow's run at the "refined" Trocadero in Chicago, the Brothers Houdini appeared for several weeks along the Midway at the Columbian Exposition. But soon Hyman struck out on his own, and *his* brother Joe briefly joined Harry in the act, until a genuine Weiss brother, Theo, replaced him. Then in the summer of 1894 this partnership, too, dissolved after Harry, in the space of a few weeks, met and married a member of a song-and-dance act, Wilhelmina Beatrice Rahner. Known as Bess, she was a petite eighteen-year-old Brooklynite from a German Catholic family. With their marriage, he took another step away from Jewish orthodoxy, and she immediately replaced Theo as part of a new magic act, the Houdinis.

Though the shift was fortuitous, it decisively transformed key elements of the performance. As part of a brother act, such as with Theo, who was taller and sturdier than he, Harry Houdini could not play the role of the commanding male nearly so effectively as when offset by his diminutive wife. Gradually Houdini forged his body into a muscular instrument of escape, but as yet he appeared slight and boyish. He was also short—though he sometimes seemed determined to will himself taller. On passport applications over the course of his career, he declared himself variously as five feet four inches, five five and a quarter, five six, and five seven.[26] (The first was undoubtedly nearest the mark.) Because Bess was less than five feet tall and weighed ninety pounds, she was an ideal partner.[27]

The importance of the change is most evident in a trunk trick that

Stages in the Houdinis' "Metamorphosis." Library of Congress

had originally been a staple of the Brothers Houdini and that Harry and Bess performed many times throughout their careers. "Metamorphosis," as Harry billed the trick with Bess, created a drama of simultaneous entrance and escape. Volunteers from the audience were invited onstage to examine an ordinary-looking box or trunk, into which a crouching person might fit, and a large cloth sack. Then, as an early promotional bill described the feat:

> Mons[ieur] Houdini's hands are fastened behind his back, [he] is secur[e]ly tied in a bag[,] and the knots are sealed, then placed in a massive box which is locked and strapped[;] the box is then rolled into a small [curtained] cabinet, and Mlle. Houdini draws the curtain and claps her hands three times[.] [A]t the last clap of her hands the curtain is drawn open by Mons. Houdini and Mlle. Houdini has disappeared, and upon the box being opened she is found in his place in the bag, the seals unbroken and her hands tied in precisely the same manner as were Mons. Houdini's when first entering the bag.

The basic trick was familiar among magicians. J. N. Maskelyne had presented a version in England as early as 1865, and the French conjurer Bernard Marius "Le Commandeur" Cazeneuve made a rendition with his wife one of his most brilliant effects. In describing the basic feat, an 1897 book on magic noted, "The whole credit of the trick is due to the cabinet maker who constructed the trunk." Although volunteers might not detect anything remarkable, one of the trunk's ends, "instead of being nailed, is secured by a pivot to the two long sides, so that it can swing. The swinging motion is arrested by a spring plate bolt. When the person in the interior presses upon a point corresponding to this bolt, the pivot turns freely and the end of the trunk swings."[28]

Nonetheless, no successful magic feat depends on apparatus alone. Presentation is everything. As Houdini boasted at the bottom of the bill promoting the trick: "Just think over this, the time consumed in making the change is THREE SECONDS! We challenge the World to produce an act . . . with greater Mystery, Speed, or Dexterity." Houdini gradually added refinements, such as beginning by borrowing a coat from a member of the audience and using a smaller

trunk, but even in the 1890s the couple's speed and showmanship drew audiences. The exchange also deeply fascinated Houdini himself, making him feel as if he had left his own body.[29]

The illusion of "Metamorphosis" could be read in at least two ways. First, it might be viewed as a man's magical release from redoubled confinement—and a woman's corresponding capture. In the zero-sum stakes of this game, only one could be free, and the Houdinis clearly knew which result audiences would find most dramatically satisfying. Second, and still more magical, the trick might be viewed as a bodily and sex change between Houdini and his wife. The French titles that the performers assumed—Monsieur and *Mademoiselle* Houdini rather than Monsieur and *Madame*—further suggested that the two were potentially one person in different sexual guises rather than a husband and wife. (Bess's page-boy appearance in tights and flowing blouse—what Houdini called her "boy[']s suit"— only accentuated this aspect.[30]) In such ways "Metamorphosis" played with the boundaries of gender and the mystery of gender differences. It seemed to affirm the rightness of clear sexual divisions (with man unbound and woman dependent) but simultaneously suggested that such boundaries might collapse with startling speed.[31]

THE METAMORPHOSIS OF JULIAN ELTINGE

To appreciate its significance, we must understand the Houdinis' "Metamorphosis," like all Houdini's performances, as highly compressed popular theater. The fascination with gender boundaries and their crossing characterized much of American theater around the turn of the century. Henry Dixey was still spoofing gender roles in *Adonis*. A still more illuminating—and arresting—series of performances of gender differences and gender crossings began when Julian Eltinge (originally William Dalton, 1883–1941) launched his career as the "World's foremost [male] delineator of the fair sex."

In 1904 Eltinge made his New York debut in the musical comedy *Mr. Wix of Wickham*. In a plot reminiscent of *Charley's Aunt* (1892), he played a young college man compelled by circumstances to impersonate a pretty girl. Productions of this sort had customarily based the farce on the transparent absurdity of the disguise, but Eltinge aston-

ished viewers with the charming plausibility of his performance and his mastery of "the many little details of apparel with which women are very familiar."[32] During the next few years he achieved spectacular success on the vaudeville circuit as a female impersonator, depicting various contemporary and historical "types," including the Bathing Girl, the Bride, Salome, and Marie Antoinette. Then he returned to Broadway to win still greater acclaim in a series of plays of gender disguise beginning with the musical comedy *The Fascinating Widow* (1910). His star shone so brightly that a New York theater named in his honor opened on Forty-second Street in September 1912. He continued to tour the country as a headliner for another decade and appeared in several films.

Eltinge fascinated men and women with what one critic called his "ambisextrous" abilities.[33] As an illusionist of femininity, he attracted a remarkably broad audience. In Cincinnati a reporter eavesdropped on theatergoers' excited conversations as they awaited an Eltinge matinee. Young women gushed to one another, without intentional irony, "I think he is the loveliest girl" and "the prettiest woman I ever saw." One woman hoped "to get a few new ideas on the latest gowns." A man in line fully shared their admiration: "I want to see him because I think he's the swellest looking dame that ever wore down the boards, tripping the light fantastic."[34] Theater critics smiled and squirmed at the gender confusions inherent in these remarks. They felt an anxious need to distinguish between Eltinge's illusions and the reality of his sex and to direct all desires in safely heterosexual channels. The completeness of his gender transformations seemed an unsettling feat of magic. A critic for *Variety* wrote, "Eltinge is a good-looking fellow on the street; well-built and perhaps a little beyond the ordinary attractive man to an impressionable young woman. As a girl on the stage any man would rave over the genuine reproduction of Eltinge's impersonation. . . . To those who know him, how he accomplishes these impersonations is marvellous. Eltinge is as great an artist in his line as any artist is or has been in any other."[35]

Like a magician eschewing sorcery, Eltinge insisted that his illusions were based on prolonged and meticulous study rather than unnatural gifts. He prided himself on his knowledge of fashion, his skill with makeup, and his expertise in all the accoutrements of femininity. And just as magicians often described a few elementary tricks, he dis-

Eltinge as a dapper young man. Theatre Arts
Collection, Harry Ransom Humanities Research Center, The University of Texas at Austin

Julian Eltinge in costume, 1905. Theatre
Arts Collection, Harry Ransom Humanities Research Center, The University of Texas at Austin

pensed advice on dress and beauty secrets to women directly in interviews and in the short-lived *Julian Eltinge Magazine* that was sold at
his performances. Such success involved considerable paradox. As a
man who could claim to have mastered femininity from the outside,
he instructed women in how to be modish in their dress yet thoroughly traditional in their concept of femininity. Reinforcing gender
stereotypes, he noted the rise of woman suffrage to defuse it playfully
in a song:

> *I've set the heads of men a-whirl,*
> *Since I was but a little girl.*
> *I lead the world of fashion, yet*
> *I'm just a Suffragette.*
> *Look me over carefully*
> *And with them you'll agree.*[36]

Eltinge also gently satirized women's new athleticism in his vaudeville song "The Modern Sandow Girl." Performing calisthenics in a
stylish gym slip, he sang of the gender reversals caused by modern
feminism:

> *In the days gone by all the girls were shy*
> *And domestic in their way,*
> *They would never roam, they would stay at home*
> *And they'd sew and they'd cook all day. . . .*
> *But the girl of to-day is a wonder, they say*
> *She goes in for athletics and sport. . . .*
> *Years ago the man saved the drowning maid*
> *Now-a-days the maid will save him. . . .* [37]

Here the ironies flew thick and fast as a feminized man satirized the
masculinized woman. Eltinge assumed women's roles ultimately to
instruct women in their duties to be charming and alluring to men.
Though men might find the degree of his success as a female impersonator disconcerting, they also discovered in it consoling proof of
male power and control. "It takes a man after all," one critic exulted,
"to show women the path to beauty." [38]

Yet as Eltinge himself knew best of all, this power could only be
accepted if his stage illusions were anchored in a thoroughly masculine demeanor offstage. He seems to have studied the arts of masculinity as carefully as those of femininity, only with the former
he never acknowledged the degree to which his was a conscious
performance. Contrasting his position with that of other female impersonators, whom he kept at a great distance, and elaborately con-
cealing his homosexuality, he maintained, "Off the stage I do not
have to try to be a man." [39] In fact, he tried hard and succeeded
well. He grew adept in striking strong, manly poses for the camera
and emphasized his love of boxing, rowing, and outdoor activities,
as well as his fondness for gambling. He often spoke in a bluff manner, swore freely in a baritone voice, and, to anyone who questioned
his masculinity, delivered well-publicized two-fisted rebukes. Indeed,
Eltinge and his spokesmen occasionally confided to reporters that he
believed his specialty was something a real man should move beyond—if only he weren't so good at it. As one journalist wrote:

The idea of a man masquerading in women's clothes is repellent to normally constituted people, and, according to this actor's manager, Mr. Eltinge himself is not in sympathy with his work. In private life he is a manly fellow, ready, if necessary, to back up an argument with his fists, and he is ambitious to gain legitimate honors as a player of romantic roles. He assumes feminine garb merely because he is successful in impersonating the fair sex and because of the considerable money there is in it.[40]

The magic of the Houdinis' exchange in "Metamorphosis" emphasized speed. As Eltinge performed his own magical metamorphosis from a robust he-man to a curvaceous feminine beauty before reporters in his dressing room, he emphasized (as Houdini was to do in some of his future escapes) the effort and time required. Over ninety minutes, he shaved and applied greasepaint and powders to his face, artfully prepared his eyes and lashes, rouged his lips, moistened and powdered his arms and shoulders, and applied still more powder, paint, rouge, polish, and pencil to his hands to make them look smaller. To shrink his waist required considerably more exertion. Eltinge's height of five feet eight and a half inches and normal weight of 185 pounds, it is startling to realize, virtually matched Eugen Sandow's. For his stage appearances he strove to reach 178 pounds, although this goal became increasingly difficult. Nevertheless, he managed to squeeze into a corset (one he commercially endorsed but privately called "Old Ironsides"). When tightly laced and breathing only from his upper chest, he achieved an hourglass figure by squeezing a thirty-eight-inch waist to twenty-six inches.[41] Whereas Houdini escaped from tight confinement as an emblem of male freedom, Eltinge painfully entered it in pursuit of femininity. Like Cinderella's stepsisters but more successfully, he then jammed his feet into tiny satin shoes. As a crowning touch, he carefully styled and donned his wig, and his metamorphosis was complete.

Julian Eltinge was but one of many female impersonators to emerge on the American vaudeville circuit. His unrivaled success stemmed from his unique ability to present dramas of gender crossing without a disturbing sense of transgression. He carefully preserved a normalizing framework of traditional gender oppositions to the satis-

ELTINGE'S METAMORPHOSIS

"Penciling the Eyebrows," in the *Chicago Tribune*, September 27, 1908. The University of North Carolina at Chapel Hill

"Beading the Eyelashes." The University of North Carolina at Chapel Hill

"Pressed into Shape." The University of North Carolina at Chapel Hill

faction of men and women alike. By rooting his performances, on-stage and off, in gender stereotypes and by reassuring his public that for the "real" Julian Eltinge, sex and gender, biology and appropriate social roles were one, he could evoke fantasies of possessing both male and female powers while muting their attendant anxieties. He was then in a position to work as an escape artist in reverse. Eltinge, in effect, entered the female body in order to assert male mastery over its secrets. But he did so in such a way as to garb the Freudian figure of the phallic mother—herself a male fantasy of a woman who combines female and male powers, breasts and a penis—in modish fashions that made her safe for the multitude. As sexologists, reform-ers, and the police patrolled with increasing vigilance for signs of sex-ual deviancy, Eltinge eluded their grasp. Denying any pleasure in his feminine masquerade and shielding his sexual orientation behind talk of marriage, he insisted that his metamorphosis started and stopped at the dressing-room door.

FROM DIME-MUSEUM MAGICIAN TO ESCAPE ARTIST

What Eltinge did for female impersonation, Houdini was to do for es-cape art. Just as Eltinge enacted the female body and claimed mas-tery over the secrets of femininity, Houdini made his ability to triumph over any threat to the male body the central theme of his ca-reer. And just as Eltinge neatly skated over the thin ice of sexual de-viancy, Houdini made elements that in other contexts would have been deemed perverse—exhibitionism, bondage, mutilation, entrap-ment, suffocation, criminality, insanity, flirtations with death—the stuff of manly spectacle and riveting popular entertainment.

But these developments did not happen all at once. Only gradu-ally did Houdini learn how to tap his own deep concerns and to pre-sent them in ways that held audiences spellbound. Indeed, his success came within an ace of not happening at all. Through the first four and a half years of his marriage and partnership with Bess, Harry struggled to distinguish his act from the scores of similar acts that jostled for a step on the lowest rungs of the business.[42] Far from specializing in es-cape art at this time, he did various tasks as entertainer. In 1895 he and Bess served a stint in Pennsylvania with the Welsh Brothers Cir-

IN THE CIRCUS. THE HOUDINIS ARE AT THE RIGHT OF THE FRONT ROW. MRS. HOUDINI WEARS A LORD FAUNTLEROY SUIT.

Harry and Bess Houdini (seated on right) with the Welsh Brothers Circus. Library of Congress

cus, which offered a series of acts (but no animals) under a single tent: Houdini worked as a magician, barker, puppeteer, and, briefly, "Wild Man," and Bess as a singing clown. Then for roughly half a year, beginning in September, Houdini served as co-owner and manager of a traveling burlesque troupe, the American Gaiety Girls, in which he not only put on "Metamorphosis" with Bess but also acted in farcical skits. When that venture sank in debts, Harry and Bess leaped on one shaky venture after another, only to see each collapse. They joined a short-lived troupe doing magic tricks in the Canadian provinces; they shunted through obscure variety theaters and dime museums, attempting new acts, revamping the old, trying to stay on their feet. As the Rahners (after Bess's maiden name), they briefly became a comedy act. As "Cardo," Harry offered an evening of card magic; as "Professor Murat," he was a hypnotist. During the winter and spring of 1898, as part of a medicine show slogging through Kansas and the Oklahoma Territory, Houdini offered spiritualist effects, including communicating messages from beyond the grave. After the show itself died, the couple attempted to continue on their own. Their mixed bill of magic and spiritualism won praise in St. Joseph, Missouri:

In sleight-of-hand work Prof. Houdini is very clever. His card
tricks, palming and shifts are unsurpassed by any magician on
the stage today. The "spirit work," if you wish to account for
his feats in that way, was good. Slate writing and reading and
answering unseen questions which had been written by the audience were successful. The professor was quickly released
from several pairs of handcuffs which had been brought in by
people in the audience and locked upon his wrists. This was
done in a cabinet, and the agency by which it was accomplished was left for the audience to decide—whether spirit
force or his own cleverness. The entertainment concluded with
his trick mystery, called "Metamorphosis." In this he was as-
sisted by Mrs. Houdini.[43]

Despite this notice and other spiritualist effects of the sort Houdini
would later condemn, the Houdinis could not survive on their own.
They rejoined for a new season the Welsh Brothers Circus. This time,
in addition to performing "Metamorphosis," Bess played skits and
Harry served as an acrobat and clown.

Houdini learned from these years of struggle, first, discipline and
craft. "[W]hen I was playing Dime Museums, and being classed a
'freak,' " he later recalled, "i [sic] generally kept very quiet, and tried
to make a living, not knowing that I was developing my dexterity by
working ten to fifteen times daily."[44] He also learned from other performers, the "freaks" especially—sword swallowers and fire-eaters,
"legless wonders," spirit mediums, and sleight-of-hand artists. Whenever he saw someone do a trick that interested him, he studied it intently. One accomplished sideshow performer gave him a lesson in
how to swallow objects and bring them up again, beginning with a
small potato attached to a long string (a technique highly useful in
sleight-of-hand tricks and escapes). Strongmen such as William Le
Roy, "the Human Claw-Hammer," who could hold a nail in his teeth
and push it through an inch-thick plank or draw one out from a depth
of two inches, held a special fascination.[45] From such performers,
Houdini learned to develop his body's resources for his own special
effects.

Nonetheless, by the end of 1898 the hardships and vexations had
grown "so bad," he later recalled, that he "contemplated quitting

show business," taking a conventional day job, and running a school of magic in the evenings, in which he would sell the secrets of his act.[46] His dream of escaping the fate of his father by becoming a master magician seemed near an end. Still, he sought new bookings.

Then, in the spring of 1899, his persistence was rewarded. Houdini's career took an astonishing turn, beginning his dizzying ascent from minor vaudeville houses, dime museums, medicine shows, ten-cent circuses, and rented halls to international stardom. These small-time houses, in which performers typically played three to six times daily in short bills and brief engagements, were distinctly inferior to the big-time theaters. Big-time engagements ran an entire week or more, with the players generally appearing twice daily, in a matinee and evening bill of at least eight acts, including a main attraction or headliner. The major vaudeville theaters throughout the country were organized into circuits controlled by theater owners and booking associations. The two largest syndicates worked together to create a network that stretched across the United States and Canada, with an eastern circuit controlled by B. F. Keith and Edward F. Albee, and the Orpheum circuit, extending from Chicago to the West Coast, managed by Martin Beck. While performing at a beer hall in St. Paul, Minnesota, Houdini was "discovered" by Beck himself. Up to this point, Houdini had aimed to be a generalist conjurer. In a diffuse act with various props, he produced pigeons and silk handkerchiefs and performed card tricks, as well as "Metamorphosis." Still, Beck saw the escape artist struggling to get out. Big-time vaudeville emphasized specialties in conjuring as in everything else. He urged Houdini to make "Metamorphosis" and his handcuff escapes the focus of his act and offered him a trial booking on the Orpheum circuit. Soon the Houdinis had a contract with Beck and vaulted to the top vaudeville theaters across the country.[47]

THE HANDCUFF KING

Houdini brilliantly exploited his new prominence. Now a "theme" act instead of an all-purpose magician, he intimately engaged his larger audiences as he performed dramatic challenges to his body. Almost immediately, he introduced the needle-swallowing trick, which

"The Handcuff King."
Library of Congress

became a staple of his act for the rest of his career. The basic trick was simple enough, but Houdini performed it with consummate showmanship. First, he invited members of the audience onstage to inspect a set of sewing needles. He chewed the set noisily, swallowed, and opened his mouth to prove they were consumed. Next, he asked the audience members to inspect a long thread, which one of their number knotted distinctively. Placing one end in his mouth, he gradually swallowed the thread until only the other end was visible in his throat. Then he triumphantly pulled the thread out to display the identical sewing needles neatly strung on it.

Yet Houdini never grabbed headlines by swallowing needles. What distinguished him at this time and soon made him famous were his handcuff escapes—onstage and off. Magicians had been performing handcuff escapes for at least two centuries, and up to this time Houdini had had difficulty injecting new drama into the feat. The release took place out of sight in his curtained cabinet, and initially some theater managers had refused to let him perform the trick.[48] To heighten interest and to prove that the cuffs were not rigged, he challenged members of the audience to place their own regulation handcuffs on him. Almost from the beginning, too, he occasionally sought to fan publicity by inviting local police to restrain him with their toughest handcuffs and allow him only a moment's privacy to escape. He had issued such challenges during the engagement that Beck witnessed in St. Paul. As Houdini later recounted the event, Beck himself had responded to Houdini's challenge by purchasing several pairs of handcuffs, from which Houdini escaped.[49] Meanwhile, the *Minneapolis Times* reported his visit to the local police station, where he defied the authorities to hold him with their best handcuffs and shackles.[50]

On the Orpheum circuit, Houdini became bolder in his handcuff escapes. A month after his fateful meeting with Beck, instead of retiring to the curtained cabinet to remove his handcuffs, Houdini slipped them off within full view of the audience. In a diary he noted with satisfaction, "1st time I took off cuffs with curtain open was the hit of act."[51] Offstage he scored equal successes. MANACLES DO NOT HOLD HIM, marveled a headline in *The Kansas City Times*. The story recounted another police-station challenge. On this occasion the police captain pasted a specially marked postage stamp over each keyhole

"so that it would be easy to tell if the stamp had been removed" and the lock picked. Houdini shed the cuffs with the stamps intact.[52]

Houdini persisted in these challenges to the police, making them a frequent and vital accompaniment to his performances onstage. Such challenges appear to have been especially gratifying to him. He was by temperament highly competitive, and he enjoyed nothing more than annihilating a rival or amazing a skeptic. Handcuff escapes gave him the opportunity to create a new kind of metamorphosis: from impotent victim of authorities to manly victor over them. They allowed him to cast himself in the role of the underdog—a modern David pitted against institutional Goliaths—and to come out on top.

The police seem never to have failed to play their part as foils to Houdini. They, too, wanted to publicize their manly prowess. The rise of a uniformed police force superseding the older constable-watch system was a historic innovation of the second half of the nine-teenth century. More recently, around the 1890s, municipal police forces shifted from concentration on the "dangerous classes"—those perceived as defective, dependent, or delinquent (including the poor, homeless, transient, and ill)—to professional crime control more generally. The new emphasis reflected a growing corporate ideal of urban safety and efficiency.[53] Mastery over the criminal's body lay at the heart of the police's power and symbolized their efficient command. Time after time, police officers swaggered before the short, slight young man and boasted of their invincibility—only to be stupefied moments later.

In these police-station challenges, Houdini ingeniously varied the terms and raised the stakes. When he arrived in San Francisco in June 1899, he demonstrated his usual wizardry before police officials and two hundred patrolmen. He submitted to a formidable array of re-straints: four varieties of handcuffs (including three with double springs) and two sets of leg irons, with the cuffs and irons linked by yet another pair of handcuffs. "This brought him to a crouching pos-ture," a reporter observed sympathetically, "and made him to all ap-pearances helpless to use a key even if he had one."[54] He escaped in seven minutes, gleefully reappearing with the cuffs snapped together to form a long chain.

Houdini's success, like Sandow's, brought forth rivals and detrac-

tors. A touring English magician, "Professor" Benzon, ridiculed Houdini's handcuff escapes in William Randolph Hearst's *San Francisco Examiner* and purported to reveal his methods. Relatively few keys were sufficient to unlock all handcuffs made, he asserted. These Houdini "keeps conveniently about him." The way to foil this "professor of trickery," he advised, was to bring to the theater "a pair with a newfangled lock and key." As a parting shot, Benzon offered a general description of the trick behind "Metamorphosis."[55]

This challenge gave Houdini the chance to gain additional publicity and to crush a rival at the same time, and he leaped at it. Not only did he deride Benzon's explanations, but he offered to demonstrate that he needed no cabinet or secret key. Four days after Benzon's article appeared, Houdini once again swept into the San Francisco police station with reporters in tow. This time he demanded that before being handcuffed he be stripped naked and thoroughly searched. (He had undergone a similar strip search by Chicago police the previous December, but this and later searches generated far more publicity.) A police surgeon examined Houdini from head to toe and "certified that it would be an impossibility for him to have any key, wire or other article concealed about him." To ensure that the master needle swallower hid nothing in his mouth or throat, his lips were sealed with adhesive plaster. The police then energetically set to work. They pinioned his arms with handcuffs, attaching them from his wrists up to his elbows. They shackled his ankles, then chained his wrists to the ankles, forcing him into a subservient bow. Weighed down with ten pairs of cuffs, Houdini was shut in a closet. Then, as the presiding police sergeant explained to reporters "the utter impossibility of the feat," the naked and now unbound Houdini blithely strode in with all the handcuffs locked together in a daisy chain. The police surgeon examined the plaster over Houdini's mouth and declared it had not been disturbed in any way.[56]

As if this were not impressive enough, Houdini proposed another trial. He challenged the superintendent of the local insane asylum, who was present, to secure him in a straitjacket. Such jackets had been devised to restrain violent patients from injuring themselves or their guards. Reversing a conventional jacket's design, they were solid in front, fastened in back. The patient's arms were thrust into two

closed sleeves, each of which ended in a thick strap. The arms were pulled tightly across the chest and buckled in the rear. Some included a crotch strap.

Houdini had never seen or heard of these devices until three years earlier, when, performing in St. John, New Brunswick, he was invited to tour the local insane asylum. One sight he never forgot:

> Through the small bars of the cell door, I saw a maniac struggling on the canvas padded floor, rolling about and struggling each and every muscle in a vain attempt to get his hands over his head and striving in every conceivable manner to free himself from his canvas restraint, which I later on learned was called a strait-jacket. Entranced, I watched the efforts of this man, whose struggles caused the beads of perspiration to roll off him. . . . But as the straps were drawn tight, the more he struggled, the tighter his restraint encircled him, and eventually he lay exhausted, panting and powerless to move. . . . [The sight] left so vivid an impression on my mind that I hardly slept that night, and in such moments as I slept I saw nothing but strait-jackets, maniacs and padded cells![57]

From this time on, Houdini endeavored to find ways of making this struggle as compelling for audiences as it had been for himself.

Strapped into such a straitjacket in the San Francisco police station, Houdini again retired to a closet (as, up to this time, he retreated behind a curtain onstage). He soon emerged "with the belt in his hand and intact."[58] He left the station bearing a signed affidavit of his escapes.

In an exultant account of his feats in *The San Francisco Examiner*, Houdini, like a heavyweight champion after a prize bout, announced that he was still "king of handcuffs." Though he refused to divulge his secrets—and crowed that all self-styled exposers had been wide of the mark—he stressed that it was a trick others could master. Significantly, Houdini suggested that the strip search and handcuff and straitjacket escapes came at the demands of the police, not on his own initiative. Thus he cast himself in the role of one forced to undergo these trials in order to prove his abilities and to clear his name of slander. Accompanying the article, five photographs recording the stages

Houdini "Handcuffed, Elbow-Ironed, and Thumbscrewed by the Berlin Police, October 1900," in *The Adventurous Life of a Versatile Artist*, p. 11. Library of Congress

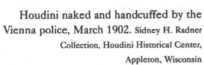

Houdini naked and handcuffed by the Vienna police, March 1902. Sidney H. Radner Collection, Houdini Historical Center, Appleton, Wisconsin

by which he achieved his escape showed a virtually naked Houdini (in the first two, his black loincloth is obscured in shadows). Henceforth, such publicity photographs became key images, widely distributed through handbills, programs, and newspapers. Although he could not perform naked onstage, he fixed the image of his naked and shackled body, making it one of the most famous in the world.[59]

Through the rest of 1899 and into the following spring, Houdini repeated his coup in city after city: sweeping into police stations, stripping off his clothes, escaping from handcuffs, manacles, and straitjackets, and carrying away affidavits of his feats. In April 1900 he again raised the stakes, performing nude escapes not just from handcuffs but also from locked prison cells.

Soon afterward, in his first trip overseas as a performer, he showed how brilliantly he could adapt his escapes to European authorities and audiences. In London, he earned a place on the leading music-hall stage after releasing himself from the cuffs of Scotland Yard. A few months later, he appeared in Dresden, where he was photographed handcuffed and manacled by the municipal police, and in Berlin, where authorities obligingly "handcuffed, elbow-ironed, and thumbscrewed" the naked escape artist.[60] In both cities he scored his greatest hits to date. He made such tactics a central element in his European campaign. In every town he played, Houdini declared, "The first thing was to break out of jail."[61]

Indeed, Houdini's success in Europe made his career's trajectory the exact inverse of Sandow's a decade earlier. Whereas the Prussian-born strongman first won fame in Britain, then scored his greatest successes in the United States, Houdini enjoyed such acclaim in Europe that he returned home only for brief respites during the next five years. As he wrote proudly to a Boston friend in 1903, "It may be a long time ere we will work America, as I am actually asking for $1000 weekly salary, and to tell you the truth, I am not even anxious to accept that work at that salary. Over here I stay one, two and even 6 months in one City, and have a G R E A T reputation, and in America it means every week jump to another city!"[62]

THE PRISON DEFIER

When at last he did return to the United States for extensive appearances beginning in October 1905, the "Handcuff King" had become the international "Prison Defier" as well. Abroad he had been escaping from the cells of notorious criminals, then from entire jails. He devised comparable exploits for American audiences. Rapidly he added to his previous escapes in Chicago and Kansas City a string of more than a dozen jailbreaks in eastern cities.[63] Three instances from early 1906 are typical.

In Washington, D.C., during a run at B. F. Keith's Chase Theatre, Houdini defied not one but two prisons. On January 1, he appeared at the Tenth Precinct police station, where he was "stripped and treated as thoroughly as an arch murderer." Then, handcuffed with an "invincible bracelet" used by the Secret Service, he was conducted to a modern steel cell, which had been searched for "any spook assistants or hidden keys." With Houdini securely inside, the police shut the "heavy, barred door with a bar lock that is first set to lock three times. A lever throws another lock, and a Yale padlock completes the quintet of locks. A wire network around the padlock prevents a hand being thrust from inside the cell." One reporter wrote, "Every policeman believed Houdini would give up after an effort. As the minutes crept on, this confidence increased, and there was talk of bets." This complacency burst, however, when, eighteen minutes after the test began, a fully clothed Houdini appeared among them. "This baffles me," confessed the Washington police chief. By Houdini's own count, it was his sixty-second jail-cell escape.[64]

Houdini's success on this occasion triggered numerous challenges from police forces determined to foil him. One came from the warden of Washington's federal prison, a "cathedral-like" structure beside the Potomac. When Houdini arrived, the warden's office was crammed with visitors, police officials, and three jail physicians. They conducted Houdini to the most secure wing of the prison, the massive brick cells of "murderers' row," each of which had a heavily barred door and an intricate lock. He was "stripped stark naked, thoroughly searched," then locked into the cell that a quarter century earlier had held President James Garfield's insane assassin, Charles Guiteau. Not only did Houdini almost immediately escape, but, while still naked,

he playfully switched each of the other nine inmates into a different cell. When he presented himself before the authorities, "their amazement passed all bounds." He left proudly bearing the warden's written testimony of his achievement.[65]

Houdini topped even this exploit two months later in Boston. The city police regarded their Somerset Street prison, popularly known as the Tombs, as absolutely "escape proof." Houdini was determined to test it. In a ground-floor cell in front of many witnesses, he shed "every stitch of his clothing," which was then locked inside the cell. On the second floor, the police superintendent and a number of witnesses searched Houdini from the hair on his head to the soles of his feet. The superintendent clamped the department's best handcuffs on Houdini, fastening his left wrist high on the cell door and his right one down at knee level. The superintendent shackled Houdini's ankles "so tightly that the iron sank into the flesh," then locked the cell

Houdini locked in a prison cell in the Boston Tombs, March 1906. Library of Congress

Houdini's escape route as published in *The Boston Journal*, March 20, 1906. Library of Congress

door and led the witnesses to his office, confident of the security of his restraints. Yet only sixteen minutes later, a few reporters waiting outside saw Houdini, now fully clothed, scale the outer wall of the prison yard, vault the iron railing, and jump down to a waiting car. According to one account, from his dressing room at Keith's Theatre, Houdini telephoned the startled superintendent, who thought he was still snugly locked in jail.[66] Police and reporters discovered that Houdini had unlocked not only the cell in which he was incarcerated and the one that held his clothes but also five other cells. He said later that he had planned to scramble the prisoners in different cells, as he had at the federal prison in Washington, until he realized he was the sole inmate. Adding a shiver of excitement, he boasted to reporters, "Were I to turn burglar tomorrow, I feel that I could plan and carry out to a successful end any number of big robberies right here in Boston, for I don't think there is a lock or a safe, guarding valuables in this city, which I couldn't break into and mysteriously dispose of the contents."[67]

Such exploits multiplied many times over made Houdini a celeb-

rity, even a legend. Still in his early thirties and only a few years beyond the obscurity of the traveling medicine show and ten-cent circus, he was one of the most famous entertainers in the world.

MARVELS AND MYSTERIES OF THE
IMPRISONED MALE BODY

What did these escapes mean? Why did they so capture the public's imagination in city after city, country after country? As Houdini himself was keenly aware, there was nothing inevitably captivating about handcuff or straitjacket escapes. His first performances of each had stirred little interest. Furthermore, none of his rivals and imitators ever enjoyed a fraction of his fame.

Houdini's achievement rested on his unique ability to dramatize the challenges to his body and to his masculinity. His escape art was exquisitely attuned to the mass media of his time and their affinity for spectacle—the synergistic combination of inexpensive, widely accessible vaudeville theater, competitive daily newspapers eager for sensational stories, and theatrical and newspaper photography. It was also exquisitely attuned to the aspirations and anxieties of millions of people aroused by the spectacle of the naked male body on trial.

That body had become an impressive one. By the time of his Boston Tombs jailbreak, Houdini had forged it into a powerful instrument of escape. Within a few years the slight young man of the early 1890s had transformed himself into a thickly muscled figure. In a gesture reminiscent of Sandow, he frequently invited people to feel his body. When in 1904 the future novelist Edna Ferber, then a young newspaperwoman, obliged by touching his forearm, she declared it "amazing, as massive and hard as a granite pillar. His neck, too," she noted approvingly, "is large, and corded."[68] He had acquired not only strength but remarkable adroitness as well. Houdini's immensely strong fingers could work through the thickest canvas. With constant training, his toes acquired the dexterity of fingers, and he could open knots and buckles with his teeth. He developed a broad, deep chest by training himself to stay for long periods underwater, even in extreme cold.

Yet these physical attainments were the preconditions, not the

essence, of his art. If a magician is an enactor of miracles and a holder of secrets, then an escape artist is a special case: an enactor of the miracles and secrets of his own body. Houdini turned the possibilities created by Sandow and others for the unclad male body to spectacular dramatic effects. Not only did he make his body the nexus of challenges, but, crucial to his success, he made it a subject to investigate and a symbol to interpret, a bearer of meaning and a source of mystery.

The newspaper accounts of his naked jail escapes in Washington and Boston only heightened this bodily drama. On one level, the reporters described contests of literal and metaphoric bodies: Houdini offers his naked body to the police, challenging their ability to hold him; he is innocent of any crime but willing to place himself literally in the position of the most feared and reviled criminals. For their part, the police stand as trusty guardians of law and order, the strong right arm of the metaphoric body of society at large whose central task is to confine and restrain the bodies of accused and convicted criminals, those who threaten to injure that metaphoric body. They appear to relish this job and to be very good at it. The record of dreaded criminals past and present—from the assassin Guiteau to cold-blooded murderers awaiting execution—testifies to their success. They welcome Houdini precisely because they are so confident of their unbreachable cells, formidable clamps, intricate locks—instruments and symbols of their power. How could Houdini possibly escape from such resolute officials and such proven restraints?

This drama of the naked citizen and the uniformed officials of the state was richly evocative for Houdini's contemporaries—and it remains so today. In many respects, it distilled the central elements of earlier melodramatic narratives in which, as the literary critic Peter Brooks has observed, "[t]he body sequestered and enchained, unable to assert its innocence and its right to freedom," is a dominant image. Such melodramas cannot reach their denouement "until the virtuous bodies have been freed" from often nightmarish gothic spaces and their innocence recognized.[69] One such melodrama was Dumas's novel *The Count of Monte Cristo* (1844–1845), and when Houdini read it for the first time, in 1920, while making movies, he wrote excitedly in his diary, "This part was made for me."[70]

At times, Houdini suggested other melodramatic possibilities—for

example, a master criminal foiling legitimate authorities: "Suppose the innate and inherent integrity of character that Houdini possesses in common with most men brought up within the circle of a mother's sweet influence, were to be swept aside by the desire for riches not his own." Stoking resentment of the rich, he added, "There are many men of many millions to-day whose money is not their own." Or, in further narrative twists: "Suppose he should be captured by a band of desperate men determined to wrest from Houdini this secret worth millions. Suppose a great hypnotist were to obtain dominance over his mystery-enveloped genius and use his baneful powers for evil designs. What then?"[71] Houdini's naked escapes gained power by leaving such narrative possibilities unresolved and enlisting the viewers' imaginations to complete them.

Behind Houdini's police challenges stood the often sadomasochistic contests between torturers and victims that so fascinated the melodramatic imagination. Another Houdini favorite, Edgar Allan Poe, created tales such as "The Pit and the Pendulum," with its pitiless "black-robed judges" who condemn the narrator to death in a torture chamber.[72] Such punishing figures preoccupied Houdini's contemporaries, among them the fellow German-speaking Jew Franz Kafka. Indeed, it is possible to recognize in the Boston police superintendent who so tightly manacled Houdini a distant relative of the officer in Kafka's short story "In the Penal Colony." The latter worships a machine that executes a prisoner by slowly inscribing on his naked body, with elaborate scrolls and flourishes, a commandment such as HONOR THY SUPERIORS! When the executing machine fails to work properly on an uncomprehending prisoner, the officer administers the punishment on his own body instead.[73]

Houdini's jail and straitjacket escapes anticipated to a degree the themes of Michel Foucault and other historians who have identified prisons and asylums as key institutions in the rigorous disciplining of individual bodies that distinguishes the rise of modern society. Houdini felt a kinship with the inmates of these institutions, visiting them and offering benefit performances throughout his life. In his escapes, he brought the tension between individual liberty and official coercion to stark dramatic confrontation. From the time of the ancient Greeks, Western philosophers have conceived of political freedom in terms of (male) bodily freedom and of political independence in

terms of personal autonomy. Houdini was no political philosopher, but what he enacted was the plight of the individual citizen stripped of dignity, imprisoned, immobilized, placed in the position of the most abject slave. Houdini's crouching, inspected, manacled naked body symbolized the consequences of giving the political order free rein over its enemies. Seen in such a light, his challenges to and defeats of the authorities' most strenuous efforts to hold him prisoner constitute a one-man revolution.

Little wonder, then, that Houdini's escapes stirred such popular excitement throughout North America and Europe. And official responses to him offer a rough index of political liberalism in different nations. Police and prison officials in the United States virtually stood in line to accept Houdini's challenges. In Great Britain, except in the largest cities, officials were usually cooperative. On the Continent, however, authorities regarded him more sternly, and when he journeyed to Russia in 1903, he found them deeply suspicious, and he thought the entire country had the atmosphere of a prison. "It does seem strange," Houdini observed in a letter from Paris, "that the people over here especially Germany, France, Saxony, and Bohemia fear the Police so much, in fact the Police are all mighty, and I am the first man that has ever dared them, that is my success."[74]

Beyond these possible political implications, Houdini's display of the unclad male body held deeply personal meanings. In one sense, his stripping and offering his body as an object to be searched was an extension of his rolling up his sleeves for his onstage handcuff escapes—a gesture of disclosure. In an all-male environment, he felt no hesitancy in appearing naked—and apparently neither did such audiences in viewing him—even when concealment was not an issue. (When, for example, he arrived for a performance of his milk-can escape at the Harvard Union in 1908 with only a blue bathing suit—the color of rival Yale College—he offered to perform naked instead, and the male audience readily accepted.)[75] But his nakedness was not incidental to the strip searches and jail escapes, or it would not have been so elaborately stressed in newspaper accounts and publicized in photographs and programs (albeit sometimes with trunks drawn on). He exposed his naked body in situations that highlighted its vulnerability and sought to arouse the curiosity of the police and the public.

That curiosity included specific questions, most immediately

whether he concealed a pick, wire, or other device, and if so, where. The effect was to encourage a detailed search, not limited to hair and skin but including orifices and cavities. Newspaper accounts displayed a certain reticence in these matters. Though they emphasized that he was "stark naked" and searched from head to toe, they never described the search *between* head and toe, focusing instead on the examination of Houdini's mouth. Privately it was possible to be more frank. After attending a special handcuff escape before a group of Boston physicians, one doctor wrote Houdini a letter speculating in detail on the ways in which a device might be concealed and retrieved from the nasal and sinus cavities, the mouth and throat, and "many portions of the genito-urinary and rectal regions." ("The urethra could easily be used to hide one or more small keys. . . . The lower colon, above the rectum, will easily learn to tolerate inoffensive foreign material.") The doctor asked not to be publicly identified.[76]

Such speculations inevitably suggest larger psychological, sexual, and gender issues. These searches encouraged Houdini's public to inspect his body for themselves and to imagine secrets—whether special powers or hiding places—within. In effect, Houdini carried the gender dynamics of the substitution trunk trick "Metamorphosis" to a much more daring level. He placed himself in what might be regarded as an especially provocative feminized position: naked, bound, bent over, inspected, even to a degree penetrated. His victimization was thus not only political (a loss of freedom) but gendered (a loss of masculinity). Then, with an extraordinary bit of magic, he confounded his foes and regained at once his liberty and his masculinity. In a sense, Houdini's escapes worked as spectacular practical jokes in which he appeared to be trapped in a position of humiliating gender defeat—unmanned—only to achieve a grandiose masculine triumph. As he put it in his own breathless prose: "He is the man to whom the shrewdest police, the sharpest detectives, and the most watchful jail wardens look with awe and anxiety. . . . [B]uried in the brain of Houdini lies the secret of an unknown power he alone possesses."[77] Houdini appears to have taken the scripts from unconscious performances of male sexual and gender anxieties—exhibitionism and bondage, most conspicuously—and transformed them into brilliant spectacle. A Freudian might see in his mixture of elation and transgression—as a master criminal defying moral authorities—a further element derived

from the enactment of private perversions.[78] The great mystery never directly confronted but always implicit in these performances was gender difference: What did it mean if women's bodies were different from men's? What secrets did they conceal? In a period of narrowing gender definitions and widespread anxiety over threats to masculinity, Houdini's performances had enormous cultural resonance.

CHALLENGES OF MODERNITY

The audacious Tombs escape brought Houdini's career as "Handcuff King" and "Prison Defier" to a climax. Beginning in the spring of 1906, simple handcuff escapes onstage and prison escapes offstage fell away. Instead, Houdini embarked on a new series of onstage challenges and offstage escapes that involved ingenious contrivances of all sorts. During the next two and a half years, until his departure for another extensive European tour in August 1908, these would command headlines in cities across the country and pack vaudeville houses wherever he appeared. One of the first was his escape from a wicker hamper at Keith's Theatre in Boston, shortly before his jailbreak from the Tombs. Many of its dramatic elements would recur again and again.

A wicker hamper might seem to hold little drama compared with a prison, but Houdini proved otherwise. The Tombs and similar jail escapes had emphasized speed and fixed the image of Houdini's naked body in the public imagination. With the hamper escape he stressed a long, unseen struggle as he took the formula from "Metamorphosis" and, paradoxically, heightened its effect by turning the feat from one lasting seconds to one lasting more than an hour. Assuring his audience, "There is nothing supernatural about the escapes I make," he stepped into the hamper wearing three pairs of handcuffs. The hamper itself resembled the picnic basket of a paranoid giant. Made of tightly woven rattan, it was held by three thick steel bands and secured by huge padlocks, thick ropes, and an iron chain. The keyhole of each padlock bore a seal signed by members of the audience. Then his assistants concealed the hamper behind a curtain. And the audience waited.

The actual escape, like most of Houdini's, took place outside the

spectators' view. While the band played, he made his audience imagine his struggle and squirm with anxiety about his safety and success.
Some of his previous escapes abroad had lasted even longer. In 1902
in Blackburn, England, a strongman locked him in specially devised
handcuffs from which he took two hours and forty minutes and "the
fight of my life" to escape. A straitjacket release in Hanover, Germany, took "90 minutes . . . and nearly drove me crazy with pain."[79]
Still, these were exceptions, and viewers knew that the hardest stage
trick he had hitherto performed in Boston lasted only nineteen minutes. As the clock ticked on, fear of his defeat grew. Finally, sixty-two
minutes after he had begun, a freed Houdini pulled back the curtains,
revealing the hamper still bound and locked. Every aspect of his appearance testified to the supreme effort of the feat:

> His eye was dim and tired, and all his life and vigor seemed to
> have departed. His frock coat was dusty, wrinkled and crushed;
> his linen was soiled, the collar and cuffs were carried in his
> hands; and his whole appearance was that of a man who has

The audience at Keith's Theatre for a Houdini performance, Boston, March 2, 1906.
Harvard Theatre Collection

been through a terrific ordeal. Traces of blood were upon his neck and wrists, and several scratches were clearly to be seen.

"Three cheers for Houdini!!" shouted a man in the balcony, and the audience "simply went wild."[80]

By the time Houdini returned to Boston the following year, he was offering a dizzying array of such challenges. Indeed, he promised a new stunt at every one of his twelve weekly appearances (matinees at four o'clock and evening performances at quarter to ten, Monday through Saturday). Individually compelling, these challenges collectively made him a legend. For the Monday matinee on February 11, 1907, he warmed up with a handcuff escape while bound and nailed to a door. That evening he accepted a challenge from employees of a local boiler works who dared him to escape from a standard galvanized-iron hot-water tank, which had been placed on display in front of Keith's Theatre. Handcuffed and shackled, Houdini crawled feetfirst into the tank as it lay on its side. Six workers then capped, bolted, and, wielding flaming blowtorches, riveted it shut before the curtains of Houdini's cabinet enclosed the whole. When Houdini emerged fifty-five minutes later, "pale, weak and trembling," his "suit . . . torn and dirty, his face . . . bloody and his hands bruised," the audience "rose and wildly applauded him for his success."[81]

Tuesday's matinee brought another challenge, this time to escape from a giant football onstage without disturbing the lacings. On Thursday afternoon he freed himself from a "crazy crib" furnished by an insane asylum. That evening workers from the Derby Desk Company enacted a clerk's nightmare as they locked the handcuffed Houdini inside a massive rolltop desk. He emerged triumphant in fifty minutes. On Friday he escaped from a formidably locked glass box. Then he offered his signature straitjacket escape on Saturday, now performed within full view of spectators, who were moved to feverish excitement and tumultuous applause, even parading him around the theater on their shoulders.

In city after city across the country, Houdini provoked equally demanding and frequently bizarre challenges. Just as he had once invited individual challengers with their handcuffs, police and prison officials, and asylum superintendents, he now appeared ready to take on all comers. Manufacturers and department stores seeking public-

Recalling the Weed Chain challenge. Library of Congress

ity, as well as male clubs and teams, responded with alacrity. Challenges frequently came from male workers eager to display their prowess and skills despite the impersonal corporate economy that surrounded them. Usually they issued printed challenges, which Houdini accepted in writing, circulating the documents as handbills. The contests took on aspects of a formal duel, albeit fought with unorthodox weapons.

For example, on April 10, 1908, in New York City, Houdini submitted to a challenge from the Weed Chain Tire Grip Company, a manufacturer of automobile tire chains to prevent skidding in snow and ice. The company proposed to bind him with its product so that he could not slip away. When workers had completed their installation on the stage of Keith & Proctor's 125th Street Theatre, Houdini's plight was both grotesque and pitiable. They had handcuffed his wrists, shackled his ankles, wrapped his body with six padlocked tire chains, and chained an automobile wheel and tire at both his neck and legs. The entire apparatus weighed four hundred pounds. One spectator exclaimed, "All he needs to run a hardware store is a kitchen stove!" He had to be carried into his curtained cabinet. A few

minutes later the audience heard "a shrieking cry for help" as Houdini complained a tire was choking him. It was adjusted, and his struggle resumed. "For many minutes," a reporter noted, "it seemed he would fail in his test." When the curtains were opened again twenty-five minutes later, Houdini had but one tire and a few chains left. He completed his escape within full view of the spectators. "When he appeared again before the audience in answer to cheers," wrote a reporter, "he could not speak and reeled off the stage with an attendant holding him up."[82]

The following month the Weed company demanded a rematch, citing "letters from motorists and others questioning the legitimacy of the test." This time the company proposed to use eight rather than six chains together with two automobile tires, a pair of leg irons, and as many handcuffs and padlocks as it desired, all in "a new and more difficult position." Houdini accepted and triumphed again.[83]

Such challenges permitted numerous variations. In dramas that merged the gothic with the surreal, Houdini struggled against an extraordinary array of objects and situations. The objects might appear formidable (for example, a zinc-lined piano box), macabre (a coffin nailed shut by members of the audience), utilitarian (a long ladder to which he was shackled and chained), startling (a standard Postal Service mailbag), whimsical (the world's largest envelope), intricate (a web of cord and fishing line that took an hour and forty-five minutes to tie), or absurd (a gigantic sausage skin). Whatever their guise, all were converted into the menacing, phantasmagoric materials of a nightmare of modern life. A challenge from the Pittsburg Auto Vise and Tool Company required Houdini to be locked in four vises "designed solely for holding the heaviest type of machinery." Handbills promised that "the contest will be filled with the greatest excitement in the war between MAN AND MACHINE."[84] Some of the challenges that Houdini rejected as impossible carried still further this feel of a modern nightmare: to escape from a gigantic incandescent lightbulb without breaking the glass or from padlocks attached to the bottom of a trip-hammer that struck twice a second. Clearly, part of the dramatic power of many of these escapes was their play with scale, as objects of large or exaggerated size threatened to engulf the individual, who ultimately proved, however, that he could not be defeated.

A Houdini lobby display, from the Salem Theatre, 1906, with (left) pairs of handcuffs, (center) wicker hamper, and (right) packing case. Library of Congress

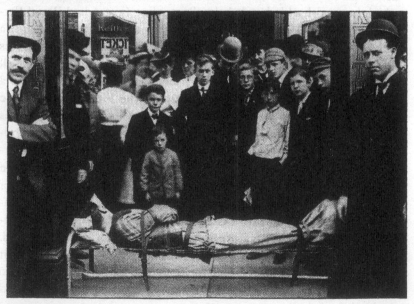

Houdini strapped to a cot. Library of Congress

Houdini regularly encouraged audiences to participate in these challenges. In addition to inviting volunteers onstage to authenticate equipment and procedures, he frequently displayed the device constituting the challenge in the theater lobby for public inspection prior to his performance. With every escape, he kept the question buzzing, How did he do it? His extraordinary success in this regard placed him in a tradition of American entertainers practiced in the arts of pleasurable deception—a tradition extending back to P. T. Barnum, who had invited mid-nineteenth-century viewers to decide which of his attractions were genuine and which hoaxes. Barnum's popular aesthetic was cunningly suited to the antebellum market economy, in which exaggeration and deception thrived. Houdini's operational aesthetic, by contrast, appealed to the amateur's desire to understand technical processes in a secularized corporate age when technology often lay outside the average individual's understanding or control. He invited viewers to look inside the works of his escapes and to match wits with him, all the better to astound them.[85]

This operational aesthetic was largely masculine, and Houdini's cultivation of a supremely masculine persona was essential to its promotion. Significantly, some of the toughest escapes he attempted lacked this critical element and did not become celebrated. These included being swathed to a cot with wet bandages—getting out of bed is not the stuff of legend—and being tied with tarred ropes by Toledo high-school boys. "Hurt like hell," Houdini noted in his diary after the latter.[86] What set him apart from other escape artists of his day was not simply his skill and strength but the remarkable intensity he created in every performance. Though he could be mildly ironical, he permitted no humor at his expense. With each new challenge, he wanted his audience to feel that his entire career—indeed, the entire masculine persona of invincibility he had constructed—was hanging in the balance. At the same time, he communicated absolute fearlessness. He simply would not be defeated.

His enormous celebrity and enduring fame suggest how greatly these qualities appealed to the emotional needs of viewers. At a time when individual male freedom seemed threatened on many fronts, Houdini's dramas were centrally concerned with issues of masculinity and the male body. Intuiting that the primacy of the body may be most dramatically expressed when that body is most at risk,[87] he,

more than any other figure of his day, repeatedly and ingeniously put the imperiled male body, agonizingly on the brink of failure, at the center of his art. Eugen Sandow invoked the victorious Hercules, but Houdini's closest analogue in classical mythology was Laocoön, the Trojan priest writhing in the coils of giant sea serpents. Houdini freed himself, of course, and his efforts to do so, the marks of which frequently covered his face and body, elicited a powerful emotional catharsis. Although audience members participated in his confinement, even helping to nail him inside a coffin, they keenly identified with his plight and fixed their hearts on his success. He appealed to both a skeptical rationalism and a deep-seated desire for magical transformation. Dramatic and psychological symbolism conjoined as he moved from vulnerability and impotence, degradation and confinement to a liberation that seemed nothing short of miraculous. In achieving his freedom, he realized fantasies of omnipotent abilities and supernatural powers. Newspaper accounts repeatedly noted the mounting tension that accompanied many of Houdini's challenge escapes and the near hysteria that greeted his triumphs. His celebrated boast spoke to broad public needs and aspirations: "Nothing on earth can hold him a prisoner."[88]

"NEARLY DYING FOR A LIVING"

For roughly the first half of Houdini's career, his feats stressed his powers as an escape artist but not as a daredevil. Then, beginning in the fall of 1906, in tandem with his challenge escapes, and escalating over the next decade, he staged an ingenious variety of challenges to pain, injury, and death itself. Instead of relying on newspaper coverage of prison breaks to generate publicity for his vaudeville appearances, he began his celebrated bridge jumps, in which he leaped, handcuffed and chained, into a river as thousands watched. Onstage he offered new escapes in which spectators feared not simply for his success but for his life. And among his challenge escapes, situations of torture and bodily risk grew prominent. In 1914 and 1915, he capped these feats by introducing his most suspenseful onstage and offstage escapes—the "Chinese Water Torture Cell" and the aerial straitjacket

release—in which death itself seemed to have become the jailer in whose clutches he placed himself.

Such feats sprang from Houdini's intense professional ambition and, quite possibly, his equally intense inner demands. The fascination with bodily injury and violent death that captivated him as a boy watching the cut-up man in "Palingenesia" continued to grip him as an adult. He collected articles and photographs of grotesquely mutilated bodies and was grimly attracted to the sites of such casualties. While performing in Cleveland in March 1908, for example, he recorded in his diary a trip to view the remains of schoolchildren whose "arms and legs [had been] burnt off" in a fire.[89] Other males (particularly those with enveloping mothers and emotionally absent fathers) have experienced similar fascination with and dread of mutilation,[90] and if such concerns in fact preoccupied Houdini, then he brilliantly converted them to his professional advantage. As an escape artist, he increasingly made it his business not only to free himself from seemingly inescapable contrivances but to give male anxieties and even terrors powerfully dramatic shape and to triumph over them. He was the self-proclaimed "Handcuff King" and mysterious "Prison Defier," but he aspired to achieve even more. As he declared in a 1910 interview:

> I want to be first. I vehemently want to be first. First in my profession, in my speciality in my profession. For that I give all the thought, all the power that is in me. . . . When I can no longer, goodbye the joy of life for me! So I have struggled and fought. I have done and abstained; I have tortured my body and risked my life only for that—to have one plank on the stage where the imitators cannot come, and one spot where they all fall back and cry, "Master!"[91]

His achievements indeed sealed Houdini's enduring fame as a master magician, fearless defier of death, greatest "self-liberator" of the age. They also brought to a climax an extraordinary career of spectacular performances of masculinity unrivaled among popular entertainers of the day. The innovations he launched reward close examination.

The Harvard Bridge Jump, 1908.
(ABOVE) Houdini just before the
jump. (CENTER) Houdini in the
middle of the jump, legs apart.
Note the spectators on poles,
packed along the bridge and
below it, and on the boats.
(BELOW) Houdini as he nears
the water. Library of Congress

They started with his bridge jumps. To leap from a high city bridge into the water below is generally the act of a suicide. To do so manacled would seem the act of a madman. Yet beginning in the fall of 1906, Houdini made such leaps repeatedly, staying underwater until he released himself. Crowds, mostly men and boys, routinely numbering ten thousand and reaching as many as forty thousand, flocked to these events.

One of his first and most famous jumps took place at Detroit's Belle Isle Bridge on November 27, 1906. Stripping down to his trousers, then being fettered by manacles and two sets of handcuffs, he leaped twenty-five feet to the water as onlookers gasped. After twice surfacing and disappearing again under the water, he gaily held the released bonds aloft. Later accounts by Houdini and others exaggerated the story, turning the chilly water into thick ice, locking Houdini in a trunk, and having him conduct an excruciating search for a hole in the ice to find his way to the surface. (The 1953 film *Houdini* outrageously stretched even these accounts: in it Houdini is directed toward an opening in the ice by his mother's voice—only to learn later that she died in New York at that precise moment, seven years before her actual death.)

Even without such embellishments, Houdini's jumps aroused considerable suspense, and he performed them throughout the country in 1907 and 1908—in Rochester, Pittsburgh, Denver, San Francisco, Los Angeles, New Orleans, Boston, and Atlantic City. Keenly alert to publicity, he offered a prize of ten dollars for the best photograph of each jump. In May 1908 in Philadelphia he plunged forty-four feet into the murky Schuylkill River and remained underwater for an agonizing seventy-nine seconds. As one journalist reported: "The very air seemed surcharged with excitement and apprehension. . . . [S]trong men began to shudder, and women's shrieks of fear filled the air." When at last he surfaced, proudly displaying the unlocked handcuffs and chains, the reporter continued,

how those excited thousands of spectators did cheer and the tug[boats]s added their noises to the din. It was a spontaneous outburst of relief, and it could not have been heartier if this man . . . had been the blood brother of every man of the joy-mad thousands. After all, there is nothing in life, paradoxically,

perhaps, which man so loves to see as his fellow-man risk his
life in an encounter with danger and death.[92]

Houdini keenly appreciated this paradox. He appealed to a desire
for momentousness and risk felt by those caught up in predictable urban routines. Devising new games of challenge and escape, he moved
from hide-and-seek to Russian roulette. As he later wrote in an article
titled "Nearly Dying for a Living":

> [T]he easiest way to attract a crowd is to let it be known that at
> a given time and a given place some one is going to attempt
> something that in the event of failure will mean sudden death.
> That's what attracts us to the man who paints the flagstaff on
> the tall building, or to the "human fly" who scales the walls of
> the same building.
> If we knew that there was no possibility of either one of
> them falling or, if they did fall, that they wouldn't injure them-
> selves in any way, we wouldn't pay any more attention to them
> than we do a nurse-maid wheeling a baby carriage.

Danger was a masculine realm, his language suggests, safety the
sphere of women and infants. Houdini walked a fine line as he sought
to heighten the drama of his feats and at the same time keep spectators from recoiling in horror. He reassured them that he possessed secrets on how to survive mortal danger but cautioned that if for some
reason these secrets failed, all was lost.[93]

Was Houdini actually risking his life? He certainly sought to give
that impression. Before the bridge jump in Detroit, he flamboyantly
scrawled a one-sentence will on the back of an envelope—"I leave all
to Bess"—and handed it to his assistant.[94] Adding to the drama, on
this and other occasions, Bess skillfully played the role of anxious
wife. Yet privately Houdini wrote to a friend prior to a similar jump,
"I have not a single fear of the result, if I had I would not GO!"[95] On
still other occasions, he vaguely acknowledged an element of risk, for
example, after a jump in Rochester, New York, on May 6, 1907, at
which his mother was present: he wanted her there, he said, because
"I thought something might happen." That she beheld his triumph
also elated him: "Ma saw me jump!" he wrote in his diary.[96] Houdini

claimed that the cuffs and manacles he used were never fixed, and he stressed that releasing them underwater was "dangerous business at best." Nonetheless, at the very jump his mother attended, one pair of handcuffs had flown off by the time he hit the water.[97] Perhaps the actual jumps involved as great a risk, because the water was often shallow. Generally, he jumped feetfirst. When in Atlantic City he dived from a pier, he hit his head against the ocean floor.

As in his bridge jumps, in his vaudeville act Houdini devised new ways of satisfying his fellowman's hunger to watch him in encounters with death. In December 1907 he initiated his milk-can escape, his most frightening feat to date. His private description of it expressed pride, not fear: "The new Can trick is the best that I have ever invented. In this I am submerged in a large can, that has been filled with water, and the lid is placed on and locked with 6 padlocks, and in 3 minutes I am free. It is a fine looking trick, and almost defies detection."[98] The trick was accomplished through the ingenious construction of the can rather than through the use of special tools. The can

Houdini in the milk can with police officers.
Library of Congress

contained an inner lining that when turned released a catch. As for the impressive locks on which he focused the audience's attention, they were superfluous because the entire top of the can separated from the base at the shoulder well beneath them.[99]

Houdini performed the feat so as to wring out every last drop of suspense. As a showman, he intuitively grasped the dictum of Leopold von Sacher-Masoch (from whose name the word "masochism" derives): "Everything must be stated, promised, announced, and carefully described before being accomplished."[100] When he left the stage to put on a tank suit, uniformed assistants filled the can to the brim. Upon his return, he invited the audience to make a simple test with him before he attempted his escape. At the moment when he climbed into the can and submerged himself, everyone should hold his breath. Most gasped for air within thirty seconds; a very few lasted slightly longer than a minute. Well after the last had quit the effort, Houdini emerged smiling. Having impressed everyone with the difficulty of remaining underwater for long, he then began the actual feat. Assistants handcuffed his wrists and poured additional pails of water into the tank as he submerged himself inside. They fastened the lid with an ominous clank, attached six padlocks to the hasps, then enclosed the can with Houdini's curtained cabinet. With gallows humor, the band played "Asleep in the Deep."[101] Members of the audience nervously studied their pocket watches. (As he refined the feat, Houdini installed a huge stopwatch onstage for everyone to see.) Then it became a drama of time. A minute passed, then ninety seconds—longer than anyone in the audience had managed to hold his breath. An assistant marched onstage with an ax in hand and stood by the curtained cabinet, listening intently; in an emergency, Houdini had explained, that man would break open the can. Two minutes elapsed, two and a half, then three. Many spectators were now visibly agitated, convinced that something had gone terribly wrong. The assistant himself appeared concerned and lifted his ax to strike—only to see the curtains suddenly swept open to reveal Houdini, panting, dripping wet, but free. The audience burst into a loud ovation.[102]

In tours in Europe and the United States over the next few years, Houdini varied the script to keep interest high. Responding to challenges from dairies, he had the can filled with milk instead of water; to satisfy brewers, he filled it with beer. In 1910, after being locked in

a tank of Yorkshire ale, he was so overpowered by the carbon dioxide fumes that he almost passed out in the middle of his escape. He called quietly to an assistant for help and completed his feat without the audience's knowledge of his actual danger.

In 1912 both the bridge jumps and the onstage milk-can escape were superseded by new death-defying feats. Instead of leaping manacled from bridges, he now submitted to the usual handcuffs and elbow irons, then had himself locked in an iron-weighted wooden trunk that was nailed shut and fastened with iron bands. At a signal from Houdini's assistant, the trunk was lowered into a body of water. This was, of course, a variation of the old trick of "Metamorphosis," and in both cases part of the trick was to have virtually completed his escape before spectators were aware it had even begun. (Here, as in so much of Houdini's escape art, the role of his assistants was crucial.) Houdini intended to inaugurate this feat off New York City's East River pier to fan publicity for his opening at Hammerstein's Roof Garden in July 1912, but for once the police refused him permission. Undeterred, he twice performed the feat beyond local jurisdiction in New York harbor—with the press corps eagerly bobbing alongside and thousands of spectators watching from ferryboats. Since, unlike most theaters, Hammerstein's Roof Garden boasted a large pool, he repeated the feat onstage each night.

Two months later, while on tour in Berlin, he unveiled the successor to his milk-can escape, the "Chinese Water Torture Cell." The following summer, he introduced it to American audiences, again at Hammerstein's Roof Garden in New York. It was Houdini's most compelling stage escape, one that he repeated hundreds of times, including in some of the last performances before his death in 1926. What most distinguished the "Chinese Water Torture Cell" from the milk-can escape was that it allowed Houdini to create a spectacle out of his body, which was visible through all the preparations, though the actual escape remained hidden from view. Over the next few years, Houdini refined the trick to enhance this effect.

He began by displaying onstage an imposing metal-lined mahogany cabinet, less than six feet high and less than three feet square, with an inch-thick plate-glass window in front. He solemnly explained its features and how he would attempt an escape under seemingly impossible conditions: locked upside down inside, his ankles

Houdini being lowered into the "Chinese Water Torture Cell," c. 1913. Library of Congress

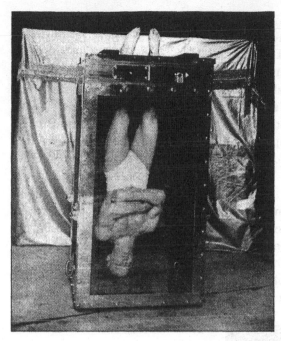

Houdini submerged in a later version of the "Water Torture Cell." Sidney H. Radner Collection, Houdini Historical Center, Appleton, Wisconsin

shackled, and completely immersed in water. He would forfeit a thousand dollars to anyone who could prove he received air inside the tank. "We all know accidents will happen—and when least expected," he continued, heightening the tension, so, "should anything go wrong," one of his assistants would stand ready with an ax to smash the glass front of the cabinet. Houdini would be protected from the broken glass by a full-length steel grill inside the tank, but this cage ostensibly further restricted his movements and made his escape still more difficult. (In a later version, he removed the grill to provide a more unobstructed view of his body underwater.)[103]

Then, while Houdini changed into a bathing suit offstage, volunteers from the audience examined the tank, and his assistants, wearing boots and slickers, filled it to the brim with water. After he returned, his ankles were secured in heavy mahogany stocks, which in turn were fitted into a solid steel frame. Slowly and dramatically, he was hoisted aloft and lowered headfirst into the cell, his entire body visible underwater through the glass. Assistants quickly locked the frame in place, fastened the tank with padlocked steel bands, then

curtained off the entire cabinet from view. Thenceforth, the feat followed the script of the milk-can escape. Once again, the orchestra played "Asleep in the Deep." A minute passed, two minutes, as many as three. Spectators invited to hold their breath from the moment Houdini was immersed had long since given up. Once again, a stalwart assistant, wearing fireman's gear, anxiously raised a large ax. Suddenly Houdini thrust the curtain aside and strode forward, dripping wet but smiling triumphantly. The empty cell behind him stood as strongly locked as before. He was inevitably greeted by thunderous applause.

Although Houdini insisted there was "nothing supernatural" about the feat, a prominent British exponent of "psychic science," J. Hewat McKenzie, asserted that to perform such tricks, Houdini dematerialized himself and oozed out. This explanation was embraced by other spiritualist adherents, including Sir Arthur Conan Doyle, the creator of Sherlock Holmes. The exact workings of the water-torture cell remain a mystery, although some biographers have speculated

Detail of a poster for the "Water Torture Cell," Cardiff, Wales, 1913. Library of Congress

that the grill allowed Houdini to work his head and shoulders to the top of the tank and to release the catch on the stocks, pull them out like a drawer, and so escape. Later, when he eliminated the grill, the catch may have been automatically released when the water reached a certain level.[104]

The "Chinese Water Torture Cell" also made explicit what had been a growing theme in Houdini's challenges and escapes: torture. (In one poster a gigantic black fiend holding Houdini within the cell made this theme especially lurid.) Many of the modern devices from which Houdini escaped carried strong suggestions of pain and even terror, and he often finished scratched, bleeding, and apparently on the brink of collapse. Other outmoded restraints were occasionally revived to test Houdini's mettle, and these allowed modern spectators to look back with horror at the barbarities of the past. They included a cruel iron body cage used to punish witches in colonial New England; a still more pitiless Scottish body cage, by which criminals "were hung in midair until death released them from their misery";[105] and, in Dover, England, "an old and obsolete Padded Cell Suit, a restraint which has been abolished on account of its extremely cruel nature in holding the criminal insane."[106] Challengers from Liverpool described with sadistic relish ship irons once used to hold mutineers on the high seas. The men proposed to "manacle and truss you up in the old fashioned PUNISHMENT method; you to lay on your back, your hands manacled to your knees, a staff placed behind your knees and between your arms, holding you in an immovable position, also heavy lead leg irons locked on your ankles."[107]

In freeing himself from such antique devices, Houdini seemed to escape from the clutches of history itself and to defeat at last the oppressive authorities that had tortured individuals with impunity. He made these connections explicit in his 1913 escape from the HMS *Success*, the infamous British ship that had supposedly carried many convicts to Australia in the late eighteenth and early nineteenth centuries without ever yielding a prisoner. Moored at a pier in New York City as a floating museum and plentifully equipped with whipping posts, cat-o'-nine-tails, manacles, branding irons, "and other fiendish inventions of men's brutality to his fellow man," it offered Houdini the opportunity to become the first man in history to escape from the cells deep in its hold.[108]

In such escapes, Houdini simultaneously flattered spectators' sense of moral superiority over those who meted out harsh punishments in earlier times and offered them the spectacle of corporeal punishment and even execution that modern Western governments had either outlawed or moved behind closed doors. Whatever personal meanings these cultivated encounters with pain, injury, and death held for Houdini, he demonstrated again and again their fascination for a broad international public. He brilliantly gave the manifold challenges to individual freedom—and, more specifically, to the male body—tangible shape. In moving beyond mere physical privations, such as handcuffs, jail cells, and prisons, to direct confrontations with pain and death, he challenged what the literary critic Elaine Scarry has called the two most intense forms of human negation.[109] In many of his escapes, he turned the process of torture inside out. He gave fear and pain, in both their stark ancient forms and their more diffuse modern guises, compelling dramatic shape and then defied their power either to torment his body or to subdue his spirit. As with his earlier handcuff and jail-cell escapes, such triumphs over torture carried important if unspecified political implications. By dramatizing the isolated male's ability to confront and defeat the most palpable threats to his body, he became a powerful symbol of individual resistance to intimidation and domination. That is why his acts of "self-liberation" assumed an almost messianic character.

Houdini's single most spectacular self-inflicted torture still remained: his aerial straitjacket escape, which quickly superseded all his other outdoor feats and drew the largest crowds of his career. He appears first to have executed this escape in Kansas City on September 8, 1915. By this time he had been wriggling out of straitjackets for almost twenty years but never before while suspended upside down over a city street in full view of thousands. For days *The Kansas City Post*, known for its sensational journalism, had trumpeted the coming event to its readers. The Kansas City police department furnished its "best and strongest straitjacket" for the occasion, and two of its detectives tightened the "straps to the very last ounce of their strength." "If you get out of that you can get out of anything," one told Houdini. Dangling by his ankles, the illusionist was slowly hoisted twenty-five feet above the street by a block and tackle attached to the roof of the *Post* building. As five thousand onlookers

craned their necks upward, he began to contort his body wildly. Like a great fish on a line fighting for its life, he put every muscle into the effort. Within seconds, he began to inch his arms under the tight canvas and leather straps. Then with surprising swiftness, he tugged the jacket down toward his shoulders, wrenched it off, and flung it to the pavement.[110]

Houdini performing an upside-down aerial straitjacket escape, suspended from Keith's Theatre across from the U.S. Treasury Building, Washington, D.C., 1922.
Library of Congress

During the next three years he repeated this escape across the country in virtually every city in which he performed that had a tall office building (at times he made do with a crane or tower). He continued to perform the feat at less frequent intervals into the 1920s. Shrewdly, he chose a newspaper building whenever possible, so that reporters were sure to publicize the event. He attracted numerous still and movie photographers as well. His favorite time was half past noon, the middle of the lunch hour. Often he ascended to much greater heights than in his initial effort. "String me up just as high as you can," he told police officials in one city. "If I drop I want to be sure it's going to be the finish. I'd rather have a lilly [sic] in my hand than go through life crippled and a burden to others."[111]

These suspended straitjacket escapes offer striking comparisons with his youthful beginnings. The man who as a boy grandiosely dreamed of becoming "Ehrich, the Prince of the Air," could truthfully boast, as he did after one performance in Boston, "My eye was the axis of the town."[112] The onetime medicine-show and circus performer who had offered free acts to lure small-town customers now turned great cities into his stage. Where once he pitched his feats to indifferent bystanders, now he drew as many as eighty thousand rapt spectators.

Women and especially men and boys streamed to the sites, clogging sidewalks and streets for blocks. Thicker than pigeons, they perched at the windows and roofs of neighboring buildings, drawn by a spirit that mixed Fourth of July festivities, a circus parade, and a hanging.[113] They watched expectantly as police or insane asylum officials vigorously tightened the jacket around Houdini. As his successes mounted, so did the ambition of officials to be the first to defeat him. A San Antonio police chief declared, "We know that he has baffled the officers in other cities, but we have hopes we can turn the trick here."[114] After these men had completed their work, Houdini's assistants carefully raised him aloft. When he reached the desired height, his body became a blur of motion. The sight of a man writhing wildly to free himself from an immobilizing restraint while suspended as much as 150 feet above the pavement, his every movement exaggerated by the swaying rope, offered not just a giddy acrobatic exhibition but an unforgettable example of manly determination and courage. Stiff as his straitjacket was, it served as an elastic metaphor for every-

RIGHT: Soldiers tightening Houdini into a straitjacket, in the *Ladies' Home Journal*, May 1918. The University of North Carolina at Chapel Hill

Note My Square Shoulders and Expanded Chest as the Soldiers Pull Tight the Straps of the Jacket at the Back

PHOTOGRAPHS BY WHITE STUDIO

3
I Have Dropped My Shoulders and De-flated My Chest; Note the Changed Relation of the Arms

5
It's Easy Enough Now to Reach Up and Unfasten the Buckles at the Back of the Jacket

1
This is the First Position. Ob-serve the Placement of the Arms in Relation to Each Other Here

4
I Have Put My Head Through My Arms and They are Free

6
And So, in Less Than a Min-ute I Am Free. Simple, Isn't It? What You Know I do?

Stages in Houdini's straitjacket escape, in the *Ladies' Home Journal*, May 1918. The University of North Carolina at Chapel Hill

thing that restrained human movement, liberty, and aspiration. Similarly, his victorious upside-down salute to the crowd—both arms outstretched as he remained suspended high over the city—proclaimed his triumph over privation, officialdom, fear, and death. It renewed hope that in the rising skyscraper civilization, the heroic individual could still claim victory against all odds.

The drama of the aerial straitjacket escapes was unparalleled; and ever since Houdini performed them, people have debated their actual difficulties and risks. Just as Houdini had mastered fear of dark, airless enclosures, he now defied dizzying heights in which a slip would mean certain death. To shed the straitjacket, he tried to gain as much slack as possible, then twist vigorously as he maneuvered inside it. The upside-down position slightly aided in both these efforts. It

lengthened his body somewhat and permitted considerable contortions. But the performer paid a heavy price, even assuming he had no fear of heights. His ankles could easily be strained in the process, and rushing blood could cloud his brain. The ropes could snarl, the pulley stick, and he might swing into the side of a building. All these difficulties Houdini encountered on one occasion or another. Only extreme vigilance on his part and that of his assistants prevented more serious or fatal accidents.[115]

MASCULINE VERSUS FEMININE MAGIC

Houdini attempted several more metamorphoses in his career. Though he remained a man of extraordinary physical energy and endurance, the strain of escapes on a now middle-aged body took its toll. As early as April 1911, his wife, Bess, anxiously observed in a letter, "Harry is worked to death, he looks so old." He absorbed numerous punishments over the years. His first lasting injury occurred seven months after that letter, in November 1911, when, freeing himself from a bag tied by longshoremen in Detroit, he ruptured a blood vessel in one of his kidneys.[116] On a number of occasions during this period, publicly and privately, he had wondered how long he could go on performing his strenuous feats.

Also, in July 1913 while on tour in Copenhagen, he suffered the greatest emotional blow of his life, from which he never entirely recovered. There he received news of his mother's fatal stroke. She was seventy-two; Houdini, thirty-nine. Just as Houdini's father's death had defined his entrance to adulthood, his mother's death marked his passage to middle age. She had been unquestionably the greatest love of his life. As he wrote to his brother Theo: "[M]y Heart will AL- WAYS ACHE FOR OUR DARLING MOTHER. . . . [M]y very Existence seems to have expired with her." Then he added, "Must try and cheer up and be a man."[117] Against the finality of death, he desperately craved some sort of reunion with her. Ultimately, the struggle between this longing for authentic communion and the bitterness of sham contact, the desire for maternal comfort and the fear of being deceived by a rival's illusions led to his passionate battle against spiritualist frauds in the 1920s. But even before this point, in 1916, expressing his desire to

move in new directions, he told a *Washington Times* reporter, "As an escapist extraordinary I feel that I'm about through." "For the last thirty years, or thereabouts," he explained, "I've been getting out of all sorts of things human ingenuity has devised to confine a human being. Hereafter, I intend to work entirely with my brain."[118]

Houdini never abandoned escape art, but the spectacular innovations he had made famous for two decades were at an end. Other developments besides physical and emotional demands contributed to this shift. Even though he was at the height of his career in vaudeville and variety, he felt the looming shadow of the movies, which by then usually closed his vaudeville bills and ultimately, in tandem with radio, eclipsed vaudeville as an institution. In addition, the war had suspended his practice of alternating tours between America and Europe. Seeking new and less taxing outlets, he determined to become both a movie star and an industry mogul. Beginning in 1916, he poured a great deal of time, energy, and money into the Film Development Corporation, a company working to improve processing methods. He went on to make seven films between 1918 and 1923, including *The Master Mystery*, in which he battles a robotic villain, and *Terror Island*, in which (as in a Tarzan film) he foils a tribe of spear-waving black cannibals. But as brilliant as Houdini had been in the compressed dramas of his live-action escapes, he proved a poor writer and a worse actor in these flaccid melodramas. The immediacy, power, mystery, and suspense of his stage and street feats were dissipated on film. As he ruefully concluded: "*No* illusion is good in a Film, as we simply resort to *camera* trix, and the deed is did."[119]

Houdini attempted other metamorphoses as well. Long a passionate collector of materials on magic and magic history, he became a major collector in these and related fields, including theater, mystery, and spiritualism. In the process, he repurchased some of the books his father had long ago been forced to sell and eagerly sought the prestige of a bibliophile and scholar. When the United States entered the war in 1917, the child of German speakers also turned himself into a 100 percent American. Passed over for military service at age forty-three, he threw himself into the war effort: entertaining American troops and performing in a patriotic revue called *Cheer Up*. He also sought to put his knowledge of escape to the national defense. He wrote to the secretary of war offering secrets on how soldiers and

sailors might rescue themselves from sinking vessels, and during intermissions of *Cheer Up*, he proposed to teach American servicemen how to escape from German manacles. "Any one can be taught to escape from them," he confided, "if he is willing to endure a little pain in the process."[120]

After almost two decades of specialization as an escape artist, Houdini developed a new and less physically punishing role as a master magician. He had offered a general magic show in 1914, when he was emotionally exhausted after his mother's death. In his performances in *Cheer Up* in 1918, he introduced a new illusion in which he made an elephant disappear, and in the 1920s he offered other magical illusions to supplement his famous escapes.

The most consuming metamorphosis of Houdini's later career, however, was as a crusader against spiritualism. The contest brought many personal and cultural elements into play, including Houdini's skepticism, his longing for emotional comfort, the prestige of science, the lure of the supernatural—and a battle of the sexes. Professional magic was (and remains) overwhelmingly a male preserve—escape art, almost exclusively so. The drama of submission and release, bodily risk and mastery goes deeply to issues of masculine prowess and identity. Spiritualism attracted both sexes, but from its beginnings, women were especially prominent as mediums and as believers. Mediumship offered a means by which women could gain power, attention, and income; it enabled them to accept the tightest bonds of femininity—passivity, spirituality, and suffering—and then slip them off. Such women practiced a form of feminine magic that was in important respects the mirror image of Houdini's masculine escape art.[121]

Modern spiritualism began in 1848 in Hydesville, New York, possibly as a girlish hoax. Two young sisters, Catherine and Margaret Fox, claimed to establish contact with a mysterious spirit in their house that communicated through strange rappings. Soon, joined by their older sister Leah, they were charging admission and became celebrities. Countless other mediums quickly discovered similar gifts, including the brothers Ira and William Davenport of nearby Buffalo, New York. Beginning in the 1850s, spiritualism swept across the country and across the Atlantic to Britain and Europe, leaving its mark on many religious and social issues, from women's rights and

The Davenport brothers with an assistant in their spirit cabinet.

Library of Congress

abolitionism to health reform. At a time when women could not publicly address mixed audiences with propriety, women mediums became, in effect, lay ministers when they took to the stage to perform spirit trances. Spiritualism appeared to offer "scientific" confirmation of immortality without doctrinal complications such as original sin, atonement, final judgment, and hell—all of which it blithely dismissed. It thus provided an optimistic, democratic alternative to sin-sick torment and the dread of damnation. Death had no sting for spirits who merely passed from earthly life to the "Summerland" beyond—from which they might visit the living at will. No soul was truly departed; each continued to grow in body and personality as well as spirit as it advanced through heavenly spheres to ultimate rest.[122]

The dramatic demonstrations of spirit communication inevitably drew investigators and detractors, not only clergymen, scientists, and physicians but also professional magicians. From the eighteenth century through Robert-Houdin's writings, numerous magicians had exposed those who used magic tricks in the name of the supernatural, and the advent of spiritualism intensified this rivalry. As early as 1852, during his first American tour, the celebrated Scottish magician John

Henry Anderson challenged spiritualists directly. He demonstrated their hidden methods so that all could see: "I caused my table to rap as loudly and as intelligently as theirs."[123] Many other prominent British magicians, including Robert Heller and H. S. Lynn, emulated his example. The English conjurer J. N. Maskelyne ridiculed spiritualists' pretensions in his book *Modern Spiritualism* (1876) and exposed their effects onstage. As a volunteer from the audience, he claimed to catch the Davenport brothers red-handed as they slipped their rope bonds inside a spirit cabinet to rattle tambourines, ring bells, and play a tune on the violin and guitar.[124] Similarly, the leading American magician in the generation before Houdini, Harry Kellar, who had worked as an assistant to the Davenport brothers in the early 1870s, launched his own international career by employing and exposing spiritualist methods, especially the Davenports' signature rope-tie release.[125]

Houdini had early learned lessons in escape from such spiritualist-magicians, and, in company with other conjurers, he regarded the Davenport brothers as among the great escape artists of the nineteenth century. He even briefly offered spiritualist effects in the 1890s and saw firsthand their electric result.[126] Yet after his mother's death he came himself to crave the comforts of direct contact with the departed that spiritualism promised. And the extraordinary resurgence of interest in spiritualism following the Great War rekindled Houdini's maternal longing. It also aroused his masculine ire, however. Sir Arthur Conan Doyle sought to convert Houdini to his self-styled virile brand of spiritualism, for which he had become a fervent evangelist after the death of his son in the war. But, flattered as Houdini was by this friendship, their radically different stances toward spiritualism ultimately erupted into a highly public quarrel. After these diverse experiences, beginning in the early 1920s, Houdini devoted considerable energy to unmasking spiritualist charlatans with all the drama and publicity at his command. Wearing disguises, he attended séances and caught mediums in the act. In various publications, including his book *A Magician among the Spirits* (1924), he debunked spiritualist tricks; on the lecture circuit and in stage performances he duplicated their effects for all to see.

Houdini's most formidable antagonist, and the one who most strikingly exposed the gender war at the center of the magic, was a Boston

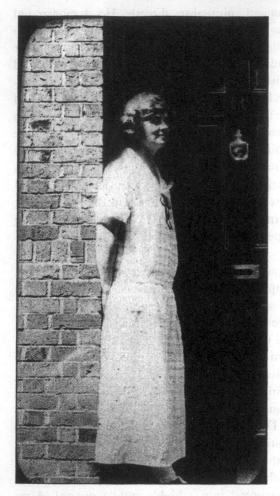

"Margery" (Mina Crandon),
1924. Library of Congress

medium known as Margery. His encounter with her came in response
to a contest conducted by *Scientific American*. The venerable monthly
magazine of science and technology had offered prizes, ultimately
raised to five thousand dollars, for "an authentic spirit photograph"
and for "the first physical manifestation of a psychic nature produced
under scientific conditions." The magazine's editor appointed a committee of supposed experts to conduct tests and verify results. A diverse lot, they included Dr. William McDougall, the chairman of
Harvard's Department of Psychology and president of the American

Society for Psychic Research; Hereward Carrington, an energetic investigator into psychic phenomena and an amateur magician; Dr. Daniel F. Comstock, an industrial engineer and former professor of physics at the Massachusetts Institute of Technology; Dr. Walter Franklin Prince, the chief research officer for the American Society for Psychic Research, a psychologist, former clergyman, and member of the Society of American Magicians; and Houdini.

During the spring of 1924 a number of mediums, both men and women, came forward to claim the prize, only to be quickly discredited. Margery, however, distinguished herself from her competitors in her social credentials, her amateur status, her aversion to the limelight, and her range of apparent psychic effects. Indeed, the name Margery was a pseudonym intended to shield her during *Scientific American*'s investigations from the publicity her rivals craved—though journalists quickly revealed her true identity. She was Mina Crandon, a blue-eyed, honey-haired woman in her mid-thirties who charmed many psychic investigators and reporters with her beauty and vivacity. In 1917 she had met a prominent, middle-aged Boston surgeon, Le Roi Crandon, whom she soon married. (It was her second marriage and her husband's third.) A former instructor at Harvard Medical School, Dr. Crandon was an ardent rationalist with a dignified, scholarly demeanor. In the early 1920s, he had read and grown excited about spiritualist phenomena, and beginning in the spring of 1923, his wife rapidly discovered her own psychic gifts. The couple began holding frequent, at times nightly, séances within their fashionable social and medical circles at their Beacon Hill home. In December 1923, during a whirlwind trip abroad, Margery astounded leading spiritualist proponents, including the physiologist (and 1913 Nobel laureate) Charles-Robert Richet in France and Sir Arthur Conan Doyle in England. In the summer of 1924, on both sides of the Atlantic, her partisans were already declaring her the most important medium of the twentieth century.

Most mediums specialized in either psychic communications or physical manifestations of spirits; Margery displayed astonishing powers in both domains. Tilting the table at her first séance in late May 1923, she quickly became a medium for coded rappings from spirits. Soon she fluently transcribed messages from the spirit world, includ-

ing lines in Latin, Italian, French, German, Swedish, Dutch, Greek, and ideographic Chinese. Even as she was claiming to be in contact with the spirit world, her corporeal presence stressed a heightened erotic allure: at her séances, she usually wore just a loose dressing gown, silk stockings, and slippers. To monitor her movements, the sitters not only took her hand but occasionally held her legs in their laps as well. At times during a deep trance, she fell into violent seizures as if possessed. At the end of 1924, after the investigations by Houdini and *Scientific American* had concluded and the controversy over them was at its height, she drew still more attention to her body by producing ectoplasm, which spiritualists regarded as the ultimate proof of ghostly presence. When a spirit's power grew sufficiently strong, they believed, it partially rematerialized through the medium's bodily orifices. In Margery's case, these included her mouth, nose, ears, navel, and vagina. First and last, however, what integrated many of Margery's phenomena and most fascinated spiritualist adherents, investigators, and the public was the personality of the figure called her spirit-control, or principal contact and guide to the world beyond, her dead older brother Walter.

Walter had died in 1911 at the age of twenty-eight, crushed between a railroad car and a tender while working as a fireman on the New York, New Haven, and Hartford Railroad. He was five years older than Margery and still spoke of her, when his hoarse, whispering voice was heard in her séances, as "the Kid." He usually whistled to announce his presence, at times rendering a popular song. He became the star of the show. A lusty, irreverent, and often profane young man, he would banter with the séance circle. When someone greeted his presence familiarly, "Hello, Walter. Where have you been?" he replied jauntily, "Oh, I had to take my girl to a strawberry festival." "Can you read my mind?" another asked. "Yes," he said, "but you wouldn't want me to tell *that*!" "Walter," a third ventured, "when you are relaxed, do you surround yourself with youth and beauty?" Walter would laugh heartily at the lofty sentiment and pat the speaker's head. "No, I'm not relaxed when youth and beauty are around. I'm under fifty!"[127] Wielding props—both supplied and unseen—around the séance room and chuckling like a low vaudeville comedian, he frequently mocked the guests' propriety and hushed expectancy. He recited limericks and parodied hymns:

Onward, psychic soldiers,
Marching as to war,
With the cross of Science
Going on before . . .[128]

He also produced impressive special effects. These extended from commonplace ghostly efforts, such as starting and stopping a record player or a clock and moving furniture around the house, to his own parlor magic: inventorying the contents of sitters' pockets, producing flowers and, on one occasion, a live pigeon. He played many instruments, including the ukulele, harmonica, tambourine, and bass drum, at times whistling an accompaniment in what he once called his own "jazz band." When sitters expressed surprise that he and his spirit crowd should know current popular tunes, "the explanation was offered that they go everywhere to our theaters as to other places." At the conclusion of a séance in 1925, he congratulated himself in terms that made the comparison with vaudeville explicit: "Continuous performance, good as Keith's."[129]

The presence of Walter and his spirit friends seemed still more palpable at Margery's séances because of a variety of touches bestowed on individual sitters, ranging from kisses to kicks, feelings of a powder puff to a hard fist. Occasionally regular participants saw Walter's body parts, such as an eye, hand, or finger, luminously displayed. In response to scientific investigators, Walter could be helpfully interested and occasionally truculent. When so inclined, he patiently participated in experiments, often making suggestions and modifications, like a psychic engineer. But in testier moods, he reminded people that a spirit's life was no bed of roses. In response to a request that he operate an intricate mechanical device brought by one investigator, he snapped, "I have to experiment and work out things in my sphere just as you do in yours. . . . If you think I'm here just to wander around the room making demonstrations, you're damn mistaken."[130]

Walter was, of course, Margery's version of "Metamorphosis," her substitution trunk trick (stuffed full of gender politics) in which she left her body to change positions and sexes in ways that mystified her audience. Inverting the drama in which Houdini assumed a feminized position and released himself, Margery simulated the swagger-

ing masculine presence of Walter while appearing never to escape the clasped hands of her fellow sitters around the table. (Her husband usually sat beside her.) Walter's "vigorous and virile" character (in Conan Doyle's phrase) seemed to many to testify to her authenticity as a medium precisely because they could not imagine that this "most charming and cultivated lady" could step into the disembodied but vividly palpable personality of a rough-and-tumble young man. (In fact, since the mid-nineteenth century, many female mediums, under the influence of their masculine spirit-controls, had assumed the personas of swearing sailors, Indian warriors, and lusty suitors.)[131]

Houdini had no such difficulties. Although he came late to the *Scientific American* investigations of Margery, after thirty sessions had taken place, he approached the case as another challenge. Antagonistic from the outset, he offered to pay one thousand dollars if he could not "detect her in fraud."[132] For their part, the Crandons had already been spoken for by Walter in his singsong taunt "Harry Houdini, he sure is a Sheeny."[133] During their first session together, in late July 1924, Houdini, sitting on Margery's left while her husband sat on her right, tried to control at least her left hand and foot. Walter appeared, ringing an electric bell apparatus designed to measure the psychic force between Houdini's feet and knocking over a screen behind Margery. Most dramatically, he picked up a megaphone and spoke: "Have Houdini tell me where to throw it." When Houdini asked that it be thrown to him, the megaphone immediately landed at his feet.[134]

"All fraud—every bit of it," Houdini announced to his co-investigators after he reached the street.[135] As a magician who performed with his body, he believed that he had detected how Margery performed with her own. In preparation for the evening, he had worn a rubber bandage that made his right leg swollen and sensitive; at the séance he pulled up his trouser leg and pressed his ankle to Margery's. He maintained that he felt her leg slide and her tendons contract just as the bell rang between his feet and he felt her lunge to tip the screen behind her. As for the megaphone, he confessed some grudging admiration: it was "the '*slickest*' ruse I have ever detected." At first he thought it depended on a confederate, but, he concluded, Margery had taken advantage of a moment when someone left the room to place the megaphone over her head like an over-

Houdini in the cabinet he devised for Margery. Library of Congress

size dunce cap. Then it was easy to flip it in whatever direction Houdini asked.[136]

In their second session together, Walter produced some dramatic table tipping, but Houdini groped underneath the table with his hand and discovered Margery's head. She lamely explained she was retrieving some dropped hairpins.[137]

These preliminary sessions were followed in August 1924 by official ones for the *Scientific American* contest. In these the investigation committee, heeding Houdini's suggestions, sought to control Margery's movements by devising a wooden cabinet with armholes and

hinged flaps at the top that could be fastened and locked around her neck. In the following séance, Walter taunted Houdini more directly than ever: "You think you're smart, don't you? How much are they paying you for stopping phenomena here?" When Houdini replied, "I don't know what you're talking about; it's costing me $2,500 a week to be here," Walter seemed remarkably knowledgeable about the vaudeville business in the slack summer season. "Where did you turn down a $2,500 contract in August?" he challenged.[138] The session ended without any psychic phenomena.

Before the next session, Margery took a page out of Houdini's playbook by offering to submit to a full anatomic search by a physician or, if he wished, Houdini himself—or so her supporters later claimed. Houdini reported that she asked him (perhaps challengingly, perhaps flirtatiously), "Do you want to search me?" to which he replied, "No, never mind, let it go. I am not a physician."[139] This time Houdini and a fellow committee member, Walter Prince, controlled Margery's hands as she sat in the cabinet, so that, as Houdini declared during the session, if she took out a concealed device by which to ring the bell apparatus on the table in front of her, it would be exposed when the cabinet was searched. When Walter "arrived," he spoke not in his usual hoarse whisper but in a loud, clear voice, strongly insinuating that Houdini or his assistant had planted a carpenter's folding ruler (with which Margery might ring the bell) in the cabinet under his kid sister's feet. "Houdini, you Goddamned son of a bitch," he raged, "get the Hell out of here and never come back. If you don't, I will."[140] The explosion, Houdini wrote, "just expressed Mrs. Crandon's feelings toward me, as she knew I had her trapped."[141] When inspected, the cabinet did indeed contain a folding ruler. For the final session, another member of the investigating committee devised a knee-high compartment to use as a control device in place of Houdini's wooden cabinet. With Houdini and another member tightly holding Margery's hands, nothing remarkable occurred.

By his own account, Houdini both exposed Margery as a magician and triumphed in this battle of the sexes: "I charge Mrs. Crandon with practicing her feats daily like a professional conjuror. Also that because of her training as a secretary, her long experience as a professional musician [she played the cello, piano, and cornet], and her athletic build she is not simple and guileless but a shrewd, cunning

woman, resourceful in the extreme, and taking advantage of every opportunity to produce a 'manifestation.' "[142] The manifestations she produced, of course, were not simply spiritualist but masculine. Walter's brash whistle and taunting voice, irreverence, and aggressiveness suggested that a swaggering male sexuality lay within her as well. In exposing Margery's fraud, Houdini also exposed her as a woman who, despite all her guides and talents, could only sham the phallus.

Although the *Scientific American* committee deliberated the Margery case for several more months, ultimately all but Carrington were unconvinced of her powers. In the next few years, other investigators and erstwhile partisans challenged her claims. Nonetheless, she remained the single most sensational medium of her time, retaining loyalists within the American Society for Psychic Research as well as finding new partisans, including the writer Hamlin Garland and the poet William Butler Yeats. As Margery lay dying in 1941, a would-be confidante encouraged her to reveal both how she had achieved her spiritualist effects and, equally pressing, why she had done so. But she adhered to her own magician's code and reportedly replied, "All you psychic investigators can go to hell."[143]

AN UNSOUGHT CHALLENGE

Following the Margery investigations, Houdini continued to make exposures of spiritualist frauds a major part of his activities both on and offstage. For their part, spiritualists railed against him, and Walter warned darkly that Houdini had a year or less to live. Characteristically, Houdini shrugged off this threat: "In the last 10 years my death has been predicted dozens of times, and if the spiritualists (?) guess often enough some time they will guess correctly."[144]

On October 22, 1926, three days after giving a lecture on spiritualist frauds at McGill University, Houdini was visited by three McGill students in his dressing room at the Princess Theatre in Montreal. One of these, a strapping young man named Whitehead, itched to test Houdini's fortitude. "Is it true," he asked, "that you can resist the hardest blow struck to the abdomen?" It was a question more appropriately put to a Sandow than to an escape artist who had never made such a public boast. According to the best eyewitness account, Hou-

dini tried to dodge the issue, inviting Whitehead to feel his forearm and back muscles instead. But the young man persisted, finally asking, "Would you mind if I delivered a few blows to your abdomen, Mr. Houdini?" Houdini reluctantly agreed, and before he could rise from his couch, Whitehead pummeled him with "four or five terribly forcible, deliberate, well-directed blows."[145]

In pain, Houdini completed his final Montreal appearance the following day. He proceeded to Detroit—only to collapse at the end of his evening performance. Three days after the assault, he entered Detroit's Grace Hospital. He wanted to walk from his bed to the operating room where surgeons would remove his ruptured appendix, and when physicians insisted on a stretcher, he bristled. For almost his entire career he had bested police officials, insane asylum attendants, and other authorities. In his aerial straitjacket escapes, he routinely urged a brace of husky men to strap him in as tightly as they could. Now his serene humor was gone, but his tough defiance remained. "Say," he challenged the orderlies, "I can still lick the two of you."[146] He died of peritonitis six days later on Halloween.

Although magic is an ancient art, Houdini demonstrated its appeal for the modern world. At a time when new technologies seemed imbued with magic, he affirmed the presence of magic within the body and spirit of the individual man. In an age of often bewildering obstacles and intimidating authorities, he dramatized the ability of a lone figure to triumph over the most formidable restraints and the most implacable foes and against the most impossible odds.

In such ways, he extended the sense of the male body's special powers that Eugen Sandow had pioneered. Stripping off his clothes in an instant, Sandow delighted in displaying the strength and dexterity of his extraordinary muscles. Houdini, too, was proud of his strength (a pride that may have contributed to his fatal injury), but the masculine power he embodied was a claim of invincibility, which is why news of his death carried a special shock. Whereas Sandow spoke to fears of enervating weakness and hopes of commanding strength and virility, Houdini appealed to nightmares of entrapment and dreams of triumphant release. Making their often unclad bodies the subject of suspenseful challenges and contests, both affirmed the possibilities

of individual male heroism in the modern world. Their metamorphoses ultimately emphasized not the fluidity but the stability of gender divisions. Sandow appealed to a male ideal purportedly rooted in both ancient sculpture and modern science. Houdini cultivated illusion in order to reaffirm traditional verities of masculinity. The distance between strongman and escape artist was often surprisingly short.

A third overwhelmingly popular embodiment of masculinity brought these figures into even closer conjunction. Though he, too, ultimately appeared in newspapers, magazines, and films, he first emerged not in dime museums or on the vaudeville and music-hall stage, as did Sandow and Houdini, but from the pen of a frustrated businessman, Edgar Rice Burroughs.

THREE

"STILL A WILD BEAST AT HEART"

EDGAR RICE BURROUGHS

AND THE DREAM OF *TARZAN*

In March 1912, at the beginning of his career as a popular author, Edgar Rice Burroughs wrote to a magazine editor with his latest idea for a yarn:

> The story I am on now is of the scion of a noble English house—of the present time—who was born in tropical Africa where his parents died when he was about a year old. The infant was found and adopted by a huge she-ape, and was brought up among a band of fierce anthropoids.
>
> The mental development of this ape-man in spite of every handicap of how he learned to read English without knowledge of the spoken language, of the way in which his inherent reasoning faculties lifted him high above his savage jungle friends and enemies, of his meeting with a white girl, how he came at last to civilization and to his own[,] makes most fascinating writing and I think will prove interesting reading, as I am especially adapted to the building of the "damphool" species of narrative.[1]

It was, the editor replied, a "crackerjack" idea. "You certainly have the most remarkable imagination."[2]

Edgar Rice Burroughs, 1912. © 1975 EDGAR RICE BURROUGHS, INC.

When Burroughs wrote *Tarzan of the Apes* he was thirty-six years old, married with two young children, and living in Chicago, the city of his birth. He was a sturdy though not especially imposing man, roughly five feet nine inches tall, with strong arms and hands.[3] Far from living a life of rugged individualism, he worked in a minor position, giving professional advice to clients for *System*, "The Magazine

of Business." "I knew little or nothing about business," Burroughs later recalled, "had failed in every enterprise I had ever attempted and could not have given valuable advice to a peanut vendor." To mesmerize clients, he took refuge in vague, portentous pronouncements and impressive if irrelevant charts and graphs. "Ethically," he admitted, "it was about two steps below the patent medicine business," in which he had also worked until the passage of the Pure Food and Drug Law in 1906 shut the enterprise down. To make matters worse, his boss was, in Burroughs's words, "an overbearing, egotistical ass with the business morality of a peep show proprietor."[4]

Burroughs thus wrote *Tarzan* as an act of self-liberation. He hoped to cast off the humiliations of a frustrated, insignificant white-collar worker for the independence of a commercial author with a mass readership. But more than merely a means of making money, the story, he hoped, would serve as an imaginative escape for himself and his readers. After he had become one of the most widely read (if never the highest paid) writers of his day, he made this point explicit. Speaking of the appeal of the Tarzan stories, he declared:

> We wish to escape not alone the narrow confines of city streets for the freedom of the wilderness, but the restrictions of man made laws, and the inhibitions that society has placed upon us. We like to picture ourselves as roaming free, the lords of ourselves and of our world; in other words, we would each like to be Tarzan. At least I would; I admit it.[5]

In his own way, then, Burroughs was as much an escape artist as Houdini. The Tarzan escape emphasized not only freedom but also wildness, not only challenge but also combat, and it proved one of the twentieth century's most popular and durable, performed by Burroughs himself in twenty-three additional Tarzan books, which were translated into a host of languages, as well as in magazine articles and newspaper serials, and by others in films, radio and television programs, cartoons, games, and toys.

As Tarzan carried escape art into the realm of fictional adventure, his body recalled Sandow's. Tarzan represented Burroughs's conception of the perfect man, a spectacular nude figure of strength, beauty, virility, violence, and command who extended many of the

themes popularized by Sandow. Like Sandow's feats and Houdini's escapes, Burroughs's creation must be understood in historical context. Ubiquitous as the name Tarzan has become, the circumstances of his creation have been largely forgotten. If, however, we see both Burroughs's situation and his protagonist's in historical context, then we also see more clearly the pressures on manhood in the modern world and the urge to recover a primitive freedom and wildness.

BURROUGHS'S BELATEDNESS

Edgar Rice Burroughs never invited the confusion between creator and character that, as vaudeville headliners, Sandow and Houdini did. Instead, he was always acutely conscious of the gulf between his life as an author and the adventures of his alter ego, Tarzan. He was still more aware that until he was nearly thirty-six (an age at which the major portion of Sandow's and Houdini's careers was over) he was not a writer at all and might easily have never written a word of the Tarzan books or the other sixty-eight books, numerous short stories, and articles that he composed before his death in 1950. Had he died in the summer of 1911, just as he attempted his first professional fiction and five months before he started *Tarzan of the Apes*, he would have been virtually unknown. Even within his extended family, he may well have been regarded as a disappointment. Certainly he was a failure in his own eyes.

"Nothing interesting ever happened to me in my life," Burroughs wrote in 1929, in the midst of his success. "I never went to a fire but that it was out before I arrived. None of my adventures ever happened. They should have because I went places and did things that invited disaster; yet the results were always blah."[6] This sense of belatedness, which his rueful humor could not disguise, dogged Burroughs from his childhood. Like many men who came of age in the 1880s and 1890s, he seemed born too late. The great adventures of his father's generation, even of his elder brothers', were over before he came on the scene. If young Ehrich Weiss had to struggle against the undertow of his father's decline, young Ed Burroughs felt the pressure to match his father's success. The very first sentence of the

Burroughs when a boy of about ten.
© 1975 EDGAR RICE BURROUGHS, INC.

unfinished autobiography in which he bemoaned his unexciting life declared, "My father, Major George T. Burroughs, was a cavalry officer during the Civil War."[7] George Burroughs's early adult life certainly did not lack excitement. As part of the Union troops at Bull Run, he had felt a bullet pierce his blouse but, fortunately, not his skin. Four years later, with his new wife, Mary, he watched the bombardment of Richmond in April 1865, and left the service as a brevet major. Three years later he moved his family to Chicago, unquestionably the greatest American city for adventure in the late nineteenth century. In 1871, from the roof of their West Side town house near fashionable Union Park, he saw the most calamitous fire in American history tear through the heart of the city. Seizing on Chicago's position as the capital of the nation's grain market, George Burroughs entered the distillery business and quickly grew wealthy. After a fire in 1885 devastated his distillery, he shifted his enterprise to the American Battery Company, which made storage batteries, and ultimately assumed the position of president.

Ed Burroughs was born on September 1, 1875 (one year after Houdini, eight years after Sandow), into a decidedly masculine household.

Three elder brothers—ages nine, eight, and three—loomed over him. Two other brothers who died in infancy cast shadows as well: Arthur, born in 1874, who survived only twelve days; and Charles, almost six years younger than Ed, who lived five months. "The earliest event in my life that I can recall clearly," Burroughs later said, "is the sudden death of an infant brother in my mother's arms."[8] As the youngest surviving child, Ed aroused considerable anxiety with his boyhood illnesses, which tightened his close bonds to his mother. He made up his first stories and told them to her during the times when he was confined to bed. Burroughs's father valued a strict Victorian order in his household: meals were punctually served to the sound of a gong; all lights were extinguished when he went to bed. So too did he favor a conservative order in society at large. A staunch Republican, as his son would become in his turn, he attended the trial of the Haymarket bombers in 1887 and received a special permit to witness their execution as the city trembled in fear of violent insurrection—another great if grim adventure.[9]

Ed grew up a straggler, always far to the rear of his father's expectations and his brothers' example. In stature and in substance, he never seemed to measure up. His father stood six feet high, and his brothers were tall as well. The two eldest, George and Harry, graduated from Yale in 1889 and dutifully joined their father at American Battery. Almost immediately, however, Harry developed a serious cough from battery fumes, and a physician recommended a change of climate. The tonic of ranch life in the West was the great restorative for many men at this time, including Theodore Roosevelt, the novelist Owen Wister, and the painter Frederic Remington. The two brothers teamed up with a Yale classmate, Lew Sweetser, whose father and uncle ranked among the leading cattle barons in Idaho; backed by their respective fathers, the young men bought land for a cattle ranch in the southeastern portion of the newly admitted state. In the spring of 1892, sixteen-year-old Ed joined his brothers in what was certainly the most exhilarating six months of his youth. Sent west to escape an influenza epidemic, he seemed to step into the pages of a dime novel. Although the romantic days of the great cattle drives had waned, he could at least bask in their afterglow. He joined in roundups, learned to ride all day and all night, and returned brimming with stories of ornery horses (including one that "Sandow himself

Burroughs in Western garb, Idaho. © 1975 EDGAR RICE BURROUGHS, INC.

Burroughs in a football uniform, sporting a mustache, at Michigan Military Academy, 1895. © 1975 EDGAR RICE BURROUGHS, INC.

could not have held . . . when he took it into his head to bolt") and "likable murderers."[10]

He at least glimpsed possibilities of self-transformation as well. A photograph from the time shows him looking at the photographer with the cockiness of a young cowboy, bulked up by his western garb, hand on hip, broad-brimmed hat shading his eyes as if the photographer's studio were a dusty street in Dodge City.

Ed's father wanted less rambunctious models for his youngest son, however. He shipped Ed off to Phillips Academy in Andover, Massachusetts, where another older brother, Coleman, was already enrolled. Ed flunked out after a single semester. His father then sent him to Michigan Military Academy, where Ed chafed under the tight discipline. As a plebe, he excelled chiefly in devising pranks and accumulating punishments. He rode in cavalry drill and played football, exaggerating his height by an inch and a half in a team description. He studied not only military tactics and mathematics but languages and literature as well. A drawing he made of Joan of Arc on the flyleaf of his French text gives us a glimpse of his inner imaginings. No

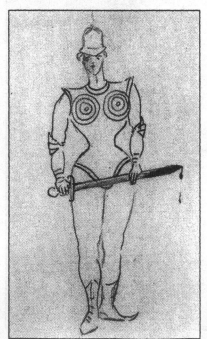

Burroughs's drawing of Joan of Arc, 1895.
© 2001 EDGAR RICE BURROUGHS, INC.

slight maid, she is a formidable woman warrior with massive iron breastplates, an hourglass waist, ample thighs, and a conspicuously phallic sword dripping with blood.

Once Burroughs was graduated from Michigan Military Academy in 1895, it was time to gallop on a career, and though he had become an excellent rider, in this effort he found himself bucked and thrown again and again. The military offered the most obvious course, one that might please his father as well as fulfill his own youthful dreams. So when Burroughs failed the examination for West Point (as did the great majority of applicants), the wound to his pride cut deep. He returned briefly to Michigan Military Academy as assistant commandant. Then with impulsive bravado he enlisted in the army, requesting a cavalry assignment in "the worst post in the United States."[11] He got his wish and quickly regretted it. Burroughs may have thought he could recapture his father's Civil War experience and also the Western cavalry's glory days (gained at horrific cost to Plains Indians) as he rose in the ranks. But despite occasional chases of renegade Apaches, garrison duty at the Seventh U.S. Cavalry at Fort Grant in the Arizona Territory resembled convict labor far more than it did Buffalo Bill's Wild West. After a bout of dysentery, Burroughs called on his father to pull the necessary strings to gain an early discharge. His military career had lasted ten months.

From 1897 until the appearance of *Tarzan of the Apes* in *The All-Story* magazine fifteen years later, Burroughs seemed inexorably pulled back to Chicago and to the world of business, try as he might to escape it. He took up his harness at American Battery under his father. A year later, when the Spanish-American War broke out in Cuba, he sought a commission. At one point he wrote directly to Theodore Roosevelt to join his Rough Riders, but he was turned down. (His dreams of military glory died hard: as late as 1906 he was inquiring about a position in the Chinese army.) Seeking then the escape route of his elder brothers and to recover the intoxicating summer of his adolescence, he returned on several occasions to Idaho—only to discover that his brothers' cattle and gold-dredging operations represented not frontier adventure but a financial noose tightening around their necks. He briefly ran a stationery shop in Pocatello, Idaho, then gladly sold it back to its previous owner, concluding, "God never intended me for a retail merchant."[12] His marriage in 1900 to Emma

Hulbert, daughter of a prominent Chicago hotel manager, only increased the pressures of career. He made a final attempt to fit into his father's designs at American Battery, where he served as treasurer, then fled west once again, with his wife, in an abortive effort to start a new life with his brothers or on his own. Even two decades later, he wrote, "It gives me a distinct sensation of nausea, accompanied by acute depression every time I think of my experience at the plant." He added sarcastically, "I have about the same pleasant recollections of each and every business connection I had in the past."[13]

Back in Chicago after 1904, Burroughs struggled like a character in an O. Henry short story or, more desperately, a Dreiser novel to stay afloat amid the hordes of scrambling white-collar workers who by the end of the decade represented one-fifth of the entire male labor force.[14] He started as timekeeper on a construction site, then took "a series of horrible jobs" as salesman. "I sold electric light bulbs to janitors, candy to drug stores and [multivolume sets of the author John L.] Stoddard's Lectures from door to door. . . . My main object in life was to get my foot in somebody's door and then recite my sales talk like a sick parrot."[15] He put in longer stints as an office manager for one firm and then "as a very minor cog in the machinery" of Sears, Roebuck's enormous mail-order business, supervising a large group of (mostly female) stenographers as they cranked out thousands of letters a day.[16] None of these positions suited his restless, independent nature. Attempts to start a small business and thrive as his father had done—in advertising, patent medicine, a correspondence course in "scientific salesmanship"—all failed miserably. The birth of his first two children in 1908 and 1909 quickened his downward plunge. He felt near bottom, financially and emotionally. "I had worked steadily for six years without a vacation," he later wrote, "and for fully half of my working hours . . . I had suffered tortures from headaches. Economize as we would, the expenses of our little family were far beyond our income. Three cents worth of ginger snaps constituted my daily lunches for months." He pawned his wife's jewelry and his watch to buy food. He "loathed poverty" and loathed himself for being in it. With the damning judgment of a conservative businessman, he wrote: "It is an indication of inefficiency, and nothing more."[17]

Burroughs's frustrations were shared by countless millions; indeed, they would become a prominent theme in twentieth-century Ameri-

can literature: from Theodore Dreiser's *Sister Carrie* to Saul Bellow's *Seize the Day*. Willy Loman's son Biff voiced them at mid-century in Arthur Miller's play *Death of a Salesman* when he exclaims: "It's a measly manner of existence. To get on that subway on the hot mornings in summer. To devote your whole life to keeping stock, or making phone calls, or selling or buying. To suffer fifty weeks of the year for the sake of a two-week vacation, when all you really desire is to be outdoors, with your shirt off. And always to have to get ahead of the next fella."[18]

Burroughs tried other, almost parodically marginal businesses with no better success: a sales agency for lead-pencil sharpeners; then, under his brother Coleman, a manufacturer of scratch pads. In the office doldrums, he tried another moneymaking scheme that might have seemed still more chimerical: writing commercial fiction for the "pulps."

Pulp magazines were so called because of the inexpensive, porous paper on which they were printed. They specialized in stories that were formulaic concoctions, long on twisting plot, offered in double-columned monthly installments to a mass readership. Tales of adventure, mystery, war, the Wild West, and science fiction were their stock-in-trade. These attracted a predominantly male following of adolescent boys and both blue- and white-collar men, as well as a significant number of women, as readers' letters attest. They were read at home, especially on Sundays, while traveling to and from work, and in idle moments on the job. In some respects, writers for the pulps might be compared to performers in the small-time vaudeville in which Harry Houdini began his career. Both worked hard for low wages and tried to entertain a diverse, unpretentious public. If vaudeville was industrialized in its specialized acts, systematized format, and centralized management, pulp magazines were fiction factories dominated by big publishers that demanded from authors a combination of literary facility, stamina, and speed. Pulp writers received as little as a tenth of a cent per word. And just as small-time vaudevillians dreamed of hitting the big-time houses, many pulp writers aspired to break into the "slicks," the more prestigious mass-circulation magazines printed on smooth stock, such as *Collier's* and *The Saturday Evening Post*, that paid thousands of dollars for a single story. Vaudeville achieved its height between the 1890s and the Great War. But as

successors to the cheap story papers of the nineteenth century, pulp magazines early in the second decade of the twentieth century were just entering their golden age, which continued through the 1930s.[19]

Burroughs himself derided pulp fiction and claimed to have stooped to it only because he needed the money. Keenly aware of the divide between "good" literature addressing a "gentle reader" and sensational fiction with no cultural pretensions, he knew that the pulps were not aesthetically respectable. In fact, he said he became acquainted with their contents by happenstance, though his quick mastery of their formulas suggests a longer and deeper acquaintance. Because one of his shaky business ventures took advertising in their pages, the office received copies of magazines to check the ads. Burroughs brought some of them home to read. "It was at that time," he later recalled, "that I made up my mind that if people were paid for writing rot such as I read in some of those magazines that I could write stories just as rotten."[20]

His first novel, *A Princess of Mars*, begun in July 1911 on leftover stationery from his failed enterprises, portrays the adventures of John Carter, a Virginia gentleman, Civil War veteran, and Indian fighter who falls into a trance in Arizona and wakes up on Mars. Carter was a kind of dream self into whom Burroughs poured many of the masculine endowments and accomplishments he most admired:

> a splendid specimen of manhood, standing a good two inches over six feet, broad of shoulder and narrow of hip, with the carriage of the trained fighting man. His features were regular and clear cut, his hair black and closely cropped, while his eyes were a steel gray, reflecting a strong and loyal character, filled with fire and initiative. His manners were perfect, and his courtliness was that of a typical southern gentleman of the highest type.

His Mars is inhabited by two races: a reddish one, who resemble earthly humans; and a hideous green one, whose warriors are fifteen feet tall, with an extra set of limbs and curved tusks. Except for ornaments, all go naked, as does Carter himself. He soon falls in love with a beautiful copper-skinned princess, and the first-person account describes his swashbuckling adventures on behalf of her and her people

as he seeks to save her from the cruel, lustful monster who commands the green race. Finally, after slaying multitudes and proving himself the finest warrior on the planet, he has the satisfactions of restoring order, being proclaimed a hero, and marrying the princess. "Was there ever such a man!" she marvels. "Alone, a stranger, hunted, threatened, persecuted, you have done in a few short months what in all the past ages [on Mars] . . . no man has ever done." Though the tale ends on a note of longing, its great theme is manly triumph both in combat and in romance.[21]

So self-conscious was Burroughs about setting down such an extravagant fantasy and about being a writer at all that he wrote surreptitiously and under the pen name Normal Bean (that is, normal brain). He sent the first forty-three thousand words of the story to the editors of *The Argosy*, one of several magazines in the publishing stable of Frank Munsey, the man who started the modern pulp-magazine revolution. Ten days later, he received a highly encouraging letter from Thomas Metcalf, an editor of *The All-Story*, a sister publication. Spurred by Metcalf, Burroughs finished the story the following month and sold it for four hundred dollars. This amounted to barely more than half a cent a word, but in his autobiographical sketch Burroughs still savored the thrill of this, "the first big event in my life."[22]

Clearly, such writing tapped both a talent and a need in Burroughs. Aside from a crude "historical fairy-tale" called "Minidoka" that he had concocted for his nephew and niece in Idaho a decade earlier, he appears not to have written fiction before and certainly none of any length. Now it seemed he could not stop. Already, while Metcalf deliberated over the Martian romance, Burroughs wrote a second novel-length story, a medieval swashbuckler called "The Outlaw of Torn." Then, with an office manager's precision, he noted that on December 1, 1911, at eight in the evening he began to write the novel that would become *Tarzan of the Apes*.

MANLINESS IN THE PAGES OF *SYSTEM*

To appreciate fully the meaning of Burroughs's dreams of manly triumph in Africa, we should first look more closely at the magazine he so eagerly left to plunge into pulp fiction. After the scratch-pad busi-

ness, like the lead-pencil sharpener agency, collapsed, Burroughs took what turned out to be his last job other than that as a self-employed writer. From shortly after he began writing stories in the summer of 1911 until early in 1913, when he felt his sales could support his growing family, he worked as manager of the business service department of *System*, a business magazine run by A. W. Shaw. Though Burroughs had almost nothing good to say about any business in which he worked, the experience at *System* aroused by far his sharpest invective. "I never so thoroughly disliked any employer as I did Shaw," he remembered, as if rubbing a wound that refused to heal. Perhaps at the root of Burroughs's disgust lay his sense of fraudulence and incompetence in dispensing business advice in response to individual requests, a service the magazine provided for an annual fee of fifty dollars. "I recall one milling company in Minneapolis or St. Paul who submitted a bunch of intricate business problems for me to solve. Had God asked me to tell Him how to run heaven, I would have known just as much about it." His boss's indifference to Burroughs's lack of qualifications only confirmed the fraud. Burroughs scornfully remembered, "Shaw also had a young man about nineteen giving advice to bankers. This lad's banking experience consisted in his having beaten his way around the world."[23]

In three crucial respects, *System* was the mirror image of the masculine world of pulp magazines in which Burroughs sought refuge and profit. First, to a startling degree, issues of manliness suffused its depiction of modern business. To read its pages is to discover an ethic of intense work and competition that both shaped and repelled Burroughs—to discover, that is, the "iron cage," in the sociologist Max Weber's phrase, from which he strove to escape.[24] If magazines such as *The All-Story* divulged a world of primarily (though not exclusively) masculine fantasy, offering satisfactions denied on the job, *System* presented an alternative world in which masculine adventure lay at the core of business competition. Second, *System* proposed a hierarchy of masculine worth and ability that emerged from competition. Whether this hierarchy was due to differences in training and environment or innate differences (an issue that Burroughs explored in *Tarzan of the Apes*) was a question to which it offered an equivocal response. Third, *System* was also a magazine of stories. Though all the incidents described in its articles were allegedly true, much of the writing was ei-

ther about decisive actions that businessmen had taken or about tales of adventure in the context of modern business.

Many of the narrative devices in the *System* articles borrowed from fiction. A problem would be introduced by a remark or exchange in direct, "manly" speech, and the story then proceeded with rapid-paced action to a clear outcome with a business moral. This was not a magazine concerned primarily with impersonal business processes and economic forces, though it did promise to extract underlying principles that readers could apply to their own situations. Rather, it concerned men who had the power to assess problems, chart their courses, and control events, coming out on top as one of the "big men." One might well suspect that writers contrived details, concocted dialogue, occasionally invented an informant, or even made up much of the supposedly true accounts of business advice. But even if authentic to the last detail, its stories shared a clear house style designed to appeal to readers seeking entertainment as well as information.

The November 1911 issue of *System* is one which Burroughs would have seen and, quite possibly, read just as he prepared to put his first Tarzan story on paper. Consider the title. "System" was a word that glittered with magic in the early twentieth century. It carried the promise of a scientific modern order. New system builders were eager to apply methods of rationalization, coordination, centralization, and supervision to ever-larger organizations of people and machines, including vast new office bureaucracies, immense factories, and far-flung financial empires. By this time, the great investment banker J. Pierpont Morgan, Jr., had consolidated and expanded corporations such as United States Steel (1901), International Harvester (1902), and American Telephone and Telegraph (1906). In 1911 Frederick Winslow Taylor, articulating his vision of maximum industrial efficiency, declared, "In the past, the man has been first; in the future the system must be first." In Highland Park, Michigan, Henry Ford was developing his revolutionary system of production for the Model T car. The skyscraper was the cathedral of this emerging corporate order, the modern electrified factory its palace. And regimented, synchronized movement increasingly constituted its dance. At the very same time that Ford was developing his assembly-line system, Broadway choreographers were creating its inverted image in

the modern chorus line. "It is system, system, system, with me," declared a leading choreographer, Ned Wayburn, in 1913. "I believe in numbers and straight lines."[25]

How was one to operate within this modern, urban world of business and stand out? The answer of *System*'s November 1911 issue began on its cover, which shows a crowd, principally of men, walking in a business district. The man in the forefront, more fully drawn than the others, models the characteristics of the exemplary businessman thriving in the urban corporate world. Well dressed but not ostentatious, bowler snug as a helmet, newspaper furled, and walking stick at the ready, he does not need to look at the clock behind him to know that time is money. Unlike the messenger just to the right, or the stoop-shouldered man at the very center retreating down the street, or the boy with hand in pocket walking into the left margin of the picture, he strides full of purpose on his mission.

The opening article offered inspiring accounts of individual business success as part of a series, "Ideas That Have Been Put to Work." Breathlessly, the piece begins: "In a flying spark that bridged a broken wire, Edison saw not merely a manifestation of electricity, but the possibility of electric light. In the steam escaping from a kettle of water, Watt saw a power that he harnessed for the development of our industries. So many of the world's greatest ideas have been suggested by trivial observations that have been adapted to the needs of the hour."[26] The article proposed to apply this heroic view of flashing genius to the world of modern business, with vignettes demonstrating breakthroughs using analogical thinking, even as it stressed the importance of interdependence, systematization, standardization, supervision, and expansion. For example, a manufacturer discovers how to make his sales force a more cooperative team by watching a football game. A store manager at the theater notes the use of a revolving stage and realizes he can apply it to his shopwindows, vastly expanding his possibilities of exhibiting goods with a four-part revolving display. A baker learns from the success of packaged laundry starch to emphasize the hygienic values of packaged bread. These are anecdotes about active, decisive, inventive men, often (though not exclusively) attuned to machinery and certainly to organization. They are adult Tom Swifts, eager to scale the business ladder.

"What Are Profits?" asks the next article, at first glance a dusty

The cover of *System*, November 1911. The University of North Carolina at Chapel Hill

disquisition by F. W. Taussig of Harvard's economics department. Its real subject, however, is the meaning of manliness in a modern capitalist society. A leading economist, Taussig was the son of a successful physician and businessman who had immigrated to the United States from Prague. He quickly described the hierarchy of manly achievement in the business world and directly addressed the issue of why some men succeed and others fail:

> Some men seem to have a golden touch. Everything to which they turn their hand yields miraculously. They are the captains of industry, the "big men," admired, feared and followed by the business community. Others, of slightly lower degree, prosper generously, though not so miraculously—the select class of "solid business men." Thence, by imperceptible gradations, there is a descent in the industrial and social hierarchy until we

reach the small tradesman who is, indeed, a business man, but whose income is modest and whose position is not very different from that of the mechanic or the clerk.

Taussig went on to consider whether such varieties in position stem from "differences in inborn abilities" or from "training and environment." (If Burroughs were reading, his eyes must have widened with interest.) With some qualifications, Taussig answered that at the highest level they are indeed innate: "Captains of industry are doubtless born. So are great poets, musicians, men of science, lawyers. Though there may be occasional suppressed geniuses among the poorer classes, ability of the highest order usually works its way to the fore." Not surprisingly, he believed that merit thrives in a laissez-faire economy. Still, for those not touched with genius, he acknowledged, other qualities were critical, including "the advantages of capital and connection," "imagination and judgment," administrative ability, "courage," and a body "vigorous in its capacity to endure prolonged application and severe nervous strain." Surveying the various types of men who succeeded in the business world, he concluded, "Among all these different sorts of persons, a process very like natural selection is at work."[27] Implicitly, this process affirmed the essential rightness of business and other social hierarchies, which he believed reflected fundamental and progressive hierarchies of nature.

After an item on making money from waste, "What's Your Scrapheap Worth?" there was a piece by Henry Beach Needham, "How to Select the Right College Man." One might fairly say that *System* was fascinated with processes of selection—whether of kinds of scrap or kinds of men—with distinguishing the exceptional individual from the mass. The college article noted that a higher proportion of college men were going into business and quoted business leaders who wanted college graduates for executive positions. (One imagines Burroughs squirming, since he was among the more than 95 percent of American men at this time who never attended college.[28]) The article at one point casually observed that the college man "has survived [in various capacities in Western Electric] because he is 'the fittest.'" The Darwinian analogy was clearly becoming a commonplace. Enos Barton, chairman of the board of Western Electric and recently retired as its president, declared, "The college . . . is a sort of

sieve—a coarse sieve wherein the best men are sifted out. . . . By our method of selection the loafers and the sports are eliminated."[29]

In the following piece, "Players in the Great Game," the subject remains the "big men," the "men who are factors in the march of progress." The first figure discussed is Irving T. Bush, who by sticking to one thing (Burroughs squirms again) is worth twenty-six million dollars at the age of forty-three. "Physically, too, Mr. Bush is big—in all some six feet and two inches, with a heart of proportionate size." He has just given a check for ten thousand dollars to his sales manager. Another "player" in the "Great Game" is Edward R. Stettinius, president of Diamond Match (and later a partner in J. P. Morgan and a key industrialist in the Allied effort during the Great War). He "sits behind his big desk in his big office. . . . As the conversation progresses, Mr. Stettinius directs it, using a half-burned cigar as a baton. . . . [H]is movements are quick and vigorous."[30] (Burroughs crunches a gingersnap.)

As a whole, the articles in *System* depicted a world of big, energetic, masterly leaders—and, implicitly, of smaller, unexceptional followers. It was a view cogently if smugly expressed by one of the largest manufacturers of the day, Cyrus McCormick, Jr., a man born with a silver reaper in his mouth. In answer to a query, "Upon what ideals, policies, programs, or specific purposes should Americans place most stress in the immediate future?" this commander of fifteen thousand workers replied: "Civilization needs leaders, but it is equally essential there should be followers. Nature has so provided that for one man capable of the larger task of brain or brawn, tens of thousands are unequal to it. In the frank recognition of this natural law, and the acceptance of it, and obedience to it, much depends."[31]

A different but equally telling perspective emerges from the advertising section of *System*. The advertisements may also be read as narratives of manliness, which directly speak to readers concerned about their inadequacy. No talent is simply innate, they seemed to say; any man can benefit from training, advice, or nostrums. The *System* articles focused on the "big men," but the advertisements promised to aid those who had fallen behind. Many offered correspondence courses and other instruction by mail. (Burroughs would hardly have glanced at these, given that one of his many failed ventures had been a correspondence course in "scientific salesmanship.")

SYSTEM for NOVEMBER—ADVERTISING SECTION

How big a man are you?

Your weekly pay envelope will answer this question.

The dollars per week you earn prove your bigness or littleness—your importance or unimportance—whether trained or untrained.

The American School offers you a chance to become a trained man, to get a better salary and live in a better home—in fact, to change your entire life, if you only have ambition and grit and will follow our advice and instruction.

The American School makes it as easy as possible for every man to get an education who really wants one. This School was founded for just such men as you—men who have the ambition, but lack time and money.

If you want to be a *big man*, write today for our *New Deferred Tuition Plan*. Let us tell you how you can obtain the training you need—how you can pay for the tuition after your salary has been raised.

Fill in and mail the coupon. Let this coupon be your *start*—your foundation for a *big man*—a better job and a bigger salary. An agent won't bother you at your home or work. We'll send you all information by mail. We obtain our students in the same manner that we teach—by correspondence.

AMERICAN SCHOOL OF CORRESPONDENCE
CHICAGO, U. S. A.

Please mention SYSTEM when writing to advertisers

"How big a man are you?" an advertisement for a correspondence school in *System*, November 1911. The University of North Carolina at Chapel Hill

"Walled in, Old Man?" an advertisement in *System*, November 1911. The University of North Carolina at Chapel Hill

"How big a man are you?" one ad demanded. A large, prosperous, and distinguished-looking man, with his suit coat open to reveal a vest and massive watch chain and with his hand cradling a watch, stands staring down on a smaller, thinner, balding, rumpled, and rather cringing figure. The copy declared: "Your weekly pay envelope will answer this question. The dollars per week you earn prove your bigness or littleness—your importance or unimportance—whether trained or untrained." The American School of Correspondence promised to make the difference.

Helping hands stretch forth in other advertisements for similar services. "Walled In, Old Man?" inquires one in which a clerk sits on his stool, shut in a corner of high brick walls, while from the top of the picture a strong hand reaches down. "Grasp the helping hand that has lifted thousands from the High Stool of Salaried Uncertainty to the Arm Chair of Successful Business Ownership." "Go," exhorts another as a man in suit and tie helps a more modestly dressed man up a rocky, thorny slope, and, by implication, to an office desk and a solidly middle-class life.

"Go," an advertisement for
another correspondence school
in *System*, November 1911. The
University of North Carolina at Chapel Hill

Burroughs wanted to escape his job at *System* and the entire world it represented—in many respects, the world of his father's values, honed to a sharp competitive edge—but he was profoundly shaped by it. And though he claimed to hate business, he approached his new career in commercial fiction like a character out of the pages of *System*. The magazine celebrated charts and graphs as indexes of scientific efficiency, and from the time he began writing, Burroughs kept a graph of his word output over his desk. (It quickly rose to a peak in 1913, the first year he wrote full-time, with 413,000 words.[32]) He proved a canny bargainer with magazine editors, publishers, and film companies; a shrewd marketer of syndication and subsidiary rights; and, beginning in 1923, the successful owner of his own corporation, Edgar Rice Burroughs, Inc.

The story that made this new career possible was *Tarzan of the Apes*. Writing it, Burroughs discovered his potential as a commercial author and the possibility of a new life (his unpublished autobiogra-

phy essentially ends with this new birth). More important, he discovered a rich cluster of themes with immense cultural as well as personal resonance. Their continuing fascination contributes much to Tarzan's enduring fame.

MASCULINE REVITALIZATION AND THE REASSERTION OF HIERARCHY

On every side in the early twentieth century, age-old questions about the basis of individual merit and social hierarchy demanded new answers. Reformers and radicals of various stripes questioned the legitimacy of special privilege and entrenched power. Swept by a flood tide of immigrants, the nation swirled with an unprecedented diversity of ethnicities, religions, and cultures. Extremes of wealth and poverty, power and impotence challenged egalitarian beliefs. The sense that American society was a sharp pyramid, with figures scrambling to reach its summit or at least advance up its steep slopes—the idea projected in the pages of *System*—pervaded all classes. Those who felt themselves rightfully on top strenuously justified their positions by appeals to hierarchies, particularly those of race (whiteness), gender (masculinity), religion (Protestant Christianity), and putative superiority of body, mind, character, and merit, and they did their best to repel all radical and leveling forces. From their high fortresses, they rolled boulders down on new immigrants, African Americans, agrarian and industrial radicals, feminists, socialists, and anarchists.

Yet their assaults were not merely defensive. The contest between conservatives and reformers over the shape of the American social and economic order took place against a larger international backdrop in which new hierarchies were being violently asserted. Burroughs's generation had grown up during the great wave of European imperial expansion, when a fifth of the world's landmass (excluding Antarctica) and a tenth of its population had been seized by European powers, great and small. Britain, whose national symbol, appropriately, was the lion, claimed the largest share: one-quarter of the land and one-third of the people on the globe.[33] With the United States' own frontier exhausted, the excitement of a new global land rush with immense prizes to the victors was hard for many Americans to resist.

Particularly in the flush of the nation's triumph in the Spanish-American War, expansionists jubilantly proposed to revitalize their numbers by carrying the battle to new realms of empire. The Indiana Republican Albert Beveridge perfectly captured this spirit in his jingoistic paean on the floor of the U.S. Senate in 1899: "God has not been preparing the English-speaking and Teutonic peoples for a thousand years for nothing but vain and idle self-contemplation and self-admiration. No! He has made us *the* master organizers of the world to establish system where chaos reigns. . . . He has made us adept in government that we may administer government among savage and senile peoples." "We will renew our youth at the fountain of new and glorious deeds," Beveridge declared. Here was "system" with a vengeance.[34]

This dream of white Anglo-American revitalization and conquest not only transformed American foreign relations; it also profoundly affected American thinking, as is evident in popular fiction. Conspicuous in many popular novels of the early twentieth century are concerns with what might be called geographies of rugged masculinity: regions within which white men of northern European stock reassert their dominance over physical and moral "inferiors," including incompetents, malefactors, weaklings, and cowards.

One such realm was the West, in which Owen Wister placed his immensely popular and influential novel *The Virginian* (1902). A historical romance, the story celebrates the adventures of a homegrown noble savage, "a slim young giant, more beautiful than pictures," who is twice compared to a Bengal tiger. Like so many Westerns (and, as we shall see, other works), it both glories in wildness as the basis of masculine freedom and insists on the necessity of imposing social order. In the heyday of the cowboy in the Wyoming territory, that order was established by the individual man. The code of this society is simple: whether in bets, card games, or horse trades, "a man must take care of himself." If this code is violated, the gun and the rope are the modes of redress, lynch law and the duel the courts of justice. As the title character declares, "[E]quality is a great big bluff. . . . [A] man has got to prove himself my equal before I'll believe him." Being equal to the occasion is the only kind of equality that counts. Burroughs, who did not remark on many literary works, called *The Virginian* "one of the greatest American novels ever written."[35]

If the Western was one popular genre of masculine adventure, what might be called the Southern became another. Here the most influential work was Thomas Dixon's *The Clansman* (1905), a book immediately controversial and now infamous for its vehement espousal of white supremacy and glorification of the Ku Klux Klan. Adapted as a play, it helped to spark wholesale assaults on African Americans in the terrible race riot in Atlanta in 1906. D. W. Griffith created his brilliant, disturbing film version, *The Birth of a Nation*, in 1915.

The novel has a number of points in common with Wister's *The Virginian*: it is also a historical romance with a slender, handsome, raven-haired white Southern hero who reaffirms his manliness in mortal combat in a plot in which lynch law figures conspicuously. Here, too, the story ends with marriages symbolizing the reunion of regions—New England and the West in *The Virginian*, the North and the South in *The Clansman*. Unlike *The Virginian*, however, *The Clansman* associates wildness and animality not with natural nobility but with African American savagery and immorality. The most flagrant instance occurs in Dixon's description of the rape of a white Southern virgin by the evil mulatto Gus. The author could not decide which wild beast to invoke:

> Gus stepped closer, with an ugly leer, his flat nose dilated, his sinister bead-eyes wide apart gleaming ape-like as he laughed. . . . The girl uttered a cry, long, tremulous, heart-rending, piteous.
>
> A single tiger-spring, and the black claws of the beast sank into the soft white throat and she was still.[36]

At the novel's conclusion, of course, the men whom Dixon regarded as the South's and the nation's proper white leaders reassert their authority against such usurpers. Anything else, Dixon made clear, would pervert morality, politics, religion, history, and biology. In a fair fight, he believed, their triumph was inevitable: "The breed to which the Southern white man belongs has conquered every foot of soil on this earth their feet have pressed for a thousand years. A handful of them hold in subjection three hundred million in India. Place a dozen of them in the heart of Africa, and they will rule the continent unless you kill them."[37] In Dixon's fervid imagination, the rise of the "invis-

ible empire" of the KKK was part of the march of visible white empires across the globe.

The far North was a third testing ground of masculinity in the novels and stories of Jack London. A year younger than Burroughs, London had virtually completed his extraordinary career as a writer of popular fiction before Burroughs even got started. He began publishing stories about Alaska in pulp magazines in his early twenties and wrote fifty-one books before his death at the age of forty in 1916. Burroughs both admired London's fiction and was fascinated by his turbulent life.[38] He would certainly have known *The Call of the Wild* (1903), London's first great popular success.

Buck, the hero of *The Call of the Wild*, is a dog rather than a man, a shift in species that allowed London to explore themes of savagery, violence, and primitivism with special power and directness. Half Saint Bernard and half Scotch shepherd, Buck has previously lived as a "sated aristocrat" on a California ranch, "with nothing to do but loaf and be bored." In the novel's opening pages, however, he is stolen and sent north to satisfy the demand for sled dogs created by the Klondike gold rush of 1897: "He had been suddenly jerked from the heart of civilization and flung into the heart of things primordial." The fierce demands of the life of a pack dog in the harsh Northland transform him physically, morally, and spiritually:

> His muscles became hard as iron, and he grew callous to all ordinary pain. . . . He could eat anything, no matter how loathsome or indigestible; and . . . [build] it into the toughest and stoutest of tissues. Sight and scent became remarkably keen, while his hearing developed such acuteness that in his sleep he heard the faintest sound and knew whether it heralded peace or peril.

At the same time, Buck increasingly recovers the instincts of his wild ancestors and, in reveries, the memory of his primeval companion, early man: "The hairy man could spring up into the trees and travel ahead as fast as on the ground, swinging by the arms from limb to limb, sometimes a dozen feet apart, letting go and catching, never falling, never missing his grip. In fact, he seemed as much at home among the trees as on the ground." Buck learns to compete in the

"ruthless struggle for existence," "the law of club and fang." "He must master or be mastered; while to show mercy was a weakness."[39] Just as the Virginian must ultimately duel the evil cowpuncher Trampas, Buck must engage in a fight to the death with the treacherous husky Spitz. Unlike the Virginian, however, he has no Vermont schoolmarm pleading with him not to fight, and he easily learns to glory in the joy of the kill.

In the course of the story, the Northland pitilessly exposes both animal and human incompetence and weakness. Buck achieves his position as lead dog through his willingness to fight rivals to the death and maintains it through his incomparable strength and sagacity. Dogs are no more created equal in London's tale than men are in Wister's.

Like Wister and Dixon, London gave readers a romance, in his case between Buck and his "ideal master," John Thornton. Thornton, too, has joined the quest for gold, though apparently animated more by delight in the wilderness and joy in the quest than by the riches to be gained. As Buck increasingly responds to the ancestral "call of the wild," only his love of Thornton holds him back. He hungers for tougher challenges, bigger game. He kills a bear, then a moose, and when he discovers Thornton slain by members of the Yeehat tribe, he kills man, "the noblest game of all." At the novel's conclusion, he has been transmuted to legend, the great Ghost Dog fabled by the Yeehats who runs at the head of a wolf pack, "leaping gigantic above his fellows, his great throat a-bellow as he sings a song of the younger world."[40]

BURROUGHS'S LITERARY EXPERIMENT

When Burroughs dropped his infant "scion of a noble English house" into tropical Africa, another harsh and savage realm that would test the character of modern masculinity, he was adapting a well-known theme. As he later recalled, "I was mainly interested in playing with the idea of a contest between heredity and environment. For this purpose I selected an infant child of a race strongly marked by hereditary characteristics of the finer and nobler sort and at an age at which he could not have been influenced by associations with creatures of his

own kind. I threw him into an environment as diametrically opposite that to which he had been born as I might well conceive."[41]

To a conservative white American of Burroughs's background and training, the jungle of Equatorial Africa brought together the starkest possible conjunction of "primitive" indigenous peoples, exotic wilderness, savage animals, and both noble and venal colonial explorers. Burroughs knew little about Africa at this point and later declared that he wrote *Tarzan* with the aid of only Henry Stanley's *In Darkest Africa* (1890) and a fifty-cent Sears dictionary.[42] Probably, his deepest direct contact with African culture had occurred on the Midway at the 1893 Chicago world's fair as he drove by the Dahomey Village in a "horseless surrey" sponsored by his father's American Battery Company. He would have grown up reading accounts of romantic European explorers, even though he was aware that in the years since his birth, Africa had quickly passed from being the object of the most lofty professions of philanthropy to being the target of the most rapacious imperial greed. More particularly, he would have read extensive newspaper accounts of one of the first modern mass atrocities, the enslavement and death of millions in the Congo Free State under the aegis of King Leopold II of Belgium. Still, Burroughs's *Tarzan* remains much more in the tradition of R. M. Ballantyne's 1862 novel for young readers, *The Gorilla Hunters* ("I say, boys, isn't it jolly to be out here living like savages?"), than in that of Joseph Conrad's *Heart of Darkness* (1902).[43] Despite Conrad's searing depiction of evil at the core of the "civilizing" enterprise, tropical Africa remained in Burroughs's and the public's imagination a great arena for white male adventure, one of the last wild places on earth.

To carry the "hereditary characteristics of the finer and nobler sort" into this demanding environment, Burroughs, who took great pride in his Anglo-Saxon ancestry, selected members of the British nobility, John and Alice Clayton, Lord and Lady Greystoke. The story opens in 1888 with John Clayton and his young, pregnant wife bound for West Africa, where he plans to investigate reports that Britain's native subjects are being exploited and enslaved by another European power (sounding much like Belgium) in pursuit of ivory and rubber. Burroughs cast Clayton from the same mold as his previous hero, John Carter, in *A Princess of Mars*. Above average height, with a military bearing and regular features, he is "a strong, virile

man—mentally, morally, and physically." By contrast, the crew of the small vessel on which John and Alice sail from Freetown on the West African coast toward their final destination typify the lowest elements of society, socially, morally, biologically. The officers are "coarse, illiterate," "swarthy bullies" led by a "brute" of a captain, and the crew that mutiny against their thuggish command are even more villainous and animalistic.[44] In their atavistic appearance and savage proclivities, they virtually step from the pages of Cesare Lombroso's highly influential *Criminal Man*.[45] In Burroughs's description, their leader, Black Michael, "a huge beast of a man, with fierce black mustachios, and a great bull neck set between massive shoulders," anticipates the apes that will play such a prominent part in the story. Burroughs poured ice water into Clayton's veins, allowing him to stroll across the deck of the ship in the midst of the mutiny as casually as he might stroll across the polished floor of a drawing room. After the crew murder the officers, Black Michael sets Lord and Lady Greystoke, together with abundant supplies and provisions, "alone upon . . . [the] wild and lonely shore," castaways in a savage land.[46]

In this setting, English nobility and apes alike respond according to their innate abilities and what Burroughs understood as the nature of their sex. "I am but a woman," Lady Alice admits, "seeing with my heart rather than my head, and all that I can see is too horrible, too unthinkable to put into words." Lord Greystoke tries to stiffen her upper lip with the reminder that they carry within themselves both the blood of triumphant forebears and the brains of enlightened Victorians: "Hundreds of thousands of years ago our ancestors of the dim and distant past faced the same problems which we must face, possibly in these same primeval forests. That we are here today evidences their victory. . . . What they accomplished . . . with instruments and weapons of stone and bone, surely that may we accomplish also." He erects a strong haven for their little family. Nonetheless, in the trauma of an attack by a bull ape, Lady Alice's mind gives way. Throughout the first year of their baby son's life (and the last of their own), she imagines them back in England and their time in Africa as merely a hideous dream. She dies as peacefully as a fading flower. Lord Greystoke, by contrast, is violently murdered by the huge king ape, Kerchak, who has led a cluster of apes to the Greystoke cabin. These apes belong to a species supposedly superior to the gorilla; yet

within it, as within the human species, Burroughs emphasized innate differences. Lacking nobility of character, intelligence, or appearance, Kerchak rules over his tribe by virtue of his immense strength and fierce temper: "His forehead was extremely low and receding, his eyes bloodshot, small and close set to his coarse, flat nose; his ears large and thin, but smaller than most of his kind." By contrast, another member of the raiding party, the she-ape Kala, is "a splendid, clean-limbed animal, with a round, high forehead, which depicted more intelligence than most of her kind possessed."[47] Having just lost her offspring, she snatches the Clayton heir from the cradle and claims him for her own. In this way, Burroughs set up a plot with both mythic resonance and modern pertinence. When Kala becomes a mother to the noble waif, a host of issues rushes to the fore of Burroughs's story: nature and nurture, primate affinities and human capacities, savagery and civilization.

WILD BOYS AND MEN

Tarzan was the exemplary fictitious feral child of Burroughs's and his readers' time—as he has remained for the ninety years since. Although the fascination with them is age-old, "wild" children have exerted a special interest for Western societies since the eighteenth century, precisely because they seemed to offer special insight into the relationship between human nature and nurture. When, for example, "a naked, brownish, black-haired creature . . . about the size of a boy of twelve" emerged from the woods in northern Germany in 1724, the discovery was heralded as "more remarkable than the discovery of Uranus." He appeared alert and seemed to have especially keen hearing and sense of smell. He did not care for clothes but gradually learned to wear them. Dubbed Wild Peter, he became the pet of the royal house of Hanover, then of the duke of Hanover, King George I of England, and subsequently of his daughter, Princess Caroline. The Scottish physician and writer John Arbuthnot eagerly examined him, hoping that Peter might learn to talk, relate his feral experiences, and thus communicate the nature of the human mind in a pure state, uncontaminated by society. Arbuthnot quickly con-

cluded, however, that Peter was an "imbecile," incapable of speech due to severe mental retardation.[48]

In 1799, seventy-five years after the discovery of Wild Peter, another feral boy of similar age was flushed by hunters in the forest near Aveyron in southern France. Like Peter, he was unaccustomed to clothes and did not speak; unlike Peter, he appeared dull rather than acute in all his senses, especially hearing and sight. The next year he was presented in Paris to the young physician Jean-Marc-Gaspard Itard, who became a pioneer in the education of the deaf and the mentally retarded. Although the Parisian public had flocked to the "savage of Aveyron" expecting to find in him the embodiment of Rousseau's noble savage, Itard encountered someone quite different: "a disgustingly dirty child affected with spasmodic movements, and often convulsions, who swayed back and forth ceaselessly like certain animals in a zoo, who bit and scratched those who opposed him, who showed no affection for those who took care of him, and who was, in short, indifferent to everything and attentive to nothing." Itard gave him the name Victor and sought to develop his senses, intellect, and emotions as well as to determine from his deficiencies what humankind owed to education and civilization. He spent five years in this effort, far longer than did Dr. Arbuthnot or any of Peter's other examiners, and though Itard claimed some successes, Victor remained profoundly a captive of his stunted early life.[49]

More immediate to Burroughs's time than this pair of "wild" boys were a pair of "wild" men. At the end of August 1911, a few months before Burroughs began writing *Tarzan*, butchers at a slaughterhouse near Oroville in north-central California discovered a "wild" man cornered by their dogs. Superficially, at least, his situation resembled Wild Peter's and Victor's when they were found. Except for a ragged scrap of canvas, which he wore like a poncho, and a frayed undershirt, he was naked. He was also fatigued, frightened, and starving. And he spoke no language that his captors could recognize. He was not a boy of twelve, however, but a man who appeared perhaps sixty years old. (He was, in fact, about fifty.) But the greatest difference that immediately set his case apart from the feral children's, long before his intelligence could be assessed or his emotional development determined, was race. When the local sheriff arrived, he perceived the "wild" man

as an Indian. To hold him and at the same time to shield him from the curious stares of people streaming to the jail at Oroville, the sheriff locked him up in a cell for the insane. Despite this setting, his appeared to be a striking case not of individual isolation and retardation, as with Wild Peter and Victor, but of cultural primitivism and isolation from the modern world. Newspapers trumpeted news of this last wild Indian, a figure who seemed to have stepped directly from the Stone Age into the age of airplanes.[50]

When Alfred Kroeber and Thomas Waterman, two anthropologists at the University of California at Berkeley, read these stories, they thought this "wild" man might be a survivor of the Yahi tribe whose last recorded members had been massacred almost a half century earlier. Two days after the "discovery" of the strange man, Waterman traveled to the Oroville jail. He sat in the inmate's cell and read down a list of phonetically transcribed Yana words, until at last, with *siunini*, yellow pine, the man's face lit up. He was, it gradually emerged, the last surviving member of the Yahi, a southern tribe of the Yana.[51] Almost his entire life, he had lived in concealment as part of a tiny and ever dwindling remnant in the foothills of Mount Lassen. For three years, since the death of his mother, sister, and an old man, he had existed entirely on his own. Now he was officially a ward of the federal government. Wearing a shirt, coat, and trousers provided for him but spurning shoes, he traveled with Waterman by train and ferry from Oroville to San Francisco. Until his death from tuberculosis four and a half years later, he lived in the University of California's new Anthropological Museum near Golden Gate Park, where he demonstrated Yahi crafts such as arrowhead making on Sunday afternoons and worked as a janitor's assistant during the week. He never revealed his name, but Kroeber called him Ishi, which means man in Yana.

With his gentle, friendly disposition, Ishi played the role of Rousseauian noble savage far better than had Wild Peter or Victor. His reactions to modern civilization aroused keen interest. Traveling around San Francisco shortly after his arrival, he was unnerved by the crowds. The exclamation *"Hansi saltu!"* burst from his lips: "Many white people, many white people!"[52] A few days later, a reporter invited Ishi to attend a vaudeville performance. From his box seat, during the first two acts, Ishi watched the audience exclusively, which to his mind was far more interesting than anything onstage. In time, he

learned white San Franciscans' names for the people around him: "English, Chinaman, Japanese, Wild Indian, Nigger, Irishman, Dutchman, policeman." He appeared impressed less with airplanes than with technologies nearer at hand and of direct use to him—matches, running water, roller window shades. According to those close to him, he blamed contemporary illnesses on "the excessive amount of time men spent cooped up in automobiles, in offices, and in their own houses. It is not a man's nature to be too much indoors and especially in his own house with women constantly about," he believed.[53]

Ishi appealed to the modern longing for a more rugged, "primitive" existence that would revitalize masculinity. This longing emerged most vividly when he returned to his home ground in May 1914, almost three years after his emergence near Oroville. The im-

Ishi in Oroville, California, August 1911. Photograph by Hogan. Phoebe A. Hearst Museum of Anthropology, University of California at Berkeley

Ishi with bow and arrow, Deer Creek, 1914.
Phoebe A. Hearst Museum of Anthropology, University of California at Berkeley

petus for the trip came not from Ishi, who was at first reluctant to re-visit the place of his ancestors, but from Kroeber and Waterman and their physician-friend Saxton Pope. Ultimately, Ishi agreed, and the outing took on the aspect of a male-bonding retreat as much as an ethnographic study. Once back in his homeland, Ishi, who had re-fused to be photographed without Western dress in San Francisco, re-verted to his native breechcloth. Still he refused to shed clothing entirely, even while swimming, unlike his "civilized" companions, all of whom reveled in their nakedness and the opportunity to "play In-dian."[54] As he demonstrated his great skills as hunter and fisherman and his deep reverence for the natural world, he seemed a time trav-eler from an ancient and alien realm.

The desire to strip off civilization with one's clothes and to experi-ence primitive life firsthand in contact with nature was, of course, a masculine Romantic impulse that recurred with astonishing force and variety in the late nineteenth and early twentieth centuries—from

the French artist Paul Gauguin's removal to Tahiti to the German nudist movement. In addition, at the time Ishi was discovered, millions of buttoned-up American boys and men were taking to the woods in organizations such as the Sierra Club and the Boy Scouts of America. Ernest Thompson Seton declared, in the first Boy Scout handbook, "Those live longest who live nearest to the ground, . . . who live the simple life of primitive times, divested, however, of the evils that ignorance in those times begot." Seton proposed that everyone spend at least one month a year outdoors.[55]

Perhaps the American figure who most grandiosely struck the primitivist pose in this period was a minor Boston illustrator, Joseph Knowles. Beginning in early August 1913, Knowles conducted an "experiment" that both reversed Ishi's passage from wilderness to modern technological civilization and, more than any contemporary effort, paralleled Edgar Rice Burroughs's literary experiment in *Tarzan of the Apes*. What Knowles proposed was to test whether a modern man, stripped naked and without any implements, could enter the woods and live the primitive life successfully, depending solely upon his own individual resources.[56] The wilderness he chose was not in Equatorial Africa but in darkest Maine, and he was not a noble foundling but an experienced woodsman and guide on the eve of his forty-fourth birthday. Even so, the rather pudgy, cigarette-smoking Knowles made an unlikely exemplar of savage virility. The surprising celebrity he achieved testifies to how much a public adapting to modern technological civilization craved the reassurance that the urban white man could face the elements on his own and triumph.

Knowles's experiment recalls Sandow's and Houdini's feats, even as it resonates with *Tarzan*. Knowles sought the limelight as assiduously as any vaudevillian, though even he was dazzled by his success. As if conducting a Houdini escape, on August 4, 1913, he stripped off his clothes before reporters and photographers near the Spencer Mountains in northeastern Maine, vowing to stay in the wilderness for two months. He had arranged with the *Boston Sunday Post* to file weekly reports, written with charcoal on birch bark, chronicling his adventures. The week before, Harvard's Dudley A. Sargent, the physical-culture expert who twenty years earlier accorded Sandow the title "perfect man," had examined him. The best Sargent could say

Joseph Knowles stripping for his wilderness experiment, 1913. From *Alone in the Wilderness.* The University of North Carolina at Chapel Hill

Knowles bidding his friends goodbye. From *Alone in the Wilderness.* The University of North Carolina at Chapel Hill

was that Knowles "showed considerable fat, which will aid him in resisting cold." Still, the doctor struck exactly the note of cultural urgency that Knowles desired: "There is no question that in our advancement from primeval life we have dropped through disuse a great deal of natural knowledge; our artificial life has robbed us of some of our greatest powers and has stunted others." Under the circumstances, he applauded Knowles's "attempt to live like a primeval man" as being of both scientific interest and practical value.[57]

Over the next two months, the activities of the "forest man" became headline news in the *Boston Post*. Readers learned of his struggle to build a fire, catch trout, and contrive leggings out of moss. On August 24, the *Post* excitedly titled his dispatch "Knowles Catches Bear in Pit." The painter turned primitivist furnished readers with a blow-by-blow description of how he caught and killed a young black bear so that he might have its skin as a covering at night and as clothing when he finally reemerged to civilization. Later, he reported how he killed a small deer, grabbing it by its horns and breaking its neck. These exploits were double-edged. On the one hand, they testified to Knowles's prowess as primordial man, recapitulating the Darwinian struggle by which his ancestors had ascended the ladder of civilization. ("In the wilderness," he declared, "the one great law is the survival of the fittest."[58]) On the other hand, these kills violated the Maine game laws, from which Knowles had unsuccessfully sought an exemption. During his last weeks, he grew worried that game wardens might seek him out and arrest him; he spent his last days in the wild fleeing across the Canadian border so that he would not be taken prematurely.

When, scratched, bruised, thirty pounds lighter, and garbed in animal skins, Knowles emerged on October 4 near Megantic, in Quebec, he looked like primordial man come to life. He seemed to have transformed his very race in the process: a reporter described him as "tanned like an Indian, almost black." The size and enthusiasm of the waiting crowd stunned him. When he came down the steps from his train, he thought the horde "would tear the skins from [his] body." It was a foretaste of the tremendous receptions to come. All the way through Maine and down to Boston, crowds cheered his passage. Schools released their charges so that they might glimpse the great man. When he arrived in Boston, once again clad in animal skins,

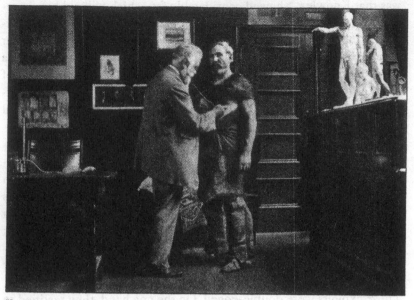

Knowles in wilderness garb as examined by Dudley A. Sargent. From *Alone in the
Wilderness.* The University of North Carolina at Chapel Hill

crowds mobbed him. For a celebration on Boston Common, they
swelled to an estimated fifteen to twenty thousand people. At Harvard, Dr. Sargent examined Knowles again and pronounced him
stronger in every respect than before he entered the woods. Afterward, the staff of Filene's Men's Store promised to turn him into a
modern man once more through "barbering, manicuring, chiropody
and complete outfitting in new and fashionable clothes."

Knowles's metamorphoses from civilized to primitive man and
back again seemed to fascinate the public as much as had Houdini's
great magical metamorphoses. At a lavish banquet honoring Knowles,
Sargent declared, "A dress shirt is not becoming to him with such a
splendid body hidden away underneath." Yet it was Knowles's ability
to inhabit both worlds that captured the public's imagination. He
served as a primitive proxy for modern men, who liked to imagine
that they, too, had splendid bodies hidden underneath their dress
shirts. Two months after his return, he completed a book based on his
dispatches to the *Post* called *Alone in the Wilderness.* A rival newspaper,
William Randolph Hearst's *Boston American*, charged that Knowles

was a fraud who actually bought his celebrated bearskin and slept in a snug, secret cabin while in the woods, but it failed to prick the bubble of his celebrity. Knowles briefly toured on the vaudeville circuit retelling his feat, and his book sold 300,000 copies.[59]

PRIMATE RELATIONS

Burroughs's "wild child" was of course a fictional hero in an adventure story rather than a historical object of scientific examination. It is doubtful that Burroughs knew of Wild Peter, Victor, or other feral children when he wrote *Tarzan*. Nor does he appear to have been aware of Ishi or, in the interval between *Tarzan*'s publication in *The All-Story* and in book form, to have remarked on the feat of Joseph Knowles. As he later said, the legend of Romulus and Remus suckled by a wolf and of Kipling's animal stories came more to his mind.[60] In time, Burroughs did learn more about the fate of feral children and acknowledged that Tarzan's adventures were fictional entertainments, not literal possibilities. He wrote in 1927:

> I do not believe that any human infant or child, unprotected by adults of its own species, could survive a fortnight in such an African environment as I describe in the Tarzan stories, and if he did, he would develop into a cunning, cowardly beast, as he would have to spend most of his waking hours fleeing for his life. He would be under-developed from lack of proper and sufficient nourishment, from exposure to the inclemencies of the weather, and from lack of sufficient restful sleep.

Burroughs intended Tarzan as "merely an interesting experiment in the mental laboratory which we call imagination."[61]

Even with this retrospective caveat, Burroughs's story could be read in two alternative yet overlapping ways. It might be understood, first, as a novel diversion, an experiment in storytelling that aimed only to entertain. At the same time, *Tarzan* could be read as an allegory that in miniature recounted and explained why its hero (and those like him) triumphed where others failed. In this sense, the workings of the narrative revealed truths about the reader's world, not

just the fictional characters'. Although he denied that the events in his imaginative laboratory could literally happen (which many a reader of *Tarzan* has contested), Burroughs still permitted a considerable area within which the story might be understood to be true.[62]

In this imaginative laboratory, Burroughs created a figure whose hereditary advantages, as he conceived them, are severely tested in the harsh environment of the African jungle. At the outset his situation in some ways reverses that of Wild Peter and of Victor. Apes rather than cultured savants regard him as developmentally backward, and both his foster father, Tublat, and the tribal leader, Kerchak, argue that he should be abandoned as hopeless. By the age of ten, he can claim some accomplishments, including superior cunning and ability on the ground, but he remains ashamed of his deficiencies, such as his hairless body, "pinched nose," and "puny white teeth."[63] The name the apes give him marks his difference (and, ultimately, Burroughs believed, his superiority): Tarzan means white skin.

In this way Burroughs sought to test the nature of white Anglo-Saxon masculinity. A literary fantasy rather than a scientific inquiry, *Tarzan* nonetheless resonated with the social and natural sciences of the day, which were, of course, much more deeply implicated in Western cultural fantasies than their practitioners realized. What was the nature of the human species, and how was it related to other higher primates? And within the human species, was modern Anglo-Saxon man's putative superiority intrinsic (biological) or extrinsic (the product of collective social and cultural achievements)? Taken out of their environments, how would modern man fare in the wild and "primitive" man fare in modern civilization? Was primitive man, as exemplified by Ishi, passing with the rise of modern civilization? Or was the racial stock that had created modern man in the first place passing? This last view was exemplified by Theodore Roosevelt's dire warnings of "race suicide" and Madison Grant's still more extremist *The Passing of the Great Race* (1916).[64] Each view—and at times a combination of both—was widely embraced by European and American scientists at the time. Relations between humans and their fellow primates and between modern and "primitive" man were especially topical when Burroughs was writing.

In many respects, interest in higher primates picked up where interest in feral children left off. (Indeed, both etymologically and bio-

logically, the line between the two frequently blurred.[65]) Especially after the publication of Charles Darwin's *On the Origin of Species* (1859) and *The Descent of Man* (1871), determining human nature became intimately connected with humanity's relation to fellow primates and their ongoing struggle for existence. What was distinctively human, it appeared, could be illuminated by determining what was common to members of the primate order. How human beings learned could be clarified by discovering how other primates learned in the wild—and, perhaps, in the laboratory. Comparisons were hampered, however, by the difficulty Western scientists experienced in studying chimpanzees and especially gorillas, which were hard to locate, capture, tame, and maintain in captivity.

A pioneering effort in this regard was made by Richard L. Garner, an early researcher of animal speech who claimed to have observed more chimpanzees and gorillas in their natural state than any other white man. In his desire to forge intellectual and emotional links with these primates—and in his persistent adherence to racial categories— he provides to some degree a flesh-and-blood anticipation of Tarzan. Garner, who was born in Virginia in 1848, declared, "From childhood, I have believed that all kinds of animals have some mode of speech by which they can talk among their own kind, and I have often wondered why man has never tried to learn it."[66] Largely on his own, in 1884 he started to study the speech of monkeys and the comparatively few apes (including orangutans, gibbons, gorillas, and chimpanzees) available in American zoological gardens and circuses. He conceived of this task "as very much the same as learning [the speech] of some strange race of mankind—more difficult in the degree of its inferiority, but less in volume."[67] In this effort he made the first phonograph recordings of monkeys and played them to other monkeys to observe their reactions. Reasoning that the primates with the greatest physical development would display the greatest linguistic development as well, he set sail in 1892 for what was then French Gabon and French Congo in Equatorial Africa to study chimpanzees and gorillas "in a state of freedom."[68]

To discover firsthand how chimpanzees and gorillas behaved in the wild, outside human cages, Garner placed himself in a cage. He built a small cubicle, six feet six inches on each side, out of steel mesh, painted it a dingy green, covered it with bamboo leaves, and

dubbed it "Fort Gorilla."[69] For 112 days in 1893, he made observations from this outpost. He did not prove so inconspicuous as he had hoped, however, and ultimately he had to rely on secondhand reports to augment his researches.

In his account of this expedition, *Gorillas and Chimpanzees* (1896), Garner stressed the kinship between apes and humans as well as their essential differences. He granted that if one measured an ape's intelligence along a human scale, its "mental horizon" would resemble a one-year-old child's. "But," he continued, with a twist that Burroughs would have appreciated, "if the operation were reversed, and man were placed under the natural conditions of the ape, the comparison would be much less in his favour. There is no common mental unit between them." Garner cast a skeptical eye on a number of previous reports about the gorilla, especially his belligerent assaults on human beings: "He is shy and timid, and shrinks alike from man and other large animals. I have no doubt that when he is in a rage he is both fierce and powerful, but his ferocity and strength are rated above their true value."[70] Nonetheless, with his interest in speech, Garner concentrated on chimpanzees, finding them more sociable, easier to teach, and more manageable. They also had a considerably larger vocabulary than gorillas, he believed, though still "not more than twenty words." (He could discern only two among gorillas.) He claimed to learn about ten of these words well enough to speak to chimpanzees in their native tongue. He went one step further. Although he emphasized that the true test of an animal's intelligence is its ability not to learn a human trick but to solve a new problem using its powers of reasoning, he could not resist teaching a chimpanzee to talk.

His pupil in this experiment had been found orphaned in a swamp, and so Garner named him Moses. In a way that recalls Itard's relation to Victor and Kala's to Tarzan, Garner became Moses's tutor and foster father. "I designed to bring Moses up in the way that good chimpanzees ought to be brought up," he wrote, "so I began to teach him good manners in the hope that some day he would be a shining light to his race, and aid me in my work among them." One senses Garner's dry humor here, as well as a hint of the "white man's burden." But if a paternalistic twinkle shines through his description of Moses's tutelage, so does a serious desire to determine to what degree

the chimpanzee might be instructed in the refinements of civilization, down to the niceties of table manners. Garner gave Moses "a tin plate and a wooden spoon, but he did not like to use the latter, and seemed to think that it was pure affectation for any one to eat with such an awkward thing," though Garner kept trying to break Moses of the habit of "putting his fingers in the dish to help himself." Ultimately, Garner claimed that Moses "was the first of his race that ever spoke a word of human speech," though in fact the most the animal ever accomplished was to repeat uncomprehendingly two or three chimpanzee sounds that vaguely approximated words known to Garner (none of them English). Garner quickly developed a great affection for Moses and treasured signs of the animal's devotion to him. If he did not fully succeed in creating an intellectual bond, he certainly established an emotional one.[71]

After Moses's death Garner acquired two other chimpanzees, Aaron, whom he prized and loved, and Elisheba, whom he disliked but tolerated. In his homeward voyage he took both to Liverpool, England, where their response to civilized Western dress surprised him. As he opened their cage in the waiting room at the pier and "they beheld the throng of huge figures with white faces, long skirts and big coats, they were almost frantic with fear. They had never before seen anything like it, and they crouched back in the corner of the cage, clinging to each other and screaming in terror." "In their own country," Garner explained, "they had never seen any thing like this, for the natives to whom they were accustomed wear no clothing as a rule, except a small piece of cloth tied round the waist, and the few white men they had seen were mostly dressed in white; but here was a great crowd in skirts and overcoats, and I have no doubt that to them it was a startling sight for the first time."[72]

Though in moments such as this Garner was able to see the clothes and bodies of Westerners through new eyes, he was never tempted to "go native" himself. Indeed, in the photographs illustrating his account, his appearance is iconic of the commanding, masculine Western explorer. The image captioned "Starting for a Stroll," for example, shows him standing in front of his cage with a native boy whose name, unlike those of many of the chimpanzees and some of the gorillas, is never given. The boy is covered from waist to just below the knees by a piece of cloth tied in front. He wears a pendant on

his neck and chest. He carries a spear, held in his lowered left hand and his raised right. Garner towers over him. The white man protects himself with a pith helmet, a jacket tightly buttoned at wrist and neck, and trousers tucked into high boots. He holds what appears to be a double-barreled rifle in a fashion roughly symmetrical to the boy's spear. Together, the two embody the types of "primitive" and "civilized" man in paternalistic colonial relationship, and except for the backdrop, they might as well be the British-American explorer Henry Stanley and his native servant in a similar illustration from the period.

Just as Garner left his native servant unnamed, though the two spent a great deal of time together in and out of the cage, he said little about the native peoples of the areas in which he worked. Nonetheless, his attitudes toward them appear highly conventional (much more so than his scientific researches). Although he sought to qualify a patronizingly hierarchical view of apes, he clearly retained one of *Homo sapiens*, with white men on top. Indeed, this conviction of white superiority over blacks served as a template as he considered differences among the apes he encountered. Speaking of two distinct types of chimpanzees (the *kulu* and the *ntyigo*) that others had considered separate species, for example, he invoked the analogies of race and caste: "I believe them to be two well-defined varieties of the same species; they are the white man and the negro of a common stock. They are the patrician and plebeian of one race, or the nobility and yeomanry of one tribe. . . . The *kulu-kamba* is simply a high order of chimpanzee."[73] Garner's research, like Burroughs's *Tarzan of the Apes*, suggests that when white Westerners around the turn of the century thought about their relation to apes, they could not avoid thinking about their relation to their fellowmen or resist reasserting supposedly natural hierarchies in which they stood at the summit. Though Garner was tempted to hang portraits of chimpanzees in his gallery of family relations, metaphorically speaking, he expressed no similar inclination with regard to black Africans.

A comparable attitude may be seen in Burroughs's *Tarzan of the Apes*. The story appeals powerfully to the fantasy of a reunion with the natural world and hence with one's authentic self. Growing up amid apes in the African jungle, Tarzan achieves a healing of the "bitter bifurcation" of modern Western culture: between civilization and

Richard Garner and an
unidentified African boy
"Starting for a Stroll."
From *Gorillas and
Chimpanzees*. The University
of North Carolina at Chapel Hill

Henry Stanley and an African
boy. From Stanley's *How I Found
Livingston* (New York: Scribner's,
1899). The University of North Carolina
at Chapel Hill

nature, man and animal, mind and body, thought and feeling, idea and act. He exults in the immediate, palpable challenges of the wild, in which "life was never monotonous or stale." Such an existence prepares him to be an exemplary savage and, ultimately, to become a superb bearer of white Anglo-Saxon civilization. As Burroughs conceived his character, both these capacities were innate, and the jungle environment made them especially robust. Discovering the cabin erected by his father and examining its books as a boy of ten, Tarzan gradually teaches himself to read and to write. In so doing, he recapitulates what Burroughs took to be the process of civilization. The narrator makes sure no reader misses the point:

> Squatting upon his haunches on the table top in the cabin his father had built—his smooth, brown, naked little body bent over the book which he rested in his strong slender hands, and his great shock of long, black hair falling about his well shaped head and bright, intelligent eyes—Tarzan of the apes, little primitive man, presented a picture filled, at once, with pathos and with promise—an allegorical figure of the primordial groping through the black night of ignorance toward the light of learning.[74]

More immediately, Tarzan's innate capacities allow him to rise above the physically more powerful apes and other animals and to become lord of the jungle. Descended from "the best of a race of mighty fighters," he delights in battle and the pleasure of the kill. Being from "a race of meat-eaters," he "craves flesh." another sign of his vigorous masculinity and racial superiority. Burroughs's stress on this appetite accords with the view of the physician Woods Hutchinson, who contended that "vegetarianism is the diet of the enslaved, stagnant, and conquered races, and a diet rich in meat is that of the progressive, the dominant, and the conquering strains." Tarzan enthusiastically devours raw gorilla and lion meat; and when he first sees a black native cook a boar, he cannot imagine "ruin[ing] good meat in any such foolish manner." Tarzan proves a mighty hunter through his innate intelligence and facility with rope and knife and, later, bow and arrow. His easy mastery of the noose to trap his enemies recalls Burroughs's own experience in the West as well as those

described in novels such as *The Virginian* and *The Clansman*. With such weapons, Tarzan triumphs over rivals within the colony and the colony's most feared enemies: other apes, a lion, and his fellowmen.[75]

TARZAN AND THE REDISCOVERY OF
WHITE MALE IDENTITY

The degree to which they *are* his fellowmen and the obligations of such fellowship become the great driving questions of the novel. Like Dumas's *The Man in the Iron Mask* and similar melodramas of a captive denied the knowledge of his noble birth, this is essentially a story of Tarzan's unfolding realization of his identity as a white Anglo-Saxon and, more specifically, as the rightful Lord Greystoke. The reader is in on the secret from the beginning, of course, but as Burroughs develops his plot, Tarzan must discover the nature of his "own kind" and the truth of his noble ancestry. He answers the first of these questions largely intuitively, though his uncertainty whether he is truly a man or the son of Kala and perhaps "a strange white ape" adds a titillation not completely dispelled until the book's final pages.[76]

Growing up in a Darwinian Eden, glorying in the struggle for existence, Tarzan nibbles on the apple that will provide the knowledge of his humanity in his father's cabin. First from an illustrated primer, then from other books, he sees pictures of white boys and men and gradually realizes why he is different from the apes around him. Like Adam, with this knowledge he becomes aware of his nakedness; yet he feels no shame. He proudly displays his "sleek skin" and covets clothing only as an ungainly emblem of human superiority over other animals.[77]

From Tarzan's first sight of another live human being, however, his sense of commonality is checked by visceral racial antipathy. A remnant of a once powerful tribe moves into the area, fleeing the brutal oppression wrought by King Leopold II of Belgium. Burroughs's initial description of the black warriors anticipates Tarzan's response:

> On their backs were oval shields, in their noses huge rings, while from the kinky wool of their heads protruded tufts of gay feathers.

Across their foreheads were tattooed three parallel lines of color, and on each breast three concentric circles. Their yellow teeth were filed to sharp points, and their great protruding lips added still further to the low and bestial brutishness of their appearance.

Almost immediately, Kulonga, their chief's son, slays Tarzan's foster mother, Kala. Without knowing the nature of Kala's killer, Tarzan determines to avenge her death. Kulonga is the first human he has encountered since infancy; still, when Tarzan sees him, he immediately identifies him from his father's books as "the *negro*," "so like him in form and yet so different in face and color." He tracks the black warrior to the edge of his village, then throws a "quick noose" over his head and, acting as a one-man vigilante party, lynches him:

> Hand over hand Tarzan drew the struggling black until he had him hanging by his neck in midair; then Tarzan climbed to a larger branch drawing the still threshing victim well up into the sheltering verdure of the tree.
>
> Here he fastened the rope securely to a stout branch, and then descending, plunged his hunting knife into Kulonga's heart. Kala was avenged.[78]

Whatever Burroughs's intentions were in this graphic description (reiterated when Tarzan kills other natives), it recalls in especially disturbing ways the racial lynchings that raged across the South from the 1880s through the 1920s.

Tarzan strips the dead body of possessions. Then, following apes' custom in dealing with slain enemies from outside their tribe, he prepares to eat the corpse. At this crucial moment, however, a minimal sense of shared humanity, fortified by ancestral instinct, overcomes both the chasm of race and the training of apes. For Burroughs, this instinct is by no means universal; rather, it flows from Tarzan's Anglo-Saxon blood. Kulonga's people have no such inhibitions, readers soon learn: to torture and devour their enemies are their greatest delights. Spying on their cannibal revels from a perch high in a tree, Tarzan "saw that these people were more wicked than his own apes" and "began to hold his own kind in but low esteem." Except for his admi-

ration of their body ornaments, Tarzan's view of black Africans seems little different from the views of most whites of his day: he is repulsed by their cruelty, contemptuous of their superstitions, and happy to terrorize them for his amusement and to steal from them whatever he wants. In *The Descent of Man* (a book in Burroughs's library), Darwin consoled his readers with the thought that mankind's fellow primates were in many respects ancestors as noble as present-day savages: "For my own part, I would as soon be descended from that heroic little monkey, who braved his dreaded enemy in order to save the life of his keeper, . . . as from a savage who delights to torture his enemies, offers up bloody sacrifices, practices infanticide without remorse, treats his wives like slaves, knows no decency, and is haunted by the grossest superstitions." These natives may be of a common species, but they are not truly Tarzan's kind at all.[79]

Still, Tarzan is a climber both of trees and of the evolutionary and social ladder. Shortly after he kills Kulonga and sends a wave of fright into the native village, he stabs the great ape-king Kerchak in a fierce fight and assumes command of the colony. Although he rules wisely, ape administration proves dull work. Even the excitement of defeating a challenger such as his stepbrother Terkoz cannot curb his restlessness. He abdicates his throne to search for "other white men like himself."[80]

Coincidentally, another mutiny is brewing nearby, remarkably similar to the one that cast Tarzan's parents onshore twenty years earlier. In their swarthy, bestial appearance, the mutineers are virtual copies of the earlier crew, except that this time the giant stand-in for Black Michael is immediately shot by a rat-faced little villain named Snipes. To Tarzan these men seem "no different from the black men" in their lack of civilization, and he feels no kinship toward them.[81]

The five hapless passengers, however, form a different category. Tarzan finds ample reason to consider them stupid and ridiculous, although to a great extent these are faults of overcivilization. The most absurd of the lot is Archimedes Q. Porter, an elderly, pedantic professor who wears a frock coat and silk hat even in the African jungle and constantly loses both his train of thought and his way. His assistant, the fussy Samuel T. Philander, is scarcely more practical. The professor's daughter, however, provides the novel's love interest and Tarzan's reason for caring about them. She is Jane Porter, a beautiful,

The cover of the October 1912 issue of *The All-Story*, featuring *Tarzan of the Apes: A Romance of the Jungle*. Illustration by Clinton Pettee. Edgar Rice Burroughs Memorial Collection, University of Louisville

golden-haired, snowy-white Southern belle almost exactly Tarzan's age. Her immense black mammy, a minstrel caricature named Esmeralda who spouts malaprop nonsense and faints in every crisis, accompanies her. Fifth, and last, wearing white ducks as if plucked from a lawn-tennis match, is Jane's English suitor, the tall, handsome, and proper William Cecil Clayton, who just happens to be the son of the current Lord Greystoke and so is Tarzan's first cousin.

At last, then, Tarzan discovers his own kind, the race, class, and even kin from which he springs, though he does not learn the secret of his birth until virtually the last page. Even so, differences divide them: not only differences of language (Tarzan can read and write in English but knows only animal speech) but, more important, immense differences between Tarzan's brute training and modern Anglo-American civilization. That this contrast works overwhelmingly to Tarzan's advantage constitutes the great twist and appeal of Burroughs's story. Faced with the basic challenges of survival in the wild, the passengers' education proves worthless. The jungle that is an open book to Tarzan is to them an unknown and frightening hieroglyph. Most especially, due to the fateful combination of his innate attributes and his savage upbringing, Tarzan possesses virile virtues to a peerless degree. None can match him in physical prowess, sensory keenness, quick thinking, courage, or selflessness. The difference between Tarzan and his cousin measures the exact degree to which he has been shaped by the jungle. The two have virtually the same heredity but completely different training. Whereas Clayton has become pampered and privileged, Tarzan is the ultimate self-taught, self-made man. In ordinary company Clayton would stand out, but next to this paragon of primal masculinity he is utterly eclipsed.

Indeed, for the rest of the book, Tarzan's chief occupation is to rescue these characters from one near disaster after another. Their assignment, in turn, is to admire his beautiful and powerful body while he does so. Burroughs has already held that body up for his readers' admiration many times, insisting that here at last is truly the perfect man, a Sandovian combination of Hercules and Adonis: "His straight and perfect figure, muscled as the best of the ancient Roman gladiators must have been muscled, and yet with the soft and sinuous curves of a Greek god, told at a glance the wondrous combination of enormous strength with suppleness and speed." In lieu of wearing a

fig leaf, Tarzan has donned a doeskin breechcloth (stripped from another black native he has killed) and meets members of the Porter party with minimally decent attire. He drops in on Cecil Clayton first, to save him from an attacking lion. A "naked giant," "the embodiment of physical perfection," he leaps from a tree directly onto the lion's back. Through Clayton's eyes, Burroughs's description continues: "With lightning speed an arm that was banded layers of iron muscle encircled the huge neck, and the great beast was raised from behind, roaring and pawing the air—raised as easily as Clayton would have lifted a pet dog." Not surprisingly, the *All-Story* illustrator Clinton Pettee chose this scene for the cover of the *Tarzan* issue.[82]

At this point Burroughs starts releasing lions as rapidly as a dispatcher does taxis in a thunderstorm. Back at Tarzan's cabin, another lion (originally a tiger in the *All-Story* version) is crawling through the window to devour Jane Porter and the hysterical Esmeralda. With Clayton in tow, Tarzan races back, pulls the beast out the window by the tail, and gets it in a full nelson. Clayton stands ineffectually to the side, as if taking notes: "At last Clayton saw the immense muscles of Tarzan's shoulders and biceps leap into corded knots beneath the silver moonlight. There was a long sustained and supreme effort on the ape-man's part—and the vertebrae of Sabor's neck parted with a sharp snap." Such a feat calls for a little celebration, and, as is his custom, Tarzan sounds "the bull ape's savage roar of victory," the African analogue to Buck's call of the wild. Then, leaving everyone within earshot quivering with fright from his yell, he is off to rescue Professor Porter and his assistant from yet another lion.[83]

The first time Jane sees Tarzan for herself, however, he is saving her from a more titillating and fearful menace. Tarzan's old rival Terkoz has been driven out of the ape colony, only to discover Jane and Esmeralda in the jungle. The "horrible man-like beast" carries Jane off, intending her for the first of his new harem, "a fate a thousand times worse than death." Here, within the conventions of melodrama, Burroughs transformed fears of the predatory black rapist and the specter of miscegenation into fears of hybridity between human beings and apes. Although nineteenth-century European naturalists stressed the "law" of nature by which animals refused to mate with those not of their kind, a fascination with exceptions persisted. In 1865 the British Anthropological Society republished a summary of

travelers' reports that described "lascivious male apes attack[ing] women," who "perish miserably in the brutal embraces of their ravishers."[84] Other popular accounts, such as Paul Du Chaillu's *Explorations and Adventures in Equatorial Africa* (1861), reported similar legends, if only to debunk them.[85] (As with miscegenation, there was a double standard at work in these fears; the thought that Tarzan's mother might be an ape was apparently far less dreadful than the idea of his having been fathered by an ape and a white woman.) In Burroughs's story, of course, Tarzan intercepts the abductor in the nick of time, and the two square off for a duel to the death. Burroughs charges the violent scene with eroticism. Jane breathlessly watches the struggle, "her lithe, young form flattened against the trunk of a great tree, her hands tight pressed against her rising and falling bosom, and her eyes wide with mingled horror, fascination, fear, and admiration." The sight of Tarzan's body, locked in mortal combat with the monstrous ape, proves irresistible:

> As the great muscles of the man's back and shoulders knotted beneath the tension of his efforts, and the huge biceps and forearm held at bay those mighty tusks, the veil of centuries of civilization and culture was swept from the blurred vision of the Baltimore girl.
>
> When the long knife drank deep a dozen times of Terkoz' heart's blood, and the great carcass rolled lifeless upon the ground, it was a primeval woman who sprang forward with outstretched arms toward the primeval man who had fought for her and won her.[86]

Where will this romance between wild man and professor's daughter end? That is the question for the rest of the novel. In reality, wild boys and men rarely if ever brimmed with sexual passion and allure. Both Wild Peter's and Victor's examiners noted their indifference to women; and Ishi, who had very little sexual experience, "blushed furiously" whenever the subject of sex cropped up. Yet Tarzan, Burroughs assured his readers, is a "red-blooded man"; so, with Jane, he experiences a conflict between his savage training and his innate nobility comparable to his deliberation over whether to dine on Kulonga: "The order of the jungle [was] for the male to take his mate by

force; but could Tarzan be guided by the laws of the beasts?" Only after wringing every delicious drop of suspense from the situation does Burroughs conclude, No. With inborn courtliness, Tarzan protects Jane and returns her to her father and friends unharmed.[87]

Jane's response is more conflicted and confused. After she first throws herself into his arms, her "outraged conscience" compels her to repulse him. When, nonetheless, Tarzan carries her off into the forest, she feels blissfully secure in the arms of her "forest god." She has fallen deeply in love. Cecil Clayton feels the shift in her affections and jealously taunts her that Tarzan is "some half-demented castaway," "beast of the jungle," or savage cannibal. These are in fact her own fears as well. When she tries to imagine Tarzan with her in civilized society—eating like an animal on an ocean liner, acting like an uncouth illiterate in front of her friends—she shudders with disgust. Can a girl from a genteel Baltimore family truly find happiness with "this jungle waif"? Still, he appeals to "the primeval woman in her nature," and she longs to be possessed by him; if need be, she will plunge into the jungle with him forever.[88]

It is not necessary to follow all the twists and turns of Burroughs's plot to the story's end. Suffice it to say that Tarzan determines to win Jane any way he can, even if it means becoming civilized. Thus he accomplishes one more astonishing metamorphosis: from savage noble to suave socialite. As yet he cannot speak English, though he can read and write it fluently. In a matter of weeks, a French navy lieutenant, Paul D'Arnot (whose life he also saves), coaches him (as Itard did Victor and Garner did Moses) with dazzling success. Tarzan quickly acquires the French language and manners (though, like Garner's Moses, he longs at times to throw his cutlery aside and to attack his food with hands and teeth). D'Arnot also teaches him not to kill every black man he meets as the two make their way to an African port. Now "Monsieur Tarzan," he dons shirt and trousers, although he is happy to shed them on a bet and, naked, to slay a lion. Swinging through the trees once more, he strongly feels the call of the wild and, even more intensely, the constrictions of civilization: "This was life! Ah! how he loved it! . . . At last he was free. He had not realized what a prisoner he had been."[89] What holds him for the moment to civilization is the hope of marrying Jane. Finally, in a dizzying rush of events, he digs up the buried treasure that Professor Porter has sought, fol-

lows Jane to America, and rescues her from a Wisconsin forest fire, swinging through the trees as of old.

But problems remain. To satisfy her father's financial obligation, Jane has reluctantly agreed to marry a scheming businessman twice her age. Still, Tarzan, who has fought Terkoz for Jane, is not about to lose her to this polished villain. "I am still a wild beast at heart," he reminds her. Gripping his rival by the throat, he persuades him to release Jane from her promise. Yet no sooner is his back turned than Jane pledges herself to his cousin Cecil Clayton, the safe, "civilized" choice. What's a jungle lord to do? The noble thing, of course. He forbears showing Clayton the proof he has just obtained that he is indeed the rightful Lord Greystoke. When Clayton naively asks him how he came to be in the African jungle in the first place, Tarzan replies, "I was born there. . . . My mother was an Ape, and of course she couldn't tell me much about it. I never knew who my father was." And it's back to the jungle once more.[90]

The selfless renunciation at the story's end provided the final hook for many readers. Knowing that they would "read for the ending," Burroughs deliberately withheld the anticipated romantic union of Tarzan and Jane. Letters poured into *The All-Story* demanding a sequel. Yet, as an American soldier in Panama wrote to the editor on behalf of "hundreds" in his unit, some regretted that Tarzan "lost the girl—while others wonder if he can get used to living in 'civilization.' "[91]

They were right to wonder. Burroughs intended *Tarzan of the Apes* as a romantic adventure story, not as a formal meditation on civilization and its discontents. Nevertheless, his tale gave powerful narrative force to a widespread sense that modern technological civilization created restrictions, frustrations, ordinariness that entailed special losses for men. Like Wister and London, Theodore Roosevelt and Frederick Jackson Turner in his own time, and like earlier American writers such as James Fenimore Cooper, Ralph Waldo Emerson, Henry David Thoreau, and Herman Melville, Burroughs celebrated untamed masculine individualism. More particularly, he created in Tarzan a figure who embodied the enduring impulse, in Emerson's words, to "enjoy an original relation to the universe," to raw nature, with all its primal, anarchic force. The desire for unmediated contact with nature and occasions to test oneself against it constitutes an overriding element of American masculine identity. It is hardly sur-

prising that in the early twentieth century, when an increasingly impersonal, bureaucratic, and corporate society dominated the everyday life of individual citizens, that desire flared with new brightness and heat.[92]

What is more problematic in Burroughs's story and in the works of many of his contemporaries is that this assertion of masculine wildness is often explicitly tied to whiteness. Earlier writers were hardly free from bigotry, but to a notable extent writers such as Emerson and Thoreau at least tried to put their affirmations of individual wildness in the service of democratic inclusiveness and against systems of oppression, of which slavery was the most glaring and hateful.[93] In Burroughs's *Tarzan* as in Wister's *The Virginian*, however, all men are not created equal. True, Tarzan does not depend on outward hereditary privilege; indeed, the book ends with his refusing to claim his title and estate. As a self-made man, he could appeal to many readers. Yet Burroughs, in line with the predominant thought of influential whites of his time, believed that Tarzan carries his most valuable hereditary privilege, his innate superiority, in his very blood. He could be strengthened rather than degraded by the wild precisely because he holds the best of Western civilization within him. Others less favored by heredity, such as the African natives and atavistic crew members, in Burroughs's eyes do not.

If for Burroughs and his readers wildness enhanced white Anglo-Saxons but debased black Africans, it also enhanced masculinity—but not, in the same way, femininity. Tarzan's murmured statement to Jane in the story's concluding pages, "I am still a wild beast at heart," is as much a reassurance as a warning. His wildness is the basis of his virility, power, and authority, and for him to become truly civilized, to lock himself within the "iron cage" of modern capitalist society, would be tantamount to emasculation. With Jane it is another story. Burroughs allows her to submit to her awakened primal passions only in fleeting and fantastic moments. Perhaps he sensed that to make her as wild as Tarzan would be to replace her teasing oscillation between submission and resistance with an independent sexuality less acceptable to his readers and, perhaps, to himself. The metamorphosis that accompanied moving between civilization and the wild remained, above all, a masculine performance. Just as Houdini's substitute trunk trick ended with him free and Bess locked inside,

the drama of Tarzan's escape art shines most brilliantly if Jane remains locked within the conventions of civilization and is released only on his initiative. It is lucky for him, then, that she plays it safe and chooses Clayton. To continue as Burroughs's "perfect man" at the top of the natural hierarchy, Tarzan must be free and unencumbered, alone and in the wild.

The gender issues of wildness may be further illuminated by considering *Tarzan* in relation to a novel published three years later, Charlotte Perkins Gilman's *Herland*. Even though we have no evidence that Gilman, the most prominent feminist theorist of this period, ever read *Tarzan*, we may regard her novel as a kind of rejoinder to it. Though a socialist as well as a feminist, Gilman had much in common with Burroughs in her views on race. Indeed, she pursued far more seriously than he did the subjects of primitivism, evolution, eugenics, and the superiority of white Anglo-Saxon civilization. She differed markedly, however, in one respect: she was convinced that the sharp division between the sexes and women's dependence on men—far from being hallmarks of advanced civilization—were perversions that led to social and racial decadence.[94] Undoubtedly, she would have distrusted Burroughs's hypermasculine ideal of Tarzan, believing as she did that primitive man behaved more like the rapist Terkoz than like the chivalrous "forest god." Certainly, too, she would have seized on the character of Jane Porter as a damning example of an overly delicate woman, economically, socially, and psychologically dependent on men. Gilman presented her startling ideas in *Women and Economics* (1898), *The Man-Made World* (1911), and many other writings. Then in *Herland*, a story serialized in Gilman's self-authored monthly *The Forerunner* in 1915, she set forth her own fictional geography of feminism, a utopian view that stands as a retort to the works of Wister, London, and Burroughs.

Gilman's story begins as another tale about white males exploring an exotic and uncharted territory. Three young American bachelors on a scientific expedition learn from neighboring "savages" of an isolated mountain country where "no men lived—only women and girl children."[95] Equipped with a private yacht, motorboat, and biplane, they set out to discover Herland for themselves. Although close friends and former classmates, the three differ in both their training and their attitudes toward women. Jeff Margrave, a physician, is a

dewy-eyed idealist who longs to place women on a pedestal and worship at their feet. Terry Nicholson, a rich explorer who finances the excursion, prefers to seduce and dominate women. In a country of women, he jokes, he will be crowned king in no time. The narrator of the story, Vandyck Jennings, tries to steer a middle course. A sociologist, he sees himself as an open-minded investigator, although he enters Herland doubting the very possibility of women's independence.

What the three discover confounds their expectations—and challenges the very notion of savage virility on which *Tarzan* was based. Far from a primitive wilderness, the entire land appears to them "an enormous garden," perfectly cultivated, immaculately ordered, utterly devoid of wild beasts—or wildness of any kind. The population is equally well tended. Two thousand years earlier, after the country was sealed off by a volcanic eruption, its men died out, but through a miraculous mutation, women developed the capacity for virgin birth, producing only girls. Gradually they created a eugenic utopia, limiting the population and choosing mothers of the finest Aryan stock so as to avoid the "degenerate" and "unfit" and to breed out "the lowest types." The result is a "clean-bred, vigorous lot," a race as remarkable for its intelligence as for its health, strength, and beauty. There has not been a criminal for six hundred years. With only one sex, there is no sense of what is "manly" and what "womanly," a situation that unnerves the male visitors. With no predatory beasts to slay, no savages to kill, no villains to foil, no helpless women to rescue or even assist, no struggle of any kind, there is no opportunity to display white masculine prowess. As Terry complains: "I like Something Doing. Here it's all done."[96]

The contrast between *Tarzan* and *Herland* emerges most vividly in the stories' attempted rapes. The dark, hairy ape Terkoz provides an occasion for Tarzan to display the courage, strength, chivalry, and sexual self-restraint that supposedly distinguished the finest Anglo-Saxons from the darker races and beasts. In Gilman's story, the situation is quite different. The arrival of the three men gives Herland the opportunity to reestablish its ancient bisexual order and to rejoin with other lands. By permitting the three men to marry local women and to conceive children, the nation also hopes to enlarge its ethic of Motherhood to include a new Fatherhood and Brotherhood

as well. The men eagerly assent, but, once wed, they discover that Herland's idea of marriage is very different from theirs. Their wives still live apart, and they limit sexual relations to the minimum for procreation. Van and Jeff gradually adjust to the new order, but Terry cannot. He believes that a woman wishes to be mastered, and, like a hunter, he approaches her as "some quarry he was pursuing, something to catch and conquer." However, his wife, Alima, even if she has an "atavistic" element of femininity, is no swooning, delicate "girl" but "a big, handsome creature, rather exceptionally strong even in that race of strong women." In a desperate effort to reassert his mastery and what he regards as his conjugal rights, Terry tries to rape her. Alima fights back, kicking him in the groin. Two or three women aid her in repulsing his attack. They easily force him to the floor, tie him "hand and foot, and then, in sheer pity for his futile rage, . . . anesthetize him."[97] Here is a metamorphosis indeed, in which man is tied up and rendered unconscious like a captured animal (or as in a Houdini nightmare) and women are free and in power. Alima initially wants Terry killed—Terkoz's fate—but the court banishes him instead. Though Herland apparently continues with its "Great Change" to heterosexuality, some readers may have wondered why.

THE *TARZAN* MACHINE

Herland reached only loyal readers of Gilman's slender magazine in 1915. By that time, through Burroughs's unflagging efforts, Tarzan had already found millions of fans. His success developed from the bottom up, beginning with magazine and newspaper readers and rising like an irresistible tide to the book-buying public. After the tale appeared in its entirety in the October 1912 issue of *The All-Story*, which had a circulation of perhaps 200,000, Burroughs approached several publishers, including A. C. McClurg, Bobbs-Merrill, Reilly & Britton, and Dodd, Mead, seeking a book contract. All turned him down flat. However, the Munsey Company, publishers of *The All-Story*, arranged with the New York *Evening World* for *Tarzan* to be serialized in that and other newspapers across the country. *Tarzan* thus reached an enormous readership, including members of the working

The title page of the first edition of *Tarzan of the Apes* (1914), adapted from a drawing by Fred J. Arting. Edgar Rice Burroughs Memorial Collection, University of Louisville

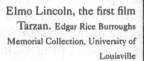

Elmo Lincoln, the first film Tarzan. Edgar Rice Burroughs Memorial Collection, University of Louisville

class, immigrants, and ethnic minorities. Its hero became a cultural icon before the story ever appeared in book form and for readers who would never enter a bookshop.

Though Burroughs was of mixed minds about attempting a sequel, at the urging of *The All-Story*'s editor Thomas Metcalf, he completed *The Return of Tarzan* in January 1913. Here the formerly laconic jungle lord, having tasted civilization, moralizes freely about its effeminacy and corruption as he foils dastardly villains on several continents, escapes from a tomb in a manner reminiscent of Houdini, and, once again, rescues a marooned Jane Porter on the African coast. Giving readers the satisfaction he had withheld in the first Tarzan novel, Burroughs contrived to marry Tarzan and Jane in the tale's closing lines. But inevitable as were Tarzan's triumphs within his fictional realm, he still encountered formidable challenges within the harsh world of publishing. The enthusiastic Metcalf, who had trumpeted the original Tarzan story to readers ("Zowie! but things happen!") and elaborately whetted their appetites for a sequel, rejected Burroughs's tale outright. It suffered from "lack of balance," he explained cryptically, a charge particularly unsettling for Burroughs, who worried how far to let his imagination carry him. "A well balanced mind would not turn out my kind of stuff," he replied defensively. But a rival pulp magazine, *New Story*, snapped up Burroughs's sequel with the rapacity of a crocodile and paid him one thousand dollars, far more than he had expected from *The All-Story*.[98]

With this crowning success, Burroughs finally quit his job at *System* to work in the "fiction factory" full-time and to become a veritable Tarzan machine. Early the next year he dashed off *The Beasts of Tarzan* in just over a month and sold it to *The All-Story* for twenty-five hundred dollars, the most the magazine had ever paid for a story. Then at last he found a book publisher for the original *Tarzan of the Apes*, McClurg and Company, which repented its earlier decision. The novel appeared in June 1914, illustrated by Fred J. Arting, who depicted Tarzan in silhouette with a Plains Indian profile and a posture both languid and alert. Tarzan still had to struggle for readers. The print run of the first edition was ten thousand copies. Although the novel never topped the sales charts in any one year, it achieved remarkable success over time both in the United States and abroad with sales that swelled into the millions before Burroughs's death.[99]

A succession of film versions powered the Tarzan machine, beginning with the release of the first *Tarzan of the Apes* in January 1918. With a coordinated publicity campaign of film distribution, newspaper serialization, and book sales, the movie proved one of the most profitable in the history of the nascent industry, and sales of Burroughs's Tarzan books soared. The film's star, barrel-chested Elmo Lincoln, attempted to embody the Arting illustration with the help of a wig. Reviewers generally applauded his efforts, though Burroughs thought he looked more like a "prize bear."[100]

For a quarter century, from 1914 to 1939, Burroughs turned out a new Tarzan book virtually every year. In failing health, he produced his last in 1947, three years before his death. During his lifetime, he also published eleven Martian adventures, four stories set on Venus, six "Pellucidar" tales taking place within Earth, several Westerns, and numerous other works. "I want to be known as Edgar Rice Burroughs the author, not Edgar Rice Burroughs the author of *Tarzan*," he declared, but he never truly got his wish. Instead, for all his success, he found himself a captive of his fictional creation. Ironically, in committing himself to manufacture a never-ending series of adventures celebrating masculine wildness and freedom, he discovered that he had exchanged one punishing regimen for another, albeit much more profitable, one. As early as December 1919, he was complaining, "I feel now that I can never write another Tarzan story and I . . . do not see how the reading public can stand for any more of them. . . . I have said and re-said a dozen times everything that there is to say about Tarzan—this is why the work is so hard." Similar moans accompanied the writing of later Tarzan adventures. Twenty years after the initial appearance of *Tarzan of the Apes*, at the height of his success, he wrote, "The only thing about the marketing of my stories that ever surprises me is when they sell. I have never written a story yet but that deep down in my heart I was positive that it would be refused."[101] Though he commanded his literary empire with stern authority and claimed a "big" man's income, he never escaped the self-doubt and tedium of the walled-in clerk.

CONCLUSION

It is easiest to say what happened to their bodies.

Sandow died first, in October 1925. After funeral services at a Baptist church in Holland Park, his body was buried in a cemetery at Putney Vale, near London. Yet surprisingly, given his immense fame and prosperity, no stone ever marked his grave. Wrapping herself in a tight silence, his widow appears to have forbidden any memorial.[1]

Houdini made sure he would not suffer a similar fate. That any great magician, let alone himself, might not have a suitable grave site deeply disturbed him, and over the course of his career he spent considerable effort and expense refurbishing the graves of other conjurers, including John Henry Anderson, Bartolomeo Bosco, William Davenport, Robert Heller, and "the Great Lafayette" (Sigmund Neuberger). He lavished still greater care over the arrangements for his own family. As early as 1904 he had exhumed the bodies of his father and half brother to rebury them in a family plot he had purchased at Machpelah Cemetery in Queens, New York. Always fascinated with the macabre, he wrote in his diary, "Saw what was left of poor father and Hermann. Nothing but skull and bones. Hermann's teeth were in splendid condition."[2] After the death in 1913 of his mother, with whom his identity was so intensely bound, he began to plan his own

Houdini's widow, Bess, and his brother Theo at his grave, c. 1928. Library of Congress

grave site in earnest. With an ostentatious display of graven images
that is startling in a Jewish cemetery, he erected a massive granite
monument, ornamented with figures carved from Italian marble. To
cap the structure, he arranged for a commanding bronze bust of himself. Ever the headliner, he had written in large letters above the
Weiss name HOUDINI. Among his meticulous instructions for his
own burial, he specified that all his mother's letters be interred with
him as a pillow for his head.

Tarzan, of course, never died. As for Burroughs, he was the only
one of the three to live to "damn[ed] old age."[3] His heart ailed for
years and finally gave out on March 19, 1950, when he was seventy-
four. After his death, in obedience to his instructions, his body was
cremated and his ashes buried next to his mother's remains under a
black walnut tree outside the offices of Edgar Rice Burroughs, Inc., in
the Los Angeles suburb that bears the name of his most famous creation, Tarzana, California.

The larger cultural legacies of Sandow, Houdini, and Burroughs

are much more difficult to specify. Even in their lifetimes, their presentations of the triumphant white male body evolved significantly, and each figure showed notable agility in adapting his message to changing circumstances.

Undoubtedly, the greatest change, to which all three responded, was the coming of the Great War. Sandow, now retired from performing and living in England, faced it first. Even when the war lay several years in the future, he contributed time, prizes, and his immense prestige to training eleven thousand recruits to guard the English home front. Once again, reporters marveled at the bodily metamorphosis he achieved by his training and competitions. *The Times* of London reported, "Each of the 104 prize-winners added no less than 12 inches to their combined neck, chest, and leg measurements, while the winner of the first prize of £500 obtained in all an improvement of 27½ inches, 5¾ inches being added to his chest girth." Throughout the war, Sandow urged the importance of physical training and gloried in his status as "the greatest 'recruiting sergeant' the Army has ever had."[4]

When the United States entered the war in April 1917, Houdini immediately registered for military service, exulting, "HURRAH, now I am one of the boys." Despite his many performances in Germany, he declared, "WE MUST WIN, and that is all there is to it." Although he was too old to serve directly, he contributed both his talents as entertainer and some of his stratagems as escape artist to support the cause.

A year younger than Houdini, Burroughs also found himself too old for active duty. Instead, he joined the Illinois reserve militia and rose to the rank of captain. With his pen, he was still more bellicose. Targeting German Americans in the drive to sell Liberty bonds, for example, he declared, "Each and every one of us pines to go over the top and spear a Hun. . . . Next to sticking a bayonet through a Hun's gizzard, you can inflict the greatest pain upon him by jabbing him in the pocket-book." Workers who thought this a "rich man's war" equally aroused his ire. He contemptuously described one who declined to join the militia because of its history of brutally repressing workers as a "narrow chested, pimple-faced, chinless, anthropoid creature." Indeed, even at the conclusion of the war, he itched to purge subversive elements at home: "We have thrashed the trouble

makers of Europe and it is within the range of possibilities that we may have to deal with similar cattle here."[5]

Tarzan fully shared Burroughs's rabid anti-German sentiments. At the outset of *Tarzan the Untamed*, the major Tarzan novel written during the war, a sadistic German officer apparently kills Tarzan's Jane (in response to pleas from his editor and his wife, Burroughs ultimately revived her). This brutal assault sets the spring for a plot in which Tarzan pursues an insatiable appetite for revenge, sadistically reveling in each German death and hungering for the next: "[N]ever could she be entirely avenged. Life was too short and there were too many Germans." A few years later, as Burroughs contemplated losing German royalties with the translation of his wartime Tarzan tales, he wrote to his editor, "How would it be to make the Germans Austrians, or will these volumes circulate also in Austria . . . ?"[6]

The war offered scant opportunity for the kinds of individual heroism, freedom, and prowess that Sandow, Houdini, and Burroughs had celebrated. On the contrary, it represented the powers of modern depersonalization and mechanization at their most ghastly. Overall, approximately 10 million died in the conflict, including more than 112,000 Americans. In the war's aftermath a new generation of writers, preeminently Ernest Hemingway, attempted to put manly courage back together again. To do so, they endeavored to purge its emphasis on romantic patriotism and heroic transcendence in favor of private tests and qualified triumphs.

Nonetheless, key elements in the work of Sandow, Houdini, and Burroughs endure. Sandow offered a compelling if controversial new standard of masculine strength, muscular development, and beauty to face the challenges of modern life, and Houdini had an aura of courage, miraculous powers, and invincibility. To these Burroughs added a narrative of the unclad white male body filled with wildness, engaged in violent combat, and inviting romance. Together, these three figures helped to shape conceptions of manliness and the white male body that proved immensely popular in their own day and have shown remarkable resilience.

History never repeats itself, but it is an avid recycler. With the end of the Vietnam War and the advent of an information-based, global economy in the 1970s, as well as new waves of immigration, the emergence of modern feminism, and other developments, came a new

"crisis" of masculinity. Responses to that crisis have taken many forms, but no cultural observer could miss the reemergence of body-building, stage magic, and adventure stories and films. Often with a high degree of self-consciousness, new popular heroes assumed the places of the old: Arnold Schwarzenegger as the great heir to Sandow; David Copperfield and Doug Henning among the many rivals for Houdini's legacy; Miles O'Keeffe and Christopher Lambert as new Tarzan hopefuls. The cultural needs at the turn of the twentieth century remain very much with us as we enter a new millennium.

The value of this legacy remains highly controversial, though. The bodily spectacles offered by Sandow, Houdini, and Burroughs always existed in dialogue with audiences who brought their own imaginative concerns and experiences to the entertainments, so that the meanings of their work are necessarily fluid. They appealed to immense and diverse publics, across class, across nation, across gender. Clearly, they spoke powerfully to individual aspirations for palpable challenge and heroic achievement. They offered compelling dramas of bodily risk as a means of self-realization. Yet their work easily fortified images of white male superiority that were used to dominate women, people of color, and less technologically advanced societies. To some degree, all spoke to the longing for a restitution of manly authority and power that appeared threatened by the coming of a more impersonal modern order. By stressing the centrality of the unclad white male body, each in effect reasserted that gender and racial divisions were fundamentally based on innate and natural differences. At the same time, each appealed to the dream of masculine metamorphosis, the possibilities for bodily transformation and, by implication, for a transformation of self and of social standing. The challenge that remains is to conceive of transformations in which freedom, wholeness, and heroism are available to all.

NOTES

INTRODUCTION

1. Theodore Roosevelt, *An Autobiography* (New York: Charles Scribner's Sons, 1920).
2. Carleton Putnam, *Theodore Roosevelt*, vol. 1, *The Formative Years* (New York: Charles Scribner's Sons, 1958), 198; Edmund Morris, *The Rise of Theodore Roosevelt* (New York: Coward, McCann, and Geoghegan, 1979), 129; David McCullough, *Mornings on Horseback* (New York: Simon and Schuster, 1981), 229.
3. See "Snap-Shots of the Presidential Candidates," *Harper's Weekly*, July 30, 1904, 1174–75.
4. Max Weber, *The Protestant Ethic and the Spirit of Capitalism*, trans. Talcott Parsons (New York: Charles Scribner's Sons, 1958); originally published in essay form in German, 1904–1905.
5. Theodore Roosevelt to Edgar Rice Burroughs, San Antonio, Tex., May 19, 1898, Irwin Porges Papers, Edgar Rice Burroughs Memorial Collection, University of Louisville, Louisville, Ky. (This letter is reproduced in Irwin Porges, *Edgar Rice Burroughs: The Man Who Created Tarzan* [Provo, Utah: Brigham Young University Press, 1975], 70.) David L. Chapman, *Sandow the Magnificent: Eugen Sandow and the Beginnings of Bodybuilding* (Urbana: University of Illinois Press, 1994), 151; Kenneth Silverman, *Houdini!!! The Career of Ehrich Weiss* (New York: HarperCollins, 1996), 189–90.
6. Kristin L. Hoganson, *Fighting for American Manhood: How Gender Politics Provoked the Spanish-American and Philippine-American Wars* (New Haven, Conn.: Yale University Press, 1998).

7. Francis A. Walker, *Discussions in Economics and Statistics*, ed. Davis R. Dewey (1899; reprint, New York: Augustus M. Kelley, 1971), 2:446–47.

8. Harvey Green, *Fit for America: Health, Fitness, Sport, and American Society* (New York: Pantheon, 1986), 224–25.

9. George M. Beard, *American Nervousness, Its Causes and Consequence* (1881; reprint, New York: Arno Press, 1972), esp. 96–138.

10. See esp. Alfred D. Chandler, Jr., *The Visible Hand: The Managerial Revolution in American Business* (Cambridge, Mass.: Belknap Press of Harvard University Press, 1977).

11. Olivier Zunz, *Making America Corporate, 1870–1920* (Chicago: University of Chicago Press, 1990), 126–27; "The Fate of the Salaried Man," *Independent*, Aug. 20, 1903, 2002–3.

12. William D. Haywood and Frank Bohn, *Industrial Socialism* (Chicago, n.d.), 25, quoted in David Montgomery, *Workers' Control in America: Studies in the History of Work, Technology, and Labor Struggle* (Cambridge, U.K.: Cambridge University Press, 1979), 9.

13. Alfred D. Chandler, Jr., *"Fin de Siècle*: Industrial Transformation," in Mikuláš Teich and Roy Porter, eds., *Fin de Siècle and Its Legacy* (Cambridge, U.K.: Cambridge University Press, 1990), 28, 31.

14. Reed Ueda, *Postwar Immigrant America: A Social History* (Boston: Bedford Books of St. Martin's Press, 1994), 2.

15. D. W. Meinig, *The Shaping of America*, vol. 3, *Transcontinental America, 1850–1915* (New Haven, Conn.: Yale University Press, 1998), 278.

16. Howard P. Chudacoff, *The Age of the Bachelor: Creating an American Subculture* (Princeton, N.J.: Princeton University Press, 1999), esp. 48, 217–50; George Chauncey, *Gay New York: Gender, Urban Culture, and the Making of the Gay Male World, 1890–1940* (New York: Basic Books, 1994); Elliott J. Gorn, *The Manly Art: Bare-Knuckle Prize Fighting in America* (Ithaca, N.Y.: Cornell University Press, 1986), esp. 179–247.

17. Caroline Ticknor, "The Steel-Engraving Lady and the Gibson Girl," *Atlantic Monthly*, July 1901, 106; Peter G. Filene, *Him/Her/Self: Gender Identities in Modern America*, 3rd ed. (Baltimore, Md.: Johns Hopkins University Press, 1998), 19–22; Nancy F. Cott, *The Grounding of Modern Feminism* (New Haven, Conn.: Yale University Press, 1987), esp. 9.

18. Edwin Milton Royle, "The Vaudeville Theatre," *Scribner's*, Oct. 1899, 489.

19. Duffield Osborne, "A Defense of Pugilism," *North American Review*, Apr. 1888, 433–35.

20. For a cogent overview of sports in this period, see Elliott J. Gorn and Warren Goldstein, *A Brief History of American Sports* (New York: Hill and Wang, 1993), 98–182.

21. Frank Luther Mott, *American Journalism: A History, 1690–1960*, 3rd ed. (New York: Macmillan, 1962), esp. 436, 547, 549.

22. Frank Luther Mott, *A History of American Magazines, 1885–1905* (Cambridge, Mass.: Belknap Press of Harvard University Press, 1957), 5–6; John Tebbell, *The*

American Magazine: A Compact History (New York: Hawthorn Books, 1969), 106–81. See Frank A. Munsey, "Impressions by the Way," *Munsey's Magazine*, Oct. 1903, 51–52; "Cheap Magazines," *Independent*, June 27, 1895, 867.

23. Mott, *American Journalism*, 593; James Collins, testimony before congressional committee, quoted in Jackson Lears, *Fables of Abundance: A Cultural History of American Advertising* (New York: Basic Books, 1994), 201.

24. Neil Harris, "Iconography and Intellectual History: The Halftone Effect," in *Cultural Excursions: Marketing Appetites and Cultural Tastes in Modern America* (Chicago: University of Chicago Press, 1990), 304–17.

25. Robert C. Allen, *Horrible Prettiness: Burlesque and American Culture* (Chapel Hill: University of North Carolina Press, 1991); Susan A. Glenn, *Female Spectacle: The Theatrical Roots of Modern Feminism* (Cambridge, Mass.: Harvard University Press, 2000).

1. WHO IS THE PERFECT MAN?

1. For this famous distinction, see Kenneth Clark, *The Nude: A Study in Ideal Form* (Princeton, N.J.: Bollingen Series XXXV [2], Princeton University Press, 1956), esp. 3. See also Kenneth R. Dutton, *The Perfectible Body: The Western Ideal of Male Physical Development* (New York: Continuum, 1995), esp. 101; Emmanuel Cooper, *Fully Exposed: The Male Nude in Photography*, 2nd ed. (New York: Routledge, 1995), 8–71.

2. On gender as performance, see especially Judith Butler, *Gender Trouble: Feminism and the Subversion of Identity* (New York: Routledge, 1990).

3. Rudolph Aronson, *Theatrical and Musical Memoirs* (New York: McBridge, Nast and Company, 1913), 82–83; Harold U. Faulkner, *Politics, Reform, and Expansion, 1890–1900* (New York: Harper & Brothers, 1959), 141–81.

4. Lewis C. Strang, *Celebrated Comedians of Light Opera and Musical Comedy in America* (Boston: L. C. Page, 1901), 191. For a discussion of *Adonis* and the text of the play, see Gerald Bordman, *American Musical Comedy: From "Adonis" to "Dreamgirls"* (New York: Oxford University Press, 1982), chap. 2 and app. 2, from which my quotations from the play are taken.

5. On this point, see David Scobey, "Nymphs and Satyrs: Sex and the Bourgeois Public Sphere in Victorian New York," unpublished essay.

6. "The Strongest Man in the World," *New York World*, June 18, 1893, 16; George C. D. Odell, *Annals of the New York Stage*, vol. 15, *1891–1894* (New York: Columbia University Press, 1949), 333; *New York Herald*, June 18, 1893; "The Strongest Man in the World," *Frank Leslie's Illustrated Weekly*, July 6, 1893, 7.

7. "Strongest Man in the World," *Leslie's Weekly*, 7; *New York Herald*, June 18, 1893, 23. The latter gives the figure of twenty-six hundred pounds; the writer for *Leslie's* estimates the weight as "nearly a ton."

8. See George Chauncey, *Gay New York: Gender, Urban Culture, and the Making of the Gay Male World, 1890–1940* (New York: Basic Books, 1994), esp. 1–127.

9. G. Mercer Adam, *Sandow on Physical Training; A Study in the Perfect Type of the Human Form* (New York: J. Selwin Tait & Sons, 1894).

10. *Chicago Tribune*, Aug. 20, 1893, 16; compare with *San Francisco Examiner*, Apr. 17, 1894, 9. But note that in one of the first newspaper pieces on Sandow after his New York debut, he described himself as so "delicate" that "his parents feared that he would not grow into manhood" (*New York Herald*, June 18, 1893, 23).

11. Theodore Roosevelt, *An Autobiography* (New York: Charles Scribner's Sons, 1920), 13, 27–28, 122.

12. George Butler and Charles Gaines, *Yours in Perfect Manhood: Charles Atlas* (New York: Simon and Schuster, 1982), 17, 19–20.

13. Eugen Sandow, "My Reminiscences," *Strand Magazine*, Feb. 1910, 144. See also "Strongest Man in the World," *New York World*, 16; and Adam, *Sandow on Physical Training*, 24–25.

14. Sandow, "My Reminiscences," 145. See Horst Ueberhorst, *Friedrich Ludwig Jahn, 1778/1978* (Munich: Moos, 1978).

15. On *tableaux vivants*, also known as "model artists," see Timothy J. Gilfoyle, *City of Eros: New York City, Prostitution, and the Commercialization of Sex, 1790–1920* (New York: W. W. Norton, 1992), 124.

16. This is the reverse side of the analysis of class and the female body offered by T. J. Clark, *The Painting of Modern Life: Paris in the Art of Manet and His Followers* (New York: Knopf, 1984), esp. 118.

17. David L. Chapman, *Sandow the Magnificent: Eugen Sandow and the Beginnings of Bodybuilding* (Urbana: University of Illinois Press, 1994), 9.

18. On challenges and boxing, see Elliott J. Gorn, *The Manly Art: Bare-Knuckle Prize Fighting in America* (Ithaca, N.Y.: Cornell University Press, 1986), 99–100.

19. Chapman, *Sandow the Magnificent*, 23–30.

20. "Strongest Man in the World," *New York World*, 16; "Great Gnarls of Muscle," *San Francisco Examiner*, Apr. 17, 1894, 9. The reporter for the *New York World*, however, noted that Sandow's clothes failed to conceal his physical development altogether: "His coat bulges out about the chest and back, in curious contrast to the waist, which is as small as a woman's."

21. For Sandow's dimensions, see "Sandow a Mighty Man of Muscle," *New York Herald*, June 18, 1893, 23; for the comparisons with Langtry and Cleveland and the reporter's description of the size of Sandow's muscles, see "Strongest Man in the World," *New York World*, 16.

22. "Sandow a Mighty Man of Muscle," *New York Herald*, 23.

23. John L. Sullivan, *Life and Reminiscences of a 19th Century Gladiator* (Boston: Jas. A. Hearn, 1892), 29.

24. *New York Herald*, Dec. 22, 1885; on Sullivan's career, see especially Michael T. Isenberg, *John L. Sullivan and His America* (Urbana: University of Illinois Press, 1988); Gorn, *Manly Art*, 210–47.

25. Roberta J. Park, "Healthy, Moral, and Strong: Educational Views of Exercise and Athletics in Nineteenth-Century America," in Kathryn Grover, ed., *Fitness*

in American Culture: Images of Health, Sport, and the Body, 1830–1940 (Amherst: University of Massachusetts Press and Margaret Woodbury Strong Museum, 1989), 151–52.

26. D. A. Sargent, "The Physical Proportions of the Typical Man," in D. A. Sargent, et al., *Athletic Sports* (New York: Charles Scribner's Sons, 1897), 16–17; *Statistics, Medical and Anthropological of the Provost-Marshal-General Bureau, Washington, D.C.,* quoted in D. A. Sargent, "The Physical Characteristics of the Athlete," *Scribner's Magazine,* Nov. 1887, 558; David J. Mrozek, *Sport and American Mentality, 1880–1919* (Knoxville: University of Tennessee Press, 1983), 194.

27. Sargent, "Physical Characteristics of Athlete," 542.

28. Mrozek, *Sport and American Mentality,* 219.

29. Gorn, *Manly Art,* 225–29.

30. "Report of Dr. D. A. Sargent's Examination," in Sullivan, *Life and Reminiscences,* 286, 294.

31. Ibid., 290.

32. In 1897 Sandow claimed a height of five feet nine and a quarter inches. See Eugen Sandow, *Strength and How to Obtain It* (London: Gale & Polden, 1897), 157.

33. *New York World,* June 25, 1893, 21.

34. Sargent's opinion was later supported by a similar examination of Sandow in San Francisco by Dr. Leverett Sweany. See "Sandow Examined," *San Francisco Examiner,* May 6, 1894, 4.

35. "Strongest Man in the World," *New York World,* 16.

36. "Lurline Lashes Sandow," *New York World,* July 2, 1893; "Lurline Whipped Eugene Sandow," *New York Herald,* July 2, 1893, 22; "Attila against Sandow," *New York Times,* July 25, 1893, 9.

37. *National Police Gazette,* Feb. 18, 1893, 14, 15.

38. Stephen D. Boyd, Jr., diary, Jan. 23, 1898, quoted in Edward L. Ayers, *The Promise of the New South* (New York: Oxford University Press, 1992), 182–83.

39. "Mirth and Muscle," *Boston Daily Globe,* July 18, 1893, 3; "Muscle and Music," *Boston Home Journal,* July 4, 1893, newspaper clipping in Dudley Sargent Papers, Harvard University Archives.

40. *Chicago Tribune,* Aug. 27, 1893, 29.

41. [Amy Leslie], "The Muscles of Sandow," *Chicago Daily News,* Aug. 2, 1893, 4; the Chicago spectator, Hunter McLean, is quoted in Chapman, *Sandow the Magnificent,* 64.

42. "Sandow in Plaster of Paris," *Strand Magazine,* Oct. 1901, 461; "Sandow Cast in Plaster," unidentified newspaper clipping in Sargent Papers.

43. Sandow, *Strength and How to Obtain It,* 124–25.

44. *New York Herald,* June 18, 1893. Another reported Sandow in the bath immediately after a performance taking his visitor's hand and placing it on Sandow's heart, "which had lately helped to support three horses." Sandow "called attention to the fact that there was no violent beating. In fact, the action of the heart could not be felt at all through the thick coating of muscle" ("Strongest Man in the World," *New York World,* 16).

45. [Leslie], "Muscles of Sandow," 4; Bertha Palmer's experience is recounted in Randolph Carter, *The World of Flo Ziegfeld* (New York: Praeger, 1974), 11.

46. David Chapman insists that Sandow had homosexual liaisons as well but offers ambiguous evidénce. For example, if a *New York World* reporter's description of Sandow's relationship to his "bosom friend" the piano accompanist Martinus Sieveking truly pointed to their sexual intimacy, it seems highly unlikely that Sandow would have permitted the article's inclusion in Adam, *Sandow on Physical Training* (p. 110), the next year. See Chapman, *Sandow the Magnificent*, 19, 51–52, 189. In any case, George Chauncey's work in *Gay New York* would suggest caution in projecting modern conceptions of homosexuality back on Sandow and his time.

47. *National Police Gazette*, Jan. 27, 1894. This double legitimation is discussed in Dutton, *Perfectible Body*, 253.

48. The magistrate lectured the seven offenders, "You ought to have more respect for the women and children" ("Heat of 89.3 Here Sets Year's Mark as Summer Begins," *New York Times*, June 22, 1934, 1, 3). Similar laws prevailed in England until the late 1930s. By contrast, in 1918 the Young Men's Christian Association (YMCA) decreed that suits need not be worn in swimming pools (Cooper, *Fully Exposed*, 77–78).

49. On these tensions in the nineteenth-century female nude in art, see Clark, *Painting of Modern Life*, esp. 129–30.

50. H. P. M., "The Latest Society Fad," *Frank Leslie's Illustrated Weekly*, Mar. 29, 1894, 206.

51. For a similar instánce of Sandow's posing before a group of socially prominent women, in an account charged with sexual innuendo, see "Posed for the Ladies," *San Francisco Chronicle*, May 17, 1894, 12.

52. See Samuel Wilson Fussell's discussion of the acceptability of the first pose among bodybuilders in the 1980s and their suspicion of the second as homoerotic in *Muscle: Confessions of an Unlikely Bodybuilder* (New York: Avon, 1991), 191.

53. Geraldine A. Johnson, "Introduction," 10; Michael Hatt, "Eakins's Arcadia: Sculpture, Photography, and the Redefinition of the Classical Body," 62–65; and Tamar Garb, "Modeling the Body: Photography, Physical Culture, and the Classical Ideal in Fin-de-Siècle France," 86–99, all in Geraldine A. Johnson, ed., *Sculpture and Photography: Envisioning the Third Dimension* (Cambridge, U.K.: Cambridge University Press, 1998).

54. These were the prices charged by Sarony in 1893; see Ben L. Bassham, *The Theatrical Photographs of Napoleon Sarony* (Kent, Ohio: Kent State University Press, 1978), 14.

55. Paul Bourget, *Outre-Mer: Impressions of America* (New York: Charles Scribner's Sons, 1895), 61. John Addington Symonds to Edmund Gosse, Dec. 25, 1899, in *The Letters of John Addington Symonds*, ed. Herbert M. Schueller and Robert L. Peters (Detroit: Wayne State University Press, 1969), 3:1779; Anthony Comstock, *Traps for the Young* (1883; reprint, Cambridge, Mass.: Belknap Press

of Harvard University Press, 1967), 171; Greg Mullins, "Nudes, Prudes, and Pigmies: The Desirability of Disavowal in *Physical Culture*," *Discourse* 15 (Fall 1992): 30.

56. Dutton, *Perfectible Body*, 142, 161–62.

57. John Mack Faragher, ed., *Rereading Frederick Jackson Turner* (New York: Henry Holt, 1994), 33–34.

58. For example, *The Christian Martyrs' Last Prayer* was commissioned by William Walters in 1863 and finished in 1883; *Pollice Verso*, one of the most celebrated of all the artist's works, was purchased by A. T. Stewart in 1875. See Gerald M. Ackerman, *La vie et l'oeuvre de Jean-Léon Gérôme* (Paris: ACR Édition, 1986), 252, 232.

59. Carlin A. Barton, "The Scandal of the Arena," *Representations* 27 (Summer 1989): 1–36, esp. 14. Barton notes a contemporary analogue in Martin Scorsese's *Raging Bull* (1980).

60. For "Spartacus Sullivan," see Sullivan, *Life and Reminiscences*, 29.

61. "Where Is the Perfect Man?" *San Francisco Examiner*, May 27, 1894, 24.

62. On the first impostor, see "Eugene Sandow's Great Strength," *Chicago Times*, July 30, 1893, 9. Of Miller, a reporter for the *Chicago Tribune*, Aug. 11, 1893, wrote, he "gives a good exhibition, but he is not in Sandow's class." For the Sampson quotation, see *Chicago Tribune*, Aug. 27, 1893, 29.

63. "A Lion Is a Rank Coward," *San Francisco Examiner*, May 13, 1894.

64. Long after the event, keeping the pretense of heroic contest to the last, Sandow, in "My Reminiscences," called this "perhaps the greatest, certainly the most thrilling, of all my experiences" (p. 150). In the same article, he said there were forty thousand in the audience; the *San Francisco Chronicle* gave the figure of three thousand, and *The San Francisco Examiner* estimated twenty-five hundred. For these attendance figures and descriptions of the event, see *San Francisco Chronicle*, May 23, 1894, 14, and *San Francisco Examiner*, May 23, 1894, 12.

65. Advertisement for "Sandow's Mail System of Teaching Physical Culture," *Collier's*, Feb. 28, 1903; Dudley A. Sargent, letter to editor, *New York Herald*, c. 1902, quoted in Chapman, *Sandow the Magnificent*, 139.

66. Eugen Sandow, *Life Is Movement* (London: National Health Press, n.d. [c. 1918]), esp. x, 5, 12; Chapman, *Sandow the Magnificent*, 176–77.

67. "Sandow, Famous Strong Man, Dead," *New York Times*, Oct. 15, 1925, 23. David Chapman questions this explanation of Sandow's death, noting that his cause of death was officially recorded as "aortic aneurysia." He speculates that Sandow really died of syphilis. See Chapman, *Sandow the Magnificent*, 185–88.

2. THE MANLY ART OF ESCAPE

1. Bronislaw Malinowski, "Culture," in Edwin R. A. Seligman, ed., *Encyclopedia of the Social Sciences* (New York: Macmillan, 1931), 638; Malinowski quoted in Keith Thomas, *Religion and the Decline of Magic* (New York: Charles Scribner's Sons, 1971), 647.

2. The most complete and authoritative biography is Kenneth Silverman, *Houdini!!! The Career of Ehrich Weiss* (New York: HarperCollins, 1996), which is supplemented by Kenneth Silverman, *Notes to Houdini!!!* (Washington, D.C.: Kaufman & Greenberg, 1996). Among earlier biographies, the most useful are Harold Kellock, *Houdini: His Life-Story* (New York: Harcourt, Brace, 1928); and Milbourne Christopher, *Houdini: The Untold Story* (New York: Thomas Y. Crowell, 1969).

3. The best accounts of this sort are Walter B. Gibson, *Houdini's Escapes* (New York: Harcourt, Brace, 1930); and J. C. Cannell, *The Secrets of Houdini* (1931; reprint, New York: Dover, 1973).

4. The most determinedly psychological (though not always the most illuminating) of these have been: Bernard C. Meyer, *Houdini: A Mind in Chains: A Psychoanalytic Portrait* (New York: E. P. Dutton, 1976); Raymond Fitzsimons, *Death and the Magician: The Mystery of Houdini* (New York: Atheneum, 1981); and Ruth Brandon, *The Life and Many Deaths of Harry Houdini* (London: Secker & Warburg, 1993).

5. James Randi and Bert Randolph Sugar, *Houdini: His Life and Art* (New York: Grosset & Dunlap, 1976), 19.

6. Harry Houdini, "Harry Houdini," *Magician Annual* 3 (1909–1910): 16.

7. Quoted in Silverman, *Houdini!!!* 8. The faulty German spelling is presumably Houdini's.

8. Houdini to Quincy Kilby, Brooklyn, May 26, 1916, Quincy Kilby Scrapbook, Harvard Theatre Collection, Harvard University (hereafter cited as QKSB, HTC).

9. Christopher, *Houdini: The Untold Story*; Harry Houdini, *A Magician among the Spirits* (New York: Harper, 1924), 151.

10. Houdini's account of these efforts, *A Magician among the Spirits*, bears the dedication: "In worshipful homage I dedicate this book to the memory of my sainted mother. If God in His infinite wisdom ever sent an angel upon earth in human form, it was my mother."

11. See Houdini's account in unidentified magazine article, probably from Houdini souvenir program, c. Sept. 1926, p. 5, in Houdini Collection, Harry Ransom Humanities Center, University of Texas at Austin (hereafter cited as HRHC).

12. Undated postcard from Ehrich Weiss to Cecilia Weiss, McManus-Young Scrapbook, Library of Congress, Washington, D.C. (hereafter cited as LC); unidentified magazine article, c. Sept. 1926, in HRHC; Harry Houdini, *The Right Way to Do Wrong: An Exposé of Successful Criminals* (1906; reprint, Mattituck, N.Y.: Amereon House, n.d.), 94; Silverman, *Notes to Houdini!!!* 14.

13. This account, like all of Houdini's about his childhood, cannot be regarded uncritically. As Manny Weltman speculates, Houdini may in fact have seen an imitation of Lynn's act by a traveling medicine show and, quite possibly, without his father. Nonetheless, Houdini's account of the act—and of his father's presence—has a significance independent of scrupulous accuracy. See Manny Welt-

man, *Houdini: Escape into Legend, the Early Years, 1862–1900* (Van Nuys, Calif.: Finders/Seekers, 1993), 10–11.

14. In 1914 Houdini bought the apparatus for the trick from Lynn's son, together, he claimed, with the world rights to perform it (Silverman, *Notes to Houdini!!!* 169–70).

15. Christopher, *Houdini: The Untold Story*, 12; Meyer, *Houdini*, 11–12; for comment on Dr. Lynn's act, see also Albert A. Hopkins, *Magic: Stage Illusions and Scientific Diversions, Including Trick Photographs* (1897; reprint, New York: Arno Press, 1977), 63–64; and Edwin A. Dawes, *The Great Illusionists* (Secaucus, N.J.: Chartwell Books, 1979), 163.

16. See Meyer, *Houdini*, 130, 140–41; Louise J. Kaplan, *The Family Romance of the Impostor-Poet Thomas Chatterton* (New York: Atheneum, 1988), 157.

17. The edition he read was titled *Robert-Houdin, the Great Wizard: Celebrated French Conjurer, Author, and Ambassador*, trans. Lascelles Wraxall, introduction and index by R. Shelton Mackenzie (Philadelphia: Charles Desilver, 1859); for a modern English edition, see *Memoirs of Robert-Houdin*, trans. Lascelles Wraxall, ed. Milbourne Christopher (New York: Dover, 1964).

18. Harry Houdini, *The Unmasking of Robert-Houdin* (London: George Routledge, 1909), 7.

19. Interestingly, Houdini dedicated the book in which he attacked Robert-Houdin to his own father, bestowing on him a Ph.D. and LL.D. that he never possessed and lauding him as one "who instilled in me love of study and patience in research" (ibid., xi).

20. "Un prestidigitateur n'est point un jongleur; c'est un acteur jouant un rôle de magicien . . ." (italics added); Jean-Eugène Robert-Houdin, *Comment on devient sorcier: Les secrets de la prestidigitation et de la magie* (1878; reprint, Paris: Slatkine Reprints, 1980), 29.

21. *The Boy's Own Conjuring Book* (New York: Dick and Fitzgerald, [1860?]).

22. Kaplan, *Chatterton*, 216–17. Houdini's career as an escape artist has many aspects in common with the psychology of the impostor.

23. Houdini to John E. Waitte, Munich, Sept. 8, 1902, HTC.

24. Quotation from L. R. C. Crandon to Arthur Conan Doyle, in Silverman, *Houdini!!!* 325.

25. Quoted in Robert W. Snyder, *The Voice of the City: Vaudeville and Popular Culture in New York* (New York: Oxford University Press, 1989), 46.

26. Silverman, *Houdini!!!* 132; Silverman, *Notes to Houdini!!!* 68.

27. Kellock, *Houdini*, 59.

28. Hopkins, *Magic*, 44.

29. Fitzsimons, *Death and the Magician*, 30, 54.

30. Silverman, *Notes to Houdini!!!* 18.

31. Other substitution tricks in the 1890s also developed narratives in which a man was released and a woman confined. In one of the most famous, "Strobeika," a young Russian woman takes the place of her imprisoned fiancé and is discov-

ered shackled and tied to a horizontal plank. A New York performance by the celebrated magician Alexander Herrmann (1843–1896) is described in "Strobeika's Secret All Laid Bare," *New York Herald*, Dec. 21, 1890, 13. At this same time, the husband-and-wife team Mildred and Rouclere (Mildred May Searing and Harry Rouclere), in a spiritualist program as "Ellington and Cook," performed a variation of the substitution trick as a spirit phenomenon rather than an escape. A few years later, Horace Goldin presented an illusion, "Dreyfus Escape from Devil's Island," in which he was released from a cage, leaving a young woman in his place. See David Price, *Magic: A Pictorial History of Conjurers in the Theater* (New York: Cornwall Books, 1985), 165–66, 175, 223.

32. *New York Dramatic Mirror*, quoted in Laurence Senelick, "Lady and the Tramp: Drag Differentials in the Progressive Era," in Laurence Senelick, ed., *Gender in Performance: The Representation of Difference in the Performing Arts* (Hanover, N.H.: University Press of New England, 1992), 27.

33. Percy Hammond, quoted in Senelick, "Lady and the Tramp," 29. See also unidentified clipping, Robinson Locke Scrapbooks, New York Public Library for the Performing Arts (hereafter cited as RLSB, NYPL).

34. "Girls and More Girls Cut Work to Form Waiting Line," *Cincinnati Times Star*, Mar. 7, 1912, RLSB, NYPL.

35. *Variety*, Apr. 24, 1909, 12.

36. Rennold Wolf, "The Sort of Fellow Julian Eltinge Really Is," *Green Book Magazine*, Nov. 1913, 802. The lyrics were by Eltinge.

37. Harry B. Smith and Gus Edwards, "The Modern Sandow Girl" (New York: Gus Edwards Music Pub. Co., 1907), quoted in Senelick, "Lady and the Tramp," 29. I have slightly altered the punctuation.

38. Sharon R. Ullman, *Sex Seen: The Emergence of Modern Sexuality in America* (Berkeley: University of California Press, 1997), 53; Ullman is here apparently quoting from *The New York Dramatic Mirror*, Apr. 11, 1912.

39. "Eltinge Says He Didn't," *Variety*, Jan. 6, 1906, 12.

40. Unidentified clipping, HRHC.

41. Wolf, "Eltinge," 794; Joan N. Vale, "Tintype Ambitions: Three Vaudevillians in Search of Hollywood Fame" (master's thesis, University of San Diego, 1985), 25.

42. On this subject, see Fred Siegel, "The Vaudeville Conjuring Act" (Ph.D. diss., New York University, 1993).

43. *St. Joseph Herald*, Mar. 1, 1898, clipping in HRHC.

44. Houdini to Kilby, June 27, 1916, QKSB, HTC.

45. Kellock, *Houdini*, 135.

46. Houdini, "Harry Houdini," 17. See his pamphlet *Magic Made Easy*, c. 1898; reprinted in Walter B. Gibson, *The Original Houdini Scrapbook* (New York: Corwin Sterling, 1976), 79–95. "Metamorphosis" is item 61.

47. On the variety of conjuring acts in vaudeville, see Siegel, "Vaudeville Conjuring Act."

48. Houdini, "Harry Houdini," 16.

49. Ibid., 17.

50. *Minneapolis Times*, Feb. 21, 1899, clipping in HRHC.

51. Houdini diary, Apr. 24, 1899, quoted in Silverman, *Houdini!!!* 25.

52. *Kansas City Times*, Apr. 15, 1899, clipping in QKSB, HTC.

53. Eric H. Monkkonen, *Police in Urban America, 1860–1920* (Cambridge, U.K.: Cambridge University Press, 1981), esp. 158–60.

54. "Irons Could Not Hold Him," *San Francisco Chronicle*, June 3, 1899, 12.

55. "Exposé of Houdini's Trunk and Handcuff Trick," *San Francisco Examiner Magazine*, July 9, 1899, 25.

56. *San Francisco Report*, July 14, 1899, clipping in QKSB, HTC.

57. Harry Houdini, *Handcuff Secrets* [bound with *Unmasking of Robert-Houdin*], 81.

58. *San Francisco Report*, July 14, 1899, clipping in QKSB, HTC.

59. Harry Houdini, "Secrets of My Handcuff Tricks," *San Francisco Examiner Magazine*, July 23, 1899, 29.

60. Harry Houdini, *The Adventurous Life of a Versatile Artist*, rev. ed. (New York?: n.p., 1922), 11.

61. "A Talk with Houdini," *New York Dramatic Mirror*, June 25, 1904.

62. Houdini to Waitte, Mischi-Mowgorod, Russia, Aug. 11, 1903, HTC.

63. Houdini, *Adventurous Life of a Versatile Artist*, 14.

64. "Expert Jail Breaker Walks through Locks and Manacles," *Washington Post*, Jan. 2, 1906.

65. *Washington Post*, Jan. 7, 1906, reprinted in Houdini, *Adventurous Life of a Versatile Artist*, 25–30.

66. "Houdini Escapes from City Prison," *Boston Daily Globe*, Mar. 19, 1906, clipping in HTC; "Houdini Breaks from City Prison," *Boston Post*, Mar. 20, 1906, clipping in HTC; Milbourne Christopher, *Houdini: A Pictorial Life* (New York: Thomas Y. Crowell, 1976), 1–4.

67. "He Could Be Biggest Burglar in World," *Boston Post*, Mar. 21, 1906, clipping in HTC.

68. "Is Master of Locks and Bolts," *Appleton (Wis.) Crescent*, July 23, 1904.

69. Peter Brooks, *Body Work: Objects of Desire in Modern Narrative* (Cambridge, Mass.: Harvard University Press, 1993), 64.

70. Kellock, *Houdini*, 272.

71. Houdini, *Adventurous Life of a Versatile Artist*, 1.

72. *Complete Tales and Poems of Edgar Allan Poe* (New York: Modern Library, Random House, 1938), 246; Silverman, *Houdini!!!* 263.

73. Franz Kafka, *The Complete Stories*, ed. Nathum N. Glatzer (New York: Schocken Books, 1971), 144.

74. Houdini to Waitte, Paris, Nov. 31 [*sic*], 1901, HTC.

75. "Houdini at Harvard," *Boston Herald*, May 7, 1908, clipping in Microfilmed Scrapbook, Houdini Historical Center, Appleton, Wis. (hereafter cited as MSB, HHC). A few days earlier, at the request of audience members, he had stripped in full view of male spectators at the Boston Athletic Club before performing an

escape. "Houdini Escapes from Glass Case," *Boston Herald*, May 4, 1908, clipping in MSB, HHC.

76. "A member of the Eclectic Medical Society" [as the writer asked to be identified] to Houdini, Jan. 27, 1906, HTC. For an instance in which a prison attendant detected a concealed device under Houdini's right foot, see "Houdini Meets His Waterloo," *Boston Herald*, Sept. 10, 1906, clipping in HTC.

77. Houdini, *Adventurous Life of a Versatile Artist*, 1.

78. See Louise J. Kaplan, *Female Perversions: The Temptations of Emma Bovary* (New York: Doubleday, 1991), 11–12.

79. "A Talk with Houdini," *New York Dramatic Mirror*; Houdini to Waitte, Hanover, Germany, Feb. 22, 1903, HTC.

80. Description and quotations are drawn from three unidentified newspaper clippings, HTC.

81. "Houdini Victor in Supreme Test," unidentified newspaper clipping in HTC.

82. "Slippery Man Scorns 400 Pounds of Chains," *New York Press*, Apr. 11, 1908, clipping in MSB, HHC.

83. Handbill with challenge from Weed Chain Tire Grip Company, New York City, and Houdini's acceptance, 1908, McManus-Young Collection, LC.

84. "Houdini vs. the Pittsburg Vise," broadside in MSB, HHC.

85. Neil Harris, *Humbug: The Art of P. T. Barnum* (Boston: Little, Brown, 1973), 59–89; James W. Cook, Jr., *The Arts of Deception: Playing with Fraud in the Age of Barnum* (Cambridge, Mass.: Harvard University Press, 2001), esp. chap. 2, "The 'Feejee Mermaid' and the American Market Revolution."

86. Kellock, *Houdini*, 196.

87. I here paraphrase Peter Brooks's observation, "Since as the primacy of the body may be most dramatically felt in its failure: the deathbed is a privileged literary place" (*Body Work*, 5).

88. Houdini, *Adventurous Life of a Versatile Artist*, 5.

89. Silverman, *Houdini!!!* 162.

90. Kaplan, *Chatterton*, esp. 216–17.

91. Sydney *Daily Telegraph*, Apr. 16, 1910, quoted in Brandon, *Life and Many Deaths of Houdini*, 24.

92. "Houdini Shackled, Leaps into River, Almost Drowned," Philadelphia *North American*, May 15, 1908, 1–2. The *Philadelphia Record* for the same date reported he stayed underwater only fifty-seven seconds.

93. Harry Houdini, "Nearly Dying for a Living," *Hearst's Magazine*, Dec. 1919, 40 [?], clipping in HRHC.

94. "Shackled, Dives from the Bridge," *Detroit Journal*, Nov. 27, 1906, clipping in HTC.

95. Houdini to Waitte, New Orleans, Nov. 17, 1907, HTC.

96. Houdini diary, May 4, 1907, quoted in Silverman, *Houdini!!!* 182.

97. "Handcuffed, Houdini Goes into Canal," *Rochester Union and Advertiser*, May 7, 1907, 9. A film of this jump confirms the reporter's account; see Silverman, *Houdini!!!* 114–15.

98. Houdini to Waitte, Chicago, Feb. 12, 1908, HTC.

99. Cannell, *Secrets of Houdini*, 61–62.

100. Quoted in Mark Seltzer, *Bodies and Machines* (New York: Routledge, 1992), 160.

101. The lyrics would have been known to all Houdini's audience: "Loudly the bell in the old tower rings,/Bidding us list to the warning it brings,/Sailor, take care! . . . /Danger is near thee, Beware! . . . /Many brave hearts are asleep in the deep, so beware!"

102. Christopher, *Houdini: The Untold Story*, 105–6.

103. Houdini recording on Edison wax cylinder, Oct. 29, 1914, Flatbush, N.Y., copy at HHC, and transcription by George N. Gordon of second wax cylinder made on the same occasion in Kenneth Silverman Papers, HHC; Silverman, *Notes to Houdini!!!* 81.

104. Houdini recording on wax cylinder; J. Hewat McKenzie, *Spirit Intercourse* (London: Smith, Marshall, Hamilton Kent, 1916), 86–87; Brandon, *Life and Many Deaths of Houdini*, 157.

105. Challenge, Glasgow, Oct. 19, 1909, MSB, HHC.

106. Challenge from Grant Staff Barracks, June 3, 1904, HRHC.

107. Challenge from Liverpool Seamen, Oct. 20, 1914, MSB, HHC.

108. In fact, *Success* was never used to transport convicts to Australia and was not built until 1840. See Charles Bateson, *The Convict Ships, 1787–1868* (Glasgow: Brown, Son & Ferguson, 1959), 257–58 and illustration facing 240.

109. Elaine Scarry, *The Body in Pain: The Making and Unmaking of the World* (New York: Oxford University Press, 1985), 31.

110. *Kansas City Post*, Sept. 8, 1915, 2. Brandon describes Houdini's Kansas City aerial straitjacket escape but misdates the year as 1914. Silverman dates Houdini's first such escape as September 29, 1915, in Minneapolis (*Houdini!!!* 194). The *Kansas City Post* had been bought by the yellow-journalist publishers Fred C. Bonfils and Harry H. Tammen in 1908. See Frank Luther Mott, *American Journalism: A History, 1690–1960*, 3rd ed. (New York: Macmillan, 1962), 568.

111. *San Antonio Express*, Feb. 1, 1916, 5.

112. Transcript of Houdini lecture, Symphony Hall, Boston, Jan. 3, 1925, bound volume titled "Lectures, Articles on Spiritualism," McManus-Young Collection, LC, quoted in Silverman, *Houdini!!!* 197.

113. A Houdini imitator, Henry Huber, made the analogy to hanging explicit in his aerial straitjacket escapes with such announcements as "Man Hanged at 2:30 Today" (Price, *Magic*, 240).

114. *San Antonio Express*, Feb. 1, 1916, 5.

115. James Randi, "A Peek behind the Curtain," in Randi and Sugar, *Houdini*, 173–74; Silverman, *Houdini!!!* 196–97; see also John A. Novak, *The Art of Escape*, vol. 4, *Escapes from a Strait Jacket* (Calgary, Alberta: Micky Hades, 1979).

116. Beatrice Houdini to Theo "Dash" Weiss, Apr. 21, 1911, Sidney H. Radner Collection, HHC; on Houdini's kidney ailment, see Houdini to Waitte, Pittsburgh, Nov. 16, 1911, and Houdini to Waitte, New York, Nov. 23, 1911, both in HTC.

117. Houdini to Theo "Dash" Weiss, Nürnberg, Sept. 23, 1913, Sidney H. Radner Collection, HHC.

118. *Washington Times*, Apr. 19, 1916, 2.

119. Houdini to Karl Germain, Pittsburgh, Mar. 7, 1922, quoted in Christopher, *Houdini: The Untold Story*, 311.

120. "Houdini Secrets for U.S. Soldiers," New York *Evening Sun*, Feb. 26, 1918, clipping in MSB, HHC.

121. R. Laurence Moore, *In Search of White Crows: Spiritualism, Parapsychology, and American Culture* (New York: Oxford University Press, 1977), 102–27.

122. See Ann Braude, *Radical Spirits: Spiritualism and Women's Rights in Nineteenth-Century America* (Boston: Beacon Press, 1989).

123. Thomas Frost, *The Lives of the Conjurors* (London: Chatto & Windus, 1881), 250; Charles J. Pecor, "John Henry Anderson, the Great Wizard of the North; Nineteenth-Century Magician, Actor, Publicist," *Theatre Studies* 24/25 (1977/78–1978/79): 51–52.

124. John Nevil Maskelyne, *Modern Spiritualism* (1876), reprinted in James Webb, ed., *The Mediums and the Conjurors* (New York: Arno Press, 1976); Frost, *Lives of Conjurors*, 332–33.

125. Harry Kellar, *A Magician's Tour* (Chicago: Donohue, Henneberry, 1897), *passim*.

126. In his early pamphlet *Magic Made Easy*, Houdini offered lessons in spiritualist effects. See reprint in Gibson, *Original Houdini Scrapbook*, 85 and *passim*.

127. Thomas R. Tietze, *Margery* (New York: Harper & Row, 1973), 1. This remains the best single account of Mina Crandon's extraordinary career.

128. Mark W. Richardson, L. R. G. Crandon, et al., *Margery Harvard Veritas: A Study in Psychics* (Boston: Blanchard, 1925), 46.

129. J. Malcolm Bird, *"Margery" the Medium* (Boston: Small, Maynard, 1925), 378, 231. The reference to Keith's appears in Richardson, Crandon, et al., *Margery Harvard Veritas*, 43. This was one of the Emerson Hall sittings at Harvard in 1925.

130. J. Malcolm Bird, "Our Next Psychic," *Scientific American*, July 1924, 28ff.; *Boston Herald*, Dec. 19, 1924, quoted in Brandon, *Life and Many Deaths of Houdini*, 258.

131. Arthur Conan Doyle, quoted in "Margery Genuine, Says Conan Doyle," *Boston Herald*, Jan. 26, 1925, in Edward Saint, comp., Scrapbooks of Mounted Clippings, vol 1., Rare Book Division, LC. See also Hamlin Garland's description of Walter's personality in a 1927 séance in *Forty Years of Psychic Research* (New York: Macmillan, 1936), 309–11. On female mediums and masculine spirit-controls in the nineteenth century, see Moore, *In Search of White Crows*, 111.

132. Silverman, *Houdini!!!* 325.

133. See Le Roi Crandon's reference to "this low-minded Jew," cited in ibid., 325.

134. Harry Houdini, *Houdini Exposes the Tricks Used by the Boston Medium "Margery"* . . . (New York: Adams Press, 1924), 6–7.

135. Bird, *"Margery" the Medium*, 413.

136. Houdini, *Houdini Exposes*, 6–8.

137. Ibid., 10.

138. Bird, *"Margery" the Medium*, 430.

139. Houdini, *Houdini Exposes*, 17.

140. Bird, *"Margery" the Medium*, 433. Bird indicates the term of abuse indirectly by referring to a famous exchange in Owen Wister, *The Virginian* (1902; reprint, New York: Penguin Books, 1988), 22. Tietze gives the quotation as "bastard," perhaps misunderstanding Bird.

141. Houdini, *Houdini Exposes*, 17.

142. Ibid., 23.

143. Tietze, *Margery*, 184.

144. "Houdini Answers Prof. McDougall . . . ," *Boston Herald*, Sept. 22, 1924, clipping in Saint, comp., Scrapbooks of Mounted Clippings, vol. 1, LC.

145. Samuel J. Smilov.tz [S. J. Smiley, pseud.], "Was Houdini Killed?" undated typescript, Fulton Oursler, Sr., Collection, Georgetown University.

146. Kellock, *Houdini*, 382.

3. "STILL A WILD BEAST AT HEART"

1. Burroughs to Thomas Newell Metcalf, Mar. 6, 1912, quoted in Irwin Porges, *Edgar Rice Burroughs: The Man Who Created Tarzan* (Provo, Utah: Brigham Young University Press, 1975), 123–24; John Taliaferro, *Tarzan Forever: The Life of Edgar Rice Burroughs* (New York: Scribner, 1999), 72. These two works are the best biographies of Burroughs, and I have relied on them throughout this chapter. Although I have examined photocopies of Edgar Rice Burroughs's papers in the Irwin Porges Papers, Edgar Rice Burroughs Memorial Collection, University of Louisville, Louisville, Ky., I have cited Porges, *Burroughs*, for the convenience of the reader whenever they are quoted within.

2. Metcalf to Burroughs, Mar. 11, 1912, quoted in Porges, *Burroughs*, 125–27.

3. At age nineteen as captain of the football team at Michigan Military Academy, Burroughs's height was given as five feet ten and a half inches. The next season it was reported as five feet ten inches. When he enlisted in the army a few months later, his height was listed as five feet nine inches. His son Hulbert Burroughs later said he was close to five feet nine inches. His weight was also variously reported. At his enlistment he was recorded as weighing 153 pounds stripped. Less than five months earlier, Burroughs wrote his weight in a notebook as 175 pounds, dressed. See Porges, *Burroughs*, 2–3, 38, 54.

4. Edgar Rice Burroughs, "Autobiography," typescript, Edgar Rice Burroughs Memorial Collection, 56–57.

5. Edgar Rice Burroughs, "The Tarzan Theme," *Writer's Digest*, June 1932, 31.

6. Burroughs, "Autobiography," 19.

7. Ibid., 1.

8. Burroughs appears to have misremembered the year, however, estimating that he was "in my second or third year," instead of six (Porges, *Burroughs*, 774).

9. Ibid., 13–14, 774–77.

10. Burroughs, "Autobiography," 6. On Burroughs's experiences in the West, see Phil Burger, "Glimpses of a World Past: Edgar Rice Burroughs, the West, and the Birth of an American Writer" (master's thesis, Utah State University, 1987).

11. Burroughs, "Autobiography," 23.

12. Ibid., 43.

13. Burroughs to brother Harry Burroughs, Mar. 19, 1921, quoted in notes, Porges Papers.

14. Peter G. Filene, *Him/Her/Self: Gender Identities in Modern America*, 3rd ed. (Baltimore, Md.: Johns Hopkins University Press, 1998), 78.

15. Burroughs, "Autobiography," 51.

16. Burroughs to Mr. M. R. Werner, Mar. 3, 1937, quoted in Porges Papers.

17. Burroughs, "Autobiography," 53–54.

18. Arthur Miller, *Death of a Salesman* (1949; reprint, New York: Viking Press, 1958), 22.

19. Quentin Reynolds, *Fiction Factory* (New York: Random House, 1955); Ron Goulart, *Cheap Thrills: An Informal History of the Pulp Magazines* (New Rochelle, N.Y.: Arlington House, 1972); Lee Server, *Danger Is my Business: An Illustrated History of the Fabulous Pulp Magazines* (San Francisco: Chronicle Books, 1993).

20. Burroughs, "Autobiography," 55.

21. Edgar Rice Burroughs, *A Princess of Mars* (1912; reprint, New York: Ballantine, 1963), 147.

22. Burroughs, "Autobiography," 56. The story first appeared in the magazine as "Under the Moons of Mars."

23. Ibid., 57.

24. Max Weber, *The Protestant Ethic and the Spirit of Capitalism*, trans. Talcott Parsons (New York: Charles Scribner's Sons, 1958); originally published in essay form in German, 1904–1905.

25. Frederick Winslow Taylor, *The Principles of Scientific Management* (1911; reprint, New York: W. W. Norton, 1967), 7; Wayburn quoted in Mary Morgan, "Handling Humanity in the Mass," *Theatre Magazine*, May 1913, 146. This last point is further developed in John F. Kasson, "Dances of the Machine in Early Twentieth-Century America," in Townsend Ludington, ed., *A Modern Mosaic: Art and Modernism in the United States* (Chapel Hill: University of North Carolina Press, 2000), 153–74.

26. *System*, Nov. 1911, 451.

27. Ibid., 460–63.

28. As late as 1900 only one in twenty-five men between the ages of eighteen and twenty-one was enrolled in college; in 1870, it had been one in sixty. See Burton J. Bledstein, *The Culture of Professionalism: The Middle Class and the Development of Higher Education in America* (New York: W. W. Norton, 1976), 278.

29. *System*, 470, 480.

30. Ibid., 489, 491.

31. Cyrus McCormick, Jr., to Albion Small, Feb. 3, 1915, quoted in Olivier Zunz,

Making America Corporate, 1870–1920 (Chicago: University of Chicago Press, 1990), 199.

32. Burroughs, "Autobiography," 58.
33. Scott B. Cook, *Colonial Encounters in the Age of Imperialism* (New York: Harper-Collins, 1998), 1.
34. *Congressional Record*, Jan. 9, 1900, 711, 712.
35. Owen Wister, *The Virginian: A Horseman of the Plains* (1902; reprint, New York: Penguin Books, 1988), 3, 179, 230, 111, 112. Burroughs's tribute appeared in an article he wrote for Thomas Ford, literary editor, *Los Angeles Times*, in 1922; see Porges, *Burroughs*, 368.
36. Thomas Dixon, *The Clansman: An Historical Romance of the Ku Klux Klan* (New York: Doubleday, Page, 1905), 304.
37. Ibid., 186.
38. When Burroughs heard of London's death, he briefly considered writing a biography of him. See Porges, *Burroughs*, 278.
39. Jack London, *The Call of the Wild* (1903; reprint, New York: Macmillan, 1915), 18, 43, 61, 199, 59, 60, 167.
40. Ibid., 223, 231.
41. Burroughs, "Tarzan Theme," 99–100.
42. Dolph Sharp, "Edgar Rice Burroughs, Inc.," *Writer's Digest*, Aug. 1949, 14.
43. R. M. Ballantyne, *The Gorilla Hunters* (London: Collins' Clear-Type Press, n.d.), 22.
44. Edgar Rice Burroughs, *Tarzan of the Apes* (1914; reprint, New York: Dover Books, 1997), 2, 4, 3.
45. See Gina Lombroso-Ferrero, *Criminal Man according to the Classification of Cesare Lombroso* (1911; reprint, Montclair, N.J.: Patterson Smith, 1972), esp. 3–51.
46. Burroughs, *Tarzan of the Apes*, 4, 13.
47. Ibid., 15, 25.
48. Robert M. Zingg, "Feral Man and Cases of Extreme Isolation of Individuals," in J. A. L. Singh and Robert M. Zingg, *Wolf-Children and Feral Man* (1942; reprint, Hamden, Conn.: Archon Books, 1966), 183, 195; Douglas Keith Candland, *Feral Children and Clever Animals: Reflections on Human Nature* (New York: Oxford University Press, 1993), 9–12.
49. Candland, *Feral Children and Clever Animals*, 17–37; quotation from Itard in Harlan Lane, *The Wild Boy of Aveyron* (Cambridge, Mass.: Harvard University Press, 1976), 4.
50. Robert F. Heizer and Theodora Kroeber, eds., *Ishi, the Last Yahi: A Documentary History* (Berkeley: University of California Press, 1979), 92; Theodora Kroeber, *Ishi in Two Worlds* (Berkeley: University of California Press, 1961), 3–4.
51. Heizer and Kroeber, eds., *Ishi, the Last Yahi*, 130.
52. Ibid., 121.
53. Saxton T. Pope, "Characteristics of Ishi," in ibid., 231; Kroeber, *Ishi in Two Worlds*, 138, 176.

54. Kroeber, *Ishi in Two Worlds*, 210; Heizer and Kroeber, eds., *Ishi, the Last Yahi*, 99, 122, 227. I am indebted to Eric Combest for this point.

55. Ernest Thompson Seton, *Boy Scouts of America: Official Handbook of Woodcraft, Scouting, and Life-Craft* (New York: Doubleday, Page, 1910), 1.

56. Joseph Knowles, *Alone in the Wilderness* (Boston: Small, Maynard, 1913), 226.

57. Ibid., 229–31.

58. Ibid., 127.

59. *Boston Post*, Oct. 5, 1913, Oct. 10, 1913, Oct. 12, 1913; Knowles, *Alone in the Wilderness*, 282; *Boston American*, Dec. 2, 1913; Roderick Nash, *Wilderness and the American Mind* (New Haven, Conn.: Yale University Press, 1967), 141–43.

60. Burroughs to Rudolph Altrocchi, Mar. 31, 1937, Porges Papers; see Porges, *Burroughs*, 132.

61. Burroughs to *Daily Maroon*, Mar. 30, 1927, quoted in Porges, *Burroughs*, 135.

62. On allegory as a mode of reading popular fiction, see Michael Denning, *Mechanic Accents: Dime Novels and Working-Class Culture in America* (New York: Verso, 1987), 72–73.

63. Burroughs, *Tarzan of the Apes*, 32.

64. Madison Grant, *The Passing of the Great Race* (New York: Scribner's, 1916).

65. The word "gorilla," for example, derives from an alleged African name for a wild or hairy man; "orangutan" from the Malaysian for man of the woods; q.v. *Oxford English Dictionary*. The Swedish naturalist Carolus Linnaeus in the definitive edition of his *Systema naturae* (1758) included two species within the genus *Homo: Homo sapiens* and *Homo troglyte*.

66. R. L. Garner, *The Speech of Monkeys* (New York: Charles L. Webster, 1892), 3. On Garner, see Candland, *Feral Children and Clever Animals*, 207–26; and Georg Schwidetzky, *Do You Speak Chimpanzee?* trans. from the German by Margaret Gardiner (London: George Routledge, 1932), 44–47.

67. Garner, *Speech of Monkeys*, 5.

68. R. L. Garner, *Gorillas and Chimpanzees* (London: Osgood, McIlvaine, 1896), 14.

69. Ibid., 15–16, 20.

70. Ibid., 61–62, 218.

71. Ibid., 77, 79–80, 101.

72. Ibid., 136–37.

73. Ibid., 42.

74. Burroughs, *Tarzan of the Apes*, 56, 43. The phrase "bitter bifurcation" is from William H. Gass, *Finding a Form* (New York: Knopf, 1996), 138.

75. Burroughs, *Tarzan of the Apes*, 38, 48, 61; Woods Hutchinson, *Instinct and Health* (New York: Dodd and Mead, 1909), 34.

76. Burroughs, *Tarzan of the Apes*, 37.

77. Ibid., 52.

78. Ibid., 57, 60, 63.

79. Ibid., 72; Charles Darwin, *The Descent of Man* (Princeton, N.J.: Princeton University Press, 1981), 2:404–5. In his copy of the second edition, Burroughs wrote

the date Jan. 1899 on the flyleaf, together with a drawing of a large monkey or ape, which he captioned "Grandpa" (Porges, *Burroughs*, 75).

80. Burroughs, *Tarzan of the Apes*, 84.

81. Ibid., 89.

82. Ibid., 86, 99. Burroughs admired Pettee's cover illustration and at one point considered purchasing the original (Porges, *Burroughs*, 159).

83. Burroughs, *Tarzan of the Apes*, 107.

84. Ibid., 135; Johann Friedrich Blumenbach, summarizing travelers' accounts in *The Anthropological Treatises . . .* , ed. and trans. Thomas Bendyshe (London: Longman, Green, Longman, Roberts, and Green for the Anthropological Society, 1865), 73, quoted in Harriet Ritvo, *The Platypus and the Mermaid and Other Figments of the Classifying Imagination* (Cambridge, Mass.: Harvard University Press, 1997), 92. Rudolph Altrocchi offers numerous other instances of human-ape unions as well as animal-raised foundlings in a variety of literary traditions, ancient and modern, in "Ancestors of Tarzan," in *Sleuthing in the Stacks* (Cambridge, Mass.: Harvard University Press, 1944), 74-124, esp. 99.

85. Paul B. Du Chaillu, *Explorations and Adventures in Equatorial Africa* (New York: Harper & Brothers, 1861), 394.

86. Burroughs, *Tarzan of the Apes*, 137.

87. On the sexuality of Wild Peter, Victor, and Ishi, see Zingg, "Feral Man," 187, 193; Candland, *Feral Children and Clever Animals*, 35; Heizer and Kroeber, eds., *Ishi, the Last Yahi*, 234; Kroeber, *Ishi in Two Worlds*, 220; Burroughs, *Tarzan of the Apes*, 137, 144.

88. Burroughs, *Tarzan of the Apes*, 138, 161, 162, 209, 181, 216.

89. Ibid., 194.

90. Ibid., 209, 218.

91. Anonymous writer on behalf of "The Soldiers of the 10th Inf[antry], U.S. Army" to Thomas Metcalf, Sept. 14, 1912, Porges Papers.

92. Ralph Waldo Emerson, *Nature*, in Robert E. Spiller and Alfred R. Ferguson, eds., *The Collected Works of Ralph Waldo Emerson* (Cambridge, Mass.: Belknap Press of Harvard University Press, 1971), 1:7; George Kateb, "Wildness and Conscience: Thoreau and Emerson" (paper presented at Sawyer Seminar, National Humanities Center, Research Triangle Park, N.C., 1999).

93. Kateb, "Wildness and Conscience."

94. Gail Bederman, *Manliness and Civilization: A Cultural History of Gender and Race in the United States, 1880-1917* (Chicago: University of Chicago Press, 1995), 138.

95. Charlotte Perkins Gilman, *Herland* (New York: Pantheon, 1979), 2.

96. Ibid., 11, 82, 71-72, 92, 99.

97. Ibid., 131, 87, 132.

98. "Table-Talk," *All-Story*, Sept. 1912, quoted in Porges, *Burroughs*, 136; Metcalf to Burroughs, Jan. 22, 1913, and Burroughs to Metcalf, Jan. 24, 1913, quoted in Porges, *Burroughs*, 150.

99. On the printing and sales of Burroughs's early Tarzan novels by A. C. McClurg,

see Alan M. Freedman, "McClurg Speaks," *Burroughs Quarterly*, n.s., no. 3 (July 1990): 2–4; and Alan M. Freedman, "McClurg Royalty Payments," *Burroughs Quarterly*, n.s., no. 4 (Oct. 1990): 13–14.

100. Burroughs to brother Harry Burroughs, quoted in Taliaferro, *Tarzan Forever*, 144.

101. For the first two quotations, see Porges, *Burroughs*, 350, 301–2. For the last quotation, see Edgar Rice Burroughs, "The Story of Tarzan" (1932), *Burroughs Bulletin*, n.s., no. 3 (July 1990): 35.

CONCLUSION

1. David L. Chapman, *Sandow the Magnificent: Eugen Sandow and the Beginnings of Bodybuilding* (Urbana: University of Illinois Press, 1994), 187.

2. Houdini diary, 1904, quoted in Kenneth Silverman, *Houdini!!! The Career of Ehrich Weiss* (New York: HarperCollins, 1996), 178.

3. Dolph Sharp, "Edgar Rice Burroughs, Inc.," *Writer's Digest*, Aug. 1949, 51.

4. Eugen Sandow, *Life Is Movement* (London: National Health Press, n.d. [c. 1918]), 10; "Territorial Physical Development Competition," London *Times*, July 24, 1909, 12. I have spelled out abbreviations.

5. Quoted in Irwin Porges, *Edgar Rice Burroughs: The Man Who Created Tarzan* (Provo, Utah: Brigham Young University Press, 1975), 288, 289.

6. The stories that formed the basis for *Tarzan the Untamed* were written in 1918 and 1919. Edgar Rice Burroughs, *Tarzan the Untamed* (1920; reprint, New York: Ballantine Books, 1963), 69; Porges, *Burroughs*, 392, 790.

INDEX

Locators in *italic* indicate illustrations and photographs.

CPSIA information can be obtained
at www.ICGtesting.com
Printed in the USA
LVOW13s2326200318

570606LV00009B/205/P

About the Author

Earl Ofari Hutchinson is the author of multiple books on race and politics in America. He is a political analyst and regular commentator on RN News. He appears frequently on MSNBC and on CNN. His books include the trilogy on the Obama Years: The Obama Legacy, How Obama Governed; The Year of Crisis and Challenge, and How Obama Won. His most recent books are the Trump Challenge to Black America, From King to Obama: Witness to a Turbulent History.

He is a weekly co-host of the Al Sharpton Show on Radio One. He is the host of the weekly Hutchinson Report on KPFK 90.7 FM Los Angeles and the Pacifica Network.

Introduction

"**H**e's dead." He's dead." The scream, the shout, and the tears that flowed like the floodwaters of a raging stream from my mother were so deafening and plaintive that I had to leave the house. It was exactly 7:05 PM, on April 4, 1968. It was a time and a day that would rank close to the day in memory as the day a quarter century earlier when the Japanese attacked Pearl Harbor. President Franklin Delano Roosevelt called that day, a day that will live in infamy.

The infamy in this case was not a sneak attack by a foreign power, and the subsequent four years of global war that America was engaged in and that cost the lives of tens millions. It reshaped the world in the second half of the 20th Century. But the murder of Dr. Martin Luther King Jr. on that raw day in Memphis, Tennessee had profound consequences, both intended and unintended, for America, that in

their own way would be just as challenging and traumatic. It was traumatic for me too.

My mother's painful sobs instantly stirred the memory I had of that warm day in May 1964. As a high schooler, I sat with my father that day in one of the front row seats at the Los Angeles Coliseum. I stared with a mix of awe and joy as the smallish, nattily-dressed man marched past me arm in arm with a phalanx of other religious leaders. He smiled broadly and graciously acknowledged the cheers from the crowd. I cheered too. The man who garnered my adulation and that of hundreds more in the crowd was King. He marched slowly, and deliberately, to a stage at the center of the football playing field. He spoke for forty minutes and struck many of the same themes that he hit on in his March on Washington speech eight months earlier—the fight against segregation, poverty, the battle for passage of the civil rights bill, and a call for mass non-violent protest against racial injustice.

Now fast forward 52 years later, another voice was heard on the King National Holiday in January 2016. It was a voice far different from the heartfelt sense of pain my mother's agonized shout conveyed. The voice this time speaking on King's place, past and present in American history, was then GOP presidential candidate Donald Trump. He had been invited by Jerry Falwell Jr. to give, of all things, a tribute to King on his national holiday in January, at of all places, the ultra-conservative Liberty University in South Carolina.

Falwell claimed he invited Trump to speak on King because he thought he'd have something thoughtful to say

about King's enduring legacy. He had the impression that Trump intended to talk solely about King. Falwell dropped an even stronger hint to Trump about the need to talk about King's importance by airing a short video on King's life before Trump spoke.

What the 10,000 students that packed the assembly hall to hear Trump discourse on King heard was something quite different. Trump barely mentioned King. He spoke in his usual disjointed manner. He spent most of the time on the stage rambling on about his favorite subject, himself, and his campaign. He bragged that he had broken the record for attendance at a speech at the University. Whether Falwell at some point gave Trump a hand signal or used body language to signal him to remember he was there to talk about King is uncertain. Trump in a lucid moment did at least remember to get another mention of King in, "So we'll dedicate that to Martin Luther King, a great man. And that's a little bit of an achievement, I will tell you."

The parenthetical mention of King came at the end of his speech.

Trump's incidental mention of King was revelatory only in the sense that even at ultra-conservative Liberty University, King was still important enough to have a man who embodied everything that King loathed and fought against pay a kind of, sort of tribute to him. However, it was my mother's plaintive scream of agony that captured the feeling of deep personal loss that millions of African-Americans, people of color, and thoughtful Americans felt at the announcement

that evening of King's death. These were the throngs who believed in, and fought for civil rights and the "beloved community" that King so eloquently and passionately believed in and fought for who felt anguish at King's passing.

✷ ✷ ✷ ✷ ✷

Dr. Martin Luther King Jr. was in many ways an accidental civil rights leader. He was the freshly minted minister of the Dexter Avenue Baptist Church in 1955. His task was to establish his ministry, boost the church, and raise a young and growing family. The Montgomery Bus Boycott, the long, protracted, and at times violent leaden struggle, abruptly changed that and King's fortunes. He and his church became the focal point of that struggle. And with the boycott's success, brought national prominence to King. The next decade he was everywhere— marches, demonstrations, lecturing, cajoling politicians and the public to dump Jim Crow America in the scrap heap of history. Equally important, the struggle for civil rights and social and economic justice, that reshaped America also reshaped King.

He began to deeply question, challenge, and probe what America should and could be in a post-civil rights America. The success in desegregating a lunch counter or motel was encapsulated in King's famous quip: what does it mean to eat at a desegregated lunch counter if a person can't afford the meal began to pale against the bigger, more intractable social problems. They were ending poverty and war, and attaining economic wealth redistribution. It was not just the evolution

of King in that period, but the evolution of King, as a radical, cutting edge, advocate of radical change.

King's moving impassioned, age defining," I Have a Dream Speech" electrified the quarter million at the March on Washington in August 1963. In time it became the kind of national anthem for the civil rights struggle, and for decades to become a source of much debate, distortion, interpretation, misinterpretation, twisting, and manipulating, for nearly every political group's agenda. By then, black leaders had already firmly staked out the moral high ground for a powerful and irresistible civil rights movement.

It was classic good versus evil. Many white Americans were sickened by the gory news scenes of baton battering racist Southern sheriffs, fire hoses, police dogs, and Klan violence unleashed against peaceful black protesters. Racial segregation was considered by just about anyone and everyone who fancied themselves as decent Americans as immoral and indefensible. The civil rights leaders were hailed as martyrs and heroes in the fight for justice.

*   *   *   *   *

As America unraveled in the 1960s in the anarchy of urban riots, campus takeovers, and anti-war street battles; the civil rights movement and its leaders fell apart, too. Many of them fell victim to their own success and failure. When they broke down the racially restricted doors of corporations, government agencies, and universities; middle class blacks, not the poor, were the ones who rushed headlong through

them. As King veered even more toward left radicalism and embraced the rhetoric of the militant anti-war movement, he became a political pariah shunned by the Lyndon Johnson White House, as well as by many mainstream white and black civil rights leaders.

King's murder in 1968 was the turning point for race relations in America. The self-destruction from within and political sabotage from outside of black organizations left the black poor organizationally fragmented and politically rudderless. The black poor lacking competitive technical skills and professional training, and shunned by many middle-class black leaders, became expendable jail and street and cemetery fodder. Some turned to gangs, guns, and drugs to survive.

50 Years Later: Why the Murder of Dr. King Still Hurts assesses what would have changed if King had lived? What was the consequence of the changes that occurred in the aftermath of his murder? How did those changes impact and influence the peace movement, the opposition to the Iraq and Afghanistan wars, immigration, gay rights and the women's movements, and Black Lives Matter? What effect would his presence on the scene have had on the fight for black political empowerment, criminal justice system reform, the problems of crime, drugs and violence in the nation's inner cities as well as the ugly racial backlash of the GOP and Trump? What relationship would he have had, and conflicts with, Presidents Reagan, Clinton, Bush and Obama? The impact of the FBI's never-ending smear campaign against King for alleged illicit sexual improprieties.

50 Years Later: Why the Murder of Dr. King Still Hurts will take a fresh look at King's murder and address why many still believe that his murder was not the work of a racist, lone nut, James Earl Ray, but that it was orchestrated by the FBI and other murky federal government agencies. It's noteworthy that fifty years after his murder, the FBI still has not formally apologized for its two decades dirty war against King.

I present the full 14 pages of FBI memos, files, notes, minutes of meetings, and letters that have rarely been fully presented and cited in their entirety: "The FBI Plans Its Campaign to Discredit Dr. King." This is the FBI's own words detailing the full scope of their plan to destroy King. Many of the details in the campaign have never been presented in complete detail for the public—the break ins, forgeries, the informants planted in SCLC, bank account seizures, poison pen letters, calls to universities, Congresspersons, and even the Nobel Prize Committee to reject King. I detail how the FBI stopped at nothing in its relentless, ruthless, no-holds barred campaign to destroy King even considering trying to turn his wife, Coretta Scott King, into an informer against him.

There are many lessons to be learned from a half century of changes and the struggle for change that King, at the time of his murder in 1968, and fifty years later still symbolizes.

The fiftieth anniversary of his assassination then is the time to reposition King once more into the mainstream of the ongoing struggle for reform, and the ills of the nation's inner cities today. King's murder by no means ended his impact and

influence on the leaders, organizations, events and changes that he envisioned and fought for. The nation continues to grapple with many of those same problems today.

CHAPTER 1

Who Killed Dr. King and Why?

"We shall overcome because the arc of the moral universe is long, but it bends toward justice." This line from King is almost as famed and quoted as the lines from his, "I Have a Dream" speech. King delivered the line in a brutal, and scathing indictment of the government for its war policy in Vietnam and its back pedal from the fight against poverty. This time King's famed line didn't come from him directly. It was a tweet from the FBI quoting King on the 49th anniversary of his assassination in April 2017.

The FBI's usurp of King's words predictably ignited a firestorm of furious, outraged tweets and digs on social media. There was more. Then FBI Director James Comey drew outrage a year earlier at a conference on civil rights at the 16th Street Baptist Church in Birmingham, Alabama. He

claimed that he kept a copy of the wiretap order and signed by then Attorney General Robert F. Kennedy in 1963, authorizing the snooping on King. Kennedy almost certainly had the approval of his brother John to issue the order.

The FBI's King tweet and Comey's frank admission that the FBI had grotesquely and illegally abused its power in its two-decade witch-hunt of King was welcomed. However, it didn't change the sordid history of that abuse then and the horrific consequences of that abuse fifty years later.

This was painfully driven home once more in November 2014. Then *The New York Times* created a mild stir when it published several newly declassified government documents that proved what had long been established beyond any dispute. The FBI and other government agencies waged a relentless, ruthless, and shameful war against King for years. The document that the *Times* printed was a poison pen letter to him in 1964. The existence of the letter was not new. The National Security Archives released the tape with the letter in 2013, and there have been many other references to it in the various investigations into the FBI's dirty war against King and the civil rights movement over the years.

The letter was written by a group of special agents mainly drawn from the Washington and Atlanta FBI offices. It was almost certainly approved by FBI Director J. Edgar Hoover. The FBI operatives called King every name in the book, "filthy," "abnormal," "fraudulent self." They capped it by demanding that he commit suicide. They even gave him a timetable for doing away with himself, 3 ½ days from the

receipt of the letter. The vicious, sordid, and gutter poison pen letter was not the first. Nor would it be the last, to hector, harass, harangue, and goad him. The letters were just one of the mountainous volumes of such documents that told the tale of the government's hectoring, haranguing, harassing, and persecuting King nearly every waking moment of his life.

It was in large part because of this sordid tale of murderous actions and intent by the government against King that his widow, Coretta Scott King never totally bought the final and official judgment of history that Ray was the lone assassin of her husband. She repeatedly expressed a burning desire to know who really killed King. That desire wasn't buried with her death in 2006. This quote from her was on the King Center website even after her passing: "There is abundant evidence that there was a high-level conspiracy in the assassination of my husband."

Coretta was hardly alone in that belief. On nearly every anniversary of King's assassination, a legion of conspiracy buffs, black skeptics, some civil rights leaders, and at time many congresspersons have demanded to know more about the circumstances of King's killing. In 2004, more than 50 House representatives endorsed a bill by then Georgia Democrat Cynthia McKinney to reopen the King assassination investigation. The bill didn't go anywhere. But the conspiracy theory about King's assassination is still very much alive and well 50 years later.

✳ ✳ ✳ ✳ ✳

Americans have always deserved to know the whole truth about the killing of King. However, there are two truths about the murder. The first is too painful for those who fervently believe that Ray was a Lee Harvey Oswald-type patsy and that the government orchestrated King's killing. Yet, the evidence is still overwhelming that Ray was the triggerman. His fingerprints were on the alleged murder weapon. He was at the crime scene and he confessed.

At different times before his death, Ray gave conflicting, confusing and muddled accounts of his activities and whereabouts at the time of the murder. His protests of innocence and frame-ups sounded like a discredited man's desperate effort to salve his conscience, grab media attention, and cash in on the notoriety of the case. It worked. Ray's public thrashing-about on the King murder sent conspiracy buffs stampeding to the barricades, shouting that the government killed King. The King family gave Ray's much belated feigning of innocence credence when Coretta took the stand on his behalf at a civil trial in Memphis in 1999.

Ray's guilt, however, has never let the government off the hook. The verdict of history stands that Ray killed King. The other truth is to know what government agencies did or didn't know about the King killing. The Senate Select Committee on Assassination that investigated King's murder in 1977 released tons of documents on the King murder. While there were many more, the door was effectively slammed shut

on getting further documents that chronicled the illegal campaign against King by the FBI when a federal judge ordered the files sealed for 50 years until 2027. They are now tucked away in the records vault at the National Archives. The files might answer many questions about the secret war the FBI waged against King from the late 1950's to his murder.

The assault on King was first and foremost the product of FBI Director J. Edgar Hoover acting out his demented, paranoid obsessions against King. "Dangerous," "evil," "colossal fraud," were the choice terms that Hoover and other top FBI officials routinely spit out during the 1950s and 1960s in their internal memos about King. They didn't stop at the name calling. They talked ominously of "neutralizing" him as an effective leader. Then there was that letter that flatly said: "King you are done," and called for him to murder himself.

There was an uglier, more ominous revelation that surfaced decades later in declassified FBI memos about the FBI's disinterest in King's safety. It came during the voter rights demonstrations in Selma in 1965. The FBI had confidential information about two alleged plots to kill King. Hoover knew of both. Yet, he scrawled an emphatic "No" on a memo querying whether the FBI should warn King. He went further and summarily ordered agents "not to tell King anything" about the alleged plots against his life. This was not smoking gun proof that the FBI had a hand in King's murder. The wiretaps, though, have always raised the legitimate question: What did the FBI know and when did it know about the possible attempts on King's life?

The government assault on King was the centerpiece of a sustained war, directed, orchestrated, and waged without stop against the Black movement. Hoover decided that the cheap and dirty way to win that war was to discredit the most respected and admired symbol of the civil rights movement. Hoover assigned Assistant FBI director William Sullivan the dirty job of getting the goods on King. Sullivan branded King as the "most dangerous Negro of the future in this nation." In his book, *My Thirty Years in Hoover's FBI,* Sullivan described the inner circle of men assigned to get King. The group was made up of special agents mainly drawn from the Washington and Atlanta FBI offices. They were the ones who wrote the "suicide" letter to King.

Their job was to monitor all of King's activities. Much of their dirty tactics have been thoroughly documented in the varied investigations, declassified documents, and memos that revealed parts of the FBI's illegal actions through the years. They deluged him with wiretaps, physical surveillance, other poison-pen letters, threats, harassment, intimidation, and leaks of smear sexual tapes to the media. Even at the time of his murder, Hoover had more plans to intensify the spy campaign against King. Decades later, Sullivan still publicly defended the FBI's war against him, and made no apology for it. We still know only the bare outline of what the FBI did toward King in his final days.

*   *   *   *   *

Even the public revelations of the FBI's illegal war

against King didn't stop the agency from plotting even more sinister and diabolical actions to destroy King and the civil rights movement. The FBI patterned its spy and harassment campaign against King on the methods used by its counter-intelligence division and internal security sections during the 1940s and '50s. The arsenal of dirty tactics they used included unauthorized wiretaps, agent provocateurs, poison-pen letters, "black-bag jobs" (breaking and entering to obtain intelligence), and the compiling of secret dossiers.

In the 1960s, the FBI recruited thousands of "ghetto informants," for their relentless campaign of harassment and intimidation against African-American groups. The bureau even organized its targets into Orwellian categories agents gave such labels as "Rabble Rouser Index," "Agitator Index," and "Security Index."

There are still a lot of dots that need to be connected in the FBI's murky onslaught against King. We do know this. The FBI officials who directed the illegal spy campaign against King and the FBI agent who played a major role in running the program in Atlanta against him were also involved in every phase of the investigation into King's assassination. The taint of the severely compromised cast of government officials that controlled the investigation five decades after his murder still raises questions about the scope, or lack thereof, of the investigation.

Then there was Army Intelligence's and the National Security Agency's war on King. They are not as well- known as the FBI's, but they were still just as prolonged and lethal.

It started in 1947 with surveillance of King who was then a
student at Morehouse College at a meeting of the Intercol-
legiate Council he attended, the group was suspected of being Communist influenced. The reports on King's activities
continued through the 1950s. As King's stature as America's
best known civil rights leaders rose in the 1960's, Army Intelligence kicked its spy campaign against him into high gear.
It went beyond mere taps and surveillance. According to declassified documents, for seven years it flew at least 26 super-
secret U2 spy flights over civil rights actions in Birmingham,
Alabama and other cities.

The NSA's spy program on King was part of a larger,
and even more sweeping snooping of leftists in the 1960s.
It even had a code name, MINARET. The cover was that it
was supposed to collect names of those who posed a threat to
the president, as well as drug peddling and domestic terror-
ism. By the time of King's murder, the NSA had thousands
of names in its alleged "threat" list. King's name continually
popped up on the NSA's spy list as a "threat" particularly as
he moved further toward the Left with his lambaste of the
Vietnam War and preachments against poverty and income
inequality.

The actual assassination investigation also had a cloud.
FBI officials who directed the illegal spy campaign against
King and the FBI agent who played a major role in running
the program in Atlanta were deeply involved in every phase
of the assassination investigation. The re-opening of any fresh
King assassination investigation likely wouldn't uncover any

smoking gun proof that the government directly issued orders to kill King. Yet, full disclosure by government agencies involved in the investigation of King's assassination at the very least could allay some of the lingering doubts and suspicions that government agencies didn't tell the complete truth about King's murder.

However, even this won't absolve the FBI of its disgraceful, destructive, and illegal campaign against King. The climate of suspicion and hostility it helped nurture toward the Civil Rights Movement made it possible for Ray to murder King.

The federal government shamefully and disgracefully with the full knowledge and assent of presidents that included Eisenhower, Kennedy, and Johnson and their attorneys general decided that the cheap and abominable way to win that war was by discrediting the most respected and admired symbol of the civil rights movement.

This is not just arcane, old news history. That war did much to destabilize, fragment, and compromise civil rights leaders and organizations then, and in the immediate years after King's murder. It bathed them with a cloud of suspicion of their actions and motives. His murder created a huge ideological and leadership vacuum which even further hastened the weakening in some cases, and break-up in others, of the old line, traditional civil rights organizations. King's murder also led to a sharp redefining of what a leader and leadership should be and what it's aims and objectives, and tactics should be. King typified the era of the nationally known leader who

could grab the news headlines, was routinely quoted as the voice of blacks, and garnered the financial backing and support of wealthy donors, and invitations to and consultation with by Presidents, and elected official. He was elevated to the perch as the "Black Leader." King's murder ended that era.

His murder also ignited the debate and fight over the goals of civil rights leaders. Should they be corporate advancement, economic empowerment, business development, ownership? Or, should they be protest, demonstrations, and other forms of in-your-face direct street action?

To give Hoover and the FBI and the many other government agencies that targeted King and the civil rights movement sole credit for hastening their slide downward is to impart a prescience that is unwarranted. They could not know that King's decline as the symbol of the movement to remake America would accomplish all of this with one man's death. However, it's no shade of the historic truth to say that the result, however unforeseen, was attained. In that sense, the hideous war against King resonated for good and ill in every decade since then.

Fifty years later there is one other fact that still stands the verdict of history. The FBI has never formally apologized for its dirty war against King. This still tells why the government's assault on King and the civil rights movement remains a hideous stain on the nation a half century later.

Sex, Lies, and Tapes

The day before the celebration of the King Holiday in January 2017, Coretta's memoir on her life within and without the civil rights movement, *My Life, My Love, My Legacy,* was released in the U.S. The press predictably honed-in on one thing in the book about King: sex and his alleged infidelities to her. Coretta made clear that she did not, nor ever did, belief the heinous, relentless, and smut leaden slander of him as a sexual reprobate. What was more revealing, though, was that nearly five decades after his death this was still an issue of debased and prurient fascination. The reasons it was during his life and, five decades later, are still instructive about how King is still viewed in some circles. The first hint of this never-let-go, smut pedaling about King came six years before the release of Coretta's book

"I can't see a picture of Martin Luther King without thinking, you know, that man's terrible," sniffed former First

Lady, Jacqueline Kennedy. Bobby had told her that King "was
calling up all these girls and arranging for a party of men and
women, I mean, sort of an orgy."

Jackie Kennedy ignited fury when she almost cavalierly
quipped this to a friend and reporter. The implication was
that King was practically an unreconstructed sex addict and
that everyone in the Kennedy circle knew it, courtesy of the
FBI wiretaps on King, that her brother-in-law, Robert F. Kennedy, as Attorney General, had authorized in 1963. This was
just one of the many bugs FBI agents planted in King's motel
and hotel rooms, wherever he traveled during the 1960s.

Some questioned what was Jackie's motive in drop-
ping this tidbit of salacious gossip to a reporter of all people,
and what purpose would it serve other than to further dirty
King's image? Her dig at King was disclosed in an oral history interview that was not released until 2011. This was more
than four decades after King's murder, and seventeen years
after her death in 1994.

The worst part is that there is really no way to know
if a word of what Jackie had to say about King is true. The
wiretaps Kennedy approved on King are sealed until 2027.
Her daughter, Caroline, attempted to shed some light on her
mother's bitter remarks about King when she finger-pointed
Hoover as the culprit. She claimed that he leaked the tapes
to Jackie with other tapes in which King allegedly took derogatory shots at her husband, JFK, for his tepid, foot-drag-
ging on civil rights legislation. The villain, then, again was
Hoover who in his clinical hatred of King would do anything

to poison the well against him. This included using Jackie as a pawn in his deadly game to vilify King.

* * * * *

Early in his brutal, no holds barred war against King, Hoover zeroed in on the one thing that he believed would bring King down. That was sex. King associates, most notably, his closest confidant during those years, Reverend Ralph Abernathy, seemed to validate Hoover's sex obsession with King when years later he claimed in his autobiography in 1989, *And the Walls Came Tumbling Down,* that King did indeed have a weakness for women, not named Coretta. King's other major biographers have lots of quotes purportedly made by King in which he supposedly boasted about his sexual prowess.

Those quotes almost exclusively came from FBI declassified wiretaps and memos. Or, from interviews with ex-FBI agents who shadowed King. One of the quotes has King boasting, "'I'm f*****g for God! I'm not a negro tonight!' The FBI tried to drive the dagger deeper by sending him one of their tapes anonymously which contained supposed tape 'highlights' of his sexual groans and dirty jokes.

The ex-agents could hardly be considered founts of objectivity. Many were unabashed racists, and like their boss, Hoover, were fiercely hostile to King. The tales they told purportedly based on the tapes of King soliciting and cavorting with white prostitutes, talking dirty, and having wild orgies, were concocted probably at the egging on of Hoover. They

have been thoroughly debunked. Even Abernathy in his supposed tell-all memoir didn't make any mention of these sexual shenanigans.

Still, it was Abernathy's claim about King's alleged rov-
ing eye that set off a wild round of finger pointing by other
King associates and friends at Abernathy. They claimed he
fabricated a dual sex life King led that was a flat out lie. They
said that the sexual hijinks that Hoover said he had on the
tapes, and Abernathy's seeming confirmation of them, were
made up whole cloth and cropped up decades later to again
smear King and his legacy. The truth about what King did or
didn't do in his private life on the road away from wife and
family as always lay somewhere in between what accusers
and defenders say about King's private life.

King was a fundamentalist Baptist minister in an era
when the role of women, especially wives, were firmly ma-
triarchal and centered in the home. It was one of the worst
kept secrets that many ministers engaged in illicit sex within
and without their churches. There was no real stigma or penalty in that era attached to their philandering. If King did
engage in extramarital sexual exploits it would have been no
surprise, and no surprise that whatever alleged affairs he may
have had would have been winked and nodded at, and ignored by friends and associates.

King's real or imagined sexual philandering was simply another weapon in Hoover's filthy attack arsenal against
him. He badly wanted to discredit King. Sex happened to be
the way that Hoover and the FBI thought was the best means

to turn the public and more particularly Presidents Kennedy, Johnson, and other major political leaders against King. The thinking went, discredit King and you discredit the civil rights movement. If King was exposed as hypocrite, cheat, and scumbag on sex, then this would wreak irreparable damage to his reputation as a principled, purer than Caesar's Wife, moral man.

It could never work for several reasons. One, was the times. In an era of rigid patriarchy, if men had affairs, they were routinely chalked up to "a man's prerogative" or "boys will be boys." Divorce then was not the ready option for women it would be decades later. Women were still largely homemakers or low paid clerical workers. They were almost totally financially dependent on their husbands, the designated breadwinners. Coretta, for instance, was a prime example. She was a housewife with four children to raise. She had scrubbed a promising career as a classically trained singer to be the family caregiver.

The more personal reason is that whatever King did or didn't do sexually on the road, he couldn't hide it from his aides and co-workers. They knew about it. So, there was really nothing to disclose to them that could shock them or besmirch King's image in their eyes. JFK and Johnson were in the same boat. John, especially, had a closet full of sexual skeletons and Johnson was suspected of having a few too. So, while they had access to Hoover's smutty tapes on King, and if they publicly revealed them they would have left themselves wide open to dirty double dealing about King, and worse, the

possibility that some snoopy reporter or gossip columnist would start looking at just what they were doing in the bedroom of someone that may not have been named Jacqueline or Lady Bird. Prudence was the best tact, on their part, and there is no evidence that Hoover's sex tapes ever influenced their willingness to meet and do business with King. Johnson, in particular, met and had phone conversations with him on several occasions especially during the fight to pass the Voting Rights Act in 1965.

＊ ＊ ＊ ＊ ＊

Yet, another reason Hoover's diabolical ploy to throttle King wouldn't work was Coretta. She was not just King's wife. She was much more. Coretta inevitably heard all the rumors and gossip flying around about her husbands alleged sexual proclivities. "'I just wouldn't have burdened him with anything so trivial', she later said. Her response gave strong hint of the pivotal role she played in the civil rights struggle. As early as 1959, she made a phone call to then Democratic presidential candidate John F. Kennedy. She asked:

"I certainly appreciate your concern, and I would appreciate anything that you can do to help." This was the dignified, but worried, request for help for King after he had been sentenced to four months of hard labor at Georgia's notorious Reidsville State Prison after being arrested on a trumped-up traffic warrant and for violating probation. The second charge stemmed from Dr. King's earlier arrest at a sit-in demonstration.

Coretta was deeply pained that King might not make it out of Reidsville alive. There had been rumors of foul play planned against him. During the tense days of his imprisonment, Coretta frantically worked the phones trying to get any help she could for his release. At the time, Kennedy was locked in a tight White House race with Republican Vice President Richard Nixon. Kennedy made the call partly out of sincere concern for Dr. King, and partly with an eye on the black vote.

Coretta's efforts paid off for King, and sunk Nixon. The Democrats turned the call into a public relations coup. Kennedy's action was credited with tipping large numbers of blacks toward the Democrats, and Nixon, the early odds-on favorite to win the presidency, lost by a narrow margin. King was soon released unharmed and the civil rights movement gained greater steam and vigor in the next couple of years. Coretta's dogged determination to save her husband energized the civil rights fight and changed the course of a presidential election and race relations in America.

It was fitting that Kennedy's life-affirming and politically profound phone call was made to Coretta. In December 1955, she and King anxiously kept watch at the front window of their home in Montgomery, Alabama, to make sure that there were no black riders on the buses. She stood, walked, and cheered arm in arm with him at countless civil rights marches, demonstrations and rallies. She endured his long absences and the gossipy rumors of his infidelities, and kept the family and the marriage together. This entailed great personal sacrifice, but equally important, she was someone

who believed in and was prepared to work alongside him to achieve the same goals as her husband.

In the decade after his murder, Coretta did not fade from the scene. She continued to storm the barricades against racial injustice, economic inequality, military adventurism, and against hate crimes and violence. She wrote countless letters, gave speeches and participated in direct action campaigns. She continued to fiercely protect King's legacy from the opportunists that twisted and sullied his words and name. This included firing back at the never-ending slurs of King on sex and marital infidelity.

The biggest reason, though, why Hoover's dirty little scheme to destroy King with sexual dirt flopped was because of King. He was simply too valued a leader of a movement and a cause that touched, energized, and mobilized millions. The events around the vicious state trooper assaults on demonstrators in Selma in 1965 was a textbook example of this. Johnson not only met with King privately at least twice before and during the bloody assault, but they almost had a tag team partnership in orchestrating and coordinating the street demonstrations and congressional support for passage of the Voting Rights Act. This was not unusual. Johnson and King spoke at least a dozen times by phone at various times during Johnson's tenure in the White House.

The mutual admiration society between the two was self-evident in this exchange transcribed from a White House tape, "We have some great challenges and opportunities ahead," said King. "And we are all with you."

"Thank you, doctor," said Johnson. "Thank you so much."

Johnson would hardly have cultivated King as a quasi-ally and informal sounding board on civil rights actions if he thought he was consorting with a sex crazed, two-bit con man, and huckster. Yes, he heard the tapes of King's alleged sexual escapades that Hoover giddily supplied to him. Whether he believed any of the rancid stuff or not was irrelevant to him. He needed to keep King as an ally in the push for passage of his civil rights and voting rights legislation.

This fact, though, didn't then, and five decades later, still doesn't stop the tongues from wagging about King's alleged unsavory sexual past. It didn't then and won't now toss any taint on his profound and enduring importance.

More Than
a Dreamer

"It must be pegged to the median income of society, not at the lowest levels of income." This was one of many pragmatic lines in King's *Where Do We Go From Here: Chaos or Community?*—a work largely ignored when published in 1967, and rarely cited in the decades since. King argued for, and spelled out in concrete terms, how a guaranteed annual income plan could be structured as a pathway out of poverty and a way to provide a living wage for millions of low income workers. The methodical and detailed measures he laid out in the book were in marked contrast to his most famous four words—"I Have a Dream." In the five decades since his murder, those four words have been a blessing and a curse for his legacy. The words were seared into the nation's consciousness at the March on Washington in 1963. Yet, those four words indelibly tagged him to many as

a hopeless utopian with lofty visions of ending war, racism, and poverty; but with no concrete programs to achieve those aims.

That was not the case then. There's still much to be learned from his pragmatic search for workable programs to deal with black ills that went far beyond fighting to stay at a motel or drink out of "whites only" water fountain. King was far more practical problem solver than dreamer. But there's a huge caveat: King can't be fitted into a neat ideological box.

There is enough paradox and ambivalence in King's positions for liberals and conservatives to praise or damn. And they have over the years.

King railed against black militants. He also embraced them. He advocated conservative self-help programs and socialist wealth distribution. He applauded violent anti-colonial and national liberation movements and championed nonviolent change.

For many of the big-ticket racial and class problems that still plague America, King's solutions are a conflicting mix of idealism and hard-nosed pragmatism. He can't be blamed for that. Five decades after his murder, the country is no closer to solving these problems. With the GOP in firm control of the White House, Congress, and most of state legislatures and governorships, they have done much to worsen the problems.

A close reading of King's fixed and evolving positions of the crisis problems then is revealing for their relevance fifty years later. The crisis in black families: King branded the black family "fragile, deprived and often psychopathic." While his

characterization accepted many of the negative myths and
stereotypes about black families, King correctly targeted ab-
sentee fathers in many black homes as a major ill. He recognized the importance of values training, discipline, hard
work, and the reduction of family violence in resolving the
family crisis. While he anticipated the finger-point of black
father absenteeism by many blacks from Bill Cosby to Denzel
Washington, legions of conservatives, in the years after his
murder, he did place the blame solely on their shoulders.

He made a big pitch for more government-funded jobs,
education, and skills training programs. Yet, he did not believe that more funds, smaller classrooms and better text-
books alone would solve the crisis in the classroom. He called
on teachers and administrators to rededicate themselves to
the ideal of quality education and on parents to get more involved in their children's education.

King's proposal for "educational parks," a kind of mul-
tifaceted complex to teach basic skills and advanced studies, anticipated the idea of magnet schools and even charter
schools.

Ensuring blacks the right to vote and electing blacks
to political office were not enough for King. He challenged
community groups to conduct continuous voter registration
and education campaigns. He asked black officeholders to be
"independent and assertive" in fighting for legislation to improve the plight of the black poor. He wanted black political
organizations to build alliances with labor and other ethnic
groups.

Black elected officials now increasingly represent districts that are no longer exclusively or in some case even majority black. Their districts have significant numbers of Hispanic, Pacific Islanders, and even whites. This has compelled them to run broad based campaigns that appeal to, and or inclusive of, other ethnic groups. This includes staffing, hiring, appointments, and working closely with Hispanic and Pacific Islander organizations

The NAACP's campaign over the years against discrimination in corporate hiring and promotion policies closely follows a four-step plan outlined by King. It included demands for more jobs and promotions, for buying campaigns, for boycotts and organized protests, for negotiations and for the monitoring of any agreement.

This ties directly into the debate and fight over economic empowerment. King often said that it was futile to integrate a lunch counter if blacks couldn't afford to buy a meal at it. He demanded huge increases in federal funding for job and skills training programs, but he also recognized that the federal government couldn't or shouldn't do it all. He called for "black dollar days" during which blacks purchased goods and services from black businesses and deposited their savings in black-owned banks. In turn, King expected black entrepreneurs to recycle those dollars into education, recreation, and social programs for the black poor.

＊　＊　＊　＊　＊

The one issue that has torn black communities, and been

the single biggest reason for the soaring prison population, and destabilized families, has been the issue of crime and violence. King understood that the destructive cycle of crime, drugs, and violence fractured black communities. While his priority was for more government-funded job and education programs, he also stressed family values, personal responsibility and discipline.

He urged black professionals to give more of their time and money to employment, educational, and recreational programs aimed at "saving" at-risk black youth. King also agreed that welfare could breed dependency and discourage personal initiative. He proposed that the government provide direct tax subsidies and tax incentives to corporations to hire and train unskilled workers. This idea was a forerunner of the federally backed enterprise and empowerment zones, touted by many conservatives as the way to reduce black poverty.

The issues that King passionately embraced above any others except civil rights was the movement to end militarism and the grotesque disparities of wealth. In his famed speech, "Beyond Vietnam" at the Riverside Church in New York City, on April 4, 1967, eerily delivered one year to the date before his murder, which is rarely cited among King's greatest speeches. He denounced the Vietnam War and branded America "the greatest purveyor of violence in the world." This got him banned from the White House, denounced by other civil rights leaders, and tagged a subversive that deserved all the foul, illegal targeting of the FBI and other government

agencies. The speech was visionary, embraced by peace activists, and stirred a wider soul search about state sponsored war, violence and terror, that came with a made in America label.

He supported struggles for racial and economic justice for Latinos, American Indians, and poor whites. These marked him as much more than a "black" or "civil rights" leader. It also was the watershed moment in the linkage of civil rights to the peace and anti-war movements.

* * * * *

It was the issue of war and peace that King set the moral template for the way he and millions more should oppose America's wars. He laid out the major points in his Riverside Church speech and in his unreserved backing for draft evaders, and other anti-Vietnam war protesters. However, there was more than morality and hatred of war behind King's aggressive anti-war stance. There was his pragmatism. In the Riverside speech, he gave "seven major reasons for bringing Vietnam into the field of my moral vision." In one of those reasons, he correctly saw that the billions spent on wars were billions that were drained from health, education, and job programs that could radically transform poor black and minority communities.

King said: "I knew that America would never invest the necessary funds or energies in rehabilitation of its poor so long as adventures like Vietnam continued to draw men and skills and money like some demonic destructive suction tube.

So, I was increasingly compelled to see the war as an enemy of the poor and to attack it as such."

Another of his reasons was his revulsion at the utter hypocrisy of pleading, cajoling, and demanding that the black poor embrace non-violence. This, while the government was killing thousands in a distant country in the name of peace and democracy.

"I knew that I could never again raise my voice against the violence of the oppressed in the ghettos." he made clear, "without having first spoken clearly to the greatest purveyor of violence in the world today—my own government. "

In the twelve months that King had to live after the Riverside speech he would repeatedly preach the twin themes of non-violence and the redistribution of public spending away from wars to America's inner cities, not to the ghetto poor, but to the federal government. It was a case of moral consistency and hard-nosed economics.

These two themes formed an early framework for what would become the standard arguments for anti-war protesters that took to the streets in 2005 to oppose then President George W. Bush's grossly ineffectual, and wasteful war against Iraq. The same protests were mounted later against then President Obama's escalation of the war in Afghanistan. No case could ever be made that King, had he lived, would have given any support to any of those wars whether waged by a conservative Republican, or a liberal, black Democratic President.

Whether it was his early and firm embrace of the peace movement, or the demand to end poverty and wealth

inequality, King put in place a workable model for battling these ills. The proof of his forward thinking about real solutions beyond protest is that almost all his proposals have been implemented, tried, discarded, or discredited.

King didn't just dream of a new world. He fought for it. In a later era when politicians and some civil rights leaders believe that grabbing a photo-op or a sound bite is leadership; King's vision and program still look and sound better than anything many of them offer.

CHAPTER 4

Getting a Piece
of the Legacy

The scramble to grab a piece of King's legacy has not diminished one bit in the fifty years since his murder. Those vying to cloak themselves in King's mantle have come from the far right to the far left and all political points in between. Conservative President Reagan was the first president to grab at the King legacy; after spending much time prior to his embrace of it in attacking it. Reagan fought tooth and nail against passage of the King holiday bill before signing it on November 2, 1983.

After insinuating that King was a Communist, Reagan signed the bill in 1983 only after Congress passed it with an overwhelming veto-proof majority (338 to 90 in the House of Representatives and 78 to 22 in the Senate). Next, Reagan reversed gears and apologized to a deeply hurt Coretta Scott King, King's widow, and effusively praised King as a

champion of freedom and democracy. Reagan said that King's struggle for equality was his struggle too.

During the furious battles that raged over affirmative action in the 1990s, conservatives snatched a flowery line from King's "I Have a Dream" speech and boasted that he would have opposed racial quotas, preferences and, by extension, affirmative action if he had lived. It was a wild stretch. King almost certainly would have been a vigorous supporter of affirmative action if he had lived.

In the late 1960s when King denounced the Vietnam war, embraced militant union struggles and barnstormed around the country blasting wealth and class privilege, the red-baiters and professional King haters branded him a Communist. The Johnson White House turned hostile after 1967. Corporate and foundation supporters slowly turned off the money spigot. The NAACP, Urban League, black Democrats, and some in King's own organization, turned their backs on him. During his last days, King spent much of his time fundraising and defending his policies against the critics within and without his organization. The backbiting of King by some of his one-time friends and supporters got worse when he railed against the penchant for lavish personal spending, luxury apartments and fancy homes by some of his group's staffers.

In his last installment on King, *At Canaan's Edge: America in the King Years, 1965-68*, Taylor Branch tells how King stormed out of a planning meeting on his Poor Peoples March in fury at the attacks at him by some of his top aides

who wanted to scrap the march. The issue of uniting masses of poor people for economic uplift smacked of class war and was just too risky and dangerous, they said. It would hopelessly alienate their Democratic Party boosters. King was unfazed by their criticism and hurled another broadside at them for their selfishness and opportunism.

King's civil rights friends weren't the only ones who took shots at him. Many black ministers joined in the King-bashing. At the National Baptist Convention in 1961, then and now the largest black religious group in America, King, and a band of dissidents, challenged the convention's leaders to give more active support to the civil rights battles. They wanted none of that. They flung un-Christian-like threats and insults at King and the civil rights advocate-ministers, engaged in fisticuffs with them and slandered King as a "hoodlum and crook."

When the dust settled, King was summarily booted out of the organization and set up a rival ministers group. Even after King's death, when he took his place among America's heroes, many black ministers remained stone silent on the assault on civil liberties protections, the gutting of job, social programs, and U.S. militarism. These were all issues that King relentlessly and loudly spoke out against when he was alive.

✶ ✶ ✶ ✶ ✶

In a sardonic, almost amusing way, King's enduring fame has made him ripe for the pickings of GOP conservatives

from time to time in the fifty years since his murder. There was no laughter, though in October 2006, when a woman in a 60 second radio ad said that "Dr. King was a Republican." The ad was bankrolled by the National Black Republican Association. It purportedly ran on several Baltimore radio stations. At first glance, the ad was a cheap political shot that stretched political lunacy far past the outer limit. But was it? The ad was not the first time that Republicans, and more specifically Republican conservatives, claimed King as one of their own.

The debate over whether King had anything in common with the GOP has raged since the 1980s. Republicans grabbed at King's famed line in his "I Have a Dream" speech at the March on Washington in August 1963, in which he called on Americans to judge individuals by the content of their character and not the color of their skin to prove that he'd be on their side against affirmative action. Supporters of affirmative action loudly protested that this deliberately distorted the spirit and intent of King's words. They have both been right.

During the fierce wars over affirmative action in the 1990's, King's words were shamelessly used to justify opposition to affirmative action. Yet, there is enough paradox and ambivalence in the few stray remarks that King uttered on the issue to give ideological ammunition to liberals and conservatives. In several speeches and articles in the 1960s, King did not demand that the government and corporations create special programs or incentives exclusively for blacks but to the disadvantaged of all races. He vaguely called for the

government and corporations to increase spending for jobs, skills training, education, and public works.

With the passage of the 1964 Civil Rights Act, King realized that ending legal segregation wasn't enough. Integrating a motel or lunch counter did not provide jobs, improved housing, or better schools for the black poor. These were stubborn and intractable problems that required massive spending on new social programs by government and business.

King felt that the bigger problem for blacks and whites was the disappearance of thousands of industry jobs to automation. He sensed that jobs were a volatile issue that could inflame blacks and whites. He claimed that black and white workers suffered equally when jobs were lost and tactfully called on labor to fight for jobs for all. But in those days affirmative action was a tool to prod employers not simply to hire and promote the disadvantaged of all races, as King insisted, but blacks. If that happened, King almost certainly knew that this would leave many whites out in the economic cold.

King's debatable ambiguity on affirmative action was only one issue that Republicans have manufactured common cause with him on. Going back to Reagan, Republican presidents slowly and grudgingly realized that they could wring maximum political mileage out of King's legacy. They have recast him in their image on civil rights, and bent and twisted his oft times public religious Puritanism on morals issues to justify GOP positions in the values wars that they wage with blacks, Democrats, and liberals.

That wouldn't have been possible if some of King's

pronouncements did not parallel the GOP's positions on crime, marriage, the family, and personal responsibility. Republicans have carefully cobbled bits and pieces from King's speeches and writings during the 1950s and early 1960s together on values issues to paint a King that is anti-big government, welfare, black crime, and an advocate of thrift, hard work, and temperance. This was not a completely politically skewered picture of King. In those speeches and writings, he took the moral high ground and lectured blacks on the value of hard work, the importance of setting personal goals, and striving to develop good character.

In countless speeches in the 1950s, he mingled the demand for civil rights, voting rights, and the government clampdown on racial violence, with a forceful call for blacks to practice thrift and self-help. King realized that government programs meant little if fathers weren't in the home, and he railed against the peril of family breakdown. This was a major social problem that civil rights leaders either ignored or downplayed. King again strongly emphasized values training, discipline, hard work, and the reduction of family violence as the key to resolve the family crisis. That crisis increasingly caught the policy attention of liberal and conservative academics and government officials.

In numerous speeches, even into the early 1960s, he continued to stress personal responsibility, economic self-help, strong families, and religious values as goals that blacks should strive to attain. The problem with this is that King at times veered into acceptance of many of the prevailing

stereotypes, then and now, about black families. Many impoverished black families, even fatherless poor families, placed a great deal of emphasis on education, and personal responsibility in raising their children. He later correctly put the blame for black family disruption squarely where it belongs on racial discrimination and poverty.

While King could never be considered a political conservative, the snippets of conservative thinking in his musings on the black family, economic uplift, and religious values blended easily with the social conservatism of many blacks, and has been deliberately twisted out of context by conservatives to paint a picture of King that suited their cynical political tastes. This evidently was more than enough for black Republicans four decades after his death to dare run a bogus and intimating that King was really one of them.

King, then, is no different than other towering historical figures, especially those that had the bad fortune to fall to an assassin's bullet. Hypocrisy, mythmaking, embellishments, and outright distortions will always swirl about them. Everyone wants a piece of the fallen legend to puff up their importance and whatever social and political ax they seek to grind. Fortunately, King's legacy is still big and wide enough to make an easy target for all to try and claim.

Ignoring a Holiday

I n January 2018, the King Holiday made news for another reason. Officials in Warner, Oklahoma were caught on tape making racial slurs about the holiday. One official purportedly said that they should honor King's assassin, James Earl Ray, instead. Now what was more revealing then the heinous remarks by the unnamed town officials was the casual response to them. Other than the pro forma promise to investigate, there was mute silence. There was absolutely no hint of any disciplinary action to be taken. The bigger question then was were the slurs just the digs from a handful of hateful, unreconstructed bigots? Or, did their rants represent the thinking of the town's white officials? It would have not have surprised if that were the case. It's not just bigoted individuals who disdain the King Holiday.

Each year, many corporations and government agencies plaster full-page ads in black newspapers that extol King on

his holiday and tout how much he's done for them. This, and the retailer's money making off King notwithstanding, the King holiday is still rock-bottom among the national holidays that business and government agencies observe. An annual survey by BNA Inc., a Washington-based business news publisher, taken prior to every King Holiday observance has revealed that about one-quarter of businesses give their workers a day off with pay.

This number pales even in comparison to the next least-celebrated holiday, Presidents Day.

In other words, the King holiday is still ignored by the majority of American businesses, the majority of organizations with a strong labor union presence, and a fair number of municipalities. Not only has there been only marginal and incremental increases in the number of businesses that officially acknowledge Martin Luther King Day in the past five years, but the number that do acknowledge it dropped from the all-time high of 33 percent of businesses that gave employees the day off in 2008. The employers and some municipalities that ignore the King holiday chalk up the failure to observe the day as simply a matter of cost, time and labor drain, instead of disrespect or any lack of appreciation for King. They argue they simply can't afford to shut down.

In part to counter that abysmal support and celebration of the holiday beyond mostly African-American communities, then President Obama and other administration officials in 2011 picked up on a call that had been made repeatedly by the King family and civil rights and social service

organizations. That is for the day to be not just about celebration, pageantry, and parades, but a day of service. Obama certainly owes a deep gratitude to King and the civil rights movement. It opened the political doors for him and a generation of other black political figures. Even so, his presidential appeals so far weren't enough to crack the lingering resistance to a full and total acknowledgement of the world altering significance of King and the movement that he led.

Still, the aim of Obama's "King initiative" for a day of service put White House muscle behind the true meaning and spirit of the day and King's life and work. However, that has only elicited at best a marginal response from anyone other than civil rights activists, educators, government officials, and service industry union officials and workers. This continuing indifference to the King Holiday strikes to the heart of the ambiguity that a wide segment of the public outside of blacks still regards King fifty years after his murder. That widespread indifference, even hostility, was evident from the very first moment that then Michigan Democrat John Conyers introduced a Martin Luther King Day bill in Congress immediately after King's assassination in April 1968.

The fight was bitter, contentious, and vicious. It took more than a decade for the bill to finally come to a vote in 1979. It failed, coming within five votes of passage. It took four more years of fierce battles in Congress, mass marches, demonstrations and countless petitions to get lawmakers to move on the legislation again.

Arch conservative then North Carolina Senator Jesse

Helms led the charge against the King holiday bill and questioned whether King was important enough to receive such an honor. He criticized King's opposition to the Vietnam war and repeatedly slurred him as an agitator, Communist, and, of course, unpatriotic. Reagan chimed in and cited cost concerns for scrapping the bill. Even after he grudgingly signed the King bill into law, it took another three years before the first Martin Luther King Day was officially observed. It would take even more bitter fights over the next quarter century before die-hard states such as Arizona, New Hampshire, and Utah finally came on board and officially recognized the holiday.

Even that hasn't ended the controversy and the infighting over the King holiday. The ploys to trivialize the accomplishments of King and the holiday have been endless and dastardly creative. One favorite is the weather. Some school districts hold classes on the King holiday to make up for the school time lost because of the inclement weather. This is one of the milder forms of subtle protests over the King Holiday

It took years of public protest and finally legislative action before Virginia in 2000 finally separated the state holiday commemorating Confederate generals and icons, Robert E. Lee and Stonewall Jackson from the King holiday. Arkansas, Alabama, Georgia, and Mississippi, fifty years later, still defiant. The states have refused to uncouple the commemoration of Lee's birthday from the King holiday. Occasionally a GOP politician will say something dumb and derisive about King on his holiday.

* * * * *

However, the greatest problem with the King holiday is that in far too many public and private circles it is still regarded as a "black holiday" or more charitably a "civil rights issue." This reinforces the chronic fiction that King was solely a black leader, and that the civil rights movement was a movement only for blacks. Therefore, his holiday should be celebrated exclusively by blacks.

King's "moral imperative" quickly stretched far past the limits of the civil rights movement. The leaders of the gay and women's rights movements were motivated by King's actions and borrowed heavily from the tactics of the civil rights movement. Cesar Chavez, who now has his own holiday in California and a few other states, repeatedly praised King and other civil rights leaders for encouraging and providing aid to the farm-worker and labor organizing battles.

The civil rights movement also had a major effect on other world struggles. It inspired activist priests in Latin America, students demonstrating against injustice in Europe, and the oppressed in South Africa fighting against apartheid.

King was the first major leader to condemn the Vietnam War and American militarism. He gave impetus and credibility to the antiwar movement and almost certainly would have been the first to hit the barricades to protest the Iraq and Afghanistan wars. The amnesia or ignorance of some about King's impassioned opposition to all wars has been on

permanent display in the virtual exorcising of King's 1967 ground breaking speech opposing the Vietnam War, and indeed all colonial and imperial wars. This is, and remains, historical revisionism with a vengeance.

King's moral vision and reach extended far beyond questions of war, peace and racial injustice. He saw that true democracy could never be realized without economic justice for the poor. He pounded away on the need to end class oppression and poverty. His Poor People's March in 1968 was a flawed but sincere effort to bring the poor of all races together to seek economic justice.

The civil rights movement, increased civil liberties protections and expanded universal voting rights together produced a vast array of legal, social and educational programs that permanently transformed American society and enriched the lives of Americans of all races and income groups, not just blacks.

Despite that rich and enduring past and present history of struggle and sacrifice, the resurgence of white nationalist and overt racist sentiment and actions stand as stark reminder to the continuing peril to civil rights gains. In the Trump era, it's even easier to see why the King holiday is still embroiled in racial rancor, and sadly blind eye, indifference, or even hostility in wide circles.

In a perverse, backdoor way, this pays tribute to the powerful emotions that King still elicits in many Americans fifty years after his murder. The King holiday will likely stand for many years to come as a bellwether of how far America

has come and how far it still must go to fulfill King's fight and vision of a racially and economically just society.

.

CHAPTER 6

Cashing in on King

"**M**LK Event Huge Savings! Up to 50% off on over 500 styles" the GAP clothing retailer tweeted and emailed this ad to thousands of customers a few days before the start of the King Holiday in January 2014. The Gap was hardly the first retailer to cash in on the King Holiday.

In fact, this will give an idea just how much of a cash cow the biggest of the big retailers see the King Holiday.

Macy's MLK Day Sale

Dates: TBA

Though Macy's hasn't announced the details of its MLK Day sale, expect it to follow a similar structure to previous Macy's holiday sales: 20 percent off sitewide with free shipping on qualifying orders. Further details are expected to be announced over the weekend.

Bloomingdale's MLK Day Sale

Dates: Jan. 12 – Jan. 16

Bloomingdale's is running a number of deals on home goods and sale items over Martin Luther King Jr. Day weekend and throughout January. Offers include:

• Up to 75 percent off linens, small appliances and other bed, bath and kitchen products.

• An extra 50 percent off sale items.

Gap MLK Day Sale

Dates: Jan. 5 – Jan. 16

Gap is clearing stores for spring fashions with a huge sale on winter merchandise. Noteworthy deals from Gap include:

• Up to 75 percent off apparel for women, men, kids, plus fitness and maternity.

• 40 percent off your order with promo code GOOD-START.

• An extra $25 in Gap cash for every $50 or more spent.

Pottery Barn MLK Day Sale

Dates: Throughout Jan. 29

Every January, Pottery Barn hosts one of the best white sales in the business. Over Martin Luther King Jr. Day weekend, the home goods retailer will take 20 percent off a wide array of bed and bath products. Visit Pottery Barn over the holiday to save on bath towels, loungewear, duvets and sheets.

Saks Fifth Avenue MLK Day Sale

Dates: Jan. 12 – Jan. 16

The Saks Fifth Avenue MLK Day sale kicks off on Thursday and runs through the long weekend. During the sale, the designer will offer bedding, bath, kitchen, and home dining products at up to 30 percent off.

There were dozens more similar ads from retailers hawking every imaginable clothing item and product during King week.

Then there were the corporate giants such as Phonevite. It got even sneakier and disguised its King Day money grab with a picture of King captioned, "Day of Service." This was an obvious play on the call by the King Center to make the day a day, not of merry making and shopping. But a day to recommit to the value of service to a community betterment cause or activity that was the very marrow of what King stood for.

✳ ✳ ✳ ✳ ✳

The King holiday by the fourth decade after his assassination had become big, and a very profitable business, for retailers. There were predictable grumbles that having sales and commercializing the King Holiday was virtually sacrilege and mocked everything that he stood for. Turning King into big business certainly did that. It was not hard to predict this would eventually happen.

Every major American holiday from Christmas on down

has been transformed into a day not of religious observance (Christmas) or historical reverence (Presidents or Memorial Days) but a chance to make a buck. The bucks that are made are often the chance for big and small businesses to pad their profit margin with stepped up merchandise sales. For others, it can mean the difference between whether they stay afloat or close their doors. Despite the protests that commercializing holidays defames the significance of them, consumers have happily given their assent to the commercial hype by packing the stores on these days. So, the buy spirit is a two-way street, retailers promote, and consumers are conditioned through years of ad pitches and price enticements to shop and purchase on those days.

The King Holiday's trajectory to becoming a commercially hyped holiday has been tortured. In the early years, it was widely shunned by a wide swatch of the public. Or, seen by many as a "black holiday." Coretta Scott King, ever sensitive, of how the King Holiday should be viewed and treated warned:" Whether you are African-American, Hispanic, or Native American, whether you are Caucasian or Asian-American, you are part of the great dream Martin Luther King, Jr. had for America. This is not a black holiday; it is a peoples' holiday. "

Major businesses, at least, in the beginning largely heeded the admonition of the King family and civil rights activists to keep their commercial hands off the holiday. It was to be celebrated as they repeatedly shouted as a day of remembrance of King's dedication and commitment to civil

rights and social change in America and globally. This was the noble, high road motive. The crasser reason was that most businesses simply did not see the day as important or popular enough to nudge large numbers of buyers into department stores. Who would think of giving a King Day gift or card?

However, as more states, counties, and cities, and private businesses acknowledged the King Holiday with a day off, things changed. Thousands more workers now had free day to engage in leisure pursuit. Retailers quickly picked up on this new sales opportunity, and now the first advertisements for King Day sales began popping up in newspapers. The lure as always was the chance to save a few dollars on the purchase of an item.

The appeal by the King Center and Obama to make the day a day of service, oddly, did not seem to conflict with the retailer's pitch to make it a day of profit for them. At no point, did the King Center or Obama expressly chide businesses for pumping the King Holiday as a day to buy. The silence while not exactly condoning the increasing commercial bent of the day, gave implicit consent that the notion of performing a service act in the name of King and making a dollar off King were not inherently incompatible.

* * * * *

The groundwork for the full throttle commercialization of King, ironically, came from another source: The King family. In 2001, an ad prominently appeared in local newspapers that showed digitally doctored footage of King's "I Have

a Dream Speech." The twist was that the ovations from the Washington D.C. crowd that August 1963 day were nowhere to be heard. Instead there was the appeal to buy an Alcatel cell phone. The commercial use of one of King's most valued speeches was approved by a spin-off operation named King Inc. It was the brainchild of a King family member. Alcatel was granted the right to use the speech of course for a price.

The word was now out that King Inc. was ready and willing to do business; the business was trading the King name for a fee. Deals were soon in the pipeline to sell King's speeches and writings to private bidders, a sale of King's home and buildings in the King Center complex to the National Park Service, and even Coretta's love letters to and from King to a New York publisher.

Other King family members and some of King's closest supporters and aides in the civil rights fights of the 1960s were appalled at the money grab in King's name. There was a round of suits and countersuits, accusations and charges of profiteering against King Inc. flew hot and heavy. The issue was money and whether King's name should be turned into a cash cow for the King family.

The attempt by some King family members to cash in on his name and fame is hardly unique to King. The heirs of George Washington, FDR, Eisenhower, Nixon and Einstein, and countless other name individuals have cut deals with private collectors, auction houses, universities and government entities for the papers, manuscripts, speeches, and other personal items belong to their famed relative; all for a hefty price.

Indeed, there is nothing morally or ethically wrong in the families of a famous figure selling the valued property to benefit the family. The King family was no exception and it would be wrong to hold them to a higher standard than other heirs that made money from their famed relatives possessions.

The problem is that in King's case, it opened the commercial floodgates for major corporations to make money off his name; and none of them made any pretense to do it because they needed the money, let alone to pay homage to his legacy of battling against racial and economic injustice.

It's no stretch to say that King would have been repelled by the morph of his name into a dollars and cents proposition. There are many quotes sprinkled throughout his speeches and writings where he repeatedly condemned the unbridled quest for profit and materialism. In his 1967 speech denouncing the Vietnam War he was explicit, and called the blind pursuit of wealth the corroded symptom of a "thing oriented" society. He went further and demanded that the nation undergo a "radical revolution of values."

It isn't just his words that give a tip as to how King regarded the unabashed pursuit of profit in his name. There was his personal life. He was an austere man and that extended to his household. He lived in a modest, rented home. It was dubbed "spartan-like simplicity." He drove a 1960 Ford with more than 70,000 miles on the odometer. There were no second cars, maids, or helpers. The burden for caring for the children fell almost exclusively on Coretta's shoulders. He

donated his speaking fees, honorariums, and royalties from book sales to SCLC.

Then there was the Nobel Prize. It carried with it a purse of $54,000. Coretta wanted some of the money used for an education fund and other family necessities. King said no. He was emphatic that the prize money be used for civil rights activities and not for his and his family's personal benefit. While King was not a pauper, by no standard could he be considered anywhere near wealthy at the time of his murder.

So, bargain sales, discounted items, and advertisements imploring shoppers to buy, buy, buy in his name are hardly the values revolution that King had in mind.

King almost certainly would not have been surprised that his name had become a commodity. He understood the fetish that a nation that put profit before people could operate in no other way than to turn anything of value into a sellable item. His murder, the holiday, and subsequent enshrinement as a towering historical figure, virtually guaranteed that one day he too would be just that; for many, namely a saleable item.

CHAPTER 7

Obama's Debt to King

I t was more than fitting that then President Barack Obama's presidential inauguration in January 2009 fell on the King holiday. It was even more fitting that he took the oath of office on the bible that King used.

More than any other resident of the White House, Obama understood that King was a big reason for his political success. Then Democratic presidential candidate Obama first publicly expressed deep gratitude to King and the civil rights movement in a speech in Selma, Alabama in March 2007. During his eight years in the White House, he referenced King many times.

An accurate, but often overlooked read of King's legacy was not just his monumental fight against racial segregation. King was also a masterful political analyst and strategist. He recognized that winning battles against segregation was much easier than breaking the strangle hold of Jim Crow

political disempowerment. White political domination and black political disfranchisement were the twin cornerstones to maintain economic and social segregation for a near century. If blacks in the South and elsewhere could not vote, they could not hold political office. If they could not hold political office, they would have absolutely no chance to change the rigid laws that entrenched segregation.

He understood that ultimately the battle for political enfranchisement didn't solely entail challenging the dominance of bigoted white Southern politicians. He also had to challenge the Democratic and Republican parties nationally. He led massive protest marches at both the 1960 Democratic convention and Republican conventions in Los Angeles and Miami. He did more. He also put forth a pointed agenda for civil rights to both conventions demanding an end to Jim Crow restrictions on voting in the South.

In the next few years, King stepped up the assault on Jim Crow politics. He coupled his mass marches against segregated public accommodations with voter registration and education drives, relentless court challenges to the poll tax, literacy tests, and political gerrymandering. These along with naked terror were the ancient weapons the white South used to chase blacks from the polls. King relentlessly pushed the Justice Department and the FBI to protect blacks that sought to register from the organized terror campaign.

King backed to the hilt the formation of the Mississippi Freedom Democratic Party in 1964, and its challenge to the seating of the lily-white Mississippi delegation at the

1964 Democratic Convention. He was instrumental in bro-
kering the deal with Lyndon Johnson and the Democratic
Party stalwarts to seat some members of the MFDP. This was
the first real crack in the armor of white political power and
dominance. It set the stage for the passage of the 1965 Voting
Rights Act that blew apart whites only political domination
and paved the way for the explosion for a time in the number
of black elected officials in the coming decades. The number
of black elected officials nationally soared from fewer than
100 to the mid-1960s to over 10,000 in 2015 but has slowed.

King also quickly realized that transforming the political
process would insure that more elected black officials could
be advocates for political equality in the South and in major
urban areas in the North where blacks increasingly were the
majority of the population. This was especially important to
King who never lost sight of the fact that the legacy of segregation, bigotry, and discrimination trapped thousands of
poor blacks that offered no easy resolution.

Obama vehemently took exception to the notion that the
civil rights movement is outdated, or worse, that he somehow
supplants the ongoing work of civil rights leaders. He did not
buy into the notion that his election signaled the nation has
reached the nirvana of a post racial society. Since the first
public acknowledgement he made of the debt of gratitude
he owed King and the civil rights movement, he repeatedly
praised past civil rights leaders for their heroic battle against
racial injustice and not just yearly during the King holiday
celebration.

This was an appropriate tribute to the civil rights movement that challenged the nation to make King's dream of justice and equality a reality. Obama faced that challenge and defied the racial odds in winning the White House. He could not have beaten the odds without the hard, patient, in the trenches effort of, and recognition by, King that political empowerment was the key to racial uplift.

The number of black elected officials nationally soared from fewer than 100 to the mid-1960s to over 10,000 in 2015.

*   *   *   *   *

There's a cautionary note about the impact King's understanding of, and push for black political empowerment had on American politics. The empowerment has been under withering assault in every one of those fifty years since King's murder. The main point of attack has been the 1965 Voting Rights Act that King did much to spur passage of in the backdrop of the national shock and revulsion over the brutal and bloody rampage by white state troopers in Selma in 1965. Since then, a succession of GOP leaders, state legislators, girded by various federal court decisions, and the reflexive rightist four, and sometimes, five U.S. Supreme Court justices, have waged relentless war on the Act. The deal in the initial passage of the Act was that it would be renewed every 25 years.

When the Act came up for renewal in 1981, hardline ultraconservatives in the administration of then President Reagan made loud threats to push Reagan to oppose its renewal. They were just that, idle threats. Reagan with no fanfare

signed the renewal legislation. When the Act came up for renewal again in 2006, the threats to thwart the law, turned into a mini-movement in Congress to delay or even block passage. A pack of House Republicans stalled the legislation for more than a week and demanded that hearings be held.

The standard attack line has always been that it punishes the South for past voting discrimination sins, and that the thousands of black and Hispanic legislators in the South, Southwest, and West is supreme proof that the crude, naked race based voter suppression ploys was a thing of a long gone past. Bush signed the renewal order. But the GOP had served notice that the early saber rattle against the Act was a just a warm-up for a full throttle frontal assault. The GOP pecked at eroding the Act with the rash of photo identifications laws that the GOP governors and GOP controlled state legislatures enacted in recent years. The aim was to discourage and damp down the number of minority and poor voters that overwhelmingly vote Democratic.

Then enter the Supreme Court. In the *Shelby County v. Holder* case in 2013, the Alabama county claimed the Act is outdated, discriminatory, and a blatant federal intrusion into state's rights. The lawsuit explicitly wants the centerpiece of the Act, Section 5 dumped. This is the provision that mandates that states get "preclearance" from the Justice Department before making any changes in voting procedures. State attorneys general in several states have endorsed the Alabama County's challenge. Chief Justice John Roberts bluntly said that things have changed in the South and that blacks

supposedly vote everywhere in the South without any barriers or prohibitions. SCOTUS Clarence Thomas, to no surprise, went even further and flatly called Section 5 of the Act unconstitutional and left no doubt when he had the chance he'd knock the Act out completely. The provision was scrapped.

GOP-controlled legislatures in six states in the South and Southwest where voting rights procedures were covered by that part of the act wasted no time in passing a slew of restrictive voting laws that the Voting Rights Act had previously blocked. This brought the total to more than 20 states that have passed tough voting restrictions, according to the Brennan Center for Justice. Even though black and Hispanic voters did vote in big numbers in the 2012 election, in many districts they still had to stand in endless lines, have their IDs thoroughly scrutinized, had no bilingual ballots, found voting hours shortened, and had to file time consuming legal challenges in state and federal courts to get injunctions to stop the more onerous of the voter suppression laws from being enforced.

This was only part of the story of the roadblocks the GOP has thrown up. A study by the Alliance for Justice, a Washington D.C. based, public interest group, documented legions of complaints and challenges filed by the Justice Department and voting rights groups to discriminatory changes that county registrars have made to eliminate or narrow down the number of voters in predominantly minority districts. The tales of supposed massive voter fraud egged on by civil rights, voter rights advocacy groups and orchestrated

by the Democrats has been just that, self-serving tales.

There has never been any evidence to support any of the GOP charges of massive voter hanky-panky. This didn't stop President Trump, who after his inauguration in January 2017, wasted no time in pandering to GOP conservatives and formed a rump committee to investigate alleged voting fraud. It was laughable and widely ridiculed. But it served as yet one more warning that wherever the GOP has its way, the emergence of new Obamas would be thwarted.

King was the driving force to meet and overcome the barriers to black political empowerment. And while his success was the big reason Obama took the oath of presidential office in 2008, and took it again in 2012, politics was only one part of the link between King and Obama.

* * * * *

Another was just how much the nation's first African-American president could do to advance King's two signature issues—jobs and the assault on poverty. The news photo was literally worth a thousand words in August 2011. There was President Obama, Daisy Bates, and a group of White House staffers gazing at the world-famous Norman Rockwell portrait prominently positioned on a West Wing wall of a black girl being escorted by federal marshals through a howling mob of enraged whites to class. The class was at Little Rock's previously segregated Central High School in 1957. Bates was one of the prime movers behind the school desegregation movement in Little Rock.

Though Obama gave no reason why he chose to hang the portrait in a conspicuous spot on a West Wing wall, it was no accident that he did. The portrait was hung there just days before he was scheduled to give his much touted and long-awaited speech at the unveiling ceremony of the Martin Luther King Jr. Monument on the National Mall. Hanging the Rockwell painting was more than symbolism.

Though the King Memorial unveiling, and Obama's speech was postponed due to a Hurricane threat at the time, the portrait was a strong signal that race would have been very much on the table in the speech he would have given at the King monument unveiling. And well it should have been. Obama was ripped at a couple of times during his White House tenure by the Congressional Black Caucus and other blacks for not doing or even saying enough about the colossal crisis of black joblessness and poverty. Polls showed that the criticism touched a nerve with many blacks. His performance rating on the jobs issue had plunged for a time among them. The tiniest chink in Obama's black support was cause for deep worry at the White House. He needed black voters to turn the 2012 presidential re-election campaign into the same, fiery holy crusade that they did in 2008. That meant a turnout in numbers, big numbers, in the key battleground states.

However, it was the color issue, namely that he was black, and therefore he was supposed to have an even greater sensitivity to the plight of the black poor. And because of that he had a special duty, obligation and even mission to use the

power and prestige of the office to do and say more for blacks.

For much of his first term, Obama walked a perilous racial tight rope. On the one hand he was hyper cautious not to give any ammunition to bigots to paint him as a race conscious or even race baiting African-American by speaking out on racial matters. On the other hand, he did what he could quietly to boost black appointments to judgeships, federal posts, and get the best deal he could from a GOP sworn to make him a one-term president, on education, jobs, and health care spending and preserve Social Security and Medicare, and Medicaid.

This only fueled criticism that Obama was not doing more to fulfill the King mission. The 1963 March on Washington that brought King world-wide attention and stamped him as a transformative leader for the ages brought thousands of persons together across gender, class, and color lines in a vocal protest against intolerance and violence. That was the hope and promise of Obama's election. It showed that millions of whites could strap racial blinders around their eyes and punch the ticket for an African-American for the world's most powerful political post. King would undoubtedly have glowed with approval at that.

Yet, the same ugly hate that King faced, Obama faced too. The racially tinged, and in some cases blatant racial vilification and ridicule of him, and even issuing veiled physical threats against him by the pack of extreme Tea Party leaders, right wing talk show gabbers, and bloggers and websites was relentless during his first couple of years in the Oval Office.

Polls then showed that a significant percentage of whites vehemently opposed Obama's policies on health care, and the economy. The slur was continually made that Obama was a closet Marxist and racial agitator. These were the exact same slurs that were repeatedly tossed at Dr. King.

The centerpiece of King's March on Washington speech and his decade of activism for racial justice and tolerance was that America could both be pushed rudely, or gently evolve, into a color-blind society. He didn't mean the phony, deliberate, and self-serving distortion of his words by many conservatives to hammer affirmative action, special programs, and initiatives and increased spending on jobs, education, and health programs for African-Americans and minorities. King never lost sight of the fact that the legacy of segregation, bigotry, and discrimination trapped thousands of poor blacks and that offered no easy resolution. Even as the King Monument was unveiled in Washington D.C. in August 2011, the black poor were still just as tightly trapped in the grip of poverty and discrimination that King warned about.

Obama decried any thought that the civil rights movement was outdated and that he supplanted the ongoing work of civil rights leaders. He made a point to tell Bates that without "you guys I might not be here." That said it. It was a fitting tribute to the civil rights movement that challenged the nation to make King's dream of justice and equality a reality. Obama firmly understood that there was still much more to overcome.

The Other Civil Rights Movement

During a planning summit in Atlanta for his Poor Peoples March in March 1968, Dr. Martin Luther King Jr. quizzically turned to one of his aides and asked, "Tijerina who?" The Tijerina in question was Reies Lopez Tijerina. A year earlier, he had rocketed to national fame when he and a band of armed men took over a courthouse in New Mexico and demanded land rights for Mexican farm workers. Though King hadn't heard of Tijerina, he eagerly sought him out. He demanded that he and other Latino leaders play a top role in the march. King wanted Latinos, blacks, American Indians and poor whites to march in lockstep for civil rights and economic justice. King, though, was virtually a lone voice calling for such an alliance.

Many in King's inner circle of black ministers and activists grumbled loudly that black leaders must call the shots

in the march. Their meaning was clear: Blacks had done the marching, picketing, demonstrating, fighting and dying for civil rights, and racism affected blacks more deeply and profoundly than any other group. To them, the struggle for land and immigrant rights was a sideshow that did not have the glitter, glamour, or poignancy of the black struggle. Latinos and other ethnic groups were at best subservient partners that were welcome if they knew their place. The most crass and cynical of King's black advisors regarded Latinos as interlopers who benefited from the black struggle, but had contributed nothing to it.

According to King biographer David Garrow, at a planning staff meeting, a campaign advisor bluntly said, "I do not think I am at the point where a Mexican can sit-in and call strategy on a steering committee." It was paternalistic, offensive, and totally denigrated Latinos and the importance of their struggle.

Tijerina and other Latino leaders chaffed at the slight, and some refused to participate. Those who came made it clear that their struggle against racism, for land and farm worker rights, and for cultural identity was just as important as that of blacks. They demanded that they be recognized and respected as leaders.

King's murder, the collapse of the civil rights movement, and the self-destruct of the black power movement brought fragmentation and disillusionment to black organizations. King and a handful of other black activists saw the fight by first- and second-generation Latinos for civil rights and

economic justice as a vital one, a struggle as important as the black civil rights battle. But they were gone now. That leadership vacuum marked the start of the retreat to race isolation.

By the 1990s, the steady rise in the number of immigrants, legal and illegal, had radically changed the shape of ethnic politics in America. The number of undocumented immigrants soared from an estimated 3 to 5 million in 1990 to double-digit numbers two decades later. Many now worked jobs in cities such as Detroit, Chicago, Washington, D.C., and Atlanta that were majority black, or where blacks made up a significant percent of the population. In those cities, Latinos made up the largest number of illegal immigrants who worked in lower-skill and low-wage jobs.

* * * * *

By 2004, Latinos had displaced blacks as the largest non-white minority in America. More blacks sounded the alarm bell. They bitterly complained that Latinos were overcrowding what had formerly been exclusively black neighborhoods and were running down achievement standards in schools. The issue that pricked the sorest spot was jobs. Blacks shouted that illegal immigrants had booted them out of unskilled entry-level jobs in hotels, restaurants, and car washes.

Generations of black students and the black unskilled had used these jobs as a stepping-stone up the economic ladder to better paying and more highly skilled jobs and professions. Immigrant rights groups countered that these were jobs that blacks wouldn't take anyway, and in bashing

Latinos, blacks were unfairly scapegoating them for their loss of economic ground.

By now, the memory of black and Latino cooperation that had marked the Poor Peoples March had long since faded. For too many blacks and Latinos, that model no longer seemed relevant.

They were wrong. Despite its gargantuan logistical problems, mishaps and ideological rifts, the march still ranked as the best effort black and Latino leaders had made to forge an alliance to fight for civil rights and economic justice. For King and the small band of black visionary activists, injustice was injustice, and it didn't matter whether the victim was an American-born black or a foreign-born Latino.

Four decades later, in the spring 2007, immigrant rights leaders again loudly demanded that civil rights groups take part in immigration marches and endorse immigration reform bills in Congress. They branded the immigration battle the new civil rights movement, and insisted that if King were still alive, he would back their claim.

It's risky to say what King would have done on that score. It's almost certain, though, that given his passionate support of the mostly Latino-led farm workers movement in California, and his glowing praise of farm worker leader Cesar Chavez, he would have regarded the immigration reform fight as a bonafide civil rights battle.

For that too-brief moment in history, the Poor Peoples March meshed the old civil rights movement for black rights with a broader movement for the civil rights of other

minorities. By then the immigrant rights movement had become the new civil rights movement. Nearly every civil rights organization, harked back to the earlier King model for outreach to, and support of, immigrant rights as an important civil rights issue.

Mainstream civil rights leaders went further and aggressively lobbied for passage of one immigration reform bill that had been sharply debated in Congress in 2006, Wade Henderson, the then chair of the civil rights organizations umbrella group, the Leadership Conference on Civil Rights, bluntly said, "I do not see this as an issue of economics, I see it as a moral one, and I believe it goes directly to our most basic understanding of civil and human rights." Henderson went further and voiced a sentiment that put him and the civil rights organizations squarely at odds with many blacks when he noted that he did not "share the simplistic and divisive view that immigrants are to blame or that they are 'stealing jobs' from any population of native born Americans."

Many blacks, though, feared just that. Some polls did show that many blacks were hostile toward illegal immigrants. The sore point with them was jobs. They blamed illegal immigrants for worsening the dire plight of young, poor African-American males. Various studies by researchers at Harvard, Columbia, and Princeton, and the Urban League's annual *State of Black America* reports confirmed that black males suffer a jobless rate double and triple that of white males in some urban areas. Their unemployment numbers are also substantially higher than those of Latino males.

Some economists and employment studies finger illegal immigration as a big cause of the economic slippage of low and marginally skilled young black males. There is some evidence that the poorest and least skilled blacks have lost jobs to illegal immigrants. However, that job loss was not unique to blacks. Unskilled workers of all ethnic groups, including white unskilled workers, lose jobs as the number of unskilled laborers increases—regardless of whether those in the expanding pool of unskilled workers are illegal immigrants or native-born.

* * * * *

This raises the larger question would King's inclusionary position during the days of the Poor Peoples Campaign to build alliances with Latino groups specifically around the anti-poverty fight translate into backing for immigration reform. In 1968, this had not become a flashpoint issue. This gave conservatives and immigration reform opponents just enough wiggle room to claim King as one of their own.

That's exactly what a group called Californians for Population Stabilization (CAPS), an anti-immigration group, did in 2014 and 2015. They bankrolled TV ads knocking Obama for signing an executive order granting work authorization to a sizable number of America's undocumented immigrants. They brashly claimed this was a slap at King's vision ending with the poignant question, "Was that Dr. King's dream?" Civil rights organizations, of course, say just the opposite that support of the rights of immigrants was very much a part of

King's dream for two incontestable reasons. The first is his reading of, an adherence to, Biblical teachings about justice and fairness to the downtrodden and dispossessed. That certainly included immigrants seeking jobs and a better life in America, and subject to jailing, deportation, and discrimination. King gave a strong hint of his thinking in his famous "Letter from a Birmingham Jail," where he flatly said:

"Injustice anywhere is a threat to justice everywhere. Anyone who lives inside the United States can never be considered an outsider anywhere within its bounds."

He was referring specifically to the charge from Birmingham city officials that he was an "outside agitator" coming into Birmingham in 1963 to lead civil rights protests. However, this admonition was as much a human-rights as a civil rights question. To attain both, no one should be excluded in the effort to achieve justice and a decent quality of life, or considered an outcast beyond the protection of the law and society.

A second reason King eagerly sought out Latino activists in his coalition for change movement was because he saw it as a broader human rights issue and one that demanded humane treatment irrespective of whether one had legal papers or not. King said as much to Cesar Chavez in a September 1966 telegram. King understood Chavez's United Farmworkers was predominantly made up of undocumented workers. Nevertheless, he wrote, "As brothers in the fight for equality.... Our struggles are really one: a struggle for freedom, for dignity and for humanity." It is beyond rational thought to think

that King would applaud Trump's name calling of undocumented workers as "rapists and terrorists," or that he would turn a blind eye to the plight of undocumented immigrant children threatened with deportation from this country.

King's ready grasp of the importance of building an all inclusive civil rights movement that spanned all ethnic groups, no matter their legal citizenship status, serve as a template then and now for building an inclusive, broad based civil rights movement that fights for the rights of all, with or without papers.

CHAPTER 9

The Poor Haven't Gone Away

Weeks before King's murder he pushed and prodded his organization, the Southern Christian
Leadership Council (SCLC) to pen an open letter to President Johnson and Congressional leaders imploring them to pass legislation that would guarantee everyone
a job. It was in part an updated version of the call that President Franklin Roosevelt had made two decades earlier in his
1944 State of the Union address that he branded "A second
Bill of Rights." He called for guaranteed jobs for all.

The other part of the SCLC economic rights call was the
total shift that King had made by that point from emphasis
on civil rights protest and legislative campaigns to what he
now viewed as the far deeper, thorny, and challenging problem of wealth and income inequality in America. King for
years had warned that civil rights without the guarantee of

jobs and a living wage would render the victories of the civil rights movement incomplete at best, and a cruel mockery at worst.

King's war against wealth inequality didn't stop there. He upped the ante by calling for unconditional cash transfers to citizens to boost their income, strengthening the activism and bargaining power of labor unions, and the guarantee of a job to everyone able to work. King summed up his economic egalitarianism this way, "I hope that a specific number of jobs is set forth, that a program will emerge to abolish unemployment, and that there will be another program to supplement the income of those whose earnings are below the poverty level."

This was a tough sell. A burned out, lame duck President Johnson would invest no more political capital in a fresh fight against poverty, and there was even less appetite for such a fight within Congress in the days before or after King's murder. There was no evidence that public opinion was any more favorable to the cause of ending poverty especially if it meant spending untold billions on that. The focus of poverty as an issue of urgency for the nation to address in effect died with King.

The poor weren't going to go away. In the decades since King's death their numbers continued to grow. As King knew a disproportionate of those sunk in poverty were blacks and Hispanics. They were nearly twice as likely as whites to be poor. Racial distinctions aside, the census figures showed that there were a lot of poor whites too, and what's become

an increasingly even more common trend many of those who tumbled into the poverty column were those who at one time were by all measures considered middle class.

Yet, as King realized, the existence of millions of poor people was never enough to push policy makers to action. In fact, it's become almost a ritual for a government report to come out yearly showing poverty on the rise. It makes the headlines one day. The next day it is forgotten. Poverty as it was in King's day, and now, has remained the taboo word on the political campaign stump, among lawmakers, the media, and the public. It remains even a taboo word among many of the poor.

Political and public references to poverty virtually disappeared from the nation's vocabulary by the end of the 1960s. The continued existence of so many poor people after a decade of civil rights gains, the rash of initiatives and programs to end poverty, and massive government spending on the poverty programs by Johnson in the 1960s, seemed ultimate proof to many that tossing money and programs at ending poverty was flawed, failed, and wasteful. It seemed to fly squarely in the face of the embedded *laissez faire* notion that the poor in America aren't poor because of any failing of the system, but because of their personal failings.

This was not just the hard-bitten attitude of GOP free market conservatives. It was the attitude of most Americans, including many of those who were poor. When poverty started to inch up in 2001, National Public Radio (NPR), the Kaiser Family Foundation, and Harvard University's Kennedy

School, conducted a national poll to find out just what Americans attributed poverty in the nation to. The terms that were bandied about by many of the respondents no matter their background was that the poor were "unmotivated," "lacked aspirations to get ahead," and "didn't work hard enough." A majority believed America was a place where with hard work and determination anyone could succeed. In other words, the loud message was that if you're poor, it's your fault, don't blame society, and especially don't look to government to be the cure.

Democratic presidents and presidential contenders took this message to heart. Still reeling from the fierce conservative backlash to the perceived failure of Johnson's war on poverty, they gingerly moved around making any public pronouncements about massive government spending hikes on welfare, income supplement, and health care programs for the next two decades. The Democrats trembled that such talk would only stir up white anger by reinforcing the old perception that Democrats tilt toward minorities, and especially blacks.

*   *   *   *   *

There was some hope during the 2008 presidential campaign that Democrats might lift the taboo about talking about the plight of the poor. Democratic presidential contender John Edwards fueled that hope when he openly talked about poverty, and that he would make the issue one of the centerpieces of his campaign. In a well-publicized appearance, Edwards launched his presidential campaign in the

front yard of a mangled brick house in New Orleans's mostly black, Katrina- and poverty-devastated Upper Ninth Ward. He talked boldly about the need to crusade against poverty.

Democratic presidential rivals Obama and Hillary Clinton, not to be outdone, also gave speeches challenging the nation to do more to alleviate poverty. The talk didn't last. Except for Edwards, whose candidacy quickly disintegrated after public revelations about his love tryst, the candidates didn't utter another word about poverty during the rest of the campaign. The GOP presidential contender, John McCain, as expected, made no mention of poverty as a policy issue either.

The mantra for the GOP and many Democrats is always deficit reduction, tax cuts, measured, narrow spending on infrastructure projects to jump start the economy. The widespread view that government should play a minimal role in assisting the poor crept through in Obama's speeches. It didn't go much further than that.

However, just as the poor weren't going away, King's proposals to deal with them and wealth inequality weren't forgotten either. King's old organization, the SCLC, in part out of tribute to King, and in part because wealth inequality and poverty still slammed hardest at blacks, made a renewal of the battle against both a central theme of its annual convention in fittingly enough in Memphis in July 2017. There was even some talk of restaging King's Poor People's Campaign as a symbolic gesture to remind the public of King's action plan to fight poverty. SCLC President Charles Steele even snatched a page from King's 1967 book *Where Do We*

Go from Here: Chaos or Community? To drive home the point that any new anti-poverty initiative rests squarely on King's work. As he put it, "I'm asked all the time, 'Where do we go from here?'" "We go back to the streets...back to non-violent protest..."

This is certainly the way King planned and envisioned his campaign's approach to getting the ear of the public and policy makers. However, there was one big difference between 1968 and 2018. There was a liberal Democratic president in the Oval Office, and Congress still had a residue of sympathy toward the civil rights movement and support for expanding civil rights protections. No such support or sympathy exists today for civil rights, let alone tackling poverty and wealth inequality, in Trump's White House or the GOP controlled Congress. Both have sprinted full speed in the exact opposite direction from King's economic fairness and justice fight by shoving even more wealth to corporations and the super-rich through massive tax giveaways to them. The result of that along with the peck away at spending on job, health and edu-cation programs will be to further widen the gap between the rich and the poor in America.

The odds are far longer to get any mention of poverty by Trump or the GOP as a compelling issue. Yet, the betting odds are that this would not deter King from trying if he were alive. This would be the kind of fight that he would relish precisely because he believed in, and was totally committed to the cause of ending poverty.

On March 31, 1968, four days before he was assassinated,

King made that quite clear. He stood in the pulpit and addressed a packed audience at National Cathedral in Washington, D.C. to deliver one of his last sermons. The title was "Remaining Awake through a Great Revolution." He warned and asked, "This is America's opportunity to help bridge the gulf between the haves and the have-nots. The question is whether America will do it."

Fifty years after he admonished the audience to make ending poverty and wealth inequality a national priority, the question as he put it still stands. Will it ever do it?

Yes to Gay Rights

"[M]y father] did not take a bullet for same-sex marriage." The speaker flatly said in a speech at a church meeting in New Zealand in 2010. She doubled down on this categorical statement in another broadside against gay marriage in the *Atlantic* magazine in August 2013, "I value marriage between a man and woman. Spiritually I value that. Psychologically I value that."

The speaker was Bernice King. The father she referenced was Dr. King. Bernice's timing in evoking her father's name to insist that he'd oppose gay marriage and the fight for gay rights was prompted in part because of her hardline evangelicalism. She was, as her father, a Baptist minister. She also was a name figure in the drive against the snow balling move by states at the time to legalize gay marriage. It was one thing though for her to oppose gay marriage and rights, that was

her right. It was a far different thing, though, to drag her father's name into it as if it was a fact that King would be on her side.

It was more than that. It was an even more insulting twist, that she, along with many other black ministers, would shamelessly evoke King's name to pound gay rights and same-sex marriage. There's not a shred of evidence that King would have been a gay rights opponent. King's wife and companion in struggle, Coretta even demanded in 1996 that one group of black minister's cease using his name to back an anti-gay referendum in Miami. In addition, virtually every one of King's closest confidants and associates, both within and without SCLC and other civil rights organizations, have been near unanimous that King's human rights based theology would have made him an advocate of gay rights. Yet, many anti-gay rights black ministers still snatch at his legacy and on several King holidays hailed King as one of their own.

Bernice, for her part, didn't relent from her insistence that King would have been an enemy of gay rights. However, it was not the first time that a King family member had sullied King's name and legacy to torpedo gay rights. In 1998, King's niece, Alveda King, barnstormed the country speaking at rallies against gay-rights legislation. In case anyone missed the King family connection, her group was named "King for America." Gay-rights groups everywhere countered King's "repent and save yourself" message to gays by quoting a public statement Coretta issued in 1996, in which she said that King would be a champion of gay rights if he were alive.

The worst part of Bernice's wrapping herself in her father's mantle to war on gays is that she and other black evangelicals that have marched, protested, and written letters and petitions denouncing gay marriages actually have spoken for many blacks. This would have posed a quandary and a fresh challenge for King if gay rights had been an issue in his day. It wasn't.

The only time known that King did pen a thought on homosexuality came in an advice column he wrote for *Ebony* magazine in 1958. He got an anonymous letter that asked:

"I am a boy," "But I feel about boys the way I ought to feel about girls. I don't want my parents to know about me. What can I do?" King simply advised him to pay "careful attention" to his feelings and suggested that the feeling was not "innate" but culturally acquired." He did add that that it was a "problem" that demanded a solution." This was a thoughtful response that was reflective of the times when homophobia was a practical article of faith and belief in American society. Even then, King did not denounce, condemn, and put down the writer.

*   *   *   *   *

In the 1960s, gay rights were invisible on America's public policy radar, and homosexuality in both black and white communities was hushed up. There's not a word about homosexuality in any of King's major speeches or writings. There's a way, however, to gauge what his feelings were on the issue, and that is the longtime personal and political relationship

that King had with Bayard Rustin. Best known as the driving force behind the historic 1963 March on Washington, Rustin was a close King associate and a known homosexual. (In 1953, Rustin was convicted on "morals" charges—the parlance, in the frozen mood of that day, for homosexual acts.) King knew this, as did top FBI officials, black elected officials, civil-rights leaders and the tight circle of black ministers around King. That didn't deter King from embracing Rustin.

At the high point of the Montgomery bus boycott in 1956 that launched King into the national spotlight, and over the vehement opposition of black ministers who called homosexuals and Rustin unsavory and evil, King invited Rustin to come to Montgomery as an adviser. A year later, King asked Rustin to draft the resolutions and the organizational charter of his fledging Southern Christian Leadership Conference. He demanded that the SCLC board, mostly composed of black ministers, hire Rustin as its coordinator and publicist. The board flatly turned him down, and though it was unstated, Rustin's homosexuality was a major reason.

The issue continued to dog King and his relationship with Rustin. Harlem Congressman Adam Clayton Powell publicly threatened to accuse King of having a homosexual affair with Rustin if he didn't call off planned demonstrations at the 1960 Democratic convention. King didn't buckle to Powell's blackmail threat and went ahead with the demonstrations anyway. During the next few years, the assault on Rustin's homosexuality, and the pressure on King to dump him, escalated. FBI Director J. Edgar Hoover publicly

released wiretaps of scurrilous remarks King associates made about Rustin's homosexuality.

On the eve of the March on Washington in 1963, South Carolina Senator Strom Thurmond denounced Rustin on the Senate floor as a sexual pervert, and inserted a copy of his 1953 arrest booking slip in the Congressional Record. President Kennedy and Attorney General Bobby Kennedy also flatly demanded that King get rid of him. King did not publicly break with Rustin. When he did eventually distance himself politically from Rustin, he gave no public hint that his homosexuality was an issue.

King risked much to work with and defend Rustin during the tumultuous battles of the civil-rights era. He valued him as an ally and a major player in the struggle. He also believed that deeply embodied in the civil-rights fight was a person's right to be whom and what he was. This likely would have included an individual's sexual preference. While King may have praised his daughter for having the courage and conviction to march for her beliefs, bigotry is still bigotry, whether it's about race or sexual orientation. He would not have marched by her side.

A New Set
of Challenges

"We might not face the same dangers as 1963, but the fierce urgency of now remains." This was only one of the many references that then President Obama made in his speech at the fiftieth anniversary of the 1963 March on Washington in August 2013 to the still unfinished work of the civil rights movement a half century earlier. While Obama's key address at the event was a highlight, there was a wave of other commemorative events that tried hard to recapture the energy and the spirit of the 1963 March. This was a tall order.

The original march punctuated by King's towering "I Have a Dream" speech acted as a powerful wrecking ball that crumbled the walls of legal segregation and ushered in an era of unbridled opportunities for many blacks. The results are unmistakable today. Blacks are better educated, more

prosperous, own more businesses, hold more positions in the professions, have more elected officials, and high ranking corporate officials, managers, and executives than ever before.

This half century of progress made was capped by the election of the first African-American president in 2008. With Obama's election, there was much talk that America now had become a "post-racial" nation where racism had faded to the point where it was almost a minor nuisance or nagging after thought. This was widely hailed as the near culmination of King's dream of a color-blind society.

However, the huge racial improvements that the 1963 March on Washington symbolized, and that included Obama's election, masked the harsh reality that the times and challenges fifty years after the March and almost fifty years after King's murder, were far different and in some ways far more daunting than what King and the civil rights leaders that organized the famed march faced.

King's murder in 1968 was the turning point for race relations in America. The self-destruction from within and political sabotage from outside of black organizations left the black poor organizationally adrift and politically rudderless. The black poor lacking competitive technical skills and professional training, and shunned by many middle-class black leaders, became expendable jail and street and cemetery fodder. Some turned to gangs, guns, and drugs to survive.

A Pew Study in August 2013, released to coincide with the 50th anniversary March on Washington celebrations,

graphically made the well-documented point that the economic and social gaps between whites and African-Americans have widened over the last few decades despite massive spending by federal and state governments, every imaginable state and federal civil rights law on the books, and two decades of affirmative action programs. The racial polarization that has been endemic between blacks and whites on everything from the George Zimmerman trial in 2015 for killing black teen Trayvon Martin to just about every other controversial case that involves black and white perceptions of the workings of the criminal justice system.

A half century later the task of redeeming King's dream meant confronting the crisis problems of family breakdown, the rash of shamefully failing public schools, racial profiling, urban police violence, and gun violence in inner cities, the obscene racial disparities in the prison and criminal justice system, as well as the HIV/AIDS crisis, immigration reform, gay marriage and gay rights. These are beguiling problems that sledgehammer the black poor, and these are the problems that King, and the civil rights movement of his day only had begun to recognize and address.

∗ ∗ ∗ ∗ ∗

Civil rights leaders today also must confront something else that King did not have to confront. King had the sympathy and goodwill of millions of whites, politicians, and business leaders, and even a president, Lyndon Johnson, who shouted the slogan of the civil rights movement, "We Shall

Overcome" in an address to Congress in 1965. Those days are long gone. Instead civil rights leaders must confront the indifference, even outright hostility, of many white and non-white Americans to affirmative action, increased spending on social programs, and civil rights marches. They confront a Trump administration that is an inherent enemy of civil rights. Civil rights leaders must maintain civility and even a working modus vivendi with Trump to have even the faintest hope of getting funds and programs for everything from job and education programs to support of minority business and Historically Black Colleges and Universities.

This points to another challenge that King only began to wrestle in his last days: the duality of two Black Americas. The rich and comfortable black America of Oprah Winfrey, Robert Johnson, Beyoncé, Colin Powell, Denzel Washington, and the legions of millionaire black athletes and entertainers, businesspeople, and professionals. They have grabbed a big slice of America's pie. They lay side by side with the far bigger other Black America of the poor that is largely isolated and ignored. Lacking competitive technical skills and professional training, and shunned by many middle-class black leaders, they have been shoved even further to the outer margins of American society.

The chronic problems of gang and drug violence, family breakdown, police abuse, the soaring incarceration rate of young black males, the mounting devastation of HIV and AIDS in black communities, and the abysmally failing inner-city public schools have made things even worse for them.

The mostly middle-class civil rights leaders at times have seemed clueless on how to get a handle on those problems.

The political rise and soaring influence of black conservatives, black evangelicals and the furious internal fights among blacks over gay marriage, gay rights, and abortion have tormented, perplexed and forced civil rights leaders, who are mostly liberal Democrats, to confront their own gender and political biases. They have tried to strike a halting, tenuous balance between their liberalism and the social conservatism of many blacks.

The endorsement of an anti-gay march by one of King's daughters was another instance of a troubling issue that King didn't have to deal with. She evoked her father's name during the march, and was gently rebuked by Coretta Scott King. Though Coretta almost certainly spoke for King in championing gay rights, he still would have been in a bind over how to deal with a family disagreement on whether gay rights was a legitimate civil rights issue.

Civil rights leaders will continue to walk a tightrope between the competing and sometimes contradictory needs of black conservatives, gay rights backers and immigration reform advocates, while still trying to be a voice for the black poor. These are weighty challenges that would perplex and frustrate King if he were alive. It was much easier when the challenge was water hoses, police dogs and brutal, bigoted white police officers brutalizing civil rights demonstrators in the South in the 1960s.

* * * * *

Then there's the reality that race matters in America can no longer be framed exclusively in black and white. Latinos and Asians have become major players in the fight for political and economic empowerment and figure big in the political strategies of Democratic and Republican presidential contenders. Today's civil rights leaders are continually challenged to figure out ways to balance the competing and contradictory needs of these and other ethnic groups and patch them into a workable coalition for change.

However, one of the most daunting problems in combatting the notion that Obama's election not only ushered in a post racial America, but that black political power had begun a dominant force in America. The supposed proof of that besides Obama in the White House were the thousands of black elected officials up and down the political food chain. The issue with King in the 1960s was that there were such a paltry number of black elected officials. In the South there were almost none, a century of poll taxes, literacy tests, naked terror and intimidation, had seen to that. This seemingly was a horrific, but long by-gone past. Like much else about race in America, looks can be badly deceiving.

In fact, the election of Obama came at a time when the number of black elected officials had been stagnant at best and, at worst, on a downhill slide. The Joint Center for Political and Economic Studies, a Washington, D.C., political think tank, in a study a year Obama was elected found the

bulk of black officeholders were still mainly concentrated in five states: Mississippi, Alabama, Illinois, Louisiana, and Georgia.

Overall, the percentage of black elected officials in relation to all elected officials had remained static in the decade before Obama's election. The slowdown was glaringly evident in Congress. The U.S. Senate then had only three, and a disputed fourth, black member since Reconstruction—Massachusetts Republican Ed Brooke and Carol Moseley-Braun, and Obama's much disputed interim replacement, Roland Burris. The year after Obama left office the number of blacks in he Senate still stood at three. In the House, the Congressional Black Caucus membership has had only a modest rise since 1996. The stagnation in black political strength has hampered the Caucus in its past efforts to get Congress and the White House to support increased commerce, trade and aid to African and Caribbean nations—as well as greater HIV/AIDS funding, strong backing for affirmative action programs, the passage of tougher anti-racial profiling and hate-crimes laws.

The stagnation in Congress has also meant that it took marches and protests by civil rights leaders to get any national attention on hate crimes, voting irregularities, police abuse, chronic black joblessness, and the gaping racial disparities in health and education. Before Obama's presidential run, the constraints on black elected officials and the treatment of black voters by top Democrats that was at times cavalier fueled rage and deepened cynicism among many blacks that

Democrats care about them only when they need their votes.

The U.S. Supreme Court's decision in 1993 on minority redistricting was another potential peril for black politicians. The court tossed out districts that had been gerrymandered to preserve black population majorities. These so-called race-based districts were mostly in the South and were deliberately drawn to ensure that black candidates would perpetually be elected to Congress.

An added dilemma for black voters was that any future increase in the number of black elected officials must come from what are currently majority white districts. Yet, with rare exceptions it was still a hard sell for blacks to triumph in non-black majority districts.

The turgidity in black political gains could also be dumped squarely on several phenomena: black voter apathy, alienation, inner-city population drops, suburban integration and displacement by Latinos and Asians who have shown a far greater willingness than blacks to split their votes more evenly among both Republican and Democratic candidates.

To overcome these daunting obstacles, civil rights and black political groups would have to borrow a page from the massive voter education and registration drives that King and civil rights leaders launched in the early and mid-1960s. It was a drive not just to increase the number of black voters, or to elect a black president or in the Trump era defeat a race hostile, race pandering white president, Trump. But a drive to elect black, Latino, or white representatives that will fight for their interests. Then hold their feet to the fire to make sure

they continue to wage that fight. At the same time, black politicians must also expand their agenda to address the needs of Latino and Asian voters. Their support will be crucial if black politicians expect to hold or win office in the future in districts that were once majority black but are fast changing to majority Latino and Asian districts.

* * * * *

King certainly was no stranger to the reality of police violence in the South during the 1960s. He had his arm bent back and was variously rough housed more than once by sadistic, and over aggressive Southern police officers and sheriff's deputies while being carted off to jail during a demonstration. He witnessed first-hand the club welding, bash their heads, and break their bones attack by sheriff's deputies and deputized white vigilantes on the Edmund Pettis Bridge in Selma during the voting rights march there in March 1965. Southern police violence was a constant fact of life for and threat to King. So much so that he made pointed reference to it in his 1963 March on Washington speech, " We can never be satisfied as long as the Negro is the victim of the unspeakable horrors of police brutality."

So, there's little doubt that the rash of police murders of Freddie Gray, Alton Sterling, Philando Castile, and Terrene Crutcher, and dozens more young blacks would almost certainly have stirred King to add yet another campaign to his protest arsenal. This one against wanton police violence. There would have been a major difference. King faced

between dressing down a club welding Southern sheriff deputy and police officer on a major urban, modern day police force who uses excessive force. The Southern cop was the object of near universal disdain, and was roundly denounced by political leaders, and much of the public. That's not the case with police officers, including those who kill under dubious circumstances.

It's an uphill battle for prosecutors to overcome both pro-police attitudes and negative racial stereotypes. Stanford University researchers in a 2014 study found that even when many whites are presented with evidence that the criminal justice system is loaded with racial bias toward blacks they are more likely to support tough, draconian laws such as three strikes, tough sentencing and increased incarceration. The galling conclusion of the researchers was that informing many whites that African-Americans are significantly over-represented in the prison population "may actually bolster support for the very policies that perpetuate the inequality."

The negative perceptions of blacks, especially black males, by much of the public are not the only problem in effecting effective legal measures against police violence. There is no ironclad standard of what is or isn't an acceptable use of force in police misconduct cases. It often comes down to a judgment call by the officer. In the Rodney King beating case in 1992 in which four LAPD officers stood trial, defense attorneys painted King as the aggressor and claimed that the level of force used against him was justified. This pattern has been evident in many celebrated cases since then.

It's made even easier to sell the notion that somehow the victims bare culpability for their deaths by dragging in their past. This is exactly what happened in the bench trial of cops in Baltimore charged with killing Freddie Gray. They harped on his drug dealing. The charged were dropped against them in 2016. Police then claim that they feared for their lives in confronting them and they use deadly force solely in self-defense. If brought to trial judges and juries routinely buy this line and acquit.

The police agencies that are on the hot seat for a dubious shooting or another act that results in the death of a civilian investigate themselves. There is almost never an independent, outside agency that will conduct a truly impartial investigation. In the rare cases that a case is bound over to a prosecutor to determine charges, the prosecutors rely heavily on the police report on why and how the officer used deadly force. Those reports are, of course, compiled, written and carefully vetted by police investigators and officials. In nearly all cases, if there is a prosecution, the officer will be charged with lesser offenses, or in some cases overcharged, which clouds the evidence and testimony. Police unions quickly step in and retain top gun defense attorneys, with lots of experience defending police officers accused of misconduct. Police unions bankroll their defense and spare no expense. Cops rarely serve any pre-trial jail time, and are released on ridiculously low bail.

If the cops are tried by a jury, police defense attorneys seek to get as many middle-class people, whites and even blacks and Latinos, on the jury as possible. The presumption

is that they are much more likely to believe the testimony of police and prosecution witnesses than black witnesses, defendants, or even the victims.

The code of silence is another powerful obstacle to convicting bad cops. Officers hide behind it and refuse to testify against other officers, or tailor their testimony to put the officer's action in the best possible light.

Prosecutors often are barred from using statements made during internal investigations of officer misconduct in court proceedings on grounds of self-incrimination. This knocks out another potentially crucial prosecution weapon.

Then there are the judges. Studies on judicial bias, both overt and implicit, have found the bench anything but impartial. Judges make decisions on bail, pretrial motions, evidentiary issues, witness credibility, and jury selection, and instructions to the jury.

King would likely have cheered Black Lives Matter's protests and in the more celebrated police shootings have joined in the protests. There was little more he could do given the hard-Blue Line that shield bad cops from prosecution. This would be an instance where King would have to step back and pass the torch on to the younger activists to press and prod police officials and prosecutors to curb police violence.

* * * * *

The other vexing problem is the confused and conflicting nature of who and what is a civil rights leader. In the years since King's murder, there' been a pronounced undertow of

disenchantment and resentment that many blacks feel toward those who designate themselves—or more likely are
designated by whites—as "Black leaders."

Many of these leaders are middle-class businesspeople
and professionals. Their agenda and top-down style of leadership is remote, distant, and often wildly out of step with the
needs of poor and working-class blacks. They often approach
tough public policy issues such as the astronomical black
imprisonment rates, the dreary plight of poor black women,
black homelessness, Black-on-Black crime and violence, the
drug crisis, gang warfare and school vouchers with a strange
blend of caution, uncertainty and wariness. They keep counsel only with those black ministers, politicians, professionals and business leaders they consider respectable and legitimate, and will blindly march in lockstep with their program.

Worst of all, more than a few have horribly disfigured
black leadership by turning it into a corporate-style competitive business in which success is measured by piling up political favors and corporate dollars. The sad thing is that it
wasn't always this way. For decades, mainstream black organizations such as the NAACP relied on the nickels and dimes
of poor and working-class blacks for their support. This
gave them complete independence and a solid constituency
to mount powerful campaigns for jobs, better housing and
quality schools, and against police violence and lynching.

The profound shift in the method and style of black leadership began in the 1970s after King. With the collapse of the
traditional civil rights organizations and the destruction and

co-optation of militant activist groups, mainstream black leaders, politicians and ministers did a sharp about-face. They quickly redefined the black agenda as: starting more and better businesses, grabbing more spots in corporations, universities and the professions, electing more Democrats, buying bigger and more expensive homes, taking more luxury vacations and gaining admission into more country clubs.

The biggest gripe many blacks have about some black leaders is that they give to themselves the sole right to speak exclusively on behalf of all blacks. Black leaders got away with this arrogant presumption because many whites regard blacks as so far outside the political and social pale that they see them as monolithic. Whites are profoundly conditioned to believe that all blacks think, act and sway to the same racial beat. They freely use the words and deeds of the chosen black leader as the standard for African American behavior.

Then, when the beleaguered chosen one makes a real or contrived misstep, he or she becomes the whipping boy for many whites. Blacks are then blamed for being rash, foolhardy, irresponsible and prone to shuffle the race card on every social ill that befalls them.

This was not the case in King's day. The NAACP, CORE, SNCC, the Urban League and King's organization, the SCLC, and the Nation of Islam had wildly different goals and tactics— integration, separatism, black self-help, black entrepreneurship, boycotts, street protests, lawsuits and litigation, corporate entrance, fighting poverty and wealth inequality. However, they also had several crucial points in common.

They had nationally identified leaders. The had coherent programs. They were activist and engaged. They had a large, and committed membership, followers and sympathizers. They had the ear and eye at times of the White House, the mass media, and the public. Each in their own way was effective in establishing a modus operandi for how leaders should lead, and organizations should be run to get results. The leadership and organizational fragmentation and collapse after King radically changed all of that.

The best that can be said is that times, as they always do, have changed. So, it's grossly unfair to expect today's civil rights leaders to be the charismatic, aggressive champions of, and martyrs for, civil rights that King was. Or to think that fifty years after King's death another March on Washington can solve the seemingly dogged problems of the black poor. The times and circumstances have changed too much for that. Still, civil rights leaders can draw strength from King's courage, vision and dedication and fight the hardest they can against racial and economic injustices that have hardly disappeared. This is still a big and significant step toward again redeeming King's dream.

King Versus Trump

Boycotts, threatened boycotts, public denunciations and demands, a march, a demonstration. These were all the familiar tactics virtually patented by King in cities and towns across the South during the heyday of the civil rights movement in the 1960s. Nearly fifty years after King's death these were the tactics used again. This time the target wasn't a Jim Crow lunch counter or voting booth. The protagonist wasn't a hardcore, violent prone racist sheriff. The target was Trump.

The protest boots were strapped on instantly when the White House announced that Trump had accepted an invitation to deliver an address at the ribbon cutting ceremony for the opening of the Civil Rights Museum in Jackson, Mississippi on December 9, 2017. This ignited a frenzy of everything from boycotts by nearly every major civil rights leader and organization, enraged denunciations and protests. Trump

got the message and opted instead to say a few words at a private event away from the main ceremony.

Trump wasn't wanted at the museum opening for a good reason. One year into his first term in the Oval Office he had done everything a president could do to try and roll back the very things that King had fought for during his life. Civil rights leaders especially gagged at Trump's claim in his remarks that King was "a man I have studied, watched, and admired for my entire life."

Trump said much the same thing, calling Dr. King "a great man" during a perfunctory photo-op with King's son, MLK III on King Day in January 2017.

During the 2016 presidential campaign Trump showed how much he "admired" King starting in the city that King had put on history's map in 1963. That city was Birmingham, Alabama. For weeks King led protests, marches, and boycotts hammering at the city's cast iron Jim Crow laws. The snarling police dogs, water hoses and blood thirsty club welding racist police assailing demonstrators made global headlines. This was the single biggest event that pushed the Kennedy administration to step up its efforts to smash the foot drag in Congress on passage of his Civil Rights Bill.

Now nearly a half century later Trump was in the city for a campaign rally. At the rally he cheered on the crowd that hooted and howled and whooped it up at the physical and verbal assault on a black protester. Trump then followed that up with a tweet on phony and doctored black crime figures that were so racist that even some staunch conservatives

cringed at the ploy. They didn't buy his lame, partial walk back excuse that he was simply retweeting what a supporter sent him.

Trump was oblivious to this. His unapologetic race baiting by then had become a big part of what rocket-launched him to the front of the GOP presidential pack and at a couple of points when he slid a bit, launched him right back to the front. The race-baiting was hardly new. The instant a multimillion-dollar settlement was announced in 2014 with the five young African-American and Latino youths falsely convicted and imprisoned for assault and rape of a jogger in New York's Central Park in 1989, Trump loudly ranted against the settlement and did everything possible to whip up another round of racial hysteria over the case. And why not? When the case broke in 1989 he shelled out $85,000 to four newspapers to splash an ad demanding the death penalty for the five. The toss of the case and the overwhelming evidence that the men were innocent meant nothing to Trump.

The record of Trump's line of naked bigotry since had been unbroken. He was ripped by the Justice Department for blatant racial discrimination in his apartment rentals and when cornered on his racist exclusion he blithely said that if he didn't his and other tenants (meaning white tenants) would flee from his units and the city.

He turned the thinly disguised racist savaging of President Obama into a fine art by stoking hard the phony, fraudulent, and bigoted Birther movement. Then he doubled down

on that by demanding that Obama produce his supposed
doctored college transcripts.

✳ ✳ ✳ ✳ ✳

His cynical but well-calculated race baiting ploy worked
to masterful perfection with the Birther issue. Trump knew
that while the issue had been thoroughly discredited and dis-
avowed by every leading GOP presidential candidate in 2012,
a significant number, if not most Republicans believed or
wanted to believe that Obama's birth was a legitimate issue to
dump back on the political table.

The only real difference in what Trump had done with
naked race baiting and what legions of other GOP presidential candidates and presidents from Nixon to George W. Bush,
and GOP state and local candidates and elected officials have
done with race is that his is blatant and in-your-face. The others were subtle, sneaky and loaded with emotional hot but-
ton code words and phrases that were designed to stoke the
racial fires to win and maintain office. They knew that no
overt mention of race was necessary to tug at the emotional
strings of the GOP's core constituency—white conservative,
rural, and blue-collar workers. A wink and a nod with the
code words on welfare cheats, entitlements, tax and spend
big government, and immigrants, and the endless wedge issues from gay marriage to abortion was more than enough to
boost their poll ratings.

Trump touched the same deep racial nerve that King
touched when he targeted Birmingham in his campaign in

1963. The nerve was white fears about the future and the direction of the country, and the horrid thought of losing grip on their numbers and power. GOP politicians in the years after King's death erected a storehouse of stock code words and phrases such as "law and order," "crime in the streets," "welfare cheats," "affirmative action hires," "bloated government spending," and so on to pander to those fears. Trump revived and updated the race baiting ploy with his Muslim bashing, and verbal broadsides against immigrants.

Trump wasted no time once in office in trying to deliver the wrecking ball to former President Obama's civil rights and economic fairness initiatives from scrapping his executive orders, appointment of unreconstructed bigots and hard line conservatives to judgeships, government agencies, and the attempted complete demolish of the Affordable Care Act.

The reform measures that Obama pushed forth, King in one form or another had fought for and attained. The outlaw of *de jure* segregation of public schools, the upholding of the equal protection clause of the 14th amendment to the United States Constitution, the Civil Rights Act of 1964 outlawed discrimination based on race, color, religion, sex, or national origin in public accommodations; including schools, housing, at the workplace, and in facilities that served the public. The Voting Rights Act of 1965 prohibited states and localities from imposing voting restrictions resulting in racial discrimination and empowered the federal Justice Department to enforce regulations.

These judicial and legislative victories still resonated

fifty years after King's death and were under attack by Trump and the GOP. In various speeches, Obama repeatedly would refer to the monumental role that King and other civil rights leaders played in preparing the ground for his and many other racial and economic reforms.

The one word that the throng of civil rights leaders and black elected officials that boycotted or protested Trump's showing his face at the civil rights museum was "insult." It was more than that. Trump at the very moment he spoke briefly at the private event had done what no president had done in the fifty years since King's death and that was to create and stoke an unabashed climate of naked raw hate and bigotry against blacks, immigrants, and Muslims.

A deadly outcrop of Trump's hate driven campaign was the murder and maiming of anti-racist protesters in Charlottesville, Virginia in August 2017. In countless speeches and his writings, King warned of the danger of the climate of hate and its inevitable horrendous and deadly consequences. This was hardly something that Trump "studied" when he claimed he studied King all his life.

MLK III gave a strong hint, though, at what his father would have said to Trump if it was he and not the son in a face-to-face meeting with him:

"I think my father would be very concerned about that fact that we have 50 to 60 million people living in poverty, and somehow we've got to create the climate for all boats to be lifted. It's insanity that we have poor people in this nation. That's unacceptable."

The words would have fallen on Trump's deaf ears. But King would not only have said them but been out in the streets and in the halls of Congress doing everything he could to make others hear them.

What if King Had Lived?

There is a huge literary growth industry in counterfactual history. Or, to put it more simply, "what if" history. In this type of fun history exercise, a historian or group of historians, will look at a cataclysmic historical fact or event, and ask the question, "What if so-so and so had happened differently?" The historian will pose a series of what if this had or hadn't happened to the individual or the historical occurrence then how would it have changed history.

Here's some of the more popular. "What if Lincoln hadn't been assassinated?" 'What if he had lost the 1864 presidential election?" Then what effect would that have had on the course of Reconstruction or the outcome of the Civil War?

"What if the Japanese had not bombed Pearl Harbor?" What effect would that have had on World War II? "What if

Columbus had sailed correctly to India, and not the America's?" Then how would that have shaped the development of the Americas? The "what if" questions such as these always ignite a furious discussion and debate among political and history buffs over the possible altered historical scenarios.

Now the what if questions are: "What if Dr. King had lived?" "What if for some reason, James Earl Ray got stuck in traffic, or was injured in an accident, or arrested for speeding on his way to his kill spot across from the Lorraine Motel on April 4, 1968?" "What if he was such a lousy shot that the assassin's bullet missed King?' "What if it had only nicked him, and he received prompt medical attention by the staff at St. Joseph's Hospital and walked out of the hospital the next day?"

This is not merely another exercise in fun, what if speculation. The question provokes much thought about what America and the world might have looked like with King alive and well, and at 39, was still a young healthy man with many good years ahead of him. Conversely, how did America and the world devolve without King? The starting point is King himself. He was in the truest sense one of a kind. That is the kind of leader who comes along once in a lifetime. He was the complete package. He had unmatched eloquence and passion. His gift for impassioned oratory and delivery could energize men and women in all walks, from workers to President and head of states. He possessed visionary insight into how to address the complex racial, social, economic ills of society and what the consequences of those solutions would

be for the future. This was not just starry eyed philosophical posturing. He was an in the trenches, hands on organization man.

He worked tirelessly to build a grassroots civil rights and social justice movement from the ground up and was the guiding force in planning, strategizing, and developing tactics for attaining the aims and objectives of his organization. He also had one other quality that all outstanding leaders have had. He had a charismatic presence that filled up a room when he entered. This meant much when it came to moving people to act on issues and problems.

✶ ✶ ✶ ✶ ✶

Take three latter day problems where his presence and charisma may have made a difference. The drug, gang, and crime problem in inner-cities. King may have been able to weld his moral imperative with pragmatic organizing in crusades to reach young, disenchanted and alienated young black males; and engage them in protest actions for increased spending on jobs, skills training, and education programs. In short, he might have fashioned a crusade to stop the violence akin to his Poor Peoples Campaign. At the very least he would have been a constant and charismatic presence in poor urban communities. This might have made a difference in a lot of young person's lives.

He demonstrated his willingness to work with jobless, alienated black youth when he went to Watts, hit the streets, and talked with and mingled with young blacks during the

1965 riots there. The next year he went to Chicago and made the rounds of the pool halls and bars talking to young blacks about their problems.

King abhorred violence, all violence. While true that King did for a brief time in the mid-1950's in Montgomery, keep a gun in his home, it was purely for self-defense. Mass killings are a far different matter. He would have been deeply pained by the spectacular and grotesque mass killings in cities from Aurora, Colorado and Newtown, Connecticut to Las Vegas. His deep concern over gun violence would also extend to the murder plague in Chicago, Baltimore and other cities. He would almost certainly have joined in the intense lobbying campaign to get Congress to pass comprehensive gun control legislation. He would bring much experience to the gun control campaign on how to use non-violent tactics as a weapon to appeal to the conscience of fence sitting Congresspersons, and even opponents, to enact meaningful gun control legislation. Then President Obama may well have reached out to King and enlisted his support in the efforts he made to prod Congress to pass tougher gun control regulations.

When Obama eventually signed a handful of executive orders that pecked at the edge of gun control in 2013, King might have been invited to witness the signing. His presence would symbolize the importance of a renewed movement to combat murder violence in America.

On this issue, King would have had the overwhelming support for any actions he took from millions of Americans.

Polls show that most Americans have consistently supported stronger gun control bans.

His presence almost certainly would have been felt on the other signature of his, namely war and peace. He would have condemned the Iraq and Afghan wars. He would have branded them ineffectual, repressive, and wasteful and a drain on vital resources that could and should go for domestic programs to aid the poor and minorities. It probably would not have made much difference that the Afghan war was largely prosecuted, and escalated, by Obama. The issue would have remained the unjustness of the war, no matter the resident of the White House.

There was some talk of King running for political office. In 1967, his name was widely floated by many on the Left to make a third-party run for president or to join a third-party antiwar ticket to run with pediatrician Benjamin Spock in the 1968 presidential election. He thought hard about it, but ultimately decided that he could be far more effective outside rather than inside electoral politics. If he had so chosen to run for a congressional post in one of the newly minted black majority districts in parts of the South, he almost certainly would have been a prohibitive favorite to win. His close friend and movement co-worker, Andrew Young did just that in grabbing the mayoral post twice in Atlanta. John Lewis took the same route in running and winning a congressional seat. Both men are regarded by many blacks as both civil rights icons and effective political leaders.

King, though, would have had to do what too many

politicians do and that's stick his finger in the wind and see which way public opinion was blowing before he took a position. King was a man who stood on and was driven by principle on an issue. That simply would not have meshed with the double speak world of politics. Still, he could have played a major role in the massive voter registration drives that sharply boosted the number of black elected officials, both North and South. This would have been crucial in the fight against the GOP's never-ending assault on the Voting Rights Act, and its endless ploys to dilute black and minority voting strength.

✶ ✶ ✶ ✶ ✶

King was not just a black American civil rights leader. He was revered as an international advocate for peace and human rights. This may have stood him well, ala Nelson Mandela. He would likely have traveled extensively outside of the country speaking at international conferences, confabs, rallies, and other global forums for peace and economic rights, and against human rights abuses in Latin America, Africa, and the Middle East. In time, King would have been regarded as the elder statesman of the human rights movement whose counsel might be sought by many foreign leaders. Martin Luther King III, is convinced that, he would have been a presence both here and abroad:

"His voice, his message, we're living every day. We're embracing more and more. We're not as close to it as I would like to see us, but we're still living it. We're still moving toward it.

So, in that way, he lives."

The one thing that King would not have been able to change was the rightward drift of the GOP and later the Democratic party. That would have been an insurmountable task even for a man of the stature of King. There were just too many powerful forces with a vested interest in halting if not reversing the momentum and direction of the country toward expanded civil rights, and labor protections, and economic fairness.

The other intractable problem which reared its ugly head again was the resurgence of overt racist sentiment, actions, and conflicts which would repeatedly give lie to the notion that America had come anywhere close to attaining the color-blind society that King envisioned. Nowhere was this more evident in the blistering and relentless race baiting of Obama.

It was brutal and unyielding from the moment that he declared his presidential candidacy in 2007. This was not simply an unorganized, spontaneous expression of bigotry. It was subtly stoked and orchestrated by the GOP with the clear political aim of disrupting, destabilizing, and rendering politically impotent his program, initiatives, and proposed legislation.

The final presidential vote in 2008 gave plenty of warning of the lethalness of the GOP's core conservative white constituency when aroused. Overall, Obama garnered slightly more than 40 percent of the white male vote. Among Southern and Heartland America white male voters, Obama made

almost no impact. The only thing that even made Obama's showing respectable in those states was the record turnout and percentage of black votes that he got. They were all Democratic votes.

A Harvard post-election assessment of the 2008 presidential vote found that race did factor into the presidential election and that it cost Obama an added three to five percent of the national popular vote. Put bluntly, if Obama had been white he would have won overwhelmingly. During the GOP presidential primary campaign that year, GOP presidential candidates made sure that race was on the public's mind about Obama. They made a stream of race-tinged references to food stamps, welfare, work ethics, and an entitlement society.

His 2012 reelection victory gave even more warning that little had changed. In fact, it got worse, he got a smaller percentage of the overall white vote than he did in 2008, and that included a small but significant defection of younger white voters who backed him in 2008.

The GOP had it both ways. Their shock troops in the streets would hurl their racist taunts at Obama, and GOP leaders could either stay mute, or engage in plausible deniability—namely it's a few lone nuts, not us, that are racist.

The racial assault on Obama simply reconfirmed the horrid fact that race baiting did not die with the disappearance of white Southern racist mobs physically attacking peaceful civil rights demonstrators or racist Southern police unleashing police dogs and fire hoses and welding clubs at

the heads of protesters. King then would have had to again spend much time leading mass protests against the GOP's race baiting maneuvers, and just as much time countering through lobbying and cajoling the Democrats, and congressional leaders to expand civil rights protections and the slash and burn of vital health, education, and job programs.

*   *   *   *   *

There is also serious question whether the majority of whites would have ever lionized King as a major national and international influential figure. Even during the height of his fame and popularity during the civil rights battles from 1960 to 1965, King was as often vilified by whites, and not just hard core bigoted Southern sheriffs and officials, as he was praised. The term "agitator" and "troublemaker" dogged King during his lifetime. The FBI and government agencies piled on by feeding the lie that King was a "communist" and "subversive." These pejoratives were as likely to be hurled at him as "admired civil rights leader." In fact, he seldom made the annual list of most admired figures compiled by several publications then.

The doubt about King's continued influence here even extends to his national holiday. If he had lived, there would not have been one in his name. It was the trauma, shock, and brutality of his murder that shamed the nation into a federal holiday for him. Even then it took nearly two decades and a gargantuan political fight to get the day. Also, there's little likelihood hundreds of schools, streets, parks, and public

buildings would have been named after him. There would not have been a permanent monument erected to him in Washington D.C.

Another issue that would have beguiled King would have been how to ensure that his organization, the SCLC, remained a vibrant, viable, pro-active organization capable of energizing legions for action. In the immediate decade after his murder, the organization was clearly on life support. It was torn by internal strife, personal jealousies, and rivalries. King's closest side kick Ralph Abernathy even endorsed Reagan for President in 1980. He later changed his mind, but the endorsement showed the confusion, gullibility, and political inexperience of the remaining leadership

The downward spiral of SCLC continued during the 1970s and 1980s with a brief revival in the 1990s when King's son, MLK III took the helm. The hope was with the son's marquee name, and his willingness to engage in the tough in the ring battles needed to keep an organization afloat and make it a real presence again on the civil rights front that good things could happen. Unfortunately, that wasn't the case. Plagued by chronic money woes, the usual personal rivalries and jealousies, and dogged by charges of corruption, the downward tumble continued. Despite the major internal woes, the organization still had a recognizable name, and a decent number of members, and had jump started

a few educational and youth programs. When King III finally bowed out, the torch passed to yet another King offspring. This time Bernice King who took the reins in 2009.

The same problems that dogged King III dogged her. In truth, the organization's slide downward in the decades after King's murder had nothing to do with who was in the top spot. The times had markedly changed. The war against legal segregation which was the issue that made King such a compelling force, by the mid-1960s was largely won, had long since ceased to be a national issue of concern.

The passage of four civil rights bills, the voting rights act within the decade of the late 1950s and 1960s, the enactment of affirmative action statues, programs, the quantum leap in the number of black elected officials, and the surge in the number of high profile black mega star millionaire TV personalities, corporate and professionals, and phenomenal expansion of the black middle class, convinced millions that the civil rights movement had achieved its goals and that the movement could now safely be tucked into the history books. It could be treated as the stuff of speeches, and sentimental memoirs, and documentaries. Other than a few isolated pockets of racism here and there, the war was over. King could have done little to change that.

He would have had to find other organizational avenues to challenge the continuing ills of poverty, wealth inequality, and the GOP's attempt to roll back the civil rights and economic gains that he and other civil rights leaders who waged the brutal battles of the 1960s to put in place. Given his superb organizing and planning skills, this may well have been possible. The only real question on this score is how much would an aging King, now in his late 70s, have left in

the tank. The decade from 1955 to 1965, the heyday of the civil rights movement, had to take a physical and mental toll on him. The pressure and focus on him during those years was enormous. He was by all accounts a man of tremendous stamina and energy. But he was human, and there are limits to the pressure a person can take.

There's little doubt, though, that King's unshakeable commitment to the cause of human rights and economic equality would not have diminished. So, it's reasonable to say that wherever there was a campaign, a march, rally, a lobbying effort, or event that his presence could boost, if health permitted, it's a safe bet that he'd be there. That's if King had lived.

50 Years Later is King's Legacy at Risk?

O n the January 2017 anniversary of the King Holiday, a group called Refuse Fascism called for thousands to take to the streets to protest the Trump presidency. The launch date for the mass action on King's birthday was more than symbolism. It was more proof, if that be needed, that King signature trademark, the mass action campaign, was still very much alive and well. The target was not just Trump taking office, but everything that Trump and the GOP stood for. The very things that King devoted a lifetime struggling against.

King and the civil rights movement of the 1960s created a moral climate in this country and a consensus that racial, social and economic injustice had no place in the tapestry of American society. Trump and the GOP seemed hell bent on reversing that progress.

The 1960s movement ended legal segregation, it spotlighted the problems of poverty, war, violence, a bloated military budget, and the first hint of the impact of sexual and gender discrimination. The civil rights movement influenced many other movements, such as the women's movement, the gay rights movement, the Latino movement, and the Native American movement.

Many times, we think of the civil rights movement as strictly domestic. But it was not. It had worldwide influence, from Nelson Mandela to the liberation priests of Latin America to European student movements and anti-colonial movements in Asia and Africa. The world is still feeling the effect of the civil rights movement in America.

Fifty years after King's murder his dream is in part fulfilled. In greater part, there's the dire threat of it being turned into a nightmare. The part that was fulfilled is the scrap of legal segregation in the dustbin of history, the legions of wealthy, influential black professionals, businesspersons, corporate heads, university presidents, NFL, NBA, Major League Baseball head coaches, general managers and owners, the A list black artists and entertainers, the thousands of black elected officials, and the election of a black president.

The nightmare is the resurgence of overt racism, the hammer by the GOP of civil rights, education, health, and job programs, the one million plus African-Americans warehoused in America's jails and prisons, the massive number of black poor, and the re-segregation of many schools and neighborhoods. The nightmare culminated in the election of

the most overtly racially hostile president, Trump, since the murder of King in 1968.

What would King do about this?

If he were alive today, he'd be one of the first to raise his voice in protest at what's going on in this country. He would also be outraged about some of the things he would see in America's inner cities: the high murder rate among young African Americans, the poverty, the lack of job development, the poor quality of education, and the police murder of young blacks.

When he was alive, he called for the American corporate structure to make room for people of color, for political forces to reorient the budget to help people in poverty and for massive increases in federal spending on social programs, jobs, and education. He'd continue to call for that. At the same time, he'd raise his voice even louder today in protest and in action campaigns and support of groups such as Black Lives Matter.

Trump and the political dominance of the GOP is going to make people more desperate, especially poor people, and it is going to increase their numbers. Judging from their rhetoric, the GOP and Trump will not do anything to strengthen laws against racial violence and discrimination. Trump's tout of white nationalists after the Charlottesville, Virginia violence in August 2017 was painful evidence of that.

King would no longer see the federal government as a friend or an ally of civil rights as it was in the 1960s. It will

not provide a reliable avenue for the redress of racial griev-
ances, health education or job development as it did then.
So, King would recognize that civil rights leaders and reform
movements would have to fall back on their own resources
and their own energies.

The other major problem that would confront King is
that there has been a fragmentation in the civil rights movement. That happened in part because of the success of King
and the civil rights leaders in the 1960s had in hastening the
end of legal segregation and opening the doors of universities, corporations, and government for some people of color.

This made some African-Americans feel that the struggle was over; that blacks had finally got their piece of the
American pie and the nation's obligation to redress racial ills
was over. Meanwhile, many whites are in collective denial.
They believe that there is no racism anymore, or that it is only
a minor nuisance. They think that if there's any failure among
blacks or people of color, it's their own fault. They are saying,
"Don't look to my tax dollars for help. The barriers have come
down and if you don't take advantage of that, you're too lazy
and stupid to do it."

The media is part of the problem because it still panders
to, reinforces and titillates racial stereotypes, especially about
black men. The obsessive focus on black crime deepens the
widespread public belief that crime in America comes with a
young black face.

On the other side, among blacks, there is often a collective paranoia. Many believe that all whites, or the majority

of them, are racists, so we should expect nothing from them. There is a feeling that racism is all-present, that everybody's out to get African-Americans. There has developed a circle-the-wagons, siege mentality.

King could have played a major role in trying to reconcile these opposites by continuing to build working coalitions with progressive activist groups and individuals. He almost certainly would have supported the efforts of progressive independents and Democrats such as Bernie Sanders and Elizabeth Warren to continue to fight against wealth inequality and given a major lift to their progressive political campaigns.

In 1955, in Montgomery, Alabama, in the early stages of the bus boycott, King didn't have many major white decisionmakers he could talk to. The sheriffs, the mayors, the legislatures, and the corporate structure initially all lined up against him at the state and federal levels. But through patient and skillful organizing and negotiating, he gradually wore down the opposition.

So, the situation is not hopeless. In Trump's America, the nation is merely going through another of many negative phases of its history. In Montgomery in 1955, King faced long odds to win victory. Fifty years later he would have faced the same long odds in a Trump White House, and a GOP controlled Congress. He would have had to confront the diminished influence, leadership and activism of civil rights organizations, and the competing interests of gays, immigrants, and women's groups. He would not have been daunted and thrown up his hands in resignation at the challenge. This

would simply have been a new set of challenges to be met and overcome. This is why his murder 50 years later still hurts.

Documenting the FBI's Dirty War Against King

133

cies to which they were disseminated. . . . I also told him if any newspapers asked about this, no comment would be made and no mention would be made that such a document existed.[219]

All copies were recovered by October 28.

Burke Marshall, Assistant Attorney General in charge of the Civil Rights Division under Robert Kennedy, told the Committee that the monograph was:

> a personal diatribe . . . a personal attack without evidentiary support on the character, the moral character and person of Dr. Martin Luther King, and it was only peripherally related to anything substantive, like whether or not there was communist infiltration or influence on the civil rights movement. . . . It was a personal attack on the man and went far afield from the charges [of possible communist influence]. [220]

Marshall recalled that he had been very "irritated" about the monograph and that the Attorney General had "thought it was outrageous." He remembered that the Attorney General had ordered the monograph withdrawn, but did not know if the Attorney General had taken any further steps to reprimand the Bureau.[221]

B. The FBI Plans Its Campaign To Discredit Dr. King: December 23, 1963

On December 23, 1963, a nine-hour conference was held at FBI headquarters to discuss Martin Luther King. In attendance were Assistant Director Sullivan, Internal Security Section Chief Frederick Baumgardner, three other FBI headquarters officials, and two agents from the FBI's Atlanta Field Office.

A prepared list of twenty-one proposals was presented and discussed. The proposals raised the possibility of "using" ministers, "disgruntled" acquaintances, "aggressive" newsmen, "colored" agents, Dr. King's housekeeper, and even suggested using Dr. King's wife or "placing a good looking female plant in King's office." [222] An account of the meeting written by William Sullivan emphasized that the Bureau must take a "discreet approach" in developing information about Dr. King for use "at an opportune time in a counterintelli-

---

[219] Memorandum from J. Edgar Hoover to Clyde Tolson, Alan Belmont, John Mohr, Cartha DeLoach, Alex Rosen, and William Sullivan, 10/25/63.

[220] Burke Marshall testimony, 3/3/76, p. 32. Carl T. Rowan, then Director of USIA, was sent a copy of the monograph. In a newspaper article in 1969, Rowan wrote, "(p)erhaps this is the time for me to reveal that I have read the FBI reports based on electronic surveillance of the late Nobel Prize-winner. I know how much dirt the FBI has dug up, and 90 percent of it is barn-yard gossip that has nothing to do with 'internal security' or 'Marxist influences.'" (Carl T. Rowan, "FBI Won't Talk About Additional Wiretappings," The Washington D.C. Evening Star, 6/20/69, p. A–13)

[221] Marshall testimony, 3/3/76, p. 34.

[222] FBI work paper, "Questions To Be Explored at Conference 12/23/63 re: Communist Influence in Racial Matters."

The Bureau subsequently considered the possibility of getting Detroit policemen to raid Dr. King's hotel room in March 1964 and kept abreast of the Miami police force's plans to raid Dr. King's hotel room in 1966 (Unsigned Bureau memorandum, "For Telephonic Briefing of Detroit Office;" Airtel, Miami Office to Director, FBI, 5/23/66).

134

gence move to discredit him." It was generally agreed that the Bureau
should make use of "all available investigative techniques coupled with
meticulous, planning, boldness, and ingenuity, tempered only with
good judgment," but that "discretion must not reach the point of
timidity." [223]

Sullivan's memorandum reported that the following decisions were
made at the conference:

(1) We must determine and check out all of the employees
of the SCLC.

(2) We must locate and monitor the funds of the SCLC.

(3) We must identify and check out the sources who con-
tribute to the SCLC.

(4) We must continue to keep close watch on King's personal activities.

(5) We will, at the proper time when it can be done without embarrassment to the Bureau, expose King as an op-
portunist who is not a sincere person but is exploiting the
racial situation for personal gain.

(6) We will explore the possibility of utilizing additional
specialized investigative techniques at the SCLC office.

Sullivan described the purpose of the meeting as

To explore how best to carry on our investigation to produce the desired results without embarrassment to the Bureau. Included in our discussion was a complete analysis of
the avenues of approach aimed at neutralizing King as an effective Negro leader and developing evidence concerning
King's continued dependence on communists for guidance
and direction. [224]

Precisely what prompted the Bureau to decide upon this drastic
new approach is still unclear.

William Sullivan was asked by the Committee whether tactics, such
as placing female "plants," were common practices of the FBI. Sullivan testified that they were:

common practice among intelligence services all over the
world. This is not an isolated phenomenon. . . . This is a
common practice, rough, tough, dirty business. Whether we
should be in it or not, that is for you folks to decide. We are
in it . . . . No holds were barred. We have used that technique
against Soviet agents. They have used it against us.

Question. The same methods were brought home?

Mr. SULLIVAN. Brought home against any organization
against which we were targeted. We did not differentiate.
This is a rough, tough business.

Senator MONDALE. Would it be safe to say that the techniques we learned in fighting . . . true espionage in World

[223] Memorandum from William Sullivan to Alan Belmont, 12/24/63. Six months
later, in April 1964, FBI headquarters was still instructing agents in the field to
"continue to gather information concerning King's personal activities . . . in
order that we may consider using this information at an opportune time in a
counterintelligence move to discredit him" and to consider the possibility of
"utilizing contracts in the news media field." (Memorandum from FBI Director
to Atlanta Office, April 1, 1964)
[224] Sullivan memorandum, 12/24/63.

135

War II came to be used against some of our own American citizens?

Mr. SULLIVAN. That would be a correct deduction.[225]

Sullivan testified that the plans formulated at the December 24, 1963 meeting were in accord with "Mr. Hoover's policy." [226] After reviewing the memoranda, Sullivan emphasized,

> I want to make this clear, this is not an isolated phenomenon, that this was a practice of the Bureau down through the years. I might say it often became a real character assassination.[227]

Sullivan was asked by the Committee whether he or any other employees of the Bureau ever objected to using these tactics. Sullivan responded:

> Not to my recollection . . . I was not ready at that time to collide with him. Everybody in the Division went right along with Hoover's policy. I do not recall anybody ever raising a question.
> . . . never once did I hear anybody, including myself, raise the question, is this course of action which we have agreed upon lawful, is it legal, is it ethical or moral? We never gave any thought to this realm of reasoning, because we were just naturally pragmatists. The one thing we were concerned about will this course of action work, will it get us what we want, will we reach the objective that we desire to reach?
> As far as legality is concerned, morals or ethics, was never raised by myself or anybody else. . . . I think this suggests really in government we are amoral.[228]

On December 29, 1963, less than a week after the FBI conference, Time magazine chose Dr. King as the "Man of the Year," describing him as the "unchallenged voice of the Negro people . . . [who] has infused the Negroes themselves with the fiber that gives their revolution its true stature." [229] Hoover wrote across the memorandum informing him of this honor: "They had to dig deep in the garbage to come up with this one." [230]

C. William Sullivan proposes a plan to promote a new negro leader: January 1964

On January 6, 1964—about two weeks after the FBI's conference to plan methods of "neutralizing" Dr. King's influence and to gather information about D. King's personal life—the FBI installed the microphone in Dr. King's room at the Willard Hotel. As explained in the preceding chapter, additional microphones soon followed;

---

[225] Sullivan, 11/1/75, p. 97.
[226] Sullivan, 11/1/75, p. 85.
[227] Sullivan, 11/1/75, p. 87.
[228] Sullivan, 11/1/75, pp. 92–93.
[229] United Press International release, 12/29/63, regarding 1/3/64 *Time* cover story.
[230] UPI release, 12/29/63.

136

physical and photographic surveillance was initiated; special
Headquarters "briefings" were held; "dry runs" were planned;
and the most sophisticated and experienced Bureau personnel were
deployed to gather information that might be used in a concerted
effort to destroy Dr. King's influence.

Two days after the installation of the Willard Hotel microphones,
Assistant Director William Sullivan proposed that the FBI select
a new "national Negro leader" as Dr. King's successor. In proposing the
plan, Sullivan stated:

> It should be clear to all of us that Martin Luther King
> must, at some propitious point in the future, be revealed to
> the people of this country and to his Negro followers as
> being what he actually is—a fraud, demagogue and scoundrel.
> When the true facts concerning his activities are presented,
> such should be enough, if handled properly, to take him off
> his pedestal and to reduce him completely in influence. When
> this is done, and it can be and will be done, obviously much
> confusion will reign, particularly among the Negro people.
> . . . The Negroes will be left without a national leader of
> sufficiently compelling personality to steer them in the proper
> direction. This is what could happen, but need not happen
> if the right kind of a national Negro leader could at this
> time be gradually developed so as to overshadow Dr. King
> and be in the position to assume the role of the leadership
> of the Negro people when King has been completely dis-
> credited.
>
> For some months I have been thinking about this matter.
> One day I had an opportunity to explore this from a philo-
> sophical and sociological standpoint with [an acquaintance]
> whom I have known for some years. . . . I asked [him] to
> give the matter some attention and if he knew any Negro of
> outstanding intelligence and ability to let me know and we
> would have a discussion. [He] has submitted to me the name
> of the above-captioned person. Enclosed with this memoran-
> dum is an outline of [the person's] biography which is truly
> remarkable for a man so young. On scanning this biography,
> it will be seen that [he] does have all the qualifications of the
> kind of a Negro I have in mind to advance to positions of na-
> tional leadership. . . .
>
> If this thing can be set up properly without the Bureau in
> any way becoming directly involved, I think it would be not
> only a great help to the FBI but would be a fine thing for
> the country at large. While I am not specifying at this
> moment, there are various ways in which the FBI could give
> this entire matter the proper direction and development.
> There are highly placed contacts of the FBI who might be
> very helpful to further such a step. These can be discussed in
> detail later when I have probed more fully into the
> possibilities [231]

When Sullivan was shown this memorandum by the Committee, he
testified:

---

[231] Memorandum from William Sullivan to Alan Belmont, 1/8/64.

137

I'm very proud of this memorandum, one of the best memoranda I ever wrote. I think here I was showing some concern for the country.[232]

Sullivan sought the Director's approval "to explore this whole matter in greater detail." The Director noted his own "o.k." and added:

I am glad to see that "light" has finally, though dismally delayed, come to the Domestic Int. Div. I struggled for months to get over the fact that the communists were taking over the racial movement but our experts here couldn't or wouldn't see it.[233]

It is uncertain whether the FBI took steps to implement Sullivan's plan. The FBI files contain no additional memoranda on the subject. The successor for Dr. King proposed in Sullivan's memorandum has told the Committee that he was never contacted by the FBI, and that he was not aware of the FBI's plans for him or of any attempts by the FBI to promote him as a civil rights leader.[234]

D. FBI Headquarters Orders the Field Offices To Intensify Efforts to Discredit Dr. King: April-August 1964

On April 1, 1964, in response to a suggestion from the Atlanta field office for another conference in Washington to plan strategy against Dr. King, FBI Headquarters ordered the Atlanta and New York offices to:

give the matter of instant investigation a thorough analysis with a view toward suggesting new avenues of investigation and intensification in areas already being explored. Bear in mind the main goals of this matter; namely, determining the extent of the communist influence in racial matters and taking such *action as is appropriate to neutralize or completely discredit the effectiveness of Martin Luther King, Jr., as a Negro leader.* . . . [235] [Emphasis added.]

Headquarters listed several areas "having potential for further inquiry":

possibilities of anonymous source contacts, possibilities of utilizing contacts in the news media field; initiating discreet checks relative to developing background information on employees of the Southern Christian Leadership Conference (SCLC); remaining alert to the possibility of capitalizing on any disgruntled SCLC employee; the possibility of developing information concerning any financial dealings of King which may be illegal; and the development of subversive information pertaining to SCLC employees.[236]

The Atlanta Office responded with several ideas for "how the effectiveness of King can be neutralized or discredited.[237]

[232] Sullivan, 11/1/75, p. 149.
[233] Sullivan memorandum, 1/8/64.
[234] Staff interview, 11/17/75. This note by Director Hoover should be read in light of his "feud" with the Domestic Intelligence Division described pp. 104 et seq.
[235] Memorandum from Director, FBI to SAC Atlanta, 4/1/64.
[236] Director, FBI memorandum, 4/1/64.
[237] Memorandum from SAC, Atlanta to Headquarters, 4/14/64, p. 11.

138

—Determining whether a "rift" was developing between Dr. King and Roy Wilkins, head of the NAACP, and if so, using newspapers friendly to the Bureau to "feed pertinent subversive connections and dealings of King to Wilkins."

—"Furnishing to friendly newspapers on an anonymous basis, certain specific leads where he may develop the necessary data so that he may further write critical news stories."

—"Discreetly investigate the background of twelve key (SCLC) employees and associates in an effort to obtain some weakness that could be used for counter-intelligence activities."

—"Injection of false information with certain discontented (SCLC) employees."

—Sending letters to SCLC's financial donors, written on SCLC stationery fabricated in the FBI laboratory and bearing Dr. King's signature, advising the donors that the IRS was checking SCLC's tax records. "It is believed that such a letter of this type from SCLC may cause considerable concern and eliminate future contributions."

—Placing a pretext call to an SCLC creditor to impress him with the "financial plight" of the SCLC so that he "may be incited into collection efforts."

—Examining Dr. King's checking accounts and credit card accounts to develop information about his financial affairs.

—Making a survey to determine whether to install a "trash cover" of the SCLC office in Atlanta.[238]

The Atlanta office also assured the Bureau that it would continue to explore the possibility of technical coverage of an Atlanta apartment frequently used by Dr. King, although coverage would involve several security problems.[239]

Shortly after these proposals were submitted, the Director expressed "the Bureau's gratitude" to the Atlanta agents for their "aggressive imagination looking toward more and better ways of meeting the problems involved" in the investigation.[240]

The New York office submitted only a few new suggestions, asserting that "It is felt that [our] coverage is adequate."[241] To this the Director replied:

> The Bureau cannot adjudge as adequate any coverage which does not positively provide to the Bureau 100 percent of the intelligence relating to the communist influence in racial mat-

---

[238] SAO, Atlanta memorandum, 4/14/64.

[239] The FBI overcame similar security problems in another city where hotel room coverage of Dr. King was desired by supplying "lead" information to newsmen "in order that they might determine if they could develop sufficient facts to cause an expose of King."

[240] Memorandum from Director, FBI to SAC, Atlanta, 4/24/64. The Domestic Intelligence Division ultimately approved taking preliminary steps for possible anonymous mailings to the newsman and to install coverage on any new apartments that King might lease. The other suggestions were rejected because they did "not appear desirable and/or feasible for direct action by the Bureau at this time." (Memorandum from Frederick Baumgardner to William Sullivan, 5/6/64.)

[241] Memorandum from SAC, New York to Director, FBI, 4/14/64, p. 2. Those suggestions essentially included increasing coverage of the New York SCLC office and sending an anonymous letter to a disaffected SCLC employee "to cause disruption in the New York office." The anonymous letter was ultimately mailed. (Memorandum from Director, FBI, to SAC, New York, 4/20/64.)

139

ters. Obviously, we are not securing all the information that is pertinent and needs to be secured. Our coverage, therefore, is not deemed adequate.[242]

With respect to the New York office's conclusions about a civil rights leader and associate of Dr. King, who was also under close Bureau scrutiny for alleged "subversive" ties, the Director wrote:

> The Bureau does not agree with the expressed belief of the New York office that [   ] is not sympathetic to the Party cause. While there may not be any direct evidence that [   ] is a communist, neither is there any substantial evidence that he is anticommunist.[243]

Surprisingly, the Bureau did not even comment on the statement of the New York office that Adviser A was "not now under CP discipline in the civil rights field." [244]

In June 1964 a special unit was established in the Bureau's Internal Security Section to handle exclusively "the over-all problem of communist penetration with the racial movement." [245] The memorandum justifying the special unit pointed out that "urgency for the FBI to 'stay ahead' of the situation is tied to pending civil rights legislation and foreseeable ramifications arising out of the complex political situations in an election year where civil rights and social disturbances will play a key role in campaign efforts and possible election results." [246]

In August the Bureau issued new instructions directing the field "to broaden its efforts relating to communist influences in the racial field." [247] The term "communist," the field was told, "should be interpreted in its broadest sense as including persons not only adhering to the principles of the CPUSA itself, but also to such splinter and offshoot groups as the Socialist Workers Party, Progressive Labor and the like." [248] The Director pointed out:

> The news media of recent months mirror the civil rights issue as probably the number one domestic issue in the political spectrum. There are clear and unmistakable signs that we are in the midst of a social revolution with the racial movement as its core. The Bureau, in meeting its responsibilities in this area, is an integral part of this revolution. . . .[249]

The Special Unit that had been established in June was made a permanent unit.

---

[242] Memorandum from Director, FBI, to SAC, New York, 4/24/64.

[243] Director, FBI memorandum, 4/24/64, p. 2.

[244] SAC, New York memorandum, 4/14/64. A detailed, comprehensive, 163-page internal Headquarters working paper, entitled "Communist Party, USA, Negro Question, Communist Influence in Racial Matters," dated April 27, 1964, includes 14 pages dealing solely with Adviser A, but does not include the information received from New York just two weeks earlier that Adviser A "is not now under CP discipline in the civil rights field."

[245] Unsigned FBI Memorandum, Addendum by Inspection Division, 6/4/64.

[246] Memorandum from Frederick Baumgardner to William Sullivan, 5/20/64, addendum by Inspection Division, p. 1.

[247] Memorandum from Frederick Baumgardner to William Sullivan, 8/25/64.

[248] Memorandum from Director, FBI, to SAC, Atlanta, 8/28/64, p. 6.

[249] Director, FBI memorandum, 8/28/64, pp. 1-2.

140

E. Steps Taken by the FBI in 1964 to Discredit Dr. King

The FBI's program to "neutralize" Martin Luther King as the leader of the civil rights movement went far beyond the planning and collection stage. The Committee has discovered the following attempts by the FBI to discredit Dr. King in 1964.

1. Attempts to Discredit Dr. King with the White House

As set forth in the preceding chapter, a memorandum summarizing the contents of the Willard Hotel tapes was shown to presidential assistant Walter Jenkins in January 1964 "inasmuch as King is seeking an appointment with President Johnson." [250] The summary of information obtained from surveillance at the Willard, Honolulu, and Los Angeles hotels was sent to the White House and to the Attorney General in March 1964 in order to "remove all doubt from the Attorney General's mind as to the type of person King is." [251] A third memorandum derived from microphone surveillance was sent to the White House in July.[252]

2. Attempts to Discredit Dr. King With the Congress

In January 1964, Director Hoover gave off-the-record testimony before the House Appropriations Committee. His precise comments are not known. The briefing paper prepared for his appearance by the Domestic Intelligence Division, however, indicates that Director Hoover was prepared to represent to the Committee that Dr. King's advisers were communists and that Dr. King engaged in improper behavior.[253]

The Director's off-the-record briefing had an immediate impact. The FBI was soon told that the members of the Committee were "very concerned regarding the background" of Dr. King, and that some members of the Committee felt that the President should be requested to instruct the USIA to withdraw a film dealing favorably with the August 1963 March on Washington. They were reported to be "particularly disturbed and irked at the fact that Martin Luther King appears to predominate the film." [254]

In March 1964 Cartha DeLoach, Assistant to the Director, reported that he had been approached by Representative Howard Smith (D-Va.), Chairman of the House Rules Committee. According to DeLoach's memorandum, Representative Smith said that he had heard about the Director's remarks before the Appropriations Committee. Congressman Smith was reported to have asked for information for a speech about Dr. King on the floor of the House. DeLoach declined to furnish the required information, but recommended to the Director

---

[250] Sullivan memorandum, 1/13/64, p. 2.
[251] Baumgardner memorandum, 3/4/64.
[252] See Chapter IV.
[253] Memorandum from Frederick Baumgardner to William Sullivan, 1/22/64.
[254] Memorandum from N. P. Callahan to John Mohr, 1/31/64.
Carl Rowan told a Committee staff member that shortly before his appointment as Director of USIA was announced, he had been invited to the White House for a Sunday evening dinner with the President and Mrs. Johnson to view the film about the March. Rowan said that when the President asked him if he was going to distribute the film, Rowan replied that if he could not, "you have to find yourself a new Director." Rowan recalled that the President replied, "That's good enough for me." Rowan recalled that after the film had been distributed, he had been called aside by Congressman Rooney, who repeated stories about Dr. King that had been given to him by the Bureau. Rowan stated that Rooney had specifically mentioned the bugging of Dr. King's suite at the Willard Hotel. (Staff Interview of Carl T. Rowan, 8/29/75)

141

that Congressman Smith might be useful in the future because a speech by him about Dr. King would be picked up by "newspapers all over the Nation."[253]

In a television interview several years later, Congressman Rooney stated:

> Now you talk about the FBI leaking something about Martin Luther King. I happen to know all about Martin Luther King, but I have never told anybody.
> INTERVIEWER. How do you know everything about Martin Luther King?
> Representative ROONEY. From the Federal Bureau of Investigation.
> INTERVIEWER. They've told you—gave you information based on tapes or other sources about Martin Luther King?
> Representative ROONEY. They did.
> INTERVIEWER. Is that proper?
> Representative ROONEY. Why not?[254]

3. Attempts to Discredit Dr. King with Universities

In early March 1964, the Bureau learned that Marquette University in Milwaukee, Wisconsin contemplated awarding Dr. King an honorary degree. A memorandum noted:

> It is shocking indeed that the possibility exists that King may receive an Honorary Degree from the same institution which honored the Director with such a degree in 1950. . . . By making pertinent information available to [a University official] at this time, on a strictly confidential basis, we will be giving the University sufficient time to enable it to take positive action in a manner which might avoid embarrassment to the University.[255]

The university official was briefed by an FBI agent on Dr. King's background and assured the Bureau that Dr. King would not be considered for an honorary degree. The result of this FBI project is unclear.

In April 1964, the FBI learned that Dr. King had been offered an honorary degree by Springfield College. DeLoach visited Senator Leverett Saltonstall, who was a member of the board of the College, in an effort to convince him to influence the College to withdraw its offer. According to DeLoach, Senator Saltonstall promised to speak with an official of the College. The College official was reported to have subsequently visited DeLoach,[256] but to have said that he would be unable to "uninvite" Dr. King because the information concerning

[253] Memorandum from Cartha DeLoach to John Mohr, 3/16/64, p. 2. Hoover wrote on DeLoach's memorandum: "Someone on Senator [sic] Rooney's committee certainly betrayed the secrecy of the 'off-the-record' testimony I gave re: King. I do *not* want anything on King given to Smith nor anyone else at this time."

[254] Interview with Congressman Rooney. NBC News' "First Tuesday." 6/1/71.

[255] Memorandum from Frederick Baumgardner to William Sullivan, 3/4/64. The officer who handled this assignment was given a letter of commendation by the Director and a monetary award.

[256] DeLoach had originally intended not to contact the College official because of his "close association with (Sargent) Shriver." Senator Saltonstall, however, requested the College official to confer with DeLoach.

142

Dr. King had to be held in confidence, and the board of trustees was governed by "liberals." [259]

4. Attempts to Discredit Dr. King with Churches

On June 12, 1964, William Sullivan wrote a memorandum stating that he had been contacted by the General Secretary of the National Council of the Churches of Christ. Sullivan reported that, "I took the liberty of advising [him] confidentally of the fact that Dr. Martin Luther King not only left a great deal to be desired from the standpoint of Communism, but also from the standpoint of personal conduct." Sullivan observed:

> I think that we have sowed an idea here which may do some good. I will follow up on the matter very discreetly to see what desirable results may emanate therefrom. [260]

Sullivan met again with the General Secretary in mid-December 1964 and reported that the General Secretary had assured him "steps have been taken by the National Council of the Churches of Christ to make certain from this time on that Martin Luther King will never get 'one single dollar' of financial support from the National Council." Sullivan reported that the Secretary stated that he had discussed Dr. King's background with some "key" protestant clergymen who were "horrified." Sullivan also noted that the Secretary said that he also intended to discuss the matter with Roy Wilkins to persuade Wilkins "that Negro leaders should completely isolate King and remove him from the role he is now occupying in civil rights activities." [261]

On December 8, 1964, the Director authorized the disclosure of information about Dr. King's personal life to an influential member of the Baptist World Alliance (BWA), so that he could pass the information along to the General Secretary of BWA, and to BWA Program Committee members, to prevent the Committee from inviting Dr. King to address the BWA's 1965 Congress in Miami Beach. The Director rejected a proposal, however, for "arranging for [certain BWA members] to listen to sources we have concerning this matter." [262]

5. Attempts to Discredit Dr. King with the Pope

On August 31, 1964, the FBI learned that Dr. King, who was going to be touring Europe in September, might have plans to visit the Pope. Internal Security Section Chief Baumgardner observed:

> It would be shocking indeed for such an unscrupulous character as King to receive an audience with the Pope. It is believed that if a plan to see the Pope is in the making, it ought to be nipped in the bud. We have considered different possibilities for meeting this problem and believe that the best one would be to have Assistant Director Malone of the New York office personally contact Francis Cardinal Spellman and on a highly confidential basis bring to the Cardinal's attention the fact that King is to visit Rome....

---

[259] Memorandum from Cartha DeLoach to John Mohr, 4/8/64. DeLoach stated that he would "deny any such information had been furnished" if the official told anyone that the FBI had briefed him.
[260] Memorandum from William Sullivan to Alan Belmont, 12/16/64.
[261] Memorandum from William Sullivan to Alan Belmont, 12/16/64.
[262] Memorandum from Milton Jones to Cartha DeLoach, 12/8/64.

143

Malone should be able to impress upon the Cardinal the likely embarrassment that may result to the Pope should he grant King an audience and King is later discredited.[203]

On September 8, Baumgardner reported:

Malone called today and stated that he had discussed the situation with Cardinal Spellman over the weekend and he said that the Cardinal took instant steps to advise the Vatican against granting any audience to King . . . Cardinal Spellman is going to Rome next week . . . and thus will be on the scene personally and further insure that the Pope is not placed in an embarrassing position through any contact with King.[264]

The FBI's efforts were to no avail. The Pope met with Dr. King. The Director wrote across the memoranda informing him of that meeting, "astounding," and "I am amazed that the Pope gave an audience to such a [excised by FBI].[265] The Director then initiated inquiries into the reason for the failure of this project.

6. The Attempt to Discredit Dr. King During His Receipt of the Nobel Peace Prize

On October 14, 1964, Martin Luther King was named to win the Nobel Peace Prize. He received the prize in Europe on December 10, 1965. The FBI took measures to dampen Dr. King's welcome, both in Europe and on his return home.

On November 22, 1964—two weeks before Dr. King's trip to receive the prize—the Domestic Intelligence Division assembled a thirteen-page updated printed version of the monograph which Attorney General Kennedy had ordered recalled in October 1963.[266] A copy was sent to Bill Moyers, Special Assistant to the President, on December 1, 1964, with a letter requesting his advice concerning whether the monograph should also be distributed to "responsible officials in the Executive Branch." [267] Moyers gave his permission on December 7,[268] and copies were distributed to the heads of several executive agencies.[269]

Information about Dr. King's private life was also made available to United Nations representatives Adlai Stevenson and Ralph Bunche, who the Bureau had learned were being considered as possible par-

---

[203] Memorandum from Frederick Baumgardner to William Sullivan, 8/31/64, p. 1.
The Chief of the Security Section recommended:
"If approved, Assistant Director Malone should personally orally brief Francis Cardinal Spellman in accordance with the attached Top Secret summary [containing information about Dr. King's private life] . . . This is the same summary we previously used in preventing King's receiving an honorary degree from Marquette University." (Baumgardner to Sullivan, 8/31/64.)
[264] Memorandum from Frederick Baumgardner to William Sullivan, 9/8/64.
[265] Director's notes on UPI release, 9/8/64, and *New York Herald Tribune*, 9/19/64.
[266] Memorandum from William Sullivan to Alan Belmont, 11/22/64. See pp. 131 et seq.
[267] Letter from J. Edgar Hoover to Bill Moyers, 12/1/64.
[268] Memorandum from Cartha DeLoach to John Mohr, 12/7/64.
[269] Copies were distributed to Acting Attorney General Nicholas Katzenbach, the Secretaries of State and Defense, the Director of the CIA, and the heads of the Military Intelligence agencies, as well as to USIA.

144

ticipants at the December 1964 "welcome home" reception for Dr. King.[270]

Three days after Vice President-elect Humphrey participated in one of the "welcome home" receptions for Dr. King in New York, the Bureau sent him a copy of the updated King monograph and a separate memorandum entitled "Martin Luther King, Jr.: His Personal Conduct." [272] On December 8, 1964, the Bureau decided to brief Governor Nelson Rockefeller about Dr. King's private life and alleged Communist associations, apparently to dissuade the Governor from taking part in ceremonies commending Dr. King for having received the Nobel Prize.[273]

Upon learning that Dr. King might meet with a certain foreign leader, FBI headquarters instructed the FBI representative in that country to brief the proper authorities about Dr. King.[274] The United States ambassadors in London and Oslo were briefed about Dr. King because "the Ambassadors might consider entertaining King while he is in Europe to receive the Nobel Peace Prize" and it might be possible to "forestall such action by the Ambassadors if they were briefed." The ambassadors in Stockholm and Copenhagen were also briefed because "King is also to visit those cities." [275]

On November 10, 1964, the FBI learned that the United States Information Agency was considering requesting Dr. King to engage in a one-week lecture tour in Europe following his receipt of the Noble Prize. Hoover approved the Domestic Intelligence Division's recommendation that USIA be furnished with the latest critical Bureau reports about Dr. King.[276]

7. Attempts to Block Dr. King's Publications

On September 11, 1964, the FBI learned that Dr. King intended to publish an article in a major national publication. The Domestic Intelligence Division noted that it did not know "what line King will take in the article or what its specific stands will be," but, nonetheless recommended that "it would be well to prevent any publication of his views." [277]

The task of preventing publication was assigned to an agent with contacts at the magazine who had "forestalled" the publication of an article by Dr. King in that magazine earlier in 1964.[278]

The agent subsequently reported that he had contacted an official of the magazine in late September. According to the agent, the official had agreed to "endeavor to assist" the FBI, and had been briefed about King, but was unable to block publication because a contractual agreement had already been made.[279] The FBI did apparently have some influence at the magazine, however, because a memorandum reporting the incident concludes:

[270] Untitled memorandum, 11/12/64.
[273] Letter from J. Edgar Hoover to Hubert Humphrey, 12/21/64.
[271] Memorandum from Frederick Baumgardner to William Sullivan, 12/8/64.
[274] Cable from Director, FBI to Legat, 11/10/64.
[275] Memorandum from Frederick Baumgardner to William Sullivan, 11/30/64.
[276] Memorandum from Frederick Baumgardner to William Sullivan, 11/12/64.
[277] Memorandum from Frederick Baumgardner to William Sullivan, 9/11/64.
[278] Baumgardner memorandum, 9/11/64.
[279] Memorandum to Cartha DeLoach, 11/3/64.

145

In connection with this [magazine] article by King, our sources have indicated that since he was awarded the Nobel Peace Prize he has attempted through some of his associates to change the [magazine] article in an effort to soften criticism made by him against other civil rights groups and leaders. King feared that such criticism would cause difficulties in the civil rights movement. The [magazine], however, has resisted King's efforts to make these changes.[280]

In February 1964, the Director alerted the field offices that Dr. King was writing a new book, and noted that "it is entirely possible that with the publication of the book the Bureau may desire to take some action, possibly in the counterintelligence area or otherwise, which may be designed to discredit King or otherwise neutralize his effectiveness . . ."[281]

The field offices were instructed to maintain information relating to the preparation and publication of the book. The FBI files indicate that this information was collected, but it is not clear whether it was ever used.

8. Attempt to Undermine the National Science Foundation's Cooperation with the SCLC

The FBI sent the National Science Foundation (NSF) a copy of the second printed monograph on King in order to convince the NSF to remove the SCLC from "the NSF program to obtain qualified Negro students from southern schools."[282]

9. Unsuccessful FBI Attempts to Locate Financial Improprieties

In early January 1964, the Chief of the Internal Security Section of the Domestic Intelligence Division, Frederick J. Baumgardner, recommended that "examination of recent income tax returns of King might well reveal information which could assist the Bureau in its efforts to discredit King or neutralize his effectiveness."[283] The Intelligence Division subsequently acquired from the Internal Revenue Service copies of income tax returns for the prior five years of Dr. King, the SCLC, and the Gandhi Society,[284] an organization which the FBI stated "augmented" the fund-raising activities of the SCLC.[285] The Intelligence Division of the IRS told the Bureau that "IRS had very carefully scrutinized King's returns in the past but had not been able to establish a cause of action against him."[286] However, the IRS assured the FBI that Dr. King's current returns would

[280] FBI memorandum, 11/3/64, p. 21.
[281] Memorandum from Director, FBI, to Special Agent in Charge, New York, 2/18/64.
[282] Memorandum from Frederick Baumgardner to William Sullivan, 12/17/64, p. 2.
[283] Memorandum from Frederick Baumgardner to William Sullivan, 1/8/64. Baumgardner observed that it was "essential that our current requests of the IRS . . . be handled in a manner which would provide for optimum security so that neither King nor any other unauthorized individuals may become aware of the Bureau's interest and so that no embarrassment may come to the Bureau."
[284] A wiretap had been placed on the Ghandi Society in July, 1963.
[285] Memorandum from Frederick Baumgardner to William Sullivan, 3/25/64.
[286] Memorandum from Daniel Brennan to William Sullivan, 3/27/64.

146

be scrutinized "very carefully to determine whether any violations appear." [287] None did.

Undeterred, the Director informed the field offices that "the Bureau believes that more than ever it would be most desirable to identify any bank where [King] may have an account . . . and consider an audit of such account." [288]

One effort to uncover derogatory information about Dr. King was conceived by the Supervisor in charge of the King case during a golf game.[289] A remote acquaintance of the Supervisor mentioned that he had heard from a friend that an acquaintance had said that Dr. King had a numbered account in a foreign bank with a balance of over one million dollars. The Supervisor suggested to Sullivan:

> If we can prove that King is hoarding large sums of money, we would have available possibly the best information to date which could be used to discredit him, especially in the eyes of his own people . . . . we may take the action to discredit King ourselves through friendly news sources, or the like, or we might turn the information over to the Internal Revenue Service for possible criminal prosecution.[290]

The plan was approved by Director Hoover and an inquiry was initiated. By December 1965, the investigation into a possible foreign bank account was described by the Director as "the most important presently pending" facet of the King investigation.[291] The investigation was dropped shortly afterward, however, when it developed that the initial source of the allegation informed the FBI that "it was merely a wild conclusion that had been previously drawn by someone whose identity he does not now recall." [292]

F. The Question of Whether Government Officials Outside of the FBI Were Aware of the FBI's Effort to Discredit Dr. King

There is no doubt that the responsible officials in the Kennedy and Johnson administrations were aware of the FBI's COMINFIL investigation involving Dr. King and the SCLC and that the wiretaps used by the FBI to collect its information were authorized under procedures existing at the time. While there is some question concerning whether officials outside of the FBI were aware that the FBI was using microphones to cover Dr. King's activities, there is no doubt that the product of the microphone surveillance was widely disseminated within the executive branch. Indeed, dissemination of the printed "monograph" about Dr. King to several executive agencies was expressly approved by Bill Moyers, President Johnson's assistant, in January 1965.

---

[287] Brennan memorandum, 3/27/64. On the bottom of this memorandum, Hoover wrote "What a farce !"

[288] Memorandum from Director, FBI to Special Agent in Charge, New York, 5/21/64.

[289] It should be noted that the Supervisor in charge of the King case is still in a high position with the FBI and handled the committee's documents requests in the King case investigation.

[290] Memorandum from Frederick Baumgardner to William Sullivan, 6/29/65.

[291] Memorandum from Director, FBI, to Special Agent in Charge, New Orleans, 12/3/65.

[292] Memorandum from Frederick Baumgardner to William Sullivan, 12/10/65.

Notes

Introduction

http://www.huffingtonpost.com/entry/donald-trump-liberty-university-martin-luther-king_us_569d1e4fe4b0778f46fa2a9a

http://twitter.com/FBI/status/849321344592470018/photo/1?ref_src=twsrc%5Etfw&ref_url=https%3A%2F%2Fwww.attn.com%2Fstories%2F16174%2Fwhy-people-are-furious-about-fbis-mlk-tribute

1
Who Killed Dr. King and Why?

http://www.attn.com/stories/16174/why-people-are-furious-about-fbis-mlk-tribute

http://www.governmentsecrets.com/fbis-suicide-letter-dr-martin-luther-king-jr-dangers-unchecked-surveillance/

http://www.thekingcenter.org/sites/default/files/KING
%20FAMILY%20TRIAL%20TRANSCRIPT.pdf

http://www.slate.com/articles/news_and_politics/ex-
plainer/1999/12/who_killed_martin_luther_king.html

http://www.washingtonpost.com/politics/mlks-
speech-attracted-fbis-intense-attention/2013/08/27/31c
8ebd4-0f60-11e3-8cdd-bcdc09410972_story.html?utm_
term=.203ad1c2d9a5

Special Agent in Charge, SAC, Detroit, to Director,
March 9, 1965; FK-1070SAC, Mobile, to Director, March 9,
1965, FDCA-487

http://www.huffingtonpost.com/2013/09/26/nsa-mar-
tin-luther-king-jr_n_3995150.html

http://www.nytimes.com/1971/01/18/archives/army-
spied-on-18000-civilians-in-2year-operation-army-fed-
names-of.html

http://www.senate.gov/artandhistory/history/common/
investigations/ChurchCommittee.htm

http://www.americanpress.com/news/informer/tran-
scripts-of-mlk-recordings-sealed-until/article_6f1682c4-
eb2c-11e7-add8-3316b6ee3085.html

2
Sex, Lies, and Tapes

http://www.huffingtonpost.com/2014/01/20/martin-lu-
ther-king-fbi_n_4631112.html

http://www.dailymail.co.uk/news/article-2407403/Sex-
tapes-FBI-smears-double-life-human-saint-The-Martin-Lu-

ther-King-story.html

http://abcnews.go.com/Politics/Jacqueline_Kennedy/
jacqueline-kennedys-feelings-martin-luther-king-jr-re-
vealed/story?id=14478321

http://www.dailymail.co.uk/news/article-4122396/Mar-
tin-Luther-King-s-wife-convinced-stayed-faithful-despite-
FBI-smear-tapes-having-sex-women.html

http://www.quora.com/What-evidence-exists-that-
Martin-Luther-King-Jr-engaged-in-orgies-with-white-pros-
titutes-and-other-women

http://www.cbsnews.com/news/contrary-to-selma-
tapes-of-lbj-show-cordiality-with-king/

3
MORE THAN A DREAMER

http://www.msnbc.com/all/mlks-fight-against-econom-
ic-inequality#49742

http://www.theatlantic.com/business/archive/2013/08/
martin-luther-kings-economic-dream-a-guaranteed-in-
come-for-all-americans/279147/

4
GETTING A PIECE OF THE LEGACY

http://defendernetwork.com/lead-story/now-dr-kings-
position-big-issues/

http://www.thenation.com/article/dr-martin-luther-
kings-economics-through-jobs-freedom/

http://www.mlkonline.net/vietnam.html

http://www.msnbc.com/all/mlks-fight-against-economic-inequality

http://www.presidency.ucsb.edu/ws/?pid=40708

https://thinkprogress.org/the-ferocious-fight-against-the-mlk-national-holiday-cc5debdbb86a/

http://www.thekingcenter.org/archive/theme/771

https://newsone.com/2069175/was-martin-luther-king-a-republican/

http://www.cnn.com/2013/01/19/us/mlk-conservative/index.html

http://thinkprogress.org/conservatives-water-down-mlk-message-5bc06907f6ce/

https://www.dailykos.com/stories/2006/10/20/259740/-

5
Ignoring a Holiday

http://kfor.com/2018/01/09/town-employees-caught-on-tape-using-racial-slurs-to-talk-about-martin-luther-king-jr-day/

htts://www.cbsnews.com/news/retailers-turn-mlk-day-into-a-shopping-bonanza/

http://www.salon.com/2014/01/19/misled_into_believing_mlk_was_a_great_man_how_some_republicans_fought_against_the_king_holiday/

http://obamawhitehouse.archives.gov/the-press-office/2017/01/13/presidential-proclamation-martin-luther-king-jr-federal-holiday-2017

http://www.blackenterprise.com/

president-obama-honored-dr-king-with-day-service/

http://www.nytimes.com/2017/01/16/us/martin-luther-king-jr-the-confederacy.html

http://www.slate.com/articles/news_and_politics/politics/2015/01/robert_e_lee_day_some_southern_states_still_celebrate_the_confederate_general.html

6
CASHING IN ON KING

http://www.thekingcenter.org/meaning-king-holiday

http://www.newsweek.com/2014/04/11/family-feud-over-martin-luther-king-jrs-legacy-248083.html

http://www.forbes.com/sites/nathanraab/2014/02/10/whats-really-behind-the-potential-sale-of-martin-luther-kings-bible-and-nobel-prize/#3ae974464a92

http://www.democracynow.org/2013/1/21/dr_martin_luther_king_in_1967

David Garrow, Bearing the Cross (New York: William Morrow & Company, 1986), 357

7
OBAMA'S DEBT TO KING

http://www.foxnews.com/politics/2013/01/10/obama-to-use-2-bibles-when-takes-oath-office.html

http://www.blackpast.org/aah/mississippi-freedom-democratic-party

http://opinionator.blogs.nytimes.com/2013/07/10/the-decline-of-black-power-in-the-south/

http://www.npr.org/templates/story/story.php?storyId=1538991

http://thehill.com/homenews/house/249959-republicans-slam-brakes-on-voting-rights-bill

http://www.nytimes.com/2013/06/26/us/supreme-court-ruling.html

http://www.afj.org/our-work/issues/supreme-court/voting-rights

http://www.huffingtonpost.com/earl-ofari-hutchinson/president-obama-can-seize_b_935919.html

http://www.politico.com/story/2013/08/barack-obama-and-martin-luther-king-jr-095866

http://www.pewresearch.org/fact-tank/2014/01/13/whos-poor-in-america-50-years-into-the-war-on-poverty-a-data-portrait/

8
THE OTHER
CIVIL RIGHTS MOVEMENT

http://www.blackpast.org/aah/poor-peoples-campaign-december-4-1967-june-19-1968

http://www.laprogressive.com/martin-luther-king-chicano-movement/

http://laprensa-sandiego.org/stories/dr-martin-luther-king-understood-chicano-movements-future-influence/

http://www.huffingtonpost.com/2013/08/25/cesar-chavez-martin-luther-king-jr_n_3813214.html

http://www.newsmax.com/Newsfront/

Obama-amnesty-MLK-immigration/2015/01/15/id/618751/

http://www.nytimes.com/2003/01/22/us/hispanics-now-largest-minority-census-shows.html

http://civilrights.org/immigration/

http://www.theatlantic.com/politics/archive/2013/04/martin-luther-kings-letter-from-birmingham-jail/274668/

http://www.huffingtonpost.com/obery-m-hendricks-jr-phd/martin-luther-king-and-im_b_9002016.html

9
THE POOR HAVEN'T GONE AWAY

http://www.msnbc.com/all/mlks-fight-against-economic-inequality#49742

http://inequality.org/research/dr-kings-nightmare-incredibly-maldistributed-wealth/

http://www.philly.com/philly/news/politics/chuck-grassley-estate-tax-hate-poor-booze-women-movies-20171207.html

http://www.nytimes.com/2015/04/19/upshot/why-americans-dont-want-to-soak-the-rich.html

http://www.salon.com/2015/04/11/why_we_hate_poor_people_partner/

http://billmoyers.com/2014/03/06/dog-whistle-politics-why-americans-hate-welfare/

http://www.commercialappeal.com/story/news/2017/07/11/martin-luther-king-jr-s-last-cause-fighting-poverty-sclcs-latest-chapter/463264001/

http://kingencyclopedia.stanford.edu/encyclopedia/

documentsentry/doc_remaining_awake_through_a_great_
revolution/

10
YES TO GAY RIGHTS

http://perezhilton.com/2013-07-31-martin-luther-king-
jr-daughter-stands-firm-against-gay-rights#.WkJ-7YwXCyI

http://religion.blogs.cnn.com/2012/01/16/what-did-mlk-
think-about-gay-people/

http://www.huffingtonpost.com/michael-g-long/coret-
ta-scott-king_b_2592049.html

http://www.advocate.com/news/2004/03/25/coretta-
scott-king-denounces-federal-marriage-amendment-11799

http://www.legacy.com/news/celebrity-deaths/article/
coretta-scott-king-20-facts

http://www.hrc.org/blog/a-problem-for-the-movement-
martin-luther-king-jr.-bayard-rustin-and-lgbt-pe

http://www.theguardian.com/world/2013/aug/23/ba-
yard-rustin-march-on-washington

11
A NEW SET OF CHALLENGES

http://50thanniversarymarchonwashington.com/

http://www.theguardian.com/world/2013/aug/28/
march-on-washington-50th-anniversary-live

http://www.cnn.com/2013/08/28/politics/obama-king-
speech-transcript/index.html

http://www.pewsocialtrends.

org/2013/08/22/50-years-after-the-march-on-washington-many-racial-divides-remain/

http://www.usatoday.com/story/news/2017/05/02/national-urban-leagues-state-black-america-shows-educational-economic-improvements/101054744/

http://jcpes.wordpress.com/2012/01/04/looking-ahead-to-2012/

http://wunc.org/post/decline-black-political-power-south#stream/0

http://www.npr.org/templates/story/story.php?storyId=94014535

http://newsone.com/3619834/majority-white-juries-decide-police-fatal-shooting-cases/

http://www.dailykos.com/stories/2014/08/09/1320288/-Stanford-Study-White-Public-Supports-Harsher-Police-Laws-If-They-Think-More-Blacks-are-Arrested

http://www.thenation.com/article/why-its-impossible-indict-cop/

http://www.eurweb.com/2013/08/earl-ofari-hutchinson-civil-rights-leaders-face-bigger-challenges-than-king-faced-fifty-years-ago/

12
KING VERSUS TRUMP

http://www.independent.co.uk/news/world/americas/us-politics/donald-trump-civil-rights-museum-mississippi-martin-luther-king-jr-a8101491.html

http://www.usatoday.com/story/news/politics/

2017/01/16/donald-trump-martin-luther-king-jr-holi-
day/96632026/

http://www.politico.com/magazine/story/2016/10/don-
ald-trump-2016-white-nationalists-alt-right-214388

http://www.huffingtonpost.com/earl-ofari-hutchinson/
donald-trumps-arch-race-b_b_5519937.html

http://abcnews.go.com/Politics/donald-trumps-
history-raising-birther-questions-president-obama/
story?id=33861832

http://www.huffingtonpost.com/entry/whats-really-
behind-trumps-clinical-fixation-with_us_5953da28e4b0
c85b96c65e70

http://theweek.com/articles/452677/what-martin-lu-
ther-king-jr-think-america-today

13
WHAT IF KING HAD LIVED?

http://www.timeshighereducation.com/books/altered
-pasts-counterfactuals-in-history-by-richard-j-evans/
2012202.article

http://www.history.com/news/alternate-take-what-if-
martin-luther-king-hadnt-been-killed

http://www.dailykos.com/stories/2013/08/28/1234462/-
Dr-King-Income-Inequality-and-the-Fight-to-Expand-So-
cial-Security

http://www.salon.com/2014/01/20/the_radical_mlk_
we_need_today/

http://www.msnbc.com/politicsnation/watch/

what-king-would-fight-for-today-122769475655

http://www.washingtonpost.com/opinions/martin-lu-ther-kings-legacy-for-today/2011/08/25/gIQAxZyykL_story.html?utm_term=.a6accee0caeb

http://www.huffingtonpost.com/adam-winkler/mlk-and-his-guns_b_810132.html

http://freakonomics.com/2011/12/02/did-racism-cost-obama-votes-in-2008/

http://www.slate.com/blogs/weigel/2011/08/26/when_martin_luther_king_was_hated_and_unpopular.html

http://www.theroot.com/the-last-gasp-of-the-sclc-1790879649

Conclusion

http://www.huffingtonpost.com/alan-singer/where-do-we-go-from-here_b_14198202.html

http://www.huffingtonpost.com/alan-singer/what-is-the-legacy-of-dr_b_8953482.html

http://thenewjournalandguide.com/2012/01/18/dr-king-s-voting-rights-legacy-under-attack/

http://articles.latimes.com/1995-01-15/news/ci-20446_1_rights-movement

Appendix

http://vault.fbi.gov/Martin%20Luther%20King,%20Jr.

http://www.aarclibrary.org/publib/church/reports/con-tents.htm

http://www.youtube.com/watch?v=i-gztpx-_20

Bibliography

Taylor Branch, *Parting the Waters: America in the King Years, 1954-1963* (New York: Simon & Schuster, 1989)

Taylor Branch, *Pillar of Fire: America in the King Years, 1963-1965* (New York: Simon & Schuster, 1999)

Taylor Branch, *At Canaan's Edge America in the King Years, 1965-1968* (New York: Simon & Schuster, 2007)

Carson, Clayborne (editor), *The Autobiography of Martin Luther King, Jr.* (New York: IPM in Association with Warner Books, 1998)

Carson, Clayborne, et al. (editors), *The Papers of Martin Luther King, Jr.—Volumes 1-6,* (Berkeley and Los Angeles: University of California Press, 1992-2007)

Carson, Clayborne and Shepard, Kris (editors), *A Call to Conscience: The Landmark Speeches of Dr. Martin Luther King, Jr.* (New York: Warner Books, 2001)

Carson, Clayborne and Holloran, Peter (editors), *A*

Testament of Hope (San Francisco: Harper & Row Publishers, 1986)

David Garrow, *Bearing the Cross: Martin Luther King Jr. and the Southern Christian Leadership Conference*, (New York: William Morrow, 1986)

Jackson, Troy, *Becoming King: Martin Luther King, Jr. and the Making of a National Leader* (Lexington, Ky.: University Press of Kentucky, 2008)

King, Coretta Scott, *My Life with Martin Luther King, Jr.* (New York: Henry Holt and Company, 1969. Revised edition copyright 1993 by Coretta Scott King.

King, Rev. Martin Luther, Sr. *Daddy King: An Autobiography* (New York: William Morrow & Co. Inc., 1980)

King, Martin Luther Jr., *Stride Toward Freedom: The Montgomery Story* (New York: Harper & Row Publishers, 1958

King, Martin Luther Jr., *Where Do We Go From Here: Chaos or Community?* (New York: Harper & Row Publishers, 1967)

King, Martin Luther Jr., *Why We Can't Wait* (New York: Harper & Row Publishers, 1963)

McKnight, Gerald, *The Last Crusade: Martin Luther King, Jr., the FBI, and the Poor People's Campaign* (Boulder, Colorado: Westview Press, 1998)

Oates, Stephen B., *Let the Trumpet Sound: The Life of Martin Luther King, Jr.* (New York: Harper & Row, 1982)

Pepper, William F., *Orders to Kill: The Truth Behind the Murder of Martin Luther King, Jr.* (New York: IPM in

Association with Warner Books, 1995)

Sides, Hampton, *Hellhound of his Trail* (New York: Doubleday, 2010)

Sullivan, William, *My Thirty Years in Hoover's FBI* (Mountain View, Cal., Ishi Press, 2011)

Yanco, Jennifer, *Misremembering Dr. King: Revisiting the Legacy of Martin Luther King Jr.* (South Bend, Indiana: Indiana University Press, 2014)

Index

50 Years Later
Why the Murder
of Dr. King Still Hurts

Table of Contents

50 Years Later: Why the Murder of Dr. King Still Hurts

Printed in the United States

Published by
Middle Passage Press
5517 Secrest Drive
Los Angeles, California 90043

Indexed by Barbara Bramwell Hutchinson
Designed by Alan Bell

Publisher's Cataloging-In-Publication Data
(Prepared by The Donohue Group, Inc.)
Names: Hutchinson, Earl Ofari.
Title: 50 years later : why the murder of Dr. King still hurts / Earl Ofari Hutchinson.
Other Titles: Fifty years later
Description: [Los Angeles, California] : [Middle Passage Press], [2018] | Includes bibliographical references and index.
Identifiers: ISBN 9781881032014
Subjects: LCSH: King, Martin Luther, Jr., 1929-1968—Assassination—Influence. | King, Martin Luther, Jr., 1929-1968—Influence. | Civil rights movements—United States. | United States—Race relations.
Classification: LCC E185.97.K5 H88 2018 | DDC 323.092—dc23

Library of Congress Control Number:
Middle Passage Press, Los Angeles, California

50 Years Later
Why the Murder of Dr. King Still Hurts

by
Earl Ofari Hutchinson

MID DLE
PASS AGE

P R E S S

50 Years Later
Why the Murder
of Dr. King Still Hurts

THE
BOOK OF MORMON

AN ACCOUNT WRITTEN BY
THE HAND OF MORMON
UPON PLATES
TAKEN FROM THE PLATES OF NEPHI

Wherefore, it is an abridgment of the record of the people of Nephi, and also of the Lamanites—Written to the Lamanites, who are a remnant of the house of Israel; and also to Jew and Gentile—Written by way of commandment, and also by the spirit of prophecy and of revelation—Written and sealed up, and hid up unto the Lord, that they might not be destroyed—To come forth by the gift and power of God unto the interpretation thereof—Sealed by the hand of Moroni, and hid up unto the Lord, to come forth in due time by way of the Gentile—The interpretation thereof by the gift of God.

An abridgment taken from the Book of Ether also, which is a record of the people of Jared, who were scattered at the time the Lord confounded the language of the people, when they were building a tower to get to heaven—Which is to show unto the remnant of the House of Israel what great things the Lord hath done for their fathers; and that they may know the covenants of the Lord, that they are not cast off forever—And also to the convincing of the Jew and Gentile that JESUS is the CHRIST, the ETERNAL GOD, manifesting himself unto all nations—And now, if there are faults they are the mistakes of men; wherefore, condemn not the things of God, that ye may be found spotless at the judgment-seat of Christ.

TRANSLATED BY JOSEPH SMITH, JUN.

Published by
The Church of Jesus Christ
of Latter-day Saints
Salt Lake City, Utah, U.S.A.

First English edition published in 1830

Printed in the United States of America 03/2002

INTRODUCTION

The Book of Mormon is a volume of holy scripture comparable to the Bible. It is a record of God's dealings with the ancient inhabitants of the Americas and contains, as does the Bible, the fulness of the everlasting gospel.

The book was written by many ancient prophets by the spirit of prophecy and revelation. Their words, written on gold plates, were quoted and abridged by a prophet-historian named Mormon. The record gives an account of two great civilizations. One came from Jerusalem in 600 B.C., and afterward separated into two nations, known as the Nephites and the Lamanites. The other came much earlier when the Lord confounded the tongues at the Tower of Babel. This group is known as the Jaredites. After thousands of years, all were destroyed except the Lamanites, and they are the principal ancestors of the American Indians.

The crowning event recorded in the Book of Mormon is the personal ministry of the Lord Jesus Christ among the Nephites soon after his resurrection. It puts forth the doctrines of the gospel, outlines the plan of salvation, and tells men what they must do to gain peace in this life and eternal salvation in the life to come.

After Mormon completed his writings, he delivered the account to his son Moroni, who added a few words of his own and hid up the plates in the hill Cumorah. On September 21, 1823, the same Moroni, then a glorified, resurrected being, appeared to the Prophet Joseph Smith and instructed him relative to the ancient record and its destined translation into the English language.

In due course the plates were delivered to Joseph Smith, who translated them by the gift and power of God. The record is now published in many languages as a new and additional witness that Jesus Christ is the Son of the living God and that all who will come unto him and obey the laws and ordinances of his gospel may be saved.

Concerning this record the Prophet Joseph Smith said: "I told the brethren that the Book of Mormon was the most correct of any book on earth, and the keystone of our religion, and a man would get nearer to God by abiding by its precepts, than by any other book."

In addition to Joseph Smith, the Lord provided for eleven others to see the gold plates for themselves and to be special witnesses of the truth and divinity of the Book of Mormon. Their written testimonies are included herewith as "The Testimony of Three Witnesses" and "The Testimony of Eight Witnesses."

We invite all men everywhere to read the Book of Mormon, to ponder in their hearts the message it contains, and then to ask God, the Eternal Father, in the name of Christ if the book is true. Those who pursue this course and ask in faith will gain a testimony of its truth and divinity by the power of the Holy Ghost. (See Moroni 10: 3–5.)

Those who gain this divine witness from the Holy Spirit will also come to know by the same power that Jesus Christ is the Savior of the world, that Joseph Smith is his revelator and prophet in these last days, and that The Church of Jesus Christ of Latter-day Saints is the Lord's kingdom once again established on the earth, preparatory to the second coming of the Messiah.

THE TESTIMONY OF THREE WITNESSES

BE IT KNOWN unto all nations, kindreds, tongues, and people, unto whom this work shall come: That we, through the grace of God the Father, and our Lord Jesus Christ, have seen the plates which contain this record, which is a record of the people of Nephi, and also of the Lamanites, their brethren, and also of the people of Jared, who came from the tower of which hath been spoken. And we also know that they have been translated by the gift and power of God, for his voice hath declared it unto us; wherefore we know of a surety that the work is true. And we also testify that we have seen the engravings which are upon the plates; and they have been shown unto us by the power of God, and not of man. And we declare with words of soberness, that an angel of God came down from heaven, and he brought and laid before our eyes, that we beheld and saw the plates, and the engravings thereon; and we know that it is by the grace of God the Father, and our Lord Jesus Christ, that we beheld and bear record that these things are true. And it is marvelous in our eyes. Nevertheless, the voice of the Lord commanded us that we should bear record of it; wherefore, to be obedient unto the commandments of God, we bear testimony of these things. And we know that if we are faithful in Christ, we shall rid our garments of the blood of all men, and be found spotless before the judgment-seat of Christ, and shall dwell with him eternally in the heavens. And the honor be to the Father, and to the Son, and to the Holy Ghost, which is one God. Amen.

OLIVER COWDERY
DAVID WHITMER
MARTIN HARRIS

THE TESTIMONY OF EIGHT WITNESSES

BE IT KNOWN unto all nations, kindreds, tongues, and people, unto whom this work shall come: That Joseph Smith, Jun., the translator of this work, has shown unto us the plates of which hath been spoken, which have the appearance of gold; and as many of the leaves as the said Smith has translated we did handle with our hands; and we also saw the engravings thereon, all of which has the appearance of ancient work, and of curious workmanship. And this we bear record with words of soberness, that the said Smith has shown unto us, for we have seen and hefted, and know of a surety that the said Smith has got the plates of which we have spoken. And we give our names unto the world, to witness unto the world that which we have seen. And we lie not, God bearing witness of it.

CHRISTIAN WHITMER	HIRAM PAGE
JACOB WHITMER	JOSEPH SMITH, SEN.
PETER WHITMER, JUN.	HYRUM SMITH
JOHN WHITMER	SAMUEL H. SMITH

TESTIMONY OF THE PROPHET JOSEPH SMITH

The Prophet Joseph Smith's own words about the coming forth of the Book of Mormon are:

"On the evening of the...twenty-first of September [1823]...I betook myself to prayer and supplication to Almighty God....

"While I was thus in the act of calling upon God, I discovered a light appearing in my room, which continued to increase until the room was lighter than at noonday, when immediately a personage appeared at my bedside, standing in the air, for his feet did not touch the floor.

"He had on a loose robe of most exquisite whiteness. It was a whiteness beyond anything earthly I had ever seen; nor do I believe that any earthly thing could be made to appear so exceedingly white and brilliant. His hands were naked, and his arms also, a little above the wrists; so, also, were his feet naked, as were his legs, a little above the ankles. His head and neck were also bare. I could discover that he had no other clothing on but this robe, as it was open, so that I could see into his bosom.

"Not only was his robe exceedingly white, but his whole person was glorious beyond description, and his countenance truly like lightning. The room was exceedingly light, but not so very bright as immediately around his person. When I first looked upon him, I was afraid; but the fear soon left me.

"He called me by name, and said unto me that he was a messenger sent from the presence of God to me, and that his name was Moroni; that God had a work for me to do; and that my name should be had for good and evil among all nations, kindreds, and tongues, or that it should be both good and evil spoken of among all people.

"He said there was a book deposited, written upon gold plates, giving an account of the former inhabitants of this continent, and the source from whence they sprang. He also said that the fulness of the everlasting Gospel was contained in it, as delivered by the Savior to the ancient inhabitants;

"Also, that there were two stones in silver bows—and these stones, fastened to a breastplate, constituted what is called the Urim and Thummim—deposited with the plates; and the possession and use of these stones were what constituted *Seers* in ancient or former times; and that God had prepared them for the purpose of translating the book.

* * * * * * * *

"Again, he told me, that when I got those plates of which he had spoken—for the time that they should be obtained was not yet fulfilled—I should not show them to any person; neither the breastplate with the Urim and Thummim; only to those to whom I should be commanded to show them; if I did I should be destroyed. While he was conversing with me about the plates, the vision was opened to my mind that I could see the place where the plates were deposited, and that so clearly and distinctly that I knew the place again when I visited it.

"After this communication, I saw the light in the room begin to gather immediately around the person of him who had been speaking to me, and it continued to do so, until the room was again left dark, except just around

him, when instantly I saw, as it were, a conduit open right up into heaven, and he ascended until he entirely disappeared, and the room was left as it had been before this heavenly light had made its appearance.

"I lay musing on the singularity of the scene, and marveling greatly at what had been told to me by this extraordinary messenger; when, in the midst of my meditation, I suddenly discovered that my room was again beginning to get lighted, and in an instant, as it were, the same heavenly messenger was again by my bedside.

"He commenced, and again related the very same things which he had done at his first visit, without the least variation; which having done, he informed me of great judgments which were coming upon the earth, with great desolations by famine, sword, and pestilence; and that these grievous judgments would come on the earth in this generation. Having related these things, he again ascended as he had done before.

"By this time, so deep were the impressions made on my mind, that sleep had fled from my eyes, and I lay overwhelmed in astonishment at what I had both seen and heard. But what was my surprise when again I beheld the same messenger at my bedside, and heard him rehearse or repeat over again to me the same things as before; and added a caution to me, telling me that Satan would try to tempt me (in consequence of the indigent circumstances of my father's family), to get the plates for the purpose of getting rich. This he forbade me, saying that I must have no other object in view in getting the plates but to glorify God, and must not be influenced by any other motive than that of building His kingdom; otherwise I could not get them.

"After this third visit, he again ascended into heaven as before, and I was again left to ponder on the strangeness of what I had just experienced; when almost immediately after the heavenly messenger had ascended from me the third time, the cock crowed, and I found that day was approaching, so that our interviews must have occupied the whole of that night.

"I shortly after arose from my bed, and, as usual, went to the necessary labors of the day; but, in attempting to work as at other times, I found my strength so exhausted as to render me entirely unable. My father, who was laboring along with me, discovered something to be wrong with me, and told me to go home. I started with the intention of going to the house; but, in attempting to cross the fence out of the field where we were, my strength entirely failed me, and I fell helpless on the ground, and for a time was quite unconscious of anything.

"The first thing that I can recollect was a voice speaking unto me, calling me by name. I looked up, and beheld the same messenger standing over my head, surrounded by light as before. He then again related unto me all that he had related to me the previous night, and commanded me to go to my father and tell him of the vision and commandments which I had received.

"I obeyed; I returned to my father in the field, and rehearsed the whole matter to him. He replied to me that it was of God, and told me to go and do as commanded by the messenger. I left the field, and went to the place where the messenger had told me the plates were deposited; and owing to the distinctness of the vision which I had had concerning it, I knew the place the instant that I arrived there.

"Convenient to the village of Manchester, Ontario county, New York, stands a hill of considerable size, and the most elevated of any in the neighborhood. On the west side of this hill, not far from the top, under a stone

of considerable size, lay the plates, deposited in a stone box. This stone was thick and rounding in the middle on the upper side, and thinner towards the edges, so that the middle part of it was visible above the ground, but the edge all around was covered with earth.

"Having removed the earth, I obtained a lever, which I got fixed under the edge of the stone, and with a little exertion raised it up. I looked in, and there indeed did I behold the plates, the Urim and Thummim, and the breastplate, as stated by the messenger. The box in which they lay was formed by laying stones together in some kind of cement. In the bottom of the box were laid two stones crossways of the box, and on these stones lay the plates and the other things with them.

"I made an attempt to take them out, but was forbidden by the messenger, and was again informed that the time for bringing them forth had not yet arrived, neither would it, until four years from that time; but he told me that I should come to that place precisely in one year from that time, and that he would there meet with me, and that I should continue to do so until the time should come for obtaining the plates.

"Accordingly, as I had been commanded, I went at the end of each year, and at each time I found the same messenger there, and received instruction and intelligence from him at each of our interviews, respecting what the Lord was going to do, and how and in what manner His kingdom was to be conducted in the last days.

* * * * * * * *

"At length the time arrived for obtaining the plates, the Urim and Thummim, and the breastplate. On the twenty-second day of September, one thousand eight hundred and twenty-seven, having gone as usual at the end of another year to the place where they were deposited, the same heavenly messenger delivered them up to me with this charge: That I should be responsible for them; that if I should let them go carelessly, or through any neglect of mine, I should be cut off; but that if I would use all my endeavors to preserve them, until he, the messenger, should call for them, they should be protected.

"I soon found out the reason why I had received such strict charges to keep them safe, and why it was that the messenger had said that when I had done what was required at my hand, he would call for them. For no sooner was it known that I had them, than the most strenuous exertions were used to get them from me. Every stratagem that could be invented was resorted to for that purpose. The persecution became more bitter and severe than before, and multitudes were on the alert continually to get them from me if possible. But by the wisdom of God, they remained safe in my hands, until I had accomplished by them what was required at my hand. When, according to arrangements, the messenger called for them, I delivered them up to him; and he has them in his charge until this day, being the second day of May, one thousand eight hundred and thirty-eight."

For the complete record, see Joseph Smith—History, in the Pearl of Great Price, and History of The Church of Jesus Christ of Latter-day Saints, volume 1, chapters 1 through 6.

The ancient record thus brought forth from the earth as the voice of a people speaking from the dust, and translated into modern speech by the gift and power of God as attested by Divine affirmation, was first published to the world in the year 1830 as THE BOOK OF MORMON.

A BRIEF EXPLANATION ABOUT
THE BOOK OF MORMON

The Book of Mormon is a sacred record of peoples in ancient America, and was engraved upon sheets of metal. Four kinds of metal record plates are spoken of in the book itself:

1. *The Plates of Nephi*, which were of two kinds: the Small Plates and the Large Plates. The former were more particularly devoted to the spiritual matters and the ministry and teachings of the prophets, while the latter were occupied mostly by a secular history of the peoples concerned (1 Nephi 9: 2–4). From the time of Mosiah, however, the large plates also included items of major spiritual importance.

2. *The Plates of Mormon*, which consist of an abridgment by Mormon from the Large Plates of Nephi, with many commentaries. These plates also contained a continuation of the history by Mormon and additions by his son Moroni.

3. *The Plates of Ether*, which present a history of the Jaredites. This record was abridged by Moroni, who inserted comments of his own and incorporated the record with the general history under the title "Book of Ether."

4. *The Plates of Brass* brought by the people of Lehi from Jerusalem in 600 B.C. These contained "the five books of Moses, . . . And also a record of the Jews from the beginning, . . . down to the commencement of the reign of Zedekiah, king of Judah; And also the prophecies of the holy prophets" (1 Nephi 5: 11–13). Many quotations from these plates, citing Isaiah and other biblical and nonbiblical prophets, appear in the Book of Mormon.

The Book of Mormon comprises fifteen main parts or divisions, known, with one exception, as books, each designated by the name of its principal author. The first portion (the first six books, ending with Omni) is a translation from the Small Plates of Nephi. Between the books of Omni and Mosiah is an insert called The Words of Mormon. This insert connects the record engraved on the Small Plates with Mormon's abridgment of the Large Plates.

The longest portion, from Mosiah to Mormon, chapter 7, inclusive, is a translation of Mormon's abridgment of the Large Plates of Nephi. The concluding portion, from Mormon, chapter 8, to the end of the volume, was engraved by Mormon's son Moroni, who, after finishing the record of his father's life, made an abridgment of the Jaredite record (as the Book of Ether) and later added the parts known as the Book of Moroni.

In or about the year A.D. 421, Moroni, the last of the Nephite prophet-historians, sealed the sacred record and hid it up unto the Lord, to be brought forth in the latter days, as predicted by the voice of God through his ancient prophets. In A.D. 1823, this same Moroni, then a resurrected personage, visited the Prophet Joseph Smith and subsequently delivered the engraved plates to him.

About this edition: Some minor errors in the text have been perpetuated in past editions of the Book of Mormon. This edition contains corrections that seem appropriate to bring the material into conformity with prepublication manuscripts and early editions edited by the Prophet Joseph Smith.

ILLUSTRATIONS

NAMES AND ORDER
OF BOOKS IN
THE BOOK OF MORMON

ABBREVIATIONS AND DESIGNATIONS
IN FOOTNOTES AND INDEX

Old Testament

Gen.	Genesis
Ex.	Exodus
Lev.	Leviticus
Num.	Numbers
Deut.	Deuteronomy
Josh.	Joshua
Judg.	Judges
Ruth	Ruth
1 Sam.	1 Samuel
2 Sam.	2 Samuel
1 Kgs.	1 Kings
2 Kgs.	2 Kings
1 Chr.	1 Chronicles
2 Chr.	2 Chronicles
Ezra	Ezra
Neh.	Nehemiah
Esth.	Esther
Job	Job
Ps.	Psalms
Prov.	Proverbs
Eccl.	Ecclesiastes
Song.	Song of Solomon
Isa.	Isaiah
Jer.	Jeremiah
Lam.	Lamentations
Ezek.	Ezekiel
Dan.	Daniel
Hosea	Hosea
Joel	Joel
Amos	Amos
Obad.	Obadiah
Jonah	Jonah
Micah	Micah
Nahum	Nahum
Hab.	Habakkuk
Zeph.	Zephaniah
Hag.	Haggai
Zech.	Zechariah
Mal.	Malachi

New Testament

Matt.	Matthew
Mark	Mark
Luke	Luke
John	John
Acts	Acts
Rom.	Romans
1 Cor.	1 Corinthians
2 Cor.	2 Corinthians
Gal.	Galatians
Eph.	Ephesians
Philip.	Philippians
Col.	Colossians
1 Thes.	1 Thessalonians
2 Thes.	2 Thessalonians
1 Tim.	1 Timothy
2 Tim.	2 Timothy
Titus	Titus
Philem.	Philemon
Heb.	Hebrews
James	James
1 Pet.	1 Peter
2 Pet.	2 Peter
1 Jn.	1 John
2 Jn.	2 John
3 Jn.	3 John
Jude	Jude
Rev.	Revelation

BD	Bible Dictionary
HC	History of the Church
JST	Joseph Smith Translation
TG	Topical Guide

Book of Mormon

1 Ne.	1 Nephi
2 Ne.	2 Nephi
Jacob	Jacob
Enos	Enos
Jarom	Jarom
Omni	Omni
W of M	Words of Mormon
Mosiah	Mosiah
Alma	Alma
Hel.	Helaman
3 Ne.	3 Nephi
4 Ne.	4 Nephi
Morm.	Mormon
Ether	Ether
Moro.	Moroni

Doctrine and Covenants

D&C	Doctrine and Covenants
OD	Official Declaration

Pearl of Great Price

Moses	Moses
Abr.	Abraham
JS-M	Joseph Smith—Matthew
JS-H	Joseph Smith—History
A of F	Articles of Faith

THE FIRST BOOK OF NEPHI

HIS REIGN AND MINISTRY

An account of Lehi and his wife Sariah, and his four sons, being called, (beginning at the eldest) Laman, Lemuel, Sam, and Nephi. The Lord warns Lehi to depart out of the land of Jerusalem, because he prophesieth unto the people concerning their iniquity and they seek to destroy his life. He taketh three days' journey into the wilderness with his family. Nephi taketh his brethren and returneth to the land of Jerusalem after the record of the Jews. The account of their sufferings. They take the daughters of Ishmael to wife. They take their families and depart into the wilderness. Their sufferings and afflictions in the wilderness. The course of their travels. They come to the large waters. Nephi's brethren rebel against him. He confoundeth them, and buildeth a ship. They call the name of the place Bountiful. They cross the large waters into the promised land, and so forth. This is according to the account of Nephi; or in other words, I, Nephi, wrote this record.

CHAPTER 1

Nephi begins the record of his people—Lehi sees in vision a pillar of fire and reads from a book of prophecy—He praises God, foretells the coming of the Messiah, and prophesies the destruction of Jerusalem—He is persecuted by the Jews.

I, NEPHI, having been ᵃborn of ᵇgoodly ᶜparents, therefore I was ᵈtaught somewhat in all the learning of my father; and having seen many ᵉafflictions in the course of my days, nevertheless, having been highly favored of the Lord in all my days; yea, having had a great knowledge of the goodness and the mysteries of God, therefore I make a ᶠrecord of my proceedings in my days.

2 Yea, I make a record in the ᵃlanguage of my father, which consists of the learning of the Jews and the language of the Egyptians.

3 And I know that the record which I make is ᵃtrue; and I make it with mine own hand; and I make it according to my knowledge.

4 For it came to pass in the commencement of the ᵃfirst year of the reign of ᵇZedekiah, king of Judah, (my father, Lehi, having dwelt at ᶜJerusalem in all his days); and in that same year there came many ᵈprophets, prophesying unto the people that they must ᵉrepent, or the great city ᶠJerusalem must be destroyed.

5 Wherefore it came to pass that my father, Lehi, as he went forth prayed unto the Lord, yea, even

1 1a ᴛɢ Birthright.
  b Prov. 22:1.
  c Mosiah 1:2 (2–3);
    D&C 68:25 (25, 28).
    ᴛɢ Honoring Father
    and Mother.
  d Enos 1:1.
    ᴛɢ Education;
    Family, Children,
    Responsibilities
    toward;
    Family, Love within.
  e ᴛɢ Affliction; Blessing;
    God, Gifts of.
  f ᴛɢ Record Keeping;
    Scriptures, Writing of.

2a Mosiah 1:4;
   Morm. 9:32 (32–33).
3a 1 Ne. 14:30;
   2 Ne. 25:20;
   Mosiah 1:6;
   Alma 3:12;
   Ether 5:3 (1–3).
4a 1 Ne. 2:4;
   Mosiah 6:4.
  b 2 Kgs. 24:18;
    2 Chr. 36:10;
    Jer. 37:1; 44:30;
    49:34; 52:3 (3–5);
    Omni 1:15.
  c 1 Chr. 9:3;

   2 Chr. 15:9;
   Alma 7:10.
  d 2 Kgs. 17:13 (13–15);
    2 Chr. 36:15 (15–16);
    Jer. 7:25; 26:20.
    ᴛɢ Prophets,
    Mission of.
  e ᴛɢ Repentance.
  f Jer. 26:18 (17–19);
    2 Ne. 1:4;
    Hel. 8:20.
    ᴛɢ Israel, Bondage of,
    in Other Lands;
    Jerusalem.

[About 600 B.C.]

with all his [a]heart, in behalf of his people.

6 And it came to pass as he prayed unto the Lord, there came a [a]pillar of fire and dwelt upon a rock before him; and he saw and heard much; and because of the things which he saw and heard he did [b]quake and tremble exceedingly.

7 And it came to pass that he returned to his own house at Jerusalem; and he cast himself upon his bed, being [a]overcome with the Spirit and the things which he had seen.

8 And being thus overcome with the Spirit, he was carried away in a [a]vision, even that he saw the [b]heavens open, and he thought he [c]saw God sitting upon his throne, surrounded with numberless concourses of angels in the attitude of singing and praising their God.

9 And it came to pass that he saw One descending out of the midst of heaven, and he beheld that his [a]luster was above that of the sun at noon-day.

10 And he also saw [a]twelve others following him, and their brightness did exceed that of the stars in the firmament.

11 And they came down and went forth upon the face of the earth; and the first came and [a]stood before my father, and gave unto him a [b]book, and bade him that he should read.

12 And it came to pass that as he read, he was filled with the [a]Spirit of the Lord.

13 And he read, saying: Wo, wo, unto Jerusalem, for I have seen thine [a]abominations! Yea, and many things did my father read concerning [b]Jerusalem—that it should be destroyed, and the inhabitants thereof; many should perish by the sword, and many should be [c]carried away captive into Babylon.

14 And it came to pass that when my father had read and seen many great and marvelous things, he did exclaim many things unto the Lord; such as: Great and marvelous are thy works, O Lord God Almighty! Thy throne is high in the heavens, and thy [a]power, and goodness, and mercy are over all the inhabitants of the earth; and, because thou art merciful, thou wilt not suffer those who [b]come unto thee that they shall perish!

15 And after this manner was the language of my father in the praising of his God; for his soul did rejoice, and his whole heart was filled, because of the things which he had seen, yea, which the Lord had shown unto him.

16 And now I, Nephi, do not make a full account of the things which my father hath written, for he hath written many things which he saw in [a]visions and in [b]dreams; and he also hath written many things which he [c]prophesied and spake

---

5a Jer. 29: 13;
  James 5: 16;
  2 Ne. 4: 24 (23–25).
6a Ex. 14: 24;
  Hel. 5: 24 (24, 43);
  D&C 29: 12;
  JS-H 1: 16, 30.
 b Isa. 6: 5 (1–5).
7a Dan. 8: 27 (26–27);
  10: 8 (8–12);
  1 Ne. 17: 47;
  Alma 27: 17;
  Moses 1: 10 (9–10).
8a 1 Ne. 3: 18 (17–18); 5: 4.
  TG Vision.
 b Ezek. 1: 1; Acts 7: 56
  (55–56); 1 Ne. 11: 14;
  Alma 36: 22; Hel. 5: 48

(45–49); D&C 137: 1.
 c TG God, Manifestations
  of; God, Privilege of
  Seeing.
9a JS-H 1: 17 (16–17),
  30 (30–32).
10a TG Apostles.
11a 1 Sam. 3: 10;
  D&C 110: 2 (2–3).
 b Ezek. 2: 9 (9–10);
  Rev. 10: 9 (2–11).
12a Gen. 41: 38;
  Mosiah 27: 24;
  Alma 18: 16.
13a 2 Kgs. 24: 19; 2 Chr.
  36: 14; Jer. 13: 27.
 b 2 Kgs. 23: 27; 24: 2;
  Jer. 13: 14; Ezek. 15:

6 (6–8); 1 Ne. 2: 13;
  3: 17.
 c 2 Kgs. 20: 17 (17–18);
  Jer. 52: 15 (3–15);
  2 Ne. 25: 10; Omni 1:
  15.
  TG Babylon.
14a TG God, Power of.
 b 2 Ne. 26: 25 (24–28);
  Alma 5: 34 (33–36);
  3 Ne. 9: 14 (13–14).
16a Ezek. 1: 1; JS-H 1: 24
  (21–25).
 b 1 Ne. 8: 2 (2–38);
  Jacob 2: 34.
 c 1 Ne. 7: 1.

unto his children, of which I shall not make a full account.

17 But I shall make an account of my proceedings in my days. Behold, I make an *a*abridgment of the record of my *b*father, upon *c*plates which I have made with mine own hands; wherefore, after I have abridged the record of my *d*father then will I make an account of mine own life.

18 Therefore, I would that ye should know, that after the Lord had shown so many marvelous things unto my father, Lehi, yea, concerning the *a*destruction of Jerusalem, behold he went forth among the people, and began to *b*prophesy and to declare unto them concerning the things which he had both seen and heard.

19 And it came to pass that the *a*Jews did *b*mock him because of the things which he testified of them; for he truly testified of their *c*wickedness and their abominations; and he testified that the things which he saw and heard, and also the things which he read in the book, manifested plainly of the coming of a *d*Messiah, and also the redemption of the world.

20 And when the Jews heard these things they were angry with him; yea, even as with the prophets of old, whom they had *a*cast out, and stoned, and slain; and they also *b*sought his life, that they might take it away. But behold, I, Nephi, will show unto you that the tender *c*mercies of the Lord are over all those whom he hath chosen, because of their faith, to make them mighty even unto the power of *d*deliverance.

CHAPTER 2

Lehi takes his family into the wilderness by the Red Sea—They leave their property—Lehi offers a sacrifice to the Lord and teaches his sons to keep the commandments—Laman and Lemuel murmur against their father—Nephi is obedient and prays in faith; the Lord speaks to him, and he is chosen to rule over his brethren.

FOR behold, it came to pass that the Lord spake unto my father, yea, even in a dream, and said unto him: Blessed art thou Lehi, because of the things which thou hast done; and because thou hast been faithful and declared unto this people the things which I commanded thee, behold, they seek to *a*take away thy *b*life.

2 And it came to pass that the Lord *a*commanded my father, even in a *b*dream, that he should *c*take his family and depart into the wilderness.

3 And it came to pass that he was *a*obedient unto the word of the Lord, wherefore he did as the Lord commanded him.

4 And it came to pass that *a*he *departed into the wilderness. And he left his house, and the land of his inheritance, and his gold, and his silver, and his precious things, and took nothing with him, save it

17a 1 Ne. 9: 2 (2–5);
    Enos 1: 13 (13, 15–18).
    TG Scriptures,
    Writing of.
  b 1 Ne. 6: 1 (1–3);
    8: 29 (29–30); 19: 1
    (1–6).
  c 1 Ne. 10: 15.
  d 2 Ne. 4: 14; 5: 33
    (29–33); D&C 10: 42.
18a 2 Ne. 25: 9; D&C 5: 20.
  b TG Prophets, Mission
    of; Prophets, Rejection
    of.
19a TG Apostasy of Israel.

  b 2 Chr. 36: 16; Jer. 25:
    4 (1–4); Ezek. 5: 6;
    1 Ne. 2: 13; 7: 14.
  c 1 Ne. 17: 22.
  d TG Jesus Christ,
    Prophecies about.
20a Jer. 13: 11; Hel. 13: 24
    (24–28).
  b Jer. 11: 19; 1 Ne. 2: 2
    (1–4); 2 Ne. 10: 20.
    TG Prophets, Rejection
    of.
  c Gen. 32: 10; Alma 34:
    38; D&C 46: 15.
  d TG Deliverance.

2 1a TG Persecution.
  b 1 Ne. 7: 14.
2a 1 Ne. 3: 16; 4: 34; 5: 8;
    17: 44; Mosiah 7: 20;
    Alma 9: 9.
    TG Called of God.
  b TG Dream.
  c Gen. 12: 1; 19: 12;
    1 Ne. 1: 20 (18–20);
    2 Ne. 10: 20; Ether 1:
    42; Abr. 2: 3.
    TG Protection, Divine.
3a TG Commitment.
4a 1 Ne. 10: 4; 19: 8.

[*600 B.C.]

were his family, and provisions, and tents, and departed into the wilderness.

5 And he came down by the borders near the shore of the ^aRed Sea; and he traveled in the wilderness in the borders which are nearer the Red Sea; and he did travel in the wilderness with his family, which consisted of my mother, Sariah, and my elder brothers, who were Laman, Lemuel, and Sam.

6 And it came to pass that when he had traveled three days in the wilderness, he pitched his tent in a ^avalley by the side of a ^briver of water.

7 And it came to pass that he built an ^aaltar of ^bstones, and made an ^coffering unto the Lord, and gave ^dthanks unto the Lord our God.

8 And it came to pass that he called the name of the river, Laman, and it emptied into the Red Sea; and the valley was in the borders near the mouth thereof.

9 And when my father saw that the waters of the river emptied into the ^afountain of the Red Sea, he spake unto Laman, saying: O that thou mightest be like unto this river, continually running into the fountain of all righteousness!

10 And he also spake unto Lemuel: O that thou mightest be like unto this valley, ^afirm and ^bsteadfast, and immovable in keeping the commandments of the Lord!

11 Now this he spake because of the ^astiffneckedness of Laman and Lemuel; for behold they did ^bmurmur in many things against their ^cfather, because he was a ^dvisionary man, and had led them out of the land of Jerusalem, to leave the land of their inheritance, and their gold, and their silver, and their precious things, to perish in the wilderness. And this they said he had done because of the foolish imaginations of his heart.

12 And thus Laman and Lemuel, being the eldest, did murmur against their ^afather. And they did ^bmurmur because they ^cknew not the dealings of that God who had ^dcreated them.

13 Neither did they ^abelieve that Jerusalem, that great city, could be ^bdestroyed according to the words of the prophets. And they were like unto the Jews who were at Jerusalem, who sought to take away the life of my father.

14 And it came to pass that my father did speak unto them in the ^avalley of Lemuel, with ^bpower, being filled with the Spirit, until their frames did ^cshake before him. And he did confound them, that they durst not utter against him; wherefore, they did as he commanded them.

15 And my father dwelt in a ^atent.

16 And it came to pass that I, Nephi, being exceedingly young, nevertheless being large in stature, and also having great desires to know of the ^amysteries of God,

---

5a 1 Ne. 16: 14; D&C 17: 1.
6a 1 Ne. 9: 1.
  b Joel 1: 20.
7a Gen. 12: 7 (7–8); 26: 25; Ex. 24: 4; Abr. 2: 17.
  b Ex. 20: 25; Deut. 27: 5 (5–6); Josh. 8: 31 (30–31).
  c TG Sacrifice.
  d TG Thanksgiving.
9a IE fount, or source, like the Gulf of Akaba, which empties into the Red Sea.
10a IE like Ezion-geber, the Hebrew roots of

which denote firmness and strength, or might of a man.
  b TG Dependability.
11a TG Stiffneckedness.
  b 1 Ne. 7: 7.
  TG Murmuring.
  c Prov. 20: 20.
  d 1 Ne. 5: 4 (2–4); 17: 20.
12a Lam. 4: 16 (16–17).
  b 1 Sam. 3: 13; Mosiah 27: 8 (7–37); Moses 5: 16.
  c Moses 4: 6.
  d Deut. 32: 6; D&C 43: 23.

TG Man, Physical Creation of.
13a Ezek. 5: 6; 1 Ne. 1: 19 (18–20).
  b Jer. 13: 14; 1 Ne. 1: 13 (4–13).
14a 1 Ne. 9: 1; 16: 6 (6, 12).
  b TG Priesthood, Power of.
  c 1 Ne. 17: 45.
15a Gen. 12: 8; 26: 17 (17, 25); 31: 25 (25, 33); 1 Ne. 4: 38; 10: 16.
16a TG Mysteries of Godliness.

wherefore, I did cry unto the Lord; and behold he did [b]visit me, and did [c]soften my heart that I did [d]believe all the words which had been spoken by my [e]father; wherefore, I did not [f]rebel against him like unto my brothers.

17 And I spake unto Sam, making known unto him the things which the Lord had manifested unto me by his Holy Spirit. And it came to pass that he believed in my words.

18 But, behold, Laman and Lemuel would not hearken unto my words; and being [a]grieved because of the hardness of their hearts I cried unto the Lord for them.

19 And it came to pass that the Lord spake unto me, saying: Blessed art thou, Nephi, because of thy [a]faith, for thou hast sought me diligently, with lowliness of heart.

20 And inasmuch as ye shall keep my commandments, ye shall [a]prosper, and shall be led to a [b]land of promise; yea, even a land which I have prepared for you; yea, a land which is choice above all other lands.

21 And inasmuch as thy brethren shall rebel against thee, they shall be [a]cut off from the presence of the Lord.

22 And inasmuch as thou shalt keep my commandments, thou shalt be made a [a]ruler and a teacher over thy brethren.

23 For behold, in that day that they shall [a]rebel against me, I will [b]curse them even with a sore curse, and they shall have no power over thy seed except they shall [c]rebel against me also.

24 And if it so be that they rebel against me, they shall be a [a]scourge unto thy seed, to [b]stir them up in the ways of remembrance.

CHAPTER 3

Lehi's sons return to Jerusalem to obtain the plates of brass—Laban refuses to give them up—Nephi exhorts and encourages his brethren—Laban steals their property and attempts to slay them—Laman and Lemuel smite Nephi and are reproved by an angel.

AND it came to pass that I, Nephi, returned from [a]speaking with the Lord, to the tent of my father.

2 And it came to pass that he spake unto me, saying: Behold I have dreamed a [a]dream, in the which the Lord hath commanded me that thou and thy brethren shall [b]return to Jerusalem.

3 For behold, Laban hath the record of the Jews and also a [a]genealogy of my forefathers, and they are [b]engraven upon plates of brass.

4 Wherefore, the Lord hath commanded me that thou and thy brothers should go unto the house of Laban, and seek the records, and bring them down hither into the wilderness.

5 And now, behold thy brothers murmur, saying it is a hard thing which I have required of them; but behold I have not required it of

16b Ps. 8: 4; 1 Ne. 3: 1;
    19: 11; Alma 17: 10;
    D&C 5: 16.
    TG Guidance, Divine.
  c 1 Kgs. 18: 37;
    Alma 5: 7.
  d 1 Ne. 11: 5.
  e TG Honoring Father
    and Mother.
  f TG Family, Love
    within.
18a Alma 31: 24;
    3 Ne. 7: 16.
19a 1 Ne. 7: 12 (9–13);
    15: 11.

20a Josh. 1: 7; 1 Ne. 4: 14;
    Mosiah 1: 7.
  b Deut. 33: 13 (13–16);
    1 Chr. 28: 8 (7–8);
    1 Ne. 5: 5 (5, 22); 7: 13;
    Moses 7: 17 (17–18).
    TG Promised Lands.
21a Josh. 23: 13; 2 Ne. 5:
    20 (20–24); Alma 9: 14
    (13–15); 38: 1.
22a Gen. 37: 8 (8–11);
    1 Ne. 3: 29.
    TG Authority.
23a Job 24: 13.
  b Deut. 11: 28; 1 Ne. 12:

22 (22–23); D&C 41: 1.
    TG Curse.
  c Josh. 22: 16;
    Mosiah 15: 26.
24a Josh. 23: 13; Judg. 2:
    22 (22–23).
  b 2 Ne. 5: 25.
3 1a 1 Ne. 2: 16.
2a TG Dream.
  b 1 Ne. 2: 4 (1–5); 7: 3.
3a 1 Ne. 3: 12; 5: 14.
  b Jer. 17: 1;
    1 Ne. 3: 24 (12, 19–24).

[Between 600 and 592 B.C.]

them, but it is a commandment of the Lord.

6 Therefore go, my son, and thou shalt be favored of the Lord, because thou hast ᵃnot ᵇmurmured.

7 And it came to pass that I, Nephi, said unto my father: I ᵃwill go and do the things which the Lord hath commanded, for I know that the Lord giveth no ᵇcommandments unto the children of men, save he shall ᶜprepare a way for them that they may accomplish the thing which he commandeth them.

8 And it came to pass that when my father had heard these words he was exceedingly glad, for he knew that I had been blessed of the Lord.

9 And I, Nephi, and my brethren took our journey in the wilderness, with our tents, to go up to the land of Jerusalem.

10 And it came to pass that when we had gone up to the land of Jerusalem, I and my brethren did consult one with another.

11 And we ᵃcast lots—who of us should go in unto the house of Laban. And it came to pass that the lot fell upon Laman; and Laman went in unto the house of Laban, and he talked with him as he sat in his house.

12 And he desired of Laban the records which were engraven upon the plates of brass, which contained the ᵃgenealogy of my father.

13 And behold, it came to pass that Laban was angry, and thrust him out from his presence; and he would not that he should have the records. Wherefore, he said unto him: Behold thou art a robber, and I will slay thee.

14 But Laman fled out of his presence, and told the things which Laban had done, unto us. And we began to be exceedingly sorrowful, and my brethren were about to return unto my father in the wilderness.

15 But behold I said unto them that: ᵃAs the Lord liveth, and as we live, we will not go down unto our father in the wilderness until we have ᵇaccomplished the thing which the Lord hath commanded us.

16 Wherefore, let us be faithful in keeping the commandments of the Lord; therefore let us go down to the land of our father's ᵃinheritance, for behold he left gold and silver, and all manner of riches. And all this he hath done because of the ᵇcommandments of the Lord.

17 For he knew that Jerusalem must be ᵃdestroyed, because of the wickedness of the people.

18 For behold, they have ᵃrejected the words of the prophets. Wherefore, if my father should dwell in the land after he hath been ᵇcommanded to flee out of the land, behold, he would also perish. Wherefore, it must needs be that he flee out of the land.

19 And behold, it is wisdom in God that we should obtain these ᵃrecords, that we may preserve unto our children the language of our fathers;

20 And also that we may ᵃpreserve unto them the words which have been spoken by the mouth of all the holy ᵇprophets, which have been delivered unto them by the Spirit and power of God, since the world began, even down unto this present time.

6a TG Sustaining Church Leaders.
  b TG Murmuring.
7a 1 Sam. 17:32; 1 Kgs. 17:15 (11–15). TG Faith; Loyalty; Obedience.
  b TG Commandments of God.
  c Gen. 18:14; Philip. 4:13; 1 Ne. 17:3, 50; D&C 5:34.
11a Neh. 10:34; Acts 1:26.

12a 1 Ne. 3:3; 5:14; Jarom 1:1.
15a TG Oath; Promise.
  b TG Commitment; Dedication.
16a 1 Ne. 2:4.
  b 1 Ne. 2:2; 4:34.
17a 2 Chr. 36:20 (16–20); Jer. 39:9 (1–9); 1 Ne. 1:13.
18a Jer. 26:23 (21–24).

TG Prophets, Rejection of.
  b 1 Ne. 5:21; 7:2; 16:8.
19a Omni 1:17; Mosiah 1:3 (2–6).
  TG Record Keeping.
20a TG Scriptures, Preservation of.
  b Zech. 7:12; Matt. 11:13; Mosiah 15:13.

[Between 600 and 592 B.C.]

21 And it came to pass that after this manner of language did I ^apersuade my brethren, that they might be faithful in keeping the commandments of God.

22 And it came to pass that we went down to the land of our inheritance, and we did gather together our ^agold, and our silver, and our precious things.

23 And after we had gathered these things together, we went up again unto the house of Laban.

24 And it came to pass that we went in unto Laban, and desired him that he would give unto us the records which were engraven upon the ^aplates of brass, for which we would give unto him our gold, and our silver, and all our precious things.

25 And it came to pass that when Laban saw our property, and that it was exceedingly great, he did ^alust after it, insomuch that he thrust us out, and sent his servants to slay us, that he might obtain our property.

26 And ^ait came to pass that we did flee before the servants of Laban, and we were obliged to leave behind our property, and it fell into the hands of Laban.

27 And it came to pass that we fled into the wilderness, and the servants of Laban did not overtake us, and we ^ahid ourselves in the cavity of a rock.

28 And it came to pass that Laman was angry with me, and also with my father; and also was Lemuel, for he hearkened unto the words of Laman. Wherefore Laman and Lemuel did speak many ^ahard words unto us, their younger brothers, and they did smite us even with a rod.

29 And it came to pass as they smote us with a rod, behold, an ^aangel of the Lord came and stood before them, and he spake unto them, saying: Why do ye smite your younger brother with a rod? Know ye not that the Lord hath chosen him to be a ^bruler over you, and this because of your iniquities? Behold ye shall go up to Jerusalem again, and the Lord will ^cdeliver Laban into your hands.

30 And after the ^aangel had spoken unto us, he departed.

31 And after the angel had departed, Laman and Lemuel again began to ^amurmur, saying: How is it possible the Lord will deliver Laban into our hands? Behold, he is a mighty man, and he can command fifty, yea, even he can slay fifty; then why not us?

CHAPTER 4

Nephi slays Laban at the Lord's command and then secures the plates of brass by stratagem—Zoram chooses to join Lehi's family in the wilderness.

AND it came to pass that I spake unto my brethren, saying: Let us go up again unto Jerusalem, and let us be ^afaithful in keeping the commandments of the Lord; for behold he is mightier than all the earth, then why not ^bmightier than Laban and his fifty, yea, or even than his tens of thousands?

2 Therefore let us go up; let us be ^astrong like unto Moses; for he truly spake unto the waters of the Red ^bSea and they divided hither and thither, and our fathers came through, out of captivity, on dry ground, and the armies of Pharaoh

---

21a TG Family, Love within; Persuade.
22a 1 Ne. 2:4.
24a 1 Ne. 3:3; 4:24 (24, 38).
25a TG Covetousness.
26a 1 Ne. 4:11.
27a Josh. 10:16 (16–17); 1 Sam. 13:6; Jer. 36: 26; Ether 13:13 (13, 22).

28a 1 Ne. 17:18.
29a 1 Ne. 4:3; 7:10.
    TG Angels.
  b Gen. 41:43 (41–43); 1 Ne. 2:22.
  c 2 Kgs. 3:18; 3 Ne. 3: 21.
30a 1 Ne. 4:3; 16:38.
31a TG Murmuring.

4 1a TG Courage; Dependability; Faithful.
  b 1 Ne. 7:11.
    TG God, Power of.
2a Deut. 11:8; Prov. 24: 10 (10–12).
  b Ex. 14:21 (18–30); Josh. 2:10; 1 Ne. 17: 26; Mosiah 7:19.

[Between 600 and 592 B.C.]

did follow and were drowned in the waters of the Red Sea.

3 Now behold ye know that this is true; and ye also know that an ᵃangel hath spoken unto you; wherefore can ye ᵇdoubt? Let us go up; the Lord is able to ᶜdeliver us, even as our fathers, and to destroy Laban, even as the Egyptians.

4 Now when I had spoken these words, they were yet wroth, and did still continue to murmur; nevertheless they did follow me up until we came without the walls of Jerusalem.

5 And it was by night; and I caused that they should hide themselves without the walls. And after they had hid themselves, I, Nephi, crept into the city and went forth towards the house of Laban.

6 And I was ᵃled by the Spirit, not ᵇknowing beforehand the things which I should do.

7 Nevertheless I went forth, and as I came near unto the house of Laban I beheld a man, and he had fallen to the earth before me, for he was ᵃdrunken with wine.

8 And when I came to him I found that it was Laban.

9 And I beheld his ᵃsword, and I drew it forth from the sheath thereof; and the hilt thereof was of pure gold, and the workmanship thereof was exceedingly fine, and I saw that the blade thereof was of the most precious steel.

10 And it came to pass that I was ᵃconstrained by the Spirit that I should kill Laban; but I said in my heart: Never at any time have I shed the blood of man. And I shrunk and would that I might not slay him.

11 And the Spirit said unto me again: Behold the ᵃLord hath ᵇdelivered him into thy hands. Yea, and I also knew that he had sought to take away mine own life; yea, and he would not hearken unto the commandments of the Lord; and he also had ᶜtaken away our property.

12 And it came to pass that the Spirit said unto me again: Slay him, for the Lord hath delivered him into thy hands;

13 Behold the Lord ᵃslayeth the ᵇwicked to bring forth his righteous purposes. It is ᶜbetter that one man should perish than that a nation should dwindle and perish in ᵈunbelief.

14 And now, when I, Nephi, had heard these words, I remembered the words of the Lord which he spake unto me in the wilderness, saying that: ᵃInasmuch as thy seed shall keep my ᵇcommandments, they shall ᶜprosper in the ᵈland of promise.

15 Yea, and I also thought that they could not keep the commandments of the Lord according to the ᵃlaw of Moses, save they should have the law.

16 And I also knew that the ᵃlaw was engraven upon the plates of brass.

17 And again, I knew that the Lord had delivered Laban into my hands for this cause—that I might obtain the records according to his commandments.

18 Therefore I did obey the voice of the Spirit, and took Laban by the hair of the head, and I smote off his head with his own ᵃsword.

19 And after I had smitten off his

3a 1 Ne. 3: 30 (29–31); 7: 10.
  b TG Doubt.
  c TG Deliverance.
6a TG Guidance, Divine; Holy Ghost, Gifts of; Inspiration.
  b Heb. 11: 8.
7a TG Drunkenness.
9a 2 Ne. 5: 14; D&C 17: 1.
10a 1 Sam. 15: 3 (3–33).
11a Deut. 3: 3; 1 Sam. 17: 46 (41–49).

b 1 Ne. 7: 11.
c 1 Ne. 3: 26.
13a Num. 25: 17; Deut. 12: 29; Ps. 139: 19; 1 Ne. 17: 37 (33–38); D&C 98: 32 (31–32).
  b TG Justice; Punishment; Wickedness.
  c Alma 30: 47. TG Life, Sanctity of.
  d TG Unbelief, Unbelievers.

14a Omni 1: 6; Mosiah 2: 22; Ether 2: 7 (7–12).
  b TG Commandments of God.
  c 1 Ne. 2: 20.
  d 1 Ne. 17: 13 (13–14); Jacob 2: 12.
15a Mosiah 1: 5 (1–6).
16a Josh. 1: 8. TG Law of Moses.
18a 1 Sam. 17: 51.

[Between 600 and 592 B.C.]

head with his own sword, I took the garments of Laban and put them upon mine own body; yea, even every whit; and I did gird on his armor about my loins.

20 And after I had done this, I went forth unto the treasury of Laban. And as I went forth towards the treasury of Laban, behold, I saw the *servant of Laban who had the keys of the treasury. And I commanded him in the voice of Laban, that he should go with me into the treasury.

21 And he supposed me to be his master, Laban, for he beheld the garments and also the sword girded about my loins.

22 And he spake unto me concerning the *elders of the Jews, he knowing that his master, Laban, had been out by night among them.

23 And I spake unto him as if it had been Laban.

24 And I also spake unto him that I should carry the engravings, which were upon the *plates of brass, to my elder brethren, who were without the walls.

25 And I also bade him that he should follow me.

26 And he, supposing that I spake of the *brethren of the *church, and that I was truly that Laban whom I had slain, wherefore he did follow me.

27 And he spake unto me many times concerning the elders of the Jews, as I went forth unto my brethren, who were without the walls.

28 And it came to pass that when Laman saw me he was exceedingly frightened, and also Lemuel and Sam. And they fled from before my presence; for they supposed it was Laban, and that he had slain me and had sought to take away their lives also.

29 And it came to pass that I called after them, and they did hear me; wherefore they did cease to flee from my presence.

30 And it came to pass that when the servant of Laban beheld my brethren he began to tremble, and was about to flee from before me and return to the city of Jerusalem.

31 And now I, Nephi, being a man large in stature, and also having received much *strength of the Lord, therefore I did seize upon the servant of Laban, and held him, that he should not flee.

32 And it came to pass that I spake with him, that if he would hearken unto my words, as the Lord liveth, and as I live, even so that if he would hearken unto our words, we would spare his life.

33 And I spake unto him, even with an *oath, that he need not fear; that he should be a *free man like unto us if he would go down in the wilderness with us.

34 And I also spake unto him, saying: Surely the Lord hath *commanded us to do this thing; and shall we not be diligent in keeping the commandments of the Lord? Therefore, if thou wilt go down into the wilderness to my father thou shalt have place with us.

35 And it came to pass that *Zoram did take courage at the words which I spake. Now Zoram was the name of the servant; and he promised that he would go down into the wilderness unto our father. Yea, and he also made an oath unto us that he would tarry with us from that time forth.

36 Now we were desirous that he should tarry with us for this cause, that the Jews might not know concerning our flight into the wilderness, lest they should pursue us and destroy us.

37 And it came to pass that when

20a 2 Ne. 1: 30.
22a 2 Sam. 17: 15; Ezek. 8: 1; Acts 25: 15.
24a 1 Ne. 3: 24 (12, 19–24); 5: 10 (10–22).
26a Ex. 2: 11; Num. 18: 6; 2 Sam. 19: 41.

b TG Church Organization.
31a TG Strength; Strengthen.
33a 2 Sam. 21: 7.
   TG Oath.
 b TG Free.

34a 1 Ne. 2: 2; 3: 16.
35a 1 Ne. 16: 7; 2 Ne. 5: 6 (5–6); Jacob 1: 13; Alma 54: 23; 4 Ne. 1: 36 (36–37).

[Between 600 and 592 B.C.]

Zoram had made an *a*oath unto us, our *b*fears did cease concerning him.

38 And it came to pass that we took the plates of brass and the servant of Laban, and departed into the wilderness, and journeyed unto the *a*tent of our father.

CHAPTER 5

Sariah complains against Lehi—Both rejoice over the return of their sons—They offer sacrifices—The plates of brass contain writings of Moses and the prophets—They identify Lehi as a descendant of Joseph—Lehi prophesies concerning his seed and the preservation of the plates.

AND it came to pass that after we had come down into the wilderness unto our father, behold, he was filled with joy, and also my mother, Sariah, was exceedingly glad, for she truly had mourned because of us.

2 For she had supposed that we had perished in the wilderness; and she also had *a*complained against my father, telling him that he was a *b*visionary man; saying: Behold thou hast led us forth from the land of our inheritance, and my sons are no more, and we perish in the wilderness.

3 And after this manner of language had my mother complained against my father.

4 And it had come to pass that my father spake unto her, saying: I know that I am a *a*visionary man; for if I had not seen the things of God in a *b*vision I should not have known the goodness of God, but had tarried at Jerusalem, and had perished with my brethren.

5 But behold, I have *a*obtained a *b*land of promise, in the which things I do rejoice; yea, and I *c*know that the Lord will deliver my sons out of the hands of Laban, and bring them down again unto us in the wilderness.

6 And after this manner of language did my father, Lehi, *a*comfort my mother, Sariah, concerning us, while we journeyed in the wilderness up to the land of Jerusalem, to obtain the record of the Jews.

7 And when we had returned to the tent of my father, behold their joy was full, and my mother was comforted.

8 And she spake, saying: Now I know of a surety that the Lord hath *a*commanded my husband to *b*flee into the wilderness; yea, and I also know of a surety that the Lord hath protected my sons, and delivered them out of the hands of Laban, and given them power whereby they could *c*accomplish the thing which the Lord hath commanded them. And after this manner of language did she speak.

9 And it came to pass that they did rejoice exceedingly, and did offer *a*sacrifice and burnt offerings unto the Lord; and they gave *b*thanks unto the God of Israel.

10 And after they had given thanks unto the God of Israel, my father, Lehi, took the records which were engraven upon the *a*plates of brass, and he did search them from the beginning.

11 And he beheld that they did contain the five *a*books of Moses, which gave an account of the creation of the world, and also of Adam and Eve, who were our first parents;

37a Ex. 22: 11 (10–11); Josh. 9: 19 (1–21).
   TG Oath; Vows.
  b TG Trustworthiness.
38a 1 Ne. 2: 15.
5 2a TG Murmuring.
  b Gen. 37: 19 (8, 19).
4a 1 Ne. 2: 11; 17: 20.
  b 1 Ne. 1: 8 (8–13); 3: 18 (17–18).
   TG Vision.

5a Eph. 1: 11; Heb. 6: 15 (13–15).
  b 1 Ne. 2: 20; 18: 8 (8, 22–23).
   TG Promised Lands.
  c TG Faith; Trust in God.
6a TG Comfort; Family, Love within.
8a 1 Ne. 2: 2.
  b Gen. 19: 14.
  c 1 Ne. 3: 7.

9a 1 Ne. 7: 22; Mosiah 2: 3; 3 Ne. 9: 19.
   TG Law of Moses.
  b TG Thanksgiving.
10a 1 Ne. 4: 24 (24, 38); 13: 23.
11a Ex. 17: 14; Deut. 31: 9; Luke 16: 29; 24: 27; 1 Ne. 19: 23; Moses 1: 41 (40–41).

[Between 600 and 592 B.C.]

12 And also a *record of the Jews from the beginning, even down to the commencement of the reign of Zedekiah, king of Judah;

13 And also the prophecies of the holy prophets, from the beginning, even down to the commencement of the reign of *Zedekiah; and also many prophecies which have been spoken by the mouth of *Jeremiah.

14 And it came to pass that my father, Lehi, also found upon the *plates of brass a *genealogy of his *fathers; wherefore he knew that he was a descendant of *Joseph; yea, even that Joseph who was the son of *Jacob, who was *sold into Egypt, and who was *preserved by the hand of the Lord, that he might preserve his father, Jacob, and all his household from perishing with famine.

15 And they were also *led out of captivity and out of the land of Egypt, by that same God who had preserved them.

16 And thus my father, Lehi, did discover the genealogy of his fathers. And Laban also was a descendant of *Joseph, wherefore he and his fathers had kept the *records.

17 And now when my father saw all these things, he was filled with the Spirit, and began to prophesy concerning his seed—

18 That these *plates of brass should go forth unto all *nations, kindreds, tongues, and people who were of his seed.

19 Wherefore, he said that these plates of brass should *never perish; neither should they be dimmed any more by time. And he prophesied many things concerning his seed.

20 And it came to pass that thus far I and my father had kept the commandments wherewith the Lord had commanded us.

21 And we had obtained the records which the Lord had commanded us, and searched them and found that they were desirable; yea, even of great *worth unto us, insomuch that we could *preserve the commandments of the Lord unto our children.

22 Wherefore, it was wisdom in the Lord that we should carry them with us, as we journeyed in the wilderness towards the land of promise.

CHAPTER 6

Nephi writes of the things of God—His purpose is to persuade men to come unto the God of Abraham and be saved.

AND now I, Nephi, do not give the genealogy of my fathers in *this part of my record; neither at any time shall I give it after upon these *plates which I am *writing; for it is given in the record which has been kept by my *father; wherefore, I do not write it in this work.

2 For it sufficeth me to say that we are descendants of *Joseph.

3 And it mattereth not to me that I am particular to give a full account of all the things of my father, for they cannot be written upon *these

12a 1 Chr. 9:1.
   TG Scriptures, Writing of.
13a 2 Kgs. 24:18; Jer. 37:1.
   b Ezra 1:1; Jer. 36:32 (17–32); 1 Ne. 7:14; Hel. 8:20.
14a Mosiah 2:34.
   b 1 Ne. 3:3, 12; Jarom 1:1.
   TG Book of Remembrance.
   c TG Israel, Origins of.
   d 2 Ne. 3:4; Alma 10:3.
   TG Israel, Joseph, People of.

e Gen. 25:26; 2 Ne. 20:21; Alma 7:25; D&C 27:10.
   f Gen. 37:36 (29–36).
   g TG Protection, Divine.
15a Gen. 15:14 (13–14); Ex. 15:13; Amos 3:1 (1–2); 1 Ne. 17:31 (23–31); 19:10; D&C 103:16 (16–18); 136:22.
16a 2 Chr. 15:9; 1 Ne. 6:2.
   TG Israel, Joseph, People of.
   b TG Record Keeping.
18a Alma 22:12.

b JS-H 1:33.
19a Alma 37:4.
21a TG Scriptures, Value of.
   b TG Scriptures, Preservation of.
6 1a 2 Ne. 4:15.
   b 1 Ne. 9:2.
   c TG Scriptures, Writing of.
   d 1 Ne. 1:17 (16–17); 19:1 (1–6).
2a 1 Ne. 5:16 (14–16).
3a Jacob 7:27; Jarom 1:2 (2, 14); Omni 1:1, 30.

[Between 600 and 592 B.C.]

plates, for I desire the room that I may write of the things of God.

4 For the fulness of mine intent is that I may [a]persuade men to [b]come unto the God of Abraham, and the God of Isaac, and the God of Jacob, and be saved.

5 Wherefore, the things which are [a]pleasing unto the world I do not write, but the things which are pleasing unto God and unto those who are not of the world.

6 Wherefore, I shall give commandment unto my seed, that they shall not occupy these plates with things which are not of worth unto the children of men.

CHAPTER 7

Lehi's sons return to Jerusalem and enlist Ishmael and his household in their cause—Laman and others rebel—Nephi exhorts his brethren to have faith in the Lord—They bind him with cords and plan his destruction—He is freed by the power of faith—His brethren ask forgiveness—Lehi and his company offer sacrifice and burnt offerings.

AND now I would that ye might know, that after my father, Lehi, had made an end of [a]prophesying concerning his seed, it came to pass that the Lord spake unto him again, saying that it was not meet for him, Lehi, that he should take his family into the wilderness alone; but that his sons should take [b]daughters to [c]wife, that they might raise up [d]seed unto the Lord in the land of promise.

2 And it came to pass that the Lord [a]commanded him that I, Nephi, and my brethren, should again return unto the land of Jerusalem, and bring down Ishmael and his family into the wilderness.

3 And it came to pass that I, Nephi, did [a]again, with my brethren, go forth into the wilderness to go up to Jerusalem.

4 And it came to pass that we went up unto the house of Ishmael, and we did gain favor in the sight of Ishmael, insomuch that we did speak unto him the words of the Lord.

5 And it came to pass that the [a]Lord did soften the heart of Ishmael, and also his household, insomuch that they took their journey with us down into the wilderness to the tent of our father.

6 And it came to pass that as we journeyed in the wilderness, behold Laman and Lemuel, and two of the [a]daughters of Ishmael, and the two [b]sons of Ishmael and their families, did [c]rebel against us; yea, against me, Nephi, and Sam, and their father, Ishmael, and his wife, and his three other daughters.

7 And it came to pass in the which rebellion, they were desirous to return unto the land of Jerusalem.

8 And now I, Nephi, being [a]grieved for the hardness of their hearts, therefore I spake unto them, saying, yea, even unto Laman and unto Lemuel: Behold ye are mine elder brethren, and how is it that ye are so hard in your hearts, and so blind in your minds, that ye have need that I, your [b]younger brother, should speak unto you, yea, and set an [c]example for you?

9 How is it that ye have not hearkened unto the word of the Lord?

10 How is it that ye have [a]forgotten that ye have seen an angel of the Lord?

4a Luke 1: 4 (3–4);
   John 20: 31 (30–31).
 b 2 Ne. 9: 41 (41, 45,
   51).
5a Gal. 1: 10; 1 Thes. 2: 4;
   Heb. 13: 21; W of
   M 1: 4.
7 1a 1 Ne. 1: 16.
 b 1 Ne. 16: 7.

 c TG Marriage.
 d Ps. 127: 3.
2a 1 Ne. 16: 8.
3a 1 Ne. 3: 2.
5a TG Guidance, Divine.
6a 1 Ne. 16: 7 (7, 17).
 b 2 Ne. 4: 10.
 c 1 Ne. 17: 18 (17–
   55).

8a Mosiah 28: 3; Alma 31:
   2; 3 Ne. 17: 14;
   Moses 7: 41.
 b 1 Chr. 29: 1; D&C 1: 19
   (19, 23).
 c TG Example.
10a Deut. 4: 9 (9–13);
   1 Ne. 4: 3.

11 Yea, and how is it that ye have forgotten what great things the Lord hath done for us, in ^adelivering us out of the hands of Laban, and also that we should obtain the record?

12 Yea, and how is it that ye have forgotten that the Lord is able to do all ^athings according to his will, for the children of men, if it so be that they exercise ^bfaith in him? Wherefore, let us be faithful to him.

13 And if it so be that we are faithful to him, we shall obtain the ^aland of promise; and ye shall know at some future period that the word of the Lord shall be fulfilled concerning the ^bdestruction of ^cJerusalem; for all things which the Lord hath spoken concerning the destruction of Jerusalem must be fulfilled.

14 For behold, the ^aSpirit of the Lord ^bceaseth soon to strive with them; for behold, they have ^crejected the prophets, and ^dJeremiah have they cast into prison. And they have sought to take away the ^elife of my father, insomuch that they have driven him out of the land.

15 Now behold, I say unto you that if ye will return unto Jerusalem ye shall also perish with them. And now, if ye have choice, go up to the land, and remember the words which I speak unto you, that if ye go ye will also perish; for thus the Spirit of the Lord constraineth me that I should speak.

16 And it came to pass that when I, Nephi, had spoken these words unto my brethren, they were angry with me. And it came to pass that they did lay their hands upon me, for behold, they were exceedingly wroth, and they did ^abind me with cords, for they sought to take away my life, that they might leave me in the wilderness to be devoured by wild beasts.

17 But it came to pass that I prayed unto the Lord, saying: O Lord, according to my faith which is in thee, wilt thou deliver me from the hands of my brethren; yea, even give me ^astrength that I may ^bburst these bands with which I am bound.

18 And it came to pass that when I had said these words, behold, the bands were loosed from off my hands and feet, and I stood before my brethren, and I spake unto them again.

19 And it came to pass that they were angry with me again, and sought to lay hands upon me; but behold, one of the ^adaughters of Ishmael, yea, and also her mother, and one of the sons of Ishmael, did plead with my brethren, insomuch that they did soften their hearts; and they did cease striving to take away my life.

20 And it came to pass that they were sorrowful, because of their wickedness, insomuch that they did bow down before me, and did plead with me that I would ^aforgive them of the thing that they had done against me.

21 And it came to pass that I did frankly ^aforgive them all that they had done, and I did exhort them that they would pray unto the Lord their God for ^bforgiveness. And it came to pass that they did so. And after they had done praying unto the Lord we did again travel on our journey towards the tent of our father.

22 And it came to pass that we did

11a 1 Ne. 4: 1 (1–38).
12a Ps. 18: 32 (32–40);
       1 Ne. 17: 50; Alma 26: 12.
   b 1 Ne. 2: 19 (18–21); 15: 11.
13a 1 Ne. 2: 20.
    TG Promised Lands.
   b 2 Kgs. 25: 4 (1–21).
   c 2 Ne. 6: 8; 25: 10;
       Omni 1: 15; Hel. 8: 21

    (20–21).
14a TG God, Spirit of.
   b Ezek. 5: 6; 1 Ne. 1: 19 (18–20); 2: 13.
   c TG Prophets, Rejection of.
   d Jer. 37: 15 (15–21).
   e 1 Ne. 2: 1.
16a 1 Ne. 18: 11 (11–15).
17a Judg. 14: 6.

   b Jacob 4: 6; Alma 14: 28 (26–28); 3 Ne. 28: 20 (19–22).
19a 1 Ne. 16: 7; 18: 19 (19–20).
20a TG Repentance.
21a TG Family, Love within.
   b TG Forgiveness.

[Between 600 and 592 B.C.]

come down unto the tent of our father. And after I and my brethren and all the house of Ishmael had come down unto the tent of my father, they did give *a*thanks unto the Lord their God; and they did offer *b*sacrifice and burnt offerings unto him.

CHAPTER 8

Lehi sees a vision of the tree of life— He partakes of its fruit and desires his family to do likewise—He sees a rod of iron, a strait and narrow path, and the mists of darkness that enshroud men—Sariah, Nephi, and Sam partake of the fruit, but Laman and Lemuel refuse.

AND it came to pass that we had gathered together all manner of *a*seeds of every kind, both of grain of every kind, and also of the seeds of fruit of every kind.

2 And it came to pass that while my father tarried in the wilderness he spake unto us, saying: Behold, I have *a*dreamed a dream; or, in other words, I have *b*seen a *c*vision.

3 And behold, because of the thing which I have seen, I have reason to rejoice in the Lord because of *a*Nephi and also of Sam; for I have reason to suppose that they, and also many of their seed, will be saved.

4 But behold, *a*Laman and Lemuel, I fear exceedingly because of you; for behold, methought I saw in my dream, a dark and dreary wilderness.

5 And it came to pass that I saw a *a*man, and he was dressed in a white *b*robe; and he came and stood before me.

6 And it came to pass that he spake unto me, and bade me follow him.

7 And it came to pass that as I followed him I beheld myself that I was in a dark and dreary waste.

8 And after I had traveled for the space of many hours in darkness, I began to pray unto the Lord that he would have *a*mercy on me, according to the multitude of his tender mercies.

9 And it came to pass after I had prayed unto the Lord I beheld a large and spacious *n*field.

10 And it came to pass that I beheld a *a*tree, whose *b*fruit was desirable to make one *c*happy.

11 And it came to pass that I did go forth and partake of the *a*fruit thereof; and I beheld that it was most sweet, above all that I ever before tasted. Yea, and I beheld that the fruit thereof was white, to exceed all the *b*whiteness that I had ever seen.

12 And as I partook of the fruit thereof it filled my soul with exceedingly great *a*joy; wherefore, I began to be *b*desirous that my family should partake of it also; for I knew that it was *c*desirable above all other fruit.

13 And as I cast my eyes round about, that perhaps I might discover my family also, I beheld a *a*river of water; and it ran along, and it was near the tree of which I was partaking the fruit.

14 And I looked to behold from whence it came; and I saw the head thereof a little way off; and at the head thereof I beheld your mother Sariah, and Sam, and *a*Nephi; and they stood as if they knew not whither they should go.

15 And it came to pass that I

22a TG Thanksgiving.
  b 1 Ne. 5: 9.
8 1a 1 Ne. 16: 11.
  2a 1 Ne. 1: 16; 10: 2.
    TG Dream; Revelation; Vision.
    b 1 Ne. 14: 29.
    c 1 Ne. 10: 17.
  3a 1 Ne. 8: 14 (14–18).
  4a 1 Ne. 8: 35.
  5a Dan. 10: 5 (2–12).

  b JS-H 1: 31 (30–32).
8a TG God, Mercy of.
9a Matt. 13: 38.
10a Gen. 2: 9; Rev. 2: 7 (1–7); 22: 2 (1–16); 1 Ne. 11: 4, 8 (8–25).
   b 1 Ne. 8: 24 (15, 20, 24); Alma 32: 42 (41–43).
   c TG Happiness.
11a 1 Ne. 15: 36; Alma 5: 34.

  b 1 Ne. 11: 8.
12a TG Joy.
   b Enos 1: 9; Alma 36: 24. TG Family, Love within.
   c Gen. 3: 6; 1 Ne. 15: 36.
13a 1 Ne. 12: 16 (16–18); 15: 26–27 (26–29).
14a 1 Ne. 8: 3 (3–4).

[Between 600 and 592 B.C.]

beckoned unto them; and I also did say unto them with a loud voice that they should come unto me, and partake of the fruit, which was desirable above all other fruit.

16 And it came to pass that they did come unto me and partake of the fruit also.

17 And it came to pass that I was desirous that Laman and Lemuel should come and partake of the fruit also; wherefore, I cast mine eyes towards the head of the river, that perhaps I might see them.

18 And it came to pass that I saw them, but they would ªnot come unto me and partake of the fruit.

19 And I beheld a ªrod of iron, and it extended along the bank of the river, and led to the tree by which I stood.

20 And I also beheld a ªstrait and narrow path, which came along by the rod of iron, even to the tree by which I stood; and it also led by the head of the fountain, unto a large and spacious field, as if it had been a ᵇworld.

21 And I saw numberless concourses of people, many of whom were ªpressing forward, that they might obtain the ᵇpath which led unto the tree by which I stood.

22 And it came to pass that they did come forth, and commence in the path which led to the tree.

23 And it came to pass that there arose a ªmist of darkness; yea, even an exceedingly great mist of darkness, insomuch that they who had commenced in the path did lose their way, that they wandered off and were ᵇlost.

24 And it came to pass that I beheld others pressing forward, and they came forth and caught hold of the end of the rod of iron; and they did press forward through the mist of darkness, ªclinging to the rod of iron, even until they did come forth and partake of the ᵇfruit of the tree.

25 And after they had partaken of the fruit of the tree they did cast their eyes about as if they were ªashamed.

26 And I also cast my eyes round about, and beheld, on the ªother side of the river of water, a great and ᵇspacious building; and it stood as it were in the ᶜair, high above the earth.

27 And it was filled with people, both old and young, both male and female; and their manner of dress was exceedingly fine; and they were in the ªattitude of ᵇmocking and pointing their fingers towards those who had come at and were partaking of the fruit.

28 And after they had ªtasted of the fruit they were ᵇashamed, because of those that were ᶜscoffing at them; and they ᵈfell away into forbidden paths and were lost.

29 And now I, Nephi, do not speak ªall the words of my father.

30 But, to be short in writing, behold, he saw other multitudes pressing forward; and they came and caught hold of the end of the ªrod of iron; and they did press their way forward, continually holding

18a 2 Ne. 5:20 (20–25).
19a Rev. 2:27; 12:5;
    19:15 (also JST Rev. 19:15); 1 Ne. 8:30;
    11:25; 15:23 (23–24).
20a Matt. 7:14; 2 Ne. 31:18 (17–20).
  b Matt. 13:38.
21a D&C 123:12.
  b TG Objectives; Path; Way.
23a Matt. 13:19 (18–19);
    2 Pet. 2:17; 1 Ne. 12:17; 15:24 (23–24).

  b TG Apostasy of Individuals.
24a TG Diligence; Perseverance.
  b 1 Ne. 8:10.
25a Rom. 1:16; 2 Tim. 1:8; Alma 46:21;
    Morm. 8:38.
26a Luke 16:26.
  b 1 Ne. 11:35 (35–36);
    12:18.
  c Eph. 2:2 (1–3).
27a TG Haughtiness; Pride.
  b Matt. 9:24 (20–26).

  TG Mocking.
28a 2 Pet. 2:20 (19–22).
  b Mark 4:17 (14–20);
    8:38; Luke 8:13 (11–15); John 12:43 (42–43); Rom. 3:3.
    TG Fearfulness.
  c TG Peer Influence.
  d TG Apostasy of Individuals.
29a 1 Ne. 1:17 (16–17).
30a 1 Ne. 8:19; 15:24 (23–24).

[Between 600 and 592 B.C.]

fast to the rod of iron, until they came forth and fell down and partook of the fruit of the tree.

31 And he also saw other [a]multitudes feeling their way towards that great and spacious building.

32 And it came to pass that many were drowned in the [a]depths of the [b]fountain; and many were lost from his view, wandering in strange roads.

33 And great was the multitude that did enter into that strange building. And after they did enter into that building they did point the finger of [a]scorn at me and those that were partaking of the fruit also; but we heeded them not.

34 These are the words of my father: For as many as [a]heeded them, had fallen away.

35 And [a]Laman and Lemuel partook not of the fruit, said my father.

36 And it came to pass after my father had spoken all the words of his dream or vision, which were many, he said unto us, because of these things which he saw in a vision, he exceedingly feared for Laman and Lemuel; yea, he feared lest they should be cast off from the presence of the Lord.

37 And he did [a]exhort them then with all the feeling of a tender parent, that they would hearken to his words, that perhaps the Lord would be merciful to them, and not cast them off; yea, my father did preach unto them.

38 And after he had preached unto them, and also prophesied unto them of many things, he bade them to keep the commandments of the Lord; and he did cease speaking unto them.

CHAPTER 9

Nephi makes two sets of records— Each is called the plates of Nephi— The larger plates contain a secular history; the smaller ones deal primarily with sacred things.

AND all these things did my father see, and hear, and speak, as he dwelt in a tent, in the [a]valley of Lemuel, and also a great many more things, which cannot be written upon these plates.

2 And now, as I have spoken concerning these plates, behold they are not the plates upon which I make a full account of the history of my people; for the [a]plates upon which I make a full account of my people I have given the name of Nephi; wherefore, they are called the plates of Nephi, after mine own name; and these plates also are called the plates of Nephi.

3 Nevertheless, I have received a commandment of the Lord that I should make these plates, for the special [a]purpose that there should be an account engraven of the [b]ministry of my people.

4 Upon the other plates should be engraven an account of the reign of the kings, and the wars and contentions of my people; wherefore these plates are for the more part of the ministry; and the [a]other plates are for the more part of the reign of the kings and the wars and contentions of my people.

31a Matt. 7:13.
32a 1 Ne. 15:29 (26–29).
  b 1 Ne. 8:14 (13–14).
33a Neh. 2:19; Alma 26: 23.
  TG Persecution; Scorn; Scorner.
34a Ex. 23:2; Prov. 19: 27; Mosiah 2:37 (33, 37).
35a 1 Ne. 8:4 (4, 17–18); 2 Ne. 5:20 (19–24).
37a TG Family, Children,

Responsibilities toward.
9 1a 1 Ne. 2:6 (4–6, 8, 14–15); 16:6 (6, 12).
  2a IE the full account is on larger plates; the special account of his ministry is on the smaller plates of Nephi. See Jacob 3:13–14. See also 1 Ne. 1:17 (16–17); 6:1; 10:1;

19:2, 4; Omni 1:1; W of M 1:3 (2–11); D&C 10:38 (38–40).
3a D&C 3:19.
  b 1 Ne. 6:3.
4a 2 Ne. 4:14; 5:33 (29–33); Jacob 1:3 (2–4); Jarom 1:14; Omni 1:18; W of M 1:10.

[Between 600 and 592 B.C.]

5 Wherefore, the Lord hath commanded me to make these plates for a *a*wise purpose in him, which purpose I know not.

6 But the Lord *a*knoweth all things from the beginning; wherefore, he prepareth a way to accomplish all his works among the children of men; for behold, he hath all *b*power unto the fulfilling of all his words. And thus it is. Amen.

CHAPTER 10

Lehi predicts the Babylonian captivity —He tells of the coming among the Jews of a Messiah, a Savior, a Redeemer—He tells also of the coming of the one who should baptize the Lamb of God—Lehi tells of the death and resurrection of the Messiah—He compares the scattering and gathering of Israel to an olive tree—Nephi speaks of the Son of God, of the gift of the Holy Ghost, and of the need for righteousness.

AND now I, Nephi, proceed to give an account upon *a*these plates of my proceedings, and my reign and ministry; wherefore, to proceed with mine account, I must speak somewhat of the things of my father, and also of my brethren.

2 For behold, it came to pass after my father had made an end of speaking the words of his *a*dream, and also of exhorting them to all diligence, he spake unto them concerning the Jews—

3 That after they should be destroyed, even that great city *a*Jerusalem, and many be *b*carried away captive into *c*Babylon, according to the own due time of the Lord, they should *d*return again, yea, even be brought back out of captivity; and after they should be brought back out of captivity they should possess again the land of their inheritance.

4 Yea, even *a*six hundred years from the time that my father left Jerusalem, a *b*prophet would the Lord God raise up among the *c*Jews —even a *d*Messiah, or, in other words, a Savior of the world.

5 And he also spake concerning the prophets, how great a number had *a*testified of these things, concerning this Messiah, of whom he had spoken, or this Redeemer of the world.

6 Wherefore, all mankind were in a *a*lost and in a *b*fallen state, and ever would be save they should rely on this Redeemer.

7 And he spake also concerning a *a*prophet who should come before the Messiah, to prepare the way of the Lord—

8 Yea, even he should go forth and cry in the wilderness: *a*Prepare ye the way of the Lord, and make his paths straight; for there standeth one among you whom ye know not; and he is mightier than I, whose shoe's latchet I am not worthy to unloose. And much spake my father concerning this thing.

9 And my father said he should

5a 1 Ne. 19: 3; W of M
  1: 7; Alma 37: 14
  (2, 12, 14).
6a Isa. 48: 3 (3–7); Moses
  1: 6, 35.
  TG God, Fore-
  knowledge of; God,
  Intelligence of; God,
  Omniscience of.
  b Matt. 28: 18.
10 1a 1 Ne. 9: 2 (1–5);
  19: 3 (1–6).
2a 1 Ne. 8: 2 (2–36).
3a Esth. 2: 6; 2 Ne. 6: 8;
  Hel. 8: 20 (20–21).
  b Ezek. 36: 12 (8–15);
  2 Ne. 25: 10.

TG Israel, Bondage of,
  in Other Lands; Israel,
  Scattering of.
  c Ezek. 24: 2; 1 Ne. 1:
  13; Omni 1: 15.
  TG Babylon.
  d Neh. 12: 1; Jer. 29: 10
  (9–10); 2 Ne. 6: 9
  (8–9); Abr. 2: 6.
4a 1 Ne. 19: 8 (8–14);
  2 Ne. 25: 19; Alma 13:
  25; 3 Ne. 1: 1.
  b 1 Ne. 22: 21 (20–21).
  c TG Israel, Judah,
  People of.
  d Jacob 1: 6.
  TG Jesus Christ, Birth

of; Jesus Christ,
  Messiah
5a Jacob 7: 11; Mosiah 13:
  33; Hel. 8: 24 (19–24);
  3 Ne. 20: 24 (23–24).
  TG Jesus Christ,
  Prophecies about.
6a Rom. 3: 23; 2 Ne. 2: 5
  (5–8).
  b TG Death, Spiritual,
  First.
7a 1 Ne. 11: 27; 2 Ne. 31:
  4 (4–18).
  TG Foreordination.
8a Isa. 40: 3; Matt. 3: 3
  (1–3); D&C 84: 26.

[Between 600 and 592 B.C.]

baptize in ᵃBethabara, beyond Jordan; and he also said he should ᵇbaptize with water; even that he should baptize the Messiah with water.

10 And after he had baptized the Messiah with water, he should behold and bear record that he had baptized the ᵃLamb of God, who should take away the sins of the world.

11 And it came to pass after my father had spoken these words he spake unto my brethren concerning the gospel which should be preached among the Jews, and also concerning the ᵃdwindling of the Jews in ᵇunbelief. And after they had ᶜslain the Messiah, who should come, and after he had been slain he should ᵈrise from the dead, and should make himself ᵉmanifest, by the Holy Ghost, unto the Gentiles.

12 Yea, even my father spake much concerning the Gentiles, and also concerning the house of Israel, that they should be compared like unto an ᵃolive-tree, whose ᵇbranches should be broken off and should be ᶜscattered upon all the face of the earth.

13 Wherefore, he said it must needs be that we should be led with one accord into the ᵃland of promise, unto the fulfilling of the word of the Lord, that we should be scattered upon all the face of the earth.

14 And after the house of ᵃIsrael should be scattered they should be ᵇgathered together again; or, in fine, after the ᶜGentiles had received the fulness of the ᵈGospel, the natural branches of the ᵉolive-tree, or the ᶠremnants of the house of ᵍIsrael, should be grafted in, or ʰcome to the knowledge of the true Messiah, their Lord and their Redeemer.

15 And after this manner of language did my father prophesy and speak unto my brethren, and also many more things which I do not write in this book; for I have written as many of them as were expedient for me in mine ᵃother book.

16 And all these things, of which I have spoken, were done as my father dwelt in a ᵃtent, in the valley of Lemuel.

17 And it came to pass after I, Nephi, having heard all the ᵃwords of my father, concerning the things which he saw in a ᵇvision, and also the things which he spake by the power of the Holy Ghost, which power he received by faith on the Son of God—and the Son of God was the ᶜMessiah who should come— I, Nephi, was ᵈdesirous also that I might see, and hear, and know of these things, by the power of the ᵉHoly Ghost, which is the ᶠgift of God unto ᵍall those who diligently seek him, as well in times of ʰold

9a John 1: 28.
  b TG Jesus Christ, Baptism of.
10a TG Jesus Christ, Lamb of God.
11a Rom. 11: 1 (1–36); Jacob 4: 15 (14–18).
  b Morm. 5: 14 (14–20). TG Unbelief, Unbelievers.
  c TG Jesus Christ, Crucifixion of; Jesus Christ, Prophecies about.
  d TG Jesus Christ, Resurrection.
  e 3 Ne. 15: 23 (21–24). TG Holy Ghost, Mission of.
12a Gen. 49: 22 (22–26);

1 Ne. 15: 12; 2 Ne. 3: 5 (4–5); Jacob 5: 3 (3–77); 6: 1 (1–7). TG Vineyard of the Lord.
  b TG Israel, Bondage of, in Other Lands.
  c Deut. 32: 26; 1 Ne. 22: 3 (3–8). TG Israel, Scattering of.
13a 1 Ne. 2: 20.
14a TG Israel, Ten Lost Tribes of.
  b TG Israel, Gathering of.
  c 1 Ne. 13: 42; D&C 14: 10.
  d TG Gospel.
  e 1 Ne. 15: 7.

f TG Israel, Remnant of.
g TG Israel, Twelve Tribes of.
h 1 Ne. 19: 15 (14–17).
15a 1 Ne. 1: 17 (16–18).
16a 1 Ne. 2: 15 (15–16).
17a Enos 1: 3; Alma 36: 17 (17–18).
  b 1 Ne. 8: 2.
  c TG Jesus Christ, Messiah.
  d 2 Ne. 4: 24.
  e 2 Pet. 1: 21.
  f TG God, Gifts of; Holy Ghost, Gift of.
  g Moro. 7: 36; 10: 7 (4–5, 7, 19).
  h D&C 20: 26.

[Between 600 and 592 B.C.]

as in the time that he should manifest himself unto the children of men.

18 For he is the *a*same yesterday, to-day, and forever; and the way is prepared for all men from the foundation of the world, if it so be that they repent and come unto him.

19 For he that diligently *a*seeketh shall find; and the *b*mysteries of God shall be unfolded unto them, by the power of the *c*Holy Ghost, as well in these times as in times of old, and as well in times of old as in times to come; wherefore, the *d*course of the Lord is one eternal round.

20 Therefore remember, O man, for all thy doings thou shalt be brought into *a*judgment.

21 Wherefore, if ye have sought to do *a*wickedly in the days of your *b*probation, then ye are found *c*unclean before the judgment-seat of God; and no unclean thing can dwell with God; wherefore, ye must be cast off forever.

22 And the Holy Ghost giveth *a*authority that I should speak these things, and deny them not.

CHAPTER 11

Nephi sees the Spirit of the Lord and is shown in vision the tree of life—He sees the mother of the Son of God and learns of the condescension of God—He sees the baptism, ministry, and crucifixion of the Lamb of God—He sees also the call and ministry of the twelve apostles of the Lamb.

FOR it came to pass after I had desired to know the things that my father had seen, and believing that the Lord was able to make them known unto me, as I sat *a*pondering in mine heart I was *b*caught away in the Spirit of the Lord, yea, into an exceedingly high *c*mountain, which I never had before seen, and upon which I never had before set my foot.

2 And the Spirit said unto me: Behold, what *a*desirest thou?

3 And I said: I desire to behold the things which my father *a*saw.

4 And the Spirit said unto me: *a*Believest thou that thy father saw the *b*tree of which he hath spoken?

5 And I said: Yea, thou knowest that I *a*believe all the words of my father.

6 And when I had spoken these words, the Spirit cried with a loud voice, saying: Hosanna to the Lord, the most high God; for he is God over all the *a*earth, yea, even above all. And blessed art thou, Nephi, because thou *b*believest in the Son of the most high God; wherefore, thou shalt behold the things which thou hast desired.

7 And behold this thing shall be given unto thee for a *a*sign, that after thou hast beheld the tree which bore the fruit which thy father tasted, thou shalt also behold a man descending out of heaven, and him shall ye witness; and after ye have witnessed him ye shall *b*bear record that it is the Son of God.

8 And it came to pass that the Spirit said unto me: Look! And I

18a Heb. 13:8; Morm.
    9:9 (9–11); D&C 20:
    12.
  TG God, Perfection of.
19a TG Objectives.
  b TG Mysteries of Godliness.
  c TG Holy Ghost, Source
    of Testimony.
  d Alma 7:20; 37:12;
    D&C 3:2; 35:1.
  TG God, Eternal
    Nature of.
20a Eccl. 12:14; Ezek. 33:
    20. TG Judgment,
    The Last.

21a Ezek. 33:9.
  b TG Probation.
  c 1 Cor. 6:9 (9–10);
    Morm. 7:7; D&C 76:
    62 (50–62); 138:20, 37;
    Moses 6:57.
22a TG Holy Ghost,
    Mission of.
11 1a D&C 76:19.
  TG Meditation.
  b Dan. 8:2; 2 Cor. 12:2
    (1–4); Rev. 21:10;
    2 Ne. 4:25;
    Moses 1:1.
  c Ex. 24:13 (12–13);
    Deut. 10:1; Ether 3:1.

2a Zech. 4:2 (1–6).
3a 1 Ne. 8:2.
4a Mosiah 5:1 (1–2).
  b 1 Ne. 8:10 (10–12);
    15:22 (21–22).
5a 1 Ne. 2:16.
6a Ex. 9:29; Deut. 10:14;
    2 Ne. 29:7; 3 Ne. 11:
    14; D&C 55:1; Moses
    6:44.
  b TG Believe.
7a TG Signs.
  b TG Testimony;
    Witnesses.

[Between 600 and 592 B.C.]

looked and beheld a tree; and it was like unto the [a]tree which my father had seen; and the [b]beauty thereof was far beyond, yea, exceeding of all beauty; and the [c]whiteness thereof did exceed the whiteness of the driven snow.

9 And it came to pass after I had seen the tree, I said unto the Spirit: I behold thou hast shown unto me the tree which is [a]precious above all.

10 And he said unto me: What desirest thou?

11 And I said unto him: To know the [a]interpretation thereof—for I spake unto him as a man speaketh; for I beheld that he was in the [b]form of a man; yet nevertheless, I knew that it was the Spirit of the Lord; and he spake unto me as a man speaketh with another.

12 And it came to pass that he said unto me: Look! And I looked as if to look upon him, and I saw him not; for he had gone from before my presence.

13 And it came to pass that I looked and beheld the great city of Jerusalem, and also other cities. And I beheld the city of Nazareth; and in the city of [a]Nazareth I beheld a [b]virgin, and she was exceedingly fair and white.

14 And it came to pass that I saw the [a]heavens open; and an angel came down and stood before me; and he said unto me: Nephi, what beholdest thou?

15 And I said unto him: A virgin, most beautiful and fair above all other virgins.

16 And he said unto me: Knowest thou the [a]condescension of God?

17 And I said unto him: I know that he loveth his children; nevertheless, I do not know the meaning of all things.

18 And he said unto me: Behold, the [a]virgin whom thou seest is the [b]mother of the Son of God, after the manner of the flesh.

19 And it came to pass that I beheld that she was carried away in the Spirit; and after she had been carried away in the [a]Spirit for the space of a time the angel spake unto me, saying: Look!

20 And I looked and beheld the virgin again, bearing a [a]child in her arms.

21 And the angel said unto me: Behold the [a]Lamb of God, yea, even the [b]Son of the Eternal [c]Father! Knowest thou the meaning of the [d]tree which thy father saw?

22 And I answered him, saying: Yea, it is the [a]love of God, which [b]sheddeth itself abroad in the hearts of the children of men; wherefore, it is the [c]most desirable above all things.

23 And he spake unto me, saying: Yea, and the most [a]joyous to the soul.

24 And after he had said these words, he said unto me: Look! And I looked, and I beheld the Son of God [a]going forth among the children of men; and I saw many fall down at his feet and worship him.

25 And it came to pass that I beheld that the [a]rod of iron, which my father had seen, was the [b]word of God, which [c]led to the fountain of [d]living waters, or to the [e]tree of life;

8a 1 Ne. 8: 10.
  b TG Beauty.
  c 1 Ne. 8: 11.
9a 1 Ne. 11: 22 (22–25).
11a Gen. 40: 8.
  b TG Spirit Body.
13a Matt. 2: 23.
  b Luke 1: 27 (26–27);
    Alma 7: 10.
14a Ezek. 1: 1; 1 Ne. 1: 8
    (6–11).
16a 1 Ne. 11: 26.
    TG Jesus Christ, Con-
    descension of.
18a Luke 1: 34 (34–35).

TG Foreordination;
  Jesus Christ,
  Prophecies about.
  b Matt. 1: 16; Mosiah 3:
    8; Alma 19: 13.
  TG Jesus Christ, Birth of.
19a Matt. 1: 20.
20a Luke 2: 16.
21a TG Jesus Christ, Lamb
    of God.
  b TG Jesus Christ, Divine
    Sonship.
  c TG God the Father—
    Elohim/Eloheim.
  d 1 Ne. 8: 10; Alma 5: 62.

22a TG God, Love of.
  b Moro. 8: 26.
  c 1 Ne. 11: 9.
23a TG Joy.
24a Luke 4: 14 (14–21).
25a See especially
    JST Rev. 2: 27.
  b 1 Ne. 8: 19.
  c TG Guidance, Divine.
  d TG Living Water.
  e Gen. 2: 9; Prov. 11: 30
    (22–30); Moses 4: 28
    (28, 31).

[Between 600 and 592 B.C.]

which waters are a representation of the love of God; and I also beheld that the tree of life was a representation of the love of God.

26 And the angel said unto me again: Look and behold the [a]condescension of God!

27 And I looked and [a]beheld the Redeemer of the world, of whom my father had spoken; and I also beheld the [b]prophet who should prepare the way before him. And the Lamb of God went forth and was [c]baptized of him; and after he was baptized, I beheld the heavens open, and the Holy Ghost come down out of heaven and abide upon him in the form of a [d]dove.

28 And I beheld that he went forth ministering unto the people, in [a]power and great glory; and the multitudes were gathered together to hear him; and I beheld that they cast him out from among them.

29 And I also beheld [a]twelve others following him. And it came to pass that they were [b]carried away in the Spirit from before my face, and I saw them not.

30 And it came to pass that the angel spake unto me again, saying: Look! And I looked, and I beheld the heavens open again, and I saw [a]angels descending upon the children of men; and they did minister unto them.

31 And he spake unto me again, saying: Look! And I looked, and I beheld the Lamb of God going forth among the children of men. And I beheld multitudes of people who were [a]sick, and who were afflicted with all manner of diseases, and with [b]devils and [c]unclean spirits; and the angel spake and showed all these things unto me. And they were [d]healed by the power of the Lamb of God; and the devils and the unclean spirits were cast out.

32 And it came to pass that the angel spake unto me again, saying: Look! And I looked and beheld the Lamb of God, that he was [a]taken by the people; yea, the Son of the everlasting God was [b]judged of the world; and I saw and bear record.

33 And I, Nephi, saw that he was [a]lifted up upon the cross and [b]slain for the sins of the world.

34 And after he was slain I saw the multitudes of the earth, that they were gathered together to [a]fight against the apostles of the Lamb; for thus were the twelve called by the angel of the Lord.

35 And the multitude of the earth was gathered together; and I beheld that they were in a large and spacious [a]building, like unto the building which my father saw. And the angel of the Lord spake unto me again, saying: Behold the world and the wisdom thereof; yea, behold the house of Israel hath gathered together to [b]fight against the twelve apostles of the Lamb.

36 And it came to pass that I saw and bear record, that the great and spacious building was the [a]pride of the world; and it [b]fell, and the fall thereof was exceedingly great. And the angel of the Lord spake unto me

26a 1 Ne. 11: 16.
    TG Jesus Christ,
    Condescension of.
27a 2 Ne. 25: 13.
  b Mal. 3: 1; Matt. 11: 10;
    John 1: 6 (6–7);
    1 Ne. 10: 7 (7–10);
    2 Ne. 31: 4 (4–18);
    D&C 35: 4.
  c TG Jesus Christ,
    Baptism of.
  d TG Holy Ghost, Dove,
    Sign of.
28a D&C 138: 26.
29a 1 Ne. 12: 9; 13: 40

(24–26, 40).
    TG Apostles.
  b 1 Ne. 14: 30.
30a TG Angels.
31a TG Sickness.
  b Mark 5: 15 (15–20);
    7: 30; Mosiah 3: 6
    (5–7); Morm. 9: 24.
  c TG Spirits, Evil or
    Unclean.
  d TG Healing.
32a TG Jesus Christ,
    Betrayal of.
  b Mark 15: 19 (17–20);
    Luke 9: 44 (44–45).

33a Luke 18: 31; 2 Ne. 10:
    3; Mosiah 3: 9 (9–10);
    3 Ne. 27: 14.
  b TG Jesus Christ,
    Atonement through;
    Jesus Christ, Death of.
34a Mark 13: 13; 1 Cor. 4:
    9 (6–13).
35a 1 Ne. 8: 26; 12: 18.
  b Micah 3: 5; D&C 121:
    38.
36a TG Pride.
  b TG Earth, Cleansing of;
    World, End of.

[Between 600 and 592 B.C.]

again, saying: Thus shall be the destruction of all nations, kindreds, tongues, and people, that shall fight against the twelve apostles of the Lamb.

CHAPTER 12

Nephi sees in vision: the land of promise; the righteousness, iniquity, and downfall of its inhabitants; the coming of the Lamb of God among them; how the twelve disciples and the twelve apostles shall judge Israel; the loathsome and filthy state of those who dwindle in unbelief.

AND it came to pass that the angel said unto me: Look, and behold thy seed, and also the seed of thy brethren. And I looked and beheld the [a]land of promise; and I beheld multitudes of people, yea, even as it were in number as many as the [b]sand of the sea.

2 And it came to pass that I beheld multitudes gathered together to battle, one against the other; and I beheld [a]wars, and rumors of wars, and great slaughters with the sword among my people.

3 And it came to pass that I beheld many generations pass away, after the manner of wars and contentions in the land; and I beheld many cities, yea, even that I did not number them.

4 And it came to pass that I saw a [a]mist of [b]darkness on the face of the land of promise; and I saw lightnings, and I heard thunderings, and earthquakes, and all manner of tumultuous noises; and I saw the earth and the rocks, that they rent; and I saw mountains tumbling into pieces; and I saw the plains of the earth, that they were [c]broken up; and I saw many cities that they were [d]sunk; and I saw many that they were burned with fire; and I saw many that did tumble to the earth, because of the quaking thereof.

5 And it came to pass after I saw these things, I saw the [a]vapor of darkness, that it passed from off the face of the earth; and behold, I saw multitudes who had not fallen because of the great and terrible judgments of the Lord.

6 And I saw the heavens open, and the [a]Lamb of God descending out of heaven; and he came down and [b]showed himself unto them.

7 And I also saw and bear record that the Holy Ghost fell upon [a]twelve others; and they were ordained of God, and chosen.

8 And the angel spake unto me, saying: Behold the twelve disciples of the Lamb, who are chosen to minister unto thy seed.

9 And he said unto me: Thou rememberest the [a]twelve apostles of the Lamb? Behold they are they who shall [b]judge the twelve tribes of Israel; wherefore, the twelve ministers of thy seed shall be judged of them; for ye are of the house of Israel.

10 And these [a]twelve ministers whom thou beholdest shall judge thy seed. And, behold, they are righteous forever; for because of their faith in the Lamb of God their [b]garments are made white in his blood.

11 And the angel said unto me: Look! And I looked, and beheld [a]three generations pass away in

---

12 1a TG Promised Lands.
  b Gen. 22: 17 (17–18);
    1 Kgs. 4: 20.
  2a Enos 1: 24; Morm. 8: 7
    (7–8).
   TG War.
  4a 1 Ne. 19: 12; Hel. 14:
    28 (20–28); 3 Ne. 10: 11.
   b 1 Ne. 19: 10;
    2 Ne. 26: 3.
   c Gen. 7: 11.
   d 3 Ne. 8: 14.

5a 3 Ne. 8: 20.
6a 2 Ne. 26: 1 (1, 9);
    3 Ne. 11: 8 (3–17).
   b 2 Ne. 32: 6; Alma 7: 8;
    16: 20.
7a 3 Ne. 11: 22; 12: 1.
9a Matt. 10: 1; Luke 6: 13;
    John 6: 70;
    1 Ne. 11: 29; 13: 40
    (24–26, 40).
   b Matt. 19: 28; D&C 29:
    12.

TG Judgment, The Last.
10a 3 Ne. 27: 27; Morm. 3:
    18–19.
   b Rev. 7: 14; 19: 8;
    Alma 5: 21 (21–27);
    13: 11 (11–13);
    3 Ne. 27: 19 (19–20);
    D&C 88: 85.
11a 2 Ne. 26: 9 (9–10);
    3 Ne. 27: 32 (30–32).

[Between 600 and 592 B.C.]

righteousness; and their garments were white even like unto the Lamb of God. And the angel said unto me: These are made white in the blood of the Lamb, because of their faith in him.

12 And I, Nephi, also saw many of the ᵃfourth generation who passed away in righteousness.

13 And it came to pass that I saw the multitudes of the earth gathered together.

14 And the angel said unto me: Behold thy seed, and also the seed of thy brethren.

15 And it came to pass that I looked and beheld the people of my seed gathered together in multitudes ᵃagainst the seed of my brethren; and they were gathered together to battle.

16 And the angel spake unto me, saying: Behold the fountain of ᵃfilthy water which thy father saw; yea, even the ᵇriver of which he spake; and the depths thereof are the depths of ᶜhell.

17 And the ᵃmists of darkness are the temptations of the devil, which ᵇblindeth the eyes, and hardeneth the hearts of the children of men, and leadeth them away into ᶜbroad roads, that they perish and are lost.

18 And the large and spacious ᵃbuilding, which thy father saw, is vain ᵇimaginations and the ᶜpride of the children of men. And a great and a terrible ᵈgulf divideth them; yea, even the word of the ᵉjustice of the Eternal God, and the Messiah who is the Lamb of God, of whom the Holy Ghost beareth record, from the beginning of the world until this time, and from this time henceforth and forever.

19 And while the angel spake these words, I beheld and saw that the seed of my brethren did contend against my seed, according to the word of the angel; and because of the pride of my seed, and the ᵃtemptations of the devil, I beheld that the seed of my brethren did ᵇoverpower the people of my seed.

20 And it came to pass that I beheld, and saw the people of the seed of my brethren that they had overcome my seed; and they went forth in multitudes upon the face of the land.

21 And I saw them gathered together in multitudes; and I saw ᵃwars and rumors of wars among them; and in wars and rumors of wars I saw ᵇmany generations pass away.

22 And the angel said unto me: Behold these shall ᵃdwindle in unbelief.

23 And it came to pass that I beheld, after they had dwindled in unbelief they became a ᵃdark, and loathsome, and a ᵇfilthy people, full of ᶜidleness and all manner of abominations.

CHAPTER 13

Nephi sees in vision: the church of the devil set up among the Gentiles; the discovery and colonizing of America; the loss of many plain and precious parts of the Bible; the resultant state of gentile apostasy; the restoration of the gospel, the coming forth of latter-day scripture, and the building up of Zion.

12a 2 Ne. 26: 9; Alma 45: 12 (10–12); Hel. 13: 10 (5, 9–10); 3 Ne. 27: 32; 4 Ne. 1: 14 (14–41).
15a Morm. 6: 7 (1–22).
16a TG Filthiness.
  b 1 Ne. 8: 13 (13–14); 15: 27 (26–29).
  c TG Hell.
17a 2 Pet. 2: 17; 1 Ne. 8: 23; 15: 24 (23–24).
  b TG Apostasy of

Individuals.
  c Prov. 4: 14; Luke 13: 24.
18a 1 Ne. 8: 26; 11: 35 (35–36).
  b Jer. 7: 24; 9: 14.
  c TG Haughtiness; Pride.
  d Luke 16: 26; 1 Ne. 15: 28 (28–30).
  e TG God, Justice of.
19a TG Temptation.

  b Jarom 1: 10; W of M 1: 2 (1–2).
21a Morm. 8: 8; Moro. 1: 2.
  b 2 Ne. 1: 18.
22a 1 Ne. 15: 13; 2 Ne. 26: 15.
23a Jacob 3: 3; Alma 3: 7 (6–19).
  b 2 Ne. 5: 22 (20–25).
  TG Filthiness.
  c TG Idleness.

[Between 600 and 592 B.C.]

AND it came to pass that the angel spake unto me, saying: Look! And I looked and beheld many nations and kingdoms.

2 And the angel said unto me: What beholdest thou? And I said: I behold many [a]nations and kingdoms.

3 And he said unto me: These are the nations and kingdoms of the Gentiles.

4 And it came to pass that I saw among the nations of the [a]Gentiles the formation of a [b]great church.

5 And the angel said unto me: Behold the formation of a [a]church which is most abominable above all other churches, which [b]slayeth the saints of God, yea, and tortureth them and bindeth them down, and yoketh them with a [c]yoke of iron, and bringeth them down into captivity.

6 And it came to pass that I beheld this [a]great and [b]abominable church; and I saw the [c]devil that he was the founder of it.

7 And I also saw [a]gold, and silver, and silks, and scarlets, and fine-twined [b]linen, and all manner of precious clothing; and I saw many harlots.

8 And the angel spake unto me, saying: Behold the gold, and the silver, and the silks, and the scarlets, and the fine-twined linen, and the precious clothing, and the harlots, are the [a]desires of this great and abominable church.

9 And also for the [a]praise of the world do they [b]destroy the saints of God, and bring them down into captivity.

10 And it came to pass that I looked and beheld many waters; and they divided the Gentiles from the seed of my brethren.

11 And it came to pass that the angel said unto me: Behold the wrath of God is upon the seed of thy brethren.

12 And I looked and beheld a man among the Gentiles, who was separated from the seed of my brethren by the many waters; and I beheld the Spirit of God, that it came down and [a]wrought upon the man; and he went forth upon the many waters, even unto the seed of my brethren, who were in the promised land.

13 And it came to pass that I beheld the Spirit of God, that it wrought upon other Gentiles; and they went forth out of captivity, upon the many waters.

14 And it came to pass that I beheld many [a]multitudes of the Gentiles upon the [b]land of promise; and I beheld the wrath of God, that it was upon the seed of my brethren; and they were [c]scattered before the Gentiles and were smitten.

15 And I beheld the Spirit of the Lord, that it was upon the Gentiles, and they did prosper and [a]obtain the [b]land for their inheritance; and I beheld that they were white, and exceedingly fair and [c]beautiful, like unto my people before they were [d]slain.

16 And it came to pass that I, Nephi, beheld that the Gentiles who had gone forth out of captivity did humble themselves before the Lord; and the power of the Lord was [a]with them.

17 And I beheld that their mother Gentiles were gathered together

13 2a TG Kings, Earthly; Nations.
4a TG Gentiles.
 b 1 Ne. 13: 26 (26, 34); 14: 10 (3, 9–17).
5a 2 Ne. 10: 16.
 b Rev. 17: 6 (3–6); 18: 24; 1 Ne. 14: 13.
 c Jer. 28: 14 (10–14). TG Bondage, Spiritual.
6a D&C 88: 94.

 b TG Devil, Church of.
 c 1 Ne. 22: 23 (22–23). TG Devil.
7a Morm. 8: 37 (36–38).
 b Ether 10: 24.
8a Rev. 18: 19 (10–24); Morm. 8: 37 (36–41).
9a Morm. 8: 38.
 b Rev. 13: 7 (4–7).
12a TG Guidance, Divine.
14a 2 Ne. 1: 11; Morm. 5:

19 (19–20).
 b TG Promised Lands.
 c 1 Ne. 22: 7. TG Israel, Scattering of.
15a Morm. 5: 19.
 b 2 Ne. 10: 19.
 c 2 Ne. 5: 21; 4 Ne. 1: 10; Morm. 9: 6.
 d Morm. 6: 19 (17–22).
16a D&C 101: 80.

[Between 600 and 592 B.C.]

upon the waters, and upon the land also, to battle against them.

18 And I beheld that the power of God was with them, and also that the wrath of God was upon all those that were gathered together ᵃagainst them to battle.

19 And I, Nephi, beheld that the Gentiles that had gone out of captivity were ᵃdelivered by the power of God out of the hands of all other nations.

20 And it came to pass that I, Nephi, beheld that they did prosper in the land; and I beheld a ᵃbook, and it was carried forth among them.

21 And the angel said unto me: Knowest thou the meaning of the book?

22 And I said unto him: I know not.

23 And he said: Behold it proceedeth out of the mouth of a Jew. And I, Nephi, beheld it; and he said unto me: The ᵃbook that thou beholdest is a ᵇrecord of the ᶜJews, which contains the covenants of the Lord, which he hath made unto the house of Israel; and it also containeth many of the prophecies of the holy prophets; and it is a record like unto the engravings which are upon the ᵈplates of brass, save there are not so many; nevertheless, they contain the covenants of the Lord, which he hath made unto the house of Israel; wherefore, they are of great worth unto the Gentiles.

24 And the angel of the Lord said unto me: Thou hast beheld that the ᵃbook proceeded forth from the mouth of a Jew; and when it proceeded forth from the mouth of a Jew it contained the fulness of the gospel of the Lord, of whom the twelve apostles bear record; and they bear record according to the truth which is in the Lamb of God.

25 Wherefore, these things go forth from the ᵃJews in purity unto the ᵇGentiles, according to the truth which is in God.

26 And after they go forth by the ᵃhand of the twelve apostles of the Lamb, from the Jews ᵇunto the Gentiles, thou seest the formation of that ᶜgreat and abominable ᵈchurch, which is most abominable above all other churches; for behold, they have ᵉtaken away from the gospel of the Lamb many parts which are ᶠplain and most precious; and also many covenants of the Lord have they taken away.

27 And all this have they done that they might pervert the right ways of the Lord, that they might blind the eyes and harden the hearts of the children of men.

28 Wherefore, thou seest that after the book hath gone forth through the hands of the great and abominable church, that there are many plain and ᵃprecious things taken away from the book, which is the book of the Lamb of God.

29 And after these plain and precious things were ᵃtaken away it goeth forth unto all the nations of the Gentiles; and after it goeth forth unto all the nations of the Gentiles, yea, even across the many waters which thou hast seen with the Gentiles which have gone forth out of captivity, thou seest—because of the many plain and precious things which have been taken out of the

18a 1 Ne. 17: 35.
19a 2 Ne. 10: 10 (10–14);
   3 Ne. 21: 4; Ether 2:
   12.
20a 1 Ne. 13: 41 (3–41);
   14: 23.
23a 1 Ne. 13: 38; 2 Ne. 29:
   6 (4–12).
   b TG Scriptures,
      Preservation of.
   c 2 Ne. 3: 12.
   d 1 Ne. 5: 10 (10–22);
      19: 22.

24a 2 Ne. 29: 3.
25a 2 Ne. 29: 4 (4–6);
   D&C 3: 16.
   TG Israel, Judah,
      People of.
   b TG Gentiles.
26a Luke 1: 1 (1–4);
   2 Tim. 4: 13.
   b Matt. 21: 43.
   c 1 Ne. 13: 4 (4–6);
      14: 10 (3, 9–17).

d TG Apostasy of the
   Early Christian
   Church.
e Morm. 8: 33; Moses 1:
   41.
   TG False Doctrine;
   Scriptures, Lost.
f 1 Ne. 14: 21 (20–26);
   A of F 8.
28a 1 Ne. 14: 23.
29a 2 Pet. 3: 16.

[Between 600 and 592 B.C.]

book, which were plain unto the understanding of the children of men, according to the plainness which is in the Lamb of God— because of these things which are taken away out of the gospel of the Lamb, an exceedingly great many do stumble, yea, insomuch that Satan hath great power over them.

30 Nevertheless, thou beholdest that the Gentiles who have gone forth out of captivity, and have been lifted up by the power of God above all other nations, upon the face of the land which is choice above all other lands, which is the land that the Lord God hath covenanted with thy father that his seed should have for the [a]land of their inheritance; wherefore, thou seest that the Lord God will not suffer that the Gentiles will utterly destroy the [b]mixture of thy [c]seed, which are among thy brethren.

31 Neither will he suffer that the Gentiles shall [a]destroy the seed of thy brethren.

32 Neither will the Lord God suffer that the Gentiles shall forever remain in that awful state of blindness, which thou beholdest they are in, because of the plain and most precious parts of the gospel of the Lamb which have been kept back by that [a]abominable church, whose formation thou hast seen.

33 Wherefore saith the Lamb of God: I will be [a]merciful unto the Gentiles, unto the visiting of the remnant of the house of Israel in great judgment.

34 And it came to pass that the angel of the Lord spake unto me, saying: Behold, saith the Lamb of God, after I have [a]visited the [b]remnant of the house of Israel— and this remnant of whom I speak is the seed of thy father—wherefore, after I have visited them in judgment, and smitten them by the hand of the Gentiles, and after the Gentiles do [c]stumble exceedingly, because of the most plain and precious parts of the [d]gospel of the Lamb which have been kept back by that abominable church, which is the mother of harlots, saith the Lamb—I will be merciful unto the [e]Gentiles in that day, insomuch that I will [f]bring forth unto them, in mine own power, much of my [g]gospel, which shall be plain and precious, saith the Lamb.

35 For, behold, saith the Lamb: I will manifest myself unto thy seed, that they shall write many things which I shall minister unto them, which shall be plain and precious; and after thy seed shall be destroyed, and dwindle in unbelief, and also the seed of thy brethren, behold, [a]these things shall be hid up, to come forth unto the Gentiles, by the gift and power of the Lamb.

36 And in them shall be written my [a]gospel, saith the Lamb, and my [b]rock and my salvation.

37 And [a]blessed are they who shall seek to bring forth my [b]Zion at that day, for they shall have the [c]gift and the [d]power of the Holy Ghost; and if they [e]endure unto the end they

30a TG Lands of Inheritance; Promised Lands.
 b 2 Ne. 29: 12 (12–13); Alma 45: 14 (10–14); D&C 3: 17.
 c 2 Ne. 3: 3.
31a 2 Ne. 4: 7; 10: 18 (18–19); Jacob 3: 6 (5–9); Hel. 15: 12 (10–17); 3 Ne. 16: 8 (4–13); Morm. 5: 20 (20–21).
32a TG Devil, Church of.
33a Isa. 42: 1 (1, 3–4).
34a D&C 124: 8; Abr. 1: 17.
 b TG Israel, Joseph,

People of.
 c 1 Ne. 14: 1 (1–3); 2 Ne. 26: 20.
 d TG Gospel.
 e TG Millennium, Preparing a People for.
 f TG Scriptures, Lost.
 g D&C 10: 62.
   TG Restoration of the Gospel.
35a 1 Ne. 14: 7; 22: 8; 2 Ne. 27: 26 (6–26); 29: 1 (1–2).
   TG Book of Mormon.
36a 3 Ne. 27: 21.
 b 3 Ne. 11: 39 (38–39).

   TG Rock.
37a Jacob 5: 75 (70–76); D&C 21: 9.
   TG Mission of Israel; Mission of Latter-day Saints.
 b TG Zion.
 c TG Holy Ghost, Gift of.
 d Luke 24: 49; 1 Ne. 14: 14; D&C 38: 38 (32–38).
 e 3 Ne. 27: 16.
   TG Endure; Perseverance; Steadfastness.

[Between 600 and 592 B.C.]

shall be ᶠlifted up at the last day, and shall be saved in the everlasting ᵍkingdom of the Lamb; and whoso shall ʰpublish peace, yea, tidings of great joy, how beautiful upon the mountains shall they be.

38 And it came to pass that I beheld the remnant of the seed of my brethren, and also the ᵃbook of the Lamb of God, which had proceeded forth from the mouth of the Jew, that it came forth from the Gentiles ᵇunto the remnant of the seed of my brethren.

39 And after it had come forth unto them I beheld ᵃother ᵇbooks, which came forth by the power of the Lamb, from the Gentiles unto them, unto the ᶜconvincing of the Gentiles and the remnant of the seed of my brethren, and also the Jews who were scattered upon all the face of the earth, that the records of the prophets and of the twelve apostles of the Lamb are ᵈtrue.

40 And the angel spake unto me, saying: These ᵃlast records, which thou hast seen among the Gentiles, shall ᵇestablish the truth of the ᶜfirst, which are of the ᵈtwelve apostles of the Lamb, and shall make known the plain and precious things which have been taken away from them; and shall make known to all kindreds, tongues, and people, that the Lamb of God is the Son of the Eternal Father, and the ᵉSavior of the world; and that all men must come unto him, or they cannot be saved.

41 And they must come according to the words which shall be established by the mouth of the Lamb; and the words of the Lamb shall be made known in the records of thy seed, as well as in the ᵃrecords of the twelve apostles of the Lamb; wherefore they both shall be established in ᵇone; for there is ᶜone God and one ᵈShepherd over all the earth.

42 And the time cometh that he shall manifest himself unto all nations, both unto the ᵃJews and also unto the Gentiles; and after he has manifested himself unto the Jews and also unto the Gentiles, then he shall manifest himself unto the Gentiles and also unto the Jews, and the ᵇlast shall be first, and the ᶜfirst shall be last.

CHAPTER 14

An angel tells Nephi of the blessings and cursings to fall upon the Gentiles —There are only two churches: the Church of the Lamb of God and the church of the devil—The saints of God in all nations are persecuted by the great and abominable church—The apostle John shall write concerning the end of the world.

AND it shall come to pass, that if the ᵃGentiles shall hearken unto the Lamb of God in that day that he shall manifest himself unto them in word, and also in ᵇpower, in very deed, unto the ᶜtaking away of their ᵈstumbling blocks—

2 And harden not their hearts

37f James 4: 10.
  g ᴛɢ Kingdom of God, in Heaven.
  h Isa. 52: 7 (7–10); Mark 13: 10; 3 Ne. 20: 40.
38a 1 Ne. 13: 23; 2 Ne. 29: 6 (4–6).
  b Morm. 5: 15; 7: 8 (8–9).
39a D&C 9: 2.
  b ᴛɢ Scriptures to Come Forth.
  c Ezek. 37: 17 (15–20); 1 Ne. 14: 2 (1–5).
  d 1 Ne. 14: 30.
40a 2 Ne. 26: 17 (16–17); 27: 6 (6–26); 29: 12.

ᴛɢ Book of Mormon.
  b ᴛɢ Scriptures, Value of.
  c See the title page of the Book of Mormon.
  ᴛɢ Bible.
  d 1 Ne. 11: 29; 12: 9.
  e Moses 1: 6.
41a 1 Ne. 13: 20 (20–28).
  b Ezek. 37: 17.
  c Deut. 6: 4; 2 Ne. 31: 21.
  d ᴛɢ Jesus Christ, Good Shepherd.
42a D&C 18: 6, 26; 19: 27; 21: 12; 90: 9 (8–9); 107: 33; 112: 4.
  b Jacob 5: 63;

Ether 13: 12.
  c Luke 13: 30; 1 Ne. 10: 14; 15: 13 (13–20); D&C 14: 10.
14 1a 1 Ne. 22: 9 (8–9); 2 Ne. 30: 3; 3 Ne. 16: 6 (6–13).
  ᴛɢ Gentiles.
  b 1 Thes. 1: 5; 1 Ne. 14: 14; Jacob 6: 2 (2–3).
  c Ether 12: 27.
  d Isa. 57: 14; Ezek. 7: 19; 1 Cor. 1: 23; 1 Ne. 13: 34 (29, 34); 2 Ne. 26: 20.

[Between 600 and 592 B.C.]

against the Lamb of God, they shall be numbered among the seed of thy father; yea, they shall be *a*numbered among the house of Israel; and they shall be a *b*blessed people upon the *c*promised land forever; they shall be no more brought down into captivity; and the house of Israel shall no more be confounded.

3 And that great *a*pit, which hath been digged for them by that great and abominable church, which was founded by the devil and his children, that he might lead away the souls of men down to hell—yea, that great pit which hath been digged for the destruction of men shall be filled by those who digged it, unto their utter destruction, saith the Lamb of God; not the destruction of the soul, save it be the casting of it into that *b*hell which hath no end.

4 For behold, this is according to the *a*captivity of the devil, and also according to the justice of God, upon all those who will work wickedness and abomination before him.

5 And it came to pass that the angel spake unto me, Nephi, saying: Thou hast beheld that if the Gentiles repent it shall be *a*well with them; and thou also knowest concerning the covenants of the Lord unto the house of Israel; and thou also hast heard that whoso *b*repenteth not must perish.

6 Therefore, *a*wo be unto the Gentiles if it so be that they harden their hearts against the Lamb of God.

7 For the time cometh, saith the Lamb of God, that I will work a great and a *a*marvelous work among the children of men; a *b*work which shall be everlasting, either on the one hand or on the other—either to the convincing of them unto *c*peace and *d*life eternal, or unto the deliverance of them to the hardness of their hearts and the blindness of their minds unto their being brought down into captivity, and also into destruction, both temporally and spiritually, according to the *e*captivity of the devil, of which I have spoken.

8 And it came to pass that when the angel had spoken these words, he said unto me: Rememberest thou the *a*covenants of the Father unto the house of Israel? I said unto him, Yea.

9 And it came to pass that he said unto me: Look, and behold that great and abominable church, which is the mother of abominations, whose founder is the *a*devil.

10 And he said unto me: Behold there are save *a*two churches only; the one is the church of the Lamb of God, and the *b*other is the church of the *c*devil; wherefore, *d*whoso belongeth not to the church of the Lamb of God belongeth to that great church, which is the mother of abominations; and she is the *e*whore of all the earth.

11 And it came to pass that I

2a Gal. 3: 7 (7, 29);
  2 Ne. 10: 18 (18–19);
3 Ne. 16: 13; 21: 6
  (6, 22); Abr. 2: 10
  (9–11).
 b 2 Ne. 6: 12; 10: 10
  (8–14); 3 Ne. 16: 6
  (6–7); 20: 27; Morm.
  5: 19.
 c TG Israel, Deliverance
  of; Israel, Restoration
  of; Lands of
  Inheritance.
3a Ps. 57: 6; Matt. 7: 2
  (1–2); 1 Ne. 22: 14
  (13–14); D&C 10: 26
  (25–27); 109: 25.
 b Alma 19: 29.

 TG Damnation; Hell.
4a TG Bondage, Spiritual.
5a 1 Ne. 13: 39 (34–42);
  22: 9.
 b TG Repentance.
6a 2 Ne. 28: 32.
7a Isa. 29: 14; 1 Ne. 13:
  35; 22: 8; 2 Ne. 27: 26;
  29: 1 (1–2); D&C 4: 1.
 TG Restoration of the
  Gospel.
 b TG God, Works of.
 c TG Peace; Peace of God.
 d Jer. 21: 8.
 TG Eternal Life.
 e 2 Ne. 2: 29 (26–29);
  Alma 12: 11 (9–11).

8a TG Abrahamic
  Covenant; Israel,
  Mission of.
9a 1 Ne. 15: 35; D&C 1:
  35.
 TG Devil, Church of.
10a 1 Ne. 22: 23; 2 Ne. 26:
  20; Morm. 8: 28
  (25–41).
 TG Church.
 b 1 Ne. 13: 4 (4–6),
  26 (26, 34).
 c TG Devil, Church of;
  False Prophets.
 d 2 Ne. 10: 16.
 e Rev. 17: 15 (5, 15).

[Between 600 and 592 B.C.]

looked and beheld the whore of all the earth, and she sat upon many *a*waters; and she had dominion over *b*all the earth, among all nations, kindreds, tongues, and people.

12 And it came to pass that I beheld the church of the Lamb of God, and its numbers were *a*few, because of the wickedness and abominations of the whore who sat upon many waters; nevertheless, I beheld that the church of the Lamb, who were the saints of God, were also upon *b*all the face of the earth; and their dominions upon the face of the earth were small, because of the wickedness of the great whore whom I saw.

13 And it came to pass that I beheld that the great mother of abominations did gather together multitudes upon the face of all the earth, among all the nations of the Gentiles, to *a*fight against the Lamb of God.

14 And it came to pass that I, Nephi, beheld the power of the Lamb of God, that it descended upon the saints of the church of the Lamb, and upon the covenant people of the Lord, who were scattered upon all the face of the earth; and they were *a*armed with *b*righteousness and with the *c*power of God in great glory.

15 And it came to pass that I beheld that the wrath of God was *a*poured out upon that great and abominable church, insomuch that there were wars and rumors of wars among all the *b*nations and kindreds of the earth.

16 And as there began to be *a*wars and rumors of wars among all the nations which belonged to the mother of abominations, the angel spake unto me, saying: Behold, the wrath of God is upon the mother of harlots; and behold, thou seest all these things—

17 And when the *a*day cometh that the *b*wrath of God is poured out upon the mother of harlots, which is the great and abominable church of all the earth, whose founder is the devil, then, at that day, the *c*work of the Father shall commence, in preparing the way for the fulfilling of his *d*covenants, which he hath made to his people who are of the house of Israel.

18 And it came to pass that the angel spake unto me, saying: Look!

19 And I looked and beheld a man, and he was dressed in a white robe.

20 And the angel said unto me: Behold *a*one of the twelve apostles of the Lamb.

21 Behold, he shall *a*see and *b*write the *c*remainder of these things; yea, and also many things which have been.

22 And he shall write also concerning the end of the world.

23 Wherefore, the things which he shall write are just and true; and behold they are written in the *a*book which thou beheld proceeding out of the mouth of the Jew; and at the time they proceeded out of the mouth of the Jew, or, at the time the book proceeded out of the mouth of the Jew, the things which were written were plain and pure, and most *b*precious and easy to the understanding of all men.

11a Jer. 51: 13 (12–14).
  b D&C 35: 11.
12a Matt. 7: 14; Jacob 5: 70; 3 Ne. 14: 14; D&C 138: 26.
  b D&C 90: 11.
13a Rev. 17: 6 (1–6); 18: 24; 1 Ne. 13: 5.
14a TG Mission of Latter-day Saints.
  b TG Deliverance; Protection, Divine.
  c Luke 24: 49; 1 Ne. 13: 37; 14: 1; Jacob 6: 2

  (2–3); D&C 38: 38 (32–38).
15a D&C 115: 6 (5–6).
  b Mark 13: 8; D&C 87: 6.
16a 1 Ne. 22: 13 (13–14); Morm. 8: 30.
  TG War.
17a TG Last Days.
  b 1 Ne. 21: 26; 22: 16 (15–16); 3 Ne. 20: 20 (19–21).
  c 3 Ne. 21: 26 (7, 20–29). TG Israel, Restoration of.

  d Morm. 8: 21 (21, 41).
  TG Abrahamic Covenant.
20a Rev. 1: 1 (1–3); 1 Ne. 14: 27.
21a Rev. 1: 1.
  b 1 Ne. 13: 24 (20–40); A of F 8.
  c Rev. 4: 1.
23a 1 Ne. 13: 20 (20–24); Morm. 8: 33; Ether 4: 16.
  b 1 Ne. 13: 28 (28–32).

24 And behold, the things which this [a]apostle of the Lamb shall write are many things which thou hast seen; and behold, the remainder shalt thou see.

25 But the things which thou shalt see hereafter thou shalt not write; for the Lord God hath ordained the apostle of the Lamb of God that he should [a]write them.

26 And also others who have been, to them hath he shown all things, and they have [a]written them; and they are [b]sealed up to come forth in their purity, according to the truth which is in the Lamb, in the own due time of the Lord, unto the house of Israel.

27 And I, Nephi, heard and bear record, that the name of the apostle of the Lamb was [a]John, according to the word of the angel.

28 And behold, I, Nephi, am forbidden that I should write the remainder of the things which I saw and heard; wherefore the things which I have written sufficeth me; and I have written but a small part of the things which I saw.

29 And I bear record that I saw the things which my [a]father saw, and the angel of the Lord did make them known unto me.

30 And now I make an end of speaking concerning the things which I saw while I was [a]carried away in the spirit; and if all the things which I saw are not written, the things which I have written are [b]true. And thus it is. Amen.

CHAPTER 15

Lehi's seed are to receive the gospel from the Gentiles in the latter days— The gathering of Israel is likened unto an olive tree whose natural branches shall be grafted in again—Nephi interprets the vision of the tree of life and speaks of the justice of God in dividing the wicked from the righteous.

AND it came to pass that after I, Nephi, had been carried away in the spirit, and seen all these things, I returned to the tent of my father.

2 And it came to pass that I beheld my brethren, and they were disputing one with another concerning the things which my father had spoken unto them.

3 For he truly spake many great things unto them, which were hard to be [a]understood, save a man should inquire of the Lord; and they being hard in their hearts, therefore they did not look unto the Lord as they ought.

4 And now I, Nephi, was grieved because of the hardness of their hearts, and also, because of the things which I had seen, and knew they must unavoidably come to pass because of the great wickedness of the children of men.

5 And it came to pass that I was overcome because of my afflictions, for I considered that mine [a]afflictions were great above all, because of the [b]destruction of my people, for I had beheld their fall.

6 And it came to pass that after I had received [a]strength I spake unto my brethren, desiring to know of them the cause of their disputations.

7 And they said: Behold, we cannot understand the words which our father hath spoken concerning the natural branches of the [a]olive-tree, and also concerning the Gentiles.

8 And I said unto them: Have ye [a]inquired of the Lord?

24a Ether 4: 16.
25a John 20: 30 (30–31); 21: 25; Rev. 1: 19.
26a TG Scriptures, Writing of.
  b Dan. 12: 9; 2 Ne. 27: 10 (6–23); 30: 17; Ether 3: 21 (21–27); 4: 5 (4–7); 12: 21; D&C 35: 18; JS-H 1: 65.

27a Rev. 1: 1 (1–3).
29a 1 Ne. 8: 2 (2–35).
30a 1 Kgs. 18: 12; 1 Ne. 11: 29 (19, 29).
  b 1 Ne. 13: 39; 2 Ne. 25: 20.
15 3a 1 Cor. 2: 11 (10–12). TG Hardheartedness; Understanding.

5a Moses 7: 44 (41–44).
  b Enos 1: 13; Morm. 6: 1.
6a Moses 1: 10; JS-H 1: 20, 48.
7a 1 Ne. 10: 14 (2–15).
8a 2 Ne. 1: 25 (24–27); Mosiah 10: 14. TG Problem-Solving.

[Between 600 and 592 B.C.]

9 And they said unto me: [a]We have not; for the Lord maketh no such thing known unto us.

10 Behold, I said unto them: How is it that ye do not keep the commandments of the Lord? How is it that ye will [a]perish, because of the hardness of your hearts?

11 Do ye not remember the things which the Lord hath said?—If ye will not harden your hearts, and [a]ask me in [b]faith, believing that ye shall receive, with diligence in keeping my commandments, surely these things shall be made known unto you.

12 Behold, I say unto you, that the house of Israel was compared unto an olive-tree, by the Spirit of the Lord which was in our father; and behold are we not broken off from the house of Israel, and are we not a [a]branch of the house of Israel?

13 And now, the thing which our father meaneth concerning the grafting in of the natural branches through the fulness of the Gentiles, is, that in the latter days, when our seed shall have [a]dwindled in unbelief, yea, for the space of many years, and many generations after the [b]Messiah shall be manifested in body unto the children of men, then shall the fulness of the [c]gospel of the Messiah come unto the Gentiles, and from the [d]Gentiles unto the remnant of our seed—

14 And at that day shall the remnant of our [a]seed [b]know that they are of the house of Israel, and that they are the [c]covenant people of the Lord; and then shall they know and

[d]come to the [e]knowledge of their forefathers, and also to the knowledge of the gospel of their Redeemer, which was ministered unto their fathers by him; wherefore, they shall come to the knowledge of their Redeemer and the very points of his doctrine, that they may know how to come unto him and be saved.

15 And then at that day will they not rejoice and give praise unto their everlasting God, their [a]rock and their salvation? Yea, at that day, will they not receive the strength and nourishment from the true [b]vine? Yea, will they not come unto the true fold of God?

16 Behold, I say unto you, Yea; they shall be remembered again among the house of Israel; they shall be [a]grafted in, being a natural branch of the olive-tree, into the true olive-tree.

17 And this is what our father meaneth; and he meaneth that it will not come to pass until after they are scattered by the Gentiles; and he meaneth that it shall come by way of the Gentiles, that the Lord may show his power unto the Gentiles, for the very cause that he shall be [a]rejected of the Jews, or of the house of Israel.

18 Wherefore, our father hath not spoken of our seed alone, but also of all the house of Israel, pointing to the covenant which should be fulfilled in the latter days; which covenant the Lord made to our father Abraham, saying: In thy [a]seed shall all the kindreds of the earth be [b]blessed.

9a D&C 58: 33.
10a TG Apostasy of Individuals.
11a James 1: 5 (5–6).
   TG Prayer.
   b 1 Ne. 2: 19 (18–21); 7: 12 (9–13).
12a Gen. 49: 22 (22–26); 1 Ne. 10: 12 (12–14); 19: 24.
   TG Israel, Joseph, People of.
13a 1 Ne. 12: 22 (22–23); 2 Ne. 26: 15.

   b TG Jesus Christ, Messiah.
   c TG Gospel; Mission of Latter-day Saints.
   d 1 Ne. 13: 42; 22: 9 (5–10); D&C 14: 10.
   TG Gentiles.
14a 2 Ne. 10: 2; 3 Ne. 5: 23 (21–26); 21: 7 (4–29).
   b 2 Ne. 3: 12; 30: 5; Morm. 7: 9 (1, 9–10).
   c TG Abrahamic Covenant.
   d Jacob 3: 6.
   e D&C 3: 18 (16–20).

   See also title page of the Book of Mormon.
15a TG Rock.
   b Gen. 49: 11; John 15: 1.
16a Jacob 5: 54 (1–77).
17a TG Jesus Christ, Betrayal of; Jesus Christ, Crucifixion of.
18a Gen. 12: 3 (1–3); Abr. 2: 11 (6–11).
   TG Seed of Abraham.
   b TG Israel, Mission of.
[Between 600 and 592 B.C.]

19 And it came to pass that I, Nephi, spake much unto them concerning these things; yea, I spake unto them concerning the ^arestoration of the Jews in the latter days.

20 And I did rehearse unto them the words of ^aIsaiah, who spake ^bconcerning the ^crestoration of the Jews, or of the house of Israel; and after they were restored they should no more be confounded, neither should they be scattered again. And it came to pass that I did speak many words unto my brethren, that they were pacified and did ^dhumble themselves before the Lord.

21 And it came to pass that they did speak unto me again, saying: What meaneth this thing which our father saw in a dream? What meaneth the ^atree which he saw?

22 And I said unto them: It was a representation of the ^atree of life.

23 And they said unto me: What meaneth the ^arod of iron which our father saw, that led to the tree?

24 And I said unto them that it was the ^aword of God; and whoso would hearken unto the word of God, and would ^bhold fast unto it, they would never perish; neither could the ^ctemptations and the fiery ^ddarts of the ^eadversary overpower them unto blindness, to lead them away to destruction.

25 Wherefore, I, Nephi, did exhort them to give ^aheed unto the word of the Lord; yea, I did exhort them with all the energies of my soul, and with all the ^bfaculty which I possessed, that they would give heed to the word of God and remember to keep his commandments always in all things.

26 And they said unto me: What meaneth the ^ariver of water which our father saw?

27 And I said unto them that the ^awater which my father saw was ^bfilthiness; and so much was his mind swallowed up in other things that he beheld not the filthiness of the water.

28 And I said unto them that it was an awful ^agulf, which separated the wicked from the tree of life, and also from the saints of God.

29 And I said unto them that it was a representation of that awful ^ahell, which the angel said unto me was prepared for the wicked.

30 And I said unto them that our father also saw that the ^ajustice of God did also divide the wicked from the righteous; and the brightness thereof was like unto the brightness of a flaming ^bfire, which ascendeth up unto God forever and ever, and hath no end.

31 And they said unto me: Doth this thing mean the torment of the body in the days of ^aprobation, or doth it mean the final state of the soul after the ^bdeath of the temporal body, or doth it speak of the things which are temporal?

32 And it came to pass that I said unto them that it was a representation of things both temporal and spiritual; for the day should come that they must be judged of their ^aworks, yea, even the works which were done by the temporal body in their days of ^bprobation.

19a Isa. 42: 22 (22–23); 1 Ne. 19: 15.
TG Israel, Gathering of; Israel, Judah, People of.
20a 1 Ne. 19: 23.
b Isa. 40: 9.
c TG Israel, Restoration of.
d 1 Ne. 16: 5 (5, 24, 39).
21a 1 Ne. 8: 10 (10–12).
22a 1 Ne. 11: 4; Moses 3: 9.
23a 1 Ne. 8: 19 (19–24).
24a 1 Ne. 8: 19.

TG Gospel.
b Prov. 4: 13.
c 1 Ne. 8: 23.
TG Temptation.
d Eph. 6: 16; D&C 3: 8; 27: 17.
e TG Devil.
25a D&C 11: 2; 32: 4; 84: 43 (43–44).
TG Scriptures, Study of.
b W of M 1: 18.
26a 1 Ne. 8: 13.
27a 1 Ne. 12: 16 (16–18).
b TG Filthiness.

28a Luke 16: 26; 1 Ne. 12: 18; 2 Ne. 1: 13.
29a 1 Ne. 8: 32 (13–14, 32).
TG Hell.
30a TG God, Justice of; Justice.
b Num. 11: 1 (1, 10); 2 Ne. 26: 6.
31a TG Probation.
b Alma 40: 11 (6–26).
32a TG Good Works.
b TG Probation.

[Between 600 and 592 B.C.]

33 Wherefore, if they should [a]die in their wickedness they must be [b]cast off also, as to the things which are spiritual, which are pertaining to righteousness; wherefore, they must be brought to stand before God, to be [c]judged of their [d]works; and if their works have been filthiness they must needs be [e]filthy; and if they be filthy it must needs be that they cannot [f]dwell in the kingdom of God; if so, the kingdom of God must be filthy also.

34 But behold, I say unto you, the kingdom of God is not filthy, and there cannot any unclean thing enter into the kingdom of God; wherefore there must needs be a place of [a]filthiness prepared for that which is filthy.

35 And there is a place prepared, yea, even that [a]awful [b]hell of which I have spoken, and the [c]devil is the preparator of it; wherefore the final state of the souls of men is to dwell in the kingdom of God, or to be cast out because of that [d]justice of which I have spoken.

36 Wherefore, the wicked are rejected from the righteous, and also from that [a]tree of life, whose fruit is most precious and most [b]desirable above all other fruits; yea, and it is the [c]greatest of all the [d]gifts of God. And thus I spake unto my brethren. Amen.

CHAPTER 16

The wicked take the truth to be hard—Lehi's sons marry the daughters of Ishmael—The Liahona guides their course in the wilderness—Messages from the Lord are written on the Liahona from time to time—Ishmael dies; his family murmur because of afflictions.

AND now it came to pass that after I, Nephi, had made an end of speaking to my brethren, behold they said unto me: Thou hast declared unto us hard things, more than we are able to bear.

2 And it came to pass that I said unto them that I knew that I had spoken [a]hard things against the wicked, according to the truth; and the righteous have I justified, and testified that they should be lifted up at the last day; wherefore, the [b]guilty taketh the [c]truth to be hard, for it [d]cutteth them to the very center.

3 And now my brethren, if ye were righteous and were willing to hearken to the truth, and give heed unto it, that ye might [a]walk uprightly before God, then ye would not murmur because of the truth, and say: Thou speakest hard things against us.

4 And it came to pass that I, Nephi, did exhort my brethren, with all diligence, to keep the commandments of the Lord.

5 And it came to pass that they did [a]humble themselves before the Lord; insomuch that I had joy and great hopes of them, that they would walk in the paths of righteousness.

6 Now, all these things were said

33a Ezek. 18:26;
   Mosiah 15:26;
   Moro. 10:26.
  b Alma 12:16; 40:26.
  c TG Jesus Christ, Judge;
   Judgment, The Last.
  d Ps. 33:15 (13–15);
   3 Ne. 27:25 (23–27).
  e 2 Ne. 9:16; D&C 88:
   35.
  f Ps. 15:1 (1–5); 24:3
   (3–4); Mosiah 15:23;
   Alma 11:37; D&C 76:
   62 (50–70); Moses 6:57
   (55–59).

34a TG Filthiness.
35a 2 Ne. 9:19; Mosiah 26:
   27.
  b TG Hell.
  c 1 Ne. 14:9; D&C 1:35.
  d TG Justice.
36a Gen. 2:9; 1 Ne. 8:11;
   2 Ne. 2:15.
  b 1 Ne. 8:12.
  c Hel. 5:8.
  d D&C 14:7.
   TG God, Gifts of.
16 2a Acts 7:54; 2 Ne. 33:
   5; Enos 1:23;

W of M 1:17.
  TG Chastening.
  b John 3:20 (19–21);
   7:7; Hel. 13:24
   (24–27).
  c Prov. 15:10; 2 Ne. 1:
   26; 9:40.
  d Acts 5:33; Mosiah 13:
   7; Moses 6:37.
3a D&C 5:21.
  TG Walking with God.
5a 1 Ne. 15:20; 16:24
   (24, 39); 18:4.

and done as my father dwelt in a tent in the ^avalley which he called Lemuel.

7 And it came to pass that I, Nephi, took one of the ^adaughters of Ishmael to ^bwife; and also, my brethren took of the ^cdaughters of Ishmael to wife; and also ^dZoram took the eldest daughter of Ishmael to wife.

8 And thus my father had fulfilled all the ^acommandments of the Lord which had been given unto him. And also, I, Nephi, had been blessed of the Lord exceedingly.

9 And it came to pass that the voice of the Lord spake unto my father by night, and commanded him that on the morrow he should take his ^ajourney into the wilderness.

10 And it came to pass that as my father arose in the morning, and went forth to the tent door, to his great astonishment he beheld upon the ground a round ^aball of curious workmanship; and it was of fine brass. And within the ball were two spindles; and the one ^bpointed the way whither we should go into the wilderness.

11 And it came to pass that we did gather together whatsoever things we should carry into the wilderness, and all the remainder of our provisions which the Lord had given unto us; and we did take ^aseed of every kind that we might carry into the wilderness.

12 And it came to pass that we did take our tents and depart into the wilderness, across the river Laman.

13 And it came to pass that we traveled for the space of four days, nearly a south-southeast direction, and we did pitch our tents again; and we did call the name of the place ^aShazer.

14 And it came to pass that we did take our bows and our arrows, and go forth into the wilderness to slay food for our families; and after we had slain food for our families we did return again to our families in the wilderness, to the place of Shazer. And we did go forth again in the wilderness, following the same direction, keeping in the most fertile parts of the wilderness, which were in the borders near the ^aRed Sea.

15 And it came to pass that we did travel for the space of many days, ^aslaying food by the way, with our bows and our arrows and our stones and our slings.

16 And we did follow the ^adirections of the ball, which led us in the more fertile parts of the wilderness.

17 And after we had traveled for the space of many days, we did pitch our tents for the space of a time, that we might again rest ourselves and obtain food for our families.

18 And it came to pass that as I, Nephi, went forth to slay food, behold, I did break my bow, which was made of fine ^asteel; and after I did break my bow, behold, my brethren were angry with me because of the loss of my bow, for we did obtain no food.

19 And it came to pass that we did return without food to our families, and being much fatigued, because of their journeying, they did suffer much for the want of food.

20 And it came to pass that Laman and Lemuel and the sons of Ishmael did begin to murmur exceedingly, because of their sufferings and afflictions in the wilderness; and also my father began to murmur against the Lord his God; yea, and they were all exceedingly sorrowful,

6a 1 Ne. 2: 14 (8, 14); 9: 1.
7a 1 Ne. 7: 1 (1, 19); 18: 19 (19-20).
 b TG Marriage.
 c 1 Ne. 7: 6.
 d 1 Ne. 4: 35; 2 Ne. 5: 6 (5-6).
8a 1 Ne. 3: 18; 5: 21; 7: 2.

9a Omni 1: 16.
10a 1 Ne. 16: 16; Alma 37: 38 (38-47).
 b Ex. 13: 21.
11a 1 Ne. 8: 1; 18: 6; Ether 1: 41; 2: 3.
13a HEB twisting, intertwining.
14a 1 Ne. 2: 5; D&C 17: 1.

15a Alma 17: 7.
16a 1 Ne. 16: 10 (10, 16, 26); 18: 12 (12, 21); 2 Ne. 5: 12; Alma 37: 38 (38-47); D&C 17: 1.
18a 2 Sam. 22: 35; Ps. 18: 34.

[Between 600 and 592 B.C.]

even that they did "murmur against the Lord.

21 Now it came to pass that I, Nephi, having been afflicted with my brethren because of the loss of my bow, and their bows having lost their "springs, it began to be exceedingly difficult, yea, insomuch that we could obtain no food.

22 And it came to pass that I, Nephi, did speak much unto my brethren, because they had hardened their hearts again, even unto "complaining against the Lord their God.

23 And it came to pass that I, Nephi, did "make out of wood a bow, and out of a straight stick, an arrow; wherefore, I did arm myself with a bow and an arrow, with a sling and with stones. And I said unto my "father: Whither shall I go to obtain food?

24 And it came to pass that he did "inquire of the Lord, for they had "humbled themselves because of my words; for I did say many things unto them in the energy of my soul.

25 And it came to pass that the voice of the Lord came unto my father; and he was truly "chastened because of his murmuring against the Lord, insomuch that he was brought down into the depths of sorrow.

26 And it came to pass that the voice of the Lord said unto him: Look upon the ball, and behold the things which are written.

27 And it came to pass that when my father beheld the things which were "written upon the ball, he did fear and tremble exceedingly, and also my brethren and the sons of Ishmael and our wives.

28 And it came to pass that I, Nephi, beheld the pointers which were in the ball, that they did work according to the "faith and diligence and heed which we did give unto them.

29 And there was also written upon them a new writing, which was plain to be read, which did give us "understanding concerning the ways of the Lord; and it was written and changed from time to time, according to the faith and diligence which we gave unto it. And thus we see that by "small means the Lord can bring about great things.

30 And it came to pass that I, Nephi, did go forth up into the top of the mountain, according to the "directions which were given upon the ball.

31 And it came to pass that I did slay wild "beasts, insomuch that I did obtain food for our families.

32 And it came to pass that I did return to our tents, bearing the beasts which I had slain; and now when they beheld that I had obtained "food, how great was their joy! And it came to pass that they did humble themselves before the Lord, and did give thanks unto him.

33 And it came to pass that we did again take our journey, traveling nearly the same course as in the beginning; and after we had traveled for the space of many days we did pitch our tents again, that we might tarry for the space of a time.

34 And it came to pass that "Ishmael died, and was buried in the place which was called "Nahom.

35 And it came to pass that the daughters of Ishmael did "mourn exceedingly, because of the loss of

---

20a TG Murmuring.
21a Gen. 49: 24.
22a Ex. 16: 8; Num. 11: 1 (1–2); D&C 29: 19.
23a TG Initiative.
  b TG Honoring Father and Mother.
24a TG Guidance, Divine; Prayer.
  b 1 Ne. 15: 20; 16: 5.
25a Ether 2: 14.

      TG Chastening; Repentance.
27a TG Warnings.
28a Alma 37: 40.
      TG Faith.
29a TG Understanding.
  b 2 Kgs. 5: 13; James 3: 4; Alma 37: 6 (6–8, 41); D&C 123: 16.
30a TG Guidance, Divine.

31a Gen. 9: 3.
32a 2 Ne. 1: 24.
      TG Food; Thanksgiving.
34a 1 Ne. 7: 2 (2–6, 19).
  b HEB probably "consolation," from verb *naham*, "be sorry, console oneself."
35a TG Mourning.

[Between 600 and 592 B.C.]

their father, and because of their [b]afflictions in the wilderness; and they did [c]murmur against my father, because he had brought them out of the land of Jerusalem, saying: Our father is dead; yea, and we have wandered much in the wilderness, and we have suffered much affliction, hunger, thirst, and fatigue; and after all these sufferings we must perish in the wilderness with hunger.

36 And thus they did murmur against my father, and also against me; and they were desirous to [a]return again to Jerusalem.

37 And Laman said unto Lemuel and also unto the sons of Ishmael: Behold, let us [a]slay our father, and also our brother Nephi, who has taken it upon him to be our [b]ruler and our teacher, who are his elder brethren.

38 Now, he says that the Lord has talked with him, and also that [a]angels have ministered unto him. But behold, we know that he lies unto us; and he tells us these things, and he worketh many things by his cunning arts, that he may deceive our eyes, thinking, perhaps, that he may lead us away into some strange wilderness; and after he has led us away, he has thought to make himself a king and a ruler over us, that he may do with us according to his will and pleasure. And after this manner did my brother Laman [b]stir up their hearts to [c]anger.

39 And it came to pass that the Lord was with us, yea, even the voice of the Lord came and did speak many words unto them, and did [a]chasten them exceedingly; and after they were chastened by the voice of the Lord they did turn away their anger, and did repent of their sins, insomuch that the Lord did bless us again with food, that we did not perish.

CHAPTER 17

Nephi is commanded to build a ship—His brethren oppose him—He exhorts them by recounting the history of God's dealings with Israel—He is filled with the power of God—His brethren are forbidden to touch him, lest they wither as a dried reed.

AND it came to pass that we did again take our journey in the wilderness; and we did travel nearly eastward from that time forth. And we did travel and [a]wade through much affliction in the wilderness; and our [b]women did bear children in the wilderness.

2 And so great were the [a]blessings of the Lord upon us, that while we did live upon [b]raw [c]meat in the wilderness, our women did give plenty of suck for their children, and were strong, yea, even like unto the men; and they began to bear their journeyings without murmurings.

3 And thus we see that the commandments of God must be fulfilled. And if it so be that the children of men keep the commandments of God he doth nourish them, and [a]strengthen them, and provide means whereby they can accomplish the thing which he has commanded them; wherefore, he did [b]provide means for us while we did sojourn in the wilderness.

4 And we did sojourn for the space of many years, yea, *even eight years in the wilderness.

5 And we did come to the land which we called [a]Bountiful, because

---

35b TG Affliction.
  c TG Murmuring.
36a Num. 14: 4 (1–5).
37a 1 Ne. 17: 44; 2 Ne. 1: 24.
  TG Murder.
  b Gen. 37: 10 (9–11); Num. 16: 13; 1 Ne. 2: 22; 8: 10.
38a 1 Ne. 3: 30 (30–31);

4: 3.
  b TG Provoking.
  c TG Anger.
39a TG Chastening.
17 1a Ps. 69: 2 (1–2, 14).
  b TG Woman.
2a TG Blessing.
  b 1 Ne. 17: 12.
  c Ex. 16: 13 (12–13); 1 Ne. 18: 6.

TG Meat.
3a Ex. 1: 19; Ezra 8: 22 (22–23); Isa. 45: 24; Mosiah 2: 41; Alma 26: 12.
  TG Strength.
  b Gen. 18: 14; 1 Ne. 3: 7.
5a Alma 22: 29 (29–33).

[*592 B.C.]

of its much fruit and also wild honey; and all these things were prepared of the Lord that we might not perish. And we beheld the sea, which we called Irreantum, which, being interpreted, is many waters.

6 And it came to pass that we did pitch our tents by the seashore; and notwithstanding we had suffered many [a]afflictions and much difficulty, yea, even so much that we cannot write them all, we were exceedingly rejoiced when we came to the seashore; and we called the place Bountiful, because of its much fruit.

7 And it came to pass that after I, Nephi, had been in the land of Bountiful for the space of many days, the voice of the Lord came unto me, saying: [a]Arise, and get thee into the mountain. And it came to pass that I arose and went up into the mountain, and cried unto the Lord.

8 And it came to pass that the Lord spake unto me, saying: Thou shalt [a]construct a ship, after the [b]manner which I shall show thee, that I may carry thy people across these waters.

9 And I said: Lord, whither shall I go that I may find ore to molten, that I may make [a]tools to construct the ship after the manner which thou hast shown unto me?

10 And it came to pass that the Lord told me whither I should go to find ore, that I might make tools.

11 And it came to pass that I, Nephi, did make a bellows wherewith to [a]blow the fire, of the skins of beasts; and after I had made a bellows, that I might have wherewith to blow the fire, I did smite two stones together that I might make fire.

12 For the Lord had not hitherto suffered that we should make much fire, as we journeyed in the wilderness; for he said: I will make thy food become sweet, that ye [a]cook it not;

13 And I will also be your [a]light in the wilderness; and I will prepare the way before you, if it so be that ye shall keep my commandments; wherefore, inasmuch as ye shall keep my commandments ye shall be led towards the [b]promised land; and ye shall [c]know that it is by me that ye are led.

14 Yea, and the Lord said also that: After ye have arrived in the promised land, ye shall [a]know that I, the Lord, am [b]God; and that I, the Lord, did [c]deliver you from destruction; yea, that I did bring you out of the land of Jerusalem.

15 Wherefore, I, Nephi, did strive to keep the [a]commandments of the Lord, and I did [b]exhort my brethren to faithfulness and diligence.

16 And it came to pass that I did [a]make tools of the ore which I did molten out of the rock.

17 And when my brethren saw that I was about to [a]build a ship, they began to [b]murmur against me, saying: Our brother is a fool, for he thinketh that he can build a ship; yea, and he also thinketh that he can cross these great waters.

18 And thus my brethren did [a]complain against me, and were desirous that they might not labor, for they did not [b]believe that I could build a ship; neither would they

6a 2 Ne. 4:20.
7a Ezek. 3:22 (22–27).
8a Gen. 6:14 (14–16).
  b Ex. 25:40; 1 Chr. 28:
    12 (11–12, 19);
    1 Ne. 18:2.
9a Deut. 8:9; 1 Kgs. 6:7;
    1 Chr. 22:3 (3, 14);
    Job 28:2; Isa. 44:12.
11a Isa. 54:16.
12a 1 Ne. 17:2.
13a Alma 5:37 (37–38);

D&C 88:66.
  b 1 Ne. 2:20; 4:14;
    Jacob 2:12.
  c Ex. 6:7; 13:21.
    TG Guidance, Divine.
14a 2 Ne. 1:4.
    TG God, Knowledge
    about; Testimony.
  b D&C 5:2.
  c TG Deliverance.
15a 1 Kgs. 2:3; Prov. 7:2.

  b Acts 14:22; Titus 2:
    15; Heb. 3:13.
16a TG Skill.
17a 1 Ne. 17:49 (8, 49–51);
    18:1 (1–6).
  b TG Murmuring.
18a 1 Ne. 3:28; 7:6
    (6–19); 18:10 (9–22).
  b TG Unbelief,
    Unbelievers.

[About 591 B.C.]

believe that I was instructed of the Lord.

19 And now it came to pass that I, Nephi, was exceedingly sorrowful because of the hardness of their hearts; and now when they saw that I began to be sorrowful they were glad in their hearts, insomuch that they did [a]rejoice over me, saying: We knew that ye could not construct a ship, for we knew that ye were lacking in judgment; wherefore, thou canst not accomplish so great a work.

20 And thou art like unto our father, led away by the foolish [a]imaginations of his heart; yea, he hath led us out of the land of Jerusalem, and we have wandered in the wilderness for these many years; and our women have toiled, being big with child; and they have borne children in the wilderness and suffered all things, save it were death; and it would have been better that they had died before they came out of Jerusalem than to have suffered these afflictions.

21 Behold, these many years we have suffered in the wilderness, which time we might have enjoyed our possessions and the land of our inheritance; yea, and we might have been happy.

22 And we know that the people who were in the land of Jerusalem were a [a]righteous people; for they kept the statutes and judgments of the Lord, and all his commandments, according to the law of Moses; wherefore, we know that they are a righteous people; and our father hath judged them, and hath

led us away because we would hearken unto his words; yea, and our brother is like unto him. And after this manner of language did my brethren murmur and complain against us.

23 And it came to pass that I, Nephi, spake unto them, saying: Do ye believe that our fathers, who were the children of Israel, would have been led away out of the hands of the [a]Egyptians if they had not hearkened unto the words of the Lord?

24 Yea, do ye suppose that they would have been led out of bondage, if the Lord had not commanded Moses that he should [a]lead them out of bondage?

25 Now ye know that the children of Israel were in [a]bondage; and ye know that they were laden with [b]tasks, which were grievous to be borne; wherefore, ye know that it must needs be a good thing for them, that they should be [c]brought out of bondage.

26 Now ye know that [a]Moses was commanded of the Lord to do that great work; and ye know that by his [b]word the waters of the Red Sea were divided hither and thither, and they passed through on dry ground.

27 But ye know that the Egyptians were [a]drowned in the Red Sea, who were the armies of Pharaoh.

28 And ye also know that they were fed with [a]manna in the wilderness.

29 Yea, and ye also know that Moses, by his word according to the power of God which was in him, [a]smote the rock, and there came

19a TG Mocking; Persecution.
20a 1 Ne. 2: 11; 5: 4 (2–4).
22a 1 Ne. 1: 19 (4, 13, 18–20).
23a Ex. 20: 2; Ps. 80: 8; Moses 1: 26.
24a Ex. 3: 10 (2–10); Hosea 12: 13 (12–14); 1 Ne. 19: 10; 2 Ne. 3: 9; 25: 20.
25a Gen. 15: 13 (13–14); Mosiah 11: 21;

D&C 101: 79.
 TG Israel, Bondage of, in Egypt.
 b Ex. 1: 11 (10–11); 2: 11; 1 Ne. 20: 10.
 c Ex. 5: 1.
26a Josh. 24: 6; Jer. 2: 2; Acts 7: 27 (22–39).
 b Ex. 14: 21 (19–31); Josh. 2: 10; Neh. 9: 11; 1 Ne. 4: 2; Mosiah 7: 19; Hel. 8: 11; D&C 8: 3; Moses 1: 25.

 TG Israel, Deliverance of.
27a Josh. 24: 6.
28a Ex. 16: 15 (4, 14–15, 35); Num. 11: 7 (7–8); Deut. 8: 3; Neh. 9: 20; Hosea 13: 6 (5–8); John 6: 49; Mosiah 7: 19.
29a Ex. 17: 6; Num. 20: 11; Deut. 8: 15; Neh. 9: 15; 1 Ne. 20: 21; 2 Ne. 25: 20.

[About 591 B.C.]

forth water, that the children of Israel might quench their thirst.

30 And notwithstanding they being led, the Lord their God, their Redeemer, going before them, [a]leading them by day and giving light unto them by night, and doing all things for them which were [b]expedient for man to receive, they hardened their hearts and blinded their minds, and [c]reviled against Moses and against the true and living God.

31 And it came to pass that according to his word he did [a]destroy them; and according to his word he did [b]lead them; and according to his word he did do all things for them; and there was not any thing done save it were by his word.

32 And after they had crossed the river Jordan he did make them mighty unto the [a]driving out of the children of the land, yea, unto the scattering them to destruction.

33 And now, do ye suppose that the children of this land, who were in the land of promise, who were driven out by our fathers, do ye suppose that they were righteous? Behold, I say unto you, Nay.

34 Do ye suppose that our fathers would have been more choice than they if they had been righteous? I say unto you, Nay.

35 Behold, the Lord esteemeth all [a]flesh in one; he that is [b]righteous is [c]favored of God. But behold, this [d]people had rejected every word of God, and they were ripe in iniquity; and the fulness of the wrath of God was upon them; and the Lord did curse the land against them, and bless it unto our fathers; yea, he did curse it against them unto their destruction, and he did bless it unto our fathers unto their obtaining power over it.

36 Behold, the Lord hath created the [a]earth that it should be [b]inhabited; and he hath created his children that they should possess it.

37 And he [a]raiseth up a righteous nation, and destroyeth the nations of the wicked.

38 And he leadeth away the righteous into precious [a]lands, and the wicked he [b]destroyeth, and curseth the land unto them for their sakes.

39 He ruleth high in the heavens, for it is his throne, and this earth is his [a]footstool.

40 And he loveth those who will have him to be their God. Behold, he loved our [a]fathers, and he [b]covenanted with them, yea, even Abraham,[c]Isaac, and[d]Jacob; and he remembered the covenants which he had made; wherefore, he did bring them out of the land of [e]Egypt.

41 And he did straiten them in the wilderness with his rod; for they [a]hardened their hearts, even as ye have; and the Lord straitened them because of their iniquity. He sent

30a Ex. 13: 18 (18, 20).
  b D&C 18: 18; 88: 64 (64–65).
  c Ex. 32: 8; Num. 14: 11 (11–12); Ezek. 20: 13 (13–16); D&C 84: 24 (23–25).
31a Num. 26: 65.
  b Ex. 15: 13; 1 Ne. 5: 15; D&C 103: 16 (16–18).
32a Ex. 34: 11; Num. 33: 52 (52–53); Josh. 11: 6; 24: 8.
35a Acts 10: 15 (15, 34); Rom. 2: 11; 2 Ne. 26: 33 (23–33).
  b Ps. 55: 22; John 15: 10;

1 Ne. 22: 17.
  c 1 Sam. 2: 30; 1 Kgs. 2: 3; Ps. 97: 10; 145: 20 (1–21); Alma 13: 4; 28: 13; D&C 82: 10 (8–10).
  d Gen. 15: 16; Ex. 23: 31 (28–31); Deut. 7: 10; Josh. 2: 24.
36a Gen. 1: 28 (26–28); Jer. 27: 5; Moses 1: 29. TG Earth, Purpose of; Man, a Spirit Child of Heavenly Father; Man, Physical Creation of.
  b Isa. 45: 18.
37a Ps. 1: 6; Prov. 14: 34;

Isa. 45: 1 (1–3); 1 Ne. 4: 13; Ether 2: 10; D&C 98: 32 (31–32); 117: 6.
38a TG Lands of Inheritance.
  b Lev. 20: 22.
39a Isa. 66: 1; Lam. 2: 1; D&C 38: 17; Abr. 2: 7.
40a TG Israel, Origins of.
  b TG Abrahamic Covenant.
  c Gen. 21: 12; D&C 27: 10.
  d Gen. 28: 4 (1–5).
  e Deut. 4: 37 (37–38).
41a 2 Kgs. 17: 7 (7–23).

[About 591 B.C.]

fiery flying [b]serpents among them; and after they were bitten he prepared a way that they might be [c]healed; and the labor which they had to perform was to look; and because of the [d]simpleness of the way, or the easiness of it, there were many who perished.

42 And they did harden their hearts from time to time, and they did [a]revile against [b]Moses, and also against God; nevertheless, ye know that they were led forth by his matchless power into the land of promise.

43 And now, after all these things, the time has come that they have become wicked, yea, nearly unto ripeness; and I know not but they are at this day about to be [a]destroyed; for I know that the day must surely come that they must be destroyed, save a few only, who shall be led away into captivity.

44 Wherefore, the Lord [a]commanded my father that he should depart into the wilderness; and the Jews also sought to take away his life; yea, and [b]ye also have sought to take away his life; wherefore, ye are murderers in your hearts and ye are like unto them.

45 Ye are [a]swift to do iniquity but slow to remember the Lord your God. Ye have seen an [b]angel, and he spake unto you; yea, ye have heard his voice from time to time; and he hath spoken unto you in a still small voice, but ye were [c]past feeling, that ye could not feel his words; wherefore, he has spoken unto you like unto the voice of thunder, which did cause the earth to shake as if it were to divide asunder.

46 And ye also know that by the [a]power of his almighty word he can cause the earth that it shall pass away; yea, and ye know that by his word he can cause the rough places to be made smooth, and smooth places shall be broken up. O, then, why is it, that ye can be so hard in your hearts?

47 Behold, my soul is rent with anguish because of you, and my heart is pained; I fear lest ye shall be cast off forever. Behold, I am [a]full of the Spirit of God, insomuch that my frame has [b]no strength.

48 And now it came to pass that when I had spoken these words they were angry with me, and were desirous to throw me into the depths of the sea; and as they came forth to lay their hands upon me I spake unto them, saying: In the name of the Almighty God, I command you that ye [a]touch me not, for I am filled with the [b]power of God, even unto the consuming of my flesh; and whoso shall lay his hands upon me shall [c]wither even as a dried reed; and he shall be as naught before the power of God, for God shall smite him.

49 And it came to pass that I, Nephi, said unto them that they should murmur no more against their father; neither should they withhold their labor from me, for God had commanded me that I should [a]build a ship.

50 And I said unto them: [a]If God had commanded me to do all things I could do them. If he should command me that I should say unto this water, be thou earth, it should be earth; and if I should say it, it would be done.

51 And now, if the Lord has such great power, and has wrought so

41b Num. 21: 6 (4–9);
    Deut. 8: 15; Alma 33:
    19 (18–22).
  c Hosea 11: 3; John 3:
    14; 2 Ne. 25: 20.
  d Alma 37: 46 (44–47);
    Hel. 8: 15.
42a Ex. 32: 23; Num. 14:
    2 (1–12). TG Reviling.
  b D&C 84: 23.
43a Hosea 7: 13.

TG Israel, Scattering of.
44a 1 Ne. 2: 2 (1–2).
  b 1 Ne. 16: 37.
45a Mosiah 13: 29.
  b 1 Ne. 4: 3.
  c Acts 17: 27; Eph. 4: 19;
    1 Ne. 2: 14.
46a Hel. 12: 10 (6–18).
47a Micah 3: 8.
  b Dan. 10: 8 (8, 17);
    1 Ne. 1: 7; 19: 20.

48a Mosiah 13: 3.
  b 2 Ne. 1: 27 (26–27).
    TG God, Power of;
    Priesthood, Power of.
  c 1 Kgs. 13: 4 (4–7);
    Moses 1: 11; 6: 47.
49a 1 Ne. 17: 17; 18: 1 (1–6).
50a Philip. 4: 13; 1 Ne. 3:
    7; D&C 24: 13.

[About 591 B.C.]

many miracles among the children of men, how is it that he cannot [a]instruct me, that I should build a ship?

52 And it came to pass that I, Nephi, said many things unto my brethren, insomuch that they were [a]confounded and could not contend against me; neither durst they lay their hands upon me nor touch me with their fingers, even for the space of many days. Now they durst not do this lest they should wither before me, so powerful was the [b]Spirit of God; and thus it had wrought upon them.

53 And it came to pass that the Lord said unto me: Stretch forth thine hand again unto thy brethren, and they shall not wither before thee, but I will [a]shock them, saith the Lord, and this will I do, that they may know that I am the Lord their God.

54 And it came to pass that I stretched forth my hand unto my brethren, and they did not wither before me; but the Lord did shake them, even according to the word which he had spoken.

55 And now, they said: We know of a surety that the Lord is [a]with thee, for we know that it is the power of the Lord that has shaken us. And they fell down before me, and were about to [b]worship me, but I would not suffer them, saying: I am thy brother, yea, even thy younger brother; wherefore, worship the Lord thy God, and honor thy father and thy mother, that thy [c]days may be long in the land which the Lord thy God shall give thee.

CHAPTER 18

The ship is finished—The births of Jacob and Joseph are mentioned—

The company embarks for the promised land—The sons of Ishmael and their wives join in revelry and rebellion—Nephi is bound, and the ship is driven back by a terrible tempest—Nephi is freed, and by his prayer the storm ceases—They arrive in the promised land.

AND it came to pass that they did [a]worship the Lord, and did go forth with me; and we did work timbers of curious [b]workmanship. And the Lord did show me from time to time after what manner I should work the timbers of the [c]ship.

2 Now I, Nephi, did not work the timbers after the manner which was learned by men, neither did I build the ship after the manner of men; but I did build it after the manner which the Lord had shown unto me; wherefore, it was not after the manner of men.

3 And I, Nephi, did go into the mount oft, and I did [a]pray oft unto the Lord; wherefore the Lord [b]showed unto me [c]great things.

4 And it came to pass that after I had finished the ship, according to the word of the Lord, my brethren beheld that it was good, and that the workmanship thereof was exceedingly fine; wherefore, they did [a]humble themselves again before the Lord.

5 And it came to pass that the voice of the Lord came unto my father, that we should arise and go down into the ship.

6 And it came to pass that on the morrow, after we had prepared all things, much fruits and [a]meat from the wilderness, and honey in abundance, and provisions according to that which the Lord had commanded us, we did go down into the ship, with all our loading and our

---

51a Gen. 6:14 (14–16);
   1 Ne. 18:1.
52a IE ashamed, overawed.
   b TG God, Spirit of.
53a IE cause to shake or
   tremble; see v. 54–55.
55a Ex. 3:12; Alma 38:4.
   b Dan. 2:46; Acts 14:

15 (11–15).
   c Ex. 20:12; Prov. 9:11;
      Mosiah 14:10; Hel. 7:
      24; D&C 5:33.
18 1a 1 Ne. 17:55.
   b TG Art.
   c 1 Ne. 17:49 (8, 17,

49–51).
3a Jer. 33:3.
   b TG Guidance, Divine.
   c 2 Ne. 1:24.
4a 1 Ne. 16:5.
6a 1 Ne. 17:2.

*b*seeds, and whatsoever thing we had brought with us, every one according to his age; wherefore, we did all go down into the *c*ship, with our wives and our children.

7 And now, my father had begat two sons in the wilderness; the elder was called *a*Jacob and the younger *b*Joseph.

8 And it came to pass after we had all gone down into the ship, and had taken with us our provisions and things which had been commanded us, we did put forth into the *a*sea and were driven forth before the wind towards the *b*promised land.

9 And after we had been *a*driven forth before the wind for the space of many days, behold, my brethren and the sons of Ishmael and also their wives began to make themselves merry, insomuch that they began to dance, and to sing, and to speak with much *b*rudeness, yea, even that they did forget by what power they had been brought thither; yea, they were lifted up unto exceeding rudeness.

10 And I, Nephi, began to fear exceedingly lest the Lord should be angry with us, and smite us because of our iniquity, that we should be swallowed up in the depths of the sea; wherefore, I, Nephi, began to speak to them with much soberness; but behold they were *a*angry with me, saying: We will not that our younger brother shall be a *b*ruler over us.

11 And it came to pass that Laman and Lemuel did take me and *a*bind me with cords, and they did treat me with much harshness; nevertheless, the Lord did suffer it that he might show forth his power, unto the ful-

filling of his word which he had *b*spoken concerning the wicked.

12 And it came to pass that after they had bound me insomuch that I could not move, the *a*compass, which had been prepared of the Lord, did cease to work.

13 Wherefore, they knew not whither they should steer the ship, insomuch that there arose a great *a*storm, yea, a great and terrible tempest, and we were *b*driven back upon the waters for the space of three days; and they began to be frightened exceedingly lest they should be drowned in the sea; nevertheless they did not loose me.

14 And on the fourth day, which we had been driven back, the tempest began to be exceedingly sore.

15 And it came to pass that we were about to be swallowed up in the depths of the sea. And after we had been driven back upon the waters for the space of four days, my brethren began to *a*see that the judgments of God were upon them, and that they must perish save that they should repent of their iniquities; wherefore, they came unto me, and loosed the bands which were upon my wrists, and behold they had swollen exceedingly; and also mine ankles were much swollen, and great was the soreness thereof.

16 Nevertheless, I did look unto my God, and I did *a*praise him all the day long; and I did not murmur against the Lord because of mine afflictions.

17 Now my father, Lehi, had said many things unto them, and also unto the sons of *a*Ishmael; but, behold, they did breathe out much

6*b* 1 Ne. 8: 1; 16: 11.
  c Gen. 7: 7.
7*a* 2 Ne. 2: 1.
  b 2 Ne. 3: 1.
8*a* Ps. 8: 8; 2 Ne. 10: 20.
  b 1 Ne. 2: 20; 5: 5 (5, 22).
  TG Promised Lands.
9*a* Ether 6: 5.
  b 2 Ne. 1: 2.
  TG Rioting and
    Reveling.

10*a* 1 Ne. 17: 18 (17–55);
    2 Ne. 4: 13 (13–14).
  b Gen. 37: 10 (9–11);
    1 Ne. 16: 37 (37–38);
    2 Ne. 1: 25 (25–27).
11*a* 1 Ne. 7: 16 (16–20).
  b Ex. 23: 7; Ps. 37: 9
    (8–13); Alma 14: 11.
12*a* 1 Ne. 16: 16 (10, 16,
    26); 2 Ne. 5: 12;
    Alma 37: 38 (38–47);

  D&C 17: 1.
13*a* Jonah 1: 4; Matt. 8: 24.
  b Mosiah 1: 17.
15*a* Hel. 12: 3.
16*a* Ezra 3: 11 (11–13);
    2 Ne. 9: 49; Mosiah 2:
    20 (20–21); Alma 36:
    28; D&C 136: 28.
17*a* 1 Ne. 7: 4 (4–20).

[About 590 B.C.]

threatenings against anyone that should speak for me; and my parents being [b]stricken in years, and having [c]suffered much grief because of their [d]children, they were brought down, yea, even upon their sick-beds.

18 Because of their grief and much sorrow, and the iniquity of my brethren, they were brought near even to be carried out of this time to meet their God; yea, their [a]grey hairs were about to be brought down to lie low in the dust; yea, even they were near to be cast with sorrow into a watery grave.

19 And Jacob and Joseph also, being young, having need of much nourishment, were grieved because of the afflictions of their mother; and also [a]my wife with her tears and prayers, and also my children, did not soften the hearts of my brethren that they would loose me.

20 And there was nothing save it were the power of God, which threatened them with destruction, could soften their [a]hearts; wherefore, when they saw that they were about to be swallowed up in the depths of the sea they repented of the thing which they had done, insomuch that they loosed me.

21 And it came to pass after they had loosed me, behold, I took the compass, and it did work whither I desired it. And it came to pass that I [a]prayed unto the Lord; and after I had prayed the winds did cease, and the storm did cease, and there was a great calm.

22 And it came to pass that I, Nephi, did guide the ship, that we sailed again towards the promised land.

23 And it came to pass that after we had sailed for the space of many days *we did arrive at the [a]promised land; and we went forth upon the land, and did pitch our tents; and we did call it the promised land.

24 And it came to pass that we did begin to till the earth, and we began to plant seeds; yea, we did put all our [a]seeds into the earth, which we had brought from the land of Jerusalem. And it came to pass that they did grow exceedingly; wherefore, we were blessed in abundance.

25 And it came to pass that we did find upon the land of promise, as we journeyed in the wilderness, that there were [a]beasts in the forests of every kind, both the cow and the ox, and the ass and the horse, and the goat and the wild goat, and all manner of wild animals, which were for the use of men. And we did find all manner of [b]ore, both of [c]gold, and of silver, and of copper.

CHAPTER 19

Nephi makes plates of ore and records the history of his people—The God of Israel will come six hundred years from the time Lehi left Jerusalem—Nephi tells of His sufferings and crucifixion—The Jews shall be despised and scattered until the latter days, when they shall return unto the Lord.

AND it came to pass that the Lord commanded me, wherefore I did make plates of ore that I might engraven upon them the [a]record of my people. And upon the plates which I made I did [b]engraven the record of my [c]father, and also our journeyings in the wilderness, and the prophecies of my father; and also many of mine own prophecies have I engraven upon them.

2 And I knew not at the time when I made them that I should be com-

---

17b Gen. 24: 1.
 c TG Suffering.
 d TG Family, Children,
   Duties of; Honoring
   Father and Mother.
18a Gen. 42: 38.
19a 1 Ne. 7: 19; 16: 7.
20a TG Hardheartedness.

21a Jonah 1: 6.
23a Mosiah 10: 13.
   TG Promised Lands.
24a 1 Ne. 8: 1.
25a Enos 1: 21.
  b 2 Ne. 5: 15 (14–
    16).
  c Deut. 33: 16 (13–17).

19 1a TG Plate; Record
     Keeping.
   b TG Scribe.
   c 1 Ne. 1: 17 (16–17);
     6: 1 (1–3); Jacob 7:
     26 (26–27).

[*Probably about 589 B.C.]

manded of the Lord to make [a]these plates; wherefore, the record of my father, and the genealogy of his fathers, and the more part of all our proceedings in the wilderness are engraven upon those first plates of which I have spoken; wherefore, the things which transpired before I made [b]these plates are, of a truth, more particularly made mention upon the first plates.

3 And after I had made these plates by way of commandment, I, Nephi, received a commandment that the ministry and the prophecies, the more plain and precious parts of them, should be written upon [a]these plates; and that the things which were written should be kept for the instruction of my people, who should possess the land, and also for other [b]wise purposes, which purposes are known unto the Lord.

4 Wherefore, I, Nephi, did make a record upon the [a]other plates, which gives an account, or which gives a greater account of the wars and contentions and destructions of my people. And this have I done, and commanded my people what they should do after I was gone; and that these plates should be handed down from one generation to another, or from one prophet to another, until further commandments of the Lord.

5 And an account of my [a]making these plates shall be given hereafter; and then, behold, I proceed accord-

ing to that which I have spoken; and this I do that the more sacred things may be [b]kept for the knowledge of my people.

6 Nevertheless, I do not [a]write anything upon plates save it be that I think it be [b]sacred. And now, if I do err, even did they err of old; not that I would excuse myself because of other men, but because of the [c]weakness which is in me, according to the flesh, I would excuse myself.

7 For the things which some men esteem to be of great worth, both to the body and soul, others set at [a]naught and trample under their feet. Yea, even the very God of Israel do men [b]trample under their feet; I say, trample under their feet but I would speak in other words—they set him at naught, and [c]hearken not to the voice of his counsels.

8 And behold he [a]cometh, according to the words of the angel, in [b]six hundred years from the time my father left Jerusalem.

9 And the world, because of their iniquity, shall judge him to be a thing of naught; wherefore they scourge him, and he suffereth it; and they smite him, and he suffereth it. Yea, they [a]spit upon him, and he suffereth it, because of his loving [b]kindness and his [c]long-suffering towards the children of men.

10 And the [a]God of our fathers, who were [b]led out of Egypt, out of bondage, and also were preserved in the wilderness by him, yea, the

---

2a 2 Ne. 5: 30; Jacob 3: 14.
 b 1 Ne. 9: 2 (1–5); Omni 1: 1.
3a 1 Ne. 10: 1; Jacob 1: 1 (1–4); 3: 13 (13–14); 4: 1 (1–4).
 b 1 Ne. 9: 5 (4–5); W of M 1: 7; D&C 3: 19 (19–20); 10: 38 (1–51).
4a 1 Ne. 9: 4 (2–5); 2 Ne. 5: 33.
5a 2 Ne. 5: 30 (28–33).
 b TG Scriptures, Preservation of.
6a TG Scriptures, Writing of.

 b See title page of the Book of Mormon. TG Sacred.
 c Morm. 8: 17 (13–17); Ether 12: 23 (23–28).
7a Num. 15: 31 (30–31); 2 Ne. 33: 2; Jacob 4: 14; D&C 3: 7 (4–13).
 b Ezek. 34: 19; D&C 76: 35. TG Blasphemy; Sacrilege.
 c TG Disobedience; Prophets, Rejection of.
8a TG Jesus Christ, Betrayal of; Jesus Christ, Birth of; Jesus Christ, Prophecies about.

 b 1 Ne. 2: 4; 10: 4 (4–11); 2 Ne. 25: 19.
9a Isa. 50: 6 (5–6); Matt. 27: 30.
 b TG Kindness.
 c TG Forbearance.
10a 2 Ne. 10: 3; 26: 12; Mosiah 7: 27; 27: 31 (30–31); Alma 11: 39 (38–39); 3 Ne. 11: 14 (14–15).
 b Gen. 15: 14 (13–14); Ex. 3: 10 (2–10); 6: 6; 1 Ne. 5: 15; 17: 24 (24, 31, 40); 2 Ne. 25: 20; D&C 136: 22.

[Between 588 and 570 B.C.]

^cGod of Abraham, and of Isaac, and the God of Jacob, ^dyieldeth himself, according to the words of the angel, as a man, into the hands of ^ewicked men, to be ^flifted up, according to the words of ^gZenock, and to be ^hcrucified, according to the words of Neum, and to be buried in a ⁱsepulchre, according to the words of ^jZenos, who he spake concerning the three days of ^kdarkness, which should be a sign given of his death unto those who should inhabit the isles of the sea, more especially given unto those who are of the ^lhouse of Israel.

11 For thus spake the prophet: The Lord God surely shall ^avisit all the house of Israel at that day, some with his ^bvoice, because of their righteousness, unto their great joy and salvation, and others with the ^cthunderings and the lightnings of his power, by tempest, by fire, and by ^dsmoke, and ^evapor of ^fdarkness, and by the opening of the ^gearth, and by ^hmountains which shall be carried up.

12 And ^aall these things must surely come, saith the prophet ^bZenos. And the ^crocks of the earth must rend; and because of the ^dgroanings of the earth, many of the kings of the isles of the sea shall be wrought upon by the Spirit of God, to exclaim: The God of nature suffers.

13 And as for those who are at Jerusalem, saith the prophet, they shall be ^ascourged by all people, because they crucify the God of Israel, and turn their hearts aside, rejecting signs and wonders, and the power and glory of the God of Israel.

14 And because they turn their hearts aside, saith the prophet, and have ^adespised the Holy One of Israel, they shall wander in the flesh, and perish, and become a ^bhiss and a ^cbyword, and be ^dhated among all nations.

15 Nevertheless, when that day cometh, saith the prophet, that they ^ano more ^bturn aside their hearts against the Holy One of Israel, then will he remember the ^ccovenants which he made to their fathers.

16 Yea, then will he remember the ^aisles of the sea; yea, and all the people who are of the house of Israel, will I ^bgather in, saith the Lord, according to the words of the prophet Zenos, from the four quarters of the earth.

17 Yea, and all the earth shall ^asee the salvation of the Lord, saith the

10c Gen. 32:9; Matt. 22: 32; Mosiah 7:19; D&C 136:21. TG Jesus Christ—Jehovah.
d TG Jesus Christ, Condescension of.
e TG Jesus Christ, Betrayal of.
f 3 Ne. 27:14; 28:6.
g BD Lost Books. See also Alma 33:15; 34:7; Hel. 8:20 (19–20); 3 Ne. 10:16 (15–16).
h Nahum 1:15; 2 Ne. 6: 9; Mosiah 3:9. TG Jesus Christ, Crucifixion of.
i Matt. 27:60; Luke 23: 53; 2 Ne. 25:13.
j Jacob 5:1; 6:1; Hel. 15:11.
k 1 Ne. 12:4 (4–5); Hel. 14:27 (20, 27);

3 Ne. 8:19 (3, 19–23); 10:9.
l 1 Ne. 16:1 (1–4).
11a D&C 5:16.
b 3 Ne. 9:1 (1–22).
c Hel. 14:21 (20–27); 3 Ne. 8:6 (5–23).
d Gen. 19:28; Ex. 19: 18; Morm. 8:29 (29–30); D&C 45:41 (40–41).
e 1 Ne. 12:5.
f Luke 23:44 (44–45). TG Darkness, Physical.
g Num. 16:32; 2 Ne. 26: 5.
h 3 Ne. 10:13 (13–14).
12a Hel. 14:28 (20–28); 3 Ne. 10:11.
b Jacob 5:1.
c Matt. 27:51 (51–54).
d Moses 7:56 (48–56).
13a Matt. 23:38 (37–39); Luke 23:28 (27–30).

14a Ps. 22:6; Mosiah 14:3 (3–6).
b Jer. 24:9; 3 Ne. 29:8 (8–9). TG Israel, Bondage of, in Other Lands.
c Deut. 28:37; 1 Kgs. 9: 7 (6–7); Joel 2:17; 3 Ne. 16:9 (8–9).
d 2 Ne. 10:6; 25:15. TG Hate.
15a 1 Ne. 15:19; 22:12 (11–12).
b TG Israel, Restoration of.
c TG Abrahamic Covenant.
16a 1 Ne. 22:4; 2 Ne. 10: 21.
b Isa. 49:22 (20–22); 60:4. TG Israel, Gathering of.
17a Isa. 40:5 (4–5).

[Between 588 and 570 B.C.]

prophet; every nation, kindred, tongue and people shall be blessed.

18 And I, Nephi, have written these things unto my people, that perhaps I might persuade them that they would ^aremember the Lord their Redeemer.

19 Wherefore, I speak unto all the house of Israel, if it so be that they should obtain ^athese things.

20 For behold, I have workings in the spirit, which doth ^aweary me even that all my joints are weak, for those who are at Jerusalem; for had not the Lord been merciful, to show unto me concerning them, even as he had prophets of old, I should have perished also.

21 And he surely did show unto the ^aprophets of old all things ^bconcerning them; and also he did show unto many concerning us; wherefore, it must needs be that we know concerning them for they are written upon the plates of brass.

22 Now it came to pass that I, Nephi, did teach my brethren these things; and it came to pass that I did read many things to them, which were engraven upon the ^aplates of brass, that they might know concerning the doings of the Lord in other lands, among people of old.

23 And I did read many things unto them which were written in the ^abooks of Moses; but that I might more fully persuade them to believe in the Lord their Redeemer I did read unto them that which was written by the prophet ^bIsaiah; for I did ^cliken all scriptures unto us, that it might be for our ^dprofit and learning.

24 Wherefore I spake unto them, saying: Hear ye the words of the prophet, ye who are a ^aremnant of the house of Israel, a ^bbranch who have been broken off; ^chear ye the words of the prophet, which were written unto all the house of Israel, and liken them unto yourselves, that ye may have hope as well as your brethren from whom ye have been broken off; for after this manner has the prophet written.

CHAPTER 20

The Lord reveals his purposes to Israel —They have been chosen in the furnace of affliction and are to go forth from Babylon—Compare Isaiah 48.

^aHEARKEN and hear this, O house of Jacob, who are called by the name of Israel, and are come forth out of the waters of Judah, or out of the waters of ^bbaptism, who ^cswear by the name of the Lord, and make mention of the God of Israel, yet they swear ^dnot in truth nor in righteousness.

2 Nevertheless, they call themselves of the ^aholy city, but they do ^bnot stay themselves upon the God of Israel, who is the Lord of Hosts; yea, the Lord of Hosts is his name.

3 Behold, I have declared the ^aformer things from the beginning; and they went forth out of my mouth, and I showed them. I did show them suddenly.

4 And I did it because I knew that thou art obstinate, and thy ^aneck is an iron sinew, and thy brow brass;

5 And I have even from the beginning declared to thee; before it came

---

18a Mosiah 13:29.
19a Enos 1:16; Morm. 5:12; 7:9 (9–10).
  TG Israel, Restoration of.
20a Dan. 10:8 (8–12); 1 Ne. 1:7; Alma 27:17; Moses 1:10 (9–10).
21a 2 Kgs. 17:13; Amos 3:7.
  TG Prophets, Mission of.
  b 3 Ne. 10:16 (16–17).
22a 1 Ne. 13:23; 22:1.

23a Ex. 17:14; 1 Ne. 5:11; Moses 1:41 (40–41).
  b Isa. 1:1; 1 Ne. 15:20; 2 Ne. 25:5 (2–6); 3 Ne. 23:1.
  c TG Scriptures, Value of.
  d 2 Ne. 4:15.
24a 2 Kgs. 19:31.
  b Gen. 49:22 (22–26); 1 Ne. 15:12 (12, 16); 2 Ne. 3:5 (4–5).
  c TG Scriptures, Study of.
20 1a Isa. 48:1 (1–22).
  b TG Baptism;

Conversion.
  c Deut. 6:13.
  d Jer. 4:2; 5:2.
2a Isa. 52:1.
  TG Jerusalem.
  b TG Hypocrisy; Prophets, Rejection of.
3a Isa. 42:9; 46:10 (9–10).
  TG God, Foreknowledge of.
4a TG Stiffneckedness.

[Between 588 and 570 B.C.]

to pass I *showed them thee; and I showed them for fear lest thou shouldst say—Mine idol hath done them, and my graven image, and my molten image hath commanded them.

6 Thou hast seen and heard all this; and will ye *not declare them? And that I have showed thee new things from this time, even hidden things, and thou didst not know them.

7 They are created now, and not from the beginning, even before the day when thou heardest them not they were declared unto thee, lest thou shouldst say—Behold I knew them.

8 Yea, and thou heardest not; yea, thou knewest not; yea, from that time thine ear was not opened; for I knew that thou wouldst deal very treacherously, and wast called a *transgressor from the womb.

9 Nevertheless, for my *name's sake will I defer mine anger, and for my praise will I refrain from thee, that I cut thee not off.

10 For, behold, I have refined thee, I have chosen thee in the furnace of *affliction.

11 For mine own sake, yea, for mine own sake will I do this, for I will not suffer my *name to be polluted, and I will *not give my glory unto another.

12 Hearken unto me, O Jacob, and Israel my called, for I am he; I am the *first, and I am also the last.

13 Mine hand hath also *laid the foundation of the earth, and my right hand hath spanned the heavens. I *call unto them and they stand up together.

14 All ye, assemble yourselves, and hear; who among them hath declared these things unto them? The Lord hath loved him; yea, and he will *fulfil his word which he hath declared by them; and he will do his pleasure on *Babylon, and his arm shall come upon the Chaldeans.

15 Also, saith the Lord; I the Lord, yea, I have spoken; yea, I have called *him to declare, I have brought him, and he shall make his way prosperous.

16 Come ye near unto me; I have not spoken in *secret; from the beginning, from the time that it was declared have I spoken; and the Lord God, and his *Spirit, hath sent me.

17 And thus saith the Lord, thy *Redeemer, the Holy One of Israel; I have sent him, the Lord thy God who teacheth thee to profit, who *leadeth thee by the way thou shouldst go, hath done it.

18 O that thou hadst hearkened to my *commandments—then had thy *peace been as a river, and thy righteousness as the waves of the sea.

19 Thy *seed also had been as the sand; the offspring of thy bowels like the gravel thereof; his name should not have been cut off nor destroyed from before me.

20 *Go ye forth of Babylon, flee ye from the *Chaldeans, with a voice of singing declare ye, tell this, utter to the end of the earth; say ye: The

5a TG God, Omniscience of; Idolatry.
6a 1 Cor. 9: 16.
8a Ps. 58: 3.
9a 1 Sam. 12: 22; Ps. 23: 3; 1 Jn. 2: 12.
10a Ex. 1: 11 (10–11); 1 Ne. 17: 25. TG Affliction.
11a Jer. 44: 26.
   b Isa. 42: 8; Moses 4: 1 (1–4).
12a Rev. 1: 17; 22: 13. TG Jesus Christ, First-

born; Jesus Christ—Jehovah.
13a Ps. 102: 25. TG God the Father—Jehovah; Jesus Christ, Creator.
   b Ps. 148: 8 (5–10).
14a 1 Kgs. 8: 56; D&C 64: 31; 76: 3.
   b TG Babylon.
15a Isa. 45: 1 (1–4).
16a Isa. 45: 19.
   b TG God, Spirit of.
17a TG Jesus Christ—

Jehovah.
   b TG Guidance, Divine.
18a Eccl. 8: 5.
   b TG Israel, Blessings of; Peace of God.
19a Gen. 22: 17 (15–19); Isa. 48: 19 (18–22); Hosea 1: 10.
20a Jer. 51: 6 (6, 44–45); D&C 133: 5 (5–14).
   b TG Israel, Bondage of, in Other Lands.

[Between 588 and 570 B.C.]

Lord hath redeemed his ^cservant Jacob.

21 And they ^athirsted not; he led them through the deserts; he caused the waters to flow out of the ^brock for them; he clave the rock also and the waters gushed out.

22 And notwithstanding he hath done all this, and greater also, there is no ^apeace, saith the Lord, unto the wicked.

CHAPTER 21

Messiah shall be a light to the Gentiles and shall free the prisoners—Israel shall be gathered with power in the last days—Kings shall be their nursing fathers—Compare Isaiah 49.

^aAND again: Hearken, O ye house of Israel, all ye that are broken off and are driven out because of the wickedness of the pastors of my people; yea, all ye that are broken off, that are scattered abroad, who are of my people, O house of Israel. Listen, O ^bisles, unto me, and hearken ye people from ^cfar; the Lord hath called me from the womb; from the bowels of my mother hath he made mention of my name.

2 And he hath made my mouth like a sharp sword; in the shadow of his hand hath he hid me, and made me a polished shaft; in his quiver hath he hid me;

3 And said unto me: Thou art my ^aservant, O Israel, in whom I will be glorified.

4 Then I said, I have labored in ^avain, I have spent my strength for naught and in vain; surely my judgment is with the Lord, and my work with my God.

5 And now, saith the Lord—that ^aformed me from the womb that I should be his servant, to bring Jacob again to him—though Israel be not gathered, yet shall I be glorious in the eyes of the Lord, and my God shall be my ^bstrength.

6 And he said: It is a light thing that thou shouldst be my servant to raise up the ^atribes of Jacob, and to restore the preserved of Israel. I will also give thee for a ^blight to the ^cGentiles, that thou mayest be my salvation unto the ends of the earth.

7 Thus saith the Lord, the Redeemer of Israel, his Holy One, to him whom man despiseth, to him whom the nations abhorreth, to servant of rulers: Kings shall see and arise, princes also shall worship, because of the Lord that is faithful.

8 Thus saith the Lord: In an acceptable time have I heard thee, O isles of the sea, and in a day of salvation have I helped thee; and I will preserve, and give thee ^amy servant for a covenant of the people, to establish the earth, to cause to inherit the desolate heritages;

9 That thou mayest say to the ^aprisoners: Go forth; to them that sit in ^bdarkness: Show yourselves. They shall feed in the ways, and their ^cpastures shall be in all high places.

10 They shall not hunger nor thirst, neither shall the heat nor the sun smite them; for he that hath mercy on them shall lead them, even by the springs of water shall he guide them.

11 And I will make all my mountains a way, and my ^ahighways shall be exalted.

20c Isa. 44: 1 (1–2, 21); 45: 4.
21a Ps. 107: 33 (33–37); Isa. 41: 18 (17–20).
  b Ex. 17: 6; Num. 20: 11; 1 Ne. 17: 29; 2 Ne. 25: 20; D&C 133: 26 (26–30).
22a Rom. 3: 17.
  TG Peace of God.
21 1a Isa. 49: 1 (1–26).
  b 1 Ne. 22: 4; 2 Ne. 10: 21 (20–22).

  c D&C 1: 1.
3a Lev. 25: 55; Isa. 41: 8; D&C 93: 46 (45–46).
4a Isa. 55: 2 (1–2).
5a Isa. 44: 24.
  b TG Strength.
6a TG Israel, Twelve Tribes of.
  b Ezek. 5: 5; D&C 103: 9 (8–9); Abr. 2: 11 (6–11).
  c 3 Ne. 21: 11.
  TG Israel, Mission of.
8a 2 Ne. 3: 11 (6–15);

3 Ne. 21: 11 (8–11); Morm. 8: 16 (16, 25).
9a TG Salvation for the Dead; Spirits in Prison.
  b 2 Ne. 3: 5.
  c Ezek. 34: 14; 1 Ne. 22: 25.
11a Isa. 62: 10; D&C 133: 27 (23–32).
  TG Jesus Christ, Second Coming.

[Between 588 and 570 B.C.]

12 And then, O house of Israel, behold, *a*these shall come from far; and lo, these from the north and from the west; and these from the land of Sinim.

13 *a*Sing, O heavens; and be joyful, O earth; for the feet of those who are in the east shall be established; and *b*break forth into singing, O mountains; for they shall be smitten no more; for the Lord hath comforted his people, and will have mercy upon his *c*afflicted.

14 But, behold, Zion hath said: The Lord hath forsaken me, and my Lord hath forgotten me—but he will show that he hath not.

15 For can a *a*woman forget her sucking child, that she should not have *b*compassion on the son of her womb? Yea, they may *c*forget, yet will I not forget thee, O house of Israel.

16 Behold, I have graven thee upon the *a*palms of my hands; thy walls are continually before me.

17 Thy children shall make haste against thy destroyers; and they that made thee *a*waste shall go forth of thee.

18 Lift up thine eyes round about and behold; all these *a*gather themselves together, and they shall come to thee. And as I live, saith the Lord, thou shalt surely clothe thee with them all, as with an ornament, and bind them on even as a bride.

19 For thy waste and thy desolate places, and the land of thy destruction, shall even now be too narrow by reason of the inhabitants; and

they that swallowed thee up shall be far away.

20 The children whom thou shalt have, after thou hast lost the first, shall *a*again in thine ears say: The place is too strait for me; give place to me that I may dwell.

21 Then shalt thou say in thine heart: Who hath begotten me these, seeing I have lost my children, and am *a*desolate, a captive, and removing to and fro? And who hath brought up these? Behold, I was left alone; these, where have they been?

22 Thus saith the Lord God: Behold, I will lift up mine hand to the *a*Gentiles, and set up my *b*standard to the people; and they shall bring thy sons in their *c*arms, and thy daughters shall be carried upon their shoulders.

23 And *a*kings shall be thy *b*nursing fathers, and their queens thy nursing mothers; they shall bow down to thee with their face towards the earth, and lick up the dust of thy feet; and thou shalt know that I am the Lord; for they shall not be ashamed that *c*wait for me.

24 For shall the prey be taken from the mighty, or the *a*lawful captives delivered?

25 But thus saith the Lord, even the captives of the mighty shall be taken away, and the prey of the terrible shall be delivered; for I will contend with him that contendeth with thee, and I will save thy children.

26 And I will *a*feed them that

12a Isa. 43: 5 (5–7).
13a Isa. 44: 23.
  b TG Earth, Renewal of.
  c 2 Sam. 22: 28; Ps. 18: 27; Isa. 49: 13.
15a TG Woman.
  b Ps. 103: 13.
  c 2 Kgs. 17: 38; Isa. 41: 17 (15–17); Alma 46: 8; D&C 61: 36; 133: 2.
16a Zech. 13: 6.
17a 3 Ne. 21: 13 (12–20).
18a Micah 4: 11 (11–13).
20a TG Israel, Gathering of.

21a Isa. 54: 1; Gal. 4: 27.
22a Isa. 66: 19 (18–20).
  TG Israel, Mission of.
  b Isa. 11: 12 (10–12); 18: 3; Zech. 9: 16.
  c 1 Ne. 22: 8; 2 Ne. 10: 8 (8–9).
23a Isa. 60: 16 (14–16).
  b 1 Ne. 22: 6.
  c Gen. 49: 18; Prov. 27: 18; 2 Ne. 6: 13; D&C 98: 2; 133: 11 (10–11, 45).
24a IE the covenant people of the Lord. See also v.

25. JST Isa. 49: 25 reads: "But thus saith the Lord; even the captives of the mighty shall be taken away, and the prey of the terrible shall be delivered, for the mighty God shall deliver his covenant people..."
26a 1 Ne. 14: 17 (15–17); 22: 13 (13–14); 2 Ne. 6: 14 (14–18).

[Between 588 and 570 B.C.]

oppress thee with their own flesh; they shall be drunken with their own blood as with sweet wine; and all flesh shall ^bknow that I, the Lord, am thy ^cSavior and thy Redeemer, the ^dMighty One of Jacob.

CHAPTER 22

Israel shall be scattered upon all the face of the earth—The gentiles shall nurse and nourish Israel with the gospel in the last days—Israel shall be gathered and saved, and the wicked shall burn as stubble—The kingdom of the devil shall be destroyed, and Satan shall be bound.

AND now it came to pass that after I, Nephi, had read these things which were engraven upon the ^aplates of brass, my brethren came unto me and said unto me: What ^bmeaneth these things which ye have read? Behold, are they to be understood according to things which are ^cspiritual, which shall come to pass according to the spirit and not the flesh?

2 And I, Nephi, said unto them: Behold they were ^amanifest unto the prophet by the voice of the ^bSpirit; for by the Spirit are all things made known unto the ^cprophets, which shall come upon the children of men according to the flesh.

3 Wherefore, the things of which I have read are things pertaining to things both ^atemporal and spiritual; for it appears that the house of Israel, sooner or later, will be ^bscattered upon all the face of the earth, and also ^camong all nations.

4 And behold, there are many who are already lost from the knowledge of those who are at Jerusalem. Yea, the more part of all the ^atribes have been ^bled away; and they are ^cscattered to and fro upon the ^disles of the sea; and whither they are none of us knoweth, save that we know that they have been led away.

5 And since they have been led away, these things have been prophesied concerning them, and also concerning all those who shall hereafter be scattered and be confounded, because of the Holy One of Israel; for against him will they ^aharden their hearts; wherefore, they shall be scattered among all nations and shall be ^bhated of all men.

6 Nevertheless, after they shall be ^anursed by the ^bGentiles, and the Lord has lifted up his hand upon the Gentiles and set them up for a standard, and their ^cchildren have been carried in their arms, and their daughters have been carried upon their shoulders, behold these things of which are spoken are temporal; for thus are the covenants of the Lord with our fathers; and it meaneth us in the days to come, and also all our brethren who are of the house of Israel.

7 And it meaneth that the time cometh that after all the house of Israel have been scattered and confounded, that the Lord God will raise up a mighty nation among the ^aGentiles, yea, even upon the face of this land; and by them shall our seed be ^bscattered.

8 And after our seed is scattered the

26b Ezek. 26: 6; Mosiah 11: 22 (20–22).
  c TG Jesus Christ, Savior.
  d TG Jesus Christ— Jehovah.
22 1a 1 Ne. 19: 22; 2 Ne. 4: 2.
  b TG Interpretation.
  c TG Spiritual.
2a 2 Pet. 1: 21 (19–21).
  b TG God, Spirit of.
  c TG Prophecy.

3a D&C 29: 34 (31–34).
  b 1 Ne. 10: 12 (12–14); 2 Ne. 25: 15 (14–16).
  TG Israel, Scattering of.
  c TG Inspiration.
4a TG Israel, Ten Lost Tribes of.
  b 2 Ne. 10: 22.
  c Ps. 107: 4; Zech. 2: 6.
  d Isa. 51: 5; 1 Ne. 21: 1; 2 Ne. 10: 8 (8, 20).

5a TG Hardheartedness.
  b Luke 23: 28–31; 1 Ne. 19: 14.
6a 1 Ne. 21: 23.
  b TG Gentiles.
  c 1 Ne. 15: 13; 2 Ne. 30: 3 (1–7).
7a 3 Ne. 20: 27.
  b Isa. 18: 7; 1 Ne. 13: 14 (12–14); 2 Ne. 1: 11.

[Between 588 and 570 B.C.]

Lord God will proceed to do a ^amarvelous work among the ^bGentiles, which shall be of great ^cworth unto our seed; wherefore, it is likened unto their being nourished by the ^dGentiles and being carried in their arms and upon their shoulders.

9 And it shall also be of ^aworth unto the Gentiles; and not only unto the Gentiles but ^bunto all the ^chouse of Israel, unto the making known of the ^dcovenants of the Father of heaven unto Abraham, saying: In thy ^eseed shall all the kindreds of the earth be ^fblessed.

10 And I would, my brethren, that ye should know that all the kindreds of the earth cannot be blessed unless he shall make ^abare his arm in the eyes of the nations.

11 Wherefore, the Lord God will proceed to make bare his arm in the eyes of all the ^anations, in bringing about his covenants and his gospel unto those who are of the house of Israel.

12 Wherefore, he will ^abring them again out of ^bcaptivity, and they shall be ^cgathered together to the lands of their ^dinheritance; and they shall be ^ebrought out of obscurity and out of ^fdarkness; and they shall know that the ^gLord is their ^hSavior

and their Redeemer, the ⁱMighty One of Israel.

13 And the blood of that great and ^aabominable church, which is the whore of all the earth, shall turn upon their own heads; for they shall ^bwar among themselves, and the sword of their ^cown hands shall fall upon their own heads, and they shall be drunken with their own blood.

14 And every ^anation which shall war against thee, O house of Israel, shall be turned one against another, and they shall ^bfall into the pit which they digged to ensnare the people of the Lord. And all that ^cfight against Zion shall be destroyed, and that great whore, who hath perverted the right ways of the Lord, yea, that great and abominable church, shall tumble to the ^ddust and great shall be the fall of it.

15 For behold, saith the prophet, the time cometh speedily that Satan shall have no more power over the hearts of the children of men; for the day soon cometh that all the proud and they who do wickedly shall be as ^astubble; and the day cometh that they must be ^bburned.

16 For the time soon cometh that the fulness of the ^awrath of God shall be poured out upon all the children

8a Isa. 29: 14; 1 Ne. 14: 7; 2 Ne. 27: 26.
   TG Restoration of the Gospel.
 b 2 Ne. 10: 10; 3 Ne. 16: 6 (4–7); Morm. 5: 19.
 c 1 Ne. 15: 14 (13–18); Jacob 3: 6; 3 Ne. 5: 23 (21–26); 21: 7 (4–29).
 d TG Mission of Latter-day Saints.
9a 1 Ne. 14: 5 (1–5); 2 Ne. 28: 2.
 b 1 Ne. 15: 13 (13–17); 2 Ne. 30: 3 (1–7).
 c 2 Ne. 29: 14 (13–14).
 d Deut. 4: 31.
 e TG Abrahamic Covenant; Seed of Abraham.
 f Gen. 12: 2; 3 Ne. 20: 25 (25, 27).

10a Isa. 52: 10.
11a TG Israel, Mission of.
12a Ps. 80: 19 (17–19); D&C 35: 25.
 b 1 Ne. 21: 25 (24–25).
 c TG Israel, Gathering of.
 d TG Lands of Inheritance.
 e TG Israel, Restoration of.
 f TG Darkness, Spiritual.
 g 1 Ne. 19: 15; 2 Ne. 6: 11 (10–15).
 h TG Jesus Christ, Prophecies about; Jesus Christ, Savior.
 i TG Jesus Christ—Jehovah.
13a Rev. 17: 16 (16–17).
   TG Devil, Church of.
 b 1 Ne. 14: 16 (3, 15–17); 2 Ne. 6: 15.

   TG War.
 c 1 Ne. 21: 26 (24–26).
14a Luke 21: 10.
 b Ps. 7: 15; Prov. 26: 27; 28: 10; Isa. 60: 12; Zech. 12: 9; 1 Ne. 14: 3; 2 Ne. 28: 8; D&C 109: 25.
 c 2 Ne. 10: 13; 27: 3 (2–3); Morm. 8: 41 (40–41); D&C 136: 36.
   TG Protection, Divine.
 d Isa. 25: 12.
15a Joel 2: 5; Mal. 4: 1; 2 Ne. 15: 24; 26: 6 (4–6); D&C 64: 24 (23–24); 133: 64.
 b Ps. 21: 9 (8–10); 3 Ne. 25: 1; D&C 29: 9.
   TG Earth, Cleansing of.
16a 1 Ne. 14: 17; 3 Ne. 20: 20 (19–21).

[Between 588 and 570 B.C.]

of men; for he will not suffer that the wicked shall destroy the righteous.

17 Wherefore, he will *a*preserve the *b*righteous by his power, even if it so be that the fulness of his wrath must come, and the righteous be preserved, even unto the destruction of their enemies by fire. Wherefore, the righteous need not fear; for thus saith the prophet, they shall be saved, even if it so be as by fire.

18 Behold, my brethren, I say unto you, that these things must shortly come; yea, even blood, and fire, and vapor of smoke must come; and it must needs be upon the face of this earth; and it cometh unto men according to the flesh if it so be that they will harden their hearts against the Holy One of Israel.

19 For behold, the righteous shall not perish; for the time surely must come that all they who fight against Zion shall be cut off.

20 And the Lord will surely *a*prepare a way for his people, unto the fulfilling of the words of Moses, which he spake, saying: A *b*prophet shall the Lord your God raise up unto you, like unto me; him shall ye hear in all things whatsoever he shall say unto you. And it shall come to pass that all those who will not hear that prophet shall be *c*cut off from among the people.

21 And now I, Nephi, declare unto you, that this *a*prophet of whom Moses spake was the Holy One of Israel; wherefore, he shall execute *b*judgment in righteousness.

22 And the righteous need not fear, for they are those who shall not be confounded. But it is the kingdom of the devil, which shall be built up among the children of men, which kingdom is established among them which are in the flesh—

23 For the time speedily shall come that all *a*churches which are built up to get gain, and all those who are built up to get power over the flesh, and those who are built up to become *b*popular in the eyes of the world, and those who seek the lusts of the flesh and the things of the world, and to do all manner of iniquity; yea, in fine, all those who belong to the kingdom of the *c*devil are they who need fear, and tremble, and *d*quake; they are those who must be brought low in the dust; they are those who must be *e*consumed as stubble; and this is according to the words of the prophet.

24 And the time cometh speedily that the righteous must be led up as *a*calves of the stall, and the Holy One of Israel must reign in dominion, and might, and power, and great *b*glory.

25 And he *a*gathereth his children from the four quarters of the earth; and he numbereth his *b*sheep, and they know him; and there shall be one fold and one shepherd; and he shall feed his sheep, and in him they shall find *e*pasture.

26 And because of the *a*righteousness of his people, *b*Satan has no power; wherefore, he cannot be loosed for the space of *c*many years; for he hath no power over the hearts

17*a* 2 Ne. 30: 10;
   3 Ne. 22: 13 (13–17);
   Moses 7: 61.
   TG Protection, Divine.
  b Ps. 55: 22;
   1 Ne. 17: 35 (33–38).
20*a* TG Millennium, Preparing a People for.
  b John 4: 19; 7: 40.
  c D&C 133: 63.
21*a* Deut. 18: 15 (15–19);
   Acts 3: 22 (20–23);
   1 Ne. 10: 4; 3 Ne. 20: 23; Moses 1: 6.
   TG Jesus Christ,

Prophecies about.
  b Ps. 98: 9; Moses 6: 57.
   TG Jesus Christ, Judge.
23*a* 1 Ne. 14: 10 (9–10);
   2 Ne. 26: 20.
   TG Covetousness;
   Priestcraft.
  b Luke 6: 26; Alma 1: 3.
  c 1 Ne. 13: 6.
  d 2 Ne. 28: 19.
  e Zeph. 1: 2 (2–3);
   2 Ne. 26: 6.
24*a* Mal. 4: 2; 3 Ne. 25: 2.
  b TG Jesus Christ,
   Glory of.

25*a* Isa. 43: 6 (5–7);
   Eph. 1: 10.
   TG Israel, Gathering of.
  b TG Jesus Christ, Good Shepherd; Sheep;
   Shepherd.
  c 1 Ne. 21: 9.
26*a* TG Millennium;
   Righteousness.
  b Rev. 20: 2; Alma 48:
   17 (16–17); D&C 43:
   31; 45: 55; 88: 110;
   101: 28. TG Devil.
  c Jacob 5: 76.

[Between 588 and 570 B.C.]

of the people, for they dwell in righteousness, and the Holy One of Israel *d*reigneth.

27 And now behold, I, Nephi, say unto you that all these things must come *a*according to the flesh.

28 But, behold, all nations, kindreds, tongues, and people shall dwell safely in the Holy One of Israel if it so be that they will *a*repent.

29 And now I, Nephi, make an end; for I durst not speak further as yet concerning these things.

30 Wherefore, my brethren, I would that ye should consider that the things which have been written upon the *a*plates of brass are true; and they testify that a man must be obedient to the commandments of God.

31 Wherefore, ye need not suppose that I and my father are the only ones that have testified, and also taught them. Wherefore, if ye shall be obedient to the *a*commandments, and endure to the end, ye shall be saved at the last day. And thus it is. Amen.

THE SECOND BOOK OF NEPHI

An account of the death of Lehi. Nephi's brethren rebel against him. The Lord warns Nephi to depart into the wilderness. His journeyings in the wilderness, and so forth.

CHAPTER 1

Lehi prophesies of a land of liberty— His seed shall be scattered and smitten if they reject the Holy One of Israel— He exhorts his sons to put on the armor of righteousness.

AND now it came to pass that after I, Nephi, had made an end of teaching my brethren, our *a*father, Lehi, also spake many things unto them, and rehearsed unto them, how great things the Lord had done for them in bringing them out of the land of Jerusalem.

2 And he spake unto them concerning their *a*rebellions upon the waters, and the mercies of God in sparing their lives, that they were not swallowed up in the sea.

3 And he also spake unto them concerning the land of promise, which they had obtained—how *a*merciful the Lord had been in *b*warning us that we should flee out of the land of Jerusalem.

4 For, behold, said he, I have *a*seen a *b*vision, in which I know that *c*Jerusalem is *d*destroyed; and had we remained in Jerusalem we should also have *e*perished.

5 But, said he, notwithstanding our afflictions, we have obtained a *a*land of promise, a land which is *b*choice above all other lands; a land which the Lord God hath *c*covenant-

---

26*d* TG Jesus Christ, Millennial Reign.
27*a* IE these things pertain to this mortal world.
28*a* TG Repentance; Forgiveness.
30*a* 1 Ne. 19:22; 2 Ne. 4:2.
31*a* Matt. 19:17. TG Commandments of God.

[2 NEPHI]
1 1*a* TG Patriarch.
2*a* Isa. 65:2 (1–5); 1 Ne. 18:9 (9–20); Alma 18:38.
3*a* Gen. 19:16.
  b TG Warnings.
4*a* 1 Ne. 17:14.
  b TG Vision.

c Jer. 26:18 (17–19); 1 Ne. 1:4 (4–18); Hel. 8:20. TG Jerusalem.
d Jer. 44:2.
e Alma 9:22.
5*a* TG Promised Lands.
  b Ether 2:10 (7–12).
  c TG Vows.

[Between 588 and 570 B.C.]

ed with me should be a land for the inheritance of my seed. Yea, the Lord hath ᵈcovenanted this land unto me, and to my children forever, and also all those who should be ᵉled out of other countries by the hand of the Lord.

6 Wherefore, I, Lehi, prophesy according to the workings of the Spirit which is in me, that there shall ᵃnone come into this land save they shall be brought by the hand of the Lord.

7 Wherefore, this ᵃland is consecrated unto him whom he shall bring. And if it so be that they shall serve him according to the commandments which he hath given, it shall be a land of ᵇliberty unto them; wherefore, they shall never be brought down into captivity; if so, it shall be because of iniquity; for if iniquity shall abound ᶜcursed shall be the land for their sakes, but unto the righteous it shall be blessed forever.

8 And behold, it is wisdom that this land should be ᵃkept as yet from the knowledge of other ᵇnations; for behold, many nations would overrun the land, that there would be no place for an inheritance.

9 Wherefore, I, Lehi, have obtained a ᵃpromise, that ᵇinasmuch as those whom the Lord God shall bring out of the land of Jerusalem shall keep his commandments, they shall ᶜprosper upon the face of this land; and they shall be kept from all other nations, that they may possess this land unto themselves. And if it so be that they shall ᵈkeep his commandments they shall be blessed upon the face of this land, and there shall be none to molest them, nor to take away the land of their ᵉinheritance; and they shall dwell safely forever.

10 But behold, when the time cometh that they shall dwindle in ᵃunbelief, after they have received so great blessings from the hand of the Lord—having a knowledge of the creation of the earth, and all men, knowing the great and marvelous works of the Lord from the creation of the world; having power given them to do all things by faith; having all the commandments from the beginning, and having been brought by his infinite goodness into this precious land of promise—behold, I say, if the day shall come that they will reject the Holy One of Israel, the true ᵇMessiah, their Redeemer and their God, behold, the judgments of him that is ᶜjust shall rest upon them.

11 Yea, he will bring ᵃother nations unto them, and he will give unto them power, and he will take away from them the lands of their possessions, and he will cause them to be ᵇscattered and smitten.

12 Yea, as one generation passeth to another there shall be ᵃbloodsheds, and great visitations among them; wherefore, my sons, I would that ye would remember; yea, I would that ye would hearken unto my words.

13 O that ye would awake; awake from a deep ᵃsleep, yea, even from the sleep of ᵇhell, and shake off the awful ᶜchains by which ye are bound, which are the chains which bind the children of men, that they are carried away captive down to the eternal ᵈgulf of misery and woe.

5d TG Covenants.
  e Ezra 8:22.
6a 2 Ne. 10:22.
7a Mosiah 29:32;
    Alma 46:10 (10–28, 34).
  b 2 Ne. 10:11. TG Liberty.
  c Alma 45:16 (10–14,
    16); Morm. 1:17;
    Ether 2:11 (8–12).
8a 3 Ne. 5:20.
  b TG Nations.
9a Jacob 1:5.

  b 2 Ne. 4:4; Alma 9:13.
  c Deut. 29:9; 30:9.
  d TG Obedience.
  e TG Inheritance.
10a TG Unbelief, Unbelievers.
  b TG Jesus Christ, Messiah.
  c TG Justice.
11a 1 Ne. 13:14 (12–20);
    Morm. 5:19 (19–20).
  b 1 Ne. 22:7.
12a Morm. 1:11 (11–19);

  4:1 (1–23); D&C 87:6
  (1–6).
13a TG Sleep.
  b TG Damnation.
  c Isa. 58:6; Alma 12:
    11 (9–11). TG Bondage,
    Spiritual.
  d 1 Ne. 12:18; 15:28
    (28–30); Alma 26:20
    (19–20); Hel. 3:29.

[Between 588 and 570 B.C.]

14 Awake! and arise from the dust, and hear the words of a trembling [a]parent, whose limbs ye must soon lay down in the cold and silent [b]grave, from whence no traveler can [c]return; a few more [d]days and I go the [e]way of all the earth.

15 But behold, the Lord hath [a]redeemed my soul from hell; I have beheld his [b]glory, and I am encircled about eternally in the [c]arms of his [d]love.

16 And I desire that ye should remember to observe the [a]statutes and the judgments of the Lord; behold, this hath been the anxiety of my soul from the beginning.

17 My heart hath been weighed down with sorrow from time to time, for I have feared, lest for the hardness of your hearts the Lord your God should come out in the fulness of his [a]wrath upon you, that ye be [b]cut off and destroyed forever;

18 Or, that a [a]cursing should come upon you for the space of [b]many generations; and ye are visited by sword, and by famine, and are hated, and are led according to the will and captivity of the [c]devil.

19 O my sons, that these things might not come upon you, but that ye might be a choice and a [a]favored people of the Lord. But behold, his will be done; for his [b]ways are righteousness forever.

20 And he hath said that: [a]Inasmuch as ye shall keep my [b]commandments ye shall [c]prosper in the land; but inasmuch as ye will not keep my commandments ye shall be cut off from my presence.

21 And now that my soul might have joy in you, and that my heart might leave this world with gladness because of you, that I might not be brought down with grief and sorrow to the grave, arise from the dust, my sons, and be [a]men, and be determined in [b]one mind and in one heart, united in all things, that ye may not come down into captivity;

22 That ye may not be [a]cursed with a sore cursing; and also, that ye may not incur the displeasure of a [b]just God upon you, unto the destruction, yea, the eternal destruction of both soul and body.

23 Awake, my sons; put on the armor of [a]righteousness. Shake off the [b]chains with which ye are bound, and come forth out of obscurity, and arise from the dust.

24 Rebel no more against your brother, whose views have been [a]glorious, and who hath kept the commandments from the time that we left Jerusalem; and who hath been an instrument in the hands of God, in bringing us forth into the land of promise; for were it not for him, we must have perished with [b]hunger in the wilderness; nevertheless, ye sought to [c]take away his

14a TG Family, Love within.
  b TG Death.
  c Job 10: 21.
  d Gen. 47: 29 (28–29); Jacob 1: 9.
  e Josh. 23: 14; 1 Kgs. 2: 2.
15a Alma 36: 28. TG Jesus Christ, Atonement through.
  b Ex. 24: 16; Lev. 9: 6 (6, 23); Ether 12: 6 (6–18). TG Jesus Christ, Glory of.
  c Isa. 59: 16; Jacob 6: 5; Alma 5: 33; 3 Ne. 9: 14.
  d Rom. 8: 39. TG God, Love of.
16a Deut. 4: 6 (5–8);

Ezek. 20: 11; 2 Ne. 5: 10 (10–11).
17a 1 Ne. 2: 23; 2 Ne. 5: 21 (21–24); Alma 3: 6 (6–19). TG God, Indignation of.
  b Gen. 6: 13; 1 Ne. 17: 31; Mosiah 12: 8; 3 Ne. 9: 9.
18a TG Curse.
  b 1 Ne. 12: 21 (20–23).
  c Rev. 12: 9 (7–9); Moses 1: 12. TG Devil.
19a TG Peculiar People.
  b Hosea 14: 9.
20a Jarom 1: 9; Omni 1: 6; Mosiah 1: 7; Alma 9: 13 (13–14); 36: 30;

37: 13; 3 Ne. 5: 22.
  b Lev. 26: 3 (3–14); Joel 2: 25 (23–26); Amos 5: 4 (4–8); Mosiah 26: 30.
  c Ps. 67: 6; Prov. 22: 4 (4–5); Mosiah 2: 24 (21–25).
21a 1 Sam. 4: 9; 1 Kgs. 2: 2.
  b Moses 7: 18.
22a TG Curse.
  b D&C 3: 4. TG Justice.
23a TG Righteousness.
  b TG Bondage, Spiritual.
24a 1 Ne. 18: 3.
  b 1 Ne. 16: 32.
  c 1 Ne. 16: 37.

[Between 588 and 570 B.C.]

life; yea, and he hath suffered much sorrow because of you.

25 And I exceedingly fear and tremble because of you, lest he shall suffer again; for behold, ye have [a]accused him that he sought power and [b]authority over you; but I know that he hath not sought for power nor authority over you, but he hath sought the glory of God, and your own eternal welfare.

26 And ye have murmured because he hath been plain unto you. Ye say that he hath used [a]sharpness; ye say that he hath been angry with you; but behold, his [b]sharpness was the sharpness of the power of the word of God, which was in him; and that which ye call anger was the truth, according to that which is in God, which he could not restrain, manifesting boldly concerning your iniquities.

27 And it must needs be that the [a]power of God must be with him, even unto his commanding you that ye must obey. But behold, it was not he, but it was the [b]Spirit of the Lord which was in him, which [c]opened his mouth to utterance that he could not shut it.

28 And now my son, Laman, and also Lemuel and Sam, and also my sons who are the sons of Ishmael, behold, if ye will hearken unto the voice of Nephi ye shall not perish. And if ye will hearken unto him I leave unto you a [a]blessing, yea, even my first blessing.

29 But if ye will not hearken unto him I take away my [a]first blessing, yea, even my blessing, and it shall rest upon him.

30 And now, Zoram, I speak unto you: Behold, thou art the [a]servant of Laban; nevertheless, thou hast been brought out of the land of Jerusalem, and I know that thou art a true [b]friend unto my son, Nephi, forever.

31 Wherefore, because thou hast been faithful thy seed shall be blessed [a]with his seed, that they dwell in prosperity long upon the face of this land; and nothing, save it shall be iniquity among them, shall harm or disturb their prosperity upon the face of this land forever.

32 Wherefore, if ye shall keep the commandments of the Lord, the Lord hath consecrated this land for the security of thy seed with the seed of my son.

CHAPTER 2

Redemption cometh through the Holy Messiah—Freedom of choice (agency) is essential to existence and progression —Adam fell that men might be— Men are free to choose liberty and eternal life.

AND now, Jacob, I speak unto you: Thou art my [a]first-born in the days of my tribulation in the wilderness. And behold, in thy childhood thou hast suffered afflictions and much sorrow, because of the rudeness of thy brethren.

2 Nevertheless, Jacob, my first-born in the wilderness, thou knowest the greatness of God; and he shall consecrate thine [a]afflictions for thy gain.

3 Wherefore, thy soul shall be blessed, and thou shalt dwell safely with thy brother, Nephi; and thy days shall be [a]spent in the service of thy God. Wherefore, I know that thou art redeemed, because of the righteousness of thy Redeemer; for thou hast [b]beheld that in the [c]fulness

25a 1 Ne. 15: 8 (8–11);
　　Mosiah 10: 14.
　b Gen. 37: 10 (9–11);
　　1 Ne. 2: 22.
26a Prov. 15: 10; 1 Ne. 16:
　　2.
　b W of M 1: 17;
　　Moro. 9: 4; D&C 121:
　　43 (41–43).

27a 1 Ne. 17: 48.
　b D&C 121: 43.
　c D&C 33: 8.
28a TG Birthright.
29a Gen. 49: 3 (3–4);
　　D&C 68: 17; Abr. 1: 3.
30a 1 Ne. 4: 20 (20, 35).
　b TG Friendship.

31a 2 Ne. 5: 6.
2 1a 1 Ne. 18: 7 (7, 19).
2a Micah 4: 13; 2 Ne. 32:
　　9. TG Affliction.
3a Enos 1: 1.
　b 2 Ne. 11: 3.
　c TG Fulness.

[Between 588 and 570 B.C.]

of time he cometh to bring salvation unto men.

4 And thou hast [a]beheld in thy youth his glory; wherefore, thou art blessed even as they unto whom he shall minister in the flesh; for the Spirit is the same, yesterday, today, and forever. And the way is prepared from the fall of man, and [b]salvation is [c]free.

5 And men are instructed sufficiently that they [a]know good from evil. And the [b]law is given unto men. And by the law no flesh is [c]justified; or, by the law men are [d]cut off. Yea, by the temporal law they were cut off; and also, by the spiritual law they perish from that which is good, and become miserable forever.

6 Wherefore, [a]redemption cometh in and through the [b]Holy [c]Messiah; for he is full of [d]grace and truth.

7 Behold, he offereth himself a [a]sacrifice for sin, to answer the ends of the law, unto all those who have a broken heart and a contrite spirit; and unto [b]none else can the [c]ends of the law be answered.

8 Wherefore, how great the importance to make these things known unto the inhabitants of the earth, that they may know that there is no flesh that can dwell in the presence of God, [a]save it be through the merits, and mercy, and grace of the Holy Messiah, who [b]layeth down his life according to the flesh, and taketh it again by the power of the Spirit, that he may bring to pass the [c]resurrection of the dead, being the first that should rise.

9 Wherefore, he is the firstfruits unto God, inasmuch as he shall make [a]intercession for all the children of men; and they that believe in him shall be saved.

10 And because of the intercession for [a]all, all men come unto God; wherefore, they stand in the presence of him, [b]judged of him according to the truth and [c]holiness which is in him. Wherefore, the ends of the law which the Holy One hath given, unto the inflicting of the [d]punishment which is affixed, which punishment that is affixed is in opposition to that of the happiness which is affixed, to answer the ends of the [e]atonement—

11 For it must needs be, that there is an [a]opposition in all things. If not so, my first-born in the wilderness, righteousness could not be brought to pass, neither wickedness, neither holiness nor misery, neither good nor bad. Wherefore, all things must needs be a compound in one; where-

4a 2 Ne. 10: 3; Jacob 7: 5.
   TG Jesus Christ,
   Appearances, Ante-
   mortal.
 b Jude 1: 3.
 c TG Grace.
5a Moro. 7: 16.
 b Gal. 2: 16; 3: 2;
   Mosiah 13: 28 (27–28).
 c Rom. 3: 20 (20–24);
   7: 5; 2 Ne. 25: 23;
   Alma 42: 14 (12–16).
   TG Justification.
 d Lev. 7: 20 (20–21);
   1 Ne. 10: 6; 2 Ne. 9: 6
   (6–38); Alma 11: 42
   (40–45); 12: 16 (16,
   24, 36); 42: 7 (6–11);
   Hel. 14: 16 (15–18).
6a 1 Ne. 10: 6; 2 Ne. 25:
   20; Mosiah 16: 5 (4–5);
   Alma 12: 22 (22–25);

   TG Jesus Christ,
   Redeemer;
   Redemption.
 b TG Holiness.
 c TG Jesus Christ,
   Messiah.
 d John 1: 17 (14, 17);
   Alma 13: 9; Moses 1: 6.
   TG Grace.
7a TG Jesus Christ,
   Atonement through;
   Sacrifice; Self-sacrifice.
 b 1 Sam. 2: 2 (1–10).
 c Rom. 10: 4.
8a 2 Ne. 25: 20; 31: 21;
   Mosiah 4: 8; 5: 8;
   Alma 21: 9; 38: 9.
 b TG Jesus Christ,
   Prophecies about.
 c 1 Cor. 15: 20; Mosiah 13:
   35; Alma 7: 12; 12: 25
   (24–25); 42: 23.

   TG Jesus Christ,
   Resurrection.
9a Isa. 53: 12 (1–12);
   Mosiah 14: 12; 15: 8;
   Moro. 7: 28 (27–28).
   TG Jesus Christ,
   Mission of.
10a Ps. 65: 2. TG Jesus
   Christ, Redeemer.
 b TG Jesus Christ, Judge.
 c TG Holiness.
 d TG Punishment.
 e 2 Ne. 9: 26 (7, 21–22,
   26); Alma 22: 14;
   33: 22; 34: 9 (8–16).
   TG Atonement.
11a Job 2: 10; Matt. 5: 45;
   D&C 29: 39; 122: 7
   (5–9); Moses 6: 55.
   TG Adversity; Agency;
   Mortality; Opposition.

[Between 588 and 570 B.C.]

fore, if it should be one body it must needs remain as dead, having no life neither death, nor corruption nor incorruption, happiness nor misery, neither sense nor insensibility.

12 Wherefore, it must needs have been created for a thing of naught; wherefore there would have been no ªpurpose in the end of its creation. Wherefore, this thing must needs destroy the wisdom of God and his eternal purposes, and also the power, and the mercy, and the ᵇjustice of God.

13 And if ye shall say there is ªno law, ye shall also say there is no sin. If ye shall say there is no sin, ye shall also say there is no righteousness. And if there be no righteousness there be no happiness. And if there be no righteousness nor happiness there be no punishment nor misery. And if these things are not ᵇthere is no God. And if there is no God we are not, neither the earth; for there could have been no creation of things, neither to act nor to be acted upon; wherefore, all things must have vanished away.

14 And now, my sons, I speak unto you these things for your profit and ªlearning; for there is a God, and he hath ᵇcreated all things, both the heavens and the earth, and all things that in them are, both things to act and things to be ᶜacted upon.

15 And to bring about his eternal

ªpurposes in the end of man, after he had ᵇcreated our first parents, and the beasts of the field and the ᶜfowls of the air, and in fine, all things which are created, it must needs be that there was an opposition; even the ᵈforbidden ᵉfruit in ᶠopposition to the ᵍtree of life; the one being sweet and the other bitter.

16 Wherefore, the Lord God gave unto man that he should ªact for himself. Wherefore, man could not ᵇact for himself save it should be that he was ᶜenticed by the one or the other.

17 And I, Lehi, according to the things which I have read, must needs suppose that an ªangel of God, according to that which is written, had ᵇfallen from heaven; wherefore, he became a ᶜdevil, having sought that which was evil before God.

18 And because he had fallen from heaven, and had become miserable forever, he ªsought also the misery of all mankind. Wherefore, he said unto Eve, yea, even that old serpent, who is the devil, who is the father of all ᵇlies, wherefore he said: Partake of the forbidden fruit, and ye shall not die, but ye shall be as God, ᶜknowing good and evil.

19 And after Adam and Eve had ªpartaken of the forbidden fruit they were driven out of the garden of ᵇEden, to till the earth.

20 And they have brought forth

12a D&C 88: 25. TG Earth, Purpose of.
  b TG God, Justice of.
13a Rom. 4: 15; 5: 13; 2 Ne. 9: 25; 11: 7.
  b Alma 42: 13.
14a TG Learning.
  b TG Creation; God, Creator; Jesus Christ, Creator.
  c D&C 93: 30.
15a Isa. 45: 18 (17–18); Matt. 5: 48; Rom. 8: 17 (14–21); Eph. 3: 11 (7–12); Alma 42: 26; D&C 29: 43 (42–44); Moses 1: 31, 39.
  TG Earth, Purpose of.
  b TG Man, Physical

Creation of.
  c Gen. 1: 20.
  d Gen. 2: 17 (16–17); Moses 3: 17.
  e Gen. 3: 6; Mosiah 3: 26; Alma 12: 22 (21–23).
  f TG Opposition.
  g Gen. 2: 9; 1 Ne. 15: 36 (22, 28, 36); Alma 12: 26 (21, 23, 26); 32: 40.
16a Alma 12: 31.
  TG Initiative.
  b 2 Ne. 10: 23.
  TG Agency.
  c D&C 29: 39 (39–40).
17a TG Council in Heaven.
  b 2 Ne. 9: 8; Moses 4: 3 (3–4); Abr. 3: 28

(27–28). TG Sons of Perdition.
  c TG Adversary; Devil; Lucifer; Satan.
18a Luke 22: 31; Rev. 13: 7; 2 Ne. 28: 20 (19–23); 3 Ne. 18: 18; D&C 10: 22 (22–27); 50: 3; 76: 29.
  b 2 Ne. 28: 8; Moses 4: 4.
  c Gen. 3: 5; Mosiah 16: 3; Alma 29: 5; Moro. 7: 16 (15–19).
19a Gen. 2: 17 (16–17); Alma 12: 31.
  TG Fall of Man.
  b TG Eden.

[Between 588 and 570 B.C.]

59 2 NEPHI 2:21-30

children; yea, even the "family of all the earth.

21 And the days of the children of "men were prolonged, according to the "will of God, that they might "repent while in the flesh; wherefore, their state became a state of "probation, and their time was lengthened, according to the commandments which the Lord God gave unto the children of men. For he gave commandment that all men must repent; for he showed unto all men that they were "lost, because of the transgression of their parents.

22 And now, behold, if Adam had not transgressed he would not have fallen, but he would have remained in the garden of Eden. And all things which were created must have remained in the same state in which they were after they were created; and they must have remained forever, and had no end.

23 And they would have had no "children; wherefore they would have remained in a state of innocence, having no "joy, for they knew no misery; doing no good, for they knew no "sin.

24 But behold, all things have been done in the wisdom of him who "knoweth all things.

25 "Adam "fell that men might be; and men "are, that they might have "joy.

26 And the "Messiah cometh in the fulness of time, that he may "redeem

the children of men from the fall. And because that they are "redeemed from the fall they have become "free forever, knowing good from evil; to act for themselves and not to be acted upon, save it be by the punishment of the "law at the great and last day, according to the commandments which God hath given.

27 Wherefore, men are "free according to the "flesh; and "all things are "given them which are expedient unto man. And they are free to "choose "liberty and eternal "life, through the great Mediator of all men, or to choose captivity and death, according to the captivity and power of the devil; for he seeketh that all men might be "miserable like unto himself.

28 And now, my sons, I would that ye should look to the great "Mediator, and hearken unto his great commandments; and be faithful unto his words, and choose eternal life, according to the will of his Holy Spirit;

29 And not choose eternal death, according to the will of the flesh and the "evil which is therein, which giveth the spirit of the devil power to "captivate, to bring you down to "hell, that he may reign over you in his own kingdom.

30 I have spoken these few words unto you all, my sons, in the last days of my probation; and I have

---

20a 1 Cor. 15: 45 (45–48); D&C 27: 11; 138: 38; Moses 1: 34. TG Adam.
21a Job 14: 1; Alma 12: 24; Moses 4: 23 (22–25).
 b TG God, Will of.
 c Alma 34: 32. TG Repentance.
 d TG Mortality; Probation.
 e Jacob 7: 12.
23a Gen. 3: 16; Moses 5: 11. TG Family,; Marriage, Motherhood.
 b TG Joy.
 c TG Sin.
24a TG God, Foreknowledge of; God, Intelligence of; God, Omni-

science of.
25a TG Adam.
 b Moses 6: 48. TG Fall of Man.
 c TG Mortality.
 d Moses 5: 10. TG Joy; Man, Potential to Become like Heavenly Father.
26a TG Jesus Christ, Messiah.
 b TG Salvation, Plan of.
 c TG Redemption.
 d Gal. 5: 1; Alma 41: 7; 42: 27; Hel. 14: 30.
 e TG God, Law of.
27a Gal. 5: 1; Hel. 14: 30 (29–30); Moses 6: 56.

 b TG Mortality.
 c 2 Ne. 26: 24; Jacob 5: 41; Alma 26: 37.
 d Alma 29: 8. TG Talents.
 e TG Initiative; Opposition.
 f TG Liberty.
 g Deut. 30: 15.
 h D&C 10: 22.
28a TG Jesus Christ, Mediator.
29a TG Evil; Sin.
 b Rom. 6: 14 (14–18); 1 Ne. 14: 7; Alma 12: 11 (9–11). TG Bondage, Spiritual.
 c TG Hell.

[Between 588 and 570 B.C.]

chosen the good part, according to the words of the prophet. And I have none other object save it be the everlasting [a]welfare of your souls. Amen.

CHAPTER 3

Joseph in Egypt saw the Nephites in vision—He prophesied of Joseph Smith, the latter-day seer; of Moses, who would deliver Israel; and of the coming forth of the Book of Mormon.

AND now I speak unto you, Joseph, my [a]last-born. Thou wast born in the wilderness of mine afflictions; yea, in the days of my greatest sorrow did thy mother bear thee.

2 And may the Lord consecrate also unto thee this [a]land, which is a most precious land, for thine inheritance and the inheritance of thy seed with thy brethren, for thy security forever, if it so be that ye shall keep the commandments of the Holy One of Israel.

3 And now, Joseph, my last-born, whom I have brought out of the wilderness of mine afflictions, may the Lord bless thee forever, for thy [a]seed shall not utterly be [b]destroyed.

4 For behold, thou art the fruit of my [a]loins; and I am a descendant of [a]Joseph who was carried [b]captive into Egypt. And great were the [c]covenants of the Lord which he made unto Joseph.

5 Wherefore, Joseph truly [a]saw our day. And he obtained a [b]promise of the Lord, that out of the fruit of his loins the Lord God would raise up a [c]righteous [d]branch unto the house of Israel; not the Messiah, but a branch which was to be broken off, nevertheless, to be remembered in the covenants of the Lord that the Messiah should be made [e]manifest unto them in the latter days, in the spirit of power, unto the bringing of them out of [f]darkness unto light —yea, out of hidden darkness and out of captivity unto freedom.

6 For Joseph truly testified, saying: A [a]seer shall the Lord my God raise up, who shall be a choice seer unto the fruit of my [b]loins.

7 Yea, Joseph truly said: Thus saith the Lord unto me: A choice [a]seer will I [b]raise up out of the fruit of thy loins; and he shall be esteemed highly among the fruit of thy loins. And unto him will I give commandment that he shall do a work for the fruit of thy loins, his brethren, which shall be of great worth unto them, even to the bringing of them to the [c]knowledge of the covenants which I have made with thy fathers.

8 And I will give unto him a commandment that he shall do [a]none other work, save the work which I shall command him. And I will make him great in mine eyes; for he shall do my work.

9 And he shall be great like unto [a]Moses, whom I have said I would raise up unto you, to [b]deliver my [c]people, O house of Israel.

10 And [a]Moses will I raise up, to deliver thy people out of the land of Egypt.

11 But a [a]seer will I raise up out of the fruit of thy loins; and unto him

---

30a TG Family, Children, Responsibilities toward.
3 1a 1 Ne. 18:7 (7, 19).
2a 1 Ne. 2:20.
  TG Promised Lands.
3a Gen. 45:7; 1 Ne. 13:30.
  b Amos 9:8; 2 Ne. 25: 21; 9:53.
4a Gen. 39:2; 45:4; 49:22 (22–26); Ps. 77: 15; 1 Ne. 5:14 (14–16).
  b Gen. 37:36 (29–36).
  c Amos 5:15.
5a JST Gen. 50:24–38; 2 Ne. 3:22; 4:2 (1–32).

b TG Promise.
c Jacob 2:25.
d Gen. 45:7 (5–7); 49: 22 (22–26); 1 Ne. 15: 12 (12, 16); 19:24; 2 Ne. 14:2.
  TG Vineyard of the Lord.
e 2 Ne. 6:14; D&C 3:18 (16–20).
f Isa. 42:16; 1 Jn. 2:8; 1 Ne. 21:9.
6a 3 Ne. 21:11 (8–11); Morm. 8:16 (16, 25); Ether 3:28 (21–28).
  TG Seer.
b D&C 132:30.

7a TG Joseph Smith.
  b TG Millennium, Preparing a People for.
  c TG Book of Mormon.
8a D&C 24:9 (8–9).
9a Moses 1:41.
  b Ex. 3:10 (7–10); 1 Ne. 17:24.
  c 2 Ne. 29:14.
10a TG Foreordination.
11a 1 Ne. 21:8; 3 Ne. 21: 11 (8–11); Morm. 8:16 (16, 25). TG Prophets, Mission of.

[Between 588 and 570 B.C.]

will I give *b*power to *c*bring forth my word unto the seed of thy loins— and not to the bringing forth my word only, saith the Lord, but to the convincing them of my word, which shall have already gone forth among them.

12 Wherefore, the fruit of thy loins shall *a*write; and the fruit of the loins of *b*Judah shall *c*write; and that which shall be written by the fruit of thy loins, and also that which shall be written by the fruit of the loins of Judah, shall grow together, unto the *d*confounding of *e*false doctrines and laying down of contentions, and establishing *f*peace among the fruit of thy loins, and *g*bringing them to the *h*knowledge of their fathers in the latter days, and also to the knowledge of my covenants, saith the Lord.

13 And out of weakness he shall be made strong, in that day when my work shall commence among all my people, unto the restoring thee, O house of Israel, saith the Lord.

14 And thus prophesied Joseph, saying: Behold, that seer will the Lord bless; and they that seek to destroy him shall be confounded; for this promise, which I have obtained of the Lord, of the fruit of my loins, shall be fulfilled. Behold, I am sure of the fulfilling of this promise;

15 And his *a*name shall be called after me; and it shall be after the *b*name of his father. And he shall be *c*like unto me; for the thing, which the Lord shall bring forth by his hand, by the power of the Lord

shall bring *d*my people unto *e*salvation.

16 Yea, thus prophesied Joseph: I am sure of this thing, even as I am sure of the promise of Moses; for the Lord hath said unto me, I will *a*preserve thy seed forever.

17 And the Lord hath said: I will raise up a Moses; and I will give power unto him in a rod; and I will give judgment unto him in writing. Yet I will not loose his tongue, that he shall speak much, for I will not make him mighty in speaking. But I will *a*write unto him my law, by the finger of mine own hand; and I will make a *b*spokesman for him.

18 And the Lord said unto me also: I will raise up unto the fruit of thy loins; and I will make for him a spokesman. And I, behold, I will give unto him that he shall write the writing of the fruit of thy loins, unto the fruit of thy loins; and the spokesman of thy loins shall declare it.

19 And the words which he shall write shall be the words which are expedient in my wisdom should go forth unto the *a*fruit of thy loins. And it shall be as if the fruit of thy loins had cried unto them *b*from the dust; for I know their faith.

20 And they shall *a*cry from the *b*dust; yea, even repentance unto their brethren, even after many generations have gone by them. And it shall come to pass that their cry shall go, even according to the simpleness of their words.

21 Because of their faith their *a*words shall proceed forth out of

11b D&C 5:4 (3–4).
 c TG Scriptures to Come Forth.
12a TG Book of Mormon.
 b 1 Ne. 13:23 (23–29); 2 Ne. 29:12.
 c TG Scriptures, Preservation of; Scriptures, Writing of.
 d Ezek. 37:17 (15–20); 1 Ne. 13:39 (38–41); 2 Ne. 29:8; 33:10 (10–11).
 e TG False Doctrine.
 f TG Peacemakers.
 g Moro. 1:4.
 h 1 Ne. 15:14; 2 Ne. 30:5; 3 Ne. 5:23; Morm. 7:9 (1, 5, 9–10).
15a D&C 18:8.
 b JS-H 1:3.
 c D&C 28:2.
 d Enos 1:13 (12–18); Alma 37:19 (1–20).
 e TG Scriptures, Value of.
16a Gen. 45:7 (1–8); D&C 107:42.
17a Deut. 10:2 (2, 4);
 Moses 2:1.
 TG Scriptures, Writing of.
 b Ex. 4:16 (14–16).
19a D&C 28:8.
 b Isa. 29:4; 2 Ne. 27:13; 33:13 (13–15); Morm. 9:30; Moro. 10:27.
20a 2 Ne. 26:16; Morm. 8:23 (23, 26).
 b TG Book of Mormon.
21a 2 Ne. 29:2.

[Between 588 and 570 B.C.]

my mouth unto their brethren who are the fruit of thy loins; and the weakness of their words will I make strong in their faith, unto the remembering of my covenant which I made unto thy fathers.

22 And now, behold, my son Joseph, after this manner did my father of old [a]prophesy.

23 Wherefore, because of this covenant thou art [a]blessed; for thy seed shall not be destroyed, for they shall [b]hearken unto the words of the book.

24 And there shall rise up [a]one mighty among them, who shall do much good, both in word and in deed, being an instrument in the hands of God, with exceeding faith, to work mighty wonders, and do that thing which is great in the sight of God, unto the bringing to pass much [b]restoration unto the house of Israel, and unto the seed of thy brethren.

25 And now, blessed art thou, Joseph. Behold, thou art little; wherefore hearken unto the words of thy brother, Nephi, and it shall be done unto thee even according to the words which I have spoken. Remember the words of thy dying father. Amen.

CHAPTER 4

Lehi counsels and blesses his posterity —He dies and is buried—Nephi glories in the goodness of God to him— Nephi puts his trust in the Lord forever.

AND now, I, Nephi, speak concerning the prophecies of which my father hath spoken, concerning [a]Joseph, who was carried into Egypt.

2 For behold, he truly prophesied concerning all his seed. And the [a]prophecies which he wrote, there are not many greater. And he prophesied concerning us, and our future generations; and they are written upon the [b]plates of brass.

3 Wherefore, after my father had made an end of speaking concerning the prophecies of Joseph, he called the children of Laman, his sons, and his daughters, and said unto them: Behold, my sons, and my daughters, who are the sons and the daughters of my [a]first-born, I would that ye should give ear unto my words.

4 For the Lord God hath said that: [a]Inasmuch as ye shall keep my commandments ye shall prosper in the land; and inasmuch as ye will not keep my commandments ye shall be cut off from my presence.

5 But behold, my sons and my daughters, I cannot go down to my grave save I should leave a [a]blessing upon you; for behold, I know that if ye are [b]brought up in the [c]way ye should go ye will not depart from it.

6 Wherefore, if ye are [a]cursed, behold, I leave my blessing upon you, that the [b]cursing may be taken from you and be answered upon the [c]heads of your parents.

7 Wherefore, because of my blessing the Lord God will [a]not suffer that ye shall perish; wherefore, he will be [b]merciful unto you and unto your seed forever.

8 And it came to pass that after my father had made an end of speaking to the sons and daughters of Laman, he caused the sons and daughters of Lemuel to be brought before him.

9 And he spake unto them, saying:

22a 2 Ne. 3: 5.
23a TG Birthright.
  b TG Obedience.
24a TG Joseph Smith.
  b TG Dispensations;
    Israel, Restoration of;
    Restoration of the
    Gospel.
4 1a Gen. 39: 2.
2a 2 Ne. 3: 5.
  b 1 Ne. 22: 30; 2 Ne. 5: 12.

3a TG Firstborn.
4a 2 Ne. 1: 9; Alma 9: 13.
5a TG Family, Patriarchal;
    Patriarchal Blessings.
  b TG Family, Children,
    Responsibilities
    toward.
  c Prov. 22: 6.
6a 1 Ne. 2: 23.
  b TG Curse.
  c D&C 68: 25 (25–29).

7a 1 Ne. 22: 7 (7–8);
    2 Ne. 30: 3 (3–6);
    Jacob 1: 5.
  TG Book of Mormon.
  b 1 Ne. 13: 31; 2 Ne. 10:
    18 (18–19); Jacob 3: 6
    (5–9); Hel. 15: 12 (10–
    17); Morm. 5: 20
    (20–21).

[Between 588 and 570 B.C.]

Behold, my sons and my daughters, who are the sons and the daughters of my second son; behold I leave unto you the same blessing which I left unto the sons and daughters of Laman; wherefore, thou shalt not utterly be destroyed; but in the end thy seed shall be blessed.

10 And it came to pass that when my father had made an end of speaking unto them, behold, he spake unto the sons of ᵃIshmael, yea, and even all his household.

11 And after he had made an end of speaking unto them, he spake unto Sam, saying: Blessed art thou, and thy ᵃseed; for thou shalt inherit the land like unto thy brother Nephi. And thy seed shall be numbered with his seed; and thou shalt be even like unto thy brother, and thy seed like unto his seed; and thou shalt be blessed in all thy days.

12 And it came to pass after my father, Lehi, had ᵃspoken unto all his household, according to the feelings of his heart and the Spirit of the Lord which was in him, he waxed ᵇold. And it came to pass that he died, and was buried.

13 And it came to pass that not many days after his death, Laman and Lemuel and the sons of Ishmael were ᵃangry with me because of the admonitions of the Lord.

14 For I, Nephi, was constrained to speak unto them, according to his word; for I had spoken many things unto them, and also my father, before his death; many of which sayings are written upon mine ᵃother plates; for a more history part are written upon mine other plates.

15 And upon ᵃthese I ᵇwrite the things of my soul, and many of the scriptures which are engraven upon the plates of brass. For my soul ᶜdelighteth in the scriptures, and my heart ᵈpondereth them, and writeth them for the ᵉlearning and the profit of my children.

16 Behold, my ᵃsoul delighteth in the things of the Lord; and my ᵇheart pondereth continually upon the things which I have seen and heard.

17 Nevertheless, notwithstanding the great ᵃgoodness of the Lord, in showing me his great and marvelous works, my heart exclaimeth: O ᵇwretched man that I am! Yea, my heart ᶜsorroweth because of my flesh; my soul grieveth because of mine iniquities.

18 I am encompassed about, because of the temptations and the sins which do so easily ᵃbeset me.

19 And when I desire to rejoice, my heart groaneth because of my sins; nevertheless, I know in whom I have ᵃtrusted.

20 My God hath been my ᵃsupport; he hath led me through mine ᵇafflictions in the wilderness; and he hath preserved me upon the waters of the great deep.

21 He hath filled me with his ᵃlove, even unto the ᵇconsuming of my flesh.

22 He hath confounded mine ᵃenemies, unto the causing of them to quake before me.

23 Behold, he hath heard my cry by

10a 1 Ne. 7: 6.
11a Jacob 1: 14 (12–14).
12a Gen. 49: 1 (1–27).
  b TG Old Age.
13a 1 Ne. 7: 6 (6–19);
    17: 18 (17–55); 18: 10
    (9–22); 2 Ne. 5: 2
    (1–25). TG Anger.
14a 1 Ne. 1: 17 (16–17);
    9: 4; 2 Ne. 5: 33 (29–
    33); D&C 10: 42.
15a 1 Ne. 6: 1 (1–6).
  b TG Scriptures, Writing
    of.

c Ps. 119: 24; Moses 6:
  59.
d TG Meditation;
  Scriptures, Study of.
e 1 Ne. 19: 23.
  TG Scriptures, Value
  of.
16a TG Spirituality;
  Thanksgiving.
  b TG Heart.
17a Ex. 34: 6 (5–7);
    2 Ne. 9: 10; D&C 86:
    11.
  b Rom. 7: 24.

c TG Poor in Spirit;
  Repentance; Sorrow.
18a Rom. 7: 21 (15–25);
    Heb. 12: 1; Alma 7:
    15.
19a TG Trust in God.
20a 2 Cor. 4: 16.
  b 1 Ne. 17: 6.
  TG Affliction; Comfort.
21a TG God, Love of.
  b D&C 84: 33.
22a Ps. 3: 7 (7–8).

[Between 588 and 570 B.C.]

day, and he hath given me knowl-
edge by visions in the night-
time.

24 And by day have I waxed bold
in mighty prayer before him; yea,
my voice have I sent up on high;
and angels came down and ministered unto me.

25 And upon the wings of his Spirit
hath my body been carried away
upon exceedingly high mountains.
And mine eyes have beheld great
things, yea, even too great for man;
therefore I was bidden that I should
not write them.

26 O then, if I have seen so great
things, if the Lord in his condescension unto the children of men
hath visited men in so much mercy,
why should my heart weep and my
soul linger in the valley of sorrow,
and my flesh waste away, and my
strength slacken, because of mine
afflictions?

27 And why should I yield to sin,
because of my flesh? Yea, why
should I give way to temptations,
that the evil one have place in my
heart to destroy my peace and
afflict my soul? Why am I angry
because of mine enemy?

28 Awake, my soul! No longer
droop in sin. Rejoice, O my heart,
and give place no more for the
enemy of my soul.

29 Do not anger again because of
mine enemies. Do not slacken my
strength because of mine afflictions.

30 Rejoice, O my heart, and cry
unto the Lord, and say: O Lord, I
will praise thee forever; yea, my

soul will rejoice in thee, my God,
and the rock of my salvation.

31 O Lord, wilt thou redeem my
soul? Wilt thou deliver me out of
the hands of mine enemies? Wilt
thou make me that I may shake at
the appearance of sin?

32 May the gates of hell be shut
continually before me, because that
my heart is broken and my spirit is
contrite! O Lord, wilt thou not shut
the gates of thy righteousness before
me, that I may walk in the path of
the low valley, that I may be strict in
the plain road!

33 O Lord, wilt thou encircle me
around in the robe of thy righteous-
ness! O Lord, wilt thou make a way
for mine escape before mine ene-
mies! Wilt thou make my path
straight before me! Wilt thou not
place a stumbling block in my way
—but that thou wouldst clear my
way before me, and hedge not up
my way, but the ways of mine
enemy.

34 O Lord, I have trusted in thee,
and I will trust in thee forever. I
will not put my trust in the arm of
flesh; for I know that cursed is he
that putteth his trust in the arm of
flesh. Yea, cursed is he that putteth
his trust in man or maketh flesh his
arm.

35 Yea, I know that God will give
liberally to him that asketh. Yea,
my God will give me, if I ask not
amiss; therefore I will lift up my
voice unto thee; yea, I will cry unto
thee, my God, the rock of my
righteousness. Behold, my voice

23a TG Knowledge.
  b 2 Chr. 26: 5. TG Dream; Vision.
24a James 5: 16; 1 Ne. 1: 5 (5–8); 10: 17.
25a 2 Cor. 12: 2 (1–4); 1 Ne. 11: 1 (1–36); Moses 1: 1.
26a Ex. 3: 16; Alma 9: 21; Morm. 1: 15.
  b TG Compassion; God, Mercy of.
  c Ps. 43: 5.
  d TG Heart.
27a Rom. 6: 13 (10–16).
  b TG Temptation.
  c TG Contentment; Peace; Peace of God.
  d TG Self-mastery.
28a Ps. 42: 11.
  b TG Adversary; Enemy.
29a TG Anger.
30a TG Heart.
  b 1 Cor. 3: 11 (9–13).
  c TG Rock.
31a Ps. 16: 10.
  b Rom. 12: 9; Alma 13: 12; 37: 32. TG Sin.
32a TG Contrite Heart.
  b TG Walking with God.
33a TG Righteousness.
  b Lev. 26: 7 (1–13);
   D&C 44: 5.
34a TG Trustworthiness.
  b TG Trust in God.
  c Ps. 33: 16; 44: 6 (6–8). TG Trust Not in the Arm of Flesh.
  d Prov. 14: 16; Jer. 17: 5; Morm. 3: 9; 4: 8.
35a James 1: 5. TG Abundant Life.
  b TG Prayer.
  c Hel. 10: 5.
  d Deut. 32: 4.
  e Ps. 4: 1.

[Between 588 and 570 B.C.]

shall forever ascend up unto thee, my rock and mine everlasting God. Amen.

CHAPTER 5

The Nephites separate themselves from the Lamanites, keep the law of Moses, and build a temple—Because of their unbelief, the Lamanites are cursed, receive a skin of blackness, and become a scourge unto the Nephites.

BEHOLD, it came to pass that I, Nephi, did cry much unto the Lord my God, because of the ᵃanger of my brethren.

2 But behold, their ᵃanger did increase against me, insomuch that they did seek to take away my life.

3 Yea, they did murmur against me, saying: Our younger brother thinks to ᵃrule over us; and we have had much trial because of him; wherefore, now let us slay him, that we may not be afflicted more because of his words. For behold, we will not have him to be our ruler; for it belongs unto us, who are the elder brethren, to ᵇrule over this people.

4 Now I do not write upon these plates all the words which they murmured against me. But it sufficeth me to say, that they did seek to take away my life.

5 And it came to pass that the Lord did ᵃwarn me, that I, ᵇNephi, should depart from them and flee into the wilderness, and all those who would go with me.

6 Wherefore, it came to pass that I, Nephi, did take my family, and also ᵃZoram and his family, and Sam, mine elder brother and his family, and Jacob and Joseph, my younger

brethren, and also my sisters, and all those who would go with me. And all those who would go with me were those who believed in the ᵇwarnings and the revelations of God; wherefore, they did hearken unto my words.

7 And we did take our tents and whatsoever things were possible for us, and did journey in the wilderness for the space of many days. And after we had journeyed for the space of many days we did pitch our tents.

8 And my people would that we should call the name of the place ᵃNephi; wherefore, we did call it Nephi.

9 And all those who were with me did take upon them to call themselves the ᵃpeople of Nephi.

10 And we did observe to keep the judgments, and the ᵃstatutes, and the commandments of the Lord in all things, according to the ᵇlaw of Moses.

11 And the Lord was with us; and we did ᵃprosper exceedingly; for we did sow seed, and we did reap again in abundance. And we began to raise flocks, and herds, and animals of every kind.

12 And I, Nephi, had also brought the records which were engraven upon the ᵃplates of brass; and also the ᵇball, or ᶜcompass, which was prepared for my father by the hand of the Lord, according to that which is written.

13 And it came to pass that we began to prosper exceedingly, and to multiply in the land.

14 And I, Nephi, did take the ᵃsword of Laban, and after the man-

5 1a 2 Ne. 4: 13; Jacob 7: 24; Enos 1: 20; Mosiah 10: 12, 15.
2a 1 Ne. 7: 6 (6–19); 17: 18 (17–55); 18: 10 (9–22); 2 Ne. 4: 13 (13–14).
3a Num. 16: 13; 1 Ne. 16: 37 (37–38); Mosiah 10: 15.
 b Alma 54: 17.
5a TG Guidance, Divine.
 b Mosiah 10: 13.

6a 1 Ne. 4: 35; 16: 7; 2 Ne. 1: 31 (30–32).
 b TG Warnings.
8a Omni 1: 12 (12, 27); Mosiah 7: 1 (1–7, 21); 9: 1 (1–6, 14); 28: 1 (1, 5); Alma 2: 24; 20: 1; 50: 8 (8, 11).
9a Jacob 1: 14.
10a Ezek. 20: 11; 2 Ne. 1: 16 (16–17).
 b 2 Ne. 11: 4. TG Law of Moses.

11a Matt. 6: 33.
12a 2 Ne. 4: 2; Mosiah 1: 3 (3–4).
 b Mosiah 1: 16.
 c 1 Ne. 16: 16 (10, 16, 26); 18: 12 (12, 21); Alma 37: 38 (38–47); D&C 17: 1.
14a 1 Ne. 4: 9; Jacob 1: 10; W of M 1: 13; Mosiah 1: 16; D&C 17: 1.

[Between 588 and 570 B.C.]

ner of it did make many *b*swords, lest by any means the people who were now called Lamanites should come upon us and destroy us; for I knew their *c*hatred towards me and my children and those who were called my people.

15 And I did teach my people to *a*build buildings, and to *b*work in all *c*manner of wood, and of *d*iron, and of copper, and of *e*brass, and of steel, and of *f*gold, and of silver, and of precious ores, which were in great abundance.

16 And I, Nephi, did *a*build a *b*temple; and I did construct it after the manner of the temple of *c*Solomon save it were not built of so many *d*precious things; for they were not to be found upon the land, wherefore, it could not be built like unto Solomon's *e*temple. But the manner of the construction was like unto the temple of *f*Solomon; and the workmanship thereof was exceedingly fine.

17 And it came to pass that I, Nephi, did cause my people to be *a*industrious, and to *b*labor with their *c*hands.

18 And it came to pass that they would that I should be their *a*king. But I, Nephi, was desirous that they should have no king; nevertheless, I did for them according to that which was in my power.

19 And behold, the words of the Lord had been fulfilled unto my brethren, which he spake concerning them, that I should be their *a*ruler and their teacher. Wherefore, I had been their ruler and their *b*teacher, according to the commandments of the Lord, until the time they sought to take away my life.

20 Wherefore, the word of the Lord was fulfilled which he spake unto me, saying that: Inasmuch as they will *a*not hearken unto thy words they shall be *b*cut off from the presence of the Lord. And behold, they were *c*cut off from his presence.

21 And he had caused the *a*cursing to come upon them, yea, even a sore cursing, because of their iniquity. For behold, they had hardened their hearts against him, that they had become like unto a flint; wherefore, as they were white, and exceedingly fair and *b*delightsome, that they might not be *c*enticing unto my people the Lord God did cause a *d*skin of *e*blackness to come upon them.

22 And thus saith the Lord God: I will cause that they shall be *a*loathsome unto thy people, save they shall repent of their iniquities.

23 And cursed shall be the seed of him that *a*mixeth with their seed; for they shall be cursed even with the same cursing. And the Lord spake it, and it was done.

24 And because of their *a*cursing which was upon them they did become an *b*idle people, full of

14*b* Jarom 1:8; Mosiah 10: 8; Alma 2:12; Hel. 1: 14; 3 Ne. 3:26.
c TG Hate.
15*a* TG Skill.
b TG Art.
c Jarom 1:8.
d Josh. 8:31; 1 Ne. 18: 25; Jacob 2:12 (12– 13); Hel. 6:9 (9–11); Ether 9:17; 10:23 (12, 23); Moses 5:46.
e Gen. 4:22.
f Ex. 31:4 (4–5); 1 Kgs. 6:21 (21–22); D&C 124:26 (26–27).
16*a* 2 Chr. 3:1 (1–17); D&C 84:5 (5, 31); 124:31 (25–55).

b 1 Kgs. 5:5; Jacob 1: 17; Mosiah 1:18; 7:17; 11:10; Alma 16:13; Hel. 3:14 (9, 14); 3 Ne. 11:1. TG Temple.
c 1 Kgs. 6:2.
d 1 Kgs. 5:17.
e 1 Kgs. 9:1.
f 1 Chr. 18:8.
17*a* TG Industry; Work, Value of.
b TG Labor.
c Prov. 31:13.
18*a* 2 Ne. 6:2; Jacob 1:9 (9, 11, 15); Jarom 1:7 (7, 14); Mosiah 1:10.
19*a* 2 Ne. 1:25 (25–27).
b TG Teacher.
20*a* 1 Ne. 8:18.

b 1 Ne. 8:35 (35–36).
c 1 Ne. 2:21; Alma 9: 14 (13–15); 38:1.
21*a* 2 Ne. 1:17; Alma 3: 6 (6–19).
b Gen. 24:16; 1 Ne. 13: 15; 4 Ne. 1:10; Morm. 9:6.
c TG Marriage, Temporal.
d 2 Ne. 30:6; 3 Ne. 2: 15 (14–16).
e Moses 7:8.
22*a* 1 Ne. 12:23.
23*a* TG Marriage, Interfaith.
24*a* TG Curse.
b Alma 22:28. TG Idleness.

[Between 588 and 570 B.C.]

mischief and subtlety, and did seek in the wilderness for beasts of prey.

25 And the Lord God said unto me: They shall be a scourge unto thy seed, to ªstir them up in remembrance of me; and inasmuch as they will not remember me, and hearken unto my words, they shall scourge them even unto destruction.

26 And it came to pass that I, Nephi, did ªconsecrate Jacob and Joseph, that they should be ᵇpriests and ᶜteachers over the land of my people.

27 And it came to pass that we lived after the manner of ªhappiness.

28 *And thirty years had passed away from the time we left Jerusalem.

29 And I, Nephi, had kept the ªrecords upon my plates, which I had made, of my people thus far.

30 And it came to pass that the Lord God said unto me: ªMake other plates; and thou shalt engraven many things upon them which are good in my sight, for the profit of thy people.

31 Wherefore, I, Nephi, to be obedient to the commandments of the Lord, went and made ªthese plates upon which I have engraven these things.

32 And I engraved that which is pleasing unto God. And if my people are pleased with the things of God they will be pleased with mine engravings which are upon these plates.

33 And if my people desire to know the more particular part of the history of my people they must search mine ªother ᵇplates.

34 And it sufficeth me to say that †forty years had passed away, and we had already had wars and contentions with our brethren.

CHAPTER 6

Jacob recounts Jewish history: Their Babylonian captivity and return; the ministry and crucifixion of the Holy One of Israel; the help received from the gentiles; and their latter-day restoration when they believe in the Messiah.

THE ªwords of Jacob, the brother of Nephi, which he spake unto the people of Nephi:

2 Behold, my beloved brethren, I, Jacob, having been called of God, and ordained after the manner of his holy ªorder, and having been consecrated by my brother Nephi, unto whom ye look as a ᵇking or a protector, and on whom ye depend for safety, behold ye know that I have spoken unto you exceedingly many things.

3 Nevertheless, I speak unto you again; for I am desirous for the ªwelfare of your souls. Yea, mine anxiety is great for you; and ye yourselves know that it ever has been. For I have exhorted you with all diligence; and I have taught you the words of my father; and I have spoken unto you concerning all things which are ᵇwritten, from the creation of the world.

4 And now, behold, I would speak unto you concerning things which are, and which are to come; wherefore, I will read you the words of ªIsaiah. And they are the words which my brother has desired that I should speak unto you. And I speak unto you for your sakes, that ye may learn and glorify the name of your God.

5 And now, the words which I shall read are they which Isaiah spake concerning all the house of Israel;

25a 1 Ne. 2: 24.
26a Lev. 16: 32; Jacob 1: 18 (18–19); Mosiah 23: 17. TG Priesthood, Authority.
  b TG Priest.
  c TG Teacher.
27a Alma 50: 23.
29a TG Record Keeping.
30a 1 Ne. 19: 5 (1–6);

Jacob 3: 14.
31a 1 Ne. 19: 3; Jacob 1: 1.
33a 1 Ne. 1: 17 (16–17); 2 Ne. 4: 14; D&C 10: 42.
  b 1 Ne. 19: 4; Jacob 1: 3.
6 1a 2 Ne. 11: 1;
  Jacob 2: 1.
2a TG Priesthood,

Melchizedek.
  b 2 Ne. 5: 18; Jacob 1: 9 (9, 11, 15); Jarom 1: 7 (7, 14); Mosiah 1: 10.
3a Jacob 2: 3; Mosiah 25: 11.
  b TG Scriptures, Value of.
4a 3 Ne. 23: 1 (1–3).

[*569 B.C. †559 B.C.]

wherefore, they may be [a]likened unto you, for ye are of the house of Israel. And there are many things which have been spoken by Isaiah which may be likened unto you, because ye are of the house of Israel.

6 And now, these are the words: [a]Thus saith the Lord God: Behold, I will lift up mine hand to the Gentiles, and set up my [b]standard to the people; and they shall bring thy sons in their arms, and thy daughters shall be carried upon their shoulders.

7 And [a]kings shall be thy nursing fathers, and their queens thy nursing mothers; they shall bow down to thee with their faces towards the earth, and lick up the dust of thy feet; and thou shalt know that [b]I am the Lord; for they shall not be ashamed that [c]wait for me.

8 And now I, Jacob, would speak somewhat concerning these words. For behold, the Lord has shown me that those who were at [a]Jerusalem, from whence we came, have been [b]slain and [c]carried away captive.

9 Nevertheless, the Lord has shown unto me that they should [a]return again. And he also has shown unto me that the Lord God, the Holy One of Israel, should manifest himself unto them in the flesh; and after he should manifest himself they should [b]scourge him and [c]crucify him, according to the words of the angel who spake it unto me.

10 And after they have [a]hardened their hearts and [b]stiffened their necks against the Holy One of Israel, behold, the [c]judgments of the Holy One of Israel shall come upon them. And the day cometh that they shall be smitten and afflicted.

11 Wherefore, after they are driven to and fro, for thus saith the angel, many shall be afflicted in the flesh, and shall not be suffered to [a]perish, because of the prayers of the faithful; they shall be scattered, and smitten, and hated; nevertheless, the Lord will be merciful unto them, that [b]when they shall come to the [c]knowledge of their Redeemer, they shall be [d]gathered together again to the [e]lands of their inheritance.

12 And blessed are the [a]Gentiles, they of whom the prophet has written; for behold, if it so be that they shall repent and fight not against Zion, and do not unite themselves to that great and [b]abominable church, they shall be saved; for the Lord God will fulfil his [c]covenants which he has made unto his children; and for this cause the prophet has written these things.

13 Wherefore, they that fight against Zion and the covenant people of the Lord shall lick up the dust of their feet; and the people of the Lord shall not be [a]ashamed. For the people of the Lord are they who [b]wait for him; for they still wait for the coming of the Messiah.

5a IE applied.
6a Isa. 49: 22 (22–26); 2 Ne. 10: 9.
 b TG Ensign.
7a Isa. 60: 16.
 b Isa. 44: 8; 45: 5 (5–22); 46: 9; 3 Ne. 24: 6; Moses 1: 6.
 c Lam. 3: 25 (25–26); D&C 133: 45.
8a Esth. 2: 6; 1 Ne. 7: 13; 10: 3; 2 Ne. 25: 6, 10; Omni 1: 15; Hel. 8: 20 (20–21).
 b Ezek. 23: 25 (24–29).
 c 2 Kgs. 24: 14 (10–16); 25: 11 (1–12); Jer. 13: 19 (19, 24).
 TG Israel, Bondage of,

in Other Lands.
9a Jer. 29: 10 (9–10); 1 Ne. 10: 3.
 b TG Jesus Christ, Betrayal of.
 c 1 Ne. 19: 10 (10, 13); Mosiah 3: 9; 3 Ne. 11: 14 (14–15).
 TG Jesus Christ, Crucifixion of.
10a TG Hardheartedness.
 b TG Stiffneckedness.
 c Matt. 27: 25 (24–25).
11a Amos 9: 8 (8–9); 2 Ne. 20: 20 (20–21).
 b 1 Ne. 22: 12 (11–12); 2 Ne. 9: 2 (1–2).
 c Hosea 3: 5; D&C 113: 10. TG Israel,

Restoration of.
 d TG Israel, Gathering of.
 e TG Lands of Inheritance.
12a 1 Ne. 14: 2 (1–5); 2 Ne. 10: 10 (8–14, 18).
 b TG Devil, Church of.
 c TG Abrahamic Covenant.
13a Joel 2: 26 (26–27); 3 Ne. 22: 4; D&C 90: 17.
 b Gen. 49: 18; Ps. 25: 5; Prov. 20: 22; 27: 18; Isa. 40: 31; 1 Ne. 21: 23; D&C 98: 2; 133: 11, 45.

[Between 559 and 545 B.C.]

14 And behold, according to the words of the prophet, the Messiah will set himself again the *a*second time to recover them; wherefore, he will *b*manifest himself unto them in power and great glory, unto the *c*destruction of their enemies, when that day cometh when they shall believe in him; and none will he destroy that believe in him.

15 And they that believe not in him shall be *a*destroyed, both by *b*fire, and by tempest, and by earthquakes, and by *c*bloodsheds, and by *d*pestilence, and by *e*famine. And they shall know that the Lord is God, the Holy One of Israel.

16 *a*For shall the prey be taken from the mighty, or the *b*lawful captive delivered?

17 But thus saith the Lord: Even the captives of the mighty shall be taken away, and the prey of the terrible shall be delivered; *a*for the *b*Mighty God shall *c*deliver his covenant people. For thus saith the Lord: I will contend with them that contendeth with thee—

18 And I will feed them that oppress thee, with their own flesh; and they shall be drunken with their own blood as with sweet wine; and all flesh shall know that I the Lord am thy Savior and thy *a*Redeemer, the *b*Mighty One of Jacob.

CHAPTER 7

Isaiah speaks Messianically—Messiah shall have the tongue of the learned—He shall give his back to the smiters—He shall not be confounded—Compare Isaiah 50.

*a*YEA, for thus saith the Lord: Have I put thee away, or have I cast thee off forever? For thus saith the Lord: Where is the *b*bill of your mother's *c*divorcement? To whom have I put thee away, or to which of my *d*creditors have I *e*sold you? Yea, to whom have I sold you? Behold, for your iniquities have ye sold yourselves, and for your transgressions is your mother put away.

2 Wherefore, when I came, there was no man; when I *a*called, yea, there was none to answer. O house of Israel, is my hand shortened at all that it cannot redeem, or have I no power to deliver? Behold, at my rebuke I *b*dry up the *c*sea, I make their *d*rivers a wilderness and their *e*fish to stink because the waters are dried up, and they die because of thirst.

3 I clothe the heavens with *a*blackness, and I make *b*sackcloth their covering.

4 The Lord God hath given me the *a*tongue of the learned, that I should know how to speak a word in season unto thee, O house of Israel. When

---

14a 2 Ne. 21:11; 25:17; 29:1.
  b 2 Ne. 3:5; D&C 3:18 (16–20).
  c 1 Ne. 21:26 (24–26); 22:13 (13–14).
15a 1 Ne. 22:13 (13–23); 2 Ne. 10:16 (15–16); 28:15 (15–32); 3 Ne. 16:8 (8–15); Ether 2:9 (8–11). TG Last Days.
  b Joel 1:19 (19–20); Jacob 5:77; 6:3.
  c TG Blood, Shedding of.
  d Luke 21:11 (10–13); Mosiah 12:4; D&C 97:26 (22–26). TG Plague.

  e TG Drought.
16a Isa. 49:24 (24–26); 2 Ne. 11:2.
  b HEB righteous captive; i.e., the covenant people of the Lord, as stated in v. 17.
17a 1 Ne. 21:25.
  b TG Jesus Christ—Jehovah.
  c 2 Kgs. 17:39; D&C 105:8. TG Jesus Christ, Prophecies about; Jesus Christ, Savior.
18a TG Jesus Christ, Redeemer.
  b Gen. 49:24; Ps. 132:2; Isa. 1:24; 60:16.
7 1a Isa. 50:1 (1–11); 2 Ne. 8:1.

  b Jer. 3:8.
  c TG Divorce.
  d 2 Kgs. 4:1; Matt. 18:25.
  e Judg. 4:2; Isa. 52:3. TG Apostasy of Israel.
2a Prov. 1:24 (24–27); Isa. 65:12; Alma 5:37.
  b Nahum 1:4.
  c Ex. 14:21 (1–31); Ps. 106:9; D&C 133:68.
  d Josh. 3:16 (15–16).
  e Ex. 7:21 (17–21).
3a Ex. 10:21.
  b Rev. 6:12.
4a Luke 21:15.

[Between 559 and 545 B.C.]

ye are weary he waketh morning by morning. He waketh mine ear to hear as the learned.

5 The Lord God hath opened mine ^aear, and I was not rebellious, neither turned away back.

6 I gave my back to the ^asmiter, and my cheeks to them that plucked off the hair. I hid not my face from ^bshame and spitting.

7 For the Lord God will help me, therefore shall I not be confounded. Therefore have I set my face like a flint, and I know that I shall not be ^aashamed.

8 And the Lord is near, and he ^ajustifieth me. Who will contend with me? Let us stand together. Who is mine adversary? Let him come near me, and I will ^bsmite him with the strength of my mouth.

9 For the Lord God will help me. And all they who shall ^acondemn me, behold, all they shall ^bwax old as a garment, and the moth shall eat them up.

10 Who is among you that feareth the Lord, that obeyeth the ^avoice of his servant, that ^bwalketh in darkness and hath no light?

11 Behold all ye that kindle fire, that compass yourselves about with sparks, walk in the light of ^ayour fire and in the sparks which ye have kindled. ^bThis shall ye have of mine hand—ye shall lie down in sorrow.

CHAPTER 8

In the last days, the Lord shall comfort Zion and gather Israel—The re- *deemed shall come to Zion amid great joy—Compare Isaiah 51 and 52 : 1–2.*

^aHEARKEN unto me, ye that follow after righteousness. Look unto the ^brock from whence ye are hewn, and to the hole of the pit from whence ye are digged.

2 Look unto Abraham, your ^afather, and unto ^bSarah, she that bare you; for I called him alone, and blessed him.

3 For the Lord shall ^acomfort ^bZion, he will comfort all her waste places; and he will make her ^cwilderness like ^dEden, and her desert like the garden of the Lord. Joy and gladness shall be found therein, thanksgiving and the voice of melody.

4 Hearken unto me, my people; and give ear unto me, O my nation; for a ^alaw shall proceed from me, and I will make my judgment to rest for a ^blight for the people.

5 My righteousness is near; my ^asalvation is gone forth, and mine arm shall ^bjudge the people. The ^cisles shall wait upon me, and on mine arm shall they trust.

6 Lift up your eyes to the ^aheavens, and look upon the earth beneath; for the heavens shall ^bvanish away like smoke, and the earth shall ^cwax old like a garment; and they that dwell therein shall die in like manner. But my salvation shall be forever, and my righteousness shall not be abolished.

7 Hearken unto me, ye that know righteousness, the people in whose heart I have written my law, ^afear

---

5a D&C 58:1.
6a Isa. 53:4; Matt. 27:26; 2 Ne. 9:5 (4–7).
 b TG Shame.
7a Rom. 9:33.
8a Rom. 8:33 (32–34).
 b Isa. 11:4.
9a Rom. 8:31.
 b Ps. 102:26.
10a D&C 1:38.
 b TG Walking in Darkness.
11a Deut. 12:8; Judg. 17:6.
 b D&C 133:70.

8 1a Isa. 51:1 (1–23); 2 Ne. 7:1.
 b IE Abraham and Sarah; see v. 2. TG Rock.
2a Gen. 17:4 (1–8); D&C 109:64; 132:49.
 b Gen. 24:36.
3a TG Israel, Restoration of.
 b TG Zion.
 c Isa. 35:2 (1–2, 6–7). TG Israel, Blessings of.
 d TG Earth, Renewal of; Eden.

4a Isa. 2:3. TG God, Law of.
 b TG Light.
5a TG Jesus Christ, Savior; Salvation.
 b TG Jesus Christ, Judge.
 c 2 Ne. 10:20.
6a 2 Pet. 3:10.
 b Isa. 13:13.
 c Ps. 102:26 (25–28).
7a Deut. 1:17; Ps. 56:4 (4, 11); 118:6; D&C 122:9. TG Peer Influence.

[Between 559 and 545 B.C.]

ye not the *b*reproach of men, neither be ye afraid of their *c*revilings.

8 For the *a*moth shall eat them up like a garment, and the worm shall eat them like wool. But my righteousness shall be forever, and my salvation from generation to generation.

9 *a*Awake, awake! Put on *b*strength, O arm of the Lord; awake as in the ancient days. Art thou not he that hath cut *c*Rahab, and wounded the *d*dragon?

10 Art thou not he who hath dried the sea, the waters of the great deep; that hath made the depths of the sea a *a*way for the ransomed to pass over?

11 Therefore, the *a*redeemed of the Lord shall *b*return, and come with *c*singing unto Zion; and everlasting joy and holiness shall be upon their heads; and they shall obtain gladness and joy; sorrow and *d*mourning shall flee away.

12 *a*I am he; yea, I am he that comforteth you. Behold, who art thou, that thou shouldst be *b*afraid of man, who shall die, and of the son of man, who shall be made like unto *c*grass?

13 And *a*forgettest the Lord thy maker, that hath *b*stretched forth the heavens, and laid the foundations of the earth, and hast feared continually every day, because of the fury of the *c*oppressor, as if he were ready to destroy? And where is the fury of the oppressor?

14 The *a*captive exile hasteneth, that he may be loosed, and that he should not die in the pit, nor that his bread should fail.

15 But I am the Lord thy God, whose *a*waves roared; the Lord of Hosts is my name.

16 And I have *a*put my words in thy mouth, and have covered thee in the shadow of mine hand, that I may plant the heavens and lay the foundations of the earth, and say unto Zion: Behold, thou art my *b*people.

17 Awake, awake, stand up, O Jerusalem, which hast drunk at the hand of the Lord the *a*cup of his *b*fury—thou hast drunken the dregs of the cup of trembling wrung out—

18 And none to guide her among all the sons she hath brought forth; neither that taketh her by the hand, of all the sons she hath brought up.

19 These two *a*sons are come unto thee, who shall be sorry for thee—thy desolation and destruction, and the famine and the sword—and by whom shall I comfort thee?

20 Thy sons have fainted, save these two; they lie at the head of all the streets; as a wild bull in a net, they are full of the fury of the Lord, the rebuke of thy God.

21 Therefore hear now this, thou afflicted, and *a*drunken, and not with wine:

22 Thus saith thy Lord, the Lord and thy God *a*pleadeth the cause of his people; behold, I have taken out of thine hand the cup of trembling, the dregs of the cup of my fury; thou shalt no more drink it again.

23 But *a*I will put it into the hand

7b TG Reproach.
  c TG Hate.
8a Isa. 50: 9.
9a Isa. 52: 1.
  b D&C 113: 8 (7–8).
    TG Israel, Restoration of.
  c Ps. 89: 10; Isa. 27: 1.
  d Ezek. 29: 3.
10a Isa. 35: 8 (8–10).
11a TG Israel, Restoration of.
  b TG Israel, Gathering of.
  c Isa. 35: 10; Jer. 31: 12 (12–13).

  d Rev. 21: 4 (2–5).
12a D&C 133: 47; 136: 22.
  b Jer. 1: 8 (7–8).
  c Isa. 40: 6 (6–8); 1 Pet. 1: 24 (24–25).
13a Jer. 23: 27 (27–39).
  b Job 9: 8.
  c IE Israel's captors, typifying evil rulers who oppress the righteous; see v. 14.
    TG Oppression.
14a Isa. 52: 2.

15a 1 Ne. 4: 2.
16a TG Israel, Mission of; Prophets, Mission of.
  b 1 Kgs. 8: 51; 2 Ne. 3: 9; 29: 14.
17a 2 Ne. 15: 15;
  b Luke 21: 24 (22–24).
19a Rev. 11: 3 (3–12).
21a 2 Ne. 27: 4.
22a Jer. 50: 34.
23a Joel 3: 16 (9–16); Zech. 12: 9 (2–3, 8–9); 14: 12 (3, 12–15).

[Between 559 and 545 B.C.]

of them that afflict thee; who have said to thy soul: Bow down, that we may go over—and thou hast laid thy body as the ground and as the street to them that went over.

24 [a]Awake, awake, put on thy [b]strength, O [c]Zion; put on thy beautiful garments, O Jerusalem, the holy city; for henceforth there shall [d]no more come into thee the uncircumcised and the unclean.

25 Shake thyself from the dust; arise, sit down, O Jerusalem; loose thyself from the [a]bands of thy neck, O captive daughter of Zion.

CHAPTER 9

Jews shall be gathered in all their lands of promise—Atonement ransoms man from the fall—The bodies of the dead shall come forth from the grave, and their spirits from hell and from paradise—They shall be judged— Atonement saves from death, hell, the devil, and endless torment—The righteous to be saved in the kingdom of God—Penalties for sins set forth— The Holy One of Israel is the keeper of the gate.

AND now, my beloved brethren, I have read these things that ye might know concerning the [a]covenants of the Lord that he has covenanted with all the house of Israel—

2 That he has spoken unto the Jews, by the mouth of his holy prophets, even from the beginning down, from generation to generation, until the time comes that they shall be [a]re-stored to the true church and fold of God; when they shall be [b]gathered home to the [c]lands of their inheritance, and shall be established in all their lands of promise.

3 Behold, my beloved brethren, I speak unto you these things that ye may rejoice, and [a]lift up your heads forever, because of the blessings which the Lord God shall bestow upon your children.

4 For I know that ye have searched much, many of you, to know of things to come; wherefore I know that ye know that our [a]flesh must waste away and die; nevertheless, in our [b]bodies we shall see God.

5 Yea, I know that ye know that in the body he shall show himself un-to those at Jerusalem, from whence we came; for it is expedient that it should be among them: for it be-hooveth the great [a]Creator that he [b]suffereth himself to become [c]subject unto man in the flesh, and [d]die for [e]all men, that all men might become subject unto him.

6 For as [a]death hath passed upon all men, to fulfil the merciful [b]plan of the great Creator, there must needs be a power of [c]resurrection, and the resurrection must needs come unto man by reason of the [d]fall; and the fall came by reason of [e]transgression; and because man became fallen they were [f]cut off from the [g]presence of the Lord.

7 Wherefore, it must needs be an [a]infinite [b]atonement—save it should be an infinite atonement this corrup-

24a Isa. 52: 1 (1–2).
  b D&C 113: 8 (7–8).
  TG Strength.
  c TG Zion.
  d Joel 3: 17; Zech. 14: 21.
25a D&C 113: 10 (9–10).
9 1a TG Abrahamic Covenant; Israel, Mission of.
2a 2 Ne. 6: 11 (10–15); 10: 7 (5–9).
  TG Israel, Restoration of; Restoration of the Gospel.
  b TG Israel, Gathering of; Mission of Latter-day Saints.

  c TG Lands of Inheri-tance.
3a Ps. 24: 7 (7–10).
4a Gen. 6: 3; Moses 8 :17.
  b Job 19: 26; Alma 11: 41 (41–45); 42: 23;
  Hel. 14: 15 (15–18);
  Morm. 9: 13. TG Body, Sanctity of.
5a TG Jesus Christ, Creator.
  b 2 Ne. 7: 6 (4–9).
  c Mark 10: 44 (43–44).
  d TG Jesus Christ, Death of; Jesus Christ, Mission of.
  e John 12: 32; 2 Ne. 26:

  24; 3 Ne. 27: 14 (14–15).
6a Eccl. 8: 8 (6–8).
  b TG Salvation, Plan of.
  c TG Jesus Christ, Resurrection.
  d TG Fall of Man.
  e TG Transgression.
  f 2 Ne. 2: 5 (5–8); Alma 11: 42 (40–45).
  g TG God, Presence of.
7a Alma 34: 10.
  b Matt. 26: 54 (52–56).
  TG Jesus Christ, Atonement through.

[Between 559 and 545 B.C.]

tion could not put on incorruption. Wherefore, the ^cfirst judgment which came upon man must needs have ^dremained to an endless duration. And if so, this flesh must have laid down to rot and to crumble to its mother earth, to rise no more.

8 O the ^awisdom of God, his ^bmercy and ^cgrace! For behold, if the ^dflesh should rise no more our spirits must become subject to that angel who ^efell from before the presence of the Eternal God, and became the ^fdevil, to rise no more.

9 And our spirits must have become ^alike unto him, and we become devils, ^bangels to a ^cdevil, to be ^dshut out from the presence of our God, and to remain with the father of ^elies, in misery, like unto himself; yea, to that being who ^fbeguiled our first parents, who ^gtransformeth himself nigh unto an ^hangel of light, and ⁱstirreth up the children of men unto ^jsecret combinations of murder and all manner of secret works of darkness.

10 O how great the ^agoodness of our God, who prepareth a way for our ^bescape from the grasp of this awful monster; yea, that monster, ^cdeath and ^dhell, which I call the death of the body, and also the death of the spirit.

11 And because of the way of ^adeliverance of our God, the Holy One of Israel, this ^bdeath, of which I have spoken, which is the temporal, shall deliver up its dead; which death is the grave.

12 And this ^adeath of which I have spoken, which is the spiritual death, shall deliver up its dead; which spiritual death is ^bhell; wherefore, death and hell must ^cdeliver up their dead, and hell must deliver up its ^dcaptive ^espirits, and the grave must deliver up its captive ^fbodies, and the bodies and the ^gspirits of men will be ^hrestored one to the other; and it is by the power of the resurrection of the Holy One of Israel.

13 O how great the ^aplan of our God! For on the other hand, the ^bparadise of God must deliver up the spirits of the righteous, and the grave deliver up the body of the righteous; and the spirit and the body is ^crestored to itself again, and all men become incorruptible, and ^dimmortal, and they are living souls, having a ^eperfect ^fknowledge like unto us in the flesh, save it be that our knowledge shall be perfect.

14 Wherefore, we shall have a ^aperfect ^bknowledge of all our ^cguilt, and our ^duncleanness, and our ^enakedness; and the righteous shall

7c Mosiah 16: 4 (4–7);
   Alma 11: 45; 12: 36;
   42: 6 (6, 9, 14).
 d Mosiah 15: 19.
8a Job 12: 13 (7–25);
   Abr. 3: 21. TG God,
   Wisdom of.
 b TG God, Mercy of.
 c TG Grace.
 d D&C 93: 34.
 e 2 Ne. 2: 17; Moses 4: 3
   (3–4); Abr. 3: 28 (27–
   28).
 f TG Devil.
9a 3 Ne. 29: 7.
 b Jacob 3: 11; Alma 5:
   25, 39; Moro. 9: 13.
 c 2 Cor. 11: 14 (13–15).
 d Rev. 12: 9 (7–9).
 e TG Lying.
 f Gen. 3: 13 (1–13);
   Mosiah 16: 3; Ether 8:
   25; Moses 4: 19 (5–19).

 g Rev. 16: 14 (13–14);
   Alma 30: 53.
 h D&C 129: 8.
 i TG Motivations.
 j TG Secret
   Combinations.
10a Ex. 34: 6 (5–7);
   2 Ne. 4: 17; D&C 86:
   11.
 b TG Death, Power over.
 c Mosiah 16: 8 (7–8);
   Alma 42: 15 (6–15).
 d TG Hell.
11a TG Deliverance.
 b TG Death.
12a TG Death, Spiritual,
   First.
 b D&C 76: 84.
 c D&C 138: 18.
 d TG Bondage, Spiritual;
   Spirits in Prison.
 e TG Spirits, Dis-
   embodied.

 f TG Body, Sanctity of.
 g TG Spirit Body.
 h TG Resurrection.
13a TG Salvation, Plan of.
 b D&C 138: 19.
   TG Paradise.
 c Alma 11: 43; 40: 23;
   41: 4 (3–5); D&C 138:
   17.
 d TG Immortality.
 e TG Perfection.
 f Eccl. 9: 10; D&C 130:
   18.
14a Mosiah 3: 25.
 b Isa. 59: 12; Alma 5: 18;
   11: 43.
 c TG Guilt.
 d TG Uncleanness.
 e Gen. 2: 25; Ex. 32: 25;
   Moses 4: 13 (13, 16–
   17).

[Between 559 and 545 B.C.]

have a perfect knowledge of their enjoyment, and their ^f righteousness, being ^g clothed with ^h purity, yea, even with the ^i robe of righteousness.

15 And it shall come to pass that when all men shall have passed from this first death unto life, insomuch as they have become immortal, they must appear before the ^a judgment-seat of the Holy One of Israel; and then cometh the ^b judgment; and then must they be judged according to the holy judgment of God.

16 And assuredly, as the Lord liveth, for the Lord God hath spoken it, and it is his eternal ^a word, which cannot ^b pass away, that they who are righteous shall be righteous still, and they who are ^c filthy shall be ^d filthy still; wherefore, they who are filthy are the ^e devil and his angels; and they shall go away into ^f everlasting fire, prepared for them; and their ^g torment is as a ^h lake of fire and brimstone, whose flame ascendeth up forever and ever and has no end.

17 O the greatness and the ^a justice of our God! For he executeth all his words, and they have gone forth out of his mouth, and his law must be ^b fulfilled.

18 But, behold, the ^a righteous, the ^b saints of the Holy One of Israel, they who have believed in the Holy One of Israel, they who have en-

dured the ^c crosses of the world, and despised the shame of it, they shall ^d inherit the ^e kingdom of God, which was prepared for them ^f from the foundation of the world, and their ^g joy shall be full ^h forever.

19 O the greatness of the mercy of our God, the Holy One of Israel! For he ^a delivereth his saints from that ^b awful monster the devil, and death, and ^c hell, and that lake of fire and brimstone, which is endless torment.

20 O how great the ^a holiness of our God! For he ^b knoweth ^c all things, and there is not anything save he knows it.

21 And he cometh into the world that he may ^a save all men if they will hearken unto his voice; for behold, he suffereth the pains of all men, yea, the ^b pains of every living creature, both men, women, and children, who belong to the family of ^c Adam.

22 And he suffereth this that the resurrection might pass upon all men, that all might stand before him at the great and judgment day.

23 And he commandeth all men that they must ^a repent, and be ^b baptized in his name, having perfect ^c faith in the Holy One of Israel, or they cannot be saved in the kingdom of God.

14f TG Righteousness.
  g Prov. 31: 25.
  h TG Purity.
  i D&C 109: 76.
15a TG Judgment, The Last.
  b Job 34: 12; Ps. 19: 9; 2 Ne. 30: 9.
16a 1 Kgs. 8: 56; Ps. 33: 11; D&C 1: 38 (37–39); Moses 1: 4.
  b D&C 56: 11.
  c Prov. 22: 8. TG Filthiness.
  d 1 Ne. 15: 33 (33–35); Alma 7: 21; Morm. 9: 14; D&C 88: 35.
  e TG Devil.
  f Mosiah 27: 28.
  g TG Punishment.
  h Rev. 19: 20; 21: 8; 2 Ne. 28: 23;

    D&C 63: 17; 76: 36.
17a TG God, Justice of; Justice.
  b Ezek. 24: 14.
18a Ps. 5: 12. TG Righteousness.
  b TG Saints.
  c Luke 14: 27.
  d Col. 1: 12; D&C 45: 58 (57–58); 84: 38 (33–38).
  e TG Exaltation.
  f Alma 13: 3 (3, 5, 7–9).
  g Matt. 5: 12 (11–12).
  h TG Eternal Life.
19a Job 23: 7; D&C 108: 8.
  b 1 Ne. 15: 35.
  c TG Hell.
20a HEB qodesh—committed, consecrated. TG Holiness.

  b Mosiah 24: 12; Alma 26: 35. TG God, Fore-knowledge of; God, Intelligence of; God, Omniscience of.
  c Prov. 5: 21; D&C 38: 2 (1–2).
21a TG Salvation.
  b D&C 18: 11; 19: 18 (15–18). TG Jesus Christ, Trials of.
  c D&C 107: 54 (53–56); 128: 21. TG Adam.
23a TG Repentance.
  b Mosiah 26: 22; D&C 76: 52 (50–52); 84: 74; 137: 6. TG Baptism, Essential.
  c TG Baptism, Qualifications for; Faith.

[Between 559 and 545 B.C.]

24 And if they will not repent and believe in his *name, and be baptized in his name, and *endure to the end, they must be *damned; for the Lord God, the Holy One of Israel, has spoken it.

25 Wherefore, he has given a *law; and where there is *no *law given there is no *punishment; and where there is no punishment there is no condemnation; and where there is no condemnation the mercies of the Holy One of Israel have claim upon them, because of the atonement; for they are delivered by the power of him.

26 For the *atonement satisfieth the demands of his *justice upon all those who *have not the *law given to them, that they are *delivered from that awful monster, death and *hell, and the devil, and the lake of fire and brimstone, which is endless torment; and they are restored to that God who gave them *breath, which is the Holy One of Israel.

27 But wo unto him that has the *law given, yea, that has all the commandments of God, like unto us, and that *transgresseth them, and that *wasteth the days of his *probation, for awful is his state!

28 O that cunning *plan of the evil one! O the *vainness, and the frailties, and the *foolishness of men! When they are *learned they think they are *wise, and they *hearken not unto the *counsel of God, for they set it aside, supposing they know of themselves, wherefore, their *wisdom is foolishness and it profiteth them not. And they shall perish.

29 But to be *learned is good if they *hearken unto the *counsels of God.

30 But wo unto the *rich, who are *rich as to the things of the *world. For because they are rich they despise the *poor, and they persecute the meek, and their *hearts are upon their treasures; wherefore, their *treasure is their god. And behold, their *treasure shall perish with them also.

31 And wo unto the deaf that will not *hear; for they shall perish.

32 Wo unto the *blind that will not see; for they shall perish also.

33 Wo unto the *uncircumcised of heart, for a knowledge of their

---

24a TG Jesus Christ, Taking the Name of.
 b TG Perseverance.
 c TG Damnation.
25a TG God, Law of.
 b Rom. 4: 15; 5: 13; 2 Ne. 2: 13.
 c John 15: 22 (22–24); Acts 17: 30; Rom. 5: 13; James 4: 17; Alma 42: 17 (12–24). TG Accountability.
 d TG Punishment.
26a Lev. 4: 20; Neh. 10: 33; 2 Ne. 2: 10. TG Atonement.
 b TG God, Justice of; Justice.
 c Mosiah 3: 11; Alma 9: 16 (15–16); 42: 21.
 d Mosiah 15: 24; D&C 137: 7. TG Ignorance.
 e TG Death, Power over.
 f TG Spirits in Prison.
 g Gen. 2: 7; 6: 17; Mosiah 2: 21; D&C 77: 2; 93: 33; Abr. 5: 7 (7–8).

27a Luke 12: 47 (47–48). TG God, Law of.
 b TG Disobedience.
 c TG Idleness; Procrastination; Waste.
 d TG Probation.
28a Alma 28: 13.
 b Job 11: 12 (11–12); Isa. 9: 9 (9–10). TG Vanity.
 c Eccl. 4: 5; 10: 12 (1–3, 12); 2 Ne. 19: 17; D&C 35: 7. TG Foolishness.
 d Luke 16: 15; 2 Ne. 26: 20; 28: 4 (4, 15). TG Education; Worldliness.
 e Prov. 14: 6; Jer. 8: 8 (8–9); Rom. 1: 22. TG Pride; Wisdom.
 f TG Walking in Darkness.
 g Prov. 15: 22; Jacob 4: 10; Alma 37: 12. TG Counsel.
 h Prov. 23: 4; Eccl. 8:

17 (16–17); Ezek. 28: 5 (4–5); D&C 76: 9. TG Knowledge.
29a D&C 67: 6. TG Learning.
 b 2 Ne. 28: 26. TG Submissiveness.
 c Jacob 4: 10. TG Counsel.
30a Jer. 17: 11; Luke 12: 34; D&C 56: 16.
 b Matt. 19: 23.
 c TG World.
 d TG Poor.
 e TG Hardheartedness.
 f TG Treasure.
 g Prov. 27: 24.
31a Ezek. 33: 31 (30–33); Matt. 11: 15; 13: 14; Heb. 5: 11 (11–14); Mosiah 26: 28; D&C 1: 14 (2, 11, 14); Moses 6: 27.
32a TG Apathy; Spiritual Blindness.
33a Rom. 2: 29 (27–29).

[Between 559 and 545 B.C.]

iniquities shall smite them at the last day.

34 Wo unto the ^aliar, for he shall be thrust down to ^bhell.

35 Wo unto the ^amurderer who deliberately ^bkilleth, for he shall ^cdie.

36 Wo unto them who commit ^awhoredoms, for they shall be thrust down to hell.

37 Yea, wo unto those that ^aworship idols, for the devil of all devils delighteth in them.

38 And, in fine, wo unto all those who die in their ^asins; for they shall ^breturn to God, and behold his face, and remain in their sins.

39 O, my beloved brethren, remember the awfulness in ^atransgressing against that Holy God, and also the awfulness of yielding to the enticings of that ^bcunning one. Remember, to be ^ccarnally-minded is ^ddeath, and to be ^espiritually-minded is ^flife ^geternal.

40 O, my beloved brethren, give ear to my words. Remember the greatness of the Holy One of Israel. Do not say that I have spoken hard things against you; for if ye do, ye will ^arevile against the ^btruth; for I have spoken the words of your Maker. I know that the words of truth are ^chard against all ^duncleanness; but the ^erighteous fear them

not, for they love the truth and are not shaken.

41 O then, my beloved brethren, ^acome unto the Lord, the Holy One. Remember that his paths are righteous. Behold, the ^bway for man is ^cnarrow, but it lieth in a straight course before him, and the keeper of the ^dgate is the Holy One of Israel; and he employeth no servant there; and there is none other way save it be by the gate; for he cannot be deceived, for the Lord God is his name.

42 And whoso ^aknocketh, to him will he open; and the ^bwise, and the learned, and they that are rich, who are puffed up because of their ^clearning, and their ^dwisdom, and their riches—yea, they are they whom he despiseth; and save they shall cast these things away, and consider themselves ^efools before God, and come down in the depths of ^fhumility, he will not open unto them.

43 But the things of the wise and the ^aprudent shall be ^bhid from them forever—yea, that happiness which is prepared for the saints.

44 O, my beloved brethren, remember my words. Behold, I take off my garments, and I shake them before you; I pray the God of my salvation that he view me with his

---

34a Prov. 19: 9. TG Gossip; Honesty; Lying.
  b TG Hell.
35a Num. 35: 16 (16–25).
  b Deut. 19: 11; 2 Sam. 12: 9; Mosiah 13: 21.
  c TG Capital Punishment.
36a 3 Ne. 12: 27 (27–32). TG Chastity; Whoredom.
37a Isa. 41: 24 (21–24). TG Idolatry.
38a Ezek. 18: 24. TG Sin.
  b Alma 40: 11.
39a TG Transgression.
  b 2 Ne. 28: 21 (20–22); 32: 8; Mosiah 2: 32; 4: 14; Alma 30: 42 (42, 53).
  c Rom. 8: 6. TG Carnal Mind.
  d TG Death; Death,

Spiritual, First; Hell.
  e Prov. 15: 24. TG Spirituality.
  f Prov. 11: 19.
  g TG Eternal Life.
40a TG Reviling.
  b Prov. 15: 10; Mosiah 13: 7. TG Truth.
  c 1 Ne. 16: 2; 2 Ne. 28: 28; 33: 5.
  d TG Uncleanness.
  e Prov. 28: 1.
41a 1 Ne. 6: 4; Jacob 1: 7; Omni 1: 26 (25–26); Alma 29: 2; 3 Ne. 21: 20; Morm. 9: 27; Ether 5: 5; Moro. 10: 30 (30–32).
  b Ex. 33: 13 (12–13); 2 Ne. 31: 21 (17–21);

Alma 37: 46; D&C 132: 22 (22, 25).
  c Luke 13: 24; 2 Ne. 33: 9; Jacob 6: 11; Hel. 3: 29 (29–30).
  d 2 Ne. 31: 9 (9, 17–18); 3 Ne. 14: 14 (13–14); D&C 22: 4; 43: 7; 137: 2.
42a TG Objectives; Study.
  b Matt. 11: 25. TG Wisdom.
  c TG Knowledge; Learning; Worldliness.
  d Ezek. 28: 5 (4–5).
  e 1 Cor. 3: 18 (18–21).
  f TG Humility; Teachable.
43a TG Prudence.
  b 1 Cor. 2: 14 (9–16).

[Between 559 and 545 B.C.]

[a]all-searching eye; wherefore, ye shall know at the last day, when all men shall be judged of their works, that the God of Israel did witness that I [b]shook your iniquities from my soul, and that I stand with brightness before him, and am [c]rid of your blood.

45 O, my beloved brethren, turn away from your sins; shake off the [a]chains of him that would bind you fast; come unto that God who is the [b]rock of your salvation.

46 Prepare your souls for that glorious day when [a]justice shall be administered unto the righteous, even the day of [b]judgment, that ye may not shrink with awful fear; that ye may not remember your awful [c]guilt in perfectness, and be constrained to exclaim: Holy, holy are thy judgments, O Lord God [d]Almighty—but I know my guilt; I transgressed thy law, and my transgressions are mine; and the devil hath [e]obtained me, that I am a prey to his awful misery.

47 But behold, my brethren, is it expedient that I should awake you to an awful reality of these things? Would I harrow up your souls if your minds were pure? Would I be plain unto you according to the plainness of the truth if ye were freed from sin?

48 Behold, if ye were holy I would speak unto you of holiness; but as ye are not holy, and ye look upon me as a [a]teacher, it must needs be expedient that I [b]teach you the consequences of sin.

49 Behold, my soul abhorreth sin, and my heart [a]delighteth in righteousness; and I will [b]praise the holy name of my God.

50 Come, my brethren, every one that [a]thirsteth, come ye to the [b]waters; and he that hath no [c]money, come buy and eat; yea, come buy wine and milk without money and without price.

51 Wherefore, do not spend money for that which is of no worth, nor your [a]labor for that which cannot [b]satisfy. Hearken diligently unto me, and remember the words which I have spoken; and come unto the Holy One of Israel, and [c]feast upon that which perisheth not, neither can be corrupted, and let your soul delight in fatness.

52 Behold, my beloved brethren, remember the words of your God; pray unto him continually by day, and give [a]thanks unto his holy name by night. Let your hearts [b]rejoice.

53 And behold how great the [a]covenants of the Lord, and how great his [b]condescensions unto the children of men; and because of his greatness, and his [c]grace and [d]mercy, he has promised unto us that our seed shall not utterly be destroyed, according to the flesh, but that he would [e]preserve them; and in future generations they shall become a righteous [f]branch unto the house of Israel.

54 And now, my brethren, I would speak unto you more; but on the morrow I will declare unto you the remainder of my words. Amen.

44a Jacob 2: 10.
  b Jacob 1: 19.
  c Jacob 2: 2 (2, 16);
    Mosiah 2: 28;
    D&C 61: 34.
45a 2 Ne. 28: 22; Alma 36: 18.
  b TG Rock.
46a TG God, Justice of.
  b TG Judgment, The Last.
  c Mosiah 3: 25.
  d Gen. 48: 3; 1 Ne. 1: 14; 3 Ne. 4: 32; Moses 2: 1.
  e TG Apostasy of Individuals.

48a 2 Ne. 5: 26.
    TG Teacher; Teaching.
  b Deut. 33: 10;
    2 Chr. 15: 3 (1–4);
    17: 9. TG Prophets, Mission of.
49a TG Desire;
    Motivations.
  b Ezra 3: 11 (11–13);
    1 Ne. 18: 16; Alma 36: 28.
50a Isa. 44: 3; 55: 1 (1–2).
  b TG Living Water.
  c Alma 5: 34; 42: 27.
51a Isa. 55: 2. TG Work, Value of.

  b Eccl. 1: 3.
  c Prov. 13: 25; Enos 1: 4; 3 Ne. 12: 6.
52a TG Thanksgiving.
  b Deut. 26: 11.
53a TG Covenants.
  b TG Jesus Christ, Condescension of.
  c TG Grace.
  d TG Compassion;
    God, Mercy of.
  e TG Protection, Divine.
  f TG Vineyard of the Lord.

[Between 559 and 545 B.C.]

CHAPTER 10

Jews shall crucify their God—They shall be scattered until they begin to believe in him—America shall be a land of liberty where no king shall rule—Be reconciled to God and gain salvation through his grace.

AND now I, Jacob, speak unto you again, my beloved brethren, concerning this righteous [a]branch of which I have spoken.

2 For behold, the [a]promises which we have obtained are promises unto us according to the flesh; wherefore, as it has been shown unto me that many of our children shall perish in the flesh because of [b]unbelief, nevertheless, God will be merciful unto many; and our children shall be [c]restored, that they may come to that which will give them the true knowledge of their Redeemer.

3 Wherefore, as I said unto you, it must needs be expedient that Christ —for in the last night the [a]angel spake unto me that this should be his name—should [b]come among the [c]Jews, among those who are the more wicked part of the world; and they shall [d]crucify him—for thus it behooveth our God, and there is none other nation on earth that would [e]crucify their [f]God.

4 For should the mighty [a]miracles be wrought among other nations they would repent, and know that he be their God.

5 But because of [a]priestcrafts and iniquities, they at Jerusalem will [b]stiffen their necks against him, that he be [c]crucified.

6 Wherefore, because of their iniquities, destructions, famines, [a]pestilences, and bloodshed shall come upon them; and they who shall not be destroyed shall be [b]scattered among all nations.

7 But behold, thus saith the [a]Lord God: [b]When the day cometh that they shall believe in me, that I am Christ, then have I covenanted with their fathers that they shall be [c]restored in the flesh, upon the earth, unto the [d]lands of their inheritance.

8 And it shall come to pass that they shall be [a]gathered in from their long dispersion, from the [b]isles of the sea, and from the four parts of the earth; and the nations of the Gentiles shall be great in the eyes of me, saith God, in [c]carrying them forth to the lands of their inheritance.

9 [a]Yea, the kings of the Gentiles shall be nursing fathers unto them, and their queens shall become nursing mothers; wherefore, the [b]promises of the Lord are great unto the Gentiles, for he hath spoken it, and who can dispute?

10 But behold, this land, said God, shall be a land of thine inheritance, and the [a]Gentiles shall be blessed upon the land.

11 And this land shall be a land of

10 1a 1 Ne. 15: 12 (12–20); 2 Ne. 3: 5; Jacob 5: 45 (43–45); Alma 46: 24 (24–25).
2a 1 Ne. 22: 8 (8–12); 3 Ne. 5: 23 (21–26); 21: 7 (4–29). TG Promise.
  b TG Doubt.
  c TG Restoration of the Gospel.
3a 2 Ne. 2: 4; 11: 3; 25: 19; Jacob 7: 5; Moro. 7: 22.
  b TG Jesus Christ, Prophecies about.
  c TG Israel, Judah, People of.
  d Luke 18: 31; 1 Ne. 11: 33; Mosiah 3: 9 (9–10).

  e Matt. 27: 22; Luke 22: 2; 23: 23 (20–24).
  f 1 Ne. 19: 10 (7, 10); 2 Ne. 26: 12.
4a TG Miracles.
5a Matt. 27: 20 (11–26); Luke 22: 2; John 11: 47 (47–53). TG Apostasy of Israel; Priestcraft.
  b TG Stiffneckedness.
  c TG Jesus Christ, Crucifixion of.
6a TG Plague.
  b 1 Ne. 19: 14 (13–14); 2 Ne. 25: 15.
    TG Israel, Bondage of, in Other Lands.
7a TG Jesus Christ, Lord.

  b 2 Ne. 9: 2 (1–2); 25: 16 (16–17).
  c Gen. 49: 10. TG Israel, Restoration of.
  d TG Lands of Inheritance.
8a TG Israel, Gathering of.
  b Isa. 51: 5; 1 Ne. 22: 4; 2 Ne. 29: 7; D&C 133: 8.
  c Isa. 11: 14; 1 Ne. 21: 22; 22: 8.
9a Isa. 49: 22 (22–23); 2 Ne. 6: 6.
  b 1 Ne. 22: 8 (1–9); Alma 9: 24; D&C 3: 20.
10a 2 Ne. 6: 12; 3 Ne. 16: 6 (4–7).

[Between 559 and 545 B.C.]

ªliberty unto the Gentiles, and there shall be no ᵇkings upon the land, who shall raise up unto the Gentiles.

12 And I will fortify this land ªagainst all other nations.

13 And he that ªfighteth against Zion shall ᵇperish, saith God.

14 For he that raiseth up a ªking against me shall perish, for I, the Lord, the ᵇking of heaven, will be their king, and I will be a ᶜlight unto them forever, that hear my words.

15 Wherefore, for this cause, that my ªcovenants may be fulfilled which I have made unto the children of men, that I will do unto them while they are in the flesh, I must needs destroy the ᵇsecret works of ᶜdarkness, and of murders, and of abominations.

16 Wherefore, he that ªfighteth against ᵇZion, both Jew and Gentile, both bond and free, both male and female, ᶜshall perish; for ᵈthey are they who are the ᵉwhore of all the earth; for ᶠthey who are ᵍnot for me are ʰagainst me, saith our God.

17 For I will ªfulfil my ᵇpromises which I have made unto the children of men, that I will do unto them while they are in the flesh—

18 Wherefore, my beloved brethren, thus saith our God: I will afflict thy seed by the hand of the Gentiles;

nevertheless, I will ªsoften the hearts of the ᵇGentiles, that they shall be like unto a father to them; wherefore, the Gentiles shall be ᶜblessed and ᵈnumbered among the house of Israel.

19 Wherefore, I will ªconsecrate this land unto thy seed, and them who shall be numbered among thy seed, forever, for the land of their inheritance; for it is a choice land, saith God unto me, above all other lands, wherefore I will have all men that dwell thereon that they shall worship me, saith God.

20 And now, my beloved brethren, seeing that our merciful God has given us so great knowledge concerning these things, let us remember him, and lay aside our sins, and not hang down our heads, for we are not cast off; nevertheless, we have been ªdriven out of the land of our inheritance; but we have been led to a ᵇbetter land, for the Lord has made the sea our ᶜpath, and we are upon an ᵈisle of the sea.

21 But great are the promises of the Lord unto them who are upon the ªisles of the sea; wherefore as it says isles, there must needs be more than this, and they are inhabited also by our brethren.

22 For behold, the Lord God has

11a ᴛɢ Liberty.
   b 2 Ne. 1: 7; Mosiah 29: 32.
12a 1 Ne. 13: 19.
13a 1 Ne. 22: 14 (14, 19).
   b Isa. 60: 10.
14a ᴛɢ Kings, Earthly.
   b Josh. 2: 11; Ps. 44: 4; Matt. 2: 2; Alma 5: 50; D&C 20: 17; 38: 21 (21–22); 128: 22 (22–23); Moses 7: 53.
   c ᴛɢ Jesus Christ, Light of the World.
15a ᴛɢ Abrahamic Covenant; Covenants.
   b Lev. 19: 26; Hel. 3: 23; 7: 25 (4–5, 21, 25).
      ᴛɢ Secret Combinations.
   c ᴛɢ Darkness, Spiritual.
16a ᴛɢ Protection, Divine.

   b ᴛɢ Zion.
   c Isa. 41: 11 (11–12).
   d 1 Ne. 13: 5.
   e ᴛɢ Devil, Church of; Whoredom.
   f 1 Ne. 14: 10.
   g 1 Ne. 22: 13 (13–23); 2 Ne. 6: 15; 28: 15 (15–32); 3 Ne. 16: 8 (8–15); Ether 2: 9 (8–11).
   h Matt. 12: 30.
17a 1 Kgs. 8: 56; D&C 1: 38; 101: 64.
   b ᴛɢ Promise.
18a 1 Ne. 13: 31; 2 Ne. 4: 7; Jacob 3: 6 (5–9); Hel. 15: 12 (10–17); Morm. 5: 20 (20–21).
   b Matt. 8: 11 (11–12); 12: 21; Luke 13: 29 (28–30); Acts 10: 45;

      D&C 45: 9 (7–30).
   c Eph. 3: 6 (1–7); 2 Ne. 33: 9; 3 Ne. 21: 14.
   d Gal. 3: 7 (7, 29); 1 Ne. 14: 2; 3 Ne. 16: 13; 21: 6 (6, 22, 25); 30: 2; Abr. 2: 10 (9–11).
19a 1 Ne. 13: 15.
20a 1 Ne. 1: 20 (18–20); 2: 2 (1–4).
   b 1 Ne. 2: 20.
      ᴛɢ Promised Lands.
   c Ps. 8: 8; 1 Ne. 18: 8 (5–23).
   d Isa. 11: 11 (11–12); 42: 4; 51: 5; Ezek. 26: 15 (3, 6–7, 15); 39: 6; 2 Ne. 8: 5.
21a Isa. 49: 1; 1 Ne. 19: 16; 21: 1; 22: 4.

[Between 559 and 545 B.C.]

[a]led away from time to time from the house of Israel, according to his will and pleasure. And now behold, the Lord remembereth all them who have been broken off, wherefore he remembereth us also.

23 Therefore, [a]cheer up your hearts, and remember that ye are [b]free to [c]act for yourselves—to [d]choose the way of everlasting death or the way of eternal life.

24 Wherefore, my beloved brethren, [a]reconcile yourselves to the [b]will of God, and not to the will of the devil and the flesh; and remember, after ye are reconciled unto God, that it is only in and through the [c]grace of God that ye are [d]saved.

25 Wherefore, may God [a]raise you from death by the power of the resurrection, and also from everlasting death by the power of the [b]atonement, that ye may be received into the [c]eternal kingdom of God, that ye may praise him through grace divine. Amen.

CHAPTER 11

Jacob saw his Redeemer—The law of Moses typifies Christ and proves he shall come.

AND now, [a]Jacob spake many more things to my people at that time; nevertheless only these things have I caused to be [b]written, for the things which I have written sufficeth me.

2 And now I, Nephi, write [a]more of the words of [b]Isaiah, for my soul delighteth in his words. For I will liken his words unto my people, and I will send them forth unto all my children, for he verily [c]saw my [d]Redeemer, even as I have seen him.

3 And my brother, Jacob, also has [a]seen him as I have seen him; wherefore, I will send their words forth unto my children to prove unto them that my words are true. Wherefore, by the words of [b]three, God hath said, I will establish my word. Nevertheless, God sendeth more [c]witnesses, and he proveth all his words.

4 Behold, my soul delighteth in [a]proving unto my people the truth of the [b]coming of Christ; for, for this end hath the [c]law of Moses been given; and all things which have been given of God from the beginning of the world, unto man, are the [d]typifying of him.

5 And also my soul delighteth in the [a]covenants of the Lord which he hath made to our fathers; yea, my soul delighteth in his [b]grace, and in his justice, and power, and mercy in the great and eternal plan of [c]deliverance from death.

6 And my soul delighteth in proving unto my people that [a]save Christ should come all men must perish.

7 For if there be [a]no Christ there be no God; and if there be no God we

22a 1 Ne. 22: 4 (4–5);
    2 Ne. 1: 6. TG Israel,
    Scattering of; Israel,
    Ten Lost Tribes of.
23a TG Cheerfulness.
   b TG Agency.
   c 2 Ne. 2: 16.
   d Deut. 30: 19 (15, 19).
24a TG Reconciliation.
   b TG God, Will of.
   c TG Grace.
   d TG Salvation;
     Salvation, Plan of.
25a TG Death, Power over;
     Resurrection.
   b TG Jesus Christ,
     Atonement through.
   c TG Eternity.

11 1a 2 Ne. 6: 1 (1–10)
    b 2 Ne. 31: 1.
  2a 2 Ne. 6: 16 (16–18).
    b 3 Ne. 23: 1.
    c 2 Ne. 16: 1. TG Jesus
      Christ, Appearances,
      Antemortal.
    d TG Jesus Christ—
      Jehovah.
  3a 2 Ne. 2: 3 (3–4); 10: 3;
      Jacob 7: 5. TG God,
      Privilege of Seeing.
    b 2 Ne. 27: 12 (12–14);
      Ether 5: 3 (2–4);
      D&C 5: 11 (11, 15).
    c TG Book of Mormon;
      Witnesses.
  4a 2 Ne. 31: 2.

    b Jacob 4: 5; Jarom 1:
      11; Alma 25: 16 (15–
      16); Ether 12: 19
      (18–19).
    c 2 Ne. 5: 10.
    d TG Jesus Christ, Types
      of, in Anticipation;
      Law of Moses.
  5a TG Abrahamic
      Covenant.
    b TG Benevolence;
      Grace.
    c TG Deliverance; Jesus
      Christ, Atonement
      through.
  6a Mosiah 3: 15.
  7a 2 Ne. 2: 13 (13–14).

[Between 559 and 545 B.C.]

are not, for there could have been no [b]creation. But there is a God, and [c]he is Christ, and he cometh in the fulness of his own time.

8 And now I write [a]some of the words of Isaiah, that whoso of my people shall see these words may lift up their hearts and rejoice for all men. Now these are the words, and ye may liken them unto you and unto all men.

CHAPTER 12

Isaiah sees the latter-day temple, gathering of Israel, and millennial judgment and peace—The proud and wicked shall be brought low at the Second Coming—Compare Isaiah 2.

[a]THE word that Isaiah, the son of Amoz, saw concerning Judah and Jerusalem:

2 And it shall come to pass in the last days, [a]when the [b]mountain of the Lord's [c]house shall be established in the top of the [d]mountains, and shall be exalted above the hills, and all nations shall flow unto it.

3 And many [a]people shall go and say, Come ye, and let us go up to the [b]mountain of the Lord, to the [c]house of the God of Jacob; and he will teach us of his ways, and we will [d]walk in his paths; for out of Zion shall go forth the law, and the word of the Lord from Jerusalem.

4 And he shall [a]judge among the nations, and shall rebuke many people: and they shall beat their swords into plow-shares, and their spears into pruning-hooks—nation shall not lift up sword against nation, neither shall they learn war any more.

5 O house of Jacob, come ye and let us walk in the light of the Lord; yea, come, for ye have all [a]gone astray, every one to his [b]wicked ways.

6 Therefore, O Lord, thou hast forsaken thy people, the house of Jacob, because they be replenished from the east, and hearken unto [a]soothsayers like the [b]Philistines, and they please themselves in the children of strangers.

7 Their land also is full of silver and gold, neither is there any end of their [a]treasures; their land is also full of horses, neither is there any end of their chariots.

8 Their land is also full of [a]idols; they worship the work of their own hands, that which their own fingers have made.

9 And the mean man [a]boweth [b]not down, and the great man humbleth himself not, therefore, forgive him not.

10 O ye wicked ones, enter into the rock, and [a]hide thee in the dust, for the fear of the Lord and the glory of his majesty shall smite thee.

11 And it shall come to pass that the [a]lofty looks of man shall be humbled, and the haughtiness of men shall be bowed down, and the Lord alone shall be exalted in that day.

12 For the [a]day of the Lord of

7b Heb. 3: 4 (3–4).
  TG Creation; God, Creator.
  c TG Jesus Christ— Jehovah.
8a See the Latter-day Saint edition of the King James Version of the Bible for other notes and cross-references on these chapters from Isaiah.
12 1a Isa. 2: 1 (1–22).
2a Comparison with the King James Bible in English shows that there are differences in

more than half of the 433 verses of Isaiah quoted in the Book of Mormon, while about 200 verses have the same wording as KJV.
  b TG Zion.
  c 3 Ne. 24: 1.
  d Gen. 49: 26; D&C 49: 25; 109: 61; 133: 31 (29–31).
3a Zech. 8: 22.
  b Joel 2: 1; 2 Ne. 30: 15 (12–18); D&C 133: 13.
  c Ps. 122: 1.
  d TG Walking with God.

4a 2 Ne. 21: 3 (2–5, 9).
5a 2 Ne. 28: 14; Mosiah 14: 6; Alma 5: 37.
  b Isa. 53: 6.
6a TG Sorcery.
  b Gen. 10: 14.
7a TG Treasure.
8a Jer. 2: 28. TG Idolatry.
9a Ex. 34: 8; Isa. 2: 9.
  b IE unto God; he worships idols instead.
10a Amos 9: 3; Rev. 6: 15 (15–16); Alma 12: 14.
11a 2 Ne. 15: 15 (15–16).
12a TG Day of the Lord.

[Between 559 and 545 B.C.]

Hosts soon cometh upon all nations, yea, upon every one; yea, upon the [b]proud and lofty, and upon every one who is lifted up, and he shall be brought low.

13 Yea, and the day of the Lord shall come upon all the [a]cedars of Lebanon, for they are high and lifted up; and upon all the oaks of Bashan;

14 And upon all the [a]high mountains, and upon all the hills, and upon all the nations which are lifted up, and upon every people;

15 And upon every [a]high tower, and upon every fenced wall;

16 And upon all the ships of the [a]sea, and upon all the ships of Tarshish, and upon all pleasant pictures.

17 And the loftiness of man shall be bowed down, and the [a]haughtiness of men shall be made low; and the Lord alone shall be exalted in [b]that day.

18 And the idols he shall utterly abolish.

19 And they shall go into the holes of the rocks, and into the caves of the earth, for the fear of the Lord shall come upon them and the [a]glory of his majesty shall smite them, when he ariseth to shake terribly the earth.

20 In that day a man shall cast his idols of silver, and his idols of gold, which he hath made for himself to worship, to the moles and to the bats;

21 To go into the clefts of the rocks, and into the tops of the ragged rocks, for the fear of the Lord shall come upon them and the majesty of his glory shall smite them, when he ariseth to shake terribly the earth.

22 Cease ye from man, whose breath is in his nostrils; for wherein is he to be accounted of?

CHAPTER 13

Judah and Jerusalem shall be punished for their disobedience—The Lord pleads for and judges his people—The daughters of Zion are cursed and tormented for their worldliness—Compare Isaiah 3.

[a]FOR behold, the Lord, the Lord of Hosts, doth take away from Jerusalem, and from Judah, the stay and the staff, the whole staff of bread, and the whole stay of water—

2 The [a]mighty man, and the man of [b]war, the judge, and the prophet, and the [c]prudent, and the ancient;

3 The captain of fifty, and the honorable man, and the counselor, and the cunning artificer, and the eloquent orator.

4 And I will give children unto them to be their princes, and babes shall rule over them.

5 And the people shall be [a]oppressed, every one by another, and every one by his neighbor; the child shall behave himself [b]proudly against the ancient, and the base against the honorable.

6 When a man shall take hold of his brother of the house of his father, and shall say: Thou hast clothing, be thou our ruler, and let not this [a]ruin come under thy hand—

7 In that day shall he swear, saying: I will not be a healer; for in my house there is neither bread nor clothing; make me not a ruler of the people.

8 For Jerusalem is [a]ruined, and Judah is [b]fallen, because their

12b Job 40: 11; Mal. 4: 1; 2 Ne. 23: 11; D&C 64: 24.
13a Isa. 37: 24; Ezek. 31: 3; Zech. 11: 1 (1–2).
14a Isa. 30: 25.
15a 3 Ne. 21: 15 (15, 18).
16a The Greek (Septuagint) has "ships of the sea." The Hebrew has "ships of Tarshish." The

Book of Mormon has both, showing that the brass plates had lost neither phrase.
17a TG Haughtiness.
 b IE the day of the Lord's coming in glory; see v. 17–21.
19a TG Jesus Christ, Glory of.
13 1a Isa. 3: 1 (1–26).

2a 2 Kgs. 24: 14.
 b 1 Chr. 28: 3.
 c TG Prudence.
5a TG Oppression.
 b TG Haughtiness.
6a Isa. 3: 6.
8a Isa. 1: 7; Jer. 9: 11; Ezek. 36: 17 (16–20).
 b Lam. 1: 3 (1–3).

[Between 559 and 545 B.C.]

^ctongues and their doings have been against the Lord, to ^dprovoke the eyes of his glory.

9 The show of their countenance doth witness against them, and doth declare their ^asin to be even as ^bSodom, and they cannot hide it. Wo unto their souls, for they have rewarded evil unto themselves!

10 Say unto the righteous that it is ^awell with them; for they shall ^beat the fruit of their doings.

11 Wo unto the wicked, for they shall perish; for the reward of their hands shall be upon them!

12 And my people, children are their oppressors, and women rule over them. O my people, they who ^alead thee cause thee to err and destroy the way of thy paths.

13 The Lord standeth up to ^aplead, and standeth to judge the people.

14 The Lord will enter into ^ajudgment with the ancients of his people and the princes thereof; for ye have eaten up the ^bvineyard and the spoil of the ^cpoor in your houses.

15 What mean ye? Ye ^abeat my people to pieces, and grind the faces of the poor, saith the Lord God of Hosts.

16 Moreover, the Lord saith: Because the daughters of Zion are ^ahaughty, and ^bwalk with stretched-forth necks and wanton eyes, walking and mincing as they go, and making a tinkling with their feet—

17 Therefore the Lord will smite with a ^ascab the crown of the head of the daughters of Zion, and the Lord will ^bdiscover their secret parts.

18 In that ^aday the Lord will take away the bravery of their tinkling ornaments, and cauls, and round tires like the moon;

19 The chains and the bracelets, and the mufflers;

20 The bonnets, and the ornaments of the legs, and the headbands, and the tablets, and the ear-rings;

21 The rings, and nose jewels;

22 The changeable suits of apparel, and the mantles, and the wimples, and the crisping-pins;

23 The glasses, and the fine linen, and hoods, and the veils.

24 And it shall come to pass, instead of sweet smell there shall be stink; and instead of a girdle, a rent; and instead of well set hair, ^abaldness; and instead of a stomacher, a girding of sackcloth; ^bburning instead of ^cbeauty.

25 Thy men shall fall by the sword and thy mighty in the war.

26 And her ^agates shall lament and ^bmourn; and she shall be desolate, and shall ^csit upon the ground.

CHAPTER 14

Zion and her daughters shall be redeemed and cleansed in the millennial day—Compare Isaiah 4.

^aAND in that day, seven women shall take hold of one man, saying: We will eat our own bread, and wear our own apparel; only let us be called by thy name to take away our ^breproach.

2 In that day shall the ^abranch of the Lord be beautiful and glorious; the fruit of the earth excellent and

---

8c Ps. 52:2.
  d TG Provoking.
9a TG Apostasy of Israel.
  b Gen. 18:20 (20–21); 19:5, 24 (24–25); 2 Ne. 23:19.
  TG Homosexuality.
10a Deut. 12:28.
  b Ps. 128:2.
12a Isa. 9:16.
  TG Leadership.
13a Micah 6:2.
14a TG Jesus Christ,

Judge.
  b Isa. 5:7.
  c Ezek. 18:12; 2 Ne. 28:13 (12–13); Hel. 4:12 (11–13).
15a Micah 3:3 (2–3).
16a TG Haughtiness.
  b TG Walking in Darkness.
17a Deut. 28:27.
  b Jer. 13:22; Nahum 3:5.
18a TG Day of the Lord.

24a Isa. 22:12; Micah 1:16.
  b 2 Ne. 14:4.
  c Lam. 1:6 (4–6).
26a Jer. 14:2.
  b Lam. 1:4 (4–6).
  c Lam. 2:10.
14 1a Isa. 4:1 (1–6).
  b TG Reproach.
2a Isa. 60:21; 61:3; 2 Ne. 3:5; Jacob 2:25.

[Between 559 and 545 B.C.]

comely to them that are escaped of Israel.

3 And it shall come to pass, they that are [a]left in Zion and remain in Jerusalem shall be called holy, every one that is written among the living in Jerusalem—

4 When the Lord shall have [a]washed away the filth of the daughters of Zion, and shall have purged the blood of Jerusalem from the midst thereof by the spirit of judgment and by the spirit of [b]burning.

5 And the [a]Lord will create upon every dwelling-place of mount Zion, and upon her assemblies, a [b]cloud and smoke by day and the shining of a flaming fire by night; for upon all the glory of Zion shall be a defence.

6 And there shall be a tabernacle for a shadow in the daytime from the heat, and for a place of [a]refuge, and a covert from storm and from rain.

CHAPTER 15

The Lord's vineyard (Israel) shall become desolate and his people shall be scattered—Woes shall come upon them in their apostate and scattered state—The Lord shall lift an ensign and gather Israel—Compare Isaiah 5.

[a]AND then will I sing to my well-beloved a song of my beloved, touching his [b]vineyard. My well-beloved hath a vineyard in a very fruitful hill.

2 And he fenced it, and gathered out the stones thereof, and planted it with the choicest [a]vine, and built a tower in the midst of it, and also made a wine-press therein; and he looked that it should bring forth grapes, and it brought forth wild grapes.

3 And now, O inhabitants of Jerusalem, and men of Judah, judge, I pray you, betwixt me and my vineyard.

4 What could have been done more to my vineyard that I have not done in it? Wherefore, when I looked that it should bring forth grapes it brought forth wild grapes.

5 And now go to; I will tell you what I will do to my vineyard—I will [a]take away the hedge thereof, and it shall be eaten up; and I will break down the wall thereof, and it shall be trodden down;

6 And I will lay it waste; it shall not be pruned nor digged; but there shall come up [a]briers and thorns; I will also command the clouds that they [b]rain no rain upon it.

7 For the [a]vineyard of the Lord of Hosts is the house of Israel, and the men of Judah his pleasant plant; and he looked for [b]judgment, and behold, [c]oppression; for righteousness, but behold, a cry.

8 Wo unto them that join [a]house to house, till there can be no place, that they may be placed alone in the midst of the earth!

9 In mine ears, said the Lord of Hosts, of a truth many houses shall be desolate, and great and fair cities without inhabitant.

10 Yea, ten acres of vineyard shall yield one [a]bath, and the seed of a homer shall yield an ephah.

11 Wo unto them that rise up early in the morning, that they may [a]follow strong drink, that continue until night, and [b]wine inflame them!

12 And the harp, and the [a]viol, the tabret, and pipe, and wine are in their feasts; but they [b]regard not

---

3a Matt. 13: 43 (41–43).
4a 2 Ne. 13: 24 (16–26).
  TG Washing.
  b Mal. 3: 2; 4: 1.
5a Isa. 60: 20 (1–3, 19–21).
  TG God, Presence of.
  b Ex. 13: 21; Zech. 2: 5.
6a Isa. 25: 4. TG Refuge.
15 1a Isa. 5: 1 (1–30).
  b TG Vineyard of the Lord.

2a Jer. 2: 21.
5a Ps. 80: 12 (8–15).
6a Isa. 7: 23 (23–24); 32: 13.
  b Lev. 26: 4; Jer. 3: 3.
7a TG Vineyard of the Lord.
  b Amos 5: 24.
  c TG Oppression.
8a Micah 2: 2.

10a BD Weights and Measures. See also Ezek. 45: 11.
11a Prov. 23: 30 (29–32).
  b TG Drunkenness; Word of Wisdom.
12a Amos 6: 5 (5–6).
  b Ps. 28: 5.
  TG Rebellion.

[Between 559 and 545 B.C.]

85

the work of the Lord, neither consider the operation of his hands.

13 Therefore, my people are gone into ᵃcaptivity, because they have no ᵇknowledge; and their honorable men are famished, and their multitude dried up with thirst.

14 Therefore, hell hath enlarged herself, and opened her mouth without measure; and their glory, and their multitude, and their pomp, and he that rejoiceth, shall descend into it.

15 And the mean man shall be ᵃbrought down, and the ᵇmighty man shall be humbled, and the eyes of the ᶜlofty shall be humbled.

16 But the Lord of Hosts shall be exalted in ᵃjudgment, and God that is holy shall be sanctified in righteousness.

17 Then shall the lambs feed after their manner, and the waste places of the ᵃfat ones shall strangers eat.

18 Wo unto them that draw iniquity with cords of ᵃvanity, and sin as it were with a cart rope;

19 That say: Let him ᵃmake speed, ᵇhasten his work, that we may ᶜsee it; and let the counsel of the Holy One of Israel draw nigh and come, that we may know it.

20 Wo unto them that ᵃcall ᵇevil good, and good evil, that put ᶜdarkness for light, and light for darkness, that put bitter for sweet, and sweet for bitter!

21 Wo unto the ᵃwise in their own eyes and ᵇprudent in their own sight!

22 Wo unto the mighty to drink ᵃwine, and men of strength to mingle strong drink;

23 Who justify the wicked for ᵃreward, and take away the righteousness of the righteous from him!

24 Therefore, as the ᵃfire devoureth the ᵇstubble, and the flame consumeth the ᶜchaff, their ᵈroot shall be rottenness, and their blossoms shall go up as dust; because they have cast away the law of the Lord of Hosts, and ᵉdespised the word of the Holy One of Israel.

25 Therefore, is the ᵃanger of the Lord kindled against his people, and he hath stretched forth his hand against them, and hath smitten them; and the hills did tremble, and their carcasses were torn in the midst of the streets. For all this his anger is not turned away, but his hand is stretched out still.

26 And he will lift up an ᵃensign to the ᵇnations from far, and will hiss unto them from the ᶜend of the earth; and behold, they shall ᵈcome with speed swiftly; none shall be weary nor stumble among them.

27 None shall slumber nor sleep; neither shall the girdle of their loins be loosed, nor the latchet of their shoes be broken;

28 Whose arrows shall be sharp, and all their bows bent, and their horses' hoofs shall be counted like flint, and their wheels like a whirlwind, their roaring like a lion.

29 They shall roar like young ᵃlions; yea, they shall roar, and lay hold of the prey, and shall carry away safe, and none shall deliver.

30 And in that ᵃday they shall roar against them like the roaring of the

13a Lam. 1: 3 (1–3).
b Isa. 1: 3; Hosea 4: 6.
TG Knowledge.
15a Isa. 2: 17 (11, 17).
b 2 Ne. 12: 11.
c TG Haughtiness.
16a TG Jesus Christ, Judge.
17a Isa. 10: 16.
18a TG Vanity.
19a Jer. 17: 15.
b TG Haste.
c TG Sign Seekers.
20a D&C 64: 16; 121: 16.
b Moro. 7: 14 (14, 18).
c 1 Jn. 1: 6.
21a Prov. 3: 7 (5–7);
2 Ne. 28: 15.
b TG Prudence.
22a Prov. 31: 4 (3–9).
23a TG Bribery.
24a Obad. 1: 18; 2 Ne. 20:
17; 3 Ne. 20: 16.
b Joel 2: 5; 1 Ne. 22:
15 (15, 23); 2 Ne. 26:
6 (4, 6); D&C 64:
24 (23–24); 133: 64.
c Luke 3: 17; Mosiah 7:
30 (29–31).
d Job 18: 16 (16–21).
e 2 Sam. 12: 9 (7–9).
25a Deut. 32: 21; D&C 63:
32; Moses 6: 27.
26a TG Ensign.
b TG Nations.
c 2 Ne. 29: 2.
d TG Israel, Gathering of.
29a 3 Ne. 21: 12 (12–13).
30a TG Day of the Lord.

[Between 559 and 545 B.C.]

sea; and if they look unto the land, behold, darkness and sorrow, and the light is darkened in the heavens thereof.

CHAPTER 16

Isaiah sees the Lord—Isaiah's sins are forgiven—He is called to prophesy —He prophesies of the rejection by the Jews of Christ's teachings—A remnant shall return—Compare Isaiah 6.

[a]IN the [b]year that king Uzziah died, I [c]saw also the Lord sitting upon a throne, high and lifted up, and his train filled the temple.

2 Above it stood the [a]seraphim; each one had six wings; with twain he covered his face, and with twain he covered his feet, and with twain he did fly.

3 And one cried unto another, and said: Holy, holy, holy, is the Lord of Hosts; the whole earth is full of his [a]glory.

4 And the posts of the door moved at the voice of him that cried, and the house was filled with smoke.

5 Then said I: Wo is unto me! for I am undone; because I am a man of unclean lips; and I dwell in the midst of a people of unclean lips; for mine eyes have [a]seen the King, the Lord of Hosts.

6 Then flew one of the seraphim unto me, having a live coal in his hand, which he had taken with the tongs from off the altar;

7 And he laid it upon my mouth, and said: Lo, this has touched thy lips; and thine [a]iniquity is taken away, and thy sin purged.

8 Also I heard the voice of the Lord, saying: [a]Whom shall I send, and who will go for us? Then I said: Here am I; send me.

9 And he said: Go and tell this people—Hear ye indeed, but they understood not; and see ye indeed, but they perceived not.

10 Make the heart of this people fat, and make their ears heavy, and shut their eyes—lest they see with their eyes, and [a]hear with their ears, and understand with their [b]heart, and be converted and be healed.

11 Then said I: Lord, how long? And he said: Until the cities be wasted without inhabitant, and the houses without man, and the land be utterly desolate;

12 And the Lord have [a]removed men far away, for there shall be a great forsaking in the midst of the land.

13 But yet there shall be a tenth, and they shall return, and shall be eaten, as a teil-tree, and as an oak whose substance is in them when they cast their leaves; so the [a]holy seed shall be the substance thereof.

CHAPTER 17

Ephraim and Syria wage war against Judah—Christ shall be born of a virgin—Compare Isaiah 7.

[a]AND it came to pass in the days of [b]Ahaz the son of [c]Jotham, the son of Uzziah, king of Judah, that [d]Rezin, king of Syria, and [e]Pekah the son of Remaliah, king of Israel, went up toward Jerusalem to war against it, but could not prevail against it.

2 And it was told the house of David, saying: Syria is confederate with Ephraim. And his heart was moved, and the heart of his people, as the trees of the wood are moved with the wind.

3 Then said the Lord unto Isaiah: Go forth now to meet Ahaz, thou

---

16 1a Isa. 6: 1 (1–13).
  b IE about 750 B.C.
  c John 12: 41; 2 Ne. 11: 2.
2a BD Seraphim.
  TG Cherubim.
3a Ps. 72: 19 (19–20).
  TG Jesus Christ, Glory of.
5a TG Jesus Christ,

Appearances, Antemortal.
7a TG Cleanse; Remission of Sins.
8a TG Called of God.
10a Matt. 13: 14 (14–15);
    John 12: 40; Acts 28: 26–27; Rom. 11: 8.
  b Prov. 2: 2.
12a 2 Kgs. 17: 18 (18, 20);

    25: 21.
13a Ezra 9: 2.
17 1a Isa. 7: 1 (1–25).
  b 2 Kgs. 16: 5;
    2 Chr. 28: 5 (5–6).
  c 2 Kgs. 15: 32.
  d 2 Kgs. 15: 37 (36–38).
  e 2 Kgs. 15: 25.
[Between 559 and 545 B.C.]

and Shearjashub thy son, at the end of the [a]conduit of the upper pool in the highway of the fuller's field;

4 And say unto him: Take heed, and be quiet; fear not, neither be faint-hearted for the two tails of these smoking firebrands, for the fierce anger of Rezin with Syria, and of the son of Remaliah.

5 Because Syria, Ephraim, and the son of Remaliah, have taken evil counsel against thee, saying:

6 Let us go up against Judah and vex it, and let us make a breach therein for us, and set a king in the midst of it, yea, the son of Tabeal.

7 Thus saith the Lord God: [a]It shall not stand, neither shall it come to pass.

8 For the head of Syria is Damascus, and the head of Damascus, Rezin; and within three score and five years shall Ephraim be [a]broken that it be not a people.

9 And the head of Ephraim is Samaria, and the head of Samaria is Remaliah's son. If ye will [a]not believe surely ye shall not be established.

10 Moreover, the Lord spake again unto Ahaz, saying:

11 Ask thee a [a]sign of the Lord thy God; ask it either in the depths, or in the heights above.

12 But Ahaz said: I will not ask, neither will I [a]tempt the Lord.

13 And he said: Hear ye now, O house of David; is it a small thing for you to weary men, but will ye weary my God also?

14 Therefore, the Lord himself shall give you a sign—Behold, a [a]virgin shall conceive, and shall bear a son, and shall call his name [b]Immanuel.

15 Butter and [a]honey shall he eat, that he may know to refuse the evil and to choose the good.

16 For [a]before the child shall know

to refuse the evil and choose the good, the land that thou abhorrest shall be forsaken of [b]both her kings.

17 The Lord shall [a]bring upon thee, and upon thy people, and upon thy father's house, days that have not come from the day that [b]Ephraim departed from Judah, the king of Assyria.

18 And it shall come to pass in that day that the Lord shall hiss for the fly that is in the uttermost part of Egypt, and for the bee that is in the land of Assyria.

19 And they shall come, and shall rest all of them in the desolate valleys, and in the holes of the rocks, and upon all thorns, and upon all bushes.

20 In the same day shall the Lord shave with a [a]razor that is hired, by them beyond the river, by the king of Assyria, the head, and the hair of the feet; and it shall also consume the beard.

21 And it shall come to pass in that day, a man shall nourish a young cow and two sheep;

22 And it shall come to pass, for the abundance of milk they shall give he shall eat butter; for butter and honey shall every one eat that is left in the land.

23 And it shall come to pass in that day, every place shall be, where there were a thousand vines at a thousand silverlings, which shall be for briers and thorns.

24 With arrows and with bows shall men come thither, because all the land shall become briers and thorns.

25 And all hills that shall be digged with the mattock, there shall not come thither the fear of briers and thorns; but it shall be for the sending forth of oxen, and the treading of lesser cattle.

3a 2 Kgs. 18:17; Isa. 36:2.
7a Prov. 21:30; Isa. 8: 10 (9–10).
8a TG Israel, Scattering of.
9a 2 Chr. 20:20. TG Unbelief, Unbelievers.
11a Judg. 6:39 (36–40). TG Signs.
12a IE test, try, or prove.
14a 2 Ne. 18:8, 10. b Isa. 8:8.
15a 2 Sam. 17:29.
16a Isa. 8:4; 2 Ne. 18:4.
b 2 Kgs. 15:30; 16:9.
17a 2 Chr. 28:19 (19–21). b 1 Kgs. 12:19 (16– 19).
20a 2 Kgs. 16:7 (7–8); 2 Chr. 28:20 (20–21).

[Between 559 and 545 B.C.]

CHAPTER 18

Christ shall be as a stone of stumbling and a rock of offense—Seek the Lord, not peeping wizards—Turn to the law and to the testimony for guidance—Compare Isaiah 8.

MOREOVER, the word of the Lord said unto me: Take thee a great *a*roll, and write in it with a man's pen, concerning *b*Maher-shalal-hash-baz.

2 And I took unto me faithful *a*witnesses to record, Uriah the priest, and Zechariah the son of Jeberechiah.

3 And I went unto the prophetess; and she conceived and bare a son. Then said the Lord to me: *a*Call his name, Maher-shalal-hash-baz.

4 For behold, *a*the child shall *b*not have knowledge to cry, My father, and my mother, before the riches of Damascus and the *c*spoil of *d*Samaria shall be taken away before the king of *e*Assyria.

5 The Lord spake also unto me again, saying:

6 Forasmuch as this people refuseth the waters of *a*Shiloah that go softly, and rejoice in *b*Rezin and Remaliah's son;

7 Now therefore, behold, the Lord bringeth up upon them the waters of the river, strong and many, even the king of *a*Assyria and all his glory; and he shall come up over all his channels, and go over all his banks.

8 And he shall pass through Judah; he shall overflow and go over, he shall *a*reach even to the neck; and the stretching out of his wings shall fill the breadth of thy land, O Immanuel.

9 *a*Associate yourselves, O ye people, and ye shall be broken in pieces; and give ear all ye of far countries; gird yourselves, and ye shall be broken in pieces; gird yourselves, and ye shall be broken in pieces.

10 Take counsel together, and it shall come to naught; speak the word, and it shall not stand; for God is with us.

11 For the Lord spake thus to me with a strong hand, and instructed me that I should not walk in the way of this people, saying:

12 Say ye not, A confederacy, to all to whom this people shall say, A *a*confederacy; neither fear ye their fear, nor be afraid.

13 Sanctify the Lord of Hosts himself, and let him be your fear, and let him be your dread.

14 And he shall be for a sanctuary; but for a *a*stone of *b*stumbling, and for a *c*rock of *d*offense to both the houses of Israel, for a gin and a *e*snare to the inhabitants of Jerusalem.

15 And many among them shall *a*stumble and fall, and be broken, and be snared, and be taken.

16 *a*Bind up the testimony, seal the law among my disciples.

17 And I will wait upon the Lord, that *a*hideth his face from the house of Jacob, and I will look for him.

18 Behold, I and the children whom the Lord hath given me are for *a*signs and for wonders in Israel from the Lord of Hosts, which dwelleth in Mount Zion.

19 And when they shall say unto you: Seek unto them that have *a*familiar spirits, and unto *b*wizards

18 1*a* Isa. 8: 1 (1–22).
  b IE destruction is imminent.
  2*a* TG Witnesses.
  3*a* 2 Ne. 18: 18.
  4*a* 2 Ne. 17: 16.
    b Isa. 8: 4.
    c 2 Kgs. 15: 29 (29–30).
    d 2 Kgs. 17: 6.
    e 2 Kgs. 16: 7 (7–18); 2 Ne. 20: 12. TG Israel, Scattering of.

6*a* Neh. 3: 15; John 9: 7.
  b Isa. 7: 1 (1–6).
  7*a* Isa. 10: 12.
  8*a* Isa. 30: 28.
  9*a* Joel 3: 9 (9–14).
  12*a* Isa. 31: 1 (1–3).
  14*c* Rom. 9: 33 (32–33). TG Cornerstone; Jesus Christ, Prophecies about.
    b Isa. 8: 14 (13–15); Luke 2: 34; 1 Pet. 2:

8 (4–8); Jacob 4: 15.
  c TG Rock.
  d Luke 7: 23.
  e Mosiah 7: 29.
  15*a* Matt. 21: 44.
  16*a* Dan. 12: 9.
  17*a* Isa. 54: 8.
  18*a* 2 Ne. 18: 3 (1–3).
  19*a* Moro. 10: 30. TG Sorcery.
    b Lev. 20: 6.

that peep and mutter—*c*should not a people seek unto their God for the living to hear from the dead?

20 To the *a*law and to the testimony; and if they speak not according to this word, it is because there is no light in them.

21 And they shall pass through it hardly bestead and hungry; and it shall come to pass that when they shall be hungry, they shall fret themselves, and curse their king and their God, and look upward.

22 And they shall look unto the earth and behold trouble, and *a*darkness, dimness of anguish, and shall be driven to darkness.

CHAPTER 19

Isaiah speaks Messianically—The people in darkness to see a great Light —Unto us a child is born—He shall be the Prince of Peace and shall reign on David's throne—Compare Isaiah 9.

*a*NEVERTHELESS, the dimness shall not be such as was in her vexation, when at first he lightly afflicted the *b*land of *c*Zebulun, and the land of *d*Naphtali, and afterwards did more grievously afflict by the way of the Red Sea beyond Jordan in Galilee of the nations.

2 The people that walked in darkness have seen a great light; they that dwell in the land of the shadow of death, upon them hath the light shined.

3 Thou hast multiplied the nation, and *a*increased the joy—they joy before thee according to the joy in harvest, and as men rejoice when they divide the spoil.

4 For thou hast broken the yoke of

*a*his burden, and the staff of his shoulder, the rod of his *b*oppressor.

5 For every battle of the warrior is with confused noise, and garments rolled in blood; but *a*this shall be with burning and fuel of fire.

6 For unto us a *a*child is born, unto us a son is given; and the *b*government shall be upon his shoulder; and his name shall be called, Wonderful, Counselor, The *c*Mighty God, The *d*Everlasting Father, The Prince of *e*Peace.

7 Of the increase of *a*government and peace *b*there is no end, upon the throne of *c*David, and upon his kingdom to order it, and to establish it with judgment and with justice from henceforth, even forever. The zeal of the Lord of Hosts will perform this.

8 The Lord sent his word unto Jacob and it hath lighted upon Israel.

9 And all the people shall know, even Ephraim and the inhabitants of Samaria, that say in the pride and stoutness of heart:

10 The bricks are fallen down, but we will build with hewn *a*stones; the sycamores are cut down, but we will change them into *b*cedars.

11 Therefore the Lord shall set up the adversaries of *a*Rezin against him, and join his enemies together;

12 The Syrians before and the Philistines behind; and they shall *a*devour Israel with open mouth. For all this his *b*anger is not turned away, but his hand is stretched out still.

13 For the people turneth not unto *a*him that smiteth them, neither do they seek the Lord of Hosts.

14 Therefore will the Lord cut off

19c 1 Sam. 28: 11 (8–20).
20a Luke 16: 29 (29–31).
22a Isa. 5: 30.
19 1a Isa. 9: 1 (1–21).
   b Matt. 4: 15 (15–16).
   c Josh. 19: 10 (10–16).
   d Josh. 19: 33 (32–39).
3a Isa. 9: 3.
4a IE Israel, the nation mentioned in v. 3.
   b TG Oppression.
5a Mal. 4: 1.

6a Isa. 7: 14; Luke 2: 11.
   b Matt. 28: 18.
   c Titus 2: 13; Mosiah 7: 27. TG Jesus Christ—Jehovah; Jesus Christ, Power of.
   d 2 Ne. 26: 12; Mosiah 3: 5; Alma 11: 39 (38–39, 44); Moro. 7: 22; 8: 18.
   e Micah 5: 5; D&C 27: 16; 111: 8.
7a TG Kingdom of God,

   on Earth.
   b Dan. 2: 44.
   c Ezek. 37: 24.
10a 1 Kgs. 5: 17.
   b 1 Kgs. 5: 6.
11a 2 Kgs. 16: 9 (7–9).
12a 2 Kgs. 17: 6 (1–18).
   b Isa. 5: 25; 10: 4; Jer. 4: 8.
13a Amos 4: 10 (6–12).

[Between 559 and 545 B.C.]

from Israel head and tail, branch and rush *a*in one day.

15 The *a*ancient, he is the head; and the prophet that teacheth lies, he is the tail.

16 For the *a*leaders of this people cause them to err; and they that are *b*led of them are destroyed.

17 Therefore the Lord shall have no joy in their young men, neither shall have *a*mercy on their fatherless and *b*widows; for *c*every one of them is a hypocrite and an *d*evildoer, and every mouth speaketh *e*folly. For all this his anger is not turned away, but his *f*hand is stretched out still.

18 For *a*wickedness burneth as the fire; it shall devour the briers and thorns, and shall kindle in the thickets of the forests, and they shall mount up like the lifting up of smoke.

19 Through the wrath of the Lord of Hosts is the *a*land darkened, and the people shall be as the fuel of the fire; *b*no man shall spare his brother.

20 And he *a*shall snatch on the right hand and be hungry; and he shall *b*eat on the left hand and they shall not be satisfied; they shall eat every man the flesh of his own arm—

21 Manasseh, *a*Ephraim; and Ephraim, Manasseh; they together shall be against *b*Judah. For all this his anger is not turned away, but his hand is stretched out still.

CHAPTER 20

Destruction of Assyria is a type of destruction of wicked at the Second Coming—Few people shall be left after the Lord comes again—Remnant of Jacob shall return in that day—Compare Isaiah 10.

*a*Wo unto them that decree *b*unrighteous decrees, and that write grievousness which they have prescribed;

2 To turn away the needy from judgment, and to take away the right from the *a*poor of my people, that *b*widows may be their prey, and that they may rob the fatherless!

3 And what will ye do in the day of visitation, and in the desolation which shall come from far? to whom will ye flee for help? and where will ye leave your glory?

4 Without me they shall bow down under the prisoners, and they shall fall under the slain. For all this his anger is not turned away, but his hand is stretched out still.

5 O Assyrian, the rod of mine anger, and the staff in their hand is *a*their indignation.

6 I will send him *a*against a hypocritical nation, and against the people of my wrath will I give him a charge to take the spoil, and to take the prey, and to tread them down like the mire of the streets.

7 Howbeit he meaneth not so, neither doth his heart think so; but in his heart it is to destroy and cut off nations not a few.

8 For he saith: Are not my *a*princes altogether kings?

9 Is not *a*Calno as *b*Carchemish? Is not Hamath as Arpad? Is not Samaria as *c*Damascus?

10 As *a*my hand hath founded the

14a Isa. 10: 17.
15a Isa. 9: 15.
16a Isa. 1: 23.
  TG Leadership.
  b TG Trust Not in the Arm of Flesh.
17a TG Mercy.
  b TG Widows.
  c Micah 7: 2 (2–3).
  d Prov. 1: 16; D&C 64: 16.
  e Eccl. 10: 12 (1–3, 12); 2 Ne. 9: 28 (28–29); D&C 35: 7.

f 2 Ne. 28: 32; Jacob 5: 47; 6: 4.
18a Mal. 4: 1.
19a Isa. 8: 22.
  b Micah 7: 2 (2–6).
20a Lev. 26: 26 (26, 29).
  b Deut. 28: 53 (53–57).
21a TG Israel, Joseph, People of.
  b TG Israel, Judah, People of.
20 1a Isa. 10: 1 (1–34).
  b TG Injustice.

2a Amos 4: 1.
  b TG Widows.
5a Isa. 10: 5.
6a IE against Israel.
  TG Hypocrisy.
8a 2 Kgs. 18: 33 (33–35); 19: 10 (10–13).
9a Amos 6: 2 (1–2).
  b 2 Chr. 35: 20.
  c 2 Kgs. 16: 9.
10a IE the king of Assyria's hand (v. 10–11).

[Between 559 and 545 B.C.]

kingdoms of the idols, and whose graven images did excel them of Jerusalem and of Samaria;

11 Shall I not, as I have done unto Samaria and her *idols, so do to Jerusalem and to her idols?

12 Wherefore it shall come to pass that when the Lord hath performed his whole work upon Mount Zion and upon Jerusalem, I will punish the fruit of the stout heart of the king of *Assyria, and the glory of his high looks.

13 For *he saith: By the strength of *my hand and by my wisdom I have done these things; for I am prudent; and I have moved the borders of the people, and have robbed their treasures, and I have put down the inhabitants like a valiant man;

14 And my hand hath found as a nest the riches of the people; and as one gathereth eggs that are left have I gathered all the earth; and there was none that moved the wing, or opened the mouth, or peeped.

15 Shall the *ax boast itself against him that heweth therewith? Shall the saw magnify itself against him that shaketh it? As if the rod should shake itself against them that lift it up, or as if the staff should lift up itself as if it were no wood!

16 Therefore shall the Lord, the Lord of Hosts, send among his fat ones, leanness; and under his glory he shall kindle a burning like the burning of a fire.

17 And the light of Israel shall be for a *fire, and his Holy One for a flame, and shall burn and shall devour his thorns and his briers in one day;

18 And shall consume the glory of his forest, and of his fruitful field, both soul and body; and they shall be as when a standard-bearer fainteth.

19 And the *rest of the trees of his forest shall be few, that a child may write them.

20 And it shall come to pass in that day, that the remnant of Israel, and such as are escaped of the *house of Jacob, shall no more again *stay upon him that smote them, but shall stay upon the Lord, the Holy One of Israel, in truth.

21 The *remnant shall return, yea, even the remnant of Jacob, unto the mighty God.

22 For though thy people *Israel be as the sand of the sea, yet a remnant of them shall *return; the *consumption decreed shall overflow with righteousness.

23 For the Lord God of Hosts shall make a *consumption, even determined in all the land.

24 Therefore, thus saith the Lord God of Hosts: O my people that dwellest in Zion, *be not afraid of the Assyrian; he shall smite thee with a rod, and shall lift up his staff against thee, after the *manner of Egypt.

25 For yet a very little while, and the *indignation shall cease, and mine anger in their destruction.

26 And the Lord of Hosts shall *stir up a scourge for him according to the slaughter of *Midian at the rock of Oreb; and as his rod was upon the sea so shall he lift it up after the manner of *Egypt.

11*a* Ezek. 36: 18 (16–20).
12*a* 2 Kgs. 16: 7 (7–18); Zeph. 2: 13; 2 Ne. 18: 4 (4–7).
13*a* IE the king of Assyria (v. 13–14).
  b Isa. 37: 24 (24–38).
15*a* IE the prophet compares the king to a tool.
17*a* Obad. 1: 18; 2 Ne. 15: 24; 3 Ne. 20: 16.
19*a* IE the remnants of the

  army of Assyria.
20*a* Amos 9: 8 (8–9); 2 Ne. 6: 11 (10–11).
  b IE depend upon. 2 Kgs. 16: 8 (7–9); 2 Chr. 28: 21 (20–21).
21*a* Isa. 11: 11. TG Israel, Remnant of.
22*a* Gen. 22: 17; Rom. 9: 27.
  b TG Israel, Gathering of.
  c Isa. 28: 22. TG World, End of.

23*a* Dan. 9: 27.
24*a* Isa. 37: 6 (6–7).
  b TG Israel, Bondage of, in Egypt; Israel, Bondage of, in Other Lands.
25*a* Isa. 10: 25; Dan. 11: 36.
26*a* 2 Kgs. 19: 35.
  b Gen. 25: 2 (1–6); Judg. 7: 25; Isa. 9: 4.
  c Ex. 14: 27 (26–27).

[Between 559 and 545 B.C.]

27 And it shall come to pass in that day that his ªburden shall be taken away from off thy shoulder, and his yoke from off thy neck, and the yoke shall be destroyed because of the ᵇanointing.

28 ªHe is come to Aiath, he is passed to Migron; at Michmash he hath laid up his carriages.

29 They are gone over the ªpassage; they have taken up their lodging at ᵇGeba; Ramath is afraid; ᶜGibeah of Saul is fled.

30 Lift up the voice, O daughter of ªGallim; cause it to be heard unto Laish, O poor ᵇAnathoth.

31 Madmenah is removed; the inhabitants of Gebim gather themselves to flee.

32 As yet shall he remain at ªNob that day; he shall shake his hand against the mount of the daughter of Zion, the hill of Jerusalem.

33 Behold, the Lord, the Lord of Hosts shall lop the bough with terror; and the ªhigh ones of stature shall be ᵇhewn down; and the ᶜhaughty shall be humbled.

34 And he shall cut down the thickets of the forests with iron, and Lebanon shall fall by a mighty one.

CHAPTER 21

Stem of Jesse (Christ) shall judge in righteousness—The knowledge of God shall cover the earth in the Millennium—The Lord shall raise an ensign and gather Israel—Compare Isaiah 11.

ªAND there shall ᵇcome forth a rod out of the ᶜstem of Jesse, and a ᵈbranch shall grow out of his roots.

2 And the ªSpirit of the Lord shall rest upon him, the spirit of ᵇwisdom and ᶜunderstanding, the spirit of counsel and might, the spirit of knowledge and of the fear of the Lord;

3 And shall make him of quick understanding in the fear of the Lord; and he shall not ªjudge after the sight of his eyes, neither reprove after the hearing of his ears.

4 But with ªrighteousness shall he ᵇjudge the poor, and reprove with equity for the ᶜmeek of the earth; and he shall ᵈsmite the earth with the ᵉrod of his mouth, and with the breath of his lips shall he slay the wicked.

5 And ªrighteousness shall be the girdle of his loins, and faithfulness the girdle of his reins.

6 The ªwolf also shall dwell with the lamb, and the leopard shall lie down with the kid, and the calf and the young lion and fatling together; and a little child shall lead them.

7 And the cow and the bear shall feed; their young ones shall lie down together; and the lion shall eat straw like the ox.

8 And the sucking child shall play on the hole of the asp, and the weaned child shall put his hand on the cockatrice's den.

9 They shall ªnot hurt nor ᵇdestroy in all my holy mountain, for the ᶜearth shall be full of the ᵈknowledge

27a Isa. 14: 25.
  b TG Jesus Christ, Messiah.
28a IE the Assyrian invasion forces introduced in v. 5 progress toward Jerusalem, v. 28–32.
29a 1 Sam. 13: 23.
  b Neh. 11: 31.
  c 1 Sam. 11: 4.
30a 1 Sam. 25: 44.
  b Josh. 21: 18.
32a 1 Sam. 21: 1; 22: 19; Neh. 11: 32.
33a Obad. 1: 3 (3–4); Hel. 4: 12 (12–13);

    D&C 101: 42.
  b Ezek. 17: 24; Amos 2: 9; D&C 112: 8 (3–8).
  c Ps. 18: 27; 3 Ne. 25: 1; D&C 29: 9.
21 1a Isa. 11: 1 (1–16).
  b Isa. 53: 2; Rev. 5: 5.
  c D&C 113: 2 (1–2).
  d TG Jesus Christ, Davidic Descent of.
2a Isa. 61: 1 (1–3).
  b 1 Kgs. 3: 28.
  c 1 Kgs. 3: 11 (10–11).
3a 2 Ne. 12: 4.
4a Ps. 50: 6; Mosiah 29: 12.

  b Ps. 72: 4 (2–4).
  TG Jesus Christ, Judge.
  c TG Meekness.
  d Ps. 2: 9.
  e 2 Thes. 2: 8; Rev. 19: 15.
5a TG Jesus Christ, Millennial Reign.
6a Isa. 65: 25.
9a Isa. 2: 4.
  b TG War.
  c Hab. 2: 14.
  d Ps. 66: 4; D&C 88: 104.
  TG Knowledge; Millennium.

[Between 559 and 545 B.C.]

of the Lord, as the waters cover the sea.

10 And in that day there shall be a [a]root of Jesse, which shall stand for an ensign of the people; to it shall the [b]Gentiles seek; and his [c]rest shall be glorious.

11 And it shall come to pass in that day that the Lord shall set his hand again the [a]second time to recover the remnant of his people which shall be left, from [b]Assyria, and from Egypt, and from Pathros, and from Cush, and from Elam, and from [c]Shinar, and from Hamath, and from the islands of the sea.

12 And he shall set up an [a]ensign for the nations, and shall assemble the [b]outcasts of Israel, and [c]gather together the dispersed of Judah from the four corners of the earth.

13 The [a]envy of Ephraim also shall depart, and the adversaries of Judah shall be cut off; Ephraim shall not [b]envy [c]Judah, and Judah shall not vex Ephraim.

14 But they shall fly upon the shoulders of the [a]Philistines towards the west; they shall spoil them of the east together; they shall lay their hand upon [b]Edom and [c]Moab; and the children of Ammon shall obey them.

15 And the Lord shall utterly [a]destroy the tongue of the Egyptian sea; and with his mighty wind he shall shake his hand over the river, and shall smite it in the seven streams, and make men go over [b]dry shod.

16 And there shall be a [a]highway for the remnant of his people which shall be left, from Assyria, like as it was to Israel in the day that he came up out of the land of Egypt.

CHAPTER 22

In the millennial day all men shall praise the Lord—He shall dwell among them—Compare Isaiah 12.

[a]AND in that day thou shalt say: O Lord, I will praise thee; though thou wast angry with me thine anger is turned away, and thou comfortedest me.

2 Behold, God is my salvation; I will [a]trust, and not be afraid; for the Lord [b]JEHOVAH is my [c]strength and my [d]song; he also has become my salvation.

3 Therefore, with joy shall ye draw [a]water out of the wells of salvation.

4 And in that day shall ye say: [a]Praise the Lord, call upon his name, declare his doings among the people, make mention that his name is exalted.

5 [a]Sing unto the Lord; for he hath done excellent things; this is known in all the earth.

6 [a]Cry out and shout, thou inhabitant of Zion; for great is the Holy One of Israel in the midst of thee.

CHAPTER 23

Destruction of Babylon is a type of destruction at Second Coming—It shall be a day of wrath and vengeance

10a Rom. 15: 12; D&C 113: 5 (5–6).
  b D&C 45: 9 (9–10).
  c D&C 19: 9. TG Earth, Renewal of.
11a 2 Ne. 6: 14; 25: 17; 29: 1.
  b Zech. 10: 10.
  c Gen. 10: 10.
12a TG Ensign.
  b 3 Ne. 15: 15; 16: 1 (1–4).
  c Neh. 1: 9; 1 Ne. 22: 12 (10–12); D&C 45: 25 (24–25).
  TG Israel, Gathering of.
13a Jer. 3: 18.
  b Ezek. 37: 22 (16–22). TG Envy.
  c TG Israel, Joseph, People of; Israel, Judah, People of.
14a Obad. 1: 19 (18–19).
  b Lam. 4: 21.
  c Gen. 19: 37 (30–38).
15a Zech. 10: 11.
  b Rev. 16: 12.
16a Isa. 11: 16; 19: 23; 35: 8 (8–10); D&C 133: 27. TG Earth, Renewal of.
22 1a Isa. 12: 1 (1–6).
  2a Ps. 36: 7 (7–8);
    Mosiah 4: 6; Hel. 12: 1.
  b Ex. 15: 2; Ps. 83: 18. TG Jesus Christ— Jehovah.
  c TG Strength.
  d TG Singing.
3a TG Living Water.
4a TG Praise; Thanksgiving.
5a Ps. 57: 7 (7–11); 108: 1 (1–5); Alma 26: 8; D&C 136: 28.
6a Isa. 54: 1 (1–8); Zeph. 3: 14 (14–20); Zech 2: 10 (10–13).

[Between 559 and 545 B.C.]

—Babylon (the world) shall fall forever—Compare Isaiah 13.

[a]THE burden of [b]Babylon, which Isaiah the son of Amoz did see.

2 Lift ye up a banner upon the high mountain, exalt the voice unto them, [a]shake the hand, that they may go into the gates of the nobles.

3 I have commanded my sanctified ones, I have also called my [a]mighty ones, for mine anger is not upon them that rejoice in my highness.

4 The noise of the multitude in the mountains like as of a great people, a tumultuous noise of the [a]kingdoms of nations [b]gathered together, the Lord of Hosts mustereth the hosts of the battle.

5 They come from a far country, from the end of heaven, yea, the Lord, and the weapons of his indignation, to destroy the whole land.

6 Howl ye, for the [a]day of the Lord is at hand; it shall come as a destruction from the Almighty.

7 Therefore shall all hands be faint, every man's heart shall [a]melt;

8 And they shall be afraid; pangs and sorrows shall take hold of them; they shall be amazed one at another; their faces shall be as flames.

9 Behold, the day of the Lord cometh, cruel both with wrath and fierce anger, to lay the land desolate; and he shall [a]destroy the sinners thereof out of it.

10 For the [a]stars of heaven and the [b]constellations thereof shall not give their [c]light; the [d]sun shall be darkened in his going forth, and the moon shall not cause her light to shine.

11 And I will [a]punish the world for evil, and the [b]wicked for their iniquity; I will cause the arrogancy of the [c]proud to cease, and will lay down the haughtiness of the terrible.

12 I will make a [a]man more precious than fine gold; even a man than the golden wedge of Ophir.

13 Therefore, I will [a]shake the heavens, and the earth shall [b]remove out of her place, in the wrath of the Lord of Hosts, and in the day of his fierce anger.

14 And it shall be as the chased roe, and as a sheep that no man taketh up; and they shall every man turn to his own people, and flee every one into his own [a]land.

15 Every one that is proud shall be thrust through; yea, and every one that is [a]joined to the wicked shall fall by the sword.

16 Their [a]children also shall be [b]dashed to pieces before their eyes; their houses shall be spoiled and their wives ravished.

17 Behold, I will stir up the [a]Medes against them, which shall not regard silver and gold, nor shall they delight in it.

18 Their bows shall also dash the young men to pieces; and they shall have no [a]pity on the fruit of the womb; their eyes shall not spare children.

19 And [a]Babylon, the glory of kingdoms, the beauty of the Chaldees' excellency, shall be as when God overthrew [b]Sodom and Gomorrah.

---

23 1a Isa. 13: 1 (1–22).
  b TG Babylon.
 2a IE wave the hand, give a signal.
 3a Joel 3: 11.
 4a Joel 3: 14 (11, 14); Zeph. 3: 8; Zech. 14: 2 (2–3).
  b Zech. 12: 3 (2–9).
 6a TG Day of the Lord.
 7a Jer. 9: 7; D&C 133: 41.
 9a TG Earth, Cleansing of.
10a Isa. 24: 23; Ezek. 32:

 7 (7–8); Rev. 6: 13 (12–13).
  b TG Astronomy.
  c Joel 3: 15.
  d TG World, End of.
11a Isa. 24: 6; Mal. 4: 1.
  b Ex. 34: 7; Prov. 21: 12.
  c Job 40: 11; 2 Ne. 12: 12; D&C 64: 24.
12a Isa. 4: 1 (1–4).
13a Hag. 2: 6 (6–7); Heb. 12: 26.
  b TG Earth, Renewal of.

14a TG Lands of Inheritance.
15a Lam. 2: 9; Alma 59: 6 (5–6).
16a Job 27: 14 (13–15).
  b Ps. 137: 9 (8–9).
17a Isa. 21: 2.
18a Lam. 2: 2 (2, 17, 21).
19a Isa. 14: 15 (4–27).
  b Gen. 19: 24 (24–25); Deut. 29: 23; Jer. 49: 18; 2 Ne. 13: 9.

[Between 559 and 545 B.C.]

20 It shall never be ᵃinhabited, neither shall it be dwelt in from generation to generation: neither shall the Arabian pitch tent there; neither shall the shepherds make their fold there.

21 But ᵃwild beasts of the desert shall lie there; and their houses shall be full of doleful creatures; and owls shall dwell there, and satyrs shall dance there.

22 And the wild beasts of the islands shall cry in their desolate houses, and dragons in their pleasant palaces; and her time is near to come, and her day shall not be prolonged. For I will destroy her speedily; yea, for I will be merciful unto my people, but the wicked shall perish.

CHAPTER 24

Israel shall be gathered and shall enjoy millennial rest—Lucifer cast out of heaven for rebellion—Israel shall triumph over Babylon (the world)—Compare Isaiah 14.

ᵃFOR the Lord will have mercy on Jacob, and will yet ᵇchoose Israel, and set them in their own land; and the ᶜstrangers shall be joined with them, and they shall cleave to the house of Jacob.

2 And the people shall take them and bring them to their place; yea, from far unto the ends of the earth; and they shall return to their ᵃlands of promise. And the house of Israel shall ᵇpossess them, and the land of the Lord shall be for ᶜservants and handmaids; and they shall take them captives unto whom they were captives; and they shall ᵈrule over their oppressors.

3 And it shall come to pass in that day that the Lord shall give thee ᵃrest, from thy sorrow, and from thy fear, and from the hard bondage wherein thou wast made to serve.

4 And it shall come to pass in that day, that thou shalt take up this proverb ᵃagainst the king of ᵇBabylon, and say: How hath the oppressor ceased, the golden city ceased!

5 The Lord hath broken the staff of the ᵃwicked, the scepters of the rulers.

6 ᵃHe who smote the people in wrath with a continual stroke, he that ruled the nations in anger, is persecuted, and none hindereth.

7 The whole earth is at ᵃrest, and is quiet; they break forth into ᵇsinging.

8 Yea, the fir-trees rejoice at thee, and also the cedars of Lebanon, saying: Since thou art laid down no feller is come up against us.

9 ᵃHell from beneath is moved for thee to meet thee at thy coming; it stirreth up the ᵇdead for thee, even all the chief ones of the earth; it hath raised up from their thrones all the kings of the nations.

10 All they shall speak and say unto thee: Art thou also become weak as we? Art thou become like unto us?

11 Thy pomp is brought down to the grave; the noise of thy viols is not heard; the worm is spread under thee, and the worms cover thee.

12 ᵃHow art thou fallen from heaven, O ᵇLucifer, son of the morning! Art thou cut down to the ground, which did weaken the nations!

13 For thou hast said in thy heart: ᵃI will ascend into heaven, I will

---

20a Jer. 50: 39 (3, 39–40); 51: 29 (29, 62).
21a Isa. 34: 14 (11–15).
24 1a Isa. 14: 1 (1–32).
  b Zech. 1: 17; 2: 12.
  c Isa. 60: 3 (3–5, 10). TG Stranger.
2a TG Promised Lands.
  b Amos 9: 12.
  c Isa. 60: 14 (10–12, 14).
  d TG Kingdom of God,

on Earth.
3a Josh. 1: 13; D&C 84: 24.
4a Hab. 2: 6 (6–8).
  b TG Babylon.
5a TG Earth, Cleansing of; Wickedness.
6a IE Babylon.
7a TG Earth, Renewal of.
  b Isa. 55: 12 (12–13).

9a Ezek. 32: 21. TG Hell.
  b TG Spirits in Prison.
12a IE the fallen king of Babylon is typified by the fallen "son of the morning," Lucifer in v. 12–15. D&C 76: 26.
  b TG Devil.
13a Moses 4: 1 (1–4).

[Between 559 and 545 B.C.]

exalt my throne above the stars of God; I will sit also upon the mount of the congregation, in the sides of the north;

14 [a]I will ascend above the heights of the clouds; I will be like the Most High.

15 Yet thou shalt be brought down to hell, to the sides of the [a]pit.

16 They that see thee shall narrowly look upon thee, and shall consider thee, and shall say: Is this the man that made the earth to tremble, that did shake kingdoms?

17 And made the world as a wilderness, and destroyed the cities thereof, and opened not the house of his prisoners?

18 All the kings of the nations, yea, all of them, lie in glory, every one of them in his own house.

19 But thou art cast out of thy grave like an abominable branch, and the remnant of those that are slain, thrust through with a sword, that go down to the stones of the pit; as a carcass trodden under feet.

20 Thou shalt not be joined with them in burial, because thou hast destroyed thy land and slain thy people; the [a]seed of [b]evil-doers shall never be renowned.

21 Prepare slaughter for his children for the [a]iniquities of their fathers, that they do not rise, nor possess the land, nor fill the face of the world with cities.

22 For I will rise up against them, saith the Lord of Hosts, and cut off from Babylon the [a]name, and remnant, and son, and [b]nephew, saith the Lord.

23 I will also make it a [a]possession for the bittern, and pools of water; and I will sweep it with the besom of destruction, saith the Lord of Hosts.

24 The Lord of Hosts hath sworn, saying: Surely as I have thought, so shall it come to pass; and as I have purposed, so shall it stand—

25 That I will bring the Assyrian in my land, and upon my mountains tread him under foot; then shall his [a]yoke depart from off them, and his burden depart from off their shoulders.

26 This is the purpose that is purposed upon the whole earth; and this is the hand that is stretched out upon all nations.

27 For the Lord of Hosts hath purposed, and who shall disannul? And his hand is stretched out, and who shall turn it back?

28 In the year that king [a]Ahaz died was this burden.

29 Rejoice not thou, whole Palestina, because the rod of him that [a]smote thee is broken; for out of the serpent's root shall come forth a cockatrice, and his [b]fruit shall be a [c]fiery flying serpent.

30 And the first-born of the poor shall feed, and the needy shall lie down in safety; and I will kill thy root with famine, and he shall slay thy remnant.

31 Howl, O gate; cry, O city; thou, whole Palestina, art dissolved; for there shall come from the north a smoke, and none shall be alone in his appointed times.

32 What shall then answer the messengers of the nations? That the Lord hath founded [a]Zion, and the [b]poor of his people shall trust in it.

CHAPTER 25

Nephi glories in plainness—Isaiah's prophecies shall be understood in the last days—The Jews shall return from Babylon, crucify the Messiah, and be scattered and scourged—They shall be restored when they believe in the

---

14a 2 Thes. 2:4.
15a Ps. 28:1; 88:4;
    1 Ne. 14:3.
20a Ps. 21:10 (10–11);
    37:28; 109:13.
  b TG Wickedness.
21a Ex. 20:5.

22a Prov. 10:7; Jer. 51:62.
  b Job 18:19.
23a Isa. 34:11 (11–15).
25a Isa. 10:27.
28a 2 Kgs. 16:20.
29a 2 Chr. 26:6.

  b 2 Kgs. 18:8 (1, 8).
  c TG Jesus Christ, Types
    of, in Anticipation.
32a TG Zion.
  b Zeph. 3:12.

[Between 559 and 545 B.C.]

Messiah—He shall first come six hundred years after Lehi left Jerusalem—Nephites keep the law of Moses and believe in Christ, who is the Holy One of Israel.

Now I, Nephi, do speak somewhat concerning the words which I have written, which have been spoken by the mouth of Isaiah. For behold, Isaiah spake many things which were [a]hard for many of my people to understand; for they know not concerning the manner of prophesying among the Jews.

2 For I, Nephi, have not taught them many things concerning the manner of the Jews; for their [a]works were works of darkness, and their doings were doings of abominations.

3 Wherefore, I write unto my people, unto all those that shall receive hereafter these things which I write, [a]that they may know the judgments of God, that they come upon all nations, according to the word which he hath spoken.

4 Wherefore, hearken, O my people, which are of the house of Israel, and give ear unto my words; for because the words of Isaiah are not plain unto you, nevertheless they are plain unto all those that are filled with the [a]spirit of [b]prophecy. But I give unto you a [c]prophecy, according to the spirit which is in me; wherefore I shall prophesy according to the [d]plainness which hath been with me from the time that I came out from Jerusalem with my father; for behold, my soul delighteth in [e]plainness unto my people, that they may learn.

5 Yea, and my soul delighteth in the words of [a]Isaiah, for I came out from Jerusalem, and mine eyes hath beheld the things of the [b]Jews, and I know that the Jews do [c]understand the things of the prophets, and there is none other people that understand the things which were spoken unto the Jews like unto them, save it be that they are taught after the manner of the things of the Jews.

6 But behold, I, Nephi, have not taught my children after the manner of the Jews; but behold, I, of myself, have dwelt at Jerusalem, wherefore I know concerning the regions round about; and I have made mention unto my children concerning the judgments of God, which [a]hath come to pass among the Jews, unto my children, according to all that which Isaiah hath spoken, and I do not write them.

7 But behold, I proceed with mine own prophecy, according to my [a]plainness; in the which I [b]know that no man can err; nevertheless, in the days that the prophecies of Isaiah shall be fulfilled men shall know of a surety, at the times when they shall come to pass.

8 Wherefore, they are of [a]worth unto the children of men, and he that supposeth that they are not, unto them will I speak particularly, and confine the words unto mine [b]own people; for I know that they shall be of great worth unto them in the [c]last days; for in that day shall they understand them; wherefore, for their good have I written them.

9 And as one generation hath been [a]destroyed among the Jews because of iniquity, even so have they been destroyed from generation to

25 1a Jacob 4: 14.
    TG Symbolism.
2a 2 Kgs. 17: 13–20.
3a TG God, Knowledge
    about; Prophets,
    Mission of; Scriptures,
    Value of.
4a TG Holy Ghost, Source
    of Testimony.
  b TG Prophecy.
  c 2 Ne. 31: 1.

  d 2 Ne. 31: 3; 33: 5;
    Jacob 2: 11; 4: 13.
  e TG Communication;
    Plainness.
5a 1 Ne. 19: 23.
  b TG Israel, Judah,
    People of.
  c Matt. 13: 11 (10–17).
6a 2 Ne. 6: 8; Hel. 8:
    20 (20–21).
7a 2 Ne. 32: 7; Alma 13:

    23; Ether 12: 39.
  b Ezek. 12: 23 (21–25).
8a TG Scriptures, Value of.
  b 2 Ne. 27: 6;
    Enos 1: 16 (13–16);
    Morm. 5: 12; D&C 3:
    20 (16–20).
  c TG Last Days.
9a Lam., chs. 1–5;
    Matt. 23: 37.

generation according to their iniquities; and never hath any of them been destroyed save it were ᵇforetold them by the prophets of the Lord.

10 Wherefore, it hath been told them concerning the destruction which should come upon them, immediately after my father left ᵃJerusalem; nevertheless, they ᵇhardened their hearts; and according to my prophecy they have been destroyed, save it be those which are ᶜcarried away ᵈcaptive into Babylon.

11 And now this I speak because of the ᵃspirit which is in me. And notwithstanding they have been carried away they shall return again, and possess the land of Jerusalem; wherefore, they shall be ᵇrestored again to the ᶜland of their inheritance.

12 But, behold, they shall have ᵃwars, and rumors of wars; and when the day cometh that the ᵇOnly Begotten of the Father, yea, even the Father of heaven and of earth, shall ᶜmanifest himself unto them in the flesh, behold, they will reject him, because of their iniquities, and the hardness of their hearts, and the stiffness of their necks.

13 Behold, they will ᵃcrucify him; and after he is laid in a ᵇsepulchre for the space of ᶜthree days he shall ᵈrise from the dead, with healing in his wings; and all those who shall believe on his name shall be saved

in the kingdom of God. Wherefore, my soul delighteth to prophesy concerning him, for I have ᵉseen his day, and my heart doth magnify his holy name.

14 And behold it shall come to pass that after the ᵃMessiah hath risen from the dead, and hath manifested himself unto his people, unto as many as will believe on his name, behold, Jerusalem shall be ᵇdestroyed again; for ᶜwo unto them that fight against God and the people of his ᵈchurch.

15 Wherefore, the ᵃJews shall be ᵇscattered among all nations; yea, and also ᶜBabylon shall be destroyed; wherefore, the Jews shall be scattered by other nations.

16 And after they have been ᵃscattered, and the Lord God hath scourged them by other nations for the space of many generations, yea, even down from generation to generation until they shall be persuaded to ᵇbelieve in Christ, the Son of God, and the atonement, which is infinite for all mankind— and when that day shall come that they shall believe in Christ, and worship the Father in his name, with pure hearts and ᶜclean hands, and look not forward any more for ᵈanother Messiah, then, at that time, the day will come that it must needs be expedient that they should believe these things.

17 And the Lord will set his hand

9b Ezek. 4: 3; Amos 3: 7; D&C 5: 20.
10a 1 Ne. 7: 13; 2 Ne. 6: 8; Omni 1: 15; Hel. 8: 21 (20–21).
  b TG Hardheartedness.
  c 2 Kgs. 24: 14 (14–15); Jer. 52: 15 (3–15); 1 Ne. 1: 13; 10: 3.
  d Lam. 1: 3 (1–3).
11a TG Teaching with the Spirit.
  b Jer. 24: 6 (5–7).
  c TG Lands of Inheritance.
12a TG War.
  b TG Jesus Christ, Divine Sonship.
  c TG Jesus Christ,

Birth of.
13a TG Jesus Christ, Crucifixion of.
  b Luke 23: 53; John 19: 41 (41–42); 1 Ne. 19: 10.
  c Mosiah 3: 10.
  d Mal. 4: 2. TG Jesus Christ, Prophecies about; Jesus Christ, Resurrection; Resurrection.
  e 1 Ne. 11: 27 (13–34).
14a TG Jesus Christ, Messiah.
  b Matt. 24: 2 (1–2); Luke 1: 24.
  c Ps. 83: 17 (2–17); D&C 71: 7; Moses 7:

15 (14–16).
  d TG Jesus Christ, Head of the Church.
15a TG Israel, Judah, People of.
  b Neh. 1: 8 (7–9); 2 Ne. 10: 6; 3 Ne. 16: 8. TG Israel, Bondage of, in Other Lands; Israel, Scattering of.
  c TG Babylon.
16a Ezek. 34: 22; Morm. 5: 14.
  b 2 Ne. 10: 7 (5–9); 30: 7 (7–8).
  c Job 17: 9; D&C 88: 86.
  d TG False Christs.

[Between 559 and 545 B.C.]

again the second time to ᵃrestore his people from their lost and fallen state. Wherefore, he will proceed to do a ᵇmarvelous work and a wonder among the children of men.

18 Wherefore, he shall bring forth ᵃhis ᵇwords unto them, which words shall ᶜjudge them at the last day, for they shall be given them for the purpose of ᵈconvincing them of the true Messiah, who was rejected by them; and unto the convincing of them that they need not look forward any more for a Messiah to come, for there should not any come, save it should be a ᵉfalse Messiah which should deceive the people; for there is save one ᶠMessiah spoken of by the prophets, and that Messiah is he who should be rejected of the Jews.

19 For according to the words of the prophets, the ᵃMessiah cometh in ᵇsix hundred years from the time that my father left Jerusalem; and according to the words of the prophets, and also the word of the ᶜangel of God, his ᵈname shall be Jesus Christ, the ᵉSon of God.

20 And now, my brethren, I have spoken plainly that ye cannot err. And as the Lord God liveth that ᵃbrought Israel up out of the land of Egypt, and gave unto Moses power that he should ᵇheal the nations after they had been bitten by the poisonous serpents, if they would cast their eyes unto the ᶜserpent which he did raise up before them, and also gave him power that he should smite the ᵈrock and the water should come forth; yea, behold I say unto you, that as these things are ᵉtrue, and as the Lord God liveth, there is none other ᶠname given under heaven save it be this Jesus Christ, of which I have spoken, whereby man can be saved.

21 Wherefore, for this cause hath the Lord God promised unto me that these things which I ᵃwrite shall be kept and preserved, and handed down unto my seed, from generation to generation, that the promise may be fulfilled unto Joseph, that his seed should never ᵇperish as long as the earth should stand.

22 Wherefore, these things shall go from generation to generation as long as the earth shall stand; and they shall go according to the will and pleasure of God; and the nations who shall possess them shall be ᵃjudged of them according to the words which are written.

23 For we labor diligently to write, to ᵃpersuade our children, and also our brethren, to believe in Christ, and to be reconciled to God; for we

17a Gen. 49: 10; 2 Ne. 21: 11; 29: 1. TG Israel, Gathering of; Israel, Restoration of; Restoration of the Gospel.
  b Isa. 29: 14; 2 Ne. 27: 26; 3 Ne. 28: 32 (31–33).
18a 3 Ne. 16: 4.
  b 2 Ne. 29: 11; 33: 14 (11, 14–15); W of M 1: 11; 3 Ne. 27: 25 (23–27); Ether 5: 4.
  c TG Judgment, The Last.
  d 2 Ne. 26: 12; Morm. 3: 21.
  e TG False Christs.
  f TG Jesus Christ, Messiah.
19a TG Jesus Christ,

    Betrayal of; Jesus Christ, Birth of.
  b 1 Ne. 10: 4; 19: 8; 3 Ne. 1: 1.
  c 2 Ne. 10: 3.
  d TG Jesus Christ, Prophecies about.
  e TG Jesus Christ, Divine Sonship.
20a Ex. 3: 10 (2–10); 1 Ne. 17: 24 (24, 31, 40); 19: 10.
  b John 3: 14; 1 Ne. 17: 41.
  c 2 Kgs. 18: 4; Alma 33: 19; Hel. 8: 14 (14–15).
  d Ex. 17: 6; Num. 20: 11; Neh. 9: 15; 1 Ne. 17: 29; 20: 21.

  e 1 Ne. 14: 30; Mosiah 1: 6.
  f Hosea 13: 4; Acts 4: 12; 1 Jn. 3: 23 (19–24); 1 Ne. 10: 6; 2 Ne. 2: 6 (5–8); Mosiah 16: 5 (4–5); Alma 12: 22 (22–25). TG Jesus Christ, Savior.
21a 2 Ne. 27: 6.
  b Amos 5: 15; Alma 46: 24 (24-27).
22a 2 Ne. 29: 11; 33: 15 (10–15); 3 Ne. 27: 25 (23–27); Ether 4: 10 (8–10).
23a TG Family, Children, Responsibilities toward.

know that it is by [b]grace that we are saved, after all we can [c]do.

24 And, notwithstanding we believe in Christ, we [a]keep the law of Moses, and look forward with steadfastness unto Christ, until the law shall be fulfilled.

25 For, for this end was the [a]law given; wherefore the law hath become [b]dead unto us, and we are made alive in Christ because of our faith; yet we keep the law because of the commandments.

26 And we [a]talk of Christ, we rejoice in Christ, we preach of Christ, we [b]prophesy of Christ, and we write according to our prophecies, that our [c]children may know to what source they may look for a [d]remission of their sins.

27 Wherefore, we speak concerning the law that our children may know the deadness of the law; and they, by knowing the deadness of the law, may look forward unto that life which is in Christ, and know for what end the law was given. And after the law is fulfilled in Christ, that they need not harden their hearts against him when the law ought to be done away.

28 And now behold, my people, ye are a [a]stiffnecked people; wherefore, I have spoken plainly unto you, that ye cannot misunderstand. And the words which I have spoken shall stand as a [b]testimony against you; for they are sufficient to [c]teach any man the [d]right way; for the right way is to believe in Christ and deny him not; for by denying ye also deny the prophets and the law.

29 And now behold, I say unto you that the right way is to believe in Christ, and deny him not; and Christ is the Holy One of Israel; wherefore ye must bow down before him, and [a]worship him with all your [b]might, mind, and strength, and your whole soul; and if ye do this ye shall in nowise be cast out.

30 And, inasmuch as it shall be expedient, ye must keep the [a]performances and [b]ordinances of God until the law shall be fulfilled which was given unto Moses.

CHAPTER 26

Christ shall minister to the Nephites—Nephi foresees the destruction of his people—They shall speak from the dust—The gentiles shall build up false churches and secret combinations—The Lord forbids men to practice priestcrafts.

AND after Christ shall have [a]risen from the dead he shall [b]show himself unto you, my children, and my beloved brethren; and the words which he shall speak unto you shall be the [c]law which ye shall do.

2 For behold, I say unto you that I have beheld that many generations shall pass away, and there shall be great wars and contentions among my people.

3 And after the Messiah shall come there shall be [a]signs given unto my people of his [b]birth, and also of his [c]death and resurrection; and great and terrible shall that day be unto the wicked, for they shall perish; and they perish because they cast

23b Ps. 130: 4 (3–4);
   Rom. 3: 20 (20–24);
   7: 5; 2 Ne. 2: 5 (4–10);
   Mosiah 13: 32;
   Alma 42: 14 (12–16);
   D&C 20: 30; 138: 4.
   TG Grace.
  c James 2: 24 (14–26).
   TG Good Works.
24a Jacob 4: 5.
25a TG Law of Moses.
  b Rom. 7: 4 (4–6);
   D&C 74: 5 (2–6).
26a Jacob 4: 12; Jarom 1:
   11; Mosiah 3: 13; 16: 6.

  b Luke 10: 24 (23–24).
  c TG Family, Children,
   Responsibilities
   toward.
  d TG Remission of Sins.
28a Mosiah 3: 14;
   Alma 9: 31.
   TG Stiffneckedness.
  b TG Testimony.
  c 1 Kgs. 8: 36; 2 Ne. 33:
   10. TG Teaching.
  d 1 Sam. 12: 23; Isa. 45:
   19; 2 Pet. 2: 15.
29a TG Worship.
  b Deut. 6: 5; Mark 12:

   30 (29–31).
30a 4 Ne. 1: 12.
  b TG Ordinance.
26 1a 3 Ne. 11: 8 (1–12).
   TG Jesus Christ,
   Resurrection.
  b 1 Ne. 11: 7; 12: 6.
  c 3 Ne. 15: 9 (2–10).
3a 1 Ne. 12: 4 (4–6).
   TG Signs.
  b TG Jesus Christ, Birth of.
  c TG Jesus Christ,
   Death of.

[Between 559 and 545 B.C.]

out the *d*prophets, and the saints, and stone them, and slay them; wherefore the cry of the *e*blood of the saints shall ascend up to God from the ground against them.

4 Wherefore, all those who are proud, and that do wickedly, the day that cometh shall *a*burn them up, saith the Lord of Hosts, for they shall be as stubble.

5 And they that kill the *a*prophets, and the saints, the depths of the earth shall *b*swallow them up, saith the Lord of Hosts; and *c*mountains shall cover them, and whirlwinds shall carry them away, and buildings shall fall upon them and crush them to pieces and grind them to powder.

6 And they shall be visited with thunderings, and lightnings, and earthquakes, and all manner of destructions, for the *a*fire of the anger of the Lord shall be kindled against them, and they shall be as stubble, and the day that cometh shall consume them, saith the Lord of Hosts.

7 *a*O the pain, and the anguish of my soul for the loss of the slain of my people! For I, Nephi, have seen it, and it well nigh consumeth me before the presence of the Lord; but I must cry unto my God: Thy ways are *b*just.

8 But behold, the righteous that hearken unto the words of the prophets, and destroy them not,

but look forward unto Christ with *a*steadfastness for the signs which are given, notwithstanding all *b*persecution—behold, they are they which shall *c*not perish.

9 But the Son of righteousness shall *a*appear unto them; and he shall *b*heal them, and they shall have *c*peace with him, until *d*three generations shall have passed away, and many of the *e*fourth generation shall have passed away in righteousness.

10 And when these things have passed away a speedy *a*destruction cometh unto my people; for, notwithstanding the pains of my soul, I have seen it; wherefore, I know that it shall come to pass; and they sell themselves for naught; for, for the reward of their pride and their *b*foolishness they shall reap destruction; for because they yield unto the devil and *c*choose works of *d*darkness rather than light, therefore they must go down to *e*hell.

11 For the Spirit of the Lord will not always *a*strive with man. And when the Spirit *b*ceaseth to strive with man then cometh speedy destruction, and this grieveth my soul.

12 And as I spake concerning the *a*convincing of the *b*Jews, that Jesus is the *c*very Christ, it must needs be that the Gentiles be convinced also that Jesus is the Christ, the *d*Eternal *e*God;

13 And that he *a*manifesteth himself unto all those who believe in

3d TG Prophets, Rejection of.
  e Gen. 4: 10; 2 Ne. 28: 10; Morm. 8: 27.
4a 3 Ne. 8: 14 (14–24); 9: 3 (3–9).
5a Ps. 105: 15.
  b Num. 16: 32; 1 Ne. 19: 11; 3 Ne. 10: 14.
  c Hosea 10: 8; Alma 12: 14.
6a 3 Ne. 8: 8; 9: 3–11.
7a Morm. 6: 17 (17–22).
  b Rom. 3: 5; Alma 42: 1 (1, 13–25).
8a TG Steadfastness.
  b TG Persecution.
  c 3 Ne. 10: 12 (12–13).

9a Alma 16: 20.
  b John 12: 40; 3 Ne. 9: 13 (13–14); 18: 32; D&C 112: 13.
  c TG Peace.
  d 1 Ne. 12: 11 (11–12); 3 Ne. 27: 32 (30–32).
  e Alma 45: 12 (10–12); Hel. 13: 10 (5, 9–10).
10a Mosiah 12: 8; Alma 45: 11 (9–14); Hel. 13: 6 (5–6).
  b TG Foolishness.
  c TG Agency.
  d Job 38: 15; John 3: 19.
  e Job 24: 24 (17–24). TG Hell.

11a Gen. 6: 3; Ether 2: 15; Moses 8: 17.
  b TG Holy Ghost, Loss of.
12a 2 Ne. 25: 18.
  b 2 Ne. 30: 7 (7–8); Morm. 5: 14 (12–14); D&C 19: 27. TG Israel, Judah, People of.
  c Morm. 3: 21.
  d 2 Ne. 19: 6; Mosiah 3: 5; Alma 11: 39 (38–39, 44); Moro. 7: 22; 8: 18.
  e 1 Ne. 19: 10 (7, 10); 2 Ne. 10: 3; Mosiah 7: 27; 27: 31 (30–31); 3 Ne. 11: 14.
13a TG God, Access to.

him, by the power of the *b*Holy Ghost; yea, unto every nation, kindred, tongue, and people, working mighty *c*miracles, signs, and wonders, among the children of men according to their *d*faith.

14 But behold, I prophesy unto you concerning the *a*last days; concerning the days when the Lord God shall *b*bring these things forth unto the children of men.

15 After my seed and the seed of my brethren shall have *a*dwindled in unbelief, and shall have been smitten by the Gentiles; yea, after the Lord God shall have *b*camped against them round about, and shall have laid siege against them with a mount, and raised forts against them; and after they shall have been brought down low in the dust, even that they are not, yet the words of the righteous shall be written, and the *c*prayers of the faithful shall be heard, and all those who have *d*dwindled in unbelief shall not be forgotten.

16 For those who shall be destroyed shall *a*speak unto them out of the ground, and their speech shall be low out of the dust, and their voice shall be as one that hath a familiar spirit; for the Lord God will give unto him power, that he may whisper concerning them, even as it were out of the ground; and their speech shall whisper out of the dust.

17 For thus saith the Lord God: They shall *a*write the things which shall be done among them, and they shall be written and *b*sealed up in a book, and those who have dwindled in *c*unbelief shall not have them, for they *d*seek to destroy the things of God.

18 Wherefore, as those who have been destroyed have been destroyed speedily; and the multitude of their *a*terrible ones shall be as *b*chaff that passeth away—yea, thus saith the Lord God: It shall be at an instant, suddenly—

19 And it shall come to pass, that those who have dwindled in unbelief shall be *a*smitten by the hand of the Gentiles.

20 And the Gentiles are lifted up in the *a*pride of their eyes, and have *b*stumbled, because of the greatness of their *c*stumbling block, that they have built up many *d*churches; nevertheless, they *e*put down the power and miracles of God, and preach up unto themselves their own wisdom and their own *f*learning, that they may get gain and grind upon the face of the poor.

21 And there are many churches built up which cause *a*envyings, and *b*strifes, and *c*malice.

22 And there are also secret *a*combinations, even as in times of old, according to the combinations of the *b*devil, for he is the founder of

13b TG Holy Ghost, Mission of.
　c TG Miracle.
　d TG Faith.
14a TG Last Days.
　b TG Restoration of the Gospel.
15a 1 Ne. 12:22 (22–23); 15:13.
　b Isa. 29:3.
　c Ex. 3:9 (7, 9); Mosiah 21:15; D&C 109:49.
　d D&C 3:18.
16a Isa. 29:4; 2 Ne. 3:20; 33:13; Morm. 8:23 (23, 26); 9:30; Moro. 10:27. TG Book of Mormon.
17a 1 Ne. 13:40 (39–42);

2 Ne. 27:6 (6–26); 29:12.
　b TG Scriptures, Preservation of.
　c TG Unbelief, Unbelievers.
　d Enos 1:14; Morm. 6:6.
18a Isa. 29:5.
　b Hosea 13:3 (1–4); Morm. 5:16 (16–18).
19a 1 Ne. 13:14; 3 Ne. 16:8 (8–9); 20:27 (27–28); Morm. 5:9.
20a Prov. 11:2; D&C 38:39. TG Pride.
　b 1 Ne. 13:34 (29, 34); 14:1 (1–3).
　TG Apostasy of the

Early Christian Church.
　c Ezek. 3:20; 14:4 (3–7).
　d 1 Ne. 14:10 (9–10); 22:23; Morm. 8:28 (25–41).
　e 2 Ne. 28:5 (4–6); Morm. 9:26 (7–26).
　f 1 Tim. 6:20; 2 Ne. 9:28; 28:4 (4, 15); D&C 1:19.
　TG Learning.
21a TG Envy.
　b Rom. 16:17 (17–18). TG Strife.
　c TG Malice.
22a TG Secret Combinations.
　b 2 Ne. 28:21.

all these things; yea, the founder of murder, and ᶜworks of darkness; yea, and he leadeth them by the neck with a flaxen cord, until he bindeth them with his strong cords forever.

23 For behold, my beloved brethren, I say unto you that the Lord God worketh not in ᵃdarkness.

24 He doeth not ᵃanything save it be for the benefit of the world; for he ᵇloveth the world, even that he layeth down his own life that he may draw ᶜall men unto him. Wherefore, he commandeth none that they shall not partake of his salvation.

25 Behold, doth he cry unto any, saying: Depart from me? Behold, I say unto you, Nay; but he saith: ᵃCome unto me all ye ᵇends of the earth, ᶜbuy milk and honey, without money and without price.

26 Behold, hath he commanded any that they should ᵃdepart out of the synagogues, or out of the houses of worship? Behold, I say unto you, Nay.

27 Hath he commanded any that they should not partake of his ᵃsalvation? Behold I say unto you, Nay; but he hath ᵇgiven it free for all men; and he hath commanded his people that they should persuade all men to ᶜrepentance.

28 Behold, hath the Lord commanded any that they should not partake of his goodness? Behold I say unto you, Nay; but ᵃall men are privileged the one ᵇlike unto the other, and none are forbidden.

29 He commandeth that there shall be no ᵃpriestcrafts; for, behold, priestcrafts are that men preach and set ᵇthemselves up for a light unto the world, that they may get ᶜgain and ᵈpraise of the world; but they seek not the ᵉwelfare of Zion.

30 Behold, the Lord hath forbidden this thing; wherefore, the Lord God hath given a commandment that all men should have ᵃcharity, which ᵇcharity is ᶜlove. And except they should have charity they were nothing. Wherefore, if they should have charity they would not suffer the laborer in Zion to perish.

31 But the ᵃlaborer in ᵇZion shall labor for Zion; for if they labor for ᶜmoney they shall perish.

32 And again, the Lord God hath ᵃcommanded that men should not murder; that they should not lie; that they should not ᵇsteal; that they should not take the name of the Lord their God in ᶜvain; that they should not ᵈenvy; that they should not have ᵉmalice; that they should not contend one with another; that they should not commit ᶠwhoredoms; and that they should do none of these things; for whoso doeth them shall perish.

33 For none of these iniquities come of the Lord; for he doeth that which is good among the children of men; and he doeth nothing save it be plain unto the children of men; and he ᵃinviteth ᵇall to ᶜcome unto him and partake of his goodness; and he ᵈdenieth none that come

22c Lev. 19: 26.
23a Isa. 48: 16 (16–18).
24a 2 Ne. 2: 27; Jacob 5: 41; Alma 26: 37.
  b John 3: 16.
  c John 12: 32; 2 Ne. 9: 5.
25a 1 Ne. 1: 14; Alma 5: 34 (33–36); 3 Ne. 9: 14 (13–14).
  b Mark 16: 15–16.
  c Isa. 55: 1.
26a Mark 9: 39 (38–40).
27a TG Salvation.
  b Eph. 2: 8.
  c TG Repentance.

28a Rom. 2: 11; Alma 13: 5.
  b 1 Ne. 17: 35 (33–35).
29a Acts 8: 9; Alma 1: 12; 3 Ne. 16: 10.
  TG Priestcraft.
  b TG Unrighteous Dominion.
  c Ezek. 22: 27.
  d D&C 58: 39; 121: 35 (34–37).
  e Ezek. 34: 3.
30a TG Charity.
  b Moro. 7: 47 (47–48).
  c TG God, Love of; Love.
31a TG Industry.
  b TG Zion.

  c Jacob 2: 18 (17–19); D&C 11: 7; 38: 39.
32a TG Commandments of God; Law of Moses.
  b TG Stealing.
  c TG Profanity.
  d TG Envy.
  e TG Malice.
  f TG Chastity; Whoredom.
33a Jude 1: 3.
  b Alma 19: 36.
  c TG God, Access to.
  d Acts 10: 28 (9–35, 44).
  TG Justice.

[Between 559 and 545 B.C.]

unto him, black and white, *e*bond and free, male and female; and he remembereth the *f*heathen; and all are alike unto God, both Jew and Gentile.

CHAPTER 27

Darkness and apostasy shall cover the earth in the last days—The Book of Mormon shall come forth—Three witnesses shall testify of the book— The learned man cannot read the sealed book—The Lord shall do a marvelous work and a wonder— Compare Isaiah 29.

BUT, behold, in the *a*last days, or in the days of the Gentiles—yea, behold all the nations of the Gentiles and also the Jews, both those who shall come upon this land and those who shall be upon other lands, yea, even upon all the lands of the earth, behold, they will be *b*drunken with iniquity and all manner of abominations—

2 And when that day shall come they shall be *a*visited of the Lord of Hosts, with thunder and with earthquake, and with a great noise, and with storm, and with tempest, and with the *b*flame of devouring fire.

3 And all the *a*nations that *b*fight against Zion, and that distress her, shall be as a dream of a night vision; yea, it shall be unto them, even as unto a hungry man which dreameth, and behold he eateth but he awaketh and his soul is empty; or like unto a thirsty man which dreameth, and behold he drinketh but he awaketh and behold he is faint, and

his soul hath appetite; yea, even so shall the multitude of all the nations be that fight against Mount Zion.

4 For behold, all ye that doeth iniquity, stay yourselves and wonder, for ye shall cry out, and cry; yea, ye shall be *a*drunken but not with wine, ye shall stagger but not with strong drink.

5 For behold, the Lord hath poured out upon you the spirit of deep sleep. For behold, ye have closed your *a*eyes, and ye have *b*rejected the prophets; and your rulers, and the seers hath he covered because of your iniquity.

6 And it shall come to pass that the Lord God shall bring forth unto *a*you the words of a *b*book, and they shall be the words of them which have slumbered.

7 And behold the book shall be *a*sealed; and in the book shall be a *b*revelation from God, from the beginning of the world to the *c*ending thereof.

8 Wherefore, because of the things which are *a*sealed up, the things which are sealed shall not be delivered in the day of the wickedness and abominations of the people. Wherefore the book shall be kept from them.

9 But the book shall be delivered unto a man, and he shall deliver the words of the book, which are the words of those who have slumbered in the dust, and he shall deliver these words unto *a*another;

10 But the words which are *a*sealed he shall not deliver, neither shall he deliver the book. For the book shall

33*e* Rom. 2:11; 1 Ne. 17: 35 (35–40).
  f Jonah 4:11 (10–11); 2 Ne. 29:12; Alma 26: 37 (27, 37). TG Heathen.
27 1*a* TG Last Days.
  b Isa. 29:9. TG Abomination; Iniquity; Wickedness.
2*a* Isa. 29:6 (6–10); Morm. 8:29.
  b Isa. 24:6; 66:16; Jacob 6:3; 3 Ne. 25:1.
3*a* Isa. 29:7 (7–8).

b 1 Ne. 22:14. TG Protection, Divine.
4*a* Rev. 17:6 (1–6); 2 Ne. 8:21.
5*a* TG Spiritual Blindness.
  b 2 Chr. 24:19; Jer. 26: 5; 37:15; Zech. 1:4 (2–5).
6*a* Jarom 1:2; Morm. 5: 12 (12–13).
  b 2 Ne. 26:17 (16–17); 29:12. TG Book of Mormon.
7*a* Isa. 29:11 (11–12);

Ether 3:27. TG Seal.
  b Mosiah 8:19; Ether 3:25 (20–28); 4:4.
  c Ether 1:2–4; 13:1–13.
8*a* 3 Ne. 26:9 (7–12, 18); Ether 4:5; 5:1; D&C 17:6.
9*a* JS-H 1:64.
10*a* Dan. 12:9; 1 Ne. 14: 26; D&C 35:18; JS-H 1:65.

[Between 559 and 545 B.C.]

be sealed by the power of God, and the revelation which was sealed shall be kept in the book until the own due time of the Lord, that they may come forth; for behold, they *b*reveal all things from the foundation of the world unto the end thereof.

11 And the day cometh that the words of the book which were sealed shall be read upon the house tops; and they shall be read by the power of Christ; and all things shall be *a*revealed unto the children of men which ever have been among the children of men, and which ever will be even unto the end of the earth.

12 Wherefore, at that day when the book shall be delivered unto the man of whom I have spoken, the book shall be hid from the eyes of the world, that the eyes of none shall behold it save it be that *a*three *b*witnesses shall behold it, by the power of God, besides him to whom the book shall be delivered; and they shall testify to the truth of the book and the things therein.

13 And there is *a*none other which shall view it, save it be a few according to the will of God, to bear testimony of his word unto the children of men; for the Lord God hath said that the words of the faithful should speak as if it were *b*from the dead.

14 Wherefore, the Lord God will proceed to bring forth the words of the book; and in the mouth of as many witnesses as seemeth him good will he establish his word; and wo be unto him that *a*rejecteth the word of God!

15 But behold, it shall come to pass that the Lord God shall say unto him to whom he shall deliver the book: Take these words which are not sealed and deliver them to another, that he may show them unto the learned, saying: *a*Read this, I pray thee. And the learned say: Bring hither the book, and I will read them.

16 And now, because of the glory of the world and to get *a*gain will they say this, and not for the glory of God.

17 And the man shall say: I cannot bring the book, for it is sealed.

18 Then shall the learned say: I cannot read it.

19 Wherefore it shall come to pass, that the Lord God will *a*deliver again the book and the words thereof to him that is not learned; and the man that is not learned shall say: I am not learned.

20 Then shall the Lord God say unto him: The learned shall not read them, for they have rejected them, and I am *a*able to do mine own work; wherefore thou shalt read the words which I shall give unto thee.

21 *a*Touch not the things which are sealed, for I will bring them forth in mine own due time; for I will show unto the children of men that I am able to do mine own work.

22 Wherefore, when thou hast read the words which I have commanded thee, and obtained the *a*witnesses which I have promised unto thee, then shalt thou seal up the book again, and hide it up unto me, that I may preserve the words which thou hast not read, until I shall see fit in mine own *b*wisdom to *c*reveal all things unto the children of men.

23 For behold, I am God; and I am a God of *a*miracles; and I will show

10*b* Ether 4: 15. TG God, Omniscience of.
11*a* Luke 12: 3; Morm. 5: 8; D&C 121: 26–31.
12*a* 2 Ne. 11: 3; Ether 5: 3 (2–4); D&C 5: 11 (11, 15); 17: 1.
  b Deut. 19: 15.
13*a* D&C 5: 14 (3, 14).
  b 2 Ne. 3: 19 (19–20);
33: 13 (13–15); Morm. 9: 30; Moro. 10: 27.
14*a* 2 Ne. 28: 29 (29–30); Ether 4: 8.
15*a* Isa. 29: 11.
16*a* TG Priestcraft.
19*a* Isa. 29: 12.
20*a* Ex. 4: 11 (11–12);
Jer. 1: 7 (7–9).
21*a* Ether 5: 1.
22*a* TG Witnesses.
  b TG God, Wisdom of.
  c Ether 4: 7 (6–7).
   TG Mysteries of Godliness.
23*a* TG Marvelous; Miracle.

[Between 559 and 545 B.C.]

unto the [b]world that I am the same yesterday, today, and forever; and I [c]work not among the children of men save it be [d]according to their faith.

24 And again it shall come to pass that the Lord shall say unto him that shall read the words that shall be delivered him:

25 [a]Forasmuch as this people draw near unto me with their mouth, and with their lips do [b]honor me, but have removed their [c]hearts far from me, and their fear towards me is taught by the [d]precepts of men—

26 Therefore, I will proceed to do a [a]marvelous work among this people, yea, a [b]marvelous work and a wonder, for the [c]wisdom of their wise and [d]learned shall perish, and the [e]understanding of their [f]prudent shall be hid.

27 And [a]wo unto them that seek deep to hide their [b]counsel from the Lord! And their works are in the [c]dark; and they say: Who seeth us, and who knoweth us? And they also say: Surely, your turning of things upside down shall be esteemed as the [d]potter's clay. But behold, I will show unto them, saith the Lord of Hosts, that I [e]know all their works. For shall the work say of him that made it, he made me not? Or shall the thing framed say of him that framed it, he had no understanding?

28 But behold, saith the Lord of Hosts: I will show unto the children of men that it is yet a very little while and Lebanon shall be turned into a fruitful field; and the [a]fruitful field shall be esteemed as a forest.

29 [a]And in that day shall the [b]deaf hear the words of the book, and the eyes of the blind shall see out of obscurity and out of darkness.

30 And the [a]meek also shall increase, and their [b]joy shall be in the Lord, and the poor among men shall rejoice in the Holy One of Israel.

31 For assuredly as the Lord liveth they shall see that the [a]terrible one is brought to naught, and the scorner is consumed, and all that watch for iniquity are cut off;

32 And they that make a man an [a]offender for a word, and lay a snare for him that reproveth in the [b]gate, and [c]turn aside the just for a thing of naught.

33 Therefore, thus saith the Lord, who redeemed Abraham, concerning the house of Jacob: Jacob shall [a]not now be ashamed, neither shall his face now wax pale.

34 But when he [a]seeth his children, the work of my hands, in the midst of him, they shall sanctify my name, and sanctify the Holy One of Jacob, and shall fear the God of Israel.

35 They also that [a]erred in spirit shall come to understanding, and they that murmured shall [b]learn doctrine.

CHAPTER 28

Many false churches shall be built up in the last days—They shall teach false and vain and foolish doctrines— Apostasy shall abound because of false teachers—The devil shall rage in the hearts of men—He shall teach all manner of false doctrines.

AND now, behold, my brethren, I have spoken unto you, according as

23b TG World.
  c W of M 1:7.
  d Heb., ch. 11; Ether 12: 12 (7–22).
25a Isa. 29:13 (13–24).
  b Matt. 15:8 (7–9). TG Honor; Respect.
  c TG Hardheartedness.
  d 2 Ne. 28:31.
26a 1 Ne. 22:8; 2 Ne. 29:1 (1–2). TG Restoration of the Gospel.
  b Isa. 29:14; 2 Ne. 25:17.
  c TG Wisdom.
  d TG Learning.
  e TG Knowledge.
  f TG Prudence.
27a Isa. 29:15 (15–16).
  b TG Conspiracy; Counsel.
  c TG Secret Combinations.
  d Jer. 18:6.
  e TG God, Omniscience of.
28a TG Earth, Renewal of.
29a Isa. 29:18.
  b TG Deaf.
30a TG Meekness.
  b D&C 101:36.
31a Isa. 29:20.
32a Luke 11:54 (53–54); Acts 22:22. TG Offense.
  b Amos 5:10 (7, 10).
  c 2 Ne. 28:16.
33a TG Israel, Restoration of.
34a Isa. 29:23.
35a 2 Ne. 28:14; D&C 33:4.
  b Dan. 12:4 (4–10).
[Between 559 and 545 B.C.]

the Spirit hath constrained me; wherefore, I know that they must surely come to pass.

2 And the things which shall be written out of the [a]book shall be of great [b]worth unto the children of men, and especially unto our seed, which is a [c]remnant of the house of Israel.

3 For it shall come to pass in that day that the [a]churches which are built up, and not unto the Lord, when the one shall say unto the other: Behold, I, I am the Lord's; and the others shall say: I, I am the Lord's; and thus shall every one say that hath built up [b]churches, and not unto the Lord—

4 And they shall contend one with another; and their priests shall contend one with another, and they shall teach with their [a]learning, and deny the [b]Holy Ghost, which giveth utterance.

5 And they [a]deny the [b]power of God, the Holy One of Israel; and they say unto the people: Hearken unto us, and hear ye our precept; for behold there is [c]no God today, for the Lord and the Redeemer hath done his work, and he hath given his power unto men;

6 Behold, hearken ye unto my precept; if they shall say there is a miracle wrought by the hand of the Lord, believe it not; for this day he is not a God of [a]miracles; he hath done his work.

7 Yea, and there shall be many which shall say: [a]Eat, drink, and be merry, for tomorrow we die; and it shall be well with us.

8 And there shall also be many which shall say: [a]Eat, drink, and be [b]merry; nevertheless, fear God—he will [c]justify in committing a little [d]sin; yea, [e]lie a little, take the advantage of one because of his words, dig a [f]pit for thy neighbor; there is [g]no harm in this; and do all these things, for tomorrow we die; and if it so be that we are guilty, God will beat us with a few stripes, and at last we shall be saved in the kingdom of God.

9 Yea, and there shall be many which shall teach after this manner, [a]false and vain and [b]foolish [c]doctrines, and shall be puffed up in their hearts, and shall seek deep to hide their counsels from the Lord; and their works shall be in the dark.

10 And the [a]blood of the saints shall cry from the ground against them.

11 Yea, they have all gone out of the [a]way; they have become [b]corrupted.

12 Because of [a]pride, and because of [b]false teachers, and [c]false doctrine, their churches have become corrupted, and their churches are lifted up; because of pride they are puffed up.

13 They [a]rob the [b]poor because of their fine sanctuaries; they rob the poor because of their fine clothing;

28 2a TG Book of Mormon; Restoration of the Gospel.
  b 1 Ne. 13:39 (34–42); 14:5 (1–5); 22:9; 2 Ne. 30:3; 3 Ne. 21:6.
  c TG Israel, Remnant of.
3a 1 Cor. 1:13 (10–13); 1 Ne. 22:23; 4 Ne. 1:26 (25–29); Morm. 8:28 (28, 32–38).
  b TG Churches, False.
4a 2 Ne. 9:28; 26:20.
  b 1 Cor. 2:4 (1–9).
5a 2 Ne. 26:20; Morm. 9:26 (7–26).
  b 2 Tim. 3:5.
  c Alma 30:28.
6a 3 Ne. 29:7; Morm. 8:

26; 9:15 (15–26).
7a Prov. 16:25; 1 Cor. 15:32; Alma 30:17 (17–18).
8a Isa. 22:13.
  b TG Worldliness.
  c Morm. 8:31.
  d Mal. 2:17.
  e D&C 10:25; Moses 4:4. TG Lying.
  f Job 6:27; Prov. 26:27; 1 Ne. 14:3; 22:14; D&C 109:25.
  g Alma 30:17.
9a TG False Doctrine.
  b Ezek. 13:3; Hel. 13:29.
  c Matt. 15:9; Col. 2:22 (18–22).
10a Gen. 4:10; Rev. 6:10 (9–11); 18:24 (22–24);

19:2; 2 Ne. 26:3; Morm. 8:27; Ether 8:22 (22–24); D&C 87:7.
11a Hel. 6:31; D&C 132:25 (22–25).
  b Morm. 8:28 (28–41); D&C 33:4.
12a Prov. 28:25. TG Pride.
  b Jer. 23:21 (21–32); 50:6; 3 Ne. 14:15. TG False Prophets.
  c TG False Doctrine.
13a Ezek. 34:8; Morm. 8:37 (37–41).
  b Ezek. 18:12; 2 Ne. 13:14 (14–15); Hel. 4:12 (11–13).

[Between 559 and 545 B.C.]

and they persecute the meek and the poor in heart, because in their ^cpride they are puffed up.

14 They wear ^astiff necks and high heads; yea, and because of pride, and wickedness, and abominations, and ^bwhoredoms, they have all ^cgone astray save it be a ^dfew, who are the humble followers of Christ; nevertheless, they are ^eled, that in many instances they do ^ferr because they are taught by the precepts of men.

15 O the ^awise, and the learned, and the rich, that are puffed up in the ^bpride of their ^chearts, and all those who preach ^dfalse doctrines, and all those who commit ^ewhoredoms, and pervert the right way of the Lord, ^fwo, wo, wo be unto them, saith the Lord God Almighty, for they shall be thrust down to hell!

16 Wo unto them that ^aturn aside the just for a thing of naught and ^brevile against that which is good, and say that it is of no worth! For the day shall come that the Lord God will speedily visit the inhabitants of the earth; and in that day that they are ^cfully ripe in iniquity they shall perish.

17 But behold, if the inhabitants of the earth shall repent of their wickedness and abominations they shall not be destroyed, saith the Lord of Hosts.

18 But behold, that great and ^aabominable church, the ^bwhore of all the earth, must ^ctumble to the earth, and great must be the fall thereof.

19 For the kingdom of the devil must ^ashake, and they which belong to it must needs be stirred up unto repentance, or the ^bdevil will grasp them with his everlasting ^cchains, and they be stirred up to anger, and perish;

20 For behold, at that day shall he ^arage in the ^bhearts of the children of men, and stir them up to anger against that which is good.

21 And others will he ^apacify, and lull them away into carnal ^bsecurity, that they will say: All is well in Zion; yea, Zion prospereth, all is well—and thus the ^cdevil ^dcheateth their souls, and leadeth them away carefully down to hell.

22 And behold, others he ^aflattereth away, and telleth them there is no ^bhell; and he saith unto them: I am no devil, for there is none—and thus he whispereth in their ears, until he grasps them with his awful ^cchains, from whence there is no deliverance.

23 Yea, they are grasped with death, and hell; and death, and hell, and the devil, and all that have been seized therewith must stand before the throne of God, and be ^ajudged according to their works, from whence they must go into the place prepared for them, even a ^blake of fire and brimstone, which is endless torment.

24 Therefore, wo be unto him that is at ^aease in Zion!

13c Alma 5: 53; Morm. 8: 36 (36–39).
14a Prov. 21: 4.
     TG Stiffneckedness.
  b TG Whoredom.
  c 2 Ne. 12: 5; Mosiah 14: 6; Alma 5: 37.
  d Morm. 8: 36.
  e 2 Pet. 3: 17.
  f Matt. 22: 29; 2 Ne. 27: 35 (34–35); D&C 33: 4.
15a Prov. 3: 7 (5–7); 2 Ne. 15: 21.
  b TG Pride.
  c TG Hardheartedness.
  d Matt. 5: 19.
  e Mosiah 11: 2.

  f 3 Ne. 29: 5 (4–7); Morm. 9: 26.
16a 2 Ne. 27: 32.
  b Mal. 2: 17. TG Reviling.
  c Ether 2: 10 (8–11).
18a TG Devil, Church of.
  b Rev. 19: 2.
  c 1 Ne. 14: 3 (3, 17).
19a 1 Ne. 22: 23 (22–23).
  b Alma 34: 35.
  c Mosiah 23: 12; Alma 12: 11. TG Chain.
20a Rev. 13: 7; 2 Ne. 2: 18; D&C 10: 27; 76: 29.
  b Alma 8: 9; D&C 10: 20.

21a Jacob 3: 11; Alma 5: 7 (6–7); Morm. 8: 31.
  b TG Apathy.
  c 2 Ne. 9: 39; 32: 8; Alma 30: 42 (42, 53).
  d Rev. 13: 14 (11–18).
22a TG Flattery.
  b Mal. 2: 17.
  c 2 Ne. 9: 45; Alma 36: 18. TG Bondage, Spiritual.
23a TG Jesus Christ, Judge.
  b Rev. 19: 20; 21: 8; 2 Ne. 9: 16 (8–19, 26); Jacob 6: 10.
24a Amos 6: 1.

[Between 559 and 545 B.C.]

25 Wo be unto him that crieth: All is well!

26 Yea, wo be unto him that *a*hearkeneth unto the precepts of men, and denieth the power of God, and the gift of the Holy Ghost!

27 Yea, wo be unto him that saith: We have received, and we *a*need no more!

28 And in fine, wo unto all those who tremble, and are *a*angry because of *b*the truth of God! For behold, he that is built upon the *c*rock *d*receiveth it with gladness; and he that is built upon a sandy foundation trembleth lest he shall fall.

29 Wo be unto him that shall say: We have received the word of God, and we *a*need *b*no more of the word of God, for we have enough!

30 For behold, thus saith the Lord God: I will give unto the children of men line upon line, precept upon *a*precept, here a little and there a little; and blessed are those who hearken unto my precepts, and lend an ear unto my counsel, for they shall learn *b*wisdom; for unto him that *c*receiveth I will give *d*more; and from them that shall say, We have enough, from them shall be taken away even that which they have.

31 Cursed is he that putteth his *a*trust in man, or maketh flesh his arm, or shall hearken unto the *b*precepts of men, save their precepts shall be given by the power of the Holy Ghost.

32 *a*Wo be unto the Gentiles, saith the Lord God of Hosts! For notwithstanding I shall lengthen out mine arm unto them from day to day, they will deny me; nevertheless, I will be merciful unto them, saith the Lord God, if they will repent and *b*come unto me; for mine *c*arm is lengthened out all the day long, saith the Lord God of Hosts.

CHAPTER 29

Many gentiles shall reject the Book of Mormon—They shall say: We need no more Bible—The Lord speaks to many nations—He will judge the world out of the books thus written.

BUT behold, there shall be many— at that day when I shall proceed to do a *a*marvelous work among them, that I may remember my *b*covenants which I have made unto the children of men, that I may set my hand again the *c*second time to recover my people, which are of the house of Israel;

2 And also, that I may remember the promises which I have made unto thee, Nephi, and also unto thy father, that I would remember your seed; and that the *a*words of your seed should proceed forth out of my mouth unto your seed; and my words shall *b*hiss forth unto the *c*ends of the earth, for a *d*standard unto my people, which are of the house of Israel;

3 And because my words shall hiss forth—many of the Gentiles shall say: A *a*Bible! A Bible! We have

---

26a 2 Ne. 9: 29.
27a Alma 12: 10 (10–11);
    3 Ne. 26: 10 (9–10);
    Ether 4: 8.
28a 2 Ne. 9: 40; 33: 5.
    TG Rebellion, Rebel.
  b Matt. 7: 25.
  c TG Rock.
  d TG Teachable.
29a 2 Ne. 29: 10 (3–10).
  b 2 Ne. 27: 14;
    Ether 4: 8.
30a Prov. 2: 9 (9–11);
    Isa. 28: 13 (9–13);
    D&C 98: 12.
  b Prov. 14: 8.

    TG Wisdom.
  c Luke 8: 18.
  d Alma 12: 10; D&C 50:
    24.
31a D&C 1: 19 (19–20).
    TG Trust Not in the
    Arm of Flesh.
  b 2 Ne. 27: 25.
32a 1 Ne. 14: 6;
    3 Ne. 16: 8.
  b TG God, Access to.
  c 2 Ne. 19: 17 (17–21);
    Jacob 5: 47; 6: 4;
    D&C 133: 67.
29 1a 2 Ne. 27: 26.
    TG Restoration of the

    Gospel.
  b TG Abrahamic
    Covenant.
  c 2 Ne. 6: 14; 21: 11;
    25: 17.
    TG Israel, Gathering of;
    Israel, Restoration of.
2a 2 Ne. 3: 21.
  b Isa. 5: 26; Moro. 10: 28.
  c 2 Ne. 15: 26.
  d Ps. 60: 4. TG Ensign.
3a 1 Ne. 13: 24 (23–24).
    TG Bible; Book of
    Mormon.

[Between 559 and 545 B.C.]

got a Bible, and there cannot be any more Bible.

4 But thus saith the Lord God: O fools, they shall have a [a]Bible; and it shall proceed forth from the [b]Jews, mine ancient covenant people. And what [c]thank they the [d]Jews for the Bible which they receive from them? Yea, what do the Gentiles mean? Do they remember the travails, and the labors, and the pains of the Jews, and their diligence unto me, in bringing forth salvation unto the Gentiles?

5 O ye Gentiles, have ye remembered the Jews, mine ancient covenant people? Nay; but ye have [a]cursed them, and have [b]hated them, and have not sought to recover them. But behold, I will return all these things upon your own heads; for I the Lord have not forgotten my people.

6 Thou fool, that shall say: A [a]Bible, we have got a Bible, and we need no more Bible. Have ye obtained a Bible save it were by the Jews?

7 Know ye not that there are more [a]nations than one? Know ye not that I, the Lord your God, have created all men, and that I remember those who are upon the [b]isles of the sea; and that I rule in the heavens above and in the [c]earth beneath; and I bring forth my [d]word unto the children of men, yea, even upon all the nations of the earth?

8 Wherefore murmur ye, because that ye shall receive more of my word? Know ye not that the [a]testimony of [b]two nations is a [c]witness unto you that I am God, that I remember one [d]nation like unto another? Wherefore, I speak the same words unto one nation like unto another. And when the two [e]nations shall run together the testimony of the two nations shall run together also.

9 And I do this that I may prove unto many that I am the [a]same yesterday, today, and forever; and that I speak forth my [b]words according to mine own pleasure. And because that I have spoken one [c]word ye need not suppose that I cannot speak another; for my [d]work is not yet finished; neither shall it be until the end of man, neither from that time henceforth and forever.

10 Wherefore, because that ye have a Bible ye need not suppose that it contains all my [a]words; neither [b]need ye suppose that I have not caused more to be written.

11 For I command [a]all men, both in the east and in the west, and in the north, and in the south, and in the islands of the sea, that they shall [b]write the words which I speak unto them; for out of the [c]books which shall be written I will [d]judge the world, every man according to their works, according to that which is written.

12 For behold, I shall speak unto the [a]Jews and they shall [b]write it; and I shall also speak unto the

4a Rom. 3: 2 (1–3).
 b Neh. 1: 10; 1 Ne. 13: 25 (23–25); D&C 3: 16.
 c TG Ingratitude; Thanksgiving.
 d TG Israel, Judah, People of.
5a Micah 6: 16. TG Curse.
 b 3 Ne. 29: 8. TG Hate.
6a 1 Ne. 13: 23, 38.
7a TG Jesus Christ, Creator; Man, Physical Creation of; Nations.
 b Isa. 51: 5; 1 Ne. 22: 4; 2 Ne. 10: 8 (8, 20); D&C 133: 8.
 c Deut. 10: 14; 1 Ne. 11: 6; D&C 55: 1; Moses 6: 44.
 d D&C 5: 6.
8a TG Testimony.
 b Ezek. 37: 17 (15–20); 1 Ne. 13: 39 (38–41); 2 Ne. 3: 12; 33: 10 (10–11).
 c Matt. 18: 16.
 d 2 Sam. 7: 23; Alma 9: 20.
 e Hosea 1: 11.
9a Heb. 13: 8.
 b TG Word of God; Word of the Lord.
 c TG Revelation.
 d Moses 1: 4.
10a TG Scriptures to Come Forth.
 b 2 Ne. 28: 29.
11a Alma 29: 8.
 b 2 Tim. 3: 16; Moses 1: 40. TG Scriptures, Preservation of; Scriptures, Writing of.
 c TG Book of Life.
 d 2 Ne. 25: 22 (18, 22); 33: 14 (11, 14–15). TG Jesus Christ, Judge.
12a 1 Ne. 13: 23 (23–29); 2 Ne. 3: 12.
 b TG Scriptures, Lost.
[Between 559 and 545 B.C.]

Nephites and they shall ^cwrite it; and I shall also speak unto the other tribes of the house of Israel, which I have led away, and they shall write it; and I shall also speak unto ^dall nations of the earth and they shall write it.

13 And it shall come to pass that the ^aJews shall have the words of the Nephites, and the Nephites shall have the words of the Jews; and the Nephites and the Jews shall have the words of the ^blost tribes of Israel; and the lost tribes of Israel shall have the words of the Nephites and the Jews.

14 And it shall come to pass that my people, which are of the ^ahouse of Israel, shall be gathered home unto the ^blands of their possessions; and my word also shall be gathered in ^cone. And I will show unto them that fight against my word and against my ^dpeople, who are of the ^ehouse of Israel, that I am God, and that I ^fcovenanted with ^gAbraham that I would remember his ^hseed ⁱforever.

CHAPTER 30

Converted gentiles shall be numbered with the covenant people—Many Lamanites and Jews shall believe the word and become a delightsome people —Israel shall be restored and the wicked destroyed.

AND now behold, my beloved brethren, I would speak unto you; for I, Nephi, would not suffer that ye should suppose that ye are more righteous than the Gentiles shall be. For behold, except ye shall keep the commandments of God ye shall all likewise ^aperish; and because of the words which have been spoken ye need not suppose that the Gentiles are utterly destroyed.

2 For behold, I say unto you that as many of the Gentiles as will repent are the ^acovenant people of the Lord; and as many of the ^bJews as will not repent shall be ^ccast off; for the Lord ^dcovenanteth with none save it be with them that ^erepent and believe in his Son, who is the Holy One of Israel.

3 And now, I would prophesy somewhat more concerning the Jews and the Gentiles. For after the book of which I have spoken shall come forth, and be written unto the Gentiles, and sealed up again unto the Lord, there shall be many which shall ^abelieve the words which are written; and ^bthey shall carry them forth unto the ^cremnant of our seed.

4 And then shall the remnant of our seed know concerning us, how that we came out from Jerusalem, and that they are descendants of the Jews.

5 And the gospel of Jesus Christ shall be declared among ^athem; wherefore, ^bthey shall be restored unto the ^cknowledge of their fathers, and also to the knowledge of Jesus Christ, which was had among their fathers.

12c 1 Ne. 13: 40 (39–42);
  2 Ne. 26: 17 (16–17);
  27: 6 (6–26).
 d 2 Ne. 26: 33; Alma 29: 8.
13a Morm. 5: 14 (13–14).
 b TG Israel, Ten Lost Tribes of.
14a Jer. 3: 18 (17–19).
 b TG Israel, Gathering of; Lands of Inheritance.
 c Ezek. 37: 17 (16–17).
 d 1 Kgs. 8: 51; 2 Ne. 3: 9; 8: 16.
 e 1 Ne. 22: 9; 2 Ne. 30: 7 (7–8).

 f Gen. 12: 2 (1–3);
  1 Ne. 17: 40; 3 Ne. 20: 27; Abr. 2: 9.
  TG Abrahamic Covenant.
 g Micah 7: 20 (18–20).
 h Ps. 102: 28; D&C 132: 30; Moses 7: 52 (50–53).
  TG Seed of Abraham.
 i Gen. 17: 7 (5–7).
30 1a Luke 13: 3 (1–5).
 2a Gal. 3: 29 (26–29);
  Abr. 2: 10 (9–11).
 b Matt. 8: 12.
  TG Israel, Judah, People of.
 c Luke 3: 9 (3–9);

  Rom. 9: 6; Jacob 5: 6.
 d Rom. 3: 29.
 e TG Repentance.
3a 2 Ne. 28: 2; 3 Ne. 16: 6 (6–13).
 b 1 Ne. 22: 9 (5–10);
  3 Ne. 5: 25 (20–26).
 c 2 Ne. 4: 7 (7–11);
  Jacob 1: 5.
  TG Israel, Remnant of.
5a 3 Ne. 21: 5 (3–7, 24–26); Morm. 5: 15.
 b D&C 3: 20.
 c 1 Ne. 15: 14; 2 Ne. 3: 12; Morm. 7: 9 (1, 9–10).

[Between 559 and 545 B.C.]

6 And then shall they rejoice; for they shall *a*know that it is a blessing unto them from the hand of God; and their *b*scales of darkness shall begin to fall from their eyes; and many generations shall not pass away among them, save they shall be a pure and a *c*delightsome people.

7 And it shall come to pass that the *a*Jews which are scattered also shall *b*begin to believe in Christ; and they shall begin to gather in upon the face of the land; and as many as shall believe in Christ shall also become a delightsome people.

8 And it shall come to pass that the Lord God shall commence his work among all nations, kindreds, tongues, and people, to bring about the *a*restoration of his people upon the earth.

9 And with righteousness shall the *a*Lord God *b*judge the poor, and reprove with equity for the *c*meek of the earth. And he shall smite the earth with the rod of his mouth; and with the breath of his lips shall he slay the wicked.

10 For the *a*time speedily cometh that the Lord God shall cause a great *b*division among the people, and the wicked will he *c*destroy; and he will *d*spare his people, yea, even if it so be that he must *e*destroy the wicked by fire.

11 And *a*righteousness shall be the girdle of his loins, and faithfulness the girdle of his reins.

12 And then shall the wolf *a*dwell with the lamb; and the leopard shall lie down with the kid, and the calf, and the young lion, and the fatling, together; and a little child shall lead them.

13 And the cow and the bear shall feed; their young ones shall lie down together; and the lion shall eat straw like the ox.

14 And the sucking child shall play on the hole of the asp, and the weaned child shall put his hand on the cockatrice's den.

15 They shall not hurt nor destroy in all my holy *a*mountain; for the earth shall be full of the *b*knowledge of the Lord as the waters cover the sea.

16 Wherefore, the things of *a*all nations shall be made known; yea, all things shall be made *b*known unto the children of men.

17 There is nothing which is secret save it shall be *a*revealed; there is no work of darkness save it shall be made manifest in the light; and there is nothing which is sealed upon the earth save it shall be loosed.

18 Wherefore, all things which have been revealed unto the children of men shall at that *a*day be revealed; and Satan shall have power over the hearts of the children of men *b*no more, for a long time. And now, my beloved brethren, I make an end of my sayings.

CHAPTER 31

Nephi tells why Christ was baptized— Men must follow Christ, be baptized, receive the Holy Ghost, and endure to the end to be saved—Repentance and

6a Alma 3: 14.
　b TG Darkness, Spiritual; Spiritual Blindness.
　c W of M 1: 8; D&C 49: 24; 109: 65.
7a 2 Ne. 29: 14 (13–14); 3 Ne. 5: 25 (23–26). TG Israel, Judah, People of.
　b 2 Ne. 25: 16 (16–17).
8a TG Israel, Restoration of; Millennium, Preparing a People for.
9a Isa. 11: 4 (4–9).
　b Ps. 19: 9; 2 Ne. 9: 15.

c TG Meekness.
10a Jacob 5: 29; 6: 2. TG Last Days.
　b D&C 63: 54.
　c Ps. 73: 17 (3–17); D&C 29: 17; JS-M 1: 55.
　d 1 Ne. 22: 17 (15–22); 3 Ne. 22: 13 (13–17); Moses 7: 61.
　e 1 Ne. 22: 23 (15–17, 23); Jacob 5: 69. TG Earth, Cleansing of.
11a Isa. 11: 5 (5–9). TG Righteousness.

12a Isa. 65: 25. TG Earth, Renewal of.
15a Joel 2: 1.
　b TG God, Knowledge about.
16a D&C 101: 32 (32–35); 121: 28 (26–32).
　b Ether 4: 7 (6–7, 13–17).
17a Luke 12: 2 (2–3); D&C 1: 3 (1–3).
18a Acts 3: 21.
　b Rev. 20: 2 (2–3); Ether 8: 26.

[Between 559 and 545 B.C.]

baptism are the gate to the strait and narrow path—Eternal life comes to those who keep the commandments after baptism.

AND now I, Nephi, make an end of my [a]prophesying unto you, my beloved brethren. And I cannot write but a few things, which I know must surely come to pass; neither can I write but a few of the [b]words of my brother Jacob.

2 Wherefore, the things which I have written sufficeth me, save it be a few words which I [a]must speak concerning the doctrine of Christ; wherefore, I shall speak unto you plainly, according to the plainness of my prophesying.

3 For my soul delighteth in [a]plainness; for after this manner doth the Lord God work among the children of men. For the Lord God giveth light unto the [b]understanding; for he speaketh unto men according to their [c]language, unto their understanding.

4 Wherefore, I would that ye should remember that I have spoken unto you concerning that [a]prophet which the Lord showed unto me, that should baptize the [b]Lamb of God, which should take away the sins of the world.

5 And now, if the Lamb of God, he being [a]holy, should have need to be [b]baptized by water, to fulfil all righteousness, O then, how much more need have we, being unholy, to be [c]baptized, yea, even by water!

6 And now, I would ask of you, my beloved brethren, wherein the Lamb of God did fulfil all righteousness in being baptized by water?

7 Know ye not that he was holy? But notwithstanding he being holy, he showeth unto the children of men that, according to the flesh he humbleth himself before the Father, and witnesseth unto the Father that he would be [a]obedient unto him in keeping his commandments.

8 Wherefore, after he was baptized with water the Holy Ghost descended upon him in the [a]form of a [b]dove.

9 And again, it showeth unto the children of men the straitness of the path, and the narrowness of the [a]gate, by which they should enter, he having set the [b]example before them.

10 And he said unto the children of men: [a]Follow thou me. Wherefore, my beloved brethren, can we [b]follow Jesus save we shall be willing to keep the commandments of the Father?

11 And the Father said: Repent ye, repent ye, and be baptized in the name of my Beloved Son.

12 And also, the voice of the Son came unto me, saying: He that is baptized in my name, to him will the Father [a]give the Holy Ghost, like unto me; wherefore, [b]follow me, and do the things which ye have seen me do.

13 Wherefore, my beloved brethren, I know that if ye shall [a]follow the Son, with full purpose of heart, acting no [b]hypocrisy and no deception before God, but with real [c]intent, repenting of your sins, witnessing unto the Father that ye are [d]willing to take upon you the [e]name

---

31 1a 2 Ne. 25:4 (1–4).
  b 2 Ne. 11:1.
 2a 2 Ne. 11:4 (4–6).
 3a 2 Ne. 25:7 (7–8);
   32:7.
  b TG Understanding.
  c D&C 1:24.
   TG Language.
 4a 1 Ne. 10:7; 11:27.
  b TG Jesus Christ, Lamb
   of God.
 5a 1 Jn. 3:3.
  b Matt. 3:11 (11–17).
   TG Jesus Christ,
   Baptism of.

  c TG Baptism, Essential.
 7a John 5:30.
   TG Obedience.
 8a 1 Ne. 11:27.
  b TG Holy Ghost, Dove,
   Sign of.
 9a 2 Ne. 9:41; 3 Ne. 14:
   14 (13–14); D&C 22:4;
   43:7.
  b TG Example.
10a Matt. 4:19; 8:22;
   9:9.
  b Matt. 8:19; Moro. 7:
   11; D&C 56:2.
12a TG Holy Ghost, Gift of.

  b Matt. 16:24 (24–26);
   Luke 9:59 (57–62);
   John 12:26; 1 Jn. 2:6.
   TG God, the Standard
   of Righteousness.
13a TG Jesus Christ,
   Exemplar.
  b TG Hypocrisy.
  c TG Integrity; Sincerity.
  d TG Agency;
   Commitment.
  e TG Jesus Christ, Taking
   the Name of.

[Between 559 and 545 B.C.]

of Christ, by ᶠbaptism—yea, by following your Lord and your Savior down into the water, according to his word, behold, then shall ye receive the Holy Ghost; yea, then cometh the ᵍbaptism of fire and of the Holy Ghost; and then can ye speak with the ʰtongue of angels, and shout praises unto the Holy One of Israel.

14 But, behold, my beloved brethren, thus came the voice of the Son unto me, saying: After ye have repented of your sins, and witnessed unto the Father that ye are willing to keep my commandments, by the baptism of water, and have received the baptism of fire and of the Holy Ghost, and can speak with a new tongue, yea, even with the tongue of angels, and after this should ᵃdeny me, it would have been ᵇbetter for you that ye had not known me.

15 And I heard a voice from the Father, saying: Yea, the ᵃwords of my Beloved are true and faithful. He that ᵇendureth to the ᶜend, the same shall be saved.

16 And now, my beloved brethren, I know by this that unless a man shall ᵃendure to the end, in following the ᵇexample of the Son of the living God, he cannot be saved.

17 Wherefore, do the things which I have told you I have seen that your Lord and your Redeemer should do; for, for this cause have they been shown unto me, that ye might know

the gate by which ye should enter. For the gate by which ye should enter is repentance and ᵃbaptism by water; and then cometh a ᵇremission of your sins by fire and by the Holy Ghost.

18 And then are ye in this ᵃstrait and narrow ᵇpath which leads to eternal life; yea, ye have entered in by the gate; ye have done according to the commandments of the Father and the Son; and ye have received the Holy Ghost, which ᶜwitnesses of the ᵈFather and the Son, unto the fulfilling of the promise which he hath made, that if ye entered in by the way ye should receive.

19 And now, my beloved brethren, after ye have gotten into this strait and narrow ᵃpath, I would ask if all is ᵇdone? Behold, I say unto you, Nay; for ye have not come thus far save it were by the word of Christ with unshaken ᶜfaith in him, ᵈrelying wholly upon the merits of him who is mighty to ᵉsave.

20 Wherefore, ye must press forward with a ᵃsteadfastness in Christ, having a perfect brightness of ᵇhope, and a ᶜlove of God and of all men. Wherefore, if ye shall press forward, feasting upon the word of Christ, and ᵈendure to the end, behold, thus saith the Father: Ye shall have ᵉeternal life.

21 And now, behold, my beloved brethren, this is the ᵃway; and there

13f Gal. 3: 27 (26–27).
  g TG Holy Ghost, Baptism of.
  h 2 Ne. 32: 2 (2–3). TG Holy Ghost, Gifts of.
14a Matt. 10: 33 (32–33); Rom. 1: 16 (15–18); 2 Tim. 2: 12 (10–15); Alma 24: 30; D&C 101: 5 (1–5). TG Holy Ghost, Unpardonable Sin against.
  b Heb. 6: 4 (4–6); 2 Pet. 2: 21.
15a D&C 64: 31; 66: 11.
  b Jacob 6: 11 (7–11). TG Endure; Steadfastness.
  c Alma 5: 13.
16a Mark 13: 13; Alma 38:

2; D&C 20: 29; 53: 7.
  b TG Example; Jesus Christ, Exemplar.
17a Mosiah 18: 10. TG Baptism.
  b TG Holy Ghost, Mission of; Remission of Sins.
18a 1 Ne. 8: 20.
  b Prov. 4: 18. TG Gate; Path; Way.
  c TG Holy Ghost, Mission of; Holy Ghost, Source of Testimony.
  d 3 Ne. 28: 11; Moses 6: 66.
19a Hosea 14: 9 (8–9).
  b Mosiah 4: 10.
  c TG Faith.
  d Moro. 6: 4; D&C 3: 20; Moses 7: 53.

e TG Jesus Christ, Atonement through.
20a TG Commitment; Dedication; Perseverance; Steadfastness; Walking with God.
  b TG Hope.
  c TG God, Love of; Love.
  d James 5: 8 (7–11); Rev. 2: 25 (25–26); 3 Ne. 15: 9.
  e 1 Jn. 2: 25; 5: 13 (10–21). TG Objectives.
21a Ex. 33: 13 (12–13); Acts 4: 12; 2 Ne. 9: 41; Alma 37: 46; D&C 132: 22 (22, 25).

[Between 559 and 545 B.C.]

is [b]none other way nor [c]name given under heaven whereby man can be saved in the kingdom of God. And now, behold, this is the [d]doctrine of Christ, and the only and true doctrine of the [e]Father, and of the Son, and of the Holy Ghost, which is [f]one God, without end. Amen.

CHAPTER 32

Angels speak by the power of the Holy Ghost—Men must pray and gain knowledge for themselves from the Holy Ghost.

AND now, behold, my beloved brethren, I suppose that ye ponder somewhat in your hearts concerning that which ye should do after ye have entered in by the way. But, behold, why do ye ponder these things in your hearts?

2 Do ye not remember that I said unto you that after ye had [a]received the Holy Ghost ye could speak with the [b]tongue of angels? And now, how could ye speak with the tongue of angels save it were by the Holy Ghost?

3 [a]Angels speak by the power of the Holy Ghost; wherefore, they speak the words of Christ. Wherefore, I said unto you, [b]feast upon the [c]words of Christ; for behold, the words of Christ will [d]tell you all things what ye should do.

4 Wherefore, now after I have spoken these words, if ye cannot understand them it will be because ye [a]ask not, neither do ye knock;

wherefore, ye are not brought into the light, but must perish in the dark.

5 For behold, again I say unto you that if ye will enter in by the way, and receive the Holy Ghost, it will [a]show unto you all things what ye should do.

6 Behold, this is the doctrine of Christ, and there will be no more doctrine given until after he shall [a]manifest himself unto you in the flesh. And when he shall manifest himself unto you in the flesh, the things which he shall say unto you shall ye observe to do.

7 And now I, Nephi, cannot say more; the Spirit stoppeth mine utterance, and I am left to mourn because of the [a]unbelief, and the wickedness, and the ignorance, and the [b]stiffneckedness of men; for they will [c]not search [d]knowledge, nor understand great knowledge, when it is given unto them in [e]plainness, even as plain as word can be.

8 And now, my beloved brethren, I perceive that ye ponder still in your hearts; and it grieveth me that I must speak concerning this thing. For if ye would hearken unto the [a]Spirit which teacheth a man to [b]pray ye would know that ye must [c]pray; for the [d]evil spirit teacheth not a man to pray, but teacheth him that he must not pray.

9 But behold, I say unto you that ye must [a]pray always, and not faint; that ye must not perform any thing unto the Lord save in the first place ye shall [b]pray unto the Father in

---

21b 2 Ne. 25: 20;
      Mosiah 3: 17.
    c TG Jesus Christ,
      Taking the Name of.
    d Matt. 7: 28; John 7: 16.
    e TG Godhead.
    f Deut. 6: 4; Gal. 3: 20;
      1 Ne. 13: 41; 3 Ne. 28:
      10; Morm. 7: 7.
      TG Unity.
32 2a Alma 36: 24;
      3 Ne. 9: 20.
    b 2 Ne. 31: 13.
   3a TG Angels.
    b Jer. 15: 16. TG Bread
      of Life; Study.
    c Col. 3: 16.

    d Ex. 4: 15.
      TG Problem-Solving.
   4a TG Ask.
   5a 3 Ne. 16: 6; Ether 4: 11
      (11–12); D&C 28: 15;
      Moses 8: 24.
      TG Holy Ghost, Gifts
      of; Revelation.
   6a 1 Ne. 12: 6.
   7a TG Doubt; Unbelief,
      Unbelievers.
    b TG Stiffneckedness.
    c 2 Pet. 3: 5.
    d TG Knowledge.
    e 2 Ne. 25: 7 (7–8);
      31: 3; Jacob 4: 13;

      Alma 13: 23;
      Ether 12: 39.
   8a TG Discernment,
      Spiritual.
    b TG Prayer.
    c Jacob 3: 1.
    d 2 Ne. 9: 39; 28: 21
      (20–22); Mosiah 2: 32;
      4: 14; Alma 30: 42
      (42, 53). TG Spirits,
      Evil or Unclean.
   9a 1 Sam. 7: 8; Mosiah 26:
      39; 3 Ne. 20: 1.
    b Job 33: 26;
      D&C 75: 11.

[Between 559 and 545 B.C.]

the *name of Christ, that he will
*consecrate thy performance unto
thee, that thy performance may be
for the *welfare of thy soul.

CHAPTER 33

*Nephi's words are true—They testify
of Christ—Those who believe in Christ
will believe Nephi's words—They shall
stand as a witness before the judgment
bar.*

AND now I, Nephi, cannot write all
the things which were taught among
my people; neither am I *mighty
in writing, like unto speaking; for
when a man *speaketh by the power
of the Holy Ghost the power of the
Holy Ghost carrieth it unto the
hearts of the children of men.

2 But behold, there are many that
*harden their *hearts against the
Holy *Spirit, that it hath no place in
them; wherefore, they cast many
things away which are written and
esteem them as things of naught.

3 But I, Nephi, have written what
I have written, and I esteem it as of
great *worth, and especially unto
my people. For I *pray continually
for them by day, and mine *eyes
water my pillow by night, because
of them; and I cry unto my God in
faith, and I know that he will hear
my cry.

4 And I know that the Lord God
will consecrate my prayers for the
gain of my people. And the words

which I have written in weakness
will be made strong unto them; for
it *persuadeth them to do good; it
maketh known unto them of their
fathers; and it speaketh of Jesus,
and persuadeth them to believe in
him, and to endure to the end, which
is life *eternal.

5 And it speaketh *harshly against
sin, according to the *plainness of
the truth; wherefore, no man will be
angry at the words which I have
written save he shall be of the spirit
of the devil.

6 I *glory in *plainness; I glory in
truth; I glory in my Jesus, for he
hath *redeemed my soul from hell.

7 I have *charity for my people,
and great faith in Christ that I shall
meet many souls spotless at his
judgment-seat.

8 I have charity for the *Jew—I
say Jew, because I mean them from
whence I came.

9 I also have charity for the
Gentiles. But behold, for none of
*these can I hope except they shall
be *reconciled unto Christ, and
enter into the *narrow *gate, and
*walk in the *strait path which leads
to life, and continue in the path
until the end of the day of *probation.

10 And now, my beloved brethren,
and also *Jew, and all ye ends of the
earth, hearken unto these words and
*believe in Christ; and if ye believe
not in these words believe in Christ.

9c Col. 3:17; Moses 5:8.
  d Micah 4:13; 2 Ne. 2:2.
  e Alma 34:27.
33 1a Ether 12:23 (23–
     27).
  b Rom. 10:17 (13–17);
     D&C 100:8 (7–8).
     TG Holy Ghost, Gifts of.
2a Num. 15:31 (30–31);
     1 Ne. 19:7; Jacob 4:
     14; D&C 3:7 (4–13).
     TG Hardheartedness.
  b TG Spiritual Blindness.
  c TG Holy Ghost, Loss of.
3a TG Scriptures, Value
     of.
  b Gen. 20:7; Num. 21:
     7; 1 Sam. 7:5;
     Jer. 42:4; Enos 1:9

(9–12); W of M 1:8;
     Moro. 9:22.
  c Jer. 13:17; Ps. 6:6;
     Acts 20:19.
4a Ether 8:26;
     Moro. 7:13 (12–17).
     TG Motivations.
  b TG Eternal Life.
5a 1 Ne. 16:2 (1–3);
     2 Ne. 9:40; 28:28;
     Enos 1:23;
     W of M 1:17.
  b 2 Ne. 25:4; Jacob 2:
     11; 4:13.
6a Ps. 44:8 (4–8);
     D&C 76:61.
  b 2 Ne. 31:3.
  c Enos 1:27.

7a TG Charity.
8a BD Judah, Kingdom
     of. TG Israel, Judah,
     People of.
9a Eph. 3:6 (1–7);
     2 Ne. 10:18; 3 Ne. 21:
     14.
  b TG Reconciliation.
  c 2 Ne. 9:41; Hel. 3:29
     (29–30).
  d Matt. 7:14.
  e TG Walking with God.
  f D&C 132:22.
  g TG Probation.
10a TG Israel, Judah,
     People of.
  b TG Believe.

[Between 559 and 545 B.C.]

117

And if ye shall ᶜbelieve in Christ ye will believe in these ᵈwords, for they are the ᵉwords of Christ, and he hath given them unto me; and they ᶠteach all men that they should do good.

11 And if they are not the words of Christ, judge ye—for Christ will show unto you, with ᵃpower and great ᵇglory, that they are his words, at the last day; and you and I shall stand face to face before his bar; and ye shall know that I have been commanded of him to write these things, notwithstanding my weakness.

12 And I pray the Father in the name of Christ that many of us, if not all, may be saved in his ᵃkingdom at that great and last day.

13 And now, my beloved brethren, all those who are of the house of Israel, and all ye ends of the earth, I speak unto you as the voice of one ᵃcrying from the dust: Farewell until that great day shall come.

14 And you that will not partake of the goodness of God, and respect the words of the ᵃJews, and also my ᵇwords, and the words which shall proceed forth out of the mouth of the Lamb of God, behold, I bid you an everlasting farewell, for these words shall ᶜcondemn you at the last day.

15 For what I seal on earth, shall be brought against you at the ᵃjudgment bar; for thus hath the Lord commanded me, and I must ᵇobey. Amen.

THE BOOK OF JACOB

THE BROTHER OF NEPHI

The words of his preaching unto his brethren. He confoundeth a man who seeketh to overthrow the doctrine of Christ. A few words concerning the history of the people of Nephi.

CHAPTER 1

Jacob and Joseph seek to persuade men to believe in Christ and keep his commandments—Nephi dies—Wickedness prevails among the Nephites.

FOR behold, it came to pass that *fifty and five years had passed away from the time that Lehi left Jerusalem; wherefore, Nephi gave me, Jacob, a ᵃcommandment concerning the ᵇsmall plates, upon which these things are engraven.

2 And he gave me, Jacob, a commandment that I should ᵃwrite upon ᵇthese plates a few of the things which I considered to be most precious; that I should not touch, save it were lightly, concerning the history of this people which are called the people of Nephi.

3 For he said that the history of his

10c John 8: 47.
  d TG Book of Mormon.
  e Isa. 51: 16; Moro. 10: 27 (27–29); D&C 1: 24.
  f 1 Kgs. 8: 36; 2 Ne. 25: 28.
11a Ether 5: 4 (4–6); Moro. 7: 35.
  b TG Jesus Christ, Glory of.
12a TG Kingdom of God, in Heaven; Kingdom of God, on Earth.
13a Isa. 29: 4; 2 Ne. 27: 13; Morm. 8: 26.
14a TG Bible.
  b TG Book of Mormon.
  c 2 Ne. 29: 11; W of M 1: 11.
15a 2 Ne. 25: 22; 3 Ne. 27: 25 (23–27); Ether 4: 10 (8–10).
  b TG Obedience.

[JACOB]
1 1a Jacob 7: 27; Jarom 1: 15 (1–2, 15); Omni 1: 3.
  b 2 Ne. 5: 31 (28–33); Jacob 3: 13 (13–14).
2a TG Scribe; Scriptures, Writing of.
  b 1 Ne. 6: 6.

[*544 B.C.]

people should be engraven upon his [a]other plates, and that I should [b]preserve these plates and hand them down unto my seed, from generation to generation.

4 And if there were preaching which was [a]sacred, or revelation which was great, or prophesying, that I should engraven the [b]heads of them upon these plates, and touch upon them as much as it were possible, for Christ's sake, and for the sake of our people.

5 For because of faith and great anxiety, it truly had been made manifest unto us concerning our people, what things should [a]happen unto them.

6 And we also had many revelations, and the spirit of much prophecy; wherefore, we knew of [a]Christ and his kingdom, which should come.

7 Wherefore we labored diligently among our people, that we might persuade them to [a]come unto Christ, and partake of the goodness of God, that they might enter into his [b]rest, lest by any means he should swear in his wrath they should not [c]enter in, as in the [d]provocation in the days of temptation while the children of Israel were in the [e]wilderness.

8 Wherefore, we would to God that we could persuade all men [a]not to rebel against God, to [b]provoke him to anger, but that all men would believe in Christ, and view his death, and suffer his [c]cross and bear the shame of the world; wherefore, I,

Jacob, take it upon me to fulfil the commandment of my brother Nephi.

9 Now Nephi began to be old, and he saw that he must soon [a]die; wherefore, he [b]anointed a man to be a king and a ruler over his people now, according to the reigns of the [c]kings.

10 The people having loved Nephi exceedingly, he having been a great protector for them, having wielded the [a]sword of Laban in their defence, and having labored in all his days for their welfare—

11 Wherefore, the people were desirous to retain in remembrance his name. And whoso should reign in his stead were called by the people, second Nephi, third Nephi, and so forth, according to the reigns of the kings; and thus they were called by the people, let them be of whatever name they would.

12 And it came to pass that Nephi died.

13 Now the people which were not [a]Lamanites were Nephites; nevertheless, they were called Nephites, Jacobites, Josephites, [b]Zoramites, Lamanites, Lemuelites, and Ishmaelites.

14 But I, Jacob, shall not hereafter distinguish [a]them by these names, but I shall [b]call them Lamanites that seek to destroy the people of Nephi, and those who are friendly to Nephi I shall call [c]Nephites, or the [d]people of Nephi, according to the reigns of the kings.

3a 2 Ne. 5: 33 (29–33);
    Jacob 3: 13 (13–14).
  b TG Scriptures,
    Preservation of.
4a TG Sacred.
  b IE the dominant,
    important items.
5a See 1 Nephi, chapters
    12–15. See also 1 Ne. 22:
    7 (7–8); 2 Ne. 1: 9
    (5–10); 4: 7 (7–11);
    30: 3 (3–6).
6a 1 Ne. 10: 4 (4–11);
    19: 8 (8–14).
7a 2 Ne. 9: 41 (41, 45,
    51); Omni 1: 26
    (25–26).

  b TG Rest.
  c Num. 14: 23; Deut. 1:
    35 (35–37); D&C 84: 24
    (23–25).
  d Heb. 3: 8.
  e Num. 26: 65; 1 Ne. 17:
    31 (23–31).
8a TG Loyalty; Rebellion.
  b Num. 14: 11 (11–12);
    1 Kgs. 16: 33; 1 Ne. 17:
    30 (23–31); Alma 12: 37
    (36–37); Hel. 7: 18.
  c Luke 14: 27.
9a Gen. 47: 29 (28–29);
    2 Ne. 1: 14.
  b TG Anointing.

  c 2 Ne. 6: 2; Jarom 1: 7
    (7, 14).
10a 1 Ne. 4: 9; 2 Ne. 5:
    14; W of M 1: 13;
    Mosiah 1: 16;
    D&C 17: 1.
13a Enos 1: 13; Alma 23:
    17; D&C 3: 18.
  b 1 Ne. 4: 35; Alma 54:
    23; 4 Ne. 1: 36 (36–37).
14a W of M 1: 16.
  b Mosiah 25: 12;
    Alma 2: 11.
  c 2 Ne. 4: 11.
  d 2 Ne. 5: 9.

[Between 544 and 421 B.C.]

15 And now it came to pass that the people of Nephi, under the reign of the second king, began to grow hard in their hearts, and indulge themselves somewhat in wicked practices, such as like unto David of old desiring many [a]wives and [b]concubines, and also Solomon, his son.

16 Yea, and they also began to search much [a]gold and silver, and began to be lifted up somewhat in pride.

17 Wherefore I, Jacob, gave unto them these words as I taught them in the [a]temple, having first obtained mine [b]errand from the Lord.

18 For I, Jacob, and my brother Joseph had been [a]consecrated priests and [b]teachers of this people, by the hand of Nephi.

19 And we did [a]magnify our office unto the Lord, taking upon us the [b]responsibility, answering the sins of the people upon our own heads if we did not [c]teach them the word of God with all diligence; wherefore, by laboring with our might their [d]blood might not come upon our garments; otherwise their blood would come upon our garments, and we would not be found spotless at the last day.

CHAPTER 2

Jacob denounces the love of riches, pride, and unchastity—Men should seek riches to help their fellow men—Jacob condemns the unauthorized practice of plural marriage—The Lord delights in the chastity of women.

THE [a]words which Jacob, the brother of Nephi, spake unto the people of Nephi, after the death of Nephi:

2 Now, my beloved brethren, I, Jacob, according to the [a]responsibility which I am under to God, to [b]magnify mine office with [c]soberness, and that I might [d]rid my garments of your sins, I come up into the temple this day that I might declare unto you the word of God.

3 And ye yourselves know that I have hitherto been diligent in the office of my calling; but I this day am weighed down with much more desire and anxiety for the [a]welfare of your souls than I have hitherto been.

4 For behold, as yet, ye have been obedient unto the word of the Lord, which I have given unto you.

5 But behold, hearken ye unto me, and know that by the help of the all-powerful Creator of heaven and earth I can tell you concerning your [a]thoughts, how that ye are beginning to labor in sin, which sin appeareth very abominable unto me, yea, and abominable unto God.

6 Yea, it grieveth my soul and causeth me to shrink with shame before the presence of my Maker, that I must testify unto you concerning the wickedness of your hearts.

7 And also it grieveth me that I must use so much [a]boldness of speech concerning you, before your wives and your children, many of whose feelings are exceedingly tender and [b]chaste and delicate

---

15a Deut. 17:17;
    1 Sam. 25:43 (42–43);
    D&C 132:38 (38–39).
  b 2 Sam. 20:3;
    1 Chr. 3:9.
16a Mosiah 2:12.
17a 2 Ne. 5:16; Alma 16:
    13; Hel. 3:14 (9, 14);
    3 Ne. 11:1. TG Temple.
  b TG Called of God.
18a 2 Ne. 5:26.
    TG Delegation of
    Responsibility;
    Setting Apart.
  b TG Teacher.

19a Jacob 2:2; D&C 24:3.
    TG Leadership;
    Priesthood, Magnifying
    Callings within.
  b Ezek. 34:10.
    TG Accountability;
    Stewardship.
  c 1 Sam. 8:9; Moro.
    9:6.
  d Lev. 20:27; Acts
    20:26; 2 Ne. 9:44;
    Mosiah 2:27; D&C
    88:85; 112:33.
2 1a 2 Ne. 6:1.
  2a TG Stewardship.

  b Rom. 11:13; Jacob
    1:19; D&C 24:3.
  c TG Sincerity.
  d Mosiah 2:28.
3a 2 Ne. 6:3; Mosiah
    25:11.
5a Amos 4:13; Alma
    12:3 (3–7); D&C 6:16.
    TG God, Omniscience
    of.
7a Lev. 19:17; D&C
    121:43.
  b TG Chastity.

[Between 544 and 421 B.C.]

before God, which thing is pleasing unto God;

8 And it supposeth me that they have come up hither to hear the pleasing *word of God, yea, the word which healeth the wounded soul.

9 Wherefore, it burdeneth my soul that I should be constrained, because of the strict commandment which I have received from God, to *admonish you according to your crimes, to enlarge the wounds of those who are already wounded, instead of consoling and healing their wounds; and those who have not been wounded, instead of feasting upon the pleasing word of God have daggers placed to pierce their souls and wound their delicate minds.

10 But, notwithstanding the greatness of the task, I must do according to the strict *commands of God, and tell you concerning your wickedness and abominations, in the presence of the pure in heart, and the broken heart, and under the glance of the *piercing eye of the Almighty God.

11 Wherefore, I must tell you the truth according to the *plainness of the *word of God. For behold, as I inquired of the Lord, thus came the word unto me, saying: Jacob, get thou up into the temple on the morrow, and declare the word which I shall give thee unto this people.

12 And now behold, my brethren, this is the word which I declare unto you, that many of you have begun to search for gold, and for silver, and for all manner of precious *ores, in the which this land,

which is a *land of promise unto you and to your seed, doth abound most plentifully.

13 And the hand of providence hath smiled upon you most pleasingly, that you have obtained many riches; and because some of you have obtained more abundantly than that of your brethren ye are *lifted up in the pride of your hearts, and wear stiff necks and high heads because of the costliness of your apparel, and persecute your brethren because ye suppose that ye are better than they.

14 And now, my brethren, do ye suppose that God justifieth you in this thing? Behold, I say unto you, Nay. But he condemneth you, and if ye persist in these things his judgments must speedily come unto you.

15 O that he would show you that he can pierce you, and with one glance of his *eye he can smite you to the dust!

16 O that he would rid you from this iniquity and abomination. And, O that ye would listen unto the word of his commands, and let not this *pride of your hearts destroy your souls!

17 Think of your *brethren like unto yourselves, and be familiar with all and free with your *substance, that *they may be rich like unto you.

18 But *before ye seek for *riches, seek ye for the *kingdom of God.

19 And after ye have obtained a hope in Christ ye shall obtain riches, if ye seek them; and ye will seek them for the intent to *do good—

8a Micah 2:7; Alma 31:5; 36:26; Hel. 3:29 (29–30).
   TG Gospel.
9a TG Warnings.
10a TG Commandments of God.
   b 2 Ne. 9:44.
   TG God, Omniscience of.
11a 2 Ne. 25:4; 33:5; Jacob 4:13.
   b Jacob 7:5.
12a 1 Ne. 18:25; 2 Ne. 5:15 (14–16); Hel.

6:9 (9–11); Ether 9:17; 10:23 (12, 23).
   b 1 Ne. 4:14; 17:13 (13–14).
   TG Promised Lands.
13a 2 Kgs. 14:10; Alma 1:32; 31:25; Morm. 8:28 (28, 36–40).
15a TG God, Indignation of; God, Omniscience of.
16a TG Pride.
17a James 5:3 (1–6).
   b TG Almsgiving;

Generosity; Welfare.
   c Alma 4:12; 5:55; 4 Ne. 1:3 (3, 24–26).
18a Mark 10:24 (17–27).
   b 1 Kgs. 3:11 (11–13); Prov. 27:24 (24–27); 2 Ne. 26:31; Alma 39:14; D&C 6:7.
   TG Worldliness.
   c Luke 12:31 (22–31).
19a Mosiah 4:26; 3 Ne. 12:42; 4 Ne. 1:3.
   TG Good Works.

[Between 544 and 421 B.C.]

to clothe the naked, and to feed the hungry, and to liberate the captive, and administer relief to the sick and the afflicted.

20 And now, my brethren, I have spoken unto you concerning pride; and those of you which have afflicted your neighbor, and persecuted him because ye were proud in your hearts, of the things which God hath given you, what say ye of it?

21 Do ye not suppose that such things are abominable unto him who created all flesh? And the one being is as precious in his sight as the other. And all flesh is of the dust; and for the selfsame end hath he created them, that they should keep his *a*commandments and glorify him forever.

22 And now I make an end of speaking unto you concerning this pride. And were it not that I must speak unto you concerning a grosser crime, my heart would rejoice exceedingly because of you.

23 But the word of God burdens me because of your grosser crimes. For behold, thus saith the Lord: This people begin to wax in iniquity; they understand not the scriptures, for they seek to excuse themselves in committing *a*whoredoms, because of the things which were written concerning David, and Solomon his son.

24 Behold, David and *a*Solomon truly had many *b*wives and concubines, which thing was *c*abominable before me, saith the Lord.

25 Wherefore, thus saith the Lord, I have led this people forth out of the land of Jerusalem, by the power of mine arm, that I might raise up

unto me a *a*righteous branch from the fruit of the loins of Joseph.

26 Wherefore, I the Lord God will not suffer that this people shall do like unto them of old.

27 Wherefore, my brethren, hear me, and hearken to the word of the Lord: For there shall not any *a*man among you have save it be *b*one *c*wife; and concubines he shall have none;

28 For I, the Lord God, delight in the *a*chastity of women. And *b*whoredoms are an abomination before me; thus saith the Lord of Hosts.

29 Wherefore, this people shall keep my commandments, saith the Lord of Hosts, or *a*cursed be the land for their sakes.

30 For if I will, saith the Lord of Hosts, raise up *a*seed unto me, I will command my people; otherwise they shall hearken unto these things.

31 For behold, I, the Lord, have seen the sorrow, and heard the mourning of the daughters of my people in the land of Jerusalem, yea, and in all the lands of my people, because of the wickedness and *a*abominations of their *b*husbands.

32 And I will not suffer, saith the Lord of Hosts, that the cries of the fair daughters of this people, which I have led out of the land of Jerusalem, shall come up unto me against the men of my people, saith the Lord of Hosts.

33 For they shall not lead away captive the daughters of my people because of their tenderness, save I shall visit them with a sore curse, even unto destruction; for they shall not commit *a*whoredoms, like unto

21a D&C 11:20; Abr. 3:25 (25–26).
23a TG Whoredom.
24a 1 Kgs. 11:1; Neh. 13:26 (25–27).
  b Deut. 17:17 (14–17); 2 Sam. 5:13; D&C 132:39 (38–39).
  c Deut. 7:3 (1–4); 1 Kgs. 11:3; Ezra 9:2 (1–2).
25a Gen. 49:22 (22–26); Ezek. 17:22 (22–24);

Amos 5:15; 2 Ne. 3:5; 14:2; Alma 26:36. TG Israel, Joseph, People of.
27a TG Marriage, Husbands.
  b Jacob 3:5 (5–7); D&C 49:16.
    TG Marriage, Plural.
  c TG Marriage, Wives.
28a TG Chastity.
  b TG Sexual Immorality; Whoredom.

29a Ether 2:11 (8–12). TG Curse.
30a Mal. 2:15; D&C 132:63 (61–66).
31a TG Family, Children, Responsibilities toward.
  b TG Marriage, Husbands.
33a Ezek. 16:25 (20–34). TG Sensuality.

[Between 544 and 421 B.C.]

them of old, saith the Lord of Hosts.

34 And now behold, my brethren, ye know that these commandments were given to our [a]father, Lehi; wherefore, ye have known them before; and ye have come unto great condemnation; for ye have done these things which ye ought not to have done.

35 Behold, ye have done [a]greater iniquities than the Lamanites, our brethren. Ye have broken the hearts of your tender wives, and lost the confidence of your children, because of your bad examples before them; and the sobbings of their hearts ascend up to God against you. And because of the [b]strictness of the word of God, which cometh down against you, many hearts died, pierced with deep wounds.

CHAPTER 3

The pure in heart receive the pleasing word of God—Lamanite righteousness exceeds that of Nephites—Jacob warns against fornication, lasciviousness, and every sin.

BUT behold, I, Jacob, would speak unto you that are pure in heart. Look unto God with firmness of mind, and [a]pray unto him with exceeding faith, and he will [b]console you in your [c]afflictions, and he will plead your cause, and send down [d]justice upon those who seek your destruction.

2 O all ye that are pure in heart, lift up your heads and receive the pleasing word of God, and feast upon his [a]love; for ye may, if your [b]minds are [c]firm, forever.

3 But, wo, wo, unto you that are not pure in heart, that are filthy this day before God; for except ye repent the land is [a]cursed for your sakes; and the Lamanites, which are not [b]filthy like unto you, nevertheless they are [c]cursed with a sore cursing, shall scourge you even unto destruction.

4 And the time speedily cometh, that except ye repent they shall possess the land of your inheritance, and the Lord God will [a]lead away the righteous out from among you.

5 Behold, the Lamanites your brethren, whom ye hate because of their filthiness and the cursing which hath come upon their skins, are more righteous than you; for they have not [a]forgotten the commandment of the Lord, which was given unto our father—that they should have save it were [b]one wife, and [c]concubines they should have none, and there should not be [d]whoredoms committed among them.

6 And now, this commandment they observe to keep; wherefore, because of this observance, in keeping this commandment, the Lord God will not destroy them, but will be [a]merciful unto them; and one day they shall [b]become a blessed people.

7 Behold, their [a]husbands [b]love their [c]wives, and their wives love their husbands; and their husbands and their wives love their children; and their [d]unbelief and their hatred towards you is because of the iniquity of their fathers; wherefore,

34a 1 Ne. 1: 16 (16–17).
35a Jacob 3: 5 (5–7).
  b Gen. 2: 24.
3 1a 2 Ne. 32: 8.
  b TG Comfort;
    Consolation; Pure.
  c TG Affliction.
  d TG Deliverance;
    Protection, Divine.
2a TG God, Love of.
  b TG Steadfastness.
  c Alma 57: 27.
3a TG Earth, Curse of.

  b TG Filthiness.
  c 1 Ne. 12: 23.
4a Omni 1: 12 (5–7,
    12–13).
5a Jacob 2: 35.
  b Jacob 2: 27.
  c Mosiah 11: 2 (2–14);
    Ether 10: 5.
  d TG Chastity.
6a 1 Ne. 13: 31; 2 Ne.
    4: 7; 10: 18 (18–19);
    Hel. 15: 12 (10–17);
    Morm. 5: 20 (20–21).

  b 1 Ne. 15: 14 (13–18);
    22: 8.
7a TG Marriage, Hus-
    bands.
  b TG Family, Love
    within; Marriage,
    Continuing Courtship
    in.
  c TG Marriage, Wives.
  d D&C 3: 18.
    TG Unbelief,
    Unbelievers.

[Between 544 and 421 B.C.]

how much better are you than they, in the sight of your great Creator?

8 O my brethren, I fear that unless ye shall repent of your sins that their skins will be [a]whiter than yours, when ye shall be brought with them before the throne of God.

9 Wherefore, a commandment I give unto you, which is the word of God, that ye [a]revile no more against them because of the darkness of their skins; neither shall ye revile against them because of their filthiness; but ye shall remember your own filthiness, and remember that their filthiness came because of their fathers.

10 Wherefore, ye shall remember your [a]children, how that ye have grieved their hearts because of the [b]example that ye have set before them; and also, remember that ye may, because of your filthiness, bring your children unto destruction, and their sins be heaped upon your heads at the last day.

11 O my brethren, hearken unto my words; [a]arouse the faculties of your souls; shake yourselves that ye may [b]awake from the slumber of death; and loose yourselves from the pains of [c]hell that ye may not become [d]angels to the devil, to be cast into that lake of fire and brimstone which is the second [e]death.

12 And now I, Jacob, spake many more things unto the people of Nephi, [a]warning them against [b]fornication and [c]lasciviousness, and every kind of sin, telling them the awful consequences of them.

13 And a hundredth part of the proceedings of this people, which now began to be numerous, cannot be written upon [a]these plates; but

many of their proceedings are written upon the [b]larger plates, and their wars, and their contentions, and the reigns of their kings.

14 [a]These plates are called the plates of Jacob, and they were [b]made by the hand of Nephi. And I make an end of speaking these words.

CHAPTER 4

All the prophets worshipped the Father in the name of Christ—Abraham's offering of Isaac was in similitude of God and his Only Begotten—Men should reconcile themselves to God through the atonement—The Jews shall reject the foundation stone.

Now behold, it came to pass that I, Jacob, having ministered much unto my people in word, (and I cannot write but a [a]little of my words, because of the [b]difficulty of engraving our words upon plates) and we know that the things which we write upon plates must remain;

2 But whatsoever things we write upon anything save it be upon [a]plates must perish and vanish away; but we can write a few words upon plates, which will give our children, and also our beloved brethren, a small degree of knowledge concerning us, or concerning their fathers—

3 Now in this thing we do rejoice; and we labor diligently to engraven these words upon plates, hoping that our beloved brethren and our children will receive them with thankful hearts, and look upon them that they may learn with joy and not with sorrow, neither with contempt, concerning their first [a]parents.

8a 3 Ne. 2: 15.
9a TG Reviling.
10a TG Family, Children, Responsibilities toward; Family, Love within.
  b TG Example.
11a TG Apathy.
  b 2 Ne. 28: 21; Alma 5: 7 (6–7).
  c TG Hell.

d 2 Ne. 9: 9 (8–9).
  TG Spirits, Evil or Unclean.
e TG Death, Spiritual, Second.
12a TG Warnings.
  b TG Fornication.
  c TG Lust.
13a Jacob 1: 1 (1–4); 4: 1 (1–4).

b Jarom 1: 14.
14a Jarom 1: 2 (1–2).
  b 1 Ne. 19: 2 (2–3).
4 1a 1 Ne. 6: 3; Jarom 1: 14; Omni 1: 30.
  b Ether 12: 24 (23–26).
2a TG Scriptures, Preservation of.
3a TG Scriptures, Value of.

[Between 544 and 421 B.C.]

4 For, for this intent have we written these things, that they may know that we *a*knew of Christ, and we had a hope of his *b*glory many hundred years before his coming; and not only we ourselves had a hope of his glory, but also all the holy *c*prophets which were before us.

5 Behold, they believed in Christ and *a*worshiped the Father in his name, and also we worship the Father in his *b*name. And for this intent we *c*keep the *d*law of Moses, it *e*pointing our souls to him; and for this cause it is sanctified unto us for righteousness, even as it was accounted unto Abraham in the wilderness to be obedient unto the commands of God in offering up his son Isaac, which is a *f*similitude of God and his *g*Only Begotten Son.

6 Wherefore, we search the prophets, and we have many revelations and the spirit of *a*prophecy; and having all these *b*witnesses we obtain a hope, and our faith becometh unshaken, insomuch that we truly can *c*command in the *d*name of Jesus and the very trees obey us, or the mountains, or the waves of the sea.

7 Nevertheless, the Lord God showeth us our *a*weakness that we may know that it is by his *b*grace, and his great condescensions unto the children of men, that we have power to do these things.

8 Behold, great and marvelous are the *a*works of the Lord. How *b*unsearchable are the depths of the *c*mysteries of him; and it is impossible that man should find out all his ways. And no man *d*knoweth of his *e*ways save it be revealed unto him; wherefore, brethren, despise not the *f*revelations of God.

9 For behold, by the power of his *a*word *b*man came upon the face of the earth, which earth was *c*created by the power of his word. Wherefore, if God being able to speak and the world was, and to speak and man was created, O then, why not able to command the *d*earth, or the workmanship of his hands upon the face of it, according to his will and pleasure?

10 Wherefore, brethren, seek not to *a*counsel the Lord, but to take counsel from his hand. For behold, ye yourselves know that he counseleth in *b*wisdom, and in justice, and in great mercy, over all his works.

11 Wherefore, beloved brethren, be *a*reconciled unto him through the *b*atonement of Christ, his *c*Only Be-

4a TG Jesus Christ, Prophecies about; Testimony.
 b TG Jesus Christ, Glory of.
 c Luke 24: 27; 1 Pet. 1: 11; Jacob 7: 11 (11–12); Mosiah 13: 33 (33–35); D&C 20: 26.
5a Moses 5: 8.
 b Gen. 4: 26; Hel. 8: 16 (16–20). TG Name of the Lord.
 c 2 Ne. 25: 24; Jacob 7: 7; Mosiah 13: 30.
 d Jarom 1: 11; Alma 25: 15 (15–16). TG Law of Moses.
 e Gal. 3: 24; Ether 12: 19 (18–19).
 f TG Jesus Christ, Types of, in Anticipation.
 g Gen. 22: 2 (1–14); John 3: 16 (16–21); Heb. 11: 17.

TG Jesus Christ, Divine Sonship.
6a TG Prophecy.
 b TG Witnesses.
 c 3 Ne. 28: 20 (19–22). TG God, Power of.
 d Acts 3: 6 (6–16); 3 Ne. 8: 1.
7a Ether 12: 27; D&C 66: 3.
 b TG Grace.
8a Ps. 106: 2.
 b Rom. 11: 34 (33–36); Mosiah 4: 9.
 c D&C 19: 10; 76: 114 (114–116). TG Mysteries of Godliness.
 d Dan. 1: 17; 1 Cor. 2: 11 (9–16); Alma 26: 21 (21–22). TG God, Knowledge about.
 e Isa. 55: 8 (8–9).

 f D&C 3: 7.
9a Morm. 9: 17; Moses 1: 32.
 b TG Man, Physical Creation of.
 c TG Creation; God, Creator; Jesus Christ, Creator.
 d Hel. 12: 16 (8–17).
10a Josh. 9: 14; Prov. 15: 22; Isa. 45: 9; 2 Ne. 9: 28–29; Alma 37: 12, 37; D&C 3: 4, 13; 22: 4.
 b TG God, Justice of; God, Wisdom of.
11a Lev. 6: 30. TG Jesus Christ, Mission of; Reconciliation.
 b TG Jesus Christ, Atonement through.
 c TG Jesus Christ, Divine Sonship.

gotten Son, and ye may obtain a [d]resurrection, according to the [e]power of the resurrection which is in Christ, and be presented as the [f]first-fruits of Christ unto God, having faith, and obtained a good hope of glory in him before he manifesteth himself in the flesh.

12 And now, beloved, marvel not that I tell you these things; for why not [a]speak of the atonement of Christ, and attain to a perfect knowledge of him, as to attain to the knowledge of a resurrection and the world to come?

13 Behold, my brethren, he that prophesieth, let him prophesy to the understanding of men; for the [a]Spirit speaketh the [b]truth and lieth not. Wherefore, it speaketh of things as they really [c]are, and of things as they really will be; wherefore, these things are manifested unto us [d]plainly, for the salvation of our souls. But behold, we are not witnesses alone in these things; for God also [e]spake them unto prophets of old.

14 But behold, the Jews were a [a]stiffnecked people; and they [b]despised the words of [c]plainness, and [d]killed the prophets, and sought for things that they could not understand. Wherefore, because of their [e]blindness, which [f]blindness came by looking beyond the [g]mark, they must needs fall; for God hath taken away his plainness from them, and delivered unto them many things which they [h]cannot understand,

because they desired it. And because they desired it God hath done it, that they may [i]stumble.

15 And now I, Jacob, am led on by the Spirit unto prophesying; for I perceive by the workings of the Spirit which is in me, that by the [a]stumbling of the [b]Jews they will [c]reject the [d]stone upon which they might build and have safe foundation.

16 But behold, according to the scriptures, this [a]stone shall become the great, and the last, and the only sure [b]foundation, upon which the Jews can build.

17 And now, my beloved, how is it possible that these, after having rejected the sure foundation, can [a]ever build upon it, that it may become the head of their corner?

18 Behold, my beloved brethren, I will unfold this mystery unto you; if I do not, by any means, get shaken from my firmness in the Spirit, and stumble because of my over anxiety for you.

CHAPTER 5

Jacob quotes Zenos relative to the allegory of the tame and wild olive trees—They are a likeness of Israel and the gentiles—The scattering and gathering of Israel are prefigured—Allusions are made to the Nephites and Lamanites and all the house of Israel—Gentiles shall be grafted into Israel—Eventually the vineyard shall be burned.

11d TG Resurrection.
  e TG God, Power of.
  f Mosiah 15: 21 (21–23);
    18: 9; Alma 40: 16
    (16–21).
12a 2 Ne. 25: 26.
13a TG Holy Ghost,
    Mission of.
  b John 17: 17.
    TG Honesty.
  c D&C 93: 24.
  d Neh. 8: 8; Jacob 2: 11;
    Alma 13: 23.
  e TG Witness of the
    Father.
14a Deut. 9: 13; Neh.
    9: 16; 2 Ne. 25: 2.

    TG Stiffneckedness.
  b Num. 15: 31 (30–31);
    Ezek. 20: 13 (13–16);
    1 Ne. 17: 30 (30–31);
    19: 7; 2 Ne. 33: 2;
    D&C 3: 7 (4–13).
  c 2 Cor. 11: 3.
  d Zech. 1: 4 (2–5).
  e Isa. 44: 18.
  f Rom. 11: 25.
    TG Spiritual Blindness.
  g John 7: 47 (45–53).
  h 2 Ne. 25: 1.
  i Isa. 57: 14.
15a Isa. 8: 14 (13–15);
    1 Cor. 1: 23; 2 Ne.

    18: 14 (13–15).
  b TG Israel, Judah,
    People of.
  c Rom. 11: 1, 20 (1–36);
    1 Ne. 10: 11; Morm.
    5: 14 (14–20).
  d TG Cornerstone; Jesus
    Christ, Prophecies
    about; Rock.
16a Ps. 118: 22 (22–23).
  b Isa. 28: 16 (14–17);
    Hel. 5: 12.
17a Matt. 19: 30; D&C
    5: 63 (62–64); D&C
    29: 30.

[Between 544 and 421 B.C.]

BEHOLD, my brethren, do ye not remember to have read the words of the prophet ªZenos, which he spake unto the house of Israel, saying:

2 Hearken, O ye house of Israel, and hear the words of me, a prophet of the Lord.

3 For behold, thus saith the Lord, I will liken thee, O house of ªIsrael, like unto a tame ᵇolive-tree, which a man took and nourished in his ᶜvineyard; and it grew, and waxed old, and began to ᵈdecay.

4 And it came to pass that the master of the vineyard went forth, and he saw that his olive-tree began to decay; and he said: I will ªprune it, and dig about it, and nourish it, that perhaps it may shoot forth young and tender branches, and it perish not.

5 And it came to pass that he ªpruned it, and digged about it, and nourished it according to his word.

6 And it came to pass that after many days it began to put forth somewhat a little, young and tender branches; but behold, the main ªtop thereof began to perish.

7 And it came to pass that the master of the vineyard saw it, and he said unto his ªservant: It grieveth me that I should lose this tree; wherefore, go and pluck the branches from a ᵇwild olive-tree, and bring them hither unto me; and we will pluck off those main branches which are beginning to wither away, and we will cast them into the fire that they may be burned.

8 And behold, saith the Lord of the vineyard, I take ªaway many of these young and tender branches, and I will graft them ᵇwhithersoever I will; and it mattereth not that if it so be that the root of this tree will perish, I may preserve the fruit thereof unto myself; wherefore, I will take these young and tender branches, and I will graft them whithersoever I will.

9 Take thou the branches of the wild olive-tree, and graft them in, in the ªstead thereof; and these which I have plucked off I will cast into the fire and burn them, that they may not cumber the ground of my vineyard.

10 And it came to pass that the servant of the Lord of the vineyard did according to the word of the Lord of the vineyard, and grafted in the branches of the ªwild olive-tree.

11 And the Lord of the vineyard caused that it should be digged about, and pruned, and nourished, saying unto his servant: It grieveth me that I should lose this tree; wherefore, that perhaps I might preserve the roots thereof that they perish not, that I might preserve them unto myself, I have done this thing.

12 Wherefore, go thy way; watch the tree, and nourish it, according to my words.

13 And these will I ªplace in the nethermost part of my vineyard, whithersoever I will, it mattereth not unto thee; and I do it that I may preserve unto myself the natural branches of the tree; and also, that I may lay up fruit thereof against the season, unto myself; for it grieveth me that I should lose this tree and the fruit thereof.

14 And it came to pass that the Lord of the vineyard went his way, and hid the natural ªbranches of the

---

5 1a 1 Ne. 19: 12 (12, 16);
    Jacob 6: 1.
    TG Scriptures, Lost.
  3a TG Israel, Twelve
    Tribes of.
   b Ezek. 36: 8 (8–15);
    Rom. 11: 21 (1–36);
    1 Ne. 10: 12; Jacob
    6: 1 (1–7). TG Israel,
    Mission of; Vineyard
    of the Lord.

   c Matt. 21: 33 (33–41);
    D&C 101: 44.
   d TG Apostasy of Israel.
  4a TG Prophets, Mission
    of.
  5a 2 Kgs. 17: 13 (13–18).
  6a Luke 3: 9 (8–9); 2 Ne.
    30: 2. TG Chief Priest.
  7a TG Servant.
   b Rom. 11: 17 (17, 24).

  8a TG Israel, Scattering of.
   b Ezek. 17: 22 (4–10, 22).
  9a Acts 9: 15; 14: 27;
    Rom. 1: 13; Gal. 3: 14.
 10a TG Gentiles.
 13a Hosea 8: 8; 1 Ne.
    10: 12.
 14a TG Israel, Bondage of,
    in Other Lands.

[Between 544 and 421 B.C.]

tame olive-tree in the nethermost parts of the vineyard, some in one and some in another, according to his will and pleasure.

15 And it came to pass that a long time passed away, and the Lord of the vineyard said unto his servant: Come, let us go down into the vineyard, that we may *a*labor in the vineyard.

16 And it came to pass that the Lord of the vineyard, and also the servant, went down into the vineyard to labor. And it came to pass that the servant said unto his master: Behold, look here; behold the tree.

17 And it came to pass that the Lord of the vineyard looked and beheld the tree in the which the wild olive branches had been grafted; and it had sprung forth and begun to bear *a*fruit. And he beheld that it was good; and the fruit thereof was like unto the natural fruit.

18 And he said unto the servant: Behold, the branches of the wild tree have taken hold of the moisture of the root thereof, that the root thereof hath brought forth much strength; and because of the much strength of the root thereof the wild branches have brought forth tame fruit. Now, if we had not grafted in these branches, the tree thereof would have perished. And now, behold, I shall lay up much fruit, which the tree thereof hath brought forth; and the fruit thereof I shall lay up against the season, unto mine own self.

19 And it came to pass that the Lord of the vineyard said unto the servant: Come, let us go to the nethermost part of the vineyard, and behold if the natural branches of the tree have not brought forth much fruit also, that I may lay up of the fruit thereof against the season, unto mine own self.

20 And it came to pass that they went forth whither the master had hid the natural branches of the tree, and he said unto the servant: Behold these; and he beheld the *a*first that it had *b*brought forth much fruit; and he beheld also that it was good. And he said unto the servant: Take of the fruit thereof, and lay it up against the season, that I may preserve it unto mine own self; for behold, said he, this long time have I nourished it, and it hath brought forth much fruit.

21 And it came to pass that the servant said unto his master: How comest thou hither to plant this tree, or this branch of the tree? For behold, it was the poorest spot in all the land of thy vineyard.

22 And the Lord of the vineyard said unto him: Counsel me not; I knew that it was a poor spot of ground; wherefore, I said unto thee, I have nourished it this long time, and thou beholdest that it hath brought forth much fruit.

23 And it came to pass that the Lord of the vineyard said unto his servant: Look hither; behold I have planted another branch of the tree also; and thou knowest that this spot of ground was poorer than the first. But, behold the tree. I have nourished it this long time, and it hath brought forth much fruit; therefore, gather it, and lay it up against the season, that I may preserve it unto mine own self.

24 And it came to pass that the Lord of the vineyard said again unto his servant: Look hither, and behold another *a*branch also, which I have planted; behold that I have nourished it also, and it hath brought forth fruit.

25 And he said unto the servant: Look hither and behold the last. Behold, this have I planted in a *a*good spot of ground; and I have

15a TG Millennium,
    Preparing a People for.
17a Matt. 12:33; John
    15:16; Gal. 3:9 (7–9,
    29); Col. 1:6 (3–8).

20a Jacob 5:39.
  b TG Israel, Restoration
    of.
24a Ezek. 17:22 (22–24);

    Alma 16:17.
25a Ezek. 17:8; 1 Ne.
    2:20; Jacob 5:43.

[Between 544 and 421 B.C.]

nourished it this long time, and only a [b]part of the tree hath brought forth tame fruit, and the [c]other part of the tree hath brought forth wild fruit; behold, I have nourished this tree like unto the others.

26 And it came to pass that the Lord of the vineyard said unto the servant: Pluck off the branches that have not brought forth good [a]fruit, and cast them into the fire.

27 But behold, the servant said unto him: Let us prune it, and dig about it, and nourish it a little [a]longer, that perhaps it may bring forth good fruit unto thee, that thou canst lay it up against the season.

28 And it came to pass that the Lord of the vineyard and the servant of the Lord of the vineyard did nourish all the fruit of the vineyard.

29 And it came to pass that a [a]long time had passed away, and the Lord of the vineyard said unto his [b]servant: Come, let us go down into the vineyard, that we may labor again in the vineyard. For behold, the time draweth near, and the [c]end soon cometh; wherefore, I must lay up fruit against the season, unto mine own self.

30 And it came to pass that the Lord of the vineyard and the servant went down into the vineyard; and they came to the tree whose natural branches had been broken off, and the wild branches had been grafted in; and behold all [a]sorts of fruit did cumber the tree.

31 And it came to pass that the Lord of the vineyard did [a]taste of the fruit, every sort according to its number. And the Lord of the vineyard said: Behold, this long time have we nourished this tree, and I have laid up unto myself against the season much fruit.

32 But behold, this time it hath brought forth much [a]fruit, and there is [b]none of it which is good. And behold, there are all kinds of bad fruit; and it profiteth me nothing, notwithstanding all our labor; and now it grieveth me that I should lose this tree.

33 And the Lord of the vineyard said unto the servant: What shall we do unto the tree, that I may preserve again good fruit thereof unto mine own self?

34 And the servant said unto his master: Behold, because thou didst graft in the branches of the wild olive-tree they have nourished the roots, that they are alive and they have not perished; wherefore thou beholdest that they are yet good.

35 And it came to pass that the Lord of the vineyard said unto his servant: The tree profiteth me nothing, and the roots thereof profit me nothing so long as it shall bring forth evil fruit.

36 Nevertheless, I know that the roots are good, and for mine own purpose I have preserved them; and because of their much strength they have hitherto brought forth, from the wild branches, good fruit.

37 But behold, the wild branches have grown and have [a]overrun the roots thereof; and because that the wild branches have overcome the roots thereof it hath brought forth much evil fruit; and because that it hath brought forth so much evil fruit thou beholdest that it beginneth to perish; and it will soon become ripened, that it may be cast into the fire, except we should do something for it to preserve it.

38 And it came to pass that the Lord of the vineyard said unto his servant: Let us go down into the nethermost parts of the vineyard, and behold if the natural branches have also brought forth evil fruit.

39 And it came to pass that they

25b Hel. 15: 3 (3–4).
 c Alma 26: 36.
26a Matt. 7: 19 (15–20);
    Alma 5: 36; D&C 97: 7.
27a Jacob 5: 50 (50–51);
    Alma 42: 4.

29a TG Last Days.
 b D&C 101: 55; 103: 21.
 c 2 Ne. 30: 10; Jacob
    6: 2.
30a TG Apostasy.
31a TG Jesus Christ,

    Judge; Judgment.
32a Hosea 10: 1.
 b JS-H 1: 19.
37a D&C 45: 30.

[Between 544 and 421 B.C.]

went down into the nethermost parts of the vineyard. And it came to pass that they beheld that the fruit of the natural branches had become corrupt also; yea, the [a]first and the second and also the last; and they had all become corrupt.

40 And the [a]wild fruit of the last had overcome that part of the tree which brought forth good fruit, even that the branch had withered away and died.

41 And it came to pass that the Lord of the vineyard wept, and said unto the servant: [a]What could I have done more for my vineyard?

42 Behold, I knew that all the fruit of the vineyard, save it were these, had become [a]corrupted. And now these which have once brought forth good fruit have also become corrupted; and now all the trees of my vineyard are good for nothing save it be to be [b]hewn down and cast into the fire.

43 And behold this last, whose branch hath withered away, I did plant in a [a]good spot of ground; yea, even that which was choice unto me above all other parts of the land of my vineyard.

44 And thou beheldest that I also cut down that which [a]cumbered this spot of ground, that I might plant this tree in the stead thereof.

45 And thou beheldest that a [a]part thereof brought forth good fruit, and a part thereof brought forth wild fruit; and because I plucked not the branches thereof and cast them into the fire, behold, they have overcome the good branch that it hath withered away.

46 And now, behold, notwithstanding all the care which we have taken of my vineyard, the trees thereof have become corrupted, that they bring forth no good [a]fruit; and these I had hoped to preserve, to have laid up fruit thereof against the season, unto mine own self. But, behold, they have become like unto the wild olive-tree, and they are of no worth but to be [b]hewn down and cast into the fire; and it grieveth me that I should lose them.

47 But [a]what could I have done more in my vineyard? Have I slackened mine hand, that I have not nourished it? Nay, I have nourished it, and I have digged about it, and I have pruned it, and I have dunged it; and I have [b]stretched forth mine [c]hand almost all the day long, and the [d]end draweth nigh. And it grieveth me that I should hew down all the trees of my vineyard, and cast them into the fire that they should be burned. Who is it that has corrupted my vineyard?

48 And it came to pass that the servant said unto his master: Is it not the [a]loftiness of thy vineyard— have not the branches thereof overcome the roots which are good? And because the branches have overcome the roots thereof, behold they grew faster than the strength of the roots, [b]taking strength unto themselves. Behold, I say, is not this the cause that the trees of thy vineyard have become corrupted?

49 And it came to pass that the Lord of the vineyard said unto the servant: Let us go and hew down the trees of the vineyard and cast them into the fire, that they shall not cumber the ground of my vineyard, for I have done all. What could I have done more for my vineyard?

50 But, behold, the servant said unto the Lord of the vineyard: Spare it a little [a]longer.

39a Jacob 5: 20 (20, 23, 25).
40a Hel. 15: 4 (3–4).
41a Isa. 5: 4; 2 Ne. 2: 27;
    26: 24; Jacob 5: 47;
    Alma 26: 37.
42a TG Apostasy.
  b Matt. 3: 10.
43a Ezek. 17: 8; Jacob 5: 25.
44a Moro. 9: 23.
45a 1 Ne. 15: 12 (12–17);
    2 Ne. 3: 5; 10: 1;
    Alma 46: 24 (24–25).
46a Luke 3: 9.
  b Alma 5: 52; 3 Ne.
    27: 11.
47a Jacob 5: 41 (41, 49).
  b Isa. 9: 12 (12, 17, 21).
  c 2 Ne. 19: 17 (17–21);
    28: 32; Jacob 6: 4.
  d TG World, End of.
48a TG Haughtiness; Pride.
  b D&C 121: 39.
    TG Unrighteous
    Dominion.
50a Jacob 5: 27.

[Between 544 and 421 B.C.]

51 And the Lord said: Yea, I will spare it a little longer, for it grieveth me that I should lose the trees of my vineyard.

52 Wherefore, let us take of the *a*branches of these which I have planted in the nethermost parts of my vineyard, and let us graft them into the tree from whence they came; and let us pluck from the tree those branches whose fruit is most bitter, and graft in the natural branches of the tree in the stead thereof.

53 And this will I do that the tree may not perish, that, perhaps, I may preserve unto myself the roots thereof for mine *a*own purpose.

54 And, behold, the roots of the natural branches of the tree which I planted whithersoever I would are yet alive; wherefore, that I may preserve them also for mine own purpose, I will take of the *a*branches of this tree, and I will *b*graft them in unto them. Yea, I will graft in unto them the branches of their mother tree, that I may preserve the roots also unto mine own self, that when they shall be sufficiently strong perhaps they may bring forth good fruit unto me, and I may yet have glory in the fruit of my vineyard.

55 And it came to pass that they took from the natural tree which had become wild, and grafted in unto the natural trees, which also had become wild.

56 And they also took of the natural trees which had become wild, and *a*grafted into their mother tree.

57 And the Lord of the vineyard said unto the servant: Pluck not the wild branches from the trees, save it be those which are most bitter; and in them ye shall graft according to that which I have said.

58 And we will nourish again the trees of the vineyard, and we will trim up the *a*branches thereof; and we will pluck from the trees those branches which are ripened, that must perish, and cast them into the fire.

59 And this I do that, perhaps, the roots thereof may take strength because of their goodness; and because of the change of the branches, that the good may *a*overcome the evil.

60 And because that I have preserved the natural branches and the roots thereof, and that I have grafted in the natural branches again into their mother tree, and have preserved the roots of their mother tree, that, perhaps, the trees of my vineyard may bring forth again good *a*fruit; and that I may have joy again in the fruit of my vineyard, and, perhaps, that I may rejoice exceedingly that I have preserved the roots and the branches of the first fruit—

61 Wherefore, go to, and call *a*servants, that we may *b*labor diligently with our might in the vineyard, that we may *c*prepare the way, that I may bring forth again the natural fruit, which natural fruit is good and the most precious above all other fruit.

62 Wherefore, let us go to and labor with our might this last time, for behold the end draweth nigh, and this is for the last time that I shall *a*prune my vineyard.

63 Graft in the branches; begin at the *a*last that they may be first, and that the first may be *b*last, and dig about the trees, both old and young, the first and the last; and the last and the first, that all may be nourished once again for the last time.

64 Wherefore, dig about them,

52a TG Israel, Gathering of; Israel, Restoration of.
53a Ex. 19: 6; Isa. 49: 6.
54a 3 Ne. 21: 6 (5–6); Morm. 5: 15.
  b 1 Ne. 15: 16.
56a Jer. 24: 6.
58a Isa. 27: 11.

59a TG Triumph.
60a Isa. 27: 6.
61a Jacob 6:2.
  b D&C 24: 19; 39: 17; 95: 4.
  c TG Millennium, Preparing a People for.
62a D&C 75: 2.

63a Matt. 20: 16; Mark 10: 31; Luke 13: 30; 1 Ne. 13: 42; Ether 13: 12 (10–12).
  b Matt. 19: 30; Jacob 4: 17; D&C 29: 30.

[Between 544 and 421 B.C.]

and prune them, and dung them once more, for the last time, for the end draweth nigh. And if it be so that these last grafts shall grow, and bring forth the natural fruit, then shall ye prepare the way for them, that they may grow.

65 And as they begin to grow ye shall [a]clear away the branches which bring forth bitter fruit, according to the strength of the good and the size thereof; and ye shall not clear away the bad thereof all at once, lest the roots thereof should be too strong for the graft, and the graft thereof shall perish, and I lose the trees of my vineyard.

66 For it grieveth me that I should lose the trees of my vineyard; wherefore ye shall clear away the bad according as the good shall grow, that the root and the top may be equal in strength, until the good shall overcome the bad, and the bad be hewn down and cast into the fire, that they cumber not the ground of my vineyard; and thus will I sweep away the bad out of my vineyard.

67 And the branches of the natural tree will I graft in again into the natural tree;

68 And the branches of the natural tree will I graft into the natural branches of the tree; and thus will I bring them together again, that they shall bring forth the natural [a]fruit, and they shall be one.

69 And the bad shall be [a]cast away, yea, even out of all the land of my vineyard; for behold, only this once will I prune my vineyard.

70 And it came to pass that the Lord of the vineyard sent his [a]servant; and the servant went and did as the Lord had commanded him, and brought other [b]servants; and they were [c]few.

71 And the Lord of the vineyard said unto them: Go to, and [a]labor in the vineyard, with your might. For behold, this is the [b]last time that I shall [c]nourish my vineyard; for the end is nigh at hand, and the season speedily cometh; and if ye labor with your might with me ye shall have joy in the fruit which I shall lay up unto myself against the time which will soon come.

72 And it came to pass that the servants did go and labor with their mights; and the Lord of the vineyard labored also with them; and they did obey the commandments of the Lord of the vineyard in all things.

73 And there began to be the natural fruit again in the vineyard; and the natural branches began to grow and thrive exceedingly; and the wild branches began to be plucked off and to be cast away; and they did keep the root and the top thereof equal, according to the strength thereof.

74 And thus they labored, with all diligence, according to the commandments of the Lord of the vineyard, even until the bad had been cast away out of the vineyard, and the Lord had preserved unto himself that the trees had become again the natural fruit; and they became like unto [a]one body; and the fruits were equal; and the Lord of the vineyard had preserved unto himself the natural fruit, which was most precious unto him from the beginning.

75 And it came to pass that when the [a]Lord of the vineyard saw that his fruit was good, and that his vineyard was no more corrupt, he called up his servants, and said unto them: Behold, for this last time have we nourished my vineyard; and thou beholdest that I have done according to my will; and I have preserved the natural fruit, that it

65a D&C 86: 6 (6–7).
68a TG Israel, Mission of.
69a 1 Ne. 22: 23 (15–17, 23);
   2 Ne. 30: 10 (9–10).
70a D&C 101: 55; 103: 21.
   b Matt. 9: 37 (36–38).

c 1 Ne. 14: 12.
71a Matt. 21: 28; Jacob 6: 2
   (2–3); D&C 33: 3 (3–4).
   b D&C 39: 17; 43: 28
   (28–30).
   c TG Millennium,

Preparing a People for.
74a D&C 38: 27.
75a TG Jesus Christ,
   Millennial Reign.

[Between 544 and 421 B.C.]

is good, even like as it was in the beginning. And [b]blessed art thou; for because ye have been diligent in laboring with me in my vineyard, and have kept my commandments, and have brought unto me again the [c]natural fruit, that my vineyard is no more corrupted, and the bad is cast away, behold ye shall have [d]joy with me because of the fruit of my vineyard.

76 For behold, for a [a]long time will I lay up of the fruit of my vineyard unto mine own self against the season, which speedily cometh; and for the last time have I nourished my vineyard, and pruned it, and dug about it, and dunged it; wherefore I will lay up unto mine own self of the fruit, for a long time, according to that which I have spoken.

77 And when the time cometh that evil fruit shall again come into my vineyard, then will I cause the [a]good and the bad to be gathered; and the good will I preserve unto myself, and the bad will I cast away into its own place. And then cometh the [b]season and the end; and my vineyard will I cause to be [c]burned with [d]fire.

CHAPTER 6

The Lord shall recover Israel in the last days—Then the world shall be burned with fire—Men must follow Christ to avoid the lake of fire and brimstone.

AND now, behold, my brethren, as I said unto you that I would prophesy, behold, this is my prophecy—that the things which this prophet [a]Zenos spake, concerning the house of Israel, in the which he likened them unto a tame [b]olive-tree, must surely come to pass.

2 And the day that he shall set his hand again the second time to [a]recover his people, is the day, yea, even the last time, that the [b]servants of the Lord shall go forth in his [c]power, to [d]nourish and prune his [e]vineyard; and after that the [f]end soon cometh.

3 And how [a]blessed are they who have labored [b]diligently in his vineyard; and how [c]cursed are they who shall be cast out into their own place! And the [d]world shall be [e]burned with fire.

4 And how merciful is our God unto us, for he remembereth the house of [a]Israel, both roots and branches; and he stretches forth his [b]hands unto them all the day long; and they are a [c]stiffnecked and a gainsaying people; but as many as will not harden their hearts shall be saved in the kingdom of God.

5 Wherefore, my beloved brethren, I beseech of you in words of soberness that ye would repent, and come with full purpose of heart, and [a]cleave unto God as he cleaveth unto you. And while his [b]arm of mercy is extended towards you in

75b 1 Ne. 13: 37; D&C
      21: 9.
   c TG Israel, Restoration
      of.
   d D&C 6: 31; 18: 15
      (15–16).
76a 1 Ne. 22: 26.
77a D&C 86: 7.
   b Rev. 20: 3 (3–10);
      D&C 29: 22; 43: 31
      (30–31); 88: 111
      (110–112).
   c TG World, End of.
   d Joel 1: 19 (19–20);
      2 Ne. 6: 15 (14–15);
      Jacob 6: 3.
6 1a Jacob 5: 1; Alma
      33: 13 (13–15).
   TG Scriptures, Lost.

   b Rom. 11: 21 (1–36);
      1 Ne. 10: 12; Jacob
      5: 3 (3–77).
2a 1 Ne. 22: 12 (10–12);
      D&C 110: 11; 137: 6.
   TG Israel, Gathering of;
      Israel, Restoration of.
   b Jacob 5: 61.
   c 1 Ne. 14: 1, 14.
   d Jacob 5: 71; D&C
      101: 56.
   e Jer. 12: 10; D&C
      138: 56. TG Vineyard
      of the Lord.
   f 2 Ne. 30: 10; Jacob
      5: 29; D&C 43: 17
      (17–20, 28).
3a Jacob 5: 71.
   b TG Diligence;

   Perseverance.
   c D&C 41: 1.
   d TG World.
   e Isa. 24: 6; 2 Ne. 27: 2;
      3 Ne. 25: 1; Jacob
      5: 77. TG World, End of.
4a 2 Sam. 7: 24.
   b Neh. 9: 19 (18–26);
      2 Ne. 19: 17 (17–21);
      28: 32; Jacob 5: 47.
   c TG Stiffneckedness.
5a Deut. 10: 20; Josh.
      23: 8; 2 Kgs. 18: 6;
      Hel. 4: 25; D&C 11: 19.
   b Isa. 59: 16; 2 Ne.
      1: 15; Alma 5: 33;
      3 Ne. 9: 14.

[Between 544 and 421 B.C.]

the light of the day, harden not your hearts.

6 Yea, today, if ye will hear his voice, harden not your hearts; for why will ye ^adie?

7 For behold, after ye have been nourished by the good ^aword of God all the day long, will ye bring forth evil fruit, that ye must be ^bhewn down and cast into the fire?

8 Behold, will ye reject these words? Will ye reject the words of the ^aprophets; and will ye reject all the words which have been spoken concerning Christ, after so many have spoken concerning him; and ^bdeny the good word of Christ, and the power of God, and the ^cgift of the Holy Ghost, and quench the Holy Spirit, and make a ^dmock of the great plan of redemption, which hath been laid for you?

9 Know ye not that if ye will do these things, that the power of the redemption and the resurrection, which is in Christ, will bring you to stand with ^ashame and ^bawful ^cguilt before the bar of God?

10 And according to the power of ^ajustice, for justice cannot be denied, ye must go away into that ^blake of fire and brimstone, whose flames are unquenchable, and whose smoke ascendeth up forever and ever, which lake of fire and brimstone is ^cendless ^dtorment.

11 O then, my beloved brethren, repent ye, and enter in at the ^astrait gate, and ^bcontinue in the way which is narrow, until ye shall obtain eternal life.

12 O be ^awise; what can I say more?

13 Finally, I bid you farewell, until I shall meet you before the ^apleasing bar of God, which bar striketh the wicked with ^bawful dread and fear. Amen.

CHAPTER 7

Sherem denies Christ, contends with Jacob, demands a sign, and is smitten of God—All of the prophets have spoken of Christ and his atonement—The Nephites lived out their days as wanderers, born in tribulation, and hated by the Lamanites.

AND now it came to pass after some years had passed away, there came a man among the people of Nephi, whose name was ^aSherem.

2 And it came to pass that he began to preach among the people, and to declare unto them that there should be ^ano Christ. And he preached many things which were flattering unto the people; and this he did that he might ^boverthrow the doctrine of Christ.

3 And he labored diligently that he might lead away the hearts of the people, insomuch that he did lead away many hearts; and he knowing that I, Jacob, had faith in Christ who should come, he sought much opportunity that he might come unto me.

4 And he was ^alearned, that he had a perfect knowledge of the language of the people; wherefore, he could use much ^bflattery, and much power of speech, according to the ^cpower of the devil.

5 And he had hope to shake me from the faith, notwithstanding the many ^arevelations and the many things which I had seen concerning

---

6a Ezek. 18:28(26–28, 32).
7a Ps. 119:28.
  b Alma 5:52; 3 Ne. 27:11 (11–12).
8a Jer. 26:5.
  b TG Holy Ghost, Loss of.
  c TG Holy Ghost, Gift of.
  d TG Sacrilege.
9a TG Shame.
  b Jacob 7:19; Mosiah 15:26.
  c TG Guilt; Judgment, The Last.

10a TG God, Justice of; Justice.
  b Rev. 19:20; 2 Ne. 28:23; Mosiah 3:27. TG Hell.
  c Mosiah 2:33; D&C 19:11 (10–12).
  d TG Damnation.
11a 2 Ne. 9:41.
  b 2 Ne. 31:15. TG Commitment.
12a Matt. 10:16; Morm. 9:28.

13a Moro. 10:34.
  b Alma 40:14.
7 1a TG False Prophets.
  2a Alma 21:8; 30:12 (12, 22).
  b TG False Doctrine.
  4a TG Learning.
  b TG Flattery.
  c TG False Priesthoods.
  5a 2 Ne. 10:3; 11:3; Jacob 2:11.

[Between 544 and 421 B.C.]

these things; for I truly had seen [b]angels, and they had ministered unto me. And also, I had [c]heard the voice of the Lord speaking unto me in very word, from time to time; wherefore, I could not be shaken.

6 And it came to pass that he came unto me, and on this wise did he speak unto me, saying: Brother Jacob, I have sought much opportunity that I might speak unto you; for I have heard and also know that thou goest about much, preaching that which ye call the [a]gospel, or the doctrine of Christ.

7 And ye have led away much of this people that they pervert the right way of God, and [a]keep not the law of Moses which is the right way; and convert the law of Moses into the worship of a being which ye say shall come many hundred years hence. And now behold, I, Sherem, declare unto you that this is [b]blasphemy; for no man knoweth of such things; for he cannot [c]tell of things to come. And after this manner did Sherem contend against me.

8 But behold, the Lord God poured in his [a]Spirit into my soul, insomuch that I did [b]confound him in all his words.

9 And I said unto him: Deniest thou the Christ who shall come? And he said: If there should be a Christ, I would not deny him; but I know that there is no Christ, neither has been, nor ever will be.

10 And I said unto him: Believest thou the scriptures? And he said, Yea.

11 And I said unto him: Then ye do not understand them; for they truly testify of Christ. Behold, I say unto you that none of the [a]prophets have written, nor [b]prophesied, save they have spoken concerning this Christ.

12 And this is not all—it has been made manifest unto me, for I have heard and seen; and it also has been made manifest unto me by the [a]power of the Holy Ghost; wherefore, I know if there should be no atonement made all mankind must be [b]lost.

13 And it came to pass that he said unto me: Show me a [a]sign by this power of the Holy Ghost, in the which ye know so much.

14 And I said unto him: What am I that I should [a]tempt God to show unto thee a sign in the thing which thou knowest to be [b]true? Yet thou wilt deny it, because thou art of the [c]devil. Nevertheless, not my will be done; but if God shall smite thee, let that be a [d]sign unto thee that he has power, both in heaven and in earth; and also, that Christ shall come. And thy will, O Lord, be done, and not mine.

15 And it came to pass that when I, Jacob, had spoken these words, the power of the Lord came upon him, insomuch that he fell to the earth. And it came to pass that he was nourished for the space of many days.

16 And it came to pass that he said unto the people: Gather together on the morrow, for I shall die; wherefore, I desire to speak unto the people before I shall die.

17 And it came to pass that on the morrow the multitude were gathered together; and he spake plainly unto them and denied the things which he had taught them, and confessed the Christ, and the power

5b 2 Ne. 2:4.
  c Ex. 19:9 (9–13).
6a 2 Ne. 31:2.
7a Jacob 4:5.
  b TG Blasphemy.
  c Alma 30:13.
8a TG God, Spirit of;
    Holy Ghost, Mission of.
  b Ps. 97:7.
    TG Confound.
11a 1 Ne. 10:5; 3 Ne.

20:24 (23–24).
  TG Jesus Christ,
    Prophecies about.
  b 1 Pet. 1:11; Rev.
    19:10; Jacob 4:4;
    Mosiah 13:33 (33–35);
    D&C 20:26.
12a TG Holy Ghost, Gifts
    of.
  b 2 Ne. 2:21 (10–30).
13a John 6:30; Alma

30:43 (43–60); D&C
    46:9 (8–9). TG Sign
    Seekers.
14a TG Test, Try, Prove.
  b Mosiah 12:30; Alma
    30:42 (41–42).
  c Alma 30:53.
  d Num. 26:10; D&C
    124:53 (50–53).

[Between 544 and 421 B.C.]

of the Holy Ghost, and the ministering of angels.

18 And he spake plainly unto them, that he had been [a]deceived by the power of the [b]devil. And he spake of hell, and of [c]eternity, and of eternal [d]punishment.

19 And he said: I [a]fear lest I have committed the [b]unpardonable sin, for I have lied unto God; for I denied the Christ, and said that I believed the scriptures; and they truly testify of him. And because I have thus lied unto God I greatly fear lest my case shall be [c]awful; but I confess unto God.

20 And it came to pass that when he had said these words he could say no more, and he [a]gave up the [b]ghost.

21 And when the multitude had witnessed that he spake these things as he was about to give up the ghost, they were astonished exceedingly; insomuch that the power of God came down upon them, and they were [a]overcome that they fell to the earth.

22 Now, this thing was pleasing unto me, Jacob, for I had requested it of my Father who was in heaven; for he had heard my cry and answered my prayer.

23 And it came to pass that peace and the [a]love of God was restored again among the people; and they [b]searched the scriptures, and hearkened no more to the words of this wicked man.

24 And it came to pass that many means were devised to [a]reclaim and restore the Lamanites to the knowledge of the truth; but it all was [b]vain, for they delighted in [c]wars and [d]bloodshed, and they had an eternal [e]hatred against us, their brethren. And they sought by the power of their arms to destroy us continually.

25 Wherefore, the people of Nephi did fortify against them with their arms, and with all their might, trusting in the God and [a]rock of their salvation; wherefore, they became as yet, conquerors of their enemies.

26 And it came to pass that I, Jacob, began to be old; and the record of this people being kept on the [a]other plates of Nephi, wherefore, I conclude this record, declaring that I have written according to the best of my knowledge, by saying that the time passed away with us, and also our [b]lives passed away like as it were unto us a [c]dream, we being a [d]lonesome and a solemn people, [e]wanderers, cast out from Jerusalem, born in tribulation, in a wilderness, and hated of our brethren, which caused wars and contentions; wherefore, we did mourn out our days.

27 And I, Jacob, saw that I must soon go down to my grave; wherefore, I said unto my son [a]Enos: Take these [b]plates. And I told him the things which my brother Nephi had [c]commanded me, and he promised obedience unto the commands. And I make an end of my writing upon these plates, which writing has been [d]small; and to the reader I bid farewell, hoping that many of my brethren may read my words. Brethren, adieu.

18a Gal. 3:1 (1–4); Alma 30:53 (53, 60).
  b TG Deceit; Devil.
  c TG Eternity.
  d TG Punishment.
19a TG Despair.
  b TG Holy Ghost, Unpardonable Sin against; Sons of Perdition.
  c Jacob 6:9; Mosiah 15:26.
20a Jer. 28:16 (15–17); Alma 30:59 (12–60).
  b Gen. 49:33; Hel.

    14:21.
21a Alma 19:6 (1–36).
23a TG God, Love of.
  b Alma 17:2.
    TG Scriptures, Study of.
24a Enos 1:20.
  b Enos 1:14.
  c Mosiah 1:5; 10:12 (11–18); Alma 3:8; 9:16; D&C 93:39.
  d Jarom 1:6; Alma 26:24 (23–25).
  e 2 Ne. 5:1 (1–3); Mosiah 28:2.
    TG Malice.

25a TG Rock.
26a 1 Ne. 19:1 (1–6); Jarom 1:14 (1, 14–15).
  b James 4:14.
  c 1 Chr. 29:15; Ps. 144:4.
  d Alma 13:23.
  e Alma 26:36.
27a Enos 1:1.
  b Omni 1:3.
  c Jacob 1:1 (1–4).
  d 1 Ne. 6:3 (1–6); Jarom 1:2 (2, 14).

[Between 544 and 421 B.C.]

THE BOOK OF ENOS

Enos prays mightily and gains a remission of his sins—The voice of the Lord comes into his mind promising salvation for the Lamanites in a future day—Nephites sought to reclaim the Lamanites in their day—Enos rejoices in his Redeemer.

BEHOLD, it came to pass that I, *a*Enos, knowing my father that *b*he was a just man—for he *c*taught me in his language, and also in the *d*nurture and admonition of the Lord—and blessed be the name of my God for it—

2 And I will tell you of the *a*wrestle which I had before God, before I received a *b*remission of my sins.

3 Behold, I went to hunt beasts in the forests; and the words which I had often heard my father speak concerning eternal life, and the *a*joy of the saints, *b*sunk deep into my heart.

4 And my soul *a*hungered; and I *b*kneeled down before my Maker, and I *c*cried unto him in mighty *d*prayer and supplication for mine own soul; and all the day long did I cry unto him; yea, and when the night came I did still raise my voice high that it reached the heavens.

5 And there came a *a*voice unto me, saying: Enos, thy sins are *b*forgiven thee, and thou shalt be blessed.

6 And I, Enos, knew that God *a*could not lie; wherefore, my guilt was swept away.

7 And I said: Lord, how is it done?

8 And he said unto me: *a*Because of thy *b*faith in Christ, whom thou hast never before heard nor seen. And many years pass away before he shall manifest himself in the flesh; wherefore, go to, thy faith hath made thee *c*whole.

9 Now, it came to pass that when I had heard these words I began to feel a *a*desire for the *b*welfare of my brethren, the Nephites; wherefore, I did *c*pour out my whole soul unto God for them.

10 And while I was thus struggling in the spirit, behold, the voice of the Lord came into my *a*mind again, saying: I will visit thy brethren according to their diligence in keeping my commandments. I have *b*given unto them this land, and it is a holy land; and I *c*curse it not save it be for the cause of iniquity; wherefore, I will visit thy brethren according as I have said; and their *d*transgressions will I bring down with sorrow upon their own heads.

11 And after I, Enos, had heard these words, my *a*faith began to be *b*unshaken in the Lord; and I *c*prayed unto him with many long

---

1 1*a* Jacob 7 : 27.
  b 2 Ne. 2 : 3 (2–4).
  c 1 Ne. 1 : 1; Mosiah 1 : 2.
  d Eph. 6 : 4.
2*a* Gen. 32 : 24 (24–32);
    Alma 8 : 10.
    TG Repentance.
  b TG Remission of Sins.
3*a* TG Joy.
  b 1 Ne. 10 : 17 (17–19);
    Alma 36 : 17.
    TG Teachable.
4*a* 2 Ne. 9 : 51; 3 Ne. 12 : 6.
    TG Meditation;
    Motivations.
  b TG Reverence.

  c Ps. 138 : 3.
    TG Perseverance.
  d TG Prayer.
5*a* TG Revelation.
  b TG Forgiveness.
6*a* TG God, the Standard
    of Righteousness.
8*a* Ether 3 : 13 (12–13).
  b TG Faith.
  c Matt. 9 : 22.
    TG Man, New,
    Spiritually Reborn;
    Steadfastness.
9*a* 1 Ne. 8 : 12; Alma
    36 : 24.
  b Alma 19 : 29.

    TG Benevolence.
  c Num. 21 : 7; 1 Sam.
    1 : 15; 7 : 5; Jer. 42 : 4;
    2 Ne. 33 : 3; Alma
    34 : 26 (26–27).
10*a* TG Inspiration; Mind.
  b 1 Ne. 2 : 20.
  c Gen. 8 : 21 (20–22);
    Ether 2 : 9 (7–12).
  d TG Transgression.
11*a* TG Faith.
  b TG Steadfastness.
  c Gen. 20 : 7; 1 Sam. 7 : 5;
    2 Ne. 33 : 3; W of M
    1 : 8.

[Between 544 and 421 B.C.]

[d]strugglings for my brethren, the Lamanites.

12 And it came to pass that after I had [a]prayed and labored with all diligence, the Lord said unto me: I will grant unto thee according to thy [b]desires, because of thy faith.

13 And now behold, this was the desire which I desired of him—that if it should so be, that my people, the Nephites, should fall into transgression, and by any means be [a]destroyed, and the Lamanites should not be [b]destroyed, that the Lord God would [c]preserve a record of my people, the Nephites; even if it so be by the power of his holy arm, that it might be [d]brought forth at some future day unto the Lamanites, that, perhaps, they might be [e]brought unto salvation—

14 For at the present our strugglings were [a]vain in restoring them to the true faith. And they swore in their wrath that, if it were possible, they would [b]destroy our records and us, and also all the traditions of our fathers.

15 Wherefore, I knowing that the Lord God was able to [a]preserve our records, I cried unto him continually, for he had said unto me: Whatsoever thing ye shall ask in faith, believing that ye shall receive in the name of Christ, ye shall receive it.

16 And I had faith, and I did cry unto God that he would [a]preserve the [b]records; and he covenanted with me that he would [c]bring [d]them forth unto the Lamanites in his own due time.

17 And I, Enos, [a]knew it would be according to the covenant which he had made; wherefore my soul did rest.

18 And the Lord said unto me: Thy fathers have also required of me this thing; and it shall be done unto them according to their faith; for their faith was like unto thine.

19 And now it came to pass that I, Enos, went about among the people of Nephi, prophesying of things to come, and testifying of the things which I had heard and seen.

20 And I bear record that the people of Nephi did seek diligently to [a]restore the Lamanites unto the true faith in God. But our [b]labors were vain; their [c]hatred was fixed, and they were led by their evil nature that they became wild, and ferocious, and a [d]blood-thirsty people, full of [e]idolatry and [f]filthiness; feeding upon beasts of prey; dwelling in [g]tents, and wandering about in the wilderness with a short skin girdle about their loins and their heads shaven; and their skill was in the [h]bow, and in the cimeter, and the ax. And many of them did eat nothing save it was raw meat; and they were continually seeking to destroy us.

21 And it came to pass that the people of Nephi did till the land, and [a]raise all manner of grain, and of fruit, and [b]flocks of herds, and flocks of all manner of cattle of every kind, and goats, and wild goats, and also many horses.

22 And there were exceedingly

11d Eph. 6: 18.
12a Morm. 5: 21; 8: 25 (24–26); 9: 36 (36–37).
  b Ps. 37: 4; 1 Ne. 7: 12; Hel. 10: 5.
13a 1 Ne. 15: 5; Morm. 6: 1.
  b Lev. 26: 44.
  c W of M 1: 7 (6–11); Alma 37: 2.
  d 2 Ne. 3: 15; Jacob 1: 13; Alma 37: 19; Morm. 7: 9 (8–10); Ether 12: 22; D&C 3: 18.
  e Alma 9: 17; Hel. 15: 16.

14a Jacob 7: 24.
  b 2 Ne. 26: 17; Morm. 6: 6.
15a TG Scriptures, Preservation of.
16a 3 Ne. 5: 14 (13–15); D&C 3: 19 (16–20); 10: 47 (46–50).
  b TG Book of Mormon.
  c 2 Ne. 25: 8; 27: 6; Morm. 5: 12.
  d 1 Ne. 19: 19. TG Israel, Restoration of.
17a TG Trust in God.

20a Jacob 7: 24.
  b Moro. 9: 6.
  c 2 Ne. 5: 1. TG Hate.
  d Jarom 1: 6.
  e Mosiah 9: 12. TG Idolatry.
  f TG Filthiness.
  g Gen. 25: 27.
  h Mosiah 10: 8; Alma 3: 5 (4–5); 43: 20 (18–21).
21a 1 Ne. 8: 1; Mosiah 9: 9.
  b 1 Ne. 18: 25; Ether 9: 19 (18–19).

[Between 544 and 421 B.C.]

many [a]prophets among us. And the people were a [b]stiffnecked people, hard to understand.

23 And there was nothing save it was exceeding [a]harshness, [b]preaching and prophesying of wars, and contentions, and destructions, and continually [c]reminding them of death, and the duration of eternity, and the judgments and the power of God, and all these things—stirring them up [d]continually to keep them in the fear of the Lord. I say there was nothing short of these things, and exceedingly great plainness of speech, would keep them from going down speedily to destruction. And after this manner do I write concerning them.

24 And I saw [a]wars between the Nephites and Lamanites in the course of my days.

25 And it came to pass that I began to be old, *and an hundred and seventy and nine years had passed away from the time that our father Lehi [a]left Jerusalem.

26 And I saw that I [a]must soon go down to my grave, having been wrought upon by the power of God that I must preach and prophesy unto this people, and declare the word according to the truth which is in Christ. And I have declared it in all my days, and have rejoiced in it above that of the world.

27 And I soon go to the place of my [a]rest, which is with my Redeemer; for I know that in him I shall [b]rest. And I rejoice in the day when my [c]mortal shall put on [d]immortality, and shall stand before him; then shall I see his face with pleasure, and he will say unto me: Come unto me, ye blessed, there is a place prepared for you in the [e]mansions of my Father. Amen.

THE BOOK OF JAROM

The Nephites keep the law of Moses, look forward to the coming of Christ, and prosper in the land—Many prophets labor to keep them in the way of truth.

NOW behold, I, Jarom, write a few words according to the commandment of my father, Enos, that our [a]genealogy may be kept.

2 And as [a]these plates are [b]small, and as these things are [c]written for the intent of the benefit of our brethren the [d]Lamanites, wherefore, it must needs be that I write a little; but I shall not write the things of my prophesying, nor of my revelations. For what could I write more than my fathers have written? For have not they revealed the plan of salvation? I say unto you, Yea; and this sufficeth me.

3 Behold, it is expedient that much

22a W of M 1:16.
  b Jarom 1:3.
23a 1 Ne. 16:2 (1–3);
    2 Ne. 33:5; W of M
    1:17.
  b TG Preaching.
  c Hel. 12:3.
  d Jarom 1:12; Alma
    4:19; 31:5.
24a 1 Ne. 12:2 (2–3);
    Morm. 8:7 (7–8).
  TG War.

25a 1 Ne. 2:2 (2–4).
26a 1 Cor. 9:16; Ether
    12:2. TG Duty.
27a TG Rest.
  b 2 Ne. 33:6.
  c TG Mortality.
  d TG Immortality.
  e Ps. 65:4; John
    14:2 (2–3); Ether
    12:32 (32–34); D&C
    72:4; 98:18.

[JAROM]
1 1a 1 Ne. 3:12; 5:14.
  2a Jacob 3:14 (13–14);
    Omni 1:1.
  b 1 Ne. 6:3 (1–6);
    Jacob 7:27.
  c TG Scriptures, Writing of.
  d 2 Ne. 27:6; Morm.
    5:12 (12–13).

should be done among this people, because of the hardness of their hearts, and the deafness of their ears, and the blindness of their minds, and the "stiffness of their necks; nevertheless, God is exceedingly merciful unto them, and has not as yet *b*swept them off from the face of the land.

4 And there are many among us who have many "revelations, for they are not all *b*stiffnecked. And as many as are not stiffnecked and have faith, have *c*communion with the Holy Spirit, which maketh manifest unto the children of men, according to their faith.

5 And now, behold, *two hundred years had passed away, and the people of Nephi had waxed strong in the land. They observed to "keep the law of Moses and the *b*sabbath day holy unto the Lord. And they *c*profaned not; neither did they *d*blaspheme. And the *e*laws of the land were exceedingly strict.

6 And they were scattered upon "much of the face of the land, and the Lamanites also. And they were exceedingly more *b*numerous than were they of the Nephites; and they loved *c*murder and would drink the *d*blood of beasts.

7 And it came to pass that they came many times against us, the Nephites, to battle. But our "kings and our *b*leaders were mighty men in the faith of the Lord; and they taught the people the ways of the Lord; wherefore, we withstood the Lamanites and swept them away out

of *c*our lands, and began to fortify our cities, or whatsoever place of our inheritance.

8 And we multiplied exceedingly, and spread upon the face of the land, and became exceedingly rich in "gold, and in silver, and in precious things, and in fine *b*workmanship of wood, in buildings, and in *c*machinery, and also in iron and copper, and brass and steel, making all manner of tools of every kind to till the ground, and *d*weapons of war—yea, the sharp pointed arrow, and the quiver, and the dart, and the javelin, and all preparations for war.

9 And thus being prepared to meet the Lamanites, they did not prosper against us. But the word of the Lord was verified, which he spake unto our fathers, saying that: "Inasmuch as ye will keep my commandments ye shall *b*prosper in the land.

10 And it came to pass that the prophets of the Lord did threaten the people of Nephi, according to the word of God, that if they did not keep the commandments, but should fall into transgression, they should be "destroyed from off the face of the land.

11 Wherefore, the prophets, and the priests, and the "teachers, did labor diligently, exhorting the people to *b*diligence; teaching the *c*law of Moses, and the intent for which it was given; persuading them to *d*look forward unto the Messiah, and believe in him to come *e*as though he already

3a Enos 1: 22 (22–23).
 b Ether 2: 8 (8–10).
4a Alma 26: 22; Hel. 11: 23; D&C 107:19(18–19).
 b TG Stiffneckedness.
 c TG Holy Ghost; Revelation.
5a 2 Ne. 25: 24; Mosiah 2: 3; Alma 30: 3; 34: 14 (13–14).
 b Ex. 35: 2. TG Sabbath.
 c TG Profanity.
 d TG Blasphemy.
 e Alma 1: 1.

6a Hel. 11: 20 (19–20).
 b Alma 2: 27.
 c Jacob 7: 24; Enos 1: 20; Alma 26: 24 (23–25).
 d TG Blood, Eating of.
7a 2 Ne. 5: 18; 6: 2; Jacob 1: 9 (9, 11, 15); Mosiah 1: 10.
 b TG Leadership.
 c W of M 1: 14.
8a 2 Ne. 5: 15.
 b TG Art.
 c TG Skill.
 d 2 Ne. 5: 14;

Mosiah 10: 8.
9a 2 Ne. 1: 20; Omni 1: 6.
 b Josh. 1: 7; Ps. 122: 6.
10a 1 Ne. 12: 19 (19–20); Omni 1: 5.
11a TG Teacher.
 b TG Diligence.
 c Jacob 4: 5; Alma 25: 15 (15–16).
 d 2 Ne. 11: 4; Ether 12: 19 (18–19).
 e 2 Ne. 25: 26 (24–27); Mosiah 3: 13; 16: 6.

was. And after this manner did they teach them.

12 And it came to pass that by so doing they kept them from being ᵃdestroyed upon the face of the land; for they did ᵇprick their hearts with the word, ᶜcontinually stirring them up unto repentance.

13 And it came to pass that *two hundred and thirty and eight years had passed away—after the manner of wars, and ᵃcontentions, and dissensions, for the space of ᵇmuch of the time.

14 And I, Jarom, do not write more, for the plates are ᵃsmall. But behold, my brethren, ye can go to the ᵇother plates of Nephi; for behold, upon them the records of our wars are engraven, according to the writings of the ᶜkings, or those which they caused to be written.

15 And I deliver these plates into the hands of my son Omni, that they may be kept according to the ᵃcommandments of my fathers.

THE BOOK OF OMNI

Omni, Amaron, Chemish, Abinadom, and Amaleki, each in turn, keep the records—Mosiah discovers the people of Zarahemla who came from Jerusalem in the days of Zedekiah—He is made king over them—The Mulekites had discovered Coriantumr, the last of the Jaredites—King Benjamin succeeds Mosiah—Men should offer their souls as an offering to Christ.

BEHOLD, it came to pass that I, Omni, being commanded by my father, Jarom, that I should write somewhat upon ᵃthese plates, to preserve our genealogy—

2 Wherefore, in my days, I would that ye should know that I fought much with the sword to preserve my people, the Nephites, from falling into the hands of their enemies, the Lamanites. But behold, I of myself ᵃam a wicked man, and I have not kept the statutes and the commandments of the Lord as I ought to have done.

3 And it came to pass that †two hundred and seventy and six years had passed away, and we had many seasons of peace; and we had many ᵃseasons of serious war and bloodshed. Yea, and in fine, ‡two hundred and eighty and two years had passed away, and I had kept these plates according to the ᵇcommandments of my ᶜfathers; and I ᵈconferred them upon my son Amaron. And I make an end.

4 And now I, Amaron, write the things whatsoever I write, which are few, in the book of my father.

5 Behold, it came to pass that §three hundred and twenty years had passed away, and the more wicked part of the Nephites were ᵃdestroyed.

6 For the Lord would not suffer, after he had led them out of the land of Jerusalem and kept and preserved them from falling into the hands of their enemies, yea, he would not suffer that the words should not be

12a Ether 2: 10 (8–10).
  b Alma 31: 5.
  c Enos 1: 23.
13a TG Contention.
  b Omni 1: 3.
14a Jacob 4: 1 (1–2);
    Omni 1: 30.
  b Jacob 7: 26 (26–27);
    W of M 1: 3.

  c Omni 1: 11; W of M
    1: 10.
15a Jacob 1:1 (1–4);
    Omni 1: 3.

[OMNI]
1 1a Jarom 1: 2 (1–2);
    Omni 1: 9.
 2a TG Confession;
    Honesty; Humility.

3a Jarom 1: 13.
  b Jacob 1: 1 (1–4); 7: 27;
    Jarom 1: 15 (1–2, 15).
  c TG Patriarch.
  d TG Delegation of
    Responsibility.
5a Jarom 1: 10.

[*361 B.C. †323 B.C.
‡317 B.C. §279 B.C.]

verified, which he spake unto our fathers, saying that: [a]Inasmuch as ye will not keep my commandments ye shall not [b]prosper in the land.

7 Wherefore, the Lord did visit them in great judgment; nevertheless, he did spare the righteous that they should not perish, but did deliver them out of the hands of their enemies.

8 And it came to pass that I did deliver the plates unto my brother Chemish.

9 Now I, Chemish, write what few things I write, in the same book with my brother; for behold, I saw the last which he wrote, that he wrote it with his own hand; and he wrote it in the day that he delivered them unto me. And after this manner we keep the [a]records, for it is according to the commandments of our fathers. And I make an end.

10 Behold, I, Abinadom, am the son of Chemish. Behold, it came to pass that I saw much war and contention between my people, the Nephites, and the Lamanites; and I, with my own sword, have taken the lives of many of the Lamanites in the defence of my brethren.

11 And behold, the [a]record of this people is engraven upon plates which is had by the [b]kings, according to the generations; and I know of no revelation save that which has been written, neither prophecy; wherefore, that which is sufficient is written. And I make an end.

12 Behold, I am Amaleki, the son of Abinadom. Behold, I will speak unto you somewhat concerning [a]Mosiah, who was made king over the [b]land of Zarahemla; for behold, he being [c]warned of the Lord that

he should [d]flee out of the [e]land of [f]Nephi, and as many as would hearken unto the voice of the Lord should also [g]depart out of the land with him, into the wilderness—

13 And it came to pass that he did according as the Lord had commanded him. And they departed out of the land into the wilderness, as many as would hearken unto the voice of the Lord; and they were led by many preachings and prophesyings. And they were admonished continually by the word of God; and they were led by the power of his [a]arm, through the wilderness until they came down into the land which is called the [b]land of Zarahemla.

14 And they discovered a [a]people, who were called the people of Zarahemla. Now, there was great rejoicing among the people of Zarahemla; and also Zarahemla did rejoice exceedingly, because the Lord had sent the people of Mosiah with the [b]plates of brass which contained the record of the Jews.

15 Behold, it came to pass that Mosiah discovered that the people of [a]Zarahemla came out from Jerusalem at the time that [b]Zedekiah, king of Judah, was carried away captive into Babylon.

16 And they [a]journeyed in the wilderness, and were brought by the hand of the Lord across the great waters, into the land where Mosiah discovered them; and they had dwelt there from that time forth.

17 And at the time that Mosiah discovered them, they had become exceedingly numerous. Nevertheless, they had had many wars and serious contentions, and had fallen by the sword from time to time; and

6a Jarom 1:9; Mosiah
    1:7.
  b Deut. 28:29.
9a Omni 1:1. TG Record
    Keeping.
11a W of M 1:10.
  b Jarom 1:14.
12a Omni 1:19.
  b Alma 4:1.
  c TG Warnings.

 d Mosiah 11:13.
 e Omni 1:27; W of M
    1:13.
 f 2 Ne. 5:8; Mosiah 7:6
    (6–7).
 g Jacob 3:4.
13a Isa. 33:2; Mosiah
    12:24.
  b Mosiah 1:1; 2:4.
14a Mosiah 1:10.

 b 1 Ne. 3:3 (3, 19–20);
    5:10 (10–22).
15a Ezek. 17:22 (22–23);
    Mosiah 25:2 (2–4).
  b Jer. 39:4 (1–10);
    52:11 (9–11); Hel.
    8:21.
16a 1 Ne. 16:9.

[Between 279 and 130 B.C.]

their *language had become corrupted; and they had brought no *records with them; and they denied the being of their Creator; and Mosiah, nor the people of Mosiah, could understand them.

18 But it came to pass that Mosiah caused that they should be taught in his *language. And it came to pass that after they were taught in the language of Mosiah, Zarahemla gave a genealogy of his fathers, according to his memory; and they are written, but *not in these plates.

19 And it came to pass that the people of Zarahemla, and of Mosiah, did *unite together; and *Mosiah was appointed to be their king.

20 And it came to pass in the days of Mosiah, there was a large *stone brought unto him with engravings on it; and he did *interpret the engravings by the gift and power of God.

21 And they gave an account of one *Coriantumr, and the slain of his people. And Coriantumr was discovered by the people of Zarahemla; and he dwelt with them for the space of nine moons.

22 It also spake a few words concerning his fathers. And his first parents came out from the *tower, at the time the Lord *confounded the language of the people; and the severity of the Lord fell upon them according to his judgments, which are just; and their *bones lay scattered in the land northward.

23 Behold, I, Amaleki, was born in the days of Mosiah; and I have lived to see his death; and *Benjamin, *his son, reigneth in his stead.

24 And behold, I have seen, in the days of king Benjamin, a serious war and much bloodshed between the Nephites and the Lamanites. But behold, the Nephites did obtain much advantage over them; yea, insomuch that king Benjamin did drive them out of the land of Zarahemla.

25 And it came to pass that I began to be old; and, having no seed, and knowing king *Benjamin to be a just man before the Lord, wherefore, I shall *deliver up *these plates unto him, exhorting all men to come unto God, the Holy One of Israel, and believe in prophesying, and in revelations, and in the ministering of angels, and in the gift of speaking with tongues, and in the gift of interpreting languages, and in all things which are *good; for there is nothing which is good save it comes from the Lord: and that which is evil cometh from the devil.

26 And now, my beloved brethren, I would that ye should *come unto Christ, who is the Holy One of Israel, and partake of his salvation, and the power of his redemption. Yea, come unto him, and *offer your whole souls as an *offering unto him, and continue in *fasting and praying, and endure to the end; and as the Lord liveth ye will be saved.

27 And now I would speak somewhat concerning a certain *number who went up into the wilderness to *return to the *land of Nephi; for there was a large number who were desirous to possess the land of their inheritance.

28 Wherefore, they went up into

17a 1 Ne. 3:19.
   TG Language.
   b Mosiah 1:3 (2–6).
18a Mosiah 24:4.
   b 1 Ne. 9:4; W of M
   1:10.
19a Mosiah 25:13.
   b Omni 1:12.
20a Mosiah 21:28 (27–28);
   28:13.
   b Mosiah 8:13 (13–19);
   28:17. TG Urim and
   Thummim.

21a Ether 12:1 (1–2);
   13:20 (13–31); 15:32.
22a Ether 1:3 (1–6).
   b Gen. 11:7 (6–9);
   Mosiah 28:17; Ether
   1:33.
   c Mosiah 8:8 (8–12).
23a W of M 1:3.
   b Mosiah 2:11.
25a W of M 1:18 (17–18);
   Mosiah 29:13.
   b W of M 1:10.
   c 1 Ne. 10:1.

   d Alma 5:40; Ether
   4:12; Moro. 7:16
   (15–17).
26a Jacob 1:7; Alma 29:2.
   b TG Commitment;
   Self-sacrifice.
   c 3 Ne. 9:20.
   d TG Fasting.
27a Mosiah 9:3 (1–4).
   b Mosiah 7:1.
   c Omni 1:12.

[Between 279 and 130 B.C.]

the wilderness. And their leader being a strong and mighty man, and a stiffnecked man, wherefore he caused a contention among them; and they were [a]all slain, save fifty, in the wilderness, and they returned again to the land of Zarahemla.

29 And it came to pass that they also took others to a considerable number, and took their journey again into the wilderness.

30 And I, Amaleki, had a brother, who also went with them; and I have not since known concerning them. And I am about to lie down in my grave; and [a]these plates are full. And I make an end of my speaking.

THE WORDS OF MORMON

Mormon abridges their history onto the plates of Mormon—He inserts the plates of Nephi into the abridgment—King Benjamin establishes peace in the land.

AND now I, Mormon, being about to deliver up the [a]record which I have been making into the hands of my son Moroni, behold I have witnessed almost all the destruction of my people, the Nephites.

2 And it is [a]many hundred years after the coming of Christ *that I deliver these records into the hands of my son; and it supposeth me that he will witness the entire [b]destruction of my people. But may God grant that he may survive them, that he may write somewhat concerning them, and somewhat concerning Christ, that perhaps some day it may [c]profit them.

3 And now, I speak somewhat concerning that which I have written; for after I had made an [a]abridgment from the [b]plates of Nephi, down to the reign of this king Benjamin, of whom Amaleki spake, I searched among the [c]records which had been delivered into my hands, and I found these plates, which contained this small account of the prophets, from Jacob down to the reign of this king [d]Benjamin, and also many of the words of Nephi.

4 And the things which are upon these plates [a]pleasing me, because of the prophecies of the coming of Christ; and my fathers knowing that many of them have been fulfilled; yea, and I also know that as many things as have been [b]prophesied concerning us down to this day have been fulfilled, and as many as go beyond this day must surely come to pass—

5 Wherefore, I chose [a]these things, to finish my [b]record upon them, which remainder of my record I shall take from the [c]plates of Nephi; and I cannot write the [d]hundredth part of the things of my people.

6 But behold, I shall take these

28a Mosiah 9: 2 (1–4).
30a 1 Ne. 6: 3 (3–6);
   Jacob 4: 1 (1–2);
   Jarom 1: 14.

[WORDS OF MORMON]
1 1a 3 Ne. 5: 12 (9–12);
   Morm. 1: 4 (1–4);
   2: 17 (17–18); 8: 5
   (1, 4–5, 14).
 2a Morm. 6: 5 (5–6).
  b 1 Ne. 12: 19.

  c D&C 3: 19 (16–20).
 3a 1 Ne. 1: 17 (16–17);
   D&C 10: 44.
  b Jarom 1: 14; W of M
   1: 10; D&C 10: 38
   (38–40).
  c Mosiah 1: 6 (2–6);
   Hel. 3: 13 (13–15);
   Morm. 4: 23.
  d Omni 1: 23 (23–25).
 4a 1 Ne. 6: 5 (3–6).

  b TG Jesus Christ,
   Prophecies about.
 5a IE the things pleasing
   to him, mentioned in
   v. 4.
  b 3 Ne. 5: 17 (14–18);
   Morm. 1: 1.
  c 1 Ne. 9: 2.
  d Alma 13: 31; 3 Ne. 5: 8
   (8–11); 26: 6 (6–12).

[*About A.D. 385]

plates, which contain these prophesyings and revelations, and put them with the remainder of my record, for they are choice unto me; and I know they will be choice unto my brethren.

7 And I do this for a ªwise ᵇpurpose; for thus it whispereth me, according to the workings of the Spirit of the Lord which is in me. And now, I do not know all things; but the Lord ᶜknoweth all things which are to come; wherefore, he ᵈworketh in me to do according to his ᵉwill.

8 And my ªprayer to God is concerning my brethren, that they may once again come to the knowledge of God, yea, the redemption of Christ; that they may once again be a ᵇdelightsome people.

9 And now I, Mormon, *proceed to finish out my record, which I take from the plates of Nephi; and I make it according to the knowledge and the ªunderstanding which God has given me.

10 Wherefore, it came to pass that after Amaleki had ªdelivered up these plates into the hands of king Benjamin, he took them and put them with the ᵇother plates, which contained records which had been handed down by the ᶜkings, from generation to generation until the days of king Benjamin.

11 And they were handed down from king Benjamin, from generation to generation until they have fallen into ªmy hands. And I, Mormon, pray to God that they may be preserved from this time henceforth. And I know that they

will be preserved; for there are great things written upon them, out of which ᵇmy people and their brethren shall be ᶜjudged at the great and last day, according to the word of God which is written.

12 And now, concerning this king Benjamin—he had somewhat of contentions among his own people.

13 And it came to pass also that the armies of the Lamanites came down out of the ªland of Nephi, to battle against his people. But behold, king Benjamin gathered together his armies, and he did stand against them; and he did fight with the strength of his own arm, with the ᵇsword of Laban.

14 And in the ªstrength of the Lord they did contend against their enemies, until they had slain many thousands of the Lamanites. And it came to pass that they did contend against the Lamanites until they had driven them out of all the lands of their ᵇinheritance.

15 And it came to pass that after there had been false ªChrists, and their mouths had been shut, and they punished according to their crimes;

16 And after there had been ªfalse prophets, and false preachers and teachers among the people, and all these having been punished according to their crimes; and after there having been much contention and many dissensions away ᵇunto the Lamanites, behold, it came to pass that king Benjamin, with the assistance of the holy ᶜprophets who were among his people—

17 For behold, king Benjamin was

7a 1 Ne. 9: 5; 19: 3;
  Enos 1: 13 (13–18);
  Alma 37: 2; D&C 3:
  19 (9–20); 10: 34 (1–
  19, 30–47).
 b D&C 10: 40 (20–46).
 c TG God,
  Foreknowledge of;
  God, Intelligence of;
  God, Omniscience of.
 d 2 Ne. 27: 23.
 e TG God, Will of.
8a 2 Ne. 33: 3; Enos 1: 11

  (11–12); Moro. 9: 22.
 b 2 Ne. 30: 6.
9a TG Understanding.
10a Omni 1: 25 (25, 30).
 b 1 Ne. 9: 4; Omni 1: 11,
  18; W of M 1: 3;
  Mosiah 28: 11.
 c Jarom 1: 14.
11a 3 Ne. 5: 12 (8–12);
  Morm. 1: 4 (1–5).
 b Hel. 15: 3 (3–4).
 c 2 Ne. 25: 18; 29: 11;
  33: 14 (11, 14–15);

  3 Ne. 27: 25 (23–27);
  Ether 5: 4.
13a Omni 1: 12.
 b 1 Ne. 4: 9; 2 Ne. 5: 14;
  Jacob 1: 10; Mosiah
  1: 16; D&C 17: 1.
14a TG Strength.
 b Jarom 1: 7.
15a TG False Christs.
16a TG False Prophets.
 b Jacob 1: 14 (13–14).
 c Enos 1: 22.

[*About A.D. 385]

a *a*holy man, and he did reign over his people in righteousness; and there were many holy men in the land, and they did speak the word of God with *b*power and with authority; and they did use much *c*sharpness because of the stiffneckedness of the people—

18 Wherefore, with the help of these, king *a*Benjamin, by laboring with all the might of his body and the *b*faculty of his whole soul, and also the prophets, did once more establish peace in the land.

THE BOOK OF MOSIAH

CHAPTER 1

King Benjamin teaches his sons the language and prophecies of their fathers—Their religion and civilization have been preserved because of the records kept on the various plates—Mosiah is chosen as king and is given custody of the records and other things.

AND now there was no more contention in all the *a*land of Zarahemla, among all the people who belonged to king Benjamin, so that king Benjamin had continual peace all the remainder of his days.

2 And it came to pass that he had three *a*sons; and he called their names Mosiah, and Helorum, and Helaman. And he caused that they should be *b*taught in all the *c*language of his fathers, that thereby they might become men of understanding; and that they might know concerning the prophecies which had been spoken by the mouths of their fathers, which were delivered them by the hand of the Lord.

3 And he also taught them concerning the records which were engraven on the *a*plates of brass, saying: My sons, I would that ye should remember that were it not for these *b*plates, which contain these records and these commandments, we must have suffered in *c*ignorance, even at this present time, not knowing the mysteries of God.

4 For it were not possible that our father, Lehi, could have remembered all these things, to have taught them to his children, except it were for the help of these plates; for he having been taught in the *a*language of the Egyptians therefore he could read these engravings, and teach them to his children, that thereby they could teach them to their children, and so fulfilling the commandments of God, even down to this present time.

5 I say unto you, my sons, *a*were it not for these things, which have been kept and *b*preserved by the hand of God, that we might *c*read and understand of his *d*mysteries, and have his *e*commandments al-

17*a* Ex. 22:31; Alma 13:26; D&C 49:8; 107:29.
 b Alma 17:3 (2–3).
  TG God, Power of.
 c Enos 1:23; Moro. 9:4; D&C 121:43 (41–43).
18*a* Omni 1:25; Mosiah 29:13.
 b 1 Ne. 15:25.

[MOSIAH]
1 1*a* Omni 1:13;

Alma 2:15.
2*a* 1 Ne. 1:1; D&C 68:25 (25, 28).
 b Enos 1:1; Mosiah 4:15 (14–15).
 b Morm. 9:32.
3*a* 2 Ne. 5:12; Mosiah 1:16; 28:20.
 b 1 Ne. 3:19 (19–20); Omni 1:17.
 c Alma 37:8.
4*a* 1 Ne. 1:2; 3:19; Morm. 9:32 (32–33);

JS-H 1:64.
5*a* Alma 37:9.
 b TG Scriptures, Preservation of.
 c Deut. 6:6 (6–8); 2 Chr. 34:21; 1 Ne. 15:24 (23–24).
  TG Scriptures, Value of.
 d TG Mysteries of Godliness.
 e 1 Ne. 4:15.

[About 130 B.C.]

ways before our eyes, that even our fathers would have dwindled in unbelief, and we should have been like unto our brethren, the Lamanites, who know nothing concerning these things, or even do not believe them when they are taught them, because of the *traditions of their fathers, which are not correct.

6 O my sons, I would that ye should remember that these sayings are true, and also that these records are *true. And behold, also the plates of Nephi, which contain the records and the sayings of our fathers from the time they left Jerusalem until now, and they are true; and we can know of their surety because we have them before our eyes.

7 And now, my sons, I would that ye should remember to *search them diligently, that ye may profit thereby; and I would that ye should *keep the commandments of God, that ye may *prosper in the land according to the *promises which the Lord made unto our fathers.

8 And many more things did king Benjamin teach his sons, which are not written in this book.

9 And it came to pass that after king Benjamin had made an end of teaching his sons, that he waxed *old, and he saw that he must very soon go the way of all the earth; therefore, he thought it expedient that he should confer the kingdom upon one of his sons.

10 Therefore, *he had Mosiah brought before him; and these are the words which he spake unto him, saying: My son, I would that ye should make a proclamation throughout all this land among all this *people, or the people of Zarahemla, and the people of Mosiah who dwell in the land, that thereby they may be gathered together; for on the morrow I shall proclaim unto this my people out of mine own mouth that thou art a *king and a ruler over this people, whom the Lord our God hath given us.

11 And moreover, I shall give this people a *name, that thereby they may be distinguished above all the people which the Lord God hath brought out of the land of Jerusalem; and this I do because they have been a *diligent people in keeping the commandments of the Lord.

12 And I give unto them a name that never shall be blotted out, except it be through *transgression.

13 Yea, and moreover I say unto you, that if this highly favored people of the Lord should fall into *transgression, and become a wicked and an adulterous people, that the Lord will deliver them up, that thereby they become *weak like unto their brethren; and he will no more *preserve them by his matchless and marvelous power, as he has hitherto preserved our fathers.

14 For I say unto you, that if he had not extended his arm in the preservation of our fathers they must have fallen into the hands of the Lamanites, and become victims to their hatred.

15 And it came to pass that after king Benjamin had made an end of these sayings to his son, that he gave him *charge concerning all the affairs of the kingdom.

16 And moreover, he also gave him charge concerning the records which

5f Jacob 7:24; Mosiah 10:12 (11–17).
6a 1 Ne. 1:3; 14:30; 2 Ne. 25:20; Alma 3:12; Ether 5:3 (1–3).
7a TG Scriptures, Study of.
  b Lev. 25:18 (18–19); Mosiah 2:22; Alma 50:20 (20–22).
  c Josh. 1:7; Ps. 1:3
(2–3); 122:6; 1 Ne. 2:20.
  d Omni 1:6; Alma 9:13 (13–14).
9a TG Old Age.
10a Omni 1:14; Mosiah 27:35.
  b Gen. 41:43 (41–43); Jarom 1:7 (7,14); Mosiah 2:30.
11a Mosiah 5:8 (8–12).
TG Jesus Christ, Taking the Name of.
  b TG Diligence.
12a TG Transgression.
13a Heb. 6:6 (4–6).
  b Jer. 46:15 (15–17); Hel. 4:24 (24,26).
  c D&C 103:8.
15a 1 Kgs. 2:1; Ps. 72:1 (1–4).

[*About 124 B.C.]

were engraven on the [a]plates of brass; and also the plates of Nephi; and also, the [b]sword of Laban, and the [c]ball or director, which led our fathers through the wilderness, which was prepared by the hand of the Lord that thereby they might be led, every one according to the heed and diligence which they gave unto him.

17 Therefore, as they were [a]unfaithful they did not prosper nor progress in their journey, but were [b]driven back, and incurred the displeasure of God upon them; and therefore they were smitten with famine and sore [c]afflictions, to stir them up in [d]remembrance of their duty.

18 And now, it came to pass that Mosiah went and did as his father had commanded him, and proclaimed unto all the people who were in the land of Zarahemla that thereby they might gather themselves together, to go up to the [a]temple to hear the words which his father should speak unto them.

CHAPTER 2

King Benjamin addresses his people —He recounts the equity, fairness, and spirituality of his reign—He counsels them to serve their heavenly King— Those who rebel against God shall suffer anguish like unquenchable fire.

AND it came to pass that after Mosiah had done as his father had commanded him, and had made a proclamation throughout all the land, that the people [a]gathered themselves together throughout all the land, that they might go up to the [b]temple to [c]hear the [d]words which king Benjamin should speak unto them.

2 And there were a great number, even so many that they did not number them; for they had multiplied exceedingly and waxed great in the land.

3 And they also took of the [a]firstlings of their flocks, that they might offer [b]sacrifice and [c]burnt [d]offerings [e]according to the law of Moses;

4 And also that they might give thanks to the Lord their God, who had brought them out of the land of Jerusalem, and who had delivered them out of the hands of their enemies, and had [a]appointed just men to be their [b]teachers, and also a just man to be their king, who had established peace in the [c]land of Zarahemla, and who had taught them to [d]keep the commandments of God, that they might rejoice and be filled with [e]love towards God and all men.

5 And it came to pass that when they came up to the temple, they pitched their tents round about, every man according to his [a]family, consisting of his wife, and his sons, and his daughters, and their sons, and their daughters, from the eldest down to the youngest, every family being separate one from another.

6 And they pitched their tents round about the temple, every man having his [a]tent with the door thereof towards the temple, that thereby they might remain in their tents and hear the words which king Benjamin should speak unto them;

16a Mosiah 1:3.
  b Jacob 1:10; W of M
    1:13; D&C 17:1.
  c 2 Ne. 5:12.
17a TG Disobedience.
  b 1 Ne. 18:13 (12–13).
  c Lam. 1:5.
    TG Affliction.
  d Judg. 13:1; Hel. 12:3
    (2–3).
18a Ne. 5:16; Mosiah
    2:1.
2 1a TG Assembly for

Worship.
  b Mosiah 1:18.
  c 2 Chr. 34:30 (29–33).
  d Mosiah 26:1.
3a Gen. 4:4 (2–7); Ex.
    13:12 (12–13); Deut.
    12:6; Moses 5:20
    (5, 19–23).
  b Ezra 6:10. TG Sacrifice.
  c Lev. 1:3 (2–9); Deut.
    33:10.
  d Ezra 3:2 (2–5); 1 Ne.
    5:9.

  e 2 Ne. 25:24; Jarom
    1:5; Alma 30:3;
    34:14 (13–14).
4a TG Called of God.
  b Mosiah 18:18 (18–22).
  c Omni 1:13 (12–15).
  d John 15:10; D&C
    95:12.
  e Deut. 11:1. TG Love.
5a TG Family, Patriarchal.
6a Ex. 33:8 (8–10).

[About 124 B.C.]

7 For the multitude being so great that king Benjamin could not teach them all within the walls of the temple, therefore he caused a [a]tower to be erected, that thereby his people might hear the words which he should speak unto them.

8 And it came to pass that he began to speak to his people from the tower; and they could not all hear his words because of the greatness of the multitude; therefore he caused that the words which he spake should be written and sent forth among those that were not under the sound of his voice, that they might also receive his words.

9 And these are the words which he [a]spake and caused to be written, saying: My brethren, all ye that have assembled yourselves together, you that can hear my words which I shall speak unto you this day; for I have not commanded you to come up hither to [b]trifle with the words which I shall speak, but that you should [c]hearken unto me, and open your ears that ye may hear, and your [d]hearts that ye may understand, and your [e]minds that the [f]mysteries of God may be unfolded to your view.

10 I have not commanded you to come up hither that ye should fear [a]me, or that ye should think that I of myself am more than a mortal man.

11 But I am like as yourselves, subject to all manner of infirmities in body and mind; yet I have been chosen by this people, and [a]consecrated by [b]my father, and was suffered by the hand of the Lord that I should be a ruler and a king over this people; and have been kept and preserved by his matchless power,

to serve you with all the might, mind and strength which the Lord hath granted unto me.

12 I say unto you that as I have been suffered to [a]spend my days in your service, even up to this time, and have not sought [b]gold nor silver nor any manner of riches of you;

13 Neither have I suffered that ye should be confined in dungeons, nor that ye should make slaves one of another, nor that ye should murder, or plunder, or steal, or commit adultery; nor even have I suffered that ye should commit any manner of wickedness, and have taught you that ye should keep the commandments of the Lord, in all things which he hath commanded you—

14 And even I, myself, have [a]labored with mine own [b]hands that I might serve you, and that ye should not be [c]laden with taxes, and that there should nothing come upon you which was grievous to be borne—and of all these things which I have spoken, ye yourselves are witnesses this day.

15 Yet, my brethren, I have not done these things that I might [a]boast, neither do I tell these things that thereby I might accuse you; but I tell you these things that ye may know that I can answer a clear [b]conscience before God this day.

16 Behold, I say unto you that because I said unto you that I had spent my days in your service, I do not desire to boast, for I have only been in the service of God.

17 And behold, I tell you these things that ye may learn [a]wisdom; that ye may learn that when ye are in the [b]service of your [c]fellow beings

7a Gen. 35:21; Neh. 8:4 (4–5); Mosiah 11:12 (12–13).
9a Mosiah 8:3.
  b D&C 6:12; 32:5. TG Mocking.
  c TG Teachable.
  d Prov. 8:5; Mosiah 12:27; 3 Ne. 19:33.
  e TG Mind.
  f TG Mysteries of Godliness.

10a TG Humility.
11a TG Setting Apart.
  b Omni 1:23 (23–24). TG Serve; Service.
12a 1 Sam. 12:2 (1–25).
  b 2 Kgs. 5:16; Acts 20:33 (33–34); Jacob 1:16.
14a Deut. 17:17; Neh. 5:14 (14–15); 1 Cor. 9:18 (4–18). TG Self-sacrifice; Work, Value of.

  b Acts 20:34 (33–35).
  c Ezek. 46:18.
15a TG Boasting.
  b TG Conscience.
17a TG Wisdom.
  b Matt. 25:40; D&C 42:31 (30–31). TG Service.
  c TG Brotherhood and Sisterhood; Fellowshipping; Neighbor.

[About 124 B.C.]

ye are only in the service of your God.

18 Behold, ye have called me your king; and if I, whom ye call your king, do labor to ᵃserve you, then ought not ye to labor to serve one another?

19 And behold also, if I, whom ye call your king, who has spent his days in your service, and yet has been in the service of God, do merit any thanks from you, O how you ought to ᵃthank your heavenly ᵇKing!

20 I say unto you, my brethren, that if you should render all the ᵃthanks and ᵇpraise which your whole soul has power to possess, to that God who has created you, and has kept and ᶜpreserved you, and has caused that ye should ᵈrejoice, and has granted that ye should live in peace one with another—

21 I say unto you that if ye should ᵃserve him who has created you from the beginning, and is ᵇpreserving you from day to day, by lending you ᶜbreath, that ye may live and move and do according to your own ᵈwill, and even supporting you from one moment to another—I say, if ye should serve him with all your ᵉwhole souls yet ye would be ᶠunprofitable servants.

22 And behold, all that he ᵃrequires of you is to ᵇkeep his commandments; and he has ᶜpromised you that if ye would keep his commandments ye should prosper in the land; and he never doth ᵈvary from that which he hath said; therefore, if

ye do ᵉkeep his ᶠcommandments he doth bless you and prosper you.

23 And now, in the first place, he hath created you, and granted unto you your lives, for which ye are indebted unto him.

24 And secondly, he doth ᵃrequire that ye should do as he hath commanded you; for which if ye do, he doth immediately ᵇbless you; and therefore he hath paid you. And ye are still indebted unto him, and are, and will be, forever and ever; therefore, of what have ye to boast?

25 And now I ask, can ye say aught of yourselves? I answer you, Nay. Ye cannot say that ye are even as much as the dust of the earth; yet ye were ᵃcreated of the ᵇdust of the earth; but behold, it ᶜbelongeth to him who created you.

26 And I, even I, whom ye call your king, am ᵃno better than ye yourselves are; for I am also of the dust. And ye behold that I am old, and am about to yield up this mortal frame to its mother earth.

27 Therefore, as I said unto you that I had ᵃserved you, ᵇwalking with a clear conscience before God, even so I at this time have caused that ye should assemble yourselves together, that I might be found blameless, and that your ᶜblood should not come upon me, when I shall stand to be judged of God of the things whereof he hath commanded me concerning you.

28 I say unto you that I have caused that ye should assemble yourselves together that I might

---

18a Luke 22: 26.
19a 1 Chr. 16: 8.
   TG Thanksgiving.
   b TG Kingdom of God, in Heaven.
20a Job 1: 21; Ps. 34: 1 (1–3); D&C 59: 21; 62: 7; 78: 19.
   b 1 Sam. 12: 24; 1 Ne. 18: 16; D&C 136: 28.
   c D&C 63: 3.
   d Neh. 12: 43.
21a Job 22: 3 (3–4).
   b Neh. 9: 6.
   c 2 Ne. 9: 26.
   d TG Agency.

e TG Dedication.
f Luke 17: 10 (7–10); Rom. 3: 12.
22a TG God, the Standard of Righteousness.
   b Gen. 4: 7; Lev. 25: 18 (18–19); Mosiah 1: 7; Alma 50: 20 (20–22).
   c 1 Ne. 4: 14; Omni 1: 6; Ether 2: 7 (7–12).
   d TG God, Perfection of.
   e Ps. 19: 11 (9–11); 2 Ne. 1: 20; D&C 14: 7; 58: 2.
   f TG Commandments of God.

24a TG Duty.
   b Prov. 22: 4 (4–5); 2 Ne. 1: 20.
25a TG Man, Physical Creation of.
   b Jacob 2: 21; Alma 42: 2; Hel. 12: 7 (7–8); Morm. 9: 17.
   c 1 Chr. 29: 12; Mosiah 4: 22.
26a TG Equal.
27a TG Serve; Service.
   b TG Walking with God.
   c Jacob 1: 19.

[About 124 B.C.]

[superscript a]rid my garments of your blood, at this period of time when I am about to go down to my grave, that I might go down in peace, and my immortal [superscript b]spirit may join the [superscript c]choirs above in singing the praises of a just God.

29 And moreover, I say unto you that I have caused that ye should assemble yourselves together, that I might declare unto you that I can no longer be your teacher, nor your king;

30 For even at this time, my whole frame doth tremble exceedingly while attempting to speak unto you; but the Lord God doth support me, and hath suffered me that I should speak unto you, and hath commanded me that I should declare unto you this day, that my son Mosiah is a [superscript a]king and a ruler over you.

31 And now, my brethren, I would that ye should do as ye have hitherto done. As ye have kept my commandments, and also the commandments of my father, and have prospered, and have been kept from falling into the hands of your enemies, even so if ye shall keep the commandments of my son, or the commandments of God which shall be delivered unto you by him, ye shall prosper in the land, and your enemies shall have no power over you.

32 But, O my people, beware lest there shall arise [superscript a]contentions among you, and ye [superscript b]list to [superscript c]obey the evil spirit, which was spoken of by my father Mosiah.

33 For behold, there is a wo pronounced upon him who listeth to [superscript a]obey that spirit; for if he listeth to obey him, and remaineth and dieth in his [superscript b]sins, the same drinketh [superscript c]damnation to his own soul; for he receiveth for his wages an [superscript d]everlasting [superscript e]punishment, having transgressed the law of God contrary to his own knowledge.

34 I say unto you, that there are not any among you, except it be your little children that have not been taught concerning these things, but what knoweth that ye are eternally [superscript a]indebted to your heavenly Father, to render to him [superscript b]all that you have and are; and also have been taught concerning the [superscript c]records which contain the prophecies which have been spoken by the holy prophets, even down to the time our father, Lehi, left Jerusalem;

35 And also, all that has been spoken by our fathers until now. And behold, also, they spake that which was commanded them of the Lord; therefore, they are [superscript a]just and true.

36 And now, I say unto you, my brethren, that after ye have known and have been taught all these things, if ye should transgress and go [superscript a]contrary to that which has been spoken, that ye do [superscript b]withdraw yourselves from the Spirit of the Lord, that it may have no place in you to guide you in wisdom's paths that ye may be blessed, prospered, and preserved—

37 I say unto you, that the man that doeth this, the same cometh out in open [superscript a]rebellion against God; therefore he [superscript b]listeth to obey the evil spirit, and becometh an enemy to all righteousness; therefore, the Lord

---

28a 2 Ne. 9:44; Jacob 2:2 (2, 16); D&C 61:34.
  b TG Spirit Body.
  c Morm. 7:7.
30a Mosiah 1:10; 6:3 (3–4). TG Kings, Earthly.
32a Eph. 4:27 (26–27); 3 Ne. 11:29. TG Contention.
  b Alma 3:27 (26–27); 5:42 (41–42); 30:60;

D&C 29:45.
  c 2 Ne. 32:8; Mosiah 4:14; Alma 5:20.
33a TG Agency.
  b TG Accountability.
  c TG Damnation.
  d Jacob 6:10; D&C 19:11 (10–12).
  e TG Punishment.
34a Philip. 3:8 (7–10). TG Debt.
  b Rom. 12:1 (1–2).

  c 1 Ne. 5:14; Alma 33:2.
35a Rom. 7:12; Rev. 15:3.
36a TG Disobedience.
  b TG Holy Ghost, Loss of.
37a Mosiah 3:12; Hel. 8:25 (24–25). TG Holy Ghost, Unpardonable Sin against; Rebellion.
  b Prov. 19:27; 1 Ne. 8:34 (33–34).

[About 124 B.C.]

has no place in him, for he dwelleth not in ᵉunholy temples.

38 Therefore if that man ᵃrepenteth not, and remaineth and dieth an enemy to God, the demands of divine ᵇjustice do awaken his immortal soul to a lively sense of his own ᶜguilt, which doth cause him to shrink from the ᵈpresence of the Lord, and doth fill his breast with guilt, and ᵉpain, and ᶠanguish, which is like an unquenchable ᵍfire, whose flame ascendeth up forever and ever.

39 And now I say unto you, that ᵃmercy hath no claim on that man; therefore his final doom is to endure a never-ending ᵇtorment.

40 O, all ye ᵃold men, and also ye young men, and you little children who can understand my words, for I have spoken plainly unto you that ye might understand, I pray that ye should awake to a ᵇremembrance of the awful situation of those that have fallen into transgression.

41 And moreover, I would desire that ye should consider on the blessed and ᵃhappy state of those that keep the commandments of God. For behold, they are ᵇblessed in all things, both temporal and spiritual; and if they hold out ᶜfaithful to the end they are received into ᵈheaven, that thereby they may dwell with God in a state of never-ending happiness. O remember, remember that these things are true; for the Lord God hath spoken it.

CHAPTER 3

King Benjamin continues his address—The Lord Omnipotent shall minister among men in a tabernacle of clay—Blood shall come from every pore as he atones for the sins of the world—His is the only name whereby salvation comes—Men can put off the natural man and become saints through the atonement—The torment of the wicked shall be as a lake of fire and brimstone.

AND again my brethren, I would call your attention, for I have somewhat more to speak unto you; for behold, I have things to tell you concerning that which is to come.

2 And the things which I shall tell you are made known unto me by an ᵃangel from God. And he said unto me: ᵇAwake; and I awoke, and behold he stood before me.

3 And he said unto me: Awake, and hear the words which I shall tell thee; for behold, I am come to declare unto you the ᵃglad tidings of great ᵇjoy.

4 For the Lord hath heard thy prayers, and hath judged of thy ᵃrighteousness, and hath sent me to declare unto thee that thou mayest rejoice; and that thou mayest declare unto thy people, that they may also be filled with joy.

5 For behold, the time cometh, and is not far distant, that with power, the ᵃLord ᵇOmnipotent who ᶜreigneth, who was, and is from all ᵈeternity to all eternity, shall come down from heaven among the

---

37c Alma 7:21; 34:36;
    Hel. 4:24.
38a TG Repentance.
  b TG God, Justice of.
  c Mosiah 27:29 (25–29).
    TG Guilt.
  d TG God, Presence of.
  e TG Pain.
  f TG Sorrow.
  g TG Hell.
39a TG Mercy.
  b TG Damnation;
    Punishment.
40a TG Old Age.
  b Alma 5:18 (7–18).

41a Matt. 11:29 (28–30);
    Alma 50:23; 4 Ne.
    1:16 (15–18).
    TG Happiness; Joy.
  b Gen. 39:3 (1–6);
    Ps. 37:25; Matt. 6:33;
    1 Ne. 17:3 (1–5, 12–14).
  c Ps. 31:23; Ether 4:19;
    D&C 6:13; 63:47.
  d TG Heaven.
3 2a Mosiah 4:1; 5:5.
    TG Angels.
  b Zech. 4:1 (1–2).
 3a Isa. 52:7 (7–10);
    Luke 2:10 (10–11);

    Rom. 10:15; D&C
    31:3.
  b TG Joy.
4a TG Righteousness.
5a TG Jesus Christ—
    Jehovah.
  b Rev. 1:8 (7–8).
    TG Jesus Christ, Power
    of.
  c TG Jesus Christ,
    Authority of.
  d 2 Ne. 26:12; Mosiah
    16:15.

[About 124 B.C.]

children of men, and shall dwell in a *e*tabernacle of clay, and shall go forth amongst men, working mighty *f*miracles, such as healing the sick, raising the dead, causing the lame to walk, the *g*blind to receive their sight, and the deaf to hear, and curing all manner of diseases.

6 And he shall cast out *a*devils, or the *b*evil spirits which dwell in the hearts of the children of men.

7 And lo, he shall *a*suffer *b*temptations, and pain of body, *c*hunger, thirst, and fatigue, even more than man can *d*suffer, except it be unto death; for behold, *e*blood cometh from every pore, so great shall be his *f*anguish for the wickedness and the abominations of his people.

8 And he shall be called *a*Jesus *b*Christ, the *c*Son of God, the *d*Father of heaven and earth, the *e*Creator of all things from the beginning; and his *f*mother shall be called Mary.

9 And lo, he cometh unto his own, that *a*salvation might come unto the children of men even through *b*faith on his name; and even after all this they shall consider him a man, and say that he hath a *c*devil, and shall

*d*scourge him, and shall *e*crucify him.

10 And he shall *a*rise the *b*third day from the dead; and behold, he standeth to *c*judge the world; and behold, all these things are done that a righteous judgment might come upon the children of men.

11 For behold, and also his *a*blood *b*atoneth for the sins of those who have *c*fallen by the transgression of Adam, who have died not knowing the *d*will of God concerning them, or who have *e*ignorantly sinned.

12 But wo, wo unto him who knoweth that he *a*rebelleth against God! For salvation cometh to none such except it be through repentance and faith on the *b*Lord Jesus Christ.

13 And the Lord God hath sent his holy *a*prophets among all the children of men, to declare these things to every kindred, nation, and tongue, that thereby whosoever should believe that Christ should come, the same might receive *b*remission of their sins, and rejoice with exceedingly great joy, even *c*as though he had already come among them.

5e Mosiah 7:27; 15:2 (1–7); Alma 7:9 (9–13).

f Matt. 4:24 (23–24); 9:35; Acts 2:22; 1 Ne. 11:31. TG Death, Power over; Healing; Miracle.

g Matt. 9:28 (28–31); 20:30 (30–34); John 9:1 (1–4); 3 Ne. 17:9 (7–10); D&C 84:69.

6a Mark 1:34 (32–34); 1 Ne. 11:31.

b TG Spirits, Evil or Unclean.

7a Luke 12:50. TG Suffering.

b TG Jesus Christ, Temptation of; Temptation.

c Matt. 4:2 (1–2).

d D&C 19:16 (15–18).

e Matt. 26:39 (38–39); Luke 22:44.

f Isa. 53:4 (4–5).

8a TG Foreordination; Jesus Christ,

Prophecies about.

b TG Jesus Christ, Messiah.

c Mosiah 15:3; Alma 7:10; 3 Ne. 1:14.

d Mosiah 15:4; Hel. 14:12; 3 Ne. 9:15; Ether 4:7.

e TG Jesus Christ, Creator.

f Matt. 1:16; 1 Ne. 11:18 (14–21).

9a TG Jesus Christ, Mission of.

b TG Faith.

c Luke 11:15 (14–22); John 8:48; 12:37; Hel. 13:26 (26–27).

d Luke 18:31; 1 Ne. 11:33; 2 Ne. 10:3.

e 1 Ne. 19:10 (10, 13); 2 Ne. 6:9; 3 Ne. 11:14 (14–15, 33). TG Jesus Christ, Crucifixion of.

10a TG Jesus Christ, Resurrection.

b 2 Ne. 25:13; Hel.

14:20 (20–27).

c TG Jesus Christ, Judge.

11a TG Blood, Symbolism of.

b TG Jesus Christ, Redeemer; Redemption.

c TG Fall of Man.

d TG God, Will of.

e Lev. 4:13 (13–35); Num. 15:27 (2–29); 2 Ne. 9:26 (25–26); Alma 9:16 (15–16); 42:21; 3 Ne. 6:18. TG Accountability; Ignorance.

12a Mosiah 2:37 (36–38); Hel. 8:25 (24–25). TG Rebellion.

b TG Jesus Christ, Lord.

13a TG Prophets, Mission of.

b TG Remission of Sins.

c 2 Ne. 25:26 (24–27); Jarom 1:11; Mosiah 16:6.

[About 124 B.C.]

14 Yet the Lord God saw that his people were a *a*stiffnecked people, and he appointed unto them a *b*law, even the *c*law of Moses.

15 And many signs, and wonders, and *a*types, and shadows showed he unto them, concerning his coming; and also holy prophets spake unto them concerning his coming; and yet they *b*hardened their hearts, and understood not that the *c*law of Moses availeth nothing *d*except it were through the *e*atonement of his blood.

16 And even if it were possible that little *a*children could sin they could not be saved; but I say unto you they are *b*blessed; for behold, as in Adam, or by nature, they fall, even so the blood of Christ *c*atoneth for their sins.

17 And moreover, I say unto you, that there shall be *a*no other name given nor any other way nor means whereby *b*salvation can come unto the children of men, only in and through the name of Christ, the *c*Lord Omnipotent.

18 For behold he judgeth, and his judgment is just; and the infant perisheth not that dieth in his infancy; but men drink *a*damnation to their own souls except they humble themselves and *b*become as little children, and believe that *c*salvation was, and is, and is to come, in and through the *d*atoning blood of Christ, the Lord Omnipotent.

19 For the *a*natural *b*man is an *c*enemy to God, and has been from the *d*fall of Adam, and will be, forever and ever, unless he *e*yields to the enticings of the Holy *f*Spirit, and *g*putteth off the *h*natural man and becometh a *i*saint through the atonement of Christ the Lord, and becometh as a *j*child, *k*submissive, meek, humble, patient, full of love, willing to submit to all things which the Lord seeth fit to inflict upon him, even as a child doth submit to his father.

20 And moreover, I say unto you, that the time shall come when the *a*knowledge of a *b*Savior shall spread throughout *c*every nation, kindred, tongue, and people.

21 And behold, when that time cometh, none shall be found *a*blameless before God, except it be little children, only through repentance and faith on the name of the Lord God Omnipotent.

22 And even at this time, when thou shalt have taught thy people the things which the Lord thy God hath commanded thee, even then

---

14a 2 Ne. 25 : 28; Alma 9 : 31.
  TG Stiffneckedness.
  b Josh. 1 : 8; Mosiah 13 : 29 (29–32); Alma 25 : 15 (15–16); D&C 41 : 5 (4–5).
  c TG Law of Moses.
15a TG Jesus Christ, Types of, in Anticipation; Passover; Symbolism.
  b TG Hardheartedness.
  c Heb. 10 : 1; Mosiah 12 : 31; 13 : 28 (27–32); Alma 25 : 16.
  d 2 Ne. 11 : 6.
  e Lev. 4 : 20; Matt. 26 : 54 (51–56).
16a TG Conceived in Sin.
  b TG Salvation of Little Children.
  c Moro. 8 : 8 (8–9);

Moses 6 : 54 (54–56).
  TG Jesus Christ, Atonement through.
17a Acts 4 : 12 (10–12); 2 Ne. 31 : 21; Mosiah 4 : 8 (7–8); 3 Ne. 9 : 17.
  b Matt. 7 : 14 (13–14).
  TG Jesus Christ, Savior; Salvation, Plan of.
  c TG Jesus Christ, Lord.
18a 1 Cor. 11 : 29.
  b Matt. 18 : 3.
  c TG Salvation.
  d Mosiah 4 : 2; Hel. 5 : 9.
19a Gen. 8 : 21; 1 Cor. 2 : 14 (11–14); 2 Pet. 2 : 12; Mosiah 16 : 3; Alma 41 : 11; Ether 3 : 2. TG Man, Natural, Not Spiritually Reborn; Worldliness.
  b TG Mortality.
  c James 4 : 4.

TG Enemies.
  d TG Fall of Man.
  e 2 Chr. 30 : 8; Rom. 6 : 13 (12–14).
  f Rom. 8 : 4 (1–9).
  TG Guidance, Divine.
  g Alma 19 : 6.
  h Col. 3 : 9; D&C 67 : 12.
  i Luke 12 : 32 (31–38).
  TG Man, New, Spiritually Reborn; Saints; Spirituality.
  j Matt. 18 : 3; 1 Pet. 2 : 2 (1–3); 3 Ne. 9 : 22.
  k TG Self-mastery; Submissiveness.
20a D&C 3 : 16.
  b TG Jesus Christ, Savior.
  c Mosiah 16 : 1.
  TG Missionary Work.
21a Col. 1 : 22; D&C 4 : 2.
  TG Accountability.

[About 124 B.C.]

are they found no more blameless in the sight of God, only according to the words which I have spoken unto thee.

23 And now I have spoken the words which the Lord God hath commanded me.

24 And thus saith the Lord: They shall stand as a bright testimony against this people, at the judgment day; whereof they shall be judged, every man according to his [a]works, whether they be good, or whether they be evil.

25 And if they be evil they are consigned to an awful [a]view of their own guilt and abominations, which doth cause them to shrink from the presence of the Lord into a state of [b]misery and [c]endless torment, from whence they can no more return; therefore they have drunk damnation to their own souls.

26 Therefore, they have drunk out of the [a]cup of the wrath of God, which justice could no more deny unto them than it could deny that [b]Adam should fall because of his partaking of the forbidden [c]fruit; therefore, [d]mercy could have claim on them no more forever.

27 And their [a]torment is as a [b]lake of fire and brimstone, whose flames are unquenchable, and whose smoke ascendeth up [c]forever and ever. Thus hath the Lord commanded me. Amen.

CHAPTER 4

King Benjamin continues his address —Salvation comes because of the atonement—Believe in God to be saved—Retain a remission of your sins through faithfulness—Impart of your substance to the poor—Do all things in wisdom and order.

AND now, it came to pass that when king Benjamin had made an end of speaking the words which had been delivered unto him by the [a]angel of the Lord, that he cast his eyes round about on the multitude, and behold they had [b]fallen to the earth, for the [c]fear of the Lord had come upon them.

2 And they had [a]viewed themselves in their own [b]carnal state, even [c]less than the dust of the earth. And they all cried aloud with one voice, saying: O have mercy, and apply the [d]atoning blood of Christ that we may receive forgiveness of our sins, and our hearts may be [e]purified; for we believe in Jesus Christ, the Son of God, who [f]created heaven and earth, and all things; who shall come down among the children of men.

3 And it came to pass that after they had spoken these words the Spirit of the Lord came upon them, and they were filled with joy, having received a [a]remission of their sins, and having peace of [b]conscience, because of the exceeding [c]faith which they had in Jesus Christ who should come, according to the [d]words which king Benjamin had spoken unto them.

4 And king Benjamin again opened his mouth and began to speak unto them, saying: My friends and my brethren, my kindred and my people, I would again call your attention, that ye may hear and

---

24a TG Good Works.
25a 2 Ne. 9: 14, 46; Alma 5: 18; 11: 43; 12: 15 (14–15).
  b Rom. 3: 16; Morm. 8: 38.
  c TG Punishment.
26a Ps. 75: 8; Jer. 25: 15; Lam. 4: 21.
  b Morm. 9: 12; Moro. 8: 8.
  c Gen. 3: 6; 2 Ne. 2: 15 (15–19); Alma

12: 22 (21–23).
  d TG Mercy.
27a TG Hell.
  b 2 Ne. 9: 16; Jacob 6: 10; Alma 12: 17; D&C 76: 36.
  c Mosiah 5: 5.
4 1a 1 Chr. 21: 18; Mosiah 3: 2.
  b Neh. 8: 9; Alma 19: 17.
  c Jer. 36: 16; Heb. 12: 28. TG Reverence.
2a TG Poor in Spirit.

  b Neh. 9: 1 (1–3).
    TG Carnal Mind.
  c Gen. 18: 27.
  d Mosiah 3: 18; Hel. 5: 9.
  e TG Purification.
  f TG Jesus Christ, Creator.
3a TG Remission of Sins.
  b TG Conscience.
  c TG Faith.
  d Neh. 8: 12.

[About 124 B.C.]

understand the remainder of my words which I shall speak unto you.

5 For behold, if the knowledge of the goodness of God at this time has awakened you to a sense of your [a]nothingness, and your worthless and fallen state—

6 I say unto you, if ye have come to a [a]knowledge of the goodness of God, and his matchless power, and his wisdom, and his patience, and his long-suffering towards the children of men; and also, the [b]atonement which has been prepared from the [c]foundation of the world, that thereby salvation might come to him that should put his [d]trust in the Lord, and should be diligent in keeping his commandments, and continue in the faith even unto the end of his life, I mean the life of the mortal body—

7 I say, that this is the man who receiveth salvation, through the atonement which was prepared from the foundation of the world for all mankind, which ever were since the [a]fall of Adam, or who are, or who ever shall be, even unto the end of the world.

8 And this is the means whereby salvation cometh. And there is [a]none other salvation save this which hath been spoken of; neither are there any conditions whereby man can be saved except the conditions which I have told you.

9 Believe in [a]God; believe that he is, and that he [b]created all things, both in heaven and in earth; believe that he has all [c]wisdom, and all power, both in heaven and in earth;

believe that man doth not [d]comprehend all the things which the Lord can comprehend.

10 And again, believe that ye must [a]repent of your sins and forsake them, and humble yourselves before God; and ask in [b]sincerity of heart that he would [c]forgive you; and now, if you [d]believe all these things see that ye [e]do them.

11 And again I say unto you as I have said before, that as ye have come to the knowledge of the glory of God, or if ye have known of his goodness and have [a]tasted of his love, and have received a [b]remission of your sins, which causeth such exceedingly great joy in your souls, even so I would that ye should remember, and always retain in remembrance, the greatness of God, and your own [c]nothingness, and his [d]goodness and long-suffering towards you, unworthy creatures, and humble yourselves even in the depths of [e]humility, [f]calling on the name of the Lord daily, and standing [g]steadfastly in the faith of that which is to come, which was spoken by the mouth of the angel.

12 And behold, I say unto you that if ye do this ye shall always rejoice, and be filled with the [a]love of God, and always [b]retain a remission of your sins; and ye shall grow in the [c]knowledge of the glory of him that created you, or in the knowledge of that which is just and true.

13 And ye will not have a [a]mind to injure one another, but to live [b]peaceably, and to render to every

---

5a Moses 1: 10.
6a TG God, Attributes of; God, Knowledge about.
  b TG Jesus Christ, Atonement through.
  c Mosiah 15: 19; 18: 13.
  d Ps. 36: 7 (7–8); 2 Ne. 22: 2; Hel. 12: 1.
    TG Trust in God.
7a TG Fall of Man.
8a Acts 4: 12; 2 Ne. 31: 21; Mosiah 3: 17.
9a Deut. 4: 39.
  b TG God, Creator; Jesus Christ, Creator.

c Rom. 11: 34 (33–36); Jacob 4: 8 (8–13).
    TG God, Perfection of.
  d Isa. 55: 9.
10a TG Repentance.
  b TG Sincerity.
  c Ps. 41: 4; D&C 61: 2.
  d Matt. 7: 24 (24–27); Acts 16: 31 (30–31).
  e 2 Ne. 31: 19 (19–21).
11a Ps. 34: 8; Alma 36: 24 (24–26).
  b TG Remission of Sins.
  c Rom. 5: 8 (6–8); Moses 1: 10.

d Ex. 34: 6 (5–7); Moro. 8: 3.
  e TG Humility.
  f TG Prayer.
  g TG Steadfastness.
12a TG God, Love of.
  b Alma 4: 14 (13–14); 5: 26 (26–35); D&C 20: 32 (31–34).
  c TG God, Knowledge about.
13a TG Man, New, Spiritually Reborn.
  b TG Peacemakers.

[About 124 B.C.]

man according to that which is his due.

14 And ye will not suffer your ^achildren that they go hungry, or naked; neither will ye ^bsuffer that they transgress the laws of God, and fight and ^cquarrel one with another, and serve the devil, who is the master of sin, or who is the ^devil spirit which hath been spoken of by our fathers, he being an enemy to all righteousness.

15 But ye will ^ateach them to ^bwalk in the ways of truth and ^csoberness; ye will teach them to ^dlove one another, and to serve one another.

16 And also, ye yourselves will ^asuccor those that stand in need of your succor; ye will administer of your substance unto him that standeth in need; and ye will not suffer that the ^bbeggar putteth up his petition to you in vain, and turn him out to perish.

17 Perhaps thou shalt ^asay: The man has brought upon himself his misery; therefore I will stay my hand, and will not give unto him of my food, nor impart unto him of my substance that he may not suffer, for his punishments are just—

18 But I say unto you, O man, whosoever doeth this the same hath great cause to repent; and except he repenteth of that which he hath done he perisheth forever, and hath no interest in the kingdom of God.

19 For behold, are we not all ^abeggars? Do we not all depend upon the same Being, even God, for all the substance which we have, for both food and raiment, and for gold, and

for silver, and for all the riches which we have of every kind?

20 And behold, even at this time, ye have been calling on his name, and begging for a ^aremission of your sins. And has he suffered that ye have begged in vain? Nay; he has poured out his ^bSpirit upon you, and has caused that your hearts should be filled with ^cjoy, and has caused that your mouths should be stopped that ye could not find utterance, so exceedingly great was your joy.

21 And now, if God, who has created you, on whom you are dependent for your lives and for all that ye have and are, doth grant unto you whatsoever ye ask that is right, in faith, believing that ye shall receive, O then, how ye ought to ^aimpart of the substance that ye have one to another.

22 And if ye ^ajudge the man who putteth up his petition to you for your substance that he perish not, and condemn him, how much more just will be your ^bcondemnation for withholding your substance, which doth not belong to you but to God, to whom also your life ^cbelongeth; and yet ye put up no petition, nor repent of the thing which thou hast done.

23 I say unto you, wo be unto that man, for his substance shall perish with him; and now, I say these things unto those who are ^arich as pertaining to the things of this world.

24 And again, I say unto the poor, ye who have not and yet have sufficient, that ye remain from day to day; I mean all you who deny

14a 1 Tim. 5:8; D&C 83:4. TG Marriage, Fatherhood.
 b Prov. 13:24.
 c TG Contention.
 d 2 Ne. 32:8; Mosiah 2:32.
15a Mosiah 1:2; Moses 6:58 (58–63). TG Family, Children, Responsibilities toward.
 b TG Walking with God.

 c TG Sincere, Sincerity.
 d 1 Sam. 18:1; Mosiah 18:21. TG Family, Love within.
16a Prov. 19:17. TG Charity; Service; Welfare.
 b Prov. 21:13; Isa. 10:2; Luke 3:11; D&C 38:16.
17a Prov. 17:5.
19a Prov. 22:2; 1 Cor. 4:7.

20a Rom. 2:4 (1–4).
 b TG God, Spirit of.
 c TG Joy.
21a Dan. 4:27. TG Generosity; Welfare.
22a Matt. 7:2 (1–2); John 7:24.
 b 1 Jn. 3:17.
 c Mosiah 2:25.
23a Luke 21:1 (1–4); D&C 56:16.

[About 124 B.C.]

the beggar, because ye have not; I would that ye say in your hearts that: I *a*give not because I *b*have not, but if I had I would *c*give.

25 And now, if ye say this in your hearts ye remain guiltless, otherwise ye are *a*condemned; and your condemnation is just for ye covet that which ye have not received.

26 And now, for the sake of these things which I have spoken unto you—that is, for the sake of retaining a remission of your sins from day to day, that ye may *a*walk guiltless before God—I would that ye should *b*impart of your substance to the *c*poor, every man according to that which he hath, such as *d*feeding the hungry, clothing the naked, visiting the sick and administering to their relief, both spiritually and temporally, according to their wants.

27 And see that all these things are done in wisdom and *a*order; for it is not requisite that a man should run *b*faster than he has strength. And again, it is expedient that he should be diligent, that thereby he might win the prize; therefore, all things must be done in order.

28 And I would that ye should remember, that whosoever among you *a*borroweth of his neighbor should return the thing that he borroweth, according as he doth agree, or else thou shalt commit sin; and perhaps thou shalt cause thy neighbor to commit sin also.

29 And finally, I cannot tell you all the things whereby ye may commit sin; for there are divers ways and means, even so many that I cannot number them.

30 But this much I can tell you, that if ye do not *a*watch yourselves, and your *b*thoughts, and your *c*words, and your deeds, and observe the commandments of God, and *d*continue in the faith of what ye have heard concerning the coming of our Lord, even unto the end of your lives, ye must perish. And now, O man, remember, and perish not.

CHAPTER 5

The saints become the sons and daughters of Christ through faith—They are then called by the name of Christ—King Benjamin exhorts them to be steadfast and immovable in good works.

AND now, it came to pass that when king Benjamin had thus spoken to his people, he sent among them, desiring to know of his people if they *a*believed the words which he had spoken unto them.

2 And they all cried with one voice, saying: Yea, we believe all the words which thou hast spoken unto us; and also, we know of their surety and truth, because of the Spirit of the Lord Omnipotent, which has wrought a mighty *a*change in us, or in our hearts, that we have no more disposition to do *b*evil, but to do good continually.

3 And we, ourselves, also, through the infinite *a*goodness of God, and the manifestations of his Spirit, have great views of that which is to come; and were it expedient, we could prophesy of all things.

4 And it is the faith which we have had on the things which our king has spoken unto us that has brought

---

24a Deut. 16:17.
  b Acts 3:6 (5–7).
  c Mark 12:44.
25a D&C 56:17.
26a TG Walking with God.
  b Jacob 2:19 (17–19);
    Mosiah 21:17; Alma
    35:9.
  c Job 29:12; Zech.
    7:10; Luke 18:22;
    Alma 1:27.
    TG Almsgiving.

d Isa. 58:10 (9–11);
    Alma 4:12 (12–13);
    3 Ne. 12:42.
27a TG Order.
  b Eccl. 9:11; Alma
    1:26; D&C 10:4.
28a TG Borrowing; Debt;
    Honesty.
30a Deut. 4:9; Alma 12:14.
    TG Watchfulness.
  b Matt. 5:28 (27–28);
    Mark 7:23 (15–23).

c Matt. 15:18 (18–20).
    TG Gossip.
  d TG Steadfastness.
5 1a 1 Ne. 11:4 (1–5).
2a Rom. 8:2 (1–4);
    Alma 5:14; 13:12.
    TG Man, New,
    Spiritually Reborn.
  b Alma 19:33.
3a Ex. 34:6 (5–7).

[About 124 B.C.]

us to this great knowledge, whereby we do rejoice with such exceedingly great joy.

5 And we are willing to enter into a [a]covenant with our God to do his will, and to be obedient to his commandments in all things that he shall command us, all the remainder of our days, that we may not bring upon ourselves a [b]never-ending torment, as has been spoken by the [c]angel, that we may not drink out of the cup of the wrath of God.

6 And now, these are the words which king Benjamin desired of them; and therefore he said unto them: Ye have spoken the words that I desired; and the covenant which ye have made is a righteous covenant.

7 And now, because of the covenant which ye have made ye shall be called the [a]children of Christ, his sons, and his daughters; for behold, this day he hath spiritually begotten you; for ye say that your hearts are [b]changed through faith on his name; therefore, ye are [c]born of him and have become his [d]sons and his daughters.

8 And under this head ye are made [a]free, and there is [b]no other head whereby ye can be made free. There is no other [c]name given whereby salvation cometh; therefore, I would that ye should take upon you the name of Christ, all you that have entered into the covenant with God that ye should be obedient unto the end of your lives.

9 And it shall come to pass that whosoever doeth this shall be found at the right hand of God, for he shall know the name by which he is called; for he shall be called by the name of Christ.

10 And now it shall come to pass, that whosoever shall not take upon him the name of Christ must be called by some [a]other name; therefore, he findeth himself on the [b]left hand of God.

11 And I would that ye should remember also, that this is the [a]name that I said I should give unto you that never should be blotted out, except it be through transgression; therefore, take heed that ye do not transgress, that the name be not blotted out of your hearts.

12 I say unto you, I would that ye should remember to [a]retain the name written always in your hearts, that ye are not found on the left hand of God, but that ye hear and know the voice by which ye shall be called, and also, the name by which he shall call you.

13 For how [a]knoweth a man the master whom he has not served, and who is a stranger unto him, and is far from the thoughts and intents of his heart?

14 And again, doth a man take an ass which belongeth to his neighbor, and keep him? I say unto you, Nay; he will not even suffer that he shall feed among his flocks, but will drive him away, and cast him out. I say unto you, that even so shall it be among you if ye know not the name by which ye are called.

15 Therefore, I would that ye should be steadfast and immovable, always abounding in [a]good works, that Christ, the [b]Lord God Omnipo-

5a 2 Chr. 15:12 (12–15); Neh. 10:29; Mosiah 6:3. TG Commitment.
  b Mosiah 3:27 (25–27).
  c Mosiah 3:2.
7a 1 Jn. 2:12; Mosiah 15:2; 27:25 (24–26); Moses 6:68 (64–68).
  b TG Sanctification.
  c John 1:13 (12–13); Mosiah 15:10. TG Man, New,

Spiritually Reborn.
  d Matt. 12:49 (49–50); D&C 11:30.
8a Rom. 6:18 (14–22); 1 Cor. 7:22; Gal. 5:1; D&C 88:86.
  b Acts 4:12; Mosiah 4:8; Alma 21:9.
  c Gal. 3:27; Mosiah 1:11; 26:18.
10a Alma 5:39 (38–42).
  b Matt. 25:33.

11a Mosiah 1:11 (11–12). TG Jesus Christ, Taking the Name of.
12a Ps. 119:55; Num. 6:27; D&C 18:25.
13a Jer. 4:22; Mosiah 26:25 (24–27).
15a TG Good Works.
  b TG Jesus Christ— Jehovah; Jesus Christ, Lord.

[About 124 B.C.]

tent, may ^cseal you his, that you may be brought to heaven, that ye may have everlasting salvation and eternal life, through the wisdom, and power, and justice, and mercy of him who ^dcreated all things, in heaven and in earth, who is God above all. Amen.

CHAPTER 6

King Benjamin records the names of the people and appoints priests to teach them—Mosiah reigns as a righteous king.

AND now, king Benjamin thought it was expedient, after having finished speaking to the people, that he should ^atake the names of all those who had entered into a covenant with God to keep his commandments.

2 And it came to pass that there was not one soul, except it were little children, but who had entered into the covenant and had taken upon them the name of Christ.

3 And again, it came to pass that when king Benjamin had made an end of all these things, and had consecrated his son ^aMosiah to be a ruler and a king over his people, and had given him all the charges concerning the kingdom, and also had ^bappointed ^cpriests to ^dteach the people, that thereby they might hear and know the commandments of God, and to stir them up in remembrance of the ^eoath which they had made, he dismissed the multitude, and they returned, every one, according to their ^ffamilies, to their own houses.

4 And Mosiah began to reign in his father's stead. *And he began to reign in the thirtieth year of his age, making in the whole, about four hundred and seventy-six years

from the ^atime that Lehi left Jerusalem.

5 And king Benjamin lived three years† and he died.

6 And it came to pass that king Mosiah did ^awalk in the ways of the Lord, and did observe his judgments and his statutes, and did keep his commandments in all things whatsoever he commanded him.

7 And king Mosiah did cause his people that they should till the earth. And he also, himself, did till the earth, that thereby he might ^anot become burdensome to his people, that he might do according to that which his father had done in all things. And there was no contention among all his people for the space of three years.

CHAPTER 7

Ammon finds the land of Lehi-Nephi where Limhi is king—Limhi's people are in bondage to the Lamanites—Limhi recounts their history—A prophet (Abinadi) had testified that Christ is the God and Father of all things—Those who sow filthiness reap the whirlwind, and those who put their trust in the Lord shall be delivered.

AND now, it came to pass that after king Mosiah had had continual peace for the space of three years, he was desirous to know concerning the people who ^awent up to dwell in the land of ^bLehi-Nephi, or in the city of Lehi-Nephi; for his people had heard nothing from them from the time they left the land of ^cZarahemla; therefore, they wearied him with their teasings.

2 And it came to pass that ‡king Mosiah granted that sixteen of their strong men might go up to the land of Lehi-Nephi, to inquire concerning their brethren.

15c TG Election.
  d Col. 1: 16; Mosiah
    4: 2; Alma 11: 39.
6 1a D&C 128: 8.
  3a Mosiah 1: 10; 2: 30.
  b TG Priesthood,
    Ordination.

  c Mosiah 29: 42.
  d Alma 4: 7.
  e Mosiah 5: 5 (5–7).
  f Num. 1: 2; Ether 1: 41;
    D&C 48: 6.
  4a 1 Ne. 1: 4; 2: 4.
  6a TG Walking with God.

  7a 2 Cor. 11: 9.
7 1a Omni 1: 27 (27–30).
  b 2 Ne. 5: 8; Mosiah 9: 6.
  c Omni 1: 13.

  [*About 124 B.C.]
  [†About 121 B.C.]
  [‡About 121 B.C.]

3 And it came to pass that on the morrow they started to go up, having with them one [a]Ammon, he being a strong and mighty man, and a [b]descendant of Zarahemla; and he was also their leader.

4 And now, they knew not the course they should travel in the wilderness to go up to the land of Lehi-Nephi; therefore they wandered many days in the wilderness, even [a]forty days did they wander.

5 And when they had wandered forty days they came to a [a]hill, which is north of the land of [b]Shilom, and there they pitched their tents.

6 And [a]Ammon took three of his brethren, and their names were Amaleki, Helem, and Hem, and they went down into the land of [b]Nephi.

7 And behold, they met the king of the people who were in the land of Nephi, and in the land of [a]Shilom; and they were surrounded by the king's guard, and were [b]taken, and were [c]bound, and were committed to [d]prison.

8 And it came to pass when they had been in prison two days they were again brought before the king, and their bands were loosed; and they stood before the king, and were permitted, or rather [a]commanded, that they should answer the questions which he should ask them.

9 And he said unto them: Behold, I am [a]Limhi, the son of Noah, who was the son of Zeniff, who came up out of the [b]land of Zarahemla to inherit this land, which was the land of their fathers, who was made a [c]king by the [d]voice of the people.

10 And now, [a]I desire to know the cause whereby ye were so bold as to come near the walls of the city, when I, myself, was with my guards without the [b]gate?

11 And now, for this cause have I suffered that ye should be preserved, that I might inquire of you, or else I should have caused that my guards should have put you to death. Ye are permitted to speak.

12 And now, when Ammon saw that he was permitted to speak, he went forth and [a]bowed himself before the king; and rising again he said: O king, I am very thankful before God this day that I am yet alive, and am permitted to speak; and I will endeavor to speak with boldness;

13 For I am assured that if ye had known me ye would not have suffered that I should have worn these bands. For I am Ammon, and am a [a]descendant of Zarahemla, and have come up out of the [b]land of Zarahemla to inquire concerning our brethren, whom [c]Zeniff brought up out of that land.

14 And now, it came to pass that after Limhi had heard the words of Ammon, he was exceedingly [a]glad, and said: Now, I know of a surety that my brethren who were in the land of Zarahemla are [b]yet alive. And now, I will rejoice; and on the morrow I will cause that my people shall rejoice also.

15 For behold, we are in bondage to the Lamanites, and are [a]taxed with a tax which is grievous to be borne. And now, behold, our brethren will deliver us out of our [b]bondage, or out of the hands of the

3a Mosiah 8: 2.
  b Omni 1: 14.
4a Num. 13: 25 (17–25).
5a Mosiah 11: 13.
  b Mosiah 9: 14 (6, 8, 14);
    11: 12 (12–13);
    22: 11 (8, 11); Alma
    23: 12.
6a Mosiah 21: 22, 26.
  b 2 Ne. 5: 8; Omni 1: 12
    (12, 27); Mosiah 9: 1

(1, 3–4, 14); 28: 1 (1,5);
    Alma 50: 8 (8, 11).
7a Mosiah 22: 8.
  b Mosiah 21: 21.
  c Alma 17: 20.
  d Mosiah 21: 23 (22–24).
8a Alma 14: 19.
9a Mosiah 11: 1; 19: 16.
  b Omni 1: 13.
  c TG Kings, Earthly.
  d Mosiah 19: 26.

10a Mosiah 21: 23 (23–24).
  b Josh. 20: 4.
12a Alma 47: 22 (22–23).
13a Omni 1: 13.
  b Omni 1: 14.
  c Mosiah 8: 2; 9: 1.
14a Mosiah 21: 24.
  b Mosiah 21: 25 (25–26).
15a Mosiah 19: 15.
  b TG Bondage, Physical.

[About 121 B.C.]

Lamanites, and we will be their *c*slaves; for it is better that we be slaves to the Nephites than to pay tribute to the king of the Lamanites.

16 And now, king Limhi commanded his guards that they should no more bind Ammon nor his brethren, but caused that they should go to the hill which was north of Shilom, and bring their brethren into the city, that thereby they might eat, and drink, and rest themselves from the labors of their journey; for they had suffered many things; they had suffered hunger, thirst, and fatigue.

17 And now, it came to pass on the morrow that king Limhi sent a proclamation among all his people, that thereby they might gather themselves together to the *a*temple, to hear the words which he should speak unto them.

18 And it came to pass that when they had gathered themselves together that he *a*spake unto them in this wise, saying: O ye, my people, lift up your heads and be comforted; for behold, the time is at hand, or is not far distant, when we shall no longer be in subjection to our enemies, notwithstanding our many strugglings, which have been in vain; yet I trust there *b*remaineth an effectual struggle to be made.

19 Therefore, lift up your heads, and rejoice, and put your *a*trust in *b*God, in that God who was the God of Abraham, and Isaac, and Jacob; and also, that God who *c*brought the children of *d*Israel out of the land of Egypt, and caused that they should walk through the Red *e*Sea on dry ground, and fed them with *f*manna that they might not perish in the wilderness; and many more things did he do for them.

20 And again, that same God has brought our fathers *a*out of the land of Jerusalem, and has kept and preserved his people even until now; and behold, it is *b*because of our iniquities and abominations that he has brought us into bondage.

21 And ye all are witnesses this day, that Zeniff, who was made king over this people, he being *a*over-zealous to inherit the land of his fathers, therefore being deceived by the cunning and craftiness of king Laman, who having entered into a treaty with king Zeniff, and having yielded up into his hands the possessions of a part of the land, or even the city of Lehi-Nephi, and the city of Shilom; and the land round about—

22 And all this he did, for the sole purpose of *a*bringing this people into subjection or into bondage. And behold, we at this time do pay *b*tribute to the king of the Lamanites, to the amount of one half of our corn, and our barley, and even all our grain of every kind, and one half of the increase of our flocks and our herds; and even one half of all we have or possess the king of the Lamanites doth exact of us, or our lives.

23 And now, is not this grievous to be borne? And is not this, our affliction, great? Now behold, how great reason we have to *a*mourn.

24 Yea, I say unto you, great are the reasons which we have to *a*mourn; for behold how many of our brethren have been slain, and their blood has been spilt in vain, and all because of iniquity.

25 For if this people had not fallen into transgression the Lord would not have suffered that this great evil should come upon them. But behold,

---

15*c* ᴛɢ Slavery.
17*a* 2 Ne. 5: 16.
18*a* Mosiah 8: 1.
  b Mosiah 22: 1 (1–16).
19*a* ᴛɢ Trust in God.
  b Ex. 3: 6 (2–10); 1 Ne.
      19: 10; D&C 136: 21.
  c Ex. 12: 51; 1 Ne.
      17: 40; Mosiah 12: 34;

Alma 36: 28.
  d ᴛɢ Israel, Origins of.
  e Josh. 2: 10; 1 Ne. 4: 2;
      17: 26.
  f Ex. 16: 15, 35; Num.
      11: 7 (7–8); Josh.
      5: 12; John 6: 49;
      1 Ne. 17: 28.
20*a* 1 Ne. 2: 2 (1–4).

  b Deut. 28: 15 (1–2,
      15–68).
21*a* Mosiah 9: 3 (1–3).
22*a* Mosiah 9: 10; 10: 18.
  b ᴛɢ Tribute.
23*a* Prov. 29: 2.
24*a* Ezek. 24: 23; Hel. 9: 22.

they would not hearken unto his words; but there arose contentions among them, even so much that they did shed blood among themselves.

26 And a *a*prophet of the Lord have they *b*slain; yea, a chosen man of God, who told them of their wickedness and abominations, and prophesied of many things which are to come, yea, even the coming of Christ.

27 And because he said unto them that Christ was the *a*God, the Father of all things, and said that he should take upon him the *b*image of man, and it should be the *c*image after which man was created in the beginning; or in other words, he said that man was created after the image of *d*God, and that God should come down among the children of men, and take upon him flesh and blood, and go forth upon the face of the earth—

28 And now, because he said this, they did *a*put him to death; and many more things did they do which brought down the wrath of God upon them. Therefore, who wondereth that they are in bondage, and that they are smitten with sore afflictions?

29 For behold, the Lord hath said: I will not *a*succor my people in the day of their transgression; but I will hedge up their ways that they prosper not; and their doings shall be as a *b*stumbling block before them.

30 And again, he saith: If my people shall sow *a*filthiness they shall *b*reap the *c*chaff thereof in the whirlwind; and the effect thereof is poison.

31 And again he saith: If my people shall sow filthiness they shall reap the *a*east wind, which bringeth immediate destruction.

32 And now, behold, the promise of the Lord is fulfilled, and ye are smitten and afflicted.

33 But if ye will *a*turn to the Lord with full purpose of heart, and put your trust in him, and serve him with all *b*diligence of mind, if ye do this, he will, according to his own will and pleasure, deliver you out of bondage.

CHAPTER 8

Ammon teaches the people of Limhi— He learns of the twenty-four Jaredite plates—Ancient records can be translated by seers—The gift of seership exceeds all others.

AND it came to pass that after king Limhi had made an end of *a*speaking to his people, for he spake many things unto them and only a few of them have I written in this book, he told his people all the things concerning their brethren who were in the land of Zarahemla.

2 And he caused that Ammon should stand up before the multitude, and rehearse unto them all that had happened unto their brethren from the time that *a*Zeniff went up out of the land even until the time that he *b*himself came up out of the land.

3 And he also rehearsed unto them the last words which king Benjamin had *a*taught them, and explained them to the people of king Limhi, so that they might understand all the words which he spake.

26a Mosiah 17: 20 (12–20).
 b TG Prophets, Rejection of.
27a Isa. 9: 6; 2 Ne. 26: 12; Mosiah 27: 31 (30–31).
 b TG God, Body of— Corporeal Nature.
 c Gen. 1: 26 (26–28); Ether 3: 15 (14–17); D&C 20: 18 (17–18).
 d Mosiah 13: 34; 15: 2 (1–7); Alma 7: 9

(9–13).
28a Mosiah 17: 13.
29a Josh. 24: 20; 1 Sam. 12: 15; 2 Chr. 24: 20.
 b Jer. 6: 21.
30a TG Filthiness.
 b Hosea 8: 7; Gal. 6: 8 (7–8); D&C 6: 33. TG Harvest.
 c Luke 3: 17; 2 Ne. 15: 24.
31a Gen. 41: 23; Jer. 18: 17; Ezek. 27: 26;

Jonah 4: 8; Mosiah 12: 6.
33a Deut. 30: 10; Lam. 5: 21; Morm. 9: 6; D&C 98: 47.
 b TG Diligence.
8 1a Mosiah 7: 18 (18–33).
2a Mosiah 7: 13.
 b Mosiah 7: 3.
3a Mosiah 2: 9.

[About 121 B.C.]

4 And it came to pass that after he had done all this, that king Limhi dismissed the multitude, and caused that they should return every one unto his own house.

5 And it came to pass that he caused that the *plates which contained the *record of his people from the time that they left the *land of Zarahemla, should be brought before Ammon, that he might read them.

6 Now, as soon as Ammon had read the record, the king inquired of him to know if he could *interpret languages, and Ammon told him that he could not.

7 And the king said unto him: Being grieved for the afflictions of my people, I caused that *forty and three of my people should take a journey into the wilderness, that thereby they might find the land of Zarahemla, that we might appeal unto our brethren to deliver us out of bondage.

8 And they were lost in the wilderness for the space of *many days, yet they were diligent, and found not the land of Zarahemla but returned to this land, having traveled in a land among many waters, having discovered a land which was covered with *bones of men, and of beasts, and was also covered with ruins of buildings of every kind, having discovered a land which had been peopled with a people who were as numerous as the hosts of Israel.

9 And for a testimony that the things that they had said are true they have brought *twenty-four plates which are filled with engravings, and they are of pure gold.

10 And behold, also, they have brought *breastplates, which are large, and they are of *brass and of copper, and are perfectly sound.

11 And again, they have brought swords, the hilts thereof have perished, and the blades thereof were cankered with rust; and there is no one in the land that is able to interpret the language or the engravings that are on the plates. Therefore I said unto thee: Canst thou translate?

12 And I say unto thee again: Knowest thou of any one that can translate? For I am desirous that these records should be translated into our language; for, perhaps, they will give us a knowledge of a remnant of the people who have been destroyed, from whence these records came; or, perhaps, they will give us a knowledge of this very people who have been destroyed; and I am desirous to know the cause of their destruction.

13 Now Ammon said unto him: I can assuredly tell thee, O king, of a man that can *translate the records; for he has wherewith that he can look, and translate all records that are of ancient date; and it is a gift from God. And the things are called *interpreters, and no man can look in them except he be commanded, lest he should look for that he ought not and he should perish. And whosoever is commanded to look in them, the same is called *seer.

14 And behold, the king of the people who are in the land of Zarahemla is the man that is commanded to do these things, and who has this high gift from God.

15 And the king said that a *seer is greater than a prophet.

16 And Ammon said that a seer is a revelator and a prophet also; and a gift which is greater can no man

---

5a See Mosiah, chapters 9–22.
b Mosiah 9: 1; 22: 14.
c Omni 1: 13.
6a 1 Cor. 12: 10; Mosiah 21: 28.
7a Mosiah 21: 25.
8a Alma 50: 29; Hel. 3: 4

(3–4); Morm. 6: 4.
b Omni 1: 22; Mosiah 21: 26 (26–27).
9a Mosiah 21: 27; 22: 14.
10a Ex. 25: 7; Ether 15: 15.
b Ether 10: 23.
13a Dan. 5: 16; Omni 1: 20 (20–22); Mosiah

28: 17 (11–17).
b Ex. 28: 30; Mosiah 21: 28 (27–28). TG Urim and Thummim.
c TG Seer.
15a 1 Sam. 9: 9; D&C 21: 1.

[About 121 B.C.]

have, except he should possess the power of God, which no man can; yet a man may have great power given him from God.

17 But a seer can know of things which are past, and also of things which are to come, and by them shall all things be revealed, or, rather, shall secret things be made manifest, and hidden things shall come to light, and things which are not known shall be made known by them, and also things shall be made known by them which otherwise could not be known.

18 Thus God has provided a means that man, through faith, might work mighty miracles; therefore he becometh a great benefit to his fellow beings.

19 And now, when Ammon had made an end of speaking these words the king rejoiced exceedingly, and gave thanks to God, saying: Doubtless a *great mystery is contained within these plates, and these interpreters were doubtless prepared for the purpose of unfolding all such mysteries to the children of men.

20 O how marvelous are the works of the Lord, and how long doth he suffer with his people; yea, and how *blind and impenetrable are the understandings of the children of men; for they will not seek wisdom, neither do they desire that she should rule over them!

21 Yea, they are as a wild flock which fleeth from the shepherd, and scattereth, and are driven, and are devoured by the beasts of the forest.

THE RECORD OF ZENIFF—*An account of his people, from the time they left the land of Zarahemla until the time that they were delivered out of the hands of the Lamanites. Comprising chapters 9 to 22 inclusive.*

CHAPTER 9

Zeniff leads a group from Zarahemla to possess the land of Lehi-Nephi— The Lamanite king permits them to inherit the land—There is war between the Lamanites and Zeniff's people.

*a*I, *b*ZENIFF, having been taught in all the language of the Nephites, and having had a knowledge of the land of *c*Nephi, or of the land of our fathers' first inheritance, *and having been sent as a spy among the Lamanites that I might spy out their forces, that our army might come upon them and destroy them—but when I saw that which was good among them I was desirous that they should not be destroyed.

2 Therefore, I contended with my brethren in the wilderness, for I would that our ruler should make a treaty with them; but he being an austere and a blood-thirsty man commanded that I should be slain; but I was rescued by the shedding of much blood; for father fought against father, and brother against brother, until the greater number of our army was destroyed in the wilderness; and we returned, those of us that were spared, to the land of Zarahemla, to relate that tale to their wives and their children.

3 And yet, I being *a*over-zealous to inherit the land of our fathers, collected as many as were desirous to go up to possess the land, and started again on our *b*journey into the wilderness to go up to the land; but we were smitten with famine and sore afflictions; for we were slow to remember the Lord our God.

4 Nevertheless, after many days' wandering in the wilderness we pitched our tents in the place where our brethren were slain, which was near to the land of our fathers.

5 And it came to pass that I went again with four of my men into the

---

19a Ether 3:26 (21–28); 4:4 (1–8).
20a TG Spiritual Blindness.
9 1a Mosiah 8:5; 22:14.

b Mosiah 7:13.
c 2 Ne. 5:8; Omni 1:12 (12, 27); Mosiah 7:6 (6–7); 28:1 (1, 5).

3a Omni 1:27 (27–29); Mosiah 7:21.
b Mosiah 25:5.

[*About 200 B.C.]

city, in unto the king, that I might know of the disposition of the king, and that I might know if I might go in with my people and possess the land in peace.

6 And I went in unto the king, and he covenanted with me that I might possess the [a]land of Lehi-Nephi, and the land of Shilom.

7 And he also commanded that his people should depart out of the land, and I and my people went into the land that we might possess it.

8 And we began to build buildings, and to repair the walls of the city, yea, even the walls of the city of Lehi-Nephi, and the city of Shilom.

9 And we began to till the ground, yea, even with all manner of [a]seeds, with seeds of corn, and of wheat, and of barley, and with neas, and with sheum, and with seeds of all manner of fruits; and we did begin to multiply and prosper in the land.

10 Now it was the cunning and the craftiness of king [a]Laman, to [b]bring my people into bondage, that he yielded up the land that we might possess it.

11 Therefore it came to pass, that after we had dwelt in the land for the space of *twelve years that king Laman began to grow uneasy, lest by any means my people should [a]wax strong in the land, and that they could not overpower them and bring them into bondage.

12 Now they were a [a]lazy and an [b]idolatrous people; therefore they were desirous to bring us into bondage, that they might glut themselves with the labors of our hands; yea, that they might feast themselves upon the flocks of our fields.

13 Therefore it came to pass that king Laman began to stir up his people that they should contend with my people; therefore there began to be wars and contentions in the land.

14 For, in the †thirteenth year of my reign in the land of Nephi, away on the south of the land of [a]Shilom, when my people were watering and [b]feeding their flocks, and tilling their lands, a numerous host of Lamanites came upon them and began to slay them, and to take off their flocks, and the corn of their fields.

15 Yea, and it came to pass that they fled, all that were not overtaken, even into the city of Nephi, and did call upon me for protection.

16 And it came to pass that I did arm them with bows, and with arrows, with swords, and with cimeters, and with clubs, and with slings, and with all manner of weapons which we could invent, and I and my people did go forth against the Lamanites to battle.

17 Yea, in the [a]strength of the Lord did we go forth to battle against the Lamanites; for I and my people did cry mightily to the Lord that he would [b]deliver us out of the hands of our enemies, for we were awakened to a remembrance of the deliverance of our fathers.

18 And God did [a]hear our cries and did answer our prayers; and we did go forth in his might; yea, we did go forth against the Lamanites, and in one day and a night we did slay three thousand and forty-three; we did slay them even until we had driven them out of our land.

19 And I, myself, with mine own hands, did help to bury our dead. And behold, to our great sorrow and lamentation, two hundred and seventy-nine of our brethren were slain.

6a 2 Ne. 5:8; Mosiah 7:1
   (1–4, 21).
9a 1 Ne. 8:1; Enos 1:21;
   Mosiah 10:4.
10a Mosiah 24:3.
   b Mosiah 7:22; 10:18.
11a Ex. 1:9 (9–10).
12a TG Laziness.

   b Enos 1:20.
   TG Idolatry.
14a Mosiah 7:5;
   11:12 (12–13).
   b Mosiah 10:21.
17a TG Strength.
   b Josh. 21:44; Alma

   46:7.
18a Ex. 2:24 (23–24);
   Ps. 4:1 (1, 3); Dan.
   10:12; D&C 35:3;
   Abr. 1:15 (15–16).

   [*About 188 B.C.]
   [†About 187 B.C.]

CHAPTER 10

King Laman dies—His people are wild and ferocious and believe in false traditions—Zeniff and his people prevail against them.

AND it came to pass that we again began to establish the kingdom and we again began to possess the land in peace. And I caused that there should be ᵃweapons of war made of every kind, that thereby I might have weapons for my people against the time the Lamanites should come up again to war against my people.

2 And I set guards round about the land, that the Lamanites might not come up on us again unawares and destroy us; and thus I did guard my people and my flocks, and keep them from falling into the hands of our enemies.

3 And it came to pass that we did inherit the land of our fathers for many years, yea, *for the space of twenty and two years.

4 And I did cause that the men should till the ground, and raise all manner of ᵃgrain and all manner of fruit of every kind.

5 And I did cause that the women should spin, and toil, and work, and work all manner of fine linen, yea, and ᵃcloth of every kind, that we might clothe our nakedness; and thus we did prosper in the land—thus we did have continual peace in the land for the space of twenty and two years.

6 And it came to pass that king ᵃLaman died, and his son began to reign in his stead. And he began to stir his people up in rebellion against my people; therefore they began to prepare for war, and to come up to battle against my people.

7 But I had sent my spies out round about the land of ᵃShemlon, that I might discover their preparations, that I might guard against them, that they might not come upon my people and destroy them.

8 And it came to pass that they came up upon the north of the land of Shilom, with their numerous hosts, men ᵃarmed with ᵇbows, and with arrows, and with swords, and with cimeters, and with stones, and with slings; and they had their heads shaved that they were naked; and they were girded with a leathern girdle about their loins.

9 And it came to pass that I caused that the women and children of my people should be hid in the wilderness; and I also caused that all my old men that could bear arms, and also all my young men that were able to bear arms, should gather themselves together to go to battle against the Lamanites; and I did place them in their ranks, every man according to his age.

10 And it came to pass that we did go up to battle against the Lamanites; and I, even I, in my old age, did go up to battle against the Lamanites. And it came to pass that we did go up in the strength of the Lord to battle.

11 Now, the Lamanites knew nothing concerning the Lord, nor the strength of the Lord, therefore they depended upon their own strength. Yet they were a strong people, as to the ᵃstrength of men.

12 They were a ᵃwild, and ferocious, and a blood-thirsty people, believing in the ᵇtradition of their fathers, which is this—Believing that they were driven out of the land of Jerusalem because of the iniquities of their fathers, and that they were ᶜwronged in the wilderness by their brethren, and they were also wronged while crossing the sea;

13 And again, that they were

---

10 1a TG Weapon.
4a Mosiah 9:9.
5a Alma 1:29; Hel. 6:13.
TG Clothing.
6a Mosiah 9:10 (10–11);
24:3.
7a Mosiah 11:12.

8a 2 Ne. 5:14; Jarom
1:8; Alma 2:12.
b Enos 1:20; Alma 3:5
(4–5).
10a TG Strength; Trust in
God.
11a TG Trust Not in the

Arm of Flesh.
12a Alma 17:14.
b 2 Ne. 5:1 (1–3);
Mosiah 1:5; Alma 3:8.
c TG Injustice.

wronged while in the land of their ^afirst inheritance, after they had crossed the sea, and all this because that Nephi was more faithful in keeping the commandments of the Lord—therefore ^bhe was favored of the Lord, for the Lord heard his prayers and answered them, and he took the lead of their journey in the wilderness.

14 And his brethren were ^awroth with him because they ^bunderstood not the dealings of the Lord; they were also wroth with him upon the waters because they hardened their hearts against the Lord.

15 And again, they were ^awroth with him when they had arrived in the promised land, because they said that he had taken the ^bruling of the people out of their hands; and they sought to kill him.

16 And again, they were wroth with him because he departed into the wilderness as the Lord had commanded him, and took the ^arecords which were engraven on the plates of brass, for they said that he ^brobbed them.

17 And thus they have taught their children that they should hate them, and that they should murder them, and that they should rob and plunder them, and do all they could to destroy them; therefore they have an eternal hatred towards the children of Nephi.

18 For this very cause has king Laman, by his ^acunning, and lying craftiness, and his fair promises, deceived me, that I have brought this my people up into this land, that they may destroy them; yea, and we have suffered these many years in the land.

19 And now I, Zeniff, after having told all these things unto my people

concerning the Lamanites, I did stimulate them to go to battle with their might, putting their trust in the Lord; therefore, we did contend with them, face to face.

20 And it came to pass that we did drive them again out of our land; and we slew them with a great slaughter, even so many that we did not number them.

21 And it came to pass that we returned again to our own land, and my people again began to ^atend their flocks, and to till their ground.

22 And now I, being old, *did confer the kingdom upon one of my sons; therefore, I say no more. And may the Lord ^abless my people. Amen.

CHAPTER 11

King Noah rules in wickedness—He revels in riotous living with his wives and concubines—Abinadi prophesies that the people will be taken into bondage—His life is sought by King Noah.

AND now it came to pass that Zeniff conferred the kingdom upon Noah, one of his sons; therefore Noah began to reign in his stead; and he did not walk in the ways of his father.

2 For behold, he did not keep the commandments of God, but he did walk after the desires of his own heart. And he had many wives and ^aconcubines. And he did ^bcause his people to commit sin, and do that which was ^cabominable in the sight of the Lord. Yea, and they did commit ^dwhoredoms and ^eall manner of wickedness.

3 And he laid a ^atax of one fifth part of all they possessed, a fifth part of their gold and of their silver,

13a 1 Ne. 18: 23.
 b 2 Ne. 5: 5 (5–9).
14a 1 Ne. 18: 10 (10–11).
 b 1 Ne. 15: 8 (8–11);
   2 Ne. 1: 25 (24–27).
15a 2 Ne. 5: 1.
 b 2 Ne. 5: 3 (1–4).
16a 2 Ne. 5: 12; Mosiah
   28: 11.

 b Alma 20: 10 (10, 13).
18a Mosiah 9: 10;
   19: 28 (26, 28).
21a Mosiah 9: 14 (9, 14).
22a Num. 6: 24 (22–27).
11 2a Jacob 3: 5; Ether
   10: 5.
 b 1 Kgs. 14: 16; 15: 26;
   16: 2; 21: 22; 2 Kgs.

21: 2 (1–9); Mosiah
   23: 12; 29: 31.
 c Mosiah 29: 18.
 d 2 Ne. 28: 15.
 e Mosiah 23: 9.
3a Gen. 47: 24; Ether
   10: 5 (5–6).
[*Probably about 160 B.C.]

and a fifth part of their [b]ziff, and of their copper, and of their brass and their iron; and a fifth part of their fatlings; and also a fifth part of all their grain.

4 And all this did he take to [a]support himself, and his wives and his [b]concubines; and also his priests, and their wives and their concubines; thus he had changed the affairs of the kingdom.

5 For he put down all the priests that had been consecrated by his father, and consecrated new [a]ones in their stead, such as were lifted up in the pride of their hearts.

6 Yea, and thus they were supported in their laziness, and in their idolatry, and in their whoredoms, by the taxes which king Noah had put upon his people; thus did the people labor exceedingly to support iniquity.

7 Yea, and they also became idolatrous, because they were deceived by the vain and flattering words of the king and priests; for they did speak flattering things unto them.

8 And it came to pass that king Noah built many elegant and spacious buildings; and he ornamented them with fine work of wood, and of all manner of [a]precious things, of gold, and of silver, and of iron, and of brass, and of ziff, and of copper;

9 And he also built him a spacious palace, and a throne in the midst thereof, all of which was of fine wood and was ornamented with gold and silver and with precious things.

10 And he also caused that his workmen should work all manner of fine work within the walls of the [a]temple, of fine wood, and of copper, and of brass.

11 And the seats which were set apart for the [a]high priests, which were above all the other seats, he did ornament with pure gold; and he caused a breastwork to be built before them, that they might rest their bodies and their arms upon while they should speak lying and vain words to his people.

12 And it came to pass that he built a [a]tower near the temple; yea, a very high tower, even so high that he could stand upon the top thereof and overlook the land of [b]Shilom, and also the land of [c]Shemlon, which was possessed by the Lamanites; and he could even look over all the land round about.

13 And it came to pass that he caused many buildings to be built in the land Shilom; and he caused a great tower to be built on the [a]hill north of the land Shilom, which had been a resort for the children of Nephi at the time they [b]fled out of the land; and thus did he do with the riches which he obtained by the taxation of his people.

14 And it came to pass that he placed his heart upon his riches, and he spent his time in [a]riotous living with his wives and his concubines; and so did also his priests spend their time with harlots.

15 And it came to pass that he planted vineyards round about in the land; and he built wine-presses, and made [a]wine in abundance; and therefore he became a wine-bibber, and also his people.

16 And it came to pass that the Lamanites began to come in upon his people, upon small numbers, and to slay them in their fields, and while they were tending their flocks.

17 And king Noah sent guards round about the land to keep them

---

3b HEB related words: adjective, "shining"; verb, "to overlay or plate with metal."
4a Prov. 29:3.
 b TG Concubine.
5a 1 Kgs. 12:31; 2 Chr. 11:14 (13–14); Mosiah 11:11; 12:25 (17, 25).

8a Esth. 1:4.
10a 2 Ne. 5:16.
11a Mosiah 11:5 (5, 14); 12:17.
12a Gen. 35:21; Mosiah 2:7 (7–8); 19:5 (5–6).
 b Mosiah 9:14 (6, 8, 14); 22:11 (8, 11).

 c Mosiah 10:7.
13a Mosiah 7:5.
 b Omni 1:12 (12–13).
14a TG Rioting and Reveling.
15a TG Drunkenness; Wine.

off; but he did not send a sufficient number, and the Lamanites came upon them and killed them, and drove many of their flocks out of the land; thus the Lamanites began to destroy them, and to exercise their hatred upon them.

18 And it came to pass that king Noah sent his armies against them, and they were driven back, or they drove them back for a time; therefore, they returned rejoicing in their spoil.

19 And now, because of this great victory they were lifted up in the pride of their hearts; they did [a]boast in their own strength, saying that their fifty could stand against thousands of the Lamanites; and thus they did boast, and did delight in blood, and the shedding of the blood of their brethren, and this because of the wickedness of their king and priests.

20 And it came to pass that there was a man among them whose name was [a]Abinadi; *and he went forth among them, and began to prophesy, saying: Behold, thus saith the Lord, and thus hath he commanded me, saying, Go forth, and say unto this people, thus saith the Lord—Wo be unto this people, for I have seen their abominations, and their wickedness, and their whoredoms; and except they repent I will [b]visit them in mine anger.

21 And except they repent and turn to the Lord their God, behold, I will deliver them into the hands of their enemies; yea, and they shall be brought into [a]bondage; and they shall be afflicted by the hand of their enemies.

22 And it shall come to pass that they shall [a]know that I am the Lord their God, and am a [b]jealous God, visiting the iniquities of my people.

23 And it shall come to pass that except this people repent and turn unto the Lord their God, they shall be brought into bondage; and none shall [a]deliver them, except it be the Lord the Almighty God.

24 Yea, and it shall come to pass that when they shall [a]cry unto me I will be [b]slow to hear their cries; yea, and I will suffer that they be smitten by their enemies.

25 And except they repent in [a]sackcloth and ashes, and cry mightily to the Lord their God, I will not [b]hear their prayers, neither will I deliver them out of their afflictions; and thus saith the Lord, and thus hath he commanded me.

26 Now it came to pass that when Abinadi had spoken these words unto them they were wroth with him, and sought to take away his life; but the Lord [a]delivered him out of their hands.

27 Now when king Noah had heard of the words which Abinadi had spoken unto the people, he was also wroth; and he said: [a]Who is Abinadi, that I and my people should be judged of him, or [b]who is the Lord, that shall bring upon my people such great affliction?

28 I command you to bring Abinadi hither, that I may slay him, for he has said these things that he might [a]stir up my people to anger one with another, and to raise contentions among my people; therefore I will slay him.

29 Now the eyes of the people were [a]blinded; therefore they [b]hardened their hearts against the words of

19a Amos 6: 13; D&C 3: 4.
    TG Boasting.
20a See accounts of
    Abinadi in Mosiah,
    chapters 11–17.
  b TG Punishment;
    Reproof.
21a Mosiah 12: 2; D&C
    101: 79.
22a Ezek. 26: 6; 1 Ne. 21:

26 (25–26); D&C
    43: 25.
  b Ex. 20: 5; Deut. 6: 15;
    32: 21; Mosiah 13: 13.
23a Hosea 13: 10 (4, 10).
24a Micah 3: 4.
  b Ps. 10: 1; Jer. 2: 27;
    Mosiah 21: 15.
25a TG Sackcloth.
  b Isa. 1: 15 (15–17);

59: 2.
26a TG Prophets, Rejection
    of; Protection, Divine.
27a Alma 9: 6 (5–6).
  b Ex. 5: 2; Mosiah 12: 13.
28a TG Provoking.
29a 1 Kgs. 15: 26 (26–34).
    TG Spiritual Blindness.
  b TG Hardheartedness.

[*About 150 B.C.]

Abinadi, and they sought from that time forward to take him. And king Noah hardened his heart against the word of the Lord, and he did not repent of his evil doings.

CHAPTER 12

Abinadi is imprisoned for prophesying the destruction of the people and the death of King Noah—The false priests quote the scriptures and pretend to keep the law of Moses—Abinadi begins to teach them the Ten Commandments.

AND it came to pass that *after the space of two years that Abinadi came among them in disguise, that they knew him not, and began to ªprophesy among them, saying: Thus has the Lord commanded me, saying—Abinadi, go and prophesy unto this my people, for they have hardened their hearts against my words; they have repented not of their evil doings; therefore, I will ᵇvisit them in my anger, yea, in my fierce anger will I visit them in their iniquities and abominations.

2 Yea, wo be unto this generation! And the Lord said unto me: Stretch forth thy hand and prophesy, saying: Thus saith the Lord, it shall come to pass that this generation, because of their iniquities, shall be brought into ªbondage, and shall be smitten on the ᵇcheek; yea, and shall be driven by men, and shall be slain; and the vultures of the air, and the dogs, yea, and the wild beasts, shall devour their ᶜflesh.

3 And it shall come to pass that the ªlife of king Noah shall be valued even as a garment in a hot ᵇfurnace; for he shall know that I am the Lord.

4 And it shall come to pass that I will smite this my people with sore afflictions, yea, with famine and with ªpestilence; and I will cause that they shall ᵇhowl all the day long.

5 Yea, and I will cause that they shall have ªburdens lashed upon their backs; and they shall be driven before like a dumb ass.

6 And it shall come to pass that I will send forth ªhail among them, and it shall smite them; and they shall also be smitten with the ᵇeast wind; and ᶜinsects shall pester their land also, and devour their grain.

7 And they shall be smitten with a great pestilence—and all this will I do because of their ªiniquities and abominations.

8 And it shall come to pass that except they repent I will utterly ªdestroy them from off the face of the earth; yet they shall leave a ᵇrecord behind them, and I will preserve them for other nations which shall possess the land; yea, even this will I do that I may discover the abominations of this people to other nations. And many things did Abinadi prophesy against this people.

9 And it came to pass that they were angry with him; and they took him and carried him bound before the king, and said unto the king: Behold, we have brought a man before thee who has prophesied evil concerning thy people, and saith that God will destroy them.

10 And he also prophesieth evil concerning thy ªlife, and saith that thy life shall be as a garment in a furnace of fire.

11 And again, he saith that thou

12 1a TG Missionary Work.
  b Isa. 65:6 (6–7, 11);
    Jer. 9:9.
2a 1 Kgs. 8:46; Mosiah
    11:21; 20:21.
  b Lam. 3:30; Mosiah
    21:3 (3–4, 13).
  c Deut. 28:26.
3a Amos 7:11 (10–11);
    Mosiah 12:10 (10–12).

  b Mosiah 19:20.
4a Luke 21:11 (10–13);
    2 Ne. 6:15; D&C
    97:26 (22–26).
  b Mosiah 21:9 (1–15).
5a Mosiah 21:3.
6a Ex. 9:18 (13–35);
    Ezek. 13:13.
  b Jer. 18:17; Ezek.
    27:26; Mosiah 7:31.

  c Ex. 10:4 (1–12).
7a D&C 3:18.
8a Gen. 6:13; Isa.
    42:14 (14–15);
    2 Ne. 26:10 (10–11);
    Alma 45:11 (9–14).
  b Morm. 8:14 (14–16).
10a Amos 7:11 (10–11);
    Mosiah 12:3.

[*About 148 B.C.]

shalt be as a stalk, even as a dry stalk of the field, which is run over by the beasts and trodden under foot.

12 And again, he saith thou shalt be as the blossoms of a thistle, which, when it is fully ripe, if the wind bloweth, it is driven forth upon the face of the land. And he pretendeth the Lord hath spoken it. And he saith all this shall come upon thee except thou repent, and this because of thine iniquities.

13 And now, O king, what great evil hast thou done, or what great sins have thy people committed, that we should be *a*condemned of God or judged of this man?

14 And now, O king, behold, we are *a*guiltless, and thou, O king, hast not sinned; therefore, this man has *b*lied concerning you, and he has prophesied in vain.

15 And behold, we are strong, we shall not come into bondage, or be taken captive by our enemies; yea, and thou hast prospered in the land, and thou shalt also prosper.

16 Behold, here is the man, we deliver him into thy hands; thou mayest do with him as seemeth thee good.

17 And it came to pass that king Noah caused that Abinadi should be cast into prison; and he commanded that the *a*priests should gather themselves together that he might hold a council with them what he should do with him.

18 And it came to pass that they said unto the king: Bring him hither that we may question him; and the king commanded that he should be brought before them.

19 And they began to question him, that they might cross him, that thereby they might have wherewith to *a*accuse him; but he answered all their

questions, yea, to their astonishment; for he did *b*withstand them in all their questions, and did confound them in all their words.

20 And it came to pass that one of them said unto him: *a*What meaneth the words which are written, and which have been taught by our fathers, saying:

21 *a*How beautiful upon the mountains are the feet of him *b*that bringeth good tidings; that publisheth peace; that bringeth good tidings of good; that publisheth salvation; that saith unto Zion, Thy God reigneth;

22 *a*Thy watchmen shall lift up the voice; with the voice together shall they sing; for they shall see eye to eye when the Lord shall bring again Zion;

23 Break forth into joy; sing together ye waste places of Jerusalem; for the Lord hath comforted his people, he hath redeemed Jerusalem;

24 The Lord hath made bare his holy *a*arm in the eyes of all the nations, and all the ends of the earth shall see the salvation of our God?

25 And now Abinadi said unto them: Are you *a*priests, and pretend to teach this people, and to understand the spirit of prophesying, and yet desire to know of me what these things mean?

26 I say unto you, wo be unto you for perverting the ways of the Lord! For if ye understand these things ye have not taught them; therefore, ye have perverted the ways of the Lord.

27 Ye have not applied your *a*hearts to *b*understanding; therefore, ye have not been wise. Therefore, what teach ye this people?

28 And they said: We teach the law of Moses.

29 And again he said unto them:

13a Mosiah 11: 27.
14a Jer. 2: 35; Alma 21: 6.
  b Hel. 13: 26 (24–28).
17a Mosiah 11: 11.
19a John 8: 6.
  b D&C 100: 5 (5–6).

20a Mosiah 13: 3.
21a Isa. 52: 7 (7–10).
  b Mosiah 15: 14;
    27: 37 (36–37).
22a Mosiah 15: 29.
24a Isa. 33: 2; Omni 1: 13.

25a John 3: 10 (7–10);
    Mosiah 11: 5.
27a Prov. 8: 5; Mosiah 2: 9.
  b TG Understanding.

[About 148 B.C.]

If ye teach the *a*law of Moses why do ye not keep it? Why do ye set your hearts upon *b*riches? Why do ye commit whoredoms and *c*spend your strength with harlots, yea, and cause this people to commit sin, that the Lord has cause to send me to prophesy against this people, yea, even a great evil against this people?

30 Know ye not that I speak the *a*truth? Yea, ye know that I speak the truth; and you ought to tremble before God.

31 And it shall come to pass that ye shall be smitten for your iniquities, for ye have said that ye teach the law of Moses. And what know ye concerning the law of Moses? *a*Doth salvation come by the law of Moses? What say ye?

32 And they answered and said that salvation did come by the law of Moses.

33 But now Abinadi said unto them: I know if ye *a*keep the commandments of God ye shall be saved; yea, if ye keep the commandments which the Lord delivered unto Moses in the mount of *b*Sinai, saying:

34 *a*I am the Lord thy God, who hath *b*brought thee out of the land of Egypt, out of the house of bondage.

35 Thou shalt have no *a*other God before me.

36 *a*Thou shalt not make unto thee any graven image, or any likeness of any thing in heaven above, or things which are in the earth beneath.

37 Now Abinadi said unto them, Have ye done all this? I say unto you, Nay, ye have not. And have ye *a*taught this people that they should do all these things? I say unto you, Nay, ye have not.

CHAPTER 13

Abinadi is protected by divine power—He teaches the Ten Commandments—Salvation does not come by the law of Moses alone—God himself shall make an atonement and redeem his people.

AND now when the king had heard these words, he said unto his priests: Away with this fellow, and slay him; for what have we to do with him, for he is *a*mad.

2 And they stood forth and attempted to lay their hands on him; but he withstood them, and said unto them:

3 *a*Touch me not, for God shall smite you if ye lay your hands upon me, for I have not delivered the message which the Lord sent me to deliver; neither have I told you that which ye *b*requested that I should tell; therefore, God will not suffer that I shall be destroyed at this time.

4 But I must fulfil the commandments wherewith God has commanded me; and because I have told you the truth ye are angry with me. And again, because I have spoken the word of God ye have judged me that I am mad.

5 Now it came to pass after Abinadi had spoken these words that the people of king Noah durst not lay their hands on him, for the Spirit of the Lord was upon him; and his face *a*shone with exceeding luster, even as Moses' did while in the mount of Sinai, while speaking with the Lord.

6 And he spake with *a*power and authority from God; and he continued his words, saying:

7 Ye see that ye have not power to

29a TG Law of Moses.
　b Jer. 48: 7.
　c TG Sexual Immorality.
30a Jacob 7: 14; Alma 30: 42 (41–42).
31a Mosiah 3: 15; 13: 28 (27–32); Alma 25: 16.
33a Deut. 27: 1; Neh. 9: 13; 3 Ne. 25: 4.

　b Ex. 19: 18 (9, 16–20); Mosiah 13: 5.
34a Ex. 20: 2 (2–4).
　b Ex. 12: 51; 1 Ne. 17: 40; Mosiah 7: 19.
35a Hosea 13: 4.
　TG Idolatry.
36a Mosiah 13: 12.
37a Mosiah 13: 25 (25–26).

13 1a John 10: 20 (19–20).
3a 1 Ne. 17: 48.
　b Mosiah 12: 20 (20–24).
5a Ex. 34: 29 (29–35).
6a TG Priesthood, Power of; Teaching with the Spirit.

[About 148 B.C.]

slay me, therefore I finish my *message. Yea, and I perceive that it cuts you to your hearts because I tell you the truth concerning your iniquities.

8 Yea, and my words fill you with wonder and amazement, and with anger.

9 But I finish my message; and then it *matters not whither I go, if it so be that I am saved.

10 But this much I tell you, what you *do with me, after this, shall be as a *type and a shadow of things which are to come.

11 And now I read unto you the remainder of the *commandments of God, for I perceive that they are not written in your hearts; I perceive that ye have studied and taught *iniquity the most part of your lives.

12 And now, ye remember that I *said unto you: Thou shalt not make unto thee any graven image, or any likeness of things which are in heaven above, or which are in the earth beneath, or which are in the water under the earth.

13 And again: Thou shalt not *bow down thyself unto them, nor serve them; for I the Lord thy God am a jealous God, visiting the iniquities of the fathers upon the children, unto the third and fourth generations of them that hate me;

14 And showing mercy unto thousands of them that love me and keep my commandments.

15 Thou shalt not take the name of the Lord thy God in vain; for the Lord will not hold him *guiltless that taketh his name in vain.

16 Remember the *sabbath day, to keep it holy.

17 Six days shalt thou labor, and do all thy work;

18 But the seventh day, the sabbath of the Lord thy God, thou shalt not do any work, thou, nor thy son, nor thy daughter, thy man-servant, nor thy maid-servant, nor thy cattle, nor thy stranger that is within thy gates;

19 For in *six days the Lord made heaven and earth, and the sea, and all that in them is; wherefore the Lord blessed the sabbath day, and hallowed it.

20 *Honor thy *father and thy mother, that thy days may be long upon the land which the Lord thy God giveth thee.

21 Thou shalt not *kill.

22 Thou shalt not commit *adultery. Thou shalt not *steal.

23 Thou shalt not bear *false witness against thy neighbor.

24 Thou shalt not *covet thy neighbor's house, thou shalt not covet thy neighbor's wife, nor his man-servant, nor his maid-servant, nor his ox, nor his ass, nor anything that is thy neighbor's.

25 And it came to pass that after Abinadi had made an end of these sayings that he said unto them: Have ye *taught this people that they should observe to do all these things for to keep these commandments?

26 I say unto you, Nay; for if ye had, the Lord would not have caused me to come forth and to prophesy evil concerning this people.

27 And now ye have said that salvation cometh by the law of Moses. I say unto you that it is expedient that ye should *keep the law of Moses as yet; but I say unto you,

---

7a Prov. 15: 10; 1 Ne. 16: 2 (1–3); 2 Ne. 9: 40.
9a Dan. 3: 16 (16–18).
10a Alma 25: 10.
  b Jer. 26: 14; Mosiah 17: 18 (13–19).
11a Ex. 20: 1 (1–17).
  b Micah 2: 1 (1–2).
12a Mosiah 12: 36.

13a Ex. 20: 5.
15a Ex. 20: 7; Morm. 7: 7; D&C 58: 30.
16a Mosiah 18: 23.
  TG Sabbath.
19a Gen. 1: 31; Ex. 20: 11.
20a TG Honoring Father and Mother.
  b Prov. 20: 20.
21a Ex. 20: 13; Deut.

5: 17; Matt. 5: 21 (21–37); 3 Ne. 12: 21 (21–37); D&C 42: 18.
22a TG Adultery.
  b TG Stealing.
23a Prov. 24: 28.
24a TG Covetousness.
25a Mosiah 12: 37.
27a 2 Ne. 25: 24.

that the time shall come when it shall [b]no more be expedient to keep the law of Moses.

28 And moreover, I say unto you, that [a]salvation doth not come by the [b]law alone; and were it not for the [c]atonement, which God himself shall make for the sins and iniquities of his people, that they must unavoidably perish, notwithstanding the law of Moses.

29 And now I say unto you that it was expedient that there should be a law given to the children of Israel, yea, even a very [a]strict law; for they were a stiffnecked people, [b]quick to do iniquity, and slow to remember the Lord their God;

30 Therefore there was a [a]law given them, yea, a law of performances and of [b]ordinances, a law which they were to [c]observe strictly from day to day, to keep them in remembrance of God and their duty towards him.

31 But behold, I say unto you, that all these things were [a]types of things to come.

32 And now, did they [a]understand the law? I say unto you, Nay, they did not all understand the law; and this because of the hardness of their hearts; for they understood not that there could not any man be saved [b]except it were through the redemption of God.

33 For behold, did not Moses prophesy unto them concerning the coming of the Messiah, and that God should redeem his people? Yea, and even [a]all the prophets who have

prophesied ever since the world began—have they not spoken more or less concerning these things?

34 Have they not said that [a]God himself should come down among the children of men, and take upon him the form of man, and go forth in mighty power upon the face of the earth?

35 Yea, and have they not said also that he should bring to pass the [a]resurrection of the dead, and that he, himself, should be oppressed and afflicted?

CHAPTER 14

Isaiah speaks Messianically—Messiah's humiliation and sufferings are set forth—He makes his soul an offering for sin and makes intercession for transgressors—Compare Isaiah 53.

YEA, even doth not Isaiah say: Who hath [a]believed our report, and to whom is the arm of the Lord revealed?

2 For he shall grow up before him as a tender plant, and as a root out of dry ground; he hath no form nor comeliness; and when we shall see him there is no beauty that we should desire him.

3 He is [a]despised and rejected of men; a man of sorrows, and acquainted with grief; and we hid as it were our faces from him; he was despised, and we esteemed him not.

4 Surely he has [a]borne our [b]griefs, and carried our sorrows; yet we did esteem him stricken, smitten of God, and afflicted.

27b 3 Ne. 9: 19 (19–20); 15: 4 (2–10).
28a Gal. 2: 16; Mosiah 12: 31; Alma 25: 16. TG Redemption; Salvation, Plan of.
  b Rom. 7: 4 (4–25); Gal. 2: 21; 3: 2; Heb. 10: 1; 2 Ne. 2: 5; Mosiah 3: 15 (14–15).
  c TG Jesus Christ, Atonement through.
29a Josh. 1: 8; Heb. 9: 10 (8–10); Mosiah 3: 14 (14–15); Alma 25: 15

(15–16); D&C 41: 5 (4–5).
  b 1 Ne. 17: 45; Alma 46: 8.
30a Rom. 7: 1 (1–3).
  b TG Ordinance.
  c 2 Ne. 25: 24; Jacob 4: 5.
31a Mosiah 16: 14; Alma 25: 15 (15–16). TG Jesus Christ, Types of, in Anticipation; Symbolism.
32a Ps. 111: 10.
  b 2 Ne. 25: 23 (23–25).
33a 1 Pet. 1: 11; 1 Ne. 10: 5;

Jacob 4: 4; 7: 11 (11–12); Alma 25: 16 (10–16); 30: 44. TG Jesus Christ, Prophecies about.
34a Mosiah 7: 27; 15: 1; 17: 8; Alma 10: 21. TG Jesus Christ— Jehovah.
35a Isa. 26: 19; 2 Ne. 2: 8.
14 1a Isa. 53: 1 (1–12).
  3a Ps. 22: 6; 1 Ne. 19: 14.
  4a Alma 7: 11.
  b Matt. 8: 17.

[About 148 B.C.]

5 But he was *a*wounded for our *b*transgressions, he was bruised for our iniquities; the chastisement of our peace was upon him; and with his stripes we are *c*healed.

6 All we, like *a*sheep, have gone astray; we have turned every one to his own way; and the Lord hath laid on him the iniquities of us all.

7 He was oppressed, and he was afflicted, yet he *a*opened not his mouth; he is brought as a *b*lamb to the slaughter, and as a sheep before her shearers is dumb so he opened not his mouth.

8 He was taken from prison and from judgment; and who shall declare his generation? For he was cut off out of the land of the living; for the transgressions of my people was he stricken.

9 And he made his grave with the wicked, and with the *a*rich in his death; because he had done no *b*evil, neither was any deceit in his mouth.

10 Yet it pleased the Lord to *a*bruise him; he hath put him to grief; when thou shalt make his soul an offering for sin he shall see his *b*seed, he shall prolong his days, and the pleasure of the Lord shall prosper in his hand.

11 He shall see the travail of his soul, and shall be satisfied; by his knowledge shall my righteous servant justify many; for he shall *a*bear their iniquities.

12 Therefore will I divide him a portion with the *a*great, and *b*he shall divide the spoil with the strong; because he hath poured out his soul unto death; and he was numbered with the transgressors; and he bore the sins of many, and made *c*intercession for the transgressors.

CHAPTER 15

How Christ is both the Father and the Son—He shall make intercession and bear the transgressions of his people—They and all the holy prophets are his seed—He bringeth to pass the resurrection—Little children have eternal life.

AND now Abinadi said unto them: I would that ye should understand that *a*God himself shall *b*come down among the children of men, and shall *c*redeem his people.

2 And because he *a*dwelleth in *b*flesh he shall be called the *c*Son of God, and having subjected the flesh to the *d*will of the *e*Father, being the Father and the Son—

3 The Father, *a*because he was *b*conceived by the power of God; and the Son, because of the flesh; thus becoming the Father and Son—

5a TG Jesus Christ, Crucifixion of.
  b Mosiah 15:9; Alma 11:40.
  c 1 Pet. 2:24 (24–25).
6a Matt. 9:36; 2 Ne. 12:5; 28:14; Alma 5:37.
7a Isa. 53:7 (7–8); Mark 15:3 (2–14); John 19:9 (9–10); 1 Pet. 2:23 (22–23); Mosiah 15:6. TG Jesus Christ, Trial of.
  b Jer. 11:19. TG Passover.
9a Matt. 27:57 (57–60); Mark 15:46 (27, 43–46). TG Jesus Christ,

Death of.
  b John 19:4.
10a Gen. 3:15; Rom. 16:20.
  b Mosiah 15:10 (10–13).
11a Lev. 16:22 (21–22); 1 Pet. 3:18; D&C 19:16 (16–19).
12a Luke 24:26.
  b Mosiah 15:12.
  c 2 Ne. 2:9; Mosiah 15:8; Moro. 7:28 (27–28).
15 1a Isa. 54:5; 1 Tim. 3:16; Mosiah 13:34 (33–34).
  b TG God, Manifestations of.
  c TG Jesus Christ, Mission of.

2a Mosiah 3:5; 7:27; Alma 7:9 (9–13).
  b TG Jesus Christ, Condescension of.
  c John 19:7. TG Jesus Christ, Divine Sonship.
  d TG God, Will of.
  e Isa. 9:6; 64:8; John 10:30; 14:10 (8–10); Mosiah 5:7; Alma 11:39 (38–39); Ether 3:14.
3a D&C 93:4.
  b Luke 1:32 (31–33); Mosiah 3:8 (8–9); Alma 7:10; 3 Ne. 1:14. TG Jesus Christ, Divine Sonship.

[About 148 B.C.]

4 And they are *a*one God, yea, the very *b*Eternal *c*Father of heaven and of earth.

5 And thus the flesh becoming subject to the Spirit, or the Son to the Father, being one God, *a*suffereth temptation, and yieldeth not to the temptation, but suffereth himself to be mocked, and *b*scourged, and cast out, and disowned by his *c*people.

6 And after all this, after working many mighty miracles among the children of men, he shall be led, yea, even *a*as Isaiah said, as a sheep before the shearer is dumb, so he *b*opened not his mouth.

7 Yea, even so he shall be led, *a*crucified, and slain, the *b*flesh becoming subject even unto death, the *c*will of the Son being swallowed up in the will of the Father.

8 And thus God breaketh the *a*bands of death, having gained the *b*victory over death; giving the Son power to make *c*intercession for the children of men—

9 Having ascended into heaven, having the bowels of mercy; being filled with compassion towards the children of men; standing betwixt them and justice; having broken the bands of death, taken upon *a*himself their iniquity and their transgressions, having redeemed them, and *b*satisfied the demands of justice.

10 And now I say unto you, who shall declare his *a*generation? Behold, I say unto you, that when his soul has been made an offering for *b*sin he shall see his *c*seed. And now what say ye? And who shall be his seed?

11 Behold I say unto you, that whosoever has heard the words of the *a*prophets, yea, all the holy prophets who have prophesied concerning the coming of the Lord—I say unto you, that all those who have hearkened unto their words, and believed that the Lord would redeem his people, and have looked forward to that day for a remission of their sins, I say unto you, that these are his seed, or they are the heirs of the *b*kingdom of God.

12 For these are they whose sins *a*he has borne; these are they for whom he has died, to redeem them from their transgressions. And now, are they not his seed?

13 Yea, and are not the *a*prophets, every one that has opened his mouth to prophesy, that has not fallen into transgression, I mean all the holy prophets ever since the world began? I say unto you that they are his seed.

14 And these are *a*they who have published peace, who have brought good *b*tidings of good, who have *c*published salvation; and said unto Zion: Thy God reigneth!

4a Deut. 6: 4.
  TG Godhead.
 b Alma 11: 39.
 c Mosiah 3: 8; Hel.
   14: 12; 3 Ne. 9: 15;
   Ether 4: 7.
5a Luke 4: 2; Heb. 4: 15.
   TG Jesus Christ,
   Temptation of.
 b John 19: 1.
 c Matt. 21: 42; Mark
   8: 31; Luke 17: 25;
   23: 38.
6a Isa. 53: 7.
 b Luke 23: 9; John
   19: 9 (9–10); Mosiah
   14: 7. TG Jesus Christ,
   Trial of.
7a TG Jesus Christ,

   Crucifixion of.
 b Isa. 53: 10.
 c Luke 22: 42; John
   6: 38; 3 Ne. 11: 11.
8a Alma 5: 7.
 b Hosea 13: 14; 1 Cor.
   15: 57 (55–57);
   Mosiah 16: 7.
 c 2 Ne. 2: 9; Mosiah
   14: 12; Moro. 7: 28
   (27–28).
9a Mosiah 14: 5 (5–12).
   TG Self-sacrifice.
 b TG Jesus Christ,
   Mission of.
10a Isa. 53: 8.
 b Lev. 6: 25 (25–26).
 c Isa. 53: 10; Mosiah
   5: 7; 27: 25; Moro.

   7: 19. TG God the
   Father—Jehovah.
11a Luke 10: 16; D&C
   84: 36 (36–38).
 b TG Kingdom of God,
   in Heaven; Kingdom
   of God, on Earth.
12a Mosiah 14: 12; Alma
   7: 13; 11: 40 (40–
   41).
13a Zech. 7: 12; Matt.
   11: 13; 1 Ne. 3: 20.
   TG Sons and Daughters
   of God.
14a Mosiah 12: 21 (21–24);
   27: 37.
 b Isa. 52: 7.
 c TG Missionary Work.

15 And O how beautiful upon the mountains were their feet!

16 And again, how beautiful upon the mountains are the feet of those that are still publishing peace!

17 And again, how beautiful upon the mountains are the feet of those who shall hereafter publish peace, yea, from this time henceforth and forever!

18 And behold, I say unto you, this is not all. For O how beautiful upon the mountains are the ªfeet of him that bringeth good tidings, that is the founder of ᵇpeace, yea, even the Lord, who has redeemed his people; yea, him who has granted salvation unto his people;

19 For were it not for the redemption which he hath made for his people, which was prepared from the ªfoundation of the world, I say unto you, were it not for this, all mankind must have ᵇperished.

20 But behold, the bands of death shall be broken, and the Son reigneth, and hath power over the dead; therefore, he bringeth to pass the resurrection of the dead.

21 And there cometh a resurrection, even a ªfirst resurrection; yea, even a resurrection of those that have been, and who are, and who shall be, even until the resurrection of Christ—for so shall he be called.

22 And now, the resurrection of all the prophets, and all those that have believed in their words, or all those that have kept the commandments of God, shall come forth in the first resurrection; therefore, they are the first resurrection.

23 They are raised to ªdwell with God who has redeemed them; thus they have eternal life through Christ, who has ᵇbroken the bands of death.

24 And these are those who have part in the first resurrection; and these are they that have died before Christ came, in their ignorance, not having ªsalvation declared unto them. And thus the Lord bringeth about the restoration of these; and they have a part in the first resurrection, or have eternal life, being redeemed by the Lord.

25 And little ªchildren also have eternal life.

26 But behold, and ªfear, and tremble before God, for ye ought to tremble; for the Lord redeemeth none such that ᵇrebel against him and ᶜdie in their sins; yea, even all those that have perished in their sins ever since the world began, that have wilfully rebelled against God, that have known the commandments of God, and would not keep them; ᵈthese are they that have ᵉno part in the first ᶠresurrection.

27 Therefore ought ye not to tremble? For salvation cometh to none such; for the Lord hath redeemed none such; yea, neither can the Lord redeem such; for he cannot deny himself; for he cannot deny ªjustice when it has its claim.

28 And now I say unto you that the time shall come that the ªsalvation of the Lord shall be declared to every nation, kindred, tongue, and people.

29 Yea, Lord, ªthy ᵇwatchmen shall lift up their voice; with the voice together shall they sing; for

---

18a Nahum 1:15; 3 Ne.
20:40; D&C 128:19.
  b Micah 5:5 (4–7);
John 16:33. TG Peace
of God.
19a Mosiah 4:6.
  b 2 Ne. 9:7 (6–13).
21a Jacob 4:11; Alma
40:16 (16–21).
TG Firstfruits.
23a Ps. 15:1 (1–5); 24:3
(3–4); 1 Ne. 15:33 (33–
36); D&C 76:62 (50–70).

  b TG Death, Power over.
24a 2 Ne. 9:26 (25–26);
D&C 137:7.
25a D&C 29:46; 137:10.
TG Salvation of Little
Children.
26a Deut. 5:29; Jacob
6:9; 7:19.
  b Josh. 22:16; Job
24:13; Ps. 5:10;
1 Ne. 2:23 (21–24).
  c Ezek. 18:26; 1 Ne.
15:33 (32–33); Moro.

10:26.
  d Alma 40:19.
  e D&C 76:85.
  f TG Telestial Glory.
27a Alma 12:32;
34:16 (15–16); 42:1.
28a Ps. 67:2 (1–2).
TG Missionary Work.
29a Isa. 52:8 (8–10);
Mosiah 12:22 (22–24).
  b TG Watchmen.

[About 148 B.C.]

they shall see eye to eye, when the Lord shall bring again Zion.

30 Break forth into joy, sing together, ye waste places of Jerusalem; for the Lord hath comforted his people, he hath redeemed Jerusalem.

31 The Lord hath made bare his holy arm in the eyes of all the nations; and all the ends of the earth shall see the [a]salvation of our God.

CHAPTER 16

God redeems men from their lost and fallen state—Those who are carnal remain as though there was no redemption—Christ brings to pass a resurrection to endless life or to endless damnation.

AND now, it came to pass that after Abinadi had spoken these words he stretched forth his hand and said: The time shall come when all shall see the [a]salvation of the Lord; when [b]every nation, kindred, tongue, and people shall see eye to eye and shall [c]confess before God that his [d]judgments are just.

2 And then shall the [a]wicked be [b]cast out, and they shall have cause to howl, and [c]weep, and wail, and gnash their teeth; and this because they would not [d]hearken unto the voice of the Lord; therefore the Lord redeemeth them not.

3 For they are [a]carnal and devilish, and the devil has power over them;

yea, even that old serpent that did [b]beguile our first parents, which was the [c]cause of their fall; which was the cause of [d]all mankind becoming carnal, sensual, devilish, [e]knowing evil from good, [f]subjecting themselves to the devil.

4 Thus all mankind were [a]lost; and behold, they would have been endlessly lost were it not that God redeemed his people from their lost and fallen state.

5 But remember that he that persists in his own [a]carnal nature, and goes on in the ways of sin and rebellion against God, remaineth in his fallen state and the [b]devil hath all power over him. Therefore he is as though there was no [c]redemption made, being an enemy to God; and also is the [d]devil an enemy to God.

6 And now if Christ had not come into the world, speaking of things to come [a]as though they had already come, there could have been no redemption.

7 And if Christ had not risen from the dead, or have broken the bands of death that the grave should have no victory, and that death should have no [a]sting, there could have been no resurrection.

8 But there is a [a]resurrection, therefore the grave hath no victory, and the sting of [b]death is swallowed up in Christ.

9 He is the [a]light and the life of the world; yea, a light that is endless,

31a TG Salvation.
16 1a TG Salvation.
  b Mosiah 3:20 (20–21).
  c Mosiah 27:31; D&C 88:104.
  d TG Justice.
2a Ps. 91:8; Jer. 12:1; D&C 1:9 (9–10).
  b Ps. 52:5; D&C 63:54.
  c Matt. 13:42 (41–42); Luke 13:28; Alma 40:13; Moses 1:22.
  d Jer. 44:16; Ether 11:13.
3a Gal. 5:19 (16–26); Mosiah 3:19.
  b Gen. 3:13; 2 Ne. 9:9; Ether 8:25;

Moses 4:19 (5–19).
  c Moses 5:13.
  d Ps. 14:3. TG Man, Natural, Not Spiritually Reborn.
  e Gen. 3:5; 2 Ne. 2:18 (18, 26); Alma 29:5; Moro. 7:16 (15–19).
  f Alma 5:41 (41–42); D&C 29:40.
4a 2 Ne. 9:7; Alma 11:45; 12:36; 42:6 (6, 9, 14). TG Fall of Man.
5a TG Carnal Mind; Man, Natural, Not Spiritually Reborn.
  b TG Bondage, Spiritual.

  c 1 Ne. 10:6; 2 Ne. 2:6 (5–8); 25:20; Alma 12:22 (22–25).
  d TG Devil.
6a 2 Ne. 25:26 (24–27); Jarom 1:11; Mosiah 3:13.
7a Hosea 13:14; Mosiah 15:8 (8, 20).
8a 2 Ne. 9:10; Alma 42:15 (6–15).
  b 1 Cor. 15:55; Morm. 7:5.
9a Ether 3:14; Moro. 7:18; D&C 88:13 (7–13). TG Jesus Christ, Light of the World.

that can never be darkened; yea, and also a life which is endless, that there can be no more death.

10 Even this mortal shall put on ªimmortality, and this ᵇcorruption shall put on incorruption, and shall be brought to ᶜstand before the bar of God, to be judged of him according to their works whether they be good or whether they be evil—

11 If they be good, to the resurrection of ªendless life and ᵇhappiness; and if they be evil, to the resurrection of ᶜendless damnation, being delivered up to the devil, who hath subjected them, which is damnation—

12 Having gone according to their own carnal wills and desires; having never called upon the Lord while the arms of mercy were extended towards them; for the arms of mercy were extended towards them, and they would ªnot; they being warned of their iniquities and yet they would not depart from them; and they were commanded to repent and yet they would not repent.

13 And now, ought ye not to tremble and repent of your sins, and remember that only in and through Christ ye can be saved?

14 Therefore, if ye teach the ªlaw of Moses, also teach that it is a ᵇshadow of those things which are to come—

15 Teach them that redemption cometh through Christ the Lord, who is the very ªEternal Father. Amen.

CHAPTER 17

Alma believes and writes the words of Abinadi—Abinadi suffers death by fire—He prophesies disease and death by fire upon his murderers.

AND now it came to pass that when Abinadi had finished these sayings, that the king commanded that the ªpriests should take him and cause that he should be put to ᵇdeath.

2 But there was one among them whose name was ªAlma, he also being a descendant of Nephi. And he was a young man, and he ᵇbelieved the words which Abinadi had spoken, for he knew concerning the iniquity which Abinadi had testified against them; therefore he began to plead with the king that he would not be angry with Abinadi, but suffer that he might depart in peace.

3 But the king was more wroth, and caused that Alma should be cast out from among them, and sent his servants after him that they might slay him.

4 But he fled from before them and ªhid himself that they found him not. And he being concealed for many days did ᵇwrite all the words which Abinadi had spoken.

5 And it came to pass that the king caused that his guards should surround Abinadi and take him; and they bound him and cast him into prison.

6 And after three days, having counseled with his ªpriests, he caused that he should again be brought before him.

7 And he said unto him: Abinadi, we have found an accusation against thee, and thou art worthy of death.

8 For thou hast said that ªGod himself should come down among

10a Alma 40:2.
   TG Immortality.
  b 1 Cor. 15:42.
  c 3 Ne. 26:4. TG Jesus Christ, Judge.
11a Dan. 12:2 (2–3); John 5:29 (28–29).
  b TG Happiness.
  c Alma 9:11.
   TG Damnation.

12a TG Prophets, Rejection of.
14a TG Law of Moses.
  b Mosiah 13:31; Alma 25:15 (15–16).
   TG Jesus Christ, Types of, in Anticipation.
15a Mosiah 3:5.
17 1a TG False Priesthoods.
  b Jer. 26:11.

2a Mosiah 23:9.
  b Mosiah 26:15; Alma 5:11.
4a 1 Kgs. 17:3 (1–16); Ether 13:13 (13, 22).
  b TG Scriptures, Writing of.
6a Mosiah 11:5.
8a Mosiah 7:27; 13:34.

[About 148 B.C.]

the children of men; and now, for this cause thou shalt be put to death unless thou wilt recall all the words which thou hast spoken evil concerning me and my people.

9 Now Abinadi said unto him: I say unto you, I will ^anot recall the words which I have spoken unto you concerning this people, for they are true; and that ye may know of their surety I have suffered myself that I have fallen into your hands.

10 Yea, and I will ^asuffer even until death, and I will not recall my words, and they shall stand as a ^btestimony against you. And if ye slay me ye will shed ^cinnocent blood, and this shall also stand as a testimony against you at the last day.

11 And now king Noah was about to release him, for he feared his word; for he feared that the judgments of God would come upon him.

12 But the ^apriests lifted up their voices against him, and began to accuse him, saying: He has reviled the king. Therefore the king was stirred up in ^banger against him, and he delivered him up that he might be slain.

13 And it came to pass that they took him and bound him, and ^ascourged his skin with faggots, yea, even unto ^bdeath.

14 And now when the flames began to scorch him, he cried unto them, saying:

15 Behold, even as ye have done unto me, so shall it come to pass that thy ^aseed shall cause that many shall suffer the pains that I do suffer, even the pains of ^bdeath by fire; and this because ye believe in the salvation of the Lord their God.

16 And it will come to pass that ye shall be afflicted with all manner of ^adiseases because of your iniquities.

17 Yea, and ye shall be smitten on every hand, and shall be driven and scattered to and fro, even as a wild flock is driven by wild and ferocious beasts.

18 And in that day ye shall be ^ahunted, and ye shall be taken by the hand of your enemies, and then ye shall suffer, as I suffer, the pains of ^bdeath by fire.

19 Thus God executeth ^avengeance upon those that destroy his people. O God, ^breceive my soul.

20 And now, *when ^aAbinadi had said these words, he fell, having suffered death by fire; yea, having been put to death because he would not deny the commandments of God, having sealed the truth of his words by his ^bdeath.

CHAPTER 18

Alma preaches in private—He sets forth the covenant of baptism and baptizes at the waters of Mormon—He organizes the Church of Christ and ordains priests—They support themselves and teach the people—Alma and his people flee from King Noah into the wilderness.

AND now, it came to pass that Alma, who had fled from the servants of king Noah, ^arepented of his sins and iniquities, and went about privately among the people, and began to teach the words of Abinadi—

2 Yea, concerning that which was to come, and also concerning the resurrection of the dead, and the ^aredemption of the people, which was to be brought to pass through

9a TG Courage; Integrity.
10a TG Persecution.
  b TG Testimony.
  c Jer. 26: 15 (14–15);
    Lam. 4: 13; Alma
    14: 11; 60: 13.
12a Mosiah 11: 5; 12: 25
    (17, 25).
  b Prov. 20: 2.
13a Dan. 3: 6; James 5: 10

(10–11); Alma 14: 26
(20–27).
  b Mosiah 7: 28; 21: 30;
    Alma 25: 11.
15a Mosiah 13: 10; Alma
    25: 12 (7–12).
  b Alma 25: 5.
16a Deut. 28: 60 (25–60).
18a Alma 25: 8.
  b Mosiah 13: 10; 19: 20;

    Alma 25: 11 (7–12).
19a Ps. 125: 3.
  b Luke 23: 46; Acts 7: 59.
20a Mosiah 7: 26.
  b Heb. 9: 16 (16–17).
18 1a Mosiah 23: 9.
  2a TG Jesus Christ,
    Redeemer.

[*About 148 B.C.]

the power, and sufferings, and ᵇdeath of Christ, and his resurrection and ascension into heaven.

3 And as many as would hear his word he did teach. And he taught them privately, that it might not come to the knowledge of the king. And many did believe his words.

4 And it came to pass that as many as did believe him did go forth to a ᵃplace which was called Mormon, having received its name from the king, being in the ᵇborders of the land having been infested, by times or at seasons, by wild beasts.

5 Now, there was in Mormon a fountain of pure water, and Alma resorted thither, there being near the water a thicket of small trees, where he did hide himself in the daytime from the searches of the king.

6 And it came to pass that as many as believed him went thither to hear his words.

7 And it came to pass *after many days there were a goodly number gathered together at the place of Mormon, to hear the words of Alma. Yea, all were gathered together that believed on his word, to hear him. And he did ᵃteach them, and did preach unto them repentance, and redemption, and faith on the Lord.

8 And it came to pass that he said unto them: Behold, here are the waters of Mormon (for thus were they called) and now, as ye are ᵃdesirous to come into the ᵇfold of God, and to be called his people, and are willing to bear one another's burdens, that they may be light;

9 Yea, and are ᵃwilling to mourn with those that ᵇmourn; yea, and

comfort those that stand in need of comfort, and to stand as ᶜwitnesses of God at all times and in all things, and in all places that ye may be in, even until death, that ye may be redeemed of God, and be numbered with those of the ᵈfirst resurrection, that ye may have eternal life—

10 Now I say unto you, if this be the desire of your hearts, what have you against being ᵃbaptized in the ᵇname of the Lord, as a witness before him that ye have entered into a ᶜcovenant with him, that ye will serve him and keep his commandments, that he may pour out his Spirit more abundantly upon you?

11 And now when the people had heard these words, they clapped their hands for joy, and exclaimed: This is the desire of our hearts.

12 And now it came to pass that Alma took Helam, he being one of the first, and went and stood forth in the water, and cried, saying: O Lord, pour out thy Spirit upon thy servant, that he may do this work with holiness of heart.

13 And when he had said these words, the ᵃSpirit of the Lord was upon him, and he said: Helam, I baptize thee, having ᵇauthority from the Almighty God, as a testimony that ye have entered into a ᶜcovenant to serve him until you are dead as to the mortal body; and may the Spirit of the Lord be poured out upon you; and may he grant unto you eternal life, through the redemption of Christ, whom he has prepared from the ᵈfoundation of the world.

14 And after Alma had said these words, both Alma and Helam were

---

2b TG Jesus Christ, Ascension of; Jesus Christ, Death of.
4a Alma 5: 3; 3 Ne. 5: 12.
 b Mosiah 18: 31.
7a Alma 5: 13.
8a D&C 20: 36–37, 77.
 b TG Brotherhood and Sisterhood; Conversion.
9a TG Baptism, Qualifica-

tions for.
 b TG Comfort; Compassion.
 c TG Missionary Work; Witnesses.
 d Jacob 4: 11.
10a 2 Ne. 31: 17; Alma 4: 4.
 b TG Jesus Christ, Taking the Name of.
 c Neh. 10: 29.

TG Commitment.
13a TG Holy Ghost, Mission of.
 b Mosiah 21: 33; Alma 5: 3; 3 Ne. 11: 25.
 c Mosiah 21: 31.
 TG Covenants.
 d Mosiah 4: 6; Alma 12: 30 (25, 30).

[*About 147 B.C.]

[a]buried in the water; and they arose and came forth out of the water rejoicing, being filled with the Spirit.

15 And again, Alma took another, and went forth a second time into the water, and baptized him according to the first, only he did not bury [a]himself again in the water.

16 And after this manner he did baptize every one that went forth to the place of Mormon; and they were in number about two hundred and four souls; yea, and they were [a]baptized in the waters of Mormon, and were filled with the [b]grace of God.

17 And they were called the church of God, or the [a]church of Christ, from that time forward. And it came to pass that whosoever was baptized by the power and authority of God was added to his church.

18 And it came to pass that Alma, having [a]authority from God, [b]ordained priests; even one priest to every fifty of their number did he ordain to preach unto them, and to [c]teach them concerning the things pertaining to the kingdom of God.

19 And he commanded them that [a]they should [b]teach nothing save it were the things which he had taught, and which had been spoken by the mouth of the holy prophets.

20 Yea, even he commanded them that they should [a]preach nothing save it were repentance and faith on the Lord, who had redeemed his people.

21 And he commanded them that there should be no [a]contention one with another, but that they should look forward with [b]one eye, having one faith and one baptism, having their hearts [c]knit together in unity and in love one towards another.

22 And thus he commanded them to preach. And thus they became the [a]children of God.

23 And he commanded them that they should observe the [a]sabbath day, and keep it holy, and also every day they should give thanks to the Lord their God.

24 And he also commanded them that the priests whom he had ordained [a]should [b]labor with their own hands for their support.

25 And there was [a]one day in every week that was set apart that they should [b]gather themselves together to teach the people, and to worship the Lord their God, and also, as often as it was in their power, to [c]assemble themselves together.

26 And the priests were not to depend upon the people for their support; but for their labor they were to receive the [a]grace of God, that they might wax strong in the Spirit, having the [b]knowledge of God, that they might teach with power and authority from God.

27 And again Alma commanded that the people of the church should impart of their substance, [a]every one according to that which he had; if he have more abundantly he should impart more abundantly; and of him that had but little, but

14a TG Baptism,
   Immersion.
15a JS-H 1: 71 (70–71).
16a Mosiah 25: 18.
  b TG Grace.
17a Mosiah 21: 34;
   25: 22 (18–23); 26: 4;
   Alma 4: 5 (4–5);
   3 Ne. 26: 21.
   TG Jesus Christ, Head
   of the Church.
18a Mosiah 23: 16.
   TG Priesthood,
   Authority.
  b TG Priesthood, History
   of.
  c Mosiah 2: 4; 23: 14;

   24: 4 (4–8).
19a Mosiah 23: 14.
  b D&C 5: 10.
20a TG Preaching;
   Repentance.
21a TG Contention.
  b Matt. 6: 22; Morm.
   8: 15; D&C 4: 5;
   88: 68.
  c 1 Sam. 18:1; Rom.
   15: 5 (1–7); Mosiah
   4: 15; 23: 15.
22a Moses 6: 68.
23a Ex. 35: 2; Mosiah
   13: 16 (16–19).
24a Acts 20: 34 (33–35);

   Mosiah 27: 5 (3–5);
   Alma 1: 3, 26.
  b 1 Cor. 9: 18 (16–19);
   Alma 30: 32.
25a Alma 32: 11.
  b TG Meetings.
  c TG Assembly for
   Worship.
26a TG Blessing; Reward;
   Wages.
  b Neh. 10: 28 (28–31).
   TG God, Knowledge
   about.
27a Alma 16: 16; 4 Ne.
   1: 3.

[About 147 B.C.]

little should be required; and to him that had not should be given.

28 And thus they should impart of their *a*substance of their own free will and good desires towards God, and to those priests that stood in need, yea, and to every needy, naked soul.

29 And this he said unto them, having been commanded of God; and they did *a*walk uprightly before God, imparting to one another both temporally and spiritually according to their needs and their wants.

30 And now it came to pass that all this was done in Mormon, yea, by the *a*waters of Mormon, in the forest that was near the waters of Mormon; yea, the place of Mormon, the waters of Mormon, the forest of Mormon, how beautiful are they to the eyes of them who there came to the knowledge of their Redeemer; yea, and how blessed are they, for they shall *b*sing to his praise forever.

31 And these things were done in the *a*borders of the land, that they might not come to the knowledge of the king.

32 But behold, it came to pass that the king, having discovered a movement among the people, sent his servants to watch them. Therefore on the day that they were assembling themselves together to hear the word of the Lord they were discovered unto the king.

33 And now the king said that Alma was stirring up the people to rebellion against him; therefore he sent his *a*army to destroy them.

34 And it came to pass that Alma and the people of the Lord were *a*apprised of the coming of the king's army; therefore they took their tents and their families and *b*departed into the wilderness.

35 And they were in number about *a*four hundred and fifty souls.

CHAPTER 19

Gideon seeks to slay King Noah— The Lamanites invade the land— King Noah suffers death by fire— Limhi rules as a tributary monarch.

AND it came to pass that the *a*army of the king returned, having searched in vain for the people of the Lord.

2 And now behold, the forces of the king were small, having been reduced, and there began to be a division among the remainder of the people.

3 And the lesser part began to *a*breathe out threatenings against the king, and there began to be a great contention among them.

4 And now there was a man among them whose name was Gideon, and he being a strong man and an enemy to the king, therefore he drew his sword, and swore in his wrath that he would slay the king.

5 And it came to pass that he fought with the king; and when the king saw that he was about to overpower him, he fled and ran and got upon the *a*tower which was near the temple.

6 And Gideon pursued after him and was about to get upon the tower to slay the king, and the king cast his eyes round about towards the land of *a*Shemlon, and behold, the army of the Lamanites were within the borders of the land.

7 And now the king cried out in the anguish of his soul, saying: Gideon, *a*spare me, for the Lamanites are upon us, and they will destroy us; yea, they will destroy my people.

8 And now the king was not so much concerned about his people as

---

28a TG Generosity;
    Initiative.
29a TG Walking with God;
    Welfare.
30a Mosiah 26:15.
  b TG Praise; Singing.
31a Mosiah 18:4.

33a Mosiah 19:1.
34a Mosiah 23:1.
  b Mosiah 21:30; 23:13,
    36.
35a Mosiah 23:10.
19 1a Mosiah 18:33.
  3a Acts 9:1.

5a Judg. 9:51 (50–55);
    Mosiah 11:12.
6a Mosiah 10:7; 11:12;
    20:1.
7a Deut. 13:8 (6–9).

[About 145 B.C.]

he was about his *own life; never-theless, Gideon did spare his life.

9 And the king commanded the people that they should flee before the Lamanites, and he himself did go before them, and they did flee into the wilderness, with their women and their children.

10 And it came to pass that the Lamanites did pursue them, and did overtake them, and began to slay them.

11 Now it came to pass that the king commanded them that all the men should *leave their wives and their children, and flee before the Lamanites.

12 Now there were many that would not leave them, but had rather stay and perish with them. And the rest left their wives and their children and fled.

13 And it came to pass that those who tarried with their wives and their children caused that their fair daughters should stand forth and plead with the Lamanites that they would not slay them.

14 And it came to pass that the Lamanites had compassion on them, for they were charmed with the beauty of their women.

15 Therefore the Lamanites did spare their lives, and took them captives and carried them back to the land of Nephi, and granted unto them that they might possess the land, under the conditions that they would deliver up king Noah into the hands of the Lamanites, and deliver up their property, even *one half of all they possessed, one half of their gold, and their silver, and all their precious things, and thus they should pay tribute to the king of the Lamanites from year to year.

16 And now there was one of the sons of the king among those that were taken captive, whose name was *Limhi.

17 And now Limhi was desirous that his father should not be de-stroyed; nevertheless, Limhi was not ignorant of the iniquities of his father, he himself being a just man.

18 And it came to pass that Gideon sent men into the wilderness secretly, to search for the king and those that were with him. And it came to pass that they met the people in the wilderness, all save the king and his priests.

19 Now they had sworn in their hearts that they would return to the land of Nephi, and if their *wives and their children were slain, and also those that had tarried with them, that they would seek revenge, and also perish with them.

20 And the king commanded them that they should not return; and they were angry with the king, and caused that he should suffer, even unto *death by fire.

21 And they were about to take the priests also and *put them to death, and they fled before them.

22 And it came to pass that they were about to return to the land of Nephi, and they met the men of Gideon. And the men of Gideon told them of all that had happened to their wives and their children; and that the Lamanites had granted unto them that they might possess the land by paying a tribute to the Lamanites of one half of all they possessed.

23 And the people told the men of *Gideon that they had slain the king, and his *priests had fled from them farther into the wilderness.

24 And it came to pass that after they had ended the ceremony, that they returned to the land of Nephi, rejoicing, because their wives and their children were not slain; and they told Gideon what they had done to the king.

25 And it came to pass that the

8a TG Selfishness.
11a Mosiah 19: 19 (19–23).
15a Mosiah 7: 15.
16a Mosiah 7: 9; 11: 1.
19a Mosiah 19: 11.

20a Mosiah 12: 3; 13: 10;
    17: 18 (13–19); Alma
    25: 11 (7–12).
21a Mosiah 20: 3.
23a Mosiah 20: 17.

b Mosiah 17: 12 (1, 6,
  12–18); 20: 23 (3, 18,
  23).

[Between 145 and 122 B.C.]

king of the Lamanites made an [a]oath unto them, that his people should not slay them.

26 And also Limhi, being the son of the king, having the kingdom conferred upon him [a]by the people, made [b]oath unto the king of the Lamanites that his people should pay [c]tribute unto him, even one half of all they possessed.

27 And it came to pass that Limhi began to establish the kingdom and to establish [a]peace among his people.

28 And the king of the Lamanites set [a]guards round about the land, that he might [b]keep the people of Limhi in the land, that they might not depart into the wilderness; and he did support his guards out of the tribute which he did receive from the Nephites.

29 And now king Limhi did have continual peace in his kingdom for the space of two years, that the Lamanites did not molest them nor seek to destroy them.

CHAPTER 20

Lamanite daughters are abducted by the priests of Noah—The Lamanites wage war upon Limhi and his people —They are repulsed and pacified.

Now there was a place in [a]Shemlon where the daughters of the Lamanites did gather themselves together to sing, and to [b]dance, and to make themselves merry.

2 And it came to pass that there was one day a small number of them gathered together to sing and to dance.

3 And now the priests of king Noah, being ashamed to return to the city of Nephi, yea, and also fearing that the people would [a]slay them, therefore they durst not return to their wives and their [b]children.

4 And having tarried in the wilderness, and having discovered the daughters of the Lamanites, they laid and watched them;

5 And when there were but few of them gathered together to dance, they came forth out of their secret places and took them and carried them into the wilderness; yea, twenty and four of the [a]daughters of the Lamanites they carried into the wilderness.

6 And it came to pass that when the Lamanites found that their daughters had been missing, they were angry with the people of Limhi, for they thought it was the people of Limhi.

7 Therefore they sent their armies forth; yea, even the king himself went before his people; and they went up to the land of Nephi to destroy the people of Limhi.

8 And now Limhi had discovered them from the [a]tower, even all their preparations for war did he discover; therefore he gathered his people together, and laid wait for them in the fields and in the forests.

9 And it came to pass that when the Lamanites had come up, that the people of Limhi began to fall upon them from their waiting places, and began to slay them.

10 And it came to pass that the battle became exceedingly sore, for they fought like lions for their prey.

11 And it came to pass that the people of Limhi began to drive the Lamanites before them; yet they were not half so numerous as the Lamanites. But they [a]fought for their lives, and for their [b]wives, and for their children; therefore they exerted themselves and like dragons did they fight.

12 And it came to pass that they found the king of the Lamanites

---

25a Mosiah 21:3.
26a Mosiah 7:9.
  b Mosiah 20:14, 22.
  c Mosiah 22:7.
27a TG Peacemakers.
28a Mosiah 21:5; 22:6

(6–10).
  b Mosiah 7:22; 9:10.
20 1a Mosiah 19:6.
  b Judg. 21:21.
3a Mosiah 19:21.
  b Mosiah 25:12.

5a Mosiah 21:20; 23:33 (30–35).
8a Mosiah 11:12.
11a Alma 43:45.
  b Alma 46:12.

[Between 145 and 122 B.C.]

among the number of their dead; yet he was not dead, having been wounded and left upon the ground, so speedy was the flight of his people.

13 And they took him and bound up his wounds, and brought him before Limhi, and said: Behold, here is the king of the Lamanites; he having received a wound has fallen among their dead, and they have left him; and behold, we have brought him before you; and now let us slay him.

14 But Limhi said unto them: Ye shall not slay him, but bring him hither that I may see him. And they brought him. And Limhi said unto him: What cause have ye to come up to war against my people? Behold, my people have not broken the ªoath that I made unto you; therefore, why should ye break the oath which ye made unto my people?

15 And now the king said: I have broken the oath because thy people did carry away the daughters of my people; therefore, in my anger I did cause my people to come up to war against thy people.

16 And now Limhi had heard nothing concerning this matter; therefore he said: I will search among my people and whosoever has done this thing shall perish. Therefore he caused a search to be made among his people.

17 Now when ªGideon had heard these things, he being the king's captain, he went forth and said unto the king: I pray thee forbear, and do not search this people, and lay not this thing to their charge.

18 For do ye not remember the priests of thy father, whom this people sought to destroy? And are they not in the wilderness? And are not they the ones who have stolen the daughters of the Lamanites?

19 And now, behold, and tell the king of these things, that he may tell his people that they may be pacified towards us; for behold they are already preparing to come against us; and behold also there are but few of us.

20 And behold, they come with their numerous hosts; and except the king doth pacify them towards us we must perish.

21 For are not the words of Abinadi ªfulfilled, which he prophesied against us—and all this because we would not hearken unto the words of the Lord, and turn from our iniquities?

22 And now let us pacify the king, and we fulfil the ªoath which we have made unto him; for it is better that we should be in bondage than that we should lose our ᵇlives; therefore, let us put a stop to the shedding of so much blood.

23 And now Limhi told the king all the things concerning his father, and the ªpriests that had fled into the wilderness, and attributed the carrying away of their daughters to them.

24 And it came to pass that the king was pacified towards his people; and he said unto them: Let us go forth to meet my people, without arms; and I swear unto you with an ªoath that my people shall not slay thy people.

25 And it came to pass that they followed the king, and went forth without arms to meet the Lamanites. And it came to pass that they did meet the Lamanites; and the king of the Lamanites did bow himself down before them, and did plead in behalf of the people of Limhi.

26 And when the Lamanites saw the people of Limhi, that they were without arms, they had ªcompassion on them and were pacified towards them, and returned with their king in peace to their own land.

14a Mosiah 19: 26 (25–26).
17a Mosiah 19: 23 (4–8, 23);
   22: 3; Alma 1: 8 (8–9).
21a Mosiah 12: 2 (1–8);

21: 4.
22a Mosiah 19: 26.
   b TG Life, Sanctity of.
23a Mosiah 19: 23 (21, 23);

23: 9 (9, 12, 31).
24a Mosiah 21: 3.
26a TG Compassion.

[Between 145 and 122 B.C.]

CHAPTER 21

Limhi's people are smitten and defeated by the Lamanites—They meet Ammon and are converted—They tell Ammon of the twenty-four Jaredite plates.

AND it came to pass that Limhi and his people returned to the city of Nephi, and began to dwell in the land again in peace.

2 And it came to pass that after many days the Lamanites began again to be stirred up in anger against the Nephites, and they began to come into the borders of the land round about.

3 Now they durst not slay them, because of the *a*oath which their king had made unto Limhi; but they would smite them on their *b*cheeks, and exercise authority over them; and began to put heavy *c*burdens upon their backs, and drive them as they would a dumb ass—

4 Yea, all this was done that the *a*word of the Lord might be *b*fulfilled.

5 And now the afflictions of the Nephites were great, and there was no way that they could deliver themselves out of their hands, for the Lamanites had *a*surrounded them on every side.

6 And it came to pass that the people began to murmur with the king because of their afflictions; and they began to be desirous to go against them to battle. And they did afflict the king sorely with their complaints; therefore he granted unto them that they should do according to their desires.

7 And they gathered themselves together again, and put on their armor, and went forth against the Lamanites to drive them out of their land.

8 And it came to pass that the Lamanites did beat them, and drove them back, and *a*slew many of them.

9 And now there was a great *a*mourning and lamentation among the people of Limhi, the widow mourning for her husband, the son and the daughter mourning for their father, and the brothers for their brethren.

10 Now there were a great many *a*widows in the land, and they did cry mightily from day to day, for a great fear of the Lamanites had come upon them.

11 And it came to pass that their continual cries did stir up the remainder of the people of Limhi to anger against the Lamanites; and they went again to battle, but they were driven back again, suffering much loss.

12 Yea, they went again even the third time, and suffered in the like manner; and those that were not slain returned again to the city of Nephi.

13 And they did humble themselves even to the dust, subjecting themselves to the *a*yoke of bondage, *b*submitting themselves to be smitten, and to be driven to and fro, and burdened, according to the desires of their enemies.

14 And they did *a*humble themselves even in the depths of humility; and they did cry mightily to God; yea, even all the day long did they cry unto their God that he would *b*deliver them out of their afflictions.

15 And now the Lord was slow to *a*hear their cry because of their iniquities; nevertheless the Lord

---

21 3*a* Mosiah 19:25;
20:24.
b Lam. 3:30;
Mosiah 12:2.
c Ex. 1:11 (10–11);
Mosiah 12:5; 24:9.
4*a* D&C 3:19.
b Mosiah 20:21.
5*a* Mosiah 19:28; 22:6

(6–10).
8*a* Mosiah 21:29.
9*a* Mosiah 12:4.
TG Mourning.
10*a* TG Widows.
13*a* Mosiah 19:28 (26, 28);
21:36.
b TG Submissiveness.
14*a* Mosiah 29:20.

b TG Deliverance;
Protection, Divine.
15*a* 1 Sam. 8:18; Prov.
15:29; Isa. 59:2;
Jer. 7:16; 14:12
(10–12); Mosiah 11:24
(23–25); D&C 101:7
(7–9).

[Between 145 and 122 B.C.]

did hear their [b]cries, and began to soften the hearts of the Lamanites that they began to ease their burdens; yet the Lord did not see fit to deliver them out of bondage.

16 And it came to pass that they began to prosper by degrees in the land, and began to raise grain more abundantly, and flocks, and herds, that they did not suffer with hunger.

17 Now there was a great number of women, more than there was of men; therefore king Limhi commanded that every man should [a]impart to the support of the [b]widows and their children, that they might not perish with hunger; and this they did because of the greatness of their number that had been slain.

18 Now the people of Limhi kept together in a body as much as it was possible, and secured their grain and their flocks;

19 And the king himself did not trust his person without the walls of the city, unless he took his guards with him, fearing that he might by some means fall into the hands of the Lamanites.

20 And he caused that his people should watch the land round about, that by some means they might take those priests that fled into the wilderness, who had stolen the [a]daughters of the Lamanites, and that had caused such a great destruction to come upon them.

21 For they were desirous to take them that they might [a]punish them; for they had come into the land of Nephi by night, and carried off their grain and many of their precious things; therefore they laid wait for them.

22 And it came to pass that there was no more disturbance between the Lamanites and the people of Limhi, *even until the time that [a]Ammon and his brethren came into the land.

23 And the king having been without the gates of the city with his guard, [a]discovered Ammon and his brethren; and supposing them to be priests of Noah therefore he caused that they should be taken, and bound, and cast into [b]prison. And had they been the priests of Noah he would have caused that they should be put to death.

24 But when he found that they were not, but that they were his brethren, and had come from the [a]land of Zarahemla, he was filled with exceedingly great joy.

25 Now king Limhi had sent, previous to the coming of Ammon, a [a]small number of men to [b]search for the land of Zarahemla; but they could not find it, and they were lost in the wilderness.

26 Nevertheless, they did find a land which had been peopled; yea, a land which was covered with dry [a]bones; yea, a land which had been peopled and which had been destroyed; and they, having supposed it to be the land of Zarahemla, returned to the land of Nephi, having arrived in the borders of the land not many days before the [b]coming of Ammon.

27 And they brought a [a]record with them, even a record of the people whose bones they had found; and it was engraven on plates of ore.

28 And now Limhi was again filled with joy on learning from the mouth of Ammon that king Mosiah had a [a]gift from God, whereby he could [b]interpret such engravings; yea, and Ammon also did rejoice.

29 Yet Ammon and his brethren were filled with sorrow because so

15b Ex. 3:9 (7, 9); 2 Ne. 26:15; D&C 109:49.
17a Mosiah 4:26 (16, 26).
  b TG Widows.
20a Mosiah 20:5.
21a Mosiah 7:7 (7–11).
22a Mosiah 7:6 (6–13).
23a Mosiah 7:10.

b Mosiah 7:7 (6–8); Hel. 5:21.
24a Omni 1:13.
25a Mosiah 8:7.
  b Mosiah 7:14.
26a Mosiah 8:8; Hel. 3:6 (3–12).
  b Mosiah 7:6 (6–11).

27a Mosiah 8:9; 28:11.
28a Omni 1:20 (20–22); Mosiah 28:13 (11–19).
  TG God, Gifts of.
  b 1 Cor. 12:10; Mosiah 8:6 (6, 12–13).

[*About 121 B.C.]

many of their brethren had been
*a*slain;

30 And also that king Noah and
his priests had caused the people to
commit so many sins and iniquities
against God; and they also did
mourn for the *a*death of Abinadi;
and also for the *b*departure of Alma
and the people that went with him,
who had formed a church of God
through the strength and power of
God, and faith on the words which
had been spoken by Abinadi.

31 Yea, they did mourn for their
departure, for they knew not
whither they had fled. Now they
would have gladly joined with them,
for they themselves had entered
into a *a*covenant with God to serve
him and keep his commandments.

32 And now since the coming of
Ammon, king Limhi had also entered into a covenant with God, and
also many of his people, to serve
him and keep his commandments.

33 And it came to pass that king
Limhi and many of his people were
desirous to be baptized; but there
was none in the land that had
*a*authority from God. And Ammon
declined doing this thing, considering himself an unworthy servant.

34 Therefore they did not at that
time form themselves into a *a*church,
waiting upon the Spirit of the Lord.
Now they were desirous to become
even as Alma and his brethren, who
had fled into the wilderness.

35 They were desirous to be baptized as a witness and a testimony
that they were willing to serve God
with all their hearts; nevertheless
they did prolong the time; and an
account of their baptism shall be
*a*given hereafter.

36 And now all the study of Ammon and *a*his people, and king
Limhi and his people, was to deliver
themselves out of the hands of the
Lamanites and from *b*bondage.

CHAPTER 22

*Plans are made for the people to
escape from Lamanite bondage—
The Lamanites are made drunk—
The people escape, return to Zara-
hemla, and become subject to King
Mosiah.*

AND now it came to pass that
Ammon and king Limhi began to
consult with the people how they
should *a*deliver themselves out of
bondage; and even they did cause
that all the people should gather
themselves together; and this they
did that they might have the voice
of the people concerning the matter.

2 And it came to pass that they
could find no way to deliver themselves out of bondage, except it were
to take their women and children,
and their flocks, and their herds,
and their tents, and depart into the
wilderness; for the Lamanites being
so numerous, it was impossible for
the people of Limhi to contend with
them, thinking to deliver themselves out of bondage by the sword.

3 Now it came to pass that
*a*Gideon went forth and stood before
the king, and said unto him: Now
O king, thou hast hitherto hearkened unto my words many times
when we have been contending with
our brethren, the Lamanites.

4 And now O king, if thou hast not
found me to be an unprofitable servant, or if thou hast hitherto
listened to my words in any degree,
and they have been of service to
thee, even so I desire that thou
wouldst listen to my words at this
time, and I will be thy servant and
deliver this people out of bondage.

5 And the king granted unto him
that he might speak. And Gideon
said unto him:

6 Behold the back pass, through
the back wall, on the back side of
the city. The Lamanites, or the

29a Mosiah 21:8 (7–14);
   25:9.
30a Mosiah 17:13 (12–20).
  b Mosiah 18:34 (34–35).
31a Mosiah 18:13.
33a TG Baptism, Essential;
   Priesthood, Authority.
34a Mosiah 18:17.
35a Mosiah 25:18 (17–18).
36a Mosiah 7:3 (2–3).
b Mosiah 21:13.
22 1a Mosiah 7:18.
3a Mosiah 20:17; Alma
   1:8 (8–9).

[About 121 B.C.]

[a]guards of the Lamanites, by night are [b]drunken; therefore let us send a proclamation among all this people that they gather together their flocks and herds, that they may drive them into the wilderness by night.

7 And I will go according to thy command and pay the last [a]tribute of wine to the Lamanites, and they will be [b]drunken; and we will pass through the secret pass on the left of their camp when they are drunken and asleep.

8 Thus we will depart with our women and our children, our flocks, and our herds into the wilderness; and we will travel around the land of [a]Shilom.

9 And it came to pass that the king hearkened unto the words of Gideon.

10 And king Limhi caused that his people should gather their flocks together; and he sent the tribute of wine to the Lamanites; and he also sent more wine, as a present unto them; and they did drink freely of the wine which king Limhi did send unto them.

11 And it came to pass that the people of king Limhi did [a]depart by night into the wilderness with their flocks and their herds, and they went round about the land of [b]Shilom in the wilderness, and bent their course towards the land of Zarahemla, being led by Ammon and his brethren.

12 And they had taken all their gold, and silver, and their precious things, which they could carry, and also their provisions with them, into the wilderness; and they pursued their journey.

13 And after being many days in the wilderness they [a]arrived in the land of Zarahemla, and joined Mosiah's people, and became his subjects.

14 And it came to pass that Mosiah [a]received them with joy; and he also received their [b]records, and also the [c]records which had been found by the people of Limhi.

15 And now it came to pass when the Lamanites had found that the people of Limhi had departed out of the land by night, that they sent an [a]army into the wilderness to pursue them;

16 And after they had pursued them two days, they could no longer follow their tracks; therefore they were lost in the wilderness.

An account of Alma and the people of the Lord, who were driven into the wilderness by the people of King Noah. Comprising chapters 23 and 24.

CHAPTER 23

Alma refuses to be king—He serves as high priest—The Lord chastens his people, and the Lamanites conquer the land of Helam—Amulon, leader of King Noah's wicked priests, rules subject to the Lamanite monarch.

Now Alma, having been [a]warned of the Lord that the armies of king Noah would come upon them, and having made it known to his people, therefore they gathered together their flocks, and took of their grain, and [b]departed into the wilderness before the armies of king Noah.

2 And the Lord did strengthen them, that the people of king Noah could not overtake them to destroy them.

3 And they fled [a]eight days' journey into the wilderness.

4 And they came to a land, yea, even a very beautiful and pleasant land, a land of pure water.

5 And they pitched their tents, and began to till the ground, and began

6a Mosiah 19:28; 21:5.
  b Alma 55:14 (8–17).
7a Mosiah 19:26.
  b TG Drunkenness.
8a Mosiah 7:7 (5–16).
11a Mosiah 25:8.

b Mosiah 11:12 (12–13); Alma 23:12.
13a Mosiah 25:5.
14a Mosiah 24:25.
  b Mosiah 8:5; 9:1.
  c Mosiah 8:9.

15a Mosiah 23:30 (30–39).
23 1a Mosiah 18:34; Alma 5:4. TG Warnings.
  b Mosiah 27:16.
3a Mosiah 24:25.

[Between 145 and 121 B.C.]

to build buildings; yea, they were [a]industrious, and did labor exceedingly.

6 And the people were desirous that Alma should be their [a]king, for he was beloved by his people.

7 But he said unto them: Behold, it is not expedient that we should have a king; for thus saith the Lord: Ye shall [a]not esteem one flesh above another, or one man shall not think himself above another; therefore I say unto you it is not expedient that ye should have a king.

8 Nevertheless, if it [a]were possible that ye could always have just men to be your [b]kings it would be well for you to have a king.

9 But remember the [a]iniquity of king Noah and his [b]priests; and I myself was [c]caught in a snare, and did many things which were abominable in the sight of the Lord, which caused me sore [d]repentance;

10 Nevertheless, [a]after much [b]tribulation, the Lord did hear my cries, and did answer my prayers, and has made me an [c]instrument in his hands in bringing [d]so many of you to a knowledge of his truth.

11 Nevertheless, in this I do not glory, for I am unworthy to glory of myself.

12 And now I say unto you, ye have been [a]oppressed by king Noah, and have been in bondage to him and his priests, and have been [b]brought into iniquity by them; therefore ye were bound with the [c]bands of iniquity.

13 And now as ye have been delivered by the power of God out of these bonds; yea, even out of the [a]hands of king Noah and his people, and also from the [b]bonds of iniquity, even so I desire that ye should [c]stand fast in this [d]liberty wherewith ye have been made free, and that ye trust [e]no man to be a king over you.

14 And also trust no one to be your [a]teacher nor your minister, except he be a man of God, walking in his ways and keeping his commandments.

15 Thus did Alma teach his people, that every man should [a]love his [b]neighbor [c]as himself, that there should be no [d]contention among them.

16 And now, Alma was their [a]high priest, he being the founder of their church.

17 And it came to pass that none received [a]authority to preach or to teach except it were by him from God. Therefore he [b]consecrated all their priests and all their teachers; and none were consecrated except they were just men.

18 Therefore they did watch over their people, and did [a]nourish them with things pertaining to righteousness.

19 And it came to pass that they began to prosper exceedingly in the land; and they called the land [a]Helam.

20 And it came to pass that they did multiply and prosper exceedingly in the land of Helam; and they built a city, which they called the city of Helam.

21 Nevertheless the Lord seeth fit

5a TG Industry; Work, Value of.
6a 1 Sam. 8:5; 3 Ne. 6:30.
7a Mosiah 27:3 (3–5).
8a Mosiah 29:13.
  b TG Governments.
9a Prov. 16:12; Mosiah 11:2 (1–15); 29:17 (17–19).
  b Mosiah 17:12 (1, 6, 12–18).
  c Mosiah 17:2 (1–4).
  d Mosiah 18:1.
10a D&C 58:4.

  b TG Tribulation.
  c Alma 17:9 (9–11); 26:3.
  d Mosiah 18:35.
12a TG Oppression; Unrighteous Dominion.
  b Mosiah 11:2 (1–15).
  c Isa. 58:6; 2 Ne. 28:19 (19–22); Alma 12:11.
13a Mosiah 18:34 (34–35).
  b TG Bondage, Spiritual.
  c Gal. 5:1.
  d TG Liberty.
  e Mosiah 29:13 (5–36).

14a Mosiah 2:4; 18:18 (18–22).
15a TG Love.
  b TG Neighbor.
  c Mosiah 18:21.
  d 3 Ne. 11:29 (28–29).
16a Mosiah 18:18; 26:7.
17a TG Priesthood, Authority.
  b Lev. 16:32; 2 Ne. 5:26.
18a Eph. 6:4; 1 Tim. 4:6.
19a Mosiah 27:16; Alma 24:1.

[Between 145 and 121 B.C.]

to [a]chasten his people; yea, he trieth their [b]patience and their faith.

22 Nevertheless—whosoever putteth his [a]trust in him the same shall be [b]lifted up at the last day. Yea, and thus it was with this people.

23 For behold, I will show unto you that they were brought into [a]bondage, and none could deliver them but the Lord their God, yea, even the God of Abraham and Isaac and of Jacob.

24 And it came to pass that he did deliver them, and he did show forth his mighty power unto them, and great were their rejoicings.

25 For behold, it came to pass that while they were in the land of Helam, yea, in the city of Helam, while tilling the land round about, behold an army of the Lamanites was in the borders of the land.

26 Now it came to pass that the brethren of Alma fled from their fields, and gathered themselves together in the city of Helam; and they were much frightened because of the appearance of the Lamanites.

27 But Alma went forth and stood among them, and exhorted them that they should not be frightened, but that they should remember the Lord their God and he would deliver them.

28 Therefore they hushed their fears, and began to cry unto the Lord that he would soften the hearts of the Lamanites, that they would spare them, and their wives, and their children.

29 And it came to pass that the Lord did soften the hearts of the Lamanites. And Alma and his brethren went forth and delivered themselves up into their hands; and the Lamanites took possession of the land of Helam.

30 Now the [a]armies of the La-manites, which had followed after the people of king Limhi, had been lost in the wilderness for many days.

31 And behold, they had found those priests of king Noah, in a place which they called [a]Amulon; and they had begun to possess the land of Amulon and had begun to till the ground.

32 Now the name of the leader of those priests was [a]Amulon.

33 And it came to pass that Amulon did plead with the Lamanites; and he also sent forth their wives, who were the [a]daughters of the Lamanites, to plead with their brethren, that they should not destroy their husbands.

34 And the Lamanites had [a]compassion on Amulon and his brethren, and did not destroy them, because of their wives.

35 And [a]Amulon and his brethren did join the Lamanites, and they were traveling in the wilderness in search of the land of Nephi when they discovered the land of Helam, which was possessed by Alma and his brethren.

36 And it came to pass that the Lamanites promised unto Alma and his brethren, that if they would show them the [a]way which led to the land of Nephi that they would grant unto them their lives and their liberty.

37 But after Alma had shown them the way that led to the land of Nephi the Lamanites would not keep their promise; but they set [a]guards round about the land of Helam, over Alma and his brethren.

38 And the remainder of them went to the land of Nephi; and a part of them returned to the land of Helam, and also brought with them the wives and the children of the guards who had been left in the land.

21a Deut. 11: 2 (1–8);
      Hel. 12: 3; D&C 98: 21.
   TG Chastening.
   b TG Patience.
22a TG Trust in God.
   b 1 Ne. 13: 37;
      Alma 26: 7.

23a Alma 36: 2.
30a Mosiah 22: 15.
31a Mosiah 24: 1;
      Alma 23: 14.
32a Mosiah 24: 8.
33a Mosiah 20: 5; 25: 12.

34a TG Compassion.
35a Alma 25: 4.
36a Mosiah 18: 34.
37a Mosiah 24: 9 (8–15);
      Alma 5: 5.

[Between 145 and 121 B.C.]

39 And the king of the Lamanites had granted unto Amulon that he should be a king and a ruler over his people, who were in the land of Helam; nevertheless he should have no power to do anything contrary to the will of the king of the Lamanites.

CHAPTER 24

Amulon persecutes Alma and his people—They are to be put to death if they pray—The Lord makes their burdens seem light—He delivers them from bondage, and they return to Zarahemla.

AND it came to pass that Amulon did gain favor in the eyes of the king of the Lamanites; therefore, the king of the Lamanites granted unto him and his brethren that they should be appointed teachers over his people, yea, even over the people who were in the land of Shemlon, and in the land of Shilom, and in the [a]land of Amulon.

2 For the Lamanites had taken possession of all these lands; therefore, the king of the Lamanites had appointed kings over all these lands.

3 And now the name of the king of the Lamanites was [a]Laman, being called after the name of his father; and therefore he was called king Laman. And he was king over a numerous people.

4 And he appointed [a]teachers of the [b]brethren of Amulon in every land which was possessed by his people; and thus the [c]language of Nephi began to be taught among all the people of the Lamanites.

5 And they were a people friendly one with another; nevertheless they knew not God; neither did the brethren of Amulon teach them anything concerning the Lord their God, neither the law of Moses; nor did they teach them the words of Abinadi;

6 But they taught them that they should keep their record, and that they might write one to another.

7 And thus the Lamanites began to increase in riches, and began to [a]trade one with another and wax great, and began to be a cunning and a wise people, as to the wisdom of the world, yea, a very cunning people, delighting in all manner of wickedness and plunder, except it were among their own brethren.

8 And now it came to pass that [a]Amulon began to exercise [b]authority over Alma and his brethren, and began to persecute him, and cause that his children should persecute their children.

9 For Amulon knew Alma, that he had been [a]one of the king's priests, and that it was he that believed the words of Abinadi and was driven out before the king, and therefore he was wroth with him; for he was subject to king Laman, yet he exercised authority over them, and put [b]tasks upon them, and put [c]taskmasters over them.

10 And it came to pass that so great were their afflictions that they began to cry mightily to God.

11 And Amulon commanded them that they should stop their cries; and he [a]put guards over them to watch them, that whosoever should be found calling upon God should be put to death.

12 And Alma and his people did not raise their voices to the Lord their God, but did pour out their [a]hearts to him; and he did know the [b]thoughts of their hearts.

13 And it [a]came to pass that the voice of the Lord came to them in their afflictions, saying: Lift up

---

24 1a Mosiah 23:31;
      Alma 21:3 (2–4).
   3a Mosiah 9:10 (10–11);
      10:6.
   4a Mosiah 2:4;
      18:18 (18–22); 23:14.
    b Mosiah 23:9 (9, 12, 31).
    c Omni 1:18.

7a Gen. 34:10 (10–21);
   4 Ne. 1:46.
8a Mosiah 23:32.
 b D&C 121:39.
9a Mosiah 17:2 (1–4);
   23:9.
 b Mosiah 21:3 (3–6).
 c Mosiah 23:37 (37–39).

11a Dan. 6:7 (7–27).
12a TG Prayer.
  b Ps. 139:2; Matt.
    12:25.
13a Jer. 33:3 (1–3);
    Matt. 6:6.

[Between 145 and 121 B.C.]

your heads and be of good comfort, for I know of the covenant which ye have made unto me; and I will covenant with my people and deliver them out of bondage.

14 And I will also ease the *a*burdens which are put upon your shoulders, that even you cannot feel them upon your backs, even while you are in bondage; and this will I do that ye may stand as *b*witnesses for me hereafter, and that ye may know of a surety that I, the Lord God, do visit my people in their *c*afflictions.

15 And now it came to pass that the burdens which were laid upon Alma and his brethren were made light; yea, the Lord did *a*strengthen them that they could bear up their *b*burdens with ease, and they did submit cheerfully and with *c*patience to all the will of the Lord.

16 And it came to pass that so great was their faith and their patience that the voice of the Lord came unto them again, saying: Be of good comfort, for on the morrow I will deliver you out of bondage.

17 And he said unto Alma: Thou shalt go before this people, and I will go *a*with thee and deliver this people out of *b*bondage.

18 Now it came to pass that Alma and his people in the night-time gathered their flocks together, and also of their grain; yea, even all the night-time were they gathering their flocks together.

19 And in the morning the Lord caused a *a*deep sleep to come upon the Lamanites, yea, and all their task-masters were in a profound sleep.

20 And Alma and his people departed into the wilderness; and when they had traveled all day they pitched their tents in a valley, and they called the valley Alma, because he led their way in the wilderness.

21 Yea, and in the valley of Alma they poured out their *a*thanks to God because he had been merciful unto them, and eased their *b*burdens, and had delivered them out of bondage; for they were in bondage, and none could deliver them except it were the Lord their God.

22 And they gave *a*thanks to God, yea, all their men and all their women and all their children that could speak lifted their voices in the praises of their God.

23 And now the Lord said unto Alma: Haste thee and get thou and this people out of this land, for the Lamanites have awakened and do pursue thee; therefore get thee out of this land, and I will stop the Lamanites in this valley that they come no further in pursuit of this people.

24 And it came to pass that they departed out of the valley, and took their journey into the wilderness.

25 And after they had been in the wilderness *a*twelve days *they arrived in the land of Zarahemla; and king Mosiah did also *b*receive them with joy.

CHAPTER 25

The people (the Mulekites) of Zarahemla become Nephites—They learn of the people of Alma and of Zeniff—Alma baptizes Limhi and all his people—Mosiah authorizes Alma to organize the Church of God.

AND now king Mosiah caused that all the people should be gathered together.

2 Now there were not so many of the children of Nephi, or so many of those who were descendants of

---

14a Isa. 46:4 (3–4).
  b TG Witnesses.
  c TG Adversity;
    Affliction.
15a Matt. 11:28 (28–30).
  b Alma 31:38; 33:23.
  c 2 Cor. 4:16; D&C

54:10. TG Patience.
17a Ex. 3:12; 1 Ne. 17:55;
    Alma 38:4.
  b Mosiah 25:10.
    TG Bondage, Physical.
19a 1 Sam. 26:12; Alma
    55:15 (15–16).

21a TG Thanksgiving.
  b Ps. 81:6 (5–6).
22a TG Thanksgiving.
25a Mosiah 23:3.
  b Mosiah 22:14.

[*About 120 B.C.]

Nephi, as there were of the [a]people of Zarahemla, who was a descendant of [b]Mulek, and those who came with him into the wilderness.

3 And there were not so many of the people of Nephi and of the people of Zarahemla as there were of the Lamanites; yea, they were not half so numerous.

4 And now all the people of Nephi were assembled together, and also all the people of Zarahemla, and they were gathered together in two bodies.

5 And it came to pass that Mosiah did read, and caused to be read, the records of Zeniff to his people; yea, he read the records of the people of Zeniff, from the time they [a]left the land of Zarahemla until they [b]returned again.

6 And he also read the account of Alma and his brethren, and all their afflictions, from the time they left the land of Zarahemla until the time they returned again.

7 And now, when Mosiah had made an end of reading the records, his people who tarried in the land were struck with wonder and amazement.

8 For they knew not what to think; for when they beheld those that had been delivered [a]out of bondage they were filled with exceedingly great joy.

9 And again, when they thought of their brethren who had been [a]slain by the Lamanites they were filled with sorrow, and even shed many tears of sorrow.

10 And again, when they thought of the immediate goodness of God, and his power in delivering Alma and his brethren out of the hands of the Lamanites and of [a]bondage, they did raise their voices and give thanks to God.

11 And again, when they thought upon the Lamanites, who were their brethren, of their sinful and [a]polluted state, they were filled with [b]pain and anguish for the [c]welfare of their souls.

12 And it came to pass that those who [a]were the children of Amulon and his brethren, who had taken to wife the [b]daughters of the Lamanites, were displeased with the conduct of their fathers, and they would no longer be called by the names of their fathers, therefore they took upon themselves the name of Nephi, that they might be called the children of Nephi and be numbered among those who were [c]called Nephites.

13 And now all the people of Zarahemla were [a]numbered with the Nephites, and this because the kingdom had been conferred upon none but those who were descendants of Nephi.

14 And now it came to pass that when Mosiah had made an end of speaking and reading to the people, he desired that Alma should also speak to the people.

15 And Alma did speak unto them, when they were assembled together in large bodies, and he went from one body to another, preaching unto the people repentance and faith on the Lord.

16 And he did exhort the people of Limhi and his brethren, all those that had been delivered out of bondage, that they should remember that it was the Lord that did deliver them.

17 And it came to pass that after Alma had taught the people many things, and had made an end of speaking to them, that king Limhi was desirous that he might be baptized; and all his people were

25 2a Hel. 6: 10.
  b Ezek. 17: 22 (22–23);
    Omni 1: 15 (14–19).
  5a Mosiah 9: 3 (3–4).
  b Mosiah 22: 13.
  8a Mosiah 22: 11 (11–13).
  9a Mosiah 21: 29 (8, 29).

10a Mosiah 24: 17; 27: 16.
11a TG Pollution.
  b Mosiah 28: 3 (3–4);
    Alma 13: 27.
  c 2 Ne. 6: 3; Jacob 2: 3.
    TG Worth of Souls.

12a Mosiah 20: 3 (3–5).
  b Mosiah 23: 33.
  c Jacob 1: 14 (13–14);
    Alma 2: 11.
13a Omni 1: 19.

[About 120 B.C.]

desirous that they might be baptized also.

18 Therefore, Alma did go forth into the water and did [a]baptize them; yea, he did baptize them after the manner he did his brethren in the [b]waters of Mormon; yea, and as many as he did baptize did belong to the church of God; and this because of their belief on the words of Alma.

19 And it came to pass that king Mosiah granted unto Alma that he might establish [a]churches throughout all the land of Zarahemla; and gave him power to [b]ordain [c]priests and [d]teachers over every church.

20 Now this was done because there were so many people that they could not all be governed by one teacher; neither could they all hear the word of God in one assembly;

21 Therefore they did [a]assemble themselves together in different bodies, being called churches; every church having their priests and their teachers, and every priest preaching the word according as it was delivered to him by the mouth of Alma.

22 And thus, notwithstanding there being many churches they were all one [a]church, yea, even the church of God; for there was nothing preached in all the churches except it were repentance and faith in God.

23 And now there were seven churches in the land of Zarahemla. And it came to pass that whosoever were desirous to take upon them the [a]name of Christ, or of God, they did join the churches of God;

24 And they were called the [a]people of God. And the Lord did pour out his [b]Spirit upon them, and they were blessed, and prospered in the land.

CHAPTER 26

Many members of the Church are led into sin by unbelievers—Alma is promised eternal life—Those who repent and are baptized gain forgiveness—Church members in sin who repent and confess to Alma and to the Lord shall be forgiven; otherwise they shall be excommunicated.

Now it came to pass that there were many of the rising generation that could not understand the [a]words of king Benjamin, being little children at the time he spake unto his people; and they did [b]not believe the tradition of their fathers.

2 They did not believe what had been said concerning the resurrection of the dead, neither did they believe concerning the coming of Christ.

3 And now because of their [a]unbelief they could not [b]understand the word of God; and their hearts were hardened.

4 And they would not be baptized; neither would they join the [a]church. And they were a separate people as to their faith, and remained so ever after, even in their [b]carnal and sinful state; for they would not call upon the Lord their God.

5 And now in the reign of Mosiah they were not half so numerous as the people of God; but because of the [a]dissensions among the brethren they became more numerous.

6 For it came to pass that they did [a]deceive many with their [b]flattering words, who were in the church, and did cause them to commit many sins; therefore it became expedient

18a Mosiah 21:35.
  b Mosiah 18:16 (8–17).
19a Mosiah 26:17.
  b TG Priesthood.
  c TG Priest.
  d TG Teacher.
21a TG Church.
22a Mosiah 18:17; 26:4.
23a TG Jesus Christ, Taking the Name of.

24a TG Sons and Daughters of God.
  b TG God, Spirit of; Prosper.
26 1a Mosiah 2:1.
  b TG Family, Children, Duties of.
3a TG Unbelief, Unbelievers.
  b TG Understanding.

4a Mosiah 25:22 (18–23); Alma 4:5 (4–5).
  b TG Man, Natural, Not Spiritually Reborn.
5a TG Apostasy.
6a Col. 2:18 (16–23).
  TG Deceit.
  b TG Flattery.

[About 120 B.C.]

that those who committed sin, that were in the church, should be [c]admonished by the church.

7 And it came to pass that they were brought before the priests, and delivered up unto the [a]priests by the teachers; and the priests brought them before Alma, who was the [b]high priest.

8 Now king Mosiah had given Alma the [a]authority over the [b]church.

9 And it came to pass that Alma did not know concerning them; but there were many [a]witnesses against them; yea, the people stood and testified of their iniquity in abundance.

10 Now there had not any such thing happened before in the church; therefore Alma was troubled in his spirit, and he caused that they should be brought before the king.

11 And he said unto the king: Behold, here are many whom we have brought before thee, who are accused of their brethren; yea, and they have been taken in divers iniquities. And they do not repent of their iniquities; therefore we have brought them before thee, that thou mayest judge them according to their crimes.

12 But king Mosiah said unto Alma: Behold, I judge them not; therefore I [a]deliver them into thy hands to be judged.

13 And now the spirit of Alma was again troubled; and he went and inquired of the Lord what he should do concerning this matter, for he feared that he should do wrong in the sight of God.

14 And it came to pass that after he had poured out his whole soul to God, the [a]voice of the Lord came to him, saying:

15 Blessed art thou, Alma, and blessed are they who were baptized in the [a]waters of Mormon. Thou art blessed because of thy exceeding [b]faith in the words alone of my servant Abinadi.

16 And blessed are they because of their exceeding faith in the words alone which thou hast spoken unto them.

17 And blessed art thou because thou hast established a [a]church among this people; and they shall be established, and they shall be my people.

18 Yea, blessed is this people who are willing to bear my [a]name; for in my [b]name shall they be called; and they are mine.

19 And because thou hast inquired of me concerning the transgressor, thou art blessed.

20 Thou art my servant; and I covenant with thee that thou shalt have [a]eternal life; and thou shalt serve me and go forth in my name, and shalt gather together my sheep.

21 And he that will hear my voice shall be my [a]sheep; and him shall ye receive into the church, and him will I also receive.

22 For behold, [a]this is my [b]church; whosoever is [c]baptized shall be baptized unto repentance. And whomsoever ye receive shall [d]believe in my name; and him will I freely [e]forgive.

23 For it is I that taketh upon me the [a]sins of the world; for it is I that hath [b]created them; and it is I that granteth unto him that believeth

6c Alma 5: 57 (57–58);
    6: 3. TG Warnings.
7a TG Priest.
  b Mosiah 23: 16; 29: 42.
8a TG Delegation of
    Responsibility.
  b TG Church
    Organization.
9a TG Witnesses.
12a D&C 42: 87 (78–93).
14a TG Guidance, Divine.
15a Mosiah 18: 30.

  b Mosiah 17: 2; D&C
    46: 14. TG Faith.
17a Mosiah 25: 19 (19–24).
18a Mosiah 1: 11; 5: 8.
    TG Jesus Christ,
    Taking the Name of.
  b Deut. 28: 10.
20a TG Election.
21a TG Jesus Christ, Good
    Shepherd.
22a Mosiah 27: 13.
  b TG Jesus Christ, Head

    of the Church.
  c 2 Ne. 9: 23.
  d TG Baptism,
    Qualifications for.
  e TG Remission of Sins.
23a TG Jesus Christ,
    Redeemer.
  b TG Jesus Christ,
    Creator.

[Probably between
        120 and 100 B.C.]

unto the end a place at my right hand.

24 For behold, in my name are they called; and if they [a]know me they shall come forth, and shall have a place eternally at my right hand.

25 And it shall come to pass that when the [a]second trump shall sound then shall they that never [b]knew me come forth and shall stand before me.

26 And then shall they know that I am the Lord their God, that I am their Redeemer; but they would not be redeemed.

27 And then I will confess unto them that I never [a]knew them; and they shall [b]depart into [c]everlasting fire prepared for the devil and his angels.

28 Therefore I say unto you, that he that will not [a]hear my voice, the same shall ye not receive into my church, for him I will not receive at the last day.

29 Therefore I say unto you, Go; and whosoever transgresseth against me, him shall ye [a]judge [b]according to the sins which he has committed; and if he [c]confess his sins before thee and me, and [d]repenteth in the sincerity of his heart, him shall ye [e]forgive, and I will forgive him also.

30 Yea, and [a]as often as my people [b]repent will I forgive them their trespasses against me.

31 And ye shall also [a]forgive one another your trespasses; for verily I say unto you, he that forgiveth not his [b]neighbor's trespasses when he says that he repents, the same hath brought himself under condemnation.

32 Now I say unto you, Go; and whosoever will [a]not repent of his sins the same shall not be numbered among my people; and this shall be observed from this time forward.

33 And it came to pass when Alma had heard these words he [a]wrote them down that he might have them, and that he might judge the people of that church according to the commandments of God.

34 And it came to pass that Alma went and judged those that had been taken in iniquity, according to the [a]word of the Lord.

35 And whosoever repented of their sins and did [a]confess them, them he did number among the people of the church;

36 And those that would not confess their sins and repent of their iniquity, the same were not numbered among the people of the church, and their names were [a]blotted out.

37 And it came to pass that Alma did regulate all the affairs of the church; and they began again to have peace and to prosper exceedingly in the affairs of the church, walking circumspectly before God, receiving many, and baptizing many.

38 And now all these things did Alma and his [a]fellow laborers do who were over the church, [b]walking in all diligence, teaching the word of God in all things, suffering all manner of afflictions, being persecuted by all those who did not belong to the church of God.

39 And they did admonish their

24a John 17: 3.
25a Dan. 12: 2 (1–2).
   b 3 Ne. 14: 23 (21–23);
      D&C 76: 85 (81–86);
      112: 26.
27a Matt. 7: 23 (21–23).
   b Luke 13: 27.
   c 1 Ne. 15: 35 (32–36).
28a 2 Ne. 9: 31; D&C 1: 14
      (2, 11, 14); Moses 6:
      27.
29a TG Judgment.
   b TG Accountability.
   c Num. 5: 7 (6–10);

Alma 17: 4; 3 Ne.
      1: 25. TG Confession.
   d TG Repentance.
   e TG Forgiveness.
30a Moro. 6: 8.
   b Ezek. 33: 11 (11,
      15–16); Amos
      5: 4 (4–8); Acts 3: 19
      (19–20); 2 Ne. 1: 20;
      Mosiah 29: 20.
31a Col. 3: 13 (12–14);
      3 Ne. 13: 14 (14–15);
      D&C 64: 10 (9–10).
   b TG Neighbor.

32a Alma 1: 24.
      TG Excommunication.
33a TG Scriptures, Writing
      of.
34a 2 Ne. 33: 14 (13–15).
35a TG Confession.
36a Ex. 32: 33; Ps. 9: 5;
      109: 13; Alma 1: 24.
      TG Book of Life.
38a TG Church
      Organization.
   b TG Walking with God.

[Probably between
      120 and 100 B.C.]

brethren; and they were also [a]admonished, every one by the word of God, according to his sins, or to the sins which he had committed, being commanded of God to [b]pray without ceasing, and to give [c]thanks in all things.

CHAPTER 27

Mosiah forbids persecution and enjoins equality—Alma the younger and the four sons of Mosiah seek to destroy the Church—An angel appears and commands them to cease their evil course—Alma is struck dumb—All mankind must be born again to gain salvation—Alma and the sons of Mosiah declare glad tidings.

AND now it came to pass that the persecutions which were inflicted on the church by the unbelievers became so great that the church began to murmur, and complain to their leaders concerning the matter; and they did complain to Alma. And Alma laid the case before their king, Mosiah. And Mosiah [a]consulted with his priests.

2 And it came to pass that king Mosiah sent a proclamation throughout the land round about that there should not any unbeliever [a]persecute any of those who belonged to the church of God.

3 And there was a strict command throughout all the churches that there should be no [a]persecutions among them, that there should be an [b]equality among all men;

4 That they should let no pride nor haughtiness disturb their [a]peace; that every man should [b]esteem his [c]neighbor as himself, [d]laboring with their own hands for their support.

5 Yea, and all their priests and teachers [a]should [b]labor with their own hands for their support, in all cases save it were in sickness, or in much want; and doing these things, they did abound in the [c]grace of God.

6 And there began to be much peace again in the land; and the people began to be very numerous, and began to scatter abroad upon the face of the earth, yea, on the north and on the south, on the east and on the west, building large cities and villages in all quarters of the land.

7 And the Lord did [a]visit them and [b]prosper them, and they became a large and wealthy people.

8 Now the sons of Mosiah were numbered among the [a]unbelievers; and also one of the sons of Alma was numbered among them, he being called Alma, after his father; nevertheless, he became a very wicked and an [b]idolatrous man. And he was a man of many words, and did speak much [c]flattery to the people; therefore he [d]led many of the people to do after the manner of his [e]iniquities.

9 And he became a great hinderment to the prosperity of the church of God; [a]stealing away the hearts of the people; causing much dissension among the people; giving a chance for the enemy of God to exercise his [b]power over them.

10 And now it came to pass that while he was going about to [a]destroy the church of God, for he did go about secretly with the sons of Mosiah seeking to destroy the church,

39a TG Warnings.
  b 2 Ne. 32: 9 (8–9).
  c TG Thanksgiving.
27 1a TG Counsel.
2a TG Persecution.
3a TG Malice.
  b Mosiah 23: 7; 29: 32;
    Alma 30: 11.
4a TG Peace.
  b TG Love.
  c TG Neighbor.
  d TG Industry; Labor.

5a Mosiah 18: 24 (24, 26);
    Alma 1: 3, 26.
  b TG Work, Value of.
  c TG Grace.
7a Ex. 3: 16.
  b TG Prosper.
8a 1 Sam. 3: 13; 1 Ne.
    2: 12 (12–13); Moses
    5: 16. TG Unbelief,
    Unbelievers.
  b TG Idolatry.
  c TG Flattery.

d TG Peer Influence.
  e Mal. 2: 8.
9a 2 Sam. 12: 14 (1–14);
    15: 6 (1–6). TG Apostasy
    of Individuals.
  b D&C 50: 7; 93: 39
    (37, 39).
10a Acts 8: 3; Mosiah 28: 4
    (3–4).

[Probably between
                100 and 92 B.C.]

and to lead astray the people of the Lord, contrary to the commandments of God, or even the king—

11 And as I said unto you, as they were going about *a*rebelling against God, behold, the *b*angel of the Lord *c*appeared unto them; and he descended as it were in a *d*cloud; and he spake as it were with a voice of thunder, which caused the earth to shake upon which they stood;

12 And so great was their astonishment, that they fell to the earth, and understood not the words which he spake unto them.

13 Nevertheless he cried again, saying: Alma, arise and stand forth, for why persecutest thou the church of God? For the Lord hath said: *a*This is my church, and I will establish it; and nothing shall *b*overthrow it, save it is the transgression of my people.

14 And again, the angel said: Behold, the Lord hath *a*heard the prayers of his people, and also the *b*prayers of his servant, Alma, who is thy father; for he has *c*prayed with much faith concerning thee that thou mightest be brought to the *d*knowledge of the truth; therefore, for this purpose have I come to *e*convince thee of the power and authority of God, that the *f*prayers of his servants might be answered according to their faith.

15 And now behold, can ye dispute the power of God? For behold, doth not my voice shake the earth? And can ye not also *a*behold me before you? And I am sent from God.

16 Now I say unto thee: Go, and remember the captivity of thy fathers in the land of *a*Helam, and in the land of Nephi; and remember how great things he has done for them; for they were in *b*bondage, and he has *c*delivered them. And now I say unto thee, Alma, go thy way, and seek to destroy the church no more, that their prayers may be answered, and this even if thou wilt of *d*thyself be *e*cast off.

17 And now it came to pass that these were the last words which the angel spake unto Alma, and he departed.

18 And now Alma and those that were with him fell again to the earth, for great was their astonishment; for with their own eyes they had beheld an *a*angel of the Lord; and his voice was as thunder, which *b*shook the earth; and they knew that there was nothing save the power of God that could shake the earth and cause it to tremble as though it would part asunder.

19 And now the astonishment of Alma was so great that he became *a*dumb, that he could not open his mouth; yea, and he became weak, even that he could not move his hands; therefore he was taken by those that were with him, and carried helpless, even until he was laid before his father.

20 And they rehearsed unto his father all that had happened unto them; and his father rejoiced, for he knew that it was the power of God.

21 And he caused that a multitude should be gathered together that they might witness what the Lord

11a TG Disobedience; Rebellion.
  b Alma 21:5.
  c Acts 9:3 (1–9); Mosiah 27:15; Alma 8:15; 17:2.
  d Ex. 19:9 (9, 16).
13a Mosiah 26:22. TG Jesus Christ, Head of the Church.
  b Hosea 13:9. TG Apostasy of Individuals.
14a Dan. 10:12; Abr. 1:16 (15–16).
  b 2 Cor. 1:11; Alma 10:22.
  c TG Family, Love within.
  d Hosea 4:6.
  e Alma 29:10.
  f Alma 19:17; Morm. 9:36 (36–37).
15a Mosiah 27:11.
16a Mosiah 23:19; Alma 24:1.
  b Mosiah 25:10; Alma 5:5 (5–6).
  c Mosiah 23:1 (1–4).
  d Alma 30:47.
  e Micah 3:6 (1–7); Matt. 8:12 (11–12).
18a TG Angels.
  b Isa. 6:4; Alma 36:7.
19a Dan. 10:15; Luke 1:20 (20–22).

[Probably between 100 and 92 B.C.]

had done for his son, and also for those that were with him.

22 And he caused that the priests should assemble themselves together; and they began to fast, and to pray to the Lord their God that he would open the mouth of Alma, that he might speak, and also that his limbs might receive their strength—that the eyes of the people might be opened to see and know of the goodness and glory of God.

23 And it came to pass after they had fasted and prayed for the space of *two days and two nights, the limbs of Alma received their strength, and he stood up and began to speak unto them, bidding them to be of good comfort:

24 For, said he, I have repented of my sins, and have been *redeemed of the Lord; behold I am born of the Spirit.

25 And the Lord said unto me: Marvel not that all mankind, yea, men and women, all nations, kindreds, tongues and people, must be *born again; yea, *born of God, *changed from their carnal and *fallen state, to a state of righteousness, being redeemed of God, becoming his *sons and daughters;

26 And thus they become new creatures; and unless they do this, they can in *nowise inherit the kingdom of God.

27 I say unto you, unless this be the case, they must be cast off; and this I know, because I was like to be cast off.

28 Nevertheless, after *wading through much *tribulation, repenting nigh unto death, the Lord in

mercy hath seen fit to snatch me out of an *everlasting burning, and I am born of God.

29 My soul hath been *redeemed from the gall of bitterness and *bonds of iniquity. I was in the darkest abyss; but now I behold the marvelous light of God. My soul was *racked with eternal torment; but I am *snatched, and my soul is *pained no more.

30 I rejected my Redeemer, and denied that which had been spoken of by our fathers; but now that they may foresee that he will come, and that he remembereth every creature of his creating, he will make himself manifest unto *all.

31 Yea, *every knee shall bow, and every tongue confess before him. Yea, even at the last day, when all men shall stand to be *judged of him, then shall they confess that he is *God; then shall they confess, who live *without God in the world, that the judgment of an everlasting punishment is just upon them; and they shall quake, and tremble, and shrink beneath the glance of his *all-searching eye.

32 And now it came to pass that Alma began from this time forward to teach the people, and those who were with Alma at the time the angel appeared unto them, traveling round about through all the land, publishing to all the people the things which they had heard and seen, and preaching the word of God in much tribulation, being greatly persecuted by those who were unbelievers, being smitten by many of them.

23a Alma 36: 10.
24a Ps. 49: 15; Alma
   27: 25; A of F 3.
25a Rom. 6: 3 (3–11).
   TG Conversion; Man,
   New, Spiritually
   Reborn.
 b Mosiah 5: 7; Alma
   5: 14 (14, 49).
 c Moses 6: 65.
 d TG Man, Natural, Not
   Spiritually Reborn.
 e Mosiah 15: 10;

Moro. 7: 19.
26a John 3: 5.
28a 1 Kgs. 18: 21.
 b TG Tribulation.
 c 2 Ne. 9: 16.
29a Isa. 38: 17.
 b Isa. 58: 6.
 c Mosiah 2: 38.
 d HEB natzal, to snatch
   away from danger, to
   save; e.g. 2 Sam. 19: 9.
 e TG Pain.
30a D&C 84: 46 (45–46).

31a Philip. 2: 10 (9–11);
   Mosiah 16: 1 (1–2);
   D&C 88: 104; 138: 23.
 b TG Jesus Christ, Judge.
 c Mosiah 7: 27;
   Alma 11: 39 (38–39).
 d Eph. 2: 12; Alma
   41: 11.
 e TG God, Omniscience
   of.

[Probably between
                 100 and 92 B.C.]

33 But notwithstanding all this, they did impart much consolation to the church, confirming their faith, and exhorting them with long-suffering and much travail to keep the commandments of God.

34 And four of them were the [a]sons of Mosiah; and their names were Ammon, and Aaron, and Omner, and Himni; these were the names of the sons of Mosiah.

35 And they traveled throughout all the land of Zarahemla, and among all the [a]people who were under the reign of king Mosiah, [b]zealously striving to repair all the injuries which they had done to the church, [c]confessing all their sins, and publishing all the things which they had seen, and explaining the prophecies and the scriptures to all who desired to hear them.

36 And thus they were instruments in the hands of God in bringing many to the knowledge of the truth, yea, to the knowledge of their Redeemer.

37 And how blessed are they! For they did [a]publish [b]peace; they did publish good tidings of good; and they did declare unto the people that the Lord reigneth.

CHAPTER 28

The sons of Mosiah shall have eternal life—They go to preach to the Lamanites—Mosiah translates the Jaredite plates with the two seer stones.

Now it came to pass that after the [a]sons of Mosiah had done all these things, *they took a small number with them and returned to their father, the king, and desired of him that he would grant unto them

that they might, with these whom they had [b]selected, go up to the land of [c]Nephi that they might preach the things which they had heard, and that they might impart the word of God to their brethren, the Lamanites—

2 [a]That perhaps they might bring them to the knowledge of the Lord their God, and convince them of the iniquity of their fathers; and that perhaps they might cure them of their [b]hatred towards the Nephites, that they might also be brought to rejoice in the Lord their God, that they might become friendly to one another, and that there should be no more contentions in all the land which the Lord their God had given them.

3 Now they were desirous that salvation should be declared to every creature, for they could not [a]bear that any human [b]soul should [c]perish; yea, even the very thoughts that any soul should endure [d]endless torment did cause them to quake and [e]tremble.

4 And thus did the Spirit of the Lord work upon them, for they were the very [a]vilest of sinners. And the Lord saw fit in his infinite [b]mercy to spare them; nevertheless they suffered much anguish of soul because of their iniquities, suffering much and fearing that they should be cast off forever.

5 And it came to pass that they did plead with their father many days that they might go up to the land of Nephi.

6 And king Mosiah went and [a]inquired of the Lord if he should let his sons go up among the Lamanites to preach the word.

34a Mosiah 28:1; 29:3;
　　Alma 17:1.
35a Mosiah 1:10; 28:18.
　　b TG Zeal.
　　c Alma 39:13.
37a Mosiah 12:21; 15:14
　　(14–17).
　　b TG Peace of God.
28 1a Mosiah 27:34.
　　b Alma 17:8.
　　c Mosiah 9:1 (1, 3–4, 14);

　　Alma 50:8 (8, 11).
2a Alma 17:16.
　　b Jacob 7:24; Mosiah
　　　1:5; Alma 26:9.
3a 1 Ne. 7:8; Mosiah
　　　25:11; Alma 13:27
　　　(27–30); 31:2; 3 Ne.
　　　17:14; Moses 7:41.
　　b TG Worth of Souls.
　　c Matt. 18:14.

d Jacob 6:10; Moro.
　8:21; D&C 19:12
　(10–12).
e 1 Cor. 2:3.
4a Mosiah 27:10; Alma
　26:18 (17–18).
　b TG God, Mercy of.
6a Ex. 18:15; Alma
　43:23.

[*About 92 B.C.]

7 And the Lord said unto Mosiah: Let them go up, for many shall believe on their words, and they shall have eternal life; and I will [a]deliver thy sons out of the hands of the Lamanites.

8 And it came to pass that Mosiah granted that they might go and do according to their request.

9 And they [a]took their journey into the wilderness to go up to preach the word among the Lamanites; and I shall give an [b]account of their proceedings hereafter.

10 Now king Mosiah had no one to confer the kingdom upon, for there was not any of his sons who [a]would accept of the kingdom.

11 Therefore he took the records which were engraven on the plates of [a]brass, and also the plates of [b]Nephi, and all the things which he had kept and preserved according to the commandments of God, after having translated and caused to be written the records which were on the [c]plates of gold which had been found by the people of Limhi, which were delivered to him by the hand of Limhi;

12 And this he did because of the great anxiety of his people; for they were desirous beyond measure to know concerning those people [a]who had been destroyed.

13 And now he translated them by the means of those two [a]stones which were fastened into the two rims of a bow.

14 Now these things were prepared from the beginning, and were handed down from generation to generation, for the purpose of interpreting languages;

15 And they have been kept and preserved by the hand of the Lord, that he should discover to every creature who should possess the land the iniquities and abominations of his people;

16 And whosoever has these things is called [a]seer, after the manner of old times.

17 Now after Mosiah had finished [a]translating these [b]records, behold, it gave an account of the people who were [c]destroyed, from the time that they were destroyed back to the building of the [d]great tower, at the time the Lord [e]confounded the language of the people and they were scattered abroad upon the face of all the earth, yea, and even from that time back until the creation of Adam.

18 Now this account did cause the people of Mosiah to mourn exceedingly, yea, they were filled with sorrow; nevertheless it gave them much knowledge, in the which they did rejoice.

19 And this account shall be [a]written hereafter; for behold, it is expedient that all people should know the things which are written in this account.

20 And now, as I said unto you, that after king Mosiah had done these things, he took the plates of [a]brass, and all the things which he had kept, and [b]conferred them upon Alma, who was the son of Alma; yea, all the records, and also the [c]interpreters, and conferred them upon him, and commanded him that he should keep and [d]preserve them, and also keep a record of the people, handing them down from one gen-

7a Alma 17: 35; 19: 23 (22–23).
9a Alma 17: 6 (6–9); 26: 1.
  b IE in Alma, chapters 17–26.
10a Mosiah 29: 3 (1–3).
11a Mosiah 10: 16.
  b W of M 1: 10.
  c Mosiah 21: 27; Alma 37: 21 (21–31).
12a Mosiah 8: 8.
13a Ex. 28: 30; Mosiah

21: 28 (27–28); Abr. 3: 1; JS-H 1: 35.
16a Mosiah 8: 13 (13–18).
  TG Seer.
17a Omni 1: 20; Alma 9: 21.
  b TG Scriptures, Writing of.
  c Mosiah 8: 8 (7–12); Alma 22: 30.
  d Ether 1: 3 (1–5).

e Gen. 11: 7 (6–9); Omni 1: 22.
19a Ether 1:1.
20a Mosiah 1: 3 (3–4); Alma 37: 3 (3–12).
  b Alma 37: 1.
  c TG Urim and Thummim.
  d TG Scriptures, Preservation of.

[About 92 B.C.]

eration to another, even as they had been handed down from the time that Lehi left Jerusalem.

CHAPTER 29

Mosiah proposes that judges be chosen in place of a king—Unrighteous kings lead their people into sin—Alma the younger is chosen chief judge by the voice of the people—He is also the high priest over the Church—Alma the elder and Mosiah die.

Now when Mosiah had done this he sent out throughout all the land, among all the people, desiring to know their will concerning who should be their king.

2 And it came to pass that the voice of the people came, saying: We are desirous that Aaron thy son should be our king and our ruler.

3 Now Aaron had gone up to the land of Nephi, therefore the king could not confer the kingdom upon him; ªneither would Aaron take upon him the kingdom; neither were any of the ᵇsons of Mosiah ᶜwilling to take upon them the kingdom.

4 Therefore king Mosiah sent again among the people; yea, even a written word sent he among the people. And these were the words that were written, saying:

5 Behold, O ye my people, or my brethren, for I esteem you as such, I desire that ye should consider the cause which ye are called to ªconsider—for ye are desirous to have a king.

6 Now I declare unto you that he to whom the kingdom doth rightly belong has declined, and will not take upon him the kingdom.

7 And now if there should be another appointed in his stead, behold I fear there would rise ªcon-

tentions among you. And who knoweth but what my son, to whom the kingdom doth belong, should turn to be angry and ᵇdraw away a part of this people after him, which would cause wars and contentions among you, which would be the cause of shedding much blood and perverting the way of the Lord, yea, and destroy the souls of many people.

8 Now I say unto you let us be wise and consider these things, for we have no right to destroy my son, neither should we have any right to destroy another if he should be appointed in his stead.

9 And if my son should turn again to his pride and vain things he would recall the things which he had said, and claim his right to the kingdom, which would cause him and also this people to commit much sin.

10 And now let us be wise and look forward to these things, and do that which will make for the peace of this people.

11 Therefore I will be your king the remainder of my days; nevertheless, let ªus appoint ᵇjudges, to judge this people according to our law; and we will newly arrange the affairs of this people, for we will appoint wise men to be judges, that will judge this people according to the commandments of God.

12 Now it is better that a man should be ªjudged of God than of man, for the judgments of God are always just, but the judgments of man are not always just.

13 Therefore, ªif it were possible that you could have ᵇjust men to be your kings, who would establish the ᶜlaws of God, and judge this people according to his commandments, yea, if ye could have men for your

---

29 3a Alma 17:6.
  b Mosiah 27:34.
  c Mosiah 28:10.
  5a 1 Sam. 8:9 (9–19).
  7a TG Contention.
  b Judg. 8:23; 9:2 (1–55).
  11a Mosiah 29:25 (25–27,

41).
  b Ex. 18:13; Deut. 16:18; Ezra 7:25; Alma 46:4; D&C 107:74 (74, 78).
  12a 2 Sam. 23:3; 2 Chr. 1:10; Ps. 50:6; 75:7;

2 Ne. 21:4; D&C 98:9; Moses 6:57.
  TG God, Justice of.
  13a Mosiah 23:8, 13.
  b 1 Kgs. 15:14 (11–14).
  c Ex. 18:21; Neh. 7:2.

[About 92 B.C.]

kings who would do even as my father [d]Benjamin did for this people—I say unto you, if this could always be the case then it would be expedient that ye should always have kings to rule over you.

14 And even I myself have labored with all the power and faculties which I have possessed, to teach you the commandments of God, and to establish peace throughout the land, that there should be no wars nor contentions, no stealing, nor plundering, nor murdering, nor any manner of iniquity;

15 And whosoever has committed iniquity, him have I [a]punished according to the crime which he has committed, according to the law which has been given to us by our fathers.

16 Now I say unto you, that because all men are not just it is not expedient that ye should have a [a]king or kings to rule over you.

17 For behold, how much [a]iniquity doth one [b]wicked king cause to be committed, yea, and what great destruction!

18 Yea, remember king Noah, his [a]wickedness and his abominations, and also the wickedness and abominations of his people. Behold what great destruction did come upon them; and also because of their iniquities they were brought into [b]bondage.

19 And were it not for the interposition of their all-wise Creator, and this because of their sincere repentance, they must unavoidably remain in bondage until now.

20 But behold, he did deliver them because they did [a]humble themselves before him; and because they [b]cried mightily unto him he did deliver them out of bondage; and thus doth the Lord work with his power in all cases among the children of men, extending the arm of [c]mercy towards them that put their [d]trust in him.

21 And behold, now I say unto you, ye cannot dethrone an iniquitous [a]king save it be through much contention, and the shedding of much blood.

22 For behold, he has his [a]friends in iniquity, and he keepeth his guards about him; and he teareth up the laws of those who have reigned in righteousness before him; and he trampleth under his feet the commandments of God;

23 And he enacteth laws, and sendeth them forth among his people, yea, laws after the manner of his own wickedness; and whosoever doth not obey his laws he [a]causeth to be destroyed; and whosoever doth rebel against him will he send his armies against them to war, and if he can he will destroy them; and thus an unrighteous [b]king doth pervert the ways of all righteousness.

24 And now behold I say unto you, it is not expedient that such abominations should come upon you.

25 Therefore, choose you by the [a]voice of this people, judges, that ye may be [b]judged according to the [c]laws which have been given you by our fathers, which are correct, and which were given them by the hand of the Lord.

26 Now it is not common that the [a]voice of the people desireth any-

13d Omni 1:25; W of M
   1:18 (17–18).
15a Alma 1:32.
16a 1 Sam. 8:5 (4–22).
   TG Kings, Earthly.
17a 1 Kgs. 16:26 (25–26);
   Alma 46:9.
   b Prov. 16:12; Mosiah
   23:9 (8–10).
18a Mosiah 11:2 (1–15).
   b 1 Sam. 8:11 (10–18);
   Mosiah 12:2 (2–8);

Ether 6:23.
20a Mosiah 21:14.
   b Ex. 2:23 (23–25);
   Alma 43:49 (49–50).
   c Ezek. 33:11 (11,
   15–16); Mosiah 26:30.
   d TG Trust in God.
21a 1 Sam. 8:9; Prov. 25:5
   (4–5).
22a 1 Kgs. 12:8 (8–15).
23a TG Tyranny; Un-

righteous Dominion.
   b TG Kings, Earthly.
25a Mosiah 29:11; Alma
   2:3 (3–7).
   TG Citizenship.
   b Ex. 18:22 (19–27).
   c Deut. 4:8; Alma 34:11.
26a 1 Sam. 8:7; Alma
   29:4; D&C 26:2.
   TG Common Consent.

[About 92 B.C.]

thing *b*contrary to that which is right; but it is common for the lesser part of the *c*people to desire that which is not right; therefore this shall ye observe and make it your law—to do your business by the voice of the people.

27 And *a*if the time comes that the voice of the people doth choose iniquity, then is the time that the judgments of God will come upon you; yea, then is the time he will visit you with great destruction even as he has hitherto visited this land.

28 And now if ye have judges, and they do not *a*judge you according to the law which has been given, ye can cause that they may be judged of a higher judge.

29 If your higher judges do not judge righteous judgments, ye shall cause that a small number of your lower judges should be gathered together, and they shall judge your higher judges, according to the voice of the people.

30 And I command you to do these things in the fear of the Lord; and I command you to do these things, and that ye have no king; that if these people commit sins and iniquities they shall be answered upon their own heads.

31 For behold I say unto you, the sins of many people have been *a*caused by the iniquities of their kings; therefore their iniquities are answered upon the heads of their kings.

32 And now I desire that this *a*inequality should be no more in this land, especially among this my people; but I desire that this land be a land of *b*liberty, and *c*every man may enjoy his rights and privileges alike, so long as the Lord sees fit that

we may live and inherit the land, yea, even as long as any of our posterity remains upon the face of the land.

33 And many more things did king Mosiah write unto them, unfolding unto them all the trials and *a*troubles of a righteous king, yea, all the travails of soul for their people, and also all the murmurings of the people to their king; and he explained it all unto them.

34 And he told them that these things ought not to be; but that the burden should come upon all the people, that every man might *a*bear his part.

35 And he also unfolded unto them all the disadvantages they labored under, by having an unrighteous *a*king to rule over them;

36 Yea, all *a*his iniquities and abominations, and all the wars, and contentions, and bloodshed, and the stealing, and the plundering, and the committing of whoredoms, and all manner of iniquities which cannot be enumerated—telling them that these things ought not to be, that they were expressly repugnant to the commandments of God.

37 And now it came to pass, after king Mosiah had sent these things forth among the people they were *a*convinced of the truth of his words.

38 Therefore they relinquished their desires for a king, and became exceedingly anxious that every man should have an equal *a*chance throughout all the land; yea, and every man expressed a willingness to answer for his own sins.

39 Therefore, it came to pass that they assembled themselves together in bodies throughout the land, to cast in their *a*voices concerning who should be their *b*judges,

26*b* TG Disobedience.
  c TG Governments.
27*a* Alma 2: 4 (3–7); 10: 19; Hel. 4: 21 (20–24); 5: 2.
28*a* Deut. 17: 8 (8–9).
31*a* 1 Kgs. 14: 16; 15: 26; 16: 2; 21: 22; Mosiah 29: 36.
32*a* Mosiah 27: 3; Alma 30: 11. TG Injustice.
  b 2 Ne. 1: 7; 10: 11; Alma 46: 17 (10–28, 34). TG Liberty.
  c Alma 27: 9.
33*a* TG Stewardship.
34*a* TG Accountability.
35*a* TG Kings, Earthly.
36*a* Mosiah 29: 31.
37*a* 1 Sam. 8: 19.
38*a* TG Agency.
39*a* TG Common Consent.
  b Alma 62: 47.

to judge them according to the ^claw which had been given them; and they were exceedingly rejoiced because of the ^dliberty which had been granted unto them.

40 And they did wax strong in love towards Mosiah; yea, they did esteem him more than any other man; for they did not look upon him as a ^atyrant who was seeking for gain, yea, for that ^blucre which doth ^ccorrupt the soul; for he had not exacted riches of them, neither had he delighted in the shedding of blood; but he had established ^dpeace in the land, and he had granted unto his people that they should be delivered from all manner of bondage; therefore they did esteem him, yea, exceedingly, beyond measure.

41 And it came to pass that they did ^aappoint ^bjudges to rule over them, or to judge them according to the law; and this they did throughout all the land.

42 And it came to pass that Alma was appointed to be the first ^achief judge, he being also the ^bhigh priest, his father having conferred the office

upon him, and having given him the charge concerning all the affairs of the church.

43 And now it came to pass that Alma did ^awalk in the ways of the Lord, and he did keep his commandments, and he did judge righteous judgments; and there was continual peace through the land.

44 And thus *commenced the ^areign of the judges throughout all the land of Zarahemla, among all the people who were called the Nephites; and Alma was the first and chief judge.

45 And now it came to pass that his father died, being eighty and two years old, having lived to fulfil the commandments of God.

46 And it came to pass that Mosiah ^adied also, in the thirty and third year of his reign, being ^bsixty and three years old; making in the whole, five hundred and nine years from the time Lehi left Jerusalem.

47 And thus ended the reign of the kings over the people of Nephi; and thus ended the days of Alma, who was the founder of their church.

THE BOOK OF ALMA

THE SON OF ALMA

The account of Alma, who was the son of Alma, the first and chief judge over the people of Nephi, and also the high priest over the Church. An account of the reign of the judges, and the wars and contentions among the people. And also an account of a war between the Nephites and the Lamanites, according to the record of Alma, the first and chief judge.

CHAPTER 1

Nehor teaches false doctrines, establishes a church, introduces priestcraft, and slays Gideon—He is executed for his crimes—Priestcrafts and persecutions spread among the people—The priests support themselves, the people care for the poor, and the Church prospers.

39c Alma 1: 14.
  d TG Liberty.
40a TG Tyranny.
  b Titus 1: 11.
  c TG Bribery.
  d TG Peacemakers.

41a Alma 11: 4.
  b Judg. 2: 16; Mosiah 29: 11.
42a Alma 2: 16; 7: 1.
  b Mosiah 26: 7; Alma 4: 4.

43a TG Walking with God.
44a Alma 17: 6.
46a Alma 1: 1.
  b Mosiah 6: 4.

[*91 B.C.]

NOW it came to pass that in the first year of the reign of the judges over the people of Nephi, from this time forward, king Mosiah having *a*gone the way of all the earth, having warred a good warfare, walking uprightly before God, leaving none to reign in his stead; nevertheless he had established *b*laws, and they were acknowledged by the people; therefore they were obliged to abide by the *c*laws which he had made.

2 And it came to pass that in the first year of the reign of Alma in the judgment-seat, there was a *a*man brought before him to be judged, a man who was large, and was noted for his much strength.

3 And he had gone about among the people, preaching to them that which he *a*termed to be the word of God, bearing down *b*against the church; declaring unto the people that every priest and teacher ought to become *c*popular; and they ought *d*not to labor with their hands, but that they ought to be supported by the people.

4 And he also testified unto the people that *a*all mankind should be saved at the last day, and that they *b*need not fear nor tremble, but that they might lift up their heads and rejoice; for the Lord had *c*created all men, and had also *d*redeemed *e*all men; and, in the end, all men should have eternal life.

5 And it came to pass that he did teach these things so much that many did believe on his words, even so many that they began to support him and give him *a*money.

6 And he began to be lifted up in the pride of his heart, and to wear very costly *a*apparel, yea, and even began to *b*establish a *c*church after the manner of his preaching.

7 And it came to pass as he was going, to preach to those who believed on his word, he met a man who belonged to the church of God, yea, even one of their *a*teachers; and he began to contend with him sharply, that he might lead away the people of the church; but the man withstood him, admonishing him with the *b*words of God.

8 Now the name of the man was *a*Gideon; and it was he who was an instrument in the hands of God in delivering the people of Limhi out of bondage.

9 Now, because Gideon withstood him with the words of God he was wroth with Gideon, and drew his sword and began to smite him. Now Gideon being *a*stricken with many years, therefore he was not able to withstand his blows, therefore he was *b*slain by the sword.

10 And the man who slew him was taken by the people of the church, and was brought before Alma, to be *a*judged according to the crimes which he had committed.

11 And it came to pass that he stood before Alma and pleaded for himself with much boldness.

12 But Alma said unto him: Behold, this is the first time that *a*priestcraft has been introduced among this people. And behold, thou art not only guilty of priestcraft, but hast endeavored to enforce it by the sword; and were

1 1a Mosiah 29:46.
  b TG Jarom 1:5;
    Alma 4:16; 8:17;
    Hel. 4:22.
  c TG Citizenship.
2a Alma 1:15.
3a Ezek. 13:3 (1–4).
  b TG Antichrist.
  c Luke 6:26; 1 Ne.
    22:23.
  d Mosiah 18:24 (24, 26);
    27:5 (3–5).
4a Alma 15:15; 21:6;
    30:17; Morm. 8:31.
  b TG Humility; Meekness.
  c TG Jesus Christ,
    Creator; Man,
    Physical Creation of.
  d TG Jesus Christ, Redeemer; Redemption.
  e Moses 4:1 (1–4).
5a Acts 8:18 (17–23).
6a TG Apparel.
  b TG Unrighteous
    Dominion.
  c TG Devil, Church of.
7a TG Teacher.
  b TG Word of God;
    Word of the Lord.
8a Mosiah 20:17; 22:3;
    Alma 2:1.
9a Gen. 24:1; 1 Ne.18:17.
  b Alma 6:7.
10a Mosiah 29:42.
12a 2 Ne. 26:29; Alma
    2:20; 14:16.
    TG Priestcraft.

[About 91 B.C.]

[b]priestcraft to be enforced among this people it would prove their entire destruction.

13 And thou hast shed the [a]blood of a righteous man, yea, a man who has done much good among this people; and were we to spare thee his blood would come upon us for [b]vengeance.

14 Therefore thou art condemned to [a]die, according to the [b]law which has been given us by Mosiah, our last king; and it has been [c]acknowledged by this people; therefore this people must [d]abide by the law.

15 And it came to pass that they took him; and his name was [a]Nehor; and they carried him upon the top of the hill Manti, and there he was caused, or rather did acknowledge, between the heavens and the earth, that what he had taught to the people was contrary to the word of God; and there he suffered an ignominious [b]death.

16 Nevertheless, this did not put an end to the spreading of priestcraft through the land; for there were many who loved the vain things of the world, and they went forth preaching [a]false doctrines; and this they did for the sake of [b]riches and honor.

17 Nevertheless, they durst not [a]lie, if it were known, for fear of the law, for liars were punished; therefore they pretended to preach according to their belief; and now the law could have no power on any man for [b]his belief.

18 And they durst not [a]steal, for fear of the law, for such were punished; neither durst they rob, nor murder, for he that [b]murdered was punished unto [c]death.

19 But it came to pass that whosoever did not belong to the church of God began to persecute those that did belong to the church of God, and had taken upon them the name of Christ.

20 Yea, they did persecute them, and afflict them with all manner of words, and this because of their humility; because they were not proud in their own eyes, and because they did impart the word of God, one with another, without [a]money and without price.

21 Now there was a strict law among the people of the church, that there should [a]not any man, belonging to the church, arise and persecute those that did not belong to the church, and that there should be no persecution among themselves.

22 Nevertheless, there were many among them who began to be proud, and began to contend warmly with their adversaries, even unto blows; yea, they would smite one another with their [a]fists.

23 Now this was in the *second year of the reign of Alma, and it was a cause of much affliction to the church; yea, it was the cause of much trial with the church.

24 For the hearts of many were hardened, and their names were [a]blotted out, that they were remembered no more among the people of God. And also many [b]withdrew themselves from among them.

25 Now this was a great trial to those that did stand fast in the faith; nevertheless, they were [a]steadfast

12b Alma 21:4.
13a Prov. 28:17. TG Blood, Shedding of.
  b Luke 18:7; D&C 121:5. TG Vengeance.
14a TG Capital Punishment.
  b Mosiah 29:39.
  c Hel. 1:8.
  d TG Citizenship.
15a Alma 1:2; 2:1 (1, 20).

  b Deut. 13:5 (1–9).
16a TG False Doctrine.
  b TG Riches; Vanity.
17a TG Honesty; Lying.
  b Alma 30:7 (7–12); A of F 11.
18a Alma 30:10. TG Stealing.
  b TG Murder.
  c TG Capital Punishment.
20a Isa. 55:1 (1–2).
21a Alma 4:8.

  TG Persecution.
22a Ex. 21:18 (18–19); Isa. 58:4.
24a Ex. 32:33; Mosiah 26:32, 36; Alma 6:3. TG Excommunication.
  b Alma 46:7. TG Apostasy of Individuals.
25a TG Commitment; Steadfastness.

and immovable in keeping the commandments of God, and they bore with [b]patience the persecution which was heaped upon them.

26 And when the priests left their [a]labor to impart the word of God unto the people, the people also left their labors to hear the word of God. And when the priest had imparted unto them the word of God they all returned again diligently unto their labors; and the priest, not esteeming himself above his hearers, for the preacher was no better than the hearer, neither was the teacher any better than the learner; and thus they were all equal, and they did all labor, every man [b]according to his strength.

27 And they did [a]impart of their substance, every man according to that which he had, to the [b]poor, and the needy, and the sick, and the afflicted; and they did not wear costly [c]apparel, yet they were neat and comely.

28 And thus they did establish the affairs of the church; and thus they began to have continual peace again, notwithstanding all their persecutions.

29 And now, because of the steadiness of the church they began to be exceedingly [a]rich, having abundance of all things whatsoever they stood in need—an abundance of flocks and herds, and fatlings of every kind, and also abundance of grain, and of gold, and of silver, and of precious things, and abundance of [b]silk and fine-twined linen, and all manner of good homely [c]cloth.

30 And thus, in their [a]prosperous circumstances, they did not send away any who were [b]naked, or that were hungry, or that were athirst, or that were sick, or that had not been nourished; and they did not set their hearts upon [c]riches; therefore they were [d]liberal to all, both old and young, both bond and free, both male and female, whether out of the church or in the church, having no [e]respect to persons as to those who stood in need.

31 And thus they did [a]prosper and become far more wealthy than those who did not belong to their church.

32 For those who did not belong to their church did indulge themselves in [a]sorceries, and in [b]idolatry or [c]idleness, and in [d]babblings, and in [e]envyings and [f]strife; wearing costly apparel; being [g]lifted up in the pride of their own eyes; persecuting, lying, thieving, robbing, committing whoredoms, and murdering, and all manner of wickedness; nevertheless, the law was put in force upon all those who did transgress it, inasmuch as it was possible.

33 And it came to pass that by thus exercising the law upon them, every man suffering according to that which he had done, they became more still, and durst not commit any wickedness if it were known; therefore, there was much peace among the people of Nephi until the fifth year of the reign of the judges.

CHAPTER 2

Amlici seeks to be king and is rejected by the voice of the people—His followers make him king—The Amlicites

25b TG Patience.
26a Mosiah 18:24 (24, 26); 27:5 (3–5).
  b Mosiah 4:27; D&C 10:4.
27a TG Almsgiving; Consecration.
  b Luke 18:22; Acts 20:35 (33–35); Mosiah 4:26; D&C 42:30 (29–31).
  c TG Vanity.

29a TG Riches; Treasure.
  b Alma 4:6.
  c Mosiah 10:5; Hel. 6:13. TG Clothing.
30a 2 Cor. 8:14; Jacob 2:19 (17–19).
  b TG Poor.
  c Job 31:25. TG Wealth.
  d TG Generosity.
  e Deut. 10:17; Alma 16:14; D&C 1:35.

31a TG Prosper.
32a TG Sorcery.
  b TG Idolatry.
  c TG Laziness.
  d TG Gossip.
  e TG Envy.
  f TG Strife.
  g 2 Kgs. 14:10; Jacob 2:13; Alma 31:25; Morm. 8:28. TG Pride.

[About 90 B.C.]

*make war on the Nephites and are
defeated—The Lamanites and Amlicites join forces and are defeated—
Alma slays Amlici.*

AND it came to pass in the commencement of the *fifth year of their
reign there began to be a contention
among the people; for a certain
*man, being called Amlici, he being
a very cunning man, yea, a wise man
as to the wisdom of the world, he
being after the order of the man that
slew *Gideon by the sword, who was
executed according to the law—

2 Now this Amlici had, by his cunning, *drawn away much people
after him; even so much that they
began to be very powerful; and they
began to endeavor to establish
Amlici to be a king over the people.

3 Now this was alarming to the
people of the church, and also to
all those who had not been drawn
away after the persuasions of
Amlici; for they knew that according to their law that such things
must be established by the *voice of
the people.

4 Therefore, if it were possible that
Amlici should gain the voice of the
people, he, being a wicked man,
would *deprive them of their rights
and privileges of the church; for
it was his intent to destroy the
church of God.

5 And it came to pass that the
people assembled themselves together throughout all the land,
every man according to his mind,
whether it were for or against
Amlici, in separate bodies, having
much dispute and wonderful *contentions one with another.

6 And thus they did assemble
themselves together to cast in their
*voices concerning the matter; and
they were laid before the judges.

7 And it came to pass that the
*voice of the people came against
Amlici, that he was not made king
over the people.

8 Now this did cause much joy in
the hearts of those who were against
him; but Amlici did stir up those
who were in his favor to anger
against those who were not in his
favor.

9 And it came to pass that they
gathered themselves together, and
did *consecrate Amlici to be their
king.

10 Now when Amlici was made
king over them he commanded
them that they should take up arms
against their brethren; and this he
did that he might subject them to
him.

11 Now the people of Amlici were
distinguished by the name of
Amlici, being called *Amlicites; and
the remainder were *called Nephites, or the people of God.

12 Therefore the people of the
Nephites were aware of the intent
of the Amlicites, and therefore they
did prepare to meet them; yea, they
did arm themselves with swords,
and with cimeters, and with bows,
and with arrows, and with stones,
and with slings, and with all manner of *weapons of war, of every
kind.

13 And thus they were prepared to
meet the Amlicites at the time of
their coming. And there were
appointed *captains, and higher
captains, and chief captains, according to their numbers.

14 And it came to pass that Amlici
did arm his men with all manner of
weapons of war of every kind; and
he also appointed rulers and leaders
over his people, to lead them to war
against their brethren.

15 And it came to pass that the

2 1a Alma 1:15; 16:11;
   24:28 (28–30).
  b Alma 1:8.
 2a 2 Sam. 15:6 (1–10).
 3a Mosiah 29:25 (25–27);
   Alma 4:16 (16–17).
 4a Mosiah 29:27; Alma
   10:19; Hel. 5:2.
 5a 3 Ne. 11:29.
 6a TG Common Consent.
 7a Mosiah 29:25 (25–27).
 9a TG Unrighteous
   Dominion.
11a Alma 3:4.
  b Jacob 1:14 (13–14);
   Mosiah 25:12; Alma
   3:11 (11, 17).
12a Mosiah 10:8;
   Hel. 1:14.
13a Alma 16:5.

Amlicites came upon the hill Amnihu, which was east of the [a]river Sidon, which ran by the [b]land of Zarahemla, and there they began to make war with the Nephites.

16 Now Alma, being the [a]chief judge and the [b]governor of the people of Nephi, therefore he went up with his people, yea, with his captains, and chief captains, yea, at the head of his armies, against the Amlicites to battle.

17 And they began to slay the Amlicites upon the hill east of Sidon. And the Amlicites did contend with the Nephites with great strength, insomuch that many of the Nephites did fall before the Amlicites.

18 Nevertheless the Lord did strengthen the hand of the Nephites, that they slew the Amlicites with great slaughter, that they began to flee before them.

19 And it came to pass that the Nephites did pursue the Amlicites all that day, and did slay them with much slaughter, insomuch that there were [a]slain of the Amlicites twelve thousand five hundred thirty and two souls; and there were slain of the Nephites six thousand five hundred sixty and two souls.

20 And it came to pass that when Alma could pursue the Amlicites no longer he caused that his people should pitch their tents in the [a]valley of Gideon, the valley being called after that Gideon who was slain by the hand of [b]Nehor with the sword; and in this valley the Nephites did pitch their tents for the night.

21 And Alma sent spies to follow the remnant of the Amlicites, that he might know of their plans and their plots, whereby he might guard himself against them, that he might preserve his people from being destroyed.

22 Now those whom he had sent out to watch the camp of the Amlicites were called Zeram, and Amnor, and Manti, and Limher; these were they who went out with their men to watch the camp of the Amlicites.

23 And it came to pass that on the morrow they returned into the camp of the Nephites in great haste, being greatly astonished, and struck with much fear, saying:

24 Behold, we followed the [a]camp of the [b]Amlicites, and to our great astonishment, in the land of Minon, above the land of Zarahemla, in the course of the land of [c]Nephi, we saw a numerous host of the Lamanites; and behold, the Amlicites have joined them;

25 And they are upon our brethren in that land; and they are fleeing before them with their flocks, and their wives, and their children, towards our city; and except we make haste they obtain possession of our city, and our fathers, and our wives, and our children be slain.

26 And it came to pass that the people of Nephi took their tents, and departed out of the valley of Gideon towards their [a]city, which was the city of [b]Zarahemla.

27 And behold, as they were crossing the river Sidon, the Lamanites and the Amlicites, being as [a]numerous almost, as it were, as the sands of the sea, came upon them to destroy them.

28 Nevertheless, the Nephites being [a]strengthened by the hand of the Lord, having prayed mightily to him that he would deliver them out of the hands of their enemies, therefore the Lord did hear their cries, and did strengthen them, and the Lamanites and the Amlicites did fall before them.

29 And it came to pass that Alma fought with Amlici with the sword,

15a Alma 3:3.
  b Omni 1:13; Mosiah 1:1.
16a Mosiah 29:42.
  b Mosiah 1:10.
19a Alma 3:1 (1–2, 26); 4:2.
20a Alma 6:7; 8:1.
  b Alma 1:12 (7–15); 14:16.
24a Alma 3:20.
  b Alma 3:4 (4, 13–18).
  c 2 Ne. 5:8;
     Alma 20:1.
26a Alma 6:4.
  b Omni 1:14 (14, 18).
27a Jarom 1:6.
28a Deut. 31:6.

[87 B.C.]

face to face; and they did contend mightily, one with another.

30 And it came to pass that Alma, being a man of God, being exercised with much ᵃfaith, cried, saying: O Lord, have mercy and ᵇspare my life, that I may be an instrument in thy hands to save and preserve this people.

31 Now when Alma had said these words he contended again with Amlici; and he was strengthened, insomuch that he slew Amlici with the sword.

32 And he also contended with the king of the Lamanites; but the king of the Lamanites fled back from before Alma and sent his guards to contend with Alma.

33 But Alma, with his guards, contended with the guards of the king of the Lamanites until he slew and drove them back.

34 And thus he cleared the ground, or rather the bank, which was on the west of the river Sidon, throwing the bodies of the Lamanites who had been slain into the waters of Sidon, that thereby his people might have room to cross and contend with the Lamanites and the Amlicites on the west side of the river Sidon.

35 And it came to pass that when they had all crossed the river Sidon that the Lamanites and the Amlicites began to flee before them, notwithstanding they were so numerous that they could not be numbered.

36 And they fled before the Nephites towards the wilderness which was west and north, away beyond the borders of the land; and the Nephites did pursue them with their might, and did slay them.

37 Yea, they were met on every hand, and slain and driven, until they were scattered on the west, and on the north, until they had reached the wilderness, which was called Hermounts; and it was that part of the wilderness which was infested by wild and ravenous beasts.

38 And it came to pass that many died in the wilderness of their wounds, and were devoured by those beasts and also the vultures of the air; and their bones have been found, and have been heaped up on the earth.

CHAPTER 3

The Amlicites had marked themselves according to the prophetic word—The Lamanites had been cursed for their rebellion—Men bring their own curses upon themselves—The Nephites defeat another Lamanite army.

AND it came to pass that the Nephites who were not ᵃslain by the weapons of war, after having buried those who had been slain—now the number of the slain were not numbered, because of the greatness of their number—after they had finished burying their dead they all returned to their lands, and to their houses, and their wives, and their children.

2 Now many women and children had been slain with the sword, and also many of their flocks and their herds; and also many of their fields of grain were destroyed, for they were trodden down by the hosts of men.

3 And now as many of the Lamanites and the Amlicites who had been slain upon the bank of the river Sidon were cast into the ᵃwaters of Sidon; and behold their bones are in the depths of the ᵇsea, and they are many.

4 And the ᵃAmlicites were distinguished from the Nephites, for they had ᵇmarked themselves with red in their foreheads after the manner of the Lamanites; nevertheless they had not shorn their heads like unto the Lamanites.

5 Now the heads of the Lamanites were shorn; and they were ᵃnaked,

---

30a TG Faith.
  b Alma 3: 22.
3 1a Alma 2: 19; 4: 2.
  3a Alma 2: 15; 4: 4.

  b Alma 44: 22.
4a Alma 2: 11, 24.
  b Alma 3: 13 (13–19).
5a Enos 1: 20; Mosiah

10: 8; Alma 43: 20 (18–21).

[87 B.C.]

save it were skin which was girded about their loins, and also their armor, which was girded about them, and their bows, and their arrows, and their stones, and their slings, and so forth.

6 And the skins of the Lamanites were dark, according to the mark which was set upon their fathers, which was a *a*curse upon them because of their transgression and their rebellion against their brethren, who consisted of Nephi, Jacob, and Joseph, and Sam, who were just and holy men.

7 And their brethren sought to destroy them, therefore they were cursed; and the Lord God set a *a*mark upon them, yea, upon Laman and Lemuel, and also the sons of Ishmael, and Ishmaelitish women.

8 And this was done that their seed might be distinguished from the seed of their brethren, that thereby the Lord God might preserve his people, that they might not *a*mix and believe in incorrect *b*traditions which would prove their destruction.

9 And it came to pass that whosoever did mingle his seed with that of the Lamanites did bring the same curse upon his seed.

10 Therefore, whosoever suffered himself to be led away by the Lamanites was called under that head, and there was a mark set upon him.

11 And it came to pass that whosoever would not believe in the *a*tradition of the Lamanites, but believed those records which were brought out of the land of Jerusalem, and also in the tradition of their fathers, which were correct, who believed in the commandments of God and kept them, were *b*called the Nephites, or the people of Nephi, from that time forth—

12 And it is they who have kept the records which are *a*true of their people, and also of the people of the Lamanites.

13 Now we will return again to the Amlicites, for they also had a *a*mark set upon them; yea, they set the mark upon themselves, yea, even a mark of red upon their foreheads.

14 Thus the word of God is fulfilled, for these are the words which he said to Nephi: Behold, the Lamanites have I cursed, and I will set a mark on them that they and their seed may be *a*separated from thee and thy seed, from this time henceforth and forever, except they repent of their wickedness and *b*turn to me that I may have mercy upon them.

15 And again: I will set a mark upon him that mingleth his seed with thy brethren, that they may be cursed also.

16 And again: I will set a mark upon him that fighteth against thee and thy seed.

17 And again, I say he that departeth from thee shall no more be called thy seed; and I will bless thee, and whomsoever shall be called thy seed, henceforth and forever; and these were the promises of the Lord unto Nephi and to his seed.

18 Now the Amlicites knew not that they were fulfilling the words of God when they began to mark themselves in their foreheads; nevertheless they had come out in open *a*rebellion against God; therefore it was expedient that the curse should fall upon them.

19 Now I would that ye should see that they brought upon themselves the *a*curse; and even so doth every man that is cursed bring

6a 1 Ne. 2:23; 2 Ne. 5:21 (21–24).
7a 1 Ne. 12:23.
8a TG Marriage, Interfaith; Separation.
  b Mosiah 10:12 (11–18); Alma 9:16.

11a Alma 17:9 (9–11).
  b Alma 2:11.
12a Mosiah 1:6; Ether 4:11 (6–11).
13a Alma 3:4.
14a TG Separation.

  b 2 Ne. 30:6 (4–7).
18a Josh. 22:18; 4 Ne. 1:38. TG Rebellion.
19a 2 Ne. 5:21 (21–25); Alma 17:15.

upon himself his own condemnation.

20 Now it came to pass that not many days after the battle which was fought in the land of Zarahemla, by the Lamanites and the Amlicites, that there was another army of the Lamanites came in upon the people of Nephi, in the [a]same place where the first army met the Amlicites.

21 And it came to pass that there was an army sent to drive them out of their land.

22 Now Alma himself being afflicted with a [a]wound did not go up to battle at this time against the Lamanites;

23 But he sent up a numerous army against them; and they went up and slew many of the Lamanites, and drove the remainder of them out of the borders of their land.

24 And then they returned again and began to establish peace in the land, being troubled no more for a time with their enemies.

25 Now all these things were done, yea, all these wars and contentions were commenced and ended in the *fifth year of the reign of the judges.

26 And in one year were thousands and tens of thousands of souls sent to the eternal world, that they might reap their [a]rewards according to their works, whether they were good or whether they were bad, to reap eternal happiness or eternal misery, according to the spirit which they listed to obey, whether it be a good spirit or a bad one.

27 For every man receiveth [a]wages of him whom he listeth to [b]obey, and this according to the words of the spirit of prophecy; therefore let it be according to the truth.

And thus endeth the fifth year of the reign of the judges.

CHAPTER 4

Alma baptizes thousands of converts —Iniquity enters the Church, and the Church's progress is hindered— Nephihah is appointed chief judge— Alma, as high priest, devotes himself to the ministry.

Now it came to pass in the †sixth year of the reign of the judges over the people of Nephi, there were no contentions nor wars in the [a]land of Zarahemla;

2 But the people were afflicted, yea, greatly afflicted for the loss of their brethren, and also for the [a]loss of their flocks and herds, and also for the loss of their fields of grain, which were trodden under foot and destroyed by the Lamanites.

3 And so great were their afflictions that every soul had cause to mourn; and they believed that it was the judgments of God sent upon them because of their wickedness and their abominations; therefore they were [a]awakened to a remembrance of their duty.

4 And they began to establish the [a]church more fully; yea, and many were [b]baptized in the [c]waters of Sidon and were joined to the church of God; yea, they were baptized by the hand of Alma, who had been consecrated the [d]high priest over the people of the church, by the hand of his father Alma.

5 And it came to pass in the ‡seventh year of the reign of the judges there were about three thousand five hundred souls that united themselves to the [a]church of God and were baptized. And thus ended the seventh year of the reign of the judges over the people

20a Alma 2: 24.
22a Alma 2: 30 (29–33).
26a Ps. 7: 16. TG Agency; Reward.
27a Mosiah 2: 32 (32–33); Alma 5: 42 (41–42). TG Wages.
  b Rom. 6: 16 (14–18);

Hel. 14: 31 (29–31).
4 1a Omni 1: 12 (12–19).
  2a Alma 2: 19; 3:1 (1–2, 26).
  3a 1 Cor. 15: 34 (33–34).
  4a TG Church Organization.

  b Mosiah 18: 10 (10–17).
  c Alma 3: 3; 6: 7.
  d Mosiah 29: 42. TG High Priest.
  5a Mosiah 25: 22 (18–23); 3 Ne. 26: 21.

[*87 B.C †86 B.C. ‡85 B.C.]

of Nephi; and there was continual peace in all that time.

6 And it came to pass in the *eighth year of the reign of the judges, that the people of the church began to wax proud, because of their exceeding ^ariches, and their ^bfine silks, and their fine-twined linen, and because of their many flocks and herds, and their gold and their silver, and all manner of precious things, which they had obtained by their ^cindustry; and in all these things were they lifted up in the pride of their eyes, for they began to wear very costly ^dapparel.

7 Now this was the cause of much affliction to Alma, yea, and to many of the people whom Alma had consecrated to be ^ateachers, and ^bpriests, and ^celders over the church; yea, many of them were sorely grieved for the wickedness which they saw had begun to be among their people.

8 For they saw and beheld with great sorrow that the people of the church began to be lifted up in the pride of their eyes, and to set their ^ahearts upon riches and upon the vain things of the world, that they began to be scornful, one towards another, and they began to persecute those that did ^bnot believe according to their own will and pleasure.

9 And thus, in this eighth year of the reign of the judges, there began to be great ^acontentions among the people of the church; yea, there were ^benvyings, and ^cstrife, and malice, and persecutions, and pride, even to exceed the pride of those who did not belong to the church of God.

10 And thus ended the eighth year of the reign of the judges; and the wickedness of the church was a great ^astumbling-block to those who did not belong to the church; and thus the church began to fail in its progress.

11 And it came to pass in the †commencement of the ninth year, Alma saw the wickedness of the church, and he saw also that the ^aexample of the church began to lead those who were unbelievers on from one piece of iniquity to another, thus bringing on the destruction of the people.

12 Yea, he saw great inequality among the people, some lifting themselves up with their pride, despising others, turning their backs upon the ^aneedy and the naked and those who were ^bhungry, and those who were athirst, and those who were sick and afflicted.

13 Now this was a great cause for lamentations among the people, while others were abasing themselves, succoring those who stood in need of their succor, such as imparting their substance to the ^apoor and the needy, feeding the hungry, and suffering all manner of ^bafflictions, for Christ's ^csake, who should come according to the spirit of prophecy;

14 Looking forward to that day, thus ^aretaining a ^bremission of their sins; being filled with great ^cjoy because of the resurrection of the dead, according to the will and power and ^ddeliverance of Jesus Christ from the bands of death.

15 And now it came to pass that Alma, having seen the afflictions of the humble followers of God, and

---

6a TG Riches.
  b Alma 1: 29.
  c TG Industry.
  d TG Apparel.
7a Mosiah 6: 3.
  TG Teacher.
  b TG Church Organization.
  c Alma 4: 16. TG Elder.
8a TG Pride; Vanity; Worldliness.

b Alma 1: 21.
9a TG Contention.
  b TG Envy.
  c Alma 16: 18. TG Strife.
10a TG Stumblingblock.
11a 2 Sam. 12: 14; Alma 39: 11. TG Example.
12a Isa. 3: 14; Ezek. 22: 12 (6–13); Amos 3: 10; Jacob 2: 17.
  b Mosiah 4: 26.

13a TG Almsgiving.
  b TG Affliction.
  c 2 Cor. 12: 10.
14a Mosiah 4: 12; Alma 5: 26 (26–35); D&C 20: 32 (31–34).
  b TG Justification.
  c TG Joy.
  d TG Deliverance.

[*84 B.C. †83 B.C.]

the persecutions which were heaped upon them by the remainder of his people, and seeing all their [a]inequality, began to be very sorrowful; nevertheless the Spirit of the Lord did not fail him.

16 And he selected a wise man who was among the [a]elders of the church, and gave him power according to the [b]voice of the people, that he might have power to enact [c]laws according to the laws which had been given, and to put them in force according to the wickedness and the crimes of the people.

17 Now this man's name was [a]Nephihah, and he was appointed [b]chief judge; and he sat in the judgment-seat to judge and to govern the people.

18 Now Alma did not grant unto him the office of being [a]high priest over the church, but he retained the office of high priest unto himself; but he delivered the judgment-seat unto [b]Nephihah.

19 And this he did that he [a]himself might go forth among his people, or among the people of Nephi, that he might [b]preach the [c]word of God unto them, to [d]stir them up in [e]remembrance of their duty, and that he might pull down, by the word of God, all the pride and craftiness and all the contentions which were among his people, seeing no way that he might reclaim them save it were in bearing down in pure [f]testimony against them.

20 And thus in the commencement of the ninth year of the reign of the judges over the people of Nephi, Alma delivered up the judgment-seat to [a]Nephihah, and confined himself wholly to the [b]high priesthood of the holy order of God, to the [c]testimony of the word, according to the spirit of revelation and prophecy.

The words which Alma, the High Priest according to the holy order of God, delivered to the people in their cities and villages throughout the land. Comprising chapter 5.

CHAPTER 5

To gain salvation, men must repent and keep the commandments, be born again, cleanse their garments through the blood of Christ, be humble and strip themselves from pride and envy, and do the works of righteousness— The Good Shepherd calleth his people —Those who do evil works are children of the devil—Alma testifies of the truth of his doctrine and commands men to repent—Names of the righteous shall be written in the book of life.

Now it came to pass that *Alma began to [a]deliver the word of [b]God unto the people, first in the land of Zarahemla, and from thence throughout all the land.

2 And these are the words which he spake to the people in the church which was established in the city of Zarahemla, according to his own record, saying:

3 I, Alma, having been [a]consecrated by my father, Alma, to be a [b]high priest over the church of God, he having power and [c]authority from God to do these things, behold, I say unto you that he began to

15a 2 Cor. 8: 14; D&C 49: 20.
16a Alma 4: 7.
  b Alma 2: 3 (3–7); 50: 39.
  c Alma 1: 1 (1, 14, 18).
17a Alma 27: 20.
  b Alma 30: 29; 50: 37.
18a TG High Priest.
  b Alma 7: 2.
19a Alma 7: 1.

b Alma 5: 1.
c Alma 31: 5; D&C 11: 2.
d Enos 1: 23.
e 2 Chr. 35: 6; Alma 16: 16; D&C 108: 7.
f TG Testimony.
20a Alma 8: 12.
  b Mosiah 29: 42; Alma 5: 3 (3, 44, 49).

c TG Preaching.
5 1a Alma 4: 19.
  b Alma 5: 61.
3a TG Priesthood, Authority.
  b Alma 4: 20 (4, 18, 20); 8: 23 (11, 23).
  c Mosiah 18: 13; 3 Ne. 11: 25.

establish a church in the ᵈland which was in the borders of Nephi; yea, the land which was called the land of Mormon; yea, and he did baptize his brethren in the waters of Mormon.

4 And behold, I say unto you, they were ᵃdelivered out of the hands of the people of king Noah, by the mercy and power of God.

5 And behold, after that, they were brought into ᵃbondage by the hands of the Lamanites in the wilderness; yea, I say unto you, they were in captivity, and again the Lord did deliver them out of ᵇbondage by the power of his word; and we were brought into this land, and here we began to establish the church of God throughout this land also.

6 And now behold, I say unto you, my brethren, you that belong to this church, have you sufficiently retained in ᵃremembrance the captivity of your fathers? Yea, and have you sufficiently retained in remembrance his mercy and long-suffering towards them? And moreover, have ye sufficiently retained in remembrance that he has ᵇdelivered their souls from hell?

7 Behold, he changed their hearts; yea, he awakened them out of a deep sleep, and they awoke unto God. Behold, they were in the midst of darkness; nevertheless, their souls were illuminated by the light of the everlasting word; yea, they were encircled about by the ᵃbands of death, and the ᵇchains of hell, and an everlasting destruction did await them.

8 And now I ask of you, my brethren, were they destroyed? Behold, I say unto you, Nay, they were not.

9 And again I ask, were the bands of death broken, and the ᵃchains of hell which encircled them about, were they loosed? I say unto you, Yea, they were loosed, and their souls did expand, and they did ᵇsing redeeming love. And I say unto you that they are saved.

10 And now I ask of you on what conditions are they ᵃsaved? Yea, what grounds had they to hope for salvation? What is the cause of their being loosed from the bands of death, yea, and also the chains of hell?

11 Behold, I can tell you—did not my father Alma believe in the words which were delivered by the ᵃmouth of Abinadi? And was he not a holy prophet? Did he not speak the words of God, and my father Alma believe them?

12 And according to his faith there was a mighty ᵃchange wrought in his heart. Behold I say unto you that this is all true.

13 And behold, he ᵃpreached the word unto your fathers, and a mighty change was also wrought in their hearts, and they humbled themselves and put their ᵇtrust in the true and ᶜliving God. And behold, they were faithful until the ᵈend; therefore they were saved.

14 And now behold, I ask of you, my brethren of the church, have ye ᵃspiritually been ᵇborn of God? Have ye received his image in your countenances? Have ye experienced this mighty ᶜchange in your hearts?

15 Do ye exercise faith in the

3d Mosiah 18:4; 3 Ne. 5:12.
4a Mosiah 23:1 (1–3).
5a Mosiah 23:37 (37–39); 24:9 (8–15).
  b Mosiah 24:17; 25:10; 27:16.
6a 2 Pet. 3:1 (1–2).
  b TG Deliverance.
7a Mosiah 15:8.
  TG Bondage, Spiritual; Man, Natural, Not

Spiritually Reborn.
  b Alma 12:11 (9–11); D&C 138:23. TG Hell.
9a Alma 12:6.
  b Ps. 147:1 (1–7).
10a TG Save.
11a Mosiah 17:2 (2–4).
12a TG Conversion.
13a Mosiah 18:7 (1–31).
  b TG Trust in God.
  c 1 Sam. 17:26; Ps. 42:2; Morm. 9:28;

D&C 20:19.
  d 2 Ne. 31:15.
14a TG Spirituality.
  b Mosiah 27:25 (24–27); Alma 22:15.
  c Rom. 7:22; 8:11 (11–17); Col. 3:10 (9–10); Mosiah 5:2; Moses 6:65.
  TG Sanctification.

[About 83 B.C.]

redemption of him who *created you? Do you look forward with an eye of faith, and view this mortal body raised in immortality, and this corruption *raised in incorruption, to stand before God to be *judged according to the deeds which have been done in the mortal body?

16 I say unto you, can you imagine to yourselves that ye hear the voice of the Lord, saying unto you, in that day: Come unto me ye *blessed, for behold, your works have been the works of righteousness upon the face of the earth?

17 Or do ye *imagine to yourselves that ye can lie unto the Lord in that day, and *say—Lord, our works have been righteous works upon the face of the earth—and that he will save you?

18 Or otherwise, can ye imagine yourselves brought before the tribunal of God with your souls filled with guilt and remorse, having a remembrance of all your guilt, yea, a perfect *remembrance of all your wickedness, yea, a remembrance that ye have set at defiance the commandments of God?

19 I say unto you, can ye look up to God at that day with a pure heart and clean hands? I say unto you, can you look up, having the *image of God engraven upon your countenances?

20 I say unto you, can ye think of being saved when you have yielded yourselves to become *subjects to the devil?

21 I say unto you, ye will know at that day that ye cannot be *saved; for there can no man be saved except his *garments are washed white; yea, his garments must be *purified until they are cleansed from all stain, through the blood of him of whom it has been spoken by our fathers, who should come to redeem his people from their sins.

22 And now I ask of you, my brethren, how will any of you feel, if ye shall stand before the bar of God, having your garments stained with *blood and all manner of *filthiness? Behold, what will these things testify against you?

23 Behold will they not *testify that ye are murderers, yea, and also that ye are *guilty of all manner of wickedness?

24 Behold, my brethren, do ye suppose that such an one can have a place to sit down in the kingdom of God, with *Abraham, with Isaac, and with Jacob, and also all the holy prophets, whose garments are cleansed and are spotless, pure and white?

25 I say unto you, Nay; except ye make our Creator a liar from the beginning, or suppose that he is a liar from the beginning, ye cannot suppose that such can have place in the kingdom of heaven; but they shall be cast out for they are the *children of the kingdom of the devil.

26 And now behold, I say unto you, my brethren, if ye have experienced a *change of heart, and if ye have felt to sing the *song of redeeming love, I would ask, *can ye feel so now?

15a TG Jesus Christ,
        Creator.
   b TG Immortality;
        Redemption;
        Resurrection.
   c TG Jesus Christ,
        Judge; Judgment,
        The Last.
16a Matt. 25: 34 (31–46).
17a Alma 7: 3.
   b 3 Ne. 14: 22 (21–23).
18a Ezek. 20: 43; 2 Ne.

        9: 14; Mosiah 2: 40;
        3: 25; Alma 11: 43.
19a 1 Jn. 3: 2 (1–3).
20a Mosiah 2: 32.
21a TG Salvation, Plan of.
   b 1 Ne. 12: 10; Alma
        13: 11 (11–13); 3 Ne.
        27: 19 (19–20).
   c D&C 138: 59.
        TG Purification.
22a Isa. 59: 3.
   b TG Filthiness.

23a Isa. 59: 12.
   b TG Guilt.
24a Luke 13: 28.
25a Deut. 32: 5; 2 Ne. 9: 9.
26a TG Change; Conversion;
        Man, New, Spiritually
        Reborn.
   b Alma 26: 13.
   c Mosiah 4: 12; Alma
        4: 14 (13–14); D&C
        20: 32 (31–34).

[About 83 B.C.]

27 Have ye walked, keeping yourselves ᵃblameless before God? Could ye say, if ye were called to die at this time, within yourselves, that ye have been sufficiently ᵇhumble? That your garments have been ᶜcleansed and made white through the blood of Christ, who will come to ᵈredeem his people from their sins?

28 Behold, are ye stripped of ᵃpride? I say unto you, if ye are not ye are not prepared to meet God. Behold ye must prepare quickly; for the kingdom of heaven is soon at hand, and such an one hath not eternal life.

29 Behold, I say, is there one among you who is not stripped of ᵃenvy? I say unto you that such an one is not prepared; and I would that he should prepare ᵇquickly, for the hour is close at hand, and he knoweth not when the time shall come; for such an one is not found guiltless.

30 And again I say unto you, is there one among you that doth make a ᵃmock of his brother, or that heapeth upon him persecutions?

31 Wo unto such an one, for he is not prepared, and the ᵃtime is at hand that he must repent or he cannot be saved!

32 Yea, even wo unto all ye ᵃworkers of iniquity; repent, repent, for the Lord God hath spoken it!

33 Behold, he sendeth an invitation unto ᵃall men, for the ᵇarms of mercy are extended towards them, and he saith: Repent, and I will receive you.

34 Yea, he saith: ᵃCome unto me and ye shall partake of the ᵇfruit of the tree of life; yea, ye shall eat and drink of the ᶜbread and the waters of life ᵈfreely;

35 Yea, come unto me and bring forth works of righteousness, and ye shall not be hewn down and cast into the fire—

36 For behold, the time is at hand that whosoever ᵃbringeth forth not good fruit, or whosoever doeth not the works of righteousness, the same have cause to wail and mourn.

37 O ye workers of iniquity; ye that are ᵃpuffed up in the vain things of the world, ye that have professed to have known the ways of righteousness nevertheless have gone ᵇastray, as ᶜsheep having no ᵈshepherd, notwithstanding a shepherd hath ᵉcalled after you and is still calling after you, but ye will not ᶠhearken unto his voice!

38 Behold, I say unto you, that the good ᵃshepherd doth call you; yea, and in his own name he doth call you, which is the name of Christ; and if ye will not ᵇhearken unto the voice of the ᶜgood shepherd, to the ᵈname by which ye are called, behold, ye are not the sheep of the good shepherd.

39 And now if ye are not the ᵃsheep of the good shepherd, of what fold are ye? Behold, I say unto you, that the ᵇdevil is your shepherd, and ye are of his fold; and now,

27a 1 Jn. 3: 21 (19–24).
  TG Justification.
  b TG Humility.
  c Rev. 19: 8.
  d 1 Cor. 15: 3. TG Jesus Christ, Mission of.
28a TG Pride.
29a TG Envy.
  b TG Procrastination.
30a TG Backbiting; Mocking.
31a TG Procrastination.
32a Ps. 5: 5 (4–6).
33a Alma 19: 36; 3 Ne. 18: 25.
  b Isa. 59: 16; 2 Ne. 1: 15; Jacob 6: 5; 3 Ne. 9: 14.

34a 1 Ne. 1: 14; 2 Ne. 26: 25 (24–28); 3 Ne. 9: 14 (13–14).
  b 1 Ne. 8: 11; 15: 36.
  c TG Bread of Life.
  d 2 Ne. 9: 50 (50–51); Alma 42: 27.
36a Matt. 3: 10; 7: 19 (15–20); Jacob 5: 26 (26–60); 3 Ne. 14: 19; D&C 97: 7.
37a TG Worldliness.
  b 2 Ne. 12: 5; 28: 14; Mosiah 14: 6.
  c Matt. 9: 36.
  d TG Shepherd.
  e Prov. 1: 24 (24–27);

Isa. 65: 12; 1 Ne. 17: 13; 2 Ne. 7: 2.
  f 2 Chr. 33: 10; Jer. 26: 4; Alma 10: 6 (5–6).
38a TG Jesus Christ, Good Shepherd.
  b Lev. 26: 14 (14–20); D&C 101: 7.
  c 3 Ne. 15: 24; 18: 31.
  d Mosiah 5: 8; Alma 34: 38.
39a Matt. 6: 24; Luke 16: 13.
  b Mosiah 5: 10.
  TG Devil, Church of.

[About 83 B.C.]

who can deny this? Behold, I say unto you, whosoever denieth this is a ᶜliar and a ᵈchild of the devil.

40 For I say unto you that whatsoever is ᵃgood cometh from God, and whatsoever is ᵇevil cometh from the devil.

41 Therefore, if a man bringeth forth ᵃgood works he hearkeneth unto the voice of the good shepherd, and he doth follow him; but whosoever bringeth forth evil works, the same becometh a ᵇchild of the devil, for he hearkeneth unto his voice, and doth follow him.

42 And whosoever doeth this must receive his ᵃwages of him; therefore, for his ᵇwages he receiveth ᶜdeath, as to things pertaining unto righteousness, being dead unto all good works.

43 And now, my brethren, I would that ye should hear me, for I speak in the ᵃenergy of my soul; for behold, I have spoken unto you plainly that ye cannot err, or have spoken according to the commandments of God.

44 For I am called to speak after this manner, according to the ᵃholy order of God, which is in Christ Jesus; yea, I am commanded to stand and testify unto this people the things which have been spoken by our fathers concerning the things which are to come.

45 And this is not all. Do ye not suppose that I ᵃknow of these things myself? Behold, I testify unto you that I do know that these things whereof I have spoken are true. And how do ye suppose that I know of their surety?

46 Behold, I say unto you they are made ᵃknown unto me by the Holy Spirit of God. Behold, I have ᵇfasted and prayed many days that I might know these things of myself. And now I do know of myself that they are true; for the Lord God hath made them manifest unto me by his Holy Spirit; and this is the spirit of ᶜrevelation which is in me.

47 And moreover, I say unto you that it has thus been revealed unto me, that the words which have been spoken by our fathers are true, even so according to the spirit of prophecy which is in me, which is also by the manifestation of the Spirit of God.

48 I say unto you, that I know of myself that whatsoever I shall say unto you, concerning that which is to come, is true; and I say unto you, that I know that Jesus Christ shall come, yea, the Son, the Only Begotten of the Father, full of grace, and mercy, and truth. And behold, it is he that cometh to take away the sins of the world, yea, the sins of every man who steadfastly believeth on his name.

49 And now I say unto you that this is the ᵃorder after which I am called, yea, to preach unto my beloved brethren, yea, and every one that dwelleth in the land; yea, to preach unto all, both old and young, both bond and free; yea, I say unto you the aged, and also the middle aged, and the rising generation; yea, to cry unto them that they must repent and be ᵇborn again.

50 Yea, thus saith the Spirit: Repent, all ye ends of the earth, for the kingdom of heaven is soon at hand; yea, the Son of God cometh in his ᵃglory, in his might,

39c 1 Jn. 2: 22.
  d 2 Ne. 9: 9.
40a Ezra 3: 11; Ps. 85: 12;
    Omni 1: 25; Ether
    4: 12; Moro. 7: 16
    (15–17).
  b Isa. 45: 7; Amos 3: 6;
    Moro. 7: 12.
41a 3 Ne. 14: 17 (16–20).
    TG Good Works.

  b Mosiah 16: 3 (3–5);
    Alma 11: 23.
42a Alma 3: 27 (26–27);
    D&C 29: 45.
  b Rom. 6: 23.
  c Hel. 14: 18 (16–18).
43a Alma 7: 5.
44a Mosiah 29: 42.
45a Alma 36: 4.
46a 1 Cor. 2: 10 (9–16).

  b Alma 10: 7.
  c Rev. 19: 10.
49a TG Called of God;
    Priesthood.
  b TG Man, New,
    Spiritually Reborn.
50a Ps. 24: 8; 72: 19.
    TG Jesus Christ,
    Glory of.

[About 83 B.C.]

majesty, power, and dominion.
Yea, my beloved brethren, I say
unto you, that the Spirit saith:
Behold the glory of the [b]King of
all the earth; and also the King of
heaven shall very soon shine forth
among all the children of men.

51 And also the Spirit saith unto
me, yea, crieth unto me with a
mighty voice, saying: Go forth and
say unto this people—Repent, for
except ye repent ye can in nowise
inherit the [a]kingdom of [b]heaven.

52 And again I say unto you, the
Spirit saith: Behold, the [a]ax is laid
at the root of the tree; therefore
every tree that bringeth not forth
good fruit shall be [b]hewn down and
cast into the fire, yea, a fire which
cannot be consumed, even an unquenchable fire. Behold, and remember, the Holy One hath spoken
it.

53 And now my beloved brethren,
I say unto you, can ye withstand
these sayings; yea, can ye lay aside
these things, and [a]trample the Holy
One under your feet; yea, can ye be
[b]puffed up in the pride of your
hearts; yea, will ye still persist in
the wearing of [c]costly apparel and
setting your hearts upon the vain
things of the world, upon your
[d]riches?

54 Yea, will ye persist in supposing
that ye are better one than another;
yea, will ye persist in the persecution of your brethren, who humble
themselves and do walk after the
holy order of God, wherewith they
have been brought into this church,
having been [a]sanctified by the Holy
Spirit, and they do bring forth works
which are meet for repentance—

55 Yea, and will you persist in
turning your backs upon the [a]poor,
and the needy, and in withholding
your substance from them?

56 And finally, all ye that will
persist in your wickedness, I say
unto you that these are they who
shall be hewn down and cast into
the fire except they speedily repent.

57 And now I say unto you, all
you that are desirous to follow the
voice of the [a]good shepherd, come
ye out from the wicked, and be ye
[b]separate, and touch not their unclean things; and behold, their
names shall be [c]blotted out, that the
names of the wicked shall not be
numbered among the names of the
righteous, that the word of God
may be fulfilled, which saith: The
names of the wicked shall not be
mingled with the names of my
people;

58 For the names of the righteous
shall be written in the [a]book of life,
and unto them will I grant an
inheritance at my right hand. And
now, my brethren, what have ye to
say against this? I say unto you, if
ye speak against it, it matters not,
for the word of God must be fulfilled.

59 For what shepherd is there
among you having many sheep
doth not watch over them, that the
wolves enter not and devour his
flock? And behold, if a wolf enter
his [a]flock doth he not drive him
out? Yea, and at the last, if he can,
he will destroy him.

60 And now I say unto you that
the good shepherd doth call after
you; and if you will hearken unto
his voice he will bring you into his

50b Ps. 74:12; 149:2;
   Matt. 2:2; Luke 23:2;
   2 Ne. 10:14; D&C
   38:21 (21–22); 128:22
   (22–23); Moses 7:53.
   TG Jesus Christ, King;
   Kingdom of God, on
   Earth.
51a TG Kingdom of God,
   in Heaven.
  b TG Heaven.
52a Luke 3:9; D&C 97:7.

  b Jacob 5:46; 6:7;
   3 Ne. 27:11 (11–12).
53a TG Sacrilege.
  b 1 Cor. 5:2.
  c 2 Ne. 28:13 (11–14);
   Morm. 8:36 (36–39).
  d Ps. 62:10; D&C
   56:16 (16–18).
54a TG Sanctification.
55a Ps. 109:16 (15–16);
   Jacob 2:17; Hel.
   6:39 (39–40); D&C

   56:16.
57a TG Jesus Christ,
   Good Shepherd.
  b Ezra 6:21; 9:1;
   Neh. 9:2; 2 Thes.
   3:6; D&C 133:5 (5, 14).
  c Deut. 29:20; Ps.
   109:13.
58a TG Book of Life.
59a Prov. 27:23.

[About 83 B.C.]

fold, and ye are his sheep; and he commandeth you that ye suffer no ravenous wolf to enter among you, that ye may not be destroyed.

61 And now I, Alma, do command you in the language of *him who hath commanded me, that ye observe to do the words which I have spoken unto you.

62 I speak by way of command unto you that belong to the church; and unto those who do not belong to the church I speak by way of invitation, saying: Come and be baptized unto repentance, that ye also may be partakers of the fruit of the *tree of life.

CHAPTER 6

The Church in Zarahemla is cleansed and set in order—Alma goes to Gideon to preach.

AND now it came to pass that after Alma had made an end of speaking unto the people of the church, which was established in the city of Zarahemla, he *ordained priests and *belders, by laying on his *chands according to the order of God, to preside and *dwatch over the church.

2 And it came to pass that whosoever did not belong to the church who *repented of their sins were baptized unto repentance, and were received into the church.

3 And it also came to pass that whosoever did belong to the church that did not *repent of their wickedness and humble themselves before God—I mean those who were lifted up in the *bpride of their hearts—the same were rejected, and their names were *cblotted out, that their names were not numbered among those of the righteous.

4 And thus they began to establish the order of the church in the *city of Zarahemla.

5 Now I would that ye should understand that the word of God was liberal unto all, that none were deprived of the privilege of assembling themselves together to hear the word of God.

6 Nevertheless the children of God were commanded that they should gather themselves together oft, and join in *fasting and mighty prayer in behalf of the welfare of the souls of those who knew not God.

7 And now it came to pass that when Alma had made these regulations he departed from them, yea, from the church which was in the city of Zarahemla, and went over upon the east of the *river Sidon, into the *bvalley of Gideon, there having been a city built, which was called the city of Gideon, which was in the valley that was called Gideon, being called after the man who was *cslain by the hand of Nehor with the sword.

8 And Alma went and began to declare the word of God unto the church which was established in the valley of Gideon, according to the revelation of the truth of the word which had been spoken by his fathers, and according to the spirit of prophecy which was in him, according to the *testimony of Jesus Christ, the Son of God, who should come to redeem his people from their sins, and the holy order by which he was called. And thus it is written. Amen.

The words of Alma which he delivered to the people in Gideon, according to his own record. Comprising chapter 7.

61a Alma 5: 1 (1, 44).
62a 1 Ne. 8: 10; 11: 21 (21–23).
6 1a TG Ordination; Priesthood.
  b TG Elder; Priest.
  c TG Hands, Laying on of.

  d D&C 52: 39.
2a TG Baptism, Qualifications for.
3a Mosiah 26: 6.
  b 1 Cor. 5: 2.
  c Ex. 32: 33; Mosiah 26: 36; Alma 1: 24; 5: 57 (57–58).

  TG Excommunication.
4a Alma 2: 26.
6a TG Fasting.
7a Alma 4: 4; 8: 3.
  b Alma 2: 20.
  c Alma 1: 9.
8a Rev. 19: 10.

[About 83 B.C.]

CHAPTER 7

Christ shall be born of Mary—He shall loose the bands of death and bear the sins of his people—Those who repent, are baptized, and keep the commandments shall have eternal life—Filthiness cannot inherit the kingdom of God—Humility, faith, hope, and charity are required.

BEHOLD my beloved brethren, seeing that I have been permitted to come unto you, therefore I attempt to address you in my language; yea, by my [a]own mouth, seeing that it is the first time that I have spoken unto you by the words of my mouth, I having been wholly confined to the [b]judgment-seat, having had much business that I could not come unto you.

2 And even I could not have come now at this time were it not that the judgment-seat hath been [a]given to another, to reign in my stead; and the Lord in much mercy hath granted that I should come unto you.

3 And behold, I have come having great hopes and much desire that I should find that ye had humbled yourselves before God, and that ye had continued in the supplicating of his grace, that I should find that ye were blameless before him, that I should find that ye were not in the awful [a]dilemma that our brethren were in at Zarahemla.

4 But blessed be the name of God, that he hath given me to know, yea, hath given unto me the exceedingly great joy of knowing that they are established again in the way of his righteousness.

5 And I trust, according to the Spirit of God which is in me, that I shall also have joy over you; nevertheless I do not desire that my joy over you should come by the cause of so much afflictions and sorrow which I have had for the brethren at Zarahemla, for behold, my joy cometh over them after wading through much affliction and sorrow.

6 But behold, I trust that ye are not in a state of so much unbelief as were your brethren; I trust that ye are not lifted up in the pride of your hearts; yea, I trust that ye have not set your hearts upon riches and the vain things of the world; yea, I trust that you do not worship [a]idols, but that ye do worship the true and the [b]living God, and that ye look forward for the remission of your sins, with an everlasting faith, which is to come.

7 For behold, I say unto you there be many things to come; and behold, there is one thing which is of more importance than they all— for behold, the [a]time is not far distant that the Redeemer liveth and cometh among his people.

8 Behold, I do not say that he will come among us at the [a]time of his dwelling in his mortal tabernacle; for behold, the Spirit hath not said unto me that this should be the case. Now as to this thing I do not know; but this much I do know, that the Lord God hath power to do all things which are according to his word.

9 But behold, the Spirit hath said this much unto me, saying: Cry unto this people, saying—[a]Repent ye, and prepare the way of the Lord, and walk in his paths, which are straight; for behold, the kingdom of heaven is at hand, and the Son of God [b]cometh upon the face of the earth.

10 And behold, he shall be [a]born of Mary, at [b]Jerusalem which is the [c]land of our forefathers, she being a [d]virgin, a precious and chosen

7 1a Alma 4: 19.
  b Mosiah 29: 42.
2a Alma 4: 18 (16–18).
3a Alma 5: 17 (16–17).
6a 2 Ne. 9: 37; Hel. 6: 31.
  b Dan. 6: 26.
7a Alma 9: 26.

8a 1 Ne. 12: 6 (4–8);
    Alma 16: 20.
9a Matt. 3: 2 (2–3);
    Alma 9: 25 (25–26).
  b Mosiah 3: 5; 7: 27;
    15: 2 (1–7).
10a Isa. 7: 14; Luke 1: 27;

    Mosiah 3: 8.
  b Luke 2: 4.
  c 1 Chr. 9: 3; 2 Chr.
    15: 9; 1 Ne. 1: 4;
    3 Ne. 20: 29.
  d 1 Ne. 11: 13 (13–21).

[About 83 B.C.]

vessel, who shall be overshadowed and [e]conceive by the power of the Holy Ghost, and bring forth a son, yea, even the Son of God.

11 And he shall go forth, suffering pains and [a]afflictions and [b]temptations of every kind; and this that the word might be fulfilled which saith he will [c]take upon him the pains and the sicknesses of his people.

12 And he will take upon him [a]death, that he may [b]loose the bands of death which bind his people; and he will take upon him their infirmities, that his bowels may be filled with mercy, according to the flesh, that he may know according to the flesh how to [c]succor his people according to their infirmities.

13 Now the Spirit [a]knoweth all things; nevertheless the Son of God suffereth according to the [b]flesh that he might [c]take upon him the sins of his people, that he might blot out their transgressions according to the power of his deliverance; and now behold, this is the testimony which is in me.

14 Now I say unto you that ye must [a]repent, and be born again; for the Spirit saith if ye are not born again ye cannot inherit the kingdom of heaven; therefore come and be baptized unto repentance, that ye may be washed from your sins, that ye may have faith on the Lamb of God, who taketh away the sins of the world, who is mighty to save and to cleanse from all unrighteousness.

15 Yea, I say unto you come and fear not, and lay aside every sin, which easily doth [a]beset you, which doth bind you down to destruction, yea, come and go forth, and show

unto your God that ye are willing to repent of your sins and enter into a covenant with him to keep his commandments, and witness it unto him this day by going into the waters of baptism.

16 And whosoever doeth this, and keepeth the commandments of God from thenceforth, the same will [a]remember that I say unto him, yea, he will remember that I have said unto him, he shall have eternal life, according to the testimony of the Holy Spirit, which testifieth in me.

17 And now my beloved brethren, do you believe these things? Behold, I say unto you, yea, I know that ye believe them; and the way that I know that ye believe them is by the manifestation of the Spirit which is in me. And now because your faith is strong concerning that, yea, concerning the things which I have spoken, great is my joy.

18 For as I said unto you from the beginning, that I had much desire that ye were not in the state of [a]dilemma like your brethren, even so I have found that my desires have been gratified.

19 For I perceive that ye are in the paths of righteousness; I perceive that ye are in the path which leads to the kingdom of God; yea, I perceive that ye are making his [a]paths straight.

20 I perceive that it has been made known unto you, by the testimony of his word, that he cannot [a]walk in crooked paths; neither doth he vary from that which he hath said; neither hath he a shadow of turning from the right to the left, or from that which is right to that which is wrong; therefore, his course is one eternal round.

10e Matt. 1: 20; Mosiah 15: 3.
11a Isa. 53: 5 (3–5).
  b TG Jesus Christ, Temptation of.
  c Mosiah 14: 4 (3–5).
12a TG Jesus Christ, Death of.
  b Ps. 116: 16 (15–16);

2 Ne. 2: 8; Alma 12: 25 (24–25); 42: 23.
  c Heb. 2: 18; 4: 15; D&C 62: 1.
13a TG God, Omniscience of.
  b TG Jesus Christ, Condescension of.
  c Mosiah 15: 12.

14a TG Purification.
15a 2 Ne. 4: 18.
16a Ether 12: 4; Moro. 7: 3.
18a James 1: 8.
19a Matt. 3: 3.
20a 1 Ne. 10: 19; Alma 37: 12; D&C 3: 2.

[About 83 B.C.]

21 And he doth not dwell in [a]unholy temples; neither can filthiness or anything which is unclean be received into the kingdom of God; therefore I say unto you the time shall come, yea, and it shall be at the last day, that he who is [b]filthy shall remain in his filthiness.

22 And now my beloved brethren, I have said these things unto you that I might awaken you to a sense of your duty to God, that ye may walk blameless before him, that ye may walk after the holy order of God, after which ye have been received.

23 And now I would that ye should be [a]humble, and be [b]submissive and gentle; easy to be entreated; full of patience and long-suffering; being temperate in all things; being diligent in keeping the commandments of God at all times; asking for whatsoever things ye stand in need, both spiritual and temporal; always returning thanks unto God for whatsoever things ye do receive.

24 And see that ye have [a]faith, hope, and charity, and then ye will always abound in good works.

25 And may the Lord bless you, and keep your garments spotless, that ye may at last be brought to sit down with [a]Abraham, Isaac, and Jacob, and the holy prophets who have been ever since the world began, having your garments [b]spotless even as their garments are spotless, in the kingdom of heaven to go no more out.

26 And now my beloved brethren, I have spoken these words unto you according to the Spirit which testifieth in me; and my soul doth exceedingly rejoice, because of the exceeding diligence and heed which ye have given unto my word.

27 And now, may the [a]peace of God rest upon you, and upon your houses and lands, and upon your flocks and herds, and all that you possess, your women and your children, according to your faith and good works, from this time forth and forever. And thus I have spoken. Amen.

CHAPTER 8

Alma preaches and baptizes in Melek—He is rejected in Ammonihah and leaves—An angel commands him to return and cry repentance unto the people—He is received by Amulek, and the two of them preach in Ammonihah.

AND now it came to pass that Alma returned from the [a]land of Gideon, after having taught the people of Gideon many things which cannot be written, having established the [b]order of the church, according as he had before done in the land of Zarahemla, yea, he returned to his own house at Zarahemla to rest himself from the labors which he had performed.

2 And thus ended the ninth year of the reign of the judges over the people of Nephi.

3 And it came to pass in the commencement of the *tenth year of the reign of the judges over the people of Nephi, that Alma departed from thence and took his journey over into the land of [a]Melek, on the west of the [b]river Sidon, on the west by the borders of the wilderness.

4 And he began to teach the people in the land of Melek according to the [a]holy order of God, by which he had been called; and he began to teach the people throughout all the land of Melek.

5 And it came to pass that the people came to him throughout all

---

21a 1 Cor. 3:17 (16–17);
     6:19; Mosiah 2:37;
     Alma 34:36.
   b 1 Ne. 15:33 (33–35);
     2 Ne. 9:16; Morm.
     9:14; D&C 88:35.
23a Prov. 18:12.
   b TG Submissiveness.

24a 1 Cor. 13:13 (1–13);
     Ether 12:31 (30–35);
     Moro. 7:44 (33–48).
25a D&C 27:10.
   b 2 Pet. 3:14.
27a TG Peace of God.
8 1a Alma 2:20; 6:7.

   b TG Church
     Organization.
3a Alma 31:6.
   b Alma 6:7; 16:6 (6–7).
4a D&C 107:3 (2–4).
   TG Priesthood.

[*82 B.C.]

the borders of the land which was by the wilderness side. And they were baptized throughout all the land;

6 So that when he had finished his work at Melek he departed thence, and traveled three days' journey on the north of the land of Melek; and he came to a city which was called [a]Ammonihah.

7 Now it was the custom of the people of Nephi to call their lands, and their cities, and their villages, yea, even all their small villages, after the [a]name of him who first possessed them; and thus it was with the land of Ammonihah.

8 And it came to pass that when Alma had come to the city of Ammonihah he began to preach the word of God unto them.

9 Now Satan had gotten great [a]hold upon the hearts of the people of the city of Ammonihah; therefore they would not hearken unto the words of Alma.

10 Nevertheless Alma [a]labored much in the spirit, [b]wrestling with God in [c]mighty prayer, that he would pour out his Spirit upon the people who were in the city; that he would also grant that he might baptize them unto repentance.

11 Nevertheless, they hardened their hearts, saying unto him: Behold, we know that thou art Alma; and we know that thou art high priest over the church which thou hast established in many parts of the land, according to your tradition; and we are not of thy church, and we do not believe in such foolish traditions.

12 And now we know that because we are not of thy church we know that thou hast no power over us; and thou hast delivered up the judgment-seat unto [a]Nephihah; therefore thou art not the chief judge over us.

13 Now when the people had said this, and withstood all his words, and [a]reviled him, and spit upon him, and caused that he should be [b]cast out of their city, he departed thence and took his journey towards the city which was called Aaron.

14 And it came to pass that while he was journeying thither, being weighed down with sorrow, wading through much [a]tribulation and anguish of soul, because of the wickedness of the people who were in the city of Ammonihah, it came to pass while Alma was thus weighed down with sorrow, behold an [b]angel of the Lord appeared unto him, saying:

15 Blessed art thou, Alma; therefore, lift up thy head and rejoice, for thou hast great cause to rejoice; for thou hast been faithful in keeping the commandments of God from the time which thou receivedst thy first message from him. Behold, I am he that [a]delivered it unto you.

16 And behold, I am sent to [a]command thee that thou return to the city of Ammonihah, and preach again unto the people of the city; yea, preach unto them. Yea, say unto them, except they repent the Lord God will [b]destroy them.

17 For behold, they do study at this time that they may destroy the liberty of thy people, (for thus saith the Lord) which is contrary to the [a]statutes, and judgments, and commandments which he has given unto his people.

18 Now it came to pass that after Alma had received his message from the angel of the Lord he returned speedily to the land of Ammonihah. And he entered the city by another way, yea, by the way which is on the south of the city of Ammonihah.

19 And as [a]he entered the city he

6a Alma 9: 1.
7a Ether 2: 13.
9a 2 Ne. 28: 20 (19–22);
   D&C 10: 20.
10a Alma 17: 5.
   b Enos 1: 2 (1–12).
   c 3 Ne. 27: 1; 5: 24;
     29: 2.

12a Alma 4: 20.
13a 1 Cor. 4: 12.
   b Alma 8: 24.
14a TG Tribulation.
   b Mosiah 3: 2 (2–3);
     Alma 10: 20 (7–10, 20).
15a Mosiah 27: 11 (11–16).
16a Gal. 2: 2; Hel. 13: 3.

   b Alma 9: 12 (4, 12, 18,
     24).
17a Alma 1: 1 (1, 14).
   TG Commandments
     of God.
19a Alma 10: 8.

[About 82 B.C.]

was an hungered, and he said to a man: Will ye give to an humble servant of God something to eat?

20 And the man said unto him: I am a Nephite, and I know that thou art a holy prophet of God, for thou art the man whom an [a]angel said in a vision: Thou shalt receive. Therefore, go with me into my house and I will impart unto thee of my [b]food; and I know that thou wilt be a blessing unto me and my house.

21 And it came to pass that the man received him into his house; and the man was called Amulek; and he brought forth bread and meat and set before Alma.

22 And it came to pass that Alma ate bread and was filled; and he [a]blessed Amulek and his house, and he gave thanks unto God.

23 And after he had eaten and was filled he said unto Amulek: I am Alma, and am the [a]high priest over the church of God throughout the land.

24 And behold, I have been called to preach the word of God among all this people, according to the spirit of revelation and prophecy; and I was in this land and they would not receive me, but they [a]cast me out and I was about to set my back towards this land forever.

25 But behold, I have been commanded that I should turn again and prophesy unto this people, yea, and to testify against them concerning their iniquities.

26 And now, Amulek, because thou hast fed me and taken me in, thou art blessed; for I was an hungered, for I had fasted many days.

27 And Alma [a]tarried many days with Amulek before he began to preach unto the people.

28 And it came to pass that the people did wax more gross in their iniquities.

29 And the word came to Alma,

saying: Go; and also say unto my servant [a]Amulek, go forth and prophesy unto this people, saying— Repent ye, for thus saith the Lord, except ye repent I will visit this people in mine anger; yea, and I will not turn my [b]fierce anger away.

30 And Alma went forth, and also Amulek, among the people, to declare the words of God unto them; and they were filled with the Holy Ghost.

31 And they had [a]power given unto them, insomuch that they could not be confined in dungeons; neither was it possible that any man could slay them; nevertheless they did not exercise their [b]power until they were bound in bands and cast into prison. Now, this was done that the Lord might show forth his power in them.

32 And it came to pass that they went forth and began to preach and to prophesy unto the people, according to the spirit and power which the Lord had given them.

The words of Alma, and also the words of Amulek, which were declared unto the people who were in the land of Ammonihah. And also they are cast into prison, and delivered by the miraculous power of God which was in them, according to the record of Alma. Comprising chapters 9 to 14 inclusive.

CHAPTER 9

Alma commands the people of Ammonihah to repent—The Lord will be merciful to the Lamanites in the last days—If the Nephites forsake the light, they shall be destroyed by the Lamanites—The Son of God soon cometh—He shall redeem those who repent and are baptized and have faith in his name.

20a Alma 10: 7 (7–9).
  b 1 Kgs. 17: 11 (8–13).
22a Alma 10: 11.
23a Alma 5: 3 (3, 44, 49);

13: 1 (1–20).
24a Alma 8: 13.
27a Alma 10: 10.
29a Alma 10: 1.

  b Alma 9: 12, 18.
31a Alma 14: 10.
  b Alma 14: 25 (17–29).

[About 82 B.C.]

AND again, I, Alma, having been commanded of God that I should take Amulek and go forth and preach again unto this people, or the people who were in the city of *a*Ammonihah, it came to pass as I began to preach unto them, they began to contend with me, saying:

2 Who art thou? Suppose ye that we shall believe the testimony of *a*one man, although he should preach unto us that the earth should pass away?

3 Now they understood not the words which they spake; for they knew not that the earth should pass away.

4 And they said also: We will not believe thy words if thou shouldst prophesy that this great city should be destroyed in *a*one day.

5 Now they knew not that God could do such marvelous *a*works, for they were a hard-hearted and a stiffnecked people.

6 And they said: *a*Who is God, that sendeth *b*no more authority than one man among this people, to declare unto them the truth of such great and marvelous things?

7 And they stood forth to lay their hands on me; but behold, they did not. And I stood with boldness to declare unto them, yea, I did boldly testify unto them, saying:

8 Behold, O ye wicked and perverse *a*generation, how have ye forgotten the *b*tradition of your fathers; yea, how soon ye have forgotten the commandments of God.

9 Do ye not remember that our father, Lehi, was brought out of Jerusalem by the *a*hand of God? Do ye not remember that they were all led by him through the wilderness?

10 And have ye forgotten so soon how many times he *a*delivered our fathers out of the hands of their enemies, and preserved them from being destroyed, even by the hands of their own brethren?

11 Yea, and if it had not been for his matchless power, and his mercy, and his *a*long-suffering towards us, we should unavoidably have been cut off from the face of the earth long before this period of time, and perhaps been consigned to a state of *b*endless misery and woe.

12 Behold, now I say unto you that he commandeth you to repent; and except ye repent, ye can in nowise inherit the kingdom of God. But behold, this is not all—he has commanded you to repent, or he will utterly *a*destroy you from off the face of the earth; yea, he will visit you in his *b*anger, and in his *c*fierce anger he will not turn away.

13 Behold, do ye not remember the words which he spake unto Lehi, saying that: *a*Inasmuch as ye shall keep my commandments, ye shall prosper in the land? And again it is said that: Inasmuch as ye will not keep my commandments ye shall be cut off from the presence of the Lord.

14 Now I would that ye should remember, that inasmuch as the Lamanites have not kept the commandments of God, they have been *a*cut off from the presence of the Lord. Now we see that the word of the Lord has been verified in this thing, and the Lamanites have been cut off from his presence, from the beginning of their transgressions in the land.

15 Nevertheless I say unto you, that it shall be more *a*tolerable for them in the day of judgment than for you, if ye remain in your sins,

9 1a Alma 8:6.
2a Deut. 17:6.
4a Alma 16:10 (9–10).
5a TG God, Works of.
6a Ex. 5:2; Mosiah 11:27; Moses 5:16.
  b Alma 10:12.
8a Matt. 3:7; Alma 10:17 (17–25).
  b TG Birthright.
9a 1 Ne. 2:2 (1–7).
10a TG Deliver, Deliverance.
11a TG Longsuffering.
  b Mosiah 16:11.
12a Alma 8:16; 10:27 (19, 23, 27).
  b Jer. 18:10 (6–10).
  c Alma 8:29.
13a 2 Ne. 1:20; Mosiah 1:7; Alma 37:13.
14a 2 Ne. 5:20 (20–24); Alma 38:1.
15a Matt. 11:22 (22, 24).

yea, and even more tolerable for them in this life than for you, except ye repent.

16 For there are many promises which are ^{a}extended to the Lamanites; for it is because of the ^{b}traditions of their fathers that caused them to remain in their state of ^{c}ignorance; therefore the Lord will be merciful unto them and ^{d}prolong their existence in the land.

17 And at some period of time they will be ^{a}brought to believe in his word, and to know of the incorrectness of the traditions of their fathers; and many of them will be saved, for the Lord will be merciful unto all who ^{b}call on his name.

18 But behold, I say unto you that if ye persist in your wickedness that your days shall not be ^{a}prolonged in the land, for the ^{b}Lamanites shall be sent upon you; and if ye repent not they shall come in a time when you know not, and ye shall be visited with ^{c}utter destruction; and it shall be according to the fierce ^{d}anger of the Lord.

19 For he will not suffer you that ye shall live in your iniquities, to ^{a}destroy his people. I say unto you, Nay; he would rather suffer that the Lamanites might destroy all his people who are called the people of Nephi, if it were possible that they could ^{b}fall into sins and transgressions, after having had so much light and so much knowledge given unto them of the Lord their God;

20 Yea, after having been such a highly favored people of the Lord; yea, after having been favored above every other ^{a}nation, kindred,

tongue, or people; after having had all things ^{b}made known unto them, according to their desires, and their faith, and prayers, of that which has been, and which is, and which is to come;

21 Having been ^{a}visited by the Spirit of God; having conversed with angels, and having been spoken unto by the voice of the Lord; and having the spirit of prophecy, and the spirit of revelation, and also many gifts, the gift of speaking with tongues, and the gift of preaching, and the gift of the Holy Ghost, and the gift of ^{b}translation;

22 Yea, and after having been ^{a}delivered of God out of the land of Jerusalem, by the hand of the Lord; having been ^{b}saved from famine, and from sickness, and all manner of diseases of every kind; and they having waxed strong in battle, that they might not be destroyed; having been brought out of ^{c}bondage time after time, and having been kept and preserved until now; and they have been prospered until they are rich in all manner of things—

23 And now behold I say unto you, that if this people, who have received so many blessings from the hand of the Lord, should transgress ^{a}contrary to the light and knowledge which they do have, I say unto you that if this be the case, that if they should fall into transgression, it would be far more ^{b}tolerable for the Lamanites than for them.

24 For behold, the ^{a}promises of the Lord are extended to the Lamanites, but they are not unto you if ye transgress; for has not the Lord expressly

16a Alma 17:15.
  b Alma 3:8; 17:15.
  c 2 Ne. 9:26 (25–26);
    Mosiah 3:11; Alma
    42:21.
  d Deut. 11:9 (8–9);
    32:47; Hel. 15:11
    (10–11); D&C 5:33.
17a Enos 1:13.
  b Ps. 81:7; Alma 38:5;
    D&C 3:8.
18a Deut. 6:2.

  b Alma 16:3.
  c Alma 16:9.
  d Alma 8:29.
19a 1 Ne. 12:19 (15,
    19–20); Alma 45:11
    (10–14).
  b Alma 24:30.
20a 2 Sam. 7:23; Abr. 2:9.
  b TG Prophets, Mission of.
21a Ex. 3:16; 2 Ne. 4:26;
    Morm. 1:15.

  b Omni 1:20; Mosiah
    8:13 (13–19); 28:17
    (11–17).
22a 2 Ne. 1:4.
  b TG Protection, Divine.
  c Mosiah 27:16.
23a TG Disobedience.
  b Matt. 11:22 (22–24).
24a 2 Ne. 30:6 (4–7);
    D&C 3:20.

[About 82 B.C.]

promised and firmly decreed, that if ye will rebel against him that ye shall [b]utterly be destroyed from off the face of the earth?

25 And now for this cause, that ye may not be destroyed, the Lord has sent his angel to visit many of his people, declaring unto them that they must go forth and cry mightily unto this people, saying: [a]Repent ye, for the kingdom of heaven is nigh at hand;

26 And [a]not many days hence the Son of God shall come in his [b]glory; and his glory shall be the glory of the Only Begotten of the Father, full of [c]grace, equity, and truth, full of patience, [d]mercy, and long-suffering, quick to [e]hear the cries of his people and to answer their prayers.

27 And behold, he cometh to [a]redeem those who will be [b]baptized unto repentance, through faith on his name.

28 Therefore, prepare ye the way of the Lord, for the time is at hand that all men shall reap a [a]reward of their [b]works, according to that which they have been—if they have been righteous they shall [c]reap the salvation of their souls, according to the power and deliverance of Jesus Christ; and if they have been evil they shall reap the [d]damnation of their souls, according to the power and captivation of the devil.

29 Now behold, this is the voice of the angel, crying unto the people.

30 And now, my [a]beloved brethren, for ye are my brethren, and ye ought to be beloved, and ye ought to bring forth works which are meet for repentance, seeing that your hearts have been grossly hardened against the word of God, and see-ing that ye are a [b]lost and a fallen people.

31 Now it came to pass that when I, Alma, had spoken these words, behold, the people were wroth with me because I said unto them that they were a hard-hearted and a [a]stiffnecked people.

32 And also because I said unto them that they were a lost and a fallen people they were angry with me, and sought to lay their hands upon me, that they might cast me into prison.

33 But it came to pass that the Lord did not suffer them that they should take me [a]at that time and cast me into prison.

34 And it came to pass that Amulek went and stood forth, and began to preach unto them also. And now the [a]words of Amulek are not all written, nevertheless a part of his words are written in this book.

CHAPTER 10

Lehi descended from Manasseh—Amulek recounts the angelic command that he care for Alma—The prayers of the righteous cause the people to be spared—Unrighteous lawyers and judges lay the foundation of the destruction of the people.

Now these are the [a]words which [b]Amulek preached unto the people who were in the land of Ammonihah, saying:

2 I am Amulek; I am the son of Giddonah, who was the son of Ishmael, who was a descendant of Aminadi; and it was that same Aminadi who interpreted the [a]writing which was upon the wall of the temple, which was written by the finger of God.

24b Alma 16:9 (2–9);
    Morm. 6:15 (15–22).
25a Matt. 3:2 (2–3);
    Alma 7:9; Hel. 5:32.
26a Alma 7:7.
  b TG Jesus Christ, Glory
    of.
  c TG Grace.
  d TG God, Mercy of.

  e Deut. 26:7; Isa. 65:24.
27a TG Redemption.
  b TG Baptism, Essential.
28a TG Reward.
  b Job 34:11; D&C 1:10;
    6:33.
  c Ps. 7:16.
  d TG Damnation.
30a 1 Jn. 4:11.

  b Alma 12:22.
31a 2 Ne. 25:28; Mosiah
    3:14.
33a Alma 14:17 (17–18).
34a Alma 10:1 (1–11).
10 1a Alma 9:34.
  b Alma 8:29 (21–29).
2a Dan. 5:16.

3 And Aminadi was a descendant of Nephi, who was the son of Lehi, who came out of the land of Jerusalem, who was a descendant of ^aManasseh, who was the son of ^bJoseph who was ^csold into Egypt by the hands of his brethren.

4 And behold, I am also a man of no small ^areputation among all those who know me; yea, and behold, I have many kindreds and ^bfriends, and I have also acquired much riches by the hand of my ^cindustry.

5 Nevertheless, after all this, I never have known much of the ways of the Lord, and his ^amysteries and marvelous power. I said I never had known much of these things; but behold, I mistake, for I have seen much of his mysteries and his marvelous power; yea, even in the preservation of the lives of this people.

6 Nevertheless, I did harden my heart, for I was ^acalled many times and I would not ^bhear; therefore I knew concerning these things, yet I would not know; therefore I went on rebelling ^cagainst God, in the wickedness of my heart, even until the fourth day of this seventh month, which is in the tenth year of the reign of the judges.

7 As I was journeying to see a very near kindred, behold an ^aangel of the Lord appeared unto me and said: Amulek, return to thine own house, for thou shalt feed a prophet of the Lord; yea, a holy man, who is a chosen man of God; for he has ^bfasted many days because of the sins of this people, and he is an hungered, and thou shalt ^creceive him into thy house and feed him, and he shall bless thee and thy house; and the blessing of the Lord shall rest upon thee and thy house.

8 And it came to pass that I obeyed the voice of the angel, and returned towards my house. And as I was going thither I found the ^aman whom the angel said unto me: Thou shalt receive into thy house—and behold it was this same man who has been speaking unto you concerning the things of God.

9 And the angel said unto me he is a ^aholy man; wherefore I know he is a holy man because it was said by an angel of God.

10 And again, I know that the things whereof he hath testified are true; for behold I say unto you, that as the Lord liveth, even so has he sent his ^aangel to make these things manifest unto me; and this he has done while this Alma hath ^bdwelt at my house.

11 For behold, he hath ^ablessed mine house, he hath blessed me, and my women, and my children, and my father and my kinsfolk; yea, even all my kindred hath he blessed, and the blessing of the Lord hath rested upon us according to the words which he spake.

12 And now, when Amulek had spoken these words the people began to be astonished, seeing there was ^amore than one witness who testified of the things whereof they were accused, and also of the things which were to come, according to the spirit of prophecy which was in them.

13 Nevertheless, there were some among them who thought to question them, that by their cunning ^adevices they might catch them in their words, that they might ^bfind

3a Gen. 41: 51; Josh.
     17: 1; 1 Chr. 7: 14;
     9: 3; 1 Ne. 5: 14.
   b TG Israel, Joseph,
     People of.
   c Gen. 37: 36 (29–36).
4a Acts 5: 34 (34–39).
   b Alma 15: 16.
   c TG Industry; Work,
     Value of.
5a TG Mysteries of

Godliness.
6a 2 Chr. 33: 10; Isa.
     50: 2; Alma 5: 37.
   b D&C 39: 9.
   c Acts 9: 5.
7a Alma 8: 20.
   b Alma 5: 46; 6: 6.
   c Acts 10: 30 (30–35).
   TG Hospitality.
8a Alma 8:19 (19–21).
9a TG Holiness.

10a Mosiah 3: 2 (2–3);
     Alma 11:31.
   b Alma 8: 27.
11a 1 Sam. 2: 20;
     Alma 8: 22.
12a Alma 9: 6.
13a Jer. 11: 19; Lam. 3: 62
     (60–62); Alma 11: 21.
   b Mark 14: 55 (55–60).

[About 82 B.C.]

witness against them, that they might deliver them to their judges that they might be judged according to the law, and that they might be slain or cast into prison, according to the crime which they could make appear or witness against them.

14 Now it was those men who sought to destroy them, who were *a*lawyers, who were hired or appointed by the people to administer the law at their times of trials, or at the trials of the crimes of the people before the judges.

15 Now these lawyers were learned in all the arts and *a*cunning of the people; and this was to enable them that they might be skilful in their profession.

16 And it came to pass that they began to question Amulek, that thereby they might make him *a*cross his words, or contradict the words which he should speak.

17 Now they knew not that Amulek could *a*know of their designs. But it came to pass as they began to question him, he *b*perceived their thoughts, and he said unto them: O ye wicked and perverse *c*generation, ye lawyers and hypocrites, for ye are laying the foundations of the devil; for ye are laying *d*traps and snares to catch the holy ones of God.

18 Ye are laying plans to *a*pervert the ways of the righteous, and to bring down the wrath of God upon your heads, even to the utter destruction of this people.

19 Yea, well did Mosiah say, who was our last king, when he was about to deliver up the kingdom, having no one to confer it upon, causing that this people should be governed by their own voices—yea, well did he say that if the time should come that the voice of this people should *a*choose iniquity, that is, if the time should come that this people should fall into transgression, they would be ripe for destruction.

20 And now I say unto you that well doth the Lord *a*judge of your iniquities; well doth he cry unto this people, by the voice of his *b*angels: Repent ye, repent, for the kingdom of heaven is at hand.

21 Yea, well doth he cry, by the voice of his angels that: *a*I will come down among my people, with equity and justice in my hands.

22 Yea, and I say unto you that if it were not for the *a*prayers of the righteous, who are now in the land, that ye would even now be visited with utter destruction; yet it would not be by *b*flood, as were the people in the days of *c*Noah, but it would be by famine, and by pestilence, and the *d*sword.

23 But it is by the *a*prayers of the righteous that ye are spared; now therefore, if ye will *b*cast out the righteous from among you then will not the Lord stay his hand; but in his fierce anger he will come out against you; then ye shall be smitten by famine, and by pestilence, and by the sword; and the *c*time is soon at hand except ye repent.

24 And now it came to pass that the people were more angry with Amulek, and they cried out, saying: This man doth revile against our laws which are just, and our wise *a*lawyers whom we have selected.

25 But Amulek stretched forth his hand, and cried the mightier unto them, saying: O ye wicked and

14a Alma 10:24; 11:21
    (20–37); 14:18 (18,
    23); 3 Ne. 6:11.
15a Luke 20:23.
16a Mark 12:13.
17a Luke 5:22.
    b Alma 12:3; D&C 6:16.
    c Matt. 3:7; Alma 9:8.
    d D&C 10:25 (21–27).
18a Acts 13:10.

19a Mosiah 29:27;
    Alma 2:4 (3–7);
    Hel. 5:2.
20a TG Jesus Christ, Judge.
    b Alma 8:14 (14–16,
    20); 13:22.
21a Mosiah 13:34 (28–35).
22a 1 Sam. 7:9 (7–10);
    Mosiah 27:14 (14–16).
    b Gen. 8:21; 3 Ne.

22:9 (8–10). TG Flood.
    c TG Earth, Cleansing of.
    d Deut. 32:25;
    JS-H 1:45.
23a TG Prayer.
    b 2 Chr. 13:9; Moro.
    9:14.
    c TG Procrastination.
24a Alma 10:14.

[About 82 B.C.]

perverse generation, why hath Satan got such great hold upon your hearts? Why will ye yield yourselves unto him that he may have power over you, to ^ablind your eyes, that ye will not understand the words which are spoken, according to their truth?

26 For behold, have I testified against your law? Ye do not understand; ye say that I have spoken against your law; but I have not, but I have spoken in favor of your law, to your condemnation.

27 And now behold, I say unto you, that the foundation of the ^adestruction of this people is beginning to be laid by the ^bunrighteousness of your ^clawyers and your judges.

28 And now it came to pass that when Amulek had spoken these words the people cried out against him, saying: Now we know that this man is a ^achild of the devil, for he hath ^blied unto us; for he hath spoken against our law. And now he says that he has not spoken against it.

29 And again, he has reviled against our lawyers, and our judges.

30 And it came to pass that the lawyers put it into their hearts that they should remember these things against him.

31 And there was one among them whose name was Zeezrom. Now he was the foremost to ^aaccuse Amulek and Alma, he being one of the most expert among them, having much business to do among the people.

32 Now the object of these lawyers was to get gain; and they got gain ^aaccording to their employ.

CHAPTER 11

Nephite coinage set forth—Amulek contends with Zeezrom—Christ will *not save people in their sins—Only those who inherit the kingdom of heaven are saved—All men shall rise in immortality—There is no death after the resurrection.*

Now it was in the law of Mosiah that every man who was a judge of the law, or those who were appointed to be judges, should receive ^awages ^baccording to the time which they labored to judge those who were brought before them to be judged.

2 Now if a man owed another, and he would not ^apay that which he did owe, he was complained of to the judge; and the judge executed authority, and sent forth officers that the man should be brought before him; and he judged the man according to the law and the evidences which were brought against him, and thus the man was compelled to pay that which he owed, or be stripped, or be cast out from among the people as a thief and a robber.

3 And the judge received for his wages ^aaccording to his time—a ^bsenine of gold for a day, or a senum of silver, which is equal to a senine of gold; and this is according to the law which was given.

4 Now these are the names of the different pieces of their gold, and of their silver, according to their value. And the names are given by the Nephites, for they did not reckon after the ^amanner of the Jews who were at Jerusalem; neither did they measure after the manner of the Jews; but they altered their reckoning and their measure, according to the minds and the circumstances of the people, in every generation, until the reign of the judges, they having been ^bestablished by king Mosiah.

25a 2 Cor. 4: 4 (3–4);
  Alma 14: 6; Moses
  6: 27.
27a Alma 8: 16; 9: 12 (4,
  12, 18, 24).
  b TG Injustice.
  c Luke 11: 46 (45–52);

  2 Ne. 28: 16.
28a John 7: 20.
  b Alma 14: 2.
31a Alma 11: 21 (20–36).
32a Alma 11: 1 (1–3).
11 1a TG Wages.
  b Alma 10: 32.

2a TG Justice.
3a Alma 10: 32.
  b Alma 30: 33; 3 Ne.
  12: 26.
4a BD Money.
  b Mosiah 29: 41 (40–44).

[About 82 B.C.]

5 Now the reckoning is thus—a senine of gold, a seon of gold, a shum of gold, and a limnah of gold.

6 A senum of silver, an amnor of silver, an ezrom of silver, and an onti of silver.

7 A senum of silver was equal to a senine of gold, and either for a measure of barley, and also for a measure of every kind of grain.

8 Now the amount of a seon of gold was twice the value of a senine.

9 And a shum of gold was twice the value of a seon.

10 And a limnah of gold was the value of them all.

11 And an amnor of silver was as great as two senums.

12 And an ezrom of silver was as great as four senums.

13 And an onti was as great as them all.

14 Now this is the value of the lesser numbers of their reckoning—

15 A shiblon is half of a senum; therefore, a shiblon for half a measure of barley.

16 And a shiblum is a half of a shiblon.

17 And a leah is the half of a shiblum.

18 Now this is their number, according to their reckoning.

19 Now an antion of gold is equal to three shiblons.

20 Now, it was for the sole purpose to get *a*gain, because they received their wages according to their *b*employ, therefore, they did *c*stir up the people to *d*riotings, and all manner of disturbances and wickedness, that they might have more employ, that they might *e*get *f*money according to the suits which were brought before them; therefore they did stir up the people against Alma and Amulek.

21 And this Zeezrom began to question Amulek, saying: Will ye answer me a few questions which I shall ask you? Now Zeezrom was a man who was *a*expert in the *b*devices of the devil, that he might destroy that which was good; therefore, he said unto Amulek: Will ye answer the questions which I shall put unto you?

22 And Amulek said unto him: Yea, if it be according to the *a*Spirit of the Lord, which is in me; for I shall say nothing which is contrary to the Spirit of the Lord. And Zeezrom said unto him: Behold, here are six onties of silver, and all these will I *b*give thee if thou wilt deny the existence of a Supreme Being.

23 Now Amulek said: O thou *a*child of hell, why *b*tempt ye me? Knowest thou that the righteous yieldeth to no such temptations?

24 Believest thou that there is no God? I say unto you, Nay, thou knowest that there is a God, but thou lovest that *a*lucre more than him.

25 And now thou hast lied before God unto me. Thou saidst unto me—Behold these six onties, which are of great worth, I will give unto thee—when thou hadst it in thy heart to retain them from me; and it was only thy desire that I should deny the true and living God, that thou mightest have cause to destroy me. And now behold, for this great evil thou shalt have thy reward.

26 And Zeezrom said unto him: Thou sayest there is a true and living God?

27 And Amulek said: Yea, there is a true and living God.

28 Now Zeezrom said: Is there more than one God?

20a TG Selfishness.
  b Prov. 28: 8.
  c TG Provoking.
  d TG Rioting and Reveling.
  e Alma 10: 32.
  f Luke 11: 52 (45–54).
21a Alma 10: 31; 14: 7

  (6–7, 18, 23).
  b Lam. 3: 62 (60–62); Alma 10: 13.
22a TG Holy Ghost, Mission of; God, Spirit of.
  b TG Bribery.
23a Acts 13: 10 (8–12);

  Alma 5: 41.
  b TG Temptation; Test, Try, Prove.
24a Luke 16: 14; John 12: 43 (42–43); Acts 19: 27 (27, 36–38); Titus 1: 11.

[About 82 B.C.]

29 And he answered, No.

30 Now Zeezrom said unto him again: How knowest thou these things?

31 And he said: An [a]angel hath made them known unto me.

32 And Zeezrom said again: Who is he that shall come? Is it the Son of God?

33 And he said unto him, Yea.

34 And Zeezrom said again: Shall he save his people [a]in their sins? And Amulek answered and said unto him: I say unto you he shall not, for it is impossible for him to deny his word.

35 Now Zeezrom said unto the people: See that ye remember these things; for he said there is but one God; yet he saith that the Son of God shall come, but he shall [a]not save his people—as though he had authority to command God.

36 Now Amulek saith again unto him: Behold thou hast [a]lied, for thou sayest that I spake as though I had authority to command God because I said he shall not save his people in their sins.

37 And I say unto you again that he cannot save them in their [a]sins; for I cannot deny his word, and he hath said that [b]no unclean thing can inherit the [c]kingdom of heaven; therefore, how can ye be saved, except ye inherit the kingdom of heaven? Therefore, ye cannot be saved in your sins.

38 Now Zeezrom saith again unto him: Is the Son of God the very Eternal Father?

39 And Amulek said unto him: Yea, he is the very [a]Eternal Father of heaven and of earth, and [b]all things which in them are; he is the beginning and the end, the first and the last;

40 And he shall come into the [a]world to [b]redeem his people; and he shall [c]take upon him the transgressions of those who believe on his name; and these are they that shall have eternal life, and salvation cometh to none else.

41 Therefore the wicked remain as though there had been [a]no redemption made, except it be the loosing of the bands of death; for behold, the day cometh that [b]all shall rise from the dead and stand before God, and be [c]judged according to their works.

42 Now, there is a death which is called a temporal death; and the death of Christ shall loose the [a]bands of this temporal death, that all shall be raised from this temporal death.

43 The spirit and the body shall be [a]reunited again in its [b]perfect form; both limb and joint shall be restored to its proper frame, even as we now are at this time; and we shall be brought to stand before God, [c]knowing even as we know now, and have a bright [d]recollection of all our [e]guilt.

44 Now, this restoration shall come to all, both old and young, both bond and free, both male and female, both the wicked and the righteous; and even there shall not so much as a hair of their heads be lost; but every thing shall be [a]restored to its perfect frame, as it is now, or in the body, and shall be

---

31a Alma 10: 10.
34a Hel. 5: 10 (10–11).
35a Alma 14: 5.
36a Alma 12: 1.
37a 1 Cor. 6: 9 (9–10).
  b 1 Ne. 15: 33; Alma
    40: 26; 3 Ne. 27: 19.
    TG Uncleanness.
  c TG Kingdom of God,
    in Heaven.
39a Isa. 9: 6; 64: 8;
    Mosiah 15: 4 (2–4);
    Moro. 7: 22; 8: 18.

  b Col. 1: 16; Mosiah 4: 2.
40a TG World.
  b Luke 2: 34; Rom.
    11: 26 (26–27).
  c Ex. 34: 7; 1 Jn. 2: 2;
    Mosiah 14: 5 (5, 8);
    15: 12; D&C 19: 17
    (16–18); 29: 17.
41a Alma 12: 18; D&C
    88: 33.
  b Rev. 20: 13 (12–13);
    Alma 28: 12; 42: 23.
  c TG Judgment,

The Last.
42a Alma 12: 16 (16, 24, 36).
43a 2 Ne. 9: 13; Alma
    40: 23.
  b TG Perfection.
  c D&C 130: 18.
  d 2 Ne. 9: 14; Mosiah
    3: 25; Alma 5: 18.
  e Matt. 12: 36 (36–37).
    TG Guilt.
44a Rev. 20: 12 (12–15).

[About 82 B.C.]

brought and be arraigned before the bar of Christ the Son, and God the [b]Father, and the Holy Spirit, which is [c]one Eternal God, to be [d]judged according to their works, whether they be good or whether they be evil.

45 Now, behold, I have spoken unto you concerning the [a]death of the mortal body, and also concerning the [b]resurrection of the mortal body. I say unto you that this mortal body is [c]raised to an [d]immortal body, that is from death, even from the first death unto life, that they can [e]die no more; their spirits uniting with their bodies, never to be divided; thus the whole becoming [f]spiritual and immortal, that they can no more see corruption.

46 Now, when Amulek had finished these words the people began again to be astonished, and also Zeezrom began to tremble. And thus ended the words of Amulek, or this is all that I have written.

CHAPTER 12

Alma contends with Zeezrom—The mysteries of God can be given only to the faithful—Men are judged by their thoughts, beliefs, words, and works—The wicked shall suffer a spiritual death—This mortal life is a probationary state—The plan of redemption brings to pass the resurrection and, through faith, a remission of sins—The repentant have a claim on mercy through the Only Begotten Son.

Now Alma, seeing that the words of Amulek had silenced Zeezrom, for he beheld that Amulek had caught him in his [a]lying and deceiving to destroy him, and seeing that he began to tremble under a [b]consciousness of his guilt, he opened his mouth and began to speak unto him, and to establish the words of Amulek, and to explain things beyond, or to unfold the scriptures beyond that which Amulek had done.

2 Now the words that Alma spake unto Zeezrom were heard by the people round about; for the multitude was great, and he spake on this wise:

3 Now Zeezrom, seeing that thou hast been taken in thy lying and craftiness, for thou hast not lied unto men only but thou hast lied unto God; for behold, he knows all thy [a]thoughts, and thou seest that thy [b]thoughts are made known unto us by his Spirit;

4 And thou seest that we know that thy plan was a very [a]subtle plan, as to the subtlety of the devil, for to lie and to deceive this people that thou mightest set them against us, to [b]revile us and to cast us out—

5 Now this was a plan of thine [a]adversary, and he hath exercised his power in thee. Now I would that ye should remember that what I say unto thee I say unto all.

6 And behold I say unto you all that this was a [a]snare of the adversary, which he has laid to catch this people, that he might bring you into subjection unto him, that he might encircle you about with his [b]chains, that he might chain you down to everlasting destruction, according to the power of his captivity.

7 Now when Alma had spoken these words, Zeezrom began to tremble more exceedingly, for he was convinced more and more of the power of God; and he was also

---

44b TG Godhead.
c 3 Ne. 11:27 (27–28, 36). TG God, Eternal Nature of.
d 2 Pet. 2:9. TG Jesus Christ, Judge.
45a Alma 12:12.
b Alma 40:23; D&C 88:16.

c TG Death, Power over.
d TG Immortality.
e Rev. 21:4; Alma 12:18 (18, 20); D&C 63:49; 88:116.
f 1 Cor. 15:44.
12 1a Alma 11:36 (20–38).
b Alma 62:45; D&C 6:11; 18:44.

TG Conscience.
3a Jacob 2:5; D&C 6:16.
b Alma 10:17.
4a D&C 123:12.
b TG Slander.
5a TG Devil.
6a Prov. 29:6 (3–8).
b Alma 5:9 (7–10).

[About 82 B.C.]

convinced that Alma and Amulek had a knowledge of him, for he was convinced that they [a]knew the thoughts and intents of his heart; for power was given unto them that they might know of these things according to the spirit of prophecy.

8 And Zeezrom began to inquire of them diligently, that he might know more concerning the kingdom of God. And he said unto Alma: What does this mean which Amulek hath spoken concerning the resurrection of the dead, that all shall rise from the dead, both the [a]just and the unjust, and are brought to stand before God to be [b]judged according to their works?

9 And now Alma began to expound these things unto him, saying: It is given unto many to [a]know the [b]mysteries of God; nevertheless they are laid under a strict command that they shall not impart [c]only according to the portion of his word which he doth grant unto the children of men, according to the heed and diligence which they give unto him.

10 And therefore, he that will [a]harden his heart, the same receiveth the [b]lesser portion of the word; and he that will [c]not harden his heart, to him is [d]given the greater portion of the word, until it is given unto him to know the mysteries of God until he know them in full.

11 And they that will harden their hearts, to them is given the lesser [a]portion of the word until they [b]know nothing concerning his mysteries; and then they are taken captive by the devil, and led by his will down to destruction. Now this is what is meant by the [c]chains of [d]hell.

12 And Amulek hath spoken plainly concerning [a]death, and being raised from this mortality to a state of immortality, and being brought before the bar of God, to be [b]judged according to our works.

13 Then if our hearts have been hardened, yea, if we have hardened our hearts against the word, insomuch that it has not been found in us, then will our state be awful, for then we shall be condemned.

14 For our [a]words will condemn us, yea, all our works will condemn us; we shall not be found spotless; and our thoughts will also condemn us; and in this awful state we shall not dare to look up to our God; and we would fain be glad if we could command the rocks and the [b]mountains to fall upon us to [c]hide us from his presence.

15 But this cannot be; we must come forth and stand before him in his glory, and in his power, and in his might, majesty, and dominion, and acknowledge to our everlasting [a]shame that all his [b]judgments are just; that he is just in all his works, and that he is merciful unto the children of men, and that he has all power to save every man that believeth on his name and bringeth forth fruit meet for repentance.

16 And now behold, I say unto you then cometh a death, even a second [a]death, which is a spiritual death;

7a Alma 14:2.
8a Dan. 12:2.
  b TG Judgment, The Last.
9a Dan. 1:17.
  b Alma 26:22. TG Mysteries of Godliness.
  c John 16:12; Alma 29:8; 3 Ne. 26:10 (6–11); Ether 4:7 (1–7).
10a 2 Ne. 28:27; 3 Ne. 26:10 (9–10); Ether 4:8.
  b D&C 93:39.
  c TG Teachable.

d Dan. 2:21; 2 Ne. 28:30; D&C 50:24; 71:5.
11a Matt. 25:29 (29–30).
  b TG Apostasy of Individuals.
  c Prov. 5:22; John 8:34 (31–36); 2 Ne. 28:19 (19–22); Mosiah 23:12; Alma 26:14. TG Bondage, Spiritual.
  d Prov. 9:18; 1 Ne. 14:7; 2 Ne. 2:29 (26–29). TG Hell.
12a Alma 11:45 (41–45).
  b TG Judgment, The

Last.
14a Prov. 18:21; Matt. 12:36; James 3:6 (1–13); Mosiah 4:30 (29–30).
  b Hosea 10:8; 2 Ne. 26:5.
  c Job 34:22; Amos 9:3; 2 Ne. 12:10.
15a Mosiah 3:25. TG Shame.
  b 2 Pet. 2:9. TG Justice.
16a TG Death, Spiritual, Second.

then is a time that whosoever dieth in his sins, as to a temporal ᵇdeath, shall also ᶜdie a spiritual death; yea, he shall die as to things pertaining unto righteousness.

17 Then is the time when their torments shall be as a ᵃlake of fire and brimstone, whose flame ascendeth up forever and ever; and then is the time that they shall be chained down to an everlasting destruction, according to the power and captivity of Satan, he having subjected them according to his will.

18 Then, I say unto you, they shall be as though there had been ᵃno redemption made; for they cannot be redeemed according to God's justice; and they cannot ᵇdie, seeing there is no more corruption.

19 Now it came to pass that when Alma had made an end of speaking these words, the people began to be more astonished;

20 But there was one Antionah, who was a chief ruler among them, came forth and said unto him: What is this that thou hast said, that man should rise from the dead and be changed from this mortal to an ᵃimmortal state, that the soul can never die?

21 What does the scripture mean, which saith that God placed ᵃcherubim and a flaming sword on the east of the garden of ᵇEden, lest our first parents should enter and partake of the fruit of the tree of life, and live forever? And thus we see that there was no possible chance that they should live forever.

22 Now Alma said unto him: This is the thing which I was about to explain. Now we see that Adam did ᵃfall by the partaking of the forbidden ᵇfruit, according to the word of God; and thus we see, that by his fall, all mankind became a ᶜlost and fallen people.

23 And now behold, I say unto you that if it had been possible for Adam to have ᵃpartaken of the fruit of the tree of life at that time, there would have been no death, and the word would have been void, making God a liar, for he said: ᵇIf thou eat thou shalt surely die.

24 And we see that ᵃdeath comes upon mankind, yea, the death which has been spoken of by Amulek, which is the temporal death; nevertheless there was a space granted unto ᵇman in which he might repent; therefore this life became a ᶜprobationary state; a time to ᵈprepare to meet God; a time to prepare for that endless state which has been spoken of by us, which is after the resurrection of the dead.

25 Now, if it had not been for the plan of redemption, which was laid from the foundation of the world, there could have been no ᵃresurrection of the dead; but there was a plan of ᵇredemption laid, which shall bring to pass the resurrection of the dead, of which has been spoken.

26 And now behold, if it were possible that our first parents could have gone forth and partaken of the ᵃtree of life they would have been forever miserable, having no preparatory state; and thus the ᵇplan

---

16b Alma 11:42 (40–45).
 c 1 Ne. 15:33; Alma 40:26.
17a Rev. 19:20; 21:8; Mosiah 3:27; Alma 14:14.
18a Alma 11:41.
 b Rev. 21:4; Alma 11:45; D&C 63:49; 88:116.
20a TG Immortality.
21a Gen. 3:24; Alma 42:2; Moses 4:31.

 TG Cherubim.
 b TG Eden.
22a TG Fall of Man.
 b Gen. 3:6; 2 Ne. 2:15 (15–19); Mosiah 3:26.
 c Mosiah 16:5 (4–5); Alma 9:30 (30–32).
23a Alma 42:5 (2–9).
 b Gen. 2:17.
24a TG Death.
 b 2 Ne. 2:21; Moses 5:8–12.
 c 1 Pet. 2:20 (20–21).

 TG Earth, Purpose of; Probation.
 d Alma 34:32 (32–35).
25a 2 Ne. 2:8; Alma 7:12; 42:23.
 b TG Redemption.
26a Gen. 2:9; 1 Ne. 15:36 (22, 28, 36); 2 Ne. 2:15; Alma 32:40.
 b Alma 34:9 (8–16); 42:8 (6–28); Moses 6:62.

[About 82 B.C.]

of redemption would have been frustrated, and the word of God would have been void, taking none effect.

27 But behold, it was not so; but it was [a]appointed unto men that they must die; and after death, they must come to [b]judgment, even that same judgment of which we have spoken, which is the end.

28 And after God had appointed that these things should come unto man, behold, then he saw that it was expedient that man should know concerning the things whereof he had appointed unto them;

29 Therefore he sent [a]angels to converse with them, who caused men to behold of his glory.

30 And they began from that time forth to call on his name; therefore God [a]conversed with men, and made known unto them the [b]plan of redemption, which had been prepared from the [c]foundation of the world; and this he made known unto them according to their faith and repentance and their [d]holy works.

31 Wherefore, he gave [a]commandments unto men, they having first transgressed the [b]first commandments as to things which were temporal, and becoming as Gods, [c]knowing good from evil, placing themselves in a state to [d]act, or being placed in a state to act according to their wills and pleasures, whether to do evil or to do good—

32 Therefore God gave unto them commandments, after having made [a]known unto them the plan of redemption, that they should not do evil, the penalty thereof being a second [b]death, which was an everlasting [c]death as to things pertaining unto righteousness; for on such the plan of redemption could have no power, for the works of [d]justice could not be destroyed, according to the supreme [e]goodness of God.

33 But God did call on men, in the name of his Son, (this being the [a]plan of redemption which was laid) saying: If ye will [b]repent, and harden not your hearts, then will I have mercy upon you, through mine Only Begotten Son;

34 Therefore, whosoever repenteth, and hardeneth not his heart, he shall have claim on [a]mercy through mine Only Begotten Son, unto a [b]remission of his sins; and these shall enter into my [c]rest.

35 And whosoever will harden his heart and will do [a]iniquity, behold, I swear in my wrath that he shall not enter into my rest.

36 And now, my brethren, behold I say unto you, that if ye will harden your hearts ye shall not enter into the rest of the Lord; therefore your iniquity [a]provoketh him that he sendeth down his [b]wrath upon you as in the [c]first provocation, yea, according to his word in the last provocation as well as the first, to the everlasting [d]destruction of your souls; therefore, according to his word, unto the last death, as well as the first.

37 And now, my brethren, seeing we know these things, and they are true, let us repent, and harden not

27a Job 7: 1; Heb. 9: 27;
    D&C 42: 48; 121: 25.
  b TG Judgment, The
    Last.
29a Moro. 7: 25 (25, 31);
    D&C 29: 42.
30a Moses 1: 1; 5: 4 (4–5);
    6: 51 (4, 51–68).
  b TG Salvation, Plan of.
  c Gen. 2: 16 (16–17);
    Mosiah 18: 13; Alma
    13: 3 (3, 5, 7–8); Abr.
    3: 26 (24–26).
  d Luke 8: 15 (14–15).
31a TG Commandments of

    God.
  b Gen. 2: 17 (16–17);
    2 Ne. 2: 19 (18–19).
  c Gen. 3: 22; Moses
    4: 11.
  d 2 Ne. 2: 16. TG Agency.
32a Moses 5: 9 (4–9).
  b TG Death, Spiritual,
    Second.
  c TG Damnation.
  d Mosiah 15: 27; Alma
    34: 16 (15–16); 42: 15.
  e TG Goodness.
33a TG Salvation, Plan of.
  b Moses 5: 8.

34a 2 Cor. 4: 1.
  b TG Remission of Sins.
  c D&C 84: 24. TG Rest.
35a Moses 5: 15.
36a 1 Kgs. 16: 33.
    TG Provoking.
  b TG God, Indignation of.
  c Heb. 3: 8; 2 Ne. 9: 7;
    Jacob 1: 7 (7–8);
    Mosiah 16: 4 (4–7);
    Alma 11: 45; 42: 6
    (6, 9, 14).
  d TG Damnation.

[About 82 B.C.]

our hearts, that we [a]provoke not the Lord our God to pull down his wrath upon us in these his second commandments which he has given unto us; but let us enter into the [b]rest of God, which is prepared according to his word.

CHAPTER 13

Men are called as high priests because of their exceeding faith and good works—They are to teach the commandments—Through righteousness they are sanctified and enter into the rest of the Lord—Melchizedek was one of these—Angels are declaring glad tidings throughout the land—They will reveal the actual coming of Christ.

AND again, my brethren, I would cite your minds forward to the time when the Lord God gave these commandments unto his children; and I would that ye should remember that the Lord God [a]ordained priests, after his holy order, which was after the order of his Son, to teach these things unto the people.

2 And those priests were ordained after the [a]order of his Son, in a [b]manner that thereby the people might know in what manner to look forward to his Son for redemption.

3 And this is the manner after which they were ordained—being [a]called and [b]prepared from the [c]foundation of the world according to the [d]foreknowledge of God, on account of their exceeding faith and good works; in the first place being left to [e]choose good or evil; therefore they having chosen good, and

exercising exceedingly great [f]faith, are [g]called with a holy calling, yea, with that holy calling which was prepared with, and according to, a preparatory redemption for such.

4 And thus they have been [a]called to this holy calling on account of their faith, while others would reject the Spirit of God on account of the hardness of their hearts and [b]blindness of their minds, while, if it had not been for this they might have had as great [c]privilege as their brethren.

5 Or in fine, in the first place they were on the [a]same standing with their brethren; thus this holy calling being prepared from the foundation of the world for such as would not harden their hearts, being in and through the atonement of the Only Begotten Son, who was prepared—

6 And thus being called by this holy calling, and ordained unto the high priesthood of the holy order of God, to teach his commandments unto the children of men, that they also might enter into his [a]rest—

7 This high priesthood being after the order of his Son, which order was from the foundation of the world; or in other words, being [a]without beginning of days or end of years, being prepared from [b]eternity to all eternity, according to his [c]foreknowledge of all things—

8 Now they were [a]ordained after this manner—being called with a holy calling, and ordained with a holy ordinance, and taking upon them the high priesthood of the holy order, which calling, and ordinance,

37a Num. 14:11 (11–12);
   1 Ne. 17:30 (23–31);
   Jacob 1:8; Hel. 7:18.
  b Alma 13:6 (6–29);
   16:17; D&C 84:24.
13 1a Alma 8:23 (11, 23);
   D&C 84:17 (17–19);
   Moses 6:7; Abr. 2:9
   (9, 11).
  2a D&C 107:3 (2–4).
  b Alma 13:16.
  3a D&C 127:2.
   TG Election; Fore-
   ordination.
  b D&C 138:56.

  c Alma 12:30 (25, 30);
   22:13. TG Man,
   Antemortal Existence
   of.
  d TG God, Fore-
   knowledge of.
  e TG Agency.
  f TG Priesthood,
   Qualifying for.
  g TG Called of God.
  4a Ether 12:10.
  b TG Spiritual Blindness.
  c 1 Ne. 17:35 (32–35).
  5a Rom. 2:11; 2 Ne.

   26:28.
  6a Alma 12:37; 16:17.
   TG Rest.
  7a Heb. 7:3; Abr. 1:3
   (2–4).
  b TG Eternity.
  c TG God,
   Foreknowledge of;
   God, Omniscience of.
  8a TG Priesthood,
   Melchizedek; Priest-
   hood, Oath and
   Covenant.

   [About 82 B.C.]

and high priesthood, is without beginning or end—

9 Thus they become [a]high priests forever, after the order of the Son, the Only Begotten of the Father, who is without beginning of days or end of years, who is full of [b]grace, equity, and truth. And thus it is. Amen.

10 Now, as I said concerning the holy order, or this [a]high priesthood, there were many who were ordained and became high priests of God; and it was on account of their exceeding [b]faith and [c]repentance, and their righteousness before God, they choosing to repent and work righteousness rather than to perish;

11 Therefore they were called after this holy order, and were [a]sanctified, and their [b]garments were washed white through the blood of the Lamb.

12 Now they, after being [a]sanctified by the [b]Holy Ghost, having their garments made white, being [c]pure and spotless before God, could not look upon [d]sin save it were with [e]abhorrence; and there were many, exceedingly great many, who were made pure and entered into the rest of the Lord their God.

13 And now, my brethren, I would that ye should humble yourselves before God, and bring forth [a]fruit meet for repentance, that ye may also enter into that rest.

14 Yea, humble yourselves even as the people in the days of [a]Melchizedek, who was also a high priest after this same order which I have spoken, who also took upon him the high priesthood forever.

15 And it was this same Melchizedek to whom Abraham paid [a]tithes; yea, even our father Abraham paid tithes of one-tenth part of all he possessed.

16 Now these [a]ordinances were given after this [b]manner, that thereby the people might look forward on the Son of God, it being a [c]type of his order, or it being his order, and this that they might look forward to him for a remission of their sins, that they might enter into the rest of the Lord.

17 Now this Melchizedek was a king over the land of Salem; and his people had waxed strong in iniquity and abomination; yea, they had all gone astray; they were full of all manner of wickedness;

18 But Melchizedek having exercised mighty faith, and received the office of the high priesthood according to the [a]holy order of God, did preach repentance unto his people. And behold, they did repent; and Melchizedek did establish peace in the land in his days; therefore he was called the prince of peace, for he was the king of Salem; and he did reign under his father.

19 Now, there were [a]many before him, and also there were many afterwards, but [b]none were greater; therefore, of him they have more particularly made mention.

20 Now I need not rehearse the matter; what I have said may suffice. Behold, the [a]scriptures are

9a TG High Priest.
  b John 1: 17 (14, 17);
    2 Ne. 2: 6; Moses 1: 6.
    TG Grace.
10a D&C 84: 18 (6–22);
    107: 53 (40–55).
  b TG Priesthood,
    Magnifying Callings
    within.
  c TG Spirituality.
11a Lev. 8: 30; Moses
    6: 60 (59–60).
  b 1 Ne. 12: 10; Alma
    5: 21 (21–27); 3 Ne.
    27: 19 (19–20).
12a Rom. 8: 1 (1–9); D&C
    11: 12 (12–13).

    TG Sanctification.
  b TG Holy Ghost,
    Baptism of.
  c TG Purity.
  d Rom. 12: 9; 2 Ne.
    4: 31; Mosiah 5: 2;
    Alma 19: 33.
  e Prov. 8: 13; Alma
    37: 29.
13a Luke 3: 8.
14a D&C 84: 14.
    JST Gen. 14: 25–40 (in
    Appendix, Latter-day
    Saint edition of King
    James Bible).
    TG Priesthood, History
    of.

15a Gen. 14: 20 (18–20);
    Mal. 3: 10 (8–10).
    TG Tithing.
16a A of F 5. TG Ordinance.
  b Alma 13: 2.
  c TG Jesus Christ, Types
    of, in Anticipation.
18a TG Priesthood.
19a Hel. 5: 18; D&C
    84: 14 (6–16); 107: 53
    (40–55).
  b D&C 107: 2 (1–4).
20a Alma 14: 1 (1, 8, 14).
    TG Scriptures, Value
    of.

[About 82 b.c.]

before you; if ye will [b]wrest them it shall be to your own destruction.

21 And now it came to pass that when Alma had said these words unto them, he stretched forth his hand unto them and cried with a mighty voice, saying: [a]Now is the time to repent, for the day of salvation draweth nigh;

22 Yea, and the voice of the Lord, by the [a]mouth of angels, doth declare it unto all nations; yea, doth declare it, that they may have glad tidings of great joy; yea, and he doth sound these glad tidings among all his people, yea, even to them that are scattered abroad upon the face of the earth; wherefore they have come unto us.

23 And they are made known unto us in [a]plain terms, that we may understand, that we cannot err; and this because of our being [b]wanderers in a strange land; therefore, we are thus highly favored, for we have these glad tidings declared unto us in all parts of our vineyard.

24 For behold, [a]angels are declaring it unto many at this time in our land; and this is for the purpose of preparing the hearts of the children of men to receive his word in the time of his coming in his glory.

25 And now we only wait to hear the joyful news declared unto us by the mouth of angels, of his coming; for the time cometh, we [a]know not how soon. Would to God that it might be in my day; but let it be sooner or later, in it I will rejoice.

26 And it shall be made known unto [a]just and holy men, by the mouth of angels, at the time of his coming,

that the words of our fathers may be fulfilled, according to that which they have spoken concerning him, which was according to the spirit of prophecy which was in them.

27 And now, my brethren, I [a]wish from the inmost part of my heart, yea, with great [b]anxiety even unto pain, that ye would hearken unto my words, and cast off your sins, and not [c]procrastinate the day of your repentance;

28 But that ye would humble yourselves before the Lord, and call on his holy name, and [a]watch and pray continually, that ye may not be [b]tempted above that which ye can bear, and thus be [c]led by the Holy Spirit, becoming humble, [d]meek, submissive, patient, full of love and all long-suffering;

29 [a]Having faith on the Lord; having a hope that ye shall receive eternal life; having the [b]love of God always in your hearts, that ye may be lifted up at the last day and enter into his [c]rest.

30 And may the Lord grant unto you repentance, that ye may not bring down his wrath upon you, that ye may not be [a]bound down by the chains of [b]hell, that ye may not suffer the second [c]death.

31 And Alma spake many more words unto the people, which are not written in [a]this book.

CHAPTER 14

Alma and Amulek are imprisoned and smitten—The believers and their holy scriptures are burned by fire— These martyrs are received by the Lord

20b 2 Pet. 3:16; Alma 41:1.
21a TG Procrastination.
22a Alma 10:20 (7–10, 20).
23a 2 Ne. 25:7 (7–8); 31:3; 32:7; Jacob 4:13; Ether 12:39.
  b Jacob 7:26.
24a Alma 10:10; 39:19.
25a 1 Ne. 10:4; 3 Ne. 1:1.
26a Ex. 22:31; Amos 3:7; W of M 1:17; D&C 49:8; 107:29.

27a Mosiah 28:3 (3–4).
  b Mosiah 25:11.
  c TG Apathy; Procrastination.
28a TG Prayer; Watchfulness.
  b Rom. 7:23 (23–24); 1 Cor. 10:13; D&C 64:20.
  c Alma 22:1; Morm. 5:17.
  d TG Forbearance; Love; Meekness.

29a Alma 7:24.
  b Ps. 18:1; D&C 20:31; 76:116. TG God, Love of.
  c D&C 84:24.
30a TG Bondage, Spiritual.
  b TG Damnation; Hell.
  c TG Death, Spiritual, Second.
31a W of M 1:5; 3 Ne. 5:9 (8–12).

[About 82 B.C.]

*in glory—The prison walls are rent
and fall—Alma and Amulek are delivered and their persecutors are slain.*

AND it came to pass after he had
made an end of speaking unto the
people many of them did believe on
his words, and began to repent, and
to search the ªscriptures.

2 But the more part of them were
desirous that they might destroy
Alma and Amulek; for they were
angry with Alma, because of the
ªplainness of his words unto Zeezrom; and they also said that Amulek
had ᵇlied unto them, and had reviled
against their law and also against
their lawyers and judges.

3 And they were also angry with
Alma and Amulek; and because
they had ªtestified so plainly against
their wickedness, they sought to
ᵇput them away privily.

4 But it came to pass that they did
not; but they took them and bound
them with strong cords, and took
them before the chief judge of the
land.

5 And the people went forth and
witnessed against them—testifying
that they had reviled against the
law, and their lawyers and judges of
the land, and also of all the people
that were in the land; and also
testified that there was but one
God, and that he should send his
Son among the people, but he
should ªnot save them; and many
such things did the people testify
against Alma and Amulek. Now
this was done before the chief judge
of the land.

6 And it came to pass that Zeezrom
was astonished at the words which
had been spoken; and he also
knew concerning the ªblindness of
the minds, which he had caused
among the people by his ᵇlying

words; and his soul began to be
ᶜharrowed up under a ᵈconscious-
ness of his own guilt; yea, he began
to be encircled about by the pains of
hell.

7 And it came to pass that he began
to cry unto the people, saying:
Behold, I am ªguilty, and these men
are spotless before God. And he
began to plead for them from that
time forth; but they reviled him,
saying: Art thou also possessed with
the devil? And they spit upon him,
and ᵇcast him out from among them,
and also all those who believed in
the words which had been spoken
by Alma and Amulek; and they cast
them out, and sent men to cast
stones at them.

8 And they brought their wives
and children together, and whosoever believed or had been taught
to believe in the word of God they
caused that they should be ªcast
into the fire; and they also brought
forth their records which contained
the holy scriptures, and cast them
into the fire also, that they might be
ᵇburned and destroyed by fire.

9 And it came to pass that they
took Alma and Amulek, and carried
them forth to the place of ªmartyr-
dom, that they might witness the
destruction of those who were consumed by fire.

10 And when Amulek saw the pains
of the women and children who
were consuming in the fire, he also
was pained; and he said unto Alma:
How can we witness this awful
scene? Therefore let us stretch forth
our hands, and exercise the ªpower
of God which is in us, and save them
from the flames.

11 But Alma said unto him: The
Spirit constraineth me that I must
not stretch forth mine hand; for
behold the Lord receiveth them up

14 1a 2 Kgs. 22: 11 (8–13);
    Acts 17: 2 (2–3, 11);
    Alma 13: 20.
  2a Alma 12: 7 (3–7).
    b Alma 10: 28 (24–32).
  3a Prov. 26: 26; Alma
    37: 21.

  b Acts 23: 12 (12–15).
  5a Alma 11: 35 (33–37).
  6a TG Spiritual Blindness.
    b Alma 10: 31 (25–31).
    c Alma 15: 5.
    d TG Conscience.
  7a Alma 10: 31; 11: 21

  (21–36); 15: 3.
    b Alma 15: 1.
  8a Alma 15: 2.
    b Jer. 36: 23 (21–28).
  9a TG Martyrdom.
 10a Alma 8: 31 (30–31).

[About 82 B.C.]

unto himself, in ᵃglory; and he doth suffer that they may do this thing, or that the people may do this thing unto them, according to the hardness of their hearts, that the ᵇjudgments which he shall exercise upon them in his wrath may be just; and the ᶜblood of the ᵈinnocent shall stand as a witness against them, yea, and cry mightily against them at the last day.

12 Now Amulek said unto Alma: Behold, perhaps they will burn us also.

13 And Alma said: Be it according to the will of the Lord. But, behold, our work is not finished; therefore they burn us not.

14 Now it came to pass that when the bodies of those who had been cast into the fire were consumed, and also the records which were cast in with them, the chief judge of the land came and stood before Alma and Amulek, as they were bound; and he smote them with his hand upon their ᵃcheeks, and said unto them: After what ye have seen, will ye preach again unto this people, that they shall be cast into a ᵇlake of fire and brimstone?

15 Behold, ye see that ye had not power to save those who had been cast into the fire; neither has God saved them because they were of thy faith. And the judge smote them again upon their cheeks, and asked: What say ye for yourselves?

16 Now this judge was after the order and faith of ᵃNehor, who slew Gideon.

17 And it came to pass that Alma and Amulek answered him ᵃnothing; and he smote them again, and delivered them to the officers to be ᵇcast into prison.

18 And when they had been cast into prison three days, there came many ᵃlawyers, and judges, and priests, and teachers, who were of the profession of Nehor; and they came in unto the prison to see them, and they questioned them about many words; but they answered them nothing.

19 And it came to pass that the judge stood before them, and said: Why do ye not answer the words of this people? Know ye not that I have ᵃpower to deliver you up unto the flames? And he ᵇcommanded them to speak; but they answered nothing.

20 And it came to pass that they departed and went their ways, but came again on the morrow; and the judge also smote them again on their cheeks. And many came forth also, and smote them, saying: Will ye stand again and judge this people, and condemn our law? If ye have such great power why do ye not ᵃdeliver yourselves?

21 And many such things did they say unto them, gnashing their teeth upon them, and spitting upon them, and saying: How shall we look when we are damned?

22 And many such things, yea, all manner of such things did they say unto them; and thus they did ᵃmock them for many days. And they did withhold food from them that they might hunger, and water that they might thirst; and they also did take from them their clothes that they were naked; and thus they were ᵇbound with strong cords, and confined in ᶜprison.

23 And it came to pass after they had thus suffered for many days, (and it was on the twelfth day, in the tenth month, *in the tenth year of the reign of the judges over the

11a TG Exaltation.
  b Ex. 23:7; Ps. 37:9
    (8–13); Alma 60:13;
    D&C 103:3. TG Justice.
  c TG Cruelty;
    Martyrdom.
  d Lam. 4:13; Mosiah
    17:10.
14a 1 Kgs. 22:24 (14–27).

  b Alma 12:17.
    TG Damnation.
16a Alma 1:12 (7–15);
    2:20; 21:4.
17a Matt. 27:12 (12–14).
  b Alma 9:33.
18a Alma 10:14; 11:21
    (20–37).
19a John 19:10 (9–10).

  b Mosiah 7:8.
20a Matt. 27:40 (39–43).
22a TG Mocking.
  b Acts 16:23 (23–40);
    D&C 122:6.
  c Gen. 39:20; Mosiah
    7:7.

                    [*81 B.C.]

people of Nephi) that the chief judge over the land of ᵃAmmonihah and many of their teachers and their lawyers went in unto the prison where Alma and Amulek were bound with cords.

24 And the chief judge stood before them, and smote them again, and said unto them: If ye have the ᵃpower of God deliver yourselves from these bands, and then we will believe that the Lord will destroy this people according to your words.

25 And it came to pass that they all went forth and smote them, saying the same words, even until the last; and when the last had spoken unto them the ᵃpower of God was upon Alma and Amulek, and they rose and stood upon their feet.

26 And Alma cried, saying: How long shall we suffer these great ᵃafflictions, O Lord? O Lord, ᵇgive us strength according to our faith which is in Christ, even unto ᶜdeliverance. And they broke the cords with which they were bound; and when the people saw this, they began to flee, for the fear of destruction had come upon them.

27 And it came to pass that so great was their fear that they fell to the earth, and did not obtain the outer door of the ᵃprison; and the earth shook mightily, and the walls of the prison were rent in twain, so that they fell to the earth; and the chief judge, and the lawyers, and priests, and teachers, who smote upon Alma and Amulek, were slain by the fall thereof.

28 And Alma and Amulek came forth out of the prison, and they were not hurt; for the Lord had granted unto them ᵃpower, according to their faith which was in

Christ. And they straightway came forth out of the prison; and they were ᵇloosed from their ᶜbands; and the prison had fallen to the earth, and every soul within the walls thereof, save it were Alma and Amulek, was slain; and they straightway came forth into the city.

29 Now the people having heard a great noise came running together by multitudes to know the cause of it; and when they saw Alma and Amulek coming forth out of the prison, and the walls thereof had fallen to the earth, they were struck with great fear, and fled from the presence of Alma and Amulek even as a goat fleeth with her young from two lions; and thus they did flee from the presence of Alma and Amulek.

CHAPTER 15

Alma and Amulek go to Sidom and establish a church—Alma heals Zeezrom, who joins the Church—Many are baptized and the Church prospers—Alma and Amulek go to Zarahemla.

AND it came to pass that Alma and Amulek were commanded to depart out of that city; and they departed, and came out even into the land of Sidom; and behold, there they found all the people who had departed out of the land of ᵃAmmonihah, who had been ᵇcast out and stoned, because they believed in the words of Alma.

2 And they related unto them all that had happened unto their ᵃwives and children, and also concerning themselves, and of their ᵇpower of deliverance.

3 And also Zeezrom lay sick at Sidom, with a burning fever, which was caused by the great tribulations

23a Alma 8: 6; 15: 1 (1, 15–16).
24a TG Sign Seekers.
25a Alma 8: 31.
26a James 5: 10 (10–11); Mosiah 17: 13 (10–20); JS-H 1: 22.
  b Ps. 69: 14 (1–2, 14); D&C 121: 3.

c TG Deliverance.
27a Acts 12: 4 (4–6); 16: 26; Hel. 5: 21 (21–50); 3 Ne. 28: 19 (19–20); 4 Ne. 1: 30; Ether 12: 13.
28a Alma 15: 2.
  b 1 Ne. 7: 17 (17–18); Jacob 4: 6; 3 Ne.

28: 20 (19–22).
  c Alma 36: 27.
15 1a Alma 14: 23; 16: 2 (2–3, 9, 11).
  b Alma 14: 7.
2a Alma 14: 8 (8–14).
  b Alma 14: 28 (26–29).

[About 81 B.C.]

of his mind on account of his [a]wickedness, for he supposed that Alma and Amulek were no more; and he supposed that they had been slain because of his iniquity. And this great sin, and his many other sins, did harrow up his mind until it did become exceedingly sore, having no deliverance; therefore he began to be scorched with a burning heat.

4 Now, when he heard that Alma and Amulek were in the land of Sidom, his heart began to take courage; and he sent a message immediately unto them, desiring them to come unto him.

5 And it came to pass that they went immediately, obeying the message which he had sent unto them; and they went in unto the house unto Zeezrom; and they found him upon his bed, sick, being very low with a burning fever; and his mind also was [a]exceedingly sore because of his iniquities; and when he saw them he stretched forth his hand, and besought him that they would heal him.

6 And it came to pass that Alma said unto him, taking him by the hand: [a]Believest thou in the power of Christ unto salvation?

7 And he answered and said: Yea, I believe all the words that thou hast taught.

8 And Alma said: If thou believest in the redemption of Christ thou canst be [a]healed.

9 And he said: Yea, I believe according to thy words.

10 And then Alma cried unto the Lord, saying: O Lord our God, have [a]mercy on this man, and [b]heal him according to his faith which is in Christ.

11 And when Alma had said these words, [a]Zeezrom leaped upon his feet, and began to walk; and this was done to the great astonishment of all the people; and the knowledge of this went forth throughout all the land of Sidom.

12 And Alma baptized Zeezrom unto the Lord; and he began from that time forth to preach unto the people.

13 And Alma established a church in the land of Sidom, and consecrated [a]priests and [b]teachers in the land, to baptize unto the Lord whosoever were desirous to be baptized.

14 And it came to pass that they were many; for they did flock in from all the region round about Sidom, and were baptized.

15 But as to the people that were in the land of Ammonihah, they yet remained a hard-hearted and a stiffnecked people; and they repented not of their sins, [a]ascribing all the power of Alma and Amulek to the devil; for they were of the profession of [b]Nehor, and did not believe in the repentance of their sins.

16 And it came to pass that Alma and Amulek, Amulek having [a]forsaken all his gold, and silver, and his precious things, which were in the land of Ammonihah, for the word of God, he being [b]rejected by those who were once his friends and also by his father and his kindred;

17 Therefore, after Alma having established the church at Sidom, seeing a great [a]check, yea, seeing that the people were checked as to the pride of their hearts, and began to [b]humble themselves before God, and began to assemble themselves together at their [c]sanctuaries to [d]worship God before the [e]altar, [f]watching and praying continually, that they might be delivered from Satan, and from [g]death, and from destruction—

3a Alma 14:7 (6–7).
5a Alma 14:6.
6a Mark 9:23.
8a TG Administrations to the Sick; Healing.
10a TG Mercy.
  b Mark 2:11 (1–12).
11a Acts 3:8 (1–11).
13a Alma 4:20 (7, 16, 18, 20); 16:18.
  b TG Teacher.
15a Matt. 12:24 (24–27).
  b Alma 1:15 (2–15).
16a Luke 14:33; Alma 10:4.
  b TG Prophets, Rejection of.
17a Alma 16:21.
  b Ezra 10:1 (1–5).
  c Ps. 150:1; Alma 16:13.
  d TG Worship.
  e Ex. 27:1 (1–8).
  f TG Watchfulness.
  g TG Death, Spiritual, First.

[About 81 B.C.]

18 Now as I said, Alma having seen all these things, therefore he took Amulek and came over to the land of Zarahemla, and took him to his *own house, and did administer unto him in his tribulations, and *strengthened him in the Lord.

19 And thus ended the tenth year of the reign of the judges over the people of Nephi.

CHAPTER 16

The Lamanites destroy the people of Ammonihah—Zoram leads the Nephites to victory over the Lamanites—Alma and Amulek and many others preach the word—They teach that after his resurrection Christ will appear to the Nephites.

AND it came to pass in the *eleventh year of the reign of the judges over the people of Nephi, on the fifth day of the second month, there having been much peace in the land of Zarahemla, there having been no wars nor contentions for a certain number of years, even until the fifth day of the second month in the eleventh year, there was a cry of war heard throughout the land.

2 For behold, the armies of the Lamanites had come in upon the wilderness side, into the borders of the land, even into the city of *Ammonihah, and began to slay the people and destroy the city.

3 And now it came to pass, before the Nephites could raise a sufficient army to drive them out of the land, they had *destroyed the people who were in the city of Ammonihah, and also some around the borders of Noah, and taken others captive into the wilderness.

4 Now it came to pass that the Nephites were desirous to obtain those who had been carried away captive into the wilderness.

5 Therefore, he that had been appointed chief captain over the armies of the Nephites, (and his name was Zoram, and he had two sons, Lehi and Aha)—now Zoram and his two sons, knowing that Alma was high priest over the church, and having heard that he had the spirit of prophecy, therefore they went unto him and desired of him to know whither the Lord would that they should go into the wilderness in search of their brethren, who had been taken captive by the Lamanites.

6 And it came to pass that Alma *inquired of the Lord concerning the matter. And Alma returned and said unto them: Behold, the Lamanites will cross the river Sidon in the south wilderness, away up beyond the borders of the land of *Manti. And behold there shall ye meet them, on the east of the river Sidon, and there the Lord will deliver unto thee thy brethren who have been taken captive by the Lamanites.

7 And it came to pass that Zoram and his sons crossed over the river Sidon, with their armies, and marched away beyond the borders of Manti into the south wilderness, which was on the east side of the river Sidon.

8 And they came upon the armies of the Lamanites, and the Lamanites were scattered and driven into the wilderness; and they took their brethren who had been taken captive by the Lamanites, and there was not one soul had been lost that were taken captive. And they were brought by their brethren to possess their own lands.

9 And thus ended the eleventh year of the judges, the Lamanites having been driven out of the land, and the people of Ammonihah were *destroyed; yea, *every living soul

18a Alma 27: 20.
  b Zech. 10: 12 (11–12).
16 2a Alma 15: 1 (1,
   15–16); 49: 3 (1–15).
3a Alma 9: 18.

6a 2 Kgs. 6: 8–12;
   Alma 43: 23 (23–24);
   48: 16; 3 Ne. 3: 20
   (18–21).
  b Alma 17: 1; 22: 27;
   56: 14.

9a Alma 8: 16; 9: 24
   (18–24); Morm. 6: 15
   (15–22).
  b Alma 14: 11.

[*81 B.C.]

of the Ammonihahites was [c]destroyed, and also their [d]great city, which they said God could not destroy, because of its greatness.

10 But behold, in [a]one day it was left desolate; and the [b]carcases were mangled by dogs and wild beasts of the wilderness.

11 Nevertheless, after many days their [a]dead bodies were heaped up upon the face of the earth, and they were covered with a shallow covering. And now so great was the scent thereof that the people did not go in to possess the land of Ammonihah for many years. And it was called Desolation of [b]Nehors; for they were of the profession of Nehor, who were slain; and their lands remained desolate.

12 And the Lamanites did not come again to war against the Nephites *until the fourteenth year of the reign of the judges over the people of Nephi. And thus for three years did the people of Nephi have continual peace in all the land.

13 And Alma and Amulek went forth preaching repentance to the people in their [a]temples, and in their [b]sanctuaries, and also in their [c]synagogues, which were built after the manner of the Jews.

14 And as many as would hear their words, unto them they did impart the word of God, without any [a]respect of persons, continually.

15 And thus did Alma and Amulek go forth, and also many more who had been chosen for the work, to preach the word throughout all the land. And the establishment of the church became general throughout the land, in all the region round about, among all the people of the Nephites.

16 And there was [a]no inequality among them; the Lord did pour out his Spirit on all the face of the land to prepare the minds of the children of men, or to prepare their [b]hearts to receive the word which should be taught among them at the time of his coming—

17 That they might not be hardened against the word, that they might not be unbelieving, and go on to destruction, but that they might receive the word with joy, and as a [a]branch be grafted into the true vine, that they might enter into the [b]rest of the Lord their God.

18 Now those [a]priests who did go forth among the people did preach against all [b]lyings, and [c]deceivings, and [d]envyings, and [e]strifes, and malice, and revilings, and stealing, robbing, plundering, murdering, committing adultery, and all manner of lasciviousness, crying that these things ought not so to be—

19 Holding forth things which must shortly come; yea, holding forth the [a]coming of the Son of God, his sufferings and death, and also the resurrection of the dead.

20 And many of the people did inquire concerning the place where the Son of God should come; and they were taught that he would [a]appear unto them [b]after his resurrection; and this the people did hear with great joy and gladness.

21 And now after the church had been established throughout all the land—having got the [a]victory over

9c Alma 25: 2.
  d Alma 49: 3.
10a Alma 9: 4.
  b Jer. 19: 7.
11a Alma 28: 11.
  b Alma 1: 15; 2: 1 (1, 20); 24: 28 (28–30).
13a 2 Ne. 5: 16; Hel. 3: 14 (9, 14).
  b Alma 15: 17; 21: 6.
  c Alma 21: 20 (4–6, 20).
14a Deut. 10: 17; Alma 1: 30.

16a Mosiah 18: 27 (19–29); 4 Ne. 1: 3.
  b Acts 16: 14.
  TG Teachable.
17a Jacob 5: 24.
  TG Vineyard of the Lord.
  b Alma 12: 37; 13: 6 (6–29).
18a Alma 15: 13; 30: 20 (20–23, 31).
  b 3 Ne. 30: 2.

  c TG Deceit.
  d TG Envy.
  e Alma 4: 9 (8–9).
  TG Strife.
19a TG Jesus Christ, Prophecies about.
20a 2 Ne. 26: 9; 3 Ne. 11: 8 (7–14).
  b 1 Ne. 12: 6 (4–8); Alma 7: 8.
21a Alma 15: 17.

the devil, and the word of God being preached in its purity in all the land, and the Lord pouring out his blessings upon the people—thus ended the fourteenth year of the reign of the judges over the people of Nephi.

An account of the sons of Mosiah, who rejected their rights to the kingdom for the word of God, and went up to the land of Nephi to preach to the Lamanites; their sufferings and deliverance—according to the record of Alma. Comprising chapters 17 to 26 inclusive.

CHAPTER 17

The sons of Mosiah have the spirit of prophecy and of revelation—They go their several ways to declare the word to the Lamanites—Ammon goes to the land of Ishmael and becomes the servant of King Lamoni—Ammon saves the king's flocks and slays his enemies at the waters of Sebus.

AND now it came to pass that as Alma was journeying from the land of Gideon southward, away to the land of ᵃManti, behold, to his astonishment, he ᵇmet with the ᶜsons of Mosiah journeying towards the land of Zarahemla.

2 Now these sons of Mosiah were with Alma at the time the angel ᵃfirst appeared unto him; therefore Alma did rejoice exceedingly to see his brethren; and what added more to his joy, they were still his brethren in the Lord; yea, and they had waxed strong in the knowledge of the truth; for they were men of a sound understanding and they had ᵇsearched the scriptures diligently, that they might know the word of God.

3 But this is not all; they had given themselves to much prayer, and ᵃfasting; therefore they had the spirit of prophecy, and the spirit of revelation, and when they taught, they taught with ᵇpower and authority of God.

4 And they had been teaching the word of God *for the space of fourteen years among the Lamanites, having had much ᵃsuccess in bringing many to the ᵇknowledge of the truth; yea, by the power of their words many were brought before the altar of God, to call on his name and ᶜconfess their sins before him.

5 Now these are the circumstances which attended them in their journeyings, for they had many afflictions; they did suffer much, both in body and in mind, such as hunger, thirst and fatigue, and also much ᵃlabor in the spirit.

6 Now these were their journeyings: Having ᵃtaken leave of their father, Mosiah, in the ᵇfirst year of the judges; having ᶜrefused the kingdom which their father was desirous to confer upon them, and also this was the minds of the people;

7 Nevertheless they departed out of the land of Zarahemla, and took their swords, and their spears, and their bows, and their arrows, and their slings; and this they did that they might ᵃprovide food for themselves while in the wilderness.

8 And thus they departed into the wilderness with their numbers which they had ᵃselected, to go up to the land of Nephi, to preach the word of God unto the Lamanites.

9 And it came to pass that they journeyed many days in the wilderness, and they fasted much and ᵃprayed much that the Lord would grant unto them a portion of his

17 1a Alma 16:6.
  b Alma 27:16.
  c Mosiah 27:34.
  2a Mosiah 27:11 (11–17).
  b Jacob 7:23; D&C
    84:85. TG Scriptures,
    Study of.
  3a TG Fasting.
  b W of M 1:17.

TG Authority; Teaching
  with the Spirit.
4a Alma 29:14.
  b TG Missionary Work.
  c Num. 5:7 (6–10);
    Mosiah 26:29 (29,
    35); 3 Ne. 1:25.
5a Alma 8:10.
6a Mosiah 28:9 (1, 5–9);

Alma 26:1.
  b Mosiah 29:44 (41–44).
  c Mosiah 29:3.
7a 1 Ne. 16:15 (15–32).
8a Mosiah 28:1.
9a Alma 25:17.
  TG Guidance, Divine.

[*From about 91 to 77 B.C.]

Spirit to go with them, and abide with them, that they might be an [b]instrument in the hands of God to bring, if it were possible, their brethren, the Lamanites, to the knowledge of the truth, to the knowledge of the baseness of the [c]traditions of their fathers, which were not correct.

10 And it came to pass that the Lord did [a]visit them with his [b]Spirit, and said unto them: Be [c]comforted. And they were comforted.

11 And the Lord said unto them also: Go forth among the Lamanites, thy brethren, and establish my word; yet ye shall be [a]patient in long-suffering and afflictions, that ye may show forth good [b]examples unto them in me, and I will make an instrument of thee in my hands unto the salvation of many souls.

12 And it came to pass that the hearts of the sons of Mosiah, and also those who were with them, took courage to go forth unto the Lamanites to declare unto them the word of God.

13 And it came to pass when they had arrived in the borders of the land of the Lamanites, that they [a]separated themselves and departed one from another, trusting in the Lord that they should meet again at the close of their [b]harvest; for they supposed that great was the work which they had undertaken.

14 And assuredly it was great, for they had undertaken to preach the word of God to a [a]wild and a hardened and a ferocious people; a people who delighted in murdering the Nephites, and robbing and plundering them; and their hearts were set upon riches, or upon gold and silver, and precious stones; yet they sought to obtain these things by murdering and plundering, that they might not labor for them with their own hands.

15 Thus they were a very indolent people, many of whom did worship idols, and the [a]curse of God had fallen upon them because of the [b]traditions of their fathers; notwithstanding the promises of the Lord were extended unto them on the conditions of repentance.

16 Therefore, this was the [a]cause for which the sons of Mosiah had undertaken the work, that perhaps they might bring them unto repentance; that perhaps they might bring them to know of the plan of redemption.

17 Therefore they separated themselves one from another, and went forth among them, every man alone, according to the word and power of God which was given unto him.

18 Now Ammon being the chief among them, or rather he did administer unto them, and he departed from them, after having [a]blessed them according to their several stations, having imparted the word of God unto them, or administered unto them before his departure; and thus they took their several journeys throughout the land.

19 And Ammon went to the land of [a]Ishmael, the land being called after the sons of [b]Ishmael, who also became Lamanites.

20 And as Ammon entered the land of Ishmael, the Lamanites took him and [a]bound him, as was their custom to bind all the Nephites who fell into their hands, and carry them before the king; and thus it was left to the pleasure of the king to slay them, or to retain them in captivity, or to cast them into prison, or to

9b Mosiah 23: 10; Alma 26: 3.
  c Alma 3: 11.
10a 1 Ne. 2: 16; D&C 5: 16.
  b TG God, Spirit of.
  c Alma 26: 27.
11a Alma 20: 29; 26: 27.
  TG Forbearance;

    Patience.
  b TG Example.
13a Alma 21: 1.
  b Matt. 9: 37.
14a Mosiah 10: 12.
15a Alma 3: 19 (6–19);
    3 Ne. 2: 15 (15–16).
  b Alma 9: 16 (16–24);

    18: 5.
16a Mosiah 28: 2 (1–3).
18a TG Blessing.
19a Alma 21: 18 (18, 20);
    22: 1 (1, 4); 25: 13.
  b 1 Ne. 7: 6 (4–6).
20a Mosiah 7: 7 (7–10).

cast them out of his land, according to his will and pleasure.

21 And thus Ammon was carried before the king who was over the land of Ishmael; and his name was Lamoni; and he was a descendant of Ishmael.

22 And the king inquired of Ammon if it were his desire to dwell in the land among the Lamanites, or among his people.

23 And Ammon said unto him: Yea, I desire to ᵃdwell among this people for a time; yea, and perhaps until the day I die.

24 And it came to pass that king Lamoni was much pleased with Ammon, and caused that his bands should be loosed; and he would that Ammon should take one of his daughters to wife.

25 But Ammon said unto him: Nay, but I will be thy servant. Therefore Ammon became a ᵃservant to king Lamoni. And it came to pass that he was set among other servants to watch the flocks of Lamoni, according to the custom of the Lamanites.

26 And after he had been in the service of the king three days, as he was with the Lamanitish servants going forth with their flocks to the place of ᵃwater, which was called the water of Sebus, and all the Lamanites drive their flocks hither, that they may have water—

27 Therefore, as Ammon and the servants of the king were driving forth their flocks to this place of water, behold, a certain number of the Lamanites, who had been with their flocks to water, stood and ᵃscattered the flocks of Ammon and the servants of the king, and they scattered them insomuch that they fled many ways.

28 Now the servants of the king began to murmur, saying: Now the king will slay us, as he has our brethren because their flocks were scattered by the wickedness of these

men. And they began to weep exceedingly, saying: Behold, our flocks are scattered already.

29 Now they wept because of the fear of being slain. Now when Ammon saw this his heart was swollen within him with joy; for, said he, I will show forth my power unto these my fellow-servants, or the power which is in me, in restoring these flocks unto the king, that I may win the hearts of these my fellow-servants, that I may lead them to ᵃbelieve in my words.

30 And now, these were the thoughts of Ammon, when he saw the afflictions of those whom he termed to be his brethren.

31 And it came to pass that he flattered them by his words, saying: My brethren, be of good cheer and let us go in search of the flocks, and we will gather them together and bring them back unto the place of water; and thus we will preserve the flocks unto the king and he will not slay us.

32 And it came to pass that they went in search of the flocks, and they did follow Ammon, and they rushed forth with much swiftness and did head the flocks of the king, and did gather them together again to the place of water.

33 And those men again stood to scatter their flocks; but Ammon said unto his brethren: Encircle the flocks round about that they flee not; and I go and contend with these men who do scatter our flocks.

34 Therefore, they did as Ammon commanded them, and he went forth and stood to contend with those who stood by the waters of Sebus; and they were in number not a few.

35 Therefore they did not fear Ammon, for they supposed that one of their men could slay him according to their pleasure, for they knew not that the Lord had promised Mosiah that he would ᵃdeliver

23a Alma 19: 19.
25a Alma 21: 19.
26a Ex. 2: 17 (15–20).

27a Alma 18: 3 (3–7);
    19: 21 (20–21).
29a 2 Kgs. 5: 8.

35a Mosiah 28: 7; Alma
    19: 23 (22–23).

[About 90 B.C.]

his sons out of their hands; neither did they know anything concerning the Lord; therefore they delighted in the destruction of their brethren; and for this cause they stood to scatter the flocks of the king.

36 But [a]Ammon stood forth and began to cast stones at them with his sling; yea, with mighty power he did sling stones amongst them; and thus he slew a [b]certain number of them insomuch that they began to be astonished at his power; nevertheless they were angry because of the slain of their brethren, and they were determined that he should fall; therefore, seeing that they [c]could not hit him with their stones, they came forth with clubs to slay him.

37 But behold, every man that lifted his club to smite Ammon, he smote off their arms with his sword; for he did withstand their blows by smiting their arms with the edge of his sword, insomuch that they began to be astonished, and began to flee before him; yea, and they were not few in number; and he caused them to flee by the strength of his arm.

38 Now six of them had fallen by the sling, but he [a]slew none save it were their leader with his sword; and he smote off as many of their arms as were lifted against him, and they were not a few.

39 And when he had driven them afar off, he returned and they watered their flocks and returned them to the pasture of the king, and then went in unto the king, bearing the arms which had been smitten off by the sword of Ammon, of those who sought to slay him; and they were carried in unto the king for a testimony of the things which they had done.

CHAPTER 18

King Lamoni supposes that Ammon is the Great Spirit—Ammon teaches the king of the creation, of God's dealings with men, and of the redemption that comes through Christ—Lamoni believes and falls to the earth as if dead.

AND it came to pass that king Lamoni caused that his [a]servants should stand forth and testify to all the things which they had seen concerning the matter.

2 And when they had all testified to the things which they had seen, and he had learned of the faithfulness of Ammon in preserving his flocks, and also of his [a]great power in contending against those who sought to slay him, he was astonished exceedingly, and said: Surely, this is more than a man. Behold, is not this the Great Spirit who doth send such great punishments upon this people, because of their murders?

3 And they answered the king, and said: Whether he be the Great Spirit or a man, we know not; but this much we do know, that he [a]cannot be slain by the enemies of the king; neither can they [b]scatter the king's flocks when he is with us, because of his expertness and [c]great strength; therefore, we know that he is a friend to the king. And now, O king, we do not believe that a man has such great power, for we know he cannot be slain.

4 And now, when the king heard these words, he said unto them: Now I know that it is the Great Spirit; and he has come down at this time to preserve your lives, that I might not [a]slay you as I did your brethren. Now this is the Great Spirit of whom our fathers have spoken.

5 Now this was the [a]tradition of Lamoni, which he had received from

---

36a Ether 12:15.
  b Alma 18:16 (16, 20).
  c Alma 18:3.
38a Alma 19:22.

18 1a Alma 19:15.
  2a Alma 22:9 (9–11).
  3a Alma 17:36 (34–38).
    b Alma 17:27; 19:21
      (20–21).

  c Alma 22:20.
  4a Alma 17:28 (28–31).
  5a Alma 17:15; 60:32.

[About 90 B.C.]

his father, that there was a [b]Great Spirit. Notwithstanding they believed in a Great Spirit, they supposed that [c]whatsoever they did was right; nevertheless, Lamoni began to fear exceedingly, with fear lest he had done wrong in slaying his servants;

6 For he had slain many of them because their brethren had scattered their flocks at the place of water; and thus, because they had had their flocks scattered they were slain.

7 Now it was the practice of these Lamanites to stand by the [a]waters of Sebus to scatter the flocks of the people, that thereby they might drive away many that were scattered unto their own land, it being a practice of plunder among them.

8 And it came to pass that king Lamoni inquired of his servants, saying: Where is this man that has such great power?

9 And they said unto him: Behold, he is feeding thy [a]horses. Now the king had commanded his servants, previous to the time of the watering of their flocks, that they should prepare his horses and chariots, and conduct him forth to the land of Nephi; for there had been a [b]great [c]feast appointed at the land of Nephi, by the father of Lamoni, who was king over all the land.

10 Now when king Lamoni heard that Ammon was preparing his horses and his [a]chariots he was more astonished, because of the faithfulness of Ammon, saying: Surely there has not been any servant among all my servants that has been so faithful as this man; for even he doth remember all my commandments to execute them.

11 Now I surely know that this is the Great Spirit, and I would desire him that he come in unto me, but I durst not.

12 And it came to pass that when Ammon had made ready the horses and the chariots for the king and his servants, he went in unto the king, and he saw that the [a]countenance of the king was changed; therefore he was about to return out of his presence.

13 And one of the king's servants said unto him, [a]Rabbanah, which is, being interpreted, powerful or great king, considering their kings to be powerful; and thus he said unto him: Rabbanah, the king desireth thee to stay.

14 Therefore Ammon turned himself unto the king, and said unto him: What wilt thou that I should do for thee, O king? And the king answered him not for the space of an [a]hour, according to their time, for he knew not what he should say unto him.

15 And it came to pass that Ammon said unto him again: What desirest thou of me? But the king answered him not.

16 And it came to pass that Ammon, being filled with the [a]Spirit of God, therefore he perceived the [b]thoughts of the king. And he said unto him: Is it because thou hast heard that I defended thy servants and thy flocks, and slew [c]seven of their brethren with the sling and with the sword, and smote off the arms of others, in order to defend thy flocks and thy servants; behold, is it this that causeth thy marvelings?

17 I say unto you, what is it, that thy marvelings are so great? Behold, I am a [a]man, and am thy servant; therefore, whatsoever thou desirest which is right, that will I do.

18 Now when the king had heard

5b Alma 19: 25 (25–27).
  TG God, Knowledge about.
  c Alma 30: 17.
7a Alma 17: 26; 19: 20 (20–21).

9a Enos 1: 21; Alma 20: 6.
  b Alma 20: 9 (9, 12).
  c Esth. 1: 3.
10a Alma 20: 6; 3 Ne. 3: 22.
12a Dan. 5: 6.
13a John 20: 16.
14a 3 Ne. 8: 19.

16a Gen. 41: 38; 1 Ne. 1: 12; Mosiah 27: 24.
  b Alma 12: 3.
  c Alma 17: 36.
17a Dan. 2: 30.

[About 90 B.C.]

these words, he marveled again, for he beheld that Ammon could [a]discern his thoughts; but notwithstanding this, king Lamoni did open his mouth, and said unto him: Who art thou? Art thou that Great Spirit, who [b]knows all things?

19 Ammon answered and said unto him: I am not.

20 And the king said: How knowest thou the thoughts of my heart? Thou mayest speak boldly, and tell me concerning these things; and also tell me by what power ye slew and smote off the arms of my brethren that scattered my flocks—

21 And now, [a]if thou wilt tell me concerning these things, whatsoever thou desirest I will give unto thee; and if it were needed, I would guard thee with my armies; but I know that thou art more powerful than all they; nevertheless, whatsoever thou desirest of me I will grant it unto thee.

22 Now Ammon being [a]wise, yet harmless, he said unto Lamoni: Wilt thou hearken unto my words, if I tell thee by what power I do these things? And this is the thing that I desire of thee.

23 And the king answered him, and said: Yea, I [a]will believe all thy words. And thus he was caught with [b]guile.

24 And Ammon began to speak unto him with [a]boldness, and said unto him: Believest thou that there is a God?

25 And he answered, and said unto him: I do not know what that meaneth.

26 And then Ammon said: Believest thou that there is a [a]Great Spirit?

27 And he said, Yea.

28 And Ammon said: This is God.

And Ammon said unto him again: Believest thou that this Great Spirit, who is God, created all things which are in heaven and in the earth?

29 And he said: Yea, I believe that he created all things which are in the earth; but I do not know the heavens.

30 And Ammon said unto him: The heavens is a place where God dwells and all his holy angels.

31 And king Lamoni said: Is it above the earth?

32 And Ammon said: Yea, and he looketh down upon all the children of men; and he [a]knows all the thoughts and [b]intents of the heart; for by his hand were they all created from the beginning.

33 And king Lamoni said: I believe all these things which thou hast spoken. Art thou [a]sent from God?

34 Ammon said unto him: I am a [a]man; and man in the beginning was created after the image of God, and I am called by his Holy [b]Spirit to teach these things unto this people, that they may be brought to a knowledge of that which is just and true;

35 And a portion of that [a]Spirit dwelleth in me, which giveth me [b]knowledge, and also power according to my faith and desires which are in God.

36 Now when Ammon had said these words, he began at the creation of the world, and also the creation of Adam, and told him all the things concerning the fall of man, and [a]rehearsed and laid before him the [b]records and the holy scriptures of the people, which had been spoken by the [c]prophets, even down to the time that their father, Lehi, left Jerusalem.

37 And he also rehearsed unto

18a TG Discernment, Spiritual.
  b TG God, Omniscience of.
21a Dan. 5:16.
22a Gen. 41:39; Alma 48:11 (11–17).
23a Alma 18:40.
  b Josh. 9:22.
24a Alma 38:12.
26a Alma 22:9 (9–10).

32a TG God, Omniscience of.
  b Amos 4:13; 3 Ne. 28:6.
33a 2 Chr. 24:19.
34a Mosiah 7:27; Ether 3:15 (13–16).
  b TG Teaching with the Spirit.
35a TG Inspiration.
  b TG Knowledge.

36a Mosiah 1:4; Alma 22:12; 36:1; 37:9; Hel. 5:13 (1–13); Moses 6:58.
  b Alma 63:12.
    TG Scriptures, Value of.
  c Acts 3:18 (18–21); 28:23.

[About 90 B.C.]

them (for it was unto the king and to his servants) all the journeyings of their fathers in the wilderness, and all their sufferings with hunger and thirst, and their travail, and so forth.

38 And he also rehearsed unto them concerning the [a]rebellions of Laman and Lemuel, and the sons of Ishmael, yea, all their rebellions did he relate unto them; and he expounded unto them all the [b]records and scriptures from the time that Lehi left Jerusalem down to the present time.

39 But this is not all; for he [a]expounded unto them the [b]plan of redemption, which was prepared from the foundation of the world; and he also made known unto them concerning the coming of Christ, and all the works of the Lord did he make known unto them.

40 And it came to pass that after he had said all these things, and expounded them to the king, that the king [a]believed all his words.

41 And he began to cry unto the Lord, saying: O Lord, have mercy; according to thy abundant [a]mercy which thou hast had upon the people of Nephi, have upon me, and my people.

42 And now, when he had said this, he [a]fell unto the earth, [b]as if he were dead.

43 And it came to pass that his [a]servants took him and carried him in unto his wife, and laid him upon a bed; and he lay as if he were dead for the space of two days and two nights; and his wife, and his sons, and his daughters mourned over him, after the manner of the Lamanites, greatly lamenting his loss.

CHAPTER 19

Lamoni receives the light of everlasting life and sees the Redeemer—His
household fall into a trance, and some see angels—Ammon is preserved miraculously—He baptizes many and establishes a church among them.

AND it came to pass that after two days and two nights they were about to take his [a]body and lay it in a sepulchre, which they had made for the purpose of burying their dead.

2 Now the queen having heard of the fame of Ammon, therefore she sent and desired that he should come in unto her.

3 And it came to pass that Ammon did as he was commanded, and went in unto the queen, and desired to know what she would that he should do.

4 And she said unto him: The [a]servants of my husband have made it known unto me that thou art a [b]prophet of a holy God, and that thou hast [c]power to do many mighty works in his name;

5 Therefore, if this is the case, I would that ye should go in and see my husband, for he has been laid upon his bed for the space of two days and two nights; and some say that he is not dead, but others say that he is dead and that he [a]stinketh, and that he ought to be placed in the sepulchre; but as for myself, to me he doth not stink.

6 Now, this was what Ammon desired, for he knew that king Lamoni was under the power of God; he knew that the dark [a]veil of [b]unbelief was being cast away from his mind, and the [c]light which did light up his mind, which was the light of the glory of God, which was a marvelous light of his goodness—yea, this light had infused such joy into his soul, the cloud of darkness having been dispelled, and that the light of everlasting life was lit up in

38a 2 Ne. 1: 2.
  b 1 Ne. 9: 2.
39a Alma 19: 31.
   TG Missionary Work.
  b TG Salvation, Plan of.
40a Alma 18: 23.
41a TG God, Mercy of.
42a Alma 19: 1 (1,5–12).

  b Alma 22: 18.
43a Alma 19: 4 (4–5).
19 1a Alma 18: 42 (42–43).
  4a Alma 18: 43.
  b TG Prophets, Mission of.
  c D&C 3: 4.

5a John 11: 39.
6a 2 Cor. 4: 4 (3–4).
   TG Veil.
  b TG Unbelief, Unbelievers.
  c TG Light.

[About 90 B.C.]

his soul, yea, he knew that this had [d]overcome his natural frame, and he was carried away in God—

7 Therefore, what the queen desired of him was his only desire. Therefore, he went in to see the king according as the queen had desired him; and he saw the king, and he knew that he was not dead.

8 And he said unto the queen: He is not dead, but he sleepeth in God, and on the morrow he shall rise again; therefore bury him not.

9 And Ammon said unto her: [a]Believest thou this? And she said unto him: I have had no witness save thy word, and the word of our servants; nevertheless I [b]believe that it shall be according as thou hast said.

10 And Ammon said unto her: Blessed art thou because of thy exceeding faith; I say unto thee, woman, there has not been such great faith among all the people of the [a]Nephites.

11 And it came to pass that she watched over the bed of her husband, from that time even until that time on the morrow which Ammon had appointed that he should rise.

12 And it came to pass that he arose, according to the words of Ammon; and as he arose, he stretched forth his hand unto the woman, and said: Blessed be the name of God, and blessed art thou.

13 For as sure as thou livest, behold, I have [a]seen my Redeemer; and he shall come forth, and be [b]born of a [c]woman, and he shall redeem all mankind who believe on his name. Now, when he had said these words, his heart was swollen within him, and he sunk again with joy; and the queen also sunk down, being overpowered by the Spirit.

14 Now Ammon seeing the Spirit of the Lord poured out according to his [a]prayers upon the Lamanites, his brethren, who had been the cause of so much mourning among the Nephites, or among all the people of God because of their iniquities and their [b]traditions, he fell upon his knees, and began to pour out his soul in prayer and thanksgiving to God for what he had done for his brethren; and he was also overpowered with [c]joy; and thus they all three had [d]sunk to the earth.

15 Now, when the servants of the king had seen that they had fallen, they also began to cry unto God, for the fear of the Lord had come upon them also, for it was [a]they who had stood before the king and testified unto him concerning the great power of Ammon.

16 And it came to pass that they did call on the name of the Lord, in their might, even until they had all fallen to the earth, save it were one of the Lamanitish [a]women, whose name was Abish, she having been converted unto the Lord for many years, on account of a remarkable vision of her father—

17 Thus, having been converted to the Lord, and never having made it [a]known, therefore, when she saw that all the servants of Lamoni had [b]fallen to the earth, and also her mistress, the queen, and the king, and Ammon lay [c]prostrate upon the earth, she knew that it was the power of God; and supposing that this opportunity, by making known unto the people what had happened among them, that by beholding this scene it would [d]cause them to believe in the power of God, therefore she ran forth from house to house, making it known unto the people.

18 And they began to assemble themselves together unto the house

6d Jacob 7: 21; Mosiah 3: 19.
9a John 11: 26 (22–45).
  b Mosiah 26: 15 (15–16).
10a Luke 7: 9.
13a TG God, Privilege of Seeing; Jesus Christ, Appearances.
  Antemortal.
  b TG Jesus Christ, Birth of.
  c 1 Ne. 11: 18 (13–21).
14a D&C 42: 14.
  b Mosiah 1: 5.
  c TG Joy.
  d Alma 27: 17.
15a Alma 18: 1 (1–2).
16a Alma 19: 28.
17a JS-H 1: 74.
  b Mosiah 4: 1.
  c Moses 1: 9 (9–10).
  d Mosiah 27: 14.

[About 90 B.C.]

of the king. And there came a multitude, and to their astonishment, they beheld the king, and the queen, and their servants prostrate upon the earth, and they all lay there as though they were dead; and they also saw Ammon, and behold, he was a Nephite.

19 And now the people began to murmur among themselves; some saying that it was a great evil that had come upon them, or upon the king and his house, because he had suffered that the Nephite should *a*remain in the land.

20 But others rebuked them, saying: The king hath brought this evil upon his house, because he slew his servants who had had their flocks scattered at the *a*waters of Sebus.

21 And they were also rebuked by those men who had stood at the waters of Sebus and *a*scattered the flocks which belonged to the king, for they were angry with Ammon because of the number which he had slain of their brethren at the waters of Sebus, while defending the flocks of the king.

22 Now, one of them, whose brother had been *a*slain with the sword of Ammon, being exceedingly angry with Ammon, drew his sword and went forth that he might let it fall upon Ammon, to slay him; and as he lifted the sword to smite him, behold, he fell dead.

23 Now we see that Ammon could not be slain, for the *a*Lord had said unto Mosiah, his father: I will spare him, and it shall be unto him according to thy faith—therefore, Mosiah *b*trusted him unto the Lord.

24 And it came to pass that when the multitude beheld that the man had fallen dead, who lifted the sword to slay Ammon, *a*fear came upon them all, and they durst not put forth their hands to touch him

or any of those who had fallen; and they began to marvel again among themselves what could be the cause of this great power, or what all these things could mean.

25 And it came to pass that there were many among them who said that Ammon was the *a*Great Spirit, and others said he was sent by the Great Spirit;

26 But others rebuked them all, saying that he was a *a*monster, who had been sent from the Nephites to torment them.

27 And there were some who said that Ammon was sent by the Great Spirit to afflict them because of their iniquities; and that it was the Great Spirit that had always attended the Nephites, who had ever delivered them out of their hands; and they said that it was this Great Spirit who had destroyed so many of their brethren, the Lamanites.

28 And thus the contention began to be exceedingly sharp among them. And while they were thus contending, the *a*woman servant who had caused the multitude to be gathered together came, and when she saw the contention which was among the multitude she was exceedingly sorrowful, even unto tears.

29 And it came to pass that she went and took the queen by the *a*hand, that perhaps she might raise her from the ground; and as soon as she touched her hand she arose and stood upon her feet, and cried with a loud voice, saying: O blessed Jesus, who has saved me from an *b*awful hell! O blessed God, have *c*mercy on this people!

30 And when she had said this, she clasped her hands, being filled with joy, speaking many words which were not understood; and when she had done this, she took the king,

19a Alma 17: 23 (22–23).
20a Alma 17: 26; 18: 7.
21a Alma 17: 27; 18: 3.
22a Alma 17: 38.
23a Mosiah 28: 7; Alma 17: 35.

b TG Family, Love within; Trust in God.
24a Luke 7: 16; Moses 6: 39 (37–40).
25a Alma 18: 5 (2–5).
26a Moses 6: 38 (37–39).

28a Alma 19: 16.
29a Alma 22: 22.
b 1 Ne. 14: 3.
c Enos 1: 9; Alma 36: 24.

[About 90 B.C.]

Lamoni, by the hand, and behold he arose and stood upon his feet.

31 And he, immediately, seeing the contention among his people, went forth and began to rebuke them, and to teach them the [a]words which he had heard from the mouth of Ammon; and as many as heard his words believed, and were converted unto the Lord.

32 But there were [a]many among them who would not hear his words; therefore they went their way.

33 And it came to pass that when Ammon arose he also administered unto them, and also did all the servants of Lamoni; and they did all declare unto the people the self-same thing—that their hearts had been [a]changed; that they had no more desire to do [b]evil.

34 And behold, many did declare unto the people that they had seen [a]angels and had conversed with them; and thus they had told them things of God, and of his righteousness.

35 And it came to pass that there were many that did [a]believe in their words; and as many as did believe were baptized; and they became a righteous people, and they did establish a church among them.

36 And thus the work of the Lord did commence among the Lamanites; thus the Lord did begin to pour out his [a]Spirit upon them; and we see that his arm is extended to [b]all people who will repent and believe on his name.

CHAPTER 20

The Lord sends Ammon to Middoni to deliver his imprisoned brethren— Ammon and Lamoni meet Lamoni's father, who is king over all the land— Ammon compels the old king to approve the release of his brethren.

AND it came to pass that when they had established a church in that [a]land, that king Lamoni desired that Ammon should go with him to the land of Nephi, that he might show him unto his father.

2 And the voice of the Lord came to Ammon, saying: Thou shalt not go up to the land of Nephi, for behold, the king will seek thy life; but thou shalt go to the land of [a]Middoni; for behold, thy brother Aaron, and also Muloki and Ammah are in prison.

3 Now it came to pass that when Ammon had heard this, he said unto Lamoni: Behold, my brother and brethren are in prison at Middoni, and I go that I may deliver them.

4 Now Lamoni said unto Ammon: I know, in the [a]strength of the Lord thou canst do all things. But behold, I will go with thee to the land of Middoni; for the king of the land of Middoni, whose name is Antiomno, is a friend unto me; therefore I go to the land of Middoni, that I may flatter the king of the land, and he will cast thy brethren out of [b]prison. Now Lamoni said unto him: Who told thee that thy brethren were in prison?

5 And Ammon said unto him: No one hath told me, save it be God; and he said unto me—Go and deliver thy brethren, for they are in prison in the land of Middoni.

6 Now when Lamoni had heard this he caused that his servants should make ready his [a]horses and his chariots.

7 And he said unto Ammon: Come, I will go with thee down to the land of Middoni, and there I will plead with the king that he will cast thy brethren out of prison.

8 And it came to pass that as Ammon and Lamoni were journey-

31a Alma 18: 39 (36–39).
32a John 12: 37 (35–37).
33a TG Man, New,
    Spiritually Reborn.
  b Jonah 3: 8; Mosiah
    5: 2; Alma 13: 12;
    3 Ne. 20: 26.
34a TG Angels; Vision.
35a TG Baptism,
    Qualifications for.
36a TG God, Spirit of.
  b 2 Ne. 26: 33; Alma
    5: 33; 3 Ne. 18: 25.
20 1a 2 Ne. 5: 8; Alma
    2: 24.
2a Alma 21: 12 (12–13,
    18); 23: 10.
4a TG Strength.
  b Alma 20: 22; 22: 2.
6a Alma 18: 9.

ing thither, they met the father of Lamoni, who was king *a*over all the land.

9 And behold, the father of Lamoni said unto him: Why did ye *a*not come to the *b*feast on that great day when I made a feast unto my sons, and unto my people?

10 And he also said: Whither art thou going with this Nephite, who is one of the children of a *a*liar?

11 And it came to pass that Lamoni rehearsed unto him whither he was going, for he feared to offend him.

12 And he also told him all the cause of his tarrying in his own kingdom, that he did not go unto his father to the feast which he had prepared.

13 And now when Lamoni had rehearsed unto him all these things, behold, to his astonishment, his father was angry with him, and said: Lamoni, thou art going to deliver these Nephites, who are sons of a liar. Behold, he robbed our fathers; and now his children are also come amongst us that they may, by their cunning and their lyings, deceive us, that they again may rob us of our property.

14 Now the father of Lamoni commanded him that he should slay Ammon with the sword. And he also commanded him that he should not go to the land of Middoni, but that he should return with him to the land of *a*Ishmael.

15 But Lamoni said unto him: I will not slay Ammon, neither will I return to the land of Ishmael, but I go to the land of Middoni that I may release the brethren of Ammon, for I know that they are just men and holy prophets of the true God.

16 Now when his father had heard these words, he was angry with him, and he drew his sword that he might smite him to the earth.

17 But Ammon stood forth and said unto him: Behold, thou shalt not slay thy son; nevertheless, it were *a*better that he should fall than thee, for behold, he has *b*repented of his sins; but if thou shouldst fall at this time, in thine anger, thy soul could not be saved.

18 And again, it is expedient that thou shouldst forbear; for if thou shouldst *a*slay thy son, he being an innocent man, his blood would cry from the ground to the Lord his God, for vengeance to come upon thee; and perhaps thou wouldst lose thy *b*soul.

19 Now when Ammon had said these words unto him, he answered him, saying: I know that if I should slay my son, that I should shed innocent blood; for it is thou that hast sought to destroy him.

20 And he stretched forth his hand to slay Ammon. But Ammon withstood his blows, and also smote his arm that he could not use it.

21 Now when the king saw that Ammon could slay him, he began to plead with Ammon that he would spare his life.

22 But Ammon raised his sword, and said unto him: Behold, I will smite thee except thou wilt grant unto me that my brethren may be *a*cast out of prison.

23 Now the king, fearing he should lose his life, said: If thou wilt spare me I will grant unto thee whatsoever thou wilt ask, even to half of the kingdom.

24 Now when Ammon saw that he had wrought upon the old king according to his desire, he said unto him: If thou wilt grant that my brethren may be cast out of prison, and also that Lamoni may retain his kingdom, and that ye be not displeased with him, but grant that he may do according to his own desires in *a*whatsoever thing he thinketh,

---

8a Alma 22:1.
9a 1 Sam. 20:27.
 b Alma 18:9.
10a Mosiah 10:16 (12–17).
14a Alma 17:19.

17a Alma 48:23.
 b Alma 22:6.
18a TG Murder.
 b D&C 42:18.

22a Alma 20:4.
24a Alma 21:21 (21–22);
    22:1.

[About 90 B.C.]

then will I spare thee; otherwise I will smite thee to the earth.

25 Now when Ammon had said these words, the king began to rejoice because of his life.

26 And when he saw that Ammon had no desire to destroy him, and when he also saw the great *a*love he had for his son Lamoni, he was astonished exceedingly, and said: Because this is all that thou hast desired, that I would *b*release thy brethren, and suffer that my son Lamoni should retain his kingdom, behold, I will grant unto you that my son may retain his kingdom from this time and forever; and I will govern him no more—

27 And I will also grant unto thee that thy brethren may be cast out of prison, and thou and thy brethren may come unto me, in my kingdom; for I shall greatly desire to see thee. For the king was greatly astonished at the words which he had spoken, and also at the words which had been spoken by his son Lamoni, therefore he was *a*desirous to learn them.

28 And it came to pass that Ammon and Lamoni proceeded on their journey towards the land of Middoni. And Lamoni found favor in the eyes of the king of the land; therefore the brethren of Ammon were brought forth out of prison.

29 And when Ammon did meet them he was exceedingly sorrowful, for behold they were naked, and their skins were worn exceedingly because of being bound with strong cords. And they also had *a*suffered hunger, thirst, and all kinds of afflictions; nevertheless they were *b*patient in all their sufferings.

30 And, as it happened, it was their lot to have fallen into the hands of a more hardened and a more *a*stiffnecked people; therefore they would not hearken unto their words, and

they had cast them out, and had smitten them, and had driven them from house to house, and from place to place, even until they had arrived in the land of Middoni; and there they were taken and cast into prison, and bound with *b*strong cords, and kept in prison for many days, and were delivered by Lamoni and Ammon.

An account of the preaching of Aaron, and Muloki, and their brethren, to the Lamanites. Comprising chapters 21 to 26 inclusive.

CHAPTER 21

Aaron teaches the Amalekites about Christ and his atonement—Aaron and his brethren are imprisoned in Middoni—After their deliverance they teach in the synagogues and make many converts—Lamoni grants religious freedom to the people in the land of Ishmael.

Now when Ammon and his brethren *a*separated themselves in the borders of the land of the Lamanites, behold Aaron took his journey towards the land which was called by the Lamanites, *b*Jerusalem, calling it after the land of their fathers' nativity; and it was away joining the borders of Mormon.

2 Now the Lamanites and the Amalekites and the people of *a*Amulon had built a great city, which was called Jerusalem.

3 Now the Lamanites of themselves were sufficiently hardened, but the Amalekites and the Amulonites were still harder; therefore they did cause the Lamanites that they should harden their hearts, that they should wax strong in wickedness and their abominations.

4 And it came to pass that Aaron came to the city of Jerusalem, and

26a 2 Sam. 1:26.
  TG Loyalty.
  b Alma 22:2.
27a TG Teachable.
29a Alma 21:14.

  b Alma 17:11.
30a TG Stiffneckedness.
  b Alma 26:29.
21 1a Alma 17:13 (13, 17).
  b Alma 24:1; 3 Ne. 9:7.

2a Mosiah 23:31; 24:1;
  Alma 24:1 (1, 28–30);
  25:7 (4–9).

[About 90 B.C.]

first began to preach to the Amalekites. And he began to preach to them in their [a]synagogues, for they had built synagogues after the [b]order of the Nehors; for many of the Amalekites and the Amulonites were after the order of the Nehors.

5 Therefore, as Aaron entered into one of their [a]synagogues to preach unto the people, and as he was speaking unto them, behold there arose an Amalekite and began to contend with him, saying: What is that thou hast testified? Hast thou seen an [b]angel? Why do not angels appear unto us? Behold [c]are not this people as good as thy people?

6 Thou also sayest, except we repent we shall perish. How knowest thou the thought and intent of our hearts? How knowest thou that we have cause to repent? How knowest thou that we are not a [a]righteous people? Behold, we have built [b]sanctuaries, and we do assemble ourselves together to worship [c]God. We do believe that God will save all men.

7 Now Aaron said unto him: Believest thou that the Son of God shall come to redeem mankind from their sins?

8 And the man said unto him: We do not [a]believe that thou knowest any such thing. We do not believe in these foolish traditions. We do not believe that thou knowest of things to come, neither do we believe that thy fathers and also that our fathers did know concerning the things which they spake, of that which is to come.

9 Now Aaron began to open the [a]scriptures unto them concerning the coming of Christ, and also concerning the resurrection of the dead, and that there could be [b]no redemption for mankind [c]save it were through the [d]death and sufferings of Christ, and the atonement of his blood.

10 And it came to pass as he began to expound these things unto them they were angry with him, and began to [a]mock him; and they would not hear the words which he spake.

11 Therefore, when he saw that they would not hear his words, he departed out of their synagogue, and came over to a village which was called Ani-Anti, and there he found Muloki preaching the word unto them; and also Ammah and his brethren. And they contended with many about the word.

12 And it came to pass that they saw that the people would harden their hearts, therefore they departed and came over into the land of [a]Middoni. And they did preach the word unto many, and [b]few believed on the words which they taught.

13 Nevertheless, Aaron and a certain number of his brethren were taken and cast into [a]prison, and the remainder of them fled out of the land of Middoni unto the regions round about.

14 And those who were cast into prison [a]suffered many things, and they were delivered by the hand of Lamoni and Ammon, and they were fed and clothed.

15 And they went forth again to declare the word, and thus they were delivered for the first time out of prison; and thus they had suffered.

16 And they went forth whithersoever they were led by the [a]Spirit of the Lord, preaching the word of God in every synagogue of the Amalekites, or in every assembly of the Lamanites where they could be admitted.

17 And it came to pass that the

4a D&C 66: 7.
 b Alma 1: 12 (2–15);
   14: 16; 24: 28.
5a Alma 16: 13.
 b Mosiah 27: 11 (11–15).
 c Moses 8: 21.
6a Jer. 2: 35; Mosiah
   12: 14 (9–15).
 b Alma 15: 17; 16: 13;

   23: 2; Hel. 3: 14 (9, 14).
 c Alma 1: 4.
8a Jacob 7: 2 (1–7).
9a Alma 25: 6.
 b Alma 22: 14 (13–14).
 c Mosiah 5: 8; Alma
   38: 9.
 d TG Jesus Christ,
   Death of.

10a TG Mocking.
12a Alma 23: 10.
 b Matt. 7: 14.
13a Alma 20: 2.
14a Alma 20: 29.
16a Acts 16: 6; Alma 22: 1
   (1–4).

[Between 90 and 77 B.C.]

Lord began to bless them, insomuch that they brought many to the knowledge of the truth; yea, they did ^aconvince many of their sins, and of the traditions of their fathers, which were not correct.

18 And it came to pass that Ammon and Lamoni returned from the land of Middoni to the land of ^aIshmael, which was the land of their inheritance.

19 And king Lamoni would not suffer that Ammon should serve him, or be his ^aservant.

20 But he caused that there should be ^asynagogues built in the land of Ishmael; and he caused that his people, or the people who were under his reign, should assemble themselves together.

21 And he did rejoice over them, and he did teach them many things. And he did also declare unto them that they were a people who were under him, and that they were a ^afree people, that they were free from the oppressions of the king, his father; for that his father had granted unto him that he might reign over the people who were in the land of Ishmael, and in all the land round about.

22 And he also declared unto them that they might have the ^aliberty of worshiping the Lord their God according to their desires, in whatsoever place they were in, if it were in the land which was under the reign of king Lamoni.

23 And Ammon did preach unto the people of king Lamoni; and it came to pass that he did teach them all things concerning things pertaining to righteousness. And he did exhort them daily, with all diligence; and they gave heed unto his word, and they were ^azealous for keeping the commandments of God.

CHAPTER 22

Aaron teaches Lamoni's father about the creation, the fall of Adam, and the plan of redemption through Christ— The king and all his household are converted—How the land was divided between the Nephites and the Lamanites.

Now, as Ammon was thus teaching the people of Lamoni continually, we will return to the account of Aaron and his brethren; for after he departed from the land of Middoni he was ^aled by the Spirit to the land of Nephi, even to the house of the king which was ^bover all the land ^csave it were the land of Ishmael; and he was the father of Lamoni.

2 And it came to pass that he went in unto him into the king's palace, with his brethren, and bowed himself before the king, and said unto him: Behold, O king, we are the brethren of Ammon, whom thou hast ^adelivered out of ^bprison.

3 And now, O king, if thou wilt spare our lives, we will be thy servants. And the king said unto them: Arise, for I will grant unto you your lives, and I will not suffer that ye shall be my servants; but I will insist that ye shall administer unto me; for I have been somewhat ^atroubled in mind because of the ^bgenerosity and the greatness of the words of thy brother Ammon; and I desire to know the cause why he has not come up out of Middoni with thee.

4 And Aaron said unto the king: Behold, the Spirit of the Lord has called him another way; he has gone ^ato the land of Ishmael, to teach the people of Lamoni.

5 Now the king said unto them: What is this that ye have said concerning the Spirit of the Lord?

17a Alma 62:45; D&C
  18:44.
18a Alma 17:19; 22:1
  (1, 4); 25:13.
19a Alma 17:25.
20a Alma 16:13.
21a Alma 20:24; 22:1.
22a Luke 4:8; D&C

93:19; 134:4 (1–4);
  A of F 11. TG Liberty.
23a TG Zeal, Zealous.
22 1a Gen. 24:27; Acts
  16:6; Alma 21:16
  (16–17).
  b Alma 20:8.
  c Alma 20:24; 21:21

(21–22).
2a Alma 20:26.
  b Alma 20:4.
3a Acts 2:37 (37–38).
  b Alma 20:26.
4a Alma 21:18.

[Between 90 and 77 B.C.]

Behold, this is the thing which doth trouble me.

6 And also, what is this that Ammon said—^aIf ye will repent ye shall be saved, and if ye will not repent, ye shall be cast off at the last day?

7 And Aaron answered him and said unto him: Believest thou that there is a God? And the king said: I know that the Amalekites say that there is a God, and I have granted unto them that they should build sanctuaries, that they may assemble themselves together to worship him. And if now thou sayest there is a God, behold I will ^abelieve.

8 And now when Aaron heard this, his heart began to rejoice, and he said: Behold, assuredly as thou livest, O king, there is a God.

9 And the king said: Is God that ^aGreat Spirit that brought our fathers out of the land of Jerusalem?

10 And Aaron said unto him: Yea, he is that Great Spirit, and he ^acreated all things both in heaven and in earth. Believest thou this?

11 And he said: Yea, I believe that the Great Spirit created all things, and I desire that ye should tell me concerning all these things, and I will ^abelieve thy words.

12 And it came to pass that when Aaron saw that the king would believe his words, he began from the creation of Adam, ^areading the scriptures unto the king—how God ^bcreated man after his own image, and that God gave him commandments, and that because of transgression, man had fallen.

13 And Aaron did expound unto him the scriptures from the ^acreation of Adam, laying the fall of man before him, and their carnal state and also the ^bplan of ^credemption, which was prepared ^dfrom the foundation of the world, through Christ, for all whosoever would believe on his name.

14 And since man had ^afallen he could not ^bmerit anything of himself; but the sufferings and ^cdeath of Christ ^datone for their sins, through faith and repentance, and so forth; and that he breaketh the bands of death, that the ^egrave shall have no victory, and that the sting of death should be swallowed up in the hopes of glory; and Aaron did expound all these things unto the king.

15 And it came to pass that after Aaron had expounded these things unto him, the king said: ^aWhat shall I do that I may have this eternal life of which thou hast spoken? Yea, what shall I do that I may be ^bborn of God, having this wicked spirit ^crooted out of my breast, and receive his Spirit, that I may be filled with joy, that I may not be cast off at the last day? Behold, said he, I will give up ^dall that I possess, yea, I will forsake my kingdom, that I may receive this great joy.

16 But Aaron said unto him: If thou desirest this thing, if thou wilt ^abow down before God, yea, if thou wilt repent of all thy sins, and will bow down before God, and call on his name in faith, believing that ye shall receive, then shalt thou receive the ^bhope which thou desirest.

17 And it came to pass that when Aaron had said these words, the king did ^abow down before the Lord, upon his knees; yea, even he did

6a Alma 20: 17 (17–18).
7a D&C 46: 14 (13–14).
9a Alma 18: 2, 26 (18–28).
10a TG Creation.
11a TG Believe.
12a 1 Ne. 5: 18 (10–18);
    Alma 18: 36; 37: 9.
   b TG Man, Physical
    Creation of.
13a Gen. 1: 26 (26–28);
    2: 7.
   b TG Salvation, Plan of.

c TG Redemption.
d 2 Ne. 9: 18; Alma
    13: 3 (3, 5, 7–9).
14a TG Fall of Man.
   b Eph. 2: 8 (8–9);
    Alma 42: 14 (10–25).
   c TG Jesus Christ,
    Death of.
   d 2 Ne. 2: 10; Alma
    33: 22; 34: 9 (8–16).
   e Isa. 25: 8; 1 Cor. 15: 55

(34–57).
15a Acts 2: 37.
   b Alma 5: 14 (14, 49);
    36: 23 (23, 26).
   c Rom. 7: 18.
   d Matt. 13: 46 (44–46);
    19: 21 (16–22).
16a TG Conversion.
   b Ether 12: 4.
17a D&C 5: 24.

prostrate himself upon the earth, and cried *b*mightily, saying:

18 O God, Aaron hath told me that there is a God; and if there is a God, and if thou art God, wilt thou make thyself known unto me, and I will give away all my sins to know thee, and that I may be raised from the dead, and be saved at the last day. And now when the king had said these words, he was struck *a*as if he were dead.

19 And it came to pass that his servants ran and told the queen all that had happened unto the king. And she came in unto the king; and when she saw him lay as if he were dead, and also Aaron and his brethren standing as though they had been the cause of his fall, she was angry with them, and commanded that her servants, or the servants of the king, should take them and slay them.

20 Now the servants had seen the cause of the king's fall, therefore they durst not lay their hands on Aaron and his brethren; and they pled with the queen saying: Why commandest thou that we should slay these men, when behold one of them is *a*mightier than us all? Therefore we shall fall before them.

21 Now when the queen saw the fear of the servants she also began to fear exceedingly, lest there should some evil come upon her. And she commanded her servants that they should go and call the people, that they might slay Aaron and his brethren.

22 Now when Aaron saw the determination of the queen, he, also knowing the hardness of the hearts of the people, feared lest that a multitude should assemble themselves together, and there should be a great contention and a disturbance among them; therefore he put forth

his *a*hand and raised the king from the earth, and said unto him: Stand. And he stood upon his feet, receiving his strength.

23 Now this was done in the presence of the queen and many of the servants. And when they saw it they greatly marveled, and began to fear. And the king stood forth, and began to *a*minister unto them. And he did minister unto them, insomuch that his *b*whole household were *c*converted unto the Lord.

24 Now there was a multitude gathered together because of the commandment of the queen, and there began to be great murmurings among them because of Aaron and his brethren.

25 But the king stood forth among them and administered unto them. And they were *a*pacified towards Aaron and those who were with him.

26 And it came to pass that when the king saw that the people were pacified, he caused that Aaron and his brethren should stand forth in the midst of the multitude, and that they should preach the word unto them.

27 And it came to pass that the king sent a *a*proclamation throughout all the land, amongst all his people who were in all his land, who were in all the regions round about, which was bordering even to the sea, on the east and on the *b*west, and which was divided from the land of *c*Zarahemla by a narrow strip of wilderness, which ran from the sea east even to the sea west, and round about on the borders of the seashore, and the borders of the wilderness which was on the north by the land of Zarahemla, through the borders of *d*Manti, by the head of the *e*river Sidon, running from the east towards the west—and thus were the Lamanites and the Nephites divided.

17b TG Prayer.
18a Alma 18:42 (42–43).
20a Alma 18:3 (1–3).
22a Alma 19:29.
23a TG Minister; Ministration; Ministry.

b Alma 23:3.
c TG Conversion.
25a TG Peace; Peacemakers.
27a Alma 23:1 (1–4).
b Hel. 3:8; 11:20.

c Omni 1:13.
d Alma 17:1; 56:14.
e Alma 16:6 (6–7); 43:22 (22–53).

[Between 90 and 77 B.C.]

28 Now, the more [a]idle part of the Lamanites lived in the wilderness, and dwelt in tents; and they were spread through the wilderness on the west, in the land of Nephi; yea, and also on the west of the land of Zarahemla, in the borders by the seashore, and on the west in the land of Nephi, in the place of their fathers' first inheritance, and thus bordering along by the seashore.

29 And also there were many Lamanites on the east by the seashore, whither the Nephites had driven them. And thus the Nephites were nearly surrounded by the Lamanites; nevertheless the Nephites had taken possession of all the northern parts of the land bordering on the wilderness, at the head of the river Sidon, from the east to the west, round about on the wilderness side; on the north, even until they came to the land which they called [a]Bountiful.

30 And it bordered upon the land which they called [a]Desolation, it being so far northward that it came into the land which had been peopled and been destroyed, of whose [b]bones we have spoken, which was discovered by the [c]people of Zarahemla, it being the place of their [d]first landing.

31 And they came from there [a]up into the south wilderness. Thus the [b]land on the northward was called [c]Desolation, and the land on the southward was called Bountiful, it being the wilderness which is filled with all manner of wild animals of every kind, a part of which had come from the land northward for food.

32 And now, it was only the [a]distance of a day and a half's journey for a Nephite, on the line Bountiful and the land Desolation, from the east to the west sea; and thus the land of Nephi and the land of Zarahemla were nearly surrounded by water, there being a small [b]neck of land between the land northward and the land southward.

33 And it came to pass that the Nephites had inhabited the land Bountiful, even from the east unto the west sea, and thus the Nephites in their wisdom, with their guards and their armies, had hemmed in the Lamanites on the south, that thereby they should have no more possession on the north, that they might not overrun the land northward.

34 Therefore the Lamanites could have no more possessions only in the land of Nephi, and the wilderness round about. Now this was wisdom in the Nephites—as the Lamanites were an enemy to them, they would not suffer their afflictions on every hand, and also that they might have a country whither they might flee, according to their desires.

35 And now I, after having said this, return again to the account of Ammon and Aaron, Omner and Himni, and their brethren.

CHAPTER 23

Religious freedom is proclaimed— The Lamanites in seven lands and cities are converted—They call themselves Anti-Nephi-Lehies and are freed from the curse—The Amalekites and the Amulonites reject the truth.

BEHOLD, now it came to pass that the king of the Lamanites sent a [a]proclamation among all his people, that they should not lay their hands on Ammon, or Aaron, or Omner, or Himni, nor either of their brethren who should go forth preaching the word of God, in whatsoever place

---

28a 2 Ne. 5: 24 (22–25).
29a Alma 52: 9, 17, 27;
　　63: 5.
30a Alma 46: 17; 50: 34;
　　Morm. 3: 5 (5, 7);
　　4: 3 (1–3).

b Mosiah 8: 8 (7–12);
　28: 17 (11–19).
c Omni 1: 21 (20–22).
d Ether 6: 12; 7: 6.
31a Hel. 6: 10.
　b Alma 46: 17; 63: 4.

c Hel. 3: 6 (5–6).
32a Hel. 4: 7.
　b Alma 50: 34; 52: 9.
23 1a Alma 22: 27.

[Between 90 and 77 B.C.]

they should be, in any part of their land.

2 Yea, he sent a decree among them, that they should not lay their hands on them to bind them, or to cast them into prison; neither should they spit upon them, nor smite them, nor cast them out of their [a]synagogues, nor scourge them; neither should they cast stones at them, but that they should have free access to their houses, and also their temples, and their [b]sanctuaries.

3 And thus they might go forth and preach the word according to their desires, for the king had been converted unto the Lord, and [a]all his [b]household; therefore he sent his proclamation throughout the land unto his people, that the word of God might have no obstruction, but that it might go forth throughout all the land, that his people might be convinced concerning the wicked [c]traditions of their fathers, and that they might be convinced that they were all brethren, and that they ought not to murder, nor to plunder, nor to steal, nor to commit adultery, nor to commit any manner of wickedness.

4 And now it came to pass that when the king had sent forth this proclamation, that Aaron and his brethren went forth from [a]city to city, and from one house of worship to another, establishing churches, and consecrating [b]priests and teachers throughout the land among the Lamanites, to preach and to teach the word of God among them; and thus they began to have great success.

5 And [a]thousands were brought to the knowledge of the Lord, yea, thousands were brought to believe in the [b]traditions of the Nephites; and they were taught the [c]records and prophecies which were handed down even to the present time.

6 And as sure as the Lord liveth, so sure as many as believed, or as many as were brought to the knowledge of the truth, through the preaching of Ammon and his brethren, according to the spirit of revelation and of prophecy, and the power of God working [a]miracles in them—yea, I say unto you, as the Lord liveth, as many of the Lamanites as believed in their preaching, and were [b]converted unto the Lord, [c]never did fall away.

7 For they became a righteous people; they did lay down the weapons of their rebellion, that they did not fight against God any more, neither against any of their brethren.

8 Now, these are [a]they who were converted unto the Lord:

9 The people of the Lamanites who were in the land of Ishmael;

10 And also of the people of the Lamanites who were in the land of [a]Middoni;

11 And also of the people of the Lamanites who were in the city of Nephi;

12 And also of the people of the Lamanites who were in the land of [a]Shilom, and who were in the land of Shemlon, and in the city of Lemuel, and in the city of Shimnilom.

13 And these are the names of the cities of the Lamanites which were [a]converted unto the Lord; and these are they that laid down the weapons of their rebellion, yea, all their weapons of war; and they were all Lamanites.

14 And the Amalekites were not

2a Alma 21: 20 (4–6, 20);
    26: 29.
 b Hel. 3: 14 (9, 14).
3a Alma 22: 23.
 b Gen. 18: 19.
 c Alma 26: 24.
4a Luke 8: 1; D&C 66: 5;
    75: 18.
 b Alma 30: 31.
5a Alma 26: 4.
 b Alma 37: 19.
 c Alma 63: 12.
    TG Scriptures, Value of.
6a Ex. 8: 19; 1 Ne. 19: 22;
    D&C 84: 3; 121: 12.
 b TG Commitment;
    Conversion.
 c Alma 27: 27.
8a Alma 26: 3, 31.
10a Alma 20: 2; 21: 12
    (12–13, 18).
12a Mosiah 22: 11 (8, 11).
13a Alma 53: 10.

[Between 90 and 77 B.C.]

[a]converted, save only one; neither were any of the [b]Amulonites; but they did harden their hearts, and also the hearts of the Lamanites in that part of the land wheresoever they dwelt, yea, and all their villages and all their cities.

15 Therefore, we have named all the cities of the Lamanites in which they did repent and come to the knowledge of the truth, and were converted.

16 And now it came to pass that the king and those who were converted were desirous that they might have a name, that thereby they might be distinguished from their brethren; therefore the king consulted with Aaron and many of their priests, concerning the name that they should take upon them, that they might be distinguished.

17 And it came to pass that they called their names [a]Anti-Nephi-Lehies; and they were called by this name and were no more called [b]Lamanites.

18 And they began to be a very [a]industrious people; yea, and they were friendly with the Nephites; therefore, they did [b]open a correspondence with them, and the [c]curse of God did no more follow them.

CHAPTER 24

The Lamanites come against the people of God—The Anti-Nephi-Lehies rejoice in Christ and are visited by angels—They choose to suffer death rather than to defend themselves—More Lamanites are converted.

AND it came to pass that the Amalekites and the Amulonites and the Lamanites who were in the land of [a]Amulon, and also in the land of [b]Helam, and who were in the land of [c]Jerusalem, and in fine, in all the land round about, who had not been converted and had not taken upon them the name of [d]Anti-Nephi-Lehi, were stirred up by the Amalekites and by the Amulonites to anger against their brethren.

2 And their hatred became exceedingly sore against them, even insomuch that they began to rebel against their king, insomuch that they would not that he should be their king; therefore, they took up arms against the people of Anti-Nephi-Lehi.

3 Now the king conferred the kingdom upon his son, and he called his name Anti-Nephi-Lehi.

4 And the king died in that self-same year that the Lamanites began to make preparations for war against the people of God.

5 Now when Ammon and his brethren and all those who had come up with him saw the preparations of the Lamanites to destroy their brethren, they came forth to the land of Midian, and there Ammon met all his brethren; and from thence they came to the land of Ishmael that they might hold a [a]council with Lamoni and also with his brother Anti-Nephi-Lehi, what they should do to defend themselves against the Lamanites.

6 Now there was not one soul among all the people who had been converted unto the Lord that would take up arms against their brethren; nay, they would not even make any preparations for war; yea, and also their king commanded them that they should not.

7 Now, these are the words which he said unto the people concerning the matter: I thank my God, my beloved people, that our great God has in goodness sent these our brethren, the Nephites, unto us to

---

14a Alma 24:29.
 b Mosiah 23:31 (31–39).
17a Alma 24:1 (1–3, 5, 20).
 b Jacob 1:13.
18a TG Industry.
 b Alma 24:8.

c 1 Ne. 2:23; 2 Ne. 30:6 (5–6); 3 Ne. 2:15 (14–16).
24 1a Alma 21:3 (2–4); 25:7 (4–9).
 b Mosiah 23:19; 27:16.

c Alma 21:1.
 d Alma 23:17; 25:13 (1, 13).
5a Alma 27:4.

[Between 90 and 77 B.C.]

preach unto us, and to convince us of the ᵃtraditions of our wicked fathers.

8 And behold, I thank my great God that he has given us a portion of his Spirit to soften our hearts, that we have ᵃopened a correspondence with these brethren, the Nephites.

9 And behold, I also thank my God, that by opening this correspondence we have been convinced of our ᵃsins, and of the many murders which we have committed.

10 And I also thank my God, yea, my great God, that he hath granted unto us that we might repent of these things, and also that he hath ᵃforgiven us of those our many sins and murders which we have committed, and taken away the ᵇguilt from our hearts, through the merits of his Son.

11 And now behold, my brethren, since it has been all that we could do, (as we were the most lost of all mankind) to repent of all our sins and the many murders which we have committed, and to get God to ᵃtake them away from our hearts, for it was all we could do to repent sufficiently before God that he would take away our stain—

12 Now, my best beloved brethren, since God hath taken away our stains, and our swords have become bright, then let us stain our swords no more with the blood of our brethren.

13 Behold, I say unto you, Nay, let us retain our swords that they be not stained with the blood of our brethren; for perhaps, if we should stain our swords ᵃagain they can no more be ᵇwashed bright through the blood of the Son of our great God, which shall be shed for the atonement of our sins.

14 And the great God has had mercy on us, and made these things

known unto us that we might not perish; yea, and he has made these things known unto us beforehand, because he loveth our ᵃsouls as well as he loveth our children; therefore, in his mercy he doth visit us by his angels, that the ᵇplan of salvation might be made known unto us as well as unto future generations.

15 Oh, how merciful is our God! And now behold, since it has been as much as we could do to get our stains taken away from us, and our swords are made bright, let us ᵃhide them away that they may be kept bright, as a testimony to our God at the last day, or at the day that we shall be brought to stand before him to be judged, that we have not stained our swords in the blood of our brethren since he imparted his word unto us and has made us ᵇclean thereby.

16 And now, my brethren, if our brethren seek to destroy us, behold, we will hide away our swords, yea, even we will bury them deep in the earth, that they may be kept bright, as a testimony that we have never used them, at the last day; and if our brethren destroy us, behold, we shall ᵃgo to our God and shall be saved.

17 And now it came to pass that when the king had made an end of these sayings, and all the people were assembled together, they took their swords, and all the weapons which were used for the shedding of man's blood, and they did ᵃbury them up deep in the earth.

18 And this they did, it being in their view a testimony to God, and also to men, that they ᵃnever would use weapons again for the shedding of man's blood; and this they did, vouching and ᵇcovenanting with God, that rather than shed the

---

7a Mosiah 1:5.
8a Alma 23:18.
9a Micah 3:8; Hel.
   13:26; D&C 18:44.
10a Dan. 9:9.
   b TG Guilt.
11a Isa. 53:6 (4–6).

13a D&C 42:26.
   b Rev. 1:5.
14a TG Worth of Souls.
   b TG Jesus Christ,
      Prophecies about;
      Salvation, Plan of.
15a Alma 25:14; 26:32.

   b TG Purification.
16a Alma 40:11 (11–
   15).
17a Hel. 15:9.
18a Alma 53:11.
   b TG Covenants.

[Between 90 and 77 B.C.]

blood of their brethren they would *give up their own lives; and rather than take away from a brother they would give unto him; and rather than spend their days in idleness they would labor abundantly with their hands.

19 And thus we see that, when these Lamanites were brought to *believe and to know the truth, they were *firm, and would suffer even unto death rather than commit sin; and thus we see that they buried their weapons of peace, or they buried the weapons of war, for peace.

20 And it came to pass that their brethren, the Lamanites, made preparations for war, and came up to the land of Nephi for the purpose of destroying the king, and to place *another in his stead, and also of destroying the people of Anti-Nephi-Lehi out of the land.

21 Now when the people saw that they were coming against them they went out to meet them, and *prostrated themselves before them to the earth, and began to call on the name of the Lord; and thus they were in this attitude when the Lamanites began to fall upon them, and began to slay them with the sword.

22 And thus without meeting any resistance, they did slay a *thousand and five of them; and we know that they are blessed, for they have gone to dwell with their God.

23 Now when the Lamanites saw that their brethren would not flee from the sword, neither would they turn aside to the right hand or to the left, but that they would lie down and *perish, and *praised God even in the very act of perishing under the sword—

24 Now when the Lamanites saw

this they did *forbear from slaying them; and there were many whose hearts had *swollen in them for those of their brethren who had fallen under the sword, for they repented of the things which they had done.

25 And it came to pass that they threw down their weapons of war, and they would not take them again, for they were stung for the murders which they had committed; and they came down even as their brethren, relying upon the mercies of those whose arms were lifted to slay them.

26 And it came to pass that the people of God were joined that day by more than the number who had been slain; and those who had been slain were righteous people, therefore we have no reason to doubt but what they were *saved.

27 And there was not a wicked man slain among them; but there were more than a thousand brought to the knowledge of the truth; thus we see that the Lord worketh in many *ways to the salvation of his people.

28 Now the greatest number of those of the Lamanites who slew so many of their brethren were Amalekites and Amulonites, the greatest number of whom were after the *order of the *Nehors.

29 Now, among those who joined the people of the Lord, there were *none who were Amalekites or Amulonites, or who were of the order of Nehor, but they were actual descendants of Laman and Lemuel.

30 And thus we can plainly discern, that after a people have been once *enlightened by the *Spirit of God, and have had great *knowledge of things pertaining to righteousness, and then have *fallen away into

---

18c TG Self-sacrifice.
19a TG Faith.
  b TG Integrity.
20a Isa. 7:6.
21a Alma 27:3.
22a Alma 26:34.
23a Alma 26:32.
  b Mosiah 16:7.
24a Alma 25:1.
  b TG Compassion;

Repentance.
26a Isa. 57:1; Rev. 14:13.
27a 2 Kgs. 5:15; Isa.
  55:8 (8–9); Alma 37:7
  (6–7).
28a Alma 21:4.
  b Alma 1:15; 2:1 (1, 20);
  16:11.
29a Alma 23:14.
30a Matt. 12:45.

  b TG God, Spirit of.
  c Heb. 10:26 (26–27);
  Alma 47:36.
  d 2 Ne. 31:14; Alma
  9:19; 31:8; D&C
  93:19. TG Apostasy
  of Individuals; Holy
  Ghost, Loss of.

[Between 90 and 77 B.C.]

sin and transgression, they become more *e*hardened, and thus their state becomes *f*worse than though they had never known these things.

CHAPTER 25

Lamanite aggressions spread—The seed of the priests of Noah perish as Abinadi prophesied—Many Lamanites are converted and join the people of Anti-Nephi-Lehi—They believe in Christ and keep the law of Moses.

AND behold, now it came to pass that those Lamanites were more angry because they had slain their brethren; therefore they swore vengeance upon the Nephites; and they did *a*no more attempt to slay the people of *b*Anti-Nephi-Lehi at that time.

2 But they took their armies and went over into the borders of the land of Zarahemla, and fell upon the people who were in the land of Ammonihah and *a*destroyed them.

3 And after that, they had *a*many battles with the Nephites, in the which they were driven and slain.

4 And among the Lamanites who were slain were almost all the *a*seed of Amulon and his brethren, who were the priests of Noah, and they were slain by the hands of the Nephites;

5 And the remainder, having fled into the east wilderness, and having usurped the power and *a*authority over the Lamanites, caused that many of the Lamanites should *b*perish by fire because of their belief—

6 For many of *a*them, after having suffered much loss and so many afflictions, began to be stirred up in remembrance of the *b*words which Aaron and his brethren had preached to them in their land; therefore they began to disbelieve the *c*traditions of their fathers, and to believe in the Lord, and that he gave great power unto the Nephites; and thus there were many of them converted in the wilderness.

7 And it came to pass that those rulers who were the remnant of the children of *a*Amulon caused that they should be put to *b*death, yea, all those that believed in these things.

8 Now this martyrdom caused that many of their brethren should be stirred up to anger; and there began to be contention in the wilderness; and the Lamanites began to *a*hunt the seed of Amulon and his brethren and began to slay them; and they fled into the east wilderness.

9 And behold they are hunted at this day by the Lamanites. Thus the words of Abinadi were brought to pass, which he said concerning the seed of the priests who caused that he should suffer death by fire.

10 For he said unto them: What ye shall *a*do unto me shall be a type of things to come.

11 And now Abinadi was the first that suffered *a*death by fire because of his belief in God; now this is what he meant, that many should suffer death by fire, according as he had suffered.

12 And he said unto the priests of Noah that their seed should cause many to be put to death, in the like manner as he was, and that they should be scattered abroad and slain, even as a sheep having no shepherd is driven and slain by wild beasts; and now behold, these words were verified, for they were driven by the Lamanites, and they were hunted, and they were smitten.

13 And it came to pass that when

30*e* TG Hardheartedness.
  f 2 Chr. 33:9; Ezek.
    5:6; 2 Pet. 2:20
    (20–21).
25 1*a* Alma 24:24 (20–25).
  b Alma 27:2.
2*a* Alma 8:16; 16:9.

3*a* Alma 27:1.
4*a* Mosiah 23:35.
5*a* TG Authority.
  b Mosiah 17:15.
6*a* IE the Lamanites.
  b Alma 21:9 (5–12).
  c Alma 26:24.

7*a* Alma 21:3 (2–4);
    24:1 (1, 28–30).
  b TG Martyrdom.
8*a* Mosiah 17:18.
10*a* Mosiah 13:10.
11*a* Mosiah 17:13 (13–20).

[Between 90 and 77 B.C.]

the Lamanites saw that they could not overpower the Nephites they returned again to their own land; and many of them came over to dwell in the land of *a*Ishmael and the land of Nephi, and did join themselves to the people of God, who were the people of *b*Anti-Nephi-Lehi.

14 And they did also *a*bury their weapons of war, according as their brethren had, and they began to be a righteous people; and they did walk in the ways of the Lord, and did observe to keep his commandments and his statutes.

15 Yea, and they did keep the law of Moses; for it was expedient that they should keep the law of Moses as yet, for it was not all fulfilled. But notwithstanding the *a*law of Moses, they did look forward to the coming of Christ, considering that the law of Moses was a *b*type of his coming, and believing that they must keep those *c*outward *d*performances until the time that he should be revealed unto them.

16 Now they did not suppose that *a*salvation came by the *b*law of Moses; but the law of Moses did serve to strengthen their faith in Christ; and thus they did retain a *c*hope through faith, unto eternal salvation, relying upon the spirit of prophecy, which spake of those things to come.

17 And now behold, Ammon, and Aaron, and Omner, and Himni, and their brethren did rejoice exceedingly, for the success which they had had among the Lamanites, seeing that the Lord had granted unto them according to their *a*prayers, and that he had also verified his word unto them in every particular.

CHAPTER 26

Ammon glories in the Lord—The faithful are strengthened by the Lord and are given knowledge—By faith men may bring thousands of souls unto repentance—God has all power and comprehendeth all things.

AND now, these are the words of Ammon to his brethren, which say thus: My brothers and my brethren, behold I say unto you, how great reason have we to rejoice; for could we have supposed when we *a*started from the land of Zarahemla that God would have granted unto us such great blessings?

2 And now, I ask, what great blessings has he bestowed upon us? Can ye tell?

3 Behold, I answer for you; for our brethren, the Lamanites, were in darkness, yea, even in the darkest abyss, but behold, how *a*many of them are brought to behold the marvelous light of God! And this is the blessing which hath been bestowed upon us, that we have been made *b*instruments in the hands of God to bring about this great work.

4 Behold, *a*thousands of them do rejoice, and have been brought into the fold of God.

5 Behold, the *a*field was ripe, and blessed are ye, for ye did thrust in the *b*sickle, and did reap with your might, yea, all the day long did ye labor; and behold the number of your *c*sheaves! And they shall be

13*a* Alma 22: 1 (1, 4).
  b Alma 24: 1 (1–3, 5, 20); 27: 21 (2, 21, 25).
14*a* Alma 24: 15; 26: 32.
15*a* Jacob 4: 5; Jarom 1: 11.
  b Mosiah 16: 14.
    TG Jesus Christ, Types of, in Anticipation.
  c Josh. 1: 8; Mosiah 3: 14 (14–15); 13: 29

    (29–32); D&C 41: 5 (4–5).
  d TG Ordinance.
16*a* Mosiah 3: 15; 12: 31; 13: 28 (27–33).
  b 2 Ne. 11: 4; Jacob 4: 5; Jarom 1: 11; Ether 12: 19 (18–19).
  c Alma 33: 22 (19–23); 37: 46 (45–46).
17*a* Alma 17: 9 (7–11).

26 1*a* Mosiah 28: 9; Alma 17: 6 (6–11).
  3*a* Alma 23: 8 (8–13).
  b 2 Cor. 4: 5; Mosiah 23: 10.
  4*a* Alma 23: 5; 26: 31.
  5*a* John 4: 35; D&C 4: 4.
  b Joel 3: 13.
  c D&C 33: 9; 75: 5.
    TG Reward.

[Between 90 and 77 B.C.]

gathered into the garners, that they are not wasted.

6 Yea, they shall not be beaten down by the storm at the last day; yea, neither shall they be harrowed up by the whirlwinds; but when the [a]storm cometh they shall be gathered together in their place, that the storm cannot penetrate to them; yea, neither shall they be driven with fierce winds whithersoever the enemy listeth to carry them.

7 But behold, they are in the hands of the Lord of the [a]harvest, and they are his; and he will [b]raise them up at the last day.

8 [a]Blessed be the name of our God; let us [b]sing to his praise, yea, let us give [c]thanks to his holy name, for he doth work righteousness forever.

9 For if we had not come up out of the land of Zarahemla, these our dearly beloved brethren, who have so dearly beloved us, would still have been racked with [a]hatred against us, yea, and they would also have been [b]strangers to God.

10 And it came to pass that when Ammon had said these words, his brother Aaron rebuked him, saying: Ammon, I fear that thy joy doth carry thee away unto boasting.

11 But Ammon said unto him: I do not [a]boast in my own strength, nor in my own wisdom; but behold, my [b]joy is full, yea, my heart is brim with [c]joy, and I will rejoice in my God.

12 Yea, I know that I am [a]nothing; as to my strength I am weak; therefore I will [b]not boast of myself, but I will [c]boast of my God, for in his

[d]strength I can do all [e]things; yea, behold, many mighty miracles we have wrought in this land, for which we will praise his name forever.

13 Behold, how many thousands of our brethren has he loosed from the pains of [a]hell; and they are brought to [b]sing redeeming love, and this because of the power of his word which is in us, therefore have we not great reason to rejoice?

14 Yea, we have reason to praise him forever, for he is the Most High God, and has loosed our brethren from the [a]chains of hell.

15 Yea, they were encircled about with everlasting [a]darkness and destruction; but behold, he has brought them into his everlasting [b]light, yea, into everlasting salvation; and they are encircled about with the matchless bounty of his love; yea, and we have been instruments in his hands of doing this great and marvelous work.

16 Therefore, let us [a]glory, yea, we will [b]glory in the Lord; yea, we will rejoice, for our joy is full; yea, we will praise our God forever. Behold, who can glory too much in the Lord? Yea, who can say too much of his great power, and of his [c]mercy, and of his long-suffering towards the children of men? Behold, I say unto you, I cannot say the smallest part which I feel.

17 Who could have supposed that our God would have been so merciful as to have snatched us from our awful, sinful, and [a]polluted state?

18 Behold, we went forth even in

6a Hel. 5:12; 3 Ne. 14:25 (25, 27).
7a TG Harvest.
  b Mosiah 23:22; Alma 36:28.
8a Ps. 41:13.
  b Ps. 57:7 (7–11); 108:1 (1–5); 2 Ne. 22:5 (5–6).
  c TG Thanksgiving.
9a Mosiah 28:2.
  b TG Stranger.
11a 2 Cor. 7:14 (13–16).
  b 1 Thes. 3:9; D&C

  18:16 (14–16).
  c TG Joy.
12a TG Poor in Spirit.
  b Alma 29:9.
  c Jer. 9:24; Rom. 15:17.
  d Isa. 45:24; Philip. 4:13 (12–13); 1 Ne. 17:3.
  e Ps. 18:32 (32–40); 1 Ne. 7:12.
13a TG Hell.
  b Alma 5:26.

14a Alma 12:11.
15a Prov. 20:20.
  b TG Light.
16a Rom. 15:17; 1 Cor. 1:31.
  b Ps. 44:8 (4–8); 2 Cor. 10:17 (15–18); D&C 76:61.
  c Ps. 36:5 (5–6); Morm. 6:22; D&C 97:6.
17a Pollution.

[Between 90 and 77 B.C.]

wrath, with mighty threatenings to [a]destroy his church.

19 Oh then, why did he not consign us to an awful destruction, yea, why did he not let the sword of his justice fall upon us, and doom us to eternal [a]despair?

20 Oh, my soul, almost as it were, fleeth at the thought. Behold, he did not exercise his justice upon us, but in his great mercy hath brought us over that everlasting [a]gulf of death and misery, even to the salvation of our souls.

21 And now behold, my brethren, what [a]natural man is there that knoweth these things? I say unto you, there is [b]none that [c]knoweth these things, save it be the penitent.

22 Yea, he that [a]repenteth and exerciseth faith, and bringeth forth good [b]works, and prayeth continually without ceasing—unto such it is given to know the [c]mysteries of God; yea, unto such it shall be [d]given to [e]reveal things which never have been revealed; yea, and it shall be given unto such to bring thousands of souls to repentance, even as it has been given unto us to bring these our brethren to repentance.

23 Now do ye remember, my brethren, that we said unto our brethren in the land of Zarahemla, we go up to the land of Nephi, to preach unto our brethren, the Lamanites, and they [a]laughed us to scorn?

24 For they said unto us: Do ye suppose that ye can bring the Lamanites to the knowledge of the truth? Do ye suppose that ye can convince the Lamanites of the [a]incorrectness of the [b]traditions of their fathers, as [c]stiffnecked a people as they are; whose hearts delight in the [d]shedding of blood; whose days have been spent in the grossest iniquity; whose ways have been the ways of a transgressor from the beginning? Now my brethren, ye remember that this was their language.

25 And moreover they did say: Let us take up arms against them, that we destroy them and their iniquity out of the land, lest they overrun us and destroy us.

26 But behold, my beloved brethren, we came into the wilderness not with the intent to destroy our brethren, but with the intent that perhaps we might save some few of their souls.

27 Now when our hearts were depressed, and we were about to [a]turn back, behold, the Lord [b]comforted us, and said: Go amongst thy brethren, the Lamanites, and bear with [c]patience thine [d]afflictions, and I will give unto you success.

28 And now behold, we have come, and been forth amongst them; and we have been patient in our sufferings, and we have suffered every privation; yea, we have traveled from house to house, relying upon the mercies of the world—not upon the mercies of the world alone but upon the mercies of God.

29 And we have entered into their houses and taught them, and we have taught them in their streets; yea, and we have taught them upon their hills; and we have also entered into their temples and their [a]synagogues and taught them; and we have been cast out, and mocked, and spit upon, and smote upon our

18a Mosiah 27: 10;
    28: 4 (3–4); Alma 36: 6
    (6–11).
19a TG Despair.
20a 2 Ne. 1: 13; Hel. 3: 29.
21a TG Man, Natural,
    Not Spiritually Reborn.
  b Alma 36: 5.
  c 1 Cor. 2: 11 (9–16);
    Jacob 4: 8 (8–10, 13).
22a TG Repentance.
  b TG Good Works.

  c Luke 8: 10; Alma
    12: 9. TG Mysteries of
    Godliness.
  d Dan. 2: 22 (19–22, 28).
  e Jarom 1: 4; Hel.
    11: 23; D&C 107: 19
    (18–19).
23a 2 Chr. 30: 10; Neh.
    2: 19; Luke 8: 53.
    TG Laughter.
24a Mosiah 1: 5; 28: 2.
  b Alma 23: 3; 25: 6.

  c TG Stiffneckedness.
  d Jacob 7: 24; Jarom
    1: 6.
27a Hel. 13: 2 (2–3).
  b Alma 17: 10.
  c Alma 17: 11.
    TG Patience.
  d Alma 7: 5.
    TG Affliction.
29a Alma 23: 2 (2, 4).

[Between 90 and 77 B.C.]

cheeks; and we have been [b]stoned, and taken and bound with [c]strong cords, and cast into prison; and through the power and wisdom of God we have been delivered again.

30 And we have suffered all manner of afflictions, and all this, that perhaps we might be the means of saving some soul; and we supposed that our [a]joy would be full if perhaps we could be the means of saving some.

31 Now behold, we can look forth and see the [a]fruits of our labors; and are they few? I say unto you, Nay, they are [b]many; yea, and we can witness of their sincerity, because of their love towards their brethren and also towards us.

32 For behold, they had rather [a]sacrifice their lives than even to take the life of their enemy; and they have [b]buried their weapons of war deep in the earth, because of their love towards their brethren.

33 And now behold I say unto you, has there been so great love in all the land? Behold, I say unto you, Nay, there has not, even among the Nephites.

34 For behold, they would take up arms against their brethren; they would not suffer themselves to be slain. But behold how [a]many of these have laid down their lives; and we know that they have gone to their God, because of their love and of their hatred to sin.

35 Now have we not reason to rejoice? Yea, I say unto you, there never were men that had so great reason to rejoice as we, since the world began; yea, and my joy is carried away, even unto boasting in my God; for he has all [a]power, [b]all wisdom, and all understanding; he comprehendeth all things, and

he is a [c]merciful Being, even unto salvation, to those who will repent and believe on his name.

36 Now if this is [a]boasting, even so will I boast; for this is my life and my light, my joy and my salvation, and my redemption from everlasting wo. Yea, blessed is the name of my God, who has been mindful of this people, who are a [b]branch of the tree of Israel, and has been [c]lost from its body in a strange land; yea, I say, blessed be the name of my God, who has been mindful of us, [d]wanderers in a strange land.

37 Now my brethren, we see that God is [a]mindful of every [b]people, whatsoever land they may be in; yea, he numbereth his people, and his bowels of mercy are over all the earth. Now this is my joy, and my great thanksgiving; yea, and I will give thanks unto my God forever. Amen.

CHAPTER 27

The Lord commands Ammon to lead the people of Anti-Nephi-Lehi to safety—Upon meeting Alma, Ammon's joy exhausts his strength—The Nephites give them the land of Jershon—They are called the people of Ammon.

Now it came to pass that when those Lamanites who had gone to war against the Nephites had found, after their [a]many struggles to destroy them, that it was in vain to seek their destruction, they returned again to the land of Nephi.

2 And it came to pass that the Amalekites, because of their loss, were exceedingly angry. And when they saw that they could not seek revenge from the Nephites, they began to [a]stir up the people in anger

29b 2 Cor. 11 : 23 (23–29).
  c Alma 20 : 30 (29–30).
30a D&C 18 : 15 (15–16).
31a Acts 21 : 19 (19–20).
  b Alma 23 : 8 (8–13);
    26 : 4.
32a Alma 24 : 23 (20–24).
  b Alma 24 : 15 ; 25 : 14.
34a Alma 24 : 22.
35a TG God, Intelligence

of; God, Perfection of;
  God, Wisdom of.
  b D&C 88 : 41.
  c TG God, Mercy of.
36a Rom. 3 : 27.
  b Gen. 49 : 22 (22–26);
    Ezek. 17 : 22 ; Jacob
    2 : 25.
  c Jacob 5 : 25 (25,
    40–45).

d Jacob 7 : 26.
37a 2 Ne. 2 : 27 ; 26 : 24;
    Jacob 5 : 41.
  b Jonah 4 : 11 (10–11);
    Acts 10 : 35 (9–35, 44);
    2 Ne. 26 : 33.
27 1a Alma 25 : 3.
  2a Acts 13 : 50.

[Between 90 and 77 B.C.]

against their [b]brethren, the people of [c]Anti-Nephi-Lehi; therefore they began again to destroy them.

3 Now this people [a]again refused to take their arms, and they suffered themselves to be slain according to the desires of their enemies.

4 Now when Ammon and his brethren saw this work of destruction among those whom they so dearly beloved, and among those who had so dearly beloved them—for they were treated as though they were angels sent from God to save them from everlasting destruction—therefore, when Ammon and his brethren saw this great work of destruction, they were moved with compassion, and they [a]said unto the king:

5 Let us gather together this people of the Lord, and let us go down to the land of Zarahemla to our brethren the Nephites, and flee out of the hands of our enemies, that we be not destroyed.

6 But the king said unto them: Behold, the Nephites will destroy us, because of the many murders and sins we have committed against them.

7 And Ammon said: I will go and inquire of the Lord, and if he say unto us, go down unto our brethren, will ye go?

8 And the king said unto him: Yea, if the Lord saith unto us go, we will go down unto our brethren, and we will be their slaves until we repair unto them the many murders and sins which we have committed against them.

9 But Ammon said unto him: It is against the law of our brethren, which was established by my father, that there should be any [a]slaves among them; therefore let us go down and rely upon the mercies of our brethren.

10 But the king said unto him: Inquire of the Lord, and if he saith unto us go, we will go; otherwise we will perish in the land.

11 And it came to pass that Ammon went and inquired of the Lord, and the Lord said unto him:

12 Get this people [a]out of this land, that they perish not; for Satan has great hold on the hearts of the Amalekites, who do stir up the Lamanites to anger against their brethren to slay them; therefore get thee out of this land; and blessed are this people in this generation, for I will [b]preserve them.

13 And now it came to pass that Ammon went and told the king all the words which the Lord had said unto him.

14 And they gathered together all their people, yea, all the people of the Lord, and did gather together all their flocks and herds, and departed out of the land, and came into the wilderness which divided the land of Nephi from the land of Zarahemla, and came over near the borders of the land.

15 And it came to pass that Ammon said unto them: Behold, I and my brethren will go forth into the land of Zarahemla, and ye shall remain here until we return; and we will [a]try the hearts of our brethren, whether they will that ye shall come into their land.

16 And it came to pass that as Ammon was going forth into the land, that he and his brethren met Alma, over in the [a]place of which has been spoken; and behold, this was a joyful meeting.

17 Now the [a]joy of Ammon was so great even that he was full; yea, he was swallowed up in the joy of his God, even to the [b]exhausting of his strength; and he fell [c]again to the earth.

2b Alma 43:11.
  c Alma 25:1.
3a Alma 24:21 (21–26).
4a Alma 24:5 (3–5).
9a Mosiah 29:32 (32, 38, 40).
12a TG Separation.
  b TG Protection, Divine.
15a Judg. 7:4.
16a Alma 17:1 (1–4).
17a TG Joy.
  b Dan. 10:8 (8–12);
    1 Ne. 1:7.
  c Alma 19:14 (14, 17).

[Between 90 and 77 B.C.]

18 Now was not this ᵃexceeding joy? Behold, this is joy which none receiveth save it be the truly penitent and humble seeker of ᵇhappiness.

19 Now the joy of Alma in meeting his ᵃbrethren was truly great, and also the joy of Aaron, of Omner, and Himni; but behold their joy was not that to exceed their strength.

20 And now it came to pass that Alma conducted his brethren back to the land of Zarahemla; even to his ᵃown house. And they went and told the ᵇchief judge all the things that had happened unto them in the land of Nephi, among their brethren, the Lamanites.

21 And it came to pass that the chief judge sent a proclamation throughout all the land, desiring the voice of the people concerning the admitting their brethren, who were the people of ᵃAnti-Nephi-Lehi.

22 And it came to pass that the voice of the people came, saying: Behold, we will give up the ᵃland of ᵇJershon, which is on the east by the sea, which joins the land Bountiful, which is on the south of the land Bountiful; and this land Jershon is the land which we will give unto our brethren for an inheritance.

23 And behold, we will set our armies between the land Jershon and the land Nephi, that we may ᵃprotect our brethren in the land Jershon; and this we do for our brethren, on account of their fear to take up arms against their brethren lest they should commit sin; and this their great fear came because of their sore repentance which they had, on account of their many murders and their awful wickedness.

24 And now behold, this will we do

unto our brethren, that they may inherit the land Jershon; and we will guard them from their enemies with our armies, on condition that they will give us a ᵃportion of their substance to assist us that we may maintain our armies.

25 Now, it came to pass that when Ammon had heard this, he returned to the people of Anti-Nephi-Lehi, and also Alma with him, into the wilderness, where they had pitched their tents, and made known unto them all these things. And Alma also related unto them his ᵃconversion, with Ammon and Aaron, and his brethren.

26 And it came to pass that it did cause great joy among them. And they went down into the land of Jershon, and took possession of the land of Jershon; and they were called by the Nephites the ᵃpeople of Ammon; therefore they were distinguished by that name ever after.

27 And they were among the people of Nephi, and also numbered among the people who were of the church of God. And they were also distinguished for their ᵃzeal towards God, and also towards men; for they were perfectly ᵇhonest and upright in all things; and they were ᶜfirm in the faith of Christ, even unto the end.

28 And they did look upon shedding the blood of their brethren with the greatest abhorrence; and they never could be prevailed upon to take up arms against their brethren; and they never did look upon death with any degree of terror, for their hope and views of Christ and the resurrection; therefore, death was swallowed up to them by the victory of Christ over it.

29 Therefore, they would suffer

18a Alma 28: 8.
  b TG Happiness;
    Objectives.
19a TG Friendship.
20a Alma 15: 18.
  b Alma 4: 17 (16–18).
21a Alma 25: 13 (1, 13);

    43: 11.
22a Alma 43: 12.
  b Alma 28: 1 (1, 8).
23a Alma 43: 12.
24a Alma 43: 13.
25a Mosiah 27: 24 (10–25).
26a Alma 30: 1.

27a TG Zeal.
  b Prov. 19: 1; D&C
    124: 20 (15, 20).
    TG Honesty.
  c Alma 23: 6; Hel.
    15: 8 (6–10).

[Between 90 and 77 B.C.]

[a]death in the most aggravating and distressing manner which could be inflicted by their brethren, before they would take the sword or cimeter to smite them.

30 And thus they were a zealous and beloved people, a highly favored people of the Lord.

CHAPTER 28

The Lamanites are defeated in a tremendous battle—Tens of thousands are slain—The wicked are consigned to a state of endless woe; the righteous attain a never-ending happiness.

AND now it came to pass that after the people of Ammon were established in the land of [a]Jershon, and a church also established in the land of Jershon, and the armies of the Nephites were set round about the land of Jershon, yea, in all the borders round about the land of Zarahemla; behold the armies of the Lamanites had followed their brethren into the wilderness.

2 And thus there was a tremendous battle; yea, even such an one as never had been known among all the people in the land from the time Lehi left Jerusalem; yea, and tens of thousands of the Lamanites were slain and scattered abroad.

3 Yea, and also there was a tremendous slaughter among the people of Nephi; nevertheless, the Lamanites were [a]driven and scattered, and the people of Nephi returned again to their land.

4 And now this was a time that there was a great [a]mourning and lamentation heard throughout all the land, among all the people of Nephi—

5 Yea, the cry of [a]widows mourning for their husbands, and also of fathers mourning for their sons, and the daughter for the brother, yea, the brother for the father; and thus the cry of mourning was heard among all of them, mourning for their kindred who had been slain.

6 And now surely this was a sorrowful day; yea, a time of solemnity, and a time of much [a]fasting and prayer.

7 And thus endeth the fifteenth year of the reign of the judges over the people of Nephi;

8 And [a]this is the account of Ammon and his brethren, their journeyings in the land of Nephi, their sufferings in the land, their sorrows, and their afflictions, and their [b]incomprehensible joy, and the reception and safety of the brethren in the land of Jershon. And now may the Lord, the Redeemer of all men, bless their souls forever.

9 And this is the account of the wars and contentions among the Nephites, and also the wars between the Nephites and the Lamanites; *and the fifteenth year of the reign of the judges is ended.

10 And from the [a]first year to the fifteenth has brought to pass destruction of many thousand lives; yea, it has brought to pass an awful scene of bloodshed.

11 And the bodies of many thousands are laid low in the earth, while the bodies of many thousands are [a]moldering in heaps upon the face of the earth; yea, and many thousands are [b]mourning for the loss of their kindred, because they have reason to fear, according to the promises of the Lord, that they are consigned to a state of endless wo.

12 While many thousands of others truly [a]mourn for the loss of their kindred, yet they rejoice and exult in the hope, and even know, according to the [b]promises of the Lord, that

---

29a Alma 24: 23 (20–23).
28 1a Alma 27: 22; 30: 19 (1, 19).
3a Alma 30: 1.
4a TG Mourning.
5a TG Widows.
6a Matt. 5: 4; Alma

30: 2; 3 Ne. 12: 4.
8a IE the account covered in Alma, chapters 17–28.
b Alma 27: 18 (16–19).
10a IE the years recounted in Alma, chapters 1–28.

11a Alma 16: 11.
b Alma 48: 23; D&C 42: 45.
12a Gen. 50: 10.
b Alma 11: 41.

[*76 B.C.]

they are raised to dwell at the right hand of God, in a state of never-ending [c]happiness.

13 And thus we see how great the [a]inequality of man is because of sin and [b]transgression, and the power of the devil, which comes by the cunning [c]plans which he hath devised to ensnare the hearts of men.

14 And thus we see the great call of [a]diligence of men to labor in the vineyards of the Lord; and thus we see the great reason of sorrow, and also of rejoicing—sorrow because of death and destruction among men, and joy because of the [b]light of Christ unto life.

CHAPTER 29

Alma desires to cry repentance with angelic zeal—The Lord grants teachers for all nations—Alma glories in the Lord's work and in the success of Ammon and his brethren.

O THAT I were an angel, and could have the wish of mine heart, that I might go forth and speak with the [a]trump of God, with a voice to shake the earth, and cry repentance unto every people!

2 Yea, I would declare unto every soul, as with the voice of thunder, repentance and the plan of redemption, that they should repent and [a]come unto our God, that there might not be more sorrow upon all the face of the earth.

3 But behold, I am a man, and do sin in my wish; for I ought to be content with the things which the Lord hath allotted unto me.

4 I ought not to harrow up in my desires, the firm decree of a just God, for I know that he granteth

unto men according to their [a]desire, whether it be unto death or unto life; yea, I know that he allotteth unto men, yea, decreeth unto them decrees which are unalterable, according to their [b]wills, whether they be unto salvation or unto destruction.

5 Yea, and I know that good and evil have come before all men; he that knoweth not good from evil is [a]blameless; but he that [b]knoweth good and evil, to him it is given according to his desires, whether he desireth good or evil, life or death, joy or remorse of [c]conscience.

6 Now, seeing that I know these things, why should I desire more than to [a]perform the work to which I have been called?

7 Why should I desire that I were an angel, that I could speak unto all the ends of the earth?

8 For behold, the Lord doth [a]grant unto [b]all nations, of their own nation and [c]tongue, to teach his word, yea, in wisdom, all that he [d]seeth fit that they should have; therefore we see that the Lord doth counsel in wisdom, according to that which is just and true.

9 I know that which the Lord hath commanded me, and I glory in it. I do [a]not [b]glory of myself, but I glory in that which the Lord hath commanded me; yea, and this is my glory, that perhaps I may be an instrument in the hands of God to bring some soul to repentance; and this is my joy.

10 And behold, when I see many of my brethren truly penitent, and coming to the Lord their God, then is my soul filled with joy; then do I remember [a]what the Lord has done

---

12c Alma 56: 11.
13a 1 Ne. 17: 35.
  b TG Transgression.
  c 2 Ne. 9: 28.
14a TG Diligence; Vineyard of the Lord.
  b TG Light of Christ.
29 1a Isa. 58: 1; D&C 29: 4.
2a Omni 1: 26 (25–26); 3 Ne. 21: 20.

4a Ps. 21: 2; 37: 4.
  b TG Agency.
5a TG Accountability.
  b Gen. 3: 5; 2 Ne. 2: 18 (18, 26); Mosiah 16: 3; Moro. 7: 16 (15–19).
  TG Discernment, Spiritual.
  c Job 27: 6.
  TG Conscience.

6a TG Stewardship.
8a 3 Ne. 26: 8 (7–10); D&C 11: 22.
  b 2 Ne. 2: 27; 29: 12.
  c D&C 90: 11.
  d Alma 12: 9 (9–11).
9a Alma 26: 12.
  b TG Glory.
10a Mosiah 27: 14 (11–31).

[About 76 B.C.]

for me, yea, even that he hath heard my prayer; yea, then do I remember his merciful arm which he extended towards me.

11 Yea, and I also remember the captivity of my fathers; for I surely do know that the ᵃLord did deliver them out of bondage, and by this did establish his church; yea, the Lord God, the God of Abraham, the God of Isaac, and the God of Jacob, did deliver them out of bondage.

12 Yea, I have always remembered the captivity of my fathers; and that same God who ᵃdelivered them out of the hands of the Egyptians did deliver them out of ᵇbondage.

13 Yea, and that same God did establish his church among them; yea, and that same God hath called me by a ᵃholy calling, to ᵇpreach the word unto this people, and hath given me much success, in the which my joy is full.

14 But I do not joy in my own ᵃsuccess alone, but my joy is more full because of the success of my brethren, who have been up to the land of Nephi.

15 Behold, they have labored exceedingly, and have brought forth much fruit; and how great shall be their reward!

16 Now, when I think of the success of these my brethren my soul is carried away, even to the separation of it from the body, as it were, so great is my ᵃjoy.

17 And now may God grant unto these, my brethren, that they may sit down in the kingdom of God; yea, and also all those who are the fruit of their labors that they may go no more out, but that they may praise him forever. And may God grant that it may be done according to my words, even as I have spoken. Amen.

CHAPTER 30

Korihor, the antichrist, ridicules Christ, the atonement, and the spirit of prophecy—He teaches that there is no God, no fall of man, no penalty for sin, and no Christ—Alma testifies that Christ shall come and that all things denote there is a God—Korihor demands a sign and is struck dumb— The devil had appeared to Korihor as an angel and taught him what to say— He is trodden down and dies.

BEHOLD, now it came to pass that after the ᵃpeople of Ammon were established in the land of Jershon, yea, and also after the Lamanites were ᵇdriven out of the land, and their dead were buried by the people of the land—

2 Now their dead were not numbered because of the greatness of their numbers; neither were the dead of the Nephites numbered—but it came to pass after they had buried their dead, and also after the days of ᵃfasting, and ᵇmourning, and prayer, (and it was in the sixteenth year of the reign of the judges over the people of Nephi) there began to be continual peace throughout all the land.

3 Yea, and the people did observe to keep the commandments of the Lord; and they were strict in observing the ᵃordinances of God, according to the law of Moses; for they were taught to ᵇkeep the law of Moses until it should be fulfilled.

4 And thus the people did have no disturbance in all the sixteenth year of the reign of the judges over the people of Nephi.

5 And it came to pass that in the commencement of the seventeenth year of the reign of the judges, there was continual peace.

6 But it came to pass in the *latter end of the seventeenth year, there came a man into the land of Zara-

---

11a Ex. 3:6; Alma 36:2.
12a Micah 6:4.
　b Alma 5:5 (5–6);
　　36:29 (2, 29).
13a Alma 5:3.
　b TG Preaching.

14a Alma 17:4 (1–4).
16a TG Joy.
30 1a Alma 27:26.
　b Alma 28:3 (2–3).
2a Alma 28:6.
　b TG Mourning.

3a TG Ordinance.
　b 2 Ne. 25:24; Jarom
　　1:5; Mosiah 2:3;
　　Alma 34:14 (13–14).

[*74 B.C.]

hemla, and he was [a]Anti-Christ, for he began to preach unto the people [b]against the prophecies which had been spoken by the prophets, concerning the coming of Christ.

7 Now there was no law against a [a]man's [b]belief; for it was strictly contrary to the commands of God that there should be a law which should bring men on to unequal grounds.

8 For thus saith the scripture: [a]Choose ye this day, whom ye will serve.

9 Now if a man desired to serve God, it was his privilege; or rather, if he believed in God it was his privilege to serve him; but if he did not believe in him there was no law to punish him.

10 But if he [a]murdered he was punished unto [b]death; and if he [c]robbed he was also punished; and if he stole he was also punished; and if he committed [d]adultery he was also punished; yea, for all this wickedness they were punished.

11 For there was a law that men should be judged according to their crimes. Nevertheless, there was no law against a man's belief; therefore, a man was punished only for the crimes which he had done; therefore all men were on [a]equal grounds.

12 And this [a]Anti-Christ, whose name was Korihor, (and the law could have no hold upon him) began to preach unto the people that there should be [b]no Christ. And after this manner did he preach, saying:

13 O ye that are bound down under a [a]foolish and a vain hope, why do ye yoke yourselves with such foolish things? Why do ye look for a Christ? For no man can [b]know of anything which is to come.

14 Behold, these things which ye call prophecies, which ye say are handed down by holy prophets, behold, they are foolish traditions of your fathers.

15 How do ye know of their surety? Behold, ye cannot know of things which ye do not [a]see; therefore ye cannot know that there shall be a Christ.

16 Ye look forward and say that ye see a remission of your sins. But behold, it is the effect of a [a]frenzied mind; and this derangement of your minds comes because of the traditions of your fathers, which lead you away into a belief of things which are not so.

17 And many more such things did he say unto them, telling them that there could be no atonement made for the sins of men, but every man [a]fared in this life according to the management of the creature; therefore every man prospered according to his genius, and that every man conquered according to his strength; and [b]whatsoever a man did was [c]no crime.

18 And thus did he preach unto them, leading away the hearts of many, causing them to lift up their heads in their wickedness, yea, leading away many women, and also men, to commit whoredoms—telling them that when a man was dead, that was the end thereof.

19 Now this man went over to the land of [a]Jershon also, to preach these things among the people of Ammon, who were once the people of the Lamanites.

20 But behold they were more wise than many of the Nephites; for they took him, and bound him, and carried him before Ammon, who was a [a]high priest over that people.

6a TG Antichrist; False Prophets.
  b TG False Doctrine; Prophets, Rejection of.
7a Alma 1: 17.
  b Acts 18: 13.
8a Josh. 24: 15. TG Agency.
10a TG Murder.
  b TG Capital Punishment.
  c Alma 1: 18.

d TG Adultery.
11a Mosiah 27: 3; 29: 32.
12a TG Antichrist.
  b Jacob 7: 2 (2, 9); Alma 31: 16 (16, 29); 34: 5.
13a 1 Cor. 1: 25 (18–25).
  b Jacob 7: 7.
15a Hel. 16: 20; Ether 12: 5 (5–6, 19).

TG Spiritual Blindness.
16a Acts 26: 24 (24–25).
17a Prov. 16: 25; 2 Ne. 28: 7 (5–9).
  b Alma 18: 5.
  c Alma 1: 4; Morm. 8: 31.
19a Alma 28: 1 (1, 8); 31: 3.
20a Alma 46: 38.

[About 74 B.C.]

21 And it came to pass that he caused that he should be carried out of the land. And he came over into the land of Gideon, and began to preach unto them also; and here he did not have much success, for he was taken and bound and carried before the high priest, and also the chief judge over the land.

22 And it came to pass that the high priest said unto him: Why do ye go about perverting the ways of the Lord? Why do ye teach this people that there shall be no Christ, to interrupt their rejoicings? Why do ye speak against all the prophecies of the holy prophets?

23 Now the high priest's name was Giddonah. And Korihor said unto him: Because I do not teach the foolish traditions of your fathers, and because I do not teach this people to bind themselves down under the foolish ordinances and performances which are laid down by ancient priests, to usurp power and authority over them, to keep them in ignorance, that they may not lift up their heads, but be brought down according to thy words.

24 Ye say that this people is a free people. Behold, I say they are in bondage. Ye say that those ancient prophecies are true. Behold, I say that ye do not know that they are true.

25 Ye say that this people is a guilty and a fallen people, because of the transgression of a parent. Behold, I say that a child is not guilty because of its parents.

26 And ye also say that Christ shall come. But behold, I say that ye do not know that there shall be a Christ. And ye say also that he shall be slain for the *a*sins of the world—

27 And thus ye lead away this people after the foolish traditions of your fathers, and according to your own desires; and ye keep them down, even as it were in bondage, that ye may glut yourselves with the labors of their hands, that they durst not look up with boldness, and that they durst not enjoy their rights and privileges.

28 Yea, they durst not make use of that which is their own lest they should offend their priests, who do yoke them according to their desires, and have brought them to believe, by their traditions and their dreams and their whims and their visions and their pretended mysteries, that they should, if they did not do according to their words, offend some unknown being, who they say is God—a being who *a*never has been seen or known, who *b*never was nor ever will be.

29 Now when the high priest and the *a*chief judge saw the hardness of his heart, yea, when they saw that he would *b*revile even against God, they would not make any reply to his words; but they caused that he should be bound; and they delivered him up into the hands of the officers, and sent him to the land of Zarahemla, that he might be brought before Alma, and the chief judge who was governor over all the land.

30 And it came to pass that when he was brought before Alma and the chief judge, he did go on in the same manner as he did in the land of Gideon; yea, he went on to *a*blaspheme.

31 And he did rise up in great *a*swelling words before Alma, and did revile against the *b*priests and teachers, accusing them of leading away the people after the silly traditions of their fathers, for the sake of glutting on the labors of the people.

32 Now Alma said unto him: Thou knowest that we do not glut ourselves upon the labors of this people; for behold I have *a*labored even from

26a Isa. 53: 6 (4–12).
28a 2 Ne. 28: 5.
  b Alma 30: 53.
29a Alma 4: 17.

  b TG Reviling.
30a TG Blasphemy.
31a Hel. 13: 22.
  TG Boasting.

  b Alma 23: 4.
32a TG Labor; Self-sacrifice.

[About 74 B.C.]

the commencement of the reign of the judges until now, with mine [b]own hands for my support, notwithstanding my many travels round about the land to declare the word of God unto my people.

33 And notwithstanding the many labors which I have performed in the church, I have never received so much as even one [a]senine for my labor; neither has any of my brethren, save it were in the judgment-seat; and then we have received only according to law for our time.

34 And now, if we do not receive anything for our labors in the church, what doth it profit us to labor in the church save it were to declare the truth, that we may have rejoicings in the [a]joy of our brethren?

35 Then why sayest thou that we preach unto this people to get gain, when thou, of thyself, knowest that we receive no gain? And now, believest thou that we deceive this people, that [a]causes such joy in their hearts?

36 And Korihor answered him, Yea.

37 And then Alma said unto him: Believest thou that there is a God?

38 And he answered, Nay.

39 Now Alma said unto him: Will ye deny again that there is a God, and also deny the Christ? For behold, I say unto you, I know there is a God, and also that Christ shall come.

40 And now what evidence have ye that there is no [a]God, or that Christ cometh not? I say unto you that ye have none, save it be your word only.

41 But, behold, I have all things as a [a]testimony that these things are true; and ye also have all things as a testimony unto you that they are true; and will ye deny them? Believest thou that these things are true?

42 Behold, I know that thou [a]believest, but thou art possessed with a [b]lying spirit, and ye have put [c]off the Spirit of God that it may have no place in you; but the devil has power over you, and he doth carry you about, working devices that he may destroy the children of God.

43 And now Korihor said unto Alma: If thou wilt show me a [a]sign, that I may be convinced that there is a God, yea, show unto me that he hath power, and then will I be convinced of the truth of thy words.

44 But Alma said unto him: Thou hast had signs enough; will ye tempt your God? Will ye say, Show unto me a sign, when ye have the testimony of [a]all these thy brethren, and also all the holy prophets? The scriptures are laid before thee, yea, and all things denote there is a God; yea, even the [b]earth, and [c]all things that are upon the face of it, yea, and its [d]motion, yea, and also all the [e]planets which move in their regular form do witness that there is a Supreme Creator.

45 And yet do ye go about, leading away the hearts of this people, testifying unto them there is no God? And yet will ye deny against all these [a]witnesses? And he said: Yea, I will deny, except ye shall show me a sign.

46 And now it came to pass that Alma said unto him: Behold, I am grieved because of the hardness of your heart, yea, that ye will still resist the spirit of the truth, that thy soul may be destroyed.

47 But behold, it is [a]better that thy

32b Acts 20:34 (33–35);
  1 Thes. 2:9; Mosiah
  18:24.
33a Alma 11:3.
34a TG Joy.
35a Matt. 7:16.
40a Ps. 14:1.
41a TG Testimony.
42a Acts 26:27; Jacob
  7:14; Mosiah 12:30;

Alma 30:52.
  b Jer. 27:10;
  Rom. 3:3–4;
  Mosiah 2:32.
  c 1 Sam. 16:14.
43a John 6:30; Jacob
  7:13 (13–21); D&C
  46:9 (8–9). TG Sign
  Seekers.
44a Mosiah 13:33 (33–34).

  b Job 12:8 (7–10).
  TG Nature.
  c D&C 88:47.
  d Hel. 12:15 (11–15).
  e Moses 6:63.
  TG Astronomy.
45a TG Witnesses.
47a 1 Ne. 4:13.

[About 74 B.C.]

soul should be *b*lost than that thou shouldst be the means of bringing many souls down to destruction, by thy lying and by thy flattering words; therefore if thou shalt deny again, behold God shall smite thee, that thou shalt become dumb, that thou shalt never open thy mouth any more, that thou shalt not deceive this people any more.

48 Now Korihor said unto him: I do not deny the existence of a God, but I do not believe that there is a God; and I say also, that ye do not know that there is a God; and except ye show me a sign, I will not believe.

49 Now Alma said unto him: This will I give unto thee for a sign, that thou shalt be *a*struck dumb, according to my words; and I say, that in the name of God, ye shall be struck dumb, that ye shall no more have utterance.

50 Now when Alma had said these words, Korihor was struck dumb, that he could not have utterance, according to the words of Alma.

51 And now when the chief judge saw this, he put forth his hand and wrote unto Korihor, saying: Art thou convinced of the power of God? In whom did ye desire that Alma should show forth his sign? Would ye that he should afflict others, to show unto thee a sign? Behold, he has showed unto you a sign; and now will ye dispute more?

52 And Korihor put forth his hand and wrote, saying: I know that I am dumb, for I cannot speak; and I know that nothing save it were the *a*power of God could bring this upon me; yea, and I always *b*knew that there was a God.

53 But behold, the devil hath *a*deceived me; for he *b*appeared unto me in the *c*form of an angel, and said unto me: Go and reclaim this people, for they have all gone astray after

an unknown God. And he said unto me: There is *d*no God; yea, and he taught me that which I should say. And I have taught his words; and I taught them because they were pleasing unto the *e*carnal mind; and I taught them, even until I had much success, insomuch that I verily believed that they were true; and for this cause I withstood the truth, even until I have brought this great *f*curse upon me.

54 Now when he had said this, he besought that Alma should pray unto God, that the *a*curse might be taken from him.

55 But Alma said unto him: If this curse should be taken from thee thou wouldst again lead away the hearts of this people; therefore, it shall be unto thee even as the Lord will.

56 And it came to pass that the curse was not taken off of Korihor; but he was *a*cast out, and went about from house to house begging for his food.

57 Now the knowledge of what had happened unto Korihor was immediately published throughout all the land; yea, the proclamation was sent forth by the chief judge to all the people in the land, declaring unto those who had believed in the words of Korihor that they must speedily repent, *a*lest the same judgments would come unto them.

58 And it came to pass that they were all convinced of the wickedness of Korihor; therefore they were all converted again unto the Lord; and this put an end to the iniquity after the manner of Korihor. And Korihor did go about from house to house, begging food for his support.

59 And it came to pass that as he went forth among the people, yea, among a people who had separated themselves from the Nephites and called themselves *a*Zoramites, being

---

47*b* Mosiah 27: 16.
49*a* Luke 1: 20; Acts 13: 11 (8–12).
52*a* 2 Chr. 3: 20.
   b Alma 30: 42 (41–42).
53*a* Jacob 7: 14 (14, 18).

b 2 Ne. 9: 9.
c 2 Cor. 11: 14.
d Ps. 10: 4 (2–11); Alma 30: 28.
e TG Carnal Mind.
f TG Curse.

54*a* Num. 12: 13 (9–15).
56*a* Dan. 5: 21.
57*a* John 5: 14.
59*a* Alma 31: 7 (7–8).

[About 74 B.C.]

led by a man whose name was Zoram—and as he went forth amongst them, behold, he was run upon and trodden down, even until he was [b]dead.

60 And thus we see the end of him who [a]perverteth the ways of the Lord; and thus we see that the devil will not [b]support his children at the last day, but doth speedily drag them down to [c]hell.

CHAPTER 31

Alma heads a mission to reclaim the apostate Zoramites—The Zoramites deny Christ, believe in a false concept of election, and worship with set prayers—The missionaries are filled with the Holy Spirit—Their afflictions are swallowed up in the joy of Christ.

Now it came to pass that after the end of Korihor, Alma having received tidings that the Zoramites were perverting the ways of the Lord, and that Zoram, who was their leader, was leading the hearts of the people to [a]bow down to dumb [b]idols, his heart again began to [c]sicken because of the iniquity of the people.

2 For it was the cause of great [a]sorrow to Alma to know of iniquity among his people; therefore his heart was exceedingly [b]sorrowful because of the separation of the Zoramites from the Nephites.

3 Now the Zoramites had gathered themselves together in a land which they called [a]Antionum, which was east of the land of Zarahemla, which lay nearly bordering upon the seashore, which was south of the land

of [b]Jershon, which also bordered upon the wilderness south, which wilderness was full of the Lamanites.

4 Now the Nephites greatly feared that the Zoramites would enter into a [a]correspondence with the Lamanites, and that it would be the means of great loss on the part of the Nephites.

5 And now, as the [a]preaching of the [b]word had a great tendency to [c]lead the people to do that which was just—yea, it had had more powerful effect upon the minds of the people than the sword, or anything else, which had happened unto them—therefore Alma thought it was expedient that they should try the virtue of the word of God.

6 Therefore he took Ammon, and Aaron, and Omner; and Himni he did leave in the church in Zarahemla; but the former three he took with him, and also [a]Amulek and Zeezrom, who were at [b]Melek; and he also took two of his sons.

7 Now the eldest of his sons he took not with him, and his name was Helaman; but the names of those whom he took with him were [a]Shiblon and [b]Corianton; and these are the names of those who went with him among the [c]Zoramites, to preach unto them the word.

8 Now the Zoramites were [a]dissenters from the Nephites; therefore they had had the word of God preached unto them.

9 But they had [a]fallen into great errors, for they would not observe to keep the commandments of God,

59b Jer. 28: 16 (15–17); Jacob 7: 20 (1–20).
60a TG Lying.
   b Alma 3: 27 (26–27); 5: 42 (41–42); D&C 29: 45.
   c TG Hell.
31 1a Ex. 20: 5; Mosiah 13: 13.
   b 2 Ne. 9: 37. TG Idolatry.
   c Alma 35: 15.
2a 1 Ne. 7: 8; Mosiah 28: 3; 3 Ne. 17: 14; Moses 7: 41.

b Isa. 22: 4.
3a Alma 43: 5 (5, 15, 22).
   b Alma 27: 22.
4a TG Conspiracy.
5a Ex. 24: 7; Jonah 3: 5; Rom. 10: 17; Enos 1: 23; Alma 4: 19. TG Preaching.
   b 2 Kgs. 22: 11; Heb. 4: 12; Jacob 2: 8; Alma 36: 26.
   c Jarom 1: 12; Alma 45: 21; Hel. 5: 51

(50–52); D&C 11: 2. TG Gospel.
6a Hel. 5: 41.
   b Alma 8: 3; 35: 13; 45: 18.
7a Alma 31: 32; 35: 14.
   b Alma 39: 1.
   c Alma 30: 59; 38: 3.
8a Alma 24: 30; 53: 8; Hel. 1: 15; D&C 93: 19.
9a TG Apostasy of Individuals.

[About 74 B.C.]

and his statutes, according to the law of Moses.

10 Neither would they observe the [a]performances of the church, to continue in prayer and supplication to God daily, that they might not enter into temptation.

11 Yea, in fine, they did pervert the ways of the Lord in very many instances; therefore, for this cause, Alma and his brethren went into the land to preach the word unto them.

12 Now, when they had come into the land, behold, to their astonishment they found that the Zoramites had built synagogues, and that they did gather themselves together on one day of the week, which day they did call the day of the Lord; and they did [a]worship after a manner which Alma and his brethren had never beheld;

13 For they had a place built up in the center of their synagogue, a place for standing, which was high above the head; and the top thereof would only admit one person.

14 Therefore, whosoever desired to [a]worship must go forth and stand upon the top thereof, and stretch forth his hands towards heaven, and cry with a loud voice, saying:

15 Holy, holy God; we believe that thou art God, and we believe that thou art holy, and that thou wast a [a]spirit, and that thou art a spirit, and that thou wilt be a spirit forever.

16 Holy God, we believe that thou hast separated us from our brethren; and we do not believe in the tradition of our brethren, which was handed down to them by the childishness of their fathers; but we believe that thou hast [a]elected us to be thy [b]holy children; and also thou hast made it known unto us that [c]there shall be [d]no Christ.

17 But thou art the same yesterday, today, and forever; and thou hast [a]elected us that we shall be saved, whilst all around us are elected to be cast by thy wrath down to hell; for the which holiness, O God, we thank thee; and we also thank thee that thou hast elected us, that we may not be led away after the foolish traditions of our brethren, which doth [b]bind them down to a belief of Christ, which doth lead their hearts to wander far from thee, our God.

18 And again we thank thee, O God, that we are a chosen and a holy people. Amen.

19 Now it came to pass that after Alma and his brethren and his sons had heard these prayers, they were astonished beyond all measure.

20 For behold, every man did go forth and offer up these same [a]prayers.

21 Now the place was called by them Rameumptom, which, being interpreted, is the holy stand.

22 Now, from this stand they did offer up, every man, the selfsame prayer unto God, thanking their God that they were chosen of him, and that he did not lead them away after the tradition of their brethren, and that their hearts were not stolen away to believe in things to come, which they knew nothing about.

23 Now, after the people had all offered up thanks after this manner, they returned to their homes, [a]never speaking of their God again until they had assembled themselves together again to the holy stand, to offer up thanks after their manner.

24 Now when Alma saw this his heart was [a]grieved; for he saw that they were a wicked and a perverse people; yea, he saw that their hearts were set upon gold, and upon silver, and upon all manner of fine goods.

10a TG Ordinance.
12a TG Worship.
14a Matt. 6:5 (1–7).
15a Alma 18:4 (4–5).
16a Luke 18:11; Alma 38:14 (13–14).

b Isa. 65:5 (1–5).
c Alma 34:5.
d Jacob 7:2 (2, 9);
  Alma 30:12 (12, 22).
17a TG Conceit; Pride.

b TG False Doctrine.
20a Matt. 6:7.
23a James 1:22 (21–25).
24a Gen. 6:6; 1 Ne. 2:18.

[About 74 B.C.]

25 Yea, and he also saw that their hearts were [a]lifted up unto great boasting, in their pride.

26 And he lifted up his voice to heaven, and [a]cried, saying: O, how long, O Lord, wilt thou suffer that thy servants shall dwell here below in the flesh, to behold such gross wickedness among the children of men?

27 Behold, O God, they [a]cry unto thee, and yet their hearts are swallowed up in their pride. Behold, O God, they cry unto thee with their mouths, while they are [b]puffed up, even to greatness, with the vain things of the [c]world.

28 Behold, O my God, their costly apparel, and their ringlets, and their [a]bracelets, and their ornaments of gold, and all their precious things which they are ornamented with; and behold, their hearts are set upon them, and yet they cry unto thee and say—We thank thee, O God, for we are a chosen people unto thee, while others shall perish.

29 Yea, and they say that thou hast made it known unto them that there shall be no Christ.

30 O Lord God, how long wilt thou suffer that such wickedness and infidelity shall be among this people? O Lord, wilt thou give me strength, that I may [a]bear with mine infirmities. For I am infirm, and such wickedness among this people doth pain my soul.

31 O Lord, my heart is exceedingly sorrowful; wilt thou comfort my soul [a]in Christ. O Lord, wilt thou grant unto me that I may have strength, that I may suffer with patience these [b]afflictions which shall come upon me, because of the iniquity of this people.

32 O Lord, wilt thou comfort my soul, and give unto me success, and also my fellow laborers who are with me—yea, Ammon, and Aaron, and Omner, and also [a]Amulek and Zeezrom, and also my [b]two sons— yea, even all these wilt thou comfort, O Lord. Yea, wilt thou comfort their souls in Christ.

33 Wilt thou grant unto them that they may have strength, that they may [a]bear their afflictions which shall come upon them because of the iniquities of this people.

34 O Lord, wilt thou grant [a]unto us that we may have success in bringing them again unto thee in Christ.

35 Behold, O Lord, their [a]souls are precious, and many of them are our brethren; therefore, give unto us, O Lord, power and wisdom that we may bring these, our brethren, again unto thee.

36 Now it came to pass that when Alma had said these words, that he [a]clapped his [b]hands upon all them who were with him. And behold, as he clapped his hands upon them, they were filled with the Holy Spirit.

37 And after that they did separate themselves one from another, [a]taking no thought for themselves what they should eat, or what they should drink, or what they should put on.

38 And the Lord provided for them that they should hunger not, neither should they thirst; yea, and he also gave them strength, that they should suffer no manner of [a]afflictions, save it were swallowed up in the joy of Christ. Now this was according to the prayer of Alma; and this because he prayed in [b]faith.

25a 2 Kgs. 14: 10; Jacob 2: 13; Alma 1: 32.
26a Moses 7: 44 (41–58).
27a Isa. 29: 13.
  TG Hypocrisy.
  b TG Pride; Selfishness.
  c TG Worldliness.
28a Isa. 3: 19 (16–24).
30a Num. 11: 14.
31a John 16: 33.

  TG Comfort; Peace of God.
  b TG Affliction.
32a Alma 8: 21; 34: 1.
  b Alma 31: 7.
33a Rom. 15: 1.
34a 2 Ne. 26: 33.
35a TG Worth of Souls.
36a 3 Ne. 18: 37.

  b TG Hands, Laying on of.
37a Matt. 6: 25 (25–34); 3 Ne. 13: 25 (25–34).
38a Matt. 5: 10 (10–12); Mosiah 24: 15 (13–15); Alma 33: 23.
  b TG Faith.

[About 74 B.C.]

CHAPTER 32

Alma teaches the poor whose afflictions had humbled them—Faith is a hope in that which is not seen which is true—Alma testifies that angels minister to men, women, and children—Alma compares the word unto a seed—It must be planted and nourished—Then it grows into a tree from which the fruit of eternal life is picked.

AND it came to pass that they did go forth, and began to preach the word of God unto the people, entering into their synagogues, and into their houses; yea, and even they did preach the word in their streets.

2 And it came to pass that after much labor among them, they began to have success among the [a]poor class of people; for behold, they were cast out of the synagogues because of the coarseness of their apparel—

3 Therefore they were not permitted to enter into their synagogues to worship God, being esteemed as filthiness; therefore they were poor; yea, they were esteemed by their brethren as [a]dross; therefore they were [b]poor as to things of the world; and also they were poor in heart.

4 Now, as Alma was teaching and speaking unto the people upon the hill [a]Onidah, there came a great [b]multitude unto him, who were those of whom we have been speaking, of whom were [c]poor in heart, because of their poverty as to the things of the world.

5 And they came unto Alma; and the one who was the foremost among them said unto him: Behold, [a]what shall these my brethren do, for they are [b]despised of all men because of their poverty, yea, and

more especially by our priests; for they have [c]cast us out of our synagogues which we have labored abundantly to build with our own hands; and they have cast us out because of our exceeding poverty; and we have [d]no place to worship our God; and behold, [e]what shall we do?

6 And now when Alma heard this, he turned him about, his face immediately towards him, and he beheld with great joy; for he beheld that their [a]afflictions had truly [b]humbled them, and that they were in a [c]preparation to hear the word.

7 Therefore he did say no more to the other multitude; but he stretched forth his hand, and cried unto those whom he beheld, who were truly penitent, and said unto them:

8 I behold that ye are [a]lowly in heart; and if so, blessed are ye.

9 Behold thy brother hath said, What shall we do?—for we are cast out of our synagogues, that we cannot worship our God.

10 Behold I say unto you, do ye suppose that ye [a]cannot worship God save it be in your synagogues only?

11 And moreover, I would ask, do ye suppose that ye must not worship God only [a]once in a week?

12 I say unto you, it is well that ye are cast out of your synagogues, that ye may be humble, and that ye may learn [a]wisdom; for it is necessary that ye should learn wisdom; for it is because that ye are cast out, that ye are despised of your brethren because of your exceeding [b]poverty, that ye are brought to a lowliness of heart; for ye are necessarily brought to be humble.

---

32 2a Luke 6: 20; 7: 22.
  TG Poor.
 3a Luke 18: 9.
  b Alma 34: 40.
 4a Alma 47: 5.
  b TG Assembly for
    Worship.
  c TG Poor in Spirit.
 5a Prov. 18: 23.

  b TG Oppression.
  c Alma 33: 10.
  d Alma 33: 2.
  e Acts 2: 37 (37–38);
    Alma 34: 3.
 6a TG Adversity.
  b TG Humility;
    Teachable.
  c Prov. 16: 1; Alma

    16: 16 (16–17); D&C
    101: 8.
 8a Matt. 5: 5 (3–5).
10a TG Worship.
11a Mosiah 18: 25.
12a Eccl. 4: 13.
  b Prov. 16: 8; 28: 11.

[About 74 B.C.]

13 And now, because ye are compelled to be humble blessed are ye; for a man sometimes, if he is compelled to be humble, seeketh *a*repentance; and now surely, whosoever repenteth shall find mercy; and he that findeth mercy and *b*endureth to the end the same shall be saved.

14 And now, as I said unto you, that because ye were compelled to be *a*humble ye were blessed, do ye not suppose that they are more blessed who truly humble themselves because of the word?

15 Yea, he that truly humbleth himself, and repenteth of his sins, and endureth to the end, the same shall be blessed—yea, much more blessed than they who are compelled to be humble because of their exceeding poverty.

16 Therefore, blessed are they who *a*humble themselves without being *b*compelled to be humble; or rather, in other words, blessed is he that believeth in the word of God, and is baptized without *c*stubbornness of heart, yea, without being brought to know the word, or even compelled to know, before they will believe.

17 Yea, there are many who do say: If thou wilt show unto us a *a*sign from heaven, then we shall know of a surety; then we shall believe.

18 Now I ask, is this faith? Behold, I say unto you, Nay; for if a man knoweth a thing he hath no cause to *a*believe, for he knoweth it.

19 And now, how much *a*more *b*cursed is he that *c*knoweth the *d*will of God and doeth it not, than he that only believeth, or only hath cause to believe, and falleth into *e*transgression?

20 Now of this thing ye must judge.

Behold, I say unto you, that it is on the one hand even as it is on the other; and it shall be unto every man according to his work.

21 And now as I said concerning faith—*a*faith is not to have a perfect knowledge of things; therefore if ye have faith ye *b*hope for things which are *c*not seen, which are true.

22 And now, behold, I say unto you, and I would that ye should remember, that God is *a*merciful unto all who believe on his name; therefore he desireth, in the first place, that ye should believe, yea, even on his word.

23 And now, he imparteth his word by angels unto men, yea, *a*not only men but women also. Now this is not all; little *b*children do have words given unto them many times, which *c*confound the wise and the learned.

24 And now, my beloved brethren, as ye have desired to know of me what ye shall do because ye are afflicted and cast out—now I do not desire that ye should suppose that I mean to judge you only according to that which is true—

25 For I do not mean that ye all of you have been compelled to humble yourselves; for I verily believe that there are some among you who *a*would humble themselves, let them be in whatsoever circumstances they might.

26 Now, as I said concerning faith—that it was not a perfect knowledge—even so it is with my words. Ye cannot know of their surety at first, unto perfection, any more than faith is a perfect knowledge.

27 But behold, if ye will awake and arouse your faculties, even to an experiment upon my words, and

13a TG Objectives.
  b Alma 38: 2; 3 Ne.
    15: 9; 27: 6 (6–17).
    TG Perseverance;
    Steadfastness.
14a 2 Kgs. 22: 19.
16a TG Humility.
  b TG Initiative.
  c TG Stubbornness.
17a TG Sign Seekers; Signs.

18a Luke 16: 30 (27–31);
    Ether 12: 12 (12, 18).
19a D&C 41: 1.
  b TG Curse.
  c John 15: 24 (22–24).
  d TG God, Will of.
  e TG Transgression.
21a John 20: 29; Heb.
    11: 1 (1–40).
  b TG Hope.

  c Ether 12: 6.
22a TG God, Mercy of.
23a Joel 2: 29 (28–29).
  b Matt. 11: 25; Luke
    10: 21; 3 Ne. 26: 14
    (14–16); D&C 128: 18.
  c D&C 133: 58.
25a TG Initiative;
    Sincerity.

[About 74 B.C.]

exercise a particle of faith, yea, even if ye can no more than [a]desire to believe, let this desire work in you, even until ye believe in a manner that ye can give place for a portion of my words.

28 Now, we will compare the word unto a [a]seed. Now, if ye give place, that a [b]seed may be planted in your [c]heart, behold, if it be a true seed, or a good seed, if ye do not cast it out by your [d]unbelief, that ye will resist the Spirit of the Lord, behold, it will begin to swell within your breasts; and when you feel these swelling motions, ye will begin to say within yourselves—It must needs be that this is a good seed, or that the word is good, for it beginneth to enlarge my soul; yea, it beginneth to [e]enlighten my [f]understanding, yea, it beginneth to be delicious to me.

29 Now behold, would not this increase your faith? I say unto you, Yea; nevertheless it hath not grown up to a perfect knowledge.

30 But behold, as the seed swelleth, and sprouteth, and beginneth to grow, then you must needs say that the seed is good; for behold it swelleth, and sprouteth, and beginneth to grow. And now, behold, will not this strengthen your faith? Yea, it will strengthen your faith: for ye will say I know that this is a good seed; for behold it sprouteth and beginneth to grow.

31 And now, behold, are ye sure that this is a good seed? I say unto you, Yea; for every seed bringeth forth unto its own [a]likeness.

32 Therefore, if a seed groweth it is good, but if it groweth not, behold it is not good, therefore it is cast away.

33 And now, behold, because ye have tried the experiment, and planted the seed, and it swelleth and sprouteth, and beginneth to grow, ye must needs know that the seed is good.

34 And now, behold, is your [a]knowledge [b]perfect? Yea, your knowledge is perfect in that thing, and your [c]faith is dormant; and this because you know, for ye know that the word hath swelled your souls, and ye also know that it hath sprouted up, that your understanding doth begin to be enlightened, and your [d]mind doth begin to expand.

35 O then, is not this real? I say unto you, Yea, because it is [a]light; and whatsoever is light, is [b]good, because it is discernible, therefore ye must know that it is good; and now behold, after ye have tasted this light is your knowledge perfect?

36 Behold I say unto you, Nay; neither must ye lay aside your faith, for ye have only exercised your faith to plant the seed that ye might try the experiment to know if the seed was good.

37 And behold, as the tree beginneth to grow, ye will say: Let us nourish it with great care, that it may get root, that it may grow up, and bring forth fruit unto us. And now behold, if ye nourish it with much care it will get root, and grow up, and bring forth fruit.

38 But if ye [a]neglect the tree, and take no thought for its nourishment, behold it will not get any root; and when the heat of the sun cometh and scorcheth it, because it hath no root it withers away, and ye pluck it up and cast it out.

39 Now, this is not because the seed was not good, neither is it because the fruit thereof would not be desirable; but it is because your [a]ground is [b]barren, and ye will not nourish the tree, therefore ye cannot have the fruit thereof.

27a TG Motivations; Teachable.
28a Alma 33:1.
   b Luke 8:11 (11–15).
   c TG Heart.
   d TG Doubt; Unbelief, Unbelievers.
   e TG Discernment, Spiritual; Edification.
   f TG Intelligence; Testimony; Understanding.
31a Gen. 1:12 (11–12).
34a TG Knowledge.
   b Ps. 19:7.
   c Ether 3:19.
   d TG Mind.
35a TG Light.
   b Gen. 1:4.
38a TG Apostasy of Individuals.
39a Matt. 13:5 (3–8).
   b TG Barrenness.

[About 74 B.C.]

40 And thus, if ye will not nourish the word, looking forward with an eye of faith to the fruit thereof, ye can never pluck of the fruit of the [a]tree of life.

41 But if ye will nourish the word, yea, nourish the tree as it beginneth to grow, by your faith with great diligence, and with [a]patience, looking forward to the fruit thereof, it shall take root; and behold it shall be a tree [b]springing up unto everlasting life.

42 And because of your [a]diligence and your faith and your patience with the word in nourishing it, that it may take root in you, behold, by and by ye shall pluck the [b]fruit thereof, which is most precious, which is sweet above all that is sweet, and which is white above all that is white, yea, and pure above all that is pure; and ye shall feast upon this fruit even until ye are filled, that ye hunger not, neither shall ye thirst.

43 Then, my brethren, ye shall [a]reap the [b]rewards of your faith, and your diligence, and patience, and long-suffering, waiting for the tree to bring forth [c]fruit unto you.

CHAPTER 33

Zenos taught that men should pray and worship in all places, and that judgments are turned away because of the Son—Zenock taught that mercy is bestowed because of the Son—Moses had lifted up in the wilderness a type of the Son of God.

Now after Alma had spoken these words, they sent forth unto him desiring to know whether they should believe in [a]one God, that they might obtain this fruit of which he had spoken, or [b]how they should plant the [c]seed, or the word of which he had spoken, which he said must be planted in their hearts; or in what manner they should begin to exercise their faith.

2 And Alma said unto them: Behold, ye have said that ye [a]could not [b]worship your God because ye are cast out of your synagogues. But behold, I say unto you, if ye suppose that ye cannot worship God, ye do greatly err, and ye ought to search the [c]scriptures; if ye suppose that they have taught you this, ye do not understand them.

3 Do ye remember to have read what [a]Zenos, the prophet of old, has said concerning prayer or [b]worship?

4 For he said: Thou art merciful, O God, for thou hast heard my prayer, even when I was [a]in the wilderness; yea, thou wast merciful when I prayed concerning those who were mine [b]enemies, and thou didst turn them to me.

5 Yea, O God, and thou wast merciful unto me when I did cry unto thee in my [a]field; when I did cry unto thee in my prayer, and thou didst hear me.

6 And again, O God, when I did turn to my house thou didst hear me in my prayer.

7 And when I did turn unto my [a]closet, O Lord, and prayed unto thee, thou didst hear me.

8 Yea, thou art merciful unto thy children when they cry unto thee, to be heard of thee and not of men, and thou [a]wilt hear them.

9 Yea, O God, thou hast been merciful unto me, and heard my cries in the midst of thy congregations.

40a Gen. 2:9; 1 Ne.
    15:36 (22, 28, 36).
41a TG Patience.
    b Alma 33:23; D&C
    63:23.
42a TG Diligence.
    b Matt. 13:23; Col. 1:6;
    1 Ne. 8:10 (10–18);
    3 Ne. 14:16; D&C
    52:34 (18, 34).
43a TG Harvest.

  b TG Reward.
  c Alma 33:23.
33 1a 2 Ne. 31:21; Mosiah
    15:4; Alma 11:28
    (28–35).
  b Alma 33:23.
  c Alma 32:28 (28–43).
  2a Alma 32:5.
  b TG Worship.
  c Mosiah 2:34; Alma
    37:8 (3–10). TG Prayer.

3a Alma 34:7.
    TG Scriptures, Lost.
  b TG Worship.
4a 1 Kgs. 8:47 (44–52).
  b Matt. 5:44.
5a Alma 34:20 (20–25).
7a Matt. 6:6 (5–6);
    Alma 34:26 (17–27).
8a TG God, Access to.

[About 74 B.C.]

10 Yea, and thou hast also heard me when I have been *a*cast out and have been despised by mine enemies; yea, thou didst hear my cries, and wast angry with mine enemies, and thou didst *b*visit them in thine anger with speedy destruction.

11 And thou didst hear me because of mine afflictions and my *a*sincerity; and it is because of thy Son that thou hast been thus merciful unto me, therefore I will cry unto thee in all mine *b*afflictions, for in thee is my joy; for thou hast turned thy judgments away from me, *c*because of thy Son.

12 And now Alma said unto them: Do ye *a*believe those scriptures which have been written by them of old?

13 Behold, if ye do, ye must believe what *a*Zenos said; for, behold he said: Thou hast turned away thy judgments because of thy Son.

14 Now behold, my brethren, I would ask if ye have read the scriptures? If ye have, how can ye *a*disbelieve on the Son of God?

15 For it is *a*not written that Zenos alone spake of these things, but *b*Zenock also spake of these things—

16 For behold, he said: Thou art angry, O Lord, with this people, because they *a*will not understand thy mercies which thou hast bestowed upon them because of thy Son.

17 And now, my brethren, ye see that a second prophet of old has testified of the Son of God, and because the people would not understand his words they *a*stoned him to death.

18 But behold, this is not all; these are not the only ones who have spoken concerning the Son of God.

19 Behold, he was spoken of by *a*Moses; yea, and behold a *b*type was *c*raised up in the wilderness, that whosoever would look upon it might live. And many did look and live.

20 But few understood the meaning of those things, and this because of the hardness of their hearts. But there were many who were so hardened that they would not look, therefore they perished. Now the reason they would not look is because they did not believe that it would *a*heal them.

21 O my brethren, if ye could be healed by merely casting about your eyes that ye might be healed, would ye not behold quickly, or would ye rather harden your hearts in *a*unbelief, and be *b*slothful, that ye would not cast about your eyes, that ye might perish?

22 If so, wo shall come upon you; but if not so, then cast about your eyes and *a*begin to believe in the Son of God, that he will come to redeem his people, and that he shall suffer and die to *b*atone for their sins; and that he shall *c*rise again from the dead, which shall bring to pass the *d*resurrection, that all men shall stand before him, to be *e*judged at the last and judgment day, according to their *f*works.

23 And now, my brethren, I desire that ye shall *a*plant this word in your hearts, and as it beginneth to swell even so nourish it by your faith. And behold, it will become a tree, *b*springing up in you unto *c*ever-

10a Alma 32: 5.
  b Ps. 3: 7; 18: 17.
11a TG Sincerity.
  b TG Affliction.
  c TG Jesus Christ, Atonement through.
12a TG Scriptures, Value of.
13a Jacob 6: 1; Alma 34: 7.
14a John 5: 39.
15a Jacob 4: 4; Mosiah 15: 11 (11–13).
  b 1 Ne. 19: 10; Alma 34: 7.
16a 2 Pet. 3: 5 (4–5).
17a TG Martyrdom.

19a Deut. 18: 15 (15, 18); Alma 34: 7.
  b Num. 21: 9; 1 Ne. 17: 41; 2 Ne. 25: 20. TG Jesus Christ, Types of, in Anticipation; Symbolism.
  c John 3: 14; Hel. 8: 14.
20a Hosea 11: 3; 1 Ne. 17: 41 (40–41).
21a TG Doubt; Unbelief; Unbelievers.
  b TG Apathy; Laziness.
22a Alma 25: 16; 37: 46

(45–46).
  b 2 Ne. 2: 10; Alma 22: 14; 34: 9 (8–16).
  c TG Jesus Christ, Resurrection.
  d Alma 11: 44. TG Resurrection.
  e TG Jesus Christ, Judge.
  f TG Good Works.
23a Alma 33: 1; 34: 4.
  b Alma 32: 41; D&C 63: 23.
  c Alma 32: 43.

lasting life. And then may God grant unto you that your [d]burdens may be light, through the joy of his Son. And even all this can ye do if ye [e]will. Amen.

CHAPTER 34

Amulek testifies that the word is in Christ unto salvation—Unless an atonement is made, all mankind must perish—The whole law of Moses points toward the sacrifice of the Son of God—The eternal plan of redemption is based on faith and repentance—Pray for temporal and spiritual blessings—This life is the time for men to prepare to meet God—Work out your salvation with fear and trembling.

AND now it came to pass that after Alma had spoken these words unto them he sat down upon the ground, and [a]Amulek arose and began to teach them, saying:

2 My brethren, I think that it is impossible that ye should be ignorant of the things which have been spoken concerning the coming of Christ, who is taught by us to be the Son of God; yea, I know that [a]these things were taught unto you bountifully before your dissension from among us.

3 And as ye have desired of my beloved brother that he should make known unto you [a]what ye should do, because of your afflictions; and he hath spoken somewhat unto you to prepare your minds; yea, and he hath exhorted you unto faith and to patience—

4 Yea, even that ye would have so much faith as even to [a]plant the word in your hearts, that ye may try the experiment of its goodness.

5 And we have beheld that the great question which is in your minds is whether the word be in the Son of God, or whether there shall be [a]no Christ.

6 And ye also beheld that my brother has proved unto you, in many instances, that the [a]word is in Christ unto salvation.

7 My brother has called upon the words of [a]Zenos, that redemption cometh through the Son of God, and also upon the words of [b]Zenock; and also he has appealed unto [c]Moses, to prove that these things are true.

8 And now, behold, I will [a]testify unto you of myself that these things are true. Behold, I say unto you, that I do know that Christ shall come among the children of men, to take upon him the [b]transgressions of his people, and that he shall [c]atone for the sins of the world; for the Lord God hath spoken it.

9 For it is expedient that an [a]atonement should be made; for according to the great [b]plan of the Eternal God there must be an atonement made, or else all mankind must unavoidably perish; yea, all are hardened; yea, all are [c]fallen and are lost, and must perish except it be through the atonement which it is expedient should be made.

10 For it is expedient that there should be a great and last [a]sacrifice; yea, not a [b]sacrifice of man, neither of beast, neither of any manner of fowl; for it shall not be a human sacrifice; but it must be an [c]infinite and [d]eternal [e]sacrifice.

23d Mosiah 24: 15 (13–15); Alma 31: 38.
e TG Agency.
34 1a Alma 8: 21; 31: 32.
2a Alma 16: 15 (13–21).
3a Alma 32: 5.
4a Alma 33: 23.
5a Jacob 7: 2 (2, 9); Alma 30: 12 (12, 22); 31: 16 (16, 29).
6a John 1: 14 (1, 14).
7a Alma 33: 13; Hel. 8: 19.

b Alma 33: 15; Hel. 8: 20 (19–20).
c Alma 33: 19.
8a TG Testimony; Witnesses.
b TG Jesus Christ, Redeemer.
c TG Jesus Christ, Atonement through.
9a 2 Ne. 2: 10; 9: 7 (7–9); Alma 22: 14; 33: 22.
b Alma 12: 26 (22–33);

42: 8 (6–28); Moses 6: 62.
c TG Fall of Man.
10a 1 Chr. 6: 49; Moses 5: 7 (6–7).
b TG Blood, Symbolism of.
c 2 Ne. 9: 7.
d Isa. 45: 17; Heb. 5: 9.
e TG Sacrifice.

[About 74 B.C.]

11 Now there is not any man that can sacrifice his own blood which will atone for the sins of another. Now, if a man murdereth, behold will our law, which is ªjust, take the life of his brother? I say unto you, Nay.

12 But the law requireth the ªlife of him who hath ᵇmurdered; therefore there can be nothing which is short of an infinite atonement which will suffice for the sins of the world.

13 Therefore, it is expedient that there should be a great and last sacrifice, and then shall there be, or it is expedient there should be, a ªstop to the shedding of ᵇblood; then shall the ᶜlaw of Moses be fulfilled; yea, it shall be all fulfilled, every jot and tittle, and none shall have passed away.

14 And behold, this is the whole ªmeaning of the ᵇlaw, every whit ᶜpointing to that great and last ᵈsacrifice; and that great and last ᵉsacrifice will be the Son of God, yea, ᶠinfinite and eternal.

15 And thus he shall bring ªsalvation to all those who shall believe on his name; this being the intent of this last sacrifice, to bring about the bowels of mercy, which overpowereth justice, and bringeth about means unto men that they may have faith unto repentance.

16 And thus ªmercy can satisfy the demands of ᵇjustice, and encircles them in the arms of safety, while he that exercises no faith unto repentance is exposed to the whole law of the demands of ᶜjustice; therefore only unto him that has faith unto repentance is brought about the great and eternal ᵈplan of ᵉredemption.

17 Therefore may God grant unto you, my brethren, that ye may begin to exercise your ªfaith unto repentance, that ye begin to ᵇcall upon his holy name, that he would have mercy upon you;

18 Yea, cry unto him for mercy; for he is ªmighty to save.

19 Yea, humble yourselves, and continue in ªprayer unto him.

20 Cry unto him when ye are in your ªfields, yea, over all your flocks.

21 ªCry unto him in your houses, yea, over all your household, both morning, mid-day, and evening.

22 Yea, cry unto him against the power of your ªenemies.

23 Yea, ªcry unto him against the ᵇdevil, who is an enemy to all ᶜrighteousness.

24 Cry unto him over the crops of your fields, that ye may prosper in them.

25 Cry over the flocks of your fields, that they may increase.

26 But this is not all; ye must ªpour out your souls in your ᵇclosets, and your secret places, and in your wilderness.

27 Yea, and when you do not cry unto the Lord, let your ªhearts be ᵇfull, drawn out in prayer unto him continually for your ᶜwelfare, and also for the welfare of ᵈthose who are around you.

11a Deut. 24:16; Mosiah 29:25.
12a TG Blood, Shedding of; Life, Sanctity of.
  b TG Capital Punishment; Murder.
13a 3 Ne. 9:19.
  b TG Blood, Symbolism of.
  c 3 Ne. 1:24; 15:5.
14a 2 Ne. 25:24; Jarom 1:5; Mosiah 2:3; Alma 30:3.
  b TG Law of Moses.
  c TG Jesus Christ, Types of, in Anticipation.

d Ex. 12:21 (1–30).
  e D&C 138:35.
  f D&C 20:17 (17, 28).
15a TG Salvation.
16a TG Mercy.
  b TG God, Justice of.
  c Mosiah 15:27; Alma 12:32.
  d TG Salvation, Plan of.
  e TG Redemption.
17a TG Faith.
  b TG God, Access to; Prayer.
18a Heb. 7:25 (24–25).
19a TG Prayer.
20a Alma 33:5 (4–5).

21a Ps. 5:3 (1–3); Dan. 6:10; 3 Ne. 18:21.
22a TG Enemies.
23a 3 Ne. 18:15 (15, 18).
  b TG Devil.
  c TG Righteousness.
26a 1 Sam. 1:15; Enos 1:9.
  b Matt. 6:6 (5–6); Alma 33:7 (4–11).
27a TG Heart.
  b TG Meditation.
  c 2 Ne. 32:9. TG Welfare.
  d D&C 108:7.

[About 74 B.C.]

28 And now behold, my beloved brethren, I say unto you, do not suppose that this is all; for after ye have done all these things, if ye ^aturn away the ^bneedy, and the ^cnaked, and visit not the sick and afflicted, and ^dimpart of your substance, if ye have, to those who stand in need—I say unto you, if ye do not any of these things, behold, your ^eprayer is ^fvain, and availeth you nothing, and ye are as ^ghypocrites who do deny the faith.

29 Therefore, if ye do not remember to be ^acharitable, ye are as dross, which the refiners do cast out, (it being of no worth) and is trodden under foot of men.

30 And now, my brethren, I would that, after ye have ^areceived so many witnesses, seeing that the holy scriptures testify of these things, ye come forth and bring ^bfruit unto repentance.

31 Yea, I would that ye would come forth and ^aharden not your hearts any longer; for behold, now is the time and the ^bday of your ^csalvation; and therefore, if ye will repent and ^dharden not your hearts, immediately shall the great plan of redemption be brought about unto you.

32 For behold, this ^alife is the time for men to ^bprepare to meet God; yea, behold the day of ^cthis life is the day for men to perform their ^dlabors.

33 And now, as I said unto you before, as ye have had so many ^awitnesses, therefore, I beseech of you that ye do not ^bprocrastinate the day of your ^crepentance until the end; for after this day of life, which is given us to prepare for eternity, behold, if we do not improve our time while in this life, then cometh the ^dnight of ^edarkness wherein there can be no labor performed.

34 Ye cannot say, when ye are brought to that awful ^acrisis, that I will repent, that I will return to my God. Nay, ye cannot say this; for that same spirit which doth ^bpossess your bodies at the time that ye go out of this life, that same spirit will have power to possess your body in that eternal world.

35 For behold, if ye have procrastinated the day of your repentance even until death, behold, ye have become ^asubjected to the spirit of the devil, and he doth ^bseal you his; therefore, the Spirit of the Lord hath withdrawn from you, and hath no place in you, and the devil hath all power over you; and this is the final state of the wicked.

36 And this I know, because the Lord hath said he dwelleth not in ^aunholy temples, but in the ^bhearts of the ^crighteous doth he dwell; yea, and he has also said that the righteous shall sit down in his kingdom, to go no more out; but their garments should be made white through the ^dblood of the Lamb.

37 And now, my beloved brethren, I desire that ye should remember

---

28a TG Apathy.
  b TG Poor.
  c Ezek. 18: 7 (5–9).
  d TG Almsgiving; Good Works.
  e Ezek. 33: 31; Matt. 15: 8 (7–8).
  f Isa. 58: 3; Moro. 7: 6 (6–8).
  g TG Hypocrisy.
29a TG Charity; Generosity.
30a TG Witnesses.
  b Matt. 3: 8; Alma 13: 13.
31a TG Self-mastery.

  b Rom. 13: 12 (11–12).
  c Matt. 11: 20; 3 Ne. 9: 3; D&C 84: 114.
  d TG Hardheartedness.
32a TG Mortality.
  b 2 Cor. 6: 2; 2 Ne. 2: 21; Alma 12: 24; 42: 4 (4–6). TG Self-mastery.
  c D&C 138: 57.
  d TG Good Works; Industry.
33a TG Witnesses.
  b Job 27: 8; Hel. 13: 38; D&C 45: 2. TG Apathy; Idleness; Procrastination.

  c TG Repentance.
  d Eccl. 9: 10; John 9: 4.
  e TG Darkness, Spiritual.
34a Alma 40: 14 (13–14); Ether 9: 34.
  b Rom. 6: 16 (14–18).
35a 2 Ne. 28: 19 (19–23).
  b 2 Ne. 9: 9; 3 Ne. 2: 10. TG Devil; Sealing.
36a Mosiah 2: 37; Alma 7: 21; Hel. 4: 24. TG Cleanliness.
  b D&C 130: 3.
  c TG Righteousness.
  d Rev. 12: 11.

[About 74 B.C.]

these things, and that ye should ^awork out your salvation with fear before God, and that ye should no more deny the coming of Christ;

38 That ye ^acontend no more against the Holy Ghost, but that ye receive it, and take upon you the ^bname of Christ; that ye humble yourselves even to the dust, and ^cworship God, in whatsoever place ye may be in, in spirit and in truth; and that ye live in ^dthanksgiving daily, for the many ^emercies and blessings which he doth bestow upon you.

39 Yea, and I also ^aexhort you, my brethren, that ye be ^bwatchful unto prayer continually, that ye may not be led away by the ^ctemptations of the devil, that he may not overpower you, that ye may not become his subjects at the last day; for behold, he rewardeth you ^dno good thing.

40 And now my beloved brethren, I would exhort you to have ^apatience, and that ye bear with all manner of ^bafflictions; that ye do not ^crevile against those who do cast you out because of your ^dexceeding poverty, lest ye become sinners like unto them;

41 But that ye have ^apatience, and bear with those ^bafflictions, with a firm hope that ye shall one day rest from all your afflictions.

CHAPTER 35

The preaching of the word destroys the craft of the Zoramites—They expel the converts, who then join the people of Ammon in Jershon—Alma sorrows because of the wickedness of the people.

Now it came to pass that after Amulek had made an end of these words, they withdrew themselves from the multitude and came over into the land of ^aJershon.

2 Yea, and the rest of the brethren, after they had preached the word unto the ^aZoramites, also came over into the land of Jershon.

3 And it came to pass that after the more popular part of the Zoramites had consulted together concerning the words which had been preached unto them, they were angry because of the word, for it did destroy their ^acraft; therefore they would not hearken unto the words.

4 And they sent and gathered together throughout all the land all the people, and consulted with them concerning the words which had been spoken.

5 Now their rulers and their priests and their teachers did not let the people know concerning their desires; therefore they found out privily the minds of all the people.

6 And it came to pass that after they had found out the minds of all the people, those who were in favor of the words which had been spoken by Alma and his brethren were cast out of the land; and they were ^amany; and they came over also into the land of Jershon.

7 And it came to pass that Alma and his brethren did minister unto them.

8 Now the ^apeople of the Zoramites were angry with the people of Ammon who were in Jershon, and the ^bchief ruler of the Zoramites, being a very wicked man, sent over unto the people of Ammon desiring them that they should cast out of their land all those who came over from them into their land.

9 And he breathed out many

37a Philip. 2: 12 (12–16).
38a TG Holy Ghost, Loss of.
  b Mosiah 5: 8; Alma
    5: 38. TG Jesus Christ,
    Taking the Name of.
  c TG Worship.
  d Ps. 69: 30 (30–31);
    D&C 46: 7.
    TG Thanksgiving.
  e Gen. 32: 10; 1 Ne.

    1: 20; D&C 46: 15.
39a Heb. 3: 13.
  b TG Watchfulness.
  c TG Temptation.
  d Alma 30: 60.
40a TG Patience;
    Steadfastness.
  b TG Affliction.
  c TG Reviling.
  d Alma 32: 3.

41a TG Patience.
  b Job 23: 2 (2–5).
35 1a Alma 28: 1.
  2a Alma 30: 59.
  3a TG Priestcraft.
  6a Alma 35: 14.
  8a Alma 27: 26.
  b Alma 30: 59.

[About 74 B.C.]

threatenings against them. And now the people of Ammon did not fear their words; therefore they did not cast them out, but they did receive all the poor of the Zoramites that came over unto them; and they did ^anourish them, and did clothe them, and did give unto them lands for their inheritance; and they did administer unto them according to their wants.

10 Now this did ^astir up the Zoramites to ^banger against the people of Ammon, and they began to mix with the Lamanites and to stir them up also to anger against them.

11 And thus the Zoramites and the Lamanites began to make preparations for war against the people of Ammon, and also against the Nephites.

12 And thus ended the *seventeenth year of the reign of the judges over the people of Nephi.

13 And the people of Ammon departed out of the land of Jershon, and came over into the land of Melek, and gave place in the land of Jershon for the armies of the Nephites, that they might contend with the armies of the Lamanites and the armies of the Zoramites; and thus commenced a war betwixt the Lamanites and the Nephites, in the eighteenth year of the reign of the judges; and an ^aaccount shall be given of their wars hereafter.

14 And Alma, and Ammon, and their brethren, and also the ^atwo sons of Alma returned to the land of Zarahemla, after having been instruments in the hands of God of bringing ^bmany of the ^cZoramites to repentance; and as many as were brought to repentance were driven out of their land; but they have lands for their inheritance in the land of Jershon, and they have

taken up arms to defend themselves, and their wives, and children, and their lands.

15 Now Alma, being ^agrieved for the iniquity of his people, yea for the wars, and the bloodsheds, and the contentions which were among them; and having been to declare the word, or sent to declare the word, among all the people in every city; and seeing that the hearts of the people began to wax hard, and that they began to be ^boffended because of the strictness of the word, his heart was exceedingly sorrowful.

16 Therefore, he caused that his sons should be gathered together, that he might give unto them every one his ^acharge, separately, concerning the things pertaining unto righteousness. And we have an account of his commandments, which he gave unto them according to his own record.

The commandments of Alma to his son Helaman. Comprising chapters 36 and 37.

CHAPTER 36

Alma testifies to Helaman of his conversion by an angel—He suffered the pains of a damned soul; he called upon the name of Jesus, and was then born of God—Sweet joy filled his soul—He saw concourses of angels praising God—His converts have tasted and seen as he did.

MY ^ason, give ear to my words; for I swear unto you, that inasmuch as ye shall keep the commandments of God ye shall prosper in the land.

2 I would that ye should do as I have done, in remembering the captivity of our fathers; for they were in ^abondage, and none could

---

9a Mosiah 4: 26; D&C 42: 43. TG Nourish; Welfare.
10a Alma 47: 1; Hel. 1: 17.
 b TG Anger; War.
13a Alma 43: 3.
14a Alma 31: 7.

b Alma 35: 6.
c Alma 30: 59.
15a Alma 31: 1.
 b TG Prophets, Rejection of.
16a TG Stewardship.

36 1a Hel. 5: 13 (1–13); Moses 6: 58.
2a Mosiah 23: 23; 24: 17 (17–21). TG Israel, Bondage of, in Egypt.

[* 74 B.C.]

[b]deliver them except it was the [c]God of Abraham, and the God of Isaac, and the God of Jacob; and he surely did deliver them in their afflictions.

3 And now, O my son Helaman, behold, thou art in thy youth, and therefore, I beseech of thee that thou wilt hear my words and learn of me; for I do know that whosoever shall put their [a]trust in God shall be supported in their [b]trials, and their troubles, and their afflictions, and shall be [c]lifted up at the last day.

4 And I would not that ye think that I [a]know of myself—not of the temporal but of the spiritual, not of the [b]carnal mind but of God.

5 Now, behold, I say unto you, if I had not been [a]born of God I should [b]not have known these things; but God has, by the mouth of his holy [c]angel, made these things known unto me, not of any [d]worthiness of myself;

6 For I went about with the sons of Mosiah, seeking to [a]destroy the church of God; but behold, God sent his holy angel to stop us by the way.

7 And behold, he spake unto us, as it were the voice of thunder, and the whole earth did [a]tremble beneath our feet; and we all fell to the earth, for the [b]fear of the Lord came upon us.

8 But behold, the voice said unto me: Arise. And I arose and stood up, and beheld the angel.

9 And he said unto me: If thou wilt of thyself be destroyed, seek no more to destroy the church of God.

10 And it came to pass that I fell to the earth; and it was for the space of [a]three days and three nights that I could not open my mouth, neither had I the use of my limbs.

11 And the angel spake more things unto me, which were heard by my brethren, but I did [a]not hear them; for when I heard the words—If thou wilt be destroyed of thyself, seek no more to destroy the church of God— I was struck with such great fear and amazement lest perhaps I should be destroyed, that I fell to the earth and I did hear no more.

12 But I was racked with [a]eternal [b]torment, for my soul was [c]harrowed up to the greatest degree and racked with all my sins.

13 Yea, I did remember all my sins and iniquities, for which I was [a]tormented with the [b]pains of hell; yea, I saw that I had [c]rebelled against my God, and that I had not kept his holy commandments.

14 Yea, and I had [a]murdered many of his children, or rather led them away unto destruction; yea, and in fine so great had been my iniquities, that the very thought of coming into the presence of my God did rack my soul with inexpressible horror.

15 Oh, thought I, that I [a]could be banished and become extinct both soul and body, that I might not be brought to stand in the presence of my God, to be judged of my [b]deeds.

16 And now, for three days and for three nights was I racked, even with the [a]pains of a [b]damned soul.

17 And it came to pass that as I was thus [a]racked with torment, while I

2b Deut. 26:8.
  c Ex. 3:6; Alma 29:11.
3a TG Trust in God.
  b Rom. 8:28.
  c Mosiah 23:22 (21–22).
4a 1 Cor. 2:11; Alma 5:45 (45–46).
  TG Knowledge.
  b TG Carnal Mind.
5a TG Man, New, Spiritually Reborn.
  b Alma 26:21 (21–22).
  c Mosiah 27:11 (11–18).
  d TG Worthiness.
6a Mosiah 27:10; 28:4 (3–4).
7a Isa. 6:4; Mosiah 27:18.
  b Prov. 2:5. TG Fear of God.
10a Mosiah 27:23 (19–23); Alma 38:8.
11a Dan. 10:7; Acts 9:7 (3–7).
12a D&C 19:11 (11–15).
  b TG Despair.
  c TG Poor in Spirit; Repentance; Sorrow.
13a TG Guilt.
  b Moses 1:20.
  c TG Disobedience.
14a Matt. 10:28.
15a Rev. 6:16 (15–17); Alma 12:14.
  b Isa. 59:18; Alma 41:3 (2–5); 42:27; D&C 1:10 (9–10).
16a TG Pain.
  b TG Damnation.
17a Ps. 119:67.

[About 73 B.C.]

was [b]harrowed up by the [c]memory of my many sins, behold, I [d]remembered also to have heard my father prophesy unto the people concerning the coming of one Jesus Christ, a Son of God, to atone for the sins of the world.

18 Now, as my mind caught hold upon this thought, I cried within my heart: O Jesus, thou Son of God, [a]have mercy on me, who am [b]in the [c]gall of bitterness, and am encircled about by the everlasting [d]chains of [e]death.

19 And now, behold, when I thought this, I could remember my [a]pains [b]no more; yea, I was harrowed up by the memory of my sins no more.

20 And oh, what [a]joy, and what marvelous light I did behold; yea, my soul was filled with joy as exceeding as was my pain!

21 Yea, I say unto you, my son, that there could be nothing so exquisite and so bitter as were my pains. Yea, and again I say unto you, my son, that on the other hand, there can be nothing so exquisite and sweet as was my joy.

22 Yea, methought I saw, even as our father [a]Lehi saw, God sitting upon his throne, surrounded with numberless concourses of angels, in the attitude of singing and [b]praising their God; yea, and my soul did long to be there.

23 But behold, my limbs did receive their [a]strength again, and I stood upon my feet, and did manifest unto the people that I had been [b]born of God.

24 Yea, and from that time even until now, I have labored without ceasing, that I might bring souls unto [a]repentance; that I might bring them to [b]taste of the exceeding joy of which I did taste; that they might also be [c]born of God, and be [d]filled with the Holy Ghost.

25 Yea, and now behold, O my son, the Lord doth [a]give me exceedingly great joy in the fruit of my [b]labors;

26 For because of the [a]word which he has imparted unto me, behold, many have been born of God, and have [b]tasted as I have tasted, and have seen eye to eye as I have seen; therefore they do know of these things of which I have spoken, as I do know; and the knowledge which I have is of God.

27 And I have been supported under trials and troubles of every kind, yea, and in all manner of afflictions; yea, God has [a]delivered me from prison, and from bonds, and from death; yea, and I do put my trust in him, and he will still [b]deliver me.

28 And I know that he will [a]raise me up at the last day, to dwell with him in [b]glory; yea, and I will [c]praise him forever, for he has [d]brought our fathers out of Egypt, and he has swallowed up the [e]Egyptians in the Red Sea; and he led them by his power into the promised land; yea, and he has delivered them out of

17b 2 Cor. 7: 10 (8–11).
   c Alma 11: 43; D&C 18: 44.
   d 1 Ne. 10: 17 (17–19); Enos 1: 3.
18a Matt. 15: 22.
   b IE in extreme remorse.
   c Jonah 2: 2; Acts 8: 23.
   d Prov. 5: 22; 2 Ne. 9: 45; 28: 22; Alma 12: 11 (10–11); Moses 7: 26.
   e TG Death, Spiritual, First.
19a TG Peace of God.
   b Jer. 31: 34; D&C 19: 16.

20a Moses 5: 11.
   TG Forgiveness; Joy.
22a 1 Ne. 1: 8. TG God, Manifestations of.
   b Isa. 6: 3 (1–4).
23a Moses 1: 10.
   b Alma 22: 15; 38: 6.
   TG Conversion.
24a Alma 19: 29.
   b Ps. 34: 8; 1 Ne. 8: 12; Mosiah 4: 11.
   c TG Holy Ghost, Baptism of.
   d 2 Ne. 32: 2 (2, 5); 3 Ne. 9: 20. TG Holy Ghost, Mission of.
25a TG Reward.

   b TG Work, Value of.
26a Prov. 10: 11; Jacob 2: 8; Alma 31: 5; D&C 108: 7.
   b 1 Pet. 2: 3 (1–3).
27a Alma 14: 28 (26–29).
   b Ps. 34: 17.
28a Alma 26: 7; 3 Ne. 15: 1.
   b TG Exaltation.
   c Ezra 3: 11 (11–13); 2 Ne. 9: 49.
   d Mosiah 12: 34; D&C 103: 16.
   e Ex. 14: 27 (26–27).

[About 73 B.C.]

bondage and captivity from time to time.

29 Yea, and he has also brought our fathers out of the land of Jerusalem; and he has also, by his everlasting power, delivered them out of [a]bondage and captivity, from time to time even down to the present day; and I have always retained in remembrance their captivity; yea, and ye also ought to retain in remembrance, as I have done, their captivity.

30 But behold, my son, this is not all; for ye ought to know as I do know, that [a]inasmuch as ye shall keep the commandments of God ye shall [b]prosper in the land; and ye ought to know also, that inasmuch as ye will not keep the commandments of God ye shall be cut off from his presence. Now this is according to his word.

CHAPTER 37

The plates of brass and other scriptures are preserved to bring souls to salvation—The Jaredites were destroyed because of their wickedness—Their secret oaths and covenants must be kept from the people—Counsel with the Lord in all thy doings—As the Liahona guided the Nephites, so the word of Christ leads men to eternal life.

AND now, my son Helaman, I command you that ye take the [a]records which have been [b]entrusted with me;

2 And I also command you that ye keep a [a]record of this people, according as I have done, upon the plates of Nephi, and keep all these things

sacred which I have kept, even as I have kept them; for it is for a [b]wise purpose that they are kept.

3 And these [a]plates of brass, which contain these engravings, which have the records of the holy scriptures upon them, which have the [b]genealogy of our forefathers, even from the beginning—

4 Behold, it has been prophesied by our fathers, that they should be kept and [a]handed down from one generation to another, and be kept and preserved by the hand of the Lord until they should go forth unto every nation, kindred, tongue, and people, that they shall know of the [b]mysteries contained thereon.

5 And now behold, if they are kept they must retain their brightness; yea, and they will retain their brightness; yea, and also shall all the plates which do contain that which is holy writ.

6 Now ye may suppose that this is [a]foolishness in me; but behold I say unto you, that by [b]small and simple things are great things brought to pass; and small means in many instances doth confound the wise.

7 And the Lord God doth work by [a]means to bring about his great and eternal purposes; and by very [b]small means the Lord doth [c]confound the wise and bringeth about the salvation of many souls.

8 And now, it has hitherto been wisdom in God that these things should be preserved; for behold, [a]they have [b]enlarged the memory of this people, yea, and convinced many of the error of their ways, and brought them to the [c]knowledge of

---

29a Mosiah 24: 17; 25: 10; 27: 16; Alma 5: 5 (5–6); 29: 12 (11–12).
30a 2 Ne. 1: 20.
  b Mosiah 1: 7; Alma 37: 13; 50: 20.
37 1a Alma 45: 2 (2–8); 50: 38; 63: 1.
  b Mosiah 28: 20.
 2a TG Record Keeping.
  b Enos 1: 13 (13–18); W of M 1: 7 (6–11); Alma 37: 12.

TG Restoration of the Gospel.
3a Mosiah 28: 20; Alma 63: 12 (1, 11–14).
  b 1 Ne. 5: 14.
4a 1 Ne. 5: 19 (16–19); Alma 63: 13; Hel. 3: 16.
  b TG Mysteries of Godliness.
6a 2 Cor. 2: 14.
  b 1 Ne. 16: 29; D&C 64: 33; 123: 16.

7a Isa. 55: 8 (8–9); Alma 24: 27.
  b 2 Kgs. 5: 13; Alma 37: 41.
  c 1 Cor. 1: 27; D&C 133: 58 (58–59).
8a Mosiah 2: 34; Alma 33: 2.
  b Mosiah 1: 3 (3–5).
  c TG Education; Scriptures, Value of.

[About 73 B.C.]

their God unto the salvation of their souls.

9 Yea, I say unto you, [a]were it not for these things that these records do contain, which are on these plates, Ammon and his brethren could not have [b]convinced so many thousands of the Lamanites of the incorrect tradition of their fathers; yea, these records and their [c]words brought them unto repentance; that is, they brought them to the knowledge of the Lord their God, and to rejoice in Jesus Christ their Redeemer.

10 And who knoweth but what they will be the [a]means of bringing many thousands of them, yea, and also many thousands of our [b]stiffnecked brethren, the Nephites, who are now hardening their hearts in sin and iniquities, to the knowledge of their Redeemer?

11 Now these mysteries are not yet fully made known unto me; therefore I shall forbear.

12 And it may suffice if I only say they are preserved for a [a]wise purpose, which purpose is known unto God; for he doth [b]counsel in wisdom over all his works, and his paths are straight, and his course is [c]one eternal round.

13 O remember, remember, my son Helaman, how [a]strict are the commandments of God. And he said: [b]If ye will keep my commandments ye shall [c]prosper in the land— but if ye keep not his commandments ye shall be cut off from his presence.

14 And now remember, my son, that God has [a]entrusted you with these things, which are [b]sacred, which he has kept sacred, and also which he will keep and [c]preserve for

a [d]wise purpose in him, that he may show forth his power unto future generations.

15 And now behold, I tell you by the spirit of prophecy, that if ye transgress the commandments of God, behold, these things which are sacred shall be taken away from you by the power of God, and ye shall be delivered up unto Satan, that he may sift you as chaff before the wind.

16 But if ye keep the commandments of God, and do with these things which are sacred according to that which the Lord doth command you, (for you must appeal unto the Lord for all things whatsoever ye must do with them) behold, no power of earth or hell can [a]take them from you, for God is powerful to the fulfilling of all his words.

17 For he will fulfil all his [a]promises which he shall make unto you, for he has fulfilled his promises which he has made unto our fathers.

18 For he promised unto them that he would [a]preserve these things for a wise purpose in him, that he might show forth his power unto future generations.

19 And now behold, one purpose hath he fulfilled, even to the restoration of [a]many thousands of the Lamanites to the knowledge of the truth; and he hath shown forth his power in them, and he will also still show forth his power in them unto [b]future generations; therefore they shall be preserved.

20 Therefore I command you, my son Helaman, that ye be diligent in fulfilling all my words, and that ye be diligent in keeping the commandments of God as they are written.

21 And now, I will speak unto

9a Mosiah 1:5.
  b Alma 18:36; 22:12.
  c TG Gospel.
10a 2 Ne. 3:15.
  b TG Stiffneckedness.
12a Alma 37:2.
  b Prov. 15:22; 2 Ne. 9:28; Jacob 4:10.
  c 1 Ne. 10:19; Alma 7:20.
13a Luke 13:24 (22–30).
  b Alma 9:13 (13–14); 3 Ne. 5:22.
  c Ps. 122:6; Mosiah 1:7; Alma 36:30; 50:20.
14a D&C 3:5.
  b TG Sacred.
  c TG Scriptures, Preservation of.
  d 1 Ne. 9:5 (3–6).
16a JS-H 1:59.
17a 2 Kgs. 10:10. TG Promise.
18a D&C 5:9.
19a Alma 23:5 (5–13).
  b 2 Ne. 3:15; Enos 1:13 (12–18); Morm. 7:9 (8–10).

[About 73 B.C.]

you concerning those [a]twenty-four plates, that ye keep them, that the [b]mysteries and the works of darkness, and their secret works, or the secret works of those people who have been destroyed, may be made [c]manifest unto this people; yea, all their murders, and robbings, and their plunderings, and all their wickedness and abominations, may be made manifest unto this people; yea, and that ye preserve these [d]interpreters.

22 For behold, the Lord saw that his people began to work in darkness, yea, work secret murders and abominations; therefore the Lord said, if they did not repent they should be destroyed from off the face of the earth.

23 And the Lord said: I will prepare unto my servant Gazelem, a [a]stone, which shall shine forth in darkness unto light, that I may [b]discover unto my people who serve me, that I may discover unto them the works of their brethren, yea, their secret works, their works of darkness, and their wickedness and abominations.

24 And now, my son, these [a]interpreters were prepared that the word of God might be fulfilled, which he spake, saying:

25 I will [a]bring forth out of darkness unto light all their secret works and their abominations; and except they repent I will [b]destroy them from off the face of the earth; and I will bring to light all their secrets and abominations, unto every nation that shall hereafter possess the land.

26 And now, my son, we see that they did not repent; therefore they have been destroyed, and thus far the word of God has been fulfilled;

yea, their [a]secret abominations have been brought out of darkness and made known unto us.

27 And now, my son, I command you that ye retain all their oaths, and their covenants, and their agreements in their secret abominations; yea, and all their [a]signs and their wonders ye shall [b]keep from this people, that they know them not, lest peradventure they should fall into darkness also and be destroyed.

28 For behold, there is a [a]curse upon all this land, that destruction shall come upon all those workers of darkness, according to the power of God, when they are fully ripe; therefore I desire that this people might not be destroyed.

29 Therefore ye shall keep these secret plans of their [a]oaths and their covenants from this people, and only their wickedness and their murders and their abominations shall ye make known unto them; and ye shall teach them to [b]abhor such wickedness and abominations and murders; and ye shall also teach them that these people were destroyed on account of their wickedness and abominations and their murders.

30 For behold, they [a]murdered all the prophets of the Lord who came among them to declare unto them concerning their iniquities; and the blood of those whom they murdered did cry unto the Lord their God for vengeance upon those who were their murderers; and thus the judgments of God did come upon these workers of darkness and secret [b]combinations.

31 Yea, and [a]cursed be the land forever and ever unto those workers of

21a Mosiah 8: 9;
    21: 27; 28: 11; Ether
    1: 2 (1–5); 15: 33.
  b TG Secret Combinations.
  c Prov. 26: 26; Alma
    14: 3 (2–3).
  d TG Urim and Thummim.
23a Mosiah 8: 13.
  b IE reveal, make known.

24a TG Urim and
    Thummim.
25a Ps. 64: 5 (4–6); D&C
    88: 108 (108–109).
  b Mosiah 21: 26.
26a 2 Ne. 10: 15.
27a Hel. 6: 22. TG Signs.
  b Alma 63: 12.
28a Ether 2: 8 (7–12).
29a Hel. 6: 25.

  b Deut. 32: 19; Alma
    13: 12. TG Hate.
30a TG Prophets, Rejection
    of.
  b TG Secret Combinations.
31a Alma 45: 16.
    TG Earth, Curse of.

[About 73 B.C.]

darkness and secret combinations, even unto destruction, except they repent before they are fully ᵇripe.

32 And now, my son, remember the words which I have spoken unto you; trust not those secret plans unto this people, but teach them an everlasting ᵃhatred against sin and iniquity.

33 ᵃPreach unto them repentance, and faith on the Lord Jesus Christ; teach them to humble themselves and to be ᵇmeek and lowly in heart; teach them to ᶜwithstand every ᵈtemptation of the devil, with their faith on the Lord Jesus Christ.

34 Teach them to never be weary of good works, but to be meek and lowly in heart; for such shall find ᵃrest to their souls.

35 O, remember, my son, and ᵃlearn ᵇwisdom in thy ᶜyouth; yea, learn in thy youth to keep the commandments of God.

36 Yea, and ᵃcry unto God for all thy support; yea, let all thy ᵇdoings be unto the Lord, and whithersoever thou goest let it be in the Lord; yea, let all thy ᶜthoughts be directed unto the Lord; yea, let the affections of thy heart be placed upon the Lord forever.

37 ᵃCounsel with the Lord in all thy doings, and he will direct thee for ᵇgood; yea, when thou liest down at night lie down unto the Lord, that he may watch over you in your sleep; and when thou risest in the ᶜmorning let thy heart be full of thanks unto God; and if ye do these things, ye shall be lifted up at the last day.

38 And now, my son, I have somewhat to say concerning the thing which our fathers call a ball, or director—or our fathers called it ᵃLiahona, which is, being interpreted, a compass; and the Lord prepared it.

39 And behold, there cannot any man work after the manner of so curious a workmanship. And behold, it was prepared to show unto our fathers the course which they should travel in the wilderness.

40 And it did work for them according to their ᵃfaith in God; therefore, if they had faith to believe that God could cause that those spindles should point the way they should go, behold, it was done; therefore they had this miracle, and also many other miracles wrought by the power of God, day by day.

41 Nevertheless, because those miracles were worked by ᵃsmall means it did show unto them marvelous works. They were ᵇslothful, and forgot to exercise their faith and diligence and then those marvelous works ceased, and they did not progress in their journey;

42 Therefore, they tarried in the wilderness, or did ᵃnot travel a direct course, and were afflicted with hunger and thirst, because of their transgressions.

43 And now, my son, I would that ye should understand that these things are not without a ᵃshadow; for as our fathers were slothful to give heed to this compass (now these things were temporal) they

31b Gen. 15: 16; Hel. 13: 14; D&C 61: 31; 101: 11.
32a Prov. 3: 5 (5–6); 2 Ne. 4: 31; Alma 43: 7.
33a TG Mission of Early Saints; Preaching.
  b TG Meekness.
  c TG Perseverance; Self-mastery.
  d TG Temptation.
34a Matt. 11: 29 (28–30).
35a TG Education; Learning.
  b TG Wisdom.
  c Eccl. 12: 1; Lam. 3: 27.
36a TG Prayer.
  b Ps. 37: 5 (4–7).
  c TG Motivations.
37a Josh. 9: 14; Ps. 34: 4 (4, 6, 10); Lam. 3: 25; Heb. 11: 6; Jacob 4: 10; D&C 3: 4.
  b TG Abundant Life.
  c Ps. 5: 3; 1 Chr. 16: 8 (7–36); Ether
6: 9; D&C 46: 32.
38a 1 Ne. 16: 10 (10, 16, 26); 18: 12 (12, 21); 2 Ne. 5: 12; D&C 17: 1.
40a 1 Ne. 16: 28.
41a 1 Ne. 16: 29; Alma 37: 7 (6–8).
  b TG Apathy; Laziness.
42a 1 Ne. 16: 28.
43a Col. 2: 17; Heb. 8: 5; Mosiah 3: 15.

[About 73 B.C.]

did not prosper; even so it is with things which are spiritual.

44 For behold, it is as easy to give heed to the [a]word of Christ, which will point to you a straight course to eternal bliss, as it was for our fathers to give heed to this compass, which would point unto them a straight course to the promised land.

45 And now I say, is there not a [a]type in this thing? For just as surely as this director did bring our fathers, by following its course, to the promised land, shall the words of Christ, if we follow their course, carry us beyond this vale of sorrow into a far better land of promise.

46 O my son, do not let us be [a]slothful because of the [b]easiness of the [c]way; for so was it with our fathers; for so was it prepared for them, that if they would [d]look they might [e]live; even so it is with us. The way is prepared, and if we will look we may live forever.

47 And now, my son, see that ye take [a]care of these sacred things, yea, see that ye [b]look to God and live. Go unto this people and declare the word, and be sober. My son, farewell.

The commandments of Alma to his son Shiblon.

CHAPTER 38

Shiblon was persecuted for righteousness' sake—Salvation is in Christ, who is the life and the light of the world—Bridle all your passions.

MY [a]son, give ear to my words, for I say unto you, even as I said unto Helaman, that [b]inasmuch as ye shall keep the commandments of God ye shall prosper in the land; and [c]inasmuch as ye will not keep the commandments of God ye shall be [d]cut off from his [e]presence.

2 And now, my son, I trust that I shall have great joy in you, because of your [a]steadiness and your faithfulness unto God; for as you have commenced in your youth to look to the Lord your God, even so I hope that you will continue in keeping his commandments; for blessed is he that [b]endureth to the end.

3 I say unto you, my son, that I have had great joy in thee already, because of thy faithfulness and thy diligence, and thy patience and thy long-suffering among the people of the [a]Zoramites.

4 For I know that thou wast in bonds; yea, and I also know that thou wast stoned for the word's sake; and thou didst bear all these things with [a]patience because the Lord was [b]with thee; and now thou knowest that the Lord did deliver thee.

5 And now my son, Shiblon, I would that ye should remember, that as much as ye shall put your [a]trust in God even so much ye shall be [b]delivered out of your trials, and your [c]troubles, and your afflictions, and ye shall be lifted up at the last day.

6 Now, my son, I would not that ye

44a Ps. 119:105.
45a TG Jesus Christ, Types of, in Anticipation.
46a Luke 6:46 (46–49); 1 Ne. 17:41 (40–41).
  b Matt. 11:30.
  c Ex. 33:13 (12–13); 2 Ne. 9:41; 31:21 (17–21); D&C 132:22 (22, 25).
  d Alma 25:16; 33:22 (19–23).
  e John 11:25; Hel. 8:15; 3 Ne. 15:9.

47a TG Scriptures, Preservation of.
  b Amos 5:6; Ether 12:41.
38 1a Alma 31:7; 63:1.
  b Alma 60:16.
  c Alma 44:3.
  d 1 Ne. 2:21; 2 Ne. 5:20 (20–24); Alma 9:14 (13–15).
  e TG God, Presence of.
2a TG Commitment.
  b Matt. 10:22; Mark 13:13; 2 Ne. 31:16

(15–20); Alma 32:13 (13–15); 3 Ne. 15:9; 27:6 (6–17); D&C 20:29; 53:7.
3a Alma 31:7; 39:2.
4a TG Patience.
  b Ex. 3:12; 1 Ne. 17:55; Mosiah 24:17.
5a Ps. 50:15; D&C 100:17.
  b Matt. 11:28 (28–30).
  c Ps. 81:7; Alma 9:17; D&C 3:8.

[About 73 B.C.]

should think that I know these things of myself, but it is the Spirit of God which is in me which maketh these things known unto me; for if I had not been *a*born of God I should not have known these things.

7 But behold, the Lord in his great mercy sent his *a*angel to declare unto me that I must stop the work of *b*destruction among his people; yea, and I have seen an angel face to face, and he spake with me, and his voice was as thunder, and it shook the whole earth.

8 And it came to pass that I was *a*three days and three nights in the most bitter *b*pain and *c*anguish of soul; and never, until I did cry out unto the Lord Jesus Christ for mercy, did I receive a *d*remission of my sins. But behold, I did cry unto him and I did find peace to my soul.

9 And now, my son, I have told you this that ye may learn wisdom, that ye may learn of me that there is *a*no other way or means whereby man can be saved, only in and through Christ. Behold, he is the life and the *b*light of the world. Behold, he is the word of truth and *c*righteousness.

10 And now, as ye have begun to teach the word even so I would that ye should continue to teach; and I would that ye would be diligent and *a*temperate in all things.

11 See that ye are not lifted up unto pride; yea, see that ye do not *a*boast in your own wisdom, nor of your much strength.

12 Use *a*boldness, but not overbearance; and also see that ye *b*bridle all your passions, that ye may be filled with love; see that ye refrain from idleness.

13 Do not *a*pray as the Zoramites do, for ye have seen that they pray to be heard of men, and to be praised for their wisdom.

14 Do not say: O God, I thank thee that we are *a*better than our brethren; but rather say: O Lord, forgive my *b*unworthiness, and remember my brethren in mercy—yea, acknowledge your unworthiness before God at all times.

15 And may the Lord bless your soul, and receive you at the last day into his kingdom, to sit down in peace. Now go, my son, and teach the word unto this people. Be *a*sober. My son, farewell.

The commandments of Alma to his son Corianton. Comprising chapters 39 to 42 inclusive.

CHAPTER 39

Sexual sin is an abomination— Corianton's sins kept the Zoramites from receiving the word—Christ's redemption is retroactive in saving the faithful who preceded it.

AND now, my *a*son, I have somewhat more to say unto thee than what I said unto thy brother; for behold, have ye not observed the steadiness of thy brother, his faithfulness, and his diligence in keeping the commandments of God? Behold, has he not set a good *b*example for thee?

2 For thou didst not give so much heed unto my words as did thy brother, among the people of the *a*Zoramites. Now this is what I have against thee; thou didst go on unto

6a Alma 36: 23 (23, 26); D&C 5: 16. TG Holy Ghost, Baptism of; Man, Natural, Not Spiritually Reborn; Man, New, Spiritually Reborn.
7a Mosiah 27: 11 (11–17).
 b Mosiah 28: 4 (3–4); Alma 26: 18 (17–18); 36: 6 (6–11).
8a Alma 36: 10 (10, 16).

 b TG Pain.
 c TG Sorrow.
 d TG Remission of Sins.
9a Alma 21: 9.
 b TG Jesus Christ, Light of the World.
 c Ether 4: 12.
10a TG Temperance.
11a TG Boasting; Pride.
12a TG Boldness.
 b TG Priesthood, Magnifying Callings

within; Self-mastery.
13a TG Hypocrisy.
14a Alma 31: 16.
 b Luke 18: 13 (10–14). TG Ingratitude; Poor in Spirit.
15a 1 Pet. 5: 8.
39 1a Alma 31: 7.
 b TG Example.
2a Alma 38: 3.

[About 73 B.C.]

boasting in thy strength and thy wisdom.

3 And this is not all, my son. Thou didst do that which was grievous unto me; for thou didst forsake the ministry, and did go over into the land of Siron among the borders of the Lamanites, after the [a]harlot Isabel.

4 Yea, she did [a]steal away the hearts of many; but this was no excuse for thee, my son. Thou shouldst have tended to the ministry wherewith thou wast entrusted.

5 Know ye not, my son, that these things are an abomination in the sight of the Lord; yea, most [a]abominable above all sins save it be the shedding of innocent [b]blood or denying the Holy Ghost?

6 For behold, if ye [a]deny the Holy Ghost when it once has had place in you, and ye know that ye deny it, behold, this is a sin which is [b]unpardonable; yea, and whosoever murdereth against the light and knowledge of God, it is not easy for him to obtain [c]forgiveness; yea, I say unto you, my son, that it is not easy for him to obtain a forgiveness.

7 And now, my son, I would to God that ye had not been [a]guilty of so great a crime. I would not dwell upon your crimes, to harrow up your soul, if it were not for your good.

8 But behold, ye cannot [a]hide your crimes from God; and except ye repent they will stand as a testimony against you at the last day.

9 Now my son, I would that ye should repent and forsake your sins, and go no more after the [a]lusts of your eyes, but [b]cross yourself in all these things; for except ye do this ye can in nowise inherit the kingdom of God. Oh, remember, and take it upon you, and [c]cross yourself in these things.

10 And I command you to take it upon you to counsel with your elder brothers in your undertakings; for behold, thou art in thy youth, and ye stand in need to be nourished by your brothers. And give heed to their counsel.

11 Suffer not yourself to be led away by any vain or foolish thing; suffer not the devil to lead away your heart again after those wicked harlots. Behold, O my son, how great [a]iniquity ye brought upon the [b]Zoramites; for when they saw your [c]conduct they would not believe in my words.

12 And now the Spirit of the Lord doth say unto me: [a]Command thy children to do good, lest they [b]lead away the hearts of many people to destruction; therefore I command you, my son, in the fear of God, that ye [c]refrain from your iniquities;

13 That ye turn to the Lord with all your mind, might, and strength; that ye lead away the hearts of no more to do wickedly; but rather return unto them, and [a]acknowledge your faults and that wrong which ye have done.

14 [a]Seek not after riches nor the vain things of this world; for behold, you cannot carry them with you.

3a 1 Sam. 2: 22 (22–25);
   Prov. 5: 3.
   TG Sensuality.
4a Prov. 7: 18 (6–27).
5a TG Adultery;
   Fornication; Sexual
   Immorality.
 b TG Life, Sanctity of.
6a Moro. 8: 28; D&C
   76: 35. TG Holy
   Ghost, Loss of.
 b TG Holy Ghost,
   Unpardonable Sin
   against.
 c Rom. 9: 18; D&C

64: 10. TG Forgiveness.
7a TG Guilt.
8a TG God, Omniscience
   of.
9a Prov. 5: 8.
   TG Carnal Mind;
   Chastity; Covetous-
   ness; Lust.
 b TG Self-mastery.
 c 3 Ne. 12: 30.
11a 1 Sam. 2: 24 (22–25).
 b Alma 35: 14 (2–14);
   43: 4 (4–6, 13).
 c 2 Sam. 12: 14; Ezek.
   5: 5; Rom. 2: 21

(21–23); 14: 13; 1 Cor.
9: 14 (13–14); 1 Ne.
21: 6; Alma 4: 11;
D&C 103: 9 (8–9).
TG Example.
12a TG Commandments of
God; Teaching.
 b TG Peer Influence.
 c TG Abstinence.
13a Mosiah 27: 35.
14a Matt. 6: 33 (25–34);
Jacob 2: 18 (18–19);
D&C 6: 7 (6–7); 68: 31
(31–32). TG Treasure.

15 And now, my son, I would say somewhat unto you concerning the [a]coming of Christ. Behold, I say unto you, that it is he that surely shall come to take away the sins of the world; yea, he cometh to declare glad tidings of salvation unto his people.

16 And now, my son, this was the ministry unto which ye were called, to declare these glad tidings unto this people, to prepare their minds; or rather that salvation might come unto them, that they may prepare the minds of their [a]children to hear the word at the time of his coming.

17 And now I will ease your mind somewhat on this subject. Behold, you marvel why these things should be known so long beforehand. Behold, I say unto you, is not a soul at this time as precious unto God as a soul will be at the time of his coming?

18 Is it not as necessary that the plan of redemption should be [a]made known unto this people as well as unto their children?

19 Is it not as easy at this time for the Lord to [a]send his angel to declare these glad tidings unto us as unto our children, or as after the time of his coming?

CHAPTER 40

Christ bringeth to pass the resurrection of all men—The righteous dead go to paradise and the wicked to outer darkness to await the day of their resurrection—All things shall be restored to their proper and perfect frame in the resurrection.

Now my son, here is somewhat more I would say unto thee; for I perceive that thy mind is worried concerning the resurrection of the dead.

2 Behold, I say unto you, that there is no resurrection— or, I would say, in other words, that this mortal does not put on [a]immortality, this corruption does not [b]put on incorruption—[c]until after the coming of Christ.

3 Behold, he bringeth to pass the [a]resurrection of the dead. But behold, my son, the resurrection is not yet. Now, I unfold unto you a mystery; nevertheless, there are many [b]mysteries which are [c]kept, that no one knoweth them save God himself. But I show unto you one thing which I have inquired diligently of God that I might know —that is concerning the resurrection.

4 Behold, there is a time appointed that all shall [a]come forth from the dead. Now when this time cometh no one knows; but God knoweth the time which is appointed.

5 Now, whether there shall be one time, or a [a]second time, or a third time, that men shall come forth from the dead, it mattereth not; for God [b]knoweth all these things; and it sufficeth me to know that this is the case—that there is a time appointed that all shall rise from the dead.

6 Now there must needs be a space betwixt the time of death and the time of the resurrection.

7 And now I would inquire what becometh of the [a]souls of men [b]from this time of death to the time appointed for the resurrection?

8 Now whether there is more than one [a]time appointed for men to rise it mattereth not; for all do not die at once, and this mattereth not; all is

15a TG Jesus Christ, Mission of.
16a TG Family, Children, Responsibilities toward.
18a Jacob 4:4 (4–6).
19a Mosiah 3:2 (2–3).
40 2a Mosiah 16:10 (10–13). TG Immortality.

b 1 Cor. 15:53 (42–54).
c 1 Cor. 15:20 (20–23).
3a TG Resurrection.
b TG Mysteries of Godliness.
c D&C 25:4; 121:26; 124:41.
4a John 5:29 (28–29).
5a 1 Thes. 4:16; Mosiah

26:25 (24–25); D&C 43:18; 76:85.
b TG God, Omniscience of.
7a TG Soul.
b TG Spirits, Disembodied.
8a 2 Pet. 3:8. TG Time.

[About 73 B.C.]

as one day with God, and time only is measured unto men.

9 Therefore, there is a time appointed unto men that they shall rise from the dead; and there is a space between the time of death and the resurrection. And now, concerning this space of time, what becometh of the souls of men is the thing which I have inquired diligently of the Lord to know; and this is the thing of which I do know.

10 And when the time cometh when all shall rise, then shall they know that God [a]knoweth all the [b]times which are appointed unto man.

11 Now, concerning the [a]state of the soul between [b]death and the resurrection—Behold, it has been made known unto me by an angel, that the spirits of all men, as soon as they are departed from this mortal body, yea, the spirits of all men, whether they be good or evil, are [c]taken [d]home to that God who gave them life.

12 And then shall it come to pass, that the spirits of those who are righteous are received into a state of [a]happiness, which is called [b]paradise, a state of rest, a state of [c]peace, where they shall rest from all their troubles and from all care, and sorrow.

13 And then shall it come to pass, that the [a]spirits of the wicked, yea, who are evil— for behold, they have no part nor portion of the Spirit of the Lord; for behold, they chose evil works rather than good; there-

fore the spirit of the [b]devil did enter into them, and take possession of their house—and these shall be cast out into outer [c]darkness; there shall be [d]weeping, and wailing, and gnashing of teeth, and this because of their own iniquity, being led captive by the will of the devil.

14 Now this is the state of the [a]souls of the [b]wicked, yea, in darkness, and a state of awful, [c]fearful looking for the fiery [d]indignation of the wrath of God upon them; thus they remain in this [e]state, as well as the righteous in paradise, until the time of their resurrection.

15 Now, there are some that have understood that this state of happiness and this state of misery of the soul, before the resurrection, was a first resurrection. Yea, I admit it may be termed a resurrection, the [a]raising of the spirit or the soul and their consignation to happiness or misery, according to the words which have been spoken.

16 And behold, again it hath been spoken, that there is a [a]first [b]resurrection, a resurrection of all those who have been, or who are, or who shall be, down to the resurrection of Christ from the dead.

17 Now, we do not suppose that this first resurrection, which is spoken of in this manner, can be the resurrection of the souls and their [a]consignation to happiness or misery. Ye cannot suppose that this is what it meaneth.

18 Behold, I say unto you, Nay; but it meaneth the [a]reuniting of the

10a TG God, Foreknowledge of.
  b Acts 17:26.
11a John 20:17.
  b Job 14:10; Luke 16:22 (22–26); 1 Ne. 15:31 (31–36); Alma 11:45; D&C 76:73 (71–74).
  c Alma 40:15.
  d Eccl. 12:5; 2 Ne. 9:38; Alma 24:16; Hel. 8:23.
12a Isa. 51:11; Luke 16:22; D&C 138:15.

  TG Happiness.
  b TG Paradise.
  c 2 Kgs. 22:20; Alma 7:27; D&C 45:46. TG Peace of God.
13a TG Spirits in Prison.
  b TG Bondage, Spiritual.
  c TG Damnation; Darkness, Spiritual; Hell.
  d Matt. 8:12; Mosiah 16:2.
14a TG Spirits in Prison.
  b D&C 138:20.

  c Jacob 6:13; Moses 7:1.
  d TG God, Indignation of.
  e Alma 34:34.
15a Alma 40:11.
16a Jacob 4:11; Mosiah 15:21 (21–23); 18:9.
  b TG Jesus Christ, Resurrection.
17a D&C 76:17 (17, 32, 50). TG Judgment, The Last.
18a Matt. 27:52.

[About 73 B.C.]

soul with the body, of those from the days of Adam down to the resurrection of Christ.

19 Now, whether the souls and the bodies of those of whom has been spoken shall all be reunited at once, the wicked as well as the righteous, I do not say; let it suffice, that I say that they all come forth; or in other words, their resurrection cometh to pass *before the resurrection of those who die after the resurrection of Christ.

20 Now, my son, I do not say that their resurrection cometh at the resurrection of Christ; but behold, I give it as my opinion, that the souls and the bodies are reunited, of the righteous, at the resurrection of Christ, and his *ascension into heaven.

21 But whether it be at his resurrection or after, I do not say; but this much I say, that there is a *space between death and the resurrection of the body, and a state of the soul in *happiness or in *misery until the time which is appointed of God that the dead shall come forth, and be reunited, both soul and body, and be *brought to stand before God, and be judged according to their works.

22 Yea, this bringeth about the restoration of those things of which has been spoken by the mouths of the prophets.

23 The *soul shall be *restored to the *body, and the body to the soul; yea, and every limb and joint shall be restored to its body; yea, even a *hair of the head shall not be lost; but all things shall be restored to their proper and *perfect frame.

24 And now, my son, this is the restoration of which has been *spoken by the mouths of the prophets—

25 And then shall the *righteous shine forth in the kingdom of God.

26 But behold, an awful *death cometh upon the wicked; for they die as to things pertaining to things of righteousness; for they are unclean, and *no unclean thing can inherit the kingdom of God; but they are cast out, and consigned to partake of the fruits of their labors or their works, which have been evil; and they drink the dregs of a bitter *cup.

CHAPTER 41

In the resurrection men come forth to a state of endless happiness or endless misery—Wickedness never was happiness—Carnal men are without God in the world—Every person receives again in the restoration the characteristics and attributes acquired in mortality.

AND now, my son, I have somewhat to say concerning the restoration of which has been spoken; for behold, some have *wrested the scriptures, and have gone far *astray because of this thing. And I perceive that thy mind has been *worried also concerning this thing. But behold, I will explain it unto thee.

2 I say unto thee, my son, that the plan of restoration is requisite with the justice of God; for it is requisite that all things should be restored to their proper order. Behold, it is requisite and just, according to the power and resurrection of Christ,

19a Mosiah 15:26.
20a TG Jesus Christ, Ascension of.
21a Luke 23:43 (39–43).
  b TG Paradise.
  c TG Spirits in Prison.
  d Alma 42:23.
23a Ezek. 37:14 (6–14); D&C 88:15 (15–17). TG Soul.
  b 2 Ne. 9:13; Alma 11:45 (40–45).

c TG Body, Sanctity of.
d Luke 21:18; Alma 41:2; D&C 29:25.
e Philip. 3:21. TG Perfection.
24a Isa. 26:19. TG Resurrection.
25a Dan. 12:3; Matt. 13:43.
26a Ps. 94:3 (1–11); 1 Cor. 6:9 (9–10); 1 Ne.

15:33; Alma 12:16; D&C 29:41. TG Hell.
  b Eph. 5:5; Alma 11:37. TG Uncleanness.
  c Ps. 75:8.
41 1a 2 Pet. 1:20; Alma 13:20.
  b TG Apostasy of Individuals.
  c TG Problem-Solving.

[About 73 B.C.]

that the soul of man should be restored to its body, and that every [a]part of the body should be restored to itself.

3 And it is requisite with the [a]justice of God that men should be [b]judged according to their [c]works; and if their works were good in this life, and the desires of their hearts were good, that they should also, at the last day, be [d]restored unto that which is good.

4 And if their works are evil they shall be [a]restored unto them for evil. Therefore, all things shall be [b]restored to their proper order, every thing to its natural frame—[c]mortality raised to [d]immortality, [e]corruption to incorruption—raised to [f]endless happiness to [g]inherit the kingdom of God, or to endless misery to inherit the kingdom of the devil, the one on one hand, the other on the other—

5 The one raised to [a]happiness according to his desires of happiness, or good according to his desires of good; and the other to evil according to his desires of evil; for as he has desired to do evil all the day long even so shall he have his reward of evil when the night cometh.

6 And so it is on the other hand. If he hath repented of his sins, and desired righteousness until the end of his days, even so he shall be rewarded unto righteousness.

7 [a]These are they that are redeemed of the Lord; yea, these are they that are taken out, that are delivered from that endless night of darkness; and thus they stand or fall; for behold, they are their own [b]judges, whether to do good or do evil.

8 Now, the decrees of God are [a]unalterable; therefore, the way is prepared for [b]whosoever will may [c]walk therein and be saved.

9 And now behold, my son, do not risk [a]one more offense against your God upon those points of doctrine, which ye have hitherto risked to commit sin.

10 Do not suppose, because it has been spoken concerning restoration, that ye shall be restored from sin to happiness. Behold, I say unto you, [a]wickedness never was [b]happiness.

11 And now, my son, all men that are in a state of [a]nature, or I would say, in a [b]carnal state, are in the [c]gall of bitterness and in the [d]bonds of iniquity; they are [e]without God in the world, and they have gone [f]contrary to the nature of God; therefore, they are in a state contrary to the nature of happiness.

12 And now behold, is the meaning of the word restoration to take a thing of a natural state and place it in an unnatural state, or to place it in a state opposite to its nature?

13 O, my son, this is not the case; but the meaning of the word restoration is to bring back again [a]evil for evil, or carnal for carnal, or devilish for devilish—good for that which is good; righteous for that which is righteous; just for that which is just; merciful for that which is merciful.

2a Alma 40: 23.
3a TG God, Justice of; Justice.
  b TG Accountability; Judgment, The Last.
  c Isa. 59: 18; Alma 36: 15; 42: 27; D&C 1: 10 (9–10).
  d Hel. 14: 31.
4a Alma 42: 28.
  b 2 Ne. 9: 13 (10–13); D&C 138: 17. TG Resurrection.
  c TG Mortality.
  d TG Immortality.
  e 1 Cor. 15: 50 (50–53).
  f TG Eternal Life.

  g TG Exaltation.
5a TG Happiness.
7a D&C 76: 65.
  b 2 Ne. 2: 26; Alma 42: 27; Hel. 14: 30. TG Agency.
8a Morm. 9: 19.
  b Alma 42: 27.
  c TG Walking with God.
9a Prov. 26: 11; Matt. 12: 45 (43–45); D&C 42: 26 (23–28).
10a Ps. 32: 10; Isa. 57: 21; Hel. 13: 38. TG Evil; Wickedness.
  b Alma 50: 21; Morm.

  2: 13. TG Happiness; Peace of God.
11a Mosiah 3: 19. TG Man, Natural, Not Spiritually Reborn.
  b TG Carnal Mind; Fall of Man.
  c Acts 8: 23; Morm. 8: 31.
  d TG Bondage, Spiritual.
  e Eph. 2: 12; Mosiah 27: 31.
  f Hel. 13: 38.
13a Dan. 12: 10; Rev. 22: 12 (6–16).

[About 73 B.C.]

14 Therefore, my son, see that you are merciful unto your brethren; deal [a]justly, [b]judge righteously, and do [c]good continually; and if ye do all these things then shall ye receive your [d]reward; yea, ye shall have [e]mercy restored unto you again; ye shall have justice restored unto you again; ye shall have a righteous judgment restored unto you again; and ye shall have good rewarded unto you again.

15 For that which ye do [a]send out shall return unto you again, and be restored; therefore, the word restoration more fully condemneth the sinner, and justifieth him not at all.

CHAPTER 42

Mortality is a probationary time to enable man to repent and serve God— The fall brought temporal and spiritual death upon all mankind— Redemption comes through repentance—God himself atoneth for the sins of the world—Mercy is for those who repent—All others are subject to God's justice—Mercy cometh because of the atonement—Only the truly penitent are saved.

AND now, my son, I perceive there is somewhat more which doth worry your mind, which ye cannot understand—which is concerning the [a]justice of God in the [b]punishment of the sinner; for ye do try to suppose that it is [c]injustice that the sinner should be consigned to a state of misery.

2 Now behold, my son, I will explain this thing unto thee. For behold, after the Lord God sent our first parents forth from the garden of [a]Eden, to till the [b]ground, from whence they were taken—yea, he drew out the man, and he placed at the east end of the garden of Eden, [c]cherubim, and a flaming sword which turned every way, to keep the tree of life—

3 Now, we see that the man had become as God, knowing good and evil; and lest he should put forth his hand, and take also of the tree of life, and eat and live forever, the Lord God placed [a]cherubim and the flaming sword, that he should not partake of the fruit—

4 And thus we see, that there was a [a]time granted unto man to repent, yea, a [b]probationary time, a time to repent and serve God.

5 For behold, if Adam had put forth his hand immediately, and [a]partaken of the [b]tree of life, he would have lived forever, according to the word of God, having no space for repentance; yea, and also the word of God would have been void, and the great plan of salvation would have been frustrated.

6 But behold, it was appointed unto man to [a]die—therefore, as they were cut off from the tree of life they should be cut off from the face of the earth—and man became [b]lost forever, yea, they became [c]fallen man.

7 And now, ye see by this that our first parents were [a]cut off both temporally and spiritually from the [b]presence of the Lord; and thus we see they became subjects to follow after their own [c]will.

8 Now behold, it was not expedient

14a TG Honesty.
 b Matt. 7: 1 (1–5);
   D&C 11: 12.
 c TG Benevolence.
 d TG Reward.
 e TG Mercy.
15a Prov. 19: 17;
   Eccl. 11: 1; Alma
   42: 27 (27–28).
42 1a Mosiah 15: 27.
   TG God, Justice of.
 b TG Punishment.
 c Rom. 3: 5; 2 Ne. 26: 7.

 TG Injustice.
2a TG Eden.
 b Jacob 2: 21; Mosiah
   2: 25; Morm. 9: 17.
 c Gen. 3: 24; Alma
   12: 21; Moses 4: 31.
3a TG Cherubim.
4a Jacob 5: 27.
 b Alma 34: 32. TG Earth,
   Purpose of; Probation.
5a Alma 12: 23; Moses
   4: 28.
 b Gen. 2: 9; 3: 24

 (22–24); 1 Ne. 8: 10
 (10–12); Moses 3: 9.
6a TG Death.
 b 2 Ne. 9: 7; Mosiah
   16: 4 (4–7); Alma
   11: 45; 12: 36.
 c TG Fall of Man.
7a 2 Ne. 2: 5; 9: 6 (6–15);
   Hel. 14: 16 (15–18).
 b TG God, Presence of.
 c TG Agency.

[About 73 B.C.]

that man should be reclaimed from this ^atemporal death, for that would destroy the great ^bplan of happiness.

9 Therefore, as the soul could never die, and the ^afall had brought upon all mankind a spiritual ^bdeath as well as a temporal, that is, they were cut off from the presence of the Lord, it was expedient that mankind should be reclaimed from this spiritual death.

10 Therefore, as they had become ^acarnal, sensual, and devilish, by ^bnature, this ^cprobationary state became a state for them to prepare; it became a preparatory state.

11 And now remember, my son, if it were not for the plan of redemption, (laying it aside) as soon as they were dead their souls were ^amiserable, being cut off from the presence of the Lord.

12 And now, there was no means to reclaim men from this fallen state, which ^aman had brought upon himself because of his own ^bdisobedience;

13 Therefore, according to justice, the ^aplan of ^bredemption could not be brought about, only on conditions of repentance of men in this probationary state, yea, this preparatory state; for except it were for these conditions, mercy could not take effect except it should destroy the work of justice. Now the work of justice could not be destroyed; if so, God would ^ccease to be God.

14 And thus we see that all mankind were ^afallen, and they were in the grasp of ^bjustice; yea, the justice of God, which consigned them forever to be cut off from his presence.

15 And now, the plan of mercy could not be brought about except an atonement should be made; therefore God himself ^aatoneth for the sins of the world, to bring about the plan of ^bmercy, to appease the demands of ^cjustice, that God might be a ^dperfect, just God, and a ^emerciful God also.

16 Now, repentance could not come unto men except there were a ^apunishment, which also was ^beternal as the life of the soul should be, affixed ^copposite to the plan of happiness, which was as ^deternal also as the life of the soul.

17 Now, how could a man repent except he should ^asin? How could he sin if there was no ^blaw? How could there be a law save there was a punishment?

18 Now, there was a punishment affixed, and a just law given, which brought remorse of ^aconscience unto man.

19 Now, if there was no law given—if a man ^amurdered he should ^bdie—would he be afraid he would die if he should murder?

20 And also, if there was no law given against sin men would not be afraid to sin.

21 And if there was ^ano law given, if men sinned what could justice do, or mercy either, for they would have no claim upon the creature?

22 But there is a law given, and a

8a Gen. 3: 22 (22–24).
  b Alma 12: 26 (22–33);
    34: 9 (8–16); Moses
    6: 62.
9a TG Fall of Man.
  b Moses 5: 4. TG Death,
    Spiritual, First.
10a TG Carnal Mind.
  b TG Man, Natural, Not
    Spiritually Reborn.
  c TG Mortality;
    Probation.
11a 2 Ne. 9: 9 (7–9).
12a 1 Cor. 15: 22.
  b TG Disobedience.
13a TG Salvation, Plan of.

  b TG Redemption;
    Repentance.
  c 2 Ne. 2: 13 (13–14).
14a Eph. 2: 8 (8–9); Alma
    22: 14 (13–14).
  b Rom. 7: 5; 2 Ne. 2: 5
    (4–10); 25: 23.
15a 2 Ne. 9: 10; Mosiah
    16: 8 (7–8).
    TG Atonement; Jesus
    Christ, Redeemer.
  b TG Jesus Christ,
    Mission of.
  c Alma 12: 32.
    TG Justice.
  d TG God, Perfection of.

  e TG God, Mercy of.
16a TG Punishment.
  b D&C 19: 11 (10–12).
  c TG Opposition.
  d TG Eternity.
17a Rom. 7: 8 (1–25).
    TG Sin.
  b Rom. 4: 15; 5: 13;
    2 Ne. 9: 25.
18a TG Conscience.
19a TG Murder.
  b TG Blood, Shedding of.
21a 2 Ne. 9: 26 (25–26);
    Mosiah 3: 11; Alma
    9: 16 (15–16).

[About 73 B.C.]

*a*punishment affixed, and a *b*repentance granted; which repentance, mercy claimeth; otherwise, justice claimeth the creature and executeth the *c*law, and the law inflicteth the punishment; if not so, the works of justice would be destroyed, and God would cease to be God.

23 But God ceaseth not to be God, and *a*mercy claimeth the penitent, and mercy cometh because of the *b*atonement; and the atonement bringeth to pass the *c*resurrection of the dead; and the *d*resurrection of the dead bringeth *e*back men into the presence of God; and thus they are restored into his presence, to be *f*judged according to their works, according to the law and justice.

24 For behold, justice exerciseth all his demands, and also *a*mercy claimeth all which is her own; and thus, none but the truly penitent are saved.

25 What, do ye suppose that *a*mercy can rob *b*justice? I say unto you, Nay; not one whit. If so, God would cease to be God.

26 And thus God bringeth about his great and eternal *a*purposes, which were prepared *b*from the foundation of the world. And thus cometh about the salvation and the redemption of men, and also their destruction and misery.

27 Therefore, O my son, *a*whosoever will come may come and partake of the waters of life freely; and whosoever will not come the same is not compelled to come; but in the last day it shall be *b*restored unto him according to his *c*deeds.

28 If he has desired to do *a*evil, and has not repented in his days, behold, evil shall be done unto him, according to the restoration of God.

29 And now, my son, I desire that ye should let these things *a*trouble you no more, and only let your sins trouble you, with that trouble which shall bring you down unto repentance.

30 O my son, I desire that ye should deny the *a*justice of God no more. Do not endeavor to excuse yourself in the least point because of your sins, by denying the justice of God; but do you let the justice of God, and his *b*mercy, and his long-suffering have full sway in your heart; and let it bring you down to the dust in *c*humility.

31 And now, O my son, ye are called of God to *a*preach the word unto this people. And now, my son, go thy way, declare the word with truth and soberness, that thou mayest *b*bring souls unto repentance, that the great plan of mercy may have claim upon them. And may God grant unto you even according to my words. Amen.

CHAPTER 43

Alma and his sons preach the word— The Zoramites and other Nephite dissenters become Lamanites—The Lamanites come against the Nephites in war—Moroni arms the Nephites with defensive armor—The Lord

22a TG Punishment.
  b TG Repentance.
  c Gal. 3: 13; D&C 76: 48.
23a TG God, Mercy of.
  b TG Jesus Christ,
    Atonement through.
  c 2 Ne. 2: 8; Alma 7: 12;
    12: 25 (24–25).
  d 2 Ne. 9: 4; Alma
    11: 41 (41–45);
    Hel. 14: 15 (15–18);
    Morm. 9: 13.
  e Alma 40: 21 (21–24).
  f TG Jesus Christ, Judge.

24a TG God, Mercy of.
25a TG Mercy.
  b TG Justice.
26a Matt. 5: 48; Rom.
    8: 17 (14–21); 2 Ne.
    2: 15 (14–30); D&C
    29: 43 (42–44); Moses
    1: 39. TG Earth,
    Purpose of.
  b Alma 13: 3 (3, 5, 7–8);
    3 Ne. 1: 14.
27a Alma 5: 34; 41: 7
    (7–8); Hel. 14: 30.
    TG Agency.

  b Alma 41: 15.
  c Isa. 59: 18; Alma
    36: 15; D&C 1: 10
    (9–10).
28a Alma 41: 4 (2–5).
29a 2 Cor. 7: 10 (8–11);
    Morm. 2: 13.
30a TG Justice.
  b TG God, Mercy of.
  c TG Humility.
31a D&C 11: 15.
  b TG Mission of Early
    Saints.

reveals to Alma the strategy of the Lamanites—The Nephites defend their homes, liberties, families, and religion—The armies of Moroni and Lehi surround the Lamanites.

AND now it came to pass that the sons of Alma did go forth among the people, to declare the word unto them. And Alma, also, himself, could not [a]rest, and he also went forth.

2 Now [a]we shall say no more concerning their preaching, except that they preached the word, and the truth, according to the spirit of prophecy and revelation; and they preached after the [b]holy order of God by which they were called.

3 And now [a]I return to an [b]account of the wars between the Nephites and the Lamanites, in the *eighteenth year of the reign of the judges.

4 For behold, it came to pass that the [a]Zoramites became Lamanites; therefore, in the commencement of the eighteenth year the people of the Nephites saw that the Lamanites were coming upon them; therefore they made preparations for war; yea, they gathered together their armies in the land of Jershon.

5 And it came to pass that the Lamanites came with their thousands; and they came into the land of [a]Antionum, which is the land of the Zoramites; and a man by the name of [b]Zerahemnah was their leader.

6 And now, as the [a]Amalekites were of a more wicked and murderous disposition than the Lamanites were, in and of themselves, therefore, Zerahemnah appointed chief [b]captains over the Lamanites,

and they were all Amalekites and [c]Zoramites.

7 Now this he did that he might preserve their [a]hatred towards the Nephites, that he might bring them into subjection to the accomplishment of his designs.

8 For behold, his [a]designs were to [b]stir up the Lamanites to anger against the Nephites; this he did that he might usurp great power over them, and also that he might gain power over the Nephites by bringing them into [c]bondage.

9 And now the design of the Nephites was to support their lands, and their houses, and their [a]wives, and their children, that they might preserve them from the hands of their enemies; and also that they might preserve their [b]rights and their privileges, yea, and also their [c]liberty, that they might worship God according to their desires.

10 For they knew that if they should fall into the hands of the Lamanites, that whosoever should [a]worship God in [b]spirit and in truth, the true and the living God, the Lamanites would [c]destroy.

11 Yea, and they also knew the extreme hatred of the Lamanites towards their [a]brethren, who were the [b]people of Anti-Nephi-Lehi, who were called the people of Ammon—and they would not take up arms, yea, they had entered into a covenant and they would not break it—therefore, if they should fall into the hands of the Lamanites they would be destroyed.

12 And the Nephites would not suffer that they should be destroyed; therefore they gave them lands for their inheritance.

43 1*a* Ether 12: 2 (2–3).
2*a* W of M 1: 9 (1–9).
  b Alma 30: 20 (20–23, 31); 46: 38.
  TG Priesthood.
3*a* Morm. 5: 9.
  b Alma 35: 13.
4*a* Alma 30: 59; 35: 14 (2–14); 52: 33 (20, 33).
5*a* Alma 31: 3.

b Alma 44: 1.
6*a* Alma 21: 4 (2–16).
  b Alma 48: 5.
  c Alma 43: 44.
7*a* Alma 37: 32.
8*a* Alma 43: 29.
  b Alma 27: 12; 47: 1.
  c Alma 44: 2.
9*a* Alma 44: 5; 46: 12; 48: 10 (10, 24).

b TG Citizenship.
  c TG Liberty.
10*a* TG Worship.
  b John 4: 23 (23–24).
  c Dan. 6: 7 (4–17).
11*a* Alma 23: 17; 24: 1 (1–3, 5, 20); 25: 13 (1, 13); 27: 2 (2, 21–26).
  b Alma 47: 29.

[*About 74 B.C.]

13 And the people of Ammon did give unto the Nephites a large portion of their substance to ^asupport their armies; and thus the Nephites were compelled, alone, to withstand against the Lamanites, who were a compound of Laman and Lemuel, and the sons of Ishmael, and all those who had dissented from the Nephites, who were Amalekites and Zoramites, and the ^bdescendants of the priests of Noah.

14 Now those descendants were as numerous, nearly, as were the Nephites; and thus the Nephites were obliged to contend with their brethren, even unto bloodshed.

15 And it came to pass as the armies of the Lamanites had gathered together in the ^aland of Antionum, behold, the armies of the Nephites were prepared to meet them in the land of Jershon.

16 Now, the leader of the Nephites, or the man who had been ^aappointed to be the ^bchief captain over the Nephites—now the chief captain took the command of all the armies of the Nephites—and his name was Moroni;

17 And Moroni took all the command, and the government of their wars. And he was only twenty and five years old when he was appointed chief captain over the armies of the Nephites.

18 And it came to pass that he met the Lamanites in the borders of Jershon, and his people were armed with swords, and with cimeters, and all manner of ^aweapons of war.

19 And when the armies of the Lamanites saw that the people of Nephi, or that Moroni, had ^aprepared his people with ^bbreastplates and with arm-shields, yea, and also shields to defend their heads, and also they were dressed with thick clothing—

20 Now the army of Zerahemnah was not prepared with any such thing; they had only their ^aswords and their cimeters, their bows and their arrows, their ^bstones and their slings; and they were ^cnaked, save it were a skin which was girded about their loins; yea, all were naked, save it were the Zoramites and the Amalekites;

21 But they were not armed with breastplates, nor shields—therefore, they were exceedingly afraid of the armies of the Nephites because of their armor, notwithstanding their number being so much greater than the Nephites.

22 Behold, now it came to pass that they durst not come against the Nephites in the borders of Jershon; therefore they departed out of the land of Antionum into the wilderness, and took their journey round about in the wilderness, away by the head of the river Sidon, that they might come into the land of ^aManti and take possession of the land; for they did not suppose that the armies of Moroni would know whither they had gone.

23 But it came to pass, as soon as they had departed into the wilderness Moroni sent spies into the wilderness to watch their camp; and Moroni, also, knowing of the prophecies of Alma, sent certain men unto him, desiring him that he should ^ainquire of the Lord ^bwhither the armies of the Nephites should go to defend themselves against the Lamanites.

24 And it came to pass that the ^aword of the Lord came unto Alma, and Alma informed the messengers of Moroni, that the armies of the

---

13a Alma 57: 27.
  b Alma 25: 4.
15a Alma 27: 26.
16a Alma 46: 34.
  b Alma 46: 11.
18a TG Weapon.
19a TG Skill.
  b Alma 49: 24.

20a Mosiah 10: 8; Alma
    3: 5 (4–5); 44: 8.
  b 1 Ne. 16: 15; Alma
    49: 2.
  c Enos 1: 20.
22a Alma 22: 27; 56: 14.
23a Ex. 18: 15; 2 Kgs.
    6: 12 (8–18);

Mosiah 28: 6.
  b Alma 16: 6 (5–8);
    48: 16; 3 Ne. 3: 20
    (18–21).
24a Isa. 31: 5; Alma
    43: 47; D&C 134: 11.
  TG Guidance, Divine.

Lamanites were marching round about in the wilderness, that they might come over into the land of Manti, that they might commence an attack upon the weaker part of the people. And those messengers went and delivered the message unto Moroni.

25 Now Moroni, leaving a part of his army in the land of Jershon, lest by any means a part of the Lamanites should come into that land and take possession of the city, took the remaining part of his army and marched over into the land of Manti.

26 And he caused that all the people in that quarter of the land should gather themselves together to battle against the Lamanites, to defend their lands and their country, their rights and their liberties; therefore they were prepared against the time of the coming of the Lamanites.

27 And it came to pass that Moroni caused that his army should be secreted in the valley which was near the bank of the river Sidon, which was on the west of the river Sidon in the wilderness.

28 And Moroni placed spies round about, that he might know when the camp of the Lamanites should come.

29 And now, as Moroni knew the ᵃintention of the Lamanites, that it was their intention to destroy their brethren, or to ᵇsubject them and bring them into bondage that they might establish a kingdom unto themselves over all the land;

30 And he also knowing that it was the ᵃonly desire of the Nephites to preserve their lands, and their ᵇliberty, and their church, therefore he thought it no sin that he should defend them by ᶜstratagem; therefore, he found by his spies which course the Lamanites were to take.

31 Therefore, he divided his army and brought a part over into the valley, and ᵃconcealed them on the east, and on the south of the hill Riplah;

32 And the remainder he concealed in the west ᵃvalley, on the west of the river Sidon, and so down into the borders of the land Manti.

33 And thus having placed his army according to his desire, he was prepared to meet them.

34 And it came to pass that the Lamanites came up on the north of the hill, where a part of the army of Moroni was concealed.

35 And as the Lamanites had passed the hill Riplah, and came into the valley, and began to cross the river Sidon, the army which was concealed on the south of the hill, which was led by a man whose name was ᵃLehi, and he led his army forth and encircled the Lamanites about on the east in their rear.

36 And it came to pass that the Lamanites, when they saw the Nephites coming upon them in their rear, turned them about and began to contend with the army of Lehi.

37 And the work of death commenced on both sides, but it was more dreadful on the part of the Lamanites, for their ᵃnakedness was exposed to the heavy blows of the Nephites with their swords and their cimeters, which brought death almost at every stroke.

38 While on the other hand, there was now and then a man fell among the Nephites, by their swords and the loss of blood, they being shielded from the more vital parts of the body, or the more vital parts of the body being shielded from the strokes of the Lamanites, by their ᵃbreastplates, and their armshields, and their head-plates; and thus the Nephites did carry on the work of death among the Lamanites.

29a Alma 43: 8.
 b Alma 49: 7.
30a Alma 44: 5; 46: 12
   (12–20); 48: 10 (10–16).
 b Alma 46: 35.

c Judg. 7: 16 (15–25).
31a Josh. 8: 13; Alma
   52: 21 (21–31); 58: 16
   (15–21).
32a Alma 43: 41.

35a Alma 49: 16.
37a Alma 3: 5.
38a Alma 44: 9.

[About 74 B.C.]

39 And it came to pass that the Lamanites became frightened, because of the great destruction among them, even until they began to flee towards the river Sidon.

40 And they were pursued by Lehi and his men; and they were driven by Lehi into the waters of Sidon, and they crossed the waters of Sidon. And Lehi retained his armies upon the bank of the river Sidon that they should not cross.

41 And it came to pass that Moroni and his army met the Lamanites in the ªvalley, on the other side of the river Sidon, and began to fall upon them and to slay them.

42 And the Lamanites did flee again before them, towards the land of Manti; and they were met again by the armies of Moroni.

43 Now in this case the Lamanites did fight exceedingly; yea, never had the Lamanites been known to fight with such exceedingly great strength and courage, no, not even from the beginning.

44 And they were inspired by the ªZoramites and the Amalekites, who were their chief captains and leaders, and by Zerahemnah, who was their chief captain, or their chief leader and commander; yea, they did fight like dragons, and many of the Nephites were slain by their hands, yea, for they did smite in two many of their head-plates, and they did pierce many of their breast-plates, and they did smite off many of their arms; and thus the Lamanites did smite in their fierce anger.

45 Nevertheless, the Nephites were inspired by a ªbetter cause, for they were not ᵇfighting for monarchy nor power but they were fighting for their homes and their ᶜliberties, their wives and their children, and their all, yea, for their rites of worship and their church.

46 And they were doing that which they felt was the ªduty which they owed to their God; for the Lord had said unto them, and also unto their fathers, that: ᵇInasmuch as ye are not guilty of the ᶜfirst offense, neither the second, ye shall not suffer yourselves to be slain by the hands of your enemies.

47 And again, the Lord has said that: Ye shall ªdefend your families even unto ᵇbloodshed. Therefore for this cause were the Nephites contending with the Lamanites, to defend themselves, and their families, and their lands, their country, and their rights, and their religion.

48 And it came to pass that when the men of Moroni saw the fierceness and the anger of the Lamanites, they were about to shrink and flee from them. And Moroni, perceiving their intent, sent forth and inspired their hearts with these thoughts—yea, the thoughts of their lands, their liberty, yea, their freedom from bondage.

49 And it came to pass that they turned upon the Lamanites, and they ªcried with one voice ᵇunto the Lord their God, for their ᶜliberty and their freedom from bondage.

50 And they ªbegan to stand against the Lamanites with power; and in that selfsame hour that they cried unto the Lord for their freedom, the Lamanites began to flee before them; and they fled even to the waters of Sidon.

51 Now, the Lamanites were more ªnumerous, yea, by more than double the number of the Nephites; nevertheless, they were driven inso-

41a Alma 43:32.
44a Alma 43:6.
45a Alma 44:1.
  b Mosiah 20:11; Alma 44:5.
  c TG Liberty.
46a TG Duty.
  b Alma 48:14 (14–16); D&C 98:33 (23–36).

  c Luke 6:29; 3 Ne. 3:21 (20–21); Morm. 3:10 (10–11); D&C 98:23 (22–48).
47a Isa. 31:5; Alma 43:24; 61:14; Morm. 7:4; D&C 134:11. TG Family, Children, Responsibilities

    toward; War.
  b Josh 1:18.
49a Ex. 2:23 (23–25); Mosiah 29:20.
  b Ps. 59:1 (1–5).
  c TG Liberty.
50a Ex. 17:11 (8–13).
51a Alma 46:30.

much that they were gathered together in one body in the valley, upon the bank by the river Sidon.

52 Therefore the armies of Moroni encircled them about, yea, even on both sides of the river, for behold, on the east were the men of Lehi.

53 Therefore when Zerahemnah saw the men of Lehi on the east of the river Sidon, and the armies of Moroni on the west of the river Sidon, that they were encircled about by the Nephites, they were struck with terror.

54 Now Moroni, when he saw their [a]terror, commanded his men that they should stop shedding their blood.

CHAPTER 44

Moroni commands the Lamanites to make a covenant of peace or be destroyed—Zerahemnah rejects the offer, and the battle resumes—Moroni's armies defeat the Lamanites.

AND it came to pass that they did stop and withdrew a pace from them. And Moroni said unto [a]Zerahemnah: Behold, Zerahemnah, that we do [b]not desire to be men of blood. Ye know that ye are in our hands, yet we do not desire to slay you.

2 Behold, we have not come out to battle against you that we might shed your blood for power; neither do we desire to bring any one to the [a]yoke of bondage. But this is the [b]very cause for which ye have come against us; yea, and ye are angry with us because of our religion.

3 But now, ye behold that the Lord is with us; and ye behold that he has delivered you into our hands. And now I would that ye should understand that this is done unto us [a]because of our religion and our faith in Christ. And now ye see that ye cannot destroy this our faith.

4 Now ye see that this is the true faith of God; yea, ye see that God will support, and keep, and preserve us, so long as we are [a]faithful unto him, and unto our faith, and our religion; and never will the Lord suffer that we shall be destroyed except we should fall into transgression and deny our faith.

5 And now, Zerahemnah, I command you, in the name of that all-powerful God, who has strengthened our arms that we have gained power over you, [a]by our faith, by our religion, and by our [b]rites of worship, and by our church, and by the sacred support which we owe to our [c]wives and our children, by that [d]liberty which binds us to our lands and our country; yea, and also by the maintenance of the sacred word of God, to which we owe all our happiness; and by all that is most dear unto us—

6 Yea, and this is not all; I command you by all the desires which ye have for life, that ye [a]deliver up your weapons of war unto us, and we will seek not your blood, but we will [b]spare your lives, if ye will go your way and come not again to war against us.

7 And now, if ye do not this, behold, ye are in our hands, and I will command my men that they shall fall upon you, and [a]inflict the wounds of death in your bodies, that ye may become extinct; and then we will see who shall have power over this people; yea, we will see who shall be brought into bondage.

8 And now it came to pass that when Zerahemnah had heard these sayings he came forth and delivered up his [a]sword and his cimeter, and his bow into the hands of Moroni, and said unto him: Behold, here are

---

54a Alma 47:2.
44 1a Alma 43:5.
  b Alma 43:45.
  2a TG Bondage, Physical.
  b Alma 43:8.
  3a Alma 38:1.

  TG Protection, Divine.
  4a Mark 4:40 (35–41).
  5a Alma 43:45 (9, 45);
   46:12 (12–20).
  b TG Ordinance.
  c Gen. 2:24 (23–24).

  d TG Liberty.
  6a Alma 52:25 (25, 32).
  b TG Benevolence.
  7a Alma 62:11.
  8a Alma 43:20.

[About 74 B.C.]

our weapons of war; we will deliver them up unto you, but we will not suffer ourselves to take an *b*oath unto you, which we know that we shall break, and also our children; but take our weapons of war, and suffer that we may depart into the wilderness; otherwise we will retain our swords, and we will perish or conquer.

9 Behold, we are *a*not of your faith; we do not believe that it is God that has delivered us into your hands; but we believe that it is your cunning that has preserved you from our swords. Behold, it is your *b*breastplates and your shields that have preserved you.

10 And now when Zerahemnah had made an end of speaking these words, Moroni returned the sword and the weapons of war, which he had received, unto Zerahemnah, saying: Behold, we will end the conflict.

11 Now I cannot recall the words which I have spoken, therefore as the Lord liveth, ye shall not depart except ye depart with an oath that ye will not return again against us to war. Now as ye are in our hands we will spill your blood upon the ground, or ye shall submit to the conditions which I have proposed.

12 And now when Moroni had said these words, Zerahemnah retained his sword, and he was angry with Moroni, and he rushed forward that he might slay Moroni; but as he raised his sword, behold, one of Moroni's soldiers smote it even to the earth, and it broke by the hilt; and he also smote Zerahemnah that he took off his scalp and it fell to the earth. And Zerahemnah withdrew from before them into the midst of his soldiers.

13 And it came to pass that the soldier who stood by, who smote off the scalp of Zerahemnah, took up the scalp from off the ground by the

hair, and laid it upon the point of his sword, and stretched it forth unto them, saying unto them with a loud voice:

14 Even as this scalp has fallen to the earth, which is the scalp of your chief, so shall ye fall to the earth except ye will deliver up your weapons of war and depart with a covenant of peace.

15 Now there were many, when they heard these words and saw the scalp which was upon the sword, that were struck with fear; and many came forth and threw down their weapons of war at the feet of Moroni, and entered into a *a*covenant of peace. And as many as entered into a covenant they suffered to *b*depart into the wilderness.

16 Now it came to pass that Zerahemnah was exceedingly wroth, and he did stir up the remainder of his soldiers to anger, to contend more powerfully against the Nephites.

17 And now Moroni was angry, because of the stubbornness of the Lamanites; therefore he commanded his people that they should fall upon them and slay them. And it came to pass that they began to slay them; yea, and the Lamanites did contend with their swords and their might.

18 But behold, their naked skins and their bare heads were exposed to the sharp swords of the Nephites; yea, behold they were pierced and smitten, yea, and did fall exceedingly fast before the swords of the Nephites; and they began to be swept down, even as the soldier of Moroni had prophesied.

19 Now Zerahemnah, when he saw that they were all about to be destroyed, cried mightily unto Moroni, promising that he would covenant and also his people with them, if they would spare the remainder of their lives, that they

8b TG Oath.
9a TG Unbelief, Unbelievers.
b Alma 43: 38; 46: 13.
15a 1 Ne. 4: 37; Alma 50: 36.
b Hel. 1: 33.
[About 74 B.C.]

ªnever would come to war again against them.

20 And it came to pass that Moroni caused that the work of death should ªcease again among the people. And he took the weapons of war from the Lamanites; and after they had entered into a ᵇcovenant with him of peace they were suffered to depart into the wilderness.

21 Now the number of their dead was not numbered because of the greatness of the number; yea, the number of their dead was exceedingly great, both on the Nephites and on the Lamanites.

22 And it came to pass that they did cast their dead into the waters of Sidon, and they have gone forth and are buried in the depths of the ªsea.

23 And the armies of the Nephites, or of Moroni, returned and came to their houses and their lands.

24 And thus *ended the eighteenth year of the reign of the judges over the people of Nephi. And thus ended the record of Alma, which was written upon the plates of Nephi.

The account of the people of Nephi, and their wars and dissensions, in the days of Helaman, according to the record of Helaman, which he kept in his days. Comprising chapters 45 to 62 inclusive.

CHAPTER 45

Helaman believes the words of Alma—Alma prophesies the destruction of the Nephites—He blesses and curses the land—Alma is taken up by the Spirit, even as Moses—Dissension grows in the Church.

BEHOLD, now it came to pass that the people of Nephi were exceedingly rejoiced, because the Lord had

again ªdelivered them out of the hands of their enemies; therefore they gave thanks unto the Lord their God; yea, and they did ᵇfast much and pray much, and they did worship God with exceedingly great joy.

2 And it came to pass in the nineteenth year of the reign of the judges over the people of Nephi, that Alma came unto his son Helaman and said unto him: Believest thou the words which I spake unto thee concerning those ªrecords which have been kept?

3 And Helaman said unto him: Yea, I ªbelieve.

4 And Alma said again: Believest thou in Jesus Christ, who shall come?

5 And he said: Yea, I believe all the words which thou hast spoken.

6 And Alma said unto him again: Will ye ªkeep my commandments?

7 And he said: Yea, I will keep thy commandments with all my heart.

8 Then Alma said unto him: Blessed art thou; and the Lord shall ªprosper thee in this land.

9 But behold, I have somewhat to ªprophesy unto thee; but what I prophesy unto thee ye shall not make known; yea, what I prophesy unto thee shall not be made known, even until the prophecy is fulfilled; therefore write the words which I shall say.

10 And these are the words: Behold, I perceive that this very people, the Nephites, according to the spirit of revelation which is in me, in ªfour hundred years from the time that Jesus Christ shall manifest himself unto them, shall dwindle in ᵇunbelief.

11 Yea, and then shall they see wars and pestilences, yea, famines and bloodshed, even until the

---

19a Alma 47: 6.
20a Alma 46: 7.
  b Alma 55: 28; 62: 16
    (16–17).
22a Alma 3: 3.
45 1a TG Deliverance.
  b TG Fasting.

2a Alma 37: 1 (1–32);
    50: 38.
3a 1 Ne. 11: 5.
6a TG Commandments of
    God; Obedience.
8a 1 Ne. 4: 14; Alma
    48: 15, 25.

9a TG Prophecy.
10a 1 Ne. 12: 12 (10–15);
    Hel. 13: 9; Morm. 8: 6.
  b TG Apostasy of
    Individuals.

[*73 B.C.]

people of Nephi shall become *extinct—

12 Yea, and this because they shall dwindle in unbelief and fall into the works of darkness, and *lasciviousness, and all manner of iniquities; yea, I say unto you, that because they shall sin against so great light and knowledge, yea, I say unto you, that from that day, even the *fourth generation shall not all pass away before this great iniquity shall come.

13 And when that great day cometh, behold, the time very soon cometh that those who are now, or the seed of those who are now numbered among the people of Nephi, shall *no more be numbered among the people of Nephi.

14 But whosoever remaineth, and is not destroyed in that great and dreadful day, shall be *numbered among the *Lamanites, and shall become like unto them, all, save it be a few who shall be called the disciples of the Lord; and them shall the Lamanites pursue even *until they shall become extinct. And now, because of iniquity, this prophecy shall be fulfilled.

15 And now it came to pass that after Alma had said these things to Helaman, he *blessed him, and also his other sons; and he also blessed the earth for the *righteous' sake.

16 And he said: Thus saith the Lord God—*Cursed shall be the land, yea, this land, unto every nation, kindred, tongue, and people, unto destruction, which do *wickedly, when they are fully ripe; and as I have said so shall it be; for this is the cursing and the *blessing of God upon the land, for the Lord cannot

look upon sin with the *least degree of allowance.

17 And now, when Alma had said these words he blessed the *church, yea, all those who should stand fast in the faith from that time henceforth.

18 And when Alma had done this he *departed out of the land of Zarahemla, as if to go into the land of *Melek. And it came to pass that he was never heard of more; as to his death or burial we know not of.

19 Behold, this we know, that he was a righteous man; and the saying went abroad in the church that he was taken up by the *Spirit, or *buried by the hand of the Lord, even as Moses. But behold, the scriptures saith the Lord took Moses unto himself; and we suppose that he has also received Alma in the spirit, unto himself; therefore, for this cause we know nothing concerning his death and burial.

20 And now it came to pass in the *commencement of the nineteenth year of the reign of the judges over the people of Nephi, that Helaman went forth among the people to declare the *word unto them.

21 For behold, because of their wars with the Lamanites and the many little dissensions and disturbances which had been among the people, it became expedient that the *word of God should be declared among them, yea, and that a *regulation should be made throughout the church.

22 Therefore, *Helaman and his brethren went forth to establish the church again in all the land, yea, in every city throughout all the land which was possessed by the people

11a Jarom 1: 10; Hel. 13: 6 (5–19).
12a TG Lust.
   b 2 Ne. 26: 9; 3 Ne. 27: 32.
13a Hel. 3: 16.
14a Moro. 9: 24.
   b 1 Ne. 13: 30; D&C 3: 17.
   c Moro. 1: 2 (1–3).
15a Gen. 49: 1 (1–27);

Alma 8: 22.
   b Alma 46: 10; 62: 40.
16a 2 Ne. 1: 7; Alma 37: 31; Morm. 1: 17; Ether 2: 11 (8–12).
   TG Earth, Curse of.
   b Jer. 44: 5 (5–6).
   c D&C 130: 21.
   d D&C 1: 31.
17a TG Church.
18a 3 Ne. 1: 3 (2–3).

   b Alma 35: 13.
19a 2 Kgs. 2: 16.
   b Deut. 34: 6 (5–6).
   TG Translated Beings.
20a Alma 46: 1.
21a Alma 31: 5.
   b Alma 6: 7; 62: 44 (44–47).
22a Alma 48: 19.

[*73 B.C.]

of Nephi. And it came to pass that they did appoint [b]priests and [c]teachers throughout all the land, over all the churches.

23 And now it came to pass that after Helaman and his brethren had appointed priests and teachers over the churches that there arose a [a]dissension among them, and they would not give heed to the words of Helaman and his brethren;

24 But they grew proud, being lifted up in their hearts, because of their exceedingly great [a]riches; therefore they grew rich in their own eyes, and would not give heed to their words, to [b]walk uprightly before God.

CHAPTER 46

Amalickiah conspires to be king—Moroni raises the title of liberty—He rallies the people to defend their religion—True believers are called Christians—A remnant of Joseph shall be preserved—Amalickiah and the dissenters flee to the land of Nephi—Those who will not support the cause of freedom are put to death.

AND it came to pass that as many as would not hearken to the [a]words of Helaman and his brethren were gathered together against their brethren.

2 And now behold, they were exceedingly wroth, insomuch that they were determined to slay them.

3 Now the leader of those who were wroth against their brethren was a large and a strong man; and his name was [a]Amalickiah.

4 And Amalickiah was desirous to be a [a]king; and those people who were wroth were also desirous that he should be their king; and they were the greater part of them the lower [b]judges of the land, and they were seeking for power.

5 And they had been led by the [a]flatteries of Amalickiah, that if they would support him and establish him to be their king that he would make them rulers over the people.

6 Thus they were led away by Amalickiah to dissensions, notwithstanding the preaching of Helaman and his brethren, yea, notwithstanding their exceedingly great care over the church, for they were [a]high priests over the church.

7 And there were many in the church who believed in the [a]flattering words of Amalickiah, therefore they [b]dissented even from the church; and thus were the affairs of the people of Nephi exceedingly precarious and dangerous, notwithstanding their great [c]victory which they had had over the Lamanites, and their great rejoicings which they had had because of their [d]deliverance by the hand of the Lord.

8 Thus we see how [a]quick the children of men do [b]forget the Lord their God, yea, how quick to do [c]iniquity, and to be led away by the evil one.

9 Yea, and we also see the great [a]wickedness one very wicked man can cause to take place among the children of men.

10 Yea, we see that Amalickiah, because he was a man of cunning device and a man of many flattering words, that he led away the hearts of many people to do wickedly; yea, and to seek to [a]destroy the church of God, and to destroy the foundation of [b]liberty which

22b TG Church Organization.
  c TG Teacher.
23a 3 Ne. 11: 29 (28–29).
24a TG Treasure.
  b TG Pride; Walking in Darkness.
46 1a Alma 45: 20.
  3a Alma 49: 25.
  4a Alma 2: 2.

  b Mosiah 29: 11 (11–44).
5a Prov. 29: 5.
6a Alma 46: 38.
7a TG Flattery.
  b Alma 1: 24.
  c Alma 44: 20.
  d Josh. 21: 44; 1 Kgs. 5: 3; Mosiah 9: 17. TG Deliverance.
8a Ex. 32: 8; Judg.

  2: 17; Hel. 4: 26; 6: 32; 12: 2 (2, 4–5).
  b Deut. 6: 12.
  c Mosiah 13: 29.
9a 2 Kgs. 10: 29; Mosiah 29: 17 (17–18).
10a TG Tyranny.
  b 2 Ne. 1: 7; Mosiah 29: 32. TG Liberty.

[73 B.C.]

God had granted unto them, or which blessing God had sent upon the face of the land for the ᶜrighteous' sake.

11 And now it came to pass that when Moroni, who was the ᵃchief commander of the armies of the Nephites, had heard of these dissensions, he was angry with Amalickiah.

12 And it came to pass that he rent his coat; and he took a piece thereof, and wrote upon it—ᵃIn memory of our God, our religion, and freedom, and our peace, our wives, and our children—and he fastened it upon the end of a pole.

13 And he fastened on his headplate, and his ᵃbreastplate, and his shields, and girded on his armor about his loins; and he took the pole, which had on the end thereof his rent coat, (and he called it the ᵇtitle of liberty) and he ᶜbowed himself to the earth, and he prayed mightily unto his God for the blessings of liberty to rest upon his brethren, so long as there should a band of ᵈChristians remain to possess the land—

14 For thus were all the true believers of Christ, who belonged to the church of God, called by those who did not belong to the church.

15 And those who did belong to the church were ᵃfaithful; yea, all those who were true believers in Christ ᵇtook upon them, gladly, the name of Christ, or ᶜChristians as they were called, because of their belief in Christ who should come.

16 And therefore, at this time, Moroni prayed that the cause of the Christians, and the ᵃfreedom of the land might be favored.

17 And it came to pass that when he had poured out his soul to God, he named all the land which was ᵃsouth of the land ᵇDesolation, yea, and in fine, all the land, both on the ᶜnorth and on the south—A chosen land, and the land of ᵈliberty.

18 And he said: Surely God shall not ᵃsuffer that we, who are despised because we take upon us the name of Christ, shall be trodden down and destroyed, until we bring it upon us by our own ᵇtransgressions.

19 And when Moroni had said these words, he went forth among the people, waving the ᵃrent part of his garment in the air, that all might see the writing which he had written upon the rent part, and crying with a loud voice, saying:

20 Behold, whosoever will maintain this title upon the land, let them come forth in the strength of the Lord, and ᵃenter into a covenant that they will ᵇmaintain their rights, and their religion, that the Lord God may bless them.

21 And it came to pass that when Moroni had proclaimed these words, behold, the people came running ᵃtogether with their armor girded about their loins, ᵇrending their garments in token, or as a ᶜcovenant, that they would not forsake the Lord their God; or, in other words, if they should transgress the commandments of God, or fall into transgression, and be ᵈashamed to take upon them the name of Christ, the Lord should rend them even as they had rent their garments.

10c Alma 45: 15 (15–16);
  62: 40.
11a Alma 43: 16.
12a 2 Sam. 10: 12; Neh.
  4: 14 (10–14); Alma
  44: 5; 48: 10 (10, 24).
13a Alma 44: 9; 49: 6
  (6, 24).
  b Alma 51: 20.
  TG Citizenship.
  c TG Reverence.
  d Alma 48: 10.

15a TG Faithful; Loyalty.
  b TG Jesus Christ,
    Taking the Name of.
  c Acts 11: 26.
16a Alma 51: 13.
17a 3 Ne. 3: 24; Morm.
    3: 5.
  b Alma 22: 30; 50: 34.
  c Alma 22: 31; 63: 4.
  d 2 Ne. 1: 7; Mosiah
    29: 32.
18a TG Protection, Divine.

  b TG Transgression.
19a TG Ensign.
20a Alma 48: 13.
  b TG Citizenship.
21a 2 Sam. 20: 14 (11–14).
  b TG Rend, Rent.
  c TG Commitment.
  d Jer. 17: 13; Rom.
    1: 16; 2 Tim. 1: 8;
    1 Ne. 8: 25; Morm.
    8: 38.

[73 B.C.]

22 Now this was the covenant which they made, and they ^acast their garments at the feet of Moroni, saying: We ^bcovenant with our God, that we shall be destroyed, even as our brethren in the land northward, if we shall fall into transgression; yea, he may cast us at the feet of our enemies, even as we have cast our garments at thy feet to be trodden under foot, if we shall fall into transgression.

23 Moroni said unto them: Behold, we are a ^aremnant of the seed of Jacob; yea, we are a remnant of the seed of ^bJoseph, whose ^ccoat was rent by his brethren into many pieces; yea, and now behold, let us remember to keep the commandments of God, or our garments shall be rent by our brethren, and we be cast into prison, or be sold, or be slain.

24 Yea, let us preserve our liberty as a ^aremnant of Joseph; yea, let us remember the words of Jacob, before his death, for behold, he saw that a ^bpart of the ^cremnant of the coat of Joseph was ^dpreserved and had not decayed. And he said— Even as this remnant of garment of my son hath been preserved, so shall a ^eremnant of the seed of my son be preserved by the hand of God, and be taken unto himself, while the remainder of the seed of Joseph shall perish, even as the remnant of his garment.

25 Now behold, this giveth my soul sorrow; nevertheless, my soul hath joy in my son, because of that part of his seed which shall be taken unto God.

26 Now behold, this was the language of Jacob.

27 And now who knoweth but what the remnant of the seed of Joseph, which shall perish as his garment, are those who have dissented from us? Yea, and even it shall be ourselves if we do not stand fast in the faith of Christ.

28 And now it came to pass that when Moroni had said these words he went forth, and also sent forth in all the parts of the land where there were dissensions, and gathered together all the people who were desirous to maintain their liberty, to stand against Amalickiah and those who had dissented, who were called Amalickiahites.

29 And it came to pass that when Amalickiah saw that the people of Moroni were more numerous than the Amalickiahites—and he also saw that his people were ^adoubtful concerning the justice of the cause in which they had undertaken— therefore, fearing that he should not gain the point, he took those of his people who would and departed into the ^bland of Nephi.

30 Now Moroni thought it was not expedient that the Lamanites should have any more ^astrength; therefore he thought to cut off the people of Amalickiah, or to take them and bring them back, and put Amalickiah to death; yea, for he knew that he would stir up the Lamanites to anger against them, and cause them to come to battle against them; and this he knew that Amalickiah would do that he might obtain his purposes.

31 Therefore Moroni thought it was expedient that he should take his armies, who had gathered themselves together, and armed themselves, and entered into a covenant to keep the peace—and it came to pass that he took his army and marched out with his tents into the wilderness, to cut off the course of Amalickiah in the wilderness.

32 And it came to pass that he did

22a Acts 7:58; 22:20.
  b TG Commitment.
23a TG Israel, Remnant of.
  b TG Israel, Joseph, People of.
  c Gen. 37:3 (3, 31–36).
24a 2 Ne. 10:1; Jacob 5:45 (43–45).
  b Gen. 44:28.
  c 3 Ne. 5:23 (23–24); 10:17.
  d 2 Ne. 3:5 (5–24):
25:21; Ether 13:7.
  e Ether 13:6.
29a TG Doubt.
  b Alma 47:20.
30a Alma 43:51.

according to his desires, and marched forth into the wilderness, and headed the armies of Amalickiah.

33 And it came to pass that Amalickiah *fled with a small number of his men, and the remainder were delivered up into the hands of Moroni and were taken back into the land of Zarahemla.

34 Now, Moroni being a man who was *appointed by the chief judges and the voice of the people, therefore he had power according to his will with the armies of the Nephites, to establish and to exercise authority over them.

35 And it came to pass that whomsoever of the Amalickiahites that would not enter into a covenant to support the *cause of freedom, that they might maintain a free *government, he caused to be put to death; and there were but few who denied the covenant of freedom.

36 And it came to pass also, that he caused the *title of liberty to be hoisted upon every tower which was in all the land, which was possessed by the Nephites; and thus Moroni planted the standard of liberty among the Nephites.

37 And they began to have peace again in the land; and thus they did maintain peace in the land until nearly the *end of the nineteenth year of the reign of the judges.

38 And Helaman and the *high priests did also maintain order in the church; yea, even for the space of four years did they have much peace and rejoicing in the church.

39 And it came to pass that there were many who died, firmly *believing that their souls were redeemed by the Lord Jesus Christ; thus they went out of the world rejoicing.

40 And there were some who died

with fevers, which at some seasons of the year were very frequent in the land—but not so much so with fevers, because of the excellent qualities of the many *plants and roots which God had prepared to remove the cause of *diseases, to which men were subject by the nature of the climate—

41 But there were many who died with *old age; and those who died in the faith of Christ are *happy in him, as we must needs suppose.

CHAPTER 47

Amalickiah uses treachery, murder, and intrigue to become king of the Lamanites—The Nephite dissenters are more wicked and ferocious than the Lamanites.

Now we will return in our record to Amalickiah and those who had *fled with him into the wilderness; for, behold, he had taken those who went with him, and went up in the *land of Nephi among the Lamanites, and did *stir up the Lamanites to anger against the people of Nephi, insomuch that the king of the Lamanites sent a proclamation throughout all his land, among all his people, that they should gather themselves together again to go to battle against the Nephites.

2 And it came to pass that when the proclamation had gone forth among them they were exceedingly afraid; yea, they *feared to displease the king, and they also feared to go to battle against the Nephites lest they should lose their lives. And it came to pass that they would not, or the more part of them would not, obey the commandments of the king.

3 And now it came to pass that the

33a Alma 47:1.
34a Alma 43:16.
35a Alma 43:30.
  b TG Governments.
36a Alma 62:4.
38a Alma 43:2; 46:6;
  49:30.
39a Moro. 7:41 (3, 41).

40a D&C 59:17 (17–20);
  89:10.
  b Ezek. 47:12.
  TG Health; Sickness.
41a TG Old Age.
  b Rev. 14:13.
47 1a Alma 46:33.

  b 2 Ne. 5:8; Omni 1:12;
  Alma 49:10.
  c Alma 27:12; 35:10;
  43:8; Hel. 1:17.
  TG Provoking.
2a Alma 43:54 (49–54).

king was wroth because of their disobedience; therefore he gave Amalickiah the command of that part of his army which was obedient unto his commands, and commanded him that he should go forth and ^acompel them to arms.

4 Now behold, this was the desire of Amalickiah; for he being a very ^asubtle man to do evil therefore he laid the plan in his heart to ^bdethrone the king of the Lamanites.

5 And now he had got the command of those parts of the Lamanites who were in favor of the king; and he sought to gain favor of those who were not obedient; therefore he went forward to the place which was called ^aOnidah, for thither had all the Lamanites fled; for they discovered the army coming, and, supposing that they were coming to destroy them, therefore they fled to Onidah, to the place of arms.

6 And they had appointed a man to be a king and a leader over them, being fixed in their minds with a determined resolution that they would ^anot be subjected to go against the Nephites.

7 And it came to pass that they had gathered themselves together upon the top of the mount which was called Antipas, in preparation to battle.

8 Now it was not Amalickiah's intention to give them battle according to the commandments of the king; but behold, it was his intention to gain favor with the armies of the Lamanites, that he might place himself at their head and dethrone the king and take possession of the kingdom.

9 And behold, it came to pass that he caused his army to pitch their tents in the valley which was near the mount Antipas.

10 And it came to pass that when it was night he sent a secret embassy into the mount Antipas, desiring that the leader of those who were upon the mount, whose name was Lehonti, that he should come down to the foot of the mount, for he desired to speak with him.

11 And it came to pass that when Lehonti received the message he durst not go down to the foot of the mount. And it came to pass that Amalickiah sent again the second time, desiring him to come down. And it came to pass that Lehonti would not; and he sent again the third time.

12 And it came to pass that when Amalickiah found that he could not get Lehonti to come down off from the mount, he went up into the mount, nearly to Lehonti's camp; and he sent again the fourth time his message unto Lehonti, desiring that he would come down, and that he would bring his guards with him.

13 And it came to pass that when Lehonti had come down with his guards to Amalickiah, that Amalickiah desired him to come down with his army in the night-time, and surround those men in their camps over whom the king had given him command, and that he would deliver them up into Lehonti's hands, if he would make him (Amalickiah) a second ^aleader over the whole army.

14 And it came to pass that Lehonti came down with his men and surrounded the men of Amalickiah, so that before they awoke at the dawn of day they were surrounded by the armies of Lehonti.

15 And it came to pass that when they saw that they were surrounded, they plead with Amalickiah that he would suffer them to fall in with their brethren, that they might not be destroyed. Now this was the very thing which Amalickiah desired.

16 And it came to pass that he delivered his men, ^acontrary to the commands of the king. Now this was the thing that Amalickiah

---

3a Alma 47: 16 (16, 21).
4a 2 Sam. 13: 3 (3–14).
  b Alma 47: 35 (8, 35).
5a Alma 32: 4.
6a Alma 44: 19 (8, 19).
13a Alma 49: 10.
16a Alma 47: 3.

[72 B.C.

desired, that he might accomplish his designs in dethroning the king.

17 Now it was the custom among the Lamanites, if their chief leader was killed, to appoint the second leader to be their chief leader.

18 And it came to pass that Amalickiah caused that one of his servants should administer ªpoison by degrees to Lehonti, that he died.

19 Now, when Lehonti was dead, the Lamanites appointed Amalickiah to be their leader and their chief commander.

20 And it came to pass that Amalickiah marched with his armies (for he had gained his desires) to the ªland of Nephi, to the city of Nephi, which was the chief city.

21 And the king came out to meet him with his guards, for he supposed that Amalickiah had ªfulfilled his commands, and that Amalickiah had gathered together so great an army to go against the Nephites to battle.

22 But behold, as the king came out to meet him Amalickiah caused that his servants should go forth to meet the king. And they went and ªbowed themselves before the king, as if to reverence him because of his greatness.

23 And it came to pass that the king put forth his hand to raise them, as was the custom with the Lamanites, as a token of peace, which custom they had taken from the Nephites.

24 And it came to pass that when he had raised the first from the ground, behold he stabbed the king to the heart; and he fell to the earth.

25 Now the servants of the king fled; and the servants of Amalickiah raised a cry, saying:

26 Behold, the servants of the king have stabbed him to the heart, and he has fallen and they have fled; behold, come and see.

27 And it came to pass that Amalickiah commanded that his armies should march forth and see what had happened to the king; and when they had come to the spot, and found the king lying in his gore, Amalickiah pretended to be wroth, and said: Whosoever loved the king, let him go forth, and pursue his servants that they may be slain.

28 And it came to pass that all they who loved the king, when they heard these words, came forth and pursued after the servants of the king.

29 Now when the ªservants of the king saw an army pursuing after them, they were frightened again, and fled into the wilderness, and came over into the land of Zarahemla and joined the ᵇpeople of Ammon.

30 And the army which pursued after them returned, having pursued after them in vain; and thus Amalickiah, by his ªfraud, gained the hearts of the people.

31 And it came to pass on the morrow he entered the city Nephi with his armies, and took possession of the city.

32 And now it came to pass that the queen, when she had heard that the king was slain—for Amalickiah had sent an embassy to the queen informing her that the king had been slain by his servants, that he had pursued them with his army, but it was in vain, and they had made their escape—

33 Therefore, when the queen had received this message she sent unto Amalickiah, desiring him that he would spare the people of the city; and she also desired him that he should come in unto her; and she also desired him that he should bring ªwitnesses with him to testify concerning the death of the king.

34 And it came to pass that Amalickiah took the same servant that slew the king, and all them who

---

18a Alma 54: 7.
20a Alma 46: 29.
21a Alma 47: 3.
22a Mosiah 7: 12.
29a Alma 55: 5.
   b Alma 43: 11; 62: 17.
30a Alma 55: 1. TG Fraud.
33a TG Witnesses.

were with him, and went in unto the queen, unto the place where she sat; and they all [a]testified unto her that the king was slain by his own servants; and they said also: They have fled; does not this testify against them? And thus they satisfied the queen concerning the death of the king.

35 And it came to pass that Amalickiah sought the [a]favor of the queen, and took her unto him to wife; and thus by his [b]fraud, and by the assistance of his cunning servants, he [c]obtained the kingdom; yea, he was acknowledged king throughout all the land, among all the people of the Lamanites, who were [d]composed of the Lamanites and the Lemuelites and the Ishmaelites, and all the dissenters of the Nephites, from the reign of Nephi down to the present time.

36 Now these [a]dissenters, having the same instruction and the same information of the Nephites, yea, having been instructed in the same [b]knowledge of the Lord, nevertheless, it is strange to relate, not long after their dissensions they became more hardened and [c]impenitent, and more wild, wicked and ferocious than the Lamanites—drinking in with the [d]traditions of the Lamanites; giving way to [e]indolence, and all manner of lasciviousness; yea, entirely forgetting the Lord their God.

CHAPTER 48

Amalickiah incites the Lamanites against the Nephites—Moroni prepares his people to defend the cause of the Christians—He rejoiced in liberty and freedom and was a mighty man of God.

AND now it came to pass that, as soon as [a]Amalickiah had obtained the kingdom he began to [b]inspire the hearts of the Lamanites against the people of Nephi; yea, he did appoint men to speak unto the Lamanites from their [c]towers, against the Nephites.

2 And thus he did inspire their hearts against the Nephites, insomuch that in the *latter end of the [a]nineteenth year of the reign of the judges, he having accomplished his designs thus far, yea, having been made king over the Lamanites, he [b]sought also to [c]reign over all the land, yea, and all the people who were in the land, the Nephites as well as the Lamanites.

3 Therefore he had accomplished his design, for he had hardened the hearts of the Lamanites and blinded their minds, and stirred them up to anger, insomuch that he had gathered together a numerous host to go to battle against the Nephites.

4 For he was determined, because of the greatness of the number of his people, to [a]overpower the Nephites and to bring them into bondage.

5 And thus he did appoint [a]chief captains of the [b]Zoramites, they being the most acquainted with the strength of the Nephites, and their places of resort, and the weakest parts of their cities; therefore he appointed them to be chief captains over his armies.

6 And it came to pass that they took their camp, and moved forth toward the land of Zarahemla in the wilderness.

7 Now it came to pass that while Amalickiah had thus been obtaining power by fraud and deceit, Moroni, on the other hand, had been [a]pre-

34a TG False; Lying.
35a Prov. 19:6 (6–7).
  b TG Conspiracy; Tyranny.
  c Alma 47:4.
  d Jacob 1:13 (13–14).
36a TG Apostasy of Individuals.
  b Heb. 10:26 (26–27);

   Alma 24:30.
  c Jer. 8:12.
  d TG Peer Influence.
  e 3 Ne. 4:5.
48 1a Alma 52:3 (1–3); 54:15.
  b Alma 62:35.
  c Mosiah 2:8.
2a Alma 48:21.

  b D&C 121:39.
  c Alma 54:24.
4a TG Tyranny.
5a Alma 43:6; 49:5 (5, 23).
  b Alma 52:20 (20, 33).
7a Alma 49:8.

paring the minds of the people to be faithful unto the Lord their God.

8 Yea, he had been strengthening the armies of the Nephites, and erecting small [a]forts, or places of resort; throwing up banks of earth round about to enclose his armies, and also building [b]walls of stone to encircle them about, round about their cities and the borders of their lands; yea, all round about the land.

9 And in their weakest fortifications he did place the greater number of men; and thus he did fortify and strengthen the land which was possessed by the Nephites.

10 And thus he was preparing to [a]support their liberty, their lands, their wives, and their children, and their peace, and that they might live unto the Lord their God, and that they might maintain that which was called by their enemies the cause of [b]Christians.

11 And Moroni was a [a]strong and a mighty man; he was a man of a perfect [b]understanding; yea, a man that did not delight in bloodshed; a man whose soul did joy in the liberty and the freedom of his country, and his brethren from bondage and slavery;

12 Yea, a man whose heart did swell with thanksgiving to his God, for the many privileges and blessings which he bestowed upon his people; a man who did labor exceedingly for the [a]welfare and safety of his people.

13 Yea, and he was a man who was firm in the faith of Christ, and he had [a]sworn with an oath to defend his people, his rights, and his country, and his religion, even to the loss of his blood.

14 Now the Nephites were taught to defend themselves against their enemies, even to the shedding of blood if it were necessary; yea, and they were also taught [a]never to give an offense, yea, and never to raise the sword except it were against an enemy, except it were to preserve their lives.

15 And this was their [a]faith, that by so doing God would [b]prosper them in the land, or in other words, if they were faithful in keeping the commandments of God that he would prosper them in the land; yea, warn them to flee, or to prepare for war, according to their danger;

16 And also, that God would make it known unto them [a]whither they should go to defend themselves against their enemies, and by so doing, the Lord would deliver them; and this was the faith of Moroni, and his heart did glory in it; not in the [b]shedding of blood but in doing good, in preserving his people, yea, in keeping the commandments of God, yea, and resisting iniquity.

17 Yea, verily, verily I say unto you, if all men had been, and were, and ever would be, like unto [a]Moroni, behold, the very powers of hell would have been shaken forever; yea, the [b]devil would never have power over the hearts of the children of men.

18 Behold, he was a man like unto [a]Ammon, the son of Mosiah, yea, and even the other sons of Mosiah, yea, and also Alma and his sons, for they were all men of God.

19 Now behold, Helaman and his brethren were no less [a]serviceable unto the people than was Moroni; for they did preach the word of God, and they did baptize unto repent-

8a Alma 49: 13 (2–13, 18–24).
  b Deut. 3: 5.
10a Alma 44: 5; 46: 12.
  b Alma 46: 13.
11a TG Strength.
  b Alma 18: 22.
  TG Understanding.
12a TG Welfare.

13a Alma 46: 20 (20–22).
  TG Dependability.
14a Alma 43: 46 (46–47);
    3 Ne. 3: 21 (20–21);
    Morm. 3: 10 (10–11);
    D&C 98: 16.
15a TG Steadfastness.
  b Alma 45: 8.
16a Alma 16: 6 (5–8);
    43: 23 (23–24);

    3 Ne. 3: 20 (18–21).
    TG Guidance, Divine.
  b Alma 55: 19.
17a Alma 53: 2.
  b 1 Ne. 22: 26; 3 Ne.
    6: 15; D&C 35: 24.
18a Alma 28: 8.
19a Alma 45: 22.

ance all men whosoever would hearken unto their words.

20 And thus they went forth, and the people did [a]humble themselves because of their [b]words, insomuch that they were highly [c]favored of the Lord, and thus they were free from wars and contentions among themselves, yea, even for the space of four years.

21 But, as I have said, in the [a]latter end of the nineteenth year, yea, notwithstanding their peace amongst themselves, they were compelled reluctantly to contend with their brethren, the Lamanites.

22 Yea, and in fine, their wars never did cease for the space of many years with the Lamanites, notwithstanding their much reluctance.

23 Now, they were [a]sorry to take up arms against the Lamanites, because they did not delight in the shedding of blood; yea, and this was not all—they were [b]sorry to be the means of sending so many of their brethren out of this world into an eternal world, [c]unprepared to meet their God.

24 Nevertheless, they could not suffer to lay down their lives, that their [a]wives and their children should be [b]massacred by the barbarous [c]cruelty of those who were once their brethren, yea, and had [d]dissented from their church, and had left them and had gone to destroy them by joining the Lamanites.

25 Yea, they could not bear that their brethren should rejoice over the blood of the Nephites, so long as there were any who should keep the commandments of God, for the promise of the Lord was, if they should keep his commandments they should [a]prosper in the land.

CHAPTER 49

The invading Lamanites are unable to take the fortified cities of Ammonihah and Noah—Amalickiah curses God and swears to drink the blood of Moroni—Helaman and his brethren continue to strengthen the Church.

AND now it came to pass in the *eleventh month of the nineteenth year, on the tenth day of the month, the armies of the Lamanites were seen approaching towards the land of [a]Ammonihah.

2 And behold, the city had been rebuilt, and Moroni had stationed an army by the borders of the city, and they had [a]cast up dirt round about to shield them from the arrows and the [b]stones of the Lamanites; for behold, they fought with stones and with arrows.

3 Behold, I said that the city of [a]Ammonihah had been rebuilt. I say unto you, yea, that it was in part rebuilt; and because the Lamanites had destroyed it once because of the iniquity of the people, they supposed that it would again become an easy prey for them.

4 But behold, how great was their disappointment; for behold, the Nephites had dug up a [a]ridge of earth round about them, which was so high that the Lamanites could not cast their stones and their arrows at them that they might take effect, neither could they come upon them save it was by their place of [b]entrance.

5 Now at this time the chief [a]captains of the Lamanites were astonished exceedingly, because of the wisdom of the Nephites in preparing their places of security.

6 Now the leaders of the Laman-

20a TG Humility.
  b 1 Ne. 15:20; Hel. 6:5.
  c 1 Ne. 17:35.
21a Alma 48:2.
23a Alma 28:11 (11–12);
    D&C 42:45.
  b 3 Ne. 12:44.
  c Amos 4:12; Alma

20:17.
24a Alma 46:12.
  b TG Martyrdom.
  c TG Cruelty.
  d TG Apostasy of
    Individuals.
25a Alma 45:8.
49 1a Alma 8:6.

2a Alma 48:8.
  b 1 Ne. 16:15; Alma
    43:20.
3a Alma 16:2 (2–3, 9, 11).
4a Alma 48:8; 50:1.
  b Alma 49:20.
5a Alma 52:19.

[*72 B.C.]

ites had supposed, because of the greatness of their numbers, yea, they supposed that they should be privileged to come upon them as they had hitherto done; yea, and they had also prepared themselves with shields, and with ᵃbreastplates; and they had also prepared themselves with garments of skins, yea, very thick garments to cover their nakedness.

7 And being thus prepared they supposed that they should easily overpower and ᵃsubject their brethren to the yoke of bondage, or slay and massacre them according to their pleasure.

8 But behold, to their uttermost astonishment, they were ᵃprepared for them, in a manner which never had been known among the children of Lehi. Now they were prepared for the Lamanites, to battle after the manner of the instructions of Moroni.

9 And it came to pass that the Lamanites, or the Amalickiahites, were exceedingly astonished at their manner of preparation for war.

10 Now, if king Amalickiah had come down out of the ᵃland of Nephi, at the head of his army, perhaps he would have caused the Lamanites to have attacked the Nephites at the city of Ammonihah; for behold, he did care not for the blood of his people.

11 But behold, Amalickiah did not come down himself to battle. And behold, his chief captains durst not attack the Nephites at the city of Ammonihah, for Moroni had altered the management of affairs among the Nephites, insomuch that the Lamanites were disappointed in their places of retreat and they could not come upon them.

12 Therefore they retreated into the wilderness, and took their camp and marched towards the land of ᵃNoah, supposing that to be the next best place for them to come against the Nephites.

13 For they knew not that Moroni had fortified, or had built ᵃforts of security, for every city in all the land round about; therefore, they marched forward to the land of Noah with a firm determination; yea, their chief captains came forward and took an ᵇoath that they would destroy the people of that city.

14 But behold, to their astonishment, the city of Noah, which had hitherto been a weak place, had now, by the means of Moroni, become strong, yea, even to exceed the strength of the city Ammonihah.

15 And now, behold, this was wisdom in Moroni; for he had supposed that they would be frightened at the city Ammonihah; and as the city of Noah had hitherto been the weakest part of the land, therefore they would march thither to battle; and thus it was according to his desires.

16 And behold, Moroni had appointed Lehi to be chief captain over the men of that city; and it was that ᵃsame Lehi who fought with the Lamanites in the valley on the east of the river Sidon.

17 And now behold it came to pass, that when the Lamanites had found that Lehi commanded the city they were again disappointed, for they feared Lehi exceedingly; nevertheless their chief captains had ᵃsworn with an oath to attack the city; therefore, they brought up their armies.

18 Now behold, the Lamanites could not get into their forts of security by any other way save by the entrance, because of the highness of the bank which had been thrown up, and the depth of the

6a Alma 46: 13; Hel.
    1: 14.
7a Alma 43: 29.
8a Alma 48: 7 (7–10).

10a 2 Ne. 5: 8; Omni 1: 12;
    Alma 47: 1 (1, 13–24).
12a Alma 16: 3.
13a Alma 48: 8; 50: 10
    (1–6, 10).

b Alma 49: 17.
16a Alma 43: 35.
17a Alma 49: 13.

[72 B.C.]

ditch which had been dug round about, save it were by the entrance.

19 And thus were the Nephites prepared to destroy all such as should attempt to climb up to enter the fort by any other way, by casting over stones and arrows at them.

20 Thus they were prepared, yea, a body of their strongest men, with their swords and their slings, to smite down all who should attempt to come into their place of security by the place of "entrance; and thus were they prepared to defend themselves against the Lamanites.

21 And it came to pass that the captains of the Lamanites brought up their armies before the place of entrance, and began to contend with the Nephites, to get into their place of security; but behold, they were driven back from time to time, insomuch that they were slain with an immense slaughter.

22 Now when they found that they could not obtain power over the Nephites by the pass, they began to dig down their banks of earth that they might obtain a pass to their armies, that they might have an equal chance to fight; but behold, in these attempts they were swept off by the stones and arrows which were thrown at them; and instead of filling up their ditches by pulling down the banks of earth, they were filled up in a measure with their dead and wounded bodies.

23 Thus the Nephites had all power over their enemies; and thus the Lamanites did attempt to destroy the Nephites until their "chief captains were all slain; yea, and more than a thousand of the Lamanites were slain; while, on the other hand, there was not a single soul of the Nephites which was slain.

24 There were about fifty who were wounded, who had been exposed to the arrows of the Lamanites through the pass, but they were shielded by their "shields, and their breastplates, and their head-plates, insomuch that their wounds were upon their legs, many of which were very severe.

25 And it came to pass, that when the Lamanites saw that their chief captains were all slain they fled into the wilderness. And it came to pass that they returned to the land of Nephi, to inform their king, Amalickiah, who was a "Nephite by birth, concerning their great "loss.

26 And it came to pass that he was exceedingly angry with his people, because he had not obtained his desire over the Nephites; he had not subjected them to the yoke of bondage.

27 Yea, he was exceedingly wroth, and he did "curse God, and also Moroni, swearing with an "oath that he would drink his blood; and this because Moroni had kept the commandments of God in preparing for the safety of his people.

28 And it came to pass, that on the other hand, the people of Nephi did "thank the Lord their God, because of his matchless power in delivering them from the hands of their enemies.

29 And thus ended the nineteenth year of the reign of the judges over the people of Nephi.

30 Yea, and there was continual peace among them, and exceedingly great prosperity in the church because of their heed and diligence which they gave unto the word of God, which was declared unto them by Helaman, and Shiblon, and Corianton, and Ammon and his brethren, yea, and by all those who had been ordained by the "holy order of God, being baptized unto repentance, and sent forth to preach among the people.

20a Alma 49:4 (4, 18, 21, 24).
23a Alma 48:5.
24a Alma 43:19.
25a Alma 46:3.
  b Alma 51:11.
27a TG Blasphemy.
  b Acts 23:12; Alma 51:9.
28a TG Thanksgiving.
30a Alma 30:20 (20–23, 31); 43:2; 46:38.

[72 B.C.]

CHAPTER 50

Moroni fortifies the lands of the Nephites—They build many new cities—Wars and destructions befell the Nephites in the days of their wickedness and abominations—Morianton and his dissenters are defeated by Teancum—Nephihah dies and his son Pahoran fills the judgment-seat.

AND now it came to pass that Moroni did not stop making preparations for war, or to defend his people against the Lamanites; for he caused that his armies should commence in the *commencement of the twentieth year of the reign of the judges, that they should commence in digging up ªheaps of earth round about all the cities, throughout all the land which was possessed by the Nephites.

2 And upon the top of these ridges of earth he caused that there should be ªtimbers, yea, works of timbers built up to the height of a man, round about the cities.

3 And he caused that upon those works of timbers there should be a frame of pickets built upon the timbers round about; and they were strong and high.

4 And he caused towers to be erected that overlooked those works of pickets, and he caused places of security to be built upon those ªtowers, that the stones and the arrows of the Lamanites could not hurt them.

5 And they were prepared that they could cast stones from the top thereof, according to their pleasure and their strength, and slay him who should attempt to approach near the walls of the city.

6 Thus Moroni did prepare strongholds against the coming of their enemies, round about every city in all the land.

7 And it came to pass that Moroni caused that his armies should go forth into the east wilderness; yea, and they went forth and drove all the Lamanites who were in the east wilderness into their own lands, which were ªsouth of the land of Zarahemla.

8 And the land of ªNephi did run in a straight course from the east sea to the west.

9 And it came to pass that when Moroni had driven all the Lamanites out of the east wilderness, which was north of the lands of their own possessions, he caused that the inhabitants who were in the land of Zarahemla and in the land round about should go forth into the east wilderness, even to the borders by the seashore, and possess the land.

10 And he also placed armies on the south, in the borders of their possessions, and caused them to erect ªfortifications that they might secure their armies and their people from the hands of their enemies.

11 And thus he cut off all the strongholds of the Lamanites in the east wilderness, yea, and also on the west, fortifying the line between the Nephites and the Lamanites, between the land of Zarahemla and the land of Nephi, from the west sea, running by the head of the ªriver Sidon—the Nephites possessing all the land ᵇnorthward, yea, even all the land which was northward of the land Bountiful, according to their pleasure.

12 Thus Moroni, with his armies, which did increase daily because of the assurance of protection which his works did bring forth unto them, did seek to cut off the strength and the power of the Lamanites from off the lands of their possessions, that they should have no power upon the lands of their possession.

13 And it came to pass that the Nephites began the foundation of a

---

50 1a Alma 48:8; 49:4;
        52:6.
     2a Alma 53:4.
     4a 2 Chr. 14:7 (7-8).
     7a Alma 22:32.

8a 2 Ne. 5:8; Omni
        1:12 (12, 27); Mosiah
        7:6 (6-7); 9:1 (1,
        3-4, 14).
10a Alma 49:13 (13,

        18-24); 53:3 (3-7).
11a Alma 2:15; 22:29.
     b Morm. 2:3.

[*72 B.C.]

city, and they called the name of the city ^aMoroni; and it was by the east sea; and it was on the south by the line of the possessions of the Lamanites.

14 And they also began a foundation for a city between the city of Moroni and the city of Aaron, joining the borders of Aaron and Moroni; and they called the name of the city, or the land, ^aNephihah.

15 And they also began in that same year to build many cities on the north, one in a particular manner which they called ^aLehi, which was in the north by the borders of the seashore.

16 And thus ended the twentieth year.

17 And in these prosperous circumstances were the people of Nephi in the *commencement of the twenty and first year of the reign of the judges over the people of Nephi.

18 And they did prosper ^aexceedingly, and they became exceedingly rich; yea, and they did multiply and wax strong in the land.

19 And thus we see how merciful and just are all the dealings of the Lord, to the fulfilling of all his words unto the children of men; yea, we can behold that his words are verified, even at this time, which he spake unto Lehi, saying:

20 Blessed art thou and thy children; and they shall be blessed, inasmuch as they shall keep my ^acommandments they shall prosper in the land. But remember, inasmuch as they will not keep my commandments they shall be ^bcut off from the presence of the Lord.

21 And we see that these promises have been verified to the people of Nephi; for it has been their quarrelings and their contentions, yea, their murderings, and their plunderings,

their idolatry, their whoredoms, and their abominations, which were among themselves, which ^abrought upon them their wars and their destructions.

22 And those who were faithful in keeping the commandments of the Lord were delivered at all times, whilst thousands of their wicked brethren have been consigned to bondage, or to perish by the sword, or to dwindle in unbelief, and mingle with the Lamanites.

23 But behold there never was a ^ahappier time among the people of Nephi, since the days of Nephi, than in the days of Moroni, yea, even at this time, in the twenty and first year of the reign of the judges.

24 And it came to pass that the twenty and second year of the reign of the judges also ended in peace; yea, and also the twenty and third year.

25 And it came to pass that in the †commencement of the twenty and fourth year of the reign of the judges, there would also have been peace among the people of Nephi had it not been for a ^acontention which took place among them concerning the land of ^bLehi, and the land of ^cMorianton, which joined upon the borders of Lehi; both of which were on the borders by the seashore.

26 For behold, the people who possessed the land of Morianton did claim a part of the land of Lehi; therefore there began to be a warm ^acontention between them, insomuch that the people of Morianton took up arms against their brethren, and they were determined by the sword to slay them.

27 But behold, the people who possessed the land of Lehi fled to the camp of Moroni, and appealed unto

13a Alma 51: 22 (22–24);
62: 32 (32, 34); 3 Ne.
8: 9.
14a Alma 51: 24 (24–26);
59: 5; 62: 18 (14, 18,
26).
15a Alma 51: 26 (24–26);
62: 30.

18a Alma 1: 29.
20a Lev. 25: 18 (18–19);
Ps. 1: 3 (2–3); Alma
37: 13; 62: 48.
b Ps. 37: 2; D&C 1: 14.
21a Alma 41: 10.
23a 2 Ne. 5: 27; Mosiah

2: 41; 4 Ne. 1: 16
(15–18).
25a TG Contention.
b Hel. 6: 10.
c Alma 51: 26.
26a 3 Ne. 11: 29.

[*71 B.C. †68 B.C.]

him for assistance; for behold they were not in the wrong.

28 And it came to pass that when the people of Morianton, who were led by a man whose name was Morianton, found that the people of Lehi had fled to the camp of Moroni, they were exceedingly fearful lest the army of Moroni should come upon them and destroy them.

29 Therefore, Morianton put it into their hearts that they should flee to the land which was northward, which was covered with ªlarge bodies of water, and take possession of the land which was ᵇnorthward.

30 And behold, they would have carried this plan into effect, (which would have been a cause to have been lamented) but behold, Morianton being a man of much passion, therefore he was angry with one of his maid servants, and he fell upon her and beat her much.

31 And it came to pass that she fled, and came over to the camp of Moroni, and told Moroni all things concerning the matter, and also concerning their intentions to flee into the land northward.

32 Now behold, the people who were in the land Bountiful, or rather Moroni, feared that they would hearken to the words of Morianton and unite with his people, and thus he would obtain possession of those parts of the land, which would lay a foundation for serious consequences among the people of Nephi, yea, which ªconsequences would lead to the overthrow of their ᵇliberty.

33 Therefore Moroni sent an army, with their camp, to head the people of Morianton, to stop their flight into the land northward.

34 And it came to pass that they did not ªhead them until they had

come to the borders of the land ᵇDesolation; and there they did head them, by the narrow pass which led by the sea into the land northward, yea, by the sea, on the west and on the east.

35 And it came to pass that the army which was sent by Moroni, which was led by a man whose name was Teancum, did meet the people of Morianton; and so stubborn were the people of Morianton, (being inspired by his wickedness and his ªflattering words) that a battle commenced between them, in the which Teancum did ᵇslay Morianton and defeat his army, and took them prisoners, and returned to the camp of Moroni. And thus ended the twenty and fourth year of the reign of the judges over the people of Nephi.

36 And thus were the people of Morianton brought back. And upon their ªcovenanting to keep the peace they were restored to the land of Morianton, and a union took place between them and the people of Lehi; and they were also restored to their lands.

37 And it came to pass that in the same year that the people of Nephi had peace restored unto them, that Nephihah, the ªsecond chief judge, died, having filled the judgment-seat with ᵇperfect uprightness before God.

38 Nevertheless, he had refused Alma to take possession of those ªrecords and those things which were esteemed by Alma and his fathers to be most sacred; therefore Alma had conferred ᵇthem upon his son, Helaman.

39 Behold, it came to pass that the son of Nephihah was appointed to fill the judgment-seat, in the stead of his father; yea, he was appointed

29a Mosiah 8:8; Hel. 3:4 (3-4).
  b Alma 22:31 (29-31); 51:30.
32a TG Contention; Division.
  b TG Liberty.
34a Hel. 1:28 (28-30).
  b Alma 46:17; Morm. 3:5 (5, 7).
35a Mosiah 27:8; Hel. 1:7; 2:5.
  b Alma 51:29.
36a 1 Ne. 4:37; Alma
44:15.
37a Alma 4:17 (16-18).
  b TG Perfection.
38a Alma 37:1 (1-5); 45:2 (2-8).
  b 3 Ne. 1:2.

chief judge and [a]governor over the people, with an [b]oath and sacred ordinance to judge righteously, and to keep the peace and the [c]freedom of the people, and to grant unto them their sacred privileges to worship the Lord their God, yea, to support and maintain the cause of God all his days, and to bring the wicked to justice according to their crime.

40 Now behold, his name was [a]Pahoran. And Pahoran did fill the seat of his father, and did commence his reign in the end of the twenty and fourth year, over the people of Nephi.

CHAPTER 51

The king-men seek to change the law and set up a king—Pahoran and the freemen are supported by the voice of the people—Moroni compels the king-men to defend their liberty or be put to death—Amalickiah and the Lamanites capture many fortified cities—Teancum repels the Lamanite invasion and slays Amalickiah in his tent.

AND now it came to pass in the *commencement of the twenty and fifth year of the reign of the judges over the people of Nephi, they having established peace between the people of Lehi and the people of Morianton concerning their lands, and having commenced the twenty and fifth year in [a]peace;

2 Nevertheless, they did not long maintain an entire peace in the land, for there began to be a contention among the people concerning the chief judge Pahoran; for behold, there were a part of the people who desired that a few particular points of the [a]law should be altered.

3 But behold, Pahoran would not alter nor suffer the law to be altered;

therefore, he did not hearken to those who had sent in their voices with their petitions concerning the altering of the law.

4 Therefore, those who were desirous that the law should be altered were angry with him, and desired that he should no longer be chief judge over the land; therefore there arose a warm [a]dispute concerning the matter, but not unto bloodshed.

5 And it came to pass that those who were desirous that Pahoran should be dethroned from the judgment-seat were called [a]king-men, for they were desirous that the law should be altered in a manner to overthrow the free government and to establish a [b]king over the land.

6 And those who were desirous that Pahoran should remain chief judge over the land took upon them the name of [a]freemen; and thus was the [b]division among them, for the freemen had sworn or [c]covenanted to maintain their rights and the privileges of their religion by a free government.

7 And it came to pass that this matter of their contention was settled by the [a]voice of the people. And it came to pass that the voice of the people came in favor of the freemen, and Pahoran retained the judgment-seat, which caused much rejoicing among the brethren of Pahoran and also many of the people of liberty, who also put the king-men to silence, that they durst not oppose but were obliged to maintain the cause of freedom.

8 Now those who were in favor of kings were those of [a]high birth, and they sought to be [b]kings; and they were supported by those who sought power and authority over the people.

39a Alma 60:1.
 b TG Oath; Ordinance.
 c Alma 4:16 (16–17);
   Hel. 1:5 (3–5, 13).
40a Alma 59:3; 61:1;
   Hel. 1:2.
51 1a TG Peacemakers.
2a Alma 1:1.

4a TG Disputations.
5a Alma 60:16; 62:9.
   TG Kings, Earthly; Un-
   righteous Dominion.
 b 3 Ne. 6:30.
6a Alma 61:3 (3–4);
   62:6.

 b 1 Kgs. 16:21 (21–22).
 c Alma 48:13; 60:25
   (25–27).
7a Alma 4:16; Hel. 1:5.
8a TG Haughtiness; Pride.
 b TG Tyranny.

9 But behold, this was a critical time for such contentions to be among the people of Nephi; for behold, Amalickiah had again ªstirred up the hearts of the people of the Lamanites against the people of the Nephites, and he was gathering together soldiers from all parts of his land, and arming them, and preparing for war with all diligence; for he had ᵇsworn to drink the blood of Moroni.

10 But behold, we shall see that his promise which he made was ªrash; nevertheless, he did prepare himself and his armies to come to battle against the Nephites.

11 Now his armies were not so great as they had hitherto been, because of the many thousands who had been ªslain by the hand of the Nephites; but notwithstanding their great loss, Amalickiah had gathered together a wonderfully great army, insomuch that he feared not to come down to the land of Zarahemla.

12 Yea, even Amalickiah did himself come down, at the head of the Lamanites. And it was in the twenty and fifth year of the reign of the judges; and it was at the same time that they had begun to settle the affairs of their contentions concerning the chief judge, Pahoran.

13 And it came to pass that when the men who were called king-men had heard that the Lamanites were coming down to battle against them, they were glad in their hearts; and they refused to take up arms, for they were so wroth with the chief judge, and also with the ªpeople of ᵇliberty, that they would not take up arms to defend their country.

14 And it came to pass that when Moroni saw this, and also saw that the Lamanites were coming into the borders of the land, he was exceedingly wroth because of the ªstubbornness of those people whom he had labored with so much diligence to preserve; yea, he was exceedingly wroth; his soul was filled with anger against them.

15 And it came to pass that he sent a petition, with the voice of the people, unto the governor of the land, desiring that he should read it, and give him (Moroni) power to compel those dissenters to defend their country or to put them to death.

16 For it was his first care to put an end to such contentions and dissensions among the people; for behold, this had been hitherto a cause of all their destruction. And it came to pass that it was granted according to the voice of the people.

17 And it came to pass that Moroni commanded that his army should go against those king-men, to pull down their pride and their nobility and level them with the earth, or they should take up arms and support the cause of liberty.

18 And it came to pass that the armies did march forth against them; and they did pull down their pride and their nobility, insomuch that as they did lift their weapons of war to fight against the men of Moroni they were hewn down and leveled to the earth.

19 And it came to pass that there were four thousand of those ªdissenters who were hewn down by the sword; and those of their leaders who were not slain in battle were taken and ᵇcast into prison, for there was no time for their trials at this period.

20 And the remainder of those dissenters, rather than be smitten down to the earth by the sword, yielded to the standard of liberty, and were compelled to hoist the ªtitle of liberty upon their towers, and in their cities, and to take up arms in defence of their country.

9a Alma 63: 14.
  b Acts 23: 12; Alma
    49: 27 (26–27).
10a TG Rashness.
11a Alma 49: 25 (22–25).
13a Alma 46: 16 (10–16).
  b TG Liberty.
14a TG Stubbornness.
19a Alma 60: 16.
  b Alma 62: 9.
20a Alma 46: 13 (12–13).

[About 67 B.C.]

21 And thus Moroni put an end to those king-men, that there were not any known by the appellation of king-men; and thus he put an end to the stubbornness and the pride of those people who professed the blood of nobility; but they were brought down to humble themselves like unto their brethren, and to fight ^avaliantly for their freedom from bondage.

22 Behold, it came to pass that while ^aMoroni was thus breaking down the wars and contentions among his own people, and subjecting them to peace and civilization, and making regulations to prepare for war against the Lamanites, behold, the Lamanites had come into the land of Moroni, which was in the borders by the seashore.

23 And it came to pass that the Nephites were not sufficiently strong in the city of Moroni; therefore Amalickiah did drive them, slaying many. And it came to pass that Amalickiah took possession of the city, yea, possession of all their fortifications.

24 And those who fled out of the ^acity of Moroni came to the city of Nephihah; and also the people of the city of Lehi gathered themselves together, and made preparations and were ready to receive the Lamanites to battle.

25 But it came to pass that Amalickiah would not suffer the Lamanites to go against the city of Nephihah to battle, but kept them down by the seashore, leaving men in every city to maintain and defend it.

26 And thus he went on, taking possession of ^amany cities, the city of ^bNephihah, and the city of ^cLehi, and the city of ^dMorianton, and the city of Omner, and the city of ^eGid,

and the city of ^fMulek, all of which were on the east borders by the seashore.

27 And thus had the Lamanites obtained, by the cunning of Amalickiah, so many cities, by their numberless hosts, all of which were strongly fortified after the manner of the ^afortifications of Moroni; all of which afforded strongholds for the Lamanites.

28 And it came to pass that they marched to the ^aborders of the land Bountiful, driving the Nephites before them and slaying many.

29 But it came to pass that they were met by Teancum, who had ^aslain Morianton and had ^bheaded his people in his flight.

30 And it came to pass that he headed Amalickiah also, as he was marching forth with his numerous army that he might take possession of the land Bountiful, and also the land ^anorthward.

31 But behold he met with a disappointment by being repulsed by Teancum and his men, for they were great warriors; for every man of Teancum did exceed the Lamanites in their strength and in their skill of war, insomuch that they did gain advantage over the Lamanites.

32 And it came to pass that they did harass them, insomuch that they did slay them even until it was dark. And it came to pass that Teancum and his men did pitch their tents in the borders of the land Bountiful; and Amalickiah did pitch his tents in the borders on the beach by the seashore, and after this manner were they driven.

33 And it came to pass that when the night had come, Teancum and his servant stole forth and went out by night, and went into the camp of Amalickiah; and behold, sleep

---

21a TG Courage.
22a Alma 50: 13; 62: 32 (32, 34); 3 Ne. 8: 9.
24a Alma 50: 14.
26a Alma 58: 31.
  b Alma 50: 14; 62: 18

(14, 18, 26).
c Alma 50: 15; 62: 30.
d Alma 50: 25; 55: 33.
e Alma 55: 7.
f Alma 52: 2 (2, 16, 22); 53: 6 (2, 6).

27a Alma 48: 8 (8–9).
28a Alma 52: 12.
29a Alma 50: 35.
  b Hel. 1: 28 (28–30).
30a Alma 50: 29; 52: 9.

[About 67 B.C.]

had overpowered them because of their much fatigue, which was caused by the labors and heat of the day.

34 And it came to pass that Teancum stole privily into the tent of the king, and [a]put a javelin to his heart; and he did cause the [b]death of the king immediately that he did not awake his servants.

35 And he returned again privily to his own camp, and behold, his men were asleep, and he awoke them and told them all the things that he had done.

36 And he caused that his armies should stand in [a]readiness, lest the Lamanites had awakened and should come upon them.

37 And thus endeth the twenty and fifth year of the reign of the judges over the people of Nephi; and thus endeth the days of Amalickiah.

CHAPTER 52

Ammoron succeeds Amalickiah as king of the Lamanites—Moroni, Teancum, and Lehi lead the Nephites in a victorious war against the Lamanites—The city of Mulek is retaken, and Jacob the Lamanite is slain.

AND now, it came to pass in the *twenty and sixth year of the reign of the judges over the people of Nephi, behold, when the Lamanites awoke on the first morning of the first month, behold, they found Amalickiah was dead in his own tent; and they also saw that Teancum was [a]ready to give them battle on that day.

2 And now, when the Lamanites saw this they were affrighted; and they abandoned their design in marching into the land northward, and retreated with all their army into the city of [a]Mulek, and sought protection in their fortifications.

3 And it came to pass that the [a]brother of Amalickiah was appointed king over the people; and his name was [b]Ammoron; thus king Ammoron, the brother of king Amalickiah, was appointed to reign in his stead.

4 And it came to pass that he did command that his people should maintain those cities, which they had taken by the shedding of blood; for they had not taken any cities save they had lost much blood.

5 And now, Teancum saw that the Lamanites were determined to maintain those cities which they had taken, and those parts of the land which they had obtained possession of; and also seeing the enormity of their number, Teancum thought it was not expedient that he should attempt to attack them in their forts.

6 But he kept his men round about, as if making preparations for war; yea, and truly he was preparing to defend himself against them, by [a]casting up walls round about and preparing places of resort.

7 And it came to pass that he kept thus preparing for war until Moroni had sent a large number of men to strengthen his army.

8 And Moroni also sent orders unto him that he should retain all the prisoners who fell into his hands; for as the Lamanites had taken many prisoners, that he should retain all the prisoners of the Lamanites as a [a]ransom for those whom the Lamanites had taken.

9 And he also sent orders unto him that he should fortify the land [a]Bountiful, and secure the [b]narrow pass which led into the land [c]northward, lest the Lamanites should obtain that point and should have power to harass them on every side.

34a Alma 62:36.
  b Alma 54:16.
36a Alma 52:1.
52 1a Alma 51:36.
  2a Alma 51:26.
  3a Alma 48:1 (1–6);

54:5.
  b Alma 54:1; Hel. 1:16.
6a Alma 50:1; 53:3.
8a Alma 54:2 (1–2).
9a Alma 22:29; 53:3

(3–4); 63:5; Hel. 1:23.
  b Alma 22:32; Morm. 2:29.
  c Alma 51:30.

[*66 B.C.]

10 And Moroni also sent unto him, desiring him that he would be ᵃfaithful in maintaining that quarter of the land, and that he would seek every opportunity to scourge the Lamanites in that quarter, as much as was in his power, that perhaps he might take again by stratagem or some other way those cities which had been taken out of their hands; and that he also would fortify and strengthen the cities round about, which had not fallen into the hands of the Lamanites.

11 And he also said unto him, I would come unto you, but behold, the Lamanites are upon us in the borders of the land by the west sea; and behold, I go against them, therefore I cannot come unto you.

12 Now, the king (Ammoron) had ᵃdeparted out of the land of Zarahemla, and had made known unto the queen concerning the death of his brother, and had gathered together a large number of men, and had marched forth against the Nephites on the borders by the west sea.

13 And thus he was endeavoring to harass the Nephites, and to draw away a part of their forces to that part of the land, while he had commanded those whom he had left to possess the cities which he had taken, that they should also harass the Nephites on the borders by the east sea, and should take possession of their lands as much as it was in their power, according to the power of their armies.

14 And thus were the Nephites in those dangerous circumstances in the ending of the twenty and sixth year of the reign of the judges over the people of Nephi.

15 But behold, it came to pass in the *twenty and seventh year of the reign of the judges, that Teancum, by the command of Moroni—who had established armies to protect the south and the west borders of the land, and had begun his march towards the land Bountiful, that he might assist Teancum with his men in retaking the cities which they had lost—

16 And it came to pass that Teancum had received orders to make an attack upon the city of Mulek, and retake it if it were possible.

17 And it came to pass that Teancum made preparations to make an attack upon the city of Mulek, and march forth with his army against the Lamanites; but he saw that it was impossible that he could overpower them while they were in their fortifications; therefore he abandoned his designs and returned again to the city Bountiful, to wait for the coming of Moroni, that he might receive strength to his army.

18 And it came to pass that Moroni did arrive with his army at the land of Bountiful, in the latter end of the twenty and seventh year of the reign of the judges over the people of Nephi.

19 And in the †commencement of the twenty and eighth year, Moroni and Teancum and many of the chief ᵃcaptains held a council of war— what they should do to cause the Lamanites to come out against them to battle; or that they might by some means flatter them out of their strongholds, that they might gain advantage over them and take again the city of Mulek.

20 And it came to pass they sent embassies to the army of the Lamanites, which protected the city of Mulek, to their leader, whose name was Jacob, desiring him that he would come out with his armies to meet them upon the plains between the two cities. But behold, Jacob, who was a ᵃZoramite, would not come out with his army to meet them upon the plains.

21 And it came to pass that Moroni, having no hopes of meeting them upon fair grounds, therefore, he resolved upon a plan that he might

[a]decoy the Lamanites out of their strongholds.

22 Therefore he caused that Teancum should take a small number of men and march down near the seashore; and Moroni and his army, by night, marched in the wilderness, on the west of the city [a]Mulek; and thus, on the morrow, when the guards of the Lamanites had discovered Teancum, they ran and told it unto Jacob, their leader.

23 And it came to pass that the armies of the Lamanites did march forth against Teancum, supposing by their numbers to overpower Teancum because of the smallness of his numbers. And as Teancum saw the armies of the Lamanites coming out against him he began to retreat down by the seashore, northward.

24 And it came to pass that when the Lamanites saw that he began to flee, they took courage and pursued them with vigor. And while Teancum was thus leading away the Lamanites who were pursuing them in vain, behold, Moroni commanded that a part of his army who were with him should march forth into the city, and take possession of it.

25 And thus they did, and slew all those who had been left to protect the city, yea, all those who would not [a]yield up their weapons of war.

26 And thus Moroni had obtained possession of the city Mulek with a part of his army, while he marched with the remainder to meet the Lamanites when they should return from the pursuit of Teancum.

27 And it came to pass that the Lamanites did pursue Teancum until they came near the city Bountiful, and then they were met by Lehi and a small army, which had been left to protect the city Bountiful.

28 And now behold, when the chief captains of the Lamanites had beheld Lehi with his army coming against them, they fled in much confusion, lest perhaps they should not obtain the city Mulek before Lehi should overtake them; for they were wearied because of their march, and the men of Lehi were fresh.

29 Now the Lamanites did not know that Moroni had been in their rear with his army; and all they feared was Lehi and his men.

30 Now Lehi was not desirous to overtake them till they should meet Moroni and his army.

31 And it came to pass that before the Lamanites had retreated far they were surrounded by the Nephites, by the men of Moroni on one hand, and the men of Lehi on the other, all of whom were fresh and full of strength; but the Lamanites were wearied because of their long march.

32 And Moroni commanded his men that they should fall upon them until they had given up their weapons of war.

33 And it came to pass that Jacob, being their leader, being also a [a]Zoramite, and having an unconquerable spirit, he led the Lamanites forth to battle with exceeding fury against Moroni.

34 Moroni being in their course of march, therefore Jacob was determined to slay them and cut his way through to the city of Mulek. But behold, Moroni and his men were more powerful; therefore they did not give way before the Lamanites.

35 And it came to pass that they fought on both hands with exceeding fury; and there were many slain on both sides; yea, and Moroni was wounded and Jacob was killed.

36 And Lehi pressed upon their rear with such fury with his strong men, that the Lamanites in the rear delivered up their weapons of war; and the remainder of them, being much confused, knew not whither to go or to strike.

37 Now Moroni seeing their con-

21a Josh. 8:13; Alma
    43:31 (30–43); 56:30.
22a Alma 51:26; 53:6
    (2, 6).
25a Alma 44:6.
33a Alma 30:59.

[About 64 B.C.]

fusion, he said unto them: If ye will bring forth your weapons of war and deliver them up, behold we will forbear shedding your blood.

38 And it came to pass that when the Lamanites had heard these words, their chief captains, all those who were not slain, came forth and threw down their weapons of war ^aat the feet of Moroni, and also commanded their men that they should do the same.

39 But behold, there were many that would not; and those who would not deliver up their swords were taken and bound, and their weapons of war were taken from them, and they were compelled to march with their brethren forth into the land Bountiful.

40 And now the number of prisoners who were taken exceeded more than the number of those who had been slain, yea, more than those who had been slain on both sides.

CHAPTER 53

The Lamanite prisoners are used to fortify the city Bountiful—Dissensions among the Nephites give rise to Lamanite victories—Helaman takes command of the two thousand stripling sons of the people of Ammon.

AND it came to pass that they did set guards over the prisoners of the Lamanites, and did compel them to go forth and bury their dead, yea, and also the dead of the Nephites who were slain; and Moroni placed men over them to guard them while they should perform their labors.

2 And ^aMoroni went to the city of Mulek with Lehi, and took command of the city and gave it unto Lehi. Now behold, this Lehi was a man who had been with Moroni in the more part of all his battles; and he was a man like unto Moroni, and they rejoiced in each other's safety; yea, they were beloved by each other, and also beloved by all the people of Nephi.

3 And it came to pass that after the Lamanites had finished burying their dead and also the dead of the Nephites, they were marched back into the land Bountiful; and Teancum, by the orders of Moroni, caused that they should commence laboring in ^adigging a ditch round about the land, or the city, ^bBountiful.

4 And he caused that they should build a ^abreastwork of timbers upon the inner bank of the ditch; and they cast up dirt out of the ditch against the breastwork of timbers; and thus they did cause the Lamanites to labor until they had encircled the city of Bountiful round about with a strong wall of timbers and earth, to an exceeding height.

5 And this city became an exceeding stronghold ever after; and in this city they did guard the prisoners of the Lamanites; yea, even within a wall which they had caused them to ^abuild with their own hands. Now Moroni was compelled to cause the Lamanites to labor, because it was easy to guard them while at their labor; and he desired all his forces when he should make an attack upon the Lamanites.

6 And it came to pass that Moroni had thus gained a victory over one of the greatest of the armies of the Lamanites, and had obtained possession of the city of ^aMulek, which was one of the strongest holds of the Lamanites in the land of Nephi; and thus he had also built a stronghold to retain his prisoners.

7 And it came to pass that he did no more attempt a battle with the Lamanites in that year, but he did employ his men in preparing for war, yea, and in making fortifications to guard against the Lamanites, yea, and also delivering their women and their children from famine and

38a Alma 55: 23.
53 2a Alma 48: 17.
  3a Alma 52: 6.

b Alma 52: 9 (9, 17, 27);
  63: 5.
4a Alma 50: 2 (2–3).

5a Alma 55: 25 (25–26).
6a Alma 51: 26; 52: 22.

[About 64 B.C.]

affliction, and providing food for their armies.

8 And now it came to pass that the armies of the Lamanites, on the west sea, south, while in the absence of Moroni on account of some intrigue amongst the Nephites, which caused ᵃdissensions amongst them, had gained some ground over the Nephites, yea, insomuch that they had obtained possession of a number of their cities in that part of the land.

9 And thus because of ᵃiniquity amongst themselves, yea, because of dissensions and intrigue among themselves they were placed in the most dangerous circumstances.

10 And now behold, I have somewhat to say concerning the ᵃpeople of Ammon, who, in the beginning, were Lamanites; but by Ammon and his brethren, or rather by the power and word of God, they had been ᵇconverted unto the Lord; and they had been brought down into the land of Zarahemla, and had ever since been protected by the Nephites.

11 And because of their oath they had been kept from taking up arms against their brethren; for they had taken an oath that they ᵃnever would shed blood more; and according to their oath they would have perished; yea, they would have suffered themselves to have fallen into the hands of their brethren, had it not been for the pity and the exceeding love which Ammon and his brethren had had for them.

12 And for this cause they were brought down into the land of Zarahemla; and they ever had been ᵃprotected by the Nephites.

13 But it came to pass that when they saw the danger, and the many ᵃafflictions and tribulations which the Nephites bore for them, they were moved with compassion and were ᵇdesirous to take up arms in the defence of their country.

14 But behold, as they were about to take their weapons of war, they were overpowered by the persuasions of Helaman and his brethren, for they were about to ᵃbreak the ᵇoath which they had made.

15 And Helaman feared lest by so doing they should lose their souls; therefore all those who had entered into this covenant were compelled to behold their brethren wade through their afflictions, in their dangerous circumstances at this time.

16 But behold, it came to pass they had many ᵃsons, who had not entered into a covenant that they would not take their weapons of war to defend themselves against their enemies; therefore they did assemble themselves together at this time, as many as were able to take up arms, and they called themselves Nephites.

17 And they entered into a covenant to fight for the liberty of the Nephites, yea, to protect the land unto the ᵃlaying down of their lives; yea, even they covenanted that they never would give up their ᵇliberty, but they would fight in all cases to protect the Nephites and themselves from bondage.

18 Now behold, there were two thousand of those young men, who entered into this covenant and took their weapons of war to defend their country.

19 And now behold, as they never had hitherto been a disadvantage to the Nephites, they became now at this period of time also a great support; for they took their weapons of war, and they would that Helaman should be their leader.

20 And they were all young men,

8a Alma 31:8; Hel. 1:15.
9a Josh. 7:4.
10a Alma 27:26.
   b Alma 23:13 (8–13).
11a Alma 24:18 (17–19).
12a Alma 27:23.

13a TG Affliction;
   Tribulation.
   b Alma 24:18 (17–19);
   56:7.
14a Num. 30:2.
   b TG Oath.

16a Alma 57:6.
17a TG Self-sacrifice.
   b Alma 56:47.
   TG Liberty.

[About 64 B.C.]

and they were exceedingly valiant for ᵃcourage, and also for strength and activity; but behold, this was not all—they were men who were true at all times in whatsoever thing they were entrusted.

21 Yea, they were men of truth and ᵃsoberness, for they had been taught to keep the commandments of God and to ᵇwalk uprightly before him.

22 And now it came to pass that Helaman did march at the head of his ᵃtwo thousand stripling soldiers, to the support of the people in the borders of the land on the south by the west sea.

23 And thus ended the twenty and eighth year of the reign of the judges over the people of Nephi.

CHAPTER 54

Ammoron and Moroni negotiate for the exchange of prisoners—Moroni demands that the Lamanites withdraw and cease their murderous attacks—Ammoron demands that the Nephites lay down their arms and become subject to the Lamanites.

AND now it came to pass in the *commencement of the twenty and ninth year of the judges, that ᵃAmmoron sent unto Moroni desiring that he would exchange prisoners.

2 And it came to pass that Moroni felt to ᵃrejoice exceedingly at this request, for he desired the provisions which were imparted for the support of the Lamanite prisoners for the support of his own people; and he also desired his own people for the strengthening of his army.

3 Now the Lamanites had taken many women and children, and there was not a woman nor a child among all the prisoners of Moroni, or the prisoners whom Moroni had taken; therefore Moroni resolved upon a stratagem to obtain as many prisoners of the Nephites from the Lamanites as it were possible.

4 Therefore he wrote an epistle, and sent it by the servant of Ammoron, the same who had brought an epistle to Moroni. Now these are the words which he wrote unto Ammoron, saying:

5 Behold, Ammoron, I have written unto you somewhat concerning this war which ye have waged against my people, or rather which thy ᵃbrother hath waged against them, and which ye are still determined to carry on after his death.

6 Behold, I would tell you somewhat concerning the ᵃjustice of God, and the sword of his almighty wrath, which doth hang over you except ye repent and withdraw your armies into your own lands, or the land of your possessions, which is the land of Nephi.

7 Yea, I would tell you these things if ye were capable of hearkening unto them; yea, I would tell you concerning that awful ᵃhell that awaits to receive such ᵇmurderers as thou and thy brother have been, except ye repent and withdraw your murderous purposes, and return with your armies to your own lands.

8 But as ye have once rejected these things, and have fought against the people of the Lord, even so I may expect you will do it again.

9 And now behold, we are prepared to receive you; yea, and except you withdraw your purposes, behold, ye will pull down the ᵃwrath of that God whom you have rejected upon you, even to your utter destruction.

10 But, as the Lord liveth, our armies shall come upon you except ye withdraw, and ye shall soon be visited with ᵃdeath, for we will retain our cities and our lands; yea,

20a TG Courage; Dependability; Integrity.
21a TG Sobriety.
  b TG Walking with God.
22a Alma 56: 3 (1–9).
54 1a Alma 52: 3.

2a Alma 52: 8.
5a Alma 48: 1 (1–6);
  52: 3 (1–3).
6a TG God, Indignation of; God, Justice of.

7a TG Hell.
  b Alma 47: 18 (18, 22–34). TG Murder.
9a TG Punishment.
10a Alma 43: 47.

and we will maintain our religion and the cause of our God.

11 But behold, it supposeth me that I talk to you concerning these things in vain; or it supposeth me that thou art a *a*child of hell; therefore I will close my epistle by telling you that I will not exchange prisoners, save it be on conditions that ye will deliver up a man and his wife and his children, for one prisoner; if this be the case that ye will do it, I will exchange.

12 And behold, if ye do not this, I will come against you with my armies; yea, even I will arm my women and my children, and I will come against you, and I will follow you even into your own land, which is the land of *a*our first inheritance; yea, and it shall be blood for blood, yea, life for life; and I will give you battle even until you are destroyed from off the face of the earth.

13 Behold, I am in my anger, and also my people; ye have sought to *a*murder us, and we have only sought to defend ourselves. But behold, if ye seek to destroy us more we will seek to destroy you; yea, and we will seek our land, the land of our first inheritance.

14 Now I close my epistle. I am Moroni; I am a leader of the people of the Nephites.

15 Now it came to pass that Ammoron, when he had received this epistle, was angry; and he wrote another epistle unto Moroni, and these are the words which he wrote, saying:

16 I am Ammoron, the king of the Lamanites; I am the brother of Amalickiah whom ye have *a*murdered. Behold, I will avenge his blood upon you, yea, and I will come upon you with my armies for I fear not your threatenings.

17 For behold, your fathers did wrong their brethren, insomuch that they did rob them of their *a*right to the *b*government when it rightly belonged unto them.

18 And now behold, if ye will lay down your arms, and subject yourselves to be governed by those to whom the government doth rightly belong, then will I cause that my people shall lay down their weapons and shall be at war no more.

19 Behold, ye have breathed out many threatenings against me and my people; but behold, we fear not your threatenings.

20 Nevertheless, I will grant to exchange prisoners according to your request, gladly, that I may preserve my food for my men of war; and we will wage a war which shall be eternal, either to the subjecting the Nephites to our authority or to their eternal extinction.

21 And as concerning that God whom ye say we have rejected, behold, we *a*know not such a being; neither do ye; but if it so be that there is such a being, we know not but that he hath made us as well as you.

22 And if it so be that there is a devil and a hell, behold will he not send you there to dwell with my brother whom ye have murdered, whom ye have hinted that he hath gone to such a place? But behold these things matter not.

23 I am Ammoron, and a descendant of *a*Zoram, whom your fathers pressed and brought out of Jerusalem.

24 And behold now, I am a bold Lamanite; behold, this war hath been waged to avenge their wrongs, and *a*to maintain and to obtain their rights to the government; and I close my epistle to Moroni.

CHAPTER 55

Moroni refuses to exchange prisoners—The Lamanite guards are en-

11a John 8: 44 (43–44).
12a 2 Ne. 5: 8 (5–8).
13a Alma 55: 2.
16a Alma 51: 34.
17a 2 Ne. 5: 3 (1–4);

Mosiah 10: 15 (12–17).
  b TG Governments.
21a TG Unbelief,
    Unbelievers.
23a 1 Ne. 4: 35; Jacob

1: 13; 4 Ne. 1: 36
(36–37).
24a Alma 48: 2 (1–4).

[About 63 B.C.]

ticed to become drunk, and the Nephite prisoners are freed—The city of Gid is taken without bloodshed.

Now it came to pass that when Moroni had received this epistle he was more angry, because he knew that Ammoron had a perfect knowledge of his [a]fraud; yea, he knew that Ammoron knew that it was not a just cause that had caused him to wage a war against the people of Nephi.

2 And he said: Behold, I will not exchange prisoners with Ammoron save he will withdraw his [a]purpose, as I have stated in my epistle; for I will not grant unto him that he shall have any more power than what he hath got.

3 Behold, I know the place where the Lamanites do guard my people whom they have taken prisoners; and as Ammoron would not grant unto me mine epistle, behold, I will give unto him according to my words; yea, I will seek death among them until they shall sue for peace.

4 And now it came to pass that when Moroni had said these words, he caused that a search should be made among his men, that perhaps he might find a man who was a descendant of Laman among them.

5 And it came to pass that they found one, whose name was Laman; and he was [a]one of the servants of the king who was murdered by Amalickiah.

6 Now Moroni caused that Laman and a small number of his men should go forth unto the guards who were over the Nephites.

7 Now the Nephites were guarded in the city of [a]Gid; therefore Moroni appointed Laman and caused that a small number of men should go with him.

8 And when it was evening Laman went to the guards who were over the Nephites, and behold, they saw him coming and they hailed him; but he saith unto them: Fear not; behold, I am a Lamanite. Behold, we have escaped from the Nephites, and they sleep; and behold we have taken of their wine and brought with us.

9 Now when the Lamanites heard these words they received him with joy; and they said unto him: Give us of your wine, that we may drink; we are glad that ye have thus taken wine with you for we are weary.

10 But Laman said unto them: Let us keep of our wine till we go against the Nephites to battle. But this saying only made them more desirous to drink of the wine;

11 For, said they: We are weary, therefore let us take of the wine, and by and by we shall receive wine for our rations, which will strengthen us to go against the Nephites.

12 And Laman said unto them: You may do according to your desires.

13 And it came to pass that they did take of the wine freely; and it was pleasant to their taste, therefore they took of it more freely; and it was strong, having been prepared in its [a]strength.

14 And it came to pass they did drink and were merry, and by and by they were all [a]drunken.

15 And now when Laman and his men saw that they were all drunken, and were in a [a]deep sleep, they returned to Moroni and told him all the things that had happened.

16 And now this was according to the design of Moroni. And Moroni had prepared his men with weapons of war; and he went to the city Gid, while the Lamanites were in a deep sleep and drunken, and cast in [a]weapons of war unto the prisoners, insomuch that they were all armed;

17 Yea, even to their women, and all those of their children, as many as were able to use a weapon of war,

55 1a Neh. 6: 8; Alma
     47: 30 (12–35).
   2a Alma 54: 13.
   5a Alma 47: 29.

   7a Alma 51: 26.
  13a Prov. 20: 1. TG Wine.
  14a Mosiah 22: 6 (6–11).
  15a 1 Sam. 26: 12;

     Mosiah 24: 19.
  16a Alma 62: 22 (21–23).

     [About 63 B.C.]

when Moroni had armed all those prisoners; and all those things were done in a profound silence.

18 But had they awakened the Lamanites, behold they were drunken and the Nephites could have slain them.

19 But behold, this was not the desire of Moroni; he did not *a*delight in murder or bloodshed, but he delighted in the saving of his people from destruction; and for this cause he might not bring upon him injustice, he would not fall upon the Lamanites and destroy them in their drunkenness.

20 But he had obtained his desires; for he had armed those prisoners of the Nephites who were within the wall of the city, and had given them power to gain possession of those parts which were within the walls.

21 And then he caused the men who were with him to withdraw a pace from them, and surround the armies of the Lamanites.

22 Now behold this was done in the night-time, so that when the Lamanites awoke in the morning they beheld that they were surrounded by the Nephites without, and that their prisoners were armed within.

23 And thus they saw that the Nephites had power over them; and in these circumstances they found that it was not expedient that they should fight with the Nephites; therefore their chief *a*captains demanded their weapons of war, and they brought them forth and *b*cast them at the feet of the Nephites, pleading for mercy.

24 Now behold, this was the desire of Moroni. He took them prisoners of war, and took possession of the city, and caused that all the prisoners should be liberated, who were Nephites; and they did join the army of Moroni, and were a great strength to his army.

25 And it came to pass that he did cause the Lamanites, whom he had taken prisoners, that they should commence a *a*labor in strengthening the fortifications round about the city Gid.

26 And it came to pass that when he had fortified the city Gid, according to his desires, he caused that his prisoners should be taken to the city Bountiful; and he also guarded that city with an exceedingly strong force.

27 And it came to pass that they did, notwithstanding all the intrigues of the Lamanites, keep and protect all the prisoners whom they had taken, and also maintain all the ground and the advantage which they had retaken.

28 And it came to pass that the Nephites began *a*again to be victorious, and to reclaim their rights and their privileges.

29 Many times did the Lamanites attempt to encircle them about by night, but in these attempts they did lose many prisoners.

30 And many times did they attempt to administer of their wine to the Nephites, that they might destroy them with poison or with drunkenness.

31 But behold, the Nephites were not slow to *a*remember the Lord their God in this their time of affliction. They could not be taken in their snares; yea, they would not partake of their wine, save they had first given to some of the Lamanite prisoners.

32 And they were thus cautious that no poison should be administered among them; for if their wine would poison a Lamanite it would also poison a Nephite; and thus they did try all their liquors.

33 And now it came to pass that it was expedient for Moroni to make preparations to attack the city *a*Morianton; for behold, the Laman-

---

19a Alma 48: 16; 55: 30 (30–32).
23a Alma 52: 19; 56: 12.
  b Alma 52: 38.

25a Alma 53: 5 (3–5).
28a Alma 44: 20 (12–23).
31a Hosea 5: 15;

  Alma 62: 49 (49–51).
33a Alma 50: 25; 51: 26.

[About 63 B.C.]

ites had, by their labors, fortified the city Morianton until it had become an exceeding stronghold.

34 And they were continually bringing new forces into that city, and also new supplies of provisions.

35 And thus ended the twenty and ninth year of the reign of the judges over the people of Nephi.

CHAPTER 56

Helaman sends an epistle to Moroni recounting the state of the war with the Lamanites—Antipus and Helaman gain a great victory over the Lamanites—Helaman's two thousand stripling sons fight with miraculous power and none of them are slain.

AND now it came to pass in the *commencement of the thirtieth year of the reign of the judges, on the second day in the first month, ᵃMoroni received an ᵇepistle from Helaman, stating the affairs of the people in ᶜthat quarter of the land.

2 And these are the words which he wrote, saying: My dearly beloved brother, Moroni, as well in the Lord as in the tribulations of our warfare; behold, my beloved brother, I have somewhat to tell you concerning our warfare in this part of the land.

3 Behold, ᵃtwo thousand of the sons of those men whom Ammon brought down out of the land of Nephi—now ye have known that these were descendants of Laman, who was the eldest son of our father Lehi;

4 Now I need not rehearse unto you concerning their traditions or their unbelief, for thou knowest concerning all these things—

5 Therefore it sufficeth me that I tell you that two thousand of these young men have taken their weapons of war, and would that I should

be their leader; and we have come forth to defend our country.

6 And now ye also know concerning the ᵃcovenant which their fathers made, that they would not take up their weapons of war against their brethren to shed blood.

7 But in the twenty and sixth year, when they saw our afflictions and our tribulations for them, they were about to ᵃbreak the covenant which they had made and take up their weapons of war in our defence.

8 But I would not suffer them that they should break this ᵃcovenant which they had made, supposing that God would strengthen us, insomuch that we should not suffer more because of the fulfilling the ᵇoath which they had taken.

9 But behold, here is one thing in which we may have great joy. For behold, in the †twenty and sixth year, I, Helaman, did march at the head of these ᵃtwo thousand young men to the city of ᵇJudea, to assist Antipus, whom ye had appointed a leader over the people of that part of the land.

10 And I did join my two thousand ᵃsons, (for they are worthy to be called sons) to the army of Antipus, in which strength Antipus did rejoice exceedingly; for behold, his army had been reduced by the Lamanites because their forces had slain a vast number of our men, for which cause we have to mourn.

11 Nevertheless, we may console ourselves in this point, that they have died in the cause of their country and of their God, yea, and they are ᵃhappy.

12 And the Lamanites had also retained many prisoners, all of whom are chief ᵃcaptains, for none other have they spared alive. And we suppose that they are now at this

56 1a Alma 58: 35.
  b Alma 59: 1.
  c Alma 53: 22 (8, 22).
3a Alma 53: 22.
6a TG Covenants.

7a Alma 24: 18 (17–19);
    53: 13 (13–15).
8a TG Honesty.
  b TG Vows.
9a Alma 53: 22.

  b Alma 57: 11.
10a Alma 56: 17.
11a Alma 28: 12.
12a Alma 52: 19.

[*62 B.C.   †66 B.C.]

time in the land of Nephi; it is so if they are not slain.

13 And now these are the cities of which the Lamanites have obtained possession by the shedding of the blood of so many of our valiant men;

14 The land of [a]Manti, or the city of Manti, and the city of Zeezrom, and the city of [b]Cumeni, and the city of Antiparah.

15 And these are the cities which they possessed when I arrived at the city of Judea; and I found Antipus and his men toiling with their might to fortify the city.

16 Yea, and they were depressed in body as well as in spirit, for they had fought valiantly by day and toiled by night to maintain their cities; and thus they had suffered great afflictions of every kind.

17 And now they were determined to conquer in this place or die; therefore you may well suppose that this little force which I brought with me, yea, those [a]sons of mine, gave them great hopes and much joy.

18 And now it came to pass that when the Lamanites saw that Antipus had received a greater strength to his army, they were compelled by the orders of Ammoron to not come against the city of Judea, or against us, to battle.

19 And thus were we favored of the Lord; for had they come upon us in this our weakness they might have perhaps destroyed our little army; but thus were we preserved.

20 They were commanded by Ammoron to maintain those cities which they had taken. And thus ended the twenty and sixth year. And in the *commencement of the twenty and seventh year we had prepared our city and ourselves for defence.

21 Now we were desirous that the Lamanites should come upon us; for we were not desirous to make an attack upon them in their strongholds.

22 And it came to pass that we kept spies out round about, to watch the movements of the Lamanites, that they might not pass us by night nor by day to make an attack upon our other cities which were on the northward.

23 For we knew in those cities they were not sufficiently strong to meet them; therefore we were desirous, if they should pass by us, to fall upon them in their rear, and thus bring them up in the rear at the same time they were met in the front. We supposed that we could overpower them; but behold, we were disappointed in this our desire.

24 They durst not pass by us with their whole army, neither durst they with a part, lest they should not be sufficiently strong and they should fall.

25 Neither durst they march down against the city of Zarahemla; neither durst they cross the head of Sidon, over to the city of Nephihah.

26 And thus, with their forces, they were determined to maintain those cities which they had taken.

27 And now it came to pass in the second month of this year, there was brought unto us many provisions from the fathers of those my two thousand sons.

28 And also there were sent two thousand men unto us from the land of Zarahemla. And thus we were prepared with ten thousand men, and provisions for them, and also for their wives and their children.

29 And the Lamanites, thus seeing our forces increase daily, and provisions arrive for our support, they began to be fearful, and began to sally forth, if it were possible to put an end to our receiving provisions and strength.

30 Now when we saw that the Lamanites began to grow uneasy on this wise, we were desirous to bring a stratagem into effect upon them; therefore Antipus ordered that I should march forth with my

---

14a Alma 43:22.   17a Alma 56:10.
  b Alma 57:7 (7–34).

little sons to a neighboring city, [a]as if we were carrying provisions to a neighboring city.

31 And we were to march near the city of Antiparah, as if we were going to the city beyond, in the borders by the seashore.

32 And it came to pass that we did march forth, as if with our provisions, to go to that city.

33 And it came to pass that Antipus did march forth with a part of his army, leaving the remainder to maintain the city. But he did not march forth until I had gone forth with my little army, and came near the city Antiparah.

34 And now, in the city Antiparah were stationed the strongest army of the Lamanites; yea, the most numerous.

35 And it came to pass that when they had been informed by their spies, they came forth with their army and marched against us.

36 And it came to pass that we did flee before them, northward. And thus we did lead away the most powerful army of the Lamanites;

37 Yea, even to a considerable distance, insomuch that when they saw the army of Antipus pursuing them, with their might, they did not turn to the right nor to the left, but pursued their march in a straight course after us; and, as we suppose, it was their intent to slay us before Antipus should overtake them, and this that they might not be surrounded by our people.

38 And now Antipus, beholding our danger, did speed the march of his army. But behold, it was night; therefore they did not overtake us, neither did Antipus overtake them; therefore we did camp for the night.

39 And it came to pass that before the dawn of the morning, behold, the Lamanites were pursuing us. Now we were not sufficiently strong to contend with them; yea, I would not suffer that my little sons should fall into their hands; therefore we did continue our march, and we took our march into the wilderness.

40 Now they durst not turn to the right nor to the left lest they should be surrounded; neither would I turn to the right nor to the left lest they should overtake me, and we could not stand against them, but be slain, and they would make their escape; and thus we did flee all that day into the wilderness, even until it was dark.

41 And it came to pass that again, when the light of the morning came we saw the Lamanites upon us, and we did flee before them.

42 But it came to pass that they did not pursue us far before they halted; and it was in the morning of the third day of the seventh month.

43 And now, whether they were overtaken by Antipus we knew not, but I said unto my men: Behold, we know not but they have halted for the purpose that we should come against them, that they might catch us in their snare;

44 Therefore what say ye, my sons, will ye go against them to battle?

45 And now I say unto you, my beloved brother Moroni, that never had I seen [a]so great [b]courage, nay, not amongst all the Nephites.

46 For as I had ever called them my sons (for they were all of them very young) even so they said unto me: Father, behold our God is with us, and he will [a]not suffer that we should fall; then let us go forth; we would not slay our brethren if they would let us alone; therefore let us go, lest they should overpower the army of Antipus.

47 Now they never had fought, yet they did not fear death; and they did think more upon the [a]liberty of their [b]fathers than they did upon their lives; yea, they had

30a Alma 52: 21; 58: 1.
45a Alma 19: 10.
  b TG Courage.
46a Alma 61: 10 (10–11).
47a TG Birthright; Liberty.
  b Alma 53: 17 (15–18).
TG Honoring Father
and Mother.

been taught by their *mothers, that if they did not doubt, God would deliver them.

48 And they rehearsed unto me the words of their *a*mothers, saying: We *b*do not doubt our mothers knew it.

49 And it came to pass that I did return with my two thousand against these Lamanites who had pursued us. And now behold, the armies of Antipus had overtaken them, and a terrible battle had commenced.

50 The army of Antipus being weary, because of their long march in so short a space of time, were about to fall into the hands of the Lamanites; and had I not returned with my two thousand they would have obtained their purpose.

51 For Antipus had fallen by the sword, and many of his leaders, because of their weariness, which was occasioned by the speed of their march—therefore the men of Antipus, being confused because of the fall of their leaders, began to give way before the Lamanites.

52 And it came to pass that the Lamanites took courage, and began to pursue them; and thus were the Lamanites pursuing them with great vigor when *a*Helaman came upon their rear with his two thousand, and began to slay them exceedingly, insomuch that the whole army of the Lamanites halted and turned upon Helaman.

53 Now when the people of Antipus saw that the Lamanites had turned them about, they gathered together their men and came again upon the rear of the Lamanites.

54 And now it came to pass that we, the people of Nephi, the people of Antipus, and I with my two thousand, did surround the Lamanites, and did slay them; yea, insomuch that they were compelled to deliver

up their weapons of war and also themselves as prisoners of war.

55 And now it came to pass that when they had surrendered themselves up unto us, behold, I numbered those young men who had fought with me, fearing lest there were many of them slain.

56 But behold, to my great joy, there had *a*not one soul of them fallen to the earth; yea, and they had fought as if with the *b*strength of God; yea, never were men known to have fought with such miraculous strength; and with such mighty power did they fall upon the Lamanites, that they did frighten them; and for this cause did the Lamanites deliver themselves up as prisoners of war.

57 And as we had no place for our prisoners, that we could guard them to keep them from the armies of the Lamanites, therefore we sent them to the land of Zarahemla, and a part of those men who were not slain of Antipus, with them; and the remainder I took and joined them to my stripling *a*Ammonites, and took our march back to the city of Judea.

CHAPTER 57

Helaman recounts the taking of Antiparah and the surrender and later the defense of Cumeni—His Ammonite striplings fight valiantly and all are wounded, but none are slain—Gid reports the slaying and the escape of the Lamanite prisoners.

AND now it came to pass that I received an epistle from Ammoron, the king, stating that if I would deliver up those prisoners of war whom we had taken that he would deliver up the city of Antiparah unto us.

2 But I sent an epistle unto the king, that we were sure our forces were sufficient to take the city of

47c Alma 57: 21.
  TG Marriage, Motherhood.
48a TG Family, Love within.

b D&C 46: 14.
52a Morm. 6: 6.
  IE Mormon here abridges some of the material in the letter of Helaman.

56a Alma 57: 25; 58: 39.
  b TG Strength.
57a Alma 27: 26.

[About 64 B.C.]

Antiparah by our force; and by delivering up the prisoners for that city we should suppose ourselves unwise, and that we would only deliver up our prisoners on exchange.

3 And Ammoron refused mine epistle, for he would not exchange prisoners; therefore we began to make preparations to go against the city of Antiparah.

4 But the people of Antiparah did leave the city, and fled to their other cities, which they had possession of, to fortify them; and thus the city of Antiparah fell into our hands.

5 And thus ended the twenty and eighth year of the reign of the judges.

6 And it came to pass that in the *commencement of the twenty and ninth year, we received a supply of provisions, and also an addition to our army, from the land of Zarahemla, and from the land round about, to the number of six thousand men, besides sixty of the "sons of the Ammonites who had come to join their brethren, my little band of two thousand. And now behold, we were strong, yea, and we had also plenty of provisions brought unto us.

7 And it came to pass that it was our desire to wage a battle with the army which was placed to protect the city "Cumeni.

8 And now behold, I will show unto you that we soon accomplished our desire; yea, with our strong force, or with a part of our strong force, we did surround, by night, the city Cumeni, a little before they were to receive a supply of provisions.

9 And it came to pass that we did camp round about the city for many nights; but we did sleep upon our swords, and keep guards, that the Lamanites could not come upon us by night and slay us, which they attempted many times; but as many times as they attempted this their blood was spilt.

10 At length their provisions did arrive, and they were about to enter the city by night. And we, instead of being Lamanites, were Nephites; therefore, we did take them and their provisions.

11 And notwithstanding the Lamanites being cut off from their support after this manner, they were still determined to maintain the city; therefore it became expedient that we should take those provisions and send them to "Judea, and our prisoners to the land of Zarahemla.

12 And it came to pass that not many days had passed away before the Lamanites began to lose all hopes of succor; therefore they yielded up the city unto our hands; and thus we had accomplished our designs in obtaining the city Cumeni.

13 But it came to pass that our prisoners were so numerous that, notwithstanding the enormity of our numbers, we were obliged to employ all our force to keep them, or to put them to death.

14 For behold, they would break out in great numbers, and would fight with stones, and with clubs, or whatsoever thing they could get into their hands, insomuch that we did slay upwards of two thousand of them after they had surrendered themselves prisoners of war.

15 Therefore it became expedient for us, that we should put an end to their lives, or guard them, sword in hand, down to the land of Zarahemla; and also our provisions were not any more than sufficient for our own people, notwithstanding that which we had taken from the Lamanites.

16 And now, in those critical circumstances, it became a very serious matter to determine concerning these prisoners of war; nevertheless, we did resolve to send them down to the land of Zarahemla; therefore we selected a part of our men, and gave them charge over our prisoners to go down to the land of Zarahemla.

---

57 6a Alma 53:16.
7a Alma 56:14.

11a Alma 56:9.

[*63 B.C.]

17 But it came to pass that on the morrow they did return. And now behold, we did not ^ainquire of them concerning the prisoners; for behold, the Lamanites were upon us, and they returned in season to save us from falling into their hands. For behold, Ammoron had sent to their support a new supply of provisions and also a numerous army of men.

18 And it came to pass that those men whom we sent with the prisoners did arrive in season to check them, as they were about to overpower us.

19 But behold, my little band of two thousand and sixty fought most desperately; yea, they were firm before the Lamanites, and did ^aadminister death unto all those who opposed them.

20 And as the remainder of our army were about to give way before the Lamanites, behold, those two thousand and sixty were firm and undaunted.

21 Yea, and they did ^aobey and observe to perform every word of command with exactness; yea, and even according to their faith it was done unto them; and I did remember the words which they said unto me that their ^bmothers had taught them.

22 And now behold, it was these my sons, and those men who had been selected to convey the prisoners, to whom we owe this great victory; for it was they who did beat the Lamanites; therefore they were driven back to the city of Manti.

23 And we retained our city Cumeni, and were not all destroyed by the sword; nevertheless, we had suffered great loss.

24 And it came to pass that after the Lamanites had fled, I immediately gave orders that my men who had been wounded should be taken from among the dead, and caused that their wounds should be dressed.

25 And it came to pass that there were two hundred, out of my two thousand and sixty, who had fainted because of the loss of blood; nevertheless, according to the goodness of God, and to our great astonishment, and also the joy of our whole army, there was ^anot one soul of them who did perish; yea, and neither was there one soul among them who had not received many wounds.

26 And now, their ^apreservation was astonishing to our whole army, yea, that they should be spared while there was a thousand of our brethren who were slain. And we do justly ascribe it to the miraculous ^bpower of God, because of their exceeding ^cfaith in that which they had been taught to believe—that there was a just God, and whosoever did not doubt, that they should be preserved by his marvelous power.

27 Now this was the ^afaith of these of whom I have spoken; they are young, and their minds are ^bfirm, and they do put their trust in God continually.

28 And now it came to pass that after we had thus taken care of our wounded men, and had buried our dead and also the dead of the Lamanites, who were many, behold, we did inquire of Gid concerning the ^aprisoners whom they had started to go down to the land of Zarahemla with.

29 Now Gid was the chief captain over the band who was appointed to guard them down to the land.

30 And now, these are the words which Gid said unto me: Behold, we did start to go down to the land of Zarahemla with our prisoners. And it came to pass that we did meet the spies of our armies, who

---

17a Alma 57:28.
19a Alma 62:11.
21a TG Trustworthiness.
  b Alma 56:47 (47–48).
25a Alma 56:56.
26a 1 Chr. 5:20 (18–22).
  b TG God, Power of.
  c TG Faith.
27a Alma 43:13.
  b Jacob 3:2.
28a Alma 57:17 (16–17).

had been sent out to watch the camp of the Lamanites.

31 And they cried unto us, saying— Behold, the armies of the Lamanites are marching towards the city of Cumeni; and behold, they will fall upon them, yea, and will destroy our people.

32 And it came to pass that our prisoners did hear their cries, which caused them to take courage; and they did rise up in rebellion against us.

33 And it came to pass because of their rebellion we did cause that our swords should come upon them. And it came to pass that they did in a body run upon our swords, in the which, the greater number of them were slain; and the remainder of them broke through and fled from us.

34 And behold, when they had fled and we could not overtake them, we took our march with speed towards the city Cumeni; and behold, we did arrive in time that we might assist our brethren in preserving the city.

35 And behold, we are again delivered out of the hands of our enemies. And blessed is the name of our God; for behold, it is he that has delivered us; yea, that has done this great thing for us.

36 Now it came to pass that when I, Helaman, had heard these words of Gid, I was filled with exceeding joy because of the goodness of God in preserving us, that we might not all perish; yea, and I trust that the souls of them who have been slain have *entered into the rest of their God.

CHAPTER 58

Helaman, Gid, and Teomner take the city of Manti by a stratagem—The Lamanites withdraw—The sons of the people of Ammon are preserved as they stand fast in defense of their liberty and faith.

AND behold, now it came to pass that our next object was to obtain the city of Manti; but behold, there was no way that we could lead them out of the city by our small bands. For behold, they remembered that which we had hitherto done; therefore we could not *decoy them away from their strongholds.

2 And they were so much more numerous than was our army that we durst not go forth and attack them in their strongholds.

3 Yea, and it became expedient that we should employ our men to the maintaining those parts of the land which we had regained of our possessions; therefore it became expedient that we should wait, that we might receive more strength from the land of Zarahemla and also a new supply of provisions.

4 And it came to pass that I thus did send an embassy to the governor of our land, to acquaint him concerning the affairs of our people. And it came to pass that we did wait to receive provisions and strength from the land of Zarahemla.

5 But behold, this did profit us but little; for the Lamanites were also receiving great strength from day to day, and also many provisions; and thus were our circumstances at this period of time.

6 And the Lamanites were sallying forth against us from time to time, resolving by stratagem to destroy us; nevertheless we could not come to battle with them, because of their *retreats and their strongholds.

7 And it came to pass that we did wait in these difficult circumstances for the space of many months, even until we were about to *perish for the want of food.

8 But it came to pass that we did receive food, which was guarded to us by an army of two thousand men to our assistance; and this is all the assistance which we did receive, to defend ourselves and our country

---

from falling into the hands of our enemies, yea, to contend with an enemy which was innumerable.

9 And now the cause of these our embarrassments, or the cause why they did not send more strength unto us, we knew not; therefore we were grieved and also filled with fear, lest by any means the judgments of God should come upon our land, to our overthrow and utter destruction.

10 Therefore we did pour out our souls in prayer to God, that he would strengthen us and deliver us out of the hands of our enemies, yea, and also give us strength that we might retain our cities, and our lands, and our possessions, for the support of our people.

11 Yea, and it came to pass that the Lord our God did visit us with assurances that he would deliver us; yea, insomuch that he did speak peace to our souls, and did grant unto us great faith, and did cause us that we should hope for our ªdeliverance in him.

12 And we did take courage with our small force which we had received, and were fixed with a determination to conquer our enemies, and to ªmaintain our lands, and our possessions, and our wives, and our children, and the cause of our ᵇliberty.

13 And thus we did go forth with all our might against the Lamanites, who were in the city of Manti; and we did pitch our tents by the wilderness side, which was near to the city.

14 And it came to pass that on the morrow, that when the Lamanites saw that we were in the borders by the wilderness which was near the city, that they sent out their spies round about us that they might discover the number and the strength of our army.

15 And it came to pass that when they saw that we were not strong, according to our numbers, and fearing that we should cut them off from their support except they should come out to battle against us and kill us, and also supposing that they could easily destroy us with their numerous hosts, therefore they began to make preparations to come out against us to battle.

16 And when we saw that they were making preparations to come out against us, behold, I caused that Gid, with a small number of men, should ªsecrete himself in the wilderness, and also that Teomner and a small number of men should secrete themselves also in the wilderness.

17 Now Gid and his men were on the right and the others on the left; and when they had thus secreted themselves, behold, I remained, with the remainder of my army, in that same place where we had first pitched our tents against the time that the Lamanites should come out to battle.

18 And it came to pass that the Lamanites did come out with their numerous army against us. And when they had come and were about to fall upon us with the sword, I caused that my men, those who were with me, should retreat into the wilderness.

19 And it came to pass that the Lamanites did follow after us with great speed, for they were exceedingly desirous to overtake us that they might slay us; therefore they did follow us into the wilderness; and we did pass by in the midst of Gid and Teomner, insomuch that they were not discovered by the Lamanites.

20 And it came to pass that when the Lamanites had passed by, or when the army had passed by, Gid and Teomner did rise up from their secret places, and did cut off the spies of the Lamanites that they should not return to the city.

11a TG Deliverance.
12a Alma 46: 12; 3 Ne.
   2: 12; Morm. 2: 23.

b TG Liberty.
16a Josh. 8: 13; Alma
   43: 31 (30–43);

52: 21 (21–31).

[About 63 B.C.]

21 And it came to pass that when they had cut them off, they ran to the city and fell upon the guards who were left to guard the city, insomuch that they did destroy them and did take possession of the city.

22 Now this was done because the Lamanites did suffer their whole army, save a few guards only, to be led away into the wilderness.

23 And it came to pass that Gid and Teomner by this means had obtained possession of their strongholds. And it came to pass that we took our course, after having traveled much in the wilderness towards the land of Zarahemla.

24 And when the Lamanites saw that they were marching towards the land of Zarahemla, they were exceedingly afraid, lest there was a plan laid to lead them on to destruction; therefore they began to retreat into the wilderness again, yea, even back by the same way which they had come.

25 And behold, it was night and they did pitch their tents, for the chief ªcaptains of the Lamanites had supposed that the Nephites were weary because of their march; and supposing that they had driven their whole army therefore they took no thought concerning the city of Manti.

26 Now it came to pass that when it was night, I caused that my men should not sleep, but that they should march forward by another way towards the land of Manti.

27 And because of this our march in the night-time, behold, on the morrow we were beyond the Lamanites, insomuch that we did arrive before them at the city of Manti.

28 And thus it came to pass, that by this stratagem we did take possession of the city of Manti without the shedding of blood.

29 And it came to pass that when the armies of the Lamanites did arrive near the city, and saw that we were prepared to meet them, they were astonished exceedingly and struck with great fear, insomuch that they did ªflee into the wilderness.

30 Yea, and it came to pass that the armies of the Lamanites did flee out of all this quarter of the land. But behold, they have carried with them many women and children out of the land.

31 And ªthose cities which had been taken by the Lamanites, all of them are at this period of time in our possession; and our fathers and our women and our children are returning to their homes, all save it be those who have been taken prisoners and carried off by the Lamanites.

32 But behold, our armies are small to maintain so great a number of cities and so great possessions.

33 But behold, we ªtrust in our God who has given us victory over those lands, insomuch that we have obtained those cities and those lands, which were our own.

34 Now we do not know the ªcause that the government does not grant us more strength; neither do those men who came up unto us know why we have not received greater strength.

35 Behold, we do not know but what ªye are unsuccessful, and ye have drawn away the forces into that quarter of the land; if so, we do not desire to murmur.

36 And if it is not so, behold, we fear that there is some ªfaction in the government, that they do not send more men to our assistance; for we know that they are more numerous than that which they have sent.

37 But, behold, it mattereth not— we trust God will ªdeliver us, notwithstanding the weakness of our

25a Alma 59: 12.
29a Alma 59: 6.
31a Alma 51: 26 (25–27);
    59: 1.
33a TG Trust in God.
34a Alma 59: 13.
35a Alma 56: 1.
36a Alma 61: 3.
37a 2 Kgs. 17: 39.

[About 63 B.C.]

armies, yea, and deliver us out of the hands of our enemies.

38 Behold, this is the twenty and ninth year, in the latter end, and we are in the possession of our lands; and the Lamanites have fled to the land of Nephi.

39 And those sons of the people of Ammon, of whom I have so highly spoken, are with me in the city of Manti; and the Lord has supported them, yea, and kept them from falling by the sword, insomuch that even [a]one soul has not been slain.

40 But behold, they have received many wounds; nevertheless they [a]stand fast in that [b]liberty wherewith God has made them free; and they are strict to remember the Lord their God from day to day; yea, they do observe to keep his statutes, and his judgments, and his commandments continually; and their faith is strong in the prophecies concerning that which is to come.

41 And now, my beloved brother, Moroni, may the Lord our God, who has redeemed us and made us free, keep you continually in his presence; yea, and may he favor this people, even that ye may have success in obtaining the possession of all that which the Lamanites have taken from us, which was for our support. And now, behold, I close mine epistle. I am Helaman, the son of Alma.

CHAPTER 59

Moroni asks Pahoran to strengthen the forces of Helaman—The Lamanites take the city of Nephihah—Moroni is angry with the government.

Now it came to pass in the *thirtieth year of the reign of the judges over the people of Nephi, after Moroni had received and had read Helaman's [a]epistle, he was exceed-

ingly rejoiced because of the welfare, yea, the exceeding success which Helaman had had, in obtaining [b]those lands which were lost.

2 Yea, and he did make it known unto all his people, in all the land round about in that part where he was, that they might rejoice also.

3 And it came to pass that he immediately sent [a]an epistle to [b]Pahoran, desiring that he should cause men to be gathered together to strengthen Helaman, or the armies of Helaman, insomuch that he might with ease maintain that part of the land which he had been so miraculously prospered in regaining.

4 And it came to pass when Moroni had sent this epistle to the land of Zarahemla, he began again to lay a plan that he might obtain the remainder of those possessions and cities which the Lamanites had taken from them.

5 And it came to pass that while Moroni was thus making preparations to go against the Lamanites to battle, behold, the people of [a]Nephihah, who were gathered together from the city of Moroni and the city of Lehi and the city of Morianton, were attacked by the Lamanites.

6 Yea, even those who had been [a]compelled to flee from the land of Manti, and from the land round about, had come over and joined the Lamanites in this part of the land.

7 And thus being exceedingly numerous, yea, and receiving strength from day to day, by the command of Ammoron they came forth against the people of Nephihah, and they did begin to slay them with an exceedingly great slaughter.

8 And their armies were so numerous that the remainder of the people of [a]Nephihah were [b]obliged to flee before them; and they came even and joined the army of Moroni.

39a Alma 56: 56.
40a Alma 61: 21.
   TG Trustworthiness.
   b TG Liberty.
59 1a Alma 56: 1.

b Alma 58: 31 (31, 41).
3a Alma 60: 1 (1–3).
b Alma 50: 40.
5a Alma 50: 14.

6a Alma 58: 29 (29–30).
8a Alma 62: 26.
b Alma 60: 17.

9 And now as Moroni had supposed that there [a]should be men sent to the city of Nephihah, to the assistance of the people to maintain that city, and knowing that it was easier to keep the city from falling into the hands of the Lamanites than to retake it from them, he supposed that they would easily maintain that city.

10 Therefore he retained all his force to maintain those places which he had recovered.

11 And now, when Moroni saw that the city of Nephihah was [a]lost he was exceedingly sorrowful, and began to doubt, because of the wickedness of the people, whether they should not fall into the hands of their brethren.

12 Now this was the case with all his chief captains. They doubted and marveled also because of the wickedness of the people, and this because of the success of the Lamanites over them.

13 And it came to pass that Moroni was angry with the government, because of their [a]indifference concerning the freedom of their country.

CHAPTER 60

Moroni complains to Pahoran of the government's neglect of the armies—The Lord suffers the righteous to be slain—The Nephites must use all of their power and means to deliver themselves from their enemies—Moroni threatens to fight against the government unless help is supplied to his armies.

AND it came to pass that he wrote [a]again to the governor of the land, who was Pahoran, and these are the words which he wrote, saying: Behold, I direct mine epistle to Pahoran, in the city of Zarahemla, who is the chief judge and the [b]governor over the land, and also to all those who have been chosen by this people to govern and manage the affairs of this war.

2 For behold, I have somewhat to say unto them by the way of [a]condemnation; for behold, ye yourselves know that ye have been appointed to gather together men, and arm them with swords, and with cimeters, and all manner of weapons of war of every kind, and send forth against the Lamanites, in whatsoever parts they should come into our land.

3 And now behold, I say unto you that myself, and also my men, and also Helaman and his men, have suffered exceedingly great [a]sufferings; yea, even hunger, thirst, and fatigue, and all manner of afflictions of every kind.

4 But behold, were this all we had suffered we would not murmur nor complain.

5 But behold, great has been the slaughter among our people; yea, thousands have fallen by the sword, while it might have otherwise been if ye had rendered unto our armies sufficient strength and succor for them. Yea, great has been your neglect towards us.

6 And now behold, we desire to know the cause of this exceedingly great neglect; yea, we desire to know the cause of your thoughtless state.

7 Can you think to sit upon your thrones in a state of thoughtless [a]stupor, while your enemies are spreading the work of death around you? Yea, while they are murdering thousands of your brethren—

8 Yea, even they who have looked up to you for protection, yea, have placed you in a situation that ye might have succored them, yea, ye might have sent armies unto them, to have strengthened them, and have saved thousands of them from falling by the sword.

9a Alma 60: 15.
11a Alma 62: 14.
13a Alma 58: 34; 61: 3.

60 1a Alma 59: 3.
 b Alma 50: 39.
2a TG Reproof.

3a Alma 61: 2.
7a TG Apathy.

[About 62 B.C.]

9 But behold, this is not all—ye have withheld your provisions from them, insomuch that many have fought and bled out their lives because of their great desires which they had for the welfare of this people; yea, and this they have done when they were about to ^aperish with hunger, because of your exceedingly great neglect towards them.

10 And now, my beloved brethren—for ye ought to be beloved; yea, and ye ought to have stirred yourselves more diligently for the welfare and the freedom of this people; but behold, ye have neglected them insomuch that the blood of thousands shall come upon your heads for vengeance; yea, for ^aknown unto God were all their cries, and all their sufferings—

11 Behold, could ye suppose that ye could sit upon your thrones, and because of the exceeding goodness of God ye could do nothing and he would deliver you? Behold, if ye have supposed this ye have supposed in vain.

12 Do ye ^asuppose that, because so many of your brethren have been killed it is because of their wickedness? I say unto you, if ye have supposed this ye have supposed in vain; for I say unto you, there are many who have fallen by the sword; and behold it is to your condemnation;

13 For the Lord suffereth the ^arighteous to be slain that his justice and ^bjudgment may come upon the wicked; therefore ye need not suppose that the righteous are lost because they are slain; but behold, they do enter into the rest of the Lord their God.

14 And now behold, I say unto you, I fear exceedingly that the judgments of God will come upon this people, because of their exceeding ^aslothfulness, yea, even the slothfulness of our government, and their exceedingly great neglect towards their brethren, yea, towards those who have been slain.

15 For were it not for the wickedness which first commenced at our head, we ^acould have withstood our enemies that they could have gained no power over us.

16 Yea, had it not been for the war which broke out ^aamong ourselves; yea, were it not for these ^bking-men, who caused so much bloodshed among ourselves; yea, at the time we were contending among ourselves, if we had united our strength as we hitherto have done; yea, had it not been for the desire of power and authority which those king-men had over us; had they been true to the cause of our freedom, and united with us, and gone forth against our enemies, instead of taking up their swords against us, which was the cause of so much bloodshed among ourselves; yea, if we had gone forth against them in the strength of the Lord, we should have dispersed our enemies, for it would have been done, according to the ^cfulfilling of his word.

17 But behold, now the Lamanites are coming upon us, taking ^apossession of our lands, and they are murdering our people with the sword, yea, our women and our children, and also carrying them away captive, causing them that they should suffer all manner of afflictions, and this because of the great wickedness of those who are seeking for power and authority, yea, even those king-men.

18 But why should I say much concerning this matter? For we know not but what ye yourselves are seeking for authority. We know not but what ye are also ^atraitors to your country.

9a Alma 58: 7 (7–9).
10a Ex. 3: 9; Ps. 9: 12.
12a Luke 13: 2 (1–2).
13a Lam. 4: 13; D&C 42: 46.
b Alma 14: 11 (10–11); D&C 103: 3.
14a TG Laziness.
15a Alma 59: 9.
16a Alma 51: 19 (5–7, 13–27).
b Alma 62: 9.
c Alma 38: 1.
17a Alma 59: 8 (5–8).
18a Alma 62: 1.

[About 62 B.C.]

19 Or is it that ye have neglected us because ye are in the heart of our country and ye are ^asurrounded by security, that ye do not cause food to be sent unto us, and also men to strengthen our armies?

20 Have ye forgotten the commandments of the Lord your God? Yea, have ye forgotten the captivity of our fathers? Have ye forgotten the many times we have been delivered out of the hands of our enemies?

21 Or do ye suppose that the Lord ^awill still deliver us, while we sit upon our thrones and do not make use of the means which the Lord has provided for us?

22 Yea, will ye sit in idleness while ye are surrounded with thousands of those, yea, and tens of thousands, who do also sit in idleness, while there are thousands round about in the borders of the land who are falling by the sword, yea, wounded and bleeding?

23 Do ye suppose that God will look upon you as guiltless while ye sit still and behold these things? Behold I say unto you, Nay. Now I would that ye should remember that God has said that the ^ainward vessel shall be ^bcleansed first, and then shall the outer vessel be cleansed also.

24 And now, except ye do repent of that which ye have done, and begin to be up and doing, and send forth food and men unto us, and also unto Helaman, that he may support those parts of our country which he has regained, and that we may also recover the remainder of our possessions in these parts, behold it will be expedient that we contend no more with the Lamanites until we have first cleansed our inward vessel, yea, even the great head of our government.

25 And except ye grant mine epistle, and come out and show unto me a true ^aspirit of freedom, and strive to strengthen and fortify our armies, and grant unto them food for their support, behold I will leave a part of my freemen to maintain this part of our land, and I will leave the strength and the blessings of God upon them, that none other power can operate against them—

26 And this because of their exceeding faith, and their patience in their ^atribulations—

27 And I will come unto you, and if there be any among you that has a desire for freedom, yea, if there be even a spark of freedom remaining, behold I will stir up insurrections among you, even until those who have desires to usurp power and authority shall become extinct.

28 Yea, behold I do not fear your power nor your authority, but it is my ^aGod whom I fear; and it is according to his commandments that I do take my sword to defend the cause of my country, and it is because of your iniquity that we have suffered so much loss.

29 Behold it is time, yea, the time is now at hand, that except ye do bestir yourselves in the defence of your country and your little ones, the ^asword of justice doth hang over you; yea, and it shall fall upon you and visit you even to your utter destruction.

30 Behold, I wait for assistance from you; and, except ye do administer unto our relief, behold, I come unto you, even in the land of Zarahemla, and smite you with the sword, insomuch that ye can have no more power to impede the progress of this people in the cause of our freedom.

31 For behold, the Lord will not suffer that ye shall live and wax strong in your iniquities to destroy his righteous people.

32 Behold, can you suppose that the Lord will spare you and come

---

19a TG Apathy.
21a 1 Ne. 17:23 (23–35).
23a Matt. 23:26 (25–26).
  b TG Purification.
25a Alma 51:6 (6–7);
    61:15.
26a TG Tribulation.
28a Acts 5:29 (26–29).
29a Isa. 1:20 (19–20);
    Hel. 13:5; 3 Ne. 2:19.

[About 62 B.C.]

out in judgment against the Lamanites, when it is the *a*tradition of their
fathers that has caused their hatred,
yea, and it has been redoubled by
those who have dissented from
us, while your iniquity is for the
cause of your love of glory and the
vain things of the world?

33 Ye know that ye do transgress
the laws of God, and ye do know
that ye do trample them under your
feet. Behold, the Lord saith unto
me: If those whom we have appointed your governors do not
repent of their sins and *a*iniquities,
ye shall *b*go up to battle against
them.

34 And now behold, I, Moroni, am
constrained, according to the covenant which I have made to keep the
commandments of my God; therefore I would that ye should adhere
to the word of God, and send speedily unto me of your provisions and
of your men, and also to Helaman.

35 And behold, if ye will not do
this I come unto you speedily; for
behold, God will not suffer that we
should perish with hunger; therefore he will give unto us of your food,
even if it must be by the sword.
Now see that ye fulfil the word of
God.

36 Behold, I am Moroni, your chief
captain. I *a*seek not for power, but
to pull it down. I *b*seek not for honor
of the world, but for the glory of my
God, and the freedom and welfare of
my country. And thus I close mine
epistle.

CHAPTER 61

*Pahoran tells Moroni of the insur-
rection and rebellion against the government—The king-men take Zarahemla and are in league with the
Lamanites—Pahoran asks for military aid against the rebels.*

BEHOLD, now it came to pass that
soon after Moroni had sent his
epistle unto the chief governor, he
received an epistle from *a*Pahoran,
the chief governor. And these are
the words which he received:

2 I, Pahoran, who am the chief
governor of this land, do send these
words unto Moroni, the chief captain
over the army. Behold, I say unto
you, Moroni, that I do not joy in
your great *a*afflictions, yea, it grieves
my soul.

3 But behold, there are those who
do joy in your afflictions, yea, insomuch that they have risen up in
*a*rebellion against me, and also those
of my people who are *b*freemen, yea,
and those who have risen up are
exceedingly numerous.

4 And it is those who have sought
to take away the judgment-seat
from me that have been the cause of
this great iniquity; for they have
used great *a*flattery, and they have
*b*led away the hearts of many people,
which will be the cause of sore
affliction among us; they have
withheld our provisions, and have
daunted our *c*freemen that they
have not come unto you.

5 And behold, they have driven me
out before them, and I have fled to
the land of Gideon, with as many men
as it were possible that I could get.

6 And behold, I have sent a proclamation throughout this part of
the land; and behold, they are
*a*flocking to us *b*daily, to their arms,
in the defence of their country and
their *c*freedom, and to avenge our
*d*wrongs.

7 And they have come unto us,
insomuch that those who have risen
up in rebellion against us are set at
defiance, yea, insomuch that they
do fear us and durst not come out
against us to battle.

32*a* Alma 17: 15.
33*a* Alma 61: 18.
   b Alma 61: 20.
36*a* Alma 61: 9; D&C
      121: 39.
   b TG Motivations.

61 1*a* Alma 50: 40.
     2*a* Alma 60: 3 (3–9).
     3*a* Alma 58: 36; 59: 13.
       b Alma 51: 6 (6–7).
     4*a* TG Flattery.
       b TG Peer Influence.
       c Alma 51: 6 (6–7);

        62: 6.
     6*a* Alma 62: 5.
       b Acts 2: 47.
       c TG Liberty.
       d TG Injustice.

                    [About 62 B.C.]

8 They have ªgot possession of the land, or the city, of Zarahemla; they have appointed a ᵇking over them, and he hath written unto the king of the Lamanites, in the which he hath joined an alliance with him; in the which alliance he hath agreed to maintain the city of Zarahemla, which maintenance he supposeth will enable the Lamanites to conquer the remainder of the land, and he shall be placed king over this people when they shall be conquered ᶜunder the Lamanites.

9 And now, in your epistle you have ªcensured me, but it mattereth not; I am not angry, but do rejoice in the greatness of your heart. I, Pahoran, do not ᵇseek for power, save only to retain my judgment-seat that I may preserve the rights and the liberty of my people. My soul standeth fast in that liberty in the which God hath made us ᶜfree.

10 And now, behold, we will resist wickedness even unto bloodshed. We would ªnot shed the blood of the Lamanites if they would stay in their own land.

11 We would not shed the blood of our brethren if they would not rise up in rebellion and take the sword against us.

12 We would subject ourselves to the ªyoke of bondage if it were requisite with the justice of God, or if he should command us so to do.

13 But behold he doth not command us that we shall subject ourselves to our enemies, but that we should put our ªtrust in him, and he will deliver us.

14 Therefore, my beloved brother, Moroni, let us resist evil, and whatsoever evil we cannot resist with our ªwords, yea, such as rebellions and dissensions, let us ᵇresist them

with our swords, that we may retain our freedom, that we may rejoice in the great privilege of our church, and in the cause of our Redeemer and our God.

15 Therefore, come unto me speedily with a few of your men, and leave the remainder in the charge of Lehi and Teancum; give unto them power to conduct the ªwar in that part of the land, according to the ᵇSpirit of God, which is also the ᶜspirit of freedom which is in them.

16 Behold I have sent a few provisions unto them, that they may not perish until ye can come unto me.

17 Gather together whatsoever force ye can upon your march hither, and we will go speedily against those dissenters, in the strength of our God according to the faith which is in us.

18 And we will ªtake possession of the city of Zarahemla, that we may obtain more food to send forth unto Lehi and Teancum; yea, we will go forth against them in the strength of the Lord, and we will put an end to this great iniquity.

19 And now, Moroni, I do joy in receiving your epistle, for I was somewhat worried concerning what we should do, whether it should be just in us to go against our brethren.

20 But ye have said, except they repent the Lord ªhath commanded you that ye should go against them.

21 See that ye ªstrengthen Lehi and Teancum in the Lord; tell them to fear not, for God will deliver them, yea, and also all those who ᵇstand fast in that liberty wherewith God hath made them free. And now I close mine epistle to my beloved brother, Moroni.

8a Alma 61:18.
 b Alma 62:6.
   TG Tyranny.
 c Mosiah 7:21.
9a D&C 101:5.
   TG Reproof.
 b Alma 60:36;
   D&C 121:39.
 c John 8:36; Gal. 5:1;

D&C 88:86.
10a TG Alma 56:46.
12a TG Bondage, Physical;
   Submissiveness.
13a TG Trust in God.
14a TG Reproof.
 b Alma 43:47.
15a TG War.

 b 2 Cor. 3:17. TG God,
   Spirit of.
 c Alma 60:25.
18a Alma 61:8.
20a Alma 60:33.
21a Zech. 10:12.
 b Alma 58:40.

[About 62 B.C.]

CHAPTER 62

Moroni marches to the aid of Pahoran in the land of Gideon—The king-men who refuse to defend their country are put to death—Pahoran and Moroni retake Nephihah—Many Lamanites join the people of Ammon—Teancum slays Ammoron and is in turn slain—The Lamanites are driven from the land, and peace is established—Helaman returns to the ministry and builds up the Church.

AND now it came to pass that when Moroni had received this epistle his heart did take courage, and was filled with exceedingly great joy because of the faithfulness of Pahoran, that he was not also a [a]traitor to the freedom and cause of his country.

2 But he did also mourn exceedingly because of the iniquity of those who had driven Pahoran from the judgment-seat, yea, in fine because of those who had rebelled against their country and also their God.

3 And it came to pass that Moroni took a small number of men, according to the desire of Pahoran, and gave Lehi and Teancum command over the remainder of his army, and took his march towards the land of Gideon.

4 And he did raise the [a]standard of [b]liberty in whatsoever place he did enter, and gained whatsoever force he could in all his march towards the land of Gideon.

5 And it came to pass that thousands did [a]flock unto his standard, and did take up their swords in the defence of their freedom, that they might not come into bondage.

6 And thus, when Moroni had gathered together whatsoever men he could in all his march, he came to the land of Gideon; and uniting his forces with those of Pahoran they became exceedingly strong, even stronger than the men of Pachus,

who was the [a]king of those dissenters who had driven the [b]freemen out of the land of Zarahemla and had taken possession of the land.

7 And it came to pass that Moroni and Pahoran went down with their armies into the land of Zarahemla, and went forth against the city, and did meet the men of Pachus, insomuch that they did come to battle.

8 And behold, Pachus was slain and his men were taken prisoners, and Pahoran was restored to his judgment-seat.

9 And the men of Pachus received their trial, according to the law, and also those king-men who had been taken and [a]cast into prison; and they were [b]executed according to the law; yea, those men of Pachus and those [c]king-men, whosoever would not take up arms in the defence of their country, but would fight against it, were put to death.

10 And thus it became expedient that this law should be strictly observed for the safety of their country; yea, and whosoever was found denying their freedom was speedily [a]executed according to the law.

11 And thus ended the thirtieth year of the reign of the judges over the people of Nephi; Moroni and Pahoran having restored peace to the land of Zarahemla, among their own people, having [a]inflicted death upon all those who were not true to the cause of freedom.

12 And it came to pass in the *commencement of the thirty and first year of the reign of the judges over the people of Nephi, Moroni immediately caused that provisions should be sent, and also an army of six thousand men should be sent unto Helaman, to assist him in preserving that part of the land.

13 And he also caused that an

---

62 1a Alma 60: 18.
  4a Alma 46: 36 (12–13, 36).
    b TG Liberty.
  5a Alma 61: 6.
  6a Alma 61: 8 (4–8).

    b Alma 51: 6 (6–7).
  9a Alma 51: 19.
    b TG Capital
      Punishment.
    c Alma 51: 5 (5, 17, 21);

       60: 16.
  10a 1 Kgs. 2: 46.
  11a Alma 44: 7; 57: 19.

[*61 B.C.]

army of six thousand men, with a sufficient quantity of food, should be sent to the armies of Lehi and Teancum. And it came to pass that this was done to fortify the land against the Lamanites.

14 And it came to pass that Moroni and Pahoran, leaving a large body of men in the land of Zarahemla, took their march with a large body of men towards the land of Nephihah, being determined to ᵃoverthrow the Lamanites in that city.

15 And it came to pass that as they were marching towards the land, they took a large body of men of the Lamanites, and slew many of them, and took their provisions and their weapons of war.

16 And it came to pass after they had taken them, they caused them to enter into a ᵃcovenant that they would no more take up their weapons of war against the Nephites.

17 And when they had entered into this covenant they sent them to ᵃdwell with the people of Ammon, and they were in number about four thousand who had not been slain.

18 And it came to pass that when they had sent them away they pursued their march towards the land of ᵃNephihah. And it came to pass that when they had come to the city of Nephihah, they did pitch their tents in the plains of Nephihah, which is near the city of Nephihah.

19 Now Moroni was desirous that the Lamanites should come out to battle against them, upon the plains; but the Lamanites, knowing of their exceedingly great courage, and beholding the greatness of their numbers, therefore they durst not come out against them; therefore they did not come to battle in that day.

20 And when the night came, Moroni went forth in the darkness of the night, and came upon the top of the wall to spy out in what part of the city the Lamanites did camp with their army.

21 And it came to pass that they were on the east, by the entrance; and they were all asleep. And now Moroni returned to his army, and caused that they should prepare in haste strong cords and ladders, to be let down from the top of the ᵃwall into the inner part of the wall.

22 And it came to pass that Moroni caused that his men should march forth and come upon the top of the wall, and let ᵃthemselves down into that part of the city, yea, even on the west, where the Lamanites did not camp with their armies.

23 And it came to pass that they were all let down into the city by night, by the means of their strong cords and their ladders; thus when the morning came they were all within the walls of the city.

24 And now, when the Lamanites awoke and saw that the armies of Moroni were within the walls, they were affrighted exceedingly, insomuch that they did flee out by the pass.

25 And now when Moroni saw that they were fleeing before him, he did cause that his men should march forth against them, and slew many, and surrounded many others, and took them prisoners; and the remainder of them fled into the land of Moroni, which was in the borders by the seashore.

26 Thus had Moroni and Pahoran obtained the ᵃpossession of the city of Nephihah without the loss of one soul; and there were many of the Lamanites who were slain.

27 Now it came to pass that many of the Lamanites that were prisoners were desirous to ᵃjoin the people of Ammon and become a free people.

28 And it came to pass that as many as were desirous, unto them it was granted according to their desires.

29 Therefore, all the prisoners of

14a Alma 59: 11 (5–11).
16a Alma 44: 15, 20;
   3 Ne. 5: 4.
17a Alma 47: 29.

18a Alma 50: 14; 51: 26
   (24–26).
21a Alma 49: 13 (13,18–24).
22a Alma 55: 16.

26a Alma 59: 8.
27a Alma 24: 26 (25–27).

[About 61 B.C.]

the Lamanites did join the people of Ammon, and did begin to labor exceedingly, tilling the ground, raising all manner of grain, and flocks and herds of every kind; and thus were the Nephites relieved from a great burden; yea, insomuch that they were relieved from all the prisoners of the Lamanites.

30 Now it came to pass that Moroni, after he had obtained possession of the city of Nephihah, having taken many prisoners, which did reduce the armies of the Lamanites exceedingly, and having regained many of the Nephites who had been taken prisoners, which did strengthen the army of Moroni exceedingly; therefore Moroni went forth from the land of Nephihah to the land of [a]Lehi.

31 And it came to pass that when the Lamanites saw that Moroni was coming against them, they were again frightened and fled before the army of Moroni.

32 And it came to pass that [a]Moroni and his army did pursue them from city to city, until they were met by Lehi and Teancum; and the Lamanites fled from Lehi and Teancum, even down upon the borders by the seashore, until they came to the land of Moroni.

33 And the armies of the Lamanites were all gathered together, insomuch that they were all in one body in the land of Moroni. Now Ammoron, the king of the Lamanites, was also with them.

34 And it came to pass that Moroni and Lehi and Teancum did encamp with their armies round about in the borders of the land of Moroni, insomuch that the Lamanites were encircled about in the borders by the wilderness on the south, and in the borders by the wilderness on the east.

35 And thus they did encamp for the night. For behold, the Nephites and the Lamanites also were weary because of the greatness of the march; therefore they did not resolve upon any stratagem in the night-time, save it were Teancum; for he was exceedingly angry with Ammoron, insomuch that he considered that Ammoron, and Amalickiah his brother, had been the [a]cause of this great and lasting war between them and the Lamanites, which had been the cause of so much war and bloodshed, yea, and so much famine.

36 And it came to pass that Teancum in his anger did go forth into the camp of the Lamanites, and did let himself down over the walls of the city. And he went forth with a cord, from place to place, insomuch that he did find the king; and he did [a]cast a javelin at him, which did pierce him near the heart. But behold, the king did awaken his servants before he died, insomuch that they did pursue Teancum, and slew him.

37 Now it came to pass that when Lehi and Moroni knew that Teancum was dead they were exceedingly sorrowful; for behold, he had been a man who had [a]fought valiantly for his country, yea, a true friend to liberty; and he had suffered very many exceedingly sore afflictions. But behold, he was dead, and had gone the way of all the earth.

38 Now it came to pass that Moroni marched forth on the morrow, and came upon the Lamanites, insomuch that they did slay them with a great slaughter; and they did drive them out of the land; and they did flee, even that they did not return at that time against the Nephites.

39 And thus *ended the thirty and first year of the reign of the judges over the people of Nephi; and thus they had had wars, and bloodsheds, and famine, and affliction, for the space of many years.

40 And there had been murders,

30a Alma 50: 15; 51: 26 (24–26).
32a Alma 50: 13; 51: 22 (22–23); 3 Ne. 8: 9.
35a Alma 48: 1.
36a Alma 51: 34.
37a IE throughout the Amalickiah–Ammoron
wars, Alma 50: 35; 51: 29–34; 52; 61; 62: 3–37.

[*60 B.C.]

and contentions, and dissensions, and all manner of iniquity among the people of Nephi; nevertheless for the ^arighteous' sake, yea, because of the prayers of the righteous, they were spared.

41 But behold, because of the exceedingly great length of the war between the Nephites and the Lamanites many had become hardened, because of the exceedingly great length of the war; and many were softened because of their ^aafflictions, insomuch that they did humble themselves before God, even in the depth of humility.

42 And it came to pass that after Moroni had fortified those parts of the land which were most exposed to the Lamanites, until they were sufficiently strong, he returned to the city of Zarahemla; and also Helaman returned to the place of his inheritance; and there was once more peace established among the people of Nephi.

43 And Moroni yielded up the ^acommand of his armies into the hands of his son, whose name was ^bMoronihah; and he retired to his own house that he might spend the remainder of his days in peace.

44 And Pahoran did return to his judgment-seat; and Helaman did take upon him again to preach unto the people the word of God; for because of so many wars and contentions it had become expedient that a ^aregulation should be made again in the church.

45 Therefore, Helaman and his brethren went forth, and did declare the word of God with much power unto the ^aconvincing of many people of their wickedness, which did cause them to repent of their sins and to be baptized unto the Lord their God.

46 And it came to pass that they did establish again the church of God, throughout all the land.

47 Yea, and regulations were made concerning the law. And their ^ajudges, and their chief judges were chosen.

48 And the people of Nephi began to ^aprosper again in the land, and began to multiply and to wax exceedingly strong again in the land. And they began to grow exceedingly rich.

49 But notwithstanding their riches, or their strength, or their prosperity, they were not lifted up in the pride of their eyes; neither were they ^aslow to remember the Lord their God; but they did humble themselves exceedingly before him.

50 Yea, they did remember how great things the Lord had done for them, that he had ^adelivered them from death, and from bonds, and from prisons, and from all manner of ^bafflictions, and he had ^cdelivered them out of the hands of their enemies.

51 And they did pray unto the Lord their God continually, insomuch that the Lord did bless them, according to his word, so that they did wax strong and ^aprosper in the land.

52 And it came to pass that all these things were done. And ^aHelaman died, in the *thirty and fifth year of the reign of the judges over the people of Nephi.

CHAPTER 63

Shiblon and later Helaman take possession of the sacred records— Many Nephites travel to the land northward—Hagoth builds ships, which sail forth in the west sea— Moronihah defeats the Lamanites in battle.

40a Alma 45: 15 (15–16);
     46: 10.
41a TG Adversity;
     Affliction.
43a Hel. 4: 16 (10, 16).
  b Alma 63: 15.
44a Alma 45: 21.

45a Alma 21: 17;
     D&C 18: 44.
47a Mosiah 29: 39.
48a Alma 50: 20.
49a Alma 55: 31.
50a 2 Cor. 11: 26 (24–33).
  b TG Adversity.

c TG Deliver,
   Deliverance.
51a Gen. 26: 22.
   TG Prosper.
52a His great career spans
   Alma chapters 31–62.

[*57 B.C.]

AND it came to pass in the *commencement of the thirty and sixth year of the reign of the judges over the people of Nephi, that *Shiblon took possession of those *sacred things which had been delivered unto Helaman by Alma.

2 And he was a just man, and he did walk uprightly before God; and he did observe to do good continually, to keep the commandments of the Lord his God; and also did his brother.

3 And it came to pass that *Moroni died also. And thus ended the thirty and sixth year of the reign of the judges.

4 And it came to pass that in the †thirty and seventh year of the reign of the judges, there was a large company of men, even to the amount of five thousand and four hundred men, with their wives and their children, departed out of the land of Zarahemla into the land which was *northward.

5 And it came to pass that Hagoth, he being an *exceedingly curious man, therefore he went forth and built him an exceedingly large ship, on the borders of the land *Bountiful, by the land Desolation, and launched it forth into the west sea, by the *narrow neck which led into the land northward.

6 And behold, there were many of the Nephites who did enter therein and did sail forth with much provisions, and also many women and children; and they took their course northward. And thus ended the thirty and seventh year.

7 And in the thirty and eighth year, this man built *other ships. And the first ship did also return, and many more people did enter

into it; and they also took much provisions, and set out again to the land northward.

8 And it came to pass that they were never heard of more. And we suppose that they were drowned in the depths of the sea. And it came to pass that one other ship also did sail forth; and whither she did go we know not.

9 And it came to pass that in this year there were many people who went forth into the land *northward. And thus ended the thirty and eighth year.

10 And it came to pass in the ‡thirty and ninth year of the reign of the judges, *Shiblon died also, and Corianton had gone forth to the land northward in a ship, to carry forth provisions unto the people who had gone forth into that land.

11 Therefore it became expedient for *Shiblon to confer those sacred things, before his death, upon the son of *Helaman, who was called *Helaman, being called after the name of his father.

12 Now behold, all those *engravings which were in the possession of Helaman were written and sent forth among the children of men throughout all the land, save it were those parts which had been commanded by Alma should *not go forth.

13 Nevertheless, these things were to be kept sacred, and *handed down from one generation to another; therefore, in this year, they had been conferred upon Helaman, before the death of Shiblon.

14 And it came to pass also in this year that there were some dissenters who had gone forth unto the

63 1a Alma 38: 1 (1–2);
      49: 30.
   b Mosiah 1: 3;
      Alma 37: 1 (1–12).
      TG Sacred.
  3a See Alma chapters
      43–63 for his great
      contributions.
  4a Alma 22: 31; 46: 17;
      Hel. 3: 3.

  5a Hel. 3: 10 (10, 14).
   b Alma 53: 3 (3–4);
      Hel. 1: 23.
   c Alma 22: 32; Morm. 2:
      29; Ether 10: 20.
  7a Hel. 3: 10.
  9a Hel. 3: 12 (11–12);
      6: 6.
 10a Alma 31: 7.

 11a Alma 63: 1.
   b See heading to the
      book of Helaman.
   c Hel. 3: 37.
 12a Alma 18: 36; 3 Ne.
      1: 2.
   b Alma 37: 27 (27–32).
 13a Alma 37: 4.

[*56 B.C. †55 B.C. ‡53 B.C.]

Lamanites; and they were *a*stirred up again to anger against the Nephites.

15 And also in this same year they came down with a numerous army to war against the people of *a*Moronihah, or against the army of Moronihah, in the which they were beaten and driven back again to their own lands, suffering great loss.

16 And thus ended the thirty and ninth year of the reign of the judges over the people of Nephi.

17 And thus ended the account of *a*Alma, and Helaman his son, and also Shiblon, who was his son.

THE BOOK OF HELAMAN

An account of the Nephites. Their wars and contentions, and their dissensions. And also the prophecies of many holy prophets, before the coming of Christ, according to the records of Helaman, who was the son of Helaman, and also according to the records of his sons, even down to the coming of Christ. And also many of the Lamanites are converted. An account of their conversion. An account of the righteousness of the Lamanites, and the wickedness and abominations of the Nephites, according to the record of Helaman and his sons, even down to the coming of Christ, which is called the book of Helaman.

CHAPTER 1

Pahoran the second becomes chief judge and is murdered by Kishkumen—Pacumeni fills the judgment-seat—Coriantumr leads the Lamanite armies, takes Zarahemla, and slays Pacumeni—Moronihah defeats the Lamanites and retakes Zarahemla, and Coriantumr is slain.

AND now behold, it came to pass in the *commencement of the fortieth year of the reign of the judges over the people of Nephi, there began to be a serious difficulty among the people of the Nephites.

2 For behold, *a*Pahoran had died, and gone the way of all the earth; therefore there began to be a serious contention concerning who should have the judgment-seat among the brethren, who were the sons of Pahoran.

3 Now these are their names who did contend for the judgment-seat, who did also cause the people to contend: Pahoran, Paanchi, and Pacumeni.

4 Now these are not all the sons of Pahoran (for he had many), but these are they who did contend for the judgment-seat; therefore, they did cause three *a*divisions among the people.

5 Nevertheless, it came to pass that Pahoran was appointed by the *a*voice of the people to be chief judge and a governor over the people of Nephi.

6 And it came to pass that Pacumeni, when he saw that he could not obtain the judgment-seat, he did *a*unite with the voice of the people.

7 But behold, Paanchi, and that part of the people that were desirous that he should be their governor, was exceedingly wroth; therefore,

---

14*a* Alma 51:9; Hel. 4:4.
15*a* Alma 62:43.
17*a* Alma 1:2 (1–2).

[HELAMAN]
1 2*a* Alma 50:40.
4*a* Matt. 12:25.

5*a* Mosiah 29:11;
   Alma 51:7; Hel. 5:2.
6*a* TG Unity.

[*52 B.C.]

he was about to ^aflatter away those people to rise up in rebellion against their brethren.

8 And it came to pass as he was about to do this, behold, he was taken, and was tried according to the ^avoice of the people, and condemned unto death; for he had raised up in rebellion and sought to destroy the ^bliberty of the people.

9 Now when those people who were desirous that he should be their governor saw that he was condemned unto death, therefore they were angry, and behold, they sent forth one ^aKishkumen, even to the judgment-seat of Pahoran, and murdered Pahoran as he sat upon the judgment-seat.

10 And he was pursued by the servants of Pahoran; but behold, so speedy was the flight of Kishkumen that no man could overtake him.

11 And he went unto those that sent him, and they all entered into a covenant, yea, ^aswearing by their everlasting Maker, that they would tell no man that Kishkumen had murdered Pahoran.

12 Therefore, Kishkumen was not known among the people of Nephi, for he was in disguise at the time that he murdered Pahoran. And Kishkumen and his band, who had covenanted with him, did mingle themselves among the people, in a manner that they all could not be found; but as many as were found were condemned unto ^adeath.

13 And now behold, Pacumeni was appointed, according to the ^avoice of the people, to be a chief judge and a governor over the people, to reign in the stead of his brother Pahoran; and it was according to his right. And all this was done in the fortieth year of the reign of the judges; and it had an end.

14 And it came to pass in the *forty and first year of the reign of the judges, that the Lamanites had gathered together an innumerable army of men, and ^aarmed them with swords, and with cimeters and with bows, and with arrows, and with head-plates, and with breastplates, and with all manner of shields of every kind.

15 And they came down again that they might pitch battle against the Nephites. And they were led by a man whose name was ^aCoriantumr; and he was a descendant of Zarahemla; and he was a ^bdissenter from among the Nephites; and he was a large and a mighty man.

16 Therefore, the king of the Lamanites, whose name was Tubaloth, who was the son of ^aAmmoron, supposing that Coriantumr, being a mighty man, could stand against the Nephites, with his strength and also with his great ^bwisdom, insomuch that by sending him forth he should gain power over the Nephites—

17 Therefore he did ^astir them up to anger, and he did gather together his armies, and he did appoint Coriantumr to be their leader, and did cause that they should march down to the land of Zarahemla to battle against the Nephites.

18 And it came to pass that because of so much contention and so much difficulty in the government, that they had not kept sufficient guards in the land of Zarahemla; for they had supposed that the Lamanites durst not come into the heart of their lands to attack that great city Zarahemla.

19 But it came to pass that Coriantumr did march forth at the head of his numerous host, and came upon the inhabitants of the city, and their march was with such exceedingly great speed that there

7a Mosiah 27 : 8; Alma 50 : 35; Hel. 2 : 5; Ether 8 : 2.
8a Alma 1 : 14 (10–15).
  b TG Liberty.
9a Hel. 2 : 3.
11a Gen. 24 : 3; Ether 8 : 14 (13–14).
12a TG Capital Punishment.
13a Hel. 1 : 5; 2 : 2.
14a Alma 2 : 12; 49 : 6 (6, 24).
15a Hel. 1 : 30.
  b Alma 31 : 8; 53 : 8; Hel. 4 : 8.
16a Alma 52 : 3.
  b Ezek. 28 : 5 (4–5).
17a Alma 35 : 10; 47 : 1.

[*51 B.C.]

was no time for the Nephites to gather together their armies.

20 Therefore Coriantumr did cut down the watch by the entrance of the city, and did march forth with his whole army into the city, and they did slay every one who did oppose them, insomuch that they did take possession of the whole city.

21 And it came to pass that Pacumeni, who was the chief judge, did flee before Coriantumr, even to the walls of the city. And it came to pass that Coriantumr did smite him against the wall, insomuch that he died. And thus ended the days of Pacumeni.

22 And now when Coriantumr saw that he was in possession of the city of Zarahemla, and saw that the Nephites had fled before them, and were slain, and were taken, and were cast into prison, and that he had obtained the possession of the strongest hold in all the land, his heart [a]took courage insomuch that he was about to go forth against all the land.

23 And now he did not tarry in the land of Zarahemla, but he did march forth with a large army, even towards the city of [a]Bountiful; for it was his determination to go forth and cut his way through with the sword, that he might obtain the north parts of the land.

24 And, supposing that their greatest strength was in the center of the land, therefore he did march forth, giving them no time to assemble themselves together save it were in small bodies; and in this manner they did fall upon them and cut them down to the earth.

25 But behold, this march of Coriantumr through the center of the land gave Moronihah great advantage over them, notwithstanding the greatness of the number of the Nephites who were slain.

26 For behold, Moronihah had

supposed that the Lamanites durst not come into the center of the land, but that they would attack the cities round about in the borders as they had hitherto done; therefore Moronihah had caused that their strong armies should maintain those parts round about by the borders.

27 But behold, the Lamanites were not frightened according to his desire, but they had come into the center of the land, and had taken the capital city which was the city of Zarahemla, and were marching through the most capital parts of the land, slaying the people with a great slaughter, both men, women, and children, taking possession of many cities and of many strongholds.

28 But when Moronihah had discovered this, he immediately sent forth Lehi with an army round about to [a]head them before they should come to the land Bountiful.

29 And thus he did; and he did head them before they came to the land Bountiful, and gave unto them battle, insomuch that they began to retreat back towards the land of Zarahemla.

30 And it came to pass that Moronihah did head them in their retreat, and did give unto them battle, insomuch that it became an exceedingly bloody battle; yea, many were slain, and among the number who were slain [a]Coriantumr was also found.

31 And now, behold, the Lamanites could not retreat either way, neither on the north, nor on the south, nor on the east, nor on the west, for they were surrounded on every hand by the Nephites.

32 And thus had Coriantumr plunged the Lamanites into the midst of the Nephites, insomuch that they were in the power of the Nephites, and he himself was slain, and the Lamanites did [a]yield themselves into the hands of the Nephites.

22a TG Pride.
23a Alma 22: 29.
28a Alma 50: 34; 51: 29

(29–30).
30a Hel. 1: 15.

32a Hel. 4: 3.

[About 51 B.C.]

33 And it came to pass that Moronihah took possession of the city of Zarahemla again, and caused that the Lamanites who had been taken prisoners should depart out of the land in ᵃpeace.

34 And thus ended the forty and first year of the reign of the judges.

CHAPTER 2

Helaman the second becomes chief judge—Gadianton leads the band of Kishkumen — Helaman's servant slays Kishkumen, and the Gadianton band flees into the wilderness.

AND it came to pass in the *forty and second year of the reign of the judges, after Moronihah had established again peace between the Nephites and the Lamanites, behold there was no one to fill the judgment-seat; therefore there began to be a contention again among the people concerning who should fill the judgment-seat.

2 And it came to pass that ᵃHelaman, who was the son of Helaman, was appointed to fill the judgment-seat, by the ᵇvoice of the people.

3 But behold, ᵃKishkumen, who had murdered Pahoran, did lay wait to destroy Helaman also; and he was upheld by his band, who had entered into a covenant that no one should know his wickedness.

4 For there was one ᵃGadianton, who was exceedingly expert in many words, and also in his craft, to carry on the secret work of murder and of robbery; therefore he became the leader of the band of Kishkumen.

5 Therefore he did ᵃflatter them, and also Kishkumen, that if they would place him in the judgment-seat he would grant unto those who belonged to his band that they should be placed in power and authority among the people; therefore Kishkumen sought to destroy Helaman.

6 And it came to pass as he went forth towards the judgment-seat to destroy Helaman, behold one of the servants of Helaman, having been out by night, and having obtained, through disguise, a knowledge of those plans which had been laid by this band to destroy Helaman—

7 And it came to pass that he met Kishkumen, and he gave unto him a sign; therefore Kishkumen made known unto him the object of his desire, desiring that he would conduct him to the judgment-seat that he might murder Helaman.

8 And when the servant of Helaman had known all the heart of Kishkumen, and how that it was his ᵃobject to murder, and also that it was the object of all those who belonged to his band to murder, and to rob, and to gain power, (and this was their ᵇsecret plan, and their combination) the servant of Helaman said unto Kishkumen: Let us go forth unto the judgment-seat.

9 Now this did please Kishkumen exceedingly, for he did suppose that he should accomplish his design; but behold, the servant of Helaman, as they were going forth unto the judgment-seat, did stab Kishkumen even to the heart, that he fell dead without a groan. And he ran and told Helaman all the things which he had seen, and heard, and done.

10 And it came to pass that Helaman did send forth to take this band of robbers and ᵃsecret murderers, that they might be executed according to the law.

11 But behold, when Gadianton had found that Kishkumen did not return he feared lest that he should be destroyed; therefore he caused that his band should follow him. And they took their flight out of

33a Alma 44:15.
2 2a Hel. 3:20.
  b Hel. 1:13.
 3a Hel. 1:9.
 4a Hel. 3:23; 6:18
   (18, 29).
5a Mosiah 27:8; Alma
   50:35; Hel. 1:7;
   Ether 8:2.
   TG Flattery.
8a TG Conspiracy.
 b 2 Ne. 10:15; Moses
5:31 (18–31).
TG Secret
Combinations.
10a Hel. 3:23.

[*50 B.C.]

the land, by a secret way, into the wilderness; and thus when Helaman sent forth to take them they could nowhere be found.

12 And more of this Gadianton shall be spoken hereafter. And thus ended the forty and second year of the reign of the judges over the people of Nephi.

13 And behold, in the end of this book ye shall see that this [a]Gadianton did prove the overthrow, yea, almost the entire destruction of the people of Nephi.

14 Behold I do not mean the end of the [a]book of Helaman, but I mean the end of the book of Nephi, from which I have taken all the account which I have written.

CHAPTER 3

Many Nephites migrate to the land northward—They build houses of cement and keep many records—Tens of thousands are converted and baptized—The word of God leads men to salvation—Nephi the son of Helaman fills the judgment seat.

AND now it came to pass in the *forty and third year of the reign of the judges, there was no contention among the people of Nephi save it were a little pride which was in the church, which did cause some little dissensions among the people, which affairs were settled in the ending of the forty and third year.

2 And there was no contention among the people in the forty and fourth year; neither was there much contention in the forty and fifth year.

3 And it came to pass in the †forty and sixth, yea, there was much contention and many dissensions; in the which there were an exceedingly great many who departed out of the land of Zarahemla, and went forth unto the land [a]northward to inherit the land.

4 And they did travel to an exceedingly great distance, insomuch that they came to [a]large bodies of water and many rivers.

5 Yea, and even they did spread forth into all parts of the land, into whatever parts it had not been rendered desolate and without timber, because of the many inhabitants who had before inherited the land.

6 And now no part of the land was desolate, save it were for timber; but because of the greatness of the [a]destruction of the people who had before inhabited the land it was called [b]desolate.

7 And there being but little timber upon the face of the land, nevertheless the people who went forth became exceedingly [a]expert in the working of cement; therefore they did build houses of cement, in the which they did dwell.

8 And it came to pass that they did multiply and spread, and did go forth from the land southward to the land northward, and did spread insomuch that they began to cover the face of the whole earth, from the sea south to the sea north, from the sea [a]west to the sea east.

9 And the people who were in the land northward did dwell in [a]tents, and in houses of cement, and they did suffer whatsoever tree should spring up upon the face of the land that it should grow up, that in time they might have timber to build their houses, yea, their cities, and their temples, and their [b]synagogues, and their sanctuaries, and all manner of their buildings.

10 And it came to pass as timber was exceedingly scarce in the land northward, they did send forth much by the way of [a]shipping.

13a Hel. 6: 18; 3 Ne. 4: 1.
14a W of M 1: 9;
   3 Ne. 5: 10.
3 3a Alma 63: 4.
 4a Mosiah 8: 8; Alma
   50: 29; Morm. 6: 4.

6a Mosiah 8: 8; 21: 26
   (26–27).
 b Alma 22: 31.
7a TG Skill.
8a Alma 22: 27 (27,
   32–33); Hel. 11: 20.

9a Gen. 25: 27; Ether
   2: 13.
 b Alma 16: 13.
10a Alma 63: 7 (5–8).

[*49 B.C. †46 B.C.]

11 And thus they did enable the people in the land northward that they might build many cities, both of wood and of cement.

12 And it came to pass that there were many of the [a]people of Ammon, who were Lamanites by birth, did also go forth into this land.

13 And now there are many [a]records kept of the proceedings of this people, by many of this people, which are particular and very large, concerning them.

14 But behold, a [a]hundredth part of the proceedings of this people, yea, the account of the Lamanites and of the Nephites, and their wars, and contentions, and dissensions, and their preaching, and their prophecies, and their shipping and their building of ships, and their building of [b]temples, and of synagogues and their [c]sanctuaries, and their righteousness, and their wickedness, and their murders, and their robbings, and their plundering, and all manner of abominations and whoredoms, cannot be contained in this work.

15 But behold, there are many books and many [a]records of every kind, and they have been kept chiefly by the Nephites.

16 And they have been [a]handed down from one generation to another by the Nephites, even until they have fallen into transgression and have been murdered, plundered, and hunted, and driven forth, and slain, and [b]scattered upon the face of the earth, and mixed with the Lamanites until they are [c]no more called the Nephites, becoming wicked, and wild, and ferocious, yea, even becoming Lamanites.

17 And now I return again to mine account; therefore, what I have spoken had passed after there had been great contentions, and disturbances, and wars, and dissensions, among the people of Nephi.

18 The forty and sixth year of the reign of the judges ended;

19 And it came to pass that there was still great contention in the land, yea, even in the *forty and seventh year, and also in the forty and eighth year.

20 Nevertheless [a]Helaman did fill the judgment-seat with justice and equity; yea, he did observe to keep the statutes, and the judgments, and the commandments of God; and he did do that which was right in the sight of God continually; and he did walk after the ways of his father, insomuch that he did prosper in the land.

21 And it came to pass that he had two sons. He gave unto the eldest the name of [a]Nephi, and unto the youngest, the name of [b]Lehi. And they began to grow up unto the Lord.

22 And it came to pass that the wars and contentions began to cease, in a small degree, among the people of the Nephites, in the latter end of the forty and eighth year of the reign of the judges over the people of Nephi.

23 And it came to pass in the †forty and ninth year of the reign of the judges, there was continual peace established in the land, all save it were the [a]secret combinations which [b]Gadianton the robber had established in the more settled parts of the land, which at that time were not known unto those who were at the head of government; therefore they were not destroyed out of the land.

24 And it came to pass that in this same year there was exceedingly great prosperity in the church, insomuch that there were thousands who did [a]join themselves unto the

12a Alma 27: 26; 63: 9
    (4–9); Hel. 6: 6.
13a W of M 1: 3 (1–11).
14a 3 Ne. 5: 8; 26: 6
    (6–11).
  b 2 Ne. 5: 16; Jacob
    1: 17; 3 Ne. 11: 1.
  c Alma 23: 2.

15a 3 Ne. 5: 9; 4 Ne. 1: 48.
16a 1 Ne. 5: 18 (16–19);
    Alma 37: 4.
  b Ezek. 36: 19 (16–20).
  c Alma 45: 13 (12–14).
20a Hel. 2: 2.
21a Hel. 4: 14; 5: 5;
    3 Ne. 1: 2.

  b Hel. 3: 37.
23a 2 Ne. 10: 15; Hel.
    2: 10 (8–10); 7: 25
    (4–5, 21, 25).
  b Hel. 2: 4; 6: 18.
24a Mosiah 25: 23.

            [*45 B.C.   †43 B.C.]

church and were baptized unto repentance.

25 And so great was the prosperity of the church, and so many the blessings which were poured out upon the people, that even the high priests and the teachers were themselves astonished beyond measure.

26 And it came to pass that the work of the Lord did prosper unto the baptizing and uniting to the church of God, many souls, yea, even tens of thousands.

27 Thus we may see that the Lord is merciful unto all who will, in the sincerity of their hearts, call upon his holy name.

28 Yea, thus we see that the *a*gate of heaven is open unto *b*all, even to those who will believe on the name of Jesus Christ, who is the Son of God.

29 Yea, we see that whosoever will may lay hold upon the *a*word of God, which is *b*quick and powerful, which shall *c*divide asunder all the cunning and the snares and the wiles of the devil, and lead the man of Christ in a strait and *d*narrow course across that everlasting *e*gulf of misery which is prepared to engulf the wicked—

30 And land their souls, yea, their immortal souls, at the *a*right hand of God in the kingdom of heaven, to sit down with Abraham, and Isaac, and with Jacob, and with all our holy fathers, to go no more out.

31 And in this year there was continual rejoicing in the land of Zarahemla, and in all the regions round about, even in all the land which was possessed by the Nephites.

32 And it came to pass that there was peace and exceedingly great joy in the remainder of the forty and ninth year; yea, and also there was continual peace and great joy in the fiftieth year of the reign of the judges.

33 And in the *fifty and first year of the reign of the judges there was peace also, save it were the pride which began to enter into the church —not into the church of God, but into the hearts of the people who *a*professed to belong to the church of God—

34 And they were lifted up in *a*pride, even to the persecution of many of their brethren. Now this was a great evil, which did cause the more humble part of the people to suffer great persecutions, and to wade through much affliction.

35 Nevertheless they did *a*fast and *b*pray oft, and did wax stronger and stronger in their *c*humility, and firmer and firmer in the faith of Christ, unto the filling their souls with joy and consolation, yea, even to the *d*purifying and the *e*sanctification of their hearts, which sanctification cometh because of their *f*yielding their hearts unto God.

36 And it came to pass that the fifty and second year ended in peace also, save it were the exceedingly great pride which had gotten into the hearts of the people; and it was because of their exceedingly great *a*riches and their prosperity in the land; and it did grow upon them from day to day.

37 And it came to pass in the †fifty and third year of the reign of the judges, *a*Helaman died, and his eldest son *b*Nephi began to reign in his stead. And it came to pass that he did fill the judgment-seat with justice and equity; yea, he did keep

---

28a Isa. 26: 2.
  b Acts 10: 28 (9–35, 44); Rom. 2: 11 (10–11).
29a Micah 2: 7; Jacob 2: 8; D&C 11: 2; 33: 1. TG Gospel.
  b Heb. 4: 12; D&C 27: 1.
  c D&C 6: 2.
  d 2 Ne. 9: 41; 33: 9.

  e 1 Ne. 12: 18; 15: 28 (28–30).
30a Matt. 25: 34 (31–46).
33a D&C 112: 26.
34a TG Pride.
35a TG Fasting.
  b TG Prayer.
  c TG Humility.
  d TG Cleanliness; Purification; Purity.

  e TG Sanctification.
  f 2 Chr. 30: 8; Rom. 6: 13 (12–14).
  TG Submissiveness; Teachable.
36a TG Treasure.
37a Alma 63: 11; Hel. 16: 25.
  b Hel. 3: 21; 5: 1.

[*41 B.C.   †39 B.C.]

the commandments of God, and did walk in the ways of his father.

CHAPTER 4

Nephite dissenters and the Lamanites join forces and take the land of Zarahemla—The Nephites' defeats come because of their wickedness—The Church dwindles and the people become weak like the Lamanites.

AND it came to pass in the *fifty and fourth year there were many dissensions in the church, and there was also a [a]contention among the people, insomuch that there was much bloodshed.

2 And the rebellious part were slain and driven out of the land, and they did go unto the king of the Lamanites.

3 And it came to pass that they did endeavor to stir up the Lamanites to [a]war against the Nephites; but behold, the Lamanites were [b]exceedingly afraid, insomuch that they would not hearken to the words of those dissenters.

4 But it came to pass in the fifty and sixth year of the reign of the judges, there were [a]dissenters who went up from the Nephites unto the Lamanites; and they succeeded with those others in [b]stirring them up to anger against the Nephites; and they were all that year preparing for war.

5 And in the †fifty and seventh year they did come down against the Nephites to battle, and they did commence the work of death; yea, insomuch that in the fifty and eighth year of the reign of the judges they succeeded in obtaining [a]possession of the land of Zarahemla; yea, and also all the lands, even unto the land which was near the land Bountiful.

6 And the Nephites and the armies of Moronihah were driven even into the land of Bountiful;

7 And there they did fortify against the Lamanites, from the west sea, even unto the east; it being a [a]day's journey for a Nephite, on the line which they had fortified and stationed their armies to defend their north country.

8 And thus those [a]dissenters of the Nephites, with the help of a numerous army of the Lamanites, had obtained all the possession of the Nephites which was in the land southward. And all this was done in the fifty and eighth and ninth years of the reign of the judges.

9 And it came to pass in the sixtieth year of the reign of the judges, Moronihah did succeed with his armies in obtaining many parts of the land; yea, they regained many cities which had fallen into the hands of the Lamanites.

10 And it came to pass in the ‡sixty and first year of the reign of the judges they succeeded in regaining even the half of all their possessions.

11 Now this great loss of the Nephites, and the great slaughter which was among them, [a]would not have happened had it not been for their [b]wickedness and their abomination which was among them; yea, and it was among those also who professed to belong to the church of God.

12 And it was because of the [n]pride of their hearts, because of their exceeding [b]riches, yea, it was because of their oppression to the [c]poor, withholding their food from the hungry, withholding their clothing from the naked, and smiting their humble brethren upon the cheek, making a [d]mock of that which was sacred, denying the spirit of prophecy and of revelation, murdering, plundering, lying, stealing,

---

4 1a 3 Ne. 11:29.
3a Hel. 11:24.
  b Hel. 1:32 (30–33).
4a Hel. 5:17.
  b Alma 63:14.
5a Hel. 5:16, 52.
7a Alma 22:32.

8a Hel. 1:15.
11a D&C 82:10.
  b Mosiah 27:13.
12a Obad. 1:3 (3–4); 2 Ne. 20:33; D&C 101:42.
  b 1 Tim. 6:17; 2 Ne. 9:42; 3 Ne. 6:12

(10–16).
  c Ezek. 18:12; Zech. 7:10; D&C 42: 30 (30–39, 71).
  d TG Mocking; Sacrilege.

[*38 B.C. †35 B.C. ‡31 B.C.]

committing adultery, rising up in great contentions, and deserting away into the land of Nephi, among the Lamanites—

13 And because of this their great wickedness, and their [a]boastings in their own strength, they were left in their own strength; therefore they did not prosper, but were afflicted and smitten, and driven before the Lamanites, until they had lost possession of almost all their lands.

14 But behold, Moronihah did [a]preach many things unto the people because of their iniquity, and also [b]Nephi and Lehi, who were the sons of Helaman, did preach many things unto the people, yea, and did prophesy many things unto them concerning their iniquities, and what should come unto them if they did not repent of their sins.

15 And it came to pass that they did repent, and inasmuch as they did repent they did begin to prosper.

16 For when Moronihah saw that they did repent he did venture to [a]lead them forth from place to place, and from city to city, even until they had regained the one-half of their property and the one-half of all their lands.

17 And thus ended the sixty and first year of the reign of the judges.

18 And it came to pass in the *sixty and second year of the reign of the judges, that Moronihah could obtain no more possessions over the Lamanites.

19 Therefore they did abandon their design to obtain the remainder of their lands, for so numerous were the Lamanites that it became impossible for the Nephites to obtain more power over them; therefore Moronihah did employ all his armies in maintaining those parts which he had taken.

20 And it came to pass, because of the greatness of the number of the Lamanites the Nephites were in great fear, lest they should be overpowered, and trodden down, and slain, and destroyed.

21 Yea, they began to remember the [a]prophecies of Alma, and also the [b]words of Mosiah; and they saw that they had been a [c]stiffnecked people, and that they had set at [d]naught the commandments of God;

22 And that they had altered and trampled under their feet the [a]laws of Mosiah, or that which the Lord commanded him to give unto the people; and they saw that their laws had become corrupted, and that they had become a wicked people, insomuch that they were wicked even like unto the Lamanites.

23 And because of their iniquity the church had begun to [a]dwindle; and they began to disbelieve in the spirit of prophecy and in the spirit of revelation; and the judgments of God did stare them in the face.

24 And they saw that they had become [a]weak, like unto their brethren, the Lamanites, and that the Spirit of the Lord did no more preserve them; yea, it had withdrawn from them because the Spirit of the Lord doth not [b]dwell in [c]unholy [d]temples—

25 Therefore the Lord did cease to preserve them by his miraculous and matchless power, for they had fallen into a state of [a]unbelief and awful wickedness; and they saw that the Lamanites were exceedingly more numerous than they, and except they should [b]cleave unto the Lord their God they must unavoidably perish.

26 For behold, they saw that the strength of the Lamanites was as

13a Ezek. 35: 13.
  TG Boasting; Trust Not in the Arm of Flesh.
14a Hel. 5: 17 (14–20).
  b Hel. 3: 21.
16a Alma 62: 43.
21a Alma 5: 53 (1–62).
  b Mosiah 29: 27.

c TG Stiffneckedness.
d Prov. 1: 25.
22a Alma 1: 1.
23a TG Apostasy.
24a Jer. 46: 15 (15–17);
  Mosiah 1: 13.
  b TG Holy Ghost, Loss of.
  c Mosiah 2: 37; Alma

7: 21; 34: 36.
d TG Temple.
25a TG Unbelief,
  Unbelievers.
  b Josh. 23: 8; Jacob
  6: 5; D&C 11: 19.

[*30 B.C.]

great as their strength, even man for man. And thus had they fallen into this great transgression; yea, thus had they become ªweak, because of their transgression, in the space of ᵇnot many years.

CHAPTER 5

Nephi and Lehi devote themselves to preaching—Their names invite them to pattern their lives after their forebears—Christ redeems those who repent—Nephi and Lehi make many converts and are imprisoned, and fire encircles them—A cloud of darkness overshadows three hundred people—The earth shakes and a voice commands men to repent—Nephi and Lehi converse with angels, and the multitude are encircled by fire.

AND it came to pass that in this *same year, behold, ªNephi ᵇdelivered up the judgment-seat to a man whose name was ᶜCezoram.

2 For as their ᵈlaws and their governments were established by the ªvoice of the people, and they who ᵇchose ᶜevil were ᶜmore numerous than they who chose good, therefore they were ᵈripening for destruction, for the laws had become corrupted.

3 Yea, and this was not all; they were a ªstiffnecked people, insomuch that they could not be governed by the law nor justice, save it were their destruction.

4 And it came to ... of God all ... it upon ... had beg... ... the remainder judgm...

5 For they remembered the words which their ªfather Helaman spake unto them. And these are the words which he spake:

6 Behold, my sons, I desire that ye should remember to keep the commandments of God; and I would that ye should declare unto the people these words. Behold, I have given unto you the names of our first ªparents who came out of the land of Jerusalem; and this I have done that when you remember your names ye may remember them; and when ye remember them ye may remember their works; and when ye remember their works ye may know how that it is said, and also written, that they were good.

7 Therefore, my sons, I would that ye should do that which is good, that it may be said of you, and also written, even as it has been said and written of them.

8 And now my sons, behold I have somewhat more to desire of you, which desire is, that ye may not do these things that ye may boast, but that ye may do these things to lay up for yourselves a ªtreasure in heaven, yea, which is eternal, and which fadeth not away; yea, that ye may have that ᵇprecious gift of eternal life, which ... given to our ...

9 O remember, remember, my sons, the words which king Benjamin spake unto his people; yea, remember that there is no other way nor means whereby man can be saved, only through the ᵇatoning blood of Jesus Christ, who shall come; yea, remember that he cometh to ᶜredeem the ᵈworld.

... 19: 8 (6–9).
ª Weak, Weaker.
Alma 46: 8; Hel. 6: 32; 7: 6; 11: 26; 12: 2.
5 1a Hel. 3: 37.
b Alma 4: 20 (15–20).
c Hel. 6: 15.
2a Mosiah 29: 25 (25–27); Hel. 1: 5 (3–5, 13).
b Alma 10: 19.

c 4 Ne. 1: 40.
d Hel. 6: 40; 10: 11; D&C 18: 6; 61: 31.
3a TG Stiffneckedness.
5a Hel. 3: 21 (21, 37).
6a 1 Ne. 1: 4 (1, 4).
b 2 Ne. 4: 12; 33: 3 (1–15); Jacob 1: 10 (9–12).
8a Hel. 8: 25; 3 Ne. 13: 20 (19–21).

TG Treasure.
b 1 Ne. 15: 36.
9a Mosiah 2: 9.
b Mosiah 3: 18; 4: 2. TG Jesus Christ, Atonement through.
c TG Jesus Christ, Redeemer.
d TG World.

10 And remember also the words which Amulek spake unto Zeezrom, [a]in the city of Ammonihah; for he said unto him that the Lord surely should come to redeem his people, but that he should not come to redeem them in their sins, but to redeem them from their sins.

11 And he hath power given unto him from the Father to redeem them from their sins because of repentance; therefore he hath [a]sent his angels to declare the tidings of the conditions of repentance, which bringeth unto the power of the Redeemer, unto the salvation of their souls.

12 And now, my sons, remember, remember that it is upon the [a]rock of our Redeemer, who is Christ, the Son of God, that ye must build your [b]foundation; that when the devil shall send forth his mighty winds, yea, his shafts in the whirlwind, yea, when all his hail and his mighty [c]storm shall beat upon you, it shall have no power over you to drag you down to the gulf of misery and endless wo, because of the rock upon which ye are built, which is a sure foundation, a foundation whereon if men build they cannot fall.

13 And it came to pass that [a]were the words to pass that Helaman taught to his sons, [a]yea, did teach them many things which are not written, and also many things which are written.

14 And they did remember his words; and therefore they went forth, keeping the commandments of God, to teach the word of God among all the people of Nephi, beginning at the city Bountiful;

15 And from thenceforth to the city of Gid; and from the city of Gid to the city of Mulek;

16 And even from one city to another, until they had gone forth [a]among all the people of Nephi who were in the land southward; and from thence into the land of Zarahemla, among the Lamanites.

17 And it came to pass that they did [a]preach with great [b]power, insomuch that they did confound many of those [c]dissenters who had gone over from the Nephites, insomuch that they came forth and did confess their sins and were baptized unto repentance, and immediately returned to the Nephites to endeavor to repair unto them the wrongs which they had done.

18 And it came to pass that Nephi and Lehi did preach unto the Lamanites with such great power and authority, for they had power and authority given unto them that they might [a]speak, and they also had what they should speak given unto them—

19 Therefore they did speak unto the great astonishment of the Lamanites, to the convincing them, insomuch that there were eight thousand of the Lamanites who were in the land of Zarahemla and round about [a]baptized unto repentance, and were convinced of the their [c]traditions of [b]dness of the traditions of their fathers.

20 And it came to pass that Nephi and Lehi did proceed from thence to the [a]land of Nephi.

21 And it came to pass that they were cast by an army of the Lamanites and were cast into [a]prison; yea, even in that [a]same prison in which Ammon and his brethren were cast by the servants of Limhi.

10a Alma 11:34.
11a Alma 13:24 (24–25); 39:19.
12a Ps. 71:3; Matt. 7:24 (24–27); D&C 6:34; Moses 7:53.
  TG Cornerstone; Rock.
 b Isa. 28:16 (14–17); Jacob 4:16.
 c Alma 26:6; 3 Ne. 14:25 (25, 27).
13a Mosiah 1:4; Alma 18:36; 36:1; Moses 6:58.
16a Hel. 4:5.
17a Hel. 4:14.
 b TG Teaching with the Spirit.
 c Hel. 4:4 (2, 4).
18a D&C 24:6; 100:5
19a TG Mission, son in
 b Mal. 2:6.
 c Hel. 15:4.
20a Alma 22:1.
21a Mosiah 7:7 (6–8); 21:23 (22–24).

[About 30 B.C.]

10 And remember also the words which Amulek spake unto Zeezrom, [a]in the city of Ammonihah; for he said unto him that the Lord surely should come to redeem his people, but that he should not come to redeem them in their sins, but to redeem them from their sins.

11 And he hath power given unto him from the Father to redeem them from their sins because of repentance; therefore he hath [a]sent his angels to declare the tidings of the conditions of repentance, which bringeth unto the power of the Redeemer, unto the salvation of their souls.

12 And now, my sons, remember, remember that it is upon the [a]rock of our Redeemer, who is Christ, the Son of God, that ye must build your [b]foundation; that when the devil shall send forth his mighty winds, yea, his shafts in the whirlwind, yea, when all his hail and his mighty [c]storm shall beat upon you, it shall have no power over you to drag you down to the gulf of misery and endless wo, because of the rock upon which ye are built, which is a sure foundation, a foundation whereon if men build they cannot fall.

13 And it came to pass that these were the words which Helaman [a]taught to his sons; yea, he did teach them many things which are not written, and also many things which are written.

14 And they did remember his words; and therefore they went forth, keeping the commandments of God, to teach the word of God among all the people of Nephi, beginning at the city Bountiful;

15 And from thenceforth to the city of Gid; and from the city of Gid to the city of Mulek;

16 And even from one city to another, until they had gone forth [a]among all the people of Nephi who were in the land southward; and from thence into the land of Zarahemla, among the Lamanites.

17 And it came to pass that they did [a]preach with great [b]power, insomuch that they did confound many of those [c]dissenters who had gone over from the Nephites, insomuch that they came forth and did confess their sins and were baptized unto repentance, and immediately returned to the Nephites to endeavor to repair unto them the wrongs which they had done.

18 And it came to pass that Nephi and Lehi did preach unto the Lamanites with such great power and authority, for they had power and authority given unto them that they might [a]speak, and they also had what they should speak given unto them—

19 Therefore they did speak unto the great astonishment of the Lamanites, to the convincing them, insomuch that there were eight thousand of the Lamanites who were in the land of Zarahemla and round about [a]baptized unto repentance, and were convinced of the [b]wickedness of the [c]traditions of their fathers.

20 And it came to pass that Nephi and Lehi did proceed from thence to go to the [a]land of Nephi.

21 And it came to pass that they were taken by an army of the Lamanites and cast into [a]prison; yea, even in that same prison in which Ammon and his brethren were cast by the servants of Limhi.

10a Alma 11: 34.
11a Alma 13: 24 (24–25); 39: 19.
12a Ps. 71: 3; Matt. 7: 24 (24–27); D&C 6: 34; Moses 7: 53.
  TG Cornerstone; Rock.
  b Isa. 28: 16 (14–17); Jacob 4:16.
  c Alma 26: 6; 3 Ne.

14: 25 (25, 27).
13a Mosiah 1: 4; Alma 18: 36; 36: 1; Moses 6: 58.
16a Hel. 4: 5.
17a Hel. 4: 14.
  b TG Teaching with the Spirit.
  c Hel. 4: 4 (2, 4).
18a D&C 24: 6; 100: 5

(5–8). TG Prophets, Mission of.
19a TG Missionary Work.
  b Mal. 2: 6.
  c Hel. 15: 4.
20a Alma 22: 1.
21a Mosiah 7: 7 (6–8); 21: 23 (22–24).

[About 30 B.C.]

great as their strength, even man for man. And thus had they fallen into this great transgression; yea, thus had they become [a]weak, because of their transgression, in the space of [b]not many years.

CHAPTER 5

Nephi and Lehi devote themselves to preaching—Their names invite them to pattern their lives after their forebears—Christ redeems those who repent—Nephi and Lehi make many converts and are imprisoned, and fire encircles them—A cloud of darkness overshadows three hundred people—The earth shakes and a voice commands men to repent—Nephi and Lehi converse with angels, and the multitude are encircled by fire.

AND it came to pass that in this *same year, behold, [a]Nephi [b]delivered up the judgment-seat to a man whose name was [c]Cezoram.

2 For as their laws and their governments were established by the [a]voice of the people, and they who [b]chose evil were [c]more numerous than they who chose good, therefore they were [d]ripening for destruction, for the laws had become corrupted.

3 Yea, and this was not all; they were a [a]stiffnecked people, insomuch that they could not be governed by the law nor justice, save it were to their destruction.

4 And it came to pass that Nephi had become weary because of their iniquity; and he yielded up the judgment-seat, and took it upon him to preach the word of God all the remainder of his days, and his brother Lehi also, all the remainder of his days;

5 For they remembered the words which their [a]father Helaman spake unto them. And these are the words which he spake:

6 Behold, my sons, I desire that ye should remember to keep the commandments of God; and I would that ye should declare unto the people these words. Behold, I have given unto you the names of our first [a]parents who came out of the land of Jerusalem; and this I have done that when ye remember your names ye may remember them; and when ye remember them ye may remember their works; and when ye remember their works ye may know how that it is said, and also written, that they were [b]good.

7 Therefore, my sons, I would that ye should do that which is good, that it may be said of you, and also written, even as it has been said and written of them.

8 And now my sons, behold I have somewhat more to desire of you, which desire is, that ye may not do these things that ye may boast, but that ye may do these things to lay up for yourselves a [a]treasure in heaven, yea, which is eternal, and which fadeth not away; yea, that ye may have that [b]precious gift of eternal life, which we have reason to suppose hath been given to our fathers.

9 O remember, remember, my sons, the [a]words which king Benjamin spake unto his people; yea, remember that there is no other way nor means whereby man can be saved, only through the [b]atoning blood of Jesus Christ, who shall come; yea, remember that he cometh to [c]redeem the [d]world.

26a Ezek. 19: 8 (6–9).
    TG Weak, Weaker.
  b Alma 46: 8; Hel.
    6: 32; 7: 6; 11: 26;
    12: 2.
5 1a Hel. 3: 37.
  b Alma 4: 20 (15–20).
  c Hel. 6: 15.
2a Mosiah 29: 25 (25–27);
    Hel. 1: 5 (3–5, 13).
  b Alma 10: 19.

  c 4 Ne. 1: 40.
  d Hel. 6: 40; 10: 11;
    D&C 18: 6; 61: 31.
3a TG Stiffneckedness.
5a Hel. 3: 21 (21, 37).
6a 1 Ne. 1: 4 (1, 4).
  b 2 Ne. 4: 12; 33: 3
    (1–15); Jacob 1: 10
    (9–12).
8a Hel. 8: 25; 3 Ne.
    13: 20 (19–21).

  TG Treasure.
  b 1 Ne. 15: 36.
9a Mosiah 2: 9.
  b Mosiah 3: 18; 4: 2.
    TG Jesus Christ,
    Atonement through.
  c TG Jesus Christ,
    Redeemer.
  d TG World.

CHAPTER 6

The righteous Lamanites preach to the wicked Nephites—Both peoples prosper during an era of peace and plenty—Lucifer, the author of sin, guides the Gadianton robbers in their murders and wickedness—They take over the Nephite government.

AND it came to pass that when the sixty and second year of the reign of the judges *had ended, all these things had happened and the Lamanites had become, the more part of them, a righteous people, insomuch that their ªrighteousness did exceed that of the Nephites, because of their firmness and their steadiness in the faith.

2 For behold, there were many of the Nephites who had become ªhardened and impenitent and grossly wicked, insomuch that they did reject the word of God and all the preaching and prophesying which did come among them.

3 Nevertheless, the people of the church did have great joy because of the conversion of the Lamanites, yea, because of the church of God, which had been established among them. And they did ªfellowship one with another, and did rejoice one with another, and did have great joy.

4 And it came to pass that many of the Lamanites did come down into the land of Zarahemla, and did declare unto the people of the Nephites the manner of their ªconversion, and did exhort them to faith and repentance.

5 Yea, and many did ªpreach with exceedingly great power and authority, unto the bringing down many of them into the depths of humility, to be the humble followers of God and the Lamb.

6 And it came to pass that many of the Lamanites did go into the land northward; and also ªNephi and ᵇLehi went into the ᶜland northward, to preach unto the people. And thus ended the sixty and third year.

7 And behold, there was peace in all the land, insomuch that the Nephites did go into whatsoever part of the land they would, whether among the Nephites or the Lamanites.

8 And it came to pass that the Lamanites did also go whithersoever they would, whether it were among the Lamanites or among the Nephites; and thus they did have free intercourse one with another, to ªbuy and to sell, and to get gain, according to their desire.

9 And it came to pass that they became exceedingly rich, both the Lamanites and the Nephites; and they did have an exceeding plenty of ªgold, and of silver, and of all manner of precious metals, both in the land south and in the land north.

10 Now the land south was called ªLehi, and the land north was called ᵇMulek, which was after the ᶜson of Zedekiah; for the Lord did bring Mulek into the land north, and Lehi into the land south.

11 And behold, there was all manner of gold in both these lands, and of silver, and of precious ore of every kind; and there were also curious workmen, who did ªwork all kinds of ore and did refine it; and thus they did become rich.

12 They did raise grain in abundance, both in the north and in the south; and they did flourish exceedingly, both in the north and in the

6 1a Hel. 13 : 1.
  2a Rom. 1 : 28 (28–32);
    Hel. 6 : 21.
    TG Hardheartedness.
  3a TG Fellowshipping.
  4a TG Conversion,
    Convert.
  5a 1 Ne. 15 : 20;
    Alma 48 : 20.
  6a Hel. 7 : 1.

    b Hel. 5 : 44 (36–44);
      11 : 19.
    c Alma 63 : 9 (4–9);
      Hel. 3 : 12 (11–12).
  8a 3 Ne. 6 : 11.
  9a 1 Ne. 18 : 25; 2 Ne.
      5 : 15 (14–16);
      Jacob 2 : 12 (12–13);
      Ether 9 : 17; 10 : 23
      (12, 23).

  10a Alma 50 : 25.
    b Omni 1 : 14; Mosiah
      25 : 2 (2–4);
      Hel. 8 : 21.
    c Jer. 39 : 6; 52 : 10;
      Ezek. 17 : 22 (22–23);
      Alma 22 : 31.
  11a TG Industry.

south. And they did multiply and wax exceedingly strong in the land. And they did raise many flocks and herds, yea, many fatlings.

13 Behold their women did toil and spin, and did *a*make all manner of *b*cloth, of fine-twined linen and cloth of every kind, to clothe their nakedness. And thus the sixty and fourth year did pass away in peace.

14 And in the *sixty and fifth year they did also have great joy and peace, yea, much preaching and many prophecies concerning that which was to come. And thus passed away the sixty and fifth year.

15 And it came to pass that in the †sixty and sixth year of the reign of the judges, behold, *a*Cezoram was murdered by an unknown hand as he sat upon the judgment-seat. And it came to pass that in the same year, that his son, who had been appointed by the people in his stead, was also murdered. And thus ended the sixty and sixth year.

16 And in the ‡commencement of the sixty and seventh year the people began to grow exceedingly wicked again.

17 For behold, the Lord had blessed them so long with the *a*riches of the world that they had not been stirred up to anger, to wars, nor to bloodshed; therefore they began to set their hearts upon their riches; yea, they began to seek to get gain that they might be lifted up one above another; therefore they began to commit *b*secret murders, and to rob and to plunder, that they might get gain.

18 And now behold, those murderers and plunderers were a band who had been formed by Kishkumen and *a*Gadianton. And now it had come to pass that there were many, even among the Nephites, of Gadianton's band. But behold, they were more numerous among the more wicked part of the Lamanites. And they were called Gadianton's robbers and murderers.

19 And it was they who did murder the chief judge *a*Cezoram, and his son, while in the judgment-seat; and behold, they were not found.

20 And now it came to pass that when the Lamanites found that there were robbers among them they were exceedingly sorrowful; and they did use every means in their power to destroy them off the face of the earth.

21 But behold, Satan did stir up the *a*hearts of the more part of the Nephites, insomuch that they did unite with those bands of robbers, and did enter into their covenants and their oaths, that they would protect and preserve one another in whatsoever difficult circumstances they should be placed, that they should not suffer for their murders, and their plunderings, and their *b*stealings.

22 And it came to pass that they did have their signs, yea, their *a*secret signs, and their *b*secret words; and this that they might distinguish a brother who had entered into the covenant, that whatsoever wickedness his brother should do he should not be injured by his brother, nor by those who did belong to his band, who had taken this covenant.

23 And thus they might murder, and plunder, and steal, and commit *a*whoredoms and all manner of wickedness, contrary to the laws of their country and also the laws of their God.

24 And whosoever of those who belonged to their band should reveal unto the world of their *a*wickedness and their abominations, should be

---

13a TG Art.
  b Mosiah 10:5;
    Alma 1:29.
15a Hel. 5:1; 6:19.
17a TG Treasure.
  b 3 Ne. 6:23; 9:9.

18a Hel. 2:4 (4, 12–13, 23).
19a Hel. 6:15.
21a Hel. 6:2.
  b TG Stealing.
22a Alma 37:27.
    TG Secret

Combinations.
  b Hel. 11:2; 3 Ne. 3:7.
23a TG Whoredom.
24a TG Wickedness.

[*27 B.C. †26 B.C. ‡25 B.C.]

tried, not according to the laws of their country, but according to the laws of their wickedness, which had been given by Gadianton and Kishkumen.

25 Now behold, it is these secret ªoaths and covenants which Alma commanded his son should not go forth unto the world, lest they should be a means of bringing down the people unto destruction.

26 Now behold, those ªsecret oaths and covenants did not come forth unto Gadianton from the ᵇrecords which were delivered unto Helaman; but behold, they were put into the heart of ᶜGadianton by that ᵈsame being who did entice our first parents to partake of the forbidden fruit—

27 Yea, that same being who did plot with ªCain, that if he would murder his brother Abel it should not be known unto the world. And he did plot with Cain and his followers from that time forth.

28 And also it is that same being who put it into the hearts of the people to ªbuild a tower sufficiently high that they might get to heaven. And it was that same being who led on the people who came from that tower into this land; who spread the works of darkness and abominations over all the face of the land, until he dragged the people down to an ᵇentire destruction, and to an everlasting hell.

29 Yea, it is that same being who put it into the heart of ªGadianton to still carry on the work of darkness, and of secret murder; and he has brought it forth from the beginning of man even down to this time.

30 And behold, it is he who is the ªauthor of all sin. And behold, he doth carry on his works of darkness and secret murder, and doth hand down their plots, and their oaths, and their covenants, and their plans of awful wickedness, from generation to generation according as he can get hold upon the hearts of the children of men.

31 And now behold, he had got great hold upon the hearts of the Nephites; yea, insomuch that they had become exceedingly wicked; yea, the more part of them had turned out of the ªway of righteousness, and did ᵇtrample under their feet the commandments of God, and did turn unto their own ways, and did build up unto themselves ᶜidols of their gold and their silver.

32 And it came to pass that all these iniquities did come unto them in the space of ªnot many years, insomuch that a more part of it had come unto them in the sixty and seventh year of the reign of the judges over the people of Nephi.

33 And they did grow in their iniquities in the *sixty and eighth year also, to the great sorrow and lamentation of the righteous.

34 And thus we see that the ªNephites did begin to dwindle in unbelief, and grow in wickedness and abominations, while the Lamanites began to grow exceedingly in the knowledge of their God; yea, they did begin to keep his statutes and commandments, and to walk in truth and uprightness before him.

35 And thus we see that the Spirit of the Lord began to ªwithdraw from the Nephites, because of the wickedness and the hardness of their hearts.

36 And thus we see that the Lord began to pour out his ªSpirit upon the Lamanites, because of their easi-

---

25a Alma 37: 29 (27–32).
26a 3 Ne. 3: 9; Ether 8: 9
    (9–19); Moses 5: 29
    (29, 49–52).
  b 3 Ne. 6: 28.
  c Hel. 8: 28.
  d Moses 4: 6 (6–12).
27a Moses 5: 25 (18–33).
28a Gen. 11: 4 (1–4);

Ether 1: 3.
  b Ether 8: 21 (9, 15–25).
29a Hel. 2: 4 (4–13).
30a Alma 5: 40 (39–42);
    Moro. 7: 12 (12, 17);
    Moses 4: 4.
31a Gen. 6: 12; 2 Ne. 28: 11.
  b 1 Ne. 19: 7.
  c Judg. 2: 17;

2 Ne. 9: 37; Alma 7: 6.
32a Alma 46: 8; Hel.
    4: 26; 7: 6; 11: 26.
34a Moro. 9: 20.
35a Matt. 13: 15; Mosiah
    2: 36; D&C 121: 37.
36a TG God, Spirit of.

[*24 B.C.]

ness and ^bwillingness to believe in his words.

37 And it came to pass that the Lamanites did hunt the band of robbers of Gadianton; and they did preach the word of God among the more wicked part of them, insomuch that this band of robbers was utterly destroyed from among the Lamanites.

38 And it came to pass on the other hand, that the Nephites did build them up and support them, beginning at the more wicked part of them, until they had overspread all the land of the Nephites, and had seduced the more part of the righteous until they had come down to believe in their works and partake of their spoils, and to join with them in their secret murders and combinations.

39 And thus they did obtain the sole management of the government, insomuch that they did trample under their feet and smite and rend and turn their backs upon the ^apoor and the meek, and the humble followers of God.

40 And thus we see that they were in an awful state, and ^aripening for an everlasting destruction.

41 And it came to pass that thus ended the sixty and eighth year of the reign of the judges over the people of Nephi.

THE PROPHECY OF NEPHI, THE SON OF HELAMAN—*God threatens the people of Nephi that he will visit them in his anger, to their utter destruction except they repent of their wickedness. God smiteth the people of Nephi with pestilence; they repent and turn unto him. Samuel, a Lamanite, prophesies unto the Nephites. Comprising chapters 7 to 16 inclusive.*

CHAPTER 7

Nephi is rejected in the north and returns to Zarahemla—He prays upon his garden tower and then calls upon the people to repent or perish.

BEHOLD, now it came to pass in the *sixty and ninth year of the reign of the judges over the people of the Nephites, that Nephi, the son of Helaman, ^areturned to the land of Zarahemla from the land northward.

2 For he had been forth among the people who were in the land northward, and did preach the word of God unto them, and did prophesy many things unto them;

3 And they did ^areject all his words, insomuch that he could not stay among them, but returned again unto the land of his nativity.

4 And seeing the people in a state of such awful wickedness, and those Gadianton robbers filling the judgment-seats—having ^ausurped the power and authority of the land; laying aside the commandments of God, and not in the least aright before him; doing no justice unto the children of men;

5 Condemning the righteous because of their righteousness; letting the guilty and the wicked go ^aunpunished because of their ^bmoney; and moreover to be held in office at the head of government, to rule and do according to their wills, that they might get gain and glory of the ^cworld, and, moreover, that they might the more easily commit adultery, and steal, and kill, and do according to their own wills—

6 Now this great iniquity had come upon the Nephites, in the space of ^anot many years; and when Nephi saw it, his heart was swollen with sorrow within his breast; and he did exclaim in the agony of his soul:

36b Ex. 25: 2 (1–7).
39a Ps. 109: 16 (15–16);
  Ezek. 22: 7 (7–13);
  Amos 5: 12; Alma
  5: 55 (54–56);
  D&C 56: 16.
40a Hel. 5: 2; 11: 37;
  D&C 18: 6; 61: 31.

7 1a Hel. 6: 6.
3a TG Prophets,
  Rejection of.
4a TG Tyranny;
  Unrighteous
  Dominion.
5a Job 12: 6; 21: 7;

  Ps. 73: 12.
  b TG Bribery.
  c Matt. 13: 22;
  D&C 39: 9.
6a IE six years; see Hel.
  4: 26; 6: 6, 32; 11: 26.

[*23 B.C.]

7 Oh, that I could have had my days in the days when my father Nephi first came out of the land of Jerusalem, that I could have ^ajoyed with him in the promised land; then were his people easy to be entreated, ^bfirm to keep the commandments of God, and slow to be led to do iniquity; and they were quick to hearken unto the words of the Lord—

8 Yea, if my days could have been in those days, then would my soul have had joy in the righteousness of my brethren.

9 But behold, I am consigned that these are my days, and that my soul shall be filled with ^asorrow because of this the wickedness of my brethren.

10 And behold, now it came to pass that it was upon a tower, which was in the ^agarden of Nephi, which was by the highway which led to the chief market, which was in the city of Zarahemla; therefore, Nephi had bowed himself upon the tower which was in his garden, which tower was also near unto the garden gate by which led the highway.

11 And it came to pass that there were certain men passing by and saw Nephi as he was pouring out his soul unto God upon the ^atower; and they ran and told the people what they had seen, and the people came together in multitudes that they might know the cause of so great mourning for the wickedness of the people.

12 And now, when Nephi arose he beheld the multitudes of people who had gathered together.

13 And it came to pass that he opened his mouth and said unto them: Behold, ^awhy have ye gathered yourselves together? That I may tell you of your iniquities?

14 Yea, because I have got upon my tower that I might pour out my soul unto my God, because of the exceeding sorrow of my heart, which is because of your iniquities!

15 And because of my ^amourning and lamentation ye have gathered yourselves together, and do marvel; yea, and ye have great need to marvel; yea, ye ought to marvel because ye are given away that the devil has got so great hold upon your hearts.

16 Yea, how could you have given way to the enticing of him who is seeking to hurl away your souls down to ^aeverlasting misery and endless wo?

17 O repent ye, repent ye! ^aWhy will ye die? Turn ye, turn ye unto the Lord your God. Why has he forsaken you?

18 It is because you have hardened your hearts; yea, ye will not ^ahearken unto the voice of the ^bgood shepherd; yea, ye have ^cprovoked him to anger against you.

19 And behold, instead of ^agathering you, except ye will repent, behold, he shall scatter you forth that ye shall become meat for dogs and wild beasts.

20 O, how could you have ^aforgotten your God in the very day that he has delivered you?

21 But behold, it is to get ^again, to be ^bpraised of men, yea, and that ye might get gold and silver. And ye have set your hearts upon the ^criches and the vain things of this world, for the which ye do murder, and plunder, and steal, and bear ^dfalse witness against your neighbor, and do all manner of iniquity.

22 And for this cause ^awo shall come unto you except ye shall re-

7a 2 Ne. 5: 27 (26–28).
  b D&C 5: 22.
9a Jer. 9: 1 (1–3).
10a Hel. 9: 8.
11a Alma 50: 4.
13a Matt. 3: 7 (5–8).
15a TG Mourning.
16a Alma 26: 20.
17a Isa. 1: 5 (5–6); Ezek. 18: 23 (23, 32).

18a TG Disobedience.
  b Ezek. 34: 12; John 10: 14; Alma 5: 60 (38–60). TG Jesus Christ, Good Shepherd.
  c Num. 14: 11 (11–12); 1 Ne. 17: 30 (23–31); Jacob 1: 8; Alma 12: 37 (36–37).

19a 3 Ne. 10: 4 (4–7).
20a Isa. 17: 10 (4–11).
21a TG Selfishness.
  b TG Peer Influence.
  c TG Treasure.
  d Matt. 15: 19 (19–20). TG Slander.
22a Rev. 8: 13; D&C 5: 5.

[Between 23 and 20 B.C.]

pent. For if ye will not repent, behold, this [b]great city, and also all those great cities which are round about, which are in the land of our possession, shall be taken away that ye shall have no place in them; for behold, the Lord will not grant unto you [c]strength, as he has hitherto done, to withstand against your enemies.

23 For behold, thus saith the Lord: I will not show unto the wicked of my strength, to one more than the other, save it be unto those who repent of their sins, and hearken unto my words. Now therefore, I would that ye should behold, my brethren, that it shall be [a]better for the Lamanites than for you except ye shall repent.

24 For behold, they are more righteous than you, for they have not sinned against that great knowledge which ye have received; therefore the Lord will be merciful unto them; yea, he will [a]lengthen out their days and increase their seed, even when thou shalt be utterly [b]destroyed except thou shalt repent.

25 Yea, wo be unto you because of that great abomination which has come among you; and ye have united yourselves unto it, yea, to that [a]secret band which was established by Gadianton!

26 Yea, [a]wo shall come unto you because of that pride which ye have suffered to enter your hearts, which has lifted you up beyond that which is good because of your exceedingly great riches!

27 Yea, wo be unto you because of your wickedness and abominations!

28 And except ye repent ye shall perish; yea, even your lands shall be taken from you, and ye shall be destroyed from off the face of the earth.

29 Behold now, I do not say that these things shall be, of myself, because it is not of myself that I [a]know these things; but behold, I [b]know that these things are true because the Lord God has made them known unto me, therefore I testify that they shall be.

CHAPTER 8

Corrupt judges seek to incite the people against Nephi—Abraham, Moses, Zenos, Zenock, Ezias, Isaiah, Jeremiah, Lehi, and Nephi all testified of Christ—By inspiration Nephi announces the murder of the chief judge.

AND now it came to pass that when Nephi had said these words, behold, there were men who were judges, who also belonged to the secret band of Gadianton, and they were angry, and they cried out against him, saying unto the people: Why do ye not seize upon this man and bring him forth, that he may be condemned according to the crime which he has done?

2 Why seest thou this man, and hearest him revile against this people and against our law?

3 For behold, Nephi had spoken unto them concerning the corruptness of their law; yea, many things did Nephi speak which cannot be written; and nothing did he speak which was contrary to the commandments of God.

4 And those judges were angry with him because he [a]spake plainly unto them concerning their secret works of darkness; nevertheless, they durst not lay their own hands upon him, for they feared the people lest they should cry out against them.

5 Therefore they did cry unto the people, saying: Why do you suffer this man to revile against us? For behold he doth condemn all this

---

22b Hel. 8: 5.
  c Mosiah 7: 29.
23a Hel. 15: 14 (11–15).
24a Ex. 20: 12; 1 Ne.
     17: 55; Alma 9: 16;

D&C 5: 33.
  b Alma 9: 19; Hel.
     10: 14.
25a 2 Ne. 10: 15;
     Hel. 3: 23.

26a Isa. 5: 8 (8–25).
29a Hel. 8: 8.
  b Hel. 8: 12.
8 4a 1 Ne. 16: 2 (2–3).

[Between 23 and 20 B.C.]

people, even unto destruction; yea, and also that these our [a]great cities shall be taken from us, that we shall have no place in them.

6 And now we know that this is impossible, for behold, we are [a]powerful, and our cities great, therefore our enemies can have no power over us.

7 And it came to pass that thus they did [a]stir up the people to anger against Nephi, and raised contentions among them; for there were some who did cry out: [b]Let this man alone, for he is a good man, and those things which he saith will surely come to pass except we repent;

8 Yea, behold, all the judgments will come upon us which he has testified unto us; for we know that he has testified aright unto us concerning our iniquities. And behold they are many, and he [a]knoweth as well all things which shall befall us as he knoweth of our iniquities;

9 Yea, and behold, if he had not been a prophet he could not have [a]testified concerning those things.

10 And it came to pass that those people who sought to destroy Nephi were compelled because of their fear, that they did not lay their hands on him; therefore he began again to speak unto them, seeing that he had gained favor in the eyes of some, insomuch that the remainder of them did fear.

11 Therefore he was constrained to speak more unto them saying: Behold, my brethren, have ye not read that God gave power unto one man, even Moses, to smite upon the waters of the Red [a]Sea, and they parted hither and thither, insomuch that

the Israelites, who were our fathers, came through upon dry ground, and the waters closed upon the armies of the Egyptians and swallowed them up?

12 And now behold, if God gave unto this man such power, then why should ye dispute among yourselves, and say that he hath given unto me no power whereby I may [a]know concerning the judgments that shall come upon you except ye repent?

13 But, behold, ye not only deny my words, but ye also deny all the words which have been spoken by our fathers, and also the words which were spoken by this man, Moses, who had such great power given unto him, yea, the words which he hath spoken concerning the coming of the Messiah.

14 Yea, did he not bear record that the Son of God should come? And as he [a]lifted up the brazen serpent in the wilderness, even so shall he be lifted up who should come.

15 And as many as should look upon that serpent should [a]live, even so as many as should look upon the Son of God with faith, having a contrite spirit, might [b]live, even unto that life which is eternal.

16 And now behold, Moses did not only testify of these things, but also [a]all the holy prophets, from his days even to the days of Abraham.

17 Yea, and behold, [a]Abraham saw of his coming, and was filled with gladness and did rejoice.

18 Yea, and behold I say unto you, that Abraham not only knew of these things, but there were [a]many before the days of Abraham who were called by the [b]order of God;

5a Hel. 7: 22.
6a Moses 8: 21 (20–22).
7a TG Provoking.
  b Acts 5: 38 (37–40).
8a Hel. 7: 29. TG God,
  Foreknowledge of.
9a TG Testimony.
11a Ex. 14: 16; Josh.
  2: 10; Neh. 9: 11;
  1 Ne. 17: 26; Mosiah
  7: 19; D&C 8: 3;

Moses 1: 25.
12a Hel. 7: 29 (28–29).
14a Num. 21: 9 (6–9);
  2 Ne. 25: 20; Alma
  33: 19 (19–22).
  TG Jesus Christ,
  Types of, in
  Anticipation.
15a 1 Ne. 17: 41; Alma
  37: 46 (46–47); 3 Ne.
  15: 9.

  b John 11: 25.
16a Luke 24: 27; Rev.
  19: 10; Jacob 4: 4
  (4–5); 7: 11.
17a Gen. 22: 8 (8–14);
  John 8: 56 (53, 56).
18a Alma 13: 19; D&C
  84: 14 (6–16); 136: 37.
  b TG Priesthood.

[Between 23 and 20 B.C.]

yea, even after the order of his Son; and this that it should be shown unto the people, a great many thousand years before his coming, that even redemption should come unto them.

19 And now I would that ye should know, that even since the days of Abraham there have been many prophets that have testified these things; yea, behold, the prophet *Zenos did testify boldly; for the which he was slain.

20 And behold, also *Zenock, and also *Ezias, and also *Isaiah, and *Jeremiah, (Jeremiah being that same prophet who testified of the destruction of *Jerusalem) and now we know that Jerusalem was destroyed according to the words of Jeremiah. O then why not the Son of God come, according to his prophecy?

21 And now will you dispute that *Jerusalem was destroyed? Will ye say that the *sons of Zedekiah were not slain, all except it were *Mulek? Yea, and do ye not behold that the seed of Zedekiah are with us, and they were driven out of the land of Jerusalem? But behold, this is not all—

22 Our father Lehi was driven out of Jerusalem because he *testified of these things. Nephi also testified of these things, and also almost all of our fathers, even down to this time; yea, they have testified of the *coming of Christ, and have looked forward, and have rejoiced in his day which is to come.

23 And behold, he is God, and he is

*with them, and he did manifest himself unto them, that they were redeemed by him; and they gave unto him glory, because of that which is to come.

24 And now, seeing ye know these things and cannot deny them except ye shall lie, therefore in this ye have sinned, for ye have rejected all these things, notwithstanding so many *evidences which ye have received; yea, even ye have received *all things, both things in heaven, and all things which are in the earth, as a witness that they are true.

25 But behold, ye have rejected the truth, and *rebelled against your holy God; and even at this time, instead of laying up for yourselves *treasures in heaven, where nothing doth corrupt, and where nothing can come which is unclean, ye are heaping up for yourselves wrath against the day of *judgment.

26 Yea, even at this time ye are ripening, because of your murders and your *fornication and wickedness, for everlasting destruction; yea, and except ye repent it will come unto you soon.

27 Yea, behold it is now even at your doors; yea, go ye in unto the judgment-seat, and search; and behold, your judge is murdered, and he *lieth in his blood; and he hath been murdered *by his brother, who seeketh to sit in the judgment-seat.

28 And behold, they both belong to your secret band, whose *author is Gadianton and the evil one who seeketh to destroy the souls of men.

19a Alma 34: 7; Hel. 15:11.
20a 1 Ne. 19: 10; Alma 33: 15; 34: 7; 3 Ne. 10: 16 (15–16).
   b TG Scriptures, Lost.
   c Isa. 53: 2 (1–12).
   d 1 Ne. 5: 13; 7: 14.
   e Jer. 26: 18 (17–19); 1 Ne. 1: 4 (4–18); 2 Ne. 6: 8; 25: 6.
21a Omni 1: 15.

   b 2 Kgs. 25: 7; Jer. 39: 6; 52: 10.
   c Ezek. 17: 22 (22–23); Hel. 6: 10; Morm. 7: 2.
22a D&C 138: 49.
   b TG Jesus Christ, Prophecies about.
23a Alma 40: 11 (11–12).
24a 2 Kgs. 17: 13; 1 Ne. 10: 5.
   b Alma 30: 44; Moses 6: 63.

25a Ps. 5: 10; Mosiah 2: 37 (36–38); 3: 12.
   b Hel. 5: 8; 3 Ne. 13: 20 (19–21). TG Treasure.
   c Ps. 109: 7 (3–7); D&C 10: 23 (20–23); 121: 24 (23–25).
26a TG Fornication.
27a Hel. 9: 3, 15.
   b Hel. 9: 6 (6, 26–38).
28a Hel. 6: 26 (26–30).

[Between 23 and 20 B.C.]

CHAPTER 9

Messengers find the chief judge dead at the judgment seat—They are imprisoned and later released—By inspiration Nephi identifies Seantum as the murderer—Nephi is accepted by some as a prophet.

BEHOLD, now it came to pass that when Nephi had spoken these words, certain men who were among them ran to the judgment-seat; yea, even there were ªfive who went, and they said among themselves, as they went:

2 Behold, now we will know of a surety whether this man be a prophet and God hath commanded him to prophesy such marvelous things unto us. Behold, we do not ªbelieve that he hath; yea, we do not believe that he is a prophet; nevertheless, if this thing which he has said concerning the chief judge be true, that he be dead, then will we believe that the other words which he has spoken are true.

3 And it came to pass that they ran in their might, and came in unto the judgment-seat; and behold, the chief judge had fallen to the earth, and did ªlie in his blood.

4 And now behold, when they saw this they were astonished exceedingly, insomuch that they fell to the earth; for they had not believed the words which Nephi had spoken concerning the chief judge.

5 But now, when they saw they believed, and fear came upon them lest all the judgments which Nephi had spoken ªshould come upon the people; therefore they did quake, and had fallen to the earth.

6 Now, immediately when the judge had been murdered—he being stabbed by his brother by a garb of secrecy, and he fled, and the servants ran and told the people, raising the cry of murder among them;

7 And behold the people did gather themselves together unto the place of the judgment-seat—and behold, to their astonishment they saw those ªfive men who had fallen to the earth.

8 And now behold, the people knew nothing concerning the multitude who had gathered together at the ªgarden of Nephi; therefore they said among themselves: These men are they who have murdered the judge, and God has smitten them that they could not flee from us.

9 And it came to pass that they laid hold on them, and bound them and cast them into prison. And there was a proclamation sent abroad that the judge was slain, and that the murderers had been taken and were cast into prison.

10 And it came to pass that on the morrow the people did assemble themselves together to ªmourn and to ᵇfast, at the burial of the great chief judge who had been slain.

11 And thus also those judges who were at the garden of Nephi, and heard his words, were also gathered together at the burial.

12 And it came to pass that they inquired among the people, saying: Where are the five who were sent to inquire concerning the chief judge whether he was dead? And they answered and said: Concerning this five whom ye say ye have sent, we know not; but there are five who are the murderers, whom we have cast into prison.

13 And it came to pass that the judges desired that they should be brought; and they were brought, and behold they were the five who were sent; and behold the judges inquired of them to know concerning the matter, and they told them all that they had done, saying:

14 We ran and came to the place of the judgment-seat, and when we saw all things even as Nephi had testified, we were astonished inso-

9 1a Hel. 9: 7 (7, 12).
2a Dan. 2: 9.
3a Hel. 8: 27.

5a 2 Kgs. 22: 13 (8–20).
7a Hel. 9: 1.
8a Hel. 7: 10 (10–11, 14).

10a TG Mourning.
  b TG Fasting.

[Between 23 and 20 B.C.]

much that we fell to the earth; and when we were recovered from our astonishment, behold they cast us into [a]prison.

15 Now, as for the murder of this man, we know not who has done it; and only this much we know, we ran and came [a]according as ye desired, and behold he was dead, according to the words of Nephi.

16 And now it came to pass that the judges did expound the matter unto the people, and did cry out against Nephi, saying: Behold, we know that this Nephi must have agreed with some one to slay the judge, and then he might declare it unto us, that he might convert us unto his faith, that he might raise himself to be a great man, chosen of God, and a prophet.

17 And now behold, we will detect this man, and he shall confess his fault and make known unto us the true murderer of this judge.

18 And it came to pass that the five were liberated on the day of the burial. Nevertheless, they did rebuke the judges in the words which they had spoken against Nephi, and did contend with them one by one, insomuch that they did confound them.

19 Nevertheless, they caused that Nephi should be taken and bound and brought before the multitude, and they began to question him in divers ways that they might cross him, that they might accuse him to death—

20 Saying unto him: Thou art confederate; who is this man that hath done this murder? Now tell us, and acknowledge thy fault; saying, Behold here is [a]money; and also we will grant unto thee thy life if thou wilt tell us, and acknowledge the agreement which thou hast made with him.

21 But Nephi said unto them:

O ye [a]fools, ye uncircumcised of heart, ye blind, and ye [b]stiffnecked people, do ye know how long the Lord your God will suffer you that ye shall go on in this your way of sin?

22 O ye ought to begin to howl and [a]mourn, because of the great destruction which at this time doth await you, except ye shall repent.

23 Behold ye say that I have agreed with a man that he should murder Seezoram, our chief judge. But behold, I say unto you, that this is because I have testified unto you that ye might know concerning this thing; yea, even for a witness unto you, that I did know of the wickedness and abominations which are among you.

24 And because I have done this, ye say that I have agreed with a man that he should do this thing; yea, because I showed unto you this sign ye are angry with me, and seek to destroy my life.

25 And now behold, I will show unto you another sign, and see if ye will in this thing seek to destroy me.

26 Behold I say unto you: Go to the house of Seantum, who is the [a]brother of Seezoram, and say unto him—

27 Has Nephi, the pretended prophet, who doth prophesy so much evil concerning this people, agreed with thee, in the which ye have murdered Seezoram, who is your brother?

28 And behold, he shall say unto you, Nay.

29 And ye shall say unto him: Have ye murdered your brother?

30 And he shall stand with fear, and wist not what to say. And behold, he shall deny unto you; and he shall make as if he were astonished; nevertheless, he shall declare unto you that he is innocent.

31 But behold, ye shall examine

14a Gen. 39: 20.
15a Hel. 8: 27.
20a 1 Sam. 8: 3 (1–4);
    Ether 9: 11.
  TG Bribery.
21a Ps. 75: 4; Luke
    24: 25; Acts 7: 51.
  b TG Stiffneckedness.
22a Ezek. 24: 23;
    Mosiah 7: 24.
26a Hel. 8: 27.

[Between 23 and 20 B.C.]

him, and ye shall find blood upon the skirts of his cloak.

32 And when ye have seen this, ye shall say: From whence cometh this blood? Do we not know that it is the blood of your brother?

33 And then shall he tremble, and shall look pale, even as if death had come upon him.

34 And then shall ye say: Because of this fear and this paleness which has come upon your face, behold, we know that thou art guilty.

35 And then shall greater fear come upon him; and then shall he confess unto you, and deny no more that he has done this murder.

36 And then shall he say unto you, that I, Nephi, know nothing concerning the matter save it were given unto me by the power of God. And then shall ye know that I am an honest man, and that I am sent unto you from God.

37 And it came to pass that they went and did, even according as Nephi had said unto them. And behold, the words which he had said were true; for according to the words he did deny; and also according to the words he did confess.

38 And he was brought to prove that he himself was the very murderer, insomuch that the five were set at liberty, and also was Nephi.

39 And there were some of the Nephites who believed on the words of Nephi; and there were some also, who believed because of the testimony of the five, for they had been converted while they were in prison.

40 And now there were some among the people, who said that Nephi was a prophet.

41 And there were others who said: Behold, he is a god, for except he was a god he could not *a*know of all things. For behold, he has told us

the thoughts of our hearts, and also has told us things; and even he has brought unto our knowledge the true murderer of our chief judge.

CHAPTER 10

The Lord gives Nephi the sealing power—He is empowered to bind and loose on earth and in heaven—He commands the people to repent or perish—The Spirit carries him from congregation to congregation.

AND it came to pass that there arose a division among the people, insomuch that they divided hither and thither and went their ways, leaving Nephi alone, as he was standing in the midst of them.

2 And it came to pass that Nephi went his way towards his own house, *a*pondering upon the things which the Lord had shown unto him.

3 And it came to pass as he was thus pondering—being much cast down because of the wickedness of the people of the Nephites, their secret works of darkness, and their murderings, and their plunderings, and all manner of iniquities—and it came to pass as he was thus pondering in his heart, behold, a *a*voice came unto him saying:

4 *a*Blessed art thou, Nephi, for those things which thou hast done; for I have beheld how thou hast with *b*unwearyingness declared the word, which I have given unto thee, unto this people. And thou hast not feared them, and hast not sought thine *c*own life, but hast sought my *d*will, and to keep my commandments.

5 And now, because thou hast done this with such unwearyingness, behold, I will bless thee forever; and I will make thee mighty in word and in deed, in faith and in works; yea, even that *a*all things shall be *b*done

---

41a TG God, Omniscience of.
10 2a TG Meditation.
  3a TG Guidance, Divine.
  4a Acts 23:11.
    b Acts 20:31.
    TG Dedication;

Dependability;
Priesthood,
Magnifying Callings
within; Steadfastness.
c TG Self-sacrifice.
d Mosiah 24:15;

3 Ne. 11:11.
5a 3 Ne. 18:20;
   D&C 88:64 (63–65).
  b Ex. 33:17.

unto thee according to thy ᶜword, for thou shalt ᵈnot ask that which is contrary to my will.

6 Behold, thou art Nephi, and I am God. Behold, I declare it unto thee in the presence of mine angels, that ye shall have power over this people, and shall smite the earth with ᵃfamine, and with pestilence, and destruction, according to the wickedness of this people.

7 Behold, I give unto you ᵃpower, that whatsoever ye shall ᵇseal on earth shall be sealed in heaven; and whatsoever ye shall loose on earth shall be loosed in heaven; and thus shall ye have power among this people.

8 And thus, if ye shall say unto this temple it shall be rent in twain, it shall be done.

9 And if ye shall say unto this ᵃmountain, Be thou cast down and become smooth, it shall be done.

10 And behold, if ye shall say that God shall smite this people, it shall come to pass.

11 And now behold, I command you, that ye shall go and declare unto this people, that thus saith the Lord God, who is the Almighty: Except ye repent ye shall be smitten, even unto ᵃdestruction.

12 And behold, now it came to pass that when the Lord had spoken these words unto Nephi, he did stop and did not go unto his own house, but did return unto the multitudes who were scattered about upon the face of the land, and began to declare unto them the word of the Lord which had been spoken unto him, concerning their destruction if they did not repent.

13 Now behold, ᵃnotwithstanding that great miracle which Nephi had done in telling them concerning the death of the chief judge, they did harden their hearts and did not hearken unto the words of the Lord.

14 Therefore Nephi did declare unto them the word of the Lord, saying: Except ye repent, thus saith the Lord, ye shall be ᵃsmitten even unto destruction.

15 And it came to pass that when Nephi had declared unto them the word, behold, they did still harden their hearts and would not hearken unto his words; therefore they did ᵃrevile against him, and did seek to lay their hands upon him that they might cast him into prison.

16 But behold, the power of God was with him, and they could not take him to cast him into prison, for he was taken by the Spirit and ᵃconveyed away out of the midst of them.

17 And it came to pass that thus he did go forth in the Spirit, from multitude to multitude, declaring the word of God, even until he had declared it unto them all, or sent it forth among all the people.

18 And it came to pass that they would not hearken unto his words; and there began to be contentions, insomuch that they were divided against themselves and began to slay one another with the sword.

19 And thus ended the seventy and first year of the reign of the judges over the people of Nephi.

CHAPTER 11

Nephi persuades the Lord to replace their war with a famine—Many people perish—They repent, and Nephi importunes the Lord for rain—Nephi and Lehi receive many revelations—The Gadianton robbers entrench themselves in the land.

5c 1 Kgs. 17: 1; Enos 1: 12.
    d James 4: 3 (1–3); 2 Ne. 4: 35; D&C 46: 30.
6a Hel. 11: 4 (4–18). TG Drought.
7a Hel. 11: 18.
    b Matt. 16: 19. TG Priesthood, Authority.
9a Matt. 17: 20; Jacob 4: 6; Morm. 8: 24; Ether 12: 30.
11a Hel. 5: 2; 11: 8.
13a Mark 6: 6 (4–6).
14a Hel. 7: 24.
15a TG Reviling.
16a Acts 8: 39 (39–40).

[Between 23 and 20 B.C.]

AND now it came to pass in the *seventy and second year of the reign of the judges that the contentions did increase, insomuch that there were wars throughout all the land among all the people of Nephi.

2 And it was this ^asecret band of robbers who did carry on this work of destruction and wickedness. And this war did last all that year; and in the †seventy and third year it did also last.

3 And it came to pass that in this year Nephi did cry unto the Lord, saying:

4 O Lord, do not suffer that this people shall be destroyed by the sword; but O Lord, rather ^alet there be a ^bfamine in the land, to stir them up in remembrance of the Lord their God, and perhaps they will repent and turn unto thee.

5 And so it was done, according to the words of Nephi. And there was a great famine upon the land, among all the people of Nephi. And thus in the ‡seventy and fourth year the famine did continue, and the work of destruction did cease by the sword but became sore by famine.

6 And this work of destruction did also continue in the §seventy and fifth year. For the earth was smitten that it was ^adry, and did not yield forth grain in the season of grain; and the whole earth was smitten, even among the Lamanites as well as among the Nephites, so that they were smitten that they did perish by thousands in the more wicked parts of the land.

7 And it came to pass that the people saw that they were about to perish by famine, and they began to ^aremember the Lord their God; and they began to remember the words of Nephi.

8 And the people ^abegan to plead with their chief judges and their leaders, that they would say unto Nephi: Behold, we know that thou art a man of God, and therefore cry unto the Lord our God that he turn away from us this famine, lest all the words which thou hast spoken concerning our ^bdestruction be fulfilled.

9 And it came to pass that the judges did say unto Nephi, according to the words which had been desired. And it came to pass that when Nephi saw that the people had ^arepented and did humble themselves in sackcloth, he cried again unto the Lord, saying:

10 O Lord, behold this people repenteth; and they have swept away the band of Gadianton from amongst them insomuch that they have become extinct, and they have concealed their secret plans in the earth.

11 Now, O Lord, because of this their humility wilt thou turn away thine anger, and let thine anger be appeased in the destruction of those wicked men whom thou hast already destroyed.

12 O Lord, wilt thou turn away thine anger, yea, thy fierce anger, and cause that this famine may cease in this land.

13 O Lord, wilt thou hearken unto me, and cause that it may be done according to my words, and send forth ^arain upon the face of the earth, that she may bring forth her fruit, and her grain in the season of grain.

14 O Lord, thou didst hearken unto ^amy words when I said, Let there be a famine, that the pestilence of the sword might cease; and I know that thou wilt, even at this time, hearken unto my words, for thou saidst that: If this people repent I will spare them.

15 Yea, O Lord, and thou seest that they have repented, because of the famine and the pestilence and

---

11 2a Hel. 6: 22 (18–24);
   11: 26 (25–26).
  4a Hel. 11: 14.
    b 1 Kgs. 8: 35; 1 Chr.
    21: 12; Hel. 10: 6.
    TG Famine.

6a TG Drought.
7a Amos 4: 7 (6–10);
   Hel. 12: 3.
8a Ex. 10: 7.
  b Hel. 10: 11 (11–14).
9a Morm. 2: 12.

13a 1 Kgs. 18: 41 (1,
   41–46).
14a Hel. 11: 4.

[*20 B.C. †19 B.C. ‡18 B.C.
              §17 B.C.]

destruction which has come unto them.

16 And now, O Lord, wilt thou turn away thine anger, and try again if they will serve thee? And if so, O Lord, thou canst bless them according to thy words which thou hast said.

17 And it came to pass that in the *seventy and sixth year the Lord did turn away his anger from the people, and caused that ^arain should fall upon the earth, insomuch that it did bring forth her fruit in the season of her fruit. And it came to pass that it did bring forth her grain in the season of her grain.

18 And behold, the people did rejoice and glorify God, and the whole face of the land was filled with rejoicing; and they did no more seek to destroy Nephi, but they did esteem him as a ^agreat prophet, and a man of God, having great power and authority given unto him from God.

19 And behold, Lehi, his brother, was not a ^awhit behind him as to things pertaining to righteousness.

20 And thus it did come to pass that the people of Nephi began to prosper again in the land, and began to build up their waste places, and began to multiply and spread, even until they did ^acover the whole face of the land, both on the northward and on the southward, from the sea west to the sea east.

21 And it came to pass that the seventy and sixth year did end in peace. And the seventy and seventh year began in peace; and the ^achurch did spread throughout the face of all the land; and the more part of the people, both the Nephites and the Lamanites, did belong to the church; and they did have exceedingly great peace in the land; and thus ended the seventy and seventh year.

22 And also they had peace in the seventy and eighth year, save it were a few contentions concerning the points of doctrine which had been laid down by the prophets.

23 And in the †seventy and ninth year there began to be much strife. But it came to pass that Nephi and Lehi, and many of their brethren who knew concerning the true points of doctrine, having many ^arevelations daily, therefore they did preach unto the people, insomuch that they did put an end to their strife in that same year.

24 And it came to pass that in the ‡eightieth year of the reign of the judges over the people of Nephi, there were a certain number of the dissenters from the people of Nephi, who had some years before gone over unto the Lamanites, and taken upon themselves the name of Lamanites, and also a certain number who were real descendants of the Lamanites, being stirred up to anger by them, or by those dissenters, therefore they commenced a ^dwar with their brethren.

25 And they did commit murder and plunder; and then they would retreat back into the mountains, and into the wilderness and secret places, hiding themselves that they could not be discovered, receiving daily an addition to their numbers, inasmuch as there were dissenters that went forth unto them.

26 And thus in time, yea, even in the space of ^anot many years, they became an exceedingly great band of robbers; and they did search out all the ^bsecret plans of Gadianton; and thus they became robbers of Gadianton.

27 Now behold, these robbers did make great havoc, yea, even great destruction among the people of Nephi, and also among the people of the Lamanites.

17a Deut. 11:14 (13–17); Ether 2:24; D&C 117:1.
18a Hel. 10:7 (5–11).
19a Hel. 5:44 (36–44); 6:6.
20a Jarom 1:6; Alma 22:27 (27, 32–33); Hel. 3:8; 3 Ne. 1:17.
21a TG Church; Peace.
23a Jarom 1:4; Alma
26:22; D&C 107:19.
24a Hel. 4:3.
26a Hel. 4:26; 6:32; 7:6.
  b Hel. 11:2.

[*16 B.C. †13 B.C. ‡12 B.C.]

28 And it came to pass that it was expedient that there should be a stop put to this work of destruction; therefore they sent an army of strong men into the wilderness and upon the mountains to search out this band of robbers, and to destroy them.

29 But behold, it came to pass that in that same year they were driven back even into their own lands. And thus ended the eightieth year of the reign of the judges over the people of Nephi.

30 And it came to pass in the *commencement of the eighty and first year they did go forth again against this band of robbers, and did destroy many; and they were also visited with much destruction.

31 And they were again obliged to return out of the wilderness and out of the ᵃmountains unto their own lands, because of the exceeding greatness of the numbers of those robbers who infested the mountains and the wilderness.

32 And it came to pass that thus ended this year. And the robbers did still increase and wax strong, insomuch that they did defy the whole armies of the Nephites, and also of the Lamanites; and they did cause great fear to come unto the people upon all the face of the land.

33 Yea, for they did visit many parts of the land, and did do great destruction unto them; yea, did kill many, and did carry away others captive into the wilderness, yea, and more especially their women and their children.

34 Now this great evil, which came unto the people because of their iniquity, did stir them up again in ᵃremembrance of the Lord their God.

35 And thus ended the eighty and first year of the reign of the judges.

36 And in the eighty and second year they began again to ᵃforget the Lord their God. And in the eighty and third year they began to wax strong in iniquity. And in the eighty and fourth year they did not mend their ways.

37 And it came to pass in the †eighty and fifth year they did wax stronger and stronger in their pride, and in their wickedness; and thus they were ᵃripening again for destruction.

38 And thus ended the eighty and fifth year.

CHAPTER 12

Men are unstable and foolish and quick to do evil—The Lord chastens his people—The nothingness of men compared with the power of God—In the day of judgment men shall gain everlasting life or everlasting damnation.

AND thus we can behold how false, and also the unsteadiness of the hearts of the children of men; yea, we can see that the Lord in his great infinite goodness doth bless and ᵃprosper those who put their ᵇtrust in him.

2 Yea, and we may see at the very ᵃtime when he doth ᵇprosper his people, yea, in the increase of their fields, their flocks and their herds, and in gold, and in silver, and in all manner of ᶜprecious things of every kind and art; sparing their lives, and delivering them out of the hands of their enemies; softening the hearts of their enemies that they should not declare wars against them; yea, and in fine, doing all things for the welfare and happiness of his people; yea, then is the time that they do ᵈharden their hearts, and do ᵉforget the Lord their God, and do ᶠtrample under their feet the

---

31a 3 Ne. 1:27.
34a Hosea 5:15.
36a Mosiah 13:29.
37a Hel. 6:40.
12 1a 2 Chr. 26:5;
    Ps. 1:3 (2–3).
  b Ps. 36:7 (7–8); 2 Ne.

22:2; Mosiah 4:6.
  TG Trust in God.
2a Alma 46:8; Hel. 4:26;
  6:32.
  b Ps. 62:10.
  c TG Treasure.

d TG Apostasy of
  Individuals.
e Deut. 8:11 (10–20).
f Alma 5:53; 3 Ne.
  28:35. TG Sacrilege.

[*11 B.C. †7 B.C.]

Holy One—yea, and this because of their ease, and their exceedingly great prosperity.

3 And thus we see that except the Lord doth *a*chasten his people with many afflictions, yea, except he doth visit them with *b*death and with terror, and with famine and with all manner of pestilence, they will not *c*remember him.

4 O how *a*foolish, and how vain, and how evil, and devilish, and how *b*quick to do iniquity, and how slow to do good, are the children of men; yea, how quick to hearken unto the words of the evil one, and to set their *c*hearts upon the vain things of the world!

5 Yea, how quick to be lifted up in *a*pride; yea, how quick to *b*boast, and do all manner of that which is iniquity; and how slow are they to remember the Lord their God, and to give ear unto his counsels, yea, how slow to *c*walk in wisdom's paths!

6 Behold, they do not desire that the Lord their God, who hath *a*created them, should *b*rule and reign over them; notwithstanding his great goodness and his mercy towards them, they do set at *c*naught his counsels, and they will not that he should be their guide.

7 O how great is the *a*nothingness of the children of men; yea, even they are *b*less than the dust of the earth.

8 For behold, the dust of the earth moveth hither and thither, to the dividing asunder, at the command of our great and everlasting God.

9 Yea, behold at his *a*voice do the hills and the mountains tremble and *b*quake.

10 And by the *a*power of his voice they are broken up, and become smooth, yea, even like unto a valley.

11 Yea, by the power of his voice doth the *a*whole earth shake;

12 Yea, by the power of his voice, do the foundations rock, even to the very center.

13 Yea, and if he say unto the earth—Move—it is moved.

14 Yea, if he say unto the *a*earth—Thou shalt *b*go back, that it *c*lengthen out the day for many hours—it is done;

15 And thus, according to his word the *a*earth goeth back, and it appeareth unto man that the *b*sun standeth still; yea, and behold, this is so; for surely it is the earth that moveth and not the sun.

16 And behold, also, if he say unto the *a*waters of the great deep—*b*Be thou dried up—it is done.

17 Behold, if he say unto this mountain—Be thou raised up, and *a*come over and fall upon that city, that it be buried up—behold it is done.

18 And behold, if a man *a*hide up a treasure in the earth, and the Lord shall say—Let it be *b*accursed, because of the iniquity of him who hath hid it up—behold, it shall be accursed.

19 And if the Lord shall say—Be thou accursed, that no man shall find thee from this time henceforth and forever—behold, no man getteth it henceforth and forever.

3*a* Deut. 11: 2 (1–8);
  Ezek. 20: 26; Mosiah
  23: 21; D&C 98: 21;
  101: 8.
 b Ps. 78: 34.
 c Amos 4: 6 (6–11);
  Jonah 2: 7;
  Mosiah 1: 17.
4*a* TG Foolishness.
 b Ex. 32: 8; Judg. 2: 17;
  Isa. 59: 7; Jer. 4: 22.
 c Gen. 6: 5; Matt.
  15: 19; Heb. 3: 12.
5*a* Prov. 29: 23.
 b TG Boasting.
 c TG Walking in

Darkness; Walking
  with God.
6*a* Isa. 45: 9 (9–10);
  D&C 58: 30.
 b Judg. 8: 23 (22–23);
  D&C 60: 4.
 c Jer. 8: 7.
7*a* Isa. 40: 17 (15, 17);
  Dan. 4: 35; Moses
  1: 10.
 b Gen. 18: 27.
9*a* Ezek. 1: 24.
 b Judg. 5: 5; 3 Ne.
  22: 10.
10*a* 1 Ne. 17: 46.
11*a* Morm. 5: 23;

Ether 4: 9.
14*a* Josh. 10: 12 (12–14).
  b Isa. 38: 8 (7–8).
  c 2 Kgs. 20: 9 (8–11).
15*a* Alma 30: 44.
  b Hab. 3: 11.
16*a* Matt. 8: 27 (23–27);
  Jacob 4: 9.
  b Isa. 44: 27; 51: 10.
17*a* 3 Ne. 8: 10 (10, 25);
  9: 8 (5–6, 8).
18*a* Hel. 13: 18 (18–23);
  Morm. 1: 18 (17–19).
  b Hel. 13: 17.

[About 7 B.C.]

20 And behold, if the Lord shall say unto a man—Because of thine iniquities, thou shalt be accursed ^aforever—it shall be done.

21 And if the Lord shall say—Because of thine iniquities thou shalt be ^acut off from my presence—he will cause that it shall be so.

22 And wo unto him to whom he shall say this, for it shall be unto him that will do iniquity, and he cannot be ^asaved; therefore, for this cause, that men might be saved, hath repentance been declared.

23 Therefore, blessed are they who will repent and hearken unto the voice of the Lord their God; for these are they that shall be saved.

24 And may God grant, in his great fulness, that men might be brought unto repentance and good works, that they might be restored unto grace for ^agrace, according to their works.

25 And I would that all men might be saved. But we read that in the ^agreat and last day there are some who shall be cast out, yea, who shall be cast off from the ^bpresence of the Lord;

26 Yea, who shall be consigned to a state of endless misery, fulfilling the words which say: They that have done good shall have ^aeverlasting life; and they that have done evil shall have everlasting ^bdamnation. And thus it is. Amen.

The prophecy of Samuel, the Lamanite, to the Nephites. Comprising chapters 13 to 15 inclusive.

CHAPTER 13

Samuel the Lamanite prophesies the destruction of the Nephites unless they repent—*They and their riches are cursed*—*They reject and stone the prophets, are encircled about by demons, and seek for happiness in doing iniquity.*

AND now it came to pass in the *eighty and sixth year, the Nephites did still remain in wickedness, yea, in great wickedness, while the ^aLamanites did observe strictly to keep the commandments of God, according to the law of Moses.

2 And it came to pass that in this year there was one ^aSamuel, a ^bLamanite, came into the land of Zarahemla, and began to preach unto the people. And it came to pass that he did preach, many days, repentance unto the people, and they did ^ccast him out, and he was about to ^dreturn to his own land.

3 But behold, the ^avoice of the Lord came unto him, that he should return again, and prophesy unto the people whatsoever things should come into his ^bheart.

4 And it came to pass that they would not suffer that he should enter into the city; therefore he went and got upon the ^awall thereof, and stretched forth his hand and cried with a loud voice, and ^bprophesied unto the people whatsoever things the Lord put into his heart.

5 And he said unto them: Behold, I, Samuel, a Lamanite, do speak the words of the Lord which he doth put into my heart; and behold he hath put it into my heart to say unto this people that the ^asword of justice hangeth over this people; and four hundred years pass not away save the sword of justice falleth upon this people.

6 Yea, heavy ^adestruction awaiteth

20a Mosiah 27: 31.
21a Jer. 23: 39 (39–40);
     D&C 63: 4.
22a TG Salvation.
24a TG Grace.
25a Mal. 4: 5; 3 Ne. 26: 4.
  b TG God, Presence of.
26a Dan. 12: 2 (2–3);
     D&C 19: 7.

  b TG Damnation.
13 1a Hel. 6: 1; 15: 5.
  2a Hel. 14: 1; 3 Ne.
     23: 9 (9–10).
  b Hel. 16: 7.
  c Hel. 14: 10.
  d Alma 26: 27.
  3a Gal. 2: 2; Alma 8: 16;
     20: 2; 3 Ne. 1: 12.

  b D&C 100: 5.
  4a Hel. 14: 11; 16: 1.
  b TG Teaching with the
     Spirit.
  5a Alma 60: 29; 3 Ne.
     2: 19.
  6a Alma 45: 11 (10–14);
     Hel. 15: 17.

this people, and it surely cometh unto this people, and nothing can save this people save it be repentance and faith on the Lord Jesus Christ, who surely shall come into the world, and shall suffer many things and shall be slain for his people.

7 And behold, an ^aangel of the Lord hath declared it unto me, and he did bring ^bglad tidings to my soul. And behold, I was sent unto you to declare it unto you also, that ye might have glad tidings; but behold ye would ^cnot receive me.

8 Therefore, thus saith the Lord: Because of the hardness of the hearts of the people of the Nephites, except they repent I will take away my word from them, and I will ^awithdraw my Spirit from them, and I will suffer them no longer, and I will turn the hearts of their brethren against them.

9 And ^afour hundred years shall not pass away before I will cause that they shall be smitten; yea, I will visit them with the sword and with famine and with pestilence.

10 Yea, I will visit them in my fierce anger, and there shall be those of the ^afourth generation who shall live, of your enemies, to behold your utter destruction; and this shall surely come except ye repent, saith the Lord; and those of the fourth generation shall visit your destruction.

11 But if ye will repent and ^areturn unto the Lord your God I will turn away mine anger, saith the Lord; yea, thus saith the Lord, blessed are they who will repent and turn unto me, but wo unto him that repenteth not.

12 Yea, ^awo unto this great city of Zarahemla; for behold, it is because of those who are righteous that it is saved; yea, wo unto this great city, for I perceive, saith the Lord, that there are many, yea, even the more part of this great city, that will harden their hearts against me, saith the Lord.

13 But blessed are they who will repent, for them will I spare. But behold, if it were not for the righteous who are in this great city, behold, I would cause that ^afire should come down out of heaven and ^bdestroy it.

14 But behold, it is for the righteous' sake that it is spared. But behold, the time cometh, saith the Lord, that when ye shall cast out the righteous from among you, then shall ye be ^aripe for destruction; yea, wo be unto this great city, because of the wickedness and abominations which are in her.

15 Yea, and wo be unto the city of Gideon, for the wickedness and abominations which are in her.

16 Yea, and wo be unto all the cities which are in the land round about, which are possessed by the Nephites, because of the wickedness and abominations which are in them.

17 And behold, a ^acurse shall come upon the land, saith the Lord of Hosts, because of the peoples' sake who are upon the land, yea, because of their wickedness and their abominations.

18 And it shall come to pass, saith the Lord of Hosts, yea, our great and true God, that whoso shall ^ahide up treasures in the earth shall find them again no more, because of the great curse of the land, save he be a righteous man and shall hide it up unto the Lord.

19 For I will, saith the Lord, that they shall hide up their ^atreasures

7a Alma 13: 26; Hel.
  14: 26 (9, 26, 28).
  b Isa. 52: 7.
  c TG Prophets, Rejection
    of.
8a Ex. 23: 21 (20–21).
9a Alma 45: 10.
10a 1 Ne. 12: 12; 2 Ne.
  26: 9; Alma 45: 12;
  3 Ne. 27: 32.
11a 1 Sam. 7: 3; 3 Ne.
  10: 6 (5–7).
12a 3 Ne. 8: 24 (8, 24);
  9: 3.
13a 2 Kgs. 1: 10 (9–16);
  3 Ne. 9: 11.
  b Gen. 18: 23; 1 Ne.
  22: 16; D&C 64: 24.
14a Gen. 15: 16; Alma
  37: 31; D&C 61: 31;
  101: 11.
17a Hel. 12: 18.
18a Morm. 1: 18 (17–19).
19a Prov. 13: 11.

[About 6 B.C.]

unto me; and cursed be they who hide not up their treasures unto me; for none hideth up their treasures unto me save it be the righteous; and he that hideth not up his treasures unto me, cursed is he, and also the treasure, and none shall redeem it because of the curse of the land.

20 And the day shall come that they shall hide up their treasures, because they have set their hearts upon riches; and because they have set their hearts upon their riches, and will hide up their treasures when they shall flee before their enemies; because they will not hide them up unto me, cursed be they and also their treasures; and in that day shall they be smitten, saith the Lord.

21 Behold ye, the people of this great city, and hearken unto my words; yea, hearken unto the words which the Lord saith; for behold, he saith that ye are ᵃcursed because of your riches, and also are your riches cursed because ye have set your hearts upon them, and have not ᵇhearkened unto the words of him who gave them unto you.

22 Ye do not remember the Lord your God in the things with which he hath blessed you, but ye do always remember your ᵃriches, not to thank the Lord your God for them; yea, your hearts are not drawn out unto the Lord, but they do swell with great pride, unto ᵇboasting, and unto great ᶜswelling, ᵈenvyings, strifes, malice, persecutions, and murders, and all manner of iniquities.

23 For this cause hath the Lord God caused that a curse should come upon the land, and also upon your riches, and this because of your iniquities.

24 Yea, wo unto this people, because of this time which has arrived, that ye do ᵃcast out the prophets, and do mock them, and cast stones at them, and do slay them, and do all manner of iniquity unto them, even as they did of old time.

25 And now when ye talk, ye say: If our days had been in the days of our ᵃfathers of old, we would not have ᵇslain the prophets; we would not have stoned them, and cast them out.

26 Behold ye are worse than they; for as the Lord liveth, if a ᵃprophet come among you and declareth unto you the word of the Lord, which testifieth of your ᵇsins and iniquities, ye are ᶜangry with him, and cast him out and seek all manner of ways to destroy him; yea, you will say that he is a ᵈfalse ᵉprophet, and that he is a sinner, and of the devil, because he ᶠtestifieth that your deeds are evil.

27 But behold, if a man shall come among you and shall say: Do this, and there is no iniquity; do that and ye shall not suffer; yea, he will say: ᵃWalk after the pride of your own hearts; yea, walk after the pride of your eyes, and do whatsoever your heart desireth—and if a man shall come among you and say this, ye will receive him, and say that he is a ᵇprophet.

28 Yea, ye will lift him up, and ye will give unto him of your substance; ye will give unto him of your gold, and of your silver, and ye will clothe him with costly apparel; and because he speaketh ᵃflattering words unto you, and he saith that all is

---

21a TG Curse.
  b TG Disobedience.
22a Luke 12:34.
  b TG Boasting.
  c Alma 30:31.
  d TG Envy.
24a 2 Chr. 36:16 (15–16);
    Neh. 9:26; Jer. 20:2;
    1 Ne. 1:20; Hel. 16:6.

25a Matt. 23:32; Acts
    7:51 (51–52).
  b TG Prophets, Rejection
    of.
26a 2 Chr. 18:7; Luke
    16:31 (19–31).
  b Micah 3:8.
  c Isa. 30:9 (9–10).
  d Mosiah 12:14.
  e Luke 11:15 (14–22);

Mosiah 3:9 (9–12).
  f Gal. 4:16.
27a TG Walking in
    Darkness.
  b Lam. 2:14; 4:13;
    Micah 2:11. TG False
    Prophets.
28a 2 Tim. 4:3 (3–4).

[About 6 B.C.]

well, then ye will not find fault with him.

29 O ye wicked and ye perverse generation; ye hardened and ye [a]stiffnecked people, how long will ye suppose that the Lord will suffer you? Yea, how long will ye suffer yourselves to be led by [b]foolish and [c]blind guides? Yea, how long will ye [d]choose darkness rather than [e]light?

30 Yea, behold, the anger of the Lord is already kindled against you; behold, he hath cursed the land because of your iniquity.

31 And behold, the time cometh that he curseth your riches, that they become [a]slippery, that ye cannot hold them; and in the days of your poverty ye cannot retain them.

32 And in the days of your poverty ye shall cry unto the Lord; and in vain shall ye cry, for your desolation is already come upon you, and your destruction is made sure; and then shall ye weep and howl in that day, saith the Lord of Hosts. And then shall ye lament, and say:

33 O [a]that I had repented, and had not killed the prophets, and [b]stoned them, and cast them out. Yea, in that day ye shall say: O that we had remembered the Lord our God in the day that he gave us our riches, and then they would not have become slippery that we should lose them; for behold, our riches are gone from us.

34 Behold, we lay a tool here and on the morrow it is gone; and behold, our swords are taken from us in the day we have sought them for battle.

35 Yea, we have hid up our [a]treasures and they have slipped away from us, because of the curse of the land.

36 O that we had repented in the day that the word of the Lord came unto us; for behold the land is cursed, and all things are become slippery, and we cannot hold them.

37 Behold, we are surrounded by [a]demons, yea, we are encircled about by the angels of him who hath sought to destroy our souls. Behold, our iniquities are great. O Lord, canst thou not turn away thine anger from us? And this shall be your language in those days.

38 But behold, your [a]days of probation are past; ye have [b]procrastinated the day of your salvation until it is everlastingly too late, and your destruction is made sure; yea, for ye have sought all the days of your lives for that which ye could not obtain; and ye have sought for [c]happiness in doing iniquity, which thing is [d]contrary to the nature of that righteousness which is in our great and Eternal Head.

39 O ye people of the land, that ye would hear my words! And I pray that the anger of the Lord be turned away from you, and that ye would repent and be saved.

CHAPTER 14

Samuel predicts light during the night and a new star at Christ's birth—Christ redeems men from temporal and spiritual death—The signs of his death include three days of darkness, the rending of the rocks, and great upheavals of nature.

AND now it came to pass that [a]Samuel, the Lamanite, did prophesy a great many more things which cannot be written.

2 And behold, he said unto them: Behold, I give unto you a sign; for [a]five years more cometh, and behold, then cometh the Son of God to

---

29a TG Stiffneckedness.
  b Ezek. 13: 3;
    2 Ne. 28: 9.
  c Matt. 15: 14; 23: 16.
  d John 3: 19.
  e Job 24: 13 (2–16).
31a Jer. 48: 36 (35–36);
    Morm. 1: 18 (17–19).
33a Morm. 2: 10 (10–15).

  b Matt. 23: 37.
35a TG Treasure.
37a Mosiah 2: 32.
38a Morm. 2: 15 (10–15).
    TG Probation.
  b Alma 34: 33 (33–34).
    TG Apathy;
    Procrastination.
  c Alma 41: 10.

    TG Abundant Life;
    Happiness.
  d Alma 41: 11 (10–12).
14 1a Hel. 13: 2; 3 Ne.
    23: 9 (9–10).
2a Hel. 16: 4; 3 Ne.
    1: 5 (5–21).

[About 6 B.C.]

redeem all those who shall believe on his name.

3 And behold, this will I give unto you for a *sign at the time of his coming; for behold, there shall be great lights in heaven, insomuch that in the night before he cometh there shall be no darkness, insomuch that it shall appear unto man as if it was day.

4 Therefore, there shall be one *day and a night and a day, as if it were one day and there were no night; and this shall be unto you for a sign; for ye shall know of the rising of the sun and also of its setting; therefore they shall know of a surety that there shall be two days and a night; nevertheless the night shall not be darkened; and it shall be the night before he is *born.

5 And behold, there shall a new *star arise, such an one as ye never have beheld; and this also shall be a sign unto you.

6 And behold this is not all, there shall be many *signs and wonders in heaven.

7 And it shall come to pass that ye shall all be amazed, and wonder, insomuch that ye shall *fall to the earth.

8 And it shall come to pass that whosoever shall *believe on the Son of God, the same shall have everlasting life.

9 And behold, thus hath the Lord commanded me, by his angel, that I should come and tell this thing unto you; yea, he hath commanded that I should prophesy these things unto you; yea, he hath said unto me: Cry unto this people, repent and prepare the way of the Lord.

10 And now, because I am a Lamanite, and have spoken unto you the words which the Lord hath commanded me, and because it was hard against you, ye are angry with me and do seek to destroy me, and have *cast me out from among you.

11 And ye shall *hear my words, for, for this intent have I come up upon the walls of this city, that ye might hear and know of the judgments of God which do await you because of your iniquities, and also that ye might know the conditions of repentance;

12 And also that ye might know of the coming of Jesus Christ, the Son of God, the *Father of heaven and of earth, the Creator of all things from the beginning; and that ye might know of the signs of his coming, to the intent that ye might believe on his name.

13 And if ye *believe on his name ye will repent of all your sins, that thereby ye may have a remission of them through his *merits.

14 And behold, again, another sign I give unto you, yea, a sign of his *death.

15 For behold, he surely must die that *salvation may come; yea, it behooveth him and becometh expedient that he *dieth, to bring to pass the *resurrection of the dead, that thereby men may be brought into the *presence of the Lord.

16 Yea, behold, this death bringeth to pass the *resurrection, and *redeemeth all mankind from the first death—that spiritual death; for all mankind, by the *fall of Adam being *cut off from the presence of

3a Hel. 16:13; 3 Ne. 1:15 (8–20).
4a 3 Ne. 1:8.
  b TG Jesus Christ, Birth of.
5a Matt. 2:2 (1–2); 3 Ne. 1:21.
  TG Astronomy.
6a 3 Ne. 2:1.
7a 3 Ne. 1:16 (16–17).
8a John 3:16.
10a Hel. 13:2 (2–7).
11a Ezek. 2:7 (6–7).

12a Mosiah 3:8; 15:4; 3 Ne. 9:15; Ether 4:7.
  TG Jesus Christ, Creator.
13a Acts 16:31 (30–31).
  b D&C 19:16 (16–20).
14a TG Jesus Christ, Death of.
15a TG Jesus Christ, Savior.
  b 1 Cor. 15:36.
  c 2 Ne. 9:4; Alma

42:23; Morm. 9:13.
  TG Resurrection.
  d TG God, Presence of.
16a John 20:9; D&C 18:12 (11–12).
  b TG Salvation, Plan of.
  c TG Fall of Man.
  d 2 Ne. 2:5; 9:6 (6–15); Alma 11:42 (40–45); 12:16 (16, 24, 36); 42:7 (6–11).

[About 6 B.C.]

the Lord, are considered as [e]dead, both as to things temporal and to things spiritual.

17 But behold, the resurrection of Christ [a]redeemeth mankind, yea, even all mankind, and bringeth them back into the presence of the Lord.

18 Yea, and it bringeth to pass the condition of repentance, that whosoever repenteth the same is not [a]hewn down and cast into the fire; but whosoever repenteth not is hewn down and cast into the fire; and there cometh upon them again a [b]spiritual death, yea, a second death, for they are cut off again as to things pertaining to righteousness.

19 Therefore repent ye, repent ye, lest by knowing these things and not doing them ye shall suffer yourselves to come under condemnation, and ye are brought down unto this second death.

20 But behold, as I said unto you concerning another [a]sign, a sign of his death, behold, in that day that he shall suffer death the sun shall be darkened and refuse to give his [b]light unto you; and also the moon and the stars; and there shall be no light upon the face of this land, even from the time that he shall suffer death, for the space of [c]three days, to the time that he shall rise again from the dead.

21 Yea, at the time that he shall yield up the [a]ghost there shall be [b]thunderings and lightnings for the space of many hours, and the earth shall shake and tremble; and the [c]rocks which are upon the face of this earth, which are both above the earth and beneath, which ye know

at this time are solid, or the more part of it is one solid mass, shall be [d]broken up;

22 Yea, they shall be rent in twain, and shall ever after be [a]found in seams and in cracks, and in broken fragments upon the face of the whole earth, yea, both above the earth and beneath.

23 And behold, there shall be great [a]tempests, and there shall be many mountains laid low, like unto a valley, and there shall be many places which are now called [b]valleys which shall become mountains, whose height is great.

24 And [a]many highways shall be broken up, and many cities shall become desolate.

25 And many [a]graves shall be opened, and shall yield up many of their dead; and many saints shall appear unto many.

26 And behold, thus hath the [a]angel spoken unto me; for he said unto me that there should be thunderings and lightnings for the space of many hours.

27 And he said unto me that while the thunder and the lightning lasted, and the tempest, that these things should be, and that [a]darkness should cover the face of the whole earth for the space of three days.

28 And the angel said unto me that many shall see greater things than these, to the intent that they might believe that [a]these signs and these wonders should come to pass upon all the face of this land, to the intent that there should be no cause for unbelief among the children of men—

29 And this to the intent that whosoever will believe might be saved,

---

16e TG Death, Spiritual, First.
17a TG Redemption.
18a Luke 13:7.
  b TG Death, Spiritual, Second.
20a 3 Ne. 8:5 (5–25); 11:2.
  b Luke 23:44.
  c Mosiah 3:10.
21a Matt. 27:50 (50–54).

b 1 Ne. 19:11; 3 Ne. 8:6 (5–23).
c 3 Ne. 10:9.
d Gen. 7:11; 1 Ne. 12:4.
22a 3 Ne. 8:18.
23a 3 Ne. 10:14.
  b Isa. 40:4; Luke 3:5; D&C 49:23; 109:74.
24a 3 Ne. 8:14 (8–10, 14); 9:12 (3–12); 10:7.

25a Matt. 27:52 (52–53); 3 Ne. 23:11 (7–13).
26a Alma 13:26; Hel. 13:7.
27a 1 Ne. 19:10; 3 Ne. 8:3; 10:9.
28a 1 Ne. 12:4 (4–5); 19:12 (10–12); 3 Ne. 10:11.

[About 6 B.C.]

and that whosoever will not believe, a *righteous judgment might come upon them; and also if they are condemned they bring upon themselves their own condemnation.

30 And now remember, remember, my brethren, that whosoever perisheth, perisheth unto *himself; and whosoever doeth iniquity, doeth it unto himself; for behold, ye are *free; ye are permitted to act for yourselves; for behold, God hath given unto you a *knowledge and he hath made you free.

31 He hath given unto you that ye might *know good from evil, and he hath given unto you that ye might *choose life or death; and ye can do good and be *restored unto that which is good, or have that which is good restored unto you; or ye can do evil, and have that which is evil restored unto you.

CHAPTER 15

The Lord chastened the Nephites because he loved them—Converted Lamanites are firm and steadfast in the faith—The Lord will be merciful unto the Lamanites in the latter days.

AND now, my beloved brethren, behold, I declare unto you that except ye shall repent your houses shall be left unto you *desolate.

2 Yea, except ye repent, your women shall have great cause to mourn in the day that they shall give suck; for ye shall attempt to flee and there shall be no place for *refuge; yea, and wo unto them which are *with child, for they shall be heavy and cannot flee; therefore, they shall be trodden down and shall be left to perish.

3 Yea, wo unto this *people who are called the *people of Nephi except they shall repent, when they shall see all these signs and wonders which shall be showed unto them; for behold, they have been a chosen people of the Lord; yea, the people of Nephi hath he loved, and also hath he *chastened them; yea, in the days of their iniquities hath he chastened them because he loveth them.

4 But behold my brethren, the *Lamanites hath he hated because their deeds have been evil continually, and this because of the iniquity of the *tradition of their fathers. But behold, salvation hath come unto them through the preaching of the Nephites; and for this intent hath the Lord *prolonged their days.

5 And I would that ye should behold that the *more part of them are in the path of their duty, and they do walk circumspectly before God, and they do observe to keep his commandments and his statutes and his judgments according to the law of Moses.

6 Yea, I say unto you, that the more part of them are doing this, and they are striving with *unwearied diligence that they may bring the remainder of their brethren to the knowledge of the truth; therefore there are many who do add to their numbers daily.

7 And behold, ye do know of yourselves, for ye have witnessed it, that as many of them as are brought to the knowledge of the truth, and to know of the wicked and abominable traditions of their fathers, and are led to believe the holy scriptures, yea, the prophecies of the holy prophets, which are written, which

29a TG Judgment.
30a 3 Ne. 3:11.
  b Gal. 5:1; 2 Ne. 2:27
    (26–27); Alma 41:7;
    Moses 6:56. TG Agency.
  c TG Knowledge.
31a Moro. 7:16.
  b Rom. 6:16 (14–18);
    Alma 3:27 (26–27).

  c Alma 41:3 (1–15).
15 1a Isa. 5:9; Matt. 23:
    38.
2a TG Refuge.
  b Matt. 24:19.
3a W of M 1:11.
  b Jacob 5:25.
  c Prov. 3:12; Heb.
    12:6 (5–11);

D&C 95:1.
4a Jacob 5:40.
  b Ezek. 20:18; Hel.
    5:19. TG Traditions
    of Men.
  c Alma 9:16.
5a Hel. 13:1; 16:6.
6a TG Dedication.

[About 6 B.C.]

leadeth them to faith on the Lord, and unto repentance, which faith and repentance bringeth a "change of heart unto them—

8 Therefore, as many as have come to this, ye know of yourselves are "firm and steadfast in the faith, and in the thing wherewith they have been made free.

9 And ye know also that they have "buried their weapons of war, and they fear to take them up lest by any means they should sin; yea, ye can see that they fear to sin—for behold they will suffer themselves that they be trodden down and slain by their enemies, and will not lift their swords against them, and this because of their "faith in Christ.

10 And now, because of their "steadfastness when they do believe in that thing which they do believe, for because of their firmness when they are once enlightened, behold, the Lord shall bless them and prolong their days, notwithstanding their iniquity—

11 Yea, even if they should dwindle in unbelief the Lord shall "prolong their days, until the time shall come which hath been spoken of by our fathers, and also by the prophet "Zenos, and many other prophets, concerning the "restoration of our brethren, the Lamanites, again to the knowledge of the truth—

12 Yea, I say unto you, that in the latter times the "promises of the Lord have been extended to our brethren, the Lamanites; and notwithstanding the many afflictions which they shall have, and notwithstanding they shall be "driven to and fro upon the face of the earth, and be hunted, and shall be smitten

and scattered abroad, having no place for "refuge, the Lord shall be "merciful unto them.

13 And this is according to the prophecy, that they shall again be "brought to the true knowledge, which is the knowledge of their Redeemer, and their great and true "shepherd, and be numbered among his "sheep.

14 Therefore I say unto you, it shall be "better for them than for you except ye repent.

15 For behold, "had the mighty works been shown unto them which have been shown unto you, yea, unto them who have dwindled in unbelief because of the traditions of their fathers, ye can see of yourselves that they never would again have dwindled in unbelief.

16 Therefore, saith the Lord: I will not utterly destroy them, but I will cause that in the day of my wisdom they shall "return again unto me, saith the Lord.

17 And now behold, saith the Lord, concerning the people of the Nephites: If they will not repent, and observe to do my will, I will utterly "destroy them, saith the Lord, because of their unbelief notwithstanding the many mighty works which I have done among them; and as surely as the Lord liveth shall these things be, saith the Lord.

CHAPTER 16

The Nephites who believe Samuel are baptized by Nephi—Samuel cannot be slain with their arrows and stones—Some harden their hearts, and others see angels—The unbelievers say it is not reasonable to believe in Christ and his coming in Jerusalem.

7a TG Conversion.
8a Alma 23: 6; 27: 27;
    3 Ne. 6: 14.
9a Alma 24: 17 (17–26).
  b Mark 5: 34 (34–36).
10a TG Steadfastness.
11a Deut. 11: 9 (8–9);
    Alma 9: 16.
  b Hel. 8: 19; 3 Ne. 10: 16.

c Morm. 5: 12 (9, 12);
    7: 1.
12a Enos 1: 13 (12–13).
  b Morm. 5: 15.
  c TG Refuge.
  d 1 Ne. 13: 31; 2 Ne.
    4: 7; 10: 18 (18–19);
    Jacob 3: 6 (5–9);
    Morm. 5: 20 (20–21).
13a 3 Ne. 16: 12.

b TG Jesus Christ,
    Good Shepherd.
  c TG Sheep.
14a Hel. 7: 23.
15a Matt. 11: 21 (20–24).
16a Enos 1: 13.
17a Hel. 13: 6 (5–10);
    Morm. 3: 2.

[About 6 B.C.]

AND now, it came to pass that there were many who heard the words of Samuel, the Lamanite, which he spake upon the "walls of the city. And as many as believed on his word went forth and sought for Nephi; and when they had come forth and found him they confessed unto him their sins and denied not, desiring that they might be *baptized unto the Lord.

2 But as many as there were who did not believe in the words of Samuel were "angry with him; and they cast stones at him upon the wall, and also many shot arrows at him as he stood upon the wall; but the Spirit of the Lord was with him, insomuch that they could not hit him with their stones neither with their arrows.

3 Now when they saw that they could not hit him, there were many more who did believe on his words, insomuch that they went away unto Nephi to be baptized.

4 For behold, Nephi was baptizing, and prophesying, and preaching, crying repentance unto the people, showing signs and wonders, working "miracles among the people, that they might know that the Christ must *shortly come—

5 Telling them of things which must shortly come, that they might know and remember at the time of their coming that they had been made known unto them beforehand, to the intent that they might believe; therefore as many as believed on the words of Samuel went forth unto him to be baptized, for they came repenting and confessing their sins.

6 But the "more part of them did not believe in the words of Samuel; therefore when they saw that they could not hit him with their stones and their arrows, they cried unto their captains, saying: *Take this

fellow and bind him, for behold he 'hath a devil; and because of the power of the devil which is in him we cannot hit him with our stones and our arrows; therefore take him and bind him, and away with him.

7 And as they went forth to lay their hands on him, behold, he did cast himself down from the wall, and did flee out of their lands, yea, even unto his own country, and began to preach and to prophesy "among his own people.

8 And behold, he was never heard of more among the Nephites; and thus were the affairs of the people.

9 And thus ended the eighty and sixth year of the reign of the judges over the people of Nephi.

10 And thus ended also the *eighty and seventh year of the reign of the judges, the more part of the people remaining in their pride and wickedness, and the lesser part walking more circumspectly before God.

11 And these were the conditions also, in the eighty and eighth year of the reign of the judges.

12 And there was but little alteration in the affairs of the people, save it were the people began to be more hardened in iniquity, and do more and more of that which was "contrary to the commandments of God, in the eighty and ninth year of the reign of the judges.

13 But it came to pass in the †ninetieth year of the reign of the judges, there were "great signs given unto the people, and wonders; and the words of the prophets *began to be fulfilled.

14 And "angels did appear unto men, wise men, and did declare unto them glad tidings of great joy; thus in this year the scriptures began to be fulfilled.

15 Nevertheless, the people began to harden their hearts, all save it were the most believing part of them, both of the Nephites and also of the

16 1a Hel. 13: 4.
  b Alma 9: 27.
2a Prov. 29: 10.
4a TG Miracle.
  b Hel. 14: 2.

6a Hel. 15: 5; 3 Ne. 1: 22.
  b Hel. 13: 24.
  c John 7: 20.
7a Hel. 13: 2.
12a TG Disobedience.

13a 3 Ne. 1: 4.
  b Hel. 14: 3 (3-7).
14a Alma 13: 26.

[*5 B.C. †2 B.C.]

Lamanites, and began to depend upon their ᵃown strength and upon their own wisdom, saying:

16 Some things they may have guessed right, among so many; but behold, we know that all these great and marvelous works cannot come to pass, of which has been spoken.

17 And they began to reason and to contend among themselves, saying:

18 That it is ᵃnot reasonable that such a being as a Christ shall come; if so, and he be the Son of God, the Father of heaven and of earth, as it has been spoken, why will he not show himself unto us as well as unto them who shall be at Jerusalem?

19 Yea, why will he not show himself in this land as well as in the land of Jerusalem?

20 But behold, we know that this is a wicked ᵃtradition, which has been handed down unto us by our fathers, to cause us that we should believe in some great and marvelous thing which should come to pass, but not among us, but in a land which is far distant, a land which we know not; therefore they can keep us in ignorance, for we cannot ᵇwitness with our own eyes that they are true.

21 And they will, by the cunning and the mysterious arts of the evil one, work some great mystery which we cannot understand, which will keep us down to be servants to their words, and also servants unto them, for we depend upon them to teach us the word; and thus will they keep us in ignorance if we will yield ourselves unto them, all the days of our lives.

22 And many more things did the people ᵃimagine up in their hearts, which were foolish and ᵇvain; and they were much disturbed, for Satan did stir them up to do iniquity continually; yea, he did go about spreading ᶜrumors and contentions upon all the face of the land, that he might harden the hearts of the people against that which was good and against that which should come.

23 And notwithstanding the signs and the wonders which were wrought among the people of the Lord, and the many miracles which they did, Satan did get great hold upon the hearts of the people upon all the face of the land.

24 And thus *ended the ninetieth year of the reign of the judges over the people of Nephi.

25 ᵃAnd thus ended the book of Helaman, according to the record of Helaman and his sons.

THIRD NEPHI

THE BOOK OF NEPHI

THE SON OF NEPHI, WHO WAS THE SON OF HELAMAN

And Helaman was the son of Helaman, who was the son of Alma, who was the son of Alma, being a descendant of Nephi who was the son of Lehi, who came out of Jerusalem in the first year of the reign of Zedekiah, the king of Judah.

CHAPTER 1

Nephi the son of Helaman departs out of the land, and his son Nephi keeps the records—Though signs and wonders abound, the wicked plan to slay the righteous—The night of Christ's birth arrives—The sign is

---

15a Isa. 5: 21.
18a Alma 30: 53.
20a TG Traditions of Men.

b Alma 30: 15; Ether
12: 5 (5–6, 19).
22a Gen. 6: 5.
b 4 Ne. 1: 43.

c Prov. 6: 18 (16–19).
25a Hel. 3: 37.

[*1 B.C.]

given and a new star arises—Lyings and deceivings increase, and the Gadianton robbers slaughter many.

NOW it came to pass that the *ninety and first year had passed away and it was "six hundred years from the time that Lehi left Jerusalem; and it was in the year that *b*Lachoneus was the chief judge and the governor over the land.

2 And *a*Nephi, the son of Helaman, had departed out of the land of Zarahemla, giving charge unto his son *b*Nephi, who was his eldest son, concerning the *c*plates of brass, and *d*all the records which had been kept, and all those things which had been kept sacred from the departure of Lehi out of Jerusalem.

3 Then he *a*departed out of the land, and *b*whither he went, no man knoweth; and his son Nephi did keep the records in his stead, yea, the record of this people.

4 And it came to pass that in the commencement of the ninety and second year, behold, the prophecies of the prophets began to be fulfilled more fully; for there began to be *a*greater signs and greater miracles wrought among the people.

5 But there were some who began to say that the time was past for the words to be fulfilled, which were *a*spoken by Samuel, the Lamanite.

6 And they began to *a*rejoice over their brethren, saying: Behold, the time is past, and the words of Samuel are not fulfilled; therefore, your joy and your faith concerning this thing hath been vain.

7 And it came to pass that they did make a great uproar through-

out the land; and the people who believed began to be very sorrowful, lest by any means those things which had been spoken might not come to pass.

8 But behold, they did watch steadfastly for *a*that day and that night and that day which should be as one day as if there were no night, that they might *know* that their faith had not been vain.

9 Now it came to pass that there was a day set apart by the *a*unbelievers, that all those who believed in those traditions should be *b*put to death except the *c*sign should come to pass, which had been given by Samuel the prophet.

10 Now it came to pass that when Nephi, the son of Nephi, saw this wickedness of his people, his heart was exceedingly sorrowful.

11 And it came to pass that he went out and bowed himself down upon the earth, and cried mightily to his God in behalf of his people, yea, those who were about to be destroyed because of their faith in the tradition of their fathers.

12 And it came to pass that he cried mightily unto the Lord *a*all that day; and behold, the *b*voice of the Lord came unto him, saying:

13 Lift up your head and be of good cheer; for behold, the time is at hand, and on this night shall the *a*sign be given, and on the *b*morrow come I into the world, to show unto the world that I will fulfil all that which I have caused to be *c*spoken by the mouth of my holy prophets.

14 Behold, I *a*come unto my own, to *b*fulfil all things which I have made known unto the children of men from the *c*foundation of the

1 1*a* 2 Ne. 25: 19;
      Alma 13: 25.
   b 3 Ne. 3: 1; 6: 19.
2*a* Hel. 3: 21 (20–21).
   b 3 Ne. 7: 15 (15, 20, 23).
   c Alma 37: 3 (3–12);
      63: 12 (1, 11–14).
   d Alma 50: 38.
3*a* Alma 45: 18 (18–19).
   b 3 Ne. 2: 9.
4*a* Hel. 16: 13 (13, 23).

5*a* Hel. 14: 2.
6*a* TG Mocking.
8*a* Hel. 14: 4 (3–4).
9*a* TG Unbelief,
      Unbelievers.
   b 3 Ne. 1: 16.
      TG Martyrdom.
   c Hel. 14: 3 (2–7).
12*a* Enos 1: 4; Alma 5: 46.
   b Alma 20: 2; Hel. 13: 3.

13*a* Matt. 2: 2.
   b Luke 2: 11 (10–11).
   c TG Jesus Christ,
      Prophecies about.
14*a* John 1: 11.
   b Matt. 5: 17 (17–18);
      Luke 24: 44.
   c Alma 42: 26; 3 Ne.
      26: 5.

world, and to do the *a*will, *c*both *f*of the Father and of the Son—of the Father because of me, and of the Son because of my flesh. And behold, the time is at hand, and this night shall the sign be given.

15 And it came to pass that the words which came unto Nephi were fulfilled, according as they had been spoken; for behold, at the going down of the *a*sun there was *b*no darkness; and the people began to be astonished because there was no darkness when the night came.

16 And there were many, who had not believed the words of the prophets, who *a*fell to the earth and became as if they were dead, for they knew that the great *b*plan of destruction which they had laid for those who believed in the words of the prophets had been frustrated; for the sign which had been given was already at hand.

17 And they began to know that the Son of God must shortly appear; yea, in fine, all the people upon the face of the whole earth from the *a*west to the east, both in the land north and in the land south, were so exceedingly astonished that they fell to the earth.

18 For they knew that the prophets had testified of these things for many years, and that the sign which had been given was already at hand; and they began to fear because of their iniquity and their unbelief.

19 And it came to pass that there was no darkness in all that night, but it was as light as though it was mid-day. And it came to pass that the sun did rise in the morning again, according to its proper order; and they knew that it was the day that the Lord should be *a*born, because of the *b*sign which had been given.

20 And it had come to pass, yea, all things, every whit, according to the words of the prophets.

21 And it came to pass also that a new *a*star did appear, according to the word.

22 And it came to pass that from this time forth there began to be *a*lyings sent forth among the people, by Satan, to harden their hearts, to the intent that they might not believe in those *b*signs and wonders which they had seen; but notwithstanding these lyings and deceivings the *c*more part of the people did believe, and were converted unto the Lord.

23 And it came to pass that Nephi went forth among the people, and also many others, baptizing unto repentance, in the which there was a great *a*remission of sins. And thus the people began again to have peace in the land.

24 And there were no contentions, save it were a few that began to preach, endeavoring to prove by the *a*scriptures that it was no more expedient to observe the law of Moses. Now in this thing they did err, having not understood the scriptures.

25 But it came to pass that they soon became converted, and were convinced of the error which they were in, for it was made known unto them that the law was not yet *a*fulfilled, and that it must be fulfilled in every whit; yea, the word came unto them that it must be fulfilled; yea, that one jot or tittle should not pass away till it should all be fulfilled; therefore in this same year were they brought to a knowledge of their error and did *b*confess their faults.

26 And thus the ninety and second

14d TG God, Will of.
  e D&C 93: 4 (4, 14).
  f Mosiah 15: 3.
15a Josh. 10: 13.
  b Hel. 14:3.
16a Hel. 14: 7.
  b 3 Ne. 1: 9 (9, 11).
17a Hel. 11: 20.

19a TG Jesus Christ,
    Birth of.
  b Hel. 14: 3.
21a Matt. 2: 2 (1–2);
    Hel. 14: 5.
22a Moses 5: 13.
  b TG Signs.
  c Hel. 16: 6.

23a TG Remission of Sins.
24a Alma 34: 13.
25a Matt. 5: 18; 2 Ne.
    25: 24.
  b Num. 5: 7 (6–10);
    Mosiah 26: 29 (29, 35);
    Alma 17: 4.

[A.D. 1]

year did pass away, bringing "glad tidings unto the people because of the signs which did come to pass, according to the words of the prophecy of all the holy prophets.

27 And it came to pass that the ninety and third year did also pass away in peace, save it were for the Gadianton robbers, who dwelt upon the "mountains, who did infest the land; for so strong were their holds and their secret places that the people could not overpower them; therefore they did commit many murders, and did do much slaughter among the people.

28 And it came to pass that in the ninety and fourth year they began to increase in a great degree, because there were many dissenters of the Nephites who did flee unto them, which did cause much sorrow unto those Nephites who did remain in the land.

29 And there was also a cause of much sorrow among the Lamanites; for behold, they had many children who did grow up and began to wax strong in years, that they became for themselves, and were "led away by some who were "Zoramites, by their lyings and their flattering words, to join those Gadianton robbers.

30 And thus were the Lamanites afflicted also, and began to decrease as to their faith and righteousness, because of the wickedness of the "rising generation.

CHAPTER 2

Wickedness and abominations increase among the people—The Nephites and Lamanites unite to defend themselves against the Gadianton robbers—Converted Lamanites become white and are called Nephites.

AND it came to pass that thus passed away the ninety and fifth year also, and the people began to forget those "signs and wonders which they had heard, and began to be less and less astonished at a sign or a wonder from heaven, insomuch that they began to be hard in their hearts, and blind in their minds, and began to disbelieve all which they had heard and seen—

2 "Imagining up some vain thing in their hearts, that it was wrought by men and by the power of the devil, to lead away and "deceive the hearts of the people; and thus did Satan get possession of the hearts of the people again, insomuch that he did blind their eyes and lead them away to believe that the doctrine of Christ was a "foolish and a vain thing.

3 And it came to pass that the people began to wax strong in wickedness and abominations; and they did not believe that there should be any more signs or wonders given; and Satan did "go about, leading away the hearts of the people, tempting them and causing them that they should do great wickedness in the land.

4 And thus did pass away the ninety and sixth year; and also the ninety and seventh year; and also the ninety and eighth year; and also the ninety and ninth year;

5 And also an hundred years had passed away since the days of "Mosiah, who was king over the people of the Nephites.

6 And six hundred and nine years had passed away since Lehi left Jerusalem.

7 And nine years had passed away from the time when the sign was given, which was spoken of by the prophets, that Christ should come into the world.

8 Now the Nephites began to "reckon their time from this period

26a Luke 2: 10.
27a Hel. 11: 31 (25–31);
    3 Ne. 2: 11.
29a TG Peer Influence.
   b Alma 30: 59; 43: 4.

30a Judg. 2: 10.
2 1a Hel. 14: 6.
  2a Heb. 3: 12.
   b TG Deceit.
   c 1 Cor. 1: 23 (23–25);

   Alma 30: 13 (12–18).
3a Job 1: 7; D&C 10: 27.
5a Mosiah 29: 46 (46–47).
8a 3 Ne. 5: 7; 8: 2.

[A.D. 3—9]

when the sign was given, or from the coming of Christ; therefore, nine years had passed away.

9 And Nephi, who was the father of Nephi, who had the charge of the records, [a]did not return to the land of Zarahemla, and could nowhere be found in all the land.

10 And it came to pass that the people did still [a]remain in wickedness, notwithstanding the much preaching and prophesying which was sent among them; and thus passed away the tenth year also; and the eleventh year also passed away in iniquity.

11 And it came to pass in the thirteenth year there began to be wars and contentions throughout all the land; for the [a]Gadianton robbers had become so [b]numerous, and did slay so many of the people, and did lay waste so many cities, and did spread so much death and carnage throughout the land, that it became expedient that all the people, both the Nephites and the Lamanites, should take up arms against them.

12 Therefore, all the Lamanites who had become converted unto the Lord did unite with their brethren, the Nephites, and were compelled, for the [a]safety of their lives and their women and their children, to take up arms against those Gadianton robbers, yea, and also to maintain their rights, and the privileges of their church and of their worship, and their freedom and their [b]liberty.

13 And it came to pass that before this thirteenth year had passed away the Nephites were threatened with utter destruction because of this war, which had become exceedingly sore.

14 And it came to pass that those Lamanites who had united with the Nephites were numbered among the Nephites;

15 And their [a]curse was taken from them, and their skin became [b]white like unto the Nephites;

16 And their young men and their daughters became exceedingly fair, and they were numbered among the Nephites, and were called Nephites. And thus ended the thirteenth year.

17 And it came to pass in the commencement of the fourteenth year, the war between the robbers and the people of Nephi did continue and did become exceedingly sore; nevertheless, the people of Nephi did gain some advantage of the robbers, insomuch that they did drive them back out of their lands into the mountains and into their secret places.

18 And thus ended the fourteenth year. And in the *fifteenth year they did come forth against the people of Nephi; and because of the wickedness of the people of Nephi, and their many contentions and dissensions, the Gadianton robbers did gain many advantages over them.

19 And thus ended the fifteenth year, and thus were the people in a state of many afflictions; and the [a]sword of destruction did hang over them, insomuch that they were about to be smitten down by it, and this because of their iniquity.

CHAPTER 3

Giddianhi, the Gadianton leader, demands that Lachoneus and the Nephites surrender themselves and their lands—Lachoneus appoints Gidgiddoni as chief captain of the armies—The Nephites assemble in Zarahemla and Bountiful to defend themselves.

AND now it came to pass that in the sixteenth year from the coming of Christ, [a]Lachoneus, the governor of the land, received an epistle from

9a 3 Ne. 1: 3 (2–3).
10a Alma 34: 35.
11a 3 Ne. 1: 27.
  b Morm. 2: 8.
12a Alma 58: 12;
3 Ne. 3: 2.
  b TG Liberty.
15a Alma 17: 15; 23: 18.
  b 2 Ne. 5: 21; 30: 6;
    Jacob 3: 8.
19a Alma 60: 29; Hel.
    13: 5; 3 Ne. 3: 3.
3 1a 3 Ne. 1: 1; 6: 6.

the leader and the governor of this band of robbers; and these were the words which were written, saying:

2 Lachoneus, most noble and chief governor of the land, behold, I write this epistle unto you, and do give unto you exceedingly great praise because of your firmness, and also the firmness of your people, in [a]maintaining that which ye suppose to be your right and [b]liberty; yea, ye do stand well, as if ye were supported by the hand of a god, in the defence of your liberty, and your property, and your country, or that which ye do call so.

3 And it seemeth a pity unto me, most noble Lachoneus, that ye should be so foolish and vain as to suppose that ye can stand against so many brave men who are at my command, who do now at this time stand in their arms, and do await with great anxiety for the word— Go down upon the Nephites and [a]destroy them.

4 And I, knowing of their unconquerable spirit, having proved them in the field of battle, and knowing of their everlasting hatred towards you because of the many wrongs which ye have done unto them, therefore if they should come down against you they would visit you with utter destruction.

5 Therefore I have written this epistle, sealing it with mine own hand, feeling for your welfare, because of your firmness in that which ye believe to be right, and your noble spirit in the field of battle.

6 Therefore I write unto you, desiring that ye would yield up unto this my people, your cities, your lands, and your possessions, rather than that they should visit you with the sword and that destruction should come upon you.

7 Or in other words, yield your-selves up unto us, and unite with us and become acquainted with our [a]secret works, and become our brethren that ye may be like unto us—not our slaves, but our brethren and partners of all our substance.

8 And behold, I [a]swear unto you, if ye will do this, with an oath, ye shall not be destroyed; but if ye will not do this, I swear unto you with an oath, that on the morrow month I will command that my armies shall come down against you, and they shall not stay their hand and shall spare not, but shall slay you, and shall let fall the sword upon you even until ye shall become extinct.

9 And behold, I am [a]Giddianhi; and I am the governor of this the [b]secret society of Gadianton; which society and the works thereof I know to be [c]good; and they are of [d]ancient date and they have been handed down unto us.

10 And I write this epistle unto you, Lachoneus, and I hope that ye will deliver up your lands and your possessions, without the shedding of blood, that this my people may recover their rights and [a]government, who have dissented away from you because of your wickedness in retaining from them their rights of government, and except ye do this, I will avenge their wrongs. I am Giddianhi.

11 And now it came to pass when Lachoneus received this epistle he was exceedingly astonished, because of the boldness of Giddianhi demanding the possession of the land of the Nephites, and also of threatening the people and avenging the wrongs of those that had received no wrong, save it were they had [a]wronged themselves by dissenting away unto those wicked and abominable robbers.

12 Now behold, this Lachoneus,

2a 3 Ne. 2: 12.
 b TG Liberty.
3a 3 Ne. 2: 19.
7a Hel. 6: 22 (22–26).
8a Hel. 1: 11; Ether
   8: 14 (13–14).

9a 3 Ne. 4: 14.
 b TG Secret
   Combinations.
 c Alma 30: 53.
 d Hel. 6: 26 (26–30);
   Ether 8: 9 (9–19);

   Moses 5: 29 (29,
   49–52).
10a TG Governments.
11a Hel. 14: 30.

[A.D. 16]

the governor, was a just man, and could not be frightened by the demands and the threatenings of a ªrobber; therefore he did not hearken to the epistle of Giddianhi, the governor of the robbers, but he did cause that his people should cry unto the Lord for ᵇstrength against the time that the robbers should come down against them.

13 Yea, he sent a proclamation among all the people, that they should ªgather together their women, and their children, their flocks and their herds, and all their substance, save it were their land, unto one place.

14 And he caused that ªfortifications should be built round about them, and the strength thereof should be exceedingly great. And he caused that armies, both of the Nephites and of the Lamanites, or of all them who were numbered among the Nephites, should be placed as guards round about to watch them, and to guard them from the robbers day and night.

15 Yea, he said unto them: As the Lord liveth, except ye repent of all your iniquities, and cry unto the Lord, ye will in nowise be ªdelivered out of the hands of those Gadianton robbers.

16 And so great and marvelous were the words and prophecies of Lachoneus that they did cause fear to come upon all the people; and they did exert themselves in their might to do according to the words of Lachoneus.

17 And it came to pass that Lachoneus did appoint chief captains over all the armies of the Nephites, to command them at the time that the robbers should come down out of the wilderness against them.

18 Now the chiefest among all the chief captains and the great commander of all the armies of the Nephites was appointed, and his name was ªGidgiddoni.

19 Now it was the custom among all the Nephites to appoint for their chief captains, (save it were in their times of wickedness) some one that had the ªspirit of revelation and also prophecy; therefore, this Gidgiddoni was a great prophet among them, as also was the chief judge.

20 Now the people said unto Gidgiddoni: ªPray unto the Lord, and let us go up upon the mountains and into the wilderness, that we may fall upon the robbers and destroy them in their own lands.

21 But Gidgiddoni saith unto them: The Lord ªforbid; for if we should go up against them the Lord would ᵇdeliver us into their hands; therefore we will prepare ourselves in the center of our lands, and we will gather all our armies together, and we will not go against them, but we will wait till they shall come against us; therefore as the Lord liveth, if we do this he will deliver them into our hands.

22 And it came to pass in the *seventeenth year, in the latter end of the year, the proclamation of Lachoneus had gone forth throughout all the face of the land, and they had taken their ªhorses, and their chariots, and their cattle, and all their flocks, and their herds, and their grain, and all their substance, and did march forth by thousands and by tens of thousands, until they had all gone forth to the ᵇplace which ᶜhad been appointed that they should gather themselves together, to defend themselves against their enemies.

23 And the ªland which was ap-

12a 1 Kgs. 20: 3 (2–3);
    Alma 54: 7 (5–11).
  b TG Strength.
13a 3 Ne. 3: 22; 4: 1.
14a Morm. 2: 4.
15a TG Deliver,
    Deliverance;
    Protection, Divine.

18a 3 Ne. 4: 13 (13, 24,
    26); 6: 6.
19a TG Guidance, Divine.
20a Alma 16: 6 (5–8);
    43: 23 (23–24); 48: 16.
21a Alma 43: 46 (46–47);
    48: 14; Morm. 3: 10
    (10–11).

  b 1 Sam. 14: 12; 2 Kgs.
    3: 18; 1 Ne. 3: 29.
22a 3 Ne. 4: 4.
  b Morm. 2: 7.
  c 3 Ne. 3: 13.
23a 3 Ne. 4: 16.

[*A.D. 17]

pointed was the land of Zarahemla, and the land which was between the land Zarahemla and the land [b]Bountiful, yea, to the line which was between the [c]land Bountiful and the land Desolation.

24 And there were a great many thousand people who were called Nephites, who did gather themselves together in this land. Now Lachoneus did cause that they should gather themselves together in the land [a]southward, because of the great curse which was upon the [b]land northward.

25 And they did fortify themselves against their enemies; and they did dwell in one land, and in one body, and they did fear the words which had been spoken by Lachoneus, insomuch that they did repent of all their sins; and they did put up their [a]prayers unto the Lord their God, that he would deliver them in the time that their enemies should come down against them to battle.

26 And they were exceedingly sorrowful because of their enemies. And Gidgiddoni did cause that they should make [a]weapons of war of every kind, and they should be strong with armor, and with shields, and with bucklers, after the manner of his instruction.

CHAPTER 4

The Nephite armies defeat the Gadianton robbers—Giddianhi is slain, and his successor, Zemnarihah, is hanged—The Nephites praise the Lord for their victories.

AND it came to pass that in the latter end of the eighteenth year those armies of [a]robbers had prepared for battle, and began to come down and to sally forth from the hills, and out of the mountains, and the wilderness, and their strongholds, and their [b]secret places, and began to take possession of the lands, both which were in the land south and which were in the land north, and began to take possession of all the lands which had been [c]deserted by the Nephites, and the cities which had been left desolate.

2 But behold, there were no wild beasts nor [a]game in those lands which had been deserted by the Nephites, and there was no game for the robbers save it were in the wilderness.

3 And the robbers could not exist save it were in the wilderness, for the want of food; for the Nephites had left their lands desolate, and had gathered their flocks and their herds and all their substance, and they were in one body.

4 Therefore, there was no chance for the robbers to plunder and to obtain food, save it were to come up in open battle against the Nephites; and the Nephites being in one body, and having so great a number, and having reserved for themselves provisions, and [a]horses and cattle, and flocks of every kind, that they might subsist for the space of [b]seven years, in the which time they did hope to destroy the robbers from off the face of the land; and thus the eighteenth year did pass away.

5 And it came to pass that in the nineteenth year Giddianhi found that it was expedient that he should go up to battle against the Nephites, for there was [a]no way that they could subsist save it were to plunder and rob and murder.

6 And they durst not spread themselves upon the face of the land insomuch that they could raise grain, lest the Nephites should come upon

---

23b Alma 22: 29; 3 Ne. 11: 1.
  c Morm. 3: 7; 4: 2.
24a Alma 46: 17; Morm. 3: 5.
  b Alma 22: 31 (30–31).
25a TG Trust in God.
26a 2 Ne. 5: 14; Jarom

1: 8; Mosiah 10: 8; Alma 2: 12; Hel. 1: 14.
4 1a Hel. 2: 13 (11–13).
  b Alma 58: 6.
  c 3 Ne. 3: 13 (13–14, 22).
2a 1 Ne. 18. 25;

2 Ne. 5: 24; 3 Ne. 4: 20.
4a 3 Ne. 3: 22; 6: 1 (1–2).
  b Gen. 41: 36 (29–36); 3 Ne. 4: 18.
5a Alma 47: 36.

them and slay them; therefore Giddianhi gave commandment unto his armies that in this year they should go up to battle against the Nephites.

7 And it came to pass that they did come up to battle; and it was in the sixth month; and behold, great and terrible was the day that they did come up to battle; and they were girded about after the manner of robbers; and they had a lamb-skin about their loins, and they were dyed in blood, and their heads were shorn, and they had headplates upon them; and great and terrible was the appearance of the armies of Giddianhi, because of their armor, and because of their being dyed in blood.

8 And it came to pass that the armies of the Nephites, when they saw the appearance of the army of Giddianhi, had all fallen to the earth, and did lift their cries to the Lord their God, that he would spare them and deliver them out of the hands of their enemies.

9 And it came to pass that when the armies of Giddianhi saw this they began to shout with a loud voice, because of their joy, for they had supposed that the Nephites had fallen with fear because of the terror of their armies.

10 But in this thing they were disappointed, for the Nephites did not *a*fear them; but they did fear their God and did supplicate him for *b*protection; therefore, when the armies of Giddianhi did rush upon them they were prepared to meet them; yea, in the strength of the Lord they did receive them.

11 And the battle commenced in this the sixth month; and great and terrible was the battle thereof, yea, great and terrible was the *a*slaughter thereof, insomuch that there never was known so great a slaughter among all the people of Lehi since he left Jerusalem.

12 And notwithstanding the *a*threatenings and the oaths which Giddianhi had made, behold, the Nephites did beat them, insomuch that they did fall back from before them.

13 And it came to pass that *a*Gidgiddoni commanded that his armies should pursue them as far as the borders of the wilderness, and that they should not spare any that should fall into their hands by the way; and thus they did pursue them and did slay them, to the borders of the wilderness, even until they had fulfilled the commandment of Gidgiddoni.

14 And it came to pass that Giddianhi, who had stood and fought with boldness, was pursued as he fled; and being weary because of his much fighting he was overtaken and slain. And thus was the end of Giddianhi the robber.

15 And it came to pass that the armies of the Nephites did return again to their place of security. And it came to pass that this nineteenth year did pass away, and the robbers did not come again to battle; neither did they come again in the twentieth year.

16 And in the *twenty and first year they did not come up to battle, but they came up on all sides to lay siege round about the people of Nephi; for they did suppose that if they should cut off the people of Nephi from their *a*lands, and should hem them in on every side, and if they should cut them off from all their outward privileges, that they could cause them to yield themselves up according to their wishes.

17 Now they had appointed unto themselves another leader, whose name was Zemnarihah; therefore it was Zemnarihah that did cause that this siege should take place.

18 But behold, this was an advantage to the Nephites; for it was impossible for the robbers to lay

---

10a TG Reverence.
  b Jer. 17: 17 (17–18).
11a Alma 28: 11 (8–12).

12a 3 Ne. 3: 8 (4–10).
13a 3 Ne. 3: 18.

16a 3 Ne. 3: 23.

siege sufficiently long to have any effect upon the Nephites, because of their ªmuch ᵇprovision which they had laid up in store,

19 And because of the scantiness of provisions among the robbers; for behold, they had nothing save it were meat for their subsistence, which meat they did obtain in the wilderness;

20 And it came to pass that the ªwild game became scarce in the wilderness insomuch that the robbers were about to perish with hunger.

21 And the Nephites were continually marching out by day and by night, and falling upon their armies, and cutting them off by thousands and by tens of thousands.

22 And thus it became the desire of the people of Zemnarihah to withdraw from their design, because of the great destruction which came upon them by night and by day.

23 And it came to pass that Zemnarihah did give command unto his people that they should withdraw themselves from the siege, and march into the furthermost parts of the land northward.

24 And now, Gidgiddoni being aware of their design, and knowing of their weakness because of the want of food, and the great slaughter which had been made among them, therefore he did send out his armies in the night-time, and did cut off the way of their retreat, and did place his armies in the way of their retreat.

25 And this did they do in the night-time, and got on their march beyond the robbers, so that on the morrow, when the robbers began their march, they were met by the armies of the Nephites both in their front and in their rear.

26 And the robbers who were on the south were also cut off in their places of retreat. And all these things were done by command of Gidgiddoni.

27 And there were many thousands who did yield themselves up prisoners unto the Nephites, and the remainder of them were slain.

28 And their leader, Zemnarihah, was taken and hanged upon a tree, yea, even upon the top thereof until he was dead. And when they had hanged him until he was dead they did fell the tree to the earth, and did cry with a loud voice, saying:

29 May the Lord preserve his people in righteousness and in holiness of heart, that they may cause to be felled to the earth all who shall seek to slay them because of power and secret combinations, even as this man hath been felled to the earth.

30 And they did rejoice and cry again with one voice, saying: May the ªGod of Abraham, and the God of Isaac, and the God of Jacob, protect this people in righteousness, so long as they shall ᵇcall on the name of their God for ᶜprotection.

31 And it came to pass that they did break forth, all as one, in singing, and ªpraising their God for the great thing which he had done for them, in preserving them from falling into the hands of their enemies.

32 Yea, they did cry: Hosanna to the Most High God. And they did cry: Blessed be the name of the Lord God ªAlmighty, the Most High God.

33 And their hearts were swollen with joy, unto the gushing out of many tears, because of the great goodness of God in delivering them out of the hands of their enemies; and they knew it was because of their repentance and their humility that they had been delivered from an everlasting destruction.

18a 3 Ne. 4:4.
  b Gen. 41:36 (33–57);
    D&C 4:4.
20a 1 Ne. 18:25;
    2 Ne. 5:24; 3 Ne. 4:2.

30a Alma 29:11.
  b Gen. 4:26; Ether
    4:15; Moro. 2:2.
  c TG Protection, Divine.

31a Alma 26:8.
  TG Thanksgiving.
32a 1 Ne. 1:14.

[A.D. 21—22]

CHAPTER 5

The Nephites repent and forsake their sins—Mormon writes the history of his people and declares the everlasting word to them—Israel shall be gathered in from her long dispersion.

AND now behold, there was not a living soul among all the people of the Nephites who did [a]doubt in the least the words of all the holy prophets who had spoken; for they knew that it must needs be that they must be fulfilled.

2 And they knew that it must be expedient that Christ had come, because of the many signs which had been given, according to the words of the prophets; and because of the things which had come to pass already they knew that it must needs be that all things should come to pass according to that which had been spoken.

3 Therefore they did forsake all their sins, and their abominations, and their whoredoms, and did serve God with all diligence day and night.

4 And now it came to pass that when they had taken all the robbers prisoners, insomuch that none did escape who were not slain, they did cast their prisoners into prison, and did cause the word of God to be preached unto them; and as many as would repent of their sins and [a]enter into a [b]covenant that they would murder no more were set at [c]liberty.

5 But as many as there were who did not enter into a covenant, and who did still continue to have those [a]secret murders in their hearts, yea, as many as were found breathing out threatenings against their brethren were condemned and punished according to the law.

6 And thus they did put an end to all those wicked, and secret, and abominable combinations, in the which there was so much wickedness, and so many murders committed.

7 And thus had the [a]twenty and second year passed away, and the twenty and third year also, and the twenty and fourth, and the twenty and fifth; and thus had *twenty and five years passed away.

8 And there had many things transpired which, in the eyes of some, would be great and marvelous; nevertheless, they cannot all be written in this book; yea, this book cannot contain even a [a]hundredth part of what was done among so many people in the space of twenty and five years;

9 But behold there are [a]records which do contain [b]all the proceedings of this people; and a [c]shorter but true account was given by Nephi.

10 Therefore I have made my [a]record of these things according to the record of Nephi, which was engraven on the plates which were called the [b]plates of Nephi.

11 And behold, I do make the record on plates which I have made with mine own hands.

12 And behold, I am called [a]Mormon, being called after the [b]land of Mormon, the land in which Alma did establish the church among the people, yea, the first church which was established among them after their transgression.

13 Behold, I am a disciple of Jesus Christ, the Son of God. I have been [a]called of him to declare his word among his people, that they might have everlasting life.

14 And it hath become expedient that I, according to the will of God, that the prayers of those who have

---

5 1a TG Doubt.
4a 3 Ne. 6: 3.
  b Alma 44: 15;
    62: 16 (16–17).
  c TG Liberty.
5a 2 Ne. 10: 15.
7a 3 Ne. 2: 8.
8a W of M 1: 5; 3 Ne.

26: 6 (6–12).
9a Hel. 3: 15 (13–15).
  b W of M 1: 5;
    Alma 13: 31.
  c Morm. 2: 18.
10a Hel. 2: 14.
  b W of M 1: 1; Morm.
    1: 4 (1–4); 2: 17

(17–18); 8: 5 (1, 4–5,
    14).
12a W of M 1: 11.
  b Mosiah 18: 4;
    Alma 5: 3.
13a 3 Ne. 30: 1; Moro. 7: 2.

[*A.D. 21––26]

gone hence, who were the holy ones, should be fulfilled according to their faith, should make a [a]record of these things which have been done—

15 Yea, a [a]small record of that which hath taken place from the time that Lehi left Jerusalem, even down until the present time.

16 Therefore I do make my record from the accounts which have been given by those who were before me, until the commencement of my day;

17 And then I do make a [a]record of the things which I have seen with mine own eyes.

18 And I know the record which I make to be a just and a true record; nevertheless there are many things which, according to our [a]language, we are not able to [b]write.

19 And now I make an end of my saying, which is of myself, and proceed to give my account of the things which have been before me.

20 I am Mormon, and a pure [a]descendant of Lehi. I have reason to bless my God and my Savior Jesus Christ, that he brought our fathers out of the land of Jerusalem, (and [b]no one knew it save it were himself and those whom he brought out of that land) and that he hath given me and my people so much knowledge unto the salvation of our souls.

21 Surely he hath [a]blessed the house of [b]Jacob, and hath been [c]merciful unto the seed of Joseph.

22 And [a]insomuch as the children of Lehi have kept his commandments he hath blessed them and prospered them according to his word.

23 Yea, and surely shall he again bring a [a]remnant of the seed of Joseph to the [b]knowledge of the Lord their God.

24 And as surely as the Lord liveth, will he [a]gather in from the four quarters of the earth all the remnant of the [b]seed of Jacob, who are scattered abroad upon all the face of the earth.

25 And as he hath [a]covenanted with all the house of Jacob, even so shall the covenant wherewith he hath covenanted with the house of Jacob be fulfilled in his own due time, unto the [b]restoring all the house of Jacob unto the knowledge of the covenant that he hath covenanted with them.

26 And then shall they [a]know their Redeemer, who is Jesus Christ, the Son of God; and then shall they be gathered in from the four quarters of the earth unto their own lands, from whence they have been dispersed; yea, as the Lord liveth so shall it be. Amen.

CHAPTER 6

The Nephites prosper—Pride, wealth, and class distinctions arise—The Church is rent with dissensions—Satan leads the people in open rebellion—Many prophets cry repentance and are slain—Their murderers conspire to take over the government.

AND now it came to pass that the people of the Nephites did all return to their own lands in the *twenty and sixth year, every man, with his family, his flocks and his herds, his [a]horses and his cattle, and all

---

14a Enos 1: 16 (13–18);
      D&C 3: 19; 10: 47
      (46–50).
15a Morm. 7: 9; 8: 12.
17a W of M 1: 5;
      Morm. 1: 1.
18a TG Language.
   b 3 Ne. 19: 32 (32–34);
      Morm. 9: 33 (32–33);
      Ether 12: 25 (24–25);
      D&C 76: 116.
20a Morm. 1: 5; 8: 13.

   b 1 Ne. 4: 36; 3 Ne.
      15: 14.
21a TG Israel, Blessings of.
   b Gen. 32: 28 (24–32);
      Ps. 135: 4;
      D&C 49: 24 (23–25).
   c Ps. 98: 3.
22a 2 Ne. 1: 20; Jarom
      1: 9; Omni 1: 6;
      Mosiah 1: 7; Alma
      9: 13 (13–14); 37: 13.
23a Alma 46: 24;
      3 Ne. 10: 17.

   b 2 Ne. 3: 12;
      Morm. 7: 5 (5, 10).
24a TG Israel, Gathering
      of.
   b Gen. 46: 8.
25a 3 Ne. 15: 8; 16: 5.
   b 2 Ne. 30: 3 (1–6);
      3 Ne. 16: 13 (6–13).
26a 2 Ne. 30: 7 (7–8);
      3 Ne. 20: 31 (29–34).
6 1a 3 Ne. 3: 22 (21–23).

                                    [*A.D. 26]

things whatsoever did belong unto them.

2 And it came to pass that they had ^anot eaten up all their provisions; therefore they did take with them all that they had not devoured, of all their grain of every kind, and their gold, and their silver, and all their precious things, and they did return to their own lands and their possessions, both on the north and on the south, both on the land northward and on the land southward.

3 And they granted unto those robbers who had ^aentered into a covenant to keep the peace of the land, who were desirous to remain Lamanites, lands, according to their numbers, that they might have, with their labors, wherewith to subsist upon; and thus they did establish peace in all the land.

4 And they began again to prosper and to wax great; and the twenty and sixth and seventh years passed away, and there was great ^aorder in the land; and they had formed their laws according to equity and justice.

5 And now there was nothing in all the land to hinder the people from prospering continually, except they should fall into transgression.

6 And now it was ^aGidgiddoni, and the judge, ^bLachoneus, and those who had been appointed leaders, who had established this great peace in the land.

7 And it came to pass that there were many cities built anew, and there were many old cities repaired.

8 And there were many ^ahighways cast up, and many roads made, which led from city to city, and from land to land, and from place to place.

9 And thus passed away the twenty and eighth year, and the people had continual peace.

10 But it came to pass in the twenty and ninth year there began to be some disputings among the people; and some were lifted up unto pride and ^aboastings because of their exceedingly great riches, yea, even unto great persecutions;

11 For there were many ^amerchants in the land, and also many ^blawyers, and many officers.

12 And the people began to be distinguished by ranks, according to their ^ariches and their chances for learning; yea, some were ^bignorant because of their poverty, and others did receive great ^clearning because of their riches.

13 Some were lifted up in pride, and others were exceedingly humble; some did return railing for railing, while others would receive railing and ^apersecution and all manner of ^bafflictions, and would not turn and ^crevile again, but were humble and penitent before God.

14 And thus there became a great inequality in all the land, insomuch that the church began to be broken up; yea, insomuch that in the thirtieth year the church was broken up in all the land save it were among a few of the Lamanites who were converted unto the true faith; and ^athey would not depart from it, for they were firm, and steadfast, and immovable, willing with all ^bdiligence to keep the commandments of the Lord.

15 Now the cause of this iniquity of the people was this—^aSatan had great ^bpower, unto the stirring up of the people to do all manner of iniquity, and to the puffing them up

2a 3 Ne. 4: 4.
3a 3 Ne. 5: 4.
4a TG Order.
6a 3 Ne. 3: 18.
  b 3 Ne. 3: 1.
8a 3 Ne. 8: 13.
10a TG Boasting.
11a Hel. 6: 8.
  b Alma 10: 14 (14–17, 27); 14: 5 (5, 18–27).

12a 1 Tim. 6: 17; Hel. 4: 12 (11–13).
  b TG Ignorance.
  c TG Learning.
13a TG Persecution.
  b TG Affliction.
  c 3 Ne. 12: 39; 4 Ne. 1: 34; D&C 98: 23 (23–27).

  TG Reviling.
14a Alma 23: 6; 27: 27; Hel. 15: 8 (5–16).
  b TG Dedication; Diligence.
15a Moses 6: 15.
  b 1 Ne. 22: 26; Alma 48: 17.

with pride, tempting them to seek for power, and authority, and ᶜriches, and the vain things of the world.

16 And thus Satan did lead away the hearts of the people to do all manner of iniquity; therefore they had enjoyed peace but a few years.

17 And thus, in the commencement of the thirtieth year—the people having been ᵃdelivered up for the space of a long time to be carried about by the ᵇtemptations of the devil whithersoever he desired to carry them, and to do whatsoever iniquity he desired they should— and thus in the commencement of this, the thirtieth year, they were in a state of awful wickedness.

18 Now they did not sin ᵃignorantly, for they knew the ᵇwill of God concerning them, for it had been taught unto them; therefore they did wilfully ᶜrebel against God.

19 And now it was in the days of Lachoneus, the son of ᵃLachoneus, for Lachoneus did fill the seat of his father and did govern the people that year.

20 And there began to be men ᵃinspired from heaven and sent forth, standing among the people in all the land, preaching and testifying boldly of the sins and iniquities of the people, and testifying unto them concerning the redemption which the Lord would make for his people, or in other words, the resurrection of Christ; and they did testify boldly of his ᵇdeath and sufferings.

21 Now there were many of the people who were exceedingly angry because of those who testified of these things; and those who were angry were chiefly the chief judges, and they who ᵃhad been high priests and lawyers; yea, all those who were

lawyers were angry with those who testified of these things.

22 Now there was no lawyer nor judge nor high priest that could have power to condemn any one to death save their condemnation was signed by the governor of the land.

23 Now there were many of those ᵃwho testified of the things pertaining to Christ who testified boldly, who were taken and put to death ᵇsecretly by the judges, that the knowledge of their death came not unto the governor of the land until after their death.

24 Now behold, this was contrary to the laws of the land, that any man should be put to death except they had power from the governor of the land—

25 Therefore a complaint came up unto the land of Zarahemla, to the governor of the land, against these judges who had condemned the prophets of the Lord unto ᵃdeath, not according to the law.

26 Now it came to pass that they were taken and brought up before the judge, to be judged of the crime which they had done, according to the ᵃlaw which had been given by the people.

27 Now it came to pass that those judges had many friends and kindreds; and the remainder, yea, even almost all the lawyers and the high priests, did gather themselves together, and unite with the kindreds of those judges who were to be tried according to the law.

28 And they did enter into a ᵃcovenant one with another, yea, even into that covenant which was given by them of old, which covenant was given and administered by the ᵇdevil, to combine against all righteousness.

15c ᴛɢ Selfishness.
17a Moses 5: 23.
  b ᴛɢ Temptation.
18a Num. 15: 27 (2–29);
    Mosiah 3: 11.
    ᴛɢ Ignorance.
  b ᴛɢ God, Will of.
  c ᴛɢ Rebellion.
19a 3 Ne. 1: 1.

20a ᴛɢ Inspiration;
    Prophets, Mission of.
  b ᴛɢ Jesus Christ, Death of.
21a D&C 121: 37.
    ᴛɢ Apostasy of Individuals.
23a 3 Ne. 7: 14.
  b Hel. 6: 17 (17–38).

25a 3 Ne. 9: 9.
26a Mosiah 29: 25;
    Alma 1: 14.
28a ᴛɢ Secret Combinations.
  b Hel. 6: 26; Ether 8: 9 (9, 15–16).

[A.D. 29—30]

29 Therefore they did combine against the people of the Lord, and enter into a covenant to destroy them, and to deliver those who were guilty of murder from the grasp of justice, which was about to be administered according to the law.

30 And they did set at defiance the law and the rights of their country; and they did covenant one with another to destroy the governor, and to establish a "king over the land, that the land should no more be at ᵇliberty but should be subject unto kings.

CHAPTER 7

The chief judge is murdered, the government is overthrown, and the people divide into tribes—Jacob, an antichrist, becomes king of a league of tribes—Nephi preaches repentance and faith in Christ—Angels minister to him daily, and he raises his brother from the dead—Many repent and are baptized.

Now behold, I will show unto you that they did not establish a king over the land; but in this same year, yea, the thirtieth year, they did destroy upon the judgment-seat, yea, did murder the chief judge of the land.

2 And the people were divided one against another; and they did "separate one from another into tribes, every man according to his family and his kindred and friends; and thus they did destroy the government of the land.

3 And every tribe did appoint a chief or a leader over them; and thus they became tribes and leaders of tribes.

4 Now behold, there was no man among them save he had much family and many kindreds and friends; therefore their tribes became exceedingly great.

5 Now all this was done, and there were no wars as yet among them; and all this iniquity had come upon the people "because they did ᵇyield themselves unto the power of Satan.

6 And the regulations of the government were destroyed, because of the "secret combination of the friends and kindreds of those who murdered the prophets.

7 And they did cause a great contention in the land, insomuch that the more righteous part of the people had nearly all become wicked; yea, there were but few righteous men among them.

8 And thus six years had not passed away since the more part of the people had turned from their righteousness, like the dog to his "vomit, or like the sow to her wallowing in the mire.

9 Now this secret combination, which had brought so great iniquity upon the people, did gather themselves together, and did place at their head a man whom they did call Jacob;

10 And they did call him their king; therefore he became a king over this wicked band; and he was one of the chiefest who had given his voice against the prophets who testified of Jesus.

11 And it came to pass that they were not so strong in number as the tribes of the people, who were united together save it were their leaders did establish their laws, every one according to his tribe; nevertheless they were enemies; notwithstanding they were not a righteous people, yet they were united in the hatred of those who had entered into a covenant to "destroy the government.

12 Therefore, Jacob seeing that their enemies were more numerous than they, he being the king of the band, therefore he commanded his

---

30a 1 Sam. 8:5; Alma
    51:5; 3 Ne. 7:12.
    TG Tyranny.
  b TG Liberty.
7 2a TG Unity.

5a Moses 4:6.
  b Rom. 6:16 (13–20);
    Alma 10:25.
6a 2 Ne. 9:9.

8a Prov. 26:11;
    2 Pet. 2:22.
11a 3 Ne. 9:9.

[A.D. 29—30]

people that they should take their flight into the northernmost part of the land, and there build up unto themselves a "kingdom, until they were joined by dissenters, (for he flattered them that there would be many dissenters) and they become sufficiently strong to contend with the tribes of the people; and they did so.

13 And so speedy was their march that it could not be impeded until they had gone forth out of the reach of the people. And thus ended the thirtieth year; and thus were the affairs of the people of Nephi.

14 And it came to pass in the thirty and first year that they were divided into tribes, every man according to his family, kindred and friends; nevertheless they had come to an agreement that they would not go to war one with another; but they were not united as to their laws, and their manner of government, for they were established according to the minds of those who were their chiefs and their leaders. But they did establish very strict laws that one tribe should not trespass against another, insomuch that in some degree they had peace in the land; nevertheless, their hearts were turned from the Lord their God, and they did stone the "prophets and did cast them out from among them.

15 And it came to pass that "Nephi—having been visited by angels and also the voice of the Lord, therefore having seen angels, and being eye-witness, and having had power given unto him that he might know concerning the ministry of Christ, and also being eye-witness to their quick return from righteousness unto their wickedness and abominations;

16 Therefore, being "grieved for the hardness of their hearts and the blindness of their minds—went forth among them in that same year, and began to testify, boldly, repentance and remission of sins through faith on the Lord Jesus Christ.

17 And he did minister many things unto them; and all of them cannot be written, and a part of them would not suffice, therefore they are not written in this book. And Nephi did minister with "power and with great authority.

18 And it came to pass that they were angry with him, even because he had greater power than they, for it were "not possible that they could disbelieve his words, for so great was his faith on the Lord Jesus Christ that angels did minister unto him daily.

19 And in the name of Jesus did he cast out devils and "unclean spirits; and even his "brother did he 'raise from the dead, after he had been stoned and suffered death by the people.

20 And the people saw it, and did witness of it, and were angry with him because of his power; and he did also do "many more miracles, in the sight of the people, in the name of Jesus.

21 And it came to pass that the thirty and first year did pass away, and there were but few who were converted unto the Lord; but as many as were converted did truly signify unto the people that they had been "visited by the power and "Spirit of God, which was in Jesus Christ, in whom they believed.

22 And as many as had devils cast out from them, and were "healed of their sicknesses and their infirmities, did truly manifest unto the

---

12a 3 Ne. 6: 30.
14a 3 Ne. 6: 23 (23–25).
15a 3 Ne. 1: 2 (2–3, 10); 11: 18.
16a Gen. 6: 6; 1 Ne. 2: 18; Alma 31: 24; Moses 8: 25.

17a TG Priesthood, Power of.
18a Alma 4: 19.
19a TG Spirits, Evil or Unclean.
  b 3 Ne. 19: 4.
  c TG Death, Power over.

20a 3 Ne. 8: 1.
21a TG God, Manifestations of.
  b TG God, Spirit of.
22a Mark 2: 11 (11–12); Acts 8: 7.

[A.D. 31—32]

people that they had been wrought upon by the Spirit of God, and had been healed; and they did show forth signs also and did do some miracles among the people.

23 Thus passed away the thirty and second year also. And Nephi did cry unto the people in the commencement of the thirty and third year; and he did preach unto them repentance and remission of sins.

24 Now I would have you to remember also, that there were none who were brought unto ªrepentance who were not baptized with water.

25 Therefore, there were ordained of Nephi, men unto this ministry, that all such as should come unto them should be ªbaptized with water, and this as a witness and a testimony before God, and unto the people, that they had repented and received a ᵇremission of their sins.

26 And there were many in the commencement of this year that were baptized unto repentance; and thus the more part of the year did pass away.

CHAPTER 8

Tempests, earthquakes, fires, whirlwinds, and physical upheavals attest the crucifixion of Christ—Many people are destroyed—Darkness covers the land for three days—Those who remain bemoan their fate.

AND now it came to pass that according to our record, and we know our record to be ªtrue, for behold, it was a ᵇjust man who did keep the record—for he truly did ᶜmany ᵈmiracles in the ᵉname of Jesus; and there was not any man who could do a miracle in the name of Jesus save he were cleansed every whit from his iniquity—

2 And now it came to pass, if there was no mistake made by this man in the reckoning of our time, the ªthirty and third year had passed away;

3 And the people began to look with great earnestness for the sign which had been given by the prophet Samuel, the Lamanite, yea, for the time that there should be ªdarkness for the space of three days over the face of the land.

4 And there began to be great ªdoubtings and ᵇdisputations among the people, notwithstanding so many signs had been given.

5 And it came to pass in the ªthirty and fourth year, in the first month, on the fourth day of the month, there arose a great ᵇstorm, such an one as never had been known in all the land.

6 And there was also a great and terrible tempest; and there was terrible ªthunder, insomuch that it did ᵇshake the whole earth as if it was about to divide asunder.

7 And there were exceedingly sharp lightnings, such as never had been known in all the land.

8 And the ªcity of Zarahemla did take fire.

9 And the city of ªMoroni did ᵇsink into the depths of the sea, and the inhabitants thereof were drowned.

10 And the earth was carried up upon the city of ªMoronihah, that in the place of the city there became a great ᵇmountain.

24a TG Baptism,
　　Qualifications for.
25a TG Baptism.
　　b D&C 20: 37.
　　TG Remission of Sins.
8 1a John 21: 24.
　　b 3 Ne. 23: 7.
　　c 3 Ne. 7: 20 (19–20).
　　d John 6: 14; Morm.
　　　9: 18 (18–19).
　　e Acts 3: 6 (6–16);
　　　Jacob 4: 6.

2a 3 Ne. 2: 8.
3a 1 Ne. 19: 10; Hel.
　　14: 27 (20, 27);
　　3 Ne. 10: 9.
　　TG Darkness, Physical.
4a TG Doubt.
　　b TG Disputations.
5a Hel. 14: 20 (20–27);
　　3 Ne. 11: 2.
　　b TG Jesus Christ,
　　Crucifixion of; Jesus
　　Christ, Death of.

6a 1 Ne. 19: 11;
　　Hel. 14: 21 (20–27).
　　b Matt. 27: 51 (45,
　　　50–51).
8a 4 Ne. 1: 8.
9a Alma 50: 13.
　　b 3 Ne. 9: 4 (4–5).
10a 3 Ne. 8: 25.
　　b Hel. 12: 17;
　　　3 Ne. 9: 8 (6–8).

[A.D. 32—34]

prophets and stoned them not; and it was they who had not shed the blood of the saints, who were spared—

13 And they were spared and were not sunk and buried up in the earth; and they were not drowned in the depths of the sea; and they were not burned by fire, neither were they fallen upon and crushed to death; and they were not carried away in the whirlwind; neither were they overpowered by the vapor of smoke and of darkness.

14 And now, whoso readeth, let him understand; he that hath the scriptures, let him ªsearch them, and see and behold if all these deaths and destructions by fire, and by smoke, and by ᵇtempests, and by whirlwinds, and by the ᶜopening of the earth to receive them, and all these things are not unto the fulfilling of the prophecies of many of the holy prophets.

15 Behold, I say unto you, Yea, many have testified of these things at the coming of Christ, and were ªslain because they testified of these things.

16 Yea, the prophet ªZenos did testify of these things, and also Zenock spake ᵇconcerning these things, because they testified particularly concerning us, who are the remnant of their seed.

17 Behold, our father Jacob also testified concerning a ªremnant of the seed of Joseph. And behold, are not we a remnant of the seed of Joseph? And these things which testify of us, are they not written upon the plates of brass which our father Lehi brought out of Jerusalem?

18 And it came to pass that in the ending of the thirty and fourth year, behold, I will show unto you that the people of Nephi who were

spared, and also those who had been called ªLamanites, who had been spared, did have great favors shown unto them, and great ᵇblessings poured out upon their heads, insomuch that soon after the ᶜascension of Christ into heaven he did truly manifest himself unto them—

19 ªShowing his body unto them, and ministering unto them; and an account of his ministry shall be given hereafter. Therefore for this time I make an end of my sayings.

Jesus Christ did show himself unto the people of Nephi, as the multitude were gathered together in the land Bountiful, and did minister unto them; and on this wise did he show himself unto them. Comprising chapters 11 to 26 inclusive.

CHAPTER 11

The Father testifies of his Beloved Son—Christ appears and proclaims his atonement—The people feel the wound marks in his hands and feet and side—They cry Hosanna—He sets forth the mode and manner of baptism—The spirit of contention is of the devil—Christ's doctrine is that men should believe and be baptized and receive the Holy Ghost.

AND now it came to pass that there were a great multitude ªgathered together, of the people of Nephi, round about the temple which was in the land ᵇBountiful; and they were marveling and wondering one with another, and were showing one to another the ᶜgreat and marvelous change which had taken place.

2 And they were also conversing about this Jesus Christ, of whom the ªsign had been given concerning his death.

14a ᴛɢ Scriptures, Study of.
  b Hel. 14: 23.
  c Num. 16: 32; 1 Ne. 19: 11; 2 Ne. 26: 5.
15a ᴛɢ Martyrdom.
16a Hel. 8: 20 (19–20).

  b 1 Ne. 19: 21.
17a Alma 46: 24; 3 Ne. 5: 23 (23–24).
18a 4 Ne. 1: 20.
  b ᴛɢ Blessing.
  c Acts 1: 9 (9–11).
19a 3 Ne. 11: 12 (12–15).

11 1a Hel. 3: 14 (9, 14).
  b Alma 22: 29; 3 Ne. 3: 23.
  c 3 Ne. 8: 12 (11–14).
2a Hel. 14: 20 (20–27); 3 Ne. 8: 5 (5–25).

3 And it came to pass that while they were thus conversing one with another, they heard a ^avoice as if it came out of heaven; and they cast their eyes round about, for they understood not the voice which they heard; and it was not a harsh voice, neither was it a loud voice; nevertheless, and notwithstanding it being a ^bsmall voice it did ^cpierce them that did hear to the center, insomuch that there was no part of their frame that it did not cause to quake; yea, it did pierce them to the very soul, and did cause their hearts to burn.

4 And it came to pass that again they heard the voice, and they ^aunderstood it not.

5 And again the third time they did hear the voice, and did ^aopen their ears to hear it; and their eyes were towards the sound thereof; and they did look steadfastly towards heaven, from whence the sound came.

6 And behold, the third time they did understand the voice which they heard; and it said unto them:

7 Behold my ^aBeloved Son, ^bin whom I am well pleased, in whom I have glorified my name—hear ye him.

8 And it came to pass, as they understood they cast their eyes up again towards heaven; and behold, they ^asaw a Man ^bdescending out of heaven; and he was clothed in a white robe; and he came down and stood in the midst of them; and the eyes of the whole multitude were turned upon him, and they durst not open their mouths, even one to another, and wist not what it meant, for they thought it was an angel that had appeared unto them.

9 And it came to pass that he stretched forth his hand and spake unto the people, saying:

10 Behold, I am Jesus Christ, whom the prophets testified shall come into the world.

11 And behold, I am the ^alight and the life of the world; and I have drunk out of that bitter ^bcup which the Father hath given me, and have glorified the Father in ^ctaking upon me the sins of the world, in the which I have suffered the ^dwill of the Father in all things from the beginning.

12 And it came to pass that when Jesus had spoken these words the whole multitude ^afell to the earth; for they remembered that it had been ^bprophesied among them that Christ should ^cshow himself unto them after his ascension into heaven.

13 And it came to pass that the ^aLord spake unto them saying:

14 Arise and come forth unto me, that ye may ^athrust your hands into my side, and also that ye may ^bfeel the prints of the nails in my hands and in my feet, that ye may know that I am the ^cGod of Israel, and the God of the whole ^dearth, and have been slain for the sins of the world.

15 And it came to pass that the multitude went forth, and thrust their hands into his side, and ^adid feel the prints of the nails in his hands and in his feet; and this they

3a Deut. 4: 33; Ezek. 1: 24; Hel. 5: 29 (28–36).
b 1 Kgs. 19: 12 (11–13); D&C 85: 6.
c 1 Sam. 3: 11; Jer. 20: 9.
4a Ezek. 1: 24 (24–28); 1 Cor. 14: 2.
5a Job 36: 15; D&C 101: 92.
7a Matt. 3: 17; 17: 5; JS-H 1: 17. TG Witness of the Father.

b 3 Ne. 9: 15.
8a 1 Ne. 12: 6; 2 Ne. 26: 1 (1, 9); Alma 16: 20; Ether 3: 17 (17–18).
b Acts 1: 9 (9–11).
11a TG Jesus Christ, Light of the World.
b John 18: 11.
c John 1: 29.
d Mark 14: 36 (32–42); Luke 22: 42; John 6: 38; Hel. 10: 4; D&C 19: 2.

12a TG Reverence.
b Alma 16: 20.
c 3 Ne. 10: 19.
13a TG Jesus Christ, Lord.
14a John 20: 27.
b Luke 24: 39 (36–39).
c Isa. 45: 3; 3 Ne. 15: 5; D&C 36: 1; 127: 3.
d Ex. 9: 29; 1 Ne. 11: 6.
15a 3 Ne. 18: 25. TG Jesus Christ, Appearances, Postmortal.

[A.D. 34]

did do, going forth one by one until they had all gone forth, and did see with their eyes and did feel with their hands, and did know of a surety and did bear record, that it was he, of whom it was written by the prophets, that should come.

16 And when they had all gone forth and had witnessed for themselves, they did cry out with one accord, saying:

17 Hosanna! Blessed be the name of the Most High God! And they did fall down at the feet of Jesus, and did [a]worship him.

18 And it came to pass that he spake unto [a]Nephi (for Nephi was among the multitude) and he commanded him that he should come forth.

19 And Nephi arose and went forth, and [a]bowed himself before the Lord and did [b]kiss his feet.

20 And the Lord commanded him that he should [a]arise. And he arose and stood before him.

21 And the Lord said unto him: I give unto you [a]power that ye shall [b]baptize this people when I am again ascended into heaven.

22 And again the Lord called [a]others, and said unto them likewise; and he gave unto them power to baptize. And he said unto them: On this wise shall ye baptize; and there shall be [b]no disputations among you.

23 Verily I say unto you, that whoso repenteth of his sins through your [a]words, and [b]desireth to be baptized in my name, on this wise shall ye baptize them—Behold, ye shall go down and [c]stand in the water, and in my name shall ye baptize them.

24 And now behold, these are the words which ye shall say, calling them by name, saying:

25 Having [a]authority given me of Jesus Christ, I baptize you in the name of the [b]Father, and of the Son, and of the Holy Ghost. Amen.

26 And then shall ye [a]immerse them in the water, and come forth again out of the water.

27 And after this manner shall ye [a]baptize in my name; for behold, verily I say unto you, that the Father, and the Son, and the Holy Ghost are [b]one; and I am in the Father, and the Father in me, and the Father and I are one.

28 And according as I have commanded you thus shall ye baptize. And there shall be no [a]disputations among you, as there have hitherto been; neither shall there be disputations among you concerning the points of my doctrine, as there have hitherto been.

29 For verily, verily I say unto you, he that hath the spirit of [a]contention is not of me, but is of the [b]devil, who is the father of contention, and he stirreth up the hearts of men to contend with anger, one with another.

30 Behold, this is not my doctrine, to stir up the hearts of men with anger, one against another; but this

---

17a TG Worship.
18a 3 Ne. 1: 2 (2–3, 10);
   7: 15 (15, 20, 23).
19a Ex. 34: 8; Ether 6: 12.
  b 3 Ne. 17: 10.
20a Josh. 7: 10; Ezek.
   2: 1 (1–2).
21a TG Church
   Organization;
   Priesthood, Authority.
  b TG Baptism, Essential.
22a 1 Ne. 12: 7;
   3 Ne. 12: 1.
  b 1 Cor. 11: 16 (16–19);
   3 Ne. 18: 34.
  TG Disputations.

23a Mosiah 26: 15 (15–16);
   3 Ne. 12: 2.
  b TG Baptism,
   Qualifications for.
  c 3 Ne. 19: 11 (10–13).
25a Mosiah 18: 13;
   Alma 5: 3; D&C
   20: 73. TG Delegation
   of Responsibility;
   Priesthood, Authority.
  b TG Godhead.
26a Moses 6: 52.
  TG Baptism, Immersion; Jesus Christ,
  Types of, in Memory.
27a TG Baptism.

  b Alma 11: 44; 3 Ne.
   28: 10; Morm. 7: 7;
   D&C 20: 28.
28a Acts 4: 32; 1 Cor.
   1: 10 (10–13);
   Eph. 4: 13 (11–14);
   D&C 38: 27.
  TG Disputations.
29a 2 Tim. 2: 24 (23–24);
   Mosiah 23: 15.
  TG Contention.
  b Eph. 4: 27 (26–27);
   Mosiah 2: 32 (32–33);
   Alma 2: 5; 45: 23;
   Hel. 4: 1.

is my doctrine, that such things *should be done away.

31 Behold, verily, verily, I say unto you, I will declare unto you my *doctrine.

32 And this is my *doctrine, and it is the doctrine which the Father hath given unto me; and I bear *record of the Father, and the Father beareth record of me, and the *Holy Ghost beareth record of the Father and me; and I bear record that the Father commandeth all men, everywhere, to repent and believe in me.

33 And whoso believeth in me, and is *baptized, the same shall be *saved; and they are they who shall *inherit the kingdom of God.

34 And whoso believeth not in me, and is not *baptized, shall be damned.

35 Verily, verily, I say unto you, that this is my doctrine, and I bear record of it from the Father; and whoso *believeth in me believeth in the Father also; and unto him will the Father bear record of me, for he will visit him *with fire and with the *Holy Ghost.

36 And thus will the Father bear record of me, and the *Holy Ghost will bear record unto him of the Father and me; for the Father, and I, and the Holy Ghost are *one.

37 And again I say unto you, ye must repent, and *become as a *little child, and be baptized in my name, or ye can in nowise receive these things.

38 And again I say unto you, ye must repent, and be baptized in my name, and become as a little *child, or ye can in nowise inherit the kingdom of God.

39 Verily, verily, I say unto you, that this is my *doctrine, and whoso *buildeth upon this buildeth upon my rock, and the *gates of hell shall not prevail against them.

40 And whoso shall *declare more or less than this, and establish it for my doctrine, the same cometh of evil, and is not built upon my rock; but he buildeth upon a *sandy foundation, and the gates of hell stand open to receive such when the floods come and the winds beat upon them.

41 Therefore, go forth unto this people, and declare the words which I have spoken, unto the ends of the earth.

CHAPTER 12

Jesus calls and commissions the Twelve—He delivers to the Nephites a discourse similar to the Sermon on the Mount—He speaks the Beatitudes —His teachings transcend and take precedence over the law of Moses— Men are commanded to be perfect even as he and his Father are perfect— Compare Matthew 5.

*AND it came to pass that when Jesus had spoken these words unto Nephi, and to those who had been called, (now the number of them who had been called, and received power and authority to *baptize, was *twelve) and behold, he stretched forth his hand unto the multi-

30a Mark 9: 50;
    John 16: 33.
31a John 18: 37; 2 Ne.
    31: 21 (2–21).
32a TG Jesus Christ,
    Teaching Mode of.
  b 1 Jn. 5: 7 (6–9).
    TG Jesus Christ,
    Relationships with
    the Father.
  c 3 Ne. 28: 11; Ether
    5: 4; Moses 1: 24.
33a Mark 16: 16.
    TG Baptism, Essential.
  b TG Salvation, Plan of.

  c TG Exaltation.
34a TG Baptism.
35a Ether 4: 12.
  b 3 Ne. 9. 20; 12: 2.
  c TG Holy Ghost,
    Baptism of.
36a TG Holy Ghost,
    Source of Testimony.
  b TG Godhead; Unity.
37a Mark 10: 15; Luke
    18: 17.
  b 3 Ne. 9: 22.
38a TG Baptism,
    Qualifications for.
39a Mark 4: 2.

  b Matt. 7: 24 (24–29);
    1 Pet. 2: 6 (4–8);
    1 Ne. 13: 36. TG Rock.
  c Matt. 16: 18; 3 Ne.
    18: 13 (12–13);
    D&C 17: 8.
40a Rom. 16: 17 (17–19);
    1 Tim. 1: 3.
  b 3 Ne. 14: 26 (24–27).
12 1a Matt. 5: 1 (1–48).
  b Mark 16: 16 (15–16);
    John 4: 2 (1–2).
  c 3 Ne. 11: 22; 13: 25.
                [A.D. 34]

tude, and cried unto them, saying: [d]Blessed are ye if ye shall give heed unto the words of these twelve whom I have [e]chosen from among you to minister unto you, and to be your servants; and unto them I have given power that they may baptize you with water; and after that ye are baptized with water, behold, I will baptize you with fire and with the Holy Ghost; therefore blessed are ye if ye shall believe in me and be baptized, after that ye have seen me and know that I am.

2 And again, more blessed are they who shall [a]believe in your words because that ye shall testify that ye have seen me, and that ye know that I am. Yea, blessed are they who shall [b]believe in your [c]words, and [d]come down into the depths of humility and be baptized, for they shall be visited [e]with fire and with the Holy Ghost, and shall receive a remission of their sins.

3 Yea, blessed are the [a]poor in spirit who [b]come unto me, for theirs is the kingdom of heaven.

4 And again, blessed are all they that [a]mourn, for they shall be [b]comforted.

5 And blessed are the [a]meek, for they shall inherit the [b]earth.

6 And blessed are all they who do [a]hunger and [b]thirst after [c]righteousness, for they shall be [d]filled with the Holy Ghost.

7 And blessed are the [a]merciful, for they shall obtain mercy.

8 And blessed are all the [a]pure in heart, for they shall [b]see God.

9 And blessed are all the [a]peacemakers, for they shall be called the [b]children of God.

10 And blessed are all they who are [a]persecuted for my name's sake, for theirs is the kingdom of heaven.

11 And blessed are ye when men shall [a]revile you and persecute, and shall say all manner of evil against you falsely, for my sake;

12 For [a]ye shall have great joy and be exceedingly glad, for great shall be your [b]reward in heaven; for so [c]persecuted they the prophets who were before you.

13 Verily, verily, I say unto you, I give unto you to be the [a]salt of the earth; but if the salt shall lose its savor wherewith shall the earth be salted? The salt shall be thenceforth good for nothing, but to be cast out and to be trodden under foot of men.

14 Verily, verily, I say unto you, I give unto you to be the light of this people. A city that is set on a hill cannot be hid.

15 Behold, do men light a [a]candle and put it under a bushel? Nay, but on a candlestick, and it giveth light to all that are in the house;

16 Therefore let your [a]light so shine before this people, that they may see your good works and [b]glorify your Father who is in heaven.

17 Think not that I am come to destroy the law or the prophets.

1d TG Blessing.
 e TG Called of God.
2a TG Teachable.
 b Mosiah 26: 15 (15–16); D&C 46: 14.
 c 3 Ne. 11: 23.
 d Ether 4: 1.
 e 3 Ne. 11: 35; 19: 13 (13–14).
3a Ps. 86: 1; Eccl. 4: 13 (13–14); Matt. 5: 3; D&C 56: 18 (17–18). TG Poor in Spirit.
 b Matt. 11: 28 (28–30).
4a Morm. 2: 11 (11–14). TG Mourning.
 b Matt. 5: 4; Alma 28: 6. TG Comfort.

5a Zeph. 2: 3 (1–3); Rom. 12: 16. TG Meekness.
 b TG Earth, Destiny of.
6a Matt. 5: 6; 2 Ne. 9: 51; Enos 1: 4.
 b Jer. 29: 13.
 c Prov. 21: 21.
 d TG Spirituality.
7a TG Mercy.
8a TG Purity.
 b TG God, Privilege of Seeing.
9a TG Peacemakers.
 b TG Sons and Daughters of God.
10a Matt. 5: 10;

   D&C 122: 5 (5–9).
11a TG Reviling.
12a Matt. 5: 12.
 b TG Reward.
 c 2 Cor. 7: 4. TG Prophets, Rejection of.
13a 2 Chr. 13: 5; Matt. 5: 13; D&C 101: 39 (39–40). TG Mission of Early Saints; Salt.
15a Luke 8: 16.
16a 3 Ne. 18: 24. TG Example.
 b John 11: 4 (1–4); Ether 12: 4.

[A.D. 34]

I am not come to destroy but to fulfil;

18 For verily I say unto you, one jot nor one tittle ^ahath not passed away from the ^blaw, but in me it hath all been fulfilled.

19 And behold, I have given you the law and the commandments of my Father, that ye shall believe in me, and that ye shall repent of your sins, and come unto me with a ^abroken heart and a contrite spirit. Behold, ye have the commandments before you, and the ^blaw is fulfilled.

20 Therefore ^acome unto me and be ye saved; for verily I say unto you, that except ye shall keep my ^bcommandments, which I have commanded you at this time, ye shall in no case enter into the kingdom of heaven.

21 Ye have heard that it hath been said by them of old time, and it is also written before you, that thou shalt not ^akill, and whosoever shall kill shall be in danger of the judgment of God;

22 But I say unto you, that whosoever is ^aangry with his brother shall be in danger of his judgment. And whosoever shall say to his brother, Raca, shall be in danger of the council; and whosoever shall say, Thou fool, shall be in danger of hell fire.

23 Therefore, ^aif ye shall come unto me, or shall desire to come unto me, and rememberest that thy brother hath aught against thee—

24 Go thy way unto thy brother, and first be ^areconciled to thy brother, and then come unto me

with full ^bpurpose of heart, and I will receive you.

25 ^aAgree with thine adversary quickly while thou art in the way with him, lest at any time he shall get thee, and thou shalt be cast into prison.

26 Verily, verily, I say unto thee, thou shalt by no means come out thence until thou hast paid the uttermost senine. And while ye are in prison can ye pay even one ^asenine? Verily, verily, I say unto you, Nay.

27 Behold, it is written by them of old time, that thou shalt not commit ^aadultery;

28 But I say unto you, that whosoever looketh on a woman, to ^alust after her, hath committed adultery already in his heart.

29 Behold, I give unto you a commandment, that ye suffer ^anone of these things to enter into your ^bheart;

30 For it is better that ye should deny yourselves of these things, wherein ye will take up your ^across, than that ye should be cast into hell.

31 It hath been written, that whosoever shall put away his wife, let him give her a writing of ^adivorcement.

32 Verily, verily, I say unto you, that whosoever shall ^aput away his wife, saving for the cause of ^bfornication, causeth her to commit ^cadultery; and whoso shall marry her who is divorced committeth adultery.

33 And again it is written, thou shalt not ^aforswear thyself, but

---

18a Matt. 5: 18.
  b TG Law of Moses.
19a 3 Ne. 9: 20.
  TG Contrite Heart.
  b 3 Ne. 9: 17.
20a Isa. 55: 3.
  b 3 Ne. 15: 10.
21a Ex. 20: 13 (13–17);
  Deut. 5: 17 (17–21);
  Matt. 5: 21;
  Mosiah 13: 21 (21–24);
  D&C 42: 18.

TG Life, Sanctity of.
22a Matt. 5: 22.
23a Matt. 5: 23.
24a TG Forgiveness;
  Reconciliation.
  b 3 Ne. 18: 29 (28–33);
  D&C 46: 4.
25a Matt. 5: 25 (25–26).
26a Alma 11: 3; 30: 33.
27a Matt. 5: 27; 2 Ne.
  9: 36; D&C 59: 6.
28a TG Lust.
29a D&C 42: 23.

  b Acts 8: 22.
30a Matt. 10: 38; 16: 24;
  Luke 9: 23; 14: 27;
  D&C 23: 6.
31a TG Divorce.
32a Matt. 5: 32; Mark 10:
  11 (11–12);
  Luke 16: 18.
  b TG Fornication.
  c TG Adultery.
33a TG Swearing.
                    [A.D. 34]

shalt *b*perform unto the Lord thine *c*oaths;

34 But verily, verily, I say unto you, *a*swear not at all; neither by heaven, for it is God's throne;

35 Nor by the earth, for it is his footstool;

36 Neither shalt thou swear by thy head, because thou canst not make one hair black or white;

37 But let your *a*communication be *b*Yea, yea; Nay, nay; for whatsoever cometh of more than these is evil.

38 And behold, it is written, an *a*eye for an eye, and a tooth for a tooth;

39 But I say unto you, that ye shall not *a*resist evil, but whosoever shall smite thee on thy right *b*cheek, *c*turn to him the other also;

40 And if any man will sue thee at the law and take away thy coat, *a*let him have thy cloak also;

41 And whosoever shall compel thee to *a*go a mile, go with him twain.

42 *a*Give to him that asketh thee, and from him that would *b*borrow of thee turn thou not away.

43 And behold it is written also, that thou shalt love thy neighbor and hate thine enemy;

44 But behold I say unto you, love your *a*enemies, bless them that curse you, do *b*good to them that hate you, and *c*pray for them who despitefully use you and persecute you;

45 That ye may be the children of your Father who is in heaven; for

he maketh his sun to rise *a*on the evil and on the good.

46 Therefore those things which were of old time, which were under the law, in me are all *a*fulfilled.

47 *a*Old things are done away, and all things have become *b*new.

48 Therefore I would that ye should be *a*perfect even as I, or your Father who is in heaven is perfect.

CHAPTER 13

Jesus teaches the Nephites the Lord's Prayer—They are to lay up treasures in heaven—The Twelve in their ministry are commanded to take no thought for temporal things—Compare Matthew 6.

*a*VERILY, verily, I say that I would that ye should do alms unto the poor; but take heed that ye do not your alms before men to be seen of them; otherwise ye have no reward of your Father who is in heaven.

2 Therefore, when ye shall do your alms do not sound a trumpet before you, as will hypocrites do in the synagogues and in the streets, that they may have *a*glory of men. Verily I say unto you, they have their reward.

3 But when thou doest alms let not thy left hand know what thy right hand doeth;

4 That thine alms may be in secret; and thy Father who seeth in secret, himself shall reward thee openly.

5 And when thou *a*prayest thou shalt not do as the *b*hypocrites, for

33b TG Dependability.
  c TG Oath.
34a Lev. 5: 4; Morm. 3: 14.
  TG Profanity.
37a TG Communication.
  b TG Honesty.
38a Lev. 24: 20;
  Matt. 5: 38 (38–42).
  TG Punishment.
39a 3 Ne. 6: 13; 4 Ne. 1: 34;
  D&C 98: 23 (23–27).
  TG Submissiveness.
  b Lam. 3: 30.
  c TG Forbearance;
  Patience.
40a TG Charity; Initiative.

41a TG Generosity.
42a Jacob 2: 19 (17–19);
  Mosiah 4: 26.
  b TG Borrowing.
44a Prov. 24: 17; 25: 21
  (21–22); Alma 48: 23.
  TG Enemies.
  b TG Benevolence.
  c Acts 7: 60 (59–60);
  2 Tim. 4: 16.
45a Matt. 5: 45.
46a Heb. 8: 13.
47a 3 Ne. 9: 17; 15: 2
  (2, 7); D&C 22: 1.
  b Jer. 31: 31 (31–33);
  Ether 13: 9.

48a Matt. 5: 48; 3 Ne.
  19: 29 (28–29); 27: 27.
  TG God, Perfection of;
  God, the Standard of
  Righteousness; Jesus
  Christ, Exemplar;
  Man, New, Spiritually
  Reborn; Man,
  Potential to Become
  like Heavenly Father.
13 1a Matt. 6: 1 (1–34).
  TG Almsgiving.
2a D&C 121: 35 (34–35).
5a TG Prayer.
  b TG Hypocrisy.

they love to pray, standing in the synagogues and in the corners of the streets, that they may be seen of men. Verily I say unto you, they have their reward.

6 But thou, when thou prayest, enter into thy closet, and when thou hast ªshut thy door, pray to thy Father who is in secret; and thy Father, who ᵇseeth in secret, shall reward thee openly.

7 But when ye pray, use not ªvain repetitions, as the ᵇheathen, for they think that they shall be heard for their much speaking.

8 Be not ye therefore like unto them, for your Father ªknoweth what things ye have need of before ye ᵇask him.

9 After this ªmanner therefore ᵇpray ye: Our ᶜFather who art in heaven, hallowed be thy name.

10 Thy will be done on earth as it is in heaven.

11 And forgive us our debts, as we forgive our debtors.

12 And ªlead us not into temptation, but deliver us from evil.

13 For thine is the kingdom, and the power, and the glory, forever. Amen.

14 For, if ye ªforgive men their trespasses your heavenly Father will also forgive you;

15 But if ye forgive not men their trespasses neither will your Father forgive your trespasses.

16 Moreover, when ye ªfast be not as the ᵇhypocrites, of a sad countenance, for they disfigure their faces that they may appear unto men to fast. Verily I say unto you, they have their reward.

17 But thou, when thou fastest, anoint thy head, and ªwash thy face;

18 That thou appear not unto men to fast, but unto thy Father, who is in ªsecret; and thy Father, who seeth in secret, shall reward thee openly.

19 Lay not up for yourselves treasures upon earth, where ªmoth and rust doth corrupt, and thieves break through and steal;

20 But lay up for yourselves ªtreasures in heaven, where neither moth nor rust doth corrupt, and where thieves do not break through nor steal.

21 For where your treasure is, there will your heart be also.

22 The ªlight of the body is the ᵇeye; if, therefore, thine eye be ᶜsingle, thy whole body shall be full of light.

23 But if thine eye be evil, thy whole body shall be full of darkness. If, therefore, the light that is in thee be darkness, how great is that darkness!

24 No man can ªserve ᵇtwo masters; for either he will hate the one and love the other, or else he will hold to the one and despise the other. Ye cannot serve God and Mammon.

25 And now it came to pass that when Jesus had spoken these words he looked upon the ªtwelve whom he had chosen, and said unto them: Remember the words which I have spoken. For behold, ye are they whom I have chosen to ᵇminister unto this people. Therefore I say unto you, ᶜtake no thought for your

6a 2 Kgs. 4: 33.
  b TG God, Omniscience of.
7a TG Sincerity.
  b TG Heathen.
8a D&C 84: 83.
  b Ezek. 36: 37.
9a Matt. 6: 9 (9–13).
  b TG Prayer.
  c TG God the Father—Elohim.
12a See JST Matt. 6: 14 in footnote for Matt. 6: 13.
14a Mosiah 26: 31.

TG Forgiveness.
16a Isa. 58: 5 (5–7);
    Zech. 7: 5 (5–6).
  TG Fasting.
  b TG Hypocrisy.
17a TG Washing.
18a Isa. 45: 15; D&C 38: 7.
19a 3 Ne. 27: 32.
20a Hel. 5: 8; 8: 25.
  TG Treasure.
22a Ezra 9: 8.
  b Matt. 6: 22 (20–25).
  c D&C 88: 67.
  TG Dedication.

24a 1 Sam. 7: 3;
    Alma 5: 41 (39–42);
    Moses 1: 15.
  b Hosea 10: 2.
25a Matt. 6: 25;
    3 Ne. 12: 1; 15: 11.
  b TG Church Organization; Delegation of Responsibility.
  c Alma 31: 37;
    D&C 84: 81 (79–85).

                    [A.D. 34]

life, what ye shall eat, or what ye shall drink; nor yet for your body, what ye shall put on. Is not the life more than meat, and the body than [d]raiment?

26 Behold the [a]fowls of the air, for they sow not, neither do they reap nor gather into barns; yet your heavenly Father feedeth them. Are ye not much better than they?

27 Which of you by taking thought can add one cubit unto his stature?

28 And why take ye thought for raiment? Consider the [a]lilies of the field how they grow; they toil not, neither do they spin;

29 And yet I say unto you, that even Solomon, in all his glory, was not arrayed like one of these.

30 Wherefore, if God so clothe the grass of the field, which today is, and tomorrow is cast into the oven, even so will he clothe you, if ye are not of little faith.

31 Therefore take no thought, saying, What shall we eat? or, What shall we drink? or, Wherewithal shall we be clothed?

32 For your heavenly Father knoweth that ye have need of all these things.

33 But [a]seek ye first the [b]kingdom of God and his righteousness, and all these things shall be added unto you.

34 Take therefore no thought for the morrow, for the morrow shall take thought for the things of itself. [a]Sufficient is the day unto the evil thereof.

CHAPTER 14

Jesus commands: Judge not; ask of God; beware of false prophets— He promises salvation to those who do the will of the Father—Compare Matthew 7.

[a]AND now it came to pass that when Jesus had spoken these words he turned again to the multitude, and did open his mouth unto them again, saying: Verily, verily, I say unto you, Judge not, that ye be not judged.

2 [a]For with what judgment ye judge, ye shall be judged; and with what measure ye mete, it shall be measured to you again.

3 And why beholdest thou the mote that is in thy brother's eye, but considerest not the beam that is in thine own eye?

4 Or how wilt thou say to thy brother: Let me pull the mote out of thine eye—and behold, a beam is in thine own eye?

5 Thou [a]hypocrite, first cast the [b]beam out of thine own eye; and then shalt thou see clearly to cast the mote out of thy brother's eye.

6 Give not that which is [a]holy unto the dogs, neither cast ye your pearls before swine, lest they trample them under their feet, and turn again and rend you.

7 [a]Ask, and it shall be given unto you; [b]seek, and ye shall find; knock, and it shall be opened unto you.

8 For every one that asketh, receiveth; and he that seeketh, findeth; and to him that knocketh, it shall be opened.

9 Or what man is there of you, who, if his son ask bread, will give him a stone?

10 Or if he ask a fish, will he give him a serpent?

11 If ye then, being evil, know how to give good gifts unto your children, how much more shall your Father who is in heaven give good things to them that ask him?

12 Therefore, all things whatsoever ye would that men should do to you, [a]do ye even so to them, for this is the law and the prophets.

25d Job 27: 16 (16–17).
26a D&C 117: 6.
28a TG Nature.
33a TG Commitment.
  b Luke 12: 31 (22–34).
  TG Objectives.
34a Matt. 6: 34.

14 1a Matt. 7: 1 (1–27). See also footnote to Matt. 7: 1.
2a Morm. 8: 19.
5a TG Hypocrisy.
  b John 8: 7 (3–11).
6a TG Holiness.
7a 3 Ne. 27: 29.

  TG Prayer.
  b TG Initiative; Objectives.
12a TG Benevolence; Compassion; Courtesy.

[A.D. 34]

13 Enter ye in at the "strait gate; for wide is the gate, and *broad* is the way, which leadeth to destruction, and many there be who go in thereat;

14 Because strait is the "gate, and *narrow* is the way, which leadeth unto life, and *few* there be that find it.

15 Beware of "false prophets, who come to you in sheep's clothing, but inwardly they are ravening wolves.

16 Ye shall know them by their "fruits. Do men gather grapes of thorns, or figs of thistles?

17 Even so every "good tree bringeth forth good fruit; but a corrupt tree bringeth forth evil fruit.

18 A good tree cannot bring forth evil fruit, neither a corrupt tree bring forth good fruit.

19 Every tree that "bringeth not forth good fruit is hewn down, and cast into the fire.

20 Wherefore, by their "fruits ye shall know them.

21 Not every one that saith unto me, Lord, Lord, shall "enter into the kingdom of heaven; but he that doeth the will of my Father who is in heaven.

22 Many will "say to me in that day: Lord, Lord, have we not prophesied in thy name, and in thy name have cast out devils, and in thy name done many wonderful works?

23 And then will "I profess unto them: I never *knew* you; *depart* from me, ye that work iniquity.

24 Therefore, whoso heareth these sayings of mine and doeth them, I will liken him unto a wise man, who built his house upon a "rock—

25 And the "rain descended, and the floods came, and the winds blew, and beat upon that house; and it *fell* not, for it was founded upon a rock.

26 And every one that heareth these sayings of mine and doeth them not shall be likened unto a "foolish man, who built his house upon the *sand*—

27 And the rain descended, and the floods came, and the winds blew, and beat upon that house; and it fell, and great was the fall of it.

CHAPTER 15

Jesus announces that the law of Moses is fulfilled in him—The Nephites are the other sheep of whom he spake in Jerusalem—Because of iniquity the Lord's people in Jerusalem do not know of the scattered sheep of Israel.

AND now it came to pass that when Jesus had ended these sayings he cast his eyes round about on the multitude, and said unto them: Behold, ye have heard the things which I "taught before I ascended to my Father; therefore, whoso remembereth these sayings of mine and *doeth* them, him will I *raise* up at the last day.

2 And it came to pass that when Jesus had said these words he perceived that there were some among them who marveled, and wondered what he would concerning the law

---

13a Luke 13:24;
   3 Ne. 27:33.
 b D&C 132:25.
14a 2 Ne. 9:41; 31:9 (9, 17–18); D&C 22:4.
 b 1 Ne. 8:20.
 c Matt. 7:14;
   1 Ne. 14:12.
15a Jer. 23:21 (21–32);
   2 Ne. 28:12 (9, 12, 15).
   TG False Prophets.
16a Col. 1:6;
   Alma 32:42 (28–42);
   D&C 52:34 (18, 34).

17a Alma 5:41.
19a Matt. 3:10;
   Alma 5:36 (36–41);
   D&C 97:7.
20a Matt. 7:17 (16–20);
   12:33; Luke 6:43
   (43–45); Moro. 7:5.
21a 1 Jn. 2:17.
22a Alma 5:17.
23a Matt. 7:23.
 b Mosiah 5:13; 26:25
   (24–27); D&C 112:26.
 c Ps. 119:115;
   Luke 13:27.

24a TG Rock.
25a Alma 26:6; Hel. 5:12.
 b Prov. 12:7.
26a TG Foolishness.
 b 3 Ne. 11:40.
15 1a IE in Galilee and
   Judea.
 b James 1:22 (22–24).
 c John 6:39; 1 Ne.
   13:37; Mosiah 23:22;
   Alma 26:7;
   D&C 5:35.

[A.D. 34]

of Moses; for they understood not the saying that [a]old things had passed away, and that all things had become new.

3 And he said unto them: Marvel not that I said unto you that old things had passed away, and that all things had become [a]new.

4 Behold, I say unto you that the [a]law is fulfilled that was given unto Moses.

5 Behold, [a]I am he that gave the law, and I am he who covenanted with my people Israel; therefore, the law in me is fulfilled, for I have come to [b]fulfil the law; therefore it hath an end.

6 Behold, I do [a]not destroy the prophets, for as many as have not been fulfilled in me, verily I say unto you, shall all be fulfilled.

7 And because I said unto you that old things have passed away, I do not destroy that which hath been spoken concerning things which are to come.

8 For behold, the [a]covenant which I have made with my people is not all fulfilled; but the law which was given unto Moses hath an end in me.

9 Behold, I am the [a]law, and the [b]light. Look unto me, and endure to the end, and ye shall [c]live; for unto him that [d]endureth to the end will I give eternal life.

10 Behold, I have given unto you the [a]commandments; therefore keep my commandments. And this is the law and the prophets, for they truly [b]testified of me.

11 And now it came to pass that when Jesus had spoken these words, he [a]said unto those twelve whom he had chosen:

12 Ye are my [a]disciples; and ye are a [b]light unto this people, who are a remnant of the house of [c]Joseph.

13 And behold, this is the [a]land of your inheritance; and the Father hath given it unto you.

14 And not at any time hath the Father given me commandment that I should [a]tell it unto your brethren at Jerusalem.

15 Neither at any time hath the Father given me commandment that I should tell unto them concerning the [a]other tribes of the house of Israel, whom the Father hath led away out of the land.

16 This much did the Father [a]command me, that I should tell unto them:

17 That other sheep I have which are not of this fold; them also I must bring, and they shall hear my voice; and there shall be one fold, and one [a]shepherd.

18 And now, because of [a]stiffneckedness and [b]unbelief they [c]understood not my word; therefore I was commanded to say no more of the [d]Father concerning this thing unto them.

19 But, verily, I say unto you that the Father hath commanded me, and I tell it unto you, that ye were [a]separated from among them because of their iniquity; therefore it

2a 3 Ne. 12:47 (46–47).
3a Heb. 8:13;
   Ether 13:9.
4a Mosiah 13:27 (27–31);
   3 Ne. 9:17 (17–20).
5a 1 Cor. 10:4 (1–4);
   3 Ne. 11:14. TG Jesus
   Christ—Jehovah.
  b Alma 34:13. TG Jesus
   Christ, Mission of.
6a 3 Ne. 20:11 (11–12);
   23:3 (1–3).
8a 3 Ne. 5:25 (24–26);
   16:5. TG Covenants;
   Restoration of the
   Gospel.
9a 2 Ne. 26:1.
  b TG Jesus Christ,

   Light of the World.
  c Lev. 18:5; John 11:
   25; D&C 84:44.
  d Matt. 10:22 (22–33);
   Mark 13:13;
   2 Ne. 31:20;
   Alma 32:13 (13–15);
   3 Ne. 27:6 (6–17).
10a 3 Ne. 12:20.
  b Mosiah 13:33.
11a 3 Ne. 13:25;
   Moro. 2:1.
12a TG Church
   Organization.
  b TG Example;
   Leadership.
  c TG Israel, Joseph,

   People of.
13a 1 Ne. 18:23;
   3 Ne. 16:16.
14a 3 Ne. 5:20.
15a 2 Ne. 21:12; 3 Ne.
   16:1 (1–4). TG Israel,
   Ten Lost Tribes of.
16a John 15:15; 16:12.
17a TG Shepherd.
18a TG Stiffneckedness.
  b TG Doubt; Unbelief,
   Unbelievers.
  c D&C 10:59.
  d John 12:50.
19a 1 Kgs. 8:53;
   John 17:6 (6–22).

                              [A.D. 34]

is because of their iniquity that they know not of you.

20 And verily, I say unto you again that the other tribes hath the Father separated from them; and it is because of their iniquity that they know not of them.

21 And verily I say unto you, that ye are they of whom I said: [a]Other sheep I have which are not of this fold; them also I must bring, and they shall hear my voice; and there shall be one fold, and one [b]shepherd.

22 And they understood me not, for they supposed it had been the [a]Gentiles; for they understood not that the Gentiles should be [b]converted through their preaching.

23 And they understood me not that I said they shall hear my voice; and they understood me not that the [a]Gentiles should not at any time hear my voice—that I should not manifest myself unto them save it were by the [b]Holy Ghost.

24 But behold, ye have both heard [a]my voice, and seen me; and ye are my sheep, and ye are numbered among those whom the Father hath [b]given me.

CHAPTER 16

Jesus will visit others of the lost sheep of Israel—In the latter days the gospel will go to the Gentiles and then to the house of Israel—The Lord's people shall see eye to eye when he brings again Zion.

AND verily, verily, I say unto you that I have [a]other sheep, which are not of this land, neither of the land of Jerusalem, neither in any parts of that land round about whither I have been to minister.

2 For they of whom I speak are they who have not as yet heard my voice; neither have I at any time manifested myself unto them.

3 But I have received a [a]commandment of the Father that I shall go unto them, and that they shall [b]hear my voice, and shall be numbered among my sheep, that there may be one fold and one shepherd; therefore I go to show myself unto them.

4 And I command you that ye shall [a]write these sayings after I am gone, that if it so be that my people at Jerusalem, they who have seen me and been with me in my ministry, do not ask the Father in my name, that they may receive a knowledge of you by the Holy Ghost, and also of the other tribes whom they know not of, that these sayings which ye shall write shall be kept and shall be manifested unto the [b]Gentiles, that through the fulness of the Gentiles, the remnant of their seed, who shall be scattered forth upon the face of the earth because of their [c]unbelief, may be brought in, or may be brought to a [d]knowledge of me, their Redeemer.

5 And then will I [a]gather them in from the four quarters of the earth; and then will I fulfil the [b]covenant which the Father hath made unto all the people of the [c]house of Israel.

6 And blessed are the [a]Gentiles, because of their belief in me, in and of the Holy Ghost, which [b]wit-

---

21a John 10: 16 (14–16).
  b TG Jesus Christ, Good Shepherd.
22a TG Gentiles.
  b Acts 10: 45 (34–48).
23a Matt. 15: 24.
  b 1 Ne. 10: 11. TG Holy Ghost, Mission of.
24a Alma 5: 38; 3 Ne. 16: 3 (1–5); 18: 31.
  b John 6: 37; D&C 27: 14.
16 1a 1 Ne. 19: 10; 2 Ne. 21: 12; 3 Ne. 15: 15. TG Israel,

Ten Lost Tribes of.
3a 3 Ne. 18: 27.
  b 3 Ne. 17: 4.
4a 2 Ne. 25: 18.
  TG Scriptures to Come Forth.
  b 1 Ne. 10: 14; 3 Ne. 21: 6 (1–11).
  c TG Unbelief, Unbelievers.
  d Ezek. 20: 42 (42–44); Micah 7: 9 (8–9); 3 Ne. 20: 13. TG Israel, Restoration of.

5a TG Israel, Gathering of.
  b 3 Ne. 5: 25 (24–26); 15: 8.
  c 1 Ne. 22: 9; 3 Ne. 21: 27 (26–29).
6a 1 Ne. 13: 39 (23, 30–42); 2 Ne. 30: 3; 3 Ne. 20: 27.
  b 2 Ne. 32: 5; 3 Ne. 11: 32 (32, 35–36). TG Holy Ghost, Source of Testimony, which.

nesses unto them of me and of the Father.

7 Behold, because of their belief in me, saith the Father, and because of the unbelief of you, O house of Israel, in the ªlatter day shall the truth come unto the ᵇGentiles, that the fulness of these things shall be made known unto them.

8 But wo, saith the Father, unto the ªunbelieving of the Gentiles—for notwithstanding they have come forth upon the face of this land, and have ᵇscattered my people who are of the house of Israel; and my people who are of the house of Israel have been ᶜcast out from among them, and have been trodden under feet by them;

9 And because of the mercies of the Father unto the Gentiles, and also the judgments of the Father upon my people who are of the house of Israel, verily, verily, I say unto you, that after all this, and I have caused my people who are of the house of Israel to be smitten, and to be afflicted, and to be ªslain, and to be cast out from among them, and to become ᵇhated by them, and to become a hiss and a byword among them—

10 And thus commandeth the Father that I should say unto you: At that day when the Gentiles shall ªsin against my gospel, and shall reject the fulness of my gospel, and shall be ᵇlifted up in the pride of their hearts above all nations, and above all the people of the whole earth, and shall be filled with all manner of lyings, and of deceits, and of mischiefs, and all manner of hypocrisy, and ᶜmurders, and ᵈpriestcrafts, and whoredoms, and of secret abominations; and if they shall do all those things, and shall ᵉreject the fulness of my gospel, behold, saith the Father, I will bring the fulness of my gospel from among them.

11 And then will I ªremember my covenant which I have made unto my people, O house of Israel, and I will bring my gospel unto them.

12 And I will show unto thee, O house of Israel, that the Gentiles shall not have power over you; but I will remember my covenant unto you, O house of Israel, and ye shall come unto the ªknowledge of the fulness of my gospel.

13 But if the Gentiles will repent and return unto me, saith the Father, behold they shall be ªnumbered among my people, O house of Israel.

14 And I will not suffer my people, who are of the house of Israel, to go through among them, and tread them down, saith the Father.

15 But if they will not turn unto me, and hearken unto my voice, I will suffer them, yea, I will suffer my people, O house of Israel, that they shall go through among them, and shall ªtread them down, and they shall be as salt that hath lost its savor, which is thenceforth good for nothing but to be cast out, and to be trodden under foot of my people, O house of Israel.

16 Verily, verily, I say unto you, thus hath the Father commanded

7a ᴛɢ Restoration of the Gospel.
  b D&C 19: 27; 107: 33.
    ᴛɢ Mission of Latter-day Saints.
8a 2 Ne. 6: 15; 28: 15 (15–32); Ether 2: 9 (8–11).
  b 1 Ne. 13: 14; 2 Ne. 26: 19; Morm. 5: 9 (9, 15).
  c 3 Ne. 20: 28.
9a Amos 9: 1 (1–4).
  b Jer. 23: 40; Lam. 2: 16 (15–16); Joel 2: 17; 1 Ne. 19: 14.
10a 3 Ne. 20: 15.
  b Morm. 8: 36 (35–41).
  c 3 Ne. 30: 2; Morm. 8: 31.
  d 2 Ne. 26: 29.
    ᴛɢ Priestcraft.
  e 3 Ne. 20: 28 (27–28); D&C 6: 31.
11a Isa. 44: 21; 3 Ne. 20: 29 (28–31); 21: 4 (1–11); Morm. 5: 20.
12a Hel. 15: 13.
    ᴛɢ Israel, Restoration of; Knowledge.
13a Gal. 3: 7 (7, 29); 1 Ne. 15: 13 (13–17); 22: 9 (5–10); 2 Ne. 10: 18 (18–19); 3 Ne. 30: 2; Abr. 2: 10 (9–11).
15a Micah 5: 8 (8–15); 3 Ne. 20: 16; 21: 12 (12–21); D&C 87: 5.

[A.D. 34]

me—that I should give unto "this people this land for their inheritance.

17 And then the "words of the prophet Isaiah shall be fulfilled, which say:

18 "Thy bwatchmen shall lift up the voice; with the voice together shall they sing, for they shall see eye to eye when the Lord shall bring again Zion.

19 Break forth into joy, sing together, ye waste places of Jerusalem; for the Lord hath comforted his people, he hath redeemed Jerusalem.

20 The Lord hath made bare his holy arm in the eyes of all the nations; and all the ends of the earth shall see the salvation of God.

CHAPTER 17

Jesus directs the people to ponder his words and pray for understanding— He heals their sick—He prays for the people, using language that cannot be written—Angels minister to and fire encircles their little ones.

BEHOLD, now it came to pass that when Jesus had spoken these words he looked round about again on the multitude, and he said unto them: Behold, my "time is at hand.

2 I "perceive that ye are weak, that ye cannot bunderstand all my words which I am commanded of the Father to speak unto you at this time.

3 Therefore, go ye unto your homes, and "ponder upon the things which I have said, and ask of the Father, in my name, that ye may understand, and bprepare your minds for the cmorrow, and I come unto you again.

4 But now I "go unto the Father, and also to bshow myself unto the lost tribes of Israel, for they are not clost unto the Father, for he knoweth whither he hath taken them.

5 And it came to pass that when Jesus had thus spoken, he cast his eyes round about again on the multitude, and beheld they were "in tears, and did look steadfastly upon him as if they would ask him to tarry a little longer with them.

6 And he said unto them: Behold, my bowels are filled with "compassion towards you.

7 Have ye any that are "sick among you? Bring them hither. Have ye any that are lame, or blind, or halt, or maimed, or bleprous, or that are withered, or that are deaf, or that are afflicted in any manner? Bring them hither and I will cheal them, for I have compassion upon you; my bowels are filled with mercy.

8 For I perceive that ye desire that I should show unto you what I have done unto your brethren at Jerusalem, for I see that your "faith is bsufficient that I should heal you.

9 And it came to pass that when he had thus spoken, all the multitude, with one accord, did go forth with their sick and their afflicted, and their lame, and with their "blind, and with their dumb, and with all them that were afflicted in any manner; and he did heal them every one as they were brought forth unto him.

16a 3 Ne. 15: 13.
17a 3 Ne. 20: 11.
18a Isa. 52: 8 (8–10);
    3 Ne. 20: 32.
  b Ezek. 33: 2 (2, 7);
    D&C 101: 45 (45,
    53–54).
  TG Watchmen.
17 1a IE to return to the
    Father. See v. 4.
 2a TG Jesus Christ,
    Teaching Mode of.
  b John 16: 12; D&C 50:

40; 78: 18 (17–18).
 3a TG Meditation.
  b Ezra 7: 10;
    D&C 29: 8; 132: 3.
  c 3 Ne. 19: 2.
 4a 3 Ne. 18: 39.
  b 3 Ne. 16: 3.
    TG Jesus Christ,
    Appearances,
    Postmortal.
  c TG Israel, Ten Lost
    Tribes of.
 5a TG God, Love of.

6a TG Compassion.
 7a TG Sickness.
  b TG Leprosy.
  c TG Administrations
    to the Sick; Healing.
 8a Matt. 8: 10 (1–17);
    Luke 18: 42.
  b 2 Ne. 27: 23;
    Ether 12: 12.
 9a Matt. 9: 28 (28–31);
    Mosiah 3: 5; 3 Ne.
    26: 15; D&C 84: 69.

[A.D. 34]

10 And they did all, both they who had been healed and they who were whole, bow down at his feet, and did worship him; and as many as could come for the multitude did *kiss his feet, insomuch that they did bathe his feet with their tears.

11 And it came to pass that he commanded that their *little children should be brought.

12 So they brought their little children and set them down upon the ground round about him, and Jesus stood in the midst; and the multitude gave way till they had all been brought unto him.

13 And it came to pass that when they had all been brought, and Jesus stood in the midst, he commanded the multitude that they should *kneel down upon the ground.

14 And it came to pass that when they had knelt upon the ground, Jesus groaned within himself, and said: Father, I am *troubled because of the wickedness of the people of the house of Israel.

15 And when he had said these words, he himself also *knelt upon the earth; and behold he *prayed unto the Father, and the things which he prayed cannot be written, and the multitude did bear record who heard him.

16 And after this manner do they bear record: The *eye hath never seen, neither hath the ear heard, before, so great and marvelous things as we saw and heard Jesus speak unto the Father;

17 And no *tongue can speak, neither can there be written by any man, neither can the hearts of men conceive so great and marvelous things as we both saw and heard

Jesus speak; and no one can conceive of the joy which filled our souls at the time we heard him pray for us unto the Father.

18 And it came to pass that when Jesus had made an end of praying unto the Father, he arose; but so great was the *joy of the multitude that they were overcome.

19 And it came to pass that Jesus spake unto them, and bade them arise.

20 And they arose from the earth, and he said unto them: Blessed are ye because of your faith. And *now behold, my joy is full.

21 And when he had said these words, he *wept, and the multitude bare record of it, and he took their little children, one by one, and *blessed them, and prayed unto the Father for them.

22 And when he had done this he wept again;

23 And he spake unto the multitude, and said unto them: Behold your little ones.

24 And as they looked to behold they cast their eyes towards heaven, and they saw the heavens open, and they saw angels descending out of heaven as it were in the midst of fire; and they came down and *encircled those little ones about, and they were encircled about with fire; and the angels did minister unto them.

25 And the multitude did see and *hear and bear record; and they know that their record is true for they all of them did see and hear, every man for himself; and they were in number about two thousand and five hundred souls; and they did consist of men, women, and children.

10a Luke 7: 38 (38, 45);
　　3 Ne. 11: 19.
11a Matt. 19: 13 (13–14);
　　Mark 10: 13;
　　3 Ne. 26: 14 (14, 16).
　　TG Children.
13a Acts 9: 40; 20: 36;
　　3 Ne. 19: 6 (6, 16–17).
14a Mosiah 28: 3; Alma 31:
　　2; 3 Ne. 17: 20;
　　27: 32; Moses 7: 41.

15a 3 Ne. 19: 19 (19, 27).
　　b TG Jesus Christ,
　　Relationships with
　　the Father.
16a Isa. 64: 4; 1 Cor.
　　2: 9; 3 Ne. 19: 32
　　(30–36); D&C 76: 10,
　　116 (114–119).
17a 2 Cor. 12: 4; 3 Ne.
　　19: 34 (32–34).

18a TG Joy.
20a 3 Ne. 17: 14.
21a John 11: 35.
　　TG Sincerity.
　　b Mark 10: 16 (14–16).
24a Hel. 5: 43 (23–24,
　　43–45); 3 Ne. 19: 14.
　　TG Transfiguration.
25a Ex. 19: 9 (9–13).

[A.D. 34]

CHAPTER 18

Jesus institutes the sacrament among the Nephites—They are commanded to pray always in his name—Those who eat his flesh and drink his blood unworthily are damned—The disciples are given power to confer the Holy Ghost.

AND it came to pass that Jesus commanded his disciples that they should bring forth some *a*bread and wine unto him.

2 And while they were gone for bread and wine, he commanded the multitude that they should sit themselves down upon the earth.

3 And when the disciples had come with *a*bread and wine, he took of the bread and brake and blessed it; and he gave unto the disciples and commanded that they should eat.

4 And when they had eaten and were filled, he commanded that they should give unto the multitude.

5 And when the multitude had eaten and were filled, he said unto the disciples: Behold there shall one be *a*ordained among you, and to him will I give power that he shall *b*break *c*bread and bless it and give it unto the people of my *d*church, unto all those who shall believe and be baptized in my name.

6 And this shall ye always observe to *a*do, even as I have done, even as I have broken bread and blessed it and given it unto you.

7 And this shall ye do in *a*remembrance of my *b*body, which I have shown unto you. And it shall be a testimony unto the Father that ye do always remember me. And if ye do always remember me ye shall have my Spirit to be with you.

8 And it came to pass that when he said these words, he commanded his disciples that they should take of the *a*wine of the cup and drink of it, and that they should also give unto the multitude that they might drink of it.

9 And it came to pass that they did so, and did drink of it and were filled; and they gave unto the multitude, and they did drink, and they were filled.

10 And when the disciples had done this, Jesus said unto them: Blessed are ye for this thing which ye have done, for this is fulfilling my commandments, and this doth witness unto the Father that ye are *a*willing to do that which I have commanded you.

11 And this shall ye always do to those who repent and are baptized in my name; and ye shall do it in *a*remembrance of my *b*blood, which I have shed for you, that ye may witness unto the Father that ye do always remember me. And if ye do always remember me ye shall have my Spirit to be with you.

12 And I give unto you a commandment that ye shall do these things. And if ye shall always do these things blessed are ye, for ye are built upon my *a*rock.

13 But whoso among you shall do *a*more or less than these are not built upon my rock, but are built upon a sandy foundation; and when the rain descends, and the floods come, and the winds blow, and beat upon them, they shall *b*fall, and the *c*gates of hell are ready open to receive them.

14 Therefore blessed are ye if ye shall keep my commandments, which the Father hath commanded me that I should give unto you.

---

18 1a Matt. 26: 26; 3 Ne.
  20: 3 (3–9); 26: 13.
3a TG Jesus Christ,
  Types of, in Memory.
5a TG Church
  Organization.
  b Moro. 4: 1.
  c Matt. 14: 19 (19–21);
  3 Ne. 20: 6 (6–7).
  d TG Church.

6a TG Jesus Christ,
  Exemplar.
7a 3 Ne. 20: 8; Moro.
  4: 3. TG Sacrament.
  b TG Bread of Life.
8a Matt. 26: 27 (27–29).
  TG Jesus Christ,
  Types of, in Memory.
10a TG Commitment.
11a Moro. 5: 1.

  b TG Blood, Symbolism
  of.
12a TG Rock.
13a Josh. 1: 7; D&C 3: 2.
  b TG Apostasy of
  Individuals.
  c Matt. 16: 18;
  3 Ne. 11: 39.

[A.D. 34]

15 Verily, verily, I say unto you, ye must watch and *a*pray always, lest ye be tempted by the devil, and ye be led away captive by him.

16 And as I have prayed among you even so shall ye pray in my *a*church, among my people who do repent and are baptized in my name. Behold I am the *b*light; I have set an *c*example for you.

17 And it came to pass that when Jesus had spoken these words unto his disciples, he turned again unto the multitude and said unto them:

18 Behold, verily, verily, I say unto you, ye must watch and pray always lest ye enter into temptation; for *a*Satan desireth to have you, that he may sift you as wheat.

19 Therefore ye must always pray unto the Father in my name;

20 And *a*whatsoever ye shall ask the Father in my name, which is right, believing that ye shall receive, behold it shall be given unto you.

21 *a*Pray in your families unto the Father, always in my name, that your wives and your children may be blessed.

22 And behold, ye shall *a*meet together oft; and ye shall not forbid any man from coming unto you when ye shall meet together, but suffer that they may come unto you and forbid them not;

23 But ye shall *a*pray for them, and shall not cast them out; and if it so be that they come unto you oft ye shall pray for them unto the Father, in my name.

24 Therefore, hold up your *a*light that it may shine unto the world. Behold I am the *b*light which ye shall hold up—that which ye have seen me do. Behold ye see that I have prayed unto the Father, and ye all have witnessed.

25 And ye see that I have commanded that *a*none of you should go away, but rather have commanded that ye should come unto me, that ye might *b*feel and see; even so shall ye do unto the world; and whosoever breaketh this commandment suffereth himself to be led into temptation.

26 And now it came to pass that when Jesus had spoken these words, he turned his eyes again upon the *a*disciples whom he had chosen, and said unto them:

27 Behold verily, verily, I say unto you, I give unto you another commandment, and then I must go unto my *a*Father that I may fulfil *b*other commandments which he hath given me.

28 And now behold, this is the commandment which I give unto you, that ye shall not suffer any one knowingly to *a*partake of my flesh and blood *b*unworthily, when ye shall minister it;

29 For whoso eateth and drinketh my flesh and *a*blood *b*unworthily eateth and drinketh damnation to his soul; therefore if ye know that a man is unworthy to eat and drink of my flesh and blood ye shall forbid him.

30 Nevertheless, ye shall not *a*cast him out from among you, but ye

---

15a Alma 34: 23;
    D&C 93: 49.
16a TG Jesus Christ, Head
    of the Church.
  b TG Jesus Christ,
    Light of the World.
  c TG God, the Standard
    of Righteousness;
    Jesus Christ,
    Exemplar.
18a Luke 22: 31;
    2 Ne. 2: 18 (17–18);
    D&C 10: 22 (22–27).
20a Isa. 58: 9 (8–9);
    Matt. 21: 22 (21–22);
    Mark 11: 24;

Hel. 10: 5; Morm. 9:
21; Moro. 7: 26;
D&C 88: 64 (63–65).
21a Alma 34: 21.
    TG Family, Children,
    Responsibilities
    toward.
22a TG Meetings.
23a 3 Ne. 18: 30.
    TG Missionary Work.
24a TG Jesus Christ,
    Light of the World.
  b Matt. 5: 16; Mark
    4: 21; 3 Ne. 12: 16.
25a Alma 5: 33; 19: 36.
  b 3 Ne. 11: 15 (14–16).

26a 3 Ne. 13: 25.
27a TG God the Father—
    Elohim.
  b 3 Ne. 16: 3.
28a Ex. 12: 43; 1 Cor.
    11: 27 (27–30);
    4 Ne. 1: 27.
  b Lev. 7: 18;
    Morm. 9: 29.
29a TG Blood, Symbolism
    of.
  b 3 Ne. 12: 24 (23–26);
    D&C 46: 4.
30a D&C 46: 3.

[A.D. 34]

shall *b*minister unto him and shall pray for him unto the Father, in my name; and if it so be that he repenteth and is baptized in my name, then shall ye receive him, and shall minister unto him of my flesh and blood.

31 But if he repent not he shall not be numbered among my people, that he may not destroy my people, for behold I *a*know *b*my sheep, and they are numbered.

32 Nevertheless, ye shall not cast him out of your *a*synagogues, or your places of worship, for unto such shall ye continue to minister; for ye know not but what they will return and repent, and come unto me with full purpose of heart, and I shall *b*heal them; and ye shall be the means of bringing salvation unto them.

33 Therefore, keep these sayings which I have commanded you that ye come not under *a*condemnation; for wo unto him whom the Father condemneth.

34 And I give you these commandments because of the disputations which have been among you. And blessed are ye if ye have *a*no disputations among you.

35 And now I go unto the Father, because it is expedient that I should go unto the Father *a*for your sakes.

36 And it came to pass that when Jesus had made an end of these sayings, he touched with his *a*hand the *b*disciples whom he had chosen, one by one, even until he had touched them all, and spake unto them as he touched them.

37 And the multitude heard not the words which he spake, therefore they did not bear record; but the disciples bare record that he gave them *a*power to give the *b*Holy Ghost. And I will show unto you *c*hereafter that this record is true.

38 And it came to pass that when Jesus had touched them all, there came a *a*cloud and overshadowed the multitude that they could not see Jesus.

39 And while they were overshadowed he *a*departed from them, and ascended into heaven. And the disciples saw and did bear record that he ascended again into heaven.

CHAPTER 19

The Twelve Disciples minister unto the people and pray for the Holy Ghost—They are baptized and receive the Holy Ghost and the ministering of angels—Jesus prays using words that cannot be written—He attests to the exceedingly great faith of these Nephites.

AND now it came to pass that when Jesus had ascended into heaven, the multitude did disperse, and every man did take his wife and his children and did return to his own home.

2 And it was noised abroad among the people immediately, before it was yet dark, that the multitude had seen Jesus, and that he had ministered unto them, and that he would also show himself on the *a*morrow unto the multitude.

3 Yea, and even all the night it was noised abroad concerning Jesus; and insomuch did they send forth unto the people that there were many, yea, an exceedingly great number, did labor exceedingly all that night, that they might be on the morrow in the place where Jesus should show himself unto the multitude.

30*b* 3 Ne. 18: 23.
31*a* D&C 27: 14.
   b John 10: 14; Alma 5: 38; 3 Ne. 15: 24.
32*a* Alma 16: 13; Moro. 7: 1.
   b Jer. 3: 22; 3 Ne. 9: 13 (13–14); D&C 112: 13.
33*a* TG Condemnation.
34*a* 3 Ne. 11: 28 (28–30).
   TG Disputations.
35*a* 1 Jn. 2: 1; 2 Ne. 2: 9; Moro. 7: 28 (27–28); D&C 29: 5.
36*a* TG Hands, Laying on of.
   b 1 Ne. 12: 7; 3 Ne. 15: 11; 19: 4 (4–12).
37*a* TG Holy Ghost, Gift
of; Priesthood, Authority.
   b Alma 31: 36.
   c Moro. 2: 2 (2–3).
38*a* Ex. 19: 9 (9, 16); 2 Chr. 5: 14 (11–14).
39*a* 3 Ne. 17: 4.
19 2*a* 3 Ne. 17: 3.

[A.D. 34]

4 And it came to pass that on the morrow, when the multitude was gathered together, behold, Nephi and his *a*brother whom he had raised from the *b*dead, whose name was Timothy, and also his son, whose name was Jonas, and also Mathoni, and Mathonihah, his brother, and Kumen, and Kumenonhi, and Jeremiah, and Shemnon, and Jonas, and Zedekiah, and Isaiah—now these were the names of the *d*disciples whom Jesus had chosen—and it came to pass that they went forth and stood in the midst of the multitude.

5 And behold, the multitude was *a*so great that they did cause that they should be separated into twelve bodies.

6 And the twelve did teach the multitude; and behold, they did cause that the multitude should *a*kneel down upon the face of the earth, and should pray unto the Father in the name of Jesus.

7 And the disciples did pray unto the Father also in the name of Jesus. And it came to pass that they arose and ministered unto the people.

8 And when they had ministered those same words which Jesus had spoken—nothing varying from the words which Jesus had spoken—behold, they knelt again and prayed to the Father in the name of Jesus.

9 And they did pray for that which they most desired; and they desired that the *a*Holy Ghost should be given unto them.

10 And when they had thus prayed they went down unto the water's edge, and the multitude followed them.

11 And it came to pass that Nephi went down *a*into the water and was *b*baptized.

12 And he came up out of the water and began to baptize. And he baptized all those whom Jesus had chosen.

13 And it came to pass when they were all baptized and had come *a*up out of the water, the *b*Holy Ghost did fall upon them, and they were filled with the Holy Ghost and with fire.

14 And behold, they were *a*encircled about as if it were by fire; and it came down from heaven, and the multitude did witness it, and did bear record; and angels did come down out of heaven and did minister unto them.

15 And it came to pass that while the angels were ministering unto the disciples, behold, Jesus came and stood in the midst and ministered unto them.

16 And it came to pass that he spake unto the multitude, and commanded them that they should kneel down again upon the earth, and also that his disciples should kneel down upon the earth.

17 And it came to pass that when they had all knelt down upon the earth, he commanded his disciples that they should pray.

18 And behold, they began to pray; and they did pray unto Jesus, calling him their Lord and their God.

19 And it came to pass that Jesus departed out of the midst of them, and went a little way off from them and *a*bowed himself to the earth, and he said:

20 Father, I thank thee that thou hast given the Holy Ghost unto these whom I have *a*chosen; and it is because of their belief in me that I have chosen them out of the world.

21 Father, I pray thee that thou wilt give the Holy Ghost unto all them that shall believe in their words.

4a 3 Ne. 7:19.
 b TG Death, Power over.
 c 3 Ne. 28:25.
 d 3 Ne. 18:36 (36–37);
   26:17.
5a Mosiah 2:7.
6a 3 Ne. 17:13.

9a 3 Ne. 9:20.
11a 3 Ne. 11:23.
 b Matt. 3:14 (13–15);
   JS-H 1:71 (70–71).
13a TG Baptism,
   Immersion.
 b 3 Ne. 12:2; Morm. 7:
   10. TG Holy Ghost,

Baptism of.
14a Hel. 5:43 (23–24,
   43–45); 3 Ne. 17:24.
19a 3 Ne. 17:15.
20a TG Church
   Organization.

[A.D. 34]

22 Father, thou hast given them the Holy Ghost because they believe in *a*me; and thou seest that they believe in me because thou hearest them, and they pray unto me; and they pray unto me because I am with them.

23 And now Father, I *a*pray unto thee for them, and also for all those who shall believe on their words, that they may believe in me, that I may be in them *b*as thou, Father, art in me, that we may be *c*one.

24 And it came to pass that when Jesus had thus prayed unto the Father, he came unto his disciples, and behold, they did still continue, without ceasing, to pray unto him; and they did not *a*multiply many words, for it was given unto them what they should *b*pray, and they were filled with desire.

25 And it came to pass that Jesus blessed them as they did pray unto him; and his *a*countenance did smile upon them, and the light of his *b*countenance did *c*shine upon them, and behold they were as *d*white as the countenance and also the garments of Jesus; and behold the whiteness thereof did exceed all the whiteness, yea, even there could be nothing upon earth so white as the whiteness thereof.

26 And Jesus said unto them: Pray on; nevertheless they did not cease to pray.

27 And he turned from them again, and went a little way off and bowed himself to the earth; and he prayed again unto the Father, saying:

28 Father, I thank thee that thou hast *a*purified those whom I have chosen, because of their faith, and I pray for them, and also for them who shall believe on their words, that they may be purified in me, through faith on their words, even as they are purified in me.

29 Father, I pray not for the world, but for those whom thou hast given me *a*out of the world, because of their faith, that they may be purified in me, that I may be in them as thou, Father, art in me, that we may be one, that I may be glorified in them.

30 And when Jesus had spoken these words he came again unto his disciples; and behold they did pray steadfastly, without ceasing, unto him; and he did smile upon them again; and behold they were *a*white, even as Jesus.

31 And it came to pass that he went again a little way off and prayed unto the Father;

32 And tongue cannot speak the words which he prayed, neither can be *a*written by man the words which he prayed.

33 And the multitude did hear and do bear record; and their *a*hearts were open and they did understand in their hearts the words which he prayed.

34 Nevertheless, so great and marvelous were the words which he prayed that they cannot be written, neither can they be *a*uttered by man.

35 And it came to pass that when Jesus had made an end of praying he came again to the disciples, and said unto them: *a*So great *b*faith have I never seen among all the Jews; wherefore I could not show unto them so great *c*miracles, because of their *d*unbelief.

22a Acts 7:59.
23a TG Jesus Christ, Relationships with the Father.
  b 3 Ne. 9:15; 11:27.
  c John 17:22 (1–22); 1 Cor. 6:17.
24a Matt. 6:7.
  b Hel. 10:5; D&C 46:30.
25a Num. 6:25 (23–27).

  b Ps. 4:6.
  c Dan. 9:17.
  d TG Transfiguration.
28a Neh. 12:30; Moro. 7:48; D&C 50:29 (28–29); 88:74 (74–75). TG Purity.
29a John 17:6.
30a Matt. 17:2.
32a 3 Ne. 5:18; D&C 76:116.
33a Prov. 2:2; 8:5;

    Isa. 44:18; Mosiah 2:9; 12:27.
34a 2 Cor. 12:4; 3 Ne. 17:17.
35a Matt. 8:10.
  b TG Faith.
  c John 11:47 (47–48).
  d Matt. 13:58. TG Doubt; Unbelief, Unbelievers.

[A.D. 34]

36 Verily I say unto you, there are none of them that have seen so great things as ye have seen; neither have they heard so great things as ye have heard.

CHAPTER 20

Jesus provides bread and wine miraculously and again administers the sacrament unto them—The remnant of Jacob shall come to the knowledge of the Lord their God and shall inherit the Americas—Jesus is the prophet like unto Moses, and the Nephites are children of the prophets—Others of the Lord's people shall be gathered to Jerusalem.

AND it came to pass that he commanded the multitude that they should [a]cease to [b]pray, and also his disciples. And he commanded them that they should not cease to pray in their hearts.

2 And he commanded them that they should arise and stand up upon their feet. And they arose up and stood upon their feet.

3 And it came to pass that he [a]brake [b]bread again and blessed it, and gave to the disciples to eat.

4 And when they had eaten he commanded them that they should break bread, and give unto the multitude.

5 And when they had given unto the multitude he also gave them wine to drink, and commanded them that they should give unto the multitude.

6 Now, there had been no [a]bread, neither wine, brought by the disciples, neither by the multitude;

7 But he truly [a]gave unto them bread to eat, and also wine to drink.

8 And he said unto them: He that eateth this bread eateth of [a]my body to his soul; and he that drinketh of this wine drinketh of my blood to his soul; and his soul shall never hunger nor thirst, but shall be filled.

9 Now, when the multitude had all eaten and drunk, behold, they were filled with the Spirit; and they did cry out with one voice, and gave glory to Jesus, whom they both saw and heard.

10 And it came to pass that when they had all given glory unto Jesus, he said unto them: Behold now I finish the commandment which the Father hath commanded me concerning this people, who are a remnant of the house of Israel.

11 Ye remember that I spake unto you, and said that when the [a]words of [b]Isaiah should be fulfilled—behold they are written, ye have them before you, therefore search them—

12 And verily, verily, I say unto you, that when they shall be fulfilled then is the fulfilling of the [a]covenant which the Father hath made unto his people, O house of Israel.

13 And then shall the [a]remnants, which shall be [b]scattered abroad upon the face of the earth, be [c]gathered in from the east and from the west, and from the south and from the north; and they shall be brought to the [d]knowledge of the Lord their God, who hath redeemed them.

14 And the Father hath [a]commanded me that I should give unto you this [b]land, for your inheritance.

15 And I say unto you, that if the Gentiles do not [a]repent after the

---

20 1*a* 1 Sam. 7: 8;
　　　2 Ne. 32: 9.
　　b Mosiah 24: 12.
　3*a* Mark 6: 41 (36–44).
　　b 3 Ne. 18: 1; 26: 13.
　6*a* Matt. 14: 19 (19–21).
　7*a* John 6: 14.
　8*a* John 6: 51 (50–58);
　　　1 Cor. 11: 24 (20–26);
　　　3 Ne. 18: 7; Moro. 4: 3.

11*a* 3 Ne. 16: 17 (17–20);
　　　23: 3 (1–3).
　　b 2 Ne. 25: 5 (1–5);
　　　Morm. 8: 23.
12*a* Gen. 17: 11 (9–12);
　　　3 Ne. 15: 7.
13*a* 3 Ne. 16: 13 (6–13);
　　　21: 3 (2–7).
　　b TG Israel, Scattering of.
　　c Jer. 46: 27 (2–28);

3 Ne. 22: 7 (6–17).
TG Israel, Gathering of.
　d Ezek. 20: 42 (42–44);
　　　3 Ne. 16: 4 (4–5).
14*a* TG Jesus Christ, Authority of.
　　b TG Promised Lands.
15*a* 3 Ne. 16: 10 (10–14).

[A.D. 34]

ᵇblessing which they shall receive, after they have scattered my people—

16 Then shall ye, who are a ᵃremnant of the house of Jacob, go forth among them; and ye shall be in the midst of them who shall be many; and ye shall be among them as a lion among the beasts of the forest, and as a young ᵇlion among the flocks of sheep, who, if he goeth through both ᶜtreadeth down and teareth in pieces, and none can deliver.

17 Thy hand shall be lifted up upon thine adversaries, and all thine enemies shall be cut off.

18 And I will ᵃgather my people together as a man gathereth his sheaves into the floor.

19 For I will make my ᵃpeople with whom the Father hath covenanted, yea, I will make thy ᵇhorn iron, and I will make thy hoofs brass. And thou shalt ᶜbeat in pieces many people; and I will consecrate their gain unto the Lord, and their substance unto the Lord of the whole earth. And behold, I am he who doeth it.

20 And it shall come to pass, saith the Father, that the ᵃsword of my justice shall hang over them at that day; and except they repent it shall fall upon them, saith the Father, yea, even upon all the nations of the Gentiles.

21 And it shall come to pass that I will establish my ᵃpeople, O house of Israel.

22 And behold, this ᵃpeople will I establish in this land, unto the fulfilling of the ᵇcovenant which I made with your father Jacob; and it shall be a ᶜNew Jerusalem. And the ᵈpowers of heaven shall be in the midst of this people; yea, even ᵉI will be in the midst of you.

23 Behold, I am he of whom Moses spake, saying: ᵃA prophet shall the Lord your God raise up unto you of your brethren, like unto me; him shall ye hear in all things whatsoever he shall say unto you. And it shall come to pass that every soul who will not hear that prophet shall be cut off from among the people.

24 Verily I say unto you, yea, and ᵃall the prophets from Samuel and those that follow after, as many as have spoken, have testified of me.

25 And behold, ye are the ᵃchildren of the prophets; and ye are of the house of Israel; and ye are of the ᵇcovenant which the Father made with your fathers, saying unto Abraham: And ᶜin thy seed shall all the kindreds of the earth be blessed.

26 The Father having raised me up unto you first, and sent me to ᵃbless you in ᵇturning away every one of you from his iniquities; and this because ye are the children of the covenant—

27 And after that ye were blessed then fulfilleth the Father the covenant which he made with Abraham, saying: ᵃIn thy seed shall all the kindreds of the earth be blessed— unto the pouring out of the Holy

15b 3 Ne. 20: 27.
16a TG Israel, Remnant of.
  b Gen. 49: 9; Morm. 5:
    24; D&C 87: 5
    (4–5); 109: 65 (65–67).
    TG Israel, Deliverance
    of.
  c Micah 5: 8 (8–9);
    3 Ne. 16: 15 (14–15);
    21: 12 (11–21).
18a Micah 4: 12.
19a Lev. 26: 12; D&C
    63: 1 (1–6).
  b TG Last Days.
  c Micah 4: 13.
20a 1 Ne. 14: 17; 22: 16
    (15–16); 3 Ne. 29: 4.

21a 1 Kgs. 8: 51;
    3 Ne. 16: 8 (8–15);
    21: 23 (12–24).
22a TG Israel, Joseph,
    People of.
  b Gen. 49: 26 (22–26).
  c Isa. 2: 3 (2–5);
    3 Ne. 21: 23 (23–24);
    Ether 13: 3 (1–12);
    D&C 84: 2 (2–4).
    TG Jerusalem, New.
  d 3 Ne. 21: 25.
  e Isa. 59: 20 (20–21);
    3 Ne. 24: 1.
23a Deut. 18: 15 (15–19);
    Acts 3: 22 (22–23);
    1 Ne. 22: 20 (20–21);

    D&C 133: 63.
24a Acts 3: 24 (24–26); 1 Ne.
    10: 5; Jacob 7: 11.
25a Rom. 4: 24 (23–24).
  b TG Abrahamic
    Covenant.
  c Gen. 12: 3 (1–3);
    22: 18 (9, 18).
    TG Seed of Abraham.
26a TG Israel, Blessings of.
  b Prov. 16: 6;
    Alma 19: 33.
27a Gen. 12: 2 (1–3);
    Gal. 3: 8 (7–29);
    2 Ne. 29: 14; Abr. 2: 9.

                    [A.D. 34]

Ghost through me upon the Gentiles, which *b*blessing upon the *c*Gentiles shall make them mighty above all, unto the *d*scattering of my people, O house of Israel.

28 And they shall be a *a*scourge unto the people of this land. Nevertheless, when they shall have received the fulness of my gospel, then if they shall harden their hearts against me I will return their *b*iniquities upon their own heads, saith the Father.

29 And I will *a*remember the covenant which I have made with my people; and I have covenanted with them that I would *b*gather them together in mine own due time, that I would give unto them again the *c*land of their fathers for their inheritance, which is the land of Jerusalem, which is the promised land unto them forever, saith the Father.

30 And it shall come to pass that the time cometh, when the fulness of my gospel shall be preached unto them;

31 And they shall *a*believe in me, that I am Jesus Christ, the Son of God, and shall pray unto the Father in my name.

32 Then shall their *a*watchmen lift up their voice, and with the voice together shall they sing; for they shall see eye to eye.

33 Then will the Father gather them together again, and give unto them *a*Jerusalem for the *b*land of their inheritance.

34 Then shall they break forth into joy—*a*Sing together, ye waste places of Jerusalem; for the Father hath comforted his people, he hath redeemed Jerusalem.

35 The Father hath made bare his holy arm in the eyes of all the nations; and all the ends of the earth shall see the salvation of the Father; and the Father and I are one.

36 And then shall be brought to pass that which is written: *a*Awake, awake again, and put on thy strength, O Zion; put on thy beautiful garments, O Jerusalem, the holy city, for henceforth there shall no more come into thee the uncircumcised and the unclean.

37 Shake thyself from the dust; arise, sit down, O Jerusalem; loose thyself from the bands of thy neck, O captive daughter of Zion.

38 For thus saith the Lord: Ye have sold yourselves for naught, and ye shall be redeemed without money.

39 Verily, verily, I say unto you, that my people shall know my name; yea, in that day they shall know that I am he that doth speak.

40 And then shall they say: *a*How beautiful upon the mountains are the feet of him that bringeth good tidings unto them, that *b*publisheth peace; that bringeth good tidings unto them of good, that publisheth salvation; that saith unto Zion: Thy God reigneth!

41 And then shall a cry go forth: *a*Depart ye, depart ye, go ye out from thence, touch not that which is *b*unclean; go ye out of the midst of her; be ye *c*clean that bear the vessels of the Lord.

27*b* 3 Ne. 20: 15.
  c 3 Ne. 16: 6 (6–7);
    Morm. 5: 19.
  d 3 Ne. 16: 8 (8–9);
    Morm. 5: 9.
28*a* Josh. 23: 13; 1 Ne. 2:
    24; 3 Ne. 16: 8 (8–10).
  b Isa. 51: 23.
29*a* Isa. 44: 21; 3 Ne.
    16: 11 (11–12).
  b TG Israel, Gathering of.
  c Amos 9: 15; Alma 7:
    10; D&C 133: 24.
    TG Israel, Land of.

31*a* 3 Ne. 5: 26 (21–26);
    21: 26 (26–29).
32*a* Isa. 52: 8 (8–9); 3 Ne.
    16: 18 (18–20).
    TG Watchmen.
33*a* Isa. 18: 7; D&C 84: 2.
    TG Jerusalem.
  b Deut. 11: 11.
    TG Israel, Land of;
    Lands of Inheritance.
34*a* Isa. 54: 1.
36*a* Isa. 52: 1 (1–3);
    D&C 113: 7 (7–10).

    TG Priesthood,
    Power of.
40*a* Isa. 52: 7; Nahum
    1: 15; Mosiah 15: 18
    (13–18);
    D&C 128: 19.
  b Mark 13: 10; 1 Ne.
    13: 37.
41*a* Isa. 52: 11 (11–15).
  b TG Uncleanness.
  c D&C 133: 5.
    TG Cleanliness.

                                    [A.D. 34]

42 For ye shall [a]not go out with [b]haste nor go by flight; for the Lord will go before you, and the God of Israel shall be your rearward.

43 Behold, my servant shall deal prudently; he shall be exalted and extolled and be very high.

44 As many were astonished at thee—his visage was so marred, more than any man, and his form more than the sons of men—

45 So shall he [a]sprinkle many nations; the kings shall shut their mouths at him, for that which had not been told them shall they see; and that which they had not heard shall they [b]consider.

46 Verily, verily, I say unto you, all these things shall surely come, even as the Father hath commanded me. Then shall this covenant which the Father hath covenanted with his people be fulfilled; and then shall [a]Jerusalem be inhabited again with my people, and it shall be the land of their inheritance.

CHAPTER 21

Israel shall be gathered when the Book of Mormon comes forth—The Gentiles shall be established as a free people in America—They shall be saved if they believe and obey; otherwise they shall be cut off and destroyed—Israel shall build the New Jerusalem, and the lost tribes shall return.

AND verily I say unto you, I give unto you a [a]sign, that ye may know the [b]time when these things shall be about to take place—that I shall gather in, from their long dispersion, my people, O house of Israel, and shall establish again among them my Zion;

2 And behold, this is the thing which I will give unto you for a sign—for verily I say unto you that [a]when these things which I declare unto you, and which I shall declare unto you hereafter of myself, and by the power of the Holy Ghost which shall be given unto you of the Father, shall be made known unto the Gentiles that they may know concerning this people who are a remnant of the house of Jacob, and concerning this my people who shall be scattered by them;

3 Verily, verily, I say unto you, when these things shall be made [a]known unto them of the Father, and shall come forth of the Father, [b]from them unto you;

4 For it is wisdom in the Father that they should be established in this land, and be set up as a [a]free people by the power of the Father, that these things might come forth from them unto a remnant of your seed, that the [b]covenant of the Father may be fulfilled which he hath covenanted with his people, O house of Israel;

5 Therefore, when these works and the works which shall be wrought among you hereafter shall come forth [a]from the Gentiles, unto your [b]seed which shall dwindle in unbelief because of iniquity;

6 For thus it behooveth the Father that it should come forth from the [a]Gentiles, that he may show forth his power unto the Gentiles, for this cause that the Gentiles, if they will not harden their hearts, that they may repent and come unto me and

---

42a 3 Ne. 21: 29.
  b TG Haste; Rashness.
45a Lev. 1: 5; Isa. 52: 15; Ezek. 36: 25.
  b 3 Ne. 21: 8; D&C 101: 94.
46a Joel 2: 18; Ether 13: 5 (5, 11).
21 1a Isa. 66: 19.
  b TG Last Days.
 2a 1 Ne. 10: 14; Ether 4:

17; D&C 20: 9 (8–11); JS-H 1: 34.
3a TG Witness of the Father.
  b 3 Ne. 20: 13; Morm. 5: 15 (10–21).
4a John 8: 32 (32–36); 1 Ne. 13: 19 (17–19); D&C 101: 77 (77–80).
  b Ps. 89: 35; 3 Ne.

16: 11 (8–12); Morm. 5: 20. TG Abrahamic Covenant.
5a 3 Ne. 26: 8.
  b 2 Ne. 30: 5; Morm. 5: 15; D&C 3: 18.
6a 1 Ne. 10: 14; Jacob 5: 54; 3 Ne. 16: 4 (4–7); 21: 24 (24–26); Morm. 5: 15.

[A.D. 34]

they see; and that which they had not heard shall they [a]consider.

9 For in that day, for my sake shall the Father [a]work a work, which shall be a great and a [b]marvelous [c]work among them; and there shall be among them those who will not believe it, although a man shall declare it unto them.

10 But behold, the life of my servant shall be in my hand; therefore they shall not hurt him, although he shall be [a]marred because of them. Yet I will heal him, for I will show unto them that [b]my wisdom is greater than the cunning of the devil.

11 Therefore it shall come to pass that whosoever will not believe in my words, who am Jesus Christ, which the Father shall cause [a]him to bring forth unto the [b]Gentiles, and shall give unto him power that he shall bring them forth unto the Gentiles, (it shall be done even as Moses said) they shall be [c]cut off

... from among my people who are of ... covenant.

... and my people who are a rem-... Jacob shall be among the ... sea, in the midst of the beasts of the ... ng lion among the ... if he go through ... and teareth in ...

... father, that I will cut off thy horses out of the midst of thee, and I will destroy thy [b]chariots;

15 And I will cut off the cities of thy land, and throw down all thy [a]strongholds;

16 And I will cut off [a]witchcrafts out of thy land, and thou shalt have no more soothsayers;

17 Thy [a]graven images I will also cut off, and thy standing images out of the midst of thee, and thou shalt no more worship the works of thy hands;

18 And I will pluck up thy [a]groves out of the midst of thee; so will I destroy thy cities.

19 And it shall come to pass that all [a]lyings, and deceivings, and envyings, and strifes, and priest-crafts, and whoredoms, shall be done away.

20 For it shall come to pass, saith the Father, that at that [a]day whosoever will not repent and come unto my Beloved Son, them will I

6b Gal. 3: 7 (7, 29); 2 Ne. 30: 3; 3 Ne. 16: 13; Abr. 2: 10 (9–11).
7a 3 Ne. 5: 23 (21–26); 21: 26.
8a 3 Ne. 20: 45.
9a TG God, Works of.
 b 1 Ne. 22: 8.
 TG Restoration of the Gospel.
 c Acts 13: 41 (40–41).
10a D&C 135: 1 (1–3).
 b D&C 10: 43.
11a 2 Ne. 3: 11 (6–15);

Morm. 8: 16 (16, 25); Ether 3: 28 (21–28).
 b 1 Ne. 21: 6.
 c D&C 1: 14; 133: 63.
12a Isa. 5: 29; Micah 5: 8 (8–15); Mal. 4: 3; 2 Ne. 15: 29; 3 Ne. 16: 15 (7–15); 20: 16; 25: 3; D&C 87: 5.
13a 1 Ne. 21: 17 (17–19).
14a Eph. 3: 6 (1–7); 2 Ne. 10: 18; 33: 9.
 b Lev. 26: 22 (21–22); Hel. 14: 24.

15a 2 Ne. 12: 15.
16a TG Sorcery; Superstitions.
17a Ex. 20: 4 (3–4, 23); Isa. 41: 29 (24, 29); Mosiah 13: 12; D&C 1: 16. TG Idolatry.
18a 1 Kgs. 16: 33 (32–33).
19a 3 Ne. 30: 2; D&C 109: 30.
20a Amos 5: 18; Alma 29: 2; Morm. 9: 27.

[A.D. 34]

[b]cut off from [a]house of Israel.

21 And I [a]will [b]fury [b]the the heath[c]ered among heard.

22 But[a] of Jacob, unto hearke[b]harge given this land for [a]est[b]ve inheritance;

23 And they shall assist my [a]people, the remnant of Jacob, and also as many of the house of Israel as [b]shall come, that they may build a city, which shall be called the [b]New Jerusalem.

24 And then shall [a]they assist my people that they may be gathered in, who are scattered upon all the face of the land, in unto the New Jerusalem.

25 And then shall the [a]power of heaven come down among them; and [b]I also will be in the midst.

26 And then shall the work of the Father commence at that day, even [a]when this gospel shall be preached among the remnant of [b]this people. Verily I say unto you, at that day shall the work of the Father commence among all the dispersed of my people, yea, even the tribes which have been [c]lost, which the Father hath led away out of Jerusalem.

27 Yea, the work shall commence among all the [a]dispersed of my

... the work ... Father among ... preparing the way ..., his people may be [a]gathered home to the land of their inheritance.

29 And they shall go out from all nations; and they shall [a]not go out in [b]haste, nor go by flight, for I will go before them, saith the Father, and I will be their rearward.

CHAPTER 22

In the last days, Zion and her stakes shall be established, and Israel shall be gathered in mercy and tenderness— They shall triumph—Compare Isaiah 54.

AND then shall that which is written come to pass: Sing, O [a]barren, thou that didst not bear; break forth into [b]singing, and cry aloud, thou that didst not travail with child; for more are the children of the [c]desolate than the children of the married wife, saith the Lord.

2 Enlarge the place of thy tent, and let them stretch forth the curtains of thy habitations; spare not, lengthen thy cords and strengthen thy [a]stakes;

3 For thou shalt break forth on the right hand and on the left, and thy seed shall [a]inherit the [b]Gentiles and make the desolate cities to be inhabited.

20b Jer. 44: 8 (6–8).
21a Isa. 34: 8; 61: 2; Jer. 23: 19 (19–20); Mal. 4: 1 (1, 3); D&C 97: 26 (25–28).
  b Ezek. 21: 17 (14–17).
22a TG Hardheartedness.
  b 1 Ne. 14: 12 (12, 14). TG Dispensations; Millennium, Preparing a People for.
  c 2 Ne. 10: 18 (18–19); 3 Ne. 16: 13; 30: 2.
  d TG Lands of Inheritance.

23a 3 Ne. 16: 8 (8–15).
  b 3 Ne. 20: 22 (21–22, 39); Ether 13: 3 (1–12). TG Jerusalem, New.
24a 3 Ne. 21: 6.
25a 1 Ne. 13: 37; 3 Ne. 20: 22.
  b Isa. 2: 2 (2–4); 59: 20 (20–21); 3 Ne. 24: 1.
26a 3 Ne. 20: 31 (29–34); Morm. 5: 14.
  b 1 Ne. 14: 17; 3 Ne. 21: 6 (6–7).
  c TG Israel, Ten Lost

Tribes of.
27a 3 Ne. 16: 5 (4–5).
  b TG Israel, Restoration of.
28a TG Israel, Gathering of.
29a 3 Ne. 20: 42.
  b Isa. 52: 12 (11–12).
22 1a Isa. 54: 1 (1–17).
  b TG Singing.
  c Isa. 49: 21.
2a TG Stakes.
3a Obad. 1: 19 (19–21).
  b TG Gentiles.

[A.D. 34]

4 Fear not, for thou shalt not be ashamed; neither be thou confounded, for thou shalt not be put to [a]shame; for thou shalt forget the [b]shame of thy youth, and shalt not remember the [c]reproach of thy youth, and shalt not remember the reproach of thy widowhood any more.

5 For thy maker, thy [a]husband, the Lord of Hosts is his name; and thy Redeemer, the Holy One of Israel—the God of the whole earth shall he be called.

6 For the Lord hath called thee [a]as a woman forsaken and grieved in spirit, and a wife of youth, when thou wast refused, saith thy God.

7 For a small moment have I [a]forsaken thee, but with great mercies will I gather thee.

8 In a little wrath I hid my face from thee for a moment, but with everlasting [a]kindness will I have [b]mercy on thee, saith the Lord thy Redeemer.

9 For this, the [a]waters of Noah unto me, for as I have sworn that the waters of Noah should no more go over the earth, so have I sworn that I would not be wroth with thee.

10 For the [a]mountains shall depart and the hills be removed, but my [b]kindness shall not [c]depart from thee, neither shall the covenant of my peace be removed, saith the Lord that hath mercy on thee.

11 O thou afflicted, tossed with tempest, and not comforted! Behold, I will lay thy [a]stones with fair colors, and lay thy foundations with sapphires.

12 And I will make thy windows of agates, and thy gates of carbuncles, and all thy borders of pleasant stones.

13 And [a]all thy children shall be taught of the Lord; and great shall be the [b]peace of thy children.

14 In [a]righteousness shalt thou be established; thou shalt be far from oppression for thou shalt not fear, and from terror for it shall not come near thee.

15 Behold, they shall surely gather together [a]against thee, not by me; whosoever shall gather together against thee shall fall for thy sake.

16 Behold, I have created the smith that bloweth the coals in the fire, and that bringeth forth an instrument for his work; and I have created the waster to destroy.

17 No weapon that is formed against thee shall prosper; and every tongue that shall revile against thee in judgment thou shalt condemn. This is the heritage of the [a]servants of the Lord, and their righteousness is of me, saith the Lord.

CHAPTER 23

Jesus approves the words of Isaiah— He commands the people to search the prophets—The words of Samuel the Lamanite concerning the resurrection are added to their records.

AND now, behold, I say unto you, that ye ought to [a]search these things. Yea, a commandment I give unto you that ye search these things diligently; for great are the words of [b]Isaiah.

2 For surely he spake as touching all things concerning my people which are of the house of Israel;

4a Joel 2: 26 (26–27);
  2 Ne. 6: 13 (7, 13).
  b TG Shame.
  c TG Reproach.
5a Hosea 3: 5 (4–5).
6a Isa. 62: 4.
7a Jer. 46: 27 (2–28);
  3 Ne. 20: 13 (11–13).
8a TG Kindness.
  b TG God, Mercy of.
9a Gen. 8: 21; Matt.
  24: 37 (36–38);

Alma 10: 22.
  TG Earth, Cleansing of.
10a Isa. 40: 4 (4–5).
  TG Earth, Renewal of.
  b TG Israel, Blessings of.
  c Ps. 94: 14; D&C
  35: 25.
11a Rev. 21: 19 (18–21).
  TG Rock.
13a Isa. 60: 21; Jer.
  31: 34 (33–34).
  b 1 Ne. 22: 17 (15–22);

2 Ne. 30: 10;
  Moses 7: 61.
14a TG Righteousness.
15a 1 Ne. 22: 14.
17a TG Servant.
23 1a TG Scriptures, Study of.
  b Isa. 1: 1; 2 Ne.
  25: 5 (1–5); 3 Ne.
  20: 11; Morm. 8: 23.

[A.D. 34]

[a]therefore it must needs be that he must speak also to the Gentiles.

3 And all things that he spake have been and [a]shall be, even according to the words which he spake.

4 Therefore give heed to my words; write the things which I have told you; and according to the time and the will of the Father [a]they shall go forth unto the Gentiles.

5 And whosoever will hearken unto my words and repenteth and is baptized, the same shall be saved. Search the [a]prophets, for many there be that testify of these things.

6 And now it came to pass that when Jesus had said these words he said unto them again, after he had expounded all the scriptures unto them which they had received, he said unto them: Behold, other scriptures I would that ye should write, that ye have not.

7 And it came to pass that he said unto [a]Nephi: Bring forth the record which ye have kept.

8 And when Nephi had brought forth the records, and laid them before him, he cast his eyes upon them and said:

9 Verily I say unto you, I commanded my servant [a]Samuel, the Lamanite, that he should testify unto this people, that at the day that the Father should glorify his name in me that there were [b]many [c]saints who should [d]arise from the dead, and should appear unto many, and should minister unto them. And he said unto them: Was it not so?

10 And his disciples answered him and said: Yea, Lord, Samuel did prophesy according to thy words, and they were all fulfilled.

11 And Jesus said unto them: How be it that ye have not [a]written this thing, that many [b]saints did arise and appear unto many and did minister unto them?

12 And it came to pass that Nephi remembered that this thing had not been written.

13 And it came to pass that Jesus commanded that it should be [a]written; therefore it was written according as he commanded.

14 And now it came to pass that when Jesus had [a]expounded all the scriptures in one, which they had written, he commanded them that they should [b]teach the things which he had expounded unto them.

CHAPTER 24

The Lord's messenger shall prepare the way for the Second Coming—Christ shall sit in judgment—Israel is commanded to pay tithes and offerings—A book of remembrance is kept—Compare Malachi 3.

AND it came to pass that he commanded them that they should write the words which the Father had given unto Malachi, which he should tell unto them. And it came to pass that after they were written he expounded them. And these are the words which he did tell unto them, saying: Thus said the Father unto Malachi—Behold, I will [a]send my [b]messenger, and he shall prepare the way before me, and the Lord whom ye seek shall suddenly [c]come to his temple, even the [d]messenger of the covenant, whom ye delight in; behold, he shall come, saith the Lord of Hosts.

2 But who may [a]abide the day of his coming, and who shall stand when he appeareth? For he is like

2*a* Isa. 49:6.
3*a* 3 Ne. 15:6; 20:11 (11–12).
4*a* Morm. 8:26.
5*a* Luke 24:27 (25–27).
7*a* 3 Ne. 8:1; 4 Ne. 1:19.
9*a* Hel. 13:2.
  b Hel. 14:25 (1, 21–26).

c TG Saints.
d TG Resurrection.
11*a* TG Jesus Christ, Teaching Mode of.
  b Matt. 27:52 (52–53).
13*a* TG Record Keeping.
14*a* Luke 24:44 (27, 44).
  b TG Scriptures, Study of; Teaching.

24 1*a* Mal. 3:1 (1–18).
  b D&C 45:9.
  c Isa. 59:20 (20–21); 3 Ne. 20:22; 21:25.
  d TG Jesus Christ, Messenger of the Covenant.
2*a* 3 Ne. 25:1.

a *b*refiner's fire, and like fuller's soap.

3 And he shall sit as a refiner and purifier of silver; and he shall *a*purify the *b*sons of Levi, and purge them as gold and silver, that they may *c*offer unto the Lord an offering in righteousness.

4 Then shall the offering of Judah and Jerusalem be pleasant unto the Lord, as in the days of old, and as in former years.

5 And I will come *a*near to you to judgment; and I will be a swift witness against the *b*sorcerers, and against the adulterers, and against false *c*swearers, and against those that *d*oppress the hireling in his wages, the widow and the *e*fatherless, and that turn aside the *f*stranger, and fear not me, saith the Lord of Hosts.

6 For *a*I am the Lord, I change not; therefore ye sons of Jacob are not consumed.

7 Even from the days of your fathers ye are gone away from mine *a*ordinances, and have not kept them. *b*Return unto me and I will return unto you, saith the Lord of Hosts. But ye say: Wherein shall we return?

8 Will a man rob God? Yet ye have robbed me. But ye say: Wherein have we robbed thee? In *a*tithes and *b*offerings.

9 Ye are cursed with a curse, for ye have robbed me, even this whole nation.

10 Bring ye all the *a*tithes into the storehouse, that there may be *b*meat in my house; and prove me now herewith, saith the Lord of Hosts, if I will not open you the *c*windows of heaven, and pour you out a *d*blessing that there shall not be room enough to receive it.

11 And I will rebuke the *a*devourer for your sakes, and he shall not destroy the fruits of your ground; neither shall your vine cast her fruit before the time in the fields, saith the Lord of Hosts.

12 And all nations shall call you blessed, for ye shall be a delightsome land, saith the Lord of Hosts.

13 Your words have been stout against me, saith the Lord. Yet ye say: What have we spoken against thee?

14 Ye have *a*said: It is *b*vain to serve God, and what doth it profit that we have kept his *c*ordinances and that we have walked mournfully before the Lord of Hosts?

15 And now we call the proud happy; yea, they that work wickedness are set up; yea, they that tempt God are even delivered.

16 Then they that feared the Lord *a*spake often one to another, and the Lord hearkened and heard; and a book of *b*remembrance was written before him for them that feared the Lord, and that thought upon his name.

17 And they shall be *a*mine, saith the Lord of Hosts, in that day when I *b*make up my jewels; and I will

---

2b Deut. 4: 24; Zech.
   13: 9; D&C 128: 24.
   TG Earth, Cleansing
   of; Jesus Christ,
   Second Coming.
3a TG Purification.
   b Deut. 10: 8; D&C
   84: 31 (31–34);
   128: 24.
   c D&C 13: 1.
5a Ezek. 43: 7 (1–7).
   b TG Sorcery.
   c Hosea 10: 4; D&C
   104: 5 (4–5).
   TG Swearing.
   d Ps. 94: 6.

e Ps. 10: 14; 68: 5;
   James 1: 27; D&C
   136: 8.
   f TG Stranger.
6a 2 Ne. 6: 7; Moses
   1: 6.
7a TG Ordinance.
   b 1 Sam. 7: 3; Hel.
   13: 11; 3 Ne. 10: 6
   (5–7); Moro. 9: 22.
8a TG Tithing.
   b Neh. 10: 32.
   TG Sacrifice.
10a D&C 64: 23; 119: 4
   (1–7).
   b TG Food.

c Gen. 7: 11.
   d TG Blessing.
11a D&C 85: 3.
14a Job 16: 11 (11–17);
   Jer. 20: 7 (7–8);
   Hab. 1: 2 (1–4).
   b Mal. 3: 14 (14–15).
   c TG Ordinance.
16a 4 Ne. 1: 12; Moro.
   6: 5 (5–6).
   b D&C 85: 9 (7–9);
   Moses 6: 5. TG Book
   of Remembrance.
17a Lev. 20: 26.
   b D&C 101: 3.

spare them as a man spareth his own son that serveth him.

18 Then shall ye return and [a]discern between the righteous and the wicked, between him that serveth God and him that serveth him not.

CHAPTER 25

At the Second Coming the proud and wicked shall be burned as stubble— Elijah shall return before that great and dreadful day—Compare Malachi 4.

[a]FOR behold, the day cometh that shall [b]burn as an oven; and all the [c]proud, yea, and all that do wickedly, shall be stubble; and the day that cometh shall burn them up, saith the Lord of Hosts, that it shall leave them neither root nor branch.

2 But unto you that fear my name, shall the [a]Son of Righteousness arise with healing in his wings; and ye shall go forth and [b]grow up as [c]calves in the stall.

3 And ye shall [a]tread down the wicked; for they shall be ashes under the soles of your feet in the day that I shall do this, saith the Lord of Hosts.

4 Remember ye the law of Moses, my servant, which I commanded unto him in [a]Horeb for all Israel, with the statutes and judgments.

5 Behold, I will send you [a]Elijah the prophet before the coming of the great and dreadful [b]day of the Lord;

6 And he shall [a]turn the heart of the [b]fathers to the children, and the heart of the children to their fathers, lest I come and [c]smite the earth with a curse.

CHAPTER 26

Jesus expounds all things from the beginning to the end—Babes and children utter marvelous things which cannot be written—Those in the Church of Christ have all things in common among them.

AND now it came to pass that when Jesus had told these things he expounded them unto the multitude; and he did expound all things unto them, both great and small.

2 And he saith: [a]These scriptures, which ye had not with you, the Father commanded that I should give unto you; for it was wisdom in him that they should be given unto future generations.

3 And he did expound all things, even from the beginning until the [a]time that he should come in his [b]glory—yea, even all things which should come upon the face of the earth, even until the [c]elements should melt with fervent heat, and the earth should be [d]wrapt together as a scroll, and the heavens and the earth should pass away;

4 And even unto the [a]great and last day, when all people, and all kindreds, and all nations and tongues shall [b]stand before God, to be

18a TG Discernment, Spiritual.
25 1a Mal. 4: 1 (1–6).
  b Ps. 21: 9 (8–10); Isa. 24: 6; 66: 16; 1 Ne. 22: 15; 3 Ne. 24: 2; D&C 29: 9; 64: 23 (23–24); 133: 64; JS-H 1: 37. TG Earth, Cleansing of.
  c Ps. 18: 27; 2 Ne. 20: 15. TG Pride.
  2a Ps. 84: 11; Mal. 4: 2; Ether 9: 22.
  b D&C 45: 58.
  c 1 Ne. 22: 24.
  3a 3 Ne. 21: 12.
  4a Ex. 3: 1; 19: 18 (9,

16–20); 1 Kgs. 19: 8; Neh. 9: 13; Mosiah 12: 33; 13: 5.
  5a 2 Kgs. 2: 2; D&C 2: 1; 35: 4; 110: 13 (13–16); 128: 17 (17–18). TG Genealogy and Temple Work.
  b TG Day of the Lord.
  6a D&C 98: 16 (16–17).
  b TG Family, Eternal; Salvation for the Dead.
  c Mal. 4: 6; D&C 110: 15 (13–16).
26 2a IE Mal. chapters 3 and 4, quoted in 3 Ne.

chapters 24 and 25.
  3a TG Day of the Lord.
  b Ps. 72: 19. TG Jesus Christ, Glory of.
  c Amos 9: 13; 2 Pet. 3: 10 (10, 12); Morm. 9: 2. TG Earth, Cleansing of; Earth, Destiny of; World, End of.
  d Morm. 5: 23.
  4a Mal. 4: 5; Hel. 12: 25; 3 Ne. 28: 31.
  b Mosiah 16: 10 (1–2, 10–11). TG Judgment, The Last.

judged of their works, whether they be good or whether they be evil—

5 If they be good, to the ᵃresurrection of everlasting life; and if they be evil, to the resurrection of damnation; being on a parallel, the one on the one hand and the other on the other hand, according to the mercy, and the ᵇjustice, and the holiness which is in Christ, who was ᶜbefore the world began.

6 And now there cannot be written in this book even a ᵃhundredth part of the things which Jesus did truly teach unto the people;

7 But behold the ᵃplates of Nephi do contain the more part of the things which he taught the people.

8 And these things have I written, which are a ᵃlesser part of the things which he taught the people; and I have written them to the intent that they may be brought again unto this people, ᵇfrom the Gentiles, according to the words which Jesus hath spoken.

9 And when they shall have received this, which is expedient that they should have first, to try their faith, and if it shall so be that they shall believe these things then shall the ᵃgreater things be made manifest unto them.

10 And if it so be that they will not believe these things, then shall the ᵃgreater things be ᵇwithheld from them, unto their condemnation.

11 Behold, I was about to write them, all which were engraven upon the plates of Nephi, but the Lord ᵃforbade it, saying: I will ᵇtry the faith of my people.

12 Therefore I, ᵃMormon, do write the things which have been commanded me of the Lord. And now I, ᵇMormon, make an end of my sayings, and proceed to write the things which have been commanded me.

13 Therefore, I would that ye should behold that the Lord truly did teach the people, for the space of three days; and after that he did ᵃshow himself unto them oft, and did break ᵇbread oft, and bless it, and give it unto them.

14 And it came to pass that he did teach and minister unto the ᵃchildren of the multitude of whom hath been spoken, and he did ᵇloose their ᶜtongues, and they did speak unto their fathers great and marvelous things, even greater than he had revealed unto the people; and he loosed their tongues that they could utter.

15 And it came to pass that after he had ascended into heaven—the second time that he showed himself unto them, and had gone unto the Father, after having ᵃhealed all their sick, and their lame, and opened the eyes of their blind and unstopped the ears of the deaf, and even had done all manner of cures among them, and raised a man from the ᵇdead, and had shown forth his power unto them, and had ascended unto the Father—

16 Behold, it came to pass on the morrow that the multitude gathered themselves together, and they both saw and heard these children; yea, even ᵃbabes did open their mouths

5a Dan. 12:2.
  b TG God, Justice of; Justice.
  c 3 Ne. 1:14; Ether 3:14. TG Man, Antemortal Existence of.
6a John 21:25; W of M 1:5; 3 Ne. 5:8 (8–11); Ether 15:33.
7a Jarom 1:14; 4 Ne. 1:19.
8a 3 Ne. 28:33; D&C 11:22.
  b 3 Ne. 21:5 (5–6).
9a John 16:12; 2 Ne. 27:8 (7–11, 21); Morm. 8:12; Ether 4:8 (4–10).
10a Ether 4:7 (1–8).
  b 2 Ne. 28:27; Alma 12:10 (9–11); D&C 6:26 (26–27).
11a 3 Ne. 26:18.
  b Ether 12:6.
12a 3 Ne. 28:24.
  b W of M 1:1 (1–2).
13a John 21·14; 3 Ne. 27:2.
  b 3 Ne. 18:1; 20:3
(3–9). TG Bread; Sacrament.
14a Luke 10:21; Alma 32:23; 3 Ne. 17:11; D&C 128:18.
  b D&C 23:3.
  c 3 Ne. 19:32; 28:14 (14, 16).
15a 3 Ne. 17:9. TG Administrations to the Sick; Healing.
  b TG Death, Power over.
16a Matt. 11:25.

and utter marvelous things; and the things which they did utter were *b*forbidden that there should not any man write them.

17 And it came to pass that the *a*disciples whom Jesus had chosen began *b*from that time forth to *c*baptize and to teach as many as did come unto them; and as many as were baptized in the name of Jesus were filled with the Holy Ghost.

18 And many of them saw and heard unspeakable things, which are *a*not lawful to be written.

19 And they taught, and did *a*minister one to another; and they had *b*all things *c*common among them, every man dealing justly, one with another.

20 And it came to pass that they did do all things even as Jesus had commanded them.

21 And they who were baptized in the name of Jesus were called the *a*church of Christ.

CHAPTER 27

Jesus commands them to call the Church in his name—His mission and atoning sacrifice constitute his gospel—Men are commanded to repent and be baptized that they may be sanctified by the Holy Ghost—They are to be even as Jesus is.

AND it came to pass that as the disciples of Jesus were journeying and were preaching the things which they had both heard and seen, and were baptizing in the name of Jesus, it came to pass that the disciples were gathered together and were *a*united in *b*mighty prayer and *c*fasting.

2 And Jesus again *a*showed himself unto them, for they were pray-ing unto the Father in his name; and Jesus came and stood in the midst of them, and said unto them: What will ye that I shall give unto you?

3 And they said unto him: Lord, we will that thou wouldst tell us the *a*name whereby we shall call this church; for there are disputations among the people concerning this matter.

4 And the Lord said unto them: Verily, verily, I say unto you, why is it that the people should murmur and dispute because of this thing?

5 Have they not read the scriptures, which say ye must take upon you the *a*name of Christ, which is my name? For by this name shall ye be called at the last day;

6 And whoso taketh upon him my name, and *a*endureth to the end, the same shall be saved at the last day.

7 Therefore, whatsoever ye shall do, ye shall do it in my name; therefore ye shall call the church in my name; and ye shall call upon the Father in my name that he will bless the church for my sake.

8 And how be it *a*my *b*church save it be called in my name? For if a church be called in Moses' name then it be Moses' church; or if it be called in the name of a man then it be the church of a man; but if it be called in my name then it is my church, if it so be that they are built upon my gospel.

9 Verily I say unto you, that ye are built upon my gospel; therefore ye shall call whatsoever things ye do call, in my name; therefore if ye call upon the Father, for the church, if it be in my name the Father will hear you;

10 And if it so be that the church

16*b* 3 Ne. 27: 23.
17*a* 3 Ne. 19: 4 (4–12);
    4 Ne. 1: 14.
  b Ether 12: 31.
  c 4 Ne. 1: 1.
18*a* 3 Ne. 26: 11.
19*a* TG Benevolence.
  b 4 Ne. 1: 3 (3, 25–26).
  c TG Consecration.
21*a* Mosiah 18: 17; Alma 4:

  5 (4–5). TG Church.
27 1*a* D&C 29: 6; 84: 1.
  b Alma 8: 10; D&C
    5: 24; 29: 2.
  c Mosiah 27: 22; Alma 5:
    46; 6: 6. TG Fasting.
2*a* 3 Ne. 26: 13. TG Jesus
    Christ, Appearances,
    Postmortal.
3*a* D&C 1: 1; 20: 1.

5*a* TG Jesus Christ,
    Taking the Name of.
6*a* Alma 32: 13 (13–15);
    38: 2; 3 Ne. 15: 9.
8*a* 1 Cor. 1: 12 (11–13);
    D&C 115: 4.
  b TG Jesus Christ, Head
    of the Church.

[A.D. 34—35]

is built upon my gospel then will the Father show forth his own works in it.

11 But if it be not built upon my gospel, and is built upon the works of men, or upon the works of the devil, verily I say unto you they have joy in their works for a season, and by and by the end cometh, and they are *a*hewn down and cast into the *b*fire, from whence there is no return.

12 For their works do *a*follow them, for it is because of their works that they are hewn down; therefore remember the things that I have told you.

13 Behold I have given unto you my *a*gospel, and this is the gospel which I have given unto you—that I came into the world to do the *b*will of my Father, because my Father sent me.

14 And my Father sent me that I might be *a*lifted up upon the *b*cross; and after that I had been lifted up upon the *c*cross, that I might *d*draw all men unto me, that as I have been lifted up by men even so should men be lifted up by the Father, to stand before me, to be *e*judged of their works, whether they be good or whether they be evil—

15 And for this cause have I been *a*lifted up; therefore, according to the power of the Father I will draw all men unto me, that they may be judged according to their *b*works.

16 And it shall come to pass, that whoso *a*repenteth and is baptized in my *b*name shall be filled; and if he *c*endureth to the end, behold, him will I hold guiltless before my Father at that day when I shall stand to judge the world.

17 And he that endureth not unto the end, the same is he that is also hewn down and cast into the fire, from whence they can no more return, because of the *a*justice of the Father.

18 And this is the word which he hath given unto the children of men. And for this cause he fulfilleth the words which he hath given, and he lieth not, but fulfilleth all his words.

19 And *a*no unclean thing can enter into his kingdom; therefore nothing entereth into his *b*rest save it be those who have *c*washed their garments in my blood, because of their faith, and the repentance of all their sins, and their faithfulness unto the end.

20 Now this is the commandment: *a*Repent, all ye ends of the earth, and come unto me and be *b*baptized in my name, that ye may be *c*sanctified by the reception of the Holy Ghost, that ye may stand *d*spotless before me at the last day.

21 Verily, verily, I say unto you, this is my *a*gospel; and ye know the things that ye must *b*do in my church; for the works which ye have seen me do that shall ye also do; for that which ye have seen me do even that shall ye do;

11a Jacob 5: 46; 6: 7;
    Alma 5: 52; D&C
    132: 13.
  b TG Hell.
12a Rev. 14: 13; D&C
    59: 2.
13a Acts 10: 36 (36–40);
    D&C 76: 40 (40–42).
    TG Gospel.
  b John 6: 39. TG Jesus
    Christ, Mission of.
14a 3 Ne. 15: 1; Morm.
    2: 19.
  b Moses 7: 55.
  c Luke 9: 44 (44–45);
    1 Ne. 11: 32.
  d John 6: 44; 2 Ne. 9: 5;

    D&C 17: 8; 27: 18.
  e TG Jesus Christ,
    Judge.
15a TG Jesus Christ,
    Atonement through.
  b 1 Sam. 2: 3.
16a TG Repentance.
  b TG Baptism,
    Qualifications for.
  c 1 Ne. 13: 37.
    TG Endure; Steadfast-
    ness.
17a TG God, Justice of.
19a Alma 11: 37.
    TG Uncleanness.
  b D&C 84: 24.
    TG Rest.

  c Rev. 1: 5 (1–6); 7: 14;
    1 Ne. 12: 10; Alma
    5: 21 (21–27); 13: 11
    (11–13).
20a Ether 4: 18; Moro.
    7: 34.
  b TG Baptism,
    Essential.
  c TG Sanctification.
  d 1 Cor. 1: 8;
    D&C 4: 2.
21a 1 Ne. 13: 36.
    TG Gospel;
    Salvation, Plan of.
  b TG Jesus Christ,
    Exemplar.

22 Therefore, if ye do these things blessed are ye, for ye shall be lifted up at the last day.

23 *Write the things which ye have seen and heard, save it be those which are *forbidden.

24 Write the works of this people, which shall be, even as hath been written, of that which hath been.

25 For behold, out of the books which have been written, and which shall be written, shall this people be *judged, for by them shall their *works be known unto men.

26 And behold, all things are *written by the Father; therefore out of the books which shall be written shall the world be judged.

27 And know ye that *ye shall be *judges of this people, according to the judgment which I shall give unto you, which shall be just. Therefore, what *manner of men ought ye to be? Verily I say unto you, even *as I am.

28 And now I *go unto the Father. And verily I say unto you, whatsoever things ye shall ask the Father in my name shall be given unto you.

29 Therefore, *ask, and ye shall receive; knock, and it shall be opened unto you; for he that asketh, receiveth; and unto him that knocketh, it shall be opened.

30 And now, behold, my joy is great, even unto fulness, because of you, and also this generation; yea, and even the Father rejoiceth, and also all the holy angels, because of you and this generation; for *none of them are lost.

31 Behold, I would that ye should understand; for I mean them who are *now alive of *this generation; and none of them are lost; and in them I have fulness of *joy.

32 But behold, it *sorroweth me because of the *fourth generation from this generation, for they are led away captive by him even as was the *son of perdition; for they will sell me for silver and for gold, and for that which *moth doth corrupt and which thieves can break through and steal. And in that day will I visit them, even in turning their works upon their own heads.

33 And it came to pass that when Jesus had ended these sayings he said unto his disciples: Enter ye in at the *strait gate; for strait is the gate, and narrow is the way that leads to life, and few there be that find it; but wide is the gate, and broad the way which leads to death, and many there be that travel therein, until the night cometh, wherein no man can work.

CHAPTER 28

Nine of the Twelve desire and are promised an inheritance in Christ's kingdom when they die—The Three Nephites desire and are given power over death so as to remain on the earth until Jesus comes again—They are translated and see things not lawful to utter, and they are now ministering among men.

AND it came to pass when Jesus had said these words, he spake unto his disciples, one by one, saying unto them: What is it that ye *desire of

23a TG Record Keeping.
  b 3 Ne. 26: 16 (16, 18).
25a 2 Ne. 33: 15 (10–15);
    W of M 1: 11.
  b Ps. 33: 15 (13–15);
    1 Ne. 15: 33 (26–36).
26a 3 Ne. 24: 16. TG Book
    of Life.
27a 1 Ne. 12: 10 (9–10);
    Morm. 3: 19.
  b Rev. 20: 4 (4–6).
  c 2 Pet. 3: 11.
    TG Godliness; Jesus
    Christ, Exemplar; Man,

Potential to Become
like Heavenly Father.
  d Matt. 5: 48; 3 Ne.
    12: 48.
28a John 16: 10; 20: 17.
29a Matt. 7: 7; 3 Ne. 14: 7.
30a John 17: 12.
31a 3 Ne. 9: 13 (11–13);
    10: 12.
  b 3 Ne. 28: 23.
  c TG Joy.
32a Gen. 6: 6; 3 Ne. 17: 14.
  b 1 Ne. 12: 11 (11–12);
    2 Ne. 26: 9 (9–10);

Alma 45: 12 (10, 12);
    Hel. 13: 6 (5–19).
  c John 17: 12; 3 Ne.
    29: 7.
  d Matt. 6: 19; 3 Ne.
    13: 19 (19–21).
33a Matt. 7: 13 (13–14);
    Luke 13: 24;
    3 Ne. 14: 13;
    D&C 22: 4 (1–4).
28 1a 2 Chr. 1: 7(7–12);
    D&C 7: 1 (1–8).

[A.D. 34—35]

me, after that I am gone to the Father?

2 And they all spake, save it were three, saying: We desire that after we have lived unto the age of man, that our ministry, wherein thou hast called us, may have an end, that we may speedily come unto thee in thy kingdom.

3 And he said unto them: Blessed are ye because ye desired this thing of me; therefore, after that ye are ᵃseventy and two years old ye shall come unto me in my ᵇkingdom; and with me ye shall find ᶜrest.

4 And when he had spoken unto them, he turned himself unto the three, and said unto them: What will ye that I should do unto you, when I am gone unto the Father?

5 And they sorrowed in their hearts, for they durst not speak unto him the thing which they desired.

6 And he said unto them: Behold, I ᵃknow your thoughts, and ye have desired the thing which ᵇJohn, my beloved, who was with me in my ministry, before that I was lifted up by the Jews, desired of me.

7 Therefore, more blessed are ye, for ye shall ᵃnever taste of ᵇdeath; but ye shall live to behold all the doings of the Father unto the children of men, even until all things shall be fulfilled according to the will of the Father, when I shall come in my glory with the ᶜpowers of heaven.

8 And ye shall never endure the pains of death; but when I shall come in my glory ye shall be changed in the twinkling of an eye from ᵃmortality to ᵇimmortality; and then shall ye be blessed in the kingdom of my Father.

9 And again, ye shall not have pain while ye shall dwell in the flesh, neither sorrow save it be for the ᵃsins of the world; and all this will I do because of the thing which ye have desired of me, for ye have desired that ye might ᵇbring the souls of men unto me, while the world shall stand.

10 And for this cause ye shall have ᵃfulness of joy; and ye shall sit down in the kingdom of my Father; yea, your joy shall be full, even as the Father hath given me fulness of joy; and ye shall be even as I am, and I am even as the Father; and the Father and I are ᵇone;

11 And the ᵃHoly Ghost beareth record of the Father and me; and the Father giveth the Holy Ghost unto the children of men, because of me.

12 And it came to pass that when Jesus had spoken these words, he touched every one of them with his finger save it were the ᵃthree who were to tarry, and then he departed.

13 And behold, the heavens were opened, and they were ᵃcaught up into heaven, and saw and heard unspeakable things.

14 And it was ᵃforbidden that they should utter; neither was it given unto them ᵇpower that they could utter the things which they saw and heard;

15 And whether they were in the body or out of the body, they could not tell; for it did seem unto them like a ᵃtransfiguration of them, that

3a 4 Ne. 1: 14.
 b TG Election.
 c TG Rest.
6a Amos 4: 13;
   Alma 18: 32.
 b John 21: 22 (21–23);
   D&C 7: 3 (1–8).
7a 4 Ne. 1: 37 (14, 37);
   Morm. 8: 10 (10–12);
   Ether 12: 17.
 b Luke 9: 27.
   TG Translated Beings.
 c 3 Ne. 20: 22.

8a 3 Ne. 28: 36 (36–40).
   TG Mortality.
 b TG Immortality.
9a 4 Ne. 1: 44;
   Morm. 8: 10.
 b Philip. 1: 24 (23–24);
   3 Ne. 28: 27; D&C
   7: 5 (1–8).
10a John 16: 15; D&C
   76: 59; 84: 38 (37–38).
 b Deut. 6: 4; Gal. 3: 20;
   2 Ne. 31: 21; 3 Ne.
   11: 27 (27–28, 36);

   Morm. 7: 7; D&C
   20: 28.
11a 2 Ne. 31: 18 (17–21);
   3 Ne. 11: 32; Ether
   5: 4; Moses 6: 66.
12a 4 Ne. 1: 14 (14, 37);
   Morm. 1: 13.
13a 2 Cor. 12: 4 (2–4).
14a D&C 76: 115.
 b 3 Ne. 19: 32; 26: 14.
15a Moses 1: 11.
   TG Transfiguration.

they were changed from this body of flesh into an immortal state, that they could behold the things of God.

16 But it came to pass that they did again minister upon the face of the earth; nevertheless they did not minister of the things which they had heard and seen, because of the commandment which was given them in heaven.

17 And now, whether they were mortal or immortal, from the day of their transfiguration, I know not;

18 But this much I know, according to the record which hath been given—they did go forth upon the face of the land, and did minister unto all the people, uniting as many to the church as would believe in their preaching; baptizing them, and as many as were baptized did receive the Holy Ghost.

19 And they were cast into prison by them who did not belong to the church. And the ªprisons could not hold them, for they were rent in twain.

20 And they were cast down into the earth; but they did smite the earth with the word of God, insomuch that by his ªpower they were delivered out of the depths of the earth; and therefore they could not dig pits sufficient to hold them.

21 And thrice they were cast into a ªfurnace and received no harm.

22 And twice were they cast into a ªden of wild beasts; and behold they did play with the beasts as a child with a suckling lamb, and received no harm.

23 And it came to pass that thus they did go forth among all the people of Nephi, and did preach the ªgospel of Christ unto all people upon the face of the land; and they were

converted unto the Lord, and were united unto the church of Christ, and thus the people of ᵇthat generation were blessed, according to the word of Jesus.

24 And now I, ªMormon, make an end of speaking concerning these things for a time.

25 Behold, I was about to write the ªnames of those who were never to taste of death, but the Lord forbade; therefore I write them not, for they are hid from the world.

26 But behold, ªI have seen them, and they have ministered unto me.

27 And behold they will be ªamong the Gentiles, and the Gentiles shall know them not.

28 They will also be among the Jews, and the Jews shall know them not.

29 And it shall come to pass, when the Lord seeth fit in his wisdom that they shall minister unto all the ªscattered tribes of Israel, and unto all nations, kindreds, tongues and people, and shall bring out of them unto Jesus many souls, that their desire may be fulfilled, and also because of the convincing power of God which is in them.

30 And they are as the ªangels of God, and if they shall pray unto the Father in the name of Jesus they can show themselves unto whatsoever man it seemeth them good.

31 Therefore, great and marvelous works shall be wrought by them, before the ªgreat and coming day when all people must surely stand before the judgment-seat of Christ;

32 Yea even among the Gentiles shall there be a ªgreat and marvelous work wrought by them, before that judgment day.

33 And if ye had ªall the scriptures which give an account of all the

19a Acts 16:26; Alma 14:27 (26–28); 4 Ne. 1:30; Morm. 8:24.
20a 1 Ne. 7:17 (17–18); Jacob 4:6.
21a Dan. 3:25; 4 Ne. 1:32; Morm. 8:24.
22a Dan. 6:16 (16–27);
4 Ne. 1:33.
23a TG Gospel.
 b 3 Ne. 27:31 (30–31).
24a 3 Ne. 26:12.
25a 3 Ne. 19:4.
26a Morm. 8:11.
27a 3 Ne. 28:9.
29a TG Israel, Scattering of; Israel, Ten Lost
Tribes of.
30a TG Angels.
31a Mal. 4:5; Hel. 12:25; 3 Ne. 26:4; Morm. 9:2.
32a 2 Ne. 25:17.
33a 3 Ne. 26:8 (6–12).

marvelous works of Christ, ye would, according to the words of Christ, know that these things must surely come.

34 And wo be unto him that will ^anot hearken unto the words of Jesus, and also to them whom he hath chosen and ^bsent among them; for whoso ^creceiveth not the words of Jesus and the words of those whom he hath sent receiveth not him; and therefore he will not receive them at the last day;

35 And it would be better for them if they had not been born. For do ye suppose that ye can get rid of the justice of an ^aoffended God, who hath been ^btrampled under feet of men, that thereby salvation might come?

36 And now behold, as I spake concerning those whom the Lord hath chosen, yea, even three who were caught up into the heavens, that I knew not whether they were ^acleansed from ^bmortality to immortality—

37 But behold, since I wrote, I have inquired of the Lord, and he hath made it manifest unto me that there must needs be a change wrought upon their bodies, or else it needs be that they must taste of death;

38 Therefore, that they might not taste of death there was a ^achange wrought upon their bodies, that they might not ^bsuffer pain nor sorrow save it were for the sins of the world.

39 Now this change was not equal to that which shall take place at the last day; but there was a change wrought upon them, insomuch that Satan could have no power over them, that he could not ^atempt them; and they were ^bsanctified in the flesh, that they were ^choly, and

that the powers of the earth could not hold them.

40 And in this state they were to remain until the judgment day of Christ; and at that day they were to receive a greater change, and to be received into the kingdom of the Father to go no more out, but to dwell with God eternally in the heavens.

CHAPTER 29

The coming forth of the Book of Mormon is a sign that the Lord has commenced to gather Israel and fulfill his covenants—Those who reject his latter-day revelations and gifts shall be cursed.

AND now behold, I say unto you that when the Lord shall see fit, in his wisdom, that these sayings shall ^acome unto the Gentiles according to his word, then ye may know that the ^bcovenant which the Father hath made with the children of Israel, concerning their restoration to the ^clands of their inheritance, is already beginning to be fulfilled.

2 And ye may know that the words of the Lord, which have been spoken by the holy prophets, shall all be fulfilled; and ye need not say that the Lord ^adelays his coming unto the children of Israel.

3 And ye need not imagine in your hearts that the words which have been spoken are vain, for behold, the Lord will remember his covenant which he hath made unto his people of the house of Israel.

4 And when ye shall see these sayings coming forth among you, then ye need not any longer spurn at the doings of the Lord, for the ^asword of his ^bjustice is in his right hand;

34a Ether 4: 8 (8–12).
  b Matt. 10: 5 (5–42).
  c TG Prophets,
    Rejection of.
35a TG Blasphemy.
  b Hel. 12: 2.
36a TG Purification.
  b 3 Ne. 28: 8 (8–9).
    TG Immortality;

Mortality.
38a TG Translated Beings.
  b TG Suffering.
39a TG Temptation;
    Test, Try, Prove.
  b TG Sanctification.
  c TG Holiness.
29 1a 2 Ne. 30: 3 (3–8);
    Morm. 3: 17.

  b Ezek. 20: 37; Morm.
    5: 14 (14, 20).
  c TG Lands of
    Inheritance.
2a Matt. 24: 48; Luke
    12: 45.
4a 3 Ne. 20: 20.
  b TG Justice.

and behold, at that day, if ye shall spurn at his doings he will cause that it shall soon overtake you.

5 ᵃWo unto him that ᵇspurneth at the doings of the Lord; yea, wo unto him that shall ᶜdeny the Christ and his works!

6 Yea, ᵃwo unto him that shall deny the revelations of the Lord, and that shall say the Lord no longer worketh by revelation, or by prophecy, or by ᵇgifts, or by tongues, or by healings, or by the power of the Holy Ghost!

7 Yea, and wo unto him that shall say at that day, to get ᵃgain, that there can be ᵇno miracle wrought by Jesus Christ; for he that doeth this shall become ᶜlike unto the son of perdition, for whom there was no mercy, according to the word of Christ!

8 Yea, and ye need not any longer ᵃhiss, nor ᵇspurn, nor make game of the ᶜ Jews, nor any of the remnant of the house of Israel; for behold, the Lord remembereth his covenant unto them, and he will do unto them according to that which he hath sworn.

9 Therefore ye need not suppose that ye can turn the right hand of the Lord unto the left, that he may not execute judgment unto the fulfilling of the covenant which he hath made unto the house of Israel.

CHAPTER 30

The latter-day Gentiles are commanded to repent and come unto Christ and be numbered with the house of Israel.

HEARKEN, O ye Gentiles, and hear the words of Jesus Christ, the Son of the living God, which he hath ᵃcommanded me that I should speak concerning you, for, behold he commandeth me that I should write, saying:

2 Turn, all ye ᵃGentiles, from your wicked ways; and ᵇrepent of your evil doings, of your ᶜlyings and deceivings, and of your whoredoms, and of your secret abominations, and your idolatries, and of your ᵈmurders, and your ᵉpriestcrafts, and your ᶠenvyings, and your strifes, and from all your wickedness and abominations, and come unto me, and be baptized in my name, that ye may receive a remission of your sins, and be filled with the Holy Ghost, that ye may be ᵍnumbered with my people who are of the house of Israel.

5a 2 Ne. 28:15;
  Morm. 9:26.
 b Morm. 8:17; Ether
  4:8 (8–10).
 c Matt. 10:33 (32–33);
  Moro. 1:3.
6a Morm. 9:7 (7–11, 15).
 b TG Holy Ghost,
  Gifts of.
7a TG Priestcraft.
 b 2 Ne. 28:6 (4–6);
  Morm. 8:26;

 9:15 (15–26).
 c 2 Ne. 9:9; 3 Ne.
  27:32. TG Sons of
  Perdition.
8a 1 Ne. 19:14.
 b 2 Ne. 29:5 (4–5).
  TG Backbiting.
 c TG Israel, Judah,
  People of.
30 1a 3 Ne. 5:13 (12–13).
2a Rom. 15:10 (8–21).
 b TG Repentance.

 c Alma 16:18; 3 Ne.
  21:19 (19–21).
 d 3 Ne. 16:10;
  Morm. 8:31.
 e TG Priestcraft.
 f TG Envy.
 g Gal. 3:29 (27–29);
  2 Ne. 10:18 (18–19);
  3 Ne. 21:22 (22–25);
  Abr. 2:10.

[A.D. 34—35]

FOURTH NEPHI
THE BOOK OF NEPHI

WHO IS THE SON OF NEPHI—ONE OF THE DISCIPLES OF JESUS CHRIST

An account of the people of Nephi, according to his record.

The Nephites and the Lamanites are all converted to the Church of Christ—They have all things in common, work miracles, and prosper in the land—After two centuries divisions, evils, false churches, and persecutions arise—After three hundred years both the Nephites and the Lamanites are wicked—Ammaron hides up the sacred records.

AND it came to pass that the thirty and fourth year passed away, and also the thirty and fifth, and behold the disciples of Jesus had formed a church of Christ in all the lands round about. And as many as did come unto them, and did truly repent of their sins, were ^abaptized in the name of Jesus; and they did also receive the Holy Ghost.

2 And it came to pass in the thirty and sixth year, the people were all converted unto the Lord, upon all the face of the land, both Nephites and Lamanites, and there were no contentions and disputations among them, and every man did deal justly one with another.

3 And they had ^aall things common among them; therefore there were not rich and poor, bond and free, but they were all made free, and partakers of the heavenly ^bgift.

4 And it came to pass that the thirty and seventh year passed away also, and there still continued to be ^apeace in the land.

5 And there were great and marvelous works wrought by the disciples of Jesus, insomuch that they did ^aheal the sick, and ^braise the dead, and cause the lame to walk, and the blind to receive their sight, and the deaf to hear; and all manner of ^cmiracles did they work among the children of men; and in nothing did they work miracles save it were in the name of Jesus.

6 And thus did the thirty and eighth year pass away, and also the thirty and ninth, and forty and first, and the forty and second, yea, even until forty and nine years had passed away, and also the fifty and first, and the fifty and second; yea, and even until fifty and nine years had passed away.

7 And the Lord did prosper them exceedingly in the land; yea, insomuch that they did build cities again where there had been cities burned.

8 Yea, even that great ^acity Zarahemla did they cause to be built again.

9 But there were many cities which had been ^asunk, and waters came up in the stead thereof; therefore these cities could not be renewed.

10 And now, behold, it came to pass that the people of Nephi did wax strong, and did multiply exceedingly fast, and became an exceedingly ^afair and delightsome people.

---

1 1a 3 Ne. 26: 17.
3a Jacob 2: 19 (17–19);
Mosiah 4: 26; 18: 27
(19–29); Alma 16: 16;
3 Ne. 12: 42; 26: 19.
TG Consecration.
b TG God, Gifts of.
4a TG Peace.
5a TG Healing.
b TG Death, Power over.
c John 14: 12 (12–14).
TG Miracle.
8a 3 Ne. 8: 8 (8, 24).
9a 3 Ne. 9: 4 (4, 7).
10a 1 Ne. 13: 15; 2 Ne.
5: 21; Morm. 9: 6.

[A.D. 36—60]

11 And they were married, and given in marriage, and were blessed according to the multitude of the ᵃpromises which the Lord had made unto them.

12 And they did not walk any more after the ᵃperformances and ᵇordinances of the ᶜlaw of Moses; but they did walk after the commandments which they had received from their Lord and their God, continuing in ᵈfasting and prayer, and in meeting together oft both to pray and to hear the word of the Lord.

13 And it came to pass that there was no contention among all the people, in all the land; but there were mighty miracles wrought among the disciples of Jesus.

14 And it came to pass that the *seventy and first year passed away, and also the seventy and second year, yea, and in fine, till the seventy and ninth year had passed away; yea, even an hundred years had passed away, and the ᵃdisciples of Jesus, whom he had chosen, had all gone to the ᵇparadise of God, save it were the ᶜthree who should tarry; and there were other ᵈdisciples ᵉordained in their stead; and also many of that ᶠgeneration had passed away.

15 And it came to pass that there was no ᵃcontention in the land, because of the ᵇlove of God which did dwell in the hearts of the people.

16 And there were no ᵃenvyings, nor ᵇstrifes, nor ᶜtumults, nor whoredoms, nor lyings, nor murders, nor any manner of ᵈlasciviousness; and surely there could not be a ᵉhappier people among all the people who had been created by the hand of God.

17 There were no robbers, nor murderers, neither were there Lamanites, nor any manner of -ites; but they were in ᵃone, the children of Christ, and heirs to the kingdom of God.

18 And how blessed were they! For the Lord did bless them in all their doings; yea, even they were blessed and prospered until †an hundred and ten years had passed away; and the first generation from Christ had passed away, and there was no contention in all the land.

19 And it came to pass that ᵃNephi, he that kept this last record, (and he kept it upon the ᵇplates of Nephi) died, and his son Amos kept it in his stead; and he kept it upon the plates of Nephi also.

20 And he kept it eighty and four years, and there was still peace in the land, save it were a small part of the people who had revolted from the church and taken upon them the name of Lamanites; therefore there began to be ᵃLamanites again in the land.

21 And it came to pass that ᵃAmos died also, (and it was an hundred and ninety and four years from the coming of Christ) and his son Amos kept the record in his stead; and he also kept it upon the plates of Nephi; and it was also written in the book of Nephi, which is this book.

22 And it came to pass that ‡two hundred years had passed away; and the second generation had all passed away save it were a few.

23 And now I, Mormon, would that ye should know that the people had multiplied, insomuch that they were spread upon all the face of the land,

---

11a TG Promise.
12a 2 Ne. 25:30.
  b TG Ordinance.
  c 3 Ne. 9:19; 15:4 (2–8).
    TG Law of Moses.
  d Moro. 6:5; D&C
    88:76.
14a 3 Ne. 28:3;
    Morm. 3:19.
  b TG Paradise.
  c 3 Ne. 28:12.
    TG Translated Beings.

d TG Apostles.
e TG Priesthood,
  History of.
f 1 Ne. 12:12.
15a TG Contention.
  b TG God, Love of.
16a TG Envy.
  b TG Strife.
  c TG Rioting and
    Reveling.
  d TG Lust.
  e Prov. 14:34;

Mosiah 2:41; Alma 50:
23. TG Happiness.
17a John 17:21 (21–23).
  TG Zion.
19a 3 Ne. 23:7.
  b 3 Ne. 26:7.
20a 3 Ne. 10:18;
  Morm. 1:9.
21a 4 Ne. 1:47.

[*A.D. 72 †A.D. 111
‡A.D. 201]

and that they had become exceedingly [a]rich, because of their prosperity in Christ.

24 And now, in this *two hundred and first year there began to be among them those who were lifted up in [a]pride, such as the wearing of costly apparel, and all manner of fine pearls, and of the fine things of the world.

25 And from that time forth they did have their goods and their substance no more [a]common among them.

26 And they began to be divided into classes; and they began to build up [a]churches unto themselves to get [b]gain, and began to deny the true church of Christ.

27 And it came to pass that when †two hundred and ten years had passed away there were many churches in the land; yea, there were many churches which professed to know the Christ, and yet they did [a]deny the more parts of his gospel, insomuch that they did receive all manner of wickedness, and did administer that which was sacred unto him to whom it had been [b]forbidden because of unworthiness.

28 And this church did multiply exceedingly because of iniquity, and because of the power of [a]Satan who did get hold upon their [b]hearts.

29 And again, there was another church which denied the Christ; and they did [a]persecute the true [b]church of Christ, because of their humility and their belief in Christ; and they did despise them because of the many miracles which were wrought among them.

30 Therefore they did exercise power and authority over the disciples of Jesus who did tarry with them, and they did cast them into [a]prison; but by the power of the word of God, which was in them, the prisons were rent in twain, and they went forth doing mighty miracles among them.

31 Nevertheless, and notwithstanding all these miracles, the people did harden their hearts, and did seek to kill them, even as the Jews at Jerusalem sought to kill Jesus, according to his word.

32 And they did cast them into [a]furnaces of [b]fire, and they came forth receiving no harm.

33 And they also cast them into [a]dens of wild beasts, and they did play with the wild beasts even as a child with a lamb; and they did come forth from among them, receiving no harm.

34 Nevertheless, the people did harden their hearts, for they were led by many priests and [a]false prophets to build up many churches, and to do all manner of iniquity. And they did [b]smite upon the people of Jesus; but the people of Jesus did not smite again. And thus they did dwindle in unbelief and wickedness, from year to year, even until two hundred and thirty years had passed away.

35 And now it came to pass in this year, yea, in the ‡two hundred and thirty and first year, there was a great division among the people.

36 And it came to pass that in this year there arose a people who were called the [a]Nephites, and they were true believers in Christ; and among them there were those who were called by the Lamanites—Jacobites, and Josephites, and [b]Zoramites;

37 Therefore the true believers in Christ, and the true worshipers of

23a TG Treasure.
24a TG Pride; Selfishness.
25a TG Consecration.
26a 1 Ne. 22: 23; 2 Ne. 28: 3 (3–32); Morm. 8: 28 (28, 32–38).
  b Ezek. 22: 27; D&C 10: 56.
  TG Priestcraft.

27a TG Apostasy of Individuals.
  b 3 Ne. 18: 28 (28–29).
28a TG Devil, Church of.
  b TG Hardheartedness.
29a TG Persecution.
  b TG Jesus Christ, Head of the Church.
30a 3 Ne. 28: 19 (19–20).
32a 3 Ne. 28: 21.

  b Dan. 3: 27.
33a 3 Ne. 28: 22.
34a TG False Prophets.
  b 3 Ne. 6: 13; 12: 39; D&C 98: 23 (23–27).
36a Morm. 1: 8.
  b Jacob 1: 13.

[*A.D. 201 †A.D. 211
‡A.D. 231]

Christ, (among whom were the ᵃthree disciples of Jesus who should tarry) were called Nephites, and Jacobites, and Josephites, and Zoramites.

38 And it came to pass that they who rejected the gospel were called Lamanites, and Lemuelites, and Ishmaelites; and they did not dwindle in ᵃunbelief, but they did ᵇwilfully rebel against the gospel of Christ; and they did teach their children that they should not believe, even as their fathers, from the beginning, did dwindle.

39 And it was because of the wickedness and abomination of their fathers, even as it was in the beginning. And they were ᵃtaught to hate the children of God, even as the Lamanites were taught to ᵇhate the children of Nephi from the beginning.

40 And it came to pass that *two hundred and forty and four years had passed away, and thus were the affairs of the people. And the ᵃmore wicked part of the people did wax strong, and became exceedingly more numerous than were the people of God.

41 And they did still continue to build up churches unto themselves, and adorn them with all manner of precious things. And thus did two hundred and fifty years pass away, and also two hundred and sixty years.

42 And it came to pass that the wicked part of the people began again to build up the secret oaths and ᵃcombinations of Gadianton.

43 And also the people who were called the people of Nephi began to be proud in their hearts, because of their exceeding riches, and become ᵃvain like unto their brethren, the Lamanites.

44 And from this time the disciples began to sorrow for the ᵃsins of the world.

45 And it came to pass that when three hundred years had passed away, both the people of Nephi and the Lamanites had become exceedingly wicked one like unto another.

46 And it came to pass that the robbers of ᵃGadianton did spread over all the face of the land; and there were none that were righteous save it were the disciples of Jesus. And gold and silver did they lay up in store in abundance, and did ᵇtraffic in all manner of traffic.

47 And it came to pass that after †three hundred and five years had passed away, (and the people did still remain in wickedness) ᵃAmos died; and his brother, Ammaron, did keep the record in his stead.

48 And it came to pass that when ‡three hundred and twenty years had passed away, ᵃAmmaron, being constrained by the Holy Ghost, did ᵇhide up the ᶜrecords which were ᵈsacred—yea, even all the sacred records which had been handed down from generation to generation, which were sacred—even until the three hundred and twentieth year from the coming of Christ.

49 And he did hide them up unto the Lord, that they might ᵃcome again unto the remnant of the house of Jacob, according to the prophecies and the promises of the Lord. And thus is the end of the record of Ammaron.

37a 3 Ne. 28: 7; Morm.
    8: 10 (10–12).
38a TG Unbelief,
    Unbelievers.
  b Josh. 22: 18;
    Morm. 1: 16.
39a Mosiah 10: 17.
  b TG Hate; Malice.
40a Hel. 5: 2.
42a TG Secret

Combinations.
43a Hel. 16: 22.
44a Eccl. 3: 16 (16–17);
    3 Ne. 28: 9; Morm.
    8: 10 (9–10).
46a Morm. 2: 8;
    Ether 8: 20.
  b Mosiah 24: 7;
    Ether 10: 22.
47a 4 Ne. 1: 21.

48a Morm. 1: 2.
  b Morm. 2: 17.
  c TG Scriptures,
    Preservation of.
  d Hel. 3: 15 (13, 15–16).
49a Enos 1: 13;
    Morm. 5: 9.

[*A.D. 245 †A.D. 306
‡A.D. 321]

THE BOOK OF MORMON

CHAPTER 1

Ammaron instructs Mormon concerning the sacred records—War commences between the Nephites and the Lamanites—The Three Nephites are taken away—Wickedness, unbelief, sorceries, and witchcraft prevail.

AND now I, Mormon, make a ^arecord of the things which I have both seen and heard, and call it the ^bBook of Mormon.

2 And about the time that ^aAmmaron hid up the records unto the Lord, he came unto me, (I being about ten years of age, and I began to be ^blearned somewhat after the manner of the learning of my people) and Ammaron said unto me: I perceive that thou art a ^csober child, and art quick to observe;

3 Therefore, when ye are about twenty and four years old I would that ye should remember the things that ye have observed concerning this people; and when ye are of that age go to the ^aland Antum, unto a hill which shall be called ^bShim; and there have I deposited unto the Lord all the sacred engravings concerning this people.

4 And behold, ye shall take the ^aplates of Nephi unto yourself, and the remainder shall ye leave in the place where they are; and ye shall engrave on the plates of Nephi all the things that ye have observed concerning this people.

5 And I, Mormon, being a descendant of ^aNephi, (and my father's name was Mormon) I remembered the things which Ammaron commanded me.

6 And it came to pass that I, being *eleven years old, was carried by my father into the land southward, even to the land of Zarahemla.

7 The whole face of the land had become covered with buildings, and the people were as numerous almost, as it were the sand of the sea.

8 And it came to pass in this year there began to be a war between the ^aNephites, who consisted of the Nephites and the Jacobites and the Josephites and the Zoramites; and this war was between the Nephites, and the Lamanites and the Lemuelites and the Ishmaelites.

9 Now the ^aLamanites and the Lemuelites and the Ishmaelites were called Lamanites, and the two parties were Nephites and Lamanites.

10 And it came to pass that the war began to be among them in the borders of Zarahemla, by the waters of Sidon.

11 And it came to pass that the Nephites had gathered together a great number of men, even to exceed the number of thirty thousand. And it came to pass that they did have in this same year a number of ^abattles, in which the Nephites did beat the Lamanites and did slay many of them.

12 And it came to pass that the Lamanites withdrew their design, and there was peace settled in the land; and peace did remain for the space of about four years, that there was no bloodshed.

13 But wickedness did prevail upon the face of the whole land, insomuch that the Lord did take away his ^abeloved disciples, and the work of miracles and of healing did cease because of the iniquity of the people.

14 And there were no ^agifts from

---

1 1a 3 Ne. 5: 11 (11–18);
   Morm. 8: 5.
  b W of M 1: 5; Morm. 5: 9.
2a 4 Ne. 1: 48 (47–49).
  b Enos 1: 1; Mosiah
   1: 3 (3–5).
  c TG Sobriety, Sober,
   Soberness;

Trustworthiness.
3a Morm. 2: 17.
  b Morm. 4: 23; Ether 9: 3.
4a W of M 1: 1 (1, 11);
  3 Ne. 5: 10 (9–12);
  Morm. 2: 17 (17–18);
  8: 5 (1, 4–5, 14).
5a 3 Ne. 5: 20 (12, 20).

8a 4 Ne. 1: 36.
9a 4 Ne. 1: 20.
11a 2 Ne. 1: 12; Morm.
  4: 1 (1–23).
13a 3 Ne. 28: 12 (2, 12).
14a 1 Sam. 3: 1.

[*About A.D. 322]

the Lord, and the [b]Holy Ghost did not come upon any, because of their wickedness and [c]unbelief.

15 And I, *being [a]fifteen years of age and being somewhat of a [b]sober mind, therefore I was [c]visited of the Lord, and [d]tasted and knew of the goodness of Jesus.

16 And I did endeavor to preach unto this people, but my mouth was shut, and I was forbidden that I should preach unto them; for behold they had [a]wilfully rebelled against their God; and the beloved disciples were [b]taken away out of the land, because of their iniquity.

17 But I did remain among them, but I was forbidden to [a]preach unto them, because of the hardness of their hearts; and because of the hardness of their hearts the land was [b]cursed for their sake.

18 And these Gadianton robbers, who were among the Lamanites, did infest the land, insomuch that the inhabitants thereof began to [a]hide up their [b]treasures in the earth; and they became slippery, because the Lord had cursed the land, that they could not hold them, nor retain them again.

19 And it came to pass that there were [a]sorceries, and witchcrafts, and magics; and the power of the evil one was wrought upon all the face of the land, even unto the fulfilling of all the words of Abinadi, and also [b]Samuel the Lamanite.

CHAPTER 2

Mormon leads the Nephite armies—Blood and carnage sweep the land—The Nephites lament and mourn with the sorrowing of the damned—Their day of grace is passed—Mormon obtains the plates of Nephi—Wars continue.

AND it came to pass in that same year there began to be a war again between the Nephites and the Lamanites. And notwithstanding I being [a]young, was large in stature; therefore the people of Nephi appointed me that I should be their leader, or the leader of their armies.

2 Therefore it came to pass that †in my sixteenth year I did go forth at the head of an army of the Nephites, against the Lamanites; therefore three hundred and twenty and six years had passed away.

3 And it came to pass that in the three hundred and twenty and seventh year the Lamanites did come upon us with [a]exceedingly great power, insomuch that they did frighten my armies; therefore they would not fight, and they began to retreat towards the [b]north countries.

4 And it came to pass that we did come to the city of Angola, and we did take possession of the city, and make preparations to defend ourselves against the Lamanites. And it came to pass that we did [a]fortify the city with our might; but notwithstanding all our fortifications the Lamanites did come upon us and did drive us out of the city.

5 And they did also drive us forth out of the land of David.

6 And we marched forth and came to the land of Joshua, which was in the borders west by the seashore.

7 And it came to pass that we did gather in our people as fast as it were

14b TG Holy Ghost, Loss of.
  c TG Unbelief,
    Unbelievers.
15a Morm. 2: 1 (1–2).
  b TG Sobriety.
  c Ex. 3: 16; 2 Ne. 4: 26;
    Alma 9: 21.
  d Ps. 34: 8.
16a 4 Ne. 1: 38.
  TG Rebellion.
  b Morm. 8: 10.

17a Micah 3: 6 (5–7).
  b 2 Ne. 1: 7; Alma
    45: 16 (10–14, 16);
    Ether 2: 11 (8–12).
18a Hel. 12: 18; Morm.
    2: 10 (10–14); Ether
    14: 1 (1–2).
  b Hel. 13: 18–23, 30–37.
  TG Treasure.
19a TG Sorcery.
  b Morm. 2: 10 (10–15).

2 1a Morm. 1: 15 (12,
    15–16).
  3a Morm. 4: 13 (13–17);
    5: 6.
  b Alma 50: 11;
    Morm. 2: 29.
  4a 3 Ne. 3: 14 (14, 25);
    Morm. 2: 21.

[*About A.D. 326
†A.D. 327—328]

possible, that we might get them together in ᵃone body.

8 But behold, the land was ᵃfilled with ᵇrobbers and with Lamanites; and notwithstanding the great destruction which hung over my people, they did not repent of their evil doings; therefore there was blood and carnage spread throughout all the face of the land, both on the part of the Nephites and also on the part of the Lamanites; and it was one complete revolution throughout all the face of the land.

9 And now, the Lamanites had a king, and his name was ᵃAaron; and he came against us with an army of forty and four thousand. And behold, I withstood him with forty and two thousand. And it came to pass that I beat him with my army that he fled before me. And behold, all this was done, and *three hundred and thirty years had passed away.

10 And it came to pass that the Nephites began to repent of their iniquity, and began to cry even as had been prophesied by Samuel the prophet; for behold no man could ᵃkeep that which was his own, for the thieves, and the robbers, and the murderers, and the magic art, and the witchcraft which was in the land.

11 Thus there began to be a ᵃmourning and a lamentation in all the land because of these things, and more especially among the people of Nephi.

12 And it came to pass that when I, Mormon, saw their lamentation and their ᵃmourning and their sorrow before the Lord, my heart did begin to rejoice within me, knowing the mercies and the long-suffering of the Lord, therefore supposing that he would be merciful unto them that they would ᵇagain become a righteous people.

13 But behold this my joy was vain, for their ᵃsorrowing was not unto repentance, because of the goodness of God; but it was rather the ᵇsorrowing of the ᶜdamned, because the Lord would not always suffer them to take ᵈhappiness in sin.

14 And they did not come unto Jesus with broken ᵃhearts and contrite spirits, but they did ᵇcurse God, and wish to die. Nevertheless they would struggle with the sword for their lives.

15 And it came to pass that my sorrow did return unto me again, and I saw that the ᵃday of ᵇgrace ᶜwas passed with them, both temporally and spiritually; for I saw thousands of them hewn down in open ᵈrebellion against their God, and heaped up as ᵉdung upon the face of the land. And thus †three hundred and forty and four years had passed away.

16 And it came to pass that in the three hundred and forty and fifth year the Nephites did begin to flee before the Lamanites; and they were pursued until they came even to the land of Jashon, before it was possible to stop them in their retreat.

17 And now, the city of Jashon was near the ᵃland where Ammaron had ᵇdeposited the records unto the Lord, that they might not be destroyed. And behold I had gone according to the word of Ammaron, and taken the ᶜplates of Nephi, and did make a record according to the words of Ammaron.

18 And upon the plates of Nephi I

7a 3 Ne. 3: 22 (22–25).
8a 3 Ne. 2: 11.
  b 4 Ne. 1: 46; Morm. 8: 9;
    Ether 8: 20.
9a Moro. 9: 17.
10a Hel. 12: 18;
    13: 18 (17–23);
    Morm. 1: 18 (17–19);
    Ether 14: 1 (1–2).
11a 3 Ne. 12: 4.

12a TG Mourning.
  b Hel. 11: 9 (8–17).
13a 2 Cor. 7: 10;
    Alma 42: 29.
  b Hosea 7: 14;
    Ether 8: 7.
  c TG Damnation.
  d Alma 41: 10.
14a TG Contrite Heart.
  b TG Blasphemy.

15a Hel. 13: 38.
  b TG Grace.
  c Jer. 8: 20.
  d TG Rebellion.
  e Jer. 8: 2 (1–3).
17a Morm. 1: 3 (1–4).
  b 4 Ne. 1: 48 (48–49).
  c Morm. 8: 5 (1, 4–5, 14).

[*A.D. 331 †A.D. 345]

did make a full account of all the wickedness and abominations; but upon ªthese plates I did forbear to make a full account of their wickedness and abominations, for behold, a continual scene of wickedness and abominations has been before mine eyes ever since I have been sufficient to behold the ways of man.

19 And wo is me because of their wickedness; for my heart has been filled with sorrow because of their wickedness, all my days; nevertheless, I know that I shall be ªlifted up at the last day.

20 And it came to pass that in this year the people of Nephi again were hunted and driven. And it came to pass that we were driven forth until we had come northward to the land which was called Shem.

21 And it came to pass that we did ªfortify the city of Shem, and we did gather in our people as much as it were possible, that perhaps we might save them from destruction.

22 And it came to pass in the *three hundred and forty and sixth year they began to come upon us again.

23 And it came to pass that I did speak unto my people, and did urge them with great energy, that they would stand boldly before the Lamanites and ªfight for their ᵇwives, and their children, and their houses, and their homes.

24 And my words did arouse them somewhat to vigor, insomuch that they did not flee from before the Lamanites, but did stand with boldness against them.

25 And it came to pass that we did contend with an army of thirty thousand against an army of fifty thousand. And it came to pass that we did stand before them with such firmness that they did flee from before us.

26 And it came to pass that when they had fled we did pursue them with our armies, and did meet them again, and did ªbeat them; nevertheless the ᵇstrength of the Lord was not with us; yea, we were left to ourselves, that the Spirit of the Lord did not abide in us; therefore we had become weak like unto our brethren.

27 And my heart did sorrow because of this the great calamity of my people, because of their wickedness and their abominations. But behold, we did go forth against the Lamanites and the robbers of Gadianton, until we had again taken possession of the lands of our inheritance.

28 And the †three hundred and forty and ninth year had passed away. And in the three hundred and fiftieth year we made a treaty with the Lamanites and the robbers of Gadianton, in which we did get the lands of our inheritance divided.

29 And the Lamanites did give unto us the land ªnorthward, yea, even to the ᵇnarrow passage which led into the land southward. And we did give unto the Lamanites all the land southward.

CHAPTER 3

Mormon cries repentance unto the Nephites—They gain a great victory and glory in their own strength—Mormon refuses to lead them, and his prayers for them are without faith—The Book of Mormon invites the twelve tribes of Israel to believe the gospel.

AND it came to pass that the Lamanites did not come to battle again ‡until ten years more had passed away. And behold, I had employed my people, the Nephites, in preparing their lands and their arms against the time of battle.

2 And it came to pass that the Lord did say unto me: Cry unto this

18a 3 Ne. 5: 15 (8–20).
19a Mosiah 23: 22;
　　Ether 4: 19.
21a Morm. 2: 4.
23a Alma 58: 12.

b Ether 14: 2.
26a Morm. 3: 8 (7–8, 13).
　b TG God, Spirit of;
　　Strength.
29a Morm. 2: 3.

b Alma 22: 32; 52: 9;
　63: 5.

[*A.D. 346 †A.D. 350
‡A.D. 360]

people—Repent ye, and come unto me, and be ye baptized, and build up again my church, and ye shall be *a*spared.

3 And I did cry unto this people, but it was *a*in vain; and they did *b*not realize that it was the Lord that had spared them, and granted unto them a chance for repentance. And behold they did harden their hearts against the Lord their God.

4 And it came to pass that after this tenth year had passed away, making, in the whole, three hundred and sixty years from the coming of Christ, the king of the Lamanites sent an epistle unto me, which gave unto me to know that they were preparing to come again to battle against us.

5 And it came to pass that I did cause my people that they should gather themselves together at the land *a*Desolation, to a city which was in the borders, by the narrow pass which led into the land *b*southward.

6 And there we did place our armies, that we might stop the armies of the Lamanites, that they might not get possession of any of our lands; therefore we did fortify against them with all our force.

7 And it came to pass that in the three hundred and sixty and first year the Lamanites did come down to the *a*city of Desolation to battle against us; and it came to pass that in that year we did beat them, insomuch that they did return to their own lands again.

8 And in the *three hundred and sixty and second year they did come down *a*again to battle. And we did beat them again, and did slay a great number of them, and their dead were cast into the sea.

9 And now, because of this great thing which my people, the Nephites, had done, they began to *a*boast in their own strength, and began to swear before the heavens that they would avenge themselves of the blood of their brethren who had been slain by their enemies.

10 And they did *a*swear by the heavens, and also by the throne of God, that they *b*would go up to battle against their enemies, and would cut them off from the face of the land.

11 And it came to pass that I, Mormon, did utterly *a*refuse from this time forth to be a commander and a leader of this people, because of their wickedness and abomination.

12 Behold, I had led them, notwithstanding their wickedness I had led them many times to battle, and had loved them, according to the *a*love of God which was in me, with all my heart; and my soul had been poured out in prayer unto my God all the day long for them; nevertheless, it was *b*without faith, because of the *c*hardness of their hearts.

13 And *a*thrice have I delivered them out of the hands of their enemies, and they have repented not of their sins.

14 And when they had sworn by all that had been *a*forbidden them by our Lord and Savior Jesus Christ, that they would go up unto their enemies to battle, and avenge themselves of the blood of their brethren, behold the voice of the Lord came unto me, saying:

15 *a*Vengeance is mine, and I will

---

3 2a Hel. 15: 17 (16–17);
    Morm. 6: 11 (11–15).
3a Morm. 4: 18.
  b TG Hardheartedness;
    Ingratitude.
5a Alma 50: 34;
    Morm. 4: 3 (1–3).
  b Ether 9: 31 (31–32);
    10: 21.
7a 3 Ne. 3: 23;
    Morm. 4: 2 (2, 19).

8a Morm. 2: 26; 3: 13.
9a Prov. 14: 16;
    2 Ne. 4: 34;
    Morm. 4: 8.
10a TG Swearing.
  b Alma 43: 46 (46–47);
    48: 14; 3 Ne.
    3: 21 (20–21);
    Morm. 4: 4.
11a Morm. 5: 1.

12a TG God, Love of.
  b James 1: 6;
    Morm. 5: 2.
  c Neh. 9: 16 (16–17).
13a Morm. 2: 26;
    3: 8 (7–8).
14a 3 Ne. 12: 34.
15a Isa. 35: 4; Rom. 12: 19.
    TG Vengeance.

[b]repay; and because this people repented not after I had delivered them, behold, they shall be cut off from the face of the earth.

16 And it came to pass that I utterly refused to go up against mine enemies; and I did even as the Lord had commanded me; and I did stand as an idle witness to manifest unto the world the things which I saw and heard, according to the manifestations of the Spirit which had testified of things to come.

17 Therefore I write [a]unto you, Gentiles, and also unto you, house of Israel, when the work shall commence, that ye shall be about to prepare to return to the land of your inheritance;

18 Yea, behold, I write unto all the ends of the earth; yea, unto you, twelve tribes of Israel, who shall be [a]judged according to your works by the twelve whom Jesus chose to be his disciples in the land of Jerusalem.

19 And I write also unto the remnant of this people, who shall also be judged by the [a]twelve whom Jesus chose in this land; and they shall be judged by the other twelve whom Jesus chose in the land of Jerusalem.

20 And these things doth the Spirit manifest unto me; therefore I write unto you all. And for this cause I write unto you, that ye may know that ye must all stand before the [a]judgment-seat of Christ, yea, every soul who belongs to the whole human [b]family of Adam; and ye must stand to be judged of your works, whether they be good or evil;

21 And also that ye may [a]believe the gospel of Jesus Christ, which ye shall [b]have among you; and also that the [c]Jews, the covenant people

of the Lord, shall have other [d]witness besides him whom they saw and heard, that Jesus, whom they slew, was the [e]very Christ and the very God.

22 And I would that I could persuade [a]all ye ends of the earth to repent and prepare to stand before the judgment-seat of Christ.

CHAPTER 4

War and carnage continue—The wicked punish the wicked—Greater wickedness prevails than ever before in all Israel—Women and children are sacrificed to idols—The Lamanites begin to sweep the Nephites before them.

AND now it came to pass that in the *three hundred and sixty and third year the Nephites did go up with their armies to [a]battle against the Lamanites, out of the land Desolation.

2 And it came to pass that the armies of the Nephites were driven back again to the land of Desolation. And while they were yet weary, a fresh army of the Lamanites did come upon them; and they had a sore battle, insomuch that the Lamanites did take possession of the [a]city Desolation, and did slay many of the Nephites, and did take many prisoners.

3 And the remainder did flee and join the inhabitants of the city Teancum. Now the city Teancum lay in the borders by the seashore; and it was also near the city [a]Desolation.

4 And it was [a]because the armies of the Nephites went up unto the Lamanites that they began to be

15b 2 Sam. 16:12 (9–12); D&C 82:23. TG God, Justice of.
17a 2 Ne. 30:3 (3–8); 3 Ne. 29:1.
18a Matt. 19:28; Luke 22:30 (29–30); D&C 29:12.
19a 1 Ne. 12:10 (9–10); 3 Ne. 27:27.
20a TG Jesus Christ, Judge; Judgment, The Last.
b D&C 27:11.
21a D&C 3:20.
b 1 Ne. 13:23 (20–29, 41).
c TG Israel, Judah, People of.
d 2 Ne. 25:18.
e 2 Ne. 26:12; Mosiah 7:27.
22a Alma 29:1.
4 1a 2 Ne. 1:12; Morm. 1:11 (11–19).
2a 3 Ne. 3:23; Morm. 3:7.
3a Morm. 3:5.
4a Morm. 3:10 (10–11).

smitten; for were it not for that, the Lamanites could have had no power over them.

5 But, behold, the judgments of God will overtake the *awicked; and it is by the wicked that the wicked are *bpunished; for it is the wicked that stir up the hearts of the children of men unto bloodshed.

6 And it came to pass that the Lamanites did make preparations to come against the city Teancum.

7 And it came to pass in the three hundred and sixty and fourth year the Lamanites did come against the city Teancum, that they might take possession of the city Teancum also.

8 And it came to pass that they were repulsed and driven back by the Nephites. And when the Nephites saw that they had driven the Lamanites they did again *aboast of their own strength; and they went forth in their own might, and took possession again of the city Desolation.

9 And now all these things had been done, and there had been thousands slain on both sides, both the Nephites and the Lamanites.

10 And it came to pass that the three hundred and sixty and sixth year had passed away, and the Lamanites came again upon the Nephites to battle; and yet the Nephites repented not of the evil they had done, but persisted in their wickedness continually.

11 And it is impossible for the tongue to describe, or for man to write a perfect description of the horrible scene of the blood and carnage which was among the people, both of the Nephites and of the Lamanites; and every heart was hardened, so that they *adelighted in the shedding of blood continually.

12 And there never had been so great *awickedness among all the children of Lehi, nor even among all the house of Israel, according to the words of the Lord, as was among this people.

13 And it came to pass that the Lamanites did take possession of the city Desolation, and this because their *anumber did exceed the number of the Nephites.

14 And they did also march forward against the city Teancum, and did drive the inhabitants forth out of her, and did take many prisoners both women and children, and did offer them up as *asacrifices unto their idol gods.

15 And it came to pass that in the three hundred and sixty and seventh year, the Nephites being angry because the Lamanites had sacrificed their women and their children, that they did go against the Lamanites with exceedingly great anger, insomuch that they did beat again the Lamanites, and drive them out of their lands.

16 And the Lamanites did not come again against the Nephites until the three hundred and seventy and fifth year.

17 And in this year they did come down against the Nephites with all their powers; and they were not numbered because of the greatness of their number.

18 And *afrom this time forth did the Nephites gain no power over the Lamanites, but began to be swept off by them even as a dew before the sun.

19 And it came to pass that the Lamanites did come down against the *acity Desolation; and there was an exceedingly sore battle fought in the land Desolation, in the which they did beat the Nephites.

5a Nahum 1: 3.
 b 2 Pet. 2: 12;
    D&C 63: 33.
8a Morm. 3: 9.
11a Moro. 9: 5 (5, 23).
 TG Blood,
    Shedding of.
12a Gen. 6: 5 (5–6);
    3 Ne. 9: 9; D&C
    112: 23; Moses
    7: 36 (36–37);
    8: 22 (22, 28–30).
13a Morm. 2: 3; 5: 6.
14a Jer. 19: 5; Alma
    17: 15; Abr. 1: 8
    (6–14).
 TG Idolatry;
    Sacrifice.
18a Morm. 3: 3.
19a Morm. 3: 7.

[A.D. 364—375]

20 And they fled again from before them, and they came to the city Boaz; and there they did stand against the Lamanites with exceeding boldness, insomuch that the Lamanites did not beat them until they had come again the second time.

21 And when they had come the second time, the Nephites were driven and slaughtered with an exceedingly great slaughter; their women and their ᵃchildren were again sacrificed unto idols.

22 And it came to pass that the Nephites did again flee from before them, taking all the inhabitants with them, both in towns and villages.

23 And now I, Mormon, seeing that the Lamanites were about to overthrow the land, therefore I did go to the hill ᵃShim, and did take up all the ᵇrecords which Ammaron had hid up unto the Lord.

CHAPTER 5

Mormon again leads the Nephite armies in battles of blood and carnage —The Book of Mormon shall come forth to convince all Israel that Jesus is the Christ—The Lamanites shall be a dark, filthy, and loathsome people— They shall receive the gospel from the Gentiles in the latter days.

AND it came to pass that I did go forth among the Nephites, and did repent of the ᵃoath which I had made that I would no more assist them; and they gave me command again of their armies, for they looked upon me as though I could deliver them from their afflictions.

2 But behold, I was ᵃwithout hope, for I knew the judgments of the Lord which should come upon them; for they repented not of their iniquities, but did struggle for their lives without calling upon that Being who created them.

3 And it came to pass that the Lamanites did come against us as we had fled to the city of Jordan; but behold, they were driven back that they did not take the city at that time.

4 And it came to pass that they came against us again, and we did maintain the city. And there were also other cities which were maintained by the Nephites, which strongholds did cut them off that they could not get into the country which lay before us, to destroy the inhabitants of our land.

5 But it came to pass that whatsoever lands we had passed by, and the inhabitants thereof were not gathered in, were destroyed by the Lamanites, and their towns, and villages, and cities were burned with fire; and thus three hundred and seventy and nine years passed away.

6 And it came to pass that in the three hundred and eightieth year the Lamanites did come again against us to battle, and we did stand against them boldly; but it was all in vain, for so ᵃgreat were their numbers that they did tread the people of the Nephites under their feet.

7 And it came to pass that we did again take to flight, and those whose flight was swifter than the Lamanites' did escape, and those whose flight did not exceed the Lamanites' were swept down and destroyed.

8 And now behold, I, Mormon, do not desire to harrow up the souls of men in casting before them such an awful scene of blood and carnage as was laid before mine eyes; but I, knowing that these things must surely be made known, and that all things which are hid must be ᵃrevealed upon the house-tops—

9 And also that a knowledge of these things must ᵃcome unto the remnant of these people, and also

---

21a 2 Kgs. 17:31.
  TG Idolatry.
23a Morm. 1:3; Ether 9:3.
  b W of M 1:3.
5 1a Morm. 3:11 (11, 16).

TG Vows.
2a Morm. 3:12.
6a Morm. 2:3; 4:13 (13–17).
8a Matt. 10:26 (26–33);

Luke 12:3; 2 Ne. 27: 11; D&C 1:3; 88:108.
9a 4 Ne. 1:49.

[A.D. 375—380]

unto the Gentiles, who the Lord hath said should [b]scatter this people, and this people should be counted as naught among them—therefore [c]I write a [d]small abridgment, daring not to give a full account of the things which I have seen, because of the commandment which I have received, and also that ye might not have too great sorrow because of the wickedness of this people.

10 And now behold, this I speak unto their seed, and also to the Gentiles who have care for the house of Israel, that realize and know from whence their blessings come.

11 For I know that such will sorrow for the calamity of the house of Israel; yea, they will sorrow for the destruction of this people; they will sorrow that this people had not repented that they might have been clasped in the arms of Jesus.

12 Now [a]these things are [b]written unto the [c]remnant of the house of Jacob; and they are written after this manner, because it is known of God that wickedness will not bring them forth unto them; and they are to be [d]hid up unto the Lord that they may come forth in his own due time.

13 And this is the commandment which I have received; and behold, they [a]shall come forth according to the commandment of the Lord, when he shall see fit, in his wisdom.

14 And behold, they shall go unto the [a]unbelieving of the [b]Jews; and for this intent shall they go—that they may be [c]persuaded that Jesus is the Christ, the Son of the living God; that the Father may bring about, through his most Beloved, his great and eternal purpose, in restoring the Jews, or all the house of Israel, to the [d]land of their inheritance, which the Lord their God hath given them, unto the fulfilling of his [e]covenant;

15 And also that the seed of [a]this people may more fully believe his gospel, which shall [b]go forth unto them from the Gentiles; for this people shall be [c]scattered, and shall [d]become a dark, a filthy, and a loathsome people, beyond the description of that which ever hath been amongst us, yea, even that which hath been among the Lamanites, and this because of their unbelief and idolatry.

16 For behold, the Spirit of the Lord hath already ceased to [a]strive with their fathers; and they are without Christ and God in the world; and they are driven about as [b]chaff before the wind.

17 They were once a delightsome people, and they had Christ for their [a]shepherd; yea, they were led even by God the Father.

18 But now, behold, they are [a]led about by Satan, even as chaff is driven before the wind, or as a vessel is tossed about upon the waves, without sail or anchor, or without anything wherewith to steer her; and even as she is, so are they.

19 And behold, the Lord hath reserved their blessings, which they

9b 3 Ne. 16: 8 (8–9).
  c Alma 43: 3.
  d Morm 1: 1.
12a 1 Ne. 19: 19; Enos 1: 16; Hel. 15: 11 (11–13); Morm. 7: 1 (1, 9–10).
  b TG Book of Mormon; Scriptures to Come Forth.
  c 2 Ne. 25: 8; 27: 6; Jarom 1: 2; D&C 3: 20 (16–20).
  d Morm. 8: 4 (4, 13–14); Moro. 10: 2 (1–2). TG Scriptures, Preservation of.

13a 2 Ne. 3: 18.
14a Rom. 11: 20 (1–36); 1 Ne. 10: 11; Jacob 4: 15 (15–18). TG Unbelief, Unbelievers.
  b 2 Ne. 26: 12; 29: 13; 30: 7 (7–8). TG Israel, Judah, People of.
  c John 20: 31; 2 Ne. 25: 16 (16–17). TG Israel, Restoration of.
  d TG Lands of Inheritance.
  e Ezek. 20: 37; 3 Ne. 29: 1 (1–?).

15a 2 Ne. 30: 5; 3 Ne. 21: 5 (3–7, 24–26).
  b 1 Ne. 13: 38 (20–29, 38); Morm. 7: 8 (8–9).
  c 1 Ne. 10: 12 (12–14); 3 Ne. 16: 8.
  d 1 Ne. 2: 23; Alma 3: 19 (6–19).
16a Gen. 6: 3; Ether 2: 15; Moro. 8: 28.
  b Ps. 1: 4 (1–4); Hosea 13: 3 (1–4).
17a TG Jesus Christ, Good Shepherd.
18a 2 Ne. 28: 21.

[A.D. 380—384]

might have received in the land, for the ^aGentiles who shall possess the land.

20 But behold, it shall come to pass that they shall be driven and scattered by the Gentiles; and after they have been driven and scattered by the Gentiles, behold, then will the Lord ^aremember the ^bcovenant which he made unto Abraham and unto all the house of Israel.

21 And also the Lord will remember the ^aprayers of the righteous, which have been put up unto him for them.

22 And then, O ye Gentiles, how can ye stand before the power of God, except ye shall repent and turn from your evil ways?

23 Know ye not that ye are in the ^ahands of God? Know ye not that he hath all power, and at his great command the ^bearth shall be ^crolled together as a scroll?

24 Therefore, repent ye, and humble yourselves before him, lest he shall come out in justice against you—lest a ^aremnant of the seed of Jacob shall go forth among you as a ^blion, and tear you in pieces, and there is none to deliver.

CHAPTER 6

The Nephites gather to the land of Cumorah for the final battles—Mormon hides the sacred records in the hill Cumorah—The Lamanites are victorious, and the Nephite nation is destroyed—Hundreds of thousands are slain with the sword.

AND now I finish my record concerning the ^adestruction of my people, the Nephites. And it came to pass that we did march forth before the Lamanites.

2 And I, Mormon, wrote an epistle unto the king of the Lamanites, and desired of him that he would grant unto us that we might gather together our people unto the ^aland of ^bCumorah, by a hill which was called Cumorah, and there we could give them battle.

3 And it came to pass that the king of the Lamanites did grant unto me the thing which I desired.

4 And it came to pass that we did march forth to the land of Cumorah, and we did pitch our tents round about the hill Cumorah; and it was in a land of ^amany waters, rivers, and fountains; and here we had hope to gain advantage over the Lamanites.

5 And *when ^athree hundred and eighty and four years had passed away, we had gathered in all the remainder of our people unto the land Cumorah.

6 And it came to pass that when we had gathered in all our people in one to the land of Cumorah, behold I, Mormon, began to be old; and knowing it to be the last struggle of my people, and having been commanded of the Lord that I should not suffer the records which had been handed down by our fathers, which were ^asacred, to fall into the hands of the Lamanites, (for the Lamanites would ^bdestroy them) therefore I made ^cthis record out of the plates of Nephi, and ^dhid up in the hill Cumorah all the records which had been entrusted to me by the hand of the Lord, save it were ^ethese few plates which I gave unto my son ^fMoroni.

19a 3 Ne. 20: 27.
20a 1 Ne. 13: 31; 3 Ne. 16: 11 (8–12).
  b TG Abrahamic Covenant.
21a Enos 1: 12 (12–18); Morm. 8: 25 (24–26); 9: 36 (36–37).
23a Ether 1: 1; D&C 87: 6 (6–7).
  b Hel. 12: 11 (8–18); Morm. 9: 2.

c 3 Ne. 26: 3.
24a TG Israel, Remnant of.
  b 3 Ne. 20: 16 (15–16).
6 1a 1 Ne. 12: 19 (19–20); Jarom 1: 10; Alma 45: 11 (9–14); Hel. 13: 5 (5–11).
2a Ether 9: 3.
  b Morm. 8: 2; D&C 128: 20.
4a Mosiah 8: 8; Alma 50: 29; Hel. 3: 4 (3–4).

5a W of M 1: 2.
6a TG Sacred.
  b 2 Ne. 26: 17; Enos 1: 14.
  c Morm. 2: 18.
  d Ether 15: 11.
  e Moro. 9: 24; 10: 2; D&C 17: 1; JS-H 1: 52.
  f Morm. 8: 1.

[*A.D. 385]

7 And it came to pass that my people, with their wives and their children, did now behold the *a*armies of the Lamanites marching towards them; and with that awful *b*fear of death which fills the breasts of all the wicked, did they await to receive them.

8 And it came to pass that they came to battle against us, and every soul was filled with terror because of the greatness of their numbers.

9 And it came to pass that they did fall upon my people with the sword, and with the bow, and with the arrow, and with the ax, and with all manner of weapons of war.

10 And it came to pass that my men were hewn down, yea, even my *a*ten thousand who were with me, and I fell wounded in the midst; and they passed by me that they did not put an end to my life.

11 And when they had gone through and hewn down *a*all my people save it were twenty and four of us, (among whom was my son Moroni) and we having survived the dead of our people, did behold on the morrow, when the Lamanites had returned unto their camps, from the top of the hill Cumorah, the ten thousand of my people who were hewn down, being led in the front by me.

12 And we also beheld the ten thousand of my people who were led by my son Moroni.

13 And behold, the ten thousand of Gidgiddonah had fallen, and he also in the midst.

14 And Lamah had fallen with his ten thousand; and Gilgal had fallen with his ten thousand; and Limhah had fallen with his ten thousand; and Jeneum had fallen with his ten thousand; and Cumenihah, and Moronihah, and Antionum, and Shiblom, and Shem, and Josh, had fallen with their ten thousand each.

15 And it came to pass that there were ten more who did fall by the sword, with their ten thousand each; yea, even *a*all my people, save it were those twenty and four who were with me, and also a *b*few who had escaped into the south countries, and a few who had deserted over unto the Lamanites, had fallen; and their flesh, and bones, and blood lay upon the face of the earth, being left by the hands of those who slew them to molder upon the land, and to crumble and to return to their mother earth.

16 And my soul was rent with *a*anguish, because of the slain of my people, and I cried:

17 *a*O ye fair ones, how could ye have departed from the ways of the Lord! O ye fair ones, how could ye have rejected that Jesus, who stood with open arms to receive you!

18 Behold, if ye had not done this, ye would not have fallen. But behold, ye are fallen, and I *a*mourn your loss.

19 O ye *a*fair sons and daughters, ye fathers and mothers, ye husbands and wives, ye fair ones, how is it that ye could have *b*fallen!

20 But behold, ye are gone, and my sorrows cannot bring your return.

21 And the day soon cometh that your mortal must put on immortality, and these bodies which are now moldering in corruption must soon become *a*incorruptible bodies; and then ye must stand before the judgment-seat of Christ, to be judged according to your works; and if it so be that ye are righteous, then are ye blessed with your fathers who have gone before you.

22 O that ye had repented before this great *a*destruction had come upon you. But behold, ye are gone,

7a 1 Ne. 12: 15.
  b TG Fearfulness.
10a Judg. 1: 4.
11a 1 Ne. 12: 19 (19–20);
    Hel. 15: 17 (16–17);
    Morm. 3: 2.

15a Alma 9: 24.
  b Morm. 8: 2.
16a TG Despair;
    Mourning; Sorrow.
17a 2 Ne. 26: 7.
18a Lam. 2: 11.

19a Ether 13: 17.
  b 1 Ne. 13: 15.
21a 1 Cor. 15: 53 (53–54).
22a 2 Sam. 1: 27 (17–27).

[A.D. 385]

and the Father, yea, the Eternal Father of heaven, [b]knoweth your state; and he doeth with you according to his [c]justice and [d]mercy.

CHAPTER 7

Mormon invites the Lamanites of the latter days to believe in Christ, accept his gospel, and be saved—All who believe the Bible will also believe the Book of Mormon.

AND now, behold, I would speak somewhat unto the [a]remnant of this people who are spared, if it so be that God may give unto them my words, that they may know of the things of their fathers; yea, I speak unto you, ye remnant of the house of Israel; and these are the words which I speak:

2 Know ye that ye are of the [a]house of Israel.

3 Know ye that ye must come unto repentance, or ye cannot be saved.

4 Know ye that ye must lay down your weapons of war, and delight no more in the shedding of blood, and take them not again, save it be that God shall [a]command you.

5 Know ye that ye must come to the [a]knowledge of your fathers, and repent of all your sins and iniquities, and [b]believe in Jesus Christ, that he is the Son of God, and that he was slain by the Jews, and by the power of the Father he hath risen again, whereby he hath gained the [c]victory over the grave; and also in him is the sting of death swallowed up.

6 And he bringeth to pass the [a]resurrection of the dead, whereby man must be raised to stand before his [b]judgment-seat.

7 And he hath brought to pass the [a]redemption of the [b]world, whereby he that is found [c]guiltless before him at the judgment day hath it given unto him to [d]dwell in the presence of God in his kingdom, to sing ceaseless praises with the [e]choirs above, unto the Father, and unto the Son, and unto the Holy Ghost, which are [f]one God, in a state of [g]happiness which hath no end.

8 Therefore repent, and be baptized in the name of Jesus, and lay hold upon the [a]gospel of Christ, which shall be set before you, not only in this record but also in the record which shall come unto the Gentiles [b]from the Jews, which record shall come from the Gentiles [c]unto you.

9 For behold, [a]this is [b]written for the intent that ye may [c]believe that; and if [d]ye believe that ye will believe this also; and if ye believe this ye will know concerning your fathers, and also the marvelous works which were wrought by the power of God among them.

10 And ye will also know that ye are a [a]remnant of the seed of Jacob; therefore ye are numbered among the people of the first covenant; and if it so be that ye believe in Christ, and are baptized, first [b]with water, then with fire and with the Holy Ghost, following the [c]example of

---

22b 2 Sam. 7:20;
    D&C 6:16.
  c TG God, Justice of.
  d Ps. 36:5 (5–6);
    Alma 26:16;
    D&C 97:6.
7 1a Hel. 15:11 (11–13);
    Morm. 5:12 (9, 12).
  2a 1 Ne. 5:14;
    Alma 10:3; Hel.
    6:10; 8:21.
  4a Alma 43:47.
  5a 2 Ne. 3:12; 3 Ne.
    5:23.
  b TG Faith.
  c Mosiah 16:8 (7–8);
    Alma 24:23.

6a TG Resurrection.
  b TG Jesus Christ, Judge.
7a TG Redemption.
  b TG World.
  c Mosiah 13:15;
    D&C 58:30.
    TG Justification.
  d Ps. 27:4; 1 Ne.
    10:21; D&C 76:62
    (50–62); Moses 6:57.
  e Mosiah 2:28.
  f Deut. 6:4; Gal. 3:20;
    D&C 20:28.
  g TG Happiness.
8a TG Gospel.
  b 2 Ne. 29:4 (4–13).
  c 1 Ne. 13:38 (20–29,

38); Morm. 5:15.
9a 1 Ne. 19:19; Enos
    1:16 (12–18); 3 Ne.
    5:15 (12–17);
    Morm. 5:12. TG Israel,
    Restoration of.
  b TG Book of Mormon.
  c 1 Ne. 13:40 (38–42).
  d 2 Ne. 3:15 (12–15);
    Alma 37:19 (1–20).
10a Israel, Remnant of.
  b 3 Ne. 19:13 (13–14);
    Ether 12:14.
  c TG God, the Standard
    of Righteousness.

[About A.D. 385]

our Savior, according to that which he hath commanded us, it shall be well with you in the day of judgment. Amen.

CHAPTER 8

The Lamanites seek out and destroy the Nephites—The Book of Mormon shall come forth by the power of God— Woes pronounced upon those who breathe out wrath and strife against the work of the Lord—The Nephite record shall come forth in a day of wickedness, degeneracy, and apostasy.

BEHOLD I, ªMoroni, do finish the ᵇrecord of my father, Mormon. Behold, I have but few things to write, which things I have been commanded by my father.

2 And now it came to pass that after the ªgreat and tremendous battle at Cumorah, behold, the Nephites who had escaped into the country southward were hunted by the ᵇLamanites, until they were all destroyed.

3 And my father also was killed by them, and I even ªremain ᵇalone to write the sad tale of the destruction of my people. But behold, they are gone, and I fulfil the commandment of my father. And whether they will slay me, I know not.

4 Therefore I will write and ªhide up the records in the earth; and whither I go it mattereth not.

5 Behold, my father hath made ªthis record, and he hath written the intent thereof. And behold, I would write it also if I had room upon the ᵇplates, but I have not; and ore I have none, for I am alone. My father hath been slain in battle, and all my kinsfolk, and I have not friends nor whither to go; and ᶜhow

long the Lord will suffer that I may live I know not.

6 Behold, ª*four hundred years have passed away since the coming of our Lord and Savior.

7 And behold, the Lamanites have hunted my people, the Nephites, down from city to city and from place to place, even until they are no more; and great has been their ªfall; yea, great and marvelous is the destruction of my people, the Nephites.

8 And behold, it is the hand of the Lord which hath done it. And behold also, the Lamanites are at ªwar one with another; and the whole face of this land is one continual round of murder and bloodshed; and no one knoweth the end of the war.

9 And now, behold, I say no more concerning them, for there are none save it be the Lamanites and ªrobbers that do exist upon the face of the land.

10 And there are none that do know the true God save it be the ªdisciples of Jesus, who did tarry in the land until the wickedness of the people was so great that the Lord would not suffer them to ᵇremain with the people; and whether they be upon the face of the land no man knoweth.

11 But behold, my ªfather and I have seen ᵇthem, and they have ministered unto us.

12 And whoso receiveth ªthis record, and shall not condemn it because of the imperfections which are in it, the same shall know of ᵇgreater things than these. Behold, I am Moroni; and were it possible, I would make all things known unto you.

---

8 1a Morm. 6: 6;
    Moro. 9: 24.
  b TG Record Keeping.
2a Morm. 6: 15 (2–15).
  b D&C 3: 18.
3a Moro. 9: 22.
  b Ether 4: 3.
4a Morm. 5: 12;
    Moro. 10: 2 (1–2).
5a Morm. 2: 17 (17–18).

  b Morm. 6: 6.
  c Moro. 1: 1; 10: 1 (1–2).
6a Alma 45: 10.
7a 1 Ne. 12: 2 (2–3);
    Enos 1: 24.
8a 1 Ne. 12: 21 (20–23).
9a 4 Ne. 1: 46; Morm.
    2: 8 (8, 28);
    Ether 8: 20.
10a 3 Ne. 28: 7; 4 Ne.

    1: 37 (14, 37);
    Ether 12: 17.
  b Morm. 1: 16.
11a 3 Ne. 28: 26.
  b TG Translated Beings.
12a 3 Ne. 5: 15 (8–18).
  b John 16: 12; 3 Ne.
    26: 9 (6–11);
    D&C 42: 15.

13 Behold, I make an end of speaking concerning this people. I am the son of Mormon, and my father was a ªdescendant of Nephi.

14 And I am the same who ªhideth up this record unto the Lord; the plates thereof are of no worth, because of the commandment of the Lord. For he truly saith that no one shall have them ᵇto get gain; but the record thereof is of ᶜgreat worth; and whoso shall bring it to light, him will the Lord bless.

15 For none can have power to bring it to light save it be given him of God; for God wills that it shall be done with an ªeye single to his glory, or the welfare of the ancient and long dispersed covenant people of the Lord.

16 And blessed be ªhe that shall bring this thing to light; for it shall be ᵇbrought out of darkness unto light, according to the word of God; yea, it shall be brought out of the earth, and it shall shine forth out of darkness, and come unto the knowledge of the people; and it shall be done by the power of God.

17 And if there be ªfaults they be the faults of a man. But behold, we know no fault; nevertheless God knoweth all things; therefore, he that ᵇcondemneth, let him be aware lest he shall be in danger of hell fire.

18 And he that saith: Show unto me, or ye shall be ªsmitten—let him beware lest he commandeth that which is forbidden of the Lord.

19 For behold, the same that ªjudgeth ᵇrashly shall be judged rashly again; for according to his works shall his wages be; therefore, he that smiteth shall be smitten again, of the Lord.

20 Behold what the scripture says—man shall not ªsmite, neither shall he ᵇjudge; for judgment is mine, saith the Lord, and vengeance is mine also, and I will repay.

21 And he that shall breathe out ªwrath and ᵇstrifes against the work of the Lord, and against the ᶜcovenant people of the Lord who are the house of Israel, and shall say: We will destroy the work of the Lord, and the Lord will not remember his covenant which he hath made unto the house of Israel—the same is in danger to be hewn down and cast into the fire;

22 For the eternal ªpurposes of the Lord shall roll on, until all his promises shall be fulfilled.

23 Search the prophecies of ªIsaiah. Behold, I cannot write them. Yea, behold I say unto you, that those saints who have gone before me, who have possessed this land, shall ᵇcry, yea, even from the dust will they cry unto the Lord; and as the Lord liveth he will remember the covenant which he hath made with them.

24 And he knoweth their ªprayers, that they were in behalf of their brethren. And he knoweth their faith, for in his name could they remove ᵇmountains; and in his name could they cause the earth to shake; and by the power of his word did they cause ᶜprisons to tumble to the earth; yea, even the fiery furnace could not harm them, neither wild

13a Alma 10: 3;
   3 Ne. 5: 20.
14a Ether 4: 3; Moro.
   10: 2 (1–2).
   b JS-H 1: 53.
   TG Scriptures,
   Preservation of.
   c 2 Ne. 3: 7 (6–9).
15a Matt. 6: 22; D&C 4: 5.
16a 3 Ne. 21: 11 (8–11);
   Ether 3: 28 (21–28).
   b TG Scriptures to
   Come Forth.

17a 1 Ne. 19: 6; Morm.
   9: 31 (31, 33); Ether
   12: 23 (22–28, 35).
   b 3 Ne. 29: 5 (1–9);
   Ether 4: 8 (8–10).
18a JS-H 1: 60 (60–61).
19a 3 Ne. 14: 2; Moro.
   7: 14. TG Gossip.
   b TG Rashness.
20a TG Violence.
   b James 4: 12 (11–12).
21a Prov. 19: 19.
   b TG Strife.

   c 1 Ne. 14: 17.
22a D&C 3: 3.
23a Isa. 29: 4;
   3 Ne. 20: 11;
   23: 1 (1–3).
   b 2 Ne. 3: 20; 26: 16.
24a Enos 1: 13 (12–18);
   Morm. 9: 36 (34–37);
   D&C 10: 46 (46–49).
   b Jacob 4: 6; Hel. 10:
   9.
   c 3 Ne. 28: 19 (19–21).

[Between A.D. 400 and 421]

beasts nor poisonous serpents, because of the power of his word.

25 And behold, their [a]prayers were also in behalf of him that the Lord should suffer to bring these things forth.

26 And no one need say they shall not come, for they surely shall, for the Lord hath spoken it; for [a]out of the earth shall they come, by the hand of the Lord, and none can stay it; and it shall come in a day when it shall be said that [b]miracles are done away; and it shall come even as if one should speak [c]from the dead.

27 And it shall come in a day when the [a]blood of saints shall cry unto the Lord, because of secret [b]combinations and the works of darkness.

28 Yea, it shall come in a day when the power of God shall be [a]denied, and [b]churches become defiled and be [c]lifted up in the pride of their hearts; yea, even in a day when leaders of churches and teachers shall rise in the pride of their hearts, even to the envying of them who belong to their churches.

29 Yea, it shall come in a day when [a]there shall be heard of fires, and tempests, and [b]vapors of smoke in foreign lands;

30 And there shall also be heard of [a]wars, rumors of wars, and earthquakes in divers places.

31 Yea, it shall come in a day when there shall be great [a]pollutions upon the face of the earth; there shall be [b]murders, and robbing, and lying, and deceivings, and whoredoms, and all manner of abominations; when there shall be many who will say, Do this, or do that, and it [c]mattereth not, for the Lord will [d]uphold such at the last day. But wo unto such, for they are in the [e]gall of bitterness and in the [f]bonds of iniquity.

32 Yea, it shall come in a day when there shall be [a]churches built up that shall say: Come unto me, and for your money you shall be forgiven of your sins.

33 O ye wicked and perverse and [a]stiffnecked people, why have ye built up churches unto yourselves to get [b]gain? Why have ye [c]transfigured the holy word of God, that ye might bring [d]damnation upon your souls? Behold, look ye unto the [e]revelations of God; for behold, the time cometh at that day when all these things must be fulfilled.

34 Behold, the Lord hath shown unto me great and marvelous things concerning that which must shortly come, at that day when these things shall come forth among you.

35 Behold, I speak unto you as if ye were present, and yet ye are not. But behold, Jesus Christ hath shown you unto me, and I know your doing.

36 And I know that ye do [a]walk in the pride of your hearts; and there are none save a few only who do not [b]lift themselves up in the pride of their hearts, unto the wearing of [c]very fine apparel, unto envying,

25a Morm. 5:21.
26a Ne. 23:4.
  b 3 Ne. 29:7; Morm. 9:15 (15–26); Moro. 7:37 (27–37).
  c 2 Ne. 26:16 (15–16); 33:13; Morm. 9:30; Moro. 10:27.
27a Gen. 4:10; Rev. 6:10 (1, 10); 2 Ne. 28:10; Ether 8:22 (22–24); D&C 87:7.
  b TG Secret Combinations.
28a TG Unbelief, Unbelievers.
  b 2 Tim. 3:1 (1–7); 1 Ne. 14:10 (9–10); 2 Ne. 28:

3 (3–32); D&C 33:4.
  c 2 Kgs. 14:10; Jacob 2:13.
29a Joel 2:30 (28–32); 2 Ne. 27:2 (1–3).
  b 1 Ne. 19:11; D&C 45:41 (40–41).
30a Matt. 24:6; 1 Ne. 14:16 (15–17).
31a TG Pollution.
  b 3 Ne. 16:10; 30:2.
  c 2 Ne. 28:21; Alma 1:4; 30:17.
  d 2 Ne. 28:8.
  e Acts 8:23; Alma 41:11.
  f TG Bondage, Spiritual.

32a TG Devil, Church of.
33a D&C 5:8.
  b TG Priestcraft.
  c 1 Ne. 13:26 (20–41). TG Apostasy of the Early Christian Church.
  d TG Damnation.
  e 1 Ne. 14:23 (18–27); Ether 4:16.
36a TG Walking in Darkness.
  b Jacob 2:13; 3 Ne. 16:10.
  c 2 Ne. 28:13 (11–14); Alma 5:53.

[Between A.D. 400 and 421]

and strifes, and malice, and persecutions, and all manner of iniquities; and your churches, yea, even every one, have become polluted because of the pride of your hearts.

37 For behold, ye do love [a]money, and your substance, and your fine apparel, and the adorning of your churches, more than ye love the poor and the needy, the sick and the afflicted.

38 O ye pollutions, ye hypocrites, ye teachers, who sell yourselves for that which will canker, why have ye polluted the holy church of God? Why are ye [a]ashamed to take upon you the name of Christ? Why do ye not think that greater is the value of an endless happiness than that [b]misery which never dies—because of the [c]praise of the world?

39 Why do ye adorn yourselves with that which hath no life, and yet suffer the hungry, and the needy, and the naked, and the sick and the afflicted to pass by you, and notice them not?

40 Yea, why do ye build up your [a]secret abominations to get gain, and cause that widows should mourn before the Lord, and also orphans to mourn before the Lord, and also the blood of their fathers and their husbands to cry unto the Lord from the ground, for vengeance upon your heads?

41 Behold, the sword of vengeance hangeth over you; and the time soon cometh that he avengeth the [a]blood of the saints upon you, for he will not suffer their cries any longer.

CHAPTER 9

Moroni calls upon those who do not believe in Christ to repent—He proclaims a God of miracles, who gives revelations and pours out gifts and signs upon the faithful—Miracles cease because of unbelief—Signs follow those who believe—Men are exhorted to be wise and keep the commandments.

AND now, I speak also concerning those who do not believe in Christ.

2 Behold, will ye believe in the day of your visitation—behold, when the Lord shall come, yea, even that [a]great day when the [b]earth shall be rolled together as a scroll, and the elements shall [c]melt with fervent heat, yea, in that great day when ye shall be brought to stand before the Lamb of God—then will ye say that there is no God?

3 Then will ye longer deny the Christ, or can ye behold the Lamb of God? Do ye suppose that ye shall dwell with him under a [a]consciousness of your guilt? Do ye suppose that ye could be happy to dwell with that holy Being, when your souls are racked with a consciousness of guilt that ye have ever abused his laws?

4 Behold, I say unto you that ye would be more miserable to dwell with a holy and just God, under a consciousness of your [a]filthiness before him, than ye would to dwell with the [b]damned souls in [c]hell.

5 For behold, when ye shall be brought to see your [a]nakedness before God, and also the glory of God, and the [b]holiness of Jesus Christ, it will kindle a flame of unquenchable fire upon you.

6 O then ye [a]unbelieving, [b]turn ye unto the Lord; cry mightily unto the Father in the name of Jesus, that perhaps ye may be found spotless,

---

37a Ezek. 34: 8; 1 Ne. 13: 7; 2 Ne. 28: 13 (9–16).
38a Rom. 1: 16; 2 Tim. 1: 8; 1 Ne. 8: 25; Alma 46: 21.
  b Rom. 3: 16; Mosiah 3: 25.
  c 1 Ne. 13: 9.
40a TG Secret Combinations.
41a 1 Ne. 22: 14; D&C 136: 36.
9 2a Mal. 4: 5; 3 Ne. 28: 31.
  b Morm. 5: 23; D&C 63: 21 (20–21). TG World, End of.
  c Amos 9: 13; 3 Ne. 26: 3.
3a TG Conscience; Guilt.
4a TG Filthiness.
  b TG Damnation.
  c TG Hell.
5a Ex. 32: 25; 2 Ne. 9: 14.
  b TG Holiness.
6a TG Unbelief, Unbelievers.
  b Ezek. 18: 23, 32; D&C 98: 47.

[c]pure, fair, and white, having been cleansed by the blood of the [d]Lamb, at that great and last day.

7 And again I speak unto you who [a]deny the revelations of God, and say that they are done away, that there are no revelations, nor prophecies, nor gifts, nor healing, nor speaking with tongues, and the [b]interpretation of tongues;

8 Behold I say unto you, he that denieth these things knoweth not the [a]gospel of Christ; yea, he has not read the scriptures; if so, he does not [b]understand them.

9 For do we not read that God is the [a]same [b]yesterday, today, and forever, and in him there is no [c]variableness neither shadow of changing?

10 And now, if ye have imagined up unto yourselves a god who doth vary, and in whom there is shadow of changing, then have ye imagined up unto yourselves a god who is not a God of miracles.

11 But behold, I will show unto you a God of [a]miracles, even the God of Abraham, and the God of Isaac, and the God of Jacob; and it is that same [b]God who created the heavens and the earth, and all things that in them are.

12 Behold, he created Adam, and by [a]Adam came the [b]fall of man. And because of the fall of man came Jesus Christ, even the Father and the Son; and because of Jesus Christ came the [c]redemption of man.

13 And because of the redemption of man, which came by Jesus Christ, they are brought back into the [a]presence of the Lord; yea, this is wherein all men are redeemed, because the death of Christ bringeth to pass the [b]resurrection, which bringeth to pass a redemption from an endless [c]sleep, from which sleep all men shall be awakened by the power of God when the trump shall sound; and they shall come forth, both small and great, and all shall stand before his bar, being redeemed and loosed from this eternal [d]band of death, which death is a temporal death.

14 And then cometh the [a]judgment of the Holy One upon them; and then cometh the time that he that is [b]filthy shall be filthy still; and he that is righteous shall be righteous still; he that is happy shall be happy still; and he that is unhappy shall be unhappy still.

15 And now, O all ye that have imagined up unto yourselves a god who can do [a]no miracles, I would ask of you, have all these things passed, of which I have spoken? Has the end come yet? Behold I say unto you, Nay; and God has not ceased to be a God of miracles.

16 Behold, are not the things that God hath wrought marvelous in our eyes? Yea, and who can comprehend the marvelous [a]works of God?

17 Who shall say that it was not a miracle that by his [a]word the heaven and the earth should be; and by the power of his word man was [b]created of the [c]dust of the earth; and by the power of his word have miracles been wrought?

6c TG Cleanliness; Purification.
  d TG Jesus Christ, Lamb of God.
7a 3 Ne. 29: 6.
  b 1 Cor. 12: 10; A of F 7.
8a TG Gospel.
  b Matt. 22: 29.
9a Heb. 13: 8; 1 Ne. 10: 18 (18–19); Alma 7: 20; Moro. 8:18; D&C 20: 12.
  b TG God, Eternal Nature of.
  c TG God, Perfection of.

11a TG God, Power of.
  b Gen. 1: 1; Mosiah 4: 2; D&C 76: 24 (20–24).
12a Mosiah 3: 26; Moro. 8: 8.
  b TG Fall of Man.
  c TG Jesus Christ, Redeemer.
13a TG God, Presence of.
  b Hel. 14: 15 (15–18).
  c Dan. 12: 2; D&C 43: 18.
  d Alma 36: 18; D&C 138: 16.
14a TG Judgment, The Last.

  b Alma 7: 21; D&C 88: 35.
15a Morm. 8: 26; Moro. 7: 35; D&C 35: 8. TG Miracle.
16a Ps. 40: 5; 92: 5; D&C 76: 114; Moses 1: 4 (3–5).
17a Jacob 4: 9.
  b TG Man, Physical Creation of.
  c Gen. 2: 7; Mosiah 2: 25; D&C 77: 12; 93: 35 (33–35).

[Between A.D. 400 and 421]

18 And who shall say that Jesus Christ did not do many mighty [a]miracles? And there were many [b]mighty miracles wrought by the hands of the apostles.

19 And if there were [a]miracles wrought then, why has God ceased to be a God of miracles and yet be an unchangeable Being? And behold, I say unto you he [b]changeth not; if so he would cease to be God; and he ceaseth not to be God, and is a God of miracles.

20 And the reason why he ceaseth to do [a]miracles among the children of men is because that they dwindle in unbelief, and depart from the right way, and know not the God in whom they should [b]trust.

21 Behold, I say unto you that whoso believeth in Christ, doubting nothing, [a]whatsoever he shall ask the Father in the name of Christ it shall be granted him; and this [b]promise is unto all, even unto the ends of the earth.

22 For behold, thus said Jesus Christ, the Son of God, unto his disciples who should tarry, yea, and also to [a]all his disciples, in the hearing of the multitude: Go ye into all the world, and preach the gospel to every creature;

23 And he that [a]believeth and is baptized shall be saved, but he that believeth not shall be [b]damned;

24 And [a]these signs shall follow them that believe—in my name shall they cast out [b]devils; they shall speak with new tongues; they shall take up serpents; and if they drink any deadly thing it shall not hurt them; they shall lay [c]hands on the sick and they shall recover;

25 And whosoever shall believe in my name, doubting nothing, unto him will I [a]confirm all my words, even unto the ends of the earth.

26 And now, behold, who can stand [a]against the works of the Lord? [b]Who can deny his sayings? Who will rise up against the almighty power of the Lord? Who will despise the works of the Lord? Who will despise the children of Christ? Behold, all ye who are [c]despisers of the works of the Lord, for ye shall wonder and perish.

27 O then despise not, and wonder not, but hearken unto the words of the Lord, and ask the Father in the name of Jesus for what things soever ye shall stand in need. [a]Doubt not, but be believing, and begin as in times of old, and [b]come unto the Lord with all your [c]heart, and [d]work out your own salvation with fear and trembling before him.

28 Be [a]wise in the days of your [b]probation; strip yourselves of all uncleanness; ask not, that ye may consume it on your [c]lusts, but ask with a firmness unshaken, that ye will yield to no temptation, but that ye will serve the true and [d]living God.

29 See that ye are not baptized [a]unworthily; see that ye partake not of the sacrament of Christ [b]unworthily; but see that ye do all

---

18a John 6: 14; 3 Ne. 8: 1.
  b Mark 6: 5.
19a Rom. 15: 19 (18–19);
    D&C 63: 10 (7–10).
  b TG God, Perfection of.
20a Judg. 6: 13 (11–13);
    Ether 12: 12 (12–18);
    Moro. 7: 37.
  b TG Trust in God.
21a Matt. 21: 22 (18–22);
    3 Ne. 18: 20.
  b TG Promise.
22a Mark 16: 15.
    TG Missionary Work;
    World.
23a Mark 16: 16.
  b TG Damnation.

24a Mark 16: 17 (17–18).
    TG Signs.
  b Mark 5: 15 (15–20);
    1 Ne. 11: 31.
  c TG Administrations to
    the Sick; Hands,
    Laying on of.
25a TG Testimony.
26a 2 Ne. 26: 20; 28: 5
    (4–6, 15).
  b 3 Ne. 29: 5 (4–7).
  c Prov. 13: 13.
27a TG Doubt.
  b 3 Ne. 21: 20; Ether
    5: 5; Moro. 10: 30
    (30–32).

  c Josh 22: 5; D&C
    64: 34 (22, 34).
    TG Commitment.
  d Philip. 2: 12 (12–16).
28a Matt. 10: 16;
    Jacob 6: 12.
  b TG Probation.
  c TG Covetousness;
    Lust.
  d Alma 5: 13.
29a TG Baptism,
    Qualifications for.
  b Lev. 22: 3; 1 Cor.
    11: 27 (27–30);
    3 Ne. 18: 29 (28–32).

things in *c*worthiness, and do it in the name of Jesus Christ, the Son of the living God; and if ye do this, and endure to the end, ye will in nowise be cast out.

30 Behold, I speak unto you as though I *a*spake from the dead; for I know that ye shall have my words.

31 Condemn me not because of mine *a*imperfection, neither my father, because of his imperfection, neither them who have written before him; but rather give thanks unto God that he hath made manifest unto you our imperfections, that ye may learn to be more wise than we have been.

32 And now, behold, we have written this record according to our knowledge, in the characters which are called among us the *a*reformed Egyptian, being handed down and altered by us, according to our manner of speech.

33 And if our plates had been *a*sufficiently large we should have written in Hebrew; but the Hebrew hath been altered by us also; and if we could have written in Hebrew, behold, ye would have had no *b*imperfection in our record.

34 But the Lord knoweth the things which we have written, and also that none other people knoweth our language; and because that none other people knoweth our language, therefore he hath prepared *a*means for the interpretation thereof.

35 And these things are written that we may rid our garments of the blood of our *a*brethren, who have dwindled in unbelief.

36 And behold, these things which we have *a*desired concerning our brethren, yea, even their restoration to the knowledge of Christ, are according to the prayers of all the saints who have dwelt in the land.

37 And may the Lord Jesus Christ grant that their prayers may be answered according to their faith; and may God the Father remember the covenant which he hath made with the house of Israel; and may he bless them forever, through faith on the name of Jesus Christ. Amen.

THE BOOK OF ETHER

The record of the Jaredites, taken from the twenty-four plates found by the people of Limhi in the days of king Mosiah.

CHAPTER 1

Moroni abridges the writings of Ether —Ether's genealogy set forth—The language of the Jaredites is not confounded at the Tower of Babel—The Lord promises to lead them to a choice land and make them a great nation.

AND now I, Moroni, proceed to give an *a*account of those ancient inhabitants who were destroyed by the *b*hand of the Lord upon the face of this north country.

2 And I take mine account from the *a*twenty and four plates which

---

29c TG Worthiness.
30a Morm. 8: 26;
   Moro. 10: 27.
31a Morm. 8: 17; Ether
   12: 23 (22–28, 35).
32a 1 Ne. 1: 2; Mosiah
   1: 2 (2–4).
33a Jarom 1: 14 (2, 14).

b 3 Ne. 5: 18.
34a Mosiah 8: 13 (13–18);
   Ether 3: 23 (23, 28);
   D&C 17: 1.
35a 2 Ne. 26: 15.
36a Morm. 5: 21; 8: 24
   (24–26); D&C
   10: 46 (46–49).

[ETHER]
1 1a Mosiah 28: 19.
   b 1 Sam. 5: 9; Morm.
   5: 23; D&C 87: 6 (6–7).
2a Alma 37: 21 (21–31);
   Ether 15: 33.

were found by the people of Limhi, which is called the Book of Ether.

3 And as I suppose that the [a]first part of this record, which speaks concerning the creation of the world, and also of Adam, and an account from that time even to the great [b]tower, and whatsoever things transpired among the children of men until that time, is had among the Jews—

4 Therefore I do not write those things which transpired from the days of [a]Adam until that time; but they are had upon the plates; and whoso findeth them, the same will have power that he may get the full account.

5 But behold, I give not the full account, but a [a]part of the account I give, from the tower down until they were destroyed.

6 And on this wise do I give the account. He that wrote this record was [a]Ether, and he was a descendant of Coriantor.

7 Coriantor was the son of Moron.

8 And Moron was the son of Ethem.

9 And Ethem was the son of Ahah.

10 And Ahah was the son of Seth.

11 And Seth was the son of Shiblon.

12 And Shiblon was the son of Com.

13 And Com was the son of Coriantum.

14 And Coriantum was the son of Amnigaddah.

15 And Amnigaddah was the son of Aaron.

16 And Aaron was a descendant of Heth, who was the son of Hearthom.

17 And Hearthom was the son of Lib.

18 And Lib was the son of Kish.

19 And Kish was the son of Corom.

20 And Corom was the son of Levi.

21 And Levi was the son of Kim.

22 And Kim was the son of Morianton.

23 And Morianton was a descendant of Riplakish.

24 And Riplakish was the son of Shez.

25 And Shez was the son of Heth.

26 And Heth was the son of Com.

27 And Com was the son of Coriantum.

28 And Coriantum was the son of Emer.

29 And Emer was the son of Omer.

30 And Omer was the son of Shule.

31 And Shule was the son of Kib.

32 And [a]Kib was the son of [b]Orihah, who was the son of Jared;

33 Which [a]Jared came forth with his brother and their families, with some others and their families, from the great tower, at the time the Lord [b]confounded the language of the people, and swore in his wrath that they should be scattered upon all the [c]face of the earth; and according to the word of the Lord the people were scattered.

34 And the [a]brother of Jared being a large and mighty man, and a man highly favored of the Lord, Jared, his brother, said unto him: Cry unto the Lord, that he will not confound us that we may not [b]understand our words.

35 And it came to pass that the brother of Jared did cry unto the Lord, and the Lord had compassion upon Jared; therefore he did not confound the [a]language of Jared; and Jared and his brother were not confounded.

36 Then Jared said unto his brother: Cry again unto the Lord, and it may be that he will turn away his anger from them who are our [a]friends, that he confound not their language.

37 And it came to pass that the brother of Jared did cry unto the Lord, and the Lord had compassion

3a Ether 8:9.
  b Gen. 11:4 (1–9);
    Omni 1:22; Mosiah
    28:17; Hel. 6:28.
4a IE covering same
    period as Genesis,
    chapters 1–10.

5a Ether 3:17; 15:33.
6a Ether 11:23; 12:2;
    15:34.
32a Ether 7:3.
  b Ether 6:27.
33a Gen. 11:9 (6–9).
  b Omni 1:22.

  c Mosiah 28:17.
34a Alma 8:7; Ether
    2:13; 6:1.
  b TG Communication.
35a Zeph. 3:9; Ether
    3:24; Moses 6:6 (5–6).
36a Ether 2:1.

upon their friends and their families also, that they were not confounded.

38 And it came to pass that Jared spake again unto his brother, saying: Go and [a]inquire of the Lord whether he will drive us out of the land, and if he will drive us out of the land, cry unto him whither we shall go. And who knoweth but the Lord will carry us forth into a land which is [b]choice above all the earth? And if it so be, let us be faithful unto the Lord, that we may receive it for our inheritance.

39 And it came to pass that the brother of Jared did cry unto the Lord according to that which had been spoken by the mouth of Jared.

40 And it came to pass that the Lord did hear the brother of Jared, and [a]had compassion upon him, and said unto him:

41 Go to and gather together thy [a]flocks, both male and female, of every kind; and also of the [b]seed of the earth of every kind; and [c]thy [d]families; and also Jared thy brother and his family; and also thy [e]friends and their families, and the friends of Jared and their families.

42 And when thou hast done this thou shalt [a]go at the head of them down into the valley which is northward. And there will I meet thee, and I will go [b]before thee into a land which is [c]choice above all the lands of the earth.

43 And there will I bless thee and thy seed, and raise up unto me of thy seed, and of the seed of thy brother, and they who shall go with thee, a great nation. And [a]there shall be none [b]greater than the nation which I will raise up unto me of thy seed, upon all the face of the earth.

And thus I will do unto thee because this long time ye have cried unto me.

CHAPTER 2

The Jaredites prepare for their journey to a promised land—It is a choice land whereon men must serve Christ or be swept off—The Lord talks to the brother of Jared for three hours—They build barges—The Lord asks the brother of Jared to propose how the barges shall be lighted.

AND it came to pass that Jared and his brother, and their families, and also the [a]friends of Jared and his brother and their families, went down into the valley which was northward, (and the name of the valley was [b]Nimrod, being called after the mighty hunter) with their [c]flocks which they had gathered together, male and female, of every kind.

2 And they did also lay snares and catch [a]fowls of the air; and they did also prepare a vessel, in which they did carry with them the fish of the waters.

3 And they did also carry with them deseret, which, by interpretation, is a honey bee; and thus they did carry with them [a]swarms of bees, and all manner of that which was upon the face of the land, [b]seeds of every kind.

4 And it came to pass that when they had come down into the valley of Nimrod the Lord came down and talked with the brother of Jared; and he was in a [a]cloud, and the brother of Jared saw him not.

5 And it came to pass that the Lord commanded them that they should [a]go forth into the wilderness, yea,

---

38a 2 Chr. 18: 4 (4–7).
  b 1 Ne. 2: 20. TG Lands of Inheritance.
40a Ether 3: 3.
41a Ether 2: 1 (1–3).
  b 1 Ne. 8: 1; 16: 11; Ether 9: 17.
  c Ether 6: 20.
  d Num. 1: 2; Mosiah 6: 3; D&C 48: 6.
  e Ether 6: 16.

42a Gen. 12: 1; Num. 9: 17; 1 Ne. 2: 2; Ether 2: 5; Abr. 2: 3.
  b Judg. 4: 14; D&C 84: 88 (87–88).
  c 1 Ne. 13: 30.
43a Gen. 26: 3; Deut. 28: 8.
  b Ether 15: 2.
2 1a Ether 1: 36.
  b Gen. 10: 8;

1 Chr. 1: 10.
  c Ether 1: 41; 6: 4; 9: 18 (18–19).
2a Gen. 7: 3 (1–3).
3a 1 Ne. 17: 5; 18: 6.
  b 1 Ne. 16: 11.
4a Num. 11: 25; D&C 34: 7 (7–9); JS-H 1: 68 (68–71).
5a Num. 9: 17; Ether 1: 42.

into that quarter where there never had man been. And it came to pass that the Lord did go before them, and did talk with them as he stood in a [b]cloud, and gave [c]directions whither they should travel.

6 And it came to pass that they did travel in the wilderness, and did [a]build [b]barges, in which they did cross many waters, being directed continually by the hand of the Lord.

7 And the Lord would not suffer that they should stop beyond the sea in the wilderness, but he would that they should come forth even unto the [a]land of promise, which was choice above all other lands, which the Lord God had [b]preserved for a righteous people.

8 And he had sworn in his wrath unto the brother of Jared, that whoso should possess this land of promise, from that time henceforth and forever, should [a]serve him, the true and only God, or they should be [b]swept off when the fulness of his wrath should come upon them.

9 And now, we can behold the decrees of God concerning this land, that it is a land of promise; and whatsoever nation shall possess it shall serve God, or they shall be [a]swept off when the fulness of his [b]wrath shall come upon them. And the fulness of his wrath cometh upon them when they are [c]ripened in iniquity.

10 For behold, this is a land which is choice above all other lands; wherefore he that doth possess it shall serve God or shall be [a]swept off; for it is the everlasting decree of God. And it is not until the [b]fulness of iniquity among the children of the land, that they are [c]swept off.

11 And this cometh unto you, O ye [a]Gentiles, that ye may know the decrees of God—that ye may repent, and not continue in your iniquities until the fulness come, that ye may not bring down the fulness of the [b]wrath of God upon you as the inhabitants of the land have hitherto done.

12 Behold, this is a choice land, and whatsoever nation shall possess it shall be [a]free from bondage, and from captivity, and from all other nations under heaven, if they will but [b]serve the God of the land, who is Jesus Christ, who hath been manifested by the things which we have written.

13 And now I proceed with my record; for behold, it came to pass that the Lord did bring Jared and his brethren forth even to that great sea which divideth the lands. And as they came to the sea they pitched their tents; and they called the name of the place Moriancumer; and they dwelt in [b]tents, and dwelt in tents upon the seashore for the space of four years.

14 And it came to pass at the end of four years that the Lord came again unto the brother of Jared, and stood in a cloud and [a]talked with him. And for the space of three hours did the Lord talk with the brother of Jared, and [b]chastened him because he remembered not to [c]call upon the name of the Lord.

15 And the brother of Jared repented of the evil which he had done, and did call upon the name of the Lord for his brethren who were with him. And the Lord said unto him: I will forgive thee and thy brethren of their sins; but thou shalt not sin

5b Ex. 13:21.
  c TG Guidance, Divine.
6a TG Skill.
  b Gen. 6:14 (14–15);
    Ether 2:16.
7a TG Promised Lands.
  b 1 Ne. 4:14.
8a Ether 13:2.
  b Jarom 1:3 (3, 10);
    Alma 37:28;
    Ether 9:20.

9a 2 Ne. 6:15.
  b TG God, Indignation of.
  c Gen. 15:16;
    1 Ne. 14:6.
10a Jarom 1:12.
  b 2 Ne. 28:16.
  c 1 Ne. 17:37.
11a 1 Ne. 14:6;
    2 Ne. 28:32.
  b Alma 45:16 (10–14,
    16); Morm. 1:17.

12a 1 Ne. 13:19.
  TG Liberty.
  b Isa. 60:12.
13a Alma 8:7; Ether 1:34.
  b Gen. 25:27; Hel. 3:9.
14a Ex. 25:22.
  b 1 Ne. 16:25.
  TG Chastening;
    Reproof.
  c TG Prayer.

any more, for ye shall remember that my ªSpirit will not always ᵇstrive with man; wherefore, if ye will sin until ye are fully ripe ye shall be cut off from the presence of the Lord. And these are my ᶜthoughts upon the land which I shall give you for your inheritance; for it shall be a land ᵈchoice above all other lands.

16 And the Lord said: Go to work and build, after the manner of ªbarges which ye have hitherto built. And it came to pass that the brother of Jared did go to work, and also his brethren, and built barges after the manner which they had built, according to the ᵇinstructions of the Lord. And they were small, and they were light upon the water, even like unto the lightness of a fowl upon the water.

17 And they were built after a manner that they were exceedingly ªtight, even that they would hold water like unto a dish; and the bottom thereof was tight like unto a dish; and the sides thereof were tight like unto a dish; and the ends thereof were peaked; and the top thereof was tight like unto a dish; and the length thereof was the length of a tree; and the door thereof, when it was shut, was tight like unto a dish.

18 And it came to pass that the brother of Jared cried unto the Lord, saying: O Lord, I have performed the work which thou hast commanded me, and I have made the barges according as thou hast directed me.

19 And behold, O Lord, in them there is no light; whither shall we steer? And also we shall perish, for in them we cannot breathe, save it is the air which is in them; therefore we shall perish.

20 And the Lord said unto the brother of Jared: Behold, thou shalt make a hole in the top, and also in the bottom; and when thou shalt suffer for air thou shalt unstop the hole and receive air. And if it be so that the water come in upon thee, behold, ye shall stop the hole, that ye may not perish in the flood.

21 And it came to pass that the brother of Jared did so, according as the Lord had commanded.

22 And he cried again unto the Lord saying: O Lord, behold I have done even as thou hast commanded me; and I have prepared the vessels for my people, and behold there is no light in them. Behold, O Lord, wilt thou suffer that we shall cross this great water in darkness?

23 And the Lord said unto the brother of Jared: What will ye that I should do that ye may have light in your vessels? For behold, ye cannot have ªwindows, for they will be dashed in pieces; neither shall ye take fire with you, for ye shall not go by the light of fire.

24 For behold, ye shall be as a ªwhale in the midst of the sea; for the mountain waves shall dash upon you. Nevertheless, I will bring you up again out of the depths of the sea; for the ᵇwinds have gone forth ᶜout of my mouth, and also the ᵈrains and the floods have I sent forth.

25 And behold, I prepare you against these things; for ye cannot cross this great deep save I prepare you against the waves of the sea, and the winds which have gone forth, and the floods which shall come. Therefore what will ye that I should prepare for you that ye may have light when ye are swallowed up in the depths of the sea?

15a TG God, Spirit of.
  b Gen. 6: 3; 2 Ne.
    26: 11; Morm. 5: 16;
    Moses 8: 17.
  c TG Earth, Purpose of.
  d Ether 9: 20.
16a Ether 2: 6.
  b Ex. 25: 40; Prov.
    16: 9; 1 Ne.
    17: 51 (50–51).
17a Ether 6: 7.
23a Gen. 6: 16.
24a Gen. 1: 21; Ether
    6: 10.
  b Ether 6: 5.
  c Job 37: 2 (2-13).
  d Ps. 148: 8; D&C
    117: 1.

CHAPTER 3

The brother of Jared sees the finger of
the Lord as he touches the sixteen
stones—Christ shows his spirit body
to the brother of Jared—Those who
have a perfect knowledge cannot be
kept from within the veil—Interpre-
ters are provided to bring the Jaredite
record to light.

AND it came to pass that the brother of Jared, (now the number of the vessels which had been prepared was eight) went forth unto the ^amount, which they called the mount ^bShelem, because of its exceeding height, and did ^cmolten out of a rock sixteen small stones; and they were white and clear, even as transparent ^dglass; and he did carry them in his hands upon the top of the mount, and cried again unto the Lord, saying:

2 O Lord, thou hast said that we must be encompassed about by the floods. Now behold, O Lord, and do not be ^aangry with thy servant because of his weakness before thee; for we know that thou art holy and dwellest in the heavens, and that we are ^bunworthy before thee; because of the ^cfall our ^dnatures have become evil continually; neverthe-less, O Lord, thou hast given us a commandment that we must call upon thee, that from thee we may receive according to our desires.

3 Behold, O Lord, thou hast smit-ten us because of our iniquity, and hast driven us forth, and for these many years we have been in the wilderness; nevertheless, thou hast been ^amerciful unto us. O Lord, look upon me in pity, and turn away thine anger from this thy people, and suffer not that they shall go

forth across this raging deep in darkness; but behold these ^bthings which I have molten out of the rock.

4 And I know, O Lord, that thou hast all ^apower, and can do whatso-ever thou wilt for the benefit of man; therefore touch these stones, O Lord, with thy ^bfinger, and prepare them that they may shine forth in darkness; and they shall shine forth unto us in the vessels which we have prepared, that we may have ^clight while we shall cross the sea.

5 Behold, O Lord, thou canst do this. We know that thou art able to show forth great power, which ^alooks small unto the understanding of men.

6 And it came to pass that when the brother of Jared had said these words, behold, the ^aLord stretched forth his hand and touched the stones one by one with his ^bfinger. And the ^cveil was taken from off the eyes of the brother of Jared, and he saw the finger of the Lord; and it was as the finger of a man, like unto flesh and blood; and the brother of Jared ^dfell down before the Lord, for he was struck with ^efear.

7 And the Lord saw that the brother of Jared had fallen to the earth; and the Lord said unto him: Arise, why hast thou fallen?

8 And he saith unto the Lord: I saw the finger of the Lord, and I feared lest he should ^asmite me; for I knew not that the Lord had flesh and blood.

9 And the Lord said unto him: Because of thy faith thou hast seen that I shall take upon me ^aflesh and blood; and never has man come before me with ^bsuch exceeding faith as thou hast; for were it not so ye

3 1a Ex. 24: 13 (12–13);
　　　Deut. 10: 1; 1 Ne.
　　　11: 1.
　　b Ether 4: 1.
　　c TG Skill.
　　d Rev. 21: 11.
2a Gen. 18: 32 (25–33).
　　b Moses 1: 10.
　　c TG Fall of Man.
　　d Mosiah 3: 19.

3a Ether 1: 40 (34–43).
　　b Ether 6: 2 (2–3, 10).
4a TG God, Power of.
　　b Ether 12: 20 (19–21).
　　c TG Light.
5a Isa. 55: 8 (8–9).
6a TG Jesus Christ, Lord.
　　b Dan. 5: 5; Abr.
　　　3: 12 (11–12).
　　c Ether 12: 19 (19, 21).

d Ezek. 1: 28;
　　Acts 9: 4 (3–5).
e Ex. 3: 6; JS-H 1: 32.
8a Moses 1: 11.
9a TG Flesh and Blood;
　　Jesus Christ,
　　Condescension of.
　　b Matt. 8: 10;
　　Alma 19: 10.

could not have seen my finger. Sawest thou more than this?

10 And he answered: Nay; Lord, [a]show thyself unto me.

11 And the Lord said unto him: [a]Believest thou the words which I shall speak?

12 And he answered: Yea, Lord, I know that thou speakest the truth, for thou art a God of truth, and [a]canst not lie.

13 And when he had said these words, behold, the Lord [a]showed himself unto him, and said: [b]Because thou knowest these things ye are redeemed from the fall; therefore ye are brought back into my [c]presence; therefore I [d]show myself unto you.

14 Behold, I am he who was [a]prepared from the foundation of the world to [b]redeem my people. Behold, I am Jesus Christ. I am the [c]Father and the Son. In me shall all mankind have [d]life, and that eternally, even they who shall believe on my name; and they shall become my [e]sons and my daughters.

15 And never have I [a]showed myself unto man whom I have created, for never has man [b]believed in me as thou hast. Seest thou that ye are created after mine own [c]image? Yea, even all men were created in the beginning after mine own image.

16 Behold, this [a]body, which ye now [b]behold, is the [c]body of my [d]spirit; and man have I created after the body of my spirit; and even as I appear unto thee to be in the spirit will I appear unto my people in the flesh.

17 And now, as I, Moroni, said I could [a]not make a full account of these things which are written, therefore it sufficeth me to say that Jesus showed himself unto this man in the spirit, even after the manner and in the likeness of the same body even as he [b]showed himself unto the Nephites.

18 And he ministered unto him even as he ministered unto the Nephites; and all this, that this man might know that he was God, because of the many great works which the Lord had showed unto him.

19 And because of the [a]knowledge of this man he could not be kept from beholding within the [b]veil; and he saw the finger of Jesus, which, when he saw, he fell with fear; for he knew that it was the finger of the Lord; and he had [c]faith no longer, for he knew, nothing [d]doubting.

20 Wherefore, having this perfect knowledge of God, he could [a]not be kept from within the veil; therefore he [b]saw Jesus; and he did minister unto him.

21 And it came to pass that the Lord said unto the brother of Jared: Behold, thou shalt not suffer these things which ye have seen and heard to go forth unto the world, until the [a]time cometh that I shall glorify my name in the flesh; wherefore, ye shall [b]treasure up the things which ye have seen and heard, and show it to no man.

10a Ex. 33: 18 (17–18).
11a 1 Ne. 11: 4 (4–5).
12a Num. 23: 19;
   Heb. 6: 18.
13a 1 Sam. 3: 21; D&C
   67: 11 (11–12).
  b Enos 1: 8 (6–8).
  c TG God, Presence of;
   God, Privilege of
   Seeing.
  d TG Jesus Christ,
   Appearances,
   Antemortal.
14a TG Jesus Christ,
   Foreordained.
  b TG Jesus Christ,
   Redeemer.

  c Mosiah 15: 2.
  d Mosiah 16: 9; D&C
   88: 13 (7–13).
  e TG Sons and
   Daughters of God.
15a Ex. 3: 6; 33: 20
   (11–23); John 1: 18;
   D&C 107: 54;
   Moses 1: 2. TG God,
   Privilege of Seeing.
  b TG Faith.
  c Gen. 1: 26 (26–28);
   Mosiah 7: 27; D&C
   20: 18 (17–18).
   TG God, Body of—
   Corporeal Nature.
16a TG God,

   Manifestations of.
  b D&C 17: 1.
  c TG Spirit Body.
  d TG Man, Antemortal
   Existence of.
17a Ether 1: 5; 15: 33.
  b 3 Ne. 11: 8 (8–16).
19a TG Knowledge.
  b TG Veil.
  c Alma 32: 34.
  d TG Doubt.
20a Ether 12: 21 (19–21).
  b TG Jesus Christ,
   Appearances,
   Antemortal.
21a Ether 4: 1.
  b Luke 2: 19 (17–20).

22 And behold, when ye shall come unto me, ye shall write them and shall seal them up, that no one can interpret them; for ye shall write them in a ªlanguage that they cannot be read.

23 And behold, these ªtwo stones will I give unto thee, and ye shall seal them up also with the things which ye shall write.

24 For behold, the ªlanguage which ye shall write I have confounded; wherefore I will cause in my own due time that these stones shall magnify to the eyes of men these things which ye shall write.

25 And when the Lord had said these words, he ªshowed unto the brother of Jared ᵇall the inhabitants of the earth which had been, and also all that would be; and he ᶜwithheld them not from his sight, even unto the ends of the earth.

26 For he had said unto him in times before, that ªif he would ᵇbelieve in him that he could show unto him ᶜall things—it should be shown unto him; therefore the Lord could not withhold anything from him, for he knew that the Lord could show him all things.

27 And the Lord said unto him: Write these things and ªseal them up; and I will show them in mine own due time unto the children of men.

28 And it came to pass that the Lord commanded him that he should seal up the two ªstones which he had received, and show them not, until the Lord should show them unto the children of ᵇmen.

CHAPTER 4

Moroni is commanded to seal up the writings of the brother of Jared— They shall not be revealed until men have faith even as the brother of Jared —Christ commands men to believe his words and those of his disciples—Men are commanded to repent and believe the gospel and be saved.

AND the Lord commanded the brother of Jared to go down out of the ªmount from the presence of the Lord, and ᵇwrite the things which he had seen; and they were forbidden to come unto the children of men ᶜuntil after that he should be lifted up upon the cross; and for this cause did king Mosiah keep them, that they should not come unto the world until after Christ should show himself unto his people.

2 And after Christ truly had showed himself unto his people he commanded that they should be made manifest.

3 And now, after that, they have all dwindled in unbelief; and there is ªnone save it be the Lamanites, and they have rejected the gospel of Christ; therefore I am commanded that I should ᵇhide them up again in the earth.

4 Behold, I have written upon these plates the ªvery things which the brother of Jared saw; and there never were ᵇgreater things made manifest than those which were made manifest unto the brother of Jared.

5 Wherefore the Lord hath commanded me to write them; and I have written them. And he com-

22a Mosiah 8: 11 (11–12).
  TG Language.
23a Mosiah 8: 13 (13–18);
  Morm. 9: 34;
  D&C 17: 1.
  TG Urim and
  Thummim.
24a Ether 1: 35.
25a 2 Ne. 27: 7.
  TG God, Omniscience
  of; Revelation.
  b Moses 1: 8.

c Luke 24: 16 (10–24);
  D&C 25: 4.
26a Ether 3: 11–13.
  b TG Believe.
  c 2 Ne. 27: 7 (7–8,
  10–11); Mosiah 8: 19;
  Ether 4: 4 (1–8).
27a 2 Ne. 27: 7 (6–23).
28a D&C 17: 1.
  b 2 Ne. 3: 6; 3 Ne.
  21: 11 (8–11); Morm.
  8: 16 (16, 25).

4 1a Ether 3: 1.
  b Ether 12: 24.
  TG Record Keeping;
  Scriptures, Writing of.
  c Ether 3: 21.
3a Morm. 8: 3 (2–3).
  b Morm. 8: 14.
  TG Scriptures,
  Preservation of.
4a Ether 5: 1.
  b 2 Ne. 27: 7 (7–8,
  10–11); Mosiah 8: 19;
  Ether 3: 26 (21–28).

manded me that I should *seal them up; and he also hath commanded that I should seal up the interpretation thereof; wherefore I have sealed up the *interpreters, according to the commandment of the Lord.

6 For the Lord said unto me: They shall not go forth unto the Gentiles until the day that they shall repent of their iniquity, and become clean before the Lord.

7 And in that day that they shall exercise *faith in me, saith the Lord, even as the brother of Jared did, that they may become *sanctified in me, then will I *manifest unto them the things which the brother of Jared saw, even to the unfolding unto them all my *revelations, saith Jesus Christ, the Son of God, the *Father of the heavens and of the earth, and all things that in them are.

8 And he that will *contend against the word of the Lord, let him be accursed; and he that shall *deny these things, let him be accursed; for unto them will I show *no greater things, saith Jesus Christ; for I am he who speaketh.

9 And at my command the heavens are opened and are *shut; and at my word the *earth shall shake; and at my command the inhabitants thereof shall pass away, even so as by fire.

10 And he that believeth not my words believeth not my disciples; and if it so be that I do not speak, judge ye; for ye shall know that it is I that speaketh, at the *last day.

11 But he that *believeth these

things which I have spoken, him will I visit with the manifestations of my Spirit, and he shall *know and bear record. For because of my Spirit he shall *know that these things are *true; for it persuadeth men to do good.

12 And whatsoever thing persuadeth men to do good is of me; for *good cometh of none save it be of me. I am the same that leadeth men to all good; he that will *not believe my words will not believe me—that I am; and he that will not believe me will not believe the Father who sent me. For behold, I am the Father, I am the *light, and the *life, and the *truth of the world.

13 *Come unto me, O ye Gentiles, and I will show unto you the greater things, the knowledge which is hid up because of unbelief.

14 Come unto me, O ye house of Israel, and it shall be made *manifest unto you how great things the Father hath laid up for you, from the foundation of the world; and it hath not come unto you, because of unbelief.

15 Behold, when ye shall rend that veil of unbelief which doth cause you to remain in your awful state of wickedness, and hardness of heart, and blindness of mind, then shall the great and marvelous things which have been *hid up from the foundation of the world from you— yea, when ye shall *call upon the Father in my name, with a broken heart and a contrite spirit, then shall ye know that the Father hath

5a Dan. 12: 9; 3 Ne. 26: 9 (7–12, 18); Ether 5: 1; D&C 17: 6; 35: 18; JS-H 1: 65.
b Morm. 6: 6; D&C 17: 1; JS-H 1: 52. TG Urim and Thummim.
7a D&C 5: 28.
b TG Sanctification.
c 2 Ne. 30: 16; Alma 12: 9; 3 Ne. 26: 10 (6–11).
d 2 Ne. 27: 22.
e Mosiah 3: 8.
8a Job 9: 3 (1–4); 3 Ne.

29: 5 (1–9); Morm. 8: 17.
b 2 Ne. 27: 14; 28: 29 (29–30, 34).
c Alma 12: 10 (10–11); 3 Ne. 26: 10 (9–10).
9a 1 Kgs. 8: 35; D&C 77: 8.
b Hel. 12: 11 (8–18); Morm. 5: 23.
10a 2 Ne. 25: 22; 33: 15 (10–15); 3 Ne. 27: 25 (23–27).
11a D&C 5: 16.
b 2 Ne. 32: 5; 3 Ne. 16: 6.

c TG Testimony.
d Alma 3: 12; Ether 5: 3 (1–4); Moro. 10: 4 (1–5).
12a Omni 1: 25; Alma 5: 40; Moro. 7: 16 (12–17).
b 3 Ne. 11: 35; 28: 34.
c TG Jesus Christ, Light of the World.
d Col. 3: 4.
e Alma 38: 9.
13a 3 Ne. 12: 2 (2–3).
14a D&C 121: 26 (26–29).
15a 2 Ne. 27: 10.
b Gen. 4: 26; Moro. 2: 2.

remembered the covenant which he made unto your fathers, O house of Israel.

16 And then shall my ^arevelations which I have caused to be written by my servant John be unfolded in the eyes of all the people. Remember, when ye see these things, ye shall know that the time is at hand that they shall be made manifest in very deed.

17 Therefore, ^awhen ye shall receive this record ye may know that the work of the Father has commenced upon all the face of the land.

18 Therefore, ^arepent all ye ends of the earth, and come unto me, and believe in my gospel, and be ^bbaptized in my name; for he that believeth and is baptized shall be saved; but he that believeth not shall be damned; and ^csigns shall follow them that believe in my name.

19 And blessed is he that is found ^afaithful unto my name at the last day, for he shall be ^blifted up to dwell in the kingdom prepared for him ^cfrom the foundation of the world. And behold it is I that hath spoken it. Amen.

CHAPTER 5

Three witnesses and the work itself shall stand as a testimony of the truthfulness of the Book of Mormon.

AND now I, Moroni, have written the words which were commanded me, according to my memory; and I have told you the things which I have ^asealed up; therefore touch them not in order that ye may translate; for that thing is forbidden you, except by and by it shall be wisdom in God.

2 And behold, ye may be privileged that ye may show the plates unto ^athose who shall assist to bring forth this work;

3 And unto ^athree shall they be shown by the power of God; wherefore they shall ^bknow of a surety that these things are ^ctrue.

4 And in the mouth of three ^awitnesses shall these things be established; and the ^btestimony of three, and this work, in the which shall be shown forth the power of God and also his word, of which the Father, and the Son, and the Holy Ghost bear record—and all this shall stand as a testimony against the world at the last day.

5 And if it so be that they repent and ^acome unto the Father in the name of Jesus, they shall be received into the kingdom of God.

6 And now, if I have no authority for these things, judge ye; for ye shall know that I have authority when ye shall see me, and we shall stand before God at the last day. Amen.

CHAPTER 6

The Jaredite barges are driven by the winds to the promised land—The people praise the Lord for his goodness—Orihah is appointed king over them—Jared and his brother pass away in death.

AND now I, Moroni, proceed to give the record of ^aJared and his brother.

2 For it came to pass after the Lord had prepared the ^astones which the brother of Jared had carried up into the mount, the brother of Jared

16a Rev. 1: 1; 1 Ne. 14: 23 (18–27).
17a 3 Ne. 21: 2 (1–11, 28).
18a 3 Ne. 27: 20; Moro. 7: 34.
  b John 3: 5 (3–5).
    TG Baptism, Essential.
  c TG Holy Ghost, Gifts of.
19a Ps. 31: 23; Mosiah 2: 41; D&C 6: 13; 63: 47. TG Jesus

Christ, Taking the Name of.
  b Morm. 2: 19.
  c 2 Ne. 9: 18; Alma 42: 26; Ether 3: 14.
5 1a 2 Ne. 27: 8 (7–11, 21); Ether 4: 5 (4–7); D&C 17: 6.
2a 2 Ne. 27: 14 (13–14); D&C 5: 15 (1–16).
3a 2 Ne. 11: 3; 27: 12 (12–14); D&C 17: 3

    (3–5).
  b D&C 5: 25.
  c Ether 4: 11 (6–11); Moro. 10: 4 (1–4).
4a 2 Ne. 27: 12 (12–14); D&C 14: 8; 17: 1.
  b 2 Ne. 25: 18; 29: 11.
5a Morm. 9: 27; Moro. 10: 30 (30–32).
6 1a Ether 1: 34.
2a Ether 3: 3.

came down out of the mount, and he did put forth the stones into the vessels which were prepared, one in each end thereof; and behold, they did give light unto the vessels.

3 And thus the Lord caused stones to shine in darkness, to give light unto men, women, and children, that they might not cross the great waters in darkness.

4 And it came to pass that when they had prepared all manner of *a*food, that thereby they might subsist upon the water, and also food for their flocks and herds, and *b*whatsoever beast or animal or fowl that they should carry with them—and it came to pass that when they had done all these things they got aboard of their vessels or barges, and set forth into the sea, commending themselves unto the Lord their God.

5 And it came to pass that the Lord God caused that there should be a *a*furious wind blow upon the face of the waters, *b*towards the promised land; and thus they were tossed upon the waves of the sea before the wind.

6 And it came to pass that they were many times buried in the depths of the sea, because of the mountain waves which broke upon them, and also the great and terrible tempests which were caused by the fierceness of the wind.

7 And it came to pass that when they were buried in the deep there was no water that could hurt them, their vessels being *a*tight like unto a dish, and also they were tight like unto the *b*ark of Noah; therefore when they were encompassed about by many waters they did cry unto the Lord, and he did bring them forth again upon the top of the waters.

8 And it came to pass that the wind did never cease to blow towards the promised land while they were upon the waters; and thus they were *a*driven forth before the wind.

9 And they did *a*sing praises unto the Lord; yea, the brother of Jared did sing praises unto the Lord, and he did *b*thank and praise the Lord all the day long; and when the night came, they did not cease to praise the Lord.

10 And thus they were driven forth; and no monster of the sea could break them, neither *a*whale that could mar them; and they did have light continually, whether it was above the water or under the water.

11 And thus they were driven forth, *a*three hundred and forty and four days upon the water.

12 And they did *a*land upon the shore of the *b*promised land. And when they had set their feet upon the shores of the promised land they bowed themselves down upon the face of the land, and did humble themselves before the Lord, and did shed tears of joy before the Lord, because of the multitude of his *c*tender mercies over them.

13 And it came to pass that they went forth upon the face of the land, and began to till the earth.

14 And Jared had four *a*sons; and they were called Jacom, and Gilgah, and Mahah, and Orihah.

15 And the brother of Jared also begat sons and daughters.

16 And the *a*friends of Jared and his brother were in number about twenty and two souls; and they also begat sons and daughters before they came to the promised land; and therefore they began to be many.

17 And they were taught to *a*walk

4a TG Food.
  b Ether 2: 1; 9: 18 (18–19).
5a Ether 2: 24 (24–25).
  b 1 Ne. 18: 9.
7a Ether 2: 17.
  b Gen. 6: 14;
    Moses 7: 43.
8a 1 Ne. 18: 13 (8–13).
9a TG Singing.
  b 1 Chr. 16: 8 (7–36);
    Ps. 34: 1 (1–3); Alma 37: 37; D&C 46: 32.
10a Gen. 1: 21; Ether 2: 24.
11a Gen. 7: 11; 8: 13.
12a Ether 7: 16.
  b Alma 22: 30 (29–34);
    Ether 7: 6.
  c Ether 7: 27; 10: 2.
14a Ether 6: 27.
16a Ether 1: 41.
17a TG Walking with God.

humbly before the Lord; and they were also [b]taught from on high.

18 And it came to pass that they began to spread upon the face of the land, and to multiply and to till the earth; and they did wax strong in the land.

19 And the brother of Jared began to be old, and saw that he must soon go down to the grave; wherefore he said unto Jared: Let us gather together our people that we may number them, that we may know of them what they will desire of us before we go down to our graves.

20 And accordingly the people were gathered together. Now the number of the sons and the daughters of the brother of Jared were twenty and two souls; and the number of sons and daughters of Jared were twelve, he having four sons.

21 And it came to pass that they did number their people; and after that they had numbered them, they did desire of them the things which they would that they should do before they went down to their graves.

22 And it came to pass that the people desired of them that they should [a]anoint one of their sons to be a king over them.

23 And now behold, this was grievous unto them. And the brother of Jared said unto them: Surely this thing [a]leadeth into captivity.

24 But Jared said unto his brother: Suffer that they may have a king. And therefore he said unto them: Choose ye out from among our sons a king, even whom ye will.

25 And it came to pass that they chose even the firstborn of the brother of Jared; and his name was Pagag. And it came to pass that he refused and would not be their [a]king. And the people would that his father should constrain him, but his father would not; and he commanded them

that they should constrain no man to be their king.

26 And it came to pass that they chose all the brothers of Pagag, and they would not.

27 And it came to pass that neither would the [a]sons of Jared, even all save it were one; and [b]Orihah was anointed to be king over the people.

28 And he began to reign, and the people began to [a]prosper; and they became exceedingly rich.

29 And it came to pass that Jared died, and his brother also.

30 And it came to pass that Orihah did walk humbly before the Lord, and did remember how great things the Lord had done for his father, and also taught his people how great things the Lord had done for their fathers.

CHAPTER 7

Orihah reigns in righteousness—Amid usurpation and strife the rival kingdoms of Shule and Cohor are set up—Prophets condemn the wickedness and idolatry of the people, who then repent.

AND it came to pass that Orihah did execute judgment upon the land in righteousness all his days, whose days were exceedingly many.

2 And he begat sons and daughters; yea, he begat thirty and one, among whom were twenty and three sons.

3 And it came to pass that he also begat [a]Kib in his [b]old age. And it came to pass that Kib reigned in his stead; and Kib begat Corihor.

4 And when Corihor was thirty and two years old he rebelled against his father, and went over and dwelt in the land of Nehor; and he begat sons and daughters, and they became exceedingly fair; wherefore Corihor drew away many people after him.

5 And when he had gathered together an army he came up unto the

17b TG Guidance, Divine; Revelation.
22a TG Anointing.
23a 1 Sam. 8:11 (10–18);
Mosiah 29:18 (16–23); Ether 7:5.
25a TG Kings, Earthly.
27a Ether 6:14.
  b Ether 1:32.
28a TG Prosper.
7 3a Ether 1:32 (31–32).
  b Gen. 18:12 (11–12);
Ether 7:26; 9:23.

land of ^aMoron where the king dwelt, and took him captive, which ^bbrought to pass the saying of the brother of Jared that they would be brought into captivity.

6 Now the ^aland of Moron, where the king dwelt, was near the land which is called Desolation by the Nephites.

7 And it came to pass that Kib dwelt in ^acaptivity, and his people under Corihor his son, until he became exceedingly old; nevertheless Kib begat Shule in his old age, while he was yet in captivity.

8 And it came to pass that Shule was angry with his brother; and Shule waxed strong, and became mighty as to the strength of a man; and he was also mighty in judgment.

9 Wherefore, he came to the hill Ephraim, and he did molten out of the hill, and made swords out of ^asteel for those whom he had drawn away with him; and after he had armed them with swords he returned to the city Nehor, and gave battle unto his brother Corihor, by which means he obtained the kingdom and restored it unto his father Kib.

10 And now because of the thing which Shule had done, his father bestowed upon him the kingdom; therefore he began to reign in the stead of his father.

11 And it came to pass that he did execute judgment in righteousness; and he did spread his kingdom upon all the face of the land, for the people had become exceedingly numerous.

12 And it came to pass that Shule also begat many sons and daughters.

13 And Corihor repented of the many evils which he had done; wherefore Shule gave him power in his kingdom.

14 And it came to pass that Corihor had many sons and daughters. And among the sons of Corihor there was one whose name was Noah.

15 And it came to pass that Noah rebelled against Shule, the king, and also his father Corihor, and drew away Cohor his brother, and also all his brethren and many of the people.

16 And he gave battle unto Shule, the king, in which he did obtain the land of their ^afirst inheritance; and he became a king over that part of the land.

17 And it came to pass that he gave battle again unto Shule, the king; and he took Shule, the king, and carried him away captive into Moron.

18 And it came to pass as he was about to put him to death, the sons of Shule crept into the house of Noah by night and slew him, and broke down the door of the prison and brought out their father, and placed him upon his throne in his own kingdom.

19 Wherefore, the son of Noah did build up his kingdom in his stead; nevertheless they did not gain power any more over Shule the king, and the people who were under the reign of Shule the king did prosper exceedingly and wax great.

20 And the country was ^adivided; and there were two kingdoms, the kingdom of Shule, and the kingdom of Cohor, the son of Noah.

21 And Cohor, the son of Noah, caused that his people should give battle unto Shule, in which Shule did beat them and did slay Cohor.

22 And now Cohor had a son who was called Nimrod; and Nimrod gave up the kingdom of Cohor unto Shule, and he did gain favor in the eyes of Shule; wherefore Shule did bestow great favors upon him, and he did do in the kingdom of Shule according to his desires.

23 And also in the reign of Shule there came ^aprophets among the people, who were sent from the Lord, prophesying that the wickedness and ^bidolatry of the people was bringing a curse upon the land, and they should be destroyed if they did not repent.

5a Ether 14: 6 (6, 11).
 b Ether 6: 23.
6a Ether 6: 12.
7a Ether 8: 4 (3–4);
   10: 14.
9a 1 Ne. 16: 18.
16a Ether 6: 12.
20a 2 Ne. 5: 7 (1–14).
23a Ether 9: 28; 11: 1
   (1, 12, 20).
 b TG Idolatry.

24 And it came to pass that the people did ᵃrevile against the prophets, and did mock them. And it came to pass that king Shule did execute judgment against all those who did revile against the prophets.

25 And he did execute a law throughout all the land, which gave power unto the prophets that they should go whithersoever they would; and by this cause the people were brought unto repentance.

26 And because the people did repent of their iniquities and idolatries the Lord did spare them, and they began to prosper again in the land. And it came to pass that Shule ᵃbegat sons and daughters in his old age.

27 And there were no more wars in the days of Shule; and he remembered the great things that the Lord had done for his fathers in bringing them ᵃacross the great deep into the promised land; wherefore he did execute judgment in righteousness all his days.

CHAPTER 8

There is strife and contention over the kingdom—Akish forms an oath-bound secret combination to slay the king—Secret combinations are of the devil and result in the destruction of nations—Modern Gentiles are warned against the secret combination which shall seek to overthrow the freedom of all lands, nations, and countries.

AND it came to pass that he begat Omer, and Omer reigned in his stead. And Omer begat Jared; and Jared begat sons and daughters.

2 And Jared rebelled against his father, and came and dwelt in the land of Heth. And it came to pass that he did ᵃflatter many people, because of his cunning words, until he had gained the half of the kingdom.

3 And when he had gained the half of the kingdom he gave battle unto his father, and he did carry away his father into captivity, and did make him serve in captivity;

4 And now, in the days of the reign of Omer he was in ᵃcaptivity the half of his days. And it came to pass that he begat sons and daughters, among whom were Esrom and Coriantumr;

5 And they were exceedingly angry because of the doings of Jared their brother, insomuch that they did raise an army and gave battle unto Jared. And it came to pass that they did give battle unto him by night.

6 And it came to pass that when they had slain the army of Jared they were about to slay him also; and he plead with them that they would not slay him, and he would give up the kingdom unto his father. And it came to pass that they did grant unto him his life.

7 And now Jared became exceedingly ᵃsorrowful because of the loss of the kingdom, for he had set his heart upon the kingdom and upon the glory of the world.

8 Now the daughter of Jared being exceedingly expert, and seeing the sorrows of her father, thought to devise a plan whereby she could redeem the kingdom unto her father.

9 Now the daughter of Jared was exceedingly fair. And it came to pass that she did talk with her father, and said unto him: Whereby hath my father so much sorrow? Hath he not read the ᵃrecord which our fathers brought across the great deep? Behold, is there not an ᵇaccount concerning them of ᶜold, that they by their ᵈsecret plans did obtain kingdoms and great glory?

10 And now, therefore, let my father send for Akish, the son of

---

24a Mosiah 27: 2 (1–3).
  TG Prophets,
  Rejection of; Reviling.
26a Ether 7: 3 (3, 7);
  9: 23.

27a Ether 6: 12 (1–12).
8 2a Hel. 1: 7; 2: 5.
4a Ether 7: 7 (5–7);
  10: 14.
7a Morm. 2: 13.
9a Ether 1: 3.

b 3 Ne. 6: 28.
c Hel. 6: 26 (26–30);
  3 Ne. 3: 9.
d Hel. 6: 27; Ether
  13: 18; Moses
  5: 30 (18–52).

Kimnor; and behold, I am fair, and I will dance before him, and I will please him, that he will desire me to wife; wherefore if he shall desire of thee that ye shall give unto him me to wife, then shall ye say: I will give her if ye will bring unto me the [a]head of my father, the king.

11 And now Omer was a friend to Akish; wherefore, when Jared had sent for Akish, the daughter of Jared danced before him that she pleased him, insomuch that he desired her to wife. And it came to pass that he said unto Jared: Give her unto me to wife.

12 And Jared said unto him: I will give her unto you, if ye will bring unto me the head of my father, the king.

13 And it came to pass that Akish gathered in unto the house of Jared all his kinsfolk, and said unto them: Will ye swear unto me that ye will be faithful unto me in the thing which I shall desire of you?

14 And it came to pass that they all [a]sware unto him, by the God of heaven, and also by the heavens, and also by the earth, and by their heads, that whoso should vary from the assistance which Akish desired should lose his head; and whoso should divulge whatsoever thing Akish made known unto them, the same should lose his life.

15 And it came to pass that thus they did agree with [a]Akish. And Akish did administer unto them the oaths which were given by them of old who also sought power, which had been handed down even from [b]Cain, who was a murderer from the beginning.

16 And they were kept up by the [a]power of the devil to administer these oaths unto the people, to keep them in darkness, to help such as sought power to gain power, and to murder, and to plunder, and to lie, and to commit all manner of wickedness and whoredoms.

17 And it was the daughter of Jared who put it into his heart to search up these things of old; and Jared put it into the heart of Akish; wherefore, Akish administered it unto his kindred and friends, leading them away by fair promises to do whatsoever thing he desired.

18 And it came to pass that they formed a secret [a]combination, even as they of old; which combination is most abominable and wicked above all, in the sight of God;

19 For the Lord worketh not in secret combinations, neither doth he will that man should shed blood, but in all things hath forbidden it, from the beginning of man.

20 And now I, Moroni, do not write the manner of their oaths and combinations, for it hath been made known unto me that they are had [a]among all people, and they are had among the Lamanites.

21 And they have caused the [a]destruction of this people of whom I am now speaking, and also the destruction of the people of Nephi.

22 And whatsoever [a]nation shall uphold such secret combinations, to get power and gain, until they shall spread over the nation, behold, they shall be destroyed; for the Lord will not suffer that the [b]blood of his saints, which shall be shed by them, shall always cry unto him from the ground for [c]vengeance upon them and yet he avenge them not.

23 Wherefore, O ye Gentiles, it is wisdom in God that these things should be shown unto you, that thereby ye may repent of your sins, and suffer not that these murderous combinations shall get above you,

10a Mark 6: 24 (22–28).
14a Hel. 1: 11; 3 Ne. 3: 8.
  TG Swearing.
15a Ether 9: 1.
  b Gen. 4: 7 (7–8);
    Moses 5: 25.
16a Moses 4: 6; 5: 13.

18a TG Secret
    Combinations.
20a 4 Ne. 1: 46; Morm.
    2: 8; 8: 9.
21a Hel. 6: 28; D&C
    38: 13 (13–16).

22a TG Governments.
  b Rev. 6: 10 (1–11);
    19: 2; 2 Ne. 28: 10;
    Morm. 8: 27 (27,
    40–41); D&C 87: 7.
  c TG God, Justice of;
    Vengeance.

which are built up to get ªpower and gain—and the work, yea, even the work of ᵇdestruction come upon you, yea, even the sword of the justice of the Eternal God shall fall upon you, to your overthrow and destruction if ye shall suffer these things to be.

24 Wherefore, the Lord commandeth you, when ye shall see these things come among you that ye shall awake to a sense of your awful situation, because of this ªsecret combination which shall be among you; or wo be unto it, because of the blood of them who have been slain; for they cry from the dust for vengeance upon it, and also upon those who built it up.

25 For it cometh to pass that whoso buildeth it up seeketh to overthrow the ªfreedom of all lands, nations, and countries; and it bringeth to pass the destruction of all people, for it is built up by the devil, who is the father of all lies; even that same liar who ᵇbeguiled our first parents, yea, even that same liar who hath caused man to commit murder from the beginning; who hath ᶜhardened the hearts of men that they have ᵈmurdered the prophets, and stoned them, and cast them out from the beginning.

26 Wherefore, I, Moroni, am commanded to write these things that evil may be done away, and that the time may come that Satan may have ªno power upon the hearts of the children of men, but that they may be ᵇpersuaded to do good continually, that they may come unto the fountain of all ᶜrighteousness and be saved.

CHAPTER 9

The kingdom passes from one to another by descent and intrigue and murder—Emer saw the Son of Righteousness—Many prophets cry repentance—A famine and poisonous serpents plague the people.

AND now I, Moroni, proceed with my record. Therefore, behold, it came to pass that because of the ªsecret combinations of Akish and his friends, behold, they did overthrow the kingdom of Omer.

2 Nevertheless, the Lord was merciful unto Omer, and also to his sons and to his daughters who did not seek his destruction.

3 And the Lord ªwarned Omer in a dream that he should depart out of the land; wherefore Omer ᵇdeparted out of the land with his family, and traveled many days, and came over and passed by the hill of ᶜShim, and came over by the place ᵈwhere the Nephites were destroyed, and from thence eastward, and came to a place which was called Ablom, by the seashore, and there he pitched his tent, and also his sons and his daughters, and all his household, save it were Jared and his family.

4 And it came to pass that Jared was anointed king over the people, by the hand of wickedness; and he gave unto Akish his daughter to wife.

5 And it came to pass that Akish ªsought the life of his father-in-law; and he applied unto those whom he had sworn by the ᵇoath of oath of the ancients, and they obtained the head of his father-in-law, as he sat upon his throne, giving audience to his people.

6 For so great had been the spreading of this wicked and secret society that it had corrupted the hearts of all the people; therefore Jared was murdered upon his throne, and Akish reigned in his stead.

23a Moses 6: 15.
  b Luke 13: 3 (1–5).
24a D&C 42: 64.
25a TG Liberty.
  b Gen. 3: 13 (1–13);
    2 Ne. 9: 9; Mosiah
    16: 3; Moses 4: 19
    (5–19).

  c TG Hardheartedness.
  d TG Prophets,
    Rejection of.
26a 2 Ne. 30: 18.
  b 2 Ne. 33: 4; Moro.
    7: 13 (12–17).
  c TG Righteousness.

9 1a Ether 8: 15 (13–17).
3a TG Dream; Warnings.
  b Ether 9: 13.
  c Morm. 1: 3; 4: 23.
  d Morm. 6: 2 (1–15).
5a Esth. 2: 21.
  b TG Oath.

7 And it came to pass that Akish began to be [a]jealous of his son, therefore he shut him up in prison, and kept him upon little or no food until he had suffered death.

8 And now the brother of him that suffered death, (and his name was Nimrah) was angry with his father because of that which his father had done unto his brother.

9 And it came to pass that Nimrah gathered together a small number of men, and fled out of the land, and came over and dwelt with Omer.

10 And it came to pass that Akish begat other sons, and they won the hearts of the people, notwithstanding they had sworn unto him to do all manner of iniquity according to that which he desired.

11 Now the people of Akish were desirous for gain, even as Akish was desirous for [a]power; wherefore, the sons of Akish did offer them [b]money, by which means they drew away the more part of the people after them.

12 And there began to be a war between the sons of Akish and Akish, which lasted for the space of many years, yea, unto the destruction of nearly all the people of the kingdom, yea, even all, save it were thirty souls, and they who fled with the house of Omer.

13 Wherefore, Omer was restored again to the [a]land of his inheritance.

14 And it came to pass that Omer began to be old; nevertheless, in his old age he begat Emer; and he anointed Emer to be king to reign in his stead.

15 And after that he had anointed Emer to be king he saw peace in the land for the space of two years, and he died, having seen exceedingly many days, which were full of sorrow. And it came to pass that Emer did reign in his stead, and did fill the steps of his father.

16 And the Lord began again to take the curse from off the land, and the house of Emer did prosper exceedingly under the reign of Emer; and in the space of sixty and two years they had become exceedingly strong, insomuch that they became exceedingly rich—

17 Having [a]all manner of fruit, and of grain, and of [b]silks, and of fine linen, and of [c]gold, and of silver, and of precious things;

18 And also [a]all manner of cattle, of oxen, and cows, and of sheep, and of swine, and of goats, and also many other kinds of animals which were useful for the food of man.

19 And they also had [a]horses, and asses, and there were elephants and cureloms and cumoms; all of which were useful unto man, and more especially the elephants and cureloms and cumoms.

20 And thus the Lord did pour out his blessings upon this land, which was [a]choice above all other lands; and he commanded that whoso should possess the land should possess it unto the Lord, or they should be [b]destroyed when they were ripened in iniquity; for upon such, saith the Lord: I will pour out the fulness of my wrath.

21 And Emer did execute judgment in righteousness all his days, and he begat many sons and daughters; and he begat Coriantum, and he anointed Coriantum to reign in his stead.

22 And after he had anointed Coriantum to reign in his stead he lived four years, and he saw peace in the land; yea, and he even saw the [a]Son of Righteousness, and did rejoice and glory in his day; and he died in peace.

23 And it came to pass that Coriantum did walk in the steps of his father, and did build many mighty cities, and did administer that which was good unto his people in all his

---

7a TG Jealousy.
11a TG Tyranny.
  b 1 Sam. 8: 3 (1–4);
    Hel. 9: 20.
    TG Bribery.
13a Ether 9: 3.
17a Ether 1: 41.
  b Ether 10: 24.
  c Hel. 6: 9 (9–11);
    Ether 10: 12 (12, 23).
18a Ether 6: 4.
19a 1 Ne. 18: 25; Enos
    1: 21; 3 Ne. 6: 1.
20a Ether 2: 15.
  b Deut. 31: 4 (4–5);
    Ether 2: 8 (8–11).
22a 3 Ne. 25: 2.

days. And it came to pass that he had no children even until he was exceedingly *a*old.

24 And it came to pass that his wife died, being an hundred and two years old. And it came to pass that Coriantum took to wife, in his old age, a young maid, and begat sons and daughters; wherefore he lived until he was an hundred and forty and two years old.

25 And it came to pass that he begat Com, and Com reigned in his stead; and he reigned forty and nine years, and he begat Heth; and he also begat other sons and daughters.

26 And the people had spread again over all the face of the land, and there began again to be an exceedingly great wickedness upon the face of the land, and *a*Heth began to embrace the secret plans again of old, to destroy his father.

27 And it came to pass that he did dethrone his father, for he slew him with his own sword; and he did reign in his stead.

28 And there came prophets in the land *a*again, crying repentance unto them—that they must prepare the way of the Lord or there should come a curse upon the face of the land; yea, even there should be a great famine, in which they should be destroyed if they did not repent.

29 But the people believed not the words of the prophets, but they cast them out; and some of them they cast into *a*pits and left them to perish. And it came to pass that they did all these things according to the commandment of the king, Heth.

30 And it came to pass that there began to be a great *a*dearth upon the land, and the inhabitants began to be destroyed exceedingly fast because of the dearth, for there was no rain upon the face of the earth.

31 And there came forth *a*poisonous serpents also upon the face of the land, and did poison many people. And it came to pass that their flocks began to flee before the poisonous serpents, towards the land *b*southward, which was called by the Nephites *c*Zarahemla.

32 And it came to pass that there were many of them which did perish by the way; nevertheless, there were some which fled into the land southward.

33 And it came to pass that the Lord did cause the *a*serpents that they should pursue them no more, but that they should hedge up the way that the people could not pass, that whoso should attempt to pass might fall by the poisonous serpents.

34 And it came to pass that the people did follow the course of the beasts, and did devour the *a*carcasses of them which fell by the way, until they had devoured them all. Now when the people saw that they must *b*perish they began to *c*repent of their iniquities and cry unto the Lord.

35 And it came to pass that when they had *a*humbled themselves sufficiently before the Lord he did send rain upon the face of the earth; and the people began to revive again, and there began to be fruit in the north countries, and in all the countries round about. And the Lord did show forth his power unto them in preserving them from famine.

CHAPTER 10

One king succeeds another—Some of the kings are righteous; others are wicked—When righteousness prevails, the people are blessed and prospered by the Lord.

AND it came to pass that Shez, who was a descendant of Heth—for

23*a* Ether 7: 3 (3, 7).
26*a* Ether 10: 1.
28*a* Ether 7: 23;
    11: 1 (1, 12, 20).
29*a* Jer. 38: 6 (4–13).

30*a* TG Drought; Famine.
31*a* Ether 10: 19.
  b Morm. 3: 5; Ether
    10: 21.
  c Omni 1: 13.
33*a* Deut. 8: 15; 1 Ne.

17: 41. TG Plague.
34*a* Jer. 7: 33 (32–33).
  b Alma 34: 34.
  c D&C 101: 8.
35*a* D&C 5: 24.

^aHeth had perished by the famine, and all his household save it were Shez—wherefore, Shez began to build up again a broken people.

2 And it came to pass that Shez did remember the destruction of his fathers, and he did build up a righteous kingdom; for he remembered what the Lord had done in bringing Jared and his brother ^aacross the deep; and he did walk in the ways of the Lord; and he begat sons and daughters.

3 And his eldest son, whose name was Shez, did ^arebel against him; nevertheless, Shez was smitten by the hand of a robber, because of his exceeding riches, which brought peace again unto his father.

4 And it came to pass that his father did build up many cities upon the face of the land, and the people began again to spread over all the face of the land. And Shez did live to an exceedingly old age; and he begat Riplakish. And he died, and Riplakish reigned in his stead.

5 And it came to pass that Riplakish did not do that which was right in the sight of the Lord, for he did have many wives and ^aconcubines, and did lay that upon men's shoulders which was grievous to be borne; yea, he did ^btax them with heavy taxes; and with the taxes he did build many spacious buildings.

6 And he did erect him an exceedingly beautiful throne; and he did build many prisons, and whoso would not be subject unto taxes he did ^acast into prison; and whoso was not able to pay taxes he did cast into prison; and he did cause that they should labor continually for their support; and whoso refused to labor he did cause to be put to death.

7 Wherefore he did obtain all his fine work, yea, even his fine ^agold he did cause to be refined in prison; and all manner of fine ^bworkmanship he did cause to be wrought in prison. And it came to pass that he did afflict the people with his whoredoms and abominations.

8 And when he had reigned for the space of forty and two years the people did rise up in rebellion against him; and there began to be war again in the land, insomuch that Riplakish was killed, and his descendants were driven out of the land.

9 And it came to pass after the space of many years, Morianton, (he being a descendant of Riplakish) gathered together an army of outcasts, and went forth and gave battle unto the people; and he gained power over many cities; and the war became exceedingly sore, and did last for the space of many years; and he did gain power over all the land, and did establish himself king over all the land.

10 And after that he had established himself king he did ease the burden of the people, by which he did gain favor in the eyes of the people, and they did anoint him to be their king.

11 And he did do justice unto the people, but not unto himself because of his many ^awhoredoms; wherefore he was cut off from the presence of the Lord.

12 And it came to pass that Morianton built up many cities, and the people became exceedingly rich under his reign, both in buildings, and in ^agold and silver, and in raising grain, and in flocks, and herds, and such things which had been restored unto them.

13 And Morianton did live to an exceedingly great age, and then he begat Kim; and Kim did reign in the stead of his father; and he did reign eight years, and his father died. And it came to pass that Kim did ^anot reign in righteousness,

---

10 1a Ether 9: 26 (25–29).
2a Ether 6: 12 (1–12).
3a Mosiah 10: 6.
5a Esth. 2: 14; Jacob 3: 5; Mosiah 11: 2

(2–14).
b Gen. 47: 24.
6a TG Oppression; Tyranny.
7a Esth. 1: 4.

b TG Art.
11a TG Whoredom.
12a Ether 9: 17 (17–18).
13a 1 Ne. 17: 35 (34–35).

wherefore he was not favored of the Lord.

14 And his brother did rise up in rebellion against him, by which he did bring him into ^acaptivity; and he did remain in captivity all his days; and he begat sons and daughters in captivity, and in his old age he begat Levi; and he died.

15 And it came to pass that Levi did serve in captivity after the death of his father, for the space of forty and two years. And he did make war against the king of the land, by which he did obtain unto himself the kingdom.

16 And after he had obtained unto himself the kingdom he did that which was right in the sight of the Lord; and the people did prosper in the land; and he did live to a good ^aold age, and begat sons and daughters; and he also begat Corom, whom he anointed king in his stead.

17 And it came to pass that Corom did that which was good in the sight of the Lord all his days; and he begat many sons and daughters; and after he had seen many days he did pass away, even like unto the rest of the earth; and Kish reigned in his stead.

18 And it came to pass that Kish passed away also, and Lib reigned in his stead.

19 And it came to pass that Lib also did that which was good in the sight of the Lord. And in the days of Lib the ^apoisonous serpents were destroyed. Wherefore they did go into the land southward, to hunt food for the people of the land, for the land was covered with animals of the forest. And Lib also himself became a great ^bhunter.

20 And they built a great city by the ^anarrow neck of land, by the place where the sea divides the land.

21 And they did preserve the land ^asouthward for a wilderness, to get game. And the whole face of the land northward was covered with inhabitants.

22 And they were exceedingly ^aindustrious, and they did buy and sell and ^btraffic one with another, that they might get gain.

23 And they did ^awork in all manner of ^bore, and they did make gold, and silver, and ^ciron, and ^dbrass, and all manner of metals; and they did dig it out of the earth; wherefore, they did cast up mighty heaps of earth to get ore, of gold, and of silver, and of iron, and of copper. And they did ^ework all manner of fine work.

24 And they did have ^asilks, and fine-twined ^blinen; and they did work all manner of ^ccloth, that they might clothe themselves from their nakedness.

25 And they did make all manner of tools to till the earth, both to plow and to sow, to reap and to hoe, and also to thrash.

26 And they did make all manner of tools with which they did work their beasts.

27 And they did make all manner of ^aweapons of war. And they did work all manner of work of exceedingly curious workmanship.

28 And never could be a people more blessed than were they, and more prospered by the hand of the Lord. And they were in a land that was choice above all lands, for the Lord had spoken it.

29 And it came to pass that Lib did live many years, and begat sons and daughters; and he also begat Hearthom.

14a Ether 7:7; 8:4 (3–4); 10:30 (30–31).
16a TG Old Age.
19a Ether 9:31.
  b Gen. 25:27; Ether 2:1.
20a Alma 63:5.
21a Morm. 3:5; Ether 9:31 (31–32).

22a TG Industry.
  b Gen. 34:10 (10–21); Mosiah 24:7; 4 Ne. 1:46.
23a TG Skill.
  b Hel. 6:9 (9–11); Ether 9:17.
  c 2 Ne. 5:15; Moses 5:46.

d Gen. 4:22; Mosiah 8:10.
e TG Art.
24a Ether 9:17.
  b Ex. 25:4 (4–5); 1 Ne. 13:7 (7–8).
  c TG Clothing.
27a Ether 15:15.

30 And it came to pass that Hearthom reigned in the stead of his father. And when Hearthom had reigned twenty and four years, behold, the kingdom was taken away from him. And he served many years in ªcaptivity, yea, even all the remainder of his days.

31 And he begat Heth, and Heth lived in captivity all his days. And Heth begat Aaron, and Aaron dwelt in captivity all his days; and he begat Amnigaddah, and Amnigaddah also dwelt in captivity all his days; and he begat Coriantum, and Coriantum dwelt in captivity all his days; and he begat Com.

32 And it came to pass that Com drew away the half of the kingdom. And he reigned over the half of the kingdom forty and two years; and he went to battle against the king, Amgid, and they fought for the space of many years, during which time Com gained power over Amgid, and obtained power over the remainder of the kingdom.

33 And in the days of Com there began to be robbers in the land; and they adopted the old plans, and administered ªoaths after the manner of the ancients, and sought again to destroy the kingdom.

34 Now Com did fight against them much; nevertheless, he did not prevail against them.

CHAPTER 11

Wars, dissensions, and wickedness dominate Jaredite life—Their prophets predict the utter destruction of the Jaredites unless they repent—The people reject the words of the prophets.

AND there came also in the days of Com many ªprophets, and prophesied of the destruction of that great people except they should repent, and turn unto the Lord, and forsake their murders and wickedness.

2 And it came to pass that the prophets were ªrejected by the people, and they fled unto Com for protection, for the people sought to destroy them.

3 And they prophesied unto Com many things; and he was blessed in all the remainder of his days.

4 And he lived to a good old age, and begat Shiblom; and Shiblom reigned in his stead. And the brother of Shiblom rebelled against him, and there began to be an exceedingly great war in all the land.

5 And it came to pass that the brother of Shiblom caused that all the prophets who prophesied of the destruction of the people should be put to ªdeath;

6 And there was great calamity in all the land, for they had testified that a great curse should come upon the land, and also upon the people, and that there should be a great destruction among them, such an one as never had been upon the face of the earth, and their bones should become as ªheaps of earth upon the face of the land except they should repent of their wickedness.

7 And they hearkened not unto the voice of the Lord, because of their wicked combinations; wherefore, there began to be wars and ªcontentions in all the land, and also many famines and pestilences, insomuch that there was a great destruction, such an one as never had been known upon the face of the earth; and all this came to pass in the days of Shiblom.

8 And the people began to repent of their iniquity; and inasmuch as they did the Lord did have ªmercy on them.

9 And it came to pass that Shiblom was slain, and Seth was brought into ªcaptivity, and did dwell in captivity all his days.

10 And it came to pass that Ahah,

30a Ether 10:14; 11:9.
33a TG Secret
       Combinations.
11 1a Ether 7:23; 9:28.

2a TG Prophets,
       Rejection of.
5a TG Persecution.
6a Omni 1:22;
       Ether 14:21.

7a TG Contention.
8a TG Mercy.
9a Ether 10:30;
       11:18 (18–19).

his son, did obtain the kingdom; and he did reign over the people all his days. And he did do all manner of iniquity in his days, by which he did cause the shedding of much blood; and few were his days.

11 And Ethem, being a descendant of Ahah, did obtain the kingdom; and he also did do that which was wicked in his days.

12 And it came to pass that in the days of Ethem there came many prophets, and prophesied again unto the people; yea, they did prophesy that the Lord would utterly ᵃdestroy them from off the face of the earth except they repented of their iniquities.

13 And it came to pass that the people hardened their hearts, and would not ᵃhearken unto their words; and the prophets ᵇmourned and withdrew from among the people.

14 And it came to pass that Ethem did execute judgment in wickedness all his days; and he begat Moron. And it came to pass that Moron did reign in his stead; and Moron did that which was wicked before the Lord.

15 And it came to pass that there arose a ᵃrebellion among the people, because of that secret ᵇcombination which was built up to get power and gain; and there arose a mighty man among them in iniquity, and gave battle unto Moron, in which he did overthrow the half of the kingdom; and he did maintain the half of the kingdom for many years.

16 And it came to pass that Moron did overthrow him, and did obtain the kingdom again.

17 And it came to pass that there arose another mighty man; and he was a descendant of the brother of Jared.

18 And it came to pass that he did overthrow Moron and obtain the kingdom; wherefore, Moron dwelt in ᵃcaptivity all the remainder of his days; and he begat Coriantor.

19 And it came to pass that Coriantor dwelt in captivity all his days.

20 And in the days of Coriantor there also came many prophets, and prophesied of great and marvelous things, and cried repentance unto the people, and except they should repent the Lord God would execute ᵃjudgment against them to their utter destruction;

21 And that the Lord God would send or bring forth ᵃanother people to possess the ᵇland, by his power, after the manner by which he brought their fathers.

22 And they did ᵃreject all the words of the prophets, because of their ᵇsecret society and wicked abominations.

23 And it came to pass that Coriantor begat ᵃEther, and he died, having dwelt in captivity all his days.

CHAPTER 12

The prophet Ether exhorts the people to believe in God—Moroni recounts the wonders and marvels done by faith—Faith enabled the brother of Jared to see Christ—The Lord gives men weaknesses that they may be humble—The brother of Jared moved Mount Zerin by faith—Faith, hope, and charity are essential to salvation—Moroni saw Jesus face to face.

AND it came to pass that the days of Ether were in the days of ᵃCoriantumr; and Coriantumr was king over all the land.

2 And ᵃEther was a prophet of the Lord; wherefore Ether came forth

---

12a Ether 12: 3.
13a Jer. 44: 16;
  Mosiah 16: 2.
  b TG Mourning.
15a TG Rebellion.
  b TG Secret
  Combinations.
18a Ether 11: 9.

20a TG Judgment.
21a Omni 1: 21; Ether
  13: 21 (20–21).
  b Deut. 29: 28.
22a TG Prophets,
  Rejection of.
  b TG Secret

Combinations.
23a Ether 1: 6; 12: 2;
  15: 34 (33–34).
12 1a Omni 1: 21; Ether
  13: 20 (13–31).
2a Ether 1: 6; 11: 23;
  15: 34 (33–34).

in the days of Coriantumr, and began to prophesy unto the people, for he could not be [b]restrained because of the Spirit of the Lord which was in him.

3 For he did [a]cry from the [b]morning, even until the going down of the sun, exhorting the people to believe in God unto repentance lest they should be [c]destroyed, saying unto them that [d]by [e]faith all things are fulfilled—

4 Wherefore, whoso believeth in God might with [a]surety [b]hope for a better world, yea, even a place at the right hand of God, which [c]hope cometh of [d]faith, maketh an [e]anchor to the souls of men, which would make them sure and steadfast, always abounding in [f]good works, being led to [g]glorify God.

5 And it came to pass that Ether did prophesy great and marvelous things unto the people, which they did not believe, because they [a]saw them not.

6 And now, I, Moroni, would speak somewhat concerning these things; I would show unto the world that [a]faith is things which are [b]hoped for and [c]not seen; wherefore, dispute not because ye see not, for ye receive no [d]witness until after the [e]trial of your faith.

7 For it was by faith that Christ showed himself unto our fathers, after he had risen from the dead; and he showed not himself unto them until after they had faith in him; wherefore, it must needs be

that some had faith in him, for he showed himself [a]not unto the world.

8 But because of the faith of men he has shown himself unto the world, and glorified the name of the Father, and prepared a way that thereby others might be partakers of the heavenly gift, that they might hope for those things which they have not seen.

9 Wherefore, ye may also have hope, and be partakers of the gift, if ye will but have faith.

10 Behold it was by faith that they of old were [a]called after the holy order of God.

11 Wherefore, by faith was the law of Moses given. But in the [a]gift of his Son hath God prepared a more [b]excellent way; and it is by faith that it hath been fulfilled.

12 For if there be no [a]faith among the children of men God can do no [b]miracle among them; wherefore, he showed not himself until after their faith.

13 Behold, it was the faith of Alma and Amulek that caused the [a]prison to tumble to the earth.

14 Behold, it was the faith of Nephi and Lehi that wrought the [a]change upon the Lamanites, that they were baptized with fire and with the [b]Holy Ghost.

15 Behold, it was the faith of [a]Ammon and his brethren which [b]wrought so great a miracle among the Lamanites.

16 Yea, and even all they who

2b Jer. 20: 9; Enos 1: 26;
    Alma 43: 1.
3a D&C 112: 5.
  b Jer. 26: 5.
  c Ether 11: 12 (12,
    20–22).
  d Heb. 11: 7 (1–40).
  e 1 Cor. 13: 13 (1–13);
    Moro. 7: 1; 8: 14;
    10: 20 (20–23).
4a Heb. 7: 22.
  b Alma 7: 16; 22: 16;
    Moro. 7: 3; D&C
    25: 10; 138: 14.
  c Heb. 11: 1; Moro.
    7: 40.
  d Luke 7: 50.

e Heb. 6: 19.
f 1 Cor. 15: 58;
  1 Tim. 2: 10.
g John 11: 4 (1–4);
  3 Ne. 12: 16.
5a Heb. 11: 3; Alma
  30: 15; Hel. 16: 20.
6a Heb. 11: 1.
  b Rom. 8: 25 (24–25).
  c Alma 32: 21.
  d Lev. 9: 6 (6, 23);
    2 Ne. 1: 15. TG
    Sign Seekers.
  e 3 Ne. 26: 11.
    TG Test, Try, Prove.
7a Acts 10: 41.

10a Alma 13: 4 (3–4).
   TG Authority.
11a TG God, Gifts of.
  b 1 Cor. 12: 31.
12a Luke 16: 30 (27–31);
    Alma 32: 18 (17–18);
    Moro. 7: 37.
  b Ps. 78: 41; Matt.
    13: 58; Morm. 9: 20.
13a Alma 14: 27 (26–29).
14a Hel. 5: 50 (50–52).
  b Hel. 5: 45; 3 Ne.
    9: 20.
15a Alma 17: 29 (29–39).
  b IE as told in Alma,
    chapters 17–26.

wrought [a]miracles wrought them by [b]faith, even those who were before Christ and also those who were after.

17 And it was by faith that the three disciples obtained a promise that they should [a]not taste of death; and they obtained not the promise until after their faith.

18 And neither at any time hath any wrought miracles until after their faith; wherefore they first believed in the Son of God.

19 And there were many whose faith was so exceedingly strong, even [a]before Christ came, who could not be kept from within the [b]veil, but truly saw with their eyes the things which they had beheld with an eye of faith, and they were glad.

20 And behold, we have seen in this record that one of these was the brother of Jared; for so great was his faith in God, that when God put forth his [a]finger he could not hide it from the sight of the brother of Jared, because of his word which he had spoken unto him, which word he had obtained by faith.

21 And after the brother of Jared had beheld the finger of the Lord, because of the [a]promise which the brother of Jared had obtained by faith, the Lord could not withhold anything from his sight; wherefore he showed him all things, for he could no longer be kept without the [b]veil.

22 And it is by faith that my fathers have obtained the [a]promise that these things should come unto their brethren through the Gentiles; therefore the Lord hath commanded me, yea, even Jesus Christ.

23 And I said unto him: Lord, the Gentiles will [a]mock at these things, because of our [b]weakness in writing; for Lord thou hast made us [c]mighty in word by faith, but thou hast not made us mighty in writing; for thou hast made all this people that they could speak much, because of the Holy Ghost which thou hast given them;

24 And thou hast made us that we could write but little, because of the [a]awkwardness of our hands. Behold, thou hast not made us mighty in [b]writing like unto the brother of Jared, for thou madest him that the things which he [c]wrote were mighty even as thou art, unto the overpowering of man to read them.

25 Thou hast also made our words powerful and great, even that we [a]cannot write them; wherefore, when we write we behold our [b]weakness, and stumble because of the placing of our words; and I fear lest the Gentiles shall [c]mock at our words.

26 And when I had said this, the Lord spake unto me, saying: [a]Fools [b]mock, but they shall mourn; and my grace is sufficient for the meek, that they shall take no advantage of your weakness;

27 And if men come unto me I will show unto them their [a]weakness. I [b]give unto men weakness that they may be humble; and my [c]grace is sufficient for all men that [d]humble themselves before me; for if they humble themselves before me, and have faith in me, then will I make [e]weak things become strong unto them.

16a TG Miracle.
  b Heb. 11: 7 (7–40).
17a 3 Ne. 28: 7; 4 Ne.
    1: 37 (14, 37); Morm.
    8: 10 (10–12).
19a 2 Ne. 11: 4; Jacob
    4: 5; Jarom 1: 11;
    Alma 25: 16 (15–16).
  b Ether 3: 6. TG Veil.
20a Ether 3: 4.
21a Ether 3: 26 (25–26).
  b Ether 3: 20; D&C
    67: 10 (10–13).
22a Enos 1: 13.

23a Ether 12: 36.
  b 1 Cor. 2: 3 (1–5);
    1 Ne. 19: 6; Morm.
    8: 17 (13–17); 9: 31
    (31, 33).
  c 2 Ne. 33: 1.
24a Jacob 4: 1.
  b TG Language.
  c Ether 4: 1.
25a 3 Ne. 5: 18.
  b Ether 12: 37.
  c 1 Cor. 2: 14.
26a Prov. 14: 9; 20: 3.
  b Gal. 6: 7; D&C

124: 71. TG Mocking;
    Offense.
27a Jacob 4: 7.
  b Ex. 4: 11; 1 Cor.
    1: 27 (26–31).
  c TG Grace.
  d D&C 1: 28. TG
    Humility; Teachable.
  e Deut. 11: 8; Joel
    3: 10; Luke 9: 48
    (46–48); 18: 14
    (10–14); 2 Cor. 12: 9
    (7–10); Heb. 11: 34;
    1 Ne. 14: 1.

28 Behold, I will show unto the Gentiles their weakness, and I will show unto them that ªfaith, hope and charity bringeth unto me—the fountain of all ᵇrighteousness.

29 And I, Moroni, having heard these words, was ªcomforted, and said: O Lord, thy righteous will be done, for I know that thou workest unto the children of men according to their faith;

30 For the brother of Jared said unto the mountain Zerin, ªRemove—and it was removed. And if he had not had faith it would not have moved; wherefore thou workest after men have faith.

31 For thus didst thou manifest thyself unto thy disciples; for ªafter they had ᵇfaith, and did speak in thy name, thou didst show thyself unto them in great power.

32 And I also remember that thou hast said that thou hast prepared a house for man, yea, even among the ªmansions of thy Father, in which man might have a more excellent ᵇhope; wherefore man must hope, or he cannot receive an inheritance in the place which thou hast prepared.

33 And again, I remember that thou hast said that thou hast ªloved the world, even unto the laying down of thy life for the world, that thou mightest take it again to prepare a place for the children of men.

34 And now I know that this ªlove which thou hast had for the children of men is charity; wherefore, except men shall have charity they cannot inherit that place which thou hast prepared in the mansions of thy Father.

35 Wherefore, I know by this thing which thou hast said, that if the Gentiles have not ªcharity, because of our weakness, that thou wilt prove them, and ᵇtake away their ᶜtalent, yea, even that which they have received, and give unto them who shall have more abundantly.

36 And it came to pass that I prayed unto the Lord that he would give unto the Gentiles ªgrace, that they might have charity.

37 And it came to pass that the Lord said unto me: If they have not charity it mattereth not unto thee, thou hast been faithful; wherefore, thy garments shall be made ªclean. And because thou hast seen thy ᵇweakness thou shalt be made strong, even unto the sitting down in the place which I have prepared in the mansions of my Father.

38 And now I, Moroni, bid farewell unto the Gentiles, yea, and also unto my brethren whom I love, until we shall meet before the ªjudgment-seat of Christ, where all men shall know that my ᵇgarments are not spotted with your blood.

39 And then shall ye know that I have ªseen Jesus, and that he hath talked with me ᵇface to face, and that he told me in ᶜplain humility, even as a man telleth another in mine own language, concerning these things;

40 And only a few have I written, because of my weakness in writing.

41 And now, I would commend you to ªseek this Jesus of whom the

28a Alma 7: 24.
  b TG God, the Standard of Righteousness.
29a TG Comfort.
30a Matt. 17: 20; Jacob 4: 6; Hel. 10: 9.
  TG God, Power of.
31a 3 Ne. 26: 17 (17–21).
  b 1 Cor. 13: 13 (1–13); Moro. 7: 44 (33–48).
32a John 14: 2; Enos 1: 27; D&C 72: 4; 98: 18.
  b TG Hope.
33a John 3: 16 (16–18).

34a Moro. 7: 47.
  TG Love.
35a 1 Cor. 13: 2 (1–2).
  b Matt. 25: 28 (14–30).
  c TG Talents.
36a Ether 12: 23.
  TG Grace.
37a Job 15: 14; 25: 4; D&C 38: 42; 88: 74 (74–75); 135: 5 (4–5).
  TG Cleanliness; Purification.
  b Ether 12: 25 (25–27).
38a TG Jesus Christ, Judge.

  b Acts 20: 26; Jacob 1: 19.
39a TG Jesus Christ, Appearances, Postmortal.
  b Gen. 32: 30; Ex. 33: 11; Num. 12: 8.
  c 2 Ne. 32: 7; Alma 13: 23.
41a Ezra 8: 22 (22–23); Ps. 27: 8; Amos 5: 6; Alma 37: 47; D&C 88: 63; 101: 38.

prophets and apostles have written, that the grace of God the Father, and also the Lord Jesus Christ, and the Holy Ghost, which beareth [b]record of them, may be and abide in you forever. Amen.

CHAPTER 13

Ether speaks of a New Jerusalem to be built in America by the seed of Joseph—He prophesies, is cast out, writes the Jaredite history, and foretells the destruction of the Jaredites— War rages over all the land.

AND now I, Moroni, proceed to finish my record concerning the destruction of the people of whom I have been writing.

2 For behold, they rejected all the words of Ether; for he truly told them of all things, from the beginning of man; and that after the waters had [a]receded from off the face of this [b]land it became a choice land above all other lands, a chosen land of the Lord; wherefore the Lord would have that all men should [c]serve him who dwell upon the face thereof;

3 And that it was the place of the [a]New Jerusalem, which should [b]come down out of heaven, and the holy sanctuary of the Lord.

4 Behold, Ether saw the days of Christ, and he spake concerning a [a]New Jerusalem upon this land.

5 And he spake also concerning the house of Israel, and the [a]Jerusalem from whence [b]Lehi should come— after it should be destroyed it should be built up again, a [c]holy city unto the Lord; wherefore, it could not be a new Jerusalem for it had

been in a time of old; but it should be built up again, and become a holy city of the Lord; and it should be built unto the house of Israel—

6 And that a [a]New Jerusalem should be built up upon this land, unto the remnant of the seed of [b]Joseph, for which things there has been a [c]type.

7 For as Joseph brought his father down into the land of [a]Egypt, even so he died there; wherefore, the Lord brought a remnant of the seed of Joseph out of the land of Jerusalem, that he might be merciful unto the seed of Joseph that they should [b]perish not, even as he was merciful unto the father of Joseph that he should perish not.

8 Wherefore, the remnant of the house of Joseph shall be built upon this [a]land; and it shall be a land of their inheritance; and they shall build up a holy [b]city unto the Lord, like unto the Jerusalem of old; and they shall [c]no more be confounded, until the end come when the earth shall pass away.

9 And there shall be a [a]new heaven and a new earth; and they shall be like unto the old save the old have passed away, and all things have become new.

10 And then cometh the New Jerusalem; and blessed are they who dwell therein, for it is they whose garments are [a]white through the blood of the Lamb; and they are they who are numbered among the remnant of the seed of Joseph, who were of the house of Israel.

11 And then also cometh the [a]Jerusalem of old; and the inhabitants thereof, blessed are they, for

---

41b 3 Ne. 11: 32 (32, 36).
13 2a Gen. 8: 3; 7: 19 (11–24).
  b TG Earth, Dividing of.
  c Ether 2: 8.
3a 3 Ne. 20: 22;
    21: 23 (23–24). TG
    Jerusalem, New.
  b Rev. 3: 12; 21: 2.
4a TG Zion.
5a TG Jerusalem.
  b 1 Ne. 1: 18 (18–20); 2: 2.
  c Joel 2: 18; Rev.

21: 10 (10–27); 3 Ne.
20: 46 (29–36, 46).
6a D&C 42: 9; 45: 66
    (66–67); 84: 2 (2–5);
    A of F 10.
  b Ezek. 48: 5 (4–5);
    D&C 28: 8. TG Israel,
    Joseph, People of.
  c Alma 46: 24 (24–26).
    TG Symbolism.
7a Gen. 46: 6 (2–7); 47: 6.
  b 2 Ne. 3: 5 (5–24).

8a TG Promised Lands.
  b Rev. 21: 10 (10–27).
  c Moro. 10: 31.
9a Heb. 8: 13; 2 Pet.
    3: 13 (10–13); Rev.
    21: 1; 3 Ne. 12: 47
    (46–47); 15: 3 (2–10);
    D&C 101: 25 (23–25).
10a Rev. 7: 14.
11a TG Israel, Gathering
    of; Israel, Land of;
    Jerusalem.

they have been washed in the blood of the Lamb; and they are they who were scattered and gathered in from the four quarters of the earth, and from the [b]north countries, and are partakers of the fulfilling of the covenant which God made with their father, [c]Abraham.

12 And when these things come, bringeth to pass the scripture which saith, there are they who were [a]first, who shall be last; and there are they who were last, who shall be first.

13 And I was about to write more, but I am forbidden; but great and marvelous were the prophecies of Ether; but they esteemed him as naught, and cast him out; and he [a]hid himself in the cavity of a rock by day, and by night he went forth viewing the things which should come upon the people.

14 And as he dwelt in the cavity of a rock he made the [a]remainder of this record, viewing the destructions which came upon the people, by night.

15 And it came to pass that in that same year in which he was cast out from among the people there began to be a great war among the people, for there were many who rose up, who were mighty men, and sought to destroy Coriantumr by their secret plans of wickedness, of which hath been spoken.

16 And now Coriantumr, having studied, himself, in all the arts of war and all the cunning of the world, wherefore he gave battle unto them who sought to destroy him.

17 But he repented not, neither his [a]fair sons nor daughters; neither the fair sons and daughters of Cohor; neither the fair sons and daughters of Corihor; and in fine, there were none of the fair sons and daughters

upon the face of the whole earth who repented of their sins.

18 Wherefore, it came to pass that in the first year that Ether dwelt in the cavity of a rock, there were many people who were slain by the sword of those [a]secret combinations, fighting against Coriantumr that they might obtain the kingdom.

19 And it came to pass that the sons of Coriantumr fought much and bled much.

20 And in the second year the word of the Lord came to Ether, that he should go and [a]prophesy unto [b]Coriantumr that, if he would repent, and all his household, the Lord would give unto him his kingdom and spare the people—

21 Otherwise they should be destroyed, and all his household save it were himself. And he should only live to see the fulfilling of the prophecies which had been spoken concerning [a]another people receiving the land for their inheritance; and Coriantumr should receive a burial by them; and every soul should be destroyed save it were [b]Coriantumr.

22 And it came to pass that Coriantumr repented not, neither his household, neither the people; and the wars ceased not; and they sought to [a]kill Ether, but he fled from before them and hid again in the cavity of the rock.

23 And it came to pass that there arose up Shared, and he also gave battle unto Coriantumr; and he did beat him, insomuch that in the third year he did bring him into captivity.

24 And the sons of Coriantumr, in the fourth year, did beat Shared, and did obtain the kingdom again unto their father.

25 Now there began to be a war

11b D&C 133: 26 (26–35).
  TG Israel, Ten Lost
    Tribes of.
  c Isa. 27: 6.
12a Mark 10: 31; Luke
    13: 30; 1 Ne. 13: 42;
    Jacob 5: 63; D&C

18: 26 (26–27); 90: 9.
13a 1 Kgs. 17: 3 (1–16);
    1 Ne. 3: 27; Mosiah
    17: 4 (1–4).
14a Ether 15: 33 (13, 33).
17a Morm. 6: 19 (16–22).
18a Ether 8: 9 (9–26).

20a Ether 15: 1.
  b Omni 1: 21;
    Ether 12: 1 (1–2).
21a Ether 11: 21.
  b Ether 14: 24; 15: 29
    (29–32).
22a Prov. 29: 10.

upon all the face of the land, "every man with his band fighting for that which he desired.

26 And there were robbers, and in fine, all manner of wickedness upon all the face of the land.

27 And it came to pass that Coriantumr was exceedingly angry with Shared, and he went against him with his armies to battle; and they did meet in great anger, and they did meet in the valley of Gilgal; and the battle became exceedingly sore.

28 And it came to pass that Shared fought against him for the space of three days. And it came to pass that Coriantumr beat him, and did pursue him until he came to the plains of Heshlon.

29 And it came to pass that Shared gave him battle again upon the plains; and behold, he did beat Coriantumr, and drove him back again to the valley of Gilgal.

30 And Coriantumr gave Shared battle again in the valley of Gilgal, in which he beat Shared and slew him.

31 And Shared wounded Coriantumr in his thigh, that he did not go to battle again for the space of two years, in which time all the people upon the face of the land were shedding blood, and there was none to restrain them.

CHAPTER 14

The iniquity of the people brings a curse upon the land—Coriantumr engages in warfare against Gilead, then Lib, and then Shiz—Blood and carnage cover the land.

AND now there began to be a great "curse upon all the land because of the iniquity of the people, in which, if a man should lay his tool or his sword upon his shelf, or upon the place whither he would keep it, behold, upon the morrow, he could not find it, so great was the curse upon the land.

2 Wherefore every man did cleave unto that which was his own, with his hands, and would not borrow neither would he lend; and every man kept the hilt of his sword in his right hand, in the "defence of his property and his own life and of his wives and children.

3 And now, after the space of two years, and after the death of Shared, behold, there arose the brother of Shared and he gave battle unto Coriantumr, in which Coriantumr did beat him and did pursue him to the wilderness of Akish.

4 And it came to pass that the brother of Shared did give battle unto him in the wilderness of Akish; and the battle became exceedingly sore, and many thousands fell by the sword.

5 And it came to pass that Coriantumr did lay siege to the wilderness; and the brother of Shared did march forth out of the wilderness by night, and slew a part of the army of Coriantumr, as they were drunken.

6 And he came forth to the land of "Moron, and placed himself upon the throne of Coriantumr.

7 And it came to pass that Coriantumr dwelt with his army in the wilderness for the space of two years, in which he did receive great strength to his army.

8 Now the brother of Shared, whose name was Gilead, also received great strength to his army, because of secret combinations.

9 And it came to pass that his high priest murdered him as he sat upon his throne.

10 And it came to pass that one of the secret combinations murdered him in a secret pass, and obtained unto himself the kingdom; and his name was Lib; and Lib was a man of great stature, more than any other man among all the people.

11 And it came to pass that in the first year of Lib, Coriantumr came up unto the land of Moron, and gave battle unto Lib.

25a TG Covetousness; Selfishness.
14 1a Hel. 12:18; 13:18
(17–23); Morm. 1:18 (17–19); 2:10 (10–14).
2a Morm. 2:23.
6a Ether 7:5.

12 And it came to pass that he fought with Lib, in which Lib did smite upon his arm that he was wounded; nevertheless, the army of Coriantumr did press forward upon Lib, that he fled to the borders upon the seashore.

13 And it came to pass that Coriantumr pursued him; and Lib gave battle unto him upon the seashore.

14 And it came to pass that Lib did smite the army of Coriantumr, that they fled again to the wilderness of Akish.

15 And it came to pass that Lib did pursue him until he came to the plains of Agosh. And Coriantumr had taken all the people with him as he fled before Lib in that quarter of the land whither he fled.

16 And when he had come to the plains of Agosh he gave battle unto Lib, and he smote upon him until he died; nevertheless, the brother of Lib did come against Coriantumr in the stead thereof, and the battle became exceedingly sore, in the which Coriantumr fled again before the army of the brother of Lib.

17 Now the name of the brother of Lib was called Shiz. And it came to pass that Shiz pursued after Coriantumr, and he did overthrow many cities, and he did slay both women and children, and he did burn the cities.

18 And there went a fear of Shiz throughout all the land; yea, a cry went forth throughout the land— Who can stand before the army of Shiz? Behold, he sweepeth the earth before him!

19 And it came to pass that the people began to flock together in armies, throughout all the face of the land.

20 And they were divided; and a part of them fled to the army of Shiz, and a part of them fled to the army of Coriantumr.

21 And so great and lasting had been the war, and so long had been the scene of bloodshed and carnage, that the whole face of the land was covered with the ᵃbodies of the ᵇdead.

22 And so swift and speedy was the war that there was none left to bury the dead, but they did march forth from the shedding of ᵃblood to the shedding of blood, leaving the bodies of both men, women, and children strewed upon the face of the land, to become a prey to the ᵇworms of the flesh.

23 And the ᵃscent thereof went forth upon the face of the land, even upon all the face of the land; wherefore the people became troubled by day and by night, because of the scent thereof.

24 Nevertheless, Shiz did ᵃnot cease to pursue Coriantumr; for he had sworn to avenge himself upon Coriantumr of the blood of his brother, who had been slain, and the word of the Lord which came to Ether that Coriantumr should not fall by the sword.

25 And thus we see that the Lord did visit them in the fulness of his ᵃwrath, and their wickedness and abominations had prepared a way for their everlasting destruction.

26 And it came to pass that Shiz did pursue Coriantumr eastward, even to the borders by the seashore, and there he gave battle unto Shiz for the space of three days.

27 And so terrible was the destruction among the armies of Shiz that the people began to be frightened, and began to flee before the armies of Coriantumr; and they fled to the land of Corihor, and swept off the inhabitants before them, all them that would not join them.

28 And they pitched their tents in the valley of Corihor; and Coriantumr pitched his tents in the valley of Shurr. Now the valley of Shurr was near the hill Comnor; where-

21a Ether 11:6.
b Ezek. 35:8.
22a Hosea 4:2 (1–3).
b Isa. 14:11 (9–11).
23a Alma 16:11 (9–11).
24a Ether 13:21.
25a TG God,
Indignation of.

fore, Coriantumr did gather his armies together upon the hill Comnor, and did sound a trumpet unto the armies of Shiz to invite them forth to battle.

29 And it came to pass that they came forth, but were driven again; and they came the second time, and they were driven again the second time. And it came to pass that they came again the third time, and the battle became exceedingly sore.

30 And it came to pass that Shiz smote upon Coriantumr that he gave him many deep wounds; and Coriantumr, having lost his blood, fainted, and was carried away as though he were dead.

31 Now the loss of men, women and children on both sides was so great that Shiz commanded his people that they should not pursue the armies of Coriantumr; wherefore, they returned to their camp.

CHAPTER 15

Millions of the Jaredites are slain in battle—Shiz and Coriantumr assemble all the people to mortal combat—The Spirit of the Lord ceases to strive with them—The Jaredite nation is utterly destroyed—Only Coriantumr remains.

AND it came to pass when Coriantumr had recovered of his wounds, he began to remember the ^awords which Ether had spoken unto him.

2 He saw that there had been slain by the sword already nearly ^atwo millions of his people, and he began to sorrow in his heart; yea, there had been slain two millions of mighty men, and also their wives and their children.

3 He began to repent of the evil which he had done; he began to remember the words which had been spoken by the mouth of all the prophets, and he saw them that they were fulfilled thus far, every whit; and his soul ^amourned and refused to be ^bcomforted.

4 And it came to pass that he wrote an epistle unto Shiz, desiring him that he would spare the people, and he would give up the kingdom for the sake of the lives of the people.

5 And it came to pass that when Shiz had received his epistle he wrote an epistle unto Coriantumr, that if he would give himself up, that he might slay him with his own sword, that he would spare the lives of the people.

6 And it came to pass that the people repented not of their iniquity; and the people of Coriantumr were stirred up to anger against the people of Shiz; and the people of Shiz were stirred up to anger against the people of Coriantumr; wherefore, the people of Shiz did give battle unto the people of Coriantumr.

7 And when Coriantumr saw that he was about to fall he fled again before the people of Shiz.

8 And it came to pass that he came to the waters of Ripliancum, which, by interpretation, is large, or to exceed all; wherefore, when they came to these waters they pitched their tents; and Shiz also pitched his tents near unto them; and therefore on the morrow they did come to battle.

9 And it came to pass that they fought an exceedingly sore battle, in which Coriantumr was wounded again, and he fainted with the loss of blood.

10 And it came to pass that the armies of Coriantumr did press upon the armies of Shiz that they beat them, that they caused them to flee before them; and they did flee southward, and did pitch their tents in a place which was called Ogath.

11 And it came to pass that the army of Coriantumr did pitch their tents by the hill Ramah; and it was that same hill where my father Mormon did ^ahide up the records unto the Lord, which were sacred.

15 1a Ether 13:20 (20–21).   2a Ether 1:43.   3a TG Mourning.   b Gen. 37:35; Moses   7:44. TG Comfort.   11a Morm. 6:6.

12 And it came to pass that they did gather together all the people upon all the face of the land, who had not been slain, save it was Ether.

13 And it came to pass that Ether did [a]behold all the doings of the people; and he beheld that the people who were for Coriantumr were gathered together to the army of Coriantumr; and the people who were for Shiz were gathered together to the army of Shiz.

14 Wherefore, they were for the space of four years gathering together the people, that they might get all who were upon the face of the land, and that they might receive all the strength which it was possible that they could receive.

15 And it came to pass that when they were all gathered together, every one to the army which he would, with their wives and their children—both men, women and children being armed with [a]weapons of war, having shields, and [b]breastplates, and head-plates, and being clothed after the manner of war—they did march forth one against another to battle; and they fought all that day, and conquered not.

16 And it came to pass that when it was night they were weary, and retired to their camps; and after they had retired to their camps they took up a howling and a [a]lamentation for the loss of the slain of their people; and so great were their cries, their howlings and lamentations, that they did rend the air exceedingly.

17 And it came to pass that on the morrow they did go again to battle, and great and terrible was that day; nevertheless, they conquered not, and when the night came again they did rend the air with their cries, and their howlings, and their mournings, for the loss of the slain of their people.

18 And it came to pass that

Coriantumr wrote again an epistle unto Shiz, desiring that he would not come again to battle, but that he would take the kingdom, and spare the lives of the people.

19 But behold, the [a]Spirit of the Lord had ceased striving with them, and [b]Satan had full power over the [c]hearts of the people; for they were given up unto the hardness of their hearts, and the blindness of their minds that they might be destroyed; wherefore they went again to battle.

20 And it came to pass that they fought all that day, and when the night came they slept upon their swords.

21 And on the morrow they fought even until the night came.

22 And when the night came they were [a]drunken with anger, even as a man who is drunken with wine; and they slept again upon their swords.

23 And on the morrow they fought again; and when the night came they had all fallen by the sword save it were fifty and two of the people of Coriantumr, and sixty and nine of the people of Shiz.

24 And it came to pass that they slept upon their swords that night, and on the morrow they fought again, and they contended in their might with their swords and with their shields, all that day.

25 And when the night came there were thirty and two of the people of Shiz, and twenty and seven of the people of Coriantumr.

26 And it came to pass that they ate and slept, and prepared for death on the morrow. And they were large and mighty men as to the strength of men.

27 And it came to pass that they fought for the space of three hours, and they fainted with the loss of blood.

28 And it came to pass that when the men of Coriantumr had received

---

13a Ether 13: 14.
15a Ether 10: 27.
  b Mosiah 8: 10.

16a TG Mourning.
19a TG God, Spirit of;
    Holy Ghost, Loss of.

  b TG Devil.
  c TG Hardheartedness.
22a Moro. 9: 23.

sufficient strength that they could walk, they were about to flee for their lives; but behold, Shiz arose, and also his men, and he swore in his wrath that he would slay Coriantumr or he would perish by the sword.

29 Wherefore, he did pursue them, and on the morrow he did overtake them; and they fought again with the sword. And it came to pass that when they had *all fallen by the sword, save it were Coriantumr and Shiz, behold Shiz had fainted with the loss of blood.

30 And it came to pass that when Coriantumr had leaned upon his sword, that he rested a little, he smote off the head of Shiz.

31 And it came to pass that after he had smitten off the head of Shiz, that Shiz raised up on his hands and *fell; and after that he had struggled for breath, he died.

32 And it came to pass that *Coriantumr fell to the earth, and became as if he had no life.

33 And the Lord spake unto Ether, and said unto him: Go forth. And he went forth, and beheld that the words of the Lord had all been fulfilled; and he *finished his *record; (and the *hundredth part I have not written) and he hid them in a manner that the people of Limhi did find them.

34 Now the last words which are written by *Ether are these: Whether the Lord will that I be translated, or that I suffer the will of the Lord in the flesh, it mattereth not, if it so be that I am *saved in the kingdom of God. Amen.

THE BOOK OF MORONI

CHAPTER 1

Moroni writes for the benefit of the Lamanites—The Nephites who will not deny Christ are put to death.

NOW I, Moroni, after having made an end of abridging the account of the people of Jared, I had supposed *not to have written more, but I have not as yet perished; and I make not myself known to the Lamanites lest they should destroy me.

2 For behold, their *wars are exceedingly fierce among themselves; and because of their *hatred they *put to death every Nephite that will not deny the Christ.

3 And I, Moroni, will not *deny the Christ; wherefore, I wander whithersoever I can for the safety of mine own life.

4 Wherefore, I write a few more things, contrary to that which I had supposed; for I had supposed not to have written any more; but I write a few more things, that perhaps they may be of *worth unto my brethren, the Lamanites, in some future day, according to the will of the Lord.

CHAPTER 2

Jesus gave the Nephite apostles power to confer the gift of the Holy Ghost.

29a Ether 13:21.
31a Judg. 5:27 (26–27).
32a Omni 1:21 (20–22).
33a Ether 13:14.
  b Mosiah 8:9; 21:27; 28:11; Alma 37:21 (21–31); Ether 1:2 (1–5).
  c 3 Ne. 26:6; Ether 3: 17.
34a Ether 1:6; 11:23; 12:2.
  b Mosiah 13:9.

[MORONI]
1 1a Morm. 8:5; Moro. 10:1 (1–2).

2a 1 Ne. 12:21 (20–23).
  b TG Hate.
  c Alma 45:14.
3a Matt. 10:33 (32–33); 3 Ne. 29:5.
4a 2 Ne. 3:12 (11–12, 19).

[Between A.D. 400 and 421]

THE words of Christ, which he spake unto his *a*disciples, the twelve whom he had chosen, as he laid his hands upon them—

2 And he called them by name, saying: Ye shall *a*call on the Father in my name, in mighty prayer; and after ye have done this ye shall have *b*power that to him upon whom ye shall lay your *c*hands, *d*ye shall give the Holy Ghost; and in my name shall ye give it, for thus do mine apostles.

3 Now Christ spake these words unto them at the time of his first appearing; and the multitude heard it not, but the disciples heard it; and on as many as they *a*laid their hands, fell the Holy Ghost.

CHAPTER 3

Elders ordain priests and teachers by the laying on of hands.

THE manner which the disciples, who were called the *a*elders of the church, *b*ordained *c*priests and teachers—

2 After they had prayed unto the Father in the name of Christ, they *a*laid their hands upon them, and said:

3 In the name of Jesus Christ I ordain you to be a priest, (or, if he be a *a*teacher) I ordain you to be a teacher, to preach repentance and *b*remission of sins through Jesus Christ, by the endurance of faith on his name to the end. Amen.

4 And after this manner did they *a*ordain priests and teachers, according to the *b*gifts and callings of God

unto men; and they ordained them by the *c*power of the Holy Ghost, which was in them.

CHAPTER 4

How the elders and priests administer the sacramental bread.

THE *a*manner of their *b*elders and *c*priests administering the flesh and blood of Christ unto the church; and they administered it *d*according to the commandments of Christ; wherefore we know the manner to be true; and the elder or priest did minister it—

2 And they did kneel down with the *a*church, and pray to the Father in the name of Christ, saying:

3 O God, the Eternal Father, we ask thee in the name of thy Son, Jesus Christ, to bless and *a*sanctify this *b*bread to the souls of all those who partake of it; that they may eat in *c*remembrance of the body of thy Son, and witness unto thee, O God, the Eternal Father, that they are willing to take upon them the *d*name of thy Son, and always remember him, and keep his commandments which he hath given them, that they may always have his *e*Spirit to be with them. Amen.

CHAPTER 5

The mode of administering the sacramental wine is set forth.

THE *a*manner of administering the wine—Behold, they took the cup, and said:

2 O God, the Eternal Father, we

2 1*a* 3 Ne. 13:25; 15:11.
2*a* Gen. 4:26;
Ether 4:15.
b Matt. 10:1.
TG Priesthood,
Melchizedek.
c TG Hands, Laying on of.
d 3 Ne. 18:37.
3*a* Acts 19:6.
3 1*a* Alma 6:1.
TG Elder.
b TG Church Organization.

c Mosiah 6:3. TG Priest.
2*a* TG Hands, Laying on of.
3*a* TG Teacher.
b TG Remission of Sins.
4*a* D&C 18:32;
20:39 (39, 60).
TG Priesthood;
Priesthood, History of.
b TG God, Gifts of.
c 1 Ne. 13:37;
Moro. 6:9.
4 1*a* 3 Ne. 18:5 (1–7).
b TG Elder.

c TG Priest.
d D&C 20:76.
2*a* TG Church.
3*a* 1 Sam. 21:4.
b TG Sacrament.
c Luke 22:19; 3 Ne. 18:7; 20:8.
d TG Jesus Christ, Taking the Name of.
e TG God, Spirit of.
5 1*a* 3 Ne. 18:11 (8–11);
D&C 20:78.

[Between A.D. 400 and 421]

ask thee, in the name of thy Son, Jesus Christ, to bless and sanctify this ªwine to the souls of all those who drink of it, that they may do it in ᵇremembrance of the ᶜblood of thy Son, which was shed for them; that they may witness unto thee, O God, the Eternal Father, that they do always remember him, that they may have his ᵈSpirit to be with them. Amen.

CHAPTER 6

Repentant persons are baptized and fellowshipped—Church members who repent are forgiven—Meetings are conducted by the power of the Holy Ghost.

AND now I speak concerning baptism. Behold, elders, priests, and teachers were baptized; and they were not baptized save they brought forth ªfruit meet that they were ᵇworthy of it.

2 Neither did they receive any unto baptism save they came forth with a ªbroken ᵇheart and a contrite spirit, and witnessed unto the church that they truly repented of all their sins.

3 And none were received unto baptism save they ªtook upon them the name of Christ, having a determination to serve him to the end.

4 And after they had been received unto baptism, and were wrought upon and ªcleansed by the power of the Holy Ghost, they were num-

bered among the people of the ᵇchurch of Christ; and their ᶜnames were taken, that they might be remembered and nourished by the good word of God, to keep them in the right way, to keep them continually ᵈwatchful unto prayer, ᵉrelying alone upon the merits of Christ, who was the author and the finisher of their faith.

5 And the ªchurch did meet together ᵇoft, to ᶜfast and to pray, and to speak one with another concerning the welfare of their souls.

6 And they did ªmeet together oft to partake of bread and wine, in ᵇremembrance of the Lord Jesus.

7 And they were strict to observe that there should be ªno iniquity among them; and whoso was found to commit iniquity, and ᵇthree witnesses of the church did condemn them before the ᶜelders, and if they repented not, and ᵈconfessed not, their names were ᵉblotted out, and they were not ᶠnumbered among the people of Christ.

8 But ªas oft as they repented and sought forgiveness, with real ᵇintent, they were ᶜforgiven.

9 And their meetings were ªconducted by the church after the manner of the workings of the Spirit, and by the ᵇpower of the Holy Ghost; for as the power of the Holy Ghost led them whether to preach, or to exhort, or to pray, or to supplicate, or to sing, even so it was done.

2a TG Sacrament.
  b Luke 22: 20; 1 Cor. 11: 25.
  c D&C 27: 2 (2–4).
  d TG Spirituality.
6 1a TG Baptism, Qualifications for.
  b TG Worthiness.
2a TG Poor in Spirit.
  b TG Contrite Heart.
3a 2 Ne. 9: 23. TG Jesus Christ, Taking the Name of.
4a TG Purification.
  b TG Jesus Christ, Head of the Church.
  c D&C 20: 82;

47: 1 (1–4).
  d D&C 20: 53.
    TG Watchfulness.
  e 2 Ne. 31: 19; D&C 3: 20.
5a Acts 1: 14 (13–14).
    TG Church.
  b 3 Ne. 24: 16.
  c 4 Ne. 1: 12; D&C 88: 76.
6a TG Assembly for Worship; Meetings.
  b TG Sacrament.
7a D&C 20: 54.
  b D&C 42: 80 (80–81).
    TG Witnesses.

c Ex. 4: 29; Josh. 20: 4; Alma 6: 1. TG Elder.
  d TG Confession.
  e Ex. 32: 33; D&C 20: 83.
    TG Excommunication.
  f TG Book of Life.
8a Mosiah 26: 30 (30–31).
  b TG Sincerity.
  c TG Forgiveness.
9a D&C 20: 45; 46: 2.
  b 1 Ne. 13: 37; Moro. 3: 4. TG Holy Ghost, Gifts of; Teaching with the Spirit.

[Between A.D. 400 and 421]

CHAPTER 7

*An invitation to enter into the rest of
the Lord—Pray with real intent—
The Spirit of Christ enables men to
know good from evil—Satan persuades men to deny Christ and do
evil—The prophets manifest the coming of Christ—By faith miracles are
wrought and angels minister—Men
should hope for eternal life and cleave
unto charity.*

AND now I, Moroni, write a few of
the words of my father Mormon,
which he spake concerning ᵃfaith,
hope, and charity; for after this
manner did he speak unto the
people, as he taught them in the
ᵇsynagogue which they had built
for the place of worship.

2 And now I, Mormon, speak unto
you, my beloved brethren; and it is
by the ᵃgrace of God the Father,
and our Lord Jesus Christ, and his
holy will, because of the gift of his
ᵇcalling unto me, that I am permitted to speak unto you at this
time.

3 Wherefore, I would speak unto
you that are of the ᵃchurch, that are
the ᵇpeaceable followers of Christ,
and that have obtained a sufficient
ᶜhope by which ye can enter into
the ᵈrest of the Lord, from this time
henceforth until ye shall rest with
him in heaven.

4 And now my brethren, I judge
these things of you because of your
peaceable ᵃwalk with the children
of men.

5 For I remember the word of God
which saith by their ᵃworks ye shall
know them; for if their works be
good, then they are good also.

6 For behold, God hath said a man
being ᵃevil cannot do that which is
good; for if he ᵇoffereth a gift, or
ᶜprayeth unto God, except he shall
do it with real ᵈintent it profiteth
him nothing.

7 For behold, it is not counted
unto him for righteousness.

8 For behold, if a man being ᵃevil
giveth a gift, he doeth it ᵇgrudg-
ingly; wherefore it is counted unto
him the same as if he had retained
the gift; wherefore he is counted
evil before God.

9 And likewise also is it counted
evil unto a man, if he shall pray and
not with ᵃreal intent of heart; yea,
and it profiteth him nothing, for
God receiveth none such.

10 Wherefore, a man being evil
cannot do that which is good;
neither will he give a good gift.

11 For behold, a bitter ᵃfountain
cannot bring forth good water;
neither can a good fountain bring
forth bitter water; wherefore, a
man being a servant of the devil
cannot follow Christ; and if he
ᵇfollow Christ he cannot be a
ᶜservant of the devil.

12 Wherefore, all things which are
ᵃgood cometh of God; and that
which is ᵇevil cometh of the devil;
for the devil is an enemy unto God,
and fighteth against him continually, and inviteth and enticeth

---

7 1a 1 Cor. 13:13 (1–13);
　　Ether 12:3 (3–37);
　　Moro. 8:14; 10:20
　　(20–23).
　b Alma 16:13; 3 Ne.
　　18:32.
2a TG Grace.
　b 3 Ne. 5:13.
　　TG Called of God.
3a TG Jesus Christ,
　　Head of the Church.
　b Acts 13:16; Rom.
　　16:20.
　c Alma 7:16; Ether
　　12:4; D&C 138:14.
　d TG Rest.

4a 1 Jn. 2:6; D&C 19:23.
5a 3 Ne. 14:20 (15–20).
6a Matt. 7:16 (15–18).
　b Lev. 17:8 (8–9);
　　D&C 132:9.
　c Prov. 28:9; Alma
　　34:28. TG Prayer.
　d Lev. 19:5.
　　TG Hypocrisy;
　　Motivations;
　　Sincerity.
8a Prov. 15:8.
　b 1 Chr. 29:9; D&C
　　64:34.
9a James 1:6 (6–7); 5:16;
　　Moro. 10:4.

　　TG Sincerity.
11a Prov. 13:14;
　　James 3:11.
　b Matt. 6:24; 8:19;
　　2 Ne. 31:10 (10–13);
　　D&C 56:2.
　c TG Servant.
12a Gen. 1:31; James
　　1:17 (17–21); 1 Jn.
　　4:1 (1–6); 3 Jn.
　　1:11 (1–14); Ether
　　4:12; D&C 59:17
　　(16–20); Moses 2:31.
　b Isa. 45:7; 2 Cor. 4:4.
　　TG Evil.

[Between A.D. 400 and 421]

to ^{c}sin, and to do that which is evil continually.

13 But behold, that which is of God inviteth and enticeth to do ^{a}good continually; wherefore, every thing which inviteth and ^{b}enticeth to do ^{c}good, and to love God, and to serve him, is ^{d}inspired of God.

14 Wherefore, take heed, my beloved brethren, that ye do not judge that which is ^{a}evil to be of God, or that which is good and of God to be of the devil.

15 For behold, my brethren, it is given unto you to ^{a}judge, that ye may know good from evil; and the way to judge is as plain, that ye may know with a perfect knowledge, as the daylight is from the dark night.

16 For behold, the ^{a}Spirit of Christ is given to every ^{b}man, that he may ^{c}know good from evil; wherefore, I show unto you the way to judge; for every thing which inviteth to do good, and to persuade to believe in Christ, is sent forth by the power and gift of Christ; wherefore ye may know with a perfect knowledge it is of God.

17 But whatsoever thing persuadeth men to do ^{a}evil, and believe not in Christ, and deny him, and serve not God, then ye may know with a perfect knowledge it is of the devil; for after this manner doth the devil work, for he persuadeth no man to do good, no, not one; neither do his angels; neither do they who subject themselves unto him.

18 And now, my brethren, seeing that ye know the ^{a}light by which ye may judge, which light is the light of Christ, see that ye do not judge wrongfully; for with that same ^{b}judgment which ye judge ye shall also be judged.

19 Wherefore, I beseech of you, brethren, that ye should search diligently in the ^{a}light of Christ that ye may know good from evil; and if ye will lay hold upon every good thing, and condemn it not, ye certainly will be a ^{b}child of Christ.

20 And now, my brethren, how is it possible that ye can lay hold upon every good thing?

21 And now I come to that faith, of which I said I would speak; and I will tell you the way whereby ye may lay hold on every good thing.

22 For behold, God ^{a}knowing all things, being from ^{b}everlasting to everlasting, behold, he sent ^{c}angels to minister unto the children of men, to make manifest concerning the coming of Christ; and in Christ there should come every good thing.

23 And God also declared unto prophets, by his own mouth, that Christ should come.

24 And behold, there were divers ways that he did manifest things unto the children of men, which were good; and all things which are good cometh of Christ; otherwise men were ^{a}fallen, and there could no good thing come unto them.

12c Alma 5: 40 (39–42);
     Hel. 6: 30. TG Sin.
13a D&C 35: 12; 84: 47
     (47–51).
  b 2 Ne. 33: 4; Ether
     8: 26.
  c TG Benevolence.
  d TG Inspiration.
14a Isa. 5: 20; 2 Ne. 15:
     20; D&C 64: 16;
     121: 16.
15a Ezek. 44: 24.
     TG Discernment,
     Spiritual.
16a TG Conscience; God,
     Spirit of; Light of
     Christ.

  b TG Mortality.
  c Gen. 3: 5; Amos 5: 14
     (14–15); Matt. 12: 33
     (33–37); 2 Ne. 2: 5
     (5, 18, 26); Mosiah
     16: 3; Alma 29: 5;
     Hel. 14: 31; Ether
     4: 12 (11–12).
17a TG Sin.
18a Mosiah 16: 9; Ether
     3: 14; D&C 50: 24;
     88: 13 (7–13).
     TG Light of Christ.
  b Luke 6: 37.
19a D&C 84: 45; 88: 7
     (6–13).

  b Mosiah 15: 10; 27: 25.
     TG Sons and
     Daughters of God.
22a TG God,
     Foreknowledge of;
     God, Omniscience of.
  b 2 Ne. 19: 6; 26: 12;
     Mosiah 3: 5; Alma
     11: 39 (38–39, 44);
     Moro. 8: 18. TG God,
     Eternal Nature of.
  c Acts 10: 3 (3, 22);
     2 Ne. 10: 3; 11: 3;
     Jacob 7: 5.
24a 2 Ne. 2: 5.

[Between A.D. 400 and 421]

25 Wherefore, by the ministering of [a]angels, and by every word which proceeded forth out of the mouth of God, men began to exercise faith in Christ; and thus by faith, they did lay hold upon every good thing; and thus it was until the coming of Christ.

26 And after that he came men also were [a]saved by faith in his name; and by faith, they become the [b]sons of God. And as surely as Christ liveth he spake these words unto our fathers, saying: [c]Whatsoever thing ye shall ask the Father in my name, which is good, in faith believing that ye shall receive, behold, it shall be done unto you.

27 Wherefore, my beloved brethren, have [a]miracles ceased because Christ hath ascended into heaven, and hath sat down on the right hand of God, to [b]claim of the Father his rights of mercy which he hath upon the children of men?

28 For he hath answered the ends of the law, and he claimeth all those who have faith in him; and they who have faith in him will [a]cleave unto every good thing; wherefore he [b]advocateth the cause of the children of men; and he dwelleth eternally in the heavens.

29 And because he hath done this, my beloved brethren, have miracles ceased? Behold I say unto you, Nay; neither have [a]angels ceased to minister unto the children of men.

30 For behold, they are subject unto him, to minister according to the word of his command, showing themselves unto them of strong faith and a firm mind in every form of [a]godliness.

31 And the office of their ministry is to call men unto repentance, and to fulfil and to do the work of the covenants of the Father, which he hath made unto the children of men, to prepare the way among the children of men, by declaring the word of Christ unto the [a]chosen vessels of the Lord, that they may bear testimony of him.

32 And by so doing, the Lord God prepareth the way that the [a]residue of men may have [b]faith in Christ, that the Holy Ghost may have place in their hearts, according to the power thereof; and after this manner bringeth to pass the Father, the covenants which he hath made unto the children of men.

33 And Christ hath said: [a]If ye will have [b]faith in me ye shall have power to do whatsoever thing is [c]expedient in me.

34 And he hath said: [a]Repent all ye ends of the earth, and come unto me, and be baptized in my name, and have faith in me, that ye may be saved.

35 And now, my beloved brethren, if this be the case that these things are true which I have spoken unto you, and God will show unto you, with [a]power and great glory at the last [b]day, that they are true, and if they are true has the day of miracles ceased?

36 Or have angels ceased to appear unto the children of men? Or has he [a]withheld the power of the Holy Ghost from them? Or will he, so

25a Alma 12: 29 (28–30); Moses 5: 58.
26a D&C 3: 20.
  b TG Sons and Daughters of God.
  c 3 Ne. 18: 20. TG Prayer.
27a TG Miracle.
  b Isa. 53: 12 (11–12); 2 Ne. 2: 9.
28a TG Motivations.
  b 1 Jn. 2: 1; 2 Ne. 2: 9; Mosiah 14: 12; 15: 8; 3 Ne. 18: 35.

TG Jesus Christ, Relationships with the Father.
29a Judg. 13: 3; Luke 1: 26; Acts 5: 19 (19–20). TG Angels; Miracle.
30a TG Godliness.
31a D&C 20: 10.
32a Acts 15: 17; Moses 7: 28.
  b Acts 16: 5; D&C 46: 14.

33a Moro. 10: 23.
  b Gal. 2: 16. TG Faith.
  c D&C 88: 64 (64–65).
34a 3 Ne. 27: 20; Ether 4: 18.
35a 2 Ne. 33: 11; Ether 5: 4 (4–6).
  b Morm. 9: 15; D&C 35: 8.
36a 1 Ne. 10: 17 (17–19); Moro. 10: 7 (4–5, 7, 19).

[Between A.D. 400 and 421]

long as time shall last, or the earth shall stand, or there shall be one man upon the face thereof to be saved?

37 Behold I say unto you, Nay; for it is by faith that ᵃmiracles are wrought; and it is by faith that angels appear and minister unto men; wherefore, if these things have ceased wo be unto the children of men, for it is because of ᵇunbelief, and all is vain.

38 For no man can be saved, according to the words of Christ, save they shall have faith in his name; wherefore, if these things have ceased, then has faith ceased also; and awful is the state of man, for they are as though there had been no redemption made.

39 But behold, my beloved brethren, I judge better things of you, for I judge that ye have faith in Christ because of your meekness; for if ye have not faith in him then ye are not ᵃfit to be numbered among the people of his church.

40 And again, my beloved brethren, I would speak unto you concerning ᵃhope. How is it that ye can attain unto faith, save ye shall have hope?

41 And what is it that ye shall ᵃhope for? Behold I say unto you that ye shall have ᵇhope through the atonement of Christ and the power of his resurrection, to be raised unto life ᶜeternal, and this because of your faith in him according to the promise.

42 Wherefore, if a man have ᵃfaith he ᵇmust needs have hope; for without faith there cannot be any hope.

43 And again, behold I say unto you that he cannot have faith and hope, save he shall be ᵃmeek, and lowly of heart.

44 If so, his ᵃfaith and hope is vain, for none is ᵇacceptable before God, save the ᶜmeek and lowly in heart; and if a man be meek and lowly in heart, and ᵈconfesses by the power of the Holy Ghost that Jesus is the Christ, he must needs have charity; for if he have not charity he is nothing; wherefore he must needs have charity.

45 And ᵃcharity suffereth long, and is ᵇkind, and ᶜenvieth not, and is not puffed up, seeketh not her own, is not easily ᵈprovoked, thinketh no evil, and rejoiceth not in iniquity but rejoiceth in the truth, beareth all things, believeth all things, hopeth all things, endureth all things.

46 Wherefore, my beloved brethren, if ye have not charity, ye are nothing, for charity never faileth. Wherefore, cleave unto charity, which is the greatest of all, for all things must fail—

47 But ᵃcharity is the pure ᵇlove of Christ, and it endureth ᶜforever; and whoso is found possessed of it at the last day, it shall be well with him.

48 Wherefore, my beloved brethren, ᵃpray unto the Father with all the energy of heart, that ye may be filled with this love, which he hath bestowed upon all who are true ᵇfollowers of his Son, Jesus Christ; that ye may become the sons of God; that when he shall appear we

37a Matt. 13: 58; Morm.
  8: 26; 9: 20; Ether
  12: 12 (12–18).
  b Moro. 10: 19 (19–27).
39a TG Worthiness.
40a Heb. 11: 1; Ether
  12: 4. TG Hope.
41a D&C 138: 14.
  b Zech. 9: 12 (11–12);
  Titus 1: 2; Jacob
  2: 19; Alma 46: 39.
  c TG Eternal Life.
42a TG Faith.

  b Moro. 10: 20.
43a TG Humility.
44a 1 Cor. 13: 13 (1–13);
  Alma 7: 24; Ether
  12: 31 (28–35).
  b Lev. 10: 19.
  c TG Meekness.
  d Luke 12: 8 (8–9).
  TG Holy Ghost, Gifts
  of; Testimony.
45a 1 Cor. 13: 4 (1–13).
  b TG Kindness.
  c TG Envy.

  d TG Provoking.
47a Rom. 13: 10;
  2 Ne. 26: 30.
  TG Charity.
  b Josh. 22: 5; Ether
  12: 34; Moro. 7: 48.
  TG Love.
  c TG Eternity.
48a TG Communication;
  Prayer.
  b TG Jesus Christ,
  Exemplar.

[Between A.D. 400 and 421]

shall *c*be like him, for we shall see him as he is; that we may have this hope; that we may be *d*purified even as he is pure. Amen.

CHAPTER 8

Infant baptism is an evil abomination—Little children are alive in Christ because of the atonement—Faith, repentance, meekness and lowliness of heart, receiving the Holy Ghost, and enduring to the end lead to salvation.

AN epistle of my *a*father Mormon, written to me, Moroni; and it was written unto me soon after my calling to the ministry. And on this wise did he write unto me, saying:

2 My beloved son, Moroni, I rejoice exceedingly that your Lord Jesus Christ hath been mindful of you, and hath called you to his ministry, and to his holy work.

3 I am mindful of you always in my prayers, continually praying unto God the Father in the name of his Holy Child, Jesus, that he, through his infinite *a*goodness and *b*grace, will keep you through the endurance of faith on his name to the end.

4 And now, my son, I speak unto you concerning that which grieveth me exceedingly; for it grieveth me that there should *a*disputations rise among you.

5 For, if I have learned the truth, there have been disputations among you concerning the baptism of your little children.

6 And now, my son, I desire that ye should labor diligently, that this gross error should be removed from among you; for, for this intent I have written this epistle.

7 For immediately after I had learned these things of you I inquired of the Lord concerning the matter. And the *a*word of the Lord came to me by the power of the Holy Ghost, saying:

8 *a*Listen to the words of Christ, your Redeemer, your Lord and your God. Behold, I came into the world not to call the righteous but sinners to repentance; the *b*whole need no physician, but they that are sick; wherefore, little *c*children are *d*whole, for they are not capable of committing *e*sin; wherefore the curse of *f*Adam is taken from them in me, that it hath no power over them; and the law of *g*circumcision is done away in me.

9 And after this manner did the Holy Ghost manifest the word of God unto me; wherefore, my beloved son, I know that it is solemn *a*mockery before God, that ye should baptize little children.

10 Behold I say unto you that this thing shall ye teach—repentance and baptism unto those who are *a*accountable and capable of committing sin; yea, teach parents that they must repent and be baptized, and humble themselves as their little *b*children, and they shall all be saved with their little children.

11 And their little *a*children need no repentance, neither baptism. Behold, baptism is unto repentance to the fulfilling the commandments unto the *b*remission of sins.

12 But little *a*children are alive in Christ, even from the foundation of the world; if not so, God is a partial

48c 1 Jn. 3: 2 (1–3);
    3 Ne. 27: 27.
  d 3 Ne. 19: 28 (28–29).
    TG Cleanliness;
    Purity.
8 1a W of M 1: 1.
  3a Ex. 34: 6 (5–7);
    Mosiah 4: 11.
  b TG Grace.
  4a TG Disputations.
  7a TG Word of the Lord.
  8a D&C 15: 1.

  b Mark 2: 17.
  c Mark 10: 14 (13–16).
    TG Conceived in Sin.
  d Mosiah 3: 16; D&C
    29: 46; 74: 7.
  e TG Sin.
  f Mosiah 3: 26;
    Morm. 9: 12.
  g Gen. 17: 11 (10–27);
    Acts 15: 24.
    TG Circumcision.
  9a 2 Ne. 31: 13.

10a TG Accountability.
  b TG Family, Children,
    Responsibilities
    toward; Family,
    Love within.
11a TG Baptism,
    Qualifications for;
    Children.
  b TG Remission of Sins.
12a D&C 29: 46; 93: 38.

[Between A.D. 400 and 421]

God, and also a changeable God, and a *b*respecter to persons; for how many little children have died without baptism!

13 Wherefore, if little children could not be saved without baptism, these must have gone to an endless hell.

14 Behold I say unto you, that he that supposeth that little children need baptism is in the gall of bitterness and in the bonds of iniquity; for he hath neither *a*faith, hope, nor charity; wherefore, should he be cut off while in the thought, he must go down to hell.

15 For awful is the wickedness to suppose that God saveth one child because of baptism, and the other must perish because he hath no baptism.

16 Wo be unto them that shall pervert the ways of the Lord after this manner, for they shall perish except they repent. Behold, I speak with boldness, having *a*authority from God; and I fear not what man can do; for *b*perfect *c*love *d*casteth out all fear.

17 And I am filled with *a*charity, which is everlasting love; wherefore, all children are alike unto me; wherefore, I love little children with a perfect love; and they are all alike and *b*partakers of salvation.

18 For I know that God is not a partial God, neither a changeable being; but he is *a*unchangeable from *b*all eternity to all eternity.

19 Little *a*children cannot repent; wherefore, it is awful wickedness to deny the pure mercies of God unto

them, for they are all alive in him because of his *b*mercy.

20 And he that saith that little children need baptism denieth the mercies of Christ, and setteth at naught the *a*atonement of him and the power of his redemption.

21 Wo unto such, for they are in danger of death, *a*hell, and an *b*endless torment. I speak it boldly; God hath commanded me. Listen unto them and give heed, or they stand against you at the *c*judgment-seat of Christ.

22 For behold that all little children are *a*alive in Christ, and also all they that are without the *b*law. For the power of *c*redemption cometh on all them that have *d*no law; wherefore, he that is not condemned, or he that is under no condemnation, cannot repent; and unto such baptism availeth nothing—

23 But it is mockery before God, denying the mercies of Christ, and the power of his Holy Spirit, and putting trust in *a*dead works.

24 Behold, my son, this thing ought not to be; for *a*repentance is unto them that are under condemnation and under the curse of a broken law.

25 And the first fruits of *a*repentance is *b*baptism; and baptism cometh by faith unto the fulfilling the commandments; and the fulfilling the commandments bringeth *c*remission of sins;

26 And the remission of sins bringeth *a*meekness, and lowliness of heart; and because of meekness and lowliness of heart cometh the visita-

12*b* Eph. 6: 9; D&C 38: 16.
14*a* 1 Cor. 13: 13 (1–13);
    Ether 12: 3 (3–37);
    Moro. 7: 1; 10: 20
    (20–23).
16*a* TG Authority.
    b TG Perfection.
    c TG Love.
    d 1 Jn. 4: 18.
17*a* TG Charity.
    b Mosiah 3: 16 (16–19).
18*a* Alma 7: 20; Morm.
    9: 9. TG God,

Perfection of.
    b Moro. 7: 22.
19*a* Luke 18: 16 (15–17).
    b TG God, Mercy of.
20*a* TG Jesus Christ,
    Atonement through;
    Salvation, Plan of.
21*a* TG Hell.
    b Jacob 6: 10; Mosiah
    28: 3; D&C 19: 12
    (10–12).
    c TG Jesus Christ, Judge.
22*a* TG Salvation of Little

Children.
    b Acts 17: 30.
    c TG Redemption.
    d TG Accountability.
23*a* D&C 22: 2.
24*a* TG Repentance.
25*a* TG Baptism,
    Qualifications for.
    b Moses 6: 60.
    c D&C 76: 52.
    TG Remission of Sins.
26*a* TG Meekness.

[Between A.D. 400 and 421]

tion of the [b]Holy Ghost, which [c]Comforter [d]filleth with hope and perfect [e]love, which love endureth by [f]diligence unto [g]prayer, until the end shall come, when all the [h]saints shall dwell with God.

27 Behold, my son, I will write unto you again if I go not out soon against the Lamanites. Behold, the [a]pride of this nation, or the people of the Nephites, hath proven their destruction except they should repent.

28 Pray for them, my son, that repentance may come unto them. But behold, I fear lest the Spirit hath [a]ceased [b]striving with them; and in this part of the land they are also seeking to put down all power and authority which cometh from God; and they are [c]denying the Holy Ghost.

29 And after rejecting so great a knowledge, my son, they must perish soon, unto the fulfilling of the prophecies which were spoken by the prophets, as well as the words of our Savior himself.

30 Farewell, my son, until I shall write unto you, or shall meet you again. Amen.

CHAPTER 9

The second epistle of Mormon to his son Moroni.

Both the Nephites and the Lamanites are depraved and degenerate—They torture and murder each other—Mormon prays that grace and goodness may rest upon Moroni forever.

My beloved son, I write unto you again that ye may know that I am yet alive; but I write somewhat of that which is grievous.

2 For behold, I have had a sore battle with the Lamanites, in which we did not conquer; and Archeantus has fallen by the sword, and also Luram and Emron; yea, and we have lost a great number of our choice men.

3 And now behold, my son, I fear lest the Lamanites shall destroy this people; for they do not repent, and Satan stirreth them up continually to [a]anger one with another.

4 Behold, I am laboring with them continually; and when I speak the word of God with [a]sharpness they tremble and anger against me; and when I use no sharpness they [b]harden their hearts against it; wherefore, I fear lest the Spirit of the Lord hath ceased [c]striving with them.

5 For so exceedingly do they anger that it seemeth me that they have no fear of death; and they have lost their love, one towards another; and they [a]thirst after blood and revenge continually.

6 And now, my beloved son, notwithstanding their hardness, let us labor [a]diligently; for if we should cease to [b]labor, we should be brought under condemnation; for we have a labor to perform whilst in this tabernacle of clay, that we may conquer the enemy of all righteousness, and rest our souls in the kingdom of God.

7 And now I write somewhat concerning the sufferings of this people.

26b TG Holy Ghost, Baptism of.
  c TG Holy Ghost, Comforter; Holy Ghost, Mission of.
  d 1 Ne. 11: 22 (22–25). TG Hope.
  e 1 Pet. 1: 22.
  f TG Diligence; Perseverance.
  g TG Prayer.
  h TG Saints.
27a D&C 38: 39.

  TG Pride.
28a TG Holy Ghost, Loss of.
  b Morm. 5: 16; Moro. 9: 4.
  c Alma 39: 6. TG Holy Ghost, Unpardonable Sin against.
9 3a TG Anger.
4a 2 Ne. 1: 26 (26–27); W of M 1: 17; D&C 121: 43 (41–43).
  b TG Hardheartedness.

  c Moro. 8: 28; D&C 1: 33.
5a Morm. 4: 11 (11–12).
6a TG Dedication; Diligence; Perseverance.
  b 1 Sam. 8: 9; 2 Cor. 5: 9; Jacob 1: 19; Enos 1: 20. TG Duty; Priesthood, Magnifying Callings within.

[Between A.D. 400 and 421]

For according to the knowledge which I have received from Amoron, behold, the Lamanites have many prisoners, which they took from the tower of Sherrizah; and there were men, women, and children.

8 And the husbands and fathers of those women and children they have slain; and they feed the women upon the [a]flesh of their husbands, and the children upon the flesh of their fathers; and no water, save a little, do they give unto them.

9 And notwithstanding this great [a]abomination of the Lamanites, it doth not exceed that of our people in Moriantum. For behold, many of the daughters of the Lamanites have they taken prisoners; and after [b]depriving them of that which was most dear and precious above all things, which is [c]chastity and [d]virtue—

10 And after they had done this thing, they did murder them in a most [a]cruel manner, torturing their bodies even unto death; and after they have done this, they devour their flesh like unto wild beasts, because of the hardness of their hearts; and they do it for a token of bravery.

11 O my beloved son, how can a people like this, that are without civilization—

12 (And only a few years have passed away, and they were a civil and a delightsome people)

13 But O my son, how can a people like this, whose [a]delight is in so much abomination—

14 How can we expect that God will [a]stay his hand in judgment against us?

15 Behold, my heart cries: Wo unto this people. Come out in judgment, O God, and hide their sins, and wickedness, and abominations from before thy face!

16 And again, my son, there are many [a]widows and their daughters who remain in Sherrizah; and that part of the provisions which the Lamanites did not carry away, behold, the army of Zenephi has carried away, and left them to wander whithersoever they can for food; and many old women do faint by the way and die.

17 And the army which is with me is weak; and the armies of the Lamanites are betwixt Sherrizah and me; and as many as have fled to the army of [a]Aaron have fallen victims to their awful brutality.

18 O the depravity of my people! They are without [a]order and without mercy. Behold, I am but a man, and I have but the [b]strength of a man, and I cannot any longer enforce my commands.

19 And they have become strong in their perversion; and they are alike brutal, sparing none, neither old nor young; and they delight in everything save that which is good; and the suffering of our women and our children upon all the face of this land doth exceed everything; yea, tongue cannot tell, neither can it be written.

20 And now, my son, I dwell no longer upon this horrible scene. Behold, thou knowest the wickedness of this people; thou knowest that they are without principle, and past feeling; and their wickedness doth [a]exceed that of the Lamanites.

21 Behold, my son, I cannot recommend them unto God lest he should smite me.

22 But behold, my son, I recommend thee unto God, and I trust in Christ that thou wilt be saved; and I [a]pray unto God that he will [b]spare thy life, to witness the return of his

8a Lev. 26:29; 1 Ne. 21:26.
9a TG Body, Sanctity of.
  b TG Sensuality.
  c TG Chastity.
  d TG Virtue.
10a TG Cruelty.
13a 2 Ne. 9:9 (8–9); Jacob 3:11.
14a 2 Sam. 24:16; Alma 10:23.
16a Mosiah 21:10 (10, 17). TG Widows.
17a Morm. 2:9.
18a TG Order.
  b TG Strength.
20a Hel. 6:34 (18–35).
22a W of M 1:8.
  b Morm. 8:3.

people unto him, or their utter destruction; for I know that they must perish except they ᶜrepent and return unto him.

23 And if they perish it will be like unto the ᵃJaredites, because of the wilfulness of their hearts, ᵇseeking for blood and ᶜrevenge.

24 And if it so be that they perish, we know that many of our brethren have ᵃdeserted over unto the Lamanites, and many more will also desert over unto them; wherefore, write somewhat a few things, if thou art spared and I shall perish and not see thee; but I trust that I may see thee soon; for I have sacred records that I would ᵇdeliver up unto thee.

25 My son, be faithful in Christ; and may not the things which I have written grieve thee, to weigh thee down unto ᵃdeath; but may Christ lift thee up, and may his sufferings and death, and the showing his body unto our fathers, and his mercy and ᵇlong-suffering, and the hope of his glory and of eternal life, rest in your ᶜmind forever.

26 And may the grace of God the Father, whose throne is high in the heavens, and our Lord Jesus Christ, who sitteth on the ᵃright hand of his power, until all things shall become subject unto him, be, and abide with you forever. Amen.

CHAPTER 10

A testimony of the Book of Mormon comes by the power of the Holy Ghost—The gifts of the Spirit are dispensed to the faithful—Spiritual gifts always accompany faith—Moroni's words speak from the dust—Come unto Christ, be perfected in him, and sanctify your souls.

Now I, Moroni, write somewhat as seemeth me good; and I write unto my brethren, the ᵃLamanites; and I would that they should know that *more than ᵇfour hundred and twenty years have passed away since the sign was given of the coming of Christ.

2 And I ᵃseal up ᵇthese records, after I have spoken a few words by way of exhortation unto you.

3 Behold, I would exhort you that when ye shall read these things, if it be wisdom in God that ye should read them, that ye would remember how ᵃmerciful the Lord hath been unto the children of men, from the creation of Adam even down until the time that ye shall receive these things, and ᵇponder it in your ᶜhearts.

4 And when ye shall receive these things, I would exhort you that ye would ᵃask God, the Eternal Father, in the name of Christ, if these things are not ᵇtrue; and if ye shall ask with a ᶜsincere heart, with ᵈreal intent, having ᵉfaith in Christ, he will ᶠmanifest the ᵍtruth of it unto you, by the power of the Holy Ghost.

5 And by the power of the Holy Ghost ye may ᵃknow the ᵇtruth of all things.

6 And whatsoever thing is good is

22c 1 Sam. 7: 3; Hel.
    13: 11; 3 Ne. 10: 6
    (5–7); 24: 7.
23a Jacob 5: 44.
  b Morm. 4: 11 (11–12).
  c Ether 15: 22 (15–31).
24a Alma 45: 14.
  b Morm. 6: 6; 8: 1.
25a TG Jesus Christ,
    Death of.
  b TG Forbearance.
  c TG Mind.
26a TG Jesus Christ,
    Relationships with
    the Father.

10 1a D&C 10: 48.
  b Morm. 8: 5; Moro. 1: 1.
2a Morm. 5: 12; 8: 4
    (4, 13–14).
  TG Scriptures,
    Preservation of; Seal.
  b Morm. 6: 6.
3a Gen. 19: 16.
  b Deut. 11: 18.
  TG Meditation; Study.
  c Deut. 6: 6.
4a TG Prayer.
  b 1 Ne. 13: 39; 14: 30;
    Mosiah 1: 6; Alma
    3: 12; Ether 4: 11
    (6–11); 5: 3 (1–4).

  TG Book of Mormon.
  c TG Honesty; Sincerity.
  d James 1: 6 (6–7);
    Moro. 7: 9.
  e TG Faith.
  f TG Revelation.
  g Ps. 145: 18.
  TG Guidance, Divine;
    Truth.
5a D&C 35: 19.
  TG Discernment,
    Spiritual; Holy Ghost,
    Source of Testimony.
  b John 8: 32.

[*About A.D. 421]

just and true; wherefore, nothing that is good denieth the Christ, but acknowledgeth that he is.

7 And ye may [a]know that he is, by the power of the Holy Ghost; wherefore I would exhort you that ye deny not the power of God; for he worketh by power, [b]according to the faith of the children of men, the same today and tomorrow, and forever.

8 And again, I exhort you, my brethren, that ye deny not the [a]gifts of God, for they are many; and they come from the same God. And there are [b]different ways that these gifts are administered; but it is the same God who worketh all in all; and they are given by the manifestations of the [c]Spirit of God unto men, to profit them.

9 [a]For behold, to one is given by the Spirit of God, that he may [b]teach the word of wisdom;

10 And to another, that he may [a]teach the word of [b]knowledge by the same Spirit;

11 And to another, exceedingly great [a]faith; and to another, the gifts of [b]healing by the same Spirit;

12 And again, to another, that he may work mighty [a]miracles;

13 And again, to another, that he may prophesy concerning all things;

14 And again, to another, the beholding of angels and ministering spirits;

15 And again, to another, all kinds of tongues;

16 And again, to another, the interpretation of [a]languages and of divers kinds of tongues.

17 And all these gifts come by the Spirit of Christ; and they come unto every man severally, according as he will.

18 And I would exhort you, my beloved brethren, that ye remember that [a]every good [b]gift cometh of Christ.

19 And I would exhort you, my beloved brethren, that ye remember that he is the [a]same yesterday, today, and forever, and that all these gifts of which I have spoken, which are spiritual, never will be done away, even as long as the world shall stand, only according to the [b]unbelief of the children of men.

20 Wherefore, there must be [a]faith; and if there must be faith there must also be hope; and if there must be hope there must also be charity.

21 And except ye have [a]charity ye can in nowise be saved in the kingdom of God; neither can ye be saved in the kingdom of God if ye have not faith; neither can ye if ye have no hope.

22 And if ye have no hope ye must needs be in [a]despair; and despair cometh because of iniquity.

23 And Christ truly said unto our fathers: [a]If ye have faith ye can do all things which are expedient unto me.

24 And now I speak unto all the ends of the earth—that if the day cometh that the power and gifts of God shall be done away among you, it shall be [a]because of [b]unbelief.

25 And wo be unto the children of men if this be the case; for there shall be [a]none that doeth good among you, no not one. For if there

---

7a TG Testimony.
  b 1 Ne. 10:17 (17–19);
    Moro. 7:36.
8a TG God, Gifts of;
    Holy Ghost, Gifts of.
  b D&C 46:15.
  c TG God, Spirit of.
9a 1 Cor. 12:8 (8–11);
    D&C 46:12 (8–30).
  b Ex. 35:34; D&C
    38:23; 88:77 (77–79,
    118); 107:85 (85–89).

10a TG Education.
  b 1 Cor. 12:8.
    TG Learning.
11a TG Faith.
  b TG Healing.
12a TG Miracle.
16a TG Language.
18a James 1:17.
  b TG Talents.
19a Heb. 13:8.
  b Moro. 7:37.
    TG Doubt.
20a 1 Cor. 13:13 (1–13);

Ether 12:3 (3–37);
  Moro. 7:1, 42 (42–44);
  8:14.
21a TG Charity.
22a TG Despair.
23a Moro. 7:33.
24a Moro. 7:37.
  b TG Doubt; Unbelief,
    Unbelievers.
25a Ps. 14:3; Rom.
  3:12.

[About A.D. 421]

be one among you that doeth good, he shall work by the power and gifts of God.

26 And wo unto them who shall do these things away and die, for they [a]die in their [b]sins, and they cannot be saved in the kingdom of God; and I speak it according to the words of Christ; and I lie not.

27 And I exhort you to remember these things; for the time speedily cometh that ye shall know that I lie not, for ye shall see me at the bar of God; and the Lord God will say unto you: Did I not declare my [a]words unto you, which were written by this man, like as one [b]crying from the dead, yea, even as one speaking out of the [c]dust?

28 I declare these things unto the fulfilling of the prophecies. And behold, they shall proceed forth out of the mouth of the everlasting God; and his word shall [a]hiss forth from generation to generation.

29 And God shall show unto you, that that which I have written is [a]true.

30 And again I would exhort you that ye would [a]come unto Christ, and lay hold upon every good [b]gift, and [c]touch not the evil gift, nor the [d]unclean thing.

31 And [a]awake, and arise from the dust, O Jerusalem; yea, and put on thy beautiful garments, O daughter of [b]Zion; and [c]strengthen thy [d]stakes and enlarge thy borders forever, that thou mayest [e]no more be confounded, that the covenants of the Eternal Father which he hath made unto thee, O house of Israel, may be fulfilled.

32 Yea, [a]come unto Christ, and be [b]perfected in him, and [c]deny yourselves of all ungodliness; and if ye shall deny yourselves of all ungodliness, and [d]love God with all your might, mind and strength, then is his grace sufficient for you, that by his grace ye may be [e]perfect in Christ; and if by the grace of God ye are perfect in Christ, ye can in nowise deny the power of God.

33 And again, if ye by the grace of God are perfect in Christ, and deny not his power, then are ye [a]sanctified in Christ by the grace of God, through the shedding of the [b]blood of Christ, which is in the covenant of the Father unto the remission of your [c]sins, that ye become [d]holy, without spot.

34 And now I bid unto all, farewell. I soon go to [a]rest in the [b]paradise of God, until my [c]spirit and body shall again [d]reunite, and I am brought forth triumphant through the [e]air, to meet you before the [f]pleasing bar of the great [g]Jehovah, the Eternal [h]Judge of both quick and dead. Amen.

26a Ezek. 18: 26; 1 Ne. 15: 33 (32–33); Mosiah 15: 26.
  b TG John 8: 21 (21–24).
27a Isa. 51: 16; 2 Ne. 33: 10 (10–11); D&C 1: 24.
  b 2 Ne. 3: 19 (19–20); 27: 13; 33: 13 (13–15); Morm. 9: 30.
  c Isa. 29: 4.
28a 2 Ne. 29: 2.
29a TG Book of Mormon.
30a 1 Ne. 6: 4; Morm. 9: 27; Ether 5: 5.
  b TG Talents.
  c 2 Ne. 18: 19.
  d TG Uncleanness.
31a Isa. 52: 1 (1–2).
  TG Israel, Restoration of.
  b TG Zion.
  c Isa. 54: 2. TG Priesthood, Power of.
  d TG Stakes.
  e Ether 13: 8.
32a Rev. 22: 17 (17–21). TG Teachable.
  b Gal. 3: 24; Philip. 3: 15 (14–15). TG Man, New, Spiritually Reborn; Worthiness.
  c Rom. 12: 1 (1–3). TG Perseverance.
  d Deut. 11: 1; Mosiah 2: 4; D&C 20: 19; 59: 5 (5–6). TG Commitment; Dedication.
  e Rom. 6: 6 (1–7). TG Perfection.
33a TG Sanctification.
  b TG Jesus Christ, Atonement through.
  c Ex. 34: 7.
  d TG Holiness.
34a TG Rest.
  b TG Paradise.
  c TG Spirit Body.
  d TG Resurrection.
  e 1 Thes. 4: 17.
  f Jacob 6: 13.
  g TG Jesus Christ—Jehovah.
  h TG Jesus Christ, Judge.

[About A.D. 421]

THE END

PRONOUNCING GUIDE

KEY TO SYMBOLS USED

a	about		ĭ	it, him, mirror
ă	ask, pat, map		ī	idle, fine, deny
ā	able, bake, way		ō	over, bone, know
ä	alms, father, call		ou	about
ĕ	ebb, met, second		u	jump
ē	eat, mete, me		ū	rule, boot, two
er	permit			

Aaron ĕr'an
Abel ā'bul
Abinadi a-bĭn'a-dī
Abinadom a-bĭn'a-dum
Abish ā'bĭsh
Ablom ăb'lum
Abraham ā'bra-hăm
Adam ăd'um
Agosh ā'gäsh
Aha ā'hä
Ahah ā'hä
Ahaz ā'häz
Aiath ī'uth
Akish ā'kĭsh
Alma ăl'ma
Alpha ăl'fa
Amaleki a-măl'a-kī
Amalekite a-măl'a-kīt
Amalickiah a-măl'a-kī'a
Amalickiahite a-măl'a-kī'a-īt
Amaron a-mā'rän
Amgid ăm'gĭd
Aminadab a-mĭn'a-dăb
Aminadi a-mĭn'a-dī
Amlici ăm'lĭ-sī
Amlicite ăm'li-sīt
Ammaron ăm'a-rän
Ammon ăm'un
Ammonite ăm'a-nīt
Ammonihah ăm-a-nī'hä
Ammonihahite ăm-a-nī'hä-īt
Ammoron ăm'ōr-än
Amnah ăm'nä
Amnigaddah ăm-nĭ-găd'ä
Amnihu ăm-nī'hū
Amnor ăm'nōr

Amoron a-mōr'än
Amos ā'mus
Amoz ā'muz
Amulek ăm'yū-lĕk
Amulon ăm'yū-län
Amulonites ăm'ya-län'īts
Anathoth ăn'a-tōth
Angola ăn-gō'la
Ani-Anti ăn'ī—ăn'tī
Anti-Nephi-Lehi ăn'tī—nē'fī—lē'hī
Anti-Nephi-Lehies ăn'tī—nē'fī—lē'hīz
Antiomno ăn-tē-äm'nō
Antion ăn'tē-än
Antionah ăn-tē-än'a
Antionum ăn-tē-ō'num
Antiparah ăn-tĭ-pär'a
Antipas ăn'tĭ-päs
Antipus ăn'tĭ-pus
Antum ăn'tum
Archeantus är-kē-ăn'tus
Arpad är'păd
Assyria a-sĭr'ē-a

Babylon băb'ĭ-län
Bashan bā'shän
Benjamin bĕn'ja-mĭn
Bethabara bĕth-ăb'a-ra
Boaz bō'äz
Bountiful boun'tĭ-ful

Cain kān
Calno kăl'nō
Carchemish kär-kĕm'ish
Cezoram sē-zōr'um

Chaldeans   kăl-dē′unz
Chaldees   kăl-dēz′
Chemish   kĕm′ĭsh
Cherubim   chĕr′a-bĭm
Cohor   kō′hōr
Com   kōm
Comnor   kōm′nōr
Corianton   kōr-ē-ăn′tun
Coriantor   kōr-ē-ăn′tōr
Coriantum   kōr-ē-ăn′tum
Coriantumr   kōr-ē-ăn′ta-mer
Corihor   kōr′ĭ-hōr
Corom   kōr′um
Cumeni   kū′ma-nī
Cumenihah   kū-ma-nī′hä
Cumom   kū′mum
Cumorah   ka-mōr′a
Curelom   kū-rē′lum

Deseret   dĕz-a-rĕt′
Desolation   dĕs-ō-lā′shun

Edom   ē′dum
Egypt   ē′jĭpt
Egyptian   ē-jĭp′shun
Elam   ē′lum
Elijah   ē-lī′ja
Emer   ē′mer
Emron   ĕm′rän
Enos   ē′nus
Ephah   ē′fä
Ephraim   ē′frĕm or ē′frum
Esrom   ĕz′rum
Ethem   ē′thum
Ether   ē′ther
Eve   ēv
Ezias   ē-zī′us
Ezrom   ĕz′rum

Gad   găd
Gadiandi   găd-ē-ăn′dī
Gadianton   găd-ē-ăn′tun
Gadiomnah   găd-ē-äm′na
Gallim   găl′ĭm
Gazelem   ga-zā′lĭm
Geba   gē′ba
Gebim   gē′bĭm
Gibeah   gĭb′ē-a
Gid   gĭd
Giddonah   gĭd-dō′nä
Giddianhi   gĭd-ē-ăn′hī
Gideon   gĭd′ē-un
Gidgiddonah   gĭd-gĭd-dō′nä
Gidgiddoni   gĭd-gĭd-dō′nī
Gilead   gĭl′ē-ud
Gilgah   gĭl′gä

Gilgal   gĭl′gäl
Gimgimno   gĭm-gĭm′nō
Gomorrah   ga-mōr′a

Hagoth   hā′gäth
Hamath   hā′muth
Hearthom   hē-är′thum
Helam   hē′lum
Helaman   hē′la-mun
Helem   hē′lĕm
Helorum   hē-lōr′um
Hem   hĕm
Hermounts   her′mounts
Heshlon   hĕsh′län
Heth   hĕth
Himni   hĭm′nī
Horeb   hōr′ĕb

Immanuel   ĭm-măn′yū-ĕl
Irreantum   ĭ-rē-ăn′tum
Isaac   ī′zĭk
Isabel   ĭz′a-bĕl
Isaiah   ī-zā′a
Ishmael   ĭsh′mul or ĭsh′mĕl
Ishmaelite   ĭsh′mul-īt or ĭsh′mĕl-īt
Israel   ĭz′rĕl or ĭz′rul
Israelite   ĭz′rĕl-īt or ĭz′rul-īt

Jacob   jā′kub
Jacobite   jā′kub-īt
Jacobugath   jā′ka-bū′gäth
Jacom   jā′kum
Jared   jĕr′ud
Jaredite   jĕr′a-dīt
Jarom   jĕr′um
Jashon   jā′shän
Jeberechiah   jĕb-a-ra-kī′a
Jehovah   jē-hō′va
Jeneum   jĕn′ē-um
Jeremiah   jĕr-a-mī′a
Jershon   jĕr′shän
Jerusalem   ja-rū′sa-lĕm
Jesse   Jĕs′ē
Jew   jū
John   jän
Jonas   jō′nus
Jordan   jōr′dun
Joseph   jō′zĕf
Josephite   jō′zĕf-īt
Josh   jäsh
Joshua   jäsh′ū-wa
Jothan   jō′thun
Judah   jū′da
Judea   jū-dē′a

Kib   kĭb

Kim kĭm
Kimnor kĭm′nōr
Kish kĭsh
Kishkumen kĭsh-kū′mun
Korihor kō′rĭ-hōr
Kumen kū′mun
Kumenonhi kū′ma-nän′hī

Laban lā′bun
Lachoneus la-kō′nē-us
Laish lā′ĭsh
Lamah lā′mä
Laman lā′mun
Lamanite lā′mun-īt
Lamoni la-mō′nī
Lebanon lĕb′a-nän
Lehi lē′hī
Lehi-Nephi lē′hī—nē′fī
Lehonti lē-hän′tī
Lemuel lĕm′yūl
Lemuelite lĕm′yūl-īt
Levi lē′vī
Liahona lē′a-hō′na
Lib lĭb
Limhah lĭm′hä
Limher lĭm′her
Limhi lĭm′hī
Limnah lĭm′nä
Luram lūr′um

Madmenah măd-mĕn′a
Mahah mā′hä
Maher-shalal-hash-baz
  mā′her—shăl-ăl—häsh′bäz
Mahonri ma-hän′rī
Malachi măl′a-kī
Manasseh ma-năs′a
Manti măn′tī
Mary mĕ′rē
Mathoni ma-thō′nī
Mathonihah măth-ō-nī′hä
Medes mēdz
Melchizedek mĕl-kĭz′a-dĭk
Melek mē′lĕk
Michmash mĭk′măsh
Middoni mĭd-dō′nī
Midian mĭd′ē-un
Migron mī′grän
Minon mī′nän
Moab mō′ăb
Mocum mō′kum
Moriancumer mōr-ē-ăn′ka-mer
Morianton mōr-ē-ăn′tun
Moriantum mōr-ē-ăn′tum
Mormon mōr′mun
Moron mōr′un

Moroni mō-rō′nī
Moronihah mō-rō-nī′hä
Moses mō′zus
Mosiah mō-sī′a or mō-zī′a
Mulek myū′lĕk
Muloki myū′la-kī

Nahom nā′hum
Naphtali năf′ta-lī
Nazareth năz′a-rĕth
Neas nē′äs
Nehor nē′hōr
Nephi nē′fī
Nephihah nē-fī′hä
Nephite nē′fīt
Neum nē′um
Nimrah nĭm′rä
Nimrod nĭm′räd
Noah nō′a

Ogath ō′găth
Omega ō-mā′ga
Omer ō′mer
Omner äm′ner
Omni äm′nī
Onidah ō-nī′da
Onihah ō-nī′hä
Onti än′tī
Opher ō′fer
Oreb ōr′ĕb
Orihah ō-rī′hä

Paanchi pā-ăn′kī
Pachus pā′kus
Pacumeni pā-kyū′mĕn-ī
Pagag pā′gäg
Pahoran pa-hōr′un
Palestina păl-a-stī′na
Pathros pā′thrōs
Pekah pē′kä
Pharaoh fā′rō or fĕ′rō
Philistine fĭl′a-stēn

Rabbanah ra-băn′a
Rahab rā′hăb
Ramah rä′mä
Ramath rā′muth
Rameumptom răm-ē-ump′tum
Remaliah rĕm-a-lī′a
Rezin rē′zĭn
Riplah rĭp′lä
Riplakish rĭp-lā′kĭsh
Ripliancum rĭp-lē-ăn′kum

Salem sā′lĕm
Sam săm

Samaria sa-mĕr'ē-a
Samuel săm'yū-ĕl
Sarah sĕr'a
Sariah sa-rī'a
Saul säl
Seantum sē-ăn'tum
Sebus sē'bus
Seezoram sē-zōr'um
Senine sē'nĭn
Senum sē'num
Seraphim sĕr'a-fĭm
Seth sĕth
Shared shā'rud
Shazer shā'zer
Shearjashub shĭr-jā'shub
Shelem shē'lĕm
Shem shĕm
Shemlon shĕm'län
Shemnon shĕm'nän
Sherem shĕr'um
Sherrizah shĕr-ī'za
Sheum shē'um
Shez shĕz
Shiblom shĭb'lum
Shiblon shĭb'lun
Shiblum shĭb'lum
Shiloah shī-lō'a
Shilom shī'lum
Shim shĭm
Shimnilon shĭm-nī'län
Shinar shī'när
Shiz shĭz
Shule shūl
Shum shum
Shurr sher

Sidom sī'dum
Sidon sī'dun
Sinai sī'nī
Sinim sī'nĭm
Siron sī'run
Syria sĭr'ē-a

Tarshish tär'shĭsh
Teancum tē-ăn'kum
Teomner tē-äm'ner
Thummim thum'ĭm
Timothy tĭm'a-thē
Tubaloth tū'ba-läth

Uriah yū-rī'a
Urim yūr'ĭm
Uzziah yū-zī'a

Zarahemla zĕr-a-hĕm'la
Zebulun zĕb'yū-lun
Zechariah zĕk'a-rī'a
Zedekiah zĕd'a-kī'a
Zeezrom zē-ĕz'rum
Zemnarihah zĕm-na-rī'hä
Zenephi zēn'a-fī
Zeniff zē'nĭf
Zenoch zē'nuk
Zenos zē'nus
Zerahemnah zĕr-a-hĕm'nä
Zeram zē'rum
Zerin zē'rĭn
Ziff zĭf
Zion zī'un
Zoram zōr'um
Zoramite zōr'um-īt

INDEX

AARON¹—*brother of Moses* (see BD Aaron)
No references in Book of Mormon.

AARON²—*Jaredite king*

    Ether 1: 16 descendant of Heth²;
10: 31 dwells in captivity.

AARON³—*son of Mosiah²* [c. 100 B.C.] (see
also Mosiah², Sons of)

    Mosiah 27: 8–10 an unbeliever,
seeks to destroy church; 27: 32 converted
by angel; 27: 34 named among sons of
King Mosiah²; 27: 35–37 preaches gospel;
28: 1–9 is allowed to preach in land of
Nephi; 29: 3 (28: 10; Alma 17: 6) refuses
to become king; **Alma** 17: 1–3 (27: 16–
19) meets Alma² with joy; 21: 1–4 goes
to land of Jerusalem; 21: 4–10 Amalekites contend as he preaches about atonement; 21: 11 goes to Ani-Anti, meets
Muloki and Ammah; 21: 12–14 (20: 2, 28)
goes to Middoni, preaches, is imprisoned,
is delivered by Ammon² and Lamoni; 21:
15–17 preaches in synagogues, converts
many; 22: 1 is led by Spirit to land of
Nephi; 22: 2–16 teaches Lamanite king;
22: 17–22 raises fallen king; 23: 1 is protected by proclamation; 23: 4 establishes
churches in cities; 23: 16–17 consulted by
king in naming Anti-Nephi-Lehies; 24: 5
travels with brothers in lands of Midian
and Ishmael; 26: 6 people are stirred up
to remember A's words; 26: 10 rebukes
Ammon²; 31: 6–7 goes with Ammon²
and Alma² to Zoramites; 35: 14 returns
to Zarahemla.

AARON⁴—*king of Lamanites* [c. A.D. 330]

    Morm. 2: 9 is defeated by armies of
Mormon²; 3: 4 sends epistle to Mormon²;
Moro. 9: 17 many Nephites fall to A's
army.

AARON, CITY OF [possibly two different
cities]

    Alma 8: 13–14 was in vicinity of
Ammonihah; 50: 14 near cities of Moroni
and Nephihah.

ABEL—*son of Adam* (see also BD Abel)

    Hel. 6: 27 Satan plots with Cain to
murder A.

ABHOR, ABHORRENCE (see also Allowance; Despise; Hate)

    2 Ne. 9: 49 my soul a. sin; **Alma**
13: 12 those sanctified cannot look upon

sin save with a.; 27: 28 Anti-Nephi-
Lehies look upon shedding of blood with
a.; 37: 29 teach them to a. such wickedness.

ABIDE (see also Dwell; Obedience;
Remain)

    1 Ne. 11: 27 Holy Ghost a. upon the
Lamb in form of dove; **Alma** 1: 1 people
obliged to a. by laws of Mosiah²; **3 Ne.**
24: 2 who may a. day of the Lord's
coming; **Morm.** 2: 26 Spirit a. not with
Nephite army; **Ether** 12: 41 (Moro. 9: 26)
grace a. in you forever.

ABINADI—*Nephite prophet* [c. 150 B.C.]

    Mosiah 11: 20 prophesies afflictions
of people of King Noah³; 11: 26–29
Noah³ angry over A's words; 12: 1–8
comes in disguise, commanded to prophesy; 12: 16–18 is delivered to king,
imprisoned, questioned; 12: 19–37 confounds and challenges questioners; 12:
34–36 (13: 12–24) quotes Ten Commandments; 13: 1–5 protected by Spirit;
13: 27–28 teaches salvation not by Mosaic
law alone, but also by atonement; 14:
1–12 (15: 6) quotes Isaiah; 15: 1–9
prophesies that God will come among
men, redeem them; 16: 1–15 preaches
Christ only Redeemer, teaches resurrection and judgment; 17: 1 condemned
to death; 17: 2–4 (24: 9; 26: 15; Alma
5: 11) Alma¹ believes and writes A's
words; 17: 5–7 imprisoned and accused;
17: 15–19 prophesies priests' death by
fire; 17: 20 is burned to death; 18: 1
Alma¹ teaches A's words; 20: 21 (25: 9;
Morm. 1: 19) A's words fulfilled; 21: 30
A's death mourned; 24: 5 A's words not
taught by Amulon.

ABINADOM—*Nephite historian, son of
Chemish* [between 279 and 130 B.C.]

    Omni 1: 10 participates in war; 1:
11 writes on plates; 1: 12 is father of
Amaleki¹.

ABISH—*Lamanite woman, servant of Lamoni*

    Alma 19: 16 converted to the Lord;
19: 17 calls people to king's house; 19: 28
grieves because of tumult; 19: 29 raises
queen.

ABLOM—*Jaredite city*

    Ether 9: 3 Omer flees to A. by sea-
shore.

ABOMINATION, ABOMINABLE (see also Church, Great and Abominable; Church of the Devil; Evil; Sin; TG Abomination; BD Abomination of Desolation)

Jacob 2: 21 pride is *a.* in sight of the Lord; **Mosiah** 3: 25 the wicked are consigned to view of own *a.*; **Alma** 13: 17 Melchizedek's people waxed strong in *a.*; 39: 5 unchastity is most *a.* above all sins save murder and denying Holy Ghost; **Hel.** 4: 11 (13: 14; 3 Ne. 9: 2) slaughter of Nephites caused by *a.*; **3 Ne.** 5: 6 (Hel. 7: 25; 3 Ne. 16: 10; Ether 8: 18; 11: 22) secret and *a.* combinations; 16: 10 Gentiles to receive gospel when they are full of secret *a.*; **Ether** 11: 22 Jaredites reject prophets because of *a.*; 14: 25 Jaredites' *a.* prepared way for destruction; **Moro.** 9: 8–9 *a.* of Lamanites and Nephites during war.

ABOUND

Mosiah 5: 15 (Alma 7: 24; Ether 12: 4) always *a.* in good works; 27: 5 Nephites *a.* in grace of God.

ABRAHAM—*father of faithful* (see also Abrahamic Covenant; BD Abraham)

2 Ne. 8: 2 look unto A., your father; 27: 33 the Lord redeemed A.; **Jacob** 4: 5 A. obedient in offering Isaac; **Alma** 5: 24 (7: 25; Hel. 3: 30) murderers cannot sit in kingdom with A.; 13: 15 A. paid tithes to Melchizedek; **Hel.** 8: 16–17 A. and prophets testified of the Son.

ABRAHAMIC COVENANT (see also Israel; TG Abrahamic Covenant; BD Abraham, Covenant of)

1 Ne. 15: 18 covenant with A. to be fulfilled; 17: 40 (22: 9; 2 Ne. 29: 14; 3 Ne. 20: 25, 27; Morm. 5: 20; Ether 3: 11) God covenants with A.

ABRIDGMENT, ABRIDGE (see also Record)

Title Page Book of Mormon an *a.* of Nephite record and Book of Ether; **1 Ne.** 1: 17 Nephi[1] *a.* father's record; **W of M** 1: 3 Mormon *a.* record of Nephi[1]; **Morm.** 5: 9 Mormon[2] makes small *a.* of things he has seen; **Moro.** 1: 1 Moroni *a.* Jaredites' record.

ABYSS

Mosiah 27: 29 Alma[2] in darkest *a.*; **Alma** 26: 3 Lamanites in darkest *a.*

ACCEPTABLE

Moro. 7: 44 none is *a.* before God except meek and lowly.

ACCOMPLISH (see also Do; Fulfill; Perform)

1 Ne. 3: 7 (17: 3) the Lord prepares way to *a.* that which he commands; 9: 6 the Lord prepares way to *a.* all his works.

ACCOUNT (see also Accountable; History; Record)

1 Ne. 1: 16–17 (6: 3) Nephi[1] does not make full *a.* on small plates; 9: 2–4 large plates of Nephi contain *a.* of secular history; 10: 1 Nephi[1] records *a.* of his ministry on small plates.

ACCOUNTABILITY, AGE OF (see also Accountable)

Moro. 8: 5–26 little children need no repentance, neither baptism.

ACCOUNTABLE (see also Accountability, Age of; Responsibility; TG Accountability)

Moro. 8: 10 teach repentance and baptism unto those *a.*

ACCURSED (see also Curse; Slippery)

Hel. 12: 18 hidden treasure to be *a.* because of iniquity; **Ether** 4: 8 he who contends against word of the Lord shall be *a.*

ACCUSE (see also Condemn)

2 Ne. 1: 25 brothers of Nephi[1] *a.* him of seeking power; **Mosiah** 2: 15 Benjamin does not *a.* his people; 12: 19 priests question Abinadi that they might *a.* him; **Alma** 10: 31 Zeezrom foremost to *a.* Amulek and Alma[2]; 30: 31 Korihor *a.* priests of leading people away; **Hel.** 9: 19 judges question Nephi[2] that they might *a.* him to death.

ACKNOWLEDGE (see also Confess)

Alma 1: 1 laws of Mosiah[2] are *a.* by people; 1: 15 Nehor *a.* false teachings; 38: 14 *a.* your unworthiness before God; 39: 13 *a.* your faults; **Moro.** 10: 6 that which is good *a.* that Christ is.

ACT (see also Agency; Deed; Walk; Work [noun])

2 Ne. 2: 13 if no God, there could have been no creation of things, neither to *a.* nor to be *a.* upon; 2: 16 (Hel. 14: 30) God gave unto man to *a.* for himself; 2: 26 because of atonement men become free to *a.* for themselves and not to be *a.* upon; 31: 13 to receive Holy Ghost, men must *a.* no hypocrisy or deception before God; **Alma** 12: 31 through transgression man was placed in state to *a.* according to his will.

ADAM—*first man created on earth* (see also Eden, Garden of; Eve; Fall of Man; Man; TG Adam; BD Adam)

1 Ne. 5: 11 A. and Eve our first parents; **2 Ne.** 2: 19 driven from garden; 2: 22 if A. had not transgressed, he would

not have fallen; 2: 25 A. fell that men might be; 9: 21 Holy One suffered pains of all who belong to family of A.; **Mosiah** 3: 11 Christ's blood atones for all who have fallen by transgression of A.; 3: 16 as in A., or by nature, men fall; 3: 19 natural man an enemy to God since fall of A.; 3: 26 justice could not deny A. should fall because of partaking of forbidden fruit.

ADD (*see also* Increase)

3 Ne. 13: 27 who can a. one cubit to his stature; 13: 33 all things shall be a. unto you.

ADHERE (*see also* Keep)

Alma 60: 34 a. to word of God.

ADMINISTRATION, ADMINISTER (*see also* Impart; Minister [verb])

Jacob 2: 19 seek riches to a. relief to sick and afflicted; **Mosiah** 4: 16 a. of your substance to those in need; 4: 26 to retain remission of sins, a. relief to needy; **Alma** 10: 14 lawyers hired to a. law at trials; 15: 18 Alma² a. to Amulek in his tribulations; 35: 9 Ammonites a. unto Zoramites according to their wants; **3 Ne.** 6: 28 covenant of secret combinations a. by devil; **4 Ne.** 1: 27 wicked churches a. that which was sacred unto the unworthy; **Ether** 10: 33 robbers a. oaths after manner of the ancients; **Moro.** 4: 1 elders and priests a. flesh and blood of Christ unto church; 5: 1–2 manner of a. sacrament wine.

ADMONISH, ADMONITION (*see also* Rebuke; Warn, Warning)

Jacob 2: 9 Jacob² sorrows that he is commanded to a. people according to crimes; **Enos** 1: 1 father of Enos² taught him in nurture and a. of the Lord; **Omni** 1: 13 people of Mosiah² were a. continually by word of God; **Mosiah** 26: 6, 39 church members who committed sin were a. by the church; **Alma** 1: 7 Gideon a. Nehor with word of God.

ADORN (*see also* Pride; Vanity)

4 Ne. 1: 41 (Morm. 8: 37) Nephites a. churches with precious things; **Morm.** 8: 39 why do ye a. yourselves with that which hath no life.

ADULTERY, ADULTERER (*see also* Chastity, Chaste; Fornication; Lust; Whore; TG Adulterer, Adultery; Sexual Immorality; BD Adultery)

Mosiah 13: 22 thou shalt not commit a.; **Alma** 16: 18 priests preach against a.; 23: 3 Lamanite king teaches people not to commit a.; 30: 10 those who commit a. are punished; 39: 3–5 a. is most abominable above all sins save murder and denying Holy Ghost; **Hel.** 4: 11–12

slaughter of Nephites caused by committing a.; 7: 5 Nephites rule that they might more easily commit a.; **3 Ne.** 12: 28 (Matt. 5: 28) whoso lusts after a woman has already committed a. in heart; 12: 32 (Matt. 5: 32) whoso puts away his wife causes her to commit a.

ADVANTAGE (*see also* Gain)

2 Ne. 28: 8 the wicked to say, Take a. of one because of words; **Ether** 12: 26 fools shall take no a. of your weakness.

ADVERSARY (*see also* Devil)

1 Ne. 15: 24 fiery darts of a. cannot overpower those who hearken to God's word; **Alma** 12: 5 Zeezrom's plan is plan of the a.; **3 Ne.** 12: 25 (Matt. 5: 25) agree with thine a. quickly.

ADVERSITY (*see* Affliction; Infirmity; Opposition; Oppression; Patience; Persecution; Sorrow; Suffering; Tempt; Trial; Tribulation; Wind)

ADVOCATE (*see* Jesus Christ—Advocate)

AFFECTION (*see also* Love)

Alma 37: 36 let a. of heart be placed upon the Lord forever.

AFFIXED (*see* Punish, Punishment)

AFFLICTED (*see also* Affliction)

1 Ne. 21: 13 the Lord will have mercy upon his a.; **Jacob** 2: 19 administer relief to the a.; **Mosiah** 14: 4, 7 (Isa. 53: 4) we did esteem him smitten of God, and a.; **Alma** 1: 27 Nephites impart substance to the a.; 34: 28 if ye turn away the a., your prayer is vain; **3 Ne.** 17: 9 Nephites brought their a. for the Savior's blessing; **Morm.** 8: 39 why do ye suffer the a. to pass by you without notice.

AFFLICTION (*see also* Afflicted; Chasten; Needy; Oppression; Pain; Suffering; Trial; Tribulation)

1 Ne. 15: 5 Nephi¹ is overcome because of a.; **2 Ne.** 2: 2 God shall consecrate thine a. for thy gain; 4: 26 why should my strength slacken because of mine a.; **Jacob** 3: 1 God will console you in your a.; **Mosiah** 24: 13–14 the Lord visits his people in their a.; **Alma** 1: 23 (4: 6–7) pride a cause of great a. to church; 7: 11 Son of God to go forth suffering a.; 17: 11 (26: 27; 31: 31; 34: 41) be patient in a.; 32: 6 a. of poor Zoramites humble them; 33: 11 the Lord hears Alma² because of his a.; 61: 4 those who try to take away judgment-seat are cause of sore a.; 62: 41 many are softened because of their a.; **Hel.** 3: 34 (3 Ne. 6: 13) the proud cause the humble to wade through much a.; 12: 3 except the Lord

chastens his people with *a.*, they will not remember him.

AGAINST

2 Ne. 10: 16 they who are not for God are *a.* him.

AGE (*see also* Accountability, Age of; Old)

Mosiah 10: 9 men placed in army ranks according to *a.*

AGENCY, AGENT (*see also* Accountable; Act; Choose; Evil; Fall of Man; Freedom; Fruit, Forbidden; Knowledge; Law; Liberty; Obedience; Opposition; Tempt; Transgression; Will; TG Agency)

2 Ne. 2: 11 opposition in all things; 2: 16 man could not act for himself save he was enticed by good and evil; 2: 27 men are free to choose; 10: 23 ye are free to act for yourselves; 26: 10 those who choose works of darkness must go down to hell; **Mosiah** 2: 21 God preserves men that they may do according to their own will; 5: 8 under Christ's head, men are made free; **Alma** 12: 31 having transgressed temporal commandments, men placed themselves in state to act according to their own wills; 13: 3 man left to choose good or evil; 30: 8 choose ye this day; 41: 7 the redeemed are their own judges, whether to do good or evil; **Hel.** 14: 30 ye are free, ye are permitted to act for yourselves; **Moro.** 7: 15 it is given unto you to judge, that ye may know good from evil.

AGOSH—*Jaredite area*

Ether 14:15–16 Lib[2] pursues Coriantumr[2] to plains of A.

AGREE (*see also* Unite)

3 Ne. 12: 25 *a.* with thine adversary quickly.

AHA—*Nephite military officer* [c. 80 B.C.]

Alma 16: 5–6 son of Zoram[2], frees captive Nephites.

AHAH—*Jaredite king, son of Seth[2]*

Ether 1: 9 father of Ethem; 11: 10 commits iniquity while king.

AIATH [possibly Ai] (*see also* BD Ai)

2 Ne. 20: 28 (Isa. 10: 28) Assyrians have come to A.

AKISH—*Jaredite king, son of Kimnor*

Ether 8: 10 daughter of Jared[3] conspires to marry A.; 8: 11–13 A. agrees to kill the king; 8: 14–18 initiates secret combination; 9: 1 overthrows kingdom of Omer; 9: 4 marries daughter of Jared[3]; 9: 5 causes death of Jared[3] and obtains kingdom; 9: 6–7 reigns, kills own son; 9: 12 has war with other sons, kingdom destroyed.

AKISH, WILDERNESS OF

Ether 14: 3–4, 14 scene of battles of Coriantumr[2].

ALIKE (*see also* Equal, Equality; Respect; Respecter; Same)

2 Ne. 26: 33 all are *a.* unto God; **Mosiah** 29: 32 every man may enjoy his rights and privileges *a.*; **Moro.** 8: 17 all children are *a.* unto me.

ALIVE (*see also* Living; Quicken)

2 Ne. 25: 25 we are made *a.* in Christ; **Jacob** 5: 34 roots of wild olive-tree are *a.*; **Moro.** 8: 12, 19, 22 little children are *a.* in Christ.

ALLOT (*see also* Give)

Alma 29: 3–4 the Lord *a.* unto men according to their wills.

ALLOWANCE (*see also* Abhor)

Alma 45: 16 the Lord cannot look upon sin with least degree of *a.*

ALMA[1]—*Nephite prophet, founder of the church* [c. 173-91 B.C.]

Mosiah 17: 1–2 priest of Noah[3], descendant of Nephi[1]; 17: 2 (24: 9) believes Abinadi; 17: 3–4 cast out by king, flees, hides, writes words of Abinadi; 18: 1 repents, teaches words of Abinadi; 18: 5 hides by waters of Mormon; 18: 7–11 people gather to hear A.; 18: 12–14 baptizes Helam; 18: 15–16 baptizes 204 souls; 18: 17 (21: 30) organizes church; 18: 18 has authority from God, ordains priests; 18: 19–26 instructs priests; 18: 27–29 commands people to share substance; 18: 34 (23: 1) is warned of approaching army, departs into wilderness; 21: 30 departure of A. is mourned; 21: 34 people want to become like A.; 23: 1 account of A. begins; 23: 6–7 declines to be king; 23: 8–25 teaches people; 23: 16 high priest, founder of church; 23: 17 consecrates priests and teachers; 23: 26 flees with brethren to city of Helam; 23: 27–29 surrenders to Lamanites; 23: 35 discovered by Amulon; 23: 36–37 is deceived by Lamanites; 24: 8 is oppressed by Amulon; 24: 12–15 pours out heart to the Lord; 24: 16–20 A. and people are delivered through faith; 24: 23 is warned to flee in haste; 24: 25 arrives in Zarahemla, meets Mosiah[2]; 25: 6 account of A. is read to people; 25: 14–16 preaches repentance; 25: 17–18 baptizes Limhi and people; 25: 19–24 establishes churches; 26: 7 dissenters brought before A.; 26: 8 is given authority over church; 26: 20 is promised eternal life; 26: 21–33 is instructed concerning wrong-doers and unbelievers; 26: 34–39 judges, regulates church, walks in diligence, teaches, suffers afflictions; 27: 1 people complain to A.; 27: 8 son of

A. an unbeliever; 27: 14 prays for son; 29: 42 (Alma 4: 4; 5: 3) ordains son high priest; 29: 45 dies; **Alma** 5: 11 son lauds A's beliefs.

ALMA²—*son of Alma¹, first chief judge, high priest* [c. 100-73 B.C.]

Mosiah 27: 8–10 seeks to destroy church; 27: 11 (Alma 36: 6–10) with sons of Mosiah² sees angel; 27: 19 becomes helpless and dumb; 27: 20 father rejoices over him; 27: 23 is revived; 27: 24–31 (Alma 36: 5–24) relates experience; 27: 32 teaches people; 28: 20 receives records and interpreters; 29: 42 (Alma 4: 4; 5: 3) is appointed chief judge and high priest; **Alma** 1: 11–15 sentences Nehor; 2: 16 leads Nephite army; 2: 30 asks the Lord for mercy to save people; 2: 31 slays Amlici; 2: 32–38 contends with Lamanites and Amlicites; 4: 4 baptizes in river Sidon; 4: 7 (6: 1; 15: 3) consecrates teachers, priests, elders; 4: 11–13 sees great wickedness in church; 4: 16–17 resigns judgment-seat to Nephihah; 4: 18 retains office of high priest; 5: 1–2 preaches in Zarahemla; 5: 3–61 preaches about his mighty change in heart; 5: 62 speaks by way of commandment; 6: 7–8 preaches in valley of Gideon; 7: 1–27 preaches about coming of Redeemer; 8: 1 leaves Gideon for Zarahemla; 8: 3–5 teaches and baptizes in Melek; 8: 6–8 preaches at Ammonihah; 8: 10 wrestles with God in mighty prayer; 8: 11–13 is reviled and cast out of Ammonihah; 8: 14 is visited by angel; 8: 16–18 returns to Ammonihah; 8: 19–21 meets Amulek; 8: 27 tarries many days; 8: 30–32 with Amulek, goes forth with power; 9: 1–7 people of Ammonihah contend with A.; 9: 8–30 boldly testifies; 10: 31 with Amulek, is accused by Zeezrom; 12: 1–18 speaks to Zeezrom; 12: 20 is questioned by Antionah; 12: 21–37 teaches of tree of life, fall, probationary state, commandments, plan of redemption; 13: 1–20 teaches of holy priesthood, responsibilities, foreknowledge, Melchizedek; 13: 21, 27–30 calls people to repent; 13: 22–26 teaches joyful news of salvation; 14: 2–4 with Amulek, bound, taken before judge; 14: 9–10 sees converts burned; 14: 11 is constrained by Spirit; 14: 13 cannot be burned till work is finished; 14: 17–24 imprisoned, mistreated; 14: 26–28 (Ether 12: 13) freed from prison; 15: 1 goes to Sidom with Amulek; 15: 10–12 heals and baptizes Zeezrom; 15: 13 establishes church in Sidom; 15: 18 takes Amulek to Zarahemla; 16: 5 sons of Zoram² ask for A's counsel in battles; 16: 13 preaches repentance with Amulek; 17: 1–2 (27: 16, 19) meets sons of Mosiah² journeying to Gideon; 27: 20 takes brethren back to Zarahemla; 27: 25 returns to wilderness

with Ammon²; 29: 1–3 desires to be angel; 29: 8 teaches that the Lord grants in wisdom to all nations; 30: 29–30 confronts Korihor; 30: 33 labors in ministry not for pay; 30: 49–50 strikes Korihor dumb; 31: 1–2 sorrowful because of Zoramites; 31: 6–7 takes several brethren to preach to Zoramites; 31: 12–38 grieves over use of Rameumptom, prays for people; 32: 4 preaches on hill Onidah; 32: 12 preaches to the poor; 32: 13–43 teaches about faith; 33: 2–15 urges reading of scripture; 33: 17–23 encourages faith in the Son; 35: 1 goes to Jershon with brethren; 35: 14 returns to Zarahemla; 35: 15 grieves over people's iniquity; 36: 1–30 gives charge to Helaman¹; 37: 1–18 (50: 38) gives Helaman¹ records; 37: 21 speaks of twenty-four plates; 37: 24–47 further instructs Helaman¹; 38: 1–15 gives commandments and instructions to his son Shiblon; 39: 1 gives commandments to his son Corianton; 39: 5–6 teaches about unpardonable sin; 40: 11–15 describes state of soul between death and resurrection; 40: 16–24 (41: 1–15) teaches about restoration of body and soul; 42: 1–31 teaches of Fall, probationary state, temporal death, spiritual death, plan of mercy, plan of happiness, law, punishment, justice, and salvation; 42: 31 sends Corianton to preach; 43: 1 goes forth to preach; 43: 24 receives word of the Lord for Moroni¹; 45: 2 instructs Helaman¹; 45: 9–16 prophesies about wickedness and destruction of people; 45: 16–17 blesses land and church; 45: 18 departs, not heard of again; 45: 19 taken up by Spirit or buried by the Lord, as Moses; **Hel.** 4: 21 people remember A's prophecies; 5: 41 A's teachings cited by Aminadab.

ALMA, VALLEY OF—*a day's travel north of city of Helam*

Mosiah 24: 20 named after Alma¹; 24: 21 people poured out thanks in A.

ALMIGHTY (*see* God, Power of)

ALMS (*see also* Charity; Impart; Needy; Poor; Relief; TG Almsgiving; BD Almsgiving)

3 Ne. 13: 1 ye should do *a.* unto the poor; 13: 2–4 *a.* should be in secret.

ALONE

1 Ne. 7: 1 not meet for Lehi¹ to take family into wilderness *a.*; **Jacob** 4: 13 Nephites are not witnesses *a.*; **Mosiah** 13: 28 salvation comes not by law *a.*

ALPHA (*see also* TG Omega; BD Alpha; Omega)

3 Ne. 9: 18 Christ is A. and Omega.

ALTAR (*see also* Idolatry; Offering; Sacrifice; Worship; BD Altar)

1 Ne. 2: 7 Lehi[1] builds *a.* of stones; Alma 15: 17 people gather in sanctuaries to worship God before *a.*; 17: 4 sons of Mosiah[2] bring many before *a.* of God.

ALTER (*see also* Change)

Alma 51: 2–5 some desire that law be *a.* to overthrow free government; Hel. 4: 22 Nephites had *a.* laws of Mosiah[2]; Morm. 9: 32–33 Nephites' written language *a.* according to speech.

AMALEKI[1]—*Nephite record keeper* [c. 130 B.C.]

Omni 1: 12 son of Abinadom; 1: 12–22 records doings of Mosiah[1]; 1: 23–24 records beginning of Benjamin's reign; 1: 25 will deliver records to Benjamin; 1: 26 calls brethren to come unto Christ; 1: 27–30 records expedition that returns to land of Nephi; W of M 1: 10 delivered plates to Benjamin.

AMALEKI[2]—*part of expedition that seeks Zeniff's group* [c. 121 B.C.] (*see also* Ammon[1])

Mosiah 7: 6 accompanies Ammon[1] in returning to land of Nephi.

AMALEKITES—*group of Nephite apostates*

Alma 21: 2 help build city of Jerusalem; 21: 3 more hardened than Lamanites; 21: 4 after order of Nehors; 21: 5 contend with Aaron[3]; 22: 7 say there is a God; 23: 14 only one A. is converted; 24: 1 stir up Lamanites against Anti-Nephi-Lehies; 43: 6 are appointed captains because of murderous dispositions; 43: 13 dissenters from Nephites; 43: 20 better armed than Lamanites; 43: 44 inspire Lamanites to fight.

AMALICKIAH—*Nephite traitor* [c. 70 B.C.]

Alma 46: 3 leader of revolt against Helaman[2]; 46: 4 desires to be king; 46: 4–10 leads people from church by flattery; 46: 11 angers Moroni[1]; 46: 28–33 flees with followers; 47: 1 stirs up Lamanites in land of Nephi; 47: 3 heads Lamanite army; 47: 4 seeks overthrow of Lamanite king; 47: 10–12 sends messages to Lehonti; 47: 13 conspires with Lehonti; 47: 17–19 poisons Lehonti, becomes Lamanite commander; 47: 21–24 has king slain; 47: 35 takes king's wife and kingdom; 48: 1 stirs up Lamanites against Nephites; 48: 5 appoints Zoramites as captains; 48: 7 obtains power by fraud; 49: 10–11 does not himself come to battle; 49: 27 enraged over defeat of his army; 51: 12 heads army in person; 51: 23 takes city of Moroni; 51: 26 takes other

cities; 51: 29 meets Teancum; 51: 34 slain by Teancum; 52: 3 brother of A. is made king.

AMALICKIAHITES—*followers of Amalickiah*

Alma 46: 28 are dissenters; 46: 35 refuse covenant, put to death; 49: 9 astonished by Nephite preparation.

AMARON—*son of Omni, Nephite record keeper*

Omni 1: 3 receives plates; 1: 8 delivers plates to Chemish.

AMGID—*Jaredite king*

Ether 10: 32 overthrown by Com[2].

AMINADAB—*Nephite dissenter living among Lamanites* [c. 30 B.C.]

Hel. 5: 35–37 sees faces of Nephi[2] and Lehi[4] shining in prison; 5: 39–41 tells Lamanites to repent.

AMINADI—*descendant of Nephi[1], ancestor of Amulek*

Alma 10: 2–3 interprets writings on temple wall.

AMISS

2 Ne. 4: 35 God will give me, if I ask not *a.*

AMLICI—*Nephite dissenter* [c. 87 B.C.] (*see also* Amlicites)

Alma 2: 1 incites people to contention and attempts to become king by cunning ways; 2: 4 would deny privileges of church; 2: 7 voice of people comes against A.; 2: 9 is consecrated king by dissenters; 2: 11 A's followers are called Amlicites; 2: 31 slain by Alma[2].

AMLICITES—*Nephite faction desiring king*

Alma 2: 11 followers of Amlici; 2: 12–13 Nephites prepare to meet A.; 2: 24 join Lamanites; 2: 35 are defeated; 3: 3 the slain are thrown in waters of Sidon; 3: 4, 13 mark foreheads like Lamanites; 3: 18 are in open rebellion against God and are cursed.

AMMAH—*missionary companion of Aaron[3]*

Alma 20: 2 imprisoned at Middoni; 21: 11–17 preaches at Ani-Anti and Middoni.

AMMARON—*Nephite record keeper* [c. A.D. 306]

4 Ne. 1: 47 brother of Amos[2], keeps records; 1: 48 hides all records; Morm. 1: 2–4 tells Mormon[2] how and when to hide the plates; 2: 17 deposits records near city of Jashon.

AMMON[1]—*leader of expedition to land of Nephi* [c. 121 B.C.]

Mosiah 7: 3 strong and mighty man, descendant of Zarahemla; 7: 6 leads brethren to land of Nephi; 7: 7 is imprisoned by king Limhi; 7: 8 is brought before king; 7: 16 is honored; 8: 2 addresses people; 8: 6 reads record of Limhi; 8: 8–11 is told of ancient relics and twenty-four gold plates; 8: 13–17 tells of Mosiah², seer who can translate; 21: 23 is suspected of being a priest of Noah³; 21: 33 declines to baptize king; 22: 11 leads Limhi and people to freedom.

AMMON²—*son of Mosiah², missionary to Lamanites* [c. 100 B.C.] (*see also* Ammon², People of; Mosiah², Sons of)

Mosiah 27: 8 unbeliever; 27: 10 seeks to destroy church; 27: 11 angel appears to A.; 27: 32 begins preaching word of God; 27: 34–35 with brethren, travels throughout Zarahemla; 28: 1–8 desires mission to Lamanites; 28: 10 (29: 3) refuses to be king; **Alma** 17: 1–4 with brethren, meets Alma²; 17: 6–8 departs for land of Nephi; 17: 13 separates from brethren; 17: 18 chief among missionaries; 17: 20–21 taken bound to Lamoni; 17: 25 becomes servant; 17: 26–39 saves king's flocks; 18: 2–4 Lamoni believes A. is Great Spirit; 18: 10 prepares chariots; 18: 16 discerns king's thoughts; 18: 22–32 teaches king, recites history; 19: 2 is called before queen; 19: 14 thanks God, overpowered with joy; 19: 22–23 cannot be slain, according to the Lord's promises; 19: 33 revives, ministers to people; 20: 1 organizes church; 20: 2 is commanded to go to Middoni; 20: 8 meets Lamoni's father; 20: 14–18 is threatened, but saves Lamoni; 20: 20–21 overpowers king; 20: 22–28 frees brethren from prison; 21: 18 returns with Lamoni to land of Ishmael; 21: 23 teaches Lamoni's people; 23: 1 proclamation for A's protection; 23: 6 A's converts never fall away; 24: 5 with brethren, holds council with Lamoni and his brother; 26: 1–34 reviews success; 26: 10 is rebuked by Aaron³; 26: 35 praises God; 27: 5 proposes migration to Zarahemla; 27: 10–15 leads his people toward Zarahemla; 27: 16 (17: 1–4) with brethren, meets Alma²; 27: 17 is swallowed up in joy; 27: 25 returns with Alma²; 30: 20 is high priest over Ammonites; 30: 21 banishes Korihor; 31: 5 goes with Alma² on mission to Zoramites; 31: 32 Alma² prays for his success; 31: 37–38 is provided for through faith; 35: 1 returns to Jershon; 35: 14 returns to Zarahemla; 37: 9 needs plates for missionary work; 48: 18 a man of God; **Ether** 12: 15 A's faith wrought miracle among Lamanites.

AMMON, CHILDREN OF—*people in Pal-*

estine descended from Lot (*see also* BD Ammon, Ammonites)

2 Ne. 21: 14 (Isa. 11: 14) to obey gathered Israel.

AMMON², PEOPLE OF—*converted Lamanites; also known as Anti-Nephi-Lehies or Ammonites* (*see also* Helaman², Sons of)

Alma 21: 23 (23: 4–5) thousands of Lamanites converted by sons of Mosiah²; 23: 6 after conversion, never fall away; 23: 16–17 (24: 1) take the name of Anti-Nephi-Lehies; 23: 18 friendly to Nephites, curse no longer follows them; 24: 1–2 unconverted Lamanites take up arms against them; 24: 6 will not take up arms; 24: 12–19 refuse to shed blood, bury weapons; 24: 20–22 do not resist Lamanite attack, and 1005 are slain; 24: 24–27 over one thousand Lamanites converted through example; 24: 28 slain mainly by Amalekites and Amulonites; 25: 13 joined by many Lamanites; 25: 15 (30: 3) observe law of Moses; 25: 16 look forward to Christ; 27: 2 Amalekites stir up Lamanites again to slay them; 27: 8 offer to become slaves to Nephites; 27: 14 depart into wilderness near Zarahemla; 27: 21–25 are given land of Jershon by Nephites; 27: 23 (28: 1; 43: 12) protected by Nephites; 27: 26 called people of Ammon²; 27: 27 numbered with church, distinguished for zeal; 35: 8 Zoramites angry with them; 35: 9 accept converted Zoramites; 35: 11 Zoramites prepare for war with them; 35: 13 remove to Melek; 43: 11 hated by Lamanites; 43: 11 will not break covenant; 43: 13 give great substance to Nephites; 47: 29 joined by Lehonti's servants; 53: 10–14 willing to break oath, dissuaded by Helaman²; 53: 16–19 their sons prepare for war, choose Helaman² as their leader; 56: 54 sons of A. defeat Lamanites; 56: 55–56 sons of A. miraculously saved from death; 62: 16–17 joined by four thousand Lamanites who enter covenant; **Hel.** 3: 12 may go to land northward.

AMMONIHAH, CITY OF—*in West, near cities of Melek, Noah, and Aaron*

Alma 8: 6–8 (9:1) Alma² preaches at A.; 8: 7 land of A. named after first possessor; 8: 9–13 Alma² cast out of A.; 8: 16–18 Alma² returns to A.; ch. 9–14 words of Alma² and Amulek to people at A.; 10: 23 destruction of people predicted; 14: 8 people at A. burn scriptures, slay believers; 14: 22 Alma² and Amulek are imprisoned; 14: 27 falling prison walls slay leaders; 14: 28 Alma² and Amulek are freed; 14: 29 people flee from prophets; 15: 1 Alma² and Amulek banished from A.; 15: 15 people remain hard-hearted; 16: 2–3, 9 (25: 2) Lamanites destroy

people of A.; 16: 11 called Desolation of Nehors; 49: 3 rebuilt; 49: 10–11 Lamanites dare not attack A.

AMMONIHAH, LAND OF—*to the west of River Sidon* (*see* Ammonihah, City of)

AMMONIHAHITES (*see* Ammonihah, City of)

AMMONITES (*see* Ammon[2], People of)

AMMORON—*Nephite traitor, brother of Amalickiah, descendant of Zoram[1]* [c. 66-61 B.C.]

Alma 52: 3 appointed king of Lamanites; 52: 12 attacks Nephites; 54: 1 proposes prisoner exchange; 54: 4–14 receives epistle from Moroni[1]; 54: 16–24 A's reply; 55: 1 knows his cause is not just; 55: 2 Moroni[1] refuses prisoner exchange with A.; 56: 18 abandons attack; 57: 1 offers to deliver city of Antiparah in exchange for prisoners; 57: 17 sends new provisions; 59: 7 strengthens Lamanites; 62: 33 is with combined Lamanite armies; 62: 36 is slain by Teancum.

AMNIGADDAH—*Jaredite king*

Ether 1: 14–15 son of Aaron[2], father of Coriantum[2]; 10: 31 dwells in captivity.

AMNIHU—*hill on east of River Sidon*

Alma 2: 15 where Amlicites fight Nephites.

AMNOR[1]—*spy for Nephites* [c. 87 B.C.]

Alma 2: 22 sent to watch camp of Amlicites.

AMNOR[2]—*Nephite coin*

Alma 11: 6 a. of silver; 11: 11 equal to two senums.

AMORON—*a Nephite* [c. A.D. 400-421]

Moro. 9: 7 reports to Mormon.

AMOS[1]—*Nephite record keeper* [c. A.D. 110-194]

4 Ne. 1: 19–20 son of Nephi[4], keeps records; 1: 21 gives records to his son.

AMOS[2]—*Nephite record keeper* [c. A.D. 194-306]

4 Ne. 1: 21 receives records from his father, Amos[1]; 1: 47 gives records to Ammaron.

AMOZ—*father of Isaiah[1]* [c. 8th century B.C.]

2 Ne. 12: 1 (23: 1; Isa. 2: 1; 13: 1) Isaiah[1], son of A.

AMULEK—*missionary companion of Alma[2]* [c. 82-74 B.C.]

Alma 8: 20 (10: 7) visited by angel; 8: 21 receives Alma[2]; 8: 31–32 goes forth with power; 10: 1–11 preaches to people in Ammonihah; 10: 2–3 son of Giddonah, grandson of Ishmael[2], descendant of Aminadi, Nephi[1], Lehi[2], and Manasseh; 10: 4 man of reputation, friends, riches; 10: 5–6 had rebelled against God; 10: 8 obeys angel; 10: 11 family and kindred blessed by Alma[2]; 10: 12 a second witness; 10: 17 perceives questioners' thoughts; 10: 22 prophesies destruction of Ammonihahites; 10: 31 accused by Zeezrom; 11: 20 judges stir up people against A.; 11: 21–33 questioned by Zeezrom; 11: 39–40 testifies of Redeemer; 11: 41–45 teaches of resurrection, judgment, and restoration; 12: 1 words silence Zeezrom; 12: 8–18 Alma[2] explains the words of A.; 12: 24 speaks of temporal death; 14: 2 people desire his destruction; 14: 10 wants to stop martyrdom of believers; 14: 17 imprisoned with Alma[2]; 14: 18 refuses to answer judge; 14: 26 breaks bonds by faith; 14: 26–27 people flee, persecutors slain; 15: 1 with Alma[2], commanded to leave city; 15: 16 rejected by relatives and friends; 15: 18 goes with Alma[2] to Zarahemla; 16: 13 preaches repentance; 31: 6 among missionaries to Zoramites; 31: 32 Alma[2] prays for A's success; 34: 1 teaches the poor; 34: 10–16 explains great and last sacrifice, meaning of law, mercy, justice; 34: 17 teaches about prayer; 34: 32 warns against procrastination; 35: 1 goes to Jershon; Hel. 5: 10 quoted on redemption; Ether 12: 13 faith of Alma[2] and A. causes prison walls to tumble.

AMULON—*leader of priests of Noah[3], tributary monarch under Laman[3]* (*see also* Amulon, Children of; Amulon, Land of; Amulonites; Noah[3], Priests of)

Mosiah 23: 32 leader of priests of Noah[3]; 23: 33 pleads with Lamanites for life; 23: 35 joins Lamanites, discovers land of Helam; 23: 39 made king; 24: 1 A. and brethren made teachers over people of Alma[1]; 24: 8 exercises authority over Alma[1] and people; 24: 11 threatens believers with death.

AMULON, CHILDREN OF—*children of priests of Noah[3]* (*see also* Amulonites)

Mosiah 25: 12 children of A. and brethren want to be called Nephites.

AMULON, LAND OF—*settled by Amulon and priests, between Zarahemla and Nephi*

Mosiah 23: 31 priests of Noah[3] are found in A.; 24: 1 Amulon and brethren appointed teachers in A.

AMULONITES—*descendants and followers of Amulon and priests of Noah[3]* (*see also* Noah[3], Priests of)

Alma 21: 3 are more wicked than Lamanites; 21: 4 after order of Nehors;

23: 14 (24: 29) none converted; 24: 1 stir up Lamanites; 24: 2 rebel against king, take up arms against Ammonites; 24: 28 (25: 7) slay believers; 25: 4 slain by Nephites; 25: 5 usurp leadership and persecute Lamanites; 25: 8 hunted, slain by Lamanites; 25: 9 Abinadi's prophecy fulfilled.

ANATHOTH—*Levite city near old Jerusalem*

2 **Ne.** 20: 30 (Isa. 10: 30) O poor A.

ANCIENT (*see also* Old)

2 **Ne.** 13: 2 (Isa. 3: 2) the Lord takes the *a.* away from Jerusalem; 19: 15 the *a.*, he is the head; 29: 4–5 (Morm. 8: 15) Jews are the Lord's *a.* covenant people; **Mosiah** 8: 13 Mosiah² can translate all records of *a.* date; **Ether** 9: 5 (10: 33) oaths of the *a.*

ANGEL (*see also* Angels, Ministering of; Angels of the Devil; Messenger; TG Angels; BD Angels)

1 **Ne.** 1: 8 (Alma 36: 22) numberless concourses of *a.* praising God; 3: 29 (17: 45) *a.* reproves Laman¹ and Lemuel¹; 11: 14—14: 30 (15: 29; 19: 8, 10) *a.* of the Lord shows Nephi¹ vision interpreting father's dream; 2 **Ne.** 10: 3 *a.* reveals Christ's name to Jacob²; 32: 3 *a.* speak by power of Holy Ghost; **Mosiah** 3: 2—4: 1 *a.* speaks to Benjamin; 27: 11–18, 32 (Alma 17: 2; 36: 5; 38: 7) *a.* of the Lord appears to Alma² and sons of Mosiah²; **Alma** 8: 14–18 (9: 19–30) *a.* gives Alma² instructions; 10: 7 (11: 31) *a.* appears to Amulek; 13: 29 voice of the Lord declares repentance by mouth of *a.* unto all nations; 18: 30 heaven is place where God and *a.* dwell; 19: 34 many Lamanites see and converse with *a.*; 21: 5 an Amalekite asks why *a.* do not appear unto them; 27: 4 Anti-Nephi-Lehies treat Ammon² and brothers as *a.*; 29: 1 O that I were an *a.*; 32: 23 God imparts his word by *a.*; 39: 19 as easy for the Lord to send *a.* at this time as to our children; 40: 11 *a.* teaches Alma² about existence between death and resurrection; **Hel.** 5: 36 faces of Nephi² and Lehi⁴ shine as faces of *a.*; 13: 7 *a.* taught Samuel the Lamanite; 16: 14 *a.* appear unto wise men to declare glad tidings; 3 **Ne.** 7: 15, 18 Nephi³ is visited by *a.*; 11: 8 Nephites think Christ is *a.* descending; 28: 30 three Nephites are as *a.* of God; **Moro.** 7: 22–25 *a.* sent to teach men of Christ's coming; 7: 37 it is by faith that *a.* appear and minister unto men.

ANGELS, MINISTERING OF (*see also* Angel; TG Angels, Ministering)

Jacob 7: 5 *a.* ministered to Jacob²; 7: 17 Sherem confesses power of Holy Ghost and ministering of *a.*; **Omni** 1: 25 Amaleki exhorts all men to believe in ministering of *a.*; 3 **Ne.** 7: 18 *a.* minister unto Nephi³ daily; 17: 24 *a.* minister to Nephite children; **Moro.** 7: 25 by ministering of *a.*, men begin to exercise faith in Christ; 7: 29 *a.* have not ceased to minister unto men; 7: 37 by faith *a.* appear and minister unto men.

ANGELS OF THE DEVIL (*see also* Demon; Devil; Devils)

2 **Ne.** 2: 17 (9: 8) *a.* of God fell from heaven, became devil; 9: 8–9 without resurrection, men's spirits must become *a.* to devil; 9: 9 (Alma 30: 53) Satan transformed himself into *a.* of light; 9: 16 the filthy shall be devil and his *a.*; **Jacob** 3: 11 loose yourselves from pains of hell that ye become not *a.* to devil; **Mosiah** 26: 27 everlasting fire prepared for devil and his *a.*; **Hel.** 13: 37 people will say, We are surrounded by devil's *a.*

ANGER (*see also* Fury; Indignation; Offend; Passion; Provoke; Rage; Wrath)

3 **Ne.** 11: 29 devil stirs men up to contend with *a.*; **Ether** 15: 22 Jaredites drunken with *a.*; **Moro.** 9: 3 Satan stirs Lamanites up continually to *a.*

ANGOLA—*Nephite City*

Morm. 2: 4 Nephites take possession of A.

ANGUISH (*see also* Misery; Pain; Remorse; Sorrow; Suffering; Torment)

1 **Ne.** 17: 47 (Morm. 6: 16) my soul is rent with *a.*; **Mosiah** 2: 38 awareness of guilt fills breast with *a.*; 3: 7 Christ's *a.* will cause blood to come from every pore; 25: 11 Nephites filled with *a.* for welfare of Lamanites' souls; 28: 4 sons of Mosiah² suffered much *a.* of soul because of their iniquities; **Alma** 38: 8 Alma² passed three days and nights in bitter *a.* of soul.

ANI-ANTI—*Lamanite village in land of Nephi*

Alma 21: 11 Aaron³ finds Muloki and brethren preaching in A.

ANIMAL (*see also* Ass; Bear; Beast; Bee; Calf, Calves; Cattle; Chickens; Cow; Creature; Cummoms; Cureloms; Dog; Dove; Dragon; Elephant; Fish; Flock; Food; Fowl; Game; Goat; Hen; Horse; Insect; Lamb; Meat; Ox, Oxen; Serpent; Sheep; Swine; Vultures; BD Animals)

1 **Ne.** 18: 25 beasts of every kind found during journey through wilderness; 2 **Ne.** 5: 11 Nephites begin to raise *a.* of every kind; **Alma** 22: 31 Bountiful filled with wild *a.* of every kind; **Ether** 9: 18 Jaredites raise many kinds of *a.* useful for food; 10: 19 land southward covered with *a.* of the forest.

ANOINTING, ANOINT (see also Consecrate; Ordinance; TG Anointing; BD Anoint)

2 Ne. 20: 27 (Isa. 10: 27) yoke shall be destroyed because of the *a*.; **Jacob** 1: 9 Nephi¹ is *a*. king; 3 Ne. 13: 17 (Matt. 6: 17) when thou fastest, *a*.

ANSWER (see also Open; Prayer; Receive)

2 Ne. 2: 7 Christ a sacrifice to *a*. ends of law; 2: 10 punishment affixed to *a*. ends of atonement; **Mosiah** 29: 38 every man expresses willingness to *a*. for own sins; **Alma** 9: 26 Son quick to *a*. prayers of his people; **Morm.** 9: 37 may the Lord grant that their prayers be *a*. according to their faith.

ANTICHRIST (see also Prophets, False; TG Antichrist; BD Antichrist)

Jacob 7: 1–2 Sherem; **Alma** 1: 2–15 Nehor; 30: 6–21 Korihor.

ANTI-NEPHI-LEHI—*a brother of Lamoni, king over converted Lamanites*

Alma 24: 3 name given son of Lamanite king, receives kingdom; 24: 5 holds council with Ammon² and Lamoni.

ANTI-NEPHI-LEHIES (see Ammon², People of)

ANTIOMNO—*Lamanite king* [early first century B.C.]

Alma 20: 4 king in land of Middoni, friend of Lamoni.

ANTION—*Nephite coin* (see also Coin)

Alma 11: 19 *a*. of gold equal to three shiblons.

ANTIONAH—*a chief ruler in Ammonihah*

Alma 12: 20 questions Alma².

ANTIONUM—*Nephite commander* [c. A.D. 385]

Morm. 6: 14 falls with his ten thousand.

ANTIONUM, LAND OF—*east of Sidon*

Alma 31: 3 Zoramites gathered in A.; 43: 5 Lamanites arrive under Zerahemnah; 43: 22 Lamanites retire from A.

ANTIPARAH—*Nephite city*

Alma 56: 14 possessed by Lamanites; 56: 31–34 Helaman² decoys Lamanite forces in A.; 57: 1–4 regained by Nephites.

ANTIPAS, MOUNT

Alma 47: 7 Lamanites gather on A.; 47: 10 Amalickiah sends message to Lehonti, leader of Lamanites on A.

ANTIPUS—*Nephite commander* [c. 65 B.C.]

Alma 56: 9 appointed a leader; 56: 10 A's army reduced by Lamanites; 56: 15 fortifies city of Judea; 56: 18 strength of A's army feared; 56: 30–33 orders Helaman² and sons to march; 56: 37 pursues Lamanites; 56: 51 is slain; 56: 57 remainder of A's men join Ammonite striplings.

ANTUM, LAND OF

Morm. 1: 3 place of hill Shim and records.

ANXIETY, ANXIOUS, ANXIOUSLY (see also Fear; Trouble; Worry)

2 Ne. 1: 16 *a*. of Lehi¹ that his people observe the Lord's statutes; 6: 3 great *a*. of Jacob for welfare of his people's souls; **Jacob** 1: 5 future manifested unto Nephi¹ and Jacob² because of *a*. for people; **Mosiah** 29: 38 Nephites *a*. that every man have equal chance; **Alma** 13: 27 Alma² wishes with *a*. unto pain that people of Ammonihah hearken to his words; 3 Ne. 3: 3 robbers wait with *a*. to destroy Nephites.

APOSTASY (see also Ammonihah, City of; Antichrist; Church, Great and Abominable; Church of the Devil; Darkness, Spiritual; Dissenter; Doctrine, False; Gadianton Robbers; Priestcraft; Prophets, False; Sin; Transgression; Unbelief; Zoramites²; TG Apostasy of Individuals)

1 Ne. 8: 23 (12: 17) those who commence path lose way in mist; 8: 28 those who partake of fruit fall into forbidden paths because of shame of world; 15: 10 (17: 45) Nephi¹ warns brothers about hardheartedness; 2 Ne. ch. 28 prophecies of Nephi¹ regarding corrupt churches in latter days; **Jacob** ch. 2–3 Jacob² denounces Nephites' sins; **Mosiah** 11: 1–7 Noah³ leads his people into *a*.; **Alma** 4: 6–12 pride, contention, wickedness grow in church, lead unbelievers astray; 24: 30 those enlightened by Spirit who fall into transgression become more hardened; ch. 31 Zoramites have fallen into great errors; 37: 27 knowledge of secret oaths to be kept from Nephites lest they fall into darkness; **Hel.** 3: 33–34 (4: 11–13; 5: 2–3) many members of church become proud, wicked, less righteous than Lamanites; 12: 2 when the Lord prospers his people, they harden hearts and forget him; 13: 38 Nephites have sought happiness in doing iniquity; 3 Ne. 2: 1–3 Nephites forget signs, harden hearts, fall under Satan's power; 14: 24–27 (18: 13; Matt. 7: 24–27) parable of houses built on rock and on sand; 18: 15 watch and pray lest ye be tempted and led away by

devil; **4 Ne.** 1: 24–34, 38–39 Nephites fall away from truth, build false churches; **Morm.** 8: 28, 31–33 Mormon² prophesies about corrupt churches in latter days.

APOSTLE (*see also* Disciple; TG Apostles; BD Apostle)

1 Ne. 1: 10–11 Lehi¹ sees twelve in vision; 11: 29 Nephi¹ sees twelve in vision; 11: 34–36 multitudes to fight against *a.* of the Lamb; 12: 9 twelve *a.* shall judge twelve tribes of Israel, twelve Nephite disciples; 13: 24 twelve *a.* to bear record of the Lamb; 13: 26, 39–41 record of gospel to go forth by hand of twelve *a.*; **Morm.** 9: 18 many mighty miracles wrought by *a.*; **Ether** 12: 41 prophets and *a.* have written of Jesus; **Moro.** 2: 2 Nephite disciples to give Holy Ghost, as do the Lord's *a.*

APPAREL (*see also* Clothing; Garment; Raiment; TG Apparel)

Jacob 2: 13 (Alma 1: 6, 32; 4: 6; 5: 53; 31: 28; 4 Ne. 1: 24; Morm. 8: 36) Nephites proud because of costly *a.*; **Alma** 1: 27 church members do not wear costly *a.*; 32: 2 poor Zoramites cast out of synagogues because of coarse *a.*; **Hel.** 13: 28 the wicked clothe false prophets in costly *a.*

APPEAL (*see also* Plead)

Alma 37: 16 you must *a.* unto the Lord.

APPEAR, APPEARANCE (*see also* Jesus Christ, Appearances of; Show)

2 Ne. 4: 31 wilt thou make me shake at *a.* of sin; **Mosiah** 27: 11 angel *a.* to Alma² and sons of Mosiah²; **Alma** 8: 14 angel *a.* to Alma² on road from Ammonihah; 10: 7 angel *a.* to Amulek; 21: 5 why do not angels *a.* unto us; 30: 53 devil *a.* to Korihor in form of angel; **Hel.** 12: 15 it *a.* to man that sun stands still; 14: 3 because of lights in heavens, night shall *a.* as day; 14: 25 (3 Ne. 25: 11) risen saints shall *a.* to many; 16: 14 angels *a.* to wise men to fulfill scriptures; **Moro.** 7: 37 it is by faith that angels *a.*

APPEASE (*see also* Satisfy)

Alma 42: 15 atonement *a.* demands of justice; **Hel.** 11: 11 may the Lord's anger be *a.* in destruction of wicked already destroyed.

APPLY

Mosiah 4: 2 *a.* the atoning blood of Christ; 12: 27 ye have not *a.* your hearts to understanding.

APPOINT (*see also* Ordain)

2 Ne. 24: 31 none shall be alone in his *a.* times; **Mosiah** 2: 4 the Lord *a.* just

men to be teachers; 29: 11 let us *a.* judges; **Alma** 12: 27 (42: 6) it was *a.* unto men that they must die; 40: 4–5, 7–9 time *a.* for all to come forth from the dead; 40: 4–5, 10 God knows the time *a.* for the resurrection.

ARCHEANTUS—*Nephite military officer* [c. A.D. 385]

Moro. 9: 2 falls by sword.

ARISE (*see also* Rise)

3 Ne. 23: 11 many saints did *a.*

ARK (*see also* BD Ark)

Ether 6: 7 Jaredite vessels were tight like *a.* of Noah¹.

ARM (*see also* Armed; Arms; Might; Strength; TG Trust Not in the Arm of Flesh)

1 Ne. 22: 10 kindreds of earth cannot be blessed unless the Lord makes bare his *a.*; **2 Ne.** 1: 15 I am encircled eternally in *a.* of the Lord's love; 4: 34 I will not trust in *a.* of flesh; 8: 5 (Isa. 51: 5) the Lord's *a.* shall judge the people, and isles shall trust on his *a.*; 28: 31 cursed is he who makes flesh his *a.*; **Jacob** 6: 5 (Alma 5: 33) the Lord's *a.* of mercy is extended; **Omni** 1: 13 Nephites led by power of the Lord's *a.*; **Alma** 17: 37 Ammon² smites off Lamanites' *a.* with sword; 20: 20 Ammon² smites *a.* of Lamoni's father; 34: 16 mercy encircles the repentant in *a.* of safety; **Morm.** 5: 11 Nephites might have been clasped in *a.* of Jesus.

ARMED (*see also* Arms)

1 Ne. 14: 14 saints *a.* with righteousness.

ARMOR (*see also* Breastplate)

1 Ne. 4: 19 Nephi¹ girds on Laban's *a.*; **2 Ne.** 1: 23 put on *a.* of righteousness; **Alma** 43: 21 Lamanites fear Nephite armies because of *a.*; **3 Ne.** 4: 7 appearance of Giddianhi's army is terrible because of their *a.*

ARMS (*see also* Weapon)

Alma 51: 13 (62: 9) king-men refuse to take up *a.* against Lamanites; 53: 11 because of oath, Ammonites do not take up *a.*; 53: 16 sons of Ammonites take up *a.*

ARMY, ARMIES (*see also* Battle; Soldier; War)

1 Ne. 4: 2 (17: 27; Hel. 8: 11) *a.* of Pharaoh drowned in Red Sea.

AROUSE (*see also* Awake; Prick; Stir)

Jacob 3: 11 (Alma 32: 27) *a.* the faculties of your souls; **Morm.** 2: 24 words of Mormon² *a.* Nephites to vigor.

ARRAIGN

Alma 11: 44 every soul to be *a.* before bar of Godhead to be judged.

ARROW (*see also* Bow; Weapon)

1 Ne. 16: 23 Nephi[1] makes *a.* out of straight stick.

ART (*see also* Skill)

Alma 10: 15 lawyers are learned in all *a.* and cunning; **Hel.** 12: 2 the Lord prospers his people in precious things of every kind and *a.*; 16: 21 wicked Nephites fear prophets work some great mystery by *a.* of the evil one; **Morm.** 2: 10 no man could keep that which was his own, because of magic *a.* in land; **Ether** 13: 16 Coriantumr[2] studies all *a.* of war.

ASCEND (*see also* Rise)

2 Ne. 24: 13–14 Lucifer claims he will *a.* into heaven; **Jacob** 2: 35 sobbings of wives and children *a.* to God against Nephites.

ASHAMED (*see also* Shame)

1 Ne. 8: 25–28 those who partake of fruit are *a.* because of scoffers; 21: 23 (2 Ne. 6: 7; Isa. 49: 23) they shall not be *a.* who wait for the Lord; **2 Ne.** 6: 13 people of the Lord shall not be *a.*; 7: 7 (Isa. 50: 7) I know that I shall not be *a.*; **Alma** 46: 21 if Nephites become *a.* to take name of Christ, the Lord shall rend them; **3 Ne.** 22: 4 fear not, for thou shalt not be *a.*; **Morm.** 8: 38 why are ye *a.* to take upon you name of Christ.

ASHES (*see also* Sackcloth)

Mosiah 11: 25 except Noah's people repent in sackcloth and *a.*, the Lord will not hear prayers; **3 Ne.** 25: 3 wicked shall be *a.* under feet of those who fear God.

ASK (*see also* Inquire; Knock; Pray; Question; Seek; TG Prayer)

1 Ne. 15: 11 (Moro. 10: 4) if ye *a.* the Lord in faith, he will make things known; **2 Ne.** 4: 35 (3 Ne. 14: 7; 18: 20; James 1: 5) God will give liberally to him that *a.*; 4: 35 God will give if I *a.* not amiss; 32: 4 if people cannot understand words of Nephi[1], it is because they *a.* not; **Enos** 1: 15 (3 Ne. 18: 20; 27: 29; Moro. 7: 26) whatsoever ye *a.* in faith ye shall receive; **Mosiah** 4: 10 *a.* in sincerity of heart that God forgive you; 4: 21 (3 Ne. 18: 20; Moro. 7: 26) God grants whatsoever men *a.* that is right; **Hel.** 10: 5 Nephi[2] would not *a.* what is contrary to the Lord's will; **3 Ne.** 13: 8 the Father knows what men need before they *a.*; 14: 7 (18: 20) *a.*, and it shall be given; 14: 8 every one who *a.* receives; 17: 3 (18: 20; 27: 28; Morm. 9: 21; Moro. 7: 26) *a.* the Father in Christ's

name; **Morm.** 9: 28 *a.* not that ye may consume it on your lusts, but *a.* with firmness unshaken that ye will yield to no temptation; **Moro.** 10: 4 *a.* God if these things are true.

ASLEEP (*see* Sleep)

ASS (*see also* Animal)

1 Ne. 18: 25 Nephites find *a.* in wilderness; **Mosiah** 5: 14 doth a man take neighbor's *a.* and keep him; 12: 5 (21: 3) people of Noah[3] shall be driven like dumb *a.*; **Ether** 9: 19 Jaredites have *a.*

ASSEMBLE (*see also* Church of God; Meet, Meeting; Worship)

Mosiah 18: 25 one day in week set apart for people to *a.* to be taught and to worship; 25: 21 Nephites *a.* in different bodies, called churches; **Alma** 6: 5 none are deprived of privilege of *a.* to hear God's word; 15: 17 Nephites in Sidom *a.* in sanctuaries to worship.

ASSYRIA—*country in western Asia* (*see also* Assyrian; BD Assyria and Babylonia)

2 Ne. 17: 17 (Isa. 7: 17) king of A. attacks Judah; 17: 18 (Isa. 7: 18) the Lord to hiss for bee in land of A.; 17: 20 (Isa. 7: 20) king of A. brings terror; 18: 4 (Isa. 8: 4) riches of Damascus and spoils of Samaria to be taken before king of A.; 18: 7 (Isa. 8: 7) king of A. and his glory shall come up over his channels; 20: 12 (Isa. 10: 12) the Lord will punish fruit of stout heart of king of A.; 21: 11, 16 (Isa. 11: 11, 16) the Lord to recover his people from A.

ASSYRIAN—*native of Assyria* (*see also* Assyria; BD Assyria)

2 Ne. 20: 5 (Isa. 10: 5) O A., rod of the Lord's anger; 20: 24 (Isa. 10: 24) people in Zion not to be afraid of A.; 24: 25 (Isa. 14: 25) the Lord will tread A. under foot.

ASTRAY (*see also* Apostasy; Err; Lose, Lost; Wander)

2 Ne. 12: 5 house of Jacob have all gone *a.*; 28: 14 false churches have all gone *a.*; **Mosiah** 14: 6 (Isa. 53: 6) all we, like sheep, have gone *a.*; 27: 10 Alma[2] seeks to lead *a.* the Lord's people; **Alma** 5: 37 unrighteous have gone *a.*, as sheep having no shepherd; 13: 17 Melchizedek's people had all gone *a.*; 30: 53 devil tells Korihor people have gone *a.* after unknown God; 41: 1 some have gone far *a.* because of wresting the scriptures.

ASTRONOMY (*see also* Moon; Star; Sun; World)

Alma 30: 44 motion of earth and planets in regular form witness Supreme Creator; **Hel.** 12: 15 earth moves, not

sun; 14: 5 (3 Ne. 1: 21) new star to arise as sign of Christ's birth.

ATE (see Eat)

ATHIRST (see also Thirst)

Alma 1: 30 Nephites do not send away those who are a.; 4: 12 some church members turn backs on those who are a.

ATONE, ATONEMENT (see Jesus Christ, Atonement through)

AUTHOR (see also Founder)

Hel. 6: 30 Satan is a. of all sin; 8: 28 a. of secret band is Gadianton and the evil one; **Moro.** 6: 4 Christ is a. and finisher of members' faith.

AUTHORITY (see also Calling; Dominion; Office; Ordain; Ordinance; Power; Priesthood; Reign; Rule; Scepter; TG Authority)

1 Ne. 10: 22 Holy Ghost gives a. to speak; **2 Ne.** 1: 25 brothers of Nephi¹ accuse him of seeking a.; **Mosiah** 13: 6 Abinadi speaks with a. from God; 18: 13 Alma¹ baptizes, having a. from God; 21: 33 none in Limhi's land have a. to baptize; 23: 17 none receive a. to teach except by Alma¹ from God; 26: 8 (Alma 5: 3) Alma² has a. over church; **Alma** 9: 6 who is God that sendeth no more a. than one man among this people; 17: 3 sons of Mosiah² teach with a. of God; 25: 5 Amulon's followers usurp a. over Lamanites; 30: 23 Korihor accuses ancient priests of usurping a.; **Hel.** 5: 18 Nephi² and Lehi⁴ preach to Lamanites with great a.; 7: 4 Gadianton robbers usurp a.; 11: 18 (3 Ne. 7: 17) Nephi² a man of God, having great a. from God; **3 Ne.** 6: 15 Satan tempts people to seek power and a.; 11: 25 (12: 1) baptism performed by a. of Christ; **Moro.** 8: 16 Moroni² preaches with boldness, having a. from God.

AVAIL (see also Profit)

Mosiah 3: 15 law of Moses a. nothing except through Christ's atonement; **Alma** 34: 28 without charity toward the needy, prayer a. nothing; **Moro.** 8: 22 baptism a. nothing unto him who is under no condemnation.

AVENGE (see also Revenge; Vengeance)

Alma 54: 16 Ammoron threatens to a. his brother's blood on Nephites; 61: 6 Nephites flock to army to a. their wrongs; **Morm.** 3: 9 Nephites swear to a. themselves of brethren's blood; 8: 41 God will a. saints' blood upon the wicked; **Ether** 8: 22 the Lord will not suffer saints' blood to cry for vengeance without a. them; 14: 24 Shiz swears to a. himself upon Coriantumr² of his brother's blood.

AWAKE, AWAKEN (see also Arouse; Consciousness; Rise)

2 Ne. 4: 28 a., my soul; 9: 47 expedient that I should a. you to awful reality of these things; 27: 3 those who oppose Zion shall be as hungry man who a. from dream of eating and soul is empty; **Jacob** 3: 11 shake yourselves that ye may a. from slumbers of death; **Mosiah** 2: 38 divine justice a. the unrepentant to sense of guilt; 2: 40 a. to remembrance of awful situation of those fallen into transgression; 4: 5 God's goodness a. man to sense of his own nothingness; **Alma** 4: 3 Nephites are a. to remembrance of duty by afflictions; 5: 7 church members a. unto God; 7: 22 Alma² teaches that he might a. people to sense of duty to God; 32: 27 Alma² warns people to a.; **Morm.** 9: 13 all men shall be a. from endless sleep by power of God; **Ether** 8: 24 when they see secret combinations come among them, Gentiles are to a. to sense of awful situation.

AWKWARDNESS

Ether 12: 24 Nephites can write but little because of a. of hands.

AX

Enos 1: 20 (Morm. 6: 9) Lamanites have skill with a.; **Alma** 5: 52 a. is laid at root of tree.

BABBLINGS

Alma 1: 32 those who do not belong to church indulge themselves in b.

BABE (see also Child; Infant)

2 Ne. 13: 4 (Isa. 3: 4) b. shall rule over Judah; **3 Ne.** 26: 16 during Christ's visit b. utter marvelous things.

BABEL, TOWER OF (see Tower)

BABYLON—capital of Babylonia, in southwest Asia (see also Assyria; Church of the Devil; TG Babylon; BD Babylon)

1 Ne. 1: 13 (10: 3; 2 Ne. 25: 10; Omni 1: 15) Jerusalem to be carried captive into B.; 20: 14 (Isa. 48: 14) the Lord will do his pleasure on B.; 20: 20 (Isa. 48: 20) go ye forth of B.; **2 Ne.** 23: 1 (Isa. 13: 1) burden of B., which Isaiah¹ saw; 23: 19 (Isa. 13: 19) B. shall be as when God overthrew Sodom and Gomorrah; 24: 4 (Isa. 14: 4) take up proverb against king of B.; 24: 22 (Isa. 14: 22) the Lord will cut off from B. the name; 25: 15 B. shall be destroyed.

BACK

Alma 4: 12 (5: 55; Hel. 6: 39) the proud turn their b. upon the needy.

BAD (see also Evil; Worse)

2 Ne. 2: 11 opposition necessary that good and b. may be brought to pass; Jacob 5: 65–77 good and b. branches in the vineyard; Alma 3: 26 the dead reap rewards according to works, whether good or b.

BALL (see Liahona)

BAND (see also Bind; Chain; Cord; Gadianton Robbers)

Mosiah 15: 8 (Alma 11: 41–42; Morm. 9: 13) through Christ, God breaks b. of temporal death; 23: 12 people of Noah³ are bound with b. of iniquity; Alma 5: 7 the fathers were encircled by b. of death; 14: 24 chief judge commands Alma² and Amulek to deliver themselves from b.

BANISHED

Alma 36: 15 oh, that I could be b. and not be brought before God to be judged.

BANNER (see also Title of Liberty)

2 Ne. 23: 2 (Isa. 13: 2) lift a b. upon high mountain.

BAPTISM, BAPTIZE (see also Accountability, Age of; Born of God; Church of God; Conversion; Faith; Fire; Forgive; Grave; Holy Ghost; Holy Ghost, Baptism of; Immersion; Name of the Lord; Ordinance; Remission; Repentance; Sacrament; Salvation; Wash; Water; Witness; TG Baptism; Baptism, Essential; Baptism, Immersion; Baptism, Qualifications for; BD Baptism)

1 Ne. 10: 9–10 John the Baptist to b. Messiah; 20: 1 (Isa. 48: 1) house of Jacob comes forth out of waters of Judah, or out of waters of b.; 2 Ne. 9: 23 God commands all men to repent and be b. in his name; 31: 4–12 Nephi¹ explains why Messiah must be b.; 31: 11 (3 Ne. 11. 37–38; 18: 16; 21: 6; 27: 20; Morm. 3: 2; 7: 8; Ether 4: 18; Moro. 7: 34) repent and be b. in name of the Son; 31: 12–13 (3 Ne. 26: 17) he who is b. shall receive Holy Ghost; Mosiah 18: 8–10 Alma¹ describes qualities of those to be b. in name of the Lord; 18: 12–16 Alma¹ b. Helam and others at Waters of Mormon; 18: 17 (3 Ne. 18: 16) those who are b. by authority of God are added to his church; 21: 35 Limhi's people desire to be b. as witness they are willing to serve God; Alma 5: 62 Alma² invites nonmembers to be b. unto repentance; 9: 27 the Son redeems those who are b. unto repentance through faith; 15: 6–12 Alma² b. Zeezrom; 32: 16 blessed is he who believes and is b. without stubbornness; Hel. 5: 19 (3 Ne. 9: 20; Ether 12: 14) eight thousand Lamanites

are b. with water and fire; 3 Ne. 7: 24 -25 none are brought to repentance who are not b. with water; 7: 25 Nephi³ ordains men to b. as witness that people have repented and received remission of sins; 9: 20 (12: 1–2; Morm. 7: 10) Christ will b. with fire those who come to him with broken heart; 11: 21–22 (12: 1) the Lord gives Nephite disciples power to b.; 11: 23–28 (Moro. 6: 1–4) conditions and mode of b.; 11: 33–34 (Morm. 9: 23; Ether 4: 18) only those who believe and are b. shall be saved; 18: 5, 11, 30 sacrament to be given to those who are b.; 19: 11–13 Nephi³ and other disciples are b.; 21: 6 Gentiles who repent and are b. may be numbered among the Lord's people; 26: 17 Nephite disciples b. those who come unto them; 27: 16 whoso repents and is b. shall be filled; Morm. 7: 10 if ye believe and are b. with water and fire, it shall be well in day of judgment; 9: 29 see that ye are not b. unworthily; Moro. 8: 5, 8, 10–15, 20–22 b. of little children is unnecessary; 8: 25 first fruits of repentance is b.

BAR (see also Judgment; Judgment-Seat)

2 Ne. 33: 11 (Jacob 6: 13; Moro. 10: 27, 34) you and I shall stand face to face before Christ's b.; Jacob 6: 9 (Morm. 9: 13) power of redemption will bring wicked before b. of God; Mosiah 16: 10 mortal shall put on immortality and be brought before b. of God to be judged; Alma 5: 22 how will you feel to stand before the b. of God with stained garments; 11: 44 everything shall be restored and arraigned before b. of Son, Father, and Holy Spirit.

BARE

1 Ne. 22: 10–11 (Mosiah 12: 24; 15: 31; 3 Ne. 16: 20; Isa. 52: 10) the Lord makes b. his holy arm; 3 Ne. 20: 35 Father hath made b. his holy arm.

BARGE (see also Dish; Ship; Vessel)

Ether 2: 6, 16–18 Jaredites build b.; 6: 4 Jaredites aboard b.

BARREN

Alma 32: 39 if you neglect tree, your ground is b.; 3 Ne. 22: 1 (Isa. 54: 1) sing, O b., thou that didst not bear.

BATHE (see Tears)

BATTLE (see also Army; Carnage; Fight; Slaughter; War; TG God to Fight Our Battles)

1 Ne. 12: 2 Nephi¹ sees multitudes gathered together to b.; Jarom 1: 7 Lamanites come many times against Nephites to b.; Mosiah 9: 16 Zeniff and his people go forth against Lamanites to b.; 10: 6 Lamanites prepare to come to

b. against Zeniff's people; **Alma** 2: 16 Alma² goes at head of armies against Amlicites to *b.*; 28: 2 tremendous *b.* between Nephites and Lamanites; 43: 26 Moroni¹ gathers people to *b.* against Lamanites; 62: 19 Lamanites do not come to *b.* because of Nephites' great courage and numbers; **3 Ne.** 4: 1 armies of robbers prepare to *b.*; 4: 4 armies of robbers do not come to *b.* against Laman; **Morm.** 4: 1 Nephite armies go up to *b.* against Lamanites; 8: 2 after great *b.* at Cumorah, Nephites hunted by Lamanites; **Ether** 15: 15 Jaredites march forth one against another to *b.*; **Moro.** 9: 2 Mormon² has sore *b.* with Lamanites.

BEAM (*see* Mote)

BEAR [noun] (*see also* Animal)
   2 Ne. 21: 7 (30: 13; Isa. 11: 7) cow and *b.* shall be fed.

BEAR, BORE, BORNE (*see also* Born; Burden; Carry; Endure; Record; Tolerable)
   1 Ne. 11: 20 Nephi¹ beholds virgin *b.* child in arms; 16: 1 thou has declared hard things, more than we are able to *b.*; **2 Ne.** 17: 14 a virgin shall conceive, and shall *b.* a son; **Mosiah** 10: 9 all old and young men willing to *b.* arms gather for battle; 13: 23 (Hel. 7: 21; Ex. 20: 16) thou shalt not *b.* false witness; 26: 18 blessed is this people who are willing to *b.* the Lord's name; **Alma** 4: 19 Alma² sees no way to reclaim people save in *b.* down in pure testimony against them; 13: 28 pray that ye be not tempted above that which ye can *b.*; 26: 27 (34: 40; 38: 4) *b.* with patience thine afflictions; **3 Ne.** 20: 41 be ye clean that *b.* the vessels of the Lord.

BEAST (*see also* Animal)
   1 Ne. 7: 16 Laman¹ and Lemuel seek to leave Nephi¹ in the wilderness to be devoured by wild *b.*; 16: 31 Nephi¹ slays wild *b.* for food; 18: 25 Lehites find *b.* in forest of every kind; **Enos** 1: 3 Enos² hunts *b.* in forests; **Jarom** 1: 6 Lamanites drink blood of *b.*; **Alma** 34: 10 great and last sacrifice not to be sacrifice of *b.*; **3 Ne.** 4: 2 no wild *b.* in lands deserted by Nephites; 20: 16 (21: 12) house of Jacob¹ to be among Gentiles as lion among *b.* of forest; 28: 22 (4 Ne. 1: 33) disciples cast into den of wild *b.*; **Morm.** 8: 24 wild *b.* could not harm saints; **Ether** 10: 26 Jaredites make tools with which they work their *b.*; **Moro.** 9: 9–10 Nephites devour flesh of Lamanite daughters like wild *b.*

BEAT (*see also* Smite; Strike)
   2 Ne. 28: 8 God will *b.* us with a few stripes; **3 Ne.** 20: 19 (Micah 4: 13) thou shalt *b.* in pieces many people.

BEATITUDES (*see also* BD Beatitudes)
   3 Ne. 12: 3–12 (Matt. 5: 5–2) the Savior teaches B. to Nephites.

BEAUTY, BEAUTIFUL (*see also* Comely; Delightsome; Fair)
   1 Ne. 11: 8 *b.* of tree exceeds all *b.*; 11: 15 Nephi¹ sees virgin, most *b.*; 13: 37 (Mosiah 12: 21; 15: 15–18; 3 Ne. 20: 40; Isa. 52: 7) how *b.* upon the mountain are they who publish peace; **2 Ne.** 8: 24 (3 Ne. 20: 36; Moro. 10: 31) Zion to put on *b.* garments; 14: 2 branch of the Lord shall be *b.* and glorious; **Mosiah** 14: 2 (Isa. 53: 2) when we shall see him there is no *b.* that we should desire him; 18: 30 how *b.* are the environs of Mormon to those who came to knowledge of the Redeemer.

BEE (*see also* Animal)
   2 Ne. 17: 18 (Isa. 7: 18) the Lord shall hiss for *b.* in Assyria; **Ether** 2: 3 deseret is interpreted as honey *b.*; 2: 3 Jaredites carry swarms of *b.*

BEFOREHAND
   1 Ne. 4: 6 Nephi¹ led by Spirit, not knowing *b.* what he should do.

BEG, BEGGAR (*see also* Plead; Poor)
   Mosiah 4: 16–25 ye will not suffer the *b.* to put up his petition to you in vain; 4: 20 Nephites *b.* the Lord for forgiveness; **Alma** 30: 56 Korihor *b.* from house to house for food.

BEGINNING (*see also* Creation; End)
   1 Ne. 5: 12–13 (Alma 37: 3) brass plates contain record of Jews from *b.*; 9: 6 (Acts 15: 18) the Lord knows all things from *b.*; 12: 18 Holy Ghost bears record of Lamb from *b.* of world; 20: 3, 5, 16 (Isa. 48: 3, 5, 16) the Lord has declared former things from *b.*; **2 Ne.** 9: 2 the Lord has spoken through his prophets from *b.*; 11: 4 all things given of God from *b.* typify Christ; 27: 7 sealed book shall be revelation from God, from *b.* of world to end; **Mosiah** 3: 8 (Hel. 14: 12) Christ the Creator of all things from *b.*; 7: 27 (Ether 3: 15–16) Christ to take image after which man was created in *b.*; 28: 14 Urim and Thummim were prepared from *b.*; **Alma** 11: 39 (3 Ne. 9: 18; Rev. 1: 8) Son is the *b.* and the end; 13: 7–8 (Heb. 7: 1–3) priesthood is without *b.* of days or end of years; 13: 9 Only Begotten is without *b.* of days or end of years; 18: 32 by God's hand men were all created from *b.*; 18: 34 (Ether 3: 15) man in *b.* was created after image of God; 26: 24 Lamanites' ways have been ways of transgressor from *b.*; **Hel.** 6: 29 devil has brought forth works of darkness from *b.* of man; **3 Ne.** 9: 15 (John 1: 1–2) Christ was with Father from *b.*; 11: 11 Christ has suffered

will of Father in all things from *b.*; 26: 3 Christ expounds all things from *b.*; **4 Ne.** 1: 38 fathers dwindled from *b.*; 1: 39 Lamanites taught to hate Nephites from *b.*; **Ether** 8: 15 Cain a murderer from *b.*; 8: 19 the Lord has forbidden secret combinations from *b.* of man; 8: 25 devil has caused people to murder and to cast out prophets from *b.*; 13: 2 Ether tells Jaredites of all things from *b.* of man.

BEGOTTEN (*see also* Born of God; Children of God; Jesus Christ — Only Begotten Son; Son)

Mosiah 5: 7 Christ hath spiritually *b.* his people.

BEGUILE (*see also* Deceit; Lying)

2 Ne. 9: 9 (Mosiah 16: 3; Ether 8: 25) devil *b.* our first parents.

BEHOLD, BEHELD (*see also* Look; See; View)

Ether 3: 19 brother of Jared² could not be kept from *b.* within the veil; **Moro.** 10: 14 gift of *b.* of angels.

BEING [noun]

2 Ne. 9: 9 devil is that *b.* who beguiled first parents; **Jacob** 2: 21 one *b.* is as precious in God's sight as other; 7: 7 Sherem claims people should not worship a *b.* who is to come in hundreds of years; **Mosiah** 2: 17 when ye are in service of fellow *b.* ye are in service of God; 8: 18 God provides means that man can become great benefit to fellow *b.*; **Alma** 26: 35 God is a merciful *b.*; **Hel.** 16: 18 people claim it is not reasonable that a *b.* such as Christ should come; **Moro.** 8: 18 God is not a changeable *b.*

BELIEF, BELIEVE, BELIEVING (*see also* Believer; Doubt; Faith; Opinion; Religion; Unbelief; TG Belief)

1 Ne. 2: 13 Laman¹ and Lemuel do not *b.* Jerusalem could be destroyed; 15: 11 (Enos 1: 15; Mosiah 4: 21; Alma 22: 16; 3 Ne. 18: 20; Moro. 7: 26) if ye ask, *b.* that ye shall receive, these things shall be made known to you; **2 Ne.** 2: 9 (3 Ne. 11: 33–35) they who *b.* in Christ shall be saved; 5: 6 those who go with Nephi¹ *b.* in God's warnings; 6: 14 (25: 16; 30: 7; 3 Ne. 20: 31) day cometh when Messiah's people shall *b.* in him; 6: 14 Messiah will destroy none who *b.* in him; 9: 18 saints who have *b.* in Holy One shall inherit kingdom of God; 25: 16 Jews will be persecuted until persuaded to *b.* in Christ; 25: 28 right way is to *b.* in Christ; 28: 6 false churches teach not to *b.* in miracles; 30: 7 scattered Jews shall also begin to *b.* in Christ; 33: 10 hearken unto these words and *b.* in Christ; 33: 10 if ye *b.* in Christ, ye shall *b.* in these words; **Jacob**

4: 5 all prophets *b.* in Christ; 7: 10 *b.* thou the scriptures; **Jarom** 1: 11 priests teach people to *b.* in Messiah as though he had already come; **Mosiah** 4: 9 *b.* in God, *b.* that he is; 4: 10 *b.* that ye must repent of sins; 4: 10 if ye *b.* these things, see that ye do them; 15: 22 those who *b.* words of prophets will come forth in first resurrection; 26: 22 whosoever is baptized shall *b.* in the Lord's name; **Alma** 1: 17 false priests pretend to teach according to *b.*; 4: 8 people of church persecute those who do not *b.* according to their will; 11: 40 the Son will take upon him transgressions of those who *b.* on his name; 18: 24, 26, 28 *b.* thou that there is a God, a Great Spirit; 21: 7 *b.* thou that the Son shall come to redeem mankind from sins; 22: 11 Lamanite king *b.* that the Great Spirit created all things; 24: 19 when brought to *b.*, converted Lamanites were firm; 30: 7 no law against a man's *b.*; 30: 42 Alma² knows that Korihor *b.*; 31: 17 Zoramites claim traditions bind brethren down to *b.* in Christ; 32: 16 blessed is he who *b.* in word of God without being compelled to know word before he will *b.*; 32: 18 if a man knows a thing, he has no cause to *b.*; 32: 27 if ye can no more than desire to *b.*, let this desire work in you; 33: 20 few looked upon Moses' serpent because they did not *b.* it would heal them; 33: 22 cast about your eyes and begin to *b.* in the Son; 46: 15 believers called Christians because of *b.* in Christ; **Hel.** 14: 13 if ye *b.* on Christ's name ye will repent; 15: 10 the Lord will prolong days of Ammonites because of steadfastness when they *b.*; **3 Ne.** 11: 35 whoso *b.* in Christ *b.* in the Father also; 12: 1 blessed are ye if ye *b.* in me after ye have seen me; 12: 2 more blessed are those who shall *b.* in your words; 16: 6–7 blessed are Gentiles because of *b.* in Christ; 18: 20 whatsoever ye ask, *b.* that ye shall receive, it shall be given; 19: 20 Christ chooses disciples because of their *b.* in him; **4 Ne.** 1: 29 church persecuted because of *b.* in Christ; **Morm.** 3: 20–21 Mormon writes so that people will *b.* gospel; 9: 27 doubt not, but be *b.*; **Ether** 3: 11 *b.* thou the words I shall speak; 3: 15 never has man *b.* in the Lord as brother of Jared²; 4: 12 he who will not *b.* Christ's words will not *b.* Christ, will not *b.* the Father; 12: 18 men first *b.* in the Son before working miracles; **Moro.** 7: 16 everything which persuades to *b.* in Christ is sent by power of Christ; 7: 17 whatsoever persuades not to *b.* in Christ is of devil; 7: 45 (1 Cor. 13: 7) charity *b.* all things.

BELIEVER (*see also* Christian; Saint; Worshipper)

Alma 46: 14–15 true *b.* in Christ are

called Christians; **4 Ne.** 1: 36–37 true *b.* in Christ are called Nephites.

BELLOWS

1 Ne. 17: 11 Nephi¹ makes a *b.*

BELOVED (*see also* Jesus Christ—Son of God; John the Beloved)

BENEFIT (*see also* Blessing, Gain; Profit)

Mosiah 8: 18 God provides means that man can become great *b.* to fellow beings.

BENJAMIN—*Nephite prophet-king* [c. 120 B.C.]

Omni 1: 23 B., son of Mosiah¹, begins reign; 1: 24 (W of M 1: 13–14) drives out Lamanites; 1: 25 (W of M 1: 10) given plates by Amaleki¹; **W of M 1:** 11 hands down plates; 1: 13 uses sword of Laban against Lamanites; 1: 16–18 (Mosiah 1: 1) holy man, establishes peace; **Mosiah** 1: 2 sons of B. named; 1: 3 teaches concerning records; 1: 10, 15 (2: 30; 6: 3) confers kingdom on Mosiah²; 1: 16 gives Mosiah² records and artifacts; 2: 9—4: 30 addresses people from tower; 2: 12–14 serve , labors with hands; 2: 17 urges service to fellow men; 3: 7 teaches of Jesus' suffering; 3: 15–19 teaches about atonement; 3: 18–27 teaches about judgment; 4: 16–19 teaches people to help beggars, for all are beggars; 5: 5 B's people covenant with the Lord; 6: 1 takes names of those who enter covenant; 6: 3 consecrates Mosiah², appoints priests; 6: 5 dies; 8: 2–3 B's word rehearsed by Ammon¹; 26: 1 rising generation do not understand B's words; 29: 13 if people could have kings like B., it would be well; **Hel.** 5: 9 Helaman³ asks sons to remember words of B.

BESET

2 Ne. 4: 18 I am encompassed about because of sins which so easily *b.* me; **Alma** 7: 15 lay aside every sin which easily doth *b.* you.

BETHABARA (*see also* BD Bethabara)

1 Ne. 10: 9 John to baptize Messiah in B.

BETTER (*see also* Good; Well)

1 Ne. 4: 13 *b.* that one man perish than nation dwindle in unbelief; **2 Ne.** 31: 14 it would have been *b.* for you that ye had not known me; **Jacob** 2: 13 some Nephites persecute brethren because they suppose they are *b.*; **Mosiah** 29: 12 *b.* that a man be judged of God than of man; **Alma** 1: 26 preacher and teacher no *b.* than hearer and learner; 37: 45 words of Christ shall carry us into far *b.* land of promise; 43: 45 Nephites inspired by *b.*

cause; **3 Ne.** 12: 30 *b.* to deny yourselves of these things than to be cast into hell; 28: 35 it would be *b.* for them if they had not been born; **Ether** 12: 4 whoso believeth in God might hope for *b.* world.

BIBLE (*see also* Book; Scriptures; BD Bible)

2 Ne. 29: 3–10 Gentiles shall say, A B., we have got a B.

BIND, BOUND (*see also* Band; Bondage; Priesthood; Seal)

2 Ne. 1: 13 awful chains *b.* men that they are carried captive to gulf of misery; 9: 45 shake off chains of him who would *b.* you; 26: 22 devil leads men with flaxen cord until he *b.* them; **Alma** 7: 15 lay aside every sin which doth *b.* you down to destruction; 44: 5 liberty *b.* Nephites to lands and country.

BIRTH (*see* Bear, Bore, Borne; Born; Jesus Christ, First Coming of)

BIRTHRIGHT (*see* Heir; Inherit; BD Birthright)

BITTER, BITTERNESS (*see also* Taste)

2 Ne. 2: 15 tree of life, being sweet, is in opposition to forbidden fruit, being *b.*; 15: 20 (Isa. 5: 20) wo unto them that put *b.* for sweet; **Jacob** 5: 52, 57, 65 *b.* fruit of olive-trees; **Mosiah** 27: 29 (Alma 36: 18) Alma² redeemed from gall of *b.*; **Alma** 36: 21 nothing could be so *b.* as pains of Alma²; 41: 11 (Morm. 8: 31) men in carnal state are in gall of *b.*; **3 Ne.** 11: 11 Christ has drunk out of the *b.* cup; **Moro.** 7: 11 *b.* fountain cannot bring forth good water; 8: 14 he who supposes little children need baptism is in gall of *b.*

BLACK, BLACKNESS (*see also* Darkness, Physical)

2 Ne. 5: 21 skin of *b.* to come upon brethren of Nephi¹; 7: 3 the Lord clothes heavens with *b.*; 26: 33 the Lord denies none who come unto him, *b.* and white; **3 Ne.** 12: 36 thou canst not make one hair *b.* or white.

BLAMELESS (*see also* Guiltless; Innocence; Spotless)

Mosiah 3: 21 none shall be found *b.* before God except little children; **Alma** 5: 27 have ye kept yourselves *b.* before God; 7: 3 Alma² hopes to find people of Gideon *b.* before God; 29: 5 he who knows not good from evil is *b.*

BLASPHEMY, BLASPHEME (*see also* TG Blaspheme; BD Blasphemy)

Jacob 7: 7 Sherem claims teachings about Christ are *b.*; **Alma** 30: 30 Korihor *b.*

BLESSING, BLESS (see also Benefit; Blessed [adj.]; Indebted; Obedience; Ordinance; Privilege; Reward)

1 Ne. 15: 18 (22: 9; 3 Ne. 20: 25, 27; Gen. 12: 3) in Abraham's seed shall all kindreds of earth be b.; 17: 2 great b. of the Lord upon family of Lehi[1] in wilderness; 17: 35 the Lord b. land unto Israelites; 19: 17 every nation, kindred, tongue, and people shall be b.; 22: 10 kindreds of earth cannot be b. unless the Lord makes bare his arm; 2 Ne. 1: 28 Lehi[1] leaves first b. if sons will hearken unto Nephi[1]; 4: 3–11 Lehi[1] leaves b. upon children of Laman[1] and Lemuel; Mosiah 2: 24 if men do what the Lord commands, he immediately b. them; 2: 41 those who keep commandments are b. in all things; 13: 19 the Lord b. sabbath day; Alma 45: 16 the cursing and b. of God upon the land; Hel. 12: 1 the Lord b. and prospers those who put trust in him; 3 Ne. 10: 18 great b. poured out upon Nephites and Lamanites; 12: 44 (Matt. 5: 44) b. them that curse you; 17: 21 Christ b. little children; 18: 3, 5 (26: 13) Christ b. bread, gives power to b. it; 20: 26 Father sent Christ to b. people by turning them away from iniquities; Ether 1: 43 the Lord will b. brother of Jared[2] in choice land; 10: 28 never could be a people more b. than Jaredites; Moro. 4: 3 (5: 2) prayers to b. and sanctify bread and wine.

BLESSED [adj.] (see also Bless; Happiness; BD Beatitudes)

1 Ne. 13: 37 b. are they who seek to bring forth Zion; 2 Ne. 3: 23 because of covenant Joseph[1] is b.; Jacob 6: 3 b. are they who have labored in vineyard; Enos 1: 1 (Alma 26: 8; 57: 35; 3 Ne. 4: 32; 11: 17) b. be name of my God; Mosiah 3: 16 little children are b.; Alma 32: 13–16 b. are they who humble themselves; 38: 2 b. is he who endures to end; 3 Ne. 9: 14 b. are those who come unto Christ; 12: 1 b. are they who give heed to disciples; 12: 1 b. are those who believe in Christ, having seen him; 12: 2 more b. are they who believe testimony of others; 12: 3–12 (Matt. 5: 3–12) the Beatitudes; 17: 20 b. are ye because of your faith; 27: 22 if ye do these things b. are ye.

BLINDNESS, BLIND (see also Darkness, Spiritual; Ignorance; BD Blindness)

1 Ne. 7: 8 Nephi[1] asks brethren why they are so b. in minds; 12: 17 mists of darkness, devil's temptations, b. eyes; 13: 27 abominable church perverts right ways of the Lord to b. men's eyes; 13: 32 the Lord will not allow Gentiles to remain in awful state of b.; 14: 7 men will be delivered to b. of their minds; 15: 24 adversary cannot overpower unto b. those who hold to iron rod; 17: 30 Israelites b.

their minds; 2 Ne. 9: 32 wo unto the b. who will not see; 27: 29 (Isa. 29: 18) the b. shall see out of obscurity; Jacob 4: 14 Jews' b. came from looking beyond the mark; Jarom 1: 3 much to be done among people because of b. of minds; Mosiah 3: 5 (3 Ne. 17: 9; 26: 15) the Lord will cause the b. to receive their sight; 11: 29 eyes of the people were b.; Alma 10: 25 people give Satan power to b. their eyes; 13: 4 men reject Spirit on account of b. of minds; 14: 6 Zeezrom knows concerning b. of minds he has caused; 4 Ne. 1: 5 the Lord's disciples cause the b. to receive sight; Ether 4: 15 veil of unbelief causes Israelites to remain in b. of mind; 15: 19 Jaredites given up to b. of minds that they might be destroyed.

BLOCK (see Stumbling Block)

BLOOD (see also Blood, Shedding of; Blood-thirsty; Jesus Christ, Atonement through; Sacrament; Sacrifice; TG Blood; Blood, Eating of; Blood, Shedding of; Blood, Symbolism of; BD Blood)

1 Ne. 12: 10 (Ether 13: 10) garments of righteous made white in b. of Lamb; 22: 13 (2 Ne. 6: 18) abominable church to be drunk with own b.; 2 Ne. 26: 3 (28: 10; 3 Ne. 9: 5–9, 11, 19; Morm. 8: 27; Ether 8: 22) b. of saints to cry up to God; Jacob 1: 19 (Mosiah 2: 27–28) the Lord's servants magnify offices, that people's b. might not come upon their garments; Jarom 1: 6 Lamanites drink b. of beasts; Mosiah 3: 7 Christ will suffer so greatly that b. will come from every pore; 3: 11 Christ's b. atones for sins of those who have fallen by Adam's transgression or sinned ignorantly; 4: 2 apply the atoning b. of Christ; 7: 27 God will take upon him flesh and b.; Alma 5: 21 garments cleansed from stain through b. of him who comes to redeem his people; 5: 22 how will ye feel to stand before God having garments stained with b.; 14: 11 b. of innocent shall stand as witness against people of Ammonihah; 24: 13 b. of Son to be shed for atonement of sins; 34: 11 no man can sacrifice own b. to atone for another's sins; Hel. 9: 31 b. will be found upon skirts of murderer's cloak; 3 Ne. 9: 5, 7–9, 11, 19 (Morm. 8: 41; Ether 8: 22) the Lord avenges b. of saints; 18: 11 (20: 8; Moro. 5: 2) wine in remembrance of the Lord's b.; 18: 28–30 the unworthy are not to partake of the Lord's b. unless they repent; 27: 19 only those who wash garments in the Lord's b. enter his rest; Ether 3: 6, 8–9 finger of the Lord appears like unto flesh and b.; 13: 10 garments of those in New Jerusalem made white in b. of Lamb; Moro. 4: 1—5: 2 manner of administering flesh and b. of the Lord; 10: 33 men are sanctified through shedding of b. of Christ.

BLOOD, SHEDDING OF (see also Blood; Kill; Martyrdom; Murder; Sacrifice; War; TG Blood, Shedding of)

1 Ne. 4: 10 Nephi[1] has never shed b. of man; 2 Ne. 1: 12 Lehi[1] predicts bloodshed and great visitations; 6: 15 they who believe not in Christ will be destroyed by bloodshed; 10: 6 because of Jews' iniquities, bloodshed shall come upon them; Mosiah 17: 10 (Alma 14: 11) b. of the innocent shall stand as witness against the wicked; Alma 24: 12–13, 15, 18 converted Lamanites refuse to stain swords with b. of brethren; 24: 13 b. of Son to be shed for atonement of sins; 24: 17–18 converted Lamanites bury all weapons used for shedding of b.; 34: 13 shedding of b. to stop after last and great sacrifice; 39: 3–5 shedding of innocent b. more abominable than whoredom; 43: 47 ye shall defend your families even unto bloodshed; 48: 11 (55: 19) Moroni[1] does not delight in bloodshed; 48: 14 Nephites taught to defend themselves against enemies, even to shedding of b.; 48: 23 Nephites do not delight in shedding of b.; 51: 9 Amalickiah has sworn to drink b. of Moroni[1]; 53: 11 converted Lamanites to take oath never to shed b.; 61: 10 Nephites will resist wickedness even unto bloodshed; Hel. 9: 31 b. will be found upon skirts of murderer's cloak; 3 Ne. 10: 12 those who did not shed b. of saints are spared; 18: 11 (Moro. 5: 2) wine in remembrance of b. which Christ shed for men; Moro. 10: 33 men are sanctified through shedding of Christ's b.

BLOOD-THIRSTY (see also Blood; Blood, Shedding of)

Enos 1: 20 (Mosiah 10: 12) Lamanites a b-thirsty people; Mosiah 9: 2 ruler is austere and b-thirsty man; Moro. 9: 5 Nephites thirst after b. and revenge continually.

BLOT (see also Cast; Cut; Excommunication)

Mosiah 1: 12 (5: 11) Benjamin gives his people a name that shall never be b. out; 26: 36 (Alma 1: 24; 5: 57; Moro. 6: 7) names of the unrighteous are b. out.

BOAST, BOASTING (see also Pride; TG Boast, Boasting)

Mosiah 2: 15 Benjamin does not do things to b.; 11: 19 people of Noah[3] b. in own strength; Alma 26: 12 Ammon[2] will not b. of himself; 26: 36 if this is b., even so will I b.; 38: 11 see that ye do not b. in your own wisdom; Hel. 4: 13 because of b., Nephites are left to own strength; 5: 8 Helaman[3] counsels sons not to do things to b.; 12: 5 how quick are men to b.; 13: 22 Nephites' hearts swell with pride unto b.; 3 Ne. 6: 10 pride and b. among

Nephites because of riches; Morm. 3: 9 (4: 8) Nephites b. in own strength.

BOAZ, CITY OF

Morm. 4: 20–21 Nephites flee to B. and are slaughtered.

BODY, BODIES (see also Death, Physical; Flesh; Resurrection; Soul; Tabernacle; TG Body; Body, Sanctity of; Spirit Body)

1 Ne. 15: 13 Messiah shall be manifested in b.; 15: 31–32 torment of b. or final state of soul after death of temporal b.; 2 Ne. 1: 22 warning against incurring God's displeasure unto eternal destruction of soul and b.; 4: 25 b. of Nephi[1] carried away on wings of Spirit; 9: 4 in b. we shall see God; 9: 10 God prepares way for escape from death of b.; 9: 13 grave must deliver up b. of righteous; Mosiah 3: 7 the Lord will suffer pain of b.; 4: 6 salvation comes to him who continues in faith unto end of life of mortal b.; 18: 13 baptism a covenant to serve God until man is dead as to mortal b.; Alma 5: 15 (11: 45) mortal b. to be raised in immortality; 11: 43–45 spirit and b. to be reunited in perfect form; 29: 16 soul of Alma[2] carried away from b. because of great joy; 34: 34 same spirit that possesses mortal b. will possess b. in eternal world; 36: 15 oh that I could become extinct both soul and b.; 40: 11–14 state of soul after it leaves mortal b.; 40: 18 first resurrection means reuniting of soul with b. of those from Adam to Christ's resurrection; 40: 21 space between death and resurrection of b.; 40: 23 soul shall be restored to b.; 41: 2 every part of b. to be restored; 3 Ne. 10: 19 Christ shows b. unto Nephites; 13: 22 (Matt. 6: 22) light of b. is the eye; 18: 7 (20: 8; Moro. 4: 3) broken bread is in remembrance of Christ's b.; 28: 15, 37 three Nephites seem to be transfigured from b. of flesh into immortal state; Morm. 6: 21 b. moldering in corruption must soon become incorruptible b.; Ether 3: 16–17 brother of Jared[2] sees b. of the Lord's spirit; Moro. 10: 34 b. and spirit shall soon reunite.

BOLDNESS, BOLDLY

Jacob 2: 7 Jacob[2] grieved that he must use b. of speech; Alma 38: 12 use b., but not overbearance; 3 Ne. 6: 20 inspired men testify b. of sins; Moro. 8: 16 Mormon[2] speaks with b., having authority from God.

BOND (see also Bondage; Freedom)

2 Ne. 10: 16 (26: 33; Alma 1: 30; 5: 49; 11: 44; 4 Ne. 1: 3) both b. and free; Mosiah 23: 13 people of Alma[1] delivered by power of God out of b.; 27: 29 (Alma 36: 27) soul of Alma[2] redeemed from b. of iniquity; Alma 38: 4 Shiblon was in b.

among Zoramites; 41: 11 all men that are in a carnal state are in *b.* of iniquity; **Morm.** 8: 31 those who say the Lord will uphold sinner are in *b.* of iniquity; **Moro.** 8: 14 he who supposes little children need baptism is in *b.* of iniquity.

BONDAGE (*see also* Blindness; Bond; Captive, Captivity; Liberty; Prison; Slavery; Subject; Yoke; TG Bondage, Physical; Bondage, Spiritual)

1 **Ne.** 17: 25 children of Israel were in *b.*; 19: 10 (Alma 29: 12; 36: 28) the Lord leads his people out of *b.* in Egypt; **Mosiah** 7: 15 Limhi's people in *b.* to Lamanites; 12: 2 (29: 18) because of iniquities, this generation shall be brought into *b.*; 21: 36 (22: 1) Limhi's people study how to deliver themselves from *b.*; 23: 12 (29: 18) people of Noah³ had been in *b.* to him and his priests; 24: 17, 21 the Lord to deliver people of Alma² out of *b.*; 29: 18–20 the Lord delivers people of Noah³ from *b.* because of humility and repentance; 29: 40 Mosiah² grants that his people be delivered from all manner of *b.*; **Alma** 9: 22 (36: 29) Nephites are brought out of *b.* time after time; 30: 24, 27 Korihor claims Nephites are in *b.* to foolish traditions; 36: 2 only God of Abraham could deliver the fathers from *b.*; 43: 8 Zerahemnah seeks to bring Nephites into *b.*; 48: 4 Amalickiah seeks to bring Nephites into *b.*; 48: 11 Moroni¹ finds joy in freedom of brethren from *b.*; 61: 12 Nephites would subject themselves to yoke of *b.* if requisite with justice of God; 62: 5 Nephites take up swords that they might not come into *b.*; **Ether** 2: 12 nation that possesses this land shall be free from *b.*

BONE (*see also* Body)

Omni 1: 22 (Mosiah 8: 8; 21: 26–27; Alma 22: 30) Jaredites' *b.* lie scattered in land northward; **Ether** 11: 6 prophets testify that Jaredites' *b.* will become as heaps of earth upon land.

BOOK (*see also* Bible; Book of Mormon; Read; Record; Scriptures; Write; TG Book; Book of Life; Book of Remembrance; Education; BD Book of Life; Lost Books)

1 **Ne.** 1: 11, 19 first angel gives Lehi¹ a *b.*; 5: 11 brass plates contain five *b.* of Moses; 10: 15 Nephi¹ does not write all prophecies of Lehi¹ in *b.*; 13: 23–29 (14: 23) Nephi¹ beholds *b.* going from Jews to Gentiles; 13: 39 other *b.* to come forth from Gentiles to seed of Nephi¹; 19: 23 Nephi¹ reads to his people things written in *b.* of Moses; 2 **Ne.** 3: 23 seed of Joseph² will not be destroyed, for they shall hearken to words of *b.*; 26: 17 history of Nephites to be written and sealed up in

b.; 27: 6–22 Nephi¹ sees coming forth of sealed *b.*; 28: 2 things written in *b.* shall be of great worth to children of men; 29: 11 (3 Ne. 27: 25–26) out of *b.* will the Lord judge world; 30: 3 many shall believe words of *b.* and carry them forth to seed of Nephi¹; **Omni** 1: 4 Amaron writes in *b.* of his father; 1: 9 Chemish writes in same *b.* with brother; **Mosiah** 1: 8 Benjamin teaches sons many things not written in *b.*; 8: 1 only a few of Limhi's words are recorded in *b.*; **Alma** 5: 58 names of righteous shall be written in *b.* of life; 9: 34 only part of Amulek's words are written in *b.*; 13: 31 many words of Alma² not written in *b.*; **Hel.** 2: 13–14 in end of *b.* of Nephi, Gadianton will prove the overthrow of Nephites; 3: 15 many *b.* and records kept by Nephites; 3 **Ne.** 5: 8 (26: 6) not all marvelous things can be written in *b.*; 24: 16 *b.* of remembrance written for them who fear the Lord; 26: 6, 9 when Gentiles believe things written in *b.*, greater things shall be revealed.

BOOK OF MORMON (*see also* Book; Record; Scriptures; Smith, Joseph, Jr.; Translation, Translate; Witnesses, Three; TG Book of Mormon; BD Ephraim, Stick of)

Title Page abridgment of record of Nephites and Jaredites, written to testify of Christ; 1 **Ne.** 13: 40 last records shall establish truth of the first; 2 **Ne.** 3: 12 (Ezek. 37: 15–20) writings of descendants of Joseph¹ and of Judah shall grow together to bring knowledge of covenants; 3: 19–20 descendants of Joseph¹ shall cry from dust; 25: 18 the Lord will bring his word to Jews to convince them of true Messiah; 25: 23 we write to persuade our children and brethren to believe in Christ; 26: 14–18 (Isa. 29: 4) those who have been destroyed will whisper out of dust; 27: 6–26 (Isa. 29: 9–14) prophecy concerning coming forth of B. *of* M.; 27: 29 (Isa. 29: 18) deaf shall hear words of *b.*; 29: 8 testimony of two nations is witness that the Lord is God; 29: 12–14 the Lord will speak to Jews, Nephites, other tribes, and they shall write; 33: 10 if ye believe in Christ, ye shall believe in these words; **Enos** 1: 16 the Lord covenants to bring records to Lamanites; **Morm.** 5: 12 record to be hid up to come forth in the Lord's due time; 8: 16 (Ps. 85: 11) record to be brought out of earth to shine forth out of darkness; **Ether** 2: 11 writings to come unto Gentiles that they may know decrees of God and repent; 5: 4 (2 Ne. 27: 12–14) in mouth of three witnesses shall these things be established; **Moro.** 10: 4 ask God if these things are not true; 10: 29 God shall show unto you that that which I have written is true.

BORN (see also Bear, Bore, Borne; Born of God; Firstborn; Jesus Christ, First Coming of)

1 Ne. 1: 1 Nephi[1] b. of goodly parents; **2 Ne.** 3: 1 Joseph[2] is last-b. of Lehi[1]; **3 Ne.** 28: 35 better for those who do not receive Jesus not to have been b.

BORN OF GOD (see also Baptism; Begotten; Change; Children of God; Conversion; Faith; Fire; Holy Ghost, Baptism of; Remission; Spirit, Holy/Spirit of the Lord; TG Man, New, Spiritually Reborn)

Mosiah 5: 7 those who enter covenant are b. of Christ; 27: 25 (Alma 5: 49) all people must be b. again, b. of God; 27: 28 (Alma 36: 23) Alma[2] is b. of God; **Alma** 5: 14 Alma[2] asks, Have ye spiritually been b. of God; 22: 15 what shall I do that I may be b. of God; 36: 5 (38: 6) if Alma[2] had not been b. of God, he would not have known these things.

BORNE (see Bear, Bore, Borne)

BORROW

Mosiah 4: 28 he who b. should return it; **3 Ne.** 12: 42 (Matt. 5: 42) from him that would b. of thee turn thou not away; **Ether** 14: 2 Jaredites would not b. or lend.

BOUGHT (see Buy, Bought)

BOUND (see Bind, Bound)

BOUNTIFUL, CITY OF—Nephite city in land of Bountiful[2] (see also Bountiful, Land of[2])

Alma 52: 15, 17 Teancum is based in B.; 52: 27 Lamanites attack B.; 53: 3 ditch dug around B.; 53: 4 B. is encircled with timber wall; 55: 26 prisoners taken to B.; **Hel.** 1: 23 Coriantumr[3] marches toward B.; 5: 14 people taught, beginning at B.

BOUNTIFUL, LAND OF[1]—area in southern Arabia, near sea

1 Ne. 17: 5 Lehites come to land they called B. because of fruit and honey; 17: 7 voice of the Lord comes to Nephi[1] in B.

BOUNTIFUL, LAND OF[2]—Nephite territory north of Zarahemla (see also Bountiful, Land of[1])

Alma 22: 29 Nephites take possession of B.; 22: 31 B. lies south of land of Desolation; 22: 33 B. runs from east to west sea; 27: 22 B. is joined on southeast by Jershon; 50: 11 Nephites possess land north of B.; 50: 32 Moroni[1] fears people in B. will hearken to Morianton; 51: 28 Nephites driven to borders of B.; 51: 30–

32 Amalickiah repulsed from B.; 52: 9 Moroni[1] orders B. fortified; 52: 15, 18 Moroni[1] marches toward B.; 52: 39 Lamanite prisoners taken to B.; 63: 5 Hagoth builds ships in B.; **Hel.** 1: 28 Lehi[3] sent to defend B.; 4: 6 Nephites driven into B.; **3 Ne.** 3: 23 Nephites prepare to defend B.; 11: 1 Christ appears to people gathered at temple in B.

BOUNTY

Alma 26: 15 converted Lamanites encircled with matchless b. of God's love.

BOW [noun] (see also Arrow; Weapon)

1 Ne. 16: 18 Nephi[1] breaks his b.; 16: 23 Nephi[1] makes b. out of wood, arms himself with b. and arrows; **Mosiah** 9: 16 Zeniff arms his people with b.; **Alma** 2: 12 Nephites arm themselves with b.; 43: 20 army of Zerahemnah armed with b.; **Hel.** 1: 14 Lamanite army armed with b.; **Morm.** 6: 9 Lamanites fall upon Nephites with sword, b., arrow.

BOW, BOWED [verb] (see also Worship)

1 Ne. 7: 20 brethren of Nephi[1] b. before him; 21: 23 (Isa. 49: 23) kings and queens shall b. to house of Israel; **Mosiah** 13: 13 (Ex. 20: 5) thou shalt not b. down thyself unto graven images; 27: 31 every knee shall b. before Redeemer; **Alma** 22: 16 if Lamanite king b. before the Lord, he will receive desired hope; 31: 1 Zoram[3] leads Zoramites to b. to dumb idols; **3 Ne.** 17: 10 Nephites b. down at Savior's feet.

BOWELS (see also Mercy)

Mosiah 15: 9 the Son has b. of mercy; **Alma** 7: 12 the Son takes their infirmities that his b. may be filled with mercy; **3 Ne.** 17: 6–7 the Savior's b. filled with compassion, mercy.

BRANCH (see also Israel; Root; Tree; TG Branch; Jesus Christ, Davidic Descent of; Vineyard of the Lord)

1 Ne. 10: 12 Lehi[1] compares Israel to olive-tree whose b. are broken off; 10: 14 (15: 7, 13, 16) natural b. of olive-tree to be grafted in; 15: 12 (19: 24; 2 Ne. 3: 5; 9: 53; Alma 26: 36) Lehites are b. of house of Israel; **2 Ne.** 3: 5 (9: 53; 10: 1; Jacob 2: 25) the Lord would raise righteous b., from descendants of Joseph[1], Nephites; 14: 2 (Isa. 4: 2) b. of the Lord shall be beautiful and glorious; 21: 1 (Isa. 11: 1) b. shall grow out of Jesse's roots; **Jacob** 5: 3–77 parable of natural and wild b. of olive-trees; 6: 4 God remembers house of Israel, both roots and b.; **Alma** 16: 17 word preached among Nephites that as b. they might be grafted into true vine; **3 Ne.** 25: 1 day of the Lord shall leave the proud neither root nor b.

BRASS (*see also* Plates, Brass)

1 Ne. 16: 10 Liahona made of fine *b*.; 2 Ne. 5: 15 (Jarom 1: 8) Nephi[1] teaches people to work in *b*.; Mosiah 8: 7–10 people of Ammon[1] discover breastplates of *b*.; 11: 8, 10 Noah[3] ornaments buildings and temple with *b*.; Ether 10: 23 Jaredites make *b*.

BRAZEN SERPENT (*see* Serpent)

BREAD (*see also* Sacrament; TG Bread; Bread of Life)

2 Ne. 14: 1 (Isa. 4: 1) seven women shall say, We will eat own *b*., only let us be called by thy name; Alma 5: 34 come unto me and ye shall eat *b*. of life freely; 3 Ne. 18: 1–7 (20: 3–9; 26: 13) Christ administers *b*. and wine of sacrament to Nephites; 18: 7 (Moro. 4: 3) *b*. is in remembrance of Christ's body; Moro. 4: 1–3 manner of administering sacrament *b*.; 6: 6 Nephite church partakes oft of *b*. and wine of sacrament.

BREAK, BRAKE, BROKEN (*see also* Broken Heart and Contrite Spirit)

1 Ne. 12: 4 in vision Nephi[1] sees plains *b*. up; 16: 18 Nephi[1] *b*. his bow; 2 Ne. 3: 5 righteous branch raised from loins of Joseph[1] will be *b*. off; Jacob 2: 35 unrighteous Nephites have *b*. wives' hearts; Mosiah 15: 8–9, 20, 23 (16: 7; Alma 5: 9) Christ *b*. bands of death; 20: 14 Limhi's people have not *b*. oath made to Lamanites; Alma 43: 11 Anti-Nephi-Lehies would not *b*. oath; Hel. 14: 21–22, 24 (3 Ne. 8: 13, 18) rocks and highways *b*. up at Christ's death; 3 Ne. 6: 14 church *b*. up because of inequality; 13: 19–20 (27: 32; Matt. 6: 19) lay not up treasures on earth, where thieves *b*. through and steal; 18: 25 whosoever *b*. commandment to come unto Christ suffers himself to be led into temptation; Ether 6: 10 no monster of sea could *b*. Jaredite vessels.

BREAST (*see also* Breastplate; Heart)

Mosiah 2: 38 justice fills *b*. of the unrepentant with guilt; Alma 22: 15 what shall I do to have wicked spirit rooted out of my *b*.; 32: 28 true seed will swell within *b*.; Morm. 6: 7 Lamanite armies fill *b*. of wicked with fear.

BREASTPLATE (*see also* BD Breastplate)

Mosiah 8: 10 Limhi's people have found large *b*. in wilderness; Alma 43: 19–21, 38, 44 (44: 9) Nephite armies wear *b*., Lamanites do not; 49: 6 (Hel. 1: 14) Lamanites wear *b*.; Ether 15: 15 Jaredite armies armed with *b*.

BREATH, BREATHE (*see also* TG Breath of Life)

2 Ne. 9: 26 God gave men *b*.; 21: 4

(30: 9; Isa. 11: 4) with *b*. of lips shall the Lord slay the wicked; Mosiah 2: 21 God preserves men from day to day by lending them *b*.; Ether 2: 19 Jaredites fear they cannot *b*. in vessels.

BRETHREN (*see* Brother)

BRIDE (*see also* TG Bride; BD Bride, Bridegroom)

1 Ne. 21: 18 (Isa. 49: 18) Israel shall bind her destroyers on even as a *b*.

BRIDLE

Alma 38: 12 *b*. all your passions.

BRIGHTNESS, BRIGHTER (*see also* Light)

1 Ne. 1: 10 *b*. of twelve followers exceeds stars; 15: 30 *b*. of God's justice is like *b*. of flaming fire; 2 Ne. 9: 44 Jacob[1] to stand with *b*. before God; 31: 20 press forward, having perfect *b*. of hope; Alma 37: 5 (1 Ne. 5: 19) brass plates will retain *b*.

BRIMSTONE (*see* Lake; BD Brimstone)

BRING, BROUGHT

1 Ne. 13: 37 blessed are they who seek to *b*. forth Zion; 2 Ne. 1: 7 land is consecrated unto him whom the Lord shall *b*.; 4: 5 (Prov. 22: 6) if ye are *b*. up in way ye should go, ye will not depart from it; 32: 4 because men ask not, they are not *b*. into light; Mosiah 2: 17 perhaps thou shalt say, The man has *b*. upon himself his misery; 12: 22 (15: 29; 3 Ne. 16: 18) they shall see eye to eye when the Lord shall *b*. again Zion; Alma 46: 18 God will not suffer believers to be destroyed until they *b*. it upon themselves by transgressions; Hel. 15: 7 faith and repentance *b*. change of heart; 3 Ne. 15: 17, 21 (John 10: 16) other sheep I have, them also I must *b*.

BROAD (*see also* Wide)

1 Ne. 12: 17 mists of darkness are temptations of devil, which lead men away into *b*. roads; 3 Ne. 14: 13 (Matt. 7: 13) *b*. is way which leads to destruction; 27: 33 *b*. is way which leads to death.

BROKEN HEART AND CONTRITE SPIRIT (*see also* Humble; Offering; Sacrifice; TG Contrite Heart)

2 Ne. 2: 7 Christ's sacrifice answers ends of law unto all who have *b.h.* and contrite spirit; 4: 32 may gates of hell be shut before me, because my heart is *b*. and spirit is contrite; Jacob 2: 10 Jacob[2] must tell people of wickedness in presence of the *b.h.*; 3 Ne. 9: 20 offer for sacrifice unto the Lord a *b.h.* and contrite spirit; 12: 19 come unto Christ with *b.h.* and contrite spirit; Morm. 2: 14 Nephites do not come unto Jesus with *b.h.* and contrite

spirits; **Ether** 4: 15 call upon the Father with *b.h.* and contrite spirit; **Moro.** 6: 2 only those with *b.h.* and contrite spirit are received unto baptism.

BROTHER, BRETHREN (*see also* Family; Jared², Brother of; Neighbor; TG Brethren; Brother; Brotherhood and Sisterhood)

1 Ne. 2: 5 elder *b.* of Nephi¹ are Laman¹, Lemuel, and Sam; 2: 22 Nephi¹ to be made ruler and teacher over *b.*; 4: 26 Zoram¹ supposes Nephi¹ speaks of *b.* of church; 22: 6 prophecies of Nephi¹ refer to *b.* who are of house of Israel; **2 Ne.** 4: 11 Sam's inheritance shall be like his *b.* Nephi¹; 25: 23 we write to persuade our *b.* to believe in Christ; **Jacob** 2: 17 think of your *b.* like unto yourselves; **Mosiah** 9: 2 *b.* fights against *b.* among Nephite expedition; **Alma** 10: 3 Joseph¹ sold into Egypt by his *b.*; 13: 4–5 except for hardheartedness, the unfaithful might have had as great privilege as their faithful *b.*; 24: 6 converted Lamanites refuse to take up arms against *b.*; **3 Ne.** 3: 7 Giddianhi tempts Nephite leaders to become *b.* with robbers; 7: 19 (19: 4) Nephi³ raises *b.* from dead; 12: 22 (Matt. 5: 22) he who is angry with his *b.* is in danger of judgment; 14: 3 (Matt. 7: 3) why beholdest thou the mote in thy *b.*'s eye; 15: 14 Father has not commanded Christ to tell *b.* at Jerusalem about Nephites.

BRUISE (*see also* Wound)

Mosiah 14: 5 (Isa. 53: 5) the Lord *b.* for our iniquities; 14: 10 (Isa. 53: 10) it pleased the Lord to *b.* Messiah.

BUILD, BUILT (*see also* Building [noun]; Church of God; Foundation; House; Rock)

1 Ne. 18: 2 Nephi¹ does not *b.* ship after manner of men; 22: 22–23 kingdom of devil shall be *b.* up among men; **Ether** 13: 5 Jerusalem to be *b.* up again; 13: 6, 8 New Jerusalem to be *b.* upon this land; 13: 8 remnant of house of Jacob shall be *b.* upon this land.

BUILDING [noun] (*see also* Build; House; Palace; Sanctuary; Synagogue; Tabernacle; Temple; Tower)

1 Ne. 8: 26–33 (11: 35–36; 12: 18) great and spacious *b.* in dream of Lehi¹; **2 Ne.** 5: 15 Nephi¹ teaches people to build *b.*; **Mosiah** 9: 8 Zeniff's people begin to build *b.*; 11: 8–15 Noah³ builds many elegant *b.*; 23: 5 people of Alma begin to build *b.*; **Hel.** 3: 14 hundredth part of Nephites' *b.* of ships, temples, synagogues cannot be contained in record; **3 Ne.** 8: 14 *b.* fall to earth at Christ's death; **Ether** 10: 5–6 Riplakish builds spacious *b.*

BURDEN, BURDENSOME (*see also* Affliction; Bear; Laden; Oppression; Suffering; Task; Weigh)

Mosiah 6: 7 Mosiah² tills earth, that he might not become *b.* to people; 18: 8–10 those willing to bear one another's *b.* should be baptized; 21: 3 Lamanites put heavy *b.* on backs of Limhi's people; 24: 14–15, 21 the Lord eases *b.* placed on Alma¹ and his people; 29: 34 *b.* should come upon all, that every man might bear his part; **Alma** 33: 23 may God grant that your *b.* be light, through joy of the Son; **Ether** 10: 10 Morianton¹ eases *b.* of people.

BURN, BURNT, BURNING (*see also* Destruction; Devour; Fire; Hell; Oven; Stubble; BD Burnt Offering)

1 Ne. 5: 9 (7: 22; Mosiah 2: 3) Nephites offer *b.* offerings according to law of Moses; 12: 4 (3 Ne. 8: 14; 9: 3, 9–10) many cities are *b.* with fire; 22: 15 (2 Ne. 26: 4; 3 Ne. 25: 1) day comes that wicked must be *b.*; **2 Ne.** 14: 4 the Lord purges by spirit of *b.*; 19: 18 wickedness *b.* as the fire; **Jacob** 5: 7, 9 main branches of olive-tree cast into fire and *b.*; 5: 47 the Lord grieved that trees should be cut down and *b.*; 5: 77 the Lord will cause vineyard to be *b.*; 6: 3 world shall be *b.* with fire; **Mosiah** 27: 28 the Lord has seen fit to snatch Alma² out of everlasting *b.*; **Alma** 14: 12–13 Alma² and Amulek not to be *b.* because work not finished; **Hel.** 5: 23–24 Nephi² and Lehi⁴ are encircled by fire, but not *b.*; **3 Ne.** 9: 19 the Lord will no longer accept *b.* offerings; 10: 13 more righteous part of people are not *b.*; 11: 3 voice from heaven causes hearts to *b.*; 25: 1 (Mal. 4: 10) day cometh that shall *b.* as oven; **4 Ne.** 1: 7 Nephites build cities where cities had been *b.*; **Morm.** 5: 5 Nephite cities *b.* by Lamanites; **Ether** 14: 17 Shiz *b.* cities.

BURY, BURIAL (*see also* Earth; Grave; BD Burial)

Mosiah 18: 14–15 Alma¹ and Helam *b.* in water at baptism; **Alma** 24: 19 (25: 14; 26: 32; Hel. 15: 9) converted Lamanites *b.* weapons; 45: 19 Alma² said to be *b.* by hand of the Lord; **3 Ne.** 8: 25 if Nephites had repented, families would not have been *b.* in great city; 9: 6, 8 the Lord causes inhabitants of cities to be *b.* in earth; 10: 13 righteous part of Nephites are not *b.* in earth; **Ether** 6: 6–7 Jaredite vessels are *b.* in depths of sea; 14: 22 no Jaredites left to *b.* the dead.

BUSHEL (*see* Candle)

BUSINESS (*see also* Gain; Merchants; Trade; Traffic)

Mosiah 29: 26 law to do *b*. by voice of people; **Alma** 10: 31 Zeezrom has much *b*. to do among the people.

BUY, BOUGHT

2 Ne. 9: 50 (26: 25; Isa. 55: 1) he who has no money, come *b*. and eat; **Hel.** 6: 8 Lamanites and Nephites have free intercourse to *b*. and sell; **Ether** 10: 22 Jaredites *b*., sell, and traffic one with another.

BY-WORD (see Hiss)

CAIN—son of Adam (see also BD Cain)

Hel. 6: 27 plotted with Lucifer; **Ether** 8: 15 murderer, handed down oaths.

CALAMITY (see also Destruction; Tribulation; Trouble)

Morm. 2: 27 Mormon² sorrows because of Nephites' *c*.; 5: 11 Gentiles will sorrow for *c*. of Israel.

CALF, CALVES (see also Animal; BD Calves)

1 Ne. 22: 24 righteous to be led up as *c*. of stall; **2 Ne.** 21: 6 (30: 12; Isa. 11: 6) leopard shall lie down with kid and *c*.; **3 Ne.** 25: 2 (Mal. 4: 2) they who fear the Lord shall grow up as *c*. in a stall.

CALL (see also Calling; Name; Ordain; Prayer; TG Called of God)

2 Ne. 3: 15 name of latter-day seer shall be *c*. after Joseph¹; 15: 20 (Isa. 5: 20) wo unto them that *c*. evil good; **Mosiah** 3: 8 (15: 21) he shall be *c*. Jesus Christ, his mother shall be *c*. Mary; 4: 11 *c*. on the name of the Lord daily; 5: 9 (3 Ne. 27: 5) the obedient shall know name by which he is *c*., shall be *c*. by name of Christ; 5: 12 retain in your hearts name by which the Lord shall *c*. you; 16: 11–12 those delivered to devil have never *c*. upon the Lord; 18: 17 (Alma 46: 14–15; 3 Ne. 26: 21) those baptized are *c*. the church of Christ; 25: 12 children of Amulon and his brethren would no longer be *c*. by fathers' names; 25: 21 Nephites assemble in different bodies, *c*. churches; 26: 4 rising generation would not *c*. upon the Lord; **Alma** 3: 17 he that departeth from thee shall no more be *c*. thy seed; 5: 37–38, 60 good shepherd hath *c*. and is still *c*. you in his own name; 5: 49 (6: 8; 8: 4; 43: 2) Alma² preaches according to holy order by which he was *c*.; 9: 17 the Lord will be merciful unto all who *c*. on his name; 10: 6 Amulek was *c*. many times but would not hear; 12: 30 after angels' visits, men began to *c*. on God's name; 12: 33 God did *c*. on men, in name of the Son; 13: 3 priests were *c*. and prepared from foundations of world; 13:

27–28 *c*. upon the Lord's holy name that ye be not tempted above that which ye can bear; 18: 34 (22: 4) Ammon² is *c*. by Holy Spirit to teach people; 22: 16 if thou wilt *c*. upon God's name in faith, thou shalt receive hope desired; 28: 14 great *c*. of diligence to labor in the Lord's vineyards; 29: 6 why should I desire more than to perform the work to which I have been *c*.; 46: 14–15 true believers in Christ are *c*. Christians; **Hel.** 8: 18 many before days of Abraham were *c*. by order of Son of God; **3 Ne.** 4: 30 Nephites ask God to protect people so long as they *c*. on his name for protection; 11: 23–25 person being baptized should be *c*. by name during prayer; 12: 1 number of disciples who had been *c*. by Christ was twelve; 12: 9 (Matt. 5: 9) peacemakers shall be *c*. children of God; 21: 27 dispersed shall *c*. on the Father in Christ's name; 22: 5 Holy One shall be *c*. God of whole earth; 27: 7–9 church should be *c*. in the Lord's name; 27: 8 if church be *c*. in name of man, it is church of man; 27: 9 ye shall *c*. whatsoever things ye do *c*. in my name; **Ether** 2: 14–15 brother of Jared² chastised because he did not remember to *c*. upon name of the Lord; 4: 15 when men *c*. upon the Father, they shall know he remembers covenant; 12: 10 by faith that they of old were *c*. after holy order of God; **Moro.** 2: 2 disciples to *c*. upon the Father in Christ's name to bestow Holy Ghost; 3: 1 Nephite disciples were *c*. elders of church; 7: 29–31 office of angels' ministry is to *c*. men unto repentance; 8: 2 Christ has *c*. Moroni² to his ministry; 8: 8 Christ came not to *c*. righteous but sinners to repentance.

CALLING (see also Authority; Call; Errand; Inspire, Inspiration; Ministry; Office; TG Called of God; Calling)

Jacob 2: 3 Jacob² has been diligent in office of his *c*.; **Alma** 13: 3–8 priests are called with a holy *c*.; 29: 13 God has called Alma² with a holy *c*.; **Moro.** 3: 4 priests and teachers are ordained according to gifts and *c*. of God unto men; 7: 2 Mormon² permitted to speak because of gift of Christ's *c*. unto him.

CALM (see also Peace)

1 Ne. 18: 21 after Nephi¹ prays, great *c*. on sea.

CALNO—possibly town near Babylon

2 Ne. 20: 9 (Isa. 10: 9) is not C. as Carchemish.

CALVES (see Calf, Calves)

CAMP

2 Ne. 26: 15 the Lord shall *c*. against seed of Nephi¹ and his brethren.

CANDLE (*see also* Candlestick; Light)

3 Ne. 8: 21 because of vapor of darkness there could be no c.; 12: 15 (Matt. 5: 15) do men light a c. and put it under a bushel.

CANDLESTICK

3 Ne. 12: 15 (Matt. 5: 15) men put lighted candle on c. and it giveth light.

CANKER (*see also* Corrupt)

Mosiah 8: 11 blades of swords are c. with rust; Morm. 8: 38 ye hypocrites who sell yourselves for that which will c.

CAPITAL PUNISHMENT (*see also* Blood, Shedding of; Death, Physical; Executed; Hang; Kill; Murder; TG Capital Punishment)

2 Ne. 9: 35 murderer who deliberately kills shall die; Alma 1: 13–14 Nehor condemned to die because he shed blood of righteous man; 1: 18 (30: 10) he who murders is punished unto death; 34: 12 law requires the life of him who has murdered.

CAPTAIN (*see also* Commander)

Mosiah 20: 17 Gideon is king's c.; Alma 2: 13 c. appointed among Nephites; 16: 5 Zoram² is appointed chief c. over Nephite armies; 43: 6 Zerahemnah appoints chief c. over Lamanites; 43: 16–17 (60: 36; 61: 2) Moroni¹ is appointed chief c. over all Nephite armies; 48: 5 Amalickiah appoints Zoramites as chief c. over his armies; 49: 5 chief c. of Lamanites are astonished at wisdom of Nephites; 49: 16 Moroni¹ appoints Lehi³ chief c. of men of city of Noah; 52: 19 chief c. of Nephites hold council of war; 57: 29 Gid is chief c. over band appointed to guard prisoners; 3 Ne. 3: 17 Lachoneus¹ appoints chief c. over Nephite armies; 3: 18–19 Gidgiddoni is appointed chief c. and chief judge; 3: 19 Nephites appoint men of revelation as chief c.

CAPTIVATE, CAPTIVATION (*see also* Captive, Captivity; Seduce)

2 Ne. 2: 29 will of flesh gives devil power to c.; Alma 9: 28 those who have been evil shall reap damnation according to power and c. of devil.

CAPTIVE, CAPTIVITY (*see also* Bondage; Captivate; Destruction; Ensnare; Freedom; Prison; Sin; Slavery; TG Captivity)

1 Ne. 1: 13 (10: 3; 2 Ne. 6: 8; 25: 10; Omni 1: 15) inhabitants of Jerusalem to be carried away c. into Babylon; 13: 5 abominable church brings saints down into c.; 13: 13 Gentiles to go forth out of c., upon the many waters; 14: 4, 7 (2 Ne. 1: 18; Alma 12: 6, 17) the wicked will be

brought down into c. of devil; 22: 12 the Lord will bring house of Israel again out of c.; 2 Ne. 2: 27 men are free to choose liberty and eternal life or c. and death; 3: 4 Joseph¹ is carried c. into Egypt; 9: 12 hell must deliver up its c. spirits; 25: 10 Jews have been destroyed, except those carried c. into Babylon; Omni 1: 15 people of Zarahemla came from Jerusalem when Zedekiah was carried c. into Babylon; Mosiah 27: 16 (Alma 5: 6; 29: 11–12; 36: 1, 2, 29) remember the c. of your fathers; Alma 12: 11 they who harden hearts are taken c. by devil; 16: 3 Lamanites take some Nephites c. into wilderness; Hel. 11: 33 robbers carry many c. into wilderness; 3 Ne. 18: 15 pray always, lest ye be tempted and led away c. by devil; 27: 32 fourth generation led away c. by devil; Ether 6: 23 to have a king leads into c.; 7: 17 (8: 4; 10: 14–15, 30–31; 11: 9, 18-19) Jaredite kings in c.

CARCASS (*see also* Body)

Alma 16: 10 c. of inhabitants of Ammonihah mangled by dogs and wild beasts; Ether 9: 34 people devour c. of them which fell by the way.

CARE (*see also* Carefully)

Alma 32: 37 if ye nourish seed with great c., it will get root; 37: 47 Alma² admonishes Helaman¹ to take great c. of sacred things; 40: 12 paradise a state of rest from all c.; Morm. 5: 10 Mormon² speaks to Gentiles who have c. for house of Israel.

CAREFULLY

2 Ne. 28: 21 devil leads souls c. down to hell.

CARNAGE (*see also* Battle; Slaughter; War)

3 Ne. 2: 11 Gadianton robbers spread great c. throughout land; Morm. 2: 8 because people do not repent, blood and c. spread among Nephites and Lamanites; 4: 11 impossible for tongue to describe horrible scene of c.; 5: 8 Mormon² does not desire to harrow up souls by describing scene of c.; Ether 14: 21 so long had been scene of c. that whole land is covered with dead bodies.

CARNAL, CARNALLY (*see also* Devilish; Evil; Fall of Man; Flesh; Lasciviousness; Law of Moses; Lust; Nature, Natural; Sensual; Temporal; Wicked; World)

2 Ne. 9: 39 (Rom. 8: 6) to be c-minded is death; 28: 21 devil lulls men away into c. security; Mosiah 4: 2 Benjamin's people view themselves in c. state; 16: 3 (Alma 42: 10) the wicked are c. and devilish; 16: 3 Fall caused all mankind to become c.; 16: 5 he who persists in his c. nature remains in his fallen state;

16: 12 those delivered up to damnation have gone according to their own c. wills; 26: 4 many in rising generation refuse baptism and remain in c. state; 27: 25 those born of God are changed from c. and fallen state to state of righteousness; **Alma** 22: 13 Aaron[2] explains fall of man and c. state; 30: 53 Korihor teaches devil's words because they are pleasing to c. mind; 36: 4 knowledge of Alma[2] comes not of c. mind but of God; 41: 11 all men in c. state are in gall of bitterness; 41: 13 restoration is to bring back c. for c.

CARRY (*see also* Bear, Bore, Borne; Catch)

1 **Ne.** 1: 8 (14: 30) Lehi[1] is c. away in vision; 11: 29 the twelve are c. away in Spirit; 21: 22 (22: 6, 8; 2 **Ne.** 6: 6; Isa. 49: 22) daughters of the Lord's people shall be c. upon Gentiles' shoulders; **2 Ne.** 33: 1 when man speaks by Holy Ghost, power of Holy Ghost c. it into men's hearts; **Alma** 37: 45 words of Christ shall c. us beyond vale of sorrow; 3 **Ne.** 6: 17 people delivered for long time to be c. about by temptations of devil.

CAST (*see also* Blot; Cut; Devils; Excommunication; Fire; Throw; Thrust; Toss)

1 **Ne.** 1: 20 Jews c. out prophets; 15: 33 those who die in wickedness must be c. off; **2 Ne.** 26: 3 (Hel. 13: 24; 3 **Ne.** 8: 25; 9: 10–11) wicked shall perish because they c. out prophets; 30: 2 (Hel. 14: 18) Jews who do not repent shall be c. off; **Mosiah** 16: 2 (Alma 40: 13, 26) wicked shall be c. out; 28: 4 Lamanites suffer much, fearing they should be c. off forever; **Alma** 10: 23 (Hel. 13: 14) if people c. out the righteous, the Lord will not stay his hand; 11: 2 man in debt must pay or be c. out from people; 22: 15 Lamanite king asks what he should do to avoid being c. off at last day; 32: 28 if ye do not c. out good seed by unbelief, it will swell; 32: 32 if seed does not grow, it is c. away; 32: 38 neglected tree withers, is c. out; **Hel.** 12: 25 in last days some shall be c. off from God's presence; 3 **Ne.** 18: 23, 30, 32 the unworthy should not be c. out from places of worship; 24: 11 (Mal. 3: 11) neither shall your vine c. her fruit before the time; **Ether** 8: 25 devil causes men to c. out prophets; 13: 13 Jaredites c. Ether out.

CATCH, CAUGHT (*see also* Carry; Ensnare)

1 **Ne.** 11: 1 Nephi[1] c. away in Spirit into high mountain; **Alma** 10: 13 lawyers try to c. Alma[2] and Amulek in their words; 12: 1 Amulek c. Zeezrom in his lying; 12: 6 adversary had laid a snare to c. people of Ammonihah; 18: 23 Ammon[2]

c. Lamoni with guile; 3 **Ne.** 28: 13 disciples c. up into heaven.

CATTLE (*see also* Animal; Beast; Herd; Ox)

Enos 1: 21 Nephites raise c.; 3 **Ne.** 3: 22 (4: 4) Nephites gather c. to defend themselves; 6: 1 Nephites return to land, with c.; **Ether** 9: 18 Jaredites have all manner of c.

CAUSE (*see also* Reason)

2 **Ne.** 8: 22 (Moro. 1: 28) God pleads the c. of his people; **Mosiah** 16: 3 serpent's beguiling of our first parents was c. of fall; 29: 5 consider the c. which ye are called to consider; **Alma** 11: 25 Zeezrom seeks c. to destroy Amulek; 19: 14 Lamanites have been c. of much mourning among Nephites; 32: 18 if a man knoweth a thing, he hath no c. to believe; 43: 45 Nephites inspired by better c.; 46:16 Moroni[1] prays that c. of Christians might be favored; 46: 35 Amalickiahites who will not support c. of freedom are put to death; 46: 40 God prepared plants and roots to remove c. of diseases; 48: 10 Nephites prepare to maintain what enemies call c. of Christians; 50: 39 chief judge appointed with oath to maintain c. of God; 51: 7, 17 king-men obliged to maintain c. of freedom; 54: 10 Nephites will maintain their religion and c. of their God; 56: 11 Nephites have died in c. of their country and their God; 58: 12 Nephites fixed with determination to maintain c. of liberty; 60: 16 if all Nephites had been true to c. of freedom, they would have dispersed their enemies; 60: 28 Moroni[1] defends c. of his country according to God's commandments; 61: 14 Pahoran rejoices in c. of his Redeemer and his God; 62: 1 Pahoran not a traitor to c. of his country; 62: 11 death inflicted upon those who are not true to c. of freedom; **Hel.** 14: 28 signs given that there should be no c. for unbelief; **Moro.** 7: 28 Christ advocates c. of children of men.

CAVITY

1 **Ne.** 3: 27 sons of Lehi[1] hide themselves in c. of rock; **Ether** 13: 13–14, 18, 22 Ether hides in c. of rock.

CEASE (*see also* Miracle; Refrain; Stop; Strive)

2 **Ne.** 23: 11 (Isa. 13: 11) the Lord will cause the arrogancy of the proud to c.; **Mosiah** 26: 39 (3 Ne. 19: 26, 30) pray without c.; **Alma** 42: 13, 22–23, 25 if justice were destroyed, God would c. to be God; **Morm.** 9: 19 if God changed he would c. to be God.

CEDARS (*see* Lebanon)

CEMENT

Hel. 3: 7, 9, 11 Nephites become expert in working c.

CENTER

1 Ne. 16: 2 truth cuts the guilty to c.; **Hel.** 12: 12 by power of the Lord's voice do foundations rock to c.; **3 Ne.** 11: 3 small voice pierces Nephites to c.

CEZORAM—*wicked chief judge of Nephites* [c. 30 B.C.]

Hel. 5: 1 receives judgment-seat; 6: 15–19 murdered, as is his son, who is appointed in his stead.

CHAFF

2 Ne. 15: 24 (Isa. 5: 24) as flame consumeth the c.; 26: 18 multitude of terrible ones shall be as c. that passes away; **Mosiah** 7: 30 if people sow filthiness, they shall reap c.; **Alma** 37: 15 Satan to sift the transgressor as c. before wind; **Morm.** 5: 16, 18 Nephites driven about as c. before wind.

CHAIN (*see also* Band; Captivate; Hell; TG Bondage, Spiritual)

2 Ne. 1: 13 (9: 45) shake off awful c. by which ye are bound; 28: 19 devil will grasp the wicked with his everlasting c.; **Alma** 5: 7, 9–10 fathers loosed from c. of hell that encircled them; 12: 6 adversary lays snares that he might encircle people with his c.; 12: 11 c. of hell means to be taken captive by devil and led by his will; 12: 17 those who die in their sins shall be c. down to everlasting destruction; 13: 30 may the Lord grant unto you repentance, that ye not be bound down by c. of hell; 36: 18 have mercy on me, who am encircled by c. of death.

CHALDEA, CHALDEAN, CHALDAIC (*see also* Language; BD Chaldea)

1 Ne. 20: 14 (Isa. 48: 14) the Lord's arm to come upon C.; 20: 20 (Isa. 48: 20) flee ye from the C.; 2 Ne. 23: 19 (Isa. 13: 19) Babylon, beauty of C's excellency, shall be as when God overthrew Sodom.

CHANCE

Mosiah 29: 38 Nephites are anxious that every man have equal c.; **3 Ne.** 6: 12 people distinguished by ranks, according to c. for learning.

CHANGE, CHANGING (*see also* Alter; Born of God; Changeable; Conversion; God, Eternal Nature of; Heart; Mend; Repentance; Transfigure, Transfiguration; Transform; Translated Beings; Unchangeable; Vary)

1 Ne. 16: 29 writing on Liahona c. from time to time; **Mosiah** 5: 7 hearts are c. through faith; 27: 25 all mankind must be c. from fallen state to state of righteousness; 5: 2 Spirit has wrought mighty c. in Benjamin's people; **Alma** 5: 12–13 mighty c. wrought in hearts of Alma[1] and his people; 5: 14–26 have ye experienced this mighty c. in your hearts; 12: 20 man to be c. from mortal to immortal state; 19: 33 Lamoni and household declare their hearts have been c.; **Hel.** 15: 7 repentance brings c. of heart; **3 Ne.** 8: 12 whole face of land is c.; 24: 6 I am the Lord, I c. not; 28: 8, 15 three Nephites c. from mortality to immortality; 28: 37–40 c. wrought upon bodies of three Nephites; **Morm.** 9: 9–10 no shadow of c. in God; 9: 19 if God c., he would cease to be God; **Ether** 12: 14 faith of Nephi[2] and Lehi[4] wrought c. upon Lamanites.

CHANGEABLE (*see also* Change)

Moro. 8: 12 if little children were not alive in Christ, God would be a c. God; 8: 18 God is not a c. being.

CHARACTERS (*see also* Language; Writing)

Morm. 9: 32 record written in c. known as reformed Egyptian.

CHARGE (*see also* Instruction)

Mosiah 1: 15–16 Benjamin gives Mosiah[2] c. concerning affairs of kingdom, records; 29: 42 Alma[2] gives Alma[2] c. concerning affairs of church; **Alma** 35: 16 Alma[2] gathers sons to give them his c.

CHARIOT (*see also* BD Chariot)

Alma 18: 9 (20: 6) Lamoni commands servants to prepare horses and c.; 18: 10, 12 Ammon[2] prepares Lamoni's c.; **3 Ne.** 3: 22 Nephites gather with horses and c.; 21: 14 (Micah 5: 10) the Father will destroy c. of Gentiles.

CHARITY, CHARITABLE (*see also* Alms; Compassion; God, Love of; Impart; Love; Needy; Neighbor; Relief; Substance; TG Charity; BD Charity)

2 Ne. 26: 30 the Lord has commanded that all men should have c.; 26: 30 c. is love; 26: 30 (Moro. 7: 44, 46) except men have c. they are nothing; 26: 30 if men have c., they will not suffer laborer in Zion to perish; 33: 7–9 Nephi[1] has c. for his people, the Jew, and the Gentiles; **Alma** 7: 24 see that ye have faith, hope, and c.; 13: 29 have faith, hope, the love of God in your hearts; 34: 29 if ye do not remember to be c., ye are as dross; **Ether** 12: 28 faith, hope, and c. bring unto the Lord; 12: 34 love that the Lord has for men is c.; 12: 34 (Moro. 10: 20–21) without c. men cannot inherit place prepared in the Father's mansions; 12: 35–37 if Gentiles have not c., the Lord will prove

them; **Moro.** 7: 1 Moroni² writes words of Mormon² on faith, hope, and c.; 7: 44 if man is meek and confesses Christ, he must have c.; 7: 45 (1 Cor. 13: 4–7) qualities of c. described; 7: 46 (1 Cor. 13: 8) c. never faileth; 7: 46 cleave unto c., which is the greatest of all; 7: 47 (8: 17) c. is pure love of Christ and endures forever; 10: 20–21 except ye have c., ye can in nowise be saved in the kingdom of God.

CHASTEN, CHASTISEMENT (*see also* Affliction; Persecution; Prove; Punishment; Rebuke; Refine; Reprove; Scourge; Suffering; Trial; Tribulation; Warn; TG Chastening)

1 Ne. 16: 25 Lehi¹ c. because of murmuring against the Lord; 16: 39 voice of the Lord c. Laman¹ and Lemuel; **Mosiah** 14: 5 (Isa. 53: 5) the c. of our peace was upon Messiah; 23: 21 the Lord sees fit to c. his people; **Hel.** 12: 3 except the Lord c. his people, they will not remember him; 15: 3 the Lord has c. Nephites because he loves them; **Ether** 2: 14 brother of Jared² is c. because he remembered not to call upon the Lord.

CHASTITY, CHASTE (*see also* Adultery; Clean; Fornication; Lust; Purity; Virtue; TG Chastity, Chaste)

Jacob 2: 7 feelings of Nephites' wives and children are tender and c.; 2: 28 the Lord delights in c. of women; **Moro.** 9: 9 Nephites deprive Lamanites' daughters of that which is most precious, c.

CHEAT (*see also* Deceit)

2 Ne. 28: 21 devil c. men's souls.

CHECK (*see also* Restrain)

Alma 15: 17 people are c. as to pride.

CHEEK (*see* Smite)

CHEER (*see also* Cheerful; Happiness; Joy; TG Cheer)

2 Ne. 10: 23 c. up your hearts; **Alma** 17: 31 (3 Ne. 1: 13) be of good c.

CHEERFULLY (*see also* Cheer; TG Cheerful, Cheerfulness)

Mosiah 24: 15 Alma¹ and his followers submit c. to will of the Lord.

CHEMISH—*Nephite record keeper, son of Omni*

Omni 1: 8 receives plates from brother, Amaron; 1: 9 writes few things; 1: 10 father of Abinadom.

CHERUBIM (*see also* TG Cherubim; BD Cherubim)

Alma 12: 21 (42: 2–3; Gen. 3: 24) God placed c. and flaming sword east of Eden.

CHICKENS (*see also* Animal; Hen)

3 Ne. 10: 4–6 (Matt. 23: 37) the Lord would have gathered people as a hen gathers c.

CHIEF (*see also* Captain; Judge, Chief)

3 Ne. 7: 3, 14 every tribe appoints c.

CHILD, CHILDREN (*see also* Babe; Children of God; Daughter; Son; TG Child; Children; Family; Children, Duties of; Family, Children, Responsibilities toward; Honoring Father and Mother; Salvation of Little Children)

1 Ne. 5: 21 (Mosiah 1: 4) brass plates of great worth in preserving the Lord's commandments unto c.; 11: 20 Nephi¹ sees virgin bearing c. in arms; 14: 3 abominable church founded by devil and his c.; 17: 1–2 women bear c. in wilderness; 22: 6, 8 (21: 22; Isa. 49: 22) c. of Jews to be carried in Gentiles' arms; **2 Ne.** 2: 23 without fall, Adam and Eve would have had no c.; 4: 15 Nephi¹ writes scriptures for learning and profit of his c.; 13: 12 (Isa. 3: 12) c. to be oppressors of the Lord's people; 19: 6 (Isa. 9: 6) for unto us a c. is born; 21: 6 (30: 12; Isa. 11: 6) leopard, kid, calf, lion to lie down together, and little c. shall lead them; 25: 26–27 Nephites write of Christ, that c. may know source of remission of sins; **Jacob** 2: 35 (3: 10) Nephites have lost confidence of c. because of bad example; **Mosiah** 3: 16 (Moro. 8: 8–24) blood of Christ atones for sins of little c.; 3: 18 men drink damnation to souls except they become as little c.; 3: 19 c. is submissive, humble, full of love; 3: 21 none shall be found blameless except little c.; 4: 14 ye will not suffer your c. to go hungry, to transgress, to quarrel, to serve devil; 6: 2 all except little c. enter covenant; 15: 25 little c. have eternal life; **Alma** 5: 25, 38–41 the wicked are c. of devil; 30: 25 Korihor says c. not guilty because of parents; 30: 60 devil will not support his c.; 32: 23 words given to little c. which confound the wise and learned; 39: 12 command thy c. to do good; 43: 45 (48: 10; 58: 12) Nephites fight for homes, wives, c.; **Hel.** 15: 2 wo unto them which are with c., for they shall be heavy and cannot flee; 3 Ne. 9: 22 the Lord will receive those who repent and come unto him as little c.; 11: 37–38 men must become as little c. or they cannot inherit kingdom of God; 17: 11–12, 21–23 Christ blesses c.; 17: 24–25 angels minister to Nephite c.; 18: 21 pray in your families that your wives and c. may be blessed; 22: 1 (Isa. 54: 1) more are the c. of the desolate than the c. of the married wife; 22: 13 (Isa. 54: 13) all thy c. shall be taught of the Lord, and great shall be peace of thy c.; 26: 14 Christ

teaches and ministers to c. of multitude, looses their tongues; 28: 22 (4 Ne. 1: 33) Nephite disciples play with beasts as c. with lamb; **4 Ne.** 1: 38 those who reject gospel teach c. they should not believe; **Morm.** 1: 2 Mormon² a sober c.; 4: 12 there never had been so great wickedness among all c. of Lehi¹; **Moro.** 8: 3 Father's Holy C., Jesus; 8: 8–24 little c. do not need repentance or baptism; 8: 12, 22 (Mosiah 3: 16) little c. are alive in Christ; 8: 15 wickedness to suppose God saves one c. because of baptism and the other must perish; 8: 17 all c. are alike unto the Lord; 8: 17 the Lord loves little c. with perfect love.

CHILDREN OF GOD (*see also* Begotten; Born of God; Heir; Inherit; Saint; Son; TG Children of Light)

1 Ne. 11: 17 God loves his c.; 17: 36 the Lord has created his c. that they should possess earth; **Alma** 36: 14 Alma² had led many of God's c. to destruction; **3 Ne.** 12: 9 (Matt. 5: 9) peacemakers shall be called c. of God; 12: 44–45 (Matt. 5: 44–45) love your enemies, that you may be c. of Father in heaven; **Moro.** 7: 19 lay hold upon every good thing and you will be c. of Christ.

CHOICE (*see also* Choose; Chosen [adj.]; Precious; Promised Land)

2 Ne. 1: 19 Lehi¹ wishes that sons might be a c. people of the Lord; 3: 6–7 the Lord will raise up c. seer from loins of Joseph¹; **Jacob** 5: 43 branch planted in c. spot in vineyard; **W of M** 1: 6 Mormon² puts plates containing c. revelations with remainder of record.

CHOOSE, CHOSE, CHOSEN (*see also* Agency; Chosen [adj.])

1 Ne. 12: 7 the twelve were ordained of God and c.; 20: 10 (Isa. 48: 10) I have c. thee in the furnace of affliction; **2 Ne.** 2: 27–29 (10: 23; Hel. 14: 31) men are free to c. liberty and eternal life or captivity and death; 2: 30 I have c. the good part; 17: 16 (Isa. 7: 16) before child knows to c. good, land shall be forsaken of both kings; 26: 10 (Alma 40: 13) because Nephites c. works of darkness, they must go down to hell; **Mosiah** 29: 25 c. judges by voice of people; 29: 27 (Alma 10: 19) if voice of people c. iniquity, judgments will come; **Alma** 13: 3 those foreordained were left to c. good or evil; 13: 3, 10 having c. good and exercised faith, priests were called with holy calling; 30: 8 (Josh. 24: 15) c. ye this day whom ye will serve; **Hel.** 5: 2 they who c. evil were more numerous than they who c. good; 13: 29 how long will ye c. darkness rather than light; **3 Ne.** 12: 1 Christ c.

twelve to minister unto Nephites; 19: 20 Christ c. Nephite disciples because of their belief in him.

CHOSEN [adj.] (*see also* Choice; Choose; Covenant)

Mosiah 7: 26 Abinadi a c. man of God; **Alma** 7: 10 Mary a precious and c. vessel; 10: 7 Alma² a c. man of God; 46: 17 (Ether 13: 2) all the land on the north and the south a c. land.

CHRIST (*see* Jesus Christ)

CHRISTIAN (*see also* Believer; Saint; Worshipper; TG Christian; BD Christians)

Alma 46: 13, 16 Moroni¹ prays for blessings of liberty as long as C. remain to possess land; 46: 14–15 true believers are called C.; 48: 10 cause of liberty is called cause of C.

CHRISTS, FALSE (*see also* Prophets, False)

2 Ne. 25: 18 not any Messiah come save false Messiah; **W of M** 1: 15–16 are punished according to crimes.

CHURCH (*see also* Church, Great and Abominable; Church of God; Church of the Devil; Churches, False; TG Church)

1 Ne. 4: 26 Zoram¹ supposes Nephi¹ speaks of brethren of c.

CHURCH, GREAT AND ABOMINABLE (*see also* Church of the Devil; Churches, False; Harlot; Whore)

1 Ne. 13: 5, 9 abominable c. slays saints; 13: 6 (14: 3, 9, 17) devil is founder of great and abominable c.; 13: 7–8 precious clothing and harlots are desires of great and abominable c.; 13: 26–28, 32, 34 great and abominable c. takes away plain and precious parts of gospel; 14: 3 (22: 14) great and abominable c. digs pit for saints; 14: 9–10, 13, 16 great and abominable c. is mother of abominations; 14: 10 those who do not belong to c. of Lamb belong to great c.; 14: 17 wrath of God to be poured out on great and abominable c.; 22: 13 blood of great and abominable c. shall turn upon their own heads; 22: 14 (2 Ne. 28: 18) great and abominable c. shall tumble to dust; **2 Ne.** 6: 12 if Gentiles do not unite themselves to great and abominable c., they shall be saved.

CHURCH OF CHRIST (*see* Church of God)

CHURCH OF GOD (*see also* Assemble; Baptism; Build; Flock; Kingdom of God; Officer; Priesthood; Religion; Saint; Stake; TG Church; Church, Name of; Church before Christ; Church Organization; BD Church)

1 Ne. 14: 10 only two *c.*, *c.* of Lamb and *c.* of devil; 14: 12, 14 *c.* of Lamb are saints of God; **2 Ne.** 9: 2 Jews shall be restored to true *c.* of God; 25: 14 wo unto those who fight against God and people of his *c.*; **Mosiah** 18: 17 (25: 18; 26: 22; Alma 4: 5; 3 Ne. 26: 21; 28: 23; Moro. 6: 4) those baptized are called *c.* of God, or *c.* of Christ; 21: 30 (23: 16; 25: 18; 29: 47) Alma¹ and his people form *c.* of God; 25: 18–19 (29: 47; Alma 4: 7; 6: 1) Mosiah² grants that Alma¹ might establish *c.* throughout land and ordain priests and teachers over every *c.*; 25: 22 notwithstanding many *c.*, they are all one *c.*; 26: 8 Mosiah² gives Alma¹ authority over *c.*; 26: 22 this is my *c.*; 27: 1–2 (Alma 1: 19) great persecutions inflicted on *c.*; 27: 9–10 (36: 6, 9, 11) Alma² seeks to destroy *c.* of God; 27: 13 angel asks Alma², Why persecutest thou *c.* of God; 29: 42 (Alma 4: 4; 5: 3) Alma¹ gives son, Alma², charge concerning all affairs of *c.*; **Alma** 1: 30 members of *c.* do not send away any, whether out of *c.* or in the *c.*; 1: 31 members of *c.* prosper more than those who do not belong; 2: 4 Amlici seeks to destroy *c.*; 4: 4–5 (5: 5) *c.* established more fully through many baptisms; 4: 11 wickedness in *c.* leads unbelievers to further iniquity; 5: 5 (8: 23) Alma² high priest over *c.*; 6: 4 (8: 1) order of *c.* established; 45: 22 (62: 46) Helaman² and brethren go forth to establish *c.* again; 46: 10 Amalickiah seeks to destroy *c.* of God; 46: 13–14 true believers who belong to *c.* are called Christians; **Hel.** 3: 33 pride enters hearts of those who profess to belong to *c.*; 4: 11 wickedness among those who profess to belong to *c.*; 11: 21 *c.* spreads throughout land; 3 **Ne.** 6: 14 *c.* begins to be broken up; 18: 5 one to be ordained with power to give broken bread to people of *c.*; 18: 16 prayers in *c.* to follow Savior's pattern; 21: 22 if they will repent, I will establish my *c.* among them; 27: 3–11 those who build upon gospel should call *c.* in Christ's name; 27: 21 ye know the things that ye must do in my *c.*; 28: 18 disciples unite as many to *c.* as believe in their preaching; **4 Ne.** 1: 1 disciples form *c.* of Christ in all lands; 1: 26 Nephites begin to build up *c.* to get gain, and deny true *c.* of Christ; 1: 27–29 *c.* that deny Christ's gospel persecute true *c.*; **Morm.** 8: 38 O ye hypocrites, why have ye polluted the holy *c.* of God; **Moro.** 3: 1 disciples are called elders of *c.*; 4: 2 (5: 2; D&C 20: 76) elders and priests kneel down with *c.* and pray over bread and wine; 6: 5 *c.* meets oft to fast, pray, speak; 7: 39 if ye have not faith in Christ, ye are not fit to be numbered among people of his *c.*

CHURCH OF THE DEVIL (*see also* Church, Great and Abominable; Churches, False; Devil; TG Devil, Church of)

1 Ne. 13: 6 (14: 3, 9, 17) devil is founder of great and abominable *c.*; 14: 10 only two *c.*, *c.* of Lamb and *c.* of devil; **Alma** 5: 39 if ye are not sheep of good shepherd, devil is your shepherd; **3 Ne.** 27: 11 those who build *c.* upon works of devil have joy for season, then comes the end.

CHURCH OF THE LAMB (*see* Church of God)

CHURCHES, FALSE (*see also* Church, Great and Abominable; Church of the Devil; Denominations; Doctrine, False; Priestcraft; Priests, False; Prophets, False; Tradition)

1 Ne. 22: 23 *c.* built up to get gain or power shall be brought low; **2 Ne.** 26: 20 Gentiles shall stumble because they build many *c.*; 28: 3–4 *c.* built by men shall contend against each other; **3 Ne.** 27: 8 if *c.* is called in name of man, it is *c.* of man; 27: 11 those who build *c.* upon works of men will have joy for season, then comes the end; **4 Ne.** 1: 26 *c.* built up to get gain deny true *c.*; 1: 27 many *c.* in land deny parts of gospel; 1: 28 false *c.* multiplies because of iniquity and power of Satan; 1: 29–30 *c.* denies Christ and persecutes true *c.*; **Morm.** 8: 28 *c.* will become defiled and leaders will rise up in pride; 8: 32 *c.* will forgive sins for money.

CIMETER (*see also* Sword; Weapon)

Enos 1: 20 Lamanites skilled in *c.*; **Mosiah** 9: 16 (10: 8; Alma 2: 12; 43: 18, 20, 37; 60: 2; Hel. 1: 14) *c.* used in wars between Nephites and Lamanites.

CIRCUMCISION (*see also* Uncircumcised; TG Circumcision; BD Circumcision)

Moro. 8: 8 law of *c.* done away in Christ.

CIRCUMSPECTLY

Mosiah 26: 37 (Hel. 15: 5; 16: 10) walk *c.* before God.

CITIZENSHIP (*see also* Government, Civil)

Mosiah 2: 17 when in service of fellow beings ye are in service of God; 4: 13 live peaceably, and render to every man his due; 29: 25 choose judges by voice of people; **Alma** 1: 1, 14 people are obliged to abide by laws; 43: 9, 26, 47 (55: 28) Nephites fight to defend rights, privileges, liberty; 46: 20 (48: 13; 51: 6) Nephites and converted Lamanites enter covenant to preserve rights and free government.

CITY (*see also* Jerusalem; Jerusalem, New; Town; Villages; Zarahemla, City of[1])

1 Ne. 12: 4 (3 Ne. 8: 14–16) in vision, Nephi[1] sees many *c.* destroyed; **2 Ne.** 16: 8–11 (Isa. 6: 8–11) Isaiah[1] is called to preach until *c.* be wasted without inhabitants; **Alma** 8: 7 Nephite custom to call *c.* after him who first possessed them; 50: 1 Nephite armies dig up heaps of earth round about all *c.*; 62: 32 (Hel. 4: 16; Morm. 8: 7) battles fought from *c.* to *c.*; **Hel.** 3: 9 trees allowed to grow for timber to build *c.*; 8: 6 Nephites do not believe they can be destroyed because *c.* are great; **3 Ne.** 6: 7 many *c.* are built anew and many old *c.* are repaired; 8: 8–10, 14–15 (9: 3–10) many *c.* destroyed at time of Crucifixion; 12: 14 (Matt. 5: 14) *c.* set on hill cannot be hid; 21: 15 (Micah 5: 11) I will cut off the *c.* of thy land; **4 Ne.** 1: 7–9 many *c.* are rebuilt; **Ether** 9: 23 Coriantum[1] builds many mighty *c.*; 13: 5 Jerusalem to be built up again and become holy *c.*

CIVIL (*see also* Government, Civil)

Moro. 9: 12 Nephites were a *c.* people.

CIVILIZATION

Alma 51: 22 Moroni[1] subjects his people to peace and *c.*; **Moro.** 9: 11 Nephites are without *c.*

CLAIM (*see also* Justice; Mercy; Profess)

Mosiah 29: 9 Mosiah[2] fears son might later *c.* right to kingdom; **Moro.** 7: 28 Christ *c.* all those who have faith in him.

CLAP (*see also* Hands, Laying on of)

Alma 31: 36 Alma[2] *c.* his hands upon them, and they were filled with Spirit.

CLASS (*see also* Ranks)

4 Ne. 1: 26 Nephites began to be divided into *c.*

CLAY (*see also* Tabernacle)

2 Ne. 27: 27 (Isa. 29: 16) turning of things upside down shall be esteemed as potter's *c.*

CLEAN, CLEANLINESS (*see also* Chastity; Cleanse; Holy; Purify; Virtue; White; Worthy; TG Cleanliness)

2 Ne. 25: 16 worship the Father with pure hearts and *c.* hands; **Alma** 5: 19 can ye look to God with pure heart and *c.* hands; 24: 15 God imparted his word and has made us *c.* thereby; **3 Ne.** 20: 41 (Isa. 52: 11) be ye *c.* that bear vessels of the Lord; **Ether** 4: 6 Gentiles shall not receive interpreters until they repent of sins and become *c.* before the Lord; 12: 37 thy garments shall be made *c.*

CLEANSE (*see also* Baptism; Clean; Fire; Purify; Rid; Sanctification; Spotless; Wash)

Alma 5: 21 no man can be saved except his garments are *c.* from all stain; 5: 24 garments of all holy prophets are *c.*; 5: 27 if called to die, could you say your garments have been *c.*; 7: 14 the Lamb is mighty to save and *c.* from all unrighteousness; 60: 23 inward vessel to be *c.* first, then outward vessel; 60: 24 Nephites not to contend with Lamanites until they have *c.* their inward vessel; **3 Ne.** 8: 1 no man could do miracle in Jesus' name save he were *c.* from iniquity; 28: 36 Mormon[2] did not know whether three Nephites had been *c.* from mortality to immortality; **Morm.** 9: 6 turn unto Father that ye might be *c.* by blood of Lamb; **Moro.** 6: 4 after baptism people are *c.* by Holy Ghost.

CLEAR (*see also* Plain)

2 Ne. 4: 33 wilt thou *c.* my way before me; **Jacob** 5: 65 ye shall *c.* away branches which bring forth bitter fruit.

CLEAVE, CLAVE [join] (*see also* Join; Mount; Rock)

Jacob 6: 5 *c.* unto God as he *c.* unto you; **Hel.** 4: 25 except Nephites *c.* unto the Lord, they must perish; **3 Ne.** 10: 10 earth *c.* together again; **Ether** 14: 2 every man *c.* unto that which was his; **Moro.** 7: 28 they who have faith in Christ will *c.* unto every good thing; 7: 46 *c.* unto charity.

CLIMATE

Alma 46: 40 men subject to diseases by nature of *c.*

CLOAK

3 Ne. 12: 40 (Matt. 5: 40) if any man will take away thy coat, let him have *c.* also.

CLOSET (*see also* Private; Secret)

Alma 33: 7 when I turned unto my *c.*, and prayed, the Lord did hear me; 34: 26 pour out your souls in your *c.*; **3 Ne.** 13:6 when thou prayest, enter into thy *c.*

CLOTH (*see also* Clothe; Clothing; Linen; Silk)

Mosiah 10: 5 (Hel. 6: 13) Nephite women work all manner of *c.*; **Alma** 1: 29 church becomes rich, having all manner of good homely *c.*; **Ether** 10: 24 Jaredites work all manner of *c.*

CLOTHE (*see also* Clothing)

2 Ne. 7: 3 (Isa. 50: 3) the Lord *c.*

heavens with blackness; 9: 14 the righteous shall be c. with purity; **Jacob** 2: 19 obtain riches to c. the naked; **Mosiah** 4: 26 impart of your substance to the poor, c. the naked; 10: 5 (Hel. 6: 13) women work cloth that Nephites might c. their nakedness; **Alma** 35: 9 people of Ammon² c. poor Zoramites; **Hel.** 13: 28 people will c. false prophet in costly apparel; **3 Ne.** 11: 8 Christ c. in white robe.

CLOTHING, CLOTHES (see also Apparel; Cloak; Coat; Garment; Raiment; Robe)

1 Ne. 13: 7–8 Nephi¹ sees precious c. in abominable church; **2 Ne.** 13: 6 (Isa. 3: 6) men shall say, Thou hast c., be thou our ruler; 28: 13 latter-day churches will rob the poor because of fine c.; **Alma** 14: 22 people of Ammonihah take away c. of Alma² and Amulek; 43: 19 Nephite army dressed with thick c.; **Hel.** 4: 12 Nephites withhold c. from the naked; **3 Ne.** 14: 15 (Matt. 7: 15) beware of false prophets, who come in sheep's c.

CLOUD (see also Smoke; Vapor)

2 Ne. 14: 5 (Isa. 4: 5) the Lord will create upon every dwelling-place of mount Zion a c. and smoke by day; 15: 6 (Isa. 5: 6) the Lord will command c. that they rain no rain; 24: 14 (Isa. 14: 14) the Lord will ascend above heights of c.; **Mosiah** 27: 11 angel descended as in c.; **Alma** 19: 6 light of God's glory dispels c. of darkness in Lamoni's mind; **Hel.** 5: 28 those in prison are overshadowed with c. of darkness; **3 Ne.** 18: 38 c. overshadows multitude, that they cannot see Jesus; **Ether** 2: 4–5, 14 the Lord speaks with brother of Jared² in c.

COAT (see also Clothing)

Alma 46: 12 Moroni¹ rends c. to make title of liberty; 46: 24 remnant of c. of Joseph¹ was preserved; **3 Ne.** 12: 40 (Matt. 5: 40) if any man will take away thy c., let him have thy cloak also.

COHOR¹—brother of Noah²

Ether 7: 15 drawn away by brother.

COHOR²—early Jaredite king

Ether 7: 20 son ot Noah², rules one of two kingdoms; 7: 21 slain by Shule in battle; 7: 22 father of Nimrod², who gives up kingdom.

COHOR³—late Jaredite

Ether 13: 17 sons and daughters of C. are unrepentant.

COIN (see also Amnor; Ezrom; Limnah; Money; Onti; Senine; Senum; Seon; Shiblon; Shiblum; Shum)

Alma 11: 1–9 Nephite c. and measures explained.

COM¹—early Jaredite king

Ether 1: 26–27 (9: 25) father of Heth¹, son of Coriantum¹; 9: 25 reigns in father's stead.

COM²—late Jaredite king

Ether 1: 12–13 (10: 31) son of Coriantum², father of Shiblon¹; 10: 32 reigns over half of kingdom; 10: 33–34 fails to prevail over robbers; 11: 1 many prophets come in C's days; 11: 2–3 blessed for protecting prophets.

COMBINATION (see Secret Combination)

COME, CAME (see also Enter; Jesus Christ, First Coming of; Jesus Christ, Second Coming of)

1 Ne. 6: 4 intent of Nephi¹ to persuade men to c. unto God; 13: 40 all men must c. unto the Son, or they cannot be saved; **2 Ne.** 2: 10 because of intercession for all, all men c. unto God; 9: 45 c. unto that God who is rock of your salvation; 9: 51 (Omni 1: 26) c. unto the Holy One of Israel; 26: 33 the Lord invites all to c. to him, denies none that c.; 28: 32 the Lord will be merciful unto Gentiles if they repent and c. unto him; **Jacob** 6: 5 c. with full purpose of heart, and cleave unto God; **Alma** 5: 16 can you imagine hearing the Lord's voice say, C. unto me; 5: 34 c. unto me and ye shall partake of fruit of tree of life; 5:35 c. unto me and bring forth works of righteousness; 12: 15 we must c. forth and stand before God in his glory; **3 Ne.** 12: 3 (Matt. 5: 3) blessed are poor in spirit who c. unto the Lord; 12: 20 c. unto me and be ye saved; 12: 24 first be reconciled and c. unto me; 21: 27 work to commence among dispersed to prepare way whereby they may c. unto Christ; **Morm.** 9: 27 c. unto the Lord with all your heart; **Ether** 12: 27 if men will c. unto the Lord, he will show them their weaknesses; 13: 3 New Jerusalem to c. down out of heaven; **Moro.** 10: 32 c. unto Christ, and be perfected in him.

COMELY, COMELINESS (see also Beauty)

2 Ne. 14: 2 (Isa. 4: 2) fruit of earth shall be c. to them that are escaped of Israel; **Mosiah** 14: 2 (Isa. 53: 2) he hath no form nor c.; **Alma** 1: 27 Nephites do not wear costly apparel, yet they are neat and c.

COMFORT (see also Consolation; Holy Ghost—Comforter; Mourn; Rest)

2 Ne. 8: 12 I am he that c. you; **Mosiah** 12: 23 (15: 30; Alma 17: 10; 3 Ne. 16: 19; 20: 34; Isa. 52: 9) the Lord

hath c. his people; 18: 9 those baptized should be willing to c. those in need of c.; **Alma** 31: 31 wilt thou c. my soul in Christ; **3 Ne.** 12: 4 (Matt. 5: 4) blessed are they that mourn, for they shall be c.; **Ether** 15: 3 soul of Coriantumr² refused to be c.

COMFORTER (see Holy Ghost—Comforter)

COMFORTER, SECOND (see TG Jesus Christ—Second Comforter)

COMING (see Jesus Christ, First Coming of; Jesus Christ, Second Coming of)

COMMAND (see also Commandments of God; Decree; Instruction; Require)

    1 Ne. 17: 48 Nephi¹ c. brothers not to touch him; **Mosiah** 18: 19–24, 27, 29 Alma¹ c. priests how church should be administered; 27: 3 strict c. throughout all churches that there should be no persecution; **Alma** 11: 35–36 Zeezrom claims Amulek speaks as though he had authority to c. God; 37: 27 (Hel. 6: 25) Alma² c. Helaman² to retain secret oaths and covenants.

COMMANDER (see also Captain)

    Alma 43: 44 Zerahemnah chief c. of Lamanites; 46: 11 Moroni¹ chief c. of Nephites; 47: 19 Amalickiah is appointed chief c. of Lamanites; **3 Ne.** 3: 18 Gidgiddoni, great c. of all Nephite armies; **Morm.** 3: 11 Mormon² refuses to be c. of Nephite armies.

COMMANDMENTS OF GOD (see also Decree; Forbid; Law; Law of Moses; Obedience; Precept; Require; Sayings; Scriptures; Statute; Ten Commandments; TG Commandments of God)

    Title Page book written by way of c.; **1 Ne.** 2: 10 Lehi¹ prays that Laman¹ might be immovable as valley in keeping c.; 3: 7 I will go and do things that the Lord has c.; 3: 7 the Lord gives no c. save he prepares a way to accomplish it; 5: 21 brass plates enable people to preserve c. unto children; 15: 25 Nephi¹ exhorts brethren to remember God's c. always in all things; 17: 3 c. of God must be fulfilled; 22: 31 those who are obedient to c. shall be saved; **2 Ne.** 1: 9 (4: 4; Jarom 1: 9; Mosiah 2: 22, 31; Alma 9: 13; 50: 20) if those brought out of Jerusalem keep the Lord's c., they shall prosper; 2: 21 the Lord gives c. that all men must repent; 9: 27 wo unto him that has all c. of God and transgresses them; 25: 25 Nephites keep law of Moses because of the c.; 26: 24 the Lord c. none that they shall not partake of salvation; 26: 29 the Lord c. that there shall be no priestcrafts; 26: 32 the Lord has c. that men should not murder; 29: 11 the Lord c. all men to

write words he speaks to them; 30: 1 except ye keep c. of God, ye shall perish; **Jacob** 2: 10 I must do according to strict c. of God; 2: 30 if the Lord will raise up seed, he will c. his people; 4: 6 our faith becometh unshaken insomuch that we can c. trees, mountains, waves to obey; **Mosiah** 2: 22 all that God requires of you is to keep his c.; 2: 41 consider the blessed and happy state of those who keep c. of God; 5: 5 Benjamin's people willing to be obedient in all things the Lord shall c.; 12: 33—13: 25 Abinadi reviews Ten C.; 18: 10 baptism a covenant to serve God and keep his c.; 23: 14 trust no man to be your teacher except he be a man of God, keeping his c.; **Alma** 5: 18 can ye imagine yourselves brought before God's tribunal with perfect remembrance that ye have set at defiance his c.; 5: 44 Alma² is c. to testify of things to come as spoken by fathers; 5: 61–62 I, Alma², c. you in language of him who hath c. me; 6: 6 children of God are c. to gather together oft; 12: 9 those who know mysteries are under strict c. to impart only that which God grants unto children of men; 12: 31–32 God gave c. to men, they having first transgressed the first c.; 12: 37 let us not provoke God to pull down his wrath upon us in these his second c.; 29: 9 I know that which the Lord has c. me; 37: 35 learn in thy youth to keep the c.; **Hel.** 4: 22 Nephites trample under feet that which the Lord c. Mosiah¹ to give them; 6: 31 more part of Nephites trample under feet the c. of God; 7: 7 in days of Nephi¹, the Lord's people were firm to keep c.; 14: 9–10 (3 Ne. 23: 9) the Lord c. Samuel the Lamanite to preach repentance; **3 Ne.** 15: 16, 18–19 Father c. Christ what to speak; 16: 4 (23: 13) Christ c. Nephites to write his sayings after he is gone; 16: 16 (20: 14) the Father c. Christ to give land for inheritance; 18: 3, 8, 12 the Lord gives c. to administer bread and wine to those who have repented and been baptized; 18: 27–28 the Lord gives c. not to suffer any one unknowingly to partake of bread and wine unworthily; 23: 14 Jesus c. Nephites to teach what he has expounded; 26: 2 the Father c. Christ to give Nephites scriptures they do not have; **Morm.** 5: 23 at God's great c., earth shall be rolled together as scroll; 7: 4 Lamanites should not take weapons of war save God c. them; **Ether** 4: 9 at Christ's c., inhabitants of earth shall pass away; **Moro.** 8: 25 baptism comes by faith unto fulfilling the c., which brings remission of sins.

COMMIT (see Adultery; Murder; Sin)

COMMON

    Mosiah 29: 26 not c. that voice of

people desires anything contrary to what is right; **3 Ne.** 26: 19 (4 Ne. 1: 3, 25) Nephites have all things c. among them.

COMMUNICATION (*see also* Correspondence; Hearken; Heed; Language; Prayer; Speak; Think; Understand; Word; TG Communication)

3 Ne. 12: 37 let your c. be Yea, yea.

COMMUNION, COMMUNE (*see also* TG Sacrament; BD Communion)

Jarom 1: 4 as many as are not stiffnecked and have faith c. with Spirit.

COMNOR—*hill near Valley of Shur*

Ether 14: 28 Coriantumr² gathers armies near hill C.

COMPASS (*see* Liahona)

COMPASSION (*see also* Charity; God, Love of; Kindness; Love; Mercy; Pity; TG Compassion)

1 Ne. 21: 15 (Isa. 49: 15) can woman forget sucking child, that she have not c. on son of her womb; **Mosiah** 15: 9 the Son is filled with c. toward children of men; 19: 14 (20: 26) Lamanites have c. on people of Limhi; 23: 34 Lamanites have c. on Amulon and brethren; **Alma** 27: 4 Ammon² and brethren moved with c. by destruction among people; **3 Ne.** 17: 6 Christ's bowels are filled with c. toward Nephites; **Ether** 1: 35 the Lord had c. upon Jared².

COMPEL (*see also* Agency; Constrain; Dominion; Liberty)

Alma 32: 13–16 blessings of those who are humble because they are c. or are not c.; 42: 27 whosoever will not come to waters of life is not c. to come; 47: 3 Lamanite king commands Amalickiah to c. reluctant soldiers to arms; 51: 15, 20 Moroni¹ requests permission to c. dissenters to defend country; **3 Ne.** 2: 12 converted Lamanites are c. to take up arms against robbers; 12: 41 (Matt. 5: 41) whosoever shall c. thee to go a mile, go with him twain.

COMPLAIN (*see also* Murmur; Reproach)

1 Ne. 5: 2–3 Sariah c. against Lehi¹; 17: 18 brethren c. against Nephi¹; **Mosiah** 27: 1 church c. against leaders because of persecution; **Alma** 60: 4 were this all we had suffered we would not c.

COMPREHEND (*see also* God, Omniscience of; Know; Learn; Perceive; Understand)

Mosiah 4: 9 man doth not c. all things which the Lord can c.; **Alma** 26:

35 God c. all things; **Morm.** 9: 16 who can c. works of God.

CONCEIVE (*see also* Bear, Bore, Borne; TG Conceived in Sin)

2 Ne. 17: 14 (18: 3; Alma 7: 10; Isa. 7: 14; 8: 3) virgin shall c. and shall bear a son; **Mosiah** 15: 3 Christ is called Father because he was c. by power of God; **3 Ne.** 17: 17 hearts cannot c. marvelous things Nephites heard Jesus speak.

CONCUBINE (*see also* Adultery; Chastity; Wife; TG Concubine)

Jacob 1: 15 (2: 24) David and Solomon desired c.; 2: 27 Nephites not to have c.; 3: 5 Lamanites do not have c.; **Mosiah** 11: 2, 4, 14 Noah³ has c.; **Ether** 10: 5 Riplakish has c.

CONDEMN, CONDEMNATION (*see also* Accuse; Judge [verb]; Spurn)

Title Page c. not the things of God; **2 Ne.** 7: 9 (Isa. 50: 9) all who c. God shall wax old as garment; 9: 25 where no punishment, there is no c.; 9: 25 where no c., mercies of Holy One have claim; 33: 14 (Alma 12: 14) words shall c. men at last day; **Mosiah** 4: 22 c. of those who withhold their substance will be just; 26: 31 he who forgives not brings himself under c.; **Alma** 3: 19 every man who is cursed brings upon himself his own c.; 41: 15 the word restoration more fully c. the sinner; 60: 2 Moroni¹ writes to civil leaders by way of c.; **Hel.** 7: 5 people c. the righteous because of their righteousness; 8: 1 wicked judges want to c. Nephi²; 14: 19 by knowing things and not doing them, men come under c.; 14: 29 those who do not believe bring upon themselves their own c.; **3 Ne.** 6: 22 people could be c. to death only with signature of governor; 6: 25 judges c. prophets to death; 22: 17 (Isa. 54: 17) every tongue that shall rise against thee in judgment thou shalt c.; **Morm.** 8: 12 record not to be c. because of imperfections; 9: 31 c. me not for my imperfection; **Moro.** 6: 7 three witnesses are needed to c. transgressor; 7: 19 lay hold upon every good thing and c. it not; 8: 22 he who is under no c. cannot repent; 9: 6 if we cease to labor, we will be brought under c.

CONDESCENSION (*see* Jesus Christ, Condescension of)

CONDUCT (*see* Lead)

CONFER (*see also* Give; Ordain; Ordinance)

Omni 1: 3 Omni c. plates upon Amaron; **Mosiah** 28: 20 Mosiah² c. records on Alma²; 29: 42 Alma¹ c. office

of high priest upon Alma²; **Alma** 63: 11 Shiblon c. sacred things upon Helaman².

CONFESS (*see also* Acknowledge; Confession of Sins; TG Confess)

Jacob 7: 17 Sherem c. Christ; **Mosiah** 16: 1 every nation shall c. before God that his judgments are just; 26: 27 (Matt. 7: 23) the Lord will c. he never knew those who never knew him; 27: 31 every tongue shall c. before Redeemer; **Moro.** 7: 44 if man is meek and c. Christ, he must have charity.

CONFESSION OF SINS (*see also* Forgive; Humble; Repentance; TG Confession)

Mosiah 26: 29, 35 transgressor who c. his sins shall be forgiven; 26: 36 (Moro. 6: 7) those who do not c. sins are not numbered among church; **Alma** 17: 4 by power of words of sons of Mosiah² many Lamanites c. sins; **3 Ne.** 1: 25 Nephites come to knowledge of error and c. faults.

CONFIDENCE (*see also* Faith; Trust)

Jacob 2: 35 Nephites lose c. of children through bad example.

CONFIRM (*see also* Establish; Hands, Laying on of; Holy Ghost, Gift of; BD Confirmation)

Mosiah 27: 33 Alma² and sons of Mosiah² c. faith; **Morm.** 9: 25 unto whosoever believes in his name will the Lord c. his words.

CONFOUND (*see also* Rebuke)

1 Ne. 14: 2 (15: 20; Ether 13: 8; Moro. 10: 31) Israel shall no more be c.; 17: 52 Nephi¹ c. his brethren; 22: 5, 7 Israel shall be scattered and c.; 22: 22 the righteous shall not be c.; **2 Ne.** 3: 12 writing shall grow unto c. of false doctrines; 3: 14 they who seek to destroy latter-day seer shall be c.; **Jacob** 7: 8 Jacob² c. Sherem; **Omni** 1: 22 (Mosiah 28: 17; Ether 1: 33–37) the Lord c. language at time of tower; **Mosiah** 12: 19 Abinadi c. priests; **Alma** 32: 23 children given words that c. the wise; 37: 6–7 by small means the Lord c. the wise; **Hel.** 5: 17 Nephi² and Lehi⁴ c. dissenters; **Ether** 1: 34–37 the Lord does not c. language of Jared² and his family; 3: 24 the Lord c. language written by brother of Jared².

CONQUER, CONQUEROR (*see also* Overcome; Prevail; Subject; Win)

Jacob 7: 25 trusting in God, Nephites become c. of enemies; **Alma** 30: 17 Korihor claims every man c. according to his strength; 44: 8 if swords not taken, Lamanites will perish or c.; **Moro.** 9: 6 labor to c. enemy of all righteousness.

CONSCIENCE (*see also* Light; TG Conscience; BD Conscience)

Mosiah 2: 27 Benjamin teaches people so that he can answer God with clear c.; 4: 3 Benjamin's people have peace of c. because of faith in Christ; **Alma** 29: 5 to him who knows good and evil is given according to his desires, whether joy or remorse of c.; 42: 18 punishment and just law bring remorse of c.

CONSCIOUSNESS (*see also* Awake; Knowledge)

Alma 12: 1 (14: 6) Zeezrom trembles under c. of guilt; **Morm.** 9: 3–4 man cannot dwell with God under c. of guilt.

CONSECRATE (*see also* Anointing; Ordain; Sanctification)

2 Ne. 1: 7, 32 (3: 2; 10: 19) land is c. unto him whom the Lord brings to it; 2: 2 God shall c. thy afflictions for thy gain; 5: 26 (Jacob 1: 18) Nephi¹ c. Jacob² and Joseph² as priests; 32: 9 pray that the Father will c. thy performance unto thee; 33: 4 the Lord will c. prayers of Nephi¹ for gain of his people; **Mosiah** 2: 11 Benjamin c. by Mosiah¹; 6: 3 Benjamin c. Mosiah² to be ruler; 23: 17 Alma¹ c. just men as priests; **Alma** 5: 3 Alma¹ c. son, Alma², to be high priest; 15: 13 Alma² c. priests; 23: 4 Aaron³ and brethren c. priests among Lamanites.

CONSEQUENCES (*see also* Reward; Wages)

2 Ne. 9: 48 (Jacob 3: 12) because people are unholy, Jacob² must teach c. of sin.

CONSIDER (*see also* Think)

Mosiah 3: 9 his people shall c. Christ a man; **Hel.** 14: 16 by the fall, all mankind are c. dead, temporally and spiritually; **3 Ne.** 20: 45 (21: 8) that which kings had not heard shall they c.

CONSIGN (*see also* Condemn; Judgment)

Mosiah 3: 25 the evil are c. to awful view of own guilt; **Alma** 9: 11 except for God's power, man would be c. to state of endless misery; 26: 19 why did God not c. us to awful destruction; 28: 11 mourners fear that dead are c. to state of endless wo; 40: 26 wicked are c. to partake of fruits of their labors; 42: 1 Corianton supposes injustice that sinner is c. to state of misery; 42: 14 justice c. fallen mankind to be cut off; **Hel.** 12: 26 those cast off shall be c. to state of endless misery.

CONSOLATION, CONSOLE (*see also* Comfort)

Jacob 3: 1 God will c. you in your

afflictions; Mosiah 27: 33 Alma² and sons of Mosiah² impart *c.* to church; **Alma** 56: 11 we may *c.* ourselves that we have died in cause of country and God; **Hel.** 3: 35 firmer faith in Christ fills souls with joy and *c.*

CONSTRAIN, CONSTRAINT (*see also* Compel)

1 Ne. 4: 10 Nephi¹ is *c.* by Spirit to kill Laban; 7: 15 (2 Ne. 4: 14; 28: 1) Spirit *c.* Nephi¹ to speak; **Alma** 14: 11 Spirit *c.* Alma² not to stretch forth hand on behalf of martyrs; **4 Ne.** 1: 48 Ammaron is *c.* by Spirit to hide up records.

CONSUME, CONSUMING, CONSUMPTION (*see also* Devour; Eat)

1 Ne. 17: 48 Nephi¹ is filled with power of God, even unto *c.* of flesh; 22: 23 churches built up for gain will be *c.* as stubble; **2 Ne.** 4: 21 God has filled Lehi¹ with his love, even unto *c.* of flesh; 26: 6 the wicked shall be *c.*; 26: 7 loss of the slain well nigh *c.* Nephi¹ before presence of the Lord; 27: 31 the scorner is *c.*; **Alma** 5: 52 tree that bringeth not forth good fruit will be cast into fire which cannot be *c.*

CONTENTION, CONTEND (*see also* Devil; Disputations; Dissension; Doctrine, False; Hardheartedness; Murmur; Prophets, False; Quarrel; Rebel; Stir; Strife; TG Contention)

1 Ne. 9: 4 (19:4) account of *c.* of people engraven on other plates; 12: 3 (Jarom 1: 13) Nephi¹ beholds many generations pass away after manner of wars and *c.*; 21: 25 (2 Ne. 6: 17; Isa. 49: 25) the Lord will *c.* with him who *c.* with Israel; **2 Ne.** 26: 2 (4 Ne. 1: 24–39) several generations after Christ's visit, wars and *c.* arise; 26: 32 the Lord commands that men not *c.* one with another; 28: 4 churches shall *c.* one with another; **Omni** 1: 17 Mulekites had had many wars and serious *c.*; **W of M** 1: 12 Benjamin had somewhat of *c.* among his own people; **Mosiah** 2: 32 beware lest *c.* arise among you; 9: 13 Laman² stirs up Lamanites to wars and *c.* with people of Zeniff; 18: 21 Alma¹ commands no *c.* among church members; 29: 7 Mosiah² fears that giving kingdom to someone other than son might raise *c.*; **Alma** 2: 5 people have much dispute and wonderful *c.* regarding Amlici; 4: 9 great *c.* arise among people of church; 19: 28 *c.* regarding Ammon² among household of Lamanite king; 34: 38 Amulek admonishes people not to *c.* against Holy Ghost; 50: 25 *c.* among Nephites concerning land of Lehi; 51: 9 critical time for *c.* because Amalickiah stirs up Lamanites; **Hel.** 16: 22 Satan spreads rumors and *c.*; **3 Ne.** 2:

11 wars and *c.* throughout land because of Gadianton robbers; 11: 29 devil is father of *c.*, stirs up men to *c.* with anger; **4 Ne.** 1: 2, 13, 15, 18 no *c.* in land because of love of God; **Ether** 4: 8 he who *c.* against word of the Lord will be accursed; 11: 7 wars and *c.* among Jaredites because of wicked combinations.

CONTINUE, CONTINUATION (*see also* Endure; Eternal Life; Faint; Increase)

2 Ne. 33: 9 *c.* in path until end of day of probation; **Jacob** 6: 11 *c.* in the way which is narrow; **Ether** 2: 11 people to know God's decrees, that they may not *c.* in iniquities.

CONTRARY

Mosiah 2: 36 if men go *c.* to what they have been taught, they withdraw themselves from Spirit; 29: 26 not common that voice of people desireth anything *c.* to that which is right; **Alma** 11: 22 Amulek will say nothing *c.* to the Spirit of the Lord; **Hel.** 8: 3 Nephi² speaks nothing *c.* to God's commandments; 10: 5 Nephi² will not seek that which is *c.* to the Lord's will; 13: 38 to seek happiness in doing iniquity is *c.* to nature of righteousness of God; 16: 12 people begin to do more of that which is *c.* to God's commandments.

CONTRITE (*see* Broken Heart and Contrite Spirit; Meek; TG Contrite Heart)

CONTROVERSY (*see* Contention; Disputations)

CONVERSION, CONVERT (*see also* Baptism; Born of God; Change; Convince; Fire; Heart; Holy Ghost; Repentance; TG Conversion, Convert; BD Conversion)

1 Ne. 2: 16 *c.* of Nephi¹; **2 Ne.** 16: 10 (Isa. 6: 10) make the heart of this people fat lest they be *c.* and healed; **Jacob** 7: 7 Sherem claims Nephites *c.* law of Moses into worship of being which shall come many hundred years hence; **Enos** 1: 2–4 *c.* of Enos; **Mosiah** 5: 1–5 *c.* of King Benjamin's people; 18: 1 (Alma 5: 11) *c.* of Alma¹; 18: 7–11 *c.* of people of Alma¹; 25: 14–17 *c.* of Limhi; 27: 11–32 (Alma 36: 6–24) *c.* of Alma²; 27: 33–35 *c.* of sons of Mosiah²; **Alma** 5: 12–14, 26 *c.* of people of Zarahemla; 15: 5–12 *c.* of Zeezrom; 18: 40–41 *c.* of Lamoni; 19: 16–17 *c.* of Abish; 22: 15 *c.* of Lamoni's father; 22: 23 *c.* of Lamoni's household; 23: 14 only one Amalekite is *c.*; 53: 10 people of Ammon² are *c.* by word and power of God; **Hel.** 5: 49–50 (6: 3) *c.* of Lamanites; **3 Ne.** 1: 22 notwithstanding Satan's lyings, most Nephites are *c.* unto the Lord; 7: 21 those who are *c.* have been visited by Spirit; 7: 26 (28: 23; 4 Ne. 1: 2) *c.* of Nephites; 9: 13 be *c.* that the Lord

may heal you; 15: 22 Gentiles to be c. through preaching of Jews.

CONVINCE, CONVINCING (see also Conversion; Persuade; Witness; BD Convince)

Title Page (2 Ne. 25: 18; 26: 12) Book of Mormon written to the c. of Jew and Gentile that Jesus is the Christ; **Alma** 21: 17 (24: 7; 26: 24; 37: 9; Hel. 5: 19) Nephite missionaries c. many Lamanites of wickedness of fathers' traditions; 37: 8–9 records c. many of error of their ways; **3 Ne.** 1: 25 those who preached to no longer observe law of Moses are c. of error.

COPPER (see also Metal; Ore)

1 Ne. 18: 25 (2 Ne. 5: 15; Jarom 1: 8; Mosiah 11: 3, 8, 10) Nephites use c.; **Mosiah** 8: 10 (Ether 10: 23) Jaredites use c.

CORD (see also Band)

1 Ne. 7: 16 (18: 11) brethren of Nephi[1] bind him with c.; **2 Ne.** 26: 22 devil leads the wicked by neck with flaxen c.; **Alma** 14: 4, 22–23, 26 Alma[2] and Amulek bound with c.; 62: 21, 23 Moroni[1] has army prepare c. and ladders to enter city; **3 Ne.** 22: 2 (Isa. 54: 2) lengthen thy c. and strengthen thy stakes.

CORIANTON—son of Alma[2] [c. 75 B.C.]

Alma 31: 7 goes to Zoramites; 39: 3 had forsaken ministry to go after harlot; 39: 11 because of C's conduct, Zoramites do not believe words of Alma[2]; ch. 39–42 Alma[2] instructs C. on state of soul after death, on resurrection, probation, redemption, justice, atonement, repentance, and agency; 42: 31 is called to preach again; 63: 10 sails northward.

CORIANTOR—a late Jaredite

Ether 1: 6–7 (11: 18, 23) son of Moron; 11: 19 lives in captivity; 11: 20 many prophets in C's days.

CORIANTUM[1]—early Jaredite king

Ether 1: 27–28 (9: 21–25) son of Emer, father of Com[1]; 9: 21 is anointed king; 9: 23 righteous reign, great builder; 9: 24 begets sons and daughters, lives to 142 years.

CORIANTUM[2]—middle Jaredite

Ether 1: 13–14 (10: 31) son of Amnigaddah, father of Com[2]; 10: 31 lives in captivity.

CORIANTUMR[1]—early Jaredite

Ether 8: 4 son of Omer; 8: 5–6 restores kingdom to father, spares brother.

CORIANTUMR[2]—Jaredite king, last Jaredite survivor

Omni 1: 21 discovered by people of Zarahemla; **Ether** 12: 1–2 king over all land in days of Ether; 13: 15 many seek to destroy C.; 13: 16 skilled in warfare; 13: 20 warned by Ether; 13: 21 to be buried by another people; 13: 23 captured by Shared; 13: 24 liberated by sons; 13: 28–31 meets Shared in battle, wounded; 14: 3–5 battles with brother of Shared; 14: 6 C's throne is taken by Gilead; 14: 12 battles with Lib[2]; 14: 14–15 is pursued to Agosh; 14: 16 slays Lib[2], battles with Shiz; 14: 17 flees from Shiz; 14: 24 not to fall by sword; 14: 30 wounded by Shiz; 15: 3 repents; 15: 4, 18 writes to Shiz; 15: 11 camps at hill Ramah; 15: 13 is watched by Ether; 15: 15 final battle; 15: 30 slays Shiz; 15: 32 falls wounded.

CORIANTUMR[3]—apostate Nephite, commander of Lamanite forces [c. 51 B.C.]

Hel. 1: 15 descendant of Zarahemla, Nephite dissenter; 1: 17 leads Lamanites against Zarahemla; 1: 20 takes Zarahemla; 1: 21 kills judge; 1: 23 marches toward Bountiful; 1: 30 is killed; 1: 32 C's army is captured.

CORIHOR[1]—early Jaredite rebel

Ether 7: 3 son of Kib; 7: 4 rebels against father; 7: 5 takes father captive; 7: 9 brother, Shule, restores kingdom to Kib; 7: 13 repents and gains favor.

CORIHOR[2]—late Jaredite

Ether 13: 17 sons and daughters of C. repent not.

CORIHOR, LAND AND VALLEY OF—Jaredite area

Ether 14: 27–28 scene of battles of Coriantumr[2] with Shiz.

COROM—middle Jaredite king

Ether 1: 19–20 (10: 15–16) son of Levi[2], father of Kish; 10: 16 anointed king; 10: 17 righteous ruler, succeeded by son.

CORRESPONDENCE (see also Communication)

Alma 23: 18 (24: 8–9) Anti-Nephi-Lehies open c. with Nephites; 31: 4 Nephites fear Zoramites will enter c. with Lamanites.

CORRUPT, CORRUPTION (see also Canker; Corruptness; Defile; Filthiness; Pervert; Pollute; Unclean; Wickedness)

2 Ne. 2: 11 without opposition, body must remain as dead, having neither c. nor incorruption; 9: 7 without infinite atonement, c. could not put on incorruption; 9: 51 feast upon that which

cannot be c.; 28: 11–12 churches will become c.; **Jacob** 5: 39 fruit of natural branches become c.; 5: 42, 46–48 fruit of vineyard has become c.; 5: 75 vineyard is no more c.; **Omni** 1: 17 language of Mulekites had become c.; **Mosiah** 16: 10 this c. shall put on incorruption; 29: 40 Mosiah[2] does not seek lucre which c. soul; **Alma** 5: 15 do you view this c. raised in incorruption; 40: 2 this c. does not put on incorruption until after resurrection of Christ; 41: 4 all things shall be restored to proper order, c. to incorruption; **Hel.** 4: 22 laws of Nephites had become c.; 8: 25 (3 Ne. 13: 20) nothing c. treasures of heaven; **3 Ne.** 13: 19–20 (Matt. 6: 19–20) lay not up for yourselves treasures upon earth, where moth and rust c.; 14: 17–18 (Matt. 7: 17–18) c. tree brings forth evil fruit; **Morm.** 6: 21 bodies moldering in c. must soon become incorruptible bodies; **Ether** 9: 6 wicked and secret society c. hearts of Jaredites.

CORRUPTNESS (*see also* Corrupt)

   Hel. 8: 3 Nephi[2] speaks of c. of laws.

COSTLY, COSTLINESS (*see* Apparel; Pride)

COUNCIL

   Alma 52: 19 chief captains hold c. of war; **3 Ne.** 12: 22 (Matt. 5: 22) whosoever shall say unto his brother, Raca, shall be in danger of c.

COUNSEL (*see also* Guide; Instruction; God, Wisdom of)

   1 Ne. 19: 7 men hearken not to voice of God's c.; **2 Ne.** 9: 28 when men are learned, they think they are wise and hearken not unto God's c.; 9: 29 to be learned is good, if they hearken to c. of God; 27: 27 (28: 9) wo unto them that seek deep to hide their c. from the Lord; 28: 30 blessed are those who lend ear unto the Lord's c.; **Jacob** 4: 10 seek not to c. the Lord, but to take c. from his hand; **Alma** 29: 8 (37: 12) the Lord c. in wisdom; 37: 37 c. with the Lord in all thy doings; 39: 10 Corianton is commanded to c. with elder brothers; **Hel.** 12: 5 how slow are men to give ear unto the Lord's c.; 12: 6 notwithstanding God's goodness and mercy, men set at naught his c.

COUNSELOR

   2 Ne. 19: 6 (Isa. 9: 6) Messiah's name shall be called, Wonderful, C.

COUNTENANCE (*see also* Face; Visage)

   2 Ne. 13: 9 (Isa. 3: 9) show of their c. witnesses against them; **Alma** 5: 14, 19 have ye received God's image in your c.; **3 Ne.** 13: 16 (Matt. 6: 16) when ye fast,

be not as the hypocrites, of sad c.; 19: 25 light of Jesus' c. smiles upon disciples.

COUNTRY, COUNTRIES (*see also* Government, Civil; Land; Nation; North)

   Alma 43: 26, 47 (56: 11; 58: 8; 61: 6; Hel. 4: 7; Morm. 5: 4) Nephites fight to defend c.; 48: 11–13 (60: 36) Moroni[1] swears oath to defend freedom of c.; 51: 13, 15, 20 (62: 9–10) dissenters are compelled to defend c.; 53: 13, 18 (56: 5) Ammonites desire to take up arms in defense of c.; 60: 28 according to God's commandments, Moroni[1] takes sword to defend c.

COURAGE (*see also* Faith; Fear; Strength; Valiant)

   Alma 15: 4 Zeezrom's heart begins to take c.; 53: 20 (56: 45) 2,000 stripling warriors are exceedingly valiant for c.; 62: 19 because of Nephites' c., Lamanites dare not come to battle.

COURSE (*see also* Direction; Lead; Path)

   1 Ne. 10: 19 (Alma 7: 20; 37: 12) c. of the Lord is one eternal round; **Mosiah** 7: 4 Nephite expedition knows not c. to travel in wilderness; **Alma** 37: 42 Lehites do not travel direct c., because of transgressions; 37: 44–45 (Hel. 3: 29) word of Christ points straight c. to eternal bliss.

COVENANT (*see also* Abraham; Abrahamic Covenant; Chosen; Gospel; Inherit; Israel; Oath; Promise; Promised Land; Sacrament; TG Covenants; Priesthood, Oath and Covenant; Seed of Abraham; BD Abrahamic Covenant; Covenant)

   1 Ne. 13: 23 book is record of Jews, contains c. of the Lord; 13: 26 abominable church takes away from gospel many c.; 14: 14 power of the Lamb descends upon c. people of the Lord; 15: 18 (3 Ne. 15: 8; 16: 5, 11–12; 20: 12, 25–27, 29; 21: 7; Morm. 5: 20; 8: 23; 9: 37; Ether 4: 15; 13: 11) c. made to Abraham to be fulfilled in latter days; 17: 40 the Lord c. with Abraham, Isaac, Jacob; 17: 40 the Lord remembered c. made to fathers and brought them out of Egypt; 19: 15 when Jews no more turn aside hearts from Holy One, he will remember c. made to fathers; 22: 9 marvelous work among Gentiles shall make known Father's c. unto Abraham; **2 Ne.** 1: 5 the Lord c. with Nephi[1] that land should be inheritance to his seed; 6: 12 if Gentiles fight not against Zion, the Lord will fulfill c. made unto his children; 9: 1 Jacob[2] reads Isaiah[1] that brethren might know the Lord's c. with Israel; 10: 7 Christ has c. with fathers that Jews will be restored to lands of inheritance when they believe in

him; 10: 15 the Lord must destroy secret works of darkness so c. may be fulfilled; 11: 5 Jacob² delights in c. of the Lord made unto fathers; 29: 1 the Lord will do marvelous work, that he may remember c.; 29: 4 Jews are the Lord's ancient c. people; 29: 14 (3 Ne. 20: 25, 27) the Lord c. with Abraham to remember his seed forever; **Mosiah** 5: 5 Benjamin's people are willing to enter c. with God to do his will; 18: 13 baptism a testimony that man has entered c. to serve God; **Alma** 24: 18 Ammonites c. to give own lives rather than shed blood; 37: 27 Helaman¹ to hold back c. of secret combinations; 43: 11 (24: 15–18; 56: 6) Ammonites enter c. not to take up arms; 46: 20 those who will maintain title of liberty should enter c. to maintain their rights; 51: 6 freemen c. to maintain rights of religion by free government; 53: 16–18 sons of Ammonites enter c. to fight for liberty of Nephites; **Hel.** 6: 21–26 (3 Ne. 6: 28–29) robbers enter c. to protect and preserve one another; 6: 26–30 (3 Ne. 6: 28) secret oaths and c. are handed down by Satan; **3 Ne.** 5: 4–5 (6: 3) robbers who enter c. to murder no more are set at liberty; 6: 27–29 (7: 11) judges, lawyers, high priests enter c. to combine against all righteousness, destroy government; 20: 26 ye are children of c.; 21: 4 Gentiles to be established as free people in land so that c. unto Israel may be fulfilled; 22: 10 c. of peace shall not be removed; **Moro.** 7: 31–32 angels do work of c. of the Father; 10: 33 Christ's blood is in c. of the Father unto remission of sins.

COVET, COVETOUSNESS (see also Desire; Envy; Jealous; Lust; TG Covet, Covetousness)

Mosiah 4: 25 your condemnation is just for ye c. that which ye have not received; 13: 24 (Ex. 20: 17; Deut. 5: 21) thou shalt not c. thy neighbor's house, wife.

COW (see also Animal; Cattle)

1 Ne. 18: 25 Lehites find c. in wilderness; **2 Ne.** 21: 7 (30: 13; Isa. 11: 7) c. and bear shall feed; **Ether** 9: 18 Jaredites have c.

CRAFTINESS, CRAFT (see also Art; Cunning; Deceit; Guile; Profession; Skill; Subtlety)

Mosiah 7: 21 (9: 10; 10: 18) Zeniff deceived by c. of King Laman²; **Alma** 4: 19 Alma² seeks to pull down, by word of God, the c. among his people; 12: 3 Zeezrom taken in lying and c.; 35: 3 Amulek's words destroy c. of Zoramites; **Hel.** 2: 4 Gadianton exceedingly expert in his c. of murder and robbery.

CREATION, CREATE (see also Adam; Beginning; Creature; Earth; Framed [verb]; God—Creator; Heaven; Jesus Christ—Creator; Make; Man; Work [noun]; World; TG Creation, Create; Earth, Purpose of; Man, Physical Creation of; Spirit Creation)

1 Ne. 5: 11 books of Moses give account of c. of world; 17: 36 the Lord has c. earth that it should be inhabited; **2 Ne.** 1: 10 those coming from Jerusalem have received great blessings, having knowledge of c.; 2: 12–13 there would have been no purpose in end of its c.; 2: 14 (Alma 18: 28; 22: 10; Morm. 9: 11) God has c. all things; 11: 7 if there be no God, there could have been no c.; 29: 7 the Lord has c. all men; Jacob 2: 21 God has c. all flesh that they should keep his commandments and glorify him forever; 4: 9 earth c. by power of God's word; **Mosiah** 2: 20–24 God hath c. you and granted unto you your lives; 2: 25 ye were c. of dust of earth; 4: 9 believe in God, that he c. all things; 7: 27 God to take upon himself the image after which man was c. in beginning; 28: 17 (Ether 1: 3) Jaredite records give account of people back to c. of Adam; **Alma** 18: 36 Ammon² teaches Lamoni, beginning at c. of world; 22: 12–13 Aaron² begins from c. of Adam, reading scriptures to Lamanite king; **3 Ne.** 9: 15 Christ c. heavens and earth; **Morm.** 9: 12 God c. Adam; **Ether** 3: 15–16 all men were c. in beginning after the Lord's own image; **Moro.** 10: 3 remember how merciful the Lord has been, from c. of Adam to present.

CREATOR (see God—Creator; Jesus Christ—Creator)

CREATURE

Mosiah 28: 3 sons of Mosiah² desire that gospel be declared to every c.; **Alma** 42: 21–22 mercy claims repentance, otherwise justice claims the c.; **Morm.** 9: 22 (Matt. 28: 19) go ye into all the world, and preach the gospel to every c.

CRIME (see also Law; Law, Civil; Offense; Punishment; Sin; Transgression)

Jacob 2: 9 Jacob² is constrained to admonish people according to c.; 2: 22–23 Jacob must speak concerning grosser c. than pride—whoredom; **Mosiah** 26: 11 unbelievers are brought before Alma¹ to be judged according to c.; 29: 15 he who commits iniquity is punished according to c.; **Alma** 10: 13 people seek to slay or imprison Alma² and Amulek according to c. they could make appear against them; 30: 17 Korihor claims that whatsoever a man does is not c.; 39: 7 I would not dwell upon your c. to harrow up your soul if it were not for your good; 39: 8 ye cannot

hide your c. from God; 50: 39 chief judge takes oath to bring the wicked to justice according to c.; **3 Ne.** 6: 26 judges who condemned prophets to be judged of c. according to law.

CRISIS

Alma 34: 34 ye cannot say, when ye are brought to that awful c., I will repent.

CROOKED (*see also* Straight)

Alma 7: 20 God cannot walk in c. paths.

CROP (*see also* Grain)

Alma 34: 24 cry unto God over c. of fields.

CROSS (*see also* Jesus Christ, Death of)

2 Ne. 9: 18 righteous saints who have endured c. of world shall inherit kingdom of God; **Jacob** 1: 8 we would to God that all men would believe in Christ and suffer his c.; **Mosiah** 12: 19 priests question Abinadi that they might c. him; **Alma** 10: 16 lawyers question Amulek that they might make him c. his words; 39: 9 c. yourself in all these things; **Hel.** 9: 19 judges question Alma² that they might c. him; **3 Ne.** 12: 30 better to deny yourselves of these things, wherein ye take up your c.

CRUCIFIXION, CRUCIFY (*see* Cross; Jesus Christ, Death of)

CRY (*see also* Lament; Mourn; Plead; Prayer; Wail; Weep)

1 Ne. 2: 16 (17: 7; 2 Ne. 5: 1; 33: 3) Nephi¹ c. unto the Lord; 10: 7–8 prophet to prepare way before Messiah, c. in wilderness; **2 Ne.** 26: 3 (28: 10; Morm. 8: 27) blood of saints shall c. to God from ground; 33: 13 I speak unto you as voice of one c. from dust; **Enos** 1: 4 Enos² c. unto his Maker in mighty prayer; **Mosiah** 11: 24 except they repent, the Lord will be slow to hear his people's c.; 21: 14 Limhi's people c. mightily to God to deliver them out of afflictions; **Alma** 9: 26 Son quick to hear c. of his people; 31: 27 Zoramites c. unto God, but hearts are swallowed up in pride; 34: 20–25 c. unto God over household, against enemies and devil, over crops and flocks; 34: 27 when ye do not c. unto God, let your hearts be full; 36: 18 Alma² c. within his heart unto Jesus; 37: 36 c. unto God for all thy support; 43: 49–50 Nephites c. unto the Lord for liberty and freedom from bondage; **Morm.** 3: 2 c. unto this people, Repent ye; **Ether** 12: 3 Ether c. from morning to sunset, exhorting people to believe in God; 15: 16 great were Jaredites' c. for loss of the slain; **Moro.** 9: 15 my heart c., Wo unto this people.

CUMENI, CITY OF—*Nephite city to southwest*

Alma 56: 13–14 captured by Lamanites; 57: 7–8, 12 recaptured by Helaman¹; 57: 23 retained; 57: 31 Lamanites march toward; 57: 34 is preserved.

CUMENIHAH—*Nephite commander* [c. A.D. 385]

Morm. 6: 14 fell with his ten thousand.

CUMMOMS—*unidentified animals* (*see also* Animal)

Ether 9: 19 useful to man, abundant in days of Emer.

CUMORAH, LAND AND HILL OF (*see also* Ramah, Hill)

Morm. 6: 2–4 Nephites gather at C.; 6: 4 land of many waters; 6: 5 Nephites at C. by A.D. 385; 6: 6 records hidden; 6: 11 all but 24 Nephites slain at C.; 8: 2 aftermath of battle.

CUNNING (*see also* Craftiness; Deceit; Device; Lying; Subtlety; Wiles)

2 Ne. 9: 28 O that c. plan of the evil one; **Mosiah** 24: 7 Lamanites begin to be c. and wise people; **Alma** 2: 2 by c., Amlici draws away many; 10: 13, 15 lawyers try to catch Alma² and Amulek by c. devices; 28: 13 power of devil comes by c.; 46: 10 (51: 27) Amalickiah a man of c. device; **Hel.** 3: 29 word of God shall divide c. of devil; 16: 21 the hardhearted fear they will work some great mystery by c. of evil one; **3 Ne.** 21: 10 Father will show that his wisdom is greater than c. of devil.

CUP (*see also* Drink)

2 Ne. 8: 17 Jerusalem has drunk c. of the Lord's fury; **Mosiah** 3: 26 (5: 5) the evil will drink out of c. of God's wrath; **Alma** 40: 26 the wicked drink dregs of bitter c.; **3 Ne.** 11: 11 Christ has drunk out of bitter c. which the Father gave him; 18: 8 disciples commanded to take wine of c. and drink it; **Moro.** 5: 1 those administering sacrament should take c. and offer prayer.

CURE (*see also* Heal; Restoration, Restore)

Mosiah 3: 5 the Lord will come down among men and c. all manner of diseases; 28: 2 sons of Mosiah² seek to c. Lamanites of hatred; **3 Ne.** 26: 15 Christ does all manner of c. among Nephites.

CURELOMS—*unidentified animals* (*see also* Animal)

Ether 9: 19 useful to man, abundant in days of Emer.

CURIOUS (*see* Workmanship)

CURSE, CURSING (*see also* Accursed;

Cursed [adj.]; Destruction; Insect; Mark; Punishment; TG Curse)

1 Ne. 2: 23 the Lord will c. brothers of Nephi[1] because of rebellion; 17: 35 the Lord c. land against house of Israel because of iniquity; **2 Ne.** 1: 7 (Jacob 2: 29; Hel. 13: 17–19, 23, 30, 35; Morm. 1: 17–18; Ether 14: 1) land is c. because of people's wickedness; 4: 6 c. to be taken from grandchildren of Lehi[1] and answered upon parents' heads; 5: 21–24 (Jacob 3: 3, 5; Alma 3: 6) the Lord causes sore c. to come upon Lamanites' skin because of iniquity; 29: 5 Gentiles have c. Jews; **Jacob** 2: 33 the Lord will visit with sore c. those who lead away captive the daughters of his people; **Alma** 17: 15 c. had fallen upon Lamanites because of traditions of fathers; 23: 18 (3 Ne. 2: 15) c. of God no more follows Lamanites; 30: 50, 53–56 Korihor brought upon himself the c. of being stricken dumb; 45: 16 this is the c. and blessing of God upon the land; 49: 27 Amalickiah c. God; **3 Ne.** 3: 24 great c. upon land northward; 25: 6 (Mal. 4: 6) Elijah shall turn hearts of fathers and children to each other lest earth be smitten with c.; **Ether** 14: 1 great c. upon land because of Jaredites' iniquity; **Moro.** 8: 8 c. of Adam is taken from little children in Christ; 8: 24 repentance is made unto them who are under c. of broken law.

CURSED [adj.] (see also Accursed; Curse)

2 Ne. 1: 7 (Jacob 2: 29) if iniquity abound, c. be land for people's sake; 4: 34 (28: 31) c. is he who puts trust in arm of flesh; 5: 23 c. shall be seed of him who mixes with Lamanites' seed; **Alma** 32: 19 how much more c. is he who knows God's will and does it not; 37: 31 c. be land forever unto workers of darkness; **Hel.** 13: 19–21 c. are people because they set hearts upon riches.

CURTAIN (see also Veil)

3 Ne. 22: 2 (Isa. 54: 2) let them stretch forth the c. of thy habitations.

CUSTOM (see also Tradition)

Alma 8: 7 c. of Nephites to call lands, cities, villages after him who first possessed them; 17: 20 Lamanite c. to bind all Nephites who fall into their hands; 47: 17 c. among Lamanites, if chief leader killed, to appoint second leader as chief; **3 Ne.** 3: 19 c. among Nephites to appoint as chief captains men who have spirit of revelation.

CUT (see also Blot; Cast; Excommunication; God, Presence of; Hew; Prune)

1 Ne. 2: 21 (2 Ne. 5: 20) if brothers of Nephi[1] rebel, they shall be c. off from

the Lord's presence; 16: 2 truth c. the guilty to center; 22: 19 all who fight against Zion shall be c. off; **2 Ne.** 1: 20 (4: 4; Alma 9: 13–14; 36: 30; 37: 13; 38: 1; 50: 20; Hel. 12: 21) if people do not keep commandments, they shall be c. off from the Lord's presence; 2: 5 by law men are c. off; 27: 31 all who watch for iniquity shall be c. off; **Alma** 42: 6 Adam and Eve c. off from tree of life; 42: 7 Adam and Eve c. off temporally and spiritually from presence of the Lord; **3 Ne.** 21: 13–17 (Micah 5: 8–13) all Israel's enemies shall be c. off; 21: 20 whosoever will not repent and come unto Son will the Lord c. off; **Ether** 2: 15 if ye will sin until fully ripe ye shall be c. off from the Lord's presence; **Moro.** 8: 14 man who thinks little children need baptism to be c. off.

DAMNATION, DAMNED (see also Condemn, Condemnation; Death, Spiritual; Hell; Punishment; Torment; BD Damnation)

2 Ne. 9: 24 (3 Ne. 11: 34; Morm. 9: 23; Ether 4: 18) if men will not repent, believe in Christ's name, be baptized, and endure to end, they must be d.; **Mosiah** 2: 33 (3: 25) if man obeys evil spirit and dies in sins, he drinketh d. to his soul; 3: 18 men bring d. to their souls except they humble themselves; 16: 11 to be delivered up to devil is d.; **Alma** 3: 28 if men have been evil, they shall reap d. of their souls; 36: 16 Alma[2] was wracked with pains of d. soul; **Hel.** 12: 26 they who have done evil shall have everlasting death; **3 Ne.** 18: 29 whoso eateth and drinketh Christ's flesh and blood unworthily eateth and drinketh d. to his soul; 26: 5 if men be evil, they are brought forth to resurrection of d.; **Morm.** 2: 13 Nephites' sorrowing is sorrowing of the d.; 8: 33 why have ye transfigured the holy word of God, that ye might bring d. upon your souls.

DANCE, DANCING (see also BD Dancing)

1 Ne. 18: 9 followers of Lehi[1] begin to make merry, d., sing; **Mosiah** 20: 1 daughters of Lamanites gather themselves together to sing, d.; **Ether** 8: 10 daughter of Jared[2] will d. before Akish.

DANGER (see also Threaten)

3 Ne. 12: 21 (Matt. 5: 21) he who kills shall be in d. of judgment; 12: 22 (Matt. 5: 22) he who says, Thou fool, shall be in d. of hell fire; **Morm.** 8: 17 he who condemns should be aware lest he be in d. of hell fire; **Moro.** 8: 20–21 he who says little children need baptism is in d. of hell.

DARK, DARKEN (see Darkness, Physical; Darkness, Spiritual; Light)

DARKNESS, PHYSICAL (see also Black; Darkness, Spiritual; Light; Night; Skin)

1 Ne. 8: 4, 7–8 in dream, Lehi¹ travels in d.; 12: 4–5 (19: 11) mist of d. to cover land at Christ's death; 12: 23 (Alma 3: 6; Morm. 5: 15) Lamanites become d. and loathsome people; 19: 10 (Hel. 14: 20, 27; 3 Ne. 8: 3, 19–23; 10: 9) three days of d. to be sign of Christ's death; **Jacob** 3: 9 commandment not to revile against Lamanites because of d. of skins; **Hel.** 5: 28–43 cloud of d. overshadows prison of Nephi² and Lehi⁴; 14: 3–4 (3 Ne. 1: 15, 19) no d. in night before Christ's birth; **3 Ne.** 10: 12–13 more righteous part of people are not overpowered by vapor of d.; **Ether** 6: 3 the Lord causes stones to shine in d.

DARKNESS, SPIRITUAL (see also Apostasy; Blindness; Ignorance; Light; Mist; Night; Obscurity; Sin; Spirit World; Wicked, Wickedness; Withdraw; TG Darkness, Spiritual; Walking in Darkness; BD Darkness)

1 Ne. 8: 23–24 (12: 17) mist of d. in dream of Lehi¹ is temptations of devil; 21: 9 go forth to them that sit in d.; 22: 12 Israel shall be brought out of obscurity and d.; 2 Ne. 3: 5 Messiah to be made manifest unto branch of Israel to bring them out of hidden d. unto light; 10: 15 the Lord will destroy secret works of d.; 15: 20 (Isa. 5: 20) wo unto them that put d. for light and light for d.; 26: 10 because the Lord's people choose d. rather than light, they must go down to hell; 26: 23 God winks not in d.; 27: 27 (28: 9) wo unto people whose works are in d.; 27: 29 deaf shall hear words of book, and blind shall see out of obscurity and d.; 30: 6 scales of d. shall fall from Lamanites' eyes; 30: 17 no work of d. save it shall be made manifest; 32: 4 those who ask not must perish in d.; **Alma** 5: 7 fathers were in midst of d.; 19: 6 d. veil of unbelief is cast from Lamoni's mind; 26: 3 Lamanites in d. abyss before brought to light of God; 34: 33 if we do not improve our time in this life, then cometh night of d.; 37: 23–24 the Lord will prepare stone which shall shine forth in d. unto light; 37: 23, 25–26 the Lord will bring forth secret works out of d. unto light; 37: 27 Helaman² to hold back secret covenants lest people fall into d.; 37: 28, 30 curse upon land, judgments of God, destruction upon workers of d.; 40: 13–14 spirits of the wicked to be cast into outer d.; 41: 7 the repentant are delivered from endless night of d.; **Hel.** 6: 28–30 devil is the being who spreads works of d.; 13: 29 how long will ye choose d. rather than

light; 3 Ne. 13: 23 (Matt. 6: 23) if eye be evil, whole body shall be full of d.; **Morm.** 8: 16 record shall be brought out of d. unto light, shall shine forth in d.

DART (see also Spear; Weapon)

1 Ne. 15: 24 fiery d. of adversary cannot overpower those who hold fast to word of God; **Jarom** 1: 8 Nephites make weapons of war, arrow, d.

DAUGHTER (see also Child; Family; Woman)

1 Ne. 7: 6 two d. of Ishmael¹ rebel with Laman¹ and Lemuel; 16: 7 Nephi¹ and brothers take d. of Ishmael¹ to wife; 21: 22 (22: 6; Isa. 49: 22) Israel's d. shall be carried on Gentiles' shoulders; 2 Ne. 4: 3–9 Lehi¹ calls sons and d. of Laman¹ together; 13: 16 (Isa. 3: 16) d. of Zion are haughty; 14: 4 (Isa. 4: 4) the Lord shall wash away filth of d. of Zion; **Jacob** 2: 31–33 the Lord has heard mourning of d. of his people in Jerusalem; **Mosiah** 5: 7 (Ether 3: 14) because of covenant, ye shall be called sons and d. of Christ; 20: 4–5 priests of Noah³ carry off d. of Lamanites; 3 Ne. 2: 16 d. of converted Lamanites become exceedingly fair; **Ether** 8: 8–17 d. of Jared² conspires to save his kingdom; **Moro.** 9: 9–10 Nephites murder many d. of Lamanites; 10: 31 put on thy beautiful garments, O d. of Zion.

DAVID—king of Israel (see also BD David)

2 Ne. 19: 7 (Isa. 9: 7) no end to throne of D.; **Jacob** 1: 15 (2: 23–24) D's practice of having many wives and concubines was abominable before the Lord.

DAY (see also Day of the Lord; Daylight; Judgment; Light; Sabbath; Time; BD Day of Atonement)

2 Ne. 2: 21 d. of children of men were prolonged, that they might repent while in flesh; 2: 26 men are free to not be acted upon save by punishment at last d.; 3: 5 Joseph¹ truly saw our d.; 33: 9 men must continue in path until end of d. of probation; **W of M** 1: 11 people shall be judged out of records at last d.; **Alma** 33: 22 all shall stand before God to be judged at last d.; 34: 31 now is d. of your salvation; 34: 32 d. of this life is d. for men to perform labors; 34: 33 do not procrastinate d. of repentance until end; 40: 8 all is as one d. with God; 41: 5 those who desire to do evil all d. shall have reward of evil when night comes; 45: 13–14 d. to come when those now numbered among Nephites shall be numbered among Lamanites; **Hel.** 4: 7 from west sea to east is a d's journey; 12: 14 if God say unto earth to lengthen the d. for many hours, it is done; 12: 25 in last d. some

shall be cast out; 14: 4 (3 Ne. 1: 8, 19) sign of Christ's birth to be one d. and a night and d. as one d.; **3 Ne.** 1: 9 d. set apart that believers should be put to death except sign be given; 8: 24 O that we had repented before this great and dreadful d.; 13: 34 (Matt. 6: 34) sufficient is d. unto evil thereof; 16: 7 in latter d. shall truth come unto Gentiles; 25: 1 (Mal. 4: 1) d. cometh that shall burn as oven; **Ether** 13: 13 Ether hid himself in cavity of rock by d.

DAY OF THE LORD (*see also* Day; Jesus Christ, Second Coming of; Judgment; Last Days; Millennium; TG Day of the Lord)

2 Ne. 12: 12–13 (Isa. 2: 12–13) d. of the Lord shall come upon the proud and lofty; 23: 6, 9 (Isa. 13: 6) d. of the Lord is at hand; **3 Ne.** 24: 2 (Mal. 3: 2) who may abide d. of the Lord's coming; 25: 1 (Mal. 4: 1) d. cometh that shall burn as oven; 25: 5 (Mal. 4: 5) Elijah to be sent before coming of great and dreadful d. of the Lord.

DAYLIGHT (*see also* Light)

Moro. 7: 15 way to judge is as plain as d. is from dark night.

DEAD, DEADNESS (*see also* Death, Physical; Death, Spiritual; Jesus Christ, Resurrection of; Raise; Resurrection)

2 Ne. 18: 19 should not a people seek unto their God for the living to hear from the d.; 25: 25 the law hath become d. unto us; 25: 27 by knowing d. of the law, men may look forward to that life which is in Christ; 27: 13 (Morm. 8: 26; 9: 30; Moro. 10: 27) words of the faithful shall speak as if it were from the d.; **Mosiah** 18: 13 baptism a covenant to serve God until d. as to mortal body; **Alma** 5: 41–42 he that becomes a child of the devil is d. unto all good works; 18: 43—19: 8, 18 Lamoni lies as though d. for two days and nights; 30: 18 Korihor claims that when a man is d., that is the end; **Hel.** 14: 16 all mankind, being cut off from presence of the Lord by fall of Adam, are considered as d.; **Moro.** 8: 23 it is mockery before God, putting trust in d. works; 10: 34 Jehovah, the Eternal Judge of both quick and d.

DEAF, DEAFNESS (*see also* Heal; Hear)

2 Ne. 9: 31 wo unto the d. that will not hear; 27: 29 the d. shall hear words of book; **Jarom** 1: 3 much should be done among Nephites because of d. of ears; **Mosiah** 3: 5 (3 Ne. 17: 7–9; 26: 15) Christ will cause the d. to hear; **4 Ne.** 1: 5 Christ's disciples cause the d. to hear.

DEARTH (*see* Famine)

DEATH, PHYSICAL (*see also* Body; Capital Punishment; Dead; Death, Spiritual; Die; Fall of Man; Grave; Immortality; Jesus Christ, Death of; Jesus Christ, Resurrection of; Kill; Life; Martyrdom; Paradise; Raise; Resurrection; Slay; Sleep; Spirit World; TG Death; Death, Power over)

1 Ne. 15: 31 doth this thing mean the final state of the soul after d. of temporal body; **2 Ne.** 9: 6 as d. has passed upon all men, there must be a power of resurrection; 9: 10, 19 God prepares way for escape from monster, d. and hell, d. of body and of spirit; 9: 11–12 temporal and spiritual d. shall deliver up their dead; 10: 25 may God raise you from d. by power of resurrection; **Mosiah** 15: 8 (16: 7) Christ breaks bands of d.; 16: 8–9 (Alma 22: 14; 27: 28; Morm. 7: 5) sting of d. is swallowed up in Christ, and there can be no more d.; 27: 28 Alma² repents nigh unto d.; **Alma** 1: 18 he who murders is punished unto d.; 7: 12 (11: 42) Christ to take upon him d. that he may loose the bands of temporal d.; 11: 45 mortal body is raised from first d. unto life; 12: 23–24 because Adam partook of forbidden fruit, temporal d. comes upon mankind; 15: 17 people pray continually that they might be delivered from Satan and d.; 27: 28 people of Ammon² never look upon d. with any degree of terror; 40: 11–14 state of soul between d. and resurrection; 42: 9 (Hel. 14: 16) fall brought upon mankind both a spiritual d. and a temporal d.; 55: 3 Moroni¹ will seek d. among Lamanites until they sue for peace; **Hel.** 12: 3 except the Lord visits his people with d., they will not remember him; **3 Ne.** 27: 7–8, 25, 37–38 (Ether 12: 17) three Nephite disciples shall never taste of d.

DEATH, SPIRITUAL (*see also* Damnation; Dead; Death, Physical; Die; Fall of Man; God, Presence of; Hell; Redemption; Repentance; Sin; Sleep; Sons of Perdition; Spirit World; TG Death, First; Death, Spiritual, Second)

2 Ne. 2: 27 (10: 23; Alma 29: 5; Hel. 14: 31) men are free to choose eternal life or d.; 9: 10 God prepares way for escape from monster, d. and hell, d. of body and of spirit; 9: 11–12 temporal and spiritual d. shall deliver their dead; 9: 39 (Rom. 8: 6) to be carnally-minded is d.; **Jacob** 3: 11 shake yourselves that ye awake from slumber of d.; 3: 11 lake of fire and brimstone is second d.; **Mosiah** 15: 8–9 (Alma 7: 12) Christ breaks bands of d.; **Alma** 5: 7 fathers encircled by bands of d., chains of hell; 12: 16 whosoever dies in sin shall suffer second d., which is spiritual d.; 12: 32 penalty for doing evil

is second *d.*, which is everlasting *d.*; 13: 30 may the Lord grant unto you repentance, that you may not suffer second *d.*; 15: 17 people pray continually that they might be delivered from Satan and *d.*; 29: 5 unto him who knows good and evil is given according to his desires, life or *d.*; 36: 18 Alma² was encircled by everlasting bands of *d.*; 40: 26 awful *d.* comes upon the wicked, for they die as to things of righteousness; 42: 9 (Hel. 14: 16) fall brought upon mankind a spiritual *d.* as well as temporal *d.*; Hel. 14: 16 (Morm. 9: 13) Christ's *d.* redeems all mankind from first *d.*, that spiritual *d.*; 14: 18 those who do not repent suffer again a spiritual *d.*, a second *d.*

DEBT (*see also* Indebted; Trespass; TG Debt)

3 **Ne.** 13: 11 (Matt. 6: 12) forgive us our *d.* as we forgive our debtors.

DECEIT, DECEIVE (*see also* Beguile; Cheat; Craftiness; Cunning; Deception; Device; False, Falsehood; Flatter; Fraud; Guile; Hypocrisy; Lying; Pretend; Sincerity; Wicked; Wiles)

1 **Ne.** 16: 38 Laman¹ claims Nephi¹ tries to *d.* their eyes; 2 **Ne.** 9: 41 the Lord cannot be *d.*; 25: 18 no other Messiah to come, save false Messiah which should *d.* people; **Jacob** 7: 18 Sherem confesses he was *d.* by power of devil; **Mosiah** 7: 21 (10: 18) Zeniff is *d.* by cunning of king Laman²; 11: 7 people of Noah³ are *d.* by flattering words of king and priests; 14: 9 (Isa. 53: 9) no *d.* in Messiah's mouth; 26: 6 unbelievers *d.* many with flattering words; **Alma** 12: 1 Amulek catches Zeezrom in *d.*; 16: 18 priests preach against all *d.*; 20: 13 Lamanites believe Nephites seek to *d.* them; 30: 47 Korihor shall not *d.* people any more; 30: 53 Korihor confesses that devil has *d.* him; 48: 7 Amalickiah obtains power by fraud and *d.*; 3 **Ne.** 2: 1–2 Nephites imagine that signs are wrought by power of devil to *d.*; 16: 10 Gentiles shall be filled with all manner of lyings and *d.*; 21: 19 all *d.* shall be done away; 30: 2 repent of your lyings and *d.*; **Morm.** 8: 31 it shall come in a day when there is lying and *d.*

DECEPTION (*see also* Deceit)

2 **Ne.** 31: 13 if ye follow the Son, acting no *d.* before God, ye shall receive Holy Ghost.

DECLARE (*see also* Preach; Proclamation; Prophecy; Publish; Tell)

Mosiah 15: 10 (Isa. 53: 8) who shall *d.* Son's generation; 3 **Ne.** 11: 40 whoso shall *d.* more or less than this as the Lord's doctrine comes of evil.

DECOY (*see also* Stratagem)

Alma 52: 21 Moroni¹ resolves upon plan to *d.* Lamanites out of strongholds; 58: 1 Nephites could not *d.* Lamanites from strongholds because they remembered former plan.

DECREE (*see also* Command; Commandments of God; Consume, Consumption; Law; Ordain; Proclaim; Statute)

2 **Ne.** 20: 1 (Isa. 10: 1) wo unto them that *d.* unrighteous *d.*; **Alma** 23: 2 Lamanite king sends *d.* not to lay hands on sons of Mosiah²; 29: 4 I ought not to harrow up in my desires the firm *d.* of a just God; 41: 8 *d.* of God are unalterable; **Ether** 2: 9 *d.* of God that this is a promised land; 2: 10 everlasting *d.* of God that those who possess land must serve him; 2: 11 this message comes unto Gentiles, that they may know *d.* of God.

DEED (*see also* Act; Do; Doing; Judgment; Work [noun])

Mosiah 4: 30 if ye do not watch words and *d.*, ye must perish; **Alma** 5: 15 (36: 15) men will be judged according to *d.* done in mortal body; 42: 27 in last day it shall be restored unto him according to his *d.*; **Hel.** 10: 5 the Lord will make Nephi² mighty in word and *d.*; 13: 26 Nephites would call a prophet false because he testified their *d.* were evil; 15: 4 the Lord has hated Lamanites because their *d.* have been evil.

DEFENCE, DEFENSE, DEFEND (*see also* Fight; Maintain; Preserve; Safe; Security)

2 **Ne.** 14: 5 (Isa. 4: 5) glory of Zion shall be a *d.*; **Alma** 35: 14 converted Zoramites take up arms to *d.* families and lands; 43: 47 ye shall *d.* your families even unto bloodshed; 48: 13 Moroni¹ swears oath to *d.* people, country, religion; 48: 14 Nephites taught to *d.* themselves against enemies; 48: 16 God reveals to Nephites where they should go to *d.* themselves; 51: 13 king-men would not take up arms to *d.* country; 54: 13 Nephites have only sought to *d.* themselves; 60: 28 Moroni¹ takes up sword to *d.* country according to God's commandments; 61: 6 (62: 5) Nephites take up arms in *d.* of country; 3 **Ne.** 3: 2 ye do stand well, as if ye were supported by hand of a god in *d.* of your liberty; **Ether** 14: 2 every man keeps sword in right hand in *d.* of property and family.

DEFIANCE (*see also* Rebel)

Alma 5: 18 can ye imagine yourselves brought before God with remembrance that ye have set at *d.* his commandments; 3 **Ne.** 6: 30 judges set at *d.* the law and rights of their country.

DEFILE (*see also* Corrupt; Filthiness; Pollute; Unclean)

Morm. 8: 28 churches shall become *d.*

DELAY (*see also* Procrastinate)

3 Ne. 29: 2 ye need not say the Lord *d.* his coming.

DELICATE (*see* Tender)

DELIGHT (*see also* Delightsome; Happiness; Joy; Pleased; Pleasure)

2 Ne. 4: 15–16 (11: 2, 4–6; 25: 5) Nephi[1] *d.* in scriptures, in things of the Lord; 9: 37 devil *d.* in those who worship idols; 9: 49 my heart *d.* in righteousness; 9: 51 let your soul *d.* in fatness; 25: 4 (31: 3) Nephi[1] *d.* in plainness; 25: 13 Nephi[1] *d.* to prophesy concerning Christ; **Jacob** 2: 28 God *d.* in chastity; **Alma** 48: 11 Moroni[1] does not *d.* in bloodshed; **Moro.** 9: 19 Nephites *d.* in everything save that which is good.

DELIGHTSOME (*see also* Beauty; Fair)

2 Ne. 5: 21 (Morm. 5: 17) Lamanites were fair and *d.* people; 30: 6–7 (W of M 1: 8) Lamanites and Jews who believe in Christ shall become *d.* people; **3 Ne.** 24: 12 ye shall be a *d.* land; **4 Ne.** 1: 10 Nephites become fair and *d.* people; **Moro.** 9: 12 few years have passed since Nephites were civil and *d.* people.

DELIVER, DELIVERANCE (*see also* Escape; Freedom; Give; Help; Loose; Ransom; Reclaim; Redemption; Salvation; Save; Snatch)

1 Ne. 1: 20 the Lord makes those he has chosen mighty unto power of *d.*; 3: 29 the Lord will *d.* Laban into brothers' hands; 4: 3 the Lord is able to *d.* us; 17: 14 the Lord *d.* Lehites from destruction in Jerusalem; **2 Ne.** 9: 11–12 temporal and spiritual deaths must *d.* up their dead; 9: 19 God *d.* his saints from awful monster of death; 11: 5 mercy of God in eternal plan of *d.* from death; 27: 9–22 book shall be *d.* unto a man; **Mosiah** 9: 17 Zeniff's people are awakened to remembrance of *d.* of their fathers; **Alma** 4: 14 resurrection of the dead according to *d.* of Christ from bands of death; 7: 13 Son blots out transgressions according to power of his *d.*; 9: 28 righteous shall reap salvation according to *d.* of Christ; 14: 26 give us strength according to our faith in Christ, even unto *d.*; 15: 2 those cast out of Ammonihah relate power of *d.*; 46: 7 Nephites' great rejoicing because of *d.* by hand of the Lord; 58: 11 the Lord causes that Nephites hope for *d.* in him; 58: 37 we trust God will *d.* us; **3 Ne.** 13: 12 (Matt. 6: 13) *d.* us from evil.

DEMANDS (*see* Justice)

DEMON (*see also* Angels of the Devil; Devils; Spirit, Evil)

Hel. 13: 37 we are surrounded by *d.*

DENY (*see also* Refuse; Reject; Resist)

2 Ne. 26: 33 the Lord *d.* none who come unto him; 28: 4 churches shall *d.* Holy Ghost; 31: 14 if men receive Holy Ghost and then *d.* Christ, better that they had not known him; **Jacob** 6: 8 will ye *d.* good word of Christ; 7: 9 *d.* thou the Christ who shall come; 7: 19 Sherem fears he has committed unpardonable sin by *d.* Christ; **Omni** 1: 17 Mulekites *d.* the being of their Creator; **Mosiah** 4: 24 they who *d.* beggar should say, If I had, I would give; 17: 20 Abinadi put to death because he would not *d.* God's commandments; **Alma** 30: 39 Alma[2] asks Korihor whether he will again *d.* God and Christ; 39: 6 to *d.* Holy Ghost when it once has had place in you is unpardonable sin; 46: 35 few *d.* covenant of freedom; **Hel.** 8: 24 ye cannot *d.* these things except ye shall lie; **3 Ne.** 12: 30 *d.* yourselves of these things; 29: 6 wo unto him that shall *d.* revelations of the Lord; **4 Ne.** 1: 27 churches profess to know Christ, but *d.* more parts of gospel; 1: 29 false church *d.* Christ; **Morm.** 9: 7–8 he who *d.* revelations and spiritual gifts knows not gospel of Christ; **Moro.** 1: 2 Lamanites put to death every Nephite who will not *d.* Christ; 10: 7 *d.* not the power of God; 10: 32 *d.* yourselves of all ungodliness.

DEPART (*see also* Die; Flight; Go; Journey; Leave)

1 Ne. 2: 2–4 (3: 18) Lehi[1] and family *d.* into wilderness; **2 Ne.** 5: 5–7 Nephi[1] and followers *d.* into wilderness; **Omni** 1: 12–14 Mosiah[1] and his people *d.* into wilderness; **3 Ne.** 20: 41 cry to go forth, *D.* ye, *d.* ye.

DEPEND, DEPENDENT (*see also* Rely; Trust)

Mosiah 4: 19, 21 do we not all *d.* upon God for substance and life; 10: 11 Lamanites *d.* upon own strength; 18: 26 priests not to *d.* upon people for support; **Hel.** 16: 15 people *d.* upon own strength.

DEPRAVITY (*see also* Wicked)

Moro. 9: 18 O the *d.* of my people.

DEPRESSED (*see also* Despair)

Alma 26: 27 when our hearts were *d.*, the Lord comforted us; 56: 16 Nephite soldiers are *d.* in body as well as in spirit.

DEPRIVE (*see also* Take)

Alma 2: 4 Amlici would *d.* people of their rights and privileges of church; 6: 5 none are *d.* of privilege of assembling to

hear word of God; **Moro.** 9: 9 Nephites d. Lamanite daughters of chastity and virtue.

DEPTH

1 Ne. 12: 16 d. of fountain of filthy water are d. of hell; 16: 25 Lehi[1] brought down into d. of sorrow for murmuring; **2 Ne.** 9: 42 (Mosiah 4: 11; Alma 62: 41; Hel. 6: 5; 3 Ne. 12: 2) men must humble themselves in d. of humility; 17:11 (Isa. 7: 11) ask a sign of the Lord, either in d. or in heights; 26: 5 d. of earth shall swallow up those who kill prophets and saints; **Jacob** 4: 8 how unsearchable are d. of mysteries of the Lord.

DESCEND (see also Descendant; Fall; Jesus Christ, Condescension of; Jesus Christ, Second Coming of)

1 Ne. 1: 19 (11: 7; 12: 6; 3 Ne. 11: 8) Lehi[1] and Nephi[1] see Christ d. out of heaven; 11: 30 (3 Ne. 17: 24) Nephi[1] sees angels d. out of heaven to minister to men.

DESCENDANT (see also Genealogy; Loins; Seed)

1 Ne. 5: 14 (6: 1–2; 2 Ne. 3: 4; Alma 10: 3) Lehi[1] a d. of Joseph[1]; 5: 16 Laban a d. of Joseph[1]; **2 Ne.** 30: 4 Nephites' seed shall know they are d. of Jews; **Mosiah** 7: 3, 13 Ammon[1] a d. of Zarahemla; 25: 2 among Nephites, fewer d. of Nephi[1] than people of Zarahemla; 25: 2 Zarahemla a d. of Mulek; 25: 13 kingdom conferred on none but d. of Nephi[1]; **Alma** 10: 3 Lehi[1] a d. of Manasseh; 17: 21 Lamoni a d. of Ishmael[1]; 24: 29 (56: 3) Lamanites who join Nephites are actual d. of Laman[1] and Lemuel, not of dissenters; 43: 13 Lamanite armies include d. of priests of Noah[3]; **Hel.** 11: 24 group of Nephite dissenters and real d. of Laman[1] commence war with Nephites; **3 Ne.** 10: 4 how oft has the Lord wanted to gather d. of Jacob[1] as hen gathereth chickens; **Morm.** 1: 5 (8: 13) Mormon[2] a d. of Nephi[1]; **Ether** 1: 6 Ether a d. of Coriantor; 10: 8 d. of Riplakish driven out of land; 11: 17–18 d. of brother of Jared[2] overthrows Moron and obtains kingdom.

DESERET

Ether 2: 3 Jaredites carry with them d., by interpretation, a honey bee.

DESIRABLE (see also Desire)

1 Ne. 8: 15 (15: 36) fruit of the tree of life is d. above all other fruit; 11: 22 love of God is most d. above all other things; **Alma** 32: 38–39 tree withers, but not because fruit would not be d.

DESIRE (see also Covet; Desirable; Intent;

List; Lust; Pleasure; Purpose; Search; Seek; Will; Willing; Wish)

Enos 1: 9 Enos feels d. for welfare of Nephites; **Mosiah** 18: 10–11 d. of Benjamin's people is to be baptized; **Alma** 29: 4 God grants unto men according to their d.; 32: 27 if ye can no more than d. to believe, let this d. work in you; 41: 5 man will be raised to happiness, goodness, or evil according to d.; **3 Ne.** 18: 18 Satan d. to have you.

DESOLATION, DESOLATE (see also Desolation, City of; Desolation, Land of; Destruction; Empty; Ruin; Waste; Wilderness)

Hel. 3: 5 Nephites spread into parts of land that have not been rendered d.; 14: 24 (3 Ne. 4: 1) many cities to become d.; **3 Ne.** 10: 7 places of Israel's dwellings shall become d. until fulfilling of covenant; 22: 3 (Isa. 54: 3) Israel's seed shall make d. cities to be inhabited.

DESOLATION, CITY OF—Nephite city to the north

Morm. 3: 7 Lamanites come to D. to battle; 4: 2 possessed by Lamanites; 4: 3 near city of Teancum; 4: 8 regained by Nephites; 4: 13 possessed again by Lamanites; 4: 19 great battle of D.

DESOLATION, LAND OF—north of the land Bountiful

Alma 22: 30–31 land far northward that had been peopled and destroyed; 22: 30 place of first landing of people of Zarahemla; 22: 32 day and a half journey from east to west sea; 46: 17 Moroni[1] names land south of D. a land of liberty; 50: 33–34 Nephites overtake Morianton in D.; 63: 5 Hagoth's ships built near D.; **3 Ne.** 3: 23 land appointed for gathering extends to line between Bountiful and D.; **Morm.** 3: 5 Mormon[2] causes people to gather in D.; 4: 1–2, 19 Lamanites possess D.; **Ether** 7: 6 near land of Moron.

DESOLATION OF NEHORS (see Ammonihah, City of)

DESPAIR (see also Depressed; Mourn; Sorrow; Suffering; Torment; Tribulation; TG Despair)

Alma 26: 19 why did God not doom us to eternal d.; **Moro.** 10: 22 if ye have no hope, ye must needs be in d.

DESPISE (see also Abhor; Despisers; Despitefully; Hate; Malice)

1 Ne. 19: 14 because Jews have d. Holy One, they shall wander; **2 Ne.** 9: 30 the rich d. the poor; 9: 42 the rich and proud are they whom God d.; 15: 24 the

Lord's anger is kindled against his people because they d. word of Holy One; **Jacob 4:** 8 d. not the revelations of God; **Mosiah 14:** 3 (Isa. 53: 3) Messiah is d. and rejected of men; **Alma 46:** 18 surely God shall not suffer that we, who are d. because we take upon us Christ's name, shall be destroyed; **3 Ne. 13:** 24 (Matt. 6: 24) man with two masters will hold to one and d. the other; **4 Ne. 1:** 29 false church d. true church because of miracles; **Morm.** 9: 26–27 who will d. works of the Lord.

DESPISERS (see also Despise)

Morm. 9: 26 d. of the Lord's works shall wonder and perish.

DESPITEFULLY (see also Despise)

3 Ne. 12: 44 (Matt. 5: 44) pray for them who d. use you.

DESTROY (see Destruction)

DESTRUCTION (see also Burn; Calamity; Captive, Captivity; Chasten; Earthquake; Famine; Fire; Flood; Hail; Iniquity; Judgment; Last Days; Lightning; Overthrow; Pestilence; Ruin; Scatter; Scourge; Slaughter; Slay; Smite; Sweep; Tempest; Thrash; Throw; Tribulation; Vengeance; War; Waste; Wrath)

1 Ne. 1: 4 (7: 13; 17: 43; 2 Ne. 1: 4; Hel. 8: 20–21) Jerusalem must be d.; **13:** 8–9 abominable church d. saints of God; **14:** 7 the hardhearted to be brought down to d., both temporally and spiritually; **17:** 32, 35 the Lord curses land against children of land unto their d.; **17:** 37–38 the Lord d. nations of the wicked; **22:** 14 all who fight against Zion shall be d.; **22:** 16 God shall not suffer that the wicked d. the righteous; **2 Ne. 1:** 22 Lehi[1] exhorts sons to unity, that they not incur God's displeasure unto d.; **3:** 3 seed of Joseph[2] shall not utterly be d.; **4:** 9 seed of Lemuel shall not utterly be d.; **6:** 15 they that believe not in Messiah shall be d.; **10:** 6 (25: 9) because of iniquities, d. shall come upon Jews; **21:** 9 (30: 15; Isa. 11: 9) they shall not hurt or d. in all my holy mountain; **25:** 9 d. of Jews from generation to generation always foretold by prophets; **25:** 14 after Messiah rises from dead, Jerusalem shall be d. again; **26:** 5–6 they who kill prophets shall be visited with all manner of d.; **26:** 8 the righteous who d. not the prophets shall not perish; **30:** 10 the Lord will d. the wicked, even by fire; **Enos 1:** 23 (Ether 11: 1) prophets prophesy of d. among people; **Mosiah 27:** 10 (Alma 36: 6) Alma[2] and sons of Mosiah[2] seek to d. church; **29:** 27 (Alma 10: 18–19) when voice of people chooses iniquity, God will visit them with d.; **Alma 1:** 12 priestcraft would prove

entire d. of Nephites; **2:** 4 Amlici's intent is to d. church; **10:** 22 (Hel. 13: 13) if not for prayers of righteous, people would be visited now with d.; **10:** 27 foundation of d. of people is laid by unrighteous lawyers and judges; **12:** 17, 36 those who die in sins will be chained down to everlasting d.; **35:** 3 the word d. craft of Zoramites; **36:** 9 if thou wilt of thyself be d., seek no more to d. church; **36:** 14 Alma[2] had murdered many, or led them away unto d.; **42:** 8 to reclaim man from temporal death would d. plan of happiness; **42:** 13 work of justice could not be d.; **46:** 10 Amalickiah seeks to d. church; **Hel. 5:** 2 (6: 40; 11: 37) Nephites are ripening for d. because laws are corrupt; **6:** 28 devil dragged Jaredites down to d.; **13:** 14 when people cast out the righteous, they are ripe for d.; **13:** 32, 38 your d. is made sure; **3 Ne. 9:** 12 many great d. has the Lord caused to come upon Nephites because of iniquity; **10:** 14 see if all these d. are not unto fulfilling of prophecies; **12:** 17 (Matt. 5: 17) Christ came not to d. law or prophets, but to fulfill; **24:** 11 (Mal. 3: 11) the Lord will rebuke the devourer and he shall not d. fruits; **Morm.** 6: 22 O that you had repented before this great d. came upon you; **8:** 3 Moroni[2] remains alone to write tale of his people's d.; **Ether 1:** 5 Moroni[2] gives account of Jaredites from tower to d.; **7:** 23 Jaredites to be d. if they do not repent; **8:** 21 secret combinations have caused d. of Jaredites and Nephites; **8:** 23 suffer not that murderous combinations bring work of d. upon you; **9:** 20 those who possess land to be d. when ripened in iniquity; **13:** 14 Ether views d. which came upon Jaredites; **15:** 19 Jaredites given up to hardness of hearts, that they might be d.

DETERMINE, DETERMINATION

2 Ne. 1: 21 be d. in one mind, united in all things; **Moro.** 6: 3 none baptized save they have d. to serve Christ to end.

DEVICE (see also Cunning; Deceit)

Alma 11: 21 Zeezrom is expert in d. of devil; **30:** 42 devil uses d. that he may destroy children of God.

DEVIL (see also Adversary; Angels of the Devil; Church of the Devil; Contention; Devilish; Devils; Evil; Hell; Lucifer; Lying; Perdition; Rebel; Satan; Serpent; Spirit, Evil; Tempt; Wicked; TG Devil; BD Devil)

1 Ne. 12: 17 mists of darkness in vision are temptations of d.; **12:** 19 Lamanites to contend against Nephites because of temptations of d.; **13:** 6 (14: 3, 9, 17) d. is founder of abominable church; **14:** 7 (2 Ne. 1: 18) the wicked are brought

down to captivity of d.; 14: 10 only two churches—church of Lamb and church of d.; 15: 35 d. is preparator of hell; **2 Ne.** 2: 17 (9: 8) angel of God fell, became d.; 2: 18 (9: 9; Mosiah 16: 3; Hel. 6: 26; Ether 8: 25) d. beguiled our first parents; 9: 8–9 except for resurrection our spirits should become like d. and we should become angels to d.; 9: 16 they who are filthy are d. and his angels; 9: 37 d. of all devils delights in those who worship idols; 26: 22 (Hel. 6: 26, 30; 8: 28; Ether 8: 16) d. is founder of secret combinations; 28: 19 kingdom of d. must shake; 28: 20–23 d. will rage, pacify, flatter; **Jacob** 7: 18 Sherem confesses he had been deceived by d.; **Omni** 1: 25 (Alma 5: 40; Moro. 7: 12, 17) that which is evil comes from d.; **Mosiah** 2: 32 beware lest contentions arise and ye obey evil spirit; 4: 14 (Alma 34: 23; Hel. 6: 30; Moro. 7: 17) d. is master of sin, enemy to righteousness; 16: 3, 5 d. has power over the wicked; **Alma** 5: 39 if ye are not sheep of good shepherd, d. is your shepherd; 9: 28 the evil shall reap damnation according to captivation of d.; 30: 53 Korihor confesses that d. deceived him; 30: 60 d. will not support his children; 34: 23 cry unto God against d.; 34: 39 pray continually that ye may not be led away by temptations of d.; 40: 13 spirit of d. takes possession of spirits of the wicked; 48: 17 if all men were like Moroni[1], d. would never have power over them; **Hel.** 5: 12 build your foundation, that d's mighty storm shall have no power over you; 6: 30 d. is author of all sin; 8: 28 d. seeks to destroy souls of men; **3 Ne.** 11: 29 he who has spirit of contention is of the d.; **Ether** 8: 25 d. is father of all lies; **Moro.** 7: 12 d. is an enemy to God; 7: 17 whatsoever persuadeth men not to believe in Christ is of d.

DEVILISH (see also Carnal; Devil)

Mosiah 16: 3 the wicked are carnal and d.; 16: 3 (Alma 42: 9–10) fall caused all mankind to become carnal, sensual, d.; **Alma** 41: 13 meaning of restoration is to bring back d. for d.; **Hel.** 12: 4 how d. are children of men.

DEVILS (see also Angels of the Devil; Demon; Devil; Spirit, Evil)

1 Ne. 11: 31 (Mosiah 3: 6) Lamb casts out d.; **2 Ne.** 9: 8–9 without resurrection we would have become d., angels to devil; **Jacob** 3: 11 d. to be cast into lake of fire and brimstone; **3 Ne.** 7: 19 Nephi[3] casts out d. in name of Lamb; 14: 22 (Matt. 7: 22) many will say they have cast out d. in the Lord's name; **Morm.** 9: 24 believers shall cast out d. in the Lord's name.

DEVOTE, DEVOTION (see Consecration, Law of; Worship)

DEVOUR (see also Burn; Consume; Eat; Fire)

Alma 5: 59 shepherd watches flocks, that wolf does not d.; **Moro.** 9: 10 Nephites d. human flesh like wild beasts.

DIE (see also Death, Physical; Death, Spiritual; Depart; Jesus Christ, Death of; Lay; Perish)

2 Ne. 2: 18 partake of forbidden fruit, and ye shall not d.; 9: 35 murderer who deliberately kills shall d.; 28: 7–8 (Isa. 22: 13; 1 Cor. 15: 32) eat, drink, and be merry, for tomorrow we d.; **Jacob** 2: 35 because of strictness of word of God against Nephites, many hearts d.; **Mosiah** 15: 26 the Lord redeems none who rebel against him and d. in their sins; **Alma** 12: 16 (40: 26) those who d. in sins shall d. second death, d. as pertaining to righteousness; **Morm.** 2: 14 Nephites curse God and wish to d.; 8: 38 greater is value of endless happiness than misery which never d.; **Moro.** 10: 26 those who d. in sins cannot be saved in kingdom of God.

DIG (see also Pit)

Jacob 5: 5, 11, 27, 63–64 master d. about trees in vineyard.

DILIGENCE, DILIGENT, DILIGENTLY (see also Endure; Faithful; Neglect; Obedience; Single; Slothful; Steadfast; Valiant; Zeal)

1 Ne. 10: 19 he who d. seeks shall find; 16: 28–29 (Mosiah 1: 16) pointers and writing on Liahona affected by d. of people; **Jacob** 1: 19 priests answer sins of people on own heads if they do not teach with d.; **Mosiah** 1: 7 (3 Ne. 23: 1) search records d., that ye may profit thereby; 1: 11 Benjamin's people have been d. in keeping commandments; 4: 27 man should be d., that thereby he might win prize; 7: 33 if ye will serve God with all d. of mind, he will deliver you; **Alma** 7: 23 I would that ye should be d. in keeping commandments; 12: 9 men are granted portion of mysteries according to d. they give God; 17: 2 sons of Mosiah[2] wax strong in knowledge of truth, for they searched scriptures d.; 32: 42–43 because of d. in nourishing word, ye may pluck fruit; 38: 10 be d. and temperate; 40: 3 Alma[2] has inquired d. of God regarding mystery of resurrection; 49: 30 Nephites enjoy peace and prosperity because of d. they give unto word of God; **3 Ne.** 6: 14 a few of converted Lamanites still willing with d. to keep commandments; **Moro.** 8: 26 love endures by d. unto prayer.

DIMMED

1 **Ne.** 5: 19 brass plates should never be *d.* by time.

DIRECT [adj.] (*see* Course; Straight)

Alma 37: 42 fathers did not travel *d.* course in wilderness because of transgressions.

DIRECTION, DIRECT [verb] (*see also* Course; Guide; Lead; Liahona; Path; Way)

1 **Ne.** 16: 16, 30 Lehites follow *d.* on Liahona; **Alma** 37: 36 let all thoughts be *d.* unto the Lord; 37: 37 counsel with the Lord, and he will *d.* thee for good; **Ether** 2: 5–6 the Lord gives Jaredites *d.* where to travel.

DISCERN (*see also* Discernible; Enlighten; Light; Perceive; Tell; TG Discernment, Spiritual)

Alma 18: 18 Ammon² can *d.* king's thoughts; 3 **Ne.** 24: 18 (Mal. 3: 18) ye shall *d.* between him that serveth God and him that serveth him not.

DISCERNIBLE

Alma 32: 35 whatsoever is light is good, because it is *d.*

DISCIPLE (*see also* Apostle; Follow, Follower; Servant; Three Nephite Disciples; TG Disciple; BD Disciple)

1 **Ne.** 12: 8 Nephi¹ sees twelve *d.* of Lamb chosen to minister to his seed; 12: 10 (Morm. 3: 19) twelve *d.* shall judge Nephites; **Alma** 45: 14 all shall be like Lamanites except *d.* of the Lord; 3 **Ne.** 5: 13 Mormon² is *d.* of Christ; 11: 22 Christ calls *d.* and gives power to baptize; 12: 1 (15: 11) number of those called and given authority is twelve; 15: 12 ye are my *d.*, and ye are a light to this people; 18: 26–34 Christ gives *d.* instructions on sacrament; 18: 37 (Moro. 2: 1–3) *d.* bear record that Christ gave them power to give Holy Ghost; 18: 39 *d.* bear record that Christ ascended into heaven; 19: 4 names of twelve *d.*; 19: 5–6 twelve *d.* teach multitude in twelve groups; 28: 1 Christ asks *d.*, one by one, what they desire; 28: 4–10 three *d.* shall not taste of death; 28: 26 (Morm. 8: 11) three *d.* minister unto Nephi³, Mormon², Moroni²; 4 **Ne.** 1: 1 disciples of Jesus form church of Christ; 1: 5 miracles wrought by *d.* of Jesus; 1: 30 false church exercises authority over three *d.* of Jesus; 1: 31–33 people try to kill three *d.*; 1: 37 three *d.* are among true believers; **Morm.** 1: 13 the Lord takes away his beloved *d.* because of people's wickedness; 8: 10 none know true God, save *d.* of Jesus; **Ether** 12: 17 it was by faith that three *d.* obtained promise not to taste of death;

Moro. 3: 1–4 manner in which *d.* ordained priests and teachers.

DISEASE (*see also* Infirmity; Leprous; Sick, Sickness)

1 **Ne.** 11: 31 (Mosiah 3: 5; 3 Ne. 17: 7) Lamb heals multitudes afflicted with *d.*; **Mosiah** 17: 16 people of Noah³ to be afflicted with *d.* because of iniquities; **Alma** 9: 22 Nephites saved from all manner of *d.*; 46: 40 God had prepared plants and roots to remove cause of *d.*

DISGUISE

Mosiah 12: 1 Abinadi comes among people in *d.*; **Hel.** 1: 12 Kishkumen in *d.* when he murders Pahoran²; 2: 6 servant obtains, by *d.*, knowledge of Kishkumen's plan to murder Helaman³.

DISH (*see also* Barge)

Ether 2: 17 (6: 7) Jaredite vessels are tight like *d.*

DISOBEDIENCE (*see also* Murmur; Obedience; Rebel; Reject; Sin; Trample; Transgression; Unfaithful; Wicked; TG Disobedience, Disobey)

Alma 42: 12 man had brought fallen state upon himself because of *d.*

DISPERSE, DISPERSION (*see also* Israel, Scattering of; Scatter; TG Israel, Scattering of; BD Dispersions)

2 **Ne.** 10: 8 (3 Ne. 21: 1) Jews shall be gathered from long *d.*; 21: 12 (3 Ne. 5: 26; Isa. 11: 12) the Lord shall gather *d.* of Israel; 3 **Ne.** 21: 26 work of the Father to commence among *d.* tribes; **Morm.** 8: 15 records to be brought forth for welfare of long *d.* covenant people.

DISPLEASURE, DISPLEASED (*see also* Indignation; Wrath)

2 **Ne.** 1: 21–22 be united, that ye may not incur *d.* of God; **Mosiah** 1: 17 followers of Lehi¹ were unfaithful and incurred *d.* of God; 25: 12 children of Amulon and his brethren are *d.* with conduct of their fathers.

DISPOSITION (*see also* Nature; Will)

Mosiah 5: 2 Benjamin's people experience mighty change and have no more *d.* to do evil; 9: 5 Zeniff goes to Lamanite king to learn his *d.*; **Alma** 43: 6 Amalekites are of more wicked and murderous *d.* than Lamanites.

DISPUTATIONS, DISPUTE (*see also* Contention; Dissension)

3 **Ne.** 8: 4 there began to be *d.* among the people; 11: 22, 28 the Lord commands that there be no *d.* regarding baptism or other points of doctrine; 18:

34 Christ gives commandments because of d. among people; 27: 3 d. among people regarding name of church; 4 Ne. 1: 2 no contentions or d. among Nephites; Ether 12: 6 d. not because ye see not; Moro. 8: 4–5 Mormon² is grieved because of d. regarding baptism of little children.

DISSENSION (see also Contention; Dissenter, Dissent; Divide; Murmur)

Mosiah 26: 5 because of d. among members, unbelievers become more numerous; 27: 9 Alma² causes much d. among people; Alma 46: 6 those who desire king are led away by Amalickiah to d.; 53: 8–9 intrigue amongst Nephites causes d., places them in dangerous circumstances; Hel. 4: 1 many d. in church; 3 Ne. 2: 18 because of d. among Nephites, Gadianton robbers gain advantages.

DISSENTER, DISSENT (see also Amalekites; Amalickiah; Ammonihah, City of; Amulonites; Apostasy; Kingmen; Prophets, False; Rebel; Revolt, Revolution; Unbelief; Zoramites²)

Alma 1: 21–25 many in church harden hearts, withdraw from people of God; 24: 29–30 no d., only Lamanites, join people of the Lord; 31: 8 Zoramites are d. from Nephites; 43: 13 (47: 35) Lamanite armies consist of Lamanites and those who had d. from Nephites; 43: 13 d. include Amalekites, Zoramites, and descendants of priests of Noah³; 48: 24 Nephites protect families from barbarous cruelties of those who had d. from church and joined Lamanites; 51: 15–20 d. compelled to defend country; 62: 6 Pachus is king of d.; Hel. 1: 15 Coriantumr³, d. from among Nephites, leads Lamanite army; 5: 35–41 Aminadab, who had d. from church, calls Lamanites to repent; 3 Ne. 3: 11 robbers had wronged themselves by d.; Moro. 9: 24 a few Nephite survivors d. over to Lamanites.

DISTINGUISH

Mosiah 1: 11 Benjamin gives his people a name to d. them; Alma 2: 11 people of Amlici are d. by name of Amlici; 3: 4 Amlicites d. themselves from Nephites with red mark on foreheads; 23: 16 Anti-Nephi-Lehies desire a name to d. them from their brethren; 27: 26 people of Ammon² d. by that name ever after; 27: 27 people of Ammon² are d. for their zeal toward God; 3 Ne. 6: 12 people began to be d. by ranks.

DIVIDE, DIVISION (see also Dissension)

1 Ne. 4: 2 (17: 26) waters of Red Sea were d.; 12: 18 terrible gulf d. spacious building and tree of life; 13: 10 many waters d. Gentiles from seed of Lamanites; 2 Ne. 30: 10 the Lord will cause great d. among the people; Mosiah 19: 2 d. among people of Noah³; Alma 11: 45 spirits will be united with bodies, never to be d.; 51: 6 great d. between freemen and king-men; Hel. 1: 4 sons of Pahoran¹ cause three d. among the people; 3 Ne. 7: 2 (4 Ne. 1: 35) people were d. one against another; 7: 14 Nephites d. into tribes; 4 Ne. 1: 26 people are d. into classes; Ether 2: 13 the Lord brings Jaredites to great sea which d. the lands.

DIVORCE, DIVORCEMENT (see also Marriage; BD Divorce)

2 Ne. 7: 1 (Isa. 50: 1) where is the bill of your mother's d.; 3 Ne. 12: 31–32 (Matt. 5: 31–32) Savior teaches concerning d.

DO, DID, DONE (see also Accomplish; Deed; Doing, Doings; Labor; Obedience; Perform; Undertake; Walk; Work [verb]; Wrought)

1 Ne. 3: 7 I will go and d. the things which the Lord hath commanded; 17: 30 the Lord d. all things for Israel that were expedient for man to receive; 17: 50 if God had commanded me to d. all good things, I could d. them; 2 Ne. 25: 23 by grace we are saved, after all we can d.; 26: 24 the Lord d. not anything save for benefit of world; 26: 33 God d. nothing save it be plain unto men; Enos 1: 7 Lord, how is it d.; Alma 32: 19 how muc' more cursed is he who knows God's will and d. it not; Hel. 14: 30 whosoever d. iniquity d. it unto himself; 3 Ne. 14: 24 (Matt. 7: 24; Luke 6: 47–48) whoso hears sayings and d. them is like man who built house upon rock; 18: 6 this shall ye always observe to d., even as I have d.; 27: 21 ye know the things ye must d. in my church.

DOCTRINE (see also Doctrine, False; Gospel; Plan; Precept; Principle)

1 Ne. 15: 14 Lamanites shall come to knowledge of Redeemer and points of his d.; 2 Ne. 31: 21 (32: 6) this is the d. of Christ; Jacob 7: 2 Sherem seeks to overthrow d. of Christ; Alma 41: 9 do not risk one more offense against God upon points of d.; Hel. 11: 22–23 those who know d. through revelation put an end to contentions; 3 Ne. 2: 2 Satan leads men to believe d. of Christ is foolish; 11: 28 there shall be no disputations concerning points of d.; 11: 30 it is not Christ's d. to stir up hearts of men with anger; 11: 32, 35, 39 this is my d.; 11: 40 whoso establishes more or less for Christ's d. comes of evil; 21: 6 Gentiles to know true points of d.

DOCTRINE, FALSE (*see also* Antichrist; Apostasy; Churches, False; Contention; Err, Error; Prophets, False)

2 Ne. 3: 12 writings of descendants of Joseph¹ and Judah shall confound false d.; 28: 9 many shall teach vain, foolish, false d.; 28: 12 because of false d., churches will be corrupted; **Alma** 1: 16 many go forth preaching false d. for riches and honor.

DOG (*see also* Animal; BD Dog)

3 Ne. 7: 8 people turned from righteousness as d. to his vomit; 14: 6 (Matt. 7: 6) give not that which is holy unto d.

DOING, DOINGS (*see also* Deed; Do)

1 Ne. 10: 20 for all thy d. thou shalt be brought into judgment; 2 Ne. 25: 2 d. of Jews were d. of abominations; **Alma** 37: 36 let all thy d. be unto the Lord; **Morm.** 8: 35 Christ hath shown you unto me, and I know your d.

DOMINION (*see also* Authority; Kingdom; Power; Reign; Rule; Scepter; Throne)

1 Ne. 14: 12 d. of church of God will be small; **Alma** 5: 50 Son cometh in his majesty, power, d.

DOOR (*see also* Gate)

Hel. 8: 26–27 destruction is even now at your d.; 3 Ne. 13: 6 (Matt. 6: 6) when thou hast shut d. of closet, pray to the Father.

DORMANT (*see also* Sleep)

Alma 32: 34 your faith is d.

DOUBT, DOUBTINGS (*see also* Belief; Faith; Hardheartedness; Unbelief; TG Doubt, Doubtful)

Alma 56: 47 (57: 26) stripling warriors were taught God would deliver them if they did not d.; 56: 48 striplings do not d. mothers; 3 Ne. 5: 1 none of Nephites d. words of prophets; 8: 4 great d. among people notwithstanding many signs; **Morm.** 9: 21 whoso believes in Christ, d. nothing, shall be granted whatsoever he asks; 9: 25 the Lord will confirm his words to those who believe in his name, d. nothing; 9: 27 d. not, but be believing; **Ether** 3: 19 brother of Jared² has faith no longer, for he knows, nothing d.

DOVE (*see also* Holy Ghost; TG Holy Ghost, Sign of; BD Dove; Dove, Sign of)

1 Ne. 11: 27 (2 Ne. 31: 8) Holy Ghost abides upon Lamb in form of d.

DRAGON (*see also* TG Dragon; BD Dragon)

2 Ne. 8: 9 (Isa. 51: 9) art thou not he that wounded the d.; 23: 22 (Isa. 13: 22)

d. shall cry in their pleasant palaces; **Mosiah** 20: 11 (Alma 43: 44) people of Limhi fight like d.

DRAW, DREW, DRAWN

2 Ne. 26: 24 (3 Ne. 27: 14–15) the Lord lays down his life that he may d. men unto him; 27: 25 (Isa. 29: 13) this people d. near the Lord with mouth, but have removed hearts from him; **Alma** 34: 27 let your hearts be full, d. out in prayer unto the Lord; 42: 2 after God sent first parents from Eden, he d. out the man; **Hel.** 13: 22 hearts of Nephites not d. out unto the Lord.

DREADFUL (*see* Day; Day of the Lord)

DREAM (*see also* Revelation; Vision; BD Dreams)

1 Ne. 1: 16 Lehi¹ has written many things which he saw in d.; 2: 1–2 the Lord speaks to Lehi¹ in d.; 3: 2 (8: 2) I have d. a d.; 8: 36 (10: 2) Lehi¹ speaks words of d.; 15: 21 what means this thing our father saw in d.; 2 Ne. 27: 3 (Isa. 29: 7) nations that fight against Zion shall be as d. of night vision; **Jacob** 7: 26 our lives passed away as a d.; **Alma** 30: 28 Korihor claims priests bring people to believe, by traditions and d., that they should offend some unknown being; **Ether** 9: 3 the Lord warns Omer in a d.

DRESS (*see also* Apparel; Clothing)

1 Ne. 8: 4, 7 d. of those in spacious building is exceeding fine.

DRINK, DRUNK (*see also* Cup; Drunk, Drunken; Eat; Partake; Sacrament; Thirst; Wine)

2 Ne. 27: 4 they who do iniquity shall stagger, but not with strong d.; **Mosiah** 2: 33 (3: 18, 25) he who dies in his sins d. damnation to his soul; **Alma** 5: 34 come unto me and ye shall d. of waters of life freely; 49: 27 (51: 9) Amalickiah swears to d. blood of Moroni¹; **Morm.** 9: 24 believers shall d. any deadly thing and it shall not hurt them.

DROSS

Alma 32: 3 the poor are esteemed by their brethren as d.; 34: 29 if ye do not remember to be charitable, ye are as d.

DROUGHT (*see* Famine)

DROWNED

1 Ne. 4: 2 (17: 27; Alma 36: 28; Hel. 8: 11) Egyptians d. in Red Sea; 8: 32 many d. in depths of fountain; **Alma** 63: 8 those who left in ships are supposed to be d.; 3 Ne. 8: 9 inhabitants of Moroni are d. in sea.

DRUNK, DRUNKEN, DRUNKENNESS
(see also Wine; TG Drunkenness)

1 Ne. 4: 7 Nephi¹ finds Laban d. with wine; 21: 26 (22: 13; Isa. 49: 26) those who oppress the Lord's people shall be d. with own blood; 2 Ne. 8: 21 hear this, thou d., and not with wine; 27: 1 in last days Gentiles and Jews shall be d. with iniquity; Mosiah 22: 7 Lamanites will be d., so that Limhi's people can escape; Alma 55: 14 Nephites cause Lamanites to become d.; 55: 19 Nephites would not destroy Lamanites in their d.; 55: 30 Lamanites try to destroy Nephites with poison or d.; Ether 15: 22 Jaredites d. with anger, as man who is d. with wine.

DUMB (see also Heal)

Mosiah 12: 5 (21: 3) people of Noah³ shall be driven like d. ass; 14: 7 (15: 6; Isa. 53: 7) as a sheep before her shearers is d., so he opened not his mouth; 27: 19 astonishment of Alma¹ was so great that he became d.; Alma 30: 49–50 Korihor is struck d.; Hel. 5: 25 Lamanites stand as if struck d. with amazement; 3 Ne. 17: 9 Christ heals the d.

DUNG

Jacob 5: 64 Lord of vineyard commands servant to d. trees once more; Morm. 2: 15 thousands hewn down and heaped up as d.

DUNGEON (see also Prison)

Mosiah 2: 13 neither have I suffered that ye should be confined in d.; Alma 8: 31 Alma² and Amulek could not be confined in d.

DUST (see also Ashes; Earth; Ground)

1 Ne. 21: 23 (2 Ne. 6: 7, 13; Isa. 49: 23) kings and queens shall lick up d. of thy feet; 22: 14 abominable church shall tumble to d.; 2 Ne. 1: 14 (Moro. 10: 31) awake and arise from the d.; 3: 19–20 fruit of loins of Nephi¹ to cry as from d.; 26: 15 Nephites and Lamanites to be brought low in d.; 26: 16 (Isa. 29: 4) speech of those who are destroyed shall be low out of d.; 27: 9 words of book are words of those who have slumbered in d.; 33: 13 Nephi¹ speaks as voice of one crying from d.; Jacob 2: 21 all flesh is of the d.; Mosiah 2: 25 (Morm. 9: 17) men were created of d. of earth; Alma 34: 38 humble yourselves even to d.; Hel. 12: 7 (Mosiah 2: 25) children of men are less than d. of earth; Morm. 8: 23 saints who have gone before will cry, even from the d.; Moro. 10: 27 Moroni² declares his words like one speaking out of dust.

DUTY (see also Obedience; Office; Perform; Responsibility; Serve)

Mosiah 1: 17 Lehites smitten with

afflictions to stir them up in remembrance of d.; 13: 30 law of performances and ordinances to keep Israel in remembrance of d. toward God; Alma 4: 19 (7: 22) Alma² preaches to stir Nephites up in remembrance of d.; 43: 46 Nephites were doing what they felt was d. they owed to God; Hel. 15: 5 more part of Lamanites are in path of d.

DWELL, DWELLING (see also Abide; God, Presence of; Home; Inhabit; Live; Sojourn)

1 Ne. 10: 21 no unclean thing can d. with God; 15: 33 if men are filthy, they cannot d. in kingdom of God; 22: 28 all nations shall d. safely in Holy One if they repent; 2 Ne. 2: 8 no flesh can d. in presence of God save through grace of Messiah; 21: 6 (30: 12; Isa. 11: 6) wolf shall d. with lamb; Mosiah 2: 37 (Alma 7: 21; 34: 36; Hel. 4: 24) the Lord d. not in unholy temples; 2: 41 those who keep commandments d. with God in never-ending happiness; 3: 5 (Alma 7: 8) the Lord shall come down and d. in tabernacle of clay; 3: 6 the Lord shall cast out evil spirits that d. in men's hearts; 15: 23 prophets are raised to d. with God, who has redeemed them; Alma 18: 35 portion of Spirit d. in Ammon²; 34: 36 the Lord d. in hearts of the righteous; 39: 7 Alma² would not d. upon Corianton's sins if it were not for his good; 3 Ne. 28: 9 disciples shall not have pain while they d. in flesh; 4 Ne. 1: 15 love of God d. in Nephites' hearts; Morm. 7: 7 he who is found guiltless shall d. in presence of God; 9: 3–4 men could not d. with Christ with consciousness of guilt; Ether 13: 2 all men who d. upon land should serve the Lord; 13: 10 blessed are they who d. in New Jerusalem; Moro. 8: 26 all saints shall d. with God.

DWINDLE, DWINDLING (see Unbelief)

EAR (see also Hear)

1 Ne. 20: 8 (Isa. 48: 8) from that time thine e. was not opened; 2 Ne. 7: 4–5 (Isa. 50: 4–5) the Lord waketh mine e. to hear; 16: 10 (Isa. 6: 10) make the e. of this people heavy; 28: 22 devil whispers in men's e. until he grasps them; Jarom 1: 3 much should be done among Nephites because of deafness of their e.; Mosiah 2: 9 open your e. that ye may hear; 3 Ne. 11: 5 survivors open e. to hear voice from heaven; 17: 16 e. has not heard such great things as Jesus spoke unto Father; 26: 15 Christ unstopped e. of the deaf.

EARTH (see also Bury; Creation; Dust; Earthquake; Ground; Land; World; TG Earth; Earth, Cleansing of; Earth, Curse

of; Earth, Destiny of; Earth, Dividing of; Earth, Purpose of; Earth, Renewal of)

1 Ne. 4: 1 the Lord is mightier than all the *e.*; 11: 6 (3 Ne. 11: 14; 22: 5) the Lord is God over all the *e.*; 13: 41 one Shepherd over all the *e.*; 17: 36 (Mosiah 4: 2; 13: 19; Morm. 9: 17) the Lord hath created the *e.*; 19: 17 all the *e.* shall see salvation of the Lord; **2 Ne.** 8: 6 (Isa. 51: 6) *e.* to wax old like a garment; 21: 4 (Isa. 11: 4) the Lord shall smite *e.* with rod of his mouth; 23: 13 (Isa. 13: 13) *e.* shall remove out of her place; **Jacob** 4: 9 by power of the Lord's word, *e.* was created and man came upon *e.*; **Alma** 5: 50 behold the glory of the King of all the *e.*; 11: 39 the Son is Eternal Father of heaven and *e.*; **Hel.** 12: 13–15 (Jacob 4: 9) if the Lord say unto *e.*, Move, it is moved; 12: 18 (13: 18; Morm. 1: 18) whoso shall hide treasure in *e.* shall find it no more; **3 Ne.** 8: 17 whole *e.* becomes deformed; 10: 9 *e.* ceases to tremble; 12: 5 (Matt. 5: 5) meek shall inherit the *e.*; 13: 10 (Matt. 6: 10) thy will be done on *e.* as it is in heaven; 26: 3 (Morm. 5: 23; 9: 2; Ether 13: 9) *e.* to be wrapt together as scroll, and heaven and *e.* to pass away; **Ether** 13: 9 a new heaven and new *e.*; **Moro.** 7: 36 will God withhold power of Holy Ghost as long as *e.* shall stand.

EARTHQUAKE (*see also* Earth; Quake; Shake; Tremble; TG Earthquake)

1 Ne. 12: 4 in dream Nephi[1] hears thunderings and *e.*; **2 Ne.** 6: 15 unbelievers will be destroyed in *e.*; 26: 6 they who kill prophets shall be visited with *e.*; 27: 2 Jews and Gentiles shall be visited with *e.*; **Morm.** 8: 30 wars and *e.* in divers places.

EASE (*see also* Comfort; Easiness)

2 Ne. 28: 24 wo unto him who is at *e.* in Zion; **Hel.** 12: 2 people harden hearts because of their *e.*

EASINESS, EASY (*see also* Light, Lightly [adj.]; Simple)

1 Ne. 14: 23 things written in book were *e.* to understand; 17: 41 because of *e.* of requirement for healing, many perished; **Alma** 7: 23 be *e.* to be entreated; 37: 44 *e.* to give heed to word of Christ; 37: 46 do not be slothful because of *e.* of way; 39: 6 not *e.* for man who has denied Holy Ghost to obtain forgiveness; **Hel.** 6: 36 the Lord pours out Spirit on Lamanites because of their *e.* to believe; 7: 7 earlier Nephites were *e.* to be entreated.

EAT, EATEN (*see also* Consume; Devour; Drink; Food; Partake; Taste)

2 Ne. 13: 10 (Isa. 3: 10) the righteous

shall *e.* fruit of their doings; 14: 1 (Isa. 4: 1) we will *e.* our own bread; 19: 20 every man shall *e.* flesh of his own arm; 21: 7 (30: 12; Isa. 11: 7) lion shall *e.* straw like ox; 28: 7–8 *e.*, drink, and be merry; **Alma** 31: 37 (3 Ne. 13: 25, 31; Matt. 6: 25, 31) missionaries take no thought for what they should *e.* or drink; 42: 3 God placed cherubim and flaming sword lest man should *e.* of tree of life; **3 Ne.** 18: 29 whoso *e.* Christ's flesh unworthily *e.* damnation to his soul; 20: 8 he that *e.* this bread *e.* Christ's body to his soul; **Moro.** 4: 3 *e.* sacrament bread in remembrance of body of Son.

EDEN, GARDEN OF—*home of Adam and Eve* (*see also* Adam; Fruit, Forbidden; BD Eden, Garden of)

2 Ne. 2: 19 (Alma 42: 2) Adam and Eve are driven out of *E.*; 2: 22 if Adam had not transgressed, he would have remained in *E.*; 8: 3 (Isa. 51: 3) the Lord will make Zion's wilderness like *E.*; **Alma** 12: 21 (42: 3) God placed cherubim and flaming sword on east of *E.*

EFFECT

Mosiah 7: 30 *e.* of reaping whirlwind is poison; **Alma** 12: 26 if first parents could have partaken of tree of life, word of God would have been void, taking none *e.*; 31: 5 preaching of word has more powerful *e.* on people than sword.

EGYPT—*land of Israel's captivity* (*see also* Egyptian; BD Egypt)

1 Ne. 5: 14 (2 Ne. 3: 4; 4: 1; Alma 10: 3) Joseph[1] sold into *E.*; 5: 15 (17: 40; 19: 10; 2 Ne. 3: 10; 21: 16; 25: 20; Mosiah 7: 19; 12: 34; Alma 36: 28) God led Israel out of captivity, out of *E.*; **2 Ne.** 17: 18 (Isa. 7: 18) the Lord shall hiss for fly in uttermost part of *E.*; 20: 24, 26 (Isa. 10: 24, 26) Assyrian shall lift up staff against Zion after manner of *E.*; 21: 11 (Isa. 11: 11) the Lord shall set his hand the second time to recover remnant of his people left in *E.*; **Ether** 13: 7 Joseph[1] brought father into *E.*

EGYPTIAN (*see also* Egypt; Language)

1 Ne. 1: 2 language of Lehi[1] consists of learning of Jews and language of *E.*; 4: 3 the Lord is able to destroy Laban, even as *E.*; 17: 27 (Alma 36: 28; Hel. 8: 11) the Lord swallowed up *E.* in Red Sea; 17: 23 (Alma 29: 12) would fathers have been led out of hands of *E.* if they had not hearkened to the Lord's words; **2 Ne.** 21: 15 (Isa. 11: 15) the Lord destroys tongue of *E.* sea; **Mosiah** 1: 4 Lehi[1] could read engravings because he had been taught in language of *E.*; **Morm.** 9: 32 record written in characters called reformed *E.*

ELDER (*see also* Priesthood; TG Elder; Elder—Melchizedek Priesthood; BD Elders)

1 Ne. 4: 22, 27 Zoram¹ speaks with Nephi¹ concerning *e.* of Jews; **Alma** 4: 7 (6: 1) Alma² consecrates *e.* over church; 4: 16 Alma² gives one of *e.* power to enact laws; **Moro.** 3: 1 disciples are called *e.* of church; 4: 1 *e.* and priests administer sacrament; 6: 1 *e.*, priests, and teachers are baptized; 6: 7 those who commit iniquity are brought before *e.*

ELECT (*see also* Choose; Chosen)

Alma 31: 16–17 Zoramites believe God has *e.* them to be his holy children.

ELEMENT (*see also* Materials; Matter)

3 Ne. 26: 3 (Morm. 9: 2) *e.* shall melt with fervent heat.

ELEPHANT (*see also* Animal; BD Elephant)

Ether 9: 19 Jaredites have *e.*

ELIJAH—*prophet of Israel* [ca. 900 B.C.] (*see also* BD Elijah)

3 Ne. 25: 5 (Mal. 4: 5) I will send you E. the prophet.

EMER—*early Jaredite king*

Ether 1: 28–29 son of Omer, father of Coriantum¹; 9: 14 anointed king; 9: 15–16 has peaceful, prosperous reign; 9: 21 executes judgment in righteousness.

EMPLOY

2 Ne. 9: 41 Holy One *e.* no servant at the gate; **Alma** 10: 32 (11: 20) lawyers got gain according to their *e.*

EMPTY

2 Ne. 27: 3 (Isa. 29: 8) enemies of Zion shall be as hungry man who dreams he eats, but soul is *e.*

EMRON—*Nephite soldier*

Moro. 9: 2 is slain.

END, ENDS, ENDING (*see also* Beginning; Endless; Endure; Final; Finish; Last; Last Days; Pass; Purpose; TG World, End of)

1 Ne. 14: 3 casting of soul into that hell which hath no *e.*; 14: 22 John the Beloved to write of *e.* of world; **2 Ne.** 2: 7 (Moro. 7: 28) Christ offers himself a sacrifice for sin, to answer *e.* of law; 2: 12 without opposition, no purpose in *e.* of its creation; 2: 22 except for Adam's fall, all things must have had no *e.*; 25: 25 law of Moses given for *e.* of preparing for Christ; 26: 25 (3 Ne. 9: 22) come unto me, all ye *e.* of earth; 27: 7 sealed book shall be revelation from God, from begin-

ning of world to *e.*; 31: 21 Godhead is one God, without *e.*; 33: 9 continue in straight path until *e.* of day of probation; **Mosiah** 26: 23 the Lord grants unto him that believeth unto the *e.* a place at right hand; **Alma** 5: 13 because fathers were faithful unto *e.*, they were saved; 27: 27 Ammonites are firm in faith of Christ unto *e.*; 30: 12, 18 Korihor claims that when man is dead, that is *e.*; 41: 6 he who desires righteousness until *e.* is rewarded unto righteousness; **3 Ne.** 16: 20 (20: 35) all *e.* of earth to see salvation of God; **Morm.** 7: 7 he who is found guiltless will dwell in state of happiness which hath no *e.*; **Moro.** 6: 3 (Mosiah 18: 9) those received unto baptism must have determination to serve Christ to *e.*; 8: 26 love endures by diligence unto prayer, until *e.* come.

ENDLESS (*see also* End; Eternal; Everlasting; God, Eternal Nature of; Infinite; Misery; Torment)

Mosiah 16: 9 Christ is light and life of world, a light and life that is *e.*; 16: 11 (Alma 41: 4; Hel. 12: 26) the good are resurrected to *e.* life and happiness, the evil to *e.* damnation; **Alma** 12: 24 life a time to prepare for *e.* state after resurrection; **Hel.** 7: 16 devil seeks to hurl souls down to *e.* wo; **Morm.** 8: 38 greater is value of *e.* happiness than misery that never dies; 9: 13 resurrection brings to pass redemption from *e.* sleep.

ENDURE, ENDURANCE (*see also* Bear; Continue; Diligence; Faint; Faithful; Firmness; Obedience; Probation; Steadfast)

1 Ne. 13: 37 those who *e.* to end shall be lifted up; 22: 31 (2 Ne. 31: 15; Omni 1: 26; Alma 5: 13; 32: 13; 3 Ne. 27: 6) those who *e.* to end shall be saved; **Alma** 32: 15 (38: 2) blessed is he who *e.* to end; **3 Ne.** 15: 9 *e.* to end, and ye shall live; 27: 16 he who *e.* to end will be held guiltless; **Morm.** 9: 29 those who *e.* to end shall not be cast out; **Moro.** 3: 3 (8: 3) remission of sins, through Christ, by *e.* of faith on his name to end; 7: 45 charity *e.* all things; 8: 26 love *e.* by diligence unto prayer.

ENEMY (*see also* Adversary; Oppressor)

2 Ne. 4: 28 give place no more for *e.* of my soul; **Mosiah** 2: 31 if Nephites keep commandments, *e.* shall have no power over them; 2: 37 man who transgresses against what he has been taught becomes *e.* to righteousness; 3: 19 (16: 5) natural man is *e.* to God; 4: 14 (16: 5) Alma 34: 23; Moro. 7: 12; 9: 6) devil is *e.* to all righteousness, *e.* to God; **Alma** 26: 6 those who are gathered shall not be driven whithersoever *e.* listeth to carry

them; 58: 10 Nephites pray that God will deliver them from e.; **Hel.** 8: 6 corrupt judges do not believe e. can have power over them; **3 Ne.** 12: 43–44 (Matt. 5: 43–44) love your e.

ENGRAVE, ENGRAVEN, ENGRAVINGS (see also Plates, Brass; Plates of Ether; Plates of Nephi, Large; Plates of Nephi, Small; Record; Write)

Jacob 4: 1–3 difficulty of e. on plates; **Omni** 1: 20 large stone with e. on it brought to Mosiah² to be translated; **Mosiah** 21: 28 Mosiah² has gift of God whereby he can interpret e.; **Alma** 5: 19 can ye look up, having image of God e. on countenances; 63: 12 all e. in possession of Helaman¹ are sent forth among people; **Morm.** 1: 3 Ammaron had deposited sacred e. in hill Shim.

ENJOY (see Enjoyment; Rights)

ENJOYMENT

2 Ne. 9: 14 the righteous shall have perfect knowledge of their e.

ENLARGE (see also Grow; Increase)

Jacob 2: 9 it burdens soul of Jacob² to e. wounds of those already wounded; **Alma** 32: 28 word must be good, for it begins to e. my soul; **3 Ne.** 22: 2 (Isa. 54: 2) e. the place of thy tent; **Moro.** 10: 31 e. thy borders forever.

ENLIGHTEN (see also Discern; Illuminate; Inspire; Light; Quick [=living]; Shine)

Alma 24: 30 people once e. by Spirit who have fallen into sin become more hardened; 32: 28 word must be good, for it begins to e. my understanding.

ENOS¹—*grandson of Adam* (see also BD Enos)

No references in Book of Mormon.

ENOS²—*Nephite prophet, record keeper*

Jacob 7: 27 son of Jacob², given plates; **Enos** 1: 1, 3 is taught by father; 1: 2 wrestles before God to receive remission of sins; 1: 4 prays all day; 1: 5–8 hears voice of the Lord, sins forgiven through faith in Christ; 1: 9 concerned for welfare of Nephites; 1: 19 prophesies and testifies; **Jarom** 1: 1 gives plates to son, Jarom.

ENSIGN (see also Standard)

2 Ne. 15: 26 (21: 12; Isa. 5: 26; 11: 12) the Lord will lift an e. to the nations; 21: 10 root of Jesse shall stand for e.

ENSNARE (see also Captive; Catch; Snare)

1 Ne. 22: 14 nations which war against Israel shall fall into pit digged to e. people of the Lord; **Alma** 28: 13 devil devises cunning plans to e. hearts of men.

ENTER (see also Come; Gate; Rest)

1 Ne. 15: 34 (10: 21; 3 Ne. 27: 19) no unclean thing can e. kingdom of God; **2 Ne.** 32: 5 e. in by the way and Holy Ghost will show what to do; **Mosiah** 5: 5 Benjamin's people willing to e. covenant with God; **Alma** 40: 13 spirit of devil e. into spirits of wicked; **3 Ne.** 14: 21 (Matt. 7: 21) not every one that saith Lord, Lord, shall e. kingdom of heaven; 18: 18 pray always lest ye e. into temptation.

ENTICE, ENTICINGS (see also Agency; Invite; Tempt)

2 Ne. 2: 16 man could not act for himself save he should be e. by the sweet or the bitter; 5: 21 Lamanites given skin of blackness that they might not be e. to Nephites; 9: 39 remember the awfulness of yielding to the e. of cunning one; **Mosiah** 3: 19 natural man will be enemy to God until he yields to e. of Spirit; **Hel.** 6: 26 Satan e. parents to partake of forbidden fruit; 7: 16 how could you have given way to e. of devil; **Moro.** 7: 12 devil e. to sin; 7: 13 that which is of God e. to do good continually.

ENTREAT (see also Exhort)

Alma 7: 23 be easy to be e.; **Hel.** 7: 7 people of Nephi were easy to be e.

ENTRUSTED (see also Give)

Alma 37: 14 Helaman¹ e. with sacred things; 39: 4 Corianton should have tended to ministry with which he was e.; 53: 20 sons of Helaman² are true in all they are e.; **Morm.** 6: 6 Mormon² hides records e. to him by the Lord.

ENVY, ENVYING (see also Covet; Jealous; Pride; TG Envy)

2 Ne. 21: 13 (Isa. 11: 13) e. of Ephraim shall depart; 26: 21 (Morm. 8: 28) false churches will cause e.; 26: 32 the Lord has commanded that men should not e.; **Alma** 1: 32 those who do not belong to church indulge in e.; 4: 9 e. among people of church; 5: 29 is there one among you who is not stripped of e.; 16: 18 priests preach against e.; **Hel.** 13: 22 hearts of Nephites swell with great pride, unto e.; **3 Ne.** 30: 2 Mormon² calls Gentiles to repent of e.; **4 Ne.** 1: 16 no e. among people after Christ's visit; **Morm.** 8: 28 in latter days teachers and leaders of churches will lift themselves up in pride, unto e.

EPHRAIM—*kingdom of Israel* (see also Israel; Joseph¹, Seed of; BD Ephraim; Israel; Israel, Kingdom of; Joseph, People of)

2 Ne. 17: 2, 5 (Isa. 7: 2, 5) Syria is confederate with *E.*; 17: 8 (Isa. 7: 8) *E.* to be broken that it be not a people; 17: 9 (Isa. 7: 9) Samaria is head of *E.*; 17: 17 (Isa. 7: 17) the Lord shall bring upon house of David days that have not come from the day that *E.* departed from Judah; 19: 8–9 (Isa. 9: 8–9) all people, even *E.*, to know the Lord's word; 19: 21 (Isa. 9: 21) Manasseh and *E.* shall be against Judah; 21: 13 (Isa. 11: 13) *E.* shall not envy Judah, and Judah shall not vex *E.*

EPHRAIM, HILL OF

Ether 7: 9 iron ore for swords obtained from hill *E.*

EPISTLE

Alma 54: 4, 15 Moroni[1] writes *e.* to Ammoron; 54: 15 (55: 1) Ammoron writes *e.* to Moroni[1]; 56: 1 Moroni[1] receives *e.* from Helaman[2]; 57: 1 Helaman[2] had received *e.* from Ammoron; 57: 2 Helaman[2] wrote *e.* to Ammoron; 59: 3 Moroni[1] writes *e.* to Pahoran[1]; 60: 1 Moroni[1] writes second *e.* to Pahoran[1]; 61: 1 (62: 1) Moroni[1] receives *e.* from Pahoran[1]; 3 Ne. 3: 1–2, 11 Lachoneus[1] receives *e.* from leader of robbers; **Morm.** 3: 4 Lamanite king sends *e.* to Mormon[2]; 6: 2 Mormon[2] writes *e.* to Lamanite king; Ether 15: 4–5 Coriantumr[2] sends *e.* to Shiz; 15: 5 Shiz writes *e.* to Coriantumr[2]; 15: 18 Coriantumr[2] writes second *e.* to Shiz; **Moro.** ch. 8–9 Moroni[1] records two *e.* from Mormon[2].

EQUAL, EQUALITY (*see also* Alike; Equity; Inequality; Judgment; Respect; Respecter; Same)

Jacob 5: 66, 73 root and top of tree should be *e.* in strength; 5: 74 fruits of trees become *e.*; **Mosiah** 27: 3 commandment throughout all churches that there should be *e.* among all men; 29: 38 every man should have *e.* chance; Alma 1: 26 teacher and learner are all *e.*; 30: 11 all men are on *e.* grounds before law; 3 Ne. 28: 39 change in three Nephite disciples not *e.* to change to take place at last day.

EQUITY (*see also* Equal; Justice)

2 Ne. 21: 4 (30: 9; Isa. 11: 4) the Lord will reprove with *e.* for the meek; Alma 9: 26 (10: 21; 13: 9) the Lord is full of grace, *e.*; **Hel.** 3: 20 Helaman[2] and Nephi[2] fill judgment-seat with *e.*; 3 Ne. 6: 4 Nephites form laws according to *e.*

ERR, ERROR (*see also* Astray; Doctrine; False; Sin; Stumble; Transgression; Wander)

2 Ne. 13: 12 (19: 16; 28: 14; Isa. 3:

12; 9: 16) they who lead the Lord's children cause them to *e.*; 25: 20 (Alma 5: 43; 13: 23) the Lord's word is taught plainly, so that people cannot *e.*; 27: 35 they who *e.* in spirit shall come to understanding; 28: 14 people *e.* because they are taught precepts of men; Alma 37: 8 sacred records convince many of *e.* of their ways; 3 Ne. 1: 25 those who preach against law of Moses are convinced of their *e.*; **Moro.** 8: 6 gross *e.* that little children need baptism.

ERRAND (*see also* Calling)

Jacob 1: 17 Jacob[2] first obtained his *e.* from the Lord.

ESCAPE (*see also* Deliver; Flight; Refuge; Salvation)

2 Ne. 9: 10 God prepares *e.* from grasp of death and hell; 14: 2 (Isa. 4: 2) fruit of earth shall be comely to them that are *e.* of Israel.

ESROM—*early Jaredite*

Ether 8: 4–6 son of Omer, helps return kingdom to father.

ESTABLISH, ESTABLISHMENT (*see also* Confirm; Prepare)

1 Ne. 13: 40 last records shall *e.* truth of the first; 2 Ne. 12: 2 (Isa. 2: 2) mountain of the Lord's house shall be *e.* in top of mountains; Alma 1: 6 Nehor *e.* church; 2: 3 king must be *e.* by voice of people; 8: 1 Alma[2] *e.* order of church; **Hel.** 5: 2 laws and government *e.* by voice of people; 3 Ne. 7: 11, 14 laws and government *e.* by chiefs and leaders of tribes; 11: 40 whoso shall declare more or less than this and *e.* it for Christ's doctrine comes of evil; 21: 1 the Lord will *e.* Zion again among house of Israel; 21: 22 the Lord will *e.* his church among house of Israel if they will hearken; Ether 5: 4 in mouth of three witnesses shall these things be *e.*

ESTEEM (*see also* Love; Value; Worth)

1 Ne. 17: 35 the Lord *e.* all flesh in one; 19: 7 things which some *e.* to be of great worth, others set at naught; 2 Ne. 3: 7 choice seer will be *e.* highly among descendants of Joseph[1]; 33: 2 many things written are *e.* as things of naught by those who harden hearts; 33: 3 Nephi[1] *e.* things he has written as of great worth; **Mosiah** 14: 4 (Isa. 53: 4) we did *e.* Messiah stricken and afflicted; 23: 7 ye shall not *e.* one flesh above another; 27: 4 every man should *e.* his neighbor as himself; 29: 40 people of Mosiah[2] *e.* him more than any other man; Alma 1: 26 priest does not *e.* himself above hearers; **Hel.** 11: 18 people *e.* Nephi[2] as great

prophet; **Ether** 13: 13 Jaredites e. Ether as naught.

ETERNAL, ETERNALLY (see also Endless; Eternal Life; Eternity; Everlasting; God, Eternal Nature of; Infinite)

1 Ne. 10: 19 (Alma 7: 20) course of the Lord is one e. round; **2 Ne.** 1: 13 men carried captive down to e. gulf of misery; **Mosiah** 2: 34 ye are e. indebted to the Father; **Alma** 3: 26 in one year tens of thousands of souls sent to e. world; 3: 26 men reap e. happiness, e. misery, according to spirit they obey; 34: 10 great and last sacrifice must be infinite and e. sacrifice; 37: 44 word of Christ will point straight course to e. bliss; 42: 16 repentance could not come except there were a punishment which also was e. as life of soul; **3 Ne.** 28: 40 three Nephites will dwell with God e.; **Ether** 3: 14 in Christ shall mankind have light e.; **Moro.** 7: 28 Christ dwells e. in the heavens.

ETERNAL FATHER, GOD THE (see God, Eternal Nature of; God the Father)

ETERNAL LIFE (see also Continue, Continuation; Immortality; Live; Redemption; Resurrection; Salvation; TG Eternal Life)

2 Ne. 2: 27–29 (10: 23) men are free to choose e. life or e. death; 9: 39 to be spiritually minded is life e.; 31: 18 those who repent and are baptized are in narrow path which leads to e. life; 33: 4 to believe in Christ and endure to end is life e.; **Jacob** 6: 11 continue in narrow way until ye obtain e. life; **Enos** 1: 3 Jacob² taught Enos² concerning e. life; **Mosiah** 26: 20 the Lord covenants with Alma¹ that he shall have e. life; **Alma** 19: 6 light of everlasting life lit up Lamoni's soul; 28: 14 great reason of rejoicing because of light of Christ unto life; **Hel.** 12: 26 (3 Ne. 26: 5) they who have done good shall have everlasting life; 14: 31 God has given unto man to choose life or death; **3 Ne.** 5: 13 Mormon² declares Christ's word, so that his people might have everlasting life; 15: 9 unto him who endures to end shall the Lord give e. life; **Ether** 3: 14 in Christ shall mankind have life; **Moro.** 7: 41 ye shall have hope, through atonement and resurrection, to be raised unto life e.

ETERNITY (see also Eternal; God, Eternal Nature of; Time)

Jacob 7: 18 Sherem speaks of e. and eternal punishment; **Mosiah** 3: 5 the Lord was and is from all e. to all e.; **Alma** 13: 7 high priesthood prepared from e. to all e.; 34: 33 this day of life given to prepare for e.; **Moro.** 8: 18 God is unchangeable from all e. to all e.

ETHEM—later Jaredite king

Ether 1: 8–9 son of Ahah, father of Moron; 11: 11, 14 executes judgment in wickedness; 11: 12 many prophets during E's reign.

ETHER—last great Jaredite prophet, record keeper

Ether 1: 2, 6 record on twenty-four gold plates called Book of E.; 1: 6 (11: 23) son of Coriantor; 12: 1–2 prophet in days of Coriantumr²; 12: 5 prophesies great and marvelous things; 13: 2 is rejected; 13: 4 speaks of Christ and New Jerusalem; 13: 13–14, 18 hides in cave, views destruction of Jaredites; 13: 20–22 calls Coriantumr² to repentance; 13: 21, 24 E's prophecies are fulfilled; 15: 1 E's words remembered by Coriantumr²; 15: 12–13 watches, but does not join others; 15: 33 finishes and hides record; 15: 34 last words.

EVE—mother of all living (see also Adam; Eden, Garden of; Parent; Woman; BD Eve)

1 Ne. 5: 11 brass plates give account of Adam and E.; **2 Ne.** 2: 15–20 tempted, partakes of forbidden fruit; **Alma** 42: 2, 7 cut off temporally and spiritually from presence of God.

EVERLASTING, EVERLASTINGLY (see also Endless; Eternal; Eternal Life; God, Eternal Nature of)

1 Ne. 14: 7 the Lord will do a work among men which will be e.; **Alma** 26: 15 Lamanites were encircled with e. darkness, but God has brought them into e. light; 37: 32 teach this people an e. hatred against sin and iniquity; **Hel.** 13: 38 ye have procrastinated day of salvation until e. too late; **Ether** 2: 10 e. decree of God that those who inhabit land must serve him or be swept off; **Moro.** 8: 17 charity is e. love.

EVIDENCE (see also Witness)

Alma 11: 2 judges judge according to law and e.; 30: 40 what e. have ye that there is no God; **Hel.** 5: 50 Lamanites are convinced because of greatness of e.; 8: 24 corrupt judges have rejected truth notwithstanding many e. they have received.

EVIL (see also Abomination; Agency; Bad; Carnal; Devil; Filthiness; Iniquity; Sin; Spirit, Evil; Transgression; Unclean; Wicked; Wrong)

2 Ne. 2: 5 (Hel. 14: 31; Moro. 7: 16) men are instructed sufficiently that they know good from e.; 2: 17 fallen angel became devil, having sought that which was e.; 2: 18 (Alma 12: 31) ye shall be as God, knowing good and e.; 2: 26 because men are redeemed from fall, they have

become free, knowing good from e.; 2: 29 not choose eternal death, according to will of flesh and e. therein; 15: 20 (Isa. 5: 20) wo unto them that call e. good, and good e.; **Jacob** 5: 37–38 trees in vineyard have brought forth e. fruit; 5: 59 because of the change of branches, the good may overcome the e.; **Omni** 1: 25 (Alma 5: 40; Moro. 7: 12, 17) that which is e. comes from devil; **Mosiah** 5: 2 (Alma 19: 33) the Spirit has wrought mighty change in Benjamin's people, that they have no more disposition to do e.; **Alma** 12: 31 through the fall, men are in position to act according to wills, whether to do e. or good; 29: 5 he who knows not good from e. is blameless; 29: 5 to him who knows good from e. is given according to his desires; 40: 13 spirits of wicked have no portion of Spirit, for they choose e. works rather than good; 41: 4–5 (Hel. 14: 31) e. works shall be restored unto men for e.; 41: 5 if man has desired e. all day long, he shall have reward of e. when night comes; 41: 7 those who repent and desire righteousness are their own judges, whether to do good or e.; 41: 13 word restoration means to bring back e. for e.; **Hel.** 12: 4 how e. and devilish are children of men; 15: 4 e. the Lord has hated Laman-ites because their deeds have been e. continually; **3 Ne.** 13: 12 (Matt. 6: 13) deliver us from e.; **Ether** 3: 2 because of fall, men's natures have become e. con-tinually; **Moro.** 7: 6 man being e. cannot do that which is good; 7: 8 if a man being e. gives a gift, he does it grudgingly; 7: 9 it is counted e. unto a man if he pray without real intent; 7: 17 whatsoever thing persuadeth men to do e. comes of devil; 7: 45 (1 Cor. 13: 5) charity thinketh no e.

EXALT, EXALTED (see also Raise; TG Exalt)

2 **Ne.** 12: 2 (Isa. 2: 2) mountain of the Lord's house shall be e. above the hills; 24: 13 (Isa. 14: 13) I will e. my throne above the stars.

EXAMPLE (see also Ensign; Follow; Light; Standard; TG Example)

1 **Ne.** 7: 8 Nephi[1] must set e. for elder brethren; 2 **Ne.** 31: 9 (3 Ne. 18: 16; Morm. 7: 10) Christ's baptism sets e.; 31: 16 unless a man endures to end in follow-ing the e. of the Son, he cannot be saved; **Jacob** 2: 35 (3: 10) Nephites have lost confidence of children because of bad e.; **Alma** 4: 11 e. of church leads unbelievers into iniquity; 17: 11 the Lord admonishes sons of Mosiah[2] to show good e. unto Lamanites; 39: 1 Shiblon has set good example for Corianton; 3 **Ne.** 18: 16 Christ has set e. for men.

EXCELLENT

Ether 12: 11 God prepared a more e. way; 12: 32 in Father's mansions, man may have more e. hope.

EXCOMMUNICATION (see also Blot; Cast; Cut)

3 **Ne.** 18: 31 he who repents not should not be numbered among the Lord's people.

EXCUSE

1 **Ne.** 19: 6 Nephi[1] does not e. him-self because of other men, but because of own weakness; **Jacob** 2: 23 Nephites seek to e. themselves in committing whoredoms because of David and Solomon; **Alma** 39: 4 Isabel stole away hearts of many, but this is no e. for Corianton; 42: 30 do not endeavor to e. yourself by denying justice of God.

EXECUTED (see also Capital Punishment)

Alma 2: 1 (1: 15) Nehor e. according to law; 11: 2 judge e. authority; 62: 9–10 king-men and many others who deny free-dom are e. according to law; **Hel.** 2: 12 Helaman[2] tries to take robbers, that they might be e.

EXERCISE (see Dominion; Faith; Power)

EXHORT, EXHORTATION (see also Entreat; Persuade; Preach; Urge; Warn)

1 **Ne.** 8: 37 Lehi[1] e. sons to hearken; 17: 15 Nephi[1] e. his brethren to faithful-ness; **Jarom** 1: 11 prophets e. people to diligence; **Omni** 1: 25 Amaleki[1] e. all men to come unto God; **Alma** 34: 40 Amulek e. Zoramites to have patience; **Hel.** 6: 4 Lamanites e. Nephites to faith and repentance; **Moro.** 10: 2 Moroni[2] speaks by way of e.; 10: 3 Moroni[2] e. readers to remember God's mercy; 10: 4 Moroni[2] e. readers to ask God whether writings are true.

EXPEDIENT

1 **Ne.** 17: 30 the Lord did for Israel-ites all things e. for man to receive; 2 **Ne.** 2: 27 all things are given unto men which are e.; **Moro.** 7: 33 (10: 23) if ye have faith in Christ, ye shall have power to do whatsoever is e. in him.

EXPERIMENT

Alma 32: 27, 33, 36 (34: 4) Alma[2] exhorts Zoramites to try e. to know whether seed is good.

EXPERT, EXPERTNESS (see also Skill)

Alma 10: 31 Zeezrom one of most e. lawyers in Ammonihah; 11: 21 Zeezrom e. in devices of devil; 18: 3 Lamoni's flocks cannot be scattered because of e.

of Ammon²; **Hel.** 2: 4 Gadianton is *e.* in many words; 3: 7 Nephites become *e.* in working of cement; **Ether** 8: 8 daughter of Jared² is exceedingly *e.*

EXPOUND (*see also* Preach; Teach)

Alma 18: 38 Ammon² *e.* all records and scriptures since time of Lehi¹; 22: 13 Aaron² *e.* all scriptures from creation of Adam; **3 Ne.** 23: 14 Christ *e.* all scriptures in one; 26: 3 Christ *e.* all things from creation to his coming in glory.

EXQUISITE

Alma 36: 21 nothing so *e.* and bitter as pains of Alma².

EXTINCT

Alma 36: 15 oh that I could become *e.* both soul and body; 45: 11 Nephites shall become *e.*; **Hel.** 11: 10 band of Gadianton have become *e.*; **3 Ne.** 3: 8 Giddianhi threatens to slay Nephites until they become *e.*

EYE (*see also* See; Sight)

1 Ne. 22: 23 churches built up to become popular in *e.* of world; **2 Ne.** 9: 44 Nephi¹ prays that God will view him with all-searching *e.*; 15: 21 (Isa. 5: 21) wo unto the wise in their own *e.*; 16: 10 (Isa. 6: 10) shut *e.* of this people, lest they see with their *e.*; 27: 12 book shall be hid from *e.* of world; 27: 29 (Isa. 29: 18) *e.* of blind shall see out of obscurity; **Jacob** 2: 10 Jacob² must tell Nephites of their wickedness under glance of piercing *e.* of God; **Mosiah** 12: 22 (15: 29; 16: 1; Alma 36: 26; 3 Ne. 16: 18; 20: 32; Isa. 52: 8) they shall see *e.* to *e.*; 18: 21 Alma¹ commands that there should be no contention, but that people look forward with one *e.*; 27: 22 priests pray that Alma² might receive strength, that *e.* of people might be opened to goodness of God; **Alma** 5: 15 (32: 40) look forward with *e.* of faith; **3 Ne.** 2: 2 Satan blinds people's *e.*; 12: 38 (Ex. 21: 24; Lev. 24: 20; Matt. 5: 38) it is written, an *e.* for an *e.*; 13: 22 (Matt. 6: 22) light of body is the *e.*; 14: 3 (Matt. 7: 3) why beholdest thou the mote in brother's *e.*, but not beam in own *e.*; 26: 15 Christ opens *e.* of the blind; 28: 8 three Nephites to be changed in twinkling of *e.*; **Morm.** 8: 15 plates to be brought to light with *e.* single to God's glory; **Ether** 12: 19 many see with their *e.* things which they behold with *e.* of faith.

EZIAS—*a prophet*

Hel. 8: 20 testified of Christ.

EZROM—*silver coin* (*see also* Coin)

Alma 11: 6, 12 as great as four senums.

FACE (*see also* Countenance; God, Presence of; Visage)

2 Ne. 9: 38 those who die in their sins shall return to God, see his *f.*; 23: 8 (Isa. 13: 8) men's *f.* shall be as flames; 33: 11 you and I shall stand *f.* to *f.* before Christ's bar; **Mosiah** 13: 5 Abinadi's *f.* shines as Moses on mount Sinai; **Hel.** 5: 36 *f.* of Nephi² and Lehi⁴ shine as *f.* of angels; **3 Ne.** 9: 11 the Lord destroys cities to hide their wickedness from before his *f.*; 13: 16 (Matt. 6: 16) when hypocrites fast, they disfigure their *f.*

FACULTY

1 Ne. 15: 25 Nephi¹ exhorts his brethren with all his *f.*; **Jacob** 3: 11 (Alma 32: 27) arouse the *f.* of your souls; **W of M** 1: 18 by laboring with *f.* of his whole soul, Benjamin establishes peace.

FAIL

Alma 4: 15 Spirit of the Lord does not *f.* Alma²; **Moro.** 7: 46 charity never *f.*

FAINT (*see also* Continue; Endure)

2 Ne. 32: 9 (Luke 18: 1) ye must pray always, and not *f.*

FAIR (*see also* Beauty; Delightsome)

1 Ne. 11: 13, 15 virgin is exceedingly *f.*; 13: 15 Gentiles who obtain land will be exceedingly *f.*; **3 Ne.** 2: 16 young men and daughters of Lamanites become exceedingly *f.*; **4 Ne.** 1: 10 Nephites become exceedingly *f.* people; **Morm.** 9: 6 cry unto Father that ye may be found *f.*

FAITH (*see also* Baptism; Belief; Born of God; Confidence; Doubt; Faithful; Forgive, Forgiveness; Gospel; Hope; Knowledge; Miracle; Obedience; Prayer; Religion; Repentance; Salvation; Sanctification; Sign; Testimony; Trial; Trust; TG Faith; BD Faith)

1 Ne. 7: 12 the Lord is able to do all things for men if they exercise *f.* in him; 10: 17 Lehi¹ received Holy Ghost by *f.* on the Son; 12: 10 because of *f.* in the Lamb, apostles' garments are made white; 16: 28 pointers in Liahona work according to *f.*; **2 Ne.** 1: 10 power given to do all things by *f.*; 9: 23 men are commanded to be baptized, having *f.* in the Holy One; 25: 25 Nephites made alive in Christ because of *f.*; 26: 13 (27: 23; Ether 12: 12; Moro. 7: 27–29, 34–38) Christ works miracles according to men's *f.*; 31: 19 ye have not come thus far save by word of Christ with unshaken *f.* in him; **Jacob** 4: 6 our *f.* becomes unshaken; **Enos** 1: 8 sins forgiven because of *f.* in Christ; **Jarom** 1: 4

as many as have *f.* have communion with Holy Spirit; 1: 4 Holy Spirit makes manifest among men according to their *f.*; **Mosiah** 3: 9, 12 (Moro. 7: 26, 38) salvation comes through *f.* on Christ's name; 5: 4 *f.* on things spoken by Benjamin brings his people to knowledge; 5: 7 hearts of Benjamin's people are changed through *f.* on the Lord's name; 21: 30 Alma¹ and his people form church through *f.* on Abinadi's words; 25: 15 (Alma 37: 33) preach repentance and *f.* on the Lord; 26: 15 Alma¹ is blessed because of *f.* in words of Abinadi; 27: 14 the Lord hears prayers of Alma¹ because of his *f.*; **Alma** 1: 24–25 withdrawal of many from church is great trial to those who stand fast in the *f.*; 2: 30 being exercised with much *f.*, Alma² cries unto the Lord to preserve his people; 7: 6 look forward for remission of your sins with everlasting *f.*; 14: 26 give us strength according to our *f.* in Christ; 15: 10 heal this man according to his *f.* in Christ; 18: 35 Spirit gives knowledge and power according to *f.*; 22: 16 if thou wilt call on God's name in *f.*, thou shalt receive the hope thou desirest; 26: 22 unto him who exercises *f.* is given to know mysteries; 32: 18 (Ether 3: 19) if a man knows a thing, he has no cause to have *f.*; 32: 21 *f.* is not a perfect knowledge; 32: 21 (Ether 12: 6) *f.* is hope for things which are not seen; 32: 36 (34: 4) exercise your *f.* to plant the seed; 32: 40 if ye will not nourish the word, looking forward with eye of *f.* to fruit, ye can never pluck fruit of tree of life; 33: 23 as word begins to swell, nourish it by *f.*; 44: 5 Nephites gain power over Lamanites by *f.*; 48: 13 Moroni¹ is firm in *f.* of Christ; 48: 15–16 *f.* that God will prosper Nephites if they fight only in defense; 57: 26–27 stripling warriors spared because of *f.* in what they had been taught; 61: 17 Nephites march against dissenters in strength of God, according to *f.*; **Hel.** 5: 47 peace be unto you because of *f.* in Well Beloved; 8: 15 those who look upon Son with *f.* will have life eternal; 13: 6 nothing can save Nephites from destruction save repentance and *f.* on Christ; 3 **Ne.** 7: 18 so great is *f.* of Nephi³ that angels minister unto him daily; 13: 30 (Matt. 6: 30) even so will God clothe you, if ye are not of little *f.*; 17: 8 your *f.* is sufficient that I should heal you; 19: 35 so great *f.* have I never seen among all the Jews; 26: 9 Lamanites to have record to try their *f.*; 26: 11 Nephi³ is commanded not to write all from plates of Nephi, in order to try people's *f.*; 27: 19 none enter the Lord's rest save those who wash garments in Christ's blood because of *f.*; **Morm.** 9: 37 may the Lord grant that prayers be answered according to *f.*; **Ether** 3: 19

brother of Jared² has *f.* no longer, because he knows; 4: 7 when Gentiles exercise *f.* in the Lord, they may become sanctified; 12: 4 hope comes of *f.*; 12: 6 receive no witness until after trial of *f.*; 12: 7 by *f.* Christ showed himself; 12: 10 by *f.* were they of old called after holy order; 12: 11 by *f.* was law of Moses given; 12: 12 without *f.* among men, God can do no miracle among them; 12: 14–15 *f.* of missionaries caused change among Lamanites; 12: 28 *f.*, hope, charity bring men unto the Lord; 12: 30 the Lord works after men have *f.*; **Moro.** 3: 3 remission of sins comes through Christ, by endurance of *f.* on his name; 6: 4 Christ is author and finisher of *f.*; ch. 7 letter of Mormon² on *f.*, hope, charity; 7: 26 by *f.* men become sons of God; 7: 26 whatsoever ye ask in *f.*, believing that ye shall receive, it shall be done; 7: 33 (10: 23) if ye have *f.* in Christ, ye shall have power to do whatsoever is expedient in him; 7: 41 hope to be raised unto life eternal because of *f.* in Christ; 7: 42 without *f.* there cannot be any hope; 7: 43 man cannot have *f.* and hope save he shall be meek; 10: 4 if ye ask with *f.* in Christ, God will manifest truth unto you.

FAITHFUL, FAITHFULNESS (*see also* Diligence; Faith; Obedience; Righteousness; Steadfast; Work [noun]; Worthy; Zeal)

1 **Ne.** 3: 16 let us be *f.* in keeping the Lord's commandments; 2 **Ne.** 6: 11 many shall not be suffered to perish, because of prayers of the *f.*; 21: 5 (30: 11; Isa. 11: 5) *f.* shall be the girdle of his reins; 26: 15 prayers of the *f.* shall be heard; **Mosiah** 2: 41 if the righteous hold out *f.* to end, they are received into heaven; 10: 13 Nephi¹ is favored of the Lord because more *f.* in keeping commandments; **Alma** 5: 13 fathers saved because they were *f.* until end; 3 **Ne.** 27: 19 garments washed in Christ's blood because of *f.* unto end; **Ether** 4: 19 he who is found *f.* unto the Lord's name shall dwell in kingdom.

FALL, FELL, FALLEN (*see also* Apostasy; Descend; Fall of Man; Tumble)

1 **Ne.** 12: 7 Holy Ghost *f.* upon twelve apostles; 22: 13 sword of abominable church shall *f.* upon own heads; 22: 14 those who fight against Zion shall *f.* into pit digged to ensnare the Lord's people; 2 **Ne.** 2: 17 (24: 12; Luke 10: 18; Isa. 14: 12) angel had *f.* from heaven; **Hel.** 13: 5 (3 Ne. 20: 20) within four hundred years sword of justice shall *f.* upon this people; 3 **Ne.** 11: 12, 17 when Jesus had spoken these words, multitude *f.* to earth; 14: 24–27 (18: 13; Matt. 7: 24–27) house built upon sand *f.*; 19: 13

Holy Ghost *f.* upon Nephite disciples; **Ether** 3: 6 brother of Jared² *f.* down before the Lord; **Moro.** 2: 3 Holy Ghost *f.* on those on whom disciples laid hands.

FALL OF MAN (*see also* Adam; Carnal; Death, Physical; Death, Spiritual; Fruit, Forbidden; Jesus Christ, Atonement through; Nature, Natural; Resurrection; Sin; Transgression; TG Fall of Man; BD Fall of Adam)

 1 **Ne.** 10: 6 all mankind were in a lost and fallen state; **2 Ne.** 2: 4 the way is prepared from the *f.* of man; 2: 19 after partaking of forbidden fruit, Adam and Eve were driven from Eden; 2: 25 Adam fell that men might be; 9: 6 resurrection must come unto man by reason of the *f.*; 9: 6 the *f.* came by reason of transgression; **Mosiah** 3: 11 Christ's blood atones for sins of those who have fallen by transgression of Adam; 3: 16 in Adam, or by nature, children *f.*; 3: 19 natural man has been enemy to God since *f.* of Adam; 4: 5 knowledge of God's goodness awakens men to sense of fallen state; 4: 7 atonement prepared for all mankind since *f.* of Adam; 16: 3 *f.* caused by serpent's beguiling of first parents; 16: 4 mankind would have been endlessly lost, had not God redeemed his people from lost and fallen state; **Alma** 12: 22 by Adam's *f.* all mankind become lost and fallen; 18: 36 Ammon² teaches Lamoni many things concerning *f.* of man; 22: 13 Aaron³ expounds scriptures, laying *f.* of man before Lamanite king; 22: 14 since man had fallen, he could not merit anything of himself; 34: 9 all mankind are fallen and lost; 42: 6–7 first parents become fallen man, cut off temporally and spiritually; 42: 9 the *f.* brought upon mankind spiritual death as well as temporal; **Hel.** 14: 16 mankind, being cut off from presence of the Lord by *f.* of Adam, are dead as to things spiritual and temporal; **Morm.** 9: 12 by Adam came the *f.* of man; **Ether** 3: 2 because of the *f.* our natures have become evil continually.

FALLEN (*see* Fall, Fell, Fallen; Fall of Man)

FALSE, FALSEHOOD (*see also* Christs, False; Churches, False; Deceit; Doctrine, False; Incorrect; Lying; Prophets, False; Wrong)

 2 **Ne.** 25: 18 no other Messiah shall come, save *f.* Messiah; **Mosiah** 13: 23 (Ex. 20: 16; Hel. 7: 21) thou shalt not bear *f.* witness; **3 Ne.** 24: 5 (Mal. 3: 5) the Lord will be swift witness against *f.* swearers.

FALSE CHRISTS (*see* Christs, False)

FALSE DOCTRINE (*see* Doctrine, False)

FALSE PRIESTHOODS (*see* Priestcraft; TG False Priesthoods)

FALSE PROPHETS (*see* Prophets, False)

FAMILIAR (*see also* Spirit, Evil)

 2 **Ne.** 18: 19 (Isa. 8: 19) they shall say, Seek unto them that have *f.* spirits; 26: 16 (Isa. 29: 4) voice shall be as one that hath a *f.* spirit; **Jacob** 2: 17 be *f.* with all.

FAMILY (*see also* Brother; Child; Daughter; Father; Household; Husband; Mother; Sister; Son; Wife; TG Family, Children, Duties of; Family, Children, Responsibilities toward; Family, Eternal; Family, Love within; Family, Patriarchal; BD Family)

 1 **Ne.** 2: 2 the Lord commands Lehi¹ to take his *f.* and depart into wilderness; **2 Ne.** 2: 20 Adam and Eve have brought forth the *f.* of all the earth; **Alma** 43: 47 ye shall defend your *f.* even unto bloodshed; **3 Ne.** 7: 14 tribes organized according to *f.*; 18: 21 pray in your *f.*; **Morm.** 3: 20 every soul who belongs to human *f.* shall stand before judgment-seat; **Ether** 1: 41 Jared² and friends to gather their *f.*

FAMINE (*see also* Destruction; Hunger; Rain)

 2 **Ne.** 1: 18 (Mosiah 1: 17) because of hardness of hearts, Nephites may be visited by *f.*; 6: 15 they who believe not on Messiah shall be destroyed by *f.*; 24: 30 (Isa. 14: 30) I will kill thy root with *f.*; **Mosiah** 9: 3 Zeniff's people smitten with *f.*; **Alma** 9: 22 the Lord has saved Israel from *f.*; 10: 22 if it were not for prayers of righteous, ye would be visited now by *f.*; 53: 7 Moroni¹ delivers women and children from *f.*; 62: 35, 39 war between Nephites and Lamanites causes much *f.*; **Hel.** 10: 6 Nephi² is given power to smite earth with *f.*; 11: 4 let there be *f.* in land to stir people up in remembrance of the Lord; 13: 9 four hundred years will not pass away before the Lord visits Nephites with *f.*; **Ether** 9: 28 great *f.* to destroy people if they do not repent; 9: 30 great dearth upon the land.

FAR

 2 **Ne.** 27: 25 (Isa. 29: 13) this people draw near the Lord with lips, but remove hearts *f.* from him; **Mosiah** 5: 13 how knoweth a man the stranger who is *f.* from thoughts of heart.

FAST (*see also* Faster; Fasting; Firmness; Steadfast)

 1 **Ne.** 8: 30 many hold *f.* to rod of iron; **Alma** 1: 24–25 withdrawal of some

is great trial to those that stand *f.* in the faith.

FASTER (*see also* Swift)

Mosiah 4: 27 not requisite that man run *f.* than he has strength.

FASTING, FAST (*see also* Humble; Prayer; TG Fasting; BD Fasts)

Omni 1: 26 (4 Ne. 1: 12) continue in *f.* and prayer; **Mosiah** 27: 22 priests *f.* and pray for Alma²; **Alma** 5: 46 Alma² has *f.* and prayed many days to know things of himself; 6: 6 children of God are commanded to gather together oft and join in *f.* and prayer; 17: 3, 9 sons of Mosiah² had given themselves to much *f.* and prayer to obtain Spirit; 45: 1 Nephites *f.* much and pray much; **Hel.** 3: 34–35 humble part of people *f.* and pray oft; **3 Ne.** 13: 16–18 (Matt. 6: 16–18) when ye *f.*, be not as hypocrites, but appear not unto men to *f.*; 27: 1 disciples unite in mighty prayer and *f.*

FATHER (*see also* Abraham; Family; Forefathers; God the Father; Husband; Mother; Parent; Son; TG Honoring Father and Mother; Marriage, Fatherhood; Fatherhood)

1 Ne. 1: 1 Nephi¹ is taught in learning of his *f.*; 15: 18 the Lord made covenant with *f.* Abraham; 17: 55 (Mosiah 13: 20; Ex. 20: 12) honor thy *f.* and thy mother; 21: 23 (2 Ne. 6: 7; 10: 9; Isa. 49: 23) kings shall be Israel's nursing *f.*; 2 Ne. 2: 18 (9: 9; Ether 8: 25) devil is *f.* of all lies; 8: 2 look unto Abraham, your *f.*; 24: 21 (Isa. 14: 21) prepare slaughter for the Lord's children for iniquities of their *f.*; **Enos** 1: 1 Enos knows his *f.* is just man; **Mosiah** 13: 13 (Ex. 20: 5) the Lord visits iniquities of *f.* upon children; **Alma** 28: 5 cries heard of *f.* mourning for sons, brother for *f.*; 3 Ne. 11: 29 devil is *f.* of contention; 25: 6 (Mal. 4: 6; D&C 110: 15; JS-H 1: 39) the Lord will turn hearts of *f.* to children and hearts of children to *f.*; **Moro.** 9: 8 Lamanites kill husbands and *f.* and feed flesh to wives and children.

FATHERLESS (*see* Orphan)

FAULT (*see also* Transgression; Weak, Weakness)

Alma 39: 13 acknowledge your *f.*; 3 Ne. 1: 25 those who had ceased practicing law of Moses confess their *f.*; **Morm.** 8: 17 if there be *f.* in record, they be *f.* of man.

FAVORED (*see also* Blessing; Please)

1 Ne. 1: 1 Nephi¹ highly *f.* of the Lord; 17: 35 he who is righteous is *f.* of God; 2 Ne. 1: 19 O that ye might be a choice and *f.* people of the Lord; **Alma** 9: 20 Nephites have been *f.* above every other nation; **Ether** 1: 34 brother of Jared² a man highly *f.* of the Lord.

FEAR, FEARFUL (*see also* Anxiety; Courage; Fear of God; Quake; Shake; Terror; Tremble; Worry)

2 Ne. 8: 7 (Isa. 51: 7) *f.* not the reproach of men; **Jacob** 7: 19 Sherem *f.* he has committed unpardonable sin; **Alma** 1: 18 many durst not steal for *f.* of law; 14: 26 inhabitants of Ammonihah flee, for *f.* of destruction; **Morm.** 6: 7 awful *f.* of death fills breasts of the wicked; **Moro.** 8: 16 *f.* not what man can do; 8: 16 perfect love casteth out *f.*

FEAR OF GOD (*see also* Obedience; Worship; TG Fear of God)

2 Ne. 12: 10 (Isa. 2: 10) *f.* of the Lord shall smite the wicked; 21: 1–2 (Isa. 11: 1–2) spirit of knowledge and *f.* of the Lord shall rest upon branch from Jesse's roots; 27: 34 children of Jacob¹ shall *f.* God of Israel; **Enos** 1: 23 prophecies of war and destruction keep Nephites in *f.* of the Lord; **Mosiah** 4: 1 Benjamin's people fall to earth, for *f.* of the Lord; 29: 30 Nephites are commanded to handle judicial matters in *f.* of the Lord; **Alma** 19: 15 *f.* of the Lord comes upon Lamoni's household; 36: 7 Alma² and sons of Mosiah² fell to earth, for *f.* of the Lord came upon them; 39: 12 Alma² commands Corianton, in *f.* of the Lord, to refrain from iniquities; 60: 28 Moroni¹ does not *f.* civil authority but he *f.* God; 3 Ne. 4: 10 Nephites do not *f.* robbers, but they *f.* God; 25: 2 unto those who *f.* the Lord's name will Son of Righteousness arise with healing in wings; **Morm.** 9: 27 work out your salvation with *f.* and trembling before the Lord; **Ether** 3: 6 brother of Jared is struck with *f.* when he sees the Lord's finger.

FEAST (*see also* Partake)

2 Ne. 9: 51 *f.* upon that which perisheth not; 31: 20 (32: 3) press forward, *f.* upon word of Christ; **Jacob** 2: 9 those who have been wounded have daggers to pierce their souls, instead of *f.* upon word of God; 3: 2 *f.* upon God's love.

FEED (*see also* Eat; Food; Nourish)

2 Ne. 21: 7 (30: 13: Isa. 11: 7) cow and bear shall *f.*; **Jacob** 2: 19 seek riches for intent to do good—to *f.* the hungry; **Mosiah** 4: 26 to retain remission of sins, men must impart of substance, *f.* the hungry; **Alma** 4: 13 some Nephites *f.* the hungry; 3 Ne. 13: 26 (Matt. 6: 26) Father *f.* fowls of the air; **Moro.** 9: 8 Lamanites *f.* women upon flesh of husbands.

FEEL, FELT (*see also* Feeling; Touch)

1 Ne. 17: 45 Laman[1] and Lemuel cannot *f.* words of still small voice; **Alma** 5: 26 if ye have *f.* to sing song of redeeming love, can ye *f.* so now; 26: 16 Ammon[2] cannot say smallest part which he *f.*; 32: 28 when ye *f.* swelling motions, ye will say seed is good; **3 Ne.** 8: 20 inhabitants of land can *f.* vapor of darkness; 11: 14–15 (18: 25) multitude *f.* prints of nails in Christ's hands.

FEELING (*see also* Feel; Passion)

1 Ne. 8: 37 Lehi[1] exhorts Laman[1] and Lemuel with *f.* of tender parent; 17: 45 (Moro. 9: 20) Laman[1] and Lemuel are past *f.*, cannot feel words of still small voice; **2 Ne.** 4: 12 Lehi[1] speaks according to *f.* of heart; **Jacob** 2: 7 *f.* of wives and children are tender and chaste.

FEET (*see* Foot, Feet)

FELL (*see* Fall, Fell, Fallen)

FELLOWSHIP (*see also* TG Brotherhood and Sisterhood; Fellowship; Fellowshipping)

Hel. 6: 3 Nephites and Lamanites *f.* one with another.

FELT (*see* Feel, Felt)

FEMALE (*see also* Woman)

1 Ne. 8: 27 spacious building filled with people, both male and *f.*; **2 Ne.** 10: 16 those who fight against Zion, both male and *f.*, shall perish; 26: 33 the Lord denies none who come unto him, male and *f.*; **Alma** 1: 30 Nephites are liberal to all, both male and *f.*; 11: 44 restoration shall come to all, both male and *f.*; **Ether** 1: 41 (2: 1) Jaredites gather flocks, both male and *f.*

FEROCIOUS (*see also* Fury; Wild)

Enos 1: 20 (Mosiah 10: 12) Lamanites led by evil nature to become *f.*; **Mosiah** 17: 17 people of Noah[3] shall be driven, even as wild flock is driven by *f.* beasts; **Alma** 17: 14 sons of Mosiah[2] preach to hardened and *f.* people; 47: 36 dissenters become more wicked and *f.* than Lamanites; **Hel.** 3: 16 Nephites are no more called Nephites, becoming wicked and *f.*

FERVENT (*see* Heat)

FEVER (*see also* Disease; Sick)

Alma 15: 3, 5 Zeezrom sick with *f.*; 46: 40 God prepares plants and roots to treat *f.*

FEW (*see also* Scarce)

1 Ne. 14: 12 numbers of church of Lamb were *f.*; 17: 43 *f.* Jews not destroyed

shall be led into captivity; **2 Ne.** 28: 14 latter-day churches are all gone astray, save a *f.*; **Alma** 21: 12 *f.* believe on words of missionaries; 33: 19–26 *f.* understood prophecies and types of Christ; **3 Ne.** 7: 7 *f.* righteous men among Nephites; 7: 21 *f.* are converted unto the Lord; 14: 14 (27: 33; Matt. 7: 14) narrow is the way, and *f.* that find it; **Morm.** 8: 36 none save a *f.* who do not lift themselves up in pride.

FIELD

1 Ne. 8: 9, 20 Lehi[1] beholds large *f.* in dream; **2 Ne.** 27: 28 Lebanon to be turned into fruitful *f.*; **Alma** 26: 5 *f.* was ripe and missionaries thrust in sickle; 33: 5 God was merciful when Alma[2] cried unto him in *f.*; 34: 20, 24–25 cry unto God in your *f.*

FIERCENESS (*see* Wrath)

FIERY (*see* Dart; Fire; Furnace; Serpent)

FIG (*see also* Tree; BD Fig Tree)

3 Ne. 14: 16 (Matt. 7: 16) do men gather *f.* of thistles.

FIGHT, FOUGHT (*see also* Battle; Persecution; Struggle; War)

1 Ne. 11: 34–35 (14: 13) multitudes of earth shall *f.* against apostles; 11: 36 (2 Ne. 10: 16) those who *f.* against apostles shall be destroyed; 22: 14, 19 (2 Ne. 6: 13; 10: 13–16) all who *f.* against Zion shall be destroyed; **2 Ne.** 6: 12 blessed are Gentiles if they *f.* not against Zion; 25: 14 wo unto them who *f.* against God and his church; 27: 3 (Isa. 29: 8) all who *f.* against Zion shall be as dream of night vision; 29: 14 the Lord will show unto them who *f.* against Zion that he is God; **Mosiah** 4: 14 ye will not suffer your children to *f.* one with another; 20: 11 people of Limhi *f.* for their lives; **Alma** 23: 7 Lamanites do not *f.* against God any more; 43: 45 Nephites inspired by better cause *f.* for homes and families; 51: 21 those who profess nobility are brought to *f.* for freedom; 53: 17 sons of Ammonites enter covenant to *f.* for liberty of Nephites; 56: 56 sons of Ammonites *f.* with strength of God.

FILL (*see also* Full)

1 Ne. 1: 12 as Lehi[1] reads book, he is *f.* with Spirit; 14: 3 pit shall be *f.* by those who digged it; **Mosiah** 2: 4 by keeping commandments, Nephites might be *f.* with love toward God and men; **Alma** 8: 30 Alma[2] and Amulek are *f.* with Holy Ghost; 38: 12 bridle passions, that ye may be *f.* with love; **3 Ne.** 12: 6 (Matt. 5: 6) blessed are those who hunger and thirst after righteousness, for they shall be *f.* with Holy Ghost; 18: 5, 9 when

multitude has partaken of bread and wine, they are f.; 19: 13 those baptized are f. with Holy Ghost and fire; 20: 9 when multitude has partaken of bread and wine, they are f. with Spirit; 27: 16 whoso repents and is baptized shall be f.; **Moro.** 7: 47–48 pray unto Father that ye may be f. with pure love of Christ; 8: 26 Comforter f. with hope and perfect love.

FILTHINESS, FILTHY (see also Corrupt; Defile; Evil; Pollute; Spot; Stain; Unclean; Wicked)

1 Ne. 12: 16 (15: 27) Nephi[1] sees fountain of f. water in vision; 12: 23 (Enos 1: 20) Lamanites to become f. people; 15: 33–34 (Alma 7: 21) kingdom of God is not f.; **2 Ne.** 9: 16 (Morm. 9: 14) they who are f. shall be f. still; **Jacob** 3: 3 land to be cursed for sake of those who are f. before God; 3: 3, 5 Lamanites are not f. like Nephites; 3: 5 Nephites hate Lamanites because of their f.; **Mosiah** 7: 29 if the Lord's people sow f., they shall reap chaff in whirlwind; **Alma** 5: 22 how will you feel to stand before bar of God with garments stained in f.; 7: 21 no f. can be received into kingdom of God; 32: 3 the poor are esteemed as f. by Zoramites; **Morm.** 5: 15 descendants of Lehites shall become f. people.

FINAL (see also End; Last)

1 Ne. 15: 35 f. state of men's souls is to dwell in kingdom of God or to be cast out; **Mosiah** 2: 38–39 f. doom of those who repent not is to endure never-ending torment; **Alma** 34: 35 f. state of the wicked is that devil has all power over them.

FIND, FOUND (see also Blameless; Spotless; Unclean)

1 Ne. 10: 19 (3 Ne. 14: 7; Matt. 7: 7) he who diligently seeks shall f.; **Jacob** 4: 8 impossible that man should f. out all the Lord's ways; **Mosiah** 5: 8–9 whosoever enters covenant with God and is obedient shall be f. at his right hand; **Alma** 32: 13 whosoever repents shall f. mercy; **3 Ne.** 14: 14 (27: 33; Matt. 7: 14) narrow is the way, and few that f. it; **Moro.** 6: 7 whoso is f. to commit iniquity is brought before elders.

FINGER

Alma 10: 2 writing on wall of temple written by f. of God; **Ether** 3: 6–9, 19 (12: 20–21) brother of Jared sees f. of the Lord.

FINISH (see also End; Finisher)

Alma 14: 13 work of Alma[2] and Amulek is not f.

FINISHER

Moro. 6: 4 Christ is author and f. of believers' faith.

FIRE (see also Born of God; Burn; Cleanse; Destruction; Flame; Furnace; Hell; Holy Ghost, Baptism of; Purify; Remission; TG Earth, Cleansing of; Fire, Baptism of; Holy Ghost, Baptism of; BD Fire)

1 Ne. 1: 6 pillar of f. comes down and dwells on rock before Lehi[1]; 15: 30 brightness of God's justice is like brightness of f.; **2 Ne.** 6: 15 they who believe not in Messiah shall be destroyed by f.; 9: 16 (Mosiah 26: 27) the filthy shall go away into everlasting f.; 9: 16, 19 (28: 23); Jacob 3: 11; 6: 10; Mosiah 3: 27; Alma 12: 17; 14: 14) lake of f. and brimstone; 15: 24 (Isa. 5: 24) as f. devoureth stubble, root of the wicked shall be rottenness; 19: 18 (Isa. 9: 18) wickedness burneth as the f.; 20: 17 (Isa. 10: 17) light of Israel shall be for a f.; 30: 10 the Lord will spare his people even if he must destroy the wicked by f.; 31: 13–14 (3 Ne. 9: 20; 12: 1; 19: 13; Ether 12: 14) baptism of f.; Jacob 5: 26, 37, 42, 45–47, 49, 58, 66 branches that do not bring forth good fruit are cast into f.; 5: 77 the Lord will cause vineyard to be burned with f.; 6: 3 world shall be burned with f.; **Mosiah** 2: 38 (Morm. 9: 5) awareness of guilt fills the breast with anguish like unquenchable f.; 19: 20 Noah[3] suffers death by f.; **Alma** 5: 35, 52 those who bring forth works of righteousness shall not be cast into f.; 25: 5 Amulonites cause many believing Lamanites to perish by f.; **Hel.** 5: 23 Nephi[2] and Lehi[4] encircled as by flaming f.; 13: 13 (3 Ne. 9: 11) except for the righteous in city, the Lord would destroy it by f.; **3 Ne.** 12: 22 (Matt. 5: 22) whosoever shall say to his brother, Thou fool, shall be in danger of hell f.; 24: 2 (Mal. 3: 2) he is like a refiners' f.; 27: 11 those who build church on works of men or devil will be cast into f.; 27: 17 he who endures not to end shall be cast into f.; **4 Ne.** 1: 32 disciples cast into furnaces of f.; **Morm.** 8: 17 he who condemns shall be in danger of hell f.; 9: 5 when ye are brought to see your nakedness before glory of God, it will kindle unquenchable f. in you.

FIRMNESS, FIRM, FIRMER (see also Endure; Fast; Fixed; Immoveable; Steadfast; Unshaken)

1 Ne. 2: 10 Lehi[1] admonishes Lemuel to be f. like valley; **Jacob** 3: 1 look unto God with f. of mind; 3: 2 if minds are f., ye may feast upon God's love forever; 4: 18 Jacob[2] will unfold mysteries if not shaken from f. in spirit; **Alma** 24: 19 when Lamanites were brought to believe truth, they were f.; 27: 27 Ammonites

are *f.* in faith of Christ; 34: 41 bear with afflictions with *f.* hope that ye shall one day rest from afflictions; 48: 13 Moroni[1] is *f.* in faith of Christ; 57: 27 minds of Ammonites are *f.*; **Hel.** 3: 35 more humble part of people wax *f.* and *f.* in faith of Christ; 6: 1 Lamanites' righteousness exceeds that of Nephites because of *f.*; 7: 7 earlier Nephites were *f.* to keep commandments; 15: 7–8 those who come to change of heart are *f.* in faith; 15: 10 because of Lamanites' *f.*, God will bless them; **3 Ne.** 6: 14 church broken up, except for a few Lamanites who are *f.*; **Morm.** 2: 25 Nephite army stands before Lamanite army with *f.*; 9: 28 ask with *f.* unshaken that ye will yield to no temptation; **Moro.** 7: 30 miracles and angels show themselves unto them of strong faith and *f.* mind.

FIRST (*see also* Death, Spiritual; Firstborn; Fruit; Resurrection)

1 Ne. 5: 11 (Mosiah 16: 3) Adam and Eve our *f.* parents; 13: 42 (Ether 13: 12) last shall be *f.* and *f.* shall be last; 20: 12 (Isa. 48: 12) I am the *f.* and I am the last; **2 Ne.** 1: 29 if brethren of Nephi[1] do not hearken unto him, Lehi[1] will take *f.* blessing and give it to him; **Jacob** 1: 17 Jacob[2] *f.* obtains errand from the Lord before teaching; 5: 63 (Ether 13: 12) begin at the last, that they may be *f.*, and the *f.* may be last; **Alma** 11: 38–39 Son is the *f.* and the last; 12: 36 hardheartedness provokes the Lord to send down destruction, unto the last death as well as the *f.*; 43: 46 if not guilty of *f.* or second offense, ye shall not suffer yourselves to be slain by enemies; **3 Ne.** 13: 33 (Matt. 6: 33) seek ye *f.* the kingdom of God; 20: 26 the Father raised Christ up unto men *f.*; **Ether** 12: 18 men *f.* believe in the Son, then work miracles.

FIRSTBORN (*see also* Firstling; BD Firstborn)

2 Ne. 2: 1 Jacob[2], my *f.* in days of tribulation; 4: 3 Lehi[1] speaks to children of his *f.* Laman[1].

FIRST-FRUITS (*see* Fruit)

FISH (*see also* Animal; Whale)

3 Ne. 14: 9–10 (Matt. 7: 10) if son ask a *f.*, what man will give him a serpent; **Ether** 2: 2 Jaredites carry *f.* with them in vessel.

FIXED (*see also* Firmness)

Enos 1: 20 Lamanites' hatred is *f.*; **Alma** 47: 6 disobedient Lamanites are *f.* in their minds with a determination not to go against Nephites; 58: 12 small Nephite force is *f.* with determination to conquer enemies.

FLAME (*see also* Fire; Sword)

2 Ne. 20: 17 (Isa. 10: 17) Holy One shall be for a *f.*; 23: 8 (Isa. 13: 8) their faces shall be as *f.*; **Jacob** 6: 10 (Mosiah 3: 27) lake of fire and brimstone, whose *f.* are unquenchable; **Mosiah** 2: 38 sense of guilt fills breast with anguish, whose *f.* ascends forever; **Morm.** 9: 5 to see our nakedness before glory of God will kindle a *f.* of unquenchable fire.

FLATTER, FLATTERING, FLATTERY (*see also* Deceit; Hypocrisy; Lying)

2 Ne. 28: 22 devil *f.* men that there is no hell; **Jacob** 7: 4 Sherem uses much *f.*; **Mosiah** 11: 7 people deceived by *f.* and vain words of Noah[3] and priests; 26: 6 unbelievers deceive many with *f.* words; 27: 8 Alma[2] and sons of Mosiah[2] speak *f.* to lead people into iniquity; **Alma** 17: 31 Ammon[2] *f.* fellow-servants by his words; 30: 47 better that Korihor's soul be lost than that he bring down many to destruction by *f.* words; 46: 7 many in church believe *f.* words of Amalickiah; 61: 4 those who seek judgment-seat use much *f.* to lead away hearts; **3 Ne.** 7: 12 Jacob[4] *f.* dissenters that many would join his band.

FLEE (*see* Flight)

FLESH (*see also* Body; Carnal; Man; Mankind; Mortal; Nature, Natural; Sacrament; Sensual; Temporal; Word; TG Flesh; Flesh and Blood; Trust Not in the Arm of Flesh; BD Flesh)

1 Ne. 17: 35 the Lord esteems all *f.* in one; 22: 18 destruction comes unto men according to *f.* if they harden hearts; 22: 22 kingdom of devil established among them which are in the *f.*; 22: 23 all who seek lusts of the *f.* shall be brought low; **2 Ne.** 2: 5 by law no *f.* is justified; 2: 27 men are free according to the *f.* to choose life or death; 4: 17 my heart sorrows because of my *f.*; 4: 34 I will not put trust in arm of *f.*; 9: 4–7 *f.* must waste away and die; 9: 53 Nephites' seed shall not be utterly destroyed according to the *f.*; 10: 24 reconcile yourselves to will of God and not to will of devil and the *f.*; 28: 31 cursed is he who makes *f.* his arm; **Jacob** 2: 21 pride is abominable unto him who created all *f.*; **Mosiah** 7: 27 (Ether 3: 6, 8–9) God will take upon him *f.* and blood; 15: 2–3 because the Lord dwells in *f.*, he shall be called the Son; 15: 2 the Son shall subject the *f.* to will of Father; 23: 7 ye shall not esteem one *f.* above another; **Alma** 7: 13 Son suffers according to the *f.*; **3 Ne.** 18: 28–30 whoso eats and drinks Christ's *f.* and blood unworthily eats and drinks damnation to soul; 28: 15, 39 three Nephites are sanctified in *f.*, transfigured

from body of *f.* into immortal state; **Ether** 15: 34 it matters not whether Ether is translated or suffers will of the Lord in *f.*; **Moro.** ch. 4–5 manner of administering Christ's *f.* and blood to church; 9: 8 Nephite women are fed *f.* of husbands.

FLIGHT, FLEE, FLED (*see also* Depart; Escape; Journey; Leave)

1 **Ne.** 4: 36 sons of Lehi¹ do not want Jews to know of *f.*; 2 **Ne.** 1: 3 the Lord has been merciful in warning Lehites to *f.* Jerusalem; **Mosiah** 20: 12 speedy *f.* of Limhi's people; **Alma** 50: 33 Moroni¹ sends army to head *f.* of people of Morianton²; **Hel.** 1: 10 speedy was *f.* of Kishkumen; 2: 11 Gadianton's band takes *f.* out of land; 15: 2 ye shall attempt to *f.*, and there shall be no refuge; 3 **Ne.** 1: 28 Nephite dissenters *f.* to robbers; 7: 12 Jacob⁴ orders his band to take *f.* into northernmost part of land; 20: 42 (21: 29; Isa. 52: 12) ye shall not go out with haste nor go by *f.*; **Morm.** 5: 7 those whose *f.* was swifter than Lamanites escape.

FLOCK (*see also* Church of God; Fold; Sheep)

2 **Ne.** 5: 11 (Enos 1: 21) Nephites begin to raise *f.*; **Mosiah** 2: 3 Nephites take firstlings of *f.* to offer sacrifice; 8: 21 children of men are wild *f.* which fleeth from shepherd; 9: 12 Lamanites bring people of Zeniff into bondage, to feast on *f.*; 10: 2 Zeniff guards his people and *f.*; 17: 17 people of Noah³ shall be driven as wild *f.* is driven by wild beasts; **Alma** 5: 59 if wolf enter *f.* doth not shepherd drive him out; 17: 25 Ammon² set to watch Lamoni's *f.*; 18: 2 faithfulness of Ammon² in defending *f.* astonishes Lamoni; 34: 20, 25 cry unto the Lord over all your *f.*; 3 **Ne.** 4: 4 Nephites reserve *f.* and provisions for seven years' subsistence; 20: 16 (21: 12; Micah 5: 8) remnant of Jacob¹ shall be among Gentiles as young lion among *f.* of sheep; **Ether** 1: 41 Jaredites are commanded to gather *f.*; 10: 12 people of Morianton¹ become exceeding rich in *f.*

FLOOD (*see also* Destruction; Noah¹; Sea; Water; TG Flood, Noah's)

Alma 10: 22 people would not be destroyed by *f.*, but by famine, pestilence, sword; 3 **Ne.** 11: 40 (14: 26–27; 18: 13) when *f.* come, gates of hell stand open to receive those built upon sandy foundation; **Ether** 2: 24–25 Jaredites could not cross sea, save the Lord prepared them against *f.*; 3: 2 Jaredites to be encompassed about by *f.*; 13: 2 after waters receded, land became choice.

FLYING SERPENTS (*see* Serpent)

FOLD (*see also* Flock; Sheep)

1 **Ne.** 15: 15 will not Israel come into true *f.* of God; 22: 25 (3 **Ne.** 16: 3; John 10: 16) one *f.* and one shepherd; 2 **Ne.** 9: 2 Jews to be restored to true church and *f.* of God; **Mosiah** 18: 8–10 those who desire to come unto *f.* of God should be baptized; **Alma** 5: 39 if ye are not sheep of good shepherd, of what *f.* are ye; 26: 4 thousands of Lamanites have been brought into *f.* of God; 3 **Ne.** 15: 17–21 (John 10: 16) the Lord has other sheep not of same *f.*

FOLLOW, FOLLOWER (*see also* Disciple; Example; Obedience; Saint)

2 **Ne.** 28: 14 all have gone astray save a few humble *f.* of Christ; 10 the Lamb says, F. me; 31: 10 can we *f.* Jesus save we keep Father's commandments; 31: 12 *f.* me, and do the things ye have seen me do; 31: 13 by *f.* Son down into water ye shall receive Holy Ghost; 31: 16 unless a man endure to end, in *f.* Christ's example, he cannot be saved; **Alma** 4: 15 Alma² sees afflictions of humble *f.* of God; 5: 41 if man brings forth good works, he *f.* the good shepherd; 5: 57 all who desire to *f.* good shepherd must come out from among the wicked; 37: 45 if we *f.* Christ's words, they will carry us to far better land of promise; 42: 7 first parents became subject to *f.* after own will; **Hel.** 6: 5 many brought down to depths of humility to be humble *f.* of God and the Lamb; 3 **Ne.** 27: 10–12 works of churches built upon works of men or devil *f.* them; **Morm.** 9: 24 (Ether 4: 18) signs *f.* them who believe; **Moro.** 7: 3 peaceable *f.* of Christ shall enter rest of the Lord; 7: 11 servant of devil cannot *f.* Christ; 7: 48 pure love of Christ bestowed upon all true *f.* of the Son.

FOLLY (*see also* Fool; Foolish)

2 **Ne.** 19: 17 (Isa. 9: 17) every mouth speaketh *f.*

FOOD (*see also* Eat; Feed; Grain; Meat; Nourish)

1 **Ne.** 16: 31–32 Nephi¹ obtains *f.*; **Mosiah** 4: 19 do we not all depend upon God for *f.*; **Alma** 8: 20 Amulek imparts *f.* to Alma²; 14: 22 people of Ammonihah withhold *f.* from Alma² and Amulek; 30: 56 Korihor goes from house to house, begging for *f.*; 58: 7 Nephite armies about to perish for want of *f.*; **Hel.** 4: 12 Nephites withhold *f.* from the hungry; 5: 22 Nephi² and Lehi⁴ cast into prison many days without *f.*; 3 **Ne.** 4: 3 robbers could not exist for want of *f.*; **Ether** 6: 4 Jaredites prepare all manner of *f.* for journey; **Moro.** 9: 16 because of armies, widows and daughters wander whithersoever they can for *f.*

FOOL (*see also* Folly; Foolish)

1 Ne. 17: 17 brethren call Nephi[1] a *f.*; **2 Ne.** 9: 42 the Lord will not open to those puffed up in learning, save they consider themselves *f.* before him; 29: 6 *f.* shall say, We need no more Bible; **Hel.** 9: 21 ye *f.*, how long will the Lord suffer you to go on in this way of sin; **3 Ne.** 12: 22 (Matt. 5: 22) whosoever shall say, Thou *f.*, shall be in danger of hell fire; **Ether** 12: 26 *f.* mock, but they shall mourn.

FOOLISH, FOOLISHNESS (*see also* Doctrine, False; False; Folly; Fool)

1 Ne. 2: 11 elder sons believe Lehi[1] is led away by *f.* imaginations of his heart; **2 Ne.** 9: 28 O the *f.* of men; 26: 10 for reward of their *f.*, Nephites shall reap destruction; 28: 9 many shall teach *f.* doctrines; **Alma** 8: 11 (21: 8; 30: 13–14, 23, 27; 31: 17) dissenters believe church teaches *f.* traditions; 37: 6 ye suppose this is *f.* in me; **Hel.** 12: 4 how *f.* are children of men; 13: 29 how long will ye suffer yourselves to be led by *f.*; **3 Ne.** 14: 26 (Matt. 7: 26) those who hear Christ's sayings but do them not are likened to *f.* man who builds house upon sand.

FOOT, FEET (*see also* Footstool; Trample; Tread)

1 Ne. 11: 24 (3 Ne. 17: 10) many will fall down at Son's *f.* and worship; **Mosiah** 12: 21 (15: 14–18; 3 Ne. 20: 40; Isa. 52: 7) how beautiful upon mountains are *f.* of him who brings good tidings; **Alma** 36: 7 earth trembles under *f.* of Alma[2] and friends; 46: 22 God may cast us at enemies' *f.*, even as we cast garments at thy *f.*, if we transgress; **3 Ne.** 11: 14–15 multitude feels prints of nails in Christ's *f.*

FOOTSTOOL

1 Ne. 17: 39 (3 Ne. 12: 35; Isa. 66: 1; Matt. 5: 35) earth is God's *f.*

FORBID, FORBADE, FORBIDDEN (*see also* Commandments of God; Fruit, Forbidden; Hinder)

1 Ne. 8: 28 those who are ashamed fall away into *f.* paths; 14: 28 Nephi[1] is *f.* to write remainder of what he saw; **2 Ne.** 26: 28 none are *f.* to partake of God's goodness; **3 Ne.** 18: 22 ye shall not *f.* any man from coming into meeting; 18: 29 (4 Ne. 1: 27) *f.* the unworthy from partaking sacrament; 26: 11 Christ *f.* Nephi[3] to write all things from plates of Nephi; 26: 16 (27: 23; 28: 14) men are *f.* to write all of marvelous things uttered or heard; 28: 25 the Lord *f.* Nephi[3] to write names of three Nephites; **Morm.** 1: 16–17 Mormon[2] is *f.* to preach unto people; **Ether** 4: 1 things written by brother of Jared[2] were *f.* to come unto men until after Crucifixion; 5: 1 to translate sealed things is *f.*; 8: 18–19 God has *f.* that men work in secret combinations; 13: 13 Moroni[2] is *f.* to write more of Ether's prophecies.

FOREFATHERS (*see also* Father)

1 Ne. 3: 3 (5: 14; Alma 37: 3) brass plates contain genealogy of *f.*; 15: 14 Lamanites to come to knowledge of *f.*; **Alma** 7: 10 Jerusalem, the land of our *f.*

FOREHEAD

Alma 3: 4 Amlicites mark themselves with red in *f.*

FOREKNOWLEDGE (*see* God, Foreknowledge of)

FOREORDINATION (*see* Calling; Elect; God, Foreknowledge of; Premortal Existence; TG Foreordination; Jesus Christ, Foreordained; Man, Antemortal Existence of)

FORGET, FORGOT, FORGOTTEN (*see also* Forgive; Remember; Remembrance)

1 Ne. 21: 15 (Isa. 49: 15) can woman *f.* her sucking child; 21: 15 (2 Ne. 29: 5) the Lord will not *f.* Israel; **Alma** 37: 41 because miracles were worked by small means, forefathers *f.* to exercise faith; 46: 8 (Hel. 11: 36; 12: 2) how quick do men *f.* the Lord; 47: 36 dissenters entirely *f.* the Lord; **Hel.** 7: 20 (12: 2) how could you have *f.* your God in very day he has delivered you; **3 Ne.** 2: 1 people begin to *f.* signs and wonders given at Christ's birth; 22: 4 (Isa. 54: 4) thou shalt *f.* shame of thy youth.

FORGIVE, FORGIVEN, FORGIVENESS (*see also* Baptism; Confession of Sins; Forsake; Jesus Christ, Atonement through; Reconcile; Remission; Repentance; TG Forgive, Forgiven)

1 Ne. 7: 21 Nephi[1] frankly *f.* brethren; **Enos** 1: 5 sins of Enos[2] are *f.*; **Mosiah** 4: 2 apply atoning blood of Christ that we may receive *f.* of sins; 4: 10 (Moro. 6: 8) ask in sincerity of heart that God would *f.* you; 26: 22 whosoever is baptized will the Lord freely *f.*; 26: 29–30 whosoever confesses and repents should be *f.*; 26: 31 *f.* one another your trespasses; 26: 31 (3 Ne. 13: 14–15) he who *f.* not his neighbor's trespasses brings himself under condemnation; **Alma** 39: 6 not easy for those who deny Holy Ghost or murder against light of God to receive *f.*; **3 Ne.** 13: 11 (Matt. 6: 12) *f.* us our debts, as we *f.* our debtors; 13: 14–15 (Matt. 6: 14–15) if ye *f.* men their trespasses, Father will *f.* you; **Morm.** 8: 32 churches will *f.* sins for money.

FORM [noun] (*see also* Frame [noun]; Image; TG Holy Ghost, Dove, Sign of)

1 Ne. 11: 11 Spirit in *f.* of man; 11: 27 (2 Ne. 31: 8) Holy Ghost will abide upon Christ in *f.* of dove; **Mosiah** 13: 34 God shall take upon himself *f.* of man; 14: 2 (Isa. 53: 2) Messiah hath no *f.* or comeliness; **Alma** 11: 43 spirit and body shall be reunited in perfect *f.*; 30: 44 all planets which move in regular *f.* witness there is a Supreme Creator; 30: 53 devil appeared unto Korihor in *f.* of angel; 3 Ne. 20: 44 (Isa. 52: 14) Messiah's *f.* was more marred than sons of men; **Moro.** 7: 30 angels show themselves in every *f.* of godliness.

FORMATION (*see also* Foundation; Founder)

1 Ne. 13: 4 Nephi[1] sees *f.* of great church among Gentiles.

FORMED [verb] (*see also* Creation; Formation; Framed [verb]; Make)

1 Ne. 21: 5 the Lord *f.* me from womb; 3 Ne. 22: 17 (Isa. 54: 17) no weapon that is *f.* against thee shall prosper.

FORNICATION, FORNICATOR (*see also* Adultery; Chastity; Lust; Whore; TG Fornication; Sexual Immorality)

Jacob 3: 12 Jacob[2] warns Nephites against *f.*; **Hel.** 8: 26 Nephites are ripening for destruction because of murders and *f.*; 3 Ne. 12: 32 (Matt. 5: 32) whosoever puts away his wife, save for *f.*, causes her to commit adultery.

FORSAKE, FORSAKEN (*see also* Forgive, Forgiveness; Leave; Repentance)

Mosiah 4: 10 (Alma 39: 9) repent of your sins and *f.* them; **Alma** 46: 21 Nephites enter covenant that they would not *f.* their Lord; 3 Ne. 22: 7 (Isa. 54: 7) for a small moment have I *f.* thee.

FORT, FORTIFY (*see also* Defence, Defense; Protect)

2 Ne. 10: 12 the Lord will *f.* land against all other nations; 26: 15 the Lord shall raise *f.* against seed of Nephi[1] and brethren.

FOUGHT (*see* Fight, Fought)

FOUND (*see* Find, Found; Founded; Founder)

FOUNDATION (*see also* Formation; Founded; Founder; Preparator; Rock)

2 Ne. 28: 28 he who is built upon sandy *f.* trembles lest he fall; **Jacob** 4: 15–17 Jews to reject only stone upon which they might build safe *f.*; **Alma** 10: 17–27 lawyers and hypocrites are laying *f.* of devil; 13: 3 those ordained were

called and prepared from *f.* of world; **Hel.** 5: 12 upon rock of Redeemer ye must build *f.*; 3 Ne. 11: 40 whoso declares more or less than Christ's doctrine builds upon sandy *f.*; 18: 13 those who do more or less than these are built upon sandy *f.*

FOUNDED (*see also* Build; Foundation; Founder)

1 Ne. 14: 3 great and abominable church *f.* by devil; 3 Ne. 14: 25 (Matt. 7: 25) house *f.* upon rock does not fall because of floods, winds, rain.

FOUNDER (*see also* Author; Devil; Foundation; Founded; Preparator)

1 Ne. 13: 6 (14: 9, 17) devil is *f.* of great and abominable church; 2 Ne. 26: 22 devil is *f.* of secret combinations, works of darkness; **Mosiah** 15: 18 how beautiful upon mountains are feet of *f.* of peace; 23: 16 (29: 47) Alma[1] *f.* of church.

FOUNTAIN (*see also* River; Spring; Water)

1 Ne. 2: 9 Lehi[1] exhorts Lemuel to be like river, continually running into *f.* of righteousness; 8: 20 straight and narrow path leads by head of *f.*; 11: 25 iron rod leads to *f.* of living waters; 12: 16 *f.* of filthy waters is depths of hell; **Mosiah** 18: 5 Alma[1] hides by *f.* of pure water in Mormon; **Ether** 8: 26 Moroni[2] writes so that men may come to *f.* of all righteousness; 12: 28 the Lord is the *f.* of all righteousness; **Moro.** 7: 11 bitter *f.* cannot bring forth good water, nor good *f.* bitter water.

FOWL (*see also* Animal)

2 Ne. 2: 15 God created *f.* of air; **Ether** 2: 16 Jaredite barges are light like *f.* upon water.

FRAME [noun] (*see also* Body)

1 Ne. 17: 47 Nephi[1] is full of Spirit, so that his *f.* has no strength; **Mosiah** 2: 26 Benjamin about to yield mortal *f.* to mother earth; **Alma** 11: 43 (40: 23; 41: 4) limb and joint shall be restored to proper *f.*; 19: 6 light of everlasting life has overcome Lamoni's natural *f.*; 3 Ne. 11: 3 no part of people's *f.* that small voice does not cause to quake.

FRAMED [verb] (*see also* Creation; Formed [verb])

2 Ne. 27: 27 shall the thing *f.* say of him that *f.* it, he had no understanding.

FRAUD (*see also* Deceit; Lying)

Alma 47: 30, 35 (48: 7) Amalickiah obtains power by *f.*; 55: 1 Ammoran has perfect knowledge of his *f.*

FREEDOM, FREE (*see also* Agency; Bond-

age; Captive; Deliver; Freely; Freemen; Government, Civil; King-men; Liberty; Redemption; Salvation)

2 Ne. 2: 4 salvation is *f.*; 2: 26 because men are redeemed from fall, they have become *f.* forever; 2: 27 men are *f.* to choose eternal life through great Redeemer; 3: 5 Messiah to be made manifest unto seed of Joseph[1] unto bringing them out of captivity unto *f.*; 10: 23 (Hel. 14: 30) men are *f.* to act for themselves; **Jacob** 2: 17 be *f.* with your substance; **Mosiah** 5: 8 under this head ye are made *f.*, and there is no other head whereby ye can be made *f.*; **Alma** 30: 24 Korihor claims Nephites are not a *f.* people; 43: 48 Moroni[1] inspires his men with thoughts of *f.*; 46: 35 Amalickiahites required to enter covenant to support cause of *f.*; 48: 11 Moroni[1] delights in *f.* of his country; 48: 20 because Nephites humble themselves, they are *f.* from wars and dissension; 50: 39 chief judge given oath to keep peace and *f.*; 51: 6 freemen swear to maintain privileges of religion by *f.* government; 51: 7 king-men are obliged to maintain cause of *f.*; 60: 36 Moroni[1] seeks not honor of world, but *f.* of his country; 61: 6 Nephites flock to army in defense of *f.*; 61: 15 Spirit of God is Spirit of *f.*; 62: 1 Pahoran[1] not a traitor to *f.* of his country; **3 Ne.** 2: 12 converted Lamanites take up arms against robbers to maintain *f.*; 21: 4 Gentiles set up as *f.* people by power of the Father; **Ether** 2: 12 nations that possess this land shall be *f.* from bondage; 8: 25 they who build secret combinations seek to overthrow *f.* of all lands.

FREELY

Mosiah 26: 22 whosoever is baptized unto repentance will the Lord *f.* forgive; **Alma** 5: 34 (42: 27) partake of waters of life *f.*

FREEMEN—*Nephite group vowing to defend freedom* [c. 67 B.C.]

Alma 51: 6–7 *f.* save judgment-seat for Pahoran[1]; 60: 25 *f.* serve in army of Moroni[1]; 61: 3–4 *f.* of Pahoran[1] are daunted by dissenters, that they do not come unto Moroni[1]; 62: 6 *f.* are driven out of Zarahemla.

FRIEND, FRIENDSHIP (*see also* TG Brotherhood and Sisterhood; Fellowshipping)

2 Ne. 1: 30 Zoram[1] a true *f.* to Nephi[1]; **Mosiah** 29: 22 iniquitous king has his *f.* in iniquity; **Alma** 15: 16 Amulek is rejected by those who were once his *f.*; 62: 37 Teancum a true *f.* to liberty; **Morm.** 8: 5 Moroni[2] has no *f.*; **Ether** 1: 36 Jared[1] pleads that the Lord might have compassion on *f.*

FRUIT, FRUITFUL (*see also* Food; Fruit, Forbidden; Tree; Tree of Life; Work [noun])

1 Ne. 8: 10–35 Lehi[1] beholds tree whose *f.* is desirable to make one happy; 15: 36 *f.* of tree of life is most precious and desirable above all other *f.*; **2 Ne.** 2: 9 Messiah is first-*f.* unto God; **Jacob** 4: 11 be presented as first-*f.* of Christ unto God; 5: 3–77 Zenos's parable of vineyard with good and evil *f.*; 5: 18 wild branches grafted into tame roots bring forth tame *f.*; 5: 26 branches that have not brought forth good *f.* shall be cast into fire; 5: 25–26 wild branches overcome tame branches, so that corrupted tree brings forth no good *f.*; 5: 64 if grafted branches bring forth natural *f.*, tree shall be spared; 5: 65 branches bringing forth bitter *f.* shall be cleared away; 5: 74 trees become again natural *f.*, and the Lord preserves unto himself the natural *f.*; 6: 7 after ye have been nourished by word of God, will ye bring forth evil *f.*; **Alma** 5: 36 whosoever brings not forth good *f.* shall have cause to mourn; 5: 62 be baptized unto repentance that ye may be partakers of *f.* of tree of life; 12: 15 (13: 13; 34: 30) bring forth *f.* meet for repentance; 26: 30–31 Ammon[2] and brethren can see *f.* of labors; 29: 17 may God grant that those who are *f.* of missionaries' labors may go no more out; 32: 40 if ye will not nourish the word, ye can never pluck of *f.* of tree of life; 36: 25 the Lord gives Alma[2] great joy in *f.* of labors; 40: 26 the wicked are consigned to partake of *f.* of their works; 42: 3 the Lord places cherubim and flaming sword so that Adam should not partake of *f.* of tree of life; **Hel.** 11: 13, 17 Nephi[2] prays the Lord to send rain, that earth may bring forth *f.*; **3 Ne.** 14: 16, 20 (Matt. 7: 16, 20) ye shall know them by their *f.*; 14: 17–18 (Matt. 7: 17–18) good tree brings forth good *f.*, evil tree evil *f.*; 24: 11 (Mal. 3: 11) the Lord will rebuke devourer that he shall not destroy *f.* of ground; **Moro.** 6: 1 elders, priests, teachers not baptized save they brought forth *f.* meet that they are worthy; 8: 25 first *f.* of repentance is baptism.

FRUIT, FORBIDDEN (*see also* Agency; Eden, Garden of; Fall of Man; Tree)

2 Ne. 2: 15 *f. f.* set in opposition to tree of life; 2: 18–19 (Hel. 6: 26) devil beguiled Adam and Eve into partaking of *f. f.*; **Mosiah** 3: 26 justice could not deny that Adam should fall because he took of *f. f.*; **Alma** 12: 22 Adam fell by partaking of *f. f.*

FRUSTRATED (*see also* Hinder)

Alma 12: 26 (42: 5) if first parents

Fulfil

could have partaken of tree of life, plan of redemption would have been *f.*; **3 Ne.** 1: 16 plan of destruction laid for believers is *f.*

FULFIL, FULFILL (*see also* Accomplish; Perform)

1 Ne. 20: 14 the Lord will *f.* his word; **2 Ne.** 9: 17 (25: 24; Alma 34: 13; 3 Ne. 1: 25) God's law must be *f.*; 10: 17 the Lord will *f.* his promises; 25: 7 (3 Ne. 16: 17; 20: 11) prophecies of Isaiah shall be *f.*; 25: 24 Nephites look forward to Christ until law shall be *f.*; 31: 5 Lamb baptized by water to *f.* all righteousness; **Alma** 34: 13 great and last sacrifice shall *f.* law of Moses; **Hel.** 16: 13–14 words of prophets, scriptures begin to be *f.*; **3 Ne.** 1: 25 law not yet *f.*; 5: 14 prayers of holy ones shall be *f.* according to their faith; 9: 17 (12: 46; 15: 5) in Christ is the law of Moses *f.*; 28: 7 three Nephite disciples to live until all things shall be *f.*; **Ether** 12: 3 by faith all things are *f.*

FULL (*see also* Fill; Fulness)

1 Ne. 1: 16 (6: 3) Nephi[1] does not make *f.* account; **Jacob** 6: 5 (3 Ne. 10: 6; 12: 24; 18: 32; Acts 11: 23) come unto the Lord with *f.* purpose of heart; **Alma** 12: 10 he who hardens not his heart shall know mysteries until he knows them in *f.*; 34: 27 let your hearts be *f.*, drawn out in prayer unto the Lord; **Morm.** 2: 18 (5: 9) Mormon[2] makes *f.* account on plates of Nephi, not upon these plates; **Ether** 3: 17 Moroni[2] does not make *f.* account; 15: 19 Satan has *f.* power over hearts.

FULLER [noun]

3 Ne. 24: 2 (Mal. 3: 2) the Lord is like refiner's fire and *f*'s soap.

FULNESS (*see also* Full; Gospel)

1 Ne. 17: 35 *f.* of God's wrath was upon those who inhabited promised land before Israel; 22: 16 time will come when *f.* of God's wrath shall be poured out; 22: 17 God will preserve the righteous if *f.* of his wrath must come; **2 Ne.** 1: 17 because of hardness of hearts, God may come out in *f.* of his wrath; 2: 3 in *f.* of time Redeemer comes to bring salvation unto men; 11: 7 Christ comes in *f.* of his own time; **3 Ne.** 27: 30 Christ's joy is great, even unto *f.*; 28: 10 disciples shall have *f.* of joy; **Ether** 2: 10 not until *f.* of iniquity are children of land swept off.

FURNACE (*see also* Fire; Oven)

1 Ne. 20: 10 (Isa. 48: 10) I have chosen thee in *f.* of affliction; **Mosiah** 12: 3 life of Noah[3] shall be valued as garment in hot *f.*; **3 Ne.** 28: 21 (4 Ne. 1: 32; Morm. 8: 24) Nephite disciples cast into fiery *f.*, without harm.

FURY (*see also* Anger; Ferocious; Passion; Wrath)

2 Ne. 8: 13 (Isa. 51: 13) thou hast feared continually every day because of *f.* of oppressor; 8: 20 (Isa. 51: 20) as wild bull in net, thy two sons are full of *f.* of the Lord; **Alma** 52: 33 Jacob[3] leads Lamanites to battle with exceeding *f.*; **3 Ne.** 21: 21 Father will execute *f.* upon those who do not come unto Son.

GAD, CITY OF

3 Ne. 9: 10 burned because inhabitants cast out prophets.

GADIANI, CITY OF

3 Ne. 9: 8 destroyed because of iniquity.

GADIANTON—*leader of robber bands* [c. 50 B.C.] (*see also* Gadianton Robbers)

Hel. 2: 4 expert in wickedness, becomes leader of robber band; 2: 11 flees with band; 2: 13 almost proves destruction of Nephites; 6: 24 gave wicked laws; 6: 26, 29 received secret oaths and covenants from devil.

GADIANTON ROBBERS (*see also* Gadianton; Kishkumen; Rob, Robbery; Secret Combination)

Hel. 2: 4 Gadianton becomes leader of band of Kishkumen; 2: 11 flee out of land by secret way, into wilderness; 3: 23 unknown to government, therefore not destroyed; 6: 18 (7: 25) include many Nephites, more numerous among wicked part of Lamanites; 6: 18 called G's robbers and murderers; 6: 24 those who reveal their wickedness unto world are tried according to laws given by G. and Kishkumen; 6: 26–29 secret oaths and covenants given to G. by devil; 6: 37 Lamanites hunt robbers, preach word of God, destroy band of G. among Lamanites; 7: 4 (8: 1, 27–28) fill judgment-seats, usurp power and authority; 11: 10 Nephites sweep away band of G.; 11: 24–26 dissenters form new band, become robbers of G.; **3 Ne.** 1: 27 robbers dwell in mountains, cannot be overpowered; 1: 29 Lamanite children are led away by Zoramites to join G. robbers; 2: 11 robbers spread death and carnage; 2: 12 converted Lamanites and Nephites unite against robbers; 2: 18 robbers gain many advantages because of people's iniquity; 3: 9 secret society of G. is of ancient date; 3: 15 unless people repent and cry unto the Lord, they will not be delivered from G. robbers; 4 **Ne.** 1: 42, 46 robbers of G. spread again over the land; **Morm.** 1: 18 people try to hide treasures because G. robbers infest the land; 2: 27–28 Nephites regain some lands from robbers of G.

GADIOMNAH, CITY OF

3 **Ne.** 9: 8 is sunk, hills and valleys in place.

GAIN (*see also* Advantage; Benefit; Business; Profit; Riches; Wealth)

1 **Ne.** 22: 23 (4 **Ne.** 1: 26) churches built up to get g. will be consumed; 2 **Ne.** 26: 29 priestcrafts are that men preach to get g.; 27: 15–16 the learned shall say, Bring book and I will read, to get g.; **Alma** 11: 3, 20 judges stir people up to wickedness to get g.; 30: 35 (Mosiah 2: 14; Alma 1: 26) missionaries receive no g.; **Hel.** 6: 8 Nephites and Lamanites have free intercourse to get g.; 7: 4–5 Gadianton robbers fill judgment-seats to get g.; 7: 21 Nephites have forgotten God to get g.; 3 **Ne.** 29: 7 wo unto him who shall say to get g. that there can be no miracle; **Morm.** 8: 14 no one shall have plates to get g.; 8: 40 (Ether 8: 16, 22–23; 11: 15) secret combinations built up to get g.; **Ether** 10: 22 Jaredites traffic one with another to get g.

GALL (*see* Bitter, Bitterness; BD Gall)

GAME (*see also* Animal)

3 **Ne.** 4: 2 Nephites leave no g. for robbers in deserted lands; 4: 20 wild g. in wilderness becomes scarce; 29: 8 ye need not any longer make g. of Jews; **Ether** 10: 21 Jaredites preserve land southward for wilderness, to get g.

GARDEN (*see also* Eden, Garden of)

2 **Ne.** 8: 3 the Lord will make Zion's desert like a g. of the Lord; **Hel.** 7: 10 Nephi² prays upon tower in g.

GARMENT (*see also* Apparel; Clothing; Raiment; Robe)

1 **Ne.** 4: 19 Nephi¹ puts on Laban's g.; 12: 10 g. made white in blood of Lamb; 2 **Ne.** 7: 9 (Isa. 50: 9) all who condemn the Lord shall wax old as a g.; 8: 6 (Isa. 51: 6) earth shall wax old like a g.; 8: 24 (Isa. 52: 1; 3 **Ne.** 20: 36) put on beautiful g., O Jerusalem; **Jacob** 1: 19 Jacob² and Joseph² labor that people's blood might not come upon their g.; 2: 2 Jacob² under responsibility to magnify office, that he might rid g. of his people's sins; **Mosiah** 12: 3 life of Noah³ to be valued as g. in hot furnace; **Alma** 5: 21 no man can be saved except g. are washed white; 7: 25 may the Lord bless you and keep your g. spotless; 46: 24 as remnant of g. of Joseph¹ was preserved, so shall remnant of his seed be preserved; 3 **Ne.** 27: 19 only those who wash g. in Christ's blood can enter Father's rest; **Morm.** 9: 35 these things are written that we may rid g. of blood of our brethren; **Ether** 12: 37 g. of Moroni² shall be made clean.

GATE (*see also* Door; Way)

2 **Ne.** 4: 32 may g. of hell be shut continually before me; 9: 41 keeper of g. is Holy One of Israel; 27: 32 (Isa. 29: 21) they who lay snare for him that reproves in g. shall be cut off; 31: 8–9 Christ's baptism shows men narrowness of g.; 31: 17–18 baptism and repentance are g. by which men should enter; 33: 9 men cannot be reconciled unto Christ except they enter narrow g.; **Jacob** 6: 11 (3 **Ne.** 14: 13; 27: 33; Matt. 7: 13) enter in at the strait g.; **Hel.** 3: 28 g. of heaven is open unto all who believe on Christ; 3 **Ne.** 11: 39 (Matt. 16: 18) g. of hell shall not prevail upon those built on rock of Christ; 14: 13 (27: 33; Matt. 7: 13–14) wide is g. which leads to destruction; 14: 14 (27: 33; Matt. 7: 14) strait is g. which leads to life; 18: 13 g. of hell are open to receive those not built on rock of Christ.

GATHER (*see also* Assemble; Israel, Gathering of; Recover; Remnant; Restoration; Return; Scatter; Zion)

1 **Ne.** 22: 25 (3 **Ne.** 16: 5) Holy One g. his children from four quarters of earth; 2 **Ne.** 10: 8 (3 **Ne.** 21: 1) the Lord will g. in Israel from long dispersion; 21: 12 (Isa. 11: 12) the Lord shall g. the dispersed of Judah from four corners of earth; 23: 4 (Isa. 13: 4) tumultuous noise of kingdoms g. together; 29: 14 Israel shall be g. home unto lands of possessions, and the Lord's word shall be g. in one; **Mosiah** 18: 25 one day in week set apart for people to g. to worship; **Alma** 6: 6 children of God are commanded to g. oft in fasting and prayer; 3 **Ne.** 10: 6 (Matt. 23: 37; Luke 13: 34) how oft will I g. you as a hen g. her chickens; 13: 26 (Matt. 6: 26) behold the fowls, for they do not g. into barns; 20: 18 the Lord will g. his people as a man g. his sheaves.

GAZELEM—*name given to servant of God*

Alma 37: 23 the Lord will prepare unto his servant G. a stone.

GENEALOGY (*see also* Descendant; Father; Forefather; TG Genealogy and Temple Work; BD Genealogy)

1 **Ne.** 3: 3, 12 (5: 14, 16; Alma 37: 3) brass plates contain g. of forefathers; **Jarom** 1: 1 (Omni 1: 1) Jarom writes, that g. may be kept; **Omni** 1: 18 Zarahemla gives g. of fathers.

GENERATION

1 **Ne.** 12: 11–12 (2 **Ne.** 26: 9; Alma 45: 12; 3 **Ne.** 27: 32; 4 **Ne.** 1: 22–24) Nephites to pass into third and fourth g.

after Christ's appearance before iniquity arises; **2 Ne.** 4: 2 Lehi[1] prophesies about future g.; 9: 53 in future g. seed of Nephites shall become righteous branch unto Israel; **Mosiah** 13: 13 (Deut. 5: 9) God visits iniquities of fathers upon children unto third and fourth g.; 14: 8 (15: 10; Isa. 53: 8) who shall declare his g.; **Alma** 9: 8 (10: 17, 25; Hel. 13: 29) O ye wicked and perverse g.; 37: 14, 18–19 the Lord will preserve records, that he might show his power unto future g.; **Hel.** 13: 10 fourth g. of enemies shall visit Nephites' destruction; **3 Ne.** 26: 2 Christ gives Nephites scriptures so that future g. will have them; **Moro.** 10: 28 God's word shall hiss forth from g. to g.

GENEROSITY (see TG Generosity)

GENTILE (see also Heathen; Nation; BD Gentile)
Title Page book written to convince Jew and G. that Jesus is the Christ; **1 Ne.** 10: 11 risen Messiah to manifest himself unto G. by Holy Ghost; 13: 3 Nephi[1] sees nations and kingdoms of G.; 13: 4, 26 formation of abominable church among G.; 13: 12 Nephi[1] beholds man among G. who goes forth upon many waters unto Lamanites; 13: 15 G. prosper in promised land; 13: 25 (Morm. 7: 8) book containing gospel goes from Jews in purity unto G.; 13: 29 after plain and precious parts are taken from gospel, it goes unto nations of G.; 13: 32 the Lord will not suffer G. to remain in blindness; 13: 35 Nephite writings shall come unto G.; 13: 42 Lamb shall manifest unto Jews and G., then unto G. and Jews; 14: 1 if G. hearken unto Lamb, he shall manifest himself; 15: 13, 17 grafting in of natural branches through fulness of G. means fulness of gospel shall come to G.; 15: 17 (2 Ne. 10: 18; 26: 15–19) Lamanites shall be scattered by G.; 22: 6 (1 Ne. 21: 22–23; 2 Ne. 6: 7; 10: 9; Isa. 49: 23) G. to nurse Israel, be set up as standard; 22: 7 the Lord will raise up mighty nation among G. upon this land; 22: 8 (3 Ne. 28: 32) the Lord will do marvelous work among G.; **2 Ne.** 10: 11 this land shall be land of liberty among G.; 10: 16 he who fights against Zion, both Jew and G., shall perish; 10: 18 G. shall be like father to Lamanites, shall be numbered among house of Israel; 26: 33 all are alike unto God, both Jew and G.; 29: 3 many G. shall say, A Bible! A Bible! we have a Bible; 30: 3 (3 Ne. 21: 5; 26: 8; Morm. 5: 15; 7: 8) G. shall carry gospel, book unto Lamanites; **3 Ne.** 15: 22 G. to be converted through preaching of Jews; 16: 10 when G. reject fulness of gospel, Father will bring gospel from among them; 21: 12 (Micah 5: 8) remnant of Jacob[1] shall be among G. as lion

among beasts of forest; 28: 27 three Nephites shall be among G., and G. shall know them not; **Morm.** 3: 17 Mormon[2] writes unto G.; **Ether** 12: 23 Moroni[2] fears G. will mock these writings because of Nephites' weakness in writing; 12: 36 Moroni[2] prays the Lord will give G. grace, that they might have charity.

GENTLE (see also Kindness; Meek; Tender)
Alma 7: 23 be humble, submissive, g.

GHOST (see also Holy Ghost; Spirit)
Jacob 7: 20 Sherem gives up the g.; **Hel.** 14: 21 when Christ yields up the g., there shall be thunderings and lightnings.

GID—Nephite military officer [c. 63 B.C.] (see also Gid, City of)
Alma 57: 28–29 chief captain over band appointed to guard prisoners; 57: 30–35 reports death and escape of rebellious prisoners; 58: 16–23 takes part in strategy to capture Lamanite cities.

GID, CITY OF
Alma 51: 26 possessed by Amalickiah; 55: 7–24 Moroni[1] takes G. without bloodshed; 55: 25–26 Lamanite prisoners labor to fortify G.

GIDDIANHI—chief Gadianton robbers [c. A.D. 16-21]
3 Ne. 3: 9 governor of secret society; 3: 10–12 demands Nephite lands; 4: 5–6 commands armies to go to battle against Nephites; 4: 10–12 Nephites defeat G's army; 4: 14 is slain.

GIDDONAH[1]—Amulek's father
Alma 10: 2–3 descendant of Nephi[1].

GIDDONAH[2]—high priest in Gideon [c. 75 B.C.]
Alma 30: 21–29 is challenged by Korihor.

GIDEON—Nephite patriot [c. 145-91 B.C.]
Mosiah 19: 4 strong man, enemy to king Noah[3]; 19: 5–8 fights with king, spares king's life; 19: 18–24 sends men into wilderness to search for king and priests; 20: 17–22 counsels with Limhi regarding dealings with Lamanite king; 22: 3–9 proposes plan for escaping from Lamanites; **Alma** 1: 7–8 a teacher in the church, withstands Nehor; 1: 9 (2: 1, 20; 6: 7; 14: 16) is slain by Nehor; 2: 20 valley named after G.; 6: 7 city named after G.

GIDEON, CITY OF—east of River Sidon
Alma 6: 7 built in valley of G.; **Hel.** 13: 15 wo unto city of G. for wickedness.

GIDEON, LAND AND VALLEY OF—*east of River Sidon*

Alma 2: 20–26 people of Alma² pitch tents in valley of G.; 6: 7—8: 1 Alma² preaches in G., establishes church; 17: 1 Alma² meets sons of Mosiah² while journeying from G.; 30: 21 Korihor preaches in land of G. without success; 61: 5 Pahoran¹ flees to land of G.; 62: 3–6 Moroni¹ unites with Pahoran¹ in land of G.

GIDGIDDONAH—*Nephite commander* [c. A.D. 385]

Morm. 6: 13 is fallen with his ten thousand.

GIDGIDDONI—*Nephite commander* [c. A.D. 16]

3 Ne. 3: 18 great commander of armies; 3: 19 has spirit of revelation and prophecy; 3: 20–21 refuses people's petition for offensive campaign against robbers; 3: 26 causes Nephites to make weapons; 4: 13–14 defeats robbers; 4: 24–26 cuts off robbers' retreat; 6: 6 establishes great peace.

GIFT (*see also* Give; Holy Ghost, Gift of; Spirit; Tongue; TG God, Gifts of)

Title Page (1 Ne. 13: 35) book to come forth by g. and power of God; **1 Ne.** 10: 17 power of Holy Ghost is g. of God unto all who diligently seek him; 15: 36 fruit of tree of life is greatest of all the g. of God; **Omni** 1: 20 Mosiah¹ interprets engravings on stones by g. and power of God; 1: 25 Amaleki¹ exhorts all men to believe in g. of speaking with tongues; **Mosiah** 8: 16 no man can have g. greater than to be seer; **Alma** 9: 21 Nephites have had many g., g. of speaking with tongues, of preaching, of Holy Ghost, of translation; **Hel.** 5: 8 Helaman² admonishes his sons to do good, that they may have g. of eternal life; **3 Ne.** 29: 6 wo unto him who says the Lord no longer works by g.; **4 Ne.** 1: 3 Nephites have all things in common, so that all are partakers of heavenly g.; **Morm.** 1: 14 Nephites have no g. from the Lord, because of their wickedness; 9: 7–8 he who says there are no g. knows not the gospel of Christ; **Ether** 12: 8 Christ prepared a way that others might be partakers of heavenly g.; 12: 9 ye may be partakers of heavenly g. if ye have faith; **Moro.** 7: 8 if a man being evil gives a g., he does it grudgingly; 10: 8 deny not the g. of God; 10: 8 different ways that g. are administered, but all are given by manifestations of Spirit; 10: 18 every good g. cometh of Christ; 10: 24 if g. of God are ever done away, it shall be because of unbelief; 10: 30 lay hold upon every good g., touch not the evil g.

GILEAD—*Jaredite military commander*

Ether 14: 3–5 is defeated by Coriantumr²; 14: 6 places himself upon throne of Coriantumr²; 14: 8 army of G. is strengthened by secret combinations; 14: 8–9 is murdered by his high priest.

GILGAH—*early Jaredite*

Ether 6: 14 one of four sons of Jared²; 6: 24–27 refuses to be king.

GILGAL—*Nephite commander* [c. A.D. 385]

Morm. 6: 14 is slain with army.

GILGAL, CITY OF

3 Ne. 9: 6 sinks into depths of earth.

GILGAL, VALLEY OF

Ether 13: 27–30 site of battle between Shared and Coriantumr².

GIMGIMNO, CITY OF

3 Ne. 9: 8 sinks into depths of earth.

GIVE, GIVEN (*see also* Confer; Deliver; Gift; Grant; Impart; Mete; Provide; Render)

2 Ne. 2: 27 all things are g. men that are expedient unto man; 4: 35 God will g. liberally to him that asketh; 4: 35 my God will g. me if I ask not amiss; **Mosiah** 4: 24 those who do not g. to the beggar should be able to say, I g. not because I have not; **3 Ne.** 14: 7 (Matt. 7: 7) ask and it shall be g. unto you; 14: 11 (Matt. 7: 11) how much more shall Father in heaven g. good things to them that ask him; **Morm.** 8: 15 none can have power to bring record to light save it be g. him of God.

GLASS (*see also* BD Glass)

Ether 3: 1 brother of Jared² brings the Lord sixteen stones, transparent as g.

GLORIFY (*see also* Exalt; Glorious; Glory; Honor; Praise; Sanctification)

2 Ne. 6: 4 Jacob² speaks so that people may learn and g. name of God; **3 Ne.** 12: 16 (Matt. 5: 16) let light so shine that they see good works and g. Father; 23: 9 Father to g. his name in Christ; **Ether** 3: 21 the Lord shall g. his name in the flesh; 12: 4 hope makes men abound in good works, being led to g. God; 12: 8 because of faith of men, Christ has shown himself, g. name of Father.

GLORIOUS (*see also* Glorify; Glory)

1 Ne. 21: 5 (Isa. 49: 5) yet shall I be g. in eyes of the Lord; **2 Ne.** 9: 46 prepare for g. day when justice shall be administered; 14: 2 (Isa. 4: 2) branch of the Lord shall be g.; 21: 10 (Isa. 11: 10) his rest shall be g.

GLORY [noun] (*see also* Eternal Life;

Glorify; Glory [verb]; Glory of the World; Light; Majesty; Power; Reward; Transfigure, Transfiguration; TG Glory; God, Glory of)

1 Ne. 22: 24 Holy One of Israel to reign in great g.; **2 Ne.** 1: 15 Nephi[1] has beheld the Lord's g.; 1: 25 Nephi[1] has sought the Lord's g.; 12: 19 (Isa. 2: 19) g. of the Lord's majesty shall smite them; 16: 3 (Isa. 6: 3) whole earth is full of the Lord's g.; **Jacob** 4: 4 not only Nephites, but all holy prophets, have hope of Christ's g.; **Mosiah** 4: 12 grow in knowledge of g. of him who created you; **Alma** 5: 50 (9: 26; 13: 24; 3 Ne. 26: 3; 28: 7–8) Son to come in g.; 5: 50 g. of King of all the earth shall soon shine forth; 14: 11 the Lord receives martyrs unto himself in g.; 19: 6 Lamoni's mind is enlightened by light of g. of God; 36: 28 I know that the Lord will raise me up at last day, to dwell with him in g.; 60: 36 Moroni[1] seeks not honor of world, but g. of God; **3 Ne.** 13: 13 (Matt. 6: 13) thine is the kingdom, the power, and the g. forever; 20: 9–10 multitude gives g. to Jesus; **Morm.** 8: 15 bringing forth of record must be done with eye single to g. of God.; 9: 5 when ye are brought to see g. of God, it will kindle unquenchable fire in you; **Moro.** 9: 25 may hope of Christ's g. rest in your mind forever.

GLORY [verb]

2 Ne. 33: 6 Nephi[1] g. in plainness, in truth, in Jesus; **Mosiah** 23: 11 Alma[1] is not worthy to g. of himself; **Alma** 26: 16 who can g. too much in the Lord; 29: 9 I do not g. of myself, but I g. in that which the Lord hath commanded me; 48: 16 heart of Moroni[1] g. in his faith.

GLORY OF THE WORLD

2 Ne. 27: 15–16 the learned will offer to read book for g. of world; **Hel.** 7: 5 robbers rule in government to get g. of world; **3 Ne.** 13: 2 (Matt. 6: 2) hypocrites give alms to have g. of men; **Ether** 8: 7 Jared[3] had set heart upon kingdom and g. of world.

GNASH, GNASHING (see also Hell; Torment)

Mosiah 16: 2 (Alma 40: 13) the wicked shall have cause to g. teeth; **Alma** 14: 21 people of Ammonihah g. teeth upon Alma[2] and Amulek.

GO

1 Ne. 3: 7 I will g. and do the things which the Lord hath commanded; 21: 9 (Isa. 49: 9) say to prisoners, G. forth; **2 Ne.** 12: 3 (Isa. 2: 3) let us g. up to mountain of the Lord; 12: 3 (Isa. 2: 3) out of Zion shall g. forth the law; **3 Ne.** 12: 41 (Matt. 5: 41) whosoever shall

compel thee to g. a mile, g. with him twain; 17: 4 (18: 27) Christ g. unto the Father; **Morm.** 9: 22 (Matt. 28: 19) g. ye into world and preach gospel to every creature; **Ether** 1: 42 the Lord will g. before Jaredites into choice land.

GOAT (see also Animal)

1 Ne. 18: 25 (Enos 1: 21) Nephites find g. upon land; **Alma** 14: 29 people flee Alma[2] and Amulek as g. fleeth with her young from two lions; **Ether** 9: 18 Jaredites have g.

GOD (see also Born of God; Children of God; Church of God; Commandments of God; Faith; Fear of God; Gift; Glory [noun]; God, Body of; God—Creator; God, Eternal Nature of; God, Foreknowledge of; God, Goodness of; God, Love of; God, Manifestations of; God, Omniscience of; God, Power of; God, Presence of; God, Wisdom of; God the Father; Godhead; Godliness; Gods; Grace; Holy Ghost; Indignation; Jesus Christ; Jesus Christ—Creator; Jesus Christ—Holy One of Israel; Jesus Christ—Jehovah; Jesus Christ—Lord; Judgment; Justice; Kingdom of God; Knowledge; Law; Mercy; Mystery; Name of the Lord; Praise; Prayer; Redemption; Spirit, Holy/Spirit of the Lord; Trust; Will; Word of God/Word of the Lord; Work [noun]; Worship; Wrath; TG God; BD God)

Title Page condemn not the things of God; **1 Ne.** 5: 9–10 (19: 7, 13; 20: 1–2; 2 Ne. 27: 34; 3 Ne. 11: 14) G. of Israel; 5: 15 (19: 10) G. preserved Israel, led them from Egypt; 6: 3–5 (2 Ne. 5: 32) Nephi[1] writes things pleasing to G. upon plates; 6: 4 (Mosiah 7: 19; 23: 23; Alma 29: 11; 36: 2; 3 Ne. 4: 30; Morm. 9: 11) G. of Abraham, Isaac, and Jacob[1]; 10: 21 no unclean thing can dwell with G.; 11: 6 (3 Ne. 11: 14; 22: 5) the Lord is G. over all the earth; 13: 41 there is one G., and one Shepherd over all the earth; 17: 14 ye shall know that I, the Lord, am G.; 17: 30 (2 Ne. 1: 10) G. is the Redeemer of Israel; 17: 30 (31: 16; Alma 5: 13; 7: 6; 11: 25–27; 43: 20; 3 Ne. 30: 1; Morm. 5: 14; 9: 28–29) the living G.; 17: 40 the Lord loves those who will have him to be their G.; 18: 16 (Jacob 3: 1) look unto G.; 19: 10 G. of our fathers; 19: 12 G. of nature suffers; 21: 5 (Isa. 49: 5) my G. shall be my strength; **2 Ne.** 2: 2 thou knowest greatness of G.; 2: 10 (2 Ne. 9: 38; Alma 40: 11; 42: 23) all men come unto G.; 2: 13 if there is no law, sin, righteousness, happiness, punishment, there is no G.; 2: 14 there is a G.; 2: 18 (Alma 42: 3) through the fall, man became as G., knowing good and evil; 2: 21 G. gave commandment that all men

must repent; 4: 20 my G. hath been my support; 4: 30 (Jacob 7: 25) my G. and rock of my salvation; 4: 35 (James 1: 5) G. will give liberally to him that asketh; 6: 15 they who believe not shall know that the Lord is G.; 6: 17 Mighty G. shall deliver his covenant people; 8: 22 thy G. pleadeth the cause of his people; 9: 4 in our bodies we shall see G.; 11: 3 G. proveth all his words; 11: 4 all things given of G. from beginning are the typifying of Christ; 11: 7 if there be no Christ, there be no G.; 15: 16 (Isa. 5: 16) G. that is holy shall be sanctified in righteousness; 18: 10 (Isa. 8: 10) G. is with us; 19: 6 (Isa. 9: 6) Messiah shall be called, The Mighty G.; 26: 17 those who have dwindled in unbelief seek to destroy the things of G.; 26: 33 all are alike unto G.; 27: 23 I am G., and I am a G. of miracles; 28: 6 churches will say G. is not a G. of miracles; 29: 8 testimony of two nations is witness that I am G.; 31: 21 (Mosiah 15: 1–5; Alma 11: 44) Father, Son, and Holy Ghost are one G.; 2: 5 sin appears abominable unto G.; 4: 5 Abraham's offering up of Isaac is in similitude of G. and his Only Begotten Son; 6: 5 cleave unto G.; **Enos** 1: 6 (Ether 3: 12) G. could not lie; **Mosiah** 2: 16–19 when ye are in service of fellow beings, ye are in service of G.; 4: 22 your substance and your life belong to G.; 5: 5, 8 (6: 1; 21: 31–32; Alma 46: 22; Ether 13: 11) enter covenant with G.; 5: 15 G. is above all; 7: 27 Christ is the G., the Father of all things; 8: 18 G. has provided means for man to become great benefit to fellow beings; 11: 21, 23 (Hel. 7: 17) turn to G.; 11: 22 (13: 13) they shall know that I am the Lord their G., and am a jealous G.; 12: 21 (15: 14; 3 Ne. 20: 40) G. reigneth; 12: 24 (15: 31) all ends of earth shall see salvation of our G.; 12: 30 you ought to tremble before G.; 12: 35 (Ex. 20: 3) thou shalt have no other G. before me; 13: 28 (Alma 42: 15) G. himself shall make atonement for sins of his people; 13: 32–33 (15: 23; 16: 4) G. to redeem his people; 13: 34 (15: 1; 17: 8) prophets have prophesied that G. would come down and take form of man; 15: 8 G. breaks the bands of death; 17: 19 G. executes vengeance; 21: 35 baptism a testimony that they were willing to serve G.; 24: 5 Lamanites know not G.; 27: 15 I am sent from G.; 27: 31 all men shall confess that he is G.; **Alma** 5: 19 can ye look up to G. at day of judgment with pure heart and clean hands; 5: 28 if ye are not stripped of pride, ye are not prepared to meet G.; 5: 40 (Moro. 7: 12) good comes from G.; 9: 5 (16: 9) people of Ammonihah knew not that G. could do such marvelous works; 11: 24 thou knowest there is a G.; 11: 28–29 there is no more than one G.; 12:

24 (34: 32; 42: 4) life a probationary time to prepare to meet G.; 12: 30 G. conversed with men and made known the plan of redemption; 12: 33 G. called on men in name of the Son; 12: 37 provoke not G.; 18: 24–28 Ammon[2] teaches Lamoni about G.; 18: 30 G. dwells in the heavens; 18: 34 (22: 12) man was created after image of G.; 22: 7–11 Aaron[3] teaches Lamanite king about Great Spirit, who is G.; 22: 18 if thou art G., wilt thou make thyself known to me; 24: 12 G. has taken away our stains; 26: 37 G. is mindful of every people; 27: 4 (36: 6) angels sent from G.; 30: 37–39 Alma[2] testifies to Korihor that there is a G.; 30: 44 what evidence have you there is no G.; 30: 44 will ye tempt G.; 30: 48, 52 Korihor does not deny existence of G.; 30: 53 devil said there is no G.; 37: 12 records preserved for wise purpose known unto G.; 37: 47 (38: 2) look to G. and live; 39: 8 ye cannot hide your crimes from G.; 39: 17 souls always precious unto G.; 40: 4–5, 10, 21 G. knows time appointed for all to come forth from the dead; 40: 8 all is as one day with G.; 41: 8 G's decrees are unalterable; 41: 11 the wicked are without G. in the world and have gone contrary to nature of G.; 42: 13, 22–23, 25 if work of justice could be destroyed, G. would cease to be G.; 42: 26 G. brings about his great and eternal purposes; 44: 4 G. will support the faithful; 46: 10 foundation of liberty granted by G.; 48: 10 Moroni[1] prepares to support liberty, that Nephites might live unto G.; 58: 11 G. visited Nephites with assurances he would deliver them; 58: 40 (61: 9, 21; Hel. 14: 30) Ammonite youth stand fast in liberty wherewith G. has made them free; 60: 10 sufferings are known unto G.; **Hel.** 3: 35 sanctification comes because of yielding hearts unto G.; 7: 20 how could you have forgotten your G. in very day he has delivered you; 9: 21 how long will G. suffer us to remain in sin; 12: 2 when G. prospers his people they forget him; 13: 11 return unto G.; 3 **Ne.** 11: 14 Christ is G. of whole earth; 13: 24 (Matt. 6: 24) ye cannot serve G. and Mammon; **Morm.** 3: 21 Jews to have witnesses that that Jesus whom they slew was the very G.; 5: 17 Lamanites were once led by G.; 8: 10 none know true G. save disciples of Jesus; 8: 15 none can have power to bring record to light save it be given him of G.; 9: 2 in day of visitation will ye say there is no G.; 9: 9 G. is same yesterday, today, forever; 9: 16 are not the things G. hath wrought marvelous; **Ether** 2: 8–12 whoso possesses this land should serve G.; 3: 12 thou art a G. of truth; 3: 15 Christ ministers unto brother of Jared[2] that he might know he is G.; 12: 11 G.

prepared a more excellent way; 12: 12 G. can do no miracle among the faithless; **Moro.** 7: 12 devil an enemy to G.; 7: 13–16 that which is of G. invites and entices to do good; 7: 14, 17 that which persuades to do evil is not of G.; 7: 23 G. declared unto prophets that Christ should come; 7: 35 (10: 4–5, 29) G. will show things that are true; 7: 44 only meek and lowly are acceptable before G.; 8: 12–18 G. is not a changeable G.

GOD, BODY OF (see also TG God, Body of—Corporeal Nature)

Mosiah 3: 5 (Alma 7: 8) the Lord shall dwell in tabernacle of clay; 7: 27 Christ to take upon himself image of man, flesh and blood; 7: 27 (Ether 3: 15; Gen. 1: 26–27) man created after image of G.; **3 Ne.** 11: 14–15 Nephites feel Christ's resurrected body; **Ether** 3: 15–16 Christ shows brother of Jared² body of his spirit, which appears as body he will have in flesh.

GOD—CREATOR (see also Creation; Jesus Christ—Creator; TG God, Creator)

1 Ne. 17: 36 the Lord has created earth and his children to possess it; **2 Ne.** 2: 14 (Mosiah 4: 9; Alma 18: 28; 22: 10; Morm. 9: 11) G. created all things in heaven and earth; 8: 13 (Isa. 51: 13) the Lord thy maker stretched forth the heavens, laid foundations of earth; 9: 40 I have spoken words of your Maker; 11: 7 if there were no G., there could have been no creation; 29: 7 G. has created all men; **Jacob** 2: 6 Nephites' sins make Jacob² shrink before his Maker; 2: 21 G. has created men to keep his commandments and glorify him; 4: 9 earth was created by power of G's word; **Enos** 1: 4 Enos² kneels before his Maker; **Omni** 1: 17 people of Zarahemla deny being of their Creator; **Mosiah** 2: 20–23 G. has created you and granted unto you your lives; 29: 19 except for interposition of all-wise Creator, people of Noah³ must remain in bondage; **Alma** 30: 44 all things witness there is a Supreme Creator; **Morm.** 9: 11–12 G. of Abraham, Isaac, and Jacob created heavens and earth.

GOD, ETERNAL NATURE OF (see also God the Father; TG God, Eternal Nature of)

Title Page (2 Ne. 26: 12) Jesus is the Christ, the Eternal G.; **1 Ne.** 10: 19 (Alma 7: 20) the course of the Lord is one eternal round; 11: 21 (13: 40; Mosiah 15: 4; 16: 15; Alma 11: 38–39; Morm. 6: 22; Moro. 4: 3; 5: 2; 10: 4, 31) the Eternal Father; 11: 32 (15: 15; 2 Ne. 4: 35; Hel. 12: 8; Moro. 10: 28) the Everlasting G.; 12: 18 (2 Ne. 9: 8; Alma 34: 9; Ether 8: 23) the Eternal G.; **2 Ne.** 19: 6

(Isa. 9: 6) Messiah shall be called, The Everlasting Father; **Mosiah** 16: 9 Christ is the light of the world, a light that is endless; **Alma** 11: 44 Godhead is one eternal G.; 13: 9 Only Begotten is without beginning of days or end of years; **Hel.** 1: 11 everlasting Maker; 13: 38 (Alma 41: 10–11) to seek happiness in iniquity is contrary to nature of righteousness which is in our Eternal Head; **3 Ne.** 24: 6 (Moro. 8: 18) the Lord changes not; **Morm.** 9: 9 G. is same yesterday, today, forever; 9: 9–10 no variableness or shadow of changing in G.; 9: 19 G. changes not, or he would cease to be G.; **Moro.** 7: 22 G. knows all things, being from everlasting to everlasting; 10: 34 Jehovah, the Eternal Judge of both quick and dead.

GOD, FOREKNOWLEDGE OF (see also Elect; God, Omniscience of; TG God, Foreknowledge of)

1 Ne. 20: 5 before it came to pass I showed them thee; **2 Ne.** 27: 10 G. reveals all things from foundation of world to end; **W of M** 1: 7 the Lord knows all things which are to come; **Alma** 13: 3 priests were called and ordained from foundation of world according to foreknowledge of G.; 13: 7 high priesthood prepared from eternity to eternity according to G's foreknowledge of all things; 40: 4–5, 10, 21 G. knows time when all shall come forth from the dead; 40: 10 G. knows all the times appointed unto man.

GOD, GOODNESS OF (see also Kindness)

1 Ne. 1: 1 Nephi¹ has great knowledge of goodness of G.; 5: 4 except for vision, Lehi¹ would not have known goodness of G.; **2 Ne.** 9: 10 how great the goodness of G.; 33: 14 you that will not partake of goodness of G., I bid you an everlasting farewell; **Jacob** 1: 7 we labored diligently to persuade our people to partake of goodness of G.; **Mosiah** 4: 5–6 knowledge of goodness of G. awakens man to sense of nothingness; 5: 3 through goodness of G. we have great views of things to come; 25: 10 G's goodness in delivering people of Alma¹; **Alma** 12: 32 justice could not be destroyed, according to supreme goodness of G.; 57: 25 goodness of G. preserves stripling Ammonites; **3 Ne.** 4: 33 Nephites weep because of goodness of G.; **Morm.** 2: 13 Nephites' sorrowing was not unto repentance because of goodness of G.

GOD, LOVE OF (see also Charity; Compassion; Love; Mercy; TG God, Love of)

1 Ne. 11: 17 G. loveth his children; 11: 22, 25 tree of life represents love of G.; 11: 25 waters are representation of love of G.; 17: 40 the Lord loveth those

who will have him to be their G.; **2 Ne.**
1: 15 Lehi¹ is encircled eternally in arms
of G's love; 4: 21 G. hath filled me with
his love; 26: 24 the Lord loveth the world,
layeth down life; **Jacob** 3: 2 feast upon
G's love; **Mosiah** 4: 11–12 if ye retain in
remembrance the greatness of G., ye shall
be filled with his love; **Alma** 24: 14 G.
has made gospel known to Lamanites
because he loves them; **Hel.** 15: 3 the
Lord has chastened Nephites because he
loves them; **Ether** 12: 34 the Lord's love
is charity; **Moro.** 7: 47 charity is pure
love of Christ.

GOD, MANIFESTATIONS OF (*see also*
Dream; God, Presence of; Jesus Christ,
Appearances of; Jesus Christ, Second
Coming of; Revelation; Vision; Voice; TG
God, Manifestations of; God, Privilege
of Seeing)

1 Ne. 1: 8 (5: 4; Alma 36: 22) Lehi¹
is carried away in vision and sees G. on
throne; 10: 11 Messiah to rise from dead
and *m.* himself to Gentiles; **2 Ne.** 2: 4
(11: 3) Jacob² has beheld Redeemer's
glory in his youth; 9: 4 in our bodies we
shall see G.; 11: 2 Isaiah¹ saw Redeemer,
as did Nephi²; 26: 13 Christ manifests
himself to all who believe in him; **Alma**
19: 6 light of glory of G. lights up Lamoni's
mind and he is carried away in G.; 19: 13
Lamoni has seen his Redeemer; **3 Ne.**
11: 8 Nephites see Man descending from
heaven; 12: 8 (Matt. 5: 8) the pure in
heart shall see G.; 28: 37 Mormon² inquires of the Lord and he makes truth
manifest; **Ether** 3: 13–16 Christ shows
himself to brother of Jared²; 12: 39
Moroni² talked with Jesus face to face.

GOD, OMNISCIENCE OF (*see also* God,
Foreknowledge of; God, Wisdom of;
Knowledge; TG God, Omniscience of)

2 Ne. 2: 24 all things done in wisdom
of him who knoweth all things; 9: 20
(Morm. 8: 17) G. knows all things, there is
not anything except he knows it; 27: 10
G's revelation reveals all things from
foundation of world to end; 27: 27 the
Lord knows all works in dark; **Jacob** 2: 5
by help of Creator Jacob² can tell his
people their thoughts; **Alma** 7: 13 Spirit
knoweth all things; 18: 32 G. knows all
thoughts and intents of heart; 26: 35 G.
comprehends all things; 26: 37 G. is mindful of every people; 39: 8 ye cannot hide
your crimes from G.; 40: 4–5, 10, 21 G.
knows time when all shall come forth
from the dead; 60: 10 known unto G. were
all their cries and sufferings; **3 Ne.** 28: 6
Christ knows his disciples' thoughts;
Ether 3: 25 the Lord shows brother of
Jared² all inhabitants of earth who had
been or would be; **Moro.** 7: 22 G. knows

all things, being from everlasting to everlasting.

GOD, POWER OF

1 Ne. 1: 14 (17: 48; Mosiah 11: 23;
18: 13; Hel. 10: 11; 3 Ne. 4: 32) G.
Almighty; 1: 14 the Lord's power is over
all inhabitants of earth; 4: 1 the Lord is
mightier than all the earth; 7: 12 the
Lord is able to do all things; 9: 6 the Lord
has all power unto fulfilling all his words;
11: 31 the afflicted are healed by power of
Lamb; 13: 18–19, 30 (Mosiah 23: 13)
Gentiles in promised land delivered by
power of G. out of hands of all other
nations; 17: 46 by power of his almighty
word G. can cause earth to pass away;
17: 48 Nephi¹ filled with power of G.; 17:
51 the Lord has such great power and
has wrought so many miracles; 18: 20
(Alma 30: 52) only power of G. threatening destruction could soften hearts; 21:
26 (22: 12; 2 Ne. 6: 18) the Lord is the
Mighty One of Jacob; **2 Ne.** 6: 17 Mighty
G. shall deliver his covenant people; 10:
25 may G. raise you by power of resurrection and by power of atonement; 19: 16
(Isa. 9: 16) Messiah's name shall be
called, The Mighty God; 26: 20 false
churches will put down power and miracles of G.; 27: 10 book shall be sealed by
power of G.; 27: 12 (Ether 5: 3–4) three
witnesses shall behold book by power of
G.; 27: 20 the Lord is able to do his own
work; 28: 3–5, 26 (Jacob 6: 8; Morm. 8:
28) churches shall deny power of G.; 31:
19 rely upon merits of him who is mighty
to save; **Jacob** 2: 5 by help of all-powerful
Creator, I can tell you your thoughts;
4: 11 power of resurrection which is in
Christ; 7: 21 power of G. comes down
upon multitude; **Enos** 1: 26 (Alma 37:
40; Morm. 7: 9) Enos² wrought upon by
power of G., that he must preach and
prophesy; **Mosiah** 3: 5, 17–18, 21 (5: 2,
15) the Lord Omnipotent; 4: 9 believe
that G. has all power in heaven and
earth; 8: 16 no man can have greater gift
than to be seer, except he possess power
of G.; 11: 23 none to deliver this people
except the Almighty G.; 15: 3 Christ is
called the Father because he was conceived by power of G.; 21: 30 Alma¹ and
his people form church through power of
G.; 27: 14 angel comes to convince Alma²
of power of G.; 27: 15 can ye dispute the
power of G.; 27: 18 nothing save power of
G. could make earth tremble as though it
would part asunder; **Alma** 5: 50 Son
cometh in his might, majesty, power; 7:
8 G. has power to do all things according
to his word; 9: 28 the righteous shall reap
salvation according to power of Christ;
14: 10 Amulek asks Alma² to exercise
power of G. on behalf of martyrs; 14: 24
if ye have power of G., deliver yourselves;

19: 6, 17 Lamoni is under power of G.; 23: 6 power of G. works miracles in Ammon² and his brethren; 26: 35 (Morm. 5: 23; Ether 3: 4) G. has all power; 30: 51–52 Korihor knows he is struck dumb by power of G.; 31: 5 preaching of word of G. has powerful effect upon minds; 34: 18 G. is mighty to save; 37: 15 if ye transgress, sacred things shall be taken away by power of G.; 37: 16 G. is powerful to fulfilling his words; 44: 5 the all-powerful G.; 56: 56 stripling Ammonites fight with strength of G.; 57: 26 stripling Ammonites are preserved by miraculous power of G.; **Hel.** 5: 11 Father gives the Lord power to redeem men from their sins; 9: 36 Nephi² knows nothing concerning murder of chief judge save given by power of G.; 12: 10–12 by power of G's voice, whole earth shakes; **3 Ne.** 13: 13 (Matt. 6: 13) thine is the kingdom, the power, and the glory; **Morm.** 5: 22 how can ye stand before power of G.; 7: 5 believe that Christ has risen by power of Father; 8: 16 bringing forth of record shall be by power of G.; 9: 13 all men shall be awakened from endless sleep by power of G.; **Ether** 3: 4 the Lord has all power and can do whatsoever he will for benefit of man; **Moro.** 7: 16 everything which invites to do good is sent by power of Christ; 7: 35 G. will show with power that these things are true; 10: 7, 32–33 deny not the power of G.; 10: 7 G. works by power according to men's faith.

GOD, PRESENCE OF (*see also* Death, Spiritual; Redemption; Resurrection)

1 **Ne.** 10: 21 no unclean thing can dwell with G.; **2 Ne.** 2: 8 no flesh can dwell in presence of G. save through mercy and grace of Messiah; 2: 10 (9: 38; Alma 40: 11; 42: 23) all men will stand in presence of G. to be judged; 9: 6 because man became fallen, they were cut off from presence of the Lord; 9: 8 angel fell from presence of Eternal G.; 9: 8–9 except for resurrection, spirits must be shut out from presence of G.; **Mosiah** 2: 38 sense of guilt causes man to shrink from presence of the Lord; 2: 41 those who keep commandments dwell with God in state of never-ending happiness; 15: 23 prophets and believers are raised to dwell with God; **Alma** 36: 14–15 thought of standing in presence of G. racks Alma² with horror; 36: 30 (38: 1) those who keep not commandments are cut off from G's presence; 42: 7 first parents were cut off temporally and spiritually from presence of the Lord; 42: 23 (Hel. 14: 15) resurrection brings men back into G's presence; **Hel.** 12: 25 in last day some shall be cast off from presence of the Lord; **Morm.** 9: 4–5 the miserable to dwell with G. under consciousness of filthiness; 9: 13

(Ether 3: 13) because of redemption, men are brought back into presence of the Lord.

GOD, WISDOM OF (*see also* God, Omniscience of; TG God, Wisdom of)

1 **Ne.** 9: 5 (W of M 1: 7) the Lord commands Nephi¹ to make plates for wise purpose; **2 Ne.** 2: 24 all things have been done in wisdom of him who knows all things; 9: 8 O the wisdom of G.; 27: 22 sealed book to be revealed when the Lord sees fit in his wisdom; **Jacob** 4: 10 (Alma 29: 8; 37: 12) the Lord counsels in wisdom; **Mosiah** 4: 9 (Alma 26: 35) believe that G. has all wisdom; 29: 19 the all-wise Creator; **Alma** 37: 2 record to be kept for a wise purpose; **3 Ne.** 28: 29 when the Lord sees fit in wisdom, three Nephites will minister to scattered tribes; 29: 1 (Morm. 5: 13) writings to come forth when the Lord sees fit in his wisdom.

GOD THE FATHER (*see also* Children of God; Jesus Christ—Creator; TG God the Father—Elohim/Eloheim; God the Father—Jehovah; Man, a Spirit Child of Heavenly Father)

1 **Ne.** 11: 21 (13: 40) Lamb of God is Son of Eternal Father; 14: 8 remember covenants of Father unto house of Israel; **2 Ne.** 19: 6 (Isa. 9: 6) Messiah shall be called, The Everlasting Father; 25: 16 Jews shall worship Father in Christ's name; 31: 21 (Alma 11: 44; 3 Ne. 11: 27; Morm. 7: 7) Father, Son, and Holy Ghost are one God; 32: 9 (3 Ne. 18: 19–20; 21: 27; Morm. 9: 27; Ether 4: 15; Moro. 2: 2; 7: 26; 8: 3; 10: 4) pray unto Father in name of Christ; **Jacob** 4: 5 prophets worshipped Father in Christ's name; **Mosiah** 2: 34 ye are eternally indebted to heavenly Father; 3: 8 (15: 4; 16: 15; Alma 11: 38–39; Hel. 14: 12; 16: 18; Ether 4: 7) Jesus Christ is Father of heaven and earth; 7: 27 Christ is Father of all things; 15: 2 (Morm. 9: 12; Ether 3: 14) Christ is Father and Son; 15: 3 Christ is the Father because he was conceived by power of God; **3 Ne.** 1: 14 Christ comes to do will both of Father and of Son; 9: 15 Christ was with Father from beginning; 9: 15 (11: 27) Christ is in Father, and Father in Christ; 9: 15 in Christ has Father glorified his name; 11: 25 baptism performed in name of Father, Son, and Holy Ghost; 11: 32 Father, Son, and Holy Ghost bear record of each other; 12: 48 (Matt. 5: 48) be perfect even as Christ, or Father in heaven, is perfect; 13: 6 (Matt. 6: 6) pray to thy Father who is in secret; 13: 9 (Matt. 6: 9) our Father who art in heaven; 13: 14–15 (Matt. 6: 14–15) if ye forgive men their trespasses, heavenly Father will forgive you; 13: 26 fowls sow not, yet heavenly Father feeds them; 13: 32 Heavenly Father knows ye

have need of all these things; 14: 21 (Matt. 7: 21) he who does will of Father will enter kingdom of heaven; 17: 15–18 Jesus speaks marvelous things in prayer to Father; 18: 21 pray in your families unto Father; 18: 27 Christ must go to Father to fulfill other commandments; 28: 11 Father gives Holy Ghost unto men because of Christ; **Morm.** 6: 22 the Eternal Father knows your state; **Moro.** 4: 3 (5: 2) O God, the Eternal Father; 10: 4 ask God, the Eternal Father, if these things are true; 10: 31 covenants of Eternal Father to house of Israel shall be fulfilled.

GODHEAD (see also God; God the Father; Holy Ghost; Jesus Christ; TG Godhead)

2 Ne. 31: 21 doctrine of Christ is only true doctrine of Father, Son, Holy Ghost; 31: 21 (Mosiah 15: 2–5; Alma 11: 44; 3 Ne. 11: 27, 36; Morm. 7: 7) Father, Son, and Holy Ghost are one God; **Alma** 11: 44 all must be arraigned before bar of Christ the Son, God the Father, and Holy Ghost; **Morm.** 7: 7 sing unto Father, Son, and Holy Ghost; **Ether** 12: 41 grace of Father, Christ, Holy Ghost to abide in you forever.

GODLINESS, GODLY (see also TG Godliness; Mysteries of Godliness)

Moro. 7: 30 miracles are shown unto them of strong faith in every form of g.

GODS (see also Idolatry)

Alma 12: 31 having transgressed first commandments, first parents became as G., knowing good from evil; **Morm.** 4: 14 Lamanites offer women and children as sacrifices unto their idol g.

GOLD (see also Metal; Ore)

1 Ne. 13: 7 Nephi[1] sees g. and silver in abominable church; 18: 25 Nephites find g. in promised land; 2 Ne. 23: 12 (Isa. 13: 12) I will make a man more precious than fine g.; **Jacob** 2: 12 many Nephites have begun to search for g.; **Mosiah** 2: 12 Benjamin has not sought g. of his people for his service; 19: 15 Limhi's people must give Lamanites half their g. as tribute; **Alma** 1: 29 (Hel. 6: 9) Nephites have abundance of g.; 3 Ne. 24: 3 (Mal. 3: 3) the Lord shall purge sons of Levi[1] as g. and silver; **Ether** 10: 5–7 Riplakish causes fine g. to be refined in prison.

GOOD (see also Better; God, Goodness of; Tidings; Work [noun])

2 Ne. 2: 5 (Hel. 14: 31) men are instructed sufficiently that they know g. from evil; 2: 18 (Alma 12: 31) Satan tells Eve partaking of forbidden fruit will make her as God, knowing g. and evil; 2: 26 because men are redeemed from fall,

they have become free forever, knowing g. and evil; 2: 30 I have chosen the g. part; 15: 20 (Isa. 5: 20) wo unto them that call evil g. and g. evil; 17: 15 (Isa. 7: 15) butter and honey shall he eat, that he may know to refuse evil and choose g.; 33: 4, 10 words of Jacob[2] persuade men to do g.; **Jacob** 2: 19 seek riches for the intent to do g.; 5: 25, 43 trees planted in g. spot of ground; **Omni** 1: 25 believe in all things which are g.; **Mosiah** 5: 2 Benjamin's people experience mighty change of heart to do g. continually; 16: 3 (Alma 12: 31) fall is cause of mankind's knowing g. from evil; **Alma** 5: 40 whatsoever is g. cometh of God; 29: 5 he that knoweth not g. from evil is blameless; 32: 35 whatsoever is light is g.; 37: 37 counsel with the Lord in all thy doings and he will direct thee for g.; 41: 13 restoration means to bring back g. for g.; 41: 14 do g. continually; **Hel.** 12: 4 children of men are slow to do g.; 14: 31 ye can do g. and be restored unto g.; 3 Ne. 12: 44 (Matt. 5: 44) do g. to them that hate you; 14: 17 (Matt. 7: 17) every g. tree bringeth forth g. fruit; **Ether** 4: 11 Spirit persuadeth men to do g.; 4: 12 whatsoever persuadeth men to do g. is of Christ, for g. cometh of none save Christ; **Moro.** 7: 12 all things which are g. come of God; 7: 13, 16 that which is of God inviteth to do g. continually; 7: 19 search diligently in the light of Christ that ye may know g. from evil; 7: 19 if ye lay hold upon every g. thing, ye will be child of Christ; 10: 6 nothing that is g. denieth Christ, but acknowledgeth that he is.

GOOD SHEPHERD (see Jesus Christ—Good Shepherd)

GOODLY

1 Ne. 1: 1 Nephi[1] born of g. parents.

GOSPEL (see also Baptism; Covenant; Faith; Holy Ghost, Gift of; Jesus Christ; Obedience; Plan; Religion; Repentance; Salvation; Tidings; Truth; Word of God/Word of the Lord)

1 Ne. 10: 14 (15: 13) after Gentiles receive fulness of g. Israel shall come to knowledge of Messiah; 13: 24 when book proceeded from Jews, it had fulness of g.; 13: 26, 32, 34 plain and precious parts of g. kept back by abominable church; 2 Ne. 30: 5 g. of Christ shall be declared among Lamanites; 3 Ne. 16: 10–12 when Gentiles reject fulness of g., it shall come to Israel; 27: 10 if church is built upon Christ's g., Father will show his works in it; 27: 13–21 this is my g.; 28: 23 disciples preach g. of Christ unto all people; 4 Ne. 1: 38 those who reject g. are called Lamanites; **Morm.** 9: 8 he that denieth these things knoweth not the g. of Christ; 9: 22 (Matt.

28: 19) go ye into world and preach g. to every creature; **Ether** 4: 18 repent all ye ends of the earth, and believe in my g.

GOSSIP (*see also* Babbling; Backbiting; Lying; Slander)

Hel. 16: 22 Satan spreads rumors and contentions.

GOVERN, GOVERNMENT (*see also* Government, Civil; Order; Regulate; Rule)

2 Ne. 19: 6 (Isa. 9: 6) unto us a child is born, and the g. shall be upon his shoulders; 19: 7 (Isa. 9: 7) of the increase of g. and peace there is no end.

GOVERNMENT, CIVIL (*see also* Country; Freedom; Governor; Governor; Law, Civil; Liberty; Nation; Right [noun]; Tax; TG Governments)

Alma 43: 17 Moroni[1] takes command and g. of wars; 46: 35 Amalickiahites who will not covenant to maintain free g. are put to death; 51: 5 king-men desire to alter law to overthrow free g.; 54: 17, 24 Ammoron claims Nephites' fathers robbed their brethren of right to g.; 58: 36 Helaman[2] fears some faction in g. does not send more men; 59: 13 Moroni[1] is angry with g.; 60: 14 Moroni[1] fears God's judgments will come because of slothfulness of g.; 60: 24 necessary to cleanse g. before contending with Lamanites; **Hel.** 1: 18 because of contention in g. Nephites do not keep sufficient guards in Zarahemla; 5: 2 laws and g. established by voice of people; 6: 39 robbers obtain sole management of g.; 7: 5 robbers held in office at head of g. to get gain; **3 Ne.** 3: 10 Giddianhi claims he desires to help his people recover g.; 7: 2, 6 people separate into tribes and destroy g. of land; 7: 11 tribes united in hatred of those who entered covenant to destroy g.; 7: 14 tribes not united as to laws and manner of g.; 9: 9 people of king Jacob[4] destroy peace and g. of land.

GOVERNOR (*see also* Government, Civil; Judge, Chief; Ruler)

Alma 2: 16 Alma[2] is g. of Nephites; 50: 39 (61: 1) Pahoran[1] is appointed g.; **3 Ne.** 1: 1 Lachoneus[1] is g.

GRACE (*see also* Jesus Christ, Atonement through; Mercy; Redemption; Salvation; Work [noun]; BD Grace)

2 Ne. 2: 6 (Alma 5: 48; 9: 26; 13: 9) Messiah is full of g. and truth; 9: 8 O the wisdom of God, his mercy and g.; 9: 53 because of g. and mercy, the Lord has promised that Nephites' seed shall not be destroyed; 10: 24 only in and through g. of God that men are saved; 11: 5 my soul delighteth in the Lord's g.; 25: 23 by g. we are saved, after all we can do; **Jacob**

4: 7 the Lord showeth us our weakness that we may know it is by his g. that we have power; **Mosiah** 18: 16 people of Alma[1] are baptized and filled with g. of God; 18: 26 (27: 5) for their labor priests were to receive g. of God; **Alma** 7: 3 continue in supplicating of the Lord's g.; **Hel.** 12: 24 men should repent that they might be restored unto g. for g.; **Morm.** 2: 15 day of g. is past with Nephites; **Ether** 12: 26–27 the Lord's g. is sufficient for the meek; 12: 36, 41 Moroni[2] prays the Lord will give the Gentiles g.; **Moro.** 7: 2 by g. of Father and Christ Mormon[2] is permitted to speak; 8: 3 continually praying that God, through infinite g., will keep you; 10: 32–33 ye may be perfect in Christ, by his g.

GRAFT

1 Ne. 10: 14 (15: 13–18; Jacob 5: 3–77; Alma 16: 17) after Gentiles receive gospel, natural branches or remnant of Israel should be g. in, or come to knowledge of Messiah.

GRAIN (*see also* Food; Wheat)

Hel. 11: 17 the Lord causes rain to fall, that earth brings forth g.

GRANT (*see also* Give)

Mosiah 26: 23 the Lord g. unto him that believeth unto end a place at his right hand; **Alma** 17: 9 sons of Mosiah[2] pray that the Lord g. them portion of Spirit; 29: 4 God g. unto men according to their desire; 42: 4 probationary time g. unto man to repent; 42: 22 law given, a punishment affixed, a repentance g.

GRAPE (*see also* Vineyard; Wine)

2 Ne. 15: 2 (Isa. 5: 2) well-beloved's vineyard brought forth wild g.; **3 Ne.** 14: 16 (Matt. 7: 16) do men gather g. of thorns.

GRAVE (*see also* Baptism; Bury; Death, Physical; Resurrection; Sepulchre)

2 Ne. 1: 14 hear words of parent, whose limbs ye must soon lay down in g.; 9: 11–13 g. must deliver up its dead; **Mosiah** 16: 7–8 (Alma 22: 14) because of resurrection, g. hath no victory; **Hel.** 14: 25 many g. shall be opened at time of Christ's resurrection; **Morm.** 7: 5 Christ hath gained victory over g.

GRAVEN (*see* Engrave; Image)

GREAT, GREATER, GREATEST (*see also* Day of the Lord; Mighty)

1 Ne. 7: 11 ye have forgotten what g. things the Lord hath done for us; 15: 36 fruit of tree of life is g. of all gifts of God; **2 Ne.** 3: 9 latter-day seer shall be g. like Moses; 12: 9 (Isa. 2: 9) g. man humbleth

himself not, therefore forgive him not; **Alma** 18: 2–21 (19: 25) Lamoni mistakes Ammon² for G. Spirit; 18: 22–35 Ammon² teaches Lamoni about G. Spirit; **Morm.** 9: 13 when trump shall sound, all shall come forth, both small and g.; **Ether** 7: 27 Shule remembers g. things the Lord hath done for forefathers in bringing them across g. deep.

GRIEVE (see also Lament; Mourn; Remorse; Sorrow)

1 **Ne.** 2: 18 (15: 4) Nephi¹ g. because of hardness of brothers' hearts; **Jacob** 5: 7, 11, 32, 46–47, 51, 66 the Lord g. that he must lose trees; 3 **Ne.** 7: 16 Nephi³ g. for hardness of hearts.

GROSS, GROSSER, GROSSEST

Jacob 2: 22 Jacob² must speak to his people concerning g. crime; **Alma** 8: 28 people wax more g. in iniquities; 26: 24 Lamanites' days spent in g. iniquities.

GROUND (see also Dust; Earth; Grounds)

1 **Ne.** 4: 2 (17: 26; Mosiah 7: 19; Hel. 8: 11) fathers come through Red Sea on dry g.; 2 **Ne.** 26: 16 those who shall be destroyed shall speak out of g.; **Jacob** 5: 22 tree planted in poor spot of g. brings forth much fruit; 5: 23 tree planted in poorer spot of g. also brings forth much fruit; 5: 25, 43 tree planted in good spot of g. brings forth tame and wild fruit; **Alma** 32: 39 if neglected tree withers, it is because g. is barren.

GROUNDS (see also Ground)

Alma 5: 10 what g. had fathers to hope for salvation; 30: 7, 11 law should not bring men on to unequal g.

GROW (see also Enlarge; Increase; Multiply; Spread; Swell; Wax)

Alma 32: 28–41 word compared to good seed which will g. if planted in heart; 3 **Ne.** 25: 2 (Mal. 4: 2) ye shall g. up as calves in stall.

GRUDGINGLY

Moro. 7: 8 if a man being evil giveth a gift, he doeth it g.

GUIDE (see also Counsel; Direction; Enlighten; God, Wisdom of; Holy Ghost; Inspire; Reveal; TG Guidance, Divine)

Mosiah 2: 36 if ye transgress, Spirit shall have no place in you to g. you in wisdom's paths; **Hel.** 13: 29 how long will ye be led by blind g.

GUILE

Alma 18: 23 Ammon² catches king with g.

GUILT, GUILTY (see also Bondage; Re-

pentance; Shame; Sin; Spot; Stain; Torment; Transgression)

1 **Ne.** 16: 2 the g. take truth to be hard; 2 **Ne.** 9: 14 we shall have perfect knowledge of all our g.; 28: 8 if we are g., God will beat us with a few stripes; **Jacob** 6: 9 resurrection will bring you to stand with awful g. before God; **Enos** 1: 6 my g. was swept away; **Mosiah** 2: 38 justice awakens soul to lively sense of g.; 3: 25 those who have done evil works are consigned to awful view of own g.; **Alma** 1: 12 Nehor is g. of priestcraft; 5: 18 can ye imagine yourselves brought before God's tribunal filled with g.; 5: 23 these things will testify ye are g. of all manner of wickedness; 11: 43 we shall be brought to stand before God with bright recollection of all our g.; 12: 1 Zeezrom trembles under consciousness of g.; 14: 7 Zeezrom confesses he is g.; 24: 10 God has forgiven us and taken away g. from hearts; 30: 25 Korihor says child is not g. because of parents; 39: 7 I would to God ye had not been g. of so great a crime; 43: 46 inasmuch as ye are not g. of first or second offense, ye shall not suffer yourselves to be slain by enemies; **Hel.** 7: 5 wicked judges let the g. go unpunished; 3 **Ne.** 6: 29 lawyers and judges enter covenant to deliver those g. of murder from grasp of justice; **Morm.** 9: 3 can ye dwell with God under consciousness of your g.

GUILTLESS (see also Blameless; Spotless)

Mosiah 4: 25–26 that ye may walk g. before God, impart of your substance to the poor; 13: 15 (Ex. 20: 7) the Lord will not hold him g. that taketh his name in vain; 3 **Ne.** 27: 16 whoso repents, is baptized, and endures to end will Christ hold g. before the Father.

GULF (see also Hell; Misery)

1 **Ne.** 12: 18 (15: 28) awful g. separates the wicked from tree of life; 2 **Ne.** 1: 13 (Alma 26: 20; Hel. 5: 12) chains bind men captive down to eternal g. of misery and woe; **Hel.** 3: 29 word leads man of Christ across g. of misery.

HAGOTH—*Nephite ship builder* [c. 55 B.C.]

Alma 63: 5–8 builds and launches many ships.

HAIL (see also Destruction; Storm)

Mosiah 12: 6 the Lord will smite people of Noah³ with h.; **Hel.** 5: 12 devil shall send forth h.

HAIR (see also Head; Shave)

2 **Ne.** 13: 24 (Isa. 3: 24) instead of well-set h. there shall be baldness; **Alma** 11: 44 (40: 23) not so much as h. of head shall be lost in restoration; 3 **Ne.** 12: 36

(Matt. 5: 36) neither shalt thou swear by head, for thou canst not make one *h.* black or white.

HALLOWED (*see also* Holy)

Mosiah 13: 19 (Ex. 20: 11) the Lord blessed sabbath day and *h.* it; **3 Ne.** 13: 9 (Matt. 6: 9) our Father who art in heaven, *h.* be thy name.

HAND (*see also* Hand of the Lord; Hands, Laying on of; Labor; Right Hand)

1 Ne. 1: 3 Nephi¹ makes record with own *h.*; 17: 54 Nephi¹ stretches *h.* unto brethren, and the Lord shakes them; **2 Ne.** 25: 16 worship Father in Christ's name with pure hearts and clean *h.*; **Alma** 5: 19 can ye look up to God with pure heart and clean *h.*; 5: 28, 50 (10: 20; Hel. 5: 32) kingdom of heaven is soon at *h.*; **3 Ne.** 11: 14–15 Christ invites Nephites to thrust *h.* into his side, feel nail prints in *h.* and feet.

HAND OF THE LORD

1 Ne. 5: 14 Joseph¹ preserved by *h.* of the Lord; 21: 22 (2 Ne. 6: 6; Isa. 49: 22) the Lord will lift up *h.* to Gentiles; **2 Ne.** 1: 5 land covenanted unto all those led out of other countries by *h.* of the Lord; 1: 6 (Omni 1: 16) none shall come into land save they who were brought by *h.* of the Lord; 1: 10 (Alma 9: 23) Nephites receive great blessings from *h.* of the Lord; 1: 24 (Mosiah 23: 10; Alma 1: 8; 2: 30; 17: 9; 26: 3; 29: 9; 35: 14) instrument in *h.* of the Lord; 5: 12 (Mosiah 1: 16) compass prepared for Lehi¹ by *h.* of the Lord; 7: 2 (Isa. 50: 2) is the Lord's *h.* shortened that it cannot redeem; 8: 17 Jerusalem has drunk at *h.* of the Lord the cup of his fury; 15: 25 (19: 12, 21; 20: 4; Isa. 5: 25; 9: 12, 21; 10: 4) the Lord's *h.* is outstretched still; 21: 11 (25: 17; 29: 1; Jacob 6: 2; Isa. 11: 11) the Lord shall set his *h.* second time to recover his people; 28: 6 churches shall deny miracle wrought by *h.* of the Lord; **Jacob** 5: 47 has the Lord slackened his *h.* that he has not nourished his vineyard; 6: 4 the Lord stretches forth his *h.* unto house of Israel all the day long; **Mosiah** 1: 2 prophecies delivered to fathers by *h.* of the Lord; 2: 11 Benjamin made ruler by *h.* of the Lord; 28: 15 (Alma 37: 4) records preserved by *h.* of the Lord; **Alma** 2: 28 Nephites strengthened by *h.* of the Lord; 9: 22 Nephites delivered out of Jerusalem by *h.* of the Lord; 26: 3, 7 converted Lamanites are in *h.* of the Lord; 45: 19 Alma² buried by *h.* of the Lord; 46: 7 Nephites delivered by *h.* of the Lord; **4 Ne.** 1: 16 no happier people among all created by *h.* of God; **Morm.** 5: 23 know ye not that ye are in *h.* of the Lord; 6: 6 records had been entrusted to

Mormon² by *h.* of the Lord; 8: 8 *h.* of the Lord has brought destruction on Nephites; 8: 26 none can stay *h.* of the Lord; **Ether** 1: 1 Jaredites destroyed by *h.* of the Lord; 2: 6 Jaredites continually directed by *h.* of the Lord; 3: 6 the Lord stretches forth his *h.* and touches stones with finger; 10: 28 Jaredites blessed and prospered by *h.* of the Lord.

HANDS, LAYING ON OF (*see also* Anointing; Confirm; Heal; Holy Ghost, Gift of; Ordain; Ordinance; Priesthood; TG Hands, Laying on of; BD Laying on of Hands)

Alma 6: 1 Alma² ordains priests and elders by laying on his *h.*; 31: 36 Alma² claps his *h.* upon those with him, and they are filled with Holy Ghost; **3 Ne.** 18: 36–37 Christ gives disciples Holy Ghost by laying on of *h.*; **Morm.** 9: 24 believers shall lay *h.* on the sick, and they shall recover; **Moro.** 2: 2 disciples given power to bestow Holy Ghost by laying on of *h.*; 3: 1–2 disciples ordain priests and teachers by laying on of *h.*

HANG (*see also* Capital Punishment; Sword)

3 Ne. 4: 28 Zemnarihah is *h.* upon tree until dead.

HAPPINESS, HAPPY, HAPPIER (*see also* Blessed [adj.]; Cheer; Delight; Joy; Merry; Pleased; Pleasure)

1 Ne. 8: 10 fruit of tree of life is desirable to make one *h.*; **2 Ne.** 2: 13 if there be no righteousness, there be no *h.*; **Mosiah** 2: 41 those who keep commandments unto the end shall dwell with God in state of never-ending *h.*; 16: 11 the good are resurrected to endless life of *h.*; **Alma** 3: 26 those whose works are good reap eternal *h.*; 27: 18 none receive joy of God save penitent and humble seeker of *h.*; 28: 12 survivors of war rejoice that dead may be raised to dwell with God in state of never-ending *h.*; 40: 12–17 spirits of those who are righteous are received into state of *h.*; 41: 5 souls will be raised to *h.* according to their desires of *h.*; 41: 10 (Hel. 13: 38) ye shall not be restored from sin to *h.*; 41: 10 wickedness never was *h.*; 42: 16 punishment affixed opposite plan of *h.*; 44: 5 Nephites owe all their *h.* to sacred word of God; 46: 41 those who die in faith of Christ are *h.* in him; 50: 23 there never was *h.* time among Nephites than in days of Moroni¹; **Hel.** 12: 2 at very time when Lord does all things for welfare and *h.* of his people they harden their hearts; 13: 38 Nephites have sought for *h.* in doing iniquity; **4 Ne.** 1: 16 could not be a *h.* people among all those created by God; **Morm.**

2: 13 the Lord would not always suffer Nephites to take *h.* in sin; 7: 7 he that is found guiltless shall dwell in state of *h.* which hath no end.

HARD (*see also* Hardheartedness; Harsh)

1 **Ne.** 3: 28 Laman¹ and Lemuel speak *h.* words unto younger brothers; 15: 3 Lehi¹ spoke many things that were *h.* to understand; 16: 2 the guilty take the truth to be *h.*; 2 **Ne.** 9: 40 words of truth are *h.* against all uncleanness; **Hel.** 14: 10 Nephites seek to destroy Samuel the Lamanite because his words are *h.* against them.

HARDHEARTEDNESS (*see also* Contention; Doubt; Hate; Pride; Rebel; Resist; Soften; Stiffnecked; Stubbornness; Unbelief; Wicked; TG Hardheartedness)

1 **Ne.** 2: 18 (7: 8) Nephi¹ grieves for hardness of brothers' hearts; 12: 17 temptations of devil harden hearts of men; 13: 27–28 abominable church takes away plain parts of gospel to harden hearts of men; 14: 7 men to be delivered to hardness of their hearts; 15: 3 being hard in hearts, Laman¹ and Lemuel look not to God for understanding; 15: 11 if ye harden not hearts and ask in faith, these things shall be made known; 22: 5 (2 **Ne.** 6: 10; 25: 10; **Mosiah** 3: 15) Jews will harden hearts against Holy One; 2 **Ne.** 33: 2 many harden hearts against Holy Spirit; **Jacob** 6: 4–5 those of house of Israel who harden not hearts shall be saved in kingdom of God; **Mosiah** 11: 29 people of Noah³ harden hearts against Abinadi's words; **Alma** 12: 10 he who hardens heart receives lesser portion of word; 12: 34 whoso repenteth and hardeneth not his heart shall have claim on mercy; 12: 37 let us repent and harden not our hearts lest we provoke the Lord to wrath; 13: 4 men reject Spirit because of hardness of hearts; 21: 3 dissenters are harder than Lamanites, cause Lamanites to harden hearts; 24: 30 enlightened people who fall into sin become more hardened; 33: 21 if ye could be healed by merely casting about your eyes, would ye harden your hearts in unbelief and not cast about your eyes; 34: 31 come forth and harden not your hearts any longer; 37: 10 Nephites harden hearts in sin and iniquities; **Hel.** 6: 35 (13: 8) Spirit withdraws from Nephites because of hardness of hearts; 13: 8 because of Nephites' hardness of heart, the Lord will withdraw his word; 16: 12 people become more hardened in iniquity; 3 **Ne.** 1: 22 lyings sent forth among people by Satan to harden their hearts; 20: 28 if Gentiles harden hearts against him, the Lord will return their iniquities upon their own

heads; 21: 22 if Israel will repent and harden not hearts, the Lord will establish church among them; **Morm.** 3: 2 Mormon² prays for Nephites, but without faith because of their *h.*; **Ether** 8: 25 devil hardens men's hearts, that men murder prophets; **Moro.** 9: 4 when Mormon² uses no sharpness, Nephites harden hearts against God's word.

HARLOT (*see also* Adultery; Church, Great and Abominable; Fornication; Whore)

1 **Ne.** 13: 7–8, 34 (14: 16–17) abominable church is mother of *h.*; **Mosiah** 11: 14 (12: 29) priests of Noah³ spend their time with *h.*; **Alma** 39: 3 Corianton goes after *h.* Isabel.

HARM (*see also* Harmless; Hurt; Mischief)

Hel. 5: 44 Nephi² and Lehi⁴ encircled by fire, yet it *h.* them not; 3 **Ne.** 28: 21 (4 **Ne.** 1: 32–33; **Morm.** 8: 24) Nephite disciples cast into furnace and den of wild beasts and receive no *h.*

HARMLESS

Alma 18: 22 Ammon² is wise, yet *h.*

HARROW (*see also* Terror; Torment)

2 **Ne.** 9: 47 would I *h.* up your souls if your minds were pure; **Alma** 15: 3 Zeezrom's sins *h.* up his mind; 39: 7 Alma² would not dwell upon Corianton's sins, to *h.* up his soul, if it were not for his good; **Morm.** 5: 8 Mormon² does not desire to *h.* up men's souls in describing carnage.

HARSH, HARSHLY, HARSHNESS (*see also* Hard)

2 **Ne.** 33: 5 record speaks *h.* against sin; **Enos** 1: 23 prophets preach and prophesy in *h.*; 3 **Ne.** 11: 3 voice from heaven is not *h.*

HARVEST (*see also* Reap; Thrash)

Alma 17: 13 sons of Mosiah² trust that they shall meet at close of their *h.*; 26: 7 converts are in hands of the Lord of the *h.*

HASTE, HASTEN (*see also* Rash)

2 **Ne.** 15: 19 (Isa. 5: 19) wo unto them that say, Let him *h.* his work; 3 **Ne.** 20: 42 (Isa. 52: 12) ye shall not go out with *h.*, for the Lord will go before you.

HATE, HATRED (*see also* Abhor; Despise; Malice; Persecution; Revile)

1 **Ne.** 19: 14 (2 **Ne.** 6: 10–11; 3 **Ne.** 16: 9) because Jews have despised the Holy One, they shall be *h.* among all nations; 2 **Ne.** 5: 14 (Jacob 7: 24; Enos 1: 20) *h.* of Lamanites against Nephites; 29: 5 Gentiles have *h.* Jews and not sought to recover them; **Mosiah** 10: 17

(4 Ne. 1: 39) Lamanites are taught to *h.* children of God; 13: 13 (Ex. 20: 5) the Lord visits iniquities of fathers upon children unto third and fourth generation of them that *h.* him; **Alma** 24: 1–2 *h.* of Lamanites against people of Anti-Nephi-Lehi becomes sore; 37: 32 teach an everlasting *h.* against sin and iniquity; **Hel.** 5: 51 converted Lamanites lay down their *h.*; **3 Ne.** 7: 11 tribes united in *h.* of robbers; 12: 43–44 (Matt. 5: 43–44) do good to them that *h.* you; 13: 24 (Matt. 6: 24) man who serves two masters will *h.* one and love other; **Moro.** 1: 2 because of *h.*, Lamanites put to death every Nephite who will not deny Christ.

HAVOC

Hel. 11: 27 robbers make great *h.*

HEAD (*see also* Hair)

1 **Ne.** 22: 13 blood of abominable church shall turn upon own *h.*; **2 Ne.** 4: 6 cursing taken from you and answered upon *h.* of parents; **Jacob** 4: 17 is it possible for Jews to build upon rejected foundation that it may become *h.* of their corner; **Mosiah** 5: 8 under this *h.* ye are made free; 10: 8 (Alma 3: 5; 3 Ne. 4: 7) warriors shave their *h.*; 29: 30 sins shall be answered upon people's *h.*; **Alma** 3: 4–5 Amlicites do not shave *h.* like Lamanites; **3 Ne.** 1: 13 lift up your *h.* and be of good cheer; 12: 36 (Matt. 5: 36) thou shalt not swear by the *h.*; 20: 28 Father will return Gentiles' iniquities upon their own *h.*

HEAL, HEALING (*see also* Cure; Deaf; Dumb; Hands, Laying on of; Jesus Christ, Atonement through; Miracle; Ordinance; Raise; Recover; Save; Sick; TG Heal, Healing)

1 **Ne.** 11: 31 multitudes of sick and afflicted *h.* by Lamb; 17: 41 the Lord prepared way that Israelites might be *h.* of serpent bites; **2 Ne.** 16: 10 (Isa. 6: 10; Acts 28: 27) make people's heart fat, lest they understand, be converted and *h.*; 25: 20 the Lord gave Moses power to *h.* nations after being bitten by serpents; **Jacob** 2: 8 pleasing word of God *h.* wounded soul; **Mosiah** 14: 5 (Isa. 53: 5) with his stripes we are *h.*; **Alma** 15: 8 if thou believest in redemption of Christ, thou canst be *h.*; 33: 20 Israelites would not look upon serpent because they did not believe it would *h.* them; 33: 21–22 if ye could be *h.* by casting about your eyes, would ye not behold quickly; **3 Ne.** 7: 22 those who are *h.* manifest unto people that they have been wrought upon by Spirit; 9: 13 repent of your sins and be converted, that I may *h.* you; 17: 9 Christ *h.* all Nephite sick who are brought to

him; 18: 32 those who repent and come unto Christ will be *h.*

HEAR, HEARD (*see also* Communication; Deaf; Ear; Hearken; Heed; Listen)

1 **Ne.** 10: 17 Nephi[1] desires to see, *h.* things seen by his father; 17: 45 Laman[1] and Lemuel have *h.* God's voice from time to time; 19: 24 Nephi[1] admonishes people to *h.* words of Moses; 22: 20 latter-day prophet shall ye *h.* in all things he shall say unto you; **2 Ne.** 9: 31 wo unto the deaf that will not *h.*; 16: 10 (Isa. 6: 10; Matt. 13: 13–15) make ears of this people heavy lest they *h.* and be converted; 27: 29 (Isa. 29: 18) the deaf shall *h.* words of book; **Jacob** 7: 5 Jacob[2] *h.* voice of the Lord from time to time; **Mosiah** 9: 18 God *h.* cries of Zeniff's people; 11: 23–24 (21: 15) except this people repent, the Lord will be slow to *h.* their cries; 26: 28 he who will not *h.* the Lord's voice shall not be received in his church; 27: 14 the Lord hath *h.* prayers of his people; **3 Ne.** 11: 3 voice from heaven pierces them that *h.*; 14: 24 (Matt. 7: 24) whoso *h.* Christ's sayings and doeth them is like wise man who built house upon rock; 15: 17, 21–23 (John 10: 16) other sheep not of this fold shall *h.* Christ's voice; 17: 16 ear hath not *h.* so marvelous things as Nephites *h.* Jesus speak unto Father; 17: 25 multitude did see, *h.*, bear record; 27: 9 if ye call upon Father in Christ's name, Father will *h.* you; **Ether** 1: 40 the Lord *h.* brother of Jared[2]; **Moro.** 2: 3 multitude did not *h.* Jesus give disciples authority to bestow Holy Ghost.

HEARKEN (*see also* Communication; Hear; Heed; Listen; Obedience)

1 **Ne.** 14: 2 if Gentiles *h.* unto Lamb, they shall be numbered among Israel; 19: 7 men *h.* not unto God's counsels; **2 Ne.** 8: 1 (Isa. 51: 1) *h.* unto me, ye that follow after righteousness; 9: 29 to be learned is good if they *h.* unto counsels of God; 26: 8 the righteous that *h.* unto words of prophets shall not perish; 28: 26, 31 wo unto him that *h.* unto precepts of men; 32: 8 if ye *h.* unto Spirit which teacheth man to pray, ye would know that ye must pray; **Alma** 5: 38 (Hel. 7: 18) if ye will not *h.* unto voice of good shepherd, ye are not his sheep; 5: 41 if a man bringeth forth good works, he *h.* unto voice of good shepherd; **3 Ne.** 28: 34 wo unto him who will not *h.* unto words of Jesus.

HEART (*see also* Breast; Broken Heart and Contrite Spirit; Change; Conversion; Hardheartedness; Humble; Intent; Lowliness; Pride; Purpose)

1 **Ne.** 17: 44 elder sons of Lehi[1] are

murderers in *h.*; 18: 20 only power of God threatening destruction could soften *h.* of brothers of Nephi[1]; 22: 26 Satan has no power over people's *h.* because they dwell in righteousness; **2 Ne.** 1: 21 Lehi[1] exhorts sons to be determined in one mind and one *h.*; 4: 16 *h.* of Nephi[1] ponders continually upon what he has seen and heard; 4: 26 why should my *h.* weep; 4: 28, 30 rejoice, O my *h.*; 9: 30 the *h.* of the rich are upon their treasures; 9: 49 my *h.* delighteth in righteousness; 16: 10 (Isa. 6: 10) make *h.* of this people fat lest they understand with their *h.* and be converted; 25: 16 Israel shall worship Father in Christ's name with pure *h.* and clean hands; 27: 25 (Isa. 29: 13) people draw near the Lord with mouth, but have removed *h.* far from him; 28: 20 devil shall rage in *h.* of men; 33: 1 when a man speaks by power of Holy Ghost, it carries unto *h.* of men; **Jacob** 2: 35 Nephites have broken *h.* of tender wives; **Mosiah** 2: 9 Benjamin admonishes people to open *h.* that they may understand; 4: 2 apply atoning blood of Christ that our *h.* may be purified; 5: 12 remember to retain the name written always in *h.*; 12: 27 ye have not applied *h.* to understanding; 18: 8–12 if this be the desire of your *h.*, what have you against being baptized; 18: 21 people of church should have *h.* knit together in unity; 24: 12 Alma[1] and his people pour out *h.* to God; **Alma** 5: 7 the Lord changed fathers' *h.*; 5: 19 can ye look to God with pure *h.* and clean hands; 5: 26 if ye have experienced a change of *h.*, can ye feel so now; 13: 29 have love of God always in *h.*; 16: 16 the Lord pours out Spirit to prepare *h.* to receive word; 32: 16 blessed is he that believeth and is baptized without stubbornness of *h.*; 32: 28 plant seed in your *h.*; 34: 27 when ye do not cry unto the Lord, let your *h.* be full; 37: 37 let thy *h.* be full of thanks unto God; **Hel.** 3: 35 sanctification of *h.*, which cometh of yielding *h.* unto God; 6: 17 Nephites begin to set *h.* upon riches; 6: 30 Satan hands down works of darkness as he can get hold upon *h.* of men; 12: 4 how quick are men to set *h.* upon vain things of world; 13: 2–4 Samuel prophesies whatsoever things the Lord puts into his *h.*; **3 Ne.** 11: 3 voice from heaven causes *h.* to burn; 11: 30 not Christ's doctrine to stir up *h.* with anger; 12: 28 (Matt. 5: 28) whoso looketh upon woman to lust after her hath committed adultery in *h.*; 12: 29 suffer none of these things to enter *h.*; 19: 33 multitude understands in their *h.* the words Jesus prays; 25: 6 (Mal. 4: 6) Elijah shall turn *h.* of fathers to children and *h.* of children to fathers; **4 Ne.** 1: 28 (Ether 15: 19) Satan gets hold upon *h.* of church; **Morm.**

9: 27 come unto the Lord with all your *h.*; **Moro.** 7: 48 pray unto Father with all energy of *h.*; 10: 3 ponder these things in your *h.*

HEARTHOM—*early Jaredite king*

Ether 1: 16–17 (10: 16) father of Heth[1], son of Lib[1]; 10: 30 reigns twenty-four years, taken into captivity.

HEAT

2 Ne. 14: 6 (Isa. 4: 6) tabernacle shall be shadow in daytime from *h.*; **3 Ne.** 26: 3 (Morm. 9: 2; 2 Pet. 3: 10, 12) elements shall melt with fervent *h.*

HEATHEN (*see also* Gentile)

2 Ne. 26: 33 the Lord remembereth the *h.*; **3 Ne.** 13: 7 (Matt. 6: 7) use not vain repetitions, as the *h.*; 21: 21 the Lord will execute vengeance and fury upon the unrepentant, as upon the *h.*

HEAVEN (*see also* Astronomy; Creation; God—Creator; Heavenly; Jesus Christ—Creator; Kingdom of God; Paradise; BD Heaven)

1 Ne. 1: 8 Lehi[1] sees *h.* open; 11: 14, 27, 30 (12: 6) Nephi[1] sees *h.* open; **2 Ne.** 7: 3 (Isa. 50: 3) the Lord clothes the *h.* with blackness; 23: 13 (Isa. 13: 13) the Lord will shake the *h.*; 24: 13 (Isa. 14: 13) Lucifer says, I will ascend into *h.*; **Mosiah** 2: 41 those who keep commandments unto end are received into *h.*; **Alma** 18: 30 *h.* is a place where God dwells; **Hel.** 3: 28 gate of *h.* is open unto all; 5: 8 (3 Ne. 13: 20; Matt. 6: 20) lay up for yourselves treasures in *h.*; 5: 48 Nephi[2] and Lehi[4] behold *h.* open; 14: 3, 6 signs in *h.* at Christ's coming; **3 Ne.** 11: 3 Nephites hear voice as if it comes out of *h.*; 13: 10 (Matt. 6: 10) thy will be done on earth as it is in *h.*; 28: 7 Christ shall come in glory with powers of *h.*; 28: 13–16, 36 three Nephites caught up into *h.*; **Ether** 13: 9 (Isa. 65: 17) there shall be a new *h.* and a new earth.

HEAVENLY (*see also* Heaven)

4 Ne. 1: 3 (Ether 12: 8) all made partakers of the *h.* gift.

HEAVENLY FATHER (*see* God the Father)

HEBREW (*see also* Language; BD Hebrew)

Morm. 9: 33 Nephites have altered the *H.*; 9: 33 if Nephites could have written in *H.*, there would have been no imperfections in record.

HEDGE (*see also* Punishment)

2 Ne. 4: 33 Lord, *h.* not up my way, but the ways of mine enemy; **Mosiah** 7: 29 in day of their transgression, the Lord

will h. up his people's ways that they prosper not.

HEED (*see also* Communication; Hear; Hearken; Listen; Notice; Obedience)

1 Ne. 15: 25 give h. unto word of the Lord; **Mosiah** 1: 16 Liahona would lead the people according to the h. they gave the Lord; 5: 11 take h. that ye do not transgress; **Alma** 12: 9 portion of word granted unto men according to h. they give the Lord; 37: 43 fathers slothful to give h. to compass; 37: 44 it is easy to give h. to word of Christ.

HEIR (*see also* Children of God; Elect; Inherit; Seed)

Mosiah 15: 11 those who hearken unto prophets and look forward to remission of sins are h. of kingdom of God; **4 Ne.** 1: 17 people are in one, children of Christ and h. of kingdom of God.

HELAM—*convert from among people of Noah³* [c. 147 B.C.]

Mosiah 18: 12–14 baptized by Alma¹.

HELAM, CITY OF (*see also* Helam, Land of)

Mosiah 23: 20 built by people of Alma¹ in land of Helam; 23: 25–26 people flee to H. when Lamanites come.

HELAM, LAND OF—*land inhabited by people of Alma¹*

Mosiah 23: 3–4 beautiful land, eight days' journey from land of Nephi; 23: 19 given name; 23: 20 people multiply, prosper, build city of H.; 23: 25 Lamanites invade; 23: 29 Lamanites take possession of H.; 23: 35 Amulon and his brethren discover H. while searching for land of Nephi; 23: 37 Lamanites set guards around H.; 23: 38 Lamanites bring families to H.; 23: 39 Amulon appointed king over H.; 24: 18–20 people of Alma¹ flee from H.; 27: 16 remember the captivity of thy fathers in land of H.; **Alma** 24: 1 Amalekites and Amulonites stir up Lamanites in H. against people of Anti-Nephi-Lehi.

HELAMAN¹—*son of King Benjamin* [c. 130 B.C.]

Mosiah 1: 2 taught in language and prophecies by father.

HELAMAN²—*son of Alma², prophet, military commander* [c. 74 B.C.]

Alma 31: 7 eldest son of Alma², not taken to preach to Zoramites; ch. 36–37 commandments of Alma² to H.; 37: 1–2 (45: 2–3; 50: 38) is entrusted with plates, to keep record; 37: 21 is given twenty-four plates of Jaredites; 37: 21, 23–24 is commanded to preserve Urim and Thummim; ch. 45–62 H's account of the Nephites; 45: 2–8 is blessed because of belief; 45: 9–14 to write prophecy of Nephite destruction; 45: 15 is blessed by father; 45: 20 (48: 19; 62: 44) preaches; 45: 22 reestablishes church; 45: 23 appoints priests; 46: 1 is opposed by unrepentant; 46: 6 a high priest over church; 46: 38 maintains order in church; 49: 30 people have peace and prosperity because they heed H.; 53: 14 persuades Ammonites not to break oath; 53: 19, 22 young Ammonites ask H. to be their leader; ch. 56–58 writes letter to Moroni¹; 56: 9 assists Antipus; 56: 30–54 armies of H. and Antipus defeat Lamanites by means of decoy; 57: 1–3 receives letter from Ammoron and sends reply; 57: 7–12 surrounds city Cumeni, intercepts Lamanites' provisions, obtains city; 57: 17–27 H. and two thousand stripling Ammonites battle Lamanites, are preserved by faith; 58: 7 complains of rulers' indifference; 58: 13–29 takes possession of Manti by decoying Lamanites from city; 60: 3 H. and his men have suffered much; 62: 12 receives six thousand additional soldiers; 62: 42 returns to Zarahemla; 62: 45 causes many to repent; 62: 52 dies.

HELAMAN³—*son of Helaman², record keeper, chief judge* [c. 53 B.C.]

Alma 63: 11 receives records; **Hel.** 2: 2 is appointed chief judge; 2: 3–5 Kishkumen plots to murder H.; 2: 6–9 is saved by servant; 2: 14 takes his account from book of Nephi; 3: 20 serves righteously; 3: 37 dies; 5: 5–13 H's instructions to his sons.

HELAMAN², SONS OF—*children of converted Lamanites known as Ammonites* [c. 64 B.C.] (*see also* Ammon², People of)

Alma 53: 14–15 H. convinces Lamanites not to break oath, never to shed blood; 53: 16 sons had not entered covenant, assemble, call themselves Nephites; 53: 17–18 two thousand enter covenant to protect liberty; 53: 19 ask H. to be their leader; 53: 20–21 (56: 46–47) are courageous, obedient to commandments; 53: 22 (56: 57) march to support of people in borders; 56: 3 H. tells Moroni¹ about sons of Ammonites; 56: 10 H. calls them his sons; 56: 45 have greatest courage among Nephites; 56: 47–48 were taught not to doubt by their mothers; 56: 52–54 defeat Lamanites; 56: 55–56 none slain; 57: 6 sixty additional sons of Ammonites join H.; 57: 19–21 fight valiantly; 57: 22 are selected to convey prisoners; 57: 24 (58: 39) two hundred wounded, none perish; 57: 26

are preserved by faith; 58: 39 in city of Manti with H.

HELEM—*brother of Ammon*[1]

Mosiah 7: 6 accompanies Ammon[1] on expedition to land of Nephi.

HELL (*see also* Captive, Captivity; Damnation; Darkness, Spiritual; Death, Spiritual; Devil; Jesus Christ, Atonement through; Lake; Redemption; Resurrection; Torment; Wicked; TG Hell; BD Hell)

1 Ne. 12: 16 (15: 26–29) depths of fountain of filthy water are depths of h.; 14: 3 abominable church founded by devil, that he might lead souls down to h.; 15: 35 devil is preparator of h.; 2 Ne. 1: 13 O that ye would awake from deep sleep of h.; 2: 29 will of flesh giveth devil power to bring men down to h.; 9: 10 God prepareth a way for escape from death and h.; 9: 12 spiritual death is h.; 9: 12 death and h. must deliver up dead; 9: 26 atonement delivereth those who have not law from death and h.; 9: 34 liar shall be thrust down to h.; 28: 15 those who are proud, preach false doctrines, commit whoredoms, pervert right way of the Lord shall be thrust down to h.; 28: 21 devil lulls some into carnal security and leads them away carefully down to h.; 28: 22 devil tells men there is no h.; 33: 6 I glory in my Jesus, for he hath redeemed my soul from h.; Jacob 3: 11 loose yourselves from pains of h.; Alma 5: 7 chains of h. awaited fathers; 12: 11 chains of h. means to be taken captive by devil; 13: 30 the Lord grant unto you repentance, that you may not be bound down by chains of h.; 26: 13 how many thousands of our brethren has God loosed from pains of h.; 30: 60 devil will not support his children, but speedily drags them down to h.; 48: 17 if all men would be like unto Moroni[1], powers of h. would be shaken forever; 54: 7 awful h. awaits murderers; Hel. 6: 28 devil dragged Jaredites down to destruction, to everlasting h.; 3 Ne. 11: 39 (Matt. 16: 18) gates of h. shall not prevail against those who build on Christ's doctrine; 11: 40 gates of h. stand open to receive those who declare more or less than Christ's doctrine; 12: 22 (Matt. 5: 22) he who says to brother, Thou fool, is in danger of h. fire; Morm. 8: 17 he who condemns shall be in danger of h. fire; 9: 4 more miserable to dwell with God under consciousness of filthiness than to dwell with damned in h.; Moro. 8: 20–21 he that saith little children need baptism is in danger of h.

HELORUM—*son of Benjamin* [c. 130 B.C.]

Mosiah 1: 2–3 taught in language of fathers, that he might become man of understanding and know prophecies.

HELP (*see also* Deliver; Relief; Serve; Succor; Support; BD Help)

Jacob 2: 5 by h. of Creator I can tell you your thoughts; W of M 1: 18 with h. of holy men, Benjamin establishes peace; Mosiah 1: 4 Lehi[1] could not have taught all these things without h. of brass plates; Ether 8: 16 oaths of secret combinations administered to h. those who sought power to gain power.

HEM—*brother of Ammon*[1]

Mosiah 7: 6 accompanies Ammon[1] on expedition to land of Nephi.

HEN (*see also* Animal; Chickens)

3 Ne. 10: 4–6 (Matt. 23: 37; Luke 13: 34) the Lord would gather Israel as h. gathers her chickens.

HERD (*see also* Animal; Cattle; Flock)

2 Ne. 5: 11 (Enos 1: 21; Hel. 6: 12) Nephites begin to raise h.; Mosiah 7: 22 Limhi's people give one half their h. as tribute to Lamanites; Alma 1: 29 because of steadiness of church, Nephites have abundance of h.; 62: 29 prisoners of Lamanites join Ammonites in raising h.; 3 Ne. 3: 13 Nephites gather h. in one place; Ether 6: 4 Jaredites prepare food for h. during journey; 10: 12 Jaredites become exceeding rich in raising h.

HERITAGE (*see also* Inherit)

1 Ne. 21: 8 (Isa. 49: 8) isles of sea to inherit desolate h.; 3 Ne. 22: 17 h. of the Lord's servants is to be preserved from weapons, tongues.

HERMOUNTS—*wilderness on west and north*

Alma 2: 37 Lamanites driven until they reach wilderness called H.

HESHLON, PLAINS OF

Ether 13: 28 Coriantumr[2] pursues Shared until he comes to plains of H.

HETH[1]—*early Jaredite*

Ether 1: 16 ancestor of Aaron[2], son of Hearthom; 10: 31 lives in captivity.

HETH[2]—*middle Jaredite*

Ether 1: 25–26 son of Com[1], father of Shez; 9: 26 embraces secret plots; 9: 29 commands persecution of prophets; 10: 1 perishes by famine.

HEW, HEWN (*see also* Cut)

Jacob 5: 42 all trees of vineyard good for nothing save to be h. down; 5: 66 bad trees shall be h. down; Alma 5: 35 bring forth works of righteousness and ye shall not be h. down; 5: 52 (3 Ne. 14: 19; Matt. 7: 19) every tree that bringeth not

forth good fruit shall be *h*. down; 5: 56 they who persist in wickedness shall be *h*. down; **Hel.** 14: 18 whoso repents shall not be *h*. down; 3 **Ne.** 27: 11–12 churches built upon works of men or devil shall be *h*. down; 27: 17 he who endures not to end shall be *h*. down.

HIDE, HID, HIDDEN (*see also* Secret)

2 **Ne.** 9: 43 things of the wise and prudent shall be *h*.; 27: 12 book shall be *h*. from world; 27: 22 after book has been read, it should be sealed and *h*. up unto the Lord; 27: 26 (Isa. 29: 14) understanding of their prudent shall be *h*.; 27: 27 (28: 9; Isa. 29: 15) wo unto them that seek deep to *h*. counsel from the Lord; **Jacob** 5: 14, 20 the Lord of vineyard *h*. natural branches of tame olive-tree; **Mosiah** 8: 17 *h*. things shall come to light; 14: 3 (Isa. 53: 3) we *h*. our faces from him; **Alma** 39: 8 ye cannot *h*. your crimes from God; **Hel.** 13: 18–20 (Morm. 1: 18) if men *h*. treasures in earth, they shall find them no more; 13: 19 men should *h*. up their treasures unto the Lord; 3 **Ne.** 9: 5 the Lord has covered city of Moronihah with earth to *h*. iniquities from his face; 12: 14 (Matt. 5: 14) city set on hill cannot be *h*.; 28: 25 names of those who should never taste death are *h*. from world; **Morm.** 5: 8 all things which are *h*. must be revealed upon housetops; **Ether** 4: 3 Moroni² is commanded to *h*. writings again in earth; **Moro.** 9: 15 come out in judgment, O God, and *h*. this people's sins from before thy face.

HIGH, HIGHER, HIGHEST (*see also* High Priest; Highway; Pride)

1 **Ne.** 11: 6 the Lord, the most *h*. God; 2 **Ne.** 24: 14 (Isa. 14: 14) I will be like unto the most *H*.; **Alma** 51: 8 those who are in favor of kings are those of *h*. birth; 3 **Ne.** 11: 17 blessed be the name of the Most *H*. God.

HIGH PRIEST (*see also* Priesthood; TG High Priest — Melchizedek Priesthood; BD High Priest)

Mosiah 23: 16 (26: 7) Alma¹ the *h.p.* over the people; **Alma** 4: 4 Alma² consecrated *h.p.* by father; 4: 18 Alma² retains office of *h.p.*; 13: 1–11 *h.p.* ordained unto high priesthood after order of Son; 30: 20 Ammon² a *h.p.* over Ammonites; 46: 6 Helaman² and his brethren are *h.p.* over church; 3 **Ne.** 6: 20–21 they who had been *h.p.* are angry with men who preach against sins of people.

HIGH PRIESTHOOD (*see* Priesthood)

HIGHWAY (*see also* Path; Road; Street; Way)

2 **Ne.** 21: 16 (Isa. 11: 16) there shall be a *h*. for remnant of the Lord's people; **Hel.** 14: 24 (3 Ne. 6: 8; 8: 13) many *h*. to be broken up in destruction at Christ's death.

HILL (*see also* Cumorah, Land and Hill of; Ephraim, Hill of; Mount, Mountain; Ramah, Hill; Riplah, Hill; Shim, Hill)

2 **Ne.** 20: 32 (Isa. 10: 32) he shall shake his hand against the mount of daughter of Zion, the *h*. of Jerusalem; 3 **Ne.** 12: 14 (Matt. 5: 14) city set on *h*. cannot be hid.

HIMNI—*son of Mosiah²* [c. 100-74 B.C.] (*see also* Mosiah², Sons of)

Mosiah 27: 8 an unbeliever; 27: 10 seeks to destroy church; 27: 32 is converted by angel; 27: 34–35 travels through Zarahemla with brothers to repair injuries they had done to church; 28: 1–9 Mosiah² allows sons to preach to Lamanites; 28: 10 (29: 3; Alma 17: 6) refuses to be king; **Alma** 23: 1–7 *H's* successful missionary efforts among Lamanites; 25: 17 rejoices with brethren for success among Lamanites; 27: 16–19 *H's* great joy at reunion with Alma²; 31: 6 is left in charge of church when Alma² and companions begin missionary journey.

HINDER (*see also* Forbid; Frustrated; Restrain; Stay; Stop; Withhold)

3 **Ne.** 6: 5 nothing to *h*. people from prospering except transgression.

HISS (*see also* Whisper)

1 **Ne.** 19: 14 (3 Ne. 16: 9) because Jews despise the Holy One, they shall become *h*. and by-word; 2 **Ne.** 15: 26 (Isa. 5: 26) the Lord will *h*. unto Israel from end of earth; 17: 18 (Isa. 7: 18) the Lord shall *h*. for fly that is in uttermost part of Egypt; 29: 2 the Lord's words shall *h*. forth unto ends of earth; 3 **Ne.** 29: 8 ye need not any longer *h*. nor spurn Jews; **Moro.** 10: 28 God's word shall *h*. forth generation to generation.

HISTORY (*see also* Account; Record)

1 **Ne.** 9: 2 (2 Ne. 4: 14; 5: 33; Jacob 1: 3) account of *h*. of Nephites recorded on large plates of Nephi; **Jacob** 1: 2 small plates touch but lightly on *h*. of Nephites.

HOLD (*see also* Keep; Power; Retain; Withhold)

1 **Ne.** 15: 24 whoso would *h*. fast to word of God would not perish; **Alma** 8: 9 (27: 15) Satan has great *h*. upon hearts; 30: 12 law could have no *h*. upon Korihor; **Hel.** 3: 29 whosoever will may lay *h*. upon word of God; 13: 31 riches to become slippery, that men cannot *h*. them; 4 **Ne.**

1: 28 false church multiplies because Satan gets *h.* upon hearts; **Moro.** 7: 19 lay *h.* upon every good thing; 10: 30 lay *h.* upon every good gift.

HOLE

2 **Ne.** 8: 1 (Isa. 51: 1) look unto the *h.* of the pit whence ye are digged; **Ether** 2: 20 Jaredites to make *h.* in tops and bottoms of vessels for air.

HOLINESS (*see also* Holy; Purity; Righteousness; Sacred; Sanctification)

2 **Ne.** 2: 10 men to be judged according to truth and *h.* which is in God; 9: 20 how great the *h.* of our God; **Mosiah** 18: 12 pour out thy Spirit upon thy servant, that he may do work with *h.* of heart; 3 **Ne.** 26: 5 men resurrected to everlasting life or damnation, according to mercy, justice, and *h.* of Christ; **Morm.** 9: 5 when ye are brought to see your nakedness and the *h.* of Christ, it will kindle unquenchable fire.

HOLY (*see also* Holiness; Holy Ghost; Order; Spirit, Holy)

1 **Ne.** 20: 2 (Isa. 48: 2) house of Jacob call themselves of the *h.* city; **2 Ne.** 31: 5 Lamb of God, being *h.*, had need to be baptized; **Jarom** 1: 5 Nephites keep sabbath *h.* unto the Lord; **W of M** 1: 17 Benjamin a *h.* man; 1: 17 many *h.* men among Nephites speak word of God with sharpness; **Mosiah** 13: 16 (Ex. 20: 8) remember the sabbath day, to keep it *h.*; **Alma** 10: 9 Alma² is a *h.* man; 12: 30 plan of redemption made known unto men according to faith, repentance, and *h.* works; 13: 1–11 high priests called with *h.* calling, ordained with *h.* ordinance unto high priesthood; 13: 26 news of Christ's coming to be made known unto *h.* men by angels; 3 **Ne.** 28: 39 three Nephites sanctified in the flesh, that they are *h.*; **Ether** 13: 5 Jerusalem to be built again, a *h.* city; **Moro.** 8: 3 continually pray unto Father in name of his **H.** Child, Jesus.

HOLY GHOST (*see also* Holy Ghost, Baptism of; Holy Ghost—Comforter; Holy Ghost, Gift of; Spirit, Gifts of; Holy/Spirit of the Lord; TG God, Spirit of; Holy Ghost; Holy Ghost, Dove, Sign of; Holy Ghost, Gifts of; Holy Ghost, Loss of; Holy Ghost, Mission of; Holy Ghost, Source of Testimony; Holy Ghost, Unpardonable Sin against; Holy Spirit; Lord, Spirit of; Spirit; BD Holy Ghost)

1 **Ne.** 10: 11 Messiah shall manifest himself to Gentiles by *H.G.*; 10: 17 *H.G.* is gift of God unto all who diligently seek him; 10: 19 mysteries of God shall be unfolded by power of *H.G.*; 10: 22 *H.G.* gives

Nephi¹ authority to speak these things; 11: 27 (2 Ne. 31: 8) after baptism of Christ, *H.G.* comes down from heaven and abides upon him in form of dove; 12: 7 *H.G.* falls upon the twelve ordained of God; 12: 18 *H.G.* beareth record of Messiah; 13: 37 those who seek to bring forth Zion shall have gift and power of *H.G.*; 1 **Ne.** 26: 13 Christ manifests himself unto believers by power of *H.G.*; 28: 4 priests shall deny *H.G.*, which gives utterance; 28: 26 wo unto him that denieth the gift of the *H.G.*; 28: 31 cursed is he who hearkens to precepts of men, save given by power of *H.G.*; 31: 18 (3 Ne. 11: 32, 36; 16: 6; 28: 11) *H.G.* bears record of Father and Son; 31: 21 (Mosiah 15: 2–5; Alma 11: 44; 3 Ne. 11: 27, 36; Morm. 7: 7) Father, Son, and *H.G.* are one God; 32: 2 speaking with tongues of angels comes by *H.G.*; 32: 3 angels speak by power of *H.G.*; 33: 1 when man speaks by power of *H.G.*, power of *H.G.* carries it unto hearts of man; **Jacob** 6: 8 will ye reject the gift of the *H.G.* and quench the **H.** Spirit; 7: 12 Jacob² testifies of Christ by power of *H.G.*; 7: 13 Sherem asks for sign by power of *H.G.*; 7: 17 Sherem confesses Christ and power of *H.G.*; **Alma** 7: 10 Mary shall conceive by power of *H.G.*; 8: 30–31 Alma² and Amulek are filled with *H.G.* and given power; 34: 38 contend no more against *H.G.*; 39: 6 to deny *H.G.* when it has had place in you is unpardonable sin; 3 **Ne.** 11: 25 I baptize you in name of the Father, Son, and *H.G.*; 15: 23 Christ does not manifest himself unto Gentiles, save by *H.G.*; 20: 27 in Abraham's seed shall all kindreds of earth be blessed, unto pouring out of *H.G.* through Christ upon Gentiles; 21: 2 things which Jesus declared are by power of *H.G.*; 29: 6 wo unto him who says the Lord no longer works by power of *H.G.*; 4 **Ne.** 1: 48 Ammaron is constrained by *H.G.* to hide up sacred records; **Morm.** 1: 14 *H.G.* does not come upon any of Nephites because of their wickedness and unbelief; **Ether** 12: 23 Nephites could speak much because of *H.G.*; **Moro.** 3: 4 disciples ordain priests and teachers by power of *H.G.*; 6: 9 meetings conducted by power of *H.G.*; 7: 32 God prepares way that men may have faith, that *H.G.* may have place in their hearts; 7: 36 has God withheld power of *H.G.* from men; 7: 44 if a man confesses by power of *H.G.* that Jesus is the Christ, he must have charity; 8: 7 word of the Lord comes unto Mormon² by power of *H.G.*; 8: 9 *H.G.* manifests word of God; 8: 26 because of meekness and lowliness of heart cometh visitation of *H.G.*; 8: 28 Spirit ceaseth to strive with Nephites because they are denying *H.G.*; 10: 4–5 by power of *H.G.*

ye may know the truth of all things; 10: 7 ye may know that Christ is by power of H.G.

HOLY GHOST, BAPTISM OF (see also Born of God; Conversion; Fire; Holy Ghost, Gift of; Remission; Sanctification; TG Holy Ghost, Baptism of)

2 **Ne.** 31: 13–14 (3 Ne. 12: 1–2; 19: 13; 26: 17; 28: 18; 4 Ne. 1: 1; Morm. 7: 10) after baptism of water comes baptism of fire and H.G.; 31: 17 after repentance and baptism by water cometh remission of sins by fire and H.G.; **Mosiah** 4: 3 Spirit comes upon Nephites, and they are filled with joy, having received remission of sins; **Alma** 13: 12 after being sanctified by H.G., high priests could not look upon sin without abhorrence; 36: 24 Alma² labors that men might be born of God and filled with H.G.; **3 Ne.** 9: 20 whoso comes unto Christ will be baptized with fire and H.G.; 11: 35 whoso believes in Christ will Father visit with fire and H.G.; 19: 9–13, 20–22 after Nephite disciples are baptized, H.G. falls upon them and they are filled with H.G. and fire; 27: 20 repent and be baptized, that ye may be sanctified by reception of H.G.; **Ether** 12: 14 after mighty change wrought upon Lamanites, they are baptized with fire and H.G.; **Moro.** 6: 4 after baptism, the people are cleansed by power of H.G.

HOLY GHOST—COMFORTER (see also Holy Ghost; TG Holy Ghost, Comforter; BD Comforter)

Moro. 8: 26 H.G., Comforter which fills with hope and perfect love.

HOLY GHOST, GIFT OF (see also Confirm; Gift; Gospel; Hands, Laying on of; Holy Ghost; Holy Ghost, Baptism of; Ordinance; Spirit, Gifts of; TG Holy Ghost, Gift of)

2 **Ne.** 31: 12 to him who is baptized will Father give H.G.; **Alma** 9: 21 Nephites have been visited by Spirit with many gifts, including gift of H.G.; **3 Ne.** 18: 36–37 (Moro. 2: 1–3) Christ gives disciples power to bestow H.G.

HOLY ONE (see Jesus Christ—Holy One of Israel)

HOME (see also Dwell, Dwelling)

2 **Ne.** 9: 2 (29: 14; 3 Ne. 21: 28) Jews shall be gathered h. to lands of inheritance; **Alma** 40: 11 when spirits depart mortal body, they are taken h. to God.

HONEST (see also Uprightness; TG Honesty)

Alma 27: 27 Ammonites are perfectly h.

HONEY (see also Bee)

1 **Ne.** 17: 5 land called Bountiful because of much fruit and wild h.; 18: 6 Lehites prepare h. in abundance for voyage; 2 **Ne.** 17: 15, 22 (Isa. 7: 15) butter and h. shall Messiah eat, that he may know to refuse evil and choose good; 26: 25 buy milk and h. without money and without price.

HONOR (see also Esteem; Glorify; Glory; Honorable; Praise; Respect)

1 **Ne.** 17: 55 (Mosiah 13: 20; Ex. 20: 12) h. thy father and thy mother; **Alma** 1: 16 men preach false doctrines for sake of riches and h.; 60: 36 Moroni¹ seeks not for h. of world.

HOPE (see also Faith; Trust)

2 **Ne.** 31: 20 press forward, having perfect brightness of h.; **Jacob** 2: 19 after ye have obtained h. in Christ, ye shall obtain riches; 4: 4 Nephites have h. of Christ's glory many hundred years before his coming; **Alma** 7: 24 see that ye have faith, h., and charity; 30: 13 Korihor claims Nephites are bound down under foolish and vain h.; 32: 21 (Ether 12: 6; Heb. 11: 11) faith is to h. for things not seen which are true; **Ether** 12: 4 whoso believeth in God might with surety h. for better world; 12: 4 h. cometh of faith; 12: 28 faith, h. and charity bringeth unto the Lord; 12: 32 house prepared in Father's mansions in which man might have more excellent h.; 12: 32 without h. man cannot receive inheritance in place prepared; **Moro.** ch. 7 teaching of Mormon² on faith, h., and charity; 7: 40 how can ye attain unto faith save ye shall have h.; 7: 41 ye shall have h., through atonement and resurrection of Christ, to be raised unto life eternal; 7: 42 without faith there cannot be any h.; 7: 45 charity h. all things; 8: 14 he who supposeth little children need baptism hath neither faith, h., nor charity; 8: 26 the Comforter filleth with h.; 10: 20 if there must be faith there must be h., if there must be h. there must be charity.

HORROR (see also Fear of God; Terror; Torment)

Alma 36: 14 thought of coming into presence of God racked soul of Alma² with inexpressible h.

HORSE (see also Animal)

1 **Ne.** 18: 25 Lehites find h. in wilderness; 2 **Ne.** 12: 7 (Isa. 2: 7) their land is full of h.; **Enos** 1: 21 Nephites raise many h.; **Alma** 18: 9–12 Ammon² prepares Lamoni's h. and chariots; **3 Ne.** 3: 22

Nephites gather with *h*. and other possessions in one place; 21: 14 (Micah 5: 10) I will cut off thy *h*. out of midst of thee; **Ether** 9: 19 Jaredites have *h*.

HOSANNA (*see also* BD Hosanna)

1 Ne. 11: 6 (3 Ne. 4: 32; 11: 17) *h*. to the Lord, the most high God.

HOUR (*see also* Time; BD Hour)

Alma 5: 29 *h*. is close at hand.

HOUSE (*see also* Household; Housetop; Israel; Jacob, House of; Temple; BD House)

2 Ne. 12: 2 (Isa. 2: 2) mountain of the Lord's *h*. shall be established in top of mountains; 12: 3 (Isa. 2: 3) let us go up to *h*. of the God of Jacob; **Mosiah** 13: 24 (Ex. 20: 17) thou shalt not covet thy neighbor's *h*.; **Alma** 30: 56 Korihor goes from *h*. to *h*. begging; **3 Ne.** 14: 24–27 (Matt. 7: 24–27) parable of those who build *h*. upon rock and sand.

HOUSEHOLD (*see also* Family)

Alma 22: 23 whole *h*. of Lamanite king is converted unto the Lord; 34: 21 cry unto the Lord over all your *h*.

HOUSETOP

2 Ne. 27: 11 words of sealed book to be read on *h*.; **Morm.** 5: 8 all hidden things must be revealed on *h*.

HUMAN (*see also* Man; Mankind)

Mosiah 28: 3 sons of Mosiah² cannot bear that any *h*. soul should perish; **Alma** 34: 10 great and last sacrifice shall not be *h*. sacrifice; **Morm.** 3: 20 every soul who belongs to whole *h*. family of Adam must stand before judgment-seat of Christ.

HUMBLE, HUMILITY (*see also* Boast; Broken Heart and Contrite Spirit; Fasting; Low, Lowliness; Poor; Submissive; Weak; TG Humility, Humble)

1 Ne. 13: 16 Gentiles *h*. themselves before the Lord; 15: 20 (16: 5, 32; 18: 4) brethren of Nephi¹ *h*. themselves before the Lord; **2 Ne.** 9: 42 save they come down in depths of *h*., the Lord will not open to the proud: 12: 11 (Isa. 2: 11) lofty looks of man shall be *h*.; 15: 15 (Isa. 5: 15) the mighty man shall be *h*.; 20: 33 the haughty shall be *h*.; 28: 14 all have gone astray, save a few *h*. followers of Christ; 31: 7 by baptism, Christ *h*. himself before the Father; **Mosiah** 3: 19 natural man is enemy to God unless he becometh as child, *h*.; 4: 11 *h*. yourselves, even in depths of *h*.; **Alma** 5: 27 could ye say that ye have been sufficiently *h*.; 32: 13 blessed is he who is compelled to be *h*.; 32: 14–15 more blessed is he that *h*.

himself without being compelled; 37: 33 Helaman² is admonished to teach people to *h*. themselves; 48: 20 people *h*. themselves because of words of Helaman² and brethren; **Hel.** 3: 34 more *h*. part of people suffer great persecutions; 3: 35 (6: 39) *h*. part of people fast and pray oft, and wax stronger in *h*.; 6: 5 powerful preachers bring many down into depths of *h*., to be *h*. followers of Christ; **3 Ne.** 6: 13 some Nephites lifted up in pride, others exceedingly *h*.; 12: 2 blessed are they who shall believe in your words and come down into depths of *h*.; **4 Ne.** 1: 29 false church persecutes true church because of their *h*.; **Ether** 6: 12 when Jaredites land in promised land, they *h*. themselves before the Lord; 9: 35 when Jaredites have sufficiently *h*. themselves, the Lord sends rain; 12: 27 the Lord gives men weakness that they may be *h*.; 12: 39 Jesus told Moroni² these things in plain *h*.; **Moro.** 8: 10 parents must *h*. themselves as their little children.

HUNGER, HUNGRY (*see also* Charity; Famine)

2 Ne. 27: 3 (Isa. 29: 8) nations that fight against Zion shall be like *h*. man who dreams he eats, but soul is empty; **Jacob** 2: 19 leave riches to feed the *h*.; **Enos** 1: 4 soul of Enos² is *h*.; **Mosiah** 3: 7 Christ shall suffer *h*.; 4: 26 impart our substance to the poor, such as feeding the *h*.; **Alma** 4: 12 some lift themselves up in pride, turning their backs upon the *h*.; 8: 26 (10: 7) Alma² was an *h*. when Amulek took him in; 32: 42 feast upon word until ye are filled, that ye *h*. not; **3 Ne.** 4: 20 robbers about to perish with *h*.; 12: 6 (Matt. 5: 6) blessed are they who *h*. and thirst after righteousness; 20: 8 soul of him who partakes of Christ's flesh and blood shall never *h*.; **Morm.** 8: 39 why do ye adorn yourselves with that which hath no life, yet suffer the *h*. to pass by you.

HUSBAND (*see also* Family; Marriage; Wife; TG Husband; Marriage, Husband)

Jacob 2: 31 daughters of the Lord's people mourn because of wickedness of *h*.; 3: 7 Lamanite *h*. love wives, and wives love *h*.; **Moro.** 9: 8 Lamanites feed Nephite women upon flesh of *h*.

HYPOCRISY, HYPOCRITE (*see also* Deceit; Guile; Lying; Sincerity; Wicked; BD Hypocrite)

2 Ne. 31: 13 if ye follow Son, acting no *h*., ye shall receive Holy Ghost; **Alma** 10: 17 lawyers and *h*. are laying foundation of devil; 34: 28 if saints turn away the needy, they are as *h*. who deny the faith; **3 Ne.** 13: 2 (Matt. 6: 2) when ye do your alms, do not sound trumpet as *h*. do; 13: 5 (Matt. 6: 5) when thou prayest,

thou shalt not do as *h.*; 16: 10 when Gentiles are full of *h.*, the Lord will bring gospel from among them; **Morm.** 8: 38 *h.* sell themselves for that which will canker, pollute church of God.

IDLENESS, IDLE, IDLER (*see also* Industry; Labor; Laziness; Procrastinate; Sleep; Slothful)

1 Ne. 12: 23 (2 Ne. 5: 24) Lamanites become an *i.* people; **Alma** 1: 32 those who do not belong to church indulge in *i.*; 22: 28 more *i.* part of Lamanites live in wilderness in tents; 24: 18 converted Lamanites covenant that they will labor rather than spend days in *i.*; 38: 12 refrain from *i.*

IDOLATRY, IDOLATROUS, IDOL (*see also* Altar; Gods; Image; Priests, False; Sacrifice; BD Idol)

2 Ne. 9: 37 wo unto those who worship *i.*; 12: 8 (Isa. 2: 8) land is full of *i.*; **Enos** 1: 20 (Mosiah 9: 12; Alma 17: 15) Lamanites are full of *i.*; **Mosiah** 11: 6 priests of Noah³ are supported in *i.* by taxes; 11: 7 people of Noah³ become *i.* because of flattery of king and priests; 12: 35 (Ex. 20: 3) thou shalt have no other God before me; 13: 12–13 (Ex. 20: 4–5) thou shalt not make unto thee any graven image; 27: 8 Alma² became a wicked and *i.* man; **Alma** 1: 32 those who do not belong to church indulge in *i.*; 31: 1 Zoram³ leads his people to bow down to dumb *i.*; 50: 21 *i.* brings wars and destructions upon Nephites; **Hel.** 6: 31 Nephites build *i.* of gold and silver; **Morm.** 4: 14, 21 Lamanites offer Nephite women and children as sacrifices to *i.*; 5: 15 Nephites to become loathsome people because of *i.*; **Ether** 7: 23 prophets testify that *i.* will bring curse upon land.

IGNORANCE, IGNORANT, IGNORANTLY (*see also* Accountable; Blindness; Darkness, Spiritual; Knowledge)

Mosiah 1: 3 except for records, Nephites must have suffered in *i.*; 3: 11 Christ's blood atoneth for those who have *i.* sinned; 15: 24 those who died in *i.* before Christ came shall come forth in first resurrection; 19: 17 Limhi not *i.* of father's iniquities; **Alma** 34: 2 impossible that Zoramites are *i.* of prophecies of Christ's coming; **3 Ne.** 6: 12 some are *i.* because of poverty; 6: 18 people do not sin *i.*, for they know will of God.

ILLUMINATE (*see also* Enlighten)

Alma 5: 7 fathers' souls were *i.* by light of everlasting word.

IMAGE (*see also* Creation; Form [noun]; Idolatry; Likeness)

Mosiah 7: 27 Christ to take upon himself the *i.* of man; 7: 27 (Alma 18: 34; 22: 12; Ether 3: 15) man created in *i.* of God; 12: 36 (13: 12–13) thou shalt not make unto thee any graven *i.*; **Alma** 5: 14, 19 have ye received God's *i.* in your countenances; **3 Ne.** 21: 17 (Micah 5: 13) thy graven *i.* I will cut off.

IMAGINATION, IMAGINE (*see also* Think; Thoughts)

1 Ne. 2: 11 (17: 20) elder sons murmur that Lehi¹ follows foolish *i.* of heart; 12: 18 spacious building is vain *i.* of men; **Alma** 5: 16–18 can you *i.* you hear the Lord's voice calling you; **Hel.** 16: 22 (3 Ne. 2: 2) Nephites *i.* up foolish and vain things in hearts; **3 Ne.** 29: 3 ye need not *i.* that words spoken are vain; **Morm.** 9: 10, 15 if ye have *i.* a changing God, he is not a God of miracles.

IMMANUEL (*see* Jesus Christ—Immanuel)

IMMERSION, IMMERSE (*see also* Baptism; Water; TG Baptism, Immersion)

Mosiah 18: 14 Alma¹ and Helam are buried in water in baptism; 18: 14–16 Alma¹ baptizes by burying in water; **3 Ne.** 11: 26 during baptism, disciples should *i.* person in water; 19: 11–13 Nephi³ goes down into water to baptize.

IMMORTALITY, IMMORTAL (*see also* Body; Death, Physical; Eternal Life; Incorruptible; Jesus Christ, Resurrection of; Life; Live; Mortal; Redemption; Resurrection; TG Immortality)

2 Ne. 9: 13 all men shall become *i.*; 9: 15 when men have become *i.*, they must appear before judgment-seat; **Enos** 1: 27 (Mosiah 16: 10; Alma 5: 15; 12: 12; 41: 4; Morm. 6: 21) mortal must put on *i.*; **Alma** 11: 45 mortal body to be raised to *i.* body; 40: 2 mortal does not put on *i.* until after Christ's coming; **3 Ne.** 28: 8, 17 three Nephites shall be changed in twinkling of eye from mortality to *i.*

IMMOVABLE (*see also* Firmness; Steadfast)

1 Ne. 2: 10 Lehi¹ exhorts Lemuel to be *i.* in keeping commandments; **Mosiah** 5: 15 I would that ye should be steadfast and *i.*; **Alma** 1: 25 those who stand fast in the faith are *i.* in keeping commandments; **3 Ne.** 6: 14 church broken up, save few Lamanites who are *i.*

IMPART (*see also* Alms; Charity; Give; Poor)

Mosiah 4: 21, 26 (18: 27–28; 21: 17; Alma 1: 27; 34: 28) saints commanded to *i.* of substance for support of needy; 28: 1 sons of Mosiah² desire to *i.* word of God to Lamanites; **Alma** 12: 9 men commanded

to *i.* only that portion of word which God grants unto men; 16: 14 Alma² and Amulek *i.* word of God without any respect of persons; 32: 23 God *i.* his word by angels unto men.

IMPOSSIBLE

Jacob 4: 8 *i.* that man should find out all God's ways; **Alma** 11: 34 *i.* for God to deny his word; **Hel.** 8: 5–6 Nephite judges believe destruction is *i.*; **Morm.** 4: 11 *i.* to write perfect description of carnage.

IMPROVE (*see also* Increase)

Alma 34: 33 if we do not *i.* our time while in this life, then cometh night of darkness.

INCORRECT (*see also* False)

Alma 3: 8 (9: 17; 26: 24; 37: 9) *i.* traditions of Lamanites.

INCORRUPTIBLE (*see also* Immortality)

2 Ne. 9: 13 all men shall become *i.*; **Morm.** 6: 21 bodies moldering in corruption must become *i.*

INCORRUPTION (*see* Corrupt, Corruption)

INCREASE (*see also* Add; Continue, Continuation; Enlarge; Grow; Improve; Lengthen; Multiply; Prolong; Reward; Seed; Spread; Swell; Wax)

2 Ne. 19: 3 (Isa. 9: 3) thou hast *i.* in the joy; 19: 7 (Isa. 9: 7) of *i.* of government and peace there is no end; 27: 30 the meek also shall *i.*; **Alma** 32: 28–29 would not the swelling of the seed *i.* your faith.

INDEBTED (*see also* Blessing; Debt; Owe)

Mosiah 2: 23 ye are *i.* unto God for creating you; 2: 24 ye will forever be *i.* unto God because of his blessings; 2: 34 ye are eternally *i.* to heavenly Father to render to him all that you have and are.

INDIGNATION (*see also* Anger; Displeasure; Judgment; Provoke; Punishment; Wrath)

2 Ne. 20: 25 (Isa. 10: 25) *i.* shall cease; **Alma** 40: 14 souls of wicked look for fiery *i.* of wrath of God upon them.

INDUSTRY, INDUSTRIOUS (*see also* Idleness; Labor; Work [verb]; TG Industry; Work, Value of)

2 Ne. 5: 17 Nephi¹ causes his people to be *i.*; **Mosiah** 23: 5 people of Alma¹ are *i.*; **Alma** 4: 6 people of church prosper by their *i.*; 10: 4 Amulek has acquired much riches by his *i.*; 23: 18 Anti-Nephi-Lehies become very *i.* people; **Ether** 10: 22 Jaredites are exceedingly *i.*

INEQUALITY (*see also* Equal; Pride; Ranks)

Mosiah 29: 32 *i.* should be no more in land; **Alma** 4: 12, 15 great *i.* among Nephites; 16: 16 no *i.* among Nephites; 28: 13 how great the *i.* of man is because of sin; **3 Ne.** 6: 14 great *i.* in all the land.

INFANT (*see also* Accountability, Age of; Babe; Child)

Mosiah 3: 18 the *i.* perisheth not that dieth in infancy.

INFINITE (*see also* Endless; Eternal; God, Eternal Nature of)

2 Ne. 1: 10 (Mosiah 5: 3; Hel. 12: 1; Moro. 8: 3) *i.* goodness of God; 9: 7 (25: 16; Alma 34: 10–14) atonement must be *i.*; **Mosiah** 28: 4 the Lord in *i.* mercy spares sons of Mosiah².

INFIRMITY (*see also* Disease; Suffering; Weak)

Mosiah 2: 11 like all men, Benjamin is subject to *i.* in body and mind; **Alma** 7: 12 Son will take upon him the *i.* of his people; 31: 30 O Lord, wilt thou give me strength, that I may bear my *i.*; **3 Ne.** 17: 22 those healed of *i.* manifest that they had been wrought upon by Spirit.

INFLICT

2 Ne. 2: 10 (Alma 42: 22) law given unto *i.* of punishment; **Mosiah** 3: 19 man must be willing to submit to all which the Lord seeth fit to *i.* upon him.

INHABIT, INHABITANT (*see also* Dwell; Possess)

1 Ne. 17: 36 the Lord created earth that it should be *i.*; 21: 19 (Isa. 49: 19) desolate places shall be too narrow by reason of *i.*; **2 Ne.** 20: 46 (Zech. 12: 6) Jerusalem shall be *i.* again; 22: 3 (Isa. 54: 3) desolate cities to be *i.*

INHERIT, INHERITANCE (*see also* Children of God; Covenant; Heir; Heritage; Kingdom of God; Possess; Promised Land; BD Inheritance)

1 Ne. 21: 8 (Isa. 49: 8) I will give thee my servant for covenant of the people, to cause to *i.* desolate heritages; 22: 12 (2 Ne. 25: 11) Israel shall be gathered into lands of *i.*; **2 Ne.** 1: 5 the Lord covenants with Lehi¹ to give his seed land of *i.*; 1: 9 if those coming out of Jerusalem keep commandments, none shall take away land of *i.*; 3: 2 may the Lord consecrate this land unto thee for thine *i.*; 9: 18 righteous saints shall *i.* kingdom of God; 10: 7 Jews to be restored to lands of *i.* when they believe in Christ; **Jacob** 3: 4 unless Nephites repent, Lamanites will possess land of *i.*; **Omni**

1: 27 (Mosiah 9: 1, 3) Zeniff and others desire to possess land of first *i.*; **Mosiah** 27: 26 unless they become new creatures, mankind cannot *i.* kingdom of God; **Alma** 5: 51 (9: 12; 39: 9; 3 Ne. 11: 38) except ye repent, ye cannot *i.* kingdom of heaven; 5: 58 unto the righteous will the Lord grant *i.* at right hand; 40: 26 no unclean thing can *i.* kingdom of God; 41: 4 those raised to endless happiness *i.* kingdom of God, those raised to endless misery *i.* kingdom of devil; **3 Ne.** 11: 33 whoso believeth in Christ and is baptized shall *i.* kingdom of God; 12: 5 (Matt. 5: 5) blessed are the meek, for they shall *i.* earth; 16: 16 (20: 14) Nephites to be given this land for *i.*; 22: 3 (Isa. 54: 3) thy seed shall *i.* the Gentiles; **Ether** 2: 15 Jaredites to be given this land for *i.*; 7: 16 Noah² obtains land of first *i.*; 12: 34 except men have charity, they cannot *i.* place prepared in Father's mansions.

INIQUITY, INIQUITOUS (*see also* Destruction; Evil; Judgment; Rebel; Sin; Transgression; Trespass; Ungodliness; Unrighteous; Wicked; TG Iniquity)

1 Ne. 17: 35 Canaanites driven out because they were ripe in *i.*; 17: 41 the Lord straitened Israel in wilderness because of *i.*; 17: 45 (Mosiah 13: 29; Alma 46: 8; Hel. 12: 4) ye are swift to do *i.*, but slow to remember the Lord; **2 Ne.** 1: 7 if *i.* abound, land to be cursed; 1: 31 nothing save *i.* shall disturb prosperity; 7: 1 (Isa. 50: 1) for your *i.* have ye sold yourselves; 25: 9 Jews have been destroyed from generation to generation according to *i.*; 27: 31 (Isa. 29: 20) all who watch for *i.* shall be cut off; 28: 16 when inhabitants of earth are fully ripe in *i.*, they shall perish; **Mosiah** 11: 22 the Lord visits the *i.* of his people; 13: 11 priests of Noah³ have studied and taught *i.*; 14: 5 (Isa. 53: 5) Messiah was bruised for our *i.*; 14: 6 (Isa. 53: 6) the Lord hath laid on Messiah the *i.* of us all; 14: 11 (Isa. 53: 11) Messiah shall bear their *i.*; 21: 15 the Lord is slow to hear cries of Limhi's people because of *i.*; 27: 29 soul of Alma² has been redeemed from bonds of *i.*; 29: 17 how much *i.* doth one wicked king cause; 29: 21 ye cannot dethrone *i.* king save through contention and bloodshed; **Alma** 26: 24 Lamanites' days have been spent in grossest *i.*; 41: 11 all men in state of nature, or carnal state, are in bonds of *i.*; **Hel.** 7: 7 early Nephites were slow to be led to do *i.*; 13: 38 ye have sought happiness in doing *i.*; **3 Ne.** 9: 5 the Lord has covered city with earth to hide *i.*; 14: 23 (Matt. 7: 23) depart from me, ye that work *i.*; 20: 28 if Gentiles harden hearts against the Lord, he will return their *i.* upon their own heads;

Ether 2: 9 (9: 20) God's wrath shall come upon inhabitants of land when they are ripened in *i.*; **Moro.** 6: 7 church members strict to observe that there should be no *i.* among them; 7: 45 (1 Cor. 13: 6) charity rejoiceth not in *i.*; 10: 22 despair cometh because of *i.*

INJUSTICE (*see* Justice; Malice; Persecution; Unjust; Unlawful)

INNOCENCE, INNOCENT (*see also* Blameless; Blood, Shedding of; Guiltless; Purity; Righteousness; Spotless)

2 Ne. 2: 23 Adam and Eve would have remained in state of *i.*

INQUIRE (*see also* Ask; Prayer; Question; Seek)

1 Ne. 15: 3 words hard to understand save a man *i.* of God; 15: 8 have ye *i.* of the Lord; 16: 23–24 Lehi¹ *i.* of the Lord where Nephi¹ should hunt; **Jacob** 2: 11 as Jacob² *i.* of the Lord, his word came; **Mosiah** 28: 6 Mosiah² *i.* of the Lord whether sons should preach to Lamanites; **Alma** 27: 7 Ammon² *i.* of the Lord whether Ammonites should go to Nephites; 40: 3, 9 Alma² has *i.* diligently of the Lord to know concerning resurrection; 43: 23 Moroni¹ asks Alma² to *i.* of the Lord whether Nephites should defend themselves against Lamanites; **3 Ne.** 28: 37 Mormon² *i.* of the Lord regarding three Nephites; **Ether** 1: 38 Jared² asks brother to *i.* of the Lord whether he will drive them out of land; **Moro.** 8: 7 Mormon² *i.* of the Lord regarding baptism of little children.

INSECT (*see also* Curse; Judgment)

Mosiah 12: 6 *i.* shall pester land of people of Noah³.

INSPIRE, INSPIRATION (*see also* Calling; Enlighten; Holy Ghost; Revelation; Spirit, Holy/Spirit of the Lord; TG Inspiration)

Alma 43: 45 Nephites are *i.* by better cause; **3 Ne.** 6: 20 men *i.* from heaven are sent forth to preach; **Moro.** 7: 13 everything which inviteth to do good, love God, and serve him is *i.* of God.

INSTRUCTION, INSTRUCT (*see also* Charge; Command; Counsel; Revelation; Teach)

1 Ne. 17: 18 Nephi¹ *i.* of the Lord to build ship; 19: 3 things written on plates should be kept for *i.* of people; **2 Ne.** 2: 5 men are sufficiently *i.* that they know good from evil; 18: 11 (Isa. 8: 11) the Lord *i.* me that I should not walk in way of this people; **Alma** 47: 36 dissenters, who have been *i.* in knowledge of the Lord,

become more hardened than Lamanites; 49: 8 Nephites prepared to battle after manner of *i.* of Moroni[1]; **3 Ne.** 3: 26 Gidgiddoni causes Nephites to make armor after manner of his *i.*; **Ether** 2: 16 Jaredites build barges according to *i.* of the Lord.

INSTRUMENT, INSTRUMENTALITY

2 Ne. 1: 24 (3: 24; Mosiah 23: 10; 27: 36; Alma 1: 8; 2: 30; 17: 9, 11; 26: 3, 15; 29: 9; 35: 14; 3 Ne. 22: 16) *i.* in hands of God.

INTENT (*see also* Desire; Purpose; Sincerity; Thoughts; Will)

1 Ne. 6: 4 fulness of mine *i.* is to persuade men to come unto God; **2 Ne.** 31: 13 if ye follow Son with real *i.*, ye shall receive Holy Ghost; **Jacob** 2: 19 seek riches for *i.* to do good; 4: 5 Nephites keep law of Moses for *i.* of pointing souls to Christ; **Mosiah** 5: 13 how knoweth a man the master who is far from *i.* of his heart; **Alma** 18: 32 God knows thoughts and *i.* of heart; 34: 15 *i.* of last sacrifice is to bring about bowels of mercy; **Moro.** 6: 8 as oft as they repented with real *i.*, they were forgiven; 7: 6 except a man offereth a gift with real *i.*, it profiteth him nothing; 7: 9 if a man prays without real *i.*, it profiteth him nothing; 10: 4 if ye ask God with real *i.*, he will manifest the truth unto you.

INTERCESSION (*see* Jesus Christ—Mediator)

INTEREST

Mosiah 4: 18 unrepentant have no *i.* in kingdom of God.

INTERPRETATION, INTERPRET (*see also* Interpreters; Language; Spirit, Gifts of; Tongue; Translation)

1 Ne. 11: 10–11 Nephi[1] desires to know *i.* of father's dream; 17: 5 Irreantum, being *i.*, is many waters; **Omni** 1: 20 Mosiah[1] *i.* engravings by gift and power of God; 1: 25 Amaleki[1] exhorts all men to believe in gift of *i.* of languages; **Mosiah** 8: 11 no one among Limhi's people can *i.* language on plates; 28: 13–14 two stones prepared for purpose of *i.* languages; **Alma** 10: 2 Aminadi *i.* writing upon temple wall; 18: 13 Rabbanah, being *i.*, is powerful or great king; 31: 21 Rameumptom, being *i.*, is holy stand; 37: 38 Liahona, being *i.*, is a compass; **Morm.** 9: 7 who can say there are no speaking with tongues and *i.* of tongues; **Ether** 2: 3 deseret, by *i.*, is honey bee; 3: 22 brother of Jared[2] shall seal record of experience, and no one can *i.* it; 4: 5 the Lord has commanded Moroni[2] to seal up *i.* of what brother of Jared[2] saw; 15: 8 Ripliancum,

by *i.*, is large, or to exceed all; **Moro.** 10: 16 (1 Cor. 12: 10) to another is given the *i.* of languages.

INTERPRETERS (*see also* Interpretation; Seer; Translation; **BD** Urim and Thummim)

Mosiah 8: 13 *i.* a gift of God to seer for translating all ancient records; 8: 19 (Alma 37: 24–25) *i.* prepared for unfolding mysteries; 28: 20 Mosiah[2] confers *i.* upon Alma[2]; **Alma** 37: 21 Alma[2] admonishes Helaman[2] to preserve *i.*; **Ether** 4: 5 Moroni[2] commanded to seal up *i.*

INVENT

Mosiah 9: 16 Zeniff arms his people with all manner of weapons they can *i.*

INVITE (*see also* Entice; Lead)

2 Ne. 26: 33 God *i.* all to come unto him; **Moro.** 7: 12 devil *i.* to sin; 7: 13 that which is of God *i.* to do good; 7: 13, 16 every thing which *i.* to do good is of God.

INWARD, INWARDLY (*see* Prophets, False; Vessel)

IRON (*see also* Metal; Ore; Rod; Steel; Yoke)

2 Ne. 5: 15 Nephi[1] teaches his people to work in all manner of *i.*; 20: 34 (Isa. 10: 34) he shall cut down thickets of forests with *i.*; **Jarom** 1: 8 Nephites become rich in workmanship in *i.*; **Mosiah** 11: 8 Noah[3] ornaments buildings with all manner of *i.*; **Ether** 10: 23 Jaredites work in all manner of *i.*

IRREANTUM—*probably an arm of Indian Ocean off southeastern Arabia*

1 Ne. 17: 5 Lehites behold sea, which they call I.

ISAAC—*son of Abraham* (*see also* **BD** Isaac)

1 Ne. 6: 4 (19: 10; Mosiah 7: 19; 23: 23; Alma 29: 11; 36: 2; 3 Ne. 4: 30; Morm. 9: 11) God of Abraham, I., and Jacob; 17: 40 God covenanted with Abraham, I., and Jacob; **Jacob** 4: 5 Abraham's offering of I. is similitude of God and Son; **Alma** 5: 24 (7: 25; Hel. 3: 30) righteous shall sit down in kingdom of God with Abraham, I., and Jacob.

ISABEL—*harlot in land of Siron* [c. 73 B.C.]

Alma 39: 3 Corianton forsakes ministry and goes after harlot I.

ISAIAH[1]—*Hebrew prophet* [c. eighth century B.C.] (*see also* **BD** Isaiah)

1 Ne. 15: 20 Nephi[1] rehearses to his brethren the words of I.; 19: 23 Nephi[1] reads prophecies of I. to persuade his people to believe in Redeemer; **2 Ne.** 6: 4 Jacob[2] speaks of things to come by read-

ing words of *I*.; 6: 5 *I*. spake concerning all house of Israel; 11: 2 *I*. saw Redeemer; 11: 8 Jacob[2] writes words of *I*. to lift hearts; 25: 1 *I*. spake things hard to understand; 25: 4 *I*'s words plain to those with spirit of prophecy; 25: 5 my soul delighteth in words of *I*.; 25: 6 judgments spoken of by *I*. have come to pass; 25: 7 men shall know when prophecies of *I*. are fulfilled; **Mosiah** 15: 6 Messiah shall be led as sheep before shearer, as *I*. said; **Hel.** 8: 18–20 *I*. testified of redemption; **3 Ne.** 16: 17–20 words of *I*. shall be fulfilled; 20: 11–12 when words of *I*. should be fulfilling, then is fulfilling of the Father's covenant with Israel; 23: 1 (Morm. 8: 23) search these things diligently, for great are words of *I*. Compare also 1 Ne. 20/Isa. 48; 1 Ne. 21/Isa. 49; 2 Ne. 7/Isa. 50; 2 Ne. 8/Isa. 51; 2 Ne. 12/Isa. 2; 2 Ne. 13/Isa. 3; 2 Ne. 14/Isa. 4; 2 Ne. 15/Isa. 5; 2 Ne. 16/Isa. 6; 2 Ne. 17/Isa. 7; 2 Ne. 18/Isa. 8; 2 Ne. 19/Isa. 9; 2 Ne. 20/Isa. 10; 2 Ne. 21/Isa. 11; 2 Ne. 22/Isa. 12; 2 Ne. 23/Isa. 13; 2 Ne. 24/Isa. 14; 2 Ne. 27/Isa. 29; Mosiah 14/Isa. 53; Mosiah 15/parts of Isa. 52; 3 Ne. 22/Isa. 54.

ISAIAH[2]—*one of the twelve Nephite disciples* [c. A.D. 34]

3 Ne. 19: 4 chosen by Christ to minister to Nephites.

ISHMAEL[1]—*an Ephraimite from Jerusalem* [c. 600 B.C.] (*see also* Ishmael[1], Sons of; Ishmaelite)

1 Ne. 7: 2 sons of Lehi[1] return to Jerusalem to bring *I*. and family into wilderness; 7: 4–5 the Lord softens heart of *I*.; 7: 19 part of *I*'s family pleads with rebellious brethren; 7: 22 house of *I*. joins Lehites in thanking God and offering sacrifice; 16: 7 Zoram[1] and sons of Lehi[1] marry *I*'s daughters; 16: 34 dies.

ISHMAEL[2]—*grandfather of Amulek*

Alma 10: 2 father of Giddonah, descendant of Aminadi.

ISHMAEL, LAND OF—*portion of land of Nephi*

Alma 17: 19 Ammon[2] goes to land of *I*.; 17: 21 (20: 14–15) Lamoni king over land of *I*.; 21: 20–21 synagogues built and word preached in land of *I*.; 22: 4 Ammon[2] and Lamoni return to land of *I*.; 22: 4 Ammon[2] called by Spirit to teach people in land of *I*.; 23: 7–9 converted Lamanites in land of *I*. lay down arms; 24: 5 council held in land of *I*. to plan defense against Lamanites; 25: 13 other Lamanites join people of Anti-Nephi-Lehi in land of *I*.

ISHMAEL[1], SONS OF (*see also* Ishmaelite)

1 Ne. 7: 6 (18: 17) two sons of *I*. join Laman[1] and Lemuel in rebelling; 16: 20 murmuring by Laman[1], Lemuel, and sons of *I*.; 16: 37 encouraged to slay Lehi[1] and Nephi[1]; 18: 9 begin to make merry; **2 Ne.** 1: 28 admonished to hearken unto Nephi[1]; 4: 13 angry with Nephi[1]; **Alma** 3: 7 the Lord set mark upon sons of *I*.; 17: 19 became Lamanites; 43: 13 (47: 35) Lamanites consist of Laman[1], Lemuel, sons of *I*., and dissenters.

ISHMAELITE, ISHMAELITISH—*descendants of Ishmael[1]*

Alma 3: 7 mark of Lamanites also placed upon *I*. women; 47: 35 (43: 13; Morm. 1: 8–9) Lamanites composed of Lamanites, Lemuelites, Ishmaelites, and dissenters; **4 Ne.** 1: 38 willfully reject gospel.

ISLAND, ISLE

1 Ne. 19: 10 three days of darkness a sign of Christ's death to those on *i*. of sea; 22: 4 more part of all tribes have been scattered upon *i*. of sea; **2 Ne.** 10: 8 Jews shall be gathered in from long dispersion, from *i*. of sea; 10: 20 we are upon an *i*. of sea; 21: 11 (Isa. 11: 11) the Lord shall set his hand the second time to recover his people from *i*. of sea; 29: 7 the Lord remembers those upon *i*. of sea; 29: 11 the Lord commands all men, in *i*. of sea.

ISRAEL—*name of Jacob[1] and, by extension, of all his descendants* (*see also* Abrahamic Covenant; Branch; Covenant; Ephraim; Israel, Gathering of; Israel, Scattering of; Israel, Ten Lost Tribes of; Israelites; Jacob[1]; Jew; Joseph[1]; Joseph[1], Seed of; Judah; Remnant; TG Israel; Israel, Blessings of; Israel, Bondage of, in Other Lands; Israel, Deliverance of; Israel, Joseph, People of; Israel, Judah, People of; Israel, Land of; Israel, Mission of; Israel, Origins of; Israel, Remnant of; Israel, Twelve Tribes of; BD Israel; Israel, Kingdom of)

Title Page (1 Ne. 12: 9; 15: 12; 2 Ne. 6: 5; 3 Ne. 20: 10; Morm. 7: 2) Nephites and Lamanites are remnant of house of *I*.; **1 Ne.** 10: 12 (15: 12) Jacob 5: 3—6: 1) house of *I*. compared to olive-tree; 10: 14 (15: 12–18) house of *I*. to come to knowledge of true Messiah; 12: 9 (Morm. 3: 18) twelve tribes of *I*. to be judged by twelve apostles; 13: 23 (14: 5, 8, 17; 22: 6, 9, 11; 2 Ne. 9: 1; 3 Ne. 16: 5, 11–12; 20: 12, 27; 21: 4, 7; 29: 3, 8; Morm. 5: 20; 9: 37; Ether 4: 15; Moro. 10: 31) covenants with house of *I*.; 13: 33–34 (19: 11) the Lamb will visit remnant of house of *I*.; 14: 2 (2 Ne. 10: 18; 3 Ne. 16: 13–15; 21: 6; 30: 2) if Gentiles harden not hearts, they shall be numbered among house of *I*.; 14: 26 sealed writings

shall come forth unto house of I.; 15: 14 (2 Ne. 28: 2; 3 Ne. 20: 10; Morm. 7: 1) remnant of Lehites' seed shall know they are of house of I.; 15: 17 the Lord shall be rejected of Jews, or of house of I.; 17: 23 children of I. were led out of Egypt because they hearkened to the Lord; 17: 25 children of I. were in bondage; 17: 29 Moses smote rock, that children of I. might quench thirst; 19: 10 sign of Christ's death to be given house of I.; 20: 1 (Isa. 48: 1) house of Jacob are called by name of I.; 20: 12 hearken, O Jacob, and I. my called; 21: 3 (Isa. 49: 3) thou art my servant, O I.; 21: 7 (Isa. 49: 7) the Lord, the Redeemer of I.; 22: 12 those who are of house of I. shall know that the Lord is their Savior, the Mighty One of I.; 22: 14 nations that war against house of I. shall be turned one against another; 2 Ne. 3: 9 Moses raised up to deliver house of I.; 6: 5 (3 Ne. 23: 2) Isaiah[1] spake concerning all house of I.; 9: 53 our seed shall become righteous branch unto house of I.; 14: 2 (Isa. 4: 2) fruit of earth shall be comely to them that are escaped of I.; 15: 7 (Isa. 5: 7) vineyard of the Lord is house of I.; 18: 14 (Isa. 8: 14) he shall be for a rock of offense to both the houses of I.; 19: 8 (Isa. 9: 8) the Lord sent his word unto Jacob and it hath lighted upon I.; 19: 12 (Isa. 9: 12) Syrians and Philistines shall devour I.; 19: 14 (Isa. 9: 14) the Lord will cut off from I. head and tail; 20: 17 (Isa. 10: 17) the light of I. shall be for a fire; 21: 16 (Isa. 11: 16) highway shall be left, as when I. came up out of Egypt; 24: 1 (Isa. 14: 1) the Lord will have mercy on Jacob and will yet choose I.; 25: 20 the Lord brought I. up out of Egypt; 29: 2 the Lord's words shall hiss forth as standard unto house of I.; Jacob 1: 7 provocation in days of temptation while children of I. were in wilderness; Mosiah 7: 19 trust in that God who brought children of I. out of Egypt; 13: 29 expedient that law should be given to children of I.; 3 Ne. 15: 5 Christ is the one who covenanted with his people I.; 16: 7 because of unbelief of house of I., truth shall come unto Gentiles; 17: 1 Jesus troubled because of wickedness of house of I.; 21: 20 unrepentant to be cut off from house of I.; 25: 4 (Mal. 4: 4) Lord commanded law of Moses for all I.; 29: 1 covenant which Father made with children of I. shall be fulfilled; 29: 2 ye need not say the Lord delays his coming to children of I.; Morm. 5: 10–11 Gentiles who have care for house of I. will have sorrow for calamity of house of I.; 8: 21 he who breathes out wrath against house of I. is in danger to be hewn down.

ISRAEL, GATHERING OF (*see also* Israel, Scattering of; TG Israel, Gathering of; Israel, Restoration of)

1 Ne. 10: 14 (15: 12–18; 3 Ne. 16: 4, 11–12) I. to be gathered again, to come to knowledge of Messiah; 10: 14 (Jacob 5: 52–74) natural branches of olive-tree, remnants of I., to be grafted in; 15: 18–20 (2 Ne. 3: 21; 3 Ne. 10: 7; 16: 5, 11–12; 20: 12–13, 29; 21: 4, 7; 29: 1, 3, 8–9) God to remember covenant to restore I.; 19: 16 (3 Ne. 5: 24) all people who are of house of I. will the Lord gather in; 21: 5–6 (Isa. 49: 5–6) Isaiah[1] to be servant to raise up tribes of Jacob and restore preserved of I.; 21: 22 (Isa. 49: 22) Gentiles shall bring I's sons and daughters; **2 Ne.** 3: 11–13 latter-day seer to be raised up when work commences unto restoring house of I.; 3: 24 mighty one to rise up as instrument of the Lord in bringing to pass much restoration unto house of I.; 6: 14 (21: 11; 25: 17; 29: 1; Jacob 6: 2; Isa. 11: 11) Messiah will set hand second time to recover covenant people of I.; 9: 2 the Lord speaks to I. by prophets until time when they are restored to true church and gathered to lands of inheritance; 10: 2 (30: 5; Hel. 15: 11; 3 Ne. 5: 23) descendants of Nephites and Lamanites to be restored to knowledge of Christ; 20: 21–22 (Isa. 10: 21–22) remnant of Jacob shall return; 20: 22 (Isa. 10: 22) though I be as sand of sea, yet a remnant shall return; 21: 12 (Isa. 11: 12) the Lord shall assemble outcasts of I.; 24: 2 (Isa. 14: 2) house of I. to return to lands of promise; 30: 7–8 (3 Ne. 20: 31–33; Morm. 5: 14) Jews shall begin to believe in Christ, and God will commence work of restoration; **3 Ne.** 10: 4–6 (Matt. 23: 37) the Lord would gather I. as hen gathers chickens; 16: 4 through fulness of Gentiles, remnant of I. shall be brought to knowledge of Redeemer; 20: 21 the Lord will establish his people, O house of I.; 20: 29 the Lord will remember covenant to gather his people and give them Jerusalem as land of inheritance; 21: 22–24 Gentiles shall assist remnant of Jacob in gathering unto New Jerusalem; 21: 27 work to commence among the dispersed to prepare way, that they call upon Father in Christ's name; 29: 1 when scriptures come to Gentiles, Father's covenant to restore I. to lands of inheritance will be fulfilled; **Morm.** 3: 17 when work commences, I. shall be about to prepare to return to land of inheritance; 5: 14 writings to convince Jews, that Father restore house of I. to land of inheritance; **Ether** 4: 14 come unto me, ye house of I.; 13: 10 seed of Joseph[1], who are of house of I., shall dwell in New Jerusalem.

ISRAEL, SCATTERING OF (see also Destruction; Israel, Gathering of; Israel, Ten Lost Tribes of; Remnant; TG Israel, Scattering of)

1 Ne. 10: 3 Jerusalem to be carried captive into Babylon; 10: 12 (Jacob 5: 7–8, 13–14) house of I. compared to olive-tree whose branches should be broken off and scattered; 10: 13 Lehites to be scattered upon the land; 10: 14 (15: 16–17; 2 Ne. 6: 11; 10: 67; 3 Ne. 20: 13) after I. is scattered, they will be gathered; 13: 14 (22: 7; 3 Ne. 16: 8; Morm. 5: 9) seed of Lamanites to be scattered by Gentiles; 15: 20 after being gathered, I. will be scattered no more; 21: 1 house of I. are broken off and driven out because of wickedness of pastors; 22: 3, 7 (2 Ne. 25: 15) house of I. to be scattered among all nations; 22: 4 many are already lost from knowledge of those at Jerusalem; 2 Ne. 3: 5 from loins of Joseph[1] would come righteous branch to be broken off; 10: 22 God has led away from time to time from house of I.; Omni 1: 15 (Hel. 8: 21) people of Zarahemla come from Jerusalem when Zedekiah was taken captive into Babylon; 3 Ne. 10: 7 place of I's dwellings shall be desolate until fulfilling of covenant; 20: 27 Gentiles to be made mighty unto scattering of Israel; 28: 29 three Nephites to minister to scattered tribes of Israel; Ether 13: 7 the Lord brought remnant of seed of Joseph[1] out of Jerusalem.

ISRAEL, TEN LOST TRIBES OF (see also Israel, Gathering of; Israel, Scattering of; TG Israel, Ten Lost Tribes of)

1 Ne. 22: 4 many are already lost from knowledge of those at Jerusalem; 2 Ne. 29: 12 the Lord will speak to Jews, Nephites, other tribes, and they shall write; 29: 13 Jews, Nephites, and lost tribes shall have each others' writings; 3 Ne. 15: 15 Father has not commanded Christ to tell Jews about other tribes whom Father led away; 15: 20 Father separated other tribes from Jews because of iniquity; 17: 4 Christ will show himself to lost tribes; 21: 26 gospel to be preached to lost tribes; 28: 29 three Nephites shall minister unto all scattered tribes; Ether 13: 11 they who were scattered and gathered from north countries are partakers of fulfilling of covenant.

ISRAELITES (see also Israel)

Hel. 8: 11 I., who were our fathers, came through Red Sea.

-ITES

4 Ne. 1: 17 no manner of i. among the people.

JACOB[1]—father of twelve tribes, name changed to Israel [c. 1800 B.C.] (see also Israel; Jacob, House of; BD Israel; Jacob)

1 Ne. 5: 14 Lehi[1] a descendant of Joseph[1], who was son of J.; 6: 4 (19: 10; Mosiah 7: 19; 23: 23; Alma 29: 11; 36: 2; 3 Ne. 4: 30; Morm. 9: 11) God of Abraham, Isaac, and J.; 17: 40 the Lord covenanted with Abraham, Isaac, and J.; 20: 20 (Isa. 48: 20) the Lord hath redeemed his servant J.; 2 Ne. 12: 3 (Isa. 2: 3) let us go up to the house of the God of J.; 19: 8 the Lord sent his word unto J., and it hath lighted upon Israel; Alma 5: 24 (7: 25; Hel. 3: 30) the righteous shall sit down in kingdom of God with Abraham, Isaac, and J.; 46: 24–26 remember the words of J. before his death; 3 Ne. 10: 17 father J. testified concerning remnant of the seed of Joseph[1]; 20: 22 this people will Christ establish in this land unto fulfilling of covenant made with father J.

JACOB[2]—son of Lehi[1] [c. 599 B.C.] (see also Jacobites)

1 Ne. 18: 7 (2 Ne. 2: 2) elder son of Lehi[1] born in wilderness; 18: 19 is grieved by afflictions of mother; 2 Ne. 2: 1 suffered afflictions and sorrow in childhood because of brothers' rudeness; 5: 6 goes with Nephi[1] into wilderness; 5: 26 (6: 2; Jacob 1: 18) is consecrated as priest and teacher; 6: 1—11: 1 (31: 1) exhorts people, citing prophecies of Isaiah; 6: 2 called of God and ordained after his holy order; 6: 8 the Lord has shown J. that Jerusalem has been destroyed; 10: 1 speaks concerning righteous branch of Israel; 11: 3 has seen Redeemer; Jacob 1: 1–2, 8 (W of M 1: 3) given small plates and commanded to write precious things; 1: 14 distinguished between Lamanites and Nephites according to righteousness; 1: 17 teaches in temple, having first obtained errand from the Lord; 1: 19 (2: 2–3) magnifies office, taking responsibility for sins of people if he does not teach them; 2: 1—3: 14 record of J's words to people after death of Nephi[1]; 2: 11 is commanded by the Lord to declare word in temple; 3: 1 admonishes people to look unto God; 3: 12 warns against every kind of sin; 3: 14 writes on plates of J., made by Nephi[1]; 4: 1 ministers much unto his people; 4: 15 is led by Spirit to prophesy; 7: 3–15 confronts and confounds Sherem; 7: 27 gives plates to son Enos[2]; Alma 3: 6 Lamanites cursed because of rebellion against J. and his brothers.

JACOB[3]—Nephite apostate of Zoramite sect [c. 64 B.C.]

Alma 52: 20 leader of Lamanite army, refuses to fight; 52: 21–31 victim of decoy strategy by Moroni[1]; 52: 33–

34 having unconquerable spirit, leads Lamanites against Moroni[1]; 52: 35 is killed.

JACOB[4]—*apostate Nephite chosen king by secret combination* [c. 29-30 B.C.] (*see also* Jacobugath, City of)

3 Ne. 7: 9 placed at head of secret combination; 7: 12–14 king of band, commands his people to flee and establish kingdom in north; 9: 9 the Lord has burned city inhabited by people of king J.

JACOB, CITY OF

3 Ne. 9: 8 the Lord causes city of J. to sink into earth.

JACOB, HOUSE OF (*see also* Israel; Jacob[1]; Remnant)

1 Ne. 20: 1, 12 hear this, O house of J., who are called by name of Israel; 20: 20 the Lord hath redeemed his servant J.; 21: 5 Isaiah[1] to be the Lord's servant to bring tribes of J. again to him; **2 Ne.** 12: 5 (Isa. 2: 5) O house of J., let us walk in light of the Lord; 12: 6 (Isa. 2: 6) O Lord, thou hast forsaken thy people, the house of J.; 18: 17 (Isa. 8: 17) the Lord hideth his face from house of J.; 19: 8 the Lord sent his word unto J., and it hath lighted upon Israel; 20: 20 such as are escaped of house of J. shall no more stay upon him that smote them; 20: 21 remnant of J. shall return unto the mighty God; 24: 1 the Lord will have mercy on J. and strangers shall cleave to house of J.; 46: 23 (3 Ne. 20: 16; 21: 2; Morm. 7: 10) Nephites are remnant of seed of J.; **3 Ne.** 5: 24 the Lord to gather all remnant of seed of J.; 5: 25 the Lord hath covenanted with all the house of J.; 10: 4 how oft would the Lord have gathered descendants of J.; 20: 16 (21: 12; Morm. 5: 24) remnant of house of J. shall go forth among Gentiles; 21: 22 if Gentiles repent, they will be numbered among this remnant of J.; 21: 23 Gentiles to assist remnant of J. in building New Jerusalem; 24: 6 (Mal. 3: 6) ye sons of J. are not consumed; **4 Ne.** 1: 49 (Morm. 5: 12) sacred records to come again unto remnant of house of J.

JACOBITES—*descendants of Jacob*[2]

Jacob 1: 13 (4 Ne. 1: 36; Morm. 1: 8) included among Nephites; **4 Ne.** 1: 37 true believers in Christ.

JACOBUGATH—*city of followers of Jacob*[4]

3 Ne. 9: 9 the Lord causes to be burned by fire.

JACOM

Ether 6: 14 one of four sons of Jared[2]; 6: 27 refuses to be king.

JARED[1]—*father of Enoch*[2]

No references in Book of Mormon.

JARED[2]—*founder of Jaredites* (*see also* Jared[2], Brother of; Jaredites)

Ether 1: 32 father of Orihah; 1: 33— 2: 1 comes from Tower of Babel with brother and friends; 1: 34–35 asks brother to pray that the Lord will not confound their language; 1: 36–37 language not confounded; 1: 38–43 asks brother to inquire of the Lord where they should go; 2: 1 journeys to valley of Nimrod with family and friends; 2: 13 dwells in tent at Moriancumer, by seashore, for four years; 6: 4–12 sails for promised land; 6: 14, 20 has four sons, eight daughters; 6: 19–21 gathers and counts his people; 6: 24 argues that people should have king; 6: 29 dies.

JARED[3]—*early Jaredite king*

Ether 8: 1 son of Omer; 8: 2 seizes kingdom from father; 8: 5–7 battles against brothers' army, loses kingdom; 8: 8–18 accepts daughter's plan to regain kingdom through secret combination with Akish; 9: 1, 4 overthrows kingdom of Omer, anointed king; 9: 5 killed by Akish's band.

JARED[2], **BROTHER OF**—*first Jaredite prophet*

Ether 1: 34 a large and mighty man, highly favored of the Lord; 1: 34–37 asks the Lord not to confound language; 1: 38–42 (2: 7) is promised a choice land; 1: 43 posterity to be great nation; 2: 4–5 is visited and led by the Lord; 2: 14-15 is chastened by the Lord, repents, and is forgiven; 2: 16 is instructed to build barges; 3: 1 melts stones for light in barges; 3: 6, 19 (12: 20) sees finger of the Lord; 3: 13—4: 1 sees, converses with Christ because of great faith; 3: 20, 26 (12: 21) the Lord could not withhold anything from brother of J. because of faith; 3: 22, 27–28 told to write, then seal up record; 3: 23, 28 is given Urim and Thummim; 3: 25 is shown all inhabitants of earth, past, present, and future; 4: 1 writings not to come forth before Christ's resurrection; 6: 2 puts stones in vessels for light; 6: 9 sings praises to the Lord; 6: 15, 20 begets twenty-two sons and daughters; 6: 23 warns against having kings; 6: 25–26 sons refuse to be king; 6: 29 dies; 7: 5 warnings of captivity are fulfilled; 12: 24 mighty in writing; 12: 30 caused mountain Zerin to be removed.

JAREDITES—*descendants of Jared*[2], *his brother, and his friends*

Ether 1: 33–37 language not confounded at Babel; 2: 1 travel to valley of Nimrod; 2: 13 dwell in tents at Morian-

cumer, by great sea, for four years; 2: 16–17 build barges according to the Lord's instructions; 6: 4 gather food, flocks, and herds and set forth in barges; 6: 9 sing praises unto the Lord; 6: 11–12 land on shores of promised land after 344 days; 6: 13, 18 multiply upon land; 6: 17 are taught to walk humbly before Lord; 6: 22–27 desire king; 6: 28 become exceedingly rich; 7: 20 are divided into two kingdoms; 7: 23–25 prophets warn of wickedness and idolatry and are mocked, but supported by king; 7: 26–27 repent, regain prosperity and peace; 8: 13–26 secret combination founded among J.; 9: 12 wars destroy all save thirty souls; 9: 15–25 period of peace and prosperity; 9: 26 secret combinations arise again; 9: 30–33 are plagued by dearth of rain, poisonous serpents; 9: 31–32 some flee to land southward; 9: 34–35 repent, and the Lord relieves dearth; 10: 28 never could be people more blessed; 11: 1–6 prophets prophesy destruction, are rejected; 11: 7 wars and contentions; 11: 8 people repent; 11: 12–13, 20–22 prophets again warn of destruction, are rejected; ch. 13–15 final wars.

JAROM—*Nephite prophet* [c. 420 B.C.]

Jarom 1: 1 son of Enos², writes that genealogy may be kept; 1: 2, 14 writes little because plates are small; **Omni** 1: 1 commands son, Omni, to write.

JASHON, CITY AND LAND OF

Morm. 2: 16 Lamanites pursue Nephites to land of; 2: 17 is near land where Ammaron deposits records.

JAVELIN (*see also* Weapon)

Jarom 1: 8 Nephites make j.; **Alma** 51: 34 Teancum puts j. through Amalickiah's heart; 62: 36 Teancum kills Ammoron with j.

JEALOUS, JEALOUSY (*see also* Covet; Envy)

Mosiah 11: 22 (13: 13; Ex. 20: 5) the Lord is a j. God; **Ether** 9: 7 Akish j. of his son.

JEHOVAH (*see* Jesus Christ—Jehovah)

JENEAM—*Nephite commander* [c. A.D. 385]

Morm. 6: 14 had fallen with his ten thousand.

JEREMIAH¹—*Hebrew prophet, contemporary of Lehi¹* [c. end of seventh century B.C.] (*see also* BD Jeremiah)

1 Ne. 5: 13 brass plates contain prophecies of J.; 7: 14 Jews have cast J. into prison; **Hel.** 8: 20 testified of Jerusalem's destruction.

JEREMIAH²—*one of twelve Nephite disciples* [c. A.D. 34]

3 Ne. 19: 4 is chosen by Jesus to minister to Nephites.

JERSHON, LAND OF—*land on east by sea, south of land Bountiful* (*see also* Ammon², People of)

Alma 27: 22, 26 Nephites give J. to people of Ammon; 27: 23–24 (28: 1) is protected by Nephites; 28: 1 church established in J.; 28: 1–3 (30: 1) is attacked by Lamanites; 30: 19–21 Korihor teaches in J.; 35: 6, 14 outcast Zoramites come into J.; 35: 13 (43: 3, 15) Ammonites leave land so that Nephite armies can gather to fight Lamanites; 43: 18 Nephites battle Lamanites in borders of J.; 43: 25 Moroni² leaves part of army in J.

JERUSALEM¹—*chief city of Jews and surrounding area* (*see also* Jerusalem, New; Jew; BD Jerusalem; Judea)

1 Ne. 1: 4, 7 Lehi¹ dwells at J.; 1: 4, 13, 18 (2: 13; 3: 17; 7: 13; 10: 3; 2 Ne. 25: 14; Alma 9: 9; Hel. 8: 20–21; Ether 13: 5) destruction of J.; 2: 4 (17: 20; Alma 10: 3; Hel. 5: 6) Lehi¹ and family leave J.; 2: 11 (2 Ne. 1: 1, 3; Jacob 2: 25, 32; Omni 1: 6; Mosiah 2: 4; 7: 20; Alma 9: 22; 22: 9; 36: 29; 3 Ne. 5: 20; Ether 13: 7) the Lord leads Lehites out of land of J.; 3: 2—4: 38 (5: 6; 7: 2) sons of Lehi¹ return to J. for records; 5: 4 (19: 20) family of Lehi¹ would have perished if they had remained at J.; 7: 3–5 sons of Lehi¹ return to J. to get family of Ishmael¹; 7: 7, 15 (16: 35–36; 17: 20) the rebellious desire to return to land of J.; 10: 4 (19: 8) Messiah to come six hundred years after Lehi¹ left J.; 11: 13 Nephi¹ sees J. in vision; 18: 24 Lehites bring seeds from land of J.; 19: 13 (4 Ne. 1: 31) those at J. shall crucify God of Israel; 22: 4 many already lost from knowledge of those at J.; **2 Ne.** 1: 4 (6: 8) Lehi¹ sees in vision that J. is destroyed; 8: 17 (Isa. 51: 17) J. has drunk cup of the Lord's fury; 8: 24 (Isa. 52: 1) put on thy beautiful garments, O J., the holy city; 8: 25 (Isa. 52: 2) arise, sit down, O J.; 9: 5 God shall show himself to those at J.; 10: 5 those at J. shall stiffen their necks; 12: 1 (Isa. 2: 1) word Isaiah¹ saw concerning Judah and J.; 13: 1 (Isa. 3: 1) the Lord takes away from J. the stay and the staff; 13: 8 (Isa. 3: 8) J. is ruined; 14: 3 (Isa. 4: 3) they who remain in J. shall be called holy; 17: 1 (Isa. 7: 1) kings of Syria and Israel went up toward J. to war against it; 18: 14 (Isa. 8: 14) the Lord shall be for gin and snare to inhabitants of J.; 20: 32 (Isa. 10: 32) the Lord shall shake hand against mount of daughter of Zion, the hill of J.; 25: 6 Nephi¹ has dwelt at J.; 25: 11 Jews will return and possess land of J.; 30: 4 remnant of Nephites' seed

shall know they came from J.; **Jacob** 2: 31 the Lord has heard mourning of his people in land of J.; 7: 26 Nephites a lonesome people, cast out from J.; **Omni** 1: 15 people of Zarahemla came from J. when Zedekiah was carried captive into Babylon; **Mosiah** 1: 6 records contain sayings of fathers from time they came from J.; 10: 12 (Hel. 8: 21) Lamanites believe they were driven from land of J. because of fathers' iniquities; 12: 23 (15: 30; 3 Ne. 16: 19) the Lord has redeemed J.; **Alma** 3: 11 (10: 17) brass plates brought out of land of J.; 7: 10 Son shall be born at J.; **3 Ne.** 4: 11 greatest slaughter among people of Lehi[1] since he left J.; 10: 5 how oft would the Lord have gathered his people that dwell at J.; 15: 14 Christ not commanded to tell those at J. about Nephites; 16: 1 the Lord has other sheep not of this land or land of J.; 16: 4 if those at J. do not ask Father, they must learn of other tribes from writings; 17: 8 Nephites desire that Christ show what he has done unto brethren at J.; 20: 29 land of J. is Israel's promised land forever; 20: 46 J. shall be inhabited again; 21: 26 work shall commence among tribes which Father led out of J.; **Morm.** 3: 18 twelve tribes of Israel shall be judged by twelve disciples in land of J.; **Ether** 13: 8 remnant of house of Joseph[1] shall build holy city, like J. of old; 13: 11 then cometh the J. of old; **Moro.** 10: 31 awake and arise from dust, O J.

JERUSALEM[2]—*Lamanite city and land in land of Nephi*

Alma 21: 1–2 Aaron[3] journeys toward land called by Lamanites J.; 21: 2 Lamanites and dissenters had built great city, called J.; 21: 4 Aaron[3] comes to city of J.; 24: 1 dissenters stir up Lamanites in land of J. against people of Anti-Nephi-Lehi; **3 Ne.** 9: 7 the Lord causes water to come upon city of J.

JERUSALEM, NEW (*see also* Zion; TG Jerusalem, New)

3 Ne. 20: 22 the Lord will establish this people in this land, and it shall be a N.J.; 21: 23 Gentiles shall assist remnant of Israel in building N.J.; 21: 24 those scattered shall be gathered unto N.J.; **Ether** 13: 2–6 N.J. shall come down out of heaven unto this land; 13: 5 rebuilt Jerusalem could not be a new J.; 13: 10 blessed are they who dwell in N.J.

JESSE—*father of David* [c. 1100 B.C.] (*see also* BD Jesse)

2 Ne. 21: 1 (Isa. 11: 1) there shall come forth a rod out of stem of J.; 21: 10 (Isa. 11: 10) there shall be a root of J., which shall stand for an ensign.

JESUS CHRIST (*see also* Baptism; Belief;

Believe; Blood; Charity; Church of God; Day of the Lord; Faith; Fall of Man; Firstborn; Glory [noun]; God; God, Body of; God, Eternal Nature of; God, Foreknowledge of; God, Goodness of; God, Love of; God, Manifestations of; God, Omniscience of; God, Power of; God, Presence of; God, Wisdom of; God the Father; Godhead; Gospel; Grace; Hand of the Lord; Jesus Christ—Advocate; Jesus Christ, Appearances of; Jesus Christ, Atonement through; Jesus Christ, Condescension of; Jesus Christ—Creator; Jesus Christ, Death of; Jesus Christ, First Coming of; Jesus Christ—Good Shepherd; Jesus Christ—Holy One of Israel; Jesus Christ—Immanuel; Jesus Christ—Jehovah; Jesus Christ—Lamb of God; Jesus Christ—Lord; Jesus Christ—Lord of Hosts; Jesus Christ — Mediator; Jesus Christ—Messiah; Jesus Christ—Only Begotten Son; Jesus Christ—Redeemer; Jesus Christ, Resurrection of; Jesus Christ—Savior; Jesus Christ, Second Coming of; Jesus Christ—Son of God; Jesus Christ, Types of; Judgment; King; Light; Love; Mercy; Name of the Lord; Rest; Rock; Spirit, Holy/Spirit of the Lord; Word of God/Word of the Lord; TG Jesus Christ; Jesus Christ, Antemortal Existence of; Jesus Christ, Ascension of; Jesus Christ, Authority of; Jesus Christ, Baptism of; Jesus Christ, Betrayal of; Jesus Christ, Davidic Descent of; Jesus Christ, Exemplar; Jesus Christ, Family of; Jesus Christ, Firstborn; Jesus Christ, Foreordained; Jesus Christ, Glory of; Jesus Christ, Head of the Church; Jesus Christ, Judge; Jesus Christ, King; Jesus Christ, Light of the World; Jesus Christ, Messenger of the Covenant; Jesus Christ, Millennial Reign of; Jesus Christ, Mission of; Jesus Christ, Power of; Jesus Christ, Prophecies about; Jesus Christ, Relationship with the Father; Jesus Christ, Rock; Jesus Christ, Second Comforter; Jesus Christ, Spirit of; Jesus Christ, Taking Name of; Jesus Christ, Teaching Mode of; Jesus Christ, Temptation of; Jesus Christ, Trials of; BD Jesus)

Title Page (2 Ne. 26: 12) convince Jews and Gentiles that Jesus is the Christ; **1 Ne.** 10: 9 Messiah to be baptized by John in Bethabara; **2 Ne.** 10: 3 (25: 19; Mosiah 3: 8) Messiah's name to be Jesus Christ; 25: 24 (26: 8; 31: 20) look forward with steadfastness unto Christ; 25: 26 we talk of Christ, we rejoice in Christ, we preach of Christ, we prophesy of Christ; 31: 2, 21 (32: 6; Jacob 7: 6; 3 Ne. 2: 2) doctrine of Christ; 31: 10 can we follow Jesus save we are willing to keep Father's commandments; 32: 3 feast upon words of Christ, for they tell you all ye should

do; 33: 4 writings persuade people to believe in Jesus; 33: 6 I glory in my Jesus; 33: 10 if ye believe in Christ, ye will believe these words; **Jacob** 1: 6 through revelations and prophecies the Nephites know of Christ; 4: 4 Nephites' writings show they know of Christ; 4: 15 Jews reject stone upon which they might build safe foundation; 7: 11, 19 (3 Ne. 6: 23; 7: 10) scriptures and prophets testify of Christ; 7: 19 Sherem has lied to God in denying Christ; **Mosiah** 3: 7 (15: 5; Alma 7: 11) Christ to suffer temptation; 16: 9 (Alma 38: 9; 3 Ne. 9: 18; 11: 11; Ether 4: 12) Christ is light and life of world; **Alma** 5: 44 holy order of God which is in Christ Jesus; 6: 8 Alma² teaches according to testimony of Jesus Christ; 28: 14 (Moro. 7: 18–19) reason for joy because of light of Christ unto life; 31: 31–32 comfort my soul in Christ; 31: 34 Lamanites to be brought again unto Christ; 31: 38 sons of Mosiah² are swallowed up in Christ; **Hel.** 3: 29 word of God leads man of Christ across gulf of misery; 5: 12 rock of our Redeemer is Christ; **3 Ne.** 9: 15 (11: 10; Ether 3: 14) I am Jesus Christ; 28: 33 scriptures give account of marvelous works of Christ; 29: 5 wo unto him who denies Christ; **4 Ne.** 1: 27 many churches profess to know Christ, but deny his gospel; **Morm.** 3: 21 Jews to have other witnesses that Jesus, whom they slew, was the very Christ; 5: 11 if Nephites had repented, they might have been clasped in arms of Jesus; 6: 17 how could ye have rejected that Jesus, who stood with open arms to receive you; 9: 5 holiness of Jesus Christ will kindle unquenchable fire in the guilty; **Ether** 2: 12 God of this land is Jesus Christ; 3: 14 Christ was prepared from foundation of world; 4: 12 (Moro. 7: 16–17) whatsoever persuades men to do good is of Christ; 12: 41 seek this Jesus of whom the prophets have written; **Moro.** 7: 11 servant of devil cannot follow Christ, follower of Christ cannot be servant of devil; 7: 16, 18–19 light of Christ is given to every man, that he may know good from evil; 7: 44 if a man confesses by Holy Ghost that Jesus is the Christ, he must have charity; 7: 47 charity is pure love of Christ; 10: 17–18 every good gift cometh of Christ.

JESUS CHRIST—ADVOCATE (*see also* Jesus Christ, Atonement through; Jesus Christ—Mediator)

2 Ne. 2: 9 Messiah shall make intercession for all men; 8: 22 (Isa. 51: 22) the Lord pleads the cause of his people; 13: 13 (Isa. 3: 13) the Lord standeth to plead and judge the people; **Jacob** 3: 1 God will plead your cause; **Mosiah** 14: 12 (Isa.

53: 12) Messiah made intercession for transgressors; 15: 8 God gives Son power to make intercession for men; **Moro.** 7: 28 Christ advocates the cause of men.

JESUS CHRIST, APPEARANCES OF (*see also* God, Manifestations of; Vision; TG God, Manifestations of; God, Privilege of Seeing; Jesus Christ, Appearances, Antemortal; Jesus Christ, Appearances, Postmortal)

1 Ne. 13: 42 Lamb shall manifest himself in body unto all nations; **2 Ne.** 2: 4 Jacob² has beheld Redeemer; 11: 2 (16: 1, 5; Isa. 6: 1, 5) Isaiah¹ has seen Redeemer; 11: 2 Nephi¹ has seen Redeemer; 25: 14 Messiah shall rise from dead and manifest himself to his people; **Enos** 1: 8 Christ shall manifest himself in flesh; **Alma** 19: 13 Lamoni has seen Redeemer; **3 Ne.** 10: 18–19 (11: 2) Christ will show his body to those who are spared; ch. 11–28 Christ's appearances among Nephites; 11: 8 Nephites see Man descending from heaven; 16: 2 Christ has not yet manifest himself to other sheep; 17: 4 Christ will show himself to the lost tribes; 19: 15 Jesus comes again and stands in Nephites' midst; 27: 2 Jesus again shows himself to disciples; **Morm.** 1: 15 Mormon² is visited of the Lord; **Ether** ch. 3 Christ's appearance to brother of Jared²; 3: 13 the Lord has never shown himself before to man; 3: 16 as Christ appears to brother of Jared², so will he appear in flesh; 9: 22 Emer sees Son; 12: 7 it was by faith that Christ showed himself to fathers; 12: 39 Moroni² has seen Jesus and talked with him face to face; **Moro.** 7: 48 (1 Jn. 3: 2) when Christ appears, we shall be like him.

JESUS CHRIST, ATONEMENT THROUGH (*see also* Fall of Man; Firstborn; Firstborn; Forgive; Grace; Jesus Christ—Advocate; Jesus Christ, Death of; Jesus Christ, First Coming of; Jesus Christ—Lamb of God; Jesus Christ—Mediator; Jesus Christ—Messiah; Jesus Christ—Only Begotten Son; Jesus Christ—Redeemer; Jesus Christ, Resurrection of; Jesus Christ—Savior; Jesus Christ, Types of; Mercy; Merit; Offering; Plan; Reconcile; Remission; Sacrifice; Salvation; Sanctification; Transgression; TG Jesus Christ, Atonement through; BD Atonement)

1 Ne. 11: 33 Son to be lifted up upon cross and slain for sins of world; **2 Ne.** 2: 7 Messiah offers himself a sacrifice for sin, to answer ends of law; 2: 10 punishment affixed to law to answer ends of atonement; 9: 7 (25: 16) atonement must be infinite; 9: 26 atonement satisfies demands of justice; 10: 25 God raises

man from everlasting death by power of atonement; **11: 5** justice, power, and mercy in great and eternal plan of deliverance from death; **11: 6** save Christ should come, all must perish; **Jacob 4: 11** be reconciled unto God through atonement of Christ; **7: 12** (Alma 34: 9; 42: 15) if no atonement, all mankind must be lost; **Mosiah 3: 11** Christ's blood atones for sins of those fallen by Adam's transgression; **3: 15** (13: 28) law of Moses avails nothing except through atonement of Christ's blood; **4: 6–7** (Alma 13: 5) atonement prepared from foundation of world; **13: 28** (Alma 34: 9) except for atonement, all must perish, notwithstanding law of Moses; **14: 5** (Isa. 53: 5) he was wounded for our transgressions; **14: 10** (Isa. 53: 10) thou shalt make his soul an offering for sin; **Alma 7: 11** Son will take upon him pains and sicknesses of his people; **22: 14** sufferings and death of Christ atone for men's sins; **24: 13** Christ's blood shed for atonement of sins; **30: 17** Korihor teaches there could be no atonement; **34: 8** Christ shall take upon him the transgressions of his people and atone for sins of world; **34: 11** no man can sacrifice own blood which will atone for sins of another; **42: 15** plan of mercy could not be brought about without an atonement; **42: 23** mercy comes because of atonement; **42: 23** atonement brings to pass the resurrection; **Hel. 5: 9** only means whereby man can be saved is through atoning blood of Jesus Christ; **3 Ne. 11: 14** Christ has been slain for sins of world; **Moro. 7: 41** ye shall have hope through atonement of Christ; **8: 20** he who says children need baptism sets at naught Christ's atonement; **10: 33** ye are sanctified in Christ, by grace of God, through shedding of blood of Christ.

JESUS CHRIST, CONDESCENSION OF (see also TG Jesus Christ, Condescension of)
1 Ne. 11: 16 knowest thou the condescension of God; **11: 26** behold the condescension of God; **19: 10** God yieldeth himself into hands of wicked men; **2 Ne. 4: 26** the Lord in condescension has visited men; **9: 53** how great the Lord's condescension unto men; **Jacob 4: 7** by the Lord's great condescension men have power to do these things; **Alma 7: 13** Son suffers according to flesh; **19: 13** Redeemer shall be born of woman; **Ether 3: 9** Christ shall take upon him flesh and blood.

JESUS CHRIST—CREATOR (see also Creation; God—Creator; God the Father; Jesus Christ—Jehovah)
2 Ne. 9: 5 Creator to die for all men; **Mosiah 3: 8** Jesus Christ, the Creator of all things; **5: 15** man to have eternal life

through mercy of him who created all things; **26: 23** I take upon me sins of world, for I have created them; **Alma 5: 15** exercise faith in redemption of him who created you; **3 Ne. 22: 5** thy maker, thy Redeemer; **Ether 3: 16** Christ has created man after body of his spirit.

JESUS CHRIST, DEATH OF (see also Death, Physical; Jesus Christ, Resurrection of; TG Jesus Christ, Crucifixion of; Jesus Christ, Death of)
1 Ne. 10: 11 after Messiah has been slain by Jews, he shall rise from dead; **11: 33** (Alma 30: 26; 3 Ne. 11: 14) Son to be lifted up upon cross and slain for sins of world; **19: 10** God to yield himself to wicked men to be crucified; **19: 10** (Hel. 14: 14, 20, 27; 3 Ne. 8: 3, 19–23; 10: 9) three days of darkness to be sign of Christ's death; **19: 13** (2 Ne. 10: 3, 5; 25: 13; Morm. 3: 21) Jews to crucify God; **2 Ne. 2: 8** Messiah lays down life according to flesh; **6: 9** (Mosiah 3: 9) Jews will scourge and crucify Holy One, Jesus Christ; **9: 5** great Creator suffers himself to die for all men; **10: 3** no other nation would crucify their God; **26: 3** signs to be given of Messiah's birth, death, resurrection; **26: 24** (3 Ne. 27: 14) God lays down his life that he might draw men unto him; **Mosiah 14: 5** (Isa. 53: 5) he was wounded for our transgressions, bruised for our iniquities; **14: 9** (Isa. 53: 9) he made his grave with the wicked and with the rich in his death; **14: 12** (Isa. 53: 12) he has poured out his soul unto death, was numbered with transgressors, bore sins of many; **15: 7** Son shall be led, crucified, and slain; **18: 2** (Hel. 14: 16; Morm. 9: 13) resurrection and redemption brought to pass through power, sufferings, death of Christ; **Alma 7: 12** (11: 42) Son will take upon him death, that he may loose bands of death; **16: 19** priests hold forth coming, sufferings, death of Son; **21: 9** no redemption save through death and sufferings of Christ; **22: 14** sufferings and death of Christ atone for sins; **Hel. 8: 14** as Moses lifted up brazen serpent, so shall Son be lifted up; **14: 15** Son must die that salvation may come; **3 Ne. 6: 20** prophets testify boldly of Christ's death and sufferings; **9: 22** for the repentant Christ has laid down his life; **27: 14** Father sent Christ that he might be lifted up upon cross; **28: 6** before Christ was lifted up by Jews, John desired to tarry; **Morm. 9: 13** all men are redeemed because death of Christ brings to pass resurrection; **Ether 4: 1** writings of brother of Jared² not to come forth until after the Lord is lifted up upon cross; **12: 33** the Lord has loved the world, even unto laying down life for world; **Moro. 9: 25** may Christ's sufferings and death rest in your mind forever.

JESUS CHRIST, FIRST COMING OF (see also Jesus Christ, Second Coming of; TG Jesus Christ, Birth of)

1 Ne. 10: 4 (19: 8; 2 Ne. 25: 19) Messiah to come six hundred years after Lehi¹ left Jerusalem; 11: 13–14, 18–20 Nephi¹ sees virgin carried away in Spirit, mother of Son of God; **2 Ne.** 10: 3 Christ to come among Jews, more wicked part of world; 11: 6 save Christ should come, all men must perish; 17: 14 (Isa. 7: 14) virgin shall conceive and bear son, Immanuel; 19: 6 (Isa. 9: 6) unto us a child is born, unto us a son is given; **Mosiah** 3: 5 (4: 2; 7: 27; 13: 34; 15: 1; 17: 8) God shall come down from heaven among men; 3: 13 whoso should believe that Christ should come might receive remission of sins; 16: 6 if Christ did not come, there could be no redemption; **Alma** 7: 10 Son to be born of Mary at Jerusalem; **Hel.** 8: 22 Lehi¹, Nephi¹, almost all fathers have testified of coming of Christ; 14: 2 in five years comes the Son; 14: 3–6 (3 Ne. 1: 15–21) signs to be given of Christ's coming; **3 Ne.** 1: 13–14 on the morrow come I into the world; 9: 16 I came unto my own, and my own received me not; 9: 16 scriptures concerning Christ's coming are fulfilled; 12: 17 (Matt. 5: 17) Christ is come not to destroy, but to fulfill.

JESUS CHRIST—GOOD SHEPHERD

1 Ne. 13: 41 one God and one Shepherd over all; 22: 25 (3 Ne. 18: 31) Holy One numbers his sheep, and they know him; **Mosiah** 26: 21 he who will hear my voice will be my sheep; **Alma** 5: 38–39 good shepherd calls you in his own name; 5: 57 he who desires to follow good shepherd should come out from the wicked; **Hel.** 7: 18 Nephites will not hearken to voice of good shepherd; 15: 13 Lamanites to be brought to knowledge of Redeemer, great and true shepherd; **3 Ne.** 15: 21 (16: 3) one fold and one s.; **Morm.** 5: 17 Nephites once had Christ for their shepherd.

JESUS CHRIST—HOLY ONE OF ISRAEL (see also BD Holy One of Israel)

1 Ne. 19: 14 (22: 5; 2 Ne. 6: 10) because Jews have despised Holy One, they shall wander in flesh; 19: 15 when Jews no more turn hearts against Holy One, God will remember covenants; 20: 17 (21: 7) the Lord, thy Redeemer, the Holy One; 22: 18 (2 Ne. 1: 10; 6: 10, 15; 15: 24) wrath to be poured out on those who harden hearts against Holy One; 22: 21 prophet of whom Moses spoke was Holy One; 22: 24, 26 Holy One to reign in power and glory; 22: 28 all who repent will dwell safely in Holy One; **2 Ne.** 2: 10 ends of law which Holy One hath given;

3: 2 land to be consecrated unto those who keep commandments of Holy One; 6: 9 Holy One to manifest himself to Jews in flesh; 9: 11–12 temporal death to deliver its dead through power of resurrection of Holy One; 9: 15 (Morm. 9: 13–14) those resurrected must appear before judgment-seat of Holy One; 9: 18 those who have believed in Holy One shall inherit kingdom of God; 9: 19 Holy One delivers his saints from death and hell; 9: 23 men must be baptized having faith in Holy One; 9: 25 mercies of Holy One have claim because of atonement; 9: 26 all to be restored to the God who gave them breath, Holy One; 9: 41 keeper of gate is Holy One; 25: 29 (30: 2; Omni 1: 26) Christ is Holy One of Israel; 27: 34 children of Jacob¹ shall sanctify Holy One; **Hel.** 12: 2 when he prospers his people, they trample under feet the Holy One; **3 Ne.** 22: 5 (Isa. 54: 5) thy maker, thy Redeemer, the Holy One.

JESUS CHRIST—IMMANUEL (see also BD Immanuel)

2 Ne. 17: 14 (Isa. 7: 14) virgin shall conceive, bear son, call his name Immanuel.

JESUS CHRIST—JEHOVAH (see also Jesus Christ—Creator; BD Jehovah)

2 Ne. 22: 2 (Isa. 12: 2) the Lord Jehovah is my strength; **Moro.** 10: 34 meet before pleasing bar of the great Jehovah, the Eternal Judge.

JESUS CHRIST—LAMB OF GOD (see also TG Jesus Christ, Lamb of God)

1 Ne. 11: 34–36 (12: 9; 13: 26, 40–41; 14: 20, 24, 27) twelve apostles of Lamb; 12: 8, 10 twelve disciples of Lamb among Nephites; 12: 11 (Alma 13: 11; 34: 36; Morm. 9: 6; Ether 13: 10–11) garments made white in blood of Lamb; 13: 26, 29, 32, 34 truths taken away from gospel of Lamb; 13: 35 records will come to Gentiles by gift and power of Lamb; 13: 37 saved in everlasting kingdom of Lamb; 13: 39 books which came forth by power of Lamb; 13: 40 Lamb is Son of Father and Savior of world; 13: 41 words of Lamb to be made known by records; 14: 12, 14 church of Lamb; 14: 26 records will come forth according to truth which is in Lamb; **Hel.** 6: 5 preachers bring many to be humble followers of God and Lamb.

JESUS CHRIST—LORD (see also Day of the Lord; God; Jesus Christ—Lord of Hosts; Name of the Lord; Spirit, Holy/Spirit of the Lord; Word of God/Word of the Lord; TG Jesus Christ, Lord; Lord; BD Lord)

1 Ne. 3: 7 the Lord giveth no commandment save he shall prepare way that

they may accomplish it; 4: 13 slays the wicked to bring forth righteous purposes; 7: 11 ye have forgotten what great things the Lord hath done; 10: 7–8 (Alma 7: 9; Hel. 14: 9; 3 Ne. 24: 1) prepare way of the Lord; 15: 18 the Lord made covenant with Abraham; 16: 29 (Alma 37: 7) by small means the Lord brings to pass great things; 17: 14 (2 Ne. 6: 7) ye shall know that I, the Lord, am God; 17: 30 (19: 23; 2 Ne. 28: 15; Alma 28: 8) the Lord their God, their Redeemer; 17: 35 the Lord esteems all flesh in one; 17: 45 ye are slow to remember the Lord; 22: 20 the Lord will prepare way for his people; **2 Ne.** 1: 15 the Lord has redeemed my soul from hell; 2: 16 the Lord gives unto man to act for himself; 4: 16 my soul delights in things of the Lord; 6: 12 the Lord God will fulfill his covenants; 9: 16 word of the Lord God cannot pass away; 9: 41 come unto the Lord, the Holy One; 9: 41 he cannot be deceived, for the Lord God is his name; 10: 7 (Mosiah 5: 15) Christ is the Lord God; 10: 9, 21 (Alma 3: 17; 9: 24; 17: 15; 28: 11; 4 Ne. 1: 49) promises of the Lord; 31: 13 follow your Lord and Savior down into water; **Jacob** 1: 17 Jacob² first obtains his errand from the Lord; 4: 10 seek not to counsel the Lord; **Omni** 1: 25 nothing good save it comes from the Lord; **Mosiah** 3: 5, 17–18, 21 (5: 15) Christ the Lord Omnipotent reigns; 3: 12 salvation through faith on the Lord Jesus Christ; **Alma** 24: 27 the Lord works in many ways to save people; 26: 16 we will glory in the Lord; 34: 36 the Lord dwells not in unholy temples; 37: 36 let all thy doings be unto the Lord; **3 Ne.** 1: 12–14 voice of the Lord comes to Nephi³, saying, On the morrow come I into the world; 14: 21–22 (Matt. 7: 21–22) not everyone who says Lord, Lord, shall enter kingdom of heaven; 19: 18 multitude pray unto Jesus, calling him their Lord; **Ether** 3: 6–18 brother of Jared² sees the Lord, who is Jesus Christ.

JESUS CHRIST—LORD OF HOSTS (see also Jesus Christ—Lord; TG Lord of Hosts; BD Lord of Hosts)

1 Ne. 20: 2 (Isa. 48: 2) God of Israel is the Lord of Hosts; **2 Ne.** 8: 15 (Isa. 51: 15) Lord of Hosts is my name; 12: 12 (Isa. 2: 12) day of the Lord of Hosts is soon to come; 15: 7 (Isa. 5: 7) vineyard of the Lord of Hosts is the house of Israel; 15: 16 (Isa. 5: 16) the Lord of Hosts shall be exalted; 19: 13 (Isa. 9: 13) people do not seek the Lord of Hosts; 24: 22 (Isa. 14: 22) the Lord of Hosts will rise up against them; 27: 2 all nations shall be visited of the Lord of Hosts; **Jacob** 2: 30 if the Lord of Hosts will raise up seed, he will command his people; **3 Ne.** 22: 5 (Isa. 54: 5) the Lord of Hosts is name of thy

husband; 24: 7 (Mal. 3: 7) return unto me and I will return unto you, saith the Lord of Hosts; 24: 10 (Mal. 3: 10) prove me now herewith, saith the Lord of Hosts.

JESUS CHRIST—MEDIATOR (see also Jesus Christ, Atonement through; Jesus Christ—Advocate; TG Jesus Christ, Mediator)

2 Ne. 2: 27 men are free to choose eternal life through great Mediator of all men; 2: 28 look to the great Mediator.

JESUS CHRIST—MESSIAH (see also TG Jesus Christ—Messiah; BD Messiah)

1 Ne. 1: 19 things which Lehi¹ saw manifest plainly coming of Messiah; 10: 4 Messiah shall come six hundred years after Lehi¹ left Jerusalem; 10: 4 God to raise up Messiah, or in other words, a Savior; 10: 5 (Jarom 1: 11; Mosiah 13: 33; Hel. 8: 13) prophets spoke of Messiah, or Redeemer; 10: 7–10 prophet will come to prepare way of Messiah; 10: 11 Jews to slay Messiah; 10: 14 Israel to come to knowledge of true Messiah, their Redeemer; 10: 17 Son of God, the Messiah who should come; 12: 18 Messiah the Lamb of God; 15: 13 fulness of Messiah's gospel will come to Gentiles after he manifests body unto men; **2 Ne.** 1: 10 judgments to come upon people if they reject Holy One, the true Messiah, their Redeemer and God; 2: 6–8 redemption comes in and through Holy Messiah; 2: 26 Messiah comes in fulness of time; 3: 5 (25: 14) the Lord's covenant that Messiah shall appear to righteous branch of Israel; 6: 13 people of the Lord are they who wait for Messiah; 6: 14 Messiah will set himself the second time to recover his people; 25: 14 Messiah shall rise from dead; 25: 16 Israel shall believe in Christ and not look forward to another Messiah; 25: 18 Christ's words shall be given to Israel to convince them of true Messiah; 25: 18 there should not any other come, save false Messiah; 26: 3 signs to be given of Messiah's birth; **Jarom** 1: 11 prophets and teachers persuade people to look forward to Messiah; **Mosiah** 13: 33 (Hel. 8: 13) Moses spoke of coming of Messiah.

JESUS CHRIST—ONLY BEGOTTEN SON (see also Jesus Christ—Son of God; TG Jesus Christ, Only Begotten Son)

2 Ne. 25: 12 (Alma 5: 48; 9: 26) Only Begotten of the Father shall manifest himself in flesh; **Jacob** 4: 5 Abraham's offering up of Isaac is similitude of God and Only Begotten Son; 4: 11 (Alma 13: 5) be reconciled unto God through atonement of Christ, his Only Begotten Son; **Alma** 5: 48 Christ, Only Begotten, shall

come to take away sins of world; 9: 26 Son's glory shall be glory of Only Begotten; 12: 33–34 mercy comes through Only Begotten Son; 13: 9 high priests after order of Son, the Only Begotten.

JESUS CHRIST—REDEEMER (*see also* Jesus Christ, Atonement through; Jesus Christ—Savior; Redemption; TG Jesus Christ, Redeemer)

1 Ne. 10: 5 prophets have spoken of Redeemer; 10: 6 all mankind lost unless they rely on Redeemer; 11: 27 Redeemer seen by Nephi¹ in vision; 15: 14 (2 Ne. 6: 11; 10: 2; Mosiah 18: 30; 26: 26; 27: 36; Alma 37: 10; Hel. 15: 13; 3 Ne. 16: 4) seed of Nephites shall come to knowledge of Redeemer; 17: 30 Redeemer led Israel by day and gave light by night; 19: 18, 23 Nephi¹ persuades his people to believe in Redeemer; 21: 26 (2 Ne. 6: 18; Isa. 49: 26) all flesh shall know the Lord is their Redeemer; **2 Ne.** 1: 10 if those in promised land reject Redeemer, judgment shall rest upon them; 1: 15 the Lord has redeemed my soul from hell; 2: 3 Jacob² is redeemed because of righteousness of Redeemer; 2: 6 redemption comes in and through Holy Messiah; 11: 2 Isaiah¹ saw Redeemer, as did Nephi¹; 28: 5 many will say Redeemer has done his work; 31: 17 do the things the Redeemer has done; **Enos** 1: 27 my rest is with my Redeemer; **Mosiah** 15: 10 Son's soul to be made an offering for sin; 15: 24 those who die in ignorance are redeemed by the Lord; 16: 15 redemption comes through Christ, who is Eternal Father; 18: 2 redemption to be brought to pass through power, sufferings, death of Christ; 18: 30 how beautiful are waters of Mormon to those who there came to knowledge of Redeemer; 26: 25–26 they who never knew the Lord shall know he is their Redeemer; 27: 30 Alma² had rejected his Redeemer; 27: 32, 36 Alma² and companions are instruments in bringing many to knowledge of Redeemer; **Alma** 5: 27 Christ will come to redeem his people from their sins; 7: 13 (11: 40) Son of God suffers to take upon him sins of his people; 9: 27 Son comes to redeem those who will be baptized; 61: 14 Nephites resist evil, that they may rejoice in cause of Redeemer; **Hel.** 5: 9 Christ comes to redeem the world; 5: 11–12 we must build upon rock of Redeemer; 14: 16 Christ's death redeems all mankind from first spiritual death; 14: 17 resurrection of Christ redeems all mankind; **3 Ne.** 9: 17 (Morm. 9: 12) by Christ redemption comes; 10: 10 lamentations of Nephites are turned into praise of Christ, their Redeemer; 11: 11 Christ has taken upon himself the sins of the world; 22: 5 (Isa. 54: 5) thy Redeemer, the God

of the whole earth, shall he be called; **Ether** 3: 14 Christ was prepared from foundation of world to redeem his people; **Moro.** 8: 8 listen to the words of Christ, your Redeemer.

JESUS CHRIST, RESURRECTION OF (*see also* Death, Physical; Immortality; Jesus Christ, Atonement through; Jesus Christ, Death of; Jesus Christ—Redeemer; Resurrection; TG Jesus Christ, Resurrection of)

1 Ne. 10: 11 Messiah shall rise from the dead; **2 Ne.** 2: 8 (Mosiah 13: 35; 15: 20; Alma 33: 22; 40: 3; Hel. 14: 15) Christ lays down life, takes it up again, to bring to pass resurrection of dead; 9: 11–12 (Alma 40: 21, 23; Moro. 10: 34) bodies and spirits of men shall be restored to one another by power of resurrection of Holy One; 26: 1 after Christ rises from dead, he will show himself to Nephites; **Jacob** 4: 11 be reconciled to God through atonement of Christ, and ye may obtain resurrection according to power of resurrection in Christ; 6: 9 power of redemption and resurrection in Christ will bring you to stand before God; **Mosiah** 15: 20 Son has power over the dead and brings to pass resurrection; 15: 21–26 (Alma 40: 15–18) those who died before Christ's resurrection will have part in first resurrection; 16: 7 if Christ had not risen from the dead, there could have been no resurrection; 16: 8 (Morm. 7: 5) sting of death is swallowed in Christ; **Alma** 11: 42 death of Christ shall loose bands of temporal death; 33: 22 (Hel. 14: 20) Son shall rise from dead to bring to pass the resurrection; **Hel.** 14: 17 resurrection of Christ redeems mankind; 14: 25 (3 Ne. 23: 9, 11) at time of Christ's resurrection many saints shall be resurrected; **3 Ne.** 6: 20 prophets testify of redemption which the Lord would make for his people, the resurrection of Christ; **Morm.** 7: 5 by power of Father, Christ has risen again; 9: 13 death of Christ brings to pass the resurrection; **Ether** 12: 7 by faith Christ showed himself to Nephites after he had risen; **Moro.** 7: 41 ye shall have hope through Christ's atonement and resurrection.

JESUS CHRIST—SAVIOR (*see also* Jesus Christ, Atonement through; Jesus Christ—Redeemer; Salvation; Save; TG Jesus Christ—Savior)

1 Ne. 10: 4 God will raise up Messiah, or in other words, Savior of world; 13: 40 Lamb is Savior; 21: 26 (22: 12; 2 Ne. 6: 18) all flesh shall know that the Lord is Savior; **2 Ne.** 6: 17 Mighty God shall deliver his covenant people; 31: 13 (Morm. 7: 10) are you willing to follow Savior into water; **Mosiah** 3: 20 know-

ledge of Savior will spread to every nation; **Hel.** 14: 15 Christ must die that salvation may come; **3 Ne.** 5: 20 Mormon² has reason to bless his Savior Jesus Christ; **Morm.** 3: 14 our Lord and Savior Jesus Christ; **Moro.** 8: 29 words of Savior will be fulfilled.

JESUS CHRIST, SECOND COMING OF (*see also* Day of the Lord; Last Days; Millennium; TG Jesus Christ, Second Coming of)

3 **Ne.** 24: 1 (Mal. 3: 1) the Lord shall suddenly come to temple; 24: 2 (Mal. 3: 2) who may abide day of the Lord's coming; 25: 5 (Mal. 4: 5) Elijah to be sent before coming of day of the Lord; 27: 16 he who endures to end will be held guiltless when Christ stands to judge world; 29: 2 ye need not say the Lord delays his coming unto Israel; **Morm.** 8: 26–32 signs of the Lord's coming in latter days.

JESUS CHRIST—SON OF GOD (*see also* God the Father; Jesus Christ—Creator; Jesus Christ—Jehovah; Jesus Christ—Lamb of God; Jesus Christ—Messiah; Jesus Christ—Only Begotten Son; TG Jesus Christ, Divine Sonship; BD Son of God)

1 **Ne.** 10: 17 Son of God is Messiah who should come; 11: 7 Nephi¹ to see, bear record of Son of God; 11: 18 virgin is mother of Son of God; 11: 21 (13: 40) Lamb of God is Son of the Eternal Father; 11: 24 Son of God to go forth among men; 2 **Ne.** 17: 14 (Isa. 7: 14) virgin shall conceive and bear a son, Immanuel; 19: 6 (Isa. 9: 6) unto us a child is born, unto us a son is given; 25: 16, 19 (Mosiah 3: 8; 4: 2; Alma 6: 8; 36: 17–18; Hel. 3: 28; 5: 12; 14: 12; 3 Ne. 5: 13, 26; 9: 15; 20: 31; Morm. 5: 14; 7: 5; Ether 4: 7) name of Son of God shall be Jesus Christ; 26: 9 (Alma 16: 20) Son of righteousness shall appear unto Nephites; 31: 11–12 be baptized in name of Son; 31: 21 (Mosiah 15: 4–5; Alma 11: 44; 3 Ne. 11: 27, 36; 28: 10; Morm. 7: 7) Father, Son, and Holy Ghost are one God; **Jacob** 4: 5 Abraham's offering up Isaac is similitude of God and Son; 4: 5, 11 (Alma 5: 48; 9: 26; 12: 33–34; 13: 5–9) Christ is the Father's Only Begotten Son; **Mosiah** 3: 8 (Alma 7: 9–10) mother of Son of God to be Mary; 15: 2–3 because he dwells in flesh, he shall be called Son of God; 15: 3 he shall be Father and Son; 15: 7 will of Son swallowed up in will of Father; 15: 8 God gives Son power to make intercession for men; **Alma** 5: 50 (9: 26) Son of God will come in his glory; 6: 8 (7: 13; 11: 40; Hel. 14: 2) Jesus Christ, the Son of God who should come to redeem his people from sins; 7: 11–13 ministry of Son foretold; 11: 32 (34: 5)

who shall come, is it Son of God; 11: 38–39 (Mosiah 15: 1–5; Hel. 16: 18) Son is the Eternal Father; 12: 33 God calls on men in name of his Son; 12: 33 (36: 18) God will have mercy upon men through Son; 13: 1–9 (Hel. 8: 18) high priesthood after order of Son; 13: 16 ordinances given that people might look forward on Son; 24: 13 blood of Son to be shed for atonement of sins; 33: 14–19 (34: 7–8; Hel. 8: 13–22) prophets have spoken of Son; 34: 2 Nephites teach that Christ is to be Son of God; 34: 10–14 great and last sacrifice will be Son of God; 36: 18 Jesus, thou Son of God, have mercy; **Hel.** 14: 2 Son of God to come in five years; 14: 8 whosoever believes on Son shall have everlasting life; 3 **Ne.** 1: 14 Christ to do will both of Father and Son; 1: 17 Son must shortly appear; 11: 7 behold my Beloved Son, in whom I am well pleased; 25: 2 (Mal. 4: 2) unto them who fear the Lord's name will Son of Righteousness arise; **Morm.** 5: 14 Jesus is the Christ, the Son of the living God; 7: 5 believe in Jesus Christ, that he is the Son of God; **Ether** 12: 18 miracles are not wrought until after men believe in Son of God.

JESUS CHRIST, TYPES OF (*see also* Type, Typify; TG Jesus Christ, Types of, in Anticipation; Jesus Christ, Types of, in Memory)

2 **Ne.** 11: 4 (Jacob 4: 5; Mosiah 13: 30–31; 16: 14; Alma 25: 15; 34: 14; Gal. 3: 24; Heb. 10: 1) law of Moses given as type pointing to Christ; 11: 4 all things given of God from beginning typify Christ; **Jacob** 4: 5 Abraham's offering up of Isaac is similitude of God and Son; **Mosiah** 3: 15 the Lord showed his people many types of his coming; **Alma** 33: 19–21 (1 Ne. 17: 41; 2 Ne. 25: 20; Hel. 8: 14–15; Num. 21: 8–9) serpent raised in wilderness a type of Christ; 37: 38–46 working of Liahona a type of word of Christ; 3 **Ne.** 18: 7, 11 bread and wine of sacrament to be taken in remembrance of body and blood of Christ.

JEW, JEWISH—*descendant of Judah, or inhabitant of kingdom of Judah* (*see also* Israel; Israel, Gathering of; Israel, Scattering of; Israelites; Jacob, House of; Jerusalem¹; Judah; Israel; TG Israel, Judah, People of; Jew, Jewish; BD Jew)

Title Page (2 Ne. 26: 12) book written to convincing of J. and Gentile that Jesus is the Christ; 1 **Ne.** 1: 2 language of Lehi¹ consists of learning of J. and language of Egyptians; 1: 19–20 J. mock Lehi¹; 2: 13 (17: 44) J. seek to kill Lehi¹; 3: 3 (5: 6) Laban has record of J.; 4: 22–37 Zoram¹ speaks to Nephi¹ concerning elders of J.; 4: 36 Lehites do not want J. to know of flight; 5: 12 (Omni

1: 14; Ether 1: 3) brass plates contain record of J. down to Zedekiah; 10: 2–4 Lehi¹ speaks to family about J.; 10: 4 the Lord will raise up Messiah among J.; 10: 11 J. to hear gospel, dwindle in unbelief; 13: 23–24, 38 (14: 23; 2 Ne. 29: 4–13) book containing record of J., covenants of the Lord to come from J.; 13: 25–26 (Morm. 7: 8) gospel goes forth in purity from J. to Gentiles; 13: 39 (2 Ne. 25: 15; 30: 7) J. to be scattered; 13: 42 Lamb shall be manifest to J., then Gentiles, to Gentiles, then J.; 15: 17 (2 Ne. 25: 18) the Lord will be rejected of J.; 15: 19–20 Nephi¹ rehearses words of Isaiah¹ concerning restoration of J.; 2 Ne. 9: 2 the Lord has spoken unto J. by mouth of prophets; 10: 3 (4 Ne. 1: 31; Morm. 7: 5) Christ to come among J., for no other nation would crucify their God; 10: 16 he who fights against Zion, both J. and Gentile, will perish; 25: 1, 5–6 difficulty of understanding manner of prophesying among J.; 25: 2 Nephi¹ has not taught many things concerning manner of J., for their works were works of darkness; 25: 9 J. have been destroyed from generation to generation according to iniquities; 26: 33 all are alike unto God, both Gentile and J.; 27: 1 in last days all nations of Gentiles and J. shall be drunken with iniquity; 29: 5 O Gentiles, have ye remembered the J.; 30: 2 J. who will not repent shall be cast off; 30: 4 remnant of Nephites' seed shall know they are descendants of J.; 33: 8 Nephi¹ has charity for J., whence he came; 33: 10 Nephi¹ admonishes J. to believe in Christ; 33: 14 words of J. will condemn those who do not accept them; Jacob 4: 14 J. a stiffnecked people; 4: 15–17 by stumbling of J., they will reject stone upon which they might build safe foundation; Alma 11: 4 Nephites do not reckon after manner of J.; 16: 13 synagogues built after manner of J.; 3 Ne. 19: 35 so great faith have I never seen among all the J.; 28: 28 three Nephites will be among J.; 29: 8 Gentiles need no longer spurn or make game of J.; Morm. 3: 21 J. shall have other witnesses that Jesus, whom they slew, is the Christ; 5: 12, 14 writings shall go unto unbelieving of J.

JEWEL

2 Ne. 13: 21 (Isa. 3: 21) the Lord will take away nose j. of daughters of Zion; 3 Ne. 24: 16–17 they who fear the Lord shall be his when he makes up his j.

JOHN THE BELOVED—*also known as the Revelator* [c. first century A.D.] (*see also* BD John)

1 Ne. 14: 19–27 Nephi¹ beholds J.

in vision; 3 Ne. 28: 4–6 three Nephite disciples desire to tarry, as did J. the beloved; Ether 4: 16 revelation written by J. to be unfolded in eyes of all people.

JOIN (*see also* Cleave; Unite)

2 Ne. 15: 8 (Isa. 5: 8) wo unto them who j. house to house; 23: 15 every one who is j. to the wicked shall fall by sword; Mosiah 25: 23 (Alma 4: 4; Hel. 3: 24) those who desire to take upon themselves name of Christ are baptized and j. churches of God.

JOINT

1 Ne. 19: 20 workings in spirit weary Nephi¹, that j. are weak; Alma 11: 43 (40: 23) both limb and j. shall be restored in resurrection.

JONAS¹—*son of Nephi³, one of twelve disciples* [c. A.D. 34]

3 Ne. 19: 4 chosen by Jesus to minister to Nephites.

JONAS²—*one of twelve disciples* [c. A.D. 34]

3 Ne. 19: 4 chosen by Jesus to minister to Nephites.

JORDAN—*river in Palestine* (*see also* BD Jordan River)

1 Ne. 10: 9 prophet shall baptize in Bethabara, beyond J.; 17: 32 after crossing river J., Israelites drove out children of land; 2 Ne. 19: 1 (Isa. 9: 1) the Lord did afflict by way of Red Sea beyond J. in Galilee.

JORDAN, CITY OF

Morm. 5: 3 Nephites flee to the city of J.

JOSEPH¹—*son of Jacob¹* [c. 1700 B.C.] (*see also* Ephraim; Israel; Joseph¹, Seed of; Manasseh; Smith, Joseph, Jr.; BD Joseph; Joseph, Stick of)

1 Ne. 5: 14 (6: 2; 2 Ne. 3: 4) Lehi¹ a descendant of J.; 5: 16 Laban a descendant of J.; 2 Ne. 3: 4 great were the covenants made unto J.; 3: 5 J. truly saw our day; 3: 6–21 J. testifies of latter-day seer named J.; 4: 1 J. is carried into Egypt; Alma 10: 3 Aminadi a descendant of J.; 46: 24 part of remnant of J. shall be preserved, as remnant of coat of J.; Ether 13: 7 J. brought his father down into Egypt.

JOSEPH²—*son of Lehi¹* [c. 595 B.C.] (*see also* Josephites)

1 Ne. 18: 7 younger son of Lehi¹ born in wilderness; 18: 19 is grieved because of mother's afflictions; 2 Ne. ch. 3 words of Lehi¹ to J.; 3: 1 thou wast born in wilderness of mine affliction; 3: 3, 23 may the Lord bless thee forever, for thy

seed shall not be destroyed; 3: 25 is admonished to hearken unto words of Nephi¹; 5: 5–6 follows Nephi¹ from land; 5: 26 (Jacob 1: 18) is consecrated a priest; **Alma** 3: 6 is a just and holy man.

JOSEPH¹, SEED OF—*descendants of Joseph¹* (*see also* Israel; Joseph¹)

2 Ne. 3: 16 (25: 21) the Lord promised J. to preserve his seed forever; **Jacob** 2: 25 Nephites to be righteous branch from loins of J.; **Alma** 46: 23 (Ether 13: 7) Nephites are remnant of seed of J.; 46: 24–27 (3 Ne. 10: 17) part of remnant of J. shall be preserved, as remnant of coat of J., remainder shall perish; **3 Ne.** 5: 21 the Lord has been merciful unto seed of J.; 5: 23 the Lord will bring remnant of seed of J. to knowledge of the Lord; 15: 12 Nephites a remnant of house of J.; **Ether** 13: 6–10 New Jerusalem to be built unto remnant of seed of J.

JOSEPHITES—*descendants of Joseph²* (*see also* Joseph²)

Jacob 1: 13 (4 Ne. 1: 36–37; Morm. 1: 8) included among Nephites.

JOSH—*Nephite commander* [c. A.D. 385]

Morm. 6: 14 had fallen with his ten thousand.

JOSH, CITY OF

3 Ne. 9: 10 is burned.

JOSHUA, LAND OF—*land in borders west, by seashore*

Morm. 2: 6 Nephites march to land of J.

JOT

Alma 34: 13 law shall be fulfilled, every j. and tittle; **3 Ne.** 1: 25 (12: 18; Matt. 5: 18) not one j. or tittle should pass away until whole law of Moses was fulfilled.

JOURNEY (*see also* Depart; Flight; Sail; Sojourn; Travel; Wander)

1 Ne. 2: 2–4 (3: 18) Lehi¹ and family depart into wilderness; 3: 9 Nephi¹ and brothers j. back to Jerusalem for records; 16: 33 Lehites j. in nearly same course as in beginning; **2 Ne.** 5: 7 Nephi¹ and followers j. many days in wilderness; **Omni** 1: 12 Mosiah¹ and his people depart into wilderness, discover people of Zarahemla; 1: 29 considerable number of Nephites j. into wilderness; **Mosiah** 1: 17 (1 Ne. 16: 28–29; Alma 37: 39–41) when Lehites were unfaithful, no progress in j.; 23: 3 people of Alma¹ flee eight days' j. into wilderness; **Alma** 8: 6 Alma² travels three days' j. to Ammonihah; 22: 32 distance of day and a half's j. from

east to west sea; **Hel.** 3: 3–5 many Nephites depart from Zarahemla and travel to land northward; 4: 7 from west sea to east is a day's j. for a Nephite.

JOY, JOYOUS (*see also* Cheer; Delight; Happiness; Pleasure; Rejoice)

1 Ne. 8: 12 (11: 21–23) fruit of tree of life fills soul with j.; 13: 37 how beautiful upon mountains shall be they who publish tidings of j.; **2 Ne.** 2: 23 if Adam had not transgressed, he would have had no j., knowing no misery; 2: 25 men are that they might have j.; 9: 18 j. of righteous saints shall be full forever; 27: 30 j. of the meek shall be in the Lord; **Mosiah** 3: 3 angel declares unto Benjamin glad tidings of j.; 4: 20 the Lord has poured out Spirit and caused hearts to be filled with j.; **Alma** 4: 14 people filled with j. because of resurrection; 19: 6 light of God's glory infuses j. into Lamoni's soul; 19: 14 Ammon² overpowered with j.; 22: 15 what shall I do to be born of God, receive Spirit, be filled with j.; 26: 11 heart of Ammon² is brim with j.; 26: 35 j. of Ammon² is carried away, unto boasting in God; 28: 8 account of incomprehensible j. of Ammon² and his brothers; 28: 14 great reason of j. because of light of Christ unto life; 29: 9 my j., that I may be instrument in hands of God to bring some soul to repentance; 29: 13–14 I do not j. in my own success, but my j. is more full because of success of brethren; 30: 34 have rejoicings in j. of our brethren; 33: 23 may God grant that your burdens be light, through j. of Son; 36: 20 soul of Alma² filled with j. as exceeding as his pain; 36: 24 Alma² labors to bring other souls to taste exceeding j. which he tasted; **3 Ne.** 17: 18 so great is j. of multitude that they are overcome; 17: 20 Christ's j. is full; 27: 11 if church is built upon works of men or devil, they have j. for season; **Morm.** 2: 13 j. of Mormon² is vain, for Nephites' sorrowing is not unto repentance; **Ether** 6: 12 when Jaredites land in promised land, they shed tears of j.

JUDAH—*southern kingdom of Israelites* (*see also* Hebrew; Israel; Jacob¹; Jacob, House of; Jerusalem¹; Jew; TG Israel, Judah, People of; BD Judah, Kingdom of)

1 Ne. 1: 4 (5: 12; Omni 1: 15) Zedekiah, king of J.; 20: 1 (Isa. 48: 1) house of Jacob are come forth out of waters of J., or waters of baptism; **2 Ne.** 3: 12 fruit of loins of J. shall write; 12: 1 (Isa. 2: 1) word that Isaiah¹ saw concerning J. and Jerusalem; 13: 8 (Isa. 3: 8) J. is fallen; 17: 6 (Isa. 7: 6) let us go up against J. and vex it; 17: 17 (Isa. 7: 17) the day that Ephraim departed from J.; 21: 13 (Isa. 11: 13) Ephraim shall not envy J., and J. shall not vex Ephraim.

JUDEA, CITY OF—*Nephite city*

    Alma 56: 9 Helaman[1] marches with two thousand stripling warriors to J.; 56: 15 Antipus and his men fortify city of J.; 56: 18 when Lamanites see Nephite reinforcements, they do not come against J.; 56: 57 Helaman[1] and stripling warriors march back to J.; 57: 11 Nephites send provisions to J.

JUDGE [noun] (*see also* Judge [verb]; Judge, Chief; Judgment; Lawyers)

    Mosiah 29: 11, 25 let us appoint j. to judge according to law; 29: 25, 39 j. chosen by voice of people; 29: 29 lower j. shall judge higher j. according to voice of people; 29: 44 commencement of reign of j. throughout land of Zarahemla; **Alma** 10: 27 foundation of destruction of Ammonihah being laid by lawyers and j.; 11: 1–3 compensation of j.; 14: 18–27 j. of Ammonihah torment of Alma[2] and Amulek; 41: 7 those who repent and desire righteousness are own j.; **3 Ne.** 6: 23–24 j. secretly put prophets to death; 6: 25–26 j. who condemned prophets to death are brought before governor; 6: 27–30 j., lawyers, and friends form secret combination; 27: 27 (1 Ne. 11: 32; Morm. 3: 19) Nephite disciples shall be j. of Nephites; **Moro.** 10: 34 great Jehovah, the Eternal J. of both quick and dead.

JUDGE [verb] (*see also* Condemn; Judge [noun]; Judgment; Justice)

    1 Ne. 11: 32 Son was j. of world; 12: 9 (Morm. 3: 18–19) twelve apostles shall j. twelve tribes of Israel, twelve Nephite disciples; 12: 10 (3 Ne. 27: 27; Morm. 3: 19) twelve Nephite disciples shall j. Nephites; 15: 32–33 (2 Ne. 9: 15; 28: 23; Mosiah 16: 10; Alma 5: 15; 11: 41; 12: 12; 41: 3; 3 Ne. 26: 4; Morm. 3: 20) men must be j. before God according to their works; **2 Ne.** 8: 5 (Isa. 51: 5) the Lord's arm shall j. the people; 25: 18 the Lord shall bring forth his word, which shall j. the Jews; 30: 9 with righteousness shall the Lord God j. the poor; **Mosiah** 4: 22 if ye j. and condemn the beggar, how much more just will be your condemnation; 26: 29 whosoever transgresseth against the Lord shall ye j. according to sins; 29: 11, 25 let us appoint judges to j. this people according to law; 29: 12 better to be j. of God than of man; 29: 29 lower judges shall j. higher judges according to voice of people; **Alma** 41: 14 deal justly, j. righteously; **3 Ne.** 14: 1 (Matt. 7: 1) j. not, that ye be not j.; 27: 16 Christ shall stand to j. the world; 27: 25–26 out of books shall world be j.; **Morm.** 8: 19 he who j. rashly shall be j. rashly; **Moro.** 7: 15 given unto you to j., that ye may know good from evil;

7: 15–18 way to j. is shown; 7: 18 j. by light of Christ; 7: 18 with that same judgment which ye j. ye shall be j.

JUDGE, CHIEF (*see also* Governor; Judge [noun])

    Mosiah 29: 42–43 (Alma 2: 16) Alma[2] appointed to be first chief j.; **Alma** 4: 16–17 (50: 37) Nephihah appointed chief j.; 14: 14–27 chief j. of land of Ammonihah, who is after order of Nehor, mocks Alma[2] and Amulek; 27: 21 chief j. asks for voice of people concerning people of Anti-Nephi-Lehi; 50: 39 Pahoran[1] succeeds father as chief j.; **Hel.** 1: 5 Pahoran[2] appointed by voice of people to be chief j.; 1: 13, 21 Pacumeni appointed by voice of people to be chief j.; 2: 2 Helaman[2] appointed to fill judgment-seat; 3: 37 Nephi[2] fills judgment seat; 5: 1 (6: 15, 19) Nephi[2] delivers judgment seat to Cezoram; 6: 15 Cezoram's son appointed in his stead and is also murdered; 8: 27 (9: 2–17, 23) Seezoram, chief j., murdered; **3 Ne.** 1: 1 Lachoneus[1] the chief j.; 3: 18–19 Gidgiddoni appointed chief captain and chief j.; 6: 19 Lachoneus[1] fills seat of his father; 7: 1 secret combination murders chief j.

JUDGMENT (*see also* Anger; Bar; Condemn, Condemnation; Day of the Lord; Destruction; Equal; Iniquity; Jesus Christ; Judge [verb]; Judgment-seat; Just; Justice; Last Days; Reward; Scourge; Thrash; Transgression; Visitation; Wicked; Wrath; TG God, Justice of; Judgment; Judgment, the Last)

    1 Ne. 10: 20 for all thy doings thou shalt be brought into j.; 12: 5 Nephi[1] beholds multitudes who had not fallen because of great and terrible j. of the Lord; 22: 21 Holy One shall execute j. in righteousness; **2 Ne.** 1: 10 if Nephites reject Holy One, the j. of him who is just shall rest upon them; 9: 7 without atonement, first j. which came upon man must have remained to endless duration; 9: 15 when all men pass from first death unto life, then comes j.; 9: 46 prepare your souls for day of j.; 18: 15 brothers of Nephi[1] see that j. of God are upon them; 25: 3 Nephi[1] writes so that people may know j. of God; Mosiah 3: 18 (29: 12; Alma 12: 15) the Lord judgeth, and his j. is just; 16: 1 every people shall confess before God that his j. are just; 17: 11 Noah[3] fears j. of God would be upon him; 29: 12 j. of God are always just, j. of men not always just; 29: 27 when voice of people chooses iniquity, j. of God will come; 29: 43 Alma[2] judges righteous j.; **Alma** 12: 27 after death, men must come to j.; 14: 11 (60: 13) the Lord suffers martyrs to die, that his j. may be just;

37: 30 j. of God come upon workers of secret combinations; 58: 9 (60: 14) Nephites filled with fear lest j. of God come upon land to destruction; Hel. 4: 23 because of iniquity, j. of God stare Nephites in face; 14: 11 j. of God await the wicked; 3 Ne. 12: 21 (Matt. 5: 21) whosoever shall kill shall be in danger of j. of God; Ether 11: 20 prophets warn Jaredites that God will execute j. to their utter destruction; Moro. 7: 18 with same j. which ye judge ye shall also be judged; 9: 14 how can we expect God will stay his hand in j. against us; 9: 15 come out in j., O God.

JUDGMENT-SEAT (*see also* Bar; Judge, Chief; Judgment; Throne; Tribunal)

Title Page condemn not the things of God that ye may be found spotless at *j-s.* of Christ; 1 Ne. 10: 21 if ye have sought to do wickedly, ye are found unclean before *j-s.* of God; 2 Ne. 9: 15 (3 Ne. 28: 31; Morm 3: 20; 6: 21; 7: 6) all men must appear before *j-s.* of Christ; 33: 7 Nephi[1] has faith he will meet many souls spotless at Christ's *j-s.*; 33: 15 what I seal on earth shall be brought against you at the *j.* bar; Alma 1: 2 (4: 17–18; 50: 39; Hel. 1: 2–9; 2:2; 3: 37; 5: 1; 6: 15; 8: 27; 3 Ne. 6: 19; 7: 1) chief judge among Nephites sits upon *j-s.*; Morm. 3: 22 all should repent and prepare to stand before *j-s.* of Christ; Ether 12: 38 Moroni[2] bids farewell until we meet before *j-s.* of Christ; Moro. 8: 20–21 listen unto them and give heed, or they stand against you at *j-s.* of Christ.

JUST, JUSTLY (*see also* Justice; Perfect; Righteousness; Uprightness)

2 Ne. 1: 10 if Nephites reject Holy One, judgments of him who is j. shall rest upon them; 1: 22 do not incur displeasure of a j. God; 26: 7 I must cry unto my God, Thy ways are j.; 27: 32 (28: 16) they who turn aside the j. for thing of naught shall be cut off; Enos 1: 1 Enos knows his father is j. man; Omni 1: 22 (Mosiah 3: 18; 16: 1; 29: 12) God's judgment is j.; Mosiah 2: 4 God appointed j. men to be Nephites' teachers; 4: 22, 25 if ye condemn the beggar, how much more j. will be your condemnation; 19: 17 Limhi is a j. man; 23: 8 (29: 13) if it were possible always to have j. men as kings, it would be well to have kings; 27: 31 (Alma 12: 15) men shall confess that judgment of everlasting punishment is j. upon them; 29: 12 God's judgments are always j., judgments of man not always j.; Alma 3: 6 Nephi[1] and followers were j. and holy men; 12: 8 all shall rise from dead, both j. and unjust; 13: 25–26 time of Christ's coming shall be made known

unto j. and holy men; 29: 4 I ought not to harrow up in my desires the firm decree of a j. God; 41: 13 restoration means to bring back j. for that which is j.; 41: 14 deal j.; 42: 15 God atoneth for sins of world so that he might be a j. and merciful God; 3 Ne. 26: 19 (4 Ne. 1: 2) every man deals j. one with another; 27: 27 ye shall be judges of this people according to j. judgment I shall give you; Morm. 9: 4 ye would be miserable to dwell with holy and j. God under consciousness of filthiness; Moro. 10: 6 whatsoever thing is good is j. and true.

JUSTICE (*see also* Equity; Judge [verb]; Judgment; Just; Mercy; Punishment; Sacrifice; Vengeance; TG God, Justice of)

1 Ne. 14: 4 j. of God will fall upon those who work wickedness; 15: 30 j. of God divides wicked from righteous; 2 Ne. 2: 11–12 absence of opposition would destroy j. of God; 9: 17 O the greatness and j. of our God; 9: 26 (Alma 42: 15) atonement satisfies demands of j.; 19: 7 (Isa. 9: 7) kingdom to be established with judgment and j.; Jacob 4: 10 God counsels in j. and great mercy; 6: 10 j. cannot be denied; Mosiah 2: 38 demands of divine j. awaken soul of unrepentant to sense of guilt; 5: 15 salvation through j. and mercy of Creator; Alma 12: 32 works of j. could not be destroyed; 41: 2–3 (61: 12) requisite with j. of God that men should be judged according to works; 42: 14 all mankind fallen and in grasp of j. of God; 42: 25 do ye suppose mercy can rob j.; 42: 30 do not excuse yourself by denying God's j., but let his j. and mercy have full sway in your heart; 54: 6 j. of God hangs over you unless you repent; 60: 13 the Lord suffereth the righteous to be slain that his j. may come upon the wicked; 3 Ne. 26: 5 the good to be resurrected to everlasting life, the evil to damnation, according to Christ's j.; 29: 4 sword of j. is in the Lord's right hand.

JUSTIFY (*see also* Jesus Christ, Atonement through; Sanctification; TG Justification)

1 Ne. 16: 2 the righteous have I j.; 2 Ne. 2: 5 by law no flesh is j.; 7: 8 the Lord is near, and he j. me; 15: 22–23 (Isa. 5: 23) wo unto the mighty who j. the wicked for reward; 28: 8 many shall say, God will j. you in committing a little sin; Mosiah 14: 11 (Isa. 53: 11) by his knowledge shall my righteous servant j. many; Alma 41: 15 the word restoration j. the sinner not at all.

KEEP, KEPT (*see also* Keeper; Maintain; Obedience; Observe; Preserve; Restrain; Retain; Withhold)

1 Ne. 19: 5 more sacred things to be

k. for knowledge of Nephites; **2 Ne.** 1: 9 (Mosiah 1: 7; 2: 22; Alma 36: 1, 30; 38: 1) if those brought out of Jerusalem *k.* commandments, they shall prosper and be *k.* from all nations; 25: 24 (Jacob 4: 5; Mosiah 13: 27–35; Alma 25: 15–16) Nephites *k.* law of Moses to look forward to Christ; **Mosiah** 2: 4 *k.* God's commandments, to be filled with love toward God and all men; 13: 16 (18: 23; Ex. 20: 8) remember the Sabbath day, to *k.* it holy; **Alma** 37: 35 learn in thy youth to *k.* commandments; 42: 2 cherubim and flaming sword placed to *k.* tree of life; **Hel.** 15: 5 more part of Lamanites *k.* commandments, according to law of Moses; **3 Ne.** 16: 4 writings shall be *k.* and manifested unto Gentiles; **Ether** 3: 19–20 (12: 21) brother of Jared[2] could not be *k.* from within veil; **Moro.** 6: 4 those baptized should be nourished by word, to *k.* them in right way; 8: 3 Mormon[2] prays that God will *k.* Moroni[2] through endurance of faith.

KEEPER

2 Ne. 9: 41 *k.* of gate is Holy One.

KIB—*early Jaredite king*

Ether 1: 31–32 (7: 3, 7) son of Orihah, father of Shule and Corihor; 7: 5, 7 taken captive by Corihor, dwells in captivity; 7: 8–9 restored to throne by Shule.

KID (*see also* Animal)

2 Ne. 21: 6 (30: 12; Isa. 11: 6) leopard shall lie down with *k.*

KILL (*see also* Blood, Shedding of; Capital Punishment; Death, Physical; Martyrdom; Murder; Slaughter; Slay; Smite)

1 Ne. 4: 10 Nephi[1] constrained by Spirit to *k.* Laban; **2 Ne.** 9: 35 murderer who deliberately *k.* shall die; 26: 5 (3 Ne. 8: 25) earth to swallow up those who *k.* prophets and saints; **Jacob** 4: 14 Jews *k.* the prophets; **Mosiah** 13: 21 (3 Ne. 12: 21; Ex. 20: 13) thou shalt not *k.*; **Hel.** 7: 5 robbers fill judgment-seat, that they might more easily *k.*; 13: 32–33 (3 Ne. 8: 25) Nephites to lament that they *k.* prophets; **4 Ne.** 1: 30–31 people seek to *k.* disciples of Jesus.

KIM—*Jaredite king*

Ether 1: 21–22 (10: 13–14) son of Morianton[1], father of Levi[2]; 10: 13 does not reign righteously; 10: 14 brought into captivity by brother.

KIMNOR—*early Jaredite*

Ether 8: 10 the father of Akish, who founded secret combination.

KINDLE (*see* Anger)

KINDNESS, KIND (*see also* Charity; Compassion; Gentle; Love)

1 Ne. 19: 9 Christ to suffer mockery because of his loving *k.*; **3 Ne.** 22: 8 (Isa. 54: 8) with everlasting *k.* will I have mercy on thee; **Moro.** 7: 45 (1 Cor. 13: 4) charity suffereth long and is *k.*

KING (*see also* Jesus Christ; Kingdom; King-men; Prince)

1 Ne. 16: 38 brothers think Nephi[1] wants to make himself *k.*; 21: 23 (2 Ne. 6: 7; 10: 9; Isa. 49: 23) *k.* of Gentiles shall be Israel's nursing fathers; **2 Ne.** 5: 18 people want Nephi[1] to be *k.*, but he desires they have no *k.*; 6: 2 Nephites look unto Nephi[1] as *k.* or protector; 10: 11 land shall be land of liberty unto Gentiles, with no *k.*; 10: 14 the Lord is *k.* of heaven; **Jacob** 1: 11 those who reign in stead of Nephi[1] are called second Nephi, third Nephi, according to reigns of *k.*; **Omni** 1: 12 Mosiah[1] made *k.* over Zarahemla; **Mosiah** 2: 19 if earthly *k.* merits any thanks, how you ought to thank heavenly *k.*; 2: 26 Benjamin, whom ye call your *k.*, is no better than ye yourselves are; 2: 30 Benjamin declares Mosiah[2] is *k.* over Nephites; 7: 9 Zeniff made *k.* by voice of people; 23: 6–7 (29: 16) Nephites ask Alma[1] to be *k.*, but he advises against *k.*; 23: 8 (29: 13, 16) if possible always to have just men as *k.*, it would be well to have *k.*; 29: 1–3 sons of Mosiah[2] not willing to become *k.*; 29: 21 ye cannot dethrone iniquitous *k.*, save through contention; 29: 22–23 unrighteous *k.* perverts ways of righteousness; 29: 31 sins of many people have been caused by iniquities of *k.*; 29: 35–36 Mosiah[2] unfolds disadvantages of having unrighteous *k.*; **Alma** 5: 50 K. of heaven shall soon shine forth among all men; 13: 17–18 Melchizedek was *k.* over land of Salem; 46: 4 Amalickiah desires to be *k.*; **3 Ne.** 6: 30 judges and lawyers covenant to destroy governor and establish *k.*; 7: 9–10 secret combination calls Jacob[4] *k.*; 20: 45 (21: 8; Isa. 52: 15) *k.* shall shut their mouths at the Lord's servant; **Ether** 6: 22–28 Jaredites desire a son of Jared[1] or his brother be anointed *k.*

KINGDOM (*see also* Church of the Devil; Dominion; Government, Civil; King; Kingdom of God; Nation)

1 Ne. 13: 1 Nephi[1] beholds many nations and *k.* in vision; 22: 22 *k.* of devil shall be built up among men; 22: 23 those who belong to *k.* of devil should fear and tremble; **2 Ne.** 20: 10 (Isa. 10: 10) my hand hath founded the *k.* of idols; 23: 4 (Isa. 13: 4) tumultuous noise of *k.* of nations gathered together; 24: 16 (Isa. 14: 16) is this the man that did shake *k.*;

28: 19 k. of devil must shake; **Mosiah** 29: 6 he to whom k. rightly belongs has declined; 29: 6–9 Mosiah[2] fears son might later claim right to k.; **Alma** 41: 4 those whose works are evil shall inherit k. of devil.

KINGDOM OF GOD (see also Church of God; Heaven; Millennium; TG Kingdom of God, in Heaven; Kingdom of God, on Earth; BD Kingdom of Heaven, or Kingdom of God)

1 Ne. 13: 37 those who seek to bring forth Zion shall be lifted up in everlasting k. of Lamb; 15: 34 k. of God is not filthy; 15: 35 righteous souls to dwell in k. of God; **2 Ne.** 9: 18 they who have endured crosses of world shall inherit k. of God, prepared from foundation of world; 9: 23 (31: 11–21; Alma 9: 12; 3 Ne. 11: 38; Moro. 10: 26) only those who repent, are baptized, and have faith can be saved in k. of God; 10: 25 may God raise up by power of resurrection and atonement to receive eternal k. of God; 25: 13 (Mosiah 15: 11; 3 Ne. 11: 33) believers shall be saved in k. of God; 33: 12 I pray that many of us, if not all, may be saved in God's k.; **Jacob** 2: 18 before ye seek riches, seek k. of God; 6: 4 those who do not harden hearts shall be saved in k. of God; **Mosiah** 4: 16–18 he who succors not the beggar has no interest in k. of God; 18: 18 priests ordained to teach things pertaining to k. of God; 27: 26 (Alma 7: 14) unless men become new creatures, they cannot inherit k. of God; **Alma** 5: 23–24 murderers cannot have place to sit down in k. of God; 5: 50 (9: 25; 10: 20; Hel. 5: 32) k. of heaven is at hand; 7: 14 if ye are not born again, ye cannot inherit k. of heaven; 7: 19 path of righteousness leads to k. of God; 7: 21 (11: 37; 40: 26) no unclean thing can be received into k. of God; 29: 17 may God grant that my brethren may sit down in k. of God; 39: 9 the unrepentant and lustful cannot inherit k. of God; 40: 25 the righteous shall shine forth in k. of God; 41: 4 all shall be raised to endless happiness to inherit k. of God or endless misery in k. of devil; **3 Ne.** 9: 22 (11: 38; Ether 5: 5) those who repent and come as little child will be received in k. of God; 12: 3 (Matt. 5: 3) blessed are poor in spirit who come unto Christ, for theirs is k. of heaven; 12: 10 (Matt. 5: 10) blessed are they who are persecuted, for theirs is k. of heaven; 13: 33 (Matt. 6: 33) seek ye first k. of God, and all these things shall be added; 14: 21 (Matt. 7: 21) not every one who says, Lord, shall enter k. of heaven; **4 Ne.** 1: 17 people are all in one, children of Christ and heirs of k. of God; **Ether** 15: 34 whether Ether is translated

or dies matters not if he is saved in k. of God; **Moro.** 9: 6 conquer enemy of all righteousness and rest souls in k. of God; 10: 21 except ye have charity, ye cannot be saved in k. of God.

KING-MEN (see also Dissenter; Freedom)

Alma 51: 5 those who desire to alter law to establish king over land are called k.; 51: 13 refuse to defend country; 51: 17–19 (60: 16) are slain by army of Moroni[1] or cast into prison; 51: 20–21 are compelled to defend country; 60: 16 prevent Nephites from dispersing enemies; 62: 9 receive trial and are executed.

KISH—Jaredite king

Ether 1: 18–19 (10: 17–18) son of Corom, father of Lib[1].

KISHKUMEN—leader of robbers (see also Gadianton Robbers)

Hel. 1: 9–10 (2: 3) murders Pahoran[2]; 1: 11–12 (2: 3) not found because of covenant of secret combination; 2: 3–9 plans to murder Helaman[3]; 2: 9 killed by servant of Helaman[3]; 6: 18, 24 cofounder of Gadianton robbers.

KISS (see also Worship)

3 Ne. 11: 19 Nephi[3] bows himself before the Lord and k. his feet; 17: 10 many of the multitude k. Christ's feet.

KNEE (see also Kneel)

Mosiah 27: 31 (Isa. 45: 23) every k. shall bow and every tongue confess before Redeemer; **Alma** 19: 14 Ammon[2] falls upon k. and pours out soul to God in thanksgiving; 22: 17 Lamanite king bows down before the Lord upon k. and prays.

KNEEL (see also Knee)

Enos 1: 4 Enos[2] k. before Maker; **3 Ne.** 17: 13 (19: 16) Jesus commands multitude to k.; **Moro.** 4: 1–2 elders and priests k. with church to offer sacrament prayer.

KNOCK (see also Ask)

2 Ne. 9: 42 (3 Ne. 14: 7; 27: 29; Matt. 7: 7) k., and it shall be opened unto you; 32: 4 if ye cannot understand, it is because ye ask not, neither do ye k.

KNOW, KNEW, KNOWN (see also Comprehend; God, Omniscience of; Knowingly; Knowledge; Learn; Perceive; Revelation, Reveal; Testimony; Understand)

1 Ne. 4: 6 Nephi[1] is led by Spirit, not k. beforehand what he should do; 9: 6 (2 Ne. 2: 24; 9: 20; W of M 1: 7; Alma 18: 18; 40: 5; Hel. 8: 8) the Lord k. all things from beginning; 15: 9 Laman[1] and Lemuel claim the Lord does not make

things k. unto them; 17: 13 ye shall k. that it is by me that ye are led; 21: 26 (22: 12) all flesh shall k. that the Lord is Savior and Redeemer; 22: 2 by Spirit all things are made k. unto prophets; **2 Ne.** 2: 18 (Alma 12: 31; 42: 3) by partaking of forbidden fruit, Adam and Eve become as God, k. good and evil; 4: 19 I k. in whom I have trusted; 9: 20 there is not anything save God k. it; 9: 28 the learned set aside God's counsel, thinking they k. of themselves; 27: 27 the Lord will show unto those who hide their counsels that he k. all their works; 31: 14 if ye deny Christ after receiving Holy Ghost, it would have been better not to have k. him; **Jacob** 1: 6 because of revelations, Nephites k. of Christ and his kingdom; 4: 4 Nephites write so that those to come will k. that they k. of Christ; 4: 8 no man k. of God's ways save it be revealed unto him; **Mosiah** 4: 11 if ye have k. of God's goodness, remember always his greatness; 5: 13 how k. a man the master whom he has not served or who is far from his thoughts; 8: 17 seer can k. of things past and future, makes k. things that could not otherwise be k.; 11: 22 people of Noah³ shall k. that I am the Lord their God; 16: 3 all mankind became carnal, k. evil from good; 26: 24 if they k. me, they shall have place eternally at my right hand; **Alma** 5: 45–46 these things are made k. by Spirit; 7: 13 Spirit k. all things; 12: 3 (18: 32) God k. all thy thoughts, and they are made k. by his Spirit; 12: 9 given unto many to k. the mysteries of God; 12: 11 to those who harden hearts is given lesser portion of word until they k. nothing of mysteries; 26: 21 what natural man k. these things; 26: 21 none k. these things save the penitent; 26: 22 unto those who repent, exercise faith, bring forth good works, and pray continually, it is given to k. mysteries of God; 29: 5 he who k. not good from evil is blameless; 32: 18 (Ether 3: 19) if a man k. a thing, he hath no cause to believe, for he k. it; 32: 19 more cursed is he who k. will of God and doeth it not; 36: 4 I would not that ye think I k. of myself, but of God; 40: 10 God k. all the times appointed unto man; **Hel.** 9: 41 some believe Nephi² is a god, otherwise he could not k. of all things; 14: 31 God has given unto you to k. good from evil; **3 Ne.** 6: 18 Nephites do not sin ignorantly, for they k. will of God; 9: 20 converted Lamanites were baptized with fire and Holy Ghost and k. it not; 11: 14 multitude feels prints of nail, to k. Christ is God of Israel; 13: 3 (Matt. 6: 3) let not left hand k. what right hand doest; 13: 8 (Matt. 6: 8) Father k. what ye have need before ye ask him; 14: 23 (Matt. 7: 23) the Lord will profess unto many, I never

k. you; 18: 31 the Lord k. his sheep; 20: 39 Christ's people shall k. his name; 21: 6 Gentiles to k. true points of Christ's doctrine; 28: 27 three Nephites will be among Gentiles, but Gentiles shall k. them not; **Morm.** 6: 22 ye are gone and the Father k. your state; **Ether** 3: 19 brother of Jared has faith no longer, for he k.; 4: 11 he who believeth these things shall be visited with Spirit, shall k. and bear record; 5: 3 three witnesses shall k. these things are true; **Moro.** 7: 15 given unto you to judge, that ye may k. good from evil; 7: 16 Spirit of Christ is given to every man, to k. good from evil; 7: 18 ye k. the light by which ye may judge; 7: 19 search diligently in light of Christ that ye may k. good from evil; 10: 5 by power of Holy Ghost ye may k. the truth of all things; 10: 7 by power of Holy Ghost ye may k. that Christ is.

KNOWINGLY

3 Ne. 18: 28 ye shall not suffer anyone k. to partake of sacrament unworthily.

KNOWLEDGE (*see also* Agency; Faith; God, Omniscience of; Holy Ghost; Ignorance; Know; Learn; Mystery; Scriptures; Study; Testimony; Truth; Understand; Wisdom; TG Knowledge; BD Knowledge)

1 Ne. 22: 4 many are already lost from k. of Jews; **2 Ne.** 4: 23 God hath given Nephi¹ k. by visions in nighttime; 6: 11 Jews shall come to k. of Redeemer; 9: 13 after the resurrection our k. shall be perfect; 9: 14 we shall have a perfect k. of guilt; 15: 13 (Isa. 5: 13) my people are gone into captivity because they have no k.; 21: 2 (Isa. 11: 2) spirit of k. shall rest upon him; 21: 9 (30: 15; Isa. 11: 9) earth shall be full of k. of the Lord; 32: 7 men will not search k., nor understand great k.; **Jacob** 4: 12 why not speak of atonement and attain perfect k. of Christ; **W of M** 1: 8 Mormon² prays his brethren may come to k. of God; **Mosiah** 3: 20 k. of Savior shall spread throughout every nation; 4: 12 ye shall grow in k. of glory of him who created you; 4: 11 (Isa. 53: 11) by his k. shall my righteous servant justify many; 18: 26 priests to wax strong in Spirit, having k. of God; 28: 1–2 (Alma 23: 5; 37: 9) sons of Mosiah² to bring Lamanites to k. of the Lord; 28: 17–18 account of Jaredites gives Nephites much k. in which they rejoice; **Alma** 9: 19 Lamanites to destroy Nephites if they fall into sin after receiving so much k. from God; 18: 35 portion of Spirit dwelleth in me, which giveth me k.; 32: 34 your k. is perfect in that thing, and your faith is dormant; 37: 8–9 sacred records

bring Lamanites to k. of the Lord; 47: 36 dissenters, who were instructed in same k. of the Lord, became more hardened; **Hel.** 6: 34 Lamanites grow in k. of God; 14: 30 God hath given you k. and hath made you free; 15: 13 Lamanites to be brought to k. of Redeemer; **3 Ne.** 5: 20 Christ has given much k. unto salvation; 5: 23 Christ to bring remnant of seed of Joseph[1] to k. of their Lord; 16: 4 if Jews do not ask for k. of Nephites, they shall receive it from writings; 20: 13 scattered remnant of Israel shall be brought to k. of Redeemer; **Ether** 3: 19–20 because of perfect k. brother of Jared[2] could not be kept from beholding within veil; 4: 13 the Lord will show unto Gentiles greater things, k. of which is hidden because of unbelief; **Moro.** 7: 15–17 way to judge is plain, that ye may know with perfect k.; 10: 10 to another is given to teach word of k. by same Spirit.

KORIHOR—*an antichrist* [c. 74 B.C.]

Alma 30: 6, 12–17 preaches against Christ; 30: 18 leads many into wickedness; 30: 19–21 tries to preach to people of Ammon[2], but is rejected; 30: 21 preaches in land of Gideon, but is bound and carried before high priest; 30: 22–29 confrontation with Giddonah, the high priest; 30: 30–55 confrontation with Alma[2]; 30: 43–48 asks for sign; 30: 49–50 is struck dumb; 30: 52–53 confesses he has been deceived by devil; 30: 54–55 Alma[2] refused to remove curse; 30: 56, 58 begs from house to house; 30: 59 is killed by Zoramites.

KUMEN—*one of twelve Nephite disciples* [c. A.D. 34]

3 Ne. 19: 4 is chosen by Jesus to minister to Nephites.

KUMENONHI—*one of twelve Nephite disciples* [c. A.D. 34]

3 Ne. 19: 4 is chosen by Jesus to minister to Nephites.

LABAN—*custodian of brass plates* [c. 600 B.C.] (*see also* Plates, Brass)

1 Ne. 3: 3 has record of Jews; 3: 4–11 sons of Lehi[1] sent to get records from; 3: 12–14 refuses to give up record; 3: 25–26 takes sons' property without giving plates of brass; 3: 29—4: 3 to be delivered into sons' hands; 4: 7–18 is slain by Nephi[1]; 4: 9, 18–19, 21 (2 Ne. 5: 14; Jacob 1: 10; W of M 1: 13; Mosiah 1: 16) sword of; 5: 16 descendant of Joseph[1].

LABOR (*see also* Do; Idleness; Industry; Laborer; Task; Travail; Wages; Work [verb])

1 Ne. 17: 41 l. which Israelites had to perform to be healed was to look; **2 Ne.** 5: 17 Nephi[1] causes his people to l. with hands; 9: 51 do not l. for that which cannot satisfy; 29: 4 do Gentiles remember the l. of the Jews; **Jacob** 1: 19 by l. with our might their blood should not come upon our garments; 5: 15, 29, 61–62, 71 servants called to l. in vineyard; **Mosiah** 2: 14 Benjamin has l. with his hands to serve his people; 13: 17 (Ex. 20: 9) six days shalt thou l. and do all thy work; 18: 24 (27: 5; Alma 1: 26) priests should l. with own hands for their support; 27: 4 every man should l. with own hands for his support; **Alma** 1: 3, 12 Nehor claims priests ought not l. with hands; 8: 10 Alma[2] l. much in spirit, wrestling with God in mighty prayer; 24: 18 converted Lamanites covenant to l. abundantly with hands rather than spend days in idleness; 29: 15 missionaries have l. exceedingly and brought forth much fruit; 30: 31 Korihor accuses priests of glutting on people's l.; 30: 32 Alma[2] has l. with own hands for support; 30: 34 if we receive nothing for l. in church, what doth it profit us to l. in church save to declare truth; 34: 32 this life is day for men to perform l.; 36: 24 Alma[2] has l., without ceasing, to bring souls unto repentance; 36: 25 the Lord gives joy in fruit of l.; **Moro.** 9: 6 if we cease to l., we should be brought under condemnation.

LABORER (*see also* Labor)

2 Ne. 26: 30 if men have charity, they would not suffer l. in Zion to perish; 26: 31 l. in Zion shall labor for Zion.

LACHONEUS[1]—*Nephite chief judge* [c. A.D. 1]

3 Ne. 1: 1 chief judge and governor over the land; 3: 1–10 receives epistle from robber leader; 3: 11–13, 22–25 gathers all the people and provisions in one place; 3: 14, 25 causes fortifications to be built; 3: 15 calls people to repentance; 3: 16 marvelous words and prophecies of L. cause people to fear; 3: 17 appoints chief captains over armies; 6: 6 helps establish peace; 6: 19 succeeded by son.

LACHONEUS[2]—*son of Lachoneus*[1] [c. A.D. 29-30]

3 Ne. 6: 19 follows father as chief judge.

LADEN (*see also* Burden)

1 Ne. 17: 25 children of Israel were l. with grievous tasks in bondage; **Mosiah** 2: 14 Benjamin labors so people will not be l. with taxes.

LAID (see Lay, Laid)

LAKE (see also Hell; Torment)

2 Ne. 9: 16 (28: 23; Jacob 3: 11; 6: 10; Mosiah 3: 27; Alma 12: 17; 14: 14) torment of the unrighteous is as *l.* of fire and brimstone; 9: 19, 26 God delivers saints and those without law from *l.* of fire and brimstone.

LAMAH—*Nephite commander* [c. A.D. 385]

Morm. 6: 14 and his ten thousand have fallen.

LAMAN¹—*eldest son of Lehi¹* [c. 600 B.C.] (see also Laman, River; Lamanite)

1 Ne. 2: 5 travels into wilderness with family; 2: 9 is admonished to be like river, continually running into fountain of all righteousness; 2: 11–12 (3: 28; 16: 36) murmurs against father; 2: 18 does not hearken unto Nephi¹; 3: 11–14 tries unsuccessfully to obtain brass plates from Laban; 3: 28 smites Nephi¹ and Sam with rod; 7: 6 rebels; 8: 35–36 does not partake of fruit of tree of life; 16: 7 takes daughter of Ishmael¹ to wife; 16: 20 murmurs because of afflictions in wilderness; 16: 37–38 stirs up Lemuel and sons of Ishmael¹ to kill Nephi¹; 17: 17–18 murmurs against desire of Nephi¹ to build ship; 18: 11–19 binds Nephi¹ in cords; **2 Ne.** 1: 24–29 Lehi¹ exhorts L. to hearken unto Nephi¹; 4: 3–7 Lehi¹ counsels L. and his family; 5: 21 (Alma 3: 7) cursing comes upon followers of L.; **Alma** 18: 38 Ammon² rehearses unto Lamanites concerning rebellion of L. and Lemuel.

LAMAN²—*Lamanite king* [c. 200 B.C.]

Mosiah 7: 21 (9: 10; 10: 18) deceives Zeniff; 9: 11–13 stirs up his people against people of Zeniff; 10: 6 dies.

LAMAN³—*son of Laman²* [c. 178 B.C.]

Mosiah 10: 6 replaces father as king; 24: 3 is called after his father, king over numerous people; 24: 9 Amulon is subject to L.

LAMAN⁴—*Nephite soldier*

Alma 55: 4 sought out by Moroni¹, who desires a descendant of Laman¹; 55: 5 (47: 29) formerly servant of Lamanite king; 55: 6–15 entices Lamanite guards into becoming drunk.

LAMAN, CITY OF

3 Ne. 9: 10 is burned at time of crucifixion.

LAMAN, RIVER—*river emptying into Red Sea* (see also Laman¹)

1 Ne. 2: 6–9 named by Lehi¹; 16: 12 Lehites cross river.

LAMANITE—*descendant of Laman¹, later any person who rejects the gospel* (see also Ammon², People of; Lamanitish)

1 Ne. 12: 20 will overcome seed of Nephi¹; 12: 23 (2 Ne. 5: 21–24; Jacob 3: 3–5; Alma 3: 6, 15–16, 19; Morm. 5: 15) cursed; **2 Ne.** 5: 14 a threat to Nephites; 5: 25 to be a scourge to Nephites; 30: 6 to be pure and delightsome people; **Jacob** 1: 13–14 seek to destroy Nephites; 2: 35 treat families better than Nephites; 3: 3 not filthy like Nephites; 7: 24 many means devised to restore L. to truth are vain; **Enos** 1: 11–13 Enos² prays for preservation of L.; 1: 16 records to be brought to L.; 1: 20 (Jarom 1: 6; Mosiah 9: 12; 10: 12) are bloodthirsty and idolatrous; 1: 24 (Jarom 1: 7; Omni 1: 10, 24; Alma 25: 3; 28: 3–10; 35: 13; 43: 3; 48: 21–22; Morm. 2: 1) wars between Nephites and L.; **Jarom** 1: 2 records written for L.; **W of M** 1: 13–14 are driven back by Nephites; **Mosiah** 1: 5 (10: 12–17; Alma 9: 16) traditions of fathers cause unbelief of L.; 7: 15, 22 Limhi's people in bondage to L.; 9: 14–15 slay Zeniff's flocks, but are driven out; 10: 8 (Alma 3: 4, 6, 15–16, 18) appearance of L.; 19: 10–22 defeat people of Noah³ and make them pay tribute; 20: 3–6 daughters of L. taken by priests of Noah³; 21: 15 the Lord softens L's hearts; 22: 10–11 Limhi's people escape from L.; 23: 29 possess land of Helam; 23: 35 priests of Noah³ join L.; 24: 4 are taught by priests of Noah³; 24: 7 prosper; 28: 1–9 (Alma ch. 17–28) sons of Mosiah² preach gospel among L.; **Alma** 2: 24 joined by Amlicites; 3: 10 dissenters marked like L.; 9: 16 the Lord extends merciful promises to L.; 16: 2–3 (25: 2) destroy city of Ammonihah; 17: 4 (19: 31–36; 23: 3–13) many L. converted; 17: 16–19 Ammon² begins ministry among L.; 19: 35–36 (23: 4–5) many L. are converted and baptized; 21: 23 converted L. are zealous for keeping commandments; 22: 27 division of land between Nephites and L.; 23: 6 after conversion, L. stand steadfast in truth; 23: 7 (24: 6) L. lay down weapons; 23: 17 (24: 3) L. converts take new name, Anti-Nephi-Lehies; 24: 1–2, 20–26 slaughter converts, more are converted; 25: 1 swear vengeance on Nephites; 25: 3 are driven and slain in battles with Nephites; 25: 4–5 many converts perish by fire; 27: 26 converted L. are called people of Ammon²; 28: 1–2 follow and slaughter converts; 28: 2–3 are slain and driven out; 43: 19, 37–38 are not as well equipped for war as Nephites; 43: 43 fight with great courage; 44: 15 make covenant of peace; 45: 14 in end, surviving Nephites will be numbered among L.; 47: 4–35

Amalickiah becomes king of L.; 49: 4 are astonished at Nephite fortifications; 49: 25 are defeated; 50: 7 are driven by army of Moroni¹; 52: 2 retreat to captured cities; 52: 8 kept prisoner for ransom by Nephites; 54: 3 take women and children as prisoners; 55: 33 fortify Morianton; 56: 12 slay all prisoners except captains; 56: 24 fear the Nephites; 57: 22 are driven to city of Manti; 58: 28 lose city of Manti; 59: 7–11 take city of Nephihah; 62: 14–15 many L. captured by Moroni¹; 62: 24–25 flee to land of Moroni; 63: 15 are driven back to own lands; **Hel.** 1: 22, 27, 33 capture and lose Zarahemla; 4: 5 recapture Zarahemla; 5: 17–19, 50 many L. are converted by sons of Helaman¹; 5: 50–52 yield up lands; 6: 1, 36 (13: 1) many L. become more righteous than Nephites; 6: 4 many L. preach to Nephites; 6: 6–8 peace between Nephites and L.; 6: 9 L. and Nephites become exceedingly rich; 6: 37 hunt Gadianton robbers and preach gospel to them; **3 Ne.** 2: 12–14 unite with and are called Nephites; 2: 15 curse taken from L. when converted; 2: 16 children become fair like Nephites; 6: 14 church broken up except among a few L.; 9: 20 baptized by fire and Holy Ghost because of faith; 10: 18 L. and Nephites receive great blessings; **4 Ne.** 1: 2–3 Nephites and L. all converted, all things held common; 1: 17 name abolished; 1: 20 name revived; 1: 38 unbelievers called L.; 1: 39 are taught to hate; **Morm.** 4: 1–2 drive Nephites to land of Desolation; 4: 11 L. and Nephites delight in shedding blood; 4: 13–14 take cities Desolation and Teancum, sacrifice women and children; 4: 18 sweep Nephites before them from this time on; 6: 7–15 slay all Nephites, except twenty-four; 7: 1–10 L. are of Israel; 8: 8 (Moro. 1: 2) dissension among L.; 8: 9 with robbers, L. possess land; **Ether** 4: 3 reject gospel of Christ; 8: 20 secret combinations among L.; **Moro.** 1: 1–2 L. put to death believers in Christ

LAMANITISH

Alma 17: 26 Ammon² tends flocks with L. servants; 19: 16 Abish a L. woman who had been converted to the Lord.

LAMB (*see also* Animal; Jesus Christ—Lamb of God; Sheep)

2 Ne. 21: 6 (30: 12; Isa. 11: 6) wolf shall dwell with l.; **Mosiah** 14: 7 (Isa. 53: 7) he is brought as l. to slaughter; **3 Ne.** 28: 22 (4 Ne. 1: 33) disciples play with wild beasts as child with l.

LAME (*see also* Heal)

Mosiah 3: 5 (3 Ne. 17: 7–9; 26: 15) the Lord shall cause the l. to walk; **4 Ne.** 1: 5 disciples of Jesus cause the l. to walk.

LAMENT, LAMENTATION (*see also* Cry; Grieve; Mourn; Sorrow; Wail; Weep)

2 Ne. 13: 26 (Isa. 3: 26) her gates shall l.; **Mosiah** 21: 9 great l. among people of Limhi; **Alma** 28: 4 time of great l. among Nephites; **Hel.** 6: 33 Nephites grow in iniquity, to great l. of the righteous; 7: 15 because of l. of Nephi² the people gather around him; 13: 32–33 in days of destruction, Nephites will l. that they did not repent; **3 Ne.** 10: 2 survivors of destruction cease to l. for loss of kindred; 10: 10 l. is turned into praise and thanksgiving unto Christ; **Morm.** 2: 11 l. in land because of robbers; **Ether** 15: 16 Jaredite survivors take up l. for loss of the slain.

LAMONI—*Lamanite king converted by Ammon²*

Alma 17: 21 descendant of Ishmael²; 17: 21–23 Ammon² carried before L.; 17: 24 offers to give Ammon² one of his daughters to wife; 17: 25–39 sets Ammon² to watch flocks; 18: 1–5, 8–12 is astonished at power of Ammon², believes him to be Great Spirit; 18: 11–15 fears Ammon²; 18: 18–21 asks Ammon² about Great Spirit; 18: 22–39 is taught by Ammon²; 18: 40–41 believes and cries unto the Lord; 18: 42–43 (19: 6) falls to earth, overcome by Spirit; 19: 12–13 arises, testifies of Redeemer, and sinks again with joy; 20: 1 asks Ammon² to go with him to land of Nephi to teach his father; 20: 2–7 journeys with Ammon² toward Middoni to free brethren from prison; 20: 8–16 meets father, who threatens to kill him for befriending a Nephite; 20: 17–25 is defended by Ammon²; 20: 28 proceeds to land of Middoni and frees brethren of Ammon² from prison; 21: 18 returns to land of Ishmael with Ammon²; 21: 20–22 builds synagogues and teaches his people; 22: 1–27 Aaron² teaches L's father; 24: 5–17 Ammon² and his brethren hold council with L. and his brother concerning defense of Anti-Nephi-Lehies.

LAND (*see also* Country; Earth; Ground; Inherit; Law, Civil; Nation; Promised Land)

1 Ne. 2: 20 (4: 14; 14: 1–2; 2 Ne. 1: 9, 20; Jarom 1: 9; Omni 1: 6; Ether 2: 8–11) if people keep commandments, they will prosper in the l.; 2: 20 (2 Ne. 1: 5; 3: 2; 10: 19; Ether 1: 38, 42; 2: 7, 10, 15; 9: 20; 10: 28; 13: 2) this l. is choice above all other lands; 17: 38 the Lord leadeth away the righteous into precious l.; **2 Ne.** 1: 7 (10: 11; Mosiah 29: 32; Ether 2: 12) this l. is to be a l. of liberty; 1: 7 if iniquity abound, l. to be cursed; 23: 14 (Isa. 13: 14) every man shall flee into his own l.; **Alma** 22: 32 small neck of l.

between *l.* northward and *l.* southward; 35: 14 (43: 47; 48: 10) Nephites fight to defend their *l.*; **3 Ne.** 8: 18 broken rocks found upon all the face of the *l.*; 20: 22 (21: 22–23; Ether 13: 4, 8) New Jerusalem to be built upon this *l.*

LANGUAGE (*see also* Chaldea, Chaldaic; Characters; Communication; Egyptian; Hebrew; Interpretation; Speak; Speech; Tongue; Translation; Word; Write; Writing; TG Language)

1 Ne. 1: 2 (Mosiah 1: 4) Nephi[1] writes in *l.* of father, which consists of learning of Jews and *l.* of Egyptians; **2 Ne.** 31: 3 the Lord speaks unto men according to their *l.*; **Omni** 1: 17 *l.* of people of Zarahemla has become corrupted; 1: 22 (Mosiah 28: 17; Ether 1: 33–37) the Lord confounded *l.* at time of tower; 1: 25 (Moro. 10: 16) believe in gift of interpreting *l.*; **Mosiah** 1: 2 Benjamin teaches his sons in all *l.* of his fathers; 1: 4 Lehi[1] could read brass plates because he had been taught in *l.* of Egyptians; 8: 11–12 Limhi desires to have twenty-four gold plates translated into his *l.*; 24: 4 *l.* of Nephi[1] is taught among Lamanites; 28: 13–14 (Morm. 9: 34–35; Ether 3: 22–23) Urim and Thummim prepared for purpose of interpreting *l.*; **Alma** 5: 61 Alma[2] commands in *l.* of him who hath commanded him; **3 Ne.** 5: 18 many things which Nephites, according to their *l.*, cannot write; **Morm.** 9: 34–35 because no other people know Nephites' *l.*, the Lord has prepared means for interpretation.

LASCIVIOUSNESS (*see also* Carnal; Lust)

Jacob 3: 12 Jacob[2] warns against *l.*; **Alma** 16: 18 priests preach against all manner of *l.*; 45: 11–12 Nephites to become extinct because of *l.*; 47: 36 dissenters give way to all manner of *l.*; **4 Ne.** 1: 16 no *l.* among people after Christ's visit.

LAST (*see also* End; Final; First; Last Days)

Alma 12: 36 the Lord sends down wrath according to his word in *l.* provocation, unto *l.* death as well as first; 34: 10–15 Son will be great and *l.* sacrifice.

LAST DAYS (*see also* Day of the Lord; Destruction; Israel, Gathering of; Jesus Christ, Second Coming of; Judgment; Lift; Millennium; Restoration; TG Last Days)

2 Ne. 25: 8 prophecies of Isaiah[1] to be of great worth in *l.* days; 26: 14 I prophesy unto you concerning *l.* days, when the Lord shall bring these things forth; 27: 1 in *l.* days, or days of Gentiles, all nations shall be drunken with iniquity;

Mosiah 26: 28 he who will not hear my voice I will not receive at *l.* day; **3 Ne.** 15: 1 (27: 22) whoso does Christ's sayings shall be lifted up at *l.* day; 16: 7 in latter day, truth shall come unto Gentiles.

LATCHET

1 Ne. 10: 8 (Mark 1: 7) John the Baptist to feel unworthy to unloose *l.* of Christ's shoe; **2 Ne.** 15: 27 (Isa. 5: 27) *l.* of their shoes shall not be broken.

LATTER DAY (*see* Last Days)

LAUGH, LAUGHTER (*see also* Scorn; TG Laughter, Laugh)

Alma 26: 23 Nephites *l.* at sons of Mosiah[2] for preaching to Lamanites; **3 Ne.** 9: 2 the devil *l.* because of the slain.

LAW (*see also* Agency; Commandments of God; Crime; Decree; Law, Civil; Law of Moses; Lawful; Obedience; Ordinance; Punishment; Statute; Transgression; TG Law)

2 Ne. 2: 5 by *l.* is not flesh justified; 2: 5 by temporal *l.* were men cut off, and by spiritual *l.* they perish from the good; 2: 26 men are free not to be acted upon, save by punishment of *l.* at last day; 8: 4 (Isa. 51: 4) *l.* shall proceed from me; 8: 7 (Isa. 51: 7) hearken unto me, ye in whose heart I have written my *l.*; 9: 25 where no *l.* is given, there is no punishment; 12: 3 (Isa. 2: 3) out of Zion shall go forth the *l.*; **Mosiah** 29: 13 if you could have just men as kings, who would establish *l.* of God, it would be expedient to have kings; **Alma** 42: 17 how could he sin if there was no *l.*; 42: 17 how could there be a *l.* save there was a punishment; 42: 21 if there was no *l.*, what could justice or mercy do; 42: 22 there is a *l.* given, and a punishment fixed; 42: 23 men will be judged according to their works, according to *l.* and justice; **Moro.** 8: 22 all they who are without *l.* are alive in Christ; 8: 22 power of redemption cometh on all them who have no *l.*

LAW, CIVIL (*see also* Crime; Government, Civil)

Mosiah 29: 15 he who commits iniquity is punished according to *l.* given by fathers; 29: 25 choose ye judges that ye may be judged according to *l.* given by fathers; **Alma** 1: 1 Mosiah[2] had established *l.* acknowledged by people; 1: 32–33 *l.* is put in force upon all who transgress it; 30: 7, 11 no *l.* among Nephites against a man's belief; 34: 12 *l.* requires life of him who has murdered; **Hel.** 4: 22 Nephites have trampled under feet the *l.* of Mosiah[2]; 5: 2 *l.* and governments established by voice of people; **3 Ne.** 6: 4 Nephites have formed their *l.* according

to equity and justice; 6: 24 contrary to *l.* of land for anyone to be put to death except power is given by governor; 6: 30 judges and lawyers set at defiance the *l.* and rights of country.

LAW OF MOSES (*see also* Carnal; Commandments of God; Jesus Christ, Types of; Law; Offering; Sacrifice)

1 Ne. 4: 16 *l.* was engraven upon brass plates; 17: 22 people of Jerusalem were righteous, kept commandments according to *l.* of Moses; **2 Ne.** 5: 10 (25: 24; Jarom 1: 5; Alma 30: 3) Nephites kept commandments according to *l.* of Moses; 11: 4 (25: 24–30; Jacob 4: 5–6; Alma 25: 15; 34: 14) *l.* of Moses has been given to point the people toward Christ; 25: 25 *l.* is dead unto us, and we are alive in Christ; 25: 25 we keep the *l.* because of the commandments; **Mosiah** 3: 14 because his people were stiffnecked, the Lord gave them *l.* of Moses; 12: 28–29 if ye teach *l.* of Moses, why do ye not keep it; 13: 30–32 *l.* of performances and ordinances given to keep people in remembrance of God; **Hel.** 13: 1 Lamanites observe commandments, according to *l.* of Moses; **3 Ne.** 1: 24–25 some teach that Nephites should not observe *l.* of Moses because Christ has been born; 9: 17 (12: 17–18; 15: 4–5; Matt. 5: 17–18) in Christ is *l.* of Moses fulfilled; 12: 17 (Matt. 5: 17) think not that I am come to destroy the *l.*; 12: 18 (Matt. 5: 18) not one jot nor one tittle hath passed away from the *l.*; 14: 12 (Matt. 7: 12) all things ye would that men should do to you, do ye to them, for this is the *l.* and the prophets; 15: 5 Christ is he that gave the *l.*; 25: 4 (Mal. 4: 4) remember ye *l.* of Moses; **4 Ne.** 1: 12 Nephites do not walk any more after performances and ordinances of *l.* of Moses; **Ether** 12: 11 by faith was *l.* of Moses given.

LAWFUL (*see also* Right [adj.])

3 Ne. 26: 18 not *l.* to write unspeakable things seen by those filled with Holy Ghost.

LAWYERS (*see also* Judge [noun])

Alma 10: 15 *l.* are learned in arts and cunning; 10: 27 foundation of destruction is being laid by unrighteousness of *l.* and judges; **3 Ne.** 6: 11 many merchants and *l.* in land; 6: 21 chief judges, *l.*, and high priests are angry with prophets; 6: 27–30 *l.* and high priests enter into secret combination.

LAY, LAID (*see also* Die; Foundation; Hands, Laying on of; Hold; Jesus Christ, Death of; Life)

2 Ne. 3: 12 writings shall *l.* down contentions; **Jacob** 5: 13, 18–20, 23, 27,

29, 71, 76 Lord of vineyard will *l.* up fruit; **Alma** 7: 15 *l.* aside every sin.

LAZINESS, LAZY (*see also* Idleness; Labor; Slothful)

Mosiah 9: 12 Lamanites are *l.* and idolatrous; 11: 6 priests of Noah³ are supported in *l.* by taxes.

LEAD, LED (*see also* Course; Direction; Guide; Inspire; Invite; Preside)

1 Ne. 4: 6 Nephi¹ is *l.* by Spirit; 14: 3 abominable church founded by devil to *l.* souls down to hell; 16: 16 directions of Liahona *l.* Lehites in more fertile parts of wilderness; 17: 24 the Lord commanded Moses to *l.* Israelites out of bondage; 17: 38 the Lord *l.* the righteous into precious lands; **2 Ne.** 10: 22 the Lord has *l.* away from time to time from house of Israel; 13: 12 (Isa. 3: 12) they who *l.* thee cause thee to err; 21: 6 (30: 12; Isa. 11: 6) little child shall *l.* them; 28: 14 they are *l.* that they do err because they are taught precepts of men; 28: 21 by lulling them into carnal security, devil *l.* men carefully down to hell; **Mosiah** 27: 8–10 Alma² and sons of Mosiah² *l.* astray people of the Lord; **Alma** 1: 7 Nehor tries to *l.* away people of church; 4: 11 because of wickedness, example of church *l.* unbelievers into iniquity; 13: 28 be *l.* by Holy Spirit; 21: 16 missionaries go forth whithersoever they are *l.* by Spirit; 34: 39 pray continually that ye be not *l.* away by temptations of devil; 36: 28 the Lord *l.* Israelites by his power into promised land; 39: 12 command thy children to do good, lest they *l.* away hearts of many; **Hel.** 3: 29 word of God *l.* man of Christ across everlasting gulf of misery; 15: 7 holy scriptures *l.* Lamanites to faith and repentance; **3 Ne.** 13: 12 (Matt. 6: 13) *l.* us not into temptation; **Morm.** 5: 17 Nephites were once *l.* by God; **Ether** 4: 12 I am the same that *l.* men to all good; **Moro.** 6: 9 Holy Ghost *l.* church whether to preach, exhort, pray, or sing.

LEADER (*see also* Lead; Ruler; TG Leadership)

2 Ne. 19: 16 (Isa. 9: 16) *l.* of this people cause them to err; **Jarom** 1: 7 Nephite *l.* were mighty men in faith of the Lord; **Omni** 1: 28 their *l.*, Zeniff, was a strong, mighty, stiffnecked man; **3 Ne.** 7: 11 *l.* of tribes establish laws; **Morm.** 2: 1 Nephites appoint Mormon² their *l.*; 8: 28 *l.* of churches shall rise in pride.

LEARN (*see also* Comprehend; Know; Learned [adj.]; Learning; Study; Teach; Understand)

2 Ne. 12: 4 (Isa. 2: 4) neither shall

they *l.* war any more; 27: 35 (Isa. 29: 24)
they that murmured shall *l.* doctrine;
Alma 32: 12 it is well that ye are cast
out of synagogues, that ye may *l.*
wisdom; 37: 35 *l.* wisdom in thy youth;
38: 9 I have told you this that ye may *l.*
wisdom; **Morm.** 9: 31 God hath manifested unto you our imperfections, that
ye may *l.* to be more wise than we have
been.

LEARNED [adj.] (*see also* Learn; Learning;
Wisdom)

2 **Ne.** 9: 29 to be *l.* is good if they
hearken to counsels of God; 9: 42 the
Lord despises the *l.* who are puffed up;
27: 15–20 prophecy concerning *l.* man
who will not read sealed book; **Jacob** 7:
4 Sherem is *l.* with perfect knowledge of
language; **Alma** 10: 15 lawyers are *l.* in
arts and cunning.

LEARNER (*see* Teacher)

LEARNING (*see also* Knowledge; Learn;
Learned [adj.]; Scriptures; Truth;
Wisdom)

1 **Ne.** 1: 1 Nephi[1] is taught in *l.* of
father; 19: 23 Nephi[1] likens scriptures
unto Nephites, to be for their *l.*; 2 **Ne.** 2:
14 I speak unto you these things for your
l.; 4: 15 Nephi[1] writes scriptures for *l.*
of his children; 26: 20 Gentiles will
preach up unto themselves their own *l.*;
3 **Ne.** 6: 12 people distinguished by ranks,
according to chances for *l.*, which depend
upon riches.

LEAST (*see also* Less)

Alma 42: 30 do not endeavor to
excuse yourself in the *l.* point; 45: 16 the
Lord cannot look upon sin with *l.* degree
of allowance.

LEAVE, LEFT (*see also* Depart; Left [adj.])

1 **Ne.** 3: 26 sons of Lehi[1] are obliged
to *l.* behind property with Laban; 2 **Ne.**
14: 3 (Isa. 4: 3) they that are *l.* in Zion
shall be called holy; **Alma** 1: 26 priests *l.*
labors to preach, and people *l.* labors to
hear; 13: 3 those called according to
God's foreknowledge are *l.* to choose good
or evil; 3 **Ne.** 25: 1 (Mal. 4: 1) day of the
Lord will *l.* the wicked neither root nor
branch; **Morm.** 2: 26 Nephites are *l.* to
themselves, that Spirit does not abide in
them.

LEBANON (*see also* BD Lebanon)

2 **Ne.** 12: 13 (Isa. 2: 13) day of the
Lord shall come upon cedars of L.; 20: 34
(Isa. 10: 34) L. shall fall by a mighty one;
24: 8 (Isa. 14: 8) cedars of L. rejoice at
thee; 27: 28 L. shall be turned into fruitful field.

LED (*see* Lead, Led)

LEFT [adj.] (*see also* Leave, Left; Right
Hand)

Mosiah 5: 10 whosoever shall not
take upon himself the name of Christ shall
find himself on *l.* hand of God.

LEHI[1]—*Hebrew prophet who led his followers
to promised land in western hemisphere* [c.
600 B.C.] (*see also* Lehi, Book of)

1 **Ne.** 1: 5 prays to the Lord on
behalf of his people; 1: 6–15 sees visions;
1: 16 writes many things he has seen in
visions and dreams; 1: 18–20 (Hel. 8: 22)
prophesies among Jews, is rejected; 2:
1–4 (Alma 9: 9; 10: 3; Hel. 8: 22; Ether
13: 5) flees Jerusalem with family; 2: 9–
14 admonishes elder sons; 2: 15 dwells in
tent; 3: 2–4 sends sons to obtain brass
plates; 5: 6 comforts Sariah; 5: 10–15
(Mosiah 1: 4) reads brass plates; 5: 14
(2 Ne. 3: 4; Alma 10: 3) a descendant of
Joseph[1]; 5: 17–19 prophesies concerning
his seed and brass plates; 7: 1–2 sends
sons to bring family of Ishmael[1] into
wilderness; 8: 2–28 explains dream of
tree of life; 10: 2–16 prophesies Babylonian captivity, coming of Christ,
future of Jews; 16: 9, 11–12 voice of the
Lord commands L. to take journey into
wilderness; 16: 10 finds Liahona; 16: 20
begins to murmur against the Lord
because of afflictions; 16: 23–31 asks the
Lord where Nephi[1] should hunt for food;
16: 25 is chastened because of murmuring
against the Lord; 18: 7 begets two sons in
wilderness; 18: 8–23 sails to promised
land; 2 **Ne.** 1: 1–3 speaks unto family
concerning great things the Lord has done
for them; 1: 4 sees in vision that Jerusalem has been destroyed; 1: 6–12
prophesies concerning promised land;
1: 13–23 admonishes sons to keep commandments; 1: 24–29 admonishes sons to
hearken unto Nephi[1]; 1: 30–32 blesses
Zoram[1]; 2: 1–30 teachings to Jacob[2]
concerning Christ, opposition, the Fall,
and redemption; 3: 1–4, 25 blesses
Joseph[2]; 3: 5–24 teaches concerning prophecy of Joseph[1]; 4: 3–11 blesses grandchildren; 4: 12 dies; **Jacob** 2: 34 commandments were given to L.; **Alma** 10: 3
descendant of Manasseh; **Hel.** 6: 10 the
Lord brought L. into land south.

LEHI[2]—*son of Zoram*[2], *possibly same as Lehi*[3]
[c. 81 B.C.]

Alma 16: 5–8 goes with father and
brother to rescue captured brethren.

LEHI[3]—*Nephite military commander* [c. 74
B.C.]

Alma 43: 35 encircles Lamanites
with his army; 43: 36–53 pursues Lamanite army; 49: 16–17 is appointed chief
captain over city of Noah; 52: 27–36
(62: 32–34) assists Moroni[1] in defeating

Lamanites; 53: 2 is given command of city of Mulek; 61: 15–21 (62: 3, 13) is left in charge of men and provisions; 62: 37 laments Teancum's death; **Hel.** 1: 28 assists Moronihah.

LEHI⁴—*son of Helaman², great missionary* [c. 45 B.C.]

Hel. 3: 21 younger son of Helaman²; 4: 14 preaches and prophesies many things; 5: 4 with brother, Nephi², preaches all his days; 5: 18–19 converts eight thousand Lamanites; 5: 20–21 goes to land of Nephi², cast into prison with Nephi²; 5: 22–25 is miraculously freed from prison; 5: 26–37 preaches to Lamanites, face shines in darkness; 5: 44 is encircled with fire, has unspeakable joy; 6: 6 goes with Nephi² to preach in land northward; 11: 19 not a whit behind Nephi² in righteousness; 11: 23 preaches, putting end to much strife; **Ether** 12: 14 by faith of Nephi² and L. was change wrought upon Lamanites.

LEHI, BOOK OF

1 Ne. 19: 1 Nephi¹ engraves record of L. on plates.

LEHI, CITY OF AND LAND OF¹—*land adjoining land of Morianton and containing city of Lehi*

Alma 50: 15 city of L. built in north by seashore; 50: 25–26 border dispute between lands of L. and Morianton; 50: 26 people of Morianton take up arms against people of L.; 50: 27–28 people of L. flee to Moroni¹; 50: 36 peace and union between people of L. and people of Morianton; 51: 24 people of L. gather, prepare for battle; 51: 26 city of L. is captured by Amalickiah; 62: 30 Moroni¹ goes to land of L. to battle Lamanites.

LEHI, LAND OF²—*apparently the entire land south*

Hel. 6: 10 the land south was called L.

LEHI-NEPHI, CITY OF AND LAND OF—*also called land of Nephi, of which it is a part* (*see also* Nephi, Land of)

Mosiah 7: 1–4 Mosiah² sends expedition to find those who had returned to land of L-N.; 9: 1, 6 Zeniff is allowed to possess land; 9: 8 Zeniff repairs walls of city of L-N.

LEHONTI—*Lamanite officer* [c. 72 B.C.]

Alma 47: 8–19 is lured into trap by Amalickiah and poisoned.

LEMUEL—*second son of Lehi¹* [c. 600 B.C.] (*see also* Lemuel, Valley of; Lemuelites)

1 Ne. 2: 5 one of four sons of Lehi¹, travels in wilderness with family; 2: 10 Lehi¹ admonishes L. to be steadfast, like valley; 2: 11–13 murmurs against father; 2: 14 is confounded by father; 2: 18 does not hearken unto Nephi¹; 2: 21, 23 is threatened with curse; 3: 4–10 is sent with brothers for brass plates; 3: 28 (2 Ne. 4: 13) angry with Nephi¹, hearkens unto Laman¹; 3: 29–31 smites younger brothers with rod, is stopped by angel; 7: 6 rebels against Nephi¹ and Lehi¹; 8: 4, 17–18, 35–36 Lehi¹ fears for L. because of dream; 16: 7 takes a daughter of Ishmael¹ to wife; 16: 20 murmurs because of afflictions; 16: 37 plots with Laman¹ against lives of father and brother; 16: 39 is chastened by voice of the Lord; 18: 11 with Laman¹, binds Nephi¹; **2 Ne.** 1: 28 Lehi¹ admonishes L. to hearken unto Nephi¹; 4: 8–9 Lehi¹ blesses L's family; 5: 21 (Alma 3: 7) is cursed because of iniquity; **Alma** 18: 38 Ammon² speaks about rebellion of L.

LEMUEL, CITY OF—*Lamanite city*

Alma 23: 12–13 inhabitants are converted to the Lord.

LEMUEL, VALLEY OF—*near borders of Red Sea*

1 Ne. 2: 10 Lehi¹ admonishes L. to be steadfast like valley; 2: 14 Lehi¹ speaks to Laman and Lemuel in valley of L.; 9: 1 (10: 16; 16: 6) family of Lehi¹ dwells in valley of L.; 16: 12 Lehites depart.

LEMUELITES—*descendants of Lemuel*

Jacob 1: 13 people called Lamanites, L., Ishmaelites; **Alma** 24: 29 those who join people of the Lord are actual descendants of Laman¹ and Lemuel; 43: 13 Lamanites are compound of Laman and Lemuel and Nephite dissenters; 47: 35 (Morm. 1: 8–9) Lamanites composed of Lamanites, L., Ishmaelites, Nephite dissenters; **4 Ne.** 1: 38 those who reject gospel are called Lamanites, L., Ishmaelites.

LEND (*see also* Borrow; Give)

2 Ne. 28: 30 blessed are they who l. ear to the Lord's counsel; **Mosiah** 2: 21 God preserves you from day to day, l. you breath; **Ether** 14: 2 people would not borrow or l.

LENGTHEN (*see also* Increase; Prolong; Stretch)

2 Ne. 2: 21 men's time was l. that they might repent in flesh; 28: 32 the Lord will l. his arm unto Gentiles; **Hel.** 7: 24 the Lord will l. Lamanites' days because they have not sinned against greater knowledge; 12: 14 if the Lord says to earth, Go back, that it l. the day, it is done; **3 Ne.** 22: 2 (Isa. 54: 2) l. thy cords and strengthen thy stakes.

LEOPARD

2 Ne. 21: 6 (30: 12; Isa. 11: 6) *l.* shall lie down with kid.

LEPROUS (*see also* Disease; Heal; BD Leper; Leprosy)

3 Ne. 17: 7 Nephites to bring the *l.* to Christ to be healed.

LESS, LESSER (*see also* Dust; Least)

Alma 12: 10–11 he who hardens heart receives *l.* portion of word; **3 Ne.** 2: 1 people become *l.* and *l.* astonished at sign or wonder from heaven; 11: 40 (18: 13) whoso declares more or *l.* than Christ's doctrine is not built upon rock.

LEVI¹—*son of Jacob¹* (*see also* BD Levi)

3 Ne. 24: 3 (Mal. 3: 3) the Lord shall purify sons of L.

LEVI²—*middle Jaredite king*

Ether 1: 20–21 (10: 14, 16) son of Kim, father of Corom; 10: 15 serves in captivity forty-two years after father's death; 10: 15 obtains kingdom by war; 10: 16 rules righteously.

LIAHONA—*compass given to Lehi¹*

1 Ne. 16: 10 Lehi¹ finds brass ball of curious workmanship, with two spindles; 16: 10 (Alma 37: 38–39) points way Lehites should go into wilderness; 16: 16 leads Lehites to more fertile parts of wilderness; 16: 26–27, 29 writing on L. gives understanding of the Lord's ways; 16: 28–29 (Mosiah 1: 16; Alma 37: 40) works according to faith and diligence; 18: 12–14 after brothers bind Nephi¹, compass ceases to work; 18: 21 when Nephi¹ is unbound, compass works; **2 Ne.** 5: 12 Nephi¹ takes compass with him; **Mosiah** 1: 16 Benjamin gives ball to Mosiah²; **Alma** 37: 38 called L., being interpreted, a compass; 37: 41–42 when Lehites were slothful, compass ceased to work and they did not progress in journey; 37: 43–45 L. a shadow or type of word of Christ.

LIB¹—*middle Jaredite king*

Ether 1: 17–18 son of Kish, father of Hearthom; 10: 18 becomes king; 10: 19 good king, great hunter, serpents destroyed during L's reign; 10: 20–29 lives long, and people prosper.

LIB²—*late Jaredite king*

Ether 14: 10 man of great stature, obtains kingdom through secret combination and murder; 14: 11–15 battles with Coriantumr²; 14: 16 is killed.

LIBERAL, LIBERALLY

2 Ne. 4: 35 (James 1: 5) God giveth

l. to him that asketh; **Alma** 1: 30 Nephites are *l.* to all in need; 6: 5 word of God is *l.* unto all.

LIBERTY (*see also* Agency; Bondage; Freedom; Freemen; Government, Civil; Promised Land; Right [noun]; TG Liberty)

2 Ne. 1: 7 (10: 11; Mosiah 29: 32; Alma 46: 17) promised land shall be land of *l.*; 2: 27 men are free to choose *l.* or captivity; **Mosiah** 23: 13 (Alma 58: 40; 61: 9) stand fast in *l.* wherewith ye have been made free; 29: 39 Nephites rejoice in *l.*; **Alma** 8: 17 people of Ammonihah study to destroy *l.*; 21: 22 Lamanites have *l.* of worshipping the Lord according to their desires; 43: 9 Nephites to preserve *l.* of worshipping God according to their desire; 43: 26, 30, 45, 48–49 (58: 12) Nephites fight to preserve their lands and *l.*; 44: 5 God strengthens Nephites, by *l.* which binds them to lands; 46: 10 Amalickiah seeks to destroy foundation of *l.*; 46: 13, 36 (51: 20; 62: 4) Moroni¹ raises title of *l.*; 46: 24 let us preserve our *l.* as a remnant of Joseph¹; 46: 28 Moroni¹ gathers all those who desire to maintain *l.*, to stand against Amalickiah; 48: 10–11 Moroni¹ prepares to support *l.*; 50: 32 Moroni¹ fears that Morianton² could cause overthrow of *l.*; 51: 7 people of *l.* rejoice in victory of freemen; 51: 13 king-men are wroth with people of *l.*; 51: 17, 20 king-men are compelled to support cause of *l.* of Nephites; 56: 47 Ammonite youth think more upon *l.* of fathers than upon their lives; 62: 37 Teancum a true friend to *l.*; **Hel.** 1: 7–8 Paanchi condemned to death for seeking to destroy *l.*; **3 Ne.** 2: 12 converted Lamanites join Nephites against robbers to maintain *l.*; 3: 2 Nephites are firm in maintaining *l.*; 5: 4 robbers who covenant to murder no more were set at *l.*

LICK (*see* Dust)

LIE, LAY, LAIN (*see also* Lying, Lie, Liar)

2 Ne. 21: 6 (30: 12; Isa. 11: 6) leopard shall *l.* down with kid; 24: 30 (Isa. 14: 30) the needy shall *l.* down in safety; **Alma** 37: 37 when thou *l.* down at night, *l.* down unto the Lord.

LIFE, LIVES (*see also* Death, Physical; Eternal Life; Immortality; Jesus Christ, Death of; Live; Mortal; Resurrection; Tree of Life; TG Breath of Life; Life; Life, Sanctity of; Life after Death; Mortality)

1 Ne. 1: 20 (2: 1) Jews seek *l.* of Lehi¹; **Jacob** 7: 26 our *l.* passed away like a dream; **Mosiah** 4: 6 continue in faith unto end of *l.* of mortal body; 7: 22 Lamanite king exacts tribute from Zeniff's people, or their *l.*; 13: 11 ye have

studied and taught iniquity the most part
of your *l.*; 16: 9 (Alma 38: 9; 3 Ne. 9: 18;
11: 11; Ether 4: 12) Christ is light and *l.*
of world; **Alma** 5: 34 ye shall eat and
drink of the bread and waters of *l.*; 5: 58
names of the righteous shall be written
in book of *l.*; 11: 45 mortal body is raised
from first death unto *l.*; 12: 24 (34: 32–
33; 42: 4) this *l.* became probationary
state; 26: 32 converted Lamanites would
rather sacrifice their *l.* than take *l.* of
enemy; 26: 36 this is my *l.* and my light;
28: 14 great reason of rejoicing because
of light of Christ unto *l.*; 34: 12 law
requireth the *l.* of him who hath murdered; 34: 33 after day of this *l.* cometh
night of darkness; 40: 11 spirits of all
men are taken home to God, who gave
them *l.*; 41: 3 if men's works were good
in this *l.*, they shall be restored unto that
which is good; 42: 16 repentance could
not come except there were punishment
as eternal as *l.* of soul; 48: 14 Nephites
are taught never to raise sword except to
preserve *l.*; 48: 24 Nephites could not
suffer to lay down *l.*, that wives and
children be massacred; 53: 17 Ammonite
youths covenant to protect land unto laying down of *l.*; 54: 12 it shall be blood for
blood, *l.* for *l.*; **3 Ne.** 13: 25 (Matt. 6: 25)
take no thought for your *l.*; **Ether** 3: 14
in Christ shall all mankind have *l.*

LIFT (*see also* Exalt; Jesus Christ, Death of;
Magnify; Pride; Raise)

1 Ne. 13: 37 they who seek to bring
forth Zion shall be *l.* up at last day; 16: 2
the righteous shall be *l.* up at last day;
18: 9 Laman[1], Lemuel, and sons of Ishmael[1] are *l.* up unto exceeding rudeness;
2 Ne. 12: 4 (Isa. 2: 4) nation shall not *l.*
up sword against nation; **Mosiah** 23: 22
(Alma 36: 3; 38: 5) whosoever puts trust
in the Lord shall be *l.* up at last day;
Alma 13: 29 have love of God always in
heart, that you may be *l.* up at last day;
31: 25 Alma[2] sees that people's hearts are
l. up unto great boasting; 37: 37 counsel
with the Lord in all your doings, and you
shall be *l.* up at last day; **Hel.** 6: 17
Nephites seek to get gain that they might
be *l.* up one above another; 8: 14 as
Moses *l.* up brazen serpent, so shall Son
be *l.* up; **Moro.** 9: 25 may Christ *l.* thee
up.

LIGHT [adj. = little] (*see also* Ease;
Easiness; Light; Little; Simple; Small)

1 Ne. 21: 6 (Isa. 49: 6) *l.* thing that
thou shouldst be my servant to raise up
tribes of Jacob.

LIGHT (*see also* Brightness; Candle; Darkness, Physical; Darkness, Spiritual; Enlighten; Example; Glory [noun]; Holy
Ghost; Illuminate; Jesus Christ; Knowl-

edge; Lamp; Shine; Spirit, Holy; Truth;
TG Light; Light of Christ; BD Light of
Christ)

1 Ne. 17: 13 the Lord will be your *l.*
in wilderness; **2 Ne.** 10: 14 the Lord will
be *l.* unto them that hear his words; 12:
5 (Isa. 2: 5) let us walk in *l.* of the Lord;
15: 20 (Isa. 5: 20) wo unto them that put
darkness for *l.* and *l.* for darkness; 18: 20
(Isa. 8: 20) if they speak not according to
this word, it is because there is no *l.* in
them; 19: 2 (Isa. 9: 2) people who walked
in darkness have seen a great *l.*; 23: 10
(Isa. 13: 10) stars of heaven shall not give
l.; 26: 10 Nephites shall reap destruction
because they choose works of darkness
rather than *l.*; 26: 29 priestcrafts are that
men set themselves up for *l.* unto world
to get gain and praise; 31: 3 the Lord
giveth *l.* unto the understanding; **Mosiah**
16: 9 (Alma 38: 9; 3 Ne. 9: 18; 11: 11;
Ether 4: 12) Christ is the *l.* and life of
world; **Alma** 9: 23 if Nephites transgress
against *l.*, it would be more tolerable for
Lamanites than for them; 19: 6 *l.* which
l. up Lamoni's mind is *l.* of God's glory,
marvelous *l.* of his goodness; 28: 14 great
cause of rejoicing because of *l.* of Christ
unto life; 32: 35 whatsoever is *l.* is good;
32: 35–36 after tasting this *l.* your
knowledge is not perfect; 36: 20 what
marvelous *l.* did Alma[2] behold; 37: 23
stone shall shine forth in darkness unto
l.; **Hel.** 13: 29 how long will ye choose
darkness rather than *l.*; 14: 3 great *l.* in
heaven shall be sign of Christ's coming;
3 Ne. 1: 19 at going down of sun there is
l. as at mid-day; 8: 21 no *l.* because of
thick darkness; 12: 16 (Matt. 5: 16) let
your *l.* so shine that they see your good
works; 15: 12 twelve disciples are *l.* unto
Nephites; 18: 16 Christ is the *l.*, has set
example; **Ether** 3: 4 (6: 2) brother of
Jared[2] asks the Lord to touch stones,
that Jaredites might have *l.*; **Moro.** 7: 18
l. by which ye should judge is *l.* of Christ;
7: 19 search diligently in *l.* of Christ that
ye may know good from evil.

LIGHTNING (*see also* Destruction;
Thunder)

1 Ne. 12: 4 (Hel. 14: 21; 3 Ne. 8: 7,
17, 19) at time of Christ's death, there
shall be great *l.*; 19: 11 the Lord will
visit house of Israel with *l.* of his power;
2 Ne. 26: 6 they who kill prophets shall
be visited with *l.*

LIKEN (*see also* Likeness; Parable; Teach)

1 Ne. 19: 23 Nephi[1] *l.* all scriptures
unto his people; 22: 8 the Lord's marvelous work is *l.* unto Israel's being nourished by Gentiles; **2 Ne.** 6: 5 (11: 2, 8) words
of Isaiah[1] concerning house of Israel may
be *l.* unto Nephites; **Jacob** 5: 3 (6: 1)

Israel is *l.* unto tame olive-tree; **3 Ne. 14:** 24 they who do Christ's sayings are *l.* unto man who built house upon rock.

LIKENESS (*see also* Image; Similitude)

Mosiah 12: 36 (13: 12; Ex. 20: 4) thou shalt not make any graven image or any *l.* of any thing in heaven or earth; **Alma** 32: 31 every seed bringeth forth unto its own *l.*; **Ether** 3: 17 Jesus shows himself to brother of Jared² in *l.* of same body he showed unto Nephites.

LILIES

3 Ne. 13: 28 (Matt. 6: 28) consider *l.* of field.

LIMHAH—*Nephite commander* [c. A.D. 385]

Morm. 6: 14 has fallen with his ten thousand.

LIMHER—*Nephite soldier* [c. 87 B.C.]

Alma 2: 22 sent out to watch camp of Amlicites; 2: 23–25 reports that Amlicites have joined large Lamanite army.

LIMHI—*king of Nephites in land of Nephi* [c. 121 B.C.] (*see also* Ammon¹; Nephi, Land of)

Mosiah 7: 7–8 (21: 22–23) commits Ammon¹ and brethren to prison; 7: 9 son of Noah³; 7: 9–11 questions Ammon¹; 7: 14 (21: 24) rejoices over news from Zarahemla; 7: 15, 21–23 is in bondage to Lamanites; 7: 17–18 gathers people to hear his words; 7: 19–20 exhorts people to put trust in God; 7: 24–33 laments over his people's transgressions; 8: 1 tells of brethren from Zarahemla; 8: 2–3 causes Ammon¹ to speak to people; 8: 5–14 (21: 25–28) brings forth twenty-four gold plates found by his people; 8: 15–18 is taught about seers by Ammon¹; 19: 17 is a just man; 19: 26 is made king by people, makes oath with Lamanite king to pay tribute; 19: 27–29 establishes peace among his people; 20: 8 discovers Lamanites and lays ambush; 20: 9–11 drives Lamanites from lands; 20: 12–16 counsels with Lamanite king; 20: 23–26 pacifies Lamanites by telling of father's priests; 21: 2–6 L's people complain to him of Lamanites' persecution; 21: 7–8, 11–12 is defeated by Lamanites three times; 21: 17 commands that every man impart to support of widows and children; 21: 19 always takes guards with him; 21: 32 enters into covenant to serve God; 21: 36—22: 2 studies how to deliver people from bondage; 22: 9–12 follows Gideon's plan to escape into wilderness; 22: 13 joins people of Mosiah²; 25: 16–18 is taught and baptized by Alma¹; 28: 11 delivers twenty-four gold plates to Mosiah².

LIMNAH (*see also* Coin)

Alma 11: 5, 10 *l.* of gold is value of all the coins.

LINE

2 Ne. 28: 30 (Isa. 28: 10) the Lord gives unto men *l.* upon *l.*

LINEN (*see also* Cloth; Clothing)

1 Ne. 13: 7–8 silks and fine-twined *l.* in abominable church; **Mosiah** 10: 5 Zeniff causes women to work all manner of fine *l.*; **Alma** 1: 29 (Hel. 6: 13) Nephites have abundance of silk and fine-twined *l.*; 4: 6 church begins to wax proud because of silks and fine-twined *l.*; **Ether** 10: 24 Jaredites have silks and fine-twined *l.*

LION (*see also* Animal; Beast)

2 Ne. 21: 7 (30: 13; Isa. 11: 7) *l.* shall eat straw like ox; **Mosiah** 20: 10 they fought like *l.* for their prey; **3 Ne.** 20: 16 (21: 12; Morm. 5: 24; Micah 5: 8) house of Jacob shall be among Gentiles as *l.* among beasts of forest.

LIPS (*see also* Mouth; Speak; Tongue; Word)

2 Ne. 16: 6 (Isa. 6: 5) I am a man of unclean *l.*; 27: 25 (Isa. 29: 13) with their *l.* this people honor the Lord; 30: 9 with breath of his *l.* the Lord shall slay the wicked.

LIST (*see also* Desire)

Mosiah 2: 32 beware lest contentions arise and ye *l.* to obey evil spirit; 2: 33, 37 whoso *l.* to obey evil spirit drinks damnation to his soul; **Alma** 3: 27 every man receiveth wages of him whom he *l.* to obey.

LISTEN (*see also* Communication; Hear; Hearken; Heed)

Jacob 2: 16 O that ye would *l.* to word of God's commands; **Mosiah** 22: 4 Gideon asks Limhi to *l.* to his words; **Moro.** 8: 8 *l.* to the words of Christ.

LITTLE (*see also* Child; Light [adj.]; Season; Small)

2 Ne. 28: 8 many shall say God justifieth in committing a *l.* sin; 28: 30 (Isa. 28: 10) the Lord gives unto men here a *l.*, there a *l.*; **Mosiah** 18: 27 of him that has but *l.*, but *l.* should be required; **3 Ne.** 13: 30 (Matt. 6: 30) so will God clothe you if ye are not of *l.* faith.

LIVE [verb] (*see also* Alive; Dwell; Eternal Life; Immortality; Inhabit; Life; Living)

Mosiah 4: 13 ye will not have a mind to injure one another, but to *l.* peaceably; 27: 31 they who *l.* without God in world shall confess that his judgment is just;

Alma 33: 19 (37: 46–47; Hel. 8: 15) type was raised in wilderness that whosoever would look upon it might *l.*; 37: 47 look to God and *l.*; 42: 3 if Adam had partaken of tree of life, he would have *l.* forever; **3 Ne.** 15: 9 look unto Christ and endure to end, and ye shall *l.*; 28: 2 disciples desire to come speedily into Christ's kingdom after they have *l.* unto age of man.

LIVING (*see also* Alive; Live; TG Living; Living Water)

    1 Ne. 11: 25 iron rod leads to fountain of *l.* waters; 17: 30 (2 Ne. 31: 16; Alma 5: 13; 7: 6; 3 Ne. 30: 1; Morm. 5: 14; 9: 28) the true and *l.* God; **2 Ne.** 9: 13 in resurrection all men will be *l.* souls.

LOATHSOME (*see also* Hate; Wicked)

    1 Ne. 12: 23 (2 Ne. 5: 22) Lamanites become *l.* people; **Morm.** 5: 15 Nephites shall become *l.* people.

LOINS (*see also* Descendant; Seed)

    2 Ne. 3: 4–22 prophecy of Joseph[1] concerning fruit of his *l.*; **Jacob** 2: 25 the Lord has led Nephites from Jerusalem to raise up righteous branch from *l.* of Joseph[1].

LONG-SUFFERING (*see also* Patience)

    1 Ne. 19: 9 Christ to suffer mockery because of his *l-s.* toward men; **Mosiah** 4: 6 come to knowledge of God and his *l-s.*; 27: 33 Alma[2] and sons of Mosiah[2] exhort people with *l-s.*; **Alma** 7: 23 be full of patience and *l-s.*; 9: 26 Son's glory shall be full of *l-s.*; 13: 28 be led by Spirit, become patient, full of all *l-s.*; 17: 11 be patient in *l-s.*; 26: 16 who can say too much of the Lord's *l-s.*; 32: 43 ye shall reap reward of your *l-s.*; 38: 3 Alma[2] has great joy in Shiblon's *l-s.* among Zoramites; 42: 30 let justice of God and his *l-s.* have full sway in your heart; **Morm.** 2: 12 Mormon[2] knows *l-s.* of God; **Moro.** 7: 45 (1 Cor. 13: 4) charity suffereth *l.*; 9: 25 may Christ's *l-s.* rest in your mind forever.

LOOK (*see also* Behold; See)

    1 Ne. 17: 40–41 (Alma 33: 19–20; Hel. 8: 14–15) labor which Israelites had to perform to be healed was to *l.* upon serpent; **2 Ne.** 2: 28 *l.* to the great Mediator; 8: 1 (Isa. 51: 1) *l.* unto rock from whence ye are hewn; 24: 16 (Isa. 14: 16) they that see thee shall narrowly *l.* upon thee; 25: 24 (26: 8) *l.* forward unto Christ; 25: 26 Nephites write of Christ, that children may know to what source they may *l.* for remission of sins; 25: 27 by knowing deadness of law, they may *l.* forward unto that life which is in Christ;

Jacob 4: 14 Jews' blindness came by *l.* beyond mark; **Jarom** 1: 11 prophets persuade men to *l.* forward unto Messiah; **Mosiah** 8: 13 Mosiah[2] has wherewith that he can *l.* and translate records; **Alma** 5: 15 *l.* forward with eye of faith and view mortal body raised in immortality; 13: 12 high priests could not *l.* upon sins save with abhorrence; 37: 47 *l.* to God and live; 45: 16 the Lord cannot *l.* upon sin with least degree of allowance; **Hel.** 8: 15 as many as *l.* upon Son might live; **3 Ne.** 12: 28 (Matt. 5: 28) whosoever *l.* on woman to lust hath committed adultery in heart.

LOOSE (*see also* Bind; Deliver)

    2 Ne. 3: 17 the Lord will not *l.* Moses' tongue; 15: 27 (Isa. 5: 27) girdle of loins shall not be *l.*; **Jacob** 3: 11 *l.* yourselves from pains of hell; **Alma** 7: 12 (11: 42) Son to take upon him death, that he might *l.* bands of death; **Hel.** 10: 7 (Matt. 16: 19) whatsoever he *l.* on earth shall be *l.* in heaven; **3 Ne.** 20: 37 *l.* thyself from bands of neck, daughter of Zion; 26: 14 Christ *l.* children's tongues; **Morm.** 9: 13 all shall be redeemed and *l.* from eternal band of death.

LORD (*see* Jesus Christ—Lord)

LORD OF HOSTS (*see* Jesus Christ—Lord of Hosts)

LORD'S DAY (*see* Day of the Lord; Sabbath)

LORD'S HOUSE (*see* House; Temple)

LORD'S PRAYER (*see also* Prayer; BD Lord's Prayer)

    3 Ne. 13: 9–13 (Matt. 6: 9–13) the Lord's Prayer given to the Nephites.

LOSE, LOST (*see also* Astray; Israel, Ten Lost Tribes of)

    1 Ne. 8: 23 those on path *l.* their way in mist of darkness; 10: 6 (Mosiah 16: 3; Alma 34: 9) all mankind were in *l.* and fallen state; **2 Ne.** 25: 17 the Lord will restore his people from *l.* and fallen state; **Jacob** 2: 35 Nephites have *l.* confidence of children because of bad example; **Mosiah** 20: 22 better that we should be in bondage than *l.* our lives; **Alma** 9: 30 people of Ammonihah are *l.* and fallen people; 16: 8 not one Nephite taken captive by Lamanites is *l.*; 30: 47 better that thy soul should be *l.* than that thou shouldst bring many down to destruction; 42: 6 man became *l.* forever; 60: 13 ye need not suppose that the righteous are *l.* because they are slain; **Hel.** 13: 33 if ye had remembered God, your riches would not have become slippery that ye *l.* them; **3 Ne.** 12: 13 (Matt. 5: 13) if salt *l.* its

savor, wherewith shall earth be salted; 16: 15 Gentiles shall be as salt that has *l.* its savor; **Moro.** 9: 5 Nephites have *l.* their love one toward another.

LOST TRIBES (*see* Israel, Ten Lost Tribes of)

LOT (*see also* BD Lots, Casting of)

    1 Ne. 3: 11 *l.* falls upon Laman[1] to visit Laban.

LOVE (*see also* Charity; Compassion; Esteem; God, Love of; TG Love)

    2 Ne. 9: 40 the righteous *l.* the truth and are not shaken; 26: 30 (Moro. 8: 17) charity is everlasting *l.*; 31: 20 (Mosiah 2: 4) press forward with steadfastness in Christ, having *l.* of God and all men; **Jacob** 3: 7 Lamanite husbands and wives *l.* each other and their children; **Mosiah** 3: 19 natural man must become a child, patient, full of *l.*; 4: 15 teach children to *l.* and serve one another; 23: 15 (Lev. 19: 18) every man should *l.* his neighbor as himself; **Alma** 5: 26 if ye have felt to sing song of redeeming *l.*, can ye feel so now; 11: 24 thou *l.* lucre more than God; 13: 28 be led by Holy Ghost, becoming patient, full of *l.*; 38: 12 bridle your passions, that ye may be filled with *l.*; **4 Ne.** 1: 15 no contention in land because of *l.* of God in hearts of people; **Morm.** 8: 37 ye *l.* your money and substance more than ye *l.* the poor and needy; **Moro.** 7: 13 every thing which inviteth to *l.* God is inspired of God; 7: 47 charity is pure *l.* of Christ; 7: 48 pray that ye may be filled with this *l.*; 8: 16 perfect *l.* casteth out fear; 8: 26 Comforter filleth with hope and perfect *l.*; 10: 32 if ye *l.* God with all your might, his grace is sufficient.

LOVING KINDNESS (*see* Kindness)

LOW, LOWER (*see also* Humble; Lowliness)

    1 Ne. 22: 23 those who belong to kingdom of devil must be brought *l.* in dust; **2 Ne.** 12: 12 (Isa. 2: 12) the proud and lofty to be brought *l.*; 12: 17 haughtiness of men shall be made *l.*; 26: 15 after Lehites' seed have been brought *l.* in dust, they shall not be forgotten; 26: 16 speech of those destroyed shall be *l.* out of dust; **Alma** 28: 11 bodies of many thousands are laid *l.* in earth; **Hel.** 14: 23 many mountains shall be laid *l.*

LOWLINESS, LOWLY (*see also* Humble; Low; Meek; Poor)

    1 Ne. 2: 19 Nephi[1] is blessed because he has sought the Lord with *l.* of heart; **Alma** 32: 8 blessed are ye if ye are *l.* in heart; 32: 12 because the poor are cast

out, they are brought to *l.* of heart; 37: 33–34 teach people to be meek and *l.* in heart; **Moro.** 7: 43 man cannot have faith and hope save he be *l.* of heart; 7: 44 none is acceptable before God save the *l.* in heart; 8: 26 remission of sins brings *l.* of heart, which brings Comforter.

LUCIFER (*see also* Devil; BD Lucifer)

    2 Ne. 24: 12 (Isa. 14: 12) how art thou fallen from heaven, L., son of morning.

LUCRE (*see also* Money; Riches)

    Mosiah 29: 40 *l.* corrupts soul; **Alma** 11: 24 Zeezrom loves *l.* more than God.

LURAM—*Nephite officer* [c. A.D. 385]

    Moro. 9: 2 has fallen by sword.

LUST (*see also* Adultery; Carnal; Chastity; Covet; Desire; Fornication; Lasciviousness; TG Lust; Sexual Immorality)

    1 Ne. 3: 25 Laban *l.* after property brought by sons of Lehi[1]; 22: 23 those who seek *l.* of flesh should fear and tremble; **Alma** 39: 9 go no more after *l.* of your eyes; **3 Ne.** 12: 28 (Matt. 5: 28) whoso looketh on woman to *l.* hath committed adultery in heart; **Morm.** 9: 28 ask not, that ye may consume it on your *l.*

LYING, LIE, LIAR (*see also* Beguile; Cunning; Deceit; Devil; False; Flatter; Fraud; Guile; Honest; Hypocrisy)

    2 Ne. 2: 18 (9: 9) devil is father of *l.*; 9: 34 *l.* shall be thrust down to hell; 28: 8 many shall say, L. a little; **Jacob** 7: 19 Sherem fears he has committed unpardonable sin by *l.* unto God; **Enos** 1: 6 (Ether 3: 12) God cannot *l.*; **Mosiah** 10: 18 Laman[3], by *l.* craftiness, deceives Zeniff; **Alma** 1: 17 *l.* are punished according to law; 5: 17 do ye imagine ye can *l.* to the Lord; 5: 25 except ye make Creator a *l.*, wicked cannot have place in heaven; 12: 1 Amulek has caught Zeezrom in his *l.*; 12: 3 thou hast not *l.* unto men only, but thou hast *l.* unto God; 12: 23 if Adam had partaken of tree of life, there would have been no death, making God a *l.*; 16: 18 priests preach against all *l.*; 30: 42 Korihor is possessed with *l.* spirit; 30: 47 better that Korihor's soul be lost than that he bring many souls to destruction by his *l.*; **Hel.** 4: 12 destruction of Nephites caused by their *l.*; 8: 24 ye cannot deny these things except ye *l.*; **3 Ne.** 1: 22 *l.* sent forth among people by Satan to harden hearts; 16: 10 when Gentiles are filled with all manner of *l.*, Father will bring gospel from among them; 21: 19 all *l.* shall be done away; 30: 2 Gentiles called to repent of *l.*; **4 Ne.** 1: 16 no *l.* among the people;

Morm. 8: 31 day of the Lord to come in day when much *l.* upon earth.

MADE

2 **Ne.** 27: 27 (Isa. 17: 27) shall the work say to him who *m.* it, he *m.* me not.

MAGIC (*see also* Sorceries, Sorcerer; Witchcraft)

Morm. 1: 19 (2: 10) *m.* art and witchcraft in the land.

MAGNIFY (*see also* Enlarge; Exalt; Lift; TG Priesthood, Magnifying Callings within)

2 **Ne.** 20: 15 (Isa. 10: 15) shall the saw *m.* itself against him that shaketh it; 25: 13 heart of Nephi[1] *m.* Only Begotten's holy name; **Jacob** 1: 19 (2: 2) Jacob[2] *m.* his office.

MAHAH

Ether 6: 14 one of four sons of Jared[2].

MAHER-SHALAL-HASH-BAZ—*son of Isaiah*[1] [c. eighth century B.C.]

2 **Ne.** 18: 1 (Isa. 8: 1) Isaiah is commanded to write concerning M.; 18: 3 (Isa. 8: 3) prophetess bears son, called M.

MAIMED (*see also* Heal)

3 **Ne.** 17: 7 Christ asks that the *m.* be brought to him.

MAINTAIN, MAINTENANCE (*see also* Defence; Keep; Preserve; Provide; Retain; Support)

Alma 44: 5 Nephites gain power over Lamanites by the *m.* of sacred word of God; 46: 20 whosoever will *m.* title of liberty should come forth; 46: 28 those desirous of *m.* liberty are gathered; 46: 35 dissenters who do not covenant to *m.* free government are put to death; 48: 10 Moroni[1] prepares people to *m.* cause of Christians; 50: 39 chief judge takes oath to *m.* cause of God; 51: 6 freemen swear to *m.* rights of religion by free government; 51: 7 king-men are obliged to *m.* cause of freedom.

MAJESTY (*see also* Glory [noun])

2 **Ne.** 12: 10, 19, 21 (Isa. 2: 10, 19, 21) glory of the Lord's *m.* shall smite wicked ones; **Alma** 5: 50 Son cometh in *m.*; 12: 15 men must stand before God in his *m.*

MAKE (*see* Made)

MAKER (*see* God—Creator; Jesus Christ—Creator)

MALACHI—*Jewish prophet* [c. late fifth century B.C.] (*see also* BD Malachi)

3 **Ne.** 24 compare Malachi 3; 3 **Ne.** 25 compare Malachi 4.

MALE (*see also* Man)

1 **Ne.** 8: 27 spacious building filled with people, both *m.* and female; 2 **Ne.** 10: 16 he who fights against Zion, both *m.* and female, shall perish; 26: 33 the Lord denies none who come to him, *m.* and female; **Alma** 1: 30 Nephites are liberal to all, both *m.* and female; 11: 44 restoration shall come to all, both *m.* and female; **Ether** 1: 41 gather thy flocks, both *m.* and female.

MALICE (*see also* Despise; Hate; Love; Mischief; Mock; Oppression; Persecution; Revile; Rudeness; Scorn)

2 **Ne.** 26: 21 churches shall cause *m.*; 26: 32 the Lord has commanded that men should not have *m.*; **Alma** 4: 9 (Hel. 13: 22; Morm. 8: 36) *m.* among the Nephites; 16: 18 priests preach against *m.*

MAMMON (*see also* Riches; BD Mammon)

3 **Ne.** 13: 24 (Matt. 6: 24) ye cannot serve God and *m.*

MAN, MEN (*see also* Adam; Agency; Body; Fall of Man; Flesh; Human; Male; Mankind; Nature, Natural; Soul; World; TG Man; Man, a Spirit Child of Heavenly Father; Man, Antemortal Existence of; Man, Natural, Not Spiritually Reborn; Man, New, Spiritually Reborn; Man, Physical Creation of; Man, Potential to Become like Heavenly Father; Man of God)

1 **Ne.** 8: 5 (14: 19) Lehi[1] sees *m.* in white robe in vision; 11: 7 (12: 6; 3 Ne. 11: 8) Nephi[1] to behold *m.* descending out of heaven; 11: 11 Nephi[1] speaks to Spirit of the Lord as a man speaks; 13: 12 Nephi[1] beholds *m.* among Gentiles who goes forth upon waters; 2 **Ne.** 1: 21 arise, my sons, and be *m.*; 2: 25 Adam fell that *m.* might be; 4: 17 O wretched *m.* that I am; 4: 34 (28: 31) cursed is he that puts trust in *m.*; 8: 7 (Isa. 51: 7) fear not the reproach of *m.*; 9: 5 Creator to become subject unto *m.* in flesh; 14: 1 (Isa. 4: 1) seven women shall take hold of one *m.*; 23: 12 (Isa. 13: 12) the Lord will make a *m.* more precious than fine gold; 26: 11 Spirit of the Lord will not always strive with *m.*; 27: 9 book to be delivered to a *m.* who will deliver it to another; 27: 25 their fear toward God is taught by precepts of *m.*; 28: 14 they err because they are taught by precepts of *m.*; 28: 26, 31 wo unto him who hearkens to precepts of *m.*; 29: 7 (Alma 1: 4) the Lord has created all *m.*; **Jacob** 2: 27 no *m.* among *m.* shall have more than one wife; 4: 8 no *m.* knows God's ways, save through revelation; 4: 9 God spoke, and *m.* was created; **Mosiah** 3: 19 natural *m.* is enemy to God; 7: 27 Christ to take upon

him image of m.; 7: 27 (Alma 18: 34; 22: 12; Ether 3: 15–16) m. was created after image of God; 8: 16 m. may have great power given him from God; **Alma** 2: 30 Alma² a m. of God; 26: 21 what natural m. knows these things; 30: 11 law that all m. should be on equal grounds; 32: 23 God imparts his words not only to m., but to women also; 40: 8 time is measured only unto m.; 41: 11 all m. in natural, carnal state, are in gall of bitterness; **Hel.** 11: 8, 18 Nephi² is esteemed a m. of God; **3 Ne.** 14: 12 (Matt. 7: 12) whatsoever ye would that m. should do to you, do to them; 27: 8 church called in name of m. is church of m.; 27: 27 what manner of m. ought ye to be; **Morm.** 9: 17 m. was created of dust; **Ether** 3: 15 never before has the Lord shown himself unto m.; 3: 16 the Lord has created m. after body of his spirit; 12: 39 Moroni² has talked with Jesus as m. talks with another; **Moro.** 8: 16 fear not what m. can do.

MANASSEH—*son of Joseph¹, father of a tribe of Israel* [c. seventeenth century B.C.]

2 Ne. 19: 21 (Isa. 9: 21) M. and Ephraim will be against Judah; **Alma** 10: 3 Lehi a descendant of M.

MANIFEST, MANIFESTATION (*see also* God, Manifestations of; Jesus Christ, Appearances of; Revelation; Show; Testify; Unfold)

1 Ne. 1: 19 vision of Lehi¹ m. coming of Messiah; **Mosiah** 8: 17 (Alma 37: 21) secret things shall be made m.; **Alma** 5: 46 the Lord m. these things to Alma² by Holy Spirit; 5: 47 spirit of prophecy is by m. of Spirit of God; **3 Ne.** 7: 22 those who are healed m. that Spirit has wrought upon them; 26: 9 if they believe, greater things shall be made m. unto them; **Ether** 2: 12 Christ has been m. by the things we have written; **Moro.** 10: 4 Father will m. truth of book by power of Holy Ghost; 10: 8 spiritual gifts are given by m. of Spirit.

MANKIND (*see also* Flesh; Human; Man)

1 Ne. 10: 6 (Alma 12: 22; 42: 14) all m. were in lost and fallen state; **2 Ne.** 2: 18 devil sought misery of all m.; **Mosiah** 16: 3 fall was cause of m. becoming carnal; **Alma** 19: 13 Redeemer shall redeem all m. who believe on his name; 34: 9 except for atonement, all m. must unavoidably perish; **Hel.** 14: 16 all m. redeemed from first death; 14: 17 Christ's resurrection redeems all m.; **Ether** 3: 14 in Christ shall all m. have light eternally.

MANNA (*see also* BD Manna)

1 Ne. 17: 28 (Mosiah 7: 19) children of Israel were fed with m. in wilderness.

MANNER

2 Ne. 25: 2 Nephi¹ has not taught his people much concerning m. of Jews; **Alma** 11: 4 Nephites do not reckon after m. of Jews; **3 Ne.** 13: 9 (Matt. 6: 9) after this m. pray ye; 27: 27 what m. of men ought ye to be.

MANSION (*see also* House)

Enos 1: 27 place is prepared for you in m. of Father; **Ether** 12: 32, 34, 37 the Lord has prepared house for man among Father's m.

MANTI—*Nephite soldier* [c. 87 B.C.]

Alma 2: 22 sent out to watch Amlicites.

MANTI, CITY OF—*chief city in land of Manti* (*see also* Manti, Land of)

Alma 56: 13–14 possessed by Lamanites; 57: 22 Lamanites driven back to M.; 58: 1 Helaman² desires to take M.; 58: 13 Nephites go forth against Lamanites in M.; 58: 39 Ammonite youth are with Helaman² in M.

MANTI, HILL OF—*near city of Zarahemla*

Alma 1: 15 Nehor put to death on M.

MANTI, LAND OF—*most southerly land of Nephites* (*see also* Manti, City of)

Alma 16: 6–7 Zoram² and sons march beyond borders of M.; 17: 1 Alma² meets sons of Mosiah² while on way to M.; 22: 27 proclamation sent to people of M.; 43: 22 head of river Sidon near M.; 43: 24–25 Nephite and Lamanite armies converge on M.; 43: 26 Moroni¹ gathers people in land to battle Lamanites; 43: 27–54 Nephites defeat Lamanites near borders of M.; 56: 13–14 Lamanites possess M.; 58: 26–30 (59: 6) Nephites march toward M. by night.

MARK (*see also* Curse; Skin)

Jacob 4: 14 Jews' blindness came by looking beyond the m.; **Alma** 3: 4, 13, 18 Amlicites m. themselves with red in forehead; 3: 6 Lamanites' skins were dark, according to m. set upon fathers; 3: 7, 14 the Lord set m. upon Laman¹, Lemuel, sons of Ishmael¹; 3: 10, 15–16, 18 those who are led away by Lamanites receive m.

MARRIAGE, MARRY (*see also* Divorce; Father; Husband; Mother; Wife; TG Marriage; Marriage, Celestial; Marriage, Continuing Courtship in; Marriage, Fatherhood; Marriage, Husbands; Marriage, Interfaith; Marriage, Motherhood;

Marriage, Plural; Marriage, Temporal; Marriage, Wives; BD Marriage)

1 Ne. 16: 7 Zoram[1] and sons of Lehi[1] take daughters of Ishmael[1] to wife; **Jacob** ch. 2 Jacob[2] denounces plurality of wives and concubines among Nephites; **3 Ne.** 12: 32 (Matt. 5: 32) whoso m. her who is divorced committeth adultery; 22: 1 (Isa. 54: 1) more are the children of the desolate than the children of the m. wife; **4 Ne.** 1: 11 Nephites are m. and given in m.

MARTYRDOM, MARTYR (see also Blood, Shedding of; Death, Physical; Kill; Murder; Persecution; TG Martyrdom; Prophets, Rejection of; BD Martyr)

Mosiah 7: 26 people of Limhi have slain a prophet; 17: 13–20 Abinadi is put to death by fire; **Alma** 14: 8–11 converted Ammonihahites are cast into fire; 24: 12–26 converted Lamanites refuse to fight, are killed, more converted; 25: 5–7 converted Lamanites put to death by children of Amulon; 25: 8 m. stirs up other Lamanites to hunt seed of Amulon; **3 Ne.** 6: 25 judges condemn prophets to death, not according to law; **Ether** 8: 25 devil has caused men to murder prophets.

MARVEL (see also Marvelous; Wonder)

Alma 22: 23 queen and others m. that Aaron[2] raises Lamanite king; **Hel.** 5: 49 converted Lamanites bidden not to m. at manifestation of Spirit; **3 Ne.** 15: 2 some m. at Jesus' words; 15: 3 m. not that I said old things have passed away.

MARVELOUS (see also Marvel; Wonderful)

1 Ne. 14: 7 (22: 8; 2 Ne. 25: 17; 27: 26; 29: 1; 3 Ne. 21: 9; 28: 31–32; Isa. 29: 14) the Lord to bring forth great and m. work among men; **Alma** 19: 6 light of God's glory, which is m. light of his goodness, enlightens Lamoni's mind; **4 Ne.** 1: 5 Jesus' disciples do great and m. works; **Ether** 4: 15 when Israel rends veil of unbelief, great and m. things shall come forth; 12: 5 (13: 13) Ether prophesies great and m. things.

MARY—mother of Jesus (see also Virgin; BD Mary)

Mosiah 3: 8 Christ's mother shall be called M.; **Alma** 7: 10 Son of God shall be born of M.

MASTER (see also Lord; Mahan)

1 Ne. 4: 21 Zoram[1] supposes Nephi[1] to be his m.; **Jacob** 5: 4 m. of vineyard goes forth; **Mosiah** 4: 14 devil is the m. of sin; 5: 13 how knoweth a man the m. he has not served; 24: 9 Amulon puts task-m. over people of Alma[1]; **3 Ne.** 13: 24 (Matt. 6: 24) no man can serve two m.

MATHONI—one of twelve Nephite disciples [c. A.D. 34]

3 Ne. 19: 4 called by Jesus to minister to Nephites.

MATHONIHAH—one of twelve Nephite disciples [c. A.D. 34]

3 Ne. 19: 4 called by Jesus to minister to Nephites.

MEANING, MEAN, MEANT (see also Interpretation; Knowledge; Means)

1 Ne. 11: 17 Nephi[1] does not know m. of all things; 11: 21 (15: 21) knowest thou m. of tree; 13: 21 knowest thou m. of book; 15: 23 what m. rod of iron; 15: 26 what m. river of water; 22: 1 what m. these things ye have read; **Mosiah** 12: 20 what m. words which are written; **Alma** 12: 11 this is what is m. by chains of hell; 34: 14 whole m. of law is to point toward Christ; 40: 18 first resurrection m. reuniting of soul with body of those from Adam to Christ; 41: 12–13 m. of word restoration is to bring back evil for evil, good for good.

MEANS (see also Meaning)

1 Ne. 16: 29 (Alma 37: 6–7) by small m. the Lord can bring about great things; **Mosiah** 28: 13 Mosiah[2] translates records by m. of two stones; **Alma** 30: 47 better that thy soul be lost than that thou shouldst be m. of bringing others to destruction; 38: 9 (Hel. 5: 9) no other m. whereby man can be saved, only in and through Christ; **3 Ne.** 18: 32 ye shall be m. of bringing salvation unto the unworthy; **Morm.** 9: 34 the Lord has prepared m. for interpretation of writings.

MEASURE (see also Mete)

Alma 11: 4 Nephites do not m. after manner of Jews; 40: 8 time is m. only unto men; **3 Ne.** 14: 2 (Matt. 7: 2) with what m. ye mete, it shall be m. unto you.

MEAT (see also Flesh; Food)

1 Ne. 17: 2 Lehites live on raw m. in wilderness; 18: 6 Lehites prepare m. for voyage; **Enos** 1: 20 many Lamanites eat nothing but raw m.; **Alma** 8: 21 Amulek sets bread and m. before Alma[2]; **3 Ne.** 4: 19 robbers have nothing save m. for their subsistence; 13: 25 (Matt. 6: 25) is not life more than m.; 24: 10 (Mal. 3: 10) bring tithes into storehouse, that there may be m. in the Lord's house.

MEDIATION, MEDIATOR (see Jesus Christ—Mediator)

MEEK, MEEKNESS (see also Contrite; Gentle; Humble; Lowliness; Poor)

2 Ne. 9: 30 (28: 13) wo unto the rich,

for they persecute the *m.*; 21: 4 (30: 9; Isa. 11: 4) the Lord will reprove with equity for the *m.*; 27: 30 the *m.* also shall increase; **Mosiah** 3: 19 natural man is enemy to God, unless he becomes *m.*; **Alma** 13: 28 be led by Holy Spirit, becoming *m.*; **Hel.** 6: 39 Nephites turn backs upon the poor and *m.*; **3 Ne.** 12: 5 (Matt. 5: 5; Ps. 37: 11) blessed are the *m.*, for they shall inherit earth; **Ether** 12: 26 my grace is sufficient for the *m.*; **Moro.** 7: 39 ye have faith in Christ because of your *m.*; 7: 44 none is acceptable before God, save the *m.*; 8: 26 remission of sins brings *m.*

MEET, MET, MEETING (*see also* Assemble; Church; Conference; Congregation; Meet [adj.]; Mete; Worship)

2 Ne. 33: 7 Nephi¹ has great faith in Christ that he will *m.* many souls spotless at judgment; **Alma** 5: 28 if ye are not stripped of pride, ye are not prepared to *m.* God; 12: 24 (34: 32) this life a time to prepare to *m.* God; 48: 23 Nephites sorry to send Lamanites into eternal world unprepared to *m.* God; **4 Ne.** 1: 12 Nephites *m.* together oft to pray and hear word of God; **Ether** 12: 38 (Moro. 10: 34) I bid farewell until we *m.* before judgment-seat; **Moro.** 6: 5–6 church *m.* together oft to fast, pray, discuss, partake of sacrament; 6: 9 *m.* are conducted after workings of Spirit.

MELCHIZEDEK—*king of Salem* (*see also* Priesthood; BD Melchizedek)

Alma 13: 14 a priest after order of Son of God; 13: 15 received Abraham's tithes; 13: 17–18 persuaded his people to repent.

MELCHIZEDEK PRIESTHOOD (*see* Priesthood, Melchizedek)

MELEK—*Nephite land west of Sidon*

Alma 8: 3–4 Alma² journeys into M. to teach; 35: 13 Ammonites come to M.; 45: 18 Alma² leaves Zarahemla as if to go to M.

MELT (*see also* Molten)

2 Ne. 23: 7 (Isa. 13: 7) every man's heart shall *m.*; **3 Ne.** 26: 3 (Morm. 9: 2; 2 Pet. 3: 10) elements to *m.* with fervent heat.

MEMORY (*see also* Remember, Remembrance)

Alma 36: 17, 19 Alma² is harrowed by *m.* of many sins; 46: 12 Moroni¹ writes on coat, In *m.* of our God.

MEN (*see* Man)

MEND (*see also* Change; Repair; Repentance)

Hel. 11: 36 Nephites do not *m.* their ways.

MENTION

1 Ne. 20: 1 (Isa. 48: 1) Israel makes *m.* of God, yet they swear not in truth; 21: 1 (Isa. 49: 1) from bowels of my mother hath the Lord made *m.* of my name; **2 Ne.** 22: 4 (Isa. 12: 4) make *m.* that the Lord's name is exalted; **Alma** 13: 19 of Melchizedek they have more particularly made *m.*

MERCHANTS (*see also* Business; Trade; Traffic)

3 Ne. 6: 11 many *m.* in the land.

MERCY, MERCIFUL (*see also* Compassion; God, Love of; Grace; Jesus Christ, Atonement through; Justice; Love; Merit; Pity; Repentance; TG Mercy, Merciful)

1 Ne. 1: 20 tender *m.* of the Lord are over all whom he has chosen; 8: 8 Lehi¹ prays the Lord will have *m.* on him; 13: 33 the Lord will be *m.* unto Gentiles; **2 Ne.** 1: 3 how *m.* the Lord was in warning Lehites to flee Jerusalem; 4: 26 the Lord has visited men in so much *m.*; 9: 25 where there is no condemnation, *m.* of Holy One have claim; 9: 53 because of his *m.*, the Lord has promised Nephites' seed will not be utterly destroyed; 19: 17 (Isa. 9: 17) the Lord shall have no *m.* on Israel's fatherless and widows; **Jacob** 6: 5 while the Lord's arm of *m.* is extended, harden not your hearts; **Mosiah** 2: 38–39 *m.* hath no claim on the unrepentant; 15: 8–9 God breaks bands of death, having bowels of *m.*; **Alma** 2: 30 Lord, have *m.* and spare my life; 5: 33 the Lord's arms of *m.* are extended to all men; 7: 12 the Lord will take upon him their infirmities, that his bowels may be filled with *m.*; 9: 11 if it had not been for the Lord's *m.* we should unavoidably have been cut off; 12: 33–34 whoso repents and hardens not his heart has claim on *m.* through Son; 15: 10 Lord, have *m.* on this man; 26: 37 the Lord's bowels of *m.* are over all the earth; 29: 10 then do I remember his *m.* arm; 32: 13 (Ether 11: 8) whoso repents shall find *m.*; 32: 22 God is *m.* unto all who believe; 34: 15 intent of last sacrifice is to bring about the bowels of *m.*, which overpowers justice; 34: 16 (42: 15) *m.* can satisfy demands of justice; 41: 14 if ye do all these things, ye shall have *m.* restored to you; 42: 15 plan of *m.* could not be brought about except an atonement be made; 42: 22 which repentance *m.* claimeth; 42: 25 do ye suppose that *m.* can rob justice; **3 Ne.** 12: 7 (Matt. 5: 7) blessed are the *m.*, for they shall obtain *m.*; 17: 7

Christ's bowels are filled with m.; 29: 7 no m. for son of perdition; **Moro.** 8: 19 awful wickedness to deny pure m. of God unto little children, for they are alive in him because of m.; 8: 20 he that saith little children need baptism denieth m. of Christ.

MERIT (see also Grace; Jesus Christ, Atonement through; Mercy; Virtue; Worth)

    2 Ne. 2: 8 no flesh can dwell in God's presence, save through m. of Messiah; 31: 19 rely wholly upon m. of him who is mighty to save; **Alma** 22: 14 since man had fallen, he could not m. anything of himself; 24: 10 God has taken away guilt from hearts through m. of his Son; **Hel.** 14: 13 have remission of sins through Christ's m.; **Moro.** 6: 4 rely alone upon m. of Christ.

MERRY (see also Glad; Happiness; Light-mindedness)

    1 Ne. 18: 9 wives begin to make themselves m.; **2 Ne.** 28: 7–8 many shall say, Eat, drink, and be m.; **Mosiah** 20: 1 Lamanite daughters gather to make themselves m.; **Alma** 55: 14 Lamanite soldiers drink and are m.

MESSENGER (see also Angel; Servant)

    3 Ne. 24: 1 (Mal. 3: 1) behold, I will send my m.

MESSIAH (see Jesus Christ—Messiah)

METAL (see also Gold; Iron; Ore; Silver; Steel)

    Hel. 6: 9 Nephites and Lamanites have all manner of precious m.; **Ether** 10: 23 Jaredites make all manner of m.

METE (see also Give; Measure)

    3 Ne. 14: 2 (Matt. 7: 2) with what measure ye m. it shall be measured to you.

MIDDONI—Lamanite land

    Alma 20: 2–3 the Lord tells Ammon² to go to M., where brethren are in prison; 20: 4–7 Lamoni offers to go with Ammon² to M. to release brethren; 20: 14–15 Lamoni refuses his father's order not to go to M.; 20: 28–30 (21: 12–13) brethren of Ammon² had been cast into prison in M., released by Ammon² and Lamoni; 21: 18 Ammon² and Lamoni return from M.; 23: 8–10 Lamanites in M. are converted unto the Lord.

MIDIAN, LAND OF—Lamanite land east of Lehi-Nephi

    Alma 24: 5 Ammon² meets his brethren in M.

MIDST

    3 Ne. 11: 8 (17: 12–13; 27: 2) Christ stands in m. of Nephites.

MIGHT (see also Arm; God, Power of; Mighty; Power; Strength)

    2 Ne. 25: 29 worship Christ with all your m.; **Jacob** 1: 19 by laboring with their m., the Lord's servants would not have people's blood on their garments; 5: 61, 71 call servants, that we may labor diligently with our m. in vineyard; 7: 25 Nephites fortify against Lamanites with all their m., trusting in God; **Mosiah** 2: 11 Benjamin has served his people with all m.; **Alma** 5: 50 Son comes in his m.; **3 Ne.** 3: 16 Nephites exert themselves in their m. to do according to words of Lachoneus; **Moro.** 10: 32 love God with all m., mind, and strength.

MIGHTY, MIGHTIER (see also God, Power of; Strong)

    1 Ne. 17: 32 the Lord makes Israelites m. unto driving out children of land; 22: 7 God will raise up a m. nation among Gentiles; **2 Ne.** 3: 24 one m. shall rise up to do much good in restoring Israel; 6: 17 (Isa. 49: 25) captives of the m. shall be taken away; 15: 15 (Isa. 5: 15) the m. shall be humbled; 31: 19 rely wholly upon merits of him who is m. to save; **Mosiah** 5: 2 the Lord has wrought m. change in Benjamin's people; **Alma** 5: 14 have ye experienced this m. change; 34: 18 cry unto God for mercy, for he is m. to save; **Hel.** 10: 5 the Lord will make Nephi² m. in word and deed; **Morm.** 9: 18 Christ and apostles did many m. miracles; **Ether** 2: 1 valley of Nimrod named after m. hunter.

MILDNESS

    Hel. 5: 29–33 still voice of perfect m. calls Lamanites to repent.

MILE

    3 Ne. 12: 41 (Matt. 5: 41) whosoever shall compel thee to go a m., go with him twain.

MILK

    2 Ne. 9: 50 (26: 25) come buy wine and m. without money.

MILLENNIUM (see also Day of the Lord; Jesus Christ, Second Coming of; Kingdom of God; Zion; TG Millennium; Millennium, Preparing a People for)

    1 Ne. 22: 26 (2 Ne. 30: 18) because of people's righteousness, Satan bound, cannot be loosed for many years.

MIND, MINDED (see also Heart; Knowledge; Mindful; Spirit)

2 **Ne.** 1: 21 my sons, to be determined in one *m.*; 9: 39 to be carnally *m.* is death, to be spiritually *m.* is life eternal; 25: 29 worship Christ with all your *m.*; **Jacob** 2: 9 instead of feasting on pleasing word of God, daggers are placed to wound their delicate *m.*; 3: 2 ye may feast upon God's love if your *m.* are firm; **Enos** 1: 10 voice of the Lord came into *m.* of Enos²; **Mosiah** 2: 9 open your *m.*, that mysteries of God may be unfolded; 4: 13 ye will not have a *m.* to injure one another; **Alma** 15: 3 Zeezrom's fever is caused by great tribulations of *m.* on account of his wickedness; 17: 5 sons of Mosiah² suffer much, both in body and *m.*; 19: 6 glory of God lights up Lamoni's *m.*; 30: 53 Korihor teaches devil's words because they are pleasing to carnal *m.*; 31: 5 word has more powerful effect upon *m.* of people than sword; 32: 34 when word swells in soul, *m.* begins to expand; 36: 4 Alma² obtains knowledge not of carnal *m.*, but of God; 36: 18 as *m.* of Alma² caught hold on Christ, he cried for mercy; 39: 13 turn to the Lord with all your *m.*; 40: 1 (41: 1) Corianton's *m.* is worried concerning resurrection; 57: 27 *m.* of Ammonite youths are firm; **Ether** 4: 15 veil of unbelief causes men to remain in blindness of *m.*; **Moro.** 7: 30 angels show themselves unto them of firm *m.* in every form of godliness; 9: 25 may Christ's mercy, long-suffering rest in your *m.* forever; 10: 32 (Matt. 22: 37) love God with all your might, *m.*

MINDFUL

Alma 26: 37 God is *m.* of every people; **Moro.** 8: 2 Christ hath been *m.* of you.

MINGLE (*see also* Mix)

Alma 3: 9 he who *m.* seed with Lamanites brings same curse on his seed; 5: 57 names of the wicked not to be *m.* with names of the Lord's people; 50: 22 wicked Nephites dwindle in unbelief and *m.* with Lamanites; **Hel.** 1: 12 robbers *m.* with people.

MINISTER [noun] (*see also* Disciple; Minister [verb], Ministration; Ministry; Officer; Preacher; Servant)

1 Ne. 12: 9–10 twelve *m.* shall judge Nephites; **Mosiah** 23: 14 trust no man to be your *m.* except he be a man of God.

MINISTER [verb], **MINISTRATION** (*see also* Administration; Angels, Ministering of; Ministry; Serve)

3 Ne. 7: 17 Nephi³ *m.* with power and great authority; 10: 19 Christ *m.* unto Nephites; 13: 25 Christ chooses twelve disciples to *m.* unto Nephites; 26: 19 disciples *m.* one to another; 28: 29 three Nephites shall administer unto

scattered tribes of Israel; **Moro.** 4: 1 elders and priests *m.* bread.

MINISTRY (*see also* Calling; Minister [noun]; Minister [verb]; Office; Preach; Serve, Service; TG Ministry; BD Ministry)

1 Ne. 9: 3 Nephi¹ to engrave on plates an account of *m.* of his people; **Alma** 39: 3 Corianton did forsake the *m.*; **3 Ne.** 7: 15 Nephi³ given power to know concerning the *m.* of Christ; **Moro.** 7: 31 office of the *m.* is to call men unto repentance; 8: 2 Christ has called Moroni² to his *m.*

MINON—*Nephite land on west bank of river Sidon*

Alma 2: 24 Nephite scouts see many Lamanites in M.

MIRACLE, MIRACULOUS (*see also* Faith; God, Manifestations of; God, Power of; Marvel; Raise; Sign; Wonder; TG Miracle; BD Miracle)

1 Ne. 17: 51 the Lord has wrought many *m.* among men; **2 Ne.** 10: 4 should mighty *m.* be wrought among other nations, they would repent; 26: 13 Christ works *m.* among men according to their faith; 27: 23 (Morm. 9: 11) I am a God of *m.*; 28: 6 (Morm. 8: 26) churches shall deny that God is God of *m.*; **Mosiah** 3: 5 (15: 6) God shall come down among men and work mighty *m.*; 8: 18 God has provided a means that man, through faith, might work mighty *m.*; **Alma** 23: 6 many Lamanites brought to knowledge of truth by power of God working *m.* in missionaries; 57: 26 preservation of Ammonite striplings ascribed to *m.* power of God; **Hel.** 4: 25 the Lord ceases to preserve Nephites by *m.* power; 16: 4 Nephi² works *m.* that people might know Christ must shortly come; **3 Ne.** 1: 4 greater *m.* wrought among the people in preparation for Christ's coming; 8: 1 no man could do *m.* in Jesus' name save he were cleansed from iniquity; 19: 35 Christ could not show so great *m.* to Jews because of their unbelief; 29: 7 wo unto him who says, to get gain, that no *m.* can be wrought by Christ; **4 Ne.** 1: 5 Jesus' disciples work all manner of *m.* in his name; **Morm.** 1: 3 *m.* cease because of iniquity; 9: 15–19 God has not ceased to be a God of *m.*; 9: 17 creation of earth and of men were *m.*; 9: 17 by power of God's word have *m.* been wrought; 9: 18 many mighty *m.* wrought by apostles; 9: 20 (Ether 12: 12) if God ceases to do *m.*, it is because of unbelief of men; **Ether** 12: 16 (Moro. 7: 37) all who work *m.* work them by faith; **Moro.** 7: 27, 29, 35–36 *m.* have not ceased because Christ ascended into heaven; 7: 37–38 if *m.* cease, it

is because faith has ceased; 10: 12 to another is given gift of working mighty m.

MIRE

2 Ne. 20: 6 (Isa. 10: 6) I will give him charge to tread them down like m. of streets; 3 Ne. 7: 8 people have turned from righteousness like sow to her wallowing in m.

MISCHIEF (*see also* Harm; Malice; Wicked)

2 Ne. 5: 24 Lamanites become idle, full of m.; 3 Ne. 16: 10 when Gentiles are filled with m., Father will bring gospel from them.

MISERY, MISERABLE (*see also* Anguish; Hell; Sorrow; Suffering; Torment; Tribulation; Unhappy; Wretched)

2 Ne. 1: 13 those bound by chains of hell are carried away to eternal gulf of m.; 2: 18 because devil became m. forever, he sought m. of all mankind; 2: 23 Adam and Eve could have had no joy, for they knew no m.; 2: 27 devil seeks that all men might be m. like himself; **Mosiah** 3: 25 view of own guilt causes wicked to shrink from the Lord into state of m.; 4: 17 perhaps thou shalt say, The man has brought upon himself his m.; **Alma** 3: 26 men will reap eternal happiness or m. according to works; 9: 11 except for the Lord's mercy, we might have been consigned to state of endless m.; 40: 15 consignation of soul to happiness or m. might be termed first resurrection; 42: 1 Corianton supposes it is unjust to consign sinner to m.; **Hel.** 3: 29 word of God leads man of Christ across everlasting gulf of m. prepared for the wicked; 5: 12 devil will have no power to drag those built in Christ's foundation down to gulf of endless m.; 12: 25–26 they who have done evil will be consigned to state of endless m.; **Morm.** 8: 38 greater is value of endless happiness than m. that never dies; 9: 4 men would be more m. to dwell with God under consciousness of filthiness than with damned souls.

MIST (*see also* Cloud; Darkness, Physical; Darkness, Spiritual; Smoke; Vapor)

1 Ne. 8: 23 m. of darkness arises in dream of Lehi[1]; 12: 4 (3 Ne. 8: 22) Nephi[1] sees m. of darkness in promised land; 12: 17 m. of darkness are temptations of devil.

MISUNDERSTAND

2 Ne. 25: 28 Nephi[1] has spoken plainly, that his people cannot m.

MIX, MIXTURE

1 Ne. 13: 30 the Lord will not suffer Gentiles to destroy m. of seed of Nephi[1]

among his brethren; 2 Ne. 5: 23 cursed shall be the seed of him who m. with Lamanites; **Alma** 3: 7–8 Lamanites are marked so that Nephites might not m. with them; 35: 10 Zoramites m. with Lamanites; **Hel.** 3: 16 Nephites m. with Lamanites until they are no longer called Nephites.

MOCK, MOCKERY (*see also* Malice; Persecution; Revile; Scorn)

1 Ne. 1: 19 Jews m. Lehi[1]; 8: 27 people in spacious building are in attitude of m.; **Jacob** 6: 8 will ye deny good word of Christ and make m. of plan of redemption; **Mosiah** 15: 5 Son suffereth himself to be m.; **Alma** 5: 30–31 he who makes m. of brother cannot be saved unless he repents; **Hel.** 4: 12 slaughter of Nephites is caused because they make m. of that which is sacred; **Ether** 7: 24 Jaredites revile against prophets and m. them; 12: 25 Moroni[2] fears Gentiles will m. his words; 12: 26 fools m., but they shall mourn; **Moro.** 8: 9, 23 solemn m. before God to baptize little children.

MOCUM, CITY OF

3 Ne. 9: 7 covered with water.

MOLTEN (*see also* Melt)

1 Ne. 17: 16 Nephi[1] makes tools with ore which he did m. out of rock; **Ether** 3: 1 brother of Jared[2] did m. out of rock sixteen small stones; 7: 9 Shule did m. out of hill and made swords.

MOMENT

3 Ne. 22: 7–8 (Isa. 54: 7–8) for small m. have I forsaken thee.

MONEY (*see also* Coin; Debt; Lucre; Mammon; Price; Riches; Tithing; Treasure; Wealth)

2 Ne. 9: 50 (Isa. 55: 1) he that hath no m., come buy and eat; 26: 25 buy milk and honey without m.; 26: 31 if laborers in Zion labor for m., they shall perish; **Alma** 1: 20 saints are persecuted because they impart word of God without m.; 11: 4–19 Nephite m. system; 11: 20 judges stir up people to disturbances, that they might get m.; **Hel.** 7: 5 the wicked go unpunished because of their m.; 9: 20 Nephi[2] is offered m. to reveal murderer; 3 Ne. 20: 38 ye shall be redeemed without m.; **Morm.** 8: 32 churches shall say, For your m. you shall be forgiven of sins; 8: 37 ye love m. more than the poor.

MOON

2 Ne. 23: 10 (Isa. 13: 10) m. shall not cause her light to shine; **Hel.** 14: 20 (3 Ne. 8: 22) as sign of Christ's death, m. shall not give light.

MORE

3 Ne. 11: 40 whoso shall declare m. or less than Christ's doctrine is not built upon his rock; 18: 13 whoso shall do m. or less than these is not built upon Christ's rock.

MORIANCUMER, LAND OF

Ether 2: 13 Jaredites camp in M.

MORIANTON¹—*Jaredite king*

Ether 1: 22–23 (10: 9, 13) descendant of Riplakish, father of Kim; 10: 9–13 gathers army of outcasts, establishes himself as king; 10: 10–11 eases people's burden, rules justly; 10: 12 builds many cities; 10: 13 lives to great age.

MORIANTON²—*founder of Nephite city* [c. 68 B.C.] (*see also* Morianton, City of and Land of; Morianton, People of)

Alma 50: 28 leader of people of Morianton; 50: 29 plans to lead his people to land northward; 50: 30–31 beats maid servant, who flees and tells Moroni¹ about plans; 50: 32 Moroni¹ fears consequences of his flight to north; 50: 35 is slain by Teancum.

MORIANTON, CITY OF AND LAND OF—*area settled by Morianton²* (*see also* Morianton²; Morianton, People of)

Alma 50: 25 land of M. next to land of Lehi, near seashore; 50: 36 people restored to land of M.; 51: 26 is possessed by Amalickiah; 55: 33 is fortified by Lamanites; 55: 33 (59: 4) Moroni¹ prepares attack; 59: 5 people flee to Nephihah, are attacked by Lamanites.

MORIANTON, PEOPLE OF—*followers of Morianton²* (*see also* Morianton, City of and Land of)

Alma 50: 26 claim part of land of Lehi, take up arms; 50: 28 fear Moroni¹ will destroy them; 50: 29–32 plan to flee to land northward; 50: 33–36 are stopped and brought back by Moroni¹; 51: 1 peace is established between people of Lehi and people of M.

MORIANTUM—*Nephite area*

Moro. 9: 9–10 people in M. take Lamanite daughters prisoner, rape and murder them.

MORMON¹ [c. A.D. 322]

Morm. 1: 5 father of Mormon².

MORMON²—*Nephite prophet, general, record keeper, abridger* [c. A.D. 333]

W of M 1: 1 is about to deliver record to Moroni²; 1: 3 after abridging large plates of Nephi, finds small plates; 1: 6 puts small plates with others; 1: 9 makes record according to understanding God has given him; 1: 11 prays plates will be preserved; **3 Ne.** 5: 12 is called after land of Mormon; 5: 20 (Morm. 1: 5) a pure descendant of Nephi¹; **Morm.** 1: 1 calls his record the Book of M.; 1: 2 when ten years old, is visited by Ammaron; 1: 3–4 is instructed to take record from hill when twenty-four; 1: 5 son of Mormon¹; 1: 6 is taken by father to Zarahemla; 1: 15 visited by the Lord; 1: 16–17 is forbidden to preach because of hardness of Nephites' hearts; 2: 12 hopes people will become righteous; 2: 17 takes large plates and makes record according to instructions; 3: 11 refuses to be leader because of people's wickedness; 3: 17 writes for future generations; 4: 23 takes all records hidden by Ammaron; 6: 2 writes epistle to Lamanite king; 6: 4–5 gathers Nephites to Cumorah; 6: 6 makes record out of plates of Nephi and places record in hill; 8: 1 record is finished by son, Moroni²; 8: 3 is killed by Lamanites; **Ether** 15: 11 hid records in hill Ramah; **Moro.** ch. 7 teachings on faith, hope, and charity; ch. 8 letter concerning baptism of little children; ch. 9 second epistle to Moroni².

MORMON, FOREST OF—*near waters of Mormon* (*see also* Mormon, Place of; Mormon, Waters of)

Mosiah 18: 30 beautiful to eyes of those who there came to knowledge of Redeemer.

MORMON, PLACE OF—*region near city of Lehi-Nephi* (*see also* Mormon, Forest of; Mormon, Waters of)

Mosiah 18: 4–7 those who believe Alma¹ go to M., where he is hiding, to hear him; 18: 5 fountain of pure water in M.; 18: 30 Alma¹ establishes order of church; 18: 31–33 people in M. are discovered by king; 18: 34–35 people depart into wilderness.

MORMON, WATERS OF—*fountain in land of Mormon*

Mosiah 18: 5 in M. a fountain of pure water; 18: 8–16, 30 (25: 18; 26: 15; Alma 5: 3) converts are baptized in waters of M.; 18: 30 beautiful to eyes of those who there came to knowledge of Redeemer.

MORNING

2 Ne. 24: 12 (Isa. 14: 12) Lucifer, son of m.; **Alma** 34: 21 cry unto the Lord m., mid-day, and evening; 37: 37 when thou risest in m., let heart be full of thanks unto God.

MORON—*late Jaredite king*

Ether 1: 7–8 (11: 14) son of Ethem, father of Coriantor; 11: 14 reigns

wickedly; 11: 15–17 battles for kingdom; 11: 18 is overthrown, dwells in captivity.

MORON, LAND OF—*north of the great land of Desolation*

Ether 7: 5–6 is invaded by Corihor[1], king taken captive; 7: 6 is near Desolation; 7: 17 Shule is carried captive into M.; 14: 6 brother of Shared places himself on throne of Coriantumr[2] in M.; 14: 11 Coriantumr[2] battles Lib[2] in M.

MORONI[1]—*righteous Nephite military commander* [c. 100 B.C.]

Alma 43: 16–17 chief captain of all Nephite armies; 43: 19–21 equips army, prepares armor for soldiers; 43: 22–23 sends spies into wilderness; 43: 24–25 marches into Manti; 43: 27–42 prepares stratagem to surround Lamanite army; 43: 47–50 inspires soldiers to fight for freedom; 43: 51–54 defeats Lamanites; 44: 1–6 demands surrender of Zerahemnah; 44: 8–12 Zerahemnah fails in attempt on M's life; 44: 16–18 commands soldiers to slay Zerahemnah's soldiers; 44: 19–20 Zerahemnah surrenders to M.; 46: 11 angered by Amalickiah's dissension; 46: 12–13 makes title of liberty; 46: 21–28 gathers army; 46: 30–33 cuts off armies of Amalickiah, who flees; 46: 34 is appointed by chief judges and voice of people; 46: 35 puts to death those who deny covenant of freedom; 46: 36 hoists title of liberty from every tower; 48: 7–10 strengthens his armies; 48: 11–18 character of M.; 49: 2–8 fortifies army with trenches; 50: 1–6 builds more fortifications; 50: 7–12 drives out Lamanites; 50: 31–36 sends army to stop flight of Morianton[2] and his people; 51: 13–21 has conflict with king-men; 52: 5–11 sends orders and reinforcements to Teancum; 52: 18–19 enters Bountiful, joins Teancum; 52: 21–26 takes city of Mulek by stratagem; 52: 35 is wounded; 52: 34–40 subdues remaining Lamanites near city of Mulek; 53: 1–5 fortifies Bountiful; 54: 4–14 epistle to Ammoron; 55: 6–15 sends Laman[4] with wine to Lamanites; 55: 16–24 arms prisoners in Gid and takes city; ch. 56–58 receives epistle from Helaman[2]; 59: 3 writes to Pahoran[1]; 59: 13 is angry with government because of indifference; ch. 60 writes second epistle to Pahoran[1]; 62: 1 is filled with joy over faithfulness of Pahoran[1]; 62: 4 raises standard of liberty wherever he goes; 62: 6, 14 joins Pahoran[1]; 62: 18–26 takes city of Nephihah; 62: 42–43 after fortifying land, yields command of army to son; 63: 3 dies.

MORONI[2]—*son of Mormon[2], last of Nephites* [c. A.D. 421]

W of M 1: 1 Mormon[2] plans to deliver record to M.; **Morm.** 6: 6 Mormon[2] stores records except few plates given to M.; 6: 11–12 one of only twenty-four remaining Nephites; 8: 1 is finishing record of his father; 8: 10–11 testifies of three Nephite disciples; 8: 12 would make all things known if possible; 8: 14 (Moro. 10: 2) seals up plates; ch. 9 address to unbelievers; **Ether** 1: 1 gives account of Jaredites; 3: 17 does not make full account of Jesus' appearance to brother of Jared[2]; 4: 5 is commanded to seal records with the interpreters; 5: 1–6 instructs future translator; 6: 1 (9: 1) continues history of Jaredites; 8: 20 does not give secret oaths; 12: 6–12 discourse on faith; 12: 23–28 not mighty in writing, fears Gentiles will mock; 12: 29 is comforted by Ether's words; 12: 38–41 bids farewell to Gentiles; 13: 1 tells of Jaredites' destruction; **Moro.** 1: 1 adds to his record; ch. 2–6 records ordinances and church discipline; ch. 7 records father's teachings on faith, hope, and charity; ch. 8 father's epistle concerning baptism of little children; ch. 9 father's second epistle; 10: 1–2 writes few more words to Lamanites before sealing records; 10: 34 to meet readers before judgment-bar of God.

MORONI, CITY OF AND LAND OF—*in southeast of Nephite lands*

Alma 50: 13 is built by Nephites near east sea, by possessions of Lamanites; 51: 22 Lamanites come into land of M.; 51: 23–24 (59: 5) Nephites are driven from city of M. to Nephihah; 62: 25 Lamanites again flee to land of M.; 62: 32–34 Lamanites encircled in land of M.; 3 Ne. 8: 9 (9: 4) city of M. sinks into sea.

MORONIHAH[1]—*righteous Nephite general, son of Moroni[1]* [c. 60 B.C.]

Alma 62: 43 Moroni[1] turns armies over to son, M.; 63: 15 drives back Lamanites; **Hel.** 1: 25–27 is surprised by Lamanite invasion; 1: 28–30 defeats and captures enemy; 1: 33 retakes city of Zarahemla; 2: 1 establishes peace, but contention arises; 4: 6 is driven into land Bountiful; 4: 9–10 regains half of Nephites' possessions; 4: 14–20 brings Lamanites to repentance, regains control over land.

MORONIHAH[2]—*Nephite general* [c. A.D. 385]

Morm. 6: 14 fallen with his ten thousand.

MORONIHAH, CITY OF—*iniquitous Nephite city*

3 Ne. 8: 10, 25 (9: 5) is buried under earth.

MORROW (see also Tomorrow)

3 Ne. 1: 13 on the m. come I into the world.

MORTAL, MORTALITY (see also Body; Flesh; Immortality; Life; Man; Probation; Temporal; World; TG Mortality)

Enos 1: 27 (Mosiah 16: 10; Morm. 6: 21) m. shall put on immortality; **Mosiah** 4: 6 continue in faith even unto end of life of m. body; **Alma** 5: 15 do you view this m. body raised in immortality; 11: 45 (12: 12, 20; 41: 4) m. body is raised to immortal body; 40: 2 this m. does not put on immortality until after coming of Christ; **3 Ne.** 28: 8, 17, 36 when Christ comes, three Nephites will be changed in twinkling of eye from m. to immortality.

MOSES—great Hebrew prophet [c. fifteenth century B.C.] (see also Law of Moses; Moses, Books of; BD Moses)

1 Ne. 4: 2 let us be strong like unto M.; 17: 24–26 (2 Ne. 3: 10) M. is commanded to lead Israel out of bondage; 17: 24 M. smote rock and water came forth; 17: 30, 42 Israelites reviled against M.; 22: 20–21 (3 Ne. 20: 23; 21: 11; Deut. 18: 15) Christ is prophet like unto M. that the Lord would raise; **2 Ne.** 3: 9–11 latter-day prophet like unto M. to be named Joseph; 25: 20 (Hel. 8: 11–13) M. was given power by God; **Mosiah** 12: 33 the Lord delivered commandments to M. in mount of Sinai; 13: 5 Abinadi's face shines even as M.; 13: 33 M. prophesied about Messiah; **Alma** 45: 19 Alma² is buried by hand of the Lord even as M.; **3 Ne.** 27: 8 if church is called by M. name, it is M. church.

MOSES, BOOKS OF

1 Ne. 5: 11 brass plates contain books of M.; 19: 23 Nephi¹ reads many things written in books of M.

MOSIAH¹—Nephite prophet, king in Zarahemla, father of Benjamin

Omni 1: 12 is warned to flee out of land of Nephi; 1: 14–15 discovers people of Zarahemla; 1: 18 causes people of Zarahemla to be taught in his language; 1: 19 is appointed king of united peoples; 1: 23 son, Benjamin, reigns after his death; **Mosiah** 2: 32 spoke of evil spirit.

MOSIAH²—Nephite king, son of Benjamin [c. 154-91 B.C.] (see also Mosiah², Sons of)

Mosiah 1: 2 son of Benjamin, taught in language of his fathers; 1: 10 (2: 30; 6: 3) is proclaimed king; 1: 18 is told to gather the people; 6: 4–7 walks in ways of his father; 7: 1–2 sends expedition to Lehi-Nephi; 21: 28 has gift of

interpretation; 22: 14 (24: 25) receives people from Lehi-Nephi with joy; 25: 1–7 reads records of Alma¹ and Zeniff; 25: 14–19 (26: 12) allows Alma¹ to establish churches; 27: 1–3 forbids unbelievers to persecute believers; 28: 11–19 translates records; 28: 20 confers records and sacred articles on Alma²; 29: 11, 25, 39 recommends that people select judges; 29: 30–36 discourses on kings; 29: 46 dies; 29: 47 last of Nephite kings; **Alma** 1: 1 accomplishments of M.; 10: 19 had warned of destruction through transgression; 11: 4 established permanent system of measures; 17: 35 (19: 23) was promised that his sons would be saved; **Hel.** 4: 21–22 words of M. were being trampled; **Ether** 4: 1 was instructed not to make experience of brother of Jared² known to people.

MOSIAH², SONS OF—great Nephite missionaries (see also Aaron²; Ammon²; Himni; Omner)

Mosiah 27: 8–10 (Alma 36: 6) among unbelievers trying to destroy church; 27: 11–12, 18–20 are rebuked by angel; 27: 32–35 preach throughout Zarahemla; 27: 34 (Alma 22: 35; 23: 1; 25: 17; 31: 6) names are Ammon², Aaron³, Omner, and Himni; 28: 1–7 obtain permission to go to preach to Lamanites; 28: 10 (29: 3; Alma 17: 6) unwilling to be king; **Alma** ch. 17–26 record of ministry among Lamanites; 17: 1 meet Alma² again; 23: 4 establish churches; 31: 6 accompany Alma² to Zoramites; 48: 18 all men of God.

MOTE

3 Ne. 14: 3 (Matt. 7: 3) why beholdest thou the m. in thy brother's eye.

MOTH

3 Ne. 13: 19–20 (27: 32; Matt. 6: 19–20) lay not up for yourselves treasures upon earth, where m. and rust corrupt.

MOTHER (see also Child; Family; Father; Marriage; Parent; Wife; TG Marriage, Motherhood; Mother)

1 Ne. 2: 5 (5: 1; 8: 14) Sariah, m. of Nephi¹; 11: 18 the virgin whom thou seest is m. of Son of God; 13: 17 m. Gentiles gather against Gentiles in promised land; 13: 34 abominable church is m. of harlots; 14: 9 abominable church is m. of abominations; 17: 55 (Mosiah 13: 20; Ex. 20: 12) honor father and m.; 18: 19 Jacob² and Joseph² are grieved because of afflictions of their m.; 21: 23 (2 Ne. 6: 7; 10: 9; Isa. 49: 23) queens shall be Israel's nursing m.; **2 Ne.** 3: 1 in days of greatest sorrow did m. bear Joseph²; 7: 1 (Isa. 50: 1) where is bill of m's divorcement, for your trans-

gressions is m. put away; 9: 7 flesh must have crumbled to m. earth; **Jacob** 5: 54 branches of m. tree grafted into roots of natural branches; 5: 56, 60 branches of natural trees grafted into roots of m. tree; **Mosiah** 2: 26 Benjamin about to yield mortal frame to m. earth; 3: 8 Christ's m. shall be called Mary; **Alma** 56: 47 (57: 21) Ammonite youths taught by m. that if they did not doubt, God would deliver them; **3 Ne.** 8: 25 if we had repented, our m. and daughters would have been spared; **Morm.** 6: 15 Nephites' bodies left to crumble and return to m. earth; 6: 19 O ye fathers and m., how is it ye could have fallen.

MOUNT, MOUNTAIN (see also Antipas, Mount; Hill; Sinai, Mount; Zerin, Mount; Zion, Mount)

1 Ne. 11: 1 Nephi¹ is caught away in Spirit into high m.; 12: 4 Nephi² beholds m. tumbling into pieces; 13: 37 (Mosiah 12: 21; 15: 15–18; 3 Ne. 20: 40; Isa. 52: 7) how beautiful upon m. are feet of them that publish peace and tidings of great joy; 16: 30 Nephi¹ goes into top of m. to hunt; 17: 7 Nephi¹ is commanded to get into m. to speak with the Lord; 18: 3 Nephi¹ goes into m. oft to pray; **2 Ne.** 12: 2–3 (Isa. 2: 2–3) m. of the Lord's house shall be established in top of m.; 21: 9 (30: 15; Isa. 11: 9) they shall not hurt nor destroy in all the Lord's holy m.; 24: 25 (Isa. 14: 25) upon my m. shall I tread the Assyrian under foot; 26: 5 m. shall cover those who kill prophets; **Jacob** 4: 6 (Morm. 8: 24; Ether 12: 30) we can command in Jesus' name and m. obey; **Alma** 12: 14 we would be glad if we could command m. to fall upon us to hide us from the Lord's presence; **Hel.** 12: 9 at the Lord's voice m. tremble; 12: 17 the Lord commands m. to fall on city, it is done; 14: 23 m. to be made low and valleys to become m. at Christ's death; **3 Ne.** 8: 10 in place of Moronihah there became a great m.; 22: 10 (Isa. 54: 10) m. shall depart and hills be removed; **Ether** 3: 1–4: 1 brother of Jared² speaks with the Lord upon m.; 12: 30 brother of Jared² tells m. to remove.

MOURN, MOURNING (see also Comfort; Cry; Grieve; Lament; Sorrow; Suffering; Wail; Weep)

2 Ne. 8: 11 (Isa. 51: 11) sorrow and m. shall flee away; 32: 7 Nephi¹ is left to m. because of wickedness of men; **Jacob** 7: 26 Nephites m. out their days; **Mosiah** 7: 23 how great reason Limhi's people have to m.; 18: 9–10 those willing to m. with those that m. should be baptized; 21: 9 (Alma 28: 4; 30: 2) great m. because of war; **Hel.** 7: 6–11 Nephi² m. for wickedness of his people; 9: 10 people

assemble to m. death of chief judge; **3 Ne.** 8: 23 great m. because of destruction; 10: 10 m. turns into joy; 12: 4 (Matt. 5: 4) blessed are all who m., for they shall be comforted; **Morm.** 2: 11–13 Nephites m. because God will not always suffer them to take happiness in sin; 6: 18 ye are fallen, and I m. your loss; 8: 40 why do ye cause widows and orphans to m. before the Lord; **Ether** 11: 13 prophets m. and withdraw from the people; 12: 26 fools mock, but they shall m.; 15: 3 Coriantumr² m. and refuses to be comforted.

MOUTH (see also Lips; Speak; Tongue; Word)

1 Ne. 21: 2 (Isa. 49: 2) he hath made my m. like a sharp sword; **2 Ne.** 27: 14 (Ether 5: 4) in m. of witnesses will the Lord establish his word; 27: 25 (Isa. 29: 13) this people draw near the Lord with mouth, but remove hearts from him; **Mosiah** 14: 7 (Isa. 53: 7) he was oppressed and afflicted, yet he opened not his m.; **Alma** 13: 22 voice of the Lord, by m. of angels, declares repentance to all nations; **3 Ne.** 20: 45 (21: 8) kings shall shut their m.; 26: 16 even babes open m. and utter marvelous things; **Ether** 5: 2–4 in m. of three witnesses shall these things be established; **Moro.** 7: 23 God declared to prophets, by own m., that Christ should come; 7: 25 by every word that proceeded out of m. of God, men began to exercise faith in Christ; 10: 28 these things shall proceed out of m. of everlasting God.

MOVE (see also Remove)

Mosiah 2: 21 God lends men breath, that they may live and m.; **Hel.** 12: 13 if the Lord says unto earth, M., it is m.; 12: 15 it is the earth that m., and not the sun; **Ether** 12: 30 if brother of Jared² had not had faith, mountain would not have m.

MULEK—*son of Jewish king Zedekiah* [c. 589 B.C.]

Mosiah 25: 2 Zarahemla a descendant of M.; **Hel.** 6: 10 son of Zedekiah was brought into land north; 8: 21 all Zedekiah's sons slain except M.

MULEK, CITY OF—*Nephite city south of Bountiful*

Alma 51: 25–26 on east borders by seashore, possessed by Amalickiah; 52: 2 Lamanite army retreats to M.; 52: 16–26 (53: 2, 6) Moroni¹ retakes M.

MULEK, LAND OF (see also Desolation, Land of)

Hel. 6: 10 land north is called M.

MULOKI—*missionary companion of Aaron³*

Alma 20: 2 imprisoned in land of Middoni; 21: 11 preaches in Ani-Anti; 21: 12 travels to Middoni with Aaron[3].

MULTIPLY (see also Enlarge; Grow; Increase)

2 Ne. 5: 13 (4 Ne. 1: 10) Nephites m. in land; 3 Ne. 19: 24 Jesus' disciples pray without m. words; Ether 6: 18 Jaredites m.

MULTITUDE (see also Nation)

1 Ne. 11: 34–35 m. of earth gathered together to fight apostles; 12: 13–15 Nephi[1] sees m. of his seed battling against seed of brethren; 13: 14 Nephi[1] beholds m. of Gentiles upon promised land; 2 Ne. 23: 4 (Isa. 13: 4) noise of m. in mountains like a great people; Mosiah 2: 7 m. of his people so great that Benjamin must speak from tower; 3 Ne. 11: 12 m. of Nephites falls to earth; 17: 18 so great is joy of m. that they are overcome; 18: 37 (Moro. 2: 3) m. does not hear Christ give disciples authority to bestow Holy Ghost.

MURDER, MURDERER, MURDEROUS (see also Blood, Shedding of; Capital Punishment; Kill; Martyrdom; Secret Combination; Slay; BD Murder)

1 Ne. 17: 44 elder sons of Lehi[1] are m. in hearts; 2 Ne. 9: 9 (Hel. 6: 29; Ether 8: 16) devil is source of secret combinations of m.; 9: 35 wo unto m. who deliberately kills; 10: 15 the Lord will destroy secret works of m.; 26: 32 (Mosiah 2: 13) the Lord commands that men should not m.; Alma 1: 18 those who practice priestcraft dare not m. for fear of law; 17: 14 Lamanites delight in m. Nephites; 30: 10 (34: 12) if a man m., he was punished unto death; 36: 14 Alma[2] had m. many, or led them unto destruction; 37: 30 secret workers of darkness m. the prophets; 39: 6 not easy for him who m. against light to gain forgiveness; 42: 19 if no law was given, would a man fear he would die if he m.; 54: 7 hell awaits m. except they withdraw m. purposes; Hel. 2: 4 Gadianton expert in craft of secret work of m.; 6: 17 Nephites begin to commit secret m.; 6: 21 robbers covenant they should not suffer for m.; 8: 26 Nephites are ripening for destruction because of m.; 3 Ne. 5: 4 robbers who covenant not to m. are set at liberty; 7: 6 government destroyed by secret combination of friends and kindred of those who m. prophets; 9: 9 people of Jacob[4] are burned because of secret m. and combinations; 16: 10 when Gentiles are filled with m., Father will bring gospel from among them; 30: 2 Mormon[2] calls Gentiles to repent of m.; Morm. 8: 8 whole face of land is one continual round of m.; Ether

8: 15 Cain was a m. from beginning; 8: 23 suffer not that m. combinations shall get above you; 8: 25 devil caused man to commit m. from beginning; Moro. 9: 10 Nephites m. Lamanite daughters in most cruel manner.

MURMUR, MURMURING (see also Complain; Contention; Disobedience; Disputations; Dissension; Hardheartedness; Rebel)

1 Ne. 2: 11 (3: 31; 16: 20; 2 Ne. 1: 26; 5: 4) Laman[1] and Lemuel m. in many things; 3: 6 Nephi[1] is favored of the Lord because he has not m.; 16: 20 Lehi[1] begins to m. against the Lord; 17: 2 Lehites begin to bear journeyings without m.; 17: 49 Nephi[1] admonishes brethren to m. no more; 2 Ne. 27: 35 they who m. shall learn doctrine; Alma 22: 24 great m. among Lamanites because of Aaron[2] and his companions.

MUSIC (see Dance; Sing)

MYSTERY (see also Godliness; Hide, Hidden; Knowledge; Secret; TG Mysteries of Godliness; BD Mystery)

1 Ne. 2: 16 Nephi[1] has great desires to know m. of God; 10: 19 m. of God shall be unfolded unto them that seek diligently, by power of Holy Ghost; Jacob 4: 8 how unsearchable are the depths of m. of God; 4: 18 (Alma 40: 3) I will unfold this m. unto you; Mosiah 1: 5 records are preserved that people might read and understand m. of God; 2: 9 open your minds that m. of God may be unfolded to your view; 8: 19 interpreters prepared for purpose of unfolding m. to men; Alma 10: 5 Amulek had never known much of the Lord's m. and marvelous power; 12: 9 given unto many to know m. of God; 26: 22 conditions for knowing God; 30: 28 Korihor claims priests yoke people with pretended m.; 37: 4 plates to go forth to every people, that they shall know m. contained thereon; 37: 11 these m. are not yet fully made known unto me, therefore I shall forbear; 37: 21 twenty-four plates to be kept, that m. and works of darkness may be made manifest; 40: 3 many m. that are kept that no one knoweth save God himself; Hel. 16: 21 people fear that prophets will work some great m. which they cannot understand.

NAHOM—place in Arabian desert

1 Ne. 16: 34 Ishmael[1] is buried at N.

NAIL

3 Ne. 11: 14–15 multitude feels prints of n. in Christ's hands and feet.

NAKED, NAKEDNESS (see also Charity; Clothing; Judgment; Needy; Poor)

2 Ne. 9: 14 we shall have perfect knowledge of our guilt and n.; **Jacob** 2: 19 seek riches to do good, to clothe the n.; **Mosiah** 4: 26 to retain remission of sin, impart substance, clothing the n.; 10: 5 (Hel. 6: 13) women work cloth, that Nephites might clothe their n.; 18: 28 Nephites are commanded to impart of substance to every needy, n. soul; **Alma** 1: 30 Nephites do not send away any who are n.; 3: 5 (43: 20) Lamanites are n. save loincloth; 14: 22 Ammonihahites take clothes from Alma² and Amulek, that they are n.; 20: 28–29 Ammon² finds brothers n. in prison; 34: 28 if ye turn away the n., your prayer is vain; **Hel.** 4: 11–12 slaughter of Nephites caused by pride, withholding clothing from n.; **Morm.** 8: 39 why do ye suffer the n. to pass by you and notice them not; 9: 5 to see your n. before glory of God will kindle unquenchable fire; **Ether** 10: 24 Jaredites work cloth to clothe themselves from n.

NAME (*see also* Call; Name of the Lord)

1 Ne. 14: 27 n. of apostle of Lamb is John; 20: 1 (Isa. 48: 1) hearken, O house of Jacob, who are called by n. of Israel; **2 Ne.** 3: 15 n. of latter-day seer shall be called after Joseph¹, and after n. of his father; **Mosiah** 1: 11–12 (5: 9–12) Benjamin gives his people a n. to distinguish them, never to be blotted out; 25: 12 children of Amulon and brethren are no longer called after n. of fathers, take n. of Nephi; 26: 36 (Alma 1: 24; 5: 57; Moro. 6: 7) n. of unrepentant transgressors are blotted out; **Alma** 5: 57 n. of wicked shall not be numbered among n. of righteous; 23: 17 converted Lamanites call their n. Anti-Nephi-Lehies; **Hel.** 5: 6 I have given you n. of first parents who came out of Jerusalem; **3 Ne.** 27: 8 if church is called in n. of man, it is church of man; 28: 25 the Lord forbids that n. of three Nephites be written.

NAME OF THE LORD (*see also* Jesus Christ; Prayer; TG Name of the Lord; BD Christ, Names of)

1 Ne. 17: 48 in n. of Almighty God I command you not to touch me; 20: 1 (Isa. 48: 1) Israel swears by n. of the Lord, but not in truth; 20: 11 (Isa. 48: 11) I will not suffer my n. to be polluted; **2 Ne.** 9: 23–24 (31: 11–12; Mosiah 18: 10; 3 Ne. 11: 23–27, 37–38; 18: 5, 11, 16, 30; 21: 6; 26: 17, 21; 27: 1, 16, 20; 30: 2; 4 Ne. 1: 1; Morm. 7: 8; Ether 4: 18; Moro. 7: 34) be baptized in n. of Christ; 9: 24 (25: 13–14; Mosiah 3: 9, 21; 5: 7; 26: 22; Alma 5: 48; 9: 27; 11: 40; 12: 15; 19: 13, 36; 22: 13; 26: 35; 32: 22; 34: 15; Hel. 3: 28; 14: 2, 12–13; 3 Ne. 9: 17–18; 5; Morm. 9: 25, 37; Ether 3: 14; 4: 18; Moro. 7: 26, 38; 8: 3) believe and have faith in Christ's n.; 9: 41 the Lord God is his n.; 10: 3 angel tells Jacob² that the Lord's n. will be Christ; 17: 14 (Isa. 7: 14) virgin shall bear a son and call his n. Immanuel; 19: 6 (Isa. 9: 6) Messiah's n. shall be called, Wonderful, Counselor, The Mighty God, The Everlasting Father, The Prince of Peace; 25: 16 (Jacob 4: 5) worship Father in Christ's n.; 25: 19 according to prophets and word of angel, Messiah's n. shall be Jesus Christ; 25: 20 (31: 21; Mosiah 3: 17; 5: 8) none other n. given, save Jesus Christ, whereby man can be saved; 26: 32 (Mosiah 13: 15; Ex. 20: 7) not take n. of the Lord thy God in vain; 27: 34 (Isa. 29: 23) they shall sanctify my n.; 31: 13 (Mosiah 5: 8; 6: 2; Alma 34: 38; 46: 18, 21; 3 Ne. 27: 5–6; Moro. 6: 3) men must take upon themselves n. of Christ; 32: 9 (33: 12; 3 Ne. 16: 4; 17: 3; 18: 19–23, 30; 19: 6–8; 20: 31; 27: 2, 7, 28; 28: 30; Morm. 9: 6, 21, 27; Ether 4: 15; Moro. 2: 2; 3: 2; 4: 2–3; 5: 2; 7: 26; 8: 3; 10: 4) pray unto Father in n. of Christ; **Jacob** 4: 6 (Morm. 8: 24) the Lord's servants can command trees or mountains in n. of Jesus; **Mosiah** 1: 11–12 (5: 9–12) Benjamin gives his people a n. to distinguish them; 4: 11 (Alma 19: 16; 24: 21; Ether 2: 15) call on n. of the Lord; 5: 9 whosoever enters covenant shall know n. by which he is called, n. of Christ; 5: 12 retain n. written always in your hearts, that ye may know n. by which ye shall be called; 26: 18 blessed is this people who are willing to bear the Lord's n., for in his n. shall they be called; **Alma** 5: 38 good shepherd calls in his own n., n. of Christ; **3 Ne.** 8: 1 no man could do miracle in n. of Jesus save he were cleansed from iniquity; 11: 17 blessed be n. of Most High God; 13: 9 (Matt. 6: 9) our Father who art in heaven, hallowed be thy n.; 14: 22 (Matt. 7: 22) in the Lord's n. many will cast out devils; 27: 5 men must take upon themselves the n. of Christ, for by that n. shall they be called; 27: 6 whoso taketh upon himself n. of Christ shall be saved; 27: 7 whatsoever ye do, do it in Christ's n.; 27: 7 church to be called in Christ's n.; **Ether** 2: 14 the Lord chastens brother of Jared² because he remembers not to call upon n. of the Lord; 3: 21 time cometh when the Lord will glorify his n. in the flesh; 4: 19 blessed is he who is found faithful unto the Lord's n. at last day; **Moro.** 4: 3 in sacrament, saints covenant to take upon themselves n. of Christ; 7: 26 men saved by faith in Christ's n.; 8: 3 the Lord will keep you through endurance of faith on his n.

NARROW (*see also* Strait)

1 Ne. 8: 20 Lehi¹ beholds straight

and *n.* path in vision; **2 Ne.** 9: 41 way for man is *n.*; 31: 18-19 (3 Ne. 14: 14; 27: 33; Matt. 7: 14) straight and *n.* path leads to eternal life; 33: 9 enter into the *n.* gate; **Jacob** 6: 11 continue in the way which is *n.*; **Alma** 50: 34 (52: 9; 63: 5; Morm. 2: 29; 3: 5; Ether 10: 20) *n.* pass leads by sea into land northward; **Hel.** 3: 29 word of God leads man of Christ in straight and *n.* course across gulf of misery.

NATION (*see also* Country; Gentile; Government, Civil; Heathen; Land; Multitude; People)

1 Ne. 5: 18 brass plates to go to every *n.*; 13: 2 Nephi[1] beholds many *n.* in vision; 13: 42 Lamb shall manifest himself unto all *n.*; 17: 37 the Lord raises up righteous *n.* and destroys *n.* of wicked; 19: 17 every *n.* shall be blessed; 22: 5 (2 Ne. 25: 15) Israel shall be scattered among all *n.*; 22: 14 every *n.* which wars against Israel shall be turned one against another; **2 Ne.** 1: 8 this land to be kept from knowledge of other *n.*; 12: 2 (Isa. 2: 2) all *n.* shall flow unto mountain of the Lord's house; 12: 12 day of the Lord soon cometh upon all *n.*; 15: 26 (Isa. 5: 26) the Lord will lift ensign to the *n.*; 25: 16 the Lord will scourge Jews by other *n.*; 27: 3 all *n.* that fight against Zion shall be as dream of night vision; 29: 7 the Lord brings his word unto all *n.*; 29: 8 testimony of two *n.* is witness that the Lord is God; 30: 8 the Lord will commence his work among all *n.*; **Mosiah** 3: 13 the Lord has sent prophets to declare these things to every *n.*; 15: 28 salvation of the Lord shall be declared to every *n.*; 16: 1 every *n.* shall confess before God that his judgments are just; **Alma** 9: 20 Nephites are favored above every other *n.*; 13: 21-22 voice of the Lord declares unto all *n.* that now is time to repent; 29: 8 the Lord grants unto all *n.*, of their own *n.* and tongue, to teach his word; 37: 4 records to go forth unto every *n.*; 45: 16 land cursed unto every *n.* that does wickedly; **3 Ne.** 28: 29 three Nephites shall minister unto all *n.*; **Ether** 2: 9 whatsoever *n.* possesses promised land should serve God or be swept off; 2: 12 whatsoever *n.* shall possess this land shall be free from all other *n.* it they serve God; 8: 22 whatsoever *n.* upholds secret combinations until they spread over the *n.* shall be destroyed; 8: 25 whoso builds secret combination seeks to overthrow freedom of all *n.*

NATURE, NATURAL (*see also* Carnal; Earth; Fall of Man; Flesh; Mortal; Temporal; World; TG Natural; Nature, Earth; Nature, Human)

1 Ne. 10: 14 (15: 7) *n.* branches of olive-tree are remnant of house of Israel; 19: 12 the God of *n.* suffers; **Jacob** 5: 3-77 parable of olive-tree, with *n.* branches and fruit; **Mosiah** 3: 16 in Adam, or by *n.*, men fall; 3: 19 *n.* man is enemy to God; 16: 5 he who persists in carnal *n.* remains in fallen state; **Alma** 19: 6 light of everlasting life overcomes Lamoni's *n.* frame; 26: 21 what *n.* man knows these things; 41: 4 every thing shall be restored to its *n.* frame; 41: 11 all men who are in state of *n.* have gone contrary to *n.* of God; 41: 12 restoration does not mean to take a thing of *n.* state and place it in unnatural state; 42: 10 men become carnal, sensual, and devilish, by *n.*; **Hel.** 13: 38 ye have sought for happiness in doing iniquity, which is contrary to *n.* of God's righteousness; **Ether** 3: 2 because of the fall our *n.* have become evil continually.

NAUGHT (*see also* Nothing; Vain)

1 Ne. 17: 48 whoso lays hands upon Nephi[1] shall be as *n.* before power of God; 19: 7-9 because of iniquity, world will judge Lord a thing of *n.*; **2 Ne.** 2: 11-12 without opposition, it must have been created for thing of *n.*; 27: 31 terrible one to be brought to *n.*; 27: 32 (28: 16) they who turn aside the just for a thing of *n.* shall be cut off; 33: 2 because they harden hearts, many cast away writings as things of *n.*; **Hel.** 4: 21 Nephites see they had set at *n.* God's commandments; 12: 6 men set at *n.* God's counsels; **3 Ne.** 20: 38 ye have sold yourselves for *n.*; **Morm.** 5: 9 this people to be counted as *n.* among Gentiles; **Ether** 13: 13 Jaredites esteem Ether as *n.*; **Moro.** 8: 20 he who says little children need baptism sets at *n.* the atonement.

NAZARETH—*city of Christ's childhood* (*see also* BD Nazareth)

1 Ne. 11: 13 Nephi[1] beholds virgin in N.

NEAR (*see also* Nigh)

2 Ne. 27: 25 (Isa. 29: 13) this people draw *n.* the Lord with mouth, but hearts are far from him.

NEAS—*unidentified plant* (*see also* Grain)

Mosiah 9: 9 people of Zeniff grow *n.*

NECK (*see also* Captive; Pride; Stiffnecked)

1 Ne. 20: 4 (Isa. 48: 4) thy *n.* is an iron sinew; **2 Ne.** 26: 22 devil leads men by *n.* with flaxen cord; **Alma** 22: 32 (50: 34; 52: 9; 63: 5; Morm. 2: 29; 3: 5; Ether 10: 20) small *n.* of land between land northward and land southward.

NEED (*see also* Needy; Want)

2 Ne. 28: 29 wo unto him that shall

say, we n. no more of word of God; **Mosiah** 4: 16 succor those that stand in n. of your succor; 18: 9 be willing to comfort those that stand in n. of comfort; **Alma** 1: 29 Nephites have abundance of all things they n.; 7: 23 (Morm. 9: 27) ask for whatsoever things ye n., spiritual and temporal; 34: 28 if ye do not impart of substance to those in n., your prayer is vain.

NEEDY (see also Afflicted; Alms; Charity; Hunger; Naked; Needs; Orphan; Poor; Relief; Widow)

2 Ne. 20: 2 (Isa. 10: 2) wo unto them that turn away the n. from judgment; 24: 30 (Isa. 14: 30) the n. shall lie down in safety; **Mosiah** 18: 28 (Alma 1: 27) Nephites should impart of substance to every n., naked soul; **Alma** 4: 12–13 (5: 55) the proud turn backs on n., the humble impart their substance to n.; 34: 28 if ye turn away the n., your prayer is vain; **Morm.** 8: 37 ye love your substance more than ye love the n.; 8: 39 why do ye adorn yourselves, yet suffer the n. to pass by.

NEGLECT (see also Diligence; Slothful)

Alma 32: 38 if ye n. the tree, it will not get any root.

NEHOR¹—brother of Abraham (see BD Nahor)

No references in Book of Mormon.

NEHOR²—Nephite apostate [c. 91 B.C.] (see also Nehors, Order of)

Alma 1: 2–3 proclaims against church; 1: 7 is withstood by Gideon; 1: 9 (2: 20) slays Gideon; 1: 14–15 is condemned by Alma² and executed.

NEHOR, CITY OF—Jaredite city

Ether 7: 9 Shule battles Corihor¹ in city of N.

NEHORS, ORDER OF—wicked combination of those who follow Nehor

Alma 14: 16–18 judge in Ammonihah is after order of N.; 15: 15 stiffnecked people of Ammonihah are of order of N.; 16: 11 many are slain on order of N.; 21: 4 Amalekites and Amulonites build synagogues after order of N.; 24: 28–29 more wicked part of Lamanites, who do not join church, are of order of N.

NEIGHBOR (see also Brother; Charity; Love)

2 Ne. 28: 8 many shall say, dig a pit for thy n.; **Mosiah** 4: 28 he who borrows from n. should return what he borrows; 5: 14 doth a man take an ass that belongs to his n. and keep it; 13: 23 (Ex. 20: 16) thou shalt not bear false witness against

thy n.; 13: 24 (Ex. 20: 17) thou shalt not covet anything that is thy n's; 23: 15 (3 Ne. 12: 43; Matt. 22: 39) every man should love his n. as himself; 26: 31 he who forgives not his n's trespasses brings himself under condemnation; 27: 4 every man should esteem his n. as himself.

NEPHI¹—son of Lehi¹, great prophet, founder of Nephites [c. 600 B.C.] (see also Nephites; Plates of Nephi, Large; Plates of Nephi, Small)

1 Ne. 1: 1 born of goodly parents; 1: 2 makes record; 1: 16–17 (8: 29) abridges father's record, will add his own account; 2: 16 character of N.; 2: 19–24 the Lord speaks to N.; 2: 19 is blessed because of faith; 2: 20 to be led to land of promise; 2: 22 chosen to be a ruler; 3: 7 will go and do things the Lord hath commanded; 3: 9 returns to Jerusalem with brothers to obtain brass plates; 3: 24 asks Laban for brass plates; 3: 27 hides in cave with brothers; 3: 28–29 is smitten by elder brothers, protected by an angel; 4: 18 slays Laban; 4: 24 obtains plates; 4: 31 is large in stature; 4: 32–35 convinces Zoram¹ to join his family; 6: 2 is a descendant of Joseph¹; 7: 2–6 returns to Jerusalem for Ishmael¹ and family; 7: 16 (18: 11) is bound by brothers; 8: 3 Lehi¹ rejoices because of N.; 8: 14–16 sees by Lehi¹ in dream; 9: 1 concludes father's account; 9: 1–5 (19: 1–2) makes two sets of plates; 9: 2–3 (19: 3) records ministry and prophecies on small plates; 9: 2, 4 (19: 4) records wars, contentions, and destructions on large plates; 10: 1 gives account of his reign and ministry; 10: 17 wants to know about our father's vision; ch. 11–14 beholds father's dream and vision of future of promised land; 11: 6 is blessed for belief in Son; 11: 32–33 in vision sees Christ crucified; 14: 28 is forbidden to write all he sees; 15: 12 explains olive-tree as symbol of house of Israel; 15: 19–20 speaks concerning restoration of Jews and words of Isaiah¹; 16: 7 marries; 16: 18, 23 breaks bow, makes another; 16: 22 speaks much to brothers; 16: 37 Laman¹ stirs the rebellious up to slay Lehi¹ and N.; 17: 8–11, 16 (18: 1–4) is commanded to build ship; 17: 15 keeps the commandments; 17: 17 is mocked by brothers; 17: 52–53 is filled with power of God; 18: 3 goes oft to mount to pray, sees great things; 18: 6–23 crosses ocean with Lehites; 18: 22 guides the ship; 19: 22 teaches from brass plates; 19: 23 reads Isaiah¹ to persuade brethren of Christ; 20: 1—21: 26 quotes Isaiah¹; 22: 1–26 expounds writings of Isaiah¹; 22: 20–21 (2 Ne. 1: 10; 25: 23; 26: 1) preaches about Christ; 2 Ne. 1: 24 Lehi¹ exhorts sons not to rebel against N.; 5: 1 cries unto Lord

because of brothers; 5: 6–7 flees from Laman¹ and Lemuel, with many followers; 5: 9 followers call themselves the people of N.; 5: 12, 14 brings plates, sword of Laban; 5: 15–16 teaches people to work, builds temple; 5: 18 people desire that N. be king; 5: 18 he recommends no king; 11: 2 writes more words of Isaiah¹; ch. 12–24 quotes Isaiah 2–14; 25: 1–6 comments on prophecies of Isaiah¹; 25: 7—31: 21 gives his own prophecies; 26: 1 teaches of Christ's resurrection; 27: 6–22 foretells coming forth of Book of Mormon; 29: 14 prophesies all records to be gathered as one; 30: 2 prophesies Gentiles to be numbered with covenant people; 31: 4–9 explains why Christ will be baptized; 32: 5 explains office of Holy Ghost; 33: 1–15 parting testimony; **Jacob** 1: 1 gives Jacob² commandment concerning small plates; 1: 12 dies; 1: 18 had consecrated Jacob² and Joseph² as priests; 3: 14 plates of Jacob made by N.; **Mosiah** 10: 13 the Lord heard and answered prayers of N.; **Hel.** 8: 22 had testified God was with Israel.

NEPHI²—*son of Helaman³, great Nephite missionary* [c. 45 B.C.]

Hel. 3: 21 elder son of Helaman³, brother of Lehi⁴; 3: 37 is appointed chief judge; 4: 14 (5: 14; 7: 2) preaches and prophesies with Lehi⁴; 5: 1 resigns position as chief judge; 5: 4 is weary over people's iniquity; 5: 18–19 preaches to Lamanites, converts eight thousand; 5: 20 goes to land of Nephi; 5: 21 is imprisoned with Lehi⁴; 5: 22–25, 43–44 is encircled with fire, protected from those who would slay them; 5: 27–31 prison is shaken, overshadowed with a cloud; 5: 36–39 converses with angels; 5: 50 converts more part of Lamanites; 6: 6 goes to land northward with Lehi⁴; 7: 1 returns to Zarahemla; 7: 4–6 sorrows over rise of Gadianton band; 7: 7 laments that he did not live in days of Lehi¹; 7: 10 prays on garden tower; 7: 12 teaches multitude from tower; 7: 19 predicts calamity unless people repent; 8: 5 arouses opposition; 8: 27 reveals secret murder of chief judge; 9: 16 is accused of the murder; 9: 26–36 identifies murderer; 9: 37–38 innocence is established; 10: 3–5 is praised by voice from heaven; 10: 6–7 is given great power; 10: 16 is conveyed away from persecutors by Spirit; 11: 4 invokes famine in land; 11: 10–16 prays for rain; 11: 17 the Lord answers N's prayer; 11: 18 is esteemed as great prophet; 11: 23 receives revelations, preaches, puts end to strife; 16: 1 Samuel's converts ask that N. baptize them; 16: 3–4 continues baptizing, prophesying, preaching repentance, working miracles; **3 Ne.** 1: 2 (2: 9) disappears.

NEPHI³—*son of Nephi², one of the twelve Nephite disciples* [c. A.D. 1] (*see also* Disciple; Nephi⁴)

3 Ne. 1: 2 eldest son of Nephi², given charge of plates; 1: 10 sorrows for wickedness of people; 1: 11–12 cries unto the Lord in behalf of his people, 1: 12–13 hears voice of the Lord, sign of Christ's birth to be given; 1: 23 performs baptisms; 5: 9–10 makes record on plates of Nephi¹; 7: 15, 18 was visited by angels and voice of the Lord; 7: 17 ministers with great power; 7: 19 (19: 4) casts out devils, raises brother from dead; 7: 20 arouses people's anger because of many miracles; 11: 18–20 Jesus calls N. forward; 11: 21–22 (12: 1) is given power to baptize; 19: 4 is called by Jesus to minister as one of twelve disciples; 19: 11–12 is baptized, baptizes other eleven disciples; 23: 7–8 is told to bring forth the records; 23: 9–13 is commanded to write missing parts of record.

NEPHI⁴—*son of Nephi³* [c. A.D. 34]

4 Ne. 1: heading—son of Nephi; 1: 19 keeps last record, dies.

NEPHI, CITY OF—*chief city in land of Nephi* (*see also* Lehi-Nephi, City of and Land of; Nephi, Land of)

Mosiah 9: 15 persecuted Nephites flee to N. for Zeniff's protection; 20: 3 priests of Noah³ are ashamed to return to N.; 21: 1, 12 Limhi and his people return to N. after battles; **Alma** 23: 8, 11 Lamanites in N. are converted; 47: 20 chief city in land of Nephi; 47: 31 Amalickiah takes possession of N.

NEPHI, LAND OF—*land of Lehites' first inheritance, also a smaller part of that land, sometimes called land of Lehi-Nephi* (*see also* Lehi-Nephi, City of and Land of¹; Limhi; Nephi, City of; Noah³; Zeniff)

2 Ne. 5: 8 named after Nephi¹; **Omni** 1: 12 Mosiah¹ flees from N. as directed; 1: 27–30 large number of Nephites return to N.; **W of M** 1: 13 Lamanite armies come from N. to battle Nephites; **Mosiah** 7: 6 Ammon² and brethren go to N.; 7: 7–8 Ammon² and brethren imprisoned in N.; 7: 9 (19: 26) Limhi, king of N.; ch. 9–22 record of Zeniff's people in land of N.; 9: 1 Zeniff has knowledge of land of N.; 9: 6 Zeniff obtains possession of land of N.; 9: 14 Lamanites invade, steal flocks; 10: 1 peace established in N.; 11: 1 Noah³ succeeds father as king in N.; 11: 20 Abinadi preaches in N.; 18: 4–5 Alma¹ teaches in Mormon, in borders of land of N.; 19: 15 Lamanites carry away Nephites' wives and children in N.; 19: 24 husbands return to N.; 20: 7 Lamanites go

to destroy Nephites in N.; 20: 11 Lamanites repulsed; 21: 1–4 Limhi's people in bondage in N.; 21: 11 Limhi's people escape from N.; 21: 21 wicked priests come into land of N. to steal; 28: 1–9 (Alma 17: 6–8) sons of Mosiah² are permitted to go on mission to N.; 29: 3 (Alma 22: 1) Aaron³ goes to N.; Alma 2: 24 Amlicites join Lamanites in N.; ch. 17–26 account of mission of sons of Mosiah to Lamanites in N.; 18: 9 Lamoni's father is king over land of N.; 20: 1 Lamoni desires Ammon² to accompany him to N.; 20: 2 the Lord tells Ammon² not to go to N.; 22: 28 idle Lamanites inhabit borders of N.; 22: 32 land of N. nearly surrounded by water; 22: 34 Nephites kept Lamanites to south in N.; 24: 20–23 Lamanites invade and slaughter many converted Lamanites in N.; 25: 13 many Lamanites join converts in N.; 27: 1 Lamanites return to N.; 27: 20 (28: 8) sons of Mosiah² tell of mission in N.; 27: 26 Ammonites leave N.; 47: 1, 20 Amalickiahites go to N.; 50: 8 land of N. runs in straight course from east sea to west; 53: 6 Moroni¹ captures city of Mulek in N.; 58: 38 Lamanites flee to N.; Hel. 4: 12 Nephite dissenters join Lamanites in N.; 5: 20 Nephi² and Lehi² go to N.

NEPHI, PEOPLE OF (see Nephites)

NEPHI, PLATES OF (see Plates of Nephi, Large; Plates of Nephi, Small)

NEPHIHAH—*second chief judge of Nephites* [c. 83 B.C.]

Alma 4: 17–18 (8: 12) Alma² delivers judgment-seat to N.; 50: 37–39 dies, son is appointed in his stead.

NEPHIHAH, CITY OF—*possibly two cities by this name*

Alma 50: 14 is built between cities of Aaron and Moroni; 51: 24 those who flee out of Moroni come to N.; 51: 26 captured by Amalickiah; 59: 5–11 is attacked by Lamanites; 62: 18–26 is retaken by Moroni¹.

NEPHIHAH, LAND OF (see also Nephihah, City of)

Alma 50: 14 Nephites call name of city, or the land, N.; 62: 14, 18 Moroni¹ goes to N.; 62: 30 Moroni¹ leaves N.

NEPHIHAH, PEOPLE OF—*residents of city or land of Nephihah*

Alma 59: 5 include people from other cities; 59: 7–8 are slaughtered and scattered.

NEPHIHAH, PLAINS OF—*near the city of Nephihah*

Alma 62: 18 Nephites pitch their tents in plains of N.

NEPHITES—*descendants of Nephi¹ and his followers, later any person who accepts gospel*

1 Ne. 12: 20 (Hel. 15: 17) to be overcome by Lamanites; 2 Ne. 5: 25 to be scourged by Lamanites; 29: 12 the Lord will speak unto N. and they shall write; 29: 13 to have Jews' words, Jews to have words of N.; Jacob 1: 13 all who are not Lamanites are N.; 2: 35 treat families worse than Lamanites; 3: 3 more filthy than Lamanites; Enos 1: 13–16 Enos prays for preservation of N. records; 1: 20 seek to restore Lamanites to faith in God; 1: 21 till earth; 1: 22 a stiffnecked people; 1: 24 (Jarom 1: 7; Omni 1: 10, 24; Alma 25: 3; 28: 3–10; 35: 13; 43: 3; 48: 21–22; Morm. 2: 1) N's wars with Lamanites; Jarom 1: 5 wax strong, observe the law; Omni 1: 2 Omni fights to preserve N.; 1: 5 more wicked part destroyed; W of M 1: 1 Mormon² witnesses destruction of most of N.; 1: 13–14 drive back Lamanites; Mosiah 19: 28 Lamanite guards supported by tribute from N.; 21: 2–5 afflicted by Lamanites; 25: 12 children of Amulonites desire to be called N.; 25: 13 people of Zarahemla all called N.; 29: 44 reign of judges commences among N.; Alma 2: 11–38 contention with Amlicites; 3: 4 dissenters marked; 8: 7 call cities and land after first possessor; 22: 27 land divided between Lamanites and N.; 25: 1 Lamanites swear vengeance on N.; 28: 1–3 defend Ammonites, great slaughter among Lamanites and N.; 30: 20 Ammonites wiser than N.; 43: 4 armies assemble in Jershon; 43: 7–9 N. fight for liberties; 43: 19, 37–38 better equipped for war; 43: 45 inspired by better cause; 45: 10–12 destruction of N. foretold; 47: 36 dissenters become more hardened; 48: 14 are taught to defend themselves; 49: 4 fortify Ammonihah; 49: 13 fortify city of Noah; 49: 21 are attacked at city of Noah; 49: 25 Amalickiah, by birth a N.; 50: 23 N. never happier than at time of Moroni¹; 52: 8 keep prisoners for ransom; 53: 2 dissension among N. gives enemy the advantage; 53: 16 sons of Ammonites call themselves N.; 55: 5–22 strategy secures release of captured N.; 56: 24 are feared by Lamanites; 58: 28 take city of Manti by stratagem; 59: 7–11 lose city of Nephihah; 62: 15 capture many prisoners; 62: 25 drive Lamanites to land of Moroni; 62: 40 are spared because of prayers of the righteous; 62: 41 many are hardened because of war, others softened from afflictions; 63: 6 many sail north; 63: 14 dissenters are stirred up against

N.; 63: 15 drive Lamanites back to own lands; **Hel.** 1: 22, 27, 33 lose and retake Zarahemla; 3: 15 many records kept by N.; 4: 11–13 slaughtered because of wickedness; 6: 2, 31 (13: 1) less righteous than Lamanites; 6: 4–5 are converted by Lamanites; 6: 6–8 peace between N. and Lamanites; 6: 9 N. and Lamanites become exceedingly rich; 6: 18–21, 38 many take Gadianton oaths and covenants; 6: 34 dwindle in unbelief; 16: 1 some repent, join church; **3 Ne.** 2: 1 become hardened after sign of Christ's birth given; 2: 8 reckon time from time of sign; 2: 12 unite with converted Lamanites; 3: 13–14, 22–25 gather in one place, fortify against robbers; 3: 19 appoint chief captains who have spirit of revelation; 4: 7–28 defeat robbers; 5: 1 believe words of prophets; 6: 1 return to own families and lands; 6: 3 have peace after subduing Gadianton band; 7: 2 have dissension and form tribes; 10: 18 N. and Lamanites receive great blessings; ch. 11–26 ministry of Jesus among N.; **4 Ne.** 1: 2–3 all are converted unto the Lord, have all things in common; 1: 7–23 prosper during reign of righteousness; 1: 24 begin to be proud; 1: 36 factions arise among N.; 1: 43 become proud and vain; **Morm.** 2: 1 appoint Mormon² leader of armies; 3: 1 prepare for battle; 3: 9–11 increase in wickedness, Mormon² refuses to lead N.; 4: 1–2 are driven to land of Desolation; 4: 11 N. and Lamanites delight to shed blood; 4: 18 gain no power over Lamanites from this time; 5: 1 Mormon² assumes command of N.; 6: 7–15 all are slain, save twenty-four; 8: 2 N. who escape are hunted, destroyed; **Moro.** 1: 2 are put to death unless they deny Christ; 9: 9 become depraved, lustful, and barbarous; 9: 11 are without civilization.

NEUM—*a Hebrew prophet quoted by Nephi¹*

1 Ne. 19: 10 God to yield himself to be crucified, according to words of N.

NEW (*see also* Jerusalem, New; Renew)

2 Ne. 31: 14 if man who can speak with n. tongue, tongue of angels, denies the Lord, it would have been better not to have known him; **Mosiah** 27: 26 those born of the Spirit become n. creatures; **Hel.** 14: 5 (3 Ne. 1: 21) n. star to appear at Christ's birth; **3 Ne.** 12: 47 (15: 2; 2 Cor. 5: 17) all things have become n.; **Morm.** 9: 24 (Mark 16: 17) they who believe shall speak with n. tongues; **Ether** 13: 9 there shall be a n. heaven and a n. earth.

NIGH (*see also* Near)

2 Ne. 15: 19 (Isa. 5: 19) let counsel of Holy One draw n.; **Jacob** 5: 47, 62, 64, 71 end draweth n.; **Mosiah** 27: 28 after

repenting n. unto death, Alma² is snatched out of everlasting burning; **Alma** 9: 25 kingdom of heaven is n. at hand; 13: 21 day of salvation draweth n.

NIGHT (*see also* Darkness, Physical; Darkness, Spiritual)

1 Ne. 16: 9 the Lord speaks unto Lehi¹ by n.; **2 Ne.** 4: 23 the Lord has given Nephi¹ knowledge by visions in n.; 27: 3 (Isa. 29: 7) all nations that fight against Zion shall be as dream of n. vision; **Alma** 34: 33 after day of this life comes n. of darkness; 41: 5 he who has desired evil all day long shall have reward of evil when n. comes; 41: 7 the redeemed shall be delivered from endless n. of darkness; **Hel.** 14: 4 (3 Ne. 1: 8, 15–19) at Christ's birth one day and n. and day shall be as one day; **3 Ne.** 27: 33 many travel broad way to death until n. cometh; **Moro.** 7: 15 way to judge is as plain as daylight is from dark n.

NIMRAH—*Jaredite, son of Akish*

Ether 9: 8–9 angry with father, flees with small group of men to Omer.

NIMROD¹—*grandson of Ham* (*see also* Nimrod, Valley of; BD Nimrod)

Ether 2: 1 valley named after N., mighty hunter.

NIMROD²—*Jaredite, son of Cohor¹*

Ether 7: 22 gives up kingdom to Shule, gains favors.

NIMROD, VALLEY OF—*in Mesopotamia*

Ether 2: 1 Jaredites travel north to valley of N.; 2: 4 the Lord talks to brother of Jared² in N.

NOAH¹—*patriarch at time of flood* (*see also* BD Noah)

Alma 10: 22 the Lord would not destroy people by flood as in days of N.; **3 Ne.** 22: 9 (Isa. 54: 9) waters of N. no more to go over earth; **Ether** 6: 7 Jaredite vessels are tight like ark of N.

NOAH²—*early Jaredite king, son of Corihor¹*

Ether 7: 14–15 rebels against his father and the king; 7: 16–17 becomes king through battle; 7: 18 is slain by sons of Shule.

NOAH³—*son of Zeniff, king over Nephites in land of Nephi* [c. 160 B.C.] (*see also* Nephi, Land of; Noah³, Priests of)

Mosiah 7: 9 father of Limhi; 11: 1 Zeniff confers kingdom on N.; 11: 2–15 commits many iniquities; 11: 16–19 N's armies drive back the Lamanites; 11: 27 angry with words of Abinadi; 12: 17 imprisons Abinadi; 13: 1 (17: 1) orders Abinadi slain; 18: 33 accuses Alma¹ of

sedition; 19: 8 life spared by Gideon; 19: 9 flees before Lamanites; 19: 11 commands men to desert wives and children; 19: 20 is burned to death; 23: 9 (29: 18) Alma[1] reminds of N's iniquities; 23: 12–13 (Alma 5: 4) people freed from bonds of N.

NOAH, CITY AND LAND OF—*in land of Zarahemla, near Ammonihah*

Alma 49: 12–13 Amalickiah marches toward N.; 49: 14–15 is strengthened by Moroni[1].

NOAH[3], PRIESTS OF—*wicked priests appointed by Noah[3]* (*see also* Amulon; Amulon, Children of; Amulonites)

Mosiah 11: 5 N. puts down priests of his father and appoints new priests; 11: 11 priests' seats are ornamented with gold; 11: 19 people lifted up in pride because of priests; 12: 17 hold council to determine Abinadi's fate; 12: 19 question Abinadi; 12: 25–37 are challenged by Abinadi; 13: 2 are withstood by Abinadi; 13: 5—16: 15 Abinadi preaches to N. and priests; 17: 1 are commanded by king to slay Abinadi; 17: 2–4 Alma[1], one of priests, is converted, flees; 17: 5–20 priests burn Abinadi to death; 17: 15–19 (Alma 25: 7–12) Abinadi prophesies future afflictions of priests' seed; 19: 21 priests flee from angry people; 20: 3 are ashamed to return to wives; 20: 4–5, 18, 23 take daughters of Lamanites for wives; 21: 20–21 Limhi desires to punish priests; 23: 9, 12 Alma[1] reminds of priests' iniquities; 23: 30–31 Lamanite army finds priests; 23: 32–35 priests join Lamanites; 24: 1, 4–6 are appointed teachers over Lamanites; **Alma** 25: 3–5 most of priests are slain in battles with Nephites.

NOBILITY (*see also* Pride; Rich)

Alma 51: 8 those of high birth are favored of kings, seek to be kings; 51: 17–18 Moroni[1] commands army to pull down pride and n. of king-men; 51: 21 Moroni[1] puts end to stubbornness and pride of those who profess n. of blood.

NOISE (*see also* Roar; Sound [noun and verb]; Tumult)

2 Ne. 23: 4 (Isa. 13: 4) n. of multitude in mountain like a great people; 27: 2 nations shall be visited of the Lord with great n.; **Alma** 14: 29 having heard great n., people see Alma[2] and Amulek walk out of fallen prison; **Hel.** 5: 30 voice calling to repentance is not voice of great tumultuous n.; **3 Ne.** 10: 9 tumultuous n. passes away.

NOON-DAY (*see also* Light)

1 Ne. 1: 9 Lehi[1] sees one descending from heaven whose luster is above sun at n.

NORTH, NORTHERN (*see also* Israel, Ten Lost Tribes of)

2 Ne. 29: 11 the Lord commands all men in east, west, n., south; **3 Ne.** 20: 13 scattered remnant shall be gathered from east, west, south, n.; **Ether** 1: 1 Jaredites are destroyed upon face of n. country; 9: 35 rain brings fruit in n. countries; 13: 11 Israel to be gathered from four quarters, from n. countries.

NOTHING, NOTHINGNESS (*see also* Avail; Humble; Naught; Profit)

1 Ne. 2: 4 Lehi[1] takes n. into wilderness save family, provisions, tents; **2 Ne.** 26: 30 (1 Cor. 13: 2) except men have charity they are n.; **Mosiah** 4: 5 knowledge of God's goodness awakens men to sense of their n.; 4: 11 always retain in remembrance the greatness of God and your own n.; **Alma** 26: 12 I know that I am n.; **Hel.** 12: 7 how great is n. of men; **3 Ne.** 12: 13 (16: 15; Matt. 5: 13) salt that has lost savor is good for n. but to be trampled under foot; **Morm.** 9: 21 believe in Christ, doubting n.; **Moro.** 10: 6 n. that is good denieth Christ.

NOTICE (*see also* Heed)

Morm. 8: 39 why do ye suffer the needy to pass by you and n. them not.

NOURISH, NOURISHMENT (*see also* Feed; Food; Nurse; Strength; Strengthen)

1 Ne. 15: 15 remnant of Nephites' seed will receive n. from true vine; 17: 3 if men keep God's commandments, he n. them; 22: 8 (21: 22–23; 22: 6; 2 Ne. 6: 6) remnant of Nephites' seed to be n. by Gentiles; **Jacob** 5: 71 last time the Lord will n. his vineyard; **Alma** 32: 37 if you n. tree with much care, it will get root; 32: 42 because of your diligence in n. the word, ye shall pluck fruit; 33: 23 plant this word in your hearts and n. it by faith; **Moro.** 6: 4 those baptized to be n. by good word of God.

NUMBER

1 Ne. 14: 12 n. of church of Lamb are few; 22: 25 (3 Ne. 18: 31) the Lord n. his sheep; **Mosiah** 14: 12 (Isa. 53: 12) Messiah was n. with transgressors; **Alma** 5: 57 (6: 3; 3 Ne. 18: 31; Moro. 6: 7) names of wicked shall not be n. among names of righteous; **3 Ne.** 16: 3 other sheep to whom Christ will go shall be n. among his sheep.

NURSE, NURSING (*see also* Care; Nourish)

1 Ne. 21: 23 (22: 6; 2 Ne. 6: 7; 10: 9;

Isa. 49: 23) kings and queens shall be Israel's *n*. fathers and mothers.

OATH (see also Covenant; Promise; Secret Combination; Swear)

1 Ne. 4: 35–37 Zoram[1] makes *o*. to tarry with Lehites; **Alma** 37: 27, 29 (Hel. 6: 25) Alma[2] commands Helaman[1] not to reveal *o*. of secret combinations; 44: 8 Zerahemnah refuses to take *o*. not to wage further wars; 49: 27 Amalickiah swears *o*. to drink blood of Moroni[1]; 50: 39 chief judge swears *o*. to keep peace and freedom; 53: 11, 14 (24: 17–19; 56: 8) Ammonites swear *o*. not to take up arms; **Hel.** 6: 21 Nephites enter *o*. of secret combinations; 6: 30 devil hands down *o*. of secret combinations; **3 Ne.** 12: 33 (Matt. 5: 33) perform unto the Lord thine *o*.; **4 Ne.** 1: 42 wicked part of people again build up secret *o*. of Gadianton; **Morm.** 5: 1 Mormon[2] repents of *o*. not to assist Nephites; **Ether** 8: 15 (9: 5) Akish administers secret *o*. handed down from Cain; 8: 20 secret *o*. and combinations have been had among all people; 10: 33 robbers administer *o*. after manner of ancients.

OBEDIENCE, OBEDIENT, OBEY (see also Abide; Agency; Baptism; Blessing; Commandments of God; Diligence; Disobedience; Do; Duty; Endure; Faith; Faithful; Fear of God; Follow; Gospel; Hearken; Heed; Humble; Keep; Law; Observe; Steadfast; Submissive; TG Obedience, Obedient, Obey)

1 Ne. 4: 18 Nephi[1] *o*. voice of Spirit; 22: 31 if ye are *o*. to commandments, ye shall be saved; **2 Ne.** 31: 7 Lamb witnesses that he would be *o*. in keeping commandments; 33: 15 thus hath the Lord commanded me, and I must *o*.; **Jacob** 7: 27 Enos[2] promises *o*. unto commands; **Mosiah** 2: 32–33, 37 he who listeth to *o*. evil spirit receiveth for wages everlasting punishment; 5: 8 all who have entered covenant to be *o*. take upon themselves name of Christ; 29: 23 he who does not *o*. iniquitous king is destroyed; **Alma** 3: 26–27 men reap their reward according to spirit they list to *o*.; 57: 20 Ammonite youth *o*. every command with exactness.

OBSCURITY (see also Darkness, Spiritual)

1 Ne. 22: 12 Israel shall be brought out of *o*.; **2 Ne.** 1: 23 Lehi[1] admonishes sons to come forth out of *o*.; 27: 29 (Isa. 29: 18) eyes of blind shall see out of *o*.

OBSERVE (see also Obedience; Perform)

2 Ne. 32: 6 when Christ manifests himself in flesh, ye shall *o*. to do the things he shall say; **Jacob** 3: 5–6 because

Nephites *o*. commandment to have only one wife, the Lord will not destroy them; **Mosiah** 13: 30 Israelites given law of performances to *o*.; 18: 23 Alma[1] commands his people to *o*. Sabbath day; **Alma** 5: 61 Alma[2] commands people to *o*. words he has spoken; 62: 10 Nephites *o*. law of putting to death king-men who do not take up arms in defence of country; **3 Ne.** 18: 6 Christ commands disciples to *o*. sacrament.

OBTAIN (see also Receive)

2 Ne. 3: 14 promise which Joseph[1] has *o*. of the Lord shall be fulfilled; 9: 46 the devil hath *o*. me; **Jacob** 1: 17 Jacob[2] *o*. his errand from the Lord; 2: 19 after ye have *o*. hope in Christ ye shall *o*. riches; **Hel.** 6: 39 secret combinations *o*. sole management of government; 13: 38 ye have sought all the days of your lives for that which ye could not *o*.; **Ether** 12: 20 brother of Jared[2] *o*. word by faith; **Moro.** 7: 3 peaceable followers of Christ have *o*. sufficient hope to enter his rest.

OFFEND, OFFENDER (see also Anger; Offense)

Alma 35: 15 people are *o*. by strictness of word of Alma[2]; **3 Ne.** 28: 35 do ye suppose ye can get rid of justice of an *o*. God.

OFFENSE (see also Crime; Offend; Transgression; Trespass)

2 Ne. 18: 14 (Isa. 8: 14) he shall be for rock of *o*. to both houses of Israel; **Alma** 41: 9 do not risk one more *o*. against God; 43: 46 if people are not guilty of first or second *o*., they should not suffer themselves to be slain; 48: 14 Nephites are taught never to give *o*.

OFFERING, OFFER (see also Altar; Broken Heart and Contrite Spirit; Gift; Give; Jesus Christ, Atonement through; Law of Moses; Sacrifice)

1 Ne. 2: 7 Lehi[1] builds altar and makes *o*. unto the Lord; 5: 9 (7: 22) Lehites *o*. sacrifice and burnt *o*. unto the Lord; **2 Ne.** 2: 7 Messiah *o*. himself a sacrifice for sin; **Jacob** 4: 5 Abraham was obedient to God's commands in *o*. up Isaac; **Omni** 1: 26 *o*. your whole souls as *o*. unto Christ; **Mosiah** 2: 3 Nephites take firstlings of flock to *o*. sacrifice according to law of Moses; 14: 10 (Isa. 53: 10) thou shalt make his soul an *o*. for sin; **Alma** 31: 23 Zoramites *o*. up thanks upon Rameumptom; **3 Ne.** 9: 19 ye shall *o*. up unto the Lord no more the shedding of blood; 24: 3 (Mal. 3: 3) sons of Levi[1] to *o*. unto the Lord an *o*. in righteousness; **Morm.** 4: 14 Lamanites *o*. women and children as sacrifices to idols.

OFFICE (see also Authority; Calling; Duty;

Ministry; Officer; Ordain; Priesthood, Melchizedek)

Jacob 1: 19 (2: 2–3) Jacob² magnifies o., that blood might not come upon his garments; **Mosiah** 29: 42 Alma¹ confers o. of high priest upon Alma²; **Alma** 4: 18 Alma² retains o. of high priest; 13: 18 Melchizedek received o. of high priesthood according to holy order of God; **Hel.** 7: 5 robbers held in o. at head of government; **Moro.** 7: 31 o. of angels' ministry is to call men to repentance.

OFFICER (*see also* Church of God; Government, Civil; Leader; Minister [noun]; Office)

Alma 11: 2 judge sends forth o. to bring man before him; 14: 17 judge delivers Alma² and Amulek to o. to be cast into prison; 30: 29 Korihor delivered into hands of o. and sent to Alma²; **3 Ne.** 6: 11 many merchants, lawyers, o. in land.

OGATH—*place near hill Ramah*

Ether 15: 10 Jaredites pitch tents in O.

OLD (*see also* Age; Ancient)

1 Ne. 1: 20 Jews angry with Lehi¹, as with prophets of o.; 8: 27 spacious building filled with people, both o. and young; **2 Ne.** 4: 12 Lehi¹ waxes o. and dies; **Mosiah** 1: 9 Benjamin waxes o.; 2: 40 all ye o. men, and young, awake to remembrance of awful situation of transgressors; 10: 10 Zeniff goes up to battle against Lamanites in o. age; 10: 22 being o., Zeniff confers kingdom upon son; **Alma** 1: 30 Nephites are liberal to all, both o. and young; 5: 49 Alma² preaches unto all, both o. and young; 11: 44 restoration shall come to all, both o. and young; 46: 41 many die of o. age; **3 Ne.** 15: 2–3, 7 o. things have passed away; **Ether** 10: 16 Levi² lives to good o. age; 13: 8 remnant of Joseph¹ shall build holy city like Jerusalem of o.; **Moro.** 9: 19 Nephites spare none, neither o. nor young.

OLIVE (*see also* Tree; BD Olive Tree)

1 Ne. 10: 12 (15: 12) house of Israel compared to o. tree; 10: 14 (15: 7, 12–13) natural branches of o. tree, remnants of Israel, to be grafted in; **Jacob** 5: 3 (6: 1) the Lord likens house of Israel to tame o. tree.

OMEGA (*see* Alpha)

OMER—*early Jaredite king*

Ether 1: 29–30 (8: 1; 9: 14) son of Shule, father of Emer; 8: 1 reigns in father's stead, begets Jared³; 8: 2 Jared³ rebels against O., gains half of kingdom; 8: 3–4 battles with Jared³, in captivity

half his days; 8: 4 begets Esrom and Coriantumr¹ in captivity; 8: 5–6 sons regain kingdom for O.; 8: 7–12 Jared³ and daughter plot with Akish to murder O.; 9: 1 secret combination of Akish overthrows kingdom of O.; 9: 2–3 escapes with family because of the Lord's warning; 9: 9 Nimrah flees to O.; 9: 12–13 is restored to land of his inheritance; 8: 14 anoints Emer king to reign in his stead.

OMNER—*son of Mosiah²* [c. 100 B.C.] (*see also* Mosiah², Sons of)

Mosiah 27: 8 an unbeliever; 27: 10 seeks to destroy church; 27: 32 is converted by angel; 27: 34 is named among sons of Mosiah²; 27: 35–37 preaches gospel; 28: 1–9 is allowed to preach in land of Nephi; 28: 10 (29: 3; Alma 17: 6) refuses to become king; **Alma** 17: 1–3 (27: 16–19) meets Alma with joy; 23: 1 is protected by proclamation of king; 24: 5 travels with brothers to Midian; 25: 17 rejoices with brethren over their success; 31: 6–7 goes with Ammon² to Zoramites; 35: 14 returns to Zarahemla.

OMNER, CITY OF—*Nephite city by seashore on east borders*

Alma 51: 26 possessed by Amalickiah.

OMNI—*Nephite record keeper* [c. 361 B.C.]

Jarom 1: 15 (Omni 1: 1) son of Jarom, is given plates; **Omni** 1: 2 fights with Lamanites, has not fully kept commandments; 1: 3 confers plates upon his son Amaron.

OMNIPOTENT (*see* God, Power of)

ONE (*see also* Unite, Unity)

1 Ne. 13: 41 records of Nephites' seed and of twelve apostles shall be established in o.; 13: 41 there is o. God over all the earth; 17: 35 the Lord esteemeth all flesh in o.; 22: 25 (3 Ne. 15: 17; 16: 3; John 10: 16) o. fold and o. shepherd; **2 Ne.** 25: 18 o. Messiah spoken of by prophets; 31: 21 (Mosiah 15: 2–5; Alma 11: 44; 3 Ne. 11: 27, 36; Morm. 7: 7) Father, Son, and Holy Ghost are o. God; **Jacob** 2: 21 the o. being is as precious in God's sight as the other; **Mosiah** 15: 4 (3 Ne. 11: 27; 19: 23, 29; 20: 35; 28: 10; John 10: 30; 17: 11, 21–22) Christ and the Father are o.; 18: 21 (Eph. 4: 4–6) Nephites should look forward with o. eye, having o. faith and o. baptism; 23: 7 ye shall not esteem o. flesh above another; **Alma** 11: 28–29, 35 (14: 5; Deut. 6: 4; Gal. 3: 20; Eph. 4: 5–6) there is only o. God; **3 Ne.** 23: 14 Jesus expounds all the scriptures in o.; **4 Ne.** 1: 17 Nephites are in o., children of Christ; **Moro.** 7: 17 devil persuades no man to do good, no, not o.

ONIDAH—*gathering place for dissatisfied Lamanites*

Alma 47: 5 Amalickiah goes to place of O.

ONIDAH, HILL—*in land of Antionum*

Alma 32: 4 Alma² speaks to multitude from hill O.

ONIHAH, CITY OF

3 **Ne.** 9: 7 destroyed at time of crucifixion.

ONLY BEGOTTEN (*see* Jesus Christ—Only Begotten Son)

ONTI—*silver coin* (*see also* Coin)

Alma 11: 6, 13 silver coin whose value is as great as them all; 11: 22 Zeezrom offers Amulek six o. to deny God.

OPEN (*see also* Answer; Openly)

1 **Ne.** 1: 8 Lehi¹ sees heavens o.; 11: 14 (12: 6) Nephi¹ sees heavens o.; **2 Ne:** 7: 5 (Isa. 50: 5) the Lord hath o. mine ear; 9: 42 (3 Ne. 14: 7–8; 27: 29; Matt. 7: 7–8) whoso knocketh, to him will the Lord o.; **Mosiah** 2: 9 o. your ears that ye may hear; 14: 7 (15: 6; Isa. 53: 7) he was afflicted, yet he o. not his mouth; 27: 22 priests fast and pray that the Lord might o. mouth of Alma² and o. eyes of people to see goodness and glory of God.

OPENLY (*see also* Open)

3 **Ne.** 13: 4, 6 (Matt. 7: 4, 6) give alms and pray in secret, that Father reward thee o.

OPINION (*see also* Belief)

Alma 40: 20 Alma² gives o. that souls and bodies are reunited at resurrection of Christ.

OPPOSITION, OPPOSITE (*see also* Agency; Probation; Sweet; Trial; Try; TG Opposition)

2 **Ne.** 2: 10 punishment that is affixed is in o. to happiness which is affixed; 2: 11, 15 o. in all things; 2: 15 forbidden fruit set in o. to tree of life; **Alma** 41: 12–13 restoration does not mean to place a thing in state o. to its nature; 42: 16 eternal punishment affixed o. plan of eternal happiness.

OPPRESSION, OPPRESS (*see also* Affliction; Malice; Oppressor; Persecution; Suffering; Trial; Try; Tribulation)

1 **Ne.** 21: 26 (Isa. 49: 26) I will feed them that o. thee with their own flesh; 2 **Ne.** 13: 5 (Isa. 3: 5) the people shall be o., every one by another; 15: 7 (Isa. 5: 7) he looked for judgment, and behold, o.; **Mosiah** 13: 35 (14: 7; Isa. 53: 7) he him-

self should be o. and afflicted; 23: 12 people of Alma¹ have been o. by king Noah³; **Hel.** 4: 11–12 great slaughter among Nephites caused by their o. to the poor; **3 Ne.** 22: 14 (Isa. 54: 14) thou shalt be far from o.; 24: 5 (Mal. 3: 5) I will be swift witness against those that o. hireling in his wages.

OPPRESSOR (*see also* Oppression)

2 **Ne.** 8: 13 (Isa. 51: 13) thou hast feared continually every day because of fury of the o.; 13: 12 (Isa. 3: 12) children are o. of the Lord's people; 19: 4 (Isa. 9: 4) thou hast broken the rod of his o.; 24: 2 (Isa. 14: 2) they shall rule over their o.

ORDAIN, ORDINATION (*see also* Appoint; Authority; Confer; Decree; Hands, Laying on of; Office; Ordinance; Priesthood; TG Priesthood, Ordination)

1 **Ne.** 12: 7 Twelve were o. and chosen; 14: 25 the Lord hath o. apostle of Lamb to write these things; **2 Ne.** 6: 2 Jacob² is o. after manner of God's holy order; **Mosiah** 18: 18 having authority from God, Alma¹ o. priests; 25: 19 Mosiah² gives Alma¹ power to o. priests and teachers over every church; **Alma** 6: 1 Alma² o. priests and teachers by laying on of hands; 13: 1–3 (49: 30) the Lord o. priests after his holy order to teach people; 13: 6–8 men are o. unto high priesthood with holy ordinances; **3 Ne.** 7: 25 Nephi³ o. men to baptize; 18: 5 one to be o. to administer sacrament to people; **4 Ne.** 1: 14 other disciples are o. instead of original disciples; **Moro.** ch. 3 manner of o. priests and teachers.

ORDER (*see also* Authority; Govern; Head; Law; Priesthood; Regulate; Unite; TG Order)

2 **Ne.** 6: 2 (Alma 5: 44; 6: 8; 13: 1–3, 6–11; 43: 2; Hel. 8: 18; Ether 12: 10) teachers are ordained after manner of God's holy o.; 19: 7 (Isa. 9: 7) of increase of government and peace there is no end upon his kingdom to o. it; **Mosiah** 4: 27 all things must be done in o.; **Alma** 4: 20 (13: 1, 6–11) high priesthood of holy o. of God; 6: 4 (8: 1) Alma² establishes o. of church; 13: 2, 6–9 (Hel. 8: 18) high priesthood after o. of the Son; 14: 16 (21: 4; 24: 28) apostates are after o. of Nehors; 41: 2 all things should be restored to proper o.; **3 Ne.** 6: 4 great o. in the land; **Moro.** 9: 18 Nephites are without o. and mercy.

ORDINANCE (*see also* Anointing; Authority; Baptism; Blessing; Confer; Confirm; Covenant; Hands, Laying on of; Heal; Holy Ghost, Gift of; Law; Ordain; Priesthood; Sacrament; Sacrifice; Statute; Temple; TG Ordinance)

2 Ne. 25: 30 keep performances and o. until law is fulfilled; **Mosiah** 13: 30 children of Israel given law of performances and o. to keep them in remembrance of God; **Alma** 13: 8 high priests ordained with holy o.; 13: 16 o. given that people might look forward on Son; 30: 3 Nephites are strict in observing o. according to law of Moses; 50: 39 chief judge appointed with sacred o. to judge righteously; **3 Ne.** 24: 7 (Mal. 3: 7) ye are gone away from mine o., 24: 14 (Mal. 3: 14) what doth it profit that we have kept God's o.; **4 Ne.** 1: 12 Nephites no longer walk after o. of law of Moses.

ORE (*see also* Copper; Gold; Iron; Metal; Silver; Stone [noun])

1 Ne. 17: 9 Nephi¹ asks the Lord where he can find o. for tools; 18: 25 Lehites find all manner of o. in wilderness; 19: 1 Nephi¹ makes plates of o.; **2 Ne.** 5: 15 Nephi¹ teaches people to work in precious o.; **Jacob** 2: 12 Nephites search for precious o.; **Mosiah** 21: 27 record of Jaredites engraven on plates of o.; **Hel.** 6: 11 precious o. of every kind in promised land; **Ether** 10: 23 Jaredites work in all manner of o.

ORIHAH—*first Jaredite king*

Ether 1: 32 (6: 27; 7: 3) son of Jared², father of Kib; 6: 27 is anointed king; 6: 28—7: 1 reigns righteously; 7: 2 begets twenty-three sons, eight daughters; 7: 3 is succeeded by son Kib.

ORPHAN (*see also* Needy)

Morm. 8: 40 why do ye cause o. to mourn before the Lord.

OUTER (*see* Darkness, Spiritual; Outward; Vessel)

OUTWARD (*see also* Temporal)

Alma 25: 15 Nephites keep o. performances until time when Christ shall be revealed; **3 Ne.** 4: 16 robbers plan to make Nephites yield by cutting them off from o. privileges.

OVEN (*see also* Furnace)

3 Ne. 13: 30 (Matt. 6: 30) grass of field tomorrow is cast into o.; 25: 1 (Mal. 4: 1) day cometh that shall burn as o.

OVERBEARANCE (*see also* Compel)

Alma 38: 12 use boldness, but not o.

OVERCOME (*see also* Conquer; Overpower; Prevail)

1 Ne. 1: 7 Lehi¹ casts himself upon bed, o. with Spirit; 12: 20 Lamanites to o. Nephites; **Jacob** 5: 59, 66 good branches may o. evil; **Alma** 19: 6 light of everlasting light had o. Lamoni's natural frame; **3 Ne.** 17: 18 so great is joy of multitude that they are o.

OVERPOWER (*see also* Overcome)

1 Ne. 15: 24 fiery darts of adversary cannot o. those who hearken to word of God; **Alma** 19: 13–14 Lamanite king and queen o. by Spirit; 34: 15 bowels of mercy o. justice; 34: 39 be watchful unto prayer continually, that devil may not o. you; 53: 14 Ammonites o. by persuasions of Helaman² not to break oath; **3 Ne.** 10: 13 righteous are not o. by vapor of smoke and darkness; **Ether** 12: 24 things written by brother of Jared² were mighty unto o. of man to read them.

OVERSHADOW

Alma 7: 10 Mary shall be o. and conceive by power of Holy Ghost; **Hel.** 5: 28, 34 Lamanites are o. with cloud of darkness; **3 Ne.** 18: 38–39 cloud o. multitude, that they cannot see Jesus.

OVERTAKE, OVERTOOK, OVERTAKEN

3 Ne. 29: 4 if ye spurn at the Lord's doings, sword of his justice will o. you; **Morm.** 4: 5 judgments of God will o. the wicked.

OVERTHROW, OVERTHREW (*see also* Conquer; Destruction; Overcome)

2 Ne. 23: 19 (Isa. 13: 19) Babylon shall be as when God o. Sodom and Gomorrah; **Jacob** 7: 2 Sherem flatters people that he might o. doctrine of Christ; **Mosiah** 27: 13 nothing shall o. God's church save transgression; **Alma** 50: 32 flight of people of Morianton² to north may lead to o. of liberty; 51: 5 king-men desire to alter law to o. free government; **Hel.** 2: 13 Gadianton proves o. of Nephites; **Ether** 8: 25 he who builds secret combinations seeks to o. freedom of all lands.

OWE (*see also* Debt; Duty; Indebted)

Alma 11: 2 if a man would not pay what he o. to another, he was complained of to judge; 44: 5 Nephites o. sacred support to wives and children; 44: 5 Nephites o. all happiness to sacred word of God; 57: 22 Nephites o. victory to Ammonite youths.

OX, OXEN (*see also* Animal; Cattle)

1 Ne. 18: 25 Lehites find o. in wilderness in promised land; **2 Ne.** 21: 7 (Isa. 11: 7) lion shall eat straw like o.; **Ether** 9: 18 Jaredites have o.

PAANCHI—*son of Pahoran¹* [c. 52 B.C.] (*see also* Pacumeni; Pahoran²)

Hel. 1: 3 contends for judgment-seat;

1: 7 plans to flatter people into rebellion; 1: 8 is tried and condemned to death.

PACHUS—*king of Nephite dissenters* [c. 61 B.C.]

Alma 62: 6 king of dissenters who had driven freemen from Zarahemla; 62: 7 battles with Moroni¹ and Pahoran¹; 62: 8 is slain.

PACIFY (*see also* Peace)

1 Ne. 15: 20 through words of Nephi¹ his brothers are *p.* and humbled; 2 Ne. 28: 21 devil will *p.* men and lull them into carnal security; Mosiah 20: 20 except Limhi *p.* Lamanites, his people perish.

PACUMENI—*son of Pahoran¹* [c. 52 B.C.] (*see also* Paanchi; Pahoran²)

Hel. 1: 3 contends for judgment-seat; 1: 6 submits to voice of people; 1: 13 is appointed chief judge and governor; 1: 21 is slain by Coriantumr³.

PAGAG—*son of brother of Jared²*

Ether 6: 25 refuses to be king.

PAHORAN¹—*third Nephite chief judge* [c. 68 B.C.]

Alma 50: 39–40 fills judgment-seat of his father, Nephihah; 51: 2–5 contends with king-men; 51: 6 P's supporters are called freemen; 51: 7 retains judgment-seat by voice of people; 51: 15–16 grants Moroni¹ power to compel dissenters to defend country; 59: 3 Moroni¹ writes to P. requesting reinforcements; ch. 60 Moroni¹ writes second epistle, complaining of neglect; ch. 61 P's reply to epistle; 61: 5, 8 is driven from Zarahemla by king-men; 61: 9 seeks not power, but to preserve rights and liberty of people; 62: 6 is joined by Moroni¹; 62: 7–8 returns to Zarahemla, is restored to judgment-seat; 62: 11 helps in restoring peace; 62: 14 marches to Nephihah; 62: 26 takes city of Nephihah without losses; 62: 34 returns to judgment-seat; Hel. 1: 2 dies.

PAHORAN²—*son of Pahoran¹, fourth Nephite chief judge* [c. 52 B.C.] (*see also* Paanchi; Pacumeni)

Hel. 1: 3 contends for judgment-seat; 1: 5 is appointed chief judge by voice of people; 1: 9 is murdered by Kishkumen.

PAID (*see* Pay, Paid)

PAIN (*see also* Affliction; Anguish; Grieve; Sorrow; Suffering; Torment)

1 Ne. 17: 47 heart of Nephi¹ is *p.* because of brothers; 2 Ne. 9: 21 God suffereth *p.* of all men; 26: 7 Nephi¹ feels *p.* for the slain of his people; Jacob 3: 11 loose yourselves from *p.* of hell; Mosiah 2: 38 demands of justice fill breast of wicked with *p.* like unquenchable fire; 3: 7 the Lord shall suffer *p.* of body; 25: 11 Nephites filled with *p.* for welfare of Lamanites' souls; 27: 29 Alma² is snatched, and his soul is *p.* no more; Alma 7: 11 Son will take upon him the *p.* of his people; 13: 27 Alma² wishes with anxiety unto *p.* that people would hearken; 14: 6 Zeezrom is encircled by *p.* of hell; 26: 13 how many thousands of Lamanites has God loosed from *p.* of hell; 31: 30 wickedness among Zoramites *p.* soul of Alma²; 36: 13, 16 (38: 8) Alma² remembered all his sins and was tormented by *p.* of hell; 36: 19–20 Alma² was filled with joy as exceeding as was his *p.*; 3 Ne. 28: 8–9, 38 three Nephites will not have *p.* in flesh or endure *p.* of death.

PALACE (*see also* Building)

2 Ne. 23: 22 (Isa. 13: 22) dragons shall cry in their pleasant *p.*; Mosiah 11: 9 Noah³ builds spacious *p.*; Alma 22: 2 Aaron³ goes to Lamanite king in his *p.*

PARABLE (*see also* Liken; BD Parables)

Jacob ch. 5 allegory of tame and wild olive-trees.

PARADISE (*see also* Death, Physical; Eden, Garden of; Heaven; Prison; Rest; Resurrection; Spirit World; TG Paradise, Paradisiacal; BD Paradise)

2 Ne. 9: 13 *p.* of God must deliver up its dead; Alma 40: 12, 14 spirits of righteous remain in state of happiness, called *p.*, until resurrection; 4 Ne. 1: 14 Jesus' disciples are gone to *p.* of God; Moro. 10: 34 Moroni² will soon go to rest in *p.* of God.

PARENT (*see also* Child; Family; Father; Mother; TG Family, Children, Responsibilities toward; Honoring Father and Mother; Marriage, Fatherhood; Marriage, Motherhood)

1 Ne. 1: 1 Nephi¹ born of goodly *p.*; 5: 11 Adam and Eve, our first *p.*; 8: 37 Lehi¹ exhorts elder sons with all the feeling of tender *p.*; 2 Ne. 1: 14 hear the words of trembling *p.*; 4: 6 Lehi¹ takes cursing from grandchildren, to be answered upon heads of *p.*; Jacob 4: 3 Nephites labor, that children may learn with joy concerning first *p.*; Omni 1: 22 first *p.* of Coriantumr² came out from tower; Alma 30: 25 child is not guilty because of *p.*; Hel. 5: 5–6 Helaman² reminds sons of names of first *p.* who came out of Jerusalem; Moro. 8: 10 teach *p.* that they must repent, be baptized, and humble themselves as their little children.

PART (see also Partake; Portion)

2 **Ne.** 2: 30 Lehi¹ has chosen the good p.; **Mosiah** 15: 24 (Rev. 20: 6) those who died before Christ came shall have p. in first resurrection; 29: 34 every man should bear his p.; **Alma** 40: 13 spirits of wicked have no p. or portion of Spirit of the Lord.

PARTAKE, PARTAKEN, PARTAKER (see also Drink; Eat; Inherit; Receive; Taste)

1 **Ne.** 8: 11–12 Lehi¹ p. of fruit of tree of life; 8: 15–16 Sariah, Sam, and Nephi¹ p. of fruit; 8: 17–18 Laman¹ and Lemuel do not p. of fruit; 8: 24 those who cling to iron rod p. of fruit; **2 Ne.** 2: 18 (Hel. 6: 26) devil tempts Eve to p. of forbidden fruit; 26: 24 the Lord commands none that they shall not p. of salvation; **Jacob** 1: 7 come unto Christ and p. of goodness of God; **Omni** 1: 26 come unto Christ and p. of his salvation; **Alma** 5: 34 come unto the Lord and you shall p. of fruit of tree of life; 5: 62 those who are baptized may be p. of fruit of tree of life; 12: 23, 26 (42: 5) if Adam had p. of tree of life, there would have been no death; 42: 27 whosoever will may come and p. of waters of life; **3 Ne.** 18: 28 (Morm. 9: 29) ye shall not suffer any one knowingly to p. of sacrament unworthily; **4 Ne.** 1: 3 Nephites are all made free, and p. of the heavenly gift; **Ether** 12: 8 Christ has prepared way by which others may be p. of heavenly gift; **Moro.** 4: 3 bread is blessed to souls of those who p.; 6: 6 saints meet together oft to p. of bread and wine; 8: 17 all children are alike and p. of salvation.

PASS (see also Cease; End; Judgment; Past; Vanish)

1 **Ne.** 17: 46 (Alma 9: 2; 3 Ne. 26: 3; Ether 13: 8; Matt. 24: 35) earth shall p. away; **3 Ne.** 1: 25 (Matt. 5: 18) not one jot or tittle should p. away until all should be fulfilled.

PASSION (see also Anger; Feeling; Fury; Rage)

Alma 38: 12 bridle all your p.; 50: 30 Morianton² a man of much p.

PAST (see also Pass; Present)

1 **Ne.** 17: 45 brothers of Nephi¹ are p. feeling; **Mosiah** 8: 17 a seer can know of things that are p.; **Hel.** 13: 38 your days of probation are p.; **3 Ne.** 1: 5–6 some say time is p. when signs of Christ's birth should be given; **Moro.** 9: 20 Nephites are without principle, and p. feeling.

PASTOR (see also Shepherd; TG Pastor)

1 **Ne.** 21: 1 Israel is broken off because of wickedness of p.

PASTURE (see Sheep)

PATH (see also Course; Direction; Highway; Road; Street; Walk; Way)

1 **Ne.** 8: 20–23 Lehi¹ beholds strait and narrow p. leading to tree of life; 8: 28 those who have tasted fruit but become ashamed fall into forbidden p.; 10: 8 (Alma 7: 19) John shall cry, Prepare way of the Lord, make his p. strait; 16: 5 Nephi¹ hopes brothers will walk in p. of righteousness; **2 Ne.** 4: 32–33 wilt thou make my p. straight before me; 12: 3 (Isa. 2: 3) God will teach us his ways, and we will walk in his p.; 13: 12 (Isa. 3: 12) they who lead the Lord's people cause them to destroy the way of their p.; 31: 9 Christ's baptism shows men the straitness of the p.; 31: 19 after ye have gotten into strait and narrow p., is all done; 33: 9 only those who walk in strait p. which leads to life have hope; **Mosiah** 2: 36 if men withdraw themselves from Spirit, it has no place to guide them in wisdom's p.; **Alma** 7: 9 repent, prepare way of the Lord, walk in his p.; 7: 19 I perceive ye are in p. of righteousness, p. which leads to kingdom of God; 7: 20 God cannot walk in crooked p.; 37: 12 God's p. are straight; **Hel.** 15: 5 more part of Lamanites are in p. of their duty.

PATIENCE, PATIENT, PATIENTLY (see also Affliction; Humble; Long-suffering)

Mosiah 3: 19 natural man is enemy to God unless he becomes as child, p.; 23: 21 the Lord tries his people's p.; 24: 15 Alma¹ and his people submit with p. to the Lord's will; **Alma** 1: 25 the faithful bear persecution with p.; 7: 23 be humble, full of p.; 9: 26 Son of God shall be full of p.; 13: 28 be led by Holy Spirit, becoming p.; 17: 11 sons of Mosiah² are commanded to be p. among Lamanites; 20: 29 brothers of Ammon² had been p. in sufferings; 26: 27 bear with p. thine afflictions; 32: 41 if ye nourish tree with p., it shall spring forth unto everlasting life; 32: 43 ye shall reap rewards of your p.; 34: 3 Alma² exhorted poor Zoramites unto faith and p.; 34: 40 Amulek exhorts poor Zoramites to have p., bear afflictions; 38: 4 Shiblon bore persecutions with p. because the Lord was with him.

PAY, PAID (see also Debt; Repay; Reward; Tax; Tithing; Tribute; Wages)

Mosiah 2: 24 the Lord will bless the obedient, therefore he hath p. them; **Alma** 11: 2 if a man did not p. another what he owed, he was taken before judge; **3 Ne.** 12: 26 (Matt. 5: 26) thou shalt not come from prison until thou hast p. the uttermost senine.

PEACE (see also Calm; Pacify; Peaceable,

Peaceably; Peacemaker; Rest; War; TG Peace of God)

1 Ne. 13: 37 (Mosiah 12: 21; 15: 15–18; 3 Ne. 20: 40; Isa. 52: 7) how beautiful upon mountains are feet of him who publishes *p.*; 14: 7 the Lord will convince men unto *p.* or deliver them to hardness of heart; 20: 18 (Isa. 48: 18) if thou hadst hearkened unto my commandment, then had thy *p.* been as a river; 20: 22 (Isa. 48: 22) there is no *p.* unto the wicked; **2 Ne.** 3: 12 writings of Nephites and Jews shall grow together unto establishing *p.*; 4: 27 why should I yield to temptation, that evil one have place in my heart to destroy my *p.*; 19: 6 (Isa. 9: 6) Messiah shall be called, The Prince of *P.*; 19: 7 (Isa. 9: 7) of increase of government and *p.* there is no end; 26: 9 (4 Ne. 1: 4) Son shall appear, and Nephites shall have *p.* until three generations have passed; **Jacob** 7: 23 (W of M 1: 18; Alma 3: 24) *p.* restored again among Nephites; **Mosiah** 4: 3 Benjamin's people receive remission of sins and have *p.* of conscience; 19: 27 Limhi establishes *p.* among his people; 27: 37 sons of Mosiah² publish *p.*; 29: 14, 40 Mosiah² has labored to establish *p.* throughout the land; **Alma** 7: 27 may *p.* of God rest upon you; 13: 18 Melchizedek established *p.*, was called prince of *p.*; 24: 19 converted Lamanites bury weapons of war for *p.*; 38: 8 after three days and nights of anguish Alma² cried unto the Lord and found *p.*; 40: 12 spirits of righteous are received into paradise, a state of *p.*; 44: 14 Nephites will slay Lamanites unless they depart with covenant of *p.*; 58: 11 the Lord speaks *p.* to our souls; **Hel.** 5: 47 *p.* be unto you because of your faith; **3 Ne.** 22: 10 covenant of *p.* shall not be removed; **4 Ne.** 1: 4 *p.* in land following Christ's visit.

PEACEABLE, PEACEABLY (*see also* Peace)

Mosiah 4: 13 ye will not have mind to injure one another, but to live *p.*; **Moro.** 7: 3–4 Mormon² speaks to *p.* followers of Christ, whom he recognizes because of their *p.* walk with men.

PEACEMAKER

3 Ne. 12: 9 (Matt. 5: 9) blessed are *p.*, for they shall be called children of God.

PEARL (*see also* Precious)

3 Ne. 14: 6 (Matt. 7: 6) cast not your *p.* before swine; **4 Ne.** 1: 24 Nephites begin to be proud, wearing fine *p.*

PENALTY (*see also* Punishment)

Alma 12: 32 *p.* of doing evil is second death.

PENETRATE (*see also* Pierce)

Alma 26: 6 storm shall not *p.* to converts.

PENITENT (*see also* Humble; Repentance)

Alma 26: 21 none knoweth these things save the *p.*; 27: 18 none receive joy of God save truly *p.* seeker of happiness; 29: 10 when I see many of my brethren truly *p.*, my soul is filled with joy; 32: 7 Alma² says no more to multitude, but cries unto *p.*; 42: 23 mercy claimeth the *p.*; 42: 24 none but truly *p.* are saved; **3 Ne.** 6: 13 some are lifted up in pride, others are humble and *p.*

PEOPLE (*see also* Nation)

1 Ne. 5: 18 brass plates to go to every *p.*; 11: 36 thus shall be destruction of all *p.* that fight against apostles; 13: 40 records shall make known to all *p.* that Lamb is Son of Father; 14: 11 whore of all the earth has dominion among all *p.*; 17: 35 this *p.* had rejected every word of God; 19: 17 (Mosiah 16: 1) every *p.* shall see salvation of the Lord; 22: 28 all *p.* shall dwell safely in Holy One if they repent; **2 Ne.** 5: 9 those who are with Nephi¹ call themselves the *p.* of Nephi; 8: 16 (Isa. 51: 16) Zion, thou art my *p.*; 23: 14 (Isa. 13: 14) every man shall turn to own *p.*; 26: 13 Christ will manifest himself unto every *p.* that believe; 29: 4–5 Jews, the Lord's ancient covenant *p.*; 29: 14 the Lord's *p.*, who are of house of Israel, shall be gathered; **Omni** 1: 14 Nephites discover a *p.* called the *p.* of Zarahemla; **Mosiah** 1: 11 Benjamin will give his *p.* a name; 3: 20 knowledge of Savior shall spread through every *p.*; 15: 28 salvation of the Lord shall be declared to every *p.*; 18: 8, 10 as ye desire to be called God's *p.*, what have ye against being baptized; 27: 25 all *p.* must be born again; **Alma** 4: 12 great inequality among the *p.*; 26: 37 God is mindful of every *p.*; **3 Ne.** 20: 39 my *p.* shall know my name; 28: 29 three Nephites shall minister unto all *p.*; **4 Ne.** 1: 16 there could not be happier *p.* among all *p.* created by God.

PERCEIVE (*see also* Comprehend; Discern; Know; See; Understand)

2 Ne. 16: 9 (Isa. 6: 9) see ye indeed, but they *p.* not; 32: 8 I *p.* that ye ponder still; **Jacob** 4: 15 Jacob² *p.* by workings of Spirit; **Mosiah** 13: 7 I *p.* that my message cuts you to your hearts; 13: 11 I *p.* that commandments are not written in your hearts; **Alma** 7: 19 I *p.* that ye are in paths of righteousness; 10: 17 Amulek *p.* lawyers' thoughts; 18: 16 Ammon², filled with Spirit, *p.* king's thoughts; 40: 1 (41: 1; 42: 1) I *p.* that thy mind is worried; 43: 48 Moroni¹ *p.* intent of his men to shrink from Lamanites; **3 Ne.**

15: 2 Jesus *p.* that some wonder concerning law of Moses; 17: 2 I *p.* that ye are weak, that ye cannot understand all my words; **Morm.** 1: 2 I *p.* that thou art a sober child.

PERFECT, PERFECTED, PERFECTION (*see also* Godliness; Just; Perfectness; Righteousness; Uprightness; TG Perfection)

2 **Ne.** 9: 13 in resurrection our knowledge shall be *p.*; 9: 14 we shall have *p.* knowledge of our guilt; 9: 23 be baptized, having *p.* faith in Holy One; 31: 20 press forward with steadfastness in Christ, having *p.* brightness of hope; **Jacob** 4: 12 attain unto *p.* knowledge of Christ; 7: 4 Sherem has *p.* knowledge of language; **Alma** 5: 18 can ye imagine yourselves brought before God with *p.* remembrance of guilt; 11: 43–44 (40: 23) spirit and body shall be reunited in *p.* form; 32: 21, 26 faith is not to have *p.* knowledge; 32: 26 ye cannot know of their surety at first unto *p.*; 32: 34 your knowledge is *p.* in that thing and your faith is dormant; 42: 15 atonement made that God might be *p.*, just, and merciful God; 48: 11 Moroni[1] a man of *p.* understanding; 50: 37 Nephihah filled judgment-seat with *p.* uprightness before God; 55: 1 Ammoron has *p.* knowledge of his fraud; **Hel.** 5: 30 those in prison hear still small voice of *p.* mildness; **3 Ne.** 12: 48 (Matt. 5: 48) I would that ye should be *p.*, even as I, or your Father is *p.*; **Ether** 3: 7, 20 having *p.* knowledge of God, brother of Jared could not be kept within veil; **Moro.** 7: 15–17 way to judge is plain, that ye may know with *p.* knowledge; 8: 16 (1 John 4: 18) *p.* love casteth out fear; 10: 32 come unto Christ and be *p.* in him; 10: 32 by God's grace ye may be *p.* in Christ.

PERFECTNESS (*see also* Perfect)

2 **Ne.** 9: 46 prepare your souls that ye may not remember your awful guilt in *p.*

PERFORM, PERFORMANCE (*see also* Accomplish; Do; Duty; Fulfil; Observe; Undertake)

1 **Ne.** 17: 41 labor which Israelites had to *p.* was to look; **2 Ne.** 25: 30 ye must keep *p.* and ordinances of God until law is fulfilled; 32: 9 ye must not *p.* any thing unto the Lord without first praying that Father consecrate thy *p.*; **Mosiah** 13: 30 Israelites given law of *p.* and ordinances to keep them in remembrance of God; **Alma** 25: 15 Nephites keep outward *p.* until Christ shall be revealed; 31: 10 Zoramites would not observe *p.* of church; 34: 32 this life is day for men to *p.* labors; 34: 33 after this life cometh night of darkness, wherein no labor can

be *p.*; 57: 21 Ammonite youth *p.* every command with exactness; **4 Ne.** 1: 12 Nephites do not walk any more after *p.* and ordinances of law of Moses; **Moro.** 9: 6 we have labor to *p.* while in tabernacle of clay.

PERISH (*see also* Destruction; Die)

1 **Ne.** 4: 13 better that one man should *p.* than nation dwindle in unbelief; 5: 19 brass plates should never *p.*; 15: 10 how is it ye will *p.* because of hardness of heart; 17: 41 (Alma 33: 20) because of simpleness of means of healing, many *p.*; 22: 19 the righteous shall not *p.*; **2 Ne.** 1: 4 if Lehites had stayed in Jerusalem, they would have *p.*; 6: 11 many Jews shall be afflicted in flesh and not suffered to *p.* because of prayers of righteous; 9: 30 treasure of the rich shall *p.* with them; 9: 51 feast upon that which *p.* not; 10: 13 they who fight against Zion shall *p.*; 25: 21 Joseph[1] received promise that his seed should never *p.*; 26: 30 if men have charity, they would not suffer laborer in Zion to *p.*; 26: 31 if laborers in Zion labor for money, they shall *p.*; 27: 26 (Isa. 29: 14) wisdom of wise and learned shall *p.*; 28: 16 when men are fully ripe in iniquity, they shall *p.*; 30: 1 except ye keep commandments of God, ye shall *p.*; **Jacob** 5: 4 master to nourish tree that it *p.* not; 5: 11 master will preserve roots, that they *p.* not; **Mosiah** 3: 18 the infant *p.* not who dies in infancy; 4: 22–23 wo unto him who withholds his substance, for it shall *p.* with him; 4: 30 O man, remember and *p.* not; 13: 28 (Alma 34: 9) except for atonement, men must unavoidably *p.*; 28: 3 sons of Mosiah[2] cannot bear that any soul should *p.*; **Alma** 53: 11 according to oath not to take up arms, Ammonites would have *p.*; **Hel.** 4: 25 except Nephites cleave unto the Lord, they must unavoidably *p.*; 14: 30 whosoever *p.*, *p.* unto himself; **Ether** 2: 19 without air in vessels, Jaredites would *p.*; **Moro.** 8: 16 they who pervert ways of the Lord shall *p.*

PERMIT (*see also* Suffer)

Mosiah 7: 8 Ammon[1] and brethren are *p.* to answer king's questions; **Hel.** 14: 30 men are *p.* to act for themselves; **Moro.** 7: 2 because of gift of his calling from the Lord, Mormon[2] is *p.* to speak to people.

PERSECUTION, PERSECUTE (*see also* Affliction; Chasten; Hate; Malice; Martyrdom; Mock; Oppression; Revile; Scourge; Smite; Spurn; Stone [verb]; Tread; Tribulation; Trial)

2 **Ne.** 9: 30 because they are rich, they *p.* the meek; 26: 8 the righteous who look forward to Christ, notwithstanding

p., shall not perish; **Jacob** 2: 13 because some have obtained more abundantly, they *p.* their brethren; **Mosiah** 26: 38 Alma¹ and fellow laborers are *p.* by those not of church; 27: 1 *p.* inflicted on church by unbelievers become so great the church murmurs; 27: 2 Mosiah² sends proclamation that no unbeliever should *p.* church member; 27: 13 why *p.* thou the church of God; 27: 32 Alma² and companions are *p.* by unbelievers; **Alma** 1: 21 strict law in church that no member should *p.* one who does not belong; 1: 25 those who stand steadfast in faith bear the *p.* with patience; 5: 54 will ye persist in *p.* your brethren; **Hel.** 3: 34 many who profess to belong to church are lifted up in pride unto *p.* their brethren; 13: 22 your hearts swell with great pride, unto *p.*; **3 Ne.** 6: 13 some receive *p.* and do not turn and revile again; 12: 10–11 (Matt. 5: 10–11) blessed are all who are *p.* for their Lord's sake, for theirs is kingdom; 12: 12 so *p.* they the prophets before you; 12: 44 (Matt. 5: 44) pray for them that *p.* you; **4 Ne.** 1: 29 other church *p.* true church of Christ; **Morm.** 8: 36 only a few do not lift themselves in pride, unto *p.*

PERSIST (*see also* Remain)

Jacob 2: 14 if ye *p.* in these things, God's judgments must speedily come upon you; **Mosiah** 16: 5 he who *p.* in carnal nature remains in fallen state; **Alma** 5: 54 will ye *p.* in persecuting brethren; 5: 55 will you *p.* in turning backs upon the needy; 5: 56 (9: 18) all who *p.* in their wickedness shall be hewn down and cast into fire; **Morm.** 4: 10 Nephites repent not and *p.* in wickedness.

PERSON (*see* Respect, Respecter)

PERSUADE, PERSUASION (*see also* Convince; Doctrine; False; Exhort; Plead; Urge)

1 Ne. 3: 21 Nephi¹ *p.* brethren to be faithful in keeping commandments; 6: 4 intent of Nephi¹ is to *p.* men to come unto God; 19: 23 (2 Ne. 25: 23; 33: 4; Morm. 5: 14) writings to *p.* people to believe in Redeemer; **2 Ne.** 26: 27 the Lord has commanded his people to *p.* all men to repentance; 33: 4 (Ether 8: 26) writings *p.* men to do good; **Jacob** 1: 8 Jacob² would *p.* all men not to rebel against God; **Jarom** 1: 11 law of Moses *p.* men to look forward to Messiah; **Morm.** 3: 22 Mormon² would *p.* all ends of earth to repent; **Ether** 4: 11 Spirit *p.* men to do good; 4: 12 whatsoever *p.* to do good is of the Lord; **Moro.** 7: 16 that which *p.* men to believe in Christ is of God; 7: 17 that which *p.* men to do evil is of devil.

PERVERT, PERVERSE, PERVERSION (*see also* Corrupt; Wrest)

1 Ne. 13: 27 (22: 14) abominable church *p.* right ways of the Lord; **2 Ne.** 28: 15 all who *p.* right way of the Lord shall be thrust down to hell; **Jacob** 7: 7 Sherem leads away people, that they *p.* right way of God; **Mosiah** 12: 26 priests of Noah³ have *p.* ways of the Lord; 29: 23 unrighteous king *p.* the ways of righteousness; **Alma** 9: 8 (10: 17, 25; Hel. 13: 29) ye wicked and *p.* generation; 10: 18 lawyers lay plans to *p.* ways of righteous; 30: 22, 60 Korihor *p.* ways of the Lord; 31: 1, 11 Zoramites *p.* ways of the Lord; 31: 24 Zoramites a wicked and *p.* people; **Morm.** 8: 33 ye wicked, *p.*, stiffnecked people; **Moro.** 8: 15–16 they who say little children need baptism *p.* ways of the Lord; 9: 19 Nephites have become strong in *p.*

PESTILENCE (*see also* Destruction)

2 Ne. 6: 15 they who believe not in Messiah shall be destroyed by *p.*; 10: 6 because of iniquities, *p.* shall come upon Jews; **Mosiah** 12: 4, 7 the Lord will smite people of Noah³ with *p.* because of iniquities; **Alma** 10: 22–23 except for prayers of the righteous, the Lord would smite people of Ammonihah with *p.*; 45: 10–11 when Nephites dwindle in unbelief, they shall see *p.*; **Hel.** 10: 6 Nephi² is given power to smite earth with *p.*; 12: 3 except the Lord chastens his people with *p.*, they will not remember him; **Ether** 11: 7 because Jaredites hearken not to the Lord, *p.* come.

PETITION (*see also* Beg; Plead)

Mosiah 4: 16 ye will not suffer beggar to put up his *p.* in vain; 4: 22 if ye condemn the man who puts his *p.* to you, how much more just will your condemnation be; **Alma** 51: 15 Moroni¹ sends *p.* to governor requesting power to compel dissenters to fight.

PHARAOH—*ruler of ancient Egypt* (*see also* BD Pharaoh)

1 Ne. 4: 2 (17: 27; Ex. 14: 26–30) armies of P. drowned in Red sea.

PHYSICIAN

Moro. 8: 8 (Matt. 9: 12) the whole need no *p.*

PIERCE, PIERCING (*see also* Penetrate)

Jacob 2: 9 those who have not been wounded must have daggers placed to *p.* their souls; 2: 10 Jacob² tells Nephites of wickedness under glance of *p.* eye of God; **Hel.** 5: 30 still voice in prison *p.* to very soul; **3 Ne.** 11: 3 survivors hear small voice that *p.* to very center.

PILLAR

1 **Ne.** 1: 6 *p.* of fire comes down before Lehi¹; **Hel.** 5: 24, 43–44 Nephi² and Lehi⁴ are encircled in *p.* of fire.

PILLOW

2 **Ne.** 33: 3 eyes of Nephi¹ water his *p.* by night because of his people.

PIT (*see also* Persecution; Snare)

1 **Ne.** 14: 3 great *p.* digged by abominable church for destruction of men; 22: 14 they shall fall into *p.* which they digged to ensnare people of the Lord; 2 **Ne.** 8: 1 (Isa. 51: 1) look to hole of *p.* from whence ye are digged; 24: 15 (Isa. 14: 15) thou shalt be brought down to hell, to sides of *p.*; 28: 8 many shall say, Dig *p.* for thy neighbor; 3 **Ne.** 28: 20 wicked could not dig *p.* sufficient to hold disciples; **Ether** 9: 29 Jaredites cast prophets into *p.* to perish.

PITY (*see also* Compassion; Mercy)

2 **Ne.** 23: 18 (Isa. 13: 18) they shall have no *p.* on fruit of womb; **Alma** 53: 11 Ammonites would allow themselves to fall into brethren's hands except for *p.* of Ammon² and brethren; **Ether** 3: 3 Lord, look upon me in *p.*

PLACE

1 **Ne.** 17: 46 (3 Ne. 8: 13) by power of his word the Lord can cause rough *p.* to be made smooth; 21: 20 (Isa. 49: 20) the *p.* is too strait for me, give *p.* to me that I may dwell; 2 **Ne.** 4: 27 why should I yield to temptation, that evil one have *p.* in my heart; 23: 13 (Isa. 13: 13) earth shall remove out of her *p.*; 28: 23 after judgment, wicked must go to *p.* prepared for them; 33: 2 many harden hearts against Spirit, that it have no *p.* in them; **Enos** 1: 27 *p.* prepared for you in mansions of Father; **Mosiah** 2: 36 if ye transgress what has been spoken, ye withdraw yourselves from Spirit, that it has no *p.* in you; 2: 37 the Lord has no *p.* in those who obey evil spirit; 12: 23 (15: 30; 3 Ne. 16: 19; 20: 34; Isa. 52: 9) ye waste *p.* of Jerusalem; 26: 24 if they know me, they shall have *p.* at my right hand; **Alma** 5: 25 ye cannot suppose the wicked have *p.* in kingdom of heaven; 20: 30 brethren of Ammon² are driven from *p.* to *p.*; 32: 27 give *p.* for portion of my words; 34: 26 pour out your souls in secret *p.*; 34: 35 if ye have procrastinated day of repentance, Spirit has withdrawn that it has no *p.* in you; 39: 6 to deny Holy Ghost when it once has had *p.* in you is unpardonable sin; **Hel.** 14: 23 many *p.* that are now valleys shall become mountains; **Morm.** 8: 30 earthquakes in divers *p.*; **Moro.** 7: 32 the Lord prepares way

that men may have faith in Christ, that Holy Ghost may have *p.* in hearts.

PLAIN, PLAINLY, PLAINNESS (*see also* Clear; Simple)

1 **Ne.** 13: 26–29, 32, 34 great and abominable church takes many *p.* and precious things from book; 13: 29 because things are taken from book which were *p.* to men's understanding, according to *p.* which is in Lamb, many stumble; 13: 34–40 the Lord will reveal many *p.* and precious parts of gospel that have been taken away; 14: 23 when book proceeded from Jews, it was *p.* and true; 2 **Ne.** 1: 26 brothers murmur because Nephi¹ has been *p.* unto them; 4: 32 may I be strict in the *p.* road; 9: 47 would I be *p.* unto you according to *p.* of truth if ye were freed from sin; 25: 4 words of Isaiah¹ are *p.* unto all who are filled with spirit of prophecy; 25: 4 (33: 6) my soul delighteth in *p.*; 25: 20 I have spoken *p.*, that ye cannot err; 26: 33 the Lord doeth nothing save it be *p.* unto men; 32: 7 men will not understand great knowledge when given them in *p.*; 33: 5 writings of Nephi¹ speak harshly against sin, according to *p.* of word of God; **Jacob** 4: 13 these things are manifested unto us *p.*, for salvation of souls; 4: 14 Jews despised words of *p.*; **Enos** 1: 23 prophets speak with great *p.* of speech; **Mosiah** 2: 40 Benjamin speaks *p.*, that his people might understand; **Alma** 13: 23 glad tidings are made known in *p.* terms; 14: 2 people are angry with Alma² because of *p.* of his words; **Moro.** 7: 15 way to judge is as *p.* as daylight is from dark night.

PLAINS (*see also* Agosh; Hershlon, Plains of; Nephihah, Plains of)

1 **Ne.** 12: 4 Nephi¹ beholds *p.* of earth broken up in vision; **Alma** 52: 20 Nephites desire to meet Jacob³ on *p.* between cities.

PLAN (*see also* Gospel; Plot; Redemption; Salvation; Secret Combination; TG Salvation, Plan of)

2 **Ne.** ch. 2, 9 (Alma ch. 12, 42) summary of *p.* of redemption; 9: 6 (Alma 12: 25) to fulfill merciful *p.* of Creator, there must be resurrection; 9: 13 how great the *p.* of our God; 9: 28 (Alma 28: 13) cunning *p.* of evil one; **Jacob** 6: 8 will ye make a mock of great *p.* of redemption; **Jarom** 1: 2 fathers have revealed *p.* of salvation on plates; **Alma** 12: 4 Zeezrom's *p.* was very subtle *p.*; 12: 25, 30 *p.* of redemption laid from foundation of world; 12: 30–32 God made *p.* of redemption known unto man; 12: 33 God called on men in name of Son, this being *p.* of redemption; 34: 9 according to great *p.* of God, atonement must be made; 34: 16 only unto him who

has faith is brought about *p.* of redemption; 37: 29, 32 trust not those secret *p.* of murder unto this people; 41: 2 *p.* of restoration is requisite with justice of God; 42: 5 if Adam had partaken of tree of life, *p.* of salvation would have been frustrated; 42: 8 to reclaim man from temporal death would destroy great *p.* of happiness; 42: 11 except for *p.* of redemption, men would be cut off from presence of the Lord; 42: 15 *p.* of mercy could not be brought about except atonement should be made; **Hel.** 2: 6 servant obtains knowledge of *p.* to destroy Helaman²; 11: 10 secret *p.* of Gadianton robbers are concealed in earth; 11: 26 great band of robbers search out secret *p.* of Gadianton; **3 Ne.** 1: 16 *p.* of destruction laid for believers has been frustrated; **Ether** 8: 8 daughter of Jared³ devises *p.* to redeem kingdom unto father.

PLANT (*see also* Grain; Seed; Sow [verb]; Till)

1 Ne. 18: 24 Lehites begin to *p.* seeds; **2 Ne.** 8: 16 (Isa. 51: 16) I have covered thee in shadow of mine hand that I may *p.* heavens; 15: 2 (Isa. 5: 2) well-beloved *p.* vineyard with choicest vine; **Jacob** 5: 21 how comest thou hither to *p.* this tree; **Mosiah** 14: 2 (Isa. 53: 2) he shall grow up before him as tender *p.*; **Alma** 32: 28, 33 (33: 23) give place, that seed may be *p.* in your heart; 32: 36 (34: 4) ye have exercised faith to *p.* seed to know if it is good; 33: 1 people ask how to *p.* seed, or word.

PLATES (*see* Book; Book of Mormon; Characters; Engrave; Plates, Brass; Plates of Ether; Plates of Jacob; Plates of Mormon; Plates of Nephi, Large; Plates of Nephi, Small; Plates of Zeniff; Record; Scriptures)

PLATES, BRASS (*see also* Laban)

1 Ne. 3: 3, 12 (19: 2) Laban has record of Jews and genealogy of fathers engraven on *b.p.*; 3: 9—4: 38 sons of Lehi¹ obtain *b.p.*; 4: 16 law is engraven upon *b.p.*; 4: 24 Nephi¹ to carry engravings on *b.p.* to brothers; 5: 10–16 (19: 23; Omni 1: 14; Alma 37: 3) *b.p.* contain five books of Moses, history of Jews to reign of Zedekiah, genealogy; 5: 18 *b.p.* to go to every people of seed of Lehi¹; 5: 19 *b.p.* should never perish; 7: 11 ye have forgotten what great things the Lord hath done that we should obtain record; 13: 23 Bible is like engravings on *b.p.*; 19: 1–2 Nephi¹ reads many scriptures engraven on *b.p.*; 19: 22—22: 1 Nephi¹ reads writings of Isaiah¹ from *b.p.*; 22: 30 writings on *b.p.* testify man must be obedient; **2 Ne.** 4: 2 prophecies of Joseph¹ are written on *b.p.*; 4: 14–15 Nephi¹ en-

graves scriptures from *b.p.* on his *p.*; 5: 12 (Mosiah 10: 16) Nephi¹ takes records engraven on *b.p.* with him; **Omni** 1: 14 Zarahemla rejoices because of *b.p.*; **Mosiah** 1: 3–4 Lehi¹ could not have taught his children all these things without *b.p.*; 1: 4 engravings on *b.p.* are in Egyptian; 1: 16 Benjamin gives *b.p.* to Mosiah²; 28: 11, 20 Mosiah² gives Alma² records engraven on *b.p.*; **Alma** 37: 1–3 Alma² gives *b.p.* to Helaman²; 37: 3 engravings on *b.p.* are records of holy scriptures; **3 Ne.** 1: 2 Nephi² gives *b.p.* to son Nephi³; 10: 17 prophecy of Jacob¹ concerning seed of Joseph¹ is on *b.p.*

PLATES OF ETHER (*see also* Ether; Jaredites)

Mosiah 8: 9 expedition from Limhi discovers twenty-four *p.* of gold filled with engravings; 21: 27 people of Limhi find Jaredite record of engraven plates or ore; 22: 14 Limhi gives record to Mosiah²; 28: 11 Mosiah² translates record on *p.* of gold found by Limhi; **Alma** 37: 21–32 twenty-four *p.* contain record of secret works of darkness of people who were destroyed; **Hel.** 6: 26 secret oaths did not come to Gadianton from record, but from devil; **Ether** 1: 2 Moroni² takes account of Jaredites from twenty-four gold *p.* found by Limhi, called Book of Ether; 3: 22 (4: 1) brother of Jared² is commanded to write what he has seen and heard, seal it; 15: 33 Ether finishes record and hides it.

PLATES OF JACOB (*see also* Jacob²; Plates of Nephi, Small)

Jacob 3: 14 Jacob² writes upon *p.* called *p.* of Jacob, made by Nephi¹.

PLATES OF MORMON (*see also* Mormon²; Moroni²)

W of M 1: 3 (Morm. 6: 6) Mormon² makes abridgment from *p.* of Nephi; 1: 6 Mormon² puts small *p.* with remainder of his record; 1: 9 Mormon² proceeds to finish his record; **3 Ne.** 5: 10–11 Mormon² makes record on *p.* he has made with own hands; **Morm.** 2: 18 upon these *p.* Mormon² does not make full account of wickedness; 6: 6 Mormon² gives Moroni² few plates; 8: 1 Moroni² finishes father's record; **Moro.** 10: 2 Moroni² seals up record.

PLATES OF NEPHI, LARGE—*secular history abridged by Mormon², whose abridgment constitutes books of Mosiah, Alma, Helaman, 3 Nephi, and 4 Nephi* (*see also* Lehi, Book of; Mormon²; Plates of Mormon; Plates of Nephi, Small)

1 Ne. 9: 2, 4 (19: 4; 2 Ne. 4: 14; 5: 29, 33; Jacob 1: 3; 3: 13; 7: 26; Mosiah 1: 6) Nephi¹ makes account of history,

kings, wars on other *p.*, also called *p.* of Nephi; **2 Ne.** 4: 14 many sayings of Lehi[1] and Nephi[1] are recorded on other *p.*; **Jacob** 1: 3 (Jarom 1: 14; Omni 1: 11) secular history to be engraven on larger *p.*; **W of M** 1: 3 after abridging larger *p.* down to reign of Benjamin, Mormon[2] finds small *p.*; **Mosiah** 1: 3 Benjamin teaches of records engraven on larger *p.*; 1: 6 Benjamin testifies *p.* of Nephi are true; **Alma** 37: 2 Alma[2] commands Helaman[2] to keep sacred record upon *p.* of Nephi; **3 Ne.** 5: 8–10 (26: 6–7) Mormon[2] gives only small part of record engraven on *p.* of Nephi; 26: 6–7 *p.* of Nephi contain more part of things Jesus taught the people; 26: 8–11 Mormon[2] is commanded not to record all Christ's sayings engraven on *p.* of Nephi; **Morm.** 1: 4 Mormon[2] is instructed to engrave on *p.* of Nephi all he observes among Nephites; 2: 18 upon *p.* of Nephi Mormon[2] makes full account of Nephites' wickedness; 6: 6 Mormon[2] makes record out of *p.* of Nephi.

PLATES OF NEPHI, SMALL—*spiritual history of Nephites, which constitutes the books of 1 Nephi, 2 Nephi, Jacob, Enos, Jarom, Omni* (*see also* Nephi[1])

1 Ne. 1: 17 (19: 1) Nephi[1] abridges record of father upon *p.* he has made; 6: 1 Nephi[1] does not include genealogy in this part of his record; 6: 3 Nephi[1] does not make full account of history on these *p.* so he can write of things of God; 9: 2–4 (10: 1; 19: 3; Jacob 1: 1–2) these *p.* do not contain full account of people, but rather an account of the ministry; 19: 1 on *p.* of ore Nephi[1] engraves father's record, journey in wilderness, father's prophecies, own prophecies; **2 Ne.** 4: 15 upon these *p.* Nephi[1] writes things of his soul and scriptures engraven on brass *p.*; 5: 30–32 Nephi[1] is commanded by the Lord to make and engrave many things for profit of his people; **Jacob** 1: 1–2, 4 Nephi[1] instructs Jacob[2] to engrave most precious, sacred things on small *p.*; 3: 13 hundredth part of Nephites' proceedings cannot be written upon these *p.*; 3: 14 *p.* of Jacob included among small *p.*; 7: 27 Jacob[2] confers *p.* upon Enos[2]; **Jarom** 1: 2, 14 Jarom writes little because *p.* are small; **Omni** 1: 1 Jarom instructs Omni to write upon *p.*; 1: 8–9 Omni delivers *p.* to Chemish; 1: 10 Abinadom writes upon *p.*; 1: 12–30 Amaleki writes upon *p.*; 1: 25 Amaleki delivers *p.* to king Benjamin; 1: 30 *p.* are full; **W of M** 1: 3 after abridging large *p.* to reign of Benjamin, Mormon[2] discovers these *p.*, which contain small account of prophets; 1: 4 small *p.* contain prophecies of coming of Christ; 1: 6 Mormon[2] puts small *p.* with remainder of his record.

PLATES OF ZENIFF (*see also* Limhi; Nephi, Land of; Noah[3]; Zeniff)

Mosiah 8: 5 Limhi brings Ammon[1] *p.* containing record of his people; 22: 14 Mosiah[2] receives with joy records of Limhi's people.

PLAY

2 Ne. 21: 8 (30: 14; Isa. 11: 8) sucking child shall *p.* on hole of asp; **3 Ne.** 28: 22 (4 Ne. 1: 33) disciples cast into den of beasts, *p.* with them.

PLEAD (*see also* Appeal; Cry; Exhort; Jesus Christ—Advocate; Persuade; Petition)

2 Ne. 8: 22 (Isa. 51: 22) the Lord *p.* cause of his people; 13: 13 (Isa. 3: 13) the Lord standeth up to *p.* and judge the people; **Jacob** 3: 1 God will *p.* your cause; **Alma** 1: 15 Nehor stands before Alma[2] and *p.* for himself with much boldness.

PLEASANT (*see also* Pleased, Pleasing)

Mosiah 23: 4, 19 people of Alma[1] come to *p.* land; **Alma** 55: 13 wine was *p.* to Lamanites' taste; **Hel.** 5: 46–47 *p.* voice whispers peace to Nephi[2] and Lehi[4]; **3 Ne.** 24: 4 (Mal. 3: 4) offering of Judah and Jerusalem shall be *p.* unto the Lord.

PLEASED, PLEASING (*see also* Delight; Favored; Happiness; Pleasant; Pleasure)

1 Ne. 6: 5 (2 Ne. 5: 32) Nephi[1] writes things *p.* unto God, not *p.* unto world; **2 Ne.** 5: 32 if Nephites are *p.* with things of God, they will be *p.* with engravings of Nephi[1]; **Jacob** 2: 7 tenderness and chasteness of feelings are *p.* unto God; 2: 8 Jacob[2] supposes people come to hear *p.* word of God; 6: 13 (Moro. 10: 34) meet before *p.* bar of God; **Mosiah** 14: 10 (Isa. 53: 10) it *p.* the Lord to bruise him; **Alma** 30: 53 Korihor taught devil's words because they were *p.* to carnal mind; **3 Ne.** 11: 7 (Matt. 3: 17) behold my Beloved Son, in whom I am well *p.*

PLEASURE (*see also* Delight; Desire; Happiness; Joy; Will)

1 Ne. 16: 38 brothers accuse Nephi[1] of desiring to be ruler, that he might do according to his *p.*; **2 Ne.** 25: 22 these things shall go according to *p.* of God; **Jacob** 4: 9 God commands earth according to his *p.*; **Enos** 1: 27 Enos[2] will see Redeemer's face with *p.*; **Mosiah** 7: 33 the Lord will deliver you out of bondage, according to *p.*; **Alma** 4: 8 people of church persecute those who do not believe according to their *p.*

PLOT (*see also* Plan)

Alma 2: 21 Alma[2] sends spies to know *p.* of Amlicites; **Hel.** 6: 30 devil,

who *p.* with Cain, hands down secret *p.* for workers of darkness.

PLOW (*see also* Till)

2 Ne. 12: 4 (Isa. 2: 4) they shall beat their swords into *p*-shares; **Ether** 10: 25 Jaredites make tools to *p.* and sow.

PLUCK (*see also* Destruction; Prune; Reap)

Jacob 5: 7, 26, 52, 57–58 branches *p.* off olive-tree; **Alma** 32: 38 if tree is not nourished, it withers and ye *p.* it up; 32: 40 if ye will not nourish word, ye can never *p.* fruit of tree of life.

PLUNDER (*see* Rob)

POINT (*see also* Direction, Direct; Doctrine)

1 Ne. 8: 33 those in building *p.* finger of scorn at partakers of fruit; **Jacob** 4: 5 (Alma 34: 14) law of Moses *p.* souls to Christ; **Alma** 34: 40 faith causes spindles to *p.* direction Lehites should go; 37: 44 word of Christ will *p.* straight course to eternal bliss; 51: 5 king-men desire that a few *p.* of law be altered.

POINTERS (*see* Liahona)

POISON, POISONOUS (*see also* Serpent)

Mosiah 7: 30 effect of whirlwind is *p.*; **Alma** 47: 18 Amalickiah causes servant to administer *p.* by degrees to Lehonti; 55: 30 Lamanites attempt to destroy Nephites with *p.*

POLLUTE, POLLUTION (*see also* Corrupt; Defile; Filthiness; Sin)

1 Ne. 20: 11 (Isa. 48: 11) the Lord will not suffer his name to be *p.*; **Mosiah** 25: 11 when Nephites think of Lamanites' *p.* state, they are filled with anguish; **Alma** 26: 17 who could have supposed God would have snatched us from *p.* state; **Morm.** 8: 31 the Lord's promises will be fulfilled in day when great *p.* are upon land; 8: 38 why have ye *p.* church of God.

POLYGAMY (*see* Marriage; Wife)

PONDER (*see also* Consider; Reasoning; Study; Think)

1 Ne. 11: 1 as Nephi[1] sits *p.*, he is caught away in Spirit; **2 Ne.** 4: 15–16 my heart *p.* the scriptures; 32: 1 brothers of Nephi[1] *p.* what to do after entering the way; **Hel.** 10: 2–3 Nephi[2] *p.* upon things the Lord has shown him; **3 Ne.** 17: 3 Christ tells people to *p.* upon what he has said; **Moro.** 10: 3 when ye read these things, *p.* them in your hearts.

POOL (*see* Water)

POOR, POORER, POOREST (*see also*

Alms; Charity; Humble; Lowliness; Meek; Naked; Needy; Poverty; Relief)

2 Ne. 9: 30 because they are rich, they despise the *p.*; 13: 15 (Isa. 3: 15) ye grind the faces of the *p.*; 21: 4 (30: 9; Isa. 11: 4) with righteousness shall the Lord judge the *p.*; 26: 20 Gentiles grind upon face of the *p.*; 27: 30 the *p.* shall rejoice in Holy One; 28: 13 false churches rob the *p.* because of fine sanctuaries; **Jacob** 5: 21 branch of tree planted in *p.* spot in all vineyard; 5: 22 the Lord knew it was *p.* spot of ground; 5: 23 the Lord has planted another branch in spot of ground *p.* than first; **Mosiah** 4: 26 impart of substance to the *p.*; **Alma** 5: 55 will you persist in turning your backs upon the *p.*; 32: 2–3 Alma[2] and missionaries have success among *p.* class of people; 32: 4 those who seek out Alma[2] are *p.* in heart because of poverty as to things of world; **Hel.** 4: 12 slaughter of Nephites is caused by their oppression of *p.*; 6: 39 robbers obtain government, turn backs upon the *p.*; **3 Ne.** 12: 3 (Matt. 5: 3) blessed are the *p.* in spirit who come unto Christ; **4 Ne.** 1: 3 Nephites have all things in common, there were not rich and *p.*; **Morm.** 8: 37 ye love money more than ye love the *p.*

POPULAR

1 Ne. 22: 23 churches built up to become *p.* in eyes of world shall be brought low; **Alma** 1: 15 Nehor declares that every priest should become *p.*; 35: 3 more *p.* part of Zoramites are angry because of word.

PORE

Mosiah 3: 7 (Luke 22: 44) blood shall come from every *p.* of Messiah.

PORTION (*see also* Part)

Mosiah 14: 12 (Isa. 53: 12) I will divide him a *p.* with the great; **Alma** 12: 10–11 he who hardens heart receives lesser *p.* of word; 17: 9 sons of Mosiah[2] pray that the Lord will grant them a *p.* of Spirit; 18: 35 *p.* of Spirit gives knowledge and power; 24: 8 Lamoni thanks God he has given converted Lamanites *p.* of Spirit; 27: 24 Nephites will defend Ammonites if they will give *p.* of substance to assist armies; 32: 27 let this desire work in you until you can give place for *p.* of my words; 40: 13 spirits of wicked have no *p.* of Spirit.

POSSESS (*see also* Inhabit)

Alma 30: 42 Korihor is *p.* with lying spirit; 34: 34 same spirit that *p.* body at death will *p.* body in eternal world; **Morm.** 5: 19 the Lord hath reserved Nephites' blessings for Gentiles who shall *p.* land; **Ether** 2: 8–10 he who *p.* land

shall serve God or be swept off; **Moro.** 7: 47 whoso is found *p.* of charity, it shall be well with him.

POTTER

2 Ne. 27: 27 your turning of things upside down shall be esteemed as *p*'s clay.

POUR

1 Ne. 14: 15 wrath of God to be *p.* out upon abominable church; **2 Ne.** 27: 5 the Lord has *p.* out upon the wicked the spirit of deep sleep; **Jacob** 7: 8 the Lord *p.* his Spirit into soul of Jacob²; **Enos** 1: 9 Enos² *p.* out whole soul unto God for Nephites; **Mosiah** 4: 20 the Lord has *p.* out his Spirit upon Benjamin's people; 14: 12 (Isa. 53: 12) he hath *p.* out his soul unto death; 18: 10 the Lord will *p.* out Spirit upon those who are baptized; 25: 24 the Lord *p.* out Spirit upon people of God; **Alma** 19: 14 Spirit is *p.* out upon Lamanites; 34: 26 *p.* out your souls in your closets; **Hel.** 3: 25 (3 Ne. 10: 18) many blessings are *p.* out upon church; **3 Ne.** 20: 27 in Abraham's seed shall all kindreds be blessed, unto *p.* out of Holy Ghost; 24: 10 (Mal. 3: 10) the Lord will open windows of heaven and *p.* out blessing; **Morm.** 3: 12 soul of Mormon² is *p.* out in prayer for Nephites; **Ether** 9: 20 the Lord *p.* out blessings upon choice land.

POVERTY (see also Poor)

Alma 32: 4 great multitude are poor in heart because of *p.* as to things of world; 34: 40 do not revile against those who cast you out because of your *p.*; **Hel.** 13: 31 in days of your *p.* ye cannot retain your riches; **3 Ne.** 6: 12 some have no chance for learning, because of *p.*

POWER, POWERFUL (see also Authority; Dominion; Glory [noun]; God, Power of; Might; Priesthood; Strength; TG God, Power of; Jesus Christ, Power of; Power; Priesthood, Power of)

1 Ne. 2: 14 (10: 17) Lehi¹ speaks with *p.*; 10: 17 Lehi¹ received *p.* by faith on Son; 10: 17 *p.* of Holy Ghost is gift of God unto all who diligently seek him; 17: 52 Spirit is so *p.*, brothers fear they should wither; 22: 15 Satan shall have no more *p.* over hearts of men; 22: 23 churches built up to get *p.* over flesh shall be brought low; 22: 26 because of righteousness of people, Satan has no *p.*; 2 **Ne.** 1: 25 elder brothers accuse Nephi¹ of seeking *p.* and authority over them; 10: 25 may God raise you from death by *p.* of resurrection and from everlasting death by *p.* of atonement; 32: 3 angels speak by *p.* of Holy Ghost; 33: 1 when a man speaks by *p.* of Holy Ghost, *p.* of Holy Ghost carries it unto hearts; **Jacob** 4: 11 ye may

obtain a resurrection according to *p.* of resurrection which is in Christ; 7: 4 Sherem's knowledge of language enables him to use much *p.* of speech; 7: 18 Sherem confesses he was deceived by *p.* of devil; **W of M** 1: 17 many holy men in land speak word of God with *p.* and authority; **Mosiah** 8: 16 man may have great *p.* given him of God; 13: 6 Abinadi speaks with *p.* and authority from God; 16: 3 (Alma 34: 35) devil has *p.* over the wicked; 23: 39 Amulon given no *p.* to do anything contrary to will of Lamanite king; 25: 19 Mosiah² gives Alma¹ *p.* to ordain priests and teachers; **Alma** 1: 17 law could have no *p.* over any man for his belief; 9: 28 the evil shall reap damnation according to *p.* of devil; 12: 5 adversary exercises *p.* in Zeezrom; 17: 3 sons of Mosiah² teach with *p.* and authority; 19: 4 Ammon² has *p.* to do many mighty works in God's name; 30: 42 devil has *p.* over Korihor; 3: 15 preaching of word has more *p.* effect than sword; 34: 34 same spirit that possesses body at death shall have *p.* to possess it in eternal world; 46: 4 lower judges seek for *p.* by declaring king; 48: 7 Amalickiah obtains *p.* by fraud and deceit; 48: 17 if all men were like Moroni,¹ *p.* of hell would be broken and devil would have no *p.*; 60: 36 Moroni¹ seeks not for *p.*, but to pull it down; **Hel.** 3: 29 word is quick and *p.*; 6: 5 many preach with great *p.* and authority; 7: 4 Gadianton robbers usurp *p.* and authority of land; 3 **Ne.** 2: 2 people imagine signs are wrought by men and *p.* of devil; 6: 15 (7: 5) cause of iniquity is that Satan has great *p.*; 7: 17 Nephi³ ministers with *p.* and great authority; 11: 21–22 Jesus gives disciples *p.* to baptize; 16: 12 Gentiles shall not have *p.* over Israel; 18: 37 (Moro. 2: 1–3) Jesus gives disciples *p.* to bestow Holy Ghost; 28: 39 three Nephites are changed, that Satan should have no *p.* over them and *p.* of earth could not hold them; 29: 6 wo unto him who says the Lord no longer works by *p.* of Holy Ghost; **Ether** 8: 16 secret combinations were kept up by *p.* of devil; 8: 22 nation that upholds secret combinations to get *p.* shall be destroyed; 8: 23 (11: 15) combinations built up to get *p.* and gain; 8: 26 Moroni² writes, that Satan may have no *p.* over men; 12: 25 God has made prophets' words *p.*; 15: 19 Satan has full *p.* over hearts of people; **Moro.** 7: 44 if a man confesses by *p.* of Holy Ghost that Jesus is the Christ, he must have charity; 8: 8 curse of Adam has no *p.* over little children; 10: 4–5 by *p.* of Holy Ghost ye may know the truth of all things.

PRAISE (see also Glorify; Honor; Rejoice; Shout; Thank; Vain; Worship)

1 Ne. 13: 9 for *p.* of world abominable church destroys saints; 18: 16 Nephi[1] *p.* God all day long; 2 Ne. 9: 49 Jacob[2] will *p.* holy name of God; 22: 4 *p.* the Lord, call upon his name; 26: 29 priestcraft is to preach to get *p.* of world; Mosiah 2: 20–21 if you surrender all *p.* to God, yet would ye be unprofitable servants; Alma 24: 23 converted Lamanites *p.* God in very act of perishing under sword; 26: 8 let us sing to God's *p.*; 38: 13 Zoramites pray to be *p.* of men; Morm. 8: 38 why are you ashamed to take upon you name of Christ, to get *p.* of world; Ether 6: 9 brother of Jared[2] did sing *p.* to the Lord.

PRAYER, PRAY (*see also* Answer; Ask; Call; Communication; Cry; Faith; Fasting; Name of the Lord; Supplicate; TG Prayer; BD Prayer)

1 Ne. 18: 3 Nephi[1] *p.* oft unto the Lord; 2 Ne. 4: 24 Lehi[1] has waxed bold in mighty *p.* unto God; 26: 15 *p.* of the faithful shall be heard; 32: 8 if ye would hearken unto Spirit which teaches man to *p.*, ye would know ye must *p.*; 32: 8 evil spirit teaches man that he must not *p.*; 32: 9 *p.* always; 33: 12 Nephi[1] *p.* that many may be saved in God's kingdom; Jacob 7: 22 Father has answered *p.* of Jacob[2]; Enos 1: 4 Enos[2] cries unto his Maker in mighty *p.*; Omni 1: 26 continue in fasting and *p.*; Mosiah 27: 14 Alma[1] has *p.* much concerning Alma[2]; 27: 22–23 Alma[1] has priests *p.* that the Lord will open mouth of Alma[2]; Alma 5: 46 Alma[2] has fasted and *p.* many days to know these things; 8: 10 Alma[2] wrestles with God in mighty *p.* that he might pour out his Spirit; 10: 22–23 people of Ammonihah are spared because of *p.* of the righteous; 17: 3 sons of Mosiah[2] teach with power because they have given themselves to much fasting and *p.*; 26: 22 to know mysteries of God, men must *p.* without ceasing; 28: 6 following tremendous slaughter is time of much fasting and *p.*; 31: 12, 22 every Zoramite offers selfsame *p.*; 34: 19 continue in *p.* unto God; 34: 27 when ye do not cry unto the Lord, let your hearts be drawn out in *p.* unto him continually; 38: 13 Zoramites *p.* to be heard of men; 45: 1 Nephites fast and *p.* much to give God thanks; 62: 51 Nephites *p.* unto the Lord continually; Hel. 3: 35 members of church fast and *p.* oft; 3 Ne. 12: 44 (Matt. 5: 44) *p.* for them that despitefully use you; 13: 5 (Matt. 6: 5) when thou *p.*, do not as the hypocrites; 13: 9 (Matt. 6: 9) after this manner therefore ye; 17: 15 Jesus *p.* unto Father; 18: 15 watch and *p.* always; 18: 16 as Jesus has *p.* among them, so should saints *p.* in church; 18: 21

p. in your families; 19: 6 twelve disciples cause multitude to kneel and *p.* to Father; 19: 17–18, 22, 24 disciples *p.* unto Jesus because he is with them; 19: 24 disciples *p.* without multiplying words; 20: 1 Jesus commands multitude to cease to *p.*, but not to cease to *p.* in hearts; 27: 1 disciples are united in mighty *p.* and fasting when Jesus appears again; Moro. 6: 4 those baptized are numbered among people of church, to keep them watchful unto *p.*; 6: 5 church meets together oft to fast and *p.*; 7: 6, 9 if man *p.* without real intent, it profits him nothing; 7: 48 *p.* unto Father with all energy of heart; 8: 26 perfect love endures by diligence unto *p.*

PREACH, PREACHING (*see also* Declare; Exhort; Gospel; Ministry; Preacher; Prophecy; Publish; Teach; Testify; Warn; TG Preaching)

2 Ne. 25: 26 Nephites *p.* of Christ; 26: 29 priestcrafts are that men *p.* for gain and praise; Enos 1: 23 prophets among Nephites *p.* of wars; Mosiah 18: 20 priests should *p.* nothing save repentance and faith; 23: 17 none receive authority to *p.* save by Alma[1] from God; Alma 1: 16 many go forth *p.* false doctrines; 9: 21 Nephites have been visited with gift of *p.*; 29: 13 God hath called me by a holy calling to *p.* word unto this people; 31: 5 *p.* of word has great tendency to lead people to do that which is just; 37: 33 Alma[2] calls Helaman[2] to *p.* repentance; 43: 2 Alma[2] and sons *p.* word according to spirit of prophecy, after holy order of God; Hel. 5: 17 Nephi[2] and Lehi[4] *p.* with great power; 3 Ne. 5: 4 word of God is *p.* to robbers in prison; 6: 20 men sent from heaven *p.* against sins of people; 20: 30 fulness of gospel shall be *p.* to the Lord's people; Morm. 1: 16 Mormon[2] endeavors to *p.*, but is forbidden; Moro. 6: 9 Holy Ghost leads church whether to *p.*, pray, sing.

PREACHER (*see also* Elder; Minister [noun]; Preach)

W of M 1: 16 false *p.* are punished according to their crimes; Alma 1: 26 *p.* is no better than hearer.

PRECEPT (*see also* Commandments of God; Doctrine; Doctrine, False; Law; Persuade, Persuasion; Principle)

2 Ne. 27: 25 (Isa. 29: 13) fear of this people toward the Lord is taught by *p.* of men; 28: 14 false churches err in many instances because they are taught by *p.* of men; 28: 26, 31 wo unto him who hearkens unto *p.* of men; 28: 30 (Isa. 28: 10) the Lord gives line upon line, *p.* upon *p.*; 28: 30 blessed are they who hearken unto the Lord's *p.*

PRECIOUS (*see also* Choice; Pearl; Value; Worth)

1 Ne. 11: 9 (15: 36; Alma 32: 42) in vision, Nephi[1] sees tree *p.* above all; 13: 7–8 abominable church has all manner of *p.* clothing; 13: 26–29, 32, 34 abominable church takes away many plain and *p.* parts of gospel; 13: 34 Gentiles to stumble because plain and *p.* parts of gospel are taken away; 13: 34–35, 40 the Lord will make known plain and *p.* truths that have been taken away; 14: 23 when writings proceed from Jew, they are most *p.*; 2 Ne. 1: 10 Nephites brought into *p.* land of promise by goodness of God; 5: 16 Nephites' temple constructed after manner of Solomon's, without so many *p.* things; Jacob 1: 2 Jacob[2] is commanded to write on plates those things he considers most *p.*; 5: 61, 74 natural fruit is most *p.* above all other fruit; Alma 7: 10 Mary a *p.* and chosen vessel; 31: 35 souls of Zoramites are *p.*; 39: 17 is not a soul at this time as *p.* unto God as a soul at the time of his coming; Hel. 5: 8 Helaman[3] desires that his sons have *p.* gift of eternal life; Moro. 9: 9 Nephites have deprived Lamanites' daughters of that which is most *p.*, chastity and virtue.

PREMORTAL EXISTENCE

Alma 13: 3 priests were called and prepared from foundation of world.

PREPARE, PREPARATION, PREPARATORY (*see also* Establish; Make; Preparator; Probation; Read)

1 Ne. 2: 20 the Lord has *p.* land for Lehites; 3: 7 (9: 6) the Lord gives not commandments save he *p.* way to accomplish them; 10: 7–8 (3 Ne. 24: 1; Mal. 3: 1) prophet shall come to *p.* way of the Lord; 10: 8 (Alma 7: 9; Hel. 14: 9) *p.* ye the way of the Lord; 10: 18 (Ether 3: 14) way is *p.* for all men from foundation of world; 15: 29 river of filthy water represents hell *p.* for the wicked; 15: 34 place of filthiness is *p.* for that which is filthy; 22: 20 the Lord will surely *p.* way for all people; 2 Ne. 9: 10 God *p.* way for escape from death and hell; 9: 43 happiness *p.* for saints shall be hid from the wise and prudent; 9: 46 *p.* your souls for day when justice shall be administered; Jacob 5: 61 call servants to labor diligently in vineyard, that we may *p.* way; Mosiah 4: 6–7 atonement *p.* from foundation of world; Alma 5: 28 if ye are not stripped of pride, ye are not *p.* to meet God and must *p.* quickly; 12: 24 (34: 32; 42: 10, 13) this life became probationary state, a *p.* state, time to *p.* to meet God; 12: 26 if first parents had partaken of tree of life, they would have had no *p.* state; 13: 3 priests are called with holy

calling which was *p.* with a *p.* redemption; 13: 5 holy calling *p.* in and through atonement of Only Begotten Son, who was *p.*; 16: 16 the Lord pours out Spirit to *p.* men's minds and hearts to receive word; 32: 6 afflictions humble poor Zoramites in *p.* to hear word; 34: 3 Alma[2] has spoken to *p.* Zoramites' minds; 37: 24–25 interpreters were *p.* that word of God might be fulfilled; 48: 15 Nephites have faith God will warn them to flee or *p.* for war; 3 Ne. 17: 3 Jesus tells Nephites to *p.* minds for morrow; 21: 27 work to commence in *p.* way whereby Father's people may come unto Christ; Ether 3: 14 Christ was *p.* from foundation of world; 9: 28 prophets cry repentance, to *p.* way of the Lord; 12: 11 God *p.* a more excellent way; Moro. 7: 31 office of angel's ministry is to *p.* way among men by declaring word unto chosen vessels; 7: 32 the Lord *p.* way that men may have faith in Christ.

PREPARATOR (*see also* Founder)

1 Ne. 15: 35 devil is *p.* of hell.

PRESENCE (*see* God, Presence of)

PRESENT [adj.]

Morm. 8: 35 Moroni[2] speaks unto readers as though they were *p.*

PRESERVE (*see also* Defence; Keep; Maintain; Protect; Safe; Spare; Support; Uphold)

1 Ne. 3: 19–20 sons of Lehi[1] should obtain brass plates to *p.* language and words of prophets; 5: 21 brass plates of great value in *p.* commandments; 22: 17 the Lord will *p.* the righteous; 2 Ne. 3: 16 the Lord covenants to *p.* seed of Joseph[1] forever; 27: 22 latter-day seer to seal up book that unread words may be *p.*; Enos 1: 15 the Lord is able to *p.* Nephites' records; Mosiah 2: 20–21 God has kept and *p.* you from day to day; Alma 37: 12–14 records are *p.* for wise purpose known unto God; 37: 21 Alma[2] commands Helaman[2] to *p.* interpreters; 46: 24 remnant of seed of Joseph[1] to be *p.* as remnant of his garment was *p.*; 57: 26 Ammonite youths believe that those who do not doubt will be *p.* by God's marvelous power; 61: 9 Pahoran[1] seeks only to *p.* rights and liberty of his people; Hel. 4: 24 Spirit no longer *p.* Nephites; Ether 2: 7 the Lord had *p.* land of promise for righteous people.

PRESIDE (*see also* Lead; Watch)

Alma 6: 1 Alma[2] ordains priests and teachers to *p.* over church.

PRESS (*see also* Wine-press)

1 Ne. 8: 24 Lehi[1] beholds others *p.*

forward through mist; **2 Ne.** 31: 20 *p.*
forward with steadfastness in Christ.

PRETEND (*see also* Deceit; False; Lying)

Mosiah 12: 12 priests say Abinadi
p. the Lord hath spoken; **Alma** 1: 17
those practicing priestcraft *p.* to preach
according to belief; 30: 28 Korihor claims
priests yoke people with *p.* mysteries;
47: 27 Amalickiah *p.* to be wroth concerning murder of king.

PREVAIL (*see also* Conquer; Overcome;
Overpower; Overthrow; Prey)

3 Ne. 11: 39 (Matt. 16: 18) gates of
hell shall not *p.* against those who build
upon Christ's doctrine.

PREY (*see also* Captive, Captivity; Prevail;
Subject)

2 Ne. 9: 46 those whom devil obtains are *p.* to his awful misery; 20: 1–2
(Isa. 10: 1–2) wo unto those who decree
unrighteous decrees that widows may be
their *p.*; **Alma** 49: 3 because Lamanites
had destroyed city of Ammonihah once,
they suppose it will be easy *p.*; **Ether**
14: 22 Jaredites leave bodies of slain upon
land to become *p.* to worms of flesh.

PRICE (*see also* Money)

2 Ne. 9: 50 (26: 25; Isa. 55: 1) come
buy wine and milk without *p.*; **Alma** 1:
20 nonbelievers persecute saints because
they impart word without *p.*

PRICK (*see also* Arouse; Stir)

Jarom 1: 12 prophets and priests *p.*
people's hearts with word.

PRIDE, PROUD (*see also* Adorn; Boast;
Envy; Hardheartedness; High; Inequality; Puffed; Rich; Stiffnecked; Stubbornness; Vanity)

1 Ne. 11: 36 (12: 18) spacious building is *p.* of world; 22: 15 (3 Ne. 25: 1;
Mal. 4: 1) the *p.* shall be as stubble; **2 Ne.**
12: 12 (Isa. 2: 12) the *p.* and lofty shall
be brought low; 26: 20 Gentiles are lifted
up in *p.* of eyes; 28: 12 because of *p.*
latter-day churches are puffed up; 28: 15
the wise, learned, and rich who are puffed
up in *p.* of hearts shall be thrust down to
hell; **Jacob** 1: 16 Nephites search much
gold and silver, begin to be lifted up in
p.; 2: 13 because some obtain more
abundantly, they are lifted up in *p.* of
heart; **Alma** 1: 6 Nehor is lifted up in *p.*
of heart; 1: 20 unbelievers persecute
saints because they are not *p.*; 4: 6 people
of church wax *p.*; 4: 12 great inequality
among people, some lifting themselves
up with *p.*; 5: 23 he who is not stripped of
p. is not prepared to meet God; 38: 11
see that ye are not lifted up unto *p.*; **Hel.**

3: 33 *p.* enters hearts of those who profess
to belong to church; 12: 5 how quick to
be lifted up in *p.* are children of men; 13:
27 people would receive man who said,
Walk after *p.* of your own hearts; **3 Ne.**
6: 10 (4 Ne. 1: 24) some of people are
lifted up unto *p.* and boastings; **Morm.**
8: 28 churches shall be lifted up in *p.*
of hearts; 8: 36 only a few do not lift
themselves up in *p.* of hearts; **Moro.**
8: 27 *p.* of Nephites has proven their
destruction.

PRIEST (*see also* High Priest; Noah³,
Priests of; Priestcraft; Priesthood;
Priests, False; TG Priest, Aaronic Priest-
hood; Priest, False; Priest, Melchizedek
Priesthood; BD Priests)

2 Ne. 5: 26 (Jacob 1: 18) Nephi¹
consecrates Jacob² and Joseph² as *p.*;
Jarom 1: 1 *p.* labor diligently exhorting people to diligence, teaching law of
Moses; **Mosiah** 6: 3 Benjamin appoints
p. to teach people; 11: 5 Noah³ puts
down *p.* consecrated by father and appoints new ones; 18: 18 (23: 17) Alma¹,
having authority from God, ordains *p.*;
18: 24, 26 (27: 5; Alma 1: 26) Alma¹ commands *p.* to labor with own hands for
support; 18: 28 people impart of substance to *p.* that stand in need; 23: 17
only just men are ordained *p.*; 25: 21
every church has *p.* and teachers; 25: 21
p. preach word as delivered by Alma¹;
26: 7 unbelievers are delivered unto *p.* by
teachers; **Alma** 1: 26 *p.* leave labors to
impart word, then return to labors; 1: 26
p. does not esteem himself above his
hearers; 4: 7 *p.* are sorely grieved by
wickedness among people; 6: 1 Alma²
ordains *p.* and elders by laying on of
hands; 13: 1–12 the Lord ordained *p.*
after his holy order, order of Son; 13:
3, 5 *p.* were called and prepared from
foundation of world; 13: 4 *p.* are called
on account of their faith; 15: 13 Alma²
consecrates *p.* and teachers to baptize;
23: 4 Aaron³ and brethren establish
churches, consecrate *p.* among Lamanites; 45: 22 Helaman² and brethren
appoint *p.* throughout land over all
churches; **Moro.** ch. 3 manner in which
disciples ordain *p.* and teachers; **Moro.**
ch. 4–5 manner in which elders and *p.*
administer sacrament; 6: 1 elders, *p.*,
teachers were baptized if fruits showed
they were worthy.

PRIESTCRAFT (*see also* Churches, False;
Nehors, Order of; Priests, False;
Prophets, False; TG Priestcraft)

2 Ne. 10: 5 because of *p.*, Jews will
crucify Christ; 26: 29 *p.* are that men
preach to get gain and praise of world;
Alma 1: 12 Nehor is first to introduce *p.*
among Nephites; 1: 12 if *p.* were en-

forced among Nephites, it would prove their destruction; 1: 16 death of Nehor does not end *p.*, for many preach false doctrines for riches and honor; **3 Ne.** 16: 10 when Gentiles are filled with *p.*, Father will bring gospel from among them; 21: 19 all *p.* shall be done away; 30: 2 Mormon[2] calls Gentiles to turn from *p.*

PRIESTHOOD (*see also* Apostle; Authority; Calling; Elder; High Priest; Minister [verb]; Ministry; Office; Officer; Ordain; Order; Ordinance; Power; Preside; Priest; Teacher; TG Priesthood; Priesthood, Aaronic; Priesthood, Authority; Priesthood, History of; Priesthood, Keys of; Priesthood, Magnifying Callings within; Priesthood, Melchizedek; Priesthood, Oath and Covenant; Priesthood, Power of; Priesthood, Qualifying for)

Alma 4: 20 Alma[2] confines himself wholly to high *p.* of holy order of God; 13: 1–12 men are ordained unto high *p.* of holy order of God, after order of Son; 13: 7–9 high *p.* after order of Son was from foundation of world, without beginning of days or end of years; 13: 14, 18 Melchizedek took upon himself the high *p.* forever.

PRIESTS, FALSE (*see also* Idolatry; Nehors, Order of; Noah[3], Priests of; Priestcraft)

2 Ne. 28: 4 *p.* of latter-day churches shall contend with one another; **Mosiah** 11: 5 Noah[3] appoints new *p.*; **Alma** 14: 18, 27 *p.* after order of Nehor question Alma[2] and Amulek in prison; **4 Ne.** 1: 34 people are led by many *p.* and false prophets to build up many churches.

PRINCE (*see also* King)

2 Ne. 13: 4 (Isa. 3: 4) I will give children unto them to be their *p.*; 19: 6 (Isa. 9: 6) Messiah shall be called, The P. of Peace; **Alma** 13: 18 Melchizedek called the *p.* of peace.

PRINCIPLE

Moro. 9: 20 Nephites are without *p.*

PRINTS (*see* Nail)

PRISON (*see also* Bondage; Captive; Dungeons; Hell; Prisoner)

1 Ne. 7: 14 Jews have cast Jeremiah[1] into *p.*; **Mosiah** 7: 7 Ammon[1] and brethren are cast into *p.*; 12: 17 Abinadi is cast into *p.*; 14: 8 (Isa. 53: 8) Messiah was taken from *p.* and from judgment; **Alma** 14: 17 Alma[2] and Amulek are cast into *p.*; 14: 27 (Ether 12: 13) walls of *p.* are rent in twain; 20: 2–7, 22–30 (21: 13–15) brethren of Ammon[2] are in *p.* in Middoni; 62: 50 Nephites had been delivered from *p.*; **Hel.** 5: 21 Nephi[2] and

Lehi[4] are cast into same *p.* in which Ammon[1] and brethren were cast; 5: 27, 31 walls of *p.* shake and tremble; 9: 39 some who believe Nephi[2] were converted in *p.*; **3 Ne.** 12: 25 (Matt. 5: 25) agree with thine adversary quickly lest thou shalt be cast into *p.*; 28: 19 (4 Ne. 1: 30) *p.* could not hold three Nephites; **Morm.** 8: 24 by power of the Lord's word saints cause *p.* to tumble; **Ether** 10: 5–6 Riplakish builds many *p.*

PRISONER (*see also* Captive; Prison)

1 Ne. 21: 9 (Isa. 49: 9) thou mayest say to *p.*, Go forth; **Alma** 52: 8 Moroni[1] orders Teancum to retain all *p.*; 53: 1 *p.* of Lamanites are compelled to bury dead; 54: 1 Ammoron desires to exchange *p.* with Moroni[1]; 54: 11 Moroni[1] sets conditions for exchanging *p.*; 55: 25 Nephites cause Lamanite *p.* to fortify city; 57: 11–18 Lamanite *p.* are sent to Zarahemla, are killed during rebellion; 62: 27–29 Lamanite *p.* join Ammonites; 62: 30 Nephites take many Lamanite *p.* and regain Nephite *p.*; **3 Ne.** 5: 4 all robbers taken *p.* and cast into prison; **Morm.** 4: 2 Lamanites take many Nephite *p.*; 4: 14 Lamanites offer women and children *p.* as sacrifices to idols; **Moro.** 9: 7–8 Lamanites take *p.*, feed wives flesh of husbands.

PRIVATE, PRIVATELY (*see also* Closet; Privily; Secret)

Mosiah 18: 1 Alma[1] teaches Abinadi's words *p.*

PRIVILEGE, PRIVILEGED (*see also* Blessing; Right [noun])

2 Ne. 26: 28 all men are *p.* to partake of God's goodness; **Mosiah** 29: 32 every man should enjoy his *p.* alike; **Alma** 2: 4 if Amlici could gain voice of people, he would deprive them of *p.* of church; 6: 5 none are denied *p.* of assembling to hear word of God; 13: 4 except for blindness of minds, those who reject Spirit might have had as great *p.* as brethren; 30: 9 if man desires to serve God, it is his *p.*; 30: 27 Korihor accuses priests of leading people away, that they durst not enjoy *p.*; 43: 9 design of Nephites is to preserve rights and *p.*; 51: 6 freemen swear to maintain *p.* of religion by free government; **3 Ne.** 2: 12 converted Lamanites and Nephites take up arms against robbers to maintain *p.* of worship; 4: 16 robbers believe they can make Nephites yield by cutting off outward *p.*

PRIVILY (*see also* Private; Secret)

Alma 14: 3 people desire to put away Alma[2] and Amulek *p.*; 35: 5 rulers of Zoramites find out *p.* the minds of the people.

PRIZE (see also Reward)

Mosiah 4: 27 man should be diligent, that thereby he might win the p.

PROBATION, PROBATIONARY (see also Endure; Mortal, Mortality; Opposition; Prepare, Preparatory; Prove; Tempt; Trial)

1 Ne. 10: 21 if men have sought to do wickedly during days of p., they are found unclean before judgment; 15: 32 men must be judged of works done in days of p.; 2 Ne. 2: 21 men's state became state of p.; 9: 27 wo unto him who wasteth days of p.; 33: 9 continue in straight and narrow path until end of day of p.; Alma 12: 24 this life became p. state; 42: 4 p. time granted to man to repent; 42: 10 p. state became state for men to prepare; 42: 13 plan of redemption can be brought about only on condition of repentance in this p. state; Hel. 13: 38 your days of p. are past; Morm. 9: 28 be wise in days of p.

PROCLAMATION (see also Declare; Decree)

Mosiah 7: 17 Limhi sends p. among people to gather; 22: 6 p. to be sent to gather flocks and drive them into wilderness by night; 27: 2 Mosiah² sends p. that unbelievers should not persecute believers; Alma 22: 27 (23: 1) Lamanite king sends p. throughout land not to harm Aaron³ and brethren; 30: 57 p. calls followers of Korihor to repent; Hel. 9: 9 p. announces murder of chief judge and capture of murderers; 3 Ne. 3: 13, 22 Lachoneus sends p. that all people should gather in one place.

PROCRASTINATE (see also Delay; Idleness; Slothful)

Alma 13: 27 (34: 33–34) do not p. day of repentance; 34: 35 if ye have p. day of repentance, ye have become subjected to spirit of devil; Hel. 13: 38 have p. day of salvation until it is everlastingly too late.

PROFESS (see also Claim; Profession)

Alma 5: 37 ye that have p. to know ways of righteousness have gone astray; 51: 21 Moroni¹ puts end to pride of those who p. blood of nobility; Hel. 3: 33 pride enters hearts of those who p. to belong to church; 4: 11 slaughter of Nephites caused by wickedness of those who p. to belong to church; 4 Ne. 1: 27 many churches p. to know Christ, but deny his gospel.

PROFESSION (see also Craftiness, Craft)

Alma 10: 15 lawyers are learned in arts and cunning that they might be skillful in their p.; 14: 18 (15: 15; 16: 11) priests of Ammonihah are of p. of Nehor.

PROFIT (see also Advantage; Avail; Benefit; Gain; Prosper; Reward)

1 Ne. 19: 23 Nephi¹ likens scriptures to Nephites, that they might be for their p.; 20: 17 (Isa. 48: 17) the Lord teacheth thee to p.; 2 Ne. 2: 14 Lehi¹ speaks to sons for their p.; 4: 15 Nephi¹ writes scriptures for learning and p. of his children; 9: 28 the wisdom of the learned p. them not; Jacob 5: 32, 35, 42 tree p. master of vineyard nothing; W of M 1: 2 writings may some day p. Nephites; Alma 30: 34 what doth it p. us to labor in church save to declare truth; 3 Ne. 24: 14 (Mal. 3: 14) what doth it p. that we have kept his ordinances; Moro. 7: 6 if evil man offers gift without real intent, it p. him nothing; 7: 6, 9 if a man prays without real intent it p. him nothing; 10: 8 gifts of Spirit are given unto men to p. them.

PROGRESS

Mosiah 1: 17 (Alma 37: 14) when Lehites were unfaithful, they did not p. on journey; Alma 4: 10 church fails to p. because of wickedness; 60: 30 Moroni¹ will strike those who impede p. of Nephites in cause of freedom.

PROLONG (see also Increase; Lengthen)

2 Ne. 2: 21 men's days were p., that they might repent while in flesh; Mosiah 14: 10 (Isa. 53: 10) he shall p. his days; Alma 9: 16 (Hel. 15: 4, 11) the Lord will p. Lamanites' existence in land; 9: 18 if Nephites persist in wickedness, their days will not be p.

PROMISE (see also Covenant; Oath; Promised; Swear)

2 Ne. 3: 5, 14 Joseph¹ obtained p. that righteous branch of Israel would rise out of fruit of his loins; 10: 2 p. which Nephites have obtained are p. according to flesh; 10: 17 (Alma 37: 17) the Lord will fulfill his p. to men; 25: 21 the Lord p. that records will be preserved; 25: 21 the Lord p. Joseph¹ his seed should never perish; Alma 9: 16, 24 many p. are extended to Lamanites; 9: 24 the Lord's p. are not extended to Nephites if they transgress; 50: 21 the Lord's p. have been verified to Nephites; 4 Ne. 1: 11 Nephites are blessed according to the multitude of p. which the Lord had made to them; Morm. 8: 22 eternal purposes of the Lord to roll on until all his p. are fulfilled; 9: 21 p. that Father will answer prayers is unto all; Ether 8: 17 Akish leads friends and kindred away by fair p.; 12: 17 by faith, three Nephites obtained p. not to taste death; Moro. 7:

41 men will be raised unto life eternal because of faith in Christ, according to the p.

PROMISED LAND (*see also* Covenant; Inherit; Land; Liberty; Zion; TG Promised Land)

1 Ne. 2: 20 (4: 14; 7: 13; 14: 1–2; 2 Ne. 1: 9, 20; Jarom 1: 9; Omni 1: 6; Ether 2: 8–11) if people keep commandments, they will prosper in land of p.; 2: 20 (5: 5; 7: 13; 2 Ne. 1: 5) Lehites are given land of p.; 2: 20 (2 Ne. 1: 5; 3: 2; 10: 19; Ether 1: 38, 42; 2: 7, 10, 15; 9: 20; 10: 28; 13: 2) p.l. is choice above all other lands; 5: 5 Lehi[1] has obtained a land of p.; 10: 13 Lehites must be led into land of p. unto fulfilling of the Lord's word that Israel should be scattered; ch. 12–14 Nephi[1] beholds vision of future of land of p.; 17: 38 the Lord leads away the righteous into precious lands; 18: 23 Lehites arrive at p.l.; 22: 12 (2 Ne. 6: 11; 9: 2; 10: 7; 25: 11; 3 Ne. 20: 33; 29: 1) Israel to be gathered to land of inheritance; **2 Ne.** 9: 2 Jews shall be established in all their lands of p.; 24: 2 (Isa. 14: 2) Israel shall return to lands of p.; **Jacob** 2: 12 land of p. abounds in precious metals; Enos 1: 10 I have given thy brethren this holy land; **Mosiah** 10: 15 brethren were wroth with Nephi[1] when they had arrived in p.l.; **3 Ne.** 20: 29 Father will remember covenant to give his people again the land of Jerusalem, which is p.l. unto them forever; 21: 22 the Lord has given land to remnant of Jacob for their inheritance; **Ether** 2: 7–15 (1: 42–43) the Lord leads Jaredites to land of p.; 6: 12 Jaredites land upon shore of land of p.

PROPERTY

1 Ne. 3: 25–26 (4: 11) Laban takes p. of sons of Lehi[1].

PROPHECY, PROPHESY (*see also* Declare; Holy Ghost; Inspire; Preach; Prophet; Revelation; TG Prophecy)

2 Ne. 25: 1 words of Isaiah[1] are hard for Nephites to understand because they know not Jew's manner of p.; 25: 4 Nephi[1] will p. with plainness; 25: 4 words of Isaiah[1] are plain to all who are filled with spirit of p.; 25: 7 Nephi[1] proceeds with his own p.; 25: 26 Nephites p. of Christ; **Jacob** 4: 6 Nephites have many revelations and spirit of p.; 4: 13 let him who p. p. to understanding of men; **W of M** 1: 4 p. of Christ's coming are pleasing to Mormon[2]; **Mosiah** 5: 3 were it expedient, Nephites could p. of all things; 12: 29 (13: 26) the Lord has sent Abinadi to p. great evil against people of Noah[3]; **Alma** 4: 20 Alma[2] confines himself wholly to testimony of the word, according to spirit of p.; 9: 4 Ammoni-

hahites will not believe his words if Alma[2] p. destruction; 17: 3 sons of Mosiah[2] have spirit of p.; 25: 16 Nephites retain hope through faith, unto eternal salvation, relying upon spirit of p.; 30: 12 Korihor preaches against p. of Christ's coming; 45: 9 that which Alma[2] p. to Helaman[2] shall not be made known until p. has been fulfilled; **Hel.** 4: 23 Nephites deny spirit of p.; 14: 1 (3 Ne. 23: 9–13) Samuel p. many things that are not written; **3 Ne.** 1: 4 p. of prophets begin to be fulfilled more fully; 29: 6 wo unto him who says the Lord no longer works by p.; **Morm.** 8: 23 search the p. of Isaiah[1]; **Ether** 12: 5 Ether p. many great things, which people do not believe; **Moro.** 10: 13 to another is given that he may p. concerning all things; 10: 28 I declare these things unto the fulfilling of p.

PROPHET (*see also* Apostle; Martyrdom; Preach; Prophecy; Prophetess; Prophets, False; Revelation; Revelator; Seer; Servant; TG Prophets, Mission of; Prophets, Rejection of; BD Prophet)

1 Ne. 3: 18 (7: 14; 2 Ne. 27: 5) Jews have rejected words of p.; 10: 4 six hundred years after Lehi[1] left Jerusalem, the Lord would raise up a p., a Messiah; 11: 27 p. should prepare way before Redeemer; 19: 20 had not the Lord shown Nephi[1] concerning Jews, as he had p. of old, he should have perished; 22: 2 by Spirit are all things made known unto p.; 22: 20–21 (3 Ne. 20: 23) the Lord will raise up p. like unto Moses, the Holy One; **2 Ne.** 25: 5 Jews understand words of p.; 25: 18 only one Messiah spoken of by p.; 26: 3 (Jacob 4: 14) Jews shall perish because they killed p.; 26: 5 depths of earth shall swallow up those who kill p.; **Jacob** 4: 6 we search the p.; 6: 8 will ye reject words of p.; **Enos** 1: 22–23 many p. among Nephites, preaching destruction; **Jarom** 1: 11 p. exhort people to diligence, teach law of Moses; **Mosiah** 7: 26 Limhi's people have slain p.; 8: 15 seer is greater than p.; 8: 16 seer is revelator and p.; **Alma** 20: 15 Lamoni knows Ammon[2] and brethren are holy p.; 37: 30 (Ether 9: 29; 11: 2) Jaredites were destroyed because they murdered p.; **Hel.** 9: 2 people do not believe Nephi[2] is p.; 13: 24 Nephites cast out p.; 13: 25–28 Nephites reject true p. and accept false p.; 13: 32–33 (3 Ne. 8: 25) Nephites will lament that they killed p.; **3 Ne.** 1: 13 on morrow Christ comes into world to fulfill that spoken by p.; 6: 23–25 (7: 6, 10) judges put p. to death secretly; 7: 14 Nephites stone the p.; 10: 12 more righteous people are saved, for they had received p.; 10: 14 destruction fulfills prophecies of many of the holy p.; 11: 10 I am Jesus Christ, whom the p. testified

shall come; 12: 11–12 (Matt. 5: 11–12) blessed are you when men persecute you, for so persecuted they the p.; 23: 5 search the p., for many testify of these things; **Ether** 7: 24 Jaredites revile against p. and mock them; 9: 28 p. come into land crying repentance; 9: 29 (11: 22) Jaredites believe not the p.; **Moro.** 7: 23 God declared unto p. that Christ should come.

PROPHETESS

2 Ne. 18: 3 (Isa. 8: 3) I went unto the p., and she conceived and bare a son.

PROPHETS, FALSE (see also Antichrist; Apostasy; Christs, False; Dissenter; Doctrine, False; Priestcraft)

W of M 1: 15–16 false p. among the people; **Hel.** 13: 25–28 Nephites reject true p. and accept false p.; **3 Ne.** 14: 15 (Matt. 7: 15) beware of false p. who come in sheep's clothing; **4 Ne.** 1: 34 Nephites are led by false p. to build many churches.

PROSPER, PROSPERITY (see also Blessing; Gain; Profit; Reward; Rich; Riches; Righteousness)

1 Ne. 2: 20 (2 Ne. 1: 9, 20, 31; Jarom 1: 9; Mosiah 1: 7; Alma 37: 13; 49: 30; 50: 20) if ye keep commandments, ye shall p.; **2 Ne.** 5: 11 Nephites p. exceedingly; 28: 21 devil will lull some, that they say, Zion p., all is well; **Jarom** 1: 9 because Nephites are prepared, Lamanites do not p. against them; **Mosiah** 7: 29 in day of transgression the Lord will hedge up people's ways that they p. not; 21: 16 people of Limhi begin to p. by degrees; 27: 7 Alma² becomes great hindrance to p. of church; **Hel.** 3: 25 so great is p. of church that high priests are astonished; 3: 26 work of the Lord p.; 12: 1 the Lord p. those who put trust in him; 12: 2 when the Lord p. his people, they harden hearts and forget him; **3 Ne.** 22: 17 (Isa. 54: 17) no weapon that is formed against thee shall p.; **4 Ne.** 1: 23 Nephites become rich because of p. in Christ.

PROTECT, PROTECTION (see also Preserve; Refuge; Safe; Security; Spare)

1 Ne. 5: 8 the Lord has p. sons of Sariah; **Mosiah** 9: 15 people call upon Zeniff for p.; **3 Ne.** 4: 10, 30 Nephites supplicate God for p.

PROUD (see Pride, Proud)

PROVE, PROVEN (see also Evidence; Probation; Reprove; Tempt; Testify; Trial; Try; Witness)

2 Ne. 11: 3 God sends witnesses to p. all his words; **Alma** 34: 6–7 Alma² has appealed to Moses to p. prophecies of Christ are true; **Hel.** 9: 38 brother of chief judge is brought to p. he is murderer;

3 Ne. 1: 24 some try to p. by scriptures that Nephites no longer need to observe law of Moses; 24: 10 (Mal. 3: 10) bring tithes into storehouse and p. the Lord; **Ether** 12: 35 if Gentiles have not charity because of Nephites' weakness, the Lord will p. them.

PROVIDE (see also Give; Maintain; Prepare)

1 Ne. 17: 3 if men keep commandments, God p. means to accomplish what is commanded; **Mosiah** 8: 18 God has p. a means that man might work mighty miracles.

PROVISION (see also Substance)

3 Ne. 4: 4, 18–19 Nephites gather all p. in one place to deny food for robbers.

PROVOKE, PROVOCATION (see also Anger; Indignation; Stir)

2 Ne. 13: 8 (Isa. 3: 8) doings of Judah have p. eyes of the Lord's glory; **Jacob** 1: 7 teachers labor diligently lest the Lord swear Nephites not enter his rest, as in p. in days of temptation; 1: 8 (Alma 12: 37) teachers persuade men not to p. God to anger; **Alma** 12: 36 your iniquity p. the Lord to send down wrath as in first p.; **Hel.** 7: 18 Nephites have p. the Lord to anger; **Moro.** 7: 45 (1 Cor. 13: 5) charity is not easily p.

PRUDENCE, PRUDENT, PRUDENTLY (see also Wisdom; Wise)

2 Ne. 9: 43 things of the wise and p. shall be hid from them; 13: 1–2 (Isa. 3: 1–2) the Lord doth take away from Judah the p.; 15: 21 (Isa. 5: 21) wo unto the p. in their own sight; 20: 13 (Isa. 10: 13) the Lord is p.; 27: 26 (Isa. 29: 14) the understanding of their p. shall be hid; **3 Ne.** 20: 43 my servant shall deal p.

PRUNE, PRUNING (see also Cut; Pluck)

2 Ne. 12: 4 (Isa. 2: 4) nations shall beat their spears into p-hooks; 15: 6 (Isa. 5: 6) vineyard shall not be p. nor digged; **Jacob** 5: 4, 27, 62, 69 the Lord p. vineyard; 6: 2 the Lord's servants to go forth last time to p. vineyard.

PUBLISH (see also Declare; Preach)

1 Ne. 13: 37 (Mosiah 12: 21; 15: 14–15; 27: 37; 3 Ne. 20: 40; Isa. 52: 7) how beautiful upon mountains are feet of those who p. peace; **Mosiah** 27: 32 Alma² and companions p. unto people things they have heard and seen; **Alma** 30: 57 knowledge of what happened to Korihor is p. throughout land.

PUFFED, PUFFING (see also Pride; Vanity)

2 Ne. 9: 42 the Lord despises those who are p. up because of learning, wisdom,

riches; 28: 9, 12–15 many shall be *p.* up in hearts and seek deep to hide counsels from the Lord; **Alma** 5: 37 those who are *p.* up in vain things of world have gone astray; 31: 27 men cry unto God with mouths while they are *p.* up with vain things of world; **3 Ne.** 6: 15 Satan *p.* people up in pride; **Moro.** 7: 45 (1 Cor. 13: 4) charity is not *p.* up.

PULL (*see also* Destruction)

Alma 4: 19 Alma² seeks to *p.* down, by preaching word, the pride and contention among his people; 12: 37 let us repent, that we provoke not the Lord to *p.* down his wrath; 51: 17–18 Moroni¹ *p.* down pride of king-men; 54: 9 Ammoron will *p.* down wrath of God to his utter destruction; 60: 36 Moroni¹ seeks not for power, but to *p.* it down; **3 Ne.** 14: 4 (Matt. 7: 4) wilt thou say to brother, Let me *p.* mote from thine eye.

PUNISHMENT, PUNISH (*see also* Chasten; Crime; Curse; Damnation; Hedge; Hell; Indignation; Justice; Law; Penalty; Sin; Transgression; Vengeance; Wrath; TG Punish, Punishment)

2 Ne. 2: 10 law given unto inflicting of *p.*; 2: 10 (Alma 42: 16) punishment affixed to law is in opposition to happiness affixed; 2: 13 if there be no righteousness nor happiness, there be no *p.* nor misery; 2: 26 men are free not to be acted upon, save by *p.* of law; 9: 25 where no law is given, no *p.*, where no *p.* no condemnation; 23: 11 the Lord will *p.* world for evil; **Jacob** 7: 18 Sherem confesses and speaks of eternal *p.*; **W of M** 1: 15 false Christs are *p.* according to crimes; **Mosiah** 2: 33 he who listeth to obey evil spirit receiveth for his wages everlasting *p.*; 29: 15 those who commit iniquity are *p.* according to law; **Alma** 1: 17 liars are *p.*; 30: 9 no law to *p.* unbelievers; 30: 10 those who murder, steal, commit adultery are *p.*; 30: 11 man is *p.* only for his crimes; 42: 1 Corianton is concerned over justice of God in *p.* of sinner; 42: 16 repentance could not come unto men except there were a *p.*; 42: 17–18 how could there be a law save there was a *p.*; 42: 18, 22 a law given and a *p.* affixed; 42: 22 the law inflicteth the *p.*; **3 Ne.** 5: 5 those who continue in secret murders and threatenings are *p.* according to law; **Morm.** 4: 5 the wicked are *p.* by the wicked.

PURGE (*see also* Purify; Refine)

3 Ne. 24: 3 (Mal. 3: 3) the Lord shall *p.* sons of Levi¹ as gold and silver.

PURIFIER

3 Ne. 24: 3 (Mal. 3: 3) he shall sit as refiner and *p.* of silver.

PURIFY (*see also* Cleanse; Fire; Purge; Purifier; Purity; Refine; Sanctification; Wash)

Mosiah 4: 2 apply atoning blood of Christ, that hearts may be *p.*; **Alma** 5: 21 no man can be saved except his garments are *p.*; **Hel.** 3: 35 saints fast and pray oft, even unto *p.* of their hearts; **3 Ne.** 19: 28–29 disciples have been *p.* and those who believe their words shall be *p.*; **Moro.** 7: 48 pray unto Father that we may be *p.* even as he is pure.

PURITY, PURE (*see also* Blameless, Chastity; Clean; Guiltless; Holiness; Innocence; Righteousness; Purify; Sanctification; Spotless; Virtue; White)

1 Ne. 13: 25 gospel goes forth in *p.* from Jews to Gentiles; 14: 26 sealed writings shall come forth in *p.*; **2 Ne.** 9: 14 the righteous shall have perfect knowledge of their righteousness, being clothed in *p.*; 9: 47 would I harrow up your souls if your minds were *p.*; 25: 16 when Jews worship Father with *p.* hearts and clean hands, they will believe in Christ; 30: 6 Lamanites to be *p.* and delightsome; **Jacob** 3: 2 ye who are *p.* in heart, receive word of God; **Alma** 4: 19 Alma² sees no way to reclaim his people save in bearing down in *p.* testimony against them; 5: 19 can ye look up to God with *p.* heart and clean hands; 13: 12 priests, being *p.* and spotless before God, could not look upon sin without abhorrence; 16: 21 word of God is preached in *p.* in all the land; 32: 42 fruit of word is *p.* above all that is *p.*; **3 Ne.** 12: 8 (Matt. 5: 8) blessed are *p.* in heart, for they shall see God; **Morm.** 9: 6 cry unto Father that ye may be found *p.*; **Moro.** 7: 47 charity is *p.* love of Christ; 7: 48 pray unto Father that we may be purified even as he is *p.*

PURPOSE (*see also* Desire; End, Ends; Intent; Reason; Will)

1 Ne. 9: 3, 5 (19: 3; W of M 1: 7; Alma 37: 2, 12, 14, 18) plates made for special *p.*; **2 Ne.** 2: 11–12 without opposition there would have been no *p.* in end of its creation; 2: 15 (Alma 37: 7; 42: 26; Morm. 8: 22) the Lord brings about his eternal *p.*; 31: 13 follow Son with full *p.* of heart; **Mosiah** 7: 33 turn to the Lord with full *p.* of heart; **Alma** 11: 20 judges stir up people for sole *p.* to get gain; **3 Ne.** 10: 6 (12: 24; 18: 32; Acts 11: 23) come unto Christ with full *p.* of heart; **Morm.** 5: 14 Father brings about eternal *p.* through Son.

PUT (*see also* Trust)

Mosiah 3: 19 natural man is enemy to God unless he *p.* off natural man; **Alma** 30: 42 ye have *p.* off Spirit, that it has no

place in you; 3 Ne. 12: 31–32 (Matt. 5: 31–32) whosoever *p.* away his wife, save for fornication, causes her to commit adultery; 13: 25 (Matt. 6: 25) take no thought for your body, what ye shall *p.* on.

QUAKE, QUAKING (see also Earthquake; Fear; Fear of God; Shake; Tremble)

1 Ne. 1: 6 because of what he sees, Lehi[1] *q.* and trembles; 12: 4 many cities to tumble to earth because of *q.*; 22: 23 all who belong to kingdom of devil need *q.*; 2 Ne. 4: 22 the Lord has confounded mine enemies, causing them to *q.*; Mosiah 28: 3 thought that any soul should endure endless torment causes sons of Mosiah[2] to *q.*; Hel. 12: 9 at the Lord's voice hills and mountains *q.*; 3 Ne. 8: 12 whole face of land is changed because of great *q.* of whole earth; 11: 3 small voice pierces to center, that no part of frame does not *q.*

QUARREL (see also Contention; Disputations)

Mosiah 4: 14 ye will not suffer your children to *q.* with each other.

QUEEN (see also King; Ruler)

1 Ne. 21: 23 (2 Ne. 6: 7; 10: 9; Isa. 49: 23) *q.* of Gentiles shall be Israel's nursing mothers; Alma 19: 2–11 Lamoni's *q.* has faith in Ammon; 19: 12–18 *q.* overcome by Spirit; 19: 29–30 *q.* is raised, praises Jesus, raises Lamoni; 47: 32–34 Amalickiah reports death of Lamanite king to *q.*; 47: 35 Amalickiah takes Lamanite *q.* to wife.

QUENCH (see also Fire; Satisfy)

1 Ne. 17: 29 Moses brings water from rock to *q.* Israelites' thirst; Jacob 6: 8 will ye reject gift of Holy Ghost and *q.* Holy Spirit.

QUESTION (see also Ask; Inquire)

Mosiah 12: 18–19 priests of Noah[3] begin to *q.* Abinadi; Alma 10: 13–14 lawyers of Ammonihah think to *q.* Alma[2] and Amulek; 34: 5 great *q.* in Zoramites' minds is whether there will be a Christ; Hel. 9: 19 multitude begins to *q.* Nephi[2] to cross him.

QUICK, QUICKLY [=fast] (see also Faster; Haste; Quick [=living]; Rash; Slow; Swift)

Mosiah 13: 29 children of Israel *q.* to do iniquity; Alma 5: 28 ye must prepare *q.*, for kingdom is at hand; 9: 26 Son is *q.* to hear cries of his people; 33: 21 if ye could be healed by casting eyes, would ye not behold *q.*; 46: 8 how *q.* men forget the Lord; Hel. 3: 29 word of God is *q.* and powerful; 12: 5 how *q.* are men to be lifted up in pride; 3 Ne. 7: 15 Nephites *q.* return from righteousness to wicked-

ness; 12: 25 (Matt. 5: 25) agree with thine adversary *q.*

QUICK [=living] (see also Alive; Living)

Moro. 10: 34 Jehovah, the Eternal Judge of both the *q.* and dead.

QUIVER

1 Ne. 21: 2 (Isa. 49: 2) in his *q.* hath the Lord hid me.

RABBANAH

Alma 18: 13 R., meaning powerful or great king.

RACA—word suggesting contempt in Aramaic and Greek

3 Ne. 12: 22 (Matt. 5: 22) whosoever says to brother, R., shall be in danger of council.

RACK

Mosiah 27: 29 (Alma 36: 12, 14) soul of Alma[2] is *r.* with eternal torment; Alma 26: 9 if Ammon[2] and brethren had not come from Zarahemla, Lamanites would still be *r.* with hatred.

RAGE (see also Fury)

2 Ne. 28: 20 devil shall *r.* in men's hearts.

RAILING (see also Revile)

3 Ne. 6: 13 some return *r.* for *r.*, others receive *r.* humbly.

RAIMENT (see also Apparel; Clothing; Garment)

Mosiah 4: 19 do we not all depend upon God for food and *r.*; 3 Ne. 13: 25 (Matt. 6: 25) is not the body more than *r.*; 13: 28 (Matt. 6: 28) why take ye thought for *r.*

RAIN (see also Destruction; Famine; Flood; BD Rain)

2 Ne. 15: 6 (Isa. 5: 6) the Lord will command clouds that they *r.* no *r.*; Hel. 11: 13, 17 Nephi[2] prays for *r.*; Ether 2: 24 *r.* and floods has the Lord sent forth; 9: 30 Jaredites begin to be destroyed because of no *r.*; 9: 35 when Jaredites have humbled themselves, the Lord sends *r.*

RAISE (see also Death, Physical; Exalt; Heal; Jesus Christ, Resurrection of; Miracle; Resurrection; Rise)

1 Ne. 7: 1 sons of Lehi[1] take wives, that they might *r.* up seed; 10: 4 the Lord will *r.* Messiah among Jews; 17: 37 the Lord *r.* up a righteous nation and destroys wicked nations; 22: 7 the Lord will *r.* up mighty nation among Gentiles; 2 Ne. 3: 5 from descendants of Joseph[1]

the Lord would r. righteous branch of Israel; 3: 7 the Lord will r. choice seer from descendants of Joseph[1]; 3: 10 the Lord will r. Moses to deliver Israel; 10: 25 may God r. you from death by power of resurrection; Jacob 2: 30 if the Lord will r. seed unto himself, he will command his people; Mosiah 3: 5 (3 Ne. 26: 15) Messiah shall r. the dead; Alma 5: 15 (11: 45) this mortal body to be r. in immortality; 11: 42 because of Christ's death, all shall be r. from temporal death; 33: 19 (Hel. 8: 14; Num. 21: 9; John 3: 14) type of Christ r. up in wilderness; 41: 4 all things shall be r. to endless happiness or endless misery; Hel. 12: 17 if the Lord says to mountain, Be r. up, it is done; 3 Ne. 7: 19 (19: 4) Nephi[3] r. brother from dead; 15: 1 the Lord will r. him who remembers these sayings; 20: 26 Father r. Christ first unto Israel; 4 Ne. 1: 5 Jesus' disciples r. the dead; Moro. 7: 41 ye shall have hope through Christ's atonement and resurrection to be r. unto life eternal.

RAMAH, HILL—*Jaredite name for Hill Cumorah (see also Cumorah, Land and Hill of)*

Ether 15: 11 army of Coriantumr[2] pitch tents by hill R., where Mormon[2] hid records.

RAMEUMPTOM—*elevated place in synagogues of Zoramites[2]*

Alma 31: 13–14 those who worship must stand upon top and recite prayer; 31: 21 R., being interpreted, is the holy stand.

RANKS (see also Inequality)

Mosiah 10: 9 men in Zeniff's army placed in r. according to age; 3 Ne. 6: 12 people distinguished by r. according to riches and chances for learning.

RANSOM (see also Deliver; Redemption)

2 Ne. 8: 10 (Isa. 51: 10) art thou not he who hath made depths of sea a way for the r. to pass over; Alma 52: 8 Moroni[1] retains Lamanite prisoners as r. for those taken by Lamanites.

RASH, RASHLY (see also Foolish; Haste; Quick, Quickly)

Alma 51: 10 Amalickiah's promise is r.; Morm. 8: 19 he who judgeth r. shall be judged r.

RAVENING, RAVENOUS (see Wolf)

RAW (see Meat)

READ (see also Book; Language; Rehearse; Scriptures; Search; Study; Word; Writing)

1 Ne. 16: 29 new writing upon Lia-

hona is plain to be r.; 19: 22–23 (ch. 20–21) Nephi[1] r. many things engraven upon brass plates; 2 Ne. 6: 4–7, 16–18 (ch. 7–8) Jacob[2] r. the words of Isaiah to Nephites; Jacob 5: 1–77 do ye not remember having r. the words of Zenos comparing Israel to tame olive-tree; Mosiah 1: 5 records preserved that people might r. and understand God's mysteries; 25: 5–6 Mosiah[2] r. to his people records of Zeniff and Alma[1]; Alma 22: 12–14 Aaron[3] r. scriptures to Lamanite king; 33: 14 if ye have r. the scriptures, how can ye disbelieve on Son of God; 3 Ne. 10: 14 whoso r., let him understand; 27: 4–5 why do the people dispute, have they not r. scriptures; Morm. 9: 8 he who denies God's revelations has not r. the scriptures; Ether 3: 22 brother of Jared[2] to record experience in language that cannot be r.; 12: 24 things written by brother of Jared[2] are mighty unto overpowering of man to r. them; Moro. 10: 3 when ye have r. these things, remember how merciful God has been to men.

READY (see also Prepare)

3 Ne. 18: 13 gates of hell are r. to receive those who build on sandy foundation.

REALITY, REAL, REALLY (see also Intent; True)

2 Ne. 9: 47 Jacob[2] must awaken brethren to awful r. of judgment; Jacob 4: 13 Spirit speaks of things as they r. are and r. will be; Alma 32: 35 is not this r.

REAP (see also Harvest; Pluck; Receive; Reward; Sow [verb]; Thrash)

Mosiah 7: 30–31 if people sow filthiness, they shall r. chaff in whirlwind; Alma 26: 5 ye did thrust in your sickle and r. with your might; 3 Ne. 13: 26 (Matt. 6: 26) fowls of air neither sow nor r.; Ether 10: 25 Jaredites make tools to r.

REASON, REASONS [noun] (see also Cause; Reasoning)

2 Ne. 9: 6 resurrection must come unto man by r. of fall; Mosiah 7: 24 great are r. which ye have to mourn; Alma 24: 26 because the slain were righteous, we have no r. to doubt they are saved; 26: 1 how great r. have we to rejoice; 28: 11 thousands mourn loss of kindred because they have r. to fear they are consigned to endless wo; 33: 20 the r. Israelites would not look upon type is that they did not believe it would heal them; 3 Ne. 5: 20 Mormon[2] has r. to bless his God; Morm. 9: 20 r. why God ceases to do miracles is unbelief.

REASONING, REASON, REASONABLE (see also Consider; Ponder; Teach; Think)

Hel. 16: 17 Nephites *r.* and contend among themselves; 16: 18 Nephites say it is not *r.* that such a being as Christ should come.

REBEL, REBELLION, REBELLIOUS (*see also* Apostasy; Contention; Defiance; Devil; Disobedience; Disputations; Dissenter; Excommunication; Hardheartedness; Iniquity; Murmur; Reject; Resist; Stiffnecked; Trample; Transgression; Unbelief; TG Rebellion)

1 Ne. 2: 21, 23–24 (7: 6) if brothers of Nephi[1] *r.*, they will be cut off; **2 Ne.** 1: 2 Lehi[1] speaks to sons concerning their *r.*; **Jacob** 1: 8 we would persuade all men not to *r.* against God; **Mosiah** 2: 36–37 man who transgresses against his knowledge comes out in open *r.* against God; 15: 26 the Lord redeems none who *r.* against him; 15: 26 those who willfully *r.* against God have no part in first resurrection; 27: 11 (Alma 36: 13) Alma[2] and sons of Mosiah[2] *r.* against God; **Alma** 3: 18 Amlicites are cursed because they come out in open *r.* against God; 23: 7 converted Lamanites lay down weapons of *r.*; 57: 32 Lamanite prisoners rise in *r.*; 62: 2 Moroni[1] mourns because of those who *r.* against country and God; **Hel.** 4: 2 the *r.* are slain and driven out of land; 8: 25 Nephites have rejected truth and *r.* against God; **3 Ne.** 6: 18 Nephites know will of God, but *r.* willfully against him; **4 Ne.** 1: 38 those who willfully *r.* against God are called Lamanites; **Morm.** 1: 16 Mormon[2] is forbidden to preach to people, because they willfully *r.* against God; 2: 15 thousands of Nephites are hewn down in open *r.* against God.

REBUKE (*see also* Admonish; Chasten; Confound; Reproach; Reprove; Warn)

2 Ne. 7: 2 (Isa. 50: 2) at his *r.*, the Lord dries up sea; 8: 20 (Isa. 51: 20) two sons are full of *r.* of God; 12: 4 (Isa. 2: 4) the Lord will judge among nations and *r.* many; **Alma** 19: 20 other Lamanites *r.* those who murmur against Ammon[2]; **3 Ne.** 24: 11 (Mal. 3: 11) the Lord will *r.* the devourer for your sakes.

RECEIVE (*see also* Answer; Obtain; Partake; Reap)

1 Ne. 17: 30 the Lord did all things for Israelites which were expedient for man to *r.*; **2 Ne.** 25: 3 Nephi[1] writes unto those who will hereafter *r.* what he writes; 28: 27 wo unto him who says, We have *r.*, and we need no more; 28: 28 he that is built upon rock *r.* it with gladness; **Jacob** 3: 2 *r.* the pleasing word of God; **Enos** 1: 15 (Mosiah 4: 21; Alma 22: 16; 3 Ne. 18: 20; Moro. 7: 26) ask, believing ye shall *r.*, and ye shall *r.* it; **Mosiah** 4: 6–7 this is the man who *r.* salvation; 22: 14 Mosiah[2]

r. Limhi's people with joy; 26: 21 he who hears the Lord's voice shall be *r.* into church and *r.* by the Lord; 26: 37 church *r.* many, baptizes many; **Alma** 5: 14 have ye *r.* God's image in your countenances; 12: 10 he who hardens heart *r.* lesser portion of words; 16: 16 the Lord pours out Spirit to prepare men to *r.* the word; 35: 9 people of Ammon[2] *r.* all the poor of the Zoramites; **3 Ne.** 9: 16 Christ came unto his own and they *r.* him not; 9: 22 whoso comes unto the Lord as little child will he *r.*; 14: 8 (Matt. 7: 8) every one who asketh *r.*; 27: 29 (Matt. 7: 7–8) ask and ye shall *r.*; **Moro.** 10: 4 when ye *r.* these things, ask God if they are true.

RECKON, RECKONING (*see also* Measure; Record; Time)

Alma 11: 4 Nephites do not *r.* after manner of Jews; 11: 5–19 system of *r.* among Nephites; **3 Ne.** 2: 8 Nephites *r.* time from period when sign of Christ's birth was given.

RECLAIM (*see also* Deliver; Recover; Restoration; Save)

Jacob 7: 24 many means were devised to *r.* Lamanites to knowledge of truth; **Alma** 4: 19 Alma[2] sees no way to *r.* his people save by bearing down in pure testimony against them; 42: 8 not expedient that man should be *r.* from temporal death; 42: 9 expedient that man should be *r.* from spiritual death; 42: 12 no means to *r.* man from fallen state; 55: 28 Nephites *r.* their rights and privileges.

RECONCILE, RECONCILIATION (*see also* Forgive; Jesus Christ, Atonement through; Satisfy; Subject; Submissive)

2 Ne. 10: 24 *r.* yourselves to will of God; 25: 23 we labor diligently to persuade men to be *r.* to God; 33: 9 for none can I hope except they shall be *r.* unto Christ; **Jacob** 4: 11 be *r.* unto God through atonement of Christ; **3 Ne.** 12: 24 (Matt. 5: 24) first be *r.* to thy brother.

RECORD (*see also* Account; Book; Book of Mormon; Engrave, Engravings; History; Plates, Brass; Plates of Ether; Plates of Mormon; Plates of Nephi, Large; Plates of Nephi, Small; Scriptures; Testify; Witness; Write)

1 Ne. 1: 1 Nephi[1] makes *r.* of his proceedings; 1: 17 Nephi[1] abridges *r.* of father; 3: 3 Laban has *r.* of Jews; 3: 19 Lehites should obtain *r.* to preserve language of fathers; 5: 12 brass plates contain *r.* of Jews from beginning to reign of Zedekiah; 5: 16 Laban and fathers had kept *r.* because they were descendants of Joseph[1]; 6: 1 *r.* of Lehi[1] gives genealogy: 10: 10 John the Baptist will bear *r.* that

he baptized Lamb; 11: 7 Nephi¹ to bear r. of Son; 12: 18 Holy Ghost bears r. of Messiah; 13: 23 Nephi¹ beholds book that is r. of Jews; 13: 24 twelve apostles bear r. according to truth which is in Lamb; 13: 41 words of Lamb shall be made known in r. of Nephites and r. of apostles; 14: 27 Nephi¹ bears r. that name of apostle was John; 19: 1 Nephi¹ is commanded to make plates that he might engrave r. of his people; 2 Ne. 5: 29 Nephi¹ kept r. upon plates; Enos 1: 13–15 Enos² desires that the Lord preserve r. of Nephites; Omni 1: 9 Nephites keep r. according to commandments of fathers; 1: 17 language of people of Zarahemla is corrupted because they brought no r. with them; W of M 1: 1 Mormon² to deliver r. to Moroni²; Mosiah 1: 16 Benjamin gives Mosiah² charge concerning r.; 8: 12–13 (21: 27) Limhi desires that r. on twenty-four gold plates be translated; 22: 14 Mosiah² receives r. of Limhi's people and r. on gold plates; 25: 5 Mosiah² reads r. of Zeniff's people to his people; 28: 20 Mosiah² confers all r. upon Alma²; Alma 18: 36 Ammon² lays before Lamoni r. of scriptures; 37: 2 Alma² commands Helaman² to keep r. of Nephites; 37: 3 brass plates contain r. of scriptures; Hel. 3: 13, 15 (3 Ne. 5: 9) many r. kept of proceedings of Nephites; 6: 26 secret covenants did not come to Gadianton from r., but from devil; 3 Ne. 5: 11 Mormon² makes r. on plates he has made; 5: 18 Mormon² testifies his r. is true; 8: 1 r. of Nephi³ is true; 11: 32, 35–36 Father, Son, and Holy Ghost bear r. of each other; 17: 25 multitude knows r. is true for they saw and heard; 21: 5 r. shall come forth from Gentiles to descendants of Nephites; 23: 7–8 Nephi³ brings r. before Jesus; 23: 9–13 Jesus instructs that missing part of r. be written; 4 Ne. 1: 19 Nephi⁴ kept r.; Morm. 1: 1 Mormon² makes r. of what he has seen and heard; 6: 6 Mormon² is commanded not to suffer r. to fall into hands of Lamanites; 8: 1 Moroni² finishes r. of Mormon²; 8: 14 (Moro. 10: 2) Moroni² hides r.; Ether 1: 6 r. of Jaredites written by Ether; 5: 4 Father, Son, and Holy Ghost bear r. of word; 13: 1 Moroni² finishes r. of destruction of Jaredites.

RECOVER (*see also* Gather; Heal; Reclaim; Restoration)

2 Ne. 6: 14 (21: 11; 29: 1; Jacob 6: 2; Isa. 11: 11) Messiah shall set himself the second time to r. his people; 3 Ne. 3: 10 Giddianhi claims his people should r. rights and government; Morm. 9: 24 (Mark 16: 18) believers shall lay hands on the sick and they shall r.

RED SEA (*see also* BD Red Sea)

1 Ne. 2: 5 (16: 14) Lehites camp near shores of R.S.; 2: 8–9 river Laman empties into R.S.; 4: 2 (17: 26–27; Mosiah 7: 19; Alma 36: 28; Hel. 8: 11) Moses divided waters of R.S.; 2 Ne. 19: 1 (Isa. 9: 1) he did more grievously afflict by way of R.S. beyond Jordan.

REDEEMER (*see* Jesus Christ — Redeemer)

REDEMPTION, REDEEM (*see also* Death, Spiritual; Deliver; Eternal Life; Freedom; Immortality; Jesus Christ — Redeemer; Plan; Ransom; Resurrection; Salvation; Save; TG Redeem, Redemption; BD Redemption)

1 Ne. 20: 20 (Isa. 48: 20) the Lord has r. his servant Jacob¹; 2 Ne. 1: 15 the Lord has r. my soul from hell; 2: 6 r. comes in and through Messiah; 2: 26 Messiah will r. men from fall; 7: 2 (Isa. 50: 2) is the Lord's hand shortened that it cannot r.; 27: 33 the Lord r. Abraham; Jacob 6: 8 will ye make a mock of great plan of r.; W of M 1: 8 Mormon² prays his brethren will come again to knowledge of r. of Christ; Mosiah 12: 23 (15: 30; 3 Ne. 16: 19; 20: 34) the Lord has r. Jerusalem; 15: 22–23 prophets and those who believe them are raised to dwell with God who has r. them; 15: 25–26 the Lord r. none who rebel against him; 16: 6 (Alma 21: 9) if Christ had not come, there could have been no r.; 18: 2 r. of people brought to pass by power, sufferings, death of Christ; 26: 26 those who never knew the Lord will know he is their Redeemer, but they would not be r.; 27: 24, 29 Alma² is r. of the Lord; Alma 5: 9 fathers did sing r. love; 5: 21 Messiah shall come to r. his people from sins; 5: 26 if ye have felt to sing song of r. love, can ye feel so now; 9: 27 Son comes to r. those who will be baptized; 11: 41 the wicked remain as though there had been no r.; 12: 18 whosoever dies in his sins cannot be r. according to God's justice; 12: 25 without plan of r., there could have been no resurrection; 13: 2 priests are ordained in manner that people might know in what manner to look forward to Son for r.; 13: 3 holy calling was prepared with, and according to, a preparatory r.; 17: 16 sons of Mosiah² to bring Lamanites to knowledge of plan of r.; 18: 39 Ammon² expounds plan of r. to Lamanite king; 26: 13 Lamanites are brought to sing r. love because of power of word; 29: 2 I would declare unto every soul with voice of thunder the plan of r.; 34: 16 only unto him who has faith unto repentance is brought about the great plan of r.; 42: 13 according to justice, plan of r. could be brought about only on conditions of repentance; Hel. 5: 9 Christ comes to r. the world; 5: 9–10 (Alma 11: 34–37) the Lord shall not r. his people in their sins,

but from their sins; 14: 16–17 (Morm. 9: 13) Christ's death and resurrection r. all men from temporal death; 3 Ne. 6: 20 prophets testify of r. which Christ would make; 9: 17 by Christ r. comes; 9: 21 Christ has come into world to bring r.; 20: 38 (Isa. 52: 3) ye shall r. without money; Morm. 7: 7 Christ has brought to pass the r. of the world; 9: 12 because of Jesus Christ came the r. of man; Ether 3: 13 brother of Jared[2] is r. from fall; Moro. 7: 38 men without faith are as though there had been no r.; 8: 22 power of r. comes on all who have no law.

REFINE, REFINER (see also Chasten; Purge; Purify)

1 Ne. 20: 10 (Isa. 48: 10) I have r. thee; Alma 34: 29 if ye are not charitable, ye are as dross which r. cast out; Hel. 6: 11 Nephites r. ore; 3 Ne. 24: 2 (Mal. 3: 2) the Lord is like r's fire; Ether 10: 7 Riplakish causes fine gold to be r. in prison.

REFORMED EGYPTIAN (see Egyptian)

REFRAIN (see also Cease)

Alma 38: 12 see that ye r. from idleness; 39: 12 Alma[1] commands Corianton to r. from iniquities.

REFUGE (see also Escape; Protect; Safe; Safety)

2 Ne. 14: 6 (Isa. 4: 6) there shall be a tabernacle for a place of r.; Hel. 15: 2 ye shall attempt to flee and there shall be no place for r.

REFUSE (see also Deny; Reject)

2 Ne. 17: 15 (Isa. 7: 15) butter and honey shall he eat, that he may know to r. evil and choose good; Mosiah 29: 1–3 (Alma 17: 6) sons of Mosiah[2] r. to be king; Alma 27: 3 (51: 13) people of Anti-Nephi-Lehi r. to take up arms; Hel. 14: 20 sun shall r. to give light; Morm. 3: 11 Mormon[2] r. to be commander of Nephites; Ether 10: 6 Riplakish puts to death those who r. to labor; 15: 3 Coriantumr[2] r. to be comforted.

REGULATE, REGULATION (see also Govern; Government, Civil; Order)

Mosiah 26: 37 Alma[1] r. all affairs of church; Alma 45: 21 (62: 44) r. made throughout church; 3 Ne. 7: 6 r. of government are destroyed.

REHEARSE (see also Read)

1 Ne. 15: 20 Nephi[1] r. words of Isaiah[1]; Mosiah 8: 3 Ammon[1] r. words of Benjamin.

REIGN (see also Authority; Dominion; King; Millennium; Power; Rule)

1 Ne. 22: 26 Holy One of Israel r.; 2 Ne. 2: 29 devil will r. over the wicked in his kingdom; Mosiah 3: 5 Lord God Omnipotent who r. shall come down among men; 6: 4 Mosiah[2] begins to r. in father's stead; 11: 1 Noah[3] begins to r. in father's stead; 12: 21 (15: 14; Isa. 52: 7) how beautiful upon mountains are feet of him that saith unto Zion, Thy God r.

REJECT (see also Apostasy; Deny; Disobedience; Rebel; Refuse; Resist; Unbelief; Withstand; TG Prophets, Rejection of)

1 Ne. 3: 18 Jews have r. words of prophets; 15: 17 the Lord will show his power unto Gentiles because Jews will r. him; 19: 13 Jews shall be scourged because they r. signs and power of God; 2 Ne. 1: 10 when those upon promised land r. Holy One, judgments shall rest upon them; 25: 12 Jews will r. Christ because of iniquities; 25: 18 word given to Israel to convince them of true Messiah, whom they r.; 27: 14 wo unto him who r. word of God; Jacob 4: 15–17 by stumbling of Jews they will r. stone upon which they might build safe foundation; Mosiah 14: 3 (Isa. 53: 3) he is despised and r. of men; 27: 30 Alma[2] r. his Redeemer; Alma 6: 3 church members who do not repent are r.; 13: 4 men r. Spirit because of hardness of heart and blindness of mind; Hel. 6: 2 many Nephites r. word of God; 3 Ne. 16: 10 when Gentiles r. fulness of gospel, Father will bring it from them; 4 Ne. 1: 38 those who r. gospel are called Lamanites; Morm. 6: 17 how could ye have r. Jesus; Ether 4: 3 Lamanites have r. gospel of Jesus Christ; 11: 22 Jaredites r. words of prophets because of secret society; Moro. 8: 29 after r. so great knowledge Nephites must soon perish.

REJOICE, REJOICING (see also Delight; Glorify; Joy; Praise; Shout; Sing; Thank)

1 Ne. 8: 3 Lehi[1] has reason to r. in the Lord because of Nephi[1] and Sam; 2 Ne. 9: 52 let your hearts r.; 25: 26 we r. in Christ; 27: 30 (Isa. 29: 19) poor among men shall r. in Holy One; Mosiah 2: 4 Benjamin teaches his people to keep commandments that they might r.; 5: 4 because of great knowledge, people r.; 18: 14 Alma[1] and Helam come forth out of water r.; Alma 46: 38 peace and r. in church for four years; 61: 9 Pahoran[1] r. in greatness of heart of Moroni[1]; Hel. 8: 22 fathers have r. in Christ's day; 3 Ne. 9: 2 devil laughs and his angels r. because of the slain.

RELIEF (see also Alms; Charity; Help; Needy; Poor; Serve; Succor)

Jacob 2: 19 obtain riches to administer r. to the needy; **Mosiah** 4: 26 to retain remission of sins, administer r. to needy, both spiritually and temporally.

RELIGION, RELIGIOUS (see also Belief; Church of God; Faith; Gospel; Worship)

Alma 43: 47 Nephites contend with Lamanites to defend their r.; 44: 2 Lamanites are angry with Nephites because of r.; 44: 5 God strengthens Nephites to gain power over Lamanites, by their faith, r.; 46: 20 those who will maintain title of liberty should covenant to maintain their rights, r.; 48: 13 Moroni[1] has sworn oath to defend his r.; 51: 6 freemen covenant to maintain privileges of r. by free government.

RELY (see also Depend; Trust)

1 Ne. 10: 6 all mankind would be lost save they r. on Redeemer; **2 Ne.** 31: 19 r. wholly upon merits of him who is mighty to save; **Alma** 24: 25 Lamanites who throw down weapons r. upon mercies of those whose arms are lifted to slay them; 25: 16 converted Lamanites r. upon spirits of prophecy; 26: 28 sons of Mosiah[2] travel from house to house, r. upon mercies of world; 27: 9 people of Anti-Nephi-Lehi r. upon mercies of Nephites; **Moro.** 6: 4 those baptized r. alone upon merits of Christ.

REMAIN (see also Abide; Persist; Sojourn; Tarry)

1 Ne. 13: 32 the Lord will not suffer Gentiles to r. in blindness; **2 Ne.** 2: 11 if it should be one body, it must r. as dead; 2: 22–23 if Adam had not transgressed, he would have r. in garden; 9: 7 without infinite atonement, first judgment must have r. endlessly; 9: 8–9 without resurrection, our spirits would have r. with devil; **Mosiah** 2: 38 if willful transgressor r. enemy to God, justice fills breast with guilt; 7: 18 Limhi trusts an effectual struggle r. to be made; 16: 5 he who persists in carnal nature r. in fallen state; **Alma** 7: 21 he who is filthy shall r. in filthiness; 9: 15 more tolerable for Lamanites if Nephites r. in sins; 15: 15 people of Ammonihah r. hardhearted; 40: 14 the wicked r. in darkness and righteous in paradise until resurrection; **3 Ne.** 28: 40 three Nephites to r. in sanctified state until judgment day.

REMEMBER, REMEMBRANCE (see also Book; Forget; Forgive; Memory; Type)

1 Ne. 2: 24 (2 Ne. 5: 25) Lamanites to scourge Nephites to stir them up in r.; 14: 8 r. Father's covenants with Israel; 15: 25 Nephi[1] exhorts brothers to r. to keep commandments; 17: 45 (Mosiah 9: 3; Alma 62: 49; Hel. 12: 5) men are slow

to r. the Lord; **2 Ne.** 3: 25 r. the words of thy dying father; 9: 39 r. awfulness in transgressing against God; 9: 40 r. greatness of Holy One; 9: 46 prepare your souls that ye may not r. your awful guilt; 29: 5 have Gentiles r. Jews; **Jacob** 1: 11 people desire to obtain name of Nephi[1] in r.; 3: 9 r. your own filthiness; **Mosiah** 1: 7 r. to search records diligently; 1: 17 Lehites smitten with afflictions to stir them up in r. of duty; 2: 40 awake to r. of awful situation of transgressors; 4: 30 r., and perish not; 27: 30 the Lord has r. every creature of his creating; **Alma** 4: 19 Alma[2] preaches to stir up people in r. of duty; 5: 6 (36: 29) have you sufficiently retained in r. the captivity of fathers; 5: 18 souls brought before God filled with remorse, having r. of guilt; 36: 13 Alma[2] r. all his sins; **Hel.** 12: 3 except the Lord chastens his people, they will not r. him; 13: 33 O that we had r. the Lord; 16: 5 Nephi[2] prophesies concerning Christ's coming, that people might r. that they had known signs beforehand; **3 Ne.** 16: 10–11 (3 Ne. 20: 29) when Gentiles reject gospel, the Lord will r. Israel; 18: 7, 11 (Moro. 4: 3; 5: 2; 6: 6) partake of sacrament in r. of Christ's flesh and blood; 24: 16 (Mal. 3: 16) book of r. written for those who fear the Lord; **Morm.** 5: 21 the Lord will r. prayers of the righteous; 8: 21 he who says the Lord r. not his covenant shall be hewn down; **Moro.** 10: 27 I exhort you to r. these things.

REMISSION, REMIT (see also Baptism; Born of God; Faith; Fire; Forgive; Holy Ghost, Baptism of; Jesus Christ, Atonement through; Mercy; Pardon; Repentance)

2 Ne. 25: 26 Nephites preach of Christ, that children may know source of r. of sins; 31: 17 (3 Ne. 12: 2; 30: 2) after baptism comes r. of sins by fire and Holy Ghost; **Enos** 1: 2 Enos[2] wrestles before God before receiving r. of sins; **Mosiah** 3: 13 those who believe Christ should come can receive r. of sins; 4: 3 Spirit comes upon Benjamin's people and they are filled with joy, having received r. of sins; 4: 11–12 always remember God's goodness in order to retain r. of sins; 4: 26 for sake of retaining r. of sins, impart substance to the poor; 15: 11 (Alma 4: 14) those who look forward to Christ's coming for r. of sins are his seed; **Alma** 7: 6 (30: 16) look forward for r. of sins with everlasting faith; 12: 34 he who repents has claim on mercy through Son, unto r. of sins; 38: 8 never until he cried out to Christ for mercy did Alma[2] receive r. of sins; **3 Ne.** 1: 23 baptism unto repentance, in which there is great r. of sins; 7: 16 Nephi[3] testifies boldly, r. of sins through faith on the

Lord; 7: 52 baptism a witness that they had repented and received r. of sins; 30: 2 be baptized, that ye may receive r. of sins and be filled with Holy Ghost; **Moro.** 3: 3 priests and teachers are ordained to preach repentance and r. of sins through Christ; 8: 11 baptism is unto repentance to fulfilling commandments unto r. of sins; 8: 26 r. of sins bringeth meekness; 10: 33 sanctification by grace through shedding of blood is Father's covenant unto r. of sins.

REMNANT (*see also* Gather; Israel; Israel, Gathering of; Israel, Scattering of; Jacob, House of; Residue)

1 **Ne.** 10: 14 (15: 12–13) natural branches of olive-tree, or r. of Israel, shall be grafted in; 13: 34 the Lord will visit r. of Israel, seed of Lehi[1]; **2 Ne.** 20: 21 (Isa. 10: 21) r. of Jacob shall return unto God; 28: 2 (Alma 46: 23; 3 Ne. 20: 16; Morm. 7: 10) Nephites' seed is r. of house of Israel, or Jacob[1]; 30: 3 Gentiles shall carry words of book to r. of Nephites' seed; **Alma** 46: 23 (3 Ne. 10: 17; 15: 12) Nephites are r. of seed of Joseph[1]; **3 Ne.** 5: 23 the Lord will again bring r. of seed of Joseph[1] to knowledge of the Lord; 5: 24 the Lord will gather all r. of seed of Jacob[1]; 21: 12 the Lord's people who are r. of Jacob[1], shall be among Gentiles; 21: 22 Gentiles can be numbered among this r. of Jacob[1], to whom the Lord has given this land; **Morm.** 5: 24 Gentiles called to repent, lest r. of Jacob[1] go among them as a lion; **Ether** 13: 7 the Lord brought r. of seed of Joseph[1] out of Jerusalem; 13: 10 those who dwell in New Jerusalem are numbered among r. of seed of Joseph[1].

REMORSE (*see also* Anguish; Grieve; Sackcloth; Sorrow; Torment)

Alma 5: 18 souls brought before God are filled with r., having remembrance of guilt; 29: 5 to him who knoweth good and evil is given according to his desire, joy or r.; 42: 18 just law brings r.

REMOVE (*see also* Move)

2 **Ne.** 16: 12 (Isa. 6: 12) the Lord will r. men far away; 23: 13 (Isa. 13: 13) earth shall r. out of her place; 27: 25 (Isa. 29: 13–14) men draw near the Lord with mouths, but have r. hearts far from him; **Alma** 46: 40 God has prepared plants and roots to r. cause of disease; **Hel.** 5: 40–41 cloud of darkness to be r. by faith; 3 **Ne.** 22: 10 (Isa. 54: 10) hills shall be r.; **Morm.** 8: 24 in the Lord's name saints could r. mountains; **Ether** 12: 30 brother of Jared[2] said to mountain, R., and it was r.

REND, RENT

1 **Ne.** 12: 4 (19: 12; Hel. 14: 22; 3 Ne. 8: 18; 10: 9) earth and rocks shall be r.; 17: 47 soul of Nephi[1] is r. with

anguish because of brothers; **Alma** 46: 12–13 Moroni[1] r. coat for title of liberty; 46: 21 Nephites r. garments as covenant not to forsake the Lord; 46: 23 let us keep commandments or our garments shall be r. by brethren; **Hel.** 6: 39 robbers obtain government, that they smite, r.; 10: 8 if Nephi[3] says to temple it should be r. in twain, it shall be done; 3 **Ne.** 14: 6 (Matt. 7: 6) cast not your pearls before swine lest they turn again and r. you; **Morm.** 6: 16 soul of Mormon[2] is r. with anguish because of the slain; **Ether** 4: 15 when Israel r. veil of unbelief, they shall know Father remembers covenants.

RENDER (*see also* Give)

Mosiah 2: 20–21 if you r. all thanks to God, ye would be unprofitable servants; 2: 34 men are eternally indebted to Father, to r. unto him all that they have and are; 4: 13 r. to every man according to his due.

RENEW (*see also* New; Repair; TG Earth, Renewal of)

4 **Ne.** 1: 9 sunken cities could not be r.

RENT (*see* Rend, Rent)

REPAIR (*see also* Mend; Renew)

Mosiah 9: 8 Nephites r. walls of cities; 27: 35 sons of Mosiah[2] strive to r. all injuries they had done to church; **Alma** 27: 8 people of Anti-Nephi-Lehi are willing to be Nephites' slaves until they have r. their many murders and sins; **Hel.** 5: 17 converted dissenters endeavor to r. wrongs they had done; 3 **Ne.** 6: 7 many old cities r.

REPAY (*see also* Pay)

Morm. 3: 15 (8: 20; Rom. 12: 19) vengeance is the Lord's, and he will r.

REPENTANCE, REPENT (*see also* Baptism; Change; Confession of Sins; Death, Spiritual; Excommunication; Faith; Forgive; Forsake; Gospel; Guilt; Mend; Mercy; Penitent; Redemption; Remission; Salvation; Work [noun]; Work [verb]; TG Repent, Repentance; BD Repentance)

1 **Ne.** 1: 4 many prophets prophesy that Jews must r. or be destroyed; 10: 18 way is prepared for all men if they r. and come unto the Lord; 14: 5 if Gentiles r., it shall be well with them; 18: 20 when they see they will be swallowed in sea, brothers of Nephi[1] r.; 22: 28 all nations shall dwell safely in Holy One if they will r.; **2 Ne.** 2: 21 days of men were prolonged, that they might r.; 2: 21 (31: 11; Alma 9: 12; 3 Ne. 11: 32) God commands that all men must r.; 6: 12 if Gentiles r., they shall be saved; 9: 23 God commands

that all must r. and be baptized; 26: 27 the Lord commands his people to persuade all men to r.; 28: 19 they who belong to devil's kingdom must be stirred up unto r.; 30: 2 (3 Ne. 16: 13) Gentiles who r. are covenant people of the Lord; 30: 2 Jews who will not r. shall be cast off; 30: 2 the Lord covenants with none save those who r.; 31: 13 those who follow Son, r. and r., shall receive Holy Ghost; 31: 17 gate by which men should enter is r. and baptism; **Jacob** 3: 3 except ye r., the land is cursed; **Mosiah** 2: 38 if willful transgressor r. not, he shall be filled with sense of guilt; 3: 12 salvation cometh to none who knowingly rebel, except through r. and faith; 3: 21 men can be found blameless before God only through r. and faith; 4: 10 believe that ye must r. of your sins; 4: 18 he who turns away beggar has great cause to r.; 18: 20 preach nothing save r. and faith; 26: 29 if transgressor confesses and r., ye shall forgive him; 26: 35–36 (3 Ne. 18: 29–32; Moro. 6: 7) only those who r. and confess sins are numbered among people of church; 27: 28 after r. nigh unto death, Alma² is snatched from everlasting burning, born of God; **Alma** 5: 31 he who persecutes his brother must r. or he cannot be saved; 5: 49 (7: 9) Alma² is called to cry unto people that they must r. and be born again; 5: 54 those sanctified by Spirit bring forth works meet for r.; 6: 2 all who r. are baptized unto r.; 7: 9 (Hel. 14: 9) r. ye, and prepare way of the Lord; 9: 12 except men r., they cannot inherit kingdom of God; 9: 25 (10: 20; Hel. 5: 32) r. ye, for kingdom of heaven is at hand; 12: 24 (42: 4) man was granted time in which he might r.; 13: 10 many are ordained high priests because they choose to r. and work righteousness rather than perish; 13: 18 Melchizedek preached r. unto his people, and they r.; 14: 1 many people begin to r. and search scriptures; 26: 22 to know mysteries of God, men must r.; 29: 1 O that I were an angel and could cry r. unto every people; 32: 13 if a man is compelled to be humble, he sometimes seeks r.; 32: 13 all who r. shall find mercy; 34: 33 do not procrastinate day of r.; 34: 34 when brought to night of darkness, men cannot say they will r.; 37: 31 cursed be land unto secret combinations except they r.; 42: 16 r. could not come unto men except there were a punishment; 42: 22 there is punishment affixed and r. granted, which r. mercy claimeth; 42: 29 only let your sins trouble you, with that trouble which shall bring you down unto r.; **Hel.** 5: 11 the Lord is given power from Father to redeem his people because of r.; 5: 11 the Lord has sent his angels to declare tidings of conditions of r.; 5: 29 r. ye, and seek no

more to destroy my servants; 5: 40–41 to remove cloud of darkness, Lamanites must r. and have faith; 12: 22 r. has been declared that men might be saved; 12: 23 (3 Ne. 23: 5) those who r. shall be saved; 13: 33, 36 (3 Ne. 8: 24–25) O that I had r. and not killed prophets; 15: 1 except ye r., your houses will be left to you desolate; 15: 7 prophecies of holy prophets lead men to faith and r., which bring change of heart; **3 Ne.** 7: 24 all who are brought unto r. are baptized; 9: 2 wo unto inhabitants of earth, except they r.; 9: 22 the Lord will receive all who r. and come unto him as little child; 16: 13 if Gentiles r., they shall be numbered among the Lord's people; 18: 32 if a man r., ye shall not cast him out; 27: 16 whoso r. and is baptized shall be filled; 30: 2 Mormon² calls Gentiles to r. of evil doings; **Ether** 2: 11 this message cometh unto Gentiles that they may r.; 11: 1 many prophets prophesy destruction of Jaredites unless they r.; **Moro.** 6: 2 only those who witness unto church that they have r. are received unto baptism; 6: 8 as oft as men r. and seek forgiveness, they are forgiven; 7: 31 office of angels' ministry is to call men to r.; 8: 8 Christ came into world to call not the righteous but sinners to r.; 8: 11, 19 little children need no r.; 8: 22 he that is under no condemnation cannot r.; 8: 24 r. is unto them that are under condemnation and under curse of broken law; 8: 25 first fruits of r. is baptism; 9: 3 Mormon² fears Lamanites will destroy Nephites, for they do not r.

REPETITION

3 Ne. 13: 7 when ye pray, use not vain r.

REPORT (*see also* Rumor)

Mosiah 14: 1 (Isa. 53: 1) who hath believed our r.

REPRESENTATION (*see also* Shadow; Type)

1 Ne. 11: 25 living waters and tree of life are r. of love of God; 15: 21–22 tree in dream of Lehi¹ was r. of tree of life; 15: 28–29 gulf separating wicked from tree of life is r. of hell; 15: 32 r. of things both temporal and spiritual.

REPROACH, REPROACHFULLY (*see also* Rebuke; Reprove; Scorn; Shame)

2 Ne. 8: 7 (Isa. 51: 7) fear not the r. of men; 14: 1 (Isa. 4: 1) seven women will want to be called by one man's name to take away r.; **3 Ne.** 22: 4 (Isa. 54: 4) not remember the r. of thy youth.

REPROVE (*see also* Prove; Punishment; Rebuke; Reproach; Warn)

2 Ne. 21: 3 (Isa. 11: 3) he shall not r.

after the hearing of his ears; 21: 4 (30: 9; Isa. 11: 4) he shall r. with equity for the meek; 27: 32 they who lay a snare for him that r. at the gate shall be cut off.

REPUGNANT (see also Loathsome; Opposition)

Mosiah 29: 36 iniquities and abominations of unrighteous king are expressly r. to commandments of God.

REQUIRE (see also Command; Commandments of God; Requisite)

1 Ne. 3: 5 brothers murmur that it is hard thing Lehi[1] r. of them; Mosiah 2: 22–24 all that God r. of men is to keep his commandments; 18: 27 of him who has but little, little is r.; Alma 34: 12 law r. the life of him who murders.

REQUISITE

Mosiah 4: 27 not r. that man should run faster than he has strength; Alma 41: 2 plan of restoration is r. with justice of God; 41: 2 r. that all things be restored to proper order; 41: 3 r. with justice of God that men be judged according to works.

RESIDUE (see also Remnant)

Moro. 7: 32 the Lord prepared way that r. of men may have faith in Christ.

RESIST (see also Deny; Hardheartedness; Rebel; Refuse; Reject; Withstand)

Alma 30: 46 Korihor r. Spirit of truth; 32: 28 if ye do not cast out seed by unbelief, that ye r. Spirit, it will swell; 48: 16 Moroni[1] glories in r. iniquity; 61: 14 whatsoever evil we cannot r. with words, let us r. with swords; 3 Ne. 12: 39 (Matt. 5: 39) ye shall not r. evil, but turn other cheek to him who smites right cheek.

RESPECT, RESPECTER (see also Alike; Equal; Esteem; Honor; Regard; Worth)

2 Ne. 33: 14 Nephi[1] bids farewell to those who will not r. words of God; Alma 1: 30 Nephites are liberal to all, having no r. to persons as to those in need; 16: 14 Alma[2] and Amulek impart word of God without any r. of persons. Moro. 8: 12 if little children need baptism, God would be r. of persons.

RESPONSIBILITY (see also Accountable; Duty)

Jacob 1: 19 priests and teachers take upon themselves r. for sins of people if they do not teach word of God; 2: 2 Jacob[2] is under r. to magnify office.

REST (see also Abide; Comfort; Paradise; Peace; Sabbath)

2 Ne. 21: 2 (Isa. 11: 2) Spirit of the Lord shall r. upon rod out of stem of Jesse; 21: 10 (Isa. 11: 10) r. of root of Jesse shall be glorious; Jacob 1: 7 we persuade our people to come unto Christ, that they might enter into his r.; Enos 1: 27 Enos[2] soon goes to place of his r.; Alma 7: 27 may peace of God r. upon you; 10: 11 the Lord's blessing has r. upon Amulek and household; 12: 34–37 only those who repent and harden not hearts shall enter the Lord's r.; 13: 6 priests are ordained to teach men, that they might enter into God's r.; 13: 12 many are made pure and enter r. of the Lord; 13: 13 humble yourselves, bring forth fruit meet for repentance, enter r. of the Lord; 13: 16 look forward to Son for remission of sins, that they may enter r. of the Lord; 13: 29 have love of God always in your hearts, that ye may enter into his r.; 16: 17 receive word with joy that they may enter r. of the Lord; 37: 34 the meek and lowly in heart shall find r. to their souls; 40: 12 righteous will be received into paradise, a state of r. and peace, where they r. from troubles; 60: 13 the righteous enter r. of the Lord; 3 Ne. 27: 19 only those who have washed garments in Christ's blood enter into Father's r.; 28: 3 disciples shall find r. with Christ in his kingdom; Moro. 7: 3 obtain sufficient hope by which ye can enter into r. of the Lord; 9: 6 we have labor to perform, that we may conquer enemy and r. our souls in kingdom of God; 9: 25 may Christ's mercy and long-suffering r. in your mind forever; 10: 34 Moroni[2] soon goes to r. in paradise of God.

RESTITUTION (see Repair)

RESTORATION, RESTORE (see also Church of God; Gather; Gospel; Israel, Gathering of; Judgment; Last Days; Reclaim; Recover; Resurrection; Return; TG Israel, Restoration of; Restoration of the Gospel; BD Restitution; Restoration)

1 Ne. 15: 19 Nephi[1] speaks concerning r. of Jews in latter days; 21: 6 (Isa. 49: 6) it is a light thing that thou shouldst be servant to r. the preserved of Israel; 2 Ne. 3: 24 mighty one shall rise up to do much good unto bringing to pass r. unto Israel; 9: 2 the Lord has spoken unto Jews by prophets, from beginning until they are r. to true church; 9: 12 (Alma 40: 23) bodies and spirits of men shall be r. to one another; 10: 2 (30: 5; Hel. 15: 11) Nephites' and Lamanites' children shall be r. to knowledge of Christ; 25: 17 the Lord will set his hand second time to r. his people; 30: 8 the Lord will commence work among all nations to bring about r. of his people; Jacob 7: 23 peace and love of God is r. again among Nephites; Enos 1: 14 Nephites' struggles are vain in r.

Lamanites to true faith; **Alma** 11: 44 this *r.* shall come to all; 11: 44 (40: 23; 41: 4) every thing shall be *r.* to its perfect frame; 40: 21–22 resurrection brings about *r.* of those things spoken by prophets; 41: 2 plan of *r.* is requisite with justice of God; 41: 4 all things shall be *r.* to proper order; 41: 10 do not suppose ye shall be *r.* from sin to happiness; 41: 12–13 meaning of *r.* is to bring back evil for evil, good for good; 41: 14 be merciful, deal justly, judge righteously, and do good, and you shall have mercy, justice, righteous judgment, and good *r.* to you; 42: 23 because of resurrection, men are *r.* to God's presence; 42: 27–28 if man has desired evil, evil shall be done unto him, according to *r.* of God; **Hel.** 12: 24 may men be brought to repentance and good works, that they might be *r.* unto grace for grace; 14: 31 ye can do good and be *r.* unto that which is good, or evil and be *r.* unto that which is evil; 3 **Ne.** 29: 1 when gospel comes to Gentiles, *r.* of Israel is beginning to be fulfilled; **Morm.** 9: 36 *r.* of Lamanites to knowledge of Christ is according to prayers of all saints.

RESTRAIN (*see also* Hinder; Keep; Stay; Stop; Withhold)

2 **Ne.** 1: 26 Nephi¹ could not *r.* the truth; **Ether** 12: 2 Ether could not be *r.* from prophesying because of Spirit.

RESURRECTION (*see also* Body; Death; Physical; Eternal Life; Fall of Man; Grave; Immortality; Jesus Christ, Resurrection of; Life; Paradise; Quick [=living]; Raise; Redemption; Restoration; Reunite; Rise; Spirit World; TG Resurrection; BD Resurrection)

2 **Ne.** 2: 8 (Mosiah 13: 35; 15: 20; Alma 33: 22; 40: 3; Hel. 14: 15) Christ lays down life, takes it up again, to bring to pass *r.* of the dead; 9: 6 *r.* must come unto man by reason of the fall; 9: 11–12 (Alma 40: 21, 23; Moro. 10: 34) bodies and spirits of men shall be restored to one another by power of *r.* of Holy One; 9: 22 *r.* will pass upon all men; 10: 25 may God raise you from death by power of the *r.*; **Jacob** 4: 11 be reconciled to God through atonement of Christ, and ye may obtain *r.* according to power of *r.* which is in Christ; 6: 9 power of redemption and *r.*, which is in Christ, will bring you to stand before God; **Mosiah** 13: 34–35 God himself shall come down and bring to pass the *r.*; 15: 20 Son hath power over the dead and bringeth to pass *r.*; 15: 21–26 (Alma 40: 15–18) those who died before Christ's *r.* will have part in first *r.*; 15: 22 all prophets and those who believe in them shall come forth in first *r.*; 15: 26 those who rebel against God shall have no part in first *r.*; 16: 7 if Christ had not

risen from dead, there could have been no *r.*; 16: 8 (Morm. 7: 5) grave has no victory, sting of death is swallowed in Christ; 18: 9–10 those who would be numbered among first *r.* must be baptized; **Alma** 11: 41 the wicked remain as though there had been no redemption, except for loosing of bands of death; 11: 42 (12: 8; 40: 4–5, 9) all shall rise from the dead; 11: 45 mortal body is raised to an immortal body; 12: 24 man given a time to prepare for endless state which is after *r.*; 21: 9 Aaron³ opens to Lamanites scriptures concerning *r.*; 33: 22 (Hel. 14: 20) Son shall rise from dead to bring to pass *r.*; 40: 4–10 time appointed that all shall come from the dead; 40: 6, 11–14 state of souls between death and *r.*; 40: 15–17 state between death and *r.* is not first *r.*; 40: 16 first *r.* includes those who died before Christ's *r.*; 40: 21 space between death and *r.*; 40: 23 soul shall be restored to body and body to soul; **Hel.** 14: 25 (3 Ne. 23: 9–13) at time of Christ's *r.* many saints shall be resurrected; 3 **Ne.** 26: 4–5 men will be judged of their works, if they be good, to *r.* of everlasting life, if evil, to *r.* of damnation; **Morm.** 9: 13 death of Christ bringeth to pass the *r.*; **Moro.** 7: 41 ye shall have hope through Christ's atonement and *r.* to be raised unto life eternal; 10: 34 I soon go to rest in paradise of God until my spirit and body shall again reunite.

RETAIN (*see also* Hold; Keep; Maintain)

Jacob 1: 11 Nephites desire to *r.* in remembrance the name of Nephi¹; **Mosiah** 4: 11–12 always *r.* in remembrance God's goodness and ye will always *r.* remission of your sins; 4: 26 to *r.* remission of sins, impart of substance to the poor; 5: 12 *r.* name of Christ written always in your heart; **Alma** 4: 14 Nephites look forward to Christ's coming, thus *r.* remission of sins; 5: 6 have you sufficiently *r.* in remembrance the captivity of your fathers; 25: 16 converted Lamanites *r.* hope through faith unto eternal salvation; 37: 5 brass plates must *r.* their brightness; **Hel.** 13: 31 (Morm. 1: 18) in days of your poverty ye cannot *r.* your riches; **Moro.** 7: 8 if man gives gift grudgingly, it is counted to him the same as if he had *r.* it.

RETURN (*see also* Gather; Israel, Gathering of; Recover; Restoration)

1 **Ne.** 10: 3 (2 Ne. 6: 9; 25: 11) Jews shall *r.* out of captivity; 2 **Ne.** 1: 14 Lehi¹ soon to lie in grave, from which no traveler can *r.*; 8: 11 (Isa. 51: 11) the redeemed of the Lord shall *r.*; 16: 13 (Isa. 6: 13) they shall *r.* and be eaten; 20: 21 (Isa. 10: 21) remnant of Jacob¹ shall *r.*; **Mosiah** 4: 28 whosoever borrows of his

neighbor should r. what he borrows; **Alma** 7: 23 always r. thanks unto God for whatsoever ye receive; 34: 34 when brought to awful crisis of night of darkness, ye cannot say I will r. to my God; **Hel.** 13: 11 if ye repent and r. to the Lord, he will turn away his anger; **3 Ne.** 6: 13 some r. railing for railing; 10: 6 Israel should repent and r. unto the Lord with full purpose of heart; 16: 13 if Gentiles will repent and r. unto Father, they shall be numbered among house of Israel; 20: 28 Father shall r. Gentiles' iniquities upon own heads; 24: 7 (Mal. 3: 7) r. unto the Lord and he will r. unto you; 27: 11 those built upon devil's works shall be cast into fire from which there is no r.; **Morm.** 6: 15 bodies of slain left to r. to mother earth; **Moro.** 9: 22 Mormon[2] prays the Lord will spare life of Moroni[2] to witness r. of his people.

REUNITE (*see also* Resurrection)

Alma 11: 43 (40: 18–21; Moro. 10: 34) spirit and body shall be r. in perfect form.

REVELATION, REVEAL (*see also* Dream; God, Manifestations of; Guide; Holy Ghost; Inspire; Instruction; Knowledge; Manifest; Prophecy; Prophet; Revelator; Scriptures; Spirit, Holy/Spirit of the Lord; Testimony; Vision; Visitation; Voice; TG Revelation; BD Revelation)

2 Ne. 5: 6 those who go with Nephi[1] are those who believe r. of God; 27: 7 in sealed book shall be r. from beginning of world to end; 27: 10 r. sealed in book r. all things from foundation of world unto end; 27: 11 (30: 18) all things shall be r. which ever have been or ever will be; 30: 17 nothing is secret save it shall be r.; **Jacob** 1: 6 (Alma 9: 21) Nephites have many r. and spirit of prophecy; 4: 8 no man knows God's ways save they are r. to him; 4: 8 despise not the r. of God; **Omni** 1: 11 Abinadom knows of no r. save those that have been written; **Mosiah** 14: 1 (Isa. 53: 1) to whom is the arm of the Lord r.; **Alma** 4: 20 (8: 24) Alma[2] confines himself to testimony of word, according to spirit of r.; 5: 46 the Lord has made manifest many things by Holy Spirit, which is spirit of r.; 17: 3 sons of Mosiah teach with spirit of prophecy and r.; 25: 15 outward ordinances must be kept until Christ is r.; 26: 22 things never r. shall be r. to those who repent, exercise faith, bring forth good works, and pray without ceasing; 43: 2 Alma[2] and sons preach according to spirit of prophecy and r.; **Hel.** 4: 12, 23 Nephites deny spirit of prophecy and r.; 11: 23 Nephi[2] and Lehi[4] have many r. daily; **3 Ne.** 3: 19 Nephites appoint as

chief captains those who have spirit of r.; 26: 14 children speak greater things than Jesus had r. to people; 29: 6 wo unto him who denies r. of the Lord and says the Lord no longer works by r.; **Morm.** 5: 8 things which are hid must be r.; 8: 33 look unto r. of God; 9: 7–8 those who deny r. know not the gospel of Christ.

REVELATOR (*see also* Prophet; Revelation; Seer)

Mosiah 8: 16 a seer is a r.

REVENGE (*see also* Avenge; Vengeance)

Mosiah 19: 19 those who fled with Noah[3] swear to return and seek r.; **Alma** 27: 2 Amalekites see they cannot seek r.; **Moro.** 9: 5, 23 Nephites thirst after blood and r. continually.

REVILE (*see also* Backbiting; Hate; Malice; Mock; Persecution; Railing; Scorn; Spit)

1 Ne. 17: 42 Israelites r. against Moses; **2 Ne.** 9: 40 if ye say I have spoken hard things against you, ye r. against truth; 28: 16 those who r. against that which is good; **Jacob** 3: 9 r. no more against Lamanites because of darkness of skin; **Alma** 8: 9, 13 people of Ammonihah r. against Alma[2]; 14: 2 people of Ammonihah claim Amulek has r. against their law; 16: 18 priests preach against all r.; 34: 40 Amulek admonishes poor Zoramites not to r. against those who cast them out; **Hel.** 10: 15 Nephites r. against Nephi[2]; **3 Ne.** 6: 13 some receive railing and do not turn and r. again; 12: 11 (Matt. 5: 11) blessed are ye when men shall r. you; 22: 17 the Lord's servants to condemn every tongue that r. against them; **Ether** 7: 24 Jaredites r. against prophets.

REVIVE

Ether 9: 35 Jaredites begin to r. after drought.

REVOLT, REVOLUTION (*see also* Dissenter; War)

4 Ne. 1: 20 small group r. from church and took name of Lamanites; **Morm.** 2: 8 one complete r. throughout all the land.

REWARD (*see also* Blessing; Increase; Judgment; Pay; Prize; Profit; Prosper; Reap; Wages; Work [noun])

2 Ne. 13: 9 (Isa. 3: 9) they have r. evil unto themselves; 15: 22–23 (Isa. 5: 23) wo unto those who justify the wicked for r.; 26: 10 for r. of their pride, Nephites will reap destruction; **Alma** 3: 26 in one year tens of thousands were sent into eternal world to reap r. according to works; 9: 28 all men shall reap r. of

works; 11: 25 for evil of bribery Zeezrom will have his r.; 29: 15 how great shall be r. of sons of Mosiah²; 32: 43 reap r. of faith and diligence; 34: 39 devil r. men no good thing; 41: 6 if man has repented and desired righteousness, he shall be r. unto righteousness; 41: 14 if you do good continually, you shall receive your r.; **3 Ne.** 12: 11–12 (Matt. 5: 11–12) great shall be r. in heaven of those who are persecuted for Christ's sake; 13: 5 (Matt. 6: 5) hypocrites, who pray to be seen of men, have their r.

RICH (*see also* Nobility; Pride; Prosper, Prosperity; Riches; Wealth)

2 Ne. 9: 30 wo unto r. who are r. as to things of world, for they despise the poor; 9: 42 the r. who are puffed up in riches are they whom the Lord despises; 28: 15 the r. who are puffed up in pride shall be thrust down to hell; **Mosiah** 4: 23 their substance shall perish with those who are r. in things of this world; 14: 9 (Isa. 53: 9) he made his grave with the r. in his death; **Alma** 1: 29 because of steadiness of church, they began to be exceedingly r.; **4 Ne.** 1: 3 Nephites have all things in common, so there are no r. or poor; 1: 23 Nephites become exceedingly r. because of prosperity in Christ.

RICHES (*see also* Gain; Lucre; Mammon; Money; Prosper, Prosperity; Rich; Treasure; Wealth)

Jacob 2: 18 before ye seek r., seek kingdom of God; 2: 19 after ye have obtained hope in Christ, ye shall obtain r. if ye seek them; 2: 19 seek r. for intent to do good; **Mosiah** 2: 12 Benjamin has not sought r. of his people; 12: 29 (Alma 5; 53; Hel. 7: 21; 13: 20) do ye set hearts upon r.; 29: 40 Mosiah² does not exact r. of his people; **Alma** 1: 30 Nephites do not set hearts upon r.; 4: 6 (45: 24; Hel. 3: 36; 4: 12; 6: 17) people of church begin to wax proud because of r.; 7: 6 I trust ye have not set your hearts upon r.; 39: 14 seek not after r.; 62: 49 in spite of r. Nephites are not lifted up in pride; **Hel.** 13: 20–21 Nephites are cursed because of r.; 13: 22 ye always remember your r., not to thank the Lord for them; 13: 31–33 (Morm. 1: 18) the Lord will curse r. that they become slippery; **3 Ne.** 6: 12 people are distinguished by ranks, according to r.; 6: 12 some receive great learning because of their r.; 6: 15 Satan tempts people to seek for r.; **Ether** 10: 3 Shez smitten by robber because of r.

RID (*see also* Cleanse)

2 Ne. 9: 44 Jacob² is r. of brethren's blood; **Jacob** 2: 2 Jacob² magnifies office to r. his garments of people's sins; 2:

16 O that God would r. you from this iniquity; **Mosiah** 2: 28 Benjamin teaches people to r. himself of their blood; **3 Ne.** 28: 35 do ye suppose ye can get r. of justice of an offended God; **Morm.** 9: 35 these things are written that we may r. our garments of blood of brethren.

RIGHT [adj.=correct], **RIGHTLY** (*see also* Right Hand; Right [noun]; True)

1 Ne. 13: 27 (22: 14) abominable church takes away parts of gospel to pervert r. ways of the Lord; **2 Ne.** 25: 28 words of Nephi¹ are sufficient to teach any man the r. way to believe in Christ; **Jacob** 7: 7 Sherem claims Jacob² has led away many, that they pervert r. way of God; 7: 7 Sherem claims law of Moses is r. way; **Mosiah** 29: 6 he to whom kingdom r. belongs has refused it; **Moro.** 6: 4 those baptized are nourished by good word of God, to keep them in r. way.

RIGHT [noun] (*see also* Government, Civil; Liberty; Privilege; Right [adj.]; Right Hand)

Mosiah 29: 32 this land should be land of liberty, that every man may enjoy r. alike; **Alma** 2: 4 Amlici would deprive people of r. and privileges of church; 30: 27 Korihor claims priests do not allow Nephites to enjoy r.; 43: 9, 26, 47 design of Nephites is to preserve r.; 48: 13 Moroni¹ had sworn oath to defend his people, his r.; 51: 6 freemen covenant to maintain their r. by free government; 61: 9 Pahoran seeks to retain judgment-seat to preserve r. of his people; **3 Ne.** 3: 10 Giddianhi claims Lamanites desire to recover their r. and government; 6: 30 secret combination sets at defiance the law and r. of country; **Moro.** 7: 27 Christ claims of Father his r. of mercy.

RIGHT HAND (*see also* Left; Right [adj.]; Right [noun])

1 Ne. 20: 13 (Isa. 48: 13) my r. hand hath spanned the heavens; **Mosiah** 5: 9 those who enter covenant will be found at r. hand of God; 26: 23 the Lord grants unto them who believe place at his r. hand; 26: 24 if men know the Lord, they shall have place at r. hand; **Alma** 5: 58 unto the righteous will the Lord grant inheritance at r. hand; 7: 20 God hath no shadow of turning from r. to left; 24: 23 converted Lamanites would not flee from sword nor turn aside to r. hand or to left; 56: 37, 40 Lamanites dare not turn to r. or left, lest they be surrounded; **3 Ne.** 12: 39 (Matt. 5: 39) whosoever shall smite thee on r. cheek, turn to him the other; 13: 3 (Matt. 6: 3) let not thy left hand know what thy r. hand doeth; 22: 3 (Isa. 54: 3) thou shalt break forth on r. hand and on

left; **Moro.** 9: 26 Christ sits on r. hand of Father's power.

RIGHTEOUSNESS, RIGHTEOUS, RIGHTEOUSLY (see also Faithful; Godliness; Holiness; Honest; Innocence; Just; Obedience; Perfect; Prosper, Prosperity; Purity; Uprightness)

1 **Ne.** 2: 9 Lehi¹ admonishes Laman¹ to be like river, continually running into fountain of r.; 14: 14 saints are armed with r.; 15: 36 the wicked are rejected from the r.; 16: 3 if ye were r., ye would not murmur; 17: 35 he who is r. is favored of God; 19: 11 the Lord will visit house of Israel because of r.; 22: 16 God will not suffer that the wicked shall destroy the r.; 22: 17, 22 the r. need not fear; 22: 26 because of r. of the Lord's people, Satan has no power; **2 Ne.** 1: 19 the Lord's ways are r. forever; 1: 23 put on armor of r.; 2: 3 Jacob² is redeemed, because of r. of Redeemer; 2: 13 if no sin, then no r., if no r., then no happiness; 4: 33 encircle me in robe of thy r.; 9: 14 the r. shall have perfect knowledge of their r., being clothed with robe of r.; 9: 16 (Morm. 9: 14) they who are r. shall be r. still; 9: 18 the r., the saints of God, shall inherit kingdom of God; 9: 40 the r. fear not words of truth; 9: 49 my heart delights in r.; 21: 4 (30: 9; Isa. 11: 4) with r. shall the Lord judge the poor; 26: 8 the r. who look forward unto Christ shall not perish; 26: 9 the Son of r. shall appear unto the r.; 31: 5–6 the Lamb is baptized to fulfill all r.; **Jacob** 2: 25 the Lord has led Nephites from Jerusalem to raise up r. branch from fruit of loins of Joseph¹; 4: 5 law of Moses is sanctified unto Nephites for r.; **Mosiah** 2: 37 man who listeth to obey evil spirit becometh enemy to all r.; 3: 10 Christ to be resurrected that r. judgment might come upon men; 4: 14 (Alma 34: 23) devil is enemy to all r.; 23: 18 priests nourish people with things pertaining to r.; 27: 25 all mankind must be born of God, changed from carnal state to state of r.; **Alma** 5: 42 whoso hearkens to devil receives wages of death as to things pertaining to r.; 5: 58 names of the r. shall be written in book of life; 7: 19 people of Gideon are in paths of r.; 12: 16 whosoever dies in sins shall die spiritual death, as to things pertaining to r.; 13: 10 many are ordained high priests on account of r.; 26: 8 the Lord works r. forever; 34: 36 in hearts of the r. doth the Lord dwell; 34: 36 the r. shall sit down in the Lord's kingdom; 38: 9 Christ is the word of truth and r.; 40: 12, 14 spirits of those who are r. are received into state of happiness; 41: 14 judge r. and you shall have r. judgment; 45: 15 Alma² blesses earth for the r's sake; 50: 39 chief judge appointed

with oath to judge r.; 60: 13 the Lord suffers the r. to be slain, that justice might come upon the wicked; 62: 40 Nephites spared because of prayers of the r.; **Hel.** 6: 1 Lamanites' r. exceeds that of Nephites; 7: 5 robbers condemn the r. because of their r.; 13: 13 were it not for the r., the Lord would destroy Zarahemla; 13: 38 ye have sought happiness in doing iniquity, which is contrary to nature of God's r.; 14: 29 signs given that r. judgment may come upon non-believers; **3 Ne.** 4: 29 may the Lord preserve his people in r.; 22: 14 (Isa. 54: 14) in r. shalt thou be established; 24: 3 (Mal. 3: 3) sons of Levi¹ to offer unto the Lord an offering in r.; 24: 18 (Mal. 3: 18) then shall ye return and discern between the r. and the wicked; 25: 2 (Mal. 4: 2) unto you that fear my name shall Son of R. arise; **4 Ne.** 1: 46 there are none who are r. save disciples of Jesus; **Morm.** 2: 12 Mormon² supposes the Lord will be merciful unto Nephites that they would again become r. people; **Ether** 2: 7 promised land preserved for r. people; 8: 26 writings to persuade people to come unto fountain of all r.; **Moro.** 7: 6–7 if man prays without real intent, it is not counted unto him for r.; 8: 8 Christ came into world to call not the r., but sinners to repentance; 9: 6 we have labor to perform to conquer enemy of all r.

RIOTINGS, RIOTOUS (see also Uproar; TG Rioting and Reveling)

Mosiah 11: 14 Noah³ spends his time in r. living; **Alma** 11: 20 judges stir people up to r.

RIPE, RIPEN

1 **Ne.** 17: 35 Jews were r. in iniquity; **2 Ne.** 28: 16 when inhabitants of earth are fully r. in iniquity, they shall perish; **Jacob** 5: 58 we will pluck from trees branches which are r.; **Mosiah** 12: 12 when blossoms of thistle are r., they are driven by wind; **Alma** 10: 19 (Hel. 5: 2) if voice of people should choose iniquity, they are r. for destruction; 26: 5 field was r. and missionaries thrust in their sickles; 37: 31 (45: 16) land to be cursed unto workers of darkness unless they repent before fully r.; **Hel.** 6: 40 (8: 26; 11: 37) Nephites are r. for everlasting destruction; 13: 14 when Nephites cast the righteous out, they will be r. for destruction; **Ether** 2: 9 (9: 20) fulness of God's wrath will come upon inhabitants of promised land when they are r. in iniquity; 2: 15 if ye sin until ye are fully r., ye shall be cut off from presence of the Lord.

RIPLAH, HILL—east of river Sidon, near land of Manti

Alma 43: 31, 35 armies of Lehi³ attack Lamanites from hill R.

RIPLAKISH—*Jaredite king*

Ether 1: 23–24 (10: 4) ancestor of Morianton¹, son of Shez; 10: 4 reigns in father's stead; 10: 5–7 reigns unrighteously, afflicts people with abominations; 10: 8 is killed in rebellion.

RIPLIANCUM, WATERS OF

Ether 15: 8 both Coriantumr² and Shiz and his people pitch tents by waters of R., which by interpretation is large, or to exceed all.

RISE, RISEN, RISING (*see also* Arise; Ascend; Awake; Jesus Christ, Resurrection of; Raise; Resurrection)

1 Ne. 10: 11 (2 Ne. 25: 13–14; 26: 1; Mosiah 3: 10; Morm. 7: 5; Ether 12: 7) Messiah to r. from dead; **2 Ne.** 2: 8 Messiah brings to pass the resurrection, being first to r. from dead; 3: 5 the Lord will r. up righteous branch from loins of Joseph¹; 9: 8 if flesh should r. no more, men become subject to devil; 9: 8 angel fell from God's presence, became devil, to r. no more; **Mosiah** 3: 10 Christ will r. the third day from the dead; 16: 7 if Christ had not r. from dead, there could have been no resurrection; 26: 1 many in r. generation do not understand Benjamin's words; **Alma** 5: 49 Alma² is called to preach to the aged, middle aged, and r. generation; 11: 41 (12: 8) all shall r. from the dead; 37: 37 when thou r. in morning, let heart be full of thanks unto God; 40: 4–10 time appointed to all men to r. from the dead; **Hel.** 14: 4 people shall know of r. of sun three nights without darkness at birth of Christ; **3 Ne.** 1: 30 Lamanites also decrease in righteousness because of wickedness of r. generation; 12: 45 (Matt. 5: 45) Father maketh his sun to r. on the evil and the good; **Morm.** 7: 5 by power of Father, Christ hath r. again; 8: 28 leaders of churches shall r. in pride of hearts.

RITES (*see* Worship)

RIVER (*see also* Fountain; Jordan; Sidon, River; Water)

1 Ne. 2: 6–9 (16: 12) Lehi¹ names r. Laman; 8: 13, 17, 19, 26 Lehi¹ beholds r. of water near tree in vision; 12: 16 (15: 26–35) Nephi¹ beholds same r., representing depths of hell; **Hel.** 3: 4 those traveling in north come to large bodies of water and many r.

ROAD (*see also* Highway; Path; Street; Way)

1 Ne. 8: 32 many are lost from view wandering in strange r.; 12: 17 mists of darkness, devil's temptations, lead men

away into broad r.; **2 Ne.** 4: 32 shut gates of thy righteousness before me, that I may be strict in plain r.; **3 Ne.** 6: 8 many r. are made, leading from city to city; 8: 13 many level r. are spoiled in destruction.

ROAR (*see also* Noise; Tumult)

2 Ne. 8: 15 (Isa. 51: 15) I am the Lord thy God, whose waves r.; 15: 29 (Isa. 5: 29) they shall r. like young lions; 15: 30 (Isa. 5: 30) they shall r. against them like r. of sea.

ROB, ROBBERY, ROBBING (*see also* Robber; Steal; Thief)

2 Ne. 28: 13 false churches r. the poor because of fine sanctuaries; **Mosiah** 10: 17 Lamanites have taught children they should r. Nephites; **Alma** 1: 18 those practicing priestcraft dare not r. for fear of law; 16: 18 priests preach against r.; 20: 13 Lamanites believe Nephi¹ r. their fathers and that Nephites will r. them of property; 37: 21 r. of secret combinations among Jaredites should be manifest to Nephites; 42: 25 do you suppose mercy can r. justice; **Hel.** 2: 4 Gadianton robbers are expert in secret craft of r. and murder; 2: 8 (3 Ne. 4: 5) object of those in Kishkumen's band is to murder, r., and gain power; 3: 14 hundredth part of Nephites' proceedings, including r., cannot be contained in record; **3 Ne.** 24: 8 (Mal. 3: 8) will a man r. God; **Morm.** 8: 31 record shall come in day when there shall be r.

ROBBER (*see also* Gadianton Robbers)

Alma 11: 2 man is compelled to pay what he owed or be cast out as thief and r.; **4 Ne.** 1: 17 no r. or murderers in land.

ROBE (*see also* Apparel; Garment)

1 Ne. 8: 5 man in white r. stands before Lehi¹; 14: 19–20 Nephi¹ beholds one of twelve apostles, dressed in white r.; **2 Ne.** 4: 33 encircle me in r. of thy righteousness; 9: 14 the righteous shall be clothed in r. of righteousness; **3 Ne.** 11: 8 Christ descends from heaven clothed in white r.

ROCK (*see also* Stone [noun]; TG Jesus Christ, Rock)

1 Ne. 12: 4 (19: 12; Hel. 14: 21; 3 Ne. 8: 18; 10: 9) Nephi¹ beholds r. rending; 13: 36 in Nephites' records shall be written the Lamb's gospel, his r. and salvation; 15: 15 will they not give praise to their God, their r. and salvation; 17: 16 Nephi¹ makes tools of ore out of r.; 17: 29 (2 Ne. 25: 20) Moses smote r. and water came forth; 20: 21 (Isa. 48: 21) the Lord clave r. and waters gushed forth;

2 **Ne.** 4: 30 my soul will rejoice in thee, my God, and r. of my salvation; 4: 35 God, r. of my righteousness; 9: 45 come unto that God who is r. of your salvation; 18: 14 (Isa. 8: 14) he shall be for r. of offense to both houses of Israel; 28: 28 he who is built upon r. receives truth with gladness; **Alma** 12: 14 the guilty would be glad if r. hid them from God's presence; **Hel.** 5: 12 upon r. of Redeemer ye must build foundation; 3 **Ne.** 11: 39–40 whoso builds upon Christ's doctrine builds upon his r.; 14: 24–27 (18: 12–13); Matt. 7: 24–28) he who does Christ's sayings is compared to wise man who built house upon r.; **Ether** 3: 1 brother of Jared[2] makes sixteen small stones out of r.

ROD

1 **Ne.** 3: 28 Laman[1] and Lemuel smite younger brothers with r.; 8: 19–20, 24, 30 Lehi[1] beholds iron r.; 11: 25 (15: 23–24) iron r. is word of God; 17: 41 the Lord straitened Israel in wilderness with his r.; 2 **Ne.** 3: 17 the Lord will give Moses power in a r.; 21: 1 (Isa. 11: 1) r. shall come forth out of stem of Jesse; 21: 4 (30: 9; Isa. 11: 4) the Lord shall smite earth with r. of his mouth.

ROLL (see also Scroll)

2 **Ne.** 18: 1 (Isa. 8: 1) take r. and write in it with pen; **Morm.** 5: 23 (9: 2) earth shall be r. together as scroll; 8: 22 purposes of the Lord shall r. on.

ROOT (see also Branch; Israel; Tree)

2 **Ne.** 15: 24 (Isa. 5: 24) their r. shall be rottenness; 21: 1 (Isa. 11: 1) branch shall grow out of Jesse's r.; 21: 10 (Isa. 11: 10) r. of Jesse shall stand for ensign; **Jacob** 5: 8 r. of this tree shall perish; 5: 18 because of strength of r., wild branches bring forth tame fruit; 5: 66, 73 r. and top of tree to be equal; **Mosiah** 14: 2 (Isa. 53: 2) he shall grow up before him as r. out of dry ground; **Alma** 5: 52 the ax is laid at r. of tree; 22: 15 what shall I do to be born of God, having wicked spirit r. out of breast; 32: 37–38, 41 if ye nourish tree, it will get r.; 32: 42 because of diligence, faith, and patience with the word, that it may take r. in you, ye shall pluck its fruit; 46: 40 God prepared plants and r. to remove cause of disease; 3 **Ne.** 25: 1 (Mal. 4: 1) day that cometh will leave the proud neither r. nor branch.

ROUGH (see Smooth)

ROUND (see also God, Eternal Nature of; Unchangeable)

1 **Ne.** 10: 19 (Alma 7: 20; 37: 12) course of the Lord is one eternal r.; **Morm.** 8: 8 whole face of land is one continual r. of murder.

RUDENESS (see also Malice; Revile)

1 **Ne.** 18: 9 elder sons of Lehi[1] and Ishmael speak with r.; 2 **Ne.** 2: 1 Jacob[2] has suffered afflictions because of r. of brethren.

RUIN (see also Desolation; Destruction; Waste)

2 **Ne.** 13: 6 (Isa. 3: 6) let not this r. come under thy hand; 13: 8 (Isa. 3: 8) Jerusalem is r.; **Mosiah** 8: 8 Limhi's people discover land covered with r. of buildings.

RULE (see also Authority; Dominion; Govern; Government, Civil; Kingdom; Kingdom of God; Millennium; Regulate; Reign; Ruler)

1 **Ne.** 17: 39 the Lord r. high in heavens; 2 **Ne.** 5: 3 elder brothers claim Nephi[1] thinks to r. over them; 13: 4, 12 (Isa. 3: 4, 12) babes and women shall r. over Judah; 24: 2 (Isa. 14: 2) Israel shall r. over oppressors; **Mosiah** 29: 13 if kings were always just men, Nephites should have kings r. over them; 29: 41 Nephites appoint judges to r. over them; **Hel.** 7: 5 robbers r. to get gain and glory; 12: 6 men do not desire that the Lord should r. over them.

RULER (see also Government, Civil; King; Leader; Rule; Tyrant)

1 **Ne.** 2: 22 (3: 29; 2 Ne. 5: 19) Nephi[1] to be made r. over brothers; 16: 37–38 (18: 10; 2 Ne. 5: 3) elder brothers do not want Nephi[1] to be r. over them; 2 **Ne.** 27: 5 your r. and seers hath the Lord covered because of your iniquity; **Mosiah** 1: 10 (2: 30) Benjamin to proclaim Mosiah[2] r. over Nephites; **Alma** 2: 14 Amlici appoints r. over his people; 12: 20 Antionah a chief r. among people of Ammonihah; 35: 8 chief r. of Zoramites a very wicked man; 46: 5 people would establish Amalickiah as king that he might make them r.

RUMOR (see also Backbiting; Report)

1 **Ne.** 12: 2, 21 (14: 15–16; 2 Ne. 25: 12; Morm. 8: 30) wars and r. of wars; **Hel.** 16: 22 Satan spreads r. and contentions upon land.

RUN

2 **Ne.** 29: 8 when two nations r. together, their testimonies shall r. together; **Mosiah** 4: 27 not requisite that man r. faster than he has strength; 12: 11 thou shalt be as dry stalk which is r. over by beasts.

RUST

Mosiah 8: 11 Limhi's people have found sword blades cankered with r.;

3 Ne. 13: 19–20 (Matt. 6: 19–20) lay not up treasures upon earth, where r. corrupts.

SABBATH (*see also* BD Sabbath)

Jarom 1: 5 Nephites keep s. day holy unto the Lord; **Mosiah** 13: 16–19 (Ex. 20: 8–11) remember the s. day, to keep it holy; 18: 23 Alma¹ commands priests to keep s. day holy.

SACKCLOTH (*see also* Darkness, Physical; Grieve; Humble; Remorse; Sorrow)

2 Ne. 7: 3 (Isa. 50: 3) I make s. the covering of the heavens; **Mosiah** 11: 25 people must repent in s. and ashes; **Hel.** 11: 9 Nephites repent and humble themselves in s.

SACRAMENT (*see also* Baptism; Blood; Bread; Flesh; Jesus Christ, Types of; Ordinance; Remember, Remembrance; Wine; TG Sacrament)

3 Ne. 18: 1–4, 8–9 (20: 3–7; 26: 13) Jesus administers s. to Nephites; 18: 5 one shall be ordained with power to administer s.; 18: 6–7 (20: 8) bread in remembrance of Christ's body; 18: 10 partaking of s. witnesses that partaker will keep commandments; 18: 11 those baptized shall receive s.; 18: 11 (20: 8) wine in remembrance of Christ's blood; 18: 28–29 the unworthy not to be allowed to partake of s.; **Moro.** 4: 3 prayer for s. bread; 5: 2 prayer for s. wine; 6: 6 Nephites meet oft to partake of bread and wine in remembrance of Jesus.

SACRED (*see also* Godliness, Godly; Holiness; Holy)

1 Ne. 19: 5–6 (Jacob 1: 4) Nephi¹ records s. things on plates; **Alma** 37: 2, 14–16, 47 (50: 38; 63: 1; 3 Ne. 1: 2; 4 Ne. 1: 48; Morm. 6: 6; Ether 15: 11; Moro. 9: 24) plates are s., to be kept s.; 44: 5 s. support owed to wives and children; 50: 39 chief judge appointed with s. ordinance to judge righteously, to grant s. privilege to worship; **Hel.** 4: 12 Nephites make mock of that which is s.; **4 Ne.** 1: 27 false churches administer that which is s. unto the unworthy.

SACRIFICE (*see also* Altar; Blood; Blood, Shedding of; Broken Heart and Contrite Spirit; Idolatry; Jesus Christ, Atonement through; Jesus Christ, Types of; Justice; Law of Moses; Mercy; Offering; Ordinance; TG Sacrifice; BD Sacrifices)

1 Ne. 5: 9 Lehites offer s. and burnt offerings; **2 Ne.** 2: 7 Messiah offers himself a s. for sin; **Mosiah** 2: 3 Nephites take firstlings and offer s. according to law of Moses; **Alma** 34: 10–15 must be great and last s., infinite and eternal; 34: 11 no man can s. own blood to atone for

another's sins; 34: 13 shedding of blood to stop after great and last s.; 34: 14 law points to great and last s. of Son; 34: 15 last s. brings about mercy, which overpowers justice; **3 Ne.** 9: 20 offer for s. to Christ a broken heart and contrite spirit; **Morm.** 4: 14–15, 21 Lamanites offer Nephite women and children as s. to idols.

SAD (*see also* Sorrow)

3 Ne. 13: 16 fast not as hypocrites, of s. countenance; **Morm.** 8: 3 Moroni² alone left to write s. tale of Nephites' destruction.

SAFE, SAFELY, SAFETY (*see also* Defence; Preserve; Protect; Refuge; Security)

1 Ne. 22: 28 all nations shall dwell s. in Holy One if they repent; **2 Ne.** 1: 9 those who keep commandments shall dwell s. in promised land; 6: 2 Nephites depend upon Nephi¹ for s.; 24: 30 (Isa. 14: 30) the needy shall lie down in s.; **Jacob** 4: 15 Jews will reject stone upon which they might build s. foundation; **Alma** 34: 16 mercy encircles the repentant in arms of s.; 48: 12 Moroni¹ labors for s. of his people; 62: 10 law strictly observed for s. of country; **3 Ne.** 2: 12 converted Lamanites and Nephites take up arms for s.; **Moro.** 1: 3 Moroni² wanders for s. of his life.

SAIL (*see also* Journey; Ship)

1 Ne. 18: 22–23 Lehites s. to promised land; **Alma** 63: 6, 8 many Nephites s. northward; **Morm.** 5: 18 Nephites are led by Satan as vessel tossed without s. or anchor.

SAINT, SAINTS (*see also* Believer; Children of God; Christian; Church of God; Flock; Sheep; TG Saints; BD Saints)

1 Ne. 13: 5, 9 abominable church slays s.; 14: 12 church of Lamb are s.; 14: 14 power of Lamb descends upon s.; 15: 28 awful gulf separates wicked from tree of life and s.; **2 Ne.** 9: 18 (Moro. 8: 26) s. shall inherit kingdom of God; 9: 19 God delivers s. from death and hell; 26: 3 (28: 10; Morm. 8: 27, 41) cry of blood of s. ascends to God against wicked; **Enos** 1: 3 words concerning joy of s. sink into heart of Enos²; **Mosiah** 3: 19 natural man is enemy to God unless he becomes s. through atonement; **Hel.** 14: 25 (3 Ne. 23: 9–13) many graves shall open, and s. shall appear; **Morm.** 8: 23 s. who have possessed land shall cry from dust; 8: 41 (Ether 8: 22) the Lord will avenge blood of s.; **Moro.** 8: 26 all s. shall dwell with God.

SALEM—*earlier name for Jerusalem in Palestine* (*see also* BD Salem)

Alma 13: 17–18 Melchizedek, king of S.

SALT (*see also* Example)

3 **Ne.** 12: 13 (Matt. 5: 13) you are *s.* of earth; 16: 15 Gentiles shall be as *s.* that has lost savor.

SALVATION (*see also* Baptism; Deliver; Escape; Eternal Life; Faith; Gospel; Grace; Jesus Christ, Atonement through; Jesus Christ—Savior; Obedience; Plan; Redemption; Repentance; Sanctification; Save; TG Salvation; Salvation, Plan of)

2 **Ne.** 2: 4 *s.* is free; 26: 24, 27 the Lord commands none not to partake of *s.*; **Enos** 1: 13 Enos prays Lamanites might be brought unto *s.*; **Mosiah** 3: 9 Christ comes unto his own that *s.* might come unto men; 3: 18 *s.* comes through atoning blood of Christ; 4: 6–8 atonement prepared that *s.* might come to those who trust in the Lord; 5: 8 no other name given whereby *s.* comes, except Christ; 12: 21 (15: 14; 3 Ne. 20: 40; Isa. 52: 7) how beautiful upon mountains are feet of him who publishes *s.*; 13: 28 *s.* comes not by law alone; 15: 26–27 *s.* comes to none who rebel against God; 15: 28 *s.* shall be declared to all; 15: 31 (16: 1; 3 Ne. 16: 20; 20: 35) all shall see *s.* of God; **Alma** 9: 28 the righteous shall reap *s.*; 11: 40 *s.* comes only to believers; 13: 21 day of *s.* draws nigh; 34: 31 now is the day of your *s.*; 34: 37 (Morm. 9: 27) work out your *s.* with fear before God; **Hel.** 13: 38 ye have procrastinated the day of your *s.*; 3 **Ne.** 18: 32 ye may be means of bringing *s.* to repentant; **Moro.** 8: 17 little children are alike and partakers of *s.*

SAM—*third son of Lehi*[1] [c. 600 B.C.]

1 **Ne.** 2: 5 third son of Lehi[1], older brother of Nephi[1]; 2: 17 is told of the Lord's manifestations by Nephi[1]; 7: 6 (Alma 3: 6) elder brothers rebel against Nephi[1] and S.; 8: 3 Lehi[1] rejoices because of S.; 2 **Ne.** 1: 28 is admonished to hearken unto Nephi[1]; 4: 11 is blessed by Lehi[1]; 5: 6 goes with Nephi[1].

SAME (*see also* Alike; Equal; Unchangeable)

1 **Ne.** 10: 18 (2 Ne. 27: 23; 29: 9; Alma 31: 17; Moro. 10: 7, 19) the Lord is *s.* yesterday, today, forever; 2 **Ne.** 2: 4 Spirit is *s.* yesterday, today, forever; 2: 22 without the fall, Adam would have stayed in *s.* state; **Alma** 34: 34 *s.* spirit shall possess body after death.

SAMUEL[1]—*Hebrew prophet* [c. 1100 B.C.] (*see also* BD Samuel)

3 **Ne.** 20: 24 S. and all prophets have testified of Christ.

SAMUEL[2]—*Lamanite prophet* [c. 6 B.C.]

Hel. ch. 13–15 prophecy of S. the

Lamanite to the Nephites; 13: 2 comes into Zarahemla; 13: 5 (3 Ne. 23: 9–10) speaks words of the Lord; 14: 2–6 foretells signs of Christ's birth; 14: 14, 20–28 foretells signs of Christ's death; 14: 15–19 teaches concerning resurrection and redemption; 16: 1, 3 those who believe S. desire baptism; 16: 2, 6 many are angry with S. and try to kill him; 16: 7 flees.

SANCTIFICATION, SANCTIFY (*see also* Born of God; Cleanse; Consecrate; Faith; Glorify; Grace; Holiness; Holy; Holy Ghost, Baptism of; Jesus Christ, Atonement through; Justify; Purify; Righteousness; Salvation; TG Sanctification, Sanctify)

2 **Ne.** 15: 16 (Isa. 5: 16) God shall be *s.* in righteousness; 18: 13 (Isa. 8: 13) *s.* the Lord himself; 27: 34 (Isa. 29: 23) they shall *s.* the Lord's name; **Jacob** 4: 5 law of Moses is *s.* unto Nephites for righteousness; **Alma** 5: 54 those brought into church have been *s.* by Holy Ghost; 13: 11–12 high priests are *s.* by Holy Ghost; **Hel.** 3: 35 *s.* comes from yielding heart to God; 3 **Ne.** 27: 20 be baptized that ye may be *s.* by reception of Holy Ghost; 28: 39 three Nephites are *s.* in flesh; **Ether** 4: 7 Gentiles shall exercise faith, that they may become *s.* in the Lord; **Moro.** 4: 3 bless and *s.* this bread; 5: 2 bless and *s.* this wine; 10: 33 if ye by grace are perfect in Christ, ye are *s.* in Christ by grace of God.

SANCTUARY (*see also* Building [noun]; Refuge; Synagogue)

2 **Ne.** 28: 13 false churches rob poor because of fine *s.*; **Alma** 15: 17 people assemble in *s.* to worship; 21: 6 Amalekites in Jerusalem have built *s.*; **Hel.** 3: 9 people in land northward use timber to build *s.*; **Ether** 13: 3 New Jerusalem the holy *s.* of the Lord.

SAND, SANDY (*see also* Innumerable; Rock)

1 **Ne.** 12: 1 multitude in promised land as many as *s.* of sea; 20: 19 (Isa. 48: 19) thy seed also had been as the *s.*; 2 **Ne.** 20: 22 (Isa. 10: 22) though Israel be as *s.* of sea, yet remnant shall return; 28: 28 (3 Ne. 11: 40; 14: 26; 18: 13) house built upon *s.* foundation; **Alma** 2: 27 Lamanites and Amlicites almost as numerous as *s.* of sea; **Morm.** 1: 7 Nephites numerous as *s.* of sea.

SARAH, SARAI—*wife of Abraham* [c. twentieth century B.C.] (*see also* BD Sarah)

2 **Ne.** 8: 2 (Isa. 51: 2) look unto S., who bare you.

SARIAH—*wife of Lehi*[1] [c. 600 B.C.]

1 **Ne.** 2: 5 accompanies Lehi[1] from Jerusalem; 5: 1, 7 rejoices over sons' return from Jerusalem; 5: 2–3 murmurs against Lehi[1]; 5: 4–6 is comforted by Lehi[1]; 8: 14–16 is seen by Lehi[1] in vision of tree of life; 18: 19 Jacob[1] and Joseph[1] are grieved because of mother's afflictions.

SATAN (*see also* Adversary; Devil; Evil; Lucifer; TG Satan; BD Satan)

1 **Ne.** 13: 29 because scriptures are missing, S. has power over men; 22: 15, 26 (2 Ne. 30: 18; Ether 8: 26) S. shall have no more power over men because of righteousness; **Alma** 8: 9 (10: 25; 27: 12; Hel. 16: 23; 3 Ne. 2: 2–3; 6: 15–16; 4 Ne. 1: 28) S. has gotten hold of people's hearts; 12: 17 S. will subject the wicked according to his will; 15: 17 people pray to be delivered from S.; 37: 15 transgressors will be delivered up unto S.; **Hel.** 6: 21 (16: 22; Moro. 9: 3) S. stirs up hearts of Nephites; 3 **Ne.** 1: 22 S. sends lyings among people; 7: 5 iniquity comes because people yield themselves to S.; 18: 18 S. desires to have you, that he may sift you as wheat; 28: 39 S. could have no power over three Nephites; **Morm.** 5: 18 Nephites are led by S. as chaff is driven before wind; **Ether** 15: 19 S. has full power over hearts of Jaredites.

SATISFY (*see also* Appease; Jesus Christ, Atonement through; Quench; Reconcile)

2 **Ne.** 9: 26 atonement s. demands of justice; 9: 51 do not spend your labor for that which cannot s.; **Mosiah** 14: 11 (Isa. 53: 11) he shall see the travail of his soul and be s.; 15: 8–9 Son s. demands of justice; **Alma** 34: 16 mercy can s. demands of justice.

SAVE (*see also* Deliver; Reclaim; Redemption; Salvation)

1 **Ne.** 6: 4 come unto God and be s.; 13: 40 all men must come unto Son or they cannot be s.; 2 **Ne.** 2: 9 they who believe in Messiah shall be s.; 9: 21 (3 Ne. 9: 21) God comes into world to s. all men if they hearken; 9: 23 those without repentance, baptism, faith cannot be s.; 25: 20 (Acts 4: 12) no name other than Jesus Christ whereby man can be s.; 25: 23 s. by grace after all we can do; 28: 8 false churches claim sinner will be beaten with few stripes, then s.; 31: 15 (Alma 32: 13) he who endures to end shall be s.; 31: 19 (Alma 7: 14; 34: 18) rely upon merits of him who is mighty to s.; **Mosiah** 4: 8 no other conditions whereby man can be s.; **Alma** 2: 30 Alma[2] asks to be

instrument in the Lord's hand to s. this people; 5: 21 no man can be s. except his garments are washed white; 11: 34–37 God will not s. his people in their sins; 12: 15 God has all power to s. every man who believes; 14: 10 Amulek would s. martyrs from flames; 26: 30 sons of Mosiah[2] suffered afflictions that they might be instruments of s. some soul; 27: 4 sons of Mosiah[2] are treated as angels sent to s. people; **Hel.** 13: 6 nothing can s. this people except repentance and faith; 13: 12 Zarahemla is s. because of the righteous; 3 **Ne.** 9: 21 Christ is come into world to s. it from sin; 11: 33 (23: 5; Morm. 9: 23; Ether 4: 18) whoso believes and is baptized shall be s.; **Morm.** 2: 21 Mormon[2] gathers people to s. them from destruction; 7: 3 ye must come unto repentance or ye cannot be s.; **Moro.** 7: 26 men are s. by faith in Christ; 8: 15 awful wickedness to suppose God s. one child because of baptism, while another perishes.

SAVIOR (*see* Jesus Christ—Savior)

SAVOR

3 **Ne.** 12: 13 (16: 15; Matt. 5: 13) if salt loses s., wherewith will earth be salted.

SAW (*see* See, Saw, Seen)

SAY (*see also* Sayings; Speak)

1 **Ne.** 21: 21 (Isa. 49: 21) then shalt thou s. in thine heart, Who hath begotten me these; **Mosiah** 2: 25 ye cannot s. ye are even as much as dust of earth.

SAYINGS (*see also* Commandments of God; Say; Teach; Word)

2 **Ne.** 4: 14 many s. of Nephi[1] and Lehi[1] are written on other plates; 30: 18 Nephi[1] makes end of his s.; **Mosiah** 1: 6 remember that these s. are true; 3 **Ne.** 15: 1 whoso remembers and does Christ's s. shall be raised up; 16: 4 Christ's s. to be written; 18: 33 keep these s. which I have commanded you; 27: 33 Jesus ends his s.; **Morm.** 9: 26 who can deny the Lord's s.

SCALES

2 **Ne.** 30: 6 s. of darkness shall begin to fall from eyes.

SCARCE (*see also* Few)

Hel. 3: 10 timber exceedingly s. in land northward; 3 **Ne.** 4: 20 wild game becomes s. in wilderness.

SCARLET

1 **Ne.** 13: 7–8 Nephi[1] beholds s. in abominable church.

SCATTER, SCATTERING (*see also* Destruction; Disperse; Gather; Israel, Scattering of; Israel, Ten Lost Tribes of; Remnant)

1 Ne. 17: 32 the Lord made Israel mighty, unto s. children of land to destruction.

SCENT

Alma 16: 11 great s. of dead bodies in Ammonihah; **Ether** 14: 23 s. of dead bodies troubles Jaredites.

SCEPTER (*see also* Authority; Dominion; Rule)

2 Ne. 24: 5 (Isa. 14: 5) the Lord has broken s. of the rulers.

SCOFF (*see also* Mock; Scorn)

1 Ne. 8: 26–28 those in spacious building s. at those partaking of fruit.

SCORN, SCORNFUL (*see also* Laugh; Malice; Mock; Reproach; Revile; Scoff)

1 Ne. 8: 33 those in spacious building point finger of s. at those partaking of fruit; **Alma** 4: 8 people of church are s. toward each other; 26: 23 Nephites laughed sons of Mosiah² to s. over preaching to Lamanites.

SCOURGE (*see also* Chasten; Destruction; Judgment; Persecution)

1 Ne. 2: 24 (2 Ne. 5: 25; Jacob 3: 3) Lamanites to be s. unto Nephites; 19: 9 (2 Ne. 6: 9; Mosiah 3: 9) world shall s. God when he comes; 19: 13 (2 Ne. 25: 16) Jews to be s. by all people for crucifying God; **Mosiah** 15: 5 Son will suffer himself to be s.; 17: 13 wicked priests s. Abinadi; **3 Ne.** 20: 28 Gentiles to be a s. to descendants of Nephites.

SCRIPTURES (*see also* Bible; Book; Book of Mormon; Commandments of God; Knowledge; Learn; Prophecy; Read; Record; Revelation; Truth; Word of God; Write; Writing; TG Scriptures; Scriptures, Lost; Scriptures, Preservation of; Scriptures, Study of; Scriptures, Value of; Scriptures, Writing of; Scriptures to Come Forth; BD Scriptures)

1 Ne. 19: 23 Nephi¹ likens s. unto Nephites; **2 Ne.** 4: 15 Nephi¹ writes on his plates many s. from brass plates; 4: 15 my soul delighteth in s.; **Jacob** 2: 23 Nephites understand not the s.; 7: 23 Nephites search s., hearken not to Sherem's words; **Alma** 12: 1 Alma² unfolds s. beyond what Amulek has done; 13: 20 (41: 1) if men wrest s., it will be to own destruction; 14: 1 repentant people of Ammonihah search s.; 18: 38 Ammon² expounds to Lamanites all s. since Lehi¹ left Jerusalem; 30: 44 s. are laid before

thee and all things denote there is a God; 33: 2 (3 Ne. 10: 14) ye ought to search the s.; 37: 3 brass plates have records of holy s. on them; **Hel.** 16: 14 s. begin to be fulfilled; **3 Ne.** 1: 24 those who use s. to preach against law of Moses have not understood s.; 9: 16 s. concerning Christ's coming are fulfilled; 10: 14 he who has s. should search them; 23: 6 Jesus expounds s. to Nephites; 23: 6 Nephites to write other s. that they have not; 23: 14 Jesus expounds all s. in one which Nephites have written; 27: 5 have they not read the s.

SCROLL (*see also* Roll)

3 Ne. 26: 3 (Morm. 5: 23; 9: 2) earth to be wrapt together as s.

SEA (*see also* Flood; Island; Isle; Red Sea; Water; Waves)

2 Ne. 7: 2 (Isa. 50: 2) at his rebuke, the Lord dries up s.; 10: 20 the Lord has made s. our path; 21: 9 (Isa. 11: 9) earth to be full of knowledge of the Lord, as waters cover s.; **Mosiah** 13: 19 in six days the Lord made heaven, earth, and s.; **Ether** 2: 13 the Lord brings Jared² and brethren to great s.

SEAL, SEALING (*see also* Bind; Elect; Hide; Marriage; Temple)

Title Page (Moro. 10: 2) Book of Mormon is s. by hand of Moroni²; **1 Ne.** 14: 26 records of visions are s. to come forth in purity; **2 Ne.** 18: 16 (Isa. 8: 16) s. the law among my disciples; 27: 7 book shall be s.; 27: 22 thou shalt s. book again and hide it unto me; 33: 15 what I s. on earth shall be brought against you at judgment bar; **Mosiah** 5: 15 abound in good works, that Christ may s. you his; 17: 20 Abinadi s. truth of his words by death; **Alma** 34: 35 if ye have procrastinated day of repentance, devil s. you his; **Hel.** 10: 7 Nephi² given power that what he s. on earth shall be s. in heaven; **Ether** 3: 22 brother of Jared² to write, s. up things seen and heard.

SEANTUM—*Nephite belonging to Gadianton band* [c. 23 B.C.]

Hel. 9: 6 murders brother, chief judge; 9: 26–36 Nephi² sends men to house of S.; 9: 37 confesses.

SEARCH, SOUGHT (*see also* Desire; Inquire; Read; Seek; Study)

1 Ne. 2: 19 Nephi¹ has s. the Lord diligently; 5: 10 Lehi¹ s. brass plates; 10: 21 if men have s. to do wickedly, they are found unclean; **2 Ne.** 1: 25 Nephi¹ has not s. for power and authority, but for glory of God; 2: 17 fallen angel became devil, having s. evil; 9: 4 many Nephites have s. much to know things to come; 9:

44 I pray God that he view me with his all-s. eye; 32: 7 men will not s. knowledge; **Jacob** 4: 6 (3 Ne. 23: 5) s. the prophets; 4: 14 Jews s. for things they could not understand; 7: 23 Nephites s. the scriptures; **W of M** 1: 3 Mormon² s. among records and finds small plates; **Mosiah** 1: 7 s. records diligently; 27: 31 those who live without God will shrink beneath glance of his all-s. eye; **Alma** 14: 1 repentant people of Ammonihah s. scriptures; 17: 2 sons of Mosiah² s. scriptures diligently to know word of God; 33: 2 (3 Ne. 10: 14; 23: 1) ye ought to s. the scriptures; **Hel.** 11: 26 robbers s. out secret plans of Gadianton; **Morm.** 8: 23 s. the prophecies of Isaiah; **Ether** 8: 17 daughter of Jared³ puts it into Akish's heart to s. out secret oaths; **Moro.** 6: 8 as oft as men s. forgiveness, they were forgiven; 7: 19 s. diligently in light of Christ to know good from evil.

SEASON (*see also* Time)

2 **Ne.** 7: 4 (Isa. 50: 4) the Lord has given me tongue of the learned that I know how to speak word in s.

SEAT (*see* Judgment-seat)

SEBUS, WATERS OF—*watering place in land of Ishmael*

Alma 17: 26 Ammon² goes where flocks are watered, called S.; 17: 34 Ammon² contends with Lamanites who stand by waters of S.; 18: 7 practice among Lamanites of scattering flocks at waters of S.; 19: 20 king slew servants whose flocks were scattered at S.

SECOND (*see also* Death, Spiritual; Jesus Christ, Second Coming of)

2 **Ne.** 6: 14 (21: 11; 25: 17; 29: 1; Jacob 6: 2) Messiah will set himself s. time to recover his people; **Mosiah** 26: 25 when s. trump sounds, they who never knew the Lord shall stand before him; **Alma** 43: 46 if ye are not guilty of first or s. offense, ye shall not suffer yourselves to be slain; **Morm.** 4: 20 Lamanites do not beat Nephites in Boaz until s. attack.

SECRET (*see also* Closet; Hide; Private; Privily; Secret Combination)

1 **Ne.** 20: 16 (Isa. 48: 16) I have not spoken in s.; 2 **Ne.** 30: 17 (Mosiah 8: 17) all things s. shall be revealed; **Alma** 34: 26 pour out your souls to the Lord in s. places; 58: 20 Gid and Teomner rise from s. places and cut off Lamanite spies; 3 **Ne.** 13: 6 (Matt. 6: 6) pray to thy Father who is in s.

SECRET COMBINATION (*see also* Gadianton Robbers; Murder; Oath; Plan)

2 **Ne.** 9: 9 (26: 22; Hel. 6: 26–30; 3 Ne. 6: 28–29; Ether 8: 15, 25; 10: 33) devil is founder of all s.c. of murder; 10: 15 Lord must destroy s. works of darkness and murder; 26: 20, 22 s.c. to be among Gentiles, as in times of old; **Alma** 37: 21 s. works of Jaredites to be made manifest; 37: 27–29 (Ether 8: 20) record of s. covenants of Jaredites not to be made manifest to Nephites; 37: 22, 25–26 the Lord destroyed Jaredites because they did not repent of s. works; 37: 23–25 the Lord will bring s. works out of darkness into light; 37: 28, 31 curse on land against s.c.; 37: 29–30 s.c. murdered prophets; 37: 30 God's judgments come upon workers of darkness and s.c.; **Hel.** 2: 8 Kishkumen's s.c. plans to murder, rob, get power; 2: 13 (Ether 8: 21) s.c. cause destruction of Nephites and Jaredites; 6: 15, 18–19 (Ether 14: 8–10) s.c. murder to get kingdom; 6: 22 robber bands have s. signs and words; 6: 22 those who enter covenant swear brother shall not be injured because of wickedness; 6: 26 s. covenants came to Gadianton not from records, but from devil; 6: 37–38 Lamanites hunt, Nephites support s.c.; 7: 25 Nephites have united themselves to s. band established by Gadianton; 3 **Ne.** 3: 9 Giddianhi, governor of s. society of Gadianton; 5: 5–6 punishment puts end to s.c.; 6: 27–30 friends of wicked judges enter covenant to combine against righteousness; 7: 6, 9 government is destroyed by s.c.; 4 **Ne.** 1: 42 wicked part of Nephites again build up s.c. of Gadianton; **Morm.** 8: 27 blood of saints will cry unto the Lord because of s.c.; 8: 40 why do ye build up your s. abominations to get gain; **Ether** 8: 13–18 Akish and followers form s.c.; 8: 19 the Lord works not in s.c.; 8: 20 s.c. are had among all people; 8: 22–23 nations that uphold s.c. shall be destroyed; 8: 24 Gentiles to awake to awful situation because of s.c.; 9: 26 Heth¹ embraces s. plans of old; 10: 33 robbers administer oaths after manner of ancients; 11: 15 rebellion arises because of s.c.; 11: 22 Jaredites reject words of prophets because of s. society; 13: 18 many are slain by sword of s.c.

SECURITY (*see also* Defence; Protect; Refuge; Safe, Safety)

2 **Ne.** 1: 32 the Lord has consecrated this land for s. of seed of Nephi¹ and Zoram¹; 28: 21 devil lulls men away into carnal s.; **Alma** 49: 13 Moroni¹ builds forts of s.; 49: 21 Lamanites contend with Nephites to get into their place of s.; 50: 4 places of s. built upon towers; 60: 19 have ye neglected us because ye are surrounded by s.; 3 **Ne.** 4: 15 Nephite armies return again to places of s.

SEDUCE (*see also* Captivate; Tempt)

Hel. 6: 38 robbers s. more part of the righteous Nephites.

SEE, SAW, SEEN (*see also* Behold; Eye; Look; Observe; Perceive; Sight; View; Vision; Watch)

1 Ne. 1: 8 Lehi¹ s. God sitting on throne; **2 Ne.** 3: 5 Joseph¹ truly s. our day; 9: 4 in our bodies we shall s. God; 9: 32 the blind that will not s. shall perish; 11: 2–3 Isaiah¹, Nephi¹, and Jacob² s. the Lord; 16: 5 (Isa. 6: 5) mine eyes have s. the King; 16: 9 (Isa. 6: 9) he said, s. ye, but they perceived not; 16: 10 (Isa. 6: 10) shut this people's eyes lest they s. and be converted; 27: 29 (Isa. 29: 18) eyes of the blind shall s. out of obscurity; **Mosiah** 15: 29 (3 Ne. 20: 32) the Lord's watchmen s. eye to eye when he brings Zion; **Alma** 19: 13 Lamoni has s. Redeemer; 30: 15 Korihor claims man cannot know of things he cannot s.; 36: 26 because of the word, many have s. eye to eye; **Hel.** 8: 17 Abraham s. of Son's coming; **3 Ne.** 11: 8 multitude s. Christ descending from heaven; 13: 6 (Matt. 6: 6) Father, who s. in secret, shall reward you openly; 17: 16–17 eye hath never s. so great and marvelous things; 17: 25 multitude bear record because each man s. for himself; 26: 18 many of those baptized s. unspeakable things; **Ether** 3: 20 brother of Jared² s. Jesus; 9: 22 Emer s. Son of Righteousness; 12: 6 faith is things hoped for and not s.; 12: 6 dispute not because ye s. not; 12: 39 Moroni² has s. Jesus.

SEED (*see also* Children of God; Descendant; Heir; Loins; Plant; BD Seed of Abraham)

1 Ne. 5: 19 (7: 1) Lehi¹ prophesies many things concerning his s.; 8: 1 (16: 11; 18: 6) Lehites gather s. of every kind; 12: 9–10 twelve ministers from s. of Nephi¹ will judge his s.; 13: 11 wrath of God to be upon s. of Lamanites; 13: 34 the Lord will manifest himself to s. of Nephi¹; 15: 13–14 remnant of s. of Nephites to receive gospel from Gentiles; 15: 18 (22: 9; 3 Ne. 20: 25) the Lord covenants with Abraham, In thy s. shall all earth be blessed; 18: 24 (2 Ne. 5: 11; Mosiah 9: 9) Lehites plant s.; 20: 19 (Isa. 48: 19) thy s. also had been as sand; **2 Ne.** 3: 3 s. of Joseph² shall not utterly be destroyed; 10: 19 the Lord to consecrate this land to s. of Lehi¹; 24: 20 (Isa. 14: 20) s. of evil-doers shall never be renowned; 29: 14 the Lord covenanted to remember Abraham's s. forever; **Jacob** 2: 30 if the Lord will raise up s., he will command his people; **Mosiah** 14: 10 (15:

10–12; Isa. 53: 10) when thou shalt make his soul an offering for sin, he shall see his s.; 15: 11–12 those who hearken to prophets are Son's s.; **Alma** 3: 9 whoever mingles his s. with Lamanites brings same curse upon his s.; 32: 28–39 word compared to s.; 46: 23 (Morm. 7: 10) Nephites are remnant of s. of Jacob¹, of Joseph¹; **Hel.** 8: 21 s. of Zedekiah are with Nephites; **3 Ne.** 5: 23 the Lord will bring remnant of s. of Joseph¹ to knowledge of God; 5: 24 the Lord will gather remnant of s. of Jacob¹; 22: 3 (Isa. 54: 3) thy s. shall inherit the Gentiles; **Ether** 1: 41 (2: 3) Jaredites gather s. of every kind; 13: 6, 10 New Jerusalem to be built unto remnant of s. of Joseph¹; 13: 7 the Lord brought remnant of s. of Joseph¹ out of Jerusalem.

SEEK, SOUGHT (*see also* Ask; Desire; Inquire; Look; Pray; Search; Watch)

1 Ne. 2: 19 Nephi¹ has s. the Lord diligently; 10: 17 power of Holy Ghost is gift of God unto all who diligently s. him; 10: 19 (3 Ne. 14: 7–8; Matt. 7: 7–8) he who diligently s. shall find; 10: 21 those who have s. to do wickedly shall be found unclean; 13: 37 blessed are they who s. to bring forth Zion; **2 Ne.** 1: 25 Nephi¹ has not s. power and authority, but glory of God; 2: 17 fallen angel became devil, having s. evil; 2: 27 devil s. that all men might be miserable; 21: 10 (Isa. 11: 10) Gentiles shall s. to ensign; 26: 29 those practicing priestcraft do not s. welfare of Zion; 27: 27 (28: 9) wo unto them that s. deep to hide counsel from the Lord; **Jacob** 2: 18 (3 Ne. 13: 33) before ye s. riches, s. kingdom of God; 2: 19 after obtaining hope in Christ, ye shall obtain riches if ye s. them; 2: 19 s. riches to do good; 4: 10 s. not to counsel the Lord, but to take counsel; 4: 14 Jews s. for things they could not understand; **Mosiah** 27: 10 (Alma 36: 6) Alma² and sons of Mosiah² s. to destroy church; **Alma** 32: 13 sometimes if man is compelled to be humble, he s. repentance; 39: 14 s. not after riches or vain things of world; 46: 10 Amalickiah leads many to s. to destroy church; 60: 36 Moroni¹ s. not for power or honor, but glory of God; **3 Ne.** 13: 33 (Matt. 6: 33) s. ye first the kingdom of God; **Ether** 8: 25 those who build up secret combinations s. to overthrow freedom of all lands; 12: 41 s. this Jesus of whom prophets have written; **Moro.** 6: 8 as oft as men s. repentance with real intent, they were forgiven; 7: 45 charity s. not her own; 8: 28 Nephites s. to put down all power and authority from God.

SEEN (*see* See, Saw, Seen)

SEER (*see also* Prophet; Revelator; Translation; BD Seer)

2 Ne. 3: 6–8, 11–15 the Lord to raise choice latter-day s. from fruit of loins of Joseph[1]; 27: 5 the Lord has covered s. because of people's iniquity; **Mosiah** 8: 13 (28: 16) whoever is commanded to look in interpreters is called s.; 8: 15–16 s. is revelator and prophet, no greater gift; 8: 17 s. can know past, future, reveal all things.

SEEZORAM—*member of Gadianton band, elected chief judge* [c. 26 B.C.]

Hel. 8: 27–28 member of Gadianton band; 9: 23 Nephi[2] is accused of murdering S.; 9: 26–37 Nephi[2] reveals S. was murdered by brother.

SELL, SOLD

1 Ne. 5: 14 (Alma 10: 3) Joseph[1] was s. into Egypt; 2 Ne. 7: 1 (Isa. 50: 1) for your iniquities you have s. yourselves; 26: 10 (3 Ne. 20: 38) Nephites s. themselves for naught; **Alma** 46: 23 let us keep commandments, or we be cast into prison or s. or slain; **Hel.** 6: 8 Nephites and Lamanites have free intercourse to buy and s.; **Hel.** 7: 32 fourth generation will s. the Lord for silver and gold; **Morm.** 8: 38 Nephites s. themselves for that which will canker; **Ether** 10: 22 Jaredites buy and s. to get gain.

SEND, SENT

2 Ne. 16: 8 (Isa. 6: 8) here am I, s. me; **Mosiah** 3: 13 the Lord has s. his holy prophets among men; 3 Ne. 20: 26 Father s. Son; 24: 1 (Mal. 3: 1) the Lord will s. messenger to prepare way; 25: 5 (Mal. 4: 5) the Lord will s. Elijah the prophet; 27: 13 Christ came into world to do Father's will because Father s. him; 28: 34 wo unto those who will not hearken to words of those whom Jesus has s. among them; **Ether** 4: 12 he who will not believe Christ will not believe Father who s. him; **Moro.** 7: 16 every thing which persuades to believe in Christ is s. by power and gift of Christ.

SENINE—*Nephite coin* (*see also* Coin)

Alma 11: 3 judges receive s. of gold for a day; 11: 3, 7 senum of silver is equal to s. of gold; 11: 5, 8 s. is half value of seon; 30: 33 Alma[2] has never received so much as one s. for labor in church; 3 Ne. 12: 26 thou shalt not come out of prison until thou hast paid the uttermost s.

SENSE

2 Ne. 2: 11 without opposition, it must have neither s. nor insensibility;

Mosiah 2: 38 justice awakens the unrepentant to lively s. of guilt; 4: 5 knowledge of God's goodness awakens s. of own nothingness; **Alma** 7: 22 Alma[2] speaks to awaken people to s. of duty toward God; **Ether** 8: 24 Jaredites will awake to s. of awful situation.

SENSUAL (*see also* Carnal; Flesh; Lust; Nature, Natural)

Mosiah 16: 3 (Alma 42: 10) because of fall, mankind became carnal, s., devilish.

SENT (*see* Send, Sent)

SENUM—*Nephite coin* (*see also* Coin)

Alma 11: 3 judges receive s. of silver each day; 11: 3, 7 s. of silver is equal to senine of gold; 11: 11 two s. equal one amnor; 11: 12 four s. equal one ezrom; 11: 15 shiblon is half of a s.

SEON—*Nephite coin* (*see also* Coin)

Alma 11: 5, 8 twice the value of senine; 11: 9 shum of gold equals two s.

SEPARATION, SEPARATE, SEPARATELY (*see also* TG Separation)

1 Ne. 13: 12 man among Gentiles is s. from Lamanites by many waters; **Mosiah** 26: 4 unbelievers in rising generations are s. people as to faith; **Alma** 3: 14 the Lord sets mark on Lamanites that they may be s. from Nephites; 5: 57 come ye out from the wicked and be s.; 29: 16 my soul is carried away, even unto s. from body, because of joy; 31: 2 Alma[2] sorrows because of s. of Zoramites from Nephites; 35: 16 Alma[2] will give charge to sons s.; **Hel.** 15: 19 Nephites were s. from Jews because of Jews' iniquity.

SEPULCHRE (*see also* Grave)

1 Ne. 19: 10 (2 Ne. 25: 13) Christ to be buried in s.; **Alma** 19: 1, 5 king Lamoni to be laid in s.

SERAPHIM (*see also* BD Seraphim)

2 Ne. 16: 2 (Isa. 6: 2) s. stand above God's throne; 16: 6–7 (Isa. 6: 6–7) s. touches lips of Isaiah[1] with coal.

SERMON ON THE MOUNT

3 Ne. ch. 12–14 (Matt. ch. 5–7) Christ teaches Nephites as he taught the Jews.

SERPENT (*see also* Devil; Jesus Christ, Types of; BD Fiery Serpents; Serpent, Brazen)

1 Ne. 17: 41 (2 Ne. 25: 20) the Lord sent fiery flying s. among Israelites and prepared way for healing; 2 Ne. 2: 18 (Mosiah 16: 3) old s., the devil, tempted Eve; 2 Ne. 24: 29 (Isa. 14: 29) out of s's

root shall come cockatrice, and his fruit shall be fiery flying s.; 25: 20 the Lord gave Moses power to heal nations bitten by poisonous s.; 25: 20 if Israelites would cast eyes unto s. raised by Moses in wilderness, they would be healed; **Hel.** 8: 14–15 (Alma 33: 19–22) brazen s. lifted up by Moses in wilderness is type of Christ; **3 Ne.** 14: 10 (Matt. 7: 10) if son asks for fish, will father give him s.; **Morm.** 8: 24 poisonous s. could not harm saints; 9: 24 those that believe shall take up s.; **Ether** 9: 31–33 poisonous s. come upon land; 10: 19 poisonous s. are destroyed.

SERVANT (see also Angel; Angels of the Devil; Disciple; Follow, Follower; Messenger; Minister [noun]; Prophet; Serve, Service)

1 Ne. 20: 20 (Isa. 48: 20) the Lord hath redeemed his s. Jacob[1]; 21: 3 (Isa. 49: 3) thou art my s., O Israel; **2 Ne.** 9: 41 Holy One employs no s. at gate; **Jacob** ch. 5 s. aids lord in caring for vineyard; **Mosiah** 2: 21 if ye serve God with whole souls, yet ye would be unprofitable s.; 14: 11 (Isa. 53: 11) the Lord's righteous s. shall justify many; 21: 33 Ammon[1] declines to baptize, considering himself unworthy s.; 22: 4 if thou hast not found me to be unprofitable s., listen to my words; **Alma** 17: 25 Ammon[2] desires to be Lamoni's s.; 17: 27–39 Ammon[2] helps king's s. tend flocks; **Hel.** 5: 29, 32 seek no more to destroy my s.; **3 Ne.** 20: 43 the Lord's s. shall deal prudently; 21: 10 life of the Lord's s. shall be in his hand; 22: 17 (Isa. 54: 17) this is the heritage of s. of the Lord; **Moro.** 7: 11 s. of devil cannot follow Christ, follower of Christ cannot be s. of devil.

SERVE, SERVICE (see also Duty; Help; Minister [verb]; Ministry; Obedience; Relief; Servant; Work [noun]; Worship)

2 Ne. 1: 7 if people s. the Lord according to his commandments, land shall have liberty; **Mosiah** 2: 12 as I have been suffered to spend my days in your s., I have not sought riches of you; 2: 17 when ye are in s. of fellow beings, ye are in s. of God; 2: 18 if king labors to s. you, ought not ye to labor to s. one another; 2: 21 if ye s. Creator with whole souls, yet are ye unprofitable servants; 4: 14 ye will not suffer children to s. devil; 5: 13 how knoweth a man the master whom he has not s.; 7: 33 if ye s. God with full diligence of mind, he will deliver you from bondage; **3 Ne.** 13: 24 (Matt. 6: 24) no man can s. two masters; **Morm.** 9: 28 ask that ye will s. the true and living God; **Ether** 2: 8 those who possess land of promise must s. God or be swept off; **Moro.** 7: 13 every thing which invites to s. God is inspired of God.

SET (see Defiance; Heart; Naught; Order)

SETH[1]—son of Adam (see BD Seth)
No references in Book of Mormon.

SETH[2]—Jaredite
Ether 1: 10–11 (11: 10) son of Shiblon, father of Ahah; 11: 9 brought into captivity all his days.

SEVEN, SEVENTH (see also Sabbath)
2 Ne. 14: 1 (Isa. 4: 1) s. women will take hold of one man; **Mosiah** 13: 18 the s. day, the sabbath, thou shalt not do any work.

SHADOW (see also Jesus Christ, Types of; Type)
1 Ne. 21: 2 (2 Ne. 8: 16; Isa. 49: 2; 51: 16) in s. of his hand he hath hid me; **2 Ne.** 14: 6 (Isa. 4: 6) tabernacle shall be for s. in daytime from heat; **Mosiah** 3: 15 the Lord shows many types and s. to his people; 13: 10 what Noah[3] will do with Abinadi shall be type and s. of things to come; 16: 1 law of Moses is s. of things to come; **Alma** 7: 20 God has no s. of turning from right to left; 37: 43 workings of Liahona are not without a s.; **Morm.** 9: 10 no s. of changing in God.

SHAFT
1 Ne. 21: 2 (Isa. 49: 2) the Lord has made me a polished s.; **Hel.** 5: 12 devil will send s. in whirlwind.

SHAKE, SHOOK, SHAKEN (see also Earthquake; Fear; Fear of God; Quake; Tremble)
1 Ne. 2: 14 Lehi[1] speaks to Laman[1] and Lemuel until their frames s.; 17: 45 (Mosiah 27: 15; Hel. 12: 11) God's voice causes earth to s.; **2 Ne.** 1: 13, 23 s. off awful chains that bind you; 4: 31 wilt thou make me s. at appearance of sin; 9: 40 the righteous love the truth and are not s. by it; 9: 44 Jacob[2] s. brethren's iniquities from his soul; 12: 19 (Isa. 2: 19) he ariseth to s. terribly the earth; 23: 13 (Isa. 13: 13) the Lord will s. the heavens; 24: 16 (Isa. 14: 16) is this the man that did s. kingdoms; 28: 19 kingdom of devil must s.; **Jacob** 7: 5 Sherem hopes to s. Jacob[2] from faith, but he cannot be s.; **Mosiah** 27: 18 (Alma 38: 7) voice of angel s. earth; **Alma** 14: 27 earth s., prison walls rent in twain; 29: 1 O that I might speak with a voice to s. the earth; 48: 17 if all men were like Moroni[1], power of hell would have been s.; **Hel.** 5: 27, 42 the Lord causes earth and prison walls to s.; **3 Ne.** 8: 6 thunder causes whole earth to s. at Christ's death; 20: 37 s. thyself from the dust, O Jerusalem;

Morm. 8: 24 in the Lord's name saints could cause earth to s.; **Ether** 4: 9 at the Lord's word, earth shall s.

SHAME (*see also* Ashamed; Guilt; Humble; Reproach)

2 Ne. 7: 6 (Isa. 50: 6) I hid not my face from s. and spitting; 9: 18 saints who have endured crosses of world and despised s. of it shall inherit kingdom; **Jacob** 1: 8 all men should suffer Christ's cross and bear s. of world; 2: 6 to testify of Nephites' wickedness causes Jacob[2] to shrink with s. before presence of Maker; 6: 9 power of resurrection will bring men to stand with s. before God; **Alma** 12: 15 men will acknowledge to their s. that God's judgments are just; **3 Ne.** 22: 4 be not confounded, for thou shalt not be put to s., shalt forget s. of youth.

SHARED—*Jaredite military leader*

Ether 13: 23–24, 27–29 gives battle to Coriantumr[2] and sons; 13: 30 is slain.

SHARED, BROTHER OF (*see* Gilead)

SHARP, SHARPNESS (*see also* Cut)

1 Ne. 21: 2 (Isa. 49: 2) he hath made my mouth like a s. sword; **2 Ne.** 1: 26 s. of words of Nephi[1] is s. of power of word of God; **3 Ne.** 8: 7 exceeding s. lightnings at Christ's death; **Moro.** 9: 4 when Mormon[2] speaks word of God with s., Nephites tremble.

SHAVE, SHAVEN (*see also* Shorn)

2 Ne. 17: 20 (Isa. 7: 20) the Lord shall s. with razor that is hired; **Enos** 1: 20 (Mosiah 10: 8) Lamanites wander about with heads s.

SHAZER—*campsite in Arabian desert*

1 Ne. 16: 13–14 Lehites camp at S.

SHEAR (*see* Shorn)

SHEARERS

Mosiah 14: 7 (15: 6; Isa. 53: 7) as sheep before s. is dumb, so Son opened not his mouth.

SHEAVES

Alma 26: 5 all the day long did ye labor, and behold the number of your s.; **3 Ne.** 20: 18 the Lord will gather his people as man gathers s. into floor.

SHED (*see also* Blood, Shedding of)

1 Ne. 11: 22 tree represents love of God, which s. itself abroad in hearts; **Mosiah** 25: 9 when Nephites think of brethren slain by Lamanites, they s. many tears of sorrow.

SHEEP (*see also* Animal; Flock; Fold; Jesus Christ—Good Shepherd; Lamb; Saint; Shepherd; BD Sheep)

1 Ne. 22: 25 the Lord numbers, feeds his s.; **Mosiah** 14: 6 (Isa. 53: 6) all we, like s., have gone astray; 14: 7 (15: 6; Isa. 53: 7) as s. before shearers is dumb, so he opened not his mouth; 26: 20 Alma[1] is called to gather the Lord's s.; 26: 21 (Alma 5: 60) he who hears the Lord's voice is his s.; **Alma** 5: 37 the wicked have gone astray, as s. having no shepherd; 5: 38–39 those who do not hearken to voice of good shepherd are not his s.; 25: 12 priests of Noah[3] to be scattered and slain as s. without shepherd; **Hel.** 15: 13 Lamanites to come to knowledge of true shepherd and be numbered among his s.; **3 Ne.** 14: 15 (Matt. 7: 15) beware of false prophets who come in s's clothing; 15: 17 (John 10: 16) other s. I have which are not of this fold; 15: 21 Nephites are the other s.; 15: 24 Nephites are numbered among the Lord's s.; 16: 1–3 the Lord has yet other s. not of this fold; 18: 31 the Lord knows his s.; 20: 16 (21: 12; Micah 5: 8) Israel shall be among Gentiles as lion among flocks of s.; **Ether** 9: 18 Jaredites have s.

SHELEM, MOUNT—*mountain in Old World named by Jaredites*

Ether 3: 1 brother of Jared[2] obtains stones in S.

SHEM[1]—*son of Noah[1]*

No references in Book of Mormon.

SHEM[2]—*Nephite commander* [c. A.D. 385]

Morm. 6: 14 has fallen with his ten thousand.

SHEM, CITY OF AND LAND OF—*Nephite land north of Antum and Jashon*

Morm. 2: 20 Nephites driven northward to land of S.; 2: 21 Nephites gather to S. and fortify it.

SHEMLON, LAND OF—*region bordering on land of Lehi-Nephi*

Mosiah 10: 7 Zeniff sends spies round about S.; 11: 12 is possessed by Lamanites; 19: 6 Lamanites come from S. to attack people of Noah[3]; 20: 1–5 Lamanites' daughters gather in S., are carried captive by priests of Noah[3]; 24: 1 Amulon and brethren are appointed teachers in S.; **Alma** 23: 8, 12 Lamanites in S. are converted to the Lord.

SHEMNON—*one of twelve Nephite disciples* [c. A.D. 34]

3 Ne. 19: 4 is called by Jesus to minister to Nephites.

SHEPHERD (see also Jesus Christ—Good Shepherd; Pastor; Sheep)

1 Ne. 13: 41 one S. over all earth; 22: 25 (3 Ne. 15: 17; 16: 3; John 10: 16) there shall be one fold and one s.; **Mosiah** 8: 21 men are as wild flock that fleeth from s.; **Alma** 5: 37 the wicked have gone astray, as sheep having no s.; 5: 39 if men are not sheep of good s., devil is their s.; 25: 12 priests of Noah[3] to be scattered and slain as sheep without s.; 15: 13 Lamanites to be brought to knowledge of true s.; **Morm.** 5: 17 Nephites once had Christ for their s.

SHEREM—antichrist [c. fifth century B.C.]

Jacob 7: 1–2 denies Christ; 7: 7 challenges Jacob[2]; 7: 13 demands a sign; 7: 15–20 is stricken and dies.

SHERRIZAH

Moro. 9: 7 Lamanites take prisoners from tower of S.; 9: 16–17 many women survivors in S.

SHEUM—unidentified crop cultivated by Nephites

Mosiah 9: 9 people of Zeniff till ground with seed of s.

SHEZ[1]—middle Jaredite king

Ether 1: 24–25 son of Heth, father of Riplakish; 10: 1–2 attempts to build up broken nation; 10: 4 builds cities, lives to old age.

SHEZ[2]—son of Shez[1]

Ether 10: 3 rebels against father, but is slain by robber.

SHIBLOM[1] [or Shiblon]—late Jaredite king

Ether 1: 11–12 son of Com[2], father of Seth[2]; 11: 4 is anointed king; 11: 5–7 great wickedness and destruction in days of S.; 11: 9 is slain.

SHIBLOM[2]—Nephite commander [c. A.D. 385]

Morm. 6: 14 falls with his ten thousand.

SHIBLON—son of Alma[2] [c. 74 B.C.] (see also Shiblom[1])

Alma 31: 7 (38: 1) second son of Alma[2], goes on mission to Zoramites; ch. 38 commandments of Alma[2] to S.; 49: 30 is successful in ministry; 63: 1 takes charge of sacred things; 63: 10–11 confers sacred things on Helaman[3], dies.

SHIBLON—Nephite coin (see also Coin)

Alma 11: 15 s. is half a senum, a s. for half a measure of barley; 11: 16 a shiblum is half a s.; 11: 19 antion of gold equals three s.

SHIBLUM—Nephite coin (see also Coin)

Alma 11: 16 s. is half a shiblon; 11: 17 leah is half a s.

SHILOAH, WATERS OF—pool near Jerusalem[1]

2 Ne. 18: 6 (Isa. 8: 6) people refuse waters of S.

SHILOM, CITY OF AND LAND OF—small region next to land of Lehi-Nephi

Mosiah 7: 7 Ammon[1] meets Lamanite king in S.; 7: 21 city of S. is given to Zeniff by Lamanite king; 9: 6 S. is possessed by Zeniff; 9: 8 walls of city of S. are repaired; 9: 14 Lamanites steal flocks in S.; 10: 8 Lamanites come upon S.; 10: 19–20 Lamanite army attacks, is repulsed; 11: 12–13 tower and buildings are built in S.; 22: 8–11 Limhi's people travel around S. during escape; 24: 1 Amulon and brethren are made teachers over people in S.; **Alma** 23: 8, 12 Lamanites in S. are converted.

SHIM, HILL—in land Antum

Morm. 1: 3 Ammaron deposited records in hill called S.; 4: 23 Mormon[2] takes records from hill S.; **Ether** 9: 3 Omer and family travel near hill of S. and place where Nephites were destroyed.

SHIMNILOM—city in land of Nephi

Alma 23: 8, 12 Lamanites in S. are converted to the Lord.

SHINE, SHINING, SHONE (see also Enlighten; Illuminate; Light)

2 Ne. 14: 5 (Isa. 4: 5) the Lord will create upon every dwelling-place of mount Zion the s. of flaming fire by night; 19: 2 (Isa. 9: 2) light has s. upon them that dwell in land of shadow of death; 23: 10 (Isa. 13: 10) moon shall not cause her light to s.; **Mosiah** 13: 5 Abinadi's face s. with exceeding luster; **Alma** 5: 50 glory of King shall soon s. forth among men; 37: 23 the Lord will prepare stone which will s. forth in darkness unto light; 40: 25 the righteous shall s. forth in kingdom of God; **Hel.** 5: 36 faces of Nephi[2] and Lehi[4] s. as faces of angels; **3 Ne.** 12: 16 (Matt. 5: 16) let your light so s. before this people; 18: 24 hold up your light that it may s. unto the world; 19: 25 light of Jesus' countenance s. upon disciples; **Morm.** 8: 16 record shall s. forth out of darkness; **Ether** 3: 1, 4 (6: 3) brother of Jared asks the Lord to make stones s.

SHIP (*see also* Barge; Sail; Vessel)

1 Ne. 17: 8, 49–51 Nephi[1] is commanded to build s.; 17: 17 elder brothers murmur at building of s.; 18: 1–3 the Lord shows Nephi[1] how to build s.; 18: 4 Nephi[1] finishes building s.; 18: 6–8 Lehites enter s. and sail to promised land; **Alma** 63: 5 Hagoth builds large s. for voyages northward; 63: 7 other s. are built; 63: 8 s. are never heard of again; **Hel.** 3: 10 much timber sent to land northward by s.; 3: 14 record does not include full account of shipping and building of s.

SHIZ—*Jaredite military leader*

Ether 14: 17 brother of Lib, pursues Coriantumr[2]; 14: 18 fear of S. goes throughout land; 14: 19–20 people are divided between Coriantumr[2] and S.; 14: 24 swears to avenge himself upon Coriantumr[2] of brother's blood; 14: 26–31 (15: 6–28) S's army battles with army of Coriantumr[2]; 15: 5 exchanges letters with Coriantumr[2]; 15: 29–31 is slain by Coriantumr[2].

SHOE (*see* Latchet)

SHORN (*see also* Shave)

Alma 3: 4–5 heads of Lamanites are s.; **3 Ne.** 4: 7 heads of robbers are s.

SHORTEN

2 Ne. 7: 2 (Isa. 50: 2) is the Lord's hand s., that he cannot redeem.

SHOULDER

1 Ne. 21: 22 (22: 6; 2 Ne. 6: 6; Isa. 49: 22) Israel's daughters shall be carried upon Gentiles' s.; **2 Ne.** 19: 6 (Isa. 9: 6) government shall be upon Messiah's s.; **Mosiah** 24: 14 the Lord will ease burdens put upon s. of people of Alma[1].

SHOUT (*see also* Praise; Rejoice)

2 Ne. 31: 13 those who receive Holy Ghost shall s. praises to Holy One.

SHOW, SHOWN (*see also* Appeal; God, Manifestations of; Jesus Christ, Appearances of; Manifest; Revelation; Sign; Unfold)

2 Ne. 32: 5 the Lord will s. all who receive Holy Ghost what they should do; 33: 11 Christ will s. that these words are his words; **Jacob** 4: 7 the Lord s. unto men their weakness; **Hel.** 7: 23 the Lord will not s. unto the wicked of his strength; **3 Ne.** 19: 35 the Lord will not s. unto Jews so great miracles because of unbelief; 28: 30 three Nephites can s. themselves to whomever it seemeth them good; **Morm.** 8: 35 Christ has s. Moroni[2] great and marvelous things to come to pass; **Ether** 3: 25 the Lord s. brother of Jared[2]

all inhabitants of earth; 4: 8 unto those who deny these things, the Lord will s. no greater things; 12: 7 Christ s. himself not to the world.

SHRINK (*see also* Withdraw)

2 Ne. 9: 46 prepare yourselves for judgment, that ye may not s. with fear; **Jacob** 2: 6 to testify of wickedness causes Jacob[2] to s. from presence of maker; **Mosiah** 2: 38 (3: 25) sense of guilt causes unrepentant to s. from presence of the Lord; 27: 31 men will s. beneath glance of God's all-piercing eye; **Alma** 43: 48 men of Moroni[1] are about to s. from Lamanites.

SHULE—*early Jaredite king*

Ether 1: 30–31 (7: 7; 8: 1) son of Kib, father of Omer; 7: 7 is born in captivity; 7: 8–9 restores kingdom to father; 7: 11, 26–27 rules righteously; 7: 12 begets many children; 7: 13 gives Corihor power in kingdom; 7: 15–16 Noah[2] rebels against S.; 7: 15–17 Noah[2] takes S. captive; 7: 18–22 sons help S. regain kingdom; 7: 23–25 S. protects the prophets.

SHUM—*Nephite coin* (*see also* Coin)

Alma 11: 5, 9 s. of gold is twice the value of a seon.

SHURR, VALLEY OF

Ether 14: 28 Coriantumr[2] and army pitch tents in S.

SHUT

2 Ne. 4: 32 may gates of hell be s. continually before me; 4: 32 wilt thou not s. gates of righteousness before me; 9: 9 except for resurrection, our spirits must have been s. out of God's presence; 16: 10 (Isa. 6: 10) s. their eyes lest they see and be converted; **3 Ne.** 13: 6 (Matt. 6: 6) when thou has s. thy door, pray to Father who is in secret; **Ether** 4: 9 at the Lord's command, heavens are opened and are s.

SICK, SICKNESS (*see also* Disease; Fever; Heal; Infirmity; Needy)

1 Ne. 11: 31 (Mosiah 3: 5) multitudes of people who are s. are healed by Lamb; **Jacob** 2: 19 seek riches to administer relief to the s.; **Alma** 1: 30 Nephites do not send away any who are s.; 7: 11 Son will take upon himself the s. of his people; 9: 22 Nephites have been saved from s. by the Lord; 15: 3 Zeezrom lies s. at Sidom; **3 Ne.** 7: 22 those healed of s. have been wrought upon by Spirit; 17: 7–9 (26: 15) Jesus heals the s. among the Nephites; **4 Ne.** 1: 5 Jesus' disciples heal the s.; **Morm.** 8: 37 ye love your money more than ye love the s.; 8: 39 why do ye

suffer the s. to pass by you without notice; 9: 24 believers shall lay hands upon the s., and they shall recover; **Moro.** 8: 8 the whole need no physician, but they who are s.

SICKLE (*see also* Reap)

Alma 26: 5 missionaries thrust in their s. and reaped.

SIDE

3 **Ne.** 11: 14–15 multitude thrust hands into Jesus' s.

SIDOM, LAND OF

Alma 15: 1 Alma² and Amulek find converts from Ammonihah in S.; 15: 3 Zeezrom lies sick in S.; 15: 10–11 Zeezrom is healed; 15: 13 Alma² establishes church in S.; 15: 14–17 people repent and are baptized.

SIDON, RIVER—*most prominent river in Nephite territory, runs north to sea* (*see also* River)

Alma 2: 15 hill Amnihu is on east of S.; 2: 34 Lamanites camp on west of S.; 4: 4 many are baptized in waters of S.; 22: 29 wilderness at S.

SIEGE

2 **Ne.** 26: 15 the Lord will lay s. with a mount against seed of Nephites and Lamanites; 3 **Ne.** 4: 16 robbers lay s. around Nephites; **Ether** 14: 5 Coriantumr² lays s. to wilderness.

SIFT

Alma 37: 15 transgressors will be delivered to Satan, that he may s. them as chaff before wind; 3 **Ne.** 18: 18 Satan desires to have you, that he may s. you as wheat.

SIGHT (*see also* Eye; See)

2 **Ne.** 15: 21 (Isa. 5: 21) wo unto the prudent in their own s.; 21: 3 (Isa. 11: 3) rod out of stem of Jesse shall not judge after s. of his eyes; **Mosiah** 3: 5 the Lord will cause the blind to receive their s.; 3 **Ne.** 7: 20 Nephi³ does many miracles in s. of people; 4 **Ne.** 1: 5 Jesus' disciples cause the blind to receive s.; **Ether** 3: 25 (12: 20–21) the Lord withholds nothing from s. of brother of Jared².

SIGN (*see also* Faith; Jesus Christ, Second Coming of; Miracle; Prophecy; Token; Wonder; TG Sign Seekers; Signs)

1 **Ne.** 11: 7 Nephi¹ given s. of man descending out of heaven as s.; 19: 10 three days of darkness to be s. of Christ's death; 2 **Ne.** 17: 14 (Isa. 7: 14) the Lord will give s., virgin shall conceive and bear son; 18: 18 (Isa. 8: 18) I and the children the Lord hath given me are for

s. in Israel; 26: 3 s. to be given of Christ's birth, death, resurrection: **Jacob** 7: 13 Sherem asks Jacob² to show him a s.; 7: 14 if God shall smite thee, let that be a s.; **Mosiah** 3: 15 the Lord shows his people many s. and types of his coming; **Alma** 30: 43–50 Korihor asks for a s., is struck dumb; 30: 44 will ye say, Show me a s., when ye have testimonies of prophets; 32: 17 many will ask for s. before they will believe; 37: 27 s. and wonders of secret combinations to be kept from people; **Hel.** 2: 7 servant of Helaman³ gives Kishkumen a s.; 6: 22 secret combinations have secret s. and words; 14: 3 Samuel the Lamanite prophesies s. of Christ's birth, night without darkness; 14: 14, 20–25 Samuel the Lamanite prophesies s. of Christ's death; 3 **Ne.** 1: 13, 16 on this night will s. be given, and on the morrow come I into world; 1: 22 Satan hardens hearts, they believe not s. they have seen; 2: 1 people begin to forget s. and wonders they have seen; 8: 3 people begin to look for s. of Christ's death; 21: 1 gathering of Israel a s. that prophecies are about to be fulfilled; **Morm.** 9: 24–25 (Ether 4: 18; Mark 16: 17) these s. shall follow them that believe.

SILENCE, SILENT

2 **Ne.** 1: 14 Lehi¹ to lie down in cold and s. grave; **Alma** 51: 7 people of liberty put king-men to s.; 55: 17 preparations for war done in profound s.; 3 **Ne.** 10: 1–2 s. in the land for many hours.

SILK (*see also* Cloth)

1 **Ne.** 13: 7 Nephi¹ sees s. in abominable church; **Alma** 1: 29 (4: 6) people have abundance of s.; **Ether** 9: 17 (10: 24) Jaredites have all manner of s.

SILLY (*see also* Foolish)

Alma 30: 31 Korihor accuses priests of leading people after s. traditions.

SILVER (*see also* Metal; Ore)

1 **Ne.** 2: 4 Lehi¹ leaves s. and precious things behind; 13: 7 gold and s. in abominable church; 18: 25 gold and s. found in promised land; 2 **Ne.** 5: 15 Nephi¹ teaches people to work in s.; **Jarom** 1: 8 (Alma 1: 29; 4: 6; Hel. 6: 9) Nephites become rich in gold and s.; **Ether** 9: 17 Jaredites have all manner of s. and precious things.

SIMILITUDE (*see also* Jesus Christ, Types of; Likeness; Shadow; Type)

Jacob 4: 5 Abraham's offering Isaac is s. of God and his Son.

SIMPLE, SIMPLENESS (*see also* Ease; Easiness; Light [adj.]; Plain)

1 **Ne.** 17: 41 Israelites would not be

healed because of s. of the way; **2 Ne.** 3: 20 descendants of Lehi[1] will cry from dust in s.; **Alma** 37: 6 by s. things are great things brought to pass.

SIN, SINFUL (*see also* Abomination; Apostasy; Captive, Captivity; Confession of Sins; Darkness, Spiritual; Death, Spiritual; Devil; Disobedience; Err; Evil; Fall of Man; Forgive; Guilt; Iniquity; Jesus Christ, Atonement through; Jesus Christ—Savior; Justice; Offense; Pollute; Punishment; Remission; Repentance; Sinner; Transgression; Trespass; Wicked; TG Sin)

2 Ne. 2: 13 if no s., then no righteousness; 2: 23 Adam could have done no good, for he knew no s.; 4: 19 heart of Nephi[1] groans because of his s.; 4: 31 wilt thou make me shake at appearance of s.; 9: 38 those who die in s. will remain in s.; 9: 45 turn away from s.; 9: 48 Jacob[2] teaches consequences of s.; 28: 8 false churches claim God will justify in committing little s.; 33: 5 sacred record speaks harshly against s.; **Jacob** 1: 19 teachers answer s. of people upon own heads if they do not teach diligently; 2: 5 Nephites begin to labor in s. which is abominable to God; 7: 19 Sherem fears he has committed unpardonable s.; **Mosiah** 2: 33 he who remains and dies in s. receives wages of everlasting punishment; 4: 14 devil is master of s.; 4: 29 I cannot tell you all the things whereby you may commit s.; 25: 11 s. and polluted state of Lamanites; **Alma** 11: 37 God cannot save men in their s.; 13: 12 those sanctified by Holy Ghost cannot look upon s. without abhorrence; 26: 17 God has snatched us from s., polluted state; 36: 17–19 Alma[2] harrowed up by memory of s.; 39: 6 to deny Holy Ghost is unpardonable s.; 41: 9–10 do not suppose ye will be restored from s. to happiness; 42: 17 how could man s. without law; 42: 20 if no law was given against s., men would not be afraid to s.; 42: 21 if no law, what could justice or mercy do for men who s.; 42: 29 only let your s. trouble you; 45: 12 fourth generation after Christ's visit will s. against great light; 45: 16 the Lord cannot look upon s. with least degree of allowance; **Hel.** 6: 30 devil is author of all s.; 7: 24 Nephites have s. against greater knowledge than Lamanites; **3 Ne.** 6: 18 wicked Nephites do not s. ignorantly; 16: 10 when Gentiles s. against gospel, Father will take it from them; 28: 38 three Nephites are changed, that they suffer no sorrow, save for s. of world; **Morm.** 8: 32 false churches will forgive s. for money; **Ether** 2: 15 I forgive thee and thy brethren their s., but thou shalt not s. any more; 2: 15 if men s.

until fully ripe, they are cut off from the Lord's presence; **Moro.** 7: 12 devil inviteth and enticeth to s.; 8: 8, 10 little children not capable of committing s.

SINAI, MOUNT (*see also* Mount, Mountain)

Mosiah 12: 33 keep commandments the Lord gave me on S.; 13: 5 Abinadi's face shines as did Moses' on S.

SINCERITY, SINCERE (*see also* Deceit; Honest; Hypocrisy; Intent)

Mosiah 4: 10 ask in s. of heart that God will forgive you; 26: 29 he who repents in s. of heart shall be forgiven; 29: 19 except for interposition of Creator and their s. repentance, people of Noah[3] must remain in bondage; **Alma** 26: 31 s. of converts is witnessed in love toward brethren; 33: 11 thou didst hear me because of my s.; **Hel.** 3: 27 the Lord is merciful to all who call upon him in s.; **Moro.** 10: 4 if ye ask with s. heart, God will manifest truth.

SING, SINGING (*see also* Praise; Rejoice)

1 Ne. 1: 8 (Alma 36: 22) God's throne surrounded by angels s. and praising God; 18: 9 the rebellious begin to dance and s.; 21: 13 (Isa. 49: 13) s., O heavens, break forth into s., O mountains; **2 Ne.** 8: 11 (Isa. 51: 11) the redeemed shall come with s. unto Zion; 15: 1 (Isa. 5: 1) then will I s. to my well-beloved a song touching his vineyard; 24: 7 (Isa. 14: 7) they break forth into s.; **Mosiah** 2: 28 Benjamin's spirit to join choirs above in s. praises of God; 12: 22 (3 Ne. 16: 18) with voice together shall watchmen s.; 20: 1 Lamanites' daughters gather in Shemlon to s. and dance; **Alma** 5: 26 if ye have felt to s. song of redeeming love, can ye feel so now; 26: 8 let us s. God's praise; 26: 13 converts are brought to s. redeeming love; **3 Ne.** 4: 31 people break forth, all as one, in s. and praising God; 22: 1 (Isa. 54: 1) s., O barren, and break forth into s.; **Morm.** 7: 7 the guiltless shall s. ceaseless praises with choirs above; **Ether** 6: 9 Jaredites s. praises unto the Lord; **Moro.** 6: 9 saints preach, pray, s. in meetings as led by Holy Ghost.

SINGLE, SINGLENESS (*see also* Diligence)

3 Ne. 13: 22 (Matt. 6: 22) if thine eye be s., thy whole body shall be full of light; **Morm.** 8: 15 record to be brought forth with eye s. to glory of God.

SINIM, LAND OF—*possibly land of China* (*see also* BD Sinim)

1 Ne. 21: 12 (Isa. 49: 12) Israel to gather from land of S.

SINK (see Sunk)

SINNER (see also Sin)

Mosiah 28: 4 sons of Mosiah[2] had been vilest of s.; **Alma** 34: 40 do not revile against those who cast you out, lest you become s. like them; 41: 15 the word restoration more fully condemns the s.; 42: 1 God's justice in condemning s. to punishment; **Hel.** 13: 26 Nephites call prophets s. because they testify of evil; **Moro.** 8: 8 Christ calls not the righteous, but s. to repentance.

SIRON, LAND OF—*land by borders of Lamanites*

Alma 39: 3 Corianton goes into land of S. after harlot.

SISTERS (see also Family)

2 Ne. 5: 6 s. of Nephi[1] go with him.

SITUATION (see also Crisis)

Mosiah 2: 40 awake to remembrance of awful s. of transgressors; **Ether** 8: 24 when secret combinations come among Gentiles, they should awake to sense of awful s.

SKILL, SKILLFUL (see also Art; Expert)

Enos 1: 20 Lamanites' s. was in bow; **Alma** 10: 15 lawyers are learned in cunning, that they might be s. in profession; 51: 31 every man of Teancum exceeds Lamanites in s. of war.

SKIN

1 Ne. 17: 11 Nephi[1] makes bellows of s. of beasts; **2 Ne.** 5: 21 (Alma 3: 6) the Lord causes s. of blackness to come upon Lamanites; **Jacob** 3: 8 Lamanites' s. will be whiter than Nephites' unless they repent; 3: 9 revile no more against Lamanites because of s.; **Enos** 1: 20 (Alma 3: 5; 43: 20; 3 Ne. 4: 7) Lamanites wear short s. girdle about loins; **Mosiah** 17: 13 priests scourge Abinadi's s. with faggots; **Alma** 20: 29 missionaries' s. is worn because of strong cords; 44: 18 Lamanites' naked s. exposed to Nephites' swords; 49: 6 Lamanites prepare thick garments of s.; **3 Ne.** 2: 15 Lamanites' s. becomes white.

SLACKEN (see also Shorten; Weak)

2 Ne. 4: 26 why should my strength s. because of my afflictions; **Jacob** 5: 47 has the Lord of vineyard s. his hand.

SLAIN (see Slay, Slew, Slain)

SLAUGHTER (see also Battle; Carnage; Kill; Slay; War)

1 Ne. 12: 2 Nephi[1] beholds great s. among his people; **Mosiah** 14: 7 (Isa. 53: 7) he is brought as lamb to s.; **Alma** 2: 18 Nephites slay Amlicites with great s.; 28: 2–3 great s. among both Lamanites and Nephites; 49: 21 (62: 38) Lamanites slain with great s.; **Hel.** 1: 27 Lamanites slay Nephites in center of land with great s.; **3 Ne.** 4: 11 great and terrible s. in battle between Nephites and robbers; **Morm.** 4: 21 Nephites driven and s.

SLAVERY, SLAVES (see also Bondage; Freedom)

Mosiah 2: 13 Benjamin has not suffered people to make s. of one another; 7: 15 Limhi's people willing to be s. of Nephites; **Alma** 27: 8 people of Anti-Nephi-Lehi willing to be Nephites' s. until they repair murders; 27: 9 against Nephites' law to have s.; 48: 11 Moroni[1] finds joy in brethren's freedom from s.; **3 Ne.** 3: 7 Giddianhi entices Nephites to become robbers' brethren, not s.

SLAY, SLEW, SLAIN (see also Death, Physical; Destruction; Jesus Christ, Death of; Jesus Christ—Lamb of God; Kill; Murder; Slaughter; Smite)

1 Ne. 1: 20 Jews had s. prophets of old; 4: 12 Spirit tells Nephi[1] to s. Laban; 4: 13 the Lord s. the wicked to bring forth righteous purposes; 13: 5 abominable church s. saints; **2 Ne.** 20: 4 (Isa. 10: 4) they shall fall under the s.; 21: 4 (30: 9) with breath of his lips shall the Lord s. the wicked; **Mosiah** 7: 26 Limhi's people have s. prophet Abinadi; **Alma** 18: 3 Lamoni's servants believe Ammon[2] cannot be s.; 19: 22–3 man who lifts sword to s. Ammon[2] falls dead; 44: 1 Nephites do not desire to s. Lamanites; 60: 13 the Lord suffers the righteous to be s. that justice might come upon the wicked; **Hel.** 1: 20 army of Coriantumr[3] s. all who oppose them; 4: 2 the rebellious are s. and driven from land; 8: 21 will ye say sons of Zedekiah were not s.; 13: 25 Nephites claim they would not have s. prophets of old; **3 Ne.** 10: 15 many have been s. for testifying of Christ's coming; 16: 9 the Lord will cause house of Israel to be s. and cast out; **Ether** 9: 27 Heth[1] s. father with sword.

SLEEP (see also Captive, Captivity; Death, Physical; Death, Spiritual; Dormant; Idleness; Slumber)

2 Ne. 1: 13 O that ye would awake from s. of hell; 27: 5 (Isa. 29: 10) the Lord pours out deep s. upon those that do iniquity; **Mosiah** 24: 19 the Lord causes deep s. to come upon Lamanites; **Alma** 5: 7 the Lord awakened fathers out of deep s.; 19: 8 Lamoni is not dead, but s. in God; 37: 37 lie down unto the Lord, that he may watch over you in your s.; 55: 15 Lamanite guards are drunken

and in deep s.; **Morm.** 9: 13 resurrection brings to pass redemption from endless s.

SLING (*see also* Weapon)

1 Ne. 16: 23 Nephi[1] arms himself with s.; **Mosiah** 9: 16 Zeniff arms people with s.; 10: 8 (Alma 3: 5; 43: 20) Lamanites armed with s.; **Alma** 2: 12 (49: 20) Nephites armed with s.; 17: 7 sons of Mosiah[2] take s. to provide food; 17: 36–38 Ammon[2] casts stones at Lamanites with s.

SLIPPERY (*see also* Accursed)

Hel. 13: 31, 33, 36 (Morm. 1: 18) the Lord will curse riches, that they become s.

SLOTHFUL, SLOTHFULNESS (*see also* Diligence; Idleness; Industry; Laziness; Neglect; Procrastinate)

Alma 33: 21 would ye be s. and not cast eyes upon the type; 37: 41 Lehites were s. and forgot to exercise faith; 60: 14 judgments of God to come upon this people because of s.

SLOW (*see also* Quick, Quickly)

1 Ne. 17: 45 (Mosiah 9: 3; 13: 29; Hel. 12: 5) ye are s. to remember the Lord; **Mosiah** 11: 24 (21: 15) the Lord will be s. to hear cries of unrepentant; **Alma** 55: 31 (62: 49) Nephites are not s. to remember the Lord; **Hel.** 7: 7 people of Nephi[1] were s. to be led to do iniquity; 12: 4 how s. are men to do good; 12: 5 how s. are men to walk in wisdom's paths.

SLUMBER (*see also* Sleep)

2 Ne. 27: 6, 9 the Lord shall bring forth words of them which have s.; **Jacob** 3: 11 awake from s. of death.

SMALL, SMALLEST (*see also* Light [adj.]; Little; Plates of Nephi, Small; Voice)

1 Ne. 14: 12 dominions of saints are s. because of wickedness of abominable church; 16: 29 by s. means the Lord can bring about great things; **2 Ne.** 17: 13 (Isa. 7: 13) s. thing to weary men, but will ye weary God; **Alma** 10: 4 Amulek a man of no s. reputation; 26: 16 Ammon[2] cannot say s. part which he feels; 37: 7 by s. means the Lord brings about salvation of many; 37: 41 because miracles were worked by s. means, Lehites forgot to exercise faith.

SMILE

Jacob 2: 13 hand of providence has s. upon Nephites; **3 Ne.** 19: 25, 30 Jesus' countenance s. upon disciples.

SMITE, SMOTE, SMITTEN (*see also* Beat; Destruction; Kill; Persecution; Slay; Strike)

1 Ne. 17: 29 Moses s. rock, and water came forth; 21: 13 Israel shall be s. no more; **2 Ne.** 7: 8 I will s. mine adversary with strength of my mouth; 9: 33 knowledge of iniquities shall s. the uncircumcised; 12: 10 fear of the Lord shall s. the wicked; 21: 4 (30: 9; Isa. 11: 4) the Lord shall s. earth with rod of his mouth; 26: 15 seed of Nephites and Lamanites to be s. by Gentiles; **Mosiah** 1: 17 as Lehites were unfaithful, they were s. with afflictions; 12: 2 because of iniquities, this generation will be s. on cheek; 12: 31 priests of Noah[3] shall be s. for iniquities; 14: 4 (Isa. 53: 4) we did esteem him s. of God; 21: 3 Lamanites s. Limhi's people on cheeks; **Alma** 14: 14 (26: 29) chief judge s. Alma[2] and Amulek; **Hel.** 4: 12 Nephites s. the poor upon cheek; 10: 6 Nephi[2] given power to s. earth with famine; **3 Ne.** 12: 39 (Matt. 5: 39) whosoever s. thee on right cheek, turn the other; 28: 20 disciples cast into pits s. earth with word of God and are delivered; **4 Ne.** 1: 34 people s. upon people of Jesus, who do not s. again; **Morm.** 8: 19 he who s. shall be s. of the Lord; 8: 20 scripture says, Man shall not s.

SMITH, JOSEPH, JR. (*see also* Book of Mormon; Joseph[1])

2 Ne. 3: 7–19 prophecy of Joseph[1] concerning latter-day seer; 3: 15 his name shall be called after Joseph[1] and after name of his father.

SMOKE (*see also* Cloud; Mist; Vapor)

1 Ne. 19: 11 the Lord will visit some of house of Israel by s.; 22: 18 vapor of s. must come upon earth; **2 Ne.** 8: 6 (Isa. 51: 6) heavens shall vanish away like s.; 14: 5 (Isa. 4: 5) the Lord will create upon Zion's assemblies a cloud and s.; 24: 31 (Isa. 14: 31) there shall come from the north a s.; **Jacob** 6: 10 (Mosiah 3: 27) s. ascends forever from lake of fire and brimstone; **3 Ne.** 10: 13 righteous are not overpowered by vapor of s.; 10: 14 deaths and destructions by s. fulfill prophecies; **Morm.** 8: 29 there shall be heard of vapors of s. in foreign lands.

SMOOTH

1 Ne. 17: 46 (3 Ne. 8: 13) rough places to be made s., s. place to be broken up; **Hel.** 10: 9 (12: 10) Nephi[2] given power to make mountain s.

SNARE (*see also* Ensnare; Guile; Pit; Trap)

2 Ne. 27: 31–32 they who lay a s. for him who reproves shall be cut off;

Mosiah 23: 9 Alma² was caught in s.; **Alma** 10: 17 lawyers of Ammonihah lay s. to catch holy ones of God; 12: 6 Zeezrom's plan was s. of the adversary; 56: 43 Helaman² warns of s. set by Lamanites; **Hel.** 3: 29 word of God divides asunder all s. of devil; **Ether** 2: 2 Jaredites lay s. to catch fowls.

SNATCH (see also Deliver; Redemption; Redeem)

Mosiah 27: 28 the Lord has s. Alma² out of everlasting burning; **Alma** 26: 17 God is merciful in s. men from sinful state.

SNOW

1 Ne. 11: 8 whiteness of tree exceeds whiteness of driven s.

SOAP

3 Ne. 24: 2 (Mal. 3: 2) the Lord is like fuller's s.

SOBERNESS, SOBER (see also Solemn)

1 Ne. 18: 10 Nephi¹ speaks with much s.; **Jacob** 2: 2 Jacob² is under responsibility to magnify office with s.; **Mosiah** 4: 15 teach children to walk in ways of s.; **Alma** 37: 47 (38: 15; 42: 31) declare the word, and be s.; 53: 21 two thousand Ammonite youths are men of s.; **Morm.** 1: 2, 15 Mormon² is s. child.

SOCIETY (see Secret Combination)

SOFTEN (see also Hardheartedness)

1 Ne. 2: 16 the Lord visits Nephi¹ and s. his heart; 18: 20 only power of God threatening destruction could s. hearts of Laman¹ and Lemuel; **2 Ne.** 10: 18 the Lord will s. Gentiles' hearts to be like father to Lamanites' seed; **Mosiah** 21: 15 the Lord s. Lamanites' hearts for Limhi's people; **Alma** 24: 8 the Lord gives portion of Spirit to s. hearts; 62: 41 many are s. because of afflictions and humble themselves; **Hel.** 12: 2 when the Lord s. hearts of enemies, his people harden their hearts.

SOJOURN (see also Dwell; Journey)

1 Ne. 17: 3 the Lord provides means for Lehites during s. in wilderness; 17: 4 Lehites s. in wilderness eight years.

SOLD (see Sell)

SOLDIER (see also Army; War)

Alma 51: 9 Amalickiah gathers s. for war with Nephites; 53: 22 Helaman² marches at head of two thousand stripling s.

SOLEMN, SOLEMNITY (see also Soberness)

Jacob 7: 26 Nephites a lonesome and s. people; **Hel.** 5: 28 s. fear comes

upon dissenters in prison because of overshadowing cloud; **Moro.** 8: 9 s. mockery before God to baptize little children.

SOLOMON—king of Israel, son of David [c. 1000 B.C.] (see also BD Solomon)

2 Ne. 5: 16 Nephi¹ builds temple after manner of temple of S.; **Jacob** 1: 15 S. had many wives and concubines; 2: 23 Nephites excuse whoredoms because of David and S.; 2: 24 practice of David and S. was abominable before the Lord; **3 Ne.** 13: 29 (Matt. 6: 29) S. in all his glory was not arrayed like lilies of field.

SON (see also Child; Children of God; Father; Jesus Christ—Only Begotten Son; Jesus Christ—Son of God; Mosiah², Sons of; Sons of Perdition)

1 Ne. 21: 22 (22: 6; 2 Ne. 6: 6; Isa. 49: 22) Gentiles will bring Israel's s. in their arms; **Jacob** 4: 5 Abraham's offering up his s., Isaac, was similitude of God and his S.; **Mosiah** 2: 30 Benjamin declares his s., Mosiah², king; 5: 7 those who enter covenant are called s. and daughters of Christ; 27: 25 those born again of God become his s. and daughters; **Alma** 20: 13 Lamanites believe Nephites are s. of a liar; 56: 5 two thousand s. of Ammonites have taken up weapons of war; **Hel.** 6: 10 land north called Mulek after s. of Zedekiah; 8: 21 s. of Zedekiah were slain, except Mulek; **3 Ne.** 14: 9 (Matt. 7: 9) what man, if s. ask bread, will given him stone; **Ether** 3: 14 those who believe on Christ's name become his s. and daughters.

SON OF GOD (see Children of God; Jesus Christ—Only Begotten Son; Jesus Christ—Son of God)

SONS OF MOSIAH (see Mosiah², Sons of)

SONS OF PERDITION (see also Death, Spiritual; Perdition; Unpardonable; TG Death, Spiritual, Second; Holy Ghost, Unpardonable Sin against; Sons of Perdition)

2 Ne. 2: 17 angel of God had fallen from heaven; **Mosiah** 2: 38–39 final doom of those who remain enemy to God is to endure never-ending torment; 16: 5 (Alma 11: 41) they who persist in carnal nature and go on in rebellion against God remain in fallen state as though no redemption had been made; **3 Ne.** 27: 32 many in fourth generation will be led captive as was s. of perdition; 29: 7 he who says Christ can work no miracle shall become like s. of perdition, for whom there was no mercy.

SOOTHSAYER (see also Prophets, False; Sorceries, Sorcerer)

2 Ne. 12: 6 (Isa. 2: 6) the Lord's people hearken unto s. like Philistines; **3 Ne.** 21: 16 (Micah 5: 12) thou shalt have no more s.

SORCERIES, SORCERER (*see also* Magic; Soothsayer)

Alma 1: 32 those who do not belong to church indulge in s.; **Morm.** 1: 19 there are s. in land.

SORE (*see also* Curse; Repentance)

Alma 15: 5 Zeezrom's mind exceedingly s. because of iniquities; **Hel.** 11: 5 work of destruction becomes s. by famine.

SORROW, SORROWFUL, SORROWING (*see also* Anguish; Despair; Grieve; Lament; Misery; Mourn; Pain; Remorse; Sad; Suffering; Torment; Tribulation; Trouble; Weep)

1 Ne. 16: 25 Lehi[1] brought down into depths of s. because of murmuring; **2 Ne.** 4: 17 heart of Nephi[1] s. because of his flesh; 4: 26 why should my soul linger in valley of s.; **Mosiah** 14: 3 (Isa. 53: 3) Messiah is man of s.; **Alma** 8: 14 Alma[2] weighed down with s. because of Nephites' wickedness; 29: 2 men should repent, that there might be no more s.; 37: 45 words of Christ can carry men beyond vale of s. to better land of promise; 40: 12 paradise a state of rest from all care and s.; **3 Ne.** 28: 5 three Nephites s. because they dare not speak their desire; 28: 38 three Nephites not to suffer s., save for sins of world; **Morm.** 2: 13 Nephites' s. was not unto repentance.

SOUGHT (*see* Seek, Sought)

SOUL (*see also* Body; Heart; Man; Mind; Spirit; TG Soul)

1 Ne. 15: 35 final state of s. is to dwell with God or be cast out; **2 Ne.** 4: 15–16 my s. delighteth in scriptures, in things of the Lord; 9: 49 my s. abhorreth sin; 11: 2 my s. delighteth in words of Isaiah[1]; 25: 4 (31: 3) my s. delighteth in plainness; 25: 29 worship Christ with whole s.; 28: 21 devil lulls men into carnal security and cheats their s.; 32: 9 ask Father to consecrate thy performance for welfare of thy s.; **Jacob** 2: 8 pleasing word of God healeth wounded s.; **Enos** 1: 4 s. of Enos[2] hungers; 1: 9 Enos[2] pours out whole s. unto God; **Omni** 1: 76 offer your whole s. as offering unto Christ; **W of M** 1: 18 Benjamin establishes peace by laboring with faculty of whole s.; **Mosiah** 14: 10 (Isa. 53: 10) thou shalt make his s. an offering for sin; 14: 12 (Isa. 53: 12) he hath poured out his s. unto death; 26: 14 Alma[1] pours out whole s. to God; 27: 29 (36: 16) s. of Alma[1] racked with eternal torment; 29: 40 Mosiah[2] seeks not lucre

which corrupts s.; **Alma** 32: 28 good seed, or word, will begin to enlarge s.; 34: 26 pour out your s. unto God in your closets; 36: 15 O that I could become extinct both s. and body; 36: 20 s. of Alma[2] is filled with joy as exceeding as his pain; 40: 7, 11–14 state of s. between death and resurrection; 40: 18 first resurrection is reuniting of s. with body of those down to resurrection of Christ; 40: 21 dead shall be reunited, body and s., to be judged; 40: 23 s. shall be restored to body and body to s.; 42: 16 repentance could not come unto men except there were punishment as eternal as life of s.; **3 Ne.** 11: 3 small voice from heaven pierces to s.; 18: 29 he who partakes of sacrament unworthily eats and drinks damnation to s.; 20: 8 he who partakes of sacrament takes Christ's body and blood to s., and s. shall never hunger nor thirst, but shall be filled; **Ether** 12: 4 hope maketh an anchor to s. of men; **Moro.** 4: 3 (5: 2) bread and wine of sacrament sanctified to s. of those who partake.

SOUND [adj.]

Alma 17: 2 sons of Mosiah[2] are men of s. understanding, having searched the scriptures.

SOUND [noun and verb] (*see also* Noise; Voice)

Mosiah 26: 25 when second trump s., they who never knew the Lord shall come before him; **3 Ne.** 11: 5 eyes of multitude are toward s. from heaven; **Morm.** 9: 13 all men shall be awakened from endless sleep when trump s.

SOUTH (*see* North)

SOW [noun] (*see also* Swine)

3 Ne. 7: 8 Nephites turn from righteousness like s. to her wallowing.

SOW [verb] (*see also* Plant; Reap)

2 Ne. 5: 11 Nephites s. seed; **Mosiah** 7: 30–31 if people s. filthiness, they shall reap chaff; **3 Ne.** 13: 26 (Matt. 6: 26) fowls of air do not s.; **Ether** 10: 25 Jaredites make tools to s.

SPACE (*see also* Time)

1 Ne. 11: 19 virgin carried away in Spirit for the s. of a time; **Alma** 40: 21 s. between death and resurrection; 42: 5 if Adam had partaken of tree of life, he would have lived forever, having no s. for repentance; **3 Ne.** 8: 3, 23 darkness for s. of three days as sign of Christ's death; 8: 19 tempest and earthquakes last for s. of three hours.

SPACIOUS (*see* Building)

SPAKE (see Speak)

SPARE (see also Preserve; Protect; Salvation; Save; Withhold)

Jacob 5: 50 servant asks the Lord to s. vineyard a little longer; **Omni** 1: 7 the Lord s. the righteous; **Mosiah** 28: 4 the Lord, in infinite mercy, s. sons of Mosiah²; **Alma** 10: 20, 23 (62: 40; Hel. 13: 14) by prayers of the righteous are the wicked s.; **3 Ne.** 8: 24 O that we had repented, then would our brethren have been s.; 10: 6 the Lord has s. house of Israel; 22: 2 (Isa. 54: 2) s. not, lengthen thy cords; **Morm.** 3: 2 repent, be baptized, build up church, and ye shall be s.; **Moro.** 9: 19 Nephites have become brutal, s. none; 9: 22 Mormon² prays the Lord will s. Moroni².

SPEAK, SPAKE, SPOKEN (see also Communication; Language; Lips; Mouth; Say; Speech; Talk; Tongue; Utter; Voice; Whisper)

1 Ne. 11: 11 Nephi¹ s. with Spirit as man s.; **2 Ne.** 25: 8 unto them who suppose records are not of worth will the Lord s. particularly; 26: 16 those who shall be destroyed will s. out of ground; 27: 13 (Moro. 10: 27) words of the faithful shall s. as if from dead; 29: 12 the Lord will s. unto Jews, Nephites, other tribes, and they shall write it; 32: 3 angels s. words of Christ by power of Holy Ghost; 33: 1 when a man s. by power of Holy Ghost, that power carries it into hearts; **Jacob** 4: 9 God being able to s. created world and man; 4: 13 Spirit s. truth and lies not; 4: 13 Spirit s. of things as they are and will be; **Mosiah** 13: 33 all prophets have s. concerning coming of Messiah; **Alma** 29: 1 O that I were an angel and could s. with trump of God; 30: 52 Korihor is dumb, cannot s.; 58: 11 the Lord s. peace to our souls; **Hel.** 5: 18 what they should s. is given to Nephi² and Lehi⁴; 5: 45 Spirit enters hearts of Nephi² and Lehi⁴, and they can s. marvelous words; **3 Ne.** 17: 17 (19: 32) no tongue can s. marvelous things Nephites heard Jesus s.; **Ether** 3: 12 brother of Jared² knows the truth; 12: 31 after disciples s. the Lord's name, he showed himself to them in power.

SPEAR (see also Dart; Javelin; Weapon)

2 Ne. 12: 4 (Isa. 2: 4) nations shall beat s. into pruning-hooks; **Alma** 17: 7 sons of Mosiah² take s. to provide food.

SPEECH (see also Communication; Language; Speak; Tongue; Voice)

2 Ne. 26: 16 (Isa. 29: 4) s. of those who are destroyed shall be low out of dust; **Jacob** 2: 7 Jacob² grieved that he must use much boldness of s.; 7: 4 Sherem has

much power of s.; **Enos** 1: 23 prophets preach with plainness of s.; **Morm.** 9: 32 reformed Egyptian characters are altered according to Nephites' manner of s.

SPIN

Mosiah 10: 5 Zeniff causes women to s. and toil; **Hel.** 6: 13 Nephite women toil and s.; **3 Ne.** 13: 28 (Matt. 6: 28) lilies of field toil not, neither do they s.

SPINDLES (see Liahona)

SPIRIT (see also Broken Heart and Contrite Spirit; Ghost; Mind; Soul; Spirit, Evil; Spirit, Holy/Spirit of the Lord; Spirit World; Spiritual; TG Spirit Body; Spirit Creation; Spirits, Disembodied; BD Spirit)

2 Ne. 9: 12 bodies and s. of men will be restored to each other; 25: 11 Nephi¹ speaks because of s. that is in him; **Mosiah** 2: 28 immortal s. to join choirs above in singing praises of God; **Alma** 3: 26 men reap eternal happiness or misery according to s. they obey; 11: 43 s. and body to be reunited in perfect form; 11: 45 s. to be united with bodies, never to be divided; 34: 34 same s. that possesses body at death will possess it in eternal world; 40: 11 after death, s. of all men are taken home to God; **3 Ne.** 12: 3 (Matt. 5: 3) blessed are poor in s. who come unto the Lord; **Ether** 3: 16 brother of Jared² sees body of Christ's s.; 3: 16 man is created after body of Christ's s.; **Moro.** 10: 14 to another is given the beholding of angels and ministering s.; 10: 34 Moroni² goes to rest in paradise until s. and body are reunited.

SPIRIT, EVIL (see also Angels of the Devil; Demon; Devil; Devils; Familiar; TG Spirits, Evil or Unclean)

1 Ne. 11: 31 (Mosiah 3: 6) Lamb casts out devils and unclean s.; **2 Ne.** 32: 8 evil s. teaches man not to pray; 33: 5 no man shall be angry with truth save he shall be of s. of devil; **Mosiah** 2: 32 beware lest contentions arise and ye list to obey evil s.; 2: 33 he who listeth to obey evil s. shall receive everlasting punishment; 2: 36-37 they who knowingly transgress obey evil s. and become enemies to all righteousness; 4: 14 ye will not suffer children to serve devil, who is evil s. spoken of by fathers; **Alma** 3: 26 men reap eternal happiness or misery according to s. they obey, whether good or evil; 22: 15 what shall I do to be born of God, having wicked s. rooted from breast and receive his S.; 40: 13 s. of devil takes possession of the wicked after death; **3 Ne.** 7: 19 Nephi³ casts out devils and unclean s.; 11: 29 he who hath s. of contention is not of Christ.

SPIRIT, GIFTS OF (see also Holy Ghost; Holy Ghost, Baptism of; Holy Ghost, Gift of; Interpretation; Sign; Spirit, Holy/Spirit of the Lord; Tongue; Translation; TG God, Gifts of; Holy Ghost, Gifts of)

1 Ne. 10: 17 Holy Ghost is gift of God unto all who diligently seek him; 13: 37 they who seek to bring forth Zion shall have gift and power of Holy Ghost; **Jacob** 6: 8 will ye deny power of God and gift of Holy Ghost and quench Holy S.; **Omni** 1: 20 (Mosiah 8: 13; 21: 28) Mosiah¹ interprets engravings by gift and power of God; **Alma** 9: 21 Nephites have received spirit of prophecy and of revelation, many gifts, gifts of speaking with tongues, preaching, gift of Holy Ghost, gift of translation; **3 Ne.** 29: 6 wo to him who says the Lord no longer works by gifts or by power of Holy Ghost: **Moro.** 10: 8 gifts are given by manifestation of S. unto men to profit them.

SPIRIT, HOLY/SPIRIT OF THE LORD (see also Born of God; Holy Ghost; Holy Ghost, Baptism of; Inspire; Light; Revelation; Spirit, Gifts of; Spiritual; Truth; TG God, Spirit of; Holy Ghost; Jesus Christ, Spirit of; Lord, Spirit of; BD Spirit, the Holy)

1 Ne. 1: 7–8 Lehi¹ is overcome with S.; 2: 17 Nephi¹ tells Sam of things manifested to him by H.S.; 3: 20 words delivered to prophets by S. of the Lord; 4: 6 Nephi¹ led by S., not knowing beforehand what he should do; 7: 14 S. of the Lord ceaseth soon to strive with Jews; 11: 1 Nephi¹ is caught away in S. into high mountain; 11: 11 Nephi¹ speaks with S. of the Lord in form of man; 13: 12–13 Gentiles wrought upon by S. of the Lord to cross many waters; 17: 49 Nephi¹ is full of S. of God, that his frame has no strength; 17: 52 S. of God is so powerful, brothers of Nephi¹ fear to touch him; 19: 12 many kings shall be wrought upon by S. of God; 20: 16 (Isa. 48: 16) the Lord God, and his S., hath sent me; 22: 2 by S. are all things made known unto prophets; **2 Ne.** 2: 4 S. is same yesterday, today, forever; 2: 28 choose eternal life according to will of H.S.; 26: 11 (Ether 2: 15) S. of the Lord will not always strive with man; 32: 8 if ye would hearken unto S. that teaches man to pray, ye would know ye must pray; 33: 2 many harden hearts against H.S., that it has no place in them; **Jacob** 4: 13 S. speaks the truth; 6: 8 will ye deny gift of Holy Ghost and quench H.S.; 7: 8 the Lord pours his S. into soul of Jacob²; **Jarom** 1: 4 those who are not stiffnecked and have faith have communion with H.S.; 1: 4 H.S. makes manifest unto men

according to faith; **Mosiah** 3: 19 natural man will remain enemy to God unless he yields to enticings of H.S.; 4: 20 God has poured out S. upon people of Benjamin; 5: 2 S. of the Lord has wrought mighty change in people of Benjamin; 18: 10 be baptized, that the Lord may pour out his S. upon you more abundantly; 27: 24 Alma² has been born of the S.; **Alma** 5: 46 teachings are made known unto Alma² by H.S. of God; 5: 46 H.S. is s. of revelation; 5: 47 prophecy is by manifestation of S. of God; 5: 54 converts have been sanctified by H.S.; 7: 5 I trust, according to S. of God which is in me, that I shall have joy over you; 8: 10 Alma² wrestles with God that he would pour out his S. upon people of Ammonihah; 9: 21 Nephites have been visited by S. of God; 11: 22 Amulek will say nothing contrary to S. of the Lord; 11: 44 (2 Ne. 31: 21; 3 Ne. 11: 27, 36; 28: 10; Morm. 7: 7) Father, Son, and H.S. are one God; 13: 4 men reject S. of God because of hardness of hearts; 13: 28 pray continually and thus be led by H.S.; 18: 16 Ammon², being filled with S. of God, perceives king's thoughts; 18: 34 Ammon² has been called by H.S. to teach these things; 19: 36 the Lord pours out his S. upon Lamanites; 24: 30 if people once enlightened by S. fall away, they become more hardened; 30: 42 Korihor has put off S. of God; 30: 46 Korihor resists s. of the truth; 31: 36 Alma² clasps hands upon fellow laborers, and they are filled with H.S.; 34: 35 if you have procrastinated day of your repentance, S. of the Lord has withdrawn from you; 38: 6 S. of God makes things known to Alma²; 40: 13 spirits of the wicked have no portion of S. of the Lord; 45: 19 Alma² is taken up by S.; 61: 15 commanders are given power to conduct war according to S. of God, which is S. of freedom; **Hel.** 4: 24 S. of the Lord no more preserves Nephites; 4: 24 S. of the Lord dwells not in unholy temples; 5: 45 H.S. enters Nephi² and Lehi⁴, that they speak marvelous words; 13: 8 because of hardness of Nephites' hearts, the Lord will withdraw his S. from them; **3 Ne.** 7: 21 converts signify they have been visited by S. of God; 18: 7, 11 (Moro. 4: 3; 5: 2) if men always remember Christ, they shall have his S.; **Moro.** 4: 3 (5: 2) those who partake of sacrament and always remember Christ will have his S.; 8: 28 (9: 4) Mormon² fears S. has ceased striving with Nephites; 10: 8, 17 gifts of God are given by manifestations of S. of God.

SPIRIT WORLD (see also Darkness, Spiritual; Death, Physical; Death, Spiritual; Hell; Paradise; Premortal Existence; Prison; Resurrection; Spirit)

Alma 40: 11 s. of all men are taken

home to God after death; 40: 12 s. of righteous are received in state of happiness, paradise; 40: 13–14 s. of the wicked are cast into outer darkness.

SPIRITUAL, SPIRITUALLY (see also Darkness, Spiritual; Death, Spiritual; Holy Ghost; Spirit; Spirit, Holy/Spirit of the Lord)

1 Ne. 14: 7 the hardhearted to be delivered unto destruction, both temporally and s.; 15: 26–32 river of filthy water is representation of things both temporal and s.; 22: 3 prophecies of Isaiah¹ pertain to things both temporal and s.; 2 Ne. 2: 5 by s. law, men perish from that which is good; 9: 39 to be s-minded is life eternal; **Mosiah** 2: 41 those who keep commandments are blessed in all things, both temporal and s.; 4: 26 administer to relief of the poor, both s. and temporally; 5: 7 Christ has s. begotten those who enter covenant; 18: 29 Nephites impart to one another both temporally and s.; **Alma** 5: 14 have ye s. been born of God; 7: 23 ask for whatsoever things ye stand in need, both temporal and s.; 11: 45 through resurrection, body and spirit become s. and immortal; 36: 4 Alma² knows these things, not of the temporal but of the s.; 37: 43 as fathers were slothful they did not prosper, so it is with s. things; **Morm.** 2: 15 day of grace is past with Nephites, both temporally and s.; **Moro.** 10: 19 s. gifts will never be done away.

SPIT, SPITTING (see also Mock; Revile; Scorn)

1 Ne. 19: 9 world shall s. upon God of Israel; 2 Ne. 7: 6 (Isa. 50: 6) I hid not my face from shame and s.; **Alma** 8: 13 people of Ammonihah s. upon Alma²; 14: 7 people s. upon Zeezrom; 26: 29 sons of Mosiah² have been s. upon.

SPOKESMAN (see also Speak)

2 Ne. 3: 17–18 the Lord will make a s. for Moses.

SPOT, SPOTTED (see also Filthiness; Guilt; Sin; Spot of Land; Spotless; Stain)

Ether 12: 38 garments of Moroni¹ not s. with Gentiles' blood; **Moro.** 10: 33 become holy, without s.

SPOT OF LAND

Jacob 5: 21–22 poorest s. of ground in vineyard; 5: 23 s. of ground poorer than first; 5: 25, 43–44 good s. of ground in vineyard.

SPOTLESS (see also Blameless; Cleanse; Guiltless; Innocence; Purity; Spot, Spotted)

2 Ne. 33: 7 Nephi¹ to meet many souls s. at judgment-seat; **Jacob** 1: 19 slothful teachers would not be found s. at last day; **Alma** 5: 24 (7: 25) garments of prophets are s.; 12: 14 our words will condemn us, and we shall not be found s.; 13: 12 after being sanctified by Holy Ghost, high priests are pure and s.; 14: 7 Zeezrom confesses Alma² and Amulek are s.; 3 Ne. 27: 20 be sanctified by Holy Ghost, that ye may stand s. before the Lord; **Morm.** 9: 6 be found s., having been cleansed by blood of Lamb.

SPREAD, SPREADING (see also Enlarge; Grow; Increase; Shed)

Mosiah 3: 20 knowledge of Savior shall s. throughout every nation; **Alma** 1: 15–16 death of Nehor does not end s. of priestcraft; **Hel.** 6: 28 devil s. works of darkness over land; 16: 22 Satan s. rumors and contentions; 3 Ne. 4: 6 robbers dare not s. themselves in land lest Nephites attack; 4 Ne. 1: 46 robbers s. over land; **Morm.** 2: 8 blood and carnage s. throughout land; **Ether** 9: 6 so great has been s. of secret society that hearts of all are corrupted; 9: 26 (10: 4) people have s. again over the land.

SPRING, SPRINGING (see also Fountain; Grow; Water)

1 Ne. 16: 21 bows have lost their s.; 21: 10 (Isa. 49: 10) he who has mercy on them shall lead them by s. of water; **Alma** 32: 41 (33: 23) nourish tree by faith and diligence, and it will s. up unto everlasting life.

SPRINKLE

3 Ne. 20: 45 (Isa. 52: 15) so shall he s. many nations.

SPURN (see also Persecution; Scorn)

3 Ne. 29: 4–5 warning not to s. doings of the Lord; 29: 8 ye need not any longer s. the Jews.

SPY

Mosiah 9: 1 Zeniff sent as s. among Lamanites; 10: 7 Zeniff sends s. around land of Shemlon; **Alma** 2: 21 Alma² sends s. to follow Amlicites; 43: 23, 28, 30 (56: 22) Moroni¹ sends s. to watch Lamanites; 58: 14 Lamanites send out s. to discover Nephites' strength.

STAFF

2 Ne. 13: 1 (Isa. 3: 1) the Lord takes from Judah whole s. of bread; 24: 5 (Isa. 14: 5) the Lord has broken s. of the wicked.

STAIN (see also Filthiness; Guilt; Sin; Spot, Spotted; Unclean)

Alma 5: 21 garments must be puri-

fied until cleansed from all s.; 5: 22 how
will you feel to stand before God with
garments s. with filthiness; 24: 11–13
since God has taken away our s., let us
s. our swords no more.

STAKE

3 Ne. 22: 2 (Moro. 10: 31; Isa. 54: 2)
strengthen thy s.

STAND, STOOD (see also Fast; Need; Rameumpton; Standing; Steadfast; Testimony; Witness)

1 Ne. 15: 33 (2 Ne. 28: 23; Alma 11:
43; Ether 5: 6) men must be brought to
s. before God to be judged; **2 Ne.** 13: 13
the Lord s. up to plead and to judge; 25:
21–22 seed of Joseph[1] shall never perish
as long as earth shall s.; **Mosiah** 18: 9 s.
as witness of God; **Alma** 5: 44 Alma[2] is
commanded to s. and testify of things to
come; 31: 21 Rameumpton, being interpreted, is holy s.; **Hel.** 12: 15 it appears to
man that sun s. still; **3 Ne.** 17: 12 (19:
15; 27: 2) Jesus s. in midst of Nephites;
27: 16 Jesus to s. to judge world; 27: 20
those sanctified by Holy Ghost may s.
before Christ at last day; **Moro.** 7: 36–37
the Lord will not withhold power of Holy
Ghost as long as earth shall s.; 10: 19
spiritual gifts shall not be done away as
long as world shall s.

STANDARD (see also Ensign; Example; Title of Liberty; TG God, the Standard of Righteousness)

1 Ne. 21: 22 (2 Ne. 6: 6; Isa. 49: 22)
the Lord will set up his s. to the people;
22: 6 the Lord will set Gentiles up for s.;
2 Ne. 20: 18 (Isa. 10: 18) they shall be as
when a s-bearer fainteth; 29: 2 the Lord's
words shall hiss forth for s. unto Israel;
Alma 46: 36 (51: 20; 62: 4–5) Moroni[1]
plants s. of liberty among Nephites.

STANDING (see also Equal)

Alma 13: 5 those called to be high
priests are on same s. with brethren.

STAR (see also Astronomy)

1 Ne. 1: 10 Lehi[1] beholds twelve
whose brightness exceeds that of s.; **2 Ne.**
24: 13 (Isa. 14: 13) Lucifer desires to
exalt his throne above s. of God; **Hel.**
14: 5 (3 Ne. 1: 21) new s. shall arise as
sign of Christ's birth; 14: 20 (3 Ne. 8: 22) s.
shall be darkened as sign of Christ's death.

STATE

1 Ne. 10: 6 all mankind in lost and
fallen s.; 15: 31, 35 final s. of souls is to
dwell with God or be cast out; **2 Ne.** 2: 21
(Alma 12: 24; 42: 10, 13) this life became
s. of probation; 25: 17 the Lord will set
his hand second time to restore his people
from lost and fallen s.; **Mosiah** 4: 2

Benjamin's people view themselves in
carnal s.; 16: 4 God redeems his people
from lost and fallen s.; 27: 25 all mankind
must be changed from carnal and fallen
s. to s. of righteousness; **Alma** 12: 31
through first transgression men placed
themselves in s. to act according to their
wills; 40: 11–14 s. of soul between death
and resurrection; 41: 11 men in s. of
nature, or carnal s., have gone contrary
to nature of God, contrary to nature of
happiness; 42: 10 probationary s. became
s. for men to prepare; **3 Ne.** 28: 15 three
Nephites seem to be transformed from
body of flesh to immortal s.

STATURE

1 Ne. 2: 16 (4: 31) Nephi[1] is large in
s.; **3 Ne.** 13: 27 (Matt. 6: 27) which of you
by taking thought can add one cubit unto
his s.; **Morm.** 2: 1 Mormon[2] is large in s.

STATUTE (see also Commandments of God; Decree; Law; Ordinance)

2 Ne. 1: 16 (5: 10; Mosiah 6: 6;
Alma 25: 14; 58: 40; Hel. 3: 20; 6: 34;
15: 5; 3 Ne. 25: 4) observe the s. and
judgments of the Lord.

STAY (see also Cease; Hinder; Restrain; Stop; Withhold)

2 Ne. 13: 1 (Isa. 3: 1) the Lord takes
away from Judah whole s. of water; 20:
20 (Isa. 10: 20) remnant of Israel shall no
longer s. upon him that smote them, but
upon the Lord; 27: 4 all ye that do
iniquity, s. yourselves and wonder;
Morm. 8: 26 records shall come by hand
of the Lord, and none can s. it.

STEADFAST, STEADFASTLY, STEADFASTNESS (see also Diligence; Endure; Faithful; Firmness; Immovable; Obedience; Steadiness; Unshaken)

1 Ne. 2: 10 Lehi[1] exhorts Lemuel to
be s. like valley; **2 Ne.** 25: 24 Nephites
look forward with s. unto Christ; 26: 8
the righteous who look forward unto
Christ with s. shall not perish; 31: 20
press forward with s. in Christ; **Mosiah**
4: 11 stand s. in faith of that which is to
come; 5: 15 be s. and immovable; **Alma**
1: 25 the faithful stand s. in keeping
commandments; 5: 48 Christ shall take
away sins of those who s. believe on his
name; **Hel.** 15: 8 converted Lamanites
are s. in faith; 15: 10 because of their s.,
the Lord will prolong Lamanites' days;
3 Ne. 1: 8 believers watch s. for sign of
Christ's birth; 6: 14 church broken up
except for few Lamanites who are s.;
Ether 12: 4 hope for better world makes
men sure and s.

STEADINESS (see also Steadfast)

Alma 38: 2 (39: 1) Alma[2] to have

great joy in Shiblon's s.; **Hel.** 6: 1 Lamanites' righteousness exceeds that of Nephites because of their s.

STEAL, STEALING, STOLEN (see also Fraud; Rob; Thief)

2 **Ne.** 26: 32 the Lord has commanded that men should not s.; **Mosiah** 2: 13 Benjamin has not suffered his people to s.; 13: 22 (Ex. 20: 15) thou shalt not s.; **Alma** 1: 18 those practicing priestcraft dare not s. for fear of law; 16: 18 priests preach against s.; 23: 3 king would convince Lamanites they ought not to s.; 39: 4 harlot Isabel s. away hearts of many; **Hel.** 4: 12 slaughter of Nephites caused by iniquities, s.; 6: 21, 23 robbers covenant they should not suffer for s.; 7: 4–5 robbers obtain management of government that they might more easily s.; 3 **Ne.** 13: 19–20 (Matt. 6: 19–20) lay not up for yourselves treasures upon earth, where thieves s.; 27: 32 fourth generation will sell the Lord for that which thieves can s.

STEEL (see also Metal)

1 **Ne.** 4: 9 Laban's sword is of most precious s.; 16: 18 Nephi[1] breaks his bow, made of fine s.; 2 **Ne.** 5: 15 (Jarom 1: 8) Nephi[1] teaches his people to work in s.; **Ether** 7: 9 Shule makes swords of s.

STEM OF JESSE

2 **Ne.** 21: 1 (Isa. 11: 1) rod shall come forth out of s. of Jesse.

STIFFNECKED, STIFFNECKEDNESS (see also Hardheartedness; Pride; Rebel; Stubbornness; Unbelief)

1 **Ne.** 2: 11 Lehi[1] speaks because of s. of elder sons; 2 **Ne.** 6: 10 (10: 5; 25: 12) Jews shall stiffen necks against Holy One; 25: 28 (Enos 1: 22; Hel. 5: 3; 9: 21; 13: 29) Nephites are s. people; 28: 14 false churches wear stiff necks and high heads; 32: 7 (3 Ne. 15: 18) Spirit stops utterance because of s. of men; **Jacob** 2: 13 rich among Nephites wear stiff necks because of costly apparel; 4: 14 (6: 4; 3 Ne. 15: 18) Jews were s. people; **Jarom** 1: 4 many among Nephites have revelations, for not all are s.; **Omni** 1: 28 Zeniff a s. man; **W of M** 1: 17 holy men speak with sharpness because of s. of people; **Mosiah** 3: 14 (13: 29) the Lord saw his people were s. and appointed unto them law of Moses; **Alma** 9: 5, 31 (15: 15) people of Ammonihah are s. people; 20: 30 Lamanites in Middoni are more s. people; 26: 24 Nephites believe Lamanites are s. people; 37: 10 records may bring thousands of s. Nephites to knowledge of Redeemer; **Hel.** 4: 21 Nephites see they

have been s.; **Morm.** 8: 33 s. people will build churches to get gain.

STILL (see also Voice)

Hel. 12: 15 it appears to man that sun stands s.

STING

Mosiah 16: 7–8 (Morm. 7: 5) s. of death is swallowed up in Christ; **Alma** 22: 14 s. of death to be swallowed up in hopes of glory.

STINK

2 **Ne.** 7: 2 (Isa. 50: 2) the Lord makes fish to s. because waters are dried up; 13: 24 (Isa. 3: 24) instead of sweet smell there shall be s.; **Alma** 19: 5 some say Lamoni s.

STIR (see also Anger; Contention; Provoke; Rebel)

Enos 1: 23 prophets s. Nephites up continually to keep them in fear of the Lord; **Mosiah** 11: 28 Abinadi s. up people; 18: 33 Noah[3] says Alma[1] is s. people up to rebellion; **Alma** 11: 20 judges s. people up to riotings to get gain; **Hel.** 6: 21 Satan s. up hearts of Nephites to unite with robbers; 16: 22 Satan s. up people to do iniquity; **Morm.** 4: 5 the wicked s. up hearts of men to bloodshed.

STONE [noun] (see also Foundation; Ore; Rock; Stone [verb])

1 **Ne.** 2: 7 Lehi[1] builds altar of s. and makes offering to the Lord; 16: 15 Lehites slay food with s. and slings; 17: 11 Nephi[1] smites two s. together to make fire; 2 **Ne.** 18: 14 (Isa. 8: 14) he shall be for s. of stumbling; 19: 10 (Isa. 9: 10) we will build with hewn s.; 26: 3 Jews s. the prophets; **Jacob** 4: 15 Jews will reject s. upon which they might build safe foundation; **Omni** 1: 20 large s. with engravings brought to Mosiah[1]; **Mosiah** 10: 8 (Alma 3: 5; 43: 20) Lamanites are armed with s. and slings; 28: 11, 13–16 Mosiah[2] translates records by means of two s.; **Alma** 2: 12 (49: 20) Nephites armed with s. and slings; 17: 14 Lamanites' hearts are set upon precious s.; 37: 23 the Lord will prepare s. which will shine forth in darkness unto light; **Hel.** 16: 2 Nephites cast s. at Samuel from the wall; **Ether** 3: 1–6 (6: 3) brother of Jared[2] makes sixteen small s. for light in vessels; 3: 23–24, 28 the Lord gives brother of Jared[2] two s. to be sealed with writings.

STONE [verb] (see also Martyrdom; Persecution; Reject; Stone [noun])

Alma 26: 29 sons of Mosiah[2] have been s.; 33: 17 second prophet of old was s. for testifying of Son; 38: 4 Shiblon was

s. for word's sake; **Hel.** 13: 33 (3 Ne. 8: 25) O that I had repented and not s. the prophets; **3 Ne.** 7: 14 people s. the prophets and cast them out; 10: 12 more righteous part of people receive prophets and s. them not; **Ether** 8: 25 devil causes men to s. prophets.

STOOD (see Stand, Stood)

STOP (see also Hinder; Restrain; Stay)

2 Ne. 32: 7 Spirit s. utterance of Nephi[1]; **Mosiah** 4: 20 the Lord has caused mouths to be s. that they cannot find utterance because of joy; **Alma** 36: 6 God sent angel to s. Alma[2] and companions by the way.

STORE (see also Storehouse)

3 Ne. 4: 18 Nephites have laid up much provision in s.; **4 Ne.** 1: 46 robbers lay up gold and silver in s.

STOREHOUSE

3 Ne. 24: 10 (Mal. 3: 10) bring ye all the tithes into the s.

STORM (see also Destruction; Tempest; Whirlwind; Wind)

1 Ne. 18: 13–21 great s. arises during voyage to promised land; **2 Ne.** 14: 6 (Isa. 4: 6) tabernacle shall be covert from s.; 27: 2 in day of iniquity Gentiles shall be visited with s.; **Alma** 26: 6 sheaves, or converts, shall not be beaten down by s.; **Hel.** 5: 12 those built upon foundation of Redeemer shall withstand s. of devil; **3 Ne.** 8: 5–19 great s. arises at death of Christ.

STRAIGHT, STRAIGHTNESS

1 Ne. 10: 8 (Alma 7: 19) make s. paths of the Lord; **2 Ne.** 9: 41 way for man is narrow, but lies in s. course; 31: 9 Christ's example shows men s. of path; **Alma** 7: 9 walk in the Lord's paths, which are s.; 37: 44 word of Christ will point s. course to eternal bliss.

STRAIT (see also Narrow; Straight; Straiten)

1 Ne. 8: 20 Lehi[1] sees s. and narrow path leading to tree; 21: 20 (Isa. 49: 20) children shall say, The place is too s. for me; **2 Ne.** 31: 18–19 s. and narrow path leads to eternal life; 33: 9 walk in the s. path; **Jacob** 6: 11 (3 Ne. 14: 13–14; 27: 33; Matt. 7: 13–14) enter in at s. gate; **Hel.** 3: 29 word of God leads in s. and narrow course across gulf of misery.

STRAITEN (see also Chasten)

1 Ne. 17: 41 the Lord s. Israel in wilderness.

STRANGE (see also Stranger; Unknown)

1 Ne. 8: 32 many in vision of Lehi[1]

are lost from view, wandering in s. paths; 8: 33 great multitude enter s. building; **Alma** 13: 23 (26: 36) Nephites are wanderers in s. land; 26: 36 Nephites a branch of tree of Israel lost from body in s. land.

STRANGER (see also BD Stranger)

Mosiah 5: 13 how knoweth a man the master who is s. unto him; 13: 18 (Ex. 20: 10) on seventh day thou shalt not do any work, nor s. within thy gates; **Alma** 26: 9 except for sons of Mosiah[2], converted Lamanites would still be s. to God; **3 Ne.** 24: 5 (Mal. 3: 5) the Lord will be swift witness against those who turn aside the s.

STRATAGEM (see also Decoy)

Alma 43: 30 Moroni[1] thinks it is no sin to defend people by s.; 52: 10 Moroni[1] encourages Teancum to take cities by s.; 54: 3 Moroni[1] resolves upon s. to obtain Nephite prisoners from Lamanites; 56: 30 Nephites desire to bring s. into effect upon Lamanites; 58: 6 Lamanites resolve by s. to destroy Nephites; 58: 28 by s. Nephites take city of Manti without bloodshed.

STRAW

2 Ne. 21: 7 (30: 13; Isa. 11: 7) lion shall eat s. like ox.

STREET (see also Highway; Path; Road; Way)

2 Ne. 8: 20 (Isa. 51: 20) two sons lie at head of all s.; **Alma** 26: 29 (32: 1) missionaries teach in s.; **3 Ne.** 13: 2 (Matt. 6: 2) when ye do alms, do not sound trumpet as hypocrites do in s.

STRENGTH (see also Arm; Courage; Might; Power; Strengthen; Strong; Virtue)

1 Ne. 4: 31 Nephi[1] receives much s. of the Lord; 21: 5 (Isa. 49: 5) my God shall be my s.; **2 Ne.** 8: 24 (3 Ne. 20: 36; Isa. 52: 1) put on thy s., O Zion; 22: 2 (Isa. 12: 2) the Lord Jehovah is my s.; **Jacob** 5: 48 branches have grown faster than s. of roots; 5: 66 root and top to be equal in s.; **Mosiah** 2: 11 Benjamin serves his people with all his s.; 4: 27 not requisite that man should run faster than he has s.; 9: 17 in s. of the Lord, Zeniff's people go to battle against Lamanites; 11: 19 people of Noah[4] boast in own s.; **Alma** 20: 4 (26: 12) in s. of the Lord, Ammon[2] can do all things; 26: 12 Ammon[2] knows that as his own s. he is weak; 39: 13 turn to the Lord with all your s.; 56: 56 Ammonite youths fight as if with s. of God; **Hel.** 4: 13 (Morm. 3: 9; 4: 8) slaughter of Nephites caused by their boasting in own s.; **3 Ne.** 3: 12

Nephites cry unto the Lord for s. against robbers; **Moro.** 9: 18 Mormon[2] has but s. of man; 10: 32 love God with all your s.

STRENGTHEN (*see also* Nourish; Strength; Strong)

1 Ne. 17: 3 if men keep commandments, God s. them; **Mosiah** 24: 15 the Lord s. people of Alma[1] to bear burdens; **Alma** 2: 28 Nephites are s. by hand of the Lord; 25: 16 law of Moses s. faith in Christ; **3 Ne.** 22: 2 (Moro. 10: 31; Isa. 54: 2) s. thy stakes.

STRETCH

1 Ne. 17: 54 Nephi[1] s. forth hand and the Lord shakes brothers; **2 Ne.** 15: 25 (19: 12, 17, 21; 20: 4; 24: 17; Jacob 6: 4; Isa. 5: 25) the Lord's hand is s. out.

STRIFE (*see also* Contention; Dissension)

2 Ne. 26: 21 many churches to be built up which cause s.; **Alma** 1: 32 those who do not belong to church indulge in envyings and s.; 4: 9 (Hel. 11: 23; 13: 22; Morm. 8: 36) s. among Nephites; 16: 18 priests preach against s.; **3 Ne.** 21: 19 all s. shall be done away; 30: 2 turn, ye Gentiles, from all your s.; **4 Ne.** 1: 16 no s. among Nephites; **Morm.** 8: 21 he who breathes out s. against work of the Lord shall be hewn down.

STRIKE, STRUCK (*see also* Beat; Smite)

Jacob 6: 13 bar of God s. wicked with fear; **Mosiah** 25: 7 Nephites are s. with wonder over records of Zeniff and Alma[1]; **Alma** 22: 18 Lamanite king is s. as if dead; 30: 50 Korihor is s. dumb; **Hel.** 5: 25 Lamanites are s. dumb with amazement over fire encircling Nephi[2] and Lehi[4].

STRIP

Alma 5: 28–29 those who are not s. of pride and envy are not prepared to meet God; 11: 2 man compelled to pay what he owes or be s.; **Morm.** 9: 28 s. yourselves of all uncleanness.

STRIPES

2 Ne. 28: 8 false churches claim sinners will be beaten with few s., then saved; **Mosiah** 14: 5 (Isa. 53: 5) with his s. are we healed.

STRIPLING (*see* Helaman[2], Sons of)

STRIVE, STRIVING (*see also* Work [verb])

1 Ne. 7: 14 Spirit ceases soon to s. with Jews; 17: 15 Nephi[1] s. to keep commandments; **2 Ne.** 26: 11 (Ether 2: 15) Spirit will not always s. with man, then comes destruction; **Mosiah** 27: 35 sons of Mosiah[2] s. to repair injuries done to church; **Hel.** 15: 6 converted Lamanites s. to bring remainder to knowledge of

truth; **Morm.** 5: 16 (Moro. 8: 28; 9: 4) Spirit hath already ceased to s. with Nephites; **Ether** 15: 19 Spirit ceases to s. with Jaredites.

STRONG, STRONGER (*see also* Mighty; Power; Strength; Strengthen)

1 Ne. 4: 2 let us be s. like unto Moses; 17: 2 women among Lehites are s. like unto men; **2 Ne.** 3: 13 out of weakness, latter-day seer shall be made s.; 15: 11 (Isa. 5: 11) wo unto those who rise early that they may follow s. drink; 27: 1 (Isa. 29: 9) ye who do iniquity shall stagger, but not with s. drink; **Mosiah** 18: 26 for their labor, priests receive grace of God, that they might wax s. in Spirit; **Alma** 17: 2 sons of Mosiah[2] have waxed s. in knowledge of truth; 48: 11 Moroni[1] a s. and mighty man; 50: 18 Nephites wax s. in land; 58: 40 faith of Ammonite youths is s. in that which is to come; **Hel.** 3: 35 humble part of Nephites wax s. and s. in humility; 11: 37 Nephites wax s. and s. in pride and wickedness; **Ether** 12: 27 the Lord makes weak things become s.; 12: 37 because thou hast seen thy weakness, thou shalt be made s.; **Moro.** 7: 30 angels show themselves unto them of s. faith.

STRONGHOLD (*see also* Fort, Fortify)

Alma 50: 6 Moroni[1] prepares s.; 52: 21 Moroni[1] plans to decoy Lamanites out of s.; 58: 2 Nephites dare not attack Lamanite s.; **Hel.** 1: 27 Lamanites capture many Nephite s.

STRUGGLE (*see also* Fight; Wrestle)

Enos 1: 10 while Enos[2] s. in spirit, the Lord's voice comes; **Mosiah** 7: 18 an effectual s. remaineth to be made.

STUBBLE

1 Ne. 22: 15, 23 (2 Ne. 26: 6; 3 Ne. 25: 1; Mal. 4: 1) they who do wickedly shall be as s., to be burned; **2 Ne.** 15: 24 (Isa. 5: 24) as fire devours s., the root of the wicked shall be rottenness.

STUBBORNNESS (*see also* Hard-heartedness; Pride; Stiffnecked)

Alma 32: 16 blessed is he who is baptized without s.; 51: 14 Moroni[1] is wroth because of s. of those he has labored to preserve.

STUDY (*see also* Knowledge; Learn; Ponder; Search)

Mosiah 13: 11 priests of Noah[3] have s. and taught iniquity.

STUMBLE (*see also* Err; Stumbling Block)

1 Ne. 13: 29, 34 many s. because parts of gospel are taken away; **2 Ne.** 26: 20 Gentiles have s. because of greatness of stumbling block, that they have built up

many churches; **Jacob** 4: 14 God has given Jews things they could not understand, that they may s.; 4: 15 by s. of Jews, they will reject stone upon which they might build safe foundation; **Ether** 12: 25 Nephite writers s. because of placing of words.

STUMBLING BLOCK (see also Stumble)

1 Ne. 14: 1 Lamb will manifest himself to Gentiles to take away their s.b.; **2 Ne.** 4: 33 wilt thou not place s.b. in my way; 18: 14 (Isa. 8: 14) he shall be for a stone of s. to both houses of Israel; 26: 20 Gentiles have stumbled because of greatness of s.b.; **Mosiah** 7: 29 doings of the Lord's people shall be as s.b.; **Alma** 4: 10 wickedness of church is s-b. to those who do not belong to church.

STUPOR

Alma 60: 7 can you sit upon thrones in thoughtless s.

SUBJECT, SUBJECTION (see also Bondage; Captive, Captivity; Conquer; Obedience; Prey; Reconcile; Submissive; Yield; Yoke)

2 Ne. 9: 5 Creator will suffer himself to become s. to man, that men might become s. to him; **Mosiah** 7: 18 Limhi's people will not be in s. to enemies; 15: 2 he shall be called Son, having s. flesh to Father's will; 15: 5 flesh to become s. to Spirit; 16: 11 (Alma 12: 17; 34: 35) spirits of the wicked delivered to devil, who hath s. them; **Alma** 5: 20 can ye think of being saved when ye have yielded yourselves to be s. to devil; 12: 6 adversary lays snare to bring people into s.; 34: 39 pray not to be led away as s. of devil; 42: 7 first parents became s. to follow after their own will; 43: 6–7 Zerahemnah appoints Nephite dissenters as captains over Lamanites, to bring them into s.; **Moro.** 7: 17 neither devil nor those who s. themselves to him persuade men to do good; 9: 26 Christ sits on right hand of power until all things become s. to him.

SUBMISSIVE, SUBMIT (see also Humble; Obedience; Patience; Reconcile; Subject; Yield)

Mosiah 3: 19 natural man is enemy to God unless he becomes as child, s., willing to s. to all things; **Alma** 7: 23 be s. and gentle; 13: 28 be led by Holy Spirit, becoming s.

SUBSTANCE (see also Charity; Property)

Jacob 2: 17 be free with your s.; **Mosiah** 4: 16–29 (18: 26–27; Alma 1: 27; 4: 13; 34: 28) administer of your s. unto those in need; **Hel.** 13: 28 Nephites would give s. to false prophet; **4 Ne.** 1: 25 Nephites no longer have s. in common;

Morm. 8: 37 ye love your s. more than ye love the poor.

SUBTLETY, SUBTLE (see also Craftiness; Cunning; Guile; Wiles)

2 Ne. 5: 24 Lamanites an idle people, full of mischief and s.; **Alma** 12: 4 Zeezrom's plan was s., as to s. of the devil; 47: 4 Amalickiah a s. man to do evil.

SUCCOR (see also Help; Relief; Strengthen)

Mosiah 4: 16 (Alma 4: 13) s. those who stand in need; 7: 29 the Lord will not s. his people in day of transgression; **Alma** 7: 12 Son to know according to flesh how to s. his people.

SUCK, SUCKING (see also Suckling)

1 Ne. 17: 2 women give plenty of s. for children; 21: 15 (Isa. 49: 15) can a woman forget her s. child; **2 Ne.** 21: 8 (30: 14; Isa. 11: 8) s. child shall play on hole of asp; **Hel.** 15: 2 women shall have great cause to mourn in day that they give s.

SUCKLING (see also Suck)

3 Ne. 28: 22 disciples play with wild beasts as child with s. lamb.

SUFFER [=allow] (see also Long-suffering; Suffering, Suffer)

1 Ne. 19: 9 (Mosiah 15: 5) world shall smite Messiah, and he shall s. it; 20: 11 (Isa. 11: 11) the Lord will not s. his name to be polluted; **2 Ne.** 26: 30 those who have charity would not s. laborer in Zion to perish; **Mosiah** 4: 14 ye will not s. your children to go hungry, to transgress; 4: 16 ye will not s. beggar to put up petition in vain; **Alma** 14: 10–11 the Lord s. the wicked to kill the righteous, that judgment might be just; **3 Ne.** 11: 11 Christ has s. will of Father in all things.

SUFFERING, SUFFER (see also Affliction; Anguish; Chasten; Despair; Infirmity; Misery; Mourn; Oppression; Pain; Sorrow; Tribulation; Trouble)

1 Ne. 18: 17 parents have s. much grief because of children; 19: 12 the God of nature s.; **2 Ne.** 9: 21–22 God s. pains of every living creature that resurrection might pass upon men; **Jacob** 1: 8 all men should s. Christ's cross; **Mosiah** 3: 7 (15: 5) the Lord shall s. temptations and pains even more than men can s.; 18: 1–2 Alma[1] teaches Abinadi's words concerning s. and death of Christ; **Alma** 7: 13 Son s. in flesh that he might take upon him his people's sins; 20: 29 brethren of Ammon[2] were patient in s.; 21: 9 no redemption for mankind, save through

death and s. of Christ; 26: 30 sons of Mosiah[2] have s. all manner of affliction that they might be means of saving one soul; 31: 38 the Lord has given his servants strength that they should s. no afflictions; **Hel.** 14: 20 on day that Christ s. death, sun shall be darkened; **3 Ne.** 6: 20 many prophets testify of Christ's death and s.; 28: 26, 38 change wrought in three Nephites that they might not s. pain or sorrow; **Moro.** 9: 25 may Christ's s. and death rest in your mind forever.

SUFFICIENT, SUFFICIENTLY

2 Ne. 2: 5 men are instructed s. that they know good from evil; 25: 28 words of Nephi[1] are s. to teach any man the right way; **Mosiah** 4: 24 those who have not and yet have s. should say, if I had I would give; **Alma** 5: 27 could ye say ye have been s. humble; 24: 11 it was all converted Lamanites could do to repent s.; **3 Ne.** 13: 34 (Matt. 6: 34) s. is the day unto the evil thereof; 17: 8 Nephites' faith is s. that Jesus should heal them; **Ether** 9: 35 when Jaredites humble themselves s., the Lord sends rain; 12: 26 the Lord's grace is s. for the meek; 12: 27 the Lord's grace is s. for all men who humble themselves; **Moro.** 10: 32 Christ's grace is s. for you to be perfect in him.

SUN (see also Astronomy)

1 Ne. 1: 9 Lehi[1] beholds one descending from heaven whose luster is above s. at noon-day; **2 Ne.** 23: 10 (Isa. 13: 10) s. shall be darkened; **Hel.** 12: 15 s. appears to stand still; 14: 4 (3 Ne. 1: 15–19) no darkness at setting of s. when Christ comes; 14: 20 (3 Ne. 8: 22) s. shall be darkened at Christ's death; **3 Ne.** 12: 45 (Matt. 5: 45) Father maketh his s. rise on the evil and the good.

SUNK

1 Ne. 12: 4 (3 Ne. 8: 14; 9: 4, 6, 8; 4 Ne. 1: 9) many cities to be s.; **3 Ne.** 10: 12–13 the righteous are spared and are not s.

SUPPLICATE, SUPPLICATION (see also Prayer)

Enos 1: 4 Enos[2] cries unto Maker in s. for his soul; **Alma** 7: 3 people of Gideon continue in s. of God's grace; 31: 10 Zoramites do not continue in s. to God daily; **3 Ne.** 4: 10 Nephites s. God for protection; **Moro.** 6: 9 saints preach, pray, s. in church meetings as led by Holy Ghost.

SUPPLY (see Provision)

SUPPORT (see also Help; Maintain; Preserve; Uphold)

2 Ne. 4: 20 my God hath been my

s.; **Mosiah** 2: 21 God s. you from one moment to another; 2: 30 the Lord doth s. me; 11: 3–4 Noah[3] taxes people for his s.; 11: 6 priests are s. in laziness by king's taxes; 18: 24 (27: 5) priests should labor with own hands for s.; 21: 17 Limhi commands that every man impart to s. of widows; **Alma** 30: 60 devil will not s. his children; 36: 3 whosoever puts trust in God shall be s. in trials; 46: 35 those who do not covenant to s. freedom are put to death; 48: 10 Moroni[1] prepares to s. liberty; 50: 39 chief judge appointed with oath to s. cause of God; 51: 17 pride of king-men to be pulled down, or they should s. cause of liberty; **Hel.** 6: 38 Nephites s. robbers; **Ether** 10: 6 Riplakish causes people to labor continually for their s.

SUPREME

Alma 11: 22 Zeezrom offers Amulek money to deny existence of S. Being; 12: 32 works of justice could not be destroyed according to s. goodness of God; 30: 44 earth and the planets witness there is a S. Creator.

SURE, SURETY

1 Ne. 5: 8 Sariah knows of s. that the Lord commanded Lehi[1] to flee; **2 Ne.** 25: 7 men shall know of s. when prophecies of Isaiah[1] come to pass; **Jacob** 4: 15–17 (Hel. 5: 12) stone rejected by Jews shall be only s. foundation; **Mosiah** 1: 6 we can know of s. of plates because we have seen them; 24: 14 people of Alma[1] to know of s. that the Lord visits his people in their afflictions; **Alma** 23: 6 as s. as the Lord liveth, converted Lamanites never fell away; 32: 17 many say they will know of s. if shown sign; 32: 26 ye cannot know of s. of words at first any more than faith is perfect knowledge; 32: 31 are you s. this is a good seed; **Hel.** 5: 12 rock of Redeemer is s. foundation; 13: 32, 38 your destruction is made s.; 14: 4 ye shall know of s. that there are two days and a night without darkness; **3 Ne.** 11: 15 after feeling Christ's wounds, multitude know of s. and bear record; **Ether** 12: 4 whoso believeth in God might with s. hope for better world; **Moro.** 7: 26 as s. as Christ liveth, he spoke these words to our fathers.

SWALLOW

1 Ne. 15: 27 mind of Lehi[1] so s. up in other things, he did not notice filthiness of river; **2 Ne.** 26: 5 earth shall s. those who kill prophets; **Mosiah** 15: 7 will of Son is s. up in will of Father; 16: 8 (Alma 22: 14; Morm. 7: 5) sting of death is s. in Christ; **Alma** 31: 27 men's hearts are s. up in pride; 31: 38 missionaries are s. up in joy of Christ; 36: 28 (Hel. 8: 11) the

Lord has s. up Egyptians in Red Sea; **Ether** 2: 25 Jaredites need light when s. in depths of sea.

SWEAR, SWARE, SWORN, SWEARING
(see also Oath; Promise; Swearer)

1 Ne. 20: 1 (Isa. 48: 1) Israel s. by name of the Lord but not in truth or righteousness; **Jacob** 1: 7 men should partake of goodness of God, lest he s. in wrath they should not enter in; **Mosiah** 19: 19 followers of Noah³ have s. they will return to land of Nephi; 20: 24 Lamanite king s. oath his people will not destroy Limhi's people; **Alma** 49: 27 Amalickiah s. oath to drink blood of Moroni¹; **Hel.** 1: 11 (Ether 8: 14) secret combination s. not to reveal murderer; **3 Ne.** 3: 8 Giddianhi s. not to destroy Nephites if they join robbers; 12: 33–37 (Matt. 5: 33–37) s. not at all; **Morm.** 3: 10, 14 Nephites s. by heavens they would go to battle against enemies; **Ether** 9: 5 secret combination s. by oath of ancients.

SWEARER

3 Ne. 24: 5 (Mal. 3: 5) the Lord will be swift witness against false s.

SWEEP, SWEPT (see also Destruction)

Jacob 5: 66 the Lord will s. away bad out of vineyard; **Enos** 1: 6 guilt of Enos¹ is s. away; **Jarom** 1: 3 God is merciful unto Nephites and has not s. them from land; **Ether** 2: 8 those in promised land who do not serve God shall be s. off; 14: 18 Shiz s. earth before him.

SWEET (see also Opposition)

1 Ne. 8: 10–11 (Alma 32: 42) fruit of tree is most s.; 17: 12 the Lord will make Lehites' food s., that they cook it not; **2 Ne.** 2: 15 forbidden fruit set in opposition to tree of life, one being s. and the other bitter; 15: 20 wo unto those who put bitter for s. and s. for bitter; **Alma** 36: 21 nothing could be so s. as joy of Alma² at being redeemed.

SWELL, SWELLING (see also Grow; Increase)

Alma 30: 31 Korihor rises up in great s. words before Alma²; 32: 30, 33 (33: 23) if seed s., ye must know it is good; 48: 12 heart of Moroni¹ s. with thanksgiving to God; **Hel.** 13: 22 your hearts s. with great pride.

SWIFT (see also Quick, Quickly)

1 Ne. 17: 45 elder brothers of Nephi¹ are s. to do iniquity; **Ether** 14: 22 so s. is war that none was left to bury dead.

SWINE (see also Sow [noun])

3 Ne. 14: 6 (Matt. 7: 6) do not cast your pearls before s.; **Ether** 9: 18 Jaredites have s.

SWORD (see also War; Weapon)

1 Ne. 1: 13 many inhabitants of Jerusalem shall perish by s.; 4: 9, 18–19 Nephi¹ cuts off Laban's head with his own s.; 21: 2 (Isa. 49: 2) the Lord hath made my mouth like sharp s.; **2 Ne.** 5: 14 (Jacob 1: 10; W of M 1: 13; Mosiah 1: 16) Nephites keep s. of Laban; 12: 4 (Isa. 2: 4) they shall beat s. into plow-shares; **Mosiah** 8: 11 Limhi's people find rusted s. in land northward; **Alma** 1: 12 Nehor has endeavored to enforce priestcraft by s.; 10: 22 Nephites would be destroyed by s. except for the righteous; 17: 37–38 Ammon² smites off Lamanites' arms with s.; 24: 12 since God has taken away stains and s. have become bright, let us stain s. no more; 24: 17 people of Anti-Nephi-Lehi bury s.; 26: 19 why did God not let s. of justice fall upon us; 42: 2–3 God placed cherubim and flaming s. to keep tree of life; 48: 14 Nephites are taught never to raise s. except against enemy; 60: 29 s. of justice hangs over you; 62: 5 thousands take up s. in defence of freedom; **Hel.** 11: 5 work of destruction ceases by s. and becomes sore by famine; 13: 5 s. of justice hangs over Nephites, to fall in four hundred years; **3 Ne.** 2: 19 s. of destruction hangs over Nephites; 20: 20 (Ether 8: 23) s. of the Lord's justice will fall upon Gentiles unless they repent; 29: 4 s. of the Lord's justice will overtake those who spurn his doings; **Morm.** 8: 41 s. of vengeance hangs over Nephites; **Ether** 7: 9 Shule makes s. of steel; 14: 4 many thousands fall by s.

SYNAGOGUE (see also Building; Sanctuary)

2 Ne. 26: 26 the Lord has not commanded any to depart out of s.; **Alma** 16: 13 Nephites build s. after manner of Jews; 21: 4, 6 Amalekites build s. after manner of Nehors; 26: 29 sons of Mosiah² have entered s. and taught Lamanites; 31: 12 Zoramites have built s.; 32: 2 Zoramites cast poor out of s.; **Hel.** 3: 9 people in land northward use timber to build s.; **3 Ne.** 13: 5 (Matt. 6: 5) hypocrites pray in s. to be seen of men; 18: 32 do not cast transgressor out of s.; **Moro.** 7: 1 Mormon² taught people in s.

TABERNACLE (see also Body; Building; BD Tabernacle)

2 Ne. 14: 6 (Isa. 4: 6) there shall be t. for shadow from heat and place of refuge; **Mosiah** 3: 5 (Alma 7: 8) God shall dwell in t. of clay; **Moro.** 9: 6 we have labor to perform while in t. of clay.

TAKE, TAKEN (see also Deprive)

1 **Ne.** 10: 10 Lamb should t. away sins of world; 13: 26–29, 40 plain and precious parts of gospel are t. away; 2 **Ne.** 26: 32 (Mosiah 13: 15; Ex. 20: 7) the Lord commands that men should not t. his name in vain; 31: 13 (Mosiah 5: 8, 10; Alma 34: 38; 46: 18, 21; 3 Ne. 27: 6; Morm. 8: 38; Moro. 4: 3) t. upon you name of Christ; **Mosiah** 7: 27 (Ether 3: 9, 16) Christ to t. upon himself image of man, t. upon himself flesh and blood; **Alma** 11: 40 (34: 8) Son shall t. upon himself transgressions of those who believe.

TALENT (see also TG Talents)

Ether 12: 35 if Gentiles have not charity, the Lord will take away their t.

TALK (see also Communication; Speak)

1 **Ne.** 16: 38 Nephi¹ says the Lord has t. with him; 2 **Ne.** 25: 26 Nephites t. of Christ; **Hel.** 5: 36 Nephi² and Lehi² are in attitude of t. to some being; **Ether** 2: 14 the Lord t. to brother of Jared² from cloud; 12: 39 Moroni² has t. with Jesus face to face.

TAME

Jacob 5: 3—6: 1 Israel likened to t. olive-tree.

TARRY (see also Abide; Remain; Wait)

1 **Ne.** 4: 35 Zoram¹ makes oath to t. with Lehites; 8: 2 Lehi¹ t. in wilderness; **Mosiah** 20: 4 priests of Noah³ t. in wilderness; 3 **Ne.** 17: 5 multitude ask Jesus to t. a little longer; 28: 4–12 (4 Ne. 1: 14, 30, 37; Morm. 8: 10; 9: 22) three Nephites allowed to t. until Christ's coming.

TASK (see also Burden; Labor)

1 **Ne.** 17: 25 children of Israel were laden with t. grievous to bear; **Jacob** 2: 10 notwithstanding greatness of t., I must do according to strict commands of God; **Mosiah** 24: 9 Amulon puts t-masters over people of Alma¹.

TASTE (see also Bitter; Eat; Partake; Sweet)

1 **Ne.** 8: 11 (11: 7) fruit of tree is sweet above all that Lehi¹ has t.; 8: 28 those who t. of fruit become ashamed; **Jacob** 5: 31 the Lord of vineyard t. of fruit; **Mosiah** 4: 11 if ye have t. of God's love, humble yourselves; **Alma** 36: 26 because of the word, many have t. as I have t.; 3 **Ne.** 28: 7, 25, 31–40 (Ether 12: 17) three Nephites shall never t. of death; **Morm.** 1: 15 Mormon² has t. of Jesus' goodness.

TAUGHT (see Teach, Taught)

TAX (see also Government, Civil; Support; Tribute)

Mosiah 2: 14 Benjamin labors with own hands, that people might not be laden with t.; **Mosiah** 7: 15 (11: 3) Limhi's people are t. with grievous t. of one-fifth of possessions; **Ether** 10: 5 Riplakish t. his people with heavy t.; 10: 6 those who would not be subject to t. are cast into prison.

TEACH, TAUGHT (see also Doctrine; Expound; Instruction, Instruct; Learn; Liken; Preach; Reasoning; Sayings; Teacher; TG Jesus Christ, Teaching Mode of; Teachable; Teaching, Teach; Teaching with the Spirit)

1 **Ne.** 1: 1 Nephi¹ was t. in learning of father; 20: 17 (Isa. 48: 17) the Lord t. thee to profit; 2 **Ne.** 25: 28 words of Nephi¹ are sufficient to t. any man right way; 28: 14 men err because they are t. precepts of men; 32: 8 hearken unto Spirit which t. men to pray; 32: 8 evil spirit t. that man must not pray; 33: 1 Nephi¹ cannot write all things t. among Nephites; 33: 10 these words t. that all men should do good; **Jacob** 1: 19 priests answer sins of people upon own heads if they do not t. diligently; **Enos** 1: 1 Jacob² t. Enos² in his language, nurture and admonition of the Lord; **Omni** 1: 18 people of Zarahemla are t. language of Mosiah¹; **Mosiah** 1: 2 Benjamin t. sons in language of fathers; 4: 15 t. children to walk in ways of soberness, to love and serve one another; 9: 1 Zeniff has been t. in language of Nephites; 13: 11 priests of Noah³ have studied and t. iniquity; 18: 26 priests to have knowledge of God, that they might t. with power and authority; **Alma** 17: 3 sons of Mosiah² t. with power and authority; 29: 8 God grants unto all nations, of their own tongue, to t. his word; 37: 34 t. them never to be weary of good works, but to be meek; 48: 14 Nephites are t. to defend themselves, t. never to give offense; 53: 21 Ammonite youths had been t. to keep commandments; 56: 47 (57: 21) Ammonite youths had been t. by mothers that God would deliver them; 3 **Ne.** 22: 13 (Isa. 54: 13) thy children shall be t. of the Lord; 26: 6 only small part of what Jesus t. can be recorded; 4 **Ne.** 1: 38 those who rebel against gospel t. children not to believe; 1: 39 Lamanites are t. to hate children of God; **Ether** 6: 17 Jaredites are t. from on high to walk humbly before the Lord; **Moro.** 10: 9 to one is given to t. word of wisdom; 10: 10 to another is given to t. word of knowledge.

TEACHER (see also Priesthood; Teach; TG Teacher)

1 **Ne.** 2: 22 (16: 37; 2 Ne. 5: 19) Nephi¹ to be made t. over brethren; 2 **Ne.** 5: 26 (Jacob 1: 18) Nephi¹ consecrates Jacob² and Joseph² as priests and t.; 9:

48 Nephites look to Jacob[2] as t.; 28: 12 churches to become corrupted because of false t.; **Jarom** 1: 11 t. labor diligently, exhorting people to diligence; **Mosiah** 2: 29 Benjamin can no longer be Nephites' t. and king; 23: 14 trust no man to be t. except he be man of God; 23: 17 (Alma 4: 7; 15: 13) Alma[1] consecrates just men as t.; 25: 19 Mosiah[2] gives Alma[1] power to ordain t. over every church; **Alma** 1: 15 Nehor declares every t. ought to become popular; 1: 26 t. is not esteemed any better than learner; 23: 4 Aaron[2] and brethren appoint t. over all churches in land of Lamanites; **Morm.** 8: 28 t. in churches shall rise in pride; **Moro.** ch. 3 manner in which elders ordained t.; 6: 1 t. are baptized.

TEANCUM—*great Nephite military leader* [c. 67 B.C.]

Alma 50: 35 slays Morianton[2]; 51: 29–32 defeats army of Amalickiah; 51: 33–34 slays Amalickiah; 52: 1–6 prepares to battle Lamanites; 52: 17–20 is ordered to attack city of Mulek; 52: 22–28 decoys Lamanites and scatters them; 53: 3 sets prisoners to work; 61: 18 (62: 13) food sought for T's army; 62: 3 T. and Lehi[3] are given command over remainder of army of Moroni[1]; 62: 35–36 slays Ammoron and is slain.

TEANCUM, CITY OF—*by seashore near City of Desolation*

Morm. 4: 3 Nephites flee to T.; 4: 6–8 Lamanites attack T., are repulsed; 4: 14 is taken by Lamanites, and women and children are sacrificed to idols.

TEARS (*see also* Joy; Sorrow; Weep)

1 Ne. 18: 19 wife and children of Nephi[1] and children do not soften brothers' hearts with t.; **Mosiah** 25: 9 Nephites shed t. of sorrow over brethren slain by Lamanites; **Alma** 19: 28 Abish sorrows unto t. over contention among Lamanites; **3 Ne.** 4: 33 Nephites' hearts are swollen with joy, unto gushing out of t.; 17: 5 multitude are in t.; 17: 10 Nephites bathe Christ's feet with t.; **Ether** 6: 12 Jaredites shed t. of joy because of the Lord's tender mercies.

TEETH (*see* Tooth, Teeth)

TELL, TOLD (*see also* Declare; Discern; Rehearse; Revelation, Reveal; Teach)

2 Ne. 28: 22 devil t. men there is no hell; 31: 17 do things I have t. you I have seen the Lord do; 32: 3 words of Christ will t. you all things ye should do; **Jacob** 2: 5 by help of Creator I can t. your thoughts; **Alma** 37: 15 Alma[2] t. Helaman[2] by spirit of prophecy that sacred things will be taken if he transgresses; **Hel.** 9: 41 Nephi[2] t. Nephites thoughts of

hearts; **3 Ne.** 20: 45 (21: 8) that which kings had not been t. them shall they see; 28: 15 whether three Nephites were in or out of body the multitude cannot t.; **Ether** 13: 2 Ether t. Jaredites of all things from beginning; **Moro.** 7: 21 I t. you the way whereby ye may lay hold on every good thing; 9: 19 tongue cannot t. of Nephites' perversion.

TEMPERATE (*see also* TG Temperance)

Alma 7: 23 (38: 10) be t. in all things.

TEMPEST (*see also* Destruction; Storm; Whirlwind; Wind)

1 Ne. 18: 13–21 great t. arises during journey to promised land; 19: 11 the Lord will visit house of Israel by t.; **2 Ne.** 6: 15 they who believe not in Messiah shall be destroyed by t.; 27: 12 all nations of Gentiles and Jews to be visited with t.; **Hel.** 14: 23 (3 Ne. 8: 6) great t. at Christ's death; **Morm.** 8: 29 there shall be heard of t. in foreign lands; **Ether** 6: 6 Jaredite vessels buried in depths of sea because of great t.

TEMPLE (*see also* Body; Building; House; Sanctuary; Tabernacle; TG Temple; Temple, House of the Lord; BD Temple)

2 Ne. 5: 16 Nephi[1] builds t. after manner of Solomon; 12: 2 (Isa. 2: 2) mountain of the Lord's house shall be established in top of mountains; 16: 1 (Isa. 6: 1) the Lord's train filled the t.; **Jacob** 1: 17 Jacob[2] teaches in t.; 2: 11 the Lord commands Jacob[2] to declare word in t.; **Mosiah** 1: 18 Benjamin gathers his people at t.; 2: 37 (Alma 7: 21; 34: 36) the Lord dwells not in unholy t.; **Alma** 10: 2 Aminadi interpreted writing upon wall of t., written by finger of the Lord; 16: 13 Alma[2] and Amulek preach in t.; 23: 2 (26: 29) sons of Mosiah[2] are given free access to Lamanites' t.; 34: 36 (Hel. 4: 24) the Lord's Spirit dwells not in unholy t.; **Hel.** 10: 8 Nephi[2] is given power to rend t. in twain; **3 Ne.** 11: 1 multitude is gathered around t. when Christ appears; 24: 1 (Mal. 3: 1) the Lord shall suddenly come to his t.

TEMPORAL, TEMPORALLY (*see also* Death, Physical; Flesh; Mortal; Nature, Natural; Outward; Spiritual, Spiritually; World)

1 Ne. 14: 7 the hardhearted shall be led down to destruction, t. and spiritually; 15: 26–32 river of filthy water is representation of things both t. and spiritual; 22: 6 these things of which are spoken are t.; **2 Ne.** 2: 5 by t. law men were cut off; **Mosiah** 2: 41 those who keep commandments are blessed in all things, both t. and spiritual; 4: 26 administer to relief of poor, both spiritually and t.; 18: 29

Nephites impart to each other both *t*. and spiritually; **Alma** 7: 23 ask for whatsoever things ye stand in need, both *t*. and spiritual; 12: 31 men first transgressed first commandments as to things which were *t*. and became as Gods, knowing good and evil; 36: 4 Alma[2] knows these things, not of the *t*. but of the spiritual; 42: 7 first parents were cut off both *t*. and spiritually; 42: 9 fall brought upon mankind spiritual death as well as *t*. death; **Hel.** 14: 16 being cut off from presence of God by fall, all mankind were dead both as to things *t*. and spiritual; **Morm.** 2: 15 day of grace is past with Nephites, both *t*. and spiritually.

TEMPT, TEMPTATION (*see also* Agency; Devil; Entice; Probation; Prove; Seduce; TG Tempt, Temptation; BD Tempt)

   1 Ne. 12: 17 mists of darkness are *t*. of devil; 12: 19 because of *t*. of devil, Lamanites' seed overpower Nephites' seed; 15: 24 *t*. of adversary cannot overpower those who hearken unto word of God; **2 Ne.** 4: 27 why should I give way to *t*., that evil one have place in my heart; 17: 12 (Isa. 7: 12) neither will I *t*. the Lord; **Jacob** 7: 14 what am I that I should *t*. God; **Mosiah** 3: 7 (15: 5; Alma 7: 11) the Lord shall suffer *t*., but shall not yield; **Alma** 11: 23 why *t*. ye me, the righteous yield to no such *t*.; 13: 28 pray that ye be not *t*. above what ye can bear; 30: 44 will ye *t*. your God; 31: 10 Zoramites do not pray that they might not enter into *t*.; 34: 39 (3 Ne. 13: 12; 18: 18; Morm. 9: 28) pray that ye may not be led away by *t*. of devil; 37: 33 teach them to withstand every *t*. of devil with faith in Christ; **3 Ne.** 2: 3 Satan leads away hearts of people, *t*. them; 6: 15 Satan causes iniquity by *t*. people to seek for power and riches; 6: 17 people had been delivered up to be carried about by *t*. of devil; 13: 12 (Matt. 6: 13) lead us not into *t*.; 18: 25 whosoever breaks this commandment suffers himself to be led into *t*.; 28: 39 change wrought in three Nephites, that Satan could not *t*. them.

TEN (*see also* Israel, Ten Lost Tribes of; Ten Commandments; Tithes)

   Morm. 1: 2 Mormon[2] is *t*. years old when Ammaron comes to him.

TEN COMMANDMENTS (*see also* Commandments of God; TG Ten Commandments; BD Commandments, the Ten)

   Mosiah 12: 33–36; 13: 12–24 Abinadi teaches T.C.

TENDER (*see also* Gentle; Mercy)

   1 Ne. 8: 37 Lehi[1] exhorts sons with all feeling of *t*. parent; **Jacob** 2: 7, 9 Jacob[2] is grieved to speak with boldness

before wives and children, whose feelings are *t*. and delicate; **Mosiah** 14: 2 (Isa. 53: 2) he shall grow up before him as *t*. plant.

TENT

   1 Ne. 2: 15 Lehi[1] dwells in *t*.; 16: 12 Lehites take *t*. and depart; 18: 23 Lehites pitch *t*. in promised land; **2 Ne.** 5: 7 Nephi[1] and followers take *t*. and depart into wilderness; **Enos** 1: 20 Lamanites dwell in *t*.; **Mosiah** 2: 5–6 Benjamin's people pitch *t*. around temple; 18: 34 Alma[1] and people take *t*. and flee into wilderness; **Alma** 2: 20 Nephite army pitch *t*. in valley of Gideon; 46: 31 Nephite army marches with *t*. into wilderness; **Ether** 2: 13 Jaredites pitch *t*. by sea; 9: 3 Omer and household pitch *t*. in Ablom by seashore; 15: 11 army of Coriantumr[2] pitch *t*. by hill Ramah.

TENTH (*see* Tithes)

TEOMNER—*Nephite military officer* [c. 63 B.C.]

   Alma 58: 16–23 takes part in successful ambush of Lamanites.

TERROR, TERRIBLE (*see also* Fear, Fearful; Harrow; Horror)

   1 Ne. 12: 5 multitudes fall because of *t*. judgments of the Lord; 12: 18 *t*. gulf divides building and tree; **2 Ne.** 20: 33 (Isa. 10: 33) the Lord shall lop bough with *t*.; **3 Ne.** 4: 7 *t*. battle between Nephites and armies of Giddianhi; 8: 6 tempest at death of Christ; 8: 24–25 O that we had repented before great and *t*. day; 22: 14 (Isa. 54: 14) *t*. for oppressions shall not come near thee; **Morm.** 6: 8 every soul filled with *t*. because of greatness of Lamanites' numbers; **Ether** 6: 6 Jaredite vessels buried in sea because of *t*. tempests.

TESTIFY (*see also* Manifest; Preach; Prove; Record; Testimony; Verified; Witness)

   1 Ne. 10: 5 (Jacob 7: 11; 3 Ne. 7: 10; 20: 24) great number of prophets have *t*. of Messiah; **2 Ne.** 3: 6–21 Joseph[1] *t*. concerning latter-day seer; 27: 12 three witnesses will *t*. to truth of book; **Jacob** 7: 11 (Alma 34: 30) scriptures *t*. of Christ; **Alma** 5: 45–46 Alma[2] *t*. to truth of what he has said; 7: 26 Alma[2] has spoken according to Spirit which *t*. in him; 14: 3 Alma[2] and Amulek have *t*. plainly concerning lawyers' wickedness; 34: 8 Amulek *t*. that words of prophets concerning Christ are true; **Hel.** 8: 9 if Nephi[2] were not a prophet, he could not *t*. concerning these things; 13: 26 Nephites would reject prophet who *t*. of their sins; **3 Ne.** 6: 20 inspired men *t*. boldly of Nephites' sins and redemption of Christ.

TESTIMONY (*see also* Faith; Holy Ghost; Know, Knowledge; Revelation; Testify; Witness; TG Testimony)

2 Ne. 18: 16 (Isa. 8: 16) bind up the *t.*; 25: 28 words of Nephi[1] to stand as *t.* against his people; 27: 13 few others will view book to bear *t.*; 29: 8 *t.* of two nations that the Lord is God will run together; **Alma** 4: 19 Alma[2] reclaims people by bearing down in pure *t.* against them; 4: 20 Alma[2] confines himself wholly to *t.* of word; 6: 8 Alma[2] declares word of God according to *t.* of Jesus Christ; 7: 13 Alma[2] bears *t.* of atonement through Son; 7: 16 whosoever keeps commandments shall have eternal life, according to *t.* of Holy Spirit; 30: 40–41 all things are *t.* that Christ's coming is true; **Ether** 5: 4 *t.* of three and this work shall stand as *t.* against world; **Moro.** 7: 31 angels declare word of Christ to chosen vessels that they may bear *t.* of him.

THANK, THANKS (*see also* Blessing; Indebted; Praise; Rejoice; Thankful; Thanksgiving)

1 Ne. 2: 7 (5: 9–10; 7: 22) Lehi[1] builds altar and gives *t.* to the Lord; **2 Ne.** 9: 52 give *t.* unto God's holy name by night; 29: 4 what *t.* the Gentiles the Jews for the Bible; **Mosiah** 2: 19 you ought to *t.* your heavenly King; 2: 20–21 if you should render all *t.* to God, yet would you be unprofitable servants; 8: 19 Limhi rejoices and gives *t.* to God; 24: 21 people of Alma[1] pour out *t.* unto God because he has been merciful to them; 26: 39 teachers are commanded to give *t.* in all things; **Alma** 7: 23 always return *t.* to God for whatsoever things you receive; 24: 7 Lamanite king *t.* God that he has sent Nephites to preach to them; 26: 8 let us give *t.* to God's holy name; 37: 37 when thou risest in morning, let thy heart be full of *t.* unto God; 49: 28 Nephites *t.* God because of his matchless power in delivering them; **Morm.** 9: 31 give *t.* unto God that he hath made manifest unto you your imperfections; **Ether** 6: 9 brother of Jared[2] *t.* the Lord all day long.

THANKFUL (*see also* Thank, Thanks; Thanksgiving)

Jacob 4: 3 teachers hope brethren and children will receive writings with *t.* hearts; **Mosiah** 7: 12 Ammon[1] is *t.* before God that he is permitted to speak.

THANKSGIVING (*see also* Thank, Thanks; Thankful)

2 Ne. 8: 3 (Isa. 51: 3) *t.* shall be found in Zion; **Alma** 19: 14 Ammon[2] pours out soul in *t.* to God; 34: 38 live in *t.* daily; 48: 12 heart of Moroni[1] swells with *t.* to God; **3 Ne.** 10: 10 Nephites' lamentations are turned in *t.* unto Christ.

THIEF, THIEVES, THIEVING (*see also* Rob; Robber; Steal)

Alma 1: 32 those who do not belong to church indulge in *t.*; 11: 2 those who do not pay what they owe are cast out as *t.*; **3 Ne.** 13: 19–20 (27: 32; Matt. 6: 19–20) lay not up treasures upon earth, where *t.* break through and steal; **Morm.** 2: 10 no man can keep what is his own because of *t.*

THINK, THOUGHT (*see also* Consider; Imagination; Intent; Ponder; Reasoning; Thoughts)

2 Ne. 9: 28 when men are learned, they *t.* they are wise; **Jacob** 2: 17 *t.* of your brethren like unto yourselves; **Mosiah** 23: 7 one man shall not *t.* himself above another; **Moro.** 7: 45 (1 Cor. 13: 5) charity *t.* no evil.

THIRD (*see also* Three)

Mosiah 3: 10 Christ shall rise from the dead the *t.* day; 13: 13 (Ex. 20: 5) the Lord visits iniquities of fathers upon children unto *t.* and fourth generation; **Hel.** 5: 33 voice comes *t.* time; **3 Ne.** 11: 5–6 multitude understand voice the *t.* time they hear it.

THIRST (*see also* Athirst; Blood-thirsty; Drink; Water)

1 Ne. 16: 35 (Alma 37: 42) Lehites have suffered *t.* in wilderness; 17: 29 Moses brings water from rock to quench Israel's *t.*; 20: 21 (Isa. 48: 21) they *t.* not; 21: 10 (Isa. 49: 10) they shall not hunger nor *t.*; **2 Ne.** 7: 2 (Isa. 50: 2) the Lord makes rivers a wilderness and they die of *t.*; 9: 50 every one that *t.*, come to waters; **Alma** 32: 42 those who feast upon fruit of tree shall not *t.*; **3 Ne.** 12: 6 (Matt. 5: 6) blessed are they who hunger and *t.* after righteousness; 20: 8 he who partakes of sacrament shall never hunger nor *t.*; **Moro.** 9: 5 Lamanites *t.* after blood and revenge continually.

THISTLE

Mosiah 12: 12 thou shalt be as blossoms of *t.*; **3 Ne.** 14: 16 (Matt. 7: 16) do men gather figs of *t.*

THORN

2 Ne. 15: 6 (Isa. 5: 6) I shall lay it waste and briers and *t.* shall come up; 17: 23 (Isa. 7: 23) every place shall be for briers and *t.*; 19: 18 (Isa. 9: 18) wickedness burns as fire, shall devour briers and *t.*; 20: 17 (Isa. 10: 17) light of Israel shall burn his *t.* and briers; **3 Ne.** 14: 16 (Matt. 7: 16) do men gather grapes of *t.*

THOUGHTS (*see also* Imagination; Think; Thought)

Jacob 2: 5 by help of Creator, Jacob[2]

can tell people's *t.*; **Mosiah** 4: 30 if ye do not watch your *t.*, ye must perish; 24: 12 the Lord knows *t.* of hearts of Alma[1] and his people; **Alma** 10: 17 Amulek perceives lawyers' *t.*; 12: 3 God knows Zeezrom's *t.* and makes them known through Spirit; 12: 14 our *t.* will condemn us; 18: 18 Ammon[2] discerns Lamoni's *t.*; 18: 32 God knows all *t.* and intents of our hearts; 31: 37 missionaries take no *t.* for themselves; 32: 38 if ye take no *t.* for nourishment of tree, it will take no root; 36: 14 *t.* of coming into God's presence racked Alma[2] with horror; 37: 36 let thy *t.* be directed unto the Lord; **Hel.** 9: 41 people believe Nephi[2] is a god because he tells their *t.*; **3 Ne.** 28: 6 Christ knows *t.* of three Nephites; **Moro.** 8: 14 he who is cut off in *t.* of baptism for little children must go down to hell.

THOUSAND (*see also* Millennium)

Hel. 8: 18 coming of redemption shown to people many *t.* years before Christ's coming; **3 Ne.** 3: 24 many *t.* Nephites gather in one place against robbers.

THRASH (*see also* Harvest; Reap)

Ether 10: 25 Jaredites make tools to *t.*

THREATEN, THREATENINGS (*see also* Danger; Warn)

1 Ne. 18: 20 nothing save power of God, which *t.* destruction, could soften hearts; **Jarom** 1: 10 prophets *t.* Nephites with destruction; **Alma** 26: 18 sons of Mosiah[2] went forth with mighty *t.* to destroy church; **3 Ne.** 2: 13 Nephites are *t.* with utter destruction because of war; 4: 12 notwithstanding Giddianhi's *t.*, Nephites beat robbers.

THREE (*see also* Third; Three Nephite Disciples; Thrice; Witnesses, Three)

1 Ne. 2: 6 Lehites travel *t.* days from Jerusalem; 12: 11 (2 Ne. 26: 9) *t.* generations to pass away in righteousness after Christ's visit; 19: 10 (Hel. 14: 20, 27; 3 Ne. 8: 3, 23; 10: 9) *t.* days of darkness a sign of Christ's death; **2 Ne.** 11: 3 (27: 12; Ether 5: 3–4) by words of *t.* will the Lord establish his word; 25: 13 (Mosiah 3: 10) Christ to rise from dead after *t.* days; **Alma** 36: 10, 16 (38: 8) Alma[2] was racked with torment for *t.* days and nights; **Hel.** 1: 4 *t.* sons of Pahoran[1] contend for judgment-seat, cause *t.* divisions among people; **3 Ne.** 8: 19 tempest for *t.* hours at Christ's death; 26: 13 Christ teaches Nephites for *t.* days; **Ether** 13: 28 Shared fights Coriantumr[2] for *t.* days; **Moro.** 6: 7 if *t.* witnesses condemn unrepentant transgressor, he should not be numbered among people of Christ.

THREE NEPHITE DISCIPLES

3 Ne. 28: 1–6 Christ grants *t.* disciples' desire to tarry until his coming; 28: 7–9 shall never taste of death, sorrow; 28: 10 shall have fulness of joy; 28: 13–17 are caught up into heaven; 28: 18, 23 minister unto people; 28: 19–22 endure persecution; 28: 25 names not given; 28: 26 (Morm. 8: 11) have ministered unto Mormon[2]; 28: 27–29 to minister to Gentiles, Jews, scattered tribes, all nations; 28: 30 can show themselves to whomever it seems to them good; 28: 32 (4 Ne. 1: 5) to do marvelous works; 28: 36–40 change wrought upon their bodies; 28: 39 are sanctified in flesh, Satan has no power over them; **4 Ne.** 1: 14 only disciples of original twelve who still tarry; **Morm.** 8: 10 are taken from people because of wickedness; 8: 11 have ministered unto Moroni[2].

THRICE (*see also* Three)

3 Ne. 28: 21 disciples *t.* cast into furnace without harm; **Morm.** 3: 13 *t.* has Mormon[2] delivered Nephites from enemies.

THRONE (*see also* Dominion; Judgment-seat; Kingdom of God)

1 Ne. 1: 8 Lehi[1] sees God sitting upon *t.*; 17: 39 (3 Ne. 12: 34; Matt. 5: 34) the heavens are God's *t.*; **2 Ne.** 16: 1 (Isa. 6: 1) Isaiah[1] sees God sitting upon *t.*; 24: 13 (Isa. 14: 13) Lucifer would exalt his *t.* above stars of God; 28: 23 spirits of the wicked must stand before *t.* of God to be judged; **Jacob** 3: 8 Lamanites' skins may be whiter than Nephites' when brought before *t.* of God; **Morm.** 3: 10 Nephites swear by *t.* of God they will defeat enemies; **Moro.** 9: 26 God's *t.* is high in the heavens.

THROW, THROWN (*see also* Cast; Destruction)

1 Ne. 17: 48 brothers desire to *t.* Nephi[1] into sea; **3 Ne.** 21: 18 (Micah 3: 15) I will *t.* down all thy strongholds.

THRUST (*see also* Cast)

2 Ne. 9: 34, 36 (28: 15) liars and those who commit whoredoms shall be *t.* down to hell; 23: 15 (Isa. 13: 15) the proud shall be *t.* through; 28: 15 those who are proud, preach false doctrine, pervert right way of the Lord shall be *t.* down to hell; **Alma** 26: 5 missionaries *t.* in sickle and reap; **3 Ne.** 11: 14–15 multitude *t.* hands into Christ's side.

THUNDER, THUNDERINGS (*see also* Lightning; Warn, Warning)

1 Ne. 12: 4 Nephi[1] beholds *t.* in promised land; 17: 45 the Lord has spoken to Laman[1] and Lemuel with voice of *t.*;

19: 11 (2 Ne. 26: 6) the Lord will visit Israel with *t*. of his power; **2 Ne.** 27: 2 Gentiles to be visited with *t*.; **Mosiah** 27: 11 (Alma 36: 7; 38: 7) angel speaks to Alma² and companions with voice of *t*.; **Hel.** 5: 30 voice of dissenters in prison was not voice of *t*.; 14: 21, 26–27 (3 Ne. 8: 6) *t*. at death of Christ.

TIDINGS (*see also* Gospel; Message)

1 Ne. 13: 37 (Mosiah 12: 21; 15: 18; 3 Ne. 20: 40; Isa. 52: 7) how beautiful upon mountains are feet of him who brings good *t*.; **Mosiah** 3: 3 angel comes to declare *t*. of great joy to Benjamin; 27: 37 sons of Mosiah² publish good *t*. of good; **Alma** 13: 22 the Lord declares day of salvation to all nations, that they might have glad *t*. of great joy; 39: 15 Christ comes to declare glad *t*. of salvation; **Hel.** 5: 29 seek no more to destroy my servant whom I have sent to declare good *t*.; 16: 14 angels appear and declare glad *t*. of great joy; **3 Ne.** 1: 26 appearance of signs brings glad *t*.

TIGHT

Ether 2: 17 (6: 7) Jaredite vessels are *t*. like dish.

TILL (*see also* Plant; Plow; Sow [verb])

1 Ne. 18: 24 Lehites begin to *t*. earth in promised land; **2 Ne.** 2: 19 (Alma 42: 2) Adam and Eve driven out of garden of Eden, to *t*. earth; **Enos** 1: 21 (Mosiah 6: 7) Nephites *t*. the land; **Jarom** 1: 8 Nephites make tools to *t*.; **Mosiah** 6: 7 Mosiah² *t*. earth to avoid burdening his people; 9: 9 (10: 4) Zeniff's people begin to *t*. ground; **Ether** 6: 13 Jaredites begin to *t*. earth in promised land; 10: 25 Jaredites make tools to *t*. earth.

TIMBER (*see also* Wood)

1 Ne. 18: 1 Nephi¹ works *t*. of ship after manner shown by the Lord; **Alma** 50: 2 (53: 4) *t*. used in fortification; **Hel.** 3: 5 Nephites spread into parts of land northward not rendered desolate and without *t*.; 3: 6–7, 9–10 *t*. scarce in land northward.

TIME (*see also* Day; Eternity; Full; Fulness; Generation; Hour; Reckon; Season; Space; Today; Tomorrow; Week; TG Time)

1 Ne. 10: 3 Jerusalem to be destroyed according to the Lord's due *t*.; 14: 26 (Morm. 5: 12) records to come forth in the Lord's due *t*.; **2 Ne.** 2: 3 in fulness of *t*. Redeemer shall come; 2: 21 (Alma 42: 4) men's *t*. was lengthened, that they might repent; 6: 14 (21: 11; 25: 17; Isa. 11: 11) Messiah will set himself the second *t*. to restore his people; 27: 10, 21 sealed revelation to be kept in book until the

Lord's due *t*.; 30: 18 Satan shall have no power for long *t*.; **Jacob** 5: 15, 29 the Lord of vineyard leaves vineyard alone for long *t*.; 5: 31 this long *t*. we have nourished this tree; 5: 76 the Lord of vineyard will lay up fruit for long *t*.; 5: 76 the Lord has nourished vineyard for last *t*.; **Alma** 12: 24 (34: 32; 42: 4) this life became *t*. to prepare to meet God; 34: 33 if we do not improve *t*. in this life, then cometh night of darkness; 40: 5–10 *t*. appointed unto all men to arise from dead; **3 Ne.** 2: 8 Nephites reckon *t*. from birth of Christ; 20: 29 the Lord will gather his people in own due *t*.; 24: 11 (Mal. 3: 11) vine shall not cast fruit before *t*. in fields.

TIMOTHY—*brother of Nephi³* [c. A.D. 34]

3 Ne. 19: 4 had been raised from dead by Nephi³, called by Jesus as one of twelve disciples.

TITHES (*see also* BD Tithe)

Alma 13: 15 Abraham paid *t*. to Melchizedek; **3 Ne.** 24: 8 (Mal. 3: 8) men have robbed God in *t*. and offerings; 24: 10 (Mal. 3: 10) bring *t*. into storehouse.

TITLE OF LIBERTY (*see also* Banner; Standard)

Alma 46: 12–13 Moroni¹ makes *t. of l*. on his rent coat; 46: 20 those who would maintain *t*. should enter covenant; 46: 36 Moroni¹ causes *t*. to be hoisted upon every tower; 51: 20 dissenters compelled to hoist *t*. upon their towers.

TITTLE (*see* Jot)

TODAY (*see also* Time)

1 Ne. 10: 18 (2 Ne. 27: 23; 29: 9; Alma 31: 17; Morm. 9: 9; Moro. 10: 19) God is same, yesterday, *t*., and forever; **2 Ne.** 2: 4 Spirit is same, yesterday, *t*., and forever; **Moro.** 10: 7 God works by power according to men's faith, same *t*., tomorrow, forever.

TOIL (*see* Spin)

TOKEN (*see also* Sign; Type)

Alma 46: 21 people rend garments as *t*. they will not forsake the Lord; 47: 23 Lamanite king puts forth hand to raise Amalickiah's servants as *t*. of peace; **Moro.** 9: 10 Nephites devour flesh as *t*. of bravery.

TOLD (*see* Tell, Told)

TOLERABLE (*see also* Bear, Bore, Borne)

Alma 9: 15 more *t*. for Lamanites at judgment unless Nephites repent.

TOMORROW (*see also* Morrow; Time; Today)

2 Ne. 28: 7–8 eat, drink, and be merry, for *t.* we die.

TONGUE (*see also* Gift; Holy Ghost; Interpretation; Language; Mouth; Nation; Speak; Speech; Spirit; Gifts of; Word; TG Tongue)

1 Ne. 5: 18 (Alma 37: 4) records to go forth to every *t.*; 11: 36 all *t.* that fight against apostles shall be destroyed; 14: 11 abominable church has dominion among all *t.*; 19: 17 (Mosiah 16: 1) every *t.* shall see salvation of the Lord; 22: 28 all *t.* to dwell safely in Holy One if they repent; **2 Ne.** 13: 8 (Isa. 3: 8) Judah is fallen because their *t.* have been against the Lord; 26: 13 Christ manifests himself to all who believe, every *t.*; 30: 8 the Lord shall commence his work among all *t.*; 31: 13–14 (32: 2) after receiving Holy Ghost, ye can speak with *t.* of angels; **Omni** 1: 25 believe in gift of speaking with *t.*; **Mosiah** 3: 13 the Lord has sent angels to declare word to every *t.*; 15: 28 salvation of the Lord to be declared to every *t.*; 27: 25 all *t.* must be born again; **Alma** 9: 20 Nephites have been favored above every other *t.*; 9: 21 Nephites have had gift of speaking with *t.*; 29: 8 the Lord grants unto all nations, of their own *t.*, to teach his word; 45: 16 land to be cursed to every *t.* which does wickedly; **3 Ne.** 17: 17 (19: 32) no *t.* can relate marvelous things Jesus spoke; 22: 17 (Isa. 54: 17) every *t.* that rises against thee thou shalt condemn; 26: 14 Jesus looses *t.* of children, that they speak marvelous things; **Morm.** 4: 11 impossible for *t.* to describe scene of carnage; 9: 7–8 he who denies speaking with *t.* knows not gospel; 9: 24 those who believe shall speak with new *t.*; **Moro.** 7: 9 who can say there is no speaking with *t.*; 9: 19 *t.* cannot tell suffering of women and children; 10: 15 to another is given all kinds of *t.*; 10: 16 to another is given interpretation of languages and divers kinds of *t.*

TOOK (*see* Take, Taken)

TOOL

1 Ne. 17: 9–10, 16 Nephi[1] makes *t.* of ore to construct ship; **Jarom** 1: 8 Nephites make all manner of *t.*; **Hel.** 13: 34 (Ether 14: 1) we lay *t.* here and on morrow it is gone; **Ether** 10: 25–26 Jaredites make all manner of *t.*

TOOTH, TEETH

Mosiah 16: 2 (Alma 40: 13) the wicked shall be cast out, to weep, wail, gnash *t.*; **Alma** 14: 21 lawyers and judges gnash *t.* upon Alma[2] and Amulek; **3 Ne.** 12: 38 (Matt. 5: 38) a *t.* for a *t.*

TOP (*see also* Housetop)

1 Ne. 16: 30 Nephi[1] goes forth into *t.* of mountain; **2 Ne.** 12: 2 (Isa. 2: 2) mountain of the Lord's house to be established in *t.* of mountains; **Jacob** 5: 66, 73 root and *t.* of tree to be equal; **Ether** 2: 17 *t.* of Jaredite vessels tight like dish; 2: 19–20 hole in *t.* and bottom of Jaredite vessels for air; 3: 1 brother of Jared[2] carries sixteen small stones upon *t.* of mount.

TORMENT (*see also* Anguish; Damnation; Despair; Gnash; Guilt; Harrow; Hell; Lake; Misery; Pain; Remorse; Sorrow)

2 Ne. 9: 16, 19, 26 (28: 23; Jacob 6: 10; Mosiah 3: 27; Alma 12: 17) endless *t.* of the wicked is like lake of fire and brimstone; **Mosiah** 2: 39 (3: 25) final doom of the unrepentant is to endure endless *t.*; 27: 29 (Alma 36: 12–13) soul of Alma[2] was racked with eternal *t.*; 28: 3 thought that any soul should suffer endless *t.* causes sons of Mosiah[2] to quake; **Moro.** 8: 20–21 he who says little children need baptism is in danger of endless *t.*

TOSS (*see also* Cast; Throw)

3 Ne. 22: 11 (Isa. 54: 11) O thou afflicted, *t.* with tempest and not comforted; **Morm.** 5: 18 Nephites are led about by Satan as vessel is *t.* upon waves; **Ether** 6: 5 Jaredite vessels are *t.* upon waves.

TOUCH (*see also* Feel; Hand)

1 Ne. 17: 48–49 Nephi[1] commands brothers not to *t.* him; **2 Ne.** 27: 21 *t.* not the things which are sealed; **Mosiah** 13: 3 Abinadi commands priests not to *t.* him; **Alma** 5: 57 (3 Ne. 20: 41; Moro. 10: 30) *t.* not unclean things of the wicked; **3 Ne.** 18: 36 Jesus *t.* each of his disciples with his hand; **Ether** 3: 6 brother of Jared[2] asks the Lord to *t.* stones.

TOWER (*see also* Building)

Omni 1: 22 (Hel. 6: 28; Ether 1: 33) first parents of Coriantumr[2] came from *t.*; **Mosiah** 2: 7 Benjamin has *t.* erected; 11: 12–13 Noah[3] builds high *t.* to watch Lamanites; 20: 8 from *t.* Limhi discovers Lamanites' preparations for war; 28: 17 (Ether 1: 3) plates of gold give account of Jaredites back to building of *t.*; **Alma** 50: 4 Moroni[1] builds *t.* as part of fortifications; **Hel.** 6: 28 devil put it into men's hearts to build *t.* high enough to reach heaven; 7: 10–11 Nephi[2] prays upon *t.*

TOWN (*see also* City; Village)

Morm. 4: 22 Nephites flee, taking all inhabitants with them, in *t.* and villages; 5: 5 *t.* and villages burned by Lamanites.

TRADE (*see also* Business; Merchants; Traffic)

    Mosiah 24: 7 Lamanites begin to *t.* one with another.

TRADITION (*see also* Custom; Doctrine, False)

    Enos 1: 14 Lamanites swear to destroy Nephites' records and *t.*; **Mosiah** 1: 5 (10: 12) Lamanites do not believe truth because of incorrect *t.* of fathers; 26: 1 many in rising generations of Nephites do not believe *t.* of fathers; **Alma** 3: 8 Nephites should not mix with Lamanites and believe incorrect *t.*; 3: 11 those who do not believe Lamanites' *t.*, but records and *t.* of fathers, are called Nephites; 9: 16 *t.* of fathers cause Lamanites to remain in ignorance; 9: 17 Lamanites will be brought to know incorrectness of *t.*; 17: 9 sons of Mosiah[2] desire to bring Lamanites to knowledge of baseness of *t.*; 24: 7 Lamanite king is thankful Nephites have convinced them of *t.* of wicked fathers; 60: 32 hatred of Lamanites caused by *t.* of fathers; **Hel.** 5: 51 (15: 7) converted Lamanites lay down hatred and *t.* of fathers; 15: 4 the Lord has hated Lamanites because of evil deeds and iniquity of *t.* of fathers.

TRAFFIC (*see also* Business; Merchants; Trade)

    4 Ne. 1: 46 robbers *t.* in all manner of *t.*; **Ether** 10: 22 Jaredites *t.* one with another to get gain.

TRAITOR (*see also* Apostasy)

    Alma 60: 18 Moroni[1] wonders whether leaders of government are *t.*; 62: 1 Moroni[1] learns that Pahoran[1] is not *t.*

TRAMPLE (*see also* Disobedience; Rebel; Tread)

    1 Ne. 19: 7 men *t.* God under feet; **Mosiah** 29: 21–22 iniquitous king *t.* under feet God's commandments; **Alma** 5: 53 can ye lay aside these things and *t.* Holy One under feet; 60: 33 (Hel. 4: 21–22; 6: 31) Nephites *t.* laws of God under their feet; **Hel.** 12: 2 when the Lord prospers his people, they forget him and *t.* him under their feet; **3 Ne.** 14: 6 (Matt. 7: 6) cast not your pearls before swine, lest they *t.* them under feet; 28: 35 do ye suppose ye can get rid of justice of offended God, who hath been *t.* under feet of men.

TRANSFIGURE, TRANSFIGURED (*see also* Change; Transform; Translated Beings; TG Transfiguration, Transfigured; Translated Beings; BD Transfiguration, Mount of)

    3 Ne. 28: 15, 17, 36–39 three Nephite disciples are *t.* from body of flesh to sanctified state; **Morm.** 8: 33 why have

ye *t.* word of God, that ye might bring damnation upon souls.

TRANSFORM (*see also* Change; Transfigure; Translated Beings)

    2 Ne. 9: 9 devil *t.* himself nigh unto angel of light.

TRANSGRESSION, TRANSGRESS (*see also* Agency; Crime; Death, Spiritual; Disobedience; Err; Evil; Fall of Man; Fault; Guilt; Iniquity; Jesus Christ, Atonement through; Judgment; Knowledge; Law; Offense; Punishment; Rebel; Sin; Transgressor; Trespass; Wicked; TG Transgress)

    2 Ne. 2: 22 if Adam had not *t.*, he would not have fallen; 9: 6 fall came by reason of *t.*; 9: 27 wo unto him that has the commandments and *t.* them; 9: 39 remember awfulness of *t.* against God; 9: 46 men will confess they have *t.* law and say, my *t.* are mine; **Enos** 1: 10 Lamanites' *t.* will the Lord bring down upon own heads; **Mosiah** 1: 12 (5: 11) new name shall never be blotted out except through *t.*; 1: 13 if Nephites fall into *t.*, the Lord will deliver them up; 2: 36–37 man who *t.* contrary to what he has been taught is in open rebellion to God; 3: 11 Christ's blood atones for sins of those who have fallen by *t.* of Adam; 4: 14 ye will not suffer your children to *t.* God's laws; 14: 5 (Isa. 53: 5) he was wounded for our *t.*; 14: 8 (Isa. 53: 8) for *t.* of my people was he stricken; 15: 9 (Alma 34: 8) Christ takes upon himself his people's *t.*; 27: 13 nothing shall overthrow church except *t.* of the Lord's people; **Alma** 7: 13 Son suffers that he might blot out his people's *t.*; 9: 19 the Lord would rather suffer that Lamanites destroy Nephites if they would fall into *t.*; 9: 23 far more tolerable for Lamanites if Nephites fall into *t.*; 10: 19 if Nephites fall into *t.*, they will be ripe for destruction; 11: 40 Christ will take upon himself *t.* of those who believe on him; 12: 31 by *t.* first commandments, men became as Gods, knowing good from evil; 24: 30 when enlightened people fall into *t.*, they become more hardened; 28: 13 how great inequality of man because of *t.*; 32: 19 how much more cursed is he who knows God's will and does it not than he who only believes and falls into *t.*; 46: 18 God will not suffer Nephites to be destroyed until they bring it upon themselves by *t.*; **Hel.** 4: 26 Nephites become weak because of *t.*

TRANSGRESSOR (*see also* Transgression, Transgress)

    1 Ne. 20: 8 (Isa. 48: 8) thou wast called a *t.* from womb; **Mosiah** 14: 12 (Isa. 53: 12) he was numbered with *t.*;

Alma 26: 24 ways of Lamanites have been ways of *t.*

TRANSLATION, TRANSLATE (*see also* Book of Mormon; Gift; Holy Ghost; Interpretation; Language; Seer; Tongue; Translated Beings)

Mosiah 8: 13 Ammon¹ tells Limhi of man who can *t.* records; 8: 13–14 (28: 13) Mosiah² has interpreters, with which he can *t.*; 28: 11, 13 Mosiah² *t.* plates of gold by means of interpreters; **Alma** 9: 21 Nephites have had gift of *t.*; **Ether** 5: 1 sealed records not to be *t.*; 15: 34 whether Ether will be *t.* matters not.

TRANSLATED BEINGS (*see also* Change; John the Beloved; Three Nephite Disciples; Transfigure; Zion)

Alma 45: 19 Alma² is said to be taken up by Spirit or buried by hand of God, as was Moses; **3 Ne.** 28: 1–9, 36–40 three Nephite disciples who desire to tarry are sanctified, never to taste death.

TRAP (*see also* Pit; Snare)

Alma 10: 17 lawyers are laying *t.* to catch holy ones of God.

TRAVAIL (*see also* Labor)

2 Ne. 29: 4 do Gentiles remember the *t.*, labors of the Jews; **Mosiah** 14: 11 (Isa. 53: 11) he shall see *t.* of his soul; 27: 33 sons of Mosiah² exhort people with much *t.* to keep commandments; 29: 33 Mosiah² unfolds all *t.* of soul for people; **Alma** 18: 37 Ammon² rehearses *t.* of fathers in wilderness; **3 Ne.** 22: 1 (Isa. 54: 1) sing, O thou that didst not *t.* with child.

TRAVEL (*see also* Depart; Flight; Journey)

1 Ne. 2: 5 (7: 21; 16: 15; 17: 1) Lehites *t.* in wilderness; **Mosiah** 8: 7–8 group of Limhi's people *t.* in land of many waters; 27: 35 sons of Mosiah² *t.* throughout Zarahemla striving to repair injuries; **Alma** 8: 6 Alma² *t.* to Ammonihah; 26: 28 missionaries *t.* from house to house, relying upon mercies of world; 30: 32 Alma² has labored for own support, notwithstanding many *t.*

TREAD, TRODDEN (*see also* Oppression; Persecution; Trample)

Alma 30: 59 Korihor is *t.* down by Zoramites; 34: 29 if ye are not charitable, ye are as dross which is *t.* under foot; **3 Ne.** 12: 13 (Matt. 5: 13) salt that has lost savor is good for nothing but to be *t.* under foot; 16: 8 Israel has been *t.* under foot by Gentiles; 16: 15 (20: 16; 21: 12) the Lord will suffer Israel to go through Gentiles and *t.* them down; 25: 3 (Mal. 4: 3) ye shall *t.* down the wicked; **Morm.** 5: 6 Lamanites *t.* Nephites under feet.

TREASURE (*see also* Money; Riches; Treasury; Value)

2 Ne. 9: 30 hearts of the rich are upon their *t.*, which is their god; 9: 30 their *t.* shall perish with them; 12: 7 (Isa. 2: 7) neither is there any end of their *t.*; **Hel.** 5: 8 lay up for yourselves *t.* in heaven; 8: 25 Nephites have rebelled against God instead of laying up *t.* in heaven; 13: 18, 20, 35 (Morm. 1: 18) he who hides *t.* shall not find it again; 13: 19 the righteous hide up their *t.* unto the Lord; **Ether** 3: 21 brother of Jared² to *t.* up things he has seen and show them to no man.

TREASURY

1 Ne. 4: 20 Nephi¹ commands Zoram¹ to go to *t.* with him.

TREATY (*see also* Covenant; Oath; Promise)

Mosiah 7: 21 (9: 2) Laman² enters *t.* with Zeniff; **Morm.** 2: 28 Nephites make *t.* with Lamanites.

TREE (*see also* Branch; Fig; Fruit; Forbidden; Olive; Root; Tree of Life)

Jacob 4: 6 saints can command in Jesus' name and very *t.* obey; **Alma** 5: 52 ax is laid at root of *t.*; 5: 52 every *t.* that brings not good fruit shall be hewn down; 26: 36 Nephites are branch of *t.* of Israel; 32: 37 if ye nourish *t.*, it will get root, bring forth fruit; 32: 38–40 if ye do not nourish *t.*, ye can never pluck fruit; **3 Ne.** 4: 28 Zemnarihah is hanged upon *t.*; 14: 17 (Matt. 7: 17) every good *t.* brings forth good fruit, corrupt *t.* brings forth evil fruit; **Ether** 2: 17 length of Jaredites' vessels is length of *t.*

TREE OF LIFE (*see also* Eden; Tree; Vision)

1 Ne. 8: 10–35 Lehi¹ beholds *t. of l.*; 11: 8–9 Nephi¹ sees *t.* seen by father; 11: 21–22, 25 *t.* represents love of God; 11: 25 (15: 22) iron rod leads to *t. of l.*; 15: 22 *t.* in vision represents *t. of l.*; 15: 28, 36 awful gulf separates the wicked from *t. of l.*; **2 Ne.** 2: 15 forbidden fruit set in opposition to *t. of l.*; **Alma** 5: 34, 62 come unto the Lord and you shall partake of fruit of *t. of l.*; 12: 21 (42: 2–6) God placed cherubim and flaming sword lest first parents partake of fruit of *t. of l.*; 12: 23 (42: 3, 5) if Adam could have partaken of fruit of *t. of l.*, there would have been no death; 12: 26 if first parents had partaken of *t. of l.*, they would have been miserable forever; 32: 40 if ye will not nourish the word, ye can never pluck fruit of *t. of l.*; 42: 6 as men were cut off from *t. of l.*, they should be cut off from face of earth.

TREMBLE, TREMBLING (*see also* Earthquake; Fear; Fear of God; Quake; Shake)

1 Ne. 1: 6 Lehi[1] *t.* because of what he has seen; **2 Ne.** 1: 14 hear the words of *t.* parent; 24: 16 (Isa. 14: 16) is this the man who made earth to *t.*; 28: 28 he who is built upon sandy foundation *t.* lest he fall; **Alma** 36: 7 earth *t.* beneath feet of Alma[2]; **Hel.** 5: 31 walls of prison *t.*; 12: 9 at the Lord's voice, mountains *t.*; 14: 21 (3 Ne. 10: 9) earth shall *t.* at Christ's death.

TRESPASS (*see also* Offense; Sin; Transgression)

Mosiah 26: 30 as often as his people repent, the Lord will forgive their *t.* against him; 26: 31 forgive one another your *t.*; **3 Ne.** 7: 14 strict laws established that one tribe should not *t.* against another; 13: 14 (Matt. 6: 14) if ye forgive men their *t.*, Father will forgive you.

TRIAL, TRY (*see also* Chasten; Faith; Opposition; Oppression; Persecution; Probation; Prove; Trial, Judicial; Tribulation; TG Test, Try, Prove)

Mosiah 23: 21 (3 Ne. 26: 11) the Lord *t.* his people's patience and faith; 29: 33 Mosiah[2] unfolds *t.* of righteous king; **Alma** 1: 22–23 contention is cause of much *t.* with church; 27: 15 Ammon[2] and brethren will *t.* Nephites' hearts, whether converted Lamanites should enter land; 31: 5 Alma[2] to *t.* virtue of word of God; 32: 36 (34: 4) *t.* experiment by planting the seed; 36: 3 (38: 5) whosoever puts trust in God will be supported in *t.*; **3 Ne.** 26: 9 Lamanites to receive account of Savior's teachings to *t.* their faith; **Ether** 12: 6 ye receive no witness until after *t.* of faith.

TRIAL, JUDICIAL (*see also* Government, Civil; Judge [noun]; Law; Law, Civil; Transgression; Transgressor; Trial, Try)

Alma 10: 14 lawyers are hired to administer laws at times of *t.*; 51: 19 dissenters thrown into prison because no time for *t.*; **Hel.** 1: 7–8 Paanchi is *t.* by voice of people and condemned to death; 6: 24 robbers who reveal wickedness to world are *t.* by laws of Gadianton; 3 **Ne.** 6: 25–27 judges who condemned prophets to death are to be *t.* according to law.

TRIBE (*see also* Israel; Israel, Ten Lost Tribes of; Jacob, House of; Judah)

3 Ne. 7: 2–4, 14 people separate into *t.*; 7: 3 each *t.* appoints leaders; 7: 11, 14 each *t.* establishes own laws; 7: 11 *t.* are united against robbers.

TRIBULATION (*see also* Affliction; Anguish; Calamity; Chasten; Despair; Destruction; Grieve; Misery; Oppression; Persecution; Sorrow; Suffering; Trial; Trouble)

2 Ne. 2: 1 Jacob[2] is firstborn in days of father's *t.*; **Jacob** 7: 26 Nephites are wanderers, born in *t.* in wilderness; **Mosiah** 23: 10 after much *t.* the Lord hears cries of Alma[1]; 27: 28 after wading through much *t.*, Alma[2] is snatched from everlasting burning; 27: 32 Alma[2] and companions preach word in much *t.*; **Alma** 8: 14 Alma[2] wades through much *t.* because of wickedness of Ammonihah; 15: 3 Zeezrom's fever caused by much *t.* of his mind; 53: 13 Ammonites are many *t.* Nephites bear for them; 60: 25–26 Nephite armies are strengthened by power of God because of patience in *t.*

TRIBUNAL (*see also* Bar; Judgment-seat)

Alma 5: 18 can ye imagine yourselves brought before God's *t.* filled with guilt.

TRIBUTE (*see also* Bondage; Tax)

Mosiah 7: 15, 22 (19: 15, 22, 26, 28) Limhi's people pay *t.* to Lamanites; 22: 7, 10 Gideon will pay last *t.* of wine to Lamanites.

TRIFLE

Mosiah 2: 9 Benjamin does not gather his people to *t.* with words.

TRODDEN (*see* Tread, Trodden)

TROUBLE (*see also* Anxiety; Calamity; Care; Sorrow; Suffering; Tribulation; Vex; Worry)

Mosiah 26: 10 Alma[2] *t.* in spirit because of false teachings; 29: 33 Mosiah[2] unfolds *t.* of righteous king; **Alma** 22: 3 Lamanite king is *t.* by generosity of Ammon[2]; 36: 3 (38: 5) those who put trust in God will be supported in *t.*; 40: 12 spirits in paradise shall rest from *t.*; 42: 29 only let your sins *t.* you with that *t.* which brings repentance; **3 Ne.** 17: 14 Jesus is *t.* because of Israel's wickedness.

TRUE (*see also* Reality; Real; Right [adj.]; Truth)

1 Ne. 10: 14 Israel to come to knowledge of *t.* Messiah; 13: 39 other books to testify that records of prophets and twelve apostles are *t.*; 15: 15 seed of Lehi[1] to receive nourishment from *t.* vine; 15: 16 seed of Lehi[1] to be grafted into *t.* olive-tree; **2 Ne.** 1: 10 if seed of Lehi[1] reject *t.* Messiah, his judgments will rest upon them; 9: 2 Jews to be restored to *t.* church and fold of God; 25: 18 words will

convince Jews of *t.* Messiah; 31: 15 words of my Beloved are *t.*; 31: 21 this is doctrine of Christ, only and *t.* doctrine of Father; **Enos** 1: 20 Nephites seek diligently to restore Lamanites to *t.* faith; **Alma** 5: 13 word was preached to fathers and they put trust in *t.* and living God; 5: 48 whatsoever I say concerning what is to come is *t.*; 16: 17 those who receive word will be grafted into *t.* vine; 32: 28 *t.* seed will swell in breast; 53: 20 Ammonite youths are *t.* in whatsoever they are entrusted; **Hel.** 11: 23 those who know *t.* points of doctrine preach to people; 15: 13 Lamanites come to *t.* knowledge of great and *t.* shepherd; **3 Ne.** 8: 1 we know our record to be *t.*; 21: 6 Gentiles may know *t.* points of Christ's doctrine; **4 Ne.** 1: 29 false church persecutes *t.* church of Christ; **Morm.** 8: 10 none know *t.* God except Jesus' disciples; 9: 28 serve the *t.* and living God; **Ether** 2: 8 those in promised land must serve *t.* and only God or be swept off; **Moro.** 10: 4 ask God if these things are not *t.*; 10: 6 whatsoever thing is good is just and *t.*; 10: 29 God will show you that what I have written is *t.*

TRUMP, TRUMPET

Mosiah 26: 25 when second *t.* sounds, those who never knew the Lord will stand before him; **Alma** 29: 1 O that I were angel and could speak with *t.* of God; **3 Ne.** 13: 2 (Matt. 6: 2) when you give alms, do not sound *t.*; **Morm.** 9: 13 all men shall be awakened from endless sleep when *t.* sounds; **Ether** 14: 28 Coriantumr² sounds *t.* to invite armies of Shiz to battle.

TRUST (*see also* Confidence; Faith; Hope; Rely; TG Trust; Trust in God; Trust Not in Arm of Flesh; Trustworthiness)

2 Ne. 4: 19 I know in whom I have *t.*; 4: 34 O Lord, I have *t.* in thee; 4: 34 I will not put *t.* in arm of flesh; 4: 34 (28: 31) cursed is he who puts *t.* in man; 8: 5 (Isa. 51: 5) on mine arm shall isles *t.*; 22: 2 (Isa. 12: 2) I will *t.* and not be afraid; 24: 32 (Isa. 14: 32) poor of the Lord's people shall *t.* in Zion; **Jacob** 7: 25 Nephites fortify against Lamanites, putting *t.* in God; **Mosiah** 4: 6 salvation to come to him who puts *t.* in the Lord; 7: 19 rejoice and put *t.* in God; 7: 33 (Alma 61: 13) if ye will put *t.* in the Lord, he will deliver you; 23: 13 *t.* no man to be king; 23: 14 *t.* no man to be teacher except he be man of God; 29: 20 the Lord extends arms of mercy to those who put *t.* in him; **Alma** 5: 13 fathers humbled themselves and put *t.* in God; 17: 13 sons of Mosiah² separate, *t.* in the Lord that they should meet again; 19: 23 Mosiah² *t.* his son unto the Lord; 36: 3 (38: 5) whoever puts *t.* in God will be supported in trials; 37: 32 *t.* not those secret plans unto this people; 57: 27 Ammonite youths put *t.* in God continually; 58: 33 we *t.* in our God, who has given us victory; **Hel.** 12: 1 the Lord prospers those who put *t.* in him; **Morm.** 9: 20 God ceases to do miracles because men know not the God in whom they should *t.*; **Moro.** 8: 22–23 to suppose little children need baptism is putting *t.* in dead works.

TRUTH (*see also* Gospel; Knowledge; Learning; Light; Mystery; Scriptures; Spirit, Holy/Spirit of the Lord; True)

1 Ne. 13: 40 last records shall establish *t.* of first; 16: 2 the guilty take the *t.* to be hard; **2 Ne.** 9: 40 words of *t.* are hard against all uncleanness; 9: 40 the righteous love the *t.*; 27: 12 three witnesses shall testify to *t.* of book; 28: 28 wo unto all who are angry because of *t.* of God; **Jacob** 4: 13 Spirit speaketh *t.*; **Alma** 9: 26 (13: 9) Only Begotten, full of grace and *t.*; 30: 41–43 Korihor resists spirit of the *t.*; 34: 38 (John 4: 24) worship God, wherever you may be, in spirit and *t.*; 38: 9 Christ is the word of *t.* and righteousness; 43: 10 whosoever worships God in spirit and *t.*, the Lamanites would destroy; **Hel.** 6: 34 Lamanites walk in *t.* and uprightness before the Lord; **3 Ne.** 16: 7 *t.* shall come unto Gentiles; **Ether** 3: 12 thou speakest the *t.*, for thou art a God of *t.*; 4: 12 (John 14: 6) Christ is light, life, and *t.* of world; **Moro.** 7: 45 (1 Cor. 13: 4, 6) charity rejoiceth in *t.*; Moro. 10: 4 Father will manifest *t.* of book by power of Holy Ghost; 10: 5 by power of Holy Ghost ye may know *t.* of all things.

TRY (*see* Trial, Try; Trial, Judicial)

TUBALOTH—*Lamanite king* [c. 51 B.C.]

Hel. 1: 16–17 son of Ammoron, appoints Coriantumr³ commander of armies.

TUMBLE (*see also* Fall)

1 Ne. 12: 4 Nephi¹ sees mountains *t.* into pieces and cities *t.* to earth; 22: 14 (2 Ne. 28: 18) abominable church must *t.* to earth; **Hel.** 5: 27, 31 prison walls about to *t.* to earth; **Morm.** 8: 24 by power of the Lord's word, saints cause prisons to *t.*; **Ether** 12: 13 (Alma 14: 27) faith causes prison to *t.* to earth.

TUMULT, TUMULTUOUS (*see also* Noise, Roar; Sound [noun and verb]; Uproar)

1 Ne. 12: 4 (3 Ne. 10: 9) Nephi¹ hears all manner of *t.* noises; **Hel.** 5: 30 voice to dissenters in prison is not voice of *t.* noise; **4 Ne.** 1: 16 no *t.* among Nephites.

TURN

1 Ne. 16: 39 after being chastened

by the Lord, the rebellious *t.* away anger; 19: 13 Jews shall be scourged because they *t.* hearts aside; 19: 15 when Jews no longer *t.* hearts against Holy One, he will remember covenants; 22: 13 blood of abominable church shall *t.* upon own heads; 22: 14 nations that war against Israel shall be *t.* against one another; **2 Ne.** 27: 32 (28: 16) they who *t.* aside the just for thing of naught shall be cut off; **Mosiah** 4: 16 ye will not *t.* beggar out to perish; 7: 33 (Alma 39: 13; Morm. 9: 6) *t.* to the Lord with full purpose of heart; **Alma** 4: 12 (5: 55) some *t.* their backs upon needy; 34: 28 if ye *t.* away the needy, your prayer is vain; 42: 2 the Lord placed flaming sword which *t.* every way, to keep tree of life; 56: 37 Lamanite army pursued by Antipus *t.* not to right or left; **3 Ne.** 6: 13 the humble receive persecution and do not *t.* and revile; 20: 26 Father sends Christ to *t.* people from iniquities; 24: 5 (Mal. 3: 5) I will be swift witness against those who *t.* aside stranger; **Ether** 1: 36 brother of Jared² to ask the Lord to *t.* away his anger.

TWAIN (*see also* Two)

Alma 14: 27 (3 Ne. 28: 19; 4 Ne. 1: 30) prison walls are rent in *t.*; **Hel.** 10: 6–8 Nephi² is given power to rend temple in *t.*; 14: 21–22 (3 Ne. 8: 18) rocks to be rent in *t.* at Christ's death; **3 Ne.** 12: 41 (Matt. 5: 41) whosoever shall compel thee to go a mile, go with him *t.*

TWINKLING

3 Ne. 28: 8 three Nephites to be changed in *t.* of eye from mortality to immortality.

TWO (*see also* Twain)

1 Ne. 14: 10 there are only *t.* churches; 16: 10 *t.* spindles within Liahona; **2 Ne.** 29: 8 testimony of *t.* nations is witness that the Lord is God; **Mosiah** 28: 10–13 Mosiah² translates record by means of *t.* stones; **Hel.** 14: 4 *t.* days and nights without darkness at Christ's birth; **3 Ne.** 13: 24 (Matt. 6: 24) no man can serve *t.* masters; **Ether** 3: 23, 28 the Lord gives brother of Jared² *t.* stones to seal up with record.

TYPE, TYPIFY (*see also* Remember, Remembrance; Representation; Shadow; Similitude; Token; TG Jesus Christ, Types of, in Anticipation; Jesus Christ, Types of, in Memory)

1 Ne. 17: 41 (2 Ne. 25: 20; Alma 33: 19–21; Hel. 8: 14–15; Num. 21: 8–9) serpent raised in wilderness a *t.* of Christ; **2 Ne.** 11: 4 all things given of God from beginning *t.* Christ; **Mosiah** 3: 15 the Lord showed his people many *t.* of his

coming; 13: 10 (Alma 25: 10) Abinadi's death a *t.* of things to come; 13: 30–31 (16: 14; Alma 25: 15; 34: 14; Gal. 3: 24; Heb. 10: 1) law of Moses a *t.* of Christ's coming; **Alma** 13: 16 ordinances given as *t.* of Son's order; 37: 38–46 working of Liahona a *t.* of word of Christ; **Ether** 13: 6 there has been a *t.* for building of New Jerusalem.

TYRANT (*see also* King; Rule; Ruler; TG Tyranny)

Mosiah 29: 40 Nephites do not look upon Mosiah² as *t.*

UNALTERABLE (*see also* Unchangeable)

Alma 41: 8 decrees of God are *u.*

UNAVOIDABLY

1 Ne. 15: 4 prophecies must *u.* come to pass because of wickedness; **Mosiah** 13: 28 except for atonement, men must *u.* perish; 29: 19 except for Creator's interposition, people of Noah³ must *u.* remain in bondage; **Alma** 9: 11 except for God's matchless power and mercy, we should *u.* have been cut off; **Hel.** 4: 25 except they cleave to the Lord, Nephites must *u.* perish in battle with Lamanites.

UNAWARES

Mosiah 10: 2 Zeniff sets guards lest Lamanites come upon them *u.*

UNBELIEF, UNBELIEVER (*see also* Apostasy; Belief; Believer; Dissenter; Doubt; Hardheartedness; Rebel; Reject; TG Unbelief, Unbelievers)

1 Ne. 4: 13 better for one man to perish than for nation to dwindle in *u.*; 10: 11 Jews to dwindle in *u.*; 12: 22–23 (2 Ne. 26: 15; Morm. 9: 35) Lamanites to dwindle in *u.*; 13: 35 (2 Ne. 26: 15; Alma 45: 10; 50: 22; Hel. 3: 16; 4 Ne. 1: 34; Ether 4: 3) Nephites dwindle in *u.*; 17: 18 brethren will not work because they do not believe Nephi¹ can build ship; **2 Ne.** 1: 10 when Nephites dwindle in *u.*, God's judgments shall rest upon them; 10: 2 many Nephites perish in flesh because of *u.*; 26: 15 all who have dwindled in *u.* shall not be forgotten; 26: 17 those who have dwindled in *u.* shall not have book; 26: 19 those who have dwindled in *u.* shall be smitten by Gentiles; 32: 7 Nephi¹ mourns because of Nephites' *u.*; **Jacob** 3: 7 Lamanites' *u.* is caused by iniquity of fathers; **Mosiah** 26: 1–3 (3 Ne. 15: 18) because of *u.*, rising generation cannot understand word of God; 27: 2 proclamation that no *u.* should persecute church; 27: 8 Alma² and sons of Mosiah² are numbered among *u.*; 27: 32 Alma² and sons of Mosiah² are persecuted by *u.*; **Alma** 4: 11 example of

church leads *u.* to iniquity; 7: 6 I trust ye are not in state of so much *u.* as your brethren; 19: 6 dark veil of *u.* being cast from Lamoni's mind; 32: 28 do not cast out seed by *u.*; 33: 21 if ye could be healed by casting eyes about, would ye harden hearts in *u.*; **Hel.** 4: 25 the Lord ceases to preserve Nephites because of *u.*; **3 Ne.** 1: 18 Nephites begin to fear because of *u.*; 1: 19 *u.* set aside day for signs of Christ's birth to be given; 16: 4 Jews to be scattered because of *u.*; 16: 8 wo unto *u.* among Gentiles; 19: 35 Jesus could not show Jews so great miracles because of *u.*; **4 Ne.** 1: 38 Lamanites do not dwindle in *u.*, but wilfully rebel against gospel; **Morm.** 1: 14 (Moro. 10: 24) gifts and Holy Ghost do not come upon any because of *u.*; 5: 14 writings to go forth among Jews; 9: 20 (Moro. 7: 37) God ceases to do miracles because of *u.*; **Ether** 4: 13 knowledge hid up because of *u.*; 4: 15 when Israel rends veil of *u.*, they shall know Father remembers covenants.

UNCHANGEABLE (*see also* Change; God, Eternal Nature of; Immutable; Round; Same; Unalterable)

Morm. 9: 19 (Moro. 8: 18) God is *u.*

UNCIRCUMCISED (*see also* Circumcision)

2 Ne. 8: 24 (3 Ne. 20: 36; Isa. 52: 1) the *u.* shall come no more to Jerusalem; 9: 33 (Hel. 9: 21) wo unto the *u.* of heart.

UNCLEAN, UNCLEANNESS (*see also* Corrupt; Defile; Evil; Filthiness; Spirit, Evil; Spot; Stain; Unholy; Wicked; TG Uncleanness, Unclean)

1 Ne. 10: 21 those who seek to do wickedly are found *u.*; 10: 21 (15: 34; Alma 7: 21; 11: 37; 40: 26; Hel. 8: 25; 3 Ne. 27: 19) no *u.* thing can dwell with God in his kingdom; **2 Ne.** 8: 24 (3 Ne. 20: 36; Isa. 52: 1) *u.* shall come no more to Jerusalem; 9: 14 we shall have perfect knowledge of our *u.*; 9: 40 truth is hard against all *u.*; **3 Ne.** 7: 17, 19 in Jesus' name Nephi[2] casts out *u.* spirits; 20: 41 (Moro. 10: 30) touch not that which is *u.*; **Morm.** 9: 28 strip yourselves of all *u.*

UNCONQUERABLE

Alma 52: 33 Jacob[3] has *u.* spirit; 3 Ne. 3: 1, 4 robbers have *u.* spirit.

UNDERSTAND, UNDERSTOOD, UNDERSTANDING (*see also* Communication; Comprehend; Know; Knowledge; Learn; Perceive; Wisdom; TG Understand; Understanding)

1 Ne. 13: 29 (14: 23) precious things taken from book were plain to *u.*; 15: 7 Laman[1] and Lemuel cannot *u.* words of Lehi[1] concerning olive-tree; 16: 29 writing on Liahona gives *u.* concerning

ways of the Lord; **2 Ne.** 21: 1–2 (Isa. 11: 1–2) spirit of *u.* shall rest upon rod from stem of Jesse; 25: 5 Jews *u.* things of prophets; 25: 8 in last days men will *u.* words of prophets; 27: 26 (Isa. 29: 14) *u.* of prudent shall be hid; 31: 3 the Lord gives light unto the *u.*; 32: 4 (3 Ne. 17: 3) if ye cannot *u.* words, it is because ye ask not; **Jacob** 2: 23–24 Nephites do not *u.* scriptures concerning wives and concubines; 4: 13 he who prophesies should prophesy to men's *u.*; 4: 14 Jews sought for things they could not *u.*; 7: 11 Sherem does not *u.* scriptures regarding Christ; **Omni** 1: 17 Mosiah[1] cannot *u.* people of Zarahemla because of corruptness of language; **W of M** 1: 9 Mormon[2] makes record according to *u.* given by God; **Mosiah** 1: 2 Mosiah[2] teaches sons language of fathers, that they might be men of *u.*; 1: 2–5 records preserved by God that men might read and *u.* prophecies, commandments, mysteries; 3: 15 Israel *u.* not that law of Moses avails nothing except for atonement; 12: 25 priests of Noah[3] pretend to *u.* spirit of prophesying; 12: 27 ye have not applied hearts to *u.*; 26: 3 (3 Ne. 15: 18) because of unbelief men cannot *u.* word of God; **Alma** 17: 2 sons of Mosiah[2] are men of sound *u.*; 26: 35 God has all *u.*; 32: 28, 34 good seed enlightens *u.*; 48: 11 Moroni[1] is man of perfect *u.*; **3 Ne.** 1: 24 those who preach against law of Moses do not *u.* scriptures; 10: 14 whoso readeth, let him *u.*; 11: 3–4 Nephites do not *u.* voice from heaven; 11: 6–8 third time, Nephites *u.* voice; 17: 2 Nephites are weak that they cannot *u.* all of Jesus' words; 17: 3 ask Father that ye may *u.*; 19: 33 multitude *u.* in hearts words Jesus prays; **Morm.** 9: 8 he who denies revelation does not *u.* scriptures; **Ether** 1: 34 brother of Jared[2] asks the Lord not to confound Jaredites that they *u.* not one another; 3: 5 the Lord is able to show forth great power, which looks small to *u.* of men.

UNDERTAKE, UNDERTAKEN (*see also* Do; Observe; Perform)

Alma 17: 13 great is work *u.* by sons of Mosiah[2]; 46: 29 Amalickiahites doubt justice of cause they have *u.*

UNEQUAL (*see also* Inequality)

Alma 30: 7 contrary to commandments that any law should bring men on *u.* grounds.

UNFAITHFUL (*see also* Disobedience)

Mosiah 1: 17 as Lehites were *u.*, they did not progress on journey.

UNFOLD (*see also* Manifest; Revelation; Show)

1 Ne. 10: 19 mysteries to be *u.* to

those who diligently seek; **Jacob** 4: 18 Jacob² will *u*. mystery; **Mosiah** 2: 9 open your hearts and minds that mysteries may be *u*. to your view; 8: 19 interpreters prepared to *u*. mysteries; 29: 33, 35 Mosiah² troubles of righteous king and disadvantages of unrighteous king; **Alma** 12: 1 Alma² *u*. scriptures to Zeezrom; **Ether** 4: 7 when Gentiles exercise faith, Christ will *u*. his revelations to them; 4: 16 revelation of John to be *u*. in eyes of all people.

UNGODLINESS (*see also* Iniquity; Wicked)

Moro. 10: 32 deny yourselves of all *u*.

UNHAPPY (*see also* Happiness; Misery)

Morm. 9: 14 he who is *u*. shall be *u*. still.

UNHOLY (*see also* Unclean; Unworthiness)

2 Ne. 31: 5 how much more need have we, being *u*., to be baptized; **Mosiah** 2: 37 (Alma 7: 21; 34: 36) the Lord dwells not in *u*. temples; **Hel.** 4: 24 Spirit dwells not in *u*. temples.

UNION (*see also* Unite, Unity)

Alma 50: 36 *u*. between people of Morianton and people of Lehi.

UNITE, UNITY (*see also* Agree; Join; One; Order; Union)

2 Ne. 1: 21 be determined in one mind and one heart, *u*. in all things; **Mosiah** 18: 21 people should have hearts knit in *u*. and love; **Alma** 4: 5 three thousand five hundred souls *u*. themselves to church in baptism; 11: 45 spirits will be *u*. with bodies, never more to be divided; **Hel.** 1: 6 when he sees he cannot obtain judgment-seat, Pacumeni *u*. with voice of people; 3: 26 work of the Lord prospers unto baptizing and *u*. with church tens of thousands; **3 Ne.** 6: 27–28 lawyers and high priests *u*. with kindred of judges to form secret combinations; 7: 11 tribes are *u*. in hatred of robbers; 7: 14 tribes not *u*. in laws; 27: 1 disciples *u*. in prayer and fasting; 28: 18, 23 three disciples *u*. as many to church as believe.

UNJUST (*see* Just)

Alma 12: 8 all shall rise from dead, the just and the *u*.

UNKNOWN (*see also* Strange)

Alma 30: 28, 53 Korihor calls God an *u*. being.

UNNATURAL (*see* Nature, Natural)

UNPARDONABLE (*see also* Sons of Perdition; TG Holy Ghost, Unpardonable Sin against)

Jacob 7: 19 Sherem fears he has committed *u*. sin; **Alma** 39: 6 to deny Holy Ghost once it has had place in you is *u*. sin.

UNPREPARED (*see also* Prepare)

Alma 48: 23 Nephites sorry to send brethren into eternal world *u*. to meet God.

UNPROFITABLE

Mosiah 2: 20–21 if ye should serve God with whole souls, ye would be *u*. servants; 22: 4 if thou hast not found me to be *u*. servant, listen to my words.

UNPUNISHED

Hel. 7: 5 robbers let wicked go *u*. because of money.

UNQUENCHABLE (*see* Fire; Flame)

UNRIGHTEOUS, UNRIGHTEOUSNESS (*see also* Iniquity; Unjust; Unworthiness; Wicked; Unrighteous Dominion)

Mosiah 29: 33, 35 Mosiah² warns of dangers of *u*. king; **Alma** 7: 14 Lamb is mighty to cleanse from all *u*.; 10: 27 foundation of destruction laid by *u*. of lawyers and judges.

UNSEARCHABLE

Jacob 4: 8 how *u*. are depths of the Lord's mysteries.

UNSHAKEN (*see also* Steadfast)

2 Ne. 31: 19 ye have not gotten into straight path save by word of Christ with *u*. faith in him; **Jacob** 4: 6 by searching scriptures our faith becomes *u*.; **Enos** 1: 11 faith of Enos¹ begins to be *u*. in the Lord.

UNSPEAKABLE

Hel. 5: 44 Nephi² and Lehi⁴ are filled with *u*. joy; **3 Ne.** 26: 18 many see and hear *u*. things; 28: 13 three Nephites are caught up into heaven, see and hear *u*. things.

UNSTEADINESS

Hel. 12: 1 we can behold the *u*. of hearts of men.

UNWEARIED, UNWEARYINGNESS (*see also* Diligence)

Hel. 10: 4–5 Nephi² declares word with *u*.; 15: 6 righteous Lamanites strive with *u*. diligence to bring brethren to knowledge of truth.

UNWISE (*see also* Foolish; Wisdom, Wise)

Alma 57: 2 by delivering up prisoners for city of Antiparah, we should suppose ourselves *u*.

UNWORTHINESS, UNWORTHY, UN-WORTHILY (*see also* Iniquity; Unholy; Unrighteous; Wicked)

Mosiah 21: 33 Ammon[1] considers himself an *u.* servant; 23: 11 Alma[1] feels *u.* to glory of himself; **Alma** 38: 14 (Ether 3: 2) acknowledge your *u.* before God at all times; **3 Ne.** 18: 28–29 he who partakes of sacrament *u.* brings damnation to his soul; 18: 28–29 (Morm. 9: 29) the *u.* should be forbidden to partake of sacrament; **4 Ne.** 1: 27 false churches administer that which is sacred to the *u.*; **Morm.** 9: 29 see that ye are not baptized *u.*

UPHOLD, UPHELD (*see also* Maintain; Preserve; Support)

Hel. 2: 3 Kishkumen is *u.* by his band; **Morm.** 8: 31 many will claim the Lord will *u.* sinners; **Ether** 8: 22 nations that *u.* secret combinations shall be destroyed.

UPRIGHTNESS, UPRIGHT, UP-RIGHTLY (*see also* Just; Righteousness)

1 Ne. 16: 3 (Mosiah 18: 29; Alma 1: 1; 45: 24; 53: 21; 63: 2; Hel. 6: 34) walk *u.* before God; **Alma** 27: 27 Ammonites are *u.* in all things; 50: 37 Nephihah[2] fills judgment-seat with perfect *u.* before God.

UPROAR (*see also* Noise; Riotings; Tumult)

3 Ne. 1: 7 great *u.* throughout land.

URGE (*see also* Exhort; Persuade)

Morm. 2: 23 Mormon[2] *u.* Nephites to stand boldly before Lamanites.

USE

3 Ne. 12: 44 (Matt. 5: 44) pray for those who despitefully *u.* you.

USURP (*see also* Overthrow)

Alma 25: 5 priests of Noah[3] *u.* power over Lamanites; 43: 8 Zerahemnah desires to *u.* power over Lamanites; 60: 27 Moroni[1] will destroy those who desire to *u.* power and authority; **Hel.** 7: 4 robbers *u.* power and authority of government.

UTTER, UTTERANCE (*see also* Speak; Word)

2 Ne. 28: 4 false churches shall deny Holy Ghost, which gives *u.*; 32: 7 Spirit stops *u.* of Nephi[1]; **Mosiah** 4: 20 people of Benjamin cannot find *u.* because of great joy; **Alma** 30: 49–50 Korihor is struck dumb, that he cannot have *u.*; **Hel.** 5: 33 voice speaks marvelous things, which cannot be *u.* by man; **3 Ne.** 19: 34 words of Jesus' prayer cannot be *u.* by

man; 26: 14, 16 Jesus looses children's tongues that they can *u.* marvelous things.

VAIN, VAINNESS (*see also* Naught; Vanity)

1 Ne. 12: 18 spacious building is *v.* imaginations of men; **2 Ne.** 9: 28 O the *v.* of men; 26: 32 (Mosiah 13: 15; Ex. 20: 7) thou shalt not take name of the Lord in *v.*; 28: 9 many shall teach false and *v.* doctrines; **Mosiah** 4: 16 ye will not suffer beggar to put up petition in *v.*; **Alma** 1: 16 (4: 8; 5: 53; Hel. 7: 21) many love, set hearts upon *v.* things of the world; 31: 27 men cry unto God while they are puffed up with *v.* things of world; 34: 28 unless you impart of substance to needy, your prayer is *v.*; 39: 14 seek not after *v.* things of world, for you cannot carry them with you; **3 Ne.** 2: 2 men imagine up some *v.* thing in hearts regarding signs; 2: 2 devil leads men to believe doctrine of Christ is *v.*; 6: 15 Satan tempts men to seek *v.* things of world; 13: 7 (Matt. 6: 7) when ye pray, use not *v.* repetitions; 24: 14 (Mal. 3: 14) ye have said, It is *v.* to serve God.

VALE (*see also* Valley; Veil)

Alma 37: 45 words of Christ carry us beyond this *v.* of sorrow into far better land of promise.

VALIANT, VALIANTLY (*see also* Courage; Diligence; Uprightness)

2 Ne. 20: 13 (Isa. 10: 13) I have put down inhabitants like a *v.* man; **Alma** 51: 21 king-men are brought down to fight *v.* for freedom; 53: 20 Ammonite youths are exceedingly *v.* for courage; 56: 13 cities obtained by shedding blood of *v.* men; 56: 16 Nephites fight *v.* by day and toil by night to maintain cities; 62: 37 Teancum fought *v.* for his country.

VALLEY (*see also* Vale)

1 Ne. 2: 10 Lehi[1] admonishes Lemuel to be steadfast like *v.*; **2 Ne.** 4: 26 why should my soul linger in *v.* of sorrow; **Hel.** 14: 23 mountains to be laid low like *v.*, *v.* to become mountains; **3 Ne.** 9: 8 *v.* made where cities stood.

VALUE (*see also* Esteem; Precious; Treasure; Worth)

Alma 11: 4–19 *v.* of Nephite coins; **Morm.** 8: 38 greater is *v.* of endless happiness than misery.

VANISH (*see also* Pass)

2 Ne. 2: 13 if there is no God, all things must have *v.* away; 8: 6 (Isa. 51: 6) heavens shall *v.* away like smoke; **Jacob** 4: 2 whatever is written upon anything other than plates will *v.*

VANITY (*see also* Pride; Vain, Vainness)

2 Ne. 15: 18 (Isa. 5: 18) wo unto those who draw iniquity with cords of v.

VAPOR (*see also* Cloud; Mist; Smoke)

1 Ne. 12: 4–5 (3 Ne. 8: 20) Nephi[1] beholds v. of darkness upon promised land; 19: 11 the Lord will visit house of Israel, some by v. of darkness; 22: 18 v. of smoke to come if men harden hearts; **Morm.** 8: 29 there shall be heard of v. of smoke in foreign lands.

VARY, VARIABLENESS (*see also* Change; God, Eternal Nature of)

Mosiah 2: 22 (Alma 7: 20) the Lord never v. from what he has said; **3 Ne.** 19: 8 disciples minister same words as Jesus spoke, nothing v.; **Morm.** 9: 9 in God there is no v.; 9: 10 a god who v. would not be a God of miracles; **Ether** 8: 14–15 combinations swear that whoso v. from what Akish desires should lose head.

VEIL (*see also* Curtain; Vale; BD Veil)

Alma 19: 6 dark v. of unbelief being cast from Lamoni's mind; **Ether** 3: 19–20 (12: 21) brother of Jared[2] could not be kept from beholding within v.; 4: 15 when Israel rends v. of unbelief, they shall know Father remembers covenants; 12: 19 many before Christ's coming had such strong faith that they could not be kept from within v.

VENGEANCE (*see also* Avenge; Destruction; Judgment; Justice; Punishment; Revenge)

Mosiah 17: 19 God executes v. upon those who destroy his people; **Alma** 1: 13 if Nehor were spared, Gideon's blood would come upon judges for v.; 37: 30 blood of murdered prophets cries to the Lord for v.; **3 Ne.** 21: 21 the Lord will execute v. and fury upon the unrepentant; **Morm.** 3: 15 (8: 20; Rom. 12: 19) v. is mine, and I will repay; 8: 41 sword of v. hangeth over you; **Ether** 8: 22 the Lord will not suffer blood of saints to cry for v. and he avenge them not.

VERIFIED (*see also* Testify; Witness)

Jarom 1: 9 (Alma 9: 14) word of the Lord is v.

VESSEL (*see also* Barge; Ship)

Alma 7: 10 Mary a precious and chosen v.; 60: 23–24 inward v. shall be cleansed first, then outer v.; **3 Ne.** 20: 41 be ye clean that bear v. of the Lord; **Morm.** 5: 18 Nephites are led by Satan as v. is tossed without anchor; **Ether** 2: 2 Jaredites prepare v. in which to carry fish; **Moro.** 7: 31 angels bear testimony to chosen v., that they may bear testimony.

VEX (*see also* Trouble)

2 Ne. 17: 6 (Isa. 7: 6) let us go up against Judah and v. it; 21: 13 (Isa. 11: 13) Judah shall not v. Ephraim.

VICTORY

Mosiah 15: 8 God gains v. over death; 16: 7–8 (Alma 22: 14) grave has no v.; **Alma** 16: 21 church established throughout land, having got v. over devil; 27: 28 death swallowed up in v. of Christ; 58: 33 God has given us v. over those lands.

VIEW (*see also* Behold; See; Sight)

2 Ne. 1: 24 rebel no more against your brother, whose v. have been glorious; 9: 44 Jacob[2] prays God to v. him with all-searching eye; 27: 13 none others shall v. book except few to bear testimony; **Mosiah** 3: 25 the wicked are consigned to awful v. of own guilt; 4: 2 Benjamin's people had v. themselves in own carnal state; **Alma** 5: 15 do you v. mortal body raised in immortality; 27: 28 converted Lamanites could never look upon death with any degree of terror for v. of Christ and his resurrection; **Ether** 13: 13–14 Ether went forth by night to v. destruction of his people.

VILEST (*see also* Wicked)

Mosiah 28: 4 sons of Mosiah[2] had been v. of sinners.

VILLAGES (*see also* City; Town)

Mosiah 27: 6 Nephites build large cities and v.; **Alma** 8: 7 v. called after him who first possessed them; **Morm.** 4: 22 Nephites flee, taking all inhabitants, both in towns and v.; 5: 5 towns and v. burned by Lamanites.

VINE (*see also* Grape; Vineyard; Wine; BD Vine)

1 Ne. 15: 15 seed of Nephites to receive nourishment from true v.; **2 Ne.** 15: 1–2 (Isa. 5: 1–2) well-beloved planted vineyard with choicest v.; **Alma** 16: 17 those who receive word are as branch grafted into true v.; **3 Ne.** 24: 11 (Mal. 3: 11) v. shall not cast her fruit before the time.

VINEYARD (*see also* Grape; Olive; Spot of Land; Vine; TG Vineyard of the Lord)

2 Ne. 15: 1–4 (Isa. 5: 1–4) well-beloved's v. brings forth wild grapes; 15: 7 (Isa. 5: 7) v. of the Lord is the house of Israel; **Jacob** ch. 5 parable of tame olive-tree in v.; ch. 6 Jacob[2] expounds parable of olive-tree in v.; **Mosiah** 11: 15 Noah[3] plants v. in land; **Alma** 13: 23 glad tidings declared in all parts of v.

VIRGIN (*see also* Jesus Christ, First Coming of; Mary

    1 Ne. 11: 13–20 Nephi[1] beholds *v.* in Nazareth, mother of Son; **2 Ne.** 17: 14 (Isa. 7: 14) *v.* shall conceive and bear son, Immanuel; **Alma** 7: 10 Christ to be born of Mary, a *v.*

VIRTUE (*see also* Chastity; Clean; Holiness; Merit; Purity; Strength; TG Virtue, Virtuous)

    Alma 31: 5 Alma[2] to try *v.* of word of God; **Moro.** 9: 9 Nephites deprive Lamanite daughters of their chastity and *v.*

VISAGE (*see also* Countenance; Face)

    3 Ne. 20: 44 his *v.* was so marred.

VISION, VISIONARY (*see also* Dream; God, Manifestations of; Revelation; See)

    1 Ne. 1: 8 Lehi[1] carried away in *v.*; 2: 11 (5: 2, 4) Lehi[1] a *v.* man; 5: 4 if Lehi[1] had not seen things of God in *v.*, he would not have known goodness of God; ch. 8 (10: 17) Lehi[1] explains what he has seen in *v.*; **2 Ne.** 1: 1, 4 Lehi[1] has seen *v.* of destruction of Jerusalem; 4: 23 the Lord has given Nephi[1] knowledge by *v.*; 27: 3 nations that fight against Zion shall be as dream of night *v.*; **Alma** 8: 20–21 in *v.* angel tells Amulek to receive Alma[2]; 19: 16 Abish is converted because of remarkable *v.* of father.

VISIT (*see also* God, Manifestations of; Judgment; Visitation)

    1 Ne. 2: 16 the Lord *v.* Nephi[1]; 13: 34 the Lord to *v.* remnant of Nephites in judgment; 19: 11 the Lord God surely will *v.* all house of Israel at that day; **2 Ne.** 4: 26 the Lord in condescension hath *v.* men in mercy; **Mosiah** 4: 26 to retain remission of sin, *v.* the sick and administer to their relief; 11: 20 (Alma 9: 12) except they repent, the Lord will *v.* this people in anger; 11: 22 the Lord is jealous God, *v.* iniquities of his people; 13: 13 (Ex. 20: 5) the Lord *v.* iniquities of fathers upon children; 27: 7 the Lord *v.* Nephites and prospers them; **Alma** 9: 21 Nephites have been *v.* by Spirit; 17: 10 the Lord *v.* sons of Mosiah[2] with Spirit; 33: 10 thou didst *v.* mine enemies in thine anger; 34: 28 if ye *v.* not the sick and afflicted, your prayer is vain; **3 Ne.** 7: 15 Nephi[3] is *v.* by angels and voice of the Lord; 7: 21 converts signify they have been *v.* by power and Spirit of God; 27: 32 in fourth generation the Lord will *v.* Nephites in turning their works upon own heads; **Morm.** 1: 15 Mormon[2] is *v.* of the Lord; **Ether** 4: 11 the Lord will *v.* believers with manifestations of Spirit.

VISITATION (*see also* Judgment; Revelation; Visit)

    2 Ne. 20: 3 (Isa. 10: 3) what will ye do in day of *v.*; **Morm.** 9: 2 will ye believe in day of your *v.*; **Moro.** 8: 26 because of meekness cometh *v.* of Holy Ghost.

VOICE (*see also* God, Manifestations of; Prayer; Preach; Revelation; Sound [noun and verb]; Speech; Warn)

    1 Ne. 4: 18 Nephi[1] obeys *v.* of Spirit in killing Laban; 16: 9, 25–26 (18: 5) *v.* of the Lord comes to Lehi[1]; 16: 39 *v.* of the Lord chastens rebellious brothers; 17: 45 the Lord has spoken to Laman[1] and Lemuel by *v.* of angel, still small *v.*, *v.* of thunder; 22: 2 prophecies were manifested upon Isaiah[1] by *v.* of Spirit; **2 Ne.** 4: 35 I will lift up my *v.* to thee, my God; 16: 8 (Isa. 6: 8) *v.* of the Lord says, Whom shall I send; 31: 12, 14 *v.* of Son comes to Nephi[1]; 33: 13 (Isa. 40: 3) I speak to you as *v.* of one crying from dust; **Jacob** 7: 5 *v.* of the Lord speaks to Jacob[2] from time to time; **Enos** 1: 5, 10 *v.* of the Lord comes into mind of Enos[2]; **Omni** 1: 12–13 those who hearken to *v.* of the Lord depart with Mosiah[1]; **Mosiah** 16: 2 (Ether 11: 7) the wicked hearken not to *v.* of the Lord; 24: 13, 16 *v.* of the Lord comes to people of Alma[1]; 26: 14 after Alma[1] pours out soul to God, *v.* of the Lord comes to him; 26: 21 (John 10: 16) he who will hear the Lord's *v.* shall be his sheep; 27: 11, 18 (Alma 36: 7–8; 38: 7) angel speaks to Alma[2] with *v.* of thunder; 29: 25 choose judges by *v.* of people; 29: 26 not common for *v.* of people to choose that which is not right, therefore, do business by *v.* of people; **Alma** 2: 7 *v.* of people comes against Amlici; 5: 16 can ye imagine ye hear *v.* of the Lord saying, Come unto me; 5: 38–39 they who will not hearken to *v.* of good shepherd are of devil's fold; 5: 41 if a man brings forth good works, he hearkens to *v.* of good shepherd; 5: 57 those desiring to follow *v.* of the good shepherd must come out from the wicked; 9: 21 Nephites have been spoken to by *v.* of the Lord; 10: 20 the Lord cries unto this people by *v.* of angels; 13: 22 *v.* of the Lord by mouth of angels declares repentance to all nations; 20: 2 *v.* of the Lord comes to Ammon[2]; 29: 2 I would declare repentance unto every soul with *v.* of thunder; **Hel.** 5: 29–31 still *v.* of perfect mildness speaks to dissenters in prison; 7: 18 ye will not hearken unto *v.* of good shepherd; 10: 3–11 *v.* of God comes to Nephi[1]; 12: 9–12 by power of the Lord's *v.* whole earth shakes; 12: 23 they who hearken to *v.* of the Lord shall be saved; 13: 3 *v.* of the Lord tells Samuel the Lamanite to return; **3 Ne.** 1: 12–14 (7: 15) *v.* of the Lord comes to

Nephi³; ch. 9 (10: 3–7) v. comes to inhabitants of land; 15: 21, 24 (John 10: 16) other sheep shall hear Christ's v.; **Morm.** 3: 14–15 v. of the Lord comes to Mormon² prophesying destruction.

VOID (see also Empty)

Alma 12: 23, 26 (42: 5) if Adam had partaken of tree of life, there would have been no death, word would have been v.

VOMIT

3 Ne. 7: 8 people turn from righteousness like dog to v.

VULTURES (see also Animal)

Mosiah 12: 2 v. shall devour flesh of this generation because of iniquity; **Alma** 2: 38 many soldiers die in wilderness and are devoured by v.

WADE (see Affliction; Anguish)

WAGES (see also Labor; Pay; Reward)

Mosiah 2: 33 he who obeys evil spirit receives for w. eternal punishment; **Alma** 3: 27 every man receives w. of him whom he obeys; 5: 41–42 whoso hearkens to devil's voice must receive w. of devil; 11: 1 judges receive w. according to time that they labored to judge; **3 Ne.** 24: 5 (Mal. 3: 5) the Lord will be swift witness against those who oppress hireling in his w.; **Morm.** 8: 19 according to works shall w. be.

WAIL (see also Cry; Lament; Mourn; Weep)

Mosiah 16: 2 the wicked shall have cause to weep and w.; **Alma** 5: 36 those who do not works of righteousness shall have cause to w. and mourn; 40: 13 weeping, w., gnashing of teeth in outer darkness; **3 Ne.** 10: 10 w. of people who are spared ceases.

WAIT (see also Watch)

1 Ne. 21: 23 (2 Ne. 6: 7; Isa. 49: 23) they shall not be ashamed who w. for the Lord; **2 Ne.** 6: 13 people of the Lord are they who w. for him; 8: 5 (Isa. 51: 5) isles shall w. upon the Lord; **Mosiah** 21: 34 Limhi's people do not form church, w. upon Spirit.

WALK (see also Act; Do; Live [verb]; Path; Way; TG Walking in Darkness; Walking with God)

1 Ne. 16: 3 (Mosiah 18: 29; Alma 1: 1; 45: 24; 53: 21; 63: 2) w. uprightly before God; 16: 5 w. in paths of righteousness; **2 Ne.** 4: 32 wilt thou not shut gates of thy righteousness, that I may w. in path of low valley; 13: 16 (Isa. 3: 16)

daughters of Zion w. with stretched-forth necks; 19: 2 (Isa. 9: 2) people that w. in darkness have seen great light; 33: 9 for none can I hope unless they w. in strait path; **Mosiah** 2: 27 Benjamin w. with clear conscience before God; 3: 5 the Lord will cause the lame to w.; 4: 15 teach children to w. in ways of truth and soberness; 4: 26 that ye may w. guiltless before God, impart substance to the poor; 6: 6 Mosiah² w. in ways of the Lord; 7: 19 the Lord caused Israelites to w. through Red Sea; 11: 1 Noah³ does not w. in father's ways; 11: 2 Noah³ w. after desires of own heart; 23: 14 trust no man to be your teacher except he w. in God's ways; 26: 37 (Hel. 15: 5) w. circumspectly before God; 26: 38 Alma¹ and fellow laborers w. in all diligence; 29: 43 Alma² w. in ways of the Lord; **Alma** 5: 27 (7: 22) have ye w., keeping yourselves blameless before God; 5: 54 (7: 22) w. after holy order of God; 7: 9 prepare way of the Lord, w. in his paths; 7: 20 God cannot w. in crooked paths; 15: 10–11 after being blessed by Alma², Zeezrom w.; 25: 14 converted Lamanites w. in ways of the Lord; 41: 8 whosoever will may w. in God's ways and be saved; **Hel.** 3: 20 Helaman³ w. in father's ways; 13: 27 false prophets teach people to w. in pride of hearts; **Ether** 6: 17, 30 Jaredites are taught to w. humbly before the Lord; 10: 2 Shez w. in ways of the Lord; **Moro.** 7: 4 Mormon² judges people of church by peaceable w. with men.

WALL

1 Ne. 4: 4 sons of Lehi¹ journey to w. of Jerusalem; **Alma** 48: 8 (52: 6) Moroni¹ builds w. of stone to encircle cities; 53: 4 w. of timbers and earth built around Bountiful; **Hel.** 13: 4 (14: 11) Samuel preaches upon w.

WALLOWING (see Sow [noun])

WANDER, WANDERERS (see also Astray; Err; Flight; Journey)

1 Ne. 8: 23 those on path w. off and are lost in mist of darkness; 16: 35 (17: 20) the rebellious murmur because they have w. in wilderness many years; 19: 14 Jews to w. in flesh; **Jacob** 7: 26 (Alma 13: 23; 26: 36) Nephites are w. in strange land; **Enos** 1: 20 Lamanites w. about in wilderness; **Mosiah** 7: 4 expedition to Lehi-Nephi w. in wilderness forty days; 27: 28 Alma² is snatched from everlasting burning; **Moro.** 1: 3 Moroni² w. for safety of his life.

WANT (see also Need)

1 Ne. 16: 19 Lehites suffer much for w. of food; **Mosiah** 4: 26 (18: 29) administer to relief of sick, both spiritually and temporally, according to their w.;

27: 5 priests labor for own support, save in cases of much *w.*; **Alma** 35: 9 Ammonites administer to outcast Zoramites according to *w.*; 58: 7 Nephite army about to perish for *w.* of food; **3 Ne.** 4: 3 robbers cannot exist save in wilderness, for *w.* of food; 4: 24 robbers become weak for *w.* of food.

WAR (*see also* Army; Battle; Blood, Shedding of; Destruction; Fight; Government, Civil; Peace; Revolt; Slaughter; Sword; Warfare; TG War; BD War in Heaven)

  1 Ne. 12: 2, 21 (14: 16; 2 Ne. 25: 12; Morm. 8: 30; Matt. 24: 6) there shall be *w.* and rumors of *w.*; 22: 13 abominable church shall *w.* among themselves; **2 Ne.** 12: 4 (Isa. 2: 4) nations shall not learn *w.* any more; 13: 1–2 (Isa. 3: 1–2) the Lord will take away from Judah the man of *w.*; 26: 2 there shall be great *w.* and contentions among Nephites; **Enos** 1: 24 (Omni 1: 10, 24; Alma 24: 20; 27: 1; 51: 9; Morm. 1: 8) *w.* between Nephites and Lamanites; **Omni** 1: 3 Nephites have many seasons of *w.*; **Alma** 50: 21 Nephites' iniquity brings *w.* upon them; 61: 15 Lehi[3] and Teancum given power to conduct *w.* according to Spirit; 62: 41 many become hardened because of great length of *w.*; **Hel.** 3: 22 *w.* and contentions begin to cease; 11: 1 contentions increase, causing *w.*; 11: 24 Nephite dissenters begin *w.* with brethren; **Morm.** 8: 8 Lamanites are at *w.* one with another; **Ether** 13: 15 great *w.* begins during reign of Coriantumr[2].

WARFARE (*see also* War)

  Alma 1: 1 Mosiah[2] has warred a good *w.*; 56: 2 Helaman[2] and Moroni[1] brothers in the Lord as in *w.*

WARN, WARNING (*see also* Admonish; Chasten; Exhort; Preach; Rebuke; Reprove; Threaten; Thunder; Voice; Watchmen)

  2 Ne. 1: 3 the Lord is merciful in *w.* Lehites to flee Jerusalem; 5: 5 the Lord *w.* Nephi[1] to depart from brethren; 5: 6 those who go with Nephi[1] believe *w.* of God; **Jacob** 3: 12 Jacob[2] *w.* people against fornication and lasciviousness; **Omni** 1: 12 Mosiah[1] is *w.* to flee out of land of Nephi; **Mosiah** 16: 12 the wicked are *w.* of iniquities, but depart not from them; 23: 1 Alma[1] is *w.* by the Lord concerning armies of Noah[3]; **Alma** 48: 15 if they keep commandments, the Lord would *w.* Nephites to flee; **Ether** 9: 3 the Lord *w.* Omer in dream.

WASH (*see also* Baptism; Cleanse; Jesus Christ, Atonement through; Purify; Sanctification)

  2 Ne. 14: 4 (Isa. 4: 4) the Lord shall *w.* away filth of daughters of Zion; **Alma** 5: 21 (3 Ne. 27: 19) no man can be saved except his garments are *w.* white; 7: 14 be baptized, that ye may be *w.* from sins; 13: 11 garments of high priests have been *w.* white through blood of Lamb; 24: 13 if we should stain swords again, perhaps they can no more be *w.* bright through blood of Son; **3 Ne.** 13: 17 (Matt. 6: 17) when thou fastest, anoint thy head and *w.* thy face; **Ether** 13: 11 inhabitants of Jerusalem shall be *w.* in blood of Lamb.

WASTE (*see also* Desolation; Destruction; Empty; Ruin; TG Waste)

  1 Ne. 8: 7 Lehi[1] dreams of dark and dreary *w.*; 21: 19 (Isa. 49: 19) *w.* places shall be too narrow because of inhabitants; **2 Ne.** 9: 27 awful is state of him who *w.* days of probation; 16: 11 (Isa. 6: 11) cities to be *w.* without inhabitants; **Mosiah** 12: 23 (15: 30; 3 Ne. 16: 19; 20: 34; Isa. 52: 9) sing together, ye *w.* places of Jerusalem; **Hel.** 11: 20 Nephites begin to build up *w.* places.

WATCH, WATCHFUL (*see also* Look; Preside; See; Seek; Wait; Watchmen)

  2 Ne. 27: 31 all who *w.* for iniquity shall be cut off; **Mosiah** 4: 30 *w.* your thoughts and deeds; **Alma** 6: 1 priests and elders ordained to *w.* over church; 13: 28 (15: 17; 3 Ne. 18: 15, 18) *w.* and pray continually; 34: 39 (Moro. 6: 4) be *w.* unto prayer continually; **3 Ne.** 1: 8 the faithful *w.* steadfastly for sign of Christ's birth.

WATCHMEN (*see also* Warn)

  Mosiah 12: 22 (15: 29; 3 Ne. 16: 18; 20: 32; Isa. 52: 8) thy *w.* shall lift up voice.

WATER (*see also* Baptism; Flood; Fountain; Immersion; Lake; Mormon, Waters of; Sea; Sebus, Waters of; Spring; Thirst; Wave)

  1 Ne. 10: 9–10 John to baptize Messiah with *w.*; 13: 10, 12–13, 17, 29 Nephi[1] beholds many *w.* separating his seed from Gentiles; 14: 11–12 abominable church sits upon many *w.*; 17: 5 Lehites call sea Irreantum, meaning many *w.*; 17: 26 (Hel. 8: 11) by Moses' word, *w.* of Red Sea were divided; 17: 29 (2 Ne. 25: 20) Moses smote rock and *w.* came forth; 20: 1 (Isa. 48: 1) come forth out of *w.* of Judah, or *w.* of baptism; **2 Ne.** 9: 50 every one that thirsteth, come to *w.*; 22: 3 (Isa. 12: 3) with joy shall ye draw *w.* out of wells of salvation; 33: 3 eyes of Nephi[1] *w.* his pillow by night because of his people; **Mosiah** 18: 14 Alma[1] and Helam are buried in *w.* in baptism; **Alma** 3: 3

slain Lamanites and Amlicites are cast into w. of Sidon; 5: 34 (42: 27) come unto the Lord and ye shall drink w. of life freely; 17: 26, 34 Ammon² tends flocks by w. of Sebus; 22: 32 lands of Nephi and Zarahemla nearly surrounded by w.; 50: 29 (Hel. 3: 4; Morm. 6: 4) land northward covered with large bodies of w.; **Hel.** 12: 16 if the Lord says to w. of deep, Be dried up, it is done; **3 Ne.** 9: 7 the Lord causes w. to come up in places of cities; **Morm.** 6: 4 Cumorah a land of many w.; **Ether** 6: 11 Jaredites driven upon w. three hundred forty and four days; 13: 2 after w. receded, this land became choice above all others; **Moro.** 7: 11 bitter fountain cannot bring forth good w., nor good fountain bitter w.

WAVES (see also Sea)

1 Ne. 20: 18 (Isa. 48: 18) thy righteousness would have been as w. of sea; **Jacob** 4: 6 saints can command in Jesus' name and w. obey; **Morm.** 5: 18 Nephites are led by Satan as vessel is tossed upon w. without anchor; **Ether** 2: 24 (6: 5–6) mountain w. shall dash upon Jaredite vessels.

WAX (see also Grow; Increase)

2 Ne. 4: 24 by day have I w. bold in mighty prayer; 7: 9 (Isa. 50: 9) those who condemn me shall w. old as garment; 8: 6 earth shall w. old like garment; **Mosiah** 18: 26 priests to receive grace of God, that they might w. strong in Spirit; **Alma** 4: 6 people of church begin to w. proud; 17: 2 sons of Mosiah² have w. strong in knowledge of truth; 50: 18 Nephites w. strong in land; **Hel.** 3: 35 the humble w. stronger and stronger in humility.

WAY (see also Direction; Example; Gate; Highway; Means; Path; Road; Street; Walk)

1 Ne. 3: 7 (9: 6) the Lord giveth no commandment save he shall prepare a w. to accomplish it; 10: 7 (3 Ne. 24: 1; Mal. 3: 1) John the Baptist to prepare w. of the Lord; 10: 8 (Alma 7: 9; 9: 28; Hel. 14: 9; Ether 9: 28; Isa. 40: 3) prepare ye w. of the Lord; 10: 18 w. is prepared for all men if they repent; 13: 27 (22: 14; 2 Ne. 28: 15; Jacob 7: 7; Mosiah 12: 26; 29: 7; Alma 30: 60; 31: 1, 11; Moro. 8: 16) the wicked pervert right w. of the Lord; 16: 10 (Alma 37: 40) one spindle in Liahona points w. to go in wilderness; 17: 13 the Lord will prepare w. in wilderness; 17: 41 the Lord prepared way that Israelites might be healed of serpents' bites; 17: 41 (Alma 37: 46) because of simpleness of w., many perish; 22: 20 the Lord will prepare w. unto fulfilling words of Moses; **2 Ne.** 2: 4 (Alma 37: 46) w. is

prepared from fall of man, and salvation is free; 4: 5 (Prov. 22: 6) if children are brought up in w. they should go, they will not depart from it; 4: 27 why should I give w. to temptations; 4: 33 Lord, wilt thou make a w. for mine escape from mine enemies; 9: 10 the Lord prepares w. for escape from death and hell; 9: 41 (3 Ne. 14: 14) w. for man is narrow; 9: 41 none other w. save by gate; 10: 23 men are free to choose w. of everlasting death or w. of eternal life; 12: 3 (Isa. 2: 3) the Lord will teach us his w.; 25: 28–29 right w. is to believe in Christ; 28: 11 they have all gone out of the w.; 31: 21 (Mosiah 3: 17; Alma 38: 9; Hel. 5: 9) none other w. whereby man can be saved; 32: 1 Nephites ponder what to do after entering w.; **Jacob** 4: 8 no man knows God's w. save they are revealed to him; 6: 11 continue in w. which is narrow; **Mosiah** 1: 9 Benjamin is soon to go w. of all earth; 14: 6 (Isa. 53: 6) we have turned every one to his own w.; 29: 23 unrighteous king perverts w. of righteousness; **Alma** 1: 1 Mosiah² has gone w. of all earth; 4: 19 Alma² sees not w. to reclaim Nephites save in bearing down in pure testimony; 37: 46 do not let us be slothful because of easiness of w.; 42: 2 flaming sword turned every w., to keep tree of life; 62: 37 Teancum has gone w. of all earth; **Hel.** 9: 21 how long will the Lord suffer you to go in your w. of sin; **3 Ne.** 14: 13 (27: 33; Matt. 7: 13) broad is w. that leads to destruction; 14: 14 (27: 33; Matt. 7: 14) narrow is w. that leads to life; 21: 27 work to commence among the dispersed to prepare w. for them to come to Christ; **Ether** 12: 11 in his Son, God has prepared more excellent w.; **Moro.** 6: 4 names of converts taken to keep them in right w.; 7: 15 w. to judge is plain; 7: 21 the w. whereby ye may lay hold upon every good thing; 7: 32 the Lord prepared w. for men to have faith in Christ.

WEAK, WEAKNESS (see also Fault; Humble; Infirmity; Slacken; Strengthen)

1 Ne. 19: 6 Nephi¹ excuses himself because of own w., not other men's; 19: 20 workings in spirit weary Nephi¹, that all his joints are w.; **2 Ne.** 3: 21 w. of their words will the Lord make strong in faith; 24: 10 (Isa. 14: 10) art thou also become w. as we; 33: 4 words which Nephi¹ has written in w. will be made strong to his people; **Jacob** 4: 7 the Lord shows Nephites w. that they may know power to do these things comes by his grace; **Mosiah** 1: 1 (Morm. 2: 26) if Nephites fall into transgression, they will become w. like brethren; 27: 19 Alma² becomes w. because of great astonishment; **Alma** 58: 37 Nephites trust God

will deliver them, notwithstanding w. of armies; **3 Ne.** 17: 2 Nephites are w., that they understand not Jesus' words; **Ether** 12: 25 Nephites behold own w. in writing; 12: 27 the Lord gives men w. that they may be humble; 12: 28 the Lord will show Gentiles their w.; 12: 35 Gentiles must have charity because of Nephites' w.; 12: 37 because thou hast seen thy w., thou shalt be made strong.

WEALTH, WEALTHY (*see also* Gain; Money; Rich; Riches; TG Wealth)

Mosiah 27: 7 Nephites become large and w. people; **Alma** 1: 31 members of church become far more w. than non-members.

WEAPON (*see also* Arms; Arrow; Bow [noun]; Cimeter; Dart; Javelin; Sling; Spear; Sword)

Jarom 1: 8 Nephites make w. of war; **Mosiah** 9: 16 Zeniff arms his people with w.; **Alma** 2: 12 (43: 18; 60: 2) Nephites arm themselves with w. of war; 23: 7 (Hel. 5: 51) converted Lamanites lay down w. of rebellion; 24: 17–19 (26: 32; 53: 11–16; 56: 6–7; Hel. 15: 9) people of Anti-Nephi-Lehi bury w.; 24: 25–26 (25: 14) other Lamanites throw down w. and are converted; 44: 14–15 soldiers of Zerahemnah throw down w.; 51: 18–19 dissenters who lift w. against Nephite army are hewn down; 52: 25, 32 Nephites fall upon Lamanites who do not give up their w.; 53: 16–19 sons of Ammonites take up w. to support Nephites; 62: 16 Lamanite prisoners enter covenant not to take up w. against Nephites; **3 Ne.** 22: 17 (Isa. 54: 17) no w. that is formed against thee shall prosper; **Morm.** 6: 7–9 Lamanites fall upon Nephites with all manner of w.; 7: 4 people must lay down w. and delight no more in bloodshed; **Ether** 10: 27 Jaredites make all manner of w. of war.

WEARY

1 Ne. 19: 20 workings in spirit w. Nephi[1]; **2 Ne.** 7: 4 (Isa. 50: 4) when ye are w., he waketh morning by morning; **Alma** 37: 34 teach people never to be w. of good works; **Hel.** 5: 4 Nephi[2] becomes w. because of Nephites' iniquity.

WEEK (*see also* Time)

Mosiah 18: 25 one day in every w. set apart for worship; **Alma** 31: 12 Zoramites set aside one day of w., called day of the Lord, for worship; 32: 11 do ye suppose ye must worship God only once in w.

WEEP, WEPT, WEEPING (*see also* Cry; Lament; Mourn; Sorrow; Wail)

2 Ne. 4: 26 if I have seen so great

things, why should my heart w.; **Jacob** 5: 41 the Lord of vineyard w.; **Mosiah** 16: 2 the wicked shall have cause to w.; **Alma** 17: 28 servants of Lamoni w. over scattering of flocks; 40: 13 in outer darkness there shall be w., wailing; **Hel.** 13: 32 (3 Ne. 8: 23; 10: 8–10) in day of destruction ye shall w. and howl; **3 Ne.** 17: 21–22 Jesus w.

WEIGH (*see also* Burden; Oppression)

2 Ne. 1: 17 heart of Lehi[1] hath been w. down with sorrow because of sons; **Jacob** 2: 3 Jacob[2] is w. down with anxiety for welfare of Nephites' souls; **Alma** 8: 14 Alma[2] is w. down with sorrow because of iniquity of Ammonihah; **Moro.** 9: 25 may not the things I have written w. thee down to death.

WELFARE (*see also* Charity; Help)

2 Ne. 1: 25 Nephi[1] seeks brothers' eternal w.; 2: 30 only object of Lehi[1] is everlasting w. of sons' souls; 6: 3 Jacob[2] is desirous for w. of his people's souls; 26: 29 those practicing priestcrafts seek not w. of Zion; 32: 9 ask Father to consecrate thy performance for w. of thy soul; **Jacob** 1: 10 Nephi[1] labored all his days for his people's w.; 2: 3 Jacob[2] is weighed down with anxiety for w. of Nephites' souls; **Enos** 1: 9 Enos[2] feels desire for w. of Nephites; **Mosiah** 25: 11 Nephites are filled with anguish for w. of Lamanites' souls; **Alma** 6: 6 Nephites pray for w. of souls of those who know not God; 34: 27 let hearts be drawn out in prayer to God continually for w.; 48: 11–12 Moroni[1] labors for w. and safety of his people; **Hel.** 12: 2 when the Lord does all things for his people's w., they harden hearts; **Morm.** 8: 15 records to come forth for w. of covenant people; **Moro.** 6: 5 church meets oft to speak one with another concerning w. of souls.

WELL [adj.] (*see also* Pleased)

2 Ne. 13: 10 (Isa. 3: 10) say unto the righteous it is w. with them; 28: 21 Satan lulls men into carnal security, saying, All is w. in Zion; 28: 25 wo unto him that crieth, All is w.; **Hel.** 13: 27–28 people accept false prophets because they say all is w.; **Morm.** 7: 10 it shall be w. with those who are baptized with water and with fire; **Moro.** 7: 47 whoso is found possessed of charity at last day, it shall be w. with him.

WHALE (*see also* Animal; BD Whale)

Ether 2: 24 Jaredite vessels shall be as w. in midst of sea; 6: 10 w. could not mar Jaredite vessels.

WHEAT (*see also* Grain)

Mosiah 9: 9 Nephites till ground with seeds of *w*.; **3 Ne.** 18: 18 Satan desires to sift you as *w*.

WHIRLWIND (*see also* Destruction; Storm; Tempest; Wind)

2 Ne. 26: 5 *w*. shall carry away those who kill prophets; **Mosiah** 7: 30 if people sow filthiness, they reap chaff in *w*.; **Alma** 26: 6 converts shall not be harrowed up by *w*.; **Hel.** 5: 12 those built upon rock of Redeemer will withstand devil's shafts in *w*.; **3 Ne.** 8: 12 whole face of land changed because of *w*.; 8: 16 some are carried away in *w*.; 10: 12–13 the righteous are not carried away in *w*.

WHISPER (*see also* Speak)

2 Ne. 26: 16 their speech shall *w*. out of dust; 28: 22 devil *w*. in men's ears until he grasps them in chains; **Hel.** 5: 30, 46 voice from heaven is perfectly mild, as a *w*.

WHITE, WHITER, WHITENESS (*see also* Brightness; Clean; Purity)

1 Ne. 8: 5 man dressed in *w*. robe stands before Lehi[1]; 8: 11 (Alma 32: 42) fruit of tree is *w*. to exceed all *w*.; 11: 13 virgin is exceedingly fair and *w*.; 12: 10–11 because of faith, garments of twelve disciples are made *w*. in Lamb's blood; 13: 15 Gentiles are *w*.; 14: 19, 27 Nephi[1] sees John the apostle dressed in *w*. robe; **2 Ne.** 5: 21 Lamanites no longer *w*., given skin of blackness; 26: 33 the Lord denies none who come unto him, black and *w*.; **Jacob** 3: 8 Lamanites' skins will be *w*. than Nephites' unless Nephites repent; **Alma** 5: 21, 24 no man can be saved unless his garments are washed *w*.; 5: 27 (Morm. 9: 6) garments must be cleansed and made *w*. through blood of Christ; **3 Ne.** 2: 15 Lamanites' skin becomes *w*. like Nephites'; 11: 8 Christ descends from heaven clothed in *w*. robe; 12: 36 (Matt. 5: 36) thou canst not make one hair black or *w*.; 19: 25 multitude are *w*. as countenance and garments of Jesus; **Ether** 3: 1 brother of Jared[2] brings sixteen small *w*. stones to the Lord; 13: 10 New Jerusalem to be inhabited by those whose garments are *w*. through Lamb's blood.

WHOLE (*see also* Soul)

Enos 1: 8 go to, thy faith hath made thee *w*.; **Alma** 11: 45 through reuniting of spirit and body the *w*. becomes spiritual and immortal; **3 Ne.** 17: 10 both those healed and those who were *w*. worship Christ; **Moro.** 8: 8 the *w*. need no physician; 8: 8 little children are *w*.

WHORE, WHOREDOM (*see also* Adultery; Fornication; Harlot; Lust; TG Sex-

ual Immorality; Whore; Whoredom)

1 Ne. 14: 10–12 (22: 13–14; 2 Ne. 10: 16; 28: 18) abominable church is *w*. of all earth; **2 Ne.** 9: 36 (28: 15) those who commit *w*. shall be thrust down to hell; 26: 32 (Jacob 3: 5) the Lord commands that men should not commit *w*.; 28: 14 because of *w*., false churches have all gone astray; **Jacob** 2: 23 Nephites excuse themselves in committing *w*. because of David and Solomon; 2: 28 *w*. are abomination before the Lord; **Mosiah** 11: 6 priests of Noah[3] are supported in *w*. by taxes; **Alma** 1: 32 those who do not belong to church indulge in *w*.; 30: 18 Korihor leads many to commit *w*.; **Hel.** 6: 22–23 (Ether 8: 16) robbers enter covenant, that they might commit *w*.; **3 Ne.** 5: 3 Nephites forsake their *w*.; 15: 10 when Gentiles are filled with *w*., Father will take gospel from them; 21: 19 all *w*. shall be done away; 30: 2 Gentiles are called to repent of *w*.; **4 Ne.** 1: 16 no *w*. among Nephites; **Ether** 10: 7 Riplakish afflicts his people with *w*.; 10: 11 Morianton[1] is cut off because of *w*.

WICKED, WICKEDLY, WICKEDNESS (*see also* Apostasy; Babylon; Carnal; Crooked; Deceit; Destruction; Devil; Disobedience; Evil; Filthiness; Hell; Hypocrisy; Iniquity; Judgment; Loathsome; Lust; Lying; Rebel; Sin; Transgression; Unclean; Ungodliness; Unholy; Unrighteous; Unworthiness; Vilest; World; TG Wickedness; Wicked)

1 Ne. 4: 13 the Lord slays the *w*. to bring forth righteous purposes; 10: 21 those who have sought to do *w*. are found unclean before God; 14: 12 numbers of church of Lamb are small because of *w*. of abominable church; 15: 36 the *w*. are rejected from the righteous; 16: 2 Nephi[1] has spoken hard things against the *w*.; 17: 37 the Lord destroys nations of the *w*.; 19: 10 God to yield himself into hands of *w*. men; 20: 22 (Isa. 48: 22) no peace unto the *w*.; 22: 16 the Lord will not suffer the *w*. to destroy the righteous; **2 Ne.** 12: 5 ye have all gone astray, every one to his *w*. ways; 15: 22–23 (Isa. 5: 22–23) wo unto those who justify the *w*. for reward; 23: 11 (Isa. 13: 11) I will punish the *w*. for their iniquity; 24: 5 (Isa. 14: 5) the Lord hath broken the staff of the *w*.; 28: 14 because of *w*., false churches have gone astray; 30: 10 the Lord will cause division among people and will destroy the *w*.; **Jacob** 6: 13 bar of God strikes the *w*. with fear; **Mosiah** 14: 9 (Isa. 53: 9) he made his grave with the *w*.; **Alma** 1: 32–33 because of law, those who do not belong to church dare not commit *w*.; 4: 3 afflictions are judgments of God because of *w*.; 5: 57 come ye out from the *w*.; 5:

57 names of the *w.* not to be numbered among the righteous; 34: 35 (40: 13) final state of the *w.* is for devil to have all power over them; 37: 29 *w.* of Jaredites to be made known, but not secret oaths; 40: 13–14 spirits of the *w.* are cast into outer darkness until resurrection; 40: 26 an awful death cometh upon the *w.*; 47: 10 *w.* never was happiness; **Hel.** 5: 19 many Lamanites are convinced of *w.* of traditions of fathers; 6: 2 many Nephites become grossly *w.*; 6: 24 members of robber band who reveal *w.* are tried according to laws of Gadianton; 7: 5 robbers in government let *w.* go unpunished because of money; **3 Ne.** 6: 17 Nephites are in state of awful *w.*; 9: 7, 9 the Lord destroys cities to hide *w.*; 17: 14 Jesus is troubled because of *w.* of Israel; 24: 15 (Mal. 3: 15) they who work *w.* are set up; 24: 18 (Mal. 3: 18) ye shall return and discern between the righteous and the *w.*; 25: 1 all who do *w.* shall be stubble; **Morm.** 4: 5 judgments of God will overtake the *w.*; 4: 5 by the *w.* are the *w.* punished; 4: 5 the *w.* stir up hearts of men unto bloodshed; 4: 12 never so great *w.* among house of Israel; **Ether** 4: 15 Israel to rend veil of unbelief which causes them to remain in state of *w.*; **Moro.** 8: 19 awful *w.* to deny pure mercies of God unto little children.

WIDE (*see also* Broad)

3 Ne. 14: 13 (27: 33; Matt. 7: 13) *w.* is gate that leads to destruction.

WIDOW, WIDOWHOOD (*see also* Needy; Orphan)

2 Ne. 19: 17 (Isa. 9: 17) the Lord shall not have mercy upon their *w.*; 20: 1–2 (Isa. 10: 2) wo unto those who make *w.* their prey; **Mosiah** 21: 10 (Alma 28: 5; Moro. 9: 16) many *w.* in land because of war; **3 Ne.** 22: 4 (Isa. 54: 4) thou shalt not remember reproach of thy *w.*; 24: 5 (Mal. 3: 5) the Lord will be swift witness against those who oppress the *w.*; **Morm.** 8: 40 secret combinations cause *w.* to mourn before the Lord.

WIFE, WIVES (*see also* Family; Husband; Marriage; Mother; Woman; TG Marriage, Wives)

1 Ne. 7: 1 sons of Lehi[1] should take *w.* to raise up seed; 16: 7 Zoram[1] and sons of Lehi[1] take daughters of Ishmael[1] to *w.*; 18: 19 *w.* of Nephi[1] cannot soften brothers' hearts; **Jacob** 1: 15 Nephites desire many *w.* and concubines; 2: 24 taking of many *w.* by David and Solomon was abominable; 2: 27 (3: 5) no man shall have more than one *w.*; 2: 35 Nephites have broken hearts of tender *w.*; 3: 7 Lamanite husbands and *w.* love each other

and their children; **Mosiah** 11: 2 Noah[3] has many *w.*; 13: 24 (Ex. 20: 17) thou shalt not covet thy neighbor's *w.*; 19: 11 Noah[3] commands all men to leave *w.* and flee from Lamanites; 19: 19–24 men return to *w.*; **Alma** 35: 14 outcast Zoramites take up arms to defend selves and *w.*; 43: 45 (46: 12; 48: 10) Nephites inspired by better cause, fighting for *w.* and children; 44: 5 sacred support owed to *w.* and children; **3 Ne.** 12: 32 (Matt. 5: 32) whosoever shall put away *w.*, save for fornication, causes her to commit adultery; 18: 21 pray in your families that *w.* and children may be blessed; **Morm.** 2: 23 Mormon[2] urges Nephites to stand boldly and fight for *w.*, children, homes.

WILD (*see also* Beast; Ferocious; Game; Wilderness)

1 Ne. 17: 5 land is called Bountiful because of fruit and *w.* honey; **2 Ne.** 15: 4 (Isa. 5: 4) what could have been done for vineyard when it brought forth *w.* grapes; **Jacob** ch. 5 parable of *w.* branches grafted into tame olive-tree; **Enos** 1: 20 (Mosiah 10: 12) Lamanites become *w.* and ferocious people; **Alma** 47: 36 Nephite dissenters become more *w.* than Lamanites; **Hel.** 3: 16 Nephites become wicked, *w.*, ferocious.

WILDERNESS (*see also* Desolate)

1 Ne. 2: 4 Lehi[1] and family depart into *w.*; 2: 5–6 Lehites travel three days in *w.* by Red Sea; 8: 4 Lehi[1] dreams of dark and dreary *w.*; 17: 4 Lehites sojourn eight years in *w.*; 18: 7 Lehi[1] begets two sons in *w.*; **2 Ne.** 2: 2 Jacob[2], firstborn in *w.*; 3: 1 Joseph[2] was born in *w.* of afflictions; 5: 5–7 the Lord warns Nephi[1] and followers to flee into *w.*; 8: 3 (Isa. 51: 3) the Lord will make Zion's *w.* like Eden; **Jacob** 1: 7 provocation in days of temptation while children of Israel were in *w.*; 4: 5 Abraham offered up Isaac in *w.*; **Mosiah** 7: 4 Ammon[1] and brethren wander forty days in *w.* looking for land of Lehi-Nephi; 21: 25 Limhi's men, searching for Zarahemla, are lost in *w.*; 23: 1, 3 Alma[1] and followers flee eight days into *w.*; **Alma** 2: 37 Lamanites flee to *w.* called Hermounts; 33: 19 (Hel. 8: 14) a type of Christ was raised in *w.*; 34: 26 pour out your souls in your secret places and *w.*; 37: 39 Liahona prepared to show way in *w.*; **Ether** 2: 5–7 Jaredites travel through *w.* to sea.

WILES (*see also* Cunning; Deceit; Subtlety)

Hel. 3: 29 word of God divides asunder all *w.* of devil.

WILFULLY (*see* Rebel)

WILL (*see also* Agency; Desire; Intent; Pleasure; Purpose; Willing; TG Will)

2 Ne. 2: 21 days of men were prolonged according to *w*. of God; 2: 28 choose eternal life according to *w*. of Holy Spirit; 2: 29 do not choose eternal death according to *w*. of flesh; 10: 24 reconcile yourselves to *w*. of God, not to *w*. of devil and flesh; 27: 13 none others shall view plates, save a few, according to *w*. of God; **Jacob** 7: 14 not my *w*. be done, if God will smite thee for a sign; 7: 14 thy *w*., O Lord, be done, and not mine; **W of M** 1: 7 the Lord works in Mormon² to do according to his *w*.; **Mosiah** 2: 21 God lends you breath, that you may do according to your own *w*.; 3: 11 Christ's blood atones for sins of those who have died not knowing *w*. of God; 15: 2 Son subjects flesh to *w*. of Father; 15: 7 *w*. of Son is swallowed up in *w*. of Father; 16: 11–12 the evil to receive eternal damnation, having gone according to own carnal *w*.; 18: 28 men should impart of their substance of own free *w*.; 24: 15 people of Alma¹ submit cheerfully to *w*. of the Lord; **Alma** 12: 31 because of transgression, men are placed in state to act according to their *w*.; 29: 4 the Lord grants unto men according to their *w*.; 32: 19 how much more cursed is he who knoweth *w*. of God and doeth it not; 40: 13 spirits of the wicked are led captive by *w*. of devil; 42: 7 first parents became subjects to follow after own *w*.; **Hel.** 7: 5 robbers obtain government that they might steal and kill and do according to own *w*.; 10: 4 Nephi² has not sought own life, but the Lord's *w*.; 10: 5 Nephi² would not ask that which is contrary to the Lord's *w*.; **3 Ne.** 1: 14 Christ comes to do *w*. both of Father and of Son; 6: 18 people do not sin ignorantly, for they know *w*. of God; 11: 11 Christ has suffered *w*. of Father in all things; 13: 10 (Matt. 6: 10) thy *w*. be done on earth as it is in heaven; 27: 13 Christ came into world to do *w*. of Father; 28: 7 three Nephites to live until all things are fulfilled according to *w*. of Father; **Morm.** 8: 14–15 God *w*. that records be brought forth with eye single to his glory; **Ether** 3: 4 God has all power and can do whatsoever he *w*. for benefit of man.

WILLING, WILLINGNESS (*see also* Desire; Will)

2 Ne. 31: 13 witness unto Father you are *w*. to take name of Christ by baptism; **Mosiah** 3: 19 natural man must become as child, *w*. to submit to all things; 18: 8–9 must *w*. to bear one another's burdens should be baptized; 21: 35 baptism a testimony that men are *w*. to serve God; 26: 18 blessed is this people who are *w*. to bear the Lord's name; 29: 3 sons of Mosiah² not *w*. to become king; 29: 38 every man expresses *w*. to answer for his own sins; **Alma** 7: 15 show God you are *w*. to enter covenant by going into waters of baptism; **Hel.** 6: 36 the Lord pours out Spirit upon Lamanites because of their *w*. to believe his words; **3 Ne.** 6: 14 Lamanites are *w*. with all diligence to keep commandments; 18: 10 (Moro. 4: 3) partaking of sacrament witnesses to Father that men are *w*. to do what they have been commanded; **Moro.** 4: 3 (5: 2) partaking of sacrament witnesses that men are *w*. to take upon themselves Christ's name and always remember him.

WIN (*see also* Conquer; Gain)

Mosiah 4: 27 men should be diligent, that they might *w*. prize; **Alma** 17: 29 Ammon² shows power in restoring flocks that he might *w*. hearts of fellow-servants; **Ether** 9: 10 sons of Akish *w*. hearts of people.

WIND (*see also* Storm; Tempest; Whirlwind)

1 Ne. 18: 8 Lehites driven before *w*. toward promised land; **Alma** 26: 6 converts shall not be driven with fierce *w*. whithersoever enemy listeth to carry them; 37: 15 (Morm. 5: 18) Satan to sift transgressor as chaff before *w*.; **Hel.** 5: 12 (3 Ne. 14: 24–25; Matt. 7: 24–25) devil's *w*. have no power over those built upon rock of Redeemer; **3 Ne.** 11: 40 (14: 26–27; 18: 13; Matt. 7: 26–27) gates of hell stand open to receive those built on sandy foundation when *w*. beat upon them; 14: 25 those built on rock do not fall when *w*. blow; **Morm.** 5: 16, 18 Nephites are driven as chaff before *w*.; **Ether** 2: 24 *w*. have gone forth out of the Lord's mouth; 6: 5–8 furious *w*. blows Jaredite vessels toward promised land.

WINDOWS

3 Ne. 24: 10 (Mal. 3: 10) the Lord will open *w*. of heaven; **Ether** 2: 23 no *w*. in Jaredite barges.

WINE (*see also* Drink; Drunk, Drunken; Grape; Sacrament; Vine; Wine-press)

1 Ne. 4: 7 Laban drunken with *w*.; 21: 26 (Isa. 49: 26) they who oppress thee shall be drunken with own blood as with sweet *w*.; **2 Ne.** 8: 21 (Isa. 51: 21) hear now this, thou drunken, and not with *w*.; 9: 50 (Isa. 55: 1) come buy *w*. and milk without money; 15: 11 (Isa. 5: 11) wo unto them that follow strong drink from early in morning until night, and *w*. inflame them; 27: 4 those who do iniquity shall be drunken, but not with *w*.; **Mosiah** 11: 15 Noah³ builds *w*-presses

and makes *w*. in abundance; 22: 7–10 Limhi sends tribute of *w*. to Lamanites to make guards drunken; **Alma** 55: 8–14 Laman⁴ takes *w*. to Lamanite guards to make them drunken; **3 Ne.** 18: 1–3, 8–9 (20: 5–9) Christ administers *w*. in sacrament to Nephites; 20: 8 (Moro. 5: 2) *w*. of sacrament in remembrance of Christ's blood; **Ether** 15: 22 Jaredites drunken with anger, as man who is drunken with *w*.; **Moro.** ch. 5. mode of administering sacramental *w*.; 6: 6 church meets oft to partake of bread and *w*. in remembrance of Jesus.

WINE-PRESS (*see also* Wine)

Mosiah 18: 15 Noah³ builds *w-p*.

WING

2 Ne. 4: 25 body of Nephi¹ is carried upon *w*. of Spirit to high mountain; 16: 1–2 (Isa. 6: 1–2) seraphim with six *w*. above God's throne; 25: 13 Christ to rise from dead with healing in *w*.; **3 Ne.** 10: 4–6 (Matt. 23: 37; Luke 13: 34) the Lord would gather Israel as hen gathers chickens under *w*.; 25: 2 Son of Righteousness to arise with healing in his *w*.

WISDOM, WISE (*see also* God, Wisdom of; Knowledge; Learned [adj.]; Learning; Prudence; Understand)

1 Ne. 9: 5 (W of M 1: 6–7) the Lord commands Nephi¹ to make plates for *w*. purpose; **2 Ne.** 9: 28 when men are learned, they think they are *w*.; 9: 28 *w*. of the learned is foolishness; 9: 42 the Lord despises those who are puffed up because of *w*.; 15: 21 (Isa. 5: 21) wo unto the *w*. in their own eyes; 21: 2 (Isa. 11: 2) spirit of *w*. and understanding shall rest upon him; 27: 26 (Isa. 29: 14) *w*. of their wise and learned shall perish; 28: 30 those who hearken to the Lord's counsel shall learn *w*.; **Jacob** 6: 12 be *w*., what can I say more; **Mosiah** 2: 17 Benjamin tells his people these things that they might learn *w*.; 2: 36 transgressors withdraw themselves from Spirit, that it has no place to guide them in *w*'s paths; 4: 27 see that all these things are done in *w*. and order; 29: 11 appoint *w*. men to be judges; **Alma** 29: 8 the Lord grants unto all nations to teach his word in *w*.; 32: 12 necessary that you should learn *w*.; 32: 23 little children are given words that confound the *w*.; 37: 2 sacred things are kept for *w*. purpose; 37: 35 learn *w*. in thy youth; 38: 9 Alma² speaks to son, that he may learn *w*.; 38: 11 do not boast in your own *w*.; **Hel.** 12: 5 how slow are men to walk in *w*'s paths; 16: 14 angels appear unto *w*. men; 16: 15 people depend upon own *w*.; **3 Ne.** 14: 24–25 (Matt. 7: 24–25) those who do Jesus' sayings are compared to *w*. man who builds house on

rock; **Morm.** 9: 28 be *w*. in days of probation; **Moro.** 10: 9 to one is given by Spirit to teach word of *w*.

WISH (*see also* Desire; Will)

Alma 13: 27 Alma² *w*. that people would hearken to his words; 29: 1 O that I were an angel and could have *w*. of my heart; 29: 3 I am a man and do sin in my *w*.; **3 Ne.** 4: 16 if robbers can cut Nephites off from outward privileges, Nephites would yield themselves up according to robbers' *w*.

WITCHCRAFT (*see also* Magic; Sorceries)

3 Ne. 21: 16 (Micah 5: 12) the Lord will cut off *w*. out of land; **Morm.** 1: 19 (2: 10) *w*. in land.

WITHDRAW (*see also* Darkness, Spiritual; Excommunication; Shrink; Spirit, Holy/Spirit of the Lord)

Mosiah 2: 36 those who transgress against knowledge *w*. themselves from Spirit; **Alma** 1: 24 many *w*. themselves from church; 34: 35 Spirit *w*. from those who become subject to spirit of devil; **Hel.** 4: 24 Spirit *w*. from Nephites; 13: 8 because of hardness of hearts, the Lord will *w*. Spirit from Nephites.

WITHER, WITHERED

Jacob 5: 40 wild branch overcomes tree, that good branch *w*.; **Alma** 32: 38 if ye do not nourish tree, it will *w*. in heat; **3 Ne.** 17: 7 bring the *w*. that the Lord may heal them.

WITHHOLD, WITHHELD (*see also* Hinder; Hold; Keep; Restrain; Retain; Stay; Stop)

1 Ne. 17: 49 brothers commanded not to *w*. labor from Nephi¹; **Mosiah** 4: 22 (Alma 5: 55) how much more just will be your condemnation for *w*. your substance; **Alma** 14: 22–23 people of Ammonihah *w*. food from Alma² and Amulek; **Hel.** 4: 11–12 slaughter of Nephites caused by *w*. food from hungry and clothing from the naked; **3 Ne.** 26: 10 if men do not believe these things, greater things shall be *w*.; **Ether** 3: 25–26 (12: 21) the Lord *w*. nothing from sight of brother of Jared²; **Moro.** 7: 36 has the Lord *w*. power of Holy Ghost.

WITHSTAND (*see also* Overcome; Reject; Resist)

Mosiah 12: 19 Abinadi *w*. priests' questions; **Alma** 5: 53 can ye *w*. these sayings; 30: 53 Korihor *w*. truth because he was deceived by devil; 37: 33 teach them to *w*. every temptation.

WITNESS (*see also* Apostle; Baptism; Convince; Evidence; Prove; Record; Revela-

tion; See; Testify; Verified; Witnesses, Three; TG Witness; Witness of the Father)

1 Ne. 11: 7 Nephi[1] to w. man descending out of heaven; **2 Ne.** 11: 3 (27: 13–14) God sends more than three w.; 13: 9 (Isa. 3: 9) show of their countenances w. against them; 18: 2 (Isa. 8: 2) Isaiah[1] takes faithful w. to record; 27: 14 in mouth of as many w. as seems good the Lord will establish his word; 27: 22 book to be sealed again after w. have been obtained; 29: 8 testimony of two nations is w. that I am God; 31: 6–7 by baptism, Christ w. to Father that he would be obedient; 31: 13–14 (Mosiah 18: 10; 3 Ne. 18: 10; Moro. 4: 3) baptism is w. to Father that you are willing to take name of Christ and keep commandments; 31: 18 (3 Ne. 16: 6) Holy Ghost w. of Father and Son; **Jacob** 4: 6 having w. of prophets and revelations, we obtain a hope; 4: 13 Nephites are not w. alone of these things; **Mosiah** 13: 23 (Ex. 20: 16) thou shalt not bear false w.; 18: 9–10 those willing to stand as w. of God should be baptized; 18: 10 baptism a w. that men have entered covenant with God; 21: 35 baptism a w. of willingness to serve God; 24: 14 people of Alma[1] to stand as w. of God; 26: 9 many w. against unbelievers; **Alma** 14: 11 blood of the innocent shall stand as w. against the wicked; 30: 45 will ye deny all these w.; 34: 30 after ye have received w., bring fruit unto repentance; 47: 33 Lamanite queen asks Amalickiah to bring w. of king's death; **Hel.** 16: 20 people do not believe what they cannot w. with own eyes; **3 Ne.** 7: 15 Nephi[3] an eye-w.; 18: 11 (Moro. 4: 3; 5: 2) partake of sacrament that Christ may w. to Father that ye always remember him; 24: 5 (Mal. 3: 5) the Lord will be swift w. against the wicked; **Ether** 12: 6 ye receive no w. until after trial of faith; **Moro.** 6: 7 transgressor condemned by three w. is not numbered among church.

WITNESSES, THREE

2 Ne. 27: 12 (Ether 5: 2–4) t.w. to see book by power of God and testify to its truth.

WIVES (see Wife)

WOLF, WOLVES (see also Animal; Prophets, False)

2 Ne. 21: 6 (30: 12; Isa. 11: 6) w. shall dwell with lamb; **Alma** 5: 59 shepherd watches that no w. enter and devour flock; 5: 60 suffer no ravenous w. to enter among you; **3 Ne.** 14: 15 (Matt. 7: 15) beware of false prophets in sheep's clothing, inwardly they are ravening w.

WOMAN, WOMEN (see also Creation; Daughter; Eve; Female; Mother; Wife; TG Woman)

1 Ne. 17: 1–2, 20 Lehite w. bear children, are strong like unto men; 21: 15 (Isa. 49: 15) can w. forget her sucking child; **2 Ne.** 9: 21 Christ to suffer pains of all men, w., children; 13: 12 (Isa. 3: 12) w. shall rule over the Lord's people; 14: 1 (Isa. 4: 1) seven w. shall ask to be called by one man's name to take away reproach; **Jacob** 2: 28 the Lord delights in chastity of w.; **Mosiah** 10: 5 (Hel. 6: 13) w. spin and toil; **Alma** 19: 16–17 Lamanitish w. named Abish makes known what has happened to Lamoni; 19: 28–29 w. servant takes queen by hand to raise her; 30: 18 Korihor leads away many w. and men to commit whoredoms; 32: 23 the Lord imparts his word by angels to men, w., children; 54: 3 Lamanites take w. and children as prisoners; **3 Ne.** 12: 28 (Matt. 5: 28) whoso looks upon a w. to lust after her has committed adultery in heart; 22: 6 (Isa. 54: 6) the Lord has called thee as a w. forsaken; **Morm.** 4: 14, 21 Lamanites offer w. and children as sacrifices to idols; **Moro.** 9: 8 Lamanites feed w. flesh of husbands; 9: 16 many old w. die from hunger.

WOMB

1 Ne. 20: 8 (Isa. 48: 8) thou wast called a transgressor from w.; 21: 1, 5 (Isa. 49: 1, 5) the Lord has called me from w.; 21: 15 (Isa. 49: 15) can woman not have compassion on son of her w.

WONDER, WONDERFUL (see also Marvel; Miracle; Sign)

1 Ne. 19: 13 Jews will reject signs and w.; **2 Ne.** 3: 24 one shall rise up to work mighty w. in restoring Israel; 19: 6 (Isa. 9: 6) Messiah shall be called W.; 25: 17 (27: 26; Isa. 29: 14) the Lord will do marvelous work and w. among men; 26: 13 the Lord works w. among men according to their faith; **Mosiah** 3: 15 the Lord showed many signs and w. to Israel; **Hel.** 14: 6 (3 Ne. 1: 22; 2: 1) many signs and w. in heavens at Christ's birth; 16: 4 Nephi[2] shows people signs and w.

WOOD (see also Timber; Waste)

1 Ne. 16: 23 Nephi[1] makes bow out of w.; **2 Ne.** 5: 15 (Jarom 1: 8) Nephites work in all manner of w.; **Mosiah** 11: 8 Noah[3] ornaments buildings with fine w.; **Hel.** 3: 10–11 Nephites ship timber to land northward to build cities of w. and cement; **3 Ne.** 8: 21 because of darkness, no fire can be kindled with fine and dry w.

WORD (see also Communication; Language; Lips; Mouth; Read; Sayings;

Tongue; Utter, Utterance; Voice; Word of God/Word of the Lord; TG Word)

1 Ne. 3: 18 Jews have rejected w. of prophets; 17: 26 by Moses' w., waters of Red Sea were divided; **2 Ne.** 3: 19–20 fruit of loins of Joseph[1] shall cry from dust according to simpleness of their w.; 3: 21 weakness of their w. will the Lord make strong in their faith; 9: 40 give ear to my w.; 9: 40 w. of truth are hard against all uncleanness; 25: 19 according to w. of prophets the Messiah comes in six hundred years after Lehi[1] left Jerusalem; 27: 6, 14 the Lord will bring forth w. of book, which shall be w. of those who have slumbered; 27: 31–32 they who make a man an offender for a w. shall be cut off; 28: 8 many shall say, take advantage of one because of his w.; 29: 2 w. of seed of Nephi[1] shall proceed out of the Lord's mouth; 33: 10 if ye believe in Christ, ye will believe in these w.; **Enos** 1: 3 w. Enos[2] had heard father speak concerning eternal life sink deep into his heart; **Mosiah** 4: 30 if ye do not watch thoughts and w., ye must perish; 15: 11 those who have hearkened to w. of prophets concerning Christ are heirs of kingdom of God; **Alma** 12: 14 our w. will condemn us; 30: 43 Korihor has no evidence that there is no God except his own w.; 32: 27 try experiment upon w. of Alma[2]; 41: 12–15 meaning of w. restoration is to bring back evil for evil, good for good; 61: 14 whatsoever evil we cannot resist with our w., let us resist with swords; **Hel.** 10: 5 the Lord will make Nephi[2] mighty in w. and deed; 12: 4 how quick are men to hearken to w. of evil one; **3 Ne.** 19: 24 disciples do not multiply many w. in prayer; **Ether** 12: 23 the Lord has made Nephites mighty in w. by faith, but not in writing; **Moro.** 10: 9 to one is given by Spirit to teach w. of wisdom; 10: 10 to another is given to teach w. of knowledge.

WORD OF GOD/WORD OF THE LORD (*see also* Gospel; Revelation; Word; TG Word of God; Word of the Lord)

1 Ne. 2: 3 Lehi[1] is obedient to w. of the Lord; 4: 14 Nephi[1] remembers w. of the Lord spoken in wilderness; 7: 4 sons of Lehi[1] speak w. of the Lord to Ishmael[1]; 7: 9 how is it ye have not hearkened to w. of the Lord; 7: 13 (10: 13; 2 Ne. 5: 19–20; Mosiah 21: 4; 3 Ne. 29: 2) w. of the Lord to be fulfilled; 11: 25 (15: 24) iron rod is w. of God; 15: 25 Nephi[1] exhorts brothers to give heed to w. of God; 17: 23 would Israel have been led out of Egypt if they had not hearkened to w. of the Lord; 17: 31 according to his w., God did all things for Israelites; 17: 31 nothing done save it were by God's w.; 17: 35

children of land had rejected every w. of God; 17: 45 ye were past feeling that ye could not feel his w.; **2 Ne.** 1: 26 sharpness of Nephi[1] is sharpness of power of w. of God; 3: 11 the Lord will give power to latter-day seer to bring forth his w. and convince people of his w.; 9: 16 God's eternal w. cannot pass away; 9: 40 Nephi[1] has spoken w. of your maker; 12: 3 (Isa. 2: 3) w. of the Lord shall go out from Jerusalem; 27: 14 wo unto him who rejects w. of God; 28: 29 wo unto him who shall say, We have received w. of God and need no more; 29: 2–3 (Moro. 10: 28) the Lord's w. shall hiss forth to ends of earth; 29: 9 the Lord speaks forth his w. according to his own pleasure; 29: 9 because the Lord has spoken one w., ye need not suppose he cannot speak another; 29: 14 the Lord's w. shall be gathered in one; 31: 15 voice from the Father says, W. of my Beloved are true; 31: 20 (32: 3) press forward, feasting upon w. of Christ; 32: 3 angels speak w. of Christ; 32: 3 w. of Christ will tell you all things you should do; **Jacob** 1: 19 teachers take responsibility for people's sins if they do not teach w. of God; 2: 4 (Morm. 7: 7) as yet, Nephites have been obedient to w. of the Lord; 2: 8 pleasing w. of God heals wounded soul; 2: 27 (Morm. 9: 27) hearken to w. of the Lord; 2: 35 because of strictness of w. of God which comes down against wicked, many hearts die pierced with deep wounds; 4: 9 by God's w. man came upon face of earth; 6: 7 after ye have been nourished by good w. of God, will ye bring forth evil fruit; **Jarom** 1: 9 (Alma 9: 14; 25: 17; 50: 19, 21) w. of the Lord is verified; **Omni** 1: 13 (Mosiah 26: 39) Nephites are admonished by w. of God; **W of M** 1: 11 people are judged out of records, according to w. of God; **Mosiah** 11: 29 Noah[3] hardens heart against w. of the Lord; 18: 32 people of Alma[1] assemble to hear w. of the Lord; 20: 21 Abinadi's prophecies are fulfilled because people would not hearken to w. of the Lord; 26: 3 because of unbelief, people could not understand w. of God; 26: 38 teachers teach w. of God in all things; 28: 1 (Alma 17: 4) sons of Mosiah[2] to impart w. of God to Lamanites; **Alma** 1: 15 Nehor acknowledges he has taught contrary to w. of God; 1: 20 members of church impart w. of God without money or price; 1: 26 priests leave labor to impart w. of God; 3: 14 w. of God is fulfilled; 3: 18 Amlicites fulfill w. of God by marking themselves in foreheads; 4: 18–19 Alma[2] gives up judgment-seat to preach w. of God; 4: 19 Alma[2] pulls down pride and contentions w. of God; 5: 7 souls of fathers were illuminated by light of everlasting w.; 5: 58 w. of God must be

fulfilled; 6: 5 *w.* of God is liberal unto all; 8: 24 Alma² is called to preach *w.* of God; 9: 30 Nephites' hearts have been hardened against *w.* of God; 12: 10 he who hardens heart receives lesser portion of *w.*; 12: 10 he who hardens not heart receives greater portion of *w.*; 12: 26–27 *w.* of God would have been void if first parents had lived forever; 16: 14 Alma² and Amulek impart *w.* of God without respect of persons; 17: 2 sons of Mosiah² search scriptures to know *w.* of God; 26: 13 Lamanites loosed from pains of hell by power of God's *w.*; 31: 5 preaching of *w.* has tendency to lead people to do that which is just; 31: 5 Alma² to try virtue of *w.* of God; 32: 23 God imparts his *w.* by angels unto men; 32: 28 if seed swells, *w.* is good; 32: 40 if ye will not nourish the *w.*, ye can never pluck fruit of tree of life; 34: 5 question in Zoramites' minds whether *w.* be in Son of God; 36: 26 because of *w.* which God has imparted to Alma², many have been born of God; 37: 44 easy to give heed to *w.* of Christ, which points straight course to eternal bliss; 43: 24 *w.* of the Lord comes to Alma², who informs Moroni¹ concerning enemies; 44: 5 Nephites owe all happiness to *w.* of God; **Hel.** 3: 29 whosoever will may lay hold upon *w.* of God; 3: 29 *w.* of God leads man of Christ in narrow course across gulf of misery; 6: 2 Nephites reject *w.* of God; 6: 37 Lamanites preach *w.* of God to robbers; 10: 12, 14 Nephi² declares *w.* of the Lord; 10: 13 Nephites do not hearken to *w.* of the Lord; 10: 15, 17 Nephi² declares or sends *w.* of God to all the people; 13: 5 Samuel the Lamanite speaks *w.* of the Lord, which he put in heart; 13: 36 O that we had repented in day when *w.* of the Lord came to us; **3 Ne.** 17: 2 Jesus perceives that Nephites are weak and cannot understand all his *w.*; 28: 20 disciples smite earth with *w.* of God and are delivered from depths; **4 Ne.** 1: 12 Nephites meet oft to hear *w.* of the Lord; **Morm.** 8: 33 why have ye transfigured holy *w.* of God; 9: 17 by power of God's *w.* heaven, earth, and man were created; 9: 17 by power of God's *w.* miracles are wrought; **Ether** 4: 8 he who contends against *w.* of the Lord shall be accursed; 4: 9 at Christ's *w.*, earth shall shake; 13: 20 (14: 24) *w.* of the Lord comes to Ether; **Moro.** 6: 4 those baptized should be nourished by good *w.* of God; 8: 7 *w.* of the Lord comes to Mormon²; 8: 9 Holy Ghost manifests *w.* of God to Mormon²; 9: 4 Mormon² speaks *w.* of God with sharpness.

WORK, WORKS [noun] (*see also* Act; Creation; Deed; Faithful; Fruit; Grace; Judgment; Repentance; Serve; Working; Workings; Workmanship)

1 Ne. 1: 14 (Jacob 4: 8) great and marvelous are thy *w.*, O Lord; 9: 6 the Lord prepares a way to accomplish all his *w.*; 14: 7 (22: 8; 2 Ne. 25: 17; 27: 26; 29: 1; 3 Ne. 21: 9; Isa. 29: 14) the Lord will work great and marvelous *w.*; 15: 32 (2 Ne. 9: 44; Mosiah 3: 24; Alma 41: 3) men must be judged of their *w.*; **2 Ne.** 4: 17 goodness of God in showing me great and marvelous *w.*; 27: 27 their *w.* are in dark; 27: 27 the Lord knows all their *w.*; 29: 9 the Lord's *w.* are not yet finished; 30: 8 the Lord will commence his *w.* among all nations to bring about restoration of his people; **Mosiah** 13: 17–18 (Ex. 20: 9–10) six days shalt thou do all thy *w.*, but on sabbath thou shalt not do any *w.*; **Alma** 5: 16 can you imagine the Lord saying, your *w.* have been *w.* of righteousness; 5: 41 if a man brings forth good *w.*, he hearkens to voice of good shepherd; 5: 41–42 he who brings forth evil *w.* is child of devil and is dead unto all good *w.*; 7: 24 (Ether 12: 4) see that ye have faith, hope, and charity, then ye will abound in good *w.*; 9: 28 men shall reap reward of their *w.*; 26: 15 sons of Mosiah² have been instruments in God's hand in doing great and marvelous *w.*; 37: 12 God counsels in wisdom over all his *w.*; 37: 34 never be weary of good *w.*; 40: 13 spirits of the wicked chose evil *w.* rather than good; 41: 3 if a man's *w.* were good in this life, he will be restored to good; 41: 4 if man's *w.* were evil, they shall be restored to him for evil; **Hel.** 15: 15 if mighty *w.* had been shown to those who dwindled in unbelief, they would not have dwindled; **3 Ne.** 12: 16 (Matt. 5: 16) let your light so shine that people will see your good *w.*; 21: 17 (Micah 5: 13) thou shalt no more worship the *w.* of thy hands; 21: 26 *w.* of Father will commence when gospel is preached to remnant of Nephites; 22: 16 (Isa. 54: 16) I have created the smith that bringeth forth an instrument for his *w.*; 27: 10 if church is built upon gospel, Father will show his *w.* in it; 27: 11 if church is built upon *w.* of men or devil, they have joy in their *w.* until cast into fire; **Morm.** 9: 16 who can comprehend the marvelous *w.* of God; **Moro.** 7: 5 by their *w.* ye shall know them; 8: 22–23 to suppose little children need baptism is putting trust in dead *w.*

WORK [verb] (*see also* Industry; Labor; Perform; Strive; Work [noun]; Working; Workings; Workmanship; Wrought; TG Work, Value of)

1 Ne. 16: 28 pointers in Liahona *w.* according to faith and diligence; **2 Ne.** 5: 15 Nephites *w.* all manner of woods and metals; 26: 13 Christ *w.* mighty miracles according to men's faith; 26: 23 the Lord *w.* not in darkness; 31: 3 the Lord *w.*

among men in plainness; **Mosiah** 3: 5 (15: 6) the Lord will go forth among men, w. mighty miracles; 10: 5 Zeniff causes women to w.; **Alma** 23: 6 power of God w. miracles in those who believe; 30: 42–43 devil w. devices in Korihor to destroy children of God; 32: 27 if ye can no more than desire to believe, let this desire w. in you; 34: 37 (Morm. 9: 27) w. out your salvation with fear before God; 37: 38, 41 because miracles were w. by small means, Liahona showed Lehites marvelous works; **Hel.** 6: 11 curious workmen w. all kinds of ore; 16: 4 Nephi² w. miracles among the people; **3 Ne.** 27: 33 many travel broad way until night comes wherein no man can w.; 29: 6 wo unto him that shall say the Lord no longer w. by revelation; **Ether** 8: 19 the Lord w. not in secret combinations; 10: 23 Jaredites w. all manner of ore, metals, fine work; 12: 30 the Lord w. after men have faith; **Moro.** 10: 7 God w. by power, according to men's faith; 10: 8 the same God w. different gifts; 10: 25 if there be one among you who does good, he shall w. by power and gifts of God.

WORKING, WORKINGS (see also Work [noun]; Work [verb])

1 Ne. 19: 20 Nephi¹ has w. in spirit which weary him; **2 Ne.** 1: 6 Lehi¹ prophesies according to w. of Spirit; **Jacob** 4: 15 Jacob² perceives by w. of Spirit that Jews will stumble; **W of M** 1: 17 I do this for wise purpose, for thus it whispereth me according to w. of Spirit; **Hel.** 3: 7 people in land northward become expert in w. of cement; **Moro.** 6: 9 church meetings conducted after manner of w. of Spirit.

WORKMANSHIP, WORKMAN

1 Ne. 4: 9 w. of Laban's sword exceedingly fine; 16: 10 (Alma 37: 38–39) Liahona a ball of curious w.; 18: 1, 4 Nephi¹ and brothers work timbers of curious w. for ship; **Jarom** 1: 8 Nephites become rich in fine w. of wood; **Hel.** 6: 11 curious w. work and refine all ore; **Ether** 10: 27 Jaredites work all manner of work of curious w.

WORLD (see also Babylon; Creation; Earth; Flesh; Man; Mortal; Nature, Natural; Spirit World; Temporal; Wicked, Wickedness; TG World; World, End of; Worldliness)

1 Ne. 6: 5 Nephi¹ writes things pleasing to God, not to w.; 8: 20 iron rod leads into spacious field, as if it were a w.; 11: 32 Son to be judged of the w.; 11: 35–36 great and spacious building is pride of w.; 13: 9 for praise of w., abominable church destroys saints; 14: 19–22, 27 John the apostle to write concerning end of w.;

19: 9 w. will judge Christ to be thing of naught; 22: 23 church built up to become popular in eyes of w. shall be brought low; 22: 23 those who seek things of w. should fear and tremble; **2 Ne.** 9: 18 saints have endured crosses of w.; 9: 18 kingdom of God prepared for saints from foundation of w.; 9: 30 wo unto those who are rich as to things of w.; 23: 11 (Isa. 13: 11) Lord will punish the w. for evil; 26: 24 the Lord does not anything save for benefit of w., for he loves w.; 26: 29 priestcrafts are that men set themselves up for light unto w. to get praise of w.; 27: 10 sealed revelations reveal all things from foundation of w. to end; 27: 23 Lord will show w. he is same yesterday, today, forever; **Jacob** 6: 3 w. shall be burned with fire; **Mosiah** 16: 9 (Alma 38: 9; 3 Ne. 9: 18; 11: 11; Ether 4: 12) Christ is light and life of w.; 27: 31 those who live without God in w. shall confess his judgment is just; **Alma** 1: 16 many who love vain things of w.; 5: 37 (31: 27) those who are puffed up in vain things of w. have gone astray; 11: 40 Christ shall come into w.; 32: 3 outcast Zoramites are poor as to things of w.; 60: 32 Nephites' iniquity is caused by love of vain things of w.; **Hel.** 5: 9 (Morm. 7: 7) Christ to come to redeem w.; 7: 5 robbers obtain government to get glory of w.; **3 Ne.** 19: 20 Christ has chosen disciples out of w.; 19: 29 Jesus prays not for w., but for those the Father has given him out of w.; 27: 16 Christ will stand to judge w.; 28: 25 names of three Nephites are hid from w.; **Morm.** 8: 38 men do not value endless happiness greater than undying misery because of praise of w.; 9: 22 go ye into all w. and preach gospel to every creature; **Ether** 4: 14 Father has laid up great things for Israel from foundation of w.; 5: 4 sacred record and witnesses shall stand as testimony against w.; 12: 4 those who believe in God might with surety hope for better w.; **Moro.** 10: 19 spiritual gifts shall not be done away as long as w. stands.

WORM (see also Corrupt, Corruption)

2 Ne. 8: 8 (Isa. 51: 8) w. shall eat men like wool; 24: 11 (Isa. 14: 11) w. is spread under thee and w. cover thee; **Ether** 14: 22 bodies of slain left to become prey to w.

WORRY (see also Anxiety, Anxious; Fear; Trouble)

Alma 40: 1 (41: 1) Corianton is w. concerning resurrection; 42: 1 Corianton is w. concerning God's justice in punishing sinner; 61: 19 Pahoran¹ w. what loyal Nephites should do.

WORSE (see also Bad)

Alma 24: 30 state of enlightened

people who fall into sin is *w*. than if they had never known; **Hel.** 13: 26 this people is *w*. than fathers of old.

WORSHIP (*see also* Assemble; Bow [verb]; Fear of God; Idolatry; Meet, Meeting; Praise; Religion; Serve; Worshipper; TG Worship)

1 Ne. 17: 55 elder brothers are about to *w*. Nephi[1], but he commands them to *w*. the Lord; 21: 7 (Isa. 49: 7) princes shall *w*. because of the Lord that is faithful; **2 Ne.** 12: 8 (Isa. 2: 8) they *w*. work of own hands; 25: 16 Jews to *w*. Father in Christ's name; 25: 29 *w*. Christ with all your might, mind, strength; **Jacob** 4: 5 prophets *w*. Father in Christ's name; **Alma** 15: 17 Nephites assemble in sanctuaries to *w*. God; 21: 22 Lamoni declares liberty of *w*. the Lord according to desires; 31: 12 Zoramites *w*. God in manner Alma[2] has never beheld; 32: 5 (33: 2) outcast Zoramites have no place to *w*. God; 34: 38 *w*. God in whatsoever place ye may be; 43: 10 Lamanites would destroy whoever *w*. God in spirit and truth; 50: 39 chief judge appointed with oath to grant sacred privileges to *w*. the Lord; **3 Ne.** 11: 17 (17: 10) Nephites fall at Jesus' feet and *w*. him; 21: 17 thou shalt no more *w*. works of thy hands; **Moro.** 7: 1 Mormon[2] teaches people in synagogue built for place of *w*.

WORSHIPPER (*see also* Believer; Worship)

4 Ne. 1: 37 true *w*. of Christ are called Nephites, Jacobites, Josephites, and Zoramites.

WORTH (*see also* Esteem; Merit; Precious; Respect; Value; Worthless; Worthy; TG Worth of Souls)

1 Ne. 5: 21 brass plates are of great *w*. in preserving commandments; 13: 23 covenants recorded in Bible are of great *w*. to Gentiles; 19: 7 things that some esteem of great *w*., others set at naught; 22: 8–9 marvelous work of the Lord to be of great *w*. to Gentiles and to all Israel; **2 Ne.** 9: 51 do not spend money for that which is of no *w*.; 25: 7–8 prophecies of Isaiah[1] are of great *w*.; 33: 3 Nephi[1] esteems what he has written to be of great *w*.; **Jacob** 5: 46 trees the Lord had hoped to preserve are of no *w*.; **Alma** 34: 29 if ye are not charitable, ye are as dross which refiners cast out, being of no *w*.; **Morm.** 8: 14 plates are of no *w*., but record is of great *w*.; **Moro.** 1: 4 Moroni[2] writes few more things that they may be of *w*. to Lamanites.

WORTHLESS

Mosiah 4: 5 knowledge of God's goodness should awaken men to sense of *w*. and fallen state.

WORTHY, WORTHINESS (*see also* Clean; Faithful; Righteousness; Uprightness)

1 Ne. 10: 8 prophet crying in wilderness feels he is not *w*. to unloose Christ's shoe latchet; **Mosiah** 17: 7 priests find Abinadi *w*. of death; **Alma** 36: 5 God has made things known to Alma[2], not of any *w*. of his; 56: 10 two thousand Ammonite youths are *w*. to be called sons; **Morm.** 9: 29 see that ye do all things in *w*.; **Moro.** 6: 1 men not baptized save they bring forth fruit meet that that they are *w*. of it.

WOUND, WOUNDED (*see also* Bruise; Stripes)

Jacob 2: 8 pleasing word of God heals the *w*. soul; 2: 9, 35 delicate minds of wives and children have been *w*.; **Mosiah** 14: 5 (Isa. 53: 5) he was *w*. for our transgressions.

WRAPT

3 Ne. 26: 3 earth to be *w*. together as scroll.

WRATH (*see also* Anger; Destruction; Displeasure; Fury; Judgment; Punishment; Rage)

1 Ne. 13: 11 *w*. of God is upon seed of Lamanites; 14: 15–17 *w*. of God poured out upon abominable church; 17: 35 fulness of *w*. of God was upon children of land; 22: 16 fulness of *w*. of God to be poured out upon all men; **2 Ne.** 1: 17 Lehi[1] fears the Lord will come out in fulness of *w*. upon sons; **Alma** 12: 36 iniquity of Ammonihah provokes God to send down *w*.; **Morm.** 8: 21 he who breathes out *w*. against work of the Lord shall be hewn down; **Ether** 2: 9 (9: 20; 14: 25) those in promised land who do not serve God will be swept off when his *w*. comes; 2: 9 fulness of the Lord's *w*. comes when people are ripened in iniquity.

WREST (*see also* Pervert)

Alma 13: 20 if ye *w*. scriptures, it will be to your destruction; 41: 1 some have *w*. scriptures and have gone far astray.

WRESTLE (*see also* Struggle)

Enos 1: 2 Enos[2] *w*. before God before receiving remission of sins; **Alma** 8: 10 Alma[2] *w*. with God in mighty prayer to pour out Spirit.

WRETCHED (*see also* Misery, Miserable)

2 Ne. 4: 17 O *w*. man that I am.

WRIT (*see also* Scriptures)

Alma 37: 5 all plates which contain holy *w*. shall retain brightness.

WRITE, WROTE, WRITTEN (*see also*

Book; Engrave; Language; Record; Scriptures; Writing)

1 Ne. 14: 25 Nephi¹ is not to *w.* what he sees, for John the apostle will *w.*; 14: 28, 30 Nephi¹ has *w.* but small part of things he saw; 14: 30 the things which Nephi¹ has *w.* are true; 19: 6 Nephi¹ *w.* only sacred things on plates; **2 Ne.** 3: 12 that which is *w.* by descendants of Joseph¹ and Judah shall grow together; 3: 17 the Lord will *w.* unto Moses his law; 4: 14 history is *w.* upon other plates; 4: 15 things of soul and scriptures *w.* upon these plates; 6: 3 Jacob² has spoken concerning all things *w.*, from creation of world; 25: 23 we labor diligently to *w.* to persuade our children to believe in Christ; 29: 11 the Lord commands all men to *w.* words he speaks to them; 29: 12 Jews, Nephites, scattered tribes, all nations shall *w.* what the Lord speaks to them; 33: 1 Nephi¹ cannot *w.* all things taught among his people; 33: 2 many cast away things that are *w.*; 33: 3 I, Nephi¹, have *w.* what I have *w.*; **Jacob** 1: 2 Nephi¹ commands Jacob² to *w.* upon plates; **Jarom** 1: 1 Jarom *w.* few words according to commandment of father; 1: 2 things *w.* on small plates are for benefit of Lamanites; **Omni** 1: 1 Omni is commanded by father to *w.* upon plates; 1: 9 Chemish *w.* in same book with brother; **W of M** 1: 2 Mormon² prays Moroni² might survive to *w.* concerning Lamanites; **Mosiah** 5: 12 retain the name *w.* always in your heart; 13: 11 Abinadi reads commandments, for they are not *w.* in priests' hearts; 24: 6 Lamanites taught to keep record, that they might *w.* one to another; **Alma** 5: 58 names of righteous shall be *w.* in book of life; 30: 52 Korihor *w.* that he is dumb; **Hel.** 3: 8 Nephi² speaks many things that cannot be *w.*; **3 Ne.** 16: 4 (23: 4) Jesus commands Nephites to *w.* his sayings after he is gone; 16: 4 (23: 4) sayings which Nephites *w.* to be manifested to Gentiles and Israel; 23: 9–13 Jesus asks why Samuel's prophecy of saints' resurrection is not *w.*; 23: 14 Jesus expounds all scriptures in one which they had *w.*; 26: 12 Mormon² *w.* things commanded of the Lord; 26: 18 many see and hear unspeakable things which are not lawful to be *w.*; 27: 23–24 Jesus commands disciples to *w.* what they have seen and heard; 27: 26 all things are *w.* by Father; 27: 26 out of books which shall be *w.* will world be judged; **Morm.** 5: 9 Mormon² *w.* small abridgment; 5: 12 these things are *w.* to remnant of house of Jacob; 5: 12 record *w.* upon plates to be hid and brought forth; 8: 4 Moroni² will *w.* and hide up records in earth; 9: 33 if plates were larger, Nephites would *w.* in Hebrew; 9:

33 if record were *w.* in Hebrew, no imperfections; **Ether** 3: 22 (4: 1) brother of Jared² to *w.* what he has seen and heard in language that cannot be read; 4: 16 revelations *w.* by John shall be unfolded to all; 12: 24 Nephites can *w.* but little because of awkwardness of hands; 12: 24 things which brother of Jared² *w.* were mighty; 12: 41 seek Jesus of whom prophets and apostles have *w.*; 15: 33 Moroni² has not *w.* hundredth part of Ether's record.

WRITING, WRITINGS (*see also* Write)

1 Ne. 13: 35–36 in hidden *w.* shall gospel be written; 16: 29 a new *w.* written upon Liahona; **2 Ne.** 3: 17 the Lord will give judgment to Moses in *w.*; 33: 1 Nephi¹ is not mighty in *w.* like unto speaking; **Jarom** 1: 14 on other plates are records of war, according to *w.* of kings; **Alma** 10: 2 Aminadi interpreted *w.* on temple wall, written by finger of God; **Ether** 12: 23–26, 40 the Lord has not made Nephites mighty in *w.*

WRONG, WRONGED, WRONGFULLY (*see also* Evil)

Mosiah 10: 12–13 (Alma 54: 17) Lamanites believe their fathers were *w.* in wilderness by brethren; 26: 13 Alma¹ fears he should do *w.* in sight of God; **Alma** 7: 20 the Lord has no shadow of turning from right to *w.*; **3 Ne.** 3: 10–11 robbers threaten to avenge *w.* of those who had received no *w.*; **Moro.** 7: 18 see that ye do not judge *w.*

WROUGHT (*see also* Do; Work [verb])

1 Ne. 13: 12 Spirit came down and *w.* upon Gentile across many waters; 17: 51 if the Lord has *w.* so many miracles, why cannot he instruct Nephi¹ to build ship; 19: 12 kings of isles of sea shall be *w.* upon by Spirit; **2 Ne.** 10: 4 if mighty miracles were *w.* among other nations, they would repent; **Mosiah** 5: 2 Spirit has *w.* mighty change in Benjamin's people; **Alma** 5: 12 mighty change was *w.* in heart of Alma¹; **3 Ne.** 7: 22 those who are healed manifest that Spirit has *w.* upon them; 28: 31 great and marvelous works shall be *w.* by three Nephites; 28: 37–38 change *w.* upon bodies of three Nephites; 29: 7 he who says no miracle can be *w.* by Christ shall be like sons of perdition; **4 Ne.** 1: 13 many mighty miracles *w.* by Jesus' disciples; **Ether** 12: 16 (Moro. 7: 37) all who *w.* miracles *w.* them by faith.

YIELD (*see also* Subject; Submissive, Submit)

1 Ne. 19: 10 God to *y.* himself into hands of wicked men to be lifted up;

2 Ne. 4: 27 why should I y. to sin; 9: 39 remember awfulness of y. to enticings of cunning one; 26: 10 Nephites to reap destruction because they y. unto devil; **Mosiah** 3: 19 natural man is enemy to God unless he y. to enticings of Holy Spirit; 15: 5 the flesh becoming subject to Spirit y. not to temptation; **Alma** 5: 20 can ye think of being saved when ye have y. yourselves to become subjects to devil; 11: 23 the righteous y. to no such temptations; 51: 20 dissenters y. to standard of liberty; **Hel.** 3: 35 sanctification comes because men y. hearts unto God.

YOKE (see also Bondage; Subject)

1 Ne. 13: 5 abominable church y. saints with y. of iron; **2 Ne.** 19: 4 (Isa. 9: 4) thou hast broken y. of his burden; 20: 27 (Isa. 10: 27) his y. shall be taken from off thy neck, and the y. shall be destroyed because of the anointing; 24: 25 (Isa. 14: 25) y. of Assyrian shall depart from the Lord's people; **Alma** 44: 2 Nephites do not desire to bring anyone to y. of bondage; 49: 7 Lamanites suppose they will easily subject brethren to y. of bondage; 61: 12 we would subject ourselves to y. of bondage if requisite with God's justice.

YOUNG, YOUNGER (see also Youth)

1 Ne. 2: 16 Nephi[1] is exceedingly y. and large in stature; 7: 8 why do elder brothers harden hearts, that y. brother must speak to them; **Mosiah** 17: 2 Alma[1] a y. man; **Alma** 1: 30 Nephites are liberal to all, both old and y.; 5: 49 Alma[2] is called to preach unto all, both old and y.; 11: 44 restoration shall come to all, both old and y.; 53: 18 (56: 46) two thousand y. Ammonite men take up weapons to defend country; **Morm.** 2: 1 Mormon[2] is y. and large in stature; **Moro.** 9: 19 Nephites are brutal, sparing none, neither old nor y.

YOUTH (see also Young)

2 Ne. 2: 4 Jacob[2] has beheld God's glory in his y.; **Alma** 37: 35 learn wisdom in thy y.; 37: 35 learn in thy y. to keep God's commandments; **3 Ne.** 22: 4 thou shalt forget shame of thy y.

ZARAHEMLA—leader of Mulek's colony (see also Zarahemla, People of)

Omni 1: 14 rejoices that the Lord has sent Nephites; 1: 18 gives genealogy of fathers; **Mosiah** 7: 3, 13 Ammon[1] is a descendant of Z.; 25: 2 Z. is a descendant of Mulek; **Hel.** 1: 15 Coriantumr[3] is a descendant of Z.

ZARAHEMLA, CITY OF—major capital of Nephites from about 200 B.C. to A.D. 300 (see also Zarahemla, Land of)

Alma 2: 26 Nephite soldiers return to city of Z.; 5: 2 (6: 1–7) church established in Z.; 7: 3–5 Alma[2] laments for condition of people in Z.; 8: 1 Alma[2] returns to Z.; 31: 6 Alma[2] leaves Himni in church in Z.; 56: 25 Lamanites dare not march against Z.; 60: 1 Moroni[1] writes to Pahoran[1] in Z.; **Hel.** 1: 18–27 Coriantumr[3] captures Z.; 1: 27–33 Z. is captured by Lamanites, retaken by Moronihah; 7: 1–6 Nephi[2] returns to Z. and sees wickedness; 13: 12 only the righteous save the wicked in Z.; **3 Ne.** 8: 8 (9: 3) Z. is burned at Christ's death; 8: 24 Z. would not have been burned if people had repented; **4 Ne.** 1: 8 Z. is rebuilt.

ZARAHEMLA, LAND OF—region around city of Zarahemla; also area from southern wilderness to land Bountiful on north

Omni 1: 12–13 Mosiah[1] made king over land of Z.; 1: 24 Benjamin drives Lamanites from Z.; 1: 28 (2: 4) expedition seeking land of Nephi returns to Z.; **Mosiah** 1: 1 (2: 4) no more contention in Z.; 1: 18 people are gathered in land of Z. to hear Benjamin; 7: 9 Zeniff came out of land of Z.; 7: 13–14 Ammon[1] comes from Z. to inquire after people of Zeniff; 21: 24–26 Limhi's expedition failed to find Z.; 22: 11–13 Limhi's people arrive in Z.; 24: 25 Alma[1] and his people arrive in Z.; 25: 19–23 Alma[1] is permitted to establish churches throughout Z.; 27: 34–35 sons of Mosiah[2] preach throughout Z. to repair injuries; 29: 44 reign of judges commences in Z.; **Alma** 2: 15–25 Lamanites and Nephites battle in Z.; 4: 1 no contentions in Z.; 5: 1 Alma[2] begins his mission in Z.; 15: 18 Alma[2] returns to Z. with Amulek; 16: 1 peace continues in Z.; 22: 32 lands of Nephi and Z. nearly surrounded by water; 27: 5–20 people of Anti-Nephi-Lehi come to Z.; 30: 12 Korihor comes into Z.; 35: 14 Alma[2] and sons of Mosiah[2] return to Z.; 59: 4 Moroni[1] sends epistle to Z.; 60: 30 Moroni[1] threatens to come to Z. and smite leaders with sword; 62: 6–8 Moroni[1] restores Pahoran to judgment-seat in Z.; **Hel.** 3: 31 continual rejoicing in Z.; 4: 5 Lamanites capture Z.; 5: 16–19 Nephi[1] and Lehi[4] convert eight thousand Lamanites in Z.; 6: 4 many converted Lamanites gather to Z.; 7: 1 Nephi[1] returns to Z.; 13: 2 Samuel the Lamanite preaches in Z.; **3 Ne.** 3: 22–23 Z. is appointed as place of gathering in defense against enemies; **Morm.** 1: 6 Mormon[2] is taken by his father to Z.

ZARAHEMLA, PEOPLE OF—*descendants of Mulek's colony*

Omni 1: 14 discovered by Nephites; 1: 15 had come from Jerusalem when Zedekiah was carried captive to Babylon; 1: 19 united with Nephites; 1: 21 discovered Coriantumr²; **Mosiah** 1: 10 Benjamin causes people of Z. and of Mosiah to gather; 25: 2–3 more numerous than Nephites, less than Lamanites; 25: 13 numbered with Nephites; **Alma** 22: 30 land of Desolation found by people of Z.

ZEAL, ZEALOUS, ZEALOUSLY (*see also* Diligence; Faithful)

Mosiah 7: 21 (9: 3) Zeniff is over-z. to inherit land of fathers; 27: 35 sons of Mosiah² strive z. to repair injuries they have done church; **Alma** 21: 23 people of Lamoni are z. in keeping commandments; 27: 27 Ammonites are distinguished for z. toward God.

ZEDEKIAH¹—*last king of Judah* [c. 600 B.C.] (*see also* BD Zedekiah)

1 Ne. 1: 4 Lehi¹ and others prophesy in first year of Z's reign; 5: 10–13 brass plates contain record of Jews to beginning of Z's reign; **Omni** 1: 15 people of Zarahemla came from Jerusalem at time Z. was taken captive to Babylon; **Hel.** 6: 10 Mulek was son of Z.; 8: 21 all Z's sons slain except Mulek.

ZEDEKIAH²—*one of twelve Nephite disciples* [c. A.D. 34]

3 Ne. 19: 4 is called by Jesus to minister to Nephites.

ZEEZROM—*lawyer in Ammonihah* [c. 82 B.C.]

Alma 10: 31 accuses Alma² and Amulek; 11: 21–38 questions Amulek; 11: 22 tries to bribe Amulek to deny God; 11: 46 trembles at words of Amulek; 12: 1–6 is caught in his lying; 12: 7 is convinced of power of God; 12: 8 inquires diligently of Alma² and Amulek to learn concerning kingdom of God; 14: 2–6 is astonished by plain words; 15: 3 is sick with fever; 15: 4–11 is healed by Alma²; 15: 12 is baptized; 31: 5–6 with Amulek in Melek, leaves on missionary journey with Alma² and others; 31: 32 Alma² prays for Z. and other companions; **Hel.** 5: 41 people are reminded of Z's teachings concerning Christ.

ZEEZROM, CITY OF—*Nephite city on southwest frontier*

Alma 56: 13–14 is captured by Lamanites.

ZEMNARIHAH—*captain of Gadianton robbers* [c. A.D. 21]

3 Ne. 4: 16–17 lays siege to Nephites; 4: 22–23 commands forces to withdraw; 4: 28 is hanged.

ZENEPHI—*Nephite commander* [c. A.D. 400]

Moro. 9: 16 army of Z. carries off provisions of widows.

ZENIFF—*first king of group of Nephites who return to land of Lehi-Nephi* [c. 200 B.C.] (*see also* Lehi-Nephi, City of and Land of)

Mosiah 7: 9 father of Noah³, grandfather of Limhi; 7: 13 Ammon¹ comes to inquire after brethren whom Z. brought from Zarahemla; 7: 21 (9: 3) overzealous to inherit land of fathers; 7: 21 is made king; 7: 21 (9: 6–13; 10: 18) is deceived by king Laman²; ch. 9–22 record of Z.; 9: 1 is sent as spy among Lamanites; 9: 2–3 becomes leader of group; 9: 6–7 covenants with King Laman² to possess land of Lehi-Nephi; 9: 13–19 (10: 19–20) drives out Lamanite invaders; 11: 1 confers kingdom on son, Noah³.

ZENOCK—*prophet of Israel*

1 Ne. 19: 10 predicted that Christ would be lifted up by wicked men; **Alma** 33: 15–16 (34: 7) Z's testimony of Son of God; **Hel.** 8: 19–20 testified with other prophets concerning Christ; **3 Ne.** 10: 16 predicted destruction at Christ's death.

ZENOS—*prophet of Israel*

1 Ne. 19: 10, 12 prophesied of Christ's burial, three days of darkness; 19: 16 predicted gathering of Israel; **Jacob** 5: 1–77 Jacob² quotes Z's parable of olive-tree; 6: 1–10 Jacob² expounds Z's allegory; **Alma** 33: 3–11 Z's words on worship and prayer; 33: 13 Z. said, Thou hast turned away judgments because of thy Son; 34: 7 taught that redemption comes through Son; **Hel.** 8: 19 slain for bold testimony; 15: 11 spoke of restoration of Lamanites; **3 Ne.** 10: 15–16 testified of destruction at Christ's death.

ZERAHEMNAH—*Lamanite commander* [c. 74 B.C.]

Alma 43: 5, 44 chief captain of Lamanite army; 43: 44 inspires soldiers to fight; 43: 53 is struck with terror when surrounded; 44: 1–6 is commanded by Moroni¹ to surrender; 44: 12 attempts to kill Moroni¹, is scalped; 44: 19 begs for mercy.

ZERAM—*Nephite military officer* [c. 87 B.C.]

Alma 2: 22 is sent to watch camp of Amlicites.

ZERIN, MOUNT

Ether 12: 30 brother of Jared² said to mountain Z., Remove, and it was removed.

ZIFF—*probably a metal used by Nephites*

Mosiah 11: 3 Noah³ lays tax of fifth part of people's z.; 11: 8 Noah³ ornaments buildings with z.

ZION—(*see also* Gather; Inherit, Inheritance; Jerusalem, New; Kingdom of God; Millennium; Promised Land; Zion, Mount; TG Zion, Sion; BD Zion)

1 Ne. 13: 37 blessed are they who shall seek to bring forth Z.; 21: 14 (Isa. 49: 14) Z. hath said, The Lord hath forsaken me; 22: 14, 19 (2 Ne. 6: 12–13; 10: 13, 16; 27: 3) all who fight against Z. shall be destroyed; **2 Ne.** 8: 3 (Isa. 51: 3) the Lord shall comfort Z.; 8: 11 (Isa. 51: 11) the redeemed shall come with singing unto Z.; 8: 16 (Isa. 51: 16) the Lord to say unto Z., Thou art my people; 8: 24 (3 Ne. 20: 36; Moro. 10: 31; Isa. 52: 1) put on thy strength and beautiful garments, O Z.; 8: 25 (3 Ne. 20: 37; Isa. 52: 2) loose thyself from bands of thy neck, O captive daughter of Z.; 12: 3 (Isa. 2: 3) out of Z. shall go forth law; 13: 16–17 (Isa. 3: 16–17) the Lord will smite haughty daughters of Z.; 14: 3–4 (Isa. 4: 3–4) those left in Z. shall be called holy, have filth washed away; 14: 5 (Isa. 4: 5) upon glory of Z. shall be a defence; 24: 32 (Isa. 14: 32) the Lord has founded Z., and the poor of his people shall trust in it; 26: 29 those practicing priestcrafts seek not welfare of Z.; 26: 30–31 laborer in Z. shall labor for Z.; 28: 21–25 devil lulls men into saying, All is well in Z.; **Mosiah** 12: 21 (15: 14; 3 Ne. 20: 40; Isa. 52: 7) how beautiful upon mountains are feet of him that saith unto Z., Thy God reigneth; 12: 22 (15: 29; 3 Ne. 16: 18; Isa. 52: 8) the Lord shall bring again Z.; **3 Ne.** 21: 1 the Lord to gather Israel and establish Z. among them again.

ZION, MOUNT (*see also* Zion)

2 Ne. 20: 12 (Isa. 10: 12) the Lord to perform his whole work upon M.Z.

ZORAM¹—*servant of Laban* [c. 600 B.C. (*see also* Zoramites¹)

1 Ne. 4: 20 has keys of treasury; 4: 21–27 thinks Nephi¹ is Laban; 4: 30 is

frightened by sight of brothers of Nephi¹; 4: 31–37 is seized, promises to accompany Lehites; 16: 7 takes eldest daughter of Ishmael¹ to wife; **2 Ne.** 1: 30–32 is blessed by Lehi¹; 1: 30 is true friend to Nephi¹; 5: 6 becomes follower of Nephi¹; **Alma** 54: 23 Ammoron is a descendant of Z.

ZORAM²—*Nephite chief captain* [c. 81 B.C.]

Alma 16: 5 is appointed chief captain, seeks counsel of Alma²; 16: 7 crosses river Sidon and defeats Lamanites.

ZORAM³—*Nephite apostate* [c. 74 B.C.] (*see also* Zoramites²)

Alma 30: 59 leads people who have separated themselves from Nephites; 31: 1 leads hearts of people to bow down to idols.

ZORAMITES¹—*descendants of Zoram¹*

Jacob 1: 13 (4 Ne. 1: 36; Morm. 1: 8) a group among the Nephites; **4 Ne.** 1: 37 are true believers in Christ.

ZORAMITES²—*apostate sect of Nephites, followers of Zoram³*

Alma 30: 59 (31: 8) dissenters, separate themselves from Nephites; 30: 58–59 trample Korihor to death; 31: 1, 9–11 pervert ways of the Lord, bow down to idols; 31: 3 gather in land of Antionum; 31: 4 Nephites fear Z. will enter into correspondence with Lamanites; 31: 5–7 Alma² and others undertake mission to Z.; 31: 9–11 Z. do not follow law of Moses or performances of church; 31: 12–23 perverted manner of worship, pray once a week from holy stand; 31: 26—34: 41 teachings of Alma² to the Z.; 35: 3–6 converts are expelled by Z.; 35: 8–11 Z. prepare for attack against Ammonites; 35: 14 Alma² and companions bring many Z. to repentance; 38: 13 do not pray to be heard of men, like the Z.; 39: 11 Corianton's bad example leads Z. not to believe Alma²; 43: 4, 6, 13 become Lamanites; 43: 43–44 inspire Lamanites to fight courageously; 48: 5 Z. are appointed chief captains among Lamanites because of knowledge of Nephites' strengths; **3 Ne.** 1: 29 children of converted Lamanites are led astray by lyings and flattery of Z.